The Broadview Anthology of

BRITISH LITERATURE

Concise Edition

Volume B

The Broadview Anthology of British Literature: Concise Edition

The Age of Romanticism
The Victorian Era
The Twentieth Century and Beyond

The Broadview Anthology of

BRITISH LITERATURE

Concise Edition
Volume B

GENERAL EDITORS

Joseph Black, University of Massachusetts
Leonard Conolly, Trent University
Kate Flint, Rutgers University
Isobel Grundy, University of Alberta
Don LePan, Broadview Press
Roy Liuzza, University of Tennessee
Jerome J. McGann, University of Virginia
Anne Lake Prescott, Barnard College
Barry V. Qualls, Rutgers University
Claire Waters, University of California, Davis

broadview press

LIBRARY AND ARCHIVES CANADA CATALOGUING IN PUBLICATION

The Broadview anthology of British literature / general editors, Joseph Black ... [et al]. — Concise ed.

Includes bibliographical references and index.
ISBN-13: 978-1-55111-868-0 (v. A.)
ISBN-13: 978-1-55111-869-7 (v. B)
ISBN-10: 1-55111-868-8 (v. A.)
ISBN-10: 1-55111-869-6 (v. B)

1. English literature. I. Black, Joseph Laurence, 1962–

PR1109.B773 2007   820.8   C2006-906191-2

Broadview Press is an independent, international publishing house, incorporated in 1985. Broadview believes in shared ownership, both with its employees and with the general public; since the year 2000 Broadview shares have traded publicly on the Toronto Venture Exchange under the symbol BDP.

We welcome comments and suggestions regarding any aspect of our publications—please feel free to contact us at the addresses below or at broadview@broadviewpress.com.

North America
PO Box 1243,
Peterborough, Ontario
Canada K9J 7H5

2215 Kenmore Ave.,
Buffalo, NY, USA 14207
TEL: (705) 743-8990
FAX: (705) 743-8353
customerservice@broadviewpress.com

UK, Ireland, and continental Europe
NBN International
Estover Road
Plymouth, UK PL6 7PY
TEL: 44 (0) 1752 202300
FAX: 44 (0) 1752 202330
enquiries@nbninternational.com

Australia and New Zealand
NewSouth Books,
c/o TL Distribution
15-23 Helles Avenue,
Moorebank, NSW, 2170
TEL: 61 2 9664 0999;
FAX: 61 2 9664 5420
orders@tldistribution.com.au

www.broadviewpress.com
Broadview Press acknowledges the financial support of the Government of Canada through the Book Publishing Industry Development Program (BPIDP) for our publishing activities.

Cover design by Lisa Brawn

PRINTED IN CANADA

Contributing Editors and Writers

MANAGING EDITOR   Don LePan
EDITORIAL COORDINATORS   Katie Dole, Jennifer McCue
DEVELOPMENTAL EDITOR   Laura Cardiff
GENERAL ACADEMIC AND TEXTUAL EDITORS   Colleen Franklin, Morgan Rooney
DESIGN COORDINATOR   Kathryn Brownsey

Contributing Editors

Katherine O. Acheson
Sandra Bell
Emily Bernhard Jackson
Joseph Black
Robert Boenig
Michael Calabrese
Laura Cardiff
Noel Chevalier
Mita Choudhury
Thomas J. Collins
Leonard Conolly
Dianne Dugaw
Michael Faletra
Christine Fitzgerald
Stephen Glosecki
Amanda Goldrick-Jones
Douglas Hayes

John Holmes
Michael Keefer
David Klausner
Scott Kleinman
Gary Kuchar
Don LePan
Roy Liuzza
Marie Loughlin
D.L. Macdonald
Hugh Magennis
Anne McWhir
Tobias Menely
Britt Mize
Robin Norris
David Oakleaf
Jude Polsky

Anne Lake Prescott
Joyce Rappaport
Herbert Rosengarten
Jason Rudy
Janice Schroeder
John T. Sebastian
Emily Steiner
David Swain
Andrew Taylor
Peggy Thompson
Fred Waage
Craig Walker
Claire Waters
David Watt
William Weaver
James Winny

Contributing Writers

Laura Cardiff
Jude Polsky
Victoria Abboud
Steven Alvarez
Lopamudra Basu
Jane Beal
Jennifer Beauvais
Rachel Bennett
Emily Bernhard Jackson
Rebecca Blasco
Julie Brennan
Andrew Bretz
Emily Cargan
Mia Chen
Adrienne Eastwood
Wendy Eberle-Sinatra
Peter Enman
Jamie Ferguson
Joanne Findon
Louise Geddes

Alina Gharabegian
Jane Grove
Isobel Grundy
Dorothy Hadfield
Camille Isaacs
Erik Isford
Andrea Jones
Stephanie King
Gabrielle L'Archeveque
Don LePan
Anna Lepine
John McIntyre
Susan McNeill-Bindon
Pia Mukherji
Carrie Nartkler
Byron Nelson
Robin Norris
Kenna Olsen
Seamus O'Malley

Kendra O'Neal Smith
Allisandra Paschkowiak
Laura Pellerine
Jason Rudy
Anne Salo
Janice Schroeder
Carrie Shanafelt
Nicole Shukin
James Soderholm
Anne Sorbie
Martha Stoddard-Holmes
Jenna Stook
Candace Taylor
Yevgeniya Traps
David van Belle
Shari Watling
Matthew Williams
bj Wray
Nicole Zylstra

LAYOUT AND TYPESETTING

Kathryn Brownsey   Susan Chamberlain

ILLUSTRATION FORMATTING AND ASSISTANCE

Cheryl Baldwin   Lisa Brawn

PRODUCTION COORDINATORS

Barbara Conolly   Leonard Conolly   Tara Lowes
Judith Earnshaw   Chris Griffin

PERMISSIONS COORDINATORS

Emily Cargan   Jennifer Elsayed   Chris Griffin
                         Amy Nimegeer

PROOFREADERS

Jennifer Bingham   Anne Hodgetts
Martin Boyne   Amy Neufeld
Lucy Conolly   Lynn Neufeld
Lynn Fraser

EDITORIAL ADVISORS

Rachel Ablow, University of Rochester
Rita Bode, Trent University
Susan Brown, University of Guelph
Catherine Burroughs, Wells College
Elizabeth Campbell, Oregon State University
Nancy Cirillo, University of Illinois, Chicago
David Cowart, University of South Carolina
Alex Dick, University of British Columbia
Len Diepeveen, Dalhousie University
Daniel Fischlin, University of Guelph
Robert Forman, St. John's University
Barbara Gates, University of Delaware
Chris Gordon-Craig, University of Alberta
Stephen Guy-Bray, University of British
    Columbia
Douglas Hayes, Lakehead University
Elizabeth Hodgson, University of British
    Columbia
John Holmes, University of Reading

Michael Keefer, University of Guelph
Gordon Kipling, University of California, Los
    Angeles
Emily Kugler, University of California, San
    Diego
William Liston, Ball State University
Peter Mallios, University of Maryland
Rod Michell, Thompson Rivers University
Byron Nelson, West Virginia University
Michael North, University of California, Los
    Angeles
Lesley Peterson, University of North Alabama
John Pollock, San Jose State University
Jason Rudy, University of Maryland
Carol Senf, Georgia Tech
Sharon Smulders, Mount Royal College
Goran Stanivukovic, St. Mary's University
Julian Yates, University of Delaware

Contents

THE AGE OF ROMANTICISM

THE VICTORIAN ERA

THE TWENTIETH CENTURY AND BEYOND

PREFACE

CONCISE EDITION

The rationale for publishing a concise edition of *The Broadview Anthology of British Literature* is, above all, pedagogical; we want to provide an alternative for those who prefer a textbook intended exclusively for use in courses that survey all of British literature over the course of two university terms. But no two academics have identical preferences as to what should be taught in such courses—and, indeed, many academics like to vary what they teach considerably from year to year. At Broadview, working with the academic general editors for the full anthology, we found it enormously difficult to make the necessary decisions to keep the larger anthology of manageable size. How should we go about trimming further to produce a two-volume concise anthology no more than two-thirds the length of the full anthology?

The natural starting point was of course to ask people who we hoped would consider the final product as a text for their own courses. Accordingly, we at Broadview conducted a wide-ranging editorial research survey inviting academics to comment not only on general matters (e.g., "how do you feel about excerpting?"), but also on specific individual selections they would prefer to see included. Over 20 academics—each of whom is listed among the special editorial advisors for the project—were kind enough to provide highly detailed responses to our survey. We have also consulted many other academics, less formally, not only as to their preferences today, but also as to trends currently taking shape that may be expected to shape pedagogy in the future.

We were pleased that a substantial majority of those we consulted shared our own feeling that it would be a shame to take an entirely "major authors" approach to a concise edition—to include *only* those authors and works already established as canonical. Obviously, the emphasis in any concise anthology will inevitably be more on the canonical than is the case with a more comprehensive anthology. But we were determined to provide some alternatives for those instructors who prefer, even within the restricted compass of a two-term British literature survey, to teach one or two lesser-known works alongside a good selection of the "greatest hits." Readers will thus find in these pages John Wilmot and Aemelia Lanyer as well as William Shakespeare and Christopher Marlowe; Eliza Haywood and Stephen Duck as well as Jonathan Swift and Alexander Pope; Augusta Webster and Algernon Charles Swinburne as well as Alfred, Lord Tennyson and Matthew Arnold; Katherine Mansfield as well as T.S. Eliot and Virginia Woolf.

Much as we have valued the wealth of advice we have received, we should also confess that in a few cases we have *not* followed the consensus that emerged from our editorial research. The research we conducted, for example, suggested very clearly that we should omit any selection of Hardy's prose fiction from the anthology. While we acknowledge the view that Hardy's fiction can only be taught adequately through a reading of his novels, we feel a strong case can be made that the outstanding qualities of his fiction may also be found in compressed form in some of his short stories—"The Son's Veto" being an outstanding example. Had we relied only on the results of our editorial research, we would also not have included Carol Ann Duffy in the concise edition. That research, however, was conducted primarily among academics in North America; in this case, our departure from the course of action suggested by the research was driven by our sense that Duffy is increasingly acknowledged within Britain itself as a poet of central importance.

We have felt it appropriate for a concise edition to take a rather different approach to excerpting than we have done in the full anthology. Notably, several longer prose works (More's *Utopia*, De Quincey's *Confessions of an Opium Eater*, Woolf's *A Room of One's Own*) that appear in their entirety in the full anthology are included here in an excerpted form.

A particularly well-received feature in the full anthology has been the inclusion of a wealth of contextual materials. Inevitably, many of these have been dropped in the concise edition, but we have resisted any impulse to cut all the "contexts" to make way for the texts themselves; even within the confines of the shorter version of the anthology, we felt it important to offer a selection of materials to help illuminate some of the historical and cultural background.

The central principles of the full anthology are of course retained in this concise edition. The introductory materials and the annotations are unchanged, as are the supplementary materials.

A FRESH APPROACH

To those with some awareness of the abundance of fresh material and lively debate in the field of English Studies in recent generations, it may seem surprising that this abundance has not been more fully reflected in the number of available anthologies. Thirty years ago there were two comprehensive anthologies designed for courses surveying British Literature: *The Norton Anthology of English Literature* and one alternative. In recent years there have been still two choices available—the *Norton* and one alternative. Over that time span *The Longman Anthology of British Literature* replaced *The Oxford Anthology of English Literature* in the role of "alternative," but there has been no expansion in range of available choices to match the expansion of content and of approach that has characterized the discipline itself. The number of available handbooks and guides to writing has multiplied steadily (to the point where there are literally hundreds of available choices), while the number of comprehensive anthologies of British literature has remained at two.

For those of us who have been working for the past three years on *The Broadview Anthology of British Literature*, it is not difficult to understand why. The very expansion of the discipline has made the task of assembling and editing an anthology that fully and vibrantly reflects the ways in which the British literary tradition is studied and taught an extraordinarily

daunting one. The sheer amount of work involved is enormous, but so too is the amount of expertise that needs to be called on. With that background very much in mind, we have charted a new course in the preparation of *The Broadview Anthology of British Literature*. Rather than dividing up the work among a relatively small number of academics, and asking each of them to handle on their own the work of choosing, annotating, and preparing introductions to texts in their own areas of specialization, we have involved a large number of contributors in the process (as the pages following the title page to this volume attest), and encouraged a high degree of collaboration at every level. First and foremost have been the distinguished academics who have served as our General Editors for the project, but in all there have literally been hundreds of people involved at various stages in researching, drafting headnotes or annotations, reviewing material, editing material, and finally carrying out the work of designing and typesetting the texts and other materials. That approach has allowed us to draw on a diverse range of talent, and to prepare a large anthology with unusual speed. It has also facilitated the maintenance of a high degree of consistency. Material has been reviewed and revised in-house at Broadview, by outside editors (chief among them Colleen Franklin, an academic with a wide-ranging background and also a superb copy editor), by a variety of academics with an extraordinarily diverse range of backgrounds and academic specialities, and by our team of General Editors for the project as a whole. The aim has been not only to ensure accuracy but also to make sure that the same standards are applied throughout the anthology to matters such as extent and coverage in author introductions, level of annotation, tone of writing, and student accessibility.

Our General Editors have throughout taken the lead in the process of making selections for the anthology. Along the way we have been guided by several core principles. We have endeavored to provide a selection that is broadly representative, while also being mindful of the importance of choosing texts that have the capacity to engage readers' interest today. Where inexpensive editions of works are available in our series of paperback Broadview Editions, we have often decided to omit them here, on the grounds that those wishing to teach one or more such works may easily order them in a combination package with the anthology; on these grounds we have decided against including *Frankenstein, Pride and Prejudice,* or *Heart of Darkness.* (However, we have included selections from *The Last Man* to represent Shelley and the first four chapters of *Pride and Prejudice* to represent Austen.)

Any discussion of what is distinctive about *The Broadview Anthology of British Literature* must focus above all on the contents. In every section of the anthology there is material that is distinctive and fresh—including not only selections by lesser-known writers but also less familiar selections from canonical writers. The anthology takes a fresh approach also to a great many canonical texts. The Medieval section of the anthology includes not only Roy Liuzza's translation of *Beowulf* (widely acclaimed as the most engaging and reliable translation available), but also new translations by Liuzza of many other works of Old English poetry and prose. Also included in the Medieval section is a new translation by Claire Waters of Marie de France's *Lanval.* The Renaissance selections include *King Lear* not only in the full Folio version but also with three key scenes from the Quarto version; readers are thus invited to engage first-hand with the question of how textual issues may substantially affect larger issues of meaning.

In a number of these cases the distinctive form of the anthology facilitates the presentation of content in an engaging and practical fashion. Notably, the adoption of a two-column format allows for some translations (the Waters translation of Marie de France's *Lanval,* the James Winny translation of *Sir Gawain and the Green Knight*) to be presented in parallel column format alongside the original texts, enabling readers to experience something of the flavor of the original while providing convenient access to an accessible translation. Similarly, scenes from the Quarto version of *King Lear* are presented alongside the comparable sections of the Folio text, and passages from four translations of the Bible are laid out parallel to one another for ready comparison.

The large trim size and two-column format also allow for greater flexibility in the presentation of visual materials. Throughout we have aimed to make this an anthology that is fully alive to the connections between literary and visual culture, from the discussion of the CHI-RHO page of the Lindisfarne Gospels in the Medieval section of the anthology (and the accompanying color illustration) to the inclusion in the twentieth-century section of several skits from "Monty Python's Flying Circus") that may be discussed in connection with film or television versions. Along the way appear several full-page illustrations from the Ellesmere manuscript of Chaucer's *Canterbury Tales* and illustrations to a wide variety of other works, such as *Robinson Crusoe* and *Gulliver's Travels.*

CONTEXTUAL MATERIALS

Visual materials are also an important part of the background materials that form a significant component of the anthology. These materials are presented in two ways. Several "Contexts" sections on particular topics or themes appear in both volumes of the anthology. Presented independent of any particular text or author, these include broadly based groupings of material on such topics as "Religion and Spiritual Life," "Print Culture, Stage Culture," "The New Art of Photography," "The Abolition of Slavery," "Work and Poverty in Victorian England," and "The Place of Women in Society." The groups of "In Context" materials each relate to a particular text or author. They range from the genealogical tables provided as a supplement to *Beowulf*; to materials on "The Eighteenth-Century Sexual Imagination" (presented in conjunction with Haywood's *Fantomina*); to the Easter 1916 Proclamation of the Irish Republic and rebellion leader Padraic Pearse's statement, which accompany W.B. Yeats's "Easter 1916." For the most part these contextual materials are, as the word suggests, included with a view to setting texts in their broader literary, historical, and cultural contexts; in some cases, however, the materials included in "Contexts" sections are themselves literary works of a high order. The autobiographical account by Eliza M. of nineteenth-century life in Cape Town, for example (included in the section in Volume 5 on "Race and Empire"), is as remarkable for its literary qualities as it is for the light it sheds on the realities of colonial life. In the inclusion of texts such as these, as well as in other ways, the anthology aims to encourage readers to explore the boundaries of the literary and the non-literary, and the issue of what constitutes a "literary text."

WOMEN'S PLACE

A central element of the broadening of the canon of British literature in recent generations has of course been a great increase in the attention paid to texts by women writers. As one might expect from a publisher that has played an important role in making neglected works by women writers widely available, this anthology reflects the broadening of the canon quantitatively, by including a substantially larger number of women writers than have earlier anthologies of British literature. But it also reflects this broadening in other ways. In many anthologies of literature (anthologies of British literature, to be sure, but also anthologies of literature of a variety of other sorts) women writers are set somewhat apart, referenced in introductions and headnotes only in relation to issues of gender, and treated as important only for the fact of their being women writers. *The Broadview Anthology* strenuously resists such segregation; while women writers are of course discussed in relation to gender issues, their texts are also presented and discussed alongside those by men in a wide variety of other contexts, including seventeenth-century religious and political controversies, the abolitionist movement, and World War I pacifism. Texts by women writers are front and center in the discussion of the development of realism in nineteenth-century fiction.

"BRITISH," "ENGLISH," "IRISH," "SCOTTISH," "WELSH," "OTHER"

The broadening of English Studies, in conjunction with the expansion and subsequent contraction of British power and influence around the world, has considerably complicated the issue of exactly how inclusive anthologies should be. In several respects this anthology (like its two main competitors) is significantly more inclusive than its title suggests, including a number of non-British writers whose works connect in important ways with the traditions of British literature. We have endeavored first of all to portray the fluid and multilingual reality of the medieval period through the inclusion not only of works in Old and Middle English but also, where other cultures interacted with the nascent "English" language and "British" culture, works in Latin, in French, and in Welsh. In later periods the word "British" becomes deeply problematic in different respects, but on balance we have preferred it to the only obvious alternative, "English." There are several objections to the latter in this context. Perhaps most obviously, "English" excludes authors or texts not only from Ireland but also from Scotland and from Wales, both of which retain to this day cultures quite distinct from that of the English. "English literature," of course, may also be taken to mean "literature written in English," but since the anthology does not cover *all* literature written in English (most obviously in excluding American literature), the ambiguity would not in this case be helpful.

The inclusion of Irish writers presents a related but even more tangled set of issues. Through most of the seventeenth, eighteenth, and nineteenth centuries almost the whole of Ireland was under British control—but for the most part unwillingly. In the period covered in the last of the six volumes Ireland was partitioned, with Northern Ireland becoming a part of the United Kingdom and the Republic of Ireland declared independent of Britain on 6 December 1921. Less than two months earlier, James Joyce had completed *Ulysses*, which was first published as a complete work the following year (in Paris, not in Britain). It would be obviously absurd to regard Joyce as a British writer up to just before the publication of *Ulysses* and an Irish writer thereafter. And arguably he and other Irish writers should never be regarded as British, whatever the politics of the day. If on no other grounds than their overwhelming influence on and connection to the body of literature written in the British Isles, however, we have included Irish writers—among them Swift, Wilde, Shaw, Beckett, and Heaney as well as Joyce— throughout this anthology. We have also endeavored to give a real sense in the six period introductions of the anthology, in the headnotes to individual authors, and in the annotations to the texts themselves, of the ways in which the histories and the cultures of England, Ireland, Scotland and Wales, much as they interact with one another, are also distinct.

Also included in this anthology are texts by writers from areas that are far removed geographically from the British Isles but that are or have been British possessions. Writers such as Olaudah Equiano and Mary Prince are included, as they spent all or most of their lives living in what were then British colonial possessions. Writers who came of age in an independent United States, on the other hand, are not included, unless (like T.S. Eliot) they subsequently put down roots in Britain and became important British literary figures. Substantial grey areas, of course, surround such issues. One might well argue, for example, that Henry James merits inclusion in an anthology of British literature, or that W.H. Auden is more an American poet than British one. But the chosen subject matter of James's work has traditionally been considered to mark him as having remained an American writer, despite having spent almost two-thirds of his life in England. And Auden so clearly made a mark in Britain before crossing the Atlantic that it would seem odd to exclude him from these pages on the grounds of his having lived the greater part of his adult life in America. One of our competitors includes Sylvia Plath in their anthology of British literature; Plath lived in England for only five of her thirty years, though, and her poetry is generally agreed to have more in common with the traditions of Lowell, Merwin, and Sexton than with the currents of British poetry in the 1950s and '60s.

As a broad principle, we have been open to the inclusion of twentieth- and twenty-first-century work in English not only by writers from the British Isles but also by writers from British possessions overseas, and by writers from countries that were once British possessions and have remained a part of the British Commonwealth. In such cases, we have often chosen selections that relate in one way or another to the tradition of British literature and the British colonial legacy. For example, the Chinua Achebe story in the anthology concerns the divide between British colonial culture and traditional Nigerian culture.

THE HISTORY OF LANGUAGE, AND OF PRINT CULTURE

Among the liveliest discussions we had at meetings of our General Editors were those concerning the issue of whether or not to bring spelling and punctuation into accord with present-day practice. We finally decided that, in the interests of making the anthology accessible to the introductory student, we should *in most cases* bring spelling and punctuation in line with present-day practice. An important exception has been made for works in which modernizing spelling and punctuation would alter the meaning or the aural and metrical qualities. In practice this means that works before the late sixteenth century tend to be presented either in their original form or in translation, whereas later texts tend to have spelling and punctuation modernized. But where spelling and punctuation choices in later texts are known (or believed on reliable authority) to represent conscious choice on the part of the author rather than simply the common practice of the time, we have in those cases, too, made an exception and retained the original spelling and punctuation. (Among these are texts by Edmund Spenser, William Cowper, Samuel Taylor Coleridge, William Blake, Emily Bronte, and George Bernard Shaw.)

Beyond this, we all agreed that we should provide for readers a real sense of the development of the language and of print culture. To that end we have included in each volume examples of texts in their original form—in some cases through the use of pages shown in facsimile, in others by providing short passages in which spelling and punctuation have not been modernized. A list of these appears near the beginning of each volume of the anthology.

We have also included a section of the history of the language as part of the introduction to each period. And throughout the anthology we include materials—visual as well as textual—relating to the history of print culture.

A DYNAMIC AND FLEXIBLE ANTHOLOGY

We at Broadview recognize that, although time constraint, make the concise anthology a practical and economical text choice for many instructors, some may nevertheless want to teach a number of non-canonical works—not all of which may be included in our concise edition. For this reason, we offer those instructors the possibility of choosing some additional texts that are included in the full, six-volume *Broadview Anthology of British Literature* but not in the concise edition. Simply visit our website, peruse the full anthology's table of contents, and provide the publisher with a list of desired selections; Broadview will then make available to students through their university bookstore a custom-made coursepack with precisely those materials included. The two volumes of the anthology may be shrink-wrapped together at a special price, and each volume may also be combined in a shrink-wrapped package with one or more of the over 200 volumes in the Broadview Editions series, for a charge of only $3.00 per edition.

THE BROADVIEW LIST

One of the reasons we have been able to bring a project of this sort to fruition in such a relatively short time is that we have been able to draw on the resources of the full Broadview list: the many titles in the Broadview Editions series, and also the considerable range of other Broadview anthologies. As the contributors' pages and the permissions acknowledgments pages indicate, a number of Broadview authors have acted as contributing editors to this volume, providing material from other volumes that has been adapted to suit the needs of the present anthology; we gratefully acknowledge their contribution.

As it has turned out, the number of cases where we have been able to draw on the resources of the Broadview list in the full sense, using in these pages texts and annotations in very much the same form in which they appear elsewhere, has been relatively small; whether because of an issue such as the level of textual modernization or one of style of annotation, we have more often than not ended up deciding that the requirements of this anthology were such that we could not use material from another Broadview source as-is. But even in these cases we often owe a debt of gratitude to the many academics who have edited outstanding editions and anthologies for Broadview. For even where we have not drawn directly from them, we have often been inspired by them—inspired to think of a wider range of texts as possibilities than we might otherwise have done, inspired to think of contextual materials in places where we might otherwise not have looked, inspired by the freshness of approach that so many of these titles exemplify.

EDITORIAL PROCEDURES AND CONVENTIONS, APPARATUS

The in-house set of editorial guidelines for *The Broadview Anthology of British Literature* now runs to over 40 pages, covering everything from conventions for the spacing of marginal notes, to the use of small caps for the abbreviations CE and BCE, to the approach we have adopted to references in author headnotes to name changes. Perhaps the most important core principle in the introductions to the various volumes, in the headnotes for each author, in the introductions in "Contexts" sections, and in annotations throughout the anthology, is to endeavor to provide a sufficient amount of information to enable students to read and interpret these texts, but without making evaluative judgments or imposing particular interpretations. In practice that is all a good deal more challenging than it sounds; it is often extremely difficult to describe why a particular author is considered to be important without using language that verges on the interpretive or the evaluative. But it is a fine line that we have all agreed is worth trying to walk; we hope that readers will find that the anthology achieves an appropriate balance.

ANNOTATION: It is also often difficult to make judgments as to where it is appropriate to provide an explanatory annotation for a word or phrase. Our policy has been to annotate where we feel that most first- or second-year students are likely to have difficulty understanding the denotative meaning. (We have made it a practice not to provide notes discussing connotative meanings.) But in practice the vocabularies and levels of verbal facility of first- and second-year students may vary enormously, both from institution to institution and within any given college or university class. On the whole, we provide somewhat more annotation than our competitors, and somewhat less interpretation. Again, we hope that readers will find that the anthology has struck a appropriate balance.

THE ETHICS AND POLITICS OF ANNOTATION: On one issue regarding annotation we have felt that principles are involved that go beyond the pedagogical. Most anthologies of British literature allow many words or phrases of a racist, sexist, anti-Semitic, or homophobic nature either to pass entirely without comment, or to be glossed with apologist comments that leave the impression that such comments were excusable in the past, and may even be unobjectionable in the present. Where derogatory comments about Jewish people and money-lending are concerned, for example, anthologies often leave the impression that money-lending was a pretty unsavory practice that Jewish people entered by choice; it has been all too rare to provide readers with any sense of the degree to which English society consistently discriminated against Jews, expelling them entirely for several centuries, requiring them to wear physical marks identifying their Jewish status, prohibiting them from entering most professions, and so on. *The Broadview Anthology* endeavors in such cases, first of all, not to allow such words and phrases to pass without comment; and second, to gloss without glossing over.

DATES: We make it a practice to include the date when a work was first made public, whether publication in print or, in the case of dramatic works, made public through the first performance of the play. Where that date is known to differ substantially from the date of composition, a note to this effect is included in parentheses. With medieval works, where there is no equivalent to the "publication" of later eras, where texts often vary greatly from one manuscript copy to another, and where knowledge as to date of original composition is usually imprecise, the date that appears at the end of each work is an estimate of the date of the work's origin in the written form included in the anthology. Earlier oral or written versions are of course in some cases real possibilities.

TEXTS: Where translations appear in this anthology, a note at the bottom of the first page indicates what translation is being used. Similar notes also address overall textual issues where choice of copy text is particularly significant. Reliable editions of all works are listed in the bibliographies for each period, which are included on *The Broadview Anthology of British Literature* website (http://www.broadviewpress.com/babl/) to facilitate ready revision. (In addition to information as to reliable editions, the bibliographies provide for each author and for

each of the six periods a select list of important or useful historical and critical works.) Copyright information for texts not in the public domain, however, is provided within the books in a section listing Permissions Acknowledgments.

INTRODUCTIONS: In addition to the introductory headnotes for each author included in the anthology, each "Contexts" section includes a substantial introduction, and each period includes an introduction to the period as a whole. These period introductions provide a sense not only of the broad picture of literary developments in the period, but also of the historical, social, and political background, and of the cultural climate. Readers should be cautioned that, while there is inevitably some overlap between information presented here and information presented in the author headnotes, an effort has been made to avoid such repetition as much as possible; the general introduction to each period should thus be read in conjunction with the author headnotes. The general introductions aim not only to provide an overview of ways in which texts and authors included in these pages may connect with one another, but also to give readers a sense of connection with a range of other writers and texts of the period.

READING POETRY: For much of the glossary and for the "Reading Poetry" section that appears as part of the appendices to each volume we have drawn on the superb material prepared by Herbert Rosengarten and Amanda Goldrick-Jones for *The Broadview Anthology of Poetry*; this section provides a concise but comprehensive introduction to the study of poetry. It includes discussions of diction, imagery, poetic figures, and various poetic forms, as well as offering an introduction to prosody.

MAPS: Also appearing within the books are maps especially prepared for this anthology, including, for each period, a map of Britain showing towns and features of relevance. Each volume also includes a map showing the counties of Britain and of Ireland, maps of both the London area and the inner city, and world maps indicating the locations of some of the significant places referenced in the anthology—and for the second volume, showing the extent of Britain's overseas territories.

GLOSSARY: Some other anthologies of British literature include both glossaries of terms and essays introducing students to various political and religious categories in British history. Similar information is included in *The Broadview Anthology of British Literature*, but we have adopted a more integrated approach, including political and religious terms along with literary ones in a convenient general glossary. While we recognize that "googling" for information of this sort is often the student's first resort (and we recognize too the value of searching the web for the wealth of background reference information available there), we also recognize that information culled from the Internet is often far from reliable; it is our intent, through this glossary, through our introductions and headnotes, and through the wealth of accessible annotation in the anthology, to provide as part of the anthology a reliable core of information in the most convenient and accessible form possible.

OTHER MATERIALS: A chart of monarchs and prime ministers is also provided within these pages. A range of other adjunct materials may be accessed through *The Broadview Anthology of British Literature* website. "Texts and Contexts" charts for each volume provide a convenient parallel reference guide to the dates of literary texts and historical developments. "British Money" provides a thumbnail sketch of the world of pounds, shillings, and pence, together with a handy guide to estimating the current equivalents of monetary values from earlier eras.

Acknowledgments

The names of those on the Editorial Board that shaped this anthology appear on the title page, and those of the many who contributed directly to the writing, editing, and production of the project on the following two pages. Special acknowledgment should go to Jennifer McCue, who as Editorial Coordinator has been instrumental in tying together all the vast threads of this project and in making it a reality; to Laura Cardiff and Jude Polsky, who have carried larger loads than any others in drafting introductory materials and annotations, and who have done so with great skill and unfailing grace; to Kathryn Brownsey, who has been responsible for design and typesetting, and has continued to do a superb job and to maintain her good spirits even when faced with near-impossible demands; to Colleen Franklin, for the range of her scholarship as well as for her keen eye as our primary copy editor for the entire project; to Emily Cargan, Jennifer Elsayed and Amy Nimegeer who have together done superb work on the vast job of clearing permissions for the anthology; and to Michelle Lobkowicz and Anna Del Col, who have ably and enthusiastically taken the lead with marketing matters.

The academic members of the Advisory Editorial Board and all of us in-house at Broadview owe an enormous debt of gratitude to the hundreds of academics who have offered assistance at various stages of this project. In particular we would like to express our appreciation and our thanks to the following:

Rachel Ablow, University of Rochester
Katherine Acheson, University of Waterloo
Bryan Alexander, Middlebury College
Sharon Alker, Whitman College
James Allard, Brock University
Ella Allen, St. Thomas University
Rosemary Allen, Georgetown College
Laurel Amtower, San Diego State University
Robert Anderson, Oakland University
Christopher Armitage, University of North Carolina, Chapel Hill
Clinton Atchley, Henderson State University
Gerry Baillargeon, University of Victoria
John Baird, University of Toronto
William Baker, Northern Illinois University
Karen Bamford, Mount Allison University
John Batchelor, University of Newcastle
Lynn Batten, University of California, Los Angeles
Alexandra Bennett, Northern Illinois University
John Beynon, California State University, Fresno
Daniel Bivona, Arizona State University
Robert E. Bjork, Arizona State University
Scott Black, Villanova University

Rita Bode, Trent University
Robert Boenig, Texas A & M University
Rick Bowers, University of Alberta
Patricia Brace, Columbus State University
David Brewer, Ohio State University
William Brewer, Appalachian State University
Susan Brown, University of Guelph
Sylvia Brown, University of Alberta
Sheila Burgar, University of Victoria
Catherine Burroughs, Wells College
Rebecca Bushnell, University of Pennsylvania
Elizabeth Campbell, Oregon State University
Gregory Castle, Arizona State University
Cynthia Caywood, University of San Diego
Jane Chance, Rice University
Ranita Chatterjee, California State University, Northridge
William Christmas, San Francisco State University
Nancy Cirillo, University of Illinois, Chicago
Eric Clarke, University of Pittsburgh
Jeanne Clegg, University of Aquila, Italy
Thomas J. Collins, University of Western Ontario
Kevin Cope, Louisiana State University

David Cowart, University of South Carolina
Catherine Craft-Fairchild, University of St. Thomas
Carol Davison, University of Windsor
Alex Dick, University of British Columbia
Len Diepeveen, Dalhousie University
Mary Dockray-Miller, Lesley College
James Doelman, Brescia University College,
    University of Western Ontario
Frank Donoghue, Ohio State University
Chris Downs, Saint James School
Alfred Drake, Chapman University
Julie Early, University of Alabama, Huntsville
Siân Echard, University of British Columbia
Garrett Epp, University of Alberta
Joshua Eyler, Columbus State University
Ruth Feingold, St. Mary's College, Maryland
Dino Franco Felluga, Perdue University
Joanne Findon, Trent University
Daniel Fischlin, University of Guelph
Christina Fitzgerald, University of Toledo
Verlyn Flieger, University of Maryland
Robert Forman, St. John's University
Allyson Foster, Hunter College
Roberta Frank, Yale University
Jeff Franklin, University of Colorado, Denver
Maria Frawley, George Washington University
Mark Fulk, Buffalo State College
Andrew Galloway, Cornell University
Michael Gamer, University of Pennsylvania
Barbara Gates, University of Delaware
Jonathan C. Glance, Mercer University
Susan Patterson Glover, Laurentian University
Daniel Gonzalez, University of New Orleans
Jan Gorak, University of Denver
Chris Gordon-Craig, University of Alberta
Ann-Barbara Graff, Georgia Tech University
Mary Griffin, Kwantlen University College
Michael Griffin, formerly of Southern Illinois University
George C. Grinnell, University of British Columbia,
    Okanagan
Elisabeth Gruner, University of Richmond
Kevin Gustafson, University of Texas at Arlington
Stephen Guy-Bray, University of British Columbia
Ruth Haber, Worcester State College
Margaret Hadley, University of Calgary
Robert Hampson, Royal Holloway University of London

Carol Hanes, Howard College
Michael Hanly, Washington State University
Lila Harper, Central Washington State University
Joseph Harris, Harvard University
Anthony Harrison, North Carolina State University
Douglas Hayes, Lakehead University
Jennifer Hellwarth, Allegheny University
David Herman, Ohio State University
Peter Herman, San Diego State University
Kathy Hickock, Iowa State University
John Hill, US Naval Academy
Thomas Hill, Cornell University
Elizabeth Hodgson, University of British Columbia
Joseph Hornsby, University of Alabama
Scott Howard, University of Denver
Sylvia Hunt, Goergian College
Tara Hyland-Russell, St. Mary's College
Catherine Innes-Parker, University of Prince Edward
    Island
Jacqueline Jenkins, University of Calgary
John Johansen, University of Alberta
Gordon Johnston, Trent University
Richard Juang, Susquehanna University
Michael Keefer, University of Guelph
Sarah Keefer, Trent University
Lloyd Kermode, California State University,
    Long Beach
Brandon Kershner, University of Florida
Jon Kertzer, University of Calgary
Helen Killoran, Ohio University
Gordon Kipling, University of California, Los Angeles
Anne Klinck, University of New Brunswick
Elizabeth Kraft, University of Georgia
Mary Kramer, University of Massachusetts, Lowell
Marilyn Lantz, East Mississippi Community College
Kate Lawson, University of Waterloo
Linda Leeds, Bellevue Community College
Mary Elizabeth Leighton, University of Victoria
Eric Lindstrom, University of Vermont
William Liston, Ball State University
Sharon Locy, Loyola Marymount University
Peter Mallios, University of Maryland
Arnold Markley, Penn State University
Louis Markos, Houston Baptist University
Pamela McCallum, University of Calgary
Patricia McCormack, Itawamba Community College

Kristen McDermott, Central Michigan University
John McGowan, University of North Carolina
Brian McHale, Ohio State University
Jim McKeown, McLennan Community College
Thomas McLean, University of Otago, New Zealand
Jodie Medd, Carleton University
Rod Michell, Thompson Rivers University
David Miller, Mississippi College
Kitty Millett, San Francisco State University
Britt Mize, Texas A&M University
Richard Moll, University of Western Ontario
Amy L. Montz, Texas A&M University
Monique Morgan, McGill University
John Morillo, North Carolina State University
Lucy Morrison, Salisbury University
Lorri Nandrea, University of Wisconsin-Steven's Point
Byron Nelson, West Virginia University
Carolyn Nelson, West Virginia University
Claudia Nelson, Southwest Texas State University
Holly Faith Nelson, Trinity Western University
John Niles, University of Wisconsin, Madison
Michael North, University of California, Los Angeles
Mary Anne Nunn, Central Connecticut State University
David Oakleaf, University of Calgary
Tamara O'Callaghan, Northern Kentucky University
Karen Odden, Assistant Editor for *Victorian Literature and Culture* (formerly of University of Wisconsin, Milwaukee)
Erika Olbricht, Pepperdine University
Patrick O'Malley, Georgetown University
Patricia O'Neill, Hamilton College
Delilah Orr, Fort Lewis College
John Pagano, Barnard College
Kirsten Parkinson, Hiram College
Diana Patterson, Mount Royal College
Cynthia Patton, Emporia State University
Russell Perkin, St. Mary's University
Marjorie G. Perloff, Stanford University
Jim Persoon, Grand Valley State University
John Peters, University of North Texas
Todd Pettigrew, Cape Breton University
Alexander Pettit, University of North Texas
Jennifer Phegley, The University of Missouri, Kansas City
John Pollock, San Jose State University
Mary Poovey, New York University

Gautam Premnath, University of Massachusetts, Boston
Regina Psaki, University of Oregon
Katherine Quinsey, University of Windsor
Geoff Rector, University of Ottawa
Margaret Reeves, Atkinson College, York University
Cedric Reverand, University of Wyoming
Gerry Richman, Suffolk University
John Rickard, Bucknell University
Michelle Risdon, Lake Tahoe Community College
David Robinson, University of Arizona
Solveig C. Robinson, Pacific Lutheran University
Laura Rotunno, Pennsylvania State University, Altoona
Brian Rourke, New Mexico State University
Nicholas Ruddick, University of Regina
Jason Rudy, University of Maryland
Donelle Ruwe, Northern Arizona University
Michelle Sauer, Minot State University
SueAnn Schatz, Lock Haven University of Pennsylvania
Dan Schierenbeck, Central Missouri State University
Norbert Schürer, California State University, Long Beach
Debora B. Schwartz, California Polytechnic University
Janelle A. Schwartz, Loyola University
John T. Sebastian, Loyola University
David Seed, University of Liverpool
Carol Senf, Georgia Tech University
Lynn Shakinovsky, Wilfred Laurier University
John Sider, Westmont College
Judith Slagle, East Tennessee State University
Johanna Smith, University of Texas at Arlington
Sharon Smulders, Mount Royal College
Malinda Snow, Georgia State University
Goran Stanivukovic, St. Mary's University
Richard Stein, University of Oregon
Eric Sterling, Auburn University Montgomery
James Stokes, University of Wisconsin, Stevens Point
Mary-Ann Stouck, Simon Fraser University
Nathaniel Strout, Hamilton College
Brad Sullivan, Western New England College
Lisa Surridge, University of Victoria
Joyce A. Sutphen, Gustavus Adolphus College
Beth Sutton-Ramspeck, Ohio State University
Nanora Sweet, University of Missouri, St. Louis
Dana Symons, Simon Fraser University
Andrew Taylor, University of Ottawa
Elizabeth Teare, University of Dayton

Doug Thorpe, University of Saskatchewan
Jane Toswell, University of Western Ontario
Herbert Tucker, University of Virginia
John Tucker, University of Victoria
Mark Turner, King's College, University of London
Eleanor Ty, Wilfrid Laurier University
Deborah Tyler-Bennett, Loughborough University
Kirsten Uszkalo, University of Alberta
Lisa Vargo, University of Saskatchewan
Gina Luria Walker, The New School, New York City
Kim Walker, Victoria University of Wellington
Miriam Wallace, New College of Florida
Hayden Ward, West Virginia State University
David Watt, University of Manitoba
Ruth Wehlau, Queen's University
Lynn Wells, University of Regina

Dan White, University of Toronto at Mississauga
Patricia Whiting, Carleton University
Thomas Willard, University of Arizona
Tara Williams, Oregon State University
Chris Willis, Birkbeck University of London
Lisa Wilson, SUNY College at Potsdam
Ed Wiltse, Nazareth College
Anne Windholz, Augustana College
Susan Wolfson, Princeton University
Kenneth Womack, Pennsylvania State University
Carolyn Woodward, University of New Mexico
Julia Wright, Wilfrid Laurier University
Julian Yates, University of Delaware
Arlene Young, University of Manitoba
Lisa Zeitz, University of Western Ontario

THE AGE OF ROMANTICISM

Perhaps more than any other era in English history, the Romantic period expressed its ongoing evolution in its clothing. When the artistic, literary, and political changes that are usually associated with Romanticism began in the 1780s, the heavy and elaborate costumes of the eighteenth century still prevailed, constricting their wearers into a rigid formality mirrored in the contemporaneous social and aesthetic structures. In the years surrounding the French Revolution, heady with the possibility of greater freedom, these stiff garments gave way to loose, flowing dresses for women, cut from muslins and patterned cottons that had been rendered relatively inexpensive by increasing British Imperial control in the East and by technological advances in weaving in Britain itself. During the same period local militiamen, sporting gorgeous military uniforms, demonstrated both Britain's growing national pride and its persistent fear of French invasion. By the time the Romantic period drew to a close in the mid-1830s, these looser fashions and glittering uniforms had themselves been superseded by the tightly-laced corsets, salt-and-pepper trousers, and bell skirts heavily supported by hoops and petticoats that are now inextricably associated with English Victorianism.

Ball dress, c. 1800.

Morning dress, c. 1800.

Richard Dighton, *George "Beau" Brummell*, 1805. Brummell, the leading "dandy" of the age, brought into fashion a new style of dress coat, pantaloons, and black evening dress for men. Brummell was fastidious about cleanliness as well as clothing, but denounced perfume for men and any form of showy display.

As the combination of freedom and militarism expressed in Romantic fashions suggests, the fifty years between the French Revolution and the reign of Queen Victoria were neither historically simple nor culturally straightforward. Despite its seeming cohesiveness and unity, the Romantic period was a complex nexus of revolution and conservatism, of bold iconoclasm and hidebound conventionality.

Revolutions played a central role in shaping the Romantic period—and continue to shape our perceptions of it. The form and structure of the British Romantic era, and of the concept "Romanticism" itself, have changed radically in recent decades. What in the mid-twentieth century was seen as a literary period centered on five or six major poets, all male, and a select number of prose writers, also all male, has gradually come to be seen as an era in which writers and thinkers of different genders, beliefs, and social backgrounds all contributed to shaping their era. Whereas students once covered British Romantic poetry by reading only William Blake, William Wordsworth, Samuel Taylor Coleridge, Lord Byron, Percy Shelley, and John Keats (collectively known as "The Big Six"), they now also hear the voices of Mary Robinson, Anna Letitia Barbauld, Felicia Hemans, and Letitia Landon—all respected and popular in their day but largely unstudied until recently. Whereas reading Romantic prose nonfiction once meant for the most part reading Coleridge, Charles Lamb, and William Hazlitt, students now explore the proto-feminist writing of Mary Wollstonecraft, the didactic prose of Hannah More and Maria Edgeworth, and myriad others. The prose fiction of the period (aside from a nod or two acknowledging Jane Austen and Sir Walter Scott) was once given short shrift, and the drama even less. Nowadays Mary Shelley's novels—particularly *Frankenstein* and *The Last Man*—receive at least as much critical attention as do the works of her spouse, with *Frankenstein* probably being read more widely than any other single work of the Romantic period; Austen's works are now seen to hold a central position in the history of the novel; and the work of other writers of fiction—from William Godwin to Mary Hays, Amelia Opie, Mary Robinson, and Charlotte Smith—has been much more fully and more favorably assessed. In the study of drama a similar if less marked shift has occurred, with the importance of the work of Hannah Cowley, Elizabeth Inchbald and Joanna Baillie, as well as that of Percy Shelley and of Byron, being newly recognized.

If recent decades have brought a substantial shift in the emphasis placed on various authors in the study of the Romantic period, they have also brought a shift in the way the period as a whole is perceived. Whereas Romantic literature in English was once discussed far more with reference to nature and to the imagination than it was with reference to politics or to ideology, a broader perspective is now almost universally acknowledged as essential to a comprehensive understanding of the period. At the same time, it is still almost universally accepted that the Romantic mind-set and the literary works it produced were shaped, above all, by the French Revolution and the Industrial Revolution.

For Romanticism, the French Revolution was epoch-making. When the Bastille fell on 14 July 1789 and the French National Assembly issued its demo-cratic, anti-monarchical *Declaration of the Rights of Man and Citizen* on August 27 of the same year, it seemed to the people of Great Britain, a mere twelve miles across the Channel, that a new dawn was on the horizon. For liberals and for many authors, artists, and intellectuals, this dawn was a rosy one, promising not only greater equality and better government in France itself, but also the beginning of a thoroughgoing transformation of the world. Mary Robinson's "Ainsi Va Le Monde" (1791) provides a vivid sense of the degree to which a fervent faith in and enthusiasm for freedom knew no bounds in the breasts of many writers of the time:

> Hark! "Freedom" echoes thro' the vaulted skies.
> The goddess speaks! O mark the blest decree,—
> Tyrants Shall Fall—Triumphant Man Be Free!

Wordsworth, present in France during the early days of the Revolution, famously wrote of it later, "Bliss was it in that dawn to be alive!", while his friend and fellow poet Robert Southey recalled that "a visionary world seemed to open ... [N]othing was dreamt of but regen-eration of the human race." Mary Wollstonecraft, who had recently published *A Vindication of the Rights of Woman*, moved to Paris in 1792, also inspired by revo-lutionary idealism. The Revolution became a central metaphor in the works of William Blake, and a central psychological influence on all the first generation Romantic writers.

The younger generation too, particularly Byron and Shelley, were stirred by revolutionary fervor. What these poets hoped for, however, was a continuation of the *spirit* of the French Revolution. For, in actuality, Words-worth's new dawn soon darkened into a terrible thun-derstorm and a rain of blood. In August of 1792, the leaders of the Revolution overthrew the French monar-chy, and a month later a Paris mob massacred more than a thousand prisoners whom they believed to be royalist conspirators. Extremist Jacobins[1] now prevailed over more moderate Girondins, and the Revolution turned into the Reign of Terror (1793–94). In January 1793, King Louis XVI went to the guillotine; Marie Antoi-nette followed him in October. France declared war on Britain in 1793, and Britain reciprocated. As the terror progressed under the guidance of Maximilien Robes-pierre, thousands of aristocrats, clergy, and alleged opponents of the Revolution were guillotined including, eventually, Robespierre himself. In 1794 France offered to support any and all revolutions abroad, and then proceeded to invade its neighbors. In 1799, Napoleon had himself named First Consul for life, and in 1804 he crowned himself Emperor. When he invaded the Iberian Peninsula in 1807, Britain intervened to aid the Spanish and Portuguese: what became known as the Napoleonic Wars did not end until Napoleon was thoroughly routed at the Battle of Waterloo in 1815.

What had begun as a movement for democracy, then, had become a military dictatorship. Looking back from a distance of twenty-four years, Byron wrote that the French made themselves a fearful monument:

> The wreck of old opinions ...
> ... the veil they rent
> And what behind it lay all earth shall view.
> But good with ill they also overthrew,
> Leaving but ruins, wherewith to rebuild
> Upon the same foundation, and renew
> Dungeons and thrones ... (*Childe Harold* 3.82)

The Revolution's promise of freedom died in a frenzy of oppression, destruction, violence, and imperi-alism, and many of Britain's intellectuals watched in horror, gradually turning from bold liberalism to a cautious conservatism they saw as both pragmatic and necessary. To use the political terminology that first developed out of the seating arrangements in the French National Constituent Assembly in 1789, they moved from the left of center to the right of center; Words-worth, Coleridge, and Southey, all radical thinkers in their youth, were firm conservatives by the end of their

---

[1] Throughout the Romantic period the terms "Jacobin" and "anti-Jacobin" were employed to describe those in sympathy with and those opposed to revolutionary ideals of the sort that had been promulgated during the French Revolution.

William Heath, *The Battle of Waterloo* (detail), 1815. British infantrymen to the right are firing into the ranks of the French cavalry. The full battle involved approximately 75,000 French troops under Napoleon; the Duke of Wellington commanded an allied force of well over 100,000. The casualties totaled over 50,000—60 per cent of them French.

lives. Others—such as Barbauld—remained politically on the left, but became disillusioned both by the course that revolution had taken in France and by the failure of the British to embrace the principles of freedom. Barbauld surveyed what seemed to her a decadent and oppressive England in "Eighteen Hundred and Eleven" —"The worm is in thy core, thy glories pass away"—and Shelley despaired in "England in 1819" at "Rulers who neither see nor feel nor know, / But leech-like to their fainting country cling."

The British government's response to the developments in France had been swift and repressive. In 1794 they suspended the right of habeas corpus, which required the state to show legitimate cause for imprisonment and to carry out trials in a timely manner. As a result, those accused of crimes could be held for an indefinite period. In 1795, Parliament passed the Treasonable Practices Act, which made criticism of the government a crime; in the same year it passed an act

that limited the size of public meetings and the places in which they could be held. The Combination Acts of 1799 and 1800 forbade workers to associate for the purposes of collective bargaining. To enforce all these restrictive measures, the government set loose a herd of spies, many of whom acted as *agents provocateurs*, infiltrating liberal and radical groups and prompting them to commit criminal acts they otherwise might not have committed. In at least one important case, that of the Cato Street Conspiracy of 1820 (a scheme to murder cabinet ministers and stage a government *coup*), these government agents first urged on and then exposed conspirators who were punished with hanging or with transportation to Australia. In Scotland and Ireland, authoritarianism could be even more severe, particularly since rebellion there required no instigating: in 1798, the United Irishmen, led by Theobald Wolfe Tone and Lord Edward Fitzgerald and assisted by French forces, attempted a country-wide uprising to achieve complete Irish independence. The rebellion ended in failure, and the oppression of the Irish under British rule became more strongly entrenched than ever.

T.W. Huffram, *Theobald Wolfe Tone*, date unknown. Tone is shown in French uniform.

James Gillray, *United Irishmen in Training*, 1798. The famous English caricaturist here portrays the Irish as cruel buffoons; they are assaulting a British uniform stuffed with straw.

If the French Revolution and the 22 years of war with France that followed produced ruinous government authoritarianism, they also acted to create for the first time a widespread and shared sense among British citizens that England, Wales, Scotland and, to a lesser extent, Ireland, formed one cohesive nation: Great Britain. Scotland had been linked to England by the Union of 1707, while union with Ireland, which had been firmly under English control since the time of Cromwell, was made official with the Act of Union in 1800. The wars with France allowed the English people to see themselves as leading a larger body defending liberty and freedom (even if that liberty and freedom were now, ironically, defined by a conservative authoritarian mind-set). At the same time, the wars raised very real threats of invasion—there were scares in 1778, 1796–98, and 1803, and Wales was actually invaded in 1797. As so often happens, threats from without acted to foster cohesion within. Foreign travel was out of the question for all but the very rich or the very brave; Great Britain turned inward and discovered itself, instead. Sir Walter Scott's collection of folk-songs and ballads, *Minstrelsy of the Scottish Border* (1802–03), Thomas Moore's *Irish Melodies* (1807–34), and Felicia Hemans's *Welsh Melodies* (1822), all gave their readers a sense of the nation's rich past, while at the same time celebrating the blend of cultures that went into making up Great Britain. Regional poets such as Robert Burns and John Clare gave proud voice to those cultures, so that the individual nations which made up the one great nation were simultaneously celebrated in and recognized as within the British fold. Long poetical works such as John Thelwall's *The Hope of Albion; or Edwin of Northumbria* (1801) expanded the sense of an epic British mythology, while collections such as Hemans's *Tales and Historic Scenes* (1819), a celebration of military valor, fostered a sense of pride in present-day accomplishments.

The sense of a larger Britain, though, did nothing to lessen the belief among the English that England was specifically and even divinely favored. Such notions were perhaps given their most memorable, if also most ambivalent, expression in the opening to William Blake's "Preface" to *Milton* (1804), in which ancient England is linked with Christ:

And did those feet in ancient time
Walk upon England's mountain's green?
And was the Holy Lamb of God
On England's pleasant pastures seen?
And did the countenance divine
Shine forth upon our clouded hills?[1]

Although Blake leaves it up to his reader to deter-mine whether the answer to these rhetorical questions is yes or no, the stanza that follows explicitly figures England as a land worthy to be the new Jerusalem (if only sometime in the future):

I will not cease from mental fight,
Nor shall my sword sleep in my hand,
Till we have built Jerusalem
In England's green and pleasant land.

Between these invocations of the divine in Britain, however, Blake inserts an insidious question, and one that began to plague English writers and citizens more and more as the Romantic period progressed: "was Jerusalem builded here/Among these dark Satanic mills?" The phrase "dark Satanic mills" has become the most famous description of the force at the center of the industrial revolution. Even as the French Revolution changed the consciousness of the British people, this other revolution in their own country had as much impact on them as did any conflagration abroad.

Beginning in the sixteenth and seventeenth centuries the British Isles, and England in particular, had been undergoing wholesale changes in economic structure. The pace of change increased dramatically as the eigh-teenth century progressed. From being a largely rural

Thomas Girtin, *Westminster from Lambeth*, c. 1800. Girtin's watercolor was one of a series of sketches for a panorama of London (now lost).

[1] *And did those feet ... clouded hills* The opening two stanzas (a total of 16 lines) were set to music by Charles H.H. Parry in 1916; under the title "Jerusalem," these verses have become an unofficial national anthem for the English.

nation with a largely agricultural economy, Britain became an urban nation with an economy based in manufacturing. James Watt's refinement of the steam engine, and James Hargreaves's invention of the Spinning Jenny (a machine that allowed cotton to be woven on several spindles simultaneously) are only the most famous of a host of changes that produced a boom in industrialization. Factories sprang up in what had once been countryside: the populations of towns and cities, particularly those associated with manufacture, swelled. At the beginning of the 1770s, about a quarter of England's population lived in urban centers, but by 1801 that proportion had risen to one third, and by the 1840s half of the English population resided in cities. In 1750, the total English population was roughly 5.5 million; by the time of the first census in 1800, it had grown to 8 million, while the population of Scotland and Ireland totaled more than 6.5 million. By 1831, the total population of Great Britain was thus approximately 14 million. This increase fueled the Industrial Revolution from both ends, supplying more consumers eager to acquire goods and more able bodies to work in factories that produced those goods.

Industrialization also contributed to an important shift in the country's social structure. The paradigm of classes and ranks that placed the nobility at the top with everyone else keeping to their places beneath had begun to change as early as the seventeenth century, as those involved in business and commerce grew wealthy enough to exert power of their own. The process was greatly accelerated in the late eighteenth and early nineteenth centuries as more and more factory owners and other men of business (they were exclusively male) amassed larger and larger fortunes. Still, the road that led from newly acquired wealth to social acceptance remained a long and circuitous one. An inherited fortune stemming from longstanding ownership of large amounts of land (and the rents thereby produced) remained the most respectable form of wealth. To possess a good deal of money as a result not of belonging to the "landed gentry" but rather of having amassed it through commercial activity was considered more than faintly disreputable. It might take two or three generations before the taint of anyone in the family having been "in trade" (a term applied to industrialists as much

Illustration of an early locomative engine, 1808.

as to tradesmen) was removed, and the source of the family fortune forgotten. The social nuances involved in such transitions are vividly captured by Jane Austen, for example, when she describes the Bingley sisters in *Pride and Prejudice*:

> They were rather handsome, had been educated in one of the first private seminaries in town, had a fortune of twenty thousand pounds, were in the habit of spending more than they ought, and of associating with people of rank; and were therefore in every respect entitled to think well of themselves, and meanly of others. They were of a respectable family in the north of England; a circumstance more deeply impressed on their memories than that their brother's fortune and their own had been acquired by trade.

Fine gradations of respectability attached to every occupation, with social position often at odds with

George and I.R. Cruikshank, *Sporting a Toe at Almacks*, 1821. Many clubs were restricted to men; Almack's was an exclusive London club controlled by a group of society women. During "the season" a fashionable ball was held at Almack's every week.

financial circumstances. Members of the clergy and their families, for instance, though sometimes impecunious, were generally respected. Whether members of the gentry or born into the working class, they often moved in elevated social circles. Physicians, defined as those medical men who had a degree from a university, could sometimes move in the "best circles" in a community, although apothecaries and surgeons, who gained their knowledge through apprenticeship, could not.

Even the Romantic literary world reflects the increased social mobility possible in the period. John Keats, for example, was the son of a stable keeper who had increased his financial standing by marrying the daughter of the stable owner. Keats trained as a surgeon-apothecary (a job that combined the duties of present-day pharmacist, general practitioner, and surgeon), but at the age of 18 he came into an inheritance and devoted himself entirely to literature. He wrote to a friend that he thought he would "be among the English poets" after his death, and as it turned out, no social barriers could prevent that from occurring. Similarly, Samuel Taylor Coleridge, a parson's son who attended a London charity school as a child, ended his life lauded and respected as "The Sage of Highgate."

The Industrial Revolution may have increased social mobility, and certainly it allowed goods to be produced more efficiently. But it also devastated large portions of England's underclasses, the agricultural laborers and peasants who had benefited, however slightly, from the land-based economy that was passing away. Wordsworth's reference in "Tintern Abbey" to "vagrant dwellers in the houseless woods" describes a very real phenomenon. In the late eighteenth and early nineteenth centuries, a series of Enclosure Acts resulted in the conversion of formerly common land into large, privately-held farms. The process of enclosure was not new; it had been occurring since the late Middle Ages, in response to population pressures and as Britain was transformed first into a largely mercantile economy and then into an industrial society. While enclosures did often result in something of an increase in agricultural production, they also often spelled ruin for thousands of small farmers. Large landholders benefitted from their enlarged acreage, but many of those who had heretofore been able to eke out a living from a tiny patch of land and sell their modest surpluses now lost all ability to support themselves. These smallholders and their families were forced either to labor for others for meager wages, to migrate to the city and enter the manufacturing workforce, or to turn to begging or thievery. Poor harvests in 1794–95, 1799–1800, and 1810–11 worsened the plight of the rural poor even further. The proliferation of vandals, vagrants, and beggars in the writing of this era reflected a growing social reality.

The leading literary figures of the day were for the most part sympathetic to the plight of the poor in a time of growing inequity, but beyond that held widely divergent attitudes concerning these developments, and concerning the commoners themselves. Barbauld was one who sought to ameliorate the inequities that had become so characteristic of English life; she cast a cold eye on the power relations involved and had harsh criticism for the privileged, but also took an un-idealized view of commoners, seeing them as prey to vice as much as virtue, in reaction to the circumstances in which they had been placed through economic hardship, lack of education, and so on. As she wrote in *Thoughts on the Inequality of Conditions* (1800),

> Power enables the indolent and the useless not only to retain, but to add to their possessions, by taking from the industrious the natural reward of their labour, and applying it to their own use ... It is not sufficiently considered how many virtues depend upon comfort, and cleanliness, and decent apparel. Destroy dirt and misery, and you will destroy at once a great many vices.

It is the very different approach of William Wordsworth, however, that has come to be seen as characteristic of British Romanticism. Wordsworth's focus was much less on the struggle to ameliorate conditions than it was on the value of recognizing the worth inherent in the hearts and minds of rural common folk—and the poetic value that they represented. In the same year as Barbauld wrote *Thoughts on the Inequality of Conditions* Wordsworth expressed his ideals in this connection in the 1800 "Preface" to *Lyrical Ballads*:

> The principal object, then, proposed in these Poems was to choose incidents and situations from common life ... Humble and rustic life was generally chosen, because, in that condition, the essential passions of the heart find a better soil in which they can attain their maturity, are less under restraint, and speak a plainer and more emphatic language; because in that condition of life our elementary feelings coexist in a state of greater simplicity, and, consequently, may be more accurately contemplated, and more forcibly communicated; because the manners of rural life germinate from those elementary feelings, and, from the necessary character of rural occupations, are more easily comprehended, and are more durable; and, lastly, because in that condition the passions of men are incorporated with the beautiful and permanent forms of nature.

Poems such as "Michael," "The Ruined Cottage," "Idiot Boy" and "Resolution and Independence" represent Wordsworth's attempt to put those ideals into practice. In "Resolution and Independence," the poet encounters an old, poor, itinerant leech-gatherer, and ends by admiring "In that decrepit Man so firm a mind." Whereas Barbauld regarded theft as a justifiable response to the oppression of extreme poverty in an iniquitous social system, Wordsworth pays homage to the old leech-gatherer for earning an "honest maintenance" despite the "many hardships" he must endure.

If the rural poor fared badly during these years, life for the workers in the cities and the unemployed poor was just as bad. In 1815, at the instigation of large land holders who stood to benefit from high prices for grain, the government passed the Corn Laws to institute a substantial tariff on imports of grain from foreign countries, making such imports much more expensive. ("Corn" in Britain denotes grain, most commonly wheat; what North Americans call "corn" is referred to in Britain as "maize.") The effect of the tariff was to protect British grain producers, and to inflate the price of bread and other foodstuffs for the consumer. The poor in the cities suffered particularly, and from 1815 until the Corn Laws were finally repealed in 1845 they remained a lightning rod for political dissent.

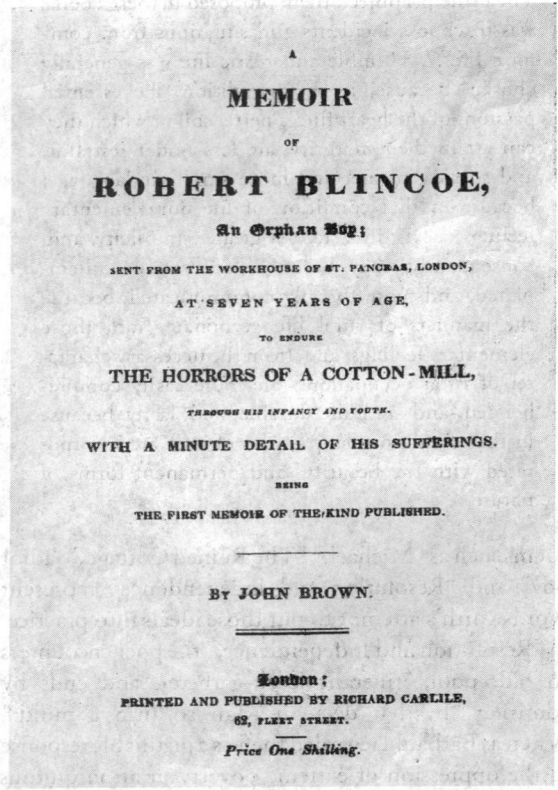

A

MEMOIR

OF

ROBERT BLINCOE,

An Orphan Boy;

SENT FROM THE WORKHOUSE OF ST. PANCRAS, LONDON,

AT SEVEN YEARS OF AGE,

TO ENDURE

THE HORRORS OF A COTTON-MILL,

THROUGH HIS INFANCY AND YOUTH,

WITH A MINUTE DETAIL OF HIS SUFFERINGS,

BEING

THE FIRST MEMOIR OF THE KIND PUBLISHED.

———

By JOHN BROWN.

———

London:

PRINTED AND PUBLISHED BY RICHARD CARLILE,
62, FLEET STREET.

Price One Shilling.

Title page, *A Memoir of Robert Blincoe*, first published in 1828, re-issued in 1832. Demonstrations in 1832 and 1833 for factory reform frequently cited the evidence of factory conditions that he had provided, and Blincoe testified before the Royal Commission that investigated the issue of child labor in 1833.

Had conditions for the urban poor been better in other respects, the Corn Laws might have had less impact. The British government, however, assured by Adam Smith's highly influential work of economic philosophy, *The Wealth of Nations* (1777), that the best way to encourage national economic success was to leave businesses free to grow without hindrance, for the most part adopted a *laissez-faire* approach to regulating treatment of employees and working conditions during this period. In practice, "laissez-faire" meant shifts of as much as 15 hours at a stretch, often for very young children. Wages were kept as low as manufacturers could manage, and injuries were common; children were the preferred workers for clearing jams in mechanized looms, for example, and the frequent result was the loss of the tiny fingers and hands that made them ideal for the job. Workers' health was often ruined by unsanitary working and living conditions (employers often owned not only the factories, but the slums in which their workers lived), and by unfettered pollution.

It is often assumed that the worst extremes of the Industrial Revolution in Britain occurred during the Victorian era, but by the time Victoria came to the throne, Parliament had already been pressed to take a succession of measures to restrict the abuse of children: the largely ineffectual Health and Morals of Apprentices Act (1802), the Regulation of Cotton Mills and Factories Act (1819), and the Act to Regulate the Labour of Children and Young Persons in the Mills and Factories of the United Kingdom (1833). Even after the passage of this last, children as young as nine could be forced to work nine hour days, and 13 year-olds to work 12 hour days, but that represented a degree of improvement from the late eighteenth and early nineteenth centuries. Robert Blincoe, for example, an orphan raised in a London workhouse and transported in 1799, at the age of seven, to work in the Lowdham Mill near Nottingham, described his life at the mill to John Brown in 1829:

> Blincoe heard the burring sound [of the machinery] before he reached the portals and smelt the fumes of the oil with which the axles of twenty-thousand wheels and spindles were bathed the moment he entered the doors. The noise appalled him, and the stench seemed intolerable. It was the custom at Lowdham Mills, as it is in most water mills, to make the apprentices work up lost time [i.e., time when the machines had been unable to run during regular working hours], by working over hours … When

children of seven years of age had to work fourteen hours every day in the week, Sundays excepted, any addition was severely felt ... Almost from the first hour [Blincoe] entered the Mill, till he arrived at a state of manhood, it was one continual round of cruel and arbitrary punishment.... I asked him if he could state the average number of times in which he might safely say he had suffered corporal punishment in a week. His answer invariably was, that his punishments were so various and so frequent, it was impossible to state with anything approaching to accuracy.... Supper consisted of milk-porridge, of a very blue complexion [together with] bread partly made of rye—very black, and so soft they could scarcely swallow it, as it stuck like bird-lime to their teeth.

If the Government addressed such outrages only with reluctance (sometimes Parliamentary committees looking into allegations would not hear any direct testimony of the workers), many citizens found them harder to ignore. Demonstrations of popular dissatisfaction were frequent and took various forms. Luddites, followers of the imaginary "General Ned Ludd," attacked and broke machinery during the years 1811–16, sometimes to force concessions from their employers but sometimes to express their dissatisfaction with creeping mechanization. After the bad harvests and the passage of the Corn Laws in 1815, food riots occurred across the country. Coercion Acts were passed in 1817 to try to stifle dissent, but they provoked strong antagonism, and both in London and in parts of Scotland some republican groups advocated revolution. Farm workers staged violent protests throughout the 1820s that culminated in mass barn-burning in 1830. Perhaps the most famous popular uprising was the 1819 gathering of nearly a hundred thousand mill workers at St. Peter's Field, near Manchester. A peaceful demonstration that ended with an address to the crowd by the radical Henry "Orator" Hunt (1773–1835), this gathering so alarmed the local gentry that they sent drunken, armed militiamen to break it up and arrest Hunt. The militiamen attacked the crowd with their sabres when it jeered them, and the ensuing melee left eleven dead, including one trampled child, and more than four hundred injured, many from sabre wounds.

"Peterloo," as it came to be dubbed by the radical press, in reference to the British victory at Waterloo four years earlier, was a seminal event in nineteenth-century politics and economics. Parliament did nothing to relieve the sufferings of these poor or the hundreds of thousands like them, but rather strengthened its repressive powers by passing the Six Acts at the end of 1819. These Acts made it a crime to demonstrate; gave magistrates the power to enter private homes to search for weapons; outlawed meetings of more than 50 people unless all those attending a meeting were residents of the parish in which the meeting was held (thus effectively curtailing any kind of large gatherings); tightened the guidelines on what could be considered blasphemous or treasonous libel; and raised the newspaper tax, thus effectively cutting the circulation of formerly inexpensive radical newspapers. The Six Acts were so repugnant to certain members of the liberal Whig party who would later become powerful politicians that they led in the long run to the liberal Reform Act of 1832. Thus, the eventual result of the massacre was a measure of relief from the extraordinarily repressive measures it had spawned.

POLITICAL PARTIES AND ROYAL ALLEGIANCES

For most of this period, the upheavals among the lower classes found little reflection in the English government, where the Tories held sway from 1783-1830, with only one short interruption. The Tories were the conservative party: they saw themselves as upholders of law and tradition, determined to preserve the prevailing political and social order. From 1793 to 1801, and again from 1804-1806, the Tories and the country were led by Prime Minister William Pitt, whose fiscal restraint and willingness to suppress political protest (sometimes with open brutality) made him a hero to some but a villain to many others. Pitt died in office in 1806, certainly of overwork and probably of alcoholism; his last words were either, "Oh, my country! how I leave my country!" or "I think I could eat one of Bellamy's veal pies," depending on the source. The Tories continued in power, on their own or in coalition, until 1830.

The Whigs, who remained the party of opposition during this time, ranged themselves against the Tories as advocates of greater civil and religious liberty. In reality, neither party would have been called "Liberals" or "Democrats" by today's standards, but the Whigs did advocate the abolition of the slave trade, Catholic emancipation (which would allow greater political participation to Catholics, heretofore barred from a role in government), and Parliamentary reform. From 1782–1806, the leader of the Whigs was the charismatic Charles James Fox, gambler, gourmand, and political colossus, whose political machinations made him as many enemies as friends. Not until 1806, a year after Fox's death, would the Whigs participate in government—and then for only a relatively short period, as part of a coalition. They would not gain power in their own right until 1830. They were then at last able to pass the Reform Act of 1832 (also known as the Great Reform Act), which extended voting rights to a broader spectrum of propertied males,[1] redistributed Parliamentary seats, and brought significantly fairer political representation.

While the politicians plotted and schemed, the British Royal Family suffered its own difficulties. George III, who had ascended the throne in 1760, embodied Toryism both politically and personally: traditionalist, ponderous, and domestic, he produced a large family, embraced conservative politics, and allegedly liked to wander the countryside incognito, chatting with farmers. In 1788, however, he suffered a bout of mental illness that lasted until early 1789. This illness, now believed to be the result of the hereditary blood disease porphyria, reappeared in 1810, leaving him permanently insane. In 1811, when it became apparent that the King would not recover, his eldest son was declared Regent.

Monarchs of the House of Hanover traditionally clashed with their eldest sons, and George III and the Prince who would become George IV were no different. Bred to wait for his father to die, growing ever fatter (at the end of his life he weighed more than 300 pounds), the Regent was a stark contrast to his thrifty father. In 1787, when he was 25, his debts totaled more than £160,000 (equivalent to about £8,000,000 today). He lived with a Roman Catholic mistress whom he later

Sir Thomas Lawrence, *The Prince Regent in Profile*, c. 1814. The Prince knighted Lawrence, the leading English portraitist of the day, in 1815, saying that he was "proud in conferring a mark of favor on one who had raised the character of British art in the estimation of all Europe."

married, secretly and unconstitutionally, before abandoning her for a series of other mistresses. Later, to secure relief from debts, he married his cousin Caroline of Brunswick, a woman he found so totally and instantly loathsome that his first words upon seeing her were, "I am not well; pray get me a glass of brandy." Although they did manage to produce one daughter, Charlotte, who later died in childbirth, the Prince and his wife never lived together, and his attempt to divorce her after his accession in 1820 was one of the great scandals of the period.

George IV was not without redeeming virtues; notably, he was a keen patron of the arts, particularly architecture. In addition to a magnificent pavilion in Brighton, he and his architects built Trafalgar Square, modified and improved Buckingham House into

---

[1] The changes are estimated to have altered the composition of the electorate to approximately one in seven males from fewer than one in ten.

Buckingham Palace, and created parks, streets, and crescents throughout London. He was an enthusiastic reader and promoter of literature, as well as a generous patron of the sciences, establishing several fellowships and prizes. Nonetheless, the Prince became a figure of increasing public contempt. Leigh Hunt described him as "a libertine head over heels in debt and disgrace, a despiser of domestic ties." Percy Shelley called him, in prose, an "overgrown bantling [infant]," and, in poetry, "the dregs of [his] dull race." When he died in 1830, *The Times* wrote, "There never was an individual less regretted by his fellow creatures than this dead King."

Sir Thomas Lawrence, *Caroline Amelia Elizabeth of Brunswick*, 1804 (detail).

IMPERIAL EXPANSION

At the same time that Britain was experiencing its own internal power struggles and upheavals, the nation was expanding its presence around the globe. Throughout the first half of the nineteenth century, Britain was well on its way to forging the Empire that would reach full flower in the Victorian period. The East India Company, founded by a group of London merchants in 1600, controlled most of Eastern India by 1765, and thereafter continued to extend their administrative and governmental control over the sub-continent. British interest in China began in the late eighteenth century, when Britain began to import the tea that would soon become a staple of the British table, and rose throughout the 1800s. Increased contact with (and domination of) various parts of the Far East led to increased fascination with its cultures, a fascination widely reflected in literature. "Eastern" influence pervades the prose and poetry of this period, from William Beckford's novel *The History of the Caliph Vathek* (1786), to Byron's *Eastern Tales* (1813–14), to Percy Shelley's *Alastor* (1816), where the protagonist makes his way

> through Arabie
> And Persia, and the wild Carmanian waste,
> And o'er the aerial mountains which pour down
> Indus and Oxus from their icy caves,
> In joy and exultation [he] held his icy way,
> Till in the vale of Cashmire …
> he stretched
> His languid limbs.

Wearing her India cotton frock, sipping her tea from Canton, coffee from Yemen, or chocolate from Mexico, the English consumer of the Romantic period felt the influence of imperial expansion not only in the commodities she purchased but in the pages she turned.

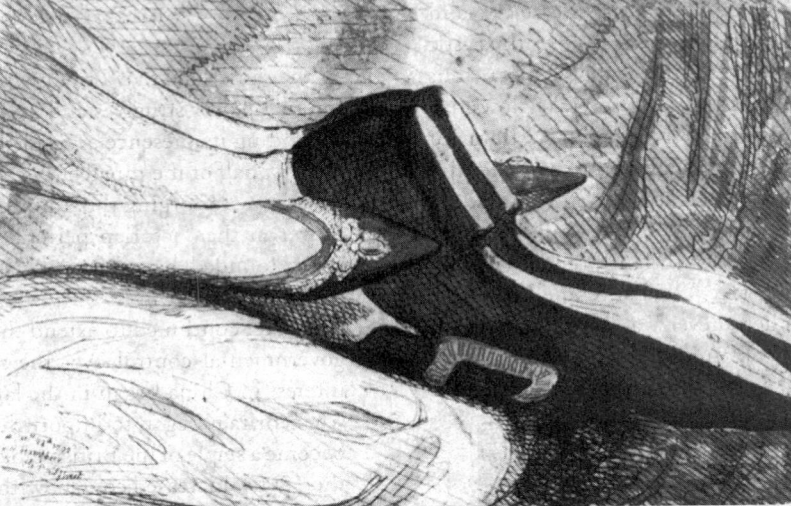

James Gillray, *Fashionable Contrasts, or the Duchess' Little Shoe Yielding to the Magnitude of the Duke's Foot*, 1792. At the time, the press had been fawning over Princess Frederica Charlotte Ulrica Catherina, who had just married Frederick Augustus, Duke of York; the daintiness of her feet had been particularly praised.

James Gillray, *The Plum Pudding in Danger*, 1805. Napoleon and British Prime Minister William Pitt are shown carving up the globe, with Napoleon skewering Europe and Pitt helping himself to the ocean. (1805 saw both the Battle of Trafalgar, at which the British under Lord Nelson established dominance at sea; and the Battle of Austerlitz, at which Napoleon defeated Russian and Austrian armies to cement his control of the Continent.)

Sir Charles D'Oyly, *The Emporium of Taylor & Co. in Calcutta*, c. 1825–28.

But if the British Empire brought rewards to the nation's citizens, it all too often entailed exploitation and horror in the colonies themselves. Chief amongst these was the slavery that fueled the economy of the British West Indies. The mass of sugar required to sweeten Britain's tea, coffee, and chocolate was cultivated, cut, and processed on these islands by slaves who worked under inhuman conditions until they literally wore out—at which point their white masters simply purchased fresh replacements. Over the course of the eighteenth century, British slavers transported some three million slaves to the West Indies and other agricultural colonies; the economic success of the port towns Bristol and Liverpool was based in large part on the important part they played in the English slave trade—and the trade in sugar from plantations that relied on slave labor. (At the start of the American Revolution, British imports from the largest sugar plantation center, Jamaica, were worth five times more than British imports from the 13 colonies.)

Arguably the strongest resistance to slavery in the West Indies came from the slaves themselves. The British invaded the formerly French island of Saint-Dominique in 1793 in order to aid in the suppression of a slave uprising led by Toussaint L'Ouverture, but withdrew five years later, having sent more troops to the West Indies over that period than they had sent to America during the War of Independence. When a subsequent effort by Napoleon also failed and the former slaves founded the Republic of Haiti in 1804, the message that emancipation was inevitable had registered widely in Britain.

Emancipation was also spurred by a widespread and effective protest movement within Britain. Between

1787, when protests first began, and 1791, abolitionists gathered 500 petitions against slavery from across Britain. In all some 400,00 signatures were collected; this was Britain's first large-scale petition campaign. The Abolitionist movement attracted support from Evangelicals, from Whig politicians, and from radicals, and has been described as the first British political movement in the modern sense. The leading figures in the movement were abolitionists Thomas Clarkson, Granville Sharp, and William Wilberforce, but it also drew considerable support from the poets of the day, among them William Cowper, Hannah More, William Blake, Mary Robinson, and Anne Cromarty Yearsley (whose *A Poem on the Inhumanity of the Slave Trade* [1788] inveighed against the very business that supported her home town of Bristol), and Anna Laetitia Barbauld.

Central to the literature of the Abolitionist movement were books written by former slaves such as Olaudah Equiano and Mary Prince, which laid out plainly the horrors of a slave's life and openly sought sympathy and fellow-feeling from readers. In his autobiography, *The Interesting Narrative of the Life of Olaudah Equiano* (1786), Equiano described conditions both in West Indies and in America. As he observed with telling effect, the system bred degradation for "free negroes" as well as for slaves:

> I have often seen slaves, particularly those who were meagre, in different islands, put into scales and weighed; and then sold from three pence to six pence to nine pence a pound. My master, however, whose humanity was shocked at this mode, used to sell by the lump. And at or after a sale it was not uncommon to see negroes taken from their wives, wives taken from their husbands, and children from their parents, and sent off to other islands, and wherever else their merciless lords chose, and probably never more during life to see each other! ...
> [Free negroes] live in constant alarm for their liberty; and even this is but nominal, for they are universally insulted and plundered without the possibility of redress; for such is the equity of West Indian laws, that no free negro's evidence will be admitted in their courts of justice.

Accounts such as these, coupled with a determined and prolonged campaign and with the effects of the growth of the Asian sugar trade, led to the abolition of the slave trade in 1806–7, and (following another uprising, this time in Jamaica in 1831–32) to an Act in 1833 that provided for the full abolition of slavery. The persecution of blacks by whites, however, continued both in the West Indies and throughout the British Empire.

Noticeably absent from the list of Abolitionist writers are several of the leading names of English Romantic poetry. Wordsworth,[1] Coleridge, Byron, Shelley and Keats were in general all sympathetic with the aims of the Abolitionist movement, and Coleridge in particular spoke out strongly both against slavery itself and against the maintenance of the slave trade, memorably writing that "a slave is a person perverted into a thing," and slavery is not so much "a deviation from justice as an absolute subversion of all morality." It has been plausibly suggested that some major works of Romantic poetry (notably Coleridge's "The Rime of the Ancient Mariner" and Keats's "Lamia") may usefully be read in relation to the slave trade. But directly pressing for the abolition of slavery through verse in the manner of Cowper, Robinson, and Yearsley was never a significant part of their poetic agenda.

THE ROMANTIC MIND AND ITS LITERARY PRODUCTIONS

It is not surprising that in a world overwhelmingly concerned with change, revolution, and freedom, the makers of literature should be similarly preoccupied; as discussed above, the French Revolution and its aftermath lent vital force to the Romantic impulse. That force, though, was not exerted on all the literary minds in the Romantic era with equal force, or in quite the same direction. For several of the leading figures of English Romanticism, the freedom that animated the poetic imagination was only tangentially related to the collectivist enterprise that the revolution in France had represented. Instead, it was very much an *individual* freedom; the freeing of the individual mind and the

---

[1] Wordsworth admitted that in the 1790s "this particular strife had wanted power / To rivet my affections." He did write two sonnets (one to Clarkson, one to Toussaint L'Ouverture) in 1807, the year in which abolition of the slave trade was accomplished.

individual soul took pride of place. Subjective experience and the role that it played in the individual's response to and experience of reality are dominant themes in the works of the Romantics. Wordsworth's "Ode: Intimations of Immortality" surveys what becomes of the "heaven-born freedom" with which every individual who enters the world is born. Percy Shelley's *Mont Blanc* is an extended exploration of power and creativity, and Keats's Odes continually express their author's fascination with the connection between physical experience and the individual human imagination. In Byron, subjectivity, creativity, and epistemological questing all find expression in a series of heroes for whom the power of the Will is a central concern. The question of what it means to be an individual looms large in the works of all these authors.

Nature became a fulcrum in the balancing of subjective and objective in the Romantic construction of reality; most of the period's leading writers remained preoccupied with the relationship between the natural world and the individual mind. Percy Shelley appealed to the wind, "Make me thy lyre, even as the forest is," and in "Tintern Abbey" Wordsworth recognized nature as

> The anchor of my purest thoughts, the nurse
> The guide, the guardian of my heart, and soul
> Of all my moral being.

This commingling of self and nature was at least in part an expression of the late eighteenth- and early nineteenth-century tendency to see the natural world in opposition to the human world. In the same poem, for example, Wordsworth describes himself as coming to nature

> more like a man
> Flying from something that he dreads than one
> Who sought the thing he loved.

Less frequently did poets of the Romantic period comment on the relationship between humans and nature as an objective reality. The focus was much more often on what non-human nature had to offer to the individual human soul than on how humans in aggregate were reshaping the natural world. Barbauld was one who saw the latter clearly; in her grim survey of England in "Eighteen Hundred and Eleven" she described how

> Science and Art urge on the useful toil,
> New mould a climate and create the soil, …
> On yielding Nature urge their new demands,
> And ask not gifts but tribute at her hands.

Such clear-eyed observations of human manipulation of nature were few and far between, however.

The importance of the subjective sense of reality to the Romantic imagination also comes out clearly in the widespread fascination in the period with the visions experienced in dreams, in nightmares, and other altered states. The question Keats poses at the end of "Ode to a Nightingale"—"Was it a vision, or a waking dream?" —is of a sort that occurs frequently in the literature of Romanticism. Among the many works of the period that touch on this theme are Coleridge's fragment "Kubla Khan" (which he claimed came to him during a drug-induced sleep); Keats's visionary *The Fall of Hyperion: A Dream*; Mary Shelley's *Frankenstein* (the story of which came to her in a dream, and in which Victor Frankenstein acquires the habit of taking "every night a small quantity of laudanum" in order to "gain the rest necessary for the preservation of life"); and De Quincey's *Confessions of an English Opium Eater*.

In the work of women writers of the period, interest in the individual and the mind often took different forms from those that engaged the interest of male writers. Many were concerned with education: Hannah More produced a series of Cheap Repository Tracts designed to enlighten the poor, while Maria Edgeworth gained fame as a children's writer and educationalist. Mary Wollstonecraft authored not only her famous *Vindication of the Rights of Woman*, but also *Thoughts on the Education of Daughters* (1787) and *The Female Reader* (1772). The Romantic period abounded in outspoken female writers who engaged with the issues of their day and sought to make a difference in their world.

In their own time, however, such authors were often derided as "bluestockings," unnatural women who revealed their prudishness through their interest in intellectual pursuits. In their own day the writings of these authors made little if any difference to the social,

J.M.W. Turner, *Melrose Abbey*, 1822. The lines in the lower left corner are (slightly misquoted) from Canto 2 of Sir Walter Scott's long poem *The Lay of the Last Minstrel* (1805): "If thou would'st view fair Melrose aright, / Go visit it by the pale moonlight."

legal, and economic position of women, who remained little more than property in the eyes of the law for many more years. But over the longer term their impact was considerable; Wollstonecraft and the Bluestockings laid the intellectual foundations for the social and political progress of women that would slowly be achieved over the next 200 years and more.

It would be a mistake to think of women writers of the Romantic period as solely concerned with women's rights and with the stereotypical "female arenas" of education and religion, however. Much of the writing by women in this period is as rich, strong, and plangent as anything produced by their male counterparts. Mary Robinson, for example—famous first as an actress and mistress of the Prince of Wales, then as a successful poet and novelist—earned the admiration of both Words-worth and Coleridge (who called her "an undoubted genius"), and preceded them in the writing of poetry concerned with the poor and disenfranchised. In her *Elegiac Sonnets* (1784), Charlotte Smith displayed all the power, control, and skill at incisive self-examination that has come to be associated with the male Romantics. Poet Felicia Hemans rivaled (indeed, perhaps surpassed) Byron in popularity. Playwright Joanna Baillie, famous for producing works that, as she put it, "delineate the progress of the higher passions in the human breast," was considered by Walter Scott to be "the best dramatic writer since the days of Shakespeare."

One area of common ground for almost all Roman-tic writers, male and female, was a strong interest in the "Imagination," the creative power by which an individual took the raw material of the physical world and transformed it into art. Although "Imagination" was recognized as being distinct from religious inspiration, descriptions of imaginative or poetic power often took on strong religious overtones, as in Blake's assertion that "One Power alone makes a Poet—Imagination, The Divine Vision." Coleridge, Blake, and Wordsworth were all deeply invested in the notion of the poet as *vates*, or prophet. And the imagination was seen as invested with moral as well as prophetic power. Like earlier ages (but unlike our own), the Romantics saw the realms of the aesthetic and the moral as being closely bound up with each other. But whereas earlier ages had tended to see literature as expressing truths emanating from elsewhere,

and to see the ethical element of literature as inhering in its ability to illustrate virtues and vices, and point out moral lessons, the leading Romantics tended to locate the moral element not only of literature but of life itself in the imagination, and tended to see the imagination as embodying truth as well as morality. "The great instru-ment of moral good," wrote Shelley in his *Defense of Poetry*, "is the imagination," while Keats proclaimed that "what the imagination seizes as beauty must be the truth."[1] More broadly, a belief took root among poets (the great male Romantic poets in particular) that the aesthetic and imaginative truths of poetry were possessed of a transcendent status, a status that placed such insights above the historical or scientific truths of the ordinary world.

Another of the several oppositions that animates the literature of the Romantic period is that between sense and sensibility—a tension with parallels to that between reason and emotion in the intellectual landscape of any age, but also one possessing elements particular to the late eighteenth and early nineteenth centuries. In this era the terms "sentiment," "sentimentality," "sentimen-talism" and "sensibility" were all widely used (and to some extent overlapped in meaning), but none more so than "sensibility." The concept of "sensibility" entailed strong emotional responsiveness—life and literary work animated by powerful feeling. Indeed, it was frequently associated with emotional excess: when Jane Austen describes Marianne's "excess of sensibility" in *Sense and Sensibility*, she is using the notion of sensibility in ways that would have been familiar to any late eighteenth- or early nineteenth-century reader:

> She was sensible and clever; but eager in every thing; her sorrows, her joys, could have no moderation. She was generous, amiable, interesting: she was every thing but prudent. The resemblance between her and her mother was strikingly great. Elinor saw, with concern, the excess of her sister's sensibility; but by Mrs. Dashwood it was valued and cherished.

---

[1] Keats's notion of the value of "negative capability—that is, when a man is capable of being in uncertainties, mysteries, doubts, without any irritable reaching after fact and reason," destabilizes in interest-ing ways the connections that he and other Romantics drew between morality and the imagination, and between the imagination and truth.

It may well be that most educated Britons of the period privileged sense over sensibility in very much the way that Austen appears to do. But it is also true that the feelings associated with the Romantic sensibility—above all, as they were expressed in poetry—became the defining passions of the age. And the poetry of sensibility carried intellectual as well as aesthetic force; for a considerable period it stood in the vanguard of the movement for social and political change.

That is not to say that the distinction separating poets of sensibility from the rest was entirely clear; far from it. Rather in the way that competing factions today will sometimes each accuse the other of being controlled by their emotions rather than their reason, many in the late eighteenth century tried to situate sensibility in a natural alliance with political views they opposed. Anti-Jacobins suggested there was a natural affinity between the supposed excesses of sensibility and those of political radicalism, while radicals often portrayed sensibility as associated with reactionary political views. In truth, the language of sensibility was used by both sides.

Also among the oppositions that occur throughout the literature of the Romantic period are the natural and the artificial, and the original and the imitative. If "artificial" is taken simply to mean "human-made," of course, the distinction between the natural and the artificial is purely a matter of physical process. But "artificial" and "natural" as matters of taste and of style have more fluid meanings. As the culture of sentiment and of sensibility grew over the course of the eighteenth century, "artificial" came to be used less and less frequently to mean "displaying special art or skill" and more and more frequently to mean "contrived, shaped in a way not spontaneous or natural," or even "not expressive of reality." The divide between natural and artificial was felt to connect with that between "novelty" of thought and expression—"originality," as we would call it—and the "servility" of the stale or overly imitative. Whereas the Neoclassical poets had proudly imitated classical models, often devoting themselves to translations of Classical works into English poetry, Romantic writers—and the leading Romantic poets in particular—had little interest in seeing the work of earlier eras as models to be imitated. They might admire the poets of earlier eras, they might be inspired by them

(by Shakespeare and by Milton above all), they might aspire to similar glory, but they had no interest in taking the same path to glory. If not entirely for the first time, then certainly to an unprecedented degree, originality came in the Romantic period to be seen as a criterion of poetic achievement in the Romantic period. Even at the beginning of the period we find judgments on poetic worth being made largely on the grounds of the originality the verse displays. A 1791 assessment of a volume of Robinson's poetry, for example, sets up an opposition between the original and the natural—two qualities often assumed to normally accompany each other:

> The attempt at originality is in all pursuits laudable. Invention is a noble attribute of the mind. But the danger is, lest, by pursuing it too intensely, we deviate so far from ease and nature, that the real object of Poetry, that of touching the heart, be lost.

A more familiar set of oppositions involving the natural and the artificial, the "original" and the imitative, is put forward by William Hazlitt in his *The Spirit of the Age* (1825), as he assesses at the end of the Romantic period the place of Wordsworth in the poetry and the intellectual life of the age:

> His popular, inartificial style gets rid (at a blow) of all the trappings of verse, of all the high places of poetry: "the cloud-capt towers, the solemn temples, the gorgeous palaces," are swept to the ground.... All the traditions of learning, all the superstitions of age, are obliterated and effaced. We begin *de novo* on a *tabula rasa* of poetry ... He chooses to have his subject a foil to his invention, to owe nothing but to himself.... Taught by political opinions to say to the vain pomp and glory of the world, "I hate ye," seeing the path of classical and artificial poetry blocked up by the cumbrous ornaments of style and turgid common-places, so that nothing more could be achieved in that direction but by the most ridiculous bombast or the tamest servility, he has ... struck into the sequestered vale of humble life, sought out the muse among sheep-cotes and hamlets, and the peasant's mountain-haunts, has discarded all the tinsel pageantry of verse, and endeavored (not in vain) to ... add the charm of novelty to the familiar.

In passages such as this one, we may see the paradigms according to which the literature of the Romantic period is still largely seen being articulated even before the period had ended. On the one side the natural, the spontaneous, the original, the fresh and the new; on the other the artificial, the studied, the imitative, the tired, and the traditional. On the one side imagination and sensibility, on the other excessive rationalism. On the one side a passion for freedom— especially, aesthetic freedom and freedom of the spirit; on the other restraint, reaction, oppression. On the one side, in short, the Romantic; on the other the Classical, the neoclassical, the conservative.

If this set of oppositions often bears some correspondence to reality, it is important to recognize that the correspondence is just as often loose and unreliable. Romantic literature, and the Romantic period itself, is filled with unexpected parallels, with surprising evolutions, with unexpected paradoxes, with outright contradictions. The Della Cruscans and their followers, for example—poets of sensibility who in the late 1780s and early 1790s took the lead in exuberantly embracing revolutionary freedom in the wake of the French Revolution—have often been taken to task for the supposed artificiality of their verse. Wordsworth, usually seen as the great poet of a natural world set apart from the oppressive workings of the human-made world of cities and factories, writes in 1833 that in "Steamboats, Viaducts, and Railways … Nature doth embrace / Her lawful offspring in Man's art." Coleridge, who in the early 1790s felt strongly the attractions of sensibility and planned to establish a community in Pennsylvania founded on revolutionary democratic ideals, became in later life as dismissive of sensibility as he was of revolutionary fervor. Byron, the paradigmatic Romantic figure, professed to reject many of the impulses at the core of the Romantic movement; in "To Romance" (1807) he vows to leave the realms of romance "for those of truth:"

> Romance! disgusted with deceit,
> Far from thy motley court I fly,
> Where Affectation holds her seat,
> And sickly Sensibility. …

Keats, for his part, is perhaps at his most enthusiastic when he exclaims not over Nature or freedom but over the experience of Classical literature ("On First Looking into Chapman's Homer") and Classical art ("On Seeing the Elgin Marbles," "Ode on a Grecian Urn"). The distinctions that are often made in attempts to define the essence of the Romantic, in short, often become elusive or indistinct when it comes to particulars—and can be downright misleading. Throughout most of the nineteenth and twentieth centuries, literary critics and theorists tended to accept very much at face value the Romantics' self-representations of the nature and importance of their work; for the past generation or more those self-representations have been more and more frequently problematized, and more and more widely challenged.

There have been few challenges, however, to the view that this was a period of revolutionary developments—or to the notion that at the center of those developments (so far as English literature is concerned) was an extraordinary body of verse. Looking back in 1832 Letitia Landon was among those who identified poetry as a particular locus of change:

> Already there is a wide gulf between the last century
> and the present. In religion, in philosophy, in
> politics, in manners, there has passed a great change;
> but in none has been worked a greater change than
> in poetry, whether as regards the art itself, or the
> general feeling towards it.

Poetic ambition was in itself central to the spirit of Romanticism. When they spoke of the confident outpouring of Romantic verse, Romantic poets did not hesitate to compare their own work to that of the great poets of the past—and to feel themselves capable of such greatness. "I would sooner fail than not be among the greatest," wrote Keats.

The tendencies of our own age, when poetry is usually taken in small doses and the lyric mode predominates, sometimes lead modern readers to place far less emphasis than did the Romantics themselves on their longer works. The shorter poems of the Romantic canon (among them Blake's "The Tyger," Wordsworth's "Ode: Intimations of Immortality," Coleridge's "Dejection: An Ode," Byron's "She Walks in Beauty," Shelley's "To a Skylark" and Keats's odes and sonnets) are justly celebrated, and Wordsworth and Coleridge's *Lyrical Ballads* is rightly seen as the era's most significant single volume of literature. But if these retain pride of place it is important to give full notice too to the vast range of the ambitions of the Romantic poets—ambitions that found their fullest expression in extended poetic work. Blake's long prophetic poems charted new territory for English verse, both in the poetry itself and in his unique marriage of the verbal and the visual. Robinson's more substantial works include the long sonnet sequence *Sapho and Phaon* and the series of longer poems on related themes that were eventually published as the sequence *The Progress of Liberty*. Over the course of some 50 years Wordsworth reworked his poetic autobiography, *The Prelude*, into an 8,000 line epic. Coleridge's narrative poems "The Rime of the Ancient Mariner" and "Christabel" are works of modest extent by comparison with these—but still long by modern standards. Byron gave extraordinary new life to the epic romance with *Childe Harold*, broke new ground poetically with what he termed the "epic satire" of *Don Juan*, and wrote seven full-length poetic dramas. Shelley's long works encompass not only the complex allegorical drama *Prometheus Unbound* but also the poems "The Mask of Anarchy" and "Adonais"and the poetic drama *The Cenci*. Keats's *Endymion* is another memorable work of epic proportions. And, though Keats abandoned both the original epic-length version of his *Hyperion* and the later *The Fall of Hyperion: A Dream*, what remains of both also constitutes a very substantial poetic achievement. Charlotte Smith's monumental poem of history, nature, and the self, "Beachy Head" (1807) is a landmark in early nineteenth-century poetry, while George Crabbe's *The Borough* memorialized village life in meticulous detail. Felicia Hemans remains best known for her short poems "Casabianca" and "The Homes of England," but her most significant works are the poetic drama *The Siege of Valencia* and the nineteen poems that together comprise *Records of Woman*.

The ambitions of the Romantic poets extended, too, to poetic theory and criticism; to an unprecedented degree the leading poets of the time were also the leading critics and theorists. Wordsworth's "Preface" to the *Lyrical Ballads*, in its various versions, Shelley's *A Defense of Poetry*, Coleridge's scattered but enormously influential body of literary theory and criticism, and the

critical insights of Keats's letters, have all long been regarded as central documents in the literature of Romanticism. But other leading writers too wrote perceptively and extensively about literature—among them Barbauld, Landon, and Elizabeth Inchbald.

The novel, dramatic writing, and the essay all flourished alongside poetry in the Romantic period, even if these genres were not accorded the same degree of respect as poetry. Barbauld commented wryly on the situation of the novel in 1810:

> A collection of novels has a better chance of giving pleasure than of commanding respect. Books of this description are condemned to the grave and despised by the fastidious; but their leaves are seldom found unopened, and they occupy the parlour and the dressing-room while productions of higher name are often gathering dust upon the shelf.

Nonetheless, the novel became increasingly popular, and the period saw changes in this form that continue to reverberate even today.

While the Romantic era saw the decline of that mainstay of eighteenth-century prose, the epistolary novel, other forms of prose fiction thrived. James Hogg produced one of the great masterpieces of psychological literature, *The Private Memoirs and Confessions of a Justified Sinner* (1824). Historical novels—especially those celebrating nationhood—became increasingly popular, among them Maria Edgeworth's *Castle Rackrent* (1800), Sydney Owenson's *The Wild Irish Girl* (1806), and Jane Porter's *Scottish Chiefs* (1810). It was Sir Walter Scott, however, who took the genre of the historical novel and made it his own. The single most influential fiction writer of the Romantic period, Scott single-handedly reshaped notions not just of "the historical novel" but of the novel itself. After beginning his career as a highly successful poet, he switched to long fiction in 1814 and produced a succession of extraordinarily popular novels, including *Waverly* (1814), *Rob Roy* (1817), and *Ivanhoe* (1819), the first modern blockbusters. Using his works to explore the ongoing political struggles of the time—the clash between traditionalism and progress, the tempting attractions of an idealized past that is really a cover for abuse and exploitation, the struggles and missteps that characterize the creation of a just society—Scott at the same time created vivid, entirely engrossing characters. Indeed, one hallmark of his writing is his ability to use these fully-realized individuals to give human expression to broad social and political issues.

Scott produced over 25 full length novels, in addition to other works. His use of dialect and his decision to set his works almost exclusively in Scotland validated the language and folklore of regional and marginalized people at a time when "British" was increasingly equated with "English." His use of editorial personae, interlocutors, mediated (sometimes twice-mediated) story presentation, and complexly constructed authorial selves raise questions about the natures of authority and authorship, the difficulty of interpretation, and the concept of truth itself. Scott not only largely created the version of "Scotland" that persists in the modern mind (a land of kilts and clans, with fierce rivalries fought out against a backdrop of misty mountains and purple heather, filled with eccentric but kind-hearted peasants); he also anticipated or pioneered many of the devices associated with modern and post-modern literature.

Many novels of the period, including Scott's, had roots in an earlier form of long prose fiction, the romance. Whereas "romance novel" today denotes a form of pulp fiction focused on romantic love as wish-fulfillment, the tradition of romance literature has its roots in medieval tales of the supernatural, of chivalry, and of courtly love, in which a sense of the extraordinary or the fantastic continually colors the narrative. The genre of romance made its influence felt in several different sorts of literary work in the Romantic era, but none more so than the Gothic. Gothic novels of the late-eighteenth and early-nineteenth centuries typically investigate human responses to supernatural occurrences—things known (thanks to the advances of science and natural history) to be "impossible." These novels tend to feature stereotypical characters and to take place in worlds temporally or geographically distanced. The surrounding landscape is often highly symbolic, reflecting the psychological world of the character that dominates the work, and the heroine's plight (the protagonist is almost without fail a heroine) is usually rendered in often highly expressive rhetoric full of rhapsodic feeling. The structures of Gothic novels frequently embody political

and social tensions resulting from the integration of ancient or historical time, preserved in castles or abbeys, into an otherwise modern world. The Gothic setting of Charlotte Smith's *Emmeline, the Orphan of the Castle*, for example, allows Smith to explore social concerns such as English laws of primogeniture and women's social status and identity within the frame of a courtship novel. Her novel illustrates the ways in which the frightening, distorted world of the Gothic could also serve as a forum for social commentary—as it also does in William Godwin's *Caleb Williams* (1794) and in Eliza Fenwick's *Secrecy* (1795). Gothic novels such as Matthew Lewis's *The Monk* (1796), Charlotte Dacre's *Zofloya, or The Moor* (1806), Charles Maturin's *Melmoth the Wanderer* (1820), and Anne Radcliffe's series of highly successful Gothic novels, including *The Romance of the Forest* (1791) and *The Mysteries of Udolpho* (1794), welcomed their readers into a world marked by sexual perversity, threatened female virtue, and grotesque sights and experiences. Concerned with revealing what lay repressed or hidden behind the mask of middle-class conformity, the Gothic also often veered into savagery and melodrama, tendencies captured perfectly in the following exchange from *The Vampyre* (1819), by John Polidori, in which a mysterious villain extracts a promise from his traveling companion:

> "Swear!" cried the dying man raising himself with exultant violence. "Swear by all your soul reveres, by all your nature fears, swear that for a year and a day you will not impart your knowledge of my crimes or death to any living being in any way, whatever may happen, or whatever you may see."—His eyes seemed bursting from their sockets; "I swear!" said Aubrey; he sunk laughing upon his pillow, and breathed no more.

If the heightened atmosphere of the Gothic novel often veers toward imaginative excess, it can also foster literary art of a high order—as *Frankenstein*, Mary Shelley's famous first novel, amply demonstrates. The story of a "monster" who turns against his creator, Victor Frankenstein, *Frankenstein* is at one level a gripping tale of adventure, written with engaging apparent simplicity. But it is also a text that brings together virtually all the great themes of the era: freedom and oppression; science and nature; society and the individual; knowledge and power; gender and sexuality; dream and reality; creation and destruction; self-deception and self-discovery; death and life; God and the universe.

If one strand of the tradition of romance literature runs through the evolution of the Gothic novel, a very different strand runs through the development of the courtship novel in the Romantic period. From Frances Burney's *Camilla* (1796) to Elizabeth Susan Ferrier's *The Inheritance* (1824), the pages of Romantic fiction are filled with young people who are misguided, thwarted, and ultimately united in love. But no author of the period was as successful with the courtship genre as was Jane Austen. Between 1811 and 1817 her six major novels were published, all of them warmly engaging yet sharply observant and often satirical novels of courtship, social class, and domestic life. Much as her novels do not engage directly or obviously with the large issues of her age, Austen reveals a shrewd awareness of both politics and economics, particularly as they concern women; her novels emphasize the limited possibilities open to women during the period in which she wrote. But within this limited frame Austen provides a vividly three-dimensional picture of the shaping of female character, of the inner world of the emotions as much as the outer world of social behavior. Austen's heroines are preoccupied with wooing, marriage, and the minutiae of income, entailment, and other details of domestic and marital economy, precisely because these dominated and defined the lives of women of the period, while her concentration on "3 or 4 Families in a country village" (as she famously remarked to her niece) draws attention to the geographical and physical constraints imposed on middle- and upper-class women during this time. Even the happy endings that have delighted generations of Austenites are undercut by the obvious and acknowledged fictionality of the novels (emphasized through authorial asides, direct appeals to the reader, and other devices), by means of which Austen suggests that all happy endings may be mere fictions.

Austen was a skilled stylist as well a keen-eyed social critic, and brought to her novels an unprecedented range of novelistic technique. With *Lady Susan* she proved herself adept at epistolary narrative; with *Sense and Sensibility*, *Pride and Prejudice* and *Emma* she brought new flexibility to the use of the third person narrative voice, demonstrating perfect pitch in a variety of ironic tones, and pioneering the technique now known as free indirect discourse. In this mode of narration the apparently independent third-person narrative voice temporarily assumes the viewpoint of one or more of the characters—or indeed of an entire social class, as is the case with the famous opening to *Pride and Prejudice*: "It is a truth universally acknowledged, that a single man in possession of a good fortune, must be in want of a wife." In her tone Austen is at a great remove from the leading poets of the Romantic period, but in the importance she places on the exercise of moral imagination—both by her characters and through her own narrative style—she is very much at one with the age.

Other Romantic novels sought to reflect the social and political concerns of the world around them in fiction more fully and more directly than did either most Gothic novels or most courtship novels; a number of writers used the novel as a means of challenging prevailing beliefs and mores. Maria Edgeworth's series of Irish novels, *Castle Rackrent* (1800), *Ennui* (1809), *The Absentee* (1812), and *Ormond* (1817), explored the colonial relationship between England and Ireland. William Godwin's *Caleb Williams* (1794) sought to reveal, in the author's words, the "perfidiousness exercised by the powerful members of the community against those who are more privileged than themselves." Hogg's *Private Memoirs* was a powerful indictment of the smug superiority that could be engendered by religious zeal. And Mary Hays's *The Victim of Prejudice*, a passionate tale of a young woman who dares to resist the pressure put upon her to marry the man who has raped her, was among those novels that spoke powerfully of injustice in a male-dominated society. Conservative voices also spoke out loudly through the medium of prose fiction; important anti-Jacobin novels of the period include Jane West's *A Tale of the Times* (1799), Elizabeth Hamilton's *Memoirs of Modern Philosophers* (1800), and Charles Lucas's *The Infernal Quixote* (1801). And a number of novelists used the novel as a means of making politically pointed connections with other parts of the world, whether to cast a critical eye on the course of European imperialism—as in Sydney

Henry Fuseli, *The Nightmare*, 1790–91. The Swiss-born artist Fuseli (1741–1825) moved to England in 1779, and soon became one of the leading artistic figures of the day. Beginning in 1781, Fuseli painted several different versions of *The Nightmare*, for which he became famous; it remains an iconic image of the Gothic sensibility, and of Romantic interest in what we now term "the unconscious."

Fuseli moved in London's artistic and intellectual circles through the 1790s, and was briefly involved romantically with Mary Wollstonecraft before her marriage to William Godwin.

William Blake, "The Sick Rose," from "Songs of Experience," 1794.

William Blake, "The Sun Standing at his Eastern Gate," illustration to John Milton's "L'Allegro."

Phillipe Jacques de Loutherbourgh, "Coalbrookdale By Night," 1801. The small Shropshire town of Coalbrookdale has been sometimes described as the birthplace of the Industrial Revolution. Located in a gorge on the River Severn, it was the site of the first ironworks that used the modern method of smelting with coke rather than charcoal (an innovation of Joseph Darby in 1709). Together with the adjacent towns of Madeley, Ironbridge, Jackfield, and Coalport, Coalbrookdale was part of an early industrial powerhouse; at the end of the eighteenth century it had a greater concentration of furnaces and forges than anywhere else in the world. Darby's son Abraham also constructed the world's first iron bridge nearby in 1779; the bridge and much of the old ironworks remain today, and the Ironbridge Gorge has been declared a World Heritage Site.

Jean-Jacques David, *Bonaparte*, 1798.

Artist unknown, *A Stoppage to a Stride over the Globe*, 1803.

Thomas Phillips, *George Gordon, Lord Byron*, 1814. Byron is wearing clothing of a sort native to the region of Epirus (then part of Albania, now part of northern Greece); he had bought this outfit while traveling through the area in 1809.

Elizabeth Levenson-Gower, Mountain, "Mountain Landscape," c. 1830. Levenson-Gower published two volumes based on her watercolor images of Scottish landscapes, the first a collection of etchings, "Views of Orkney and the North-Eastern coast of Scotland" (1807), and the second a volume of twenty aquatints, "Views on the Northern and Western Coasts of Sutherland" (1833). The artist intended that various of the wide Sutherland images be joined together to form 360 degree scenic panoramas.

J.M.W. Turner, *The Burning of the Houses of Parliament*, 1835. In the 1830s it became Turner's practice to send unfinished work (often with only rough underpainting completed) to the Royal Academy in advance of its annual exhibition. During the period devoted (in the case of other artists) to the varnishing of already-completed work, Turner would complete the painting itself, often watched by a sizeable crowd. An eyewitness, E.V. Rippingille, described Turner completing *The Burning of the Houses of Parliament* in 1835:

For [the] three hours I was there ... he never ceased to work, or even once looked or turned from the wall in which his picture was hung. A small box of colors, a few very small brushes, and a vial or two, were at this feet ... In one part of the mysterious proceedings Turner, who worked almost entirely with his palette knife, was observed to be rolling and spreading a half-transparent stuff over his picture, the size of a figure in length and thickness. As Callcott was looking on I ventured to say ... "What is that he is plastering his picture with?" to which enquiry it was replied, "should be sorry to be the man to ask him" ... Presently the work was finished: Turner gathered his tools together, put them into and shut the box, and then with his face still turned to the wall, and at the same distance from it, went sidelong off, without speaking a word to anybody ... Maclise, who stood near, remarked, "There, that's masterly, he does not stop to look at his work; he knows it is done, and he is off!"

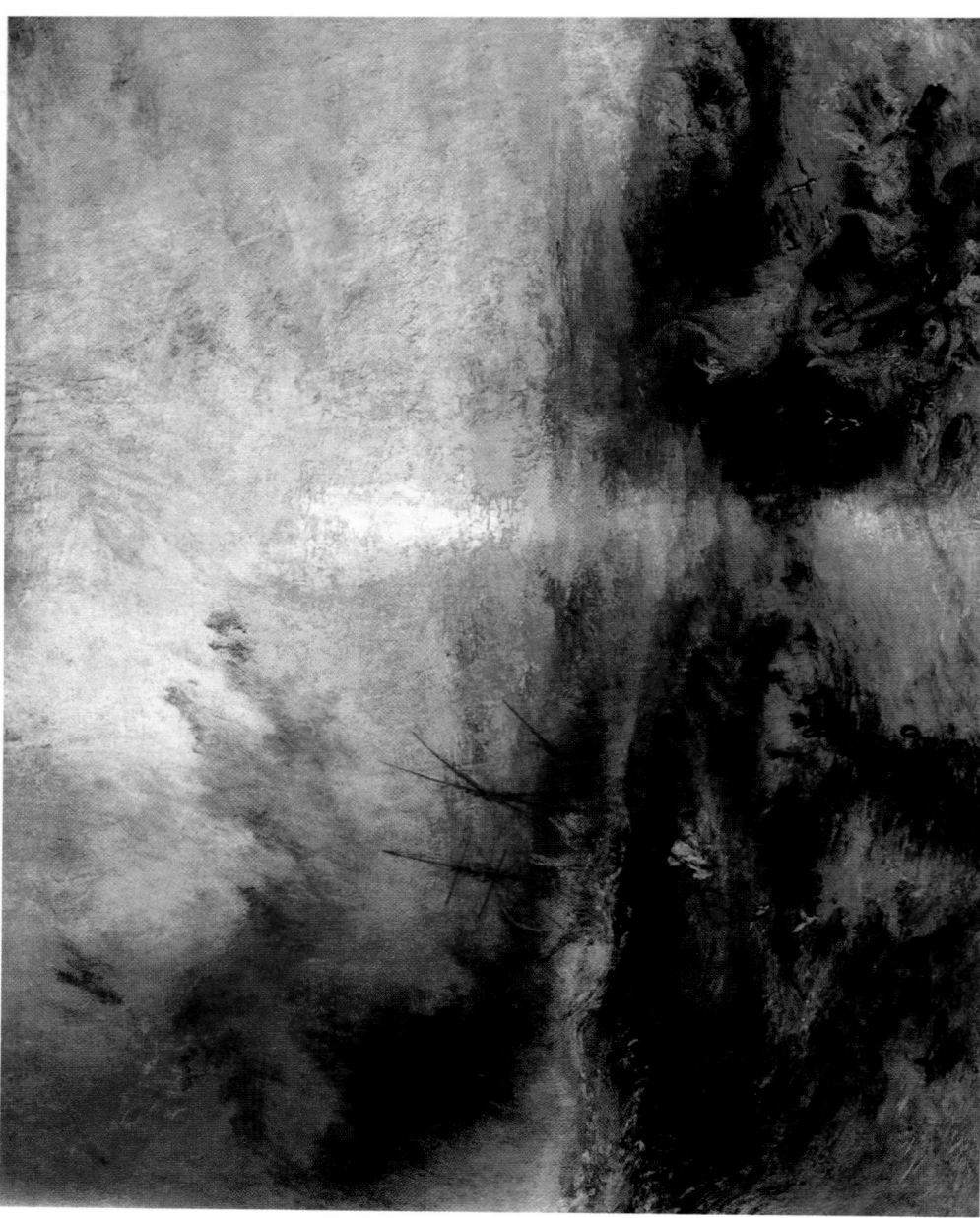

J.M.W. Turner, "Slavers Throwing Overboard the Dead and Dying—Typhoon coming on," 1840. Turner's painting depicts a 1781 incident in which Captain Luke Collingwood of the slave ship "Zong," with his ship running short of water and other supplies when it had been blown off-course during a severe storm, ordered that all sick and dying slaves be thrown overboard; 133 were killed as a result. Insurance was a factor in Collingwood's decision; compensation could be claimed for property lost or jettisoned in storms, but not for slaves killed by disease or other natural causes. The incident became widely publicized and spurred support for the abolitionist movement. In the ensuing legal case the court upheld the insurance company's financial liability; no criminal charges were brought against the captain. In the twentieth century the incident became the basis for several literary works, including a long poem by David Dabydeen and a novel by Fred D'Aguiar.

Owenson's *The Missionary* (1811)—or to criticize aspects of British society by presenting them through the view of an outsider—as in Hamilton's *Translations of the Letters of a Hindoo Rajah* (1796).

While the novel prospered and evolved, so too did the genre of non-fiction prose. With the rise of the periodical (see "The Business of Literature," below) came the rise of first critical and then more general essays, designed to engage, enlighten, and entertain the reader. William Hazlitt, originally intended for the Church and later an aspiring painter and philosopher, turned his hand to writing and became the most trenchant cultural critic of his time. His works include dramatic, literary, and art criticism, as well as political journalism, general essays, and his famous collection of pieces on important figures of the eighteenth century and the Romantic period, *The Spirit of the Age* (1824). His friend Charles Lamb rivaled Hazlitt's renown as an essayist, although his style was very different. Where Hazlitt used plain language and popular modes of construction to express his points cleanly and carefully, Lamb cultivated a more genteel style, rich in allusions and puns, the prose both thoughtful and rhetorically complex. Together, the two played a central role in the development of the essay during the Romantic period, but they were far from the only practitioners of the art. From Francis Jeffrey, whose pieces in the *Edinburgh Review* made literary criticism an exercise in stylish perspicacity, to Thomas De Quincey, whose psychological probing anticipates Freud, Romantic essay writers came in all shapes and sizes.

In the field of drama, the Romantic period is traditionally seen as an era of great "closet dramas" (plays written not for the stage but for private performance—in a private room or "closet"—or to be read). And, given that the period produced both Byron's powerful verse drama, *Manfred*, his iconoclastic meditation on sin and damnation, *Cain*, and Shelley's mythographic masterpiece, *Prometheus Unbound*, its reputation as a breeding ground for rich, multi-layered private theatricals may fairly be said to be well deserved. Other serious plays—chief among them Joanna Baillie's series of tragedies, collectively entitled *Plays on the Passions* (1798–1812), failed on the stage but were widely read and highly praised as literature. Depicting the passions "in their rise and progress in the heart" was Baillie's intent, and she believed that such drama could have a moral purpose (though she made no transcendent claims for the moral value of the imagination). The drama, in her view, "improves us by the knowledge we acquire of our own minds, from the natural desire we have to look into the thoughts, and observe the behavior of others." Baillie's explorations in psychology harked back to Enlightenment concepts, but her plays also engaged powerfully with the issues of her own day—chief among them the question of women's rights.

In Byron's view, the distaste many serious writers felt for the public theater in this period was entirely justified:

> When I first entered upon theatrical affairs, I had some idea of writing for the [play] house myself, but soon became a convert to Pope's opinion of that subject. Who would condescend to the drudgery of the stage, and enslave himself to the humours, the caprices, the taste or tastelessness, of the age? Besides, one must write for particular actors, have them continually in one's eye, sacrifice character to the personating of it, cringe to some favorite of the public, neither give him too many nor too few lines to spout …

Baillie was rather more charitable, attributing the low tolerance of audiences for serious drama to an escapism borne of a desire to find refuge from the "commercial hurricane" of the age—and locating a good deal of the problem in the poor acoustics and lighting of the theaters of the day:

> The Public have now to choose between what we shall suppose are well-written and well-acted plays, the words of which are not heard, or heard but imperfectly by two-thirds of the audience, while the finer and more pleasing traits of the acting are by a still greater proportion lost altogether; and splendid pantomime, or pieces whose chief object is to produce striking scenic effect, which can be seen and comprehended by the whole.

As both Byron's and Baillie's comments indicate, the theater in this period was, in some sense at least, thriving. People thronged to the theaters, where they saw plays by such popular and prolific playwrights as Hannah Cowley and Elizabeth Inchbald, as well as successful dramas such as Samuel Taylor Coleridge's *Remorse* and Charles Maturin's *Bertram*. The Stage Licensing Act of 1737 meant that in London only two theaters, Covent Garden and Drury Lane (and, in the summer, the Haymarket) were permitted to present "legitimate" drama, but this in no way limited theatrical production. Stage entertainments of all sorts were held in venues from pubs to tents. In cities and provinces outside London, theaters sprang up to meet the demands of an increasing audience: a survey completed in 1804 counted 280 playhouses throughout the nation. The Licensing Act also required the texts of plays to be submitted to the Lord Chamberlain for censorship before performance. As a result, many works intended for the stage were forced into the closet (perhaps the most famous example is Shelley's *The Cenci*, which features not only father-daughter incest but also parricide). Many, however, were not, and a roll call of drama produced between 1780 and 1834 features everything from light comedy to melodramatic tragedy and from pantomimes to operas, as well as spectacles that featured impressive special effects.

THE BUSINESS OF LITERATURE

The thriving literary scene of the period is intimately tied to developments in the worlds of book publishing, book selling, and book marketing. The most influential of these was the rise of the periodical. By the 1760s there were more than 30 periodicals in London alone—monthly journals, quarterly magazines, collections of reviews and essays designed to inform and stimulate their readers. This boom in the periodical press meant increased employment for those who sought to become men and women of letters; the demand for articles often outweighed the supply. For readers and publishers, it meant an ever-growing number of publications in which reviews of the latest books might appear. Published books were expensive—a three-volume novel could cost a total of nine shillings, roughly $40 today—but reviews often printed long extracts, and thus readers could experience the book through the review. Such extracts were also, of course, excellent advertisements for the books under review.

At the same time as the number of periodicals increased, so did ways to obtain books. Between 1740 and 1790 the number of outlets nearly doubled. Most obviously, books could be bought: well-established bookshops flourished in cities all over the nation. In provincial towns and villages, literature was often sold side by side with stationery, patent medicines, and even groceries. Because the cost of books put them outside the means of many readers, however, some booksellers began to lend volumes to customers for a small fee. Thus did the circulating library begin. A patron would pay a yearly fee, then borrow books as he or she pleased.

Although both circulating and subscription libraries offered good value for money, they still lay outside the financial resources of those below the lower middle-classes. For these readers, there were other alternatives. Pedlars and hawkers sold street literature that included ballads, sermons, and tracts. Those who could not afford library subscriptions but who wished to read something more than broadsheet ballads or pamphlets often formed book clubs in which a number of people contributed money to buy a single book, which they would then share. After all had read the book, it might well be sold to a local bookseller, and the proceeds put toward the price of a new one. Slightly more formally, in numerous towns and villages the local male elite came together to select and discuss books and pamphlets, usually on a controversial topic of the day. This literature, too, was sold, often by means of an auction among members at the end of the year.

Perhaps as a result of these efforts in group reading, or perhaps simply because people enjoyed it, reading aloud remained a feature of the Romantic era. The fiction and the non-fiction of the period abound in scenes of communal reading, and the visions that come down to us range from Countess Granville's admission that when her husband read *Don Juan* to her "I roared till I could neither hear nor see," to Henry Austen's description of his sister Jane as one who "read aloud with very great taste and effect. Her own works, probably, were never heard to such advantage as from her own mouth." Writers of the Romantic period were not very far removed from a time when illiteracy was more common than literacy, a time when literature was still

Thomas Rowlandson, *Dr. Syntax and a Bookseller*, 1812.

J. Bluck, after Augustus Charles Pugin, *Ackermann's Art Library* (detail), c. 1812–15. Rudolf Ackermann (1764–1834) moved to London from his native Germany and opened a print shop in London on the Strand in 1795, selling books and artist supplies as well as prints, and exhibiting paintings. He later also began to publish color-plate books, the most notable of which was *The Microcosm of London*, a three-volume set with 104 hand-colored aquatint plates by various artists (including Thomas Rowlandson and Augustus Pugin), published between 1808 and 1811.

an oral art. It is worth bearing in mind that many of them wrote to be read aloud, and many of their works gain luster from being heard.

"ROMANTIC"

Of the six periods into which the history of British literature has long been conventionally divided, the era of Romanticism is by far the briefest, extending over less than forty years. Arguably it is also the most intense, particularly during the years 1789-1815, the era not only of the French Revolution and the Napoleonic Wars but also of the era's most tumultuous literary developments—and most lasting literary achievements.

This was unquestionably an age of contradiction. It was a period in which political consciousness spread through society in unprecedented ways, with a great growth in collective awareness not only among those whose hearts resonated with revolutionary developments on the Continent but also amongst workers, the disenfranchised poor, women, and anti-slavery activists. Yet it was also a time of unprecedented growth in awareness of humans as individuals, of a rights-based political individualism, and of a Romantic individualism of the soul.

Applying a broad title to any literary or historical period is always risky. As much as any group of authors and thinkers may at first appear to have in common, deeper examination always reveals complexities. In addition, literature, like history, does not occur in isolation. One idea bleeds into another; revolutions are often old ideas returning under new names; factions develop, and their members deny that they are in any way related to the members of other factions. In its own time, Romanticism (a label never used by any of its writers, but rather first applied by the Victorians) was very frequently a house divided. "Lakers" like Wordsworth and Southey denounced the "Satanic School" of Shelley and Byron, who in turn produced vicious satires of these elders. "The Cockney School" of Londoners Leigh Hunt and John Keats was derided by critics of the day, while writers now long ignored, such as Felicia Hemans, Samuel Rogers, and Thomas Moore, were lauded for their skill and were extremely popular. The Romantic era gains richness and interest if we view it not as a perfect stream, but as what it was: a thick murmuring torrent of powerful voices that chorused and clashed, that simultaneously sought and struggled. These mingled tones together make up the voice of a movement that changed English literature.

A CHANGING LANGUAGE

Of all the places in which the political clashes of the Romantic period made themselves felt, perhaps the most surprising was in the arena of linguistics. Concern with questions of nationalism and political loyalties reached into the very language of Britain. From 1750 onward, the book market was flooded with pronunciation guides, a deluge inspired by the belief that standardized pronunciation would foster a sense of national unity. In this case, "standard" pronunciation meant the speech of educated urban dwellers. Even as many adhered to the essentially Tory belief that this supposedly standard speech was superior, there grew up a precisely opposite point of view, largely expressed by radical publishers and writers, that in the everyday speech of the common people one might find all that was best and most true about England: honesty, frankness, and English liberty given verbal form. In his 1785 *Classical Dictionary of the Vulgar Tongue*, Francis Grose transcribed and celebrated the speech of commoners in their many regional variations, and in 1818 the radical William Cobbett published his *Grammar of the English Language*, a book which explicitly treated language as a political issue. Cobbett took issue with the "false grammar" that he saw as having been put forward by eighteenth-century authorities such as Samuel Johnson, and attacked the grammatical slips as well as the privileged position of kings and nobles (chapters include "Errors and Nonsense in a King's Speech." He addressed his work to the less privileged classes, whom he believed should be enabled to participate in political discussions—"to assert with effect the rights and liberties of [their] country." As Cobbett saw it, "tyranny has no enemy so formidable as the pen."

Evidence of the Romantic celebration of "common language" can be found throughout the literature of the period. It accounts in part for the huge popularity of Robert Burns—a poet whose greatest effects come from his mixing of standard English with his native Scots dialect. But it finds its most famous expression in the Preface to the 1800 edition of *Lyrical Ballads*. There, Wordsworth writes that

> "men" in "low and rustic life" hourly communicate with the best objects from which the best part of language is originally derived; and because, from their rank in society and the sameness and narrow circle of intercourse, being less under the influence of social vanity they convey their feelings and notions in simple and unelaborated expressions. Accordingly, such language, rising out of repeated experience and regular feelings, is a more permanent, and far more philosophical language …

Even at the time Wordsworth's opinions on this point represented a minority view, and with the passage of time this Romantic belief in the "philosophical language" of "low and rustic life" became less and less widely held. Fifteen years later one finds Wordsworth's collaborator on *Lyrical Ballads*, Coleridge, writing that

> The best part of human language, properly so called, is derived from reflection on the acts of the mind itself. It is formed by a voluntary appropriation of fixed symbols to internal acts, to processes and results of imagination, the greater part of which have no place in the consciousness of the uneducated man…

As the Romantic period slid into the Victorian and the vogue for rustic or uneducated authors passed away, so the point of view represented in Coleridge's remark came to dominate, and "standard" educated English became more and more widely accepted as an ideal to which all should aspire.

Over the course of this period, the varieties of English were to some extent dissolving into the forms of standard English, many regional variations persisted—and the forms of standard English itself were far from unchanging. In pronunciation the most significant change in "standard British English" was the disappearance of the "r" sound before many consonants, and before a pause, so that in words such as "harm" or "person," for example, the "r" has since the late eighteenth century been flattened into the smooth "hahm" or "pehson" associated with modern "standard English" pronunciation. Interesting geographical variations have developed over this change, however. In Scotland and in Ireland, as in Canada and most of the United States, the "r" has continued to be sounded in such contexts; these varieties of English are referred to by linguists as "rhotic." In Australia, New Zealand, and South Africa, on the other hand, as well as in some parts of the United States, for instance in Massachusetts and some other parts of New England, non-rhotic forms have come to predominate in much the same way as they have in England.

As the rhymes of English poetry reveal, there were also changes in the sounding of some vowels in the late eighteenth century. In the early eighteenth century, for example, Alexander Pope rhymed "tea" with "obey;" rhymes also suggest that "sea" was pronounced in a manner closer to "say" than to "see." By 1797, however, Coleridge was rhyming "sea" with "free;" and by the end of the Romantic period the older pronunciations of such words had almost certainly died out.

Eighteenth-century habits of capitalization and punctuation were also largely abandoned during this period. Capitalization and typography had generally been considered the business of the compositor rather than that of the author, and the tendency in the early and mid-eighteenth century had been to capitalize (or sometimes italicize) a wide range of nouns. By the end of the century, patterns of usage were coming to approximate the conventions of modern English.

Paragraphing remained less strongly conventionalized than it is now—many writers tended to start new paragraphs very infrequently—and the conventions for writing direct speech were still unstable, with the practice of using double quotation marks surrounding the exact words spoken starting to become common at the end of the eighteenth century. (The practice of using single rather than double quotation marks did not become common in Britain until later in the nineteenth century, and did not become entirely standardized as British usage until the twentieth century.)

HISTORY OF THE LANGUAGE
AND OF PRINT CULTURE

In an effort to provide for readers a direct sense of the development of the language and of print culture, examples of texts in their original form (and of illustrations) have been provided for each period. A list of these within the Age of Romanticism appears below. Overviews of "the business of literature" and of developments in the history of language during this period appear on pp. 26–28, and a "Contexts" section on various aspects of "Reading, Writing, Publishing" appears on pp. 160–74.

Robert Burns, all poems (1785–99) in original spelling and punctuation, pp. 93–109

William Blake, all poems (1789–94) in original spelling and punctuation, pp. 42–61.

William Blake, *Songs of Innocence and of Experience*, 1789–94, title page for the full work, p. 42; "The Little Black Boy," p. 43; title page for *Songs of Experience*, p. 46; frontispiece, *Songs of Experience*, p. 46; "The Tyger," p. 48. See also the color insert pages.

William Blake, *The Marriage of Heaven and Hell*, 1793, illustrated plates, pp. 58–61.

Samuel Taylor Coleridge, all poems (1795–1836) in original spelling and punctuation, pp. 177–207.

William Blake, illustrations for John Stedman, *Narrative of Five Years' Expedition against the Revolted Negroes of Surinam*, 1796, p. 301.

William Wordsworth, all poems (1798–1850) in original spelling and punctuation, pp. 112–57.

William Wordsworth, "I wandered lonely as a Cloud," 1807, facsimile of page from *Poems in Two Volumes* with manuscript additions, pp. 144–45.

Thomas Rowlandson, *Dr. Syntax and a Bookseller*, 1812, p. 27.

J. Bluck, *Ackermann's Art Library*, c.1812–15, p. 27.

Felicia Hemans, all poems (1812–29) in original spelling and punctuation, pp. 412–20.

George Gordon, Lord Byron, all poems (1814–23) in original spelling and punctuation, pp. 308–68.

John Keats, all poems (1816–20) in original spelling and punctuation, pp. 423–55.

John Brown, *A Memoir of Robert Blincoe*, title page, 1832, p. 10.

Anna Laetitia Barbauld
1743 – 1825

William Blake admired Anna Laetitia Barbauld's poetry, as did Samuel Taylor Coleridge, who walked forty miles to meet her, and William Wordsworth, who said about the Barbauld poem "Life": "I am not in the habit of grudging people their good things, but I wish I had written those [final] lines." Although born in the provinces, Barbauld became in her own day a leading figure in London literary life. She composed innovative and influential poetry, hymns, children's literature, political pamphlets, essays, and works of literary criticism. She also established herself as a leading educator and political and social activist. By the time of her death, however, her literary reputation had begun to fade, and she was largely forgotten until recent critical work renewed interest in this talented and versatile professional writer.

Anna Laetitia Aiken was born in Leicestershire to Jane Jennings and John Aiken, a nonconformist Presbyterian minister and schoolteacher at the Warrington Dissenting Academy in Yorkshire. Schooled by her father, she was a precocious child who studied the classics early in life. In her late teens she became acquainted with the influential educator and scientist Joseph Priestley and developed a lasting friendship with him and his wife. Barbauld was inspired by Priestley's poetry, and he was impressed by hers; he eventually encouraged her to publish her first volume, *Poems* (1773). This collection of lyrics, hymns, epistles, and mock-heroic poems, published under her birth name, went through five editions in four years and received considerable critical acclaim, *The Monthly Review* calling it a "great accession to the literary world." That same year Barbauld printed *Miscellaneous Pieces in Prose* with her brother, John Aiken (later the editor of a radical journal, *Monthly Magazine*).

Living at her father's school prepared Barbauld to run her own boys' boarding school, which she started with her husband, the dissenting clergyman Rochemont Barbauld, whom she married in 1774. During this period she wrote her popular and influential *Lessons for Children* (1787–88) and *Hymns in Prose for Children* (1787), designed for the very young. Both went through many printings and continued to be read in the United States and England until the close of the century. By 1785 her husband's mental instability required them to close the school (he eventually became violent and later committed suicide), and from this point on, Barbauld committed herself solely to literary work.

In her political pamphlets and essays of the 1790s, Barbauld addressed ethics, education, and political economy, and argued for freedom of religion and conscience—a cause dear to the hearts of Dissenters. She also argued strongly for the abolition of slavery (at a moment when the movement had suffered a setback) in her verse *Epistle to William Wilberforce* (1791); and in the essay *Sins of Government, Sins of Nation* (1793) she derided the British government for its involvement in the war against France. Barbauld then turned to editorial work, producing the first collection of *The Correspondence of Samuel Richardson* (1804), which includes her biography of the author. She also published *The British Novelists* (1810), a fifty-volume collection featuring the work of 28 novelists, both male and female, along with Barbauld's biographical and critical prefaces. In her general introduction to *On the Origin and Progress of Novel-Writing*, she argued for the value of novels for both education and enjoyment. This was pioneering in its recognition of the novel as a serious genre.

In 1812 Barbauld published her final work, the prophetic poem *Eighteen Hundred and Eleven*. Written in a pessimistic tone, the poem traces the cyclical rise and fall of national empires, indicts Britain for its involvement in the war with France, and predicts the fall of the British Empire. At the end of the poem, "Genius" leaves for America, the nation Barbauld suggests will replace Britain as the new empire. The poem elicited widespread criticism for what was deemed its "anti-patriotism." John Wilson Croker's abusive attack in the *Quarterly Review* used to be credited with effectively ending Barbauld's publishing career, but this is not accurate: she continued writing into the 1820s. After her death in 1825 her niece published two collections of her works.

⌘ ⌘ ⌘

Washing Day

… and their voice,
Turning again towards childish treble, pipes
And whistles in its sound.[1]

The Muses[2] are turned gossips; they have lost
The buskined step,[3] and clear high-sounding phrase,
Language of gods. Come, then, domestic Muse,
In slipshod measure loosely prattling on
Of farm or orchard, pleasant curds and cream,
5   Or drowning flies, or shoe lost in the mire
By little whimpering boy, with rueful face;
Come, Muse, and sing the dreaded Washing-Day.
Ye who beneath the yoke of wedlock bend,
With bowed soul, full well ye ken° the day   *know*
10 Which week, smooth sliding after week, brings on
Too soon; for to that day nor peace belongs
Nor comfort; ere the first grey streak of dawn,
The red-armed washers come and chase repose.
Nor pleasant smile, nor quaint device of mirth,
15 E'er visited that day; the very cat,
From the wet kitchen scared, and reeking hearth,
Visits the parlour, an unwonted° guest.   *infrequent*

The silent breakfast meal is soon dispatched
Uninterrupted, save by anxious looks
20 Cast at the lowering sky, if sky should lower.
From that last evil, O preserve us, heavens!
For should the skies pour down, adieu to all
Remains of quiet; then expect to hear
Of sad disasters—dirt and gravel stains
25 Hard to efface, and loaded lines at once
Snapped short—and linen-horse° by dog   *clotheshorse*
    thrown down,
And all the petty miseries of life.
Saints have been calm while stretched upon the rack,
30 And Guatimozin[4] smiled on burning coals;
But never yet did housewife notable
Greet with a smile a rainy washing-day.
But grant the welkin° fair, require not thou   *sky*
Who call'st thyself perchance the master there,
35 Or study swept, or nicely dusted coat,
Or usual 'tendance; ask not, indiscreet,
Thy stockings mended, though the yawning rents
Gape wide as Erebus,[5] nor hope to find
Some snug recess impervious; should'st thou try
40 The 'customed garden walks, thine eye shall rue
The budding fragrance of thy tender shrubs,
Myrtle or rose, all crushed beneath the weight
Of coarse checked apron, with impatient hand

---

[1] *and their voice … sound* Cf. Shakespeare's *As You Like It* 2.7.161–63: "and his big manly voice, / Turning again toward childish treble, pipes / And whistles in his sound."

[2] *Muses* In classical mythology, nine goddesses who presided over learning and the arts.

[3] *buskined step* I.e., tragic mode. Actors in Athenian tragedy wore buskins, or high, thick-soled boots.

[4] *Guatimozin* Cuauhtémoc, the last Aztec emperor (c. 1495–1522), was captured and tortured by Cortés's Spanish conquistadors when they invaded the Aztec capital (now Mexico City).

[5] *Erebus* In Greek mythology, a place below the earth that the dead pass through on their way to Hades, or the underworld.

Twitched off when showers impend: or crossing lines
45   Shall mar thy musings, as the wet cold sheet
Flaps in thy face abrupt. Woe to the friend
Whose evil stars have urged him forth to claim
On such a day the hospitable rites;
Looks, blank at best, and stinted courtesy,
50   Shall he receive. Vainly he feeds his hopes
With dinner of roast chicken, savoury pie,
Or tart or pudding:—pudding he nor tart
That day shall eat; nor, though the husband try,
Mending what can't be helped, to kindle mirth
55   From cheer deficient, shall his consort's brow
Clear up propitious; the unlucky guest
In silence dines, and early slinks away.
I well remember, when a child, the awe
This day struck into me; for then the maids,
60   I scarce knew why, looked cross, and drove me from
      them;
Nor soft caress could I obtain, nor hope
Usual indulgencies; jelly or creams,
Relic of costly suppers, and set by
For me their petted one; or buttered toast,
65   When butter was forbid; or thrilling tale
Of ghost, or witch, or murder—so I went
And sheltered me beside the parlour fire:
There my dear grandmother, eldest of forms,
Tended the little ones, and watched from harm,
70   Anxiously fond, though oft her spectacles
With elfin cunning hid, and oft the pins
Drawn from her ravelled stocking, might have soured
One less indulgent.—
At intervals my mother's voice was heard,
75   Urging dispatch; briskly the work went on,
All hands employed to wash, to rinse, to wring,
To fold, and starch, and clap, and iron, and plait.[1]
Then would I sit me down, and ponder much
Why washings were. Sometimes through hollow
      bole°   *bowl*
80   Of pipe amused we blew, and sent aloft
The floating bubbles, little dreaming then
To see, Mongolfier,[2] thy silken ball
Ride buoyant through the clouds—so near approach

The sports of children and the toils of men.
85   Earth, air, and sky, and ocean, hath its bubbles,[3]
And verse is one of them—this most of all.
—1797

Eighteen Hundred and Eleven,[4] *A Poem*

Still the loud death drum, thundering from afar,
O'er the vext nations pours the storm of war:
To the stern call still Britain bends her ear,
Feeds the fierce strife, the alternate hope and fear;
5   Bravely, though vainly, dares to strive with fate,
And seeks by turns to prop each sinking state.
Colossal Power[5] with overwhelming force
Bears down each fort of freedom in its course;
Prostrate she lies beneath the despot's sway,
10   While the hushed nations curse him—and obey.
    Bounteous in vain, with frantic man at strife,
Glad Nature pours the means—the joys of life;
In vain with orange blossoms scents the gale,
The hills with olives clothes, with corn the vale;
15   Man calls to Famine,[6] nor invokes in vain,
Disease and Rapine° follow in her train;   *plunder*
The tramp of marching hosts disturbs the plough,
The sword, not sickle, reaps the harvest now,[7]
And where the soldier gleans the scant supply,
20   The helpless peasant but retires to die;
No laws his hut from licensed outrage shield,
And war's least horror is the ensanguined° field. *blood-stained*
    Fruitful in vain, the matron counts with pride

---

1 *clap* Smooth; *plait* Fold.

2 *Montgolfier* Montgolfier brothers, from Annonay, France, who invented and launched the first hot-air balloon in 1783.

3 *Earth ... bubbles* Cf. Shakespeare's *Macbeth* 1.3.83: "The earth hath bubbles, as the water has."

4 *Eighteen Hundred and Eleven* Britain's war with France, begun in 1793, would not end until the Battle of Waterloo in 1815. By 1811, Russia, Austria, and Spain, Britain's allies, had already capitulated to the strength of Napoleon's army; Britain was in financial distress; and King George III had been declared insane.

5 *Colossal Power* Napoleon Bonaparte (1769–1821), emperor of France.

6 *Famine* In 1811 there was widespread hunger in Britain and much of Europe due to crop failures in the preceding years, as well as the necessity of providing food for soldiers.

7 *The sword ... now* Napoleon sent his soldiers out unencumbered with baggage; consequently, most of them were starving and were forced to steal food.

The blooming youths that grace her honoured side;
25 No son returns to press her widow'd hand,
Her fallen blossoms strew a foreign strand.
—Fruitful in vain, she boasts her virgin race,
Whom cultured arts adorn and gentlest grace;
Defrauded of its homage, Beauty mourns,
30 And the rose withers on its virgin thorns.
Frequent, some stream obscure, some uncouth name
By deeds of blood is lifted into fame;
Oft o'er the daily page some soft one bends
To learn the fate of husband, brothers, friends,
35 Or the spread map with anxious eye explores,
Its dotted boundaries and penciled shores,
Asks where the spot that wrecked her bliss is found,
And learns its name but to detest the sound.
    And think'st thou, Britain, still to sit at ease,
40 An island queen amidst thy subject seas,
While the vext billows, in their distant roar,
But soothe thy slumbers, and but kiss thy shore?
To sport in wars, while danger keeps aloof,
Thy grassy turf unbruised by hostile hoof?
45 So sing thy flatterers; but, Britain, know,
Thou who hast shared the guilt must share the woe.
Nor distant is the hour; low murmurs spread,
And whispered fears, creating what they dread;
Ruin, as with an earthquake shock, is here,
50 There, the heart-witherings of unuttered fear,
And that sad death, whence most affection bleeds,
Which sickness, only of the soul, precedes.
Thy baseless wealth dissolves in air away,[1]
Like mists that melt before the morning ray:
55 No more on crowded mart or busy street
Friends, meeting friends, with cheerful hurry greet;
Sad, on the ground thy princely merchants bend
Their altered looks, and evil days portend,
And fold their arms, and watch with anxious breast
60 The tempest blackening in the distant West.[2]
    Yes, thou must droop; thy Midas dream is o'er;
The golden tide of Commerce leaves thy shore,

Leaves thee to prove the alternate ills that haunt
Enfeebling Luxury and ghastly Want;
65 Leaves thee, perhaps, to visit distant lands,
And deal the gifts of Heaven with equal hands.
    Yet, O my country, name beloved, revered,
By every tie that binds the soul endeared,
Whose image to my infant senses came
70 Mixt with Religion's light and Freedom's holy flame!
If prayers may not avert, if 'tis thy fate
To rank amongst the names that once were great,
Not like the dim cold crescent[3] shalt thou fade,
Thy debt to Science and the Muse unpaid;
75 Thine are the laws surrounding states revere,
Thine the full harvest of the mental year,
Thine the bright stars in Glory's sky that shine,
And arts that make it life to live are thine.
If westward streams the light that leaves thy shores,
80 Still from thy lamp the streaming radiance pours.
Wide spreads thy race from Ganges[4] to the pole,
O'er half the western world thy accents roll:
Nations beyond the Appalachian hills[5]
Thy hand has planted and thy spirit fills:
85 Soon as their gradual progress shall impart
The finer sense of morals and of art,
Thy stores of knowledge the new states shall know,
And think thy thoughts, and with thy fancy glow;
Thy Lockes, thy Paleys[6] shall instruct their youth,
90 Thy leading star direct their search for truth;
Beneath the spreading platan's[7] tent-like shade,
Or by Missouri's rushing waters laid,
"Old father Thames" shall be the poet's theme,
Of Hagley's woods[8] the enamoured virgin dream,
95 And Milton's tones the raptured ear enthrall,

---

[1] *Thy baseless wealth … away* 1810 saw the failure of many British businesses, and in 1811, the country itself was threatened with financial collapse.

[2] *The tempest … West* Relations had been strained between England and the United States since the French Revolution; Barbauld here foresees the beginning of the War of 1812.

[3] *crescent* Symbol of the Ottoman Empire, which had been in decline throughout the eighteenth and into the nineteenth century.

[4] *Ganges* Sacred river of India.

[5] *Appalachian hills* Mountain range in the eastern United States.

[6] *Lockes … Paleys* Men as eminent as John Locke and William Paley. John Locke (1632–1704), English philosopher who wrote about political, intellectual, and religious freedom and William Paley (1743–1805), English theologian and moral philosopher, who defended Christianity in many of his texts.

[7] *platan* Plane tree.

[8] *Hagley's woods* Cf. *The Seasons, "Spring,"* in which James Thomson writes about Lord Lyttleton's lush estate in Worcestershire.

Mixt with the roar of Niagara's fall;
In Thomson's glass[1] the ingenuous youth shall learn
A fairer face of Nature to discern;
Nor of the bards that swept the British lyre
100 Shall fade one laurel, or one note expire.
Then, loved Joanna,[2] to admiring eyes
Thy storied groups in scenic pomp shall rise;
Their high souled strains and Shakespeare's noble rage
Shall with alternate passion shake the stage.
105 Some youthful Basil[3] from thy moral lay
With stricter hand his fond desires shall sway;
Some Ethwald,[4] as the fleeting shadows pass,
Start at his likeness in the mystic glass;
The tragic Muse resume her just control,
110 With pity and with terror purge the soul,
While wide o'er transatlantic realms thy name
Shall live in light, and gather all its fame.

      Where wanders Fancy down the lapse of years
      Shedding o'er imaged woes untimely tears?
115 Fond moody Power! as hopes—as fears prevail,
She longs, or dreads, to lift the awful veil,
On visions of delight now loves to dwell,
Now hears the shriek of woe or Freedom's knell:
Perhaps, she says, long ages past away,
120 And set in western waves our closing day,
Night, Gothic night, again may shade the plains
Where Power is seated, and where Science reigns;
England, the seat of arts, be only known
By the gray ruin and the mouldering stone;
125 That time may tear the garland from her brow,
And Europe sit in dust, as Asia now.

      Yet then the ingenuous youth whom Fancy fires
      With pictured glories of illustrious sires,
      With duteous zeal their pilgrimage shall take
130 From the Blue Mountains,° or Ontario's lake, *in Pennsylvania*
With fond adoring steps to press the sod
By statesmen, sages, poets, heroes trod;
On Isis' banks[5] to draw inspiring air,

From Runnymede[6] to send the patriot's prayer;
135 In pensive thought, where Cam's slow waters[7] wind,
To meet those shades that ruled the realms of mind;
In silent halls to sculptured marbles bow,
And hang fresh wreaths round Newton's[8] awful brow.
Oft shall they seek some peasant's homely shed,
140 Who toils, unconscious of the mighty dead,
To ask where Avon's[9] winding waters stray,
And thence a knot of wild flowers bear away;
Anxious enquire where Clarkson,[10] friend of man,
Or all-accomplished Jones[11] his race began;
145 If of the modest mansion aught remains
Where Heaven and Nature prompted Cowper's[12] strains;
Where Roscoe, to whose patriot breast belong
The Roman virtue and the Tuscan song,
Led Ceres to the black and barren moor
150 Where Ceres never gained a wreath before:[13]
With curious search their pilgrim steps shall rove
By many a ruined tower and proud alcove,
Shall listen for those strains that soothed of yore
Thy rock, stern Skiddaw, and thy fall, Lodore;[14]
155 Feast with Dun Edin's° classic brow their sight, *Edinburgh's*
And visit "Melrose by the pale moonlight."[15]

      But who their mingled feelings shall pursue
      When London's faded glories rise to view?

---

[1] *glass* Mirror; i.e., nature as reflected in Thomson's *The Seasons*.

[2] *Joanna* Scottish playwright Joanna Baillie (1762–1851), who was often compared with Shakespeare.

[3] *Basil* Character in Baillie's tragedy *Count Basil* (1798).

[4] *Ethwald* Character in Baillie's tragedy *Ethwald* (1802).

[5] *Isis' banks* Bank of the River Thames at Oxford, known as the Isis.

[6] *Runnymede* Site where King John signed the Magna Carta (1215).

[7] *Cam* River at Cambridge.

[8] *Newton* Sir Isaac Newton (1642–1727), mathematician, physicist, and professor at Cambridge University.

[9] *Avon* River that runs through Stratford, where Shakespeare was born.

[10] *Clarkson* Thomas Clarkson (1760–1846), abolitionist, whose work helped to end the British slave trade in 1807.

[11] *Jones* Sir William Jones (1746–94), judge and scholar, who promoted Asian and Sanskrit studies.

[12] *Cowper* William Cowper (1731–1800), English poet.

[13] *Roscoe ... before* William Roscoe (1753–1831), historian and MP, who promoted the use of the moors for agriculture; *Ceres* Roman goddess of agriculture.

[14] *Skiddaw ... Lodore* Mountain and waterfall in the Lake District, England.

[15] *Melrose ... moonlight* Site of the beautiful Melrose Abbey ruins in the Scottish Borderlands; cf. Sir Walter Scott's *The Lay of the Last Minstrel* 2.1: "If thou woud'st view fair Melrose aright, / Go visit it by the pale moonlight." See also p. xxxiii in the Introduction to this volume.

160 The mighty city, which by every road,
In floods of people poured itself abroad;
Ungirt by walls, irregularly great,
No jealous drawbridge, and no closing gate;
Whose merchants (such the state which commerce brings)
165 Sent forth their mandates to dependant kings;
Streets, where the turban'd Moslem, bearded Jew,
And woolly Afric, met the brown Hindu;
Where through each vein spontaneous plenty flowed,
Where Wealth enjoyed, and Charity bestowed.
Pensive and thoughtful shall the wanderers greet
170 Each splendid square, and still, untrodden street;
Or of some crumbling turret, mined by time,
The broken stairs with perilous step shall climb,
Thence stretch their view the wide horizon round,
By scattered hamlets trace its ancient bound,
175 And, choked no more with fleets, fair Thames survey
Through reeds and sedge pursue his idle way.
    With throbbing bosoms shall the wanderers tread
The hallowed mansions of the silent dead,
Shall enter the long isle and vaulted dome
180 Where Genius and where Valour find a home;[1]
Awestruck, midst chill sepulchral marbles breathe,
Where all above is still, as all beneath;
Bend at each antique shrine, and frequent turn
To clasp with fond delight some sculptured urn,
185 The ponderous mass of Johnson's[2] form to greet,
Or breathe the prayer at Howard's[3] sainted feet.
    Perhaps some Briton, in whose musing mind
Those ages live which Time has cast behind,
To every spot shall lead his wondering guests
190 On whose known site the beam of glory rests:
Here Chatham's eloquence in thunder broke,
Here Fox persuaded, or here Garrick[4] spoke;
Shall boast how Nelson, fame and death in view,

To wonted victory led his ardent crew,
195 In England's name enforced, with loftiest tone,
Their duty—and too well fulfilled his own:[5]
How gallant Moore,[6] as ebbing life dissolved,
But hoped his country had his fame absolved.[7]
Or call up sages whose capacious mind
200 Left in its course a track of light behind;
Point where mute crowds on Davy's[8] lips reposed,
And Nature's coyest secrets were disclosed;
Join with their Franklin, Priestley's[9] injured name,
Whom, then, each continent shall proudly claim.
205   Oft shall the strangers turn their eager feet
The rich remains of ancient art to greet,
The pictured walls with critic eye explore,
And Reynolds be what Raphael[10] was before.
On spoils from every clime their eyes shall gaze,
210 Egyptian granites and the Etruscan vase;
And when midst fallen London, they survey
The stone where Alexander's ashes lay,[11]
Shall own with humbled pride the lesson just
By Time's slow finger written in the dust.
215   There walks a Spirit o'er the peopled earth,
Secret his progress is, unknown his birth;
Moody and viewless° as the changing wind,   *invisible*
No force arrests his foot, no chains can bind;

[1] *vaulted dome ... home* St. Paul's Cathedral, home to statues of eminent British men and women.

[2] *Johnson* Samuel Johnson (1709–84), scholar and author of *The Dictionary of the English Language.*

[3] *Howard* John Howard (1726–90), prison reformer and philanthropist.

[4] *Chatham* William Pitt, 1st Earl of Chatham (1708–78), prime minister and famous patriot and orator; *Fox* Charles James Fox (1749–1806), parliamentarian and orator; *Garrick* David Garrick (1717–79), famous English actor and dramatist.

[5] *Nelson ... his own* Admiral Horatio Nelson, English war hero, spoke these famous words before he died at the Battle of Trafalgar in 1805: "England expects that every man will do his duty."

[6] *Moore* Sir John Moore (1761–1809), general who led a retreat during the Napoleonic Wars; he saved his troops, but died in the process.

[7] [Barbauld's note] "I hope England will be satisfied," were the last words of General Moore.

[8] *Davy* Sir Humphrey Davy (1778–1829), physicist and chemist, whose lectures were renowned.

[9] *Franklin* Benjamin Franklin (1706–90), American scientist, inventor, and statesman; *Priestley* Joseph Priestley (1733–1804), English scientist and theologian, whose correspondence with Franklin led to Priestley's experimentation with and discoveries regarding electricity; Priestley was persecuted for his support of the French and American Revolutions, which led to his emigration from England to America.

[10] *Reynolds ... Raphael* Sir Joshua Reynolds (1723–92), eminent English portrait artist, and Raphael (1483–1520), famous Italian Renaissance painter and architect.

[11] *stone ... lay* The British Museum mistakenly believed it had purchased the tomb of Alexander the Great.

Where'er he turns, the human brute awakes,
220 And, roused to better life, his sordid hut forsakes:
He thinks, he reasons, glows with purer fires,
Feels finer wants, and burns with new desires:
Obedient Nature follows where he leads;
The steaming marsh is changed to fruitful meads;
225 The beasts retire from man's asserted reign,
And prove his kingdom was not given in vain.
Then from its bed is drawn the ponderous ore,
Then Commerce pours her gifts on every shore.
Then Babel's towers[1] and terraced gardens rise,
230 And pointed obelisks invade the skies;
The prince commands, in Tyrian purple drest,
And Egypt's virgins weave the linen vest.
Then spans the graceful arch the roaring tide,
And stricter bounds the cultured fields divide.
235 Then kindles Fancy, then expands the heart,
Then blow° the flowers of Genius and of Art;   *blossom*
Saints, Heroes, Sages, who the land adorn,
Seem rather to descend than to be born;
Whilst History, midst the rolls consigned to fame,
240 With pen of adamant inscribes their name.
    The Genius now forsakes the favoured shore,
And hates, capricious, what he loved before;
Then empires fall to dust, then arts decay,
And wasted realms enfeebled despots sway;
245 Even Nature's changed; without his fostering smile
Ophir[2] no gold, no plenty yields the Nile;
The thirsty sand absorbs the useless rill,°   *stream*
And spotted plagues from putrid fens distill.
In desert solitudes then Tadmor[3] sleeps,
250 Stern Marius then o'er fallen Carthage weeps;[4]
Then with enthusiast love the pilgrim roves
To seek his footsteps in forsaken groves,
Explores the fractured arch, the ruined tower,

Those limbs disjointed of gigantic power;
255 Still at each step he dreads the adder's sting,
The Arab's javelin, or the tiger's spring;
With doubtful caution treads the echoing ground,
And asks where Troy or Babylon[5] is found.
    And now the vagrant Power no more detains
260 The vale of Tempe, or Ausonian plains;[6]
Northward he throws the animating ray,
O'er Celtic nations bursts the mental day:
And, as some playful child the mirror turns,
Now here now there the moving lustre burns;
265 Now o'er his changeful fancy more prevail
Batavia's dykes than Arno's[7] purple vale,
And stinted suns, and rivers bound with frost,
Than Enna's plains or Baia's[8] viny coast;
Venice the Adriatic weds in vain,
270 And Death sits brooding o'er Campania's[9] plain;
O'er Baltic shores and through Hercynian groves,[10]
Stirring the soul, the mighty impulse moves;
Art plies his tools, and Commerce spreads her sail,
And wealth is wafted in each shifting gale.
275 The sons of Odin[11] tread on Persian looms,
And Odin's daughters breathe distilled perfumes;
Loud minstrel bards, in Gothic halls, rehearse
The Runic rhyme, and "build the lofty verse:"[12]
The Muse, whose liquid notes were wont to swell
280 To the soft breathings of the Aeolian[13] shell,
Submits, reluctant, to the harsher tone,
And scarce believes the altered voice her own.

---

[1] *Babel's towers* Cf. Genesis 11.3–9. The Babylonians attempted to create a tower that would reach heaven; God punished them by giving them different languages and scattering them around the earth.

[2] *Ophir* Cf. 1 Kings 9.28: "And they came to Ophir, and fetched from thence gold."

[3] *Tadmor* Biblical land in ancient Syria.

[4] *Marius … weeps* Gaius Marius (157–86 BCE), Roman Consul and general who was once called the "savior of Rome"; upon aging and falling from power, he was said to have wept among the ruins of Carthage.

[5] *Troy* Ancient city in Asia Minor, subject of the Trojan War in Homer's *Iliad*; *Babylon* Ancient Mesopotamian city known for its wealth and beauty, destroyed in 689 BCE.

[6] *vale of Tempe* Valley in Greece celebrated by ancient poets for its beauty; *Ausonian plains* Virgil called Italy "Ausonia."

[7] *Batavia* Republic, now the Netherlands; *Arno* River in Italy.

[8] *Enna* Sicilian valley; *Baia* Italian village on the Bay of Naples, celebrated for its spas in Roman times.

[9] *Campania* Italian province whose plains were marshy and malarial.

[10] *Hercynian groves* Black Forest in Germany.

[11] *Odin* Supreme Norse god.

[12] *build the lofty verse* From Milton's *Lycidas* (10–11): "He knew / Himself to sing, and build the lofty rhyme."

[13] *Aeolian* Aeolis is the ancient name of a beautiful coastal region in Asia Minor (now Turkey).

And now, where Caesar saw with proud disdain
The wattled hut and skin of azure stain,[1]
285 Corinthian columns rear their graceful forms,
And light verandas brave the wintry storms,
While British tongues the fading fame prolong
Of Tully's eloquence and Maro's[2] song.
Where once Bonduca whirled the scythed car,
290 And the fierce matrons raised the shriek of war,[3]
Light forms beneath transparent muslins float,
And tutored voices swell the artful note.
Light-leaved acacias and the shady plane
And spreading cedar grace the woodland reign;
295 While crystal walls the tenderer plants confine,
The fragrant orange and the nectared pine;
The Syrian grape there hangs her rich festoons,
Nor asks for purer air, or brighter noons:
Science and Art urge on the useful toil,
300 New mold a climate and create the soil,
Subdue the rigour of the northern Bear,[4]
O'er polar climes shed aromatic air,
On yielding Nature urge their new demands,
And ask not gifts but tribute at her hands.
305   London exults:—on London Art bestows
Her summer ices and her winter rose;
Gems of the East her mural crown adorn,
And Plenty at her feet pours forth her horn;[5]
While even the exiles her just laws disclaim,

310 People a continent, and build a name:
August she sits, and with extended hands
Holds forth the book of life to distant lands.
    But fairest flowers expand but to decay;
The worm is in thy core, thy glories pass away;
315 Arts, arms and wealth destroy the fruits they bring;
Commerce, like beauty, knows no second spring.
Crime walks thy streets, Fraud earns her unblest bread,
O'er want and woe thy gorgeous robe is spread,
And angel charities in vain oppose:
320 With grandeur's growth the mass of misery grows.
For see,—to other climes the Genius soars,
He turns from Europe's desolated shores;
And lo, even now, midst mountains wrapt in storm,
On Andes' heights he shrouds his awful form;
325 On Chimborazo's[6] summits treads sublime,
Measuring in lofty thought the march of Time;
Sudden he calls:—"'Tis now the hour!" he cries,
Spreads his broad hand, and bids the nations rise.
La Plata[7] hears amidst her torrents' roar,
330 Potosi[8] hears it, as she digs the ore:
Ardent, the Genius fans the noble strife,
And pours through feeble souls a higher life,
Shouts to the mingled tribes from sea to sea,
And swears—Thy world, Columbus, shall be free.
—1812

---

[1] *Caesar ... stain* Cf. Julius Caesar's *The Gallic Wars* 5.14: "All the Britains, indeed, dye themselves with wood, which occasions a bluish color, and thereby have a more terrible appearance in fight."

[2] *Tully* Marcus Tullius Cicero (106–43 BCE), Roman orator, philosopher, and politician; *Maro* Publius Vergilius Maro, or Virgil (70–19 BCE), Roman poet, author of the *Aeneid*.

[3] *Bonduca ... war* Queen of the ancient Iceni Celts, Boadicea (sometimes written as "Bonduca" or "Boudicca") led a massive rebellion against the Romans in about 60 CE; she committed suicide upon the failure of the mission.

[4] *northern Bear* Ursa Minor, a constellation that includes the North Star.

[5] *horn* Horn of plenty, or cornucopia, contains an abundance of the essentials and luxuries of life.

[6] *Chimborazo* Volcanic mountain in Ecuador.

[7] *La Plata* City in Argentina.

[8] *Potosi* City in Bolivia. All three countries were home to movements resistant to colonial rule. The region was famous for its gold deposits.

WILLIAM BLAKE
1757 – 1827

"I labor upwards into futurity," etched William Blake onto the back of one of the copper plates which constituted the "tablets" of his visionary art. A poet and artist whose work was sorely undervalued during his own lifetime, Blake recognized that his was a genius before its time. The mysterious and powerful poetry that he crafted to convey his vision would eventually be recognized as having revolutionary significance; for the past century or more Blake has been recognized as a great poet of the Romantic era.

Blake was born one November evening in 1757 above his parents' hosiery shop in the Soho district of London. James and Catherine Blake, religious Dissenters whose non-compromising beliefs were those of a growing number of tradespeople, allowed their son to pursue a program of self study that saved him from being schooled under the institutional authorities he instinctively abhorred. Although his parents were generally indulgent, there are hints that Blake balked even under their natural expressions of authority. He received a thrashing for declaring he had seen the face of God, and was accused of lying when he reported passing a tree bespangled with angels. Since his family could not afford the expense of artistic training, he was apprenticed at fourteen to a highly respected engraver, with whom he lived for seven years while learning the trade which would thereafter earn him his living

During the period of his apprenticeship, Blake began writing the poems that were eventually collected in *Poetical Sketches* (1783)—the only volume of his verse originally printed by letter-press rather than by the "illuminated" methods he later originated. Of his parents and three siblings, Blake retained lasting affection only for his younger brother, Robert. Blake claimed to communicate daily with the spirit of Robert after his early death from tuberculosis. Indeed, the unique style of relief etching or "Illuminated Printing" which Blake later devised was imparted, he claimed, by Robert in a visitation. Etching words backwards into copper plates so that they would reverse to normal upon printing, Blake in 1788 produced his first illuminated texts with "All Religions Are One" and "There is No Natural Religion." It was a defining moment for him, one in which words and images converged into an indivisible and prophetic expression. He soon applied his new method of printing to a larger project, the poetic and pictorial depiction of a young soul descending into the realm of matter, recounted in *The Book of Thel*.

Blake's words and designs "interanimate each other," in the words of one critic; a master of color, he, at times, achieved unearthly effects in his hand-tinted books, of which no two copies were exactly the same. Rather than reflecting the tones of the natural world, Blake's color—and indeed the vividness of his verse—aim towards the supernatural. Similarly, what separates his poetry from that of contemporaries, such as Wordsworth and Coleridge is his lack of interest in "painting Nature." For Blake, the true aim of art was to tune the senses and the imaginative faculties to the higher pitch of a spiritual reality, not to the natural world. For this reason, Blake detested what he called the "muddy" colors, nuanced shade work, and secular sensibilities of an artist such as Rembrandt, while revering the determined outlines, bright colors and unequivocal contrasts of light and dark achieved by High Renaissance painters such as Michelangelo and Raphael.

The bold, declarative and (to some modern eyes) exaggerated style which Blake admired in painting is paralleled in many of his literary preferences. His work has close associations with the declamatory traditions of prophecy, of the aphorism, of the political pamphlet, and of the proverb. *The Marriage of Heaven and Hell* (1790) contains some of his most chiseled epigrams: "The cut worm forgives the plow" and "The tigers of wrath are wiser than the horses of instruction." The Bible was a tremendous imaginative reserve upon which he drew all of his life. He admired Dante, Milton, Spenser, and Shakespeare, supplied commissioned designs for editions of Milton's *L'Allegro, Il Penseroso, Paradise Lost*, and *Paradise Regained*, and left behind an unfinished series of watercolors illustrating Dante's work. He was also influenced by the architecture and sepulchral art of Westminster Abbey and by the literary gothic of Edward Young's *Night Thoughts* and Robert Blair's *The Grave*, versions of which he illustrated. If he was in many respects an outsider to his own culture, Blake was fully a man of the times in his love of the popular "forgeries" of James Macpherson (author of the "Ossian" poems) and Thomas Chatterton, as well as in his enjoyment of works of Gothic fiction such as Ann Radcliffe's *The Mysteries of Udolpho* (1794).

On at least two occasions Blake struck out to earn a reputation as an artist in his own right. The first occasion came at the end of his apprenticeship, when he submitted a portfolio to the Royal Academy of Arts (under the presidency of Sir Joshua Reynolds—and was accepted into the Academy. Yet he failed to emerge out of obscurity, and was forced to set up an engraver's shop. For twenty years Blake would resign himself to the grueling schedule of a copy engraver, recognized only by a few of his friends as a formidably original artist, and almost wholly overlooked as a poet. In 1809, energized by a gallery showing of works by Dürer, Michelangelo, Giulio Romano, and others, Blake renewed his association with the Royal Academy to launch a solo exhibition of his own work. With the exception of a caustic review or two, the public remained unmoved by—possibly unready for—the idiosyncratic light Blake cast upon subjects such as "The Body of Abel found by Adam and Eve."

Blake found his soul mate in Catherine Boucher, the illiterate daughter of a market gardener. He taught her to read and trained her in the preparation of copper plates, the hand coloring of prints, and the stitching of pages into bound copies. Catherine was evidently a submissive, devoted wife, and some have denigrated Blake's traditional and even misogynist approach to marriage, citing his pronouncement that "the female … lives from the light of the male." At the same time, however, Blake approved of the arguments for sexual equality made by Mary Wollstonecraft in *A Vindication of the Rights of Woman* (1793). Blake radically proposed that carnal pleasure was a portal to the divine. In *Visions of the Daughters of Albion* (1793), Blake abjures sexual domination and celebrates "the moment of desire!" in a manner highly unconventional at the time. Visitors to the Blake home reported coming across the couple reading naked in a garden house in their back yard, enjoying the innocence of their private Eden and rejecting the narratives of shame and the Fall.

The rewriting of the Biblical drama of the Creation and Fall that underlies nearly all of Blake's work was influenced by radical Dissenters who celebrated nudity as a symbol of unfallen humanity. Blake was also influenced by the mystical systems of Emmanuel Swedenborg and Jacob Boehme, and tapped into veins of esoteric knowledge related to the cabbalistic teachings of the Freemasons, the Rosicrucians, and Paracelsus. He also had associations with decidedly non-mystical political movements that were bravely calling for democratic reforms at a time when the English monarchy was intent on quashing sympathizers with American War of Independence and the French Revolution.

Blake never fully participated in an organized movement of any kind, be it religious or political. His was "a voice crying in the wilderness," an unsystematizable voice urging men and women to realize their "human form divine." Unwilling to conform to any system not of his own creation, Blake's language grew increasingly esoteric and opaque in later major prophecies such as *The Four Zoas, Milton* (1804) and *Jerusalem* (1804–20).

One vision that Blake explores over and over again is that of an earthly Eden triumphing over forces of repression. This is the common theme of *The French Revolution* (1791), *America: A Prophecy* (1793), *Europe: A Prophecy* (1794), and *The Book of Urizen* (1794). When Blake summons Albion, figure of the human form divine in *Jerusalem*, to "Awake!" he is calling for a spiritual revolution in which humanity awakens to the knowledge that the republic of heaven is immanent.

Blake imagined the spiritual dimensions of the geography of London in particularly vivid detail. That the material double of his holy city was corrupt lends a sharp edge to Blake's vision. As one Blake biographer writes, "it was a time when mobs and rioters often controlled large areas of the city; there were riots by sailors, silk-weavers, coal-heavers, hatters, glass-grinders ....and bloody demonstrations over the price of bread." The biting simplicity of "The Chimney Sweeper" and "The Little Black Boy" in Blake's *Songs of Innocence and of Experience* (1789–94) are testimony to his acute sensitivity to the realities of poverty and exploitation that accompanied the "dark satanic mills" of the industrial revolution.

In this London, Blake admitted to living in fear that his artistic vision and eccentric tendency to converse with angels and ghosts would land him in trouble with the authorities—a fear horribly realized in 1803. The Blakes had been generously invited by William Hayley, an eminent poet and wealthy patron of the arts, to live in a country cottage at Felpham. One day a drunken private in the Royal Dragoons, John Scofield, fell into a heated argument with Blake at his garden gate. Blake physically evicted the abusive soldier from the premises. Scofield subsequently accused Blake of making seditious remarks against the Crown, an offense punishable by death. Hayley generously paid for his friend's bail and his defense, and Blake was eventually acquitted, to the thunderous approval of the court. However, the incident stamped itself upon his sensitive mind; he raised it to mythological proportions in the convoluted poetic symbology of *Jerusalem*, where the Law is figured as the nauseous region of "Bowlahoola," while Scofield and his cohorts appear as "ministers of evil."

As the culture around him placed increasing faith in the physical laws of natural science, Blake's insistence on the incorruptible coordinates of imaginative truth cast him as an increasing oddity. Many of Blake's contemporaries considered him insane. London was shifting to a secular orientation under the rise of industrial culture. Against the grain of the times, Blake continued producing labor-intensive printings of illuminated books, none of which proved to be a commercial success. Only twenty-eight copies of *Songs of Innocence and of Experience* are known to exist, sixteen of *The Book of Thel*, nine of *The Marriage of Heaven and Hell*, and five of *Jerusalem*.

In his last years, just as he had reconciled himself to poverty and obscurity, Blake attracted the first following he had ever enjoyed, a small group of painters called "the Ancients." Charles Lamb and a few other writers of the period also expressed admiration, but the glimmerings of a full-fledged "Blake industry" did not appear until years after his death, when his art and poetry were discovered by Dante Gabriel Rossetti and the Pre-Raphaelites. Rossetti and, later, William Butler Yeats edited volumes of Blake's poems, and appreciation grew of his powerful poetic as well as painterly achievements. By the middle of the twentieth century, academics around the world were devoting themselves to the scholarly study of Blake's work, which was also exerting a profound influence on the literary and popular culture of the time. Blake was an inspiration to the generation of Beat poets clustered around Allen Ginsberg and to many in the 'sixties counterculture who took up his call to open the "doors of perception" (words straight from *The Marriage of Heaven and Hell*), trying everything from the hallucinogenic drugs proposed by Aldous Huxley, to communal living and free love, to approximate his visionary universe. The future had finally caught up with William Blake.

⌘ ⌘ ⌘

from *Songs of Innocence and of Experience
Showing the Two Contrary States of the
Human Soul*

Title page, *Songs of Innocence and of Experience.*

from *Songs of Innocence*

Introduction

Piping down the valleys wild
Piping songs of pleasant glee
On a cloud I saw a child.
And he laughing said to me.

5   'Pipe a song about a Lamb:'
So I piped with merry chear.[1]

'Piper pipe that song again'
So I piped, he wept to hear.

'Drop thy pipe thy happy pipe
10   Sing thy songs of happy chear.'
So I sung the same again,
While he wept with joy to hear

'Piper sit thee down and write
In a book that all may read—'
15   So he vanish'd from my sight
And I pluck'd a hollow reed

And I made a rural pen,
And I stain'd the water clear,
And I wrote my happy songs
20   Every child may joy to hear
—1789

The Ecchoing Green

The Sun does arise,
And make happy the skies.
The merry bells ring
To welcome the Spring.
5   The sky-lark and thrush,
The birds of the bush,
Sing louder around,
To the bells chearful sound.
While our sports shall be seen
10   On the Ecchoing Green.
Old John with white hair
Does laugh away care,
Sitting under the oak,
Among the old folk.
15   They laugh at our play,
And soon they all say.
'Such such were the joys.
When we all girls & boys,
In our youth-time were seen.
20   On the Ecchoing Green.'

---

[1]   *chear*   The usual practice of this anthology regarding modernization of spelling and punctuation has not been followed in the case
of Blake; his idiosyncrasies have been retained.

Till the little ones weary
No more can be merry
The sun does descend,
And our sports have an end:
25   Round the laps of their mothers.
Many sisters and brothers,
Like birds in their nest,
Are ready for rest:
And sport no more seen,
30   On the darkening Green.
—1789

The Lamb

Little Lamb who made thee
  Dost thou know who made thee
Gave thee life & bid thee feed.
By the stream & o'er the mead;
5   Gave thee clothing of delight,
Softest clothing wooly bright;
Gave thee such a tender voice,
Making all the vales rejoice;
    Little Lamb who made thee
10   Dost thou know who made thee

    Little Lamb I'll tell thee,
    Little Lamb I'll tell thee:
He is called by thy name,
For he calls himself a Lamb:

15   He is meek & he is mild,[1]
He became a little child:
I a child & thou a lamb,
We are called by his name.
    Little Lamb God bless thee
20   Little Lamb God bless thee.
—1789

"The Little Black Boy."

The Little Black Boy

My mother bore me in the southern wild,
  And I am black, but O! my soul is white.
White as an angel is the English child:
But I am black as if bereav'd of light.

5   My mother taught me underneath a tree
And sitting down before the heat of day.
She took me on her lap and kissed me.
And pointing to the east began to say.

'Look on the rising sun! there God does live
10   And gives his light. and gives his heat away.
And flowers and trees and beasts and men receive
Comfort in morning joy in the noon day.

'And we are put on earth a little space.
That we may learn to bear the beams of love.
15   And these black bodies and this sun-burnt face

---

[1] *He … mild* Cf. Charles Wesley, "Gentle Jesus, meek and mild."

Is but a cloud, and like a shady grove.

'For when our souls have learn'd the heat to bear
The cloud will vanish we shall hear his voice.
Saying: "come out from the grove my love & care,
20   And round my golden tent like lambs rejoice."'

Thus did my mother say and kissed me.
And thus I say to little English boy.
When I from black and he from white cloud free,
And round the tent of God like lambs we joy:

25   Ill shade him from the heat till he can bear.
To lean in joy upon our fathers knee
And then Ill stand and stroke his silver hair.
And be like him and he will then love me.
—1789

The Chimney Sweeper [1]

When my mother died I was very young,
    And my father sold me while yet my tongue,
Could scarcely cry 'weep weep weep weep.'[2]
So your chimneys I sweep & in soot I sleep.[3]

5   Theres little Tom Dacre who cried when his head
That curl'd like a lambs back, was shav'd. so I said.
'Hush Tom never mind it, for when your head's bare.
You know that the soot cannot spoil your white hair.'

And so he was quiet, & that very night.
10   As Tom was a sleeping he had such a sight,
That thousands of sweepers Dick, Joe Ned & Jack
Were all of them lock'd up in coffins of black,

And by came an Angel who had a bright key,
And he open'd the coffins & set them all free.

15   Then down a green plain leaping laughing they run
And wash in a river and shine in the Sun.[4]

Then naked & white, all their bags left behind.
They rise upon clouds, and sport in the wind.
And the Angel told Tom if he'd be a good boy.
20   He'd have God for his father & never want joy.

And so Tom awoke and we rose in the dark
And got with our bags & our brushes to work.
Tho' the morning was cold, Tom was happy & warm.
So if all do their duty, they need not fear harm.
—1789

The Divine Image

To Mercy Pity Peace and Love,
    All pray in their distress:
And to these virtues of delight
Return their thankfulness.

5   For Mercy Pity Peace and Love.
Is God our father dear:
And Mercy Pity Peace and Love.
Is Man his child and care.

For Mercy has a human heart
10   Pity a human face:
And Love, the human form divine.
And Peace, the human dress.

Then every man of every clime,
That prays in his distress,
15   Prays to the human form divine
Love Mercy Pity Peace.

And all must love the human form,
In heathen, turk or jew.[5]

---

[1] *The Chimney Sweeper*   Children were often forced to climb up chimneys to clean them—a filthy, dangerous, and unhealthy job. A law ameliorating their working conditions was passed in 1788, but it was rarely enforced.

[2] *weep ... weep*   The child is attempting to say "sweep," the chimney-sweeper's street cry. The act of 1788 should have prevented the apprenticing of children younger than eight.

[3] *in soot I sleep*   The sweeps used their bags of soot as blankets.

[4] *And wash ... Sun*   The act of 1788 called for weekly washings for sweeps.

[5] *heathen ... jew*   Cf. Isaac Watts, "Praise for the Gospel": "Lord, I ascribe it to thy Grace / And not to Chance, as others do, / That I was born of *Christian* Race, / And not a *Heathen*, or a *Jew*." Whereas Watt's emphasis had been on the theological underpinnings for a hierarchy of birth that took for granted the inferiority of other races and religions, Blake's emphasis is on loving even those whom his

Where Mercy, Love & Pity dwell,
20 There God is dwelling too.
—1789

Holy Thursday [1]

Twas on a Holy Thursday their innocent faces clean
The children walking two & two in red & blue &
green [2]
Grey headed beadles [3] walkd before with wands as
white as snow
Till into the high dome of Pauls they like Thames
waters flow

5 O what a multitude they seemd these flowers of
London town
Seated in companies they sit with radiance all their own
The hum of multitudes was there but multitudes of
lambs
Thousands of little boys & girls raising their innocent
hands

Now like a mighty wind they raise to heaven the voice
of song
10 Or like harmonious thunderings the seats of heaven
among
Beneath them sit the aged men wise guardians of the poor
Then cherish pity, lest you drive an angel from your
door [4]
—1789

Infant Joy

I have no name
I am but two days old.—'
What shall I call thee?
'I happy am
5 Joy is my name,—'
Sweet joy befall thee!

Pretty joy!
Sweet joy but two days old,
Sweet joy I call thee;
10 Thou dost smile.
I sing the while
Sweet joy befall thee.
—1789

Nurse's Song

When the voices of children are heard on the green
And laughing is heard on the hill,
My heart is at rest within my breast
And every thing else is still

5 'Then come home my children, the sun is gone down
And the dews of night arise
Come come leave off play. and let us away
Till the morning appears in the skies.'

'No no let us play, for it is yet day
10 And we cannot go to sleep
Besides in the sky, the little birds fly
And the hills are all coverd with sheep'

'Well well go & play till the light fades away
And then go home to bed'
15 The little ones leaped & shouted & laugh'd
And all the hills ecchoed.
—1789

---

society despises.

[1] *Holy Thursday* Each year since 1782, the 6,000 children in
London's charity schools had been brought to St. Paul's Cathedral
for an annual service of thanks-giving. Though "Holy Thursday" is
the name given to Ascension Day, these services always occurred on
a Thursday, usually in May, but never on Ascension Day.

[2] *in … green* The school uniforms.

[3] *beadles* Officials.

[4] *cherish … door* Cf. Hebrews 13.2, "Be not forgetful to entertain
strangers; for thereby some have entertained angels unawares."

Title page, *Songs of Experience*.

from *Songs of Experience*

Introduction

Hear the voice of the Bard!
Who Present, Past, & Future sees
Whose ears have heard,
The Holy Word,

5   That walk'd among the ancient trees.[1]
Calling[2] the lapsed Soul
And weeping in the evening dew:
That[3] might controll
The starry pole;
10 And fallen fallen light renew!

---

[1] *Holy Word ... trees* Cf. Genesis 3.8: "And they heard the voice of the Lord God walking in the garden in the cool of the day: and Adam and his wife hid themselves from the presence of the Lord God amongst the trees of the garden."

[2] *Calling* The subject here is ambiguous, and could either be the bard or the Holy Word.

[3] *That* Most likely the referent here is the lapsed soul, but it may also be the Holy Word.

Frontispiece, *Songs of Experience*.

O Earth, O Earth return!
Arise from out the dewy grass;
Night is worn,
And the morn
15 Rises from the slumberous mass.

'Turn away no more:
Why wilt thou turn away
The starry floor[1]
The watry shore
20 Is giv'n thee till the break of day.'
—1794

The Clod & the Pebble

Love seeketh not Itself to please.
Nor for itself hath any care;
But for another gives its ease.
And builds a Heaven in Hells despair.'

5   So sang a little Clod of Clay.
Trodden with the cattles feet:
But a Pebble of the brook.
Warbled out these metres meet.

'Love seeketh only Self to please,
10 To bind another to Its delight;
Joys in anothers loss of ease,
And builds a Hell in Heavens despite.'[2]
—1794

Holy Thursday

Is this a holy thing to see.
In a rich and fruitful land,
Babes reducd to misery.
Fed with cold and usurous hand?[3]

5 Is that trembling cry a song?
Can it be a song of joy?
And so many children poor?
It is a land of poverty!

And their sun does never shine.
10 And their fields are bleak & bare.
And their ways are fill'd with thorns
It is eternal winter there.

For where-e'er the sun does shine.
And where-e'er the rain does fall:
15 Babe can never hunger there,
Nor poverty the mind appall.
—1794

The Chimney Sweeper

A little black thing among the snow:
Crying 'weep, weep,' in notes of woe!
'Where are thy father & mother? say?'
'They are both gone up to the church to pray.

5 'Because I was happy upon the heath.
And smil'd among the winters snow:
They clothed me in the clothes of death.
And taught me to sing the notes of woe.

'And because I am happy & dance & sing.
10 They think they have done me no injury:
And are gone to praise God & his Priest & King
Who make up a heaven of our misery.'
—1794

The Sick Rose

O Rose thou art sick.
The invisible worm.
That flies in the night
In the howling storm:

5 Has found out thy bed
Of crimson joy:

---

[1] *starry floor* The sky, the floor of heaven.

[2] *builds ... despite* In Milton's *Paradise Lost* (1.254–55), Satan declares, "The mind is its own place, and in itself / Can make a Heaven of Hell, a Hell of Heaven."

[3] *usurous hand* I.e., the hand of someone engaged in lending money at interest.

And his dark secret love
Does thy life destroy.
—1794

The Fly

Little Fly
Thy summers play.
My thoughtless hand
Has brush'd away.

5 Am not I
A fly like thee?[1]
Or art not thou
A man like me?

For I dance
10 And drink & sing:
Till some blind hand
Shall brush my wing.

If thought is life
And strength & breath:
15 And the want
Of thought is death;[2]

Then am I
A happy fly,
If I live,
20 Or if I die.
—1794

The Tyger

Tyger Tyger, burning bright,
In the forests of the night;
What immortal hand or eye.
Could frame thy fearful symmetry?

5 In what distant deeps or skies.
Burnt the fire of thine eyes?

On what wings dare he aspire?[3]
What the hand. dare seize the fire?[4]

And what shoulder, & what art,
10 Could twist the sinews of thy heart?
And when thy heart began to beat,
What dread hand? & what dread feet?

What the hammer? what the chain,
In what furnace was thy brain?
15 What the anvil? what dread grasp.
Dare its deadly terrors clasp!

When the stars threw down the spears[5]
And water'd heaven with their tears:

---

[1] *Am … thee* Cf. Shakespeare, *King Lear* 4.1.36–37: "As flies to wanton boys, are we to the gods, / They kill us for their sport."

[2] *If thought …death* Cf. René Descartes's statement "Cogito, ergo sum" ("I think, therefore I am").

[3] *what … aspire* In Greek mythology, Icarus fashioned wings of wax and feathers; these melted when he attempted to fly too close to the sun.

[4] *What … fire* Prometheus stole fire from heaven to give to humans.

[5] *threw down the spears* Either in surrender or as an act of rebellion —it is uncertain which.

Did he smile his work to see?
20   Did he who made the Lamb make thee?[1]

Tyger Tyger burning bright,
In the forests of the night:
What immortal hand or eye.
Dare frame thy fearful symmetry?
—1794

Ah! Sun-Flower

Ah Sun-flower! weary of time,
   Who countest the steps of the Sun:
Seeking after that sweet golden clime
Where the travellers journey is done.

5   Where the Youth pined away with desire,
And the pale Virgin shrouded in snow:
Arise from their graves and aspire.
Where my Sun-flower wishes to go.
—1794

The Garden of Love

I went to the Garden of Love.
   And saw what I never had seen:
A Chapel was built in the midst,
Where I used to play on the green.[2]

5   And the gates of this Chapel were shut,
And 'Thou shalt not'[3] writ over the door;
So I turn'd to the Garden of Love,
That so many sweet flowers bore.

And I saw it was filled with graves,
10   And tomb-stones where flowers should be:
And Priests in black gowns. were walking their
      rounds,

---

[1] *Did he … thee*   Tigers are not mentioned in the Bible.

[2] *A Chapel … green*   Possibly a reference to the erection of a chapel on South Lambeth Green in 1793.

[3] *Thou shalt not*   The phrase that introduces most of the Ten Commandments (Exodus 20.3–17).

And binding with briars.[4] my joys & desires.
—1794

London

I wander thro' each charter'd[5] street,
   Near where the charter'd Thames does flow,
And mark in every face I meet
Marks of weakness, marks of woe.

5   In every cry of every Man,
In every Infants cry of fear.
In every voice; in every ban.
The mind-forg'd manacles I hear

How the Chimney-sweepers cry
10   Every blackning Church appalls.
And the hapless Soldiers sigh
Runs in blood down Palace walls

But most thro' midnight streets I hear
How the youthful Harlots curse[6]
15   Blasts the new born Infants tear[7]
And blights with plagues the Marriage hearse.
—1794

The Human Abstract

Pity would be no more.
   If we did not make somebody Poor:
And Mercy no more could be.
If all were as happy as we;

5   And mutual fear brings peace;
Till the selfish loves increase.

---

[4] *binding with briars*   Prior to the nineteenth century, binding graves with briars was a common practice.

[5] *charter'd*   Privileged, licensed. While charters grant freedoms, they often do so for a select minority (such as merchants) and thereby simultaneously oppress the majority.

[6] *Harlots curse*   Referring both to the oaths she utters and the venereal diseases she spreads.

[7] *Blasts … tear*   A reference to the blindness caused in infants if they contract certain venereal diseases (such as gonorrhea) from the mother.

Then Cruelty knits a snare,
And spreads his baits with care.

He sits down with holy fears,
10 And waters the ground with tears;
Then Humility takes its root
Underneath his foot.

Soon spreads the dismal shade
Of Mystery over his head;
15 And the Catterpiller and Fly.
Feed on the Mystery.

And it bears the fruit of Deceit.
Ruddy and sweet to eat;
And the Raven his nest has made
20 In its thickest shade.

The Gods of the earth and sea.
Sought thro' Nature to find this Tree
But their search was all in vain:
There grows one in the Human Brain
—1794

Infant Sorrow

My mother groand! my father wept.
Into the dangerous world I leapt:
Helpless, naked. piping loud;
    Like a fiend hid in a cloud.

5 Struggling in my fathers hands:
Striving against my swadling bands:
Bound and weary I thought best
To sulk upon my mothers breast.
—1794

A Poison Tree[1]

I was angry with my friend;
    I told my wrath, my wrath did end.
I was angry with my foe:
I told it not, my wrath did grow.

5 And I waterd it in fears,
Night & morning with my tears:
And I sunned it with smiles,
And with soft deceitful wiles.

And it grew both day and night.
10 Till it bore an apple bright.
And my foe beheld it shine,
And he knew that it was mine.

And into my garden stole.
When the night had veild the pole;
15 In the morning glad I see.
My foe outstretchd beneath the tree.
—1794

[Plate 1][2]

The Marriage of Heaven and Hell[3]

[Plate 2]

The Argument[4]

Rintrah[5] roars & shakes his fires in the burdend air;
    Hungry clouds swag[6] on the deep

Once meek, and in a perilous path,
The just man kept his course along
5 The vale of death.
Roses are planted where thorns grow,
And on the barren heath
Sing the honey bees.

Then the perilous path was planted:
10 And a river, and a spring

---

[1] the Poison Tree Another version of this poem is entitled "Christian Forbearance."

[2] [Plate 1] The illustrated plates are reproduced on pp. 58–61.

[3] Marriage … Hell Blake combines the titles of two works by the Swedish visionary Emanuel Swedenborg (1688–1772), A Treatise Concerning Heaven and Hell, and of the Wonderful Things Therein, as Heard and Seen by Emanuel Swedenborg (1758, trans. 1784) and Conjugial Love (1768, trans. 1790).

[4] Argument For the imagery of "The Argument," Cf. Isaiah 5.1–7, 7.23–25, 35.1–10.

[5] Rintrah The character of Rintrah, a prophet and herald, reappears in Blake's Europe a Prophecy (1794) as well as in his Milton.

[6] swag Sag, hang heavily.

On every cliff and tomb;
And on the bleached bones[1]
Red clay[2] brought forth.

Till the villain left the paths of ease,
15   To walk in perilous paths, and drive
The just man into barren climes.

Now the sneaking serpent walks
In mild humility.
And the just man rages in the wilds
20   Where lions roam.

Rintrah roars & shakes his fires in the burdend air;
Hungry clouds swag on the deep.

[Plate 3]

    As a new heaven is begun, and it is now thirty-three years since its advent: the Eternal Hell revives.[3] And lo! Swedenborg is the Angel sitting at the tomb; his writings are the linen clothes folded up. Now is the dominion of Edom,[4] & the return of Adam into Paradise; see Isaiah XXXIV & XXXV chap.[5]

    Without Contraries is no progression. Attraction and Repulsion, Reason and Energy, Love and Hate, are necessary to Human existence.

    From these contraries spring what the religious call Good & Evil. Good is the passive that obeys Reason Evil is the active springing from Energy.

    Good is Heaven. Evil is Hell.

[Plate 4]

The Voice of the Devil

All Bibles or sacred codes have been the causes of the following errors.
1. That Man has two real existing principles Viz: a Body & a Soul.
2. That Energy. calld Evil. is alone from the Body. & that Reason. calld Good. is alone from the soul.
3. That God will torment Man in Eternity for following his Energies.
But the following Contraries to these are True
1. Man has no Body distinct from his soul for that calld Body is a portion of soul discernd by the five Senses, the chief inlets of Soul in this age
2. Energy is the only life and is from the Body and Reason is the bound or outward circumference of Energy.
3. Energy is Eternal Delight

[Plate 5]

    Those who restrain desire, do so because theirs is weak enough to be restrained; and the restrainer or reason usurps its place & governs the unwilling.

    And being restrained it by degrees becomes passive till it is only the shadow of desire.

    The history of this is written in *Paradise Lost*.[6] & the Governor or Reason is call'd Messiah.

    And the original Archangel or possessor of the command of the heavenly host, is calld the Devil or Satan and his children are call'd Sin & Death[7]

    But in the Book of Job Miltons Messiah is call'd Satan.

    For this history has been adopted by both parties

    It indeed appear'd to Reason as if Desire was cast out, but the Devils account is, that the Messiah [Plate 6] fell. & formed a heaven of what he stole from the Abyss[8]

---

[1] *bleached bones* Cf. Ezekiel 37.1–11, in which Ezekiel sees life resurrected from a valley of bones.

[2] *Red clay* Since God created Adam from "the dust of the ground" (Genesis 2.8), "Adam" is sometimes said to mean "red clay" in Hebrew.

[3] *As a … revives* Swedenborg had predicted that the Last Judgment would occur in 1757, coincidentally the year of Blake's birth. In 1790, the "now" of the poem, Blake is 33, Christ's age when He was crucified and rose again.

[4] *Edom* Cf. Genesis 27.40, in which "Edom" is another name for "Esau," whose brother Jacob stole his inheritance. Like "Adam," "Edom" suggests redness.

[5] *Isaiah XXXIV & XXXV* Prophecies of divine vengeance and restoration, respectively.

[6] *Paradise Lost* The rest of this section contains Blake's own reading of Milton's epic.

[7] *Sin & Death* Cf. *Paradise Lost* 2.746–814, in which the birth of Satan's daughter, Sin, and the son of their incestuous union, Death, are described.

[8] *It … Abyss Paradise Lost* 6.824ff. describes God's defeat of Satan, originally the Archangel Lucifer, and Satan's expulsion from heaven, along with his rebel faction.

This is shewn in the Gospel, where he prays to the Father to send the comforter[1] or Desire that Reason may have Ideas to build on, the Jehovah of the Bible being no other than he who dwells in flaming fire Know that after Christs death, he became Jehovah.

But in Milton; the Father is Destiny, the Son, a Ratio[2] of the five senses. & the Holy Ghost, Vacuum!

Note. The reason Milton wrote in fetters when he wrote of Angels & God, and at liberty when of Devils & Hell, is because he was a true Poet and of the Devils party without knowing it.

A Memorable Fancy[3]

As I was walking among the fires of hell, delighted with the enjoyments of Genius; which to Angels look like torment and insanity. I collected some of their Proverbs: thinking that as the sayings used in a nation. mark its character, so the Proverbs of Hell, shew the nature of Infernal wisdom better than any description of buildings or garments

When I came home; on the abyss of the five senses. where a flat sided steep frowns over the present world. I saw a mighty Devil folded in black clouds, hovering on the sides of the rock, with corroding [Plate 7] fires[4] he wrote the following sentence now percieved by the minds of men, & read by them on earth.

How do you know but ev'ry Bird that cuts the airy way,
Is an immense world of delight, clos'd by your
    senses five?[5]

---

[1] *he prays ... comforter* In John 14.16–17, Christ says He will pray to the Father to give mankind another comforter, the Holy Ghost.

[2] *Ratio* Sum.

[3] *Memorable Fancy* Blake's "Memorable Fancies" are modeled on the "Memorable Relations" in which Swedenborg recounts his visionary experiences.

[4] *corroding fires* A reference to Blake's use of acids to etch the copper plates from which he printed his poems. More extended accounts of the printing process occur on plates 14 and 15.

[5] *How do ... five* Cf. Thomas Chatterton, *Bristowe Tragedie, or the Dethe of Syr Charles Bawdin* (1768): "How dydd I know that ev'ry darte / That cutte the airie waie / Myghte nott find passage toe my harte / And close myne eyes for aie?" (133–36).

Proverbs of Hell[6]

In seed time learn, in harvest teach, in winter enjoy.
Drive your cart and your plow over the bones of the
    dead.
The road of excess leads to the palace of wisdom.
Prudence is a rich ugly old maid courted by Incapacity.
5 He who desires but acts not, breeds pestilence.
The cut worm forgives the plow.
Dip him in the river who loves water.
A fool sees not the same tree that a wise man sees.
He whose face gives no light, shall never become a star.
10 Eternity is in love with the productions of time.
The busy bee has no time for sorrow.
The hours of folly are measur'd by the clock, but of
    wisdom: no clock can measure.
All wholsom food is caught without a net or a trap.
Bring out number weight, & measure in a year of dearth
15 No bird soars too high. if he soars with his own wings.
A dead body. revenges not injuries.
The most sublime act is to set another before you.
If the fool would persist in his folly he would become
    wise
Folly is the cloke of knavery.
20 Shame is Prides cloke.

[Plate 8]

Prisons are built with stones of Law, Brothels with
    bricks of Religion.
The pride of the peacock is the glory of God.
The lust of the goat is the bounty of God.
The wrath of the lion is the wisdom of God.
5 The nakedness of woman is the work of God.
Excess of sorrow laughs. Excess of joy weeps.
The roaring of lions, the howling of wolves, the raging
    of the stormy sea, and the destructive sword. are
    portions of eternity too great for the eye of man.
The fox condemns the trap, not himself.
Joys impregnate. Sorrows bring forth.
10 Let man wear the fell of the lion. woman the fleece of
    the sheep.
The bird a nest. the spider a web. man friendship.

---

[6] *Proverbs of Hell* A diabolical version of the Old Testament's Book of Proverbs.

The selfish smiling fool & the sullen frowning fool.
    shall be both thought wise. that they may be a rod.
What is now proved was once only imagin'd.
The rat, the mouse, the fox, the rabbet; watch the roots,
    the lion. the tyger. the horse. the elephant. watch
    the fruits.
15 The cistern contains: the fountain overflows
One thought. fills immensity.
Always be ready to speak your mind, and a base man
    will avoid you.
Every thing possible to be believ'd is an image of truth.
The eagle never lost so much time as when he
    submitted to learn of the crow.

[Plate 9]

The fox provides for himself. but God provides for the
    lion.
Think in the morning. Act in the noon, Eat in the
    evening, Sleep in the night,
He who has sufferd you to impose on him knows you.
As the plow follows words, so God rewards prayers.
5 Thy tygers of wrath are wiser than the horses of
    instruction
Expect poison. from the standing water.
You never know what is enough unless you know what
    is more than enough.
Listen to the fools reproach! it is a kingly title!
The eyes of fire, the nostrils of air, the mouth of water,
    the beard of earth.
10 The weak in courage is strong in cunning.
The apple tree never asks the beech how he shall grow,
    nor the lion the horse, how he shall take his prey.
The thankful reciever bears a plentiful harvest.
If others had not been foolish, we should be so.
The soul of sweet delight, can never be defil'd,
15 When thou seest an Eagle. thou seest a portion of
    Genius. lift up thy head!
As the caterpiller chooses the fairest leaves to lay her
    eggs on. so the priest lays his curse on the fairest
    joys.
To create a little flower is the labour of ages.
Damn. braces. Bless relaxes.
The best wine is the oldest. the best water the newest.

20 Prayers plow not! Praises reap not!
Joys laugh not! Sorrows weep not!

[Plate 10]

The head Sublime, the heart Pathos, the genitals
    Beauty. the hands & feet Proportion.
As the air to a bird or the sea to a fish, so is contempt to
    the contemptible.
The crow wish'd every thing was black, the owl, that
    every thing was white.
Exuberance is Beauty.
5 If the lion was advised by the fox. he would be cunning.
Improvent makes strait roads, but the crooked roads
    without Improvement. are roads of Genius.
Sooner murder an infant in its cradle than nurse
    unacted desires
Where man is not nature is barren.
Truth can never be told so as to be understood. and not
    be believ'd.
                Enough! or Too much
10

[Plate 11]

    The ancient Poets animated all sensible objects with
Gods or Geniuses, calling them by the names and
adorning them with the properties of woods, rivers,
mountains, lakes, cities, nations, and whatever their
enlarged & numerous senses could perceive.
    And particularly they studied the genius of each city
& country. placing it under its mental deity.
    Till a system was formed, which some took
advantage of & enslav'd the vulgar by attempting to
realize or abstract the mental deities from their objects:
thus began Priesthood.
    Choosing forms of worship from poetic tales.
And at length they pronounced that the Gods had
ordered such things.
    Thus men forgot that All deities reside in the human
breast.

[Plate 12]

A Memorable Fancy

The Prophets Isaiah and Ezekiel dined with me, and I asked them how they dared so roundly to assert. that God spoke to them; and whether they did not think at the time, that they would be misunderstood, & so be the cause of imposition.

Isaiah answer'd. 'I saw no God. nor heard any, in a finite organical perception; but my senses discover'd the infinite in every thing, and as I was then perswaded. & remain confirm'd; that the voice of honest indignation is the voice of God, I cared not for consequences but wrote'

Then I asked: 'does a firm perswasion that a thing is so, make it so?'

He replied, 'All poets believe that it does. & in ages of imagination this firm perswasion removed mountains; but many are not capable of a firm perswasion of any thing'

Then Ezekiel said. The philosophy of the east taught the first principles of human perception some nations held one principle for the origin & some another, we of Israel taught that the Poetic Genius (as you now call it) was the first principle and all the others merely derivative, which was the cause of our despising the Priests & Philosophers of other countries, and prophecying that all Gods [Plate 13] would at last be proved to originate in ours & to be the tributaries of the Poetic Genius, it was this. that our great poet King David desired so fervently & invokes so patheticly, saying by this he conquers enemies & governs kingdoms; and we so loved our God. that we cursed in his name all the deities of surrounding nations, and asserted that they had rebelled; from these opinions the vulgar came to think that all nations would at last be subject to the jews.

'This' said he, 'like all firm perswasions, is come to pass, for all nations believe the jews code and worship the jews god, and what greater subjection can be'

I heard this with some wonder, & must confess my own conviction. After dinner I ask'd Isaiah to favour the world with his lost works, he said none of equal value was lost. Ezekiel said the same of his.

I also asked Isaiah what made him go naked and barefoot three years? he answered, 'the same that made our friend Diogenes the Grecian.'[1]

I then asked Ezekiel. why he eat dung, & lay so long on his right & left side?[2] he answered. 'the desire of raising other men into a perception of the infinite this the North American tribes practise, & is he honest who resists his genius or conscience. only for the sake of present ease or gratification?'

[Plate 14]

The ancient tradition that the world will be consumed in fire at the end of six thousand years[3] is true. as I have heard from Hell.

For the cherub with his flaming sword is hereby commanded to leave his guard at tree of life, and when he does, the whole creation will be consumed, and appear infinite. and holy whereas it now appears finite & corrupt.

This will come to pass by an improvement of sensual enjoyment.

But first the notion that man has a body distinct from his soul, is to be expunged; this I shall do, by printing in the infernal method, by corrosives, which in Hell are salutary and medicinal, melting apparent surfaces away, and displaying the infinite which was hid.[4]

If the doors of perception were cleansed every thing would appear to man as it is, infinite.

For man has closed himself up, till he sees all things thro' narrow chinks of his cavern.[5]

[Plate 15]

---

and barefoot" for three years.

[2] *why ... side* As he was instructed by the Lord in Ezekiel 4.4–6.

[3] *The ancient ... years* In Genesis 8.21, just after the Flood, God promises not to destroy the world again. The New Testament, however, contains several prophecies that it will be destroyed, this time by fire (Luke 12.49, 2 Peter 3.5–7). The traditional figure of six thousand years seems to have been obtained by combining the six days it took to make the world (Genesis 1) and the idea "that one day is with the Lord as a thousand years" (2 Peter 3.8).

[4] *this I ... hid* In conventional etching, only the lines of the design are burned away by the acid, the rest of the plate being protected by an acid-proof substance such as wax. In Blake's relief etching process, however, almost the whole surface of the plate is burned away, leaving the lines in relief.

[5] *chinks ... cavern* Cf. the allegory of the cave in Plato, *Republic*, and the image of the camera obscura in John Locke (1632–1704), *An Essay Concerning Human Understanding*.

---

[1] *Diogenes the Grecian* Founder of the Cynic school of philosophers, who advocated and practiced a lifestyle of extreme simplicity. In Isaiah 20.2–3, Isaiah is commanded by the Lord to walk "naked

A Memorable Fancy

I was in a Printing House in Hell & saw the method in which knowledge is transmitted from generation to generation

In the first chamber was a Dragon-Man. clearing away the rubbish from a caves mouth; within, a number of Dragons were hollowing the cave,

In the second chamber was a Viper folding round the rock & the cave, and others adorning it with gold silver and precious stones

In the third chamber was an Eagle with wings and feathers of air, he caused the inside of the cave to be infinite, around were numbers of Eagle like men, who built palaces in the immense cliffs.

In the fourth chamber were Lions of flaming fire raging around & melting the metals into living fluids.

In the fifth chamber were Unnam'd forms, which cast the metals into the expanse.

There they were reciev'd by Men who occupied the sixth chamber, and took the forms of books & were arranged in libraries.

[Plate 16]

The Giants who formed this world into its sensual existence and now seem to live in it in chains, are in truth. the causes of its life & the sources of all activity, but the chains are, the cunning of weak and tame minds. which have power to resist energy. according to the proverb, the weak in courage is strong in cunning.

Thus one portion of being, is the Prolific. the other, the Devouring; to the devourer it seems as if the producer was in his chains, but it is not so, he only takes portions of existence and fancies that the whole.

But the Prolific would cease to be Prolific unless the Devourer as a sea received the excess of his delights.

Some will say, 'Is not God alone the Prolific?' I answer, 'God only Acts & Is. in existing beings or Men.'

These two classes of men are always upon earth. & they should be enemies; whoever tries [Plate 17] to reconcile them seeks to destroy existence.

Religion is an endeavour to reconcile the two.

Note. Jesus Christ did not wish to unite but to seperate them, as in the Parable of sheep and goats![1] & he says 'I came not to send Peace but a Sword.'[2]

Messiah or Satan or Tempter was formerly thought to be one of the Antediluvians[3] who are our Energies.

A Memorable Fancy

An Angel came to me and said. 'O pitiable foolish young man! O horrible! O dreadful state! consider the hot burning dungeon thou art preparing for thyself to all eternity, to which thou art going in such career.'

I said. 'perhaps you will be willing to shew me my eternal lot & we will contemplate together upon it and see whether your lot or mine is most desirable'

So he took me thro' a stable & thro a church & down into the church vault at the end of which was a mill; thro' the mill; we went. and came to a cave. down the winding cavern we groped our tedious way till a void boundless as a nether sky appeard beneath us & we held by the roots of trees and hung over this immensity, but I said,' if you please we will commit ourselves to this void, and see whether providence is here also, if you will not I will?' but he answerd. 'do not presume O young-man but as we here remain behold thy lot which will soon appear when the darkness passes away'

So I remaind with him sitting in the twisted [Plate 18] root of an oak. he was suspended in a fungus which hung with the head downward into the deep;

By degrees we beheld the infinite Abyss, fiery as the smoke of a burning city; beneath us at an immense distance was the sun, black but shining round it were fiery tracks on which revolv'd vast spiders. crawling after their prey; which flew or rather swum in the infinite deep, in the most terrific shapes of animals sprung from corruption. & the air was full of them, & seemd composed of them; these are Devils. and are called Powers of the air, I now asked my companion which was my eternal lot? he said, 'between the black & white spiders'

---

[1] *Parable … goats*   Cf. Matthew 25.32–46. God divides the nations "as a shepherd divideth his sheep from his goats," placing the sheep, who are to be saved, on his right hand, and the goats, who are damned, on his left.

[2] *I … Sword*   From Matthew 10.34.

[3] *Antediluvians*   Those who existed before the Flood.

But now, from between the black & white spiders a cloud and fire burst and rolled thro' the deep blackning all beneath, so that the nether deep grew black as a sea & rolled with a terrible noise: beneath us was nothing now to be seen but a black tempest, till looking east between the clouds & the waves. we saw a cataract of blood mixed with fire and not many stones throw from us appeard and sunk again the scaly fold of a monstrous serpent at last to the east, distant about three degrees[1] appeard a fiery crest above the waves slowly it reared like a ridge of golden rocks till we discoverd two globes of crimson fire. from which the sea fled away in clouds of smoke, and now we saw, it was the head of Leviathan,[2] his forehead was divided into streaks of green & purple like those on a tygers forehead: soon we saw his mouth & red gills hang just above the raging foam tinging the black deep with beams of blood, advancing toward [Plate 19] us with all the fury of a spiritual existence.

My friend the Angel climb'd up from his station into the mill; I remain'd alone, & then this appearance was no more, but I found myself sitting on a pleasant bank beside a river by moon light hearing a harper who sung to the harp. & his theme was, 'The man who never alters his opinion is like standing water, & breeds reptiles of the mind.'

But I arose. and sought for the mill, & there I found my Angel, who surprised asked me, how I escaped?

I answered. 'All that we saw was owing to your metaphysics: for when you ran away, I found myself on a bank by moonlight hearing a harper, But now we have seen my eternal lot, shall I shew you yours?' he laughd at my proposal; but I by force suddenly caught him in my arms, & flew westerly thro' the night, till we were elevated above the earths shadow: then I flung myself with him directly into the body of the sun, here I clothed myself in white,[3] & taking in my hand Sweden-borgs volumes sunk from the glorious clime, and passed all the planets till we came to saturn, here I staid to rest & then leap'd into the void. between saturn & the fixed stars.[4]

'Here' said I! 'is your lot, in this space, if space it may be calld,' Soon we saw the stable and the church, & I took him to the altar and open'd the Bible, and lo! it was a deep pit, into which I descended driving the Angel before me, soon we saw seven houses of brick,[5] one we entred; in it were a [Plate 20] number of monkeys. baboons, & all of that species chaind by the middle, grinning and snatching at one another. but witheld by the shortness of their chains; however I saw that they sometimes grew numerous, and then the weak were caught by the strong and with a grinning aspect, first coupled with & then devourd, by plucking off first one limb and then another till the body was left a helpless trunk. this after grinning & kissing it with seeming fondness they devourd too; and here & there I saw one savourily picking the flesh off his own tail; as the stench terribly annoyd us both we went into the mill, & I in my hand brought the skeleton of a body, which in the mill was Aristotles Analytics.[6]

So the Angel said: 'thy phantasy has imposed upon me & thou oughtest to be ashamed.'

I answerd: 'we impose on one another, & it is but lost time to converse with you whose works are only Analytics.'

Opposition is True Friendship

[Plate 21]

I have always found that Angels have the vanity to speak of themselves as the only wise; this they do with a confident insolence sprouting from systematic reasoning;

Thus Swedenborg boasts that what he writes is new; tho' it is only the Contents or Index of already publish'd books

---

[1] *three degrees* Paris is three degrees east of London.

[2] *Leviathan* The beast Leviathan is described in Job 4.1, Psalms 104.26, Isaiah 27.1, Revelation 11.7, 12.9, 13.2, 20.1–3. Blake may also be thinking of Thomas Hobbes's *Leviathan; or, The Matter, Form, and Power of a Commonwealth, Ecclesiastical and Civil.*

[3] *clothed … white* Cf. Revelation 7.9, in which those who have been redeemed are clothed in white when they appear before Christ's throne.

[4] *void … stars* In the Ptolemaic world system, Saturn was the outermost planet, and bordered on the sphere of the fixed stars.

[5] *seven … brick* John addresses the book of Revelation to the "seven churches which are in Asia" (Revelation 1.4).

[6] *Analytics* Aristotle's two treatises on logic.

A man carried a monkey about for a shew. & because he was a little wiser than the monkey, grew vain. and conceiv'd himself as much wiser than seven men. It is so with Swedenborg; he shews the folly of churches & exposes hypocrites, till he imagines that all are religious. & himself the single [Plate 22] one on earth that ever broke a net.

Now hear a plain fact: Swedenborg has not written one new truth: Now hear another: he has written all the old falshoods.

And now hear the reason. He conversed with Angels who are all religious. & conversed not with Devils who all hate religion, for he was incapable thro' his conceited notions.

Thus Swedenborgs writings are a recapitulation of all superficial opinions, and an analysis of the more sublime. but no further.

Have now another plain fact: Any man of mechanical talents may from the writings of Paracelsus or Jacob Behmen,[1] produce ten thousand volumes of equal value with Swedenborg's. and from those of Dante or Shakespear. an infinite number.

But when he has done this, let him not say that he knows better than his master, for he only holds a candle in sunshine.

A Memorable Fancy

Once I saw a Devil in a flame of fire. who arose before an Angel that sat on a cloud. and the Devil uttered these words.

'The worship of God is. Honouring his gifts in other men, each according to his genius. and loving the [Plate 23] greatest men best, those who envy or calumniate great men hate God, for there is no other God.'

The Angel hearing this became almost blue but mastering himself he grew yellow, & at last white pink & smiling, and then replied,

'Thou Idolater, is not God One? & is not he visible in Jesus Christ? and has not Jesus Christ given his sanction to the law of ten commandments and are not all other men fools. sinners, & nothings?'

The Devil answer'd; 'bray a fool in a morter with wheat. yet shall not his folly be beaten out of him:[2] if Jesus Christ is the greatest man. you ought to love him in the greatest degree; now hear how he has given his sanction to the law of ten commandments: did he not mock at the sabbath,[3] and so mock the sabbaths God? murder those who were murderd because of him?[4] turn away the law from the woman taken in adultery?[5] steal the labor of others to support him?[6] bear false witness when he omitted making a defence before Pilate?[7] covet when he pray'd for his disciples, and when he bid them shake off the dust of their feet against such as refused to lodge them?[8] I tell you, no virtue can exist without breaking these ten commandments: Jesus was all virtue, and acted from im pulse.[Plate 24] not from rules.'

When he had so spoken: I beheld the Angel who stretched out his arms embracing the flame of fire & he was consumed and arose as Elijah.[9]

Note. This Angel, who is now become a Devil, is my particular friend: we often read the Bible together in its infernal or diabolical sense which the world shall have if they behave well

I have also: The Bible of Hell:[10] which the world shall have whether they will or no.

One Law for the Lion & Ox is Oppression

—1793

---

[1] *Paracelsus* Philippus Aureolus, Theophrastus Bombastus von Hohenheim (1493–1541), Swiss physician and alchemist; *Behmen* Jakob Boehme (1575–1624), German mystic.

[2] *bray … him* Proverbs 27.22. This devil can quote scripture to his purpose; *Bray* Crush.

[3] *mock … sabbath* In Exodus 20.8–11; Matthew 12.8–12; Mark 2.27, 3.2–4; Luke 14.3–5; John 5.16.

[4] *murder … him* In Exodus 20.13; see the martyrdom of Stephen (Acts 7.58–60).

[5] *turn … adultery* In Exodus 20.14; John 8.3–11.

[6] *steal … him* Cf. Exodus 20.15; Matthew 26.6–13.

[7] *bear … Pilate* Cf. Exodus 20.16; Matthew 27.11–14; Mark 15.2–5.

[8] *covet … them* Cf. Exodus 20.17; Matthew 10.14, Luke 9.5.

[9] *who … Elijah* Cf. 2 Kings 2.11: "There appeared a chariot of fire, and … Elijah went up by a whirlwind into heaven."

[10] *Bible of Hell* A reference to Blake's own work. In addition to the Proverbs of Hell (plates 7–10), this bible is sometimes said to include such later works as *The [First] Book of Urizen*, *The Book of Ahania*, and *The Book of Los* (1794–95).

1

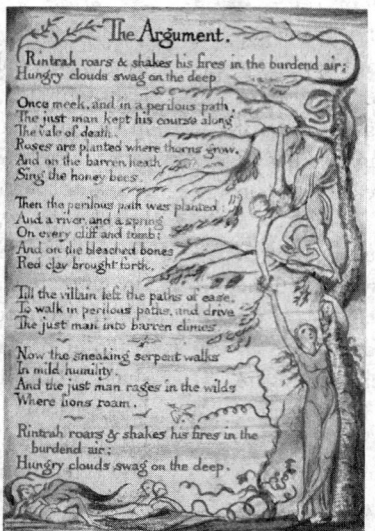

2

3

4

5

6

roding fires, he wrote the following sentence now per-
ceived by the minds of men, & read by them on earth.
How do you know but ev'ry Bird that cuts the airy way,
Is an immense world of delight, clos'd by your senses five?

Proverbs of Hell

In seed time learn, in harvest teach, in winter enjoy.
Drive your cart and your plow over the bones of the dead.
The road of excess leads to the palace of wisdom.
Prudence is a rich ugly old maid courted by Incapacity.
He who desires but acts not, breeds pestilence.
The cut worm forgives the plow.
Dip him in the river who loves water.
A fool sees not the same tree that a wise man sees.
He whose face gives no light, shall never become a star.
Eternity is in love with the productions of time.
The busy bee has no time for sorrow.
The hours of folly are measur'd by the clock, but of wis-
    dom: no clock can measure.
All wholsom food is caught without a net or a trap.
Bring out number weight & measure in a year of dearth.
No bird soars too high, if he soars with his own wings.
A dead body. revenges not injuries.
The most sublime act is to set another before you.
If the fool would persist in his folly he would become
    wise.
Folly is the cloke of knavery.
Shame is Prides cloke.

7

Proverbs of Hell
Prisons are built with stones of Law, Brothels with
    bricks of Religion.
The pride of the peacock is the glory of God.
The lust of the goat is the bounty of God.
The wrath of the lion is the wisdom of God.
The nakedness of woman is the work of God.
Excess of sorrow laughs. Excess of joy weeps.
The roaring of lions, the howling of wolves, the raging
    of the stormy sea, and the destructive sword are
    portions of eternity too great for the eye of man.
The fox condemns the trap, not himself.
Joys impregnate. Sorrows bring forth.
Let man wear the fell of the lion. woman the fleece of
    the sheep.
The bird a nest, the spider a web, man friendship.
The selfish smiling fool, & the sullen frowning fool, shall
    be both thought wise, that they may be a rod.
What is now proved was once, only imagin'd.
The rat, the mouse, the fox, the rabbet; watch the roots,
    the lion, the tyger, the horse, the elephant, watch
    the fruits.
The cistern contains; the fountain overflows.
One thought, fills immensity.
Always be ready to speak your mind, and a base man
    will avoid you.
Every thing possible to be believed is an image of truth.
The eagle never lost so much time, as when he submit-
    ted to learn of the crow.   The

8

Proverbs of Hell
The fox provides for himself, but God provides for the Lion.
Think in the morning. Act in the noon, Eat in the even-
    ing, Sleep in the night.
He who has suffer'd you to impose on him knows you.
As the plow follows words, so God rewards prayers.
The tygers of wrath are wiser than the horses of in-
struction.
Expect poison from the standing water.
You never know what is enough unless you know what is
    more than enough.
Listen to the fools reproach! it is a kingly title!
The eyes of fire, the nostrils of air, the mouth of water,
    the beard of earth.
The weak in courage is strong in cunning.
The apple tree never asks the beech how he shall grow,
    nor the lion, the horse; how he shall take his prey.
The thankful reciever bears a plentiful harvest.
If others had not been foolish, we should be so.
The soul of sweet delight, can never be defil'd.
When thou seest an Eagle, thou seest a portion of Ge-
    nius. lift up thy head!
As the catterpiller chooses the fairest leaves to lay
    her eggs on, so the priest lays his curse on
    the fairest joys.
To create a little flower is the labour of ages.
Damn, braces: Bless relaxes.
The best wine is the oldest, the best water the newest.
Prayers plow not! Praises reap not!
Joys laugh not! Sorrows weep not!

9

Proverbs of Hell
The head Sublime, the heart Pathos, the genitals Beauty,
    the hands & feet Proportion.
As the air to a bird or the sea to a fish, so is contempt
    to the contemptible.
The crow wish'd every thing was black, the owl, that eve-
    ry thing was white.
Exuberance is Beauty.
If the lion was advised by the fox, he would be cunning.
Improvent makes strait roads, but the crooked roads
    without Improvement, are roads of Genius.
Sooner murder an infant in its cradle than nurse unact-
    ed desires.
Where man is not nature is barren.
Truth can never be told so as to be understood, and
    not be believ'd.
Enough! or Too much.

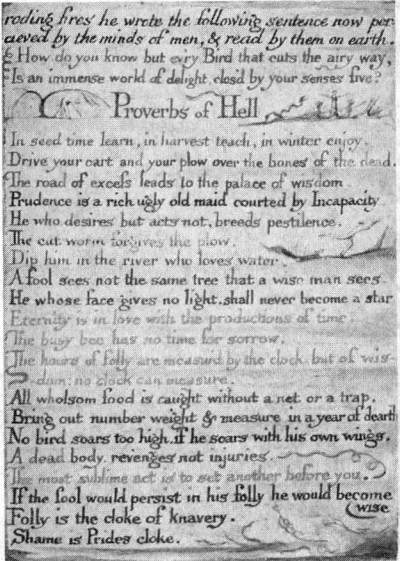

10

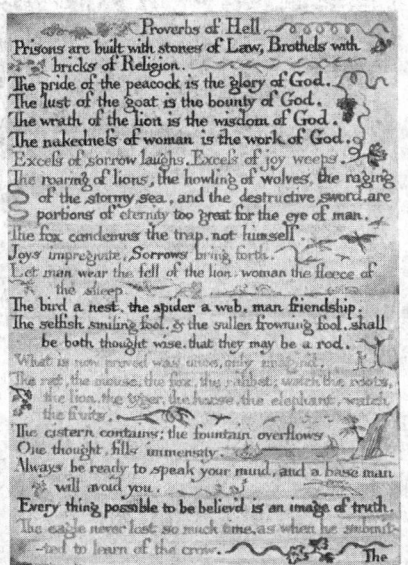

The ancient Poets animated all sensible objects
with Gods or Geniuses, calling them by the names and
adorning them with the properties of woods, rivers,
mountains, lakes, cities, nations, and whatever their
enlarged & numerous senses could perceive.
    And particularly they studied the genius of each
city & country, placing it under its mental deity.
    Till a system was formed, which some took ad-
vantage of, & enslav'd the vulgar by attempting to
realize or abstract the mental deities from their
objects: thus began Priesthood.
    Choosing forms of worship from poetic tales.
    And at length they pronounced that the Gods
had orderd such things.
    Thus men forgot that All deities reside
in the human breast.

11

A Memorable Fancy

The Prophets Isaiah and Ezekiel dined with
me, and I asked them how they dared so roundly to
assert, that God spoke to them; and whether they
did not think at the time, that they would be misunderstood, & so be the cause of imposition.
    Isaiah answer'd. I saw no God, nor heard
any, in a finite organical perception; but my senses discover'd the infinite in every thing, and as I
was then perswaded, & remain confirm'd; that the
voice of honest indignation is the voice of God, I
cared not for consequences but wrote.
    Then I asked: does a firm perswasion that a
thing is so, make it so?
    He replied. All poets believe that it does, &
in ages of imagination this firm perswasion removed mountains; but many are not capable of a
firm perswasion of any thing.
    Then Ezekiel said. The philosophy of the east
taught the first principles of human perception:
some nations held one principle for the origin &
some another, we of Israel taught that the Poetic
Genius (as you now call it) was the first principle
and all the others merely derivative, which was the
cause of our despising the Priests & Philosophers
of other countries, and prophecying that all Gods
would

12

would at last be proved, to originate in ours & to be the
tributaries of the Poetic Genius, it was this, that our
great poet King David desired so fervently & invokes
so pathetically, saying by this he conquers enemies &
governs kingdoms; and we so loved our God, that we
cursed in his name all the deities of surrounding
nations, and asserted that they had rebelled; from
these opinions the vulgar came to think that all nations would at last be subject to the jews.

This said he, like all firm perswasions, is come to
pass, for all nations believe the jews code and worship the jews god, and what greater subjection can be

I heard this with some wonder, & must confess
my own conviction. After dinner I asked Isaiah to favour the world with his last works, he said none of
equal value was last. Ezekiel said the same of his.

I also asked Isaiah what made him go naked and
barefoot three years? he answerd, the same that made
our friend Diogenes the Grecian.

I then asked Ezekiel. why he eat dung, & lay so
long on his right & left side? he answerd, the desire
of raising other men into a perception of the infinite
this the North American tribes practise. & is he honest who resists his genius or conscience. only for
the sake of present ease or gratification?

13

The ancient tradition that the world will be consumed in fire at the end of six thousand years
is true, as I have heard from Hell.

For the cherub with his flaming sword is
hereby commanded to leave his guard at tree of
life, and when he does, the whole creation will
be consumed, and appear infinite. and holy
whereas it now appears finite & corrupt.

This will come to pass by an improvement of
sensual enjoyment.

But first the notion that man has a body
distinct from his soul, is to be expunged; this
I shall do, by printing in the internal method, by
corrosives, which in Hell are salutary and medicinal, melting apparent surfaces away, and
displaying the infinite which was hid.

If the doors of perception were cleansed
every thing would appear to man as it is: Infinite.

For man has closed himself up, till he sees
all things thro' narrow chinks of his cavern.

14

A Memorable Fancy.

I was in a Printing house in Hell & saw the
method in which knowledge is transmitted from generation to generation.

In the first chamber was a Dragon-Man, clearing away the rubbish from a caves mouth; within, a
number of Dragons were hollowing the cave.

In the second chamber was a Viper folding round
the rock & the cave, and others adorning it with gold,
silver and precious stones.

In the third chamber was an Eagle with wings
and feathers of air, he caused the inside of the cave
to be infinite, around were numbers of Eagle like
men, who built palaces in the immense cliffs.

In the fourth chamber were Lions of flaming fire
raging around & melting the metals into living fluids.

In the fifth chamber were Unnam'd forms, which
cast the metals into the expanse.

There they were reciev'd by Men who occupied
the sixth chamber, and took the forms of books &
were arranged in libraries.

15

The Giants who formed this world into its
sensual existence and now seem to live in it
in chains; are in truth, the causes of its life &
the sources of all activity, but the chains
are, the cunning of weak and tame minds, which
have power to resist energy, according to the proverb, the weak in courage is strong in cunning.

Thus one portion of being, is the Prolific, the
other, the Devouring: to the devourer it seems as
if the producer was in his chains, but it is not so,
he only takes portions of existence and fancies
that the whole.

But the Prolific would cease to be Prolific
unless the Devourer as a sea received the excess
of his delights.

Some will say, Is not God alone the Prolific?
I answer, God only Acts & Is, in existing beings
or Men.

These two classes of men are always upon
earth, & they should be enemies; whoever tries

10

16

to reconcile them seeks to destroy existence.

Religion is an endeavour to reconcile the two.

Note. Jesus Christ did not wish to unite
but to separate them, as in the Parable of sheep and
goats! & he says I came not to send Peace but a
Sword.

Messiah or Satan or Tempter was formerly
thought to be one of the Antediluvians who are our
Energies.

A Memorable Fancy

An Angel came to me and said. O pitiable foolish
young man! O horrible! O dreadful state! consider
the hot burning dungeon thou art preparing for thyself
to all eternity, to which thou art going in such career.

I said, perhaps you will be willing to shew me
my eternal lot & we will contemplate together upon it
and see whether your lot or mine is most desirable.

So he took me thro' a stable & thro' a church
& down into the church vault at the end of which
was a mill: thro' the mill we went, and came to a
cave, down the winding cavern we groped our tedious way till a void boundless as a nether sky appeard beneath us & we held by the roots of trees
and hung over this immensity; but I said, if you
please we will commit ourselves to this void, and
see whether providence is here also, if you will not
I will! but he answerd, do not presume O young-
man but as we here remain behold thy lot which
will soon appear when the darkness passes away.

So I remaind with him sitting in the twisted

17

root of an oak, he was suspended in a fungus
which hung with the head downward into the deep;

By degrees we beheld the infinite Abyss, fiery
as the smoke of a burning city; beneath us at an
immense distance was the sun, black but shining
round it were fiery tracks on which revolv'd vast
spiders, crawling after their prey; which flew or
rather swum in the infinite deep, in the most terrific shapes of animals sprung from corruption.
& the air was full of them, & seemd composed
of them; these are Devils. and are called Powers
of the air. I now asked my companion which was my
eternal lot? he said, between the black & white spiders

But now, from between the black & white spiders
a cloud and fire burst and rolled thro' the deep
blackning all beneath, so that the nether deep grew
black as a sea & rolled with a terrible noise; beneath us was nothing now to be seen but a black
tempest, till looking east between the clouds & the
waves, we saw a cataract of blood mixed with fire
and not many stones throw from us appeard and
sunk again the scaly fold of a monstrous serpent;
at last to the east, distant about three degrees appeard a fiery crest above the waves slowly it reared like a ridge of golden rocks till we discoverd
two globes of crimson fire, from which the sea
fled away in clouds of smoke, and now we saw, it
was the head of Leviathan, his forehead was divided into streaks of green & purple like those on
a tigers forehead: soon we saw his mouth & red
gills hang just above the raging foam tinging the
black deep with beams of blood, advancing towards
us

18

us with all the fury of a spiritual existence.

My friend the Angel climb'd up from his station into the mill; I remaind alone, & then this appearance was no more, but I found myself sitting on a pleasant bank beside a river by moonlight hearing a harper who sung to the harp. & his theme was, The man who never alters his opinion is like standing water, & breeds reptiles of the mind.

But I arose, and sought for the mill & there I found my Angel, who surprised asked me. how I escaped?

I answerd. All that we saw was owing to your metaphysics; for when you ran away, I found myself on a bank by moonlight hearing a harper. But now we have seen my eternal lot, shall I shew you yours? he laughd at my proposal; but I by force suddenly caught him in my arms, & flew westerly thro' the night, till we were elevated above the earths shadow; then I flung myself with him directly into the body of the sun, here I clothed myself in white, & taking in my hand Swedenborgs volumes sunk from the glorious clime, and passed all the planets till we came to saturn, here I staid to rest & then leap'd into the void, between saturn & the fixed stars.

Here said I! is your lot, in this space, if space it may be call'd, Soon we saw the stable and the church, & I took him to the altar and open'd the Bible, and lo! it was a deep pit, into which I descended driving the Angel before me, soon we saw seven houses of brick, one we enterd; in it were a num[ber]

19

number of monkeys, baboons, & all of that species chaind by the middle, grinning and snatching at one another. but witheld by the shortness of their chains: however I saw that they sometimes grew numerous, and then the weak were caught by the strong and with a grinning aspect, first coupled with & then devourd, by plucking off first one limb and then another till the body was left a helpless trunk, this after grinning & kissing it with seeming fondness they devourd too; and here & there I saw one savourly picking the flesh off of his own tail; as the stench terribly annoyd us both we went into the mill, & I in my hand brought the skeleton of a body, which in the mill was Aristotles Analytics.

So the Angel said: thy phantasy has imposed upon me & thou oughtest to be ashamed.

I answerd: we impose on one another, & it is but lost time to converse with you whose works are only Analytics.

20

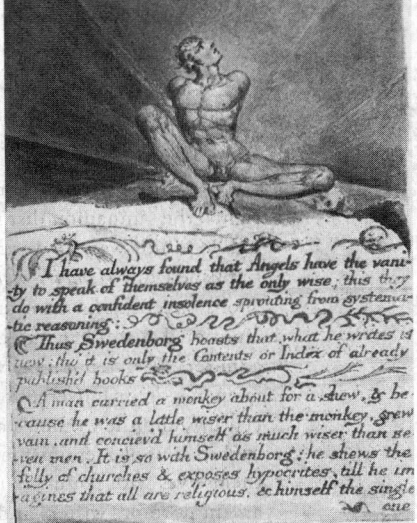

I have always found that Angels have the vanity to speak of themselves as the only wise; this they do with a confident insolence sprouting from systematic reasoning:

Thus Swedenborg boasts that what he writes is new; tho' it is only the Contents or Index of already publishd books

A man carried a monkey about for a shew, & because he was a little wiser than the monkey, grew vain, and conceivd himself as much wiser than seven men. It is so with Swedenborg; he shews the folly of churches & exposes hypocrites, till he imagines that all are religious, & himself the single one

21

one on earth that ever broke a net.

Now hear a plain fact: Swedenborg has not written one new truth: Now hear another: he has written all the old falshoods.

And now hear the reason. He conversed with Angels who are all religious, & conversed not with Devils who all hate religion, for he was incapable thro' his conceited notions.

Thus Swedenborgs writings are a recapitulation of all superficial opinions, and an analysis of the more sublime, but no further.

Have now another plain fact: Any man of mechanical talents may from the writings of Paracelsus or Jacob Behmen, produce ten thousand volumes of equal value with Swedenborgs, and from those of Dante or Shakespear, an infinite number.

But when he has done this, let him not say that he knows better than his master, for he only holds a candle in sunshine.

A Memorable Fancy

Once I saw a Devil in a flame of fire, who arose before an Angel that sat on a cloud, and the Devil utterd these words.

The worship of God is. Honouring his gifts in other men each according to his genius. and loving the greatest

22

greatest men best, those who envy or calumniate great men hate God, for there is no other God.

The Angel hearing this became almost blue but mastering himself he grew yellow, & at last white pink & smiling, and then replied,

Thou Idolater, is not God One? & is not he visible in Jesus Christ? and has not Jesus Christ given his sanction to the law of ten commandments and are not all other men fools, sinners & nothings?

The Devil answerd; bray a fool in a morter with wheat yet shall not his folly be beaten out of him; if Jesus Christ is the greatest man, you ought to love him in the greatest degree; now hear how he has given his sanction to the law of ten commandments; did he not mock at the sabbath, and so mock the sabbaths God? murder those who were murderd because of him? turn away the law from the woman taken in adultery? steal the labor of others to support him? bear false witness when he omitted making a defence before Pilate? covet when he prayd for his disciples, and when he bid them shake off the dust of their feet against such as refused to lodge them? I tell you, no virtue can exist without breaking these ten commandments: Jesus was all virtue, and acted from impulse: not from rules.

23

pulse, not from rules.

When he had so spoken: I beheld the Angel who stretched out his arms embracing the flame of fire & he was consumed and arose as Elijah.

Note. This Angel, who is now become a Devil, is my particular friend; we often read the Bible together in its infernal or diabolical sense which the world shall have if they behave well.

I have also: The Bible of Hell: which the world shall have whether they will or no.

One Law for the Lion & Ox is Oppression.

24

Mary Wollstonecraft
1759 – 1797

When Mary Wollstonecraft died in 1797 she was a literary celebrity. The most recognized female political writer of her day, Wollstonecraft tackled issues such as women and education, human rights, the "unnatural distinctions" of class, and the relationship between the sexes. Her prominent public profile was, however, severely diminished five months after her death when William Godwin published his *Memoirs of the Author of a Vindication of the Rights of Woman*. Godwin, who was Wollstonecraft's husband and intellectual companion, included controversial details of her sexual and emotional history in his book, which shocked many of her admirers. Her reputation was restored to some extent by the women's rights movement in the second half of the nineteenth century, and the women's movement of the 1970s elevated her to the status of a feminist icon. Even those who do not associate themselves with feminism now acknowledge Wollstonecraft as an important writer and thinker of the late eighteenth century—and *A Vindication of the Rights of Woman* as a core text in the Western tradition.

Wollstonecraft was born in London on 27 April 1759 to Elizabeth Dixon and Edward Wollstonecraft; she was the eldest daughter among seven children. The Wollstonecrafts were a middle-class, modestly prosperous family whose fortunes went into a gradual decline. Edward attempted to transform himself into a gentleman farmer, moving the family to Epping, Barking, and finally to Beverley in Yorkshire. These moves exacerbated the family's financial difficulties. As well, Wollstonecraft's father was a violent man. As a child, Wollstonecraft frequently intervened in her father's outbursts in order to try to protect her mother. For solace and respite, she turned to her close friend, Jane Arden. Arden's father, John, was a teacher and philosopher who encouraged Wollstonecraft's self-education and provided her with access to his library.

When Mary was 15 the Wollstonecrafts moved to Hoxton, on the outskirts of London. Here, Wollstonecraft was befriended by her next-door neighbors, the Reverend and Mrs. Clare. They became her surrogate family and were responsible for introducing her to Fanny Blood, with whom she would develop an intensely passionate and possibly romantic friendship. Years later, Wollstonecraft described her connection to Blood as "a friendship so fervent, as for years to have constituted the ruling passion of my mind." Blood became the model for Ann in Wollstonecraft's autobiographical novel, *Mary, A Fiction*.

In 1778, Wollstonecraft made the decision to leave home and earn her own living. Now 19, she took a job as a paid companion to a Mrs. Dawson, a widow in Bath. When her mother became ill in 1781, however, Mary returned to London to nurse her. After months of pain, Elizabeth Wollstonecraft died and Mary took up residence with the Bloods. Shortly afterwards Wollstonecraft's sister Eliza married Meredith Bishop, a well-to-do shipwright. After Eliza gave birth to a daughter in 1783, she fell into a deep postpartum depression that Wollstonecraft attributed to Bishop's cruelty. Wanting to rescue her sister, Wollstonecraft convinced Eliza to run away from her husband and child. (At the time, children legally belonged to the father.) Bishop eventually gave up his attempts to bring his wife back, and their daughter died just days before her first birthday.

Wollstonecraft soon realized that she and Eliza would need to find their own source of financial support. In 1784, together with Fanny Blood, they opened a school at Newington Green, north of London. Here, Wollstonecraft met Richard Price, a preacher and a leader of the Dissenters. His congregation was a Unitarian-like group whose political positions on freedom and equality influenced Wollstonecraft's developing ideas. In 1785, Fanny Blood left Newington Green to marry her long-time suitor, Hugh Skeys, in Lisbon. Wollstonecraft joined them several months later when she heard that Fanny was having trouble with her first pregnancy, but despite her efforts both Fanny and her child died a few days after the birth. Wollstonecraft returned to London where her school's financial problems had worsened during her absence. To raise money, she wrote her first book, *Thoughts on the Education of Daughters*. Joseph Johnson, a leading radical bookseller (that is, publisher) and a fellow Dissenter, published the book in 1787. The book's modest success was not enough to save the school, but it did establish Wollstonecraft in the debate on women's education.

Following the collapse of the school, Wollstonecraft became a governess to the Kingsborough family in Ireland, but it was not a happy development; she was doubtless drawing on experience when she later wrote that governesses "are not always treated in a manner calculated to render them respectable in the eyes of their pupils." She did, however, exert an apparently life-long influence on one of her pupils, who grew up to be a public champion of women's rights. Wollstonecraft soon fell into a depression that was diagnosed as nervous fever. She continued writing, though, beginning work on *Mary: A Fiction*. When she was dismissed from her position as governess, still within the year 1787, she returned to London and convinced Johnson to publish *Mary*. He also hired her as a reviewer for the *Analytical Review*, a monthly progressive periodical. Through her reviews she became an influential voice in the decade of ferment that was coming. Through Johnson, Wollstonecraft met Henry Fuseli, an artist and self-described genius. Although Fuseli was married, Wollstonecraft felt he was her soulmate and they soon began an affair.

Wollstonecraft embraced the start of the French Revolution with excitement. When Edmund Burke published his *Reflections on the Revolution in France* (1790), a treatise that attacked revolutionary ideas, Johnson urged Wollstonecraft to write a reply. She quickly crafted *A Vindication of the Rights of Man*, published anonymously less than a month after the appearance of Burke's book. A few weeks later, a second edition was published under her name, and this solidified her reputation as a radical. In early 1792, she became famous throughout Europe when her new book, *A Vindication of the Rights of Woman*, was published. Written in only six weeks, *A Vindication* presented the case for universal rights, social equality, and women's economic independence. As Wollstonecraft pointed out, the refusal of those who had espoused revolutionary principles of equality to extend rights to women represented a betrayal of those supposedly universal principles.

Eager to obtain first-hand knowledge about the Revolution, and just as eager to escape her deteriorating affair with Fuseli, Wollstonecraft traveled to France in December 1792. There she met Gilbert Imlay, an American and a fellow radical whose lover she soon became. When she discovered she was pregnant, Imlay registered her at the American Embassy as his wife, even though they were not married, so that she could claim the protection of American citizenship. In May 1794, she gave birth to a daughter whom she called Fanny, and two months later Imlay returned to England, leaving mother and child alone. Wollstonecraft's *An Historical and Moral View of the French Revolution* was published in London later that year.

Wollstonecraft's relationship with Imlay was strained, and when she returned to London in April 1795 she discovered he had been unfaithful. Distraught, she attempted suicide but was prevented by him. As a way of distancing himself from her, as well as tracking some bothersome financial losses, Imlay sent her (with Fanny) to Scandinavia on a business trip. She returned to England in September to find him living with another woman. Outraged and increasingly depressed, Wollstonecraft attempted suicide a second time by jumping off Putney Bridge into the Thames. This time, fishers pulled her out of the water.

In January 1796, Wollstonecraft published *Letters Written during a Short Residence in Sweden, Norway, and Denmark*. The book was highly successful, and the praise she received on its publication helped to restore her sense of purpose and mental health. In March, she met Imlay for the final time, and in April she began to write her next novel, *Maria, or The Wrongs of Woman*. In that month she also began a relationship with William Godwin, a leading radical writer and political philosopher to whom she had been introduced by Johnson a few years earlier. They planned a serious mutual commitment without the form of a marriage service, but when Wollstonecraft became pregnant they decided to marry for the sake of the baby. Their marriage on 29 March 1797 caused something of a scandal when it was revealed that Wollstonecraft had never been formally married to Imlay. On 30 August 1797, she gave birth to a daughter, Mary, later to become the wife of Percy Shelley and the author of *Frankenstein*. Only 38 years old, Wollstonecraft died on 10 September from complications resulting from the childbirth. Godwin was left with her manuscripts, and in 1798 published her *Posthumous Works* (which he naively expected to cement her fame) along with his controversial biography.

⌘ ⌘ ⌘

from *A Vindication of the Rights of Woman*

INTRODUCTION

After considering the historic page, and viewing the living world with anxious solicitude,[1] the most melancholy emotions of sorrowful indignation have depressed my spirits, and I have sighed when obliged to confess that either nature has made a great difference between man and man, or that the civilization which has hitherto taken place in the world has been very partial.[2] I have turned over various books written on the subject of education, and patiently observed the conduct of parents and the management of schools; but what has been the result? A profound conviction that the neglected education of my fellow-creatures is the grand source of the misery I deplore; and that women, in particular, are rendered weak and wretched by a variety of concurring[3] causes, originating from one hasty conclusion. The conduct and manners of women, in fact, evidently prove that their minds are not in a healthy state; for, like the flowers which are planted in too rich a soil, strength and usefulness are sacrificed to beauty; and the flaunting leaves, after having pleased a fastidious eye, fade, disregarded on the stalk, long before the season when they ought to have arrived at maturity. One cause of this barren blooming I attribute to a false system of education, gathered from the books written on this subject by men who, considering females rather as women than human creatures, have been more anxious to make them alluring mistresses than affectionate wives and rational mothers; and the understanding of the sex has been so bubbled[4] by this specious[5] homage that the civilized women of the present century, with a few exceptions, are only anxious to inspire love, when they ought to cherish a nobler ambition, and by their abilities and virtues exact respect.

In a treatise, therefore, on female rights and manners, the works which have been particularly written for their improvement must not be overlooked; especially when it is asserted, in direct terms, that the minds of women are enfeebled by false refinement; that the books of instruction, written by men of genius, have had the same tendency as more frivolous productions; and that,

---

[1] *solicitude* Concern.

[2] *partial* Biased.

[3] *concurring* Occurring together.

[4] *bubbled* Deluded, fooled.

[5] *specious* Superficially plausible yet misleading.

in the true style of Mahometanism,[1] they are treated as a kind of subordinate beings, and not as a part of the human species, when improvable reason is allowed to be the dignified distinction which raises men above the brute creation, and puts a natural sceptre in a feeble hand.

Yet, because I am a woman, I would not lead my readers to suppose that I mean violently to agitate the contested question respecting the equality or inferiority of the sex; but as the subject lies in my way, and I cannot pass it over without subjecting the main tendency of my reasoning to misconstruction, I shall stop a moment to deliver, in a few words, my opinion. In the government of the physical world it is observable that the female in point of strength is, in general, inferior to the male. This is the law of nature; and it does not appear to be suspended or abrogated[2] in favour of woman. A degree of physical superiority cannot, therefore, be denied—and it is a noble prerogative! But not content with this natural pre-eminence, men endeavour to sink us still lower, merely to render us alluring objects for a moment; and women, intoxicated by the adoration which men, under the influence of their senses, pay them, do not seek to obtain a durable interest in their hearts, or to become the friends of the fellow creatures who find amusement in their society.

I am aware of an obvious inference—from every quarter have I heard exclamations against masculine women; but where are they to be found? If by this appellation men mean to inveigh[3] against their ardour in hunting, shooting, and gaming,[4] I shall most cordially join in the cry; but if it be against the imitation of manly virtues, or, more properly speaking, the attainment of those talents and virtues, the exercise of which ennobles the human character, and which raise females in the scale of animal being when they are comprehensively termed mankind—all those who view them with a philosophic eye must, I should think, wish with me that they may every day grow more and more masculine.

This discussion naturally divides the subject. I shall first consider women in the grand light of human creatures who, in common with men, are placed on this earth to unfold their faculties; and afterwards I shall more particularly point out their peculiar designation.

I wish also to steer clear of an error which many respectable writers have fallen into; for the instruction which has hitherto been addressed to women has rather been applicable to ladies, if the little indirect advice that is scattered through Sandford and Merton[5] be excepted; but, addressing my sex in a firmer tone, I pay particular attention to those in the middle class because they appear to be in the most natural state. Perhaps the seeds of false-refinement, immorality, and vanity have ever been shed by the great. Weak, artificial beings, raised above the common wants and affections of their race in a premature unnatural manner, undermine the very foundation of virtue, and spread corruption through the whole mass of society! As a class of mankind they have the strongest claim to pity; the education of the rich tends to render them vain and helpless, and the unfolding mind is not strengthened by the practice of those duties that dignify the human character. They only live to amuse themselves, and by the same law that in nature invariably produces certain effects, they soon only afford barren amusement.

But as I purpose taking a separate view of the different ranks of society, and of the moral character of women in each, this hint is, for the present, sufficient; and I have only alluded to the subject because it appears to me to be the very essence of an introduction to give a cursory account of the contents of the work it introduces.

My own sex, I hope, will excuse me if I treat them like rational creatures, instead of flattering their fascinating graces and viewing them as if they were in a state of perpetual childhood, unable to stand alone. I earnestly wish to point out in what true dignity and human

---

[1] *Mahometanism* Archaic term for Islam.

[2] *abrogated* Repealed, abolished.

[3] *inveigh* Denounce.

[4] *gaming* Gambling.

[5] *Sandford and Merton* Thomas Day (1748–89), English poet, philanthropist, political essayist, and author of *The History of Sandford and Merton* (1783), a children's novel that gives expression to Day's educational theories, which are based on the work of Jean-Jacques Rousseau. Highly didactic, the novel contrasts the corrupt, conventional education of spoiled Tommy Merton, son of a Jamaican plantation owner, with the natural education of virtuous Harry Sandford, son of an honest farmer.

happiness consists: I wish to persuade women to endeavour to acquire strength, both of mind and body, and to convince them that the soft phrases, susceptibility of heart, delicacy of sentiment, and refinement of taste are almost synonymous with epithets of weakness, and that those beings who are only the objects of pity and that kind of love, which has been termed its sister, will soon become objects of contempt.

Dismissing then those pretty feminine phrases, which the men condescendingly use to soften our slavish dependence, and despising that weak elegancy of mind, exquisite sensibility, and sweet docility of manners supposed to be the sexual characteristics of the weaker vessel, I wish to show that elegance is inferior to virtue; that the first object of laudable ambition is to obtain a character as a human being, regardless of the distinction of sex; and that secondary views should be brought to this simple touchstone.

This is a rough sketch of my plan; and should I express my conviction with the energetic emotions that I feel whenever I think of the subject, the dictates of experience and reflection will be felt by some of my readers. Animated by this important object, I shall disdain to cull[1] my phrases or polish my style: I aim at being useful, and sincerity will render me unaffected; for, wishing rather to persuade by the force of my arguments than dazzle by the elegance of my language, I shall not waste my time in rounding periods,[2] or in fabricating the turgid bombast of artificial feelings, which, coming from the head, never reach the heart. I shall be employed about things, not words—and, anxious to render my sex more respectable members of society, I shall try to avoid that flowery diction which has slid from essays into novels, and from novels into familiar letters and conversation.

These pretty superlatives, dropping glibly from the tongue, vitiate[3] the taste and create a kind of sickly delicacy that turns away from simple unadorned truth; and a deluge of false sentiments and over-stretched feelings, stifling the natural emotions of the heart, render the domestic pleasures insipid that ought to sweeten the exercise of those severe duties that educate

a rational and immortal being for a nobler field of action.

The education of women has, of late, been more attended to than formerly; yet they are still reckoned a frivolous sex, and ridiculed or pitied by the writers who endeavour by satire or instruction to improve them. It is acknowledged that they spend many of the first years of their lives in acquiring a smattering of accomplishments; meanwhile strength of body and mind are sacrificed to libertine[4] notions of beauty, to the desire of establishing themselves—the only way women can rise in the world—by marriage. And this desire making mere animals of them, when they marry they act as such children may be expected to act: they dress, they paint,[5] and nickname God's creatures.[6] Surely these weak beings are only fit for a seraglio![7] Can they be expected to govern a family with judgment, or take care of the poor babes whom they bring into the world?

If then it can be fairly deduced from the present conduct of the sex, from the prevalent fondness for pleasure—which takes place of ambition and those nobler passions that open and enlarge the soul—that the instruction which women have hitherto received has only tended, with the constitution of civil society, to render them insignificant objects of desire—mere propagators of fools! If it can be proved that in aiming to accomplish them without cultivating their understandings they are taken out of their sphere of duties, and made ridiculous and useless when the short-lived bloom of beauty is over,[8] I presume that rational men will excuse me for endeavouring to persuade them to become more masculine and respectable.

---

[1]   *cull*   Choose carefully.

[2]   *rounding periods*   Crafting graceful sentences.

[3]   *vitiate*   Render impure, corrupt.

[4]   *libertine*   Licentious.

[5]   *paint*   I.e., wear makeup.

[6]   *they dress ... God's creatures*   From Shakespeare's *Hamlet* 3.1.142–46: "I have heard of your paintings, well enough. God hath given you one face, and you make yourselves another. You jig and amble, and you lisp, you nickname God's creatures and make your wantonness your ignorance."

[7]   *seraglio*   Harem.

[8]   [Wollstonecraft's note]   A lively writer, I cannot recollect his name, asks what business women turned of forty have to do in the world? [Wollstonecraft is perhaps referring to a remark made by a libertine character in Frances Burney's *Evelina*, Lord Merton.]

Indeed the word masculine is only a bugbear:[1] there is little reason to fear that women will acquire too much courage or fortitude, for their apparent inferiority with respect to bodily strength must render them, in some degree, dependent on men in the various relations of life; but why should it be increased by prejudices that give a sex to virtue and confound simple truths with sensual reveries?

Women are, in fact, so much degraded by mistaken notions of female excellence that I do not mean to add a paradox when I assert that this artificial weakness produces a propensity to tyrannize, and gives birth to cunning, the natural opponent of strength, which leads them to play off those contemptible infantine airs that undermine esteem even whilst they excite desire. Let men become more chaste and modest, and if women do not grow wiser in the same ratio, it will be clear that they have weaker understandings. It seems scarcely necessary to say that I now speak of the sex in general. Many individuals have more sense than their male relatives; and as nothing preponderates[2] where there is a constant struggle for an equilibrium without[3] it has naturally more gravity, some women govern their husbands without degrading themselves because intellect will always govern.

CHAPTER 2

The Prevailing Opinion of a Sexual Character Discussed

To account for, and excuse, the tyranny of man, many ingenious arguments have been brought forward to prove that the two sexes, in the acquirement of virtue, ought to aim at attaining a very different character: or, to speak explicitly, women are not allowed to have sufficient strength of mind to acquire what really deserves the name of virtue. Yet it should seem, allowing them to have souls, that there is but one way appointed by Providence to lead mankind to either virtue or happiness.

If then women are not a swarm of ephemeron[4] triflers, why should they be kept in ignorance under the specious name of innocence? Men complain, and with reason, of the follies and caprices[5] of our sex, when they do not keenly satirize our headstrong passions and grovelling vices. Behold, I should answer, the natural effect of ignorance! The mind will ever be unstable that has only prejudices to rest on, and the current will run with destructive fury when there are no barriers to break its force. Women are told from their infancy, and taught by the example of their mothers, that a little knowledge of human weakness, justly termed cunning, softness of temper, outward obedience, and a scrupulous attention to a puerile kind of propriety, will obtain for them the protection of man; and should they be beautiful, every thing else is needless for, at least, twenty years of their lives.

Thus Milton describes our first frail mother; though when he tells us that women are formed for softness and sweet attractive grace,[6] I cannot comprehend his meaning; unless, in the true Mahometan strain, he meant to deprive us of souls and insinuate that we were beings only designed by sweet attractive grace, and docile blind obedience, to gratify the senses of man when he can no longer soar on the wing of contemplation.

How grossly do they insult us who thus advise us only to render ourselves gentle, domestic brutes! For instance, the winning softness so warmly, and frequently, recommended that governs by obeying. What childish expressions, and how insignificant is the being—can it be an immortal one?—who will condescend to govern by such sinister methods! "Certainly," says Lord Bacon, "man is of kin to the beasts by his body; and if he be not of kin to God by his spirit, he is a base and ignoble creature!"[7] Men, indeed, appear to me to act in a very unphilosophical manner when they

---

[1] *bugbear* Imaginary creature invoked to cause fear.

[2] *preponderates* Weighs more, predominates.

[3] *without* Unless.

[4] *ephemeron* Short-lived.

[5] *caprices* Whims, fancies.

[6] *Milton ... grace* John Milton contrasts Adam and Eve, the first man and woman, in *Paradise Lost* (1667): "For contemplation he and valour formed, / For softness she and sweet attractive grace" (4.297–98).

[7] *Certainly ... creature* Francis Bacon (1561–1626), English philosopher and statesman, author of *Essays or Counsels Civil and Moral* (1625). The quotation is from Essay 16, "Of Atheism."

try to secure the good conduct of women by attempting to keep them always in a state of childhood. Rousseau[1] was more consistent when he wished to stop the progress of reason in both sexes, for if men eat of the tree of knowledge,[2] women will come in for a taste; but, from the imperfect cultivation which their understandings now receive, they only attain a knowledge of evil.

Children, I grant, should be innocent; but when the epithet is applied to men, or women, it is but a civil term for weakness. For if it be allowed that women were destined by Providence to acquire human virtues and, by the exercise of their understandings, that stability of character which is the firmest ground to rest our future hopes upon, they must be permitted to turn to the fountain of light, and not forced to shape their course by the twinkling of a mere satellite.[3] Milton, I grant, was of a very different opinion; for he only bends to the indefeasible[4] right of beauty, though it would be difficult to render two passages, which I now mean to contrast, consistent. But into similar inconsistencies are great men often led by their senses.

> To whom thus Eve with *perfect beauty* adorn'd.
> My Author and Disposer, what thou bidst
> *Unargued* I obey; so God ordains;
> God *is thy law, thou mine*: to know no more
> Is Woman's *happiest* knowledge and her *praise*.[5]

These are exactly the arguments that I have used to children; but I have added, "Your reason is now gaining strength, and, until it arrives at some degree of maturity, you must look up to me for advice—then you ought to think and only rely on God."

Yet in the following lines Milton seems to coincide with me when he makes Adam thus expostulate[6] with his Maker.

> Hast thou not made me here thy substitute,
> And these inferior far beneath me set?
> Among *unequals* what society
> Can sort, what harmony or true delight?
> Which must be mutual, in proportion due
> Giv'n and receiv'd; but in *disparity*
> The one intense, the other still remiss
> Cannot well suit with either, but soon prove
> Tedious alike: of *fellowship* I speak
> Such as I seek, fit to participate
> All rational delight—[7]

In treating, therefore, of the manners of women, let us, disregarding sensual arguments, trace what we should endeavour to make them in order to co-operate, if the expression be not too bold, with the supreme Being.

By individual education, I mean—for the sense of the word is not precisely defined—such an attention to a child as will slowly sharpen the senses, form the temper, regulate the passions as they begin to ferment, and set the understanding to work before the body arrives at maturity; so that the man may only have to proceed, not to begin, the important task of learning to think and reason.

To prevent any misconstruction, I must add that I do not believe that a private education can work the wonders which some sanguine[8] writers have attributed to it. Men and women must be educated, in a great degree, by the opinions and manners of the society they live in. In every age there has been a stream of popular opinion that has carried all before it, and given a family character, as it were, to the century. It may then fairly be inferred that until society be differently constituted, much cannot be expected from education. It is, however, sufficient for my present purpose to assert that whatever effect circumstances have on the abilities, every being may become virtuous by the exercise of its own reason; for if but one being was created with vicious inclinations that is positively bad, what can save us from

---

[1] *Rousseau* Jean-Jacques Rousseau (1712–78), Geneva born philosopher, composer and essayist.

[2] *tree of knowledge* In Genesis 2:17, God forbids Adam and Eve to eat of the tree of the knowledge of good and evil; tempted by the serpent, Eve disobeys and Adam follows suit.

[3] *satellite* Subordinate, secondary planet orbiting round a larger one.

[4] *indefeasible* Incapable of being defeated.

[5] *To whom … praise* Milton, *Paradise Lost*, 4.634–38. [Wollstonecraft's italics.]

[6] *expostulate* Remonstrate, argue.

[7] *Hast … delight* Milton, *Paradise Lost*, 8.381–91. [Wollstonecraft's italics.]

[8] *sanguine* Cheerfully optimistic.

atheism? Or, if we worship a God, is not that God a devil?

Consequently, the most perfect education, in my opinion, is such an exercise of the understanding as is best calculated to strengthen the body and form the heart. Or, in other words, to enable the individual to attain such habits of virtue as will render it independent. In fact, it is a farce to call any being virtuous whose virtues do not result from the exercise of its own reason. This was Rousseau's opinion respecting men:[1] I extend it to women, and confidently assert that they have been drawn out of their sphere by false refinement and not by an endeavour to acquire masculine qualities. Still the regal homage which they receive is so intoxicating that until the manners of the times are changed and formed on more reasonable principles, it may be impossible to convince them that the illegitimate power, which they obtain by degrading themselves, is a curse, and that they must return to nature and equality if they wish to secure the placid satisfaction that unsophisticated affections impart. But for this epoch we must wait—wait, perhaps, until kings and nobles, enlightened by reason, and preferring the real dignity of man to childish state, throw off their gaudy hereditary trappings: and if then women do not resign the arbitrary power of beauty, they will prove that they have less mind than man.

I may be accused of arrogance; still I must declare what I firmly believe: that all the writers who have written on the subject of female education and manners from Rousseau to Dr. Gregory[2] have contributed to render women more artificial, weak characters than they would otherwise have been; and, consequently, more useless members of society. I might have expressed this conviction in a lower key, but I am afraid it would have been the whine of affectation and not the faithful expression of my feelings, of the clear result which experience and reflection have led me to draw. When I come to that division of the subject, I shall advert[3] to the passages that I more particularly disapprove of in the

works of the authors I have just alluded to; but it is first necessary to observe that my objection extends to the whole purport[4] of those books, which tend, in my opinion, to degrade one half of the human species and render women pleasing at the expense of every solid virtue.

Though, to reason on Rousseau's ground, if man did attain a degree of perfection of mind when his body arrived at maturity, it might be proper, in order to make a man and his wife one, that she should rely entirely on his understanding; and the graceful ivy, clasping the oak that supported it, would form a whole in which strength and beauty would be equally conspicuous. But, alas! Husbands, as well as their helpmates, are often only overgrown children; nay, thanks to early debauchery, scarcely men in their outward form—and if the blind lead the blind,[5] one need not come from heaven to tell us the consequence.

Many are the causes that, in the present corrupt state of society, contribute to enslave women by cramping their understandings and sharpening their senses. One, perhaps, that silently does more mischief than all the rest is their disregard of order.

To do every thing in an orderly manner is a most important precept which women, who generally speaking receive only a disorderly kind of education, seldom attend to with that degree of exactness that men, who from their infancy are broken into method, observe. This negligent kind of guess-work—for what other epithet can be used to point out the random exertions of a sort of instinctive common sense, never brought to the test of reason?—prevents their generalizing matters of fact: so they do today what they did yesterday, merely because they did it yesterday.

This contempt of the understanding in early life has more baneful[6] consequences than is commonly supposed; for the little knowledge which women of strong minds attain is, from various circumstances, of a more desultory[7] kind than the knowledge of men, and it is acquired more by sheer observations on real life than

---

[1] *Rousseau's … men* Jean-Jacques Rousseau, *Émile* (1762), Book One.

[2] *Dr. Gregory* John Gregory (1724–73), Scottish physician, author of *A Father's Legacy to His Daughters* (1774), an influential conduct book for young women.

[3] *advert* Take notice.

[4] *purport* Intention.

[5] *blind lead the blind* Matthew 15:14: "And if the blind lead the blind, both shall fall into the ditch."

[6] *baneful* Destructive, poisonous.

[7] *desultory* Irregular, unmethodical.

from comparing what has been individually observed with the results of experience generalized by speculation. Led by their dependent situation and domestic employments more into society, what they learn is rather by snatches; and as learning is with them, in general, only a secondary thing, they do not pursue any one branch with that persevering ardour necessary to give vigour to the faculties and clearness to the judgment. In the present state of society, a little learning is required to support the character of a gentleman; and boys are obliged to submit to a few years of discipline. But in the education of women, the cultivation of the understanding is always subordinate to the acquirement of some corporeal accomplishment; even while enervated[1] by confinement and false notions of modesty, the body is prevented from attaining that grace and beauty which relaxed half-formed limbs never exhibit. Besides, in youth their faculties are not brought forward by emulation; and having no serious scientific study, if they have natural sagacity it is turned too soon on life and manners. They dwell on effects, and modifications, without tracing them back to causes; and complicated rules to adjust behaviour are a weak substitute for simple principles.

As a proof that education gives this appearance of weakness to females, we may instance the example of military men who are, like them, sent into the world before their minds have been stored with knowledge or fortified by principles. The consequences are similar; soldiers acquire a little superficial knowledge, snatched from the muddy current of conversation, and, from continually mixing with society, they gain what is termed a knowledge of the world; and this acquaintance with manners and customs has frequently been confounded[2] with a knowledge of the human heart. But can the crude fruit of casual observation, never brought to the test of judgment, formed by comparing speculation and experience, deserve such a distinction? Soldiers, as well as women, practice the minor virtues with punctilious[3] politeness. Where is then the sexual difference when the education has been the same? All the difference that I can discern arises from the superior advan-

tage of liberty, which enables the former to see more of life.

It is wandering from my present subject, perhaps, to make a political remark; but, as it was produced naturally by the train of my reflections, I shall not pass it silently over.

Standing armies can never consist of resolute, robust men; they may be well-disciplined machines, but they will seldom contain men under the influence of strong passions or with very vigorous faculties. And as for any depth of understanding, I will venture to affirm that it is as rarely to be found in the army as amongst women; and the cause, I maintain, is the same. It may be further observed that officers are also particularly attentive to their persons, fond of dancing, crowded rooms, adventures, and ridicule.[4] Like the fair sex, the business of their lives is gallantry. They were taught to please, and they only live to please. Yet they do not lose their rank in the distinction of sexes, for they are still reckoned superior to women, though in what their superiority consists, beyond what I have just mentioned, it is difficult to discover.

The great misfortune is this: that they both acquire manners before morals, and a knowledge of life before they have, from reflection, any acquaintance with the grand ideal outline of human nature. The consequence is natural; satisfied with common nature, they become a prey to prejudices, and taking all their opinions on credit, they blindly submit to authority. So that, if they have any sense, it is a kind of instinctive glance that catches proportions and decides with respect to manners, but fails when arguments are to be pursued below the surface, or opinions analyzed.

May not the same remark be applied to women? Nay, the argument may be carried still further, for they are both thrown out of a useful station by the unnatural distinctions established in civilized life. Riches and hereditary honours have made ciphers[5] of women to

---

[1] *enervated* Mentally weakened.

[2] *confounded* Disordered, confused.

[3] *punctilious* Carefully polite.

[4] [Wollstonecraft's note] Why should women be censured with petulant acrimony, because they seem to have a passion for a scarlet coat? Has not education placed them more on a level with soldiers than any other class of men? [See Jonathan Swift's "The Furniture of a Woman's Mind."]

[5] *ciphers* Neutral symbols which can change the value of other numbers depending on their position.

give consequence to the numerical figure; and idleness has produced a mixture of gallantry and despotism into society which leads the very men who are the slaves of their mistresses to tyrannize over their sisters, wives, and daughters. This is only keeping them in rank and file, it is true. Strengthen the female mind by enlarging it and there will be an end to blind obedience; but, as blind obedience is ever sought for by power, tyrants and sensualists are in the right when they endeavour to keep women in the dark, because the former only want slaves, and the latter a play-thing. The sensualist, indeed, has been the most dangerous of tyrants, and women have been duped by their lovers, as princes by their ministers, whilst dreaming that they reigned over them.

I now principally allude to Rousseau, for his character of Sophia[1] is, undoubtedly, a captivating one, though it appears to me grossly unnatural; however, it is not the superstructure but the foundation of her character, the principles on which her education was built, that I mean to attack; nay, warmly as I admire the genius of that able writer, whose opinions I shall often have occasion to cite, indignation always takes place of admiration, and the rigid frown of insulted virtue effaces the smile of complacency, which his eloquent periods are wont to raise when I read his voluptuous reveries. Is this the man who, in his ardour for virtue, would banish all the soft arts of peace and almost carry us back to Spartan discipline?[2] Is this the man who delights to paint the useful struggles of passion, the triumphs of good dispositions, and the heroic flights which carry the glowing soul out of itself? How are these mighty sentiments lowered when he describes the pretty foot and enticing airs of his little favourite! But, for the present, I wave the subject, and, instead of severely reprehending[3] the transient effusions of overweening[4] sensibility, I shall only observe that whoever has cast a benevolent eye on society must often have been gratified by the sight of humble mutual love, not dignified by sentiment, or strengthened by a union in intellectual pursuits. The domestic trifles of the day have afforded matters for cheerful converse, and innocent caresses have softened toils which did not require great exercise of mind or stretch of thought: yet, has not the sight of this moderate felicity excited more tenderness than respect? An emotion similar to what we feel when children are playing, or animals sporting,[5] whilst the contemplation of the noble struggles of suffering merit has raised admiration and carried our thoughts to that world where sensation will give place to reason.

Women are, therefore, to be considered either as moral beings, or so weak that they must be entirely subjected to the superior faculties of men.

Let us examine this question. Rousseau declares that a woman should never, for a moment, feel herself independent, that she should be governed by fear to exercise her natural cunning, and made a coquettish slave in order to render her a more alluring object of desire, a sweeter companion to man whenever he chooses to relax himself.[6] He carries the arguments, which he pretends to draw from the indications of nature, still further and insinuates that truth and fortitude, the corner stones of all human virtue, should be cultivated with certain restrictions, because, with respect to the female character, obedience is the grand lesson which ought to be impressed with unrelenting rigour.

What nonsense! When will a great man arise with sufficient strength of mind to puff away the fumes which pride and sensuality have thus spread over the subject! If women are by nature inferior to men, their virtues must be the same in quality, if not in degree, or virtue is a relative idea; consequently, their conduct should be founded on the same principles and have the

---

[1] *Sophia* Character in Jean-Jacques Rousseau, *Émile*, Book Five.

[2] *Spartan discipline* The militaristic Greek city-state of Sparta was infamous for its harsh laws, outlined in Plutarch's account of Lycurgus (*Lives*), which controlled nearly every aspect of the lives of its citizens.

[3] *reprehending* Finding fault with.

[4] *overweening* Arrogant.

[5] [Wollstonecraft's note] Similar feelings has Milton's pleasing picture of paradisiacal happiness ever raised in my mind; yet, instead of envying the lovely pair, I have, with conscious dignity, or Satanic pride, turned to hell for sublimer objects. In the same style, when viewing some noble monument of human art, I have traced the emanation of the Deity in the order I admired, till, descending from that giddy height, I have caught myself contemplating the grandest of all human sights;—for fancy quickly placed, in some solitary recess, an outcast of fortune, rising superior to passion and discontent.

[6] *Rousseau ... himself* See Jean-Jacques Rousseau, *Émile*, Book Five.

same aim.

Connected with man as daughters, wives, and mothers, their moral character may be estimated by their manner of fulfilling those simple duties; but the end, the grand end of their exertions should be to unfold their own faculties and acquire the dignity of conscious virtue. They may try to render their road pleasant, but ought never to forget, in common with man, that life yields not the felicity which can satisfy an immortal soul. I do not mean to insinuate that either sex should be so lost in abstract reflections or distant views as to forget the affections and duties that lie before them, and are, in truth, the means appointed to produce the fruit of life; on the contrary, I would warmly recommend them, even while I assert that they afford most satisfaction when they are considered in their true, sober light.

Probably the prevailing opinion, that woman was created for man,[1] may have taken its rise from Moses's poetical story;[2] yet, as very few, it is presumed, who have bestowed any serious thought on the subject ever supposed that Eve was, literally speaking, one of Adam's ribs,[3] the deduction must be allowed to fall to the ground; or, only be so far admitted as it proves that man, from the remotest antiquity, found it convenient to exert his strength to subjugate his companion, and his invention to show that she ought to have her neck bent under the yoke because the whole creation was only created for his convenience or pleasure.

Let it not be concluded that I wish to invert the order of things; I have already granted that, from the constitution of their bodies, men seem to be designed by Providence to attain a greater degree of virtue. I speak collectively of the whole sex; but I see not the shadow of a reason to conclude that their virtues should differ in respect to their nature. In fact, how can they, if virtue has only one eternal standard? I must, therefore, if I reason consequentially, as strenuously maintain that they have the same simple direction as that there is a God.

It follows then that cunning should not be opposed to wisdom, little cares to great exertions, or insipid softness, varnished over with the name of gentleness, to that fortitude which grand views alone can inspire.

I shall be told that woman would then lose many of her peculiar graces, and the opinion of a well-known poet might be quoted to refute my unqualified assertion. For Pope[4] has said, in the name of the whole male sex:

> Yet ne'er so sure our passion to create,
> As when she touch'd the brink of all we hate.[5]

In what light this sally[6] places men and women, I shall leave to the judicious to determine; meanwhile I shall content myself with observing that I cannot discover why, unless they are mortal, females should always be degraded by being made subservient to love or lust.

To speak disrespectfully of love is, I know, high treason against sentiment and fine feelings; but I wish to speak the simple language of truth, and rather to address the head than the heart. To endeavour to reason love out of the world would be to out Quixote Cervantes[7] and equally offend against common sense; but an endeavour to restrain this tumultuous passion, and to prove that it should not be allowed to dethrone superior powers, or to usurp the sceptre which the understanding should ever coolly wield, appears less wild.

Youth is the season for love in both sexes; but in those days of thoughtless enjoyment, provision should be made for the more important years of life when reflection takes place of sensation. But Rousseau, and most of the male writers who have followed his steps,

---

[1] *woman ... man*   Genesis 2.18–25: "And the Lord God said, It is not good that the man should be alone; I will make him an helpmeet for him" (Genesis 2:18).

[2] *Moses's ... story*   I.e., Genesis. Moses was believed to be the author of the Pentateuch, the first five books of the Bible: Genesis, Exodus, Leviticus, Numbers, and Deuteronomy.

[3] *Adam's ribs*   "And the Lord God caused a deep sleep to fall upon Adam, and he slept: and he took one of his ribs, and closed up the flesh instead thereof; And the rib, which the Lord God had taken from man, made he a woman, and brought her unto the man" (Genesis 2.22–23).

[4] *Pope*   Alexander Pope (1688–1744), English poet and satirist.

[5] *Yet ... hate*   Alexander Pope, "Epistle II: To a Lady (Of the Characters of Women)," from "Epistles to Several Persons," *Works*, 51–52 (1735).

[6] *sally*   Sudden attack on an enemy.

[7] *out Quixote Cervantes*   I.e., even more than the hero of Cervantes's picaresque novel, *Don Quixote*, be determined to carry out a lofty albeit impossible goal.

have warmly inculcated[1] that the whole tendency of female education ought to be directed to one point: to render them pleasing.

Let me reason with the supporters of this opinion who have any knowledge of human nature: do they imagine that marriage can eradicate the habitude of life? The woman who has only been taught to please will soon find that her charms are oblique sunbeams, and that they cannot have much effect on her husband's heart when they are seen every day, when the summer is passed and gone. Will she then have sufficient native energy to look into herself for comfort and cultivate her dormant faculties? Or, is it not more rational to expect that she will try to please other men; and, in the emotions raised by the expectation of new conquests, endeavour to forget the mortification her love or pride has received? When the husband ceases to be a lover— and the time will inevitably come—her desire of pleasing will then grow languid, or become a spring of bitterness; and love, perhaps, the most evanescent of all passions, gives place to jealousy or vanity.

I now speak of women who are restrained by principle or prejudice; such women, though they would shrink from an intrigue with real abhorrence, yet, nevertheless, wish to be convinced by the homage of gallantry that they are cruelly neglected by their husbands; or, days and weeks are spent in dreaming of the happiness enjoyed by congenial souls until their health is undermined and their spirits broken by discontent. How then can the great art of pleasing be such a necessary study? It is only useful to a mistress; the chaste wife, and serious mother, should only consider her power to please as the polish of her virtues, and the affection of her husband as one of the comforts that render her task less difficult and her life happier. But, whether she be loved or neglected, her first wish should be to make herself respectable, and not to rely for all her happiness on a being subject to like infirmities with herself.

The worthy Dr. Gregory fell into a similar error. I respect his heart, but entirely disapprove of his celebrated *Legacy to his Daughters*.

He advises them to cultivate a fondness for dress,[2]

because a fondness for dress, he asserts, is natural to them. I am unable to comprehend what either he or Rousseau mean when they frequently use this indefinite term. If they told us that in a pre-existent state the soul was fond of dress, and brought this inclination with it into a new body, I should listen to them with a half smile, as I often do when I hear a rant about innate elegance. But if he only meant to say that the exercise of the faculties will produce this fondness—I deny it. It is not natural; but arises, like false ambition in men, from a love of power.

Dr. Gregory goes much further; he actually recommends dissimulation,[3] and advises an innocent girl to give the lie to her feelings, and not dance with spirit, when gaiety of heart would make her feel eloquent without making her gestures immodest. In the name of truth and common sense, why should not one woman acknowledge that she can take more exercise than another? Or, in other words, that she has a sound constitution; and why, to damp innocent vivacity, is she darkly to be told that men will draw conclusions which she little thinks of? Let the libertine draw what inference he pleases; but I hope that no sensible mother will restrain the natural frankness of youth by instilling such indecent cautions. Out of the abundance of the heart the mouth speaketh;[4] and a wiser than Solomon[5] hath said that the heart should be made clean, and not trivial ceremonies observed,[6] which it is not very difficult to fulfil with scrupulous exactness when vice reigns in the heart.

Women ought to endeavour to purify their heart; but can they do so when their uncultivated understandings make them entirely dependent on their senses for employment and amusement, when no noble pursuit sets them above the little vanities of the day, or enables them to curb the wild emotions that agitate a reed over

---

[1] *inculcated* Taught through force or persistence.

[2] *fondness for dress* Gregory, *A Father's Legacy to his Daughters*, 55–57.

[3] *dissimulation* Concealment, feigning; Gregory, *A Father's Legacy to his Daughters*, 57–58.

[4] *Out of … speaketh* Matthew 12.34: "O generation of vipers, how can ye, being evil, speak good things? For out of the abundance of the heart the mouth speaketh."

[5] *a wiser than Solomon* I.e., Jesus; see Luke 11.31.

[6] *the heart … observed* Matthew 23.25: "Woe unto you, scribes and Pharisees, hypocrites! For ye make clean the outside of the cup and of the platter, but within they are full of extortion and excess."

which every passing breeze has power? To gain the affections of a virtuous man is affectation necessary? Nature has given woman a weaker frame than man; but, to ensure her husband's affections, must a wife—who, by the exercise of her mind and body whilst she was discharging the duties of a daughter, wife, and mother, has allowed her constitution to retain its natural strength, and her nerves a healthy tone—is she, I say, to condescend to use art and feign a sickly delicacy in order to secure her husband's affection? Weakness may excite tenderness and gratify the arrogant pride of man; but the lordly caresses of a protector will not gratify a noble mind that pants for and deserves to be respected. Fondness is a poor substitute for friendship!

In a seraglio, I grant that all these arts are necessary; the epicure[1] must have his palate tickled or he will sink into apathy; but have women so little ambition as to be satisfied with such a condition? Can they supinely[2] dream life away in the lap of pleasure, or the languor of weariness, rather than assert their claim to pursue reasonable pleasures and render themselves conspicuous by practising the virtues which dignify mankind? Surely she has not an immortal soul who can loiter life away, merely employed to adorn her person, that she may amuse the languid hours, and soften the cares of a fellow-creature who is willing to be enlivened by her smiles and tricks when the serious business of life is over.

Besides, the woman who strengthens her body and exercises her mind will, by managing her family and practising various virtues, become the friend and not the humble dependent of her husband; and if she, by possessing such substantial qualities, merit his regard, she will not find it necessary to conceal her affection, nor to pretend to an unnatural coldness of constitution to excite her husband's passions. In fact, if we revert to history, we shall find that the women who have distinguished themselves have neither been the most beautiful nor the most gentle of their sex.

Nature, or, to speak with strict propriety, God, has made all things right; but man has sought him out many inventions to mar the work. I now allude to that part of Dr. Gregory's treatise where he advises a wife never to let her husband know the extent of her sensibility or affection.[3] Voluptuous precaution, and as ineffectual as absurd. Love, from its very nature, must be transitory. To seek for a secret that would render it constant would be as wild a search as for the philosopher's stone, or the grand panacea:[4] and the discovery would be equally useless, or rather pernicious, to mankind. The most holy band of society is friendship. It has been well said, by a shrewd satirist, "that rare as true love is, true friendship is still rarer."[5]

This is an obvious truth, and the cause, not lying deep, will not elude a slight glance of inquiry.

Love, the common passion in which chance and sensation take place of choice and reason, is, in some degree, felt by the mass of mankind; for it is not necessary to speak, at present, of the emotions that rise above or sink below love. This passion, naturally increased by suspense and difficulties, draws the mind out of its accustomed state and exalts the affections; but the security of marriage, allowing the fever of love to subside, a healthy temperature is thought insipid only by those who have not sufficient intellect to substitute the calm tenderness of friendship, the confidence of respect, instead of blind admiration and the sensual emotions of fondness.

This is, must be, the course of nature—friendship or indifference inevitably succeeds love—and this constitution seems perfectly to harmonize with the system of government which prevails in the moral world. Passions are spurs to action and open the mind; but they sink into mere appetites, become a personal and momentary gratification, when the object is gained and the satisfied mind rests in enjoyment. The man who had some virtue whilst he was struggling for a crown often becomes a voluptuous tyrant when it graces his brow; and, when the lover is not lost in the husband, the dotard,[6] a prey

---

[1] *epicure*   One devoted to physical pleasures.

[2] *supinely*   Indolently, literally on one's back.

[3] *never to let ... affection*   Gregory, *A Father's Legacy to his Daughters*, 87–88.

[4] *wild a search ... panacea*   Alchemists believed in the existence of a philosopher's stone, a substance which could turn base metals into gold, as well as a grand panacea, a medicine that could cure all illnesses.

[5] *that rare ... rarer*   François de La Rochefoucauld (1613–80), French essayist, author of *Réflexions; ou Sentences et maximes morales* (1665).

[6] *dotard*   Senile person.

to childish caprices and fond jealousies, neglects the serious duties of life, and the caresses which should excite confidence in his children are lavished on the overgrown child, his wife.

In order to fulfil the duties of life, and to be able to pursue with vigour the various employments which form the moral character, a master and mistress of a family ought not to continue to love each other with passion. I mean to say that they ought not to indulge those emotions which disturb the order of society and engross the thoughts that should be otherwise employed. The mind that has never been engrossed by one object wants vigour—if it can long be so, it is weak.

A mistaken education, a narrow, uncultivated mind, and many sexual prejudices tend to make women more constant than men; but, for the present, I shall not touch on this branch of the subject. I will go still further and advance, without dreaming of a paradox, that an unhappy marriage is often very advantageous to a family, and that the neglected wife is, in general, the best mother. And this would almost always be the consequence if the female mind were more enlarged: for it seems to be the common dispensation[1] of Providence that what we gain in present enjoyment should be deducted from the treasure of life—experience; and that when we are gathering the flowers of the day and revelling in pleasure, the solid fruit of toil and wisdom should not be caught at the same time. The way lies before us, we must turn to the right or left; and he who will pass life away in bounding from one pleasure to another must not complain if he acquire neither wisdom nor respectability of character.

Supposing, for a moment, that the soul is not immortal, and that man was only created for the present scene; I think we should have reason to complain that love, infantine fondness, ever grew insipid and palled upon the sense. Let us eat, drink, and love, for to-morrow we die,[2] would be, in fact, the language of reason, the morality of life; and who but a fool would part with a reality for a fleeting shadow? But, if awed by observing the improbable powers of the mind, we disdain to confine our wishes or thoughts to such a comparatively mean field of action that only appears grand and important, as it is connected with a boundless prospect and sublime hopes, what necessity is there for falsehood in conduct, and why must the sacred majesty of truth be violated to detain a deceitful good that saps the very foundation of virtue? Why must the female mind be tainted by coquettish arts to gratify the sensualist and prevent love from subsiding into friendship, or compassionate tenderness, when there are not qualities on which friendship can be built? Let the honest heart show itself, and reason teach passion to submit to necessity; or, let the dignified pursuit of virtue and knowledge raise the mind above those emotions which rather embitter than sweeten the cup of life when they are not restrained within due bounds.

I do not mean to allude to the romantic passion which is the concomitant[3] of genius. Who can clip its wing? But that grand passion not proportioned to the puny enjoyments of life is only true to the sentiment and feeds on itself. The passions which have been celebrated for their durability have always been unfortunate. They have acquired strength by absence and constitutional melancholy—the fancy has hovered round a form of beauty dimly seen—but familiarity might have turned admiration into disgust; or, at least, into indifference, and allowed the imagination leisure to start fresh game. With perfect propriety, according to this view of things, does Rousseau make the mistress of his soul, Eloisa, love St. Preux[4] when life was fading before her; but this is no proof of the immortality of the passion.

Of the same complexion is Dr. Gregory's advice respecting delicacy of sentiment,[5] which he advises a woman not to acquire if she have determined to marry. This determination, however, perfectly consistent with his former advice, he calls indelicate, and earnestly persuades his daughters to conceal it, though it may govern their conduct—as if it were indelicate to have

---

[1] *dispensation* Divine ordering of the world.

[2] *Let us ... die* Isaiah 22.13.

[3] *concomitant* Accompaniment.

[4] *Eloisa ... St. Preux* Eloisa/Julie is the heroine of Rousseau's epistolary novel *Julie, ou, La Nouvelle Héloïse* (1761). Julie falls in love with her tutor, St. Preux, but is forced to marry her father's friend, Wolmar. St. Preux and Julie meet again many years later, and Julie ultimately admits on her deathbed that she has never stopped loving him.

[5] *advice ... sentiment* Gregory, *A Father's Legacy to His Daughters*, 116–119.

the common appetites of human nature.

Noble morality!, and consistent with the cautious prudence of a little soul that cannot extend its views beyond the present minute division of existence. If all the faculties of woman's mind are only to be cultivated as they respect her dependence on man; if, when a husband be obtained, she have arrived at her goal and, meanly proud, rests satisfied with such a paltry crown, let her grovel contentedly, scarcely raised by her employments above the animal kingdom; but if, struggling for the prize of her high calling, she look beyond the present scene, let her cultivate her understanding without stopping to consider what character the husband may have whom she is destined to marry. Let her only determine, without being too anxious about present happiness, to acquire the qualities that ennoble a rational being, and a rough inelegant husband may shock her taste without destroying her peace of mind. She will not model her soul to suit the frailties of her companion, but to bear with them: his character may be a trial, but not an impediment to virtue.

If Dr. Gregory confined his remark to romantic expectations of constant love and congenial feelings, he should have recollected that experience will banish what advice can never make us cease to wish for, when the imagination is kept alive at the expense of reason.

I own it frequently happens that women who have fostered a romantic, unnatural delicacy of feeling waste their lives in imagining how happy they should have been with a husband who could love them with a fervid increasing affection every day, and all day. But they might as well pine married as single—and would not be a jot more unhappy with a bad husband than longing for a good one. That a proper education or, to speak with more precision, a well stored mind would enable a woman to support a single life with dignity, I grant; but that she should avoid cultivating her taste lest her husband should occasionally shock it, is quitting a substance for a shadow. To say the truth, I do not know of what use is an improved taste if the individual be not rendered more independent of the casualties of life; if new sources of enjoyment, only dependent on the solitary operations of the mind, are not opened. People of taste, married or single, without distinction, will ever be disgusted by various things that touch not less

observing minds. On this conclusion the argument must not be allowed to hinge; but in the whole sum of enjoyment is taste to be denominated a blessing?

The question is whether it procures most pain or pleasure? The answer will decide the propriety of Dr. Gregory's advice, and show how absurd and tyrannical it is thus to lay down a system of slavery; or to attempt to educate moral beings by any other rules than those deduced from pure reason, which apply to the whole species.

Gentleness of manners, forbearance, and long-suffering are such amiable Godlike qualities[1] that in sublime poetic strains the Deity has been invested with them; and, perhaps, no representation of his goodness so strongly fastens on the human affections as those that represent him abundant in mercy and willing to pardon.[2] Gentleness, considered in this point of view, bears on its front all the characteristics of grandeur combined with the winning graces of condescension;[3] but what a different aspect it assumes when it is the submissive demeanour of dependence, the support of weakness that loves, because it wants protection, and is forbearing, because it must silently endure injuries, smiling under the lash at which it dare not snarl. Abject as this picture appears, it is the portrait of an accomplished woman, according to the received opinion of female excellence, separated by specious reasoners from human excellence. Or, they kindly restore the rib and make one moral being of a man and woman—not forgetting to give her all the "submissive charms."

How women are to exist in that state where there is to be neither marrying nor giving in marriage,[4] we are not told. For though moralists have agreed that the tenor[5] of life seems to prove that man is prepared by

---

[1] *Gentleness ... long-suffering* Galatians 5.22–23: "But the fruit of the Spirit is love, joy, peace, longsuffering, gentleness, goodness, faith, meekness, temperance: against such there is no law."

[2] *abundant ... pardon* Isaiah 55.7. "Let the wicked forsake his way, and the unrighteous man his thoughts: and let him return unto the Lord, and he will have mercy upon him; and to our God, for he will abundantly pardon."

[3] *condescension* Gracious behavior shown to a social inferior.

[4] *neither ... marriage* Matthew 22.30: "For in the resurrection they neither marry, nor are given in marriage, but are as the angels of God in heaven."

[5] *tenor* Continuous meaning.

various circumstances for a future state, they constantly concur in advising woman only to provide for the present. Gentleness, docility, and a spaniel-like affection are, on this ground, consistently recommended as the cardinal virtues of the sex; and, disregarding the arbitrary economy of nature, one writer has declared that it is masculine for a woman to be melancholy. She was created to be the toy of man, his rattle, and it must jingle in his ears whenever, dismissing reason, he chooses to be amused.

To recommend gentleness, indeed, on a broad basis is strictly philosophical. A frail being should labour to be gentle. But when forbearance confounds right and wrong, it ceases to be a virtue; and, however convenient it may be found in a companion, that companion will ever be considered as an inferior and only inspire a vapid tenderness, which easily degenerates into contempt. Still, if advice could really make a being gentle, whose natural disposition admitted not of such a fine polish, something towards the advancement of order would be attained; but if, as might quickly be demonstrated, only affectation be produced by this indiscriminate counsel, which throws a stumbling-block in the way of gradual improvement and true melioration[1] of temper, the sex is not much benefited by sacrificing solid virtues to the attainment of superficial graces, though for a few years they may procure the individuals regal sway.

As a philosopher, I read with indignation the plausible epithets which men use to soften their insults; and, as a moralist, I ask what is meant by such heterogeneous associations as fair defects, amiable weaknesses, &c.? If there be but one criterion of morals, but one archetype for man, women appear to be suspended by destiny, according to the vulgar tale of Mahomet's coffin;[2] they have neither the unerring instinct of brutes, nor are allowed to fix the eye of reason on a perfect model. They were made to be loved, and must not aim at respect, lest they should be hunted out of society as masculine.

But to view the subject in another point of view. Do passive, indolent women make the best wives? Confining our discussion to the present moment of existence, let us see how such weak creatures perform their part. Do the women who, by the attainment of a few superficial accomplishments, have strengthened the prevailing prejudice merely contribute to the happiness of their husbands? Do they display their charms merely to amuse them? And have women, who have early imbibed notions of passive obedience, sufficient character to manage a family or educate children? So far from it that, after surveying the history of woman, I cannot help agreeing with the severest satirist, considering the sex as the weakest as well as the most oppressed half of the species. What does history disclose but marks of inferiority, and how few women have emancipated themselves from the galling yoke of sovereign man? So few that the exceptions remind me of an ingenious conjecture respecting Newton: that he was probably a being of a superior order accidentally caged in a human body.[3] Following the same train of thinking, I have been led to imagine that the few extraordinary women who have rushed in eccentrical directions out of the orbit prescribed to their sex were male spirits, confined by mistake in female frames. But if it be not philosophical to think of sex when the soul is mentioned, the inferiority must depend on the organs; or the heavenly fire, which is to ferment the clay, is not given in equal portions.

But avoiding, as I have hitherto done, any direct comparison of the two sexes collectively, or frankly acknowledging the inferiority of woman, according to the present appearance of things, I shall only insist that men have increased that inferiority until women are almost sunk below the standard of rational creatures. Let their faculties have room to unfold, and their virtues to gain strength, and then determine where the whole sex must stand in the intellectual scale. Yet let it be remembered that for a small number of distinguished women I do not ask a place.

It is difficult for us purblind[4] mortals to say to what height human discoveries and improvements may arrive when the gloom of despotism subsides, which makes us

---

[1] *melioration* Betterment.

[2] *Mahomet's coffin* It was believed that Mohammed's coffin was suspended in mid-air at his tomb in Medina, Saudi Arabia.

[3] *Newton ... body* Newton and his scientific discoveries were held in extremely high regard during the eighteenth century; consider, for example, Pope's *Epitaph. Intended for Sir Isaac Newton, In Westminster-Abbey* (1730): "Nature and nature's laws lay hid in night; / God said 'Let Newton be' and all was light."

[4] *purblind* Imperfectly sighted.

stumble at every step; but, when morality shall be settled on a more solid basis, then, without being gifted with a prophetic spirit, I will venture to predict that woman will be either the friend or slave of man. We shall not, as at present, doubt whether she is a moral agent or the link which unites man with brutes. But, should it then appear that, like the brutes, they were principally created for the use of man, he will let them patiently bite the bridle and not mock them with empty praise; or, should their rationality be proved, he will not impede their improvement merely to gratify his sensual appetites. He will not, with all the graces of rhetoric, advise them to submit implicitly their understanding to the guidance of man. He will not, when he treats of[1] the education of women, assert that they ought never to have the free use of reason, nor would he recommend cunning and dissimulation to beings who are acquiring, in like manner as himself, the virtues of humanity.

Surely there can be but one rule of right, if morality has an eternal foundation; and whoever sacrifices virtue, strictly so called, to present convenience, or whose duty it is to act in such a manner,[2] lives only for the passing day and cannot be an accountable creature.

The poet then should have dropped his sneer when he says:

> If weak women go astray,
> The stars are more in fault than they.[3]

For that they are bound by the adamantine[4] chain of destiny is most certain, if it be proved that they are never to exercise their own reason, never to be independent, never to rise above opinion, or to feel the dignity of a rational will that only bows to God—and often forgets that the universe contains any being but itself and the model of perfection to which its ardent gaze is turned—to adore attributes that, softened into virtues, may be imitated in kind, though the degree overwhelms the enraptured mind.

If, I say, for I would not impress by declamation when Reason offers her sober light, if they be really capable of acting like rational creatures, let them not be treated like slaves, or like the brutes who are dependent on the reason of man when they associate with him; but cultivate their minds, give them the salutary, sublime curb of principle, and let them attain conscious dignity by feeling themselves only dependent on God. Teach them, in common with man, to submit to necessity, instead of giving, to render them more pleasing, a sex to morals.

Further, should experience prove that they cannot attain the same degree of strength of mind, perseverance, and fortitude, let their virtues be the same in kind, though they may vainly struggle for the same degree; and the superiority of man will be equally clear, if not clearer; and truth, as it is a simple principle, which admits of no modification, would be common to both. Nay, the order of society as it is at present regulated would not be inverted, for woman would then only have the rank that reason assigned her, and arts could not be practised to bring the balance even, much less to turn it.

These may be termed Utopian dreams—thanks to that Being who impressed them on my soul and gave me sufficient strength of mind to dare to exert my own reason until, becoming dependent only on him for the support of my virtue, I view, with indignation, the mistaken notions that enslave my sex.

I love man as my fellow; but his sceptre, real or usurped, extends not to me, unless the reason of an individual demands my homage; and even then the submission is to reason, and not to man. In fact, the conduct of an accountable being must be regulated by the operations of its own reason, or on what foundation rests the throne of God?

It appears to me necessary to dwell on these obvious truths because females have been insulated, as it were; and, while they have been stripped of the virtues that should clothe humanity, they have been decked with artificial graces that enable them to exercise a short-lived tyranny. Love, in their bosoms, takes the place of every nobler passion; their sole ambition is to be fair, to raise emotion instead of inspiring respect; and this ignoble desire, like the servility in absolute monarchies, destroys all strength of character. Liberty is the mother of virtue, and if women be, by their very constitution, slaves, and not allowed to breathe the sharp invigorating air of

---

[1]   *treats of* Discourses on.

[2]   *to act in such a manner* I.e., to sacrifice duty to convenience.

[3]   *If weak ... they* "Hans Carvel" (1700) by Matthew Prior.

[4]   *adamantine* Unbreakable.

freedom, they must ever languish like exotics, and be reckoned beautiful flaws in nature.

As to the argument respecting the subjection in which the sex has ever been held, it retorts on[1] man. The many have always been enthralled by the few; and monsters, who scarcely have shown any discernment of human excellence, have tyrannized over thousands of their fellow-creatures. Why have men of superior endowments submitted to such degradation? For is it not universally acknowledged that kings, viewed collectively, have ever been inferior, in abilities and virtue, to the same number of men taken from the common mass of mankind—yet have they not, and are they not still treated with a degree of reverence that is an insult to reason? China is not the only country where a living man has been made a God.[2] Men have submitted to superior strength to enjoy with impunity[3] the pleasure of the moment; women have only done the same, and therefore until it is proved that the courtier, who servilely resigns the birthright of a man, is not a moral agent, it cannot be demonstrated that woman is essentially inferior to man because she has always been subjugated.

Brutal force has hitherto governed the world; and that the science of politics is in its infancy is evident from philosophers scrupling to give the knowledge most useful to man that determinate distinction.

I shall not pursue this argument any further than to establish an obvious inference: that as sound politics diffuse liberty, mankind, including woman, will become more wise and virtuous.

from CHAPTER 3

The Same Subject Continued

… I wish to sum up what I have said in a few words, for I here throw down my gauntlet and deny the existence of sexual virtues, not excepting modesty. For man and woman, truth—if I understand the meaning of the word—must be the same; yet for the fanciful female character, so prettily drawn by poets and novelists demanding the sacrifice of truth and sincerity, virtue becomes a relative idea, having no other foundation than utility, and of that utility men pretend arbitrarily to judge, shaping it to their own convenience.

Women, I allow, may have different duties to fulfil; but they are human duties, and the principles that should regulate the discharge of them, I sturdily maintain, must be the same.

To become respectable, the exercise of their understanding is necessary; there is no other foundation for independence of character. I mean explicitly to say that they must only bow to the authority of reason instead of being the modest slaves of opinion.

In the superior ranks of life how seldom do we meet with a man of superior abilities, or even common acquirements? The reason appears to me clear: the state they are born in was an unnatural one. The human character has ever been formed by the employments that the individual, or class, pursues; and if the faculties are not sharpened by necessity, they must remain obtuse. The argument may fairly be extended to women; for, seldom occupied by serious business, the pursuit of pleasure gives that insignificancy to their character which renders the society of the great so insipid. The same want of firmness, produced by a similar cause, forces them both to fly from themselves to noisy pleasures, and artificial passions, until vanity takes place of every social affection, and the characteristics of humanity can scarcely be discerned. Such are the blessings of civil governments, as they are at present organized, that wealth and female softness equally tend to debase mankind and are produced by the same cause; but allowing women to be rational creatures, they should be incited to acquire virtues which they may call their own, for how can a rational being be ennobled by any thing that is not obtained by its own exertions?

—1792

---

[1] *retorts on* Answers back.

[2] *China … God* See A *Discourse on the Love of our Country* (1789) by Richard Price (1723–91), English philosopher and writer.

[3] *impunity* Safety from punishment.

In Context

Contemporary Reviews of *A Vindication of the Rights of Woman*

Early reviews of *The Vindication of the Rights of Woman* divided largely along party lines. Reviewers from *The Analytic Review* and *The Monthly Review*, for example, praised the work while more conservative papers such as *The Critical Review*, *The General Magazine*, and *The Gentleman's Magazine* attacked it. Excerpts from *The Analytic Review* and *The Critical Review* are reprinted below.

from *The Analytical Review* 12 (1792)

… It is with some reluctance that for the present we take our leave of this singular, and, on the whole, excellent production. The subjects which it investigates, are of the utmost importance to human nature, and we should be wanting in our engagements, and in our duty, if we passed it over too slightly. This circumstance makes it necessary to defer the further analysis to a future Review, when we shall proceed to the remaining topics of this volume.

It might have been supposed that Mrs. W. had taken advantage of the popular topic of the "Rights of Man" in calling her work "A Vindication of the Rights of Woman," had she not already published a work, one of the first answers that appeared to Mr. Burke, under the title of "A Vindication of the Rights of Man." But in reality the present work is an elaborate *treatise* of *female education*. The lesser wits will probably affect to make themselves merry at the title and apparent object of this publication; but we have no doubt if even her contemporaries should fail to do her justice, posterity will compensate the defect; and have no hesitation in declaring, that if the bulk of the great truths which this publication contains were reduced to practice, the nation would be better, wiser and happier, than it is upon the wretched, trifling, useless and absurd system of education which is now prevalent.

from *The Critical Review* 4 (1792)

One of the strictest proofs in mathematical demonstrations, is the reducing the questions to an absurdity; by allowing, for instance, that the proposition is not true, and then showing that this would lead to the most obvious inconsistencies. Miss Wollstonecraft has converted this method of proceeding with the same success: reasoning on the boasted principles of the Rights of Man, she finds they lead very clearly to the object of her work, a Vindication of the Rights of Woman; and, by the absurdity of many of her conclusions, shows, while we admit the reasoning, that the premises must be, in some respects, fallacious.

> Dismissing then those pretty feminine phrases, which the men condescendingly use to soften our slavish dependence, and despising that weak elegancy of mind, exquisite sensibility, and sweet docility of manners, supposed to be the sexual characteristics of the weaker vessel, I wish to shew that elegance is inferior to virtue, that the first object of laudable ambition is to obtain a character as a human being, regardless of the distinction of sex; and that secondary views should be brought to this simple touchstone.

This is the outline of her plan; but before she proceeds to show that this change would be suitable, useful, advantageous, it will be first necessary to prove that there is no sexual distinction of character; that the female mind is equally fitted for the more arduous mental operations; that women are equally able to pursue the toilsome road of minute, laborious, investigation; that their judgments are equally sound, their resolution equally strong. After this is done, the benefit derived must be considered; and, when all are strong, to whom must the weaker operations belong? The female Plato will find it unsuitable to "the dignity of her virtue" to dress the child, and descend to the disgusting offices of a nurse: the new Archimedes will measure the shirts by means of the altitude taken by a quadrant; and the young lady, instead of studying the softer and more amiable arts of pleasing, must contend with her lover for superiority of mind, for greater dignity of virtue; and before she condescends to become his wife, must prove herself his equal or superior.—It may be fancy, prejudice, or obstinacy, we contend not for a name, but we are infinitely better pleased with the present system; and, in truth, dear young lady, for by the appellation sometimes prefixed to your name we must suppose you to be young, endeavour to attain "the weak elegancy of mind," the "sweet docility of manners," "the exquisite sensibility," the former ornaments of your sex; we are certain you will be more pleasing, and we dare pronounce that you will be infinitely happier. Mental superiority is not an object worth contending for, if happiness be the aim. But, as this is the first female combatant in the new field of the Rights of Woman, if we smile only, we shall be accused of wishing to decline the contest; if we content ourselves with paying a compliment to her talents, it will be styled inconsistent with "true dignity," and as showing that we want to continue the "slavish dependence."—We must contend then with this new Atalanta; and who knows whether, in this modern instance, we may not gain two victories by the contest? There is more than one bachelor in our corps; and, if we should succeed, Miss Wollstonecraft may take her choice.

This work is dedicated to M. Talleyrand-Perigord, late bishop of Autun, who, in his treatise on National Education, does not seem to be perfectly convinced that the rights of man extend to woman; yet in France the diffusion of knowledge, our author asserts, is greater than in any other European nation, on account of the more unreserved communication between the sexes, though what the ladies have gained in knowledge they seem confessedly to have lost in delicacy. The following passage we must transcribe, for we confess we do not fully understand it.

Contending for the rights of woman, my main argument is built on this simple principle, that if she be not prepared by education to become the companion of man, she will stop the progress of knowledge, for truth must be common to all, or it will be inefficacious with respect to its influence on general practice. And how can woman be expected to co-operate unless she know why she ought to be virtuous! unless freedom strengthen her reason till she comprehend her duty, and see in what manner it is connected with her real good? If children are to be educated to understand the true principle of patriotism, their mother must be a patriot; and the love of mankind, from which an orderly train of virtues spring, can only be produced by considering the moral and civil interest of mankind; but the education and situation of woman, at present, shuts her out from such investigations.

In this work I have produced many arguments, which to me were conclusive, to prove that the prevailing notion respecting a sexual character was subversive of morality, and I have contended, that to render the human body and mind more perfect, chastity must more universally prevail, and that chastity will never be respected in the male world till the person of a woman is not, as it were, idolized, when little virtue or sense embellish it with the grand traces of mental beauty, or the interesting simplicity of affection.

The first sentence is erroneous in fact and in reasoning: it is contradicted by the experience of ages, the practice of different nations. The second sentence is a curious one—How can she be supposed to co-operate (we *suppose* in the progress of knowledge) unless she know why she ought to be *virtuous?* Virtuous! Here must be some mistake: what has virtue to do with the progress of knowledge? As to freedom, strengthening the reason, &c. we see no occasion for metaphysical investigation on this subject: that virtue is connected with prosperity and happiness, and vice with misfortune and misery, she might learn, not from Locke, but the New Testament. The concluding sentence of the first paragraph is still more strange. Patriotism may be very properly instilled by a *father,* and we must beg leave to differ in opinion from this lady in another point: we are confident, from frequent and extensive observation, no arguments can confute the opinion that we have formed, and we must still persist in thinking, that the education and situation of women, *at present,* really and effectually *inspire* the *love* of *mankind.* We do believe with Miss Wollstonecraft, that chastity will be respected more, when the person of a woman ceases to be idolized, and the grand traces of mental beauty are principally conspicuous. ...

from *Maria; or The Wrongs of Woman*

CHAPTER 5

"My Father," said Jemima, "seduced my mother, a pretty girl, with whom he lived fellow-servant; and she no sooner perceived the natural, the dreaded consequence, than the terrible conviction flashed on her— that she was ruined. Honesty, and a regard for her reputation, had been the only principles inculcated by her mother; and they had been so forcibly impressed that she feared shame more than the poverty to which it would lead. Her incessant importunities[1] to prevail upon my father to screen her from reproach by marrying her, as he had promised in the fervour of seduction, estranged him from her so completely that her very person became distasteful to him; and he began to hate, as well as despise me, before I was born.

"My mother, grieved to the soul by his neglect, and unkind treatment, actually resolved to famish herself and injured her health by the attempt; though she had not sufficient resolution to adhere to her project, or renounce it entirely. Death came not at her call; yet sorrow, and the methods she adopted to conceal her condition, still doing the work of a house-maid, had such an effect on her constitution that she died in the wretched garret where her virtuous mistress had forced

her to take refuge in the very pangs of labour; though my father, after a slight reproof,[2] was allowed to remain in his place—allowed by the mother of six children who, scarcely permitting a footstep to be heard during her month's indulgence,[3] felt no sympathy for the poor wretch denied every comfort required by her situation.

"The day my mother died, the ninth after my birth, I was consigned to the care of the cheapest nurse my father could find; who suckled her own child at the same time, and lodged as many more as she could get in two cellar-like apartments.

"Poverty, and the habit of seeing children die off her hands, had so hardened her heart that the office of a mother did not awaken the tenderness of a woman; nor were the feminine caresses which seem a part of the rearing of a child ever bestowed on me. The chicken has a wing to shelter under; but I had no bosom to nestle in, no kindred warmth to foster me. Left in dirt, to cry with cold and hunger till I was weary, and sleep without ever being prepared by exercise, or lulled by kindness to rest, could I be expected to become any thing but a weak and rickety babe? Still, in spite of neglect, I continued to exist, to learn to curse existence her countenance grew ferocious as she spoke, and the treatment that rendered me miserable seemed to sharpen my wits. Confined then in a damp hovel, to rock the cradle of the succeed-

---

[1] *importunities* Attempts to get attention.

[2] *reproof* Rebuke.

[3] *during her month's indulgence* I.e., during the period when she herself had been recovering after childbirth.

ing tribe, I looked like a little old woman, or a hag shriveling into nothing. The furrows of reflection and care contracted the youthful cheek, and gave a sort of supernatural wildness to the ever-watchful eye. During this period, my father had married another fellow-servant, who loved him less and knew better how to manage his passion than my mother. She likewise proving with child, they agreed to keep a shop: my stepmother—if, being an illegitimate offspring, I may venture thus to characterize her—having obtained a sum of a rich relation for that purpose.

"Soon after her lying-in,[1] she prevailed on my father to take me home, to save the expense of maintaining me, and of hiring a girl to assist her in the care of the child. I was young, it was true, but appeared a knowing little thing and might be made handy. Accordingly I was brought to her house; but not to a home—for a home I never knew. Of this child, a daughter, she was extravagantly fond; and it was a part of my employment to assist to spoil her, by humouring all her whims and bearing all her caprices. Feeling her own consequence before she could speak, she had learned the art of tormenting me, and if I ever dared to resist, I received blows, laid on with no compunctious hand,[2] or was sent to bed dinnerless, as well as supperless. I said that it was a part of my daily labour to attend this child with the servility of a slave; still it was but a part. I was sent out in all seasons, and from place to place, to carry burdens far above my strength, without being allowed to draw near the fire, or ever being cheered by encouragement or kindness. No wonder then, treated like a creature of another species, that I began to envy, and at length to hate, the darling of the house. Yet, I perfectly remember that it was the caresses, and kind expressions of my step-mother, which first excited my jealous discontent. Once, I cannot forget it, when she was calling in vain her wayward child to kiss her, I ran to her, saying, 'I will kiss you, ma'am!'; and how did my heart, which was in my mouth, sink, what was my debasement of soul, when pushed away with—'I do not want you, pert thing!' Another day, when a new gown had excited the highest good humour, and she uttered the appropriate

dear, addressed unexpectedly to me, I thought I could never do enough to please her; I was all alacrity,[3] and rose proportionally in my own estimation.

"As her daughter grew up, she was pampered with cakes and fruit, while I was, literally speaking, fed with the refuse of the table, with her leavings. A liquorish tooth[4] is, I believe, common to children, and I used to steal any thing sweet that I could catch up with a chance of concealment. When detected, she was not content to chastise me herself at the moment, but, on my father's return in the evening (he was a shopman), the principal discourse was to recount my faults, and attribute them to the wicked disposition which I had brought into the world with me, inherited from my mother. He did not fail to leave the marks of his resentment on my body, and then solaced himself by playing with my sister. I could have murdered her at those moments. To save myself from these unmerciful corrections, I resorted to falsehood, and the untruths which I sturdily maintained were brought in judgment against me, to support my tyrant's inhuman charge of my natural propensity to vice. Seeing me treated with contempt, and always being fed and dressed better, my sister conceived a contemptuous opinion of me that proved an obstacle to all affection; and my father, hearing continually of my faults, began to consider me as a curse entailed[5] on him for his sins: he was therefore easily prevailed on to bind me apprentice to one of my step-mother's friends, who kept a slop shop[6] in Wapping.[7] I was represented (as it was said) in my true colours; but she 'warranted,'[8] snapping her fingers, 'that she should break my spirit or heart.'

"My mother replied, with a whine, 'that if any body could make me better, it was such a clever woman as herself; though, for her own part, she had tried in vain, but good nature was her fault.'

"I shudder with horror when I recollect the treatment I had now to endure. Not only under the lash of my task-mistress, but the drudge of the maid, appren-

---

[1] lying-in Period of rest following childbirth.

[2] compunctious hand I.e., Jemima was beaten without pity, or indeed any concern.

[3] alacrity Readiness.

[4] liquorish tooth Sweet tooth, i.e., fondness for sweets.

[5] entailed Irrevocably attached.

[6] slop shop Shop that sold inexpensive, ready-made clothing.

[7] Wapping District of east London.

[8] warranted Guaranteed.

tices, and children, I never had a taste of human kindness to soften the rigour of perpetual labour. I had been introduced as an object of abhorrence into the family; as a creature of whom my step-mother, though she had been kind enough to let me live in the house with her own child, could make nothing. I was described as a wretch whose nose must be kept to the grinding stone—and it was held there with an iron grasp. It seemed indeed the privilege of their superior nature to kick me about like the dog or cat. If I were attentive, I was called fawning, if refractory,[1] an obstinate mule, and like a mule I received their censure on my loaded back. Often has my mistress, for some instance of forgetfulness, thrown me from one side of the kitchen to the other, knocked my head against the wall, spit in my face, with various refinements on barbarity that I forbear to enumerate, though they were all acted over again by the servant, with additional insults, to which the appellation of *bastard* was commonly added with taunts or sneers. But I will not attempt to give you an adequate idea of my situation, lest you, who probably have never been drenched with the dregs of human misery, should think I exaggerate.

"I stole now—from absolute necessity—bread; yet whatever else was taken, which I had it not in my power to take, was ascribed to me. I was the filching cat, the ravenous dog, the dumb brute who must bear all; for if I endeavoured to exculpate[2] myself, I was silenced without any enquiries being made, with 'Hold your tongue, you never tell truth.' Even the very air I breathed was tainted with scorn; for I was sent to the neighbouring shops with Glutton, Liar, or Thief written on my forehead. This was, at first, the most bitter punishment; but sullen pride, or a kind of stupid desperation, made me, at length, almost regardless of the contempt which had wrung from me so many solitary tears at the only moments when I was allowed to rest.

"Thus was I the mark of cruelty till my sixteenth year; and then I have only to point out a change of misery, for a period I never knew. Allow me first to make one observation. Now I look back, I cannot help attributing the greater part of my misery to the misfortune of having been thrown into the world without the grand support of life—a mother's affection. I had no one to love me, or to make me respected, to enable me to acquire respect. I was an egg dropped on the sand; a pauper by nature, hunted from family to family, who belonged to nobody—and nobody cared for me. I was despised from my birth, and denied the chance of obtaining a footing for myself in society. Yes; I had not even the chance of being considered as a fellow-creature—yet all the people with whom I lived, brutalized as they were by the low cunning of trade, and the despicable shifts of poverty, were not without bowels,[3] though they never yearned for me. I was, in fact, born a slave, and chained by infamy[4] to slavery during the whole of existence, without having any companions to alleviate it by sympathy, or teach me how to rise above it by their example....

"At sixteen, I suddenly grew tall, and something like comeliness[5] appeared on a Sunday, when I had time to wash my face and put on clean clothes. My master had once or twice caught hold of me in the passage; but I instinctively avoided his disgusting caresses. One day however, when the family were at a Methodist meeting, he contrived to be alone in the house with me, and by blows—yes, blows and menaces—compelled me to submit to his ferocious desire; and, to avoid my mistress's fury, I was obliged in future to comply, and skulk to my loft at his command, in spite of increasing loathing.

"The anguish which was now pent up in my bosom seemed to open a new world to me: I began to extend my thoughts beyond myself and grieve for human misery, until I discovered, with horror—ah! what horror!—that I was with child. I know not why I felt a mixed sensation of despair and tenderness, excepting that, ever called a bastard, a bastard appeared to me an object of the greatest compassion in creation.

"I communicated this dreadful circumstance to my master, who was almost equally alarmed at the intelligence; for he feared his wife and public censure at the meeting. After some weeks of deliberation had elapsed, I in continual fear that my altered shape would be noticed, my master gave me a medicine in a phial which

---

[1]   *refractory*   Stubborn, non-compliant.

[2]   *exculpate*   Clear oneself from blame.

[3]   *bowels*   Heart, compassion.

[4]   *infamy*   Scandalous reputation.

[5]   *comeliness*   Beauty.

he desired me to take, telling me, without any circumlocution,[1] for what purpose it was designed. I burst into tears, I thought it was killing myself—yet was such a self as I worth preserving? He cursed me for a fool, and left me to my own reflections. I could not resolve to take this infernal potion; but I wrapped it up in an old gown, and hid it in a corner of my box.

"Nobody yet suspected me, because they had been accustomed to view me as a creature of another species. But the threatening storm at last broke over my devoted head—never shall I forget it! One Sunday evening when I was left, as usual, to take care of the house, my master came home intoxicated, and I became the prey of his brutal appetite. His extreme intoxication made him forget his customary caution, and my mistress entered and found us in a situation that could not have been more hateful to her than me. Her husband was 'pot-valiant,'[2] he feared her not at the moment, nor had he then much reason, for she instantly turned the whole force of her anger another way. She tore off my cap, scratched, kicked, and buffeted me until she had exhausted her strength, declaring, as she rested her arm, 'that I had wheedled[3] her husband from her. But, could any thing better be expected from a wretch whom she had taken into her house out of pure charity?' What a torrent of abuse rushed out, until, almost breathless, she concluded with saying, 'that I was born a strumpet;[4] it ran in my blood, and nothing good could come to those who harboured me.'

"My situation was, of course, discovered, and she declared that I should not stay another night under the same roof with an honest family. I was therefore pushed out of doors, and my trumpery[5] thrown after me, when it had been contemptuously examined in the passage lest I should have stolen any thing.

"Behold me then in the street, utterly destitute! Whither could I creep for shelter? To my father's roof I had no claim when not pursued by shame—now I shrunk back as from death from my mother's cruel reproaches, my father's execrations.[6] I could not endure to hear him curse the day I was born, though life had been a curse to me. Of death I thought, but with a confused emotion of terror, as I stood leaning my head on a post and starting at every footstep, lest it should be my mistress coming to tear my heart out. One of the boys of the shop passing by heard my tale, and immediately repaired to his master to give him a description of my situation; and he touched the right key—the scandal it would give rise to if I were left to repeat my tale to every enquirer. This plea came home to his reason, who had been sobered by his wife's rage, the fury of which fell on him when I was out of her reach, and he sent the boy to me with half-a-guinea,[7] desiring him to conduct me to a house where beggars, and other wretches, the refuse of society, nightly lodged.

"This night was spent in a state of stupefaction, or desperation. I detested mankind, and abhorred myself.

"In the morning I ventured out, to throw myself in my master's way, at his usual hour of going abroad. I approached him, he 'damned me for a b——, declared I had disturbed the peace of the family, and that he had sworn to his wife never to take any more notice of me.' He left me; but, instantly returning, he told me that he should speak to his friend, a parish-officer,[8] to get a nurse for the brat I laid to him; and advised me, if I wished to keep out of the house of correction, not to make free with his name.

"I hurried back to my hole, and, rage giving place to despair, sought for the potion that was to procure abortion and swallowed it, with a wish that it might destroy me at the same time that it stopped the sensations of new-born life, which I felt with indescribable emotion. My head turned round, my heart grew sick, and in the horrors of approaching dissolution,[9] mental anguish was swallowed up. The effect of the medicine

[1] *circumlocution* Indirect speaking.
[2] *pot-valiant* Courageous due to the affects of alcohol.
[3] *wheedled* Seduced by flattery or gentle coaxing.
[4] *strumpet* Derogatory term for a woman who has a number of sexual partners.
[5] *trumpery* Worthless clothing goods.
[6] *execrations* Expressions of intense loathing.
[7] *half-a-guinea* Gold coin.
[8] *parish-officer* General term for person holding any one of several elected positions within a parish, including churchwarden, surveyor, overseer of the poor, constable, etc.; overseers of the poor set and collected poor rates, as well as administering benefits to those in need.
[9] *dissolution* Death.

was violent, and I was confined to my bed several days; but, youth and a strong constitution prevailing, I once more crawled out to ask myself the cruel question, 'Whither I should go?' I had but two shillings[1] left in my pocket, the rest had been expended, by a poor woman who slept in the same room, to pay for my lodging and purchase the necessaries of which she partook.

"With this wretch I went into the neighbouring streets to beg, and my disconsolate appearance drew a few pence from the idle, enabling me still to command a bed; until, recovering from my illness, and taught to put on my rags to the best advantage, I was accosted from different motives, and yielded to the desire of the brutes I met with the same detestation that I had felt for my still more brutal master. I have since read in novels of the blandishments[2] of seduction, but I had not even the pleasure of being enticed into vice.

"I shall not," interrupted Jemima, "lead your imagination into all the scenes of wretchedness and depravity which I was condemned to view, or mark the different stages of my debasing misery. Fate dragged me through the very kennels[3] of society: I was still a slave, a bastard, a common property. Become familiar with vice, for I wish to conceal nothing from you, I picked the pockets of the drunkards who abused me; and proved by my conduct that I deserved the epithets with which they loaded me at moments when distrust ought to cease.

"Detesting my nightly occupation, though valuing, if I may so use the word, my independence, which only consisted in choosing the street in which I should wander, or the roof, when I had money, in which I should hide my head, I was some time before I could prevail on myself to accept of a place in a house of ill fame[4] to which a girl, with whom I had accidentally conversed in the street, had recommended me. I had been hunted almost into a fever by the watchmen[5] of the quarter of the town I frequented; one, whom I had

unwittingly offended, giving the word to the whole pack. You can scarcely conceive the tyranny exercised by these wretches: considering themselves as the instruments of the very laws they violate, the pretext which steels their conscience hardens their heart. Not content with receiving from us, outlaws of society (let other women talk of favours), a brutal gratification gratuitously as a privilege of office, they extort a tithe[6] of prostitution, and harass with threats the poor creatures whose occupation affords not the means to silence the growl of avarice. To escape from this persecution, I once more entered into servitude.

"A life of comparative regularity restored my health; and— do not start[7]—my manners were improved in a situation where vice sought to render itself alluring, and taste was cultivated to fashion the person, if not to refine the mind. Besides, the common civility of speech, contrasted with the gross vulgarity to which I had been accustomed, was something like the polish of civilization. I was not shut out from all intercourse[8] of humanity. Still I was galled[9] by the yoke of service, and my mistress often flying into violent fits of passion made me dread a sudden dismission, which I understood was always the case. I was therefore prevailed on, though I felt a horror of men, to accept the offer of a gentleman, rather in the decline of years, to keep his house, pleasantly situated in a little village near Hampstead.[10]

"He was a man of great talents, and of brilliant wit; but, a worn-out votary of voluptuousness,[11] his desires became fastidious in proportion as they grew weak, and the native tenderness of his heart was undermined by a vitiated[12] imagination. A thoughtless career of libertinism[13] and social enjoyment had injured his health to such a degree that, whatever pleasure his conversation afforded me (and my esteem was ensured by proofs of the generous humanity of his disposition), the being his

---

[1] *shillings* Coins of small value.

[2] *blandishments* Flattering words.

[3] *kennels* Gutters.

[4] *house of ill-fame* Brothel.

[5] *watchmen* Before the Police Act of 1839, men were formally appointed to guard city and town streets from sunset to sunrise.

[6] *tithe* Tenth of one's earnings.

[7] *do not start* I.e., do not be startled, shocked.

[8] *intercourse* Social interaction or communication.

[9] *galled* Irritated, chafed.

[10] *Hampstead* North London suburb.

[11] *votary of voluptuousness* Person devoted to sensuality.

[12] *vitiated* Rendered impure, soiled.

[13] *libertinism* Unrestrained, licentious conduct.

mistress was purchasing it at a very dear rate. With such a keen perception of the delicacies of sentiment, with an imagination invigorated by the exercise of genius, how could he sink into the grossness of sensuality!

"But, to pass over a subject which I recollect with pain, I must remark to you, as an answer to your often-repeated question—'Why my sentiments and language were superior to my station?'—that I now began to read, to beguile[1] the tediousness of solitude, and to gratify an inquisitive, active mind. I had often, in my childhood, followed a ballad-singer to hear the sequel of a dismal story, though sure of being severely punished for delaying to return with whatever I was sent to purchase. I could just spell and put a sentence together, and I listened to the various arguments, though often mingled with obscenity, which occurred at the table where I was allowed to preside: for a literary friend or two frequently came home with my master to dine and pass the night. Having lost the privileged respect of my sex, my presence, instead of restraining, perhaps gave the reins to their tongues; still I had the advantage of hearing discussions from which, in the common course of life, women are excluded.

"You may easily imagine that it was only by degrees that I could comprehend some of the subjects they investigated, or acquire from their reasoning what might be termed a moral sense. But my fondness of reading increasing, and my master occasionally shutting himself up in this retreat for weeks together to write, I had many opportunities of improvement. At first, considering money ("I was right!" exclaimed Jemima, altering her tone of voice) as the only means, after my loss of reputation, of obtaining respect, or even the toleration of humanity, I had not the least scruple to secrete a part of the sums entrusted to me, and to screen myself from detection by a system of falsehood. But, acquiring new principles, I began to have the ambition of returning to the respectable part of society, and was weak enough to suppose it possible. The attention of my unassuming instructor, who, without being ignorant of his own powers, possessed great simplicity of manners, strengthened the illusion. Having sometimes caught up hints for thought from my untutored remarks, he often led me to discuss the subjects he was treating, and would read to

me his productions, previous to their publication, wishing to profit by the criticism of unsophisticated feeling. The aim of his writings was to touch the simple springs of the heart; for he despised the would-be oracles, the self-elected philosophers, who fright away fancy while sifting each grain of thought to prove that slowness of comprehension is wisdom.

"I should have distinguished this as a moment of sunshine, a happy period in my life, had not the repugnance the disgusting libertinism of my protector inspired daily become more painful. And, indeed, I soon did recollect it as such with agony, when his sudden death (for he had recourse to the most exhilarating cordials to keep up the convivial tone of his spirits) again threw me into the desert of human society. Had he had any time for reflection, I am certain he would have left the little property in his power to me: but, attacked by the fatal apoplexy[2] in town, his heir, a man of rigid morals, brought his wife with him to take possession of the house and effects before I was even informed of his death—'to prevent,' as she took care indirectly to tell me, 'such a creature as she supposed me to be from purloining[3] any of them, had I been apprized of the event in time.'

"The grief I felt at the sudden shock the information gave me, which at first had nothing selfish in it, was treated with contempt, and I was ordered to pack up my clothes; and a few trinkets and books, given me by the generous deceased, were contested, while they piously hoped, with a reprobating[4] shake of the head, 'that God would have mercy on his sinful soul!' With some difficulty, I obtained my arrears of wages; but asking—such is the spirit-grinding consequence of poverty and infamy—for a character[5] for honesty and economy, which God knows I merited, I was told by this—why must I call her woman?—'that it would go against her conscience to recommend a kept mistress.' Tears started in my eyes, burning tears; for there are situations in which a wretch is humbled by the contempt they are conscious they do not deserve.

---

[1] *beguile* Charm away.

[2] *apoplexy* Stroke.

[3] *purloining* Stealing.

[4] *reprobating* Condemning.

[5] *character* I.e., formal reference from an employer.

"I returned to the metropolis; but the solitude of a poor lodging was inconceivably dreary after the society I had enjoyed. To be cut off from human converse, now I had been taught to relish it, was to wander a ghost among the living. Besides, I foresaw, to aggravate the severity of my fate, that my little pittance would soon melt away. I endeavoured to obtain needlework; but, not having been taught early, and my hands being rendered clumsy by hard work, I did not sufficiently excel to be employed by the ready-made linen shops when so many women, better qualified, were suing[1] for it. The want of a character prevented my getting a place; for, irksome as servitude would have been to me, I should have made another trial had it been feasible. Not that I disliked employment, but the inequality of condition to which I must have submitted. I had acquired a taste for literature during the five years I had lived with a literary man, occasionally conversing with men of the first abilities of the age; and now to descend to the lowest vulgarity was a degree of wretchedness not to be imagined unfelt. I had not, it is true, tasted the charms of affection, but I had been familiar with the graces of humanity.

"One of the gentlemen, whom I had frequently dined in company with while I was treated like a companion, met me in the street and enquired after my health. I seized the occasion, and began to describe my situation; but he was in haste to join, at dinner, a select party of choice spirits; therefore, without waiting to hear me, he impatiently put a guinea into my hand, saying, 'It was a pity such a sensible woman should be in distress—he wished me well from his soul.'

"To another I wrote, stating my case and requesting advice. He was an advocate for unequivocal sincerity; and had often, in my presence, descanted[2] on the evils which arise in society from the despotism of rank and riches.

"In reply, I received a long essay on the energy of the human mind with continual allusions to his own force of character. He added, 'That the woman who could write such a letter as I had sent him could never be in want of resources, were she to look into herself and exert her powers; misery was the consequence of indolence,

and, as to my being shut out from society, it was the lot of man to submit to certain privations.'[3]

"How often have I heard," said Jemima, interrupting her narrative, "in conversation, and read in books, that every person willing to work may find employment? It is the vague assertion, I believe, of insensible[4] indolence when it relates to men; but, with respect to women, I am sure of its fallacy, unless they will submit to the most menial bodily labour; and even to be employed at hard labour is out of the reach of many whose reputation misfortune or folly has tainted.

"How writers, professing to be friends to freedom and the improvement of morals, can assert that poverty is no evil, I cannot imagine."

"No more can I," interrupted Maria, "yet they even expatiate[5] on the peculiar happiness of indigence,[6] though in what it can consist, excepting in brutal rest, when a man can barely earn a subsistence, I cannot imagine. The mind is necessarily imprisoned in its own little tenement; and, fully occupied by keeping it in repair, has not time to rove abroad for improvement. The book of knowledge is closely clasped against those who must fulfill their daily task of severe manual labour or die; and curiosity, rarely excited by thought or information, seldom moves on the stagnate lake of ignorance."

"As far as I have been able to observe," replied Jemima, "prejudices, caught up by chance, are obstinately maintained by the poor to the exclusion of improvement; they have not time to reason or reflect to any extent, or minds sufficiently exercised to adopt the principles of action, which form perhaps the only basis of contentment in every station."

"And independence," said Darnford, "they are necessarily strangers to, even the independence of despising their persecutors. If the poor are happy, or can be happy, *things are very well as they are*. And I cannot conceive on what principle those writers contend for a change of system who support this opinion. The authors on the other side of the question are much more consis-

---

[1] *suing* Asking, applying.

[2] *descanted* Commented on.

[3] *privations* Absence of comforts.

[4] *insensible* Incapable of feeling.

[5] *expatiate* Write or speak copiously on a subject.

[6] *indigence* Poverty.

tent who grant the fact; yet, insisting that it is the lot of the majority to be oppressed in this life, kindly turn them over to another, to rectify the false weights and measures of this, as the only way to justify the dispensations of Providence.[1] I have not," continued Darnford, "an opinion more firmly fixed by observation in my mind than that, though riches may fail to produce proportionate happiness, poverty most commonly excludes it by shutting up all the avenues to improvement."

"And as for the affections," added Maria, with a sigh, "how gross,[2] and even tormenting do they become, unless regulated by an improving mind! The culture of the heart ever, I believe, keeps pace with that of the mind. But pray go on," addressing Jemima, "though your narrative gives rise to the most painful reflections on the present state of society."

"Not to trouble you," continued she, "with a detailed description of all the painful feelings of unavailing[3] exertion, I have only to tell you that at last I got recommended to wash in a few families, who did me the favour to admit me into their houses without the most strict enquiry, to wash from one in the morning till eight at night for eighteen or twenty-pence a day. On the happiness to be enjoyed over a washing-tub I need not comment; yet you will allow me to observe that this was a wretchedness of situation peculiar to my sex. A man with half my industry, and, I may say, abilities, could have procured a decent livelihood and discharged some of the duties which knit mankind together; whilst I, who had acquired a taste for the rational—nay, in honest pride let me assert it, the virtuous enjoyments of life—was cast aside as the filth of society. Condemned to labour, like a machine, only to earn bread, and scarcely that, I became melancholy and desperate.

"I have now to mention a circumstance which fills me with remorse, and fear it will entirely deprive me of your esteem. A tradesman became attached to me, and visited me frequently, and I at last obtained such a power over him that he offered to take me home to his house. Consider, dear madam, I was famishing: wonder not that I became a wolf! The only reason for not taking me home immediately was the having a girl in the house with child by him; and this girl, I advised him—yes, I did! Would I could forget it!—to turn out of doors: and one night he determined to follow my advice. Poor wretch! She fell upon her knees, reminded him that he had promised to marry her, that her parents were honest! What did it avail? She was turned out.

"She approached her father's door in the skirts of London, listened at the shutters, but could not knock. A watchman had observed her go and return several times—Poor wretch! (The remorse Jemima spoke of seemed to be stinging her to the soul, as she proceeded.)

"She left it, and, approaching a tub where horses were watered, she sat down in it, and, with desperate resolution, remained in that attitude[4]—till resolution was no longer necessary!

"I happened that morning to be going out to wash, anticipating the moment when I should escape from such hard labour. I passed by, just as some men, going to work, drew out the stiff, cold corpse—let me not recall the horrid moment! I recognized her pale visage; I listened to the tale told by the spectators, and my heart did not burst. I thought of my own state, and wondered how I could be such a monster! I worked hard; and, returning home, I was attacked by a fever. I suffered both in body and mind. I determined not to live with the wretch. But he did not try[5] me; he left the neighbourhood. I once more returned to the wash tub.

"Still this state, miserable as it was, admitted of aggravation. Lifting one day a heavy load, a tub fell against my shin and gave me great pain. I did not pay much attention to the hurt until it became a serious wound, being obliged to work as usual or starve. But, finding myself at length unable to stand for any time, I thought of getting into an hospital. Hospitals, it should seem (for they are comfortless abodes for the sick), were expressly endowed for the reception of the friendless; yet I, who had on that plea a right to assistance, wanted the recommendation of the rich and respectable, and was several weeks languishing for admittance; fees were demanded on entering; and, what was still more unrea-

---

[1] *dispensations of Providence* Providential management of the world.

[2] *gross* Unrefined, lacking sensitivity.

[3] *unavailing* Of no avail, no use or hope.

[4] *attitude* Posture, bodily position.

[5] *try* Put to the test.

sonable, security for burying me—that expense not coming into the letter of the charity. A guinea was the stipulated sum—I could as soon have raised a million; and I was afraid to apply to the parish for an order, lest they should have passed me I knew not whither.[1] The poor woman at whose house I lodged, compassionating[2] my state, got me into the hospital; and the family where I received the hurt sent me five shillings, three and six-pence of which I gave at my admittance—I know not for what.

"My leg grew quickly better; but I was dismissed before my cure was completed because I could not afford to have my linen washed to appear decently, as the virago[3] of a nurse said, when the gentlemen (the surgeons) came. I cannot give you an adequate idea of the wretchedness of an hospital; everything is left to the care of people intent on gain. The attendants seem to have lost all feeling of compassion in the bustling discharge of their offices; death is so familiar to them that they are not anxious to ward it off. Everything appeared to be conducted for the accommodation of the medical men and their pupils, who came to make experiments on the poor for the benefit of the rich. One of the physicians, I must not forget to mention, gave me half-a-crown, and ordered me some wine, when I was at the lowest ebb. I thought of making my case known to the lady-like matron;[4] but her forbidding countenance prevented me. She condescended to look on the patients, and make general enquiries, two or three times a week; but the nurses knew the hour when the visit of ceremony would commence, and every thing was as it should be.

"After my dismission, I was more at a loss than ever for a subsistence, and, not to weary you with a repetition of the same unavailing attempts, unable to stand at the washing-tub, I began to consider the rich and poor as natural enemies, and became a thief from principle. I could not now cease to reason, but I hated mankind. I despised myself, yet I justified my conduct. I was taken, tried, and condemned to six months' imprisonment in a house of correction. My soul recoils with horror from the remembrance of the insults I had to endure until, branded with shame, I was turned loose in the street, penniless. I wandered from street to street until, exhausted by hunger and fatigue, I sunk down senseless at a door where I had vainly demanded a morsel of bread. I was sent by the inhabitant to the work-house, to which he had surlily bid me go, saying, he 'paid enough in conscience to the poor' when, with parched tongue, I implored his charity. If those well-meaning people who exclaim against beggars were acquainted with the treatment the poor receive in many of these wretched asylums, they would not stifle so easily involuntary sympathy by saying that they have all parishes to go to, or wonder that the poor dread to enter the gloomy walls. What are the common run of workhouses but prisons, in which many respectable old people, worn out by immoderate labour, sink into the grave in sorrow to which they are carried like dogs!"

Alarmed by some indistinct noise, Jemima rose hastily to listen, and Maria, turning to Darnford, said, "I have indeed been shocked beyond expression when I have met a pauper's funeral. A coffin carried on the shoulders of three or four ill-looking wretches, whom the imagination might easily convert into a band of assassins hastening to conceal the corpse and quarrelling about the prey on their way. I know it is of little consequence how we are consigned to the earth;[5] but I am led by this brutal insensibility, to what even the animal creation appears forcibly to feel, to advert to[6] the wretched, deserted manner in which they died."

"True," rejoined Darnford, "and until the rich will give more than a part of their wealth, until they will give time and attention to the wants of the distressed, never let them boast of charity. Let them open their hearts, and not their purses, and employ their minds in the service if they are really actuated by humanity; or charitable institutions will always be the prey of the

---

[1] *I was afraid ... whither*   One applied for poor relief from the parish in which one was last legally settled; terms of legal settlement included being born into a parish, renting property of a certain value, working for over a year and a day, serving an apprenticeship of seven years or more, marrying into the parish, etc. If one applied for poor relief without meeting the settlement requirements, one would be sent back to a parish in which one did.

[2] *compassionating*   Having compassion for.

[3] *virago*   Bold woman, scold.

[4] *matron*   Woman in charge of the nurses.

[5] *how we are consigned to the earth*   I.e., how we are buried.

[6] *advert to*   Pay attention to.

---

lowest order of knaves."

Jemima returning, seemed in haste to finish her tale. "The overseer farmed[1] the poor of different parishes, and out of the bowels of poverty was wrung the money with which he purchased this dwelling, as a private receptacle for madness. He had been a keeper at a house of the same description, and conceived that he could make money much more readily in his old occupation. He is a shrewd—shall I say it?—villain. He observed something resolute in my manner, and offered to take me with him and instruct me how to treat the disturbed minds he meant to entrust to my care. The offer of forty pounds a year, and to quit a workhouse, was not to be despised, though the condition of shutting my eyes and hardening my heart was annexed[2] to it.

"I agreed to accompany him; and four years have I been attendant on many wretches, and"—she lowered her voice—"the witness of many enormities.[3] In solitude my mind seemed to recover its force, and many of the sentiments which I imbibed in the only tolerable period of my life returned with their full force. Still, what should induce me to be the champion for suffering humanity? Who ever risked any thing for me? Who ever acknowledged me to be a fellow-creature?"

Maria took her hand, and Jemima, more overcome by kindness than she had ever been by cruelty, hastened out of the room to conceal her emotions.

Darnford soon after heard his summons, and, taking leave of him, Maria promised to gratify his curiosity, with respect to herself, at the first opportunity.

—1798

---

[1] *farmed* Contracted out care or maintenance for a fee.

[2] *annexed* Included as a condition.

[3] *enormities* Gross breaches of law or morals.

Robert Burns
1759 – 1796

There is a riddle among certain linguists: "What is the difference between a language and a dialect?" Answer: "A language is a dialect that has an army and a navy." The point is well taken and the enduring popularity of the British language across the planet no doubt is connected to the huge successes of the British navy in the last two and a half centuries. But when we sing Robert Burns's "Auld Lang Syne" on New Year's Eve we repeat a dialect piece that made good without the backing of an army or a navy. No doubt the distinctive resonance of Burns's Ayrshire dialect has helped to make the words of "Auld Lang Syne" memorable, but its popularity also rests on the degree to which it speaks the language of the heart, conveying a strong sense of mortality and of the blessings of memory itself.

Burns was born in Ayrshire, a county in southwestern Scotland, and spent his early years laboring with his father, a tenant-farmer who died in 1784. Intending to accept a position on a plantation in Jamaica, Burns gave up on this scheme when his first volume of poems, *Poems, Chiefly in the Scottish Dialect* (1786), brought him instant acclaim and the means to a more comfortable life. The Scottish dialect in which he wrote was descended from the Northumbrian dialect of Old English and had been known originally as "Inglis." In the eighteenth century it came to be called "Scots." Mostly gathered in Edinburgh, the champions of the Scottish Enlightenment attempted to be equally fluent in Scots and English. Burns owes his reputation as "Heaven-taught plowman" to his ear for his Scots dialect, but he also knew how to write using English diction.

In some of his best poems, broad Scots and formal English alternate—indeed, nearly overlap. Burns's most famous narrative poem, the mock-heroic "Tam o'Shanter," is one in which we may see and hear the double-fluency of the poet, his broad Scots dialect giving way to "pure English." Many readers, both in Burns's time and in our own, have felt some relief when the poetry gives us a brief shower of "pure English." But by not forsaking the richness of his dialect, Burns was helping to ensure his future status as Scotland's national poet—and dealing a blow to the class prejudice against him that was always present, despite the Edinburgh aristocracy's celebration of him when *Poems* first appeared.

Burns's *Poems* became known as the "Kilmarnock edition," after the place in which the book was published. Already at twenty-seven, Burns had written his most famous poems, and he spent much of the rest of his short life helping to formalize an oral tradition in Scotland, contributing many of the works collected in James Johnson's *The Scots Musical Museum* and in George Thomson's *Select Collection of Original Scottish Airs*. Although never a wealthy man, Burns refused any money for his contribution to this work.

Burns's reputation as a lover for a time rivaled his fame as a poet. Having fathered several illegitimate children, he finally settled down in 1788 with a former lover, Jean Armour, in the town of Dumfries, where he received a commission as an excise (tax) officer. Thereafter he seems to have become a good family man and to have enjoyed relative prosperity in the last years of his life. Burns's love songs often express both his love of women and his feeling for his craft, as in "Green grow the rashes": "Auld nature swears, the lovely dears / Her noblest work she classes, O: / Her prentice han' she tries on man, / An' then she made the lasses, O." Burns also collected all the bawdy songs he inherited and invented in *The Merry Muses of Caledonia*, published shortly after his death (and subjected to expurgation and suppression ever since).

A rebel in religion (he chafed against his strict Calvinist upbringing, although he attended church his entire life) and a sympathizer with the revolutions in America and France, Burns often wrote politically-charged poems. In "Robert Bruce's March to Bannockburn" (popularly known as "Scots, wha hae"), for example, we hear a war-cry for emancipation: "Lay the proud usurpers low! / Tyrants fall in every foe! / Liberty's in every blow! / Let us do, or die!" Burns could also see the world from the lowliest, humblest places, even to the point of reckoning the mischief and malice of plowing up a field mouse from its home and seeing the calamity from the mouse's point of view ("To a Mouse").

Burns drew heavily on oral tradition, using the ballad form to produce what many consider his masterpiece: "Love and Liberty: A Cantata," commonly known as "The Jolly Beggars" (published posthumously in 1799). The cantata is a series of songs sung by a group of vagabonds, who recall past events in their lives. Burns was strongly influenced by his literary predecessors—perhaps most notably the Scottish Chaucerians of the fifteenth and sixteenth centuries (Gavin Douglas, William Dunbar), and the eighteenth-century Scottish poets Allan Ramsay and Robert Fergusson, whose work supplied him with materials and forms for his comprehensive refashioning of the lyric tradition in Scotland.

Burns was only thirty-seven when he died from an attack of rheumatic fever in 1796, on the day that his wife gave birth to the couple's ninth child. He was buried in St. Michael's Churchyard, Dumfries, Scotland, but his remains were later moved to a mausoleum. Scottish people around the world continue to celebrate Burns's birthday each year on 25 January.

⌘ ⌘ ⌘

To a Mouse, On Turning Her Up in Her Nest with the Plough

Wee, sleekit, cowrin, tim'rous beastie,
   O, what a panic's in thy breastie!
Thou need na start awa sae hasty,
   Wi' bickerin' brattle![1]
5 I wad be laith° to rin an' chase thee,   *loathe*
   Wi' murd'ring pattle!°   *plough spade*

I'm truly sorry man's dominion
Has broken nature's social union,
An' justifies that ill opinion,
10   Which makes thee startle,
At me, thy poor, earth-born companion,
   An' fellow mortal!

I doubt na, whyles,° but thou may thieve;   *at times*
What then? poor beastie, thou maun° live!   *must*
15 A daimen icker in a thrave[2]
   'S a sma' request;
I'll get a blessin wi' the lave,°   *rest*
   An' never miss't!

Thy wee-bit housie, too, in ruin!
20 It's silly wa's° the win's are strewin!   *walls*
An' naething, now, to big° a new ane,   *build*
   O' foggage° green!   *moss*
An' bleak December's winds ensuin,
   Baith snell° an' keen!   *bitter*

25 Thou saw the fields laid bare an' waste,
An's weary winter comin fast,
An' cozie here, beneath the blast,
   Thou thought to dwell,

---

1 *bickerin' brattle* Hurrying scurry.

2 *A daimen icker in a thrave* The odd ear in 24 sheaves of corn.

Till crash! the cruel coulter° past   *plow blade*
30   Out thro' thy cell.

That wee-bit heap o' leaves an' stibble,
Has cost thee monie a weary nibble!
Now thou's turn'd out, for a' thy trouble,
        But° house or hald,°   *without / belongings*
35   To thole° the winter's sleety dribble,   *bear*
        An' cranreuch° cauld!   *hoar frost*

But, Mousie, thou art no thy lane,[1]
In proving foresight may be vain:
The best-laid schemes o' mice an' men
40   Gang aft agley,[2]
An' lea'e us nought but grief an' pain,
        For promis'd joy!

Still thou art blest, compar'd wi' me!
The present only toucheth thee:
45   But, Och! I backward cast my e'e
        On prospects drear!
An' forward, tho' I canna see,
        I guess an' fear!
        —1785

The Fornicator

Ye jovial boys who love the joys,
        The blissful joys of lovers;
Yet dare avow with dauntless brow,
        When th'bony lass discovers;
5   I pray draw near and lend an ear,
        And welcome in a frater,°   *brother*
For I've lately been on quarantine,
        A proven Fornicator.

Before the congregation wide
10   I pass'd the muster fairly,
My handsome Betsey by my side,
        We gat our ditty° rarely;   *sermon*
But my downcast eye by chance did spy

What made my lips to water,
15   Those limbs so clean where I, between
        Commenc'd a Fornicator.

With rueful face and signs of grace
        I pay'd the buttock–hire,[3]
The night was dark and thro the park
20   I could not but convoy her;
A parting kiss, what could I less,
        My vows began to scatter,
My Betsey fell—lal de dal lal lal,
        I am a Fornicator.

But for her sake this vow I make,
        And solemnly I swear it,
That while I own a single crown,
        She's welcome for to share it;
And my roguish boy his mother's joy,
30   And the darling of his pater,   *father*
For him I boast my pains and cost,
        Although a Fornicator.

Ye wenching blades whose hireling jades°   *prostitutes*
        Have tipt ye off blue–joram,[4]
35   I tell ye plain, I do disdain
        To rank ye in the quorum;
But a bony lass upon the grass
        To teach her esse mater,[5]
And no reward but for regard,
40   O that's a Fornicator.

Your warlike kings and heroes bold,
        Great captains and commanders;
Your mighty Caesars fam'd of old,
        And conquering Alexanders;
45   In fields they fought and laurels[6] bought
        And bulwarks strong did batter,
But still they grac'd our noble list
        And ranked Fornicator!!!
        —1785

---

[1] *no thy lane* Not alone.

[2] *Gang aft agley* Go oft awry.

[3] *buttock-hire* Church fine charged to fornicators.

[4] *tipt ye off blue-joram* Given you the pox.

[5] *esse mater* Latin: to be a mother.

[6] *laurels* Leaves of the bay laurel tree were once a symbol of victory in battle.

Halloween

Yes! let the rich deride, the proud disdain,
The simple pleasure of the lowly train;
To me more dear, congenial to my heart,
One native charm, than all the gloss of art.[1]
GOLDSMITH

1

Upon that night, when fairies light
   On Cassilis Downans[2] dance,
Or owre the lays, in splendid blaze,
   On sprightly coursers° prance;   *horses*
5 Or for Colean° the rout is ta'en,   *a cavern*
   Beneath the moon's pale beams;
There, up the cove, to stray an' rove,
   Amang the rocks and streams
      To sport that night.

2

10 Amang the bonie winding banks,
   Where Doon rins, wimplin,[3] clear;
Where Bruce[4] ance rul'd the martial ranks,
   An' shook his Carrick[5] spear;
Some merry, friendly, countra-folks
15   Together did convene,
To burn their nits, an' pou[6] their stocks,
   An' haud° their Halloween   *hold*
      Fu' blythe° that night.   *merry*

3

The lasses feat,° an' cleanly neat,   *well-dressed*
20   Mair braw° than when they're fine;   *handsome*
Their faces blythe, fu' sweetly kythe,°   *displayed*
   Hearts leal,° an' warm, an' kin':°   *loyal / kind*
The lads sae trig,° wi' wooer-babs   *neat*

Weel-knotted on their garten;[7]
25 Some unco blate,[8] an' some wi' gabs°   *mouths*
   Gar° lasses' hearts gang startin   *cause*
      Whiles fast at night.

4

Then, first an' foremost, thro' the kail,
   Their stocks maun° a' be sought ance;°   *must / once*
30 They steek° their een,° and grape an' wale   *close / eyes*
   For muckle anes,[9] an' straught anes.
Poor hav'rel° Will fell aff the drift,[10]   *half-wit*
   An' wandered thro' the bow-kail,   *cabbage*
An' pou't° for want o' better shift°   *pulled / choice*
35   A runt° was like a sow-tail   *cabbage*
      Sae bow't° that night.   *bent*

5

Then, straught or crooked, yird° or nane,°   *earth / none*
   They roar an' cry a' throu'ther;°   *recklessly*
The vera wee-things, toddlin, rin,
40   Wi' stocks out owre their shouther:
An' gif° the custock's sweet or sour,   *if / kale-stock*
   Wi' joctelegs° they taste them;   *pocketknives*
Syne° coziely, aboon° the door,   *then / above*
   Wi' cannie care, they've plac'd them
45   To lie that night.

6

The lassies staw frae[11] 'mang them a,'
   To pou their stalks o' corn;
But Rab slips out, an' jinks° about,   *dodges*
   Behint the muckle° thorn: *great*
50 He grippit Nelly hard and fast;
   Loud skirl'd° a' the lasses;   *shrieked*
But her tap-pickle[12] maist° was lost,   *most*

---

[1] *Yes!… art* From Oliver Goldsmith's *The Deserted Village* (1770) 251–54.

[2] *Cassilis Downans* Small hills in Ayrshire County, Scotland.

[3] *Doon rins, wimplin* The river Doon runs, winding.

[4] *Bruce* Scottish hero Robert the Bruce (1274–1329).

[5] *Carrick* District in Ayrshire.

[6] *nits* Nuts; *pou* Pull.

[7] *wooer-babs … garten* Garters worn in a particular way in order to announce that the wearer is wooing the person he is visiting.

[8] *unco blate* Extremely shy.

[9] *They steek … anes* They shut their eyes, and grope and choose / For big ones.

[10] *fell aff the drift* Wandered away.

[11] *staw frae* Steal from.

[12] *tap-pickle* Grain at the top of the stalk.

What kiutlan° in the fause-house[1] *fondling*
    Wi' him that night.

7

55 The auld guid-wife's° weel-hoordit° nits *landlady's / hoarded*
    Are round an' round divided,
An' mony lads an' lasses' fates
    Are there that night decided:
Some kindle couthie° side by side, *comfortably*
60   And burn thegither° trimly; *together*
Some start awa wi' saucy pride,
    An' jump out owre the chimlie° *chimney*
        Fu' high that night.

8

Jean slips in twa, wi' tentie° e'e; *watchful*
65   Wha 'twas, she wadna tell;
But this is Jock, an' this is me,
    She says in to hersel':
He bleez'd owre her, an' she owre him,
    As they wad never mair part:
70 Till fuff! he started up the lum,° *chimney*
    An' Jean had e'en a sair° heart *sore*
        To see't that night.

9

Poor Willie, wi' his bow-kail runt,
    Was brunt° wi' primsie° Mallie; *burned / prim*
75 An' Mary, nae doubt, took the drunt,[2]
    To be compar'd to Willie:
Mall's nit lap° out, wi' pridefu' fling, *leaped*
    An' her ain fit,[3] it brunt it;
While Willie lap, and swore by jing,
80   'Twas just the way he wanted
        To be that night.

10

Nell had the fause-house in her min',
    She pits hersel an' Rob in;
In loving bleeze they sweetly join,
    Till white in ase° they're sobbin: *ash*
85

Nell's heart was dancin at the view;
    She whisper'd Rob to leuk for't:
Rob, stownlins,° prie'd° her bonie mou', *stealthily / kissed*
    Fu' cozie in the neuk° for't, *nook*
90   Unseen that night.

11

But Merran sat behint their backs,
    Her thoughts on Andrew Bell:
She lea'es them gashin at their cracks,[4]
    An' slips out-by hersel';
95 She thro' the yard the nearest taks,
    An' for the kiln she goes then,
An' darklins[5] grapit for the bauks,
    And in the blue-clue[6] throws then,
        Right fear't that night.

12

100 An' ay she win't,° an' ay she swat°— *wound / sweated*
    I wat° she made nae jaukin;° *know / dawdling*
Till something held within the pat,
    Good Lord! but she was quaukin!
But whether 'twas the deil himsel,
105   Or whether 'twas a bauk-en',° *beam end*
Or whether it was Andrew Bell,
    She did na wait on talkin
        To spier that night. *inquire*

13

Wee Jenny to her graunie says,
110   "Will ye go wi' me, graunie?
I'll eat the apple at the glass,
    I gat frae uncle Johnie":
She fuff't° her pipe wi' sic a lunt,[7] *puffed*
    In wrath she was sae vap'rin,
115 She notic't na an aizle° brunt *hot ember*
    Her braw, new, worset apron
        Out thro' that night.

---

[1] *fause-house* Hollow in a large stack of corn stalks, created for drying the corn.

[2] *took the drunt* Sulked.

[3] *ain fit* Own foot.

[4] *gashin at their cracks* Gossiping.

[5] *darklins grapit for the bauks* In the darkness grabbed for the beams.

[6] *clue* Clew; ball of yarn.

[7] *lunt* Smoke column.

14

"Ye little skelpie-limmer's face!°   *naughty girl's*
  I daur you try sic sportin,
120 As seek the foul thief° ony place,   *devil*
  For him to spae° your fortune: *tell*
Nae doubt but ye may get a sight!
  Great cause ye hae to fear it;
For mony a ane has gotten a fright,
125   An' liv'd an' died deleerit,°   *delirious*
    On sic° a night.   *such*

15

"Ae hairst° afore the Sherra-moor,   *harvest*
  I mind't as weel's yestreen—
I was a gilpey° then, I'm sure   *young girl*
130   I was na past fyfteen:
The simmer had been cauld an' wat,
  An' stuff was unco green;
An' eye a rantin kirn[1] we gat,
  An' just on Halloween
135   It fell that night.

16

"Our stibble-rig° was Rab M'Graen,   *chief harvester*
  A clever, sturdy fallow;
His sin° gat Eppie Sim wi' wean,°   *son / child*
  That lived in Achmacalla:
140 He gat hemp-seed, I mind° it weel,   *remember*
  An'he made unco light o't;
But mony a day was by himsel,'
  He was sae sairly frighted
    That vera night."

17

145 Then up gat fechtin° Jamie Fleck,   *fighting*
  An' he swoor by his conscience,
That he could saw° hemp-seed a peck;   *sow*
  For it was a' but nonsense:
The auld guidman raught° down the pock,°   *reached / bag*
150   An' out a handfu' gied° him;   *gave*
Syne bad[2] him slip frae' mang the folk,
  Sometime when nae ane see'd him,
    An' try't that night.

18

He marches thro' amang the stacks,
155   Tho' he was something sturtin;°   *frightened*
The graip° he for a harrow taks,   *pitchfork*
  An' haurls° at his curpin:[3]   *drags*
And ev'ry now an' then, he says,
  "Hemp-seed I saw thee,
160 An' her that is to be my lass
  Come after me, an' draw thee
    As fast this night."

19

He wistl'd up Lord Lennox' March
  To keep his courage cherry;
165 Altho' his hair began to arch,
  He was sae fley'd° an' eerie: *terrified*
Till presently he hears a squeak,
  An' then a grane an' gruntle;
He by his shouther gae a keek,°   *glance*
170   An' tumbled wi' a wintle   *somersault*
    Out-owre that night.

20

He roar'd a horrid murder-shout,
  In dreadfu' desperation!
An' young an' auld come rinnin out,
175   An' hear the sad narration:
He swoor 'twas hilchin° Jean M'Craw,   *limping*
  Or crouchie° Merran Humphie—   *hunchbacked*
Till stop! she trotted thro' them a';
  And wha was it but grumphie°   *a pig*
180   Asteer that night!

21

Meg fain° wad to the barn gaen,°   *gladly / have gone*
  To winn° three wechts° o' naething;   *winnow / sieves*
But for to meet the deil her lane,[4]
  She pat but little faith in:
185 She gies the herd° a pickle° nits,   *shepherd / few*
  An' twa red cheekit apples,
To watch, while for the barn she sets,
  In hopes to see Tam Kipples
    That vera night.

---

[1] *rantin kirn* Boisterous party.
[2] *Syne bad* Soon bade.
[3] *at his curpin* Behind him (at his buttocks).
[4] *her lane* Alone.

22

190 She turns the key wi' cannie thraw,[1]
 An'owre the threshold ventures;
But first on Sawnie° gies a ca',   *Sandy*
 Syne baudly in she enters:
A ratton° rattl'd up the wa',   *rat*
195 An' she cry'd Lord preserve her!
An' ran thro' midden-hole° an' a', *dung pile*
 An' pray'd wi' zeal and fervour,
  Fu' fast that night.

23

They hoy't° out Will, wi' sair advice; *urged*
200 They hecht° him some fine braw ane; *promised*
It chanc'd the stack he faddom't thrice
 Was timmer-propt° for thrawin: *propped up*
He taks a swirlie auld moss-oak
 For some black, grousome carlin;° *witch*
205 An' loot a winze,[2] an' drew a stroke,
 Till skin in blypes° cam haurlin *shreds*
  Aff's nieves° that night. *fists*

24

A wanton widow Leezie was,
 As cantie° as a kittlen;° *lively / kitten*
210 But och! that night, amang the shaws,° *woods*
 She gat a fearfu' settlin!
She thro' the whins,° an' by the cairn, *gorse bushes*
 An' owre the hill gaed scrievin;° *running swiftly*
Whare three lairds' lan's met at a burn,
215 To dip her left sark°-sleeve in, *shirt*
  Was bent that night.

25

Whiles owre a linn° the burnie° plays, *waterfall / brook*
 As thro' the glen it wimpl't;
Whiles round a rocky scar° it strays, *cliff*
220 Whiles in a wiel° it dimpl't; *eddy*
Whiles glitter'd to the nightly rays,
 Wi' bickerin,' dancin' dazzle;

Whiles cookit° underneath the braes, *hidden*
 Below the spreading hazel
225   Unseen that night.

26

Amang the brachens, on the brae,
 Between her an' the moon,
The deil, or else an outler quey,[3]
 Gat up an' ga'e a croon:
230 Poor Leezie's heart maist lap the hool;[4]
 Near lav'rock°-height she jumpit, *lark*
But mist a fit, an' in the pool
 Out-owre the lugs° she plumpit, *ears*
  Wi' a plunge that night.

27

235 In order, on the clean hearth-stane,
 The luggies° three are ranged; *wooden dishes*
An' ev'ry time great care is ta'en
 To see them duly changed:
Auld uncle John, wha wedlock's joys
240 Sin' Mar's-year[5] did desire,
Because he gat the toom° dish thrice, *empty*
 He heav'd them on the fire
  In wrath that night.

28

Wi' merry sangs, an' friendly cracks,
245 I wat they did na weary;
And unco tales, an' funnie jokes—
 Their sports were cheap an' cheery:
Till butter'd sowens,[6] wi' fragrant lunt,° *steam*
 Set a' their gabs a-steerin;[7]
250 Syne, wi' a social glass o' strunt,° *liquor*
 They parted aff careerin
  Fu' blythe that night.

—1786

---

1 *cannie thraw* Careful turn.

2 *loot a winze* Cursed.

3 *outler quey* Cows in the field.

4 *maist lap the hool* Almost jumped out of her skin.

5 *Mar's-year* 1715, the year of the Jacobite Rebellion.

6 *butter'd sowens* Puddings.

7 *gabs a-steerin* Tongues wagging.

Address to the De'il[1]

O Prince, O chief of many throned pow'rs,
That led th'embattled Seraphim to war—[2]
                    MILTON

O Thou, whatever title suit thee!
Auld Hornie, Satan, Nick, or Clootie,°   *Hoofie*
Wha in yon cavern grim an' sooty
        Closed under hatches,
5   Spairges about the brunstane cootie,[3]
            To scaud° poor wretches!   *scald*

Hear me, auld Hangie,° for a wee,   *hangman*
An' let poor, damned bodies bee;
I'm sure sma' pleasure it can gie,
10   Ev'n to a de'il,
To skelp° an' scaud poor dogs like me,   *strike*
            An' hear us squeel!

Great is thy pow'r, an' great thy fame;
Far ken'd,° an' noted is thy name;   *known*
15 An' tho' yon lowan heugh's[4] thy hame,
            Thou travels far;
An' faith! thou's neither lag° nor lame,   *slow*
            Nor blate° nor scaur.°   *shy / scared*

Whyles,° ranging like a roaring lion,   *sometimes*
20 For prey, a' holes an' corners tryin;
Whyles, on the strong-wing'd tempest flyin,
            Tirlan the kirks;[5]
Whyles, in the human bosom pryin,
            Unseen thou lurks.

25 I've heard my rev'rend Graunie° say,   *grandmother*
In lanely° glens ye like to stray;   *lonely*
Or where auld, ruined castles, gray,
            Nod to the moon,

30 Ye fright the nightly wand'rer's way,
            Wi' eldritch croon.[6]

When twilight did my Graunie summon,
To say her pray'rs, douse,° honest woman,   *grave*
Aft 'yont° the dyke she's heard you bumman°   *beyond /*
            Wi' eerie drone;
35 Or, rustling, thro' the boortries° coman,   *elder shrubs*
            Wi' heavy groan.

Ae dreary, windy, winter night,
The stars shot down wi' sklentan° light,   *slanting*
Wi' you, mysel, I gat a fright
40   Ayont the lough;°   *lake*
Ye, like a rash-buss,[7] stood in sight,
            Wi' waving sugh:°   *sound*

The cudgel in my nieve° did shake,   *fist*
Each bristl'd hair stood like a stake,
45 When wi' an eldritch, stoor,° quaick, quaick,   *hoarse*
            Amang the springs,
Awa ye squatter'd° like a drake,   *fluttered*
            On whistling wings.

Let warlocks grim, an' wither'd hags,
50 Tell, how wi' you, on ragweed nags,[8]
They skim the muirs° an' dizzy crags,   *moors*
            Wi' wicked speed;
And in kirk-yards renew their leagues,
            Owre howcket° dead.   *dug up*

55 Thence, countra° wives, wi' toil an' pain,   *country*
May plunge an' plunge the kirn° in vain;   *churn*
For och! the yellow treasure's taen,°   *taken*
            By witching skill;
An' dawtit, twal-pint Hawkie's gane
60   As yell's the bill.[9]

---

[1]   *De'il* Devil.

[2]   *O Prince ... war* From *Paradise Lost* 1.128–9.

[3]   *Spairges ... cootie* Splashes about the brimstone vat.

[4]   *lowan heugh* Flaming pit.

[5]   *Tirlan the kirks* Unroofing the churches.

[6]   *eldrich croon* Ghastly moan.

[7]   *rash-buss* Bunch of rushes.

[8]   *ragweed nags* Broomsticks.

[9]   *dawtit ... bill* Pampered twelve-pint cow's gone / As milkless as the bull.

Thence, mystic knots mak great abuse,
On young guidmen,° fond, keen an' croose;°   *husbands / spirited*
When the best warklum° i' the house,   *tool*
    By cantraip° wit,   *enchanted*
65 Is instant made no worth a louse,
    Just at the bit.°   *final moment*

When thowes° dissolve the snawy hoord,°   *thaws / hoard*
An' float the jinglan° icy boord,°   *crackling / shore*
Then, water-kelpies haunt the foord,[1]
70   By your direction,
An' nighted trav'llers are allur'd
    To their destruction.

An' aft your moss-traversing spunkies°   *will-o'-the-wisps*
Decoy the wight° that late an' drunk is;   *person*
75 The bleezan,° curst, mischievous monkies   *blazing*
    Delude his eyes,
Till in some miry slough he sunk is,
    Ne'er mair to rise.

When Masons'[2] mystic word an' grip,
80 In storms an' tempests raise you up,
Some cock, or cat, your rage maun° stop,   *must*
    Or, strange to tell!
The youngest brother ye wad whip
    Aff straught to H-ll.

85 Lang syne[3] in Eden's bonie yard,
When youthfu' lovers first were pair'd,
An' all the soul of love they shar'd,
    The raptured hour,
Sweet on the fragrant, flow'ry swaird,°   *surface*
90   In shady bow'r:

Then you, ye auld, snick°-drawing dog!   *latch*
Ye cam to Paradise incog,°   *disguised*
An' play'd on a man a cursed brogue,°   *trick*
    (Black be your fa'!)
95 An' gied° the infant warld a shog,°   *gave / shock*
    'Maist° ruin'd a.'   *almost*

D'ye mind that day, when in a bizz,°   *flurry*
Wi' reeket duds, an' reestet gizz,[4]
Ye did present your smoutie phiz[5]
100   'Mang better folk,
An' sklented on the man of Uz[6]
    Your spitefu' joke?

An' how ye gat him i' your thrall,
An' brak him out o' house an' hal',
105 While scabs an' botches° did him gall,   *tumor*
    Wi' bitter claw,
An' lows'd° his ill-tongu'd, wicked scawl[7]   *loosed*
    Was warst ava?[8]

But a' your doings to rehearse,
110 Your wily snares an' fechtin° fierce,   *fighting*
Sin' that day Michael did you pierce,[9]
    Down to this time,
Wad ding° a' Lallan° tongue, or Erse,   *overcome / Lowland*
    In prose or rhyme.

115 An' now, auld cloots, I ken ye're thinkan,
A certain bardie's° rantin, drinkin,   *poet's*
Some luckless hour will send him linkan,°   *running*
    To your black pit;
But faith! he'll turn a corner jinkan,°   *ducking*
120   An' cheat you yet.

But fare you weel, auld Nickie-ben!°   *Devil*
O wad ye tak a thought an' men'!°   *mend*
Ye aiblins° might—I dinna ken—   *perhaps*
    Still hae a stake[10]—
125 I'm wae° to think upo' yon den,   *sad*
    Ev'n for your sake.
      —1786

---

[1] *water-kelpies … foord* Water spirits haunt the rivers.

[2] *Masons* Freemasons; members of an organization, formerly of stone masons, with secret codes and rites.

[3] *Lang syne* Long ago.

[4] *reeket … gizz* Smoky clothes and singed face.

[5] *smoutie phiz* Dirty face.

[6] *man of Uz* Job, the man of Uz, was a righteous man who lost everything when God and Satan challenged his faith. See Job 1.1.

[7] *scawl* Scolding wife.

[8] *warst ava* Worst of all.

[9] *Michael did you pierce* See Milton's *Paradise Lost* 6.321–5, in which Satan stabs the angel Michael with a sword.

[10] *hae a stake* Have a chance.

Flow gently, sweet Afton[1]

Flow gently, sweet Afton, among thy green
   braes!°   *banks*
Flow gently, I'll sing thee a song in thy praise!
My Mary's asleep by thy murmuring stream—
Flow gently, sweet Afton, disturb not her dream!

5 Thou stock–dove whose echo resounds thro' the glen,
Ye wild whistling blackbirds in yon thorny den,
Thou green–crested lapwing, thy screaming forbear—
I charge you, disturb not my slumbering fair!

How lofty, sweet Afton, thy neighbouring hills,
10 Far mark'd with the courses of clear, winding rills!°   *brooks*
There daily I wander, as noon rises high,
My flocks and my Mary's sweet cot° in my eye.   *cottage*

How pleasant thy banks and green valleys below,
Where wild in the woodlands the primroses blow;
15 There oft, as mild ev'ning weeps over the lea,
The sweet–scented birk° shades my Mary and me.   *birch*

Thy crystal stream, Afton, how lovely it glides,
And winds by the cot where my Mary resides!
How wanton thy waters her snowy feet lave,°   *wash*
20 As, gathering sweet flowerets, she stems thy clear wave.

Flow gently, sweet Afton, among thy green braes!
Flow gently, sweet river, the theme of my lays!°   *song*
My Mary's asleep by thy murmuring stream—
Flow gently, sweet Afton, disturb not her dream!
   —1792

Ae Fond Kiss[2]

Ae° fond kiss, and then we sever;   *one*
   Ae fareweel, alas, forever!
Deep in heart-wrung tears I'll pledge thee,

Warring sighs and groans I'll wage thee.
5 Who shall say that Fortune grieves him,
While the star of hope she leaves him?
Me, nae cheerful twinkle lights me;
Dark despair around benights me.

I'll ne'er blame my partial fancy,
10 Naething could resist my Nancy:
But to see her was to love her;
Love but her, and love forever.
Had we never lov'd sae kindly,
Had we never lov'd sae blindly,
15 Never met—or never parted,
We had ne'er been brokenhearted.

Fare-thee-weel, thou first and fairest!
Fare-thee-weel, thou best and dearest!
Thine be ilka° joy and treasure,   *every*
20 Peace, Enjoyment, Love and Pleasure!
Ae fond kiss, and then we sever!
Ae fareweel, alas, forever!
Deep in heart-wrung tears I'll pledge thee,
Warring sighs and groans I'll wage thee.
   —1792

Robert Bruce's March To Bannockburn[3]

Scots, wha hae° wi' Wallace[4] bled,   *who have*
   Scots, wham° Bruce has aften led,   *whom*
Welcome to your gory bed,
      Or to victorie!

5 Now's the day, and now's the hour;
See the front o' battle lour;°   *threaten*
See approach proud Edward's power—
      Chains and slaverie!

Wha will be a traitor knave?
10 Wha can fill a coward's grave?

---

1 *Afton*   River that runs through southwestern Scotland.

2 *Ae Fond Kiss*   Burns wrote this love song for Nancy McLehose (the two called each other "Sylvander" and "Clarinda"), when she left England to reunite with her husband in Jamaica.

3 *Robert Bruce … Bannockburn*   In 1314, Robert the Bruce, King of the Scots, fought successfully for a free Scotland in a battle against the English under Edward I at Bannockburn.

4 *Wallace*   Sir William Wallace led numerous battles against the English under King Edward I.

Wha sae base as be a slave?
            Let him turn and flee!

Wha, for Scotland's King and Law,
Freedom's sword will strongly draw,
15 Free–man stand, or Free–man fa',
            Let him on wi' me!

By Oppression's woes and pains!
By your Sons in servile chains!
We will drain our dearest veins,
20   But they shall be free!

Lay the proud usurpers low!
Tyrants fall in every foe!
Liberty's in every blow!—
            Let us Do or Die!

—1795

A Man's A Man For A' That

Is there for honest poverty
    That hings° his head, an' a'° that;   *hangs / all*
The coward slave—we pass him by,
    We dare be poor for a' that!
5 For a' that, an' a' that.
    Our toils obscure an' a' that,
The rank is but the guinea's stamp,
    The Man's the gowd° for a' that.   *gold*

What though on hamely° fare we dine,   *simple*
10   Wear hoddin grey,[1] an' a that;
Gie° fools their silks, and knaves their wine;   *give*
    A Man's a Man for a' that:
For a' that, and a' that,
    Their tinsel show, an' a' that;
15 The honest man, tho' e'er sae° poor,   *so*
    Is king o' men for a' that.

Ye see yon birkie,[2] ca'd° "a lord,"   *called*
    Wha struts, an' stares, an' a' that;

Tho' hundreds worship at his word,
20   He's but a coof° for a' that: *fool*
For a' that, an' a' that,
    His ribband,° star,[3] an' a' that: *ribbon*
The man o' independent mind
    He looks an' laughs at a' that.

25 A prince can mak a belted knight,
    A marquis, duke, an' a' that;
But an honest man's aboon° his might,   *above*
    Gude faith, he mauna fa'[4] that!
For a' that, an' a' that,
30   Their dignities an' a' that;
The pith° o' sense, an' pride o' worth,   *importance*
    Are higher rank than a' that.

Then let us pray that come it may,
    As come it will for a' that,
35 That sense and worth, o'er a' the earth,
    Shall bear the gree,[5] an' a' that.
For a' that, an' a' that,
    It's coming yet for a' that,
That Man to Man, the world o'er,
40   Shall brithers be for a' that.
—1795

Comin' thro' the Rye

CHORUS
O, Jenny's a' weet,[6] poor body,
    Jenny's seldom dry;
She draigl't[7] a' her petticoatie
    Comin thro' the rye!

5 Comin thro' the rye, poor body,
    Comin thro' the rye,
She draigl't a' her petticoatie,
    Comin thro' the rye!

---

[1] *hodden grey* Coarse, woolen peasant cloth.

[2] *birkie* Conceited, swaggering fellow.

[3] *ribband, star* Emblems of nobility.

[4] *mauna fa' that* Musn't have that befall him.

[5] *bear the gree* Have the victory.

[6] *a' weet* All wet.

[7] *draigl't* Draggled; dragged through the mud.

10   Gin° a body meet a body   *suppose*
            Comin thro' the rye;
    Gin a body kiss a body,
            Need a body cry?

    Gin a body meet a body
            Comin thro' the glen,
15   Gin a body kiss a body,
            Need the warld ken°?   *know*

            CHORUS
        O, Jenny's a' weet, poor body,
            Jenny's seldom dry;
        She draigl't a' her petticoatie
20   Comin thro' the rye!
    —1796

A Red, Red Rose

O, my luve's like a red, red rose,
    That's newly sprung in June;
O, my luve's like the melodie,
    That's sweetly play'd in tune.

5   As fair art thou, my bonie lass,
        So deep in luve am I;
    And I will luve thee still, my dear,
        Till a' the seas gang° dry.   *go*

    Till a' the seas gang dry, my dear,
10   And the rocks melt wi' the sun;
    And I will luve thee still, my dear,
        While the sands o' life shall run.

    And fare thee weel, my only luve!
        And fare thee weel, a while!
15 And I will come again, my luve,
        Tho' 'twere ten thousand mile!
    —1796

Auld Lang Syne[1]

Should auld acquaintance be forgot,
And never brought to mind?
Should auld acquaintance be forgot,
    And auld lang syne!

        CHORUS
5   For auld lang syne, my dear,
            For auld lang syne.
        We'll tak a cup o' kindness yet,
            For auld lang syne.

And surely ye'll be° your pint stowp![2]   *raise*
10 And surely I'll be mine!
And we'll tak a cup o' kindness yet,
    For auld lang syne.

        CHORUS
We twa° hae run about the braes,°   *two / hills*
And pou'd° the gowans fine;   *pulled / daisies*
15 But we've wander'd mony a weary fit,°   *foot*
Sin'° auld lang syne.   *since*

        CHORUS
We twa hae paidl'd in the burn,°   *stream*
Frae morning sun till dine;
But seas between us braid° hae roar'd   *broad*
20 Sin'° auld lang syne.   *since*

        CHORUS
And there's a hand, my trusty fiere!°   *friend*
And gie's° a hand o' thine!   *give us*
And we'll tak a right gude willie-waught,[3]
For auld lang syne.

        CHORUS
    —1796

---

[1] *Auld Lang Syne* Times long since passed.

[2] *stowp* Drinking glass.

[3] *gude willie-waught* Hearty glass of draught beer.

Love and Liberty. A Cantata[1]

RECITATIVO

When lyart° leaves bestrow the yird,°   *decayed / ground*
Or wavering like the bauckie-bird,°   *bat*
Bedim cauld Boreas' blast;[2]
When hailstanes drive wi' bitter skyte,°   *lash*
5   And infant frosts begin to bite,
In hoary cranreuch[3] drest;
Ae night at e'en a merry core°   *corps*
O' randie, gangrel° bodies,   *vagrant*
In Poosie Nansie's[4] held the splore,°   *drinking spree*
10   To drink their orra duddies;[5]
Wi' quaffing an' laughing,
They ranted an' they sang,
Wi' jumping an' thumping,
The vera girdle[6] rang,

15   First, neist° the fire, in auld red rags,   *next*
Ane sat, weel brac'd wi' mealy bags,[7]
And knapsack a' in order;
His doxy° lay within his arm;   *wench*
Wi' usquebae° an' blankets warm   *whiskey*
20   She blinkit on her sodger;
An' aye he gies the tozie drab[8]
The tither skelpin'[9] kiss,
While she held up her greedy gab,°   *mouth*
Just like an aumous° dish;   *alms*
25   Ilk° smack still, did crack still,   *each*
Just like a cadger's[10] whip;

Then staggering an' swaggering
He roar'd this ditty up—

AIR

I am a son of Mars[11] who have been in many wars,
30   And show my cuts and scars wherever I come;
This here was for a wench, and that other in a trench,
When welcoming the French at the sound of the drum.

                    Lal de daudle, &c.

My 'prenticeship I past where my leader breath'd his last,
35   When the bloody die was cast on the heights of Abram:[12]
And I served out my trade when the gallant game was play'd,
And the Moro[13] low was laid at the sound of the drum.

I lastly was with Curtis[14] among the floating batt'ries,
And there I left for witness an arm and a limb;
40   Yet let my country need me, with Elliot[15] to head me,
I'd clatter on my stumps at the sound of a drum.

And now tho' I must beg, with a wooden arm and leg,
And many a tatter'd rag hanging over my bum,
I'm as happy with my wallet, my bottle, and my callet,°   *whore*
45   As when I used in scarlet to follow a drum.

What tho' with hoary locks, I must stand the winter shocks,
Beneath the woods and rocks oftentimes for a home,

---

1   *Love and Liberty. A Cantata*   Commonly known by the title "The Jolly Beggars."

2   *Boreas' blast*   North wind (Boreas is the Greek god of the north wind).

3   *hoary cranreuch*   Hoar frost.

4   *Poosie Nansie's*   Scottish tavern where Burns found the inspiration for *The Jolly Beggars*.

5   *orra duddies*   Extra rags.

6   *vera girdle*   Very griddle.

7   *weel brac'd wi' mealy bags*   Well fed with porridge.

8   *tozie drab*   Drunken slut.

9   *tither skelpin'*   Other smacking.

10   *cadger*   Salesman who traveled with a horse and cart.

---

11   *Mars*   Roman god of war.

12   *heights of Abram*   In 1759, British general James Wolfe's troops won the Battle of the Plains of Abraham against the French in Quebec; Wolfe and the opposing general, Montcalm, both died in the battle.

13   *Moro*   El Moro was a castle on the island of Santiago, Cuba, which was stormed by the British in 1762.

14   *Curtis*   Rear Admiral Sir Roger Curtis, who took part in the battle of 1782 against the Spanish off the waters of Gibraltar.

15   *Elliot*   Sir George Augustus Elliot, who also helped defend Gibraltar.

When the t'other bag I sell, and the t'other bottle tell,
    I could meet a troop of hell, at the sound of a drum.

RECITATIVO

50 He ended; and the kebars° sheuk,   *rafters*
    Aboon° the chorus roar;   *above*
While frighted rattons° backward leuk,   *rats*
    An' seek the benmost° bore: *innermost*
A fairy fiddler frae the neuk,
55   He skirl'd out, *Encore!*
But up arose the martial chuck,°   *camp whore*
    An' laid the loud uproar.

AIR

I once was a maid, tho' I cannot tell when,
And still my delight is in proper young men;
60 Some one of a troop of dragoons was my daddie,
No wonder I'm fond of a sodger laddie,
                Sing, lal de lal, &c.

The first of my loves was a swaggering blade,
To rattle the thundering drum was his trade;
65 His leg was so tight, and his cheek was so ruddy,
Transported I was with my sodger laddie.

But the godly old chaplain left him in the lurch;
The sword I forsook for the sake of the church:
He ventur'd the soul, and I risked the body,
70 'Twas then I proved false to my sodger laddie.

Full soon I grew sick of my sanctified sot,
The regiment at large for a husband I got;
From the gilded spontoon° to the fife I was ready, *weapon*
I asked no more but a sodger laddie.

75 But the peace it reduc'd me to beg in despair,
Till I met old boy in a Cunningham fair,
His rags regimental, they flutter'd so gaudy,
My heart it rejoic'd at a sodger laddie.

And now I have liv'd—I know not how long,
80 And still I can join in a cup and a song;
But whilst with both hands I can hold the glass steady,
Here's to thee, my hero, my sodger laddie.

RECITATIVO

Poor Merry-Andrew,[1] in the neuk,
    Sat guzzling wi' a tinkler-hizzie;°   *tinker-hussy*
85 They mind't na wha the chorus teuk,
    Between themselves they were sae busy:
At length, wi' drink an' courting dizzy,
He stoiter'd° up an' made a face;   *staggered*
    Then turn'd an' laid a smack on Grizzie,
90 Syne° tun'd his pipes wi' grave grimace.   *then*

AIR

Sir Wisdom's a fool when he's fou;°   *drunk*
    Sir Knave is a fool in a session;
He's there but a 'prentice I trow,°   *trust*
    But I am a fool by profession.

95 My grannie she bought me a beuk,
    An' I held° awa to the school;   *went*
I fear I my talent misteuk,
    But what will ye hae of a fool?

For drink I would venture my neck;
100   A hizzie's the half of my craft;
But what could ye other expect
    Of ane that's avowedly daft?

I ance was tied up like a stirk,°   *young cow*
    For civilly swearing and quaffin;[2]
105 I ance was abus'd i' the kirk,°   *church*
    For towsing a lass i' my daffin.[3]

Poor Andrew that tumbles for sport,
    Let naebody name wi' a jeer;
There's even, I'm tauld, i' the Court
110   A tumbler ca'd the Premier.

Observ'd ye yon reverend lad
    Mak faces to tickle the mob;
He rails at our mountebank[4] squad—
    It's rivalship just i' the job.

---

[1] *Merry-Andrew* Clown, joker, buffoon.

[2] *quaffin* Drinking large amounts of alcohol.

[3] *towsing a lass i' my daffin* Literally, disheveling a woman in merriment; obliquely, having sex out of wedlock.

[4] *mountebank* Itinerant seller of supposed remedies.

115 And now my conclusion I'll tell,
　　For faith I'm confoundedly dry;
　　The chiel° that's a fool for himsel',　　　　　*young boy*
　　　Guid Lord! he's far dafter than I.

RECITATIVO

Then niest° outspak a raucle carlin,[1]　　　　　*next*
120 Wha kent fu' weel to cleek° the sterlin;°　　*steal / money*
For mony a pursie she had hooked,
An' had in mony a well been douked;°　　　　　*ducked*
Her love had been a Highland laddie,
But weary fa' the waefu' woodie!°　　　　　　　*dolt*
125 Wi' sighs an' sobs she thus began
To wail her braw° John Highlandman.　　　　　*handsome*

AIR

A Highland lad my love was born,
The Lalland° laws he held in scorn;　　　　　　*Lowland*
But he still was faithfu' to his clan,
130 My gallant, braw John Highlandman.

CHORUS

　Sing hey my braw John Highlandman!
　Sing ho my braw John Highlandman!
　There's not a lad in a' the lan'
　Was match for my John Highlandman.

135 With his philibeg° an' tartan plaid,　　　　　*kilt*
An' guid claymore° down by his side,　　　　　*sword*
The ladies' hearts he did trepan,°　　　　　　　*entrap*
My gallant, braw John Highlandman.
　　　　Sing hey, &c.

140 We ranged a' from Tweed to Spey,
An' liv'd like lords an' ladies gay;
For a Lalland face he feared none—
My gallant, braw John Highlandman.
　　　　Sing hey, &c.

145 They banish'd him beyond the sea.
But ere the bud was on the tree,
Adown my cheeks the pearls ran,
Embracing my John Highlandman.
　　　　Sing hey, &c.

150 But, och! they catch'd him at the last,
And bound him in a dungeon fast:
My curse upon them every one,
They've hang'd my braw John Highlandman!
　　　　Sing hey, &c.

155 And now a widow, I must mourn
The pleasures that will ne'er return:
The comfort but a hearty can,
When I think on John Highlandman.
　　　　Sing hey, &c.

RECITATIVO

160 A pigmy scraper wi' his fiddle,
Wha us'd at trystes° an' fairs to driddle.　　*markets / dawdle*
Her strappin limb and gausy° middle　　　　　　*plump*
　　(He reach'd nae higher)
Had hol'd his heartie like a riddle,
165 　　　An' blawn't° on fire.　　　　　　　　　*blown it*

Wi' hand on hainch, and upward e'e,
He croon'd his gamut, one, two, three,
Then in an arioso key,
　　　The wee Apollo[2]
170 Set off wi' allegretto glee
　　　His giga° solo.　　　　　　　　　　　　*jig*

AIR

Let me ryke° up to dight° that tear,　　　*reach / wipe*
An' go wi' me an' be my dear;
An' then your every care an' fear
175 　　May whistle owre the lave° o't.　　　　*rest*

CHORUS

　I am a fiddler to my trade,
　An' a' the tunes that e'er I played,
　The sweetest still to wife or maid,
　Was whistle owre the lave o't.

180 At kirns° an' weddins we'se be there,　　*harvest feasts*
An' O sae nicely's we will fare!
We'll bowse° about till Daddie Care　　　　　*drink*
　Sing whistle owre the lave o't.
　　　　I am, &c.

---

[1] *raucle carlin* Stout hag.

[2] *Apollo* Greek god of music.

185 Sae merrily's the banes° we'll pyke,°   bones / pick
     An' sun oursel's about the dyke;
     An' at our leisure, when ye like,
          We'll whistle owre the lave o't.
               I am, &c.

190 But bless me wi' your heav'n o' charms,
     An' while I kittle° hair on thairms,[1]   tickle
     Hunger, cauld, an' a' sic° harms,   such
          May whistle owre the lave o't.
               I am, &c.

                    RECITATIVO
195 Her charms had struck a sturdy caird,°   tinker
          As weel as poor gut-scraper;
     He taks the fiddler by the beard,
          An' draws a roosty° rapier—   rusty
     He swoor, by a' was swearing worth,
200   To speet° him like a pliver,°   pierce / plover
     Unless he would from that time forth
          Relinquish her forever.

     Wi' ghastly e'e° poor tweedle-dee   eye
          Upon his hunkers° bended,   haunches
205 An' pray'd for grace wi' ruefu' face,
          An' so the quarrel ended.
     But tho' his little heart did grieve
          When round the tinkler prest her,
     He feign'd to snirtle° in his sleeve,   snicker
210   When thus the caird address'd her:

                    AIR
     My bonie lass, I work in brass,
          A tinkler is my station:
     I've travell'd round all Christian ground
          In this my occupation;
215 I've taen the gold, an' been enrolled
          In many a noble squadron;
     But vain they search'd when off I march'd
          To go an' clout° the cauldron.   patch

     Despise that shrimp, that wither'd imp,
220   With a' his noise an' cap'rin;
     An' take a share with those that bear

---

[1] *hair on thairms* Fiddle strings.

     The budget° and the apron!   pouch
     And by that stowp!° my faith an' houp,   cup
          And by that dear Kilbaigie![2]
225 If e'er ye want, or meet wi' scant,
          May I ne'er weet° my craigie.°   wet / throat

                    RECITATIVO
     The caird prevail'd—th' unblushing fair
          In his embraces sunk;
     Partly wi' love o'ercome sae sair,
230   An' partly was she drunk:
     Sir Violino, with an air
          That show'd a man o' spunk,
     Wish'd unison between the pair,
          An' made the bottle clunk
235   To their health that night.

     But hurchin° Cupid shot a shaft,   urchin
          That play'd a dame a shavie°—   trick
     The fiddler rak'd her, fore and aft,
          Behint the chicken cavie.°   coop
240 Her lord, a wight° of Homer's craft,   creature
          Tho' limpin wi' the spavie,[3]
     He hirpl'd° up, an' lap° like daft,   limped / leapt
          An' shor'd° them Dainty Davie[4]   offered
               O' boot[5] that night.

245 He was a care-defying blade[6]
          As ever Bacchus[7] listed!
     Tho' Fortune sair upon him laid,
          His heart, she ever miss'd it.
     He had no wish but—to be glad,
250   Nor want but—when he thirsted;
     He hated nought but—to be sad,
          An' thus the muse suggested
               His sang that night.

---

[2] *Kilbaigie* Brand of whiskey.

[3] *spavie* Tumorous bone disease.

[4] *Dainty Davie* Lovemaking; Dainty Davie is the subject of a
Scottish song about David Williamson, who was said to have been
given refuge by the Laird of Cherrytrees. The Laird hid the man in
his daughter's bed, and the girl was later discovered to be pregnant.

[5] *O' boot* For free.

[6] *blade* Good-natured fellow.

[7] *Bacchus* Roman god of wine.

AIR

I am a Bard of no regard,
   Wi' gentle folks an' a' that;
But Homer—like, the glowrin byke,°   *crowd*
   Frae town to town I draw that.

CHORUS

   For a' that, an' a' that,
      An' twice as muckle's° a' that;   *much*
   I've lost but ane, I've twa behin,'
    I've wife eneugh for a' that.

I never drank the Muses'[1] stank,°   *pool*
   Castalia's[2] burn,° an' a' that;   *brewing water*
But there it streams an' richly reams,
   My Helicon[3] I ca' that.
          For a' that, &c.

Great love I bear to a' the fair,
   Their humble slave an' a' that;
But lordly will, I hold it still
   A mortal sin to thraw° that.   *thwart*
          For a' that, &c.

In raptures sweet, this hour we meet,
   Wi' mutual love an' a' that;
But for how lang the flie may stang,
   Let inclination law that.
          For a' that, &c.

Their tricks an' craft hae put me daft,
   They've taen me in, an' a' that;
But clear your decks, and here's—"The Sex!"
   I like the jads° for a' that.   *young ladies*

CHORUS

   For a' that, an' a' that,
      An' twice as muckle's a' that;

My dearest bluid,° to do them guid,   *blood*
   They're welcome till't° for a' that.   *to it*

RECITATIVO

So sang the bard — and Nansie's wa's
Shook with a thunder of applause,
   Re-echo'd from each mouth!
They toom'd° their pocks,° they pawn'd their duds, *emptied / pockets*
They scarcely left to co'er their fuds,°   *behinds*
   To quench their lowin drouth:[4]
Then owre again, the jovial thrang
   The poet did request
To lowse his pack an' wale° a sang,   *choose*
   A ballad o' the best;
     He rising, rejoicing,
      Between his twa Deborahs,[5]
     Looks round him, an' found them
      Impatient for the chorus.

AIR

See the smoking bowl before us,
   Mark our jovial ragged ring!
Round and round take up the chorus,
   And in raptures let us sing—

CHORUS

   A fig for those by law protected!
     Liberty's a glorious feast!
   Courts for cowards were erected,
     Churches built to please the priest.

What is title, what is treasure,
   What is reputation's care?
If we lead a life of pleasure,
   'Tis no matter how or where!
     A fig for, &c.

With the ready trick and fable,
   Round we wander all the day;
And at night in barn or stable,
   Hug our doxies° on the hay.   *mistresses*
     A fig for, &c.

---

[1] *Muses* In Greek mythology, the nine daughters of Zeus and Mnemosyne, each of whom presided over and provided inspiration for an aspect of learning or the arts.

[2] *Castalia* Spring on Mount Parnassus that was sacred to the Muses.

[3] *Helicon* Mountain dedicated to the Muses.

---

[4] *lowin drouth* Burning thirst.

[5] *twa Deborahs* The two Deborahs of the Bible.

Does the train-attended carriage
    Thro' the country lighter rove?
Does the sober bed of marriage
320   Witness brighter scenes of love?
       A fig for, &c.

Life is all a variorum,[1]
    We regard not how it goes;
Let them cant about decorum,
325   Who have character to lose.
       A fig for, &c.

Here's to budgets, bags and wallets!
    Here's to all the wandering train.
Here's our ragged brats and callets,°   *strumpets*
330   One and all cry out, Amen!

    A fig for those by law protected!
       Liberty's a glorious feast!
    Courts for cowards were erected,
       Churches built to please the priest.

—1799

---

[1] *variorum* Changing scene, variation.

WILLIAM WORDSWORTH
1770 – 1850

Since about 1815, William Wordsworth has been acknowledged as a central figure in the English Romantic Movement. *Lyrical Ballads*, produced in conjunction with Samuel Taylor Coleridge though largely Wordsworth's project, marks a decisive break with the formalism and neo-classicism of eighteenth-century literature. It became the touchstone of a new literary sensibility that gave its faith to the benevolence of feeling, and of the vehicle it associated most with feeling: a poetry of sincerity. And it established the idea of Nature as the measure by which to judge whether a poem's expression of feeling was genuine or not.

Wordworth's poems respond powerfully to the major developments of his day—including the French Revolution, war, and industrialization. That response, however, was marked by many tensions and contradictions. It is the play of those contradictions that give such weight and continued authority to Wordsworth's work.

Wordsworth was born in the Lake District of England, in West Cumberland, and spent his boyhood absorbing the natural beauty around him. The death of his mother when he was eight, and of his father only five years later, unsettled the lives of William and his four siblings. Their situation was worsened by the fact that the only substantial legacy their father left was a sum owed to him by his employer, Lord Lonsdale, who withheld the money until his death in 1802. Along with his three brothers, William was sent to school at Hawkshead. His sister Dorothy—later his muse, confidante, and secretary—found herself shifting among various relatives.

At Hawkshead Wordsworth and his brothers boarded at the home of Ann Tyson, who became a surrogate mother to Wordsworth, encouraging his love of nature and tolerating his habit of roaming the countryside. Wordsworth paid close attention to and frequently conversed with the town's working people. His observations would inform the representation of many of the humble rural characters who appear in his poetry. Leaving the Lake District for the first time in 1787, he entered St. John's College, Cambridge. During this period he made two walking tours with his friend Robert Jones, first through France and the Alps during a crucial period of the French Revolution, and later through Wales (excursions described in Books Six and Fourteen respectively of the 1850 *Prelude*).

These adventures quickened Wordsworth's belief in the healing powers of nature and of his own responsive imagination, and they also awakened radical sentiments. While traveling in France in 1791–1792 he was swept up in the heady excitement that followed the French Revolution (1789). Young Wordsworth also fell in love with Annette Vallon, whose politics (Royalist) and religion (Catholic) he did not share, and they produced a daughter, Caroline, out of wedlock. Too poor to remain in France, which was now at war with England, Wordsworth returned to his country a divided man, his disillusionment growing as France fell into a Reign of Terror.

Financial concerns fed Wordsworth's doubts about his political convictions and his choice of vocation. In 1795, however, Wordsworth received a legacy of £900 from a friend, Raisley Calvert, whom he had nursed through his final illness. With this sum, and a rent-free cottage in Alfoxden provided by other friends, Wordsworth was able to set up housekeeping with his sister Dorothy, with his friend Coleridge not far away at Nether Stowey. (Describing his relationship with Coleridge in an 1832 letter to a friend, Wordsworth declared, "He and my beloved sister are the two beings to whom my intellect is most indebted.") Long walks and talks with Coleridge resulted in an extraordinary literary collaboration, *Lyrical Ballads, with a few other poems* (1798), a slender, anonymously-published volume that opens with Coleridge's literary ballad "The Rime of the Ancient Mariner" and closes with Wordsworth's blank-verse meditation, "Lines, Composed a Few Miles Above Tintern Abbey." The volume sought to combat what the authors saw as the increasingly marginal position of the poet in society, and the overly artificial language on which poetry relied.

As Coleridge and Wordsworth had expected, critics attacked the tone and subject matter of the volume. In the *Preface to the Second Edition* (1800)—perhaps the most famous poetic manifesto in the language—Wordsworth explained and defended the decision he made "to choose incidents and situations from common life, and to relate or describe them, throughout, as far as was possible, in a selection of language really used by men." In poems such as "Michael" and "The Brothers" (added to the 1800 edition of *Lyrical Ballads*), Wordsworth shows the strength and dignity with which the Lake District's inhabitants endure hardship, living in harmony with the natural world, removed from the taint of urban superficiality. Wordsworth was thus in an important sense what he is often taken to be, a "poet of nature." But his main object was not to depict directly "the beautiful and permanent forms of nature" but rather to explore how "the passions of men are incorporated with" such forms, and to depict the "ennobling interchange" between the natural world and the mental world. It is the mind, ultimately, that was Wordsworth's "haunt, and the main region of my song."

After a brief, inhospitable stay in Germany in 1798–99, during which Wordsworth wrote the "Lucy" poems (the identity of "Lucy" is unknown) and Coleridge assimilated German philosophy, Wordsworth and his sister returned to England and took up residence at Dove Cottage in Grasmere. Here Dorothy kept journals that have since become famous in their own right, and Wordsworth composed some of his finest lyrics, including "Resolution and Independence," "The Solitary Reaper" (a memorial of his walking tour through Scotland), and *Ode: Intimations of Immortality from Recollections of Early Childhood*, all of which were later published in his *Poems, in Two Volumes* (1807).

In 1802, Wordsworth married a childhood friend, Mary Hutchinson, and began a period of relative tranquility and poetic fruitfulness, although these years were not without grief and disappointment. By 1812, two of his five children were dead, his brother John had been lost at sea, his friendship with Coleridge (whose health was deteriorating as his opium addiction deepened) had become strained, and *Poems, in Two Volumes* had suffered damaging reviews.

Then in 1814 Wordsworth published *The Excursion*, a long blank-verse meditation that was a forecast and first installment of his planned epic, *The Recluse*. The book was poorly reviewed, even ridiculed. Nevertheless, Wordworth by this time had gained a growing audience of devoted admirers, and his reputation from this low point began to establish itself firmly.

Like *The Excursion*, *The Prelude*, which Wordsworth had begun in 1799, was intended as a subsidiary piece that would be incorporated into *The Recluse*. He completed a two-book version of *The Prelude* in 1799 and a much expanded thirteen-book poem in 1805. He then continued to revise the poem for the rest of his life. This epic in blank verse—which Coleridge, upon hearing it, declared a "prophetic Lay"—describes the growth of the poet's mind from earliest memories to adulthood. By the end of his journey in the poem, Wordsworth reaffirms both providential design and the revolutionary potential of the imagination. *The Prelude* is a great, long lesson showing "how the mind of Man becomes / A thousand times more beautiful than the earth / On which he dwells."

In 1813, the Wordsworth household left Dove Cottage for the more expansive environs of Rydal Mount. There the poet, his beloved sister, and his wife lived out their days. The move was made possible by Wordsworth's improved financial situation, the result of a literary patronage granted by Lord Lonsdale and a position as Stamp Distributor for Westmorland. In the eyes of the younger generation (including Percy Shelley, Lord Byron, and Robert Browning), the patronage and the government position seemed to transform the once radical poet into a hypocritical and complacent hireling. As they saw it, Wordsworth had abandoned his early commitment to be the voice of the disenfranchised and the poor. Increasingly skeptical of external revolutions and political agitation, Wordsworth saw himself not as having abandoned his ideals but rather as having internalized—or spiritualized—his commitment to truth and liberty.

During his middle and old age Wordsworth wrote numerous sonnets, including *Ecclesiastical Sketches* (1822), inspired by his brother Christopher, a clergyman and scholar. Having begun as a poetic and political revolutionary, he ended his life an iconic figure of the early Victorian era. Queen Victoria crowned him her Poet Laureate in 1843, and admirers flocked to the Lake District to seek him out in his home. The influence of his poetic style remained strong until well into the twentieth century, and Victorian writers of prose and poetry alike—including Tennyson, Charles Dickens, George Eliot, and Elizabeth Gaskell—acknowledged their debt to the life he had breathed into ways of thinking about nature, poetic feeling, and the human imagination.

⌘ ⌘ ⌘

from *Lyrical Ballads, 1798*

ADVERTISEMENT

It is the honourable characteristic of Poetry that its materials are to be found in every subject which can interest the human mind. The evidence of this fact is to be sought, not in the writings of Critics, but in those of Poets themselves.

The majority of the following poems are to be considered as experiments. They were written chiefly with a view to ascertain how far the language of conversation in the middle and lower classes of society is adapted to the purposes of poetic pleasure. Readers accustomed to the gaudiness and inane phraseology of many modern writers, if they persist in reading this book to its conclusion, will perhaps frequently have to struggle with feelings of strangeness and awkwardness: they will look round for poetry, and will be induced to enquire by what species of courtesy these attempts can be permitted to assume that title. It is desirable that such readers, for their own sakes, should not suffer the solitary word Poetry, a word of very disputed meaning, to stand in the way of their gratification; but that, while they are perusing this book, they should ask themselves if it contains a natural delineation of human passions, human characters, and human incidents; and if the answer be favourable to the author's wishes, that they should consent to be pleased in spite of that most dreadful enemy to our pleasures, our own pre-established codes of decision.

Readers of superior judgment may disapprove of the style in which many of these pieces are executed. It must be expected that many lines and phrases will not exactly suit their taste. It will perhaps appear to them that, wishing to avoid the prevalent fault of the day, the author has sometimes descended too low, and that many of his expressions are too familiar, and not of sufficient dignity. It is apprehended that the more conversant the reader is with our elder writers, and with those in modern times who have been the most successful in painting manners and passions, the fewer complaints of this kind will he have to make.

An accurate taste in poetry, and in all the other arts, Sir Joshua Reynolds[1] has observed, is an acquired talent, which can only be produced by severe thought, and a long continued intercourse with the best models of composition. This is mentioned not with so ridiculous a purpose as to prevent the most inexperienced reader from judging for himself; but merely to temper the

---

[1]   *Sir Joshua Reynolds*   Renowned portrait and history painter, and first President of the Royal Academy (1723–92).

rashness of decision, and to suggest that if poetry be a subject on which much time has not been bestowed, the judgment may be erroneous, and that in many cases it necessarily will be so.

    The tale of Goody Blake and Harry Gill is founded on a well-authenticated fact which happened in Warwickshire. Of the other poems in the collection, it may be proper to say that they are either absolute inventions of the author, or facts which took place within his personal observation or that of his friends. The poem of the Thorn, as the reader will soon discover, is not supposed to be spoken in the author's own person: the character of the loquacious narrator will sufficiently show itself in the course of the story. The Rime of the Ancyent Marinere was professedly written in imitation of the style, as well as of the spirit of the elder poets; but with a few exceptions, the Author believes that the language adopted in it has been equally intelligible for these three last centuries. The lines entitled Expostulation and Reply, and those which follow, arose out of conversation with a friend who was somewhat unreasonably attached to modern books of moral philosophy.

We Are Seven

A simple child, dear brother Jim,
That lightly draws its breath,
And feels its life in every limb,
What should it know of death?

5 I met a little cottage girl,
She was eight years old, she said;
Her hair was thick with many a curl
That cluster'd round her head.

She had a rustic, woodland air,
10 And she was wildly clad;
Her eyes were fair, and very fair
—Her beauty made me glad.

"Sisters and brothers, little maid,
How many may you be?"

15 "How many? seven in all," she said,
And wondering looked at me.

"And where are they, I pray you tell?"
She answered, "Seven are we,
And two of us at Conway[1] dwell,
20 And two are gone to sea.

"Two of us in the church-yard lie,
My sister and my brother,
And in the church-yard cottage, I
Dwell near them with my mother."

25 "You say that two at Conway dwell,
And two are gone to sea,
Yet you are seven; I pray you tell
Sweet Maid, how this may be?"

Then did the little Maid reply,
30 "Seven boys and girls are we;
Two of us in the church-yard lie,
Beneath the church-yard tree."

"You run about, my little maid,
Your limbs they are alive;
35 If two are in the church-yard laid,
Then ye are only five."

"Their graves are green, they may be seen,"
The little Maid replied,
"Twelve steps or more from my mother's door,
40 And they are side by side.

"My stockings there I often knit,
My 'kerchief there I hem;
And there upon the ground I sit—
I sit and sing to them.

45 "And often after sunset, Sir,
When it is light and fair,
I take my little porringer,[2]
And eat my supper there.

[1] *Conway* Seaport of southern Wales.

[2] *porringer* Small metal or earthenware basin from which broth or porridge is eaten.

"The first that died was little Jane;
50   In bed she moaning lay,
Till God released her of her pain,
And then she went away.

"So in the church-yard she was laid,
And all the summer dry,
55   Together round her grave we played,
My brother John and I.

"And when the ground was white with snow,
And I could run and slide,
My brother John was forced to go,
60   And he lies by her side."

"How many are you then," said I,
If they two are in Heaven?"
The little Maiden did reply,
"O Master! we are seven."

65   "But they are dead; those two are dead!
Their spirits are in heaven!"
'Twas throwing words away; for still
The little Maid would have her will,
And said, "Nay, we are seven!"
—1798

Lines Written in Early Spring

I heard a thousand blended notes,
While in a grove I sat reclined,
In that sweet mood when pleasant thoughts
Bring sad thoughts to the mind.

5   To her fair works did nature link
The human soul that through me ran;
And much it griev'd my heart to think
What man has made of man.

Through primrose-tufts, in that sweet bower,
10   The periwinkle trail'd its wreathes;
And 'tis my faith that every flower
Enjoys the air it breathes.

The birds around me hopp'd and play'd:
Their thoughts I cannot measure,
15   But the least motion which they made,
It seem'd a thrill of pleasure.

The budding twigs spread out their fan,
To catch the breezy air;
And I must think, do all I can,
20   That there was pleasure there.

If I these thoughts may not prevent,
If such be of my creed the plan,
Have I not reason to lament
What man has made of man?
—1798

The Thorn[1]

1

There is a thorn;° it looks so old,   *thorn bush*
In truth you'd find it hard to say,
How it could ever have been young,
It looks so old and grey.
5   Not higher than a two-years' child,
It stands erect this aged thorn;
No leaves it has, no thorny points;
It is a mass of knotted joints,
A wretched thing forlorn.
10   It stands erect, and like a stone
With lichens it is overgrown.

2

Like rock or stone, it is o'ergrown
With lichens to the very top,
And hung with heavy tufts of moss,
15   A melancholy crop:
Up from the earth these mosses creep,
And this poor thorn they clasp it round

---

[1]   [Wordsworth's note]   Arose from my observing, on the ridge of Quantock Hill, on a stormy day a thorn which I had often passed in calm and bright weather without noticing it. I said to myself, "Cannot I by some invention do as much to make this Thorn permanently an impressive object as the storm has made it to my eyes at this moment?"

So close, you'd say that they were bent
With plain and manifest intent,
20 To drag it to the ground;
And all had joined in one endeavour
To bury this poor thorn for ever.

3

High on a mountain's highest ridge,
Where oft the stormy winter gale
25 Cuts like a scythe, while through the clouds
It sweeps from vale to vale;
Not five yards from the mountain-path,
This thorn you on your left espy;
And to the left, three yards beyond,
30 You see a little muddy pond
Of water, never dry;
I've measured it from side to side:
'Tis three feet long, and two feet wide.

4

And close beside this aged thorn,
35 There is a fresh and lovely sight,
A beauteous heap, a hill of moss,
Just half a foot in height.
All lovely colours there you see,
All colours that were ever seen,
40 And mossy network too is there,
As if by hand of lady fair
The work had woven been,
And cups,° the darlings of the eye,   *blossoms*
So deep is their vermilion° dye.   *red*

5

45 Ah me! what lovely tints are there!
Of olive-green and scarlet bright,
In spikes, in branches, and in stars,
Green, red, and pearly white.
This heap of earth o'ergrown with moss,
50 Which close beside the thorn you see,
So fresh in all its beauteous dyes,
Is like an infant's grave in size
As like as like can be:
But never, never any where,
55 An infant's grave was half so fair.

6

Now would you see this aged thorn,
This pond and beauteous hill of moss,
You must take care and choose your time
The mountain when to cross.
60 For oft there sits, between the heap
That's like an infant's grave in size,
And that same pond of which I spoke,
A woman in a scarlet cloak,
And to herself she cries,
65 "Oh misery! oh misery!
"Oh woe is me! oh misery!"

7

At all times of the day and night
This wretched woman thither goes,
And she is known to every star,
70 And every wind that blows;
And there beside the thorn she sits
When the blue day-light's in the skies,
And when the whirlwind's on the hill,
Or frosty air is keen and still,
75 And to herself she cries,
"Oh misery! oh misery!
Oh woe is me! oh misery!"

8

"Now wherefore thus, by day and night,
In rain, in tempest, and in snow,
80 Thus to the dreary mountain-top
Does this poor woman go?
And why sits she beside the thorn
When the blue day-light's in the sky,
Or when the whirlwind's on the hill,
85 Or frosty air is keen and still,
And wherefore does she cry?
Oh wherefore? wherefore? tell me why
Does she repeat that doleful cry?"

9

I cannot tell; I wish I could;
90 For the true reason no one knows,
But if you'd gladly view the spot,
The spot to which she goes;
The heap that's like an infant's grave,

The pond—and thorn, so old and grey;
95   Pass by her door—'tis seldom shut—
And if you see her in her hut,
Then to the spot away!
I never heard of such as dare
Approach the spot when she is there.

10

100 "But wherefore to the mountain-top
Can this unhappy woman go,
Whatever star is in the skies,
Whatever wind may blow?"
Nay rack your brain—'tis all in vain,
105 I'll tell you every thing I know;
But to the thorn, and to the pond
Which is a little step beyond,
I wish that you would go:
Perhaps when you are at the place
110 You something of her tale may trace.

11

I'll give you the best help I can:
Before you up the mountain go,
Up to the dreary mountain-top,
I'll tell you all I know.
115 'Tis now some two and twenty years,
Since she (her name is Martha Ray)
Gave with a maiden's true good will
Her company to Stephen Hill;
And she was blithe and gay,
120 And she was happy, happy still
Whene'er she thought of Stephen Hill.

12

And they had fix'd the wedding-day,
The morning that must wed them both;
But Stephen to another maid
125 Had sworn another oath;
And with this other maid to church
Unthinking Stephen went—
Poor Martha! on that woeful day
A cruel, cruel fire, they say,
130 Into her bones was sent:

It dried her body like a cinder,
And almost turn'd her brain to tinder.[1]

13

They say, full six months after this,
While yet the summer leaves were green,
135 She to the mountain-top would go,
And there was often seen.
'Tis said, a child was in her womb,
As now to any eye was plain;
She was with child, and she was mad,
140 Yet often she was sober sad
From her exceeding pain.
Oh me! ten thousand times I'd rather
That he had died, that cruel father!

14

Sad case for such a brain to hold
145 Communion with a stirring child!
Sad case, as you may think, for one
Who had a brain so wild!
Last Christmas when we talked of this,
Old Farmer Simpson did maintain,
150 That in her womb the infant wrought
About its mother's heart, and brought
Her senses back again:
And when at last her time drew near,
Her looks were calm, her senses clear.

15

155 No more I know, I wish I did,
And I would tell it all to you;
For what became of this poor child
There's none that ever knew:
And if a child was born or no,
160 There's no one that could ever tell;
And if 'twas born alive or dead,
There's no one knows, as I have said,
But some remember well,
That Martha Ray about this time
165 Would up the mountain often climb.

---

[1]   *tinder* Dry, flammable substance that will take fire from a spark.

16

And all that winter, when at night
The wind blew from the mountain-peak,
'Twas worth your while, though in the dark,
The church-yard path to seek:
170 For many a time and oft were heard
Cries coming from the mountain-head,
Some plainly living voices were,
And others, I've heard many swear,
Were voices of the dead:
175 I cannot think, whate'er they say,
They had to do with Martha Ray.

17

But that she goes to this old thorn,
The thorn which I've described to you,
And there sits in a scarlet cloak,
180 I will be sworn is true.
For one day with my telescope,
To view the ocean wide and bright,
When to this country first I came,
Ere I had heard of Martha's name,
185 I climbed the mountain's height:
A storm came on, and I could see
No object higher than my knee.

18

'Twas mist and rain, and storm and rain,
No screen, no fence could I discover,
190 And then the wind! in faith, it was
A wind full ten times over.
I looked around, I thought I saw
A jutting crag, and off I ran,
Head-foremost, through the driving rain,
195 The shelter of the crag to gain,
And, as I am a man,
Instead of jutting crag, I found
A woman seated on the ground.

19

I did not speak—I saw her face,
200 Her face it was enough for me;
I turned about and heard her cry,
"O misery! O misery!"
And there she sits, until the moon

Through half the clear blue sky will go,
205 And when the little breezes make
The waters of the pond to shake,
As all the country know,
She shudders and you hear her cry,
"Oh misery! oh misery!"

20

210 "But what's the thorn? and what's the pond?
And what's the hill of moss to her?
And what's the creeping breeze that comes
The little pond to stir?"
I cannot tell; but some will say
215 She hanged her baby on the tree,
Some say she drowned it in the pond,
Which is a little step beyond,
But all and each agree,
The little babe was buried there,
220 Beneath that hill of moss so fair.

21

I've heard the scarlet moss is red
With drops of that poor infant's blood;
But kill a new-born infant thus!
I do not think she could.
225 Some say, if to the pond you go,
And fix on it a steady view,
The shadow of a babe you trace,
A baby and a baby's face,
And that it looks at you;
230 Whene'er you look on it, 'tis plain
The baby looks at you again.

22

And some had sworn an oath that she
Should be to public justice brought;
And for the little infant's bones
235 With spades they would have sought.
But then the beauteous hill of moss
Before their eyes began to stir;
And for full fifty yards around,
The grass it shook upon the ground;
240 But all do still aver
The little babe is buried there,
Beneath that hill of moss so fair.

23

I cannot tell how this may be,
But plain it is, the thorn is bound
245   With heavy tufts of moss, that strive
To drag it to the ground.
And this I know, full many a time,
When she was on the mountain high,
By day, and in the silent night,
250   When all the stars shone clear and bright,
That I have heard her cry,
"Oh misery! oh misery!
"Oh woe is me! oh misery!"
—1798

Expostulation and Reply

"Why William, on that old grey stone,
Thus for the length of half a day,
Why William, sit you thus alone,
And dream your time away?

5   "Where are your books? that light bequeath'd
To beings else forlorn and blind!
Up! Up! and drink the spirit breath'd
From dead men to their kind.

"You look round on your mother earth,
10   As if she for no purpose bore you;
As if you were her first-born birth,
And none had lived before you!"

One morning thus, by Esthwaite lake,[1]
When life was sweet I knew not why,
15   To me my good friend Matthew spake,
And thus I made reply.

"The eye it cannot choose but see,
We cannot bid the ear be still;
Our bodies feel, where'er they be,
20   Against, or with our will.

"Nor less I deem that there are powers,
Which of themselves our minds impress,
That we can feed this mind of ours,
In a wise passiveness.

25   "Think you, mid all this mighty sum
Of things for ever speaking,
That nothing of itself will come,
But we must still be seeking?

"—Then ask not wherefore, here, alone,
30   Conversing as I may,
I sit upon this old grey stone,
And dream my time away."
—1798

The Tables Turned
An Evening Scene on the Same Subject

Up! up! my friend, and clear your looks,
Why all this toil and trouble?
Up! up! my friend, and quit your books,
Or surely you'll grow double.[2]

5   The sun above the mountain's head,
A freshening lustre mellow,
Through all the long green fields has spread,
His first sweet evening yellow.

Books! 'tis a dull and endless strife,
10   Come, hear the woodland linnet,
How sweet his music; on my life
There's more of wisdom in it.

And hark! how blithe the throstle° sings!   *thrush*
And he is no mean preacher;
15   Come forth into the light of things,
Let Nature be your teacher.

She has a world of ready wealth,
Our minds and hearts to bless—

---

[1] *Esthwaite lake* Located at Hawkshead (in England's Lake District), where Wordsworth attended grammar school.

[2] *double* Doubled over.

Spontaneous wisdom breathed by health,
20 Truth breathed by cheerfulness.

One impulse from a vernal wood
May teach you more of man;
Of moral evil and of good,
Than all the sages can.

25 Sweet is the lore which nature brings;
Our meddling intellect
Mishapes the beauteous forms of things
—We murder to dissect.

Enough of science and of art;
30 Close up these barren leaves;
Come forth, and bring with you a heart
That watches and receives.
—1798

Lines Written a Few Miles above Tintern Abbey

On Revisiting the Banks of the Wye during a Tour, July 13, 1798[1]

Five years have passed; five summers, with the length
Of five long winters! and again I hear
These waters, rolling from their mountain-springs
With a sweet inland murmur.[2] Once again
5 Do I behold these steep and lofty cliffs,
Which on a wild secluded scene impress
Thoughts of more deep seclusion; and connect
The landscape with the quiet of the sky.
The day is come when I again repose
10 Here, under this dark sycamore, and view
These plots of cottage-ground, these orchard-tufts,
Which, at this season, with their unripe fruits,

Among the woods and copses lose themselves,
Nor, with their green and simple hue, disturb
15 The wild green landscape. Once again I see
These hedge-rows, hardly hedge-rows, little lines
Of sportive wood run wild; these pastoral farms
Green to the very door; and wreaths of smoke
Sent up, in silence, from among the trees,
20 With some uncertain notice, as might seem,
Of vagrant dwellers in the houseless woods,
Or of some hermit's cave, where by his fire
The hermit sits alone.

        Though absent long,
25 These forms of beauty have not been to me,
As is a landscape to a blind man's eye:
But oft, in lonely rooms, and 'mid the din
Of towns and cities, I have owed to them,
In hours of weariness, sensations sweet,
30 Felt in the blood, and felt along the heart,
And passing even into my purer mind
With tranquil restoration—feelings too
Of unremembered pleasure; such, perhaps,
As may have had no trivial influence
35 On that best portion of a good man's life;
His little, nameless, unremembered acts
Of kindness and of love. Nor less, I trust,
To them I may have owed another gift,
Of aspect more sublime; that blessed mood,
40 In which the burthen of the mystery,
In which the heavy and the weary weight
Of all this unintelligible world
Is lighten'd—that serene and blessed mood,
In which the affections gently lead us on,
45 Until, the breath of this corporeal frame,
And even the motion of our human blood
Almost suspended, we are laid asleep
In body, and become a living soul:
While with an eye made quiet by the power
50 Of harmony, and the deep power of joy,
We see into the life of things.

        If this
Be but a vain belief, yet, oh! how oft,
In darkness, and amid the many shapes
55 Of joyless day-light; when the fretful stir

---

1 [Wordsworth's note] No poem of mine was composed under circumstances more pleasant for me to remember than this. I began it upon leaving Tintern, after crossing the Wye, and concluded it just as I was entering Bristol in the evening, after a ramble of 4 or 5 days, with my sister. Not a line of it was altered, and not any part of it was written down till I reached Bristol.

2 [Wordsworth's note] The river is not affected by the tides a few miles above Tintern.

Unprofitable, and the fever of the world,
Have hung upon the beatings of my heart,
How oft, in spirit, have I turned to thee
O sylvan Wye! Thou wanderer through the woods,
60   How often has my spirit turned to thee!

And now, with gleams of half-extinguish'd thought,
With many recognitions dim and faint,
And somewhat of a sad perplexity,
The picture of the mind revives again:
65   While here I stand, not only with the sense
Of present pleasure, but with pleasing thoughts
That in this moment there is life and food
For future years. And so I dare to hope
Though changed, no doubt, from what I was, when first
70   I came among these hills; when like a roe°   deer
I bounded o'er the mountains, by the sides
Of the deep rivers, and the lonely streams,
Wherever nature led; more like a man
Flying from something that he dreads, than one
75   Who sought the thing he loved. For nature then
(The coarser pleasures of my boyish days,
And their glad animal movements all gone by)
To me was all in all. I cannot paint
What then I was. The sounding cataract
80   Haunted me like a passion: the tall rock,
The mountain, and the deep and gloomy wood,
Their colours and their forms, were then to me
An appetite: a feeling and a love,
That had no need of a remoter charm,
85   By thought supplied, or any interest
Unborrowed from the eye. That time is past,
And all its aching joys are now no more,
And all its dizzy raptures. Not for this
Faint[1] I, nor mourn nor murmur: other gifts
90   Have followed, for such loss, I would believe,
Abundant recompence. For I have learned
To look on nature, not as in the hour
Of thoughtless youth, but hearing oftentimes
The still, sad music of humanity,
95   Not harsh nor grating, though of ample power
To chasten and subdue. And I have felt
A presence that disturbs me with the joy
Of elevated thoughts; a sense sublime

Of something far more deeply interfused,
100   Whose dwelling is the light of setting suns,
And the round ocean, and the living air,
And the blue sky, and in the mind of man,
A motion and a spirit, that impels
All thinking things, all objects of all thought,
105   And rolls through all things. Therefore am I still
A lover of the meadows and the woods,
And mountains; and of all that we behold
From this green earth; of all the mighty world
Of eye and ear, both what they half create,
110   And what perceive; well pleased to recognize
In nature and the language of the sense,
The anchor of my purest thoughts, the nurse,
The guide, the guardian of my heart, and soul
Of all my moral being.

115   Nor, perchance,
If I were not thus taught, should I the more
Suffer my genial° spirits to decay: creative
For thou art with me, here, upon the banks
Of this fair river; thou, my dearest Friend,[2]
120   My dear, dear Friend, and in thy voice I catch
The language of my former heart, and read
My former pleasures in the shooting lights
Of thy wild eyes. Oh! yet a little while
May I behold in thee what I was once,
125   My dear, dear Sister! And this prayer I make,
Knowing that Nature never did betray
The heart that loved her; 'tis her privilege,
Through all the years of this our life, to lead
From joy to joy: for she can so inform
130   The mind that is within us, so impress
With quietness and beauty, and so feed
With lofty thoughts, that neither evil tongues,
Rash judgments, nor the sneers of selfish men,
Nor greetings where no kindness is, nor all
135   The dreary intercourse of daily life,
Shall e'er prevail against us, or disturb
Our cheerful faith that all which we behold
Is full of blessings. Therefore let the moon
Shine on thee in thy solitary walk;
140   And let the misty mountain winds be free

---

[1] *Faint* Lose heart; grow weak.

[2] *my dearest Friend* I.e., Dorothy Wordsworth, Wordsworth's sister.

To blow against thee: and in after years,
When these wild ecstasies shall be matured
Into a sober pleasure, when thy mind
Shall be a mansion for all lovely forms,
145 Thy memory be as a dwelling-place
For all sweet sounds and harmonies; Oh! then,
If solitude, or fear, or pain, or grief,
Should be thy portion, with what healing thoughts
Of tender joy wilt thou remember me,
150 And these my exhortations! Nor, perchance,
If I should be, where I no more can hear
Thy voice, nor catch from thy wild eyes these gleams
Of past existence, wilt thou then forget
That on the banks of this delightful stream
155 We stood together; and that I, so long
A worshipper of Nature, hither came,
Unwearied in that service: rather say
With warmer love, oh! with far deeper zeal
Of holier love. Nor wilt thou then forget,
160 That after many wanderings, many years
Of absence, these steep woods and lofty cliffs,
And this green pastoral landscape, were to me
More dear, both for themselves, and for thy sake.
—1798

from *Lyrical Ballads, 1800, 1802*

PREFACE[1]

The first Volume of these Poems has already been submitted to general perusal. It was published as an experiment, which, I hoped, might be of some use to ascertain how far, by fitting to metrical arrangement a selection of the real language of men in a state of vivid sensation, that sort of pleasure and that quantity of pleasure may be imparted, which a Poet may rationally endeavour to impart.

I had formed no very inaccurate estimate of the probable effect of those Poems: I flattered myself that they who should be pleased with them would read them with more than common pleasure: and, on the other hand, I was well aware that by those who should dislike them they would be read with more than common dislike. The result has differed from my expectation in this only, that I have pleased a greater number than I ventured to hope I should please.

For the sake of variety, and from a consciousness of my own weakness, I was induced to request the assistance of a Friend,[2] who furnished me with the Poems of the *Ancient Mariner*, the *Foster-Mother's Tale*, the *Nightingale*, and the Poem entitled *Love*. I should not, however, have requested this assistance, had I not believed that the Poems of my Friend would in a great measure have the same tendency as my own, and that, though there would be found a difference, there would be found no discordance in the colours of our style; as our opinions on the subject of poetry do almost entirely coincide.

Several of my Friends are anxious for the success of these Poems from a belief that, if the views with which they were composed were indeed realized, a class of Poetry would be produced, well adapted to interest mankind permanently, and not unimportant in the multiplicity, and in the quality of its moral relations: and on this account they have advised me to prefix a systematic defence of the theory upon which the poems were written. But I was unwilling to undertake the task, because I knew that on this occasion the Reader would look coldly upon my arguments, since I might be suspected of having been principally influenced by the selfish and foolish hope of *reasoning* him into an approbation of these particular Poems: and I was still more unwilling to undertake the task, because, adequately to display my opinions, and fully to enforce my arguments, would require a space wholly disproportionate to the nature of a preface. For to treat the subject with the clearness and coherence of which I believe it susceptible, it would be necessary to give a full account of the present state of the public taste in this country, and to determine how far this taste is healthy or depraved; which, again, could not be determined without pointing out in what manner language and the human mind act and re-act on each other, and without retracing the revolutions, not of literature alone, but likewise of society itself. I have therefore altogether declined to

---

1 *Preface* This preface first appeared in the 1800 edition of *Lyrical Ballads*, and was revised for the 1802 edition.

2 *Friend* Samuel Taylor Coleridge (1772–1834). Coleridge gives his account of their plan in his *Biographia Literaria*, chapter 14.

enter regularly upon this defence; yet I am sensible that there would be some impropriety in abruptly obtruding upon the Public, without a few words of introduction, Poems so materially different from those upon which general approbation is at present bestowed.

It is supposed, that by the act of writing in verse an Author makes a formal engagement that he will gratify certain known habits of association; that he not only thus apprizes the Reader that certain classes of ideas and expressions will be found in his book, but that others will be carefully excluded. This exponent or symbol held forth by metrical language must in different areas of literature have excited very different expectations: for example, in the age of Catullus, Terence, and Lucretius and that of Statius or Claudian;[1] and in our own country, in the age of Shakespeare and Beaumont and Fletcher, and that of Donne and Cowley, or Dryden, or Pope.[2] I will not take upon me to determine the exact import of the promise which by the act of writing in verse an Author, in the present day, makes to his Reader; but, I am certain, it will appear to many persons that I have not fulfilled the terms of an engagement thus voluntarily contracted. They who have been accustomed to the gaudiness and inane phraseology of many modern writers, if they persist in reading this book to its conclusion, will, no doubt, frequently have to struggle with feelings of strangeness and awkwardness: they will look round for poetry, and will be induced to inquire by what species of courtesy these attempts can be permitted to assume that title. I hope therefore the Reader will not censure me if I attempt to state what I have proposed to myself to perform; and also (as far as the limits of a preface will permit) to explain some of the chief reasons which have determined me in the choice of my purpose: that at least he maybe spared any unpleasant feeling of disappointment, and that I myself may be protected from the most dishonorable accusation which can be brought against an Author, namely, that of an indolence which prevents him from endeavouring to ascertain what is his duty, or, when his duty is ascertained, prevents him from performing it.

The principal object, then, which I proposed to myself in these Poems was to choose incidents and situations from common life, and to relate or describe them, throughout, as far as was possible, in a selection of language really used by men; and, at the same time, to throw over them a certain colouring of imagination, whereby ordinary things should be presented to the mind in an unusual way; and, further, and above all, to make these incidents and situations interesting by tracing in them, truly though not ostentatiously, the primary laws of our nature: chiefly as far as regards the manner in which we associate ideas in a state of excitement. Low and rustic life was generally chosen because, in that condition, the essential passions of the heart find a better soil in which they can attain their maturity, are less under restraint, and speak a plainer and more emphatic language; because in that condition of life our elementary feelings co-exist in a state of greater simplicity, and, consequently, may be more accurately contemplated, and more forcibly communicated; because the manners of rural life germinate from those elementary feelings; and, from the necessary character of rural occupations, are more easily comprehended, and are more durable; and lastly, because in that condition the passions of men are incorporated with the beautiful and permanent forms of nature. The language, too, of these men is adopted (purified indeed from what appear to be its real defects, from all lasting and rational causes of dislike or disgust) because such men hourly communicate with the best objects from which the best part of language is originally derived; and because, from their rank in society and the sameness and narrow circle of their intercourse, being less under the influence of social vanity they convey their feelings and notions in simple and unelaborated expressions. Accordingly, such a language, arising out of repeated experience and regular feelings, is a more permanent, and a far more philosophical language, than that which is frequently substituted for it by Poets, who think that they are conferring honour upon themselves and their art, in proportion as they separate themselves from the sympathies of men,

---

[1] *Catullus, Terence, and Lucretius* Roman poets of the first and second centuries BCE; *Statius or Claudian* Roman epic poets of the first and fourth centuries CE, respectively.

[2] *Shakespeare and Beaumont and Fletcher* The age of Renaissance drama, during which Shakespeare, Francis Beaumont, and John Fletcher wrote; *Donne and Cowley* John Donne and Abraham Cowley, poets of the seventeenth century; *Dryden* John Dryden, Poet Laureate during the Restoration (1660–1700); *Pope* Alexander Pope, a major poet of the eighteenth century.

and indulge in arbitrary and capricious habits of expression, in order to furnish food for fickle tastes, and fickle appetites, of their own creation.[1]

I cannot, however, be insensible of the present outcry against the triviality and meanness both of thought and language, which some of my contemporaries have occasionally introduced into their metrical compositions; and I acknowledge that this defect, where it exists, is more dishonorable to the Writer's own character than false refinement or arbitrary innovation, though I should contend at the same time that it is far less pernicious in the sum of its consequences. From such verses the Poems in these volumes will be found distinguished at least by one mark of difference, that each of them has a worthy *purpose*. Not that I mean to say that I always began to write with a distinct purpose formally conceived; but I believe that my habits of meditation have so formed my feelings, as that my descriptions of such objects as strongly excite those feelings will be found to carry along with them a *purpose*. If in this opinion I am mistaken, I can have little right to the name of a Poet. For all good poetry is the spontaneous overflow of powerful feelings: but though this be true, Poems to which any value can be attached, were never produced on any variety of subjects but by a man who, being possessed of more than usual organic sensibility, had also thought long and deeply. For our continued influxes of feeling are modified and directed by our thoughts, which are indeed the representatives of all our past feelings; and, as by contemplating the relation of these general representatives to each other we discover what is really important to men, so, by the repetition and continuance of this act, our feelings will be connected with important subjects, till at length, if we be originally possessed of much sensibility, such habits of mind will be produced, that, by obeying blindly and mechanically the impulses of those habits, we shall describe objects, and utter sentiments, of such a nature and in such connection with each other, that the understanding of the being to whom we address ourselves, if he be in a healthful state of association, must necessarily be in some degree enlightened, and his affections ameliorated.

I have said that each of these poems has a purpose. I have also informed my Reader what this purpose will be found principally to be: namely to illustrate the manner in which our feelings and ideas are associated in a state of excitement. But, speaking in language somewhat more appropriate, it is to follow the fluxes and refluxes of the mind when agitated by the great and simple affections of our nature. This object I have endeavoured in these short essays to attain by various means; by tracing the maternal passion through many of its more subtle windings, as in the poems of the *Idiot Boy* and the *Mad Mother*; by accompanying the last struggles of a human being, at the approach of death, cleaving in solitude to life and society, as in the Poem of the *Forsaken Indian*; by showing, as in the Stanzas entitled *We Are Seven*, the perplexity and obscurity which in childhood attend our notion of death, or rather our utter inability to admit that notion; or by displaying the strength of fraternal, or to speak more philosophically, of moral attachment when early associated with the great and beautiful objects of nature, as in *The Brothers*; or, as in the *Incident of Simon Lee*, by placing my Reader in the way of receiving from ordinary moral sensations another and more salutary impression than we are accustomed to receive from them. It has also been part of my general purpose to attempt to sketch characters under the influence of less impassioned feelings, as in the *Two April Mornings*, *The Fountain*, *The Old Man Travelling*, *The Two Thieves*, &c., characters of which the elements are simple, belonging rather to nature than to manners, such as exist now, and will probably always exist, and which from their constitution may be distinctly and profitably contemplated. I will not abuse the indulgence of my Reader by dwelling longer upon this subject; but it is proper that I should mention one other circumstance which distinguishes these Poems from the popular Poetry of the day; it is this, that the feeling therein developed gives importance to the action and situation, and not the action and situation to the feeling. My meaning will be rendered perfectly intelligible by referring my Reader to the Poems entitled *Poor Susan* and the *Childless Father*, particularly to the last Stanza of the latter Poem.

I will not suffer a sense of false modesty to prevent

---

[1] [Wordsworth's note] It is worth while here to observe that the affecting parts of Chaucer are almost always expressed in language pure and universally intelligible even to this day.

me from asserting that I point my Reader's attention to this mark of distinction, far less for the sake of these particular Poems than from the general importance of the subject. The subject is indeed important! For the human mind is capable of being excited without the application of gross and violent stimulants; and he must have a very faint perception of its beauty and dignity who does not know this, and who does not further know that one being is elevated above another, in proportion as he possesses this capability. It has therefore appeared to me that to endeavour to produce or enlarge this capability is one of the best services in which, at any period, a Writer can be engaged; but this service, excellent at all times, is especially so at the present day. For a multitude of causes, unknown to former times, are now acting with a combined force to blunt the discriminating powers of the mind, and unfitting it for all voluntary exertion to reduce it to a state of almost savage torpor. The most effective of these causes are the great national events which are daily taking place,[1] and the increasing accumulation of men in cities, where the uniformity of their occupations produces a craving for extraordinary incident, which the rapid communication of intelligence hourly gratifies. To this tendency of life and manners the literature and theatrical exhibitions of the country have conformed themselves. The invaluable works of our elder writers, I had almost said the works of Shakespeare and Milton, are driven into neglect by frantic novels, sickly and stupid German Tragedies, and deluges of idle and extravagant stories in verse.[2] When I think upon this degrading thirst after outrageous stimulation, I am almost ashamed to have spoken of the feeble effort with which I have endeavoured to counteract it; and, reflecting upon the magnitude of the general evil, I should be oppressed with no dishonorable melancholy, had I not a deep impression of certain inherent and indestructible qualities of the human mind, and likewise of certain powers in the great and permanent objects that act upon

it which are equally inherent and indestructible; and did I not further add to this impression a belief that the time is approaching when the evil will be systematically opposed, by men of greater powers, and with far more distinguished success.

Having dwelt thus long on the subjects and aim of these Poems, I shall request the Reader's permission to apprize him of a few circumstances relating to their *style*, in order, among other reasons, that I may not be censured for not having performed what I never attempted. The Reader will find that personifications of abstract ideas rarely occur in these volumes; and, I hope, are utterly rejected as an ordinary device to elevate the style, and raise it above prose. I have proposed to myself to imitate, and, as far as is possible, to adopt, the very language of men; and assuredly such personifications do not make any natural or regular part of that language. They are, indeed, a figure of speech occasionally prompted by passion, and I have made use of them as such; but I have endeavoured utterly to reject them as a mechanical device of style, or as a family language which Writers in metre seem to lay claim to by prescription. I have wished to keep my Reader in the company of flesh and blood, persuaded that by so doing I shall interest him. I am, however, well aware that others who pursue a different track may interest him likewise; I do not interfere with their claim, I only wish to prefer a different claim of my own. There will also be found in these volumes little of what is usually called poetic diction; I have taken as much pains to avoid it as others ordinarily take to produce it; this I have done for the reason already alleged, to bring my language near to the language of men, and further, because the pleasure which I have proposed to myself to impart is of a kind very different from that which is supposed by many persons to be the proper object of poetry. I do not know how without being culpably particular I can give my Reader a more exact notion of the style in which I wished these poems to be written than by informing him that I have at all times endeavoured to look steadily at my subject; consequently, I hope that there is in these Poems little falsehood of description, and that my ideas are expressed in language fitted to their respective importance. Something I must have gained by this practice, as it is friendly to one property of all good poetry, namely, good sense;

---

[1]   *great national ... place*   I.e., the wars against France and the Irish rebellion.

[2]   *frantic novels ... verse*   References to popular Gothic novels of the time, such as Matthew Gregory Lewis's *The Monk* (1796) and the novels of Ann Radcliffe, and to the German sentimental melodramas translated and staged during the 1780s.

but it has necessarily cut me off from a large portion of phrases and figures of speech which from father to son have long been regarded as the common inheritance of Poets. I have also thought it expedient to restrict myself still further, having abstained from the use of many expressions, in themselves proper and beautiful, but which have been foolishly repeated by bad Poets, till such feelings of disgust are connected with them as it is scarcely possible by any art of association to overpower.

If in a Poem there should be found a series of lines, or even a single line, in which the language, though naturally arranged and according to the strict laws of metre, does not differ from that of prose, there is a numerous class of critics, who, when they stumble upon these prosaisms, as they call them, imagine that they have made a notable discovery, and exult over the Poet as over a man ignorant of his own profession. Now these men would establish a canon of criticism which the Reader will conclude he must utterly reject, if he wishes to be pleased with these volumes. And it would be a most easy task to prove to him that not only the language of a large portion of every good poem, even of the most elevated character, must necessarily, except with reference to the metre, in no respect differ from that of good prose, but likewise that some of the most interesting parts of the best poems will be found to be strictly the language of prose, when prose is well written. The truth of this assertion might be demonstrated by innumerable passages from almost all the poetical writings, even of Milton himself. I have not space for much quotation; but, to illustrate the subject in a general manner, I will here adduce a short composition of Gray,[1] who was at the head of those who by their reasonings have attempted to widen the space of separation betwixt Prose and Metrical composition, and was more than any other man curiously elaborate in the structure of his own poetic diction.

In vain to me the smiling mornings shine,
And reddening Phoebus[2] lifts his golden fire:
The birds in vain their amorous descant join,
Or cheerful fields resume their green attire:

These ears alas! for other notes repine;
A different object do these eyes require;
My lonely anguish melts no heart but mine;
And in my breast the imperfect joys expire;
Yet Morning smiles the busy race to cheer,
And new-born pleasure brings to happier men;
The fields to all their wonted tribute bear;
To warm their little loves the birds complain.
I fruitless mourn to him that cannot hear
And weep the more because I weep in vain.

It will easily be perceived that the only part of this Sonnet which is of any value is the lines printed in Italics: it is equally obvious that, except in the rhyme, and in the use of the single word "fruitless" for fruitlessly, which is so far a defect, the language of these lines does in no respect differ from that of prose.

By the foregoing quotation I have shown that the language of Prose may yet be well adapted to Poetry; and I have previously asserted that a large portion of the language of every good poem can in no respect differ from that of good Prose. I will go further. I do not doubt that it may be safely affirmed that there neither is, nor can be, any essential difference between the language of prose and metrical composition....

I ask what is meant by the word Poet? What is a Poet? To whom does he address himself? And what language is to be expected from him? He is a man speaking to men: a man, it is true, endued with more lively sensibility, more enthusiasm and tenderness, who has a greater knowledge of human nature, and a more comprehensive soul, than are supposed to be common among mankind; a man pleased with his own passions and volitions, and who rejoices more than other men in the spirit of life that is in him; delighting to contemplate similar volitions and passions as manifested in the goings-on of the Universe, and habitually impelled to create them where he does not find them. To these qualities he has added a disposition to be affected more than other men by absent things as if they were present; an ability of conjuring up in himself passions, which are indeed far from being the same as those produced by real events, yet (especially in those parts of the general sympathy which are pleasing and delightful) do more nearly resemble the passions produced by real events than any thing which, from the motions of their own

---

[1] *Gray* Thomas Gray (1716–71). Wordsworth quotes his *Sonnet on the Death of Richard West.*

[2] *Phoebus* Apollo, god of the sun and of poetry.

minds merely, other men are accustomed to feel in themselves; whence, and from practice, he has acquired a greater readiness and power in expressing what he thinks and feels, and especially those thoughts and feelings which, by his own choice, or from the structure of his own mind, arise in him without immediate external excitement.

But, whatever portion of this faculty we may suppose even the greatest Poet to possess, there cannot be a doubt but that the language which it will suggest to him must, in liveliness and truth, fall far short of that which is uttered by men in real life, under the actual pressure of those passions, certain shadows of which the Poet thus produces, or feels to be produced, in himself. However exalted a notion we would wish to cherish of the character of a Poet, it is obvious that, while he describes and imitates passions, his situation is altogether slavish and mechanical, compared with the freedom and power of real and substantial action and suffering. So that it will be the wish of the Poet to bring his feelings near to those of the persons whose feelings he describes—nay, for short spaces of time, perhaps, to let himself slip into an entire delusion, and even confound and identify his own feelings with theirs; modifying only the language which is thus suggested to him, by a consideration that he describes for a particular purpose, that of giving pleasure. Here, then, he will apply the principle on which I have so much insisted, namely, that of selection; on this he will depend for removing what would otherwise be painful or disgusting in the passion; he will feel that there is no necessity to trick out or to elevate nature: and, the more industriously he applies this principle, the deeper will be his faith that no words which his fancy or imagination can suggest will be to be compared with those which are the emanations of reality and truth....

It is not, then, in the dramatic parts of composition that we look for this distinction of language; but still it may be proper and necessary where the Poet speaks to us in his own person and character. To this I answer by referring my Reader to the description which I have before given of a Poet. Among the qualities which I have enumerated as principally conducting to form a Poet, is implied nothing differing in kind from other men, but only in degree. The sum of what I have there said is that the Poet is chiefly distinguished from other men by a greater promptness to think and feel without immediate external excitement, and a greater power in expressing such thoughts and feelings as are produced in him in that manner. But these passions and thoughts and feelings are the general passions and thoughts and feelings of men. And with what are they connected? Undoubtedly with our moral sentiments and animal sensations, and with the causes which excite these; with the operations of the elements and the appearances of the visible universe; with storm and sunshine, with the revolutions of the seasons, with cold and heat, with loss of friends and kindred, with injuries and resentments, gratitude and hope, with fear and sorrow. These, and the like, are the sensations and objects which the Poet describes, as they are the sensations of other men, and the objects which interest them. The Poet thinks and feels in the spirit of the passions of men. How, then, can his language differ in any material degree from that of all other men who feel vividly and see clearly? It might be *proved* that it is impossible. But supposing that this were not the case, the Poet might then be allowed to use a peculiar language when expressing his feelings for his own gratification, or that of men like himself. But Poets do not write for Poets alone, but for men. Unless therefore we are advocates for that admiration which depends upon ignorance, and that pleasure which arises from hearing what we do not understand, the Poet must descend from this supposed height, and, in order to excite rational sympathy, he must express himself as other men express themselves. To this it may be added, that while he is only selecting from the real language of men, or, which amounts to the same thing, composing accurately in the spirit of such selection, he is treading upon safe ground, and we know what we are to expect from him. Our feelings are the same with respect to metre; for, as it may be proper to remind the Reader, the distinction of metre is regular and uniform, and not like that which is produced by what is usually called poetic diction, arbitrary, and subject to infinite caprices upon which no calculation whatever can be made. In the one case, the Reader is utterly at the mercy of the Poet respecting what imagery or diction he may choose to connect with the passion, whereas, in the other, the metre obeys certain laws, to which the Poet and Reader both willingly submit because they are certain, and because no interference is made by them with the passion but such as the concurring testimony of ages has shown to heighten and improve the pleasure which co-exists with it.

It will now be proper to answer an obvious question, namely, why, professing these opinions, have I written in verse? To this, in addition to such answer as is included in what I have already said, I reply in the first place, because, however I may have restricted myself, there is still left open to me what confessedly constitutes the most valuable object of all writing whether in prose or verse, the great and universal passions of men, the most general and interesting of their occupations, and the entire world of nature, from which I am at liberty to supply myself with endless combinations of forms and imagery. Now, supposing for a moment that whatever is interesting in these objects may be as vividly described in prose, why am I to be condemned, if to such description I have endeavoured to superadd the charm which, by the consent of all nations, is acknowledged to exist in metrical language? To this, by such as are unconvinced by what I have already said, it may be answered that a very small part of the pleasure given by Poetry depends upon the metre, and that it is injudicious to write in metre, unless it be accompanied with the other artificial distinctions of style with which metre is usually accompanied, and that by such deviation more will be lost from the shock which will be thereby given to the Reader's associations than will be counterbalanced by any pleasure which he can derive from the general power of numbers. In answer to those who still contend for the necessity of accompanying metre with certain appropriate colours of style in order to the accomplishment of its appropriate end, and who also, in my opinion, greatly under-rate the power of metre in itself, it might perhaps, as far as relates to these Poems, have been almost sufficient to observe that poems are extant, written upon more humble subjects, and in a more naked and simple style than I have aimed at, which poems have continued to give pleasure from generation to generation. Now, if nakedness and simplicity be a defect, the fact here mentioned affords a strong presumption that poems somewhat less naked and simple are capable of affording pleasure at the present day; and,

what I wished *chiefly* to attempt, at present, was to justify myself for having written under the impression of this belief.

But I might point out various causes why, when the style is manly, and the subject of some importance, words metrically arranged will long continue to impart such a pleasure to mankind as he who is sensible of the extent of that pleasure will be desirous to impart. The end of Poetry is to produce excitement in co-existence with an overbalance of pleasure. Now, by the supposition, excitement is an unusual and irregular state of the mind; ideas and feelings do not in that state succeed each other in accustomed order. But, if the words by which this excitement is produced are in themselves powerful, or the images and feelings have an undue proportion of pain connected with them, there is some danger that the excitement may be carried beyond its proper bounds. Now the co-presence of something regular, something to which the mind has been accustomed in various moods and in a less excited state, cannot but have great efficacy in tempering and restraining the passion by an intertexture of ordinary feeling, and of feeling not strictly and necessarily connected with the passion. This is unquestionably true, and hence, though the opinion will at first appear paradoxical, from the tendency of metre to divest language in a certain degree of its reality, and thus to throw a sort of half consciousness of unsubstantial existence over the whole composition, there can be little doubt but that more pathetic situations and sentiments—that is, those which have a greater proportion of pain connected with them—may be endured in metrical composition, especially in rhyme, than in prose. The metre of the old Ballads is very artless; yet they contain many passages which would illustrate this opinion, and, I hope, if the following Poems be attentively perused, similar instances will be found in them....

I have said that Poetry is the spontaneous overflow of powerful feelings: it takes its origin from emotion recollected in tranquillity: the emotion is contemplated till by a species of reaction the tranquillity gradually disappears, and an emotion, kindred to that which was before the subject of contemplation, is gradually produced, and does itself actually exist in the mind. In this mood successful composition generally begins, and in a mood similar to this it is carried on; but the emotion, of whatever kind and in whatever degree, from various causes is qualified by various pleasures, so that in describing any passions whatsoever, which are voluntarily described, the mind will upon the whole be in a state of enjoyment. Now, if Nature be thus cautious in preserving in a state of enjoyment a being thus employed, the Poet ought to profit by the lesson thus held forth to him, and ought especially to take care that whatever passions he communicates to his Reader, those passions, if his Reader's mind be sound and vigorous, should always be accompanied with an overbalance of pleasure. Now the music of harmonious metrical language, the sense of difficulty overcome, and the blind association of pleasure which has been previously received from works of rhyme or metre of the same or similar construction, an indistinct perception perpetually renewed of language closely resembling that of real life, and yet, in the circumstance of metre, differing from it so widely, all these imperceptibly make up a complex feeling of delight, which is of the most important use in tempering the painful feeling which will always be found intermingled with powerful descriptions of the deeper passions. This effect is always produced in pathetic and impassioned poetry; while, in lighter compositions, the ease and gracefulness with which the Poet manages his numbers[1] are themselves confessedly a principal source of the gratification of the Reader. I might perhaps include all which it is *necessary* to say upon this subject by affirming what few persons will deny, that, of two descriptions, either of passions, manners, or characters, each of them equally well executed, the one in prose and the other in verse, the verse will be read a hundred times where the prose is read once. We see that Pope, by the power of verse alone, has contrived to render the plainest common sense interesting, and even frequently to invest it with the appearance of passion. ...

I know that nothing would have so effectually contributed to further the end which I have in view as to have shown of what kind the pleasure is, and how that pleasure is produced, which is confessedly produced by metrical composition essentially different from that which I have here endeavoured to recommend: for the Reader will say that he has been pleased by such composition; and what can I do more for him? The power of any art is limited; and he will suspect that, if I propose to furnish him with new friends, it is only upon condition of his abandoning his old friends. Besides, as I have said, the Reader is himself conscious of the pleasure which he has received from such composition, composition to which he has peculiarly attached the endearing name of Poetry; and all men feel an habitual gratitude, and something of an honorable bigotry for the objects which have long continued to please them: we not only wish to be pleased, but to be pleased in that particular way in which we have been accustomed to be pleased. There is a host of arguments in these feelings; and I should be the less able to combat them successfully, as I am willing to allow that, in order entirely to enjoy the Poetry which I am recommending, it would be necessary to give up much of what is ordinarily enjoyed. But, would my limits have permitted me to point out how this pleasure is produced, I might have removed many obstacles, and assisted my Reader in perceiving that the powers of language are not so limited as he may suppose; and that it is possible that poetry may give other enjoyments, of a purer, more lasting, and more exquisite nature. This part of my subject I have not altogether neglected; but it has been less my present aim to prove that the interest excited by some other kinds of poetry is less vivid, and less worthy of the nobler powers of the mind, than to offer reasons for presuming that, if the object which I have proposed to myself were adequately attained, a species of poetry would be produced which is genuine poetry; in its nature well adapted to interest mankind permanently, and likewise important in the multiplicity and quality of its moral relations.

From what has been said, and from a perusal of the Poems, the Reader will be able clearly to perceive the object which I have proposed to myself: he will determine how far I have attained this object; and, what is a much more important question, whether it be worth attaining; and upon the decision of these two questions will rest my claim to the approbation of the public.
—1800, 1802

---

[1] *numbers* Meter.

[*There was a Boy*]

There was a Boy, ye knew him well, ye Cliffs
  And Islands of Winander![1] many a time,
At evening, when the stars began
To move along the edges of the hills,
5 Rising or setting, would he stand alone,
Beneath the trees, or by the glimmering lake,
And there, with fingers interwoven, both hands
Press'd closely palm to palm and to his mouth
Uplifted, he, as through an instrument,
10 Blew mimic hootings to the silent owls
That they might answer him. And they would shout
Across the wat'ry vale and shout again
Responsive to his call, with quivering peals,
And long halloos, and screams, and echoes loud
15 Redoubled and redoubled, a wild scene
Of mirth and jocund din. And, when it chanced
That pauses of deep silence mock'd his skill,
Then, sometimes, in that silence, while he hung
Listening, a gentle shock of mild surprise
20 Has carried far into his heart the voice
Of mountain torrents, or the visible scene
Would enter unawares into his mind
With all its solemn imagery, its rocks,
Its woods, and that uncertain heaven, receiv'd
25 Into the bosom of the steady lake.
     Fair are the woods, and beauteous is the spot,
The vale where he was born: the Church-yard hangs
Upon a slope above the village school,[2]
And there along that bank when I have pass'd
30 At evening, I believe, that near his grave
A full half-hour together I have stood,
Mute—for he died when he was ten years old.
    —1800

[*Strange fits of passion I have known*][3]

Strange fits of passion I have known,
  And I will dare to tell,
But in the Lover's ear alone,
  What once to me befell.

5 When she I lov'd, was strong and gay
  And like a rose in June,
I to her cottage bent my way,
  Beneath the evening moon.

Upon the moon I fix'd my eye,
10 All over the wide lea;°   *meadow*
My horse trudg'd on, and we drew nigh
  Those paths so dear to me.

And now we reach'd the orchard plot,
  And, as we climb'd the hill,
15 Towards the roof of Lucy's cot°   *cottage*
  The moon descended still.

In one of those sweet dreams I slept,
  Kind Nature's gentlest boon!
And, all the while, my eyes I kept
20 On the descending moon.

My horse mov'd on; hoof after hoof
  He rais'd and never stopp'd;
When down behind the cottage roof
  At once the planet dropp'd.

25 What fond and wayward thoughts will slide
  Into a Lover's head—
"O mercy!" to myself I cried,
  "If Lucy should be dead!"[4]
    —1800

---

3 *Strange ... known*   This and the following two lyrics are part of a group of five lyrics now commonly called the "Lucy poems," all of which were composed during the winter of 1798–9, when Wordsworth and his sister were in Germany. The identity of Lucy is unknown (if she existed at all); she is not the Lucy of Wordsworth's poem *Lucy Gray* (1800). Some critics believe that in these poems Wordsworth attempts to express his feelings for his sister.

4 *If ... dead*   In an earlier manuscript version, another stanza followed: "I told her this: her laughter light / Is ringing in my ears;/ And when I think upon that night / My eyes are dim with tears."

---

1 *Winander* Windermere, the largest lake in England's Lake District.

2 *the village school* Hawkshead Grammar School in Esthwaite.

Song [*She dwelt among th'untrodden ways*]

She dwelt among th'untrodden ways
Beside the springs of Dove,[1]
A Maid whom there were none to praise
    And very few to love.

5   A violet by a mossy stone
        Half-hidden from the Eye!
    —Fair, as a star when only one
        Is shining in the sky.

    She *liv'd* unknown, and few could know
10   When Lucy ceas'd to be;
    But she is in her Grave, and Oh!
        The difference to me.
    —1800

[*A slumber did my spirit seal*][2]

A slumber did my spirit seal,
    I had no human fears:
She seem'd a thing that could not feel
    The touch of earthly years.

5   No motion has she now, no force
        She neither hears nor sees
    Roll'd round in earth's diurnal° course   *daily*
        With rocks and stones and trees!
    —1800

Lucy Gray[3]

Oft I had heard of Lucy Gray,
    And when I cross'd the Wild,
I chanc'd to see at break of day
The solitary child.

5   No Mate, no comrade Lucy knew;
    She dwelt on a wide Moor,
    The sweetest Thing that ever grew
    Beside a human door!

    You yet may spy the Fawn at play,
10   The Hare upon the Green;
    But the sweet face of Lucy Gray
    Will never more be seen.

    "To-night will be a stormy night,
    You to the Town must go,
15   And take a lantern, Child, to light
    Your Mother thro' the snow."

    "That, Father! will I gladly do;
    'Tis scarcely afternoon—
    The Minster°-clock has just struck two,   *church*
20   And yonder is the Moon!"

    At this the Father rais'd his hook,
    And snapp'd a faggot-band;[4]
    He plied his work, and Lucy took
    The lantern in her hand.

25   Not blither° is the mountain roe,   *more merry*
    With many a wanton° stroke   *frolicsome*

[1] *Dove*   Name of numerous rivers in England, one of which is in the Lake District.

[2] *A slumber … seal*   Of this poem, Coleridge wrote to a friend in April 1799: "Some months ago Wordsworth transmitted to me a most sublime epitaph. … Whether it had any reality, I cannot say. Most probably, in some gloomier moment he had fancied the moment in which his sister might die."

[3] *Lucy Gray*   Based on an account of a drowned girl told to Wordsworth by his sister. In his note, Wordsworth says that after the girl had become lost in a snowstorm, "her footsteps were traced by her parents to the middle of the lock of a canal, and no other vestige of her, backward or forward, could be traced. The body, however, was found in the canal. The way in which the incident was treated and the spiritualizing of the character might furnish hints for consulting the imaginative influences which I have endeavoured to throw over common life with Crabbe's matter of fact style of treating subjects of the same kind." (Wordsworth refers to the poet George Crabbe [1754–1832].)

[4] *faggot-band*   Cord for binding a bundle of firewood.

Her feet disperse the powd'ry snow,
That rises up like smoke.

The storm came on before its time,
30 She wander'd up and down,
And many a hill did Lucy climb:
But never reach'd the Town.

The wretched Parents all that night
Went shouting far and wide;
35 But there was neither sound nor sight
To serve them for a guide.

At day-break on a hill they stood
That overlook'd the Moor;
And thence they saw the Bridge of Wood,
40 A furlong¹ from their door.

And now they homeward turn'd, and cry'd
"In Heaven we all shall meet!"
When in the snow the Mother spied
The print of Lucy's feet.

45 Then downward from the steep hill's edge
They track'd the footmarks small;
And through the broken hawthorn-hedge,
And by the long stone-wall;

And then an open field they cross'd,
50 The marks were still the same;
They track'd them on, nor ever lost,
And to the Bridge they came.

They follow'd from the snowy bank
Those footmarks, one by one,
55 Into the middle of the plank,
And further there were none.

Yet some maintain that to this day
She is a living Child,
That you may see sweet Lucy Gray
60 Upon the lonesome Wild.

O'er rough and smooth she trips along,
And never looks behind;
And sings a solitary song
That whistles in the wind.
—1800

Nutting

It seems a day,
(I speak of one from many singled out)
One of those heavenly days which cannot die,
When forth I sallied from our cottage-door,
5 And with a wallet° o'er my shoulder slung,   knapsack
A nutting crook² in hand, I turn'd my steps
Towards the distant woods, a Figure quaint,
Trick'd out in proud disguise of Beggar's weeds°   garments
Put on for the occasion, by advice
10 And exhortation of my frugal Dame.³
Motley accoutrements! of power to smile
At thorns, and brakes,° and brambles, and,   thickets
    in truth,
More ragged than need was. Among the woods,
And o'er the pathless rocks, I forc'd my way
15 Until, at length, I came to one dear nook
Unvisited, where not a broken bough
Droop'd with its wither'd leaves, ungracious sign
Of devastation, but the hazels rose
Tall and erect, with milk-white clusters hung,
20 A virgin scene!—A little while I stood,
Breathing with such suppression of the heart
As joy delights in; and with wise restraint
Voluptuous, fearless of a rival, eyed
The banquet, or beneath the trees I sat
25 Among the flowers, and with the flowers I play'd;
A temper known to those, who, after long
And weary expectation, have been bless'd
With sudden happiness beyond all hope.
—Perhaps it was a bower beneath whose leaves
30 The violets of five seasons re-appear
And fade, unseen by any human eye,

¹ *furlong* Measurement equal to 220 yards, or one eighth of a mile.

² *nutting crook* Hooked instrument for gathering nuts.

³ *my frugal Dame* Ann Tyson, at whose house Wordsworth boarded during his school years.

Where fairy water-breaks[1] do murmur on
For ever, and I saw the sparkling foam,
And with my cheek on one of those green stones
35 That, fleec'd with moss, beneath the shady trees,
Lay round me scatter'd like a flock of sheep,
I heard the murmur and the murmuring sound,
In that sweet mood when pleasure loves to pay
Tribute to ease, and, of its joy secure
40 The heart luxuriates with indifferent things,
Wasting its kindliness on stocks° and stones,   *stumps*
And on the vacant air. Then up I rose,
And dragg'd to earth both branch and bough, with crash
And merciless ravage; and the shady nook
45 Of hazels, and the green and mossy bower
Deform'd and sullied, patiently gave up
Their quiet being: and unless I now
Confound my present feelings with the past,
Even then, when from the bower I turn'd away,
50 Exulting, rich beyond the wealth of kings
I felt a sense of pain when I beheld
The silent trees and the intruding sky.

Then, dearest Maiden![2] move along these shades
In gentleness of heart with gentle hand
55 Touch—for there is a Spirit in the woods.
—1800

Michael

Wordsworth said this pastoral poem is founded
on two real incidents, one of "the son of an
old couple having become dissolute, and run away
from his parents" and the other of "an old shepherd
having been seven years in building up a sheepfold
in a solitary valley." In combining these tales, he
said in a letter to Thomas Poole, "I have attempted
to give a picture of a man of strong mind and lively
sensibility, agitated by two of the most powerful
affections of the human heart—parental affection

and the love of property, landed property, including
the feelings of inheritance, home, and personal and
family independence." As in his poem *Brothers*,
Wordsworth writes "with a view to show that men
who do not wear fine clothes can feel deeply" and
attempts "to draw a picture of the domestic
affections, as I know they exist among a class of men
who are now almost confined to the north of
England. They are small independent proprietors of
land, here called 'states-men,' men of respectable
education, who daily labor on their own little
properties. The domestic affections will always be
strong amongst men who live in a country not
crowded with population; if these men are placed
above poverty. … Their little tract of land serves as
a kind of permanent rallying point for their
domestic feelings, as a tablet on which they are
written, which makes them objects of memory in a
thousand instances, when they would otherwise be
forgotten."

Michael, A Pastoral Poem

If from the public way you turn your steps
Up the tumultuous brook of Green-head Gill,[3]
You will suppose that with an upright path
Your feet must struggle; in such bold ascent
5   The pastoral Mountains front you, face to face.
But, courage! for beside that boisterous Brook
The mountains have all open'd out themselves,
And made a hidden valley of their own.
No habitation can be seen; but such
10 As journey thither find themselves alone
With a few sheep, with rocks and stones, and kites[4]
That overhead are sailing in the sky.

It is in truth an utter solitude,
Nor should I have made mention of this Dell
15 But for one object which you might pass by,
Might see and notice not. Beside the brook
There is a straggling heap of unhewn stones!
And to that place a story appertains,

---

[1] *water-breaks* Places where the water flow is broken by underlying rocks.

[2] *Maiden* In a longer manuscript draft of the poem, a passage originally intended to lead up to "Nutting" describes a maiden named Lucy ravaging a bower.

[3] *Gill* Steep, narrow valley with a stream running through it. Green-head Gill is near Wordsworth's cottage at Grasmere.

[4] *kites* Small falcon-like birds of prey.

Which, though it be ungarnish'd with events,
20 Is not unfit, I deem, for the fire-side,
Or for the summer shade. It was the first,
The earliest of those tales that spake to me
Of Shepherds, dwellers in the valleys, men
Whom I already lov'd, not verily
25 For their own sakes, but for the fields and hills
Where was their occupation and abode.
And hence this Tale, while I was yet a boy
Careless of books, yet having felt the power
Of Nature, by the gentle agency
30 Of natural objects led me on to feel
For passions that were not my own, and think
At random and imperfectly indeed
On man; the heart of man and human life.
Therefore, although it be a history
35 Homely and rude, I will relate the same
For the delight of a few natural hearts,
And with yet fonder feeling, for the sake
Of youthful Poets, who among these Hills
Will be my second self when I am gone.

40 Upon the Forest-side in Grasmere Vale
There dwelt a Shepherd, Michael was his name,
An old man, stout of heart, and strong of limb.
His bodily frame had been from youth to age
Of an unusual strength: his mind was keen
45 Intense and frugal, apt for all affairs,
And in his Shepherd's calling he was prompt
And watchful more than ordinary men.
Hence he had learn'd the meaning of all winds,
Of blasts of every tone, and often-times
50 When others heeded not, He heard the South[1]
Make subterraneous music, like the noise
Of Bagpipers on distant Highland hills;
The Shepherd, at such warning, of his flock
Bethought him, and he to himself would say
55 The winds are now devising work for me!
And truly at all times the storm, that drives
The Traveller to a shelter, summon'd him
Up to the mountains: he had been alone
Amid the heart of many thousand mists
60 That came to him and left him on the heights.
So liv'd he till his eightieth year was pass'd.

And grossly that man errs, who should suppose
That the green Valleys, and the Streams and Rocks
Were things indifferent to the Shepherd's thoughts.
65 Fields, where with cheerful spirits he had breath'd
The common air; the hills, which he so oft
Had climb'd with vigorous steps; which had impress'd
So many incidents upon his mind
Of hardship, skill or courage, joy or fear;
70 Which like a book preserv'd the memory
Of the dumb animals, whom he had sav'd,
Had fed or shelter'd, linking to such acts,
So grateful in themselves, the certainty
Of honorable gains; these fields, these hills
75 Which were his living Being, even more
Than his own Blood——what could they less? had laid
Strong hold on his affections, were to him
A pleasurable feeling of blind love,
The pleasure which there is in life itself.

80 He had not passed his days in singleness.
He had a Wife, a comely Matron, old
Though younger than himself full twenty years.
She was a woman of a stirring life
Whose heart was in her house: two wheels she had
85 Of antique form, this large for spinning wool,
That small for flax, and if one wheel had rest,
It was because the other was at work.
The Pair had but one Inmate in their house,
An only Child, who had been born to them
90 When Michael telling° o'er his years began   counting
To deem that he was old, in Shepherd's phrase,
With one foot in the grave. This only son,
With two brave sheep dogs tried in many a storm,
The one of an inestimable worth,
95 Made all their Household. I may truly say,
That they were as a proverb in the vale
For endless industry. When day was gone,
And from their occupations out of doors
The Son and Father were come home, even then
100 Their labour did not cease, unless when all
Turn'd to their cleanly supper-board,[2] and there
Each with a mess of pottage[3] and skimm'd milk,
Sat round their basket pil'd with oaten cakes,

---

[1] *South* South wind.

[2] *supper-board* Table.

[3] *pottage* Stew of vegetables, and sometimes meat, boiled in water.

And their plain home-made cheese. Yet when their meal
105 Was ended, LUKE (for so the Son was nam'd)
And his old Father, both betook themselves
To such convenient work, as might employ
Their hands by the fire-side; perhaps to card[1]
Wool for the House-wife's spindle, or repair
110 Some injury done to sickle, flail,[2] or scythe,
Or other implement of house or field.
Down from the ceiling by the chimney's edge,
Which in our ancient uncouth country style
Did with a huge projection overbrow°   *overhang*
115 Large space beneath, as duly as the light
Of day grew dim, the House-wife hung a lamp;
An aged utensil, which had perform'd
Service beyond all others of its kind.
Early at evening did it burn and late,
120 Surviving Comrade of uncounted Hours
Which going by from year to year had found
And left the Couple neither gay perhaps
Nor cheerful, yet with objects and with hopes
Living a life of eager industry.
125 And now, when LUKE was in his eighteenth year,
There by the light of this old lamp they sat,
Father and Son, while late into the night
The House-wife plied her own peculiar work,
Making the cottage thro' the silent hours
130 Murmur as with the sound of summer flies.
Not with a waste of words, but for the sake
Of pleasure, which I know that I shall give
To many living now, I of this Lamp
Speak thus minutely: for there are no few
135 Whose memories will bear witness to my tale.
The Light was famous in its neighbourhood,
And was a public Symbol of the life,
The thrifty Pair had liv'd. For, as it chanc'd,
Their Cottage on a plot of rising ground
140 Stood single, with large prospect North and South,
High into Easedale, up to Dunmal-Raise,
And Westward to the village near the Lake.
And from this constant light so regular
And so far seen, the House itself by all
145 Who dwelt within the limits of the vale,
Both old and young, was nam'd The Evening Star.

Thus living on through such a length of years,
The Shepherd, if he lov'd himself, must needs
Have lov'd his Help-mate; but to Michael's heart
150 This Son of his old age was yet more dear—
Effect which might perhaps have been produc'd
By that instinctive tenderness, the same
Blind Spirit, which is in the blood of all,
Or that a child, more than all other gifts,
155 Brings hope with it, and forward-looking thoughts,
And stirrings of inquietude, when they
By tendency of nature needs must fail.
From such, and other causes, to the thoughts
Of the old Man his only Son was now
160 The dearest object that he knew on earth.
Exceeding was the love he bare to him,
His Heart and his Heart's joy! For oftentimes
Old Michael, while he was a babe in arms,
Had done him female service, not alone
165 For dalliance and delight, as is the use
Of Fathers, but with patient mind enforc'd
To acts of tenderness; and he had rock'd
His cradle with a woman's gentle hand.

And in a later time, ere yet the Boy
170 Had put on Boy's attire, did Michael love,
Albeit of a stern unbending mind,
To have the young one in his sight, when he
Had work by his own door, or when he sat
With sheep before him on his Shepherd's stool,
175 Beneath that large old Oak, which near their door
Stood, and from its enormous breadth of shade
Chosen for the Shearer's covert from the sun,
Thence in our rustic dialect was call'd
The CLIPPING° TREE, a name which yet it bears.   *shearing*
180 There, while they two were sitting in the shade,
With others round them, earnest all and blithe,
Would Michael exercise his heart with looks
Of fond correction and reproof bestow'd
Upon the child, if he disturb'd the sheep
185 By catching at their legs, or with his shouts
Scar'd them, while they lay still beneath the shears.
And when by Heaven's good grace the Boy grew up
A healthy Lad, and carried in his cheek
Two steady roses that were five years old,

---

[1] *card* Comb out impurities.
[2] *flail* Tool for threshing corn.

190 Then Michael from a winter coppice[1] cut
With his own hand a sapling, which he hoop'd
With iron, making it throughout in all
Due requisites a perfect Shepherd's Staff,
And gave it to the Boy; wherewith equipp'd
195 He as a Watchman oftentimes was plac'd
At gate or gap, to stem or turn the flock,
And to his office prematurely call'd
There stood the urchin, as you will divine,
Something between a hindrance and a help,
200 And for this cause not always, I believe,
Receiving from his Father hire of praise.
Though nought was left undone which staff, or voice,
Or looks, or threatening gestures, could perform.
But soon as Luke, full ten years old, could stand
205 Against the mountain blasts, and to the heights,
Not fearing toil, nor length of weary ways,
He with his Father daily went, and they
Were as companions, why should I relate
That objects which the Shepherd loved before
210 Were dearer now? that from the Boy there came
Feelings and emanations, things which were
Light to the sun and music to the wind;
And that the Old Man's heart seemed born again?
Thus in his Father's sight the Boy grew up:
215 And now when he had reached his eighteenth year,
He was his comfort and his daily hope.

While this good household thus were living on
From day to day, to Michael's ear there came
Distressful tidings. Long before the time
220 Of which I speak, the Shepherd had been bound
In surety for his Brother's Son, a man
Of an industrious life, and ample means,
But unforeseen misfortunes suddenly
Had press'd upon him, and old Michael now
225 Was summon'd to discharge the forfeiture,
A grievous penalty, but little less
Than half his substance. This un-look'd for claim
At the first hearing, for a moment took
More hope out of his life than he supposed
230 That any old man ever could have lost.
As soon as he had gather'd so much strength
That he could look his trouble in the face,

It seem'd that his sole refuge was to sell
A portion of his patrimonial fields.
235 Such was his first resolve; he thought again,
And his heart fail'd him. "Isabel," said he,
Two evenings after he had heard the news,
"I have been toiling more than seventy years,
And in the open sunshine of God's love
240 Have we all liv'd, yet if these fields of ours
Should pass into a Stranger's hand, I think
That I could not lie quiet in my grave.
Our lot is a hard lot; the Sun itself
Has scarcely been more diligent than I,
245 And I have liv'd to be a fool at last
To my own family. An evil Man
That was, and made an evil choice, if he
Were false to us; and if he were not false,
There are ten thousand to whom loss like this
250 Had been no sorrow. I forgive him—but
'Twere better to be dumb than to talk thus.
When I began, my purpose was to speak
Of remedies and of a cheerful hope.
Our Luke shall leave us, Isabel; the land
255 Shall not go from us, and it shall be free,[2]
He shall possess it, free as is the wind
That passes over it. We have, thou knowest,
Another Kinsman, he will be our friend
In this distress. He is a prosperous man,
260 Thriving in trade, and Luke to him shall go,
And with his Kinsman's help and his own thrift,
He quickly will repair this loss, and then
May come again to us. If here he stay,
What can be done? Where every one is poor
265 What can be gain'd?" At this, the old man paus'd,
And Isabel sat silent, for her mind
Was busy, looking back into past times.
There's Richard Bateman, thought she to herself,[3]
He was a parish-boy[4]—at the church-door
270 They made a gathering for him, shillings, pence,
And halfpennies, wherewith the Neighbours bought
A Basket, which they fill'd with Pedlar's wares,

---

1 *coppice* Thicket of small trees.

2 *free* I.e., not mortgaged.

3 [Wordsworth's note] The story alluded to here is well known in the country. The chapel is called Ings Chapel and is on the road leading from Kendal to Ambleside.

4 *parish-boy* Youth cared for and supported by the parish.

And with this Basket on his arm, the Lad
Went up to London, found a Master there,
275 Who out of many chose the trusty Boy
To go and overlook his merchandise
Beyond the seas, where he grew wond'rous rich,
And left estates and monies to the poor,
And at his birth-place built a Chapel, floor'd
280 With Marble, which he sent from foreign lands.
These thoughts, and many others of like sort,
Pass'd quickly thro' the mind of Isabel,
And her face brighten'd. The Old Man was glad,
And thus resum'd. "Well! Isabel, this scheme
285 These two days has been meat and drink to me.
Far more than we have lost is left us yet.
—We have enough—I wish indeed that I
Were younger, but this hope is a good hope.
—Make ready Luke's best garments, of the best
290 Buy for him more, and let us send him forth
To-morrow, or the next day, or to-night:
—If he could go, the Boy should go to-night."

Here Michael ceas'd, and to the fields went forth
With a light heart. The House-wife for five days
295 Was restless morn and night, and all day long
Wrought on with her best fingers to prepare
Things needful for the journey of her Son.
But Isabel was glad when Sunday came
To stop her in her work; for, when she lay
300 By Michael's side, she for the last two nights
Heard him, how he was troubled in his sleep:
And when they rose at morning she could see
That all his hopes were gone. That day at noon
She said to Luke, while they two by themselves
305 Were sitting at the door, "Thou must not go,
We have no other Child but thee to lose,
None to remember—do not go away,
For if thou leave thy Father he will die."
The Lad made answer with a jocund voice,
310 And Isabel, when she had told her fears,
Recover'd heart. That evening her best fare
Did she bring forth, and all together sat
Like happy people round a Christmas fire.
Next morning Isabel resum'd her work,
315 And all the ensuing week the house appear'd
As cheerful as a grove in Spring: at length

The expected letter from their Kinsman came,
With kind assurances that he would do
His utmost for the welfare of the Boy,
320 To which requests were added that forthwith
He might be sent to him. Ten times or more
The letter was read over; Isabel
Went forth to shew it to the neighbours round:
Nor was there at that time on English land
325 A prouder heart than Luke's. When Isabel
Had to her house return'd, the Old Man said,
"He shall depart to-morrow." To this word
The House-wife answered, talking much of things
Which, if at such short notice he should go,
330 Would surely be forgotten. But at length
She gave consent, and Michael was at ease.

Near the tumultuous brook of Green-head Gill,
In that deep Valley, Michael had design'd
To build a Sheep-fold,[1] and, before he heard
335 The tidings of his melancholy loss,
For this same purpose he had gathered up
A heap of stones, which close to the brook side
Lay thrown together, ready for the work.
With Luke that evening thitherward he walk'd;
340 And soon as they had reach'd the place he stopp'd,
And thus the Old Man spake to him. "My Son,
To-morrow thou wilt leave me; with full heart
I look upon thee, for thou art the same
That wert a promise to me ere thy birth,
345 And all thy life hast been my daily joy.
I will relate to thee some little part
Of our two histories; 'twill do thee good
When thou art from me, even if I should speak
Of things thou canst not know of.———After thou
350 First cam'st into the world, as it befalls
To new-born infants, thou didst sleep away
Two days, and blessings from thy Father's tongue
Then fell upon thee. Day by day pass'd on,
And still I lov'd thee with encreasing love.
355 Never to living ear came sweeter sounds
Than when I heard thee by our own fire-side
First uttering without words a natural tune,
When thou, a feeding babe, didst in thy joy
Sing at thy Mother's breast. Month follow'd month,

---

[1] *Sheep-fold* Stone-walled pen for sheep.

360 And in the open fields my life was pass'd
And in the mountains, else I think that thou
Hadst been brought up upon thy father's knees.
—But we were playmates, Luke; among these hills,
As well thou know'st, in us the old and young
365 Have play'd together, nor with me didst thou
Lack any pleasure which a boy can know."

Luke had a manly heart; but at these words
He sobb'd aloud; the Old Man grasp'd his hand,
And said, "Nay, do not take it so—I see
370 That these are things of which I need not speak.
—Even to the utmost I have been to thee
A kind and a good Father: and herein
I but repay a gift which I myself
Receiv'd at others hands, for, though now old
375 Beyond the common life of man, I still
Remember them who lov'd me in my youth.
Both of them sleep together: here they liv'd
As all their Forefathers had done, and when
At length their time was come, they were not loth
380 To give their bodies to the family mold.
I wish'd that thou should'st live the life they liv'd.
But 'tis a long time to look back, my Son,
And see so little gain from sixty years.
These fields were burthen'd° when they   *mortgaged*
     came to me;
385 'Till I was forty years of age, not more
Than half of my inheritance was mine.
I toil'd and toil'd; God bless'd me in my work,
And 'till these three weeks past the land was free.
—It looks as if it never could endure
390 Another Master. Heaven forgive me, Luke,
If I judge ill for thee, but it seems good
That thou should'st go." At this the Old Man paus'd,
Then, pointing to the Stones near which they stood,
Thus, after a short silence, he resum'd:
395 "This was a work for us, and now, my Son,
It is a work for me. But, lay one Stone—
Here, lay it for me, Luke, with thine own hands.
Nay, Boy, be of good hope: we both may live
To see a better day. At eighty-four
400 I still am strong and stout; do thou thy part,
I will do mine. I will begin again
With many tasks that were resign'd to thee;

Up to the heights, and in among the storms,
Will I without thee go again, and do
405 All works which I was wont to do alone,
Before I knew thy face. Heaven bless thee, Boy!
Thy heart these two weeks has been beating fast
With many hopes—it should be so—yes—yes—
I knew that thou could'st never have a wish
410 To leave me, Luke, thou hast been bound to me
Only by links of love, when thou art gone
What will be left to us! But, I forget
My purposes. Lay now the corner-stone,
As I requested, and hereafter, Luke,
415 When thou art gone away, should evil men
Be thy companions, let this Sheep-fold be
Thy anchor and thy shield; amid all fear
And all temptation, let it be to thee
An emblem of the life thy Fathers liv'd,
420 Who, being innocent, did for that cause
Bestir them in good deeds. Now, fare thee well—
When thou return'st, thou in this place wilt see
A work which is not here, a covenant
'Twill be between us——but whatever fate
425 Befall thee, I shall love thee to the last,
And bear thy memory with me to the grave."

The Shepherd ended here; and Luke stoop'd down,
And as his Father had requested, laid
The first stone of the Sheep-fold; at the sight
430 The Old Man's grief broke from him, to his heart
He press'd his Son, he kissed him and wept;
And to the House together they return'd.
Next morning, as had been resolv'd, the Boy
Began his journey, and when he had reach'd
435 The public Way, he put on a bold face;
And all the Neighbours as he pass'd their doors
Came forth, with wishes and with farewell pray'rs,
That follow'd him 'till he was out of sight.
A good report did from their Kinsman come,
440 Of Luke and his well-doing; and the Boy
Wrote loving letters, full of wond'rous news,
Which, as the House-wife phrased it, were throughout
The prettiest letters that were ever seen.
Both parents read them with rejoicing hearts.
445 So, many months pass'd on: and once again
The Shepherd went about his daily work

With confident and cheerful thoughts; and now
Sometimes when he could find a leisure hour
He to that valley took his way, and there
450 Wrought at the Sheep-fold. Meantime Luke began
To slacken in his duty, and at length
He in the dissolute city gave himself
To evil courses: ignominy and shame
Fell on him, so that he was driven at last
455 To seek a hiding-place beyond the seas.

There is a comfort in the strength of love;
'Twill make a thing endurable, which else
Would break the heart: Old Michael found it so.
I have convers'd with more than one who well
460 Remember the Old Man, and what he was
Years after he had heard this heavy news.
His bodily frame had been from youth to age
Of an unusual strength. Among the rocks
He went, and still look'd up upon the sun,
465 And listen'd to the wind; and as before
Perform'd all kinds of labour for his Sheep,
And for the land his small inheritance.
And to that hollow Dell from time to time
Did he repair, to build the Fold of which
470 His flock had need. 'Tis not forgotten yet
The pity which was then in every heart
For the Old Man—and 'tis believ'd by all
That many and many a day he thither went,
And never lifted up a single stone.

475 There, by the Sheep-fold, sometimes was he seen
Sitting alone, with that his faithful Dog,
Then old, beside him, lying at his feet.
The length of full seven years from time to time
He at the building of this Sheep-fold wrought,
480 And left the work unfinished when he died.

Three years, or little more, did Isabel,
Survive her Husband: at her death the estate
Was sold, and went into a Stranger's hand.
The Cottage which was nam'd The Evening Star
485 Is gone, the ploughshare has been through the ground
On which it stood; great changes have been wrought
In all the neighbourhood, yet the Oak is left
That grew beside their Door; and the remains

Of the unfinished Sheep-fold may be seen
490 Beside the boisterous brook of Green-head Gill.
—1800

[*I Griev'd for Buonaparté*][1]

I griev'd for Buonaparté, with a vain
  And an unthinking grief! the vital blood
Of that Man's mind what can it be? What food
Fed his first hopes? What knowledge could *He* gain?
5 'Tis not in battles that from youth we train
The Governor who must be wise and good,
And temper with the sternness of the brain
Thoughts motherly, and meek as womanhood.
Wisdom doth live with children round her knees:
10 Books, leisure, perfect freedom, and the talk
Man holds with week-day man in the hourly walk
Of the mind's business: these are the degrees
By which true Sway doth mount; this is the stalk
True Power doth grow on; and her rights are these.
—1802

Ode to Duty

Stern Daughter of the Voice of God![2]
  O Duty! if that name thou love
Who art a Light to guide, a Rod
To check the erring, and reprove;
5 Thou, who art victory and law
When empty terrors overawe;
From vain temptations dost set free;
From strife and from despair; a glorious ministry.

There are who ask not if thine eye
10 Be on them; who, in love and truth,
Where no misgiving is, rely
Upon the genial° sense° of youth: *natural / vitality*

---

1 *I … Buonaparté* According to Dorothy Wordsworth, this sonnet was composed in 1802, the year that Napoleon Buonaparte declared himself First Consul of France for life.

2 *Stern … God* Cf. Milton, *Paradise Lost* 9.652–54: "God so commanded, and left that Command / Sole Daughter of His voice; the rest, we live / Law to ourselves, our Reason is our Law."

Glad Hearts! without reproach or blot;
Who do thy work, and know it not:
15   May joy be theirs while life shall last!
And Thou, if they should totter, teach them to stand
      fast!

Serene will be our days and bright,
And happy will our nature be,
When love is an unerring light,
20   And joy its own security.
And bless'd are they who in the main
This faith, even now, do entertain:
Live in the spirit of this creed;
Yet find that other strength, according to their need.

25   I, loving freedom, and untried;
No sport of every random gust,
Yet being to myself a guide,
Too blindly have reposed my trust:
Resolved that nothing e'er should press
30   Upon my present happiness,
I shoved unwelcome tasks away;
But thee I now would serve more strictly, if I may.

Through no disturbance of my soul,
Or strong compunction in me wrought,
35   I supplicate for thy control;
But in the quietness of thought:
Me this uncharter'd freedom tires;
I feel the weight of chance desires:
My hopes no more must change their name,
40   I long for a repose that ever is the same.

Yet not the less would I throughout
Still act according to the voice
Of my own wish; and feel past doubt
That my submissiveness was choice:
45   Not seeking in the school of pride
For "precepts over dignified,"
Denial and restraint I prize
No farther than they breed a second Will more wise.

Stern Lawgiver! yet thou dost wear
50   The Godhead's most benignant grace;
Nor know we anything so fair

As is the smile upon thy face:
Flowers laugh before thee on their beds;
And Fragrance in thy footing treads;
55   Thou dost preserve the Stars from wrong;
And the most ancient Heavens, through Thee are fresh
      and strong.

To humbler functions, awful Power!
I call thee: I myself commend
Unto thy guidance from this hour;
60   Oh! let my weakness have an end!
Give unto me, made lowly wise,
The spirit of self-sacrifice;
The confidence of reason give;
And in the light of truth thy Bondman let me live!
—1807

Resolution and Independence

There was a roaring in the wind all night;
      The rain came heavily and fell in floods;
But now the sun is rising calm and bright;
The birds are singing in the distant woods;
5   Over his own sweet voice the Stock-dove°   *wild pigeon*
      broods;
The Jay makes answer as the Magpie chatters;
And all the air is fill'd with pleasant noise of waters.

All things that love the sun are out of doors;
The sky rejoices in the morning's birth;
10   The grass is bright with rain-drops; on the moors
The Hare is running races in her mirth;
And with her feet she from the plashy[1] earth
Raises a mist; which, glittering in the sun,
Runs with her all the way, wherever she doth run.

15   I was a Traveller then upon the moor;
I saw the Hare that rac'd about with joy;
I heard the woods, and distant waters, roar;
Or heard them not, as happy as a Boy:
The pleasant season did my heart employ:
20   My old remembrances went from me wholly;
And all the ways of men, so vain and melancholy.

---
[1] *plashy* Having many puddles or pools of water; wet.

But, as it sometimes chanceth, from the might
Of joy in minds that can no farther go,
As high as we have mounted in delight
25 In our dejection do we sink as low,
To me that morning did it happen so;
And fears, and fancies, thick upon me came;
Dim sadness, and blind thoughts I knew not nor could
  name.

I heard the Sky-lark singing in the sky;
30 And I bethought me of the playful Hare:
Even such a happy Child of earth am I;
Even as these blissful Creatures do I fare;
Far from the world I walk, and from all care;
But there may come another day to me,
35 Solitude, pain of heart, distress, and poverty.

My whole life I have liv'd in pleasant thought,
As if life's business were a summer mood;
As if all needful things would come unsought
To genial faith, still rich in genial good;
40 But how can He expect that others should
Build for him, sow for him, and at his call
Love him, who for himself will take no heed at all?

I thought of Chatterton,[1] the marvellous Boy,
The sleepless Soul that perish'd in its pride;
45 Of Him who walk'd in glory and in joy
Behind his plough, upon the mountain-side:[2]
By our own spirits are we deified;
We Poets in our youth begin in gladness;
But thereof comes in the end despondency and
  madness.

50 Now, whether it were by peculiar grace,
A leading from above, a something given,
Yet it befel, that, in this lonely place,
When up and down my fancy thus was driven,
And I with these untoward thoughts had striven,

I saw a Man before me unawares:
55 The oldest man he seem'd that ever wore grey hairs.

My course I stopped as soon as I espied
The Old Man in that naked wilderness:
Close by a Pond, upon the further side,
60 He stood alone: a minute's space I guess
I watch'd him, he continuing motionless:
To the Pool's further margin then I drew;
He being all the while before me full in view.

As a huge Stone is sometimes seen to lie
65 Couch'd on the bald top of an eminence;
Wonder to all who do the same espy
By what means it could thither come, and whence;
So that it seems a thing endued with sense:
Like a Sea-beast crawl'd forth, which on a shelf
70 Of rock or sand reposeth, there to sun itself.

Such seem'd this Man, not all alive nor dead,
Nor all asleep; in his extreme old age:
His body was bent double, feet and head
Coming together in their pilgrimage;
75 As if some dire constraint of pain, or rage
Of sickness felt by him in times long past,
A more than human weight upon his frame had cast.

Himself he propp'd, his body, limbs, and face,
Upon a long grey Staff of shaven wood:
80 And, still as I drew near with gentle pace,
Beside the little pond or moorish flood
Motionless as a Cloud the Old Man stood;
That heareth not the loud winds when they call;
And moveth altogether, if it move at all.

85 At length, himself unsettling, he the Pond
Stirred with his Staff, and fixedly did look
Upon the muddy water, which he conn'd,°   studied
As if he had been reading in a book:
And now such freedom as I could I took;
90 And, drawing to his side, to him did say,
"This morning gives us promise of a glorious day."

A gentle answer did the Old Man make,
In courteous speech which forth he slowly drew:

---

1 *Chatterton* Poet Thomas Chatterton (1752–70), who, after
failing to make a living as a poet in London, poisoned himself at the
age of seventeen.

2 *Him who … mountain-side* Scottish poet Robert Burns (1759–
96), known as "the Ploughman Poet" because of his farming
background.

And him with further words I thus bespake,
95   "What kind of work is that which you pursue?
This is a lonesome place for one like you."
He answer'd me with pleasure and surprise;
And there was, while he spake, a fire about his eyes.

His words came feebly, from a feeble chest,
100   Yet each in solemn order follow'd each,
With something of a lofty utterance drest;
Choice word, and measured phrase; above the reach
Of ordinary men; a stately speech!
Such as grave Livers[1] do in Scotland use,
105   Religious men, who give to God and Man their dues.

He told me that he to this pond had come
To gather Leeches,[2] being old and poor:
Employment hazardous and wearisome!
And he had many hardships to endure:
110   From Pond to Pond he roam'd, from moor to moor,
Housing, with God's good help, by choice or chance:
And in this way he gain'd an honest maintenance.

The old Man still stood talking by my side;
But now his voice to me was like a stream
115   Scarce heard; nor word from word could I divide;
And the whole Body of the man did seem
Like one whom I had met with in a dream;
Or like a Man from some far region sent;
To give me human strength, and strong admonishment.

120   My former thoughts return'd: the fear that kills;
The hope that is unwilling to be fed;
Cold, pain, and labour, and all fleshly ills;
And mighty Poets in their misery dead.
And now, not knowing what the Old Man had said,
125   My question eagerly did I renew,
"How is it that you live, and what is it you do?"

He with a smile did then his words repeat;
And said that, gathering Leeches, far and wide

He travelled; stirring thus about his feet
130   The waters of the Ponds where they abide.
"Once I could meet with them on every side;
But they have dwindled long by slow decay;
Yet still I persevere, and find them where I may."

While he was talking thus, the lonely place,
135   The Old Man's shape, and speech, all troubled me:
In my mind's eye I seem'd to see him pace
About the weary moors continually,
Wandering about alone and silently.
While I these thoughts within myself pursued,
140   He, having made a pause, the same discourse renewed.

And soon with this he other matter blended,
Cheerfully uttered, with demeanour kind,
But stately in the main; and, when he ended,
I could have laugh'd myself to scorn, to find
145   In that decrepit Man so firm a mind.
"God," said I, "be my help and stay° secure;   *support*
I'll think of the Leech-gatherer on the lonely moor."
    —1807

Composed upon Westminster Bridge
Sept. 3, 1803[3]

Earth has not any thing to show more fair:
  Dull would he be of soul who could pass by
A sight so touching in its majesty:
This City now doth like a garment wear
5   This beauty of the morning; silent, bare,
Ships, towers, domes, theatres, and temples lie
Open unto the fields, and to the sky;
All bright and glittering in the smokeless air.
Never did sun more beautifully steep
10   In his first splendor valley, rock, or hill;
Ne'er saw I, never felt, a calm so deep!

---

[1] *grave Livers* I.e., those who live seriously.

[2] *Leeches* Used at this time by doctors for drawing the blood of patients. A leech gatherer would find leeches by standing in shallow water and allowing them to attach themselves to his legs.

[3] *Composed ... 1803* Wordsworth misremembered the date of composition, which was actually (according to Dorothy Wordsworth's *Grasmere Journals*) July 1802, when Wordsworth set out for a brief trip to France, where his former lover Annette Vallon lived with their daughter, Caroline.

The river glideth at his own sweet will:
Dear God! the very houses seem asleep;
And all that mighty heart is lying still!
—1807

[*The world is too much with us*]

The world is too much with us; late and soon,
 Getting and spending, we lay waste our powers:
Little we see in nature that is ours;
We have given our hearts away, a sordid boon!
5 The Sea that bares her bosom to the moon;
The Winds that will be howling at all hours
And are up-gathered now like sleeping flowers;
For this, for every thing, we are out of tune;
It moves us not. Great God! I'd rather be
10 A Pagan suckled in a creed outworn;
So might I, standing on this pleasant lea,
Have glimpses that would make me less forlorn;
Have sight of Proteus coming from the sea;
Or hear old Triton blow his wreathed horn.[1]
—1807

[*It is a beauteous Evening*]

It is a beauteous Evening, calm and free;
 The holy time is quiet as a Nun
Breathless with adoration; the broad sun
Is sinking down in its tranquillity;
5 The gentleness of heaven is on the Sea:
Listen! the mighty Being is awake
And doth with his eternal motion make
A sound like thunder—everlastingly.
Dear Child! dear Girl![2] that walkest with me here,
10 If thou appear'st untouch'd by solemn thought,
Thy nature is not therefore less divine:
Thou liest in Abraham's bosom[3] all the year;

And worshipp'st at the Temple's inner shrine,
God being with thee when we know it not.
—1807

London
1802[4]

Milton! thou should'st be living at this hour:
 England hath need of thee: she is a fen
Of stagnant waters: altar, sword, and pen,
Fireside, the heroic wealth of hall and bower,
5 Have forfeited their ancient English dower
Of inward happiness. We are selfish men;
Oh! raise us up, return to us again;
And give us manners, virtue, freedom, power.
Thy soul was like a Star and dwelt apart:
10 Thou hadst a voice whose sound was like the sea;
Pure as the naked heavens, majestic, free,
So didst thou travel on life's common way,
In cheerful godliness; and yet thy heart
The lowliest duties on itself did lay.
—1807

The Solitary Reaper[5]

Behold her, single in the field,
 Yon solitary Highland Lass!
Reaping and singing by herself;
Stop here, or gently pass!
5 Alone she cuts, and binds the grain,
And sings a melancholy strain;
O listen! for the Vale profound
Is overflowing with the sound.

---

[1] *Proteus* Shape-changing sea god; *Triton* Sea god with the head and torso of a man and the tail of a fish. He was usually depicted blowing on a conch shell.

[2] *Dear … Girl* Wordsworth's daughter Caroline.

[3] *Abraham's bosom* The resting place for souls bound for heaven. See Luke 16.22: "And it came to pass, that the beggar died, and was carried by the angels into Abraham's bosom."

[4] *London, 1802* Written immediately after Wordsworth's return from France, when he was struck by the differences between his native country and France after the Revolution. Milton died in 1674.

[5] *The Solitary Reaper* Suggested by the following passage in Thomas Wilkinson's *Tours to the British Mountains* (1824): "Passed a female who was reaping alone: she sung in Erse [a Gaelic language] as she bended over her sickle; the sweetest human voice I ever heard: her strains were tenderly melancholy, and felt delicious, long after they were heard no more."

No Nightingale did ever chaunt
10   So sweetly to reposing bands
Of Travellers in some shady haunt,
Among Arabian Sands:
No sweeter voice was ever heard
In spring-time from the Cuckoo-bird,
15   Breaking the silence of the seas
Among the farthest Hebrides.

Will no one tell me what she sings?
Perhaps the plaintive numbers° flow   verses
For old, unhappy, far-off things,
20   And battles long ago:
Or is it some more humble lay,
Familiar matter of today?
Some natural sorrow, loss, or pain,
That has been, and may be again!

25   Whate'er the theme, the Maiden sang
As if her song could have no ending;
I saw her singing at her work,

And o'er the sickle bending;
I listen'd till I had my fill:
30   And, as I mounted up the hill,
The music in my heart I bore,
Long after it was heard no more.
—1807

[*My heart leaps up*]

My heart leaps up when I behold
A Rainbow in the sky:
So was it when my life began;
So is it now I am a Man;
5   So be it when I shall grow old,
        Or let me die!
The Child is Father of the Man;
And I could wish my days to be
Bound each to each by natural piety.
—1804

In Context

"I wandered lonely as a cloud":
Stages in the Life of a Poem

The earliest version of this poem was composed in 1804 and first published in 1807. It was evidently inspired by an entry in Dorothy Wordsworth's journal from two years earlier, describing a scene at Glencoyne Bay, Ullswater, seen by Dorothy and William on their way back to Grasmere after a long ramble. Appearing below are the scene as described by Dorothy in the journal; William's first version of the poem; a facsimile copy of the page in the copy of *Poems in Two Volumes* in which William began to compose an additional stanza to the poem; a transcription of his handwritten jottings; and William's revised version, with the added stanza and some other changes (which was not published until 1815).

from Dorothy Wordsworth, *Grasmere Journal* (Thursday, 15 April 1802)

When we were in the woods beyond Gowbarrow park we saw a few daffodils close to the water side. We fancied that the lake had floated the seeds ashore and that the little colony had so sprung up. But as we went along there were more and yet more and at last under the boughs of the trees, we saw that there was a long belt of them along the shore, about the breadth of a country turnpike road. I never saw daffodils so beautiful they grew among the mossy stones about and about them, some rested their heads upon these stones as on a pillow for weariness and the rest tossed and reeled and danced and seemed as if they verily laughed with the wind that blew upon them over the lake, they looked so gay ever glancing ever changing. This wind blew directly over the lake to them. There was here and there a little knot and a few stragglers a few yards higher up but they were so few as not to disturb the simplicity and unity and life of that one busy highway.

[*I wandered lonely as a Cloud*]

I wandered lonely as a Cloud
That floats on high o'er Vales and Hills,
When all at once I saw a crowd
A host of dancing Daffodils;
Along the Lake, beneath the trees,
Ten thousand dancing in the breeze.

The waves beside them danced, but they
Outdid the sparkling waves in glee—
A Poet could not but be gay
In such a laughing company:
I gazed—and gaz'd—but little thought
What wealth the show to me had brought:

For oft when on my couch I lie
In vacant or in pensive mood,
They flash upon that inward eye
Which is the bliss of solitude,
And then my heart with pleasure fills,
And dances with the Daffodils.

—1807

I wandered lonely as a cloud[1]

                       l

A host of golden Daffodi ls

Beside

~~*Along*~~ *the Lake beneath the trees*

                        vernal

All dancing ~~*dancing*~~ *in the breeze*

 Continuous

             ed

~~*Close crowd* ~~ *ing. [?like]*

~~*As numerous*~~ *as the stars that shine*

 and twinkle

               on

At midnight, in the milky way

                a

They stretch'd in never ending line

Along the margin of a bay

Ten thousand saw I at a glance

Tossing their heads in spritely dance

[*I wandered lonely as a Cloud*]

I wandered lonely as a cloud
  That floats on high o'er vales and hills,
When all at once I saw a crowd,
A host, of golden daffodils;
5 Beside the lake, beneath the trees,
Fluttering and dancing in the breeze.

Continuous as the stars that shine
And twinkle on the milky way,
They stretched in never-ending line
10 Along the margin of a bay:
Ten thousand saw I at a glance,
Tossing their heads in sprightly dance.

The waves beside them danced, but they
Outdid the sparkling waves in glee:
15 A poet could not but be gay,
In such a jocund company;
I gazed—and gazed—but little thought
What wealth the show to me had brought:

For oft, when on my couch I lie
20 In vacant or in pensive mood,
They flash upon that inward eye

Which is the bliss of solitude;
And then my heart with pleasure fills,
And dances with the daffodils.
—1815

---

[1] *I wandered ... cloud* Transcription of Wordsworth's manuscript
(see previous page for facsimile).

Elegiac Stanzas

Suggested by a Picture of Peele Castle, in a Storm, painted by Sir George Beaumont[1]

I was thy Neighbour once, thou rugged Pile!°   castle
Four summer weeks I dwelt in sight of thee:
I saw thee every day; and all the while
Thy Form was sleeping on a glassy sea.

5   So pure the sky, so quiet was the air!
So like, so very like, was day to day!
Whene'er I look'd, thy Image still was there;
It trembled, but it never pass'd away.

How perfect was the calm! it seem'd no sleep;
10   No mood, which season takes away, or brings:
I could have fancied that the mighty Deep
Was even the gentlest of all gentle Things.

Ah! THEN, if mine had been the Painter's hand,
To express what then I saw; and add the gleam,
15   The light that never was, on sea or land,
The consecration, and the Poet's dream;

I would have planted thee, thou hoary Pile!
Amid a world how different from this!
Beside a sea that could not cease to smile;
20   On tranquil land, beneath a sky of bliss:

Thou shouldst have seem'd a treasure-house, a mine
Of peaceful years; a chronicle of heaven—
Of all the sunbeams that did ever shine
The very sweetest had to thee been given.

25   A Picture had it been of lasting ease,
Elysian[2] quiet, without toil or strife;
No motion but the moving tide, a breeze,
Or merely silent Nature's breathing life.

Such, in the fond delusion of my heart,
30   Such Picture would I at that time have made:
And seen the soul of truth in every part;
A faith, a trust, that could not be betray'd.

So once it would have been—'tis so no more;
I have submitted to a new control:
35   A power is gone, which nothing can restore;
A deep distress hath humaniz'd my Soul.

Not for a moment could I now behold
A smiling sea and be what I have been:
The feeling of my loss will ne'er be old;
40   This, which I know, I speak with mind serene.

Then, Beaumont, Friend! who would have been the
    Friend,
If he had lived, of Him whom I deplore,°   mourn
This Work of thine I blame not, but commend;
This sea in anger, and that dismal shore.

45   Oh 'tis a passionate Work!—yet wise and well;
Well chosen is the spirit that is here;
That Hulk which labours in the deadly swell,
This rueful sky, this pageantry of fear!

And this huge Castle, standing here sublime,
50   I love to see the look with which it braves,
Cased in the unfeeling armour of old time,
The light'ning, the fierce wind, and trampling waves.

Farewell, farewell the Heart that lives alone,
Hous'd in a dream, at distance from the Kind![3]
55   Such happiness, wherever it be known,
Is to be pitied; for 'tis surely blind.

---

[1] *Suggested by ... Beaumont* In 1794, Wordsworth spent a month in Rampside, Lancashire, which is located across the Morecambe Bay from the Furness Peninsula, where the ruins of Peele Castle stand. In 1806 he saw the two pictures of this castle that had been painted by Sir George Beaumont, a landscape painter who was Wordsworth's friend and patron. Wordsworth's youngest brother, a captain with the East India Company, drowned when his ship sank off the Bill of Portland in February 1805.

[2] *Elysian* Blissful. Referring to Elysium, where, according to classical mythology, the blessed reside after death.

[3] *Kind* Human race.

But welcome fortitude, and patient cheer,
And frequent sights of what is to be born!
Such sights, or worse, as are before me here.
60 Not without hope we suffer and we mourn.
—1807

Ode
[Intimations of Immortality]

In an 1843 letter to Isabella Fenwick, Wordsworth explained the experiences from his own life on which this ode is based, saying, "Nothing was more difficult for me in childhood than to admit the notion of death as a state applicable to my own being.... I used to brood over the stories of Enoch and Elijah, and almost to persuade myself that, whatever might become of others, I should be translated, in something of the same way, to heaven. With a feeling congenial to this, I was often unable to think of external things as having external existence, and I communed with all that I saw as something not apart from, but inherent in, my own immaterial nature. Many times while going to school have I grasped at a wall or tree to recall myself from this abyss of idealism to the reality. At that time I was afraid of such processes. In later periods of life I have deplored, as we have all reason to do, a subjugation of an opposite character, and have rejoiced over the remembrances, as is expressed in the lines—

        Obstinate questionings
    Of sense and outward things,
    Fallings from us, vanishings; etc."[1]

Wordsworth wrote the first four stanzas of the poem in 1802, and two years elapsed before he completed the poem in 1804. In 1815 he changed the title to "Ode: Intimations of Immortality from Recollections of Early Childhood," its more common title today. He also replaced the Latin epigram from Virgil with the last three lines from "My heart leaps up": "The Child is Father to the Man: / And I could wish my days to be / Bound each to each by natural piety."

Ode
[Intimations of Immortality
from Recollections of Early Childhood]

Paulo majora canamus.[2]

There was a time when meadow, grove, and stream,
    The earth, and every common sight,
            To me did seem
        Apparelled in celestial light,
5 The glory and the freshness of a dream.
It is not now as it has been of yore;—
        Turn wheresoe'er I may,
            By night or day,
The things which I have seen I now can see no more.

10   The Rainbow comes and goes,
        And lovely is the Rose,
        The Moon doth with delight
Look round her when the heavens are bare;
        Waters on a starry night
15   Are beautiful and fair;
        The sunshine is a glorious birth;
        But yet I know, where'er I go,
That there hath passed away a glory from the earth.

Now, while the Birds thus sing a joyous song,
20   And while the young Lambs bound
            As to the tabor's[3] sound,
To me alone there came a thought of grief:
A timely utterance gave that thought relief,
            And I again am strong.
25 The Cataracts blow their trumpets from the steep,
No more shall grief of mine the season wrong;
I hear the Echoes through the mountains throng,

---

[1] *Obstinate ... etc.* Lines 141–43.

[2] *Paulo majora canamus* Latin: "Let us sing of loftier things." From Virgil's Fourth Eclogue.

[3] *tabor* Small drum.

The Winds come to me from the fields of sleep,
    And all the earth is gay,
30   Land and sea
    Give themselves up to jollity,
    And with the heart of May
    Doth every Beast keep holiday,
    Thou Child of Joy
35 Shout round me, let me hear thy shouts, thou happy
    Shepherd Boy!

Ye blessed Creatures, I have heard the call
    Ye to each other make; I see
The heavens laugh with you in your jubilee;
    My heart is at your festival,
40   My head hath it's coronal,°   *wreath*
The fullness of your bliss, I feel—I feel it all.
      Oh evil day! if I were sullen
      While Earth herself is adorning,
        This sweet May-morning,
45   And the Children are pulling,
        On every side,
    In a thousand valleys far and wide,
    Fresh flowers; while the sun shines warm,
And the Babe leaps up on his mother's arm:—
      I hear, I hear, with joy I hear!
50   —But there's a Tree, of many one,
A single Field which I have looked upon,
Both of them speak of something that is gone:
      The Pansy at my feet
55   Doth the same tale repeat:
Whither is fled the visionary gleam?
Where is it now, the glory and the dream?

Our birth is but a sleep and a forgetting:
The Soul that rises with us, our life's Star,
60   Hath had elsewhere it's setting,
      And cometh from afar:
      Not in entire forgetfulness,
      And not in utter nakedness,
But trailing clouds of glory do we come
65   From God, Who is our home:
Heaven lies about us in our infancy!
Shades of the prison-house begin to close

      Upon the growing Boy,
But he beholds the light, and whence it flows,
70   He sees it in his joy;
The Youth, who daily farther from the East
    Must travel, still is Nature's Priest,
      And by the vision splendid
      Is on his way attended;
75 At length the Man perceives it die away,
And fade into the light of common day.

Earth fills her lap with pleasures of her own;
Yearnings she hath in her own natural kind,
And, even with something of a Mother's mind,
80   And no unworthy aim,
    The homely° Nurse doth all she can   *simple*
To make her Foster-child, her Inmate Man,
    Forget the glories he hath known,
And that imperial palace whence he came.
85 Behold the Child among his new-born blisses,
A four year's Darling of a pigmy size!
See, where 'mid work of his own hand he lies,
Fretted by sallies of his Mother's kisses,
With light upon him from his Father's eyes!
90 See, at his feet, some little plan or chart,
Some fragment from his dream of human life,
Shaped by himself with newly-learned art;
      A wedding or a festival,
      A mourning or a funeral;
95   And this hath now his heart,
      And unto this he frames his song:
      Then will he fit his tongue
To dialogues of business, love, or strife;
      But it will not be long
100   Ere this be thrown aside,
      And with new joy and pride
The little Actor cons another part,
Filling from time to time his "humourous stage"[1]
With all the Persons, down to palsied Age,
105 That Life brings with her in her Equipage;

---

[1] *humourous stage* From Elizabethan poet Samuel Daniel's *Musophilus* (1599), in reference to the different character types (defined by their dominant temperaments, or "humors") depicted in Renaissance drama.

As if his whole vocation
    Were endless imitation.

Thou, whose exterior semblance doth belie
    Thy Soul's immensity;
110 Thou best Philosopher, who yet dost keep
Thy heritage, thou Eye among the blind,
That, deaf and silent, read'st the eternal deep,
Haunted for ever by the eternal mind—
    Mighty Prophet! Seer blest!
115   On whom those truths do rest,
Which we are toiling all our lives to find;
Thou, over whom thy Immortality
Broods like the Day, a Master o'er a Slave,
A Presence which is not to be put by;
120   To whom the grave
Is but a lonely bed without the sense or sight
    Of day or the warm light,
A place of thought where we in waiting lie;
Thou little Child, yet glorious in the might
125 Of untamed pleasures, on thy Being's height,
Why with such earnest pains dost thou provoke
The Years to bring the inevitable yoke,
Thus blindly with thy blessedness at strife?
Full soon thy Soul shall have her earthly freight,
130 And custom lie upon thee with a weight,
Heavy as frost, and deep almost as life!

    O joy! that in our embers
    Is something that doth live,
    That nature yet remembers
135   What was so fugitive!
The thought of our past years in me doth breed
Perpetual benedictions: not indeed
For that which is most worthy to be blest;
Delight and liberty, the simple creed
140 Of Childhood, whether fluttering or at rest,
With new-born hope for ever in his breast:—
    Not for these I raise
    The song of thanks and praise;
    But for those obstinate questionings
145   Of sense and outward things,
    Fallings from us, vanishings;

    Blank misgivings of a Creature
Moving about in worlds not realized,[1]
High instincts, before which our mortal Nature
150 Did tremble like a guilty Thing surprised:
    But for those first affections,
    Those shadowy recollections,
     Which, be they what they may,
Are yet the fountain light of all our day,
155 Are yet a master light of all our seeing;
    Uphold us, cherish us, and make
Our noisy years seem moments in the being
Of the eternal Silence: truths that wake,
    To perish never;
160 Which neither listlessness, nor mad endeavour,
    Nor Man nor Boy,
Nor all that is at enmity with joy,
Can utterly abolish or destroy!
    Hence, in a season of calm weather,
165   Though inland far we be,
Our Souls have sight of that immortal sea
    Which brought us hither,
    Can in a moment travel thither,
And see the Children sport upon the shore,
170 And hear the mighty waters rolling evermore.

Then, sing ye Birds, sing, sing a joyous song!
    And let the young Lambs bound
    As to the tabor's sound!
We in thought will join your throng,
175   Ye that pipe and ye that play,
    Ye that through your hearts to day
    Feel the gladness of the May!
What though the radiance which was once so bright
Be now for ever taken from my sight,
180   Though nothing can bring back the hour
Of splendour in the grass, of glory in the flower;
    We will grieve not, rather find
    Strength in what remains behind,
    In the primal sympathy
185   Which having been must ever be,
    In the soothing thoughts that spring

---

[1] *realized* Seeming real.

Out of human suffering,
In the faith that looks through death,
In years that bring the philosophic mind.

190 And oh ye Fountains, Meadows, Hills, and Groves,
Think not of any severing of our loves!
Yet in my heart of hearts I feel your might;
I only have relinquished one delight
To live beneath your more habitual sway.
195 I love the Brooks which down their channels fret,
Even more than when I tripped lightly as they;
The innocent brightness of a new-born Day
        Is lovely yet;
The Clouds that gather round the setting sun
200 Do take a sober colouring from an eye
That hath kept watch o'er man's mortality;
Another race hath been, and other palms[1] are won.
Thanks to the human heart by which we live,
Thanks to its tenderness, its joys, and fears,
205 To me the meanest flower that blows can give
Thoughts that do often lie too deep for tears.
—1807

from *The Excursion*
[*The Ruined Cottage*]

This excerpt is taken from Wordsworth's nine-book epic *The Excursion, Being a Portion of The Recluse, A Poem* (1814). It was intended as the second part of the tripartite *The Recluse*, which was never completed, and *The Excursion* was the only part of the poem published during Wordsworth's lifetime. *The Prelude* was planned as an autobiographical introduction to the project. The portion from *The Excursion* reprinted here is from the end of ok ¹ which is titled "The Wanderer," and was eived and written as a poem entitled tage."

of the Wanderer (the principal , Wordsworth says, "Had I ich would have deprived me

reece, palm branches or wreaths were of foot races.)

of what is called a liberal education, it is not unlikely that, being strong in body, I should have taken to a way of life such as that in which my Pedlar passed the greater part of his days. At all events, I am here called upon freely to acknowledge that the character I have represented in his person is chiefly an idea of what I fancied my own character might have become in his circumstances," combined with observations of such figures encountered in his own youth.

[*The Ruined Cottage*]

SUPINE the Wanderer lay,
His eyes as if in drowsiness half shut,
The shadows of the breezy elms above
Dappling his face. He had not heard my steps
5 As I approached; and near him did I stand
Unnotic'd in the shade, some minutes' space.
At length I hailed him, seeing that his hat
Was moist with water-drops, as if the brim
Had newly scooped a running stream. He rose,
10 And ere the pleasant greeting that ensued
Was ended, "'Tis," said I, "a burning day;
My lips are parched with thirst, but you, I guess,
Have somewhere found relief." He, at the word,
Pointing towards a sweet-briar, bade me climb
15 The fence hard by, where that aspiring shrub
Looked out upon the road. It was a plot
Of garden-ground run wild, its matted weeds
Marked with the steps of those, whom, as they pass'd
The gooseberry trees that shot in long lank slips,
20 Or currants hanging from their leafless stems
In scanty strings, had tempted to o'erleap
The broken wall. I looked around, and there,
Where two tall hedge-rows of thick alder boughs
Joined in a cold damp nook, espied a Well
25 Shrouded with willow-flowers and plumy fern.
My thirst I slaked, and from the cheerless spot
Withdrawing, straightway to the shade returned
Where sat the Old Man on the Cottage bench;

And, while, beside him, with uncovered head,
30 I yet was standing, freely to respire,
And cool my temples in the fanning air,
Thus did he speak. "I see around me here
Things which you cannot see: we die, my Friend,
Nor we alone, but that which each man loved
35 And prized in his peculiar nook of earth
Dies with him, or is changed; and very soon
Even of the good is no memorial left.
—The Poets, in their elegies and songs
Lamenting the departed, call the groves,
40 They call upon the hills and streams to mourn,
And senseless rocks; nor idly; for they speak,
In these their invocations, with a voice
Obedient to the strong creative power
Of human passion. Sympathies there are
45 More tranquil, yet perhaps of kindred birth,
That steal upon the meditative mind,
And grow with thought. Beside yon Spring I stood,
And eyed its waters till we seemed to feel
One sadness, they and I. For them a bond
50 Of brotherhood is broken: time has been
When, every day, the touch of human hand
Dislodged the natural sleep that binds them up
In mortal stillness; and they minister'd
To human comfort. As I stooped to drink,
55 Upon the slimy foot-stone I espied
The useless fragment of a wooden bowl,
Green with the moss of years; a pensive sight
That moved my heart!—recalling former days
When I could never pass that road but She
60 Who lived within these walls, at my approach,
A Daughter's welcome gave me; and I loved her
As my own child. O Sir! the good die first,
And they whose hearts are dry as summer dust
Burn to the socket. Many a Passenger
65 Hath blessed poor Margaret for her gentle looks,
When she upheld the cool refreshment drawn
From that forsaken Spring; and no one came
But he was welcome; no one went away
But that it seemed she loved him. She is dead,
70 The light extinguished of her lonely Hut,

The Hut itself abandoned to decay,
And She forgotten in the quiet grave!

    "I speak," continued he, "of One whose stock
Of virtues bloom'd beneath this lowly roof.
75 She was a Woman of a steady mind,
Tender and deep in her excess of love,
Not speaking much, pleased rather with the joy
Of her own thoughts: by some especial care
Her temper had been framed, as if to make
80 A Being—who by adding love to peace
Might live on earth a life of happiness.
Her wedded Partner lacked not on his side
The humble worth that satisfied her heart:
Frugal, affectionate, sober, and withal
85 Keenly industrious. She with pride would tell
That he was often seated at his loom,
In summer, ere the Mower was abroad
Among the dewy grass—in early spring,
Ere the last Star had vanished. They who passed
90 At evening, from behind the garden fence
Might hear his busy spade, which he would ply,
After his daily work, until the light
Had failed, and every leaf and flower were lost
In the dark hedges. So their days were spent
95 In peace and comfort; and a pretty Boy
Was their best hope—next to the God in Heaven.

    Not twenty years ago, but you I think
Can scarcely bear it now in mind, there came
Two blighting seasons when the fields were left
100 With half a harvest. It pleased heaven to add
A worse affliction in the plague of war;
This happy Land was stricken to the heart!
A Wanderer then among the Cottages
I, with my freight of winter raiment, saw
105 The hardships of that season; many rich
Sank down, as in a dream, among the poor;
And of the poor did many cease to be
And their place knew them not. Meanwhile abridg'd
Of daily comforts, gladly reconciled
110 To numerous self-denials, Margaret

Went struggling on through those calamitous years
With cheerful hope: but ere the second autumn
Her life's true Help-mate on a sick-bed lay,
Smitten with perilous fever. In disease
115 He lingered long; and when his strength return'd,
He found the little he had stored, to meet
The hour of accident or crippling age,
Was all consumed. Two children had they now,
One newly born. As I have said, it was
120 A time of trouble; shoals of Artisans
Were from their daily labour turn'd adrift
To seek their bread from public charity,
They, and their wives and children—happier far
Could they have lived as do the little birds
125 That peck along the hedges, or the Kite[1]
That makes his dwelling on the mountain Rocks!

        A sad reverse it was for him who long
Had filled with plenty, and possess'd in peace,
This lonely Cottage. At the door he stood,
130 And whistled many a snatch of merry tunes
That had no mirth in them; or with his knife
Carved uncouth figures on the heads of sticks—
Then, not less idly, sought, through every nook
In house or garden, any casual work
135 Of use or ornament; and with a strange,
Amusing, yet uneasy novelty,
He blended, where he might, the various tasks
Of summer, autumn, winter, and of spring.
But this endured not; his good humour soon
140 Became a weight in which no pleasure was:
And poverty brought on a petted° mood   *sulky*
And a sore temper: day by day he drooped,
And he would leave his work—and to the Town,
Without an errand, would direct his steps,
145 Or wander here and there among the fields.
One while he would speak lightly of his Babes,
And with a cruel tongue: at other times
He toss'd them with a false unnatural joy:
And 'twas a rueful thing to see the looks
150 Of the poor innocent children. "Every smile,"

---
[1] *Kite* Small bird of prey of the falcon family.

Said Margaret to me, here beneath these trees,
"Made my heart bleed."
                    At this the Wanderer paused;
And, looking up to those enormous Elms,
155 He said, "'Tis now the hour of deepest noon.—
At this still season of repose and peace,
This hour, when all things which are not at rest
Are cheerful; while this multitude of flies
Is filling all the air with melody;
160 Why should a tear be in an Old Man's eye?
Why should we thus, with an untoward mind,
And in the weakness of humanity,
From natural wisdom turn our hearts away,
To natural comfort shut our eyes and ears,
165 And, feeding on disquiet, thus disturb
The calm of nature with our restless thoughts?"

He spake with somewhat of a solemn tone:
But, when he ended, there was in his face
Such easy cheerfulness, a look so mild,
170 That for a little time it stole away
All recollection, and that simple Tale
Passed from my mind like a forgotten sound.
A while on trivial things we held discourse,
To me soon tasteless. In my own despite
175 I thought of that poor Woman as of one
Whom I had known and loved. He had rehearsed
Her homely Tale with such familiar power,
With such an active countenance, an eye
So busy, that the things of which he spake
180 Seemed present; and, attention now relax'd,
There was a heart-felt chillness in my veins.—
I rose; and, turning from the breezy shade,
Went forth into the open air, and stood
To drink the comfort of the warmer sun.
185 Long time I had not staid, ere, looking round
Upon that tranquil Ruin, I return'd,
And begged of the Old Man that, for my sake,
He would resume his story.—
                              He replied,
190 "It were a wantonness, and would demand
Severe reproof, if we were Men whose hearts
Could hold vain dalliance with the misery

Even of the dead; contented thence to draw
A momentary pleasure, never marked
195 By reason, barren of all future good.
But we have known that there is often found
In mournful thoughts, and always might be found,
A power to virtue friendly; were't not so,
I am a Dreamer among men, indeed
200 An idle Dreamer! 'Tis a common Tale,
An ordinary sorrow of Man's life,
A tale of silent suffering, hardly clothed
In bodily form. But, without further bidding,
I will proceed—
205   While thus it fared with them,
To whom this Cottage, till those hapless years,
Had been a blessed home, it was my chance
To travel in a Country far remote.
And glad I was, when, halting by yon gate
210 That leads from the green lane, once more I saw
These lofty elm-trees. Long I did not rest:
With many pleasant thoughts I cheer'd my way
O'er the flat Common. Having reached the door
I knock'd—and, when I entered with the hope
215 Of usual greeting, Margaret looked at me
A little while; then turn'd her head away
Speechless, and sitting down upon a chair
Wept bitterly. I wist° not what to do,   *knew*
Or how to speak to her. Poor Wretch! at last
220 She rose from off her seat, and then—O Sir!
I cannot *tell* how she pronounced my name.
With fervent love, and with a face of grief
Unutterably helpless, and a look
That seemed to cling upon me, she enquired
225 If I had seen her Husband. As she spake
A strange surprise and fear came to my heart,
Nor had I power to answer ere she told
That he had disappear'd—not two months gone.
He left his House: two wretched days had pass'd,
230 And on the third, as wistfully she rais'd
Her head from off her pillow, to look forth,
Like one in trouble, for returning light,
Within her chamber-casement she espied
A folded paper, lying as if placed
235 To meet her waking eyes. This tremblingly

She open'd—found no writing, but therein
Pieces of money carefully enclosed,
Silver and gold. "I shuddered at the sight,"
Said Margaret, "for I knew it was his hand
240 Which placed it there; and ere that day was ended,
That long and anxious day! I learned from One
Sent hither by my Husband to impart
The heavy news—that he had joined a Troop
Of Soldiers, going to a distant Land.
245 —He left me thus—he could not gather heart
To take a farewell of me; for he fear'd
That I should follow with my Babes, and sink
Beneath the misery of that wandering Life."

This Tale did Margaret tell with many tears:
250 And when she ended I had little power
To give her comfort, and was glad to take
Such words of hope from her own mouth as served
To cheer us both—but long we had not talked
Ere we built up a pile of better thoughts,
255 And with a brighter eye she look'd around
As if she had been shedding tears of joy.
We parted. 'Twas the time of early spring;
I left her busy with her garden tools;
And well remember, o'er that fence she looked,
260 And, while I paced along the foot-way path,
Called out, and sent a blessing after me,
With tender cheerfulness; and with a voice
That seem'd the very sound of happy thoughts.

I roved o'er many a hill and many a dale,
265 With my accustomed load; in heat and cold,
Through many a wood, and many an open ground,
In sunshine and in shade, in wet and fair,
Drooping, or blithe of heart, as might befall;
My best companions now the driving winds,
270 And now the "trotting brooks" and whispering trees,
And now the music of my own sad steps,
With many a short-lived thought that pass'd between,
And disappeared. I journey'd back this way
Towards the wane of Summer; when the wheat
275 Was yellow; and the soft and bladed grass
Springing afresh had o'er the hay-field spread

Its tender verdure. At the door arrived,
I found that she was absent. In the shade,
Where now we sit, I waited her return.
280　Her Cottage, then a cheerful Object, wore
Its customary look—only, I thought,
The honeysuckle, crowding round the porch,
Hung down in heavier tufts: and that bright weed,
The yellow stone-crop, suffered to take root
285　Along the window's edge, profusely grew,
Blinding the lower panes. I turned aside,
And strolled into her garden. It appeared
To lag behind the season, and had lost
Its pride of neatness. From the border lines
290　Composed of daisy and resplendent thrift,[1]
Flowers straggling forth had on those paths encroached
Which they were used to deck: Carnations, once
Prized for surpassing beauty, and no less
For the peculiar pains they had required,
295　Declined their languid heads—without support.
The cumbrous bind-weed, with its wreaths and bells,
Had twined about her two small rows of peas,
And dragged them to the earth.—Ere this an hour
Was wasted.—Back I turned my restless steps,
300　And, as I walked before the door, it chanced
A Stranger passed; and, guessing whom I sought,
He said that she was used to ramble far.
The sun was sinking in the west; and now
I sat with sad impatience. From within
305　Her solitary Infant cried aloud;
Then, like a blast that dies away self-stilled,
The voice was silent. From the bench I rose;
But neither could divert nor soothe my thoughts.
The spot, though fair, was very desolate—
310　The longer I remained more desolate.
And, looking round, I saw the corner stones,
Till then unnotic'd, on either side the door
With dull red stains discolour'd, and stuck o'er
With tufts and hairs of wool, as if the Sheep,
315　That fed upon the Common, thither came
Familiarly; and found a couching-place
Even at her threshold. Deeper shadows fell

From these tall elms; the Cottage-clock struck eight;
I turned, and saw her distant a few steps.
320　Her face was pale and thin, her figure too
Was changed. As she unlocked the door, she said,
"It grieves me you have waited here so long,
But, in good truth, I've wandered much of late,
And, sometimes—to my shame I speak—have need
325　Of my best prayers to bring me back again."
While on the board she spread our evening meal,
She told me, interrupting not the work
Which gave employment to her listless hands,
That she had parted with her elder Child;
330　To a kind Master on a distant farm
Now happily apprenticed—"I perceive
You look at me, and you have cause; to-day
I have been travelling far; and many days
About the fields I wander, knowing this
335　Only, that what I seek I cannot find.
And so I waste my time: for I am changed;
And to myself," said she, "have done much wrong,
And to this helpless Infant. I have slept
Weeping, and weeping I have waked; my tears
340　Have flowed as if my body were not such
As others are; and I could never die.
But I am now in mind and in my heart
More easy; and I hope," said she, "that heaven
Will give me patience to endure the things
345　Which I behold at home." It would have grieved
Your very soul to see her; Sir, I feel
The story linger in my heart: I fear
'Tis long and tedious; but my spirit clings
To that poor Woman—so familiarly
350　Do I perceive her manner, and her look,
And presence, and so deeply do I feel
Her goodness, that, not seldom, in my walks
A momentary trance comes over me;
And to myself I seem to muse on One
355　By sorrow laid asleep; or borne away,
A human being destined to awake
To human life, or something very near
To human life, when he shall come again
For whom she suffered. Yes, it would have grieved
360　Your very soul to see her: evermore

---

[1] *thrift* Common plant that bears pink, white, or purple flowers.

Her eyelids drooped, her eyes were downward cast;
And, when she at her table gave me food,
She did not look at me. Her voice was low,
Her body was subdued. In every act
365 Pertaining to her house affairs, appeared
The careless stillness of a thinking mind
Self-occupied; to which all outward things
Are like an idle matter. Still she sighed,
But yet no motion of the breast was seen,
370 No heaving of the heart. While by the fire
We sate together, sighs came on my ear,
I knew not how, and hardly whence they came.

    Ere my departure to her care I gave,
For her Son's use, some tokens of regard,
375 Which with a look of welcome she received;
And I exhorted her to have her trust
In God's good love, and seek his help by prayer.
I took my staff, and, when I kissed her babe
The tears stood in her eyes. I left her then
380 With the best hope and comfort I could give;
She thanked me for my wish;—but for my hope
Methought she did not thank me.
                         I returned,
And took my rounds along this road again
385 Ere on its sunny bank the primrose flower
Peeped forth, to give an earnest of the Spring.
I found her sad and drooping; she had learned
No tidings of her Husband; if he lived
She knew not that he lived; if he were dead
390 She knew not he was dead. She seem'd the same
In person and appearance; but her House
Bespake a sleepy hand of negligence.
The floor was neither dry nor neat, the hearth
Was comfortless, and her small lot of books,
395 Which, in the Cottage window, heretofore
Had been piled up against the corner panes
In seemly order, now, with straggling leaves
Lay scattered here and there, open or shut,
As they had chanced to fall. Her Infant Babe
400 Had from its Mother caught the trick of grief,
And sighed among its playthings. Once again
I turned towards the garden gate, and saw,

More plainly still, that poverty and grief
Were now come nearer to her: weeds defaced
405 The harden'd soil, and knots of wither'd grass;
No ridges there appeared of clear black mold,
No winter greenness; of her herbs and flowers,
It seemed the better part were gnawed away
Or trampled into earth; a chain of straw,
410 Which had been twined about the slender stem
Of a young apple-tree, lay at its root;
The bark was nibbled round by truant Sheep.
—Margaret stood near, her Infant in her arms,
And, noting that my eye was on the tree,
415 She said, "I fear it will be dead and gone
Ere Robert come again." Towards the House
Together we returned; and she enquired
If I had any hope: but for her Babe
And for her little orphan Boy, she said,
420 She had no wish to live, that she must die
Of sorrow. Yet I saw the idle loom
Still in its place; his Sunday garments hung
Upon the self-same nail; his very staff
Stood undisturbed behind the door. And when,
425 In bleak December, I retraced this way,
She told me that her little Babe was dead,
And she was left alone. She now, released
From her maternal cares, had taken up
The employment common through these Wilds,
    and gain'd
430 By spinning hemp a pittance for herself;
And for this end had hired a neighbour's Boy
To give her needful help. That very time
Most willingly she put her work aside,
And walked with me along the miry road
435 Heedless how far; and, in such piteous sort
That any heart had ached to hear her, begged
That, wheresoe'er I went, I still would ask
For him whom she had lost. We parted then,
Our final parting; for from that time forth
440 Did many seasons pass ere I return'd
Into this tract again.
                  Nine tedious years;
From their first separation, nine long years,
She lingered in unquiet widowhood;

445 A Wife and Widow. Needs must it have been
A sore heart-wasting! I have heard, my Friend,
That in yon arbour oftentimes she sat
Alone, through half the vacant Sabbath-day,
And if a dog passed by she still would quit
450 The shade, and look abroad. On this old Bench
For hours she sate; and evermore her eye
Was busy in the distance, shaping things
That made her heart beat quick. You see that path,
Now faint—the grass has crept o'er its grey line;
455 There, to and fro, she paced through many a day
Of the warm summer, from a belt of hemp
That girt her waist, spinning the long drawn thread
With backward steps. Yet ever as there pass'd
A man whose garments showed the Soldier's red,
460 Or crippled Mendicant in Sailor's garb,
The little Child who sate to turn the wheel
Ceas'd from his task; and she with faltering voice
Made many a fond enquiry; and when they,
Whose presence gave no comfort, were gone by,
465 Her heart was still more sad. And by yon gate,
That bars the Traveller's road, she often stood,
And when a stranger Horseman came, the latch
Would lift, and in his face look wistfully;
Most happy, if, from aught discovered there
470 Of tender feeling, she might dare repeat
The same sad question. Meanwhile her poor Hut
Sank to decay: for he was gone—whose hand,
At the first nipping of October frost,
Closed up each chink, and with fresh bands of straw
475 Chequered the green-grown thatch. And so she lived
Through the long winter, reckless and alone;
Until her House by frost, and thaw, and rain,
Was sapped; and while she slept the nightly damps
Did chill her breast; and in the stormy day
480 Her tattered clothes were ruffled by the wind;
Even at the side of her own fire. Yet still
She loved this wretched spot, nor would for worlds
Have parted hence; and still that length of road,
And this rude bench, one torturing hope endeared,
485 Fast rooted at her heart: and here, my Friend,
In sickness she remained; and here she died,
Last human Tenant of these ruined Walls."

The Old Man ceased: he saw that I was moved;
From that low Bench, rising instinctively
490 I turn'd aside in weakness, nor had power
To thank him for the Tale which he had told.
I stood, and leaning o'er the Garden wall,
Reviewed that Woman's sufferings; and it seemed
To comfort me while with a Brother's love
495 I bless'd her—in the impotence of grief.
At length towards the Cottage I returned
Fondly, and traced with interest more mild,
That secret spirit of humanity
Which, 'mid the calm oblivious tendencies
500 Of Nature, 'mid her plants, and weeds, and flowers,
And silent overgrowings, still survived.
The Old Man, noting this, resumed, and said,
"My Friend! enough to sorrow you have given,
The purposes of wisdom ask no more;
505 Be wise and cheerful; and no longer read
The forms of things with an unworthy eye.
She sleeps in the calm earth, and peace is here.
I well remember that those very plumes,
Those weeds, and the high spear-grass on that wall,
510 By mist and silent rain-drops silver'd o'er,
As once I passed, did to my heart convey
So still an image of tranquillity,
So calm and still, and looked so beautiful
Amid the uneasy thoughts which filled my mind,
515 That what we feel of sorrow and despair
From ruin and from change, and all the grief
The passing shows of Being leave behind,
Appeared an idle dream, that could not live
Where meditation was. I turned away
520 And walked along my road in happiness."

He ceased. Ere long the sun declining shot
A slant and mellow radiance, which began
To fall upon us, while beneath the trees
We sat on that low Bench: and now we felt,
525 Admonished thus, the sweet hour coming on.
A linnet warbled from those lofty elms,
A thrush sang loud, and other melodies,
At distance heard, peopled the milder air.
The Old Man rose, and, with a sprightly mien° *countenance*

530 Of hopeful preparation, grasped his Staff:
Together casting then a farewell look
Upon those silent walls, we left the Shade;
And, ere the Stars were visible, had reached
A Village Inn—our Evening resting-place.
—1814

Surprised by Joy

Surprised by joy—impatient as the Wind
I turned to share the transport—Oh! with whom
But Thee,[1] deep buried in the silent tomb,
That spot which no vicissitude can find?
5 Love, faithful love, recalled thee to my mind—
But how could I forget thee? Through what power,
Even for the least division of an hour,
Have I been so beguiled as to be blind
To my most grievous loss?—That thought's return
10 Was the worst pang that sorrow ever bore,
Save one, one only, when I stood forlorn,
Knowing my heart's best treasure was no more;
That neither present time, nor years unborn
Could to my sight that heavenly face restore.
—1815

Mutability[2]

From low to high doth dissolution climb,
And sink from high to low, along a scale
Of awful° notes, whose concord shall not fail;   *awe-inspiring*
A musical but melancholy chime,
5 Which they can hear who meddle not with crime,
Nor avarice, nor over-anxious care.
Truth fails not; but her outward forms that bear
The longest date do melt like frosty rime,
That in the morning whitened hill and plain
10 And is no more; drop like the tower sublime
Of yesterday, which royally did wear
His crown of weeds, but could not even sustain
Some casual shout that broke the silent air,
Or the unimaginable touch of Time.
—1822

Steamboats, Viaducts, and Railways

Motions and Means, on land and sea at war
With old poetic feeling, not for this,
Shall ye, by Poets even, be judged amiss!
Nor shall your presence, howsoe'er it mar
5 The loveliness of Nature, prove a bar
To the Mind's gaining that prophetic sense
Of future change, that point of vision whence
May be discovered what in soul ye are.
In spite of all that beauty may disown
10 In your harsh features, Nature doth embrace
Her lawful offspring in Man's art; and Time,
Pleased with your triumphs o'er his brother Space,
Accepts from your bold hands the proffered crown
Of hope, and smiles on you with cheer sublime.
—1835

---

[1] *Thee* Catherine, the Wordsworths's daughter, who died in June 1812 at the age of three.

[2] *Mutability* From *Ecclesiastical Sonnets*, a sequence of poems dealing with the history of the Church of England.

IN CONTEXT

Visual Depictions of "Man's Art"

While one artistic tradition emphasized the "harsh features" of the products of the industrial revolution, many painters in the first half of the nineteenth century depicted such subjects as viaducts and railways in ways which suggested that, like Wordsworth, they saw these as nature's "lawful offspring."

John Sell Cotman, *Chirk Aqueduct* (1806–07). The aqueduct, built between 1796 and 1801, is 70 feet high.

J.M.W. Turner, *Rain, Steam and Speed* (1844).

Reading, Writing, Publishing
CONTEXTS

During the Romantic period, questions concerning the definition of literature and the nature of its role in society pervaded print culture. Among the topics debated were definitions of intellectual property, the ways in which dissemination of texts should be encouraged or restrained, and the extent to which literature could effect social or political reform. For many, particularly in light of the French Revolution, literature was felt to hold a radical potential to change the world.

Some questioned whether women or members of the laboring classes should be allowed access to political tracts, and feared that less educated or discerning minds could be easily swayed by the persuasive rhetoric of radicals. Daniel Isaac Eaton was among those whom they feared; he had been tried nine times for publishing or writing radical texts and on one occasion had been sentenced to eighteen months in jail. Here he satirizes the anti-revolutionaries' fear of the power of the press and the government's desire to control the circulation of potentially seditious material through legislation and taxes. Eaton's weekly magazine, *Politics for the People* (1793–95), was an important and popular organ of radical journalism; when he was placed in the pillory in 1812 for printing the third part of *Age of Reason*, he was cheered by a large crowd.

Thomas Spence, whose poem on the theme of repression appears next, was also well acquainted with the accusation of libel. He had been arrested four times and imprisoned twice between 1792 and 1794 alone. In the poem reproduced here, his parenthetical denials cleverly serve to protect him from such charges while simultaneously articulating radical criticism of the monarchy and aristocracy. The poem following Spence's, by an anonymous author, uses the sort of animal analogies that were commonly relied upon in political satire at the time. By exploiting traditional moral fables, writers could create poems that were clearly understood by their readers, yet were ambiguous enough to allow their authors to disavow any subversive intent.

The piece that follows emphasizes the importance of literature to revolutionary efforts. While Eaton had mocked anti-radicals' fear of the press, the anonymous author of "On the Characteristics of Poetry" links the feelings excited by poetry to powerful political action, and even to military victory.

The period was what John Stuart Mill called "a reading age"; there were more readers than ever before, and publishing was becoming a major industry. While many viewed this development as beneficial to society, others feared a proliferation of trivial works that would neither improve the minds of readers nor encourage them to pick up more challenging works. If too many books were produced each year for any one person to read, how could people hope to peruse them all and decide which were most worthy of their attention? Voicing a common fear, the anonymous correspondent to the *Monthly Magazine* whose letter is excerpted here claims that the proliferation of writers has led to a decline in literary standards and a decreased appreciation for writers of true genius. In the piece following, Samuel Pratt proposes an effective solution to this problem in the form of literary journals, whose writers can together provide readers with a balanced critical appraisal. In a slightly later article, Isaac D'Israeli proposes another solution in the form of changes to copyright laws that would reward authors of true genius rather than benefitting only the "booksellers" (publishers), who in his view sought to publish trivial works of mass appeal.

Hannah More, in *Strictures on the Modern System of Female Education*, examines what she sees as the negative effects of the abundant novels and other "alluring little works" on the morals and intellects of young women. In a later excerpt, prolific novelist Anna Laetitia Barbauld, in her introduction to her edition of *The British Novelists*, celebrates the novel's ability to divert and entertain, a characteristic more important to the average reader than moral instruction.

During this period, literature was often celebrated as a vehicle for debate, and reading was frequently a communal activity accompanied by discussion and reflection. In this manner, readers—particularly young or less educated ones—were trained to read critically. Two adaptations of Shakespeare stressed the importance of reading as a family activity. Thomas Bowdler's highly successful ten-volume *Family Shakespeare* (whose name became a component of a verb, "to bowdlerize," referring to the removal of "inappropriate" material from a literary work) did not add any new material to the original texts, but omitted "those words and expressions ... which cannot with propriety be read aloud in a family." He was also careful to alter the representation of those events that might not be suitable for younger readers. Ophelia's suicide in *Hamlet*, for example, is presented as an accidental drowning. Charles and Mary Lamb's *Tales from Shakespeare*, which recasts the plays as prose stories for younger audiences, allowed children to gain exposure to Shakespeare's plays and to discuss them with older family members, helping them gain a fuller appreciation for the plays when they were read later in life.

In the final two excerpts, John Stuart Mill and William Hazlitt express opposing views on the future of British literature and culture. Hazlitt takes a more positive view of the commodification of literature, accepting what he sees as inevitable, while Mill predicts the downfall of a culture whose integrity he feared would soon be undermined by commercial society.

⌘ ⌘ ⌘

from Daniel Isaac Eaton, *The Pernicious Effects of the Art of Printing Upon Society, Exposed* (1793)

Before this diabolical art was introduced among men, there was social order. ... In the times we are speaking of (the Golden Age), the feudal system prevailed—a system replete with blessings—by it the different orders of society were kept perfectly distinct and separate—there were kings, barons, priests, yeomanry, villains[1] or slaves; and they were, I believe, with regard to rank and power, in the order in which I have named them. The villains, or lowest class, were what Mr. Burke so elegantly terms the *Swinish Multitude*,[2] but of rights or privileges as men they had not an idea; we may with propriety style them the Jackals of the times: they tilled the earth, and performed all manual labour; but in return, their superiors allowed them sufficient of the produce for subsistence—permitted them to take some rest, in order that they might be strong. To bear hardship and fatigue took from them the trouble of thinking—indeed, from the very prudent manner in which they were brought up, I will not say educated, they were little capable of thought, of course exempt from the mental fatigues of study and reflections. The Scriptures having declared gold to be the root of every evil, they were very humanely prevented from possessing any. As to religion, the clergy taught them as much as they thought necessary, and they were without doubt the best judges, being in general good scholars. ...

Since printing has been employed as the medium of diffusing sentiments, &c. government has become more difficult—the governors are frequently and insolently called upon to give an account of the national treasure,

---

[1] *villains* I.e., villeins, serfs or peasants.

[2] *Mr. Burke ... multitude* Edmund Burke, probably in reference to a particular faction of extremists (rather than all members of the working classes), said that if learning were removed from the hierarchical social order in which it had originated, it would be "cast into the mire, and trodden down under the hoofs of a swinish multitude." Reformers took this comment as proof of the arrogance and superiority with which conservatives regarded the people.

its expenditure, &c.—and if they are in any respect tardy, or should circumstances render evasion necessary, it is astonishing, with what boldness some men will dare to revile and insult them.

The lower orders begin to have ideas of rights, as men—to think that one man is as good as another; that society is at present founded upon false principles; that hereditary honours and distinctions are absurd, unjust, and oppressive; that abilities and morals only should recommend to the first officers in a state; that no regard should be paid to rank and titles; that instruction, sufficient to qualify a man for being a member of society, is a debt due to every individual, and that it is the duty of every state to take care that he receive it; that every man has a right to a share in the government, either in his own person, or that of his representative, and that no portion of his property or labour ought to be taxed without his consent, given either by himself, or representative; that everyone should contribute to the support of the state in proportion to his ability, and that all partial exactions are oppressive; that laws should be the same to all, and that no one, whatever may be his rank or station, should be allowed to offend them with impunity; that freedom of speech is the equal right of all, and that the rich have no right to dictate to the poor what sentiments they shall adopt on any subject, or in any wise[1] prevent investigation and inquiry. This, with a great deal more such stuff, is called the rights of man—blessed fruits of the art of printing—the scum of the earth, the swinish multitude, talking of their rights! and insolently claiming, nay, almost demanding, that political liberty shall be the same to all—to the high and the low, the rich and the poor—what audacity!—what unparalleled effrontery!—it ought to meet correction. With similar mistaken notions of liberty, even many women are infatuated; and the press, that grand prolific source of evil, that fruitful mother of mischief, has already favoured the public with several female productions on this very popular subject—one in particular, called *Rights of Women*,[2] and in which, as one of their rights, a share in legislation is claimed and asserted —gracious heaven! to what will this fatal delusion lead,

and in what will it terminate! …

For all these, and numberless other evils, the natural consequence of a diffusion of knowledge and science, some remedy must be found; the present administration have made some trifling feeble attempts to check their progress, such as additional duties upon advertisements and newspapers, which almost preclude cheap publications—of the same nature I suppose the late tax upon paper to be—but these remedies are totally inadequate, at least they will be so exceedingly slow in their operation, that the present race have but little prospect of living to see any of their good effects.

To rid ourselves of such a monster, some strong efficient measure must be had recourse to, something that will strike at the root, and have an almost instantaneous effect—such a one, I think, I can point out.

Let all printing presses be committed to the flames, all letter foundries be destroyed, schools and seminaries of learning abolished, dissenters of every denominations double and treble taxed, all discourse upon government and religion prohibited, political clubs and associations of every kind suppressed—excepting those formed for the express purpose of supporting government—and lastly, issue a proclamation against reading, and burn all private libraries. To carry some part of this plan into execution, it will be necessary to employ spies and informers, which by many (Jacobins and Republicans) are thought to be signs either of a weak or wicked and corrupt government; they say that governors, conscious of acting for the public good, of having it only in view in all their measure, would scorn using such unworthy and dishonourable means. I cannot be of this opinion, but am confident that if the measures I have proposed be but speedily adopted, and rigorously pursued, the happiest consequences would soon be experienced; all the wild, idle theories with which men are at present disturbed, would soon vanish—the lower orders would mind their work, become tractable and docile, and perhaps in less than half a century that desirable state of ignorance and darkness, which formerly prevailed, might again restore to this Island that happy state of society with which it once was blessed.

---

[1] *wise* Way.

[2] *Rights of Women* Mary Wollstonecraft's *Vindication of the Rights of Woman* (1792).

from Thomas Spence, "Examples of Safe Printing," *Pig's Meat*,[1] Volume 2 (1794)

To prevent misrepresentation in these prosecuting times, it seems necessary to publish every thing relating to tyranny and oppression, though only among brutes, in the most guarded manner.

The following are meant as specimens:

That tyger, or that other salvage wight°   *savage creature*
Is so exceeding furious and fell,°   *fierce*
  As WRONG,
     [*Not meaning our most gracious sovereign*
5   *Lord the King, or the Government of this*
     country]
     when it hath arm'd himself with might;
Not fit 'mong men that do with reason mell,°   *mix*
But 'mong wild beasts and salvage woods to dwell;
10   Where still the stronger
     [*Not meaning the great men of this country*]
     doth the weak devour,
And they that most in boldness do excell,
  Are dreaded most, and feared by their power.
                 —E. Spencer[2]

from Joshua,[3] "Sonnet: The Lion," *Moral and Political Magazine*, Volume 1 (1796)

Why grace we the stern lion with the name
  That marks the chiefs of Europe? More of use
  To man's assistance do the kine° produce;   *cattle*
For bulk, behold the elephant's huge frame!
5 For agile beauty see the stately horse.
  King of the forest HE, and doomed to reign,

Like earthly monarch, o'er the Lybian plain
For fierce pre-eminence in brutal force:
  Before his tyrant rage the fleet° horse flies,   *swift*
10   The patient sheep avoids him, or he dies.
Stern bloody beast! they named thee well: thy right
  Is to this royal title just and good;
Thou gain'dst it by thy savage joy in fight,
Thy brutal fury, and thy thirst for blood.

from Anonymous, "On the Characteristics of Poetry" No. 2, *Monthly Magazine* (1797)

In the course of our last discussion, we seemed to be unanimously of opinion that the grand characteristic, the *sine qua non*[4] of poetry, consists in its capacity of pressing the mind with the most vivid pictures. Indeed, the maxim *ut pictura poesis*[5] is amply illustrated whenever poetry is in any shape the subject of investigation. The terms of the painter's art then insensibly creep into the discourse and model our phraseology.

    Pursuing, then, this idea, we may perhaps lay it down as the grand and leading end of poetry to make a strong and lively impression on the feelings. In her operations she hurries us far beyond the reach of the voice of sober judgment, and captivates by exciting the aid of the passions. Here, then, we see the cause of the mighty energy of verse, nor wonder at the efficaciousness that has been ascribed to the Muses.[6] For how easily are mankind guided by those that possess the happy art of awakening or allaying their feelings. Though all unconscious of being under the guidance of another, they turn obedient to the rein. They are roused to insurrection, or moderated to peace, by him who can touch, with a skilful hand, the master springs that regulate the motions of their minds. When Brutus ascends the rostrum, the words of truth and soberness are heard, and plain integrity convinces the judgment.

---

[1] *Pig's Meat* The title is a reference to Burke's term "swinish multitude," which many radical writers adopted as an ironic definition of the working classes.

[2] *E. Spencer* I.e., Renaissance poet Edmund Spenser (1552?–99), whom the poet imitates in order to create historical distance from the referents of the poem.

[3] *Joshua* Biblical lieutenant of Moses who led the Israelites to victory over the Canaanites (see Joshua 1–12).

[4] *sine qua non* Latin: indispensable attribute.

[5] *ut pictura poetis* Latin: "As is painting, so is poetry" (from Horace, *Ars Poetica*).

[6] *Muses* Nine daughters of Zeus and Mnemosyne, each of whom presided over and provided inspiration for an aspect of the arts and sciences.

But, when Anthony displays the bloody robe, and points to the wounds of Caesar, reminding the people that this was once their darling benefactor, the multitude are melted to sorrow, and at last roused from pity to fury and revenge.[1]

Here, then, this essay might, perhaps, with propriety, have been closed. But I must rely upon your candour for the admission of a few more observations, which may, perhaps, tend to illustrate the point to which this enquiry has led us:

The end of poetry, it is said, is an impression upon the feelings. But as there is an intimate connection between feeling and action, so that where the one appears, the other "follows hard upon," if the foregoing observations be true, we may expect to find that the actions of mankind are, in some measure, influenced by the Muses.

And if we look to the simpler ages of society, when we can best distinguish the grand outlines of the human character, where the springs that actuate the conduct of man are, in a manner, bared for inspection, we shall find this to have been the case. In the infancy of states, poetry is a method equally captivating and efficacious of forming the dispositions of the people, and kindling in their hearts that love of glory which is their country's safeguard and defence. Whether we look to the cold regions of Scandinavia, or the delicious clime of Greece, we find that when society has made a certain progress, mankind are strongly influenced by a love of song, and listen, with raptured attention, to the strains that record the tale of other times, and the deeds of heroes of old. They listen till they imbibe the enthusiasm of warfare, and in the day of battle, the hero's arm has not unfrequently been nerved by the rough energy of the early bard. ...

But, indeed, what occasion have we to search into the dust of antiquity for examples of the influence of verse upon human conduct? The transactions of our own times may teach us that as strong feelings generate poetic language, so poetic language inspires the mind with at least a temporary enthusiasm, and thus impels to action. In this country, the fervour or loyalty has of late been blown into a blaze, and for this event the parties interested are not a little indebted to the assistance of the Muses. And when the Marseillaise Hymn[2] echoed through the ranks of the French army at the field of Jemappe,[3] we need not wonder that "the spear of liberty was wielded with classic grace," and that the energy of heroism was communicated with the sound.

from Anonymous, Letter to the *Monthly Magazine* (24 October 1798)

Sir,

Literature is either less cultivated, or less valued in these days than it was in those of our ancestors, for certainly learning does not *now* receive the honours it *then* did. That it is less cultivated, cannot, I think, with any truth be asserted, because the present is denominated a learned age. It must be the universality then, with which it is diffused throughout society, that renders it less valuable—as articles grow cheap, not in proportion to their insignificancy, but their abundance. Great talents, indeed, in any condition of civilized society must inevitably confer a certain degree of power, inasmuch as they render their possessors either useful or formidable; but scarcely any literary attainments would, I apprehend, raise a writer in these days to the same degree of eminence and request as Petrarch, Erasmus, and Politiano[4] enjoyed in their respective times. We have now amongst us many scholars of great erudition (Parr, Wakefield, Professors Porson and White,[5] &c.

---

[1] *Brutus*   One of the men who assassinated Julius Caesar, who had become dictator of Rome for life; *Anthony* Marc Antony, consul who, after Caesar's assassination, aroused the mob against the conspirators, causing them to be driven from the city.

[2] *Marseillaise Hymn*   Composed by Claude Joseph Rouget de Lisle on 24 April 1792, "the Marseillaise" celebrated freedom and human rights and became a rallying cry for the French Revolutionaries. It was declared the French national anthem in 1795.

[3] *field of Jemappe*   Where a Revolutionary victory occurred in 1792.

[4] *Petrarch*   Francesco Petrarch, Italian poet and Humanist of the fourteenth century, famous for his sonnets; *Erasmus* Desidero Erasmus, Dutch Humanist (1466–1536); *Politiano* Italian poet Angelo Poliziano (1454–95), who also served as professor of Greek and Latin at the University of Florence.

[5] *Parr*   Samuel Parr (1747–1825); a Latin scholar, schoolmaster, minister, and vocal Whig supporter; *Wakefield* Gilbert Wakefield (1756–1801), a Biblical scholar and religious and political controversialist who also produced an edition of Virgil's *Georgics* (1788);

&c.), men of distinguished abilities; yet I much question, as haughty as kings were under the feudal system, if any of the princes in being would contend with the same eagerness for their favour, as we learn the various sovereigns of Europe did for that of Petrarch or Erasmus.

It has been questioned by some whether the number of publications, which are annually poured upon the world, have contributed in any proportionable ratio to the increase of literature? In my opinion, they have *not*. To a liberal and cultivated mind there is certainly no indulgence equal to the luxury of books; but, in works of learning, may not the facilities of information be increased, until the powers of application and retention be diminished? After admitting that the present is a learned age, it may appear singular to doubt whether it affords[1] individuals as profoundly learned (at least, as far as Latin and Greek go), as some who flourished in the fifteenth and sixteenth centuries.

From these remarks, I would not be understood as wishing to make invidious comparisons between the learning of different ages, or to depreciate that of our own. Upon a fair investigation, there can be no doubt, I think, to which side the scale of general literature would incline. My object simply is, to show the different direction which letters take, and the different patronage they obtain, in different periods of society. Indeed, learning may more properly be said to *lead* than to *follow* the course of the world: since, though it may, at first, bend to the spirit of the age, it will in the end assuredly direct and govern it. The general stock of genius is, perhaps, always pretty equal; the opportunities of improving it, and the support it receives, vary with the times. Petrarch and Erasmus were caressed by popes and princes; Butler, Otway, and Chatterton,[2] not much inferior in merit, were absolutely starved; and Johnson,[3]

whose moral works were calculated to delight and improve the age, lived long in distress, and at length received a scanty pension. In some ages, and upon some occasions, it must be admitted, a genius darts upon the world with intellectual powers that no industry, in the common course of things, can hope to equal. But this is a *particular* case, and is generally compensated some other way. If former times have enjoyed works of more fancy, and sublimity of imagination, than are given to us, we, in return, possess more useful acquisitions. If they have had their Spenser, Tasso, and Shakespeare, we boast Newton, Locke, and Johnson.[4] Science, taste, and correction are indeed the characteristics of the present day. Everything is refined; everything is grand. We are actually misers in luxury and taste, and have left nothing for posterity. "*Venimus ad summum fortunae*"[5]—We learn our Greek from the Pursuits of Literature,[6] and our morality from Parissot, and I do not see how we are to be outdone either in learning or in dress.

I remain, Sir, &c., &c.
Ausonius[7]

from Samuel Pratt, *Gleanings in England: Descriptive of the Countenance, Mind, and Character of the Country* (1799)

There cannot be a doubt but that while the liberty of the press, as to the freedom of publication, shall be sacred—and on this side of licentiousness, it ought to be uncontrolled—it is equally just that the sense and nonsense which indiscriminately issue from the immense vehicle of communication should be subject to

---

Professors Porson and White Richard Porson (1759–1808), Greek professor at Cambridge, and Gilbert White (1720–93), noted naturalist.

[1] *affords* Is capable of yielding.

[2] *Butler, Otway, and Chatterton* Satirical poet Samuel Butler (1612–80), tragic dramatist Thomas Otway (1652–85), and young poet Thomas Chatterton (1752–70) all lived in dire poverty.

[3] *Johnson* Samuel Johnson (1709–84), lexicographer, poet, and author of the journals *The Rambler* and *The Idler*. He struggled for financial security until 1762, when he was granted a pension for his

---

work on the *Dictionary*.

[4] *Spenser* English poet Edmund Spenser (c. 1552–99), author of *The Faerie Queene*; *Tasso* Italian poet Torquato Tasso (1544–95); *Locke* Philosopher John Locke (1632–1704); *Newton* Mathematician and natural philosopher Sir Isaac Newton (1642–1727).

[5] "*Venimus ... fortunae*" Latin: "We have come to the height of fortune" (Horace, *Epistles* 2.1).

[6] *Pursuits of Literature* Four-part satirical poem by Thomas James Mathias concerning the nature of literature. Its publication (1794–97) aroused much debate.

[7] *Ausonius* I.e., the author's pseudonym, referring to the Latin poet Dicimius Magmus Ausonius (c. 310–c. 393).

vigilant examination, otherwise the whole world would be over-run with abortions of the mind. We want the assistance of some guides who will take upon themselves the trouble of separating the good from the bad and wade through the troubled deep of literature in order, if we may be permitted a continuation of the figure, to collect the pearls and gems, and to describe the useless weeds, whether swimming on the surface or lying at the muddy bottom. A stupendous labour if we consider the great disproportion betwixt the former and the latter. Applying this to the case in point, and it is by no means inapposite, a reader unused to such arduous undertakings can image to himself no task so overwhelming as that of being left unaided to search for instruction in the mass of productions which are every year piled, mountain high, before him.... For this reason, it would be proper that there should be some professional inspectors to direct our choice, even were literary excellence and defect nearly equal. But when the average is on a ratio of at least ninety in the hundred in the scale of compositions *deadweight*, there is not, perhaps, any office so necessary as his, who, with patient circumspection, will examine the great account betwixt wisdom and folly, and settle the balance.

It is not, therefore, possible to conceive a more useful institution than that of a literary journal, when conducted with various ability and inflexible justice; nor can it be denied that a great variety of articles, in every branch of literature, have been analysed on these principles, and a due proportion of good has thence resulted to the community.

We have to boast, even at this day, of great and noble critics; and from most, indeed, in all of our literary journals, we find substantial evidence of unimpeachable judgement and unwarped integrity. It is not, however, to be expected that any human association composed of many members should be conducted on principles uniformly sagacious and correct. Were they to write apart, and consult together ultimately, there must even then often be a clash of sentiment, a dissonance of opinion.

Yet I am persuaded the critics above-described are the very persons who must reprobate the virulences[1] and regret the errors for which they are made responsible. The literary body cannot be supposed to separate, or seem to move a limb independently—much less to commit themselves, and confederate against each other, by deploring the want of candour in some of their colleagues, and of capacity in others. Thus from their not being associated by congeniality, or chosen by consent—and yet under a kind of compact to hold together, and by the good faith that should be preserved in all treaties, bound to support one another in the way of a common cause—the errors, incongruities, adulations, and virulences, which are observed occasionally to disfigure their journals, attach indiscriminately to all.

from Hannah More, *Strictures on the Modern System of Female Education* (1799)

from CHAPTER 8, ON FEMALE STUDY

Will it not be ascribed to a captious singularity, if I venture to remark that real knowledge and real piety, though they may have gained in many instances, have suffered in others from that profusion of little, amusing, sentimental books with which the youthful library overflows? Abundance has its dangers as well as scarcity. In the first place, may not the multiplicity of these alluring little works increase the natural reluctance to those more dry and uninteresting studies, of which, after all, the rudiments of every part of learning *must* consist? And, secondly, is there not some danger (though there are many honourable exceptions) that some of those engaging narratives may serve to infuse into the youthful heart a sort of spurious goodness, a confidence of virtue, a parade of charity? And that the benevolent actions with the recital of which they abound, when they are not made to flow from any source but *feeling*, may tend to inspire a self-complacency, a self-gratulation, a "stand by, for I am holier than thou?" May not the success with which the good deeds of the little heroes are uniformly crowned, the invariable reward which is made the instant concomi-

---

[1]   *virulences* Incidences of bitter hostility or antagonism.

tant of well-doing, furnish the young reader with false views of the condition of life, and the nature of the divine dealings with men? May they not help to suggest a false standard of morals, to infuse a love of popularity and an anxiety for praise, in the place of that simple and unostentatious rule of doing whatever good we do *because it is the will of God*? The universal substitution of this principle would tend to purify the worldly morality of many a popular little story. And there are few dangers which good parents will more carefully guard against than that of giving their children a mere political piety—that sort of religion which just goes to make people more respectable, and to stand well with the world; a religion which is to save appearances without inculcating realities; a religion which affects to "preach peace and good will to men," but which forgets to give "glory to God in the highest."[1]

There is a certain precocity of mind which is much helped on by these superficial modes of instruction; for frivolous reading will produce its correspondent effect in much less time than books of solid instruction; the imagination being liable to be worked upon, and the feelings to be set a going, much faster than the understanding can be opened and the judgment enlightened. A talent for conversation should be the result of instruction, not its precursor: it is a golden fruit when suffered to ripen gradually on the tree of knowledge; but if forced in the hot-bed of a circulating library, it will turn out worthless and vapid in proportion as it was artificial and premature. Girls who have been accustomed to devour a multitude of frivolous books will converse and write with a far greater appearance of skill, as to style and sentiment, at twelve or fourteen years old, than those of a more advanced age who are under the discipline of severer studies; but the former having early attained to that low standard which had been held out to them, become stationary; while the latter, quietly progressive, are passing through just gradations to a higher strain of mind; and those who early begin with talking and writing like women, commonly end with thinking and acting like children.

… Who are those ever-multiplying authors that with unparalleled fecundity are overstocking the world with their quick-succeeding progeny? They are NOVEL-WRITERS, the easiness of whose productions is at once the cause of their own fruitfulness, and of the almost infinitely numerous race of imitators to whom they give birth. Such is the frightful facility of this species of composition, that every raw girl, while she reads, is tempted to fancy that she can also write. And as Alexander, on perusing the *Iliad*, found by congenial sympathy the image of Achilles stamped on his own ardent soul, and felt himself the hero he was studying; and as Correggio, on first beholding a picture which exhibited the perfection of the graphic art, prophetically felt all his own future greatness, and cried out in rapture, "And I, too, am a painter!"[2] so a thorough-paced novel-reading Miss, at the close of every tissue of hackneyed adventures, feels within herself the stirring impulse of corresponding genius, and triumphantly exclaims, "And I, too, am an author!" The glutted imagination soon overflows with the redundance of cheap sentiment and plentiful incident, and by a sort of arithmetical proportion is enabled by the perusal of any three novels to produce a fourth; till every fresh production, like the prolific progeny of Banquo, is followed by "Another, and another, and another!"[3] Is a lady, however destitute of talents, education, or knowledge of the world, whose studies have been completed by a circulating library, in any distress of mind? the writing a novel suggests itself as the best soother of her sorrows! Does she labour under any depression of circumstances? writing a novel occurs as the readiest receipt for mending them! and she solaces her imagination with the conviction that the subscription which has been extorted by her importunity, or given to her necessities, has been offered as a homage to her genius; and this confidence instantly levies a fresh contribution for a succeeding work. Capacity and cultivation are so little taken into the account, that writing a book seems to be now considered as the only sure resource which the idle and the illiterate have always in their power.

---

[1] *preach peace … the highest* Quotations from Luke 2.14.

[2] *Alexander … ardent soul* Reference to a famous anecdote recounting Alexander the Great's sympathy with Achilles, the Greek hero of Homer's *Iliad*; *Correggio* Italian Renaissance painter Antonio Allegri (c. 1494–1534), called Correggio after his birthplace.

[3] *prolific progeny … another* See *Macbeth* 4.1, in which Macbeth is frustrated by a vision of a nearly endless line of Banquo's royal heirs.

from Charles and Mary Lamb, "Preface," *Tales from Shakespeare* (1807)[1]

The following tales are meant to be submitted to the young reader as an introduction to the study of Shakespeare, for which purpose his words are used whenever it seemed possible to bring them in; and in whatever has been added to give them the regular form of a connected story, diligent care has been taken to select such words as might least interrupt the effect of the beautiful English tongue in which he wrote: therefore, words introduced into our language since his time have been as far as possible avoided.

In those tales which have been taken from the tragedies, the young readers will perceive, when they come to see the source from which these stories are derived, that Shakespeare's own words, with little alteration, recur very frequently in the narrative as well as in the dialog; but in those made from the comedies the writers found themselves scarcely ever able to turn his words into the narrative form: therefore it is feared that, in them, dialogue has been made use of too frequently for young people not accustomed to the dramatic form of writing. But this fault, if it be a fault, has been caused by an earnest wish to give as much of Shakespeare's own words as possible; and if the "he said" and "she said," the question and the reply, should sometimes seem tedious to their young ears, they must pardon it, because it was the only way in which could be given to them a few hints and little foretastes of the great pleasure which awaits them in their elder years, when they come to the rich treasures from which these small and valueless coins are extracted; pretending to no other merit than as faint and imperfect stamps of Shakespeare's matchless image. Faint and imperfect images they must be called, because the beauty of his language is too frequently destroyed by the necessity of changing many of his excellent words into words far less expressive of his true sense, to make it read something like prose; and even in some few places, where his blank verse is given unaltered, as hoping from its simple plainness to cheat the young reader into the belief that they are reading prose, yet still, his language being transplanted from its own natural soil and wild poetic garden, it must want much of its native beauty.

It has been wished to make these tales easy reading for very young children. To the utmost of their ability the writers have constantly kept this in mind; but the subjects of most of them made this a very difficult task. It was no easy matter to give the histories of men and women in terms familiar to the apprehension of a very young mind. For young ladies too, it has been the intention chiefly to write; because boys being generally permitted the use of their fathers' libraries at a much earlier age than girls are, they frequently have the best scenes of Shakespeare by heart before their sisters are permitted to look into this manly book; and, therefore, instead of recommending these tales to the perusal of young gentlemen who can read them so much better in the originals, their kind assistance is rather requested in explaining to their sisters such parts as are hardest for them to understand. And when they have helped them to get over the difficulties, then perhaps they will read to them (carefully selecting what is proper for a young sister's ear) some passage which has pleased them in one of these stories, in the very words of the scene from which it is taken; and it is hoped they will find that the beautiful extracts, the select passages, they may choose to give their sisters in this way will be much better relished and understood from their having some notion of the general story from one of these imperfect abridgments; which, if they be fortunately so done as to prove delightful to any of the young readers, it is hoped that no worse effect will result than to make them wish themselves a little older, that they may be allowed to read the plays at full length (such a wish will be neither peevish nor irrational). When time and leave of judicious friends shall put them into their hands, they will discover in such of them as are here abridged (not to mention almost as many more, which are left untouched) many surprising events and turns of fortune, which for their infinite variety could not be contained in this little book, besides a world of sprightly and

---

[1] *Tales from Shakespeare* This first appeared under Charles's name. He wrote the first half of the preface and adapted some of the tragedies; Mary completed the rest of the collection.

cheerful characters, both men and women, the humour of which it was feared would be lost if it were attempted to reduce the length of them. ...

from an advertisement in *The Times* for Thomas Bowdler's *The Family Shakespeare* (15 December 1818)

> Bowdler's work gained little attention upon publication until, in 1812, two literary journals, *Black-wood's Magazine* and the *Edinburgh Review*, began a literary debate over the merits and achievements of Bowdler's work. The controversy sparked sales, making the work a sudden bestseller.

Entire New School Books, and New Editions, published by Longman, Hunt, Rees, Orme, and Brown, London,

1. THE FAMILY SHAKESPEARE; in which nothing is added to the original text; but those words and expressions are omitted which cannot with propriety be read aloud in a family. By THOMAS BOWDLER, Esq. ...

"My great objects in this undertaking are to remove from the writings of Shakespeare some defects which diminish their value, and at the same to present to the public an edition of his plays, which the parent, the guardian, and the instructor of youth may place without fear in the hands of the pupil; and from which the pupil may derive instruction as well as pleasure; may improve his moral principles while he refines his taste; and, without incurring the danger of being hurt with any indelicacy of expression, may learn, in the fate of Macbeth, that even a kingdom is dearly purchased, if virtue be the price of acquisition."—Preface.

Anna Laetitia Barbauld, "On the Origin and Progress of Novel-Writing" (1810)[1]

A collection of novels has a better chance of giving pleasure than of commanding respect. Books of this description are condemned by the grave, and despised by the fastidious; but their leaves are seldom found unopened, and they occupy the parlour and the dressing-room while productions of higher name are often gathering dust upon the shelf. It might not perhaps be difficult to show that this species of composition is entitled to a higher rank than has been generally assigned it. Fictitious adventures, in one form or other, have made a part of the polite literature of every age and nation. These have been grafted upon the actions of their heroes; they have been interwoven with their mythology; they have been moulded upon the manners of the age—and, in return, have influenced the manners of the succeeding generation by the sentiments they have infused and the sensibilities they have excited.

If the end and object of this species of writing be asked, many no doubt will be ready to tell us that its object is to call in fancy to the aid of reason, to deceive the mind into embracing truth under the guise of fiction:

Cosi a l'egro fanciul porgiamo aspersi
Di soave licor gli orli del vaso,
Succhi amari, ingannato in tanto ei beve,
E da l'inganno suo vita riceve,[2]

with such-like reasons equally grave and dignified. For my own part, I scruple not to confess that when I take up a novel my end and object is entertainment; and as I suspect that to be the case with most readers, I hesitate not to say that entertainment is their legitimate end and object. To read the productions of wit and genius is a very high pleasure to all persons of taste, and the avidity

---

[1] *On the ... Writing* From the introduction to Barbauld's fifty-volume edition of *The British Novelists*.

[2] *Cosi a ... riceve* Italian: "So when the draught we give to the sick child, / The vessel's edge we touch with syrup sweet; / Cheated, he swift drinks down the bitter brew, / And from the cheat receives his life anew" (from Torquato Tasso's *Gerusalemme Liberata*, 1575).

with which they are read by all such shows sufficiently that they are calculated to answer this end. Reading is the cheapest of pleasures: it is a domestic pleasure. Dramatic exhibitions give a more poignant delight, but they are seldom enjoyed in perfection, and never without expense and trouble. Poetry requires in the reader a certain elevation of mind and a practiced ear. It is seldom relished unless a taste be formed for it pretty early. But the humble novel is always ready to enliven the gloom of solitude, to soothe the languor of debility and disease, to win the attention from pain or vexatious occurrences, to take man from himself (at many seasons the worst company he can be in), and, while the moving picture of life passes before him, to make him forget the subject of his own complaints. It is pleasant to the mind to sport in the boundless regions of possibility; to find relief from the sameness of everyday occurrences by expatiating amidst brighter skies and fairer fields; to exhibit love that is always happy, valour that is always successful; to feed the appetite for wonder by a quick succession of marvelous events; and to distribute, like a ruling Providence, rewards and punishments which fall just where they ought to fall.

It is sufficient, therefore, as an end, that these writings add to the innocent pleasures of life; and if they do no harm, the entertainment they give is a sufficient good. We cut down the tree that bears no fruit, but we ask nothing of a flower beyond its scent and its colour. The unpardonable sin in a novel is dullness: however grave or wise it may be, if its author possesses no powers of amusing, he has no business to write novels; he should employ his pen in some more serious part of literature.

from Isaac D'Israeli, *The Case of Authors Stated, Including the History of Literary Property* (1812)

Johnson has dignified the booksellers as "the patrons of literature,"[1] which was generous in that great author, who had written well and lived but ill all his life on that patronage. Eminent booksellers, in their constant intercourse with the most enlightened class of the community, that is, with the best authors and the best readers, partake of the intelligence around them; their great capitals, too, are productive of good and evil in literature; useful when they carry on great works, and pernicious when they sanction indifferent ones. Yet are they but commercial men. A trader can never be deemed a patron, for it would be romantic to purchase what is not saleable; and where no favour is conferred, there is no patronage.

Authors continue poor, and booksellers become opulent; an extraordinary result! Booksellers are not agents for authors, but proprietors of their works, so that the perpetual revenues of literature are solely in the possession of the trade.[2]

Is it then wonderful that even successful authors are indigent? They are heirs to fortunes, but by a strange singularity they are disinherited at their birth; for, on the publication of their works, these cease to be their own property. Let that natural property be secured, and a good book would be an inheritance, a leasehold or a freehold, as you choose it; it might at least last out a generation, and descend to the author's blood, were they permitted to live on their father's glory, as in all other property they do on his industry. ...

The verbal and tasteless lawyers, not many years past, with legal metaphysics wrangled like the schoolmen,[3] inquiring of each other, "whether the *style* and *ideas* of an author were tangible things; or if these were *property*, how is *possession* to be taken, or any act of *occupancy* made on mere intellectual *ideas*." Nothing, said they, can be an object of property but which has a corporeal substance; the air and the light, to which they compared an author's ideas, are common to all; ideas in

---

[1] *Johnson ... literature*   According to James Boswell's *Life of Samuel Johnson* (1791), the lexicographer and author (whose father was a bookseller) referred to his publisher ("bookseller") as his "patron" in a letter to a friend. Johnson is also recorded as having said mockingly to the Earl of Chesterfield (the *Dictionary*'s intended patron, with

whom Johnson had quarreled), "Is not a patron, my lord, one who looks with unconcern on a man struggling for life in the water and when he has reached ground encumbers him with help?"

[2] *Authors continue ... trade*   The Statute of Anne (1710), generally considered the first copyright act, granted copyright protection to authors or proprietors for a fixed period of fourteen years. The law generally protected publishers rather than authors.

[3] *schoolmen*   I.e., the Scholastics, adherents of the Scholastic philosophy.

the MS[1] state were compared to birds in a cage; while the author confines them in his own dominion, none but he has a right to let them fly; but the moment he allows the bird to escape from his hand, it is no violation of property in anyone to make it his own. And to prove that there existed no property after publication, they found an analogy in the gathering of acorns, or in seizing on a vacant piece of ground; and thus degrading that most refined piece of art formed in the highest state of society, a literary production, they brought us back to a state of nature, and seem to have concluded that literary property was purely ideal; a phantom which, as its author could neither grasp nor confine to himself, he must entirely depend on the public benevolence for his reward.[2]

The ideas, that is, the work of an author, are "tangible things." "There are works," to quote the words of a near and dear relative, "which require great learning, great industry, great labour, and great capital, in their preparation. They assume a palpable form. You may fill warehouses with them, and freight ships; and the tenure by which they are held is superior to that of all other property, for it is original. It is tenure which does not exist in a doubtful title; which does not spring from any adventitious circumstances; it is not found, it is not purchased, it is not prescriptive—it is original; so it is the most natural of all titles, because it is the most simple and least artificial. It is paramount and sovereign, because it is a tenure by creation."[3]

There were indeed some more generous spirits and better philosophers fortunately found on the same bench; and the identity of a literary composition was resolved into its sentiments and language, besides what was more obviously valuable to some persons, the print and paper. On this slight principle was issued the profound award which accorded a certain term of years to any work, however immortal. They could not diminish the immortality of a book, but only its reward. In all the litigations respecting literary property, authors were little considered—except some honourable testimonies due to genius, from the sense of Willes, and the eloquence of Mansfield.[4] Literary property was still disputed, like the rights of a parish common. An honest printer, who could not always write grammar, had the shrewdness to make a bold effort in this scramble, and perceiving that even by this last favourable award all literary property would necessarily centre with the booksellers, now stood forward for his own body—the printers. This rough advocate observed that "a few persons who call themselves *booksellers*, about the number of *twenty-five*, have kept the *monopoly of books and copies* in their hands, to the entire exclusion of all others, but more especially to the *printers*, whom they have always held it a rule never to let become purchasers in *copy*." Not a word for the *authors*! As for them, they were doomed by both parties as the fat oblation: they indeed sent forth some meek bleatings; but what were authors, between judges, booksellers, and printers? The sacrificed among the sacrificers. ...

As the matter now stands, let us address an arithmetical age—but my pen hesitates to bring down my subject to an argument fitted to "these coster-monger times."[5] On the present principle of literary property, it results that an author disposes of a leasehold property of twenty-eight years, often for less than the price of one year's purchase! How many living authors are the sad witnesses of this fact, who, like so many Esaus, have sold their inheritance for a meal![6] I leave the whole school of Adam Smith to calm their calculating emotions concerning "that unprosperous race of men" (sometimes

---

[1] *MS* I.e., manuscript.

[2] [D'Israeli's note] Sir James Burrows's Reports on Literary Property.

[3] [D'Israeli's note] *Mirror of Parliament*, 3529. [*Mirror of Parliament* was a journal, founded by Sir John Barrow in 1828, that aimed to provide a record of Parliamentary debates.]

[4] *Willes* Sir John Willes (1685–1761), who was the presiding judge in several copyright cases, and who believed that authors had a right to their intellectual property; *Mansfield* William Murray, first Earl of Mansfield (1705–93), a judge who upheld authors' perpetual common-law rights to their literary property in the influential copyright case *Millar v. Taylor* (1769, overturned in *Donaldson v. Beckett*, 1774).

[5] [D'Israeli's note] A coster-monger, or Costard-monger, is "A dealer in apples, which are so called because they are shaped like a costard, i.e., a man's head."—*Stevens.* Johnson explains the phrase eloquently: "In these times when the prevalence of trade has produced that meanness that rates the merit of everything by money."

[6] *Esaus ... meal* Cf. Hebrews 12.16: "Lest there be any fornicator, or profane person, as Esau, who for one morsel of meat sold his birthright."

this master-seer calls them "unproductive") "commonly called *men of letters*," who are pretty much in the situation which lawyers and physicians would be in, were these, as he tells us, in that state when "*a scholar* and *a beggar* seem to have been very nearly *synonymous terms*"[1]—and this melancholy fact that man of genius discovered, without the feather of his pen brushing away a tear from his lid—without one spontaneous and indignant groan!

Authors may exclaim, "we ask for justice, not charity." They would not need to require any favour, nor claim any other than that protection which an enlightened government, in its wisdom and its justice, must bestow. They would leave to the public disposition the sole appreciation of their works; their book must make its own fortune; a bad work may be cried up, and a good work may be cried down; but Faction will soon lose its voice, and Truth acquire one. The cause we are pleading is not the calamities of indifferent writers, but of those whose utility or whose genius long survives that limited term which has been so hardly wrenched from the penurious hand of verbal lawyers. Every lover of literature, and every votary of humanity has long felt indignant at that sordid state and all those secret sorrows to which men of the finest genius, or of sublime industry, are reduced and degraded in society. Johnson himself, who rejected that perpetuity of literary property which some enthusiasts seemed to claim at the time the subject was undergoing the discussion of the judges, is, however, for extending the copyright to a *century*. Could authors secure this, their natural right, literature would acquire a permanent and a nobler reward; for great authors would then be distinguished by the very profits they would receive from that obscure multitude whose common disgraces they frequently participate, notwithstanding the superiority of their own genius. ...

Authors now submit to have a shorter life than their own celebrity. While the book markets of Europe are supplied with the writings of English authors, and they have a wider diffusion in America than at home, it seems a national ingratitude to limit the existence of works for their authors to a short number of years, and then to seize on their possession for ever.

William Hazlitt, "A Review of *The St. James Chronicle, The Morning Chronicle, The Times, The New Times, The Courier, &c., Cobbett's Weekly Journal, The Examiner, The Observer, The Gentleman's Magazine, The New Monthly Magazine, The London, &c. &c.*," *The Edinburgh Review* (1823)

Literature formerly was a sweet Heremitress,[2] who fed on the pure breath of Fame in silence and in solitude, far from the madding strife, in sylvan shade or cloistered hall, she trimmed her lamp or turned her hourglass, pale with studious care, and aiming only to "make the age to come her own!"[3] She gave her life to the perfecting some darling work, and bequeathed it, dying, to posterity! Vain hope, perhaps; but the hope itself was fruition—calm, serene, blissful, unearthly! Modern literature, on the contrary, is a gay Coquette, fluttering, fickle, vain; followed by a train of flatterers; besieged by a crowd of pretenders; courted, she courts again; receives delicious praise, and dispenses it; is impatient for applause; pants for the breath of popularity; renounces eternal fame for a newspaper puff; trifles with all sorts of arts and sciences; coquettes with fifty accomplishments—*mille ornatus habet, mille decenter*[4]—is the subject of polite conversation; the darling of private parties; the go-between in politics; the directress of fashion; the polisher of manners; and, like her winged prototype in Spenser,

"Now this now that, she tasteth tenderly,"[5]

---

[1] *Adam Smith ... terms* Reference to Adam Smith's *Wealth of Nations*, Book 1, Chapter 10, in which Smith discusses "that unprosperous race of men commonly called men of letters." He says these writers were generally educated for the Church, and then failed for some reason to take holy orders. "They have generally, therefore, been educated at the public expense, and their numbers are everywhere so great as commonly to reduce the price of their labor to a very paltry recompense."

[2] *Heremitress* I.e., female hermit.

[3] *make the ... own* Cf. Abraham Cowley, "The Motto" (1656), line 2.

[4] *mille ... decenter* Latin: "She has a thousand trifling things, a thousand things which are fitting to her." Reference to a quotation from the work of Roman elegiac poet Tibullus (c. 55–c. 19 BCE).

[5] *Now this ... tenderly* From Edmund Spenser's "Muiopotmos, or The Fate of the Butterflie" (1590).

glitters, flutters, buzzes, spawns, dies—and is forgotten! But the very variety and superficial polish show the extent and height to which knowledge has been accumulated, and the general interest taken in letters.

To dig to the bottom of a subject through so many generations of authors is now impossible: the concrete mass is too voluminous and vast to be contained in any single head; and therefore, we must have essences and samples as substitutes for it. We have collected a superabundance of raw materials: the grand *desideratum*[1] now is, to fashion and render them portable. Knowledge is no longer confined to the few: the object therefore is, to make it accessible and attractive to the many. The *Monachism*[2] of literature is at an end; the cells of learning are thrown open and let in the light of universal day. We can no longer be churls of knowledge, ascetics in pretension. We must yield to the spirit of change (whether for the better or worse); and "to beguile the time, look like the time."[3] A modern author may (without much imputation of his wisdom) declare for a short life and a merry one. He may be a little gay, thoughtless, and dissipated. Literary immortality is now let on short leases, and he must be contented to succeed by rotation. A scholar of the olden time had resources, had consolations to support him under many privations and disadvantages. A light (that light which penetrates the most clouded skies) cheered him in his lonely cell, in the most obscure retirement; and, with the eye of faith, he could see the meanness of his garb exchanged for the wings of the Shining Ones, and the wedding-garment of the Spouse. Again, he lived only in the contemplation of old books and old events; and the remote and future became habitually present to his imagination, like the past. He was removed from low, petty vanity by the nature of his studies, and could wait patiently for his reward till after death. We exist in the bustle of the world, and cannot escape from the notice of our contemporaries. We must please to live, and therefore should live to please. We must look to the public for support. Instead of solemn testimonies from the learned, we require the smiles of the fair and the polite. If princes scowl upon us, the broad shining face of the people may turn to us with a favorable aspect. Is not this life (too) sweet? Would we change it for the former if we could? But the great point is that *we cannot*! Therefore, let reviews[4] flourish—let magazines increase and multiply—let the daily and weekly newspapers live forever! We are optimists in literature, and hold, with certain limitations that in this respect, whatever is, is right![5]

from John Stuart Mill, "The Present State of Literature" (16 November 1827)[6]

It is the demand, in literature as in most other things, which calls forth the supply. … Assuming, therefore, as an indisputable truth, that the writers of every age are for the most part what the readers make them, it becomes important to the present question to consider who formed the reading public formerly, and who compose it now. The present age is very remarkably distinguished from all other ages by the number of persons who can read, and, what is of more consequence, by the number who do. Our working classes have learned to read, and our idle classes have learned to find pleasure in reading, and to devote a part of that time to it which they formerly spent in amusements of a grosser kind. That human nature will be a gainer, and that in a high degree, by this change, no one can be more firmly convinced than I am—but it will perhaps be found that the benefit lies rather in the ultimate than in the immediate effects. Reading is necessary, but no wise or even sensible man was ever made by reading alone. The proper use of reading is to be subservient to thinking. It is by those who read to think that knowledge is advanced, prejudices dispelled, and the physical and moral condition of mankind is improved. I cannot, however, perceive that the general diffusion (so remarkable in our own day) of the taste for reading has yet been accompanied by any marked increase in taste for the

---

[1] *desideratum* Latin: thing desired.

[2] *Monachism* Monasticism.

[3] *to beguile … like the time* From Shakespeare's *Macbeth* 1.5.62–63.

[4] *reviews* I.e., literary journals or periodicals.

[5] *whatever … right* Reference to Alexander Pope's *Essay on Man* (1733), Epistle 1, line 294: "One truth is clear: whatever is, is right."

[6] *The Present … 1827* From a speech delivered to the London Debating Society.

severer exercises of the intellect; that such will one day be its effect, may fairly be presumed, but it has not yet declared itself: and it is to the immense multiplication in the present day of those who read but do not think, that I should be disposed to ascribe what I view as the degeneracy of our literature.

In former days the literati and the learned formed a class apart, and few concerned themselves with literature and philosophy except those who had leisure and inclination to form their philosophical opinions by study and meditation, and to cultivate their literary taste by the assiduous perusal of the most approved models. Those whose sole occupation was pleasure did not seek it in books, but in the gaieties of a court, or in field sports and debauchery. The public for which authors wrote was a small but, to a very considerable degree, an instructed public; and their suffrages were only to be gained by thinking to a certain extent profoundly and by writing well. The authors who were then in highest reputation are chiefly those to whom we now look back as the ablest thinkers and best writers of their time. No doubt there were many blockheads among the reading public in those days, as well as in our own, and the blockheads often egregiously misplaced their admiration, as blockheads are wont, but the applause of the blockheads was not then the object aimed at even by those who obtained it, and they did not constitute so large and so influential a class of readers as to tempt any writer of talent to lay himself out for their admiration. If an author failed of obtaining the suffrages of men of knowledge and taste, it was for want of powers, not from the misapplication of them. The case is now altered. We live in a refined age, and there is a corresponding refinement in our amusements. It is now the height of *mauvais ton*[1] to be drunk, neither is it any longer considered decorous among gentlemen that the staple of their conversation should consist of bawdy. Reading has become one of the most approved and fashionable methods of killing time, and the number of persons who have skimmed the surface of literature is far greater than at any previous period of our history. Our writers therefore find that the greatest success is now to be obtained by writing for the many, and endeavouring all they can to bring themselves down to the level of the many, both in their matter and in the manner of expressing it.

---

[1]   *mauvais ton* French: bad form.

Samuel Taylor Coleridge
1772 – 1834

Samuel Taylor Coleridge is one of the most important figures of English Romanticism. Over the course of a few years, when in his mid-twenties, he composed poems that continue to be regarded as central to the English canon, among them "The Rime of the Ancient Mariner," "Frost at Midnight," and the fragment "Kubla Khan." He wrote few poems for the last thirty-five years of his life, as he was undermined by procrastination and an addiction to opium. Nonetheless, Coleridge's story is in the end one of success. His poetry has remained fresh and affecting for generations of readers, and his later philosophical writing earned him a place as one of the most profound thinkers of the nineteenth century.

Born in 1772, Coleridge was the youngest son of the vicar of Ottery St. Mary, the Rev. John Coleridge, and his wife, Anna Bowdon. He was a voracious reader with a mind that he described as "habituated to *the Vast*." When his father died, his mother arranged for nine-year-old Samuel to be sent to Christ's Hospital in London, a school founded to educate the promising sons of the poor. Although he received an excellent education at Christ's, Coleridge remained ambivalent about the school long after he left, continuing to feel injured by the fact that he had been a "charity boy."

In 1791, Coleridge entered Jesus College, Cambridge, where his intellectual abilities and academic success were matched only by his facility in running up debts and his increasing despair at his financial situation. He eventually attempted to escape his financial problems by enlisting (under the name Silas Tomkyn Comberbache), but he was rescued by his brother George from both the army and financial distress. In 1794 he met Robert Southey, then an Oxford undergraduate, and the two recognized a shared interest in poetry and radical political ideas. They hatched a plan to found a communitarian settlement in Pennsylvania to be run under a system they called "Pantisocracy." Both the plan and the friendship, however, foundered over the question of what role women and servants should play (Coleridge insisted on a completely egalitarian community; Southey did not). In his early exuberance for the scheme Coleridge became engaged to Sara Fricker, the sister of Southey's fiancée, and he felt bound to honor the commitment even though his feeling for her quickly waned. They married in 1795 but after a brief period of happiness they became progressively more miserable, finally separating in 1807. The marriage produced four children.

Coleridge began a short-lived liberal periodical in 1796 called *The Watchman*. He also published his first poetic collection, *Poems on Various Subjects*, which contained the poem that would later be titled "The Eolian Harp." Almost destitute, he was saved by a yearly pension granted him by Tom and Josiah Wedgwood, sons of the famous potter. The following year he met William Wordsworth and began a troubled but lifelong friendship, the first fruit of which was the joint volume *Lyrical Ballads*, which opened with Coleridge's "The Rime of the Ancyent Marinere" (revised and retitled in 1816). Shortly afterward he accompanied Wordsworth and his sister Dorothy to Germany, where he immersed himself in German philosophy.

Returning to England in 1799, Coleridge joined Wordsworth in the Lake District. Here he met Sara Hutchinson, Wordsworth's future sister-in-law, and became infatuated with her. The relationship between the two remained platonic, but it magnified Coleridge's estrangement from his wife, and the situation was made worse by his increasing dependence on laudanum, the liquid form of opium. From 1802 onward Coleridge spent only brief periods with his family. In 1804 he set off for Malta, where he took a post in the British government. From this time forth he became progressively more conservative, eventually going so far as to deny entirely his early liberal leanings. After a year and a half he returned to England penniless.

From 1808 to 1818, Coleridge intermittently delivered lectures with topics that ranged from German philosophy to current educational controversies. The highlight was a series he gave on Shakespeare and Milton, which displayed all the brilliance of his critical skills. Although frequently sidetracked onto other topics, he also offered incisive analyses of aspects of Shakespeare's plays, from a consideration of love in *Romeo and Juliet* to an anatomization of Hamlet's paradoxical psychology. He ended the series with a masterful examination of *Paradise Lost*.

Coleridge's great talents as a poet lay in his ability to combine Gothicism with complex psychological presentation and to delineate the mind as it explored itself and its relation to the larger world. His more uncanny poems, such as "The Rime of the Ancient Mariner," are haunting both because they excite tension in the reader and because the psychological complexity of the characters and relationships brings to life what might otherwise be clichéd sensationalism. Poems such as "Frost at Midnight" mingle contemplation and description to produce a richly interrelated whole, a style which influenced not only Wordsworth (specifically in "Tintern Abbey"), but poets to the present day.

From the first Coleridge was interested in newspaper writing, in which he could comment on immediate social and cultural issues. The most important of his journalistic ventures was *The Friend* (1809–10), a weekly newspaper he largely wrote himself. In 1813 his drama, *Remorse,* was staged at the Drury Lane Theatre. Three years later he took up residence in Highgate with the family of the young doctor James Gillman. He asked to stay for a month; he remained for the rest of his life. The situation offered a stable environment, and Coleridge began publishing regularly. His Gothic ballad, "Christabel," long known to other writers through private recitation (and an influence on Walter Scott's "The Lay of the Last Minstrel" and Lord Byron's "The Siege of Corinth"), was published in a collection with "Kubla Khan" and "The Pains of Sleep" in 1816, through Byron's enthusiastic support. Soon afterward Coleridge published *Sybilline Leaves*, a collection of his previous poems (including a newly revised *Ancient Mariner* with a marginal gloss) and the long work *Biographia Literaria*.

Although at times rambling and discursive, *Biographia Literaria* is a major literary and philosophical work. Its first volume is autobiographical, detailing (among other events) Coleridge's education and his first involvement with Wordsworth. This volume also begins to delve into literary analysis as, for example, in the famous passage in Chapter 13, in which Coleridge differentiates between imagination and fancy, defining the qualities of each and declaring imagination superior. The second volume consists almost entirely of literary criticism, both formal and philosophical, much of it focusing on Wordsworth's poetry. In both volumes, Coleridge anatomizes both poetry and poetic production, considering not only formal elements but also the psychology of the creative process.

Coleridge's genius and importance were gradually acknowledged by a considerable number of his contemporaries, and the "Sage of Highgate" began to be viewed as an important thinker. This opinion was cemented by the publication of *Aids to Reflection* (1825), which stressed the role of the personal in Christian faith, and *On the Constitution of Church and State* (1830), which emphasized the importance of national culture and defined the class of intellectuals needed to protect it. This latter book in particular had a profound influence on such authors as Matthew Arnold and Thomas Carlyle.

From 1832 onward Coleridge became increasingly ill, although this did not prevent him from helping to prepare *Poetical Works* (1834), a collection of his poetry—he died shortly after its publication. *Table Talk*, a posthumously-published collection of his remarks on miscellaneous topics, appeared the following year.

⌘ ⌘ ⌘

The Eolian Harp[1]

Composed at Clevedon, Somersetshire

My pensive Sara![2] thy soft cheek reclined
Thus on mine arm, most soothing sweet it is
To sit beside our Cot,° our Cot o'ergrown   cottage
With white-flower'd Jasmin, and the broad-leav'd Myrtle,
5 (Meet emblems they of Innocence and Love!)
And watch the clouds, that late were rich with light,
Slow saddening round, and mark the star of eve
Serenely brilliant (such should Wisdom be)
Shine opposite! How exquisite the scents
10 Snatch'd from yon bean-field! and the world so hush'd!
The stilly murmur of the distant Sea
Tells us of silence.

             And that simplest Lute,
Placed length-ways in the clasping casement, hark!
15 How by the desultory breeze caress'd,
Like some coy maid half yielding to her lover,
It pours such sweet upbraiding, as must needs
Tempt to repeat the wrong! And now, its strings
Boldlier swept, the long sequacious° notes   unvarying
20 Over delicious surges sink and rise,
Such a soft floating witchery of sound
As twilight Elfins make, when they at eve
Voyage on gentle gales from Fairy-Land,
Where Melodies round honey-dropping flowers,
25 Footless and wild, like birds of Paradise,[3]
Nor pause, nor perch, hovering on untam'd wing!
O! the one Life within us and abroad,
Which meets all motion and becomes its soul,
A light in sound, a sound-like power in light,
30 Rhythm in all thought, and joyance every where—
Methinks, it should have been impossible
Not to love all things in a world so fill'd;
Where the breeze warbles, and the mute still air

Is Music slumbering on her instrument.

35 And thus, my Love! as on the midway slope
Of yonder hill I stretch my limbs at noon,
Whilst through my half-clos'd eye-lids I behold
The sunbeams dance, like diamonds, on the main,
And tranquil muse upon tranquillity;
40 Full many a thought uncall'd and undetain'd,
And many idle flitting phantasies,
Traverse my indolent and passive brain,
As wild and various, as the random gales
That swell and flutter on this subject Lute!
45 And what if all of animated nature
Be but organic Harps diversely fram'd,
That tremble into thought, as o'er them sweeps
Plastic and vast, one intellectual breeze,
At once the Soul of each, and God of all?
50 But thy more serious eye a mild reproof
Darts, O belovéd Woman! nor such thoughts
Dim and unhallow'd dost thou not reject,
And biddest me walk humbly with my God.
Meek Daughter in the family of Christ!
55 Well hast thou said and holily disprais'd
These shapings of the unregenerate mind;
Bubbles that glitter as they rise and break
On vain Philosophy's aye-babbling spring.
For never guiltless may I speak of Him,
60 The Incomprehensible! save when with awe
I praise Him, and with Faith that inly feels;
Who with His saving mercies healéd me,
A sinful and most miserable man,
Wilder'd and dark, and gave me to possess
65 Peace, and this Cot, and thee, heart-honour'd Maid!
—1795

Fears In Solitude

Written in April 1798, During the Alarm of An Invasion[4]

A green and silent spot, amid the hills,
A small and silent dell! O'er stiller place

---

[1] *Eolian Harp* Musical instrument named after Æolus, Greek god of the winds; the music of the harp is created by exposure to the wind passing through it.

[2] *Sara* Sara Fricker, whom Coleridge had recently wed.

[3] *birds of Paradise* New Guinean birds of brilliant plumage, thought by Europeans to have no feet.

[4] *Invasion* By the French, who threatened an attack on Wales.

No singing sky-lark ever poised himself.
The hills are heathy, save that swelling slope,
5   Which hath a gay and gorgeous covering on,
All golden with the never-bloomless furze,°   *evergreen shrub*
Which now blooms most profusely: but the dell,
Bathed by the mist, is fresh and delicate
As vernal corn-field, or the unripe flax,
10   When, through its half-transparent stalks, at eve,
The level sunshine glimmers with green light.
O! 'tis a quiet spirit-healing nook!
Which all, methinks, would love; but chiefly he,
The humble man, who, in his youthful years,
15   Knew just so much of folly, as had made
His early manhood more securely wise!
Here he might lie on fern or withered heath,
While from the singing lark (that sings unseen
The minstrelsy that solitude loves best),
20   And from the sun, and from the breezy air,
Sweet influences trembled o'er his frame;
And he, with many feelings, many thoughts,
Made up a meditative joy, and found
Religious meanings in the forms of Nature!
25   And so, his senses gradually wrapt
In a half sleep, he dreams of better worlds,
And dreaming hears thee still, O singing lark,
That singest like an angel in the clouds!

My God! it is a melancholy thing
30   For such a man, who would full fain preserve
His soul in calmness, yet perforce must feel
For all his human brethren—O my God!
It weighs upon the heart, that he must think
What uproar and what strife may now be stirring
35   This way or that way o'er these silent hills—
Invasion, and the thunder and the shout,
And all the crash of onset; fear and rage,
And undetermined conflict—even now,
Even now, perchance, and in his native isle:
40   Carnage and screams beneath this blessed sun!
We have offended, O! my countrymen!
We have offended very grievously,
And have been tyrannous. From east to west
A groan of accusation pierces Heaven!
45   The wretched plead against us; multitudes
Countless and vehement, the sons of God,
Our brethren! like a cloud that travels on,

Steamed up from Cairo's swamps of pestilence,
Even so, my countrymen! have we gone forth
50   And borne to distant tribes slavery and pangs,
And, deadlier far, our vices, whose deep taint
With slow perdition murders the whole man,
His body and his soul! Meanwhile, at home,
All individual dignity and power
55   Engulfed in Courts, Committees, Institutions,
Associations and Societies,
A vain, speech-mounting, speech-reporting Guild,
One Benefit-Club for mutual flattery,
We have drunk up, demure as at a grace,
60   Pollutions from the brimming cup of wealth;
Contemptuous of all honourable rule,
Yet bartering freedom and the poor man's life
For gold, as at a market! The sweet words
Of Christian promise, words that even yet
65   Might stem destruction, were they wisely preached,
Are muttered o'er by men, whose tones proclaim
How flat and wearisome they feel their trade:
Rank scoffers some, but most too indolent
To deem them falsehoods, or to know their truth.
70   O! blasphemous! the Book of Life is made
A superstitious instrument, on which
We gabble o'er the oaths we mean to break,
For all must swear[1]—all and in every place,
College and wharf, council and justice-court;
75   All, all must swear, the briber and the bribed,
Merchant and lawyer, senator and priest,
The rich, the poor, the old man and the young;
All, all make up one scheme of perjury,
That faith doth reel; the very name of God
80   Sounds like a juggler's charm; and bold with joy,
Forth from his dark and lonely hiding-place,
(Portentous sight!) the owlet Atheism,
Sailing on obscene wings athwart the noon,
Drops his blue-fringèd lids, and holds them close,
85   And hooting at the glorious sun in Heaven,
Cries out, "Where is it?"

Thankless too for peace,
(Peace long preserved by fleets and perilous seas)

---

[1]   *all must swear*   According to the Test and Corporation Acts, all
public officials were required to swear allegiance to the Church of
England. (Thus there would be no Catholics, Nonconformists, or
Jews in office.)

Secure from actual warfare, we have loved
90   To swell the war-whoop, passionate for war!
Alas! for ages ignorant of all
Its ghastlier workings, (famine or blue plague,
Battle, or siege, or flight thro' wintry snows,)
We, this whole people, have been clamorous
95   For war and bloodshed; animating sports,
The which we pay for as a thing to talk of,
Spectators and not combatants! No guess
Anticipative of a wrong unfelt,
No speculation on contingency,
100   However dim and vague, too vague and dim
To yield a justifying cause; and forth,
(Stuffed out with big preamble, holy names,
And adjurations° of the God in Heaven,)   appeal
We send our mandates for the certain death
105   Of thousands and ten thousands! Boys and girls,
And women, that would groan to see a child
Pull off an insect's leg, all read of war,
The best amusement for our morning meal!
The poor wretch, who has learnt his only prayers
110   From curses, who knows scarcely words enough
To ask a blessing from his Heavenly Father,
Becomes a fluent phraseman, absolute
And technical in victories and defeats,
And all our dainty terms for fratricide;
115   Terms which we trundle smoothly o'er our tongues
Like mere abstractions, empty sounds to which
We join no feeling and attach no form!
As if the soldier died without a wound;
As if the fibres of this godlike frame
120   Were gored without a pang; as if the wretch,
Who fell in battle, doing bloody deeds,
Passed off to Heaven, translated and not killed;
As though he had no wife to pine for him,
No God to judge him! Therefore, evil days
125   Are coming on us, O my countrymen!
And what if all-avenging Providence,
Strong and retributive, should make us know
The meaning of our words, force us to feel
The desolation and the agony
130   Of our fierce doings?

                    Spare us yet awhile,
Father and God! O! spare us yet awhile!

Oh! let not English women drag their flight
Fainting beneath the burthen of their babes,
135   Of the sweet infants, that but yesterday
Laughed at the breast! Sons, brothers, husbands, all
Who ever gazed with fondness on the forms
Which grew up with you round the same fire-side,
And all who ever heard the sabbath-bells
140   Without the infidel's scorn, make yourselves pure!
Stand forth! be men! repel an impious foe,
Impious and false, a light yet cruel race,
Who laugh away all virtue, mingling mirth
With deeds of murder; and still promising
145   Freedom, themselves too sensual to be free,
Poison life's amities, and cheat the heart
Of faith and quiet hope, and all that soothes,
And all that lifts the spirit! Stand we forth;
Render them back upon the insulted ocean,
150   And let them toss as idly on its waves
As the vile sea-weed, which some mountain-blast
Swept from our shores! And oh! may we return
Not with a drunken triumph, but with fear,
Repenting of the wrongs with which we stung
155   So fierce a foe to frenzy!

                    I have told,
O Britons! O my brethren! I have told
Most bitter truth, but without bitterness.
Nor deem my zeal or factious or mistimed;
160   For never can true courage dwell with them,
Who, playing tricks with conscience, dare not look
At their own vices. We have been too long
Dupes of a deep delusion! Some, belike,
Groaning with restless enmity, expect
165   All change from change of constituted power;
As if a Government had been a robe,
On which our vice and wretchedness were tagged
Like fancy-points and fringes, with the robe
Pulled off at pleasure. Fondly these attach
170   A radical causation to a few
Poor drudges of chastising Providence,
Who borrow all their hues and qualities
From our own folly and rank wickedness,
Which gave them birth and nursed them. Others,
        meanwhile,
175   Dote with a mad idolatry; and all

Who will not fall before their images,
And yield them worship, they are enemies
Even of their country!

                        Such have I been deemed.—
180 But, O dear Britain! O my Mother Isle!
Needs must thou prove a name most dear and holy
To me, a son, a brother, and a friend,
A husband, and a father! who revere
All bonds of natural love, and find them all
185 Within the limits of thy rocky shores.
O native Britain! O my Mother Isle!
How shouldst thou prove aught else but dear and holy
To me, who from thy lakes and mountain-hills,
Thy clouds, thy quiet dales, thy rocks and seas,
190 Have drunk in all my intellectual life,
All sweet sensations, all ennobling thoughts,
All adoration of the God in nature,
All lovely and all honourable things,
Whatever makes this mortal spirit feel
195 The joy and greatness of its future being?
There lives nor form nor feeling in my soul
Unborrowed from my country! O divine
And beauteous island! thou hast been my sole
And most magnificent temple, in the which
200 I walk with awe, and sing my stately songs,
Loving the God that made me!—

                           May my fears,
My filial fears, be vain! and may the vaunts
And menace of the vengeful enemy
205 Pass like the gust, that roared and died away
In the distant tree: which heard, and only heard
In this low dell, bowed not the delicate grass.

      But now the gentle dew-fall sends abroad
The fruit-like perfume of the golden furze:
210 The light has left the summit of the hill,
Though still a sunny gleam lies beautiful,
Aslant the ivied beacon. Now farewell,
Farewell, awhile, O soft and silent spot!
On the green sheep-track, up the heathy hill,
215 Homeward I wind my way; and lo! recalled
From bodings that have well-nigh wearied me,
I find myself upon the brow, and pause

Startled! And after lonely sojourning
In such a quiet and surrounded nook,
220 This burst of prospect, here the shadowy main,
Dim tinted, there the mighty majesty
Of that huge amphitheatre of rich
And elmy fields, seems like society—
Conversing with the mind, and giving it
225 A livelier impulse and a dance of thought!
And now, belovéd Stowey![1] I behold
Thy church-tower, and, methinks, the four huge elms
Clustering, which mark the mansion of my friend;
And close behind them, hidden from my view,
230 Is my own lowly cottage, where my babe
And my babe's mother dwell in peace! With light
And quickened footsteps thitherward I tend,
Remembering thee, O green and silent dell!
And grateful, that by nature's quietness
235 And solitary musings, all my heart
Is softened, and made worthy to indulge
Love, and the thoughts that yearn for human kind.
—1798

Frost at Midnight

The Frost performs its secret ministry,
Unhelped by any wind. The owlet's cry
Came loud—and hark, again! loud as before.
The inmates of my cottage, all at rest,
5 Have left me to that solitude, which suits
Abstruser musings: save that at my side
My cradled infant slumbers peacefully.
'Tis calm indeed! so calm, that it disturbs
And vexes meditation with its strange
10 And extreme silentness. Sea, hill, and wood,
This populous village! Sea, and hill, and wood,
With all the numberless goings-on of life,
Inaudible as dreams! the thin blue flame
Lies on my low-burnt fire, and quivers not;
15 Only that film,[2] which fluttered on the grate,

---

[1] *Stowey* Nether Stowey, a village in Somerset where Coleridge lived for a few years.

[2] [Coleridge's note] In all parts of the kingdom these films are called *strangers* and supposed to portend the arrival of some absent friend.

Still flutters there, the sole unquiet thing.
Methinks, its motion in this hush of nature
Gives it dim sympathies with me who live,
Making it a companionable form,
20 Whose puny flaps and freaks the idling Spirit
By its own moods interprets, every where
Echo or mirror seeking of itself,
And makes a toy of Thought.

                But O! how oft,
25 How oft, at school, with most believing mind,
Presageful, have I gazed upon the bars,
To watch that fluttering *stranger*! and as oft
With unclosed lids, already had I dreamt
Of my sweet birth-place, and the old church-tower,
30 Whose bells, the poor man's only music, rang
From morn to evening, all the hot Fair-day,
So sweetly, that they stirred and haunted me
With a wild pleasure, falling on mine ear
Most like articulate sounds of things to come!
35 So gazed I, till the soothing things, I dreamt,
Lulled me to sleep, and sleep prolonged my dreams!
And so I brooded all the following morn,
Awed by the stern preceptor's° face, mine eye   *teacher's*
Fixed with mock study on my swimming book:
40 Save if the door half opened, and I snatched
A hasty glance, and still my heart leaped up,
For still I hoped to see the *stranger's* face,
Townsman, or aunt, or sister more beloved,
My play-mate when we both were clothed alike!

45   Dear Babe, that sleepest cradled by my side,
Whose gentle breathings, heard in this deep calm,
Fill up the interspersèd vacancies
And momentary pauses of the thought!
My babe so beautiful! it thrills my heart
50 With tender gladness, thus to look at thee,
And think that thou shalt learn far other lore,
And in far other scenes! For I was reared
In the great city, pent 'mid cloisters dim,
And saw nought lovely but the sky and stars.
55 But *thou*, my babe! shalt wander like a breeze
By lakes and sandy shores, beneath the crags
Of ancient mountain, and beneath the clouds,

Which image in their bulk both lakes and shores
And mountain crags: so shalt thou see and hear
60 The lovely shapes and sounds intelligible
Of that eternal language, which thy God
Utters, who from eternity doth teach
Himself in all, and all things in himself.
Great universal Teacher! he shall mould
65 Thy spirit, and by giving make it ask.

    Therefore all seasons shall be sweet to thee,
Whether the summer clothe the general earth
With greenness, or the redbreast sit and sing
Betwixt the tufts of snow on the bare branch
70 Of mossy apple-tree, while the nigh thatch
Smokes in the sun-thaw; whether the eave-drops fall
Heard only in the trances of the blast,
Or if the secret ministry of frost
Shall hang them up in silent icicles,
75 Quietly shining to the quiet Moon.
—1798

from *The Rime of the Ancyent Marinere,* *in Seven Parts*[1]

ARGUMENT

How a Ship having passed the Line was driven by Storms to the cold Country towards the South Pole; and how from thence she made her course to the Tropical Latitude of the Great Pacific Ocean; and of the strange things that befell; and in what manner the Ancyent Marinere came back to his own Country.

PART I

It is an ancyent Marinere,
    And he stoppeth one of three:
"By thy long grey beard and thy glittering eye,
    "Now wherefore stoppest thou me?

5 "The Bridegroom's doors are open'd wide,
    "And I am next of kin;

---

[1] *The Rime ... Parts* This is an excerpt from the version of the poem first published in Wordsworth and Coleridge's *Lyrical Ballads* (1798).

"The Guests are met, the Feast is set—
      "May'st hear the merry din."

But still he holds the wedding-guest—
10   There was a Ship, quoth he—
"Nay, if thou'st got a laughsome tale,
      "Marinere! Come with me."

He holds him with his skinny hand,
      Quoth he, there was a Ship—
15 "Now get thee hence, thou grey-beard Loon!
      "Or my Staff shall make thee skip."[1]

He holds him with his glittering eye—
      The wedding-guest stood still,
And listens like a three year's child;
20   The Marinere hath his will.[2]

The wedding-guest sate on a stone,
      He cannot chuse but hear:
And thus spake on that ancyent man,
      The bright-eyed Marinere.

25 The Ship was cheer'd, the Harbour clear'd—
      Merrily did we drop
Below the Kirk,° below the Hill,   church
      Below the Light-house top.

The Sun came up upon the left,
30   Out of the Sea came he:
And he shone bright, and on the right
      Went down into the Sea.

Higher and higher every day,
      Till over the mast at noon—
35 The wedding-guest here beat his breast,
      For he heard the loud bassoon.

The Bride hath pac'd into the Hall,
      Red as a rose is she;

Nodding their heads before her goes
40   The merry Minstralsy.

The wedding-guest he beat his breast,
      Yet he cannot chuse but hear:
And thus spake on that ancyent Man,
      The bright-eyed Marinere.

45 Listen, Stranger! Storm and Wind,
      A Wind and Tempest strong!
For days and weeks it play'd us freaks—
      Like Chaff we drove along.

Listen, Stranger! Mist and Snow,
50   And it grew wond'rous cauld:
And Ice mast-high came floating by
      As green as Emerauld.

And thro' the drifts the snowy clifts
      Did send a dismal sheen;
55 Ne shapes of men ne beasts we ken—
      The Ice was all between.

The Ice was here, the Ice was there,
      The Ice was all around:
It crack'd and growl'd, and roar'd and howl'd—
60   Like noises of a swound!

At length did cross an Albatross,
      Thorough the Fog it came;
And an° it were a Christian Soul,   as though
      We hail'd it in God's name.

65 The Marineres gave it biscuit-worms,
      And round and round it flew:
The Ice did split with a Thunder-fit;
      The Helmsman steer'd us thro.'

And a good south wind sprung up behind,
70   The Albatross did follow;
And every day for food or play
      Came to the Marinere's hollo!

In mist or cloud on mast or shroud
      It perch'd for vespers nine,

---

[1] *my staff shall make thee skip* Cf. Shakespeare's *King Lear* 5.3.275–76: "[W]ith my good biting falchion [sword] / I would have made them skip."

[2] *And listens ... will* Wordsworth claimed to have composed these two lines.

75 Whiles all the night thro' fog-smoke white
    Glimmer'd the white moon-shine.

"God save thee, ancyent Marinere!
    "From the fiends that plague thee thus—
"Why look'st thou so?"—with my Cross-bow
80   I shot the Albatross.
—1798

The Rime of the Ancient Mariner
In Seven Parts[1]

Facile credo, plures esse Naturas invisibiles quam visibiles in rerum universitate. Sed horum omnium familiam quis nobis enarrabit? et gradus et cognationes et discrimina et singulorum munera? Quid agunt? quæ loca habitant? Harum rerum notitiam semper ambivit ingenium humanum, nunquam attigit. Juvat, interea, non diffiteor, quandoque in animo, tanquam in Tabulâ, majoris et melioris mundi imaginem contemplari: ne mens assuefecta hodiernæ vitæ minutiis se contrahat nimis, & tota subsidat in pusillas cogitationes. Sed veritati interea invigilandum est, modusque servandus, ut certa ab incertis, diem a nocte, distinguamus.—T. Burnet. Archaeol. Phil. p. 68.[2]

PART I

It is an ancient Mariner,
    And he stoppeth one of three.
"By thy long grey beard and glittering eye,
Now wherefore stopp'st thou me?

5 "The Bridegroom's doors are opened wide,

An ancient Mariner meeteth three Gallants bidden to a wedding-feast, and detaineth one.

---

[1] *The Rime ... Parts* This version of the poem was published in 1817.

[2] *Facile ... distinguamus* From Thomas Burnet's *Archaeologiae Philosophicae* (1692), translated by Mead and Foxton (1736): "I can easily believe, that there are more invisible than visible beings in the universe. But who will declare to us the family of all these, and acquaint us with the agreements, differences, and peculiar talents which are to be found among them? It is true, human wit has always desired a knowledge of these things, though it has never yet attained it. I will own that it is very profitable, sometimes to contemplate in the mind, as in a draught, the image of the greater and better world, lest the soul being accustomed to the trifles of this present life, should contract itself too much, and altogether rest in mean cogitations, but, in the meantime, we must take care to keep to the truth, and observe moderation, that we may distinguish certain from uncertain things, and day from night."

And I am next of kin;
The guests are met, the feast is set:
May'st hear the merry din."

He holds him with his skinny hand,
10 "There was a ship," quoth he.
"Hold off! unhand me, grey-beard loon!"
Eftsoons[3] his hand dropt he.

He holds him with his glittering eye—
The Wedding-Guest stood still,
15 And listens like a three years' child:
The Mariner hath his will.

The wedding-guest is spellbound by the eye of the old sea-faring man, and constrained to hear his tale.

The Wedding-Guest sat on a stone:
He cannot choose but hear;
And thus spake on that ancient man,
20 The bright-eyed Mariner.

"The ship was cheered, the harbour cleared,
Merrily did we drop
Below the kirk,[4] below the hill,
Below the lighthouse top.

The Mariner tells how the ship sailed southward with a good wind and fair weather, till it reached the line.

25 "The Sun came up upon the left,
Out of the sea came he!
And he shone bright, and on the right
Went down into the sea.

Higher and higher every day,
30 Till over the mast at noon—"
The Wedding-Guest here beat his breast,
For he heard the loud bassoon.

The bride hath paced into the hall
Red as a rose is she;
35 Nodding their heads before her goes
The merry minstrelsy.

The wedding-guest heareth the bridal music; but the mariner continueth his tale.

The Wedding-Guest he beat his breast,
Yet he cannot choose but hear;

---

[3] *Eftsoons* At once.

[4] *kirk* Church.

And thus spake on that ancient man,
40 The bright-eyed Mariner.

"And now the STORM-BLAST came, and he
Was tyrannous and strong:
He struck with his o'ertaking wings,
And chased us south along.

The ship drawn by a storm toward the south pole.

45 With sloping masts and dipping prow,
As who pursued with yell and blow
Still treads the shadow of his foe,
And forward bends his head,
The ship drove fast, loud roared the blast,
50 And southward aye we fled.

And now there came both mist and snow,
And it grew wondrous cold:
And ice, mast-high, came floating by,
As green as emerald.

55 And through the drifts the snowy clifts
Did send a dismal sheen:
Nor shapes of men nor beasts we ken[1]—
The ice was all between.

The land of ice, and of fearful sounds, where no living thing was to be seen.

The ice was here, the ice was there,
60 The ice was all around:
It cracked and growled, and roared and howled,
Like noises in a swound![2]

At length did cross an Albatross,
Thorough the fog it came;
65 As if it had been a Christian soul,
We hailed it in God's name.

Till a great sea-bird, called the Albatross, came through the snow-fog, and was received with great joy and hospitality.

It ate the food it ne'er had eat,
And round and round it flew.
The ice did split with a thunder-fit;
70 The helmsman steered us through!

And a good south wind sprung up behind;
The Albatross did follow,

And every day, for food or play,
Came to the Mariner's hollo!

75 In mist or cloud, on mast or shroud,
It perched for vespers nine;[3]
Whiles all the night, through fog-smoke white,
Glimmered the white Moon-shine."

And lo! the Albatross proveth a bird of good omen, and followeth the ship as it returned northward, through fog and floating ice.

"God save thee, ancient Mariner!
80 From the fiends, that plague thee thus!—
Why look'st thou so?"—"With my cross-bow
I shot the ALBATROSS.

The ancient Mariner inhospitably killed the pious bird of good omen.

PART 2

The Sun now rose upon the right:
Out of the sea came he,
85 Still hid in mist, and on the left
Went down into the sea.

And the good south wind still blew behind,
But no sweet bird did follow,
Nor any day for food or play
90 Came to the mariners' hollo!

And I had done a hellish thing,
And it would work 'em woe:
For all averred, I had killed the bird
That made the breeze to blow.
95 Ah wretch! said they, the bird to slay,
That made the breeze to blow!

His ship mates cry out against the ancient Mariner, for killing the bird of good luck.

Nor dim nor red, like God's own head,
The glorious Sun uprist:
Then all averred, I had killed the bird
100 That brought the fog and mist.
'Twas right, said they, such birds to slay,
That bring the fog and mist.

But when the fog cleared off, they justify the same— and thus make themselves accomplices in the crime.

The fair breeze blew, the white foam flew,
The furrow followed free;
105 We were the first that ever burst
Into that silent sea.

The fair breeze continues;

[1] *ken* Recognize.
[2] *swound* Swoon.
[3] *vespers nine* I.e., nine evenings. Vespers are evening prayer.

Down dropt the breeze, the sails dropt down,
'Twas sad as sad could be;
And we did speak only to break
110 The silence of the sea!

All in a hot and copper sky,
The bloody Sun, at noon,
Right up above the mast did stand,
No bigger than the Moon.

115 Day after day, day after day,
We stuck, nor breath nor motion;
As idle as a painted ship
Upon a painted ocean.

Water, water, every where,
120 And all the boards did shrink;
Water, water, every where,
Nor any drop to drink.

The very deep did rot: O Christ!
That ever this should be!
125 Yea, slimy things did crawl with legs
Upon the slimy sea.

About, about, in reel and rout
The death-fires[1] danced at night;
The water, like a witch's oils,
130 Burnt green, and blue and white.

And some in dreams assuréd were
Of the Spirit that plagued us so;
Nine fathom deep he had followed us
From the land of mist and snow.

135 And every tongue, through utter drought,
Was withered at the root;
We could not speak, no more than if
We had been choked with soot.

Ah! well a-day! what evil looks
140 Had I from old and young!
Instead of the cross, the Albatross
About my neck was hung.

The ship enters the Pacific Ocean and sails northward, even till it reaches the Line.

The ship hath been suddenly becalmed.

And the Albatross begins to be avenged.

A spirit has followed them; one of the invisible inhabitants of this planet, neither departed souls nor angels; concerning whom the learned Jew, Josephus, and the Platonic Constantinopolitan, Michael Psellus, may be consulted, and there is no climate or element without one or more.

The shipmates in their sore distress, would fain throw the whole guilt on the ancient Mariner: in sign whereof they hang the dead sea-bird round his neck.

---

[1] *death-fires* Possibly luminescent plankton.

PART 3

There passed a weary time. Each throat
Was parched, and glazed each eye.
145 A weary time! a weary time!
How glazed each weary eye,
When looking westward, I beheld
A something in the sky.

At first it seemed a little speck,
150 And then it seemed a mist;
It moved and moved, and took at last
A certain shape, I wist.

A speck, a mist, a shape, I wist!
And still it neared and neared:
155 And as if it dodged a water-sprite,
It plunged and tacked and veered.

With throat unslacked, with black lips baked,
We could nor laugh nor wail;
Through utter drought all dumb we stood!
160 I bit my arm, I sucked the blood,
And cried, A sail! a sail!

With throat unslacked, with black lips baked,
Agape they heard me call:
Gramercy![2] they for joy did grin,
165 And all at once their breath drew in,
As they were drinking all.

See! see! (I cried) she tacks no more!
Hither to work us weal;[3]
Without a breeze, without a tide,
170 She steadies with upright keel!

The western wave was all a-flame.
The day was well nigh done!
Almost upon the western wave
Rested the broad bright Sun;
175 When that strange shape drove suddenly
Betwixt us and the Sun.

The ancient Mariner beholdeth a sign in the element afar off.

As its nearer approach, it seemeth him to be a ship; and at a dear ransom he freeth his speech from the bonds of thirst.

A flash of joy.

And horror follows. For can it be a ship that comes onward without wind or tide?

---

[2] *Gramercy* Grant mercy, i.e., may God reward you in His mercy.

[3] *us weal* Will benefit us.

And straight the Sun was flecked with bars,
(Heaven's Mother send us grace!)
As if through a dungeon-grate he peered
180 With broad and burning face.

It seemeth him but the skeleton of a ship.

Alas! (thought I, and my heart beat loud)
How fast she nears and nears!
Are those *her* sails that glance in the Sun,
Like restless gossameres?

And its ribs are seen as bars on the face of the setting Sun. The spectre-woman and her death-mate, and no other on board the skeleton-ship.

185 Are those *her* ribs through which the Sun
Did peer, as through a grate?
And is that Woman all her crew?
Is that a DEATH? and are there two?
Is DEATH that woman's mate?

190 *Her* lips were red, *her* looks were free,
Her locks were yellow as gold:
Her skin was as white as leprosy,
The Night-mare LIFE-IN-DEATH was she,
Who thicks man's blood with cold.

Like vessel, like crew! Death and Life-in-Death have diced for the ship's crew, and she (the latter) winneth the ancient Mariner.

195 The naked hulk alongside came,
And the twain were casting dice;
"The game is done! I've won! I've won!"
Quoth she, and whistles thrice.

The Sun's rim dips; the stars rush out:
200 At one stride comes the dark;
With far-heard whisper, o'er the sea,
Off shot the spectre-bark.

No twilight within the courts of the sun.

We listened and looked sideways up!
Fear at my heart, as at a cup,
205 My life-blood seemed to sip!
The stars were dim, and thick the night,
The steersman's face by his lamp gleamed white;
From the sails the dews did drip—
Till clomb above the eastern bar
210 The hornéd Moon, with one bright star
Within the nether tip.

At the rising of the Moon,

One after one, by the star-dogged Moon
Too quick for groan or sigh,
Each turned his face with a ghastly pang,
215 And cursed me with his eye.

One after another,

Four times fifty living men,
(And I heard nor sigh nor groan)
With heavy thump, a lifeless lump,
They dropped down one by one.

His ship-mates drop down dead.

220 The souls did from their bodies fly,—
They fled to bliss or woe!
And every soul, it passed me by,
Like the whiz of my cross-bow!

But Life-in-Death begins her work on the ancient Mariner.

PART 4

"I fear thee, ancient Mariner!
225 I fear thy skinny hand!
And thou art long, and lank, and brown,
As is the ribbed sea-sand.[1]

The wedding-guest feareth that a spirit is talking to him;

I fear thee and thy glittering eye,
And thy skinny hand, so brown."—
230 Fear not, fear not, thou Wedding-Guest!
This body dropt not down.

But the ancient Mariner assureth him of his bodily life, and proceed-eth to relate his horrible penance.

Alone, alone, all, all alone,
Alone on a wide wide sea!
And never a saint took pity on
235 My soul in agony.

The many men, so beautiful!
And they all dead did lie:
And a thousand thousand slimy things
Lived on; and so did I.

He despiseth the creatures of the calm,

240 I looked upon the rotting sea,
And drew my eyes away;
I looked upon the rotting deck,
And there the dead men lay.

And envieth that they *should live, and so many lie dead.*

I looked to heaven, and tried to pray;
245 But or ever a prayer had gusht,
A wicked whisper came, and made
My heart as dry as dust.

----

[1] [Coleridge's note] For the two last lines of this stanza, I am indebted to Mr. WORDSWORTH. It was on a delightful walk from Nether Stowey to Dulverton, with him and his sister, in the Autumn of 1797, that this Poem was planned, and in part composed.

I closed my lids, and kept them close,
And the balls like pulses beat;
250 For the sky and the sea, and the sea and the sky
Lay like a load on my weary eye,
And the dead were at my feet.

The cold sweat melted from their limbs,   *But the curse*
Nor rot nor reek did they: *liveth for him*
255 The look with which they looked on me   *in the eye of*
Had never passed away.   *the dead men.*

An orphan's curse would drag to hell
A spirit from on high;
But oh! more horrible than that   *In his loneliness*
260 Is the curse in a dead man's eye!   *and fixedness, he*
Seven days, seven nights, I saw that curse,   *yearneth towards*
And yet I could not die.   *the journeying Moon,*
and the stars that still
sojourn, yet still move
The moving Moon went up the sky,   *onwards; and every*
And no where did abide: *where the blue sky*
265 Softly she was going up,   *belongs to them, and*
And a star or two beside—   *is their appointed rest,*
and their native country,
and their own natural
Her beams bemocked the sultry main,   *homes, which they enter*
Like April hoar-frost spread;   *unannounced, as lords*
But where the ship's huge shadow lay,   *that are certain ex-*
270 The charmèd water burnt alway   *pected, and yet there is*
A still and awful red.   *a silent joy at their*
arrival.

Beyond the shadow of the ship,
I watched the water-snakes: *By the light of the*
They moved in tracks of shining white,   *Moon he beholdeth*
275 And when they reared, the elfish light   *God's creatures of*
Fell off in hoary flakes.   *the great calm.*

Within the shadow of the ship
I watched their rich attire:
Blue, glossy green, and velvet black,
280 They coiled and swam; and every track
Was a flash of golden fire.

O happy living things! no tongue   *Their beauty and*
Their beauty might declare: *their happiness.*
A spring of love gushed from my heart,
285 And I blessed them unaware: *He blesseth them in*
his heart.

Sure my kind saint took pity on me,
And I blessed them unaware.

The selfsame moment I could pray;   *The spell begins*
And from my neck so free   *to break.*
290 The Albatross fell off, and sank
Like lead into the sea.

PART 5

Oh sleep! it is a gentle thing,
Beloved from pole to pole!
To Mary Queen the praise be given!
295 She sent the gentle sleep from Heaven,
That slid into my soul.

The silly[1] buckets on the deck,   *By grace of the holy*
That had so long remained,   *Mother, the ancient*
I dreamt that they were filled with dew;   *Mariner is refreshed*
300 And when I awoke, it rained.   *with rain.*

My lips were wet, my throat was cold,
My garments all were dank;
Sure I had drunken in my dreams,
And still my body drank.

305 I moved, and could not feel my limbs:
I was so light—almost
I thought that I had died in sleep,
And was a blessèd ghost.

And soon I heard a roaring wind: *He heareth sounds,*
310 It did not come anear;   *and seeth strange*
But with its sound it shook the sails,   *sights and*
That were so thin and sere.   *commotions in*
the sky and the
elements.
The upper air burst into life!
And a hundred fire-flags sheen,
315 To and fro they were hurried about!
And to and fro, and in and out,
The wan stars danced between.

And the coming wind did roar more loud,
And the sails did sigh like sedge;

---

[1] *silly* Simple.

320 And the rain poured down from one black cloud;
The Moon was at its edge.

The thick black cloud was cleft, and still
The Moon was at its side:
Like waters shot from some high crag,
325 The lightning fell with never a jag,
A river steep and wide.

The loud wind never reached the ship,   The bodies of
Yet now the ship moved on!   the ship's crew
Beneath the lightning and the Moon   are inspirited,
330 The dead men gave a groan.   and the ship
    moves on;

They groaned, they stirred, they all uprose,
Nor spake, nor moved their eyes;
It had been strange, even in a dream,
To have seen those dead men rise.

335 The helmsman steered, the ship moved on;
Yet never a breeze up-blew;
The mariners all 'gan work the ropes,
Where they were wont to do;
They raised their limbs like lifeless tools—
340 We were a ghastly crew.

The body of my brother's son
Stood by me, knee to knee:
The body and I pulled at one rope,
But he said nought to me.   But not by the
    souls of the men,
345 "I fear thee, ancient Mariner!"   nor by dæmons
Be calm, thou Wedding-Guest!   of earth or
'Twas not those souls that fled in pain,   middle air, but
Which to their corses¹ came again,   by a blessed troop
But a troop of spirits blest: of angelic spirits,
    sent down by the
350 For when it dawned—they dropped their arms,   invocation of the
And clustered round the mast;   guardian saint.
Sweet sounds rose slowly through their mouths,
And from their bodies passed.

Around, around, flew each sweet sound,
355 Then darted to the Sun;

Slowly the sounds came back again,
Now mixed, now one by one.

Sometimes a-dropping from the sky
I heard the sky-lark sing;
360 Sometimes all little birds that are,
How they seemed to fill the sea and air
With their sweet jargoning!

And now 'twas like all instruments,
Now like a lonely flute;
365 And now it is an angel's song,
That makes the heavens be mute.

It ceased; yet still the sails made on
A pleasant noise till noon,
A noise like of a hidden brook
370 In the leafy month of June,
That to the sleeping woods all night
Singeth a quiet tune.

Till noon we quietly sailed on,
Yet never a breeze did breathe:
375 Slowly and smoothly went the ship,
Moved onward from beneath.

Under the keel nine fathom deep,   The lonesome spirit
From the land of mist and snow,   from the south-pole
The spirit slid: and it was he   carries on the ship as
380 That made the ship to go.   far as the line, in
The sails at noon left off their tune,   obedience to the
And the ship stood still also.   angelic troop, but
    still requireth
The Sun, right up above the mast,   vengeance.
Had fixed her to the ocean:
But in a minute she 'gan stir,
385 With a short uneasy motion—
Backwards and forwards half her length
With a short uneasy motion.

Then like a pawing horse let go,
390 She made a sudden bound:
It flung the blood into my head,
And I fell down in a swound.

---

¹ *corses* Corpses.

How long in that same fit I lay,
I have not to declare;
395 But ere my living life returned,
I heard and in my soul discerned
Two voices in the air.

"Is it he?" quoth one, "Is this the man?
By Him who died on cross,
400 With his cruel bow he laid full low
The harmless Albatross.

The spirit who bideth by himself
In the land of mist and snow,
He loved the bird that loved the man
405 Who shot him with his bow."

The other was a softer voice,
As soft as honey-dew:
Quoth he, "The man hath penance done,
And penance more will do."

PART 6

FIRST VOICE

410 "But tell me, tell me! speak again,
Thy soft response renewing—
What makes that ship drive on so fast?
What is the ocean doing?"

SECOND VOICE

"Still as a slave before his lord,
415 The ocean hath no blast;
His great bright eye most silently
Up to the Moon is cast—

If he may know which way to go;
For she guides him smooth or grim.
420 See, brother, see! how graciously
She looketh down on him."

FIRST VOICE

"But why drives on that ship so fast,
Without or wave or wind?"

> The Polar Spirit's fellow-dæmons, the invisible inhabitants of the element, take part in his wrong; and two of them relate, one to the other, that penance long and heavy for the ancient Mariner hath been accorded to the Polar Spirit, who returned southward.

SECOND VOICE

"The air is cut away before,
425 And closes from behind.

Fly, brother, fly! more high, more high!
Or we shall be belated:
For slow and slow that ship will go,
When the Mariner's trance is abated."

430 I woke, and we were sailing on
As in a gentle weather:
'Twas night, calm night, the Moon was high;
The dead men stood together.

All stood together on the deck,
435 For a charnel-dungeon[1] fitter:
All fixed on me their stony eyes,
That in the Moon did glitter.

The pang, the curse, with which they died,
Had never passed away:
440 I could not draw my eyes from theirs,
Nor turn them up to pray.

And now this spell was snapt: once more
I viewed the ocean green,
And looked far forth, yet little saw
445 Of what had else been seen—

Like one, that on a lonesome road
Doth walk in fear and dread,
And having once turned round, walks on,
And turns no more his head;
450 Because he knows, a frightful fiend
Doth close behind him tread.

But soon there breathed a wind on me,
Nor sound nor motion made:
Its path was not upon the sea,
455 In ripple or in shade.

It raised my hair, it fanned my cheek
Like a meadow-gale of spring—

> The Mariner hath been cast into a trance; for the angelic power causeth the vessel to drive northward, faster than human life could endure.

> The supernatural motion is retarded; the Mariner awakes, and his penance begins anew.

> The curse is finally expiated.

---

[1] *charnel-dungeon* Mortuary; house of death.

It mingled strangely with my fears,
Yet it felt like a welcoming.

460 Swiftly, swiftly flew the ship,
Yet she sailed softly too:
Sweetly, sweetly blew the breeze—
On me alone it blew.

Oh! dream of joy! is this indeed   And the ancient
465 The light-house top I see?   Mariner beholdeth
Is this the hill? is this the kirk?   his native country.
Is this mine own countree?

We drifted o'er the harbour-bar,
And I with sobs did pray—
470 O let me be awake, my God!
Or let me sleep alway.

The harbour-bay was clear as glass,
So smoothly was it strewn!
And on the bay the moonlight lay,
475 And the shadow of the Moon.

The rock shone bright, the kirk no less,
That stands above the rock:
The moonlight steeped in silentness
The steady weathercock.

480 And the bay was white with silent light,   The angelic spirits
Till rising from the same,   leave the dead
Full many shapes, that shadows were,   bodies,
In crimson colours came.

A little distance from the prow   And appear in their
485 Those crimson shadows were: own forms of light.
I turned my eyes upon the deck—
Oh, Christ! what saw I there!

Each corse lay flat, lifeless and flat,
And, by the holy rood!
490 A man all light, a seraph-man,[1]
On every corse there stood.

This seraph-band, each waved his hand:
It was a heavenly sight!
They stood as signals to the land,
495 Each one a lovely light;

This seraph-band, each waved his hand,
No voice did they impart—
No voice; but oh! the silence sank
Like music on my heart.

500 But soon I heard the dash of oars,
I heard the Pilot's cheer;
My head was turned perforce away
And I saw a boat appear.

The Pilot and the Pilot's boy,
505 I heard them coming fast:
Dear Lord in Heaven! it was a joy
The dead men could not blast.

I saw a third—I heard his voice:
It is the Hermit good!
510 He singeth loud his godly hymns
That he makes in the wood.
He'll shrieve[2] my soul, he'll wash away
The Albatross's blood.

PART 7

This Hermit good lives in that wood   The Hermit of
515 Which slopes down to the sea.   the Wood.
How loudly his sweet voice he rears!
He loves to talk with marineres
That come from a far countree.

He kneels at morn, and noon, and eve—
520 He hath a cushion plump:
It is the moss that wholly hides
The rotted old oak-stump.

The skiff-boat neared: I heard them talk,
"Why, this is strange, I trow![3]
525 Where are those lights so many and fair,
That signal made but now?"

---

[1] rood Cross; seraph-man Angel.

[2] shrieve Give absolution to.

[3] trow Believe.

"Strange, by my faith!" the Hermit said—
"And they answered not our cheer!
The planks look warped! and see those sails,
530 How thin they are and sere!
I never saw aught like to them,
Unless perchance it were

Brown skeletons of leaves that lag
My forest-brook along;
535 When the ivy-tod[1] is heavy with snow,
And the owlet whoops to the wolf below,
That eats the she-wolf's young."

"Dear Lord! it hath a fiendish look—
(The Pilot made reply)
540 I am a-feared"—"Push on, push on!"
Said the Hermit cheerily.

The boat came closer to the ship,
But I nor spake nor stirred;
The boat came close beneath the ship,
545 And straight a sound was heard.

Under the water it rumbled on,
Still louder and more dread:
It reached the ship, it split the bay;
The ship went down like lead.

550 Stunned by that loud and dreadful sound,
Which sky and ocean smote,
Like one that hath been seven days drowned
My body lay afloat;
But swift as dreams, myself I found
555 Within the Pilot's boat.

Upon the whirl, where sank the ship,
The boat spun round and round;
And all was still, save that the hill
Was telling of the sound.

560 I moved my lips—the Pilot shrieked
And fell down in a fit;
The holy Hermit raised his eyes,
And prayed where he did sit.

I took the oars: the Pilot's boy,
565 Who now doth crazy go,
Laughed loud and long, and all the while
His eyes went to and fro.
"Ha! ha!" quoth he, "full plain I see,
The Devil knows how to row."

570 And now, all in my own countree,
I stood on the firm land!
The Hermit stepped forth from the boat,
And scarcely he could stand.

"O shrieve me, shrieve me, holy man!"
575 The Hermit crossed his brow.
"Say quick," quoth he, "I bid thee say—
What manner of man art thou?"

Forthwith this frame of mine was wrenched
With a woful agony,
580 Which forced me to begin my tale;
And then it left me free.

Since then, at an uncertain hour,
That agony returns;
And till my ghastly tale is told,
585 This heart within me burns.

I pass, like night, from land to land;
I have strange power of speech;
That moment that his face I see,
I know the man that must hear me:
590 To him my tale I teach.

What loud uproar bursts from that door!
The wedding-guests are there:
But in the garden-bower the bride
And bride-maids singing are:
595 And hark the little vesper bell,
Which biddeth me to prayer!

O Wedding-Guest! this soul hath been
Alone on a wide wide sea:
So lonely 'twas, that God Himself
600 Scarce seeméd there to be.

Approacheth the ship with wonder.

The ship suddenly sinketh.

The ancient Mariner is saved in the Pilot's boat.

The ancient Mariner earnestly entreateth the Hermit to shrieve him; and the penance of life falls on him.

And ever and anon throughout his future life an agony constraineth him to travel from land to land.

[1] *ivy-tod* Bush.

O sweeter than the marriage-feast,
'Tis sweeter far to me,
To walk together to the kirk
With a goodly company!—

605 To walk together to the kirk,
And all together pray,
While each to his great Father bends,
Old men, and babes, and loving friends
And youth and maidens gay!

610 Farewell, farewell! but this I tell
To thee, thou Wedding-Guest!
He prayeth well, who loveth well
Both man and bird and beast.

And to teach by
his own example,
love and reverence
to all things that
God made and
loveth.

He prayeth best, who loveth best
615 All things both great and small;
For the dear God who loveth us,
He made and loveth all."

The Mariner, whose eye is bright,
Whose beard with age is hoar,[1]
620 Is gone: and now the Wedding-Guest
Turned from the bridegroom's door.

He went like one that hath been stunned,
And is of sense forlorn:
A sadder and a wiser man,
625 He rose the morrow morn.
—1817

In Context

The Origin of "The Rime of the Ancient Mariner"

from Samuel Taylor Coleridge, *Biographia Literaria*, Chapter 14 (1817)

Almost twenty years after the first publication of "The Rime of the Ancient Mariner," Coleridge gave the following account of the poem's origin and composition.

During the first year that Mr. Wordsworth and I were neighbours, our conversations turned frequently on the two cardinal points of poetry, the power of exciting the sympathy of the reader by a faithful adherence to the truth of nature, and the power of giving the interest of novelty by the modifying colours of imagination. The sudden charm, which accidents of light and shade, which moonlight or sunset diffused over a known and familiar landscape, appeared to represent the practicability of combining both. These are the poetry of nature. The thought suggested itself (to which of us I do not recollect) that a series of poems might be composed of two sorts. In the one, the incidents and agents were to be, in part at least supernatural; and the excellence aimed at was to consist in the interesting of the affections by the dramatic truth of such emotions, as would naturally accompany such situations, supposing them real. And real in *this* sense they have been to every human being who, from whatever source of delusion, has at any time believed himself under supernatural agency. For the second class, subjects were to be chosen from ordinary life; the characters and incidents were to be such, as will be found in every village and its vicinity where there is a meditative and feeling mind to seek after them, or to notice them, when they present themselves. In this idea originated the plan of the *Lyrical Ballads*; in which it was agreed, that my endeavours should be directed to persons and characters supernatural, or at least romantic; yet so as to transfer from our inward nature a human interest and a semblance of truth sufficient to procure for these shadows of imagination that willing suspension of disbelief for the moment, which constitutes poetic faith. Mr.

[1]   *hoar* White, as with frost (hoarfrost).

Wordsworth, on the other hand, was to propose to himself as his object, to give the charm of novelty to things of every day, and to excite a feeling analogous to the supernatural, by awakening the mind's attention from the lethargy of custom, and directing it to the loveliness and the wonders of the world before us; an inexhaustible treasure, but for which, in consequence of the film of familiarity and selfish solicitude we have eyes, yet see not, and hearts that neither feel or understand. With this view I wrote "The Ancient Mariner," and was preparing among other poems, "The Dark Ladie," and the "Christabel" in which I should have more nearly realized my ideal than I had done in my first attempt.

from A letter from the Rev. Alexander Dyce to Hartley Coleridge (1852)

In this letter to Samuel Taylor Coleridge's eldest son, Hartley, the Reverend Alexander Dyce quotes Wordsworth as saying the following about the inception of "The Rime of the Ancient Mariner."

"The Ancient Mariner" was founded on a strange dream, which a friend of Coleridge had, who fancied he saw a skeleton ship, with figures in it. We had both determined to write some poetry for a monthly magazine, the profits of which were to defer the expenses of a little excursion we were to make together. "The Ancient Mariner" was intended for this periodical, but was too long. I had very little share in the composition of it, for I soon found the style of Coleridge and myself would not assimilate. Beside the lines (in the fourth part) "And thou art long, and lank, and brown, / As in the ribbed sea-sand—" I wrote the stanza (in the first part) "He holds him with his glittering eye— / The Wedding-Guest stood still, / And listens like a three-years child: / The Mariner hath his will" and four or five lines more in different parts of the poem, which I could not now point out. The idea of shooting an albatross was mine; for I had been reading *Shelvocke's Voyages*, which probably Coleridge never saw. I also suggested the reanimation of the dead bodies, to work the ship.

Lime-Tree Bower My Prison[1]

Addressed to Charles Lamb,
Of the India House, London

Well, they are gone, and here must I remain,
    This lime-tree bower my prison! I have lost
Beauties and feelings, such as would have been
Most sweet to my remembrance even when age
5 Had dimm'd mine eyes to blindness! They, meanwhile,
Friends, whom I never more may meet again,
On springy heath, along the hill-top edge,
Wander in gladness, and wind down, perchance,
To that still roaring dell, of which I told;
10 The roaring dell, o'erwooded, narrow, deep,
And only speckled by the mid-day sun;
Where its slim trunk the ash from rock to rock
Flings arching like a bridge;—that branchless ash,
Unsunn'd and damp, whose few poor yellow leaves
15 Ne'er tremble in the gale, yet tremble still,
Fann'd by the water-fall! and there my friends
Behold the dark green file of long lank weeds,[2]
That all at once (a most fantastic sight!)
Still nod and drip beneath the dripping edge
20 Of the blue clay-stone.

                    Now, my friends emerge
Beneath the wide wide Heaven—and view again

---

[1] [Coleridge's note] In the June of 1797 some long-expected friends [Charles Lamb and William and Dorothy Wordsworth] paid a visit to the author's cottage; and on the morning of their arrival, he met with an accident, which disabled him from walking during the whole time of their stay. One evening, when they had left him for a few hours, he composed the following lines in the garden-bower.

[2] [Coleridge's note] The *Asplenium Scolopendrium*, called in some countries the Adder's Tongue, in others the Hart's Tongue, but Withering gives the Adder's Tongue as the trivial name of the *Ophioglossum* only.

The many-steepled tract magnificent
Of hilly fields and meadows, and the sea,
25 With some fair bark, perhaps, whose sails light up
The slip of smooth clear blue betwixt two Isles
Of purple shadow! Yes! they wander on
In gladness all; but thou, methinks, most glad,
My gentle-hearted Charles! for thou hast pined
30 And hunger'd after Nature, many a year,
In the great City pent, winning thy way
With sad yet patient soul, through evil and pain
And strange calamity!¹ Ah! slowly sink
Behind the western ridge, thou glorious Sun!
35 Shine in the slant beams of the sinking orb,
Ye purple heath-flowers! richlier burn, ye clouds!
Live in the yellow light, ye distant groves!
And kindle, thou blue Ocean! So my friend
Struck with deep joy may stand, as I have stood,
40 Silent with swimming sense; yea, gazing round
On the wide landscape, gaze till all doth seem
Less gross than bodily; and of such hues
As veil the Almighty Spirit, when yet he makes
Spirits perceive his presence.

45   A delight
Comes sudden on my heart, and I am glad
As I myself were there! Nor in this bower,
This little lime-tree bower, have I not mark'd
Much that has sooth'd me. Pale beneath the blaze
50 Hung the transparent foliage; and I watch'd
Some broad and sunny leaf, and lov'd to see
The shadow of the leaf and stem above
Dappling its sunshine! And that walnut-tree
Was richly ting'd, and a deep radiance lay
55 Full on the ancient ivy, which usurps
Those fronting elms, and now, with blackest mass
Makes their dark branches gleam a lighter hue
Through the late twilight: and though now the bat
Wheels silent by, and not a swallow twitters,
60 Yet still the solitary humble-bee
Sings in the bean-flower! Henceforth I shall know
That Nature ne'er deserts the wise and pure;
No plot so narrow, be but Nature there,
No waste so vacant, but may well employ

65 Each faculty of sense, and keep the heart
Awake to Love and Beauty! and sometimes
'Tis well to be bereft of promis'd good,
That we may lift the soul, and contemplate
With lively joy the joys we cannot share.
70 My gentle-hearted Charles! when the last rook
Beat its straight path along the dusky air
Homewards, I blest it! deeming its black wing
(Now a dim speck, now vanishing in light)
Had cross'd the mighty Orb's dilated glory,
75 While thou stood'st gazing; or, when all was still,
Flew creeking o'er thy head, and had a charm²
For thee, my gentle-hearted Charles, to whom
No sound is dissonant which tells of Life.
—1800

Christabel

PREFACE

The first part of the following poem was written in the year 1797, at Stowey, in the county of Somerset. The second part, after my return from Germany, in the year 1800, at Keswick, Cumberland. Since the latter date, my poetic powers have been, till very lately, in a state of suspended animation. But as, in my very first conception of the tale, I had the whole present to my mind, with the wholeness, no less than with the liveliness of a vision; I trust that I shall be able to embody in verse the three parts yet to come, in the course of the present year.

It is probable that if the poem had been finished at either of the former periods, or if even the first and second part had been published in the year 1800, the impression of its originality would have been much greater than I dare at present expect. But for this, I have only my own indolence to blame. The dates are mentioned for the exclusive purpose of precluding charges of plagiarism or servile imitation from myself. For there is among us a set of critics, who seem to hold, that every

---

¹ *strange calamity* Charles Lamb's sister Mary, who suffered from periods of insanity, had fatally stabbed their mother.

² [Coleridge's note]   Some months after I had written this line, it gave me pleasure to find that Bartram had observed the same circumstance of the Savanna Crane. "When these Birds move their wings in flight, their strokes are slow, moderate and regular; and even when at a considerable distance or high above us, we plainly hear the quill-feathers: their shafts and webs upon one another creek as the joints or working of a vessel in a tempestuous sea."

possible thought and image is traditional; who have no notion that there are such things as fountains in the world, small as well as great; and who would therefore charitably derive every rill[1] they behold flowing from a perforation made in some other man's tank. I am confident however, that as far as the present poem is concerned, the celebrated poets whose writings I might be suspected of having imitated,[2] either in particular passages, or in the tone and the spirit of the whole, would be among the first to vindicate me from the charge, and who, on any striking coincidence, would permit me to address them in this doggerel version of two monkish Latin hexameters:

> 'Tis mine and it is likewise yours,
> But an if this will not do;
> Let it be mine, good friend! for I
> Am the poorer of the two.

I have only to add, that the metre of the Christabel is not, properly speaking, irregular, though it may seem so from its being founded on a new principle: namely, that of counting in each line the accents, not the syllables. Though the latter may vary from seven to twelve, yet in each line the accents will be found to be only four. Nevertheless this occasional variation in the number of syllables is not introduced wantonly, or for the mere ends of convenience, but in correspondence with some transition in the nature of the imagery or passion.

PART I

'Tis the middle of night by the castle clock,
⠀⠀And the owls have awakened the crowing cock;
Tu—whit!—Tu—whoo!
And hark, again! the crowing cock,
5⠀How drowsily it crew.

Sir Leoline, the Baron rich,
Hath a toothless mastiff bitch;
From her kennel beneath the rock
She maketh answer to the clock,

10⠀Four for the quarters, and twelve for the hour;
Ever and aye,° by shine and shower,⠀⠀⠀⠀⠀⠀*always*
Sixteen short howls, not over loud;
Some say, she sees my lady's shroud.

Is the night chilly and dark?
15⠀The night is chilly, but not dark.
The thin gray cloud is spread on high,
It covers but not hides the sky.
The moon is behind, and at the full;
And yet she looks both small and dull.
20⠀The night is chill, the cloud is gray:
'Tis a month before the month of May,
And the Spring comes slowly up this way.

The lovely lady, Christabel,
Whom her father loves so well,
25⠀What makes her in the wood so late,
A furlong from the castle gate?
She had dreams all yesternight
Of her own betrothéd knight;
And she in the midnight wood will pray
30⠀For the weal° of her lover that's far away.⠀⠀*well-being*

She stole along, she nothing spoke,
The sighs she heaved were soft and low,
And naught was green upon the oak
But moss and rarest misletoe:[3]
35⠀She kneels beneath the huge oak tree,
And in silence prayeth she.

The lady sprang up suddenly,
The lovely lady, Christabel!
It moaned as near, as near can be,
40⠀But what it is she cannot tell.—
On the other side it seems to be,
Of the huge, broad-breasted, old oak tree.

The night is chill; the forest bare;
Is it the wind that moaneth bleak?
45⠀There is not wind enough in the air
To move away the ringlet curl
From the lovely lady's cheek—

---

[1] *rill* Brook.

[2] *celebrated poets … imitated* Lord Byron and Sir Walter Scott, both of whom had read "Christabel" in manuscript form and had been influenced by it in their own subsequent writings.

[3] *mistletoe* Plant considered sacred in ancient Britain when found growing on oak trees.

There is not wind enough to twirl
The one red leaf, the last of its clan,
50 That dances as often as dance it can,
Hanging so light, and hanging so high,
On the topmost twig that looks up at the sky.

Hush, beating heart of Christabel!
Jesu, Maria, shield her well!
55 She folded her arms beneath her cloak,
And stole to the other side of the oak.
        What sees she there?

There she sees a damsel bright,
Dressed in a silken robe of white,
60 That shadowy in the moonlight shone:
The neck that made that white robe wan,
Her stately neck, and arms were bare;
Her blue-veined feet unsandal'd were,
And wildly glittered here and there
65 The gems entangled in her hair.
I guess, 'twas frightful there to see
A lady so richly clad as she—
Beautiful exceedingly!

Mary mother, save me now!
70 (Said Christabel,) And who art thou?

The lady strange made answer meet,
And her voice was faint and sweet:—
Have pity on my sore distress,
I scarce can speak for weariness:
75 Stretch forth thy hand, and have no fear!
Said Christabel, How camest thou here?
And the lady, whose voice was faint and sweet,
Did thus pursue her answer meet:—

My sire is of a noble line,
80 And my name is Geraldine:
Five warriors seized me yestermorn,
Me, even me, a maid forlorn:
They choked my cries with force and fright,
And tied me on a palfrey° white.   saddle horse
85 The palfrey was as fleet as wind,
And they rode furiously behind.

They spurred amain,° their steeds were white: forcefully
And once we crossed the shade of night.
As sure as Heaven shall rescue me,
90 I have no thought what men they be;
Nor do I know how long it is
(For I have lain entranced, I wis°)   know
Since one, the tallest of the five,
Took me from the palfrey's back,
95 A weary woman, scarce alive.
Some muttered words his comrades spoke:
He placed me underneath this oak;
He swore they would return with haste;
Whither they went I cannot tell—
100 I thought I heard, some minutes past,
Sounds as of a castle bell.
Stretch forth thy hand (thus ended she),
And help a wretched maid to flee.

Then Christabel stretched forth her hand,
105 And comforted fair Geraldine:
O well, bright dame! may you command
The service of Sir Leoline;
And gladly our stout° chivalry   fierce
Will he send forth and friends withal
110 To guide and guard you safe and free
Home to your noble father's hall.

She rose: and forth with steps they passed
That strove to be, and were not, fast.
Her gracious stars the lady blest,
115 And thus spake on sweet Christabel:
All our household are at rest,
The hall is silent as the cell;
Sir Leoline is weak in health,
And may not well awakened be,
120 But we will move as if in stealth,
And I beseech your courtesy,
This night, to share your couch with me.

They crossed the moat, and Christabel
Took the key that fitted well;
125 A little door she opened straight,
All in the middle of the gate;
The gate that was ironed within and without,
Where an army in battle array had marched out.

The lady sank, belike through pain,
130 And Christabel with might and main
Lifted her up, a weary weight,
Over the threshold of the gate:
Then the lady rose again,
And moved, as she were not in pain.

135 So free from danger, free from fear,
They crossed the court: right glad they were.
And Christabel devoutly cried
To the Lady by her side,
Praise we the Virgin all divine
140 Who hath rescued thee from thy distress!
Alas, alas! said Geraldine,
I cannot speak for weariness.
So free from danger, free from fear,
They crossed the court: right glad they were.

145 Outside her kennel, the mastiff old
Lay fast asleep, in moonshine cold.
The mastiff old did not awake,
Yet she an angry moan did make!
And what can ail the mastiff bitch?
150 Never till now she uttered yell
Beneath the eye of Christabel.
Perhaps it is the owlet's scritch:
For what can aid the mastiff bitch?

They passed the hall, that echoes still
155 Pass as lightly as you will!
The brands° were flat, the brands were dying,   *burning logs*
Amid their own white ashes lying;
But when the lady passed, there came
A tongue of light, a fit of flame;
160 And Christabel saw the lady's eye,
And nothing else saw she thereby,
Save the boss of the shield of Sir Leoline tall,
Which hung in a murky old niche in the wall.
O softly tread, said Christabel,
165 My father seldom sleepeth well.

Sweet Christabel her feet doth bare,
And jealous of the listening air
They steal their way from stair to stair,
Now in glimmer, and now in gloom,

170 And now they pass the Baron's room,
As still as death, with stifled breath!
And now have reached her chamber door;
And now doth Geraldine press down
The rushes of the chamber floor.

175 The moon shines dim in the open air,
And not a moonbeam enters here.
But they without its light can see
The chamber carved so curiously,
Carved with figures strange and sweet,
180 All made out of the carver's brain,
For a lady's chamber meet:°   *suitable*
The lamp with twofold silver chain
Is fastened to an angel's feet.

The silver lamp burns dead and dim;
185 But Christabel the lamp will trim.
She trimmed the lamp, and made it bright,
And left it swinging to and fro,
While Geraldine, in wretched plight,
Sank down upon the floor below.

190 O weary lady, Geraldine,
I pray you, drink this cordial wine!
It is a wine of virtuous powers;
My mother made it of wild flowers.

And will your mother pity me,
195 Who am a maiden most forlorn?
Christabel answered—Woe is me!
She died the hour that I was born.
I have heard the gray-haired friar tell
How on her death-bed she did say,
200 That she should hear the castle-bell
Strike twelve upon my wedding-day.
O mother dear! that thou wert here!
I would, said Geraldine, she were!

But soon with altered voice, said she—
205 "Off, wandering mother! Peak and pine!
I have power to bid thee flee."
Alas! what ails poor Geraldine?
Why stares she with unsettled eye?
Can she the bodiless dead espy?

210 And why with hollow voice cries she,
    "Off, woman, off! this hour is mine—
    Though thou her guardian spirit be,
    Off, woman, off! 'tis given to me."

    Then Christabel knelt by the lady's side,
215 And raised to heaven her eyes so blue—
    Alas! said she, this ghastly ride—
    Dear lady! it hath wildered you!
    The lady wiped her moist cold brow,
    And faintly said, "'tis over now!"

220 Again the wild-flower wine she drank:
    Her fair large eyes 'gan glitter bright,
    And from the floor whereon she sank,
    The lofty lady stood upright:
    She was most beautiful to see,
225 Like a lady of a far countrée.

    And thus the lofty lady spake—
    "All they who live in the upper sky,
    Do love you, holy Christabel!
    And you love them, and for their sake
230 And for the good which me befell,
    Even I in my degree will try,
    Fair maiden, to requite you well.
    But now unrobe yourself; for I
    Must pray, ere yet in bed I lie."

235 Quoth Christabel, So let it be!
    And as the lady bade, did she.
    Her gentle limbs did she undress
    And lay down in her loveliness.

    But through her brain of weal and woe
240 So many thoughts moved to and fro,
    That vain it were her lids to close;
    So half-way from the bed she rose,
    And on her elbow did recline
    To look at the lady Geraldine.

245 Beneath the lamp the lady bowed,
    And slowly rolled her eyes around;
    Then drawing in her breath aloud,
    Like one that shuddered, she unbound

The cincure° from beneath her breast: *girdle*
250 Her silken robe, and inner vest,
    Dropt to her feet, and full in view,
    Behold! her bosom, and half her side—
    A sight to dream of, not to tell!
    O shield her! shield sweet Christabel!

255 Yet Geraldine nor speaks nor stirs;
    Ah! what a stricken look was hers!
    Deep from within she seems half-way
    To lift some weight with sick assay,°   *attempt*
    And eyes the maid and seeks delay;
260 Then suddenly as one defied
    Collects herself in scorn and pride,
    And lay down by the Maiden's side!—
    And in her arms the maid she took,
              Ah wel-a-day!
265 And with low voice and doleful look
    These words did say:
    "In the touch of this bosom there worketh a spell,
    Which is lord of thy utterance, Christabel!
    Thou knowest to-night, and wilt know to-morrow
270 This mark of my shame, this seal of my sorrow;
              But vainly thou warrest,
                  For this is alone in
              Thy power to declare,
                  That in the dim forest
275   Thou heard'st a low moaning,
    And found'st a bright lady, surpassingly fair;
    And didst bring her home with thee in love and in
        charity,
    To shield her and shelter her from the damp air."

THE CONCLUSION TO PART I

    It was a lovely sight to see
280 The lady Christabel, when she
    Was praying at the old oak tree.
              Amid the jaggéd shadows
              Of mossy leafless boughs,
              Kneeling in the moonlight,
285   To make her gentle vows;
    Her slender palms together prest,
    Heaving sometimes on her breast;

Her face resigned to bliss or bale°—   *grief*
Her face, oh call it fair not pale,
290 And both blue eyes more bright than clear.
Each about to have a tear.

With open eyes (ah, woe is me!)
Asleep, and dreaming fearfully,
Fearfully dreaming, yet, I wis,
295 Dreaming that alone, which is—
O sorrow and shame! Can this be she,
The lady, who knelt at the old oak tree?
And lo! the worker of these harms,
That holds the maiden in her arms,
300 Seems to slumber still and mild,
As a mother with her child.

A star hath set, a star hath risen,
O Geraldine! since arms of thine
Have been the lovely lady's prison.
305 O Geraldine! one hour was thine—
Thou'st had thy will! By tairn° and rill,   *mountain pool*
The night-birds all that hour were still.
But now they are jubilant anew,
From cliff and tower, tu—whoo! tu—whoo!
310 Tu—whoo! tu—whoo! from wood and fell!°   *hill*

And see! the lady Christabel
Gathers herself from out her trance;
Her limbs relax, her countenance
Grows sad and soft; the smooth thin lids
315 Close o'er her eyes; and tears she sheds—
Large tears that leave the lashes bright!
And oft the while she seems to smile
As infants at a sudden light!

Yea, she doth smile, and she doth weep,
320 Like a youthful hermitess,
Beauteous in a wilderness,
Who, praying always, prays in sleep.
And, if she move unquietly,
Perchance, 'tis but the blood so free
325 Comes back and tingles in her feet.
No doubt, she hath a vision sweet.
What if her guardian spirit 'twere,
What if she knew her mother near?

But this she knows, in joys and woes,
330 That saints will aid if men will call:
For the blue sky bends over all!

PART 2

Each matin° bell, the Baron saith,   *morning*
Knells us back to a world of death.
These words Sir Leoline first said,
335 When he rose and found his lady dead:
These words Sir Leoline will say
Many a morn to his dying day!

And hence the custom and law began
That still at dawn the sacristan,°   *church sexton*
340 Who duly pulls the heavy bell,
Five and forty beads° must tell°   *rosary beads / count*
Between each stroke—a warning knell,
Which not a soul can choose but hear
From Bratha Head to Wyndermere.[1]

345 Saith Bracy the bard, So let it knell!
And let the drowsy sacristan
Still count as slowly as he can!
There is no lack of such, I ween,°   *suppose*
As well fill up the space between.
350 In Langdale Pike and Witch's Lair,
And Dungeon-ghyll so foully rent,
With ropes of rock and bells of air
Three sinful sextons' ghosts are pent,
Who all give back, one after t'other,
355 The death-note to their living brother;
And oft too, by the knell offended,
Just as their one! two! three! is ended,
The devil mocks the doleful tale
With a merry peal from Borodale.

360 The air is still! through mist and cloud
That merry peal comes ringing loud;
And Geraldine shakes off her dread,
And rises lightly from the bed;
Puts on her silken vestments white,

---

[1] *Bratha Head ... Wyndermere* In the Lake District.

365 And tricks her hair in lovely plight,[1]
And nothing doubting of her spell
Awakens the lady Christabel.
"Sleep you, sweet lady Christabel?
I trust that you have rested well."

370 And Christabel awoke and spied
The same who lay down by her side—
O rather say, the same whom she
Raised up beneath the old oak tree!
Nay, fairer yet! and yet more fair!
375 For she belike hath drunken deep
Of all the blessedness of sleep!
And while she spake, her looks, her air
Such gentle thankfulness declare,
That (so it seemed) her girded vests
380 Grew tight beneath her heaving breasts.
"Sure I have sinn'd!" said Christabel,
"Now heaven be praised if all be well!"
And in low faltering tones, yet sweet,
Did she the lofty lady greet
385 With such perplexity of mind
As dreams too lively leave behind.

So quickly she rose, and quickly arrayed
Her maiden limbs, and having prayed
That He, who on the cross did groan,
390 Might wash away her sins unknown,
She forthwith led fair Geraldine
To meet her sire, Sir Leoline.

The lovely maid and the lady tall
Are pacing both into the hall,
395 And pacing on through page and groom,
Enter the Baron's presence-room.

The Baron rose, and while he prest
His gentle daughter to his breast,
With cheerful wonder in his eyes
400 The lady Geraldine espies,
And gave such welcome to the same,
As might beseem so bright a dame!

But when he heard the lady's tale,
And when she told her father's name,

405 Why waxed Sir Leoline so pale,
Murmuring o'er the name again,
Lord Roland de Vaux of Tryermaine?

Alas! they had been friends in youth;
But whispering tongues can poison truth;
410 And constancy lives in realms above;
And life is thorny; and youth is vain;
And to be wroth with one we love,
Doth work like madness in the brain.
And thus it chanced, as I divine,
415 With Roland and Sir Leoline.
Each spake words of high disdain
And insult to his heart's best brother:
They parted—ne'er to meet again!
But never either found another
420 To free the hollow heart from paining—
They stood aloof, the scars remaining,
Like cliffs which had been rent asunder;
A dreary sea now flows between;—
But neither heat, nor frost, nor thunder,
425 Shall wholly do away, I ween,
The marks of that which once hath been.

Sir Leoline, a moment's space,
Stood gazing on the damsel's face:
And the youthful Lord of Tryermaine
430 Came back upon his heart again.

O then the Baron forgot his age,
His noble heart swelled high with rage;
He swore by the wounds in Jesu's side,
He would proclaim it far and wide
435 With trump and solemn heraldry,
That they, who thus had wronged the dame,
Were base as spotted infamy!
"And if they dare deny the same,
My herald shall appoint a week,
440 And let the recreant traitors seek
My tourney° court—that there and then   *tournament*
I may dislodge their reptile souls
From the bodies and forms of men!"
He spake: his eye in lightning rolls!
445 For the lady was ruthlessly seized; and he kenned° *recognized*
In the beautiful lady the child of his friend!

---

[1] *plight*   I.e., plait, or braid.

And now the tears were on his face,
And fondly in his arms he took
Fair Geraldine, who met the embrace,
450 Prolonging it with joyous look.
Which when she viewed, a vision fell
Upon the soul of Christabel,
The vision of fear, the touch and pain!
She shrunk and shuddered, and saw again—
455 (Ah, woe is me! Was it for thee,
Thou gentle maid! such sights to see?)

Again she saw that bosom old,
Again she felt that bosom cold,
And drew in her breath with a hissing sound:
460 Whereat the Knight turned wildly round,
And nothing saw, but his own sweet maid
With eyes upraised, as one that prayed.

The touch, the sight, had passed away,
And in its stead that vision blest,
465 Which comforted her after-rest.
While in the lady's arms she lay,
Had put a rapture in her breast,
And on her lips and o'er her eyes
Spread smiles like light!
470   With new surprise,
"What ails then my belovéd child?"
The Baron said—His daughter mild
Made answer, "All will yet be well!"
I ween, she had no power to tell
475 Aught else: so mighty was the spell.

Yet he, who saw this Geraldine,
Had deemed her sure a thing divine:
Such sorrow with such grace she blended,
As if she feared she had offended
480 Sweet Christabel, that gentle maid!
And with such lowly tones she prayed,
She might be sent without delay
Home to her father's mansion.
                                    "Nay!
485 Nay, by my soul!" said Leoline.
"Ho! Bracy the bard, the charge be thine!
Go thou, with music sweet and loud,
And take two steeds with trappings proud,

And take the youth whom thou lov'st best
490 To bear thy harp, and learn thy song,
And clothe you both in solemn vest,
And over the mountains haste along,
Lest wandering folk, that are abroad,
Detain you on the valley road.

495 "And when he has crossed the Irthing flood,
My merry bard! he hastes, he hastes
Up Knorren Moor, through Halegarth Wood,
And reaches soon that castle good
Which stands and threatens Scotland's wastes.

500 "Bard Bracy! bard Bracy! your horses are fleet,
Ye must ride up the hall, your music so sweet,
More loud than your horses' echoing feet!
And loud and loud to Lord Roland call,
Thy daughter is safe in Langdale hall!
505 Thy beautiful daughter is safe and free—
Sir Leoline greets thee thus through me!
He bids thee come without delay
With all thy numerous array
And take thy lovely daughter home:
510 And he will meet thee on the way
With all his numerous array
White with their panting palfreys' foam:
And, by mine honour! I will say,
That I repent me of the day
515 When I spake words of fierce disdain
To Roland de Vaux of Tryermaine!—
—For since that evil hour hath flown,
Many a summer's sun hath shone;
Yet ne'er found I a friend again
520 Like Roland de Vaux of Tryermaine."

The lady fell, and clasped his knees,
Her face upraised, her eyes o'erflowing;
And Bracy replied, with faltering voice,
His gracious hail on all bestowing!—
525 "Thy words, thou sire of Christabel,
Are sweeter than my harp can tell;
Yet might I gain a boon° of thee,   *request*
This day my journey should not be,
So strange a dream hath come to me,
530 That I had vowed with music loud

To clear yon wood from thing unblest,
Warned by a vision in my rest!
For in my sleep I saw that dove,
That gentle bird, whom thou dost love,
535 And call'st by thy own daughter's name—
Sir Leoline! I saw the same
Fluttering, and uttering fearful moan,
Among the green herbs in the forest alone.
Which when I saw and when I heard,
540 I wonder'd what might ail the bird;
For nothing near it could I see,
Save the grass and herbs underneath the old tree.

"And in my dream methought I went
To search out what might there be found;
545 And what the sweet bird's trouble meant,
That thus lay fluttering on the ground.
I went and peered, and could descry
No cause for her distressful cry;
But yet for her dear lady's sake
550 I stooped, methought, the dove to take,
When lo! I saw a bright green snake
Coiled around its wings and neck.
Green as the herbs on which it couched,
Close by the dove's its head it crouched;
555 And with the dove it heaves and stirs,
Swelling its neck as she swelled hers!
I woke; it was the midnight hour,
The clock was echoing in the tower;
But though my slumber was gone by,
560 This dream it would not pass away—
It seems to live upon my eye!
And thence I vowed this self-same day,
With music strong and saintly song
To wander through the forest bare,
565 Lest aught unholy loiter there."

Thus Bracy said: the Baron, the while,
Half-listening heard him with a smile;
Then turned to Lady Geraldine,
His eyes made up of wonder and love;
570 And said in courtly accents fine,
"Sweet maid, Lord Roland's beauteous dove,
With arms more strong than harp or song,
Thy sire and I will crush the snake!"

He kissed her forehead as he spake,
575 And Geraldine in maiden wise,
Casting down her large bright eyes,
With blushing cheek and courtesy fine
She turned her from Sir Leoline;
Softly gathering up her train,
580 That o'er her right arm fell again;
And folded her arms across her chest,
And couched her head upon her breast,
And looked askance at Christabel—
Jesu, Maria, shield her well!

585 A snake's small eye blinks dull and shy;
And the lady's eyes they shrunk in her head,
Each shrunk up to a serpent's eye,
And with somewhat of malice, and more of dread,
At Christabel she looked askance!—
590 One moment—and the sight was fled!
But Christabel in dizzy trance
Stumbling on the unsteady ground
Shuddered aloud, with a hissing sound;
And Geraldine again turned round,
595 And like a thing, that sought relief,
Full of wonder and full of grief,
She rolled her large bright eyes divine
Wildly on Sir Leoline.

The maid, alas! her thoughts are gone,
600 She nothing sees—no sight but one!
The maid, devoid of guile and sin,
I know not how, in fearful wise,
So deeply had she drunken in
That look, those shrunken serpent eyes,
605 That all her features were resigned
To this sole image in her mind:
And passively did imitate
That look of dull and treacherous hate!
And thus she stood, in dizzy trance,
610 Still picturing that look askance
With forced unconscious sympathy
Full before her father's view—
As far as such a look could be
In eyes so innocent and blue!

615　And when the trance was o'er, the maid
　　　Paused awhile, and inly prayed:
　　　Then falling at the Baron's feet,
　　　"By my mother's soul do I entreat
　　　That thou this woman send away!"
620　She said: and more she could not say:
　　　For what she knew she could not tell,
　　　O'er-mastered by the mighty spell.

　　　Why is thy cheek so wan and wild,
　　　Sir Leoline? Thy only child
625　Lies at thy feet, thy joy, thy pride,
　　　So fair, so innocent, so mild;
　　　The same, for whom thy lady died!
　　　O by the pangs of her dear mother
　　　Think thou no evil of thy child!
630　For her, and thee, and for no other,
　　　She prayed the moment ere she died:
　　　Prayed that the babe for whom she died,
　　　Might prove her dear lord's joy and pride!
　　　　　That prayer her deadly pangs beguiled,
635　　　　　　　Sir Leoline!
　　　　　And wouldst thou wrong thy only child,
　　　　　　　Her child and thine?

　　　Within the Baron's heart and brain
　　　If thoughts, like these, had any share,
640　They only swelled his rage and pain,
　　　And did but work confusion there.
　　　His heart was cleft with pain and rage,
　　　His cheeks they quivered, his eyes were wild,
　　　Dishonored thus in his old age;
645　Dishonored by his only child,
　　　And all his hospitality
　　　To the wronged daughter of his friend
　　　By more than woman's jealousy
　　　Brought thus to a disgraceful end—
650　He rolled his eye with stern regard
　　　Upon the gentle minstrel bard,
　　　And said in tones abrupt, austere—
　　　"Why, Bracy! dost thou loiter here?
　　　I bade thee hence!" The bard obeyed;
655　And turning from his own sweet maid,
　　　The agèd knight, Sir Leoline,
　　　Led forth the lady Geraldine!

THE CONCLUSION TO PART 2

　　　A little child, a limber elf,
　　　Singing, dancing to itself,
660　A fairy thing with red round cheeks,
　　　That always finds, and never seeks,
　　　Makes such a vision to the sight
　　　As fills a father's eyes with light;
　　　And pleasures flow in so thick and fast
665　Upon his heart, that he at last
　　　Must needs express his love's excess
　　　With words of unmeant bitterness.
　　　Perhaps 'tis pretty to force together
　　　Thoughts so all unlike each other;
670　To mutter and mock a broken charm,
　　　To dally with wrong that does no harm.
　　　Perhaps 'tis tender too and pretty
　　　At each wild word to feel within
　　　A sweet recoil of love and pity.
675　And what, if in a world of sin
　　　(O sorrow and shame should this be true!)
　　　Such giddiness of heart and brain
　　　Comes seldom save from rage and pain,
　　　So talks as it's most used to do.
　　　　　　　　　　—1801

Dejection: An Ode[1]

　　　Late, late yestreen I saw the new Moon,
　　　With the old Moon in her arms;
　　　And I fear, I fear, my Master dear!
　　　We shall have a deadly storm.
　　　　　　　　　"Ballad of Sir Patrick Spence"[2]

1

Well! If the Bard was weather-wise, who made
　　　The grand old ballad of Sir Patrick Spence,
　　This night, so tranquil now, will not go hence
Unroused by winds, that ply a busier trade

---

[1]　*Dejection: An Ode*　Coleridge originally wrote this poem as a verse letter to Sara Hutchinson (Wordsworth's future sister-in-law), with whom he had fallen in love.

[2]　*Ballad of Sir Patrick Spence*　Anonymous; published in Thomas Percy's *Reliques of Ancient English Poetry* (1765).

5   Than those which mould yon cloud in lazy flakes,
    Or the dull sobbing draft, that moans and rakes
    Upon the strings of this Æolian lute,[1]
            Which better far were mute.
            For lo! the New-moon winter-bright!
10   And overspread with phantom light,
            (With swimming phantom light o'erspread
            But rimmed and circled by a silver thread)
    I see the old Moon in her lap, foretelling
            The coming-on of rain and squally blast.
15 And oh! that even now the gust were swelling,
            And the slant night-shower driving loud and fast!
    Those sounds which oft have raised me, whilst they awed,
            And sent my soul abroad,
    Might now perhaps their wonted° impulse give,   usual
20 Might startle this dull pain, and make it move and live!

                            2

    A grief without a pang, void, dark, and drear,
            A stifled, drowsy, unimpassioned grief,
            Which finds no natural outlet, no relief,
            In word, or sigh, or tear—
25 O Lady! in this wan and heartless mood,
    To other thoughts by yonder throstle° woo'd,   song-thrush
            All this long eve, so balmy and serene,
    Have I been gazing on the western sky,
            And its peculiar tint of yellow green:
30 And still I gaze—and with how blank an eye!
    And those thin clouds above, in flakes and bars,
    That give away their motion to the stars;
    Those stars, that glide behind them or between,
    Now sparkling, now bedimmed, but always seen:
35 Yon crescent Moon, as fixed as if it grew
    In its own cloudless, starless lake of blue;
    I see them all so excellently fair,
    I see, not feel, how beautiful they are!

                            3

            My genial spirits fail;
40   And what can these avail
    To lift the smothering weight from off my breast?
            It were a vain endeavour,

---

[1] *Æolian lute*   Musical instrument named after Æolus, Greek god
of the winds; the music of the lute, or, rather, harp, is made by
exposure to the wind passing through it.

        Though I should gaze for ever
    On that green light that lingers in the west:
45 I may not hope from outward forms to win
    The passion and the life, whose fountains are within.

                            4

    O Lady! we receive but what we give,
    And in our life alone does Nature live:
    Ours is her wedding-garment, ours her shroud!
50   And would we aught behold, of higher worth,
    Than that inanimate cold world allowed
    To the poor loveless ever-anxious crowd,
            Ah! from the soul itself must issue forth
    A light, a glory, a fair luminous cloud
            Enveloping the Earth—
    And from the soul itself must there be sent
            A sweet and potent voice, of its own birth,
    Of all sweet sounds the life and element!

                            5

    O pure of heart! thou need'st not ask of me
60 What this strong music in the soul may be!
    What, and wherein it doth exist,
    This light, this glory, this fair luminous mist,
    This beautiful and beauty-making power.
            Joy, virtuous Lady! Joy that ne'er was given,
65 Save to the pure, and in their purest hour,
    Life, and Life's effluence, cloud at once and shower,
    Joy, Lady! is the spirit and the power,
    Which wedding Nature to us gives in dower
            A new Earth and new Heaven,
70 Undreamt of by the sensual and the proud—
    Joy is the sweet voice, Joy the luminous cloud—
            We in ourselves rejoice!
    And thence flows all that charms or ear or sight,
            All melodies the echoes of that voice,
75 All colours a suffusion from that light.

                            6

    There was a time when, though my path was rough,
            This joy within me dallied with distress,
    And all misfortunes were but as the stuff
            Whence Fancy made me dreams of happiness:
80 For hope grew round me, like the twining vine,
    And fruits, and foliage, not my own, seemed mine.

But now afflictions bow me down to earth:
Nor care I that they rob me of my mirth;
    But oh! each visitation
85 Suspends what nature gave me at my birth,
    My shaping spirit of Imagination.
For not to think of what I needs must feel,
    But to be still and patient, all I can;
And haply by abstruse research to steal
90   From my own nature all the natural man—
This was my sole resource, my only plan:
Till that which suits a part infects the whole,
And now is almost grown the habit of my soul.

7

Hence, viper thoughts, that coil around my mind,
95   Reality's dark dream!
I turn from you, and listen to the wind,
    Which long has raved unnoticed. What a scream
Of agony by torture lengthened out
That lute sent forth! Thou Wind, that rav'st without,
100   Bare crag, or mountain-tairn,[1] or blasted tree,
Or pine-grove whither woodman never clomb,
Or lonely house, long held the witches' home,
    Methinks were fitter instruments for thee,
Mad Lutanist! who in this month of showers,
105 Of dark-brown gardens, and of peeping flowers,
Mak'st Devils' yule, with worse than wintry song,
The blossoms, buds, and timorous leaves among.
    Thou Actor, perfect in all tragic sounds!
Thou mighty Poet, e'en to frenzy bold!
110   What tell'st thou now about?
    'Tis of the rushing of an host in rout,
With groans, of trampled men, with smarting
    wounds—
At once they groan with pain, and shudder with the cold!
But hush! there is a pause of deepest silence!
115   And all that noise, as of a rushing crowd,
With groans, and tremulous shudderings—all is over—
    It tells another tale, with sounds less deep and loud!
    A tale of less affright,
    And tempered with delight,

120 As Otway's[2] self had framed the tender lay,—
    'Tis of a little child
    Upon a lonesome wild,
Not far from home, but she hath lost her way:
And now moans low in bitter grief and fear,
125 And now screams loud, and hopes to make her
    mother hear.

8

'Tis midnight, but small thoughts have I of sleep:
Full seldom may my friend such vigils keep!
Visit her, gentle Sleep! with wings of healing,
    And may this storm be but a mountain-birth,
130 May all the stars hang bright above her dwelling,
    Silent as though they watched the sleeping Earth!
    With light heart may she rise,
    Gay fancy, cheerful eyes,
    Joy lift her spirit, joy attune her voice;
135 To her may all things live, from the pole to pole,
Their life the eddying of her living soul!
    O simple spirit, guided from above,
Dear Lady! friend devoutest of my choice,
Thus mayest thou ever, evermore rejoice.
—1802

Work Without Hope

Lines Composed 21st February 1825

All Nature seems at work. Slugs leave their lair—
The bees are stirring—birds are on the wing—
And Winter slumbering in the open air,
Wears on his smiling face a dream of Spring!
5 And I the while, the sole unbusy thing,
Nor honey make, nor pair, nor build, nor sing.

    Yet well I ken° the banks where   *recognize*
    amaranths[3] blow,
Have traced the fount whence streams of nectar flow.
Bloom, O ye amaranths! bloom for whom ye may,
10 For me ye bloom not! Glide, rich streams, away!

---

[1] [Coleridge's note] Tairn is a small lake, generally if not always applied to the lakes up in the mountains and which are the feeders of those in the valleys. This address to the Storm-wind will not appear extravagant to those who have heard it at night and in a mountainous country.

[2] *Otway* Thomas Otway (1652–85), English playwright known for his tragedies.

[3] *amaranths* Imaginary flowers, the blossoms of which never fade.

With lips unbrightened, wreathless brow, I stroll:
And would you learn the spells that drowse my soul?
Work without hope draws nectar in a sieve,
And Hope without an object cannot live.
—1828

Kubla Khan
Or, A Vision in a Dream. A Fragment[1]

In Xanadu did Kubla Khan
A stately pleasure-dome decree:
Where Alph, the sacred river, ran

[1] [Coleridge's note] The following fragment is here published at the request of a poet [Lord Byron] of great and deserved celebrity, and as far as the Author's own opinions are concerned, rather as a psychological curiosity, than on the ground of any supposed poetic merits.

In the summer of the year 1797, the Author, then in ill health, had retired to a lonely farmhouse between Porlock and Linton, on the Exmoor confines of Somerset and Devonshire. In consequence of a slight indisposition [dysentery], an anodyne [opium] had been prescribed, from the effects of which he fell asleep in his chair at the moment that he was reading the following sentence, or words of the same substance, in *Purchas's Pilgrimage* [i.e., *Purchas his Pilgrimage* (1613, 1614, 1617, 1626)]: "Here the Khan Kubla commanded a palace to be built, and a stately garden thereunto. And thus ten miles of fertile ground were inclosed with a wall." The author continued for about three hours in a profound sleep, at least of the external senses, during which time he has the most vivid confidence, that he could not have composed less than from two to three hundred lines, if that indeed can be called composition in which all the images rose up before him as things, with a parallel production of the correspondent expressions, without any sensation or consciousness of effort. On awaking he appeared to himself to have a distinct recollection of the whole, and taking his pen, ink, and paper, instantly and eagerly wrote down the lines that are here preserved. At this moment he was unfortunately called out by a person on business from Porlock, and detained by him above an hour, and on his return to his room, found to his no small surprise and mortification, that though he still retained some vague and dim recollection of the general purpose of the vision, yet, with the exception of some eight or ten scattered lines and images, all the rest had passed away like the images on the surface of a stream into which a stone has been cast, but, alas! without the after restoration of the latter!

     Then all the charm
Is broken—all that phantom-world so fair
Vanishes, and a thousand circlets spread,
And each mis-shape the other. Stay awhile,
Poor youth! who scarcely dar'st lift up thine eyes—
The stream will soon renew its smoothness, soon

Through caverns measureless to man
    Down to a sunless sea.
So twice five miles of fertile ground
With walls and towers were girdled round:
And there were gardens bright with sinuous rills,°   *brooks*
Where blossomed many an incense-bearing tree;
And here were forests ancient as the hills,
Enfolding sunny spots of greenery.

But oh! that deep romantic chasm which slanted
Down the green hill athwart a cedarn cover!
A savage place! as holy and enchanted
As e'er beneath a waning moon was haunted
By woman wailing for her demon-lover!
And from this chasm, with ceaseless turmoil seething,
As if this earth in fast thick pants were breathing,
A mighty fountain momently was forced:
Amid whose swift half-intermitted burst
Huge fragments vaulted like rebounding hail,
Or chaffy grain beneath the thresher's flail:
And 'mid these dancing rocks at once and ever
It flung up momently the sacred river.
Five miles meandering with a mazy° motion   *labyrinthine*
Through wood and dale the sacred river ran,
Then reached the caverns measureless to man,
And sank in tumult to a lifeless ocean:
And 'mid this tumult Kubla heard from far
Ancestral voices prophesying war!
    The shadow of the dome of pleasure
    Floated midway on the waves;
    Where was heard the mingled measure
    From the fountain and the caves.
It was a miracle of rare device,
A sunny pleasure-dome with caves of ice!

The visions will return! And lo, he stays,
And soon the fragments dim of lovely forms
Come trembling back, unite, and now once more
The pool becomes a mirror.
[from Coleridge's "The Picture, or the Lover's Resolution" (1802) 69–78]

Yet from the still surviving recollections in his mind, the Author has frequently purposed to finish for himself what had been originally, as it were, given to him. Σαμερον αδιον ασω [from Theocritus's *Idyll* 1.145]: but the tomorrow is yet to come.

As a contrast to this vision, I have annexed a fragment of a very different character [Coleridge's poem "The Pains of Sleep"], describing with equal fidelity the dream of pain and disease.

A damsel with a dulcimer
In a vision once I saw:
It was an Abyssinian maid,
40   And on her dulcimer she played,
Singing of Mount Abora.
Could I revive within me
Her symphony and song,
To such a deep delight 'twould win me,
45 That with music loud and long,
I would build that dome in air,
That sunny dome! those caves of ice!
And all who heard should see them there,
And all should cry, Beware! Beware!
50 His flashing eyes, his floating hair!
Weave a circle round him thrice,
And close your eyes with holy dread,
For he on honey-dew hath fed,
And drunk the milk of Paradise.
—1816 (WRITTEN 1798)

Epitaph

Stop, Christian passerby!—Stop, child of God,
And read with gentle breast. Beneath this sod
A poet lies, or that which once seem'd he.
O, lift one thought in prayer for S.T.C.;
5 That he who many a year with toil of breath
Found death in life, may here find life in death!
Mercy for praise—to be forgiven for[1] fame
He ask'd, and hoped, through Christ. Do thou the same!
—1833

On Donne's Poetry

With Donne,[2] whose muse on dromedary trots,
Wreathe iron pokers into true-love knots;
Rhyme's sturdy cripple, fancy's maze and clue,
Wit's forge and fire-blast, meaning's press and screw.
—1836

---

[1] [Coleridge's note] "For" in the sense of "instead of,"

[2] Donne English poet John Donne (1572–1631).

from Lectures and Notes On Literature

[DEFINITION OF POETRY]

Readers may be divided into four classes:
1. Sponges, who absorb all they read, and return it nearly in the same state, only a little dirtied.
2. Sand-glasses, who retain nothing, and are content to get through a book for the sake of getting through the time.
3. Strain-bags, who retain merely the dregs of what they read.
4. Mogul diamonds, equally rare and valuable, who profit by what they read, and enable others to profit by it also.

[MECHANIC VS. ORGANIC FORM]

Are the plays of Shakespeare works of rude uncultivated genius, in which the splendour of the parts compensates, if aught can compensate, for the barbarous shapelessness and irregularity of the whole? … Or is the form equally admirable with the matter, the judgment of the great poet not less deserving of our wonder than his genius? Or to repeat the question in other words, is Shakespeare a great dramatic poet on account only of those beauties and excellencies which he possesses in common with the ancients, but with diminished claims to our love and honour to the full extent of his difference from them? Or are these very differences additional proofs of poetic wisdom, at once results and symbols of living power as contrasted with lifeless mechanism, of free and rival originality as contradistinguished from servile imitation, or more accurately, a blind copying of effects instead of a true imitation of the essential principles? Imagine not I am about to oppose genius to rules. No! the comparative value of these rules is the very cause to be tried. The spirit of poetry, like all other living powers, must of necessity circumscribe itself by rules, were it only to unite power with beauty. It must embody in order to reveal itself; but a living body is of necessity an organized one—and what is organization but the connection of parts to a whole, so that each part is at once end and means! This is no discovery of criticism; it is a necessity of the human mind—and all nations have felt and obeyed it, in the invention of meter and measured sounds as the vehicle and involucrum[1] of poetry, itself a fellow growth from the same life, even as the bark is to the tree.

No work of true genius dare want its appropriate form; neither indeed is there any danger of this. As it must not, so neither can it, be lawless! For it is even this that constitutes its genius—the power of acting creatively under laws of its own origination. How then comes it that ... whole nations have combined in unhesitating condemnation of our great dramatist, as a sort of African nature, fertile in beautiful monsters, as a wild heath where islands of fertility look greener from the surrounding waste, where the loveliest plants now shine out among unsightly weeds and now are choked by their parasitic growth, so intertwined that we cannot disentangle the weed without snapping the flower.... The true ground of the mistake, as has been well remarked by a continental critic,[2] lies in the confounding mechanical regularity with organic form. The form is mechanic when on any given material we impress a predetermined form, not necessarily arising out of the properties of the material, as when to a mass of wet clay we give whatever shape we wish it to retain when hardened. The organic form, on the other hand, is innate; it shapes as it develops itself from within, and the fullness of its development is one and the same with the perfection of its outward form. Such is the life, such the form. Nature, the prime genial artist, inexhaustible in diverse powers, is equally inexhaustible in forms. Each exterior is the physiognomy of the being within, its true image reflected and thrown out from the concave mirror. And even such is the appropriate excellence of her chosen poet, of our own Shakespeare, himself a nature humanized, a genial understanding directing self-consciously a power and an implicit wisdom deeper than consciousness.

—1811–12

---

[1]   *involucrum*   Outer membrane.

[2]   *a continental critic*   German art and literary critic August Wilhelm Schlegel (1767–1845).

from *Biographia Literaria; or Biographical Sketches of my Literary Life and Opinions*

from CHAPTER 1
Reception of the Author's First Publication

... In 1794, when I had barely passed the verge of manhood, I published a small volume of juvenile poems. They were received with a degree of favour, which young as I was, I well know was bestowed on them not so much for any positive merit, as because they were considered buds of hope, and promises of better works to come. The critics of that day, the most flattering, equally with the severest, concurred in objecting to them: obscurity, a general turgidness of diction, and a profusion of new coined double epithets.[3] ... From that period to the date of the present work I have published nothing, with my name, which could by any possibility have come before the board of anonymous criticism. Even the three or four poems, printed with the works of a friend, as far as they were censured at all, were charged with the same or similar defects, though I am persuaded not with equal justice: with an excess of ornament, in addition to strained and

---

[3]   [Coleridge's note]   The authority of Milton and Shakespeare may be usefully pointed out to young authors. In the *Comus* and other early poems of Milton there is a superfluity of double epithets, while in the *Paradise Lost* we find very few, in the *Paradise Regained* scarce any. The same remark holds almost equally true of the *Love's Labour Lost, Romeo and Juliet, Venus and Adonis*, and *Lucrece*, compared with the *Lear, Macbeth, Othello*, and *Hamlet* of our great dramatist. The rule for the admission of double epithets seems to be this: either that they should be already denizens of our language, such as blood-stained, terror-stricken, self-applauding, or when a new epithet, or one found in books only, is hazarded, that it, at least, be one word, not two words made one by mere virtue of the printer's hyphen. A language which, like the English, is almost without cases, is indeed in its very genius unfitted for compounds. If a writer, every time a compounded word suggests itself to him, would seek for some other mode of expressing the same sense, the chances are always greatly in favour of his finding a better word. *Ut tanquam scopulum sic fugias insolens verbum*, is the wise advice of Caesar to the Roman orators, and the precept applies with double force to the writers in our own language. But it must not be forgotten that the same Caesar wrote a treatise for the purpose of reforming the ordinary language by bringing it to a greater accordance with the principles of logic or universal grammar.

elaborate diction. (*Vide*[1] *the criticisms on the "Ancient Mariner" in the Monthly and Critical Reviews of the first volume of the* Lyrical Ballads.) May I be permitted to add, that, even at the early period of my juvenile poems, I saw and admitted the superiority of an austerer, and more natural style, with an insight not less clear, than I at present possess. My judgement was stronger, than were my powers of realizing its dictates; and the faults of my language, though indeed partly owing to a wrong choice of subjects, and the desire of giving a poetic colouring to abstract and metaphysical truths, in which a new world then seemed to open upon me, did yet, in part likewise, originate in unfeigned diffidence of my own comparative talent....

THE EFFECT OF CONTEMPORARY WRITERS ON YOUTHFUL MINDS

... Among those with whom I conversed, there were, of course, very many who had formed their taste, and their notions of poetry, from the writings of Mr. Pope[2] and his followers: or to speak more generally, in that school of French poetry, condensed and invigorated by English understanding, which had predominated from the last century. I was not blind to the merits of this school, yet as from inexperience of the world and consequent want of sympathy with the general subjects of these poems, they gave me little pleasure, I doubtless undervalued the *kind*, and with the presumption of youth withheld from its masters the legitimate name of poets. I saw, that the excellence of this kind consisted in just and acute observations on men and manners in an artificial state of society, as its matter and substance: and in the logic of wit, conveyed in smooth and strong epigrammatic couplets, as its *form*. Even when the subject was addressed to the fancy, or the intellect, as in *The Rape of the Lock*, or *The Essay on Man*—nay, when it was a consecutive narration, as in that astonishing product of matchless talent and ingenuity, Pope's Translation of the *Iliad*—still a *point* was looked for at the end of each second line, and the whole was as it were a sorites,[3] or, if I may exchange a logical for a grammatical metaphor, a *conjunction disjunctive*, of epigrams.[4] Meantime the matter and diction seemed to me characterized not so much by poetic thoughts, as by thoughts *translated* into the language of poetry.

... I was ... led to a conjecture, which, many years afterwards was recalled to me from the same thought having been started in conversation, but far more ably, and developed more fully, by Mr. Wordsworth; namely, that this style of poetry, which I have characterised above, as translations of prose thoughts into poetic language, had been kept up by, if it did not wholly arise from, the custom of writing Latin verses, and the great importance attached to these exercises, in our public schools. Whatever might have been the case in the fifteenth century, when the use of the Latin tongue was so general among learned men, that Erasmus[5] is said to have forgotten his native language; yet in the present day it is not to be supposed, that a youth can *think* in Latin, or that he can have any other reliance on the force or fitness of his phrases, but the authority of the writer from whence he has adopted them. Consequently he must first prepare his thoughts, and then pick out, from Virgil, Horace, Ovid,[6] or perhaps more compendiously from his *Gradus*,[7] halves and quarters of lines, in which to embody them....

BOWLES'S SONNETS

... Our genuine admiration of a great poet is a continuous *undercurrent* of feeling; it is everywhere present, but seldom anywhere as a separate excitement. I was wont boldly to affirm, that it would be scarcely more difficult to push a stone out from the pyramids

---

[1] *Vide* Latin: see.

[2] *Mr. Pope* British poet Alexander Pope (1688–1744). It is to his work that Coleridge proceeds to refer.

[3] *sorites* Type of argument in which the predicate of one thesis becomes the subject of the next.

[4] *conjunctive disjunctive, of epigrams* Connecting and disconnecting, in poems that seem to lead up to one point and then turn at the end to make another.

[5] *Erasmus* Dutch author, priest, and scholar (1466?–1536), who translated many classics into Greek and Latin.

[6] *Virgil, Horace, Ovid* Roman poets.

[7] *Gradus* Latin dictionary of verse (*Gradus ad Parnassum*) used to aid in composition.

with the bare hand, than to alter a word, or the position of a word, in Milton or Shakespeare (in their most important works at least), without making the author say something else, or something worse, than he does say. One great distinction, I appeared to myself to see plainly, between, even the characteristic faults of our elder poets, and the false beauty of the moderns. In the former, from Donne to Cowley,[1] we find the most fantastic out-of-the-way thoughts, but in the most pure and genuine mother English; in the latter, the most obvious thoughts, in language the most fantastic and arbitrary. Our faulty elder poets sacrificed the passion, and passionate flow of poetry, to the subtleties of intellect, and to the starts of wit; the moderns to the glare and glitter of a perpetual, yet broken and heterogeneous imagery, or rather to an amphibious something, made up, half of image, and half of abstract meaning. The one sacrificed the heart to the head; the other both heart and head to point and drapery.

The reader must make himself acquainted with the general style of composition that was at that time deemed poetry, in order to understand and account for the effect produced on me by the *Sonnets*, the "Monody at Matlock," and the "Hope," of Mr. Bowles;[2] for it is peculiar to original genius to become less and less *striking*, in proportion to its success in improving the taste and judgement of its contemporaries. The poems of West indeed had the merit of chaste and manly diction, but they were cold, and, if I may so express it, only *dead-coloured*; while in the best of Warton's there is a stiffness, which too often gives them the appearance of imitations from the Greek. Whatever relation therefore of cause or impulse Percy's collection of ballads[3] may bear to the most *popular* poems of the present day; yet in the more sustained and elevated style, of the then living poets, Bowles and Cowper[4] were, to

the best of my knowledge, the first who combined natural thoughts with natural diction; the first who reconciled the heart with the head. ...

from CHAPTER 4
Mr. Wordsworth's Earlier Poems

... During the last year of my residence at Cambridge, I became acquainted with Mr. Wordsworth's first publication entitled *Descriptive Sketches*,[5] and seldom, if ever, was the emergence of an original poetic genius above the literary horizon more evidently announced. In the form, style, and manner of the whole poem, and in the structure of the particular lines and periods, there is an harshness and acerbity connected and combined with words and images all aglow, which might recall those products of the vegetable world, where gorgeous blossoms rise out of the hard and thorny rind and shell, within which the rich fruit was elaborating. The language was not only peculiar and strong, but at times knotty and contorted, as by its own impatient strength, while the novelty and struggling crowd of images, acting in conjunction with the difficulties of the style, demanded always a greater closeness of attention than poetry (at all events, than descriptive poetry) has a right to claim. It not seldom therefore justified the complaint of obscurity. In the following extract I have sometimes fancied that I saw an emblem of the poem itself, and of the author's genius as it was then displayed.

'Tis storm; and hid in mist from hour to hour,
All day the floods a deepening murmur pour;
The sky is veiled, and every cheerful sight:
Dark is the region as with coming night;
And yet what frequent bursts of overpowering light!
Triumphant on the bosom of the storm,

[1] *Donne ... Cowley* English poets of the early seventeenth century.

[2] *Mr. Bowles* William Lisle Bowles (1762–1850), English poet and literary critic, who published a collection of his sonnets in 1789.

[3] *Percy's collection of ballads* Reverend Thomas Percy's *Reliques of Ancient English Poetry* (1765).

[4] [Coleridge's note] Cowper's *Task* was published some time before the *Sonnets* of Mr. Bowles; but I was not familiar with it till many years afterwards. The vein of satire which runs through that excellent poem, together with the somber hue of its religious

opinions, would probably, *at that time*, have prevented its laying any strong hold on my affections. The love of nature seems to have led Thompson to a cheerful religion; and a gloomy religion to have led Cowper to a love of nature. The one would carry his fellow men along with him into nature; the other flies to nature from his fellow men. In chastity of diction, however, and the harmony of blank verse, Cowper leaves Thompson immeasurably below him; yet still I feel the latter to have been the *born poet*.

[5] *Descriptive Sketches* Published 1793 and again in 1815 in an altered version.

Glances the fire-clad eagle's wheeling form;
Eastward, in long perspective glittering, shine
The wood-crowned cliffs that o'er the lake recline;
Wide o'er the Alps a hundred streams unfold,
At once to pillars turned that flame with gold;
Behind his sail the peasant strives to shun
The West, that burns like one dilated sun,
Where in a mighty crucible expire
The mountains, glowing hot, like coals of fire.[1]

The poetic psyche, in its process to full development, undergoes as many changes as its Greek namesake, the butterfly.[2] And it is remarkable how soon genius clears and purifies itself from the faults and errors of its earliest products; faults which, in its earliest compositions, are the more obtrusive and confluent, because as heterogeneous elements, which had only a temporary use, they constitute the very *ferment*, by which themselves are carried off. Or we may compare them to some diseases, which must work on the humours, and be thrown out on the surface, in order to secure the patient from their future recurrence. I was in my twenty-fourth year, when I had the happiness of knowing Mr. Wordsworth personally, and while memory lasts, I shall hardly forget the sudden effect produced on my mind, by his recitation of a manuscript poem, which still remains unpublished,[3] but of which the stanza, and tone of style were the same as those of "The Female Vagrant" as originally printed in the first volume of the *Lyrical Ballads*. There was here, no mark of strained thought, or forced diction, no crowd or turbulence of imagery; and, as the poet hath himself

well described in his lines "on revisiting the Wye,"[4] manly reflection, and human associations had given both variety, and an additional interest to natural objects, which in the passion and appetite of the first love they had seemed to him neither to need or permit. The occasional obscurities, which had risen from an imperfect control over the resources of his native language, had almost wholly disappeared, together with that worse defect of arbitrary and illogical phrases, at once hackneyed, and fantastic, which hold so distinguished a place in the *technique* of ordinary poetry, and will, more or less, alloy the earlier poems of the truest genius, unless the attention has been specifically directed to their worthlessness and incongruity.[5] I did not perceive anything particular in the mere style of the poem alluded to during its recitation, except indeed such difference as was not separable from the thought and manner; and the Spenserian stanza, which always, more or less, recalls to the reader's mind Spenser's own style, would doubtless have authorized, in my then opinion, a more frequent descent to the phrases of ordinary life, than could without an ill effect have been hazarded in the heroic couplet. It was not however the freedom from false taste, whether as to common defects, or to those more properly his own, which made so unusual an impression on my feelings immediately, and subsequently on my judgement. It was the union of deep feeling with profound thought; the fine balance of

---

[1] *'Tis storm ... fire* From "Descriptive Sketches Taken During a Pedestrian Tour in the Alps" (1815).

[2] [Coleridge's note] The fact that in Greek Psyche is the common name for the soul, and the butterfly is thus alluded to in the following stanzas from an unpublished poem ["The Butterfly" (1817)] of the author:
The butterfly the ancient Grecians made
The soul's fair emblem, and its only name—
But of the soul, escaped the slavish trade
Of mortal life! For in this earthly frame
Our's is the reptile's lot, much toil, much blame,
Manifold motions making little speed,
And to deform and kill the things, whereon we feed.

[3] *manuscript ... unpublished* "Guilt and Sorrow; or, Incidents Upon Salisbury Plain" (1842; written 1793-94).

[4] *"on revisiting the Wye"* From Wordsworth's "Lines Composed a Few Miles Above Tintern Abbey," 77–94.

[5] [Coleridge's note] Mr. Wordsworth, even in his two earliest, "An Evening Walk" and the "Descriptive Sketches," is more free from this latter defect than most of the young poets his contemporaries. It may, however, be exemplified, together with the harsh and obscure construction, in which he more often offended, in the following lines:
'Mid stormy vapours ever driving by,
Where ospreys, cormorants, and herons cry;
Where hardly given the hopeless waste to cheer,
Denied the bread of life, the foodful ear,
Dwindles the pear on autumn's latest spray,
And *apple sickens* pale in summer's ray;
Ev'n here content has fixed her smiling reign
With independence, child of high disdain.
I hope, I need not say, that I have quoted these lines for no other purpose than to make my meaning fully understood. It is to be regretted that Mr. Wordsworth has not republished these two poems entire.

truth in observing, with the imaginative faculty in modifying the objects observed; and above all the original gift of spreading the tone, the *atmosphere*, and with it the depth and height of the ideal world around forms, incidents, and situations, of which, for the common view, custom had bedimmed all the lustre, had dried up the sparkle and the dew drops. "To find no contradiction in the union of old and new; to contemplate the Ancient of days and all his works with feelings as fresh, as if all had then sprang forth at the first creative fiat;[1] characterizes the mind that feels the riddle of the world, and may help to unravel it. To carry on the feelings of childhood into the powers of manhood; to combine the child's sense of wonder and novelty with the appearances, which every day for perhaps forty years had rendered familiar;

> With sun and moon and stars throughout the year,
> And man and woman;[2]

this is the character and privilege of genius, and one of the marks which distinguish genius from talents. And therefore is it the prime merit of genius and its most unequivocal mode of manifestation, so to represent familiar objects as to awaken in the minds of others a kindred feeling concerning them and that freshness of sensation which is the constant accompaniment of mental, no less than of bodily, convalescence. Who has not a thousand times seen snow fall on water? Who has not watched it with a new feeling, from the time that he has read Burns' comparison of sensual pleasure

> To snow that falls upon a river
> A moment white—then gone for ever![3]

In poems, equally as in philosophic disquisitions, genius produces the strongest impressions of novelty, while it rescues the most admitted truths from the impotence caused by the very circumstance of their universal

admission. Truths of all others the most awful and mysterious, yet being at the same time of universal interest, are too often considered as so true, that they lose all the life and efficiency of truth, and lie bedridden in the dormitory of the soul, side by side with the most despised and exploded errors."—The Friend,[4] p. 76, No. 5.

This excellence, which in all Mr. Wordsworth's writings is more or less predominant, and which constitutes the character of his mind, I no sooner felt, than I sought to understand. Repeated meditations led me first to suspect (and a more intimate analysis of the human faculties, their appropriate marks, functions, and effects matured my conjecture into full conviction) that fancy and imagination were two distinct and widely different faculties, instead of being, according to the general belief, either two names with one meaning, or, at furthest, the lower and higher degree of one and the same power. It is not, I own, easy to conceive a more apposite translation of the Greek *Phantasia* than the Latin Imaginatio; but it is equally true that in all societies there exists an instinct of growth, a certain collective, unconscious good sense working progressively to desynonymize[5] those words originally of the same

---

[1] *fiat* Command.

[2] *With sun ... woman* Milton's sonnet "To Mr. Cyriack Skinner upon his Blindness" (1655) actually reads: "Of sun or moon or star throughout the year, / Or man or woman."

[3] *To snow ... for ever!* Robert Burns's "Tam O'Shanter" (1791) reads: "Or like the snow falls in the river, / A moment white—then melts for ever."

[4] [Coleridge's note] As "The Friend" was printed on stampt sheets, and sent only by the poet to a very limited number of subscribers, the author has felt less objection to quote from it, though a work of his own. To the public at large indeed it is the same as a volume in manuscript.

[5] [Coleridge's note] This is effected either by giving to the one word a general, and to the other an exclusive use; as "to put on the back" and "to indorse;" or by an actual distinction of meanings as "naturalist," and "physician"; or by difference of relation as "I" and "Me"; (each of which the rustics of our different provinces still use in all the cases singular of the first personal pronoun). Even the mere difference, or corruption, in the *pronunciation* of the same word, if it have become general, will produce a new word with a distinct signification; thus "property" and "propriety"; the latter of which, even to the time of Charles II was the *written* word for all the senses of both. Thus too "mister" and "master" both hasty pronunciations of the same word "magister," "mistress," and "miss," "if," and "give," &c. &c. There is a sort of *minim immortal* among the *animalcula infusoria* which has not naturally either birth, or death, absolute beginning, or absolute end: for at a certain period a small point appears on its back, which deepens and lengthens till the creature divides into two, and the same process recommences in each of the halves now become integral. This may be a fanciful, but it is by no means a bad emblem of the formation of words, and may facilitate the conception, how immense a nomenclature may be organized

meaning, which the conflux of dialects had supplied to the more homogeneous languages, as the Greek and German: and which the same cause, joined with accidents of translation from original works of different countries, occasion in mixed languages like our own. The first and most important point to be proved is, that two conceptions perfectly distinct are confused under one and the same word, and (this done) to appropriate that word exclusively to one meaning, and the synonym (should there be one) to the other. But if (as will be often the case in the arts and sciences) no synonym exists, we must either invent or borrow a word. In the present instance the appropriation has already begun, and been legitimated in the derivative adjective: Milton had a highly *imaginative*, Cowley a very *fanciful* mind. If therefore I should succeed in establishing the actual existences of two faculties generally different, the nomenclature would be at once determined. To the faculty by which I had characterized Milton, we should confine the term *imagination*; while the other would be contra-distinguished as *fancy*. Now were it once fully ascertained, that this division is no less grounded in nature, than that of delirium from mania, or Otway's

Lutes, lobsters, seas of milk, and ships of amber,[1]

from Shakespeare's

What! have his daughters brought him to this pass?[2]

or from the preceding apostrophe to the elements; the theory of the fine arts, and of poetry in particular, could not, I thought, but derive some additional and important light. It would in its immediate effects furnish a torch of guidance to the philosophical critic; and ultimately to the poet himself. In energetic minds,

---

from a few simple sounds by rational beings in a social state. For each new application, or excitement of the same sound, will call forth a different sensation, which cannot but affect the pronunciation. The after recollection of the sound, without the same vivid sensation, will modify it still further; till at length all trace of the original likeness is worn away.

[1] *Lutes ... amber* From Thomas Otway's play *Venice Preserved* (1682) 5.2.; Otway's version has the word "laurel" replacing "lobster."

[2] *What! ... pass?* From *King Lear* 3.4.65.

truth soon changes by domestication into power; and from directing in the discrimination and appraisal of the product, becomes influencive in the production. To admire on principle, is the only way to imitate without loss of originality. ...

from CHAPTER 11
An affectionate exortation to those who in early life feel themselves disposed to become authors

... With no other privilege than that of sympathy and sincere good wishes, I would address an affectionate exhortation to the youthful literati, grounded on my own experience. It will be but short; for the beginning, middle, and end converge to one charge: NEVER PURSUE LITERATURE AS A TRADE. With the exception of one extraordinary man, I have never known an individual, least of all an individual of genius, healthy or happy without a *profession*, i.e., some *regular* employment, which does not depend on the will of the moment, and which can be carried on so far *mechanically* that an average quantum only of health, spirits, and intellectual exertion are requisite to its faithful discharge. Three hours of leisure, unannoyed by any alien anxiety, and looked forward to with delight as a change and recreation, will suffice to realize in literature a larger product of what is truly *genial*, than weeks of compulsion. Money, and immediate reputation form only an arbitrary and accidental end of literary labour. The *hope* of increasing them by any given exertion will often prove a stimulant to industry; but the *necessity* of acquiring them will in all works of genius convert the stimulant into a *narcotic*. Motives by excess reverse their very nature, and instead of exciting, stun and stupify the mind. For it is one contradistinction of genius from talent, that its predominant end is always comprized in the means; and this is one of the many points which establish an analogy between genius and virtue. Now though talents may exist without genius, yet as genius cannot exist, certainly not manifest itself, without talents, I would advise every scholar, who feels the genial power working within him, so far to make a division between the two, as that he should devote his *talents* to the acquirement of competence in some known trade or profession, and his genius to objects of his tranquil and unbiased choice; while the consciousness of being actuated in both alike by the sincere desire to perform his duty, will alike ennoble both. My dear young friend (I would say), "Suppose yourself established in any honourable occupation. From the manufactory or counting-house, from the law-court, or from having visited your last patient, you return at evening,

> Dear tranquil time, when the sweet sense of home
> Is sweetest—[1]

to your family, prepared for its social enjoyments, with the very countenances of your wife and children brightened, and their voice of welcome made doubly welcome, by the knowledge that, as far as *they* are concerned, you have satisfied the demands of the day by the labour of the day. Then, when you retire into your study, in the books on your shelves you revisit so many venerable friends with whom you can converse. Your own spirit scarcely less free from personal anxieties than the great minds, that in those books are still living for you! Even your writing desk with its blank paper and all its other implements will appear as a chain of flowers, capable of linking your feelings as well as thoughts to events and characters past or to come; not a chain of iron which binds you down to think of the future and the remote by recalling the claims and feelings of the peremptory present. But why should I say *retire*? The habits of active life and daily intercourse with the stir of the world will tend to give you such self-command, that the presence of your family will be no interruption. Nay, the social silence, or undisturbing voices of a wife or sister will be like a restorative atmosphere, or soft music which moulds a dream without becoming its object. If facts are required to prove the possibility of combining weighty performances in literature with full and independent employment, the works of Cicero and Xenophon among the ancients; of Sir Thomas Moore, Bacon, Baxter, or to refer at once to later and contemporary instances, Darwin and Roscoe,[2] are at

once decisive of the question."

from CHAPTER 13
On the Imagination, or Esemplastic[3] Power

The IMAGINATION then I consider either as primary, or secondary. The primary IMAGINATION I hold to be the living Power and prime Agent of all human Perception, and as a repetition in the finite mind of the eternal act of creation in the infinite I AM. The secondary I consider as an echo of the former, co-existing with the conscious will, yet still as identical with the primary in the *kind* of its agency, and differing only in *degree,* and in the *mode* of its operation. It dissolves, diffuses, dissipates, in order to re-create; or where this process is rendered impossible, yet still at all events it struggles to idealize and to unify. It is essentially *vital*, even as all objects (as objects) are essentially fixed and dead.

FANCY, on the contrary, has no other counters to play with, but fixities and definites. The Fancy is indeed no other than a mode of Memory emancipated from the order of time and space; and blended with, and modified by that empirical phenomenon of the will, which we express by the word CHOICE. But equally with the ordinary memory it must receive all its materials ready made from the law of association.

Whatever more than this, I shall think it fit to declare concerning the powers and privileges of the imagination in the present work, will be found in the critical essay on the uses of the Supernatural in poetry and the principles that regulate its introduction, which the reader will find prefixed to the poem of *The Ancient Mariner*.

CHAPTER 14
Occasion of the Lyrical Ballads

During the first year that Mr. Wordsworth and I were neighbours, our conversations turned frequently on the

---

[1] *Dear ... sweetest* From Coleridge's "To William Wordsworth," 96–97.

[2] *Cicero* Roman orator, philosopher, and statesman of the first century BCE; *Xenophon* Greek historian (c. 430 BCE–c. 355 BCE); *Sir Thomas More* English statesman (1478–1535); More was

eventually beatified by the Catholic Church; *Bacon* Francis Bacon (1561–1626), English philosopher and statesman; *Baxter* Clergyman Richard Baxter (1615–91); *Darwin* Erasmus Darwin (1731–1802), physician, botanist, and author of *The Botanic Garden* (1789); *Roscoe* William Rosco (1753–1831), English lawyer, historian, and MP. All of those mentioned are also authors.

[3] *Esemplastic* Word coined by Coleridge to mean "moulded into unity."

two cardinal points of poetry, the power of exciting the sympathy of the reader by a faithful adherence to the truth of nature, and the power of giving the interest of novelty by the modifying colours of imagination. The sudden charm, which accidents of light and shade, which moonlight or sunset diffused over a known and familiar landscape, appeared to represent the practicability of combining both. These are the poetry of nature. The thought suggested itself (to which of us I do not recollect) that a series of poems might be composed of two sorts. In the one, the incidents and agents were to be, in part at least, supernatural; and the excellence aimed at was to consist in the interesting of the affections by the dramatic truth of such emotions, as would naturally accompany such situations, supposing them real. And real in *this* sense they have been to every human being who, from whatever source of delusion, has at any time believed himself under supernatural agency. For the second class, subjects were to be chosen from ordinary life; the characters and incidents were to be such, as will be found in every village and its vicinity, where there is a meditative and feeling mind to seek after them, or to notice them, when they present themselves.

In this idea originated the plan of the *Lyrical Ballads*, in which it was agreed, that my endeavours should be directed to persons and characters supernatural, or at least romantic; yet so as to transfer from our inward nature a human interest and a semblance of truth sufficient to procure for these shadows of imagination that willing suspension of disbelief for the moment, which constitutes poetic faith. Mr. Wordsworth, on the other hand, was to propose to himself as his object, to give the charm of novelty to things of every day, and to excite a feeling analogous to the supernatural, by awakening the mind's attention from the lethargy of custom, and directing it to the loveliness and the wonders of the world before us; an inexhaustible treasure, but for which in consequence of the film of familiarity and selfish solicitude we have eyes, yet see not, ears that hear not, and hearts that neither feel nor understand.[1]

With this view I wrote *The Ancient Mariner*, and was preparing among other poems, the "Dark Ladie," and the "Christabel," in which I should have more nearly realized my ideal, than I had done in my first attempt. But Mr. Wordsworth's industry had proved so much more successful, and the number of his poems so much greater, that my compositions, instead of forming a balance, appeared rather an interpolation of heterogeneous matter. Mr. Wordsworth added two or three poems written in his own character, in the impassioned, lofty, and sustained diction, which is characteristic of his genius. In this form the *Lyrical Ballads* were published; and were presented by him, as an *experiment*, whether subjects, which from their nature rejected the usual ornaments and extra-colloquial style of poems in general, might not be so managed in the language of ordinary life as to produce the pleasurable interest, which it is the peculiar business of poetry to impart. To the second edition he added a preface of considerable length, in which notwithstanding some passages of apparently a contrary import, he was understood to contend for the extension of this style to poetry of all kinds, and to reject as vicious and indefensible all phrases and forms of style that were not included in what he (unfortunately, I think, adopting an equivocal expression) called the language of *real* life. From this preface, prefixed to poems in which it was impossible to deny the presence of original genius, however mistaken its direction might be deemed, arose the whole long continued controversy. For from the conjunction of perceived power with supposed heresy I explain the inveteracy[2] and in some instances, I grieve to say, the acrimonious passions, with which the controversy has been conducted by the assailants.

Had Mr. Wordsworth's poems been the silly, the childish things, which they were for a long time described as being; had they been really distinguished from the compositions of other poets merely by meanness of language and inanity of thought; had they indeed contained nothing more than what is found in the parodies and pretended imitations of them; they must have sunk at once, a dead weight, into the slough of oblivion, and have dragged the preface along with them. But year after year increased the number of Mr. Wordsworth's admirers. They were found too not in the lower

---

[1] *we have eyes ... understand* Cf. Isaiah 6.9: "Hear ye indeed, but understand not; and see ye indeed, but perceive not." See also Matthew 13.13–14.

[2] *inveteracy* Deeply rooted prejudice.

classes of the reading public, but chiefly among young men of strong sensibility and meditative minds; and their admiration (inflamed perhaps in some degree by opposition) was distinguished by its intensity, I might almost say, by its *religious* fervour. These facts, and the intellectual energy of the author, which was more or less consciously felt, where it was outwardly and even boisterously denied, meeting with sentiments of aversion to his opinions, and of alarm at their consequences, produced an eddy of criticism, which would of itself have borne up the poems by the violence with which it whirled them round and round. With many parts of this preface in the sense attributed to them and which the words undoubtedly seem to authorise, I never concurred; but on the contrary objected to them as erroneous in principle, and as contradictory (in appearance at least) both to other parts of the same preface, and to the author's own practice in the greater number of the poems themselves. Mr. Wordsworth in his recent collection[1] has, I find, degraded this prefatory disquisition to the end of his second volume, to be read or not at the reader's choice. But he has not, as far as I can discover, announced any change in his poetic creed. At all events, considering it as the source of a controversy, in which I have been honoured, more than I deserve, by the frequent conjunction of my name with his, I think it expedient to declare once for all, in what points I coincide with his opinions, and in what points I altogether differ. But in order to render myself intelligible I must previously, in as few words as possible, explain my ideas, first, of a POEM; and secondly, of POETRY itself, in *kind*, and in *essence*.

The office of philosophical *disquisition* consists in just *distinction*; while it is the privilege of the philosopher to preserve himself constantly aware, that distinction is not division. In order to obtain adequate notions of any truth, we must intellectually separate its distinguishable parts; and this is the technical *process* of philosophy. But having so done, we must then restore them in our conceptions to the unity, in which they actually co-exist; and this is the *result* philosophy. A poem contains the same elements as a prose composition; the difference therefore must consist in different

combination of them, in consequence of a different object proposed. According to the difference of the object will be the difference of the combination. It is possible, that the object may be merely to facilitate the recollection of any given facts or observations by artificial arrangement; and the composition will be a poem, merely because it is distinguished from prose by metre, or by rhyme, or by both conjointly. In this, the lowest sense, a man might attribute the name of a poem to the well known enumeration of the days in the several months;

> Thirty days hath September,
> April, June, and November, &c.

and others of the same class and purpose. And as a particular pleasure is found in anticipating the recurrence of sounds and quantities, all compositions that have this charm superadded, whatever be their contents, *may* be entitled poems.

So much for the superficial *form*. A difference of object and contents supplies an additional ground of distinction. The immediate purpose may be the communication of truths; either of truth absolute and demonstrable, as in works of science; or of facts experienced and recorded, as in history. Pleasure, and that of the highest and most permanent kind, may *result* from the *attainment* of the end; but it is not itself the immediate end. In other works the communication of pleasure may be the immediate purpose; and though truth, either moral or intellectual, ought to be the *ultimate* end, yet this will distinguish the character of the author, not the class to which the work belongs. Blest indeed is that state of society, in which the immediate purpose would be baffled by the perversion of the proper ultimate end; in which no charm of diction or imagery could exempt the Bathyllus even of an Anacreon, or the Alexis of Virgil,[2] from disgust and aversion! But the communication of pleasure may be the immediate object of a work not metrically composed; and that object may have been in a high degree attained, as in novels and romances. Would then the mere super-

---

[1] *recent collection*   Two volumes entitled *Poems by William Wordsworth* (1815).

[2] *Ballythus ... Virgil*   Both Virgil and Anacreon wrote homoerotic poems. In this period, homosexuality was viewed unfavorably, in a way that we now consider prejudiced and unfair.

addition of metre, with or without rhyme, entitle *these* to the name of poems? The answer is, that nothing can permanently please, which does not contain in itself the reason why it is so, and not otherwise. If metre be superadded, all other parts must be made consonant with it. They must be such, as to justify the perpetual and distinct attention to each part, which an exact correspondent recurrence of accent and sound are calculated to excite. The final definition then, so deduced, may be thus worded. A poem is that species of composition, which is opposed to works of science, by proposing for its *immediate* object pleasure, not truth; and from all other species (having *this* object in common with it) it is discriminated by proposing to itself such delight from the *whole*, as is compatible with a distinct gratification from each component *part*.

Controversy is not seldom excited in consequence of the disputants attaching each a different meaning to the same word; and in few instances has this been more striking, than in disputes concerning the present subject. If a man chooses to call every composition a poem, which is rhyme, or measure, or both, I must leave his opinion uncontroverted. The distinction is at least competent to characterize the writer's intention. If it were subjoined, that the whole is likewise entertaining or affecting, as a tale, or as a series of interesting reflections, I of course admit this as another fit ingredient of a poem, and an additional merit. But if the definition sought for be that of a *legitimate* poem, I answer, it must be one, the parts of which mutually support and explain each other; all in their proportion harmonizing with, and supporting the purpose and known influences of metrical arrangement. The philosophic critics of all ages coincide with the ultimate judgment of all countries, in equally denying the praises of a just poem, on the one hand, to a series of striking lines or distichs,[1] each of which absorbing the whole attention of the reader to itself disjoins it from its context, and makes it a separate whole, instead of an harmonizing part; and on the other hand, to an unsustained composition, from which the reader collects rapidly the general result unattracted by the component parts. The reader should be carried forward, not merely or chiefly by the mechanical impulse of curiosity, or by a restless desire to arrive at the final solution; but by the pleasurable activity of mind excited by the attractions of the journey itself. Like the motion of a serpent, which the Egyptians made the emblem of intellectual power; or like the path of sound through the air; at every step he pauses and half recedes, and from the retrogressive movement collects the force which again carries him onward. *Præcipitandus est liber spiritus*,[2] says Petronius Arbiter most happily. The epithet, *liber*,[3] here balances the preceding verb; and it is not easy to conceive more meaning condensed in fewer words.

But if this should be admitted as a satisfactory character of a poem, we have still to seek for a definition of poetry. The writings of Plato, and Bishop Taylor, and the *Theoria Sacra* of Burnet,[4] furnish undeniable proofs that poetry of the highest kind may exist without metre, and even without the contra-distinguishing objects of a poem. The first chapter of Isaiah (indeed a very large proportion of the whole book) is poetry in the most emphatic sense; yet it would be not less irrational than strange to assert, that pleasure, arid not truth, was the immediate object of the prophet. In short, whatever *specific* import we attach to the word, poetry, there will be found involved in it, as a necessary consequence;, that a poem of any length neither can be, or ought to be, all poetry. Yet if an harmonious whole is to be produced, the remaining parts must be preserved *in keeping* with the poetry; and this can be no otherwise effected than by such a studies selection and artificial arrangement, as will partake of *one*, though not a *peculiar*, property of poetry. And this again can be no other than the property of exciting a more continuous and equal attention, than the language of prose aims at, whether colloquial or written.

My own conclusions on the nature of poetry, in the strictest use of the word, have been in part anticipated in the preceding disquisition on the fancy and imagination. What is poetry? is so nearly the same question with, what is a poet? that the answer to the one is

---

[1] *distichs* Poetic couplets.

[2] *Præcipitandus est liber spiritus* Latin: from the *Satyricon*: "The free spirit must be hurried along."

[3] *liber* Free.

[4] *Bishop Taylor* English theologian and author Jeremy Taylor (1613–67); *Burnet* English cleric and author Thomas Burnet (1635–1715), who wrote *Sacred Theory of the Earth*.

involved in the solution of the other. For it is a distinction resulting from the poetic genius itself, which sustains and modifies the images, thoughts, and emotions of the poet's own mind. The poet, described in *ideal* perfection, brings the whole soul of man into activity, with the subordination of its faculties to each other, according to their relative worth and dignity. He diffuses a tone, and spirit of unity, that blends, and (as it were) *fuses*, each into each, by that synthetic and magical power, to which we have exclusively appropriated the name of imagination. This power, first put in action by the will and understanding, and retained under their irremissive, though gentle and unnoticed, controul (*laxis effertur habenis*)[1] reveals itself in the balance or reconciliation of opposite or discordant qualities: of sameness, with difference; of the general, with the concrete; the idea, with the image; the individual, with the representative; the sense of novelty and freshness, with old and familiar objects; a more than usual state of emotion, with more than usual order; judgement ever awake and steady self-possession, with enthusiasm and feeling profound or vehement; and while it blends and harmonizes the natural and the artificial, still subordinates art to nature; the manner to the matter; and our admiration of the poet to our sympathy with the poetry. "Doubtless," as Sir John Davies observes of the soul (and his words may with slight alteration be applied, and even more appropriately to the poetic IMAGINATION):

Doubtless this could not be, but that she turns
Bodies to spirit by sublimation strange,
As fire converts to fire the things it burns,
As we our food into our nature change.

From their gross matter she abstracts their forms,
And draws a kind of quintessence from things;
Which to her proper nature she transforms
To bear them light, on her celestial wings.

Thus does she, when from individual states
She doth abstract the universal kinds;

Which then re-clothed in divers names and fates
Steal access through our senses to our minds.[2]

Finally, GOOD SENSE is the BODY of poetic genius, FANCY, its DRAPERY, MOTION its LIFE, and IMAGINATION the SOUL that is everywhere, and in each; and forms all into one graceful and intelligent whole.

from CHAPTER 17
Examination of the Tenets Peculiar to Mr. Wordsworth

As far then as Mr. Wordsworth in his preface contended, and most ably contended, for a reformation in our poetic diction, as far as he has evinced the truth of passion, and the *dramatic* propriety of those figures and metaphors in the original poets, which stript of their justifying reasons, and converted into mere artifices of connection or ornament, constitute the characteristic falsity in the poetic style of the moderns; and as far as he has, with equal acuteness and clearness, pointed out the process in which this change was effected, and the resemblances between that state into which the reader's mind is thrown by the pleasurable confusion of thought from an unaccustomed bain[3] of words and images; and that state which is induced by the natural language of empassioned feeling; he undertook a useful task, and deserves all praise, both for the attempt and for the execution....

My own differences from certain supposed parts of Mr. Wordsworth's theory ground themselves on the assumption, that his words had been rightly interpreted, as purporting that the proper diction for poetry in general consists altogether in a language taken, with due exceptions, from the mouths of men in real life, a language which actually constitutes the natural conversation of men under the influence of natural feelings. My objection is, first, that in *any* sense this rule is applicable only to *certain* classes of poetry; secondly, that even to these classes it is not applicable, except in such a sense, as hath never by any one (as far as I know or have read) been denied or doubted; and lastly, that as far

---

[1] *laxis effertur habenis* Latin: moved forward with loosened rein.

[2] *Doubtless ... soul* Adapted from "Nosce Teipsum: Of Human Knowledge" (1599).

[3] *bain* Vessel for water.

as, and in that degree in which it is *practicable*, yet as a *rule* it is useless, if not injurious, and therefore either need not, or ought not to be practised. The poet informs his reader, that he had generally chosen *low and rustic* life; but not *as* low and rustic, or in order to repeat that pleasure of doubtful moral effect, which persons of elevated rank and of superior refinement oftentimes derive from a happy *imitation* of the rude unpolished manners and discourse of their inferiors. For the pleasure so derived may be traced to three exciting causes. The first is the naturalness, in *fact*, of the things presented. The second is the apparent naturalness of the *representation*, as raised and qualified by an imperceptible infusion of the author's own knowledge and talent, which infusion does, indeed, constitute it an *imitation* as distinguished from a mere *copy*. The third cause may be found in the reader's conscious feeling of his superiority awakened by the contrast presented to him; even as for the same purpose the kings and great barons of yore retained, sometimes *actual* clowns and fools, but more frequently shrewd and witty fellows in that *character*. These, however, were not Mr. Wordsworth's objects. *He* chose low and rustic life, "because in that condition the essential passions of the heart find a better soil, in which they can attain their maturity, are less under restraint, and speak a plainer and more emphatic language; because in that condition of life our elementary feelings coexist in a state of greater simplicity, and consequently may be more accurately contemplated, and more forcibly communicated; because the manners of rural life germinate from those elementary feelings; and from the necessary character of rural occupations are more easily comprehended, and are more durable; and lastly, because in that condition the passions of men are incorporated with the beautiful and permanent forms of nature."[1]

Now it is clear to me, that in the most interesting of the poems, in which the author is more or less dramatic, as the "Brothers," "Michael," "Ruth," the "Mad Mother," &c. the persons introduced are by no means taken *from low or rustic life* in the common acceptation of those words; and it is not less clear, that the sentiments and language, as far as they can be conceived to have been really transferred from the minds and conversation of such persons, are attributable to causes and circumstances not necessarily connected with "their occupations and abode." The thoughts, feelings, language, and manners of the shepherd-farmers in the vales of Cumberland and Westmoreland, as far as they are actually adopted in those poems, may be accounted for from causes, which will and do produce the same results in *every* state of life, whether in town or country. As the two principal I rank that INDEPENDENCE, which raises a man above servitude, or daily toil for the profit of others, yet not above the necessity of industry and a frugal simplicity of domestic life; and the accompanying unambitious, but solid and religious EDUCATION, which has rendered few books familiar, but the Bible, and the liturgy or hymn book. To this latter cause, indeed, which is so far *accidental*, that it is the blessing of particular countries and a particular age, not the product of particular places or employments, the poet owes the shew of probability, that his personages might really feel, think, and talk with any tolerable resemblance to his representation. It is an excellent remark of Dr. Henry More's (*Enthusiasmus triumphatus*, Sec. xxxv) that "a man of confined education, but of good parts, by constant reading of the Bible will naturally form a more winning and commanding rhetoric than those that are learned; the intermixture of tongues and of artificial phrases debasing *their* style."

It is, moreover, to be considered that to the formation of healthy feelings, and a reflecting mind, *negations* involve impediments not less formidable, than sophistication intermixture. I am convinced, that for the human soul to prosper in rustic life, a certain vantage-ground is prerequisite. It is not every man, that is likely to be improved by a country life or by country labours. Education, or original sensibility, or both, must pre-exist, if the changes, forms, and incidents of nature are to prove a sufficient stimulant. And where these are not sufficient, the mind contracts and hardens by want of stimulants; and the man becomes selfish, sensual, gross, hard-hearted. Let the management of the POOR LAWS in Liverpool, Manchester, or Bristol be compared with the ordinary dispensation of the poor rates in agricultural villages, where the *farmers* are the overseers and guardians of the poor. ... [The] result would engender

[1] *"because ... nature"* From Wordsworth's "Preface" to *Lyrical Ballads* (1800).

more than skepticism concerning the desirable influences of low and rustic life in and for itself. ...

If then I am compelled to doubt the theory, by which the choice of *characters* was to be directed, not only *a priori*,[1] from grounds of reason, but both from the few instances in which the poet himself *need* be supposed to have been governed by it, and from the comparative inferiority of those instances; still more must I hesitate in my assent to the sentence which immediately follows the former citation; and which can neither admit as particular fact, or a general rule. "The language too of these men is adopted (purified indeed from what appear to be its real defects, from all lasting and rational causes of dislike or disgust) because such men hourly communicate with the best objects from which the best part of language is originally derived; and because, from their rank in society, and the sameness and narrow circle of their intercourse, being less under the action of social vanity, they convey their feelings and notions in simple and unelaborated expressions."[2] To this I reply; that a rustic's language, purified from all provincialism and grossness, and so far reconstructed as to be made consistent with the rules of grammar which are in essence no other than the laws of universal logic, applied to psychological materials will not differ from the language of any other man of commonsense, however learned or refined he may be, except as far as the notions, which the rustic has to convey, are fewer and more indiscriminate. This will become still clearer, if we add the consideration (equally important though less obvious) that the rustic, from the more imperfect development of his faculties, and from the lower state of their cultivation, aims almost solely to convey *insulated facts*, either those of his scanty experience or his traditional belief; while the educated man chiefly seeks to discover and express those *connections* of things, or those relative *hearings* of fact to fact, from which some more or less general law is deducible. For *facts* are valuable to a wise man, chiefly as they lead to the discovery of the indwelling *law*, which is the true *being* of things, the sole solution of their modes of existence, and in the knowledge of which consists our dignity and our

power. ...

Here let me be permitted to remind the reader, that the positions, which I controvert, at contained in the sentences —"*a selection of the* REAL *language of men*"—"*the language of these men* (i.e, men in low and rustic life) I *propose to myself to imitate, and as far as possible, to adopt the very language of men.*" "*Between the language of prose and that of metrical composition, there neither is, nor can be any essential difference.*"[3] It is against these exclusively, that my opposition is directed.

I object, in the very first instance, to an equivocation in the use of the word "real." Every man's language varies, according to the extent of his knowledge, the activity of his faculties, and the depth or quickness of his feelings. Every man's language has, first, its *individualities*; secondly, the common properties of the *class* to which he belongs; and thirdly, words and phrases of *universal* use. The language of Hooker,[4] Bacon, Bishop Taylor, and Burke,[5] differ from the common language of the learned class only by the superior number and novelty of the thoughts and relations which they had to convey. The language of Algernon Sidney differs not at all from that, which every well educated gentleman would wish to write, and (with due allowances for the undeliberateness, and less connected train, of thinking natural and proper to conversation) such as he would wish to talk. Neither one or the other differ half as much from the general language of cultivated society, as the language of Mr. Wordsworth's homeliest composition differs from that of a common peasant. For "real" therefore, we must substitute *ordinary*, or *lingua communis*.[6] And this, we have proved, is no more to be found in the phraseology of low and rustic life, than in that of any other class. Omit the peculiarities of each, and the result of course must be common to all. And assuredly the omissions and changes to be made in the language of rustics, before it could be transferred to any species of poem, except the drama or other professed

---

1   *a priori* Latin: without direct experience.

2   "*The language ... expressions*" From Wordsworth's "Preface" to *Lyrical Ballads* (1800).

3   "*a selection ... difference*" From Wordsworth's "Preface" to *Lyrical Ballads* (1800).

4   *Hooker* English clergyman and theologian Richard Hooker (1554–1600).

5   *Burke* British statesman and political writer Edmund Burke (1729–97).

6   *lingua communis* Latin: common language.

imitation, are at least as numerous and weighty, as would be required in adapting to the same purpose the ordinary language of tradesmen and manufacturers. Not to mention, that the language so highly extolled by Mr. Wordsworth varies in every county, nay in every village, according to the accidental character of the clergyman, the existence or non-existence of schools; or even, perhaps, as the exciseman, publican, or barber happen to be, or not to be, zealous politicians, and readers of the weekly newspaper *pro bono publico*.[1] Anterior to cultivation the lingua communis of every country, as Dante has well observed, exists everywhere in parts, and nowhere as a whole.

Neither is the case rendered at all more tenable by the addition of the words, "*in a state of excitement.*" For the nature of a man's words, when he is strongly affected by joy, grief, or anger, must necessarily depend on the number and quality of the general truths, conceptions and images, and of the words expressing them, with which his mind had been previously stored. For the property of passion is not to *create*; but to set in increased activity. At least, whatever new connections of thought or images, or (which is equally, if not more than equally, the appropriate effect of strong excitement) whatever generalizations of truth or experience, the heat of passion may produce; yet the terms of their conveyance must have pre-existed in his former conversations, and are only collected and crowded together by the unusual stimulation. It is indeed very possible to adopt in a poem the unmeaning repetitions, habitual phrases, and other blank counters, which an unfurnished or confused understanding interposes at short intervals, in order to keep hold of his subject which is still slipping from him, and to give him time for recollection; or in mere aid of vacancy, as in the scanty companies of a country stage the same player pops backwards and forwards, in order to prevent the appearance of empty spaces, in the procession of *Macbeth*, or *Henry VIII*. But what assistance to the poet, or ornament to the poem, these can supply, I am at a loss to conjecture. Nothing assuredly can differ either in origin or in mode more widely from the *apparent* tautologies[2] of intense and turbulent feeling, in which the passion is greater and of longer endurance, than to be exhausted or satisfied by a single representation of the image or incident exciting it. Such repetitions I admit to be a beauty of the highest kind; as illustrated by Mr. Wordsworth himself from the song of Deborah. "*At her feet he bowed, he fell, he lay down; at her feet he bowed, he fell; where he bowed, there he fell down dead.*"[3]

—1817

[1] *pro bono publico*   Latin: for the good of the public.

[2] *tautologies*   Repetitions.

[3] "*At her feet ... dead*"   From Wordsworth's note to "The Thorn" (1798).

JANE AUSTEN
1775 – 1817

Jane Austen is considered to be one of the finest novelists in the English language. Her six major novels, along with her shorter fictional works, juvenilia, and surviving correspondence, share a keenness of wit and irony of observation that have ensured her continued popularity among scholars and general readers alike into the twenty-first century. Her fiction scrutinizes the manners and the behavior of ordinary women of the emergent middle-class in Georgian England, who need to negotiate between feeling and duty, personal desire and social expectation. As Sir Walter Scott, the most famous novelist of Austen's time, commented in reviewing her favorably in the influential *Quarterly Review,* her writing bears "that exquisite touch which renders ordinary commonplace things and characters interesting." Her work was not as highly esteemed in the middle decades of the nineteenth century, but her popularity rose in the 1870s, and her life and work have for generations been the subject of what is often called an "industry," both scholarly and popular.

Jane Austen was born at Steventon, Hampshire, the sixth child in a family of seven, and the younger of two daughters. Her father, the Reverend George Austen, was a spirited and cultivated man who allowed his daughters free access to his extensive library. Educated mostly at home, she read broadly, including novels by Frances Burney, Laurence Sterne, Henry Fielding, and Samuel Richardson, whose *Sir Charles Grandison* was a particular favorite. Owing in part to the proximity of the boys' school run by Austen's parents from the Steventon Rectory, the household in which Austen grew up was busy and lively, and its members enjoyed and encouraged each others' literary and theatrical pursuits. The young Jane Austen's imagination was fed by family theatricals directed and performed by her elder siblings and cousins for friends and neighbors. Austen's biographer, Claire Tomalin, speculates that the young Jane may have played a minor role in the family production of Richard Brinsley Sheridan's *The Rivals* before she was ten years old. Most importantly, Austen was encouraged to read aloud from her early writing, and her family delighted in the comic stories and burlesques she produced in her teenage years. Fictions such as *Lesley Castle* and *Love & Freindship* (sic), the latter written when Austen was 14, are filled with impertinent and riotous humor, indecorous behavior on the part of young women, and an already astute sense of generic convention. Her father was particularly supportive of her writing: at the front of a notebook he had given her, in which she had composed her *History of England*, a juvenile parody of popular histories, George Austen inscribed the following appreciation: "Effusions of Fancy by a very Young Lady Consisting of Tales in a Style entirely new."

Austen lived a quiet country life among a wide network of relations, friends and neighbors, an ideal context in which to hone the skills in social observation that informed her writing. She never married, although she had at least two admirers, and even accepted a proposal of marriage in 1802 (retracting her acceptance the following day). In 1795–96 she wrote an epistolary sketch called "Elinor and Marianne," which went through several rewrites in subsequent years before taking its final form as *Sense and Sensibility*. This became Austen's first published work (1811), selling out by 1813 and receiving positive reviews. Three other novels were published in quick succession: *Pride and Prejudice* in 1813, *Mansfield Park* in 1814, and *Emma* in 1816. *Pride and Prejudice*, whose first title was "First Impressions," had initially been rejected in 1797 by the publisher Thomas Cadell, who did not even read the manuscript before returning it. When it finally did appear, *Pride and Prejudice* was an instant hit, and it has since become one of the most widely-read novels in the English language. Much of its success is due to the appeal of its heroine, Elizabeth Bennet, whose intelligence, feeling, and independence of thought Austen conveys through sparkling dialogue and pioneering use of narrative techniques that provide for flexibility of viewpoint.

The composition of Austen's major works can be divided into two distinct periods. By 1800 she had written three full-length novels, none of them published. Then followed a ten-year silence: the Austens' decision to quit the family home at Steventon and move to Bath, taking Jane and her elder sister Cassandra with them, meant a break in Austen's writing routine. The family moved often in the next several years, and with the death of several friends and family members in this period, most importantly her father in 1805, Austen seems to have experienced a depression that prevented her from writing. Tomalin points out how easily Austen's existing manuscripts in this decade could have been lost or destroyed. With her settlement at Chawton Cottage in Hampshire late in 1808 with her mother and sister, Austen again found the time and space to write, and it was here that she revised "Elinor and Marianne" into *Sense and Sensibility,* and wrote *Mansfield Park, Emma,* and *Persuasion*.

Two of Austen's six major novels were published posthumously in 1818. *Northanger Abbey* had been written under the title "Susan" in 1798–99 and sold to the publisher Richard Crosby in 1803 for the low sum of ten pounds. Although he placed advertisements for the book, he never printed it, and refused to turn over the manuscript or copyright at her request in 1809. *Persuasion*, written in 1815-16, was Austen's last completed novel. Some readers find in it a tone of melancholy, which might be attributable to the fact that she was suffering from illness when it was completed. It is also unique among her major works as the only novel for which any manuscript material survives. Many of her letters were also destroyed by her elder sister Cassandra Austen after her death. The Austen sisters were extremely close, sparing no confidence in their correspondence with each other. Many of Austen's surviving letters to her sister are characterized by harshly honest observations of others' foibles.

Lady Susan stands between Austen's juvenilia and her major work in several respects. She probably wrote most of it in 1794–95, revising and adding its abrupt conclusion by 1805, thus putting its date of composition between her last known juvenile writing and her first draft of what would become *Sense and Sensibility*. More importantly, *Lady Susan* seems to bring many of the impulses of Austen's juvenile writing to a head while displaying a sophistication that anticipates her mature work. Many critics have pointed out the novel's debt in both theme and form to the mid-eighteenth-century fiction and Restoration drama Austen grew up on, with its sexual frankness and cynical tone. The novel is in several respects anomalous in the Austen canon: it is her only mature fiction written in the epistolary form, and its eponymous heroine is a female rake—a sexual predator—who openly uses her sexual power to dominate others. Although Austen seems to have become frustrated with the limitations of the epistolary form, eventually abandoning it altogether in her adult writing, in *Lady Susan* it allows the author a moral detachment from the story's action: one is never quite sure whether Austen approved of or deplored her heroine's rebellion against accepted models of proper femininity. *Lady Susan* remained unpublished until 1871, when Austen's nephew James Austen-Leigh included it in his *Memoir of Jane Austen*.

Austen wrote fiction at a moment when women were getting their work into print in ever greater numbers, yet faced relentless pressure to think and behave in ways that militated against their attaining, or expressing, social power and authority. Although by 1816 Austen was a critical and popular success (whose most illustrious fan was the Prince Regent himself), she wore her success lightly, famously referring in a letter of that year to her nephew to the "little bit (two inches wide) of Ivory on which I work with so fine a brush." Perhaps the best known description of Austen's writing, the statement has been read by critics as both a disclaimer and a sly celebration of "women's" writing and the domestic novel. But perhaps not too much should be made of a comment made in a spirit of playful banter with a teenager. By the time she wrote this letter she was already seriously ill. She was working on a new novel around this time—*Sanditon*—but it was never finished. Jane Austen died of an undetermined illness on 18 July 1817, and was buried at Winchester Cathedral.

⌘ ⌘ ⌘

Pride and Prejudice

Pride and Prejudice, first published in 1813, has remained Austen's most popular novel. The story turns on the marriage prospects of the five daughters of Mr. And Mrs. Bennet; on the affection between the eldest, Jane, and the charming Mr. Bingley; and on the prejudice formed by Jane's sister, Elizabeth, against the proud and distant Mr. Darcy. The novel's famous opening chapters set the tone; they also provide a sense of the characteristic style of Austen's major novels.

from *Pride and Prejudice*

CHAPTER I

It is a truth universally acknowledged, that a single man in possession of a good fortune must be in want of a wife.

However little known the feelings or views of such a man may be on his first entering a neighbourhood, this truth is so well fixed in the minds of the surrounding families that he is considered as the rightful property of some one or other of their daughters.

"My dear Mr. Bennet," said his lady to him one day, "have you heard that Netherfield Park is let at last?"

Mr. Bennet replied that he had not.

"But it is," returned she; "for Mrs. Long has just been here, and she told me all about it."

Mr. Bennet made no answer.

"Do not you want to know who has taken it?" cried his wife impatiently.

"*You* want to tell me, and I have no objection to

hearing it."

This was invitation enough.

"Why, my dear, you must know, Mrs. Long says that Netherfield is taken by a young man of large fortune from the north of England; that he came down on Monday in a chaise and four[1] to see the place, and was so much delighted with it that he agreed with Mr. Morris immediately; that he is to take possession before Michaelmas,[2] and some of his servants are to be in the house by the end of next week."

"What is his name?"

"Bingley."

"Is he married or single?"

"Oh! single, my dear, to be sure! A single man of large fortune; four or five thousand a year. What a fine thing for our girls!"

"How so? how can it affect them?"

"My dear Mr. Bennet," replied his wife, "how can you be so tiresome! You must know that I am thinking of his marrying one of them."

"Is that his design in settling here?"

"Design! nonsense, how can you talk so! But it is very likely that he *may* fall in love with one of them, and therefore you must visit him as soon as he comes."

"I see no occasion for that. You and the girls may go, or you may send them by themselves, which perhaps will be still better, for as you are as handsome as any of them, Mr. Bingley might like you the best of the party."

"My dear, you flatter me. I certainly *have* had my share of beauty, but I do not pretend to be anything extraordinary now. When a woman has five grown up daughters, she ought to give over thinking of her own

---

[1] *chaise and four* Traveling carriage pulled by four horses.

[2] *Michaelmas* The feast of St. Michael, on 29 September.

beauty."

"In such cases, a woman has not often much beauty to think of."

"But, my dear, you must indeed go and see Mr. Bingley when he comes into the neighbourhood."

"It is more than I engage for,[1] I assure you."

"But consider your daughters. Only think what an establishment it would be for one of them. Sir William and Lady Lucas are determined to go, merely on that account, for in general you know they visit no newcomers. Indeed you must go, for it will be impossible for *us* to visit him, if you do not."

"You are over scrupulous, surely. I dare say Mr. Bingley will be very glad to see you; and I will send a few lines by you to assure him of my hearty consent to his marrying which ever he chooses of the girls, though I must throw in a good word for my little Lizzy."

"I desire you will do no such thing. Lizzy is not a bit better than the others, and I am sure she is not half so handsome as Jane, nor half so good humoured as Lydia. But you are always giving *her* the preference."

"They have none of them much to recommend them," replied he; "they are all silly and ignorant like other girls, but Lizzy has something more of quickness than her sisters."

"Mr. Bennet, how can you abuse your own children in such a way? You take delight in vexing me. You have no compassion on my poor nerves."

"You mistake me, my dear. I have a high respect for your nerves. They are my old friends. I have heard you mention them with consideration these twenty years at least."

"Ah! you do not know what I suffer."

"But I hope you will get over it, and live to see many young men of four thousand a year come into the neighbourhood."

"It will be no use to us if twenty such should come, since you will not visit them."

"Depend upon it, my dear, that when there are twenty, I will visit them all."

Mr. Bennet was so odd a mixture of quick parts, sarcastic humour, reserve, and caprice, that the experience of three and twenty years had been insufficient to make his wife understand his character. *Her* mind was less difficult to develop. She was a woman of mean[2] understanding, little information, and uncertain temper. When she was discontented she fancied herself nervous. The business of her life was to get her daughters married; its solace was visiting and news.

<h2>CHAPTER 2</h2>

Mr. Bennet was among the earliest of those who waited on Mr. Bingley. He had always intended to visit him, though to the last always assuring his wife that he should not go; and till the evening after the visit was paid, she had no knowledge of it. It was then disclosed in the following manner. Observing his second daughter employed in trimming a hat, he suddenly addressed her with,

"I hope Mr. Bingley will like it, Lizzy."

"We are not in a way to know *what* Mr. Bingley likes," said her mother resentfully, "since we are not to visit."

"But you forget, mama," said Elizabeth, "that we shall meet him at the assemblies, and that Mrs. Long has promised to introduce him."

"I do not believe Mrs. Long will do any such thing. She has two nieces of her own. She is a selfish, hypocritical woman, and I have no opinion[3] of her."

"No more have I," said Mr. Bennet; "and I am glad to find that you do not depend on her serving you."

Mrs. Bennet deigned not to make any reply; but unable to contain herself, began scolding one of her daughters.

"Don't keep coughing so, Kitty, for heaven's sake! Have a little compassion on my nerves. You tear them to pieces."

"Kitty has no discretion in her coughs," said her father; "she times them ill."

"I do not cough for my own amusement," replied Kitty fretfully.

"When is your next ball to be, Lizzy?"

"Tomorrow fortnight."[4]

"Aye, so it is," cried her mother, "and Mrs. Long

1 *engage for* Promise to perform.

2 *mean* Modest.

3 *have no opinion of her* I.e., have no great opinion of her; regard her as unworthy.

4 *Tomorrow fortnight* I.e., a fortnight (two weeks) from tomorrow.

does not come back till the day before; so, it will be impossible for her to introduce him, for she will not know him herself."

"Then, my dear, you may have the advantage of your friend, and introduce Mr. Bingley to *her*."

"Impossible, Mr. Bennet, impossible, when I am not acquainted with him myself; how can you be so teazing?"

"I honour your circumspection. A fortnight's acquaintance is certainly very little. One cannot know what a man really is by the end of a fortnight. But if *we* do not venture, somebody else will; and after all, Mrs. Long and her nieces must stand their chance; and therefore, as she will think it an act of kindness, if you decline the office, I will take it on myself."

The girls stared at their father. Mrs. Bennet said only, "Nonsense, nonsense!"

"What can be the meaning of that emphatic exclamation?" cried he. "Do you consider the forms of introduction, and the stress that is laid on them, as nonsense? I cannot quite agree with you *there*. What say you, Mary? for you are a young lady of deep reflection I know, and read great books, and make extracts."

Mary wished to say something very sensible, but knew not how.

"While Mary is adjusting her ideas," he continued, "let us return to Mr. Bingley."

"I am sick of Mr. Bingley," cried his wife.

"I am sorry to hear *that*; but why did not you tell me so before? If I had known as much this morning, I certainly would not have called on him. It is very unlucky, but as I have actually paid the visit, we cannot escape the acquaintance now."

The astonishment of the ladies was just what he wished; that of Mrs. Bennet perhaps surpassing the rest; though when the first tumult of joy was over, she began to declare that it was what she had expected all the while.

"How good it was in you, my dear Mr. Bennet! But I knew I should persuade you at last. I was sure you loved your girls too well to neglect such an acquaintance. Well, how pleased I am! and it is such a good joke, too, that you should have gone this morning, and never said a word about it till now."

"Now, Kitty, you may cough as much as you choose," said Mr. Bennet; and, as he spoke, he left the room, fatigued with the raptures of his wife.

"What an excellent father you have, girls," said she, when the door was shut. "I do not know how you will ever make him amends for his kindness; or me either, for that matter. At our time of life, it is not so pleasant, I can tell you, to be making new acquaintance every day; but for your sakes, we would do anything. Lydia, my love, though you *are* the youngest, I dare say Mr. Bingley will dance with you at the next ball."

"Oh!" said Lydia stoutly, "I am not afraid; for though I *am* the youngest, I'm the tallest."

The rest of the evening was spent in conjecturing how soon he would return Mr. Bennet's visit, and determining when they should ask him to dinner.

CHAPTER 3

Not all that Mrs. Bennet, however, with the assistance of her five daughters, could ask on the subject was sufficient to draw from her husband any satisfactory description of Mr. Bingley. They attacked him in various ways: with barefaced questions, ingenious suppositions, and distant surmises; but he eluded the skill of them all, and they were at last obliged to accept the second-hand intelligence of their neighbour Lady Lucas. Her report was highly favourable. Sir William had been delighted with him. He was quite young, wonderfully handsome, extremely agreeable, and to crown the whole, he meant to be at the next assembly with a large party. Nothing could be more delightful! To be fond of dancing was a certain step towards falling in love; and very lively hopes of Mr. Bingley's heart were entertained.

"If I can but see one of my daughters happily settled at Netherfield," said Mrs. Bennet to her husband, "and all the others equally well married, I shall have nothing to wish for."

In a few days Mr. Bingley returned Mr. Bennet's visit, and sat about ten minutes with him in his library. He had entertained hopes of being admitted to a sight of the young ladies, of whose beauty he had heard much; but he saw only the father. The ladies were somewhat more fortunate, for they had the advantage of ascertaining, from an upper window, that he wore a blue coat and rode a black horse.

An invitation to dinner was soon afterwards dispatched; and already had Mrs. Bennet planned the courses that were to do credit to her housekeeping, when an answer arrived which deferred it all. Mr. Bingley was obliged to be in town the following day, and consequently unable to accept the honour of their invitation, &c. Mrs. Bennet was quite disconcerted. She could not imagine what business he could have in town so soon after his arrival in Hertfordshire, and she began to fear that he might be always flying about from one place to another, and never settled at Netherfield as he ought to be. Lady Lucas quieted her fears a little by starting the idea of his being gone to London only to get a large party for the ball; and a report soon followed that Mr. Bingley was to bring twelve ladies and seven gentlemen with him to the assembly. The girls grieved over such a large number of ladies, but were comforted the day before the ball by hearing that, instead of twelve, he had brought only six with him from London, his five sisters and a cousin. And when the party entered the assembly room, it consisted of only five altogether; Mr. Bingley, his two sisters, the husband of the eldest, and another young man.

Mr. Bingley was good looking and gentlemanlike; he had a pleasant countenance, and easy, unaffected manners. His sisters were fine women, with an air of decided fashion. His brother-in-law, Mr. Hurst, merely looked the gentleman; but his friend Mr. Darcy soon drew the attention of the room by his fine, tall person, handsome features, noble mien,[1] and the report which was in general circulation within five minutes after his entrance, of his having ten thousand a year. The gentlemen pronounced him to be a fine figure of a man, the ladies declared he was much handsomer than Mr. Bingley, and he was looked at with great admiration for about half the evening, till his manners gave a disgust which turned the tide of his popularity; for he was discovered to be proud, to be above his company, and above being pleased; and not all his large estate in Derbyshire could then save him from having a most forbidding, disagreeable countenance, and being unworthy to be compared with his friend.

Mr. Bingley had soon made himself acquainted with all the principal people in the room; he was lively and unreserved, danced every dance, was angry that the ball closed so early, and talked of giving one himself at Netherfield. Such amiable qualities must speak for themselves. What a contrast between him and his friend! Mr. Darcy danced only once with Mrs. Hurst and once with Miss Bingley, declined being introduced to any other lady, and spent the rest of the evening in walking about the room, speaking occasionally to one of his own party. His character was decided. He was the proudest, most disagreeable man in the world, and everybody hoped that he would never come there again. Amongst the most violent against him was Mrs. Bennet, whose dislike of his general behaviour was sharpened into particular resentment by his having slighted one of her daughters.

Elizabeth Bennet had been obliged, by the scarcity of gentlemen, to sit down for two dances; and during part of that time, Mr. Darcy had been standing near enough for her to overhear a conversation between him and Mr. Bingley, who came from the dance for a few minutes to press his friend to join it.

"Come, Darcy," said he, "I must have you dance. I hate to see you standing about by yourself in this stupid manner. You had much better dance."

"I certainly shall not. You know how I detest it, unless I am particularly acquainted with my partner. At such an assembly as this, it would be insupportable. Your sisters are engaged, and there is not another woman in the room whom it would not be a punishment to me to stand up with."

"I would not be so fastidious as you are," cried Bingley, "for a kingdom! Upon my honour, I never met with so many pleasant girls in my life as I have this evening; and there are several of them you see uncommonly pretty."

"*You* are dancing with the only handsome girl in the room," said Mr. Darcy, looking at the eldest Miss Bennet.

"Oh! she is the most beautiful creature I ever beheld! But there is one of her sisters sitting down just behind you who is very pretty, and, I dare say, very agreeable. Do let me ask my partner to introduce you."

"Which do you mean?" and turning round, he looked for a moment at Elizabeth, till, catching her eye,

---

[1] *mien* Bearing.

he withdrew his own and coldly said, "She is tolerable; but not handsome enough to tempt *me*; and I am in no humour at present to give consequence to young ladies who are slighted by other men. You had better return to your partner and enjoy her smiles, for you are wasting your time with me."

Mr. Bingley followed his advice. Mr. Darcy walked off, and Elizabeth remained with no very cordial feelings towards him. She told the story however with great spirit among her friends; for she had a lively, playful disposition, which delighted in anything ridiculous.

The evening altogether passed off pleasantly to the whole family. Mrs. Bennet had seen her eldest daughter much admired by the Netherfield party. Mr. Bingley had danced with her twice, and she had been distinguished by his sisters. Jane was as much gratified by this as her mother could be, though in a quieter way. Elizabeth felt Jane's pleasure. Mary had heard herself mentioned to Miss Bingley as the most accomplished girl in the neighbourhood; and Catherine and Lydia had been fortunate enough to be never without partners, which was all that they had yet learnt to care for at a ball. They returned therefore in good spirits to Longbourn, the village where they lived, and of which they were the principal inhabitants. They found Mr. Bennet still up. With a book he was regardless of time; and on the present occasion he had a good deal of curiosity as to the event of an evening which had raised such splendid expectations. He had rather hoped that all his wife's views on the stranger would be disappointed; but he soon found that he had a very different story to hear.

"Oh! my dear Mr. Bennet," as she entered the room, "we have had a most delightful evening, a most excellent ball. I wish you had been there. Jane was so admired, nothing could be like it. Everybody said how well she looked; and Mr. Bingley thought her quite beautiful, and danced with her twice. Only think of *that* my dear; he actually danced with her twice, and she was the only creature in the room that he asked a second time. First of all, he asked Miss Lucas. I was so vexed to see him stand up with her; but, however, he did not admire her at all—indeed, nobody can, you know—and he seemed quite struck with Jane as she was going down the dance. So, he enquired who she was, and got introduced, and asked her for the two next. Then, the two third he

danced with Miss King, and the two fourth with Maria Lucas, and the two fifth with Jane again, and the two sixth with Lizzy, and the Boulanger."[1]

"If he had had any compassion for *me*," cried her husband impatiently, "he would not have danced half so much! For God's sake, say no more of his partners. Oh! that he had sprained his ankle in the first dance!"

"Oh! my dear," continued Mrs. Bennet, "I am quite delighted with him. He is so excessively handsome! and his sisters are charming women. I never in my life saw anything more elegant than their dresses. I dare say the lace upon Mrs. Hurst's gown—"

Here she was interrupted again. Mr. Bennet protested against any description of finery. She was therefore obliged to seek another branch of the subject, and related, with much bitterness of spirit and some exaggeration, the shocking rudeness of Mr. Darcy.

"But I can assure you," she added, "that Lizzy does not lose much by not suiting *his* fancy; for he is a most disagreeable, horrid man, not at all worth pleasing. So high and so conceited that there was no enduring him! He walked here, and he walked there, fancying himself so very great! Not handsome enough to dance with! I wish you had been there, my dear, to have given him one of your set downs. I quite detest the man."

CHAPTER 4

When Jane and Elizabeth were alone, the former, who had been cautious in her praise of Mr. Bingley before, expressed to her sister how very much she admired him.

"He is just what a young man ought to be," said she, "sensible, good humoured, lively; and I never saw such happy manners!—so much ease, with such perfect good breeding!"

"He is also handsome," replied Elizabeth, "which a young man ought likewise to be, if he possibly can. His character is thereby complete."

"I was very much flattered by his asking me to dance a second time. I did not expect such a compliment."

"Did not you? *I* did for you. But that is one great difference between us. Compliments always take *you* by

---

[1] *Boulanger* French dance, performed by a circle of couples, in which each person dances briefly with each member of the opposite sex. The boulanger was the closing dance at balls.

surprise, and *me* never. What could be more natural than his asking you again? He could not help seeing that you were about five times as pretty as every other women in the room. No thanks to his gallantry for that. Well, he certainly is very agreeable, and I give you leave to like him. You have liked many a stupider person."

"Dear Lizzy!"

"Oh! you are a great deal too apt, you know, to like people in general. You never see a fault in anybody. All the world are good and agreeable in your eyes. I never heard you speak ill of a human being in my life."

"I would wish not to be hasty in censuring anyone; but I always speak what I think."

"I know you do; and it is *that* which makes the wonder. With *your* good sense, to be honestly blind to the follies and nonsense of others! Affectation of candour is common enough; one meets it everywhere. But to be candid without ostentation or design—to take the good of everybody's character and make it still better, and say nothing of the bad—belongs to you alone. And so, you like this man's sisters too, do you? Their manners are not equal to his."

"Certainly not, at first. But they are very pleasing women when you converse with them. Miss Bingley is to live with her brother and keep his house; and I am much mistaken if we shall not find a very charming neighbour in her."

Elizabeth listened in silence, but was not convinced; their behaviour at the assembly had not been calculated to please in general; and with more quickness of observation and less pliancy of temper than her sister, and with a judgment too unassailed by any attention to herself, she was very little disposed to approve them. They were in fact very fine ladies; not deficient in good humour when they were pleased, nor in the power of being agreeable where they chose it; but proud and conceited. They were rather handsome, had been educated in one of the first private seminaries in town, had a fortune of twenty thousand pounds, were in the habit of spending more than they ought, and of associating with people of rank; and were therefore in every respect entitled to think well of themselves, and meanly of others. They were of a respectable family in the north of England, a circumstance more deeply impressed on their memories than that their brother's fortune and

their own had been acquired by trade.

Mr. Bingley inherited property to the amount of nearly an hundred thousand pounds from his father, who had intended to purchase an estate, but did not live to do it. Mr. Bingley intended it likewise, and sometimes made choice of his county; but as he was now provided with a good house and the liberty of a manor, it was doubtful to many of those who best knew the easiness of his temper, whether he might not spend the remainder of his days at Netherfield, and leave the next generation to purchase.

His sisters were very anxious for his having an estate of his own; but though he was now established only as a tenant, Miss Bingley was by no means unwilling to preside at his table, nor was Mrs. Hurst, who had married a man of more fashion than fortune, less disposed to consider his house as her home when it suited her. Mr. Bingley had not been of age two years when he was tempted by an accidental recommendation to look at Netherfield House. He did look at it and into it for half an hour, was pleased with the situation and the principal rooms, satisfied with what the owner said in its praise, and took it immediately.

Between him and Darcy there was a very steady friendship, in spite of a great opposition of character. Bingley was endeared to Darcy by the easiness, openness, ductility of his temper—though no disposition could offer a greater contrast to his own, and though with his own he never appeared dissatisfied. On the strength of Darcy's regard Bingley had the firmest reliance, and of his judgment the highest opinion. In understanding, Darcy was the superior. Bingley was by no means deficient, but Darcy was clever. He was at the same time haughty, reserved, and fastidious, and his manners, though well bred, were not inviting. In that respect his friend had greatly the advantage. Bingley was sure of being liked wherever he appeared; Darcy was continually giving offence.

The manner in which they spoke of the Meryton assembly was sufficiently characteristic. Bingley had never met with pleasanter people or prettier girls in his life; every ody had been most kind and attentive to him, there had been no formality, no stiffness, he had soon felt acquainted with all the room; and as to Miss Bennet, he could not conceive an angel more beautiful.

Darcy, on the contrary, had seen a collection of people in whom there was little beauty and no fashion, for none of whom he had felt the smallest interest, and from none received either attention or pleasure. Miss Bennet he acknowledged to be pretty, but she smiled too much.

Mrs. Hurst and her sister allowed it to be so—but still they admired her and liked her, and pronounced her to be a sweet girl, and one whom they should not object to know more of. Miss Bennet was therefore established as a sweet girl, and their brother felt authorised by such commendation to think of her as he chose.

—1811 (WRITTEN 1796-97)

WILLIAM HAZLITT
1778 – 1830

William Hazlitt is often placed alongside the major authors of the Romantic era—a remarkable association in that Hazlitt was neither a poet nor a novelist nor a playwright. He was, however, perhaps the most significant essayist of his time, writing with great facility and great energy on literature, on theater, on art, and on politics. Hazlitt won many admirers for the steadfastness of his moral stance and, even more so, for his lively and penetrating prose style; it has sometimes been claimed he changed the nature of criticism, turning it into an art form in itself. His personality was less widely admired, however. With his critical essays and "portraits" of authors, many of them disparaging, many of them passionately argued, Hazlitt made scores of enemies, and was in turn often viciously attacked by the press. According to his contemporary Thomas De Quincey, he "wilfully placed himself in collision from the first with all the interests that were in the sunshine of the world, and of all the persons that were then powerful in England."

Hazlitt came by his rebellious nature honestly: he was born in Maidstone, Kent, into a family of Dissenters, a group of independent thinkers who disagreed with the tenets of the Church of England. His father was an Irish Unitarian minister who outspokenly supported the ideals of the French and American Revolutions and moved his family first to Ireland and then to the new republic of the United States of America in 1783, where he founded its first Unitarian church. In 1787 the family returned to England and settled in Shropshire. When he was 15, Hazlitt was sent to the New Unitarian College in London to train for the ministry, but he eventually realized he had no calling. For a time he followed in his brother John's footsteps and attempted a career as a painter; he ultimately recognized that he could not make a living painting portraits, but his eye for detail would later surface in the literary "portraits" for which he would become famous.

In 1798, Hazlitt made the acquaintance of Samuel Taylor Coleridge and William Wordsworth; years later the two would become the subjects of a charming essay, "My First Acquaintance with Poets" (1823). Hazlitt began to move in literary circles, also becoming friends (and sometimes enemies) with William Godwin, Leigh Hunt, Robert Southey, Percy Bysshe Shelley, Lord Byron, and Charles Lamb (Lamb was one of the few to remain a loyal companion). Hazlitt embarked on a career as a writer himself in 1805, publishing his first book, *An Essay on the Principles of Human Action*. It was followed by various political essays and pamphlets, and in 1808 (also the year in which he began an ill-fated marriage to Sarah Stoddart) Hazlitt began writing for *The Times*. Within a few years he was writing as well for the *Morning Chronicle* and for Leigh Hunt's journal *The Examiner*; in later years the *Edinburgh Review* and *London Magazine* were added to this list. It was for the *London Magazine* that he wrote *Table-Talk* (published in book form in 1821 and 1822), a series of brilliant and sparkling essays.

In 1824 *New Monthly Magazine* began publishing Hazlitt's next series of essays, *The Spirit of the Age*, in which he created memorably biting literary portraits of such contemporary writers as Byron ("he cares little what it is he says, so that he can say it differently from others") and Sir Walter Scott ("his speculative understanding is empty, flaccid, poor, and dead"). Hazlitt established himself as a leading art, literary, and drama critic, and, through his lectures and essays on William Shakespeare, helped spark a revival of Elizabethan theater.

Hazlitt stayed true to his radical roots, and remained an ardent supporter of Napoleon and the principles of the French Revolution (Hazlitt's four-volume *The Life of Napoleon Buonaparte* was published in 1828 and 1830). This spirit caused a rift with many of his fellow writers—most notably with Wordsworth, whose writing Hazlitt would praise, but whom he would publicly accuse of being an "apostate" to the French Revolution, saying that he "turned from his beliefs of his younger days and sold out to the establishment in accepting government jobs, pensions and laurels." For these convictions Hazlitt was blasted by the conservative press, whose recriminations were often scathing (Hazlitt was prompted to bring charges of libel against *Blackwood's Magazine* in 1818).

Hazlitt wrote about an enormous variety of subjects, telling the public, as J.B. Priestley put it in 1960, "what William Hazlitt thought and felt about everything," leaving a legacy of writing that spans 21 volumes. He died of cancer in 1830; although Hazlitt claimed on his death bed that he had led "a happy life," Charles Lamb was the only one of his old friends to attend his funeral. For Hazlitt, however, a life was made happy by the power of one's convictions and the zeal with which one lived out those convictions. "The love of life" was, according to Hazlitt, "the elect not of our enjoyment, but of our passions."

⌘ ⌘ ⌘

from *The Spirit of the Age; or Contemporary Portraits*

MR. COLERIDGE

The present is an age of talkers, and not of doers; and the reason is, that the world is growing old. We are so far advanced in the Arts and Sciences, that we live in retrospect, and dote on past achievements. The accumulation of knowledge has been so great, that we are lost in wonder at the height it has reached, instead of attempting to climb or add to it; while the variety of objects distracts and dazzles the looker-on. What *niche* remains unoccupied? What path untried? What is the use of doing anything, unless we could do better than all those who have gone before us? What hope is there of this? We are like those who have been to see some noble monument of art, who are content to admire without thinking of rivalling it; or like guests after a feast, who praise the hospitality of the donor "and thank the bounteous Pan"[1]—perhaps carrying away some trifling fragments; or like the spectators of a mighty battle, who still hear its sound afar off, and the clashing of armour and the neighing of the war-horse and the shout of victory is in their ears, like the rushing of innumerable waters!

Mr. Coleridge has "a mind reflecting ages past";[2] his voice is like the echo of the congregated roar of the "dark rearward and abyss" of thought. He who has seen a mouldering tower by the side of a crystal lake, hid by the mist, but glittering in the wave below, may conceive the dim, gleaming, uncertain intelligence of his eye: he who has marked the evening clouds unrolled (a world of vapours), has seen the picture of his mind, unearthly, unsubstantial, with gorgeous tints and ever-varying forms—

---

[1] *"and thank the bounteous Pan"* From John Milton's *A Mask Presented at Ludlow Castle* ("Comus"): "In wanton dance they praise the bounteous Pan" (Greek god of shepherds and flocks).

[2] *"a mind … past"* In an 1818 lecture, Hazlitt also wrote of Shakespeare: "He had 'a mind reflecting ages past' and present."

That which was now a horse, even with a thought
The rack dislimns, and makes it indistinct
As water is in water.[1]

Our author's mind is (as he himself might express it) *tangential.* There is no subject on which he has not touched, none on which he has rested. With an understanding fertile, subtle, expansive, "quick, forgetive, apprehensive,"[2] beyond all living precedent, few traces of it will perhaps remain. He lends himself to all impressions alike; he gives up his mind and liberty of thought to none. He is a general lover of art and science, and wedded to no one in particular. He pursues knowledge as a mistress, with outstretched hands and winged speed; but as he is about to embrace her, his Daphne turns— alas! not to a laurel![3] Hardly a speculation has been left on record from the earliest time, but it is loosely folded up in Mr. Coleridge's memory, like a rich, but somewhat tattered piece of tapestry: we might add (with more seeming than real extravagance), that scarce a thought can pass through the mind of man, but its sound has at some time or other passed over his head with rustling pinions. On whatever question or author you speak, he is prepared to take up the theme with advantage—from Peter Abelard down to Thomas Moore,[4] from the subtlest metaphysics to the politics of the *Courier.* There is no man of genius, in whose praise, he descants, but the critic seems to stand above the author, and "what in him is weak, to strengthen, what is low, to raise and support": nor is there any work of genius that does not come out of his hands like an illuminated Missal,[5] sparkling even in its defects. If Mr. Coleridge had not been the most impressive talker of his age, he would probably have been the finest writer; but he lays down his pen to make sure of an auditor, and mortgages the admiration of posterity for the stare of an idler. If he had not been a poet, he would have been a powerful logician; if he had not dipped his wing in the Unitarian controversy,[6] he might have soared to the very summit of fancy. But in writing verse, he is trying to subject the Muse to *transcendental* theories: in his abstract reasoning, he misses his way by strewing it with flowers. All that he has done of moment, he had done twenty years ago: since then, he may be said to have lived on the sound of his own voice. Mr. Coleridge is too rich in intellectual wealth, to need to task himself to any drudgery: he has only to draw the sliders of his imagination, and a thousand subjects expand before him, startling him with their brilliancy, or losing themselves in endless obscurity—

And by the force of blear illusion,
They draw him on to his confusion.[7]

What is the little he could add to the stock, compared with the countless stores that lie about him, that he should stoop to pick up a name, or to polish an idle fancy? He walks abroad in the majesty of a universal understanding, eyeing the "rich strond,"[8] or golden sky above him, and "goes sounding on his way," in eloquent accents, uncompelled and free! Persons of the greatest capacity are often those, who for this reason do the least; for surveying themselves from the highest point of view, amidst the infinite variety of the universe, their own share in it seems trifling, and scarce worth a thought, and they prefer the contemplation of all that is, or has been, or can be, to the making a coil about doing what, when done, is no better than vanity. It is hard to concentrate all our attention and efforts on one pursuit, except from ignorance of others; and without this concentration of our faculties, no great progress can be made in any one effort; it does not think the effort worth making. Action is one; but thought is manifold. He whose restless eye glances through the wide compass of nature and art, will not consent to have "his own

---

[1] *That which ... water* From Shakespeare's *Antony and Cleopatra* 4.14.9–11.

[2] *"quick, forgetive, apprehensive"* From Shakespeare's *2 Henry IV,* 4.3.98–99: "Apprehensive, quick, forgetive"; *forgetive* inventive.

[3] *Daphne ... laurel* In Greek mythology, a nymph who eluded her pursuer by transforming herself into a laurel tree.

[4] *Peter Abelard* French philosopher and theologian (1079–1142); *Thomas Moore* Irish poet and composer (1779–1852).

[5] *Missal* Roman Catholic prayerbook.

[6] *Unitarian controversy* Coleridge became a Unitarian preacher in 1798; Hazlitt wrote in praise of Coleridge's lay-sermon of 1798.

[7] *And by ... confusion* From Shakespeare's *Macbeth* 3.5.28–29.

[8] *"rich strond"* Beach; from Edmund Spenser's *The Faerie Queene* 3.4.2.

nothings monstered";[1] but he must do this, before he can give his whole soul to them. The mind, after "letting contemplation have its fill," or

> Sailing with supreme dominion,
> Through the azure deep of air,[2]

sinks down on the ground, breathless, exhausted, powerless, inactive; or if it must have some vent to its feelings, seeks the most easy and obvious; is soothed by friendly flattery, lulled by the murmur of immediate applause, thinks as it were aloud, and babbles in its dreams! A scholar (so to speak) is a more disinterested and abstracted character than a mere author. The first looks at the numberless volumes of a library, and says, "All these are mine": the other points to a single volume (perhaps it may be an immortal one) and says, "My name is written on the back of it." This is a puny and groveling ambition, beneath the lofty amplitude of Mr. Coleridge's mind. No, he revolves in his wayward soul, or utters to the passing wind, or discourses to his own shadow, things mightier and more various!—Let us draw the curtain, and unlock the shrine.

Learning rocked him in his cradle, and while yet a child,

> He lisped in numbers, for the numbers came.[3]

At sixteen he wrote his *Ode on Chatterton*,[4] and he still reverts to that period with delight, not so much as it relates to himself (for that string of his own early promise of fame rather jars than otherwise) but as exemplifying the youth of a poet. Mr. Coleridge talks of himself, without being an egotist, for in him the individual is always merged in the abstract and general. He distinguished himself at school and at the University by his knowledge of the classics, and gained several prizes for Greek epigrams. How many men are there (great scholars, celebrated names in literature) who having done the same thing in their youth, have no other idea all the rest of their lives but of this achievement, of a fellowship and dinner, and who, installed in academic honours, would look down on our author as a mere strolling bard! At Christ's Hospital,[5] where he was brought up, he was the idol of those among his schoolfellows, who mingled with their bookish studies the music of thought and of humanity; and he was usually attended round the cloisters by a group of these (inspiring and inspired) whose hearts, even then, burnt within them as he talked, and where the sounds yet linger to mock ELIA[6] on his way, still turning pensive to the past! One of the finest and rarest parts of Mr. Coleridge's conversation, is when he expatiates on the Greek tragedians (not that he is not well acquainted, when he pleases, with the epic poets, or the philosophers, or orators, or historians of antiquity)—on the subtle reasonings and melting pathos of Euripides, on the harmonious gracefulness of Sophocles, tuning his love-laboured song, like sweetest warblings from a sacred grove; on the high-wrought trumpet-tongued eloquence of Æschylus,[7] whose Prometheus, above all, is like an Ode to Fate, and a pleading with Providence, his thoughts being let loose as his body is chained on his solitary rock, and his afflicted will (the emblem of mortality)

> Struggling in vain with ruthless destiny.[8]

As the impassioned critic speaks and rises in his theme, you would think you heard the voice of the Man hated by the Gods, contending with the wild winds as they roar, and his eye glitters with the spirit of Antiquity!

---

1   *"his own ... monstered"*   From Shakespeare's *Coriolanus* 3.2.81.

2   *Sailing ... air*   From Thomas Gray's *The Progress of Poesy: A Pindaric Ode* 2.116–17.

3   *He lisped ... came*   From Alexander Pope's "An Epistle to Dr. Arbuthnot" 128: "I lisped in numbers, for the numbers came."

4   *Ode on Chatterton*   "Monody on the Death of Chatterton."

5   *Christ's Hospital*   Christ's Hospital School for poor boys, founded by Edward VI.

6   *ELIA*   Pen name of essayist Charles Lamb (1775–1834). Lamb's "Elia" essays included a piece on Christ's, where he had been to school with Coleridge.

7   *Euripides*   Greek tragedian (480?–406 BCE), author of *Medea*; *Sophocles*   Greek tragedian (496?–406 BCE), author of *Oedipus Rex*; *Æschylus*   The father of the Greek tragedy (525–456 BCE), author of *Prometheus Bound*.

8   *Struggling ... destiny*   From William Wordsworth's *The Excursion* (1814) 6.557.

Next, he was engaged with Hartley's[1] tribes of mind, "etherial braid, thought-woven,"—and he busied himself for a year or two with vibrations and vibratiun-cles[2] and the great law of association that binds all things in its mystic chain, and the doctrine of Necessity (the mild teacher of Charity) and the Millennium, anticipa-tive of a life to come—and he plunged deep into the controversy on Matter and Spirit, and, as an escape from Dr. Priestley's Materialism,[3] where he felt himself imprisoned by the logician's spell, like Ariel in the cloven pine-tree,[4] he became suddenly enamoured of Bishop Berkeley's[5] fairy-world,[6] and used in all compa-nies to build the universe, like a brave poetical fiction, of fine words—and he was deep-read in Malebranche, and in Cudworth's Intellectual System (a huge pile of learning, unwieldy, enormous) and in Lord Brook's hieroglyphic theories, and in Bishop Butler's Sermons, and in the Duchess of Newcastle's fantastic folios, and in Clark and South and Tillotson, and all the fine thinkers and masculine reasoners of that age—and Leibnitz's *Pre-Established Harmony* reared its arch above his head,[7] like the rainbow in the cloud, covenanting[8]

with the hopes of man—and then he fell plump, ten thousand fathoms down (but his wings saved him harmless) into the *hortus siccus*[9] of Dissent, where he pared religion down to the standard of reason and stripped faith of mystery, and preached Christ crucified and the Unity of the Godhead, and so dwelt for a while in the spirit with John Huss and Jerome of Prague and Socinus and old John Zisca,[10] and ran through Neal's History of the Puritans, and Calamy's Non-Conform-ists' Memorial,[11] having like thoughts and passions with them—but then Spinoza[12] became his God, and he took up the vast chain of being in his hand, and the round world became the centre and the soul of all things in some shadowy sense, forlorn of meaning, and around him he beheld the living traces and the sky-pointing proportions of the mighty Pan—but poetry redeemed him from this spectral philosophy, and he bathed his heart in beauty, and gazed at the golden light of heaven, and drank of the spirit of the universe, and wandered at eve by fairy-stream or fountain,

—When he saw nought but beauty,
When he heard the voice of that Almighty One
In every breeze that blew, or wave that murmured—[13]

and wedded with truth in Plato's shade, and in the writings of Proclus and Plotinus saw the ideas of things

[1] *Hartley's* Referring to the theories of David Hartley (1705–57), English physician and materialist philosopher, who believed that all mental phenomena are functions of the brain; Hartley's ideas greatly influenced Coleridge.

[2] *vibratiuncles* Small vibrations.

[3] *Dr. Priestley's Materialism* Joseph Priestley's (1733–1804) philosophical theory: all things that exist are composed of matter.

[4] *Ariel ... pine-tree* From Shakespeare's *The Tempest* 1.2.324; the evil witch Sycorax imprisoned the spirit Ariel in a cloven pine tree.

[5] *Bishop Berkeley's* Referring to the theories of George Berkeley (1685–1753), an Anglo-Irish clergyman and idealist philosopher who argued that God thinks everything into existence.

[6] [Hazlitt's note] Mr. Coleridge named his eldest son (the writer of some beautiful sonnets) after Hartley, and the second after Berkeley. The third was called Derwent, after the river of that name. Nothing can be more characteristic of his mind than this circumstance. All his ideas indeed are like a river, flowing on for ever, and still murmuring as it flows, discharging its still waters and still replenished—"And so by many winding nooks it strays, with willing sport to the ocean world!" ["*And so by ... wild ocean*" From Shakespeare's *The Two Gentlemen of Verona* 2.7.31–32.]

[7] *Malebranche* Nicolas Malebranche (1638–1715) was a French Cartesian philosopher who argued that mind and body are separate, but God coordinates the two; *Cudworth* Ralph Cudworth (1617–88) was an English philosopher who argued against atheism

and determinism; *Lord Brook* Robert Greville, Lord Brooke (1608–43) was an English philosopher who proposed that all things are emanations from God; *Duchess of Newcastle* Margaret Caven-dish (1623–73) was an English author and materialist philosopher who argued that nothing in nature is incorporeal; *Tillotson* John Tillotson (1630–94) was an Archbishop of Canterbury who argued against atheism; *Leibniz* Gottfried Leibniz (1646–1716) was a German mathematician and rationalist philosopher who argued that there is a non-causal relationship between mind and body, and that there is a pre-existing harmony in the world established by God.

[8] *covenanting* Suiting; agreeing.

[9] *hortus siccus* Dry garden.

[10] *John Huss ... John Zisca* Church reformers, most of whom died for their beliefs.

[11] *Neal's ... Memorial* Daniel Neal (1678–1743), English historian; Edmund Calamy (1678–1732), English historian and dissenting minister.

[12] *Spinoza* Dutch determinist philosopher (1632–1677) who argued that God and nature are one and the same.

[13] *When ... murmered* From Coleridge's *Remorse* 4.2.100–02.

in the eternal mind, and unfolded all mysteries with the Schoolmen and fathomed the depths of Duns Scotus and Thomas Aquinas, and entered the third heaven with Jacob Behmen, and walked hand in hand with Swedenborg through the pavilions of the New Jerusalem, and sung his faith in the promise and in the word in his *Religious Musings*[1]—and lowering himself from that dizzy height, poised himself on Milton's wings, and spread out his thoughts in charity with the glad prose of Jeremy Taylor,[2] and wept over Bowles's Sonnets,[3] and studied Cowper's[4] blank verse, and betook himself to Thomson's Castle of Indolence,[5] and sported with the wits of Charles the Second's days and of Queen Anne, and relished Swift's[6] style and that of the John Bull (Arbuthnot's we mean, not Mr. Croker's),[7] and dallied with the British essayists and novelists, and knew all qualities of more modern writers with a learned spirit, Johnson, and Goldsmith, and Junius, and Burke, and Godwin, and the Sorrows of Werter, and Jean Jacques Rousseau, and Voltaire, and Marivaux, and Crebillon, and thousands more—now "laughed with Rabelais[8] in his easy chair" or pointed to Hogarth, or afterwards dwelt on Claude's classic scenes, or spoke with rapture of Raphael,[9] and compared the women at Rome to figures that had walked out of his pictures, or visited the Oratory of Pisa, and described the works of Giotto and Ghirlandaio and Masaccio,[10] and gave the moral of the picture of the Triumph of Death, where the beggars and the wretched invoke his dreadful dart, but the rich and mighty of the earth quail and shrink before it; and in that land of siren sights and sounds, saw a dance of peasant girls, and was charmed with lutes and gondolas,—or wandered into Germany and lost himself in the labyrinths of the Hartz Forest and of the Kantean philosophy, and amongst the cabalistic names of Fichte and Schelling and Lessing,[11] and God knows who—this was long after, but all the former while, he had nerved his heart and filled his eyes with tears, as he hailed the

---

[1] *Plato* Greek philosopher (428?–348? BCE) and author of *The Republic*, who argued that all we see in the world is a glimpse of what is ultimately a perfect "form" and that good art stimulates the passions, giving us a vision of the ideal form; *Proclus* Greek philosopher (411–85), Neoplatonist, who argued for the existence of one ultimate, original creator (reality), from whom emanates all existence in lower and lower forms; *Plotinus* Egyptian philosopher (205–270), Neoplatonist, whose theories of emanation postulated the existence of one supreme source that creates the possibility of all other existences; *Duns Scotus* Scottish philosopher and theologian (c. 1266–1308), who argued for the "univocity" or commonality of being that provides our understanding of "essential truths"; *Thomas Aquinas* Italian priest (later made a saint) and philosopher (1225–74), who said that reason can prove the existence of God; *Jacob Behmen* Sometimes spelled Jakob Boehme (1575–1634), German mystic who wrote of a Supreme reality and of humankind's struggle to choose good over evil; *Swedenborg* Emanuel Swedenborg, Swedish theologian, scientist, and philosopher (1688–1772), whose visionary writings gave rise to the Church of the New Jerusalem (or New Church); *Religious Musings* Coleridge's *Religious Musings: a Desultory Poem, written on Christmas Eve in the year of our Lord, 1794*.

[2] *Jeremy Taylor* (1613–67), clergyman.

[3] *Bowles's Sonnets* William Lyle Bowles's (1762–1850) influential *Fourteen Sonnets*.

[4] *Cowper's* Poet William Cowper's (1731–68) verse.

[5] *Thomson's Castle of Indolence* A poem by James Thomson (1700–48).

[6] *Swift's* Jonathan Swift's (1667–1745) satiric style.

[7] *John Bull ... Croker's* John Arbuthnot (1667–1735) wrote *The History of John Bull* (1727), a satire; John Wilson Croker (1780–1857), was a conservative MP, writer, and critic.

[8] *Johnson ... Rabelais* Johnson Samuel Johnson (1709–84); *Goldsmith* Oliver Goldsmith (1728–74); *Junius* A pseudonym for the author of *The Letters of Junius*, satirical polemics on English politics; *Burke* Edmund Burke (1729–97), statesman, orator, and author; *Godwin* William Godwin (1756–1836), radical philosopher; *Sorrows of Werter* *The Sorrows of Young Werther*, by Johann Wolfgang von Goethe (1749–1832); *Jean Jacques Rousseau* French philosopher (1712–78); *Voltaire* Author and philosopher (1694–1778); *Marivaux* Pierre Carlet de Marivaux (1688–1763), French dramatist; *Crebillon* P.J. de Crébillon (1674–1762), French dramatist; *Rabelais* François Rabelais (1494–1553), writer known for his humorous *La Vie de Gargantua and Pantagruel*.

[9] *Hogarth ... Raphael* Hogarth English artist William Hogarth (1697–1764); *Claude's* Referring to the paintings of Claude Lorraine, Baroque painter (c. 1600–82); *Raphael* Raffaello Sanzi, Italian artist (1483–1520).

[10] *Giotto ... Masaccio* Giotto di Bondone, Florentine painter and architect (1267–1337); *Ghirlandaio* Domenico Ghirlandio, Florentine painter (1401–27?); *Masaccio* Tommaso Cassai, Florentine painter (1401–27?).

[11] *Kantean philosophy ... Lessing* Kantean philosophy The theories of philosopher Immanuel Kant (1724–1804); *Fichte* J.G. Fichte (1762–1814), German philosopher and follower of Kant; *Schelling* Friedrich W.J. Schelling (1775–1854), German philosopher and follower of Kant; *Lessing* Gotthold Ephraim Lessing (1729–81), German critic and playwright.

rising orb of liberty, since quenched in darkness and in blood, and had kindled his affections at the blaze of the French Revolution, and sang for joy when the towers of the Bastille[1] and the proud places of the insolent and the oppressor fell, and would have floated his bark, freighted with fondest fancies, across the Atlantic wave with Southey[2] and others to seek for peace and freedom—

In Philarmonia's undivided dale![3]

Alas! "Frailty, thy name is *Genius*!"[4]—What is become of all this mighty heap of hope, of thought, of learning, and humanity? It has ended in swallowing doses of oblivion and in writing paragraphs in the *Courier*.—Such, and so little is the mind of man!

It was not to be supposed that Mr. Coleridge could keep on at the rate he set off; he could not realize all he knew or thought, and less could not fix his desultory ambition; other stimulants supplied the place, and kept up the intoxicating dream, the fever and the madness of his early impressions. Liberty (the philosopher's and the poet's bride) had fallen a victim, meanwhile, to the murderous practices of the hag, Legitimacy. Proscribed by court-hirelings, too romantic for the herd of vulgar politicians, our enthusiast stood at bay, and at last turned on the pivot of a subtle casuistry to the *unclean side:* but his discursive reason would not let him trammel himself into a poet-laureate or stamp-distributor,[5] and he stopped, ere he had quite passed that well-known "bourne from whence no traveller returns"[6]—and so has sunk into torpid, uneasy repose, tantalized by useless resources, haunted by vain imaginings, his lips idly moving, but his heart for ever still, or, as the shattered chords vibrate of themselves, making melancholy music to the ear of memory! Such is the fate of genius in an age, when in the unequal contest with sovereign wrong, every man is ground to powder who is not either a born slave, or who does not willingly and at once offer up the yearnings of humanity and the dictates of reason as a welcome sacrifice to besotted prejudice and loathsome power.

Of all Mr. Coleridge's productions, the *Ancient Mariner* is the only one that we could with confidence put into any person's hands, on whom we wished to impress a favourable idea of his extraordinary powers. Let whatever other objections be made to it, it is unquestionably a work of genius—of wild, irregular, overwhelming imagination, and has that rich, varied movement in the verse, which gives a distant idea of the lofty or changeful tones of Mr. Coleridge's voice. In the *Christabel,* there is one splendid passage on divided friendship. The *Translation of Schiller's Wallenstein* is also a masterly production in its kind, faithful and spirited. Among his smaller pieces there are occasional bursts of pathos and fancy, equal to what we might expect from him; but these form the exception, and not the rule. Such, for instance, is his affecting Sonnet to the author of the Robbers.

Schiller! that hour I would have wish'd to die,
        If through the shudd'ring midnight I had sent
        From the dark dungeon of the tower time-rent,
That fearful voice, a famish'd father's cry—
That in no after-moment aught less vast
        Might stamp me mortal! A triumphant shout
        Black horror scream'd, and all her goblin rout
From the more with'ring scene diminsh'd pass'd.
Ah! Bard tremendous in sublimity!
        Could I behold thee in thy loftier mood,
Wand'ring at eve, with finely frenzied eye,
        Beneath some vast old tempest-swinging wood!
        Awhile, with mute awe gazing, I would brood,

---

[1] *towers of … Bastille*   The Bastille, a French prison, was stormed by the people of Paris on 14 July 1789.

[2] *Southey*   Robert Southey (1774–1843), British Poet Laureate from 1813–43, collaborated with Coleridge on political and creative works, and shared an interest in the egalitarian principles of the French Revolution.

[3] *In … dale*   From Coleridge's "Monody on the Death of Chatterton" 40.

[4] *"Frailty … Genius"*   From Shakespeare's *Hamlet* 1.2.146, "Frailty, thy name is woman!"

[5] *poet-laureate or stamp-distributor*   William Wordsworth, Poet Laureate from 1843–50; when Wordsworth in 1813 took a position with the tax department as the Distributor of Stamps, many proponents of the reform came to believe that he had abandoned progressive causes.

[6] *"bourne … returns"*   From Shakespeare's *Hamlet* 3.1: "The undiscover'd country from whose bourne / No traveller returns."

Then weep aloud in a wild ecstacy.[1]

His Tragedy, entitled *Remorse*, is full of beautiful and striking passages, but it does not place the author in the first rank of dramatic writers. But if Mr. Coleridge's works do not place him in that rank, they injure instead of conveying a just idea of the man, for he himself is certainly in the first class of general intellect.

If our author's poetry is inferior to his conversation, his prose is utterly abortive. Hardly a gleam is to be found in it of the brilliancy and richness of those stores of thought and language that he pours out incessantly, when they are lost like drops of water in the ground. The principal work, in which he has attempted to embody his general views of things, is the FRIEND,[2] of which, though it contains some noble passages and fine trains of thought, prolixity and obscurity are the most frequent characteristics.

No two persons can be conceived more opposite in character or genius than the subject of the present and of the preceding sketch. Mr. Godwin, with less natural capacity, and with fewer acquired advantages, by concentrating his mind on some given object, and doing what he had to do with all his might, has accomplished much, and will leave more than one monument of a powerful intellect behind him; Mr. Coleridge, by dissipating his, and dallying with every subject by turns, has done little or nothing to justify to the World or to posterity, the high opinion which all who have ever heard him converse, or known him intimately, with one accord entertain of him. Mr. Godwin's faculties have kept at home, and plied their task in the workshop of the brain, diligently and effectually: Mr. Coleridge's have gossiped their time away, and gadded about from house to house, as if life's business were to melt the hours in listless talk. Mr. Godwin is intent on a subject, only as it concerns himself and his reputation; he works it out as a matter of duty, and discards from his mind whatever does not forward his main object as impertinent and vain. Mr. Coleridge, on the other hand, delights in nothing but episodes and digressions, ne-

glects whatever he undertakes to perform, and can act only on spontaneous impulses, without object or method. "He cannot be constrained by mastery."[3] While he should be occupied with a given pursuit, he is thinking of a thousand other things; a thousand tastes, a thousand objects tempt him, and distract his mind, which keeps open house, and entertains all comers; and after being fatigued and amused with morning calls from idle visitors, finds the day consumed and its business unconcluded. Mr. Godwin, on the contrary, is somewhat exclusive and unsocial in his habits of mind, entertains no company but what he gives his whole time and attention to, and wisely writes over the doors of his understanding, his fancy, and his senses—"No admittance except on business." He has none of that fastidious refinement and false delicacy, which might lead him to balance between the endless variety of modern attainments. He does not throw away his life (nor a single half-hour of it) in adjusting the claims of different accomplishments, and in choosing between them or making himself master of them all. He sets about his task, (whatever it may be) and goes through it with spirit and fortitude. He has the happiness to think an author the greatest character in the world, and himself the greatest author in it. Mr. Coleridge, in writing an harmonious stanza, would stop to consider whether there was not more grace and beauty in a *Pas de trois*,[4] and would not proceed till he had resolved this question by a chain of metaphysical reasoning without end. Not so Mr. Godwin. That is best to him, which he can do best. He does not waste himself in vain aspirations and effeminate sympathies. He is blind, deaf, insensible to all but the trump of Fame. Plays, operas, painting, music, ballrooms, wealth, fashion, titles, lords, ladies, touch him not—all these are no more to him than to the magician in his cell, and he writes on to the end of the chapter, through good report and evil report. *Pingo in eternitatem*[5]—is his motto. He neither envies nor admires what others are, but is contented to be what he is, and strives to do the utmost he can. Mr. Coleridge

---

[1]   *Schiller! ... ecstacy*   Coleridge's "Effusion" 20, from *Poems on Various Subjects* (1796).

[2]   *the FRIEND*   Coleridge's *The Friend* was first published in periodical form (1809–10).

[3]   *"He cannot be constrained by mastery"*   From Geoffrey Chaucer's *The Canterbury Tales*, "The Franklin's Tale" 764: "Love wol nat been constreyned by maistrye."

[4]   *Pas de trois*   Dance for three.

[5]   *Pingo in eternitatem*   Ceaselessly depict.

has flirted with the Muses[1] as with a set of mistresses: Mr. Godwin has been married twice, to Reason and to Fancy, and has to boast no short-lived progeny by each. So to speak, he has *valves* belonging to his mind, to regulate the quantity of gas admitted into it, so that like the bare, unsightly, but well-compacted steam-vessel, it cuts its liquid way, and arrives at its promised end: while Mr. Coleridge's bark, "taught with the little nautilus to sail,"[2] the sport of every breath, dancing to every wave,

> Youth at its prow, and Pleasure at its helm,[3]

flutters its gaudy pennons[4] in the air, glitters in the sun, but we wait in vain to hear of its arrival in the destined harbour. Mr. Godwin, with less variety and vividness, with less subtlety and susceptibility both of thought and feeling, has had firmer nerves, a more determined purpose, a more comprehensive grasp of his subject, and the results are as we find them. Each has met with his reward: for justice has, after all, been done to the pretensions of each; and we must, in all cases, use means to ends!

It was a misfortune to any man of talent to be born in the latter end of the last century. Genius stopped the way of Legitimacy, and therefore it was to be abated, crushed, or set aside as a nuisance. The spirit of the monarchy was at variance with the spirit of the age. The flame of liberty, the light of intellect was to be extinguished with the sword—or with slander, whose edge is sharper than the sword. The war between power and reason was carried on by the first of these abroad—by the last at home. No quarter was given (then or now) by the Government-critics, the authorised censors of the press, to those who followed the dictates of independence, who listened to the voice of the tempter, Fancy. Instead of gathering fruits and flowers, immortal fruits

and amaranthine[5] flowers, they soon found themselves beset not only by a host of prejudices, but assailed with all the engines of power, by nicknames, by lies, by all the arts of malice, interest and hypocrisy, without the possibility of their defending themselves "from the pelting of the pitiless storm,"[6] that poured down upon them from the strong-holds of corruption and authority. The philosophers, the dry abstract reasoners, submitted to this reverse pretty well, and armed themselves with patience "as with triple steel"[7] to bear discomfiture, persecution, and disgrace. But the poets, the creatures of sympathy, could not stand the frowns both of king and people. They did not like to be shut out when places and pensions, when the critic's praises, and the laurel-wreath were about to be distributed. They did not stomach being *sent to Coventry*,[8] and Mr. Coleridge sounded a retreat for them by the help of casuistry, and a musical voice.—"His words were hollow, but they pleased the ear"[9] of his friends of the Lake School, who turned back disgusted and panic-struck from the dry desert of unpopularity, like Hassan the camel driver,

> And curs'd the hour, and curs'd the luckless day,
> When first from Shiraz' walls they bent their way.[10]

They are safely enclosed there, but Mr. Coleridge did not enter with them; pitching his tent upon the barren waste without, and having no abiding place nor city of refuge.[11]

---

[1] *Muses* The nine goddesses of classical mythology who inspire learning and the arts.

[2] "*taught ... sail*" From Pope's *An Essay on Man: Epistle* (1733–34) 3.177: "Learn of the little Nautilus to sail."

[3] *Youth ... helm* From Thomas Gray's *The Bard: A Pindaric Ode* (1757) 2.2.12: "Youth on the prow, and Pleasure at the helm."

[4] *pennons* Banners.

[5] *amaranthine* Everlasting.

[6] "*from ... storm*" From Shakespeare's *King Lear* (1608) 3.4.28–29: "Poor naked wretches, whereso'er you are / That bide the pelting of this pitiless storm."

[7] "*as with triple steel*" From Milton's *Paradise Lost* (1667) 2.569.

[8] *sent to Coventry* Shunned.

[9] "*His words ... ear*" From Milton's *Paradise Lost* 2.112–17: "But all was false and hollow... yet he pleas'd the ear."

[10] *And curs'd ... way* From William Collins's *The Persian Eclogues* 11.3–4: "Eclogue the Second Hassan; or, The Camel Driver" (1742): "Sad was the hour and luckless was the day, / When first from Shiraz' walls I bent my way."

[11] *city of refuge* From Joshua 20.7–9.

MR. WORDSWORTH

Mr. Wordsworth's genius is a pure emanation of the Spirit of the Age. Had he lived in any other period of the world, he would never have been heard of. As it is, he has some difficulty to contend with the hebetude[1] of his intellect, and the meanness of his subject. With him "lowliness is young ambition's ladder":[2] but he finds it a toil to climb in this way the steep of Fame. His homely Muse can hardly raise her wing from the ground, nor spread her hidden glories to the sun. He has "no figures nor no fantasies, which busy *passion* draws in the brains of men":[3] neither the gorgeous machinery of mythologic lore, nor the splendid colours of poetic diction. His style is vernacular: he delivers household truths. He sees nothing loftier than human hopes; nothing deeper than the human heart. This he probes, this he tampers with, this he poises, with all its incalculable weight of thought and feeling, in his hands; and at the same time calms the throbbing pulses of his own heart, by keeping his eye ever fixed on the face of nature. If he can make the life-blood flow from the wounded breast, this is the living colouring with which he paints his verse: if he can assuage the pain or close up the wound with the balm of solitary musing, or the healing power of plants and herbs and "skyey influences,"[4] this is the sole triumph of his art. He takes the simplest elements of nature and of the human mind, the mere abstract conditions inseparable from our being, and tries to compound a new system of poetry from them; and has perhaps succeeded as well as any one could. "*Nihil humani a me alienum puto*"[5]—is the motto of his works. He thinks nothing low or indifferent of which this can be affirmed: every thing that professes to be more than this, that is not an absolute essence of truth and feeling, he holds to be vitiated, false, and

spurious. In a word, his poetry is founded on setting up an opposition (and pushing it to the utmost length) between the natural and the artificial; between the spirit of humanity, and the spirit of fashion and of the world!

It is one of the innovations of the time. It partakes of, and is carried along with, the revolutionary movement of our age: the political changes of the day were the model on which he formed and conducted his poetical experiments. His Muse (it cannot be denied, and without this we cannot explain its character at all) is a levelling one. It proceeds on a principle of equality, and strives to reduce all things to the same standard. It is distinguished by a proud humility. It relies upon its own resources, and disdains external show and relief. It takes the commonest events and objects, as a test to prove that nature is always interesting from its inherent truth and beauty, without any of the ornaments of dress or pomp of circumstances to set it off. Hence the unaccountable mixture of seeming simplicity and real abstruseness in the *Lyrical Ballads*. Fools have laughed at, wise men scarcely understand them. He takes a subject or a story merely as pegs or loops to hang thought and feeling on; the incidents are trifling, in proportion to his contempt for imposing appearances; the reflections are profound, according to the gravity and the aspiring pretensions of his mind.

His popular, inartificial style gets rid (at a blow) of all the trappings of verse, of all the high places of poetry: "the cloud-capt towers, the solemn temples, the gorgeous palaces," are swept to the ground, and "like the baseless fabric of a vision, leave not a wreck behind."[6] All the traditions of learning, all the superstitions of age, are obliterated and effaced. We begin *de novo,* on a *tabula rasa*[7] of poetry. The purple pall, the nodding plume of tragedy are exploded as mere pantomime and trick, to return to the simplicity of truth and nature. Kings, queens, priests, nobles, the altar and the throne, the distinctions of rank, birth, wealth, power, "the judge's robe, the marshal's truncheon, the ceremony

---

[1] *hebetude* Dullness.

[2] "*lowliness ... ladder*" From William Shakespeare's *Julius Caesar* 2.1.231–32.

[3] "*no figures ... men*" From *Julius Caesar* 2.1.231–32; Hazlitt substitutes the word "passion" for "care."

[4] "*skyey influences*" Influences of the stars. From Shakespeare's *Measure for Measure* 3.1.9.

[5] "*Nihil ... puto*" From Roman playwright Terence (195–159 BCE), "Nothing human is alien to me."

[6] "*the ... behind*" From Shakespeare's *The Tempest* 4.1.151–56: "And, like the baseless fabric of this vision, / The cloud-capp'd towers, the gorgeous palaces, / The solemn temples, the great globe itself, / Yea all which it inherit, shall dissolve / And, like this insubstantial pageant faded, / Leave not a rack behind."

[7] *de novo, on a tabula rasa* Anew, on a blank slate.

that to great ones 'longs,"[1] are not to be found here. The author tramples on the pride of art with greater pride. The Ode and Epode, the Strophe and the Antistrophe,[2] he laughs to scorn. The harp of Homer, the trump of Pindar and of Alcaeus[3] are still. The decencies of costume, the decorations of vanity are stripped off without mercy as barbarous, idle, and Gothic. The jewels in the crisped hair,[4] the diadem[5] on the polished brow are thought meretricious, theatrical, vulgar; and nothing contents his fastidious taste beyond a simple garland of flowers. Neither does he avail himself of the advantages which nature or accident holds out to him. He chooses to have his subject a foil to his invention, to owe nothing but to himself. He gathers manna in the wilderness, he strikes the barren rock for the gushing moisture. He elevates the mean by the strength of his own aspirations; he clothes the naked with beauty and grandeur from the stores of his own recollections. No cypress grove loads his verse with funeral pomp: but his imagination lends "a sense of joy"

> To the bare trees and mountains bare,
> And grass in the green field.[6]

No storm, no shipwreck startles us by its horrors: but the rainbow lifts it head in the cloud, and the breeze sighs through the withered fern. No sad vicissitude of fate, no overwhelming catastrophe in nature deforms his page: but the dew-drop glitters on the bending flower, the tear collects in the glistening eye.

> Beneath the hills, along the flowery vales,
> The generations are prepared; the pangs,
> The internal pangs, are ready; the dread strife
> Of poor humanity's afflicted will,
> Struggling in vain with ruthless destiny.[7]

As the lark ascends from its low bed on fluttering wing, and salutes the morning skies; so Mr. Wordsworth's unpretending Muse, in russet guise, scales the summits of reflection, while it makes the round earth its footstool, and its home!

Possibly a good deal of this may be regarded as the effect of disappointed views and an inverted ambition. Prevented by native pride and indolence from climbing the ascent of learning or greatness, taught by political opinions to say to the vain pomp and glory of the world, "I hate ye,"[8] seeing the path of classical and artificial poetry blocked up by the cumbrous ornaments of style and turgid *common-places*, so that nothing more could be achieved in that direction but by the most ridiculous bombast or the tamest servility; he has turned back partly from the bias of his mind, partly perhaps from a judicious policy—has struck into the sequestered vale of humble life, sought out the Muse among sheep-cotes and hamlets and the peasant's mountain-haunts, has discarded all the tinsel pageantry of verse, and endeavoured (not in vain) to aggrandise the trivial and add the charm of novelty to the familiar. No one has shown the same imagination in raising trifles into importance: no one has displayed the same pathos in treating of the simplest feelings of the heart. Reserved, yet haughty, having no unruly or violent passions, (or those passions having been early suppressed,) Mr. Wordsworth has passed his life in solitary musing, or in daily converse with the face of nature. He exemplifies in an eminent degree the power of *association*; for his poetry has no other source or character. He has dwelt among pastoral scenes, till each object has become connected with a thousand feelings, a link in the chain of thought, a fibre of his own heart. Every one is by habit and familiarity strongly attached to the place of his birth, or to objects

---

[1] *"the judge's robe ... 'longs"* From Shakespeare's *Measure for Measure* 2.2.59–61: "No ceremony that to great ones 'longs, / Not the king's crown, nor the deputed sword, / The marshal's truncheon, nor the judge's robe."

[2] *The Ode ... Antistrophe   ode* A rhymed lyric poem in the form of an address, with an irregular or varied meter; *epode* Lyric poem composed of couplets, in which a long line is followed by a short line;   *strophe* Metrically-structured section of an ode; *antistrophe* Response to strophe.

[3] *The harp ... Alcaeus* Homer: ancient Greek poet, author of the *Iliad* and the *Odyssey*; Pindar (518?–c. 438 BCE) and Alcaeus (c. 620–c. 580 BCE): Greek lyric poets.

[4] *jewels in the crisped hair   Crisped* Wavy. From William Collins's "The Manners: An Ode"; Hazlitt substitutes "the" for "his."

[5] *diadem* Jeweled crown.

[6] *a sense ... field* From Wordsworth's "To My Sister" 6–8.

[7] *Beneath ... destiny* From *The Excursion* 6.553–57; the first line should read: "Amid the groves, under the shadowy hills."

[8] *vain pomp ... ye* From Shakespeare's *Henry VIII* 3.2.365: "Vain pomp and glory of this world, I hate ye!"

that recall the most pleasing and eventful circumstances of his life. But to the author of the *Lyrical Ballads*, nature is a kind of home; and he may be said to take a personal interest in the universe. There is no image so insignificant that it has not in some mood or other found the way into his heart: no sound that does not awaken the memory of other years.—

> To him the meanest flower that blows can give
> Thoughts that do often lie too deep for tears.[1]

The daisy looks up to him with sparkling eye as an old acquaintance: the cuckoo haunts him with sounds of early youth not to be expressed: a linnet's nest startles him with boyish delight: an old withered thorn is weighed down with a heap of recollections: a grey cloak, seen on some wild moor, torn by the wind, or drenched in the rain, afterwards becomes an object of imagination to him: even the lichens on the rock have a life and being in his thoughts. He has described all these objects in a way and with an intensity of feeling that no one else had done before him, and has given a new view or aspect of nature. He is in this sense the most original poet now living, and the one whose writings could the least be spared: for they have no substitute elsewhere. The vulgar do not read them, the learned, who see all things through books, do not understand them, the great despise, the fashionable may ridicule them: but the author has created himself an interest in the heart of the retired and lonely student of nature, which can never die. Persons of this class will still continue to feel what he has felt: he has expressed what they might in vain wish to express, except with glistening eye and faultering tongue! There is a lofty philosophic tone, a thoughtful humanity, infused into his pastoral vein. Remote from the passions and events of the great world, he has communicated interest and dignity to the primal movements of the heart of man, and ingrafted his own conscious reflections on the casual thoughts of hinds[2] and shepherds. Nursed amidst the grandeur of mountain scenery, he has stooped to have a nearer view of the daisy under his feet, or plucked a branch of white-thorn from the spray: but in describing it, his mind seems imbued with the majesty and solemnity of the objects around him—the tall rock lifts its head in the erectness of his spirit; the cataract roars in the sound of his verse; and in its dim and mysterious meaning, the mists seem to gather in the hollows of Helvellyn, and the forked Skiddaw[3] hovers in the distance. There is little mention of mountainous scenery in Mr. Wordsworth's poetry; but by internal evidence one might be almost sure that it was written in a mountainous country, from its bareness, its simplicity, its loftiness and its depth!

His later philosophic productions have a somewhat different character. They are a departure from, a dereliction of his first principles. They are classical and courtly. They are polished in style, without being gaudy; dignified in subject, without affectation. They seem to have been composed not in a cottage at Grasmere,[4] but among the half-inspired groves and stately recollections of Cole-Orton.[5] We might allude in particular, for examples of what we mean, to the lines on a Picture by Claude Lorraine,[6] and to the exquisite poem, entitled *Laodamia*. The last of these breathes the pure spirit of the finest fragments of antiquity—the sweetness, the gravity, the strength, the beauty and the languor of death—

> Calm contemplation and majestic pains.[7]

Its glossy brilliancy arises from the perfection of the finishing, like that of careful sculpture, not from gaudy colouring—the texture of the thoughts has the smoothness and solidity of marble. It is a poem that might be read aloud in Elysium,[8] and the spirits of departed heroes and sages would gather round to listen to it! Mr. Wordsworth's philosophic poetry, with a less glowing aspect and less tumult in the veins than Lord Byron's on

1 *To him ... tears* From Wordsworth's "Ode: Intimations of Immortality from Recollections of Early Childhood" 11.203; Hazlitt substitutes "him" for "me."

2 *hinds* Deer.

3 *Helvellyn ... Skiddaw* Mountains in England's Lake District.

4 *Grasmere* Wordsworth's home in the Lake District.

5 *Cole-Orton* Coleorton, a village in Leicestershire.

6 *Claude Lorraine* Baroque painter (c. 1600–82).

7 *Calm ... pains* From "Laodamia" 72: "Calm pleasures there abide—majestic pains."

8 *Elysium* Paradise.

similar occasions, bends a calmer and keener eye on morality; the impression, if less vivid, is more pleasing and permanent; and we confess it (perhaps it is a want of taste and proper feeling) that there are lines and poems of our author's, that we think of ten times for once that we recur to any of Lord Byron's.[1] Or if there are any of the latter's writings, that we can dwell upon in the same way, that is, as lasting and heart-felt sentiments, it is when laying aside his usual pomp and pretension, he descends with Mr. Wordsworth to the common ground of a disinterested humanity. It may be considered as characteristic of our poet's writings, that they either make no impression on the mind at all, seem mere *nonsense-verses*, or that they leave a mark behind them that never wears out. They either

> Fall blunted from the indurated breast—[2]

without any perceptible result, or they absorb it like a passion. To one class of readers he appears sublime, to another (and we fear the largest) ridiculous. He has probably realised Milton's wish,—"and fit audience found, though few";[3] but we suspect he is not reconciled to the alternative. There are delightful passages in the EXCURSION, both of natural description and of inspired reflection (passages of the latter kind that in the sound of the thoughts and of the swelling language resemble heavenly symphonies, mournful *requiems* over the grave of human hopes); but we must add, in justice and in sincerity, that we think it impossible that this work should ever become popular, even in the same degree as the *Lyrical Ballads*. It affects a system without having any intelligible clue to one; and instead of unfolding a principle in various and striking lights, repeats the same conclusions till they become flat and insipid. Mr. Wordsworth's mind is obtuse, except as it is the organ and the receptacle of accumulated feelings; it is not analytic, but synthetic; it is reflecting, rather than theoretical. The EXCURSION, we believe, fell still-born from the press. There was something abortive, and clumsy, and ill-judged in the attempt. It was long and laboured. The personages, for the most part, were low, the fare rustic: the plan raised expectations which were not fulfilled, and the effect was like being ushered into a stately hall and invited to sit down to a splendid banquet in the company of clowns, and with nothing but successive courses of apple-dumplings served up. It was not even *toujours perdrix*![4]

Mr. Wordsworth, in his person, is above the middle size, with marked features, and an air somewhat stately and Quixotic. He reminds one of some of Holbein's heads,[5] grave, saturnine, with a slight indication of sly humour, kept under by the manners of the age or by the pretensions of the person. He has a peculiar sweetness in his smile, and great depth and manliness and a rugged harmony, in the tones of his voice. His manner of reading his own poetry is particularly imposing; and in his favourite passages his eye beams with preternatural lustre, and the meaning labours slowly up from his swelling breast. No one who has seen him at these moments could go away with an impression that he was a "man of no mark or likelihood."[6] Perhaps the comment of his face and voice is necessary to convey a full idea of his poetry. His language may not be intelligible, but his manner is not to be mistaken. It is clear that he is either mad or inspired. In company, even in a *tête-à-tête*,[7] Mr. Wordsworth is often silent, indolent, and reserved. If he is become verbose and oracular of late years, he was not so in his better days. He threw out a bold or an indifferent remark without either effort or pretension, and relapsed into musing again. He shone most (because he seemed most roused and animated) in reciting his own poetry, or in talking about it. He sometimes gave striking views of his feelings and trains of association in composing certain passages; or if one did not always understand his distinctions, still there was no want of interest—there was a latent meaning worth inquiring into, like a vein of ore that one cannot exactly hit upon at the moment, but of which there are

---

[1] *Byron's* The poems of George Gordon, Lord Byron (1788–1824).

[2] *Fall ... breast* From Oliver Goldsmith's "The Traveller" 232: "Falls blunted from each indurated heart."

[3] *"and fit ... few"* From Milton's *Paradise Lost* 7.30–1: "govern thou my Song, / Urania, and fit audience find, though few."

[4] *toujours perdrix* "Always partridge"; too much of the same thing.

[5] *Holbein's heads* The portraits of Hans Holbein (1497–1543).

[6] *"man ... likelihood"* From Shakespeare's *1 Henry IV*, 3.2.45: "A fellow of no mark no likelihood."

[7] *tête-à-tête* Private conversation between two people.

sure indications. His standard of poetry is high and severe, almost to exclusiveness. He admits of nothing below, scarcely of any thing above himself. It is fine to hear him talk of the way in which certain subjects should have been treated by eminent poets, according to his notions of the art. Thus he finds fault with Dryden's description of Bacchus in the *Alexander's Feast*, as if he were a mere good-looking youth, or boon companion—

Flushed with a purple grace, He shows his honest face—[1]

instead of representing the God returning from the conquest of India, crowned with vine-leaves, and drawn by panthers, and followed by troops of satyrs, of wild men and animals that he had tamed. You would think, in hearing him speak on this subject, that you saw Titian's picture of the meeting of *Bacchus and Ariadne*—so classic were his conceptions, so glowing his style. Milton is his great idol, and he sometimes dares to compare himself with him. His sonnets, indeed, have something of the same high-raised tone and prophetic spirit. Chaucer is another prime favourite of his, and he has been at the pains to modernize some of the Canterbury Tales. Those persons who look upon Mr. Wordsworth as a merely puerile writer, must be rather at a loss to account for his strong predilection for such geniuses as Dante and Michelangelo.[2] We do not think our author has any very cordial sympathy with Shakespeare. How should he? Shakespeare was the least of an egotist of any body in the world. He does not much relish the variety and scope of dramatic composition. "He hates those interlocutions between Lucius and Caius." Yet Mr. Wordsworth himself wrote a tragedy when he was young; and we have heard the following energetic lines quoted from it, as put into the mouth of a person smit with remorse for some rash crime:

　　—Action is momentary,
　　The motion of a muscle this way or that;
　　Suffering is long, obscure, and infinite![3]

Perhaps for want of light and shade, and the unshackled spirit of the drama, this performance was never brought forward. Our critic has a great dislike to Gray, and a fondness for Thomson and Collins. It is mortifying to hear him speak of Pope and Dryden,[4] whom, because they have been supposed to have all the possible excellences of poetry, he will allow to have none. Nothing, however, can be fairer, or more amusing, than the way in which he sometimes exposes the unmeaning verbiage of modern poetry. Thus, in the beginning of Dr. Johnson's *Vanity of Human Wishes*—

　　Let observation with extensive view
　　Survey mankind from China to Peru[5]

he says there is a total want of imagination accompanying the words, the same idea is repeated three times under the disguise of a different phraseology: it comes to this—"let *observation*, with extensive *observation, observe mankind*"; or take away the first line, and the second,

　　Survey mankind from China to Peru.

literally conveys the whole. Mr. Wordsworth is, we must say, a perfect Drawcansir[6] as to prose writers. He complains of the dry reasoners and matter-of-fact people for their want of *passion*; and he is jealous of the rhetorical declaimers and rhapsodists as trenching on the province of poetry. He condemns all French writers (as well of poetry as prose) in the lump. His list in this way is indeed small. He approves of Walton's Angler, Paley,[7] and some other writers of an inoffensive modesty of pretension. He also likes books of voyages and travels, and Robinson Crusoe.[8] In art, he greatly esteems Be-

dark."

[1]　*Flushed ... face*　From John Dryden's "Alexander's Feast," 3.5–6.

[2]　*Dante* Alighieri Dante (1265–1321); *Michelangelo* Michelangelo Buonarroti (1475–1564).

[3]　*Action ... infinite!* From Wordsworth's play *The Borderers*: "Action is transitory—a step, a blow, / The motion of a muscle—this way or that— /... / Suffering is permanent, obscure and

[4]　*Gray... Dryden*　Poets Thomas Gray (1716–71), James Thomson (1700–48), William Collins (1721–59), Alexander Pope (1688–1744), John Dryden (1631–1700).

[5]　*Let ... Peru*　"The Vanity of Human Wishes" 1–2.

[6]　*Drawcansir*　Bully, from a character in George Villiers's play *The Rehearsal*.

[7]　*Walton's Angler*　Izaak Walton's *The Compleat Angler* (1653); *Paley* William Paley (1743–1805), philosopher and theologian.

[8]　*Robinson Crusoe*　Novel by Daniel Defoe (1660–1731).

wick's woodcuts, and Waterloo's[1] sylvan etchings. But he sometimes takes a higher tone, and gives his mind fair play. We have known him enlarge with a noble intelligence and enthusiasm on Nicolas Poussin's fine landscape-compositions, pointing out the unity of design that pervades them, the superintending mind, the imaginative principle that brings all to bear on the same end; and declaring he would not give a rush for any landscape that did not express the time of day, the climate, the period of the world it was meant to illustrate, or had not this character of *wholeness* in it. His eye also does justice to Rembrandt's[2] fine and masterly effects. In the way in which that artist works something out of nothing, and transforms the stump of a tree, a common figure into an *ideal* object, by the gorgeous light and shade thrown upon it, he perceives an analogy to his own mode of investing the minute details of nature with an atmosphere of sentiment; and in pronouncing Rembrandt to be a man of genius, feels that he strengthens his own claim to the title. It has been said of Mr. Wordsworth, that "he hates conchology, that he hates the Venus of Medicis."[3] But these, we hope, are mere epigrams and *jeux-d'esprit*,[4] as far from truth as they are free from malice; a sort of running satire or critical clenches—

> Where one for sense and one for rhyme
> Is quite sufficient at one time.[5]

We think, however, that if Mr. Wordsworth had been a more liberal and candid critic, he would have been a more sterling writer. If a greater number of sources of pleasure had been open to him, he would have communicated pleasure to the world more frequently. Had he been less fastidious in pronouncing sentence on the works of others, his own would have been received more favourably, and treated more leniently. The current of his feelings is deep, but narrow; the range of his understanding is lofty and aspiring rather than discursive. The force, the originality, the absolute truth and identity with which he feels some things, makes him indifferent to so many others. The simplicity and enthusiasm of his feelings, with respect to nature, renders him bigotted and intolerant in his judgments of men and things. But it happens to him, as to others, that his strength lies in his weakness; and perhaps we have no right to complain. We might get rid of the cynic and the egotist, and find in his stead a common place man. We should "take the good the Gods provide us":[6] a fine and original vein of poetry is not one of their most contemptible gifts, and the rest is scarcely worth thinking of, except as it may be a mortification to those who expect perfection from human nature; or who have been idle enough at some period of their lives, to deify men of genius as possessing claims above it. But this is a chord that jars, and we shall not dwell upon it.

Lord Byron we have called, according to the old proverb, "the spoiled child of fortune":[7] Mr. Wordsworth might plead, in mitigation of some peculiarities, that he is "the spoiled child of disappointment." We are convinced, if he had been early a popular poet, he would have borne his honours meekly, and would have been a person of great *bonhommie*[8] and frankness of disposition. But the sense of injustice and of undeserved ridicule sours the temper and narrows the views. To have produced works of genius, and to find them neglected or treated with scorn, is one of the heaviest trials of human patience. We exaggerate our own merits when they are denied by others, and are apt to grudge and cavil[9] at every particle of praise bestowed on those to whom we feel a conscious superiority. In mere self-defence we turn against the world, when it turns against us; brood over the undeserved slights we receive; and thus the genial current of the soul is stopped, or vents itself in effusions of petulance and self-conceit. Mr.

---

[1] *Bewick* Thomas Bewick (1753–1828); *Waterloo* Anthonie Waterloo (1610–90).

[2] *Rembrandt* Rembrandt Harmenszoon van Rijn (1606–69).

[3] *"he hates ... Medicis"* Referring to Sandro Botticelli's painting *The Birth of Venus*, in which Venus is standing on a scallop shell.

[4] *jeux-d'esprit* Witticisms.

[5] *Where ... time* From Samuel Butler's *Hudibras* 2.1.29–30: "For one for sense, and one for rhyme, / I think's sufficient at one time."

[6] *"take ... provide us"* From Plautus's play *Rudens* 4.7.3: "If you are wise, be wise; keep what goods the gods provide you."

[7] *"spoiled child of fortune"* From the Latin *"fortunae filius."* After Byron's death in 1824, Thomas Moore wrote: "[Byron] was truly a spoiled child, not merely the spoiled child of his parent, but the spoiled child of nature, the spoiled child of fortune, the spoiled child of fame, the spoiled child of society."

[8] *bonhommie* Pleasant nature.

[9] *cavil* Quibble.

Wordsworth has thought too much of contemporary critics and criticism; and less than he ought of the award of posterity, and of the opinion, we do not say of private friends, but of those who were made so by their admiration of his genius. He did not court popularity by a conformity to established models, and he ought not to have been surprised that his originality was not understood as a matter of course. He has *gnawed too much on the bridle*; and has often thrown out crusts to the critics, in mere defiance or as a point of honour when he was challenged, which otherwise his own good sense would have withheld. We suspect that Mr. Wordsworth's feelings are a little morbid in this respect, or that he resents censure more than he is gratified by praise. Otherwise, the tide has turned much in his favour of late years—he has a large body of determined partisans—and is at present sufficiently in request with the public to save or relieve him from the last necessity to which a man of genius can be reduced—that of becoming the God of his own idolatry!

—1825

Thomas De Quincey
1785 – 1859

Because he published his first essay in 1821, Thomas De Quincey appears to be a contemporary of Byron, Shelley, and Keats. The sensational title of his most famous work, *Confessions of an English Opium-Eater*, adds to the case for associating him with these later Romantics. For his elegant and introspective style, however, De Quincey is better compared with Wordsworth and Coleridge, the earlier Romantics he so admired, as well as with the other major essayists of his time, Lamb and Hazlitt. Written in installments for one of the magazines popular in the day, *Confessions* was one of

the first pieces De Quincey submitted, and it brought him immediate notoriety and success. Citing St. Augustine and Rousseau as predecessors of his autobiographical "impassioned prose," De Quincey at times wrote lovingly about his addiction: "If opium-eating be a sensual pleasure, and if I am bound to confess that I have indulged in it to an excess not yet *recorded* of any other man, it is no less true that I have struggled against this fascinating enthralment with a religious zeal, and have at length accomplished what I never yet heard attributed to any other man—have untwisted, almost to its final links, the accursed chain which fettered me." Whether he ever became unfettered is in question—De Quincey seems to have remained hopelessly addicted his entire adult life—but he went on to write hundreds of essays on subjects as diverse as German philosophy and literature, Shakespearean drama, the French Revolution, economics, Christianity, and the California gold rush.

De Quincey was born in Manchester in 1785 to Elizabeth Penson and Thomas Quincey, a successful linen merchant. One of eight children, he had already experienced the loss of two sisters by the time of his father's early death in 1793. Even though these events made for a troubled childhood, De Quincey gained a reputation as a precocious student and scholar. In 1796 he entered Bath Grammar School, where he became fluent in Latin and Greek despite what he considered his ineffectual teachers. He later wrote that a headmaster once said of his brilliance as a Greek scholar, "That boy could harangue an Athenian mob better than you and I could address an English one."

In 1802 De Quincey fled the school with the thought of presenting himself to Wordsworth, whose *Lyrical Ballads* he had greatly admired. Instead he embarked on a tour of Wales and eventually arrived in London, hungry and destitute. These years, although difficult, were fodder for some of his most vivid recollections. In the *Confessions*, for example, De Quincey often recalls his relationship with a prostitute named Ann, who had befriended and housed him in London. A year later, he returned to his family and enrolled in Worcester College, Oxford, where he became known as a solitary but brilliant scholar. During his college years, he began taking laudanum—the liquid form of opium—for a toothache, and for a number of years his habit was kept under control. In 1807 he once again quit school, this time on the brink of examinations for which he had appeared to be extremely well-prepared.

De Quincey came to know Coleridge during his university years, and through Coleridge he met his idol, Wordsworth. The attraction was such that De Quincey settled in Grasmere in order to be near both poets, eventually moving into Dove Cottage, the Wordsworths' home, when Dorothy and

William moved into a larger house. After years of close friendship, De Quincey became estranged from the Wordsworths when his addiction became uncontrollable and when he chose to live out of wedlock with Margaret Simpson, a local farmer's daughter. The couple married in 1816 after the birth of their son. They eventually had eight children together during their twenty-one years of marriage.

Again destitute, De Quincey moved his family to London and began publishing the *Confessions* anonymously in *The London Magazine*. His "spiritual autobiography" is in part a paean to the glories of opium—"Thou hast the keys of Paradise, oh just, subtle, and mighty opium!"—and in part a record of the nightmares and dream visions he experienced as an addict. (He influenced both Edgar Allan Poe and Charles Baudelaire, not only in their writing, but also in their use of the drug.)

De Quincey had a sense of the importance of dreams and the unconscious that was remarkable for his time. "I feel assured," he wrote in *Confessions*, "that there is no such thing as *forgetting* possible to the mind; a thousand accidents may, and will, interpose a veil between our present consciousness and the secret inscriptions on the mind. Accidents of the same sort will also rend away this veil; but alike, whether veiled or unveiled, the inscription remains forever." De Quincey later penned *Suspiria de Profundis* (1845), a sequel to the *Confessions* in which he wrote about his dreams with considerable psychological acuity; many regard his ideas as precursors to Freud's dream theories.

Although his lifestyle was anything but conservative, the political and moral conservatism of many of his ideas was deep-seated. He was also a talented humorist, as his 1827 essay "On Murder Considered as One of the Fine Arts" well illustrates. De Quincey delineates how "drinking and Sabbath-breaking" and eventual "incivility and procrastination" follows on the "downward path" from murder. "Many a man," De Quincey writes, "dated his ruin from some murder or other that perhaps he thought little of at the time."

In the 1850s De Quincey began compiling the fourteen-volume series *Selections Grave and Gay from Writings Published and Unpublished*, which was completed in 1860, a year after his death. In the words of a review written shortly afterward in London's *Quarterly Review*, "The position of De Quincey in the literature of the present day is remarkable. We might search in vain for a writer who, with equal powers, has made an equally slight impression upon the general public. His style is superb; his powers of reasoning are unsurpassed; his imagination is warm and brilliant, and his humor … delicate." The past few decades have seen a surge of interest in De Quincey and his *Confessions of an English Opium-Eater*, which has struck a chord with many who have similarly experienced isolation and alienation from society.

⌘ ⌘ ⌘

from *Confessions of an English Opium-Eater*

TO THE READER

I here present you, courteous reader, with the record of a remarkable period in my life; according to my application of it, I trust that it will prove not merely an interesting record, but in a considerable degree useful and instructive. In *that* hope it is that I have drawn it up; and *that* must be my apology for breaking through that delicate and honourable reserve which, for the most part, restrains us from the public exposure of our own errors and infirmities. Nothing, indeed, is more revolting to English feelings than the spectacle of a human being obtruding on our notice his moral ulcers or scars, and tearing away that "decent drapery"[1] which time or indulgence to human frailty may have drawn over them; accordingly, the greater part of *our* confessions (that is, spontaneous and extra-judicial confessions) proceed

---

[1] *"decent drapery"* From Edmund Burke's *Reflections on the Revolution in France* (1790): "All the pleasing illusions … are to be dissolved by this new conquering empire of light and reason. All the decent drapery of life is to be rudely torn off."

from demi-reps,[1] adventurers, or swindlers; and for any such acts of gratuitous self-humiliation from those who can be supposed in sympathy with the decent and self-respecting part of society, we must look to French literature, or to that part of the German which is tainted with the spurious and defective sensibility of the French. All this I feel so forcibly, and so nervously am I alive to reproach of this tendency, that I have for many months hesitated about the propriety of allowing this or any part of my narrative to come before the public eye until after my death (when, for many reasons, the whole will be published); and it is not without an anxious review of the reasons for and against this step that I have at last concluded on taking it.

Guilt and misery shrink, by a natural instinct, from public notice; they court privacy and solitude; and even in their choice of a grave will sometimes sequester themselves from the general population of the church-yard, as if declining to claim fellowship with the great family of man, and wishing (in the affecting language of Mr. Wordsworth)

> —humbly to express
> A penitential loneliness.[2]

It is well, upon the whole, and for the interest of us all, that it should be so; nor would I willingly in my own person manifest a disregard of such salutary feelings, nor in act or word do anything to weaken them; but, on the one hand, as my self-accusation does not amount to a confession of guilt, so, on the other, it is possible that, if it *did*, the benefit resulting to others from the record of an experience purchased at so heavy a price might compensate, by a vast overbalance, for any violence done to the feelings I have noticed, and justify a breach of the general rule. Infirmity and misery do not of necessity imply guilt. They approach or recede from shades of that dark alliance, in proportion to the probable motives and prospects of the offender, and the palliations,[3] known or secret, of the offence, in proportion as the temptations to it were potent from the first, and the resistance to it, in act or in effort, was earnest to the last.

For my own part, without breach of truth or modesty, I may affirm that my life has been, on the whole, the life of a philosopher; from my birth I was made an intellectual creature, and intellectual in the highest sense my pursuits and pleasures have been, even from my school-boy days. If opium-eating be a sensual pleasure, and if I am bound to confess that I have indulged in it to an excess not yet *recorded*[4] of any other man, it is no less true that I have struggled against this fascinating enthralment with a religious zeal, and have at length accomplished what I never yet heard attributed to any other man—have untwisted, almost to its final links, the accursed chain which fettered me. Such a self-conquest may reasonably be set off in counterbalance to any kind or degree of self-indulgence. Not to insist that in my case the self-conquest was unquestionable, the self-indulgence open to doubts of casuistry,[5] according as that name shall be extended to acts aiming at the bare relief of pain, or shall be restricted to such as aim at the excitement of positive pleasure.

Guilt, therefore, I do not acknowledge; and if I did, it is possible that I might still resolve on the present act of confession in consideration of the service which I may thereby render to the whole class of opium-eaters. But who are they? Reader, I am sorry to say a very numerous class indeed. Of this I became convinced some years ago by computing at that time the number of those in one small class of English society (the class of men distinguished for talents, or of eminent station) who were known to me, directly or indirectly, as opium-eaters; such, for instance, as the eloquent and benevolent ——,[6] the late Dean of ——, Lord ——, Mr. —— the philosopher, a late Under-Secretary of State (who described to me the sensation which first drove him to the use of opium in the very same words as the Dean of ——, viz.,[7] "that he felt as though rats were gnawing and abrading the coats of his stomach"), Mr. ——, and

---

[1] *demi-reps* Women of dubious character.

[2] *humbly ... loneliness* From Wordsworth's "The White Doe of Rylstone, or The Fate of the Nortons" (176–77): "[G]uilt, that humbly would express / A penitential loneliness."

[3] *palliations* Concealment or alleviation of symptoms.

[4] [De Quincey's note] "Not yet *recorded*," I say; for there is one celebrated man of the present day, who, if all be true which is reported of him, has greatly exceeded me in quantity. [De Quincey is referring to Samuel Taylor Coleridge.]

[5] *casuistry* Specious rationalization used to determine morality.

[6] *benevolent*—— De Quincey entered the full names in his 1856 revision to the *Confessions*, saying that the editor of the original version deleted the names.

[7] *viz.* I.e., *Le videlicet*. Latin: that is to say.

many others hardly less known, whom it would be tedious to mention. Now, if one class, comparatively so limited, could furnish so many scores of cases (and that within the knowledge of one single inquirer), it was a natural inference that the entire population of England would furnish a proportionable number. The soundness of this inference, however, I doubted, until some facts became known to me which satisfied me that it was not incorrect. I will mention two.

(1) Three respectable London druggists, in widely remote quarters of London, from whom I happened lately to be purchasing small quantities of opium, assured me that the number of amateur opium-eaters (as I may term them) was at this time immense; and that the difficulty of distinguishing those persons to whom habit had rendered opium necessary from such as were purchasing it with a view to suicide, occasioned them daily trouble and disputes. This evidence respected London only. But,

(2) —which will possibly surprise the reader more— some years ago, on passing through Manchester, I was informed by several cotton manufacturers that their workpeople were rapidly getting into the practice of opium-eating, so much so, that on a Saturday afternoon the counters of the druggists were strewed with pills of one, two, or three grains, in preparation for the known demand of the evening. The immediate occasion of this practice was the lowness of wages, which at that time would not allow them to indulge in ale or spirits, and wages rising, it may be thought that this practice would cease; but as I do not readily believe that any man having once tasted the divine luxuries of opium will afterwards descend to the gross and mortal enjoyments of alcohol, I take it for granted

That those eat now who never ate before;
And those who always ate, now eat the more.

Indeed, the fascinating powers of opium are admitted even by medical writers, who are its greatest enemies. Thus, for instance, Awsiter, apothecary to Greenwich Hospital, in his "Essay on the Effects of Opium" (published in the year 1763), when attempting to explain why Mead[1] had not been sufficiently explicit on the properties, counteragents, &c., of this drug, expresses himself in the following mysterious terms (φωνάντα συνετοισ[2]): "Perhaps he thought the subject of too delicate a nature to be made common; and as many people might then indiscriminately use it, it would take from that necessary fear and caution which should prevent their experiencing the extensive power of this drug, *for there are many properties in it, if universally known, that would habituate the use, and make it more in request with us than with Turks themselves*, the result of which knowledge," he adds, "must prove a general misfortune." In the necessity of this conclusion I do not altogether concur; but upon that point I shall have occasion to speak at the close of my Confessions, where I shall present the reader with the moral of my narrative.

PRELIMINARY CONFESSIONS

These preliminary confessions, or introductory narrative of the youthful adventures which laid the foundation of the writer's habit of opium-eating in afterlife, it has been judged proper to premise, for three several reasons:

1. As forestalling that question, and giving it a satisfactory answer, which else would painfully obtrude itself in the course of the Opium Confessions—"How came any reasonable being to subject himself to such a yoke of misery; voluntarily to incur a captivity so servile, and knowingly to fetter himself with such a sevenfold chain?"—a question which, if not somewhere plausibly resolved, could hardly fail, by the indignation which it would be apt to raise as against an act of wanton folly, to interfere with that degree of sympathy which is necessary in any case to an author's purposes.

2. As furnishing a key to some parts of that tremendous scenery which afterwards peopled the dreams of the opium-eater.

3. As creating some previous interest of a personal sort in the confessing subject, apart from the matter of the confessions, which cannot fail to render the confessions themselves more interesting. If a man "whose talk is of oxen" should become an opium-eater, the probability is that (if he is not too dull to dream at all) he will dream about oxen; whereas, in the case before him, the reader will find that the opium-eater boasteth himself to be a philosopher, and accordingly, that the phantasma-

---

[1] *Mead* Dr. Richard Mead (1673–1754), said to be the leading physician of the age, whose patients included Queen Anne and Sir Isaac Newton.

[2] φωνάντα συνετοισ Greek: speaking to the wise.

goria of *his* dreams (waking or sleeping, daydreams or nightdreams) is suitable to one who in that character

Humani nihil a se alienum putat.[1]

For amongst the conditions which he deems indispensable to the sustaining of any claim to the title of philosopher is not merely the possession of a superb intellect in its *analytic* functions (in which part of the pretensions, however, England can for some generations show but few claimants; at least, he is not aware of any known candidate for this honour who can be styled emphatically *a subtle thinker*, with the exception of Samuel Taylor Coleridge, and in a narrower department of thought with the recent illustrious exception[2] of David Ricardo[3]) but also on such a constitution of the *moral* faculties as shall give him an inner eye and power of intuition for the vision and the mysteries of our human nature: *that* constitution of faculties, in short, which (amongst all the generations of men that from the beginning of time have deployed into life, as it were, upon this planet) our English poets have possessed in the highest degree, and Scottish professors[4] in the lowest. ...

from PART 2

THE PLEASURES OF OPIUM

It is so long since I first took opium that if it had been a trifling incident in my life I might have forgotten its date; but cardinal events are not to be forgotten, and from circumstances connected with it I remember that it must be referred to the autumn of 1804. During that season I was in London, having come thither for the first time since my entrance at college. And my introduction to opium arose in the following way. From an early age I had been accustomed to wash my head in cold water at least once a day; being suddenly seized with toothache, I attributed it to some relaxation caused by an accidental intermission of that practice, jumped out of bed, plunged my head into a basin of cold water, and with hair thus wetted went to sleep. The next morning, as I need hardly say, I awoke with excruciating rheumatic pains of the head and face, from which I had hardly any respite for about twenty days. On the twenty-first day I think it was, and on a Sunday, that I went out into the streets, rather to run away, if possible, from my torments, than with any distinct purpose. By accident I met a college acquaintance, who recommended opium. Opium! dread agent of unimaginable pleasure and pain! I had heard of it as I had of manna or of ambrosia,[5] but no further. How unmeaning a sound was it at that time; what solemn chords does it now strike upon my heart! what heart-quaking vibrations of sad and happy remembrances! Reverting for a moment to these, I feel a mystic importance attached to the minutest circumstances connected with the place and the time and the man (if man he was) that first laid open to me the Paradise of Opium-eaters. It was a Sunday afternoon, wet and cheerless, and a duller spectacle this earth of ours has not to show than a rainy Sunday in London. My road homewards lay through Oxford Street; and near "the stately Pantheon"[6] (as Mr. Wordsworth has obligingly called it) I saw a druggist's shop. The druggist—unconscious minister of celestial pleasures!—as if in sympathy with the rainy Sunday, looked dull and stupid, just as any mortal druggist might be expected to look on a Sunday; and when I asked for the tincture of opium, he gave it to me as any other man might do, and furthermore, out of my shilling returned me what seemed to be real copper halfpence, taken out of a real wooden drawer. Neverthe-

---

[1] *Humani ... putat* Latin: from Terence's *Heautontimorumenos* (163 BCE); translates to: He thinks that nothing that is human is alien to him.

[2] [De Quincey's note] A third exception might perhaps have been added; and my reason for not adding that exception is chiefly because it was only in his juvenile efforts that the writer whom I allude to [William Hazlitt] expressly addressed hints to philosophical themes; his riper powers having been all dedicated (on very excusable and very intelligible grounds, under the present direction of the popular mind in England) to criticism and the fine arts. This reason apart, however, I doubt whether he is not rather to be considered an acute thinker than a subtle one. It is, besides, a great drawback on his mastery over philosophical subjects that he has obviously not had the advantage of a regular scholastic education: he has not read Plato in his youth (which most likely was only his misfortune), but neither has he read Kant in his manhood (which is his fault).

[3] *David Ricardo* British political economist, author of *On the Principles of Political Economy, and Taxation* (1819).

[4] [De Quincey's note] I disclaim any allusion to *existing* professors, of whom indeed I know only one.

[5] *manna* Biblical food that saved the Jews in their escape from Egypt; *ambrosia* Food of the Greek gods.

[6] *"the stately Pantheon"* From Wordsworth's "Power of Music" (3); London's Pantheon was then a concert hall.

less, in spite of such indications of humanity, he has ever since existed in my mind as the beatific vision of an immortal druggist, sent down to earth on a special mission to myself. And it confirms me in this way of considering him, that when I next came up to London I sought him near the stately Pantheon, and found him not; and thus to me, who knew not his name (if indeed he had one), he seemed rather to have vanished from Oxford Street than to have removed in any bodily fashion. The reader may choose to think of him as possibly no more than a sublunary[1] druggist; it may be so, but my faith is better—I believe him to have evanesced,[2] or evaporated. So unwillingly would I connect any mortal remembrances with that hour, and place, and creature, that first brought me acquainted with the celestial drug.

Arrived at my lodgings, it may be supposed that I lost not a moment in taking the quantity prescribed. I was necessarily ignorant of the whole art and mystery of opium-taking, and what I took I took under every disadvantage. But I took it—and in an hour—oh, heavens! what a revulsion! what an upheaving, from its lowest depths, of inner spirit! what an apocalypse of the world within me! That my pains had vanished was now a trifle in my eyes; this negative effect was swallowed up in the immensity of those positive effects which had opened before me—in the abyss of divine enjoyment thus suddenly revealed. Here was a panacea, a φαρμακον νήωενθες[3] for all human woes; here was the secret of happiness, about which philosophers had disputed for so many ages, at once discovered; happiness

might now be bought for a penny, and carried in the waistcoat pocket; portable ecstacies might be had corked up in a pint bottle, and peace of mind could be sent down in gallons by the mail coach. But if I talk in this way the reader will think I am laughing, and I can assure him that nobody will laugh long who deals much with opium; its pleasures even are of a grave and solemn complexion, and in his happiest state the opium-eater cannot present himself in the character of L'Allegro; even then he speaks and thinks as becomes Il Penseroso.[4] Nevertheless, I have a very reprehensible way of jesting at times in the midst of my own misery; and unless when I am checked by some more powerful feelings, I am afraid I shall be guilty of this indecent practice even in these annals of suffering or enjoyment. The reader must allow a little to my infirm nature in this respect; and with a few indulgences of that sort I shall endeavour to be as grave, if not drowsy, as fits a theme like opium, so antimercurial as it really is, and so drowsy as it is falsely reputed.

And first, one word with respect to its bodily effects; for upon all that has been hitherto written on the subject of opium, whether by travellers in Turkey (who may plead their privilege of lying as an old immemorial right), or by professors of medicine, writing *ex cathedra*,[5] I have but one emphatic criticism to pronounce—Lies! lies! lies! I remember once, in passing a book stall, to have caught these words from a page of some satiric author: "By this time I became convinced that the London newspapers spoke truth at least twice a week, viz., on Tuesday and Saturday,[6] and might safely be depended upon for—the list of bankrupts." In like manner, I do by no means deny that some truths have been delivered to the world in regard to opium. Thus it has been repeatedly affirmed by the learned that opium is a dusky brown in colour; and this, take notice, I grant. Secondly, that it is rather dear, which also I grant, for in my time East Indian opium has been three guineas a pound, and Turkey eight. And thirdly, that if you eat a good deal of it, most probably you must do what is

---

[1]   *sublunary*   Earthly.

[2]   [De Quincey's note]   *Evanesced*: this way of going off the stage of life appears to have been well known in the 17th century, but at that time to have been considered a peculiar privilege of blood-royal, and by no means to be allowed to druggists. For about the year 1686 a poet of rather ominous name (and who, by-the-bye, did ample justice to his name), viz., Mr. *Flat-man*, in speaking of the death of Charles II expresses his surprise that any prince should commit so absurd an act as dying, because, says he, "Kings should disdain to die, and only *disappear*." They should *abscond*, that is, into the other world. [Cf. Thomas Flatman's *On the Death of our Late Sovereign Lord King Charles II of Blessed Memory: A Pindarique Ode* (1685): "*Princes* (like the wondrous *Enoch)* should be free / From death's unbounded tyranny, / And when their godlike race is run, / And nothing glorious left undone, / Never submit to fate, but only disappear."]

[3]   φαρμακον νήωενθες   Greek: soothing and healing drug.

[4]   *L'Allegro ... Il Penseroso*   Poems by Milton (1645), whose titles mean "The Happy Man" and "The Brooding Man" respectively.

[5]   *ex cathedra*   With authority (from the Latin, meaning, literally, "from the cathedral").

[6]   *Tuesday and Saturday*   Days on which the newspaper would publish a list of bankruptcies.

particularly disagreeable to any man of regular habits, viz., die.[1] These weighty propositions are, all and singular, true; I cannot gainsay them, and truth ever was, and will be, commendable. But in these three theorems I believe we have exhausted the stock of knowledge as yet accumulated by men on the subject of opium. And therefore, worthy doctors, as there seems to be room for further discoveries, stand aside, and allow me to come forward and lecture on this matter.

First, then, it is not so much affirmed as taken for granted, by all who ever mention opium, formally or incidentally, that it does or can produce intoxication. Now, reader, assure yourself, *meo perieulo*,[2] that no quantity of opium ever did or could intoxicate. As to the tincture of opium (commonly called laudanum) *that* might certainly intoxicate if a man could bear to take enough of it, but why? Because it contains so much proof spirit, and not because it contains so much opium. But crude opium, I affirm peremptorily, is incapable of producing any state of body at all resembling that which is produced by alcohol, and not in *degree* only incapable, but even in *kind*; it is not in the quantity of its effects merely, but in the quality, that it differs altogether. The pleasure given by wine is always mounting and tending to a crisis, after which it declines; that from opium, when once generated, is stationary for eight or ten hours: the first, to borrow a technical distinction from medicine, is a case of acute—the second, the chronic pleasure; the one is a flame, the other a steady and equable glow. But the main distinction lies in this, that whereas wine disorders the mental faculties, opium, on the contrary (if taken in a proper manner), introduces amongst them the most exquisite order, legislation, and harmony. Wine robs a man of his self-possession; opium greatly invigorates it. Wine unsettles and clouds the judgment, and gives a preternatural brightness and a vivid exaltation to the contempts and the admirations, the loves and the hatreds of the drinker; opium, on the contrary, communicates serenity and equipoise to all the faculties, active or passive, and with respect to the temper and moral feelings in general it gives simply that sort of vital warmth which is approved by the judgment, and which would probably always accompany a bodily constitution of primeval or antediluvian[3] health. Thus, for instance, opium, like wine, gives an expansion to the heart and the benevolent affections; but then, with this remarkable difference, that in the sudden development of kindheartedness which accompanies inebriation there is always more or less of a maudlin character, which exposes it to the contempt of the bystander. Men shake hands, swear eternal friendship, and shed tears, no mortal knows why; and the sensual creature is clearly uppermost. But the expansion of the benigner feelings incident to opium is no febrile access, but a healthy restoration to that state which the mind would naturally recover upon the removal of any deep-seated irritation of pain that had disturbed and quarrelled with the impulses of a heart originally just and good. True it is that even wine, up to a certain point and with certain men, rather tends to exalt and to steady the intellect; I myself, who have never been a great wine drinker, used to find that half a dozen glasses of wine advantageously affected the faculties—brightened and intensified the consciousness, and gave to the mind a feeling of being "*ponderibus librata suis*,"[4] and certainly it is most absurdly said, in popular language, of any man that he is *disguised* in liquor; for, on the contrary, most men are disguised by sobriety, and it is when they are drinking (as some old gentleman says in Athenaeus), that men ἑαυτοὺς ἐμφανίζουσιν οἵτινες εἰσίν—display themselves in their true complexion of character, which surely is not disguising themselves. But still, wine constantly leads a man to the brink of absurdity and extravagance, and beyond a certain point it is sure to volatilize and to disperse the intellectual energies, whereas opium always seems to compose what had been agitated, and to concentrate what had been distracted. In short, to sum up all in one word, a man who is inebriated, or tending to inebriation, is, and feels that he is, in a condition which calls up into supremacy the merely human, too often the brutal part of his nature;

---

[1] [De Quincey's note] Of this, however, the learned appear latterly to have doubted; for in a pirated edition of Buchan's *Domestic Medicine*, which I once saw in the hands of a farmer's wife, who was studying it for the benefit of her health, the doctor was made to say—"Be particularly careful never to take above five-and-twenty *ounces* of laudanum [the liquid form of opium] at once;" the true reading being probably five-and-twenty *drops*, which are held equal to about one grain of crude opium.

[2] *meo perieulo* Latin: at my risk.

[3] *antediluvian* Before the Biblical flood, hence primitive.

[4] "*ponderibus librata suis*" Latin: from Ovid's *Metamorphoses* (1.16): "[the earth, not] poised, did on its own foundations lie."

but the opium-eater (I speak of him who is not suffering from any disease or other remote effects of opium) feels that the diviner part of his nature is paramount; that is, the moral affections are in a state of cloudless serenity, and overall is the great light of the majestic intellect.

This is the doctrine of the true church on the subject of opium, of which church I acknowledge myself to be the only member—the alpha and the omega;[1] but then it is to be recollected that I speak from the ground of a large and profound personal experience, whereas most of the unscientific[2] authors who have at all treated of opium, and even of those who have written expressly on the *materia medica*, make it evident, from the horror they express of it, that their experimental knowledge of its action is none at all. I will, however, candidly acknowledge that I have met with one person who bore evidence to its intoxicating power, such as staggered my own incredulity, for he was a surgeon, and had himself taken opium largely. I happened to say to him that his enemies (as I had heard) charged him with talking nonsense on politics, and that his friends apologized for him by suggesting that he was constantly in a state of intoxication from opium. Now the accusation, said I, is not *prima facie*[3] and of necessity an absurd one; but the

defence *is*. To my surprise, however, he insisted that both his enemies and his friends were in the right. "I will maintain," said he, "that I *do* talk nonsense; and secondly, I will maintain that I do not talk nonsense upon principle, or with any view to profit, but solely and simply," said he, "solely and simply—solely and simply (repeating it three times over), because I am drunk with opium, and *that* daily." I replied that, as to the allegation of his enemies, as it seemed to be established upon such respectable testimony, seeing that the three parties concerned all agree in it, it did not become me to question it; but the defence set up I must demur to. He proceeded to discuss the matter, and to lay down his reasons; but it seemed to me so impolite to pursue an argument which must have presumed a man mistaken in a point belonging to his own profession, that I did not press him even when his course of argument seemed open to objection, not to mention that a man who talks nonsense, even though "with no view to profit," is not altogether the most agreeable partner in a dispute, whether as opponent or respondent. I confess, however, that the authority of a surgeon, and one who was reputed a good one, may seem a weighty one to my prejudice; but still I must plead my experience, which was greater than his greatest by 7,000 drops a day; and though it was not possible to suppose a medical man unacquainted with the characteristic symptoms of vinous intoxication, it yet struck me that he might proceed on a logical error of using the word intoxication with too great latitude, and extending it generically to all modes of nervous excitement, instead of restricting it as the expression for a specific sort of excitement connected with certain diagnostics. Some people have maintained in my hearing that they had been drunk upon green tea; and a medical student in London, for whose knowledge in his profession I have reason to feel great respect, assured me the other day that a patient in recovering from an illness had got drunk on a beefsteak.

Having dwelt so much on this first and leading error in respect to opium, I shall notice very briefly a second and a third, which are, that the elevation of spirits produced by opium is necessarily followed by a proportionate depression, and that the natural and even immediate consequence of opium is torpor and stagnation, animal and mental. The first of these errors I shall content myself with simply denying, assuring my reader

1   *the alpha and the omega*   The beginning and the end; from the first and last letters of the Greek alphabet.

2   [De Quincey's note]   Amongst the great herd of travellers, &c., who show sufficiently by their stupidity that they never held any intercourse with opium, I must caution my readers specially against the brilliant author [Thomas Hope] of *Anastasius* [(1819)]. This gentleman, whose wit would lead one to presume him an opium-eater, has made it impossible to consider him in that character, from the grievous misrepresentation which he gives of its effects at pp. 215–17 of vol. 1. Upon consideration it must appear such to the author himself, for, waiving the errors I have insisted on in the text, which (and others) are adopted in the fullest manner, he will himself admit that an old gentleman "with a snow-white beard," who eats "ample doses of opium," and is yet able to deliver what is meant and received as very weighty counsel on the bad effects of that practice, is but an indifferent evidence that opium either kills people prematurely or sends them into a madhouse. But for my part, I see into this old gentleman and his motives: the fact is, he was enamoured of "the little golden receptacle of the pernicious drug" which Anastasius carried about him; and no way of obtaining it so safe and so feasible occurred as that of frightening its owner out of his wits (which, by the bye, are none of the strongest). This commentary throws a new light upon the case, and greatly improves it as a story; for the old gentleman's speech, considered as a lecture on pharmacy, is highly absurd; but considered as a hoax on Anastasius, it reads excellently.

3   *prima facie*   Latin: on first impressions.

that for ten years, during which I took opium at intervals, the day succeeding to that on which I allowed myself this luxury was always a day of unusually good spirits.

With respect to the torpor supposed to follow, or rather (if we were to credit the numerous pictures of Turkish opium-eaters) to accompany the practice of opium-eating, I deny that also. Certainly opium is classed under the head of narcotics, and some such effect it may produce in the end; but the primary effects of opium are always, and in the highest degree, to excite and stimulate the system. This first stage of its action always lasted with me, during my noviciate, for upwards of eight hours, so that it must be the fault of the opium-eater himself if he does not so time his exhibition of the dose (to speak medically) as that the whole weight of its narcotic influence may descend upon his sleep. Turkish opium-eaters, it seems, are absurd enough to sit, like so many equestrian statues, on logs of wood as stupid as themselves. But that the reader may judge of the degree in which opium is likely to stupefy the faculties of an Englishman, I shall (by way of treating the question illustratively, rather than argumentatively) describe the way in which I myself often passed an opium evening in London during the period between 1804–1812. It will be seen that at least opium did not move me to seek solitude, and much less to seek inactivity, or the torpid state of self-involution ascribed to the Turks. I give this account at the risk of being pronounced a crazy enthusiast or visionary, but I regard *that* little. I must desire my reader to bear in mind that I was a hard student, and at severe studies for all the rest of my time; and certainly I had a right occasionally to relaxations as well as other people. These, however, I allowed myself but seldom. ...

Thus I have shown that opium does not of necessity produce inactivity or torpor, but that, on the contrary, it often led me into markets and theatres. Yet, in candour, I will admit that markets and theatres are not the appropriate haunts of the opium-eater when in the divinest state incident to his enjoyment. In that state, crowds become an oppression to him; music even, too sensual and gross. He naturally seeks solitude and silence, as indispensable conditions of those trances, or profoundest reveries, which are the crown and consummation of what opium can do for human nature. I, whose disease it was to meditate too much and to observe too little, and who upon my first entrance at college was nearly falling into a deep melancholy, from brooding too much on the sufferings which I had witnessed in London, was sufficiently aware of the tendencies of my own thoughts to do all I could to counteract them. I was, indeed, like a person who, according to the old legend, had entered the cave of Trophonius;[1] and the remedies I sought were to force myself into society, and to keep my understanding in continual activity upon matters of science. But for these remedies I should certainly have become hypochondriacally melancholy. In after years, however, when my cheerfulness was more fully re-established, I yielded to my natural inclination for a solitary life. And at that time I often fell into these reveries upon taking opium; and more than once it has happened to me, on a summer night, when I have been at an open window, in a room from which I could overlook the sea at a mile below me, and could command a view of the great town of L———, at about the same distance, that I have sat from sunset to sunrise, motionless, and without wishing to move. ...

INTRODUCTION TO THE PAINS OF OPIUM

... I remember about this time a little incident, which I mention because, trifling as it was, the reader will soon meet it again in my dreams, which it influenced more fearfully than could be imagined. One day a Malay[2] knocked at my door. What business a Malay could have to transact amongst English mountains I cannot conjecture, but possibly he was on his road to a seaport about forty miles distant.

The servant who opened the door to him was a young girl, born and bred amongst the mountains, who had never seen an Asiatic dress of any sort; his turban therefore confounded her not a little; and as it turned out that his attainments in English were exactly of the same extent as hers in the Malay, there seemed to be an impassable gulf fixed between all communication of ideas, if either party had happened to possess any. In this

---

[1] *cave of Trophonius* State of despair: in Greek mythology, Trophonius, who had killed his brother, was buried in a cave that became famous for its oracle that would overwhelm with melancholy all those who consulted it.

[2] *Malay* Member of a people that inhabits Malaysia, Brunei, and parts of Indonesia.

dilemma, the girl, recollecting the reputed learning of her master (and doubtless giving me credit for a knowledge of all the languages of the earth besides perhaps a few of the lunar ones), came and gave me to understand that there was a sort of demon below, whom she clearly imagined that my art could exorcise from the house. I did not immediately go down, but when I did, the group which presented itself, arranged as it was by accident, though not very elaborate, took hold of my fancy and my eye in a way that none of the statuesque attitudes exhibited in the ballets at the opera house, though so ostentatiously complex, had ever done. In a cottage kitchen, but panelled on the wall with dark wood that from age and rubbing resembled oak, and looking more like a rustic hall of entrance than a kitchen, stood the Malay—his turban and loose trousers of dingy white relieved upon the dark panelling. He had placed himself nearer to the girl than she seemed to relish, though her native spirit of mountain intrepidity contended with the feeling of simple awe which her countenance expressed as she gazed upon the tiger cat before her. And a more striking picture there could not be imagined than the beautiful English face of the girl, and its exquisite fairness, together with her erect and independent attitude, contrasted with the sallow and bilious skin of the Malay, enamelled or veneered with mahogany by marine air, his small, fierce, restless eyes, thin lips, slavish gestures and adorations. Half hidden by the ferocious-looking Malay was a little child from a neighbouring cottage who had crept in after him, and was now in the act of reverting its head and gazing upwards at the turban and the fiery eyes beneath it, whilst with one hand he caught at the dress of the young woman for protection. My knowledge of the Oriental tongues is not remarkably extensive, being indeed confined to two words—the Arabic word for barley and the Turkish for opium (*madjoon*), which I have learned from *Anastasius*; and as I had neither a Malay dictionary nor even Adelung's *Mithridates*,[1] which might have helped me to a few words, I addressed him in some lines from the *Iliad*, considering that, of such languages as I possessed, Greek, in point of longitude, came geographi-

cally nearest to an Oriental one. He worshipped me in a most devout manner, and replied in what I suppose was Malay. In this way I saved my reputation with my neighbours, for the Malay had no means of betraying the secret. He lay down upon the floor for about an hour and then pursued his journey. On his departure I presented him with a piece of opium. To him, as an Orientalist, I concluded that opium must be familiar, and the expression of his face convinced me that it was. Nevertheless, I was struck with some little consternation when I saw him suddenly raise his hand to his mouth, and, to use the schoolboy phrase, bolt the whole, divided into three pieces, at one mouthful. The quantity was enough to kill three dragoons[2] and their horses, and I felt some alarm for the poor creature, but what could be done? I had given him the opium in compassion for his solitary life, on recollecting that if he had travelled on foot from London it must be nearly three weeks since he could have exchanged a thought with any human being. I could not think of violating the laws of hospitality by having him seized and drenched with an emetic, and thus frightening him into a notion that we were going to sacrifice him to some English idol. No, there was clearly no help for it. He took his leave, and for some days I felt anxious, but as I never heard of any Malay being found dead, I became convinced that he was used to opium,[3] and that I must have done him the service I designed by giving him one night of respite from the pains of wandering....

THE PAINS OF OPIUM

—as when some great painter dips
His pencil in the gloom of earthquake and eclipse.
Shelley's *Revolt of Islam*.

---

[1] Adelung's *Mithridates*   German linguistics and grammar scholar Johann Christoph Adelung (1732–1806), author of *Mithridate or the Universal Table of Languages, with the Lord's Prayer in 500 Dialects*, a four-volume book on Oriental languages.

[2] *dragoons*   Mounted soldiers.

[3] [De Quincey's note]   This, however, is not a necessary conclusion; the varieties of effect produced by opium on different constitutions are infinite. A London magistrate (Harriott's *Struggles through Life*, vol. iii. p. 391, third edition) has recorded that, on the first occasion of his trying laudanum for the gout he took *forty* drops, the next night *sixty*, and on the fifth night *eighty*, without any effect whatever, and this at an advanced age. I have an anecdote from a country surgeon, however, which sinks Mr. Harriott's case into a trifle; and in my projected medical treatise on opium, which I will publish provided the College of Surgeons will pay me for enlightening their benighted understandings upon this subject, I will relate it; but it is far too good a story to be published gratis.

Reader, who have thus far accompanied me, I must request your attention to a brief explanatory note on three points:

1. For several reasons I have not been able to compose the notes for this part of my narrative into any regular and connected shape. I give the notes disjointed as I find them, or have now drawn them up from memory. Some of them point to their own date, some I have dated, and some are undated. Whenever it could answer my purpose to transplant them from the natural or chronological order, I have not scrupled to do so. Sometimes I speak in the present, sometimes in the past tense. Few of the notes, perhaps, were written exactly at the period of time to which they relate; but this can little affect their accuracy, as the impressions were such that they can never fade from my mind. Much has been omitted. I could not, without effort, constrain myself to the task of either recalling, or constructing into a regular narrative, the whole burden of horrors which lies upon my brain. This feeling partly I plead in excuse, and partly that I am now in London, and am a helpless sort of person, who cannot even arrange his own papers without assistance; and I am separated from the hands which are wont to perform for me the offices of an amanuensis.[1]

2. You will think perhaps that I am too confidential and communicative of my own private history. It may be so. But my way of writing is rather to think aloud, and follow my own humors, than much to consider who is listening to me; and if I stop to consider what is proper to be said to this or that person, I shall soon come to doubt whether any part at all is proper. The fact is, I place myself at a distance of fifteen or twenty years ahead of this time, and suppose myself writing to those who will be interested about me hereafter; and wishing to have some record of time, the entire history of which no one can know but myself, I do it as fully as I am able with the efforts I am now capable of making, because I know not whether I can ever find time to do it again.

3. It will occur to you often to ask, why did I not release myself from the horrors of opium by leaving it off or diminishing it? To this I must answer briefly: it might be supposed that I yielded to the fascinations of opium too easily; it cannot be supposed that any man can be charmed by its terrors. The reader may be sure, therefore, that I made attempts innumerable to reduce the quantity. I add, that those who witnessed the agonies of those attempts, and not myself, were the first to beg me to desist. But could not have I reduced it a drop a day, or, by adding water, have bisected or trisected a drop? A thousand drops bisected would thus have taken nearly six years to reduce, and that way would certainly not have answered. But this is a common mistake of those who know nothing of opium experimentally; I appeal to those who do, whether it is not always found that down to a certain point it can be reduced with ease and even pleasure, but that after that point further reduction causes intense suffering. Yes, say many thoughtless persons, who know not what they are talking of, you will suffer a little low spirits and dejection for a few days. I answer, no; there is nothing like low spirits; on the contrary, the mere animal spirits are uncommonly raised; the pulse is improved; the health is better. It is not there that the suffering lies. It has no resemblance to the sufferings caused by renouncing wine. It is a state of unutterable irritation of stomach (which surely is not much like dejection), accompanied by intense perspirations, and feelings such as I shall not attempt to describe without more space at my command....

I now pass to what is the main subject of these latter confessions, to the history and journal of what took place in my dreams, for these were the immediate and proximate cause of my acutest suffering.

The first notice I had of any important change going on in this part of my physical economy was from the reawakening of a state of eye generally incident to childhood, or exalted states of irritability. I know not whether my reader is aware that many children, perhaps most, have a power of painting, as it were upon the darkness, all sorts of phantoms. In some that power is simply a mechanical affection of the eye; others have a voluntary or semi-voluntary power to dismiss or to summon them, or, as a child once said to me when I questioned him on this matter, "I can tell them to go, and they go; but sometimes they come when I don't tell them to come." Whereupon I told him that he had almost as unlimited a command over apparitions as a Roman centurion over his soldiers. In the middle of 1817, I think it was, that this faculty became positively distressing to me: at night, when I lay awake in bed, vast

---

[1] *amanuensis* Latin: scribe or secretary.

processions passed along in mournful pomp; friezes of never-ending stories, that to my feelings were as sad and solemn as if they were stories drawn from times before Oedipus or Priam, before Tyre, before Memphis.[1] And at the same time a corresponding change took place in my dreams; a theater seemed suddenly opened and lighted up within my brain, which presented nightly spectacles of more than earthly splendour. And the four following facts may be mentioned as noticeable at this time:

1. That as the creative state of the eye increased, a sympathy seemed to arise between the waking and the dreaming states of the brain in one point—that whatsoever I happened to call up and to trace by a voluntary act upon the darkness was very apt to transfer itself to my dreams, so that I feared to exercise this faculty, for, as Midas turned all things to gold that yet baffled his hopes and defrauded his human desires,[2] so whatsoever things capable of being visually represented I did but think of in the darkness, immediately shaped themselves into phantoms of the eye; and by a process apparently no less inevitable, when thus once traced in faint and visionary colours, like writings in sympathetic[3] ink, they were drawn out by the fierce chemistry of my dreams into insufferable splendour that fretted my heart.

2. For this and all other changes in my dreams were accompanied by deep-seated anxiety and gloomy melancholy, such as are wholly incommunicable by words. I seemed every night to descend, not metaphorically, but literally to descend, into chasms and sunless abysses, depths below depths, from which it seemed hopeless that I could ever re-ascend. Nor did I, by waking, feel that I *had* re-ascended. This I do not dwell upon because the state of gloom which attended these gorgeous spectacles, amounting at last to utter darkness, as of some suicidal despondency, cannot be approached by words.

3. The sense of space, and in the end the sense of time, were both powerfully affected. Buildings, land-scapes, &c., were exhibited in proportions so vast as the bodily eye is not fitted to receive. Space swelled and was amplified to an extent of unutterable infinity. This, however, did not disturb me so much as the vast expansion of time; I sometimes seemed to have lived for 70 or 100 years in one night—nay, sometimes had feelings representative of a millennium passed in that time, or, however, of a duration far beyond the limits of any human experience.

4. The minutest incidents of childhood, or forgotten scenes of later years, were often revived; I could not be said to recollect them, for if I had been told of them when waking, I should not have been able to acknowledge them as parts of my past experience. But placed as they were before me, in dreams like intuitions, and clothed in all their evanescent circumstances and accompanying feelings, I *recognized* them instantaneously. I was once told by a near relative of mine, that having in her childhood fallen into a river, and being on the very verge of death but for the critical assistance which reached her, she saw in a moment her whole life, in its minutest incidents, arrayed before her simultaneously as in a mirror; and she had a faculty developed as suddenly for comprehending the whole and every part. This, from some opium experiences of mine, I can believe; I have indeed seen the same thing asserted twice in modern books, and accompanied by a remark which I am convinced is true, viz., that the dread book of account which the Scriptures speak of[4] is in fact the mind itself of each individual. Of this at least I feel assured, that there is no such thing as *forgetting* possible to the mind; a thousand accidents may and will interpose a veil between our present consciousness and the secret inscriptions on the mind; accidents of the same sort will also rend away this veil; but alike, whether veiled or unveiled, the inscription remains forever, just as the stars seem to withdraw before the common light of day, whereas in fact we all know that it is the light which is drawn over them as a veil, and that they are waiting to be revealed when the obscuring daylight shall have withdrawn. ...

---

[1] *Oedipus*   King of Thebes, a city in ancient Egypt; *Priam*   King of Troy, a city in ancient Greece; *Tyre*   Ancient city of Phoenicia, now Lebanon; *Memphis*   Capital of ancient Egypt.

[2] *Midas ... desires*   The Greek god Dionysus granted King Midas his wish that everything he touched be turned to gold; the king was devastated when his food, wine, and eventually his daughter were all turned to gold.

[3] *sympathetic*   Invisible.

[4] *dread ... speak of*   Cf. Revelation 20.12: "I saw the dead, small and great, stand before God; and the books were opened: and another book was opened, which is the book of life: and the dead were judged out of those things which were written in the books, according to their works."

May 1818

The Malay has been a fearful enemy for months. I have been every night, through his means, transported into Asiatic scenes. I know not whether others share in my feelings on this point, but I have often thought that if I were compelled to forego England and to live in China, and among Chinese manners and modes of life and scenery, I should go mad. The causes of my horror lie deep, and some of them must be common to others. Southern Asia in general is the seat of awful images and associations. As the cradle of the human race, it would alone have a dim and reverential feeling connected with it. But there are other reasons. No man can pretend that the wild, barbarous, and capricious superstitions of Africa, or of savage tribes elsewhere, affect him in the way that he is affected by the ancient, monumental, cruel, and elaborate religions of Indostan, &c. The mere antiquity of Asiatic things, of their institutions, histories, modes of faith, &c., is so impressive, that to me the vast age of the race and name overpowers the sense of youth in the individual. A young Chinese seems to me an antediluvian man renewed. Even Englishmen, though not bred in any knowledge of such institutions, cannot but shudder at the mystic sublimity of *castes* that have flowed apart, and refused to mix, through such immemorial tracts of time; nor can any man fail to be awed by the names of the Ganges or the Euphrates.[1] It contributes much to these feelings that southern Asia is, and has been for thousands of years, the part of the earth most swarming with human life, the great *officina gentium*.[2] Man is a weed in those regions. The vast empires also in which the enormous population of Asia has always been cast, give a further sublimity to the feelings associated with all Oriental names or images. In China, over and above what it has in common with the rest of southern Asia, I am terrified by the modes of life, by the manners, and the barrier of utter abhorrence and want of sympathy placed between us by feelings deeper than I can analyse. I could sooner live with lunatics or brute animals. All this, and much more than I can say or have time to say, the reader must enter into before he can comprehend the unimaginable horror which these dreams of Oriental imagery and mythological tortures impressed upon me. Under the connecting feeling of tropical heat and vertical sunlights I brought together all creatures, birds, beasts, reptiles, all trees and plants, usages and appearances, that are found in all tropical regions, and assembled them together in China or Indostan. From kindred feelings, I soon brought Egypt and all her gods under the same law. I was stared at, hooted at, grinned at, chattered at, by monkeys, by parroquets,[3] by cockatoos. I ran into pagodas, and was fixed for centuries at the summit or in secret rooms. I was the idol; I was the priest; I was worshipped; I was sacrificed. I fled from the wrath of Brama through all the forests of Asia; Vishnu hated me. Seeva[4] laid wait for me. I came suddenly upon Isis and Osiris. I had done a deed, they said, which the ibis and the crocodile[5] trembled at. I was buried for a thousand years in stone coffins, with mummies and sphinxes, in narrow chambers at the heart of eternal pyramids. I was kissed, with cancerous kisses, by crocodiles, and laid, confounded with all unutterable slimy things, amongst reeds and Nilotic mud.[6]

I thus give the reader some slight abstraction of my Oriental dreams, which always filled me with such amazement at the monstrous scenery that horror seemed absorbed for a while in sheer astonishment. Sooner or later came a reflux of feeling that swallowed up the astonishment, and left me not so much in terror as in hatred and abomination of what I saw. Over every form, and threat, and punishment, and dim sightless incarceration, brooded a sense of eternity and infinity that drove me into an oppression as of madness. Into these dreams only it was, with one or two slight exceptions, that any circumstances of physical horror entered. All before had been moral and spiritual terrors. But here the main agents were ugly birds, or snakes, or crocodiles, especially the last. The cursed crocodile became to me the object of more horror than almost all the rest. I was compelled to live with him, and (as was always the case almost in my dreams) for centuries. I escaped sometimes, and found myself in Chinese houses, with cane

---

[1] *Ganges or the Euphrates* Major rivers of Asia.

[2] *officina gentium* Latin: factory of nations.

[3] *parroquets* I.e., parakeets.

[4] *Brama … Seeva* The Hindu triad: the gods Brahma, Vishnu, and Shiva.

[5] *Isis … crocodile* Isis and Osiris were deities of ancient Egypt; Thoth, in the shape of an ibis, and Sobek, a crocodile, were also Egyptian gods.

[6] *Nilotic mud* I.e., mud of the river Nile.

tables, &c. All the feet of the tables, sofas, &c., soon became instinct with life; the abominable head of the crocodile, and his leering eyes, looked out at me, multiplied into a thousand repetitions, and I stood loathing and fascinated. And so often did this hideous reptile haunt my dreams that many times the very same dream was broken up in the very same way: I heard gentle voices speaking to me (I hear everything when I am sleeping), and instantly I awoke. It was broad noon, and my children were standing, hand in hand, at my bedside—come to show me their coloured shoes, or new frocks, or to let me see them dressed for going out. I protest that so awful was the transition from the damned crocodile, and the other unutterable monsters and abortions of my dreams, to the sight of innocent *human* natures and of infancy, that in the mighty and sudden revulsion of mind I wept, and could not forbear it, as I kissed their faces.

June 1819

I have had occasion to remark, at various periods of my life, that the deaths of those whom we love, and indeed the contemplation of death generally, is (*caeteris paribus*[1]) more affecting in summer than in any other season of the year. And the reasons are these three, I think: first, that the visible heavens in summer appear far higher, more distant, and (if such a solecism may be excused) more infinite; the clouds, by which chiefly the eye expounds the distance of the blue pavilion stretched over our heads, are in summer more voluminous, massed and accumulated in far grander and more towering piles. Secondly, the light and the appearances of the declining and the setting sun are much more fitted to be types and characters of the Infinite. And thirdly (which is the main reason), the exuberant and riotous prodigality of life naturally forces the mind more powerfully upon the antagonist thought of death, and the wintry sterility of the grave. For it may be observed generally, that wherever two thoughts stand related to each other by a law of antagonism, and exist, as it were, by mutual repulsion, they are apt to suggest each other. On these accounts it is that I find it impossible to banish the thought of death when I am walking alone in the endless days of summer; and any particular death, if not more affecting, at least haunts my mind more

obstinately and besiegingly in that season. Perhaps this cause, and a slight incident which I omit, might have been the immediate occasions of the following dream, to which, however, a predisposition must always have existed in my mind; but having been once roused it never left me, and split into a thousand fantastic varieties, which often suddenly reunited, and composed again the original dream.

I thought that it was a Sunday morning in May, that it was Easter Sunday, and as yet very early in the morning. I was standing, as it seemed to me, at the door of my own cottage. Right before me lay the very scene which could really be commanded from that situation, but exalted, as was usual, and solemnized by the power of dreams. There were the same mountains, and the same lovely valley at their feet; but the mountains were raised to more than Alpine height, and there was interspace far larger between them of meadows and forest lawns; the hedges were rich with white roses, and no living creature was to be seen, excepting that in the green churchyard there were cattle tranquilly reposing upon the verdant graves, and particularly round about the grave of a child whom I had tenderly loved, just as I had really beheld them, a little before sunrise in the same summer, when that child died. I gazed upon the well-known scene, and I said aloud (as I thought) to myself, "It yet wants much of sunrise, and it is Easter Sunday; and that is the day on which they celebrate the first fruits of resurrection. I will walk abroad; old griefs shall be forgotten today, for the air is cool and still, and the hills are high and stretch away to heaven; and the forest glades are as quiet as the churchyard, and with the dew I can wash the fever from my forehead, and then I shall be unhappy no longer." And I turned as if to open my garden gate, and immediately I saw upon the left a scene far different, but which yet the power of dreams had reconciled into harmony with the other. The scene was an Oriental one, and there also it was Easter Sunday, and very early in the morning. And at a vast distance were visible, as a stain upon the horizon, the domes and cupolas of a great city—an image or faint abstraction, caught perhaps in childhood from some picture of Jerusalem. And not a bowshot[2] from me, upon a stone and shaded by Judean palms, there sat a woman, and I looked, and it was—Ann! She fixed her

---

[1]   *caeteris paribus*   Latin: other things being equal.

[2]   *bowshot*   Measurement of distance: the span an arrow will fly from the bow.

eyes upon me earnestly, and I said to her at length: "So, then, I have found you at last." I waited, but she answered me not a word. Her face was the same as when I saw it last, and yet again how different! Seventeen years ago, when the lamplight fell upon her face, as for the last time I kissed her lips (lips, Ann, that to me were not polluted), her eyes were streaming with tears; the tears were now wiped away; she seemed more beautiful than she was at that time, but in all other points the same, and not older. Her looks were tranquil, but with unusual solemnity of expression, and I now gazed upon her with some awe; but suddenly her countenance grew dim, and turning to the mountains I perceived vapours rolling between us. In a moment all had vanished, thick darkness came on, and in the twinkling of an eye I was far away from mountains, and by lamplight in Oxford Street, walking again with Ann—just as we walked seventeen years before, when we were both children.

As a final specimen, I cite one of a different character, from 1820.

The dream commenced with a music which now I often heard in dreams—a music of preparation and of awakening suspense, a music like the opening of the Coronation Anthem, and which, like *that*, gave the feeling of a vast march, of infinite cavalcades filing off, and the tread of innumerable armies. The morning was come of a mighty day—a day of crisis and of final hope for human nature, then suffering some mysterious eclipse, and labouring in some dread extremity. Somewhere, I knew not where—somehow, I knew not how—by some beings, I knew not whom—a battle, a strife, an agony, was conducting, was evolving like a great drama or piece of music, with which my sympathy was the more insupportable from my confusion as to its place, its cause, its nature, and its possible issue. I, as is usual in dreams (where of necessity we make ourselves central to every movement), had the power, and yet had not the power, to decide it. I had the power, if I could raise myself to will it, and yet again had not the power, for the weight of twenty Atlantics was upon me, or the oppression of inexpiable guilt. "Deeper than ever plummet sounded,"[1] I lay inactive. Then like a chorus the passion deepened. Some greater interest was at stake, some mightier cause than ever yet the sword had plead-

ed, or trumpet had proclaimed. Then came sudden alarms, hurryings to and fro, trepidations of innumerable fugitives—I knew not whether from the good cause or the bad, darkness and lights, tempest and human faces, and at last, with the sense that all was lost, female forms, and the features that were worth all the world to me, and but a moment allowed—and clasped hands, and heartbreaking partings, and then—everlasting farewells! And with a sigh, such as the caves of Hell sighed when the incestuous mother uttered the abhorred name of death,[2] the sound was reverberated—everlasting farewells! And again and yet again reverberated—everlasting farewells!

And I awoke in struggles, and cried aloud—"I will sleep no more."[3]

But I am now called upon to wind up a narrative which has already extended to an unreasonable length. Within more spacious limits the materials which I have used might have been better unfolded, and much which I have not used might have been added with effect. Perhaps, however, enough has been given. It now remains that I should say something of the way in which this conflict of horrors was finally brought to a crisis. The reader is already aware (from a passage near the beginning of the introduction to the first part) that the opium-eater has, in some way or other, "unwound almost to its final links the accursed chain which bound him." By what means? To have narrated this according to the original intention would have far exceeded the space which can now be allowed. It is fortunate, as such a cogent reason exists for abridging it, that I should, on a maturer view of the case, have been exceedingly unwilling to injure, by any such unaffecting details, the impression of the history itself, as an appeal to the prudence and the conscience of the yet unconfirmed opium-eater—or even (though a very inferior consideration) to injure its effect as a composition. The interest of the judicious reader will not attach itself chiefly to the subject of the fascinating spells, but to the fascinating

---

[1] *"Deeper … sounded"* From Shakespeare's *The Tempest* 3.3.115.

[2] *incestuous … death* In Milton's *Paradise Lost* 2.787–89, Sin, the daughter of Satan, fled and: "cried out DEATH! / Hell trembled at the hideous name, and sighed / From all her caves, and back resounded, DEATH!"

[3] *"I will sleep no more."* From Shakespeare's *Macbeth* 2.2.46, in which the guilt-ridden Macbeth says: "Methought I heard a voice cry 'Sleep no more!'"

power. Not the opium-eater, but the opium, is the true hero of the tale, and the legitimate centre on which the interest revolves. The object was to display the marvellous agency of opium, whether for pleasure or for pain; if that is done, the action of the piece has closed.

However, as some people, in spite of all laws to the contrary, will persist in asking what became of the opium-eater, and in what state he now is, I answer for him thus: The reader is aware that opium had long ceased to found its empire on spells of pleasure; it was solely by the tortures connected with the attempt to abjure it that it kept its hold. Yet, as other tortures, no less it may be thought, attended the non-abjuration of such a tyrant, a choice only of evils was left; and *that* might as well have been adopted which, however terrific in itself, held out a prospect of final restoration to happiness. This appears true, but good logic gave the author no strength to act upon it. However, a crisis arrived for the author's life, and a crisis for other objects still dearer to him—and which will always be far dearer to him than his life, even now that it is again a happy one. I saw that I must die if I continued the opium. I determined, therefore, if that should be required, to die in throwing it off. How much I was at that time taking I cannot say, for the opium which I used had been purchased for me by a friend, who afterwards refused to let me pay him, so that I could not ascertain even what quantity I had used within the year. I apprehend, however, that I took it very irregularly, and that I varied from about fifty or sixty grains to 150 a day. My first task was to reduce it to forty, to thirty, and as fast as I could to twelve grains.

I triumphed. But think not, reader, that therefore my sufferings were ended, nor think of me as of one sitting in a *dejected* state. Think of me as one, even when four months had passed, still agitated, writhing, throbbing, palpitating, shattered, and much perhaps in the situation of him who has been racked, as I collect the torments of that state from the affecting account of them left by a most innocent sufferer[1] of the times of James I. Meantime, I derived no benefit from any medicine, except one prescribed to me by an Edinburgh surgeon of great eminence, viz., ammoniated tincture of valerian. Medical account, therefore, of my emancipation I have not much to give, and even that little, as managed by a man so ignorant of medicine as myself, would probably tend only to mislead. At all events, it would be misplaced in this situation. The moral of the narrative is addressed to the opium-eater, and therefore of necessity limited in its application. If he is taught to fear and tremble, enough has been effected. But he may say that the issue of my case is at least a proof that opium, after a seventeen years' use and an eight years' abuse of its powers, may still be renounced, and that *he* may chance to bring to the task greater energy than I did, or that with a stronger constitution than mine he may obtain the same results with less. This may be true. I would not presume to measure the efforts of other men by my own. I heartily wish him more energy. I wish him the same success. Nevertheless, I had motives external to myself which he may unfortunately want, and these supplied me with conscientious supports which mere personal interests might fail to supply to a mind debilitated by opium.

Jeremy Taylor[2] conjectures that it may be as painful to be born as to die. I think it probable; and during the whole period of diminishing the opium I had the torments of a man passing out of one mode of existence into another. The issue was not death, but a sort of physical regeneration; and I may add that ever since, at intervals, I have had a restoration of more than youthful spirits, though under the pressure of difficulties which in a less happy state of mind I should have called misfortunes.

One memorial of my former condition still remains—my dreams are not yet perfectly calm; the dread swell and agitation of the storm have not wholly subsided; the legions that encamped in them are drawing off, but not all departed; my sleep is still tumultuous, and, like the gates of Paradise to our first parents when looking back from afar, it is still (in the tremendous line of Milton)

> With dreadful faces thronged, and fiery arms.[3]

—1821

---

[1] [De Quincey's note]   William Lithgow. His book (*Travels*, &c.) is ill and pedantically written; but the account of his own sufferings on the rack at Malaga is overpoweringly affecting. [Lithgow was tortured in Malaga, Spain, after being accused of being a spy for King James I, who reigned from 1604–25.]

[2] *Jeremy Taylor*   English bishop, theologian, and author (1613–67).

[3] *"With dreadful … arms"*   From Milton's *Paradise Lost* (12.644).

MARY PRINCE
1788 – 1833

Author of the earliest extant slave narrative by a woman, Mary Prince was born into bondage in the British colony of Bermuda, where for the first twelve years of her life she was spared the cruelty that dominated her adult years. Both her parents were also slaves, the property of Charles Myners. After Myners died, Mary and her mother were sold to a Captain Williams, whose daughter Betsey treated Mary as "her little nigger," yet with relative compassion. Williams sold Prince to another family to raise money for his marriage and in 1806 she was sent to work in the salt ponds of Turks Island: "This work was perfectly new to me. I was given a half barrel and shovel, and had to stand up to my knees in the water, from four o'clock in the morning till nine, when we were given some Indian corn boiled in water, which we were obliged to swallow as fast as we could for fear the rain should come on and melt the salt."

In 1818, Prince was sold for three hundred dollars to John Wood, a plantation owner in Antigua. On the plantation Prince contracted rheumatism and became essentially crippled, her legs covered with boils; these maladies stayed with her and eventually affected her eyesight. She was also beaten and sexually abused by her master. Prince began attending meetings held at the Moravian Church, where various women taught her to read: "After we had done spelling, we tried to read in the Bible. After reading was over, the missionary gave out a hymn for us to sing." Prince was married in this church to Daniel Jones, a former slave who had purchased his own freedom. Wood horsewhipped Prince when he discovered the marriage. In 1828 Wood took Prince to London as his servant. Abolitionist sympathizers helped her escape and she found employment as a domestic servant (slavery was illegal in England) of Thomas Pringle, a Methodist and secretary of the Anti-Slavery Society.

Pringle encouraged Prince to tell the story of her life and, in 1831, he arranged for the publication of her book, *The History of Mary Prince, a West-Indian Slave, Related by Herself.* In his "Preface" to the work, Pringle wrote: "The idea of writing Mary Prince's history was first suggested by herself. She wished it to be done, she said, that good people in England might hear from a slave what a slave had felt and suffered." Mary Prince told her story to Susanna Strickland (later Moodie), who recorded it in writing. It seems improbable that Strickland—who would later come to be regarded as one of Canada's most accomplished writers in the nineteenth century—would not at a minimum have edited the dictated narrative for grammar and syntax, and some have suggested that Pringle may have had some hand in shaping the manuscript so as to better serve abolitionist ends. (His insistence that the rhetorical flourish at the end of Prince's first paragraph is "given verbatim as uttered by Mary Prince" has struck more than one reader as rather forced.) But most scholars have stopped short of suggesting that material was fabricated by Pringle and Strickland, or that this is not in essence Prince's own narrative. Strickland herself attested that she had "been writing Mr. Pringle's black Mary's life from her own dictation and for her benefit adhering to her own simple story and language without deviating to the paths of flourish or romance."

The book was a great success, and gave rise to considerable controversy. *Blackwood's Magazine* and *The Glasgow Courier* claimed it was fraudulent and propagandistic. A number of libel suits resulted, with Wood suing Pringle and Pringle counter-suing. Wood claimed that the book had "endeavored to injure the character of my family by the most vile and infamous falsehoods." Wood lost the case and the libel scandal served only to make Prince's work more widely known. It reached a third edition in the same year it was published and it has since that time retained its place as one of the most moving, detailed, and comprehensive narratives of the life of a slave.

Slavery was abolished in all British colonies in 1833. Little is known of Prince's life after the publication of her *History*, and we do not know when, where, or how she died.

⌘ ⌘ ⌘

The History of Mary Prince
A West Indian Slave
Related by Herself

PREFACE [BY THOMAS PRINGLE]

The idea of writing Mary Prince's history was first suggested by herself. She wished it to be done, she said, that good people in England might hear from a slave what a slave had felt and suffered; and a letter of her late master's, which will be found in the Supplement, induced me to accede to her wish without farther delay. The more immediate object of the publication will afterwards appear.

The narrative was taken down from Mary's own lips by a lady who happened to be at the time residing in my family as a visitor. It was written out fully, with all the narrator's repetitions and prolixities,[1] and afterwards pruned into its present shape; retaining, as far as was practicable, Mary's exact expressions and peculiar phraseology. No fact of importance has been omitted, and not a single circumstance or sentiment has been added. It is essentially her own, without any material alteration farther than was requisite to exclude redundances and gross grammatical errors, so as to render it clearly intelligible.

After it had been thus written out, I went over the whole, carefully examining her on every fact and circumstance detailed; and in all that relates to her residence in Antigua I had the advantage of being assisted in this scrutiny by Mr. Joseph Phillips, who was a resident in that colony during the same period, and had known her there.

The names of all the persons mentioned by the narrator have been printed in full, except those of Capt. I—and his wife, and that of Mr. D—, to whom conduct of peculiar atrocity is ascribed. These three individuals are now gone to answer at a far more awful tribunal than that of public opinion, for the deeds of which their former bondwoman accuses them; and to hold them up more openly to human reprobation could no longer affect themselves, while it might deeply lacerate the feelings of their surviving and perhaps innocent relatives, without any commensurate public advantage.

Without detaining the reader with remarks on other points which will be adverted to more conveniently in the Supplement, I shall here merely notice farther, that the Anti-Slavery Society have no concern whatever with this publication, nor are they in any degree responsible for the statements it contains. I have published the tract, not as their Secretary, but in my private capacity; and any profits that may arise from the sale will be exclusively appropriated to the benefit of Mary Prince herself.

THOMAS PRINGLE [2]
7, Solly Terrace, Claremont Square,
January 25, 1831

P.S. Since writing the above, I have been furnished by my friend Mr. George Stephen, with the interesting narrative of Asa-Asa, a captured African, now under his protection; and have printed it as a suitable appendix to this little history.

T.P.

The History of Mary Prince

I was born at Brackish-Pond, in Bermuda, on a farm belonging to Mr. Charles Myners. My mother was a household slave; and my father, whose name was Prince,

---

[1] *prolixities* Instances of wordiness.

[2] *Thomas Pringle* Also known as the "father of South African poetry," Pringle (1789–1834) was born in Scotland and lived in South Africa between 1820 and 1826, where he published a newspaper and a magazine. In 1826 he returned to England, where he devoted himself to the antislavery movement as secretary to the Society for the Abolition of Slavery.

was a sawyer[1] belonging to Mr. Trimmingham, a shipbuilder at Crow-Lane. When I was an infant, old Mr. Myners died, and there was a division of the slaves and other property among the family. I was bought along with my mother by old Captain Darrel, and given to his grandchild, little Miss Betsey Williams. Captain Williams, Mr. Darrel's son-in-law, was master of a vessel which traded to several places in America and the West Indies, and he was seldom at home long together.

Mrs. Williams was a kind-hearted good woman, and she treated all her slaves well. She had only one daughter, Miss Betsey, for whom I was purchased, and who was about my own age. I was made quite a pet of by Miss Betsey, and loved her very much. She used to lead me about by the hand, and call me her little nigger. This was the happiest period of my life; for I was too young to understand rightly my condition as a slave, and too thoughtless and full of spirits to look forward to the days of toil and sorrow.

My mother was a household slave in the same family. I was under her own care, and my little brothers and sisters were my play-fellows and companions. My mother had us several fine children after she came to Mrs. Williams, three girls and two boys. The tasks given out to us children were light, and we used to play together with Miss Betsey, with as much freedom almost as if she had been our sister.

My master, however, was a very harsh, selfish man; and we always dreaded his return from sea. His wife was herself much afraid of him; and, during his stay at home, seldom dared to show her usual kindness to the slaves. He often left her, in the most distressed circumstances, to reside in other female society, at some place in the West Indies of which I have forgot the name. My poor mistress bore his ill-treatment with great patience, and all her slaves loved and pitied her. I was truly attached to her, and, next to my own mother, loved her better than any creature in the world. My obedience to her commands was cheerfully given: it sprung solely from the affection I felt for her, and not from fear of the power which the white people's law had given her over me.

I had scarcely reached my twelfth year when my mistress became too poor to keep so many of us at home; and she hired me out to Mrs. Pruden, a lady who lived about five miles off, in the adjoining parish, in a large house near the sea. I cried bitterly at parting with my dear mistress and Miss Betsey, and when I kissed my mother and brothers and sisters, I thought my young heart would break, it pained me so. But there was no help; I was forced to go. Good Mrs. Williams comforted me by saying that I should still be near the home I was about to quit, and might come over and see her and my kindred whenever I could obtain leave of absence from Mrs. Pruden. A few hours after this I was taken to a strange house, and found myself among strange people. This separation seemed a sore trial to me then; but oh! 'twas light, light to the trials I have since endured!—'twas nothing—nothing to be mentioned with them; but I was a child then, and it was according to my strength.

I knew that Mrs. Williams could no longer maintain me; that she was fain to part with me for my food and clothing; and I tried to submit myself to the change. My new mistress was a passionate woman; but yet she did not treat me very unkindly. I do not remember her striking me but once, and that was for going to see Mrs. Williams when I heard she was sick, and staying longer than she had given me leave to do. All my employment at this time was nursing a sweet baby, little Master Daniel; and I grew so fond of my nursling that it was my greatest delight to walk out with him by the sea-shore, accompanied by his brother and sister, Miss Fanny and Master James.—Dear Miss Fanny! She was a sweet, kind young lady, and so fond of me that she wished me to learn all that she knew herself; and her method of teaching me was as follows:—Directly she had said her lessons to her grandmamma, she used to come running to me, and make me repeat them one by one after her; and in a few months I was able not only to say my letters but to spell many small words. But this happy state was not to last long. Those days were too pleasant to last. My heart always softens when I think of them.

At this time Mrs. Williams died. I was told suddenly of her death, and my grief was so great that, forgetting I had the baby in my arms, I ran away directly to my poor mistress's house; but reached it only in time to see the corpse carried out. Oh, that was a day of sorrow—a

---

[1] *sawyer* Worker whose job it is to saw timber.

heavy day! All the slaves cried. My mother cried and lamented her sore; and I (foolish creature!) vainly entreated them to bring my dear mistress back to life. I knew nothing rightly about death then, and it seemed a hard thing to bear. When I thought about my mistress I felt as if the world was all gone wrong; and for many days and weeks I could think of nothing else. I returned to Mrs. Pruden's; but my sorrow was too great to be comforted, for my own dear mistress was always in my mind. Whether in the house or abroad, my thoughts were always talking to me about her.

I stayed at Mrs. Pruden's about three months after this; I was then sent back to Mr. Williams to be sold. Oh, that was a sad sad time! I recollect the day well. Mrs. Pruden came to me and said, "Mary, you will have to go home directly; your master is going to be married, and he means to sell you and two of your sisters to raise money for the wedding." Hearing this I burst out a crying,—though I was then far from being sensible of the full weight of my misfortune, or of the misery that waited for me. Besides, I did not like to leave Mrs. Pruden, and the dear baby, who had grown very fond of me. For some time I could scarcely believe that Mrs. Pruden was in earnest, till I received orders for my immediate return.—Dear Miss Fanny! how she cried at parting with me, whilst I kissed and hugged the baby, thinking I should never see him again. I left Mrs. Pruden's, and walked home with a heart full of sorrow. The idea of being sold away from my mother and Miss Betsey was so frightful, that I dared not trust myself to think about it. We had been bought of Mrs. Myners, as I have mentioned, by Miss Betsey's grandfather, and given to her, so that we were by right *her* property, and I never thought we should be separated or sold away from her.

When I reached the house, I went in directly to Miss Betsey. I found her in great distress; and she cried out as soon as she saw me, "Oh, Mary! my father is going to sell you all to raise money to marry that wicked woman. You are *my* slaves, and he has no right to sell you; but it is all to please her." She then told me that my mother was living with her father's sister at a house close by, and I went there to see her. It was a sorrowful meeting; and we lamented with a great and sore crying our unfortunate situation. "Here comes one of my poor piccaninnies!"[1] she said, the moment I came in, "one of the poor slave-brood who are to be sold to-morrow."

Oh dear! I cannot bear to think of that day,— it is too much.—It recalls the great grief that filled my heart, and the woeful thoughts that passed to and fro through my mind, whilst listening to the pitiful words of my poor mother, weeping for the loss of her children. I wish I could find words to tell you all I then felt and suffered. The great God above alone knows the thoughts of the poor slave's heart, and the bitter pains which follow such separations as these. All that we love taken away from us—oh, it is sad, sad! and sore to be borne!—I got no sleep that night for thinking of the morrow; and dear Miss Betsey was scarcely less distressed. She could not bear to part with her old playmates and she cried sore and would not be pacified.

The black morning at length came; it came too soon for my poor mother and us. Whilst she was putting on us the new osnaburgs[2] in which we were to be sold, she said, in a sorrowful voice, (I shall never forget it!) "See, I am *shrouding* my poor children; what a task for a mother!"— She then called Miss Betsey to take leave of us. "I am going to carry my little chickens to market," (these were her very words) "take your last look of them; may be you will see them no more." "Oh, my poor slaves! my own slaves!" said dear Miss Betsey, "you belong to me; and it grieves my heart to part with you."—Miss Betsey kissed us all, and, when she left us, my mother called the rest of the slaves to bid us good bye. One of them, a woman named Moll, came with her infant in her arms. "Ay!" said my mother, seeing her turn away and look at her child with the tears in her eyes, "your turn will come next." The slaves could say nothing to comfort us; they could only weep and lament with us. When I left my dear little brothers and the house in which I had been brought up, I thought my heart would burst.

Our mother, weeping as she went, called me away with the children Hannah and Dinah, and we took the road that led to Hamble Town, which we reached about four o'clock in the afternoon. We followed my mother to the market-place, where she placed us in a row against

---

[1] *piccaninnies* Children, usually applied derogatively to black children.

[2] *osnaburgs* Type of coarse linen used to make clothing.

a large house, with our backs to the wall and our arms folded across our breasts. I, as the eldest, stood first, Hannah next to me, then Dinah; and our mother stood beside, crying over us. My heart throbbed with grief and terror so violently, that I pressed my hands quite tightly across my breast, but I could not keep it still, and it continued to leap as though it would burst out of my body. But who cared for that? Did one of the many bystanders, who were looking at us so carelessly, think of the pain that wrung the hearts of the negro woman and her young ones? No, no! They were not all bad, I dare say, but slavery hardens white people's hearts towards the blacks; and many of them were not slow to make their remarks upon us aloud, without regard to our grief— though their light words fell like cayenne on the fresh wounds of our hearts. Oh those white people have small hearts who can only feel for themselves.

At length the vendue[1] master, who was to offer us for sale like sheep or cattle, arrived, and asked my mother which was the eldest. She said nothing, but pointed to me. He took me by the hand, and led me out into the middle of the street, and, turning me slowly round, exposed me to the view of those who attended the vendue. I was soon surrounded by strange men, who examined and handled me in the same manner that a butcher would a calf or a lamb he was about to purchase, and who talked about my shape and size in like words—as if I could no more understand their meaning than the dumb beasts. I was then put up for sale. The bidding commenced at a few pounds, and gradually rose to fifty-seven, when I was knocked down to the highest bidder; and the people who stood by said that I had fetched a great sum for so young a slave.

I then saw my sisters led forth, and sold to different owners; so that we had not the sad satisfaction of being partners in bondage. When the sale was over, my mother hugged and kissed us, and mourned over us, begging of us to keep up a good heart, and do our duty to our new masters. It was a sad parting; one went one way, one another, and our poor mammy went home with nothing.

My new master was a Captain I—, who lived at Spanish Point. After parting with my mother and sisters, I followed him to his store, and he gave me into the

charge of his son, a lad about my own age, Master Benjy, who took me to my new home. I did not know where I was going, or what my new master would do with me. My heart was quite broken with grief, and my thoughts went back continually to those from whom I had been so suddenly parted. "Oh, my mother! my mother!" I kept saying to myself, "Oh, my mammy and my sisters and my brothers, shall I never see you again!" Oh, the trials! the trials! they make the salt water come into my eyes when I think of the days in which I was afflicted—the times that are gone; when I mourned and grieved with a young heart for those whom I loved.—It was night when I reached my new home. The house was large, and built at the bottom of a very high hill; but I could not see much of it that night. I saw too much of it afterwards. The stones and the timber were the best things in it; they were not so hard as the hearts of the owners.

Before I entered the house, two slave women, hired from another owner, who were at work in the yard, spoke to me, and asked who I belonged to? I replied, "I am come to live here." "Poor child, poor child!" they both said; "you must keep a good heart, if you are to live here."—When I went in, I stood up crying in a corner. Mrs. I— came and took off my hat, a little black silk hat Miss Pruden made for me, and said in a rough voice, "You are not come here to stand up in corners and cry, you are come here to work." She then put a child into my arms, and, tired as I was, I was forced instantly to take up my old occupation of a nurse.—I could not bear to look at my mistress, her countenance was so stern. She was a stout tall woman with a very dark complexion, and her brows were always drawn together into a frown. I thought of the words of the two slave women when I saw Mrs. I—, and heard the harsh sound of her voice.

The person I took the most notice of that night was a French Black called Hetty, whom my master took in privateering from another vessel, and made his slave. She was the most active woman I ever saw, and she was tasked to her utmost. A few minutes after my arrival she came in from milking the cows, and put the sweet-potatoes on for supper. She then fetched home the sheep, and penned them in the fold; drove home the cattle, and staked them about the pond side; fed and

[1] *vendue* Sale.

rubbed down my master's horse, and gave the hog and the fed cow their suppers; prepared the beds, and undressed the children, and laid them to sleep. I liked to look at her and watch all her doings, for her's was the only friendly face I had as yet seen, and I felt glad that she was there. She gave me my supper of potatoes and milk, and a blanket to sleep upon, which she spread for me in the passage before the door of Mrs. I——'s chamber.

I got a sad fright, that night. I was just going to sleep, when I heard a noise in my mistress's room; and she presently called out to inquire if some work was finished that she had ordered Hetty to do. "No, Ma'am, not yet," was Hetty's answer from below. On hearing this, my master started up from his bed, and just as he was, in his shirt, ran down stairs with a long cow-skin in his hand. I heard immediately after, the cracking of the thong, and the house rang to the shrieks of poor Hetty, who kept crying out, "Oh, Massa! Massa! me dead. Massa! have mercy upon me—don't kill me outright."—This was a sad beginning for me. I sat up upon my blanket, trembling with terror, like a frightened hound, and thinking that my turn would come next. At length the house became still, and I forgot for a little while all my sorrows by falling fast asleep.

The next morning my mistress set about instructing me in my tasks. She taught me to do all sorts of household work; to wash and bake, pick cotton and wool, and wash floors, and cook. And she taught me (how can I ever forget it!) more things than these; she caused me to know the exact difference between the smart of the rope, the cart-whip, and the cow-skin, when applied to my naked body by her own cruel hand. And there was scarcely any punishment more dreadful than the blows I received on my face and head from her hard heavy fist. She was a fearful woman, and a savage mistress to her slaves.

There were two little slave boys in the house, on whom she vented her bad temper in a special manner. One of these children was a mulatto, called Cyrus, who had been bought while an infant in his mother's arms; the other, Jack, was an African from the coast of Guinea, whom a sailor had given or sold to my master. Seldom a day passed without these boys receiving the most severe treatment, and often for no fault at all. Both my master and mistress seemed to think that they had a right to ill-use them at their pleasure; and very often accompanied their commands with blows, whether the children were behaving well or ill. I have seen their flesh ragged and raw with licks.—Lick—lick—they were never secure one moment from a blow, and their lives were passed in continual fear. My mistress was not contented with using the whip, but often pinched their cheeks and arms in the most cruel manner. My pity for these poor boys was soon transferred to myself; for I was licked, and flogged, and pinched by her pitiless fingers in the neck and arms, exactly as they were. To strip me naked—to hang me up by the wrists and lay my flesh open with the cow-skin, was an ordinary punishment for even a slight offence. My mistress often robbed me too of the hours that belong to sleep. She used to sit up very late, frequently even until morning; and I had then to stand at a bench and wash during the greater part of the night, or pick wool and cotton and often I have dropped down overcome by sleep and fatigue, till roused from a state of stupor by the whip, and forced to start up to my tasks.

Poor Hetty, my fellow slave, was very kind to me, and I used to call her my Aunt; but she led a most miserable life, and her death was hastened (at least the slaves all believed and said so,) by the dreadful chastisement she received from my master during her pregnancy. It happened as follows. One of the cows had dragged the rope away from the stake to which Hetty had fastened it, and got loose. My master flew into a terrible passion, and ordered the poor creature to be stripped quite naked, notwithstanding her pregnancy, and to be tied up to a tree in the yard. He then flogged her as hard as he could lick, both with the whip and cow-skin, till she was all over streaming with blood. He rested, and then beat her again and again. Her shrieks were terrible. The consequence was that poor Hetty was brought to bed before her time, and was delivered after severe labour of a dead child. She appeared to recover after her confinement, so far that she was repeatedly flogged by both master and mistress afterwards; but her former strength never returned to her. Ere long her body and limbs swelled to a great size; and she lay on a mat in the kitchen, till the water burst out of her body and she died. All the slaves said that death was a good thing for poor Hetty; but I cried very much for her death. The manner of it filled me with horror. I could not bear to think about it; yet it was always present to my mind for many a day.

After Hetty died all her labours fell upon me, in addition to my own. I had now to milk eleven cows every morning before sunrise, sitting among the damp weeds; to take care of the cattle as well as the children; and to do the work of the house. There was no end to my toils—no end to my blows. I lay down at night and rose up in the morning in fear and sorrow; and often wished that like poor Hetty I could escape from this cruel bondage and be at rest in the grave. But the hand of that God whom then I knew not, was stretched over me; and I was mercifully preserved for better things. It was then, however, my heavy lot to weep, weep, weep, and that for years; to pass from one misery to another, and from one cruel master to a worse. But I must go on with the thread of my story. One day a heavy squall of wind and rain came on suddenly, and my mistress sent me round the corner of the house to empty a large earthen jar. The jar was already cracked with an old deep crack that divided it in the middle, and in turning it upside down to empty it, it parted in my hand. I could not help the accident, but I was dreadfully frightened, looking forward to a severe punishment. I ran crying to my mistress, "O mistress, the jar has come in two." "You have broken it, have you?" she replied; "come directly here to me." I came trembling: she stripped and flogged me long and severely with the cow-skin; as long as she had strength to use the lash, for she did not give over till she was quite tired.—When my master came home at night, she told him of my fault; and oh, frightful! how he fell a swearing. After abusing me with every ill name he could think of, (too, too bad to speak in England,) and giving me several heavy blows with his hand, he said, "I shall come home to-morrow morning at twelve, on purpose to give you a round hundred." He kept his word—Oh sad for me! I cannot easily forget it. He tied me up upon a ladder, and gave me a hundred lashes with his own hand, and master Benjy stood by to count them for him. When he had licked me for some time he sat down to take breath; then after resting, he beat me again and again, until he

was quite wearied, and so hot (for the weather was very sultry), that he sank back in his chair, almost like to faint. While my mistress went to bring him drink, there was a dreadful earthquake. Part of the roof fell down, and every thing in the house went—clatter, clatter, clatter. Oh I thought the end of all things near at hand; and I was so sore with the flogging, that I scarcely cared whether I lived or died. The earth was groaning and shaking; every thing tumbling about; and my mistress and the slaves were shrieking and crying out, "The earthquake! the earthquake!" It was an awful day for us all.

During the confusion I crawled away on my hands and knees, and laid myself down under the steps of the piazza, in front of the house. I was in a dreadful state— my body all blood and bruises, and I could not help moaning piteously. The other slaves, when they saw me, shook their heads and said, "Poor child! poor child"—I lay there till the morning, careless of what might happen, for life was very weak in me, and I wished more than ever to die. But when we are very young, death always seems a great way off, and it would not come that night to me. The next morning I was forced by my master to rise and go about my usual work, though my body and limbs were so stiff and sore, that I could not move without the greatest pain.—Nevertheless, even after all this severe punishment, I never heard the last of that jar; my mistress was always throwing it in my face.

Some little time after this, one of the cows got loose from the stake, and eat one of the sweet-potato slips. I was milking when my master found it out. He came to me, and without any more ado, stooped down, and taking off his heavy boot, he struck me such a severe blow in the small of my back, that I shrieked with agony, and thought I was killed; and I feel a weakness in that part to this day. The cow was frightened by his violence, and kicked down the pail and spilt the milk all about. My master knew that this accident was his own fault, but he was so enraged that he seemed glad of an excuse to go on with his ill usage. I cannot remember how many licks he gave me then, but he beat me till I was unable to stand, and till he himself was weary.

After this I ran away and went to my mother, who was living with Mr. Richard Darrel. My poor mother was both grieved and glad to see me; grieved because I had been so ill used, and glad because she had not seen me for a long, long while. She dared not receive me into the house, but she hid me up in a hole in the rocks near, and brought me food at night, after every body was asleep. My father, who lived at Crow-Lane, over the salt-water channel, at last heard of my being hid up in the cavern, and he came and took me back to my master. Oh I was loath, loath to go back; but as there was no remedy, I was obliged to submit.

When we got home, my poor father said to Capt. I—, "Sir, I am sorry that my child should be forced to run away from her owner; but the treatment she has received is enough to break her heart. The sight of her wounds has nearly broke mine.—I entreat you, for the love of God, to forgive her for running away, and that you will be a kind master to her in future." Capt. I— said I was used as well as I deserved, and that I ought to be punished for running away. I then took courage and said that I could stand the floggings no longer; that I was weary of my life, and therefore I had run away to my mother; but mothers could only weep and mourn over their children, they could not save them from cruel masters—from the whip, the rope, and the cow-skin. He told me to hold my tongue and go about my work, or he would find a way to settle me. He did not, however, flog me that day.

For five years after this I remained in his house, and almost daily received the same harsh treatment. At length he put me on board a sloop,[1] and to my great joy sent me away to Turk's Island.[2] I was not permitted to see my mother or father, or poor sisters and brothers, to say good bye, though going away to a strange land, and might never see them again. Oh the Buckra[3] people who keep slaves think that black people are like cattle, without natural affection. But my heart tells me it is far otherwise.

We were nearly four weeks on the voyage, which was unusually long. Sometimes we had a light breeze, sometimes a great calm, and the ship made no way; so that our provisions and water ran very low, and we were put upon short allowance. I should almost have been starved had it not been for the kindness of a black man called Anthony, and his wife, who had brought their own victuals, and shared them with me.

When we went ashore at the Grand Quay, the captain sent me to the house of my new master, Mr. D—, to whom Captain I— had sold me. Grand Quay is a small town upon a sandbank; the houses low and built of wood. Such was my new master's. The first person I saw, on my arrival, was Mr. D—, a stout sulky looking man, who carried me through the hall to show me to his wife and children. Next day I was put up by the vendue master to know how much I was worth, and I was valued at one hundred pounds currency.

My new master was one of the owners or holders of the salt ponds, and he received a certain sum for every slave that worked upon his premises, whether they were young or old. This sum was allowed him out of the profits arising from the salt works. I was immediately sent to work in the salt water with the rest of the slaves. This work was perfectly new to me. I was given a half barrel and a shovel, and had to stand up to my knees in the water, from four o'clock in the morning till nine, when we were given some Indian corn boiled in water, which we were obliged to swallow as fast as we could for fear the rain should come on and melt the salt. We were then called again to our tasks, and worked through the heat of the day; the sun flaming upon our heads like fire, and raising salt blisters in those parts which were not completely covered. Our feet and legs, from standing in the salt water for so many hours, soon became full of dreadful boils, which eat down in some cases to the very bone, afflicting the sufferers with great torment. We came home at twelve; ate our corn soup, called *blawly,* as fast as we could, and went back to our employment till dark at night. We then shovelled up the salt in large heaps, and went down to the sea, where we washed the pickle from our limbs, and cleaned the barrows and shovels from the salt. When we returned to the house, our master gave us each our allowance of raw Indian corn, which we pounded in a mortar and boiled in water for our suppers. We slept in a long shed, divided into narrow slips, like the stalls used for cattle. Boards fixed upon stakes driven into the ground, without mat or covering, were our only beds. On Sundays, after we had washed the salt bags, and done

---

[1] *sloop* Small ship.

[2] *Turk's Island* The southernmost and easternmost islands of the Bahamas.

[3] *Buckra* White.

other work required of us, we went into the bush and cut the long soft grass, of which we made trusses for our legs and feet to rest upon, for they were so full of the salt boils that we could get no rest lying upon the bare boards.

Though we worked from morning till night, there was no satisfying Mr. D—. I hoped, when I left Capt. I—, that I should have been better off, but I found it was but going from one butcher to another. There was this difference between them: my former master used to beat me while raging and foaming with passion; Mr. D— was usually quite calm. He would stand by and give orders for a slave to be cruelly whipped, and assist in the punishment, without moving a muscle of his face; walking about and taking snuff with the greatest composure. Nothing could touch his hard heart—neither sighs, nor tears, nor prayers, nor streaming blood; he was deaf to our cries, and careless of our sufferings.—Mr. D— has often stripped me naked, hung me up by the wrists, and beat me with the cow-skin, with his own hand, till my body was raw with gashes. Yet there was nothing very remarkable in this; for it might serve as a sample of the common usage of the slaves on that horrible island.

Owing to the boils in my feet, I was unable to wheel the barrow fast through the sand, which got into the sores, and made me stumble at every step; and my master, having no pity for my sufferings from this cause, rendered them far more intolerable, by chastising me for not being able to move so fast as he wished me. Another of our employments was to row a little way off from the shore in a boat, and dive for large stones to build a wall round our master's house. This was very hard work; and the great waves breaking over us continually, made us often so giddy that we lost our footing, and were in danger of being drowned.

Ah, poor me!—my tasks were never ended. Sick or well, it was work—work—work!—After the diving season was over, we were sent to the South Creek, with large bills, to cut up mangoes to burn lime with. Whilst one party of slaves were thus employed, another were sent to the other side of the island to break up coral out of the sea.

When we were ill, let our complaint be what it might, the only medicine given to us was a great bowl of hot salt water, with salt mixed with it, which made us very sick. If we could not keep up with the rest of the gang of slaves, we were put in the stocks,[1] and severely flogged the next morning. Yet, not the less, our master expected, after we had thus been kept from our rest, and our limbs rendered stiff and sore with ill usage, that we should still go through the ordinary tasks of the day all the same.—Sometimes we had to work all night, measuring salt to load a vessel; or turning a machine to draw water out of the sea for the salt-making. Then we had no sleep—no rest—but were forced to work as fast as we could, and go on again all next day the same as usual. Work—work —work—Oh that Turk's Island was a horrible place! The people in England, I am sure, have never found out what is carried on there. Cruel, horrible place!

Mr. D— had a slave called old Daniel, whom he used to treat in the most cruel manner. Poor Daniel was lame in the hip, and could not keep up with the rest of the slaves; and our master would order him to be stripped and laid down on the ground, and have him beaten with a rod of rough briar till his skin was quite red and raw. He would then call for a bucket of salt, and fling upon the raw flesh till the man writhed on the ground like a worm, and screamed aloud with agony. This poor man's wounds were never healed, and I have often seen them full of maggots, which increased his torments to an intolerable degree. He was an object of pity and terror to the whole gang of slaves, and in his wretched case we saw, each of us, our own lot, if we should live to be as old.

Oh the horrors of slavery!—How the thought of it pains my heart! But the truth ought to be told of it; and what my eyes have seen I think it is my duty to relate; for few people in England know what slavery is. I have been a slave—I have felt what a slave feels, and I know what a slave knows; and I would have all the good people in England to know it too, that they may break our chains, and set us free.

Mr. D— had another slave called Ben. He being very hungry, stole a little rice one night after he came in from work, and cooked it for his supper. But his master soon discovered the theft; locked him up all night; and kept him without food till one o'clock the next day. He

---

[1] *stocks*   Device for confining the ankles and sometimes the wrists.

then hung Ben up by his hands, and beat him from time to time till the slaves came in at night. We found the poor creature hung up when we came home; with a pool of blood beneath him, and our master still licking him, but this was not the worst. My master's son was in the habit of stealing the rice and rum. Ben had seen him do this, and thought he might do the same, and when master found out that Ben had stolen the rice and swore to punish him, he tried to excuse himself by saying that Master Dickey did the same thing every night. The lad denied it to his father, and was so angry with Ben for informing against him, that out of revenge he ran and got a bayonet, and whilst the poor wretch was suspended by his hands and writhing under his wounds, he run it quite through his foot. I was not by when he did it, but I saw the wound when I came home, and heard Ben tell the manner in which it was done.

I must say something more about this cruel son of a cruel father.—He had no heart—no fear of God; he had been brought up by a bad father in a bad path, and he delighted to follow in the same steps. There was a little old woman among the slaves called Sarah, who was nearly past work; and, Master Dickey being the overseer of the slaves just then, this poor creature, who was subject to several bodily infirmities, and was not quite right in her head, did not wheel the barrow fast enough to please him. He threw her down on the ground, and after beating her severely, he took her up in his arms and flung her among the prickly-pear[1] bushes, which are all covered over with sharp venomous prickles. By this her naked flesh was so grievously wounded, that her body swelled and festered all over, and she died in a few days after. In telling my own sorrows, I cannot pass by those of my fellow-slaves—for when I think of my own griefs, I remember theirs.

I think it was about ten years I had worked in the salt ponds at Turk's Island, when my master left off business, and retired to a house he had in Bermuda, leaving his son to succeed him in the island. He took me with him to wait upon his daughters; and I was joyful, for I was sick, sick of Turk's Island, and my heart yearned to see my native place again, my mother, and my kindred.

I had seen my poor mother during the time I was a

slave in Turk's Island. One Sunday morning I was on the beach with some of the slaves, and we saw a sloop come in loaded with slaves to work in the salt water. We got a boat and went aboard. When I came upon the deck I asked the black people, "Is there any one here for me?" "Yes," they said, "your mother." I thought they said this in jest—I could scarcely believe them for joy; but when I saw my poor mammy my joy was turned to sorrow, for she had gone from her senses. "Mammy," I said, "is this you!" She did not know me. "Mammy," I said, "what's the matter?" She began to talk foolishly and said that she had been under the vessel's bottom. They had been overtaken by a violent storm at sea. My poor mother had never been on the sea before, and she was so ill, that she lost her senses, and it was long before she came quite to herself again. She had a sweet child with her—a little sister I had never seen, about four years of age, called Rebecca. I took her on shore with me, for I felt I should love her directly; and I kept her with me a week. Poor little thing! her's has been a sad life, and continues so to this day. My mother worked for some years on the island, but was taken back to Bermuda some time before my master carried me again thither.

After I left Turk's Island, I was told by some negroes that came over from it, that the poor slaves had built up a place with boughs and leaves, where they might meet for prayers, but the white people pulled it down twice, and would not allow them even a shed for prayers. A flood came down soon after and washed away many houses, filled the place with sand, and overflowed the ponds: and I do think that this was for their wickedness; for the Buckra men there were very wicked. I saw and heard much that was very very bad at that place.

I was several years the slave of Mr. D— after I returned to my native place. Here I worked in the grounds. My work was planting and hoeing sweet-potatoes, Indian corn, plaintains, bananas, cabbages, pumpkins, onions, &c. I did all the household work, and attended upon a horse and cow besides,—going also upon all errands. I had to curry the horse—to clean and feed him—and sometimes to ride him a little. I had more than enough to do—but still it was not so very bad as Turk's Island.

My old master often got drunk, and then he would

---

[1] *prickly-pear* Type of cactus.

get in a fury with his daughter, and beat her till she was not fit to be seen. I remember on one occasion, I had gone to fetch water, and when I was coming up the hill I heard a great screaming; I ran as fast as I could to the house, put down the water, and went into the chamber, where I found my master beating Miss D— dreadfully. I strove with all my strength to get her away from him; for she was all black and blue with bruises. He had beat her with his fist, and almost killed her. The people gave me credit for getting her away. He turned round and began to lick me. Then I said, "Sir, this is not Turk's Island." I can't repeat his answer, the words were too wicked—too bad to say. He wanted to treat me the same in Bermuda as he had done in Turk's Island.

He had an ugly fashion of stripping himself quite naked and ordering me then to wash him in a tub of water. This was worse to me than all the licks. Sometimes when he called me to wash him I would not come, my eyes were so full of shame. He would then come to beat me. One time I had plates and knives in my hand, and I dropped both plates and knives, and some of the plates were broken. He struck me so severely for this, that at last I defended myself, for I thought it was high time to do so. I then told him I would not live longer with him, for he was a very indecent man—very spiteful, and too indecent; with no shame for his servants, no shame for his own flesh. So I went away to a neighbouring house and sat down and cried till the next morning, when I went home again, not knowing what else to do.

After that I was hired to work at Cedar Hills, and every Saturday night I paid the money to my master. I had plenty of work to do there—plenty of washing; but yet I made myself pretty comfortable. I earned two dollars and a quarter a week, which is twenty pence a day.

During the time I worked there, I heard that Mr. John Wood was going to Antigua. I felt a great wish to go there, and I went to Mr. D—, and asked him to let me go in Mr. Wood's service. Mr. Wood did not then want to purchase me; it was my own fault that I came under him, I was so anxious to go. It was ordained to be, I suppose; God led me there. The truth is, I did not wish to be any longer the slave of my indecent master. Mr. Wood took me with him to Antigua, to the town of St. John's, where he lived. This was about fifteen years

ago. He did not then know whether I was to be sold; but Mrs. Wood found that I could work, and she wanted to buy me. Her husband then wrote to my master to inquire whether I was to be sold? Mr. D— wrote in reply, "that I should not be sold to any one that would treat me ill." It was strange he should say this, when he had treated me so ill himself. So I was purchased by Mr. Wood for 300 dollars (or £100 Bermuda currency).

My work there was to attend the chambers and nurse the child, and to go down to the pond and wash clothes. But I soon fell ill of the rheumatism, and grew so very lame that I was forced to walk with a stick. I got the Saint Anthony's fire,[1] also, in my left leg, and became quite a cripple. No one cared much to come near me, and I was ill a long long time; for several months I could not lift the limb. I had to lie in a little old out-house, that was swarming with bugs and other vermin, which tormented me greatly; but I had no other place to lie in. I got the rheumatism by catching cold at the pond side, from washing in the fresh water; in the salt water I never got cold. The person who lived in next yard, (a Mrs. Greene,) could not bear to hear my cries and groans. She was kind, and used to send an old slave woman to help me, who sometimes brought me a little soup. When the doctor found I was so ill, he said I must be put into a bath of hot water. The old slave got the bark of some bush that was good for pains, which she boiled in the hot water, and every night she came and put me into the bath, and did what she could for me; I don't know what I should have done, or what would have become of me, had it not been for her.—My mistress, it is true, did send me a little food; but no one from our family came near me but the cook, who used to shove my food in at the door, and say, "Molly, Molly, there's your dinner." My mistress did not care to take any trouble about me; and if the Lord had not put it into the hearts of the neighbours to be kind to me, I must, I really think, have lain and died.

It was a long time before I got well enough to work in the house. Mrs. Wood, in the meanwhile, hired a mulatto woman to nurse the child; but she was such a fine lady she wanted to be mistress over me. I thought

---

[1] *Saint Anthony's fire* Erysipelas or ergotism, diseases that cause intense redness, swelling of the skin, and severe pain.

it very hard for a coloured woman to have rule over me because I was a slave and she was free. Her name was Martha Wilcox; she was a saucy woman, very saucy; and she went and complained of me, without cause, to my mistress, and made her angry with me. Mrs. Wood told me that if I did not mind what I was about, she would get my master to strip me and give me fifty lashes: "You have been used to the whip," she said, "and you shall have it here." This was the first time she threatened to have me flogged; and she gave me the threatening so strong of what she would have done to me, that I thought I should have fallen down at her feet, I was so vexed and hurt by her words. The mulatto woman was rejoiced to have power to keep me down. She was constantly making mischief; there was no living for the slaves—no peace after she came.

I was also sent by Mrs. Wood to be put in the Cage one night, and was next morning flogged, by the magistrate's order, at her desire; and this all for a quarrel I had about a pig with another slave woman. I was flogged on my naked back on this occasion; although I was in no fault after all; for old Justice Dyett, when we came before him, said that I was in the right, and ordered the pig to be given to me. This was about two or three years after I came to Antigua.

When we moved from the middle of the town to the Point, I used to be in the house and do all the work and mind the children, though still very ill with the rheumatism. Every week I had to wash two large bundles of clothes, as much as a boy could help me to lift; but I could give no satisfaction. My mistress was always abusing and fretting after me. It is not possible to tell all her ill language.—One day she followed me foot after foot scolding and rating me. I bore in silence a great deal of ill words: at last my heart was quite full, and I told her that she ought not to use me so;—that when I was ill I might have lain and died for what she cared; and no one would then come near me to nurse me, because they were afraid of my mistress. This was a great affront. She called her husband and told him what I had said. He flew into a passion: but did not beat me then; he only abused and swore at me; and then gave me a note and bade me go and look for an owner. Not that he meant to sell me; but he did this to please his wife

and to frighten me. I went to Adam White, a cooper,[1] a free black who had money, and asked him to buy me. He went directly to Mr. Wood, but was informed that I was not to be sold. The next day my master whipped me.

Another time (about five years ago) my mistress got vexed with me because I fell sick and I could not keep on with my work. She complained to her husband, and he sent me off again to look for an owner. I went to a Mr. Burchell, showed him the note, and asked him to buy me for my own benefit; for I had saved about 100 dollars, and hoped with a little help, to purchase my freedom. He accordingly went to my master:—"Mr. Wood," he said, "Molly has brought me a note that she wants an owner. If you intend to sell her, I may as well buy her as another." My master put him off and said that he did not mean to sell me. I was very sorry at this, for I had no comfort with Mrs. Wood, and I wished greatly to get my freedom.

The way in which I made my money was this.— When my master and mistress went from home, as they sometimes did, and left me to take care of the house and premises, I had a good deal of time to myself and made the most of it. I took in washing, and sold coffee and yams and other provisions to the captains of ships. I did not sit still idling during the absence of my owners; for I wanted, by all honest means, to earn money to buy my freedom. Sometimes I bought a hog cheap on board ship, and sold it for double the money on shore; and I also earned a good deal by selling coffee. By this means I by degrees acquired a little cash. A gentleman also lent me some to help to buy my freedom—but when I could not get free he got it back again. His name was Captain Abbot.

My master and mistress went on one occasion into the country, to Date Hill, for a change of air, and carried me with them to take charge of the children, and to do the work of the house. While I was in the country, I saw how the field negroes are worked in Antigua. They are worked very hard and fed but scantily. They are called out to work before daybreak, and come home after dark; and then each has to heave his bundle of grass for the cattle in the pen. Then, on Sunday morning, each slave has to go out and gather a large

---

[1] *cooper* Barrel-and tub-maker.

bundle of grass; and, when they bring it home, they have all to sit at the manager's door and wait till he comes out: often have they to wait there till past eleven o'clock without any breakfast. After that, those that have yams or potatoes, or fire-wood to sell, hasten to market to buy a dog's worth[1] of salt fish, or pork, which is a great treat for them. Some of them buy a little pickle out of the shad barrels, which they call sauce, to season their yams and Indian corn. It is very wrong, I know, to work on Sunday or go to market; but will not God call the Buckra men to answer for this on the great day of judgment—since they will give the slaves no other day?

While we were at Date Hill Christmas came; and the slave woman who had the care of the place (which then belonged to Mr. Roberts the marshal), asked me to go with her to her husband's house, to a Methodist meeting for prayer, at a plantation called Winthorps. I went; and they were the first prayers I ever understood. One woman prayed; and then they all sung a hymn; then there was another prayer and another hymn; and then they all spoke by turns of their own griefs as sinners. The husband of the woman I went with was a black driver. His name was Henry. He confessed that he had treated the slaves very cruelly; but said that he was compelled to obey the orders of his master. He prayed them all to forgive him, and he prayed that God would forgive him. He said it was a horrid thing for a ranger to have sometimes to beat his own wife or sister; but he must do so if ordered by his master.

I felt sorry for my sins also. I cried the whole night, but I was too much ashamed to speak. I prayed God to forgive me. This meeting had a great impression on my mind, and led my spirit to the Moravian church; so that when I got back to town, I went and prayed to have my name put down in the Missionaries' book; and I followed the church earnestly every opportunity. I did not then tell my mistress about it; for I knew that she would not give me leave to go. But I felt I *must* go. Whenever I carried the children their lunch at school, I ran round and went to hear the teachers.

The Moravian ladies (Mrs. Richter, Mrs. Olufsen, and Mrs. Sauter) taught me to read in the class; and I got on very fast. In this class there were all sorts of people, old and young, grey headed folks and children;

but most of them were free people. After we had done spelling, we tried to read in the Bible. After the reading was over, the missionary gave out a hymn for us to sing. I dearly loved to go to the church, it was so solemn. I never knew rightly that I had much sin till I went there. When I found out that I was a great sinner, I was very sorely grieved, and very much frightened. I used to pray God to pardon my sins for Christ's sake, and forgive me for every thing I had done amiss; and when I went home to my work, I always thought about what I had heard from the missionaries, and wished to be good that I might go to heaven. After a while I was admitted a candidate for the holy Communion.—I had been baptized long before this, in August 1817, by the Rev. Mr. Curtin, of the English Church, after I had been taught to repeat the Creed and the Lord's Prayer. I wished at that time to attend a Sunday School taught by Mr. Curtin, but he would not receive me without a written note from my master, granting his permission. I did not ask my owner's permission, from the belief that it would be refused; so that I got no farther instruction at that time from the English Church.

Some time after I began to attend the Moravian Church, I met with Daniel James, afterwards my dear husband. He was a carpenter and cooper to his trade; an honest, hard-working, decent black man, and a widower. He had purchased his freedom of his mistress, old Mrs. Baker, with money he had earned whilst a slave. When he asked me to marry him, I took time to consider the matter over with myself, and would not say yes till he went to church with me and joined the Moravians. He was very industrious after he bought his freedom; and he had hired a comfortable house, and had convenient things about him. We were joined in marriage, about Christmas 1826, in the Moravian Chapel at Spring Gardens, by the Rev. Mr. Olufsen. We could not be married in the English Church. English marriage is not allowed to slaves; and no free man can marry a slave woman.

When Mr. Wood heard of my marriage, he flew into a great rage, and sent for Daniel, who was helping to build a house for his old mistress. Mr. Wood asked him who gave him a right to marry a slave of his? My husband said, "Sir, I am a free man, and thought I had a right to choose a wife; but if I had known Molly was

---

[1] *dog's worth* 72nd part of a dollar.

not allowed to have a husband, I should not have asked her to marry me." Mrs. Wood was more vexed about my marriage than her husband. She could not forgive me for getting married, but stirred up Mr. Wood to flog me dreadfully with his horsewhip. I thought it very hard to be whipped at my time of life for getting a husband—I told her so. She said that she would not have nigger men about the yards and premises, or allow a nigger man's clothes to be washed in the same tub where hers were washed. She was fearful, I think, that I should lose her time, in order to wash and do things for my husband: but I had then no time to wash for myself; I was obliged to put out my own clothes, though I was always at the wash-tub.

I had not much happiness in my marriage, owing to my being a slave. It made my husband sad to see me so ill-treated. Mrs. Wood was always abusing me about him. She did not lick me herself, but she got her husband to do it for her, whilst she fretted the flesh off my bones. Yet for all this she would not sell me. She sold five slaves whilst I was with her; but though she was always finding fault with me, she would not part with me. However, Mr. Wood afterwards allowed Daniel to have a place to live in our yard, which we were very thankful for.

After this, I fell ill again with the rheumatism, and was sick a long time; but whether sick or well, I had my work to do. About this time I asked my master and mistress to let me buy my own freedom. With the help of Mr. Burchell, I could have found the means to pay Mr. Wood; for it was agreed that I should afterwards serve Mr. Burchell a while, for the cash he was to advance for me. I was earnest in the request to my owners; but their hearts were hard—too hard to consent. Mrs. Wood was very angry—she grew quite outrageous—she called me a black devil, and asked me who had put freedom into my head. "To be free is very sweet," I said: but she took good care to keep me a slave. I saw her change colour, and I left the room.

About this time my master and mistress were going to England to put their son in school, and bring their daughters home; and they took me with them to take care of the child. I was willing to come to England: I thought that by going there I should probably get cured of my rheumatism, and should return with my master

and mistress, quite well, to my husband. My husband was willing for me to come away, for he had heard that my master would free me,—and I also hoped this might prove true; but it was all a false report.

The steward of the ship was very kind to me. He and my husband were in the same class in the Moravian Church. I was thankful that he was so friendly, for my mistress was not kind to me on the passage; and she told me, when she was angry, that she did not intend to treat me any better in England than in the West Indies—that I need not expect it. And she was as good as her word.

When we drew near to England, the rheumatism seized all my limbs worse than ever, and my body was dreadfully swelled. When we landed at the Tower, I showed my flesh to my mistress, but she took no great notice of it. We were obliged to stop at the tavern till my master got a house; and a day or two after, my mistress sent me down into the wash-house to learn to wash in the English way. In the West Indies we wash with cold water—in England with hot. I told my mistress I was afraid that putting my hands first into the hot water and then into the cold, would increase the pain in my limbs. The doctor had told my mistress long before I came from the West Indies, that I was a sickly body and the washing did not agree with me. But Mrs. Wood would not release me from the tub, so I was forced to do as I could. I grew worse, and could not stand to wash. I was then forced to sit down with the tub before me, and often through pain and weakness was reduced to kneel or to sit down on the floor, to finish my task. When I complained to my mistress of this, she only got into a passion as usual, and said washing in hot water could not hurt any one;—that I was lazy and insolent, and wanted to be free of my work; but that she would make me do it. I thought her very hard on me, and my heart rose up within me. However I kept still at that time, and went down again to wash the child's things; but the English washerwomen who were at work there, when they saw that I was so ill, had pity upon me and washed them for me.

After that, when we came up to live in Leigh Street, Mrs. Wood sorted out five bags of clothes which we had used at sea, and also such as had been worn since we came on shore, for me and the cook to wash. Elizabeth the cook told her, that she did not think that I was able to stand to the tub, and that she had better hire a woman. I also said myself, that I had come over to nurse the child, and that I was sorry I had come from Antigua, since mistress would work me so hard, without compassion for my rheumatism. Mr. and Mrs. Wood, when they heard this, rose up in a passion against me. They opened the door and bade me get out. But I was a stranger, and did not know one door in the street from another, and was unwilling to go away. They made a dreadful uproar, and from that day they constantly kept cursing and abusing me. I was obliged to wash, though I was very ill. Mrs. Wood, indeed once hired a washerwoman, but she was not well treated, and would come no more.

My master quarrelled with me another time, about one of our great washings, his wife having stirred him up to do so. He said he would compel me to do the whole of the washing given out to me, or if I again refused, he would take a short course with me: he would either send me down to the brig in the river, to carry me back to Antigua, or he would turn me at once out of doors, and let me provide for myself. I said I would willingly go back, if he would let me purchase my own freedom. But this enraged him more than all the rest: he cursed and swore at me dreadfully, and said he would never sell my freedom—if I wished to be free, I was free in England, and I might go and try what freedom would do for me, and be d——d. My heart was very sore with this treatment, but I had to go on. I continued to do my work, and did all I could to give satisfaction, but all would not do.

Shortly after, the cook left them, and then matters went on ten times worse. I always washed the child's clothes without being commanded to do it, and any thing else that was wanted in the family; though still I was very sick—very sick indeed. When the great washing came round, which was every two months, my mistress got together again a great many heavy things, such as bed-ticks, bed-coverlets, &c. for me to wash. I told her I was too ill to wash such heavy things that day. She said, she supposed I thought myself a free woman, but I was not; and if I did not do it directly I should be instantly turned out of doors. I stood a long time before I could answer, for I did not know well what to do. I knew that I was free in England, but I did not know

where to go, or how to get my living; and therefore, I did not like to leave the house. But Mr. Wood said he would send for a constable to thrust me out; and at last I took courage and resolved that I would not be longer thus treated, but would go and trust to Providence. This was the fourth time they had threatened to turn me out, and, go where I might, I was determined now to take them at their word; though I thought it very hard, after I had lived with them for thirteen years, and worked for them like a horse, to be driven out in this way, like a beggar. My only fault was being sick, and therefore unable to please my mistress, who thought she never could get work enough out of her slaves; and I told them so: but they only abused me and drove me out. This took place from two to three months, I think, after we came to England.

When I came away, I went to the man (one Mash) who used to black the shoes of the family, and asked his wife to get somebody to go with me to Hatton Garden to the Moravian Missionaries: these were the only persons I knew in England. The woman sent a young girl with me to the mission house, and I saw there a gentleman called Mr. Moore. I told him my whole story, and how my owners had treated me, and asked him to take in my truck with what few clothes I had. The missionaries were very kind to me—they were sorry for my destitute situation, and gave me leave to bring my things to be placed under their care. They were very good people, and they told me to come to the church.

When I went back to Mr. Wood's to get my trunk, I saw a lady, Mrs. Pell, who was on a visit to my mistress. When Mr. and Mrs. Wood heard me come in, they set this lady to stop me, finding that they had gone too far with me. Mrs. Pell came out to me, and said, "Are you really going to leave, Molly? Don't leave, but come into the country with me." I believe she said this because she thought Mrs. Wood would easily get me back again. I replied to her, "Ma'am, this is the fourth time my master and mistress have driven me out, or threatened to drive me—and I will give them no more occasion to bid me go. I was not willing to leave them, for I am a stranger in this country, but now I must go—I can stay no longer to be used." Mrs. Pell then went up stairs to my mistress, and told that I would go, and that she could not stop me. Mrs. Wood was very much hurt and frightened when she found I was determined to go out that day. She said, "If she goes the people will rob her, and then turn her adrift." She did not say this to me, but she spoke it loud enough for me to hear; that it might induce me not to go, I suppose. Mr. Wood also asked me where I was going to. I told him where I had been, and that I should never have gone away had I not been driven out by my owners. He had given me a written paper some time before, which said that I had come with them to England by my own desire; and that was true. It said also that I left them of my own free will, because I was a free woman in England; and that I was idle and would not do my work— which was not true. I gave this paper afterwards to a gentleman who inquired into my case.

I went into the kitchen and got my clothes out. The nurse and the servant girl were there, and I said to the man who was going to take out my trunk, "Stop, before you take up this trunk, and hear what I have to say before these people. I am going out of this house, as I was ordered; but I have done no wrong at all to my owners, neither here nor in the West Indies. I always worked very hard to please them, both by night and day; but there was no giving satisfaction, for my mistress could never be satisfied with reasonable service. I told my mistress I was sick, and yet she has ordered me out of doors. This is the fourth time; and now I am going out."

And so I came out, and went and carried my trunk to the Moravians. I then returned back to Mash the shoeblack's house, and begged his wife to take me in. I had a little West Indian money in my trunk; and they got it changed for me. This helped to support me for a little while. The man's wife was very kind to me. I was very sick, and she boiled nourishing things up for me. She also sent for a doctor to see me, and sent me medicine, which did me good, though I was ill for a long time with the rheumatic pains. I lived a good many months with these poor people, and they nursed me, and did all that lay in their power to serve me. The man was well acquainted with my situation, as he used to go to and fro to Mr. Wood's house to clean shoes and knives; and he and his wife were sorry for me.

About this time, a woman of the name of Hill told me of the Anti-Slavery Society, and went with me to their office, to inquire if they could do any thing to get me my freedom, and send me back to the West Indies. The gentlemen of the Society took me to a lawyer, who examined very strictly into my case; but told me that the laws of England could do nothing to make me free in Antigua. However they did all they could for me: they gave me a little money from time to time to keep me from want; and some of them went to Mr. Wood to try to persuade him to let me return a free woman to my husband; but though they offered him, as I have heard, a large sum for my freedom, he was sulky and obstinate, and would not consent to let me go free.

This was the first winter I spent in England, and I suffered much from the severe cold, and from the rheumatic pains, which still at times torment me. However, Providence was very good to me, and I got many friends—especially some Quaker ladies, who hearing of my case, came and sought me out, and gave me good warm clothing and money. Thus I had great cause to bless God in my affliction.

When I got better I was anxious to get some work to do, as I was unwilling to eat the bread of idleness. Mrs. Mash, who was a laundress, recommended me to a lady for a charwoman. She paid me very handsomely for what work I did, and I divided the money with Mrs. Mash; for though very poor, they gave me food when my own money was done, and never suffered me to want.

In the spring, I got into service with a lady, who saw me at the house where I sometimes worked as a charwoman. This lady's name was Mrs. Forsyth. She had been in the West Indies, and was accustomed to Blacks, and liked them. I was with her six months, and went with her to Margate. She treated me well, and gave me a good character when she left London.

After Mrs. Forsyth went away, I was again out of place, and went to lodgings, for which I paid two shillings a week, and found coals and candle. After eleven weeks, the money I had saved in service was all gone, and I was forced to go back to the Anti-Slavery office to ask a supply, till I could get another situation. I did not like to go back—I did not like to be idle. I would rather work for my living than get it for nothing. They were very good to give me a supply, but I felt shame at being obliged to apply for relief whilst I had strength to work.

At last I went into the service of Mr. and Mrs.

Pringle, where I have been ever since, and am as comfortable as I can be while separated from my dear husband, and away from my own country and all old friends and connections. My dear mistress teaches me daily to read the word of God, and takes great pains to make me understand it. I enjoy the great privilege of being enabled to attend church three times on the Sunday; and I have met with many kind friends since I have been here, both clergymen and others. The Rev. Mr. Young, who lives in the next house, has shown me much kindness, and taken much pains to instruct me, particularly while my master and mistress were absent in Scotland. Nor must I forget, among my friends, the Rev. Mr. Mortimer, the good clergyman of the parish, under whose ministry I have now sat for upwards of twelve months. I trust in God I have profited by what I have heard from him. He never keeps back the truth, and I think he has been the means of opening my eyes and ears much better to understand the word of God. Mr. Mortimer tells me that he cannot open the eyes of my heart, but that I must pray to God to change my heart, and make me to know the truth, and the truth will make me free.

I still live in the hope that God will find a way to give me my liberty, and give me back to my husband. I endeavour to keep down my fretting, and to leave all to Him, for he knows what is good for me better than I know myself. Yet, I must confess, I find it a hard and heavy task to do so.

I am often much vexed, and I feel great sorrow when I hear some people in this country say, that the slaves do not need better usage, and do not want to be free. They believe the foreign people, who deceive them, and say slaves are happy. I say, Not so. How can slaves be happy when they have the halter round their neck and the whip upon their back? and are disgraced and thought no more of than beasts?—and are separated from their mothers, and husbands, and children, and sisters, just as cattle are sold and separated? Is it happiness for a driver in the field to take down his wife or sister or child, and strip them, and whip them in such a disgraceful manner?—women that have had children exposed in the open field to shame! There is no modesty or decency shown by the owner to his slaves; men, women, and children are exposed alike. Since I have been here I have

often wondered how English people can go out into the West Indies and act in such a beastly manner. But when they go to the West Indies, they forget God and all feeling of shame, I think, since they can see and do such things. They tie up slaves like hogs—moor them up like cattle, and they lick them, so as hogs, or cattle, or horses never were flogged;—and yet they come home and say, and make some good people believe, that slaves don't want to get out of slavery. But they put a cloak about the truth. It is not so. All slaves want to be free—to be free is very sweet. I will say the truth to English people who may read this history that my good friend, Miss S—, is now writing down for me. I have been a slave myself—I know what slaves feel—I can tell by myself what other slaves feel, and by what they have told me. The man that says slaves be quite happy in slavery—that they don't want to be free—that man is either ignorant or a lying person. I never heard a slave say so. I never heard a Buckra man say so, till I heard tell of it in England. Such people ought to be ashamed of themselves. They can't do without slaves they say. What's the reason they can't do without slaves as well as in England? No slaves here—no whips—no stocks—no punishment, except for wicked people. They hire servants in England; and if they don't like them, they send them away: they can't lick them. Let them work ever so hard in England, they are far better off than slaves. If they get a bad master, they give warning and go hire to another. They have their liberty. That's just what *we* want. We don't mind hard work, if we had proper treatment, and proper wages like English servants, and proper time given in the week to keep us from breaking the Sabbath. But they won't give it; they will have work—work—work, night and day, sick or well, till we are quite done up; and we must not speak up nor look amiss, however much we be abused. And then when we are quite done up, who cares for us, more than for a lame horse? This is slavery. I tell it to let English people know the truth; and I hope they will never leave off to pray God, and call loud to the great King of England, till all the poor blacks be given free, and slavery done up for evermore.

—1831

IN CONTEXT

Mary Prince and Slavery

Mary Prince's Petition Presented to Parliament on 24 June 1829

A Petition of Mary Prince or James, commonly called Molly Wood, was presented, and read; setting forth, That the Petitioner was born a Slave in the colony of Bermuda, and is now about forty years of age; That the Petitioner was sold some years go for the sum of 300 dollars to Mr. John Wood, by whom the Petitioner was carried to Antigua, where she has since, until lately resided as a domestic slave on his establishment; that in December 1826, the Petitioner who is connected with the Moravian Congregation, was married in a Moravian Chapel at Spring Gardens, in the parish of Saint John's, by the Moravian minister, Mr. Ellesen, to a free Black of the name of Daniel James, who is a carpenter at Saint John's, in Antigua, and also a member of the same congregation; that the Petitioner and the said Daniel James have lived together ever since as man and wife; that about ten months ago the Petitioner arrived in London, with her master and mistress, in the capacity of nurse to their child; that the Petitioner's master has offered to send her back in his brig to the West Indies , to work in the yard; that the Petitioner expressed her desire to return to the West Indies, but not as a slave, and has entreated her master to sell her, her freedom on account of her services as a nurse to his child, but he has refused, and still does refuse; further stating the particulars of her case; and praying the House to take the same into their consideration, and to grant such relief as to them may, under the circumstances, appear right. Ordered, That the said Petition do lie upon the Table.

from Thomas Pringle, Supplement to *The History of Mary Prince* (1831)

It was through the auspices of Thomas Pringle that Mary Prince's narrative came to be published, and that Prince found employment in London. Pringle contributed a substantial *Supplement* to the *History* when it was first published; excerpts are reproduced below.

By the Original Editor, Thomas Pringle

L eaving Mary's narrative, for the present, without comment to the reader's reflections, I proceed to state some circumstances connected with her case which have fallen more particularly under my own notice, and which I consider it incumbent now to lay fully before the public.

About the latter end of November, 1828, this poor woman found her way to the office of the Anti-Slavery Society in Aldermanbury, by the aid of a person who had become acquainted with her situation, and had advised her to apply there for advice and assistance. After some preliminary examination into the accuracy of the circumstances related by her, I went along with her to Mr. George Stephen, solicitor, and requested him to investigate and draw up a statement of her case, and have it submitted to counsel, in order to ascertain whether or not, under the circumstances, her freedom could be legally established on her return to Antigua. On this occasion, in Mr. Stephen's presence and mine, she expressed, in very strong terms, her anxiety to return thither if she could go as a free person, and, at the same time, her extreme apprehensions of the fate that would probably await her if she returned as a slave. Her words were, "I would rather go into my grave than go back a slave to Antigua, though I wish to go back to my husband very much—very much—very much! I am much afraid my owners would separate me from my husband, and use me very hard, or perhaps sell me for a field negro;—and slavery is too too bad. I would rather go into my grave!'

The paper which Mr. Wood had given her before she left his house, was placed by her in Mr. Stephen's hands. It was expressed in the following terms:—

"I have already told Molly, and now give it her in writing, in order that there may be no misunderstanding on her part, that as I brought her from Antigua at her own request and entreaty, and that she is consequently now free, she is of course at liberty to take her baggage and go where she pleases. And, in consequence of her late conduct, she must do one of two things—either quit the house, or return to Antigua by the earliest opportunity, as she does not evince a disposition to make herself useful. As she is a stranger in London, I do not wish to turn her out, or would do so, as two female servants are sufficient for my establishment. If after this she does remain, it will be only during her good behaviour; but on no consideration will I allow her wages or any other remuneration for her services.

JOHN A. WOOD
London, 18 August 1828

This paper, though not devoid of inconsistencies, which will be apparent to any attentive reader, is craftily expressed; and was well devised to serve the purpose which the writer had obviously in view, namely, to frustrate any appeal which the friendless black woman might make to the sympathy of strangers, and thus prevent her from obtaining an asylum, if she left his house, from any respectable family. As she had no one to refer to for a character in this country except himself, he doubtless calculated securely on her being speedily driven back, as soon as the slender fund she had in her possession was expended, to throw herself unconditionally upon his tender mercies; and his disappointment in this expectation appears to have exasperated his feelings of resentment towards the poor woman, to a degree which few persons alive to the claims of common justice, not to speak of Christianity or common humanity, could easily have anticipated. Such, at least, seems the only intelligible inference that can be drawn from his subsequent conduct.

The case having been submitted, by desire of the Anti-Slavery Committee, to the consideration of Dr. Lushington and Mr. Sergeant Stephen, it was found that there existed no legal means of compelling Mary's master to grant her manumission; and that if she returned to Antigua, she would inevitably fall again under his power, or that of his attorneys, as a slave. It was, however, resolved to try what could be effected for her by amicable negotiation; and with this view Mr. Ravenscroft, a solicitor, (Mr. Stephen's relative,) called upon Mr. Wood, in order to ascertain whether he would consent to Mary's manumission on any reasonable terms, and to refer, if required, the amount of compensation for her value to arbitration. Mr. Ravenscroft with some difficulty obtained one or two interviews, but found Mr. Wood so full of animosity against the woman, and so firmly bent against any arrangement having her freedom for its object, that the negotiation was soon broken off as hopeless. The angry slave-owner declared "that he would not move a finger about her in this country, or grant her manumission on any terms whatever; and that if she went back to the West Indies, she must take the consequences."

This unreasonable conduct of Mr. Wood, induced the Anti-Slavery Committee, after several other abortive attempts to effect a compromise, to think of bringing the case under the notice of Parliament. The heads of Mary's statement were accordingly engrossed in a Petition, which Dr. Lushington offered to present, and to give notice at the same time of his intention to bring in a Bill to provide for the entire emancipation of all slaves brought to England with the owner's consent. But before this step was taken, Dr. Lushington again had recourse to negotiation with the master; and, partly through the friendly intervention of Mr. Manning, partly by personal conference, used every persuasion in his power to induce Mr. Wood to relent and let the bondwoman go free. Seeing the matter thus seriously taken up, Mr. Wood became at length alarmed,—not relishing, it appears, the idea of having the case publicly discussed in the House of Commons; and to avert this result he submitted to temporize—assumed a demeanour of unwonted civility, and even hinted to Mr. Manning (as I was given to understand) that if he was not driven to utter hostility by the threatened exposure, he would probably meet our wishes "in his own time and way." Having gained time by these manoeuvres, he adroitly endeavoured to cool the ardour of Mary's new friends, in her cause, by representing her as an abandoned and worthless woman, ungrateful towards him, and undeserving of sympathy from others; allegations which he supported by the ready affirmation of some of his West India friends, and by one or two plausible letters procured from Antigua. By these and like artifices he appears completely to have imposed on Mr. Manning, the respectable West India merchant whom Dr. Lushington had asked to negotiate with him; and he prevailed so far as to induce Dr. Lushington himself (actuated by the benevolent view of thereby best serving Mary's cause), to abstain from any remarks upon his conduct when the petition was at last presented in Parliament. In this way he dextrously contrived to neutralize all our efforts, until the close of the Session of 1829; soon after which he embarked with his family for the West Indies.

Every exertion for Mary's relief having thus failed; and being fully convinced from a twelvemonth's observation of her conduct, that she was really a well-disposed and respectable woman; I engaged her, in December 1829, as a domestic servant in my own family. In this capacity she has remained ever since; and I am thus enabled to speak of her conduct and character with a degree of confidence I could not have otherwise done....

I may here add a few words respecting the earlier portion of Mary Prince's narrative. The facts there stated must necessarily rest entirely,—since we have no collateral evidence,—upon their intrinsic claims to probability, and upon the reliance the reader may feel disposed, after perusing the foregoing pages, to place on her veracity. To my judgment, the internal evidence of the truth of her narrative appears remarkably strong. The circumstances are related in a tone of natural sincerity, and are accompanied in almost every case with characteristic and minute details, which must, I conceive, carry with them full conviction to every candid mind that this negro woman has actually seen, felt, and suffered all that she so impressively describes; and that the picture she has given of West Indian slavery is not less true than it is revolting.

But there may be some persons into whose hands this tract may fall, so imperfectly acquainted with the real character of Negro Slavery, as to be shocked into partial, if not absolute incredulity, by the acts of inhuman oppression and brutality related of Capt. I— and his wife, and of Mr. D—, the salt manufacturer of Turk's Island. Here, at least, such persons may be disposed to think, there surely must be *some* exaggeration; the facts are too shocking to be credible. The facts are indeed shocking, but unhappily not the less credible on that account. Slavery is a curse to the oppressor scarcely less than to the oppressed: its natural tendency is to brutalize both.

The Narrative of Ashton Warner

The History of Mary Prince was published in January of 1831. The following month Susanna Strickland recorded the narrative of the life of another slave, Ashton Warner, which was published March 1st. No doubt inevitably, there is some similarity in the descriptions of horrific abuse in the two narratives, but there is also a good deal to suggest that Strickland was not being disingenuous in her assertion that she was quite faithful in recording these narratives as they were related to her; certainly there are noticeable differences between the narrative style of Warner and that of Prince. (Strickland's note inviting readers to "see and converse with themselves" if they doubt that someone of Warner's background would be able to express himself so well is particularly interesting in this connection.)

Advertisement

In consequence of the unexpected decease of Ashton Warner, while this little volume was in the press, the profits that may arise from its sale will no longer be required, as was originally designed, for his personal benefit. But, in compliance with a wish expressed by the poor negro on his death-bed, it is now proposed to appropriate the proceeds to the benefit of his aged mother, and the enfranchisement (should the amount prove so considerable) of his enslaved wife and child. And I have the satisfaction of being authorized to add, for the information of benevolent individuals disposed to contribute liberally towards the objects now intimated—whether by the purchase of copies of this volume, or by pecuniary donations—that the little charitable fund thus contemplated, will be placed under the immediate management of George Stephen, Esq., Solicitor, 17, King's Arms Yard, Coleman Street, and Thomas Pringle, Esq., Secretary of the Anti-Slavery Society, 18, Aldermanbury, who have kindly undertaken to superintend its proper application.

S. STRICKLAND.

from Introduction

In writing Ashton's narrative, I have adhered strictly to the simple facts, adopting, wherever it could conveniently be done, his own language, which, for a person in his condition, is remarkably expressive and appropriate. Had I been inclined to give a recital of revolting cruelty, I should have chosen another case; and for such, unhappily, I had not far to seek. But those who wish to read such mournful narratives of human depravity will find enough for their information (far too many for the honour of human nature!) recorded in the publications of the Anti-Slavery Society.

The profits arising from the sale of this tract will be appropriated to the benefit of Ashton, who has been for the last three months in England, endeavouring to establish his claims to freedom; and who is at present suffering under severe illness, without any adequate means of subsistence.

With a view to render this Sketch of Colonial Slavery more complete, and to enable the reader to compare the details given by Ashton with those recorded by intelligent and conscientious eye-witnesses from England, I have subjoined, as an Appendix, the very important testimonies on this subject of three highly respectable clergymen of the established Church, and of an excellent Wesleyan Missionary—testimonies as yet but partially known to the public, and which comprise a mass of information equally recent and interesting.

Should this little tract assist, however feebly, in the diffusion of correct information in regard to the general condition and the feelings of the slaves, and thus tend to promote the great and good cause of justice and mercy, the writer's object will be fully accomplished. Like the widow's mite cast into the sacred treasury,[1] those who love the truth will not deem it unworthy because its value is but humble.

London, February 19, 1831.
S.S.

NEGRO SLAVERY
DESCRIBED
BY A NEGRO:
BEING

---

[1] *widow's ... treasury* See Luke 21.1–4.

THE NARRATIVE OF ASHTON WARNER,
A NATIVE OF ST. VINCENT'S.
With an Appendix,
CONTAINING THE
TESTIMONY OF FOUR CHRISTIAN MINISTERS,
RECENTLY RETURNED FROM THE COLONIES,
ON THE SYSTEM OF SLAVERY AS IT NOW EXISTS.
BY
S. STRICKLAND.

"And tears and toil have been my lot
Since I the white man's thrall became;
And sorer griefs I wish forgot—
Harsh blows and burning shame!
Oh, Englishman! thou ne'er canst know
The injured bondman's bitter woe,
When round his heart, like scorpions, cling
Black thoughts that madden while they sting!"

LONDON:
SAMUEL MAUNDER, NEWGATE STREET.
1831.

from The Narrative of Ashton Warner (1831)

I was born in the Island of St. Vincent's, and baptized by the name of Ashton Warner, in the parish church, by the Rev. Mr. Gildon. My father and mother, at the time of my birth, were slaves on Cane Grove estate, in Bucumar Valley, then the property of Mr. Ottley. I was an infant at the breast when Mr. Ottley died; and shortly after the estate was put to sale, that the property might be divided among his family. Before Cane Grove was sold, my aunt, Daphne Crosbie, took the opportunity of buying my mother and me of Mr. Ottley's trustees. My aunt had been a slave, but a favoured one. She had money left her by a coloured gentleman of the name of Crosbie, with whom she lived, and whose name she took. After his death she went to reside at Kingston. Finding it a good thing to be free, aunt Daphne wished to make all her friends free also, particularly the slaves on the estate where she was born, and with whom she had shared, in her early days, all the sorrows of negro servitude. She had a large heart, and felt great kindness for her own people; but her means were not equal to her good wishes. She bought her old parents of Mr. Jackson, Mr. Ottley's executor; and, as it was her earnest desire to make us all happy, she would have bought my uncle John Baptiste (my mother's brother) too; but Mr. Wilson, the gentleman who purchased the estate, would not sell him, His reason for refusing my aunt never knew, for my uncle was an old man then, and nearly past work. Mr. Wilson sent him away to the Island of St. Lucia, and it was some years before aunt Daphne heard any tidings of him. At last some persons, coming from St. Lucia to St. Vincent's, told her that he lay very sick on Mr. Grant's estate. My aunt was glad to find that he was still living, and she went herself to make him free. She had never crossed the water, or been on the great sea, but she overcame her fears, and hired a small boat, and went directly to St. Lucia. She found my poor uncle in a very miserable state, and in this condition she bought him of his master, and brought him back to St. Vincent's. He was ill a long, long time; it was many long weary months before he could even take up a broom to sweep the house. He was very grateful to aunt Daphne for all that she had done for him; and so were we all. She was a very good, kind woman, and a Christian, though a black woman; and we (her relations) all loved her very, very much. We had no one else to love—she was all the world to us.

Whilst I lived with my aunt at Kingston I was very happy. I had no heavy tasks to do; and she was as careful over me as if she had been my own mother, and used to keep me with her in the house, that I might not be playing about in the streets with bad companions. My mother made sausages and *souse*,[1] and I used to help her to carry them to gentlemen's houses for sale. This was light labour to her, for she had been a field slave, kept at hard work, and driven to it by the whip. I am sure our best days were spent with my dear aunt; nor did she make us alone happy; all the money she could save went to purchase the freedom of slaves who had formerly been her companions in bondage at Cane Grove, or to make their condition better. There was not a person upon the island who did not speak well of Daphne Crosbie; black or white it was all the same. She bore a good character until the day she died.

I lived with my aunt till I was ten years old, when I was claimed as a slave belonging to the Cane Grove estate, by Mr. Wilson. This was a hard and unjust claim; but Mr. Wilson said, that though my mother was sold I was not—that the best slaves had been sold off the estate—that I was *his* property, and he would claim me wherever I was to be found. Now, he was wrong in all this, and I can prove to you, in two short minutes, that I did not belong to him. When my aunt manumitted my mother and me, Mr. Wilson had not-yet bought the estate; and in the Island of St. Vincent's it has always been a customary rule that the young child at the breast is sold as one with its mother, and does not become separate property till it is five or six years old; so that Mr. Wilson's claim was very unjust and oppressive.[2]

When my aunt found Mr. Wilson bent on taking me away by force, she went to Mr. Jackson, the gentleman from whom she had purchased my mother, and told him the state of the case, and he gave her a written paper to take to the Chief Justice of the island, to prove that I belonged to Daphne Crosbie, should Mr. Wilson continue to claim me. My aunt went to the Governor and showed him this paper, and also the manumission paper she had received from Mr. Jackson. The Governor, after looking at it, said that Mr. Wilson had no legal right to claim me upon the estate, and he promised my aunt that he would write to him to that effect. But we never knew whether he did or not, for we never got an answer from him. It is of no use trusting to what the white people in the West Indies say; they always forget their promises to slaves. Before this happened, my aunt had bound me apprentice to a cooper, to learn his trade. I was bound for seven years, and had signed the indenture myself, as a free black, by making a cross for my name.

My master's name was Pierre Wynn. He was a kind good master, and I never ceased to lament the cause which parted me from him. I had been with him between two and three months, and was busy one morning at work in the cooper's yard, helping the journeyman to truss a molasses-cask, when Mr. Wilson's manager, Mr. Donald, with two coloured men, and a white named Newman, came into the yard. This man, Newman, had informed Mr. Wilson where I was, and he sent his people to take me away by force. When the manager came into the yard, he said, "Which is Ashton?" I answered, quite innocently, not suspecting any mischief, "I am Ashton." Directly I said so the manager caught hold of me by the back of my neck. I did not know why he held me. I did not know what to think—I could not get my breath to speak—I was dreadfully frightened, and trembled all over. The other men got hold of me, and held me fast. They then led me away to Mr. Dalzell, Mr. Wilson's attorney, and shut me up in his office till Mr. Wilson came. Mr. Dalzell was afraid that I

---

[1] [Strickland's note] Slices of pig's head, salted and prepared in a particular manner, and sold in the markets by the slaves.

[2] [Strickland's note] This is poor Ashton's own statement. Whether the Colonial *Slave Law* will support his claim for freedom on this ground, is a question which remains to be determined.—S. S.

would try to make my escape, and to make sure of me one man kept watch at the window and another at the door. When Mr. Wilson came in he did not know me, and asked who I was. One of the men told him that I was Ashton. He said, "Very well; keep him here till I am ready to send him down to the estate." He then came up to the place where I was standing, and examined me from head to foot; then turned to Mr. Dalzell, and began talking to him about me. I was too young, and too much frightened at being stolen away, to remember much of their discourse; but I am very sure that I shall never forget that day.

Before Mr. Wilson left the office, my mother and Daphne Crosbie came to hear what was to be done with me, and why I had been taken away. But all they said was of no use; they could do no good where there was no justice to be had. Mr. Wilson insisted that I was a slave, and *his* slave, and he would have it so, in spite of my mother's tears and my aunt's entreaties. My poor mother was greatly distressed, and cried very bitterly. She entreated Mr. Wilson, if he thought he had a just claim for me, to put me in gaol till the question as to my freedom could be fairly settled; but he refused to do this, and when she continued her entreaties he grew angry, and ordered her not to stop in the yard, but to go away directly. And she and aunt Crosbie, on finding that nothing could be done for me there, were obliged to leave me in his hands.

The manager then put me into a boat, and took me down to the estate. It was rather late in the afternoon when we got there. I had nothing given me to do that day. It was Saturday, and I was not set to work till the Monday morning. I was very sad, and wished very much to run away. I could not bear the thought of being a slave, and I was very restless and unhappy.

On the Monday morning, John, the head cooper, took me down to the sugar works to help him; but I had no heart to work—I did nothing but think how I might run away. I was not knowing enough, however, to make my escape; and, after consulting with myself a long time, I found it would be the best plan to make myself as patient as I could. But still I was always thinking of my mother and aunt, and of Pierre Wynn, and the home I had been taken from. The estate of Cane Grove was in the middle of a deep valley, near the sea shore. Mr. Wilson's house stood upon the brow of the hill, and overlooked the whole sugar plantation. He had about three hundred slaves, and was considered one of the severest masters in the whole island.

As I have spoken of the condition of the field negroes as being so much worse than that of the mechanics among whom I was ranked on the estate, I shall here endeavour to describe the manner in which the field gang were worked on Cane Grove estate. They were obliged to be in the field before five o'clock in the morning; and, as the negro houses were at the distance of from three to four miles from the cane pieces, they were generally obliged to rise as early as four o'clock, to be at their work in time. The driver is first in the field, and calls the slaves together by cracking the whip or blowing the conch shell. Before five o'clock the overseer calls over the roll; and if any of the slaves are so unfortunate as to be too late, even by a few minutes, which, owing to the distance, is often the case, the driver flogs them as they come in, with the cart-whip, or with a scourge of tamarind rods. When flogged with the whip, they are stripped and held down upon the ground, and exposed in the most shameful manner.

In the cultivation of the canes the slaves work in a row. Each person has a hoe, and the women are expected to do as much as the men. This work is so hard that any slave, newly put to it, in the course of a month becomes so weak that often he is totally unfit for labour. If he falls back behind the rest, the driver keeps forcing him up with the whip.

They work from five o'clock to nine, when they are allowed to sit down for half an hour in the field, and take such food as they have been able to prepare over night. But many have no food ready, and so fast till mid-day.

They go to work again directly after half an hour's respite, and labour till twelve o'clock, when they leave off for dinner. They are allowed two hours of mid-day intermission, out of crop time, and an hour and a half in crop time.

During this interval every slave must pick a bundle of grass to bring home for the cattle at night. The grass grows in tufts, often scattered over a great space of ground, and, when the season is dry, it is very scarce and withered, so that the slaves collect it slowly and with difficulty, and are often employed most of the time allowed them for mid-day rest, in seeking for it. I have frequently known them occupied the whole two hours in collecting it.

They work again in gang from two till seven o'clock. It is then dark. When they return home the overseer calls over the roll, and demands of every man and woman their bundles of grass. He weighs with his hand each bundle as it is given in, and, if it be too light, the person who presents it is either instantly laid down and flogged severely with the cart-whip, or is put into the stocks for the whole night. If the slaves bring home no grass, they are not only put into the stocks all night, but are more severely flogged the next morning. This grass-picking is a very sore grievance to the field slaves.

When they are manuring the ground, the slaves are forced to carry the wet manure in open baskets upon their heads. This is most unpleasant as well as severe work. It is a usual occupation for wet weather, and the moisture from the manure drips constantly down upon the faces, and over the body and clothes of the slaves. They are forced to run with their loads as fast as they can; and, if they flag, the driver is instantly at their heels with the cart-whip.

The crop-time usually commences in January and lasts till June, and, if the season is wet, till July. During this season every slave must bring in a bundle of cane-tops for the cattle, instead of a bundle of grass. They then go immediately to the sugar works, where they have to take up the *mogass* which was spread out at nine o'clock in the morning to dry for fuel to boil the sugar. This mogass is the stalks of the cane after the juice has been squeezed out by the mill. The slaves are employed till ten at night in gathering in the mogass, that it may not be wetted with the dew and rendered unfit for immediate use. The overseer then calls over the roll, and issues orders for a certain spell of them to be up and at the works at one o'clock in the morning. After this the slaves have to prepare their suppers; for, if they have no very aged parents or friends belonging to them, they must do this themselves, which occupies them another hour. Every creature that is capable of work must take a part in the labours of the crop; and no person remains at home but those who are totally unfit for work. Slaves who are too old and weak to go to the field have to make up bundles of mogass, cut grass for the stock, &c.

During this season all the mechanics on the estate are employed to pot the sugar; carpenters, coopers, masons, and rum-distillers, even the pasture-boys who tend the cattle, are called in to assist. To the little people are given small tubs to carry the sugar into the curing house; and the grown-up slaves have shovels to fill the tubs for them. When employed in potting the sugar, we did not leave off to get our breakfast till ten or eleven o'clock, and I have known it mid-day before we have tasted food.

The whole gang of field slaves are divided into spells, and every man and woman able to work has not only to endure during crop-time the severe daily labour, but to work half the night also, or three whole nights in the week. The work is very severe, and great numbers of the slaves, during this period, sink under it, and become ill; but if they complain, their complaints are not readily believed, or are considered only a pretence to escape from labour. If they are so very ill that their inability to work can be no longer doubted, they are at length sent to the sick house.

The sick-house is just like a pen to keep pigs in; if you wish to keep yourself clean and decent, you cannot. It is one of the greatest punishments to the slaves to be sent there. When we were hard pressed, and had much sugar to pot, the manager would often send to the sick-house for the people who were sick, or lame with sores, to help us. If they refused to come, and said that they were unable to work, they were taken down and severely flogged, by the manager's order, with the cart-whip. There is nothing in slavery harder to bear than this. When you are ill and cannot work, your pains are made light of, and your complaints neither listened to, nor believed. I have seen people who were so sick that they could scarcely stand, dragged out of the sick-house, and tied up to a tree, and flogged in a shocking manner; then driven with the whip to the work. I have seen slaves in this state crawl away, and lie down among the wet trash to get a little ease, though they knew that it would most likely cause their death.

The quantity of food allowed the slaves is from two pounds and a half to three pounds of salt-fish per week, for each grown person. They could easily eat this in two days, but they must make it last till they receive a fresh allowance from the overseer. The rest of their food they raise upon their provision grounds. The owner gives to each slave from thirty to forty feet square of ground; not the best ground, but such as has been over-cropped, and is no longer productive for canes. This is taken from them the next year, when, by manuring and planting with yams and other things, it has been brought round, and recovered strength for the cultivation of sugar. The slaves are likewise permitted to cultivate waste pieces of ground, and the headlands of fields, that are unfit for planting. They work this ground every Sunday. It is generally given to them in March or April, and it is taken away in December or January. Besides the Sunday, they get part of twenty-six Saturdays, out of crop-time, to cultivate their grounds. What I mean by saying they get only *part* of these Saturdays is this—that they are employed in their master's work, such as carrying out trash, &c., from five to ten o'clock in the forenoon; and in the evening they must bring each his bundle of grass to deliver as usual at the calling of the lists; so that about seven hours, even of the day which is called their own, is occupied with their owner's work. They are obliged to work on these days at the provision grounds, if they wish ever so much for a holiday. If they are absent when the overseer inspects the grounds, they are flogged, or put in the stocks. The grounds produce plantains, yams, potatoes, pumpkins, calabashes, &c. On the Sunday, at every town, a market is held, in which the slaves are allowed to sell the produce of their grounds. Those that can save a little money, buy a pig and fatten it, that, in case of any death happening among their friends, they may sell the pig to provide a few necessaries for the funeral. They bury the dead during the night, being allowed no time during the day for their funerals.

In building their houses, they are allowed as much board as will form a window and a door. They go to the woods and cut wild canes, to form the walls and roof. The huts are thatched with cane-trash or tops.

For clothing, the owner gives to each slave in the year six yards of blue stuff, called bamboo, and six yards of brown. The young people and children are given a less allowance, in proportion to their size and age; the young children getting only a small stripe to tie round the waist. For bed-clothing, they give them only a blanket once in four or five years; and they are obliged to wear this till it falls in pieces. If the slaves require other clothes, they must buy them out of their own little savings. Many of the field negroes are very badly off for clothing. A good many are always to be seen with only a rag of cloth round their loins in all weathers.

People so hardly, so harshly, treated, and so destitute of every comfort, cannot be supposed to work with a willing mind. They have no home which they can well call their own. They are worked beyond their strength, and live in perpetual fear of the whip. They are insulted, tormented, and indecently exposed and degraded; yet English people wonder that they are not contented. Some have even said that they are happy! Let such people place themselves for a few minutes under the same yoke, and see if they could bear it. Such bondage is ruin both to the soul and body of the slave; and I hope every good Englishman will daily pray to God, that the yoke of slavery may soon be broken from off the necks of my unfortunate countrymen for ever.[1]

What made me feel more deeply for the sad condition of the field slaves was the circumstance of

---

[1] [Strickland's note] Such is the impressive language in which Ashton speaks of slavery. The above are his own expressions; for, though an uneducated, he is a very intelligent negro, and speaks remarkably good English. Any reader, who wishes it, may see and converse with himself, by making application through the publisher.—S.S.

my having taken a wife from among them, after I had resided several years on Cane Grove estate. When I was about twenty-one years of age, finding my condition lonely, because I had no friends to manage for me, as the other slaves had, I wished to marry, and have a home of my own, and a kind partner to do for me. Among the field slaves there was a very respectable young woman, called Sally, for whom I had long felt a great deal of regard. At last I asked her to be my wife; and we stood up in her father's house, before her mother, and her uncle, and her sisters, and, holding each other by the hand, pledged our troth as husband and wife, and promised before God to be good and kind to each other, and to love and help each other, as long as we lived.

And so we married. And though it was not as white folks marry, before the parson, yet I considered her as much my wife, and I loved her as well, as though we had been married in the church; and she was as careful, and managed as well for me, as if she had been my mother. I could not bear to see her work in the field. It is, as I have already said, a very sad and hard condition of slavery; and the more my wife suffered, the more I wished to be free, and to make her so. When she was with child, she was flogged for not coming out early enough to work, and afterwards, when far advanced in pregnancy, she was put into the stocks by the manager, because she said she was unable to go to the field. My heart was almost broken to see her so treated, but I could do nothing to help her; and it would have made matters worse if I had attempted to speak up for her. She was twice punished in this cruel manner, though the overseer must have known that she was in no condition to work. After our child was born, she was again repeatedly flogged for not coming sooner to the field, though she had stopped merely to attend and suckle the baby. But they had no feeling for the mother or for her child, they cared only for the work. It is a dreadful thing to be a field negro; and it is scarcely less dreadful, if one's heart is not quite hardened, to have a wife, or a husband, or a child, in that condition. On this account I was often grieved that I had taken poor Sally to be my wife; for it caused her more suffering as a mother, while her cruel treatment wrung my heart, without my being able to move a finger, or utter a word, in her behalf.

The Abolition of Slavery

CONTEXTS

In the 1750s it was possible for John Newton, the author of the hymn "Amazing Grace," to write that neither he nor any of his friends had had any notion that "slavery could be considered unlawful and wrong." By 1807 the tide had turned sufficiently that the British Parliament (through the Slave Trade Act) prohibited British vessels from participating in the trading of humans. And in 1833 (through the Slavery Abolition Act) slavery in all British territory was ended.

What brought about such a vast change in such a relatively short time? In part the answer lies in the history of ideas; the Enlightenment gave birth to concepts of freedom and equality—of human rights which, as they were thought through, were widely recognized to apply to all humans, regardless of gender, regardless of race. But the abolition first of the slave trade and then of slavery itself was also the result of concerted political pressure. Some have identified the birth of the modern political movement and modern political lobbying in the campaign to abolish slavery. Certainly the Society for Effecting the Abolition of the Slave Trade, formed in 1787 and led by Thomas Clarkson and Granville Sharp, among others, played a hugely important role in acquiring and disseminating information as to the actual conditions endured by slaves, and in pressuring the government to take action. In Parliament, William Wilberforce became the *de facto* leader of the anti-slavery movement: Wilberforce, the author of *Practical Christianity*, was tireless in his efforts. The Society of Friends (also known as the Quakers) also played a leading role, both within the Society for Effecting the Abolition of the Slave Trade and independently, in shaping public opinion and pressing for change. And a number of authors—including William Wordsworth, Samuel Taylor Coleridge, Helen Maria Williams, Anna Laetitia Barbauld, and Mary Robinson—lent their voices to the cause.

The legal system too played an important role in the process. In a landmark 1772 case the owner of one James Somerset lost his legal suit to regain ownership of Somerset, who had run away from servitude while in England. Lord Mansfield, the Lord Chief Justice ruled that, according to the established principles of English law, everyone in England was free. Proponents of slavery had suggested that villeinage, the state of servitude which had existed under feudalism and which had never been declared illegal, provided sufficient legal precedent. Mansfield decided, however, that no such justification could be deemed to exist under English Common Law. If Parliament wished to legalize slavery in England, that would require specific new legislation. Despite Mansfield's *caveat* against taking his ruling to apply to British possessions overseas, abolitionists had some reason to feel confident from that point on that the law would eventually support their arguments universally and unequivocally, in Britain's colonies as well as within Britain itself.

⌘ ⌘ ⌘

from John Newton, *A Slave Trader's Journal* (1751)

John Newton (1725–1807) first went to sea at the age of ten, sailing with his father, the captain of the vessel. By the age of twenty-eight he had wide experience both of the sea and of the slave trade, and was for the first time commanding a vessel himself. The *Duke of Argyll* left England for Bassa in West Africa (in what is now Guinea Bissau) in 1750, made the "middle passage" from Bassa to Antigua in the West Indies between 22 May and 2 July, and returned to Liverpool with a cargo of sugar, arriving in November. The following excerpts are from Newton's journal of that voyage. In later life, Newton came to regret deeply his life as a slave trader (which he had given up for health reasons in 1754). He became a Christian minister and wrote that he would have left the slave trade sooner "had I considered it as I now do to be unlawful and wrong. But I never had a scruple upon this head at the time; nor was such a thought ever suggested to me by any friend." In 1770 Newton wrote the famous hymn "Amazing Grace." He became a strong advocate for the abolition of the slave trade.

Thursday 16 May
… [A] long boat came on board from Grande Bassa. I sent Billinge [the second mate] chiefly to satisfy myself of the state and price of slaves. He says the glut we heard so much of is entirely over, the Brittannia and Ranger having met very few. About Settra Crue there is still plenty (upon the account of a war very probably begun with that view) but extravagantly dear … He brought me a sample of the prices in a woman slave he bought at Bassa, which upon costing up the goods I find cost 96 bars, and I ordered him to get one upon any terms for that reason. That I might not think he gave more than usual, he brought me a list of goods he saw Saunders pay for a man which amounts to 102 bars, and the farther to leeward the dearer still. I think I have sufficient reason not to go down, for setting aside the cost, the assortments in demand there would ruin me soon.

Tuesday 28 May
Secured the after bulkhead of the men's room, for they had started almost every stantient. Their plot was exceedingly well laid, and had they been let alone an hour longer, must have occasioned us a good deal of trouble and damage. I have reason to be thankful they did not make attempts upon the coast when we had often 7 or 8 of our best men out of the ship at a time and the rest busy. They still look very gloomy and sullen and have doubtless mischief in their heads if they could find every opportunity to vent it. But I hope (by the Divine Assistance) we are fully able to overawe them now. …

Wednesday 12 June
Got the slaves up this morn. Washed them all with fresh water. They complained so much that was obliged to let them go down again when the rooms were cleaned. Buryed a man slave (No. 84) of a flux, which he has been struggling with near 7 weeks. …

Saturday 22 June
Being pretty warm, got up the men and washed all the slaves with fresh water. I am much afraid of another ravage from the flux, for we have had 8 taken within these few days. Have seen 2 or 3 tropick birds and a few flying fish.

Monday 24 June
Buried a girl slave (No. 92). In the afternoon while we were off the deck, William Cooney seduced a woman slave down into the room and lay with her brutelike in view of the whole quarter deck, for which I put him in irons.[1] I hope this has been the first affair of the kind on board and I am determined to keep them quiet if possible. If anything happens to the woman I shall impute it to him, for she was big with child. Her number is 83. …

Friday 28 June
By the favour of Divine Providence made a timely discovery today that the slaves were forming a plot for an insurrection. Surprised 2 of them attempting to get off their irons, and upon farther search in their rooms,

---

[1] *for which … irons* In contrast to Newton, some captains actively encouraged their crew to rape the female slaves, since pregnant slaves could be sold at a higher price; mulatto children were especially highly valued as house servants.

upon the information of 3 of the boys, found some knives, stones, shot, etc., and a cold chissel. Upon enquiry there appeared 8 principally concerned to move in projecting the mischief and 4 boys in supplying them with the above instruments. Put the boys in irons and slightly in the thumbscrews to urge them to a full confession. We have already 36 men out of our small number. ...

Friday 5 July
... [I]n the morning Mr. Guichard went off with me to view the slaves. When came on shore again, after comparing orders and intelligence, he judged it best for the concern to sell here, if I approved it, without which, he was pleased to say, he would do nothing, tho my letters from the owners referred me wholly to his direction. It seems by all I can learn that this is likely to prove as good a market as any of the neighbouring islands; and as for Jamaica or America, I should be extremely loth to venture so far, for we have had the men slaves so long on board that their patience is just worn out, and I am certain they would drop fast had we another passage to make. Monday is appointed for the sale.

from Quobna Ottobah Cugoano, *Thoughts and Sentiments on the Evil and Wicked Traffic of the Slavery and Commerce of the Human Species* (1787)

> Cugoano had been kidnapped in West Africa and sold into slavery in the West Indies. His owner traveled with him to England in 1772, and he declared himself a free man on English soil following the landmark Somerset case. His *Thoughts and Sentiments* is the first substantial anti-slavery work by a black writer.

But why should total abolition, and an universal emancipation of slaves, and the enfranchisement of all the Black People employed in the culture of the Colonies, taking place as it ought to do, and without any hesitation, or delay for a moment, even though it might have some seeming appearance of loss either to government or to individuals, be feared at all? Their labour, as freemen, would be as useful in the sugar colonies as any other class of men that could be found; and should it even take place in such a manner that some individuals, at first, would suffer loss as a just reward for their wickedness in slave-dealing, what is that to the happiness and good of doing justice to others; and, I must say, to the great danger, otherwise, that must eventually hang over the whole community? It is certain, that the produce of the labour of slaves, together with all the advantages of the West-India traffic, bring in an immense revenue to government; but let that amount be what it will, there might be as much or more expected from the labour of an equal increase of free people, and without the implication of any guilt attending it, and which, otherwise, must be a greater burden to bear, and more ruinous consequences to be feared from it, than if the whole national debt was to sink at once, and to rest upon the heads of all that might suffer by it. Whereas, if a generous encouragement were to be given to a free people, peaceable among themselves, intelligent and industrious, who by art and labour would improve the most barren situations, and make the most of that which is fruitful; the free and voluntary labour of many, would soon yield to any government, many greater advantages than any thing that slavery can produce. And this should be expected, wherever a Christian government is extended, and the true religion is embraced, that the blessings of liberty should be extended likewise, and that it should diffuse its influences first to fertilize the mind, and then the effects of its benignity would extend, and arise with exuberant blessings and advantages from all its operations. Was this to be the case, every thing would increase and prosper at home and abroad, and ten thousand times greater and greater advantages would arise to the state, and more permanent and solid benefit to individuals from the service of freemen, than ever they can reap, or in any possible way enjoy, by the labour of slaves. ...

from Alexander Falconbridge, *Account of the Slave Trade on the Coast of Africa* (1788)

> Falconbridge sailed aboard slave trading vessels as a surgeon in the 1780s. The work from which the

following excerpts are taken was given wide distribution by the Society for Effecting the Abolition of the Slave Trade. In 1789 Falconbridge also testified as to the horrors of the trade before the Parliamentary Committee investigating the issue.

The men negroes, on being brought aboard the ship, are immediately fastened together, two and two, by hand-cuffs on their wrists, and by irons rivetted on their legs. They are then sent down between the decks, and placed in an apartment partitioned off for that purpose. The women likewise are placed in a separate apartment between decks, but without being ironed. And an adjoining room, on the same deck, is besides appointed for the boys. Thus are they all placed in different apartments.

But at the same time, they are frequently stowed so close, as to admit of no other posture than lying on their sides. Neither will the height between decks, unless directly under the grating, permit them the indulgence of an erect posture; especially where there are platforms, which is generally the case. These platforms are a kind of shelf, about eight or nine feet in breadth, extending from the side of the ship towards the centre. They are placed nearly midway between the decks, at the distance of two or three feet from each deck. Upon these the negroes are stowed in the same manner as they are on the deck underneath.

In each of the apartments are placed three or four large buckets, of a conical form, being near two feet in diameter at the bottom, and only one foot at the top, and in depth about twenty-eight inches; to which, when necessary, the negroes have recourse. It often happens, that those who are placed at a distance from the buckets, in endeavouring to get to them, tumble over their companions, in consequence of their being shackled. These accidents, although unavoidable, are productive of continual quarrels, in which some of them are always bruised. In this distressed situation, unable to proceed, and prevented from getting to the tubs, they desist from the attempt; and, as the necessities of nature are not to be repelled, ease themselves as they lie. This becomes a fresh source of broils and disturbances, and tends to render the condition of the poor captive wretches still more uncomfortable. The nuisance arising from these circumstances, is not unfrequently increased by the tubs being much too small for the purpose intended, and their being usually emptied but once every day. The rule for doing this, however, varies in different ships, according to the attention paid to the health and convenience of the slaves by the captain …

The diet of the negroes, while on board, consists chiefly of horse-beans, boiled to the consistence of a pulp; of boiled yams and rice, and sometimes of a small quantity of beef or pork. The latter are frequently taken from the provisions laid in for the sailors. They sometimes make use of a sauce, composed of palm-oil, mixed with flour, water, and pepper, which the sailors call *slabber-sauce*. Yams are the favourite food of the Eboe, or Bight negroes, and rice or corn, of those from the Gold and Windward Coasts; each preferring the produce of their native soil …

They are commonly fed twice a day, about eight o'clock in the morning and four in the afternoon. In most ships they are only fed with their *own food* once a day. Their food is served up to them in tubs, about the size of a small water bucket. They are placed round these tubs in companies of ten to each tub, out of which they feed themselves with wooden spoons. These they soon lose, and when they are not allowed others, they feed themselves with their hands. In favourable weather they are fed upon deck, but in bad weather their food is given them below. Numberless quarrels take place among them during their meals; more especially when they are put upon short allowance … Their allowance of water is about half a pint each at every meal. It is handed round in a bucket, and given to each negroe in a pannekin; a small utensil with a strait handle, somewhat similar to a sauce-boat. …

Upon the negroes refusing to take sustenance, I have seen coals of fire, glowing hot, put on a shovel, and placed so near their lips, as to scorch and burn them. And this has been accompanied with threats, of forcing them to swallow the coals, if they any longer persisted in refusing to eat. These means have generally had the desired effect. I have also been credibly informed, that a certain captain in the slave trade, poured melted lead on such of the negroes as obstinately refused their food.

Exercise being deemed necessary for the preservation of their health, they are sometimes obliged to dance, when the weather will permit their coming on deck. If they go about it reluctantly, or do not move with agility, they are flogged; a person standing by them all the time with a cat-o'-nine-tails[1] in his hand for that purpose. Their musick, upon these occasions consists of a drum, sometimes with only one head; and when that is worn out, they do not scruple to make use of the bottom of one of the tubs before described. The poor wretches are frequently compelled to sing also; but when they do so, their songs are generally, as may naturally be expected, melancholy lamentations of their exile from their native country.…

On board some ships, the common sailors are allowed to have intercourse with such of the black women whose consent they can procure. And some of them have been known to take the inconstancy of their paramours so much to heart, as to leap overboard and drown themselves. The officers are permitted to indulge their passions among them at pleasure, and sometimes are guilty of such brutal excesses, as disgrace human nature.

Diagram showing allotment of space for slaves on two

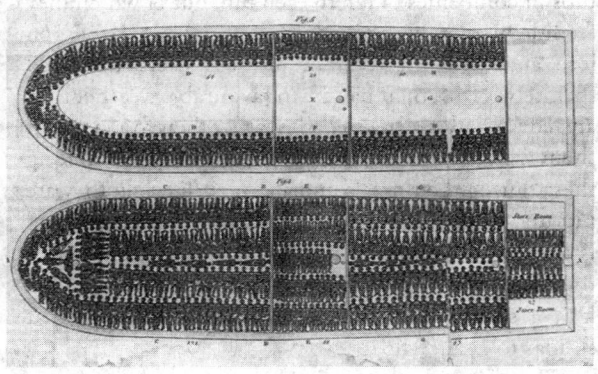

decks of a late eighteenth-century sailing ship.

---

[1] *cat-o'-nine-tails* Switch with nine ropes attached, used as a beating implement.

William Cowper, "Sweet Meat has Sour Sauce, or, The Slave-Trader in the Dumps"[2] (1788)

A trader I am to the African shore,
But since that my trading is like to be o'er,
I'll sing you a song that you ne'er heard before,
    Which nobody can deny, deny,
5   Which nobody can deny.

When I first heard the news it gave me a shock,
Much like what they call an electrical knock,
And now I am going to sell off my stock,
10   Which nobody, &c.

'Tis a curious assortment of dainty regales,
To tickle the negroes with when the ship sails,
Fine chains for the neck, and a cat with nine tails,
    Which nobody, &c.

15 Here's supple-jack plenty, and store of rat-tan,[3]
That will wind itself round the sides of a man,
As close as a hoop round a bucket or can,
    Which nobody, &c.

Here's padlocks and bolts, and screws for the thumbs,
20 That squeeze them so lovingly till the blood comes,
They sweeten the temper like comfits or plums,[4]
    Which nobody, &c.

When a negro his head from his victuals withdraws,
And clenches his teeth and thrusts out his paws,
25 Here's a notable engine to open his jaws,
    Which nobody, &c.

Thus going to market, we kindly prepare
A pretty black cargo of African ware,

---

[2] *Sweet Meat … Dumps* The poem is one of several anti-slavery poems by Cowper. The Society for Effecting the Abolition of the Slave Trade distributed his ballad "The Negro's Complaint" widely; both that poem and this were set to music and sung as well as read.

[3] *supple-jack* Climbing vine; *rat-tan* Palm stem. Both supple-jack and rattan were used for switches or canes.

[4] *comfits or plums* Sweetmeats; sugarplums: fruits preserved with sugar.

For what they must meet with when they get there,
30   Which nobody, &c.

'Twould do your heart good to see 'em below
Lie flat on their backs all the way as we go,
Like sprats on a gridiron,[1] scores in a row,
    Which nobody, &c.

35 But ah! if in vain I have studied an art
So gainful to me, all boasting apart,
I think it will break my compassionate heart,
    Which nobody, &c.

For oh! how it enters my soul like an awl![2]
40 This pity, which some people self-pity call,
Is sure the most heart-piercing pity of all,
    Which nobody, &c.

So this is my song, as I told you before;
Come buy off my stock, for I must no more
45 Carry Caesars and Pompeys[3] to Sugar-cane shore,
    Which nobody can deny, deny,
    Which nobody can deny.

from William Wilberforce, "Speech to the House of Commons," 13 May 1789

William Wilberforce began his long struggle to have the British Parliament abolish the slave trade with the speech excerpted below. In April of 1791, a bill put forward by Wilberforce was voted down by 163 votes to 88; not until 1807 were his efforts on this score successful. News of the passage of the Slavery Abolition Act reached Wilberforce on his deathbed in 1833.

A report has been made by his Majesty's Privy Council, which, I trust, every Gentleman has read, and which ascertains the Slave Trade to be just such in practice as we know, from theory, that it must be. What should we suppose must naturally be the consequence of our carrying on a Slave Trade with Africa? With a country, vast in its extent, not utterly barbarous, but civilized in a very small degree? Does any one suppose a Slave Trade would *help* their civilization? That Africa would *profit* by such an intercourse? Is it not plain, that she must *suffer* from it? That civilization must be checked; that her barbarous manners must be made more barbarous; and that the happiness of her millions of inhabitants must be prejudiced by her intercourse with Britain? Does not every one see, that a Slave Trade, carried on around her coasts, must carry violence and desolation to her very centre? That, in a Continent, just emerging from barbarism, if a Trade in Men is established—if her men are all converted into goods, and become commodities that can be bartered, it follows, they must be subject to ravage just as goods are; and this too, at a period of civilization, when there is no protecting Legislature to defend this their only sort of property, in the same manner as the rights of property are maintained by the legislature of every civilized country.

We see then, in the nature of things, how easily all the practices of Africa are to be accounted for. Her kings are never compelled to war, that we can hear of, by public principles,—by national glory—still less by the love of their people. In Europe it is the extension of commerce, the maintenance of national honor, or some great public object, that is ever the motive to war with every monarch; but, in Africa, it is the personal *avarice* and *sensuality* of their kings: these two vices of avarice and sensuality, (the most powerful and predominant in natures thus corrupt) we tempt, we stimulate in all these African Princes, and we depend upon these vices for the very maintenance of the Slave Trade....

Sir, the nature and all the circumstances of this trade are now laid open to us; we can no longer plead ignorance,—we cannot evade it,—it is now an object placed before us,—we cannot pass it; we may spurn it, we may kick it out of our way, but we cannot turn aside so as to avoid seeing it; for it is brought now so directly before our eyes, that this House must decide, and must justify to all the world, and to their own consciences, the rectitude of the grounds and principles of their decision.

A Society [the Society for Effecting the Abolition of the Slave Trade] has been established for the abolition of this trade, [in 1787] in which Dissenters, Quakers,

---

[1] *sprats on a gridiron* Small fish on a griddle or broiling-pan.

[2] *awl* Tool for piercing holes in leather.

[3] *Caesars and Pompeys* Names commonly given to African slaves.

Churchmen—in which the most conscientious of all persuasions have all united, and made a common cause in this great question. Let not Parliament be the only body that is insensible to the principles of national justice. Let us make reparation to Africa, so far as we can, by establishing a trade upon true commercial principles, and we shall soon find the rectitude of our conduct rewarded, by the benefits of a regular and a growing commerce.

Proponents of Slavery

It is often (and rightly) pointed out that appeals to Christian virtue were central to the abolitionist cause. As some of the following excerpts illustrate, appeals to Christian principles were also made on the other side of the argument—as were appeals of a variety of other sorts.

from Rev. Robert Boncher Nicholls, *Observations, Occasioned by the Attempts Made in England to Effect the Abolition of the Slave Trade* (1788)

[The author] thought it incumbent on him first to search the scriptures, to learn whether slavery was inconsistent with the revealed will of the Deity. The result of his enquiry was perfectly satisfactory to himself, and he thought it but right to point out some few of the many passages, to be found in the sacred volumes, which justify that commerce. Since the following observations went to the press the author has the great satisfaction to find, that he might have pursued his original plan without any injury to the cause he has endeavoured to support, as he has seen a pamphlet by the Rev. Mr. Harris, of Liverpool, who has so clearly proved, from the scriptures, that slavery is neither contrary to the law nor gospel, that it is scarcely possible for the most conscientious believer, who reads that tract, to doubt in future; whether the man servant or the maid servant is not as much a man's property as *"his ox or his ass, or any thing that is his."* …

About the time of Lord Mansfield's determination in the case of Mr. Stuart's negro, [those in England who were attended by slaves] … had every right to suppose they were authorised, by the laws of Great Britain, as well as those of the colonies, to consider those people as their property; and that they had a right to their services in Europe, or to send, or accompany them back to the colonies, as they judged proper: They found themselves mistaken, and that it was permitted to debauch their slaves, to encourage or entice them to run away, with impunity. The ideas of liberty, the charms of novelty, and an ignorance of the country they had got to; where they found themselves upon a perfect equality, at least, with the inferior white people, could not fail of having pernicious effects upon their minds, and great numbers ran away from their masters. They in general plunged into vice and debauchery, and many of them, who were desirous of returning to their masters and mistresses, were refused to be received. The whole of those thus lost to their owners, and as to every useful purpose, to the community, cannot have been less in number than from 15,000 to 20,000.—As most of them were prime, young seasoned, or Creole slaves, the loss to their owners, the planters, have not been less than from 1,000,000 to 1,200,000 sterling. A large sum to be sacrificed, to the mere names of *liberty and humanity!* What has been the result of thus extending *the blessings of liberty* to so many *wretched slaves.* Let any body shew scarce a single instance of any one of these people being in so happy a situation as they were before. The greater part, it is known, died miserably, in a very short time. No parish was willing to receive them, so that the survivers, after begging about the streets of London, and suffering all those evils, and inconveniencies, consequent on idleness and poverty, famine, disease, and the inclemency of the weather; attracted the attention of the public, and government was prevailed upon to undertake the transportation of them to the country from whence they or their ancestors had been ravished *by the wicked traders* of London, Liverpool, and Bristol.

Equal unhappiness would be the lot of the slaves in the islands, if they were set free; what could they do to obtain a livelihood? To suppose they would hire themselves out to work, can only enter into the imagination of those who do not know the people, or the country: What has so lately passed in England is surely sufficient to shew that there can be no idea, they will, any of them, wish to return to their own country. Thousands of negroes have been made free by their masters in the colonies, and it may, with truth, be asserted, that, notwithstanding many of them were very capable of paying for a passage to any part of Africa they thought proper; scarce a single instance can be produced of any one of them desiring to return to the place of his nativity.

The present attempt to cram liberty down the throats of people who are incapable of digesting it, can with propriety, be resembled to nothing, so well as to the account of poor Gulliver, when he was carried out of his little cabinet to the top of the house, by the Brobdignag Monkey.

from Anonymous, *Thoughts on the Slavery of Negroes, as it Affects the British Colonies in the West Indies: Humbly Submitted to the Consideration of Both Houses of Parliament* (1788)

If I am able to shew that the blacks are really happy; that their condition (if the odious name of slave could be forgotten) is preferable to the lower orders of the people in Great Britain and Ireland; and that they enjoy the necessaries, and often the luxuries of life, I trust every honest man will feel a just indignation at any attempt to mislead his judgment, and to impose upon him an opinion of cruelty, which has no existence in any of the British West India islands. …

Let us take a view of the situation of the Africans, the nature of their country, their climate and government, and the genius and disposition of its inhabitants. The appearance of the slave-coast of Africa, when it was first visited by the Europeans, strongly marked the barbarous state of the people; a rude, inhospitable country, susceptible indeed of cultivation, but almost every way covered with thick, impenetrable forests. The wild luxuriance of nature was here portrayed in rich attire. The pruning hand of man was hardly seen. The peaceful labours of agriculture were little known.

It has been observed, that those countries most favoured by nature, often make the slowest progress to civilization; and that the people always groan under the weight of a cruel despotism. "This is an effect which springs from a natural cause. Great heat enervates the strength and courage of men, while in cold climates they have a certain vigour of body and mind, which renders them capable of long, painful, great, and intrepid actions. We ought not, then, to be astonished, that the effeminacy of the people in hot climates has almost always rendered them slaves; and that the bravery of those in colder regions has enabled them to maintain their liberties."

In those countries between the tropics, and especially under the equator, "the excess of heat renders men so slothful and dispirited, that nothing but the most pressing necessity can induce them to perform any laborious duty." An unconquerable indolence is universally felt and acknowledged. Sunk into the most deplorable degeneracy, they feel no incitements beyond the present moment. In vain may we represent to them the happiness of others. In vain may we attempt to rouse them to a sense of their own weakness. The soul, unwilling to enlarge itself, becomes the prey of every ignoble passion. Strangers to every virtuous and magnanimous sentiment, they are without fame—they are without glory.

The Africans have been always represented as a cruel and perfidious people, lazy, lascivious, faithless in their engagements, innate thieves, without morals, and without any just notion of any one religious duty. Their laws are founded on such principles as naturally flow from so impure a source. The government of the slave-coast of Africa is despotic. The will of the Prince must be obeyed. There is no appeal upon earth from his awful decree. The lives and fortunes of every one are absolutely at his disposal. These tyrants have thought fit to distinguish a number of crimes, but have taken no care to proportionate their degrees of punishment. Every offence is there punished with loss of life or liberty. Captives in war are deliberately murdered, or sold as slaves, as may most indulge the sanguinary caprice of the conqueror. Those convicted of adultery or theft, lose their liberty. He who is in debt, and unable to pay must either sell himself or his children to satisfy the creditor. It may be said, that the loss of life, or liberty, only commences with the injury done to society. I answer, "that in Africa, the civil liberty is already destroyed by the political slavery." A country like this, doomed to bear the weight of human misery, will always present a history of the most shocking cruelties, and of the severest slavery upon earth.

After viewing this melancholy picture, we ought not to be surprised at the extent of the present intercourse between the Africans and Europeans. For want of proper consideration, and from the influence of certain prejudices, the slave-trade has long been considered the scandal and reproach of every nation who have been anywise engaged in it, but without sufficient reason.

Men who enjoy the benefits of civilization, and who are protected in life, liberty, and property, by the wisdom of humane and equal laws, feel that spirit of liberty, and enthusiastic love of their country, which freedom only can inspire. Talk to them of banishment, and it is more terrible than death. Not so the poor African—he has few motives for wishing any longer to behold the distresses of his country; he is, alas! perhaps, the last witness of the sad misfortunes of his house— Already deprived of family, friends, and every other tender endearment, he has no relief but in banishment or death.

It is pleasant to mark the progress of the barbarian, from the moment he is put on shore in an English colony, to the time he becomes the master of a family, and acquires property of his own. He is first of all clothed (a thing unknown to him in his own country) and then instructed in the necessity of cleanliness. When carried to the plantation, he is shewn how to work in common with others. In a little time he chooses himself a wife, and has a house given to him, much better, allowing for the difference of climate, than what the peasants have in this country. When he is sufficiently instructed in the management of ground, a certain portion is allotted to the exclusive use of himself and family, which, with a moderate share of industry, is not only sufficient to supply every personal want, but leave a considerable part to be sent to market, to be sold, or exchanged for either necessaries or luxuries. The African now, finding himself a family man, and in possession of house and land, he begins to rear hogs, poultry, and other small stock, and either sells them to his master at a fair price, or carries them to market, for which one day in the week is allowed him. …

The African, no longer remembering a country to which he owes nothing but birth, becomes attached to the soil which is so propitious to his wants, and having few cares, and few desires, that are not completely satis-

fied, there is nothing so terrible to him as a change of situation. The master is the steward, the faithful guardian of all his wants and necessities. In sickness and in health—in youth and in old age, his assiduities are undiminished. The reader will anticipate the happiness of these people—and happy they must be, while their labours are directed by equity and humanity, and not by avarice.

God forbid that I should be an advocate for slavery, or servitude of any description, that can anywise limit the extent of human happiness: at the same time let me caution my countrymen against the weakness and folly of believing that happiness can only be sought in a constitution as free as their own. The history of all nations shew how extremely improper the laws of one country would be for those of another.

from Gordon Turnbull, *An Apology of Negro Slavery; or, the West India Planters Vindicated from the Charge of Inhumanity* (1786)

As a contrast to the horrid and fictitious picture, which has been drawn of the state of the negroes in the West-Indies, I shall here exhibit a true and more pleasing representation, taken from the life.

To begin then with the period of the Guinea negroe's arrival in one of the islands.—As soon as the ship that brings them is at anchor, the master or surgeon goes on shore to procure fresh provisions, fruit, and vegetables of all kinds, which are immediately sent on board for the slaves. Parties of them are sent on shore at different times, and conducted a little way into the country, where they frequently meet with many natives of their own country, who speak the same language, and sometimes with near and dear relations, who all appear very cheerful and happy. These agreeable and unexpected meetings are truly affecting, and excite the most tender and pleasing sensations in the breasts of the by-standers. It is not uncommon for these newly arrived guests, to mingle in the dance, or to join in the song, with their country people. If any of them appear dull or desponding, the old negroes endeavour to enliven them, by the most soothing and endearing expressions, telling them, in their own tongue, not to be afraid of the white men; that the white men are very good; that they will get plenty of *yam, yam,* (their general name for victuals) and that their work will be of the easiest kind. By these means, they are perfectly reconciled to the white men, and to a change of country, and of situation, which many of them declare, to be far superior to that which they had quitted. When the day of sale arrives, they not only meet the planter's looks, and answer his enquiries, by means of an interpreter, with great firmness, but they try, by offering their stout limbs to his inspection, jumping to shew their activity, and other allurements, to induce those, whose appearance pleases them, to buy them, and to engage, if possible, a preference in their favour ...

As soon as the new negroes are brought home to the plantation, if a planter has purchased them they are properly clothed.—A sufficient quantity of wholesome food is prepared, and served to them three times a day. They are comfortably lodged in some room of the manager's own house, or in some other convenient place, where they can be immediately under his eye for a few days. During this time they are not put to any kind of labour whatever, but are regularly conducted to bathe in the river, or in the sea, if it is nigh, twice a day. In the evenings they sing and dance, after the manner of their own nation, together with the old negroes who happen to be from the same country, one or two of whom are commonly instrumental performers, in these very noisy, but very joyous assemblies. In a very short time, they are taken into the houses of the principal and best disposed negroes, who adopt one of two of these new subjects into each family, to assist them in all the little domestic offices of cookery, carrying water, wood, &c. This is almost the only work they are employed in for the first two or three months, at the expiration of which, they are put to the easiest kind of labour for some months more....

from Mary Wollstonecraft, *A Vindication of the Rights of Men* (1790)

> Wollstonecraft's more famous work, *A Vindication of the Rights of Woman*, was published two years after her much shorter work on the rights of men, which briefly discusses the issue of slavery.

Is it necessary to repeat, that there are rights which we received, at our birth, as men, when we were raised above the brute creation by the power of improving ourselves—and that we receive these not from our forefathers, but from God?

My father may dissipate his property, yet I have no right to complain;—but if he should attempt to sell me for a slave, or fetter me with laws contrary to reason; nature, in enabling me to discern good from evil, teaches me to break the ignoble chain. ...

But on what principle Mr. Burke[1] could defend American independence, I cannot conceive; for the whole tenor of his ... arguments settles slavery on an everlasting foundation. Allowing his servile reverence for antiquity, and prudent attention to self-interest, to have the force which he insists on, it ought never to be abolished; and, because our ignorant forefathers, not understanding the native dignity of man, sanctioned a traffic that outrages every suggestion of reason and religion, we are to submit to the inhuman custom, and term an atrocious insult to humanity the love of our country and a proper submission to those laws which secure our property.—Security of property! Behold, in a few words, the definition of English liberty. And to this selfish principle every nobler one is sacrificed....

Anna Laetitia Barbauld, "Epistle to William Wilberforce, Esq., on the Rejection of the Bill for Abolishing the Slave Trade" (1791)[2]

Cease, Wilberforce, to urge thy generous aim!
     Thy country knows the sin, and stands the shame!
The preacher, poet, senator in vain
Has rattled in her sight the Negro's chain;
With his deep groans assailed her startled ear,
And rent the veil that hid his constant tear;
Forced her averted eyes his stripes[3] to scan,

---

[1] *Mr. Burke* Edmund Burke (1729–97), Anglo-Irish statesman, author, and philosopher. Burke famously supported the right of the colonies to self-rule.

[2] *William Wilberforce ... Slave Trade* This poem appeared shortly after the bill put forward by Wilberforce (and supported both by the Prime Minister, William Pitt, and the leader of the Opposition, Charles Fox) was defeated by a vote of 163 to 88.

[3] *stripes* Open wounds caused by the lash.

Beneath the bloody scourge laid bare the man,
Claimed Pity's tear, urged Conscience's strong control,
10   And flashed conviction on her shrinking soul.
The Muse too, soon awaked, with ready tongue
At Mercy's shrine applausive paeans rung;
And Freedom's eager sons, in vain foretold
A new Astraean[1] reign, an age of gold:
15   She knows and she persists—Still Afric bleeds,
Unchecked, the human traffic still proceeds;
She stamps her infamy to future time,
And on her hardened forehead seals the crime.
      In vain, to thy white standard[2] gathering round,
20   Wit, Worth, and Parts° and Eloquence   *intelligence*
        are found:
In vain, to push to birth thy great design,
Contending chiefs, and hostile virtues join;
All, from conflicting ranks, of power possest
To rouse, to melt, or to inform the breast.
25   Where seasoned tools of Avarice prevail,
A nation's eloquence, combined, must fail:
Each flimsy sophistry by turns they try;
The plausive° argument, the daring lie,   *plausible*
The artful gloss,° that moral sense confounds, *explanation*
30   Th'acknowledged thirst of gain that honour wounds:
Bane of ingenuous minds, th'unfeeling sneer,
Which, sudden, turns to stone the falling tear:
They search assiduous, with inverted skill,
For forms of wrong, and precedents of ill;
35   With impious mockery wrest the sacred page,
And glean up crimes from each remoter age:
Wrung Nature's tortures, shuddering, while you tell,
From scoffing fiends bursts forth the laugh of hell;
In Britain's senate, Misery's pangs give birth
40   To jests unseemly, and to horrid mirth—[3]
Forbear!—thy virtues but provoke our doom,
And swell th'account of vengeance yet to come;
For, not unmarked in Heaven's impartial plan,
Shall man, proud worm, condemn his fellow man?
45   And injured Afric, by herself redrest,
Darts her own serpents at her tyrant's breast.

Each vice, to minds depraved by bondage known,
With sure contagion fastens on his own;
In sickly languors melts his nerveless frame,
50   And blows to rage impetuous Passion's flame:
Fermenting swift, the fiery venom gains
The milky innocence of infant veins;
There swells the stubborn will, damps learning's fire,
The whirlwind wakes of uncontrolled desire,
55   Sears the young heart to images of woe,
And blasts the buds of Virtue as they blow.
      Lo! where reclined, pale Beauty courts the breeze,
Diffused on sofas of voluptuous ease;
With anxious awe, her menial train around,
60   Catch her faint whispers of half-uttered sound;
See her, in monstrous fellowship, unite
At once the Scythian, and the Sybarite;[4]
Blending repugnant vices, misallied,
Which frugal nature purposed to divide;
65   See her, with indolence to fierceness joined,
Of body delicate, infirm of mind,
With languid tones imperious mandates urge;
With arm recumbent wield the household scourge;
And with unruffled mien,° and placid sounds,   *appearance*
70   Contriving torture, and inflicting wounds.
Nor, in their palmy walks and spicy groves,
The form benign of rural pleasure roves;
No milkmaid's song, or hum of village talk,
Soothes the lone poet in his evening walk:
75   No willing arm the flail unwearied plies,
Where the mixed sounds of cheerful labour rise;
No blooming maids, and frolic swains are seen
To pay gay homage to their harvest queen:
No heart-expanding scenes their eyes must prove
80   Of thriving industry, and faithful love:
But shrieks and yells disturb the balmy air,
Dumb sullen looks of woe announce despair,
And angry eyes through dusky features glare.
Far from the sounding lash the Muses fly,
85   And sensual riot drowns each finer joy.
      Nor less from the gay East,° on   *India*
        essenced wings,
Breathing unnamed perfumes, Contagion springs;

---

[1]   *Astraea*   Greek goddess of justice.

[2]   *standard*   Flag.

[3]   *To jests ... mirth*   Barbauld refers to some Members of Parliament
who laughed in the House of Commons upon hearing of the
suffering of slaves.

---

[4]   *Scythian*   Ancient nomadic Europeans: synonym for ferocity;
Sybarite   People from the ancient Greek city of Sybaris: synonym
for pleasure-loving.

The soft luxurious plague alike pervades
The marble palaces, and rural shades;
90 Hence, thronged Augusta° builds her rosy bowers,   *London*
And decks in summer wreaths her smoky towers;
And hence, in summer bow'rs, Art's costly hand
Pours courtly splendours o'er the dazzled land:
The manners melt—One undistinguished blaze
95 O'erwhelms the sober pomp of elder days;
Corruption follows with gigantic stride,
And scarce vouchsafes his shameless front to hide:
The spreading leprosy taints ev'ry part,
Infects each limb, and sickens at the heart.
100 Simplicity! most dear of rural maids,
Weeping resigns her violated shades:
Stern Independence from his glebe° retires,   *field*
And anxious Freedom eyes her drooping fires;
By foreign wealth are British morals changed,
105 And Afric's sons, and India's, smile avenged.
     For you, whose tempered ardour long has borne
Untired the labour, and unmoved the scorn;
In Virtue's fasti° be inscribed your fame,   *calendar*
And uttered yours with Howard's[1] honoured name,
110 Friends of the friendless—Hail, ye generous band!
Whose efforts yet arrest Heav'n's lifted hand,
Around whose steady brows, in union bright,
The civic wreath, and Christian's palm unite:
Your merit stands, no greater and no less,
115 Without, or with the varnish of success;
But seek no more to break a nation's fall,
For ye have saved yourselves—and that is all.
Succeeding times your struggles, and their fate,
With mingled shame and triumph shall relate,
120 While faithful History, in her various page,
Marking the features of this motley age,
To shed a glory, and to fix a stain,
Tells how you strove, and that you strove in vain.

William Blake, Images of Slavery

The engravings reproduced here are among sixteen
plates prepared by William Blake in 1792–93 as
illustrations for John Stedman's *Narrative of Five
Years' Expedition against the Revolted Negroes of
Surinam* (1796).

---

[1] *Howard* John Howard (1726–90), prison reformer and philanthropist.

from Samuel Taylor Coleridge, *On the Slave Trade* (1796)

The article from which this excerpt is taken was delivered as a lecture in 1795, and published in Coleridge's magazine *The Watchman* the following year.

I have dwelt anxiously on this subject, with a particular view, to the slave-trade, which, I knew, has insinuated in the minds of many, uneasy doubts respecting the existence of a beneficent Deity. And indeed the evils arising from the formation of *imaginary* wants, have in no instance been so dreadfully exemplified, as in this inhuman traffic. We receive from the West-India Islands sugars, rum, cotton, logwood, cocoa, coffee, pimento, ginger, indigo, mahogany, and conserves. Not one of these articles are necessary; indeed with the exception of cotton and mahogany we cannot truly call them even useful: and not one of them is at present attainable by the poor and labouring part of Society. In return we export vast quantities of necessary tools, raiment, and defensive weapons, with great stores of provision. So that in this trade as in most others the poor are employed with unceasing toil first to raise, and then to send away the comforts, which they themselves absolutely want, in order to procure idle superfluities for their masters. If this trade had never existed, no one human being would have been less comfortably cloathed, housed, or nourished. Such is its value—they who would estimate the price which we pay for it, may consult the evidence delivered before the House of Commons.

from William Earle, *Obi; or, the History of Three-Fingered Jack* (1800)

Earle's novel is set against the background of a slave rebellion in Jamaica; it is based on the true story of Jack Mansong, an escaped slave who was said to have gained strength to lead the rebellion from the religion of "obeah," or "obi." The epistolary novel is for the most part made up of letters from one George Stanford, "a resident of Jamaica," to Charles, "his friend in England." The excerpt that appears here is from the letter with which the book opens.

Jack is a noble fellow, and in spite of every cruel hard-hearted planter, I shall repeat the same to the last hour of my life. "Jack is a Negro," say they. "Jack is a MAN," say I.

—"He is a slave."

—"MAN cannot be a slave to MAN."

—"He is my property."

—"How did you acquire that property?"

—"By paying for it."

—"Paying! Paying whom?"

—"Him who brought him from Africa."

—"How did he get possession of him?"

—"He caught him there."

—"Caught! what? Like a wild beast?"

—"No, but he contrived means to convey him into his ship."

—"Contrived! Then he brought him without his consent?"

—"Very likely."

—"And what is become of that robber?"

—"Robber! He is a very respectable man, who has left off trade, has married the daughter of a rich planter, and now lives very comfortably, after the fatigues of an industrious life."

—"What! Do they hang a poor hard-labouring man, who, driven by despair at the sight of his numerous family ready to starve for want of a bit of bread, takes advantage of a dark night, goes on the highway and frightens the traveller out of a few pieces of gold; and shall a daring ruffian, who is openly guilty of a crime more heinous in its nature and baneful in its effects, get respected by every body and pass his days in the peaceable enjoyment of riches acquired by such infamous means?"

—"I don't understand you; I never heard that the traffic was infamous. Is it not authorised by all the nations of Europe, Asia and America? Have not regulations been made concerning it by all governments?"

—"Very true, but that does not make it more honorable."

Anti-slavery woodcut (c. 1790s).

Mary Robinson, Poems on Slavery (1798, 1800)

Robinson, one of the best-known writers of the age, published a substantial number of works devoted in whole or in part to anti-slavery themes, including "Captivity: A Poem" (1777), "The African" (1798), and "The Negro Girl" (1800). "The African" was published initially in the *Morning Post*, 2 August 1798 and later incorporated into the long poem *The Progress of Liberty*. "The Negro Girl" appeared in Robinson's collection of *Lyrical Tales*.

The African (1798)

Shall the poor AFRICAN, the passive Slave,
Born in the bland effulgence of broad day,
Cherish'd by torrid splendours, while around
The plains prolific teem with honey'd stores,
5 Sink prematurely to a grave obscure,
No tear to grace his ashes? Or suspire
To wear Submission's long and goading chain,
To drink the tear that down his swarthy cheek
Flows fast, to moisten his toil-fever'd lip
10 Parch'd by the noon-tide blaze? Shall HE endure

The frequent lash, the agonizing scourge,
The day of labour, and the night of pain;
Expose his naked limbs to burning gales;
Faint in the sun, and wither in the storm;
15 Traverse hot sands, imbibe the morbid breeze,
Wing'd with contagion; while his blister'd feet,
Scorch'd by the vertical and raging beam,
Pour the swift life-stream? Shall his frenzied eyes,
Oh! worst of mortal miseries! behold
20 The darling of his heart, his sable love,
Selected from the trembling timid throng,
By the wan TYRANT, whose licentious touch
Seals the dark fiat of the SLAVE's despair!

OH LIBERTY! From thee the suppliant claims
25 The meed of retribution! Thy pure flame
Would light the sense opaque, and warm the spring
Of boundless ecstacy: while Nature's laws,
So violated, plead immortal tongu'd,
For her dark-fated children! Lead them forth
30 From bondage infamous! Bid Reason own
The dignities of MAN, whate'er his clime,
Estate, or colour. And, O sacred TRUTH!
Tell the proud Lords of traffic, that the breast
Thrice ebon-tinted, owns a crimson tide
35 As pure,—as clear, as Europe's Sons can boast.

The Negro Girl (1800)

I

Dark was the dawn, and o'er the deep
    The boist'rous whirlwinds blew;
The Sea-bird wheel'd its circling sweep,
    And all was drear to view—
5 When on the beach that binds the western shore
The love-lorn ZELMA stood, list'ning the tempest's roar.

2

Her eager Eyes beheld the main,
    While on her DRACO dear
She madly call'd, but call'd in vain,
10   No sound could DRACO hear,
Save the shrill yelling of the fateful blast,
While ev'ry Seaman's heart, quick shudder'd as it past.

3

White were the billows, wide display'd
     The clouds were black and low;
15 The Bittern shriek'd, a gliding shade
     Seem'd o'er the waves to go!
The livid flash illum'd the clam'rous main,
While ZELMA pour'd, unmark'd, her melancholy
     strain.

4

"Be still!" she cried, "loud tempest cease!
20   O! spare the gallant souls:
The thunder rolls—the winds increase—
     The Sea, like mountains, rolls!
While, from the deck, the storm-worn victims leap,
And o'er their struggling limbs, the furious billows
     sweep.

5

25 "O! barb'rous Pow'r! relentless Fate!
     Does Heav'n's high will decree
That some should sleep on beds of state,—
     Some, in the roaring Sea?
Some, nurs'd in splendour, deal Oppression's blow,
30 While worth and DRACO pine—in Slavery and woe!

6

"Yon Vessel oft has plough'd the main
     With human traffic fraught;
Its cargo,—our dark Sons of pain—
     For worldly treasure bought!
35 What had they done?—O Nature tell me why—
Is taunting scorn the lot, of thy dark progeny?

7

"Thou gav'st, in thy caprice, the Soul
     Peculiarly enshrin'd;
Nor from the ebon Casket stole
40   The Jewel of the mind!
Then wherefore let the suff'ring Negro's breast
Bow to his fellow, MAN, in brighter colours drest.

8

"Is it the dim and glossy hue
     That marks him for despair?—

45 While men with blood their hands embrue,
     And mock the wretch's pray'r?
Shall guiltless Slaves the Scourge of tyrants feel,
And, e'en before their GOD! unheard, unpitied kneel.

9

"Could the proud rulers of the land
50   Our Sable race behold;
Some bow'd by torture's Giant hand
     And others, basely sold!
Then would they pity Slaves, and cry, with shame,
Whate'er their TINTS may be, their SOULS are still
     the same!

10

55 "Why seek to mock the Ethiop's face?
     Why goad our hapless kind?
Can features alienate the race—
     Is there no kindred mind?
Does not the cheek which vaunts the roseate hue
60 Oft blush for crimes, that Ethiops never knew?

11

"Behold! the angry waves conspire
     To check the barb'rous toil!
While wounded Nature's vengeful ire—
     Roars, round this trembling Isle!
65 And hark! her voice re-echoes in the wind—
Man was not form'd by Heav'n, to trample on his kind!

12

"Torn from my Mother's aching breast,
     My Tyrant sought my love—
But, in the Grave shall ZELMA rest,
70   E'er she will faithless prove—
No DRACO!—Thy companion I will be
To that celestial realm, where Negroes shall be free!

13

"The Tyrant WHITE MAN taught my mind—
     The letter'd page to trace;—
75 He taught me in the Soul to find
     No tint, as in the face:
He bade my Reason, blossom like the tree—
But fond affection gave, the ripen'd fruits to thee.

14

"With jealous rage he mark'd my love;
    He sent thee far away;—
80 And prison'd in the plantain grove—
    Poor ZELMA pass'd the day—
But ere the moon rose high above the main,
ZELMA, and Love contriv'd, to break the Tyrant's
    chain.

15

85 "Swift, o'er the plain of burning Sand
    My course I bent to thee;
And soon I reach'd the billowy strand
    Which bounds the stormy Sea.—
DRACO! my Love! Oh yet, thy ZELMA's soul
90 Springs ardently to thee,—impatient of controul.

16

"Again the lightning flashes white—
    The rattling cords among!
Now, by the transient vivid light,
    I mark the frantic throng!
95 Now up the tatter'd shrouds my DRACO flies—
While o'er the plunging prow, the curling billows rise.

17

"The topmast falls—three shackled slaves—
    Cling to the Vessel's side!
Now lost amid the madd'ning waves—
100   Now on the mast they ride—
See! on the forecastle my DRACO stands
And now he waves his chain, now clasps his bleeding
    hands.

18

"Why, cruel WHITE-MAN! when away
    My sable Love was torn,

105 Why did you let poor ZELMA stay,
    On Afric's sands to mourn?
No! ZELMA is not left, for she will prove
In the deep troubled main, her fond—her faithful
    LOVE."

19

The lab'ring Ship was now a wreck,
110   The Shrouds were flutt'ring wide!
The rudder gone, the lofty deck
    Was rock'd from side to side—
Poor ZELMA's eyes now dropp'd their last big tear,
While, from her tawny cheek, the blood recoil'd with
    fear.

20

115 Now frantic, on the sands she roam'd,
    Now shrieking stop'd to view
Where high the liquid mountains foam'd,
    Around the exhausted crew—
'Till, from the deck, her DRACO's well known form
120 Sprung mid the yawning waves, and buffetted the
    Storm.

21

Long, on the swelling surge sustain'd
    Brave DRACO sought the shore,
Watch'd the dark Maid, but ne'er complain'd,
    Then sunk, to gaze no more!
125 Poor ZELMA saw him buried by the wave—
And, with her heart's true Love, plung'd in a wat'ry
    grave.

GEORGE GORDON, LORD BYRON
1788 – 1824

George Gordon, Lord Byron, was one of the most influential literary figures of the nineteenth century. His works—the long poems *Childe Harold's Pilgrimage* and *Don Juan* among them —were tremendous popular successes, and the Byronic Hero has become a cultural icon. Byron himself, handsome and charming, sexually unconventional, politically iconoclastic, has been alternately celebrated and reviled from his own time to the present.

Byron's beginnings were inauspicious. He was born in near-poverty on 22 January 1788, lame in one leg (probably the result of a form of cerebral palsy). His father, Captain John ("Mad Jack") Byron, a notorious spendthrift and rake, had married Byron's mother, the Scottish heiress Catherine Gordon, for her money. This he quickly squandered, afterward fleeing to France. Byron and his mother moved to Aberdeen. Here Byron lived out his first ten years, the object of his mother's capricious mixture of love and sudden overwhelming rages, deeply conscious of his lameness, and steeped in Calvinism. Here, too, at ten years old, he was regularly molested by his nursemaid.

In 1798 Byron's great-uncle, the fifth Lord Byron, died childless, and Byron inherited the title. He and his mother moved to the family's ancestral, debt-encumbered home, Newstead Abbey, in Nottinghamshire. Byron was sent to school, first to an academy in Dulwich, then to Harrow in 1801. Around 1801 he also met for the first time his half-sister Augusta, the product of an earlier marriage of his father's. In 1805 Byron entered Trinity College, Cambridge University, where he made the most lasting friendships of his life. He also contracted huge debts to which he would only add in the future.

Byron took a degree from Cambridge in 1807. In the same year, he published his first poetry collection, *Hours of Idleness*. The book was excoriated in the press as pretentious and derivative; Byron responded in 1809 with the verse satire *English Bards and Scotch Reviewers*, in which he attacked the most notable of his critics and many of the leading poets of the day. In that same year, Byron came of age and took possession of Newstead Abbey, where he held riotous parties; as a result of carousing and redecorating, his mountain of debt grew larger. In March he made his first appearance in the House of Lords, and in July, after having incurred more debt to finance himself, he set off on a trip through Europe and the Near East, areas largely closed to the English as a result of the Napoleonic Wars. This journey began an intense attachment to Greece that would color the rest of Byron's life and writing and allowed him to fulfill the homosexual desires that he had been unable to explore in England (where sodomy was a capital crime). During this time he also began *Childe Harold's Pilgrimage,* the work that would make him a celebrity.

Featuring a journey almost identical to that which Byron himself had just completed, undertaken by a mysteriously gloomy hero, *Childe Harold's Pilgrimage*, Cantos I&II, launched both the figure of the "Byronic Hero" and the association between that figure and Byron that the poet would alternately embrace and seek to evade for the remainder of his life. The poem cunningly managed to weave elements from familiar genres such as travel writing, gothic novels, and sentimental literature with experiments in mood and tone. It enthralled its readers. Byron wrote in Spenserian stanzas, but as the poem progressed he began to bend this stiff form so that it became his own. (Harold's discoveries and the narrator's own growing observational and meditative abilities find their mirror in the rhythms of the verse.) With its panoramic focus, high-flown tone, and alluringly aloof protagonist, *Childe Harold's Pilgrimage* marked an important moment in English and European literature.

Now a celebrity, Byron played that role with gusto. He became a darling of Whig society and indulged in a series of affairs, most scandalously with Lady Caroline Lamb. In addition, some time in 1813 Byron began a sexual relationship with his half-sister Augusta. This was to prove his undoing, but it was nonetheless the deepest and most lasting attachment of his life. He also continued writing, producing a collection of hugely popular works ranging from the short lyrics of *Hebrew Melodies* to the "Eastern Tales" produced in 1813 and 1814. In this series of long narrative poems, set in the Near East, he fleshed out the anti-heroic figure he had sketched in *Childe Harold's Pilgrimage*. The protagonists of the "Tales" stood aloof from those who surround them, tortured by a mysterious but deeply-felt guilt. Brave, glamorous, and in each case devoted utterly to one woman (who herself was an idealized romantic heroine), they were nonetheless fated to be outcasts. Described most fully in the first of the "Eastern Tales," "The Giaour," the hero reached his final refinement in the last, "Lara." The public embraced this figure, and a literary type entered into the canon with a vengeance: the writing of the next hundred years would be crowded with Byronic Heroes.

In January of 1815, Byron married Annabella Millbanke, a sheltered heiress. The marriage was based on a short courtship and false hopes, and the two participants were utterly unsuited. Byron was psychologically abusive to his wife, whose piety and conventionality were a constant irritant to him. At the end of 1815, a few weeks after the birth of their daughter, Ada Augusta, Annabella left him. A public scandal, aided by unauthorized publication of Byron's poems and his wife's revelations about his incest with Augusta Leigh, followed. Now a social outcast, Byron departed for Europe, never to return. He continued to communicate with his friends in England through a voluminous and revealingly frank series of letters that detailed his sexual adventures, his political and literary beliefs, and his continued involvement with affairs in England. Even if he had written no poetry, the letters would qualify Byron for a place as one of England's foremost authors: urbane, broad-ranging, dazzling, and hilarious, they make for riveting and delightful reading.

Landing in Belgium in April of 1816, Byron made his way through scenes—including a visit to Waterloo—which he would describe in the final two cantos of *Childe Harold*. At Geneva he met Mary and Percy Shelley. They had travelled to Switzerland accompanied by Mary's stepsister Claire Clairmont, who had had a brief sexual relationship with Byron in England. The two poets formed an intimate and intellectually rich friendship, and the four lived in close proximity during the summer. Byron resumed his involvement with Claire; she bore him a daughter, Allegra, in January of 1817.

When the Shelleys departed for England in August, Byron journeyed to Venice, where he lived for the next three years. Here he flung himself into a period of promiscuity (he estimated that he had sex with over two hundred women during this time), but continued to work as well, producing his verse drama *Manfred*, the fourth canto of *Childe Harold*, and the humorous *Beppo*, written in *ottava rima*. This colloquial Italian form was fiendishly ill-adapted to English, but Byron made it his own, also using it to produce his masterpiece, *Don Juan*, which he began in July of 1818.

Don Juan is the creation of an author who has found his *métier*. It is the longest satirical poem in English, a rollicking tale of a young hero who bears the same name as the seducer but resembles him in no other way. Juan, passive and sweet-natured, is seduced by women ranging from a family friend to Catherine the Great. His adventures take him on a journey from Spain to London by way of Greece and Russia. Byron was thus able to mock not only current social mores but also his own previous poems, Don Juan standing as a kind of anti-Byronic Hero. He took as his model for the poem a slight satire written in 1817 by John Hookham Frere in *ottava rima*, but *Don Juan* is also descended from Swift's *Gulliver's Travels*, and Sterne's *Tristram Shandy*. As with the latter, the focus of Byron's poem is not so much what is narrated as its narrator, a garrulous, easily distracted gentleman who at times bears a remarkable resemblance to the author. Byron's publisher, friends, and the critical establishment condemned *Don Juan* for its immorality, but he himself relished it, asserting that he had written it only "to giggle and make giggle"—a comment typically Byronic in its attempt to deny responsibility by invoking comedy. For all its author's disclaimers, *Don Juan* is no mere comic throwaway. It is a text of great cultural and political scope and a work of questing philosophy, arguably the best of its age.

In April of 1819 Byron met Countess Teresa Guiccioli, a young Italian woman married to a much older man. Almost immediately they began a socially-sanctioned affair that would last, with reasonable fidelity, until the end of Byron's life. Through her family, Byron was drawn into nationalist schemes to free Italy from the Austrians. When the family was exiled to Pisa in 1821 as a result of this plotting, Byron followed. The Shelleys were now based in Pisa, and Byron became one of their group. Soon, however, this "Pisan circle" fell apart, first because of Shelley's anger over Byron's callous treatment of Allegra (she had joined him in Venice in 1819, only for him first to neglect her and then send her to be brought up in a convent, where she died, unvisited by him, in 1822), then because of Byron's decision to follow the Gambas to Genoa, and finally because of Shelley's own death in July 1822.

Despite these upheavals, Byron wrote at a furious pace. Between 1819 and 1823 he produced numerous works, including a series of closet dramas (including *Sardanapalus*, *The Two Foscari*, and *Cain*), and his biting satire of England under George III, *The Vision of Judgment*. He also continued *Don Juan*, finishing sixteen cantos by the end of 1823.

In 1824 Byron organized an expedition to assist the Greeks in their fight for independence from the Turks. Settled in the marsh town of Missolonghi, he financed and trained soldiers. Exhausted and worn down, he contracted a fever and died on 19 April, aged thirty-six, his death hastened by copious bloodletting performed by his incompetent doctors.

⌘ ⌘ ⌘

Sun of the Sleepless

Sun of the sleepless! melancholy star!
Whose tearful beam glows tremulously far,
That show'st the darkness thou canst not dispel,
How like art thou to joy remembered well!
5 So gleams the past, the light of other days,
Which shines, but warms not with its powerless rays;
A night-beam Sorrow watcheth to behold,
Distinct, but distant—clear—but, oh how cold!
—1814

She walks in beauty

1

She walks in beauty, like the night
Of cloudless climes and starry skies;
And all that's best of dark and bright
Meet in her aspect and her eyes:
5 Thus mellow'd to that tender light
Which heaven to gaudy day denies.

2

One shade the more, one ray the less,
Had half impair'd the nameless grace
Which waves in every raven tress,
10 Or softly lightens o'er her face;

Where thoughts serenely sweet express
　　How pure, how dear their dwelling place.

3

And on that cheek, and o'er that brow,
　　So soft, so calm, yet eloquent,
15　The smiles that win, the tints that glow,
　　But tell of days in goodness spent,
A mind at peace with all below,
　　A heart whose love is innocent!
—1815 [WRITTEN 1814]

When we two parted [1]

1

When we two parted
　　In silence and tears,
Half broken-hearted
　　To sever for years,
5　Pale grew thy cheek and cold,
　　Colder thy kiss;
Truly that hour foretold
　　Sorrow to this.

2

The dew of the morning
10　　Sunk chill on my brow—
It felt like the warning
　　Of what I feel now.
Thy vows are all broken,
　　And light is thy fame;
15　I hear thy name spoken,
　　And share in its shame.

3

They name thee before me,

A knell to mine ear;
A shudder comes o'er me—
20　　Why wert thou so dear?
They know not I knew thee,
　　Who knew thee too well:—
Long, long shall I rue thee,
　　Too deeply to tell.

4

25　In secret we met—
　　In silence I grieve,
That thy heart could forget,
　　Thy spirit deceive.
If I should meet thee
30　　After long years,
How should I greet thee!—
　　With silence and tears.
—1816

Stanzas for Music [2]

1

There's not a joy the world can give like that it
　　takes away,
When the glow of early thought declines in feeling's
　　dull decay;
'Tis not on youth's smooth cheek the blush alone,
　　which fades so fast,
But the tender bloom of heart is gone, ere youth
　　itself be past.

2

5　Then the few whose spirits float above the wreck
　　of happiness,
Are driven o'er the shoals of guilt or ocean of excess:
The magnet of their course is gone, or only points
　　in vain
The shore to which their shiver'd sail shall never
　　stretch again.

---

[1] *When we two parted*　This poem has a complex history, at least partially because Byron deliberately misdated the date of its composition as 1816, in order to hide its true subject. In fact, the lines were written in 1815, and their subject is Lady Frances Wedderburn Webster, the wife of a friend of Byron's; Byron had heard gossip about her affair with the Duke of Wellington. Byron himself had had a brief "platonic" affair with Lady Webster in 1813: a heated and exciting chase, kept secret from her husband and ending without consummation.

[2] *Stanzas for Music*　Byron wrote this poem in 1815 to commemorate the death of one of the friends of his youth, the Duke of Dorset. He referred to it in an 1816 letter as "the truest, though the most melancholy, I ever wrote."

3

Then the mortal coldness of the soul like death
    itself comes down;
10 It cannot feel for others' woes, it dare not dream
    its own;
That heavy chill has frozen o'er the fountain of
    our tears,
And tho' the eye may sparkle still, 'tis where the
    ice appears.

4

Tho' wit may flash from fluent lips, and mirth
    distract the breast,
Through midnight hours that yield no more their
    former hope of rest;
15 'Tis but as ivy-leaves around the ruin'd turret wreath,
All green and wildly fresh without but worn and
    grey beneath.

5

Oh could I feel as I have felt,—or be what I have been,
Or weep as I could once have wept, o'er many a
    vanished scene:
As springs in deserts found seem sweet, all
    brackish though they be,
20 So midst the wither'd waste of life, those tears
    would flow to me.
—1816

Darkness [1]

I had a dream, which was not all a dream.
  The bright sun was extinguish'd, and the stars
Did wander darkling in the eternal space,
Rayless, and pathless, and the icy earth

5 Swung blind and blackening in the moonless air;[2]
Morn came, and went—and came, and brought no day,
And men forgot their passions in the dread
Of this their desolation; and all hearts
Were chill'd into a selfish prayer for light:
10 And they did live by watchfires—and the thrones,
The palaces of crowned kings—the huts,
The habitations of all things which dwell,
Were burnt for beacons; cities were consumed,
And men were gathered round their blazing homes
15 To look once more into each other's face;
Happy were those who dwelt within the eye
Of the volcanos, and their mountain-torch:
A fearful hope was all the world contain'd;
Forests were set on fire—but hour by hour
20 They fell and faded—and the crackling trunks
Extinguish'd with a crash—and all was black.
The brows of men by the despairing light
Wore an unearthly aspect, as by fits
The flashes fell upon them; some lay down
25 And hid their eyes and wept; and some did rest
Their chins upon their clenched hands, and smiled;
And others hurried to and fro, and fed
Their funeral piles with fuel, and looked up
With mad disquietude on the dull sky,
30 The pall of a past world; and then again
With curses cast them down upon the dust,
And gnash'd their teeth and howl'd: the wild
    birds shriek'd,
And, terrified, did flutter on the ground,
And flap their useless wings; the wildest brutes
35 Came tame and tremulous; and vipers crawl'd
And twined themselves among the multitude,
Hissing, but stingless—they were slain for food:
And War, which for a moment was no more,
Did glut himself again;—a meal was bought
40 With blood, and each sate sullenly apart
Gorging himself in gloom: no love was left;
All earth was but one thought—and that was death,
Immediate and inglorious; and the pang
Of famine fed upon all entrails—men
45 Died, and their bones were tombless as their flesh;
The meagre by the meagre were devoured,

1 *Darkness* The dust thrown into the atmosphere in 1815 by
Mount Tamboro, an Indonesian volcano, made the summer of 1816
the coldest and wettest on record. Influenced by the weather, and
perhaps by recent warnings by an Italian astronomer that sunspots
might lead to the extinction of the sun, Byron produced this
prescient poem, which he labeled "a Fragment." The "last man"
theme was a source of fascination for the Romantics, but Byron's
poem is distinctive for its absence of a last man, its unrelentingly
bleak vision, and its representation of a typically Byronic faithful
dog.

2 *icy earth ... moonless air* Cf. Ezekiel 32.7–8; Joel 2.31; Revelation
6.12.

Even dogs assail'd their masters, all save one,
And he was faithful to a corse,[1] and kept
The birds and beasts and famish'd men at bay,
50 Till hunger clung them, or the dropping dead
Lured their lank jaws; himself sought out no food,
But with a piteous and perpetual moan
And a quick desolate cry, licking the hand
Which answered not with a caress—he died.
55 The crowd was famish'd by degrees; but two
Of an enormous city did survive,
And they were enemies; they met beside
The dying embers of an altar-place
Where had been heap'd a mass of holy things
60 For an unholy usage; they raked up,
And shivering scraped with their cold skeleton hands
The feeble ashes, and their feeble breath
Blew for a little life, and made a flame
Which was a mockery; then they lifted up
65 Their eyes as it grew lighter, and beheld
Each other's aspects—saw, and shriek'd, and died—
Even of their mutual hideousness they died,
Unknowing who he was upon whose brow
Famine had written Fiend. The world was void,
70 The populous and the powerful was a lump,
Seasonless, herbless, treeless, manless, lifeless—
A lump of death—a chaos of hard clay.
The rivers, lakes, and ocean all stood still,
And nothing stirred within their silent depths;
75 Ships sailorless lay rotting on the sea,
And their masts fell down piecemeal; as they dropp'd
They slept on the abyss without a surge—
The waves were dead; the tides were in their grave,
The moon their mistress had expired before;
80 The winds were withered in the stagnant air,
And the clouds perish'd; Darkness had no need
Of aid from them—She was the universe.
—1816

---

1 *corse* Corpse.

Prometheus[2]

Titan! to whose immortal eyes
  The sufferings of mortality,
    Seen in their sad reality,
Were not as things that gods despise;
5 What was thy pity's recompense?
A silent suffering, and intense;
The rock, the vulture, and the chain,
All that the proud can feel of pain,
The agony they do not show,
10 The suffocating sense of woe,
    Which speaks but in its loneliness,
And then is jealous lest the sky
Should have a listener, nor will sigh
    Until its voice is echoless.

2

15 Titan! to thee the strife was given
    Between the suffering and the will,
      Which torture where they cannot kill;
And the inexorable Heaven,
And the deaf tyranny of Fate,
20 The ruling principle of Hate,
Which for its pleasure doth create
The things it may annihilate,
Refused thee even the boon to die:
The wretched gift eternity
25 Was thine—and thou hast borne it well.
All that the Thunderer[3] wrung from thee
Was but the menace which flung back
On him the torments of thy rack;
The fate thou didst so well foresee
30 But would not to appease him tell;
And in thy Silence was his Sentence,
And in his Soul a vain repentance,
And evil dread so ill dissembled
That in his hand the lightnings trembled.

---

2 *Prometheus* The Titan Prometheus stole fire from heaven and
gave it to humanity. To punish him, Jupiter, King of the gods, had
him chained to a rock in the Caucasus, where a vulture (in some
versions, an eagle) tore at his liver. Each night Prometheus's liver
grew afresh, to be torn out the next day.

3 *Thunderer* Jupiter.

3

35 Thy Godlike crime was to be kind,
        To render with thy precepts less
        The sum of human wretchedness,
    And strengthen Man with his own mind;
    But baffled as thou wert from high,
40 Still in thy patient energy,
    In the endurance, and repulse
        Of thine impenetrable Spirit,
    Which Earth and Heaven could not convulse,
        A mighty lesson we inherit:
45 Thou art a symbol and a sign
        To Mortals of their fate and force;
    Like thee, Man is in part divine,
        A troubled stream from a pure source;
    And Man in portions can foresee
50 His own funereal destiny;
    His wretchedness, and his resistance,
    And his sad unallied existence:
    To which his Spirit may oppose
    Itself—an equal to all woes,
55   And a firm will, and a deep sense,
    Which even in torture can descry
        Its own concentered recompense,
    Triumphant where it dares defy,
    And making Death a Victory.
    —1816

So, we'll go no more a roving[1]

1

So, we'll go no more a roving
    So late into the night,
Though the heart be still as loving,
    And the moon be still as bright.

2

5   For the sword outwears its sheath,
        And the soul wears out the breast,
    And the heart must pause to breathe,
        And love itself have rest.

3

Though the night was made for loving,
10   And the day returns too soon,
Yet we'll go no more a roving
        By the light of the moon.
    —1817

When a man hath no freedom to fight for at home[2]

When a man hath no freedom to fight for at home,
    Let him combat for that of his neighbors;
Let him think of the glories of Greece and of Rome,
    And get knock'd on the head for his labours.

5   To do good to mankind is the chivalrous plan,
        And is always as nobly requited;
    Then battle for freedom wherever you can,
        And, if not shot or hang'd, you'll get knighted.
    —1820

---

1 *When ... home* Originally written as part of a letter from Byron to his friend Thomas Moore, 28 February 1817. Just before these lines Byron writes, "The Carnival ... knocked me up a little. But it is over—and it is now Lent, with all its abstinence and sacred music. The mumming closed with a masked ball ... and, though I did not dissipate much upon the whole, yet I find 'the sword wearing out the scabbard', though I have but just turned the corner of twenty-nine."

2 *When a man ... home* Byron first sent these lines in a letter to his friend Thomas Moore on 5 November 1820. They are based on Byron's activities with the Italian freedom-fighters, the Carbonari, and their abortive attempt to stage an uprising.

January 22nd 1842.
Missolonghi
On this day I complete my thirty sixth year [1]

1

'Tis time this heart should be unmoved
    Since others it hath ceased to move,
Yet though I cannot be beloved
    Still let me love.

2

5 My days are in the yellow leaf [2]
    The flowers and fruits of love are gone—
The worm—the canker, and the grief
    Are mine alone.

3

The fire that on my bosom preys
10   Is lone as some Volcanic Isle,
No torch is kindled at its blaze
    A funeral pile!

4

The hope, the fear, the jealous care
    The exalted portion of the pain
15 And power of Love I cannot share
    But wear the chain.

5

But 'tis not *thus*—and 'tis not *here*
    Such thoughts should shake my soul, nor *now*

    Where Glory decks the hero's bier
20   Or binds his brow.

6

The Sword—the Banner—and the Field
    Glory and Greece around us see!
The Spartan borne upon his shield [3]
    Was not more free!

7

25 Awake! (not Greece—She *is* awake!)
    Awake my spirit—think through *whom*
Thy life-blood tracks its parent lake
    And then strike home!

8

Tread those reviving passions down
30   Unworthy Manhood;—unto thee
Indifferent should the smile or frown
    Of Beauty be.

9

If thou regret'st thy youth, why *live?*
    The land of honourable Death
35 Is here—up to the Field! and give
    Away thy Breath.

10

Seek out—less often sought than found,
    A Soldier's Grave—for thee the best,
Then look around and choose thy ground
40   And take thy Rest.

—1824

Epistle to Augusta [4]

1

My Sister—my sweet Sister—if a name
    Dearer and purer were—it should be thine.
Mountains and seas divide us—but I claim

---

[1] *On this ... year* This poem was until recently most commonly known by its subtitle, but the date and place are the correct title. Byron wrote it on his 36th birthday, in Greece. A companion who was with him at the time says, "January 22.—Lord Byron came from his bedroom into the apartment ... where some friends were assembled, and said, with a smile, 'You were complaining, the other day, that I never write any poetry now:—this is my birthday, and I have just finished something which, I think, is better than what I usually write.'" The poem is informed by Byron's relationship with two people, his young Greek companion of the time, Loukas Chalandritsanos, and a Turkish girl, Hataje, whom he had taken into his care. Byron's feelings for Chalandritsanos are commonly understood to be the stronger influence of the two.

[2] *My days ... leaf* See *Macbeth* 5.3.21–22.

[3] [Byron's note] The slain were borne on their shields—witness the Spartan mother's speech to her son, delivered with his buckler—"Either *with* this or *on* this."

[4] *Augusta* Byron's sister, Augusta Leigh (1783–1857).

No tears, but tenderness to answer mine:
5   Go where I will, to me thou art the same—
        A loved regret which I would not resign—
    There yet are two things in my destiny
    A world to roam through—and a home with thee.

2

    The first were nothing—had I still the last
10   It were the haven of my happiness—
    But other claims and other ties thou hast—
        And mine is not the wish to make them less.
    A strange doom is thy father's son's and past
        Recalling—as it lies beyond redress—
15   Reversed for him our grandsire's fate of yore
    He had no rest at sea—nor I on shore.[1]

3

    If my inheritance of storms hath been
        In other elements—and on the rocks
    Of perils overlooked or unforeseen
20   I have sustained my share of worldly shocks
    The fault was mine—nor do I seek to screen
        My errors with defensive paradox—
    I have been cunning in mine overthrow
    The careful pilot of my proper woe.

4

25   Mine were my faults—and mine be their reward—
        My whole life was a contest—since the day
    That gave me being gave me that which marred
        The gift—a fate, or will that walked astray—
    And I at times have found the struggle hard
30   And thought of shaking off my bonds of clay—
    But now I fain would for a time survive
    If but to see what next can well arrive.

5

    Kingdoms and empires in my little day
        I have outlived, and yet I am not old—
35   And when I look on this, the petty spray
        Of my own years of trouble, which have rolled
    Like a wild bay of breakers, melts away:—

Something—I know not what—does still uphold
    A spirit of slight patience;—not in vain,
40   Even for its own sake—do we purchase pain.

6

    Perhaps—the workings of defiance stir
        Within me, or perhaps a cold despair—
    Brought on when ills habitually recur,—
        Perhaps a kinder clime—or purer air—
45   For even to this may change of soul refer—
        And with light armour we may learn to bear—
    Have taught me a strange quiet which was not
        The chief companion of a calmer lot.

7

    I feel almost at times as I have felt
50   In happy childhood—trees, and flowers, and brooks
    Which do remember me of where I dwelt
        Ere my young mind was sacrificed to books—
    Come as of yore upon me—and can melt
        My heart with recognition of their looks—
55   And even at moments I could think I see
    Some living thing to love—but none like thee.

8

    Here are the Alpine landscapes—which create
        A fund for contemplation;—to admire
    Is a brief feeling of a trivial date—
60   But something worthier do such scenes inspire:
    Here to be lonely is not desolate—
        For much I view which I could most desire—
    And, above all a Lake I can behold—
    Lovelier—not dearer than our own of old.

9

65   Oh that thou wert but with me!—but I grow
        The fool of my own wishes—and forget
    The solitude which I have vaunted so
        Has lost its praise in this but one regret—
    There may be others which I less may show—
70   I am not of the plaintive mood—and yet
    I feel an ebb in my philosophy
    And the tide rising in my altered eye.

[1]   *He had no ... on shore* Byron and Augusta's grandfather, Admiral
John Byron, was renowned for never making a sea voyage without
encountering a storm. He was known as "Foulweather Jack."

10

I did remind thee of our own dear lake
    By the old Hall which may be mine no more—
75 Leman's is fair—but think not I forsake
    The sweet remembrance of a dearer shore—
Sad havoc Time must with my memory make
    Ere that or thou can fade these eyes before—
Though like all things which I have loved—they are
80 Resigned for ever—or divided far.

11

The world is all before me—I but ask
    Of Nature that with which she will comply—
It is but in her Summer's sun to bask—
    To mingle with the quiet of her sky—
85 To see her gentle face without a mask
    And never gaze on it with apathy—
She was my early friend—and now shall be
My Sister—till I look again on thee.

12

I can reduce all feelings but this one,
90   And that I would not—for at length I see
Such scenes as those wherein my life begun
    The earliest—were the only paths for me.
Had I but sooner learnt the crowd to shun
    I had been better than I now can be
95 The passions which have torn me would have slept—
I had not suffered—and *thou* hadst not wept.

13

With false Ambition what had I to do?
    Little with love, and least of all with fame!
And yet they came unsought and with me grew,
100   And made me all which they can make—a Name.
Yet this was not the end I did pursue—
    Surely I once beheld a nobler aim.
But all is over—I am one the more
    To baffled millions which have gone before.

14

105 And for the future—this world's future may
    From me demand but little from my care;
I have outlived myself by many a day,
    Having survived so many things that were—
My years have been no slumber—but the prey
110   Of ceaseless vigils;—for I had the share
Of life which might have filled a century
Before its fourth in time had passed me by.

15

And for the remnants which may be to come
    I am content—and for the past I feel
115 Not thankless—for within the crowded sum
    Of struggles—happiness at times would steal
And for the present—I would not benumb
    My feelings farther—nor shall I conceal
That with all this I still can look around
120 And worship Nature with a thought profound.

16

For thee—my own sweet Sister—in thy heart
    I know myself secure—as thou in mine
We were and are—I am—even as thou art—
    Beings who ne'er each other can resign
125 It is the same together or apart
    From Life's commencement to its slow decline—
We are entwined—let death come slow or fast
The tie which bound the first endures the last.
    —1830

Don Juan

Byron worked on *Don Juan* from 1818 until his death, publishing it piecemeal from 1819 to 1824. His immediate poetic inspiration for his satirical reworking of the *Don Juan* legend was *The Monks and the Giants* (1817), by his friend John Hookham Frere. In this, he said, he discovered the power of the ottava rima rhyme scheme (abababcc) that drives his own poem. His models for *Don Juan*'s rambling episodic format were the serio-comic romances of the fifteenth- and sixteenth-century Italian writers Pulci, Ariosto, and Berni. Byron, however, did more with these influences than anyone could have hoped or dreamed. The flexible structure allowed him to range widely, moving with ease from high-flown philosophical reflections to the most trivial minutiae, and back again—sometimes within the same stanza. In the guise of a garrulous raconteur, Byron was able to comment seriously on English and European politics, the hypocrisy of sexual mores, the falseness of conventional morals, and the often painful complexities of human emotions. The philosophical aspects of *Don Juan* are only just beginning to be discussed, but they are an integral part of the poem.

At the same time, *Don Juan* remains a comic goldmine. All forms of wit—satire, wordplay, parody, just plain silliness—confront the reader, and no cultural shibboleth escapes Byron's mockery. For this reason, the poem was met with outrage and horror upon its publication. Indeed, Byron's own mistress, Teresa Guiccioli, found it immoral, but although he stopped writing it at her request in 1821, he resumed again in 1822. Friends and critics alike lamented what they saw as Byron's lack of tact, his lack of taste, and his lack of decency. He was attacked for making his personal life public (the portrait of Juan's mother, Donna Inez, in the first canto was agreed to be a satirical picture of Lady Byron), and for writing a poem "not … didactic of any thing but mischief." Byron himself famously insisted that he had written the poem only "to giggle and make giggle," and continued writing.

Byron's protagonist is a many-layered creation. The story of the great seducer was first told by Tirso de Molina (Gabriel Téllez) in *El Burlador de Sevilla y convidado di piedra* ("The Trickster of Seville and the Stone Guest," 1616?); it subsequently inspired such masterpieces as Molière's *Don Juan ou Le Festin de pierre* (1665), Thomas Shadwell's *The Libertine* (1676), and Mozart's *Don Giovanni* (1787). Apparently Byron first encountered the story in a pantomime (see Canto 1.7, below). But Byron's Don Juan (pronounced, in the English manner, Joo-an, with the stress on the first syllable), like his poem, is more than the sum of his sources. He is, first and foremost, a parody of the famous Don Juan, for he is a passive fellow, seduced and sweet-natured rather than seducing and ruthless. He is also a parodic version of the epic hero figure (including Byron's own most famous creation, Childe Harold), and by extension, of Byron himself; throughout the poem Byron uses Juan to play on the public notion of what it meant to be "Byron."

Don Juan incorporates three chronological levels: Byron wrote it from 1818-1824, using his memories of the England in which he moved from 1812–16, but Juan lives in the late eighteenth century. The narrative voice is carefully constructed; it evidently both is and is not meant to be Byron. This subversion of certainty pervades the poem at every level. Yet paradoxically, the effect it creates is often naturalistic. "Confess—you dog!" Byron wrote to his friend Douglas Kinnaird about the poem in 1819, "is it not life?—is it not the thing?"

Don Juan

"Difficile est proprie communia dicere."[1]

Horace, *Epistola ad Pisones*

DEDICATION[2]

1

Bob Southey! You're a poet—Poet Laureate,
    And representative of all the race;
Although 'tis true that you turned out a Tory[3] at
    Last—yours has lately been a common case:
5 And now, my epic renegade! what are ye at,
    With all the Lakers[4] in and out of place?
A nest of tuneful persons, to my eye
Like "four and twenty Blackbirds in a pye;[5]

2

"Which pye being opened they began to sing"
10   (This old song and new simile holds good),
"A dainty dish to set before the King,"

3

You, Bob! are rather insolent, you know,
    At being disappointed in your wish
To supersede all warblers here below,
20   And be the only Blackbird in the dish;
And then you overstrain yourself, or so,
    And tumble downward like the flying fish
Gasping on deck, because you soar too high, Bob,
And fall, for lack of moisture quite a-dry, Bob![8]

4

25 And Wordsworth, in a rather long "Excursion"
    (I think the quarto holds five hundred pages),[9]
Has given a sample from the vasty version
    Of his new system to perplex the sages;
'Tis poetry—at least by his assertion,
30   And may appear so when the dog-star rages—[10]
And he who understands it would be able
To add a story to the Tower of Babel.

5

You—Gentlemen! by dint of long seclusion
    From better company, have kept your own
35 At Keswick,[11] and, through still continued fusion
    Of one another's minds, at last have grown
To deem as a most logical conclusion,

Or Regent,[6] who admires such kind of food;
And Coleridge, too, has lately taken wing,
    But like a hawk encumbered with his hood,
15 Explaining Metaphysics to the nation—
I wish he would explain his Explanation.[7]

---

[1] *Difficile ... dicere* Latin: "It is hard to treat in your own way what is common."

[2] *Dedication* This Dedication is an attack on Robert Southey (1774–1843), then England's Poet Laureate, although Byron also makes jokes at the expense of other poets (especially Coleridge and Wordsworth). Southey had spread the rumor that Byron and Shelley participated in a "league of incest" when they were living in Switzerland (Byron was at that time conducting an affair with Mary Shelley's stepsister, Clare Clairmont. Southey believed them to be half-sisters, and further believed that both had sex with both men). Less personally, Byron felt that Southey had played the part of a traitor when he abandoned his early republican ideals and became a wholehearted supporter of the increasingly conservative government. Nonetheless, when he decided to publish the first two cantos anonymously, Byron had the Dedication omitted; he felt it was cowardly to attack Southey anonymously. The stanzas were first published in 1833.

[3] *Tory* Supporter of the Conservative party in Parliament, here opposed to a more republican political stance, which Southey once assumed.

[4] *Lakers* The name applied by *The Edinburgh Review* to Coleridge, Southey, and Wordsworth, who all resided in the Lake District at one time or another.

[5] *pye* Byron here makes a pun on the familiar nursery rhyme. Henry James Pye (1745–1813) had been Poet Laureate before Southey.

[6] *Regent* The Prince of Wales (later George IV) was appointed Prince Regent in 1811, after his father, George III, had become permanently incapacitated for ruling.

[7] *I wish ... his Explanation* Coleridge's philosophical prose was notoriously vague and hard to follow.

[8] *dry-bob* Slang for sex without ejaculation.

[9] *Wordsworth ... pages* Byron here refers to Wordsworth's *The Excursion* (1814).

[10] *dog-star* Sirius, ascendant during the hottest days of the summer, was once believed to have a maddening influence.

[11] *Keswick* Of the Lake Poets only Southey lived at Keswick, in the Lake District; Coleridge had moved there with his family in 1800, but he was no longer living there in 1819. Wordsworth lived nearby, at Grasmere.

That Poesy has wreaths for you alone:
There is a narrowness in such a notion,
40 Which makes me wish you'd change your lakes
        for Ocean.

6

I would not imitate the petty thought,
    Nor coin my self-love to so base a vice,
For all the glory your conversion brought,
    Since gold alone should not have been its price.
45 You have your salary; was't for that you wrought?
    And Wordsworth has his place in the Excise.[1]
You're shabby fellows—true—but poets still,
And duly seated on the Immortal Hill.

7

Your bays[2] may hide the baldness of your brows—
50   Perhaps some virtuous blushes—let them go—
To you I envy neither fruit nor boughs—
        And for the fame you would engross below,
The field is universal, and allows
        Scope to all such as feel the inherent glow:
55 Scott, Rogers, Campbell, Moore and Crabbe,[3] will try
'Gainst you the question with posterity.

8

For me, who, wandering with pedestrian Muses,
    Contend not with you on the winged steed,
I wish your fate may yield ye, when she chooses,
60   The fame you envy, and the skill you need;
And, recollect, a poet nothing loses
    In giving to his brethren their full meed

Of merit, and complaint of present days
Is not the certain path to future praise.

9

65 He that reserves his laurels for posterity
    (Who does not often claim the bright reversion)
Has generally no great crop to spare it, he
    Being only injured by his own assertion;
And although here and there some glorious rarity
70   Arise like Titan[4] from the sea's immersion,
The major part of such appellants go
To—God knows where—for no one else can know.

10

If, fallen in evil days on evil tongues,
    Milton appealed to the Avenger, Time,
75 If Time, the Avenger, execrates his wrongs,
    And makes the word "Miltonic" mean "sublime,"
He deigned not to belie his soul in songs,
    Nor turn his very talent to a crime;
He did not loathe the Sire to laud the Son,
80 But closed the tyrant-hater he begun.

11

Think'st thou, could he—the blind Old Man—arise
    Like Samuel from the grave,[5] to freeze once more
The blood of monarchs with his prophecies
    Or be alive again— again all hoar
85 With time and trials, and those helpless eyes,
    And heartless daughters—worn—and pale—and
        poor;[6]
Would *he* adore a sultan? *he* obey
The intellectual eunuch Castlereagh?[7]

---

[1] *Wordsworth ... Excise* In 1813, Wordsworth had been appointed Distributor of Stamps for Westmoreland (a sinecure), through the influence of his patron Lord Lonsdale. In gratitude, he dedicated *The Excursion* to Lonsdale.

[2] *bays* Bay, or laurel, leaves were awarded both to military heroes and to poets (hence the term "poet laureate"). Julius Caesar was allegedly gratified with his because they hid the fact that he was bald. Southey was not bald, and this particular insult is striking, given that Byron himself had frequently commented on Southey's good looks.

[3] *Scott ... Crabbe Scott* Sir Walter Scott, poet and novelist (1771–1832); *Rogers* Samuel Rogers, poet (1763–1855); *Campbell* Thomas Campbell, poet (1777–1844); *Moore* Thomas Moore, poet (1779–1852).

[4] *Titan* The Latin name for Helios, the Sun God.

[5] *Samuel from the grave* See 1 Samuel 28.13–14.

[6] [Byron's note] Pale, but not cadaverous:—Milton's two elder daughters are said to have robbed him of his books, besides cheating and plaguing him in the economy of his house, &c. His feelings on such an outrage, both as a parent and a scholar, must have been singularly painful. Hayley compares him to Lear. See part third, *Life of Milton*, by W. Hayley (or Hailey, as spelt in the edition before me).

[7] *Castlereagh* Conservative politician Robert Stewart, Lord Castlereagh (1769–1822).

12

Cold-blooded, smooth-faced, placid miscreant!
90   Dabbling its sleek young hands in Erin's gore,
And thus for wider carnage taught to pant,
      Transferred to gorge upon a sister shore,
The vulgarest tool that Tyranny could want,
      With just enough of talent, and no more,
95 To lengthen fetters by another fixed,
And offer poison long already mixed.

13

An orator of such set trash of phrase
      Ineffably—legitimately vile,
That even its grossest flatterers dare not praise,
100   Nor foes—all nations—condescend to smile,
Not even a sprightly blunder's spark can blaze
      From that Ixion grindstone's ceaseless toil,[1]
That turns and turns to give the world a notion
Of endless torments and perpetual motion.

14

105 A bungler even in its disgusting trade,
      And botching, patching, leaving still behind
Something of which its masters are afraid,
      States to be curbed, and thoughts to be confined,
Conspiracy or Congress to be made—
110   Cobbling at manacles for all mankind—
A tinkering slave-maker, who mends old chains,
With God and Man's abhorrence for its gains.

15

If we may judge of matter by the mind,
      Emasculated to the marrow *It*
115 Hath but two objects, how to serve, and bind,
      Deeming the chain it wears even men may fit,
Eutropius of its many masters,[2] blind
      To worth as freedom, wisdom as to Wit,
Fearless—because *no* feeling dwells in ice,
120 Its very courage stagnates to a vice.

16

Where shall I turn me not to *view* its bonds,
      For I will never *feel* them?—Italy!
Thy late reviving Roman soul desponds
      Beneath the lie this State-thing breathed o'er
            thee—
125 Thy clanking chain, and Erin's yet green wounds,
      Have voices—tongues to cry aloud for me.
Europe has slaves—allies—kings—armies still,
And Southey lives to sing them very ill.

17

Meantime—Sir Laureate—I proceed to dedicate,
130   In honest simple verse, this song to you,
And, if in flattering strains I do not predicate,
      'Tis that I still retain my "buff and blue";[3]
My politics as yet are all to educate:
      Apostasy's so fashionable, too,
135 To keep *one* creed's a task grown quite Herculean;
Is it not so, my Tory, ultra-Julian?[4]

Canto 1

1

I want a hero: an uncommon want,
      When every year and month sends forth a new one,
Till, after cloying the gazettes with cant,
      The age discovers he is not the true one;
5 Of such as these I should not care to vaunt,
      I'll therefore take our ancient friend Don Juan—
We all have seen him in the pantomime,
Sent to the devil somewhat ere his time.

2

Vernon, the butcher Cumberland, Wolfe, Hawke,
10   Prince Ferdinand, Granby, Burgoyne, Keppel, Howe,
Evil and good, have had their tithe of talk,

---

[1] *Ixion ... toil*   For attempting to rape Hera, Ixion was bound to a wheel that rolled forever through Hades.

[2] [Byron's note]   For the character of Eutropius, the eunuch and minister at the court of Arcadius, see Gibbon. [See Edward Gibbon, *The Decline and Fall of the Roman Empire*, ch. 32.]

[3] *buff and blue*   The colours of the Whig Club, and of the cover of the leading Whig periodical, the *Edinburgh Review*.

[4] [Byron's note]   I allude not to our friend Landor's hero, the traitor Count Julian, but to Gibbon's hero, vulgarly yclept "The Apostate." [The Emperor Julian was raised as a Christian, but returned to the worship of the Roman gods before becoming emperor in 361.]

And filled their sign posts then, like Wellesley now;[1]
Each in their turn like Banquo's monarchs stalk,
    Followers of fame, "nine farrow" of that sow:[2]
France, too, had Buonaparte and Dumourier[3]
Recorded in the Moniteur and Courier.

3

Barnave, Brissot, Condorcet, Mirabeau,
    Petion, Clootz, Danton, Marat, La Fayette,[4]
Were French, and famous people, as we know:
    And there were others, scarce forgotten yet,
Joubert, Hoche, Marceau, Lannes, Desaix, Moreau[5]
    With many of the military set,
Exceedingly remarkable at times,
But not at all adapted to my rhymes.

4

Nelson was once Britannia's god of war,
    And still should be so, but the tide is turned;
There's no more to be said of Trafalgar,
    'T is with our hero quietly inurned;
Because the army's grown more popular,
    At which the naval people are concerned;
Besides, the prince is all for the land-service,
Forgetting Duncan, Nelson, Howe, and Jervis.[6]

5

Brave men were living before Agamemnon[7]
    And since, exceeding valorous and sage,
A good deal like him too, though quite the same none;
    But then they shone not on the poet's page,
And so have been forgotten:—I condemn none,
    But can't find any in the present age
Fit for my poem (that is, for my new one);
So, as I said, I'll take my friend Don Juan.

6

Most epic poets plunge "in medias res"[8]
    (Horace makes this the heroic turnpike road),
And then your hero tells, whene'er you please,
    What went before—by way of episode,
While seated after dinner at his ease,
    Beside his mistress in some soft abode,
Palace, or garden, paradise, or cavern,
Which serves the happy couple for a tavern.

7

That is the usual method, but not mine—
    My way is to begin with the beginning;
The regularity of my design
    Forbids all wandering as the worst of sinning,
And therefore I shall open with a line
    (Although it cost me half an hour in spinning)

---

[1] *Vernon* Admiral Edward Vernon (1684–1757); *Cumberland* William, Duke of Cumberland (1721–65), whose victory over the Young Pretender at Culloden (1746) was marred by ferocity, and whose nickname was "Billy the Butcher"; *Wolfe* General James Wolfe (1726–59); *Hawke* Edward, Lord Admiral Hawke (1715–81); *Ferdinand* Ferdinand, Duke of Brunswick (1721–92); *Granby* John Manners, Marquess of Granby (1721–90); *Burgoyne* General John Burgoyne (d. 1792); *Keppel* Augustus, Lord Admiral Keppel (1725–86); *Howe* Richard, Lord Admiral Howe (1725–99); *Wellesley* Arthur Wellesley, Duke of Wellington. Wellington Street and Waterloo Bridge were both opened on the anniversary of Waterloo, in 1817.

[2] *Each in … sow* See Shakespeare, *Macbeth* 4.1.64–65, 112–24.

[3] *Dumourier* Charles-François Duperier Dumouriez (1739–1823), French general. The *Moniteur* and *Courier* were French newspapers.

[4] *Barnave* Antoine-Pierre-Joseph Barnave (1761–93); *Brissot* Jean-Pierre Brissot de Warville (1754–93); *Condorcet* Marie-Jean-Antoine, marquis de Condorcet (1743–94); *Mirabeau* Honoré-Gabriel Riquetti, comte de Mirabeau (1749–91); *Petion* Jérôme Petion de Villeneuve (1753–94); *Clootz* Jean-Baptiste, baron de Clootz (1755–94); *Danton* Georges-Jacques Danton (1759–94); *Marat* Jean-Paul Marat (1744–93); *La Fayette* Marie–Jean-Paul, marquis de La Fayette (1757–1834), French Revolutionaries. Mirabeau died of natural causes, Marat was assassinated, and La Fayette was still alive; the rest all perished in the Terror that followed the French Revolution. Clootz, who changed his name to Anacharsis Clootz and nominated himself "l'orateur du genre humain," is a clue to Byron's plans for the conclusion of his unfinished epic: see his letter to John Murray on 16 February 1821, in this volume.

[5] *Joubert … Moreau* For Hoche and Marceau, see note to *Childe Harold's Pilgrimage* 3.541. Barthélemi-Catherine Joubert (1769–99), Jean Lannes, duc de Montebello (1769–1809), Louis-Charles-Antoine Desaix de Voygoux (1768–1800), and Jean-Victor Moreau (1763–1813) were French Revolutionary generals.

[6] *Duncan* Adam, Lord Admiral Duncan (1731–1804); *Nelson* Horatio, Lord Admiral Nelson (1758–1805), killed at Trafalgar; *Jervis* John, Lord Admiral Jervis (1735–1823); for Howe, see note to line 12.

[7] [Byron's note] "'Vixere fortes ante Agamemnona,' &c.—HORACE." [Agamemnon was the King of the Greeks and leader of the Greek expedition against Troy in Homer's *Iliad*.]

[8] *in medias res* Latin: in the middle of things.

55 Narrating somewhat of Don Juan's father,
And also of his mother, if you'd rather.

8

In Seville was he born, a pleasant city,
    Famous for oranges and women—he
Who has not seen it will be much to pity,
60   So says the proverb—and I quite agree;
Of all the Spanish towns is none more pretty,
    Cadiz[1] perhaps —but that you soon may see:
Don Juan's parents lived beside the river,
A noble stream, and called the Guadalquivir.

9

65 His father's name was Jóse[2]—Don,[3] of course,
    A true Hidalgo,[4] free from every stain
Of Moor or Hebrew blood, he traced his source
    Through the most Gothic gentlemen of Spain;
A better cavalier ne'er mounted horse,
70   Or, being mounted, e'er got down again,
Than Jóse, who begot our hero, who
Begot—but that's to come—Well, to renew:

10

His mother was a learned lady,[5] famed
    For every branch of every science known—
75 In every Christian language ever named,
    With virtues equalled by her wit alone,
She made the cleverest people quite ashamed,
    And even the good with inward envy groan,
Finding themselves so very much exceeded
80 In their own way by all the things that she did.

11

Her memory was a mine: she knew by heart

All Calderon and greater part of Lopé,[6]
So that if any actor missed his part
    She could have served him for the prompter's copy;
85 For her Feinagle's were an useless art,[7]
    And he himself obliged to shut up shop—he
Could never make a memory so fine as
That which adorned the brain of Donna Inez.

12

Her favourite science was the mathematical,
90   Her noblest virtue was her magnanimity,
Her wit (she sometimes tried at wit) was Attic all,[8]
    Her serious sayings darkened to sublimity;
In short, in all things she was fairly what I call
    A prodigy—her morning dress was dimity,
95 Her evening silk, or, in the summer, muslin,
And other stuffs, with which I won't stay puzzling.

13

She knew the Latin—that is, "The Lord's Prayer,"
    And Greek—the alphabet—I'm nearly sure;
She read some French romances here and there,
100   Although her mode of speaking was not pure;
For native Spanish she had no great care,
    At least her conversation was obscure;
Her thoughts were theorems, her words a problem,
As if she deemed that mystery would ennoble 'em.

14

105 She liked the English and the Hebrew tongue,
    And said there was analogy between 'em;
She proved it somehow out of sacred song,
    But I must leave the proofs to those who've seen 'em,
But this I heard her say, and can't be wrong,
110   And all may think which way their judgments lean
        'em,
"'Tis strange—the Hebrew noun which means 'I am,'
The English always used to govern d—n."[9]

[1] *Cadiz* Byron anglicizes the pronunciations of his Spanish words, so that Seville is pronounced "SEVil"; Cadiz to rhyme with "ladies."

[2] *Jóse* Byron changes the stress, so that José is pronounced in the English manner, with the emphasis on the first syllable.

[3] *Don* Spanish title, denoting high rank.

[4] *Hidalgo* Gentleman, by birth.

[5] *His mother … lady* Although Byron denied that the character of Donna Inez was a satiric portrait of his wife, a perceived resemblance to her was one of the chief complaints his friends made against these cantos.

[6] *Calderon … Lopé* Calderón de la Barca (1600–81) and Lopé de Vega (1562–1635), Spanish dramatists.

[7] *Feinagle's … art* Gregor von Feinagle (1765?–1819) invented a new method of memorization.

[8] *Her wit … Attic all* Attic, that is, Grecian, wit, refined and delicate.

[9] *d—n* Cf. Exodus 3.14. Byron is referring to "God damn."

15

Some women use their tongues—she *looked* a lecture,
    Each eye a sermon, and her brow a homily,
115 An all-in-all sufficient self-director,
    Like the lamented late Sir Samuel Romilly,[1]
The Law's expounder, and the State's corrector,
    Whose suicide was almost an anomaly—
One sad example more, that "All is vanity"
120 (The jury brought their verdict in "Insanity").

16

In short, she was a walking calculation,
    Miss Edgeworth's novels stepping from their covers,
Or Mrs. Trimmer's books on education,
    Or "Cœlebs' Wife" set out in quest of lovers,[2]
125 Morality's prim personification,
    In which not Envy's self a flaw discovers,
To others' share let "female errors fall,"
For she had not even one—the worst of all.

17

Oh! she was perfect past all parallel—
130   Of any modern female saint's comparison;
So far above the cunning powers of hell,
    Her guardian angel had given up his garrison;
Even her minutest motions went as well
    As those of the best time-piece made by Harrison:[3]
135 In virtues nothing earthly could surpass her,
Save thine "incomparable oil," Macassar![4]

18

Perfect she was, but as perfection is
    Insipid in this naughty world of ours,
Where our first parents never learned to kiss
140   Till they were exiled from their earlier bowers,
Where all was peace, and innocence, and bliss
    (I wonder how they got through the twelve hours)
Don Jóse, like a lineal son of Eve,
Went plucking various fruit without her leave.

19

145 He was a mortal of the careless kind,
    With no great love for learning, or the learned,
Who chose to go where'er he had a mind,
And never dreamed his lady was concerned:
    The world, as usual, wickedly inclined
150 To see a kingdom or a house o'erturned,
Whispered he had a mistress, some said *two*,
But for domestic quarrels *one* will do.

20

Now Donna Inez had, with all her merit,
    A great opinion of her own good qualities;
155 Neglect, indeed, requires a saint to bear it,
    And such, indeed, she was in her moralities;
But then she had a devil of a spirit,
    And sometimes mixed up fancies with realities,
And let few opportunities escape
160 Of getting her liege lord into a scrape.

21

This was an easy matter with a man
    Oft in the wrong, and never on his guard;
And even the wisest, do the best they can,
    Have moments, hours, and days, so unprepared,
165 That you might "brain them with their lady's fan;"[5]
    And sometimes ladies hit exceeding hard,
And fans turn into falchions° in fair hands,   *swords*
And why and wherefore no one understands.

22

'Tis pity learned virgins ever wed
170   With persons of no sort of education,
Or gentlemen, who, though well-born and bred,

---

[1] *Romilly* Sir Samuel Romilly (1757–1818), lawyer and legal reformer, represented Lady Byron during the separation proceedings, despite having previously accepted a retainer from Byron. Byron never forgave him. Romilly's wife died in October 1818, and he committed suicide. This stanza was censored in the first edition.

[2] *Miss Edgeworth's ... lovers* Byron here refers to three female writers famous for their didactic and moral works: Maria Edgeworth (1767–1849), author of *Moral Tales* (1801) and other fiction; Sarah Trimmer (1741–1810), author of books for children and publisher of *Guardian to Education* (1802–6), and Hannah More, to whose *Coelebs in Search of a Wife* (1809) he alludes.

[3] *Harrison* John Harrison (1693–1776) invented a chronometer so accurate that it could be used to calculate longitude.

[4] [Byron's note] 'description des *vertus incomparables* de l'Huile de Macassar.'—See the Advertisement. [Macassor oil, a dressing for the hair named after an Indonesian location said to be the source of its ingredients, was very popular through the nineteenth century.]

---

[5] *brain them ... fan* Cf. Shakespeare, *1 Henry IV* 2.3.21.

Grow tired of scientific conversation:
  I don't choose to say much upon this head,
    I'm a plain man, and in a single station,
175 But—Oh! ye lords of ladies intellectual,
  Inform us truly, have they not hen-pecked you all?

23

Don Jóse and his lady quarrelled—*why*,
  Not any of the many could divine,
Though several thousand people chose to try,
180   'Twas surely no concern of theirs nor mine;
  I loathe that low vice curiosity,
    But if there's any thing in which I shine
'Tis in arranging all my friends' affairs,
Not having, of my own, domestic cares.

24

185 And so I interfered, and with the best
    Intentions, but their treatment was not kind;
  I think the foolish people were possessed,
    For neither of them could I ever find,
  Although their porter afterwards confessed—
190   But that's no matter, and the worst 's behind,
  For little Juan o'er me threw, down stairs,
  A pail of housemaid's water unawares.

25

A little curly-headed, good-for-nothing,
    And mischief-making monkey from his birth;
195 His parents ne'er agreed except in doting
    Upon the most unquiet imp on earth;
  Instead of quarrelling, had they been but both in
    Their senses, they'd have sent young master forth
To school, or had him soundly whipped at home,
200 To teach him manners for the time to come.

26

Don Jóse and the Donna Inez led
    For some time an unhappy sort of life,
  Wishing each other, not divorced, but dead;
    They lived respectably as man and wife,
205 Their conduct was exceedingly well-bred,
    And gave no outward signs of inward strife,
  Until at length the smothered fire broke out,
  And put the business past all kind of doubt.

27

For Inez called some druggists and physicians,
210   And tried to prove her loving lord was *mad*,
  But as he had some lucid intermissions,
    She next decided he was only *bad*;
  Yet when they asked her for her depositions,
    No sort of explanation could be had,
215 Save that her duty both to man and God
  Required this conduct—which seemed very odd.

28

She kept a journal, where his faults were noted,
    And opened certain trunks of books and letters,
  All which might, if occasion served, be quoted;
220   And then she had all Seville for abettors,
  Besides her good old grandmother (who doted);
    The hearers of her case became repeaters,
  Then advocates, inquisitors, and judges,
  Some for amusement, others for old grudges.[1]

29

225 And then this best and meekest woman bore
    With such serenity her husband's woes,
  Just as the Spartan ladies did of yore,
    Who saw their spouses killed, and nobly chose
  Never to say a word about them more—
230   Calmly she heard each calumny that rose,
  And saw *his* agonies with such sublimity,
  That all the world exclaimed, "What magnanimity!"

30

No doubt, this patience, when the world is damning us,
    Is philosophic in our former friends;
235 'Tis also pleasant to be deemed magnanimous,
    The more so in obtaining our own ends;
  And what the lawyers call a "*malus animus*"[2]
    Conduct like this by no means comprehends:
  Revenge in person's certainly no virtue,
240 But then 'tis not my fault, if *others* hurt you.

---

[1] *For Inez … grudges* During the months leading up to their separation, Lady Byron did, or was suspected by her husband of doing, all the things attributed to Donna Inez in these two stanzas.

[2] *malus animus* Latin: bad spirit.

31

And if our quarrels should rip up old stories,
　　And help them with a lie or two additional,
I'm not to blame, as you well know, no more is
　　Any one else—they were become traditional;
245　Besides, their resurrection aids our glories
　　By contrast, which is what we just were wishing all:
And science profits by this resurrection—
Dead scandals form good subjects for dissection.

32

Their friends had tried at reconciliation,
250　Then their relations, who made matters worse;
('Twere hard to tell upon a like occasion
　　To whom it may be best to have recourse—
I can't say much for friend or yet relation):
　　The lawyers did their utmost for divorce,
255　But scarce a fee was paid on either side
Before, unluckily, Don Jóse died.

33

He died: and most unluckily, because,
　　According to all hints I could collect
From counsel learned in those kinds of laws
260　(Although their talk's obscure and circumspect)
His death contrived to spoil a charming cause;
　　A thousand pities also with respect
To public feeling, which on this occasion
Was manifested in a great sensation.

34

265　But ah! he died; and buried with him lay
　　The public feeling and the lawyers' fees:
His house was sold, his servants sent away,
　　A Jew took one of his two mistresses,
A priest the other—at least so they say:
270　I asked the doctors after his disease,
He died of the slow fever called the tertian,
And left his widow to her own aversion.

35

Yet Jóse was an honourable man,
　　That I must say, who knew him very well;
275　Therefore his frailties I'll no further scan,
　　Indeed there were not many more to tell;

And if his passions now and then outran
　　Discretion, and were not so peaceable
As Numa's (who was also named Pompilius),[1]
280　He had been ill brought up, and was born bilious.

36

Whate'er might be his worthlessness or worth,
　　Poor fellow! he had many things to wound him,
Let's own, since it can do no good on earth;
　　It was a trying moment that which found him
285　Standing alone beside his desolate hearth,
　　Where all his household gods lay shivered round him;
No choice was left his feelings or his pride,
Save death or Doctors' Commons[2]—so he died.

37

Dying intestate, Juan was sole heir
290　To a chancery suit, and messuages, and lands,
Which, with a long minority and care,
　　Promised to turn out well in proper hands:
Inez became sole guardian, which was fair,
　　And answered but to nature's just demands;
295　An only son left with an only mother
Is brought up much more wisely than another.

38

Sagest of women, even of widows, she
　　Resolved that Juan should be quite a paragon,
And worthy of the noblest pedigree:
300　(His sire was of Castile, his dam from Aragon).
Then for accomplishments of chivalry,
　　In case our lord the king should go to war again,
He learned the arts of riding, fencing, gunnery,
And how to scale a fortress—or a nunnery.

39

305　But that which Donna Inez most desired,
　　And saw into herself each day before all
The learned tutors whom for him she hired,
　　Was, that his breeding should be strictly moral;
Much into all his studies she inquired,
310　And so they were submitted first to her, all,

---

[1] *Pompilius* The peaceable second king of Rome; see Plutarch, *Parallel Lives.*

[2] *Doctors' Commons* Divorce courts.

Arts, sciences, no branch was made a mystery
To Juan's eyes, excepting natural history.

40

The languages, especially the dead,
        The sciences, and most of all the abstruse,
315 The arts, at least all such as could be said
        To be the most remote from common use,
In all these he was much and deeply read;
        But not a page of any thing that's loose,
Or hints continuation of the species,
320 Was ever suffered, lest he should grow vicious.

41

His classic studies made a little puzzle,
        Because of filthy loves of gods and goddesses,
Who in the earlier ages raised a bustle,
        But never put on pantaloons or boddices;
325 His reverend tutors had at times a tussle,
        And for their Æneids, Iliads, and Odysseys,
Were forced to make an odd sort of apology,
For Donna Inez dreaded the mythology.

42

Ovid's a rake, as half his verses show him,
330   Anacreon's morals are a still worse sample,
Catullus scarcely has a decent poem,
        I don't think Sappho's Ode a good example,
Although Longinus tells us there is no hymn
        Where the sublime soars forth on wings more ample;[1]
335 But Virgil's songs are pure, except that horrid one
Beginning with "Formosum Pastor Corydon."[2]

43

Lucretius' irreligion is too strong
        For early stomachs, to prove wholesome food;

I can't help thinking Juvenal was wrong,
340   Although no doubt his real intent was good,
For speaking out so plainly in his song,
        So much indeed as to be downright rude;
And then what proper person can be partial
To all those nauseous epigrams of Martial?[3]

44

345 Juan was taught from out the best edition,
        Expurgated by learned men, who place,
Judiciously, from out the schoolboy's vision,
        The grosser parts; but fearful to deface
Too much their modest bard by this omission,
350   And pitying sore his mutilated case,
They only add them all in an appendix,
Which saves, in fact, the trouble of an index.[4]

45

For there we have them all at one fell swoop,
        Instead of being scattered through the pages;
355 They stand forth marshalled in a handsome troop,
        To meet the ingenuous youth of future ages,
Till some less rigid editor shall stoop
        To call them back into their separate cages,
Instead of standing staring altogether,
360 Like garden gods—and not so decent either.

46

The Missal too (it was the family Missal)
        Was ornamented in a sort of way
Which ancient mass-books often are, and this all
        Kinds of grotesques illumined; and how they,
365 Who saw those figures on the margin kiss all,
        Could turn their optics to the text and pray
Is more than I know—but Don Juan's mother
Kept this herself, and gave her son another.

---

[1] [Byron's note] See Longinus, Section 10, "*hina me hen ti peri auten pathos phainetai, pathon de sunodos*]." [See Ovid's *Amores* and *Ars Amatoria*; the erotic lyrics then attributed to Anacreon; the erotic lyrics of Catullus; and the poem by Sappho beginning "To me he seems a peer of the gods," praised by Longinus in *On the Sublime* 10.]

[2] *Formosum ... Corydon* This is the first line of Virgil's second Eclogue, which may be translated, "The shepherd Corydon [burned for] fair [Alexis, his master's darling.]" The poem is about homosexual love.

---

[3] *Lucretius' ... Martial* Byron here refers to three classical works which Inez certainly would have considered dangerous: Lucretius, *On the Nature of Things*, a philosophical poem; Juvenal, *Satires*; and Martial's epigrams, which are notoriously scurrilous and obscene.

[4] [Byron's note] Fact. There is, or was, such an edition, with all the obnoxious epigrams of Martial placed by themselves at the end. [The Delphin edition of Martial (Amsterdam, 1701) has an appendix entitled "Epigrammata Obscaena."]

47

Sermons he read, and lectures he endured,
370   And homilies, and lives of all the saints;
To Jerome and to Chrysostom[1] inured,
    He did not take such studies for restraints;
But how faith is acquired, and then insured,
    So well not one of the aforesaid paints
375 As Saint Augustine in his fine Confessions,
Which make the reader envy his transgressions.[2]

48

This, too, was a sealed book to little Juan—
    I can't but say that his mamma was right,
If such an education was the true one.
380   She scarcely trusted him from out her sight;
Her maids were old, and if she took a new one
    You might be sure she was a perfect fright,
She did this during even her husband's life—
I recommend as much to every wife.

49

385 Young Juan waxed in goodliness and grace;
    At six a charming child, and at eleven
With all the promise of as fine a face
    As e'er to man's maturer growth was given:
He studied steadily, and grew apace,
390   And seemed, at least, in the right road to heaven,
For half his days were passed at church, the other
Between his tutors, confessor, and mother.

50

At six, I said, he was a charming child,
    At twelve he was a fine, but quiet boy;
395 Although in infancy a little wild,
    They tamed him down amongst them; to destroy
His natural spirit not in vain they toiled,
    At least it seemed so; and his mother's joy

Was to declare how sage, and still, and steady,
400 Her young philosopher was grown already.

51

I had my doubts, perhaps I have them still,
    But what I say is neither here nor there:
I knew his father well, and have some skill
    In character—but it would not be fair
405 From sire to son to augur good or ill:
    He and his wife were an ill-sorted pair—
But scandal's my aversion—I protest
Against all evil speaking, even in jest.

52

For my part I say nothing—nothing—but
410   *This* I will say—my reasons are my own—
That if I had an only son to put
    To school (as God be praised that I have none)
'Tis not with Donna Inez I would shut
    Him up to learn his catechism alone,
415 No—no—I'd send him out betimes to college,
For there it was I picked up my own knowledge.

53

For there one learns—'tis not for me to boast,
    Though I acquired—but I pass over *that*,
As well as all the Greek I since have lost:
420   I say that there's the place—but "*Verbum sat.*"[3]
I think, I picked up too, as well as most,
    Knowledge of matters—but no matter *what*—
I never married—but, I think, I know
That sons should not be educated so.

54

425 Young Juan now was sixteen years of age,
    Tall, handsome, slender, but well knit; he seemed
Active, though not so sprightly, as a page;
    And every body but his mother deemed
Him almost man; but she flew in a rage,
430   And bit her lips (for else she might have screamed),
If any said so, for to be precocious
Was in her eyes a thing the most atrocious.

---

[1] *Jerome* St. Jerome (340?–420), translator of the Bible into Latin; *Chrysostom* St. John Chrysostom (347?–407); both were ascetics.

[2] [Byron's note] See his *Confessions*, lib. i. cap. ix. By the representation which Saint Augustine gives of himself in his youth, it is easy to see that he was what we should call a rake. He avoided the school as the plague; he loved nothing but gaming and public shows; he robbed his father of everything he could find; he invented a thousand lies to escape the rod, which they were obliged to make use of to punish his irregularities.

[3] *Verbum sat* Latin: a word [to the wise] is enough.

55

Amongst her numerous acquaintance, all
    Selected for discretion and devotion,
435 There was the Donna Julia, whom to call
    Pretty were but to give a feeble notion
Of many charms in her as natural
    As sweetness to the flower, or salt to ocean,
Her zone to Venus, or his bow to Cupid
440 (But this last simile is trite and stupid).

56

The darkness of her oriental eye
    Accorded with her Moorish origin;
(Her blood was not all Spanish, by the by;
    In Spain, you know, this is a sort of sin).
445 When proud Granada fell, and, forced to fly,
    Boabdil wept,[1] of Donna Julia's kin
Some went to Africa, some staid in Spain,
Her great great grandmamma chose to remain.

57

She married (I forget the pedigree)
450   With an Hidalgo, who transmitted down
His blood less noble than such blood should be;
    At such alliances his sires would frown,
In that point so precise in each degree
    That they bred *in and in*, as might be shown,
455 Marrying their cousins—nay, their aunts and nieces,
Which always spoils the breed, if it increases.[2]

58

This heathenish cross restored the breed again,
    Ruined its blood, but much improved its flesh;
For, from a root the ugliest in Old Spain
460   Sprung up a branch as beautiful as fresh;
The sons no more were short, the daughters plain:
    But there's a rumour which I fain would hush,
'Tis said that Donna Julia's grandmamma
Produced her Don more heirs at love than law.

59

465 However this might be, the race went on
    Improving still through every generation,
Until it centred in an only son,
    Who left an only daughter; my narration
May have suggested that this single one
470   Could be but Julia (whom on this occasion
I shall have much to speak about), and she
Was married, charming, chaste, and twenty-three.

60

Her eye (I'm very fond of handsome eyes)
    Was large and dark, suppressing half its fire
475 Until she spoke, then through its soft disguise
    Flashed an expression more of pride than ire,
And love than either; and there would arise
    A something in them which was not desire,
But would have been, perhaps, but for the soul
480 Which struggled through and chastened down the
    whole.

61

Her glossy hair was clustered o'er a brow
    Bright with intelligence, and fair and smooth;
Her eyebrow's shape was like the aerial bow,
    Her cheek all purple with the beam of youth,
485 Mounting, at times, to a transparent glow,
    As if her veins ran lightning; she, in sooth,
Possessed an air and grace by no means common:
Her stature tall—I hate a dumpy woman.

62

Wedded she was some years, and to a man
490   Of fifty, and such husbands are in plenty;
And yet, I think, instead of such a ONE
    'Twere better to have TWO of five-and-twenty,
Especially in countries near the sun:
    And now I think on't, "mi vien in mente,"[3]
495 Ladies even of the most uneasy virtue
Prefer a spouse whose age is short of thirty.

63

'Tis a sad thing, I cannot choose but say,
    And all the fault of that indecent sun,

---

1. *Boabdil* Mohammed XI, the last Moorish king of Granada, defeated by the Spanish in 1492.

2. *Marrying… increases* The Byron family frequently intermarried, cousins wedding cousins.

---

3. *mi … mente* Italian: "It comes into my mind."

Who cannot leave alone our helpless clay,
    But will keep baking, broiling, burning on,
500 That howsoever people fast and pray
    The flesh is frail, and so the soul undone:
What men call gallantry, and gods adultery,
Is much more common where the climate's sultry.

64

505 Happy the nations of the moral north!
    Where all is virtue, and the winter season
Sends sin, without a rag on, shivering forth;
    ('Twas snow that brought St. Anthony to reason);[1]
Where juries cast up what a wife is worth
510   By laying whate'er sum, in mulct, they please on
The lover, who must pay a handsome price,
Because it is a marketable vice.

65

Alfonso was the name of Julia's lord,
    A man well looking for his years, and who
515 Was neither much beloved, nor yet abhorred;
    They lived together as most people do,
Suffering each other's foibles by accord,
    And not exactly either *one* or *two*;
Yet he was jealous, though he did not show it,
520 For jealousy dislikes the world to know it.

66

Julia was—yet I never could see why—
    With Donna Inez quite a favourite friend;
Between their tastes there was small sympathy,
    For not a line had Julia ever penned:
525 Some people whisper (but, no doubt, they lie,
    For malice still imputes some private end)
That Inez had, ere Don Alfonso's marriage,
Forgot with him her very prudent carriage.

67

And that still keeping up the old connexion,
530   Which time had lately rendered much more chaste,
She took his lady also in affection,

---

[1] [Byron's note] For the particulars of St. Anthony's recipe for hot blood in cold weather, see Mr. Alban Butler's Lives of the Saints. [It was actually St. Francis of Assisi who was reported to have thrown himself naked into the snow to counteract the temptations of the flesh.]

And certainly this course was much the best:
She flattered Julia with her sage protection,
    And complimented Don Alfonso's taste;
535 And if she could not (who can?) silence scandal,
At least she left it a more slender handle.

68

I can't tell whether Julia saw the affair
    With other people's eyes, or if her own
Discoveries made, but none could be aware
540   Of this, at least no symptom e'er was shown;
Perhaps she did not know, or did not care,
    Indifferent from the first, or callous grown:
I'm really puzzled what to think or say,
She kept her counsel in so close a way.

69

545 Juan she saw, and, as a pretty child,
    Caressed him often, such a thing might be
Quite innocently done, and harmless styled,
    When she had twenty years, and thirteen he;
But I am not so sure I should have smiled
550   When he was sixteen, Julia twenty-three,
These few short years make wondrous alterations,
Particularly amongst sun-burnt nations.

70

Whate'er the cause might be, they had become
    Changed; for the dame grew distant, the youth shy,
555 Their looks cast down, their greetings almost dumb,
    And much embarrassment in either eye;
There surely will be little doubt with some
    That Donna Julia knew the reason why,
But as for Juan, he had no more notion
560 Than he who never saw the sea of ocean.

71

Yet Julia's very coldness still was kind,
    And tremulously gentle her small hand
Withdrew itself from his, but left behind
    A little pressure, thrilling, and so bland
565 And slight, so very slight, that to the mind
    'Twas but a doubt; but ne'er magician's wand

Wrought change with all Armida's fairy art[1]
Like what this light touch left on Juan's heart.

72

And if she met him, though she smiled no more,
570   She looked a sadness sweeter than her smile,
As if her heart had deeper thoughts in store
      She must not own, but cherished more the while,
For that compression in its burning core;
      Even innocence itself has many a wile,
575 And will not dare to trust itself with truth,
And love is taught hypocrisy from youth.

73

But passion most dissembles yet betrays
      Even by its darkness; as the blackest sky
Foretells the heaviest tempest, it displays
580   Its workings through the vainly guarded eye,
And in whatever aspect it arrays
      Itself, 'tis still the same hypocrisy;
Coldness or anger, even disdain or hate,
Are masks it often wears, and still too late.

74

585 Then there were sighs, the deeper for suppression,
      And stolen glances, sweeter for the theft,
And burning blushes, though for no transgression,
      Tremblings when met, and restlessness when left;
All these are little preludes to possession,
590   Of which young Passion cannot be bereft,
And merely tend to show how greatly Love is
Embarrassed at first starting with a novice.

75

Poor Julia's heart was in an awkward state;
      She felt it going, and resolved to make
595 The noblest efforts for herself and mate,
      For honour's, pride's, religion's, virtue's sake;
Her resolutions were most truly great,
      And almost might have made a Tarquin quake;[2]
She prayed the Virgin Mary for her grace,
600 As being the best judge of a lady's case.

---

[1] *Armida* The enchantress in Torquato Tasso's *Jerusalem Delivered*.

[2] *Tarquin* Sextus Tarquinius raped Lucretia, a Roman matron, who subsequently stabbed herself.

76

She vowed she never would see Juan more,
      And next day paid a visit to his mother,
And looked extremely at the opening door,
      Which, by the Virgin's grace, let in another;
605 Grateful she was, and yet a little sore—
      Again it opens, it can be no other,
'Tis surely Juan now—No! I'm afraid
That night the Virgin was no further prayed.

77

She now determined that a virtuous woman
610   Should rather face and overcome temptation,
That flight was base and dastardly, and no man
      Should ever give her heart the least sensation;
That is to say, a thought beyond the common
      Preference, that we must feel upon occasion,
615 For people who are pleasanter than others,
But then they only seem so many brothers.

78

And even if by chance—and who can tell?
      The devil's so very sly—she should discover
That all within was not so very well,
620   And, if still free, that such or such a lover
Might please perhaps, a virtuous wife can quell
      Such thoughts, and be the better when they're over;
And if the man should ask, 'tis but denial:
I recommend young ladies to make trial.

79

625 And then there are such things as love divine,
      Bright and immaculate, unmixed and pure,
Such as the angels think so very fine,
      And matrons, who would be no less secure,
Platonic, perfect, "just such love as mine:"
630   Thus Julia said—and thought so, to be sure,
And so I'd have her think, were I the man
On whom her reveries celestial ran.

80

Such love is innocent, and may exist
　　Between young persons without any danger,
A hand may first, and then a lip be kist;
　　For my part, to such doings I'm a stranger,
But *hear* these freedoms form the utmost list
　　Of all o'er which such love may be a ranger:
If people go beyond, 'tis quite a crime,
But not my fault—I tell them all in time.

81

Love, then, but love within its proper limits,
　　Was Julia's innocent determination
In young Don Juan's favour, and to him its
　　Exertion might be useful on occasion;
And, lighted at too pure a shrine to dim its
　　Ethereal lustre, with what sweet persuasion
He might be taught, by love and her together—
I really don't know what, nor Julia either.

82

Fraught with this fine intention, and well fenced
　　In mail of proof—her purity of soul—
She, for the future of her strength convinced,
　　And that her honour was a rock, or mole,[1]
Exceeding sagely from that hour dispensed
　　With any kind of troublesome control;
But whether Julia to the task was equal
Is that which must be mentioned in the sequel.

83

Her plan she deemed both innocent and feasible,
　　And, surely, with a stripling of sixteen
Not scandal's fangs could fix on much that's seizable,
　　Or if they did so, satisfied to mean
Nothing but what was good, her breast was peaceable—
　　A quiet conscience makes one so serene!
Christians have burnt each other, quite persuaded
That all the Apostles would have done as they did.

84

And if in the mean time her husband died,
　　But heaven forbid that such a thought should cross
Her brain, though in a dream! (and then she sighed)

Never could she survive that common loss;
　　But just suppose that moment should betide,
I only say suppose it—*inter nos.*
(This should be *entre nous,*[2] for Julia thought
In French, but then the rhyme would go for nought.)

85

I only say suppose this supposition:
　　Juan being then grown up to man's estate
Would fully suit a widow of condition,
　　Even seven years hence it would not be too late;
And in the interim (to pursue this vision)
　　The mischief, after all, could not be great,
For he would learn the rudiments of love,
I mean the seraph way[3] of those above.

86

So much for Julia. Now we'll turn to Juan,
　　Poor little fellow! he had no idea
Of his own case, and never hit the true one;
　　In feelings quick as Ovid's Miss Medea,
He puzzled over what he found a new one,
　　But not as yet imagined it could be a
Thing quite in course, and not at all alarming,
Which, with a little patience, might grow charming.

87

Silent and pensive, idle, restless, slow,
　　His home deserted for the lonely wood,
Tormented with a wound he could not know,
　　His, like all deep grief, plunged in solitude:
I'm fond myself of solitude or so,
　　But then, I beg it may be understood,
By solitude I mean a sultan's, not
A hermit's, with a haram° for a grot.   *harem*

88

"Oh Love! in such a wilderness as this,
　　Where transport and security entwine,
Here is the empire of thy perfect bliss,

---

[1]   *mole*   Massive structure, such as a pier or breakwater.

[2]   *inter nos*   Latin: between us;   *entre nous*   French: between us.

[3]   *seraph way*   I.e., angelic way.

700 And here thou art a god indeed divine."[1]
The bard I quote from does not sing amiss,
    With the exception of the second line,
For that same twining "transport and security"
Are twisted to a phrase of some obscurity.

89

705 The poet meant, no doubt, and thus appeals
    To the good sense and senses of mankind,
The very thing which every body feels,
    As all have found on trial, or may find,
That no one likes to be disturbed at meals
710   Or love.—I won't say more about "entwined"
Or "transport," as we knew all that before,
But beg "Security" will bolt the door.

90

Young Juan wandered by the glassy brooks,
    Thinking unutterable things; he threw
715 Himself at length within the leafy nooks
    Where the wild branch of the cork forest grew;
There poets find materials for their books,
    And every now and then we read them through,
So that their plan and prosody are eligible,
720 Unless, like Wordsworth, they prove unintelligible.

91

He, Juan (and not Wordsworth), so pursued
    His self-communion with his own high soul,
Until his mighty heart,[2] in its great mood,
    Had mitigated part, though not the whole
725 Of its disease; he did the best he could
    With things not very subject to control,
And turned, without perceiving his condition,
Like Coleridge, into a metaphysician.[3]

92

He thought about himself, and the whole earth,

730 Of man the wonderful, and of the stars,
    And how the deuce they ever could have birth;
    And then he thought of earthquakes, and of wars,
How many miles the moon might have in girth,
    Of air-balloons, and of the many bars
735 To perfect knowledge of the boundless skies;
And then he thought of Donna Julia's eyes.

93

In thoughts like these true wisdom may discern
    Longings sublime, and aspirations high,
Which some are born with, but the most part learn
740   To plague themselves withal, they know not why:
'Twas strange that one so young should thus concern
    His brain about the action of the sky;
If *you* think 'twas philosophy that this did,
I can't help thinking puberty assisted.

94

745 He pored upon the leaves, and on the flowers,
    And heard a voice in all the winds; and then
He thought of wood nymphs and immortal bowers,
    And how the goddesses came down to men:
He missed the pathway, he forgot the hours,
750   And when he looked upon his watch again,
He found how much old Time had been a winner—
He also found that he had lost his dinner.[4]

95

Sometimes he turned to gaze upon his book,
    Boscan, or Garcilasso;[5]—by the wind
755 Even as the page is rustled while we look,
    So by the poesy of his own mind
Over the mystic leaf his soul was shook,
    As if 'twere one whereon magicians bind
Their spells, and give them to the passing gale,
760 According to some good old woman's tale.

96

Thus would he while his lonely hours away
    Dissatisfied, nor knowing what he wanted;

---

1 [Byron's note] Campbell's Gertrude of Wyoming, (I think) the opening of Canto II; but quote from memory. [Thomas Campbell, *Gertrude of Wyoming* 3.1.1–4.]

2 *so pursued … heart* See Wordsworth, "Composed upon Westminster Bridge" (1802), 14.

3 *turned … metaphysician* See Coleridge, "Dejection: an Ode," 87–93.

---

4 *lost his dinner* I.e., was so late for dinner that he had missed it entirely.

5 *Boscan* Spanish poet Juan Boscán (1500–44); *Garcilasso* Spanish poet Garcias Lasso or Garcilaso de la Vega (1503–36).

Nor glowing reverie, nor poet's lay,
    Could yield his spirit that for which it panted,
765 A bosom whereon he his head might lay,
    And hear the heart beat with the love it granted,
With—several other things, which I forget,
Or which, at least, I need not mention yet.

97

Those lonely walks, and lengthening reveries,
770   Could not escape the gentle Julia's eyes;
She saw that Juan was not at his ease;
    But that which chiefly may, and must surprise,
Is, that the Donna Inez did not tease
    Her only son with question or surmise;
775 Whether it was she did not see, or would not,
Or, like all very clever people, could not.

98

This may seem strange, but yet 'tis very common;
    For instance—gentlemen, whose ladies take
Leave to o'erstep the written rights of woman,
780   And break the—Which commandment is't they
        break?[1]
(I have forgot the number, and think no man
    Should rashly quote, for fear of a mistake.)
I say, when these same gentlemen are jealous,
They make some blunder, which their ladies tell us.

99

785 A real husband always is suspicious,
    But still no less suspects in the wrong place,
Jealous of some one who had no such wishes,
    Or pandering blindly to his own disgrace
By harbouring some dear friend extremely vicious;
790   The last indeed's infallibly the case:
And when the spouse and friend are gone off wholly,
He wonders at their vice, and not his folly.

100

Thus parents also are at times short-sighted;
    Though watchful as the lynx, they ne'er discover,
795 The while the wicked world beholds delighted,
    Young Hopeful's mistress, or Miss Fanny's lover,

Till some confounded escapade has blighted
    The plan of twenty years, and all is over;
And then the mother cries, the father swears,
800 And wonders why the devil he got heirs.[2]

101

But Inez was so anxious, and so clear
    Of sight, that I must think, on this occasion,
She had some other motive much more near
    For leaving Juan to this new temptation;
805 But what that motive was, I shan't say here;
    Perhaps to finish Juan's education,
Perhaps to open Don Alfonso's eyes,
In case he thought his wife too great a prize.

102

It was upon a day, a summer's day;—
810   Summer's indeed a very dangerous season,
And so is spring about the end of May;
    The sun, no doubt, is the prevailing reason;
But whatsoe'er the cause is, one may say,
    And stand convicted of more truth than treason,
815 That there are months which nature grows more
      merry in,
March has its hares, and May must have its heroine.

103

'Twas on a summer's day—the sixth of June:—
    I like to be particular in dates,
Not only of the age, and year, but moon;
820   They are a sort of post-house, where the Fates
Change horses, making history change its tune,
    Then spur away o'er empires and o'er states,
Leaving at last not much besides chronology,
Excepting the post-obits[3] of theology.

104

825 'Twas on the sixth of June, about the hour
    Of half-past six—perhaps still nearer seven,
When Julia sat within as pretty a bower
    As e'er held hour in that heathenish heaven

---

1 *Which commandment … break?* They break the seventh commandment, "Thou shalt not commit adultery."

2 *got heirs* I.e., begot children, heirs to his estate.

3 *post-obits* Latin: after death; here, referring to a legacy, that which comes after a death.

Described by Mahomet, and Anacreon Moore,[1]
    To whom the lyre and laurels have been given,
With all the trophies of triumphant song—
He won them well, and may he wear them long!

105

She sate, but not alone; I know not well
    How this same interview had taken place,
And even if I knew, I should not tell—
    People should hold their tongues in any case;
No matter how or why the thing befell,
    But there were she and Juan, face to face—
When two such faces are so, 'twould be wise,
But very difficult, to shut their eyes.

106

How beautiful she looked! her conscious heart
    Glowed in her cheek, and yet she felt no wrong.
Oh Love! how perfect is thy mystic art,
    Strengthening the weak, and trampling on the
        strong,
How self-deceitful is the sagest part
    Of mortals whom thy lure hath led along—
The precipice she stood on was immense,
So was her creed in her own innocence.

107

She thought of her own strength, and Juan's youth
    And of the folly of all prudish fears,
Victorious virtue, and domestic truth,
    And then of Don Alfonso's fifty years:
I wish these last had not occurred, in sooth,
    Because that number rarely much endears,
And through all climes, the snowy and the sunny,
Sounds ill in love, whate'er it may in money.

108

When people say, "I've told you *fifty* times,"
    They mean to scold, and very often do;
When poets say, "I've written *fifty* rhymes,"

They make you dread that they'll recite them too;
    In gangs of *fifty*, thieves commit their crimes;
At *fifty* love for love is rare, 'tis true,
    But then, no doubt, it equally as true is,
A good deal may be bought for *fifty* Louis.[2]

109

Julia had honour, virtue, truth, and love
    For Don Alfonso; and she inly swore,
By all the vows below to powers above,
    She never would disgrace the ring she wore,
Nor leave a wish which wisdom might reprove;
    And while she pondered this, besides much more,
One hand on Juan's carelessly was thrown,
Quite by mistake—she thought it was her own;

110

Unconsciously she leaned upon the other,
    Which played within the tangles of her hair;
And to contend with thoughts she could not smother,
    She seemed by the distraction of her air.
'Twas surely very wrong in Juan's mother
    To leave together this imprudent pair,
She who for many years had watched her son so—
I'm very certain *mine* would not have done so.

111

The hand which still held Juan's, by degrees
    Gently, but palpably confirmed its grasp,
As if it said, "detain me, if you please;"
    Yet there's no doubt she only meant to clasp
His fingers with a pure Platonic squeeze;
    She would have shrunk as from a toad, or asp,
Had she imagined such a thing could rouse
A feeling dangerous to a prudent spouse.

112

I cannot know what Juan thought of this,
    But what he did, is much what you would do;
His young lip thanked it with a grateful kiss,
    And then, abashed at its own joy, withdrew
In deep despair, lest he had done amiss,
    Love is so very timid when 'tis new:

---

[1] *Anacreon Moore* Byron's friend Thomas Moore was known as "Anacreon" Moore because he first became famous for translating the lyric poems then attributed to the Roman poet Anacreon. The reference is to "Paradise and the Peri," one of the tales in Moore's *Lalla Rookh* (1817).

[2] *Louis* French gold coin.

895 She blushed, and frowned not, but she strove to speak,
And held her tongue, her voice was grown so weak.

113

The sun set, and up rose the yellow moon:
    The devil's in the moon for mischief; they
Who called her CHASTE, methinks, began too soon
900   Their nomenclature; there is not a day,
The longest, not the twenty-first of June,
    Sees half the business in a wicked way
On which three single hours of moonshine smile—
And then she looks so modest all the while.

114

905 There is a dangerous silence in that hour,
    A stillness, which leaves room for the full soul
To open all itself, without the power
    Of calling wholly back its self-control;
The silver light which, hallowing tree and tower,
910   Sheds beauty and deep softness o'er the whole,
Breathes also to the heart, and o'er it throws
A loving languor, which is not repose.

115

And Julia sat with Juan, half embraced
    And half retiring from the glowing arm,
915 Which trembled like the bosom where 'twas placed;
    Yet still she must have thought there was no harm,
Or else 'twere easy to withdraw her waist;
    But then the situation had its charm,
And then—God knows what next—I can't go on;
920 I'm almost sorry that I e'er begun.

116

Oh Plato! Plato! you have paved the way,
    With your confounded fantasies, to more
Immoral conduct by the fancied sway
    Your system feigns o'er the controlless core
925 Of human hearts, than all the long array
    Of poets and romancers:—You're a bore,
A charlatan, a coxcomb—and have been,
At best, no better than a go-between.

117

And Julia's voice was lost, except in sighs,

---

930 Until too late for useful conversation;
The tears were gushing from her gentle eyes,
    I wish, indeed, they had not had occasion,
But who, alas! can love, and then be wise?
    Not that remorse did not oppose temptation,
935 A little still she strove, and much repented,
And whispering "I will ne'er consent"—consented.

118

'Tis said that Xerxes[1] offered a reward
    To those who could invent him a new pleasure;
Methinks, the requisition's rather hard,
940   And must have cost His majesty a treasure:
For my part, I'm a moderate-minded bard,
    Fond of a little love (which I call leisure);
I care not for new pleasures, as the old
Are quite enough for me, so they but hold.

119

945 Oh Pleasure! you're indeed a pleasant thing,
    Although one must be damned for you, no doubt;
I make a resolution every spring
    Of reformation, ere the year run out,
But, somehow, this my vestal vow takes wing,
950   Yet still, I trust, it may be kept throughout:
I'm very sorry, very much ashamed,
And mean, next winter, to be quite reclaimed.

120

Here my chaste Muse a liberty must take—
    Start not! still chaster reader—she'll be nice
        hence—
955 Forward, and there is no great cause to quake;
    This liberty is a poetic licence,
Which some irregularity may make
    In the design, and as I have a high sense
Of Aristotle and the Rules,[2] 'tis fit
960 To beg his pardon when I err a bit.

121

This licence is to hope the reader will
    Suppose from June the sixth (the fatal day,

---

1 *Xerxes* Xerxes was King of Persia from 486 to 465 BCE.

2 *Rules* I.e., rules for literary composition set out in Aristotle's
Poetics.

Without whose epoch my poetic skill
    For want of facts would all be thrown away),
965 But keeping Julia and Don Juan still
    In sight, that several months have passed; we'll say
'Twas in November, but I'm not so sure
    About the day—the era's more obscure.

122

We'll talk of that anon.—'Tis sweet to hear
970   At midnight on the blue and moonlit deep
The song and oar of Adria's gondolier,
    By distance mellowed, o'er the waters sweep;
'Tis sweet to see the evening star appear;
    'Tis sweet to listen as the night-winds creep
975 From leaf to leaf; 'tis sweet to view on high
    The rainbow, based on ocean, span the sky.

123

'Tis sweet to hear the watch-dog's honest bark
    Bay deep-mouthed welcome as we draw near home;
'Tis sweet to know there is an eye will mark
980   Our coming, and look brighter when we come;
'Tis sweet to be awakened by the lark,
    Or lulled by falling waters; sweet the hum
Of bees, the voice of girls, the song of birds,
The lisp of children, and their earliest words.

124

985 Sweet is the vintage, when the showering grapes
    In Bacchanal profusion reel to earth
Purple and gushing: sweet are our escapes
    From civic revelry to rural mirth;
Sweet to the miser are his glittering heaps,
990   Sweet to the father is his first-born's birth,
Sweet is revenge—especially to women,
Pillage to soldiers, prize-money to seamen.

125

Sweet is a legacy, and passing sweet
    The unexpected death of some old lady
995 Or gentleman of seventy years complete,
    Who've made "us youth" wait too—too long already
For an estate, or cash, or country-seat,
    Still breaking, but with stamina so steady,

That all the Israelites are fit to mob its
1000 Next owner for their double-damned post-obits.[1]

126

'Tis sweet to win, no matter how, one's laurels
    By blood or ink; 'tis sweet to put an end
To strife; 'tis sometimes sweet to have our quarrels,
    Particularly with a tiresome friend;
1005 Sweet is old wine in bottles, ale in barrels;
    Dear is the helpless creature we defend
Against the world; and dear the schoolboy spot
We ne'er forget, though there we are forgot.

127

But sweeter still than this, than these, than all,
1010   Is first and passionate love—it stands alone,
Like Adam's recollection of his fall;
    The tree of knowledge has been plucked—all's
        known—
And life yields nothing further to recall
    Worthy of this ambrosial sin, so shown,
1015 No doubt in fable, as the unforgiven
Fire which Prometheus filched for us from heaven.

128

Man's a strange animal, and makes strange use
    Of his own nature, and the various arts,
And likes particularly to produce
1020   Some new experiment to show his parts;
This is the age of oddities let loose,
    Where different talents find their different marts;
You'd best begin with truth, and when you've lost your
Labour, there's a sure market for imposture.

129

1025 What opposite discoveries we have seen!
    (Signs of true genius, and of empty pockets.)
One makes new noses,[2] one a guillotine,
    One breaks your bones, one sets them in their
        sockets;

---

1 *post-obits* Here, loans repayable after a death; that is, when the
borrower comes into an inheritance.

2 *new noses* Benjamin Charles Perkins, an American quack, alleged
that his metallic "tractors" could cure toes afflicted with the gout, as
well as broken legs, flatulence, and red noses.

But vaccination certainly has been
1030   A kind antithesis to Congreve's rockets,[1]
With which the Doctor paid off an old pox,
By borrowing a new one from an ox.[2]

130

Bread has been made (indifferent) from potatoes;
      And galvanism has set some corpses grinning,
1035 But has not answered like the apparatus
      Of the Humane Society's beginning
By which men are unsuffocated gratis:
      What wondrous new machines have late been
            spinning!
I said the small-pox has gone out of late;
1040 Perhaps it may be followed by the great.

131

'Tis said the great came from America;
      Perhaps it may set out on its return,—
The population there so spreads, they say
      'Tis grown high time to thin it in its turn,
1045 With war, or plague, or famine,[3] any way,
      So that civilisation they may learn;
And which in ravage the more loathsome evil is—
Their real lues,° or our pseudo-syphilis?   syphilis

132

This is the patent age of new inventions
1050   For killing bodies, and for saving souls,[4]
All propagated with the best intentions;
      Sir Humphry Davy's lantern, by which coals
Are safely mined for in the mode he mentions,[5]

Timbuctoo travels, voyages to the Poles,[6]
1055 Are ways to benefit mankind, as true,
Perhaps, as shooting them at Waterloo.[7]

133

Man's a phenomenon, one knows not what,
      And wonderful beyond all wondrous measure;
'Tis pity though, in this sublime world, that
1060   Pleasure's a sin, and sometimes sin's a pleasure;
Few mortals know what end they would be at,
      But whether glory, power, or love, or treasure,
The path is through perplexing ways, and when
The goal is gained, we die, you know—and then—

134

1065 What then?—I do not know, no more do you—
      And so good night.—Return we to our story:
'Twas in November, when fine days are few,
      And the far mountains wax a little hoary,
And clap a white cape on their mantles blue;
1070   And the sea dashes round the promontory,
And the loud breaker boils against the rock,
And sober suns must set at five o'clock.

135

'Twas, as the watchmen say, a cloudy night;
      No moon, no stars, the wind was low or loud
1075 By gusts, and many a sparkling hearth was bright
      With the piled wood, round which the family
            crowd;
There's something cheerful in that sort of light,
      Even as a summer sky's without a cloud:
I'm fond of fire, and crickets, and all that,
1080 A lobster salad, and champagne, and chat.

136

'Twas midnight—Donna Julia was in bed,
      Sleeping, most probably,—when at her door
Arose a clatter might awake the dead,
      If they had never been awoke before,

---

[1] *Congreve's rockets* Sir William Congreve (1772–1828) invented the Congreve rocket, which terrified the French at the Battle of Leipzig (1813), although it did little actual harm.

[2] *old pox ... ox* Edward Jenner (1749–1823) first vaccinated against smallpox in 1796, using the related cow-pox virus as his inoculant.

[3] *war, or plague, or famine* Byron here refers to the theory propounded by Thomas Malthus in his *An Essay on the Principles of Population* (1798–1817).

[4] *killing bodies ... saving souls* The British and Foreign Bible Society was founded in 1804.

[5] *Sir Humphry ... mentions* Sir Humphrey Davy (1778–1829) invented the safety lantern in 1815.

[6] *Timbuctoo ... Poles* Byron here refers to voyages of exploration such as those recounted in James Grey Jackson, *An Account of the Empire of Marocco* (1809) and Sir John Ross (1777–1856), *A Voyage of Discovery ... for the Purpose of Exploring Baffin's Bay* (1819).

[7] *Waterloo* I.e., the Battle of Waterloo, 18 June 1815.

1085 And that they have been so we all have read,
       And are to be so, at the least, once more—
     The door was fastened, but with voice and fist
     First knocks were heard, then "Madam—Madam—
       hist!"[1]

137

     "For God's sake, Madam—Madam—here's my master,
1090   With more than half the city at his back—
     Was ever heard of such a curst disaster!
       'Tis not my fault—I kept good watch—Alack!
     Do, pray undo the bolt a little faster—
       They're on the stair just now, and in a crack
1095 Will all be here; perhaps he yet may fly—
     Surely the window's not so *very* high!"

138

     By this time Don Alfonso was arrived,
       With torches, friends, and servants in great number;
     The major part of them had long been wived,
1100   And therefore paused not to disturb the slumber
     Of any wicked woman, who contrived
       By stealth her husband's temples to encumber:[2]
     Examples of this kind are so contagious,
     Were *one* not punished, *all* would be outrageous.

139

1105 I can't tell how, or why, or what suspicion
       Could enter into Don Alfonso's head;
     But for a cavalier of his condition
       It surely was exceedingly ill-bred,
     Without a word of previous admonition,
1110   To hold a levee[3] round his lady's bed,
     And summon lackeys, armed with fire and sword,
     To prove himself the thing he most abhorred.

140

     Poor Donna Julia, starting as from sleep!
       (Mind—that I do not say—she had not slept)
1115 Began at once to scream, and yawn, and weep;

     Her maid Antonia, who was an adept,[4]
       Contrived to fling the bed-clothes in a heap,
     As if she had just now from out them crept:
     I can't tell why she should take all this trouble
1120 To prove her mistress had been sleeping double.[5]

141

     But Julia mistress, and Antonia maid,
       Appeared like two poor harmless women, who
     Of goblins, but still more of men afraid,
       Had thought one man might be deterred by two,
1125 And therefore side by side were gently laid,
       Until the hours of absence should run through,
     And truant husband should return, and say,
     "My dear, I was the first who came away."

142

     Now Julia found at length a voice, and cried,
1130   "In heaven's name, Don Alfonso, what d'ye mean?
     Has madness seized you? would that I had died
       Ere such a monster's victim I had been!
     What may this midnight violence betide,
       A sudden fit of drunkenness or spleen?
1135 Dare you suspect me, whom the thought would kill?
     Search, then, the room!"—Alfonso said, "I will."

143

     He searched, *they* searched, and rummaged every where,
       Closet and clothes'-press, chest and window-seat,
     And found much linen, lace, and several pair
1140   Of stockings, slippers, brushes, combs, complete,
     With other articles of ladies fair,
       To keep them beautiful, or leave them neat:
     Arras[6] they pricked and curtains with their swords,
     And wounded several shutters, and some boards.

144

1145 Under the bed they searched, and there they found—
       No matter what—it was not that they sought;
     They opened windows, gazing if the ground
       Had signs or footmarks, but the earth said nought;
     And then they stared each others' faces round:

---

[1] *hist!* I.e., listen!

[2] *temples to encumber* That is, to give him horns, the traditional symbol of a cuckold.

[3] *levee* Morning reception.

[4] *adept* Skilled person.

[5] *sleeping double* I.e., with Antonia.

[6] *Arras* Wall-hangings.

1150 'Tis odd, not one of all these seekers thought,
And seems to me almost a sort of blunder,
Of looking *in* the bed as well as under.

145

During this inquisition, Julia's tongue
    Was not asleep—"Yes, search and search," she cried,
1155 "Insult on insult heap, and wrong on wrong!
    It was for this that I became a bride!
For this in silence I have suffered long
    A husband like Alfonso at my side;
But now I'll bear no more, nor here remain,
1160 If there be law, or lawyers, in all Spain.

146

"Yes, Don Alfonso! husband now no more,
    If ever you indeed deserved the name,
Is't worthy of your years?—you have threescore,
    Fifty, or sixty—it is all the same—
1165 Is't wise or fitting causeless to explore
    For facts against a virtuous woman's fame?
Ungrateful, perjured, barbarous Don Alfonso,
How dare you think your lady would go on so?

147

"Is it for this I have disdained to hold
    The common privileges of my sex?
1170 That I have chosen a confessor so old
    And deaf, that any other it would vex,
And never once he has had cause to scold,
    But found my very innocence perplex
1175 So much, he always doubted I was married—
How sorry you will be when I've miscarried!

148

"Was it for this that no Cortejo[1] ere
    I yet have chosen from out the youth of Seville?
Is it for this I scarce went any where,
1180   Except to bull-fights, mass, play, rout, and revel?
Is it for this, whate'er my suitors were,
    I favoured none—nay, was almost uncivil?

Is it for this that General Count O'Reilly,
Who took Algiers, declares I used him vilely?[2]

149

1185 "Did not the Italian Musico° Cazzani   *musician*
    Sing at my heart six months at least in vain?
Did not his countryman, Count Corniani,[3]
    Call me the only virtuous wife in Spain?
Were there not also Russians, English, many?
1190   The Count Strongstroganoff I put in pain,
And Lord Mount Coffeehouse, the Irish peer,
Who killed himself for love (with wine) last year.

150

"Have I not had two bishops at my feet?
    The Duke of Ichar, and Don Fernan Nunez?
1195 And is it thus a faithful wife you treat?
    I wonder in what quarter now the moon is:
I praise your vast forbearance not to beat
    Me also, since the time so opportune is—
Oh, valiant man! with sword drawn and cocked trigger,
1200 Now, tell me, don't you cut a pretty figure?

151

"Was it for this you took your sudden journey,
    Under pretence of business indispensible
With that sublime of rascals your attorney,
    Whom I see standing there, and looking sensible
1205 Of having played the fool? though both I spurn, he
    Deserves the worst, his conduct's less defensible,
Because, no doubt, 'twas for his dirty fee,
And not from any love to you nor me.

152

"If he comes here to take a deposition,
1210   By all means let the gentleman proceed;
You've made the apartment in a fit condition:—
    There's pen and ink for you, sir, when you need—
Let every thing be noted with precision,

---

2 [Byron's note] Donna Julia here made a mistake. Count O'Reilly did not take Algiers—but Algiers very nearly took him: he and his army and fleet retreated with great loss, and not much credit, from before that city in the year 17[75]. [Alexander O'Reilly (1722–94), Irish-born Spanish general.]

3 *Cazzani … Corniani* "Cazzani" is from "cazzo" (penis); "Corniani," from "cornuto" (horned; i.e., cuckolded).

---

1 *Cortejo* The acknowledged lover of a married woman.

I would not you for nothing should be feed—
1215 But, as my maid's undrest, pray turn your spies out."
"Oh!" sobbed Antonia, "I could tear their eyes out."

153

"There is the closet, there the toilet, there
    The antechamber—search them under, over;
There is the sofa, there the great arm-chair,
1220   The chimney—which would really hold a lover.
I wish to sleep, and beg you will take care
    And make no further noise, till you discover
The secret cavern of this lurking treasure—
And when 'tis found, let me, too, have that pleasure.

154

1225 "And now, Hidalgo! now that you have thrown
    Doubt upon me, confusion over all,
Pray have the courtesy to make it known
    Who is the man you search for? how d'ye call
Him? what's his lineage? let him but be shown—
1230   I hope he's young and handsome—is he tall?
Tell me—and be assured, that since you stain
My honour thus, it shall not be in vain.

155

"At least, perhaps, he has not sixty years,
    At that age he would be too old for slaughter,
1235 Or for so young a husband's jealous fears—
    (Antonia! let me have a glass of water.)
I am ashamed of having shed these tears,
    They are unworthy of my father's daughter;
My mother dreamed not in my natal hour
1240 That I should fall into a monster's power.

156

"Perhaps 'tis of Antonia you are jealous,
    You saw that she was sleeping by my side
When you broke in upon us with your fellows:
    Look where you please—we've nothing, sir, to hide;
1245 Only another time, I trust, you'll tell us,
    Or for the sake of decency abide
A moment at the door, that we may be
Drest to receive so much good company.

157

"And now, sir, I have done, and say no more;
1250   The little I have said may serve to show
The guileless heart in silence may grieve o'er
    The wrongs to whose exposure it is slow:—
I leave you to your conscience as before,
    'Twill one day ask you *why* you used me so?
1255 God grant you feel not then the bitterest grief!
Antonia! where's my pocket-handkerchief?"

158

She ceased, and turned upon her pillow; pale
    She lay, her dark eyes flashing through their tears,
Like skies that rain and lighten; as a veil,
1260   Waved and o'ershading her wan cheek, appears
Her streaming hair; the black curls strive, but fail,
    To hide the glossy shoulder, which uprears
Its snow through all;—her soft lips lie apart,
And louder than her breathing beats her heart.

159

1265 The Senhor Don Alfonso stood confused;
    Antonia bustled round the ransacked room,
And, turning up her nose, with looks abused
    Her master, and his myrmidons,[1] of whom
Not one, except the attorney, was amused;
1270   He, like Achates,[2] faithful to the tomb,
So there were quarrels, cared not for the cause,
Knowing they must be settled by the laws.

160

With prying snub-nose, and small eyes, he stood,
    Following Antonia's motions here and there,
1275 With much suspicion in his attitude;
    For reputations he had little care;
So that a suit or action were made good,
    Small pity had he for the young and fair,
And ne'er believed in negatives, till these
1280 Were proved by competent false witnesses.

---

[1] *myrmidons* Warriors led by Achilles to the siege of Troy.

[2] *Achates* Aeneas's companion in *The Aeneid*, famous for his faithfulness.

161

But Don Alfonso stood with downcast looks,
    And, truth to say, he made a foolish figure;
When, after searching in five hundred nooks,
    And treating a young wife with so much rigour,
1285 He gained no point, except some self-rebukes,
    Added to those his lady with such vigour
Had poured upon him for the last half-hour,
Quick, thick, and heavy—as a thunder-shower.

162

At first he tried to hammer an excuse,
1290   To which the sole reply were tears and sobs,
And indications of hysterics, whose
    Prologue is always certain throes, and throbs,
Gasps, and whatever else the owners choose:—
    Alfonso saw his wife, and thought of Job's;[1]
1295 He saw too, in perspective, her relations,
And then he tried to muster all his patience.

163

He stood in act to speak, or rather stammer,
    But sage Antonia cut him short before
The anvil of his speech received the hammer,
1300   With "Pray, sir, leave the room, and say no more,
Or madam dies."—Alfonso muttered, "D—n her,"
    But nothing else, the time of words was o'er;
He cast a rueful look or two, and did,
He knew not wherefore, that which he was bid.

164

1305 With him retired his "*posse comitatus*,"[2]
    The attorney last, who lingered near the door,
Reluctantly, still tarrying there as late as
    Antonia let him—not a little sore
At this most strange and unexplained "*hiatus*"
1310   In Don Alfonso's facts, which just now wore
An awkward look; as he revolved the case,
The door was fastened in his legal face.

165

No sooner was it bolted, than—Oh shame!

Oh sin! Oh sorrow! and Oh womankind!
1315 How can you do such things and keep your fame,
    Unless this world, and t'other too, be blind?
Nothing so dear as an unfilched good name!
    But to proceed—for there is more behind:
With much heart-felt reluctance be it said,
1320 Young Juan slipped, half-smothered, from the bed.

166

He had been hid—I don't pretend to say
    How, nor can I indeed describe the where—
Young, slender, and packed easily, he lay,
    No doubt, in little compass, round or square;
1325 But pity him I neither must nor may
    His suffocation by that pretty pair;
'Twere better, sure, to die so, than be shut
With maudlin Clarence in his Malmsey butt.[3]

167

And, secondly, I pity not, because
1330 He had no business to commit a sin,
    Forbid by heavenly, fined by human laws,
At least 'twas rather early to begin;
    But at sixteen the conscience rarely gnaws
So much as when we call our old debts in
1335   At sixty years, and draw the accompts of evil,
And find a deuced balance with the devil.

168

Of his position I can give no notion:
    'Tis written in the Hebrew Chronicle,
How the physicians, leaving pill and potion,
1340   Prescribed, by way of blister, a young belle,
When old King David's blood grew dull in motion,[4]
    And that the medicine answered very well;
Perhaps 'twas in a different way applied,
For David lived, but Juan nearly died.

169

1345 What's to be done? Alfonso will be back

---

[1] *Job's* See the Biblical book of Job.

[2] *posse comitatus* Latin: literally, "the power of the county," a group of deputies.

[3] *Clarence … butt* According to rumors that passed into legend, King Richard III of England, when Duke of Gloucester, arranged for his elder brother the Duke of Clarence to be drowned in a barrel of Malmsey wine, thus moving Richard closer to the throne.

[4] *When old … motion* See 1 Kings 1.1-4.

The moment he has sent his fools away.
Antonia's skill was put upon the rack,
    But no device could be brought into play—
And how to parry the renewed attack?
1350   Besides, it wanted but few hours of day:
Antonia puzzled; Julia did not speak,
But pressed her bloodless lip to Juan's cheek.

170

He turned his lip to hers, and with his hand
    Called back the tangles of her wandering hair;
1355 Even then their love they could not all command,
    And half forgot their danger and despair:
Antonia's patience now was at a stand—
    "Come, come, 'tis no time now for fooling there,"
She whispered, in great wrath—"I must deposit
1360 This pretty gentleman within the closet.

171

"Pray, keep your nonsense for some luckier night—
    Who can have put my master in this mood?
What will become on't—I'm in such a fright,
    The devil's in the urchin, and no good—
1365 Is this a time for giggling? this a plight?
    Why, don't you know that it may end in blood?
You'll lose your life, and I shall lose my place,
My mistress all, for that half-girlish face.

172

"Had it but been for a stout cavalier
1370   Of twenty-five or thirty—(Come, make haste)
But for a child, what piece of work is here!
    I really, madam, wonder at your taste—
(Come, sir, get in)—my master must be near.
    There, for the present, at the least he's fast,
1375 And if we can but till the morning keep
Our counsel—(Juan, mind, you must not sleep.)"

173

Now, Don Alfonso entering, but alone,
    Closed the oration of the trusty maid:
She loitered, and he told her to be gone,
1380   An order somewhat sullenly obeyed;
However, present remedy was none,
    And no great good seemed answered if she staid:

Regarding both with slow and sidelong view,
She snuffed the candle, curtsied, and withdrew.

174

1385 Alfonso paused a minute—then begun
    Some strange excuses for his late proceeding;
He would not justify what he had done,
    To say the best, it was extreme ill-breeding;
But there were ample reasons for it, none
1390   Of which he specified in this his pleading:
His speech was a fine sample, on the whole,
Of rhetoric, which the learned call "*rigmarole*."

175

Julia said nought; though all the while there rose
    A ready answer, which at once enables
1395 A matron, who her husband's foible knows,
    By a few timely words to turn the tables,
Which if it does not silence still must pose,
    Even if it should comprise a pack of fables;
'Tis to retort with firmness, and when he
1400 Suspects with *one*, do you reproach with *three*.

176

Julia, in fact, had tolerable grounds,
    Alfonso's loves with Inez were well known;
But whether 'twas that one's own guilt confounds,
    But that can't be, as has been often shown,
1405 A lady with apologies abounds;
    It might be that her silence sprang alone
From delicacy to Don Juan's ear,
To whom she knew his mother's fame was dear.

177

There might be one more motive, which makes two,
1410   Alfonso ne'er to Juan had alluded,
Mentioned his jealousy, but never who
    Had been the happy lover, he concluded,
Concealed amongst his premises; 'tis true,
    His mind the more o'er this its mystery brooded;
1415 To speak of Inez now were, one may say,
Like throwing Juan in Alfonso's way.

178

A hint, in tender cases, is enough;

Silence is best, besides there is a *tact*
(That modern phrase appears to me sad stuff,
1420   But it will serve to keep my verse compact)
      Which keeps, when pushed by questions rather rough,
      A lady always distant from the fact—
The charming creatures lie with such a grace,
There's nothing so becoming to the face.

179

1425 They blush, and we believe them; at least I
      Have always done so; 'tis of no great use,
In any case, attempting a reply,
      For then their eloquence grows quite profuse;
And when at length they're out of breath, they sigh,
1430   And cast their languid eyes down, and let loose
A tear or two, and then we make it up;
And then—and then—and then—sit down and sup.

180

Alfonso closed his speech, and begged her pardon,
      Which Julia half withheld, and then half granted,
1435 And laid conditions, he thought, very hard on,
      Denying several little things he wanted:
He stood like Adam lingering near his garden,
      With useless penitence perplexed and haunted,
Beseeching she no further would refuse,
1440 When, lo! he stumbled o'er a pair of shoes.

181

A pair of shoes!—what then? not much, if they
      Are such as fit with lady's feet, but these
(No one can tell how much I grieve to say)
      Were masculine; to see them, and to seize,
1445 Was but a moment's act.—Ah! Well-a-day!
      My teeth begin to chatter, my veins freeze—
Alfonso first examined well their fashion,
And then flew out into another passion.

182

He left the room for his relinquished sword,
1450   And Julia instant to the closet flew.
"Fly, Juan, fly! for heaven's sake—not a word—
      The door is open—you may yet slip through
The passage you so often have explored—
      Here is the garden-key—Fly—fly—Adieu!

1455 Haste—haste!—I hear Alfonso's hurrying feet—
Day has not broke—there's no one in the street."

183

None can say that this was not good advice,
      The only mischief was, it came too late;
Of all experience 'tis the usual price,
1460   A sort of income-tax laid on by fate:
Juan had reached the room-door in a trice,
      And might have done so by the garden-gate,
But met Alfonso in his dressing-gown,
Who threatened death—so Juan knocked him down.

184

1465 Dire was the scuffle, and out went the light,
      Antonia cried out "Rape!" and Julia "Fire!"
But not a servant stirred to aid the fight.
      Alfonso, pommelled to his heart's desire,
Swore lustily he'd be revenged this night;
1470   And Juan, too, blasphemed an octave higher,
His blood was up; though young, he was a Tartar,
And not at all disposed to prove a martyr.

185

Alfonso's sword had dropped ere he could draw it,
      And they continued battling hand to hand,
1475 For Juan very luckily ne'er saw it;
      His temper not being under great command,
If at that moment he had chanced to claw it,
      Alfonso's days had not been in the land
Much longer.—Think of husbands', lovers' lives!
1480 And how ye may be doubly widows—wives!

186

Alfonso grappled to detain the foe,
      And Juan throttled him to get away,
And blood ('twas from the nose) began to flow;
      At last, as they more faintly wrestling lay,
1485 Juan contrived to give an awkward blow,
      And then his only garment quite gave way;
He fled, like Joseph, leaving it; but there,
I doubt, all likeness ends between the pair.[1]

---

[1] *He fled … the pair* See the story of Joseph and Potiphar's wife, Genesis 39.7–20.

187

Lights came at length, and men, and maids, who found
1490   An awkward spectacle their eyes before;
Antonia in hysterics, Julia swooned,
    Alfonso leaning, breathless, by the door;
Some half-torn drapery scattered on the ground,
    Some blood, and several footsteps, but no more:
1495 Juan the gate gained, turned the key about,
And liking not the inside, locked the out.

188

Here ends this canto.—Need I sing, or say,
    How Juan, naked, favoured by the night,
Who favours what she should not, found his way,
1500   And reached his home in an unseemly plight?
The pleasant scandal which arose next day,
    The nine days' wonder which was brought to light,
And how Alfonso sued for a divorce,
Were in the English newspapers, of course.

189

1505 If you would like to see the whole proceedings,
    The depositions, and the cause at full,
The names of all the witnesses, the pleadings
    Of counsel to nonsuit, or to annul,
There's more than one edition, and the readings
1510   Are various, but they none of them are dull,
The best is that in short-hand ta'en by Gurney,[1]
Who to Madrid on purpose made a journey.

190

But Donna Inez, to divert the train
    Of one of the most circulating scandals
1515 That had for centuries been known in Spain,
    At least since the retirement of the Vandals,
First vowed (and never had she vowed in vain)
    To Virgin Mary several pounds of candles;
And then, by the advice of some old ladies,
1520 She sent her son to be shipped off from Cadiz.

191

She had resolved that he should travel through

All European climes, by land or sea,
    To mend his former morals, or get new,
    Especially in France and Italy,
1525 (At least this is the thing most people do.)
    Julia was sent into a convent; she
Grieved, but, perhaps, her feelings may be better
Shown in the following copy of her letter:

192

"They tell me 'tis decided; you depart:
1530   'Tis wise—'tis well, but not the less a pain;
I have no further claim on your young heart,
    Mine is the victim, and would be again;
To love too much has been the only art
    I used;—I write in haste, and if a stain
1535 Be on this sheet, 'tis not what it appears,
My eyeballs burn and throb, but have no tears.

193

"I loved, I love you, for this love have lost
    State, station, heaven, mankind's, my own esteem,
And yet can not regret what it hath cost,
1540   So dear is still the memory of that dream;
Yet, if I name my guilt, 'tis not to boast,
    None can deem harshlier of me than I deem:
I trace this scrawl because I cannot rest—
I've nothing to reproach, or to request.

194

1545 "Man's love is of man's life a thing apart,
    'Tis woman's whole existence; man may range
The court, camp, church, the vessel, and the mart;
    Sword, gown, gain, glory, offer in exchange
Pride, fame, ambition, to fill up his heart,
1550   And few there are whom these cannot estrange;
Men have all these resources, we but one,
To love again, and be again undone.

195

"You will proceed in pleasure, and in pride,
    Beloved and loving many; all is o'er
1555 For me on earth, except some years to hide
    My shame and sorrow deep in my heart's core;
These I could bear, but cannot cast aside
    The passion which still rages as before,

---

1 *Gurney* William Brodie Gurney (1777–1855), official shorthand
writer to the Houses of Parliament, also reported several notorious
trials.

And so farewell—forgive me, love me—No,
1560   That word is idle now—but let it go.

196

"My breast has been all weakness, is so yet;
        But still I think I can collect my mind;
My blood still rushes where my spirit's set,
        As roll the waves before the settled wind;
1565   My heart is feminine, nor can forget—
        To all, except one image, madly blind;
So shakes the needle, and so stands the pole,
As vibrates my fond heart to my fixed soul.

197

"I have no more to say, but linger still,
1570   And dare not set my seal upon this sheet,
And yet I may as well the task fulfil,
        My misery can scarce be more complete:
I had not lived till now, could sorrow kill;
        Death shuns the wretch who fain the blow would
            meet,
1575   And I must even survive this last adieu,
And bear with life, to love and pray for you!"

198

This note was written upon gilt-edged paper
        With a neat little crow-quill, slight and new:
Her small white hand could hardly reach the taper,
1580   It trembled as magnetic needles do,
And yet she did not let one tear escape her;
        The seal a sun-flower; *"Elle vous suit partout,"*[1]
The motto, cut upon a white cornelian;
The wax was superfine, its hue vermilion.

199

1585   This was Don Juan's earliest scrape; but whether
        I shall proceed with his adventures is
Dependent on the public altogether;
        We'll see, however, what they say to this,
Their favour in an author's cap's a feather,
1590   And no great mischief's done by their caprice;
And if their approbation we experience,
Perhaps they'll have some more about a year hence.

200

My poem's epic, and is meant to be
        Divided in twelve books; each book containing,
1595   With love, and war, a heavy gale at sea,
        A list of ships, and captains, and kings reigning,
New characters; the episodes are three:
        A panorama view of hell's in training,
After the style of Virgil and of Homer,
1600   So that my name of Epic's no misnomer.[2]

201

All these things will be specified in time,
        With strict regard to Aristotle's rules,
The *Vade Mecum*[3] of the true sublime,
        Which makes so many poets, and some fools;
1605   Prose poets like blank-verse, I'm fond of rhyme,
        Good workmen never quarrel with their tools;
I've got new mythological machinery,
And very handsome supernatural scenery.

202

There's only one slight difference between
1610   Me and my epic brethren gone before,
And here the advantage is my own, I ween;
        (Not that I have not several merits more,
But this will more peculiarly be seen)
        They so embellish, that 'tis quite a bore
1615   Their labyrinth of fables to thread through,
Whereas this story's actually true.

203

If any person doubt it, I appeal
        To history, tradition, and to facts,
To newspapers, whose truth all know and feel,
1620   To plays in five, and operas in three acts;
All these confirm my statement a good deal,
        But that which more completely faith exacts
Is, that myself, and several now in Seville,
Saw Juan's last elopement with the devil.

---

[1]   *Elle ... partout* French: she follows you everywhere.

[2]   *My poem's ... no misnomer* Byron lists the traditional elements of
an epic poem. See also the letter to John Murray, February 16, 1821,
in this volume.

[3]   *Vade Mecum* Latin: literally, go with me; i.e., a guidebook.

204

1625 If ever I should condescend to prose,
 I'll write poetical commandments, which
Shall supersede beyond all doubt all those
 That went before; in these I shall enrich
My text with many things that no one knows,
1630 And carry precept to the highest pitch:
I'll call the work "Longinus o'er a Bottle,
Or, Every Poet his *own* Aristotle."[1]

205

Thou shalt believe in Milton, Dryden, Pope;
 Thou shalt not set up Wordsworth, Coleridge,
  Southey;
1635 Because the first is crazed beyond all hope,
 The second drunk, the third so quaint and mouthey:
With Crabbe it may be difficult to cope,
 And Campbell's Hippocrene[2] is somewhat
  drouthy:°   *dry*
Thou shalt not steal from Samuel Rogers, nor
1640 Commit—flirtation with the muse of Moore.

206

Thou shalt not covet Mr. Sotheby's Muse,[3]
 His Pegasus, nor any thing that's his;
Thou shalt not bear false witness like "the Blues,"[4]
 (There's *one*, at least, is very fond of this);
1645 Thou shalt not write, in short, but what I choose:
 This is true criticism, and you may kiss—
Exactly as you please, or not, the rod,
But if you don't, I'll lay it on, by G—d!

207

If any person should presume to assert
1650 This story is not moral, first, I pray,
That they will not cry out before they're hurt,
 Then that they'll read it o'er again, and say,

(But, doubtless, nobody will be so pert)
 That this is not a moral tale, though gay;
1655 Besides, in canto twelfth, I mean to show
The very place where wicked people go.

208

If, after all, there should be some so blind
 To their own good this warning to despise,
Led by some tortuosity of mind,
1660 Not to believe my verse and their own eyes,
And cry that they "the moral cannot find,"
 I tell him, if a clergyman, he lies;
Should captains the remark or critics make,
They also lie too—under a mistake.

209

1665 The public approbation I expect,
 And beg they'll take my word about the moral,
Which I with their amusement will connect,
 (So children cutting teeth receive a coral);[5]
Meantime, they'll doubtless please to recollect
1670 My epical pretensions to the laurel:
For fear some prudish readers should grow skittish,
I've bribed my grandmother's review—the British.[6]

210

I sent it in a letter to the editor,
 Who thanked me duly by return of post—
1675 I'm for a handsome article his creditor;
 Yet if my gentle Muse he please to roast,
And break a promise after having made it her,
 Denying the receipt of what it cost,
And smear his page with gall instead of honey,
1680 All I can say is—that he had the money.

211

I think that with this holy *new* alliance
 I may ensure the public, and defy
All other magazines of art or science,
 Daily, or monthly, or three monthly; I

---

[1] *Longinus ... Aristotle* Longinus, *On the Sublime*, and Aristotle, *Poetics*: two renowned works of literary theory.

[2] *Hippocrene* A fountain sacred to the Muses, which started flowing when the winged horse Pegasus (see line 1642) struck the ground with his hoof.

[3] *Sotheby* William Sotheby (1757–1833), poet.

[4] *Blues* Group of intellectual women commonly called the "Bluestockings."

[5] *coral* Teething rings were commonly made of coral.

[6] *British* William Roberts, editor of the *British Review*, took this accusation seriously and contradicted it in his review of *Don Juan*, prompting Byron to write "Letter to the Editor of my Grandmother's Review" (1822).

Have not essayed to multiply their clients,
    Because they tell me 'twere in vain to try,
And that the Edinburgh Review and Quarterly
Treat a dissenting author very martyrly.

212

"*Non ego hoc ferrem calida juventa*
    Consule Planco,"[1] Horace said, and so
Say I; by which quotation there is meant a
    Hint that some six or seven good years ago
(Long ere I dreamt of dating from the Brenta)[2]
    I was most ready to return a blow,
And would not brook at all this sort of thing
In my hot youth—when George the Third was King.

213

But now at thirty years my hair is gray—
    (I wonder what it will be like at forty?
I thought of a peruke° the other day)   *wig*
    My heart is not much greener; and, in short, I
Have squandered my whole summer while 'twas May,
    And feel no more the spirit to retort; I
Have spent my life, both interest and principal,
And deem not, what I deemed, my soul invincible.

214

No more—no more—Oh! never more on me
    The freshness of the heart can fall like dew,
Which out of all the lovely things we see
    Extracts emotions beautiful and new,
Hived in our bosoms like the bag o' the bee:
    Think'st thou the honey with those objects grew?
Alas! 'twas not in them, but in thy power
To double even the sweetness of a flower.

215

No more—no more—Oh! never more, my heart,
    Canst thou be my sole world, my universe!
Once all in all, but now a thing apart,
    Thou canst not be my blessing or my curse:
The illusion's gone for ever, and thou art
    Insensible, I trust, but none the worse,

And in thy stead I've got a deal of judgment,
Though heaven knows how it ever found a lodgement.

216

My days of love are over, me no more[3]
    The charms of maid, wife, and still less of widow,
Can make the fool of which they made before,
    In short, I must not lead the life I did do;
The credulous hope of mutual minds is o'er,
    The copious use of claret is forbid too,
So for a good old-gentlemanly vice,
I think I must take up with avarice.

217

Ambition was my idol, which was broken
    Before the shrines of Sorrow and of Pleasure;
And the two last have left me many a token
    O'er which reflection may be made at leisure:
Now, like Friar Bacon's brazen head,[4] I've spoken,
    "Time is, Time was, Time's past,"—a
        chymic° treasure   *counterfeit gold*
Is glittering youth, which I have spent betimes—
My heart in passion, and my head on rhymes.

218

What is the end of Fame? 'tis but to fill
    A certain portion of uncertain paper:
Some liken it to climbing up a hill,
    Whose summit, like all hills, is lost in vapour;
For this men write, speak, preach, and heroes kill,
    And bards burn what they call their "midnight
        taper,"
To have, when the original is dust,
A name, a wretched picture, and worse bust.[5]

---

1. *Non ... Planco* "I would not have borne with this in the heat of my youth, when Plancus was consul." Horace, *Odes* 3.14.27–28.

2. *Brenta* River flowing into the Adriatic at Venice.

3. [Byron's note] 'Me nec femina, nec puer
        Jam, nec spes animi credula mutui,
    Nec certare juvat mero;
        Nec vincire novis tempora floribus.'
[Horace, *Odes* 4.1.30: "Now neither a woman nor a boy delights me, nor confident hope of love returned, nor drinking bouts, nor binding my temples with fresh flowers."]

4. *Friar Bacon's brazen head* See Robert Greene's *Friar Bacon and Friar Bungay.*

5. Byron sat for a number of busts and disliked all the results; he also found fault with most of his portraits.

219

1745 What are the hopes of man? old Egypt's King
      Cheops erected the first pyramid
And largest, thinking it was just the thing
      To keep his memory whole, and mummy hid;
But somebody or other rummaging,
1750   Burglariously broke his coffin's lid:
Let not a monument give you or me hopes,
Since not a pinch of dust remains of Cheops.

220

But I, being fond of true philosophy,
      Say very often to myself, "Alas!
1755 All things that have been born were born to die,
      And flesh (which Death mows down to hay) is grass;[1]
You've passed your youth not so unpleasantly,
      And if you had it o'er again—'twould pass—
So thank your stars that matters are no worse,
1760 And read your Bible, sir, and mind your purse."

221

But for the present, gentle reader! and
      Still gentler purchaser! the bard—that's I—
Must, with permission, shake you by the hand,
      And so your humble servant, and good-bye!
1765 We meet again, if we should understand
      Each other; and if not, I shall not try
Your patience further than by this short sample—
'Twere well if others followed my example.

222

"Go, little book, from this my solitude!
1770   I cast thee on the waters—go thy ways!
And if, as I believe, thy vein be good,
      The world will find thee after many days."
When Southey's read, and Wordsworth, understood,
      I can't help putting in my claim to praise—
1775 The four first rhymes are Southey's every line:[2]
For God's sake, reader! take them not for mine.
                                        —1819

---

[1] *flesh ... grass* See Isaiah 40.6.

[2] *Southey's every line* From Southey, *The Lay of the Laureate*
(1816), "L'Envoy."

from *Canto 2*

In this canto, Juan, his tutor Pedrillo, his spaniel,
and three servants set sail for the Italian port of
Leghorn, where Juan plans to seek out some
relatives. Besieged by a storm, the ship sinks, and
most of the passengers perish. Juan, Pedrillo, and
the spaniel escape to a lifeboat with a number of the
crew members, but after several days without food
the spaniel is killed and eaten. Still hungry, the
sailors draw lots (using Julia's letter to Juan for
paper) to decide who will be eaten next, and Pedrillo
is chosen. The sailors who consume him, however,
soon succumb to fevers and madness. Eventually the
boat comes in sight of land and Juan, ultimately the
only survivor, swims ashore on an island in the
Cyclades. In the passages describing the shipwreck
and the cannibalistic episode, Byron relies heavily on
Shipwrecks and Disasters at Sea, edited by Sir J.G.
Dalyell (1812).

1

Oh ye! who teach the ingenuous youth of nations,
      Holland, France, England, Germany, or Spain,
I pray ye flog them upon all occasions,
      It mends their morals; never mind the pain:
5 The best of mothers and of educations
      In Juan's case were but employed in vain,
Since in a way, that's rather of the oddest, he
Became divested of his native modesty.

2

Had he but been placed at a public school,
10   In the third form, or even in the fourth,
His daily task had kept his fancy cool,
      At least, had he been nurtured in the north;
Spain may prove an exception to the rule,
      But then exceptions always prove its worth—
15 A lad of sixteen causing a divorce
Puzzled his tutors very much, of course.

3

I can't say that it puzzles me at all,
      If all things be considered: first, there was
His lady-mother, mathematical,
20   A—never mind; his tutor, an old ass;
A pretty woman—(that's quite natural,

Or else the thing had hardly come to pass);
A husband rather old, not much in unity
With his young wife—a time, and opportunity.

4

25 Well—well, the world must turn upon its axis,
    And all mankind turn with it, heads or tails,
And live and die, make love and pay our taxes,
    And as the veering wind shifts, shift our sails;
The king commands us, and the doctor quacks us,
30   The priest instructs, and so our life exhales,
A little breath, love, wine, ambition, fame,
Fighting, devotion, dust,—perhaps a name.

5

I said that Juan had been sent to Cadiz—
    A pretty town, I recollect it well—
35 'Tis there the mart of the colonial trade is,
    (Or was, before Peru learned to rebel)[1]
And such sweet girls—I mean, such graceful ladies,
    Their very walk would make your bosom swell;
I can't describe it, though so much it strike,
40   Nor liken it—I never saw the like.

6

An Arab horse, a stately stag, a barb
    New broke, a camelopard,° a gazelle,   *giraffe*
No—none of these will do;—and then their garb!
    Their veil and petticoat—Alas! to dwell
45 Upon such things would very near absorb
    A canto—then their feet and ankles—well,
Thank Heaven I've got no metaphor quite ready,
(And so, my sober Muse—come, let's be steady—

7

Chaste Muse!—well, if you must, you must)—the veil
50   Thrown back a moment with the glancing hand,
While the o'erpowering eye, that turns you pale,
    Flashes into the heart:—All sunny land
Of love! when I forget you, may I fail
    To—say my prayers—but never was there planned

55 A dress through which the eyes give such a volley,
Excepting the Venetian Fazzioli.[2]

8

But to our tale: the Donna Inez sent
    Her son to Cadiz only to embark;
To stay there had not answered her intent,
60   But why?—we leave the reader in the dark—
'Twas for a voyage the young man was meant,
    As if a Spanish ship were Noah's ark,
To wean him from the wickedness of earth,
And send him like a dove of promise forth.

9

65 Don Juan bade his valet pack his things
    According to direction, then received
A lecture and some money: for four springs
    He was to travel; and though Inez grieved,
(As every kind of parting has its stings)
70   She hoped he would improve—perhaps believed:
A letter, too, she gave (he never read it)
Of good advice—and two or three of credit.[3]

10

In the mean time, to pass her hours away,
    Brave Inez now set up a Sunday school
75 For naughty children, who would rather play
    (Like truant rogues) the devil, or the fool;
Infants of three years old were taught that day,
    Dunces were whipt, or set upon a stool:
The great success of Juan's education
80 Spurred her to teach another generation.

11

Juan embarked—the ship got under way,
    The wind was fair, the water passing rough;
A devil of a sea rolls in that Bay,
    As I, who've crossed it oft, know well enough;
85 And, standing upon deck, the dashing spray
    Flies in one's face, and makes it weather-tough:
And there he stood to take, and take again,
His first—perhaps his last—farewell of Spain.

---

1 *Peru learned to rebel* Peru rebelled against Spain in 1813, and would finally win its independence in 1824.

2 [Byron's note] *Fazzioli*—literally, little handkerchiefs—the veils most availing of St. Mark.

3 *letter … of credit* For presentation in order to procure funds.

12

I can't but say it is an awkward sight
90   To see one's native land receding through
The growing waters; it unmans one quite,
        Especially when life is rather new:
I recollect Great Britain's coast looks white,
        But almost every other country's blue,
95 When gazing on them, mystified by distance,
We enter on our nautical existence.

13

So Juan stood, bewildered, on the deck:
        The wind sung, cordage strained, and sailors swore,
And the ship creaked, the town became a speck,
100   From which away so fair and fast they bore.
The best of remedies is a beef-steak
        Against sea-sickness; try it, sir, before
You sneer, and I assure you this is true,
For I have found it answer—so may you.

…

100

The land appeared a high and rocky coast,
        And higher grew the mountains as they drew,
795 Set by a current, toward it: they were lost
        In various conjectures, for none knew
To what part of the earth they had been tost,
        So changeable had been the winds that blew;
Some thought it was Mount Ætna, some the highlands
800 Of Candia,[1] Cyprus, Rhodes, or other islands.

101

Meantime the current, with a rising gale,
        Still set them onwards to the welcome shore,
Like Charon's bark of spectres, dull and pale:[2]
        Their living freight was now reduced to four,
805 And three dead, whom their strength could not avail
        To heave into the deep with those before,
Though the two sharks still followed them, and dashed
The spray into their faces as they splashed.

102

Famine, despair, cold, thirst, and heat, had done
810   Their work on them by turns, and thinned them to
Such things a mother had not known her son
        Amidst the skeletons of that gaunt crew;
By night chilled, by day scorched, thus one by one
        They perished, until withered to these few,
815 But chiefly by a species of self-slaughter,
In washing down Pedrillo with salt water.

103

As they drew nigh the land, which now was seen
        Unequal in its aspect here and there,
They felt the freshness of its growing green,
820   That waved in forest-tops, and smoothed the air,
And fell upon their glazed eyes like a screen
        From glistening waves, and skies so hot and bare—
Lovely seemed any object that should sweep
Away the vast, salt, dread, eternal deep.

104

825 The shore looked wild, without a trace of man,
        And girt by formidable waves; but they
Were mad for land, and thus their course they ran,
        Though right ahead the roaring breakers lay:
A reef between them also now began
830   To show its boiling surf and bounding spray,
But finding no place for their landing better,
They ran the boat for shore,—and overset her.

105

But in his native stream, the Guadalquivir,
        Juan to lave° his youthful limbs was wont;   *wash*
835 And having learnt to swim in that sweet river,
        Had often turned the art to some account:
A better swimmer you could scarce see ever,
        He could, perhaps, have passed the Hellespont,
As once (a feat on which ourselves we prided)
840 Leander, Mr. Ekenhead, and I did.[3]

106

So here, though faint, emaciated, and stark,

---

1   *Candia*   Crete.

2   *Charon's bark … pale*   Charon ferried the souls of the newly dead across the river Acheron in Hades.

3   *Hellespont … did*   In imitation of the classical hero Leander, who swam across the Hellespont to reach his lover, Byron swam the Hellespont on 3 May 1810, accompanied by Lieutenant Ekenhead of the Marines. See Byron's "Written after Swimming from Sestos to Abydos."

He buoyed his boyish limbs, and strove to ply
With the quick wave, and gain, ere it was dark,
   The beach which lay before him, high and dry:
845   The greatest danger here was from a shark,
   That carried off his neighbour by the thigh;
As for the other two they could not swim,
So nobody arrived on shore but him.

107

Nor yet had he arrived but for the oar,
850   Which, providentially for him, was washed
Just as his feeble arms could strike no more,
   And the hard wave o'erwhelmed him as 'twas dashed
Within his grasp; he clung to it, and sore
   The waters beat while he thereto was lashed;
855   At last, with swimming, wading, scrambling, he
Rolled on the beach, half-senseless, from the sea.

108

There, breathless, with his digging nails he clung
   Fast to the sand, lest the returning wave,
From whose reluctant roar his life he wrung,
860   Should suck him back to her insatiate grave:
And there he lay, full length, where he was flung,
   Before the entrance of a cliff-worn cave,
With just enough of life to feel its pain,
And deem that it was saved, perhaps, in vain.

109

865 With slow and staggering effort he arose,
   But sunk again upon his bleeding knee
And quivering hand; and then he looked for those
   Who long had been his mates upon the sea,
But none of them appeared to share his woes,
870   Save one, a corpse from out the famished three,
Who died two days before, and now had found
An unknown barren beach for burial ground.

110

And as he gazed, his dizzy brain spun fast,
   And down he sunk; and as he sunk, the sand
875 Swam round and round, and all his senses passed:
   He fell upon his side, and his stretched hand
Drooped dripping on the oar, (their jury-mast)
   And, like a withered lily, on the land

His slender frame and pallid aspect lay,
880 As fair a thing as e'er was formed of clay.

111

How long in his damp trance young Juan lay
   He knew not, for the earth was gone for him,
And Time had nothing more of night nor day
   For his congealing blood, and senses dim;
885 And how this heavy faintness passed away
   He knew not, till each painful pulse and limb,
And tingling vein, seemed throbbing back to life,
For Death, though vanquished, still retired with strife.

112

His eyes he opened, shut, again unclosed,
890   For all was doubt and dizziness; methought
He still was in the boat, and had but dozed,
   And felt again with his despair o'erwrought,
And wished it death in which he had reposed,
   And then once more his feelings back were brought,
895 And slowly by his swimming eyes was seen
A lovely female face of seventeen.

113

'Twas bending close o'er his, and the small mouth
   Seemed almost prying into his for breath;
And chafing him, the soft warm hand of youth
900   Recalled his answering spirits back from death;
And, bathing his chill temples, tried to soothe
   Each pulse to animation, till beneath
Its gentle touch and trembling care, a sigh
To these kind efforts made a low reply.

114

905 Then was the cordial poured, and mantle flung
   Around his scarce-clad limbs; and the fair arm
Raised higher the faint head which o'er it hung;
   And her transparent cheek, all pure and warm,
Pillowed his death-like forehead; then she wrung
910   His dewy curls, long drenched by every storm;
And watched with eagerness each throb that drew
A sigh from his heaved bosom—and hers, too.

115

And lifting him with care into the cave,

The gentle girl and her attendant,—one
915   Young, yet her elder, and of brow less grave,
        And more robust of figure,—then begun
    To kindle fire, and as the new flames gave
        Light to the rocks that roofed them, which the sun
    Had never seen, the maid, or whatsoe'er
920   She was, appeared distinct, and tall, and fair.

116

Her brow was overhung with coins of gold,
    That sparkled o'er the auburn of her hair,
Her clustering hair, whose longer locks were rolled
    In braids behind, and though her stature were
925   Even of the highest for a female mould,
        They nearly reached her heel; and in her air
    There was a something which bespoke command,
    As one who was a lady in the land.

117

Her hair, I said, was auburn; but her eyes
930   Were black as death, their lashes the same hue,
Of downcast length, in whose silk shadow lies
        Deepest attraction, for when to the view
    Forth from its raven fringe the full glance flies,
        Ne'er with such force the swiftest arrow flew;
935   'Tis as the snake late coiled, who pours his length,
    And hurls at once his venom and his strength.

118

Her brow was white and low, her cheek's pure dye
    Like twilight rosy still with the set sun;
Short upper lip—sweet lips! that make us sigh
940   Ever to have seen such; for she was one
    Fit for the model of a statuary
        (A race of mere impostors, when all's done—
    I've seen much finer women, ripe and real,
    Than all the nonsense of their stone ideal).

119

945   I'll tell you why I say so, for 'tis just
        One should not rail without a decent cause:
    There was an Irish lady,[1] to whose bust
        I ne'er saw justice done, and yet she was

A frequent model; and if e'er she must
950   Yield to stern Time and Nature's wrinkling laws,
    They will destroy a face which mortal thought
    Ne'er compassed, nor less mortal chisel wrought.

120

And such was she, the lady of the cave:
    Her dress was very different from the Spanish,
955   Simpler, and yet of colours not so grave;
        For, as you know, the Spanish women banish
    Bright hues when out of doors, and yet, while wave
        Around them (what I hope will never vanish)
    The basquiña[2] and the mantilla, they
960   Seem at the same time mystical and gay.

121

But with our damsel this was not the case:
    Her dress was many-coloured, finely spun;
Her locks curled negligently round her face,
        But through them gold and gems profusely shone;
965   Her girdle sparkled, and the richest lace
        Flowed in her veil, and many a precious stone
    Flashed on her little hand; but, what was shocking
    Her small snow feet had slippers, but no stocking.

122

The other female's dress was not unlike,
970   But of inferior materials; she
    Had not so many ornaments to strike,
        Her hair had silver only, bound to be
    Her dowry; and her veil, in form alike,
        Was coarser; and her air, though firm, less free;
975   Her hair was thicker, but less long; her eyes
    As black, but quicker, and of smaller size.

123

And these two tended him, and cheered him both
        With food and raiment, and those soft attentions,
    Which are (as I must own) of female growth,
980   And have ten thousand delicate inventions:
    They made a most superior mess of broth,
        A thing which poesy but seldom mentions,
    But the best dish that e'er was cooked since Homer's

---

[1] *Irish lady* Perhaps a reference to Lady Adelaide Forbes (1798–1858), whom Byron compared to the Apollo Belvedere.

[2] *basquiña* Beautiful outer petticoat.

Achilles ordered dinner for new comers.[1]

124

985 I'll tell you who they were, this female pair,
 Lest they should seem princesses in disguise;
Besides, I hate all mystery, and that air
 Of clap-trap, which your recent poets prize;
And so, in short, the girls they really were
990 They shall appear before your curious eyes,
Mistress and maid; the first was only daughter
Of an old man, who lived upon the water.

125

A fisherman he had been in his youth,
 And still a sort of fisherman was he;
995 But other speculations were, in sooth,
 Added to his connexion with the sea,
Perhaps not so respectable, in truth:
 A little smuggling, and some piracy,
Left him, at last, the sole of many masters
1000 Of an ill-gotten million of piastres.[2]

126

A fisher, therefore, was he—though of men,
 Like Peter the Apostle,[3]—and he fished
For wandering merchant-vessels, now and then,
 And sometimes caught as many as he wished;
1005 The cargoes he confiscated, and gain
 He sought in the slave-market too, and dished
Full many a morsel for that Turkish trade,
By which, no doubt, a good deal may be made.

127

He was a Greek, and on his isle had built
1010 (One of the wild and smaller Cyclades)
A very handsome house from out his guilt,
 And there he lived exceedingly at ease;
Heaven knows what cash he got, or blood he spilt,
 A sad old fellow was he, if you please;
1015 But this I know, it was a spacious building,
Full of barbaric carving, paint, and gilding.

128

He had an only daughter, called Haidée,
 The greatest heiress of the Eastern Isles;
Besides, so very beautiful was she,
1020 Her dowry was as nothing to her smiles:
Still in her teens, and like a lovely tree
 She grew to womanhood, and between whiles
Rejected several suitors, just to learn
How to accept a better in his turn.

129

1025 And walking out upon the beach, below
 The cliff, towards sunset, on that day she found,
Insensible,—not dead, but nearly so,—
 Don Juan, almost famished, and half drowned;
But being naked, she was shocked, you know,
1030 Yet deemed herself in common pity bound,
As far as in her lay, "to take him in,
A stranger" dying, with so white a skin.

130

But taking him into her father's house
 Was not exactly the best way to save,
1035 But like conveying to the cat the mouse,
 Or people in a trance into their grave;
Because the good old man had so much "vous,"[4]
 Unlike the honest Arab thieves so brave,
He would have hospitably cured the stranger,
1040 And sold him instantly when out of danger.

131

And therefore, with her maid, she thought it best
 (A virgin always on her maid relies)
To place him in the cave for present rest:
 And when, at last, he opened his black eyes,
1045 Their charity increased about their guest;
 And their compassion grew to such a size,
It opened half the turnpike-gates to heaven—
(St. Paul says, 'tis the toll which must be given).

132

They made a fire, but such a fire as they
1050 Upon the moment could contrive with such
Materials as were cast up round the bay,

---

[1] *since Homer's ... comers* See Homer, *Iliad* 9.

[2] *piastres* Pieces of eight.

[3] *Like ... Apostle* Cf. Matthew 4.18–19.

[4] vous Intelligence, or, more cynically, cunning.

Some broken planks, and oars, that to the touch
Were nearly tinder, since so long they lay
    A mast was almost crumbled to a crutch;
1055 But, by God's grace, here wrecks were in such plenty,
That there was fuel to have furnished twenty.

133

He had a bed of furs, and a pelisse,
    For Haidée stripped her sables off to make
His couch; and, that he might be more at ease,
1060   And warm, in case by chance he should awake,
They also gave a petticoat apiece,
    She and her maid, and promised by day-break
To pay him a fresh visit, with a dish
For breakfast, of eggs, coffee, bread, and fish.

134

1065 And thus they left him to his lone repose:
    Juan slept like a top, or like the dead,
Who sleep at last, perhaps, (God only knows)
    Just for the present; and in his lulled head
Not even a vision of his former woes
1070   Throbbed in accursed dreams, which sometimes spread
Unwelcome visions of our former years,
Till the eye, cheated, opens thick with tears.

135

Young Juan slept all dreamless:—but the maid,
    Who smoothed his pillow, as she left the den
1075 Looked back upon him, and a moment staid,
    And turned, believing that he called again.
He slumbered; yet she thought, at least she said,
    (The heart will slip even as the tongue and pen)
He had pronounced her name—but she forgot
1080 That at this moment Juan knew it not.

136

And pensive to her father's house she went,
    Enjoining silence strict to Zoe, who
Better than her knew what, in fact, she meant,
    She being wiser by a year or two:
1085 A year or two's an age when rightly spent,
    And Zoe spent hers, as most women do,
In gaining all that useful sort of knowledge
Which is acquired in Nature's good old college.

137

The morn broke, and found Juan slumbering still
1090   Fast in his cave, and nothing clashed upon
His rest; the rushing of the neighbouring rill,
    And the young beams of the excluded sun,
Troubled him not, and he might sleep his fill;
    And need he had of slumber yet, for none
1095 Had suffered more—his hardships were comparative
To those related in my grand-dad's Narrative.[1]

138

Not so Haidée: she sadly tossed and tumbled,
    And started from her sleep, and, turning o'er,
Dreamed of a thousand wrecks, o'er which she stumbled,
1100   And handsome corpses strewed upon the shore;
And woke her maid so early that she grumbled,
    And called her father's old slaves up, who swore
In several oaths—Armenian, Turk, and Greek—
They knew not what to think of such a freak.

139

1105 But up she got, and up she made them get,
    With some pretence about the sun, that makes
Sweet skies just when he rises, or is set;
    And 'tis, no doubt, a sight to see when breaks
Bright Phoebus,[2] while the mountains still are wet
1110   With mist, and every bird with him awakes,
And night is flung off like a mourning suit
Worn for a husband, or some other brute.

140

I say, the sun is a most glorious sight,
    I've seen him rise full oft, indeed of late
1115 I have sat up on purpose all the night,
    Which hastens, as physicians say, one's fate;
And so all ye, who would be in the right
    In health and purse, begin your day to date
From day-break, and when coffined at fourscore,
1120 Engrave upon the plate, you rose at four.

---

[1] *Narrative* Byron's grandfather, Admiral John Byron (1723–86), was famous for encountering a storm each time he sailed, and hence was nicknamed "Foulweather Jack." In 1768 he published *Narrative of Great Distresses on the Shores of Patagonia.*

[2] *Phoebus* Phoebus Apollo, god of the sun; i.e., the sun.

141

And Haidée met the morning face to face;
    Her own was freshest, though a feverish flush
Had dyed it with the headlong blood, whose race
From heart to cheek is curbed into a blush,
1125 Like to a torrent which a mountain's base,
    That overpowers some Alpine river's rush,
Checks to a lake, whose waves in circles spread;
Or the Red Sea—but the sea is not red.

142

And down the cliff the island virgin came,
1130   And near the cave her quick light footsteps drew,
While the sun smiled on her with his first flame,
    And young Aurora[1] kissed her lips with dew,
Taking her for a sister; just the same
    Mistake you would have made on seeing the two,
1135 Although the mortal, quite as fresh and fair,
Had all the advantage, too, of not being air.

143

And when into the cavern Haidée stepped
    All timidly, yet rapidly, she saw
That like an infant Juan sweetly slept;
1140   And then she stopped, and stood as if in awe,
(For sleep is awful) and on tiptoe crept
    And wrapt him closer, lest the air, too raw,
Should reach his blood, then o'er him still as death
Bent, with hushed lips, that drank his scarce-drawn
    breath.

144

And thus like to an angel o'er the dying
1145   Who die in righteousness, she leaned; and there
All tranquilly the shipwrecked boy was lying,
    As o'er him lay the calm and stirless air:
But Zoe the meantime some eggs was frying,
1150   Since, after all, no doubt the youthful pair
Must breakfast, and betimes—lest they should ask it,
She drew out her provision from the basket.

145

She knew that the best feelings must have victual,
    And that a shipwrecked youth would hungry be;

1155 Besides, being less in love, she yawned a little,
    And felt her veins chilled by the neighbouring sea;
And so, she cooked their breakfast to a tittle;
    I can't say that she gave them any tea,
But there were eggs, fruit, coffee, bread, fish, honey,
1160 With Scio wine,—and all for love, not money.

146

And Zoe, when the eggs were ready, and
    The coffee made, would fain have wakened Juan;
But Haidée stopped her with her quick small hand,
    And without word, a sign her finger drew on
1165 Her lip, which Zoe needs must understand;
    And, the first breakfast spoilt, prepared a new one
Because her mistress would not let her break
That sleep which seemed as it would ne'er awake.

147

For still he lay, and on his thin worn cheek
1170   A purple hectic played like dying day
On the snow-tops of distant hills; the streak
    Of sufferance yet upon his forehead lay,
Where the blue veins looked shadowy, shrunk, and
    weak;
    And his black curls were dewy with the spray,
1175 Which weighed upon them yet, all damp and salt,
Mixed with the stony vapours of the vault.

148

And she bent o'er him, and he lay beneath,
    Hushed as the babe upon its mother's breast,
Drooped as the willow when no winds can breathe,
1180   Lulled like the depth of ocean when at rest,
Fair as the crowning rose of the whole wreath,
    Soft as the callow cygnet in its nest;
In short, he was a very pretty fellow,
Although his woes had turned him rather yellow.

149

1185 He woke and gazed, and would have slept again,
    But the fair face which met his eyes forbade
Those eyes to close, though weariness and pain
    Had further sleep a further pleasure made;
For woman's face was never formed in vain
1190   For Juan, so that even when he prayed

---

[1] *Aurora* Goddess of the dawn.

He turned from grisly saints, and martyrs hairy,
To the sweet portraits of the Virgin Mary.

150

And thus upon his elbow he arose,
    And looked upon the lady, in whose cheek
1195 The pale contended with the purple rose,
    As with an effort she began to speak;
Her eyes were eloquent, her words would pose,
    Although she told him, in good modern Greek,
With an Ionian accent, low and sweet,
1200 That he was faint, and must not talk, but eat.

151

Now Juan could not understand a word,
    Being no Grecian; but he had an ear,
And her voice was the warble of a bird,
    So soft, so sweet, so delicately clear,
1205 That finer, simpler music ne'er was heard;
    The sort of sound we echo with a tear,
Without knowing why—an overpowering tone,
Whence Melody descends as from a throne.

152

And Juan gazed as one who is awoke
1210 By a distant organ, doubting if he be
Not yet a dreamer, till the spell is broke
    By the watchman, or some such reality,
Or by one's early valet's cursed knock;
    At least it is a heavy sound to me,
1215 Who like a morning slumber—for the night
Shows stars and women in a better light.

153

And Juan, too, was helped out from his dream,
    Or sleep, or whatso'er it was, by feeling
A most prodigious appetite: the steam
1220   Of Zoe's cookery no doubt was stealing
Upon his senses, and the kindling beam
    Of the new fire, which Zoe kept up, kneeling
To stir her viands, made him quite awake
And long for food, but chiefly a beef-steak.

154

1225 But beef is rare within these oxless isles;
    Goat's flesh there is, no doubt, and kid, and mutton;

And, when a holiday upon them smiles,
    A joint upon their barbarous spits they put on;
But this occurs but seldom, between whiles,
1230   For some of these are rocks with scarce a hut on;
Others are fair and fertile, among which
This, though not large, was one of the most rich.

155

I say that beef is rare, and can't help thinking
    That the old fable of the Minotaur—
1235 From which our modern morals, rightly shrinking,
    Condemn the royal lady's taste who wore
A cow's shape for a mask—was only (sinking
    The allegory) a mere type, no more,
That Pasiphae promoted breeding cattle,
1240 To make the Cretans bloodier in battle.[1]

156

For we all know that English people are
    Fed upon beef—I won't say much of beer,
Because 'tis liquor only, and being far
    From this my subject, has no business here;
1245 We know, too, they are very fond of war,
    A pleasure—like all pleasures—rather dear;
So were the Cretans—from which I infer
That beef and battles both were owing to her.

157

But to resume. The languid Juan raised
1250   His head upon his elbow, and he saw
A sight on which he had not lately gazed,
    As all his latter meals had been quite raw,
Three or four things, for which the Lord he praised,
    And, feeling still the famished vulture gnaw,[2]
1255 He fell upon whate'er was offered, like
    A priest, a shark, an alderman, or pike.

---

[1] *Minotaur ... battle* Pasiphaë, Queen of Crete, lusted after a bull sent by Poseidon. To fulfill her desires, she had herself enclosed in a hollow model of a cow to mate with the bull. She gave birth to the Minotaur, a creature with the body of a man and the head of a bull. Her husband Minos imprisoned the monster in a labyrinth built by Daedalus.

[2] *feeling still ... gnaw* Jove sent an eagle to gnaw the vitals (guts) of Prometheus, chained to a mountainside.

158

He ate, and he was well supplied; and she,
    Who watched him like a mother, would have fed
Him past all bounds, because she smiled to see
1260   Such appetite in one she had deemed dead;
But Zoe, being older than Haidée,
    Knew (by tradition, for she ne'er had read)
That famished people must be slowly nurst,
And fed by spoonfuls, else they always burst.

159

1265 And so she took the liberty to state,
    Rather by deeds than words, because the case
Was urgent, that the gentleman, whose fate
    Had made her mistress quit her bed to trace
The sea-shore at this hour, must leave his plate,
1270   Unless he wished to die upon the place—
She snatched it, and refused another morsel,
Saying, he had gorged enough to make a horse ill.

160

Next they—he being naked, save a tattered
    Pair of scarce decent trousers—went to work,
1275 And in the fire his recent rags they scatterd,
    And dressed him, for the present, like a Turk,
Or Greek—that is, although it not much mattered,
    Omitting turban, slippers, pistols, dirk,—
They furnished him, entire except some stitches,
1280 With a clean shirt, and very spacious breeches.[1]

161

And then fair Haidée tried her tongue at speaking,
    But not a word could Juan comprehend,
Although he listened so that the young Greek in
    Her earnestness would ne'er have made an end;
1285 And, as he interrupted not, went eking
    Her speech out to her protegé and friend,
Till pausing at the last her breath to take,
She saw he did not understand Romaic.[2]

162

And then she had recourse to nods, and signs,
1290   And smiles, and sparkles of the speaking eye,
And read (the only book she could) the lines
    Of his fair face, and found, by sympathy,
The answer eloquent, where the soul shines
    And darts in one quick glance a long reply;
1295 And thus in every look she saw exprest
A world of words, and things at which she guessed.

163

And now, by dint of fingers and of eyes,
    And words repeated after her, he took
A lesson in her tongue; but by surmise,
1300   No doubt, less of her language than her look:
As he who studies fervently the skies
    Turns oftener to the stars than to his book,
Thus Juan learned his alpha beta better
From Haidée's glance than any graven letter.

164

1305 'Tis pleasing to be schooled in a strange tongue
    By female lips and eyes—that is, I mean,
When both the teacher and the taught are young,
    As was the case, at least, where I have been;
They smile so when one's right, and when one's wrong
1310   They smile still more, and then there intervene
Pressure of hands, perhaps even a chaste kiss;—
I learned the little that I know by this:

165

That is, some words of Spanish, Turk, and Greek,
    Italian not at all, having no teachers;
1315 Much English I cannot pretend to speak,
    Learning that language chiefly from its preachers,
Barrow, South, Tillotson, whom every week
    I study, also Blair,[3] the highest reachers
Of eloquence in piety and prose—
1320 I hate your poets, so read none of those.

166

As for the ladies, I have nought to say,
    A wanderer from the British world of fashion,
Where I, like other "dogs, have had my day,"[4]

---

[1] *breeches* Pronounced "britches."
[2] *Romaic* Modern Greek.

[3] *Barrow* Isaac Barrow (1630–77); *South* Robert South (1634–1716); *Tillotson* John Tillotson (1630–94); *Blair* Hugh Blair (1718–1800); British preachers.
[4] *dogs ... day* See Shakespeare, *Hamlet* 5.1.279.

Like other men, too, may have had my passion—
1325 But that, like other things, has passed away,
    And all her fools whom I *could* lay the lash on,
Foes, friends, men, women, now are nought to me
    But dreams of what has been, no more to be.

167

Return we to Don Juan. He begun
1330   To hear new words, and to repeat them; but
Some feelings, universal as the sun,
    Were such as could not in his breast be shut
More than within the bosom of a nun:
    He was in love,—as you would be, no doubt,
1335 With a young benefactress—so was she,
Just in the way we very often see.

168

And every day by day-break—rather early
    For Juan, who was somewhat fond of rest—
She came into the cave, but it was merely
1340   To see her bird reposing in his nest;
And she would softly stir his locks so curly,
    Without disturbing her yet slumbering guest,
Breathing all gently o'er his cheek and mouth,
As o'er a bed of roses the sweet south.

169

1345 And every morn his colour freshlier came,
    And every day helped on his convalescence;
'Twas well, because health in the human frame
    Is pleasant, besides being true love's essence,
For health and idleness to passion's flame
1350   Are oil and gunpowder; and some good lessons
Are also learnt from Ceres and from Bacchus,[1]
    Without whom Venus will not long attack us.

170

While Venus fills the heart (without heart really
    Love, though good always, is not quite so good),
1355 Ceres presents a plate of vermicelli,—
    For love must be sustained like flesh and blood,—
While Bacchus pours out wine, or hands a jelly:

Eggs, oysters, too, are amatory food;
    But who is their purveyor from above
1360 Heaven knows,—it may be Neptune, Pan, or Jove.

171

When Juan woke he found some good things ready,
    A bath, a breakfast, and the finest eyes
That ever made a youthful heart less steady,
    Besides her maid's, as pretty for their size;
1365 But I have spoken of all this already—
    And repetition's tiresome and unwise,—
Well—Juan, after bathing in the sea,
Came always back to coffee and Haidée.

172

Both were so young, and one so innocent,
1370   That bathing passed for nothing; Juan seemed
To her, as 'twere, the kind of being sent,
    Of whom these two years she had nightly dreamed,
A something to be loved, a creature meant
    To be her happiness, and whom she deemed
1375 To render happy; all who joy would win
Must share it,—Happiness was born a twin.

173

It was such pleasure to behold him, such
    Enlargement of existence to partake
Nature with him, to thrill beneath his touch,
1380   To watch him slumbering, and to see him wake:
To live with him forever were too much;
    But then the thought of parting made her quake:
He was her own, her ocean-treasure, cast
Like a rich wreck—her first love, and her last.

174

1385 And thus a moon rolled on, and fair Haidée
    Paid daily visits to her boy, and took
Such plentiful precautions, that still he
    Remained unknown within his craggy nook;
At last her father's prows put out to sea,
1390   For certain merchantmen upon the look,
Not as of yore to carry off an Io,[2]
But three Ragusan vessels, bound for Scio.

---

[1] *Ceres* Ceres, or Demeter, was the goddess of agriculture; *Bacchus* God of wine.

[2] *Io* A nymph spirited away by Zeus.

175

Then came her freedom, for she had no mother,
　　So that, her father being at sea, she was
1395 Free as a married woman, or such other
　　Female, as where she likes may freely pass,
Without even the incumbrance of a brother,
　　The freest she that ever gazed on glass:
I speak of Christian lands in this comparison,
1400 Where wives, at least, are seldom kept in garrison.

176

Now she prolonged her visits and her talk
　　(For they must talk), and he had learnt to say
So much as to propose to take a walk,—
　　For little had he wandered since the day
1405 On which, like a young flower snapped from the stalk,
　　Drooping and dewy on the beach he lay,—
And thus they walked out in the afternoon,
And saw the sun set opposite the moon.

177

It was a wild and breaker-beaten coast,
1410 　　With cliffs above, and a broad sandy shore,
Guarded by shoals and rocks as by an host,
　　With here and there a creek, whose aspect wore
A better welcome to the tempest-tost;
　　And rarely ceased the haughty billow's roar,
1415 Save on the dead long summer days, which make
The outstretched ocean glitter like a lake.

178

And the small ripple spilt upon the beach
　　Scarcely o'erpassed the cream of your champagne,
When o'er the brim the sparkling bumpers reach,
1420 　　That spring-dew of the spirit! the heart's rain!
Few things surpass old wine; and they may preach
　　Who please,—the more because they preach in
　　　　vain,—
Let us have wine and woman, mirth and laughter,
Sermons and soda-water the day after.

179

1425 Man, being reasonable, must get drunk;
　　The best of life is but intoxication:
Glory, the grape, love, gold, in these are sunk
　　The hopes of all men, and of every nation;

Without their sap, how branchless were the trunk
1430 　　Of life's strange tree, so fruitful on occasion:
But to return,—Get very drunk; and when
You wake with headache, you shall see what then.

180

Ring for your valet—bid him quickly bring
　　Some hock[1] and soda-water, then you'll know
1435 A pleasure worthy Xerxes the great king;
　　For not the blest sherbet, sublimed with snow,
Nor the first sparkle of the desert-spring,
　　Nor Burgundy in all its sunset glow,
After long travel, ennui, love, or slaughter,
1440 Vie with that draught of hock and soda-water.

181

The coast—I think it was the coast that I
　　Was just describing—Yes, it *was* the coast—
Lay at this period quiet as the sky,
　　The sands untumbled, the blue waves untost,
1445 And all was stillness, save the sea-bird's cry,
　　And dolphin's leap, and little billow crost
By some low rock or shelve, that made it fret
Against the boundary it scarcely wet.

182

And forth they wandered, her sire being gone,
1450 　　As I have said, upon an expedition;
And mother, brother, guardian, she had none,
　　Save Zoe, who, although with due precision
She waited on her lady with the sun,
　　Thought daily service was her only mission,
1455 Bringing warm water, wreathing her long tresses,
And asking now and then for cast-off dresses.

183

It was the cooling hour, just when the rounded
　　Red sun sinks down behind the azure hill,
Which then seems as if the whole earth it bounded,
1460 　　Circling all nature, hushed, and dim, and still,
With the far mountain-crescent half surrounded
　　On one side, and the deep sea calm and chill
Upon the other, and the rosy sky,
With one star sparkling through it like an eye.

---

[1]   *hock*   Wine from the area of Hochheim in Germany.

184

1465 And thus they wandered forth, and hand in hand,[1]
    Over the shining pebbles and the shells,
Glided along the smooth and hardened sand,
    And in the worn and wild receptacles
Worked by the storms, yet worked as it were planned,
1470   In hollow halls, with sparry roofs and cells,
They turned to rest; and, each clasped by an arm,
Yielded to the deep twilight's purple charm.

185

They looked up to the sky, whose floating glow
    Spread like a rosy ocean, vast and bright;
1475 They gazed upon the glittering sea below,
    Whence the broad moon rose circling into sight;
They heard the wave's splash, and the wind so low,
    And saw each other's dark eyes darting light
Into each other—and, beholding this,
1480 Their lips drew near, and clung into a kiss;

186

A long, long kiss, a kiss of youth, and love,
    And beauty, all concentrating like rays
Into one focus, kindled from above;
    Such kisses as belong to early days,
1485 Where heart, and soul, and sense, in concert move,
    And the blood's lava, and the pulse a blaze,
Each kiss a heart-quake,—for a kiss's strength,
I think, it must be reckoned by its length.

187

By length I mean duration; theirs endured
1490   Heaven knows how long—no doubt they never reckoned;
And if they had, they could not have secured
    The sum of their sensations to a second:
They had not spoken; but they felt allured,
    As if their souls and lips each other beckoned,
1495 Which, being joined, like swarming bees they clung—
Their hearts the flowers from whence the honey sprung.

188

They were alone, but not alone as they
    Who shut in chambers think it loneliness;
The silent ocean, and the starlight bay,
1500   The twilight glow, which momently grew less,
The voiceless sands, and dropping caves, that lay
    Around them, made them to each other press,
As if there were no life beneath the sky
Save theirs, and that their life could never die.

189

1505 They feared no eyes nor ears on that lone beach,
    They felt no terrors from the night, they were
All in all to each other: though their speech
    Was broken words, they *thought* a language there,—
And all the burning tongues the passions teach
1510   Found in one sigh the best interpreter
Of nature's oracle—first love,—that all
Which Eve has left her daughters since her fall.

190

Haidée spoke not of scruples, asked no vows,
    Nor offered any; she had never heard
1515 Of plight and promises to be a spouse,
    Or perils by a loving maid incurred;
She was all which pure ignorance allows,
    And flew to her young mate like a young bird;
And, never having dreamt of falsehood, she
1520 Had not one word to say of constancy.

191

She loved, and was beloved—she adored,
    And she was worshipped; after nature's fashion,
Their intense souls, into each other poured,
    If souls could die, had perished in that passion,—
1525 But by degrees their senses were restored,
    Again to be o'ercome, again to dash on;
And, beating 'gainst *his* bosom, Haidée's heart
Felt as if never more to beat apart.

192

Alas! they were so young, so beautiful,
1530   So lonely, loving, helpless, and the hour
Was that in which the heart is always full,
    And, having o'er itself no further power,
Prompts deeds eternity can not annul,
    But pays off moments in an endless shower
1535 Of hell-fire—all prepared for people giving
Pleasure or pain to one another living.

---

[1] *They wandered … hand* Cf. Milton, *Paradise Lost* 12.645–49.

193

Alas! for Juan and Haidée! they were
　　So loving and so lovely—till then never,
Excepting our first parents, such a pair
　　Had run the risk of being damn'd for ever;
And Haidée, being devout as well as fair,
　　Had, doubtless, heard about the Stygian river,[1]
And hell and purgatory—but forgot
Just in the very crisis she should not.

194

They look upon each other, and their eyes
　　Gleam in the moonlight; and her white arm clasps
Round Juan's head, and his around her lies
　　Half buried in the tresses which it grasps;
She sits upon his knee, and drinks his sighs,
　　He hers, until they end in broken gasps;
And thus they form a group that's quite antique,
Half naked, loving, natural, and Greek.

195

And when those deep and burning moments passed
　　And Juan sunk to sleep within her arms,
She slept not, but all tenderly, though fast,
　　Sustained his head upon her bosom's charms;
And now and then her eye to heaven is cast,
　　And then on the pale cheek her breast now warms,
Pillowed on her o'erflowing heart, which pants
With all it granted, and with all it grants.

196

An infant when it gazes on a light,
　　A child the moment when it drains the breast,
A devotee when soars the Host in sight,
　　An Arab with a stranger for a guest,
A sailor when the prize has struck in fight,
　　A miser filling his most hoarded chest,
Feel rapture; but not such true joy are reaping
As they who watch o'er what they love while sleeping.

197

For there it lies so tranquil, so beloved,
　　All that it hath of life with us is living;
So gentle, stirless, helpless, and unmoved,

And all unconscious of the joy 'tis giving;
　　All it hath felt, inflicted, passed, and proved,
　　Hushed into depths beyond the watcher's diving;
There lies the thing we love with all its errors
And all its charms, like death without its terrors.

198

The lady watched her lover—and that hour
　　Of Love's, and Night's, and Ocean's solitude,
O'erflowed her soul with their united power;
　　Amidst the barren sand and rocks so rude
She and her wave-worn love had made their bower,
　　Where nought upon their passion could intrude,
And all the stars that crowded the blue space
Saw nothing happier than her glowing face.

199

Alas! the love of women! it is known
　　To be a lovely and a fearful thing;
For all of theirs upon that die is thrown,
　　And if 'tis lost, life hath no more to bring
To them but mockeries of the past alone,
　　And their revenge is as the tiger's spring,
Deadly, and quick, and crushing; yet, as real
Torture is theirs, what they inflict they feel.

200

They are right; for man, to man so oft unjust,
　　Is always so to women; one sole bond
Awaits them, treachery is all their trust;
　　Taught to conceal, their bursting hearts despond
Over their idol, till some wealthier lust
　　Buys them in marriage—and what rests beyond?
A thankless husband, next a faithless lover,
Then dressing, nursing, praying, and all's over.

201

Some take a lover, some take drams or prayers,
　　Some mind their household, others dissipation,
Some run away, and but exchange their cares,
　　Losing the advantage of a virtuous station;
Few changes e'er can better their affairs,
　　Theirs being an unnatural situation,

---

[1] *Stygian river*   River Styx, in Hades.

From the dull palace to the dirty hovel:
Some play the devil, and then write a novel.[1]

202

Haidée was Nature's bride, and knew not this;
    Haidée was Passion's child, born where the sun
Showers triple light, and scorches even the kiss
    Of his gazelle-eyed daughters; she was one
Made but to love, to feel that she was his
    Who was her chosen: what was said or done
Elsewhere was nothing—She had nought to fear,
Hope, care, nor love beyond, her heart beat *here*.

203

And oh! that quickening of the heart, that beat!
    How much it costs us! yet each rising throb
Is in its cause as its effect so sweet,
    That Wisdom, ever on the watch to rob
Joy of its alchymy, and to repeat
    Fine truths; even Conscience, too, has a tough job
To make us understand each good old maxim,
So good—I wonder Castlereagh don't tax 'em.

204

And now 't was done—on the lone shore were plighted
    Their hearts; the stars, their nuptial torches, shed
Beauty upon the beautiful they lighted:
    Ocean their witness, and the cave their bed,
By their own feelings hallowed and united,
    Their priest was Solitude, and they were wed:
And they were happy, for to their young eyes
Each was an angel, and earth paradise.

205

Oh, Love! of whom great Caesar was the suitor,
    Titus the master, Antony the slave,[2]
Horace, Catullus, scholars, Ovid tutor,[3]

Sappho the sage blue-stocking, in whose grave
All those may leap who rather would be neuter—[4]
    (Leucadia's rock still overlooks the wave)
Oh, Love! thou art the very god of evil,
For, after all, we cannot call thee devil.

206

Thou mak'st the chaste connubial state precarious,
    And jestest with the brows of mightiest men:
Caesar and Pompey, Mahomet, Belisarius[5]
    Have much employed the muse of history's pen;
Their lives and fortunes were extremely various,
    Such worthies Time will never see again;
Yet to these four in three things the same luck holds,
They all were heroes, conquerors, and cuckolds.

207

Thou mak'st philosophers; there's Epicurus
    And Aristippus,[6] a material crew!
Who to immoral courses would allure us
    By theories quite practicable too;
If only from the devil they would insure us,
    How pleasant were the maxim, (not quite new)
"Eat, drink, and love, what can the rest avail us?"
So said the royal sage Sardanapalus.[7]

208

But Juan! had he quite forgotten Julia?
    And should he have forgotten her so soon?
I can't but say it seems to me most truly a
    Perplexing question; but, no doubt, the moon
Does these things for us, and whenever newly a

---

[1] *write a novel* Byron's former lover, Lady Caroline Lamb, published *Glenarvon*, a roman-à-clef about their relationship, in 1816. Byron's comment on the book was, "I read 'Glenarvon,' too, by Caro. Lamb / *God damn*!"

[2] *great Caesar ... slave* Caesar and Antony were lovers of Cleopatra. Titus mastered his passion for Berenice, sending her away.

[3] *tutor* Because of his didactic poem, *Ars Amatoria* (*The Art of Love*).

[4] *Sappho ... neuter* An allusion to the legend of Sappho's suicide; *neuter* is a reference to her lesbianism.

[5] *Caesar ... Belisarius* Julius Caesar divorced his third wife, Pompeia, apparently for attempted adultery. Pompey divorced his third wife, Mucia, for committing adultery with Caesar. Mohammed's favourite wife, Ayesha, was suspected of impropriety, but he received a divine revelation of her purity. Antonina, the wife of Justinian's great general Belisarius, had several lovers before she married him.

[6] *Epicurus* (342–270 BCE) Greek philosopher; *Aristippus* (c. 370 BCE), pupil of Socrates. Byron thinks of them (unfairly in the case of Epicurus) as advocating the unrestrained pursuit of pleasure.

[7] *Sardanapalus* A famously sybaritic Assyrian king. Byron wrote a tragedy about him in 1821.

Strong palpitation rises, 'tis her boon,
Else how the devil is it that fresh features
Have such a charm for us poor human creatures?

209

1665 I hate inconstancy—I loathe, detest,
Abhor, condemn, abjure the mortal made
Of such quicksilver clay that in his breast
No permanent foundation can be laid;
Love, constant love, has been my constant guest,
1670 And yet last night, being at a masquerade,
I saw the prettiest creature, fresh from Milan,
Which gave me some sensations like a villain.

210

But soon Philosophy came to my aid,
And whispered "think of every sacred tie!"
1675 "I will, my dear Philosophy!" I said,
"But then her teeth, and then, Oh heaven! her eye!
I'll just inquire if she be wife or maid,
Or neither—out of curiosity."
"Stop!" cried Philosophy, with air so Grecian,
1680 (Though she was masqued then as a fair Venetian.)

211

"Stop!" so I stopped.—But to return: that which
Men call inconstancy is nothing more
Than admiration due where nature's rich
Profusion with young beauty covers o'er
1685 Some favoured object; and as in the niche
A lovely statue we almost adore,
This sort of adoration of the real
Is but a heightening of the "beau ideal."[1]

212

'Tis the perception of the beautiful,
1690 A fine extension of the faculties,
Platonic, universal, wonderful,
Drawn from the stars, and filtered through the skies,
Without which life would be extremely dull;
In short, it is the use of our own eyes,
1695 With one or two small senses added, just
To hint that flesh is formed of fiery dust.

213

Yet 'tis a painful feeling, and unwilling,
For surely if we always could perceive
In the same object graces quite as killing
1700 As when she rose upon us like an Eve,
'Twould save us many a heartache, many a shilling,
(For we must get them any how, or grieve)
Whereas if one sole lady pleased for ever,
How pleasant for the heart, as well as liver!

214

1705 The heart is like the sky, a part of heaven,
But changes night and day too, like the sky;
Now o'er it clouds and thunder must be driven,
And darkness and destruction as on high:
But when it hath been scorched, and pierced, and riven,
1710 Its storms expire in water-drops; the eye
Pours forth at last the heart's-blood turned to tears,
Which make the English climate of our years.

215

The liver is the lazaret[2] of bile,
But very rarely executes its function,
1715 For the first passion stays there such a while,
That all the rest creep in and form a junction,
Like knots of vipers on a dunghill's soil,
Rage, fear, hate, jealousy, revenge, compunction,
So that all mischiefs spring up from this entrail,
1720 Like earthquakes from the hidden fire called "central."

216

In the mean time, without proceeding more
In this anatomy, I've finished now
Two hundred and odd stanzas as before,
That being about the number I'll allow
1725 Each canto of the twelve, or twenty-four;
And, laying down my pen, I make my bow,
Leaving Don Juan and Haidée to plead
For them and theirs with all who deign to read.

---

1 *beau ideal* French: ideal beauty.

2 *lazaret* Hospital for those with infectious diseases, particularly leprosy.

from *Canto 3*

In this canto, Haidée takes Juan to the palace of her absent father, the fierce pirate Lambro (see Canto 1.174–75, above). He returns home to find them feasting, entertained by a bard. In the figure of the bard (who "lied with such a fervour of intention / There was no doubt he earned his laureate pension"), Byron again parodies Robert Southey, but he also mocks himself (see stanzas 84–85), and all poets. Byron's own fervent commitment to the cause of a free Greece finds expression in the poet's song.

1

Hail, Muse! *et cetera.*—We left Juan sleeping,
    Pillowed upon a fair and happy breast,
And watched by eyes that never yet knew weeping,
    And loved by a young heart, too deeply blest
5 To feel the poison through her spirit creeping,
    Or know who rested there; a foe to rest,
Had soiled the current of her sinless years,
And turned her pure heart's purest blood to tears!

2

Oh, Love! what is it in this world of ours
10   Which makes it fatal to be loved? Ah why
With cypress[1] branches hast thou wreathed thy bowers,
    And made thy best interpreter a sigh?
As those who dote on odours pluck the flowers,
    And place them on their breast—but place to die—
15 Thus the frail beings we would fondly cherish
Are laid within our bosoms but to perish.

3

In her first passion woman loves her lover,
    In all the others all she loves is love,
Which grows a habit she can ne'er get over,
20   And fits her loosely—like an easy glove,
As you may find, whene'er you like to prove her:
    One man alone at first her heart can move;
She then prefers him in the plural number,
Not finding that the additions much encumber.

4

25 I know not if the fault be men's or theirs;
    But one thing's pretty sure; a woman planted—
(Unless at once she plunge for life in prayers)—
    After a decent time must be gallanted;
Although, no doubt, her first of love affairs
30   Is that to which her heart is wholly granted;
Yet there are some, they say, who have had *none,*
But those who have ne'er end with only *one.*

5

Tis melancholy, and a fearful sign
    Of human frailty, folly, also crime,
35 That love and marriage rarely can combine,
    Although they both are born in the same clime;
Marriage from love, like vinegar from wine—
    A sad, sour, sober beverage—by time
Is sharpened from its high celestial flavour
40 Down to a very homely household savour.

6

There's something of antipathy, as 'twere,
    Between their present and their future state;
A kind of flattery that's hardly fair
    Is used until the truth arrives too late—
45 Yet what can people do, except despair?
    The same things change their names at such a rate;
For instance—passion in a lover's glorious,
But in a husband is pronounced uxorious.

7

Men grow ashamed of being so very fond;
50   They sometimes also get a little tired
(But that, of course, is rare), and then despond:
    The same things cannot always be admired,
Yet 'tis "so nominated in the bond,"[2]
    That both are tied till one shall have expired.
55 Sad thought! to lose the spouse that was adorning
Our days, and put one's servants into mourning.

8

There's doubtless something in domestic doings
    Which forms, in fact, true love's antithesis;

---

[1] *cypress* Tree traditionally symbolic of mourning.

[2] *Yet ... the bond* From Shakespeare's *The Merchant of Venice* 4.1.254. Byron here uses "bond" to mean "marriage bond."

Romances paint at full length people's wooings,
60   But only give a bust of marriages;[1]
For no one cares for matrimonial cooings,
        There's nothing wrong in a connubial kiss:
Think you, if Laura had been Petrarch's wife,
He would have written sonnets all his life?[2]

9

65 All tragedies are finished by a death,
        All comedies are ended by a marriage;
The future states of both are left to faith,
        For authors fear description might disparage
The worlds to come of both, or fall beneath,
70   And then both worlds would punish their
                miscarriage;
So leaving each their priest and prayer-book ready,
They say no more of Death or of the Lady.[3]
…

70

Of all the dresses I select Haidée's:
        She wore two jelicks[4]—one was of pale yellow;
555 Of azure, pink, and white was her chemise—
        'Neath which her breast heaved like a little billow;
With buttons formed of pearls as large as peas,
        All gold and crimson shone her jelick's fellow,
And the striped white gauze baracan[5] that bound her,
560 Like fleecy clouds about the moon, flowed round her.

71

One large gold bracelet clasped each lovely arm,
        Lockless—so pliable from the pure gold
That the hand stretched and shut it without harm,
        The limb which it adorned its only mould;

So beautiful—its very shape would charm,
565   And clinging as if loath to lose its hold,
The purest ore enclosed the whitest skin
That e'er by precious metal was held in.

72

Around, as princess of her father's land,
570   A like gold bar above her instep rolled
Announced her rank; twelve rings were on her hand;
        Her hair was starred with gems; her veil's fine fold
Below her breast was fastened with a band
        Of lavish pearls, whose worth could scarce be told;
575 Her orange silk full Turkish trousers furled
About the prettiest ankle in the world.

73

Her hair's long auburn waves down to her heel
        Flowed like an Alpine torrent which the sun
Dyes with his morning light,—and would conceal
580   Her person if allowed at large to run,
And still they seem resentfully to feel
        The silken fillet's° curb, and sought to   *thin headband*
            shun
Their bonds whene'er some Zephyr[6] caught began
To offer his young pinion as her fan.

74

585 Round her she made an atmosphere of life,
        The very air seemed lighter from her eyes,
They were so soft and beautiful, and rife
        With all we can imagine of the skies,
And pure as Psyche ere she grew a wife—
590   Too pure even for the purest human ties;
Her overpowering presence made you feel
It would not be idolatry to kneel.

75

Her eyelashes, though dark as night, were tinged
        (It is the country's custom), but in vain;
595 For those large black eyes were so blackly fringed,
        The glossy rebels mocked the jetty stain,
And in their native beauty stood avenged:
        Her nails were touched with henna; but again
The power of art was turned to nothing, for
600 They could not look more rosy than before.

---

1   *Romances … marriages*   Romances detail all of courtship (as a full-length portrait does a person), but only mention marriage briefly (as a sculpted bust cuts off a person).

2   *Think … life*   Petrarch (Francesco Petrarca, 1304–74), the Italian poet, fell passionately in love with a woman named Laura, who was already married. He wrote a series of sonnets in praise of her.

3   *Death … Lady*   In the ballad *Death and the Lady*, Death demands the life of the Lady, despite her pleas. The ballad's conclusion asserts that the only hope for salvation is to have lived a moral life.

4   *jelick*   Bodice worn by Turkish women.

5   *baracan*   Byron means a veil of delicate material, but he uses the word incorrectly. The actual definition is a woolly garment.

6   *Zephyr*   Wind. Zephyrus was the Greek god of the west wind.

76

The henna should be deeply dyed to make
    The skin relieved appear more fairly fair;
She had no need of this, day ne'er will break
    On mountain tops more heavenly white than her:
605 The eye might doubt if it were well awake,
    She was so like a vision; I might err,
But Shakespeare also says 'tis very silly
"To gild refined gold, or paint the lily."[1]

77

Juan had on a shawl of black and gold,
610   But a white baracan, and so transparent
The sparkling gems beneath you might behold,
    Like small stars through the milky way apparent;
His turban, furled in many a graceful fold,
    An emerald aigrette[2] with Haidée's hair in't
615 Surmounted, as its clasp, a glowing crescent,
Whose rays shone ever trembling, but incessant.

78

And now they were diverted by their suite,
    Dwarfs, dancing girls, black eunuchs, and a poet,
Which made their new establishment complete;
620   The last was of great fame, and liked to show it:
His verses rarely wanted their due feet—
    And for his theme—he seldom sung below it,
He being paid to satirise or flatter,
As the psalm says, "inditing a good matter."[3]

79

625 He praised the present, and abused the past,
    Reversing the good custom of old days,
An Eastern Anti-Jacobin[4] at last
    He turned, preferring pudding to *no* praise—
For some few years his lot had been o'ercast
630   By his seeming independent in his lays,

But now he sung the Sultan and the Pacha[5]
With truth like Southey, and with verse like Crashaw.[6]

80

He was a man who had seen many changes,
    And always changed as true as any needle;[7]
635 His polar star being one which rather ranges,
    And not the fixed—he knew the way to wheedle:
So vile he 'scaped the doom which oft avenges;
    And being fluent (save indeed when feed ill),
He lied with such a fervour of intention—
640 There was no doubt he earned his laureate pension.

81

But he had genius,—when a turncoat has it,
    The "Vates irritabilis"[8] takes care
That without notice few full moons shall pass it;
    Even good men like to make the public stare:—
645 But to my subject—let me see—what was it?—
    Oh!—the third canto—and the pretty pair—
Their loves, and feasts, and house, and dress, and mode
Of living in their insular abode.

82

Their poet, a sad trimmer, but no less
650   In company a very pleasant fellow,
Had been the favourite of full many a mess
    Of men, and made them speeches when half mellow;
And though his meaning they could rarely guess,
    Yet still they deigned to hiccup or to bellow
655 The glorious meed of popular applause,
Of which the first ne'er knows the second cause.

83

But now being lifted into high society,
    And having picked up several odds and ends
Of free thoughts in his travels for variety,
660   He deemed, being in a lone isle, among friends,
That without any danger of a riot, he

---

[1] *To gild ... the lily* See Shakespeare's *King John* 4.2.11.

[2] *aigrette* Ornament worn on the head, consisting of gems clasping a spray of feathers. In this case, it seems, the piece incorporates some of Haidée's hair.

[3] *As the psalm ... matter* See Psalm 45.1.

[4] *Anti-Jacobin* The Anti-Jacobins fought against subversive thought brought into England after the French Revolution, urging the English to maintain conservative standards and institutions.

[5] *Pacha* In Turkey, a man of high rank or office. Usually spelt Pasha.

[6] *Crashaw* Richard Crashaw (1613–49), a poet then widely judged to have written verse of uneven quality.

[7] *needle* Compass needle.

[8] *Vates irritabilis* Latin: the irritability of men of genius.

Might for long lying make himself amends;
    And singing as he sung in his warm youth,
Agree to a short armistice with truth.

84

665 He had travelled 'mongst the Arabs, Turks, and Franks,
        And knew the self-loves of the different nations;
    And having lived with people of all ranks,
        Had something ready upon most occasions—
    Which got him a few presents and some thanks.
670   He varied with some skill his adulations;
    To "do at Rome as Romans do," a piece
    Of conduct was which he observed in Greece.

85

Thus, usually, when he was asked to sing,
        He gave the different nations something national;
675 'Twas all the same to him—"God save the King,"
        Or "Ça ira,"[1] according to the fashion all:
    His muse made increment of any thing,
        From the high lyric down to the low rational:
    If Pindar sang horse-races, what should hinder
680 Himself from being as pliable as Pindar?[2]

86

In France, for instance, he would write a chanson;[3]
        In England a six canto quarto tale;
    In Spain, heed make a ballad or romance on
        The last war—much the same in Portugal;
685 In Germany, the Pegasus heed prance on
        Would be old Goethe's—(see what says de Staël)[4]
    In Italy heed ape the "Trecentisti";[5]
    In Greece, heed sing some sort of hymn like this t'ye:

---

[1] *Ça ira* French: "It will succeed," a song of the French Revolution.

[2] *Pindar ... Pindar* The Greek poet Pindar (c. 522–443 BCE), was famous for his Odes. His first Olympian Ode celebrates the winner of a horse race.

[3] *chanson* French: "song," but here possibly a reference to the *chansons de geste*, poems in Old French detailing legends about historical figures.

[4] *De Staël* In *De l'Allemagne* (1818), Madame de Staël (1766–1817) writes that Goethe "will be able to represent the whole of German literature."

[5] *Trecentisti* Italian poets of the fourteenth century.

1

The isles of Greece, the isles of Greece!
690   Where burning Sappho loved and sung,
    Where grew the arts of war and peace,—
        Where Delos rose, and Phoebus sprung![6]
    Eternal summer gilds them yet,
    But all, except their sun, is set.

2

695   The Scian and the Teian muse,[7]
        The hero's harp, the lover's lute,
    Have found the fame your shores refuse;
        Their place of birth alone is mute
    To sounds which echo further west
700   Than your sires' "Islands of the Blest."

3

The mountains look on Marathon—
        And Marathon looks on the sea;
    And musing there an hour alone,
        I dreamed that Greece might still be free;
705 For standing on the Persians' grave,[8]
    I could not deem myself a slave.

4

A king sat on the rocky brow
        Which looks o'er sea-born Salamis;
    And ships, by thousands, lay below,
710   And men in nations;—all were his!
    He counted them at break of day—
    And when the sun set where were they?[9]

5

And where are they? and where art thou,
        My country? On thy voiceless shore
715 The heroic lay is tuneless now—
        The heroic bosom beats no more!
    And must thy lyre, so long divine,
    Degenerate into hands like mine?

---

[6] *Delos ... sprung* Delos, the mythical birthplace of Phoebus Apollo, was called out of the ocean by Poseidon.

[7] *Scian ... muse* Homer, primarily a poet of war and heroes, was born on Scio; Anacreon, famous for his poems of love, was born at Teos.

[8] *Persians' grave* The Greeks defeated the Persians at the Battle of Marathon in 490 BCE.

[9] *A king ... they* At the Battle of Salamis in 480 BCE, the Persian king Xerxes watched from a promontory as the Greeks, although vastly outnumbered, defeated his men in a sea battle.

6

'Tis something, in the dearth of fame,
    Though linked among a fettered race,
To feel at least a patriot's shame,
    Even as I sing, suffuse my face;
For what is left the poet here?
For Greeks a blush—for Greece a tear.

7

Must we but weep o'er days more blest?
    Must *we* but blush?—Our fathers bled.
Earth! render back from out thy breast
    A remnant of our Spartan dead!
Of the three hundred grant but three,
To make a new Thermopylae!¹

8

What, silent still? and silent all?
    Ah! no;—the voices of the dead
Sound like a distant torrent's fall,
    And answer, "Let one living head,
But one arise,—we come, we come!"
'Tis but the living who are dumb.

9

In vain—in vain: strike other chords;
    Fill high the cup with Samian wine!²
Leave battles to the Turkish hordes,
    And shed the blood of Scio's vine!
Hark! rising to the ignoble call—
How answers each bold Bacchanal!

10

You have the Pyrrhic dance as yet,
    Where is the Pyrrhic phalanx³ gone?
Of two such lessons, why forget
    The nobler and the manlier one?

You have the letters Cadmus⁴ gave—
Think ye he meant them for a slave?

11

Fill high the bowl with Samian wine!
    We will not think of themes like these!
It made Anacreon's song divine:
    He served—but served Polycrates—⁵
A tyrant; but our masters then
Were still, at least, our countrymen.

12

The tyrant of the Chersonese
    Was freedom's best and bravest friend;
That tyrant was Miltiades!⁶
    Oh! that the present hour would lend
Another despot of the kind!
Such chains as his were sure to bind.

13

Fill high the bowl with Samian wine!
    On Suli's rock, and Parga's shore,⁷
Exists the remnant of a line
    Such as the Doric mothers bore;
And there, perhaps, some seed is sown,
The Heracleidan⁸ blood might own.

14

Trust not for freedom to the Franks—⁹
    They have a king who buys and sells:
In native swords, and native ranks,
    The only hope of courage dwells;
But Turkish force, and Latin fraud,
Would break your shield, however broad.

15

Fill high the bowl with Samian wine!
    Our virgins dance beneath the shade—

---

¹ *Spartan ... Thermopylae* In 480 BCE the Persians slaughtered 300 Spartans in the narrow pass of Thermopylae. The Spartan sacrifice, however, halted the Persian advance into Greece.

² *Samian wine* The Greek island of Samos was famous for its Muscat wine.

³ *Pyrrhic dance* In the Pyrrhic dance, armed men perform quick acrobatic movements of attack and defense; *Pyrrhic phalanx* The Pyrrhic phalanx was a close massing of soldiers, a maneuver responsible for many Greek victories.

⁴ *Cadmus* Phoenician prince who reputedly introduced the use of letters in Greece.

⁵ *Polycrates* Greek tyrant and ruler of Samos, the island to which Anacreon fled after Teos was captured by Persians in 510 BCE.

⁶ *tyrant ... Miltiades* In the fifth century BCE, Miltiades became the ruler of Chersonesus, now the peninsula of the Dardanelles.

⁷ *Suli's rock ... Parga's shore* The Suliotes were a fierce Albanian tribe; Parga is a town on the Ionian coast.

⁸ *Heracleidan blood* The Heracleidae, supposedly descendants of Hercules, conquered the Pelopennesus.

⁹ *Franks* Western Europeans.

775   I see their glorious black eyes shine;
         But gazing on each glowing maid,
       My own the burning tear-drop laves,
         To think such breasts must suckle slaves.

                        16
       Place me on Sunium's[1] marbled steep,
780   Where nothing, save the waves and I,
       May hear our mutual murmurs sweep;
           There, swan-like, let me sing and die:
       A land of slaves shall ne'er be mine—
       Dash down yon cup of Samian wine!

                        87
785   Thus sung, or would, or could, or should have sung,
         The modern Greek, in tolerable verse;
       If not like Orpheus quite, when Greece was young,
           Yet in these times he might have done much worse:
       His strain displayed some feeling—right or wrong;
790   And feeling, in a poet, is the source
       Of others' feeling; but they are such liars,
       And take all colours—like the hands of dyers.

                        88
       But words are things, and a small drop of ink,
         Falling like dew, upon a thought, produces
795   That which makes thousands, perhaps millions, think;
         'Tis strange, the shortest letter which man uses
       Instead of speech, may form a lasting link
           Of ages; to what straits old Time reduces
       Frail man, when paper—even a rag like this,
800   Survives himself, his tomb, and all that's his.
       —1821

from *Canto 7*

In Cantos 7 and 8 Byron describes the Siege of
Ismail and Juan's participation in it. In December of
1790, Russian troops under the command of
General Alexander Suvarov besieged and overpowered the Turkish fortress of Ismail in a quick,
brutal attack. Byron's cantos vividly depict the
action, confusion, brutality, and devastation of war.

                        78
     —The work of glory still went on
         In preparations for a cannonade
     As terrible as that of Ilion,[2]
         If Homer had found mortars ready made;
5   But now, instead of slaying Priam's son,[3]
         We only can but talk of escalade,
     Bombs, drums, guns, bastions, batteries, bayonets,
         bullets;
     Hard words, which stick in the soft Muses' gullets.

                        79
     Oh, thou eternal Homer! who couldst charm
10   All ears, though long; all ages, though so short,
     By merely wielding with poetic arm
         Arms to which men will never more resort,
     Unless gunpowder should be found to harm
         Much less than is the hope of every court,
15   Which now is leagued young Freedom to annoy;
     But they will not find Liberty a Troy:—

                        80
     Oh, thou eternal Homer! I have now
         To paint a siege, wherein more men were slain,
     With deadlier engines and a speedier blow,
20   Than in thy Greek gazette of that campaign;
     And yet, like all men else, I must allow,
         To vie with thee would be about as vain
     As for a brook to cope with ocean's flood;
     But still we moderns equal you in blood;

                        81
25   If not in poetry, at least in fact;
         And fact is truth, the grand desideratum![4]
     Of which, howe'er the Muse describes each act,
         There should be ne'ertheless a slight substratum.
     But now the town is going to be attacked;
30   Great deeds are doing—how shall I relate 'em?
     Souls of immortal generals! Phoebus watches
     To colour up his rays from your despatches.
     —1823

---

1   *Sunium's*   I.e., Cape Sounion's. Cape Sounion was the site of a
temple of Poseidon.

2   *Ilion*   I.e., Troy.

3   *Priam's son*   I.e., Hector, Trojan hero and prince of Troy.

4   *desideratum*   Latin: something desired or believed to be essential.

PERCY BYSSHE SHELLEY
1792 — 1822

Even more than Blake's, Percy Bysshe Shelley's progressive social and political ideas have been an inspiration to many readers, from nineteenth-century socialists like Marx and Engels to radical thinkers of the 1960s. Although he was born into wealth and privilege, Shelley opposed the powerful, from those who teased and harassed him in school at Eton to the Tory government and press whom he believed were responsible for the oppression of the working classes. He collaborated on *The Necessity of Atheism* (1811), a pamphlet destined to alienate not only his father, but also the bishops and authorities at Oxford, to whom Shelley sent the piece. Antagonistic to kings, priests, judges, the conservative press and aristocracy, he was called "Mad Shelley" at Oxford. He earned this sobriquet not only for his radicalism but also for his intense interest in science. These intellectual passions underwrite a body of remarkable visionary poetry characterized by an elegance and complexity that is at once very wonderful and very difficult.

Shelley was born in 1792 at Field Place in Sussex, the first of the six children of Elizabeth and Timothy Shelley, a Member of Parliament who became a baronet on the death of his father, Sir Bysshe Shelley. Percy grew up in the affluence befitting his role as heir to the estate and title of his father and grandfather. He spent his early years running free on the estate and entertaining his siblings, so he was unprepared for the rules of the boys' academy he attended, or the bullying he would suffer there. Shelley later attended Eton College, and there the teasing continued, further developing his allegiance to outcasts and the disenfranchised, and nurturing his rebellious spirit. He was still a student at Eton when he published *Zastrozzi* (1810), a Gothic romance novel. He continued to publish during his short stint at Oxford University, from which he and Thomas Jefferson Hogg, his friend and the co-author of *The Necessity of Atheism*, were expelled for writing the pamphlet.

In 1813 Shelley published his first important work: *Queen Mab*, a poetic dream-vision that vilified conventional morality and institutional religion in a utopian picture of humanity returned to a condition of innocence. Shelley's greatest utopian fantasy, *Prometheus Unbound* (1820), would essentially reprise the same picture, imagining a world grown young again as human beings learn to undo the curse of their acquired historical fears and hatreds and replace it with a program based on love, which he called "the great secret" of all morality.

Shelley's personal involvements with love, fueled by his ideals, were also fraught with that inherited curse. In 1811 Shelley married Harriet Westbrook, and the couple had a daughter born to them in 1813. But before long he would fall in love with another young woman, Mary Godwin, the daughter of the radical thinkers William Godwin and Mary Wollstonecraft.

In 1814 Shelley left Harriet and traveled to the continent with Mary and her half sister Clair Clairmont for a six-week tour. When they returned to England Shelley proposed that Harriet should live with Mary and himself as free lovers. When Harriet refused, Shelley, Mary, and Clair again traveled to Europe, where the three met Lord Byron in Switzerland in June. In the meantime, Harriet gave birth to Shelley's second child, a son, in late 1814, and at the end of 1816 she committed suicide. Mary and Percy were then married.

The summer of 1816 is one of the most famous in the history of English letters. Out of it came a series of stunning literary works: Mary's great novel *Frankenstein*; Byron's third canto of *Childe Harold* as well as various apocalyptic works, especially *Manfred*; and a series of key lyric poems by Shelley including "Mont Blanc" and the "Hymn to Intellectual Beauty." Later (1818) Shelley would write "Julian and Maddalo: A Conversation," a brilliant verse dialogue representing the conversations that he and Byron had been having since they met in 1816.

Upon this return to England from Switzerland, his life bristling with personal and political scandals, Shelley was denied custody of his two children from his first marriage. In 1818 the Shelleys moved to the Continent with their baby girl Clara in the hope of joining Byron in Italy and avoiding the judgment of English society. Unfortunately, Clara died in September, and William, born in 1816, died the following year. The only child to survive would be Percy Florence, born in 1819.

Shelley wrote his lyric masterpiece *Prometheus Unbound* that same year, to show how social life might and ought to be, and he wrote the political tragedy *The Cenci* (1819), to show the way it actually was. The distance between the two works is dialectical, as Shelley later attempted to explain in his important prose work, the *Defence of Poetry* (1821). During this prolific period Shelley also responded to the Peterloo Massacre—in which eleven workers were killed at what was meant to be a peaceful rally in Manchester—by writing "The Mask of Anarchy," "Song: To the Men of England," "A Philosophical View of Reform," and "Ode to the West Wind," a revolutionary lyric that recapitulates, in miniature, the argument and structure of *Prometheus Unbound*. Shelley hoped his verse would undermine the retrograde political institutions of his time and seed the future with a promise of rejuvenation. Enjoying scant fame or immediate influence, he nevertheless concluded his *Defence of Poetry* with the now-famous pronouncement that poets are "the unacknowledged legislators of the world."

In 1822 Shelley—who could not swim—went sailing on the Bay of Spezia in Italy with his friend Edward Williams. They were caught in a sudden squall and drowned. When Shelley's body washed up on the beach a few days later, a copy of Keats's poems was found in his pocket. A funeral pyre was hastily built and his corpse cremated—except for his heart, which was snatched from the pyre by his friend Edward Trelawney.

In a letter to some of his conservative English friends Byron famously declared: "You are all brutally mistaken about Shelley who was without exception—the *best* and least selfish man I ever knew." His ashes were placed near the recently buried Keats in the Protestant Cemetery in Rome. His inconsumable heart remained in Mary Shelley's possession, wrapped in the pages of *Adonais*, Shelley's elegy for Keats, until her death. It is buried with her in her tomb at St. Peter's Churchyard in Bournemouth.

⌘ ⌘ ⌘

To Wordsworth[1]

Poet of Nature, thou hast wept to know
That things depart which never may return:
Childhood and youth, friendship and love's first glow,
Have fled like sweet dreams, leaving thee to mourn.
5 These common woes I feel. One loss is mine
Which thou too feel'st, yet I alone deplore.
Thou wert as a lone star, whose light did shine
On some frail bark in winter's midnight roar:
Thou hast like to a rock-built refuge stood
10 Above the blind and battling multitude:
In honoured poverty thy voice did weave
Songs consecrate to truth and liberty—
Deserting these, thou leavest me to grieve,
Thus having been, that thou shouldst cease to be.
—1816

Alastor; or, The Spirit of Solitude

PREFACE

The poem entitled "Alastor" may be considered as allegorical of one of the most interesting situations of the human mind. It represents a youth of uncorrupted feelings and adventurous genius[2] led forth by an imagination inflamed and purified through familiarity with all that is excellent and majestic, to the contemplation of the universe. He drinks deep of the fountains of knowledge, and is still insatiate. The magnificence and beauty of the external world sinks profoundly into the frame of his conceptions, and affords to their modifications a variety not to be exhausted. So long as it is possible for his desires to point towards objects thus infinite and unmeasured, he is joyous, and tranquil, and self-possessed. But the period arrives when these objects cease to suffice. His mind is at length suddenly awakened and thirsts for intercourse with an intelligence similar to itself. He images to himself the Being whom he loves. Conversant with speculations of the sublimest and most perfect natures, the vision in which he embodies his own imaginations unites all of wonderful, or wise, or beautiful, which the poet, the philosopher, or the lover could depicture. The intellectual faculties, the imagination, the functions of sense, have their respective requisitions[3] on the sympathy of corresponding powers in other human beings. The Poet is represented as uniting these requisitions, and attaching them to a single image. He seeks in vain for a prototype of his conception. Blasted by his disappointment, he descends to an untimely grave.

The picture is not barren of instruction to actual men. The Poet's self-centred seclusion was avenged by the furies of an irresistible passion pursuing him to speedy ruin. But that Power which strikes the luminaries of the world with sudden darkness and extinction, by awakening them to too exquisite a perception of its influences, dooms to a slow and poisonous decay those meaner spirits that dare to abjure its dominion. Their destiny is more abject and inglorious as their delinquency is more contemptible and pernicious. They who, deluded by no generous error, instigated by no sacred thirst of doubtful knowledge, duped by no illustrious superstition, loving nothing on this earth, and cherishing no hopes beyond, yet keep aloof from sympathies with their kind, rejoicing neither in human joy nor mourning with human grief; these, and such as they, have their apportioned curse. They languish, because none feel with them their common nature. They are morally dead. They are neither friends, nor lovers, nor fathers, nor citizens of the world, nor benefactors of their country. Among those who attempt to exist without human sympathy, the pure and tender-hearted perish through the intensity and passion of their search after its communities, when the vacancy of their spirit suddenly makes itself felt. All else, selfish, blind, and torpid, are those unforeseeing multitudes who constitute, together with their own, the lasting misery and loneliness of the world. Those who love not their fellow-beings live unfruitful lives, and prepare for their old age a miserable grave.

"The good die first,
And those whose hearts are dry as summer dust,
Burn to the socket!"[4]

December 14, 1815

---

[1] *To Wordsworth*   As a young man, Wordsworth identified himself as a political radical, but as his career progressed he gradually became more conservative. His 1814 poem *The Excursion* showed a marked change in his political and religious thinking, and was received with disappointment by many of his early admirers, such as Shelley.

[2] *youth of ... genius*   This protagonist is unnamed, although because of the poem's title he is often (incorrectly) assumed to be called Alastor. In his *Memoirs of Shelley*, Shelley's friend Thomas Love Peacock explains that Shelley was "at a loss for a title, and I proposed that which he adopted: Alastor, or the Spirit of Solitude. The Greek word *Alastor* is an evil genius."

[3] *requisitions*   Claims.

[4] *The ... socket*   From Wordsworth's *Excursion*, 1.500–02.

Alastor; or, The Spirit of Solitude

*Nondum amabam, et amare amabam, quaerebam quid
amarem, amans amare.*
                              —*Confess. St. August.*[1]

Earth, ocean, air, belovèd brotherhood!
If our great Mother[2] has imbued my soul
With aught of natural piety[3] to feel
Your love, and recompense the boon with mine;
5   If dewy morn, and odorous noon, and even,
With sunset and its gorgeous ministers,
And solemn midnight's tingling silentness;
If autumn's hollow sighs in the sere wood,
And winter robing with pure snow and crowns
10   Of starry ice the grey grass and bare boughs;
If spring's voluptuous pantings when she breathes
Her first sweet kisses, have been dear to me;
If no bright bird, insect, or gentle beast
I consciously have injured, but still loved
15   And cherished these my kindred; then forgive
This boast, belovèd brethren, and withdraw
No portion of your wonted favour now!

Mother of this unfathomable world!
Favour my solemn song, for I have loved
20   Thee ever, and thee only; I have watched
Thy shadow, and the darkness of thy steps,
And my heart ever gazes on the depth
Of thy deep mysteries. I have made my bed
In charnels[4] and on coffins, where black death   *cemeteries*
25   Keeps record of the trophies won from thee,
Hoping to still these obstinate questionings[5]
Of thee and thine, by forcing some lone ghost,

Thy messenger, to render up the tale
Of what we are. In lone and silent hours,
30   When night makes a weird sound of its own stillness,
Like an inspired and desperate alchemist
Staking his very life on some dark hope,
Have I mixed awful talk and asking looks
With my most innocent love, until strange tears
35   Uniting with those breathless kisses, made
Such magic as compels the charmèd night
To render up thy charge: ... and, though ne'er yet
Thou hast unveiled thy inmost sanctuary,
Enough from incommunicable dream,
40   And twilight phantasms, and deep noon-day thought,
Has shone within me, that serenely now
And moveless, as a long-forgotten lyre
Suspended in the solitary dome
Of some mysterious and deserted fane,°   *temple*
45   I wait thy breath, Great Parent, that my strain
May modulate with murmurs of the air,
And motions of the forests and the sea,
And voice of living beings, and woven hymns
Of night and day, and the deep heart of man.

50   There was a Poet whose untimely tomb
No human hands with pious reverence reared,
But the charmed eddies of autumnal winds
Built o'er his mouldering bones a pyramid
Of mouldering leaves in the waste wilderness:
55   A lovely youth—no mourning maiden decked
With weeping flowers, or votive cypress wreath,[6]
The lone couch of his everlasting sleep:
Gentle, and brave, and generous—no lorn° bard   *forlorn*
Breathed o'er his dark fate one melodious sigh:
60   He lived, he died, he sung, in solitude.
Strangers have wept to hear his passionate notes,
And virgins, as unknown he passed, have pined
And wasted for fond love of his wild eyes.
The fire of those soft orbs has ceased to burn,
65   And Silence, too enamoured of that voice,
Locks its mute music in her rugged cell.

---

[1] *Nondum ... August* Latin: "I was not yet in love, and I loved to love, I sought what I might love, loving to love." From St. Augustine's *Confessions* 3.1, in which he describes his youthful desire for sexual love, rather than the spiritual love of God that he later found.

[2] *our great Mother* Cybele, goddess of the powers of nature and fertility.

[3] *natural piety* From Wordsworth's "My Heart Leaps Up," line 9.

[4] *charnels* Houses of death, mortuaries.

[5] *obstinate questionings* From Wordsworth's "Ode: Intimations of Immortality," lines 142–43: "Those obstinate questionings / Of sense and outward things."

[6] *cypress wreath* Worn to represent mourning.

By solemn vision, and bright silver dream,
His infancy was nurtured. Every sight
And sound from the vast earth and ambient air,
70   Sent to his heart its choicest impulses.
The fountains of divine philosophy
Fled not his thirsting lips, and all of great,
Or good, or lovely, which the sacred past
In truth or fable consecrates, he felt
75   And knew. When early youth had passed, he left
His cold fireside and alienated home
To seek strange truths in undiscovered lands.
Many a wide waste and tangled wilderness
Has lured his fearless steps; and he has bought
80   With his sweet voice and eyes, from savage men,
His rest and food. Nature's most secret steps
He like her shadow has pursued, where'er
The red volcano overcanopies
Its fields of snow and pinnacles of ice
85   With burning smoke, or where bitumen° lakes   pitch
On black bare pointed islets ever beat
With sluggish surge, or where the secret caves
Rugged and dark, winding among the springs
Of fire and poison, inaccessible
90   To avarice or pride, their starry domes
Of diamond and of gold expand above
Numberless and immeasurable halls,
Frequent with crystal column, and clear shrines
Of pearl, and thrones radiant with chrysolite.[1]
95   Nor had that scene of ampler majesty
Than gems or gold, the varying roof of heaven
And the green earth lost in his heart its claims
To love and wonder; he would linger long
In lonesome vales, making the wild his home,
100   Until the doves and squirrels would partake
From his innocuous hand his bloodless food,
Lured by the gentle meaning of his looks,
And the wild antelope, that starts whene'er
The dry leaf rustles in the brake,° suspend   thicket
105   Her timid steps to gaze upon a form
More graceful than her own.

                         His wandering step
Obedient to high thoughts, has visited
The awful ruins of the days of old:

110   Athens, and Tyre, and Balbec,[2] and the waste
Where stood Jerusalem,[3] the fallen towers
Of Babylon, the eternal pyramids,
Memphis and Thebes,[4] and whatsoe'er of strange
Sculptured on alabaster obelisk,
115   Or jasper tomb, or mutilated sphynx,
Dark Æthiopia in her desert hills
Conceals. Among the ruined temples there,
Stupendous columns, and wild images
Of more than man, where marble daemons[5] watch
120   The Zodiac's brazen mystery,[6] and dead men
Hang their mute thoughts on the mute walls around,
He lingered, poring on memorials
Of the world's youth, through the long burning day
Gazed on those speechless shapes, nor, when the moon
125   Filled the mysterious halls with floating shades
Suspended he that task, but ever gazed
And gazed, till meaning on his vacant mind
Flashed like strong inspiration, and he saw
The thrilling secrets of the birth of time.

130   Meanwhile an Arab maiden brought his food,
Her daily portion, from her father's tent,
And spread her matting for his couch, and stole
From duties and repose to tend his steps—
Enamoured, yet not daring for deep awe
135   To speak her love—and watched his nightly sleep,
Sleepless herself, to gaze upon his lips
Parted in slumber, whence the regular breath
Of innocent dreams arose: then, when red morn
Made paler the pale moon, to her cold home
140   Wildered,° and wan, and panting, she returned.   bewildered

---

[1] *chrysolite* Green gemstone.

[2] *Tyre* Ancient capital of Phoenicia, located in present-day Lebanon, that was destroyed by Muslims in 1291; *Balbec* Ancient Phoenician city in eastern Lebanon that is known for its Roman ruins.

[3] *Jerusalem* Destroyed by Emperor Titus in 70 CE.

[4] *Memphis and Thebes* Ancient cities of lower and upper Egypt, respectively.

[5] *daemons* Supernatural beings, or minor deities, of Greek mythology.

[6] *Zodiac's brazen mystery* Representations of the Zodiac decorate the ceiling of the temple of Isis (goddess of fertility) at Denderah, in Egypt.

The Poet wandering on, through Arabie
And Persia, and the wild Carmanian waste,[1]
And o'er the aërial mountains which pour down
Indus and Oxus[2] from their icy caves,
145 In joy and exultation held his way;
Till in the vale of Cashmire, far within
Its loneliest dell, where odorous plants entwine
Beneath the hollow rocks a natural bower,
Beside a sparkling rivulet he stretched
150 His languid limbs. A vision on his sleep
There came, a dream of hopes that never yet
Had flushed his cheek. He dreamed a veilèd maid
Sate near him, talking in low solemn tones.
Her voice was like the voice of his own soul
155 Heard in the calm of thought; its music long,
Like woven sounds of streams and breezes, held
His inmost sense suspended in its web
Of many-coloured woof[3] and shifting hues.
Knowledge and truth and virtue were her theme,
160 And lofty hopes of divine liberty,
Thoughts the most dear to him, and poesy,
Herself a poet. Soon the solemn mood
Of her pure mind kindled through all her frame
A permeating fire: wild numbers[4] then
165 She raised, with voice stifled in tremulous sobs
Subdued by its own pathos: her fair hands
Were bare alone, sweeping from some strange harp
Strange symphony, and in their branching veins
The eloquent blood told an ineffable tale.
170 The beating of her heart was heard to fill
The pauses of her music, and her breath
Tumultuously accorded with those fits
Of intermitted song. Sudden she rose,
As if her heart impatiently endured
175 Its bursting burthen: at the sound he turned,
And saw by the warm light of their own life
Her glowing limbs beneath the sinuous veil
Of woven wind, her outspread arms now bare,
Her dark locks floating in the breath of night,

180 Her beamy bending eyes, her parted lips
Outstretched, and pale, and quivering eagerly.
His strong heart sunk and sickened with excess
Of love. He reared his shuddering limbs and quelled
His gasping breath, and spread his arms to meet
185 Her panting bosom … she drew back a while,
Then, yielding to the irresistible joy,
With frantic gesture and short breathless cry
Folded his frame in her dissolving arms.
Now blackness veiled his dizzy eyes, and night
190 Involved and swallowed up the vision; sleep,
Like a dark flood suspended in its course,
Rolled back its impulse on his vacant brain.

Roused by the shock he started from his trance—
The cold white light of morning, the blue moon
195 Low in the west, the clear and garish hills,
The distinct valley and the vacant woods,
Spread round him where he stood. Whither have fled
The hues of heaven that canopied his bower
Of yesternight? The sounds that soothed his sleep,
200 The mystery and the majesty of Earth,
The joy, the exultation? His wan eyes
Gaze on the empty scene as vacantly
As ocean's moon looks on the moon in heaven.
The spirit of sweet human love has sent
205 A vision to the sleep of him who spurned
Her choicest gifts. He eagerly pursues
Beyond the realms of dream that fleeting shade;
He overleaps the bounds. Alas! Alas!
Were limbs, and breath, and being intertwined
210 Thus treacherously? Lost, lost, for ever lost,
In the wide pathless desert of dim sleep,
That beautiful shape! Does the dark gate of death
Conduct to thy mysterious paradise,
O Sleep? Does the bright arch of rainbow clouds,
215 And pendent mountains seen in the calm lake,
Lead only to a black and watery depth,
While death's blue vault, with loathliest vapours hung,
Where every shade which the foul grave exhales
Hides its dead eye from the detested day,
220 Conducts, O Sleep, to thy delightful realms?
This doubt with sudden tide flowed on his heart,
The insatiate hope which it awakened, stung
His brain even like despair.

---

[1] *Carmanian waste* Kerman Desert, in present-day Iran.

[2] *Indus and Oxus* Rivers which flow from opposite sides of the
Hindu Kush mountains in Asia.

[3] *woof* Thread that crosses from side to side in a web of weaving.

[4] *numbers* Verses, of song or poetry.

While daylight held

225 The sky, the Poet kept mute conference
With his still soul. At night the passion came,
Like the fierce fiend of a distempered dream,
And shook him from his rest, and led him forth
Into the darkness. As an eagle, grasped
230 In folds of the green serpent, feels her breast
Burn with the poison, and precipitates
Through night and day, tempest, and calm, and cloud,
Frantic with dizzying anguish, her blind flight
O'er the wide aëry° wilderness: thus driven   *lofty*
235 By the bright shadow of that lovely dream,
Beneath the cold glare of the desolate night,
Through tangled swamps and deep precipitous dells,
Startling with careless step the moonlight snake,
He fled. Red morning dawned upon his flight,
240 Shedding the mockery of its vital hues
Upon his cheek of death. He wandered on
Till vast Aornos seen from Petra's steep[1]
Hung o'er the low horizon like a cloud;
Through Balk,[2] and where the desolated tombs
245 Of Parthian kings[3] scatter to every wind
Their wasting dust, wildly he wandered on,
Day after day a weary waste of hours,
Bearing within his life the brooding care
That ever fed on its decaying flame.
250 And now his limbs were lean; his scattered hair
Sered° by the autumn of strange suffering   *made dry*
Sung dirges in the wind; his listless hand
Hung like dead bone within its withered skin;
Life, and the lustre that consumed it, shone
255 As in a furnace burning secretly
From his dark eyes alone. The cottagers,
Who ministered with human charity
His human wants, beheld with wondering awe
Their fleeting visitant. The mountaineer,
260 Encountering on some dizzy precipice
That spectral form, deemed that the Spirit of wind
With lightning eyes, and eager breath, and feet
Disturbing not the drifted snow, had paused
In its career: the infant would conceal

265 His troubled visage in his mother's robe
In terror at the glare of those wild eyes,
To remember their strange light in many a dream
Of after-times; but youthful maidens, taught
By nature, would interpret half the woe
270 That wasted him, would call him with false names
Brother, and friend, would press his pallid hand
At parting, and watch, dim through tears, the path
Of his departure from their father's door.

At length upon the lone Chorasmian shore[4]
275 He paused, a wide and melancholy waste
Of putrid marshes. A strong impulse urged
His steps to the sea-shore. A swan was there,
Beside a sluggish stream among the reeds.
It rose as he approached, and with strong wings
280 Scaling the upward sky, bent its bright course
High over the immeasurable main.
His eyes pursued its flight—"Thou hast a home,
Beautiful bird; thou voyagest to thine home,
Where thy sweet mate will twine her downy neck
285 With thine, and welcome thy return with eyes
Bright in the lustre of their own fond joy.
And what am I that I should linger here,
With voice far sweeter than thy dying notes,
Spirit more vast than thine, frame more attuned
290 To beauty, wasting these surpassing powers
In the deaf air, to the blind earth, and heaven
That echoes not my thoughts?" A gloomy smile
Of desperate hope wrinkled his quivering lips.
For sleep, he knew, kept most relentlessly
295 Its precious charge, and silent death exposed,
Faithless perhaps as sleep, a shadowy lure,
With doubtful smile mocking its own strange charms.

Startled by his own thoughts he looked around.
There was no fair fiend near him, not a sight
300 Or sound of awe but in his own deep mind.
A little shallop[5] floating near the shore
Caught the impatient wandering of his gaze.
It had been long abandoned, for its sides
Gaped wide with many a rift, and its frail joints
305 Swayed with the undulations of the tide.

---

[1] *Aornos* Mountain on the Indus; *Petra's steep* Probably the Rock of Soghdiana in Uzbekistan. ("Petra" is Latin for "rock.")

[2] *Balk* Balkh, in present-day Afghanistan.

[3] *Parthian kings* Rulers of northern Persia.

---

[4] *Chorasmian shore* Shore of the Caspian sea.

[5] *shallop* Small open boat or dinghy.

A restless impulse urged him to embark
And meet lone Death on the drear ocean's waste;
For well he knew that mighty Shadow loves
The slimy caverns of the populous deep.

310   The day was fair and sunny, sea and sky
Drank its inspiring radiance, and the wind
Swept strongly from the shore, blackening the waves.
Following his eager soul, the wanderer
Leaped in the boat, he spread his cloak aloft
315 On the bare mast, and took his lonely seat,
And felt the boat speed o'er the tranquil sea
Like a torn cloud before the hurricane.

As one that in a silver vision floats
Obedient to the sweep of odorous winds
320 Upon resplendent clouds, so rapidly
Along the dark and ruffled waters fled
The straining boat. A whirlwind swept it on,
With fierce gusts and precipitating force,
Through the white ridges of the chafèd sea.
325 The waves arose. Higher and higher still
Their fierce necks writhed beneath the tempest's scourge
Like serpents struggling in a vulture's grasp.
Calm and rejoicing in the fearful war
Of wave ruining on wave, and blast on blast
330 Descending, and black flood on whirlpool driven
With dark obliterating course, he sate:
As if their genii were the ministers
Appointed to conduct him to the light
Of those belovèd eyes, the Poet sate
335 Holding the steady helm. Evening came on,
The beams of sunset hung their rainbow hues
High 'mid the shifting domes of sheeted spray
That canopied his path o'er the waste deep;
Twilight, ascending slowly from the east,
340 Entwined in duskier wreaths her braided locks
O'er the fair front and radiant eyes of day;
Night followed, clad with stars. On every side
More horribly the multitudinous streams
Of ocean's mountainous waste to mutual war
345 Rushed in dark tumult thundering, as to mock
The calm and spangled sky. The little boat
Still fled before the storm; still fled, like foam
Down the steep cataract of a wintry river;

Now pausing on the edge of the riven wave;
350 Now leaving far behind the bursting mass
That fell, convulsing ocean: safely fled—
As if that frail and wasted human form
Had been an elemental god.

At midnight
355 The moon arose: and lo! the ethereal cliffs
Of Caucasus,[1] whose icy summits shone
Among the stars like sunlight, and around
Whose caverned base the whirlpools and the waves
Bursting and eddying irresistibly
360 Rage and resound for ever. Who shall save?
The boat fled on—the boiling torrent drove—
The crags closed round with black and jaggèd arms,
The shattered mountain overhung the sea,
And faster still, beyond all human speed,
365 Suspended on the sweep of the smooth wave,
The little boat was driven. A cavern there
Yawned, and amid its slant and winding depths
Ingulfed the rushing sea. The boat fled on
With unrelaxing speed. "Vision and Love!"
370 The Poet cried aloud, "I have beheld
The path of thy departure. Sleep and death
Shall not divide us long!"

The boat pursued
The windings of the cavern. Daylight shone
375 At length upon that gloomy river's flow;
Now, where the fiercest war among the waves
Is calm, on the unfathomable stream
The boat moved slowly. Where the mountain, riven,
Exposed those black depths to the azure sky,
380 Ere yet the flood's enormous volume fell
Even to the base of Caucasus, with sound
That shook the everlasting rocks, the mass
Filled with one whirlpool all that ample chasm;
Stair above stair the eddying waters rose,
385 Circling immeasurably fast, and laved°   bathed
With alternating dash the gnarlèd roots
Of mighty trees, that stretched their giant arms
In darkness over it. I' the midst was left,
Reflecting, yet distorting every cloud,
390 A pool of treacherous and tremendous calm.

---

[1] *ethereal* Belonging to the upper air; *Caucasus* On the western
shore of the Caspian sea, in present-day Georgia.

Seized by the sway of the ascending stream,
With dizzy swiftness, round, and round, and round,
Ridge after ridge the straining boat arose,
Till on the verge of the extremest curve,
395 Where, through an opening of the rocky bank,
The waters overflow, and a smooth spot
Of glassy quiet mid those battling tides
Is left, the boat paused shuddering. Shall it sink
Down the abyss? Shall the reverting stress
400 Of that resistless gulf embosom it?
Now shall it fall? A wandering stream of wind,
Breathed from the west, has caught the expanded sail,
And, lo! with gentle motion, between banks
Of mossy slope, and on a placid stream,
405 Beneath a woven grove it sails, and, hark!
The ghastly torrent mingles its far roar
With the breeze murmuring in the musical woods.
Where the embowering trees recede, and leave
A little space of green expanse, the cove
410 Is closed by meeting banks, whose yellow flowers
For ever gaze on their own drooping eyes,[1]
Reflected in the crystal calm. The wave
Of the boat's motion marred their pensive task,
Which nought but vagrant bird, or wanton wind,
415 Or falling spear-grass, or their own decay
Had e'er disturbed before. The Poet longed
To deck with their bright hues his withered hair,
But on his heart its solitude returned,
And he forbore. Not the strong impulse hid
420 In those flushed cheeks, bent eyes, and shadowy frame
Had yet performed its ministry: it hung
Upon his life, as lightning in a cloud
Gleams, hovering ere it vanish, ere the floods
Of night close over it.
425   The noonday sun
Now shone upon the forest, one vast mass
Of mingling shade, whose brown° magnificence   *dark*
A narrow vale embosoms. There, huge caves,
Scooped in the dark base of their aëry rocks
430 Mocking its moans, respond and roar for ever.
The meeting boughs and implicated° leaves   *entwined*
Wove twilight o'er the Poet's path, as led

By love, or dream, or god, or mightier Death,
He sought in Nature's dearest haunt, some bank,
435 Her cradle, and his sepulchre. More dark
And dark the shades accumulate. The oak,
Expanding its immense and knotty arms,
Embraces the light beech. The pyramids
Of the tall cedar overarching, frame
440 Most solemn domes within, and far below,
Like clouds suspended in an emerald sky,
The ash and the acacia floating hang
Tremulous and pale. Like restless serpents, clothed
In rainbow and in fire, the parasites,
445 Starred with ten thousand blossoms, flow around
The grey trunks, and, as gamesome° infants' eyes, *playful*
With gentle meanings, and most innocent wiles,
Fold their beams round the hearts of those that love,
These twine their tendrils with the wedded boughs
450 Uniting their close union; the woven leaves
Make net-work of the dark blue light of day,
And the night's noontide clearness, mutable
As shapes in the weird clouds. Soft mossy lawns
Beneath these canopies extend their swells,
455 Fragrant with perfumed herbs, and eyed with blooms
Minute yet beautiful. One darkest glen
Sends from its woods of musk-rose, twined with jasmine,
A soul-dissolving odour, to invite
To some more lovely mystery. Through the dell,
460 Silence and Twilight here, twin-sisters, keep
Their noonday watch, and sail among the shades,
Like vaporous shapes half seen; beyond, a well,
Dark, gleaming, and of most translucent wave,
Images[2] all the woven boughs above,
465 And each depending leaf, and every speck
Of azure sky, darting between their chasms;
Nor aught else in the liquid mirror laves
Its portraiture, but some inconstant star
Between one foliaged lattice twinkling fair,
470 Or, painted bird, sleeping beneath the moon,
Or gorgeous insect floating motionless,
Unconscious of the day, ere yet his wings
Have spread their glories to the gaze of noon.

Hither the Poet came. His eyes beheld
475 Their own wan light through the reflected lines

---

[1] *yellow flowers* Narcissus flowers. According to Greek mythology, the handsome youth Narcissus fell in love with his own reflection in a pool of water and wasted away pining after his own image.

[2] *Images* Reflects; forms an image of.

Of his thin hair, distinct in the dark depth
Of that still fountain; as the human heart,
Gazing in dreams over the gloomy grave,
Sees its own treacherous likeness there. He heard
480 The motion of the leaves, the grass that sprung
Startled and glanced and trembled even to feel
An unaccustomed presence, and the sound
Of the sweet brook that from the secret springs
Of that dark fountain rose. A Spirit seemed
485 To stand beside him—clothed in no bright robes
Of shadowy silver or enshrining light.
Borrowed from aught the visible world affords
Of grace, or majesty, or mystery—
But, undulating woods, and silent well,
490 And leaping rivulet, and evening gloom
Now deepening the dark shades, for speech assuming,
Held commune with him, as if he and it
Were all that was,—only ... when his regard
Was raised by intense pensiveness, ... two eyes,
495 Two starry eyes, hung in the gloom of thought,
And seemed with their serene and azure smiles
To beckon him.

    Obedient to the light
That shone within his soul, he went, pursuing
500 The windings of the dell. The rivulet
Wanton and wild through many a green ravine
Beneath the forest flowed. Sometimes it fell
Among the moss with hollow harmony
Dark and profound. Now on the polished stones
505 It danced; like childhood laughing as it went:
Then, through the plain in tranquil wanderings crept,
Reflecting every herb and drooping bud
That overhung its quietness. "O stream!
Whose source is inaccessibly profound,
510 Whither do thy mysterious waters tend?
Thou imagest my life. Thy darksome stillness,
Thy dazzling waves, thy loud and hollow gulfs,
Thy searchless° fountain,° and   *undiscoverable / source*
    invisible course
Have each their type in me: and the wide sky,
515 And measureless ocean may declare as soon
What oozy cavern or what wandering cloud
Contains thy waters, as the universe
Tell where these living thoughts reside, when stretched

Upon thy flowers my bloodless limbs shall waste
520 I' the passing wind!"

    Beside the grassy shore
Of the small stream he went; he did impress
On the green moss his tremulous step, that caught
Strong shuddering from his burning limbs. As one
525 Roused by some joyous madness from the couch
Of fever, he did move; yet, not like him,
Forgetful of the grave, where, when the flame
Of his frail exultation shall be spent,
He must descend. With rapid steps he went
530 Beneath the shade of trees, beside the flow
Of the wild babbling rivulet; and now
The forest's solemn canopies were changed
For the uniform and lightsome° evening sky.   *luminous*
Grey rocks did peep from the spare moss, and stemmed
535 The struggling brook: tall spires of windlestrae[1]
Threw their thin shadows down the rugged slope,
And nought but gnarled roots[2] of ancient pines,
Branchless and blasted, clenched with grasping roots
The unwilling soil. A gradual change was here,
540 Yet ghastly. For, as fast years flow away,
The smooth brow gathers, and the hair grows thin
And white, and where irradiate° dewy eyes   *illumined*
Had shone, gleam stony orbs: so from his steps
Bright flowers departed, and the beautiful shade
545 Of the green groves, with all their odorous winds
And musical motions. Calm, he still pursued
The stream, that with a larger volume now
Rolled through the labyrinthine dell; and there
Fretted a path through its descending curves
550 With its wintry speed. On every side now rose
Rocks, which, in unimaginable forms,
Lifted their black and barren pinnacles
In the light of evening, and, its precipice
Obscuring the ravine, disclosed above,
555 Mid toppling stones, black gulfs and yawning caves,
Whose windings gave ten thousand various tongues
To the loud stream. Lo! where the pass expands
Its stony jaws, the abrupt mountain breaks,
And seems, with its accumulated crags,
560 To overhang the world: for wide expand

---

1   *windlestrae*   Windlestraw; withered grass stalks.

2   *roots*   Believed to be a misprint for "trunks" or "knots."

Beneath the wan stars and descending moon
Islanded seas, blue mountains, mighty streams,
Dim tracts and vast, robed in the lustrous gloom
Of leaden-coloured even,° and fiery hills   *evening*
565 Mingling their flames with twilight, on the verge
Of the remote horizon. The near scene,
In naked and severe simplicity,
Made contrast with the universe. A pine,
Rock-rooted, stretched athwart the vacancy
570 Its swinging boughs, to each inconstant blast
Yielding one only response, at each pause
In most familiar cadence, with the howl
The thunder and the hiss of homeless streams
Mingling its solemn song, whilst the broad river,
575 Foaming and hurrying o'er its rugged path,
Fell into that immeasurable void
Scattering its waters to the passing winds.

Yet the grey precipice and solemn pine
And torrent, were not all—one silent nook
580 Was there. Even on the edge of that vast mountain,
Upheld by knotty roots and fallen rocks,
It overlooked in its serenity
The dark earth, and the bending vault of stars.
It was a tranquil spot, that seemed to smile
585 Even in the lap of horror. Ivy clasped
The fissured stones with its entwining arms,
And did embower with leaves for ever green,
And berries dark, the smooth and even space
Of its inviolated floor, and here
590 The children of the autumnal whirlwind bore,
In wanton sport, those bright leaves, whose decay,
Red, yellow, or ethereally pale,
Rivals the pride of summer. 'Tis the haunt
Of every gentle wind, whose breath can teach
595 The wilds to love tranquillity. One step,
One human step alone, has ever broken
The stillness of its solitude; one voice
Alone inspired its echoes—even that voice
Which hither came, floating among the winds,
600 And led the loveliest among human forms
To make their wild haunts the depository
Of all the grace and beauty that endued[1]
Its motions, render up its majesty,

Scatter its music on the unfeeling storm,
605 And to the damp leaves and blue cavern mould,
Nurses of rainbow flowers and branching moss,
Commit the colours of that varying cheek,
That snowy breast, those dark and drooping eyes,

The dim and hornèd moon hung low, and poured
610 A sea of lustre on the horizon's verge
That overflowed its mountains. Yellow mist
Filled the unbounded atmosphere, and drank
Wan moonlight even to fulness: not a star
Shone, not a sound was heard; the very winds,
615 Danger's grim playmates, on that precipice
Slept, clasped in his embrace—O, storm of death!
Whose sightless speed divides this sullen night:
And thou, colossal Skeleton, that, still
Guiding its irresistible career
620 In thy devastating omnipotence,
Art king of this frail world, from the red field
Of slaughter, from the reeking hospital,
The patriot's sacred couch, the snowy bed
Of innocence, the scaffold and the throne,
625 A mighty voice invokes thee. Ruin calls
His brother Death. A rare and regal prey
He hath prepared, prowling around the world;
Glutted with which thou mayst repose, and men
Go to their graves like flowers or creeping worms,
630 Nor ever more offer at thy dark shrine
The unheeded tribute of a broken heart.

When on the threshold of the green recess
The wanderer's footsteps fell, he knew that death
Was on him. Yet a little, ere it fled,
635 Did he resign his high and holy soul
To images of the majestic past,
That paused within his passive being now,
Like winds that bear sweet music, when they breathe
Through some dim latticed chamber. He did place
640 His pale lean hand upon the rugged trunk
Of the old pine. Upon an ivied stone
Reclined his languid head, his limbs did rest,
Diffused and motionless, on the smooth brink
Of that obscurest chasm—and thus he lay,
645 Surrendering to their final impulses
The hovering powers of life. Hope and despair,

---

[1] *endued*   Were inherent in.

The torturers, slept; no mortal pain or fear
Marred his repose, the influxes of sense,
And his own being unalloyed by pain,
650 Yet feebler and more feeble, calmly fed
The stream of thought, till he lay breathing there
At peace, and faintly smiling—his last sight
Was the great moon, which o'er the western line
Of the wide world her mighty horn suspended,
655 With whose dun° beams inwoven darkness   dusky
    seemed
To mingle. Now upon the jaggèd hills
It rests, and still as the divided frame
Of the vast meteor[1] sunk, the Poet's blood,
That ever beat in mystic sympathy
660 With nature's ebb and flow, grew feebler still:
And when two lessening points[2] of light alone
Gleamed through the darkness, the alternate gasp
Of his faint respiration scarce did stir
The stagnate° night—till the minutest ray   stagnant
665 Was quenched, the pulse yet lingered in his heart.
It paused—it fluttered. But when heaven remained
Utterly black, the murky shades involved
An image, silent, cold, and motionless,
As their own voiceless earth and vacant air.
670 Even as a vapour° fed with golden beams   cloud
That ministered on sunlight, ere the west
Eclipses it, was now that wondrous frame—
No sense, no motion, no divinity—
A fragile lute, on whose harmonious strings
675 The breath of heaven did wander—a bright stream
Once fed with many-voicèd waves—a dream
Of youth, which night and time have quenched for ever,
Still, dark, and dry, and unremembered now.

    O, for Medea's wondrous alchemy,[3]
680 Which wheresoe'er it fell made the earth gleam
With bright flowers, and the wintry boughs exhale

From vernal blooms fresh fragrance! O, that God,
Profuse of poisons, would concede the chalice
Which but one living man has drained, who now,
685 Vessel of deathless wrath, a slave that feels
No proud exemption in the blighting curse
He bears, over the world wanders for ever,
Lone as incarnate death![4] O, that the dream
Of dark magician in his visioned[5] cave,
690 Raking the cinders of a crucible
For life and power, even when his feeble hand
Shakes in its last decay, were the true law
Of this so lovely world! But thou art fled
Like some frail exhalation; which the dawn
695 Robes in its golden beams—ah! thou hast fled!
The brave, the gentle, and the beautiful,
The child of grace and genius. Heartless things
Are done and said i'the world, and many worms
And beasts and men live on, and mighty Earth
700 From sea and mountain, city and wilderness,
In vesper[6] low or joyous orison,°   prayer
Lifts still its solemn voice—but thou art fled—
Thou canst no longer know or love the shapes
Of this phantasmal scene, who have to thee
705 Been purest ministers, who are, alas!
Now thou art not. Upon those pallid lips
So sweet even in their silence, on those eyes
That image sleep in death, upon that form
Yet safe from the worm's outrage, let no tear
710 Be shed—not even in thought. Nor, when those hues
Are gone, and those divinest lineaments,
Worn by the senseless° wind, shall live alone   unfeeling
In the frail pauses of this simple strain,
Let not high verse, mourning the memory
715 Of that which is no more, or painting's woe
Or sculpture, speak in feeble imagery
Their own cold powers. Art and eloquence,
And all the shows o'the world are frail and vain
To weep a loss that turns their lights to shade.

---

[1] *meteor* Formerly used to refer to any atmospheric phenomenon;
here, the moon.

[2] *two lessening points* The horns, or curved points, of the crescent
moon.

[3] *Medea's wondrous alchemy* According to Greek myth, the
sorceress Medea brewed a magic potion to restore youth to the dying
Aeson. In Ovid's version of the tale (*Metamorphosis* 7.275ff), some
of the potion spills on the ground and has the effect described in the
following lines.

---

[4] *one living … death* Reference to the legend of Ahasuerus, the
Wandering Jew, who taunted Christ on the way to His crucifixion
and as punishment was condemned to wander the earth until
Christ's second coming.

[5] *visioned* I.e., in which he has visions.

[6] *vesper* Evening prayer.

720　It is a woe too "deep for tears,"[1] when all
　　Is reft at once, when some surpassing Spirit,
　　Whose light adorned the world around it, leaves
　　Those who remain behind, not sobs or groans,
　　The passionate tumult of a clinging hope;
725　But pale despair and cold tranquillity,
　　Nature's vast frame, the web of human things,
　　Birth and the grave, that are not as they were.
　　　　—1816

Mutability

　　We are as clouds that veil the midnight moon;
　　　　How restlessly they speed, and gleam, and
　　　　　　quiver,
　　Streaking the darkness radiantly! Yet soon
　　Night closes round, and they are lost for ever:

5　Or like forgotten lyres,[2] whose dissonant strings
　　Give various response to each varying blast,
　　To whose frail frame no second motion brings
　　One mood or modulation like the last.

　　We rest—A dream has power to poison sleep;
10　We rise—One wandering thought pollutes the day;
　　We feel, conceive or reason, laugh or weep;
　　Embrace fond woe, or cast our cares away:

　　It is the same! For, be it joy or sorrow,
　　The path of its departure still is free:
15　Man's yesterday may ne'er be like his morrow;
　　Nought may endure but Mutability.
　　　　—1816

Mont Blanc
Lines Written in the Vale of Chamouni[3]

1

The everlasting universe of things
　Flows through the mind, and rolls its rapid waves,
Now dark—now glittering—now reflecting gloom—
Now lending splendour, where from secret springs
5　The source of human thought its tribute brings
Of waters—with a sound but half its own,
Such as a feeble brook will oft assume
In the wild woods, among the mountains lone,
Where waterfalls around it leap for ever,
10　Where woods and winds contend, and a vast river
Over its rocks ceaselessly bursts and raves.

2

Thus thou, Ravine of Arve—dark, deep Ravine—
Thou many-coloured, many-voicèd vale,
Over whose pines, and crags, and caverns sail
15　Fast cloud shadows and sunbeams: awful°　　　awe-inspiring
　　scene,
Where Power in likeness of the Arve comes down
From the ice gulfs that gird his secret throne,
Bursting through these dark mountains like the flame
Of lightning through the tempest—thou dost lie,
20　Thy giant brood of pines around thee clinging,
Children of elder time, in whose devotion
The chainless winds still come and ever came
To drink their odours, and their mighty swinging
To hear—an old and solemn harmony;
25　Thine earthly rainbows stretched across the sweep
Of the etherial waterfall, whose veil
Robes some unsculptured[4] image; the strange sleep
Which when the voices of the desert fail

1　*deep for tears*　From the last line of Wordsworth's "Ode: Intimations of Immortality": "Thoughts that do often lie too deep for tears."

2　*lyres*　Aeolian harps, stringed instruments that produce music when exposed to wind.

3　*Mont Blanc ... Chamouni*　Mont Blanc, located near France's border with Italy, is the highest peak in the Alps. Shelley conceived the idea for the poem when standing on a bridge over the Arve River in the Valley of Chamonix in southeastern France. Of the poem, Shelley wrote, "It was composed under the immediate impression of the deep and powerful feelings excited by the objects which it attempts to describe; and, as an indisciplined overflowing of the soul, rests its claim to approbation on an attempt to imitate the untameable wildness and inaccessible solemnity from which those feelings sprang."

4　*unsculptured*　I.e., not shaped by humans.

Wraps all in its own deep eternity—
30 Thy caverns echoing to the Arve's commotion,
A loud, lone sound no other sound can tame;
Thou art pervaded with that ceaseless motion,
Thou art the path of that unresting sound—
Dizzy Ravine! and when I gaze on thee
35 I seem as in a trance sublime and strange
To muse on my own separate fantasy,
My own, my human mind, which passively
Now renders and receives fast influencings,
Holding an unremitting interchange
40 With the clear universe of things around;
One legion of wild thoughts, whose wandering wings
Now float above thy darkness, and now rest
Where that or thou art no unbidden guest,
In the still cave of the witch Poesy,
45 Seeking among the shadows that pass by,
Ghosts of all things that are, some shade of thee,
Some phantom, some faint image; till the breast
From which they fled recalls them, thou art there!

3

Some say that gleams of a remoter world
50 Visit the soul in sleep—that death is slumber,
And that its shapes the busy thoughts outnumber
Of those who wake and live. I look on high;
Has some unknown omnipotence unfurled
The veil of life and death? or do I lie
55 In dream, and does the mightier world of sleep
Spread far around and inaccessibly
Its circles? For the very spirit fails,
Driven like a homeless cloud from steep to steep
That vanishes among the viewless° gales!   invisible
60 Far, far above, piercing the infinite sky,
Mont Blanc appears—still, snowy, and serene—
Its subject mountains their unearthly forms
Pile around it, ice and rock; broad vales between
Of frozen floods, unfathomable deeps,
65 Blue as the overhanging heaven, that spread
And wind among the accumulated steeps;
A desert peopled by the storms alone,
Save when the eagle brings some hunter's bone,
And the wolf tracks her there—how hideously
70 Its shapes are heaped around: rude, bare, and high,
Ghastly, and scarred, and riven. Is this the scene

Where the old Earthquake-daemon[1] taught her young
Ruin? Were these their toys? or did a sea
Of fire envelop once this silent snow?
75 None can reply—all seems eternal now.
The wilderness has a mysterious tongue
Which teaches awful doubt, or faith so mild,
So solemn, so serene, that man may be
But for such faith with nature reconciled;
80 Thou hast a voice, great Mountain, to repeal
Large codes of fraud and woe; not understood
By all, but which the wise, and great, and good
Interpret, or make felt, or deeply feel.

4

The fields, the lakes, the forests, and the streams,
85 Ocean, and all the living things that dwell
Within the daedal[2] earth; lightning, and rain,
Earthquake, and fiery flood, and hurricane,
The torpor of the year when feeble dreams
Visit the hidden buds, or dreamless sleep
90 Holds every future leaf and flower; the bound
With which from that detested trance they leap;
The works and ways of man, their death and birth,
And that of him and all that his may be;
All things that move and breathe with toil and sound
95 Are born and die; revolve, subside and swell.
Power dwells apart in its tranquillity
Remote, serene, and inaccessible:
And this, the naked countenance of earth,
On which I gaze, even these primeval mountains
100 Teach the adverting mind. The glaciers creep
Like snakes that watch their prey, from their far
        fountains,
Slow rolling on; there, many a precipice,
Frost and the Sun in scorn of mortal power
Have piled: dome, pyramid, and pinnacle,
105 A city of death, distinct with many a tower
And wall impregnable of beaming ice.
Yet not a city, but a flood of ruin
Is there, that from the boundaries of the sky
Rolls its perpetual stream; vast pines are strewing

---

[1] *daemon* In Greek mythology, supernatural being or minor deity
that controls some natural force.

[2] *daedal* Skillfully or intricately wrought. (From Daedalus of
classical myth, who built the famous labyrinth in Crete.)

110 Its destined path, or in the mangled soil
Branchless and shattered stand; the rocks, drawn down
From yon remotest waste, have overthrown
The limits of the dead and living world,
Never to be reclaimed. The dwelling-place
115 Of insects, beasts, and birds, becomes its spoil;
Their food and their retreat for ever gone,
So much of life and joy is lost. The race
Of man flies far in dread; his work and dwelling
Vanish, like smoke before the tempest's stream,
120 And their place is not known. Below, vast caves
Shine in the rushing torrent's restless gleam,
Which from those secret chasms in tumult welling[1]
Meet in the vale, and one majestic River,
The breath and blood of distant lands, for ever
125 Rolls its loud waters to the ocean waves,
Breathes its swift vapours to the circling air.

5

Mont Blanc yet gleams on high—the power is there,
The still and solemn power of many sights
And many sounds, and much of life and death.
130 In the calm darkness of the moonless nights,
In the lone glare of day, the snows descend
Upon that Mountain; none beholds them there,
Nor when the flakes burn in the sinking sun,
Or the star-beams dart through them. Winds contend
135 Silently there, and heap the snow with breath
Rapid and strong, but silently! Its home
The voiceless lightning in these solitudes
Keeps innocently, and like vapour broods
Over the snow. The secret strength of things
140 Which governs thought, and to the infinite dome
Of heaven is as a law, inhabits thee!
And what were thou, and earth, and stars, and sea,
If to the human mind's imaginings
Silence and solitude were vacancy?
—1817

---

1 *Which from ... welling* Cf. Coleridge's *Kubla Khan*, lines 12–24.

Hymn to Intellectual Beauty[2]

1

The awful shadow of some unseen Power
    Floats though unseen amongst us, visiting
    This various world with as inconstant wing
As summer winds that creep from flower to flower.
5 Like moonbeams that behind some piny mountain
        shower,
        It visits with inconstant glance
        Each human heart and countenance;
Like hues and harmonies of evening,
        Like clouds in starlight widely spread,
10   Like memory of music fled,
        Like aught that for its grace may be
Dear, and yet dearer for its mystery.

2

Spirit of BEAUTY, that doth consecrate
    With thine own hues all thou dost shine upon
15   Of human thought or form—where art thou gone?
Why dost thou pass away and leave our state,
This dim vast vale of tears, vacant and desolate?
        Ask why the sunlight not forever
        Weaves rainbows o'er yon mountain river,
20 Why aught should fail and fade that once is shown,
        Why fear and dream and death and birth
        Cast on the daylight of this earth
        Such gloom—why man has such a scope
For love and hate, despondency and hope?

3

25 No voice from some sublimer world hath ever
    To sage or poet these responses given—
    Therefore the name of God, and ghosts, and Heaven,
Remain the records of their vain endeavour,
Frail spells—whose uttered charm might not avail to
        sever,
30   From all we hear and all we see,

---

2 *Hymn ... Beauty* Composed during the summer of 1816, the same summer in which Shelley wrote "Mont Blanc." The concept of "intellectual beauty" is Platonic in origin and was a popular one in contemporary writing. It denotes a beauty of the soul, or the mind and its inventions, that cannot be perceived by the senses and therefore must be grasped intuitively.

Doubt, chance, and mutability.
Thy light alone—like mist o'er mountains driven,
    Or music by the night wind sent
    Through strings of some still instrument,
35   Or moonlight on a midnight stream,
Gives grace and truth to life's unquiet dream.

4

Love, Hope, and Self-esteem, like clouds depart
    And come, for some uncertain moments lent.
    Man were° immortal, and omnipotent,   *would be*
40 Didst thou,[1] unknown and awful as thou art,
Keep with thy glorious train firm state within his heart.
    Thou messenger of sympathies
    That wax and wane in lovers' eyes—
Thou—that to human thought art nourishment,
45   Like darkness to a dying flame!
    Depart not as thy shadow came,
    Depart not—lest the grave should be,
Like life and fear, a dark reality.

5

While yet a boy I sought for ghosts, and sped
50   Through many a listening chamber, cave and ruin,
    And starlight wood, with fearful steps pursuing
Hopes of high talk with the departed dead.
I called on poisonous names with which our youth is fed,
    I was not heard—I saw them not—
55   When musing deeply on the lot
Of life, at that sweet time when winds are wooing
    All vital things that wake to bring
    News of buds and blossoming—
    Sudden, thy shadow fell on me;
60 I shrieked, and clasped my hands in ecstasy!

6

I vowed that I would dedicate my powers
    To thee and thine—have I not kept the vow?
    With beating heart and streaming eyes, even now
I call the phantoms of a thousand hours
65 Each from his voiceless grave: they have in visioned
        bowers
    Of studious zeal or love's delight
    Outwatched with me the envious night—

---

[1] *Didst thou* I.e., "if thou didst."

They know that never joy illumed my brow
    Unlinked with hope that thou wouldst free
70   This world from its dark slavery,
    That thou—O awful LOVELINESS,
Wouldst give whate'er these words cannot express.

7

The day becomes more solemn and serene
    When noon is past—there is a harmony
75   In autumn, and a lustre in its sky,
Which through the summer is not heard or seen,
As if it could not be, as if it had not been!
    Thus let thy power, which like the truth
    Of nature on my passive youth
80 Descended, to my onward life supply
    Its calm—to one who worships thee,
    And every form containing thee,
    Whom, SPIRIT fair, thy spells did bind
To fear° himself, and love all human kind.   *revere*
    —1817

Ozymandias[2]

I met a traveller from an antique land
Who said: Two vast and trunkless legs of stone
Stand in the desert … Near them, on the sand,
Half sunk, a shattered visage lies, whose frown,
5 And wrinkled lip, and sneer of cold command,
Tell that its sculptor well those passions read
Which yet survive, stamped on these lifeless things,
The hand that mocked them, and the heart that fed:
And on the pedestal these words appear:
10 "My name is Ozymandias, king of kings:
Look on my works, ye Mighty, and despair!"
Nothing beside remains. Round the decay
Of that colossal wreck, boundless and bare
The lone and level sands stretch far away.
    —1818

---

[2] *Ozymandias* Greek name for King Ramses II of Egypt (1304–1237 BCE). First century BCE Greek historian Diodorus Siculus records the story of this monument (Ozymandias's tomb was in the shape of a male sphinx) and its inscription, which Diodorus says reads: "King of Kings am I, Ozymandias. If anyone would know how great I am and where I lie, let him surpass one of my exploits."

Ode to the West Wind[1]

1

O Wild West Wind, thou breath[2] of Autumn's
        being,
Thou, from whose unseen presence the leaves dead
Are driven, like ghosts from an enchanter fleeing,

Yellow, and black, and pale, and hectic° red,   *feverish*
5   Pestilence-stricken multitudes: O thou,
Who chariotest to their dark wintry bed

The winged seeds, where they lie cold and low,
Each like a corpse within its grave, until
Thine azure sister of the Spring shall blow

10 Her clarion[3] o'er the dreaming earth, and fill
(Driving sweet buds like flocks to feed in air)
With living hues and odours plain and hill:

Wild Spirit, which art moving everywhere;
Destroyer and Preserver; hear, oh, hear!

2

15 Thou on whose stream, 'mid the steep sky's commotion,
Loose clouds like earth's decaying leaves are shed,
Shook from the tangled boughs of Heaven and Ocean,

Angels° of rain and lightning: there are spread   *harbingers*
On the blue surface of thine aëry surge,
20 Like the bright hair uplifted from the head

Of some fierce Mænad,[4] even from the dim verge
Of the horizon to the zenith's height,
The locks of the approaching storm. Thou dirge

Of the dying year, to which this closing night
25 Will be the dome of a vast sepulchre,
Vaulted with all thy congregated might

Of vapours,° from whose solid atmosphere   *clouds*
Black rain, and fire, and hail will burst: oh, hear!

3

Thou who didst waken from his summer dreams
30 The blue Mediterranean, where he lay,
Lulled by the coil of his chrystàlline streams,[5]

Beside a pumice isle in Baiae's bay,[6]
And saw in sleep old palaces and towers
Quivering within the wave's intenser day,

35 All overgrown with azure moss and flowers
So sweet, the sense faints picturing them! Thou
For whose path the Atlantic's level powers

Cleave themselves into chasms, while far below
The sea-blooms and the oozy woods which wear
40 The sapless foliage of the ocean, know

Thy voice, and suddenly grow gray with fear,
And tremble and despoil themselves:[7] oh, hear!

---

[1] [Shelley's note]   This poem was conceived and chiefly written in a wood that skirts the Arno, near Florence, and on a day when that tempestuous wind, whose temperature is at once mild and animating, was collecting the vapours which pour down the autumnal rains. They began, as I foresaw, at sunset with a violent tempest of hail and rain, attended by that magnificent thunder and lightning peculiar to the Cispaline regions.

[2] *breath*   The Latin word for wind, *spiritus*, also means "breath" and "soul," and is the root of the word "inspiration."

[3] *clarion*   High-pitched trumpet.

[4] *Mænad*   Female attendant of Bacchus, the Greek god of wine.

[5] *coil … streams*   Currents of the Mediterranean, the color of which are often different from the surrounding water.

[6] *pumice*   Porous stone made from cooled lava; *Baiae's Bay*   Bay west of Naples that contains the ruins of several imperial villas.

[7] [Shelley's note]   The phenomenon alluded to at the conclusion of the third stanza is well known to naturalists. The vegetation at the bottom of the sea, of rivers, and of lakes, sympathizes with that of the land in the change of seasons, and is consequently influenced by the winds which announce it.

4

If I were a dead leaf thou mightest bear;
If I were a swift cloud to fly with thee;
45 A wave to pant beneath thy power, and share

The impulse of thy strength, only less free
Than thou, O uncontrollable! If even
I were as in my boyhood, and could be

The comrade of thy wanderings over Heaven,
50 As then, when to outstrip thy skiey speed
Scarce seemed a vision; I would ne'er have striven

As thus with thee in prayer in my sore need.
Oh! lift me as a wave, a leaf, a cloud!
I fall upon the thorns of life! I bleed!

55 A heavy weight of hours has chained and bowed
One too like thee: tameless, and swift, and proud.

5

Make me thy lyre,[1] even as the forest is:
What if my leaves are falling like its own!
The tumult of thy mighty harmonies

60 Will take from both a deep, autumnal tone,
Sweet though in sadness. Be thou, Spirit fierce,
My spirit! Be thou me, impetuous one!

Drive my dead thoughts over the universe
Like withered leaves to quicken a new birth!
65 And, by the incantation of this verse,

Scatter, as from an unextinguished hearth
Ashes and sparks, my words among mankind!
Be through my lips to unawakened Earth

The trumpet of a prophecy! O, Wind,
70 If Winter comes, can Spring be far behind?
—1820

The Cloud

I bring fresh showers for the thirsting flowers,
    From the seas and the streams;
I bear light shade for the leaves when laid
    In their noonday dreams.
5 From my wings are shaken the dews that waken
    The sweet buds every one,
When rocked to rest on their mother's breast,
    As she dances about the sun.
I wield the flail of the lashing hail,
10   And whiten the green plains under,
And then again I dissolve it in rain,
    And laugh as I pass in thunder.

I sift the snow on the mountains below,
    And their great pines groan aghast;
15 And all the night 'tis my pillow white,
    While I sleep in the arms of the blast,
Sublime on the towers of my skiey bowers,
    Lightning my pilot sits;
In a cavern under is fettered the thunder,
20   It struggles and howls at fits;[2]
Over earth and ocean, with gentle motion,
    This pilot is guiding me,
Lured by the love of the genii that move
    In the depths of the purple sea;
25 Over the rills, and the crags, and the hills,
    Over the lakes and the plains,
Wherever he dream, under mountain or stream,
    The Spirit he loves remains;
And I all the while bask in Heaven's blue smile,
30   Whilst he is dissolving in rains.

The sanguine Sunrise, with his meteor eyes,
    And his burning plumes outspread,
Leaps on the back of my sailing rack,[3]
    When the morning star shines dead;
35 As on the jag of a mountain crag,
    Which an earthquake rocks and swings,
An eagle alit one moment may sit
    In the light of its golden wings.

---

1 *lyre* Aeolian harp, a stringed instrument that produces music when exposed to wind.

2 *at fits* Fitfully.

3 *rack* Mass of clouds in the upper air.

And when Sunset may breathe, from the lit sea beneath,
40   Its ardours of rest and love,
And the crimson pall[1] of eve may fall
    From the depth of Heaven above,
With wings folded I rest, on mine aëry nest,
    As still as a brooding dove.

45 That orbèd maiden with white fire laden,
    Whom mortals call the Moon,
Glides glimmering o'er my fleece-like floor,
    By the midnight breezes strewn;
And wherever the beat of her unseen feet,
50   Which only the angels hear,
May have broken the woof° of my tent's   *weave*
    thin roof,
    The stars peep behind her and peer;
And I laugh to see them whirl and flee,
    Like a swarm of golden bees,
55 When I widen the rent in my wind-built tent,
    Till the calm rivers, lakes, and seas,
Like strips of the sky fallen through me on high,
    Are each paved with the moon and these.

I bind the Sun's throne with a burning zone,°   *belt*
60   And the Moon's with a girdle of pearl;
The volcanoes are dim, and the stars reel and swim,
    When the whirlwinds my banner unfurl.
From cape to cape, with a bridge-like shape,
    Over a torrent sea,
65 Sunbeam-proof, I hand like a roof—
    The mountains its columns be.
The triumphal arch through which I march
    With hurricane, fire, and snow,
When the Powers of the air are chained to my chair,
70   Is the million-coloured bow;
The sphere-fire[2] above its soft colours wove,
    While the moist Earth was laughing below.

I am the daughter of Earth and Water,
    And the nursing of the Sky;
75 I pass through the pores of the ocean and shores;
    I change, but I cannot die.
For after the rain, when with never a stain

    The pavilion of Heaven is bare,
And the winds and sunbeams with their convex gleams
80   Build up the blue dome of air,
I silently laugh at my own cenotaph,[3]
    And out of the caverns of rain,
Like a child from the womb, like a ghost from the tomb,
    I arise and unbuild it again.
—1820

To a Skylark[4]

Hail to thee, blithe Spirit!
  Bird thou never wert,
That from Heaven, or near it,
  Pourest thy full heart
5 In profuse strains of unpremeditated art.

Higher still and higher
  From the earth thou springest
Like a cloud of fire;
  The blue deep thou wingest,
10 And singing still dost soar, and soaring ever singest.

In the golden lightning
  Of the sunken sun,
O'er which clouds are bright'ning,
  Thou dost float and run;
15 Like an unbodied joy whose race is just begun.

The pale purple even
  Melts around thy flight;
Like a star of Heaven,
  In the broad daylight
20 Thou art unseen, but yet I hear thy shrill delight,

Keen as are the arrows
  Of that silver sphere,[5]
Whose intense lamp narrows

---

1 *pall* Rich cloth or canopy.

2 *sphere-fire* I.e., sunlight.

3 *cenotaph* Empty sepulcher; monument honoring a dead person whose body lies elsewhere.

4 *Skylark* Small bird that sings only when in flight, and often flies so high that it cannot be easily seen.

5 *silver sphere* I.e., the morning star.

In the white dawn clear
25 Until we hardly see—we feel that it is there.

All the earth and air
 With thy voice is loud,
As, when night is bare,
 From one lonely cloud
30 The moon rains out her beams, and Heaven is
 overflowed.

What thou art we know not;
 What is most like thee?
From rainbow clouds there flow not
 Drops so bright to see
35 As from thy presence showers a rain of melody.

Like a Poet hidden
 In the light of thought,
Singing hymns unbidden,
 Till the world is wrought
40 To sympathy with hopes and fears it heeded not:

Like a high-born maiden
 In a palace-tower,
Soothing her love-laden
 Soul in secret hour
45 With music sweet as love, which overflows her bower:

Like a glow-worm golden
 In a dell of dew,
Scattering unbeholden
 Its aëreal hue
50 Among the flowers and grass, which screen it from the
 view:

Like a rose embowered
 In its own green leaves,
By warm winds deflowered,
 Till the scent it gives
55 Makes faint with too much sweet these heavy-wingèd
 thieves:

Sound of vernal° showers   *springtime*
 On the twinkling grass,
Rain-awakened flowers,

All that ever was
60 Joyous, and clear, and fresh, thy music doth surpass:

Teach us, Sprite° or Bird,   *fairy*
 What sweet thoughts are thine:
I have never heard
 Praise of love or wine
65 That panted forth a flood of rapture so divine.

Chorus Hymeneal,[1]
 Or triumphal chaunt,°   *chant*
Matched with thine would be all
 But an empty vaunt,
70 A thing wherein we feel there is some hidden want.

What objects are the fountains
 Of thy happy strain?
What fields, or waves, or mountains?
 What shapes of sky or plain?
75 What love of thine own kind? what ignorance of pain?

With thy clear keen joyance
 Languor cannot be:
Shadow of annoyance
 Never came near thee:
80 Thou lovest—but ne'er knew love's sad satiety.

Waking or asleep,
 Thou of death must deem
Things more true and deep
 Than we mortals dream,
85 Or how could thy notes flow in such a crystal stream?

We look before and after,
 And pine for what is not:
Our sincerest laughter
 With some pain is fraught;
90 Our sweetest songs are those that tell of saddest thought.

Yet if we could scorn
 Hate, and pride, and fear;
If we were things born
 Not to shed a tear,
95 I know not how thy joy we ever should come near.

---

[1] *Hymeneal* Marital (Hymen is the Greek god of marriage).

Better than all measures
    Of delightful sound,
Better than all treasures
    That in books are found,
100 Thy skill to poet were, thou scorner of the ground!

Teach me half the gladness
    That thy brain must know,
Such harmonious madness
    From my lips would flow
105 The world should listen then—as I am listening now.
—1820

Adonais

In this pastoral elegy for fellow poet John Keats, Shelley calls the young poet Adonais after Adonis, the beautiful youth of classical myth who was loved by Venus and killed by a wild boar. In some versions of the story Venus asks Persephone, Queen of the underworld, to allow Adonis to return above ground for four months of every year, while in others she transforms his blood into the bright red anemone, enabling him to live on in this ever-blooming flower.

    Shelley had known Keats only casually, through their mutual acquaintance Leigh Hunt, the editor of the radical *Examiner*, but he admired his poetry and agreed with many of his political views. Hearing of Keats's serious illness in 1820, Shelley had invited Keats to spend the winter with him in Pisa. Keats did journey to Italy, but died in Rome in February of 1812, before he could reach Pisa.

    The beast whom Shelley blames for Keats's death is the anonymous critic who ridiculed Keats's *Endymion* in *The Quarterly Review* (April 1818); Shelley thus gave force to a sentimental myth that Keats's illness and death were brought on by demoralizing reviews, both in *The Quarterly Review* and *Blackwoods Magazine*. For many years after his death, it was commonly maintained that, as Byron said, Keats was "snuffed out by an article." Until the late 1840s, Keats was better known by *Adonais* and the legend of his death than by his own poetry.

Adonais
An Elegy on the Death of John Keats

Αστήρ πρὶν μὲν ἐλαμπες ενι ζῶοισιν εῶος.
    Νυν δε θανὼν, λαμπεις ἕοπερος εν φθίμενοις.
                         PLATO[1]

1

I weep for Adonais—he is dead!
O, weep for Adonais! though our tears
Thaw not the frost which binds so dear a head!
And thou, sad Hour, selected from all years
5 To mourn our loss, rouse thy obscure compeers,
And teach them thine own sorrow, say: with me
Died Adonais; till the Future dares
Forget the Past, his fate and fame shall be
An echo and a light unto eternity!

2

10 Where wert thou mighty Mother, when he lay,
When thy Son lay, pierced by the shaft which flies
In darkness? Where was lorn° Urania[2]   *forlorn*
When Adonais died? With veiled eyes,
'Mid listening Echoes, in her Paradise
15 She sate, while one, with soft enamoured breath,
Rekindled all the fading melodies,
With which, like flowers that mock the corse°   *body*
    beneath,
He had adorned and hid the coming bulk of death.

3

O, weep for Adonais—he is dead!
20 Wake, melancholy Mother, wake and weep!
Yet wherefore? Quench within their burning bed
Thy fiery tears, and let thy loud heart keep
Like his, a mute and uncomplaining sleep;
For he is gone, where all things wise and fair

---

1 Αστήρ ... *Plato* [Shelley's translation] Thou wert the morning star among the living, / Ere thy fair light had fled— / Now, having died, thou art as Hesperus, giving / New splendour to the dead. [Translation from the Greek of Plato's *Epigram on Aster*. The planet Venus appears in the sky as both the morning star, Vesper, and the evening star, Hesperus.]

2 *Urania* Muse who is invoked near the beginning of Milton's *Paradise Lost*. Urania is also an epithet for the goddess Venus, who loved Adonais.

25   Descend—oh, dream not that the amorous Deep°   *abyss*
    Will yet restore him to the vital air;
    Death feeds on his mute voice, and laughs at our
       despair.

4

    Most musical of mourners, weep again!
    Lament anew, Urania! He[1] died,
30   Who was the Sire of an immortal strain,
    Blind, old, and lonely, when his country's pride,
    The priest, the slave, and the liberticide,
    Trampled and mocked with many a loathed rite
    Of lust and blood; he went, unterrified,
35   Into the gulf of death; but his clear Sprite°   *spirit*
    Yet reigns o'er earth; the third among the sons of light.

5

    Most musical of mourners, weep anew!
    Not all to that bright station dared to climb;
    And happier they their happiness who knew,
40   Whose tapers yet burn through that night of time
    In which suns perished; others more sublime,
    Struck by the envious wrath of man or God,
    Have sunk, extinct in their refulgent° prime;   *gleaming*
    And some yet live, treading the thorny road,
45   Which leads, through toil and hate, to Fame's serene
       abode.

6

    But now, thy youngest, dearest one, has perished,
    The nursling of thy widowhood, who grew,
    Like a pale flower by some sad maiden cherished,
    And fed with true love tears, instead of dew;
50   Most musical of mourners, weep anew!
    Thy extreme hope, the loveliest and the last,
    The bloom, whose petals nipt before they blew,°   *bloomed*
    Died on the promise of the fruit, is waste;
    The broken lily lies—the storm is overpast.

7

55   To that high Capital,[2] where kingly Death
    Keeps his pale court in beauty and decay,
    He came; and bought, with price of purest breath,
    A grave among the eternal. Come away!
    Haste, while the vault of blue Italian day
60   Is yet his fitting charnel°-roof! while still   *mortuary*
    He lies, as if in dewy sleep he lay;
    Awake him not! surely he takes his fill
    Of deep and liquid rest, forgetful of all ill.

8

    He will awake no more, oh, never more!
65   Within the twilight chamber spreads apace,
    The shadow of white Death, and at the door
    Invisible Corruption waits to trace
    His extreme way to her dim dwelling-place;
    The eternal Hunger sits, but pity and awe
70   Soothe her pale rage, nor dares she to deface
    So fair a prey, till darkness, and the law
    Of mortal change, shall fill the grave which is her
       maw.°   *stomach*

9

    O, weep for Adonais! The quick° Dreams,   *living*
    The passion-winged Ministers of thought,
75   Who were his flocks, whom near the living streams
    Of his young spirit he fed, and whom he taught
    The love which was its music, wander not—
    Wander no more, from kindling brain to brain,
    But droop there, whence they sprung; and mourn their
       lot
80   Round the cold heart, where, after their sweet pain,
    They ne'er will gather strength, or find a home again.

10

    And one with trembling hands clasps his cold head,
    And fans him with her moonlight wings, and cries,
    "Our love, our hope, our sorrow, is not dead;
85   See, on the silken fringe of his faint eyes,
    Like dew upon a sleeping flower, there lies
    A tear some Dream has loosened from his brain."
    Lost Angel of a ruined Paradise!

---

1 *He* Poet John Milton (1608–74), who served in Cromwell's Parliamentary government and, as a result, was imprisoned when the monarchy was restored, although he was released quickly. At the end of this stanza, Shelley places Milton in a triumvirate with the earlier epic poets Homer and Dante ("the third among the sons of light").

2 *high Capital* Rome, where Keats died.

She knew not 'twas her own; as with no stain
90 She faded, like a cloud which had outwept its rain.

11

One from a lucid° urn of starry dew   *resplendent*
Washed his light limbs as if embalming them;
Another clipt her profuse locks, and threw
The wreath upon him, like an anadem,°   *garland*
95 Which frozen tears instead of pearls begem;
Another in her wilful grief would break
Her bow and winged reeds,° as if to stem   *arrows*
A greater loss with one which was more weak;
And dull the barbed fire against his frozen cheek.

12

100 Another Splendour on his mouth alit,
That mouth, whence it was wont to draw the breath
Which gave it strength to pierce the guarded wit,
And pass into the panting heart beneath
With lightning and with music: the damp death
105 Quenched its caress upon his icy lips;
And, as a dying meteor stains a wreath
Of moonlight vapour, which the cold night clips,° *clasps*
It flushed through his pale limbs, and passed to its
    eclipse.

13

And others came … Desires and Adorations,
110 Winged Persuasions and veiled Destinies,
Splendours, and Glooms, and glimmering Incarnations
Of hopes and fears, and twilight Phantasies;
And Sorrow, with her family of Sighs,
And Pleasure, blind with tears, led by the gleam
115 Of her own dying smile instead of eyes,
Came in slow pomp—the moving pomp might seem
Like pageantry of mist on an autumnal stream.

14

All he had loved, and moulded into thought,
From shape, and hue, and odour, and sweet sound,
120 Lamented Adonais. Morning sought
Her eastern watchtower, and her hair unbound,
Wet with the tears which should adorn the ground,
Dimmed the aerial eyes that kindle day;
Afar the melancholy thunder moaned,

125 Pale Ocean in unquiet slumber lay,
And the wild winds flew round, sobbing in their dismay.

15

Lost Echo sits amid the voiceless mountains,
And feeds her grief with his remembered lay,° *song*
And will no more reply to winds or fountains,
130 Or amorous birds perched on the young green spray,
Or herdsman's horn, or bell° at closing day; *church-bell*
Since she can mimic not his lips, more dear
Than those for whose disdain she pined away
Into a shadow of all sounds[1]—a drear
135 Murmur, between their songs, is all the woodmen hear.

16

Grief made the young Spring wild, and she threw down
Her kindling buds, as if she Autumn were,
Or they dead leaves; since her delight is flown
For whom should she have waked the sullen year?
140 To Phoebus was not Hyacinth so dear[2]
Nor to himself Narcissus, as to both
Thou Adonais: wan they stand and sere° *withered*
Amid the drooping comrades of their youth,
With dew all turned to tears; odour, to sighing ruth.° *pity*

17

145 Thy spirit's sister, the lorn nightingale
Mourns not her mate with such melodious pain;
Not so the eagle, who like thee could scale
Heaven, and could nourish in the sun's domain
Her mighty youth with morning,[3] doth complain,
150 Soaring and screaming round her empty nest,

[1] *those for … sounds* Narcissus, whom the nymph Echo loved. Echo had been robbed of her voice by the goddess Hera, and could only repeat what others said. After falling in love with Narcissus, who rejected her in favor of his own reflection, she pined away until only her echoing voice remained.

[2] *To Phoebus … dear* Phoebus Apollo, god of poetry and the sun, loved the beautiful youth Hyacinthus. When Hyacinthus was accidentally slain by a discus the god had thrown, Apollo caused the hyacinth flower to spring up from his spilt blood. It was said that Zephyrus (the west wind), a rejected suitor of Hyancinthus, blew the discus off course so that it would strike the youth. "Zephyr" was also the pen name of the reviewer of *Endymion*.

[3] *nourish … morning* According to legend, the eagle could renew her youth by flying toward the sun until its heat burnt off her old plumage and cleared the film from her eyes.

As Albion[1] wails for thee: the curse of Cain[2]
Light on his head who pierced thy innocent breast,
And scared the angel soul that was its earthly guest!

18

Ah woe is me! Winter is come and gone,
155 But grief returns with the revolving year;
The airs and streams renew their joyous tone;
The ants, the bees, the swallows reappear;
Fresh leaves and flowers deck the dead Seasons' bier;
The amorous birds now pair in every brake,°   *thicket*
160 And build their mossy homes in field and brere;°   *briar*
And the green lizard, and the golden snake,
Like unimprisoned flames, out of their trance awake.

19

Through wood and stream and field and hill and Ocean
A quickening life from the Earth's heart has burst
165 As it has ever done, with change and motion,
From the great morning of the world when first
God dawned on Chaos; in its steam immersed
The lamps of Heaven flash with a softer light;
All baser things pant with life's sacred thirst;
170 Diffuse themselves; and spend in love's delight,
The beauty and the joy of their renewed might.

20

The leprous corpse touched by this spirit tender
Exhales itself in flowers of gentle breath;
Like incarnations of the stars, when splendour
175 Is changed to fragrance, they illumine death
And mock the merry worm that wakes beneath;
Nought we know, dies. Shall that alone which knows[3]
Be as a sword consumed before the sheath
By sightless[4] lightning?—th'intense atom glows
180 A moment, then is quenched in a most cold repose.

21

Alas! that all we loved of him should be,

But for our grief, as if it had not been,
And grief itself be mortal! Woe is me!
Whence are we, and why are we? of what scene
185 The actors or spectators? Great and mean
Meet massed in death, who lends what life must borrow.
As long as skies are blue, and fields are green,
Evening must usher night, night urge the morrow,
Month follow month with woe, and year wake year to
   sorrow.

22

190 *He* will awake no more, oh, never more!
"Wake thou," cried Misery, "childless Mother, rise
Out of thy sleep, and slake,° in thy heart's core,   *ease*
A wound more fierce than his with tears and sighs."
And all the Dreams that watched Urania's eyes,
195 And all the Echoes whom their sister's song
Had held in holy silence, cried: "Arise!"
Swift as a Thought by the snake Memory stung,
From her ambrosial[5] rest the fading Splendour sprung.

23

She rose like an autumnal Night, that springs
200 Out of the East, and follows wild and drear
The golden Day, which, on eternal wings,
Even as a ghost abandoning a bier,
Had left the Earth a corpse. Sorrow and fear
So struck, so roused, so rapt Urania;
205 So saddened round her like an atmosphere
Of stormy mist; so swept her on her way
Even to the mournful place where Adonais lay.

24

Out of her secret Paradise she sped,
Through camps and cities rough with stone, and steel,
210 And human hearts, which to her aery tread
Yielding not, wounded the invisible
Palms of her tender feet where'er they fell:
And barbed tongues, and thoughts more sharp than they
Rent the soft Form they never could repel,
215 Whose sacred blood, like the young tears of May,
Paved with eternal flowers that undeserving way.

---

[1] *Albion*   England.

[2] *curse of Cain*   For murdering his brother Abel, Cain was forced to
wander the earth as a vagabond, unable to farm because no land
would yield crops for him. See Genesis 4.

[3] *that alone which knows*   I.e., the mind.

[4] *sightless*   Invisible; blind.

[5] *ambrosial*   Divine (ambrosia is the food of the gods); *the fading
Splendour*   Urania.

25

In the death chamber for a moment Death,
Shamed by the presence of that living Might,
Blushed to annihilation, and the breath
220 Revisited those lips, and life's pale light
Flashed through those limbs, so late her dear delight.
"Leave me not wild and drear and comfortless,
As silent lightning leaves the starless night!
Leave me not!" cried Urania: her distress
225 Roused Death: Death rose and smiled, and met her
        vain caress.

26

"Stay yet awhile! speak to me once again;
Kiss me, so long but as a kiss may live;
And in my heartless breast and burning brain
230 That word, that kiss shall all thoughts else survive,
With food of saddest memory kept alive,
Now thou art dead, as if it were a part
Of thee, my Adonais! I would give
All that I am to be as thou now art!
But I am chained to Time, and cannot thence depart!

27

235 "Oh gentle child, beautiful as thou wert,
Why didst thou leave the trodden paths of men
Too soon, and with weak hands though mighty heart
Dare° the unpastured dragon in his den?   *challenge*
Defenceless as thou wert, oh where was then
240 Wisdom the mirrored shield,[1] or scorn the spear?
Or hadst thou waited the full cycle, when
Thy spirit should have filled its crescent sphere,
The monsters of life's waste had fled from thee like deer.

28

"The herded wolves, bold only to pursue;
245 The obscene ravens, clamorous o'er the dead;
The vultures to the conqueror's banner true
Who feed where Desolation first has fed,
And whose wings rain contagion—how they fled,
When like Apollo, from his golden bow,

250 The Pythian of the age[2] one arrow sped
And smiled! The spoilers tempt no second blow,
They fawn on the proud feet that spurn them as they
        go.

29

"The sun comes forth, and many reptiles spawn;
He sets, and each ephemeral insect then
255 Is gathered into death without a dawn,
And the immortal stars awake again;
So is it in the world of living men:
A godlike mind soars forth, in its delight
Making earth bare and veiling heaven, and when
260 It sinks, the swarms that dimmed or shared its light
Leave to its kindred lamps the spirit's awful°   *awe-inspiring*
        night."

30

Thus ceased she: and the mountain shepherds came,
Their garlands sere, their magic mantles rent;
The Pilgrim of Eternity,[3] whose fame
265 Over his living head like Heaven is bent,
An early but enduring monument,
Came, veiling all the lightnings of his song
In sorrow; from her wilds Ierne° sent   *Ireland*
The sweetest lyrist of her saddest wrong,
270 And love taught grief to fall like music from his
        tongue.[4]

31

Midst others of less note, came one frail Form,[5]
A phantom among men; companionless
As the last cloud of an expiring storm
Whose thunder is its knell;° he, as I guess,   *funeral-bell*
275 Had gazed on Nature's naked loveliness,

---

[1] *mirrored shield* Because the stare of the Gorgon Medusa would turn men into stone, Perseus fought and defeated her by viewing her reflection in his shield.

[2] *Pythian of the age* Byron, who attacked the unfavorable reviewers of his *Hours of Idleness* in his satire *English Bards and Scotch Reviewers* (1809). The epithet "Pythian" was given to the god Apollo when he slew the dragon Python.

[3] *Pilgrim of Eternity* Byron.

[4] *The sweetest ... tongue* Poet Thomas Moore (1779–1852), whose *Irish Melodies* deals with the oppression of his native Ireland by England.

[5] *one frail Form* Shelley.

Actæon-like,[1] and now he fled astray
With feeble steps o'er the world's wilderness,
And his own thoughts, along that rugged way,
Pursued, like raging hounds, their father and their prey.

32

280 A pardlike° Spirit beautiful and swift—   *leopard-like*
A Love in desolation masked—a Power
Girt round with weakness; it can scarce uplift
The weight of the superincumbent hour;
It is a dying lamp, a falling shower,
285 A breaking billow—even whilst we speak
Is it not broken? On the withering flower
The killing sun smiles brightly: on a cheek
The life can burn in blood, even while the heart may
    break.

33

His head was bound with pansies overblown,
290 And faded violets, white, and pied, and blue;
And a light spear topped with a cypress cone,
Round whose rude shaft dark ivy tresses grew[2]
Yet dripping with the forest's noonday dew,
Vibrated, as the ever-beating heart
295 Shook the weak hand that grasped it; of that crew
He came the last, neglected and apart;
A herd-abandoned deer struck by the hunter's dart.

34

All stood aloof, and at his partial° moan   *sympathetic*
Smiled through their tears; well knew that gentle band
300 Who in another's fate now wept his own;
As in the accents of an unknown land,
He sung new sorrow; sad Urania scanned
The Stranger's mien, and murmured: "who art thou?"
He answered not, but with a sudden hand
305 Made bare his branded and ensanguined° brow,   *bloody*
Which was like Cain's or Christ's—Oh! that it should
    be so!

35

What softer voice is hushed over the dead?
Athwart what brow is that dark mantle thrown?
What form leans sadly o'er the white death-bed,
310 In mockery of monumental stone,
The heavy heart heaving without a moan?
If it be He, who, gentlest of the wise,
Taught, soothed, loved, honoured the departed one;[3]
Let me not vex, with inharmonious sighs
315 The silence of that heart's accepted sacrifice.

36

Our Adonais has drunk poison—oh!
What deaf and viperous murderer could crown
Life's early cup with such a draught of woe?
The nameless worm would now itself disown:
320 It felt, yet could escape the magic tone
Whose prelude held all envy, hate, and wrong,
But what was howling in one breast alone,
Silent with expectation of the song,
Whose master's hand is cold, whose silver lyre unstrung.[4]

37

325 Live thou, whose infamy is not thy fame!
Live! fear no heavier chastisement from me,
Thou noteless blot on a remembered name!
But be thyself, and know thyself to be!
And ever at thy season be thou free
330 To spill the venom when thy fangs o'er flow:
Remorse and Self-contempt shall cling to thee;
Hot Shame shall burn upon thy secret brow,
And like a beaten hound tremble thou shalt—as now.

38

Nor let us weep that our delight is fled
335 Far from these carrion kites[5] that scream below;
He wakes or sleeps with the enduring dead;
Thou canst not soar where he is sitting now.

---

[1] *Actæon-like*   Actaeon was a hunter who accidentally came upon Diana, goddess of chastity, bathing naked. Angered, she turned him into a stag, and his own hounds chased him down and tore him apart.

[2] *pansies overblown*   Pansies (a symbol of sorrow) past their bloom; *violets* Representing death; *light spear ... tresses grew* Thyrsus, staff borne by Dionysus, the god of fertility, and his followers.

[3] *He who ... one*   Radical journalist Leigh Hunt, to whom Keats dedicated his first volume.

[4] *silver lyre unstrung*   On Keats's tomb is engraved the image of a Greek lyre with half its strings broken. According to his friend Joseph Severn, this symbolizes "his classical genius cut off by death before its maturity."

[5] *kites*   Falcon-like birds of prey.

Dust to the dust! but the pure spirit shall flow
Back to the burning fountain whence it came,
340 A portion of the Eternal, which must glow
Through time and change, unquenchably the same,
Whilst thy cold embers choke the sordid hearth of
shame.

39

Peace, peace! he is not dead, he doth not sleep—
He hath awakened from the dream of life—
345 'Tis we who lost in stormy visions keep
With phantoms an unprofitable strife,
And in mad trance, strike with our spirit's knife
Invulnerable nothings. *We* decay
Like corpses in a charnel; fear and grief
350 Convulse us and consume us day by day,
And cold hopes swarm like worms within our living
clay.

40

He has outsoared the shadow of our night;
Envy and calumny° and hate and pain,   *slander*
And that unrest which men miscall delight,
355 Can touch him not and torture not again;
From the contagion of the world's slow stain
He is secure, and now can never mourn
A heart grown cold, a head grown grey in vain;
Nor, when the spirit's self has ceased to burn,
360 With sparkless ashes load an unlamented urn.

41

He lives, he wakes—'tis Death is dead, not he;
Mourn not for Adonais. Thou young Dawn
Turn all thy dew to splendour, for from thee
The spirit thou lamentest is not gone;
365 Ye caverns and ye forests, cease to moan!
Cease ye faint flowers and fountains, and thou Air
Which like a mourning veil thy scarf hadst thrown
O'er the abandoned Earth, now leave it bare
Even to the joyous stars which smile on its despair!

42

370 He is made one with Nature: there is heard
His voice in all her music, from the moan

Of thunder, to the song of night's sweet bird;[1]
He is a presence to be felt and known
In darkness and in light, from herb and stone,
375 Spreading itself where'er that Power may move
Which has withdrawn his being to its own;
Which wields the world with never wearied love,
Sustains it from beneath, and kindles it above.

43

He is a portion of the loveliness
380 Which once he made more lovely: he doth bear
His part, while the one Spirit's plastic° stress   *formative*
Sweeps through the dull dense world, compelling there,
All new successions to the forms they wear;
Torturing th'unwilling dross° that checks   *impure matter*
its flight
385 To its own likeness, as each mass may bear;
And bursting in its beauty and its might
From trees and beasts and men into the Heaven's light.

44

The splendours of the firmament of time
May be eclipsed, but are extinguished not;
390 Like stars to their appointed height they climb
And death is a low mist which cannot blot
The brightness it may veil. When lofty thought
Lifts a young heart above its mortal lair,
And love and life contend in it, for what
395 Shall be its earthly doom,° the dead live there   *fate*
And move like winds of light on dark and stormy air.

45

The inheritors of unfulfilled renown
Rose from their thrones, built beyond mortal thought,
Far in the Unapparent. Chatterton[2]
400 Rose pale, his solemn agony had not
Yet faded from him; Sidney,[3] as he fought
And as he fell and as he lived and loved
Sublimely mild, a Spirit without spot,

---

[1] *night's sweet bird* I.e., the nightingale, in reference to Keats's "Ode to a Nightingale."

[2] *Chatterton* Poet Thomas Chatterton, who committed suicide in 1770 at the age of 17.

[3] *Sidney* Sir Philip Sidney (1554–86), who was killed in battle when he was 32.

Arose; and Lucan,[1] by his death approved:
405 Oblivion as they rose shrank like a thing reproved.

46

And many more, whose names on Earth are dark
But whose transmitted effluence cannot die
So long as fire outlives the parent spark,
Rose, robed in dazzling immortality.
410 "Thou art become as one of us," they cry,
"It was for thee yon kingless sphere has long
Swung blind in unascended majesty,
Silent alone amid an Heaven of song.
Assume thy winged throne, thou Vesper[2] of our
       throng!"

47

415 Who mourns for Adonais? Oh come forth
Fond° wretch! and know thyself and him aright.   *foolish*
Clasp with thy panting soul the pendulous Earth;
As from a centre, dart thy spirit's light
Beyond all worlds, until its spacious might
420 Satiate the void circumference: then shrink
Even to a point within our day and night;
And keep thy heart light lest it make thee sink
When hope has kindled hope, and lured thee to the
       brink.

48

Or go to Rome, which is the sepulchre
425 O, not of him, but of our joy: 'tis nought
That ages, empires, and religions there
Lie buried in the ravage they have wrought;
For such as he can lend°——they borrow not   *bestow*
Glory from those who made the world their prey;
430 And he is gathered to the kings of thought
Who waged contention with their time's decay,
And of the past are all that cannot pass away.

49

Go thou to Rome—at once the Paradise,
The grave, the city, and the wilderness;

435 And where its wrecks like shattered mountains rise,
And flowering weeds, and fragrant copses° dress   *thickets*
The bones of Desolation's nakedness
Pass, till the Spirit of the spot shall lead
Thy footsteps to a slope of green access[3]
440 Where, like an infant's smile, over the dead,
A light of laughing flowers along the grass is spread.

50

And gray walls moulder round,[4] on which dull Time
Feeds, like slow fire upon a hoary° brand;[5]   *white*
And one keen pyramid with wedge sublime,
445 Pavilioning the dust of him who planned
This refuge for his memory, doth stand
Like flame transformed to marble; and beneath,
A field is spread, on which a newer band
Have pitched in Heaven's smile their camp of death
450 Welcoming him we lose with scarce extinguished
       breath.

51

Here pause: these graves are all too young as yet
To have outgrown the sorrow which consigned
Its charge to each; and if the seal is set,
Here, on one fountain of a mourning mind,
455 Break it not thou! too surely shalt thou find
Thine own well full, if thou returnest home,
Of tears and gall. From the world's bitter wind
Seek shelter in the shadow of the tomb.
What Adonais is, why fear we to become?

52

460 The One remains, the many change and pass;
Heaven's light forever shines, Earth's shadows fly;
Life, like a dome of many-coloured glass,
Stains the white radiance of Eternity,
Until Death tramples it to fragments. Die,
465 If thou wouldst be with that which thou dost seek!

---

[1]   *Lucan* First-century CE Roman poet Marcus Annaeus Lucan, who at the age of twenty-six killed himself to avoid being executed for conspiring against the tyrannical emperor Nero.

[2]   *Vesper* The evening star.

[3]   *slope of green access* The Protestant Cemetery in Rome, where Keats is buried. Shelley's son William, who died at age three, is also buried there.

[4]   *gray ... round* One of the boundaries of the cemetery incorporates the wall of ancient Rome, while another is formed by the pyramid-tomb of Roman tribune Caius Cestius.

[5]   *brand* Burning log.

Follow where all is fled! Rome's azure sky,
Flowers, ruins, statues, music, words, are weak
The glory they transfuse with fitting truth to speak.

53

Why linger, why turn back, why shrink, my Heart?
470 Thy hopes are gone before: from all things here
They have departed; thou shouldst now depart!
A light is past from the revolving year,
And man, and woman; and what still is dear
Attracts to crush, repels to make thee wither.
475 The soft sky smiles—the low wind whispers near:
'Tis Adonais calls! Oh, hasten thither,
No more let Life divide what Death can join together.

54

That Light whose smile kindles the Universe,
That Beauty in which all things work and move,
480 That Benediction which the eclipsing Curse
Of birth can quench not, that sustaining Love
Which through the web of being blindly wove
By man and beast and earth and air and sea,
Burns bright or dim, as[1] each are mirrors of
485 The fire for which all thirst; now beams on me,
Consuming the last clouds of cold mortality.

55

The breath whose might I have invoked in song
Descends on me; my spirit's bark is driven,
Far from the shore, far from the trembling throng
490 Whose sails were never to the tempest given;
The massy earth and sphered skies are riven!
I am borne darkly, fearfully, afar;
Whilst burning through the inmost veil of Heaven,
The soul of Adonais, like a star,
495 Beacons from the abode where the Eternal are.
—1821

from *Hellas*[2]

CHORUS[3]

Worlds on worlds are rolling ever
    From creation to decay,
Like the bubbles on a river
    Sparkling, bursting, borne away.
5   But they[4] are still immortal
    Who, through birth's orient° portal   *eastern*
And death's dark chasm hurrying to and fro,
    Clothe their unceasing flight
    In the brief dust and light
10 Gathered around their chariots as they go;
    New shapes they still may weave,
    New gods, new laws receive,
Bright or dim are they as the robes they last
    On Death's bare ribs had cast.

15 A power from the unknown God,[5]

[2] *Hellas* Classical name for Greece. Shelley's inspiration for the poem was the 1821 Greek revolt (against the Turks), which began their eleven-year war for independence. He uses as a model fifth century BCE playwright Aeschylus's *Persians*, which details the Greek defeat of Xerxes and the invading Persians at Salamis in 480 BCE. In his preface to the play, Shelley explains that his interest in Greece results from his belief that the culture, religion, and laws of his society all have their roots in Greece (a belief, common at the time, often referred to now as "Romantic Hellenism"). He also declares his wholehearted support for the Greek cause in an age characterized by "war of the oppressed against the oppressors."

[3] *Chorus* Shelley's chorus is composed of Greek women in Constantinople, the city founded by Roman Emperor Constantine the Great but conquered by the Ottoman Empire in 1435.

[4] *they* "Living and thinking beings which inhabit the planets." In a note to *Hellas*, Shelley says that in this first stanza he contrasts the immortality of these beings with "the transience of the noblest manifestations of the external world." The following verses go on, he says, to "indicate a progressive state of more or less exalted existence, according to the degree of perfection which every distinct intelligence may have attained," and to "conjecture the condition of futurity towards which we are all impelled by an inextinguishable thirst for immortality."

[5] *unknown God* God is here "unknown" because this is before the coming of Christ. Shelley goes on to compare Christ to Prometheus, the classical god who stole fire from Mount Olympus (home of the gods) and gave it to humans. For this, Zeus, King of the gods, chained him to a rock and had an eagle eat out his liver, which grew back daily only to be devoured again.

[1] *as* I.e., to the extent that.

A Promethean conqueror, came;
Like a triumphal path he trod
    The thorns of death and shame.
    A mortal shape to him
20   Was like the vapour dim
Which the orient planet[1] animates with light;
    Hell, Sin, and Slavery came,
    Like bloodhounds mild and tame,
Nor preyed, until their Lord had taken flight;
25   The moon of Mahomet[2]
    Arose, and it shall set:
While blazoned as on Heaven's immortal noon
    The cross leads generations on.[3]

Swift as the radiant shapes of sleep
30   From one whose dreams are Paradise
Fly, when the fond° wretch° wakes   *foolish / mortal*
        to weep,
    And Day peers forth with her blank eyes;
    So fleet, so faint, so fair,
    The Powers of earth and air
35 Fled from the folding-star[4] of Bethlehem:
    Apollo, Pan, and Love,
    And even Olympian Jove[5]
Grew weak, for killing Truth had glared on them;
    Our hills and seas and streams,
40   Dispeopled of their dreams,
Their waters turned to blood, their dew to tears.
    Wailed for the golden years. ...

CHORUS[6]

The world's great age begins anew,
    The golden years return,
45 The earth doth like a snake renew
    Her winter weeds outworn:
Heaven smiles, and faiths and empires gleam,
Like wrecks of a dissolving dream.

A brighter Hellas rears its mountains
50   From waves serener far;
A new Peneus[7] rolls his fountains°   *waters*
    Against the morning star.
Where fairer Tempes bloom, there sleep
Young Cyclads[8] on a sunnier deep.

55 A loftier Argo[9] cleaves the main,°   *sea*
    Fraught with a later prize;
Another Orpheus[10] sings again,
    And loves, and weeps, and dies.
A new Ulysses leaves once more
60 Calypso for his native shore.[11]

---

[6] [From Shelley's note] The final chorus is indistinct and obscure, as the event of the living drama whose arrival it foretells. Prophesies of wars, and rumours of wars, etc., may safely be made by poet or prophet in any age, but to anticipate however darkly a period of regeneration and happiness is a more hazardous exercise of the faculty which bards possess or feign. [This chorus occurs after the Greek rebels have been defeated by the Turks.]

[7] *Peneus* River in Thessaly, also known as the Salambria, which flows from Mount Pindus (one of the homes of the Muses) through the Tempe Valley; also, god of that river.

[8] *Cyclads* Islands in the Aegean Sea off the southeast shore of Greece.

[9] *Argo* Ship of classical myth in which Jason sailed in search of the Golden Fleece.

[10] *Orpheus* Celebrated Thracian musician and poet of Greek mythology. When his beloved, Eurydice, was killed by a snake, he so charmed Hades with his lyre playing that Hades allowed him to lead Eurydice back with him, provided he not look at her on the journey from the underworld. When he could not resist making sure she was behind him, she was condemned to return to Hades forever. In his grief, Orpheus spent the rest of his life as a wandering recluse until the women of Thrace, enraged at his inattention, tore him to pieces.

[11] *A new ... shore* Ulysses (Odysseus) in Homer's *Odyssey* is shipwrecked on the nymph Calypso's island on his voyage home from the Trojan War. He spends seven years with her, entranced by her charms, until finally leaving to continue his voyage home.

---

[1] *orient planet* Venus, which appears in the east as the morning star.

[2] *moon of Mahomet* Crescent moon, the emblem of Islam (which was founded by the prophet Mohammed in the sixth century CE).

[3] *While blazoned ... on* In 312 CE, Constantine is said to have beheld a flaming cross inscribed with the words "In this sign, thou shalt conquer." He converted to Christianity and won control of Rome.

[4] *folding-star* I.e., star that appears as shepherds are herding their sheep back to the pen (fold).

[5] *Apollo ... Jove* Greek and Roman gods.

Oh, write no more the tale of Troy,
    If earth Death's scroll must be!
Nor mix with Laian rage the joy
    Which dawns upon the free:
65 Although a subtler Sphinx renew
Riddles of death Thebes never knew.[1]

Another Athens shall arise,
    And to remoter time
Bequeath, like sunset to the skies,
70   The splendour of its prime;
And leave, if nought so bright may live,
All earth can take or Heaven can give.

Saturn and Love their long repose
    Shall burst, more bright and good
75 Than all who fell, than One who rose,
    Than many unsubdued:[2]
Not gold, not blood, their altar dowers,°   *dowries*
But votive tears and symbol flowers.

Oh, cease! must hate and death return?
80   Cease! must men kill and die?
Cease! drain not to its dregs the urn
    Of bitter prophecy.
The world is weary of the past,
Oh, might it die or rest at last!
—1822

---

[1] *Nor mix … knew* Laius, King of Thebes, ordered the death of his son Oedipus after it was prophesied that the boy would later kill him. Oedipus was rescued and grew up in ignorance of his origin. As a grown man he became involved in a dispute with Laius, not knowing him to be his father, and killed him. He then married Laius's widow, similarly ignorant of her identity as his mother. When he discovered what he had done, he blinded himself, and his mother committed suicide. The Sphinx was a monster who challenged travelers on the road to Thebes with riddles. If they solved the riddle (as Oedipus did) they were allowed to pass. If they did not, they were slain.

[2] [From Shelley's note] Saturn and Love were among the deities of a real or imaginary state of innocence and happiness. *All those who fell*, or the Gods of Greece, Asia and Egypt; the *One who rose*, or Jesus Christ. . .; and *the many unsubdued*, or the monstrous objects of the idolatry of China, India, the Antarctic islands, and the native tribes of America.

Mutability

1

The flower that smiles to-day
    To-morrow dies;
All that we wish to stay
    Tempts and then flies.
5 What is this world's delight?
Lightning that mocks the night,
    Brief even as bright.

2

Virtue, how frail it is!
    Friendship how rare!
10 Love, how it sells poor bliss
    For proud despair!
But we, though soon they fall,
Survive their joy, and all
    Which ours we call.

3

15 Whilst skies are blue and bright,
    Whilst flowers are gay,
Whilst eyes that change ere night
    Make glad the day;
Whilst yet the calm hours creep,
20 Dream thou—and from thy sleep
    Then wake to weep.
—1824

Stanzas
Written in Dejection – December 1818, near Naples

1

The sun is warm, the sky is clear,
  The waves are dancing fast and bright,
Blue isles and snowy mountains wear
    The purple noon's transparent might,
5   The breath of the moist earth is light,
Around its unexpanded buds;

Like many a voice of one delight,
  The winds, the birds, the ocean floods,
The City's voice itself, is soft like Solitude's.

2

10   I see the Deep's untrampled floor
  With green and purple seaweeds strown;
I see the waves upon the shore,
  Like light dissolved in star-showers,[1] thrown:
  I sit upon the sands alone—
15   The lightning of the noontide ocean
  Is flashing round me, and a tone
Arises from its measured motion,
How sweet! did any heart now share in my emotion.

3

Alas! I have nor hope nor health,
20   Nor peace within nor calm around,
Nor that content surpassing wealth
  The sage in meditation found,
  And walked with inward glory crowned—
Nor fame, nor power, nor love, nor leisure.
25   Others I see whom these surround—
  Smiling they live, and call life pleasure;—
To me that cup has been dealt in another measure.

4

Yet now despair itself is mild,
  Even as the winds and waters are;
30   I could lie down like a tired child,
  And weep away the life of care
  Which I have borne and yet must bear,
Till death like sleep might steal on me,
  And I might feel in the warm air
35   My cheek grow cold, and hear the sea
Breathe o'er my dying brain its last monotony.

5

Some might lament that I were cold.
  As I, when this sweet day is gone,
Which my lost heart, too soon grown old,
40   Insults with this untimely moan;
  They might lament—for I am one
Whom men love not—and yet regret,

Unlike this day, which, when the sun
  Shall on its stainless glory set,
45   Will linger, though enjoyed, like joy in memory yet.
—1824

Sonnet [Lift Not the Painted Veil]

Lift not the painted veil which those who live
  Call Life: though unreal shapes be pictured there,
And it but mimic all we would believe
With colours idly spread—behind, lurk Fear
5   And Hope, twin Destinies; who ever weave
Their shadows, o'er the chasm, sightless and drear.
I knew one who had lifted it—he sought,
For his lost heart was tender, things to love,
But found them not, alas! nor was there aught
10   The world contains, the which he could approve.
Through the unheeding many he did move,
A splendour among shadows, a bright blot
Upon this gloomy scene, a Spirit that strove
For truth, and like the Preacher[2] found it not.
—1824

To Night

1

Swiftly walk o'er the western wave,
    Spirit of Night!
Out of the misty eastern cave,
Where, all the long and lone daylight,
5   Thou wovest dreams of joy and fear,
Which make thee terrible and dear,
    Swift be thy flight!

2

Wrap thy form in a mantle gray,
    Star-inwrought!
10   Blind with thine hair the eyes of Day;
Kiss her until she be wearied out,
Then wander o'er city, and sea, and land,

---

[1] *star-showers* Meteor showers.

[2] *Preacher* Speaker of Ecclesiastes, who says, "I have seen all the works that are done under the sun; and, behold, all is vanity and vexation of spirit" (1.14).

Touching all with thine opiate° wand—   *sleep-inducing*
    Come, long-sought!

3

15 When I arose and saw the dawn,
    I sighed for thee;
When light rode high, and the dew was gone,
And noon lay heavy on flower and tree,
And the weary Day turned to his rest,
20 Lingering like an unloved guest,
    I sighed for thee.

4

Thy brother Death came, and cried,
    Wouldst thou me?
Thy sweet child Sleep, thy filmy-eyed,
25 Murmured like a noontide bee,
Shall I nestle near thy side?
Wouldst thou me? And I replied,
    No, not thee!

5

Death will come when thou art dead,
30   Soon, too soon—
Sleep will come when thou art fled;
Of neither would I ask the boon
I ask of thee, beloved Night—
Swift be thine approaching flight,
35   Come soon, soon!
   —1824

To ——

Music, when soft voices die,
Vibrates in the memory—
Odours, when sweet violets sicken,
Live within the sense they quicken.°   *vivify*

5 Rose leaves, when the rose is dead,
Are heaped for the beloved's bed;
And so thy thoughts, when thou art gone,
Love itself shall slumber on.
   —1824

Song to the Men of England [1]

1

Men of England, wherefore plough
    For the lords who lay ye low?
Wherefore weave with toil and care
The rich robes your tyrants wear?

2

5 Wherefore feed, and clothe, and save,
From the cradle to the grave,
Those ungrateful drones who would
Drain your sweat—nay, drink your blood?

3

Wherefore, Bees of England, forge
10 Many a weapon, chain, and scourge,
That these stingless drones may spoil
The forced produce of your toil?

4

Have ye leisure, comfort, calm,
Shelter, food, love's gentle balm?
15 Or what is it ye buy so dear
With your pain and with your fear?

5

The seed ye sow, another reaps;
The wealth ye find, another keeps;
The robes ye weave, another wears;
20 The arms ye forge, another bears.

6

Sow seed—but let no tyrant reap;
Find wealth—let no impostor heap;
Weave robes—let not the idle wear;
Forge arms—in your defence to bear.

7

25 Shrink to your cellars, holes, and cells;

---

[1] *Song ... England* Composed in 1819, during a time of economic depression and social turmoil following the end of the Napoleonic Wars. In this song, which became a hymn for the British labor movement, Shelley urges the proletariat to force change in the social and economic order.

In halls ye deck another dwells.
Why shake the chains ye wrought? Ye see
The steel ye tempered glance on[1] ye.

8

With plough and spade, and hoe and loom,
30 Trace your grave, and build your tomb,
And weave your winding-sheet, till fair
England be your sepulchre.
—1839 (1819)

England in 1819

An old, mad, blind, despised, and dying king,[2]
Princes, the dregs of their dull race, who flow
Through public scorn—mud from a muddy spring—
Rulers who neither see, nor feel, nor know,
5 But leech-like to their fainting country cling,
Till they drop, blind in blood, without a blow—
A people starved and stabbed in the untilled field[3]—
An army, which liberticide and prey
Makes as a two-edged sword to all who wield—
10 Golden and sanguine laws[4] which tempt and slay;
Religion Christless, Godless—a book sealed;
A Senate, Time's worst statute, unrepealed,[5]
Are graves, from which a glorious Phantom[6] may
Burst, to illumine our tempestuous day.
—1839

---

[1] glance on   Strike obliquely.

[2] old mad ... king   George III, who was declared insane in 1811. His sons were known for their corruption and their licentious behavior.

[3] A people ... field   Reference to the massacre at St. Peter's Field on 16 August 1819 (the Peterloo Massacre), when the militia used undue force to disperse a crowd of men, women, and children who were peacefully demonstrating for political reform. Several people were killed and hundreds more injured (see "The Mask of Anarchy").

[4] Gold ... laws   I.e., laws, bought with gold, that lead to bloodshed.

[5] Time's ... unrepealed   Laws against Catholics and Dissenters.

[6] a glorious Phantom   I.e., revolution.

A Defence of Poetry

This essay, begun in 1822 and never completed, was written in response to an 1820 essay by Shelley's friend Thomas Love Peacock called "The Four Ages of Poetry." In this partially-ironic essay, Peacock describes four cycles through which poetry passes: the first is an iron age of crude folk ballads, medieval romances, etc; the second, the gold age, contains the great epics of Homer, Dante, and Milton; the silver age contains the "derivative" poetry of the Augustan poets (who included John Dryden and Alexander Pope; and the fourth stage, the age of brass, is that of Peacock's contemporaries, whom he claimed were markedly inferior. Criticizing Romantic poets such as Byron, Coleridge, and Wordsworth, Peacock urged the men of his generation to apply themselves to new sciences, such as astronomy, economics, politics, mathematics, or chemistry, instead of poetry. Though Shelley recognized Peacock's satirical humor, he also acknowledged that Peacock had put his finger on a common bias of the time—both in the theories of Utilitarian philosophers and in general public opinion—in favor of economic growth and scientific progress over creativity and humanitarian concerns. It was this bias that he attempted to correct in his Defence.

from A Defence of Poetry,
or Remarks Suggested by an Essay Entitled "The Four Ages of Poetry"

According to one mode of regarding those two classes of mental action which are called reason and imagination, the former may be considered as mind contemplating the relations borne by one thought to another, however produced; and the latter, as mind acting upon those thoughts so as to colour them with its own light, and composing from them, as from elements, other thoughts, each containing within itself the principle of its own integrity. The one is the τὸ ποιειν,[7] or the principle of synthesis, and has for its objects those forms which are common to universal nature and

---

[7] τὸ ποιειν   Greek: making.

existence itself; the other is the τὸ λογιζειν[1] or principle of analysis, and its action regards the relations of things, simply as relations; considering thoughts, not in their integral unity, but as the algebraical representations which conduct to certain general results. Reason is the enumeration of quantities already known; imagination is the perception of the value of those quantities, both separately and as a whole. Reason respects the differences, and imagination the similitudes of things. Reason is to Imagination as the instrument to the agent, as the body to the spirit, as the shadow to the substance.

Poetry, in a general sense, may be defined to be "the expression of the Imagination": and poetry is connate with the origin of man. Man is an instrument over which a series of external and internal impressions are driven, like the alternations of an ever-changing wind over an Æolian lyre,[2] which move it by their motion to ever-changing melody. But there is a principle within the human being, and perhaps within all sentient beings, which acts otherwise than in the lyre, and produces not melody alone, but harmony, by an internal adjustment of the sounds or motions thus excited to the impressions which excite them. It is as if the lyre could accommodate its chords to the motions of that which strikes them, in a determined proportion of sound; even as the musician can accommodate his voice to the sound of the lyre. A child at play by itself will express its delight by its voice and motions; and every inflexion of tone and every gesture will bear exact relation to a corresponding antitype in the pleasurable impressions which awakened it; it will be the reflected image of that impression; and as the lyre trembles and sounds after the wind has died away, so the child seeks, by prolonging in its voice and motions the duration of the effect, to prolong also a consciousness of the cause. In relation to the objects which delight a child, these expressions are what poetry is to higher objects. The savage (for the savage is to ages what the child is to years) expresses the emotions produced in him by surrounding objects in a similar manner; and language and gesture, together with

plastic[3] or pictorial imitation, become the image of the combined effect of those objects, and of his apprehension of them. Man in society, with all his passions and his pleasures, next becomes the object of the passions and pleasures of man; an additional class of emotions produces an augmented treasure of expressions; and language, gesture, and the imitative arts become at once the representation and the medium, the pencil and the picture, the chisel and the statue, the chord and the harmony. The social sympathies, or those laws from which as from its elements society results, begin to develop themselves from the moment that two human beings coexist; the future is contained within the present as the plant within the seed; and equality, diversity, unity, contrast, mutual dependence, become the principles alone capable of affording the motives according to which the will of a social being is determined to action, inasmuch as he is social; and constitute pleasure in sensation, virtue in sentiment, beauty in art, truth in reasoning, and love in the intercourse of kind. Hence men, even in the infancy of society, observe a certain order in their words and actions, distinct from that of the objects and the impressions represented by them, all expression being subject to the laws of that from which it proceeds. But let us dismiss those more general considerations which might involve an enquiry into the principles of society itself, and restrict our view to the manner in which the imagination is expressed upon its forms.

In the youth of the world, men dance and sing and imitate natural objects, observing[4] in these actions, as in all others, a certain rhythm or order. And, although all men observe a similar, they observe not the same order, in the motions of the dance, in the melody of the song, in the combinations of language, in the series of their imitations of natural objects. For there is a certain order or rhythm belonging to each of these classes of mimetic representation, from which the hearer and the spectator receive an intenser and purer pleasure than from any other: the sense of an approximation to this order has been called taste, by modern writers. Every man in the infancy of art observes an order which approximates more or less closely to that from which this highest

[1] τὸ λογιζειν Greek: reasoning.
[2] Æolian lyre Stringed instrument that produces music when exposed to wind.

[3] plastic Formative.
[4] observing Following.

delight results: but the diversity is not sufficiently marked, as that its gradations should be sensible, except in those instances where the predominance of this faculty of approximation to the beautiful (for so we may be permitted to name the relation between this highest pleasure and its cause) is very great. Those in whom it exists in excess are poets, in the most universal sense of the word; and the pleasure resulting from the manner in which they express the influence of society or nature upon their own minds, communicates itself to others, and gathers a sort of reduplication from that community. Their language is vitally metaphorical; that is, it marks the before unapprehended relations of things, and perpetuates their apprehension, until the words which represent them, become through time signs for portions or classes of thoughts instead of pictures of integral thoughts; and then if no new poets should arise to create afresh the associations which have been thus disorganized, language will be dead to all the nobler purposes of human intercourse. These similitudes or relations are finely said by Lord Bacon to be "the same footsteps of nature impressed upon the various subjects of the world"[1]—and he considers the faculty which perceives them as the storehouse of axioms common to all knowledge. In the infancy of society every author is necessarily a poet, because language itself is poetry; and to be a poet is to apprehend the true and the beautiful, in a word the good which exists in the relation, subsisting, first between existence and perception, and secondly between perception and expression. Every original language near to its source is in itself the chaos of a cyclic poem:[2] the copiousness of lexicography and the distinctions of grammar are the works of a later age, and are merely the catalogue and the form of the creations of Poetry.

But Poets, or those who imagine and express this indestructible order, are not only the authors of language and of music, of the dance and architecture and statuary and painting: they are the institutors of laws, and the founders of civil society and the inventors of the arts of life and the teachers, who draw into a certain propinquity with the beautiful and the true that partial apprehension of the agencies of the invisible world which is called religion. Hence all original religions are allegorical, or susceptible of allegory, and like Janus have a double face of false and true.[3] Poets, according to the circumstances of the age and nation in which they appeared, were called in the earlier epochs of the world legislators or prophets:[4] a poet essentially comprises and unites both these characters. For he not only beholds intensely the present as it is, and discovers those laws according to which present things ought to be ordered, but he beholds the future in the present, and his thoughts are the germs of the flower and the fruit of latest time. Not that I assert poets to be prophets in the gross sense of the word, or that they can foretell the form as surely as they foreknow the spirit of events: such is the pretence of superstition which would make poetry an attribute of prophecy, rather than prophecy an attribute of poetry. A Poet participates in the eternal, the infinite, and the one; as far as relates to his conceptions, time and place and number are not. The grammatical forms which express the moods of time, and the difference of persons and the distinction of place, are convertible with respect to the highest poetry without injuring it as poetry, and the choruses of Æschylus, and the book of Job, and Dante's Paradise[5] would afford, more than any other writings, examples of this fact, if the limits of this essay did not forbid citation. The creations of sculpture, painting, and music are illustrations still more decisive.

Language, colour, form, and religious and civil habits of action are all the instruments and materials of poetry; they may be called poetry by that figure of

---

[1] *the same ... world*   From Francis Bacon's *Of the Advancement of Learning* (1605) 3.1.

[2] *cyclic poem*   Set of poems dealing with the same subject (though not always by the same author). The "Arthurian Cycle," a series of poems about the court of King Arthur, is one example of the genre.

[3] *like Janus ... true*   Janus, the Roman god of war, of doorways, and of beginnings and endings (after whom the month of January is named) is generally depicted with two faces, one looking forward and one back.

[4] *were called ... prophets*   Cf. Sir Philip Sidney's *Defence of Poesy* (1595), in which he points out that *vates*, the Latin word for poet, also means diviner or prophet.

[5] *Æschylus*   Greek tragic dramatist (c. 525–456 BCE);   *Dante's Paradise*   Reference to Italian poet Dante Alighieri's fourteenth-century work, *The Divine Comedy*, which describes a journey from Hell, through Purgatory, to Paradise.

speech which considers the effect as a synonym of the cause. But poetry in a more restricted sense expresses those arrangements of language, and especially metrical language, which are created by that imperial faculty whose throne is curtained within the invisible nature of man. And this springs from the nature itself of language, which is a more direct representation of the actions and passions of our internal being, and is susceptible of more various and delicate combinations, than colour, form, or motion, and is more plastic and obedient to the control of that faculty of which it is the creation. For language is arbitrarily produced by the Imagination and has relation to thoughts alone; but all other materials, instruments and conditions of art, have relations among each other, which limit and interpose between conception and expression. The former is as a mirror which reflects, the latter as a cloud which enfeebles, the light of which both are mediums of communication. Hence the fame of sculptors, painters and musicians, although the intrinsic powers of the great masters of these arts, may yield in no degree to that of those who have employed language as the hieroglyphic of their thoughts, has never equalled that of poets in the restricted sense of the term; as two performers of equal skill will produce unequal effects from a guitar and a harp. The fame of legislators and founders of religions, so long as their institutions last, alone seems to exceed that of poets in the restricted sense; but it can scarcely be a question whether, if we deduct the celebrity which their flattery of the gross opinions of the vulgar usually conciliates, together with that which belonged to them in their higher character of poets, any excess will remain.

We have thus circumscribed the meaning of the word Poetry within the limits of that art which is the most familiar and the most perfect expression of the faculty itself. It is necessary however to make the circle still narrower, and to determine the distinction between measured and unmeasured language; for the popular division into prose and verse is inadmissible in accurate philosophy. Sounds as well as thoughts have relation both between each other and towards that which they represent, and a perception of the order of those relations has always been found connected with a perception of the order of the relations of thoughts.

Hence the language of poets has ever affected a certain uniform and harmonious recurrence of sound, without which it were not poetry, and which is scarcely less indispensable to the communication of its influence, than the words themselves, without reference to that peculiar order. . . .

A poem is the very image of life expressed in its eternal truth. There is this difference between a story and a poem, that a story is a catalogue of detached facts, which have no other bond of connection than time, place, circumstance, cause and effect; the other is the creation of actions according to the unchangeable forms of human nature, as existing in the mind of the creator, which is itself the image of all other minds. The one is partial, and applies only to a definite period of time, and a certain combination of events which can never again recur; the other is universal, and contains within itself the germ of a relation to whatever motives or actions have place in the possible varieties of human nature. . . .

Poetry is ever accompanied with pleasure: all spirits on which it falls open themselves to receive the wisdom which is mingled with its delight. In the infancy of the world, neither poets themselves nor their auditors are fully aware of the excellence of poetry: for it acts in a divine and unapprehended manner, beyond and above consciousness; and it is reserved for future generations to contemplate and measure the mighty cause and effect in all the strength and splendour of their union. Even in modern times, no living poet ever arrived at the fulness of his fame; the jury which sits in judgement upon a poet, belonging as he does to all time, must be composed of his peers: it must be impanelled by Time from the selectest of the wise of many generations. A Poet is a nightingale, who sits in darkness and sings to cheer its own solitude with sweet sounds; his auditors are as men entranced by the melody of an unseen musician, who feel that they are moved and softened, yet know not whence or why. The poems of Homer and his contemporaries were the delight of infant Greece; they were the elements of that social system which is the column upon which all succeeding civilization has reposed. Homer embodied the ideal perfection of his age in human character; nor can we doubt that those who read his verses were awakened to an ambition of becoming like to Achilles, Hector and Ulysses:[1] the truth and beauty of friendship, patriotism, and persevering devotion to an object were unveiled to the depths in these immortal creations: the sentiments of the auditors must have been refined and enlarged by a sympathy with such great and lovely impersonations, until from admiring they imitated, and from imitation they identified themselves with the objects of their admiration....

The whole objection, however, of the immorality of poetry[2] rests upon a misconception of the manner in which poetry acts to produce the moral improvement of man. Ethical science[3] arranges the elements which poetry has created, and propounds schemes and proposes examples of civil and domestic life: nor is it for want of admirable doctrines that men hate, and despise, and censure, and deceive, and subjugate one another. But Poetry acts in another and diviner manner. It awakens and enlarges the mind itself by rendering it the receptacle of a thousand unapprehended combinations of thought. Poetry lifts the veil from the hidden beauty of the world, and makes familiar objects be as if they were not familiar; it reproduces[4] all that it represents, and the impersonations clothed in its Elysian[5] light stand thenceforward in the minds of those who have once contemplated them, as memorials of that gentle and exalted content which extends itself over all thoughts and actions with which it coexists. The great secret of morals is Love; or a going out of our own nature, and an identification of ourselves with the beautiful which exists in thought, action, or person not our own. A man, to be greatly good, must imagine intensely and comprehensively; he must put himself in the place of another and of many others; the pains and pleasures of his species must become his own. The great

instrument of moral good is the imagination; and poetry administers to the effect by acting upon the cause. Poetry enlarges the circumference of the imagination by replenishing it with thoughts of ever new delight, which have the power of attracting and assimilating to their own nature all other thoughts, and which form new intervals and interstices whose void for ever craves fresh food. Poetry strengthens that faculty which is the organ of the moral nature of man, in the same manner as exercise strengthens a limb. A Poet therefore would do ill to embody his own conceptions of right and wrong, which are usually those of his place and time, in his poetical creations, which participate in neither. By this assumption of the inferior office of interpreting the effect, in which perhaps after all he might acquit himself but imperfectly, he would resign the glory in a participation in the cause. There was little danger that Homer, or any of the eternal poets, should have so far misunderstood themselves as to have abdicated this throne of their widest dominion. Those in whom the poetical faculty, though great, is less intense, as Euripides, Lucan, Tasso, Spenser,[6] have frequently affected a moral aim, and the effect of their poetry is diminished in exact proportion to the degree in which they compel us to advert to this purpose....

The drama at Athens, or wheresoever else it may have approached to its perfection, coexisted with the moral and intellectual greatness of the age. The tragedies of the Athenian poets are as mirrors in which the spectator beholds himself, under a thin disguise of circumstance, stript of all but that ideal perfection and energy which every one feels to be the internal type of all that he loves, admires, and would become. The imagination is enlarged by a sympathy with pains and passions so mighty that they distend in their conception the capacity of that by which they were conceived; the good affections are strengthened by pity, indignation, terror and sorrow; and an exalted calm is prolonged from the satiety of this high exercise of them into the tumult of familiar life; even crime is disarmed of half its horror and all its contagion by being represented as the

---

1 *Achilles, Hector and Ulysses* Trojan and Greek heroes in Homer's *Iliad* and *Odyssey*.

2 *immorality of poetry* An objection voiced by Plato in his *Republic*, in which he says that poetry often depicts characters who are morally imperfect and whose actions do not provide suitable examples for readers.

3 *Ethical science* Moral philosophy.

4 *reproduces* I.e., produces or creates anew.

5 *Elysian* I.e., paradisical. From Elysium, the paradise where the blessed reside after death, according to Greek myth.

6 *Euripides* Greek tragedian of the fifth century BCE; *Lucan* Roman poet of the first century CE; *Tasso* Torquato Tasso, Italian epic poet of the sixteenth century; *Spenser* Edmund Spenser, sixteenth-century epic poet; author of *The Faerie Queene*.

fatal consequence of the unfathomable agencies of nature; error is thus divested of its wilfulness; men can no longer cherish it as the creation of their choice. In a drama of the highest order there is little food for censure or hatred; it teaches rather self-knowledge and self-respect. Neither the eye nor the mind can see itself, unless reflected upon that which it resembles. The drama, so long as it continues to express poetry, is as a prismatic and many-sided mirror, which collects the brightest rays of human nature and divides and reproduces them from the simplicity of these elementary forms, and touches them with majesty and beauty, and multiplies all that it reflects, and endows it with the power of propagating its like wherever it may fall.

But in periods of the decay of social life, the drama sympathizes with that decay. Tragedy becomes a cold imitation of the form of the great masterpieces of antiquity, divested of all harmonious accompaniment of the kindred arts; and often the very form misunderstood: or a weak attempt to teach certain doctrines, which the writer considers as moral truths; and which are usually no more than specious flatteries of some gross vice or weakness with which the author in common with his auditors are infected....

The drama being that form under which a greater number of modes of expression of poetry are susceptible of being combined than any other, the connection of poetry and social good is more observable in the drama than in whatever other form: and it is indisputable that the highest perfection of human society has ever corresponded with the highest dramatic excellence; and that the corruption or the extinction of the drama in a nation where it has once flourished, is a mark of a corruption of manners, and an extinction of the energies which sustain the soul of social life. But, as Machiavelli[1] says of political institutions, that life may be preserved and renewed, if men should arise capable of bringing back the drama to its principles. And this is true with respect to poetry in its most extended sense: all language, institution and form, require not only to be produced but to be sustained: the office and character of a poet participates in the divine nature as regards providence, no less than as regards creation.

... It is admitted that the exercise of the imagination is most delightful, but it is alleged that that of reason is more useful. Let us examine as the grounds of this distinction, what is here meant by Utility. Pleasure or good, in a general sense, is that which the consciousness of a sensitive and intelligent being seeks, and in which when found it acquiesces. There are two kinds of pleasure, one durable, universal, and permanent; the other transitory and particular. Utility may either express the means of producing the former or the latter. In the former sense, whatever strengthens and purifies the affections, enlarges the imagination, and adds spirit to sense, is useful. But the meaning in which the Author of the Four Ages of Poetry seems to have employed the word utility is the narrower one of banishing the importunity of the wants of our animal nature, the surrounding men with security of life, the dispersing the grosser delusions of superstition, and the conciliating such a degree of mutual forbearance among men as may consist with the motives of personal advantage.

Undoubtedly the promoters of utility in this limited sense have their appointed office in society. They follow the footsteps of poets, and copy the sketches of their creations into the book of common life. They make space, and give time. Their exertions are of the highest value so long as they confine their administration of the concerns of the inferior powers of our nature within the limits due to the superior ones. But whilst the sceptic destroys gross superstitions, let him spare to deface, as some of the French writers have defaced, the eternal truths charactered upon the imaginations of men. Whilst the mechanist abridges, and the political economist combines, labour, let them beware that their speculations, for want of correspondence with those first principles which belong to the imagination, do not tend, as they have in modern England, to exasperate at once the extremes of luxury and want. They have exemplified the saying, "To him that hath, more shall be given; and from him that hath not, the little that he hath shall be taken away."[2] The rich have become richer, and the poor have become poorer; and the vessel of the

[1] *Machiavelli* Niccolo Machiavelli (1469–1527), author of the political treatise *The Prince*.

[2] *To him ... away* Repeatedly said by Jesus (Matthew 25.29, Mark 4.25, Luke 8.18 and 19.26).

state is driven between the Scylla and Charybdis[1] of anarchy and despotism. Such are the effects which must ever flow from an unmitigated exercise of the calculating faculty.

It is difficult to define pleasure in its highest sense; the definition involving a number of apparent paradoxes. For, from an inexplicable defect of harmony in the constitution of human nature, the pain of the inferior is frequently connected with the pleasures of the superior portions of our being. Sorrow, terror, anguish, despair itself are often the chosen expressions of an approximation to the highest good. Our sympathy in tragic fiction depends on this principle; tragedy delights by affording a shadow of the pleasure which exists in pain. This is the source also of the melancholy which is inseparable from the sweetest melody. The pleasure that is in sorrow is sweeter than the pleasure of pleasure itself. And hence the saying, "It is better to go to the house of mourning, than to the house of mirth."[2] Not that this highest species of pleasure is necessarily linked with pain. The delight of love and friendship, the ecstasy of the admiration of nature, the joy of the perception and still more of the creation of poetry is often wholly unalloyed.

The production and assurance of pleasure in this highest sense is true utility. Those who produce and preserve this pleasure are Poets or poetical philosophers.

The exertions of Locke, Hume, Gibbon, Voltaire, Rousseau,[3] and their disciples, in favour of oppressed and deluded humanity, are entitled to the gratitude of mankind. Yet it is easy to calculate the degree of moral and intellectual improvement which the world would have exhibited, had they never lived. A little more nonsense would have been talked for a century or two; and perhaps a few more men, women, and children, burnt as heretics. We might not at this moment have been congratulating each other on the abolition of the Inquisition in Spain.[4] But it exceeds all imagination to conceive what would have been the moral condition of the world if neither Dante, Petrarch, Boccaccio, Chaucer, Shakespeare, Calderon,[5] Lord Bacon, nor Milton, had ever existed; if Raphael and Michael Angelo[6] had never been born; if the Hebrew poetry had never been translated; if a revival of the study of Greek literature had never taken place; if no monuments of ancient sculpture had been handed down to us; and if the poetry of the religion of the ancient world had been extinguished together with its belief. The human mind could never, except by the intervention of these excitements, have been awakened to the invention of the grosser sciences, and that application of analytical reasoning to the aberrations of society, which it is now attempted to exalt over the direct expression of the inventive and creative faculty itself.

… The cultivation of those sciences which have enlarged the limits of the empire of man over the external world, has, for want of the poetical faculty, proportionally circumscribed those of the internal world; and man, having enslaved the elements, remains himself a slave. To what but a cultivation of the mechanical arts in a degree disproportioned to the presence of the creative faculty, which is the basis of all knowledge, is to be attributed the abuse of all invention for abridging and combining labour, to the exasperation of the inequality of mankind? From what other cause has it arisen that the discoveries which should have lightened, have added a weight to the curse imposed on Adam? Poetry, and the principle of Self, of which money is the visible incarnation, are the God and the Mammon of the world.[7]

The functions of the poetical faculty are two-fold; by one it creates new materials of knowledge, and power

---

[1] *Scylla and Charybdis* A group of rocks and a whirlpool located at the Strait of Messina (between Sicily and mainland Italy).

[2] *It is … mirth* From Ecclesiastes 7.2.

[3] *Locke … Rousseau* John Locke, David Hume, Edward Gibbon, François-Marie Arouet Voltaire, and Jean-Jacques Rousseau, noted philosophers of the seventeenth and eighteenth centuries.

[4] *We might … Spain* The Inquisition was suspended in 1820 (the year before Shelley wrote this essay) and abolished permanently in 1834.

[5] *Petrarch* Fourteenth-century Italian poet, famous for his love lyrics; *Boccaccio* Italian poet, author of the *Decameron* (1351–3); *Calderon* Seventeenth-century Spanish poet and dramatist.

[6] *Raphael and Michael Angelo* Italian Renaissance painters.

[7] *God and … world* Cf. Matthew 6.24: "No man can serve two masters: for either he will hate the one, and love the other; or else he will hold to the one, and despise the other. Ye cannot serve God and Mammon," Mammon being the false idol of worldly possessions.

and pleasure; by the other it engenders in the mind a desire to reproduce and arrange them according to a certain rhythm and order which may be called the beautiful and the good. The cultivation of poetry is never more to be desired than at periods when, from an excess of the selfish and calculating principle, the accumulation of the materials of external life exceed the quantity of the power of assimilating them to the internal laws of human nature. The body has then become too unwieldy for that which animates it.

Poetry is indeed something divine. It is at once the centre and circumference of knowledge; it is that which comprehends all science, and that to which all science must be referred. It is at the same time the root and blossom of all other systems of thought: it is that from which all spring, and that which adorns all; and that which, if blighted, denies the fruit and the seed, and withholds from the barren world the nourishment and the succession of the scions[1] of the tree of life. It is the perfect and consummate surface and bloom of things; it is as the odour and the colour of the rose to the texture of the elements which compose it, as the form and the splendour of unfaded beauty to the secrets of anatomy and corruption. What were Virtue, Love, Patriotism, Friendship &c.—what were the scenery of this beautiful Universe which we inhabit—what were our consolations on this side of the grave—and what were our aspirations beyond it—if Poetry did not ascend to bring light and fire from those eternal regions where the owl-winged faculty of calculation dare not ever soar? Poetry is not like reasoning, a power to be exerted according to the determination of the will. A man cannot say, "I will compose poetry." The greatest poet even cannot say it: for the mind in creation is as a fading coal which some invisible influence, like an inconstant wind, awakens to transitory brightness: this power arises from within, like the colour of a flower which fades and changes as it is developed, and the conscious portions of our natures are unprophetic either of its approach or its departure. ...

Poetry is the record of the best and happiest moments of the happiest and best minds. We are aware of evanescent visitations of thought and feeling sometimes associated with place or person, sometimes regarding our own mind alone, and always arising unforeseen and departing unbidden, but elevating and delightful beyond all expression: so that even in the desire and the regret they leave, there cannot but be pleasure, participating as it does in the nature of its object. It is as it were the interpenetration of a diviner nature through our own; but its footsteps are like those of a wind over a sea, which the coming calm erases, and whose traces remain only as on the wrinkled sand which paves it. These and corresponding conditions of being are experienced principally by those of the most delicate sensibility and the most enlarged imagination; and the state of mind produced by them is at war with every base desire. The enthusiasm of virtue, love, patriotism, and friendship is essentially linked with these emotions; and whilst they last, self appears as what it is, an atom to a Universe. Poets are not only subject to these experiences as spirits of the most refined organization, but they can colour all that they combine with the evanescent hues of this ethereal world; a word, a trait in the representation of a scene or a passion, will touch the enchanted chord, and reanimate, in those who have ever experienced these emotions, the sleeping, the cold, the buried image of the past. Poetry thus makes immortal all that is best and most beautiful in the world; it arrests the vanishing apparitions which haunt the interlunations[2] of life, and veiling them or in language or in form sends them forth among mankind, bearing sweet news of kindred joy to those with whom their sisters abide— abide, because there is no portal of expression from the caverns of the spirit which they inhabit into the universe of things. Poetry redeems from decay the visitations of the divinity in man.

Poetry turns all things to loveliness; it exalts the beauty of that which is most beautiful, and it adds beauty to that which is most deformed: it marries exultation and horror, grief and pleasure, eternity and change; it subdues to union under its light yoke all irreconcilable things. It transmutes all that it touches, and every form moving within the radiance of its presence is changed by wondrous sympathy to an incarnation of the spirit which it breathes; its secret

---

[1] *scions* Shoots.

[2] *interlunations* Period between an old and a new moon; period of darkness.

alchemy turns to potable[1] gold the poisonous waters which flow from death through life; it strips the veil of familiarity from the world, and lays bare the naked and sleeping beauty which is the spirit of its forms.

All things exist as they are perceived: at least in relation to the percipient. "The mind is its own place, and of itself can make a heaven of hell, a hell of heaven."[2] But poetry defeats the curse which binds us to be subjected to the accident of surrounding impressions. And whether it spreads its own figured curtain or withdraws life's dark veil from before the scene of things, it equally creates for us a being within our being. It makes us the inhabitants of a world to which the familiar world is a chaos. It reproduces the common universe of which we are portions and percipients, and it purges from our inward sight the film of familiarity which obscures from us the wonder of our being. It compels us to feel that which we perceive, and to imagine that which we know. It creates anew the universe after it has been annihilated in our minds by the recurrence of impressions blunted by reiteration....

The first part of these remarks has related to Poetry in its elements and principles; and it has been shown, as well as the narrow limits assigned them would permit, that what is called poetry, in a restricted sense, has a common source with all other forms of order and of beauty according to which the materials of human life are susceptible of being arranged, and which is poetry in an universal sense.

The second part[3] will have for its object an application of these principles to the present state of the cultivation of Poetry, and a defence of the attempt to idealize the modern forms of manners and opinion, and compel them into a subordination to the imaginative and creative faculty. For the literature of England, an energetic development of which has ever preceded or accompanied a great and free development of the national will, has arisen as it were from a new birth. In spite of the low-thoughted envy which would undervalue contemporary merit, our own will be a memorable age in intellectual achievements, and we live among such philosophers and poets as surpass beyond comparison any who have appeared since the last national struggle for civil and religious liberty.[4] The most unfailing herald, companion, and follower of the awakening of a great people to work a beneficial change in opinion or institution, is Poetry. At such periods there is an accumulation of the power of communicating and receiving intense and impassioned conceptions respecting man and nature. The persons in whom this power resides, may often, as far as regards many portions of their nature, have little apparent correspondence with that spirit of good of which they are the ministers. But even whilst they deny and abjure, they are yet compelled to serve the Power which is seated upon the throne of their own soul. It is impossible to read the compositions of the most celebrated writers of the present day without being startled with the electric life which burns within their words. They measure the circumference and sound the depths of human nature with a comprehensive and all-penetrating spirit, and they are themselves perhaps the most sincerely astonished at its manifestations, for it is less their spirit than the spirit of the age. Poets are the hierophants[5] of an unapprehended inspiration, the mirrors of the gigantic shadows which futurity casts upon the present, the words which express what they understand not; the trumpets which sing to battle, and feel not what they inspire: the influence which is moved not, but moves.[6] Poets are the unacknowledged legislators of the World.

—1820

---

[1] *potable* Drinkable. Alchemists sought a liquid form of gold that, when consumed, would be the elixir of life.

[2] *The mind ... heaven* From Satan's speech in Milton's *Paradise Lost* 1.254–55.

[3] *The second part* Shelley did not complete a second part.

[4] *the last ... liberty* I.e., the English Civil War of the 1640s.

[5] *hierophants* Interpreters of sacred mysteries.

[6] *is moved ... moves* Reference to Greek philosopher Aristotle's description of God as the "Unmoved Mover" of the universe.

FELICIA HEMANS
1793 – 1835

Felicia Hemans was one of the first English poets to earn a living by writing. Her poetry was in many ways representative of the late Romantic and early Victorian eras, with an emphasis on religious, martial, and domestic themes, but several of her poems—perhaps most notably "Casabianca" and "The Homes of England"—remained enormously popular well into the twentieth century. Writing was in Hemans's day still widely considered incompatible with women's domestic bliss; some have argued that Hemans's own marriage failed because of her literary pursuits. It was certainly the case that, while her

work was widely read and widely praised, it was also occasionally mocked, and that gender was at the root of much of the ridicule. (Byron, for example, parodied her as "Mrs. Hewoman.")

Hemans was born Felicia Browne, the fifth of seven children of a Liverpool wine merchant and his wife, the daughter of a foreign diplomat. The failure of her father's business in 1799 caused the family to move to Wales; Felicia adored the countryside and it became the inspiration for much of her poetry. She learned several languages and a great deal about music from her mother, and benefited from a well-stocked family library. She loved Shakespeare as a child and was said to have had an excellent memory for reciting verse. Her own first published volume appeared in 1808, when she was only 14. Although *Poems* received some negative reviews, it sold 1,000 copies and she was encouraged to continue writing. Two of her brothers were then engaged in the British war against Spain and many of the poems are patriotic depictions of Britain in battle. Her brothers passed the volume on to one of their colleagues, Captain Alfred Hemans; he later became her husband. Percy Bysshe Shelley also received her first volume and began a correspondence with the young poet.

Felicia Browne married in 1812, shortly after the publication of her third volume of poetry, *The Domestic Affections and Other Poems*. She and her husband initially lived in her mother's house in Wales, a situation that would eventually prove uncomfortable for Captain Hemans. While Hemans continued to publish and become more popular, Captain Hemans became disillusioned with Wales and moved to Italy in 1818 on grounds of "ill health," never to see his wife again. From this point onwards she supported herself solely by her writing.

Hemans was one of very few British poets to have been in the prime of their writing careers in the 1810s and 1820s. She occupies something of an uneasy position between the Romantics and the Victorians. That she lived into Victoria's era and that her poetry retained a high degree of popularity through the Victorian period may have encouraged modern critics to see Hemans in the light of the standards of a later period; in the past critics perceived her poetry as characterized by powerful rhythms and powerful passions (even by emotional "gush"). And certainly the strength of form and of feeling in poems of patriotic fervor such as "The Homes of England" and "Casabianca" (both of which were learnt by heart by English schoolchildren into the twentieth century) is unquestionable. Yet in her own day, seen against the backdrop of the extravagant passions of Byron and other poets associated with the Romantic Movement, her poetry was praised for its formal and emotional restraint.

Though Hemans's most famous poems are short, she was also successful with long narrative poems, most notably *The Siege of Valencia* (1823), which recounts the epic story of Elmira after her two sons are captured by a Moorish army. And she wrote innovative linked poems, such as those in *Records of Woman* (1828). Though she is often thought of as an important poet of domesticity, Hemans focused at least as much on women acting out their lives on a larger stage.

In 1821 Hemans was awarded the Royal Society of Literature's annual prize of £52.50 (a substantial amount at the time). She was then publishing regularly in British literary magazines, and from 1823, she was earning roughly £200 per year, enough to support herself and her five sons in some comfort. Her work was never out of print, and she was widely read in Britain and in America. The death of her mother in 1827 had a devastating effect on her, however, and from that point onwards she was plagued by poor health.

In her latter years, she rivaled Byron in popularity, and was highly sought after by budding poets and autograph-seekers. She found herself caught, however, between the success she needed to support herself and the masculine characteristics attributed to it, a theme she explores in "Women and Fame." In 1831 Hemans moved to Dublin to live with one of her brothers. She died there in 1835, of a weak heart and the effects of rheumatic fever.

⌘ ⌘ ⌘

The Homes of England

Where's the coward that would not dare
To fight for such a land?
MARMION[1]

The stately Homes of England,
How beautiful they stand!
Amidst their tall ancestral trees,
O'er all the pleasant land.
5 The deer across their greensward° bound   turf
Thro' shade and sunny gleam,
And the swan glides past them with the sound
Of some rejoicing stream.

The merry Homes of England!
10 Around their hearths by night,
What gladsome looks of household love
Meet, in the ruddy° light!   red-hued
There woman's voice flows forth in song,
Or childhood's tale is told,
15 Or lips move tunefully along
Some glorious page of old.

The blessed Homes of England!
How softly on their bowers°   arbors
Is laid the holy quietness
20 That breathes from Sabbath-hours!
Solemn, yet sweet, the church-bell's chime
Floats thro' their woods at morn;
All other sounds, in that still time,
Of breeze and leaf are born.

25 The Cottage Homes of England!
By thousands on her plains,
They are smiling o'er the silvery brooks,
And round the hamlet-fanes.[2]
Thro' glowing orchards forth they peep,

[1] *Marmion* Walter Scott's *Marmion: A Tale of Flodden Field* (1808), 4.30. When first published in *Blackwood's Magazine*, the poem had instead the following epigraph from Joanna Baillie, *Ethwald: A Tragedy* (1802) 2.1.2.76–82:

A land of peace,
Where yellow fields unspoil'd, and pastures green,
Mottled with herds and flocks, who crop secure
Their native herbage, nor have ever known
A stranger's stall, smile gladly.
See through its tufted alleys to Heaven's roof
The curling smoke of quiet dwellings rise.

[2] *hamlet-fanes* Weather vanes of the village.

30 Each from its nook of leaves,
And fearless there the lowly sleep,
    As the bird beneath their eaves.

The free, fair Homes of England!
    Long, long, in hut and hall,
35 May hearts of native proof be rear'd
    To guard each hallow'd wall!
And green for ever be the groves,
    And bright the flowery sod,
Where first the child's glad spirit loves
40 Its country and its God![1]
    —1812

The Land of Dreams

And dreams, in their development, have breath,
And tears and tortures, and the touch of joy;
They leave a weight upon our waking thoughts,
They make us what we were not—what they will,
And shake us with the vision that's gone by.
                                    BYRON.[2]

Oh spirit land, thou land of dreams!
    A world thou art of mysterious gleams,
Of startling voices, and sounds at strife—
A world of the dead in the hues of life.

5 Like a wizard's magic-glass° thou art   *mirror*
When the wavy shadows float by, and part—
Visions of aspects, now loved, now strange,
Glimmering and mingling in ceaseless change.

Thou art like a city of the past
10 With its gorgeous halls into fragments cast,
Amidst whose ruins there glide and play
Familiar forms of the world's today.

Thou art like the depths where the seas have birth,
Rich with the wealth that is lost from earth—

15 All the sere° flowers of our days gone by,   *dry*
And the buried gems in thy bosom lie.

Yes, thou art like those dim sea-caves,
A realm of treasures, a realm of graves!
And the shapes through thy mysteries that come and go,
20 Are of beauty and terror, of power and woe.

But for me, oh thou picture-land of sleep,
Thou art all one world of affections deep—
And wrung from my heart is each flushing dye
That sweeps o'er thy chambers of imagery.

25 And thy bowers° are fair—even as Eden fair;   *arbors*
All the beloved of my soul are there!
The forms my spirit most pines to see,
The eyes whose love hath been life to me:

They are there, and each blessed voice I hear,
30 Kindly, and joyous, and silvery clear;
But undertones are in each, that say,
"It is but a dream; it will melt away!"

I walk with sweet friends in the sunset's glow;
I listen to music of long ago;
35 But one thought, like an omen, breathes faint through
    the lay[3]—
"It is but a dream; it will melt away!"

I sit by the hearth of my early days;
All the home-faces are met by the blaze,
And the eyes of the mother shine soft, yet say,
40 "It is but a dream; it will melt away!"

And away, like a flower's passing breath, 'tis gone,
And I wake more sadly, more deeply lone—
Oh, a haunted heart is a weight to bear!
Bright faces, kind voices, where are ye, where?

45 Shadow not forth, oh thou land of dreams,
The past, as it fled by my own blue streams!
Make not my spirit within me burn
For the scenes and the hours that may ne'er return!

---

[1] [Hemans's note]   Originally published in *Blackwood's Magazine*.
[1828.]

[2] *And dreams … Byron*   From "The Dream," by George Gordon,
Lord Byron (1788–1824).

[3] *lay*   Medieval narrative song or poem.

Call out from the future thy visions bright,
50   From the world o'er the grave, take thy solemn light,
And oh! with the loved, whom no more I see,
Show me my home as it yet may be!

As it yet may be in some purer sphere,
No cloud, no parting, no sleepless fear;
55   So my soul may bear on through the long, long day,
Till I go where the beautiful melts not away!
    —1821

Evening Prayer at a Girls' School

    Now in thy youth, beseech of Him,
        Who giveth, upbraiding° not,   *sharply scolding*
    That his light in thy heart become not dim,
        And his love be unforgot;
    And thy God, in the darkest of days, will be
    Greenness, and beauty, and strength to thee.[1]
            BERNARD BARTON.

Hush! 'tis a holy hour—the quiet room
    Seems like a temple, while yon soft lamp sheds
A faint and starry radiance, through the gloom
    And the sweet stillness, down on bright young heads,
5   With all their clust'ring locks, untouch'd by care,
And bow'd, as flowers are bow'd with night—in prayer.

Gaze on,—'tis lovely!—childhood's lip and cheek,
    Mantling[2] beneath its earnest brow of thought—
Gaze—yet what seest thou in those fair, and meek,
10   And fragile things, as but for sunshine wrought?
—Thou seest what grief must nurture for the sky,
What death must fashion for eternity!

Oh! joyous creatures, that will sink to rest,
    Lightly, when those pure orisons° are done,   *prayers*
15   As birds with slumber's honey-dew oppress'd,
    'Midst the dim folded leaves, at set of sun—
Lift up your hearts!—though yet no sorrow lies
Dark in the summer-heaven of those clear eyes;

Though fresh within your breasts th'untroubled springs
20   Of hope make melody where'er ye tread;
And o'er your sleep bright shadows, from the wings
    Of spirits visiting but youth, be spread;
Yet in those flute-like voices, mingling low,
Is woman's tenderness—how soon her woe!°   *sorrow*

25   Her lot° is on you—silent tears to weep,   *fate*
        And patient smiles to wear through suffering's hour,
And sumless riches, from Affection's deep,
        To pour on broken reeds-a wasted shower!
And to make idols, and to find them clay,[3]
30   And to bewail that worship—therefore pray!

Her lot is on you—to be found untir'd,
        Watching the stars out by the bed of pain,
With a pale cheek, and yet a brow inspir'd,
        And a true heart of hope, though hope be vain.
35   Meekly to bear with wrong, to cheer decay,
And oh! to love through all things—therefore pray!

And take the thought of this calm vesper°   *evening prayer*
    time,
        With its low murmuring sounds and silvery light,
Or through the dark days fading from their prime,
40   As a sweet dew to keep your souls from blight.
Earth will forsake—oh! happy to have given
Th'unbroken heart's first fragrance unto Heaven!
    —1825

Casabianca[4]

The boy stood on the burning deck,
    Whence all but him had fled;

---

[1] *Now in ... strength to thee* "The Ivy, Addressed to a Young Friend" (1825), 43–48, by Bernard Barton (1784–1849).

[2] *Mantling* Blushing, coloring from emotion.

[3] *And to ... clay* See Daniel 2.31–45.

[4] [Hemans's note] Young Casabianca, a boy about thirteen years old, son to the admiral of the Orient, remained at his post (in the battle of the Nile), after the ship had taken fire, and all the guns had been abandoned; and perished in the explosion of the vessel, when the flames had reached the powder. [The British fleet, commanded by Horatio Nelson, defeated Napoleon's fleet, commanded by Louis de Casabianca, at the battle of the Nile on 1 August 1798. Among those killed when the French flagship, *L'Orient*, exploded were the Admiral and his son, Giacomo Jocante Casabianca (who in fact was only ten). Hemans's source is probably Southey, *Life of Horatio, Lord Nelson* (1813). The poem was first published in the *Monthly Magazine*.]

The flame that lit the battle's wreck,
    Shone round him o'er the dead.

5   Yet beautiful and bright he stood,
    As born to rule the storm;
A creature of heroic blood,
    A proud, though child-like form.

The flames roll'd on—he would not go,
10   Without his father's word;
That father, faint in death below,
    His voice no longer heard.

He call'd aloud—"Say, father, say
    If yet my task is done?"
15 He knew not that the chieftain lay
    Unconscious of his son.

"Speak, Father!" once again he cried,
    "If I may yet be gone!"
—And but the booming shots replied,
20   And fast the flames roll'd on.

Upon his brow he felt their breath,
    And in his waving hair;
And look'd from that lone post of death,
    In still, yet brave despair.

25 And shouted but once more aloud,
    "My father! must I stay?"
While o'er him fast, through sail and shroud,
    The wreathing fires made way.

They wrapt the ship in splendor wild,
30   They caught the flag on high,
And stream'd above the gallant child,
    Like banners in the sky.

There came a burst of thunder sound—
    The boy—oh! where was he?
35 —Ask of the winds that far around
    With fragments strew'd the sea!

With mast, and helm, and pennon[1] fair,
    That well had borne their part—
But the noblest thing that perish'd there,
40   Was that young faithful heart.
—1826

Corinne at the Capitol[2]

Les femmes doivent penser qu'il est dans cette carrière bien
peu de sort qui puissent valoir la plus obscure vie d'une
femme aimée et d'une mère heureuse.

                MADAME DE STAËL.[3]

Daughter of th'Italian heaven!
  Thou, to whom its fires are given,
Joyously thy car° hath roll'd   *chariot*
Where the conqueror's pass'd of old;
5 And the festal° sun that shone,   *festive*
O'er three hundred triumphs gone,[4]
Makes thy day of glory bright,
With a shower of golden light.

Now thou tread'st th'ascending road,
10 Freedom's foot so proudly trode;[5]
While, from tombs of heroes borne,
From the dust of empire shorn,
Flowers upon thy graceful head,
Chaplets[6] of all hues, are shed,

---

[1] *pennon* Banner or flag.

[2] *Corinne at the Capitol* Based on the novel *Corinne, ou l'Italie*
(1807), by Germaine de Staël (1766–1817). Corinne is an Italian
improvisatrice—a poet who improvises verses in public. The English
Lord Nelvil first sees her when she is being honored at the Capitol,
in Rome. They fall in love and he offers to marry her, but she
declines, preferring her independence. When he marries her
half-sister instead, she dies of a broken heart. The poem was first
published in *The Literary Souvenir* for 1827 (1826) 189–91.

[3] *Les femmes … heureuse* French: "Women must reflect that there
are in this career [of glory] very few destinies that can equal in worth
the most obscure life of a beloved wife and happy mother." See Staël,
De l'Influence des passions sur le bonheur des individus et des nations
(1796) ch. 3.

[4] [Hemans's note] The trebly hundred triumphs.—Byron. [See
"Childe Harold's Pilgrimage" 4.82 (1818)]; *triumph* Ancient
Roman celebration of a military victory; there were a total of 320.

[5] *trode* Archaic past tense of "tread."

[6] *chaplets* Garlands of flowers worn on the head.

15 In a soft and rosy rain,
   Touch'd with many a gemlike stain.

   Thou hast gain'd the summit now!
   Music hails thee from below;
   Music, whose rich notes might stir
20 Ashes of the sepulchre;°   tomb
   Shaking with victorious notes
   All the bright air as it floats.
   Well may woman's heart beat high
    Unto that proud harmony!

25 Now afar it rolls—it dies—
   And thy voice is heard to rise
   With a low and lovely tone
   In its thrilling power alone;
   And thy lyre's deep silvery string,
30 Touch'd as by a breeze's wing,
   Murmurs tremblingly at first,
   Ere° the tide of rapture burst.   before

   All the spirit of thy sky
   Now hath lit thy large dark eye,
35 And thy cheek a flush hath caught
   From the joy of kindled thought;
   And the burning words of song
   From thy lip flow fast and strong,
   With a rushing stream's delight
40 In the freedom of its might.

   Radiant daughter of the sun!
   Now thy living wreath is won.
   Crown'd of Rome!—Oh! art thou not
   Happy in that glorious lot?°—   fate
45 Happier, happier far than thou,
   With the laurel on thy brow,[1]
   She that makes the humblest hearth
   Lovely but to one on earth!
   —1826

The Effigies[2]

Der rasche Kampf verewigt einen Mann:
Er falle gleich, so preiset ihn das Lied.
Allein die Thränen, die unendlichen
Der überbliebnen, der verlass'nen Frau,
Zählt keine Nachwelt.

                                        GOETHE[3]

Warrior! whose image on thy tomb,
    With shield and crested head,
Sleeps proudly in the purple gloom
    By the stain'd window shed;
5 The records of thy name and race
    Have faded from the stone,
Yet, through a cloud of years, I trace
    What thou hast been and done.

A banner, from its flashing spear,
10   Flung out o'er many a fight;
A war-cry ringing far and clear,
    And strong to turn the flight;
An arm that bravely bore the lance
    On for the holy shrine;
15 A haughty heart and a kingly glance—
    Chief! were not these things thine?

A lofty place where leaders sate°   sat
    Around the council-board;°   table
In festive halls a chair of state
20   When the blood-red wine was pour'd;
A name that drew a prouder tone
    From herald, harp, and bard;°   court poet
Surely these things were all thine own,—
    So hadst thou thy reward.

25 Woman! whose sculptur'd form at rest
    By the armed knight is laid,
With meek hands folded o'er a breast
    In matron robes array'd;

---

[1] *laurel on … brow* Poets were traditionally honored with crowns of laurel, which was sacred to Apollo.

[2] *Effigies* Sculptural representations of people, often upon their tombs.

[3] *Der rasche … Nachwelt* German: "Rash combat oft immortalizes man. / If he should fall, he is renowned in song; / But after ages reckon not the tears / Which ceaseless the forsaken woman sheds." (Goethe, *Iphigenie* 5.6. English translation by Anna Swanwick [1909-14].)

What was thy tale?—Oh! gentle mate
   Of him, the bold and free,
Bound unto his victorious fate,
   What bard hath sung of *thee*?

He woo'd a bright and burning star—
   Thine was the void, the gloom,
The straining eye that follow'd far
   His fast-receding plume;
The heart-sick listening while his steed
   Sent echoes on the breeze;
The pang—but when did *Fame* take heed
   Of griefs obscure as these?

Thy silent and secluded hours
   Thro' many a lonely day,
While bending o'er thy broider'd° flowers,   *embroidered*
   With spirit far away;
Thy weeping midnight prayers for him
   Who fought on Syrian plains,
Thy watchings till the torch grew dim—
   These fill no minstrel strains.

A still, sad life was thine!—long years
   With tasks unguerdon'd° fraught,   *unrewarded*
Deep, quiet love, submissive tears,
   Vigils of anxious thought;
Prayer at the cross in fervour pour'd,
   Alms[1] to the pilgrim given—
Oh! happy, happier than thy lord,
   In that lone path to heaven!
—1826

The Image in Lava[2]

Thou thing of years departed!
   What ages have gone by,

Since here the mournful seal was set
   By love and agony!

Temple and tower have moulder'd,
   Empires from earth have pass'd,—
And woman's heart hath left a trace
   Those glories to outlast!

And childhood's fragile image
   Thus fearfully enshrin'd,
Survives the proud memorials rear'd
   By conquerors of mankind.

Babe! wert thou brightly slumbering
   Upon thy mother's breast,
When suddenly the fiery tomb
   Shut round each gentle guest?

A strange, dark fate o'ertook you,
   Fair babe and loving heart!
One moment of a thousand pangs—
   Yet better than to part!

Haply° of that fond bosom,   *by chance*
   On ashes here impress'd,
Thou wert the only treasure, child!
   Whereon a hope might rest.

Perchance all vainly lavish'd,
   Its other love had been,
And where it trusted, nought remain'd
   But thorns on which to lean.

Far better then to perish,
   Thy form within its clasp,
Than live and lose thee, precious one!
   From that impassion'd grasp.

Oh! I could pass all relics
   Left by the pomps of old,
To gaze on this rude° monument,   *primitive*
   Cast in affection's mould.

Love, human love! what art thou?
   Thy print upon the dust
Outlives the cities of renown

---

1. *Alms* Money given in charity to the poor.
2. [Hemans's note] The impression of a woman's form, with an infant clasped to the bosom, found at the uncovering of Herculaneum. [Herculaneum and Pompeii were destroyed by the eruption of Vesuvius in 79 BCE. The image is one of the casts made during the excavations (1763–1820) by pouring plaster into the holes left in the lava by the victims' bodies. The poem was first published in the *New Monthly Magazine* in 1827.]

40 Wherein the mighty trust!
Immortal, oh! immortal
    Thou art, whose earthly glow
Hath given these ashes holiness—
    It must, it must be so!
—1827

Properzia Rossi

(Properzia Rossi,[1] a celebrated female sculptor of Bologna, possessed also of talents for poetry and music, died in consequence of an unrequited attachment.—A painting, by Ducis,[2] represents her showing her last work, a basso-relievo of Ariadne,[3] to a Roman knight, the object of her affection, who regards it with indifference.)

      —Tell me no more, no more
  Of my soul's lofty gifts! Are they not vain
  To quench its haunting thirst for happiness?
   Have I not lov'd, and striven, and fail'd to bind
  One true heart unto me, whereon my own
  Might find a resting-place, a home for all
  Its burden of affections? I depart,
  Unknown, tho' Fame goes with me; I must leave
  The earth unknown. Yet it may be that death
  Shall give my name a power to win such tears
  As would have made life precious.[4]

1

O ne dream of passion and of beauty more!
  And in its bright fulfilment let me pour
My soul away! Let earth retain a trace
Of that which lit my being, tho' its race
5 Might have been loftier far.—Yet one more dream!
From my deep spirit one victorious gleam
Ere I depart! For thee alone, for thee!
May this last work, this farewell triumph be,
Thou, loved so vainly! I would leave enshrined

10 Something immortal of my heart and mind,
That yet may speak to thee when I am gone,
Shaking thine inmost bosom with a tone
Of lost affection;—something that may prove
What she hath been, whose melancholy love
15 On thee was lavish'd; silent pang and tear,
And fervent song, that gush'd when none were near,
And dream by night, and weary thought by day,
Stealing the brightness from her life away,—
While thou—Awake! not yet within me die,
20 Under the burden and the agony
Of this vain tenderness,—my spirit, wake!
Ev'n for thy sorrowful affection's sake,
Live! in thy work breathe out!—that he may yet,
Feeling sad mastery there, perchance regret
25 Thine unrequited gift.

2

      It comes,—the power
Within me born, flows back; my fruitless dower°   *dowry*
That could not win me love. Yet once again
I greet it proudly, with its rushing train
30 Of glorious images:—they throng—they press—
A sudden joy lights up my loneliness,—
I shall not perish all![5]
      The bright work grows
Beneath my hand, unfolding, as a rose,
35 Leaf after leaf, to beauty; line by line,
I fix my thought, heart, soul, to burn, to shine,
Thro' the pale marble's veins. It grows—and now
I give my own life's history to thy brow,
Forsaken Ariadne! thou shalt wear
40 My form, my lineaments;[6] but oh! more fair,
Touch'd into lovelier being by the glow
    Which in me dwells, as by the summer-light
All things are glorified. From thee my woe
    Shall yet look beautiful to meet his sight,
45 When I am pass'd away. Thou art the mould
Wherein I pour the fervent thoughts, th'untold,
The self-consuming! Speak to him of me,
Thou, the deserted by the lonely sea,
With the soft sadness of thine earnest eye,
50 Speak to him, lorn° one! deeply, mournfully,   *forlorn*
Of all my love and grief! Oh! could I throw

---

[1] *Properzia Rossi* Properzia de'Rossi (c.1491–1530), Bolognese sculptor, painter, and poet.

[2] *Ducis* Louis Ducis (1775–1847), *Properzia de'Rossi and her Last Bas-relief*.

[3] *basso-relievo* Relief sculpture; *Ariadne* Cretan princess who helped Theseus find his way through the labyrinth and kill the Minotaur. They eloped, but he abandoned her on the island of Naxos. See Ovid (43–17 BCE), *Heroides* 10.

[4] *Tell me … precious* The epigraph is by Hemans herself.

[5] *I shall … all* Cf. Horace, *Odes* 3.30.6.

[6] *lineaments* Distinctive shapes.

Into thy frame a voice, a sweet, and low,
And thrilling voice of song! when he came nigh,
To send the passion of its melody
55 Thro' his pierced bosom—on its tones to bear
My life's deep feeling, as the southern air
Wafts the faint myrtle's[1] breath,—to rise, to swell,
To sink away in accents of farewell,
Winning but one, one gush of tears, whose flow
60 Surely my parted spirit yet might know,
If love be strong as death!

3

Now fair thou art,
Thou form, whose life is of my burning heart!
Yet all the vision that within me wrought,
65   I cannot make thee! Oh! I might have given
Birth to creations of far nobler thought,
    I might have kindled, with the fire of heaven,
Things not of such as die! But I have been
Too much alone;[2] a heart whereon to lean,
70 With all these deep affections, that o'erflow
My aching soul, and find no shore below;
An eye to be my star, a voice to bring
Hope o'er my path, like sounds that breathe of spring,
These are denied me—dreamt of still in vain,—
75 Therefore my brief aspirings from the chain,
Are ever but as some wild fitful° song,   *irregular*
Rising triumphantly, to die ere° long   *before*
In dirge-like[3] echoes.

4

Yet the world will see
80 Little of this, my parting work, in thee,
    Thou shalt have fame! Oh, mockery! give the reed
From storms a shelter,—give the drooping vine
Something round, which its tendrils may entwine,—
    Give the parch'd flower a rain-drop, and the
        meed°   *reward*
85 Of love's kind words to woman! Worthless fame!
That in *his* bosom wins not for my name
Th'abiding place it ask'd! Yet how my heart,
In its own fairy world of song and art,

Once beat for praise!—Are those high longings o'er?
90 That which I have been can I be no more?—
Never, oh! never more; tho' still thy sky
Be blue as then, my glorious Italy!
And tho' the music, whose rich breathings fill
Thine air with soul, be wandering past me still,
95 And tho' the mantle° of thy sunlight streams,   *cloak*
Unchang'd on forms, instinct with poet-dreams;
Never, oh! never more! Where'er I move,
The shadow of this broken-hearted love
Is on me and around! Too well *they* know,
100   Whose life is all within, too soon and well,
When there the blight hath settled;—but I go
    Under the silent wings of peace to dwell;
From the slow wasting, from the lonely pain,
The inward burning of those words—"*in vain*,"
105   Sear'd on the heart—I go. 'Twill soon be past.
Sunshine, and song, and bright Italian heaven,
    And thou, oh! thou, on whom my spirit cast
Unvalued wealth,—who know'st not what was given
In that devotedness,—the sad, and deep,
110 And unrepaid—farewell! If I could weep
Once, only once, belov'd one! on thy breast,
Pouring my heart forth ere I sink to rest!
But that were happiness, and unto me
Earth's gift is *fame*. Yet I was form'd to be
115 So richly blest! With thee to watch the sky,
Speaking not, feeling but that thou wert nigh;
With thee to listen, while the tones of song
Swept ev'n as part of our sweet air along,
To listen silently;—with thee to gaze
120 On forms, the deified of olden days,
This had been joy enough;—and hour by hour,
From its glad well-springs drinking life and power,
How had my spirit soar'd, and made its fame
    A glory for thy brow!—Dreams, dreams!—the fire
125 Burns faint within me. Yet I leave my name—
    As a deep thrill may linger on the lyre[4]
When its full chords are hush'd—awhile to live,
And one day haply in thy heart revive
Sad thoughts of me:—I leave it, with a sound,
130 A spell o'er memory, mournfully profound,
I leave it, on my country's air to dwell,—
Say proudly yet—"'Twas hers who lov'd me well!"
—1828

---

[1] *myrtle's* Belonging to the myrtle, a Mediterranean evergreen shrub bearing pink flowers and black berries.

[2] *Too ... alone* Cf. Byron, *Mazeppa* (1819), 839.

[3] *dirge-like* Like a funeral hymn, solemn and mournful.

[4] *lyre* Stringed instrument.

Woman and Fame

Happy—happier far than thou,
    With the laurel on thy brow;[1]
She that makes the humblest hearth,
    Lovely but to one on earth.[2]

Thou hast a charmed cup, O Fame!
    A draught that mantles[3] high,
And seems to lift this earthly frame
    Above mortality.
5   Away! to me—a woman—bring
Sweet waters from affection's spring.

Thou hast green laurel leaves, that twine
    Into so proud a wreath;
For that resplendent gift of thine,
10   Heroes have smiled in death:
Give *me* from some kind hand a flower,
The record of one happy hour!

Thou hast a voice, whose thrilling tone
    Can bid each life-pulse beat
15 As when a trumpet's note hath blown,
    Calling the brave to meet:
But mine, let mine—a woman's breast,
By words of home-born love be bless'd.

A hollow sound is in thy song,
20   A mockery in thine eye,
To the sick heart that doth but long
    For aid, for sympathy—
For kindly looks to cheer it on,
For tender accents that are gone.

25 Fame, Fame! thou canst not be the stay°   prop
    Unto the drooping reed,
The cool fresh fountain in the day
    Of the soul's feverish need:
Where must the lone one turn or flee?—
30 Not unto thee—oh! not to thee!
—1829

---

[1]   *laurel on ... brow*   Poets were traditionally honored with crowns of laurel, which was sacred to Apollo.

[2]   *Happy—happier ... earth*   Paraphrased from Hemans's own "Corinne at the Capitol" (ll. 45–8).

[3]   *mantles*   Here, foams.

JOHN KEATS
1795 – 1821

John Keats has come to epitomize the popular conception of the Romantic poet as a passionate dreamer whose intense, sensuous poetry celebrates the world of the imagination over that of everyday life. Keats published only 54 poems in his short lifetime, but his work ranges across a number of poetic genres, including sonnets, odes, romances, and epics. In each of these genres his poetry seeks beauty and truth that will transcend the world of suffering, always questioning its own process of interpretation.

The eldest of four children, John Keats was born in London on 31 October 1795. He lost both his parents by the time he was fourteen—his father in a riding accident and his mother of tuberculosis (then commonly known as consumption). After his mother's death, Keats came under the care of two guardians. He continued to attend Enfield School, a liberal institution where he first became acquainted with Leigh Hunt's radical paper *The Examiner*, and where his interest in poetry grew, particularly after reading the poetry of Edmund Spenser. Keats's friend Charles Brown said it was *The Faerie Queene* that awakened Keats's talent for expressing the "acute sense of beauty" he possessed.

After a promising but incomplete schooling, Keats apprenticed himself in 1815 to a surgeon at Guy's Hospital in London. (He remained licensed as an apothecary until 1817.) Having befriended some of the most prolific artists and critics of his day, among them radical publisher Leigh Hunt, essayist Charles Lamb, painter Benjamin Haydon, and poets John Hamilton Reynolds and Percy Shelley (later to eulogize Keats in *Adonais*), Keats was spurred to further develop his own creative abilities. In 1816, after spending a night reading a translation of Homer with his school friend Cowden Clarke, Keats wrote "On First Looking Into Chapman's Homer" (1816), a sonnet that presents a poet reflecting on poetic tradition and discovering his talent, as an explorer surveys "with a wild surmise" another ocean of possibility.

Shortly thereafter, Keats composed "Sleep and Poetry" (1817), a poetic manifesto of sorts in which he proclaims his devotion to a new type of poetry, one in the style of Wordsworth, devoted to nature and the human heart. By aligning himself with Wordsworth's naturalism, Keats ensured the condemnation of critics; nevertheless, that same year he chose to give up surgery and devote himself entirely to poetry. This decision was most likely sealed by Leigh Hunt's first "Young Poets" article (*Examiner*, December 1816), in which he identified Keats, Shelley, and Reynolds as the leaders of a new generation of poets.

Keats's first volume, *Poems* (1817), received little critical attention. The following year he published the long and ambitious romance *Endymion* (1818), about a shepherd-prince who pursues his elusive feminine ideal. The book was sharply criticized in a famous review published in the *Quarterly Review*, where Keats and his friend Hunt were ridiculed as representing "the Cockney school of poetry." Keats endured further criticism when he read "Hymn to Pan" from *Endymion* to the contemporary poet he most admired, Wordsworth; the elder poet ungenerously dismissed it as "a very pretty piece of paganism."

His hopes undimmed, Keats continued to pursue his poetic ideals. In a series of now-famous letters to Benjamin Bailey, he explored his aesthetic ideas and sought to define the purpose of literature for modern life. Keats's letters to his friends and family are justly acclaimed for their intuitions about life, suffering, and poetry. To Keats we owe the concepts of "negative capability," the "chameleon poet," and "the vale of Soul-making." He particularly admired what he saw as Shakespeare's chameleon-like ability to escape from his personality and enter fully into the being of his characters.

During this time, Keats fell in love with the lively and flirtatious Fanny Brawne, who became a kind of muse. Though they became engaged, Keats wanted to gain financial security before marrying. He had begun as well to be haunted by fears of his own early death. (Throat ulcers that had appeared during a walking tour in poor weather the previous summer had become chronic.) It was in this set of tumultuous emotional circumstances that Keats began one of the most extraordinary periods of creativity in the history of English literature. Between January and September of 1819 he composed all seven of his "great Odes"—"Ode to Psyche," "Ode to a Nightingale," "Ode on a Grecian Urn," "Ode on Indolence," "Ode on Melancholy," and "To Autumn"—as well as "The Eve of St. Agnes," "La Belle Dame sans Merci," "Lamia," and a number of sonnets. "The Eve of St. Agnes" remains Keats's best-known narrative poem. Suffused with amorous feeling and lush imagery, "The Eve of St. Agnes" recounts a romantic story with affinities to the story of Romeo and Juliet. Generations of readers have been seduced by the sensuous immediacy of this poetry.

Keats's largest poetic project was *Hyperion*, a blank-verse epic on Jupiter's dethroning of Saturn and Apollo's overthrow of Hyperion. An intense study of cultural loss, the poem is a self-consciously Miltonic exercise that Keats kept returning to but never completed. He began the poem in the autumn of 1818, but put the manuscript aside in April of the following year. (This first fragmentary version of the poem was published as "Hyperion: A Fragment" in the 1820 volume of his verse.)

In the summer he resumed work on the project, this time casting the story within the frame of a poet's dream vision, but he stopped for a second time in September. (This second version, also fragmentary, was finally published in 1856 as "The Fall of Hyperion.")

As Keats's extraordinary poetic outpouring of 1819 was coming to a close, he began to suspect himself inadequate to the task of undertaking a Miltonic epic. As he wrote to a friend John Reynolds on 21 September 1819:

I have given up Hyperion … Miltonic verse cannot be written but in an artful or rather artist's humour. I wish to give myself up to other sensations. English ought to be kept up.

Keats wrote little after September of 1819, but he published his third volume of poetry, *Lamia, Isabella, The Eve of St. Agnes, and Other Poems*, in 1820—defiantly advertising himself on the cover as "the author of *Endymion*." Critics were gradually acquiring a taste for Keats's work, but by this time Keats was very ill, having contracted tuberculosis. His lungs weakened and his throat still ulcerating, Keats in August of 1820 declined an invitation to join Shelley and his circle in Pisa, and instead went to Rome, where he died in the house at the base of the Spanish Steps that is now the Keats-Shelley Memorial House. Keats was buried in the Protestant Cemetery in Rome.

In the generations since his death many have wondered what Keats would have accomplished had he lived. Such thoughts, however, focus on the tragedy of the poet's death, rather than on the sustained richness of his achievement. Before his death, Keats asked that his epitaph be "Here lies one whose name was writ in water." (Though his friends complied, they added above, "This Grave contains all that was Mortal of a YOUNG ENGLISH POET, Who on his Death Bed in the Bitterness of his Heart at the Malicious Power of his Enemies, Desired these Words to be incised on his Tomb Stone.") On visiting his gravesite in 1877, Oscar Wilde supplied another epitaph: "A Priest of Beauty slain before his time." But the last sentences of Keats's last letter to Charles Brown are perhaps more evocative: "I can scarcely bid you good bye even in a letter. I always made an awkward bow."

⌘⌘⌘

On First Looking into Chapman's Homer[1]

Much have I travell'd in the realms of gold,
    And many goodly states and kingdoms seen;
    Round many western islands have I been
Which bards in fealty to Apollo[2] hold.
5 Oft of one wide expanse had I been told
        That deep-brow'd Homer ruled as his demesne;
        Yet never did I breathe its pure serene,
Till I heard Chapman speak out loud and bold:
Then felt I like some watcher of the skies
10   When a new planet swims into his ken;[3]
    Or like stout Cortez[4] when with eagle eyes
        He star'd at the Pacific—and all his men
Look'd at each other with a wild surmise—
        Silent, upon a peak in Darien.

—1816

On the Grasshopper and Cricket

The poetry of earth is never dead:
    When all the birds are faint with the hot sun,
    And hide in cooling trees, a voice will run
From hedge to hedge about the new-mown mead;
5 That is the Grasshopper's—he takes the lead
        In summer luxury—he has never done
        With his delights; for when tired out with fun

He rests at ease beneath some pleasant weed.
The poetry of earth is ceasing never:
10   On a lone winter evening, when the frost
        Has wrought a silence, from the stove there shrills
The Cricket's song, in warmth increasing ever,
        And seems to one in drowsiness half lost,
        The Grasshopper's among some grassy hills.

—1817

Sleep and Poetry

As I lay in my bed slepe full unmete°   unallotted
Was unto me, but why that I ne might
Rest I ne wist,° for there n'as° erthly   knew / was no
    wight°   creature
[As I suppose] had more of hertis ese°   heart's ease
Than I, for I n'ad° sicknesse nor disese.[5]   had not

CHAUCER

What is more gentle than a wind in summer?
    What is more soothing than the pretty hummer
That stays one moment in an open flower,
And buzzes cheerily from bower to bower?
5 What is more tranquil than a musk-rose
    blowing°   blossoming
In a green island, far from all men's knowing?
More healthful than the leafiness of dales?
More secret than a nest of nightingales?
More serene than Cordelia's[6] countenance?
10 More full of visions than a high romance?
What, but thee Sleep? Soft closer of our eyes!
Low murmurer of tender lullabies!
Light hoverer around our happy pillows!
Wreather of poppy buds, and weeping willows!

---

[1] *On … Homer*   Written in October 1816, on the morning after Keats and his friend and mentor Charles Cowden Clarke had stayed up all night reading the 1614 translation of Homer by George Chapman (1559–1634).

[2] *Apollo*   Greek god of poetry.

[3] *a new … ken*   William Herschel had discovered Uranus in 1781.

[4] *Cortez*   The first European to see the Pacific (from the Isthmus of Darien in Panama) was not actually Hernán Cortez (1485–1547), the conqueror of Mexico, but Vasco Nuñez de Balboa in 1513 (1475–1519).

[5] *As … disese*   From *The Floure and the Leafe* 17–21, which was then thought to have been written by Chaucer.

[6] *Cordelia*   Daughter of King Lear in Shakespeare's *King Lear*.

15 Silent entangler of a beauty's tresses!
Most happy listener! when the morning blesses
Thee for enlivening all the cheerful eyes
That glance so brightly at the new sun-rise.

But what is higher beyond thought than thee?
20 Fresher than berries of a mountain tree?
More strange, more beautiful, more smooth, more
    regal,
Than wings of swans, than doves, than dim-seen eagle?
What is it? And to what shall I compare it?
It has a glory, and naught else can share it:
25 The thought thereof is awful, sweet, and holy,
Chasing away all worldliness and folly;
Coming sometimes like fearful claps of thunder,
Or the low rumblings earth's regions under;
And sometimes like a gentle whispering
30 Of all the secrets of some wond'rous thing
That breathes about us in the vacant air;
So that we look around with prying stare,
Perhaps to see shapes of light, aërial limning,[1]
And catch soft floatings from a faint-heard hymning;
35 To see the laurel wreath,[2] on high suspended,
That is to crown our name when life is ended.
Sometimes it gives a glory to the voice,
And from the heart up-springs, "Rejoice! rejoice!"
Sounds which will reach the Framer of all things,
40 And die away in ardent mutterings.

No one who once the glorious sun has seen,
And all the clouds, and felt his bosom clean
For his great Maker's presence, but must know
What 'tis I mean, and feel his being glow:
45 Therefore no insult will I give his spirit,
By telling what he sees from native merit.

O Poesy! For thee I hold my pen
That am not yet a glorious denizen
Of thy wide heaven—Should I rather kneel
50 Upon some mountain-top until I feel

A glowing splendour round about me hung,
And echo back the voice of thine own tongue?
O Poesy! For thee I grasp my pen
That am not yet a glorious denizen
55 Of thy wide heaven; yet, to my ardent prayer,
Yield from thy sanctuary some clear air,
Smoothed for intoxication by the breath
Of flowering bays, that I may die a death
Of luxury, and my young spirit follow
60 The morning sun-beams to the great Apollo[3]
Like a fresh sacrifice; or, if I can bear
The o'erwhelming sweets, 'twill bring to me the fair
Visions of all places: a bowery nook
Will be elysium[4]—an eternal book
65 Whence I may copy many a lovely saying
About the leaves, and flowers—about the playing
Of nymphs in woods, and fountains; and the shade
Keeping a silence round a sleeping maid;
And many a verse from so strange influence
70 That we must ever wonder how, and whence
It came. Also imaginings will hover
Round my fire-side, and haply there discover
Vistas of solemn beauty, where I'd wander
In happy silence, like the clear Meander[5]
75 Through its lone vales; and where I found a spot
Of awfuller shade, or an enchanted grot,°   grotto
Or a green hill o'erspread with chequered dress
Of flowers, and fearful from its loveliness,
Write on my tablets all that was permitted,
80 All that was for our human senses fitted.
Then the events of this wide world I'd seize
Like a strong giant, and my spirit tease
Till at its shoulders it should proudly see
Wings to find out an immortality.

85 Stop and consider! Life is but a day;
A fragile dew-drop on its perilous way
From a tree's summit; a poor Indian's sleep
While his boat hastens to the monstrous steep

---

1 *limning* Painting.
2 *laurel wreath* Wreaths made of leaves of the bay laurel were traditionally bestowed upon those who distinguished themselves in poetry.

3 *Apollo* Greek god of poetry.
4 *elysium* State of perfect happiness. From the Elysium of Greek mythology, the place where the blessed reside after death.
5 *Meander* Winding river in Asia Minor.

Of Montmorenci.[1] Why so sad a moan?
90 Life is the rose's hope while yet unblown;
The reading of an ever-changing tale;
The light uplifting of a maiden's veil;
A pigeon tumbling in clear summer air;
A laughing school-boy, without grief or care,
95 Riding the springy branches of an elm.

O for ten years, that I may overwhelm
Myself in poesy; so I may do the deed
That my own soul has to itself decreed.
Then will I pass the countries that I see
100 In long perspective, and continually
Taste their pure fountains. First the realm I'll pass
Of Flora, and old Pan:[2] sleep in the grass,
Feed upon apples red, and strawberries,
And choose each pleasure that my fancy sees;
105 Catch the white-handed nymphs in shady places,
To woo sweet kisses from averted faces,
Play with their fingers, touch their shoulders white
Into a pretty shrinking with a bite
As hard as lips can make it: till agreed,
110 A lovely tale of human life we'll read
And one will teach a tame dove how it best
May fan the cool air gently o'er my rest;
Another, bending o'er her nimble tread,
Will set a green robe floating round her head,
115 And still will dance with ever varied ease,
Smiling upon the flowers and the trees:
Another will entice me on, and on
Through almond blossoms and rich cinnamon;
Till in the bosom of a leafy world
120 We rest in silence, like two gems upcurl'd
In the recesses of a pearly shell.

And can I ever bid these joys farewell?
Yes, I must pass them for a nobler life,
Where I may find the agonies, the strife
125 Of human hearts: for lo! I see afar,

O'er sailing the blue cragginess, a car°   *chariot*
And steeds with streamy manes—the charioteer
Looks out upon the winds with glorious fear:
And now the numerous tramplings quiver lightly
130 Along a huge cloud's ridge; and now with sprightly
Wheel downward come they into fresher skies,
Tipt round with silver from the sun's bright eyes.
Still downward with capacious whirl they glide,
And now I see them on the green-hill's side
135 In breezy rest among the nodding stalks.
The charioteer with wond'rous gesture talks
To the trees and mountains; and there soon appear
Shapes of delight, of mystery, and fear,
Passing along before a dusky space
140 Made by some mighty oaks: as they would chase
Some ever-fleeting music on they sweep.
Lo! how they murmur, laugh, and smile, and weep:
Some with upholden hand and mouth severe;
Some with their faces muffled to the ear
145 Between their arms; some, clear in youthful bloom,
Go glad and smilingly athwart the gloom;
Some looking back, and some with upward gaze;
Yes, thousands in a thousand different ways
Flit onward—now a lovely wreath of girls
150 Dancing their sleek hair into tangled curls;
And now broad wings. Most awfully intent
The driver of those steeds is forward bent,
And seems to listen: O that I might know
All that he writes with such a hurrying glow.

155 The visions all are fled—the car is fled
Into the light of heaven, and in their stead
A sense of real things comes doubly strong,
And, like a muddy stream, would bear along
My soul to nothingness: but I will strive
160 Against all doubtings, and will keep alive
The thought of that same chariot, and the strange
Journey it went.

Is there so small a range
In the present strength of manhood, that the high
165 Imagination cannot freely fly
As she was wont of old? prepare her steeds,
Paw up against the light, and do strange deeds
Upon the clouds? Has she not shown us all?

[1] *Montmorenci* Montmorency Falls near Québec City, Canada.

[2] *Flora ... Pan* In Greek mythology, the goddess of flowers and the shepherd god of nature, respectively. The realm of Flora and Pan is that of pastoral poesy, which, according to Virgil, should be the genre with which the aspiring poet begins, eventually working his way up to the epic.

From the clear space of ether, to the small
170 Breath of new buds unfolding? From the meaning
Of Jove's[1] large eyebrow, to the tender greening
Of April meadows? Here her altar shone,
E'en in this isle; and who could paragon
The fervid choir that lifted up a noise
175 Of harmony, to where it aye will poise
Its mighty self of convoluting sound,
Huge as a planet, and like that roll round,
Eternally around a dizzy void?
Ay, in those days the Muses[2] were nigh cloy'd
180 With honours; nor had any other care
Than to sing out and sooth their wavy hair.

Could all this be forgotten? Yes, a schism
Nurtured by foppery and barbarism,
Made great Apollo blush for this his land.
185 Men were thought wise who could not understand
His glories: with a puling infant's force
They sway'd about upon a rocking horse,
And thought it Pegasus.[3] Ah dismal soul'd!
The winds of heaven blew, the ocean roll'd
190 Its gathering waves—ye felt it not. The blue
Bared its eternal bosom, and the dew
Of summer nights collected still to make
The morning precious: beauty was awake!
Why were ye not awake? But ye were dead
195 To things ye knew not of—were closely wed
To musty laws lined out with wretched rule
And compass vile: so that ye taught a school
Of dolts to smooth, inlay, and clip, and fit,
Till, like the certain wands of Jacob's wit,[4]
200 Their verses tallied. Easy was the task:
A thousand handicraftsmen wore the mask
Of Poesy. Ill-fated, impious race!

That blasphemed the bright Lyrist[5] to his face,
And did not know it—no, they went about,
205 Holding a poor, decrepit standard out
Mark'd with most flimsy mottos, and in large
The name of one Boileau![6]

         O ye whose charge
It is to hover round our pleasant hills!
210 Whose congregated majesty so fills
My boundly[7] reverence, that I cannot trace
Your hallowed names, in this unholy place,
So near those common folk; did not their shames
Affright you? Did our old lamenting Thames°   river
215 Delight you? Did ye never cluster round
Delicious Avon,° with a mournful sound,   river
And weep? Or did ye wholly bid adieu
To regions where no more the laurel grew?
Or did ye stay to give a welcoming
220 To some lone spirits[8] who could proudly sing
Their youth away, and die? 'Twas even so:
But let me think away those times of woe:
Now 'tis a fairer season; ye have breathed
Rich benedictions o'er us; ye have wreathed
225 Fresh garlands: for sweet music has been heard
In many places—some has been upstirr'd
From out its crystal dwelling in a lake,
By a swan's ebon bill;[9] from a thick brake,°   thicket
Nested and quiet in a valley mild,
230 Bubbles a pipe;[10] fine sounds are floating wild
About the earth: happy are ye and glad.

---

[1] *Jove* Roman king of the gods.

[2] *Muses* In Greek mythology, nine daughters of Zeus and Mnemosyne, each of whom presided over and provided inspiration for an aspect of learning or the arts.

[3] *Pegasus* Great winged horse of Greek mythology. This line is a reference to William Hazlitt's essay "On Milton's Versification" (1815), in which he says, on the use of the heroic couplet by eighteenth-century poets, "Dr. Johnson and Pope would have turned [Milton's] vaulting Pegasus into a rocking-horse."

[4] *Jacob's wit* See Genesis 30.27–43, in which Jacob increases his wealth at the expense of Laban.

[5] *the bright Lyrist* I.e., Apollo.

[6] *Boileau* French literary critic Nicolas Boileau Despréaux (1636–1711), whose *L'Art Poétique* (1674), a verse treatise on literary aesthetics, was extremely influential among English poets.

[7] *boundly* Term coined by Keats, meaning either "boundless" or "bounden."

[8] *some lone spirits* Reference to poets Thomas Chatterton (1752–70), Henry White (1785–1806), and others, who died young, without receiving the critical attention their work deserved.

[9] *swan's ebon bill* Reference to William Wordsworth (1770–1850), who, along with Coleridge and Southey, was known as a "Lake Poet."

[10] *from a ... pipe* Reference to poet Leigh Hunt (1784–1859).

These things are doubtless: yet in truth we've had
Strange thunders from the potency of song;
Mingled indeed with what is sweet and strong,
235 From majesty: but in clear truth the themes
Are ugly clubs, the poets Polyphemes[1]
Disturbing the grand sea. A drainless shower
Of light is poesy; 'tis the supreme of power;
'Tis might half slumb'ring on its own right arm.
240 The very archings of her eye-lids charm
A thousand willing agents to obey,
And still she governs with the mildest sway:
But strength alone though of the Muses born
Is like a fallen angel: trees uptorn,
245 Darkness, and worms, and shrouds, and sepulchres
Delight it; for it feeds upon the burrs,
And thorns of life; forgetting the great end
Of poesy, that it should be a friend
To sooth the cares, and lift the thoughts of man.

250   Yet I rejoice: a myrtle fairer than
E'er grew in Paphos,[2] from the bitter weeds
Lifts its sweet head into the air, and feeds
A silent space with ever sprouting green.
All tenderest birds there find a pleasant screen,
255 Creep through the shade with jaunty fluttering,
Nibble the little cupped flowers and sing.
Then let us clear away the choking thorns
From round its gentle stem; let the young fawns,
Yeaned° in after times, when we are flown,   *brought forth*
260 Find a fresh sward° beneath it, overgrown   *turf*
With simple flowers: let there nothing be
More boisterous than a lover's bended knee;
Nought more ungentle than the placid look
Of one who leans upon a closed book;
265 Nought more untranquil than the grassy slopes
Between two hills. All hail delightful hopes!
As she was wont, th'imagination
Into most lovely labyrinths will be gone,
And they shall be accounted poet kings
270 Who simply tell the most heart-easing things.
O may these joys be ripe before I die.

Will not some say that I presumptuously
Have spoken? that from hastening disgrace
'Twere better far to hide my foolish face?
275 That whining boyhood should with reverence bow
Ere the dread thunderbolt could reach? How!
If I do hide myself, it sure shall be
In the very fane, the light of Poesy:
If I do fall, at least I will be laid
280 Beneath the silence of a poplar shade;
And over me the grass shall be smooth shaven;
And there shall be a kind memorial graven.
But off Despondence! miserable bane!
They should not know thee, who athirst to gain
285 A noble end, are thirsty every hour.
What though I am not wealthy in the dower
Of spanning wisdom; though I do not know
The shiftings of the mighty winds that blow
Hither and thither all the changing thoughts
290 Of man: though no great minist'ring reason sorts
Out the dark mysteries of human souls
To clear conceiving: yet there ever rolls
A vast idea before me, and I glean
Therefrom my liberty; thence too I've seen
295 The end and aim of Poesy. 'Tis clear
As any thing most true; as that the year
Is made of the four seasons—manifest
As a large cross, some old cathedral's crest,
Lifted to the white clouds. Therefore should I
300 Be but the essence of deformity,
A coward, did my very eyelids wink
At speaking out what I have dared to think.
Ah! rather let me like a madman run
Over some precipice; let the hot sun
305 Melt my Dedalian wings,[3] and drive me down
Convuls'd and headlong! Stay! an inward frown
Of conscience bids me be more calm awhile.
An ocean dim, sprinkled with many an isle,
Spreads awfully before me. How much toil!
310 How many days! what desperate turmoil!
Ere I can have explored its widenesses.

---

[1] *Polyphemes* One-eyed, club-wielding giant in Homer's *Odyssey*.

[2] *Paphos* City in Cyprus that is the site of a famous temple to Venus, goddess of love and beauty. Myrtle (line 248) is also associated with Venus.

[3] *Dedalian wings* According to Greek mythology, the sculptor Daedalus built wings of wax and feathers so that he and his son Icarus could escape from the island of Crete, where they were imprisoned. Icarus flew too close to the sun, and his wings melted, causing him to fall into the sea.

Ah, what a task! upon my bended knees,
I could unsay those—no, impossible!
Impossible!

315   For sweet relief I'll dwell
On humbler thoughts, and let this strange assay
Begun in gentleness die so away.
E'en now all tumult from my bosom fades:
I turn full hearted to the friendly aids
320 That smooth the path of honour; brotherhood,
And friendliness the nurse of mutual good.
The hearty grasp that sends a pleasant sonnet
Into the brain ere one can think upon it;
The silence when some rhymes are coming out;
325 And when they're come, the very pleasant rout:
The message certain to be done to-morrow.
'Tis perhaps as well that it should be to borrow
Some precious book from out its snug retreat,
To cluster round it when we next shall meet.
330 Scarce can I scribble on; for lovely airs
Are fluttering round the room like doves in pairs;
Many delights of that glad day recalling,
When first my senses caught their tender falling.
And with these airs come forms of elegance
335 Stooping their shoulders o'er a horse's prance,
Careless, and grand—fingers soft and round
Parting luxuriant curls—and the swift bound
Of Bacchus from his chariot, when his eye
Made Ariadne's cheek look blushingly.[1]
340 Thus I remember all the pleasant flow
Of words at opening a portfolio.

Things such as these are ever harbingers
To trains of peaceful images: the stirs
Of a swan's neck unseen among the rushes:
345 A linnet starting all about the bushes:
A butterfly, with golden wings broad parted,
Nestling a rose, convuls'd as though it smarted
With over pleasure—many, many more,
Might I indulge at large in all my store

350 Of luxuries: yet I must not forget
Sleep, quiet with his poppy coronet:[2]
For what there may be worthy in these rhymes
I partly owe to him: and thus, the chimes
Of friendly voices had just given place
355 To as sweet a silence, when I 'gan retrace
The pleasant day, upon a couch at ease.
It was a poet's house who keeps the keys
Of pleasure's temple.[3] Round about were hung
The glorious features of the bards who sung
360 In other ages—cold and sacred busts
Smiled at each other. Happy he who trusts
To clear Futurity his darling fame!
Then there were fauns and satyrs taking aim
At swelling apples with a frisky leap
365 And reaching fingers, 'mid a luscious heap
Of vine leaves. Then there rose to view a fane°   temple
Of liny° marble, and thereto a train   veined
Of nymphs approaching fairly o'er the sward:
One, loveliest, holding her white hand toward
370 The dazzling sun-rise: two sisters sweet
Bending their graceful figures till they meet
Over the trippings of a little child:
And some are hearing, eagerly, the wild
Thrilling liquidity of dewy piping.
375 See, in another picture, nymphs are wiping
Cherishingly Diana's[4] timorous limbs;
A fold of lawny mantle dabbling swims
At the bath's edge, and keeps a gentle motion
With the subsiding crystal: as when ocean
380 Heaves calmly its broad swelling smoothness o'er
Its rocky marge, and balances once more
The patient weeds; that now unshent°   unharmed
         by foam
Feel all about their undulating home.

Sappho's[5] meek head was there half smiling down
385 At nothing; just as though the earnest frown

---

[1] *Of Bacchus ... blushingly* Adriane, daughter of King Minos of Crete, was abandoned by her lover, Theseus, on the island of Naxos. Bacchus, god of wine, found her there, consoled her, and married her (Ovid, *Metamorphoses* 8.172–82). Keats would also have been familiar with the painting *Bacchus and Ariadne* (1523) by Venetian painter Titian (1490–1576).

[2] *poppy coronet* The seed capsules of some species of poppy contain opium, and therefore were associated with sleep.

[3] *It was ... temple* Poet Leigh Hunt kept a bed for Keats in his study. Hunt's cottage was filled with busts and pictures, on which the following descriptions are probably based.

[4] *Diana* Roman goddess of chastity, childbirth, and the hunt.

[5] *Sappho* Greek lyric poet of the sixth century BCE.

Of over thinking had that moment gone
From off her brow, and left her all alone.

Great Alfred's[1] too, with anxious, pitying eyes,
As if he always listened to the sighs
390 Of the goaded world; and Kosciusko's[2] worn
By horrid suffrance—mightily forlorn.

Petrarch, outstepping from the shady green,
Starts at the sight of Laura;[3] nor can wean
His eyes from her sweet face. Most happy they!
395 For over them was seen a free display
Of out-spread wings, and from between them shone
The face of Poesy: from off her throne
She overlook'd things that I scarce could tell.
The very sense of where I was might well
400 Keep Sleep aloof: but more than that there came
Thought after thought to nourish up the flame
Within my breast; so that the morning light
Surprised me even from a sleepless night;
And up I rose refresh'd, and glad, and gay,
405 Resolving to begin that very day
These lines; and howsoever they be done,
I leave them as a father does his son.
—1817

On Seeing the Elgin Marbles[4]

My spirit is too weak; mortality
Weighs heavily on me like unwilling sleep,
And each imagined pinnacle and steep
Of godlike hardship, tells me I must die

5 Like a sick Eagle looking at the sky.
    Yet 'tis a gentle luxury to weep,
    That I have not the cloudy winds to keep
Fresh for the opening of the morning's eye.
Such dim-conceived glories of the brain
10   Bring round the heart an indescribable feud;
So do these wonders a most dizzy pain,
    That mingles Grecian grandeur with the rude
Wasting of old Time—with a billowy main,°   sea
    A sun, a shadow of a magnitude.
—1817

On Sitting Down to Read
King Lear Once Again

O golden tongued Romance, with serene lute!
    Fair plumed Syren![5] Queen of far-away!
    Leave melodizing on this wintry day,
Shut up thine olden pages, and be mute:
5 Adieu! for once again the fierce dispute
    Betwixt damnation and impassion'd clay
    Must I burn through; once more humbly assay
The bitter-sweet of this Shakespearian fruit.
Chief Poet! and ye clouds of Albion,[6]
10   Begetters of our deep eternal theme,
When through the old oak forest I am gone,
    Let me not wander in a barren dream,
But when I am consumed in the fire,
Give me new Phœnix[7] wings to fly at my desire.
—1838

When I Have Fears that I May Cease to Be

When I have fears that I may cease to be
    Before my pen has glean'd my teeming brain,
Before high piled books, in charact'ry,[8]
    Hold like rich garners the full-ripen'd grain;

---

[1] *Great Alfred* Alfred the Great, King of Wessex from 871 to 899.

[2] *Kosciusko* Polish patriot Tadeusz Kosciusko (1746–1817), who led his countrymen in an uprising against Russia, and also fought for the United States Army in the American struggle for independence.

[3] *Petrarch … Laura* Italian poet Petrarch (1304–74) wrote odes and sonnets in celebration of his beloved, Laura.

[4] *Elgin Marbles* In 1806 Lord Elgin brought friezes and other sculptures that had decorated the exterior of the Parthenon, in Athens, to England. In 1816 the government purchased them for display in the British Museum, where they remain today. See the "In Context" section on this topic.

[5] *Syren* Monster of classical mythology who is half woman, half serpent, and whose enchanted singing lures sailors to their deaths.

[6] *Albion* England.

[7] *Phoenix* Mythical Egyptian bird that is consumed by fire, and then reborn, once every 500 years.

[8] *charact'ry* Symbols or characters.

5   When I behold, upon the night's starr'd face,
       Huge cloudy symbols of a high romance,
   And think that I may never live to trace
       Their shadows, with the magic hand of chance;
   And when I feel, fair creature of an hour!
10   That I shall never look upon thee more,
   Never have relish in the fairy power
       Of unreflecting love—then on the shore
   Of the wide world I stand alone, and think
   Till love and fame to nothingness do sink.
   —1848 (WRITTEN 1818)

Epistle to John Hamilton Reynolds[1]

Dear Reynolds! as last night I lay in bed,
   There came before my eyes that wonted thread
Of shapes, and shadows, and remembrances,
That every other minute vex and please:
5   Things all disjointed come from north and south—
Two witch's eyes above a cherub's mouth,
Voltaire with casque and shield and habergeon,[2]
And Alexander[3] with his night-cap on;
Old Socrates[4] a-tying his cravat,
10   And Hazlitt playing with Miss Edgeworth's cat;[5]
And Junius Brutus, pretty well so so,[6]
Making the best of's way towards Soho.[7]

   Few are there who escape these visitings—
Perhaps one or two whose lives have patent wings,
15   And through whose curtains peeps no hellish nose,
No wild-boar tushes,° and no mermaid's toes;   *tusks*

But flowers bursting out with lusty pride,
And young Æolian harps[8] personified;
Some, Titian[9] colours touch'd into real life—
20   The sacrifice goes on; the pontiff knife
Gleams in the sun, the milk-white heifer lows,
The pipes go shrilly, the libation flows:
A white sail shows above the green-head cliff,
Moves round the point, and throws her anchor stiff;
25   The mariners join hymn with those on land.

   You know the Enchanted Castle[10]—it doth stand
Upon a rock, on the border of a lake,
Nested in trees, which all do seem to shake
From some old magic like Urganda's sword.[11]
30   O Phoebus![12] that I had thy sacred word
To show this Castle, in fair dreaming wise,
Unto my friend, while sick and ill he lies!

   You know it well enough, where it doth seem
A mossy place, a Merlin's Hall,[13] a dream;
35   You know the clear lake, and the little isles,
The mountains blue, and cold near neighbour rills,
All which elsewhere are but half animate;
There do they look alive to love and hate,
To smiles and frowns; they seem a lifted mound
40   Above some giant, pulsing underground.

   Part of the building was a chosen see,°   *dwelling-place*
Built by a banish'd Santon° of Chaldee;   *holy man*
The other part, two thousand years from him,
Was built by Cuthbert de Saint Aldebrim;[14]
45   Then there's a little wing, far from the sun,

---

[1] *John Hamilton Reynolds* Poet and lawyer (1794–1852) who was a close friend of Keats. Reynolds was ill at the time, and Keats sent him this verse letter to cheer him.

[2] *Voltaire* French philosopher François-Marie Arouet de Voltaire (1694–1778); *casque* Helmet; *habergeon* Sleeveless jacket of chain mail.

[3] *Alexander* Poet Alexander Pope (1688–1744).

[4] *Socrates* Greek philosopher of the fifth century BCE.

[5] *Hazlitt* Painter and writer William Hazlitt (1778–1830); *Miss Edgeworth* Novelist Maria Edgeworth (1767–1849).

[6] *Junius Brutus* Actor Junius Brutus Booth (1796–1852); *so so* Tipsy.

[7] *Soho* Area in London, then rather disreputable.

[8] *Æolian harps* Harps that produce sound when exposed to the wind or open air. From Æolus, the Greek god of the winds.

[9] *Titian* I.e., rich; in the style of Titian, a Venetian Renaissance painter whose work was characterized by bold colors. The following lines most likely describe *Sacrifice to Apollo*, by French painter Claude Lorraine (1600–82).

[10] *the Enchanted Castle* Painting by Claude Lorraine.

[11] *Urganda's sword* Enchantress figure in *Amadis of Gaul*, a fifteenth-century romance.

[12] *Phoebus* Apollo, Greek god of poetry and of the sun.

[13] *Merlin's Hall* I.e., a hall built by magicians such as the sorcerer Merlin, from Arthurian legend.

[14] *Cuthbert ... Aldebrim* Character invented by Keats.

Built by a Lapland witch[1] turn'd maudlin nun;
And many other juts of aged stone
Founded with many a mason-devil's groan.

50 The doors all look as if they oped themselves,
The windows as if latched by fays° and elves,   *fairies*
And from them comes a silver flash of light,
As from the westward of a summer's night;
Or like a beauteous woman's large blue eyes
Gone mad through olden songs and poesies.

55 See! what is coming from the distance dim!
A golden galley all in silken trim!
Three rows of oars are lightening, moment whiles,
Into the verd'rous bosoms of those isles;
Towards the shade, under the Castle wall,
60 It comes in silence—now 'tis hidden all.
The clarion sounds, and from a postern-gate
An echo of sweet music doth create
A fear in the poor herdsman, who doth bring
His beasts to trouble the enchanted spring—
65 He tells of the sweet music, and the spot,
To all his friends, and they believe him not.

O that our dreamings all, of sleep or wake,
Would all their colours from the sunset take:
From something of material sublime,
70 Rather than shadow our own soul's daytime
In the dark void of night. For in the world
We jostle—but my flag is not unfurl'd
On the admiral-staff—and to philosophise
I dare not yet! Oh, never will the prize,
75 High reason, and the lore of good and ill,
Be my award! Things cannot to the will
Be settled, but they tease us out of thought;
Or is it that imagination brought
Beyond its proper bound, yet still confin'd,
80 Lost in a sort of Purgatory blind,
Cannot refer to any standard law
Of either earth or heaven? It is a flaw
In happiness, to see beyond our bourn—
It forces us in summer skies to mourn,
85 It spoils the singing of the nightingale.

Dear Reynolds! I have a mysterious tale,
And cannot speak it: the first page I read
Upon a lampit° rock of green sea-weed   *limpet*
Among the breakers; 'twas a quiet eve,
90 The rocks were silent, the wide sea did weave
An untumultuous fringe of silver foam
Along the flat brown sand; I was at home
And should have been most happy—but I saw
Too far into the sea, where every maw°   *throat, gullet*
95 The greater on the less feeds evermore.
But I saw too distinct into the core
Of an eternal fierce destruction,
And so from happiness I far was gone.
Still am I sick of it, and tho', to-day,
100 I've gather'd young spring-leaves, and flowers gay
Of periwinkle and wild strawberry,
Still do I that most fierce destruction see—
The shark at savage prey, the hawk at pounce,
The gentle robin, like a pard° or ounce,°   *leopard / lynx*
105 Ravening a worm—Away, ye horrid moods!
Moods of one's mind! You know I hate them well.
You know I'd sooner be a clapping bell
To some Kamschatkan[2] missionary church,
Than with these horrid moods be left i'the lurch.
110 Do you get health—and Tom the same—I'll dance,
And from detested moods in new romance[3]
Take refuge—Of bad lines a centaine[4] dose
Is sure enough—and so "here follows prose."[5]
—1848

To Homer[6]

Standing aloof in giant ignorance,
  Of thee I hear and of the Cyclades,[7]
As one who sits ashore and longs perchance

---

[1] *Lapland witch* Lapland was supposed to be the dwelling-place of witches.

[2] *Kamschatkan* From the Kamchatka Peninsula in Siberia.

[3] *new romance* Probably Keats's *Isabella* (1820), a romance based on a tale from Italian poet Giovanni Boccaccio's *Decameron* (written 1348–53).

[4] *centaine* Company of one hundred.

[5] *here follows prose* See Shakespeare's *Twelfth Night* 2.5.154.

[6] *Homer* Early Greek poet, believed to be the author of *The Iliad* and *Odyssey*.

[7] *Cyclades* Group of islands in the Aegean Sea, off the southeast coast of Greece.

To visit dolphin-coral in deep seas.
5   So thou wast blind!¹—but then the veil was rent;
For Jove² uncurtain'd Heaven to let thee live,
And Neptune³ made for thee a spumy⁴ tent,
And Pan⁵ made sing for thee his forest-hive;
Aye, on the shores of darkness there is light,
10   And precipices show untrodden green;
There is a budding morrow in midnight;
There is a triple sight in blindness keen;
Such seeing hast thou, as it once befell
To Dian, Queen of Earth, and Heaven, and Hell.⁶
—1848 (WRITTEN C.1818)

The Eve of St. Agnes⁷

1

St. Agnes' Eve—Ah, bitter chill it was!
  The owl, for all his feathers, was a-cold;
The hare limp'd trembling through the frozen grass,
And silent was the flock in woolly fold:
5   Numb were the Beadsman's⁸ fingers, while he told
His rosary, and while his frosted breath,
Like pious incense from a censer⁹ old,
Seem'd taking flight for heaven, without a death,

---

1   *thou wast blind* Homer was said to have been blind.

2   *Jove* Roman King of the gods.

3   *Neptune* Roman god of the sea.

4   *spumy* Covered in sea foam.

5   *Pan* Greek shepherd god of nature who was half goat and half man. After the nymph Syrinx turned herself into a bed of reeds in order to escape him, Pan created an instrument (the panpipe) out of the reeds.

6   *To Dian … Hell* Diana was sometimes envisioned as a three-figured goddess, presiding over the moon, childbirth, and the hunt, and hell.

7   *St. Agnes* Fourth-century Christian martyr, executed at the age of thirteen, who is the patron saint of virgins. It was tradition that young women could obtain a vision of their future husbands if they performed the proper rituals on 20 January, the night before St. Agnes's Feast Day.

8   *Beadsman* Pensioner paid to say prayers for the souls of his benefactors. He "tells," or counts, the beads of his rosary, saying a prayer at each bead.

9   *censer* Incense burner.

Past the sweet Virgin's¹⁰ picture, while his prayer he
  saith.

2

His prayer he saith, this patient, holy man;
10   Then takes his lamp, and riseth from his knees,
And back returneth, meagre, barefoot, wan,
Along the chapel aisle by slow degrees:
The sculptur'd dead, on each side, seem to freeze,
Emprison'd in black, purgatorial rails:
15   Knights, ladies, praying in dumb orat'ries,°   *chapels*
He passeth by; and his weak spirit fails
To think how they may ache in icy hoods and mails.

3

Northward he turneth through a little door,
20   And scarce three steps, ere Music's golden tongue
Flatter'd to tears this aged man and poor;
But no—already had his deathbell rung:
The joys of all his life were said and sung:
His was harsh penance on St. Agnes' Eve:
25   Another way he went, and soon among
Rough ashes sat he for his soul's reprieve,
And all night kept awake, for sinners' sake to grieve.

4

That ancient Beadsman heard the prelude soft;
And so it chanc'd, for many a door was wide,
30   From hurry to and fro. Soon, up aloft,
The silver, snarling trumpets 'gan to chide:
The level chambers, ready with their pride,
Were glowing to receive a thousand guests:
The carved angels, ever eager-eyed,
35   Star'd, where upon their heads the cornice rests,
With hair blown back, and wings put cross-wise on
  their breasts.

5

At length burst in the argent¹¹ revelry,
With plume, tiara, and all rich array,
Numerous as shadows haunting fairily
40   The brain, new stuff'd, in youth, with triumphs gay
Of old romance. These let us wish away,

---

10   *Virgin* I.e., Mary, virgin mother of Christ.

11   *argent* Adorned with silver.

And turn, sole-thoughted, to one Lady there,
Whose heart had brooded, all that wintry day,
On love, and wing'd St. Agnes' saintly care,
45 As she had heard old dames full many times declare.

6

They told her how, upon St. Agnes' Eve,
Young virgins might have visions of delight,
And soft adorings from their loves receive
Upon the honey'd middle of the night,
50 If ceremonies due they did aright;°   *arranged properly*
As, supperless to bed they must retire,
And couch supine their beauties, lily white;
Nor look behind, nor sideways, but require
Of Heaven with upward eyes for all that they desire.

7

55 Full of this whim was thoughtful Madeline:
The music, yearning like a God in pain,
She scarcely heard: her maiden eyes divine,
Fix'd on the floor, saw many a sweeping train
Pass by—she heeded not at all: in vain
60 Came many a tiptoe, amorous cavalier,
And back retir'd; not cool'd by high disdain,
But she saw not: her heart was otherwhere:
She sigh'd for Agnes' dreams, the sweetest of the year.

8

She danc'd along with vague, regardless eyes,
65 Anxious her lips, her breathing quick and short:
The hallow'd hour was near at hand: she sighs
Amid the timbrels,° and the throng'd resort   *tambourines*
Of whisperers in anger, or in sport;
'Mid looks of love, defiance, hate, and scorn,
70 Hoodwink'd° with faery fancy; all   *blindfolded*
amort,°   *dead*
Save to St. Agnes and her lambs unshorn,[1]
And all the bliss to be before to-morrow morn.

9

So, purposing each moment to retire,
She linger'd still. Meantime, across the moors,
75 Had come young Porphyro, with heart on fire

For Madeline. Beside the portal doors,
Buttress'd from moonlight, stands he, and implores
All saints to give him sight of Madeline,
But for one moment in the tedious hours,
80 That he might gaze and worship all unseen;
Perchance speak, kneel, touch, kiss—in sooth such
things have been.

10

He ventures in: let no buzz'd whisper tell:
All eyes be muffled, or a hundred swords
Will storm his heart, Love's fev'rous citadel:
85 For him, those chambers held barbarian hordes,
Hyena foemen, and hot-blooded lords,
Whose very dogs would execrations howl
Against his lineage: not one breast affords
Him any mercy, in that mansion foul,
90 Save one old beldame,[2] weak in body and in soul.

11

Ah, happy chance! the aged creature came,
Shuffling along with ivory-headed wand,°   *staff*
To where he stood, hid from the torch's flame,
Behind a broad hall-pillar, far beyond
95 The sound of merriment and chorus bland:°   *soft*
He startled her; but soon she knew his face,
And grasp'd his fingers in her palsied hand,
Saying, "Mercy, Porphyro! hie thee from this place;
They are all here to-night, the whole blood-thirsty race!"

12

100 "Get hence! get hence! there's dwarfish Hildebrand;
He had a fever late, and in the fit
He cursed thee and thine, both house and land:
Then there's that old Lord Maurice, not a whit
More tame for his gray hairs—Alas me! flit!
105 Flit like a ghost away."—"Ah, Gossip[3] dear,
We're safe enough; here in this arm-chair sit,
And tell me how"—"Good Saints! not here, not here;
Follow me, child, or else these stones will be thy bier."

13

He follow'd through a lowly arched way,
110 Brushing the cobwebs with his lofty plume,

---

1 *St. Agnes … unshorn* The Latin for lamb is *agnus*; thus the traditional association of St. Agnes with lambs, which also carry connotations of whiteness and purity.

2 *beldame* Grandmother, old woman, or elderly nurse.

3 *Gossip* Good friend; godmother.

And as she mutter'd "Well-a—well-a-day!"
He found him in a little moonlight room,
Pale, lattic'd, chill, and silent as a tomb.
"Now tell me where is Madeline," said he,
115   "O tell me, Angela, by the holy loom
Which none but secret sisterhood may see,
When they St. Agnes' wool are weaving piously."

14

"St. Agnes! Ah! it is St. Agnes' Eve—
Yet men will murder upon holy days:
120   Thou must hold water in a witch's sieve,
And be liege-lord of all the Elves and Fays,°   *fairies*
To venture so: it fills me with amaze
To see thee, Porphyro!—St. Agnes' Eve!
God's help! my lady fair the conjuror plays
125   This very night: good angels her deceive!
But let me laugh awhile, I've mickle° time to grieve.   *much*

15

Feebly she laugheth in the languid moon,
While Porphyro upon her face doth look,
Like puzzled urchin on an aged crone
130   Who keepeth clos'd a wond'rous riddle-book,
As spectacled she sits in chimney nook.
But soon his eyes grew brilliant, when she told
His lady's purpose; and he scarce could brook°   *prevent*
Tears, at the thought of those enchantments cold
135   And Madeline asleep in lap of legends old.

16

Sudden a thought came like a full-blown rose,
Flushing his brow, and in his pained heart
Made purple riot: then doth he propose
A stratagem, that makes the beldame start:
140   "A cruel man and impious thou art:
Sweet lady, let her pray, and sleep, and dream
Alone with her good angels, far apart
From wicked men like thee. Go, go!—I deem
Thou canst not surely be the same that thou didst seem."

17

145   "I will not harm her, by all saints I swear,"
Quoth Porphyro: "O may I ne'er find grace
When my weak voice shall whisper its last prayer,
If one of her soft ringlets I displace,

Or look with ruffian passion in her face:
150   Good Angela, believe me by these tears;
Or I will, even in a moment's space,
Awake, with horrid shout, my foemen's ears,
And beard° them, though they be more fang'd than   *oppose*
    wolves and bears."

18

"Ah! why wilt thou affright a feeble soul?
155   A poor, weak, palsy-stricken, churchyard thing,
Whose passing-bell may ere the midnight toll;
Whose prayers for thee, each morn and evening,
Were never miss'd."—Thus plaining,°   *complaining*
    doth she bring
A gentler speech from burning Porphyro;
160   So woeful, and of such deep sorrowing,
That Angela gives promise she will do
Whatever he shall wish, betide her weal or woe.

19

Which was, to lead him, in close secrecy,
Even to Madeline's chamber, and there hide
165   Him in a closet, of such privacy
That he might see her beauty unespied,
And win perhaps that night a peerless bride,
While legion'd fairies pac'd the coverlet,
And pale enchantment held her sleepy-eyed.
170   Never on such a night have lovers met,
Since Merlin paid his Demon all the monstrous debt.[1]

20

"It shall be as thou wishest," said the Dame:
"All cates° and dainties shall be stored there   *delicacies*
Quickly on this feast-night: by the tambour frame[2]
175   Her own lute thou wilt see: no time to spare,
For I am slow and feeble, and scarce dare
On such a catering trust my dizzy head.
Wait here, my child, with patience; kneel in prayer
The while: Ah! thou must needs the lady wed,
180   Or may I never leave my grave among the dead."

---

1   *Since ... debt* Probably a reference to the episode in Arthurian
legend in which the enchanter Merlin falls in love with the enchantress Vivien, or Nimue, who turns one of his spells against him and
imprisons him in a cave.

2   *tambour frame* Circular frame for embroidery.

21

So saying, she hobbled off with busy fear.
The lover's endless minutes slowly pass'd:
The dame return'd, and whisper'd in his ear
To follow her; with aged eyes aghast
185 From fright of dim espial. Safe at last,
Through many a dusky gallery, they gain
The maiden's chamber, silken, hush'd, and chaste;
Where Porphyro took covert, pleas'd amain.°   *completely*
His poor guide hurried back with agues°   *fever*
    in her brain.

22

190 Her falt'ring hand upon the balustrade,
Old Angela was feeling for the stair,
When Madeline, St. Agnes' charmed maid,
Rose, like a mission'd spirit, unaware:
With silver taper's light, and pious care,
195 She turn'd, and down the aged gossip led
To a safe level matting. Now prepare,
Young Porphyro, for gazing on that bed;
She comes, she comes again, like ring-dove
    fray'd° and fled.   *frightened*

23

Out went the taper° as she hurried in;   *candle*
200 Its little smoke, in pallid moonshine, died:
She clos'd the door, she panted, all akin
To spirits of the air, and visions wide:
No uttered syllable, or, woe betide!
But to her heart, her heart was voluble,
205 Paining with eloquence her balmy side;
As though a tongueless nightingale should swell
Her throat in vain, and die, heart-stifled, in her dell.

24

A casement high and triple-arch'd there was,
All garlanded with carven imag'ries
210 Of fruits, and flowers, and bunches of knot-grass,
And diamonded with panes of quaint device,
Innumerable of stains and splendid dyes,
As are the tiger-moth's deep-damask'd wings;
And in the midst, 'mong thousand heraldries,[1]
215 And twilight saints, and dim emblazonings,

A shielded scutcheon blush'd with blood of queens
    and kings.[2]

25

Full on this casement shone the wintry moon,
And threw warm gules[3] on Madeline's fair breast,
As down she knelt for heaven's grace and boon;°   *blessing*
220 Rose-bloom fell on her hands, together prest,
And on her silver cross soft amethyst,
And on her hair a glory, like a saint:
She seem'd a splendid angel, newly drest,
Save wings, for heaven—Porphyro grew faint:
225 She knelt, so pure a thing, so free from mortal taint.

26

Anon his heart revives: her vespers° done,   *evening prayers*
Of all its wreathed pearls her hair she frees;
Unclasps her warmed jewels one by one;
Loosens her fragrant boddice; by degrees
230 Her rich attire creeps rustling to her knees:
Half-hidden, like a mermaid in sea-weed,
Pensive awhile she dreams awake, and sees,
In fancy, fair St. Agnes in her bed,
But dares not look behind, or all the charm is fled.

27

235 Soon, trembling in her soft and chilly nest,
In sort of wakeful swoon, perplex'd[4] she lay,
Until the poppied° warmth of sleep oppress'd   *narcotic*
Her soothed limbs, and soul fatigued away;
Flown, like a thought, until the morrow-day;
240 Blissfully haven'd both from joy and pain;
Clasp'd like a missal[5] where swart Paynims[6] pray;
Blinded alike from sunshine and from rain,
As though a rose should shut, and be a bud again.

28

Stol'n to this paradise, and so entranced,
245 Porphyro gazed upon her empty dress,
And listen'd to her breathing, if it chanced

[1] *heraldries* Emblems of rank and genealogy.

[2] *scutcheon* I.e., escutcheon: shield; *blushed ... kings* I.e., indicates she is of royal blood.

[3] *gules* Red bars (a heraldic device).

[4] *perplexed* I.e., between sleep and waking.

[5] *missal* Christian mass- or prayer-book.

[6] *swart Paynims* Dark-skinned pagans.

To wake into a slumberous tenderness;
Which when he heard, that minute did he bless,
And breath'd himself: then from the closet crept,
250　Noiseless as fear in a wide wilderness,
And over the hush'd carpet, silent, stept,
And 'tween the curtains peep'd, where, lo!—how fast
　　she slept.

29

Then by the bed-side, where the faded moon
Made a dim, silver twilight, soft he set
255　A table, and, half anguish'd, threw thereon
A cloth of woven crimson, gold, and jet—
O for some drowsy Morphean amulet!¹
The boisterous, midnight, festive clarion,°　　　trumpet
The kettle-drum, and far-heard clarinet,
260　Affray his ears, though but in dying tone—
The hall door shuts again, and all the noise is gone.

30

And still she slept an azure-lidded sleep,
In blanched linen, smooth, and lavender'd,
While he from forth the closet brought a heap
265　Of candied apple, quince, and plum, and gourd;°　melon
With jellies soother² than the creamy curd,
And lucent° syrops, tinct° with cinnamon;　clear / imbued
Manna³ and dates, in argosy⁴ transferr'd
From Fez;⁵ and spiced dainties, every one,
270　From silken Samarkand⁶ to cedar'd Lebanon.

31

These delicates he heap'd with glowing hand
On golden dishes and in baskets bright
Of wreathed silver: sumptuous they stand
In the retired quiet of the night,
275　Filling the chilly room with perfume light.
"And now, my love, my seraph° fair, awake!　angel

Thou art my heaven, and I thine eremite:°　hermit
Open thine eyes, for meek St. Agnes' sake,
Or I shall drowse beside thee, so my soul doth ache."

32

280　Thus whispering, his warm, unnerved arm
Sank in her pillow. Shaded was her dream
By the dusk curtains—'twas a midnight charm
Impossible to melt as iced stream:
The lustrous salvers° in the moonlight gleam;　trays
285　Broad golden fringe upon the carpet lies:
It seem'd he never, never could redeem
From such a stedfast spell his lady's eyes;
So mus'd awhile, entoil'd in woofed° phantasies.　woven

33

Awakening up, he took her hollow lute—
290　Tumultuous—and, in chords that tenderest be,
He play'd an ancient ditty, long since mute,
In Provence call'd, "La belle dame sans mercy":⁷
Close to her ear touching the melody—
Wherewith disturb'd, she utter'd a soft moan:
295　He ceased—she panted quick—and suddenly
Her blue affrayed eyes wide open shone:
Upon his knees he sank, pale as smooth-sculptured
　　stone.

34

Her eyes were open, but she still beheld,
Now wide awake, the vision of her sleep:
300　There was a painful change, that nigh expell'd
The blisses of her dream so pure and deep,
At which fair Madeline began to weep,
And moan forth witless words with many a sigh;
While still her gaze on Porphyro would keep;
305　Who knelt, with joined hands and piteous eye,
Fearing to move or speak, she look'd so dreamingly.

35

"Ah, Porphyro!" said she, "but even now
Thy voice was at sweet tremble in mine ear,
Made tuneable with every sweetest vow;
310　And those sad eyes were spiritual and clear:

---

¹ *Morphean amulet* Sleep-inducing medicine or charm. (Morpheus is the god of dreams.)

² *soother* A word of Keats's own invention, meaning more soothing, softer.

³ *Manna* Dried, sweet gum taken from various plants.

⁴ *argosy* Merchant vessels.

⁵ *Fez* City in Morocco.

⁶ *Samarkand* City in Uzbekistan.

⁷ *La belle … mercy* French: "The beautiful woman without pity." Title of a long poem by medieval poet Alain Chartier (c. 1385–1433); Keats had not yet written his own poem with this title.

How chang'd thou art! how pallid, chill, and drear!
Give me that voice again, my Porphyro,
Those looks immortal, those complainings° *lamentings*
   dear!
Oh leave me not in this eternal woe,
315   For if thou diest, my Love, I know not where to go."

36

Beyond a mortal man impassion'd far
At these voluptuous accents, he arose,
Ethereal, flush'd, and like a throbbing star
Seen mid the sapphire heaven's deep repose;
320   Into her dream he melted, as the rose
Blendeth its odour with the violet—
Solution sweet: meantime the frost-wind blows
Like Love's alarum° pattering the sharp sleet   *warning bell*
Against the window-panes; St. Agnes' moon hath set.

37

325   'Tis dark: quick pattereth the flaw-blown° sleet: *gust-driven*
"This is no dream, my bride, my Madeline!"
'Tis dark: the iced gusts still rave and beat:
"No dream, alas! alas! and woe is mine!
Porphyro will leave me here to fade and pine.
330   Cruel! what traitor could thee hither bring?
I curse not, for my heart is lost in thine,
Though thou forsakest a deceived thing—
A dove forlorn and lost with sick unpruned wing."

38

"My Madeline! sweet dreamer! lovely bride!
335   Say, may I be for aye° thy vassal blest?   *ever*
Thy beauty's shield, heart-shap'd and
   vermeil° dyed?   *vermilion (red)*
Ah, silver shrine, here will I take my rest
After so many hours of toil and quest,
A famish'd pilgrim, saved by miracle.
340   Though I have found, I will not rob thy nest
Saving of thy sweet self; if thou think'st well
To trust, fair Madeline, to no rude infidel.

39

"Hark! 'tis an elfin-storm from faery land,
Of haggard° seeming, but a boon indeed: *wild*
345   Arise—arise! the morning is at hand;
The bloated wassaillers° will never heed—   *drinkers*
Let us away, my love, with happy speed;

There are no ears to hear, or eyes to see—
Drown'd all in Rhenish and the sleepy mead:[1]
350   Awake! arise! my love, and fearless be,
For o'er the southern moors I have a home for thee."

40

She hurried at his words, beset with fears,
For there were sleeping dragons all around,
At glaring watch, perhaps, with ready spears—
355   Down the wide stairs a darkling[2] way they found.
In all the house was heard no human sound.
A chain-droop'd lamp was flickering by each door;
The arras,° rich with horseman, hawk, and   *tapestries*
   hound,
Flutter'd in the besieging wind's uproar;
360   And the long carpets rose along the gusty floor.

41

They glide, like phantoms, into the wide hall;
Like phantoms, to the iron porch, they glide;
Where lay the Porter, in uneasy sprawl,
With a huge empty flaggon by his side:
365   The wakeful bloodhound rose, and shook his hide,
But his sagacious eye an inmate owns:
By one, and one, the bolts full easy slide—
The chains lie silent on the footworn stones—
The key turns, and the door upon its hinges groans.

42

370   And they are gone: ay, ages long ago
These lovers fled away into the storm.
That night the Baron dreamt of many a woe,
And all his warrior-guests, with shade and form
Of witch, and demon, and large coffin-worm,
375   Were long be-nightmar'd. Angela the old
Died palsy-twitch'd, with meagre face deform;
The Beadsman, after thousand aves[3] told,
For aye unsought for slept among his ashes cold.
—1820

---

[1] *Rhenish* Wine from the Rhine region; *mead* Alcoholic beverage made from fermented honey and water.

[2] *darkling* Obscure, gloomy.

[3] *aves* Latin: abbreviation for *Ave Marias*, or Hail Marys, prayers to the Virgin Mary.

Bright Star

Bright star, would I were steadfast as thou art—
   Not in lone splendour hung aloft the night
And watching, with eternal lids apart,
   Like nature's patient, sleepless Eremite,°   hermit
5 The moving waters at their priestlike task
   Of pure ablution[1] round earth's human shores,
Or gazing on the new soft fallen mask
   Of snow upon the mountains and the moors—
No—yet still steadfast, still unchangeable,
10   Pillow'd upon my fair love's ripening breast,
To feel for ever its soft fall and swell,
   Awake for ever in a sweet unrest,
Still, still to hear her tender-taken breath,
And so live ever—or else swoon to death.
   —1838 (WRITTEN 1819)

La Belle Dame sans Merci[2]

O what can ail thee, knight-at-arms,
   Alone and palely loitering?
The sedge[3] has wither'd from the lake,
   And no birds sing.

5 O what can ail thee, knight-at-arms,
   So haggard, and so woe-begone?
The squirrel's granary is full,
   And the harvest's done.

I see a lily[4] on thy brow,
10   With anguish moist and fever dew
And on thy cheeks a fading rose
   Fast withereth too.

I met a lady in the meads,°   meadows
   Full beautiful—a faery's child,

15 Her hair was long, her foot was light,
   And her eyes were wild.

I made a garland for her head,
   And bracelets too, and fragrant zone;°   belt
She look'd at me as she did love,
20   And made sweet moan.

I set her on my pacing steed,
   And nothing else saw all day long,
For sidelong would she bend and sing
   A faery's song.

25 She found me roots of relish sweet,
   And honey wild, and manna dew,[5]
And sure in language strange she said
   "I love thee true."

She took me to her elfin grot,°   grotto
30   And there she wept and sigh'd full sore,
And there I shut her wild wild eyes
   With kisses four.

And there she lulled me asleep,
   And there I dream'd—Ah! woe betide!
35 The latest° dream I ever dream'd   last
   On the cold hill side.

I saw pale kings and princes too,
   Pale warriors, death-pale were they all;
They cried, "La belle dame sans merci
40   Hath thee in thrall!"°   captivity

I saw their starved lips in the gloam,°   twilight
   With horrid warning gaped wide,
And I awoke, and found me here,
   On the cold hill's side.

45 And this is why I sojourn here,
   Alone and palely loitering,
Though the sedge is wither'd from the lake,
   And no birds sing.
   —1848 (WRITTEN 1819)

---

[1] *ablution* Religious ritual washing of the body.

[2] *La Belle Dame sans Merci* French: the beautiful lady without pity. This original version of the poem, found in a journal letter to George and Georgiana Keats, was first published in 1848. Keats's revised version was published in 1820.

[3] *sedge* Rush-like grass.

[4] *lily* Flower traditionally symbolic of death.

[5] *manna dew* See Exodus 16, in which God provides the Israelites with a food that falls from heaven, called manna.

La Belle Dame sans Mercy[1]

Ah, what can ail thee, wretched wight,°   *being*
    Alone and palely loitering;
The sedge[2] is wither'd from the lake,
    And no birds sing.

5 Ah, what can ail thee, wretched wight,
    So haggard and so woe-begone?
The squirrel's granary is full,
    And the harvest's done.

I see a lily[3] on thy brow,
10   With anguish moist and fever dew;
And on thy cheek a fading rose
    Fast withereth too.

I met a lady in the meads°   *meadows*
    Full beautiful, a fairy's child;
15 Her hair was long, her foot was light,
    And her eyes were wild.

I set her on my pacing steed,
    And nothing else saw all day long;
For sideways would she lean, and sing
20   A fairy's song.

I made a garland for her head,
    And bracelets too, and fragrant zone:°   *belt*
She look'd at me as she did love,
    And made sweet moan.

25 She found me roots of relish sweet,
    And honey wild, and manna[4] dew;
And sure in language strange she said,
    "I love thee true."

She took me to her elfin grot,°   *grotto*
30   And there she gaz'd and sighed deep.

And there I shut her wild sad eyes—
    So kiss'd to sleep.

And there we slumber'd on the moss,
    And there I dream'd, ah woe betide,
35 The latest dream I ever dream'd
    On the cold hill side.

I saw pale kings, and princes too,
    Pale warriors, death-pale were they all;
Who cry'd—"La belle dame sans mercy
40   Hath thee in thrall!"°   *captivity*

I saw their starv'd lips in the gloom
    With horrid warning gaped wide,
And I awoke, and found me here
    On the cold hill side.

45 And this is why I sojourn here
    Alone and palely loitering,
Though the sedge is wither'd from the lake,
    And no birds sing.
    —1820 (written 1819)

Incipit altera Sonneta[5]

I have been endeavouring to discover a better sonnet stanza than we have. The legitimate[6] does not suit the language over-well from the pouncing rhymes—the other kind appears too elegaiac—and the couplet at the end of it has seldom a pleasing effect—I do not pretend to have succeeded—it will explain itself—

If by dull rhymes our English must be chain'd
    And, like Andromeda,[7] the Sonnet sweet
Fetter'd in spite of pained loveliness;
Let us find out, if we must be constrain'd
5 Sandals more interwoven & complete

---

1 *La Belle … Mercy* French: the beautiful lady without pity. Keats's revised version was published in 1820.

2 *sedge* Rush-like grass.

3 *lily* Flower traditionally symbolic of death.

4 *manna* See Exodus 16, in which God provides the Israelites with a food that falls from heaven, called manna.

5 *Incipit Altera Sonneta* Latin: another sonnet begins.

6 *The legitimate* I.e., the Petrarchan sonnet. The "other kind" to which Keats refers is the Shakespearean sonnet.

7 *Andromeda* In Greek myth, Andromeda is tied to a rock to be devoured by a sea serpent after her mother boasts that she is more beautiful than the sea nymphs. Perseus, on his winged horse Pegasus (a symbol of poetic inspiration), rescues her.

To fit the naked foot of Poesy;
Let us inspect the Lyre,[1] & weigh the stress
Of every chord & see what may be gain'd
By ear industrious & attention meet;°   *fitting*
10   Misers of sound & syllable, no less
Than Midas of his coinage,[2] let us be
Jealous of dead leaves in the bay wreath Crown;[3]
So if we may not let the Muse[4] be free,
She will be bound with Garlands of her own.
—1836 (WRITTEN 1819)

Ode to Psyche [5]

O Goddess! hear these tuneless numbers, wrung
By sweet enforcement and remembrance dear,
And pardon that thy secrets should be sung
Even into thine own soft-conched[6] ear:
5   Surely I dreamt to-day, or did I see
The winged Psyche with awaken'd eyes?
I wander'd in a forest thoughtlessly,
And, on the sudden, fainting with surprise,
Saw two fair creatures, couched side by side
10   In deepest grass, beneath the whisp'ring roof
Of leaves and trembled blossoms, where there ran
A brooklet, scarce espied:

'Mid hush'd, cool-rooted flowers, fragrant-eyed,
Blue, silver-white, and budded Tyrian,[7]

15   They lay calm-breathing on the bedded grass;
Their arms embraced, and their pinions° too;   *wings*
Their lips touch'd not, but had not bade adieu,
As if disjoined by soft-handed slumber,
And ready still past kisses to outnumber
20   At tender eye-dawn of aurorean[8] love:
The winged boy° I knew;   *Cupid*
But who wast thou, O happy, happy dove?
His Psyche true!

O latest born and liveliest vision far
25   Of all Olympus'[9] faded hierarchy!
Fairer than Phoebe's[10] sapphire-region'd star,
Or Vesper,[11] amorous glow-worm of the sky;
Fairer than these, though temple thou hast none,
Nor altar heap'd with flowers;
30   Nor virgin-choir to make delicious moan
Upon the midnight hours;
No voice, no lute, no pipe, no incense sweet
From chain-swung censer° teeming;   *incense burner*
No shrine, no grove, no oracle, no heat
35   Of pale-mouth'd prophet dreaming.

O brightest! Though too late for antique vows,
Too, too late for the fond believing
lyre,°   *stringed instrument*
When holy were the haunted forest boughs,
Holy the air, the water, and the fire;
40   Yet even in these days so far retir'd
From happy pieties, thy lucent fans,°   *wings*
Fluttering among the faint Olympians,
I see, and sing, by my own eyes inspired.
So let me be thy choir, and make a moan
45   Upon the midnight hours;
Thy voice, thy lute, thy pipe, thy incense sweet
From swinged censer teeming;
Thy shrine, thy grove, thy oracle, thy heat
Of pale-mouth'd prophet dreaming.

50   Yes, I will be thy priest, and build a fane°   *temple*
In some untrodden region of my mind,

---

[1]   *Lyre* Stringed instrument.

[2]   *Midas … coinage* In Ovid's *Metamorphoses*, King Midas of Phrygia gets his wish that everything he touches will turn to gold.

[3]   *bay wreath Crown* Wreaths made of leaves of the bay laurel were traditionally bestowed upon those who distinguished themselves in poetry.

[4]   *Muse* One of nine daughters of Zeus and Mnemosyne, each of whom presided over and provided inspiration for an aspect of learning or the arts.

[5]   *Psyche* In classical mythology, a young woman who was beloved by Cupid, winged god of love and son of Venus. After winning over Venus, who was jealous of Psyche's beauty, Psyche was granted immortality by Jupiter. In Greek myth she is often a personification of the soul: her name in Greek means soul or mind as well as butterfly.

[6]   *soft-conched* Shaped like a conch shell, but soft.

[7]   *Tyrian* Purple. From the Phoenician city of Tyre, where purple or crimson dyes were made in ancient times.

[8]   *aurorean* I.e., dawning. Aurora was the goddess of the dawn.

[9]   *Olympus* Mount Olympus, home of the gods.

[10]   *Phoebe* Diana, goddess of the moon.

[11]   *Vesper* Venus, the evening star.

Where branched thoughts, new grown with pleasant
    pain,
    Instead of pines shall murmur in the wind:
Far, far around shall those dark-cluster'd trees
55   Fledge the wild-ridged mountains steep by steep;
And there by zephyrs,° streams, and birds,   *breezes*
    and bees,
    The moss-lain Dryads° shall be lull'd   *wood nymphs*
    to sleep;
And in the midst of quietness
A rosy sanctuary will I dress
60 With the wreath'd trellis of a working brain,
    With buds, and bells, and stars without a name,
With all the gardener Fancy e'er could feign,
    Who breeding flowers, will never breed the same:
And there shall be for thee all soft delight
65   That shadowy thought can win,
A bright torch, and a casement ope°   *window opened*
    at night,
To let the warm Love in!
—1820

Ode to a Nightingale [1]

1

My heart aches, and a drowsy numbness pains
    My sense, as though of hemlock° I had   *poison*
    drunk,
Or emptied some dull opiate to the drains
    One minute past, and Lethe-wards[2] had sunk:
5 'Tis not through envy of thy happy lot,
    But being too happy in thine happiness—

---

[1] *Ode to a Nightingale* Written about 1 May 1819. Twenty years later, Keats's friend and housemate Charles Armitage Brown remembered the composition of the poem: "In the spring of 1819 a nightingale had built her nest near my house. Keats felt a tranquil and continual joy in her song; and one morning he took his chair from the breakfast-table to the grass-plot under a plum-tree, where he sat for two or three hours. When he came into the house, I perceived he had some scraps of paper in his hand, and these he was quietly thrusting behind the books. On enquiry, I found those scraps, four or five in number, contained his poetic feeling on the song of our nightingale."

[2] *Lethe-wards* Towards Lethe, the river of forgetfulness which, in classical mythology, the dead must cross to reach Hades, the underworld.

    That thou, light-winged Dryad°   *wood-nymph*
    of the trees,
    In some melodious plot
Of beechen green, and shadows numberless,
10   Singest of summer in full-throated ease.

2

O, for a draught of vintage! that hath been
    Cool'd a long age in the deep-delved earth,
Tasting of Flora[3] and the country green,
    Dance, and Provençal song,[4] and sunburnt mirth!
15 O for a beaker full of the warm South,
    Full of the true, the blushful Hippocrene,[5]
    With beaded bubbles winking at the brim,
    And purple-stained mouth;
    That I might drink, and leave the world unseen,
20   And with thee fade away into the forest dim:

3

Fade far away, dissolve, and quite forget
    What thou among the leaves hast never known,
The weariness, the fever, and the fret
    Here, where men sit and hear each other groan;
25 Where palsy shakes a few, sad, last gray hairs,
    Where youth grows pale, and spectre-thin, and dies;
    Where but to think is to be full of sorrow
    And leaden-eyed despairs,
    Where Beauty cannot keep her lustrous eyes,
30   Or new Love pine at them beyond to-morrow.

4

Away! away! for I will fly to thee,
    Not charioted by Bacchus and his pards,[6]
But on the viewless wings of Poesy,
    Though the dull brain perplexes and retards:
35 Already with thee! tender is the night,
    And haply° the Queen-Moon is on her th
    Cluster'd around by all her starry ̶

---

[3] *Flora* Roman goddess of flowers.

[4] *Provençal song* The region of Pr
known in the Middle Ages for ir

[5] *Hippocrene* Fountain of
presided over aspects of lea.
Mount Helicon. Its waters we

[6] *Bacchus … pards* Bacchus, the g.
by pards, or leopards.

But here there is no light,
  Save what from heaven is with the breezes blown
40   Through verdurous glooms and winding mossy ways.

5

I cannot see what flowers are at my feet,
  Nor what soft incense hangs upon the boughs,
But, in embalmed° darkness, guess each sweet   *fragrant*
  Wherewith the seasonable month endows
45 The grass, the thicket, and the fruit-tree wild;
  White hawthorn, and the pastoral eglantine;
    Fast fading violets cover'd up in leaves;
      And mid-May's eldest child,
  The coming musk-rose, full of dewy wine,
50   The murmurous haunt of flies on summer eves.

6

Darkling[1] I listen; and, for many a time
  I have been half in love with easeful Death,
Call'd him soft names in many a mused rhyme,
  To take into the air my quiet breath;
55 Now more than ever seems it rich to die,
  To cease upon the midnight with no pain,
    While thou art pouring forth thy soul abroad
      In such an ecstasy!
  Still wouldst thou sing, and I have ears in vain—
60   To thy high requiem[2] become a sod.

7

Thou wast not born for death, immortal Bird!
  No hungry generations tread thee down;
The voice I hear this passing night was heard
  In ancient days by emperor and clown:°   *rustic*
Perhaps the self-same song that found a path
  Through the sad heart of Ruth, when, sick for home,
    She stood in tears amid the alien corn;[3]
      The same that oft-times hath
  Charm'd magic casements, opening on the foam
    Of perilous seas, in faery lands forlorn.

8

Forlorn! the very word is like a bell
  To toll me back from thee to my sole self!
Adieu! the fancy cannot cheat so well
  As she is fam'd to do, deceiving elf.
75 Adieu! adieu! thy plaintive anthem fades
  Past the near meadows, over the still stream,
    Up the hill-side; and now 'tis buried deep
      In the next valley-glades:
  Was it a vision, or a waking dream?
80   Fled is that music—Do I wake or sleep?
—1819

Ode on a Grecian Urn

1

Thou still unravish'd bride of quietness,
  Thou foster-child of silence and slow time,
Sylvan° historian, who canst thus express   *woodland*
  A flowery tale more sweetly than our rhyme:
5 What leaf-fring'd legend haunts about thy shape
  Of deities or mortals, or of both,
    In Tempe or the dales of Arcady?[4]
  What men or gods are these? What maidens loth?
What mad pursuit? What struggle to escape?
10   What pipes and timbrels?° What   *tambourines*
      wild ecstasy?

2

Heard melodies are sweet, but those unheard
  Are sweeter; therefore, ye soft pipes, play on;
Not to the sensual° ear, but, more endear'd,   *physical*
  Pipe to the spirit ditties of no tone:
15 Fair youth, beneath the trees, thou canst not leave
  Thy song, nor ever can those trees be bare;
    Bold Lover, never, never canst thou kiss,
Though winning near the goal—yet, do not grieve;
  She cannot fade, though thou hast not thy bliss,
20   For ever wilt thou love, and she be fair!

In the dark.

Mass sung for the dead.

Widow in the Book of Ruth (1-4) who leaves Moab
her mother-in-law Naomi because of famine.

---

[4] *Tempe* Valley in ancient Greece renowned for its beauty; *Arcady*
Ideal region of rural life, named for a mountainous district in
Greece.

3

Ah, happy, happy boughs! that cannot shed
　　Your leaves, nor ever bid the Spring adieu;
And, happy melodist, unwearied,
　　For ever piping songs for ever new;
25　More happy love! more happy, happy love!
　　For ever warm and still to be enjoy'd,
　　　　For ever panting, and for ever young;
All breathing human passion far above,
　　That leaves a heart high-sorrowful and cloy'd,
30　　　　A burning forehead, and a parching tongue.

4

Who are these coming to the sacrifice?
　　To what green altar, O mysterious priest,
Lead'st thou that heifer lowing at the skies,
　　And all her silken flanks with garlands drest?
35　What little town by river or sea shore,
　　Or mountain-built with peaceful citadel,
　　　　Is emptied of this folk, this pious morn?
And, little town, thy streets for evermore
　　Will silent be; and not a soul to tell
40　　　　Why thou art desolate, can e'er return.

5

O Attic[1] shape! Fair attitude! with brede°　　*interwoven design*
　　Of marble men and maidens overwrought,°　　*overlaid*
With forest branches and the trodden weed;
　　Thou, silent form, dost tease us out of thought
45　As doth eternity: Cold Pastoral!
　　When old age shall this generation waste,
　　　　Thou shalt remain, in midst of other woe
Than ours, a friend to man, to whom thou say'st,
　　"Beauty is truth, truth beauty,"—that is all
50　　　　Ye know on earth, and all ye need to know.[2]
—1820

---

[1] *Attic*　I.e., Greek. Attica was an ancient region of Greece that had Athens as its capital.

[2] *Beauty is … know*　The quotation marks in line 49 are present in Keats's 1820 volume of poems, but are absent in transcripts of the poem made by Keats's friends and in the version of the poem published in *Annals of the Fine Arts* in 1820. As a result, their presence has engendered much critical debate. It is unclear whether Keats meant the last line and a half to be spoken by the poet, or whether the entire final two lines are the imagined declaration of the urn.

Ode on Melancholy[3]

1

No, No, go not to Lethe,[4] neither twist
　　Wolf's-bane,[5] tight-rooted, for its poisonous
　　　　wine;
Nor suffer thy pale forehead to be kiss'd
By nightshade, ruby grape of Proserpine;[6]
5　Make not your rosary of yew-berries,[7]
　　Nor let the beetle, nor the death-moth[8] be
　　　　Your mournful Psyche,[9] nor the downy owl
A partner in your sorrow's mysteries;[10]

---

[3] *Ode on Melancholy*　In the original manuscript version, the poem opened with the following stanza:
Though you should build a bark of dead men's bones,
　　And rear a phantom gibbet for a mast,
Stitch creeds together for a sail, with groans
　　To fill it out, bloodstained and aghast;
Although your rudder be a Dragon's tail,
　　Long sever'd, yet still hard with agony,
Your cordage large uprootings from the skull
Of bald Medusa; certes you would fail
　　To find Melancholy, whether she
　　　　Dreameth in any isle of Lethe dull.
(Medusa was one of the Gorgons, three monstrous, winged sisters who had snakes for hair.)

[4] *Lethe*　River in Hades, the classical underworld, whose waters produce forgetfulness.

[5] *Wolf's-bane*　Poisonous plant native to Europe.

[6] *nightshade*　Plants with poisonous berries; *Proserpine* Daughter of Demeter who was abducted by Pluto, god of the underworld, and made queen of Hades. Her mother, goddess of the harvest, mourned for her daughter and so caused an eternal winter until Pluto was prevailed upon to allow Proserpine to return to her mother six months of every year.

[7] *yew-berries*　Poisonous berries of the yew tree, which is commonly planted in graveyards and is therefore often regarded as symbolic of death or sadness.

[8] *beetle*　The scarab, a large black beetle that Egyptians placed in their tombs as a symbol of resurrection; *death-moth* Death's-head moth, whose wings carry a mark resembling a human skull.

[9] *Psyche*　In classical mythology, a young woman who was beloved by Cupid, winged god of love and son of Venus. After winning over Venus, who was jealous of Psyche's beauty, Psyche was granted immortality by Jupiter. In Greek myth she is often a personification of the soul. Her name in Greek means butterfly as well as soul. Psyche was often represented as a butterfly flying out of a dying person's mouth.

[10] *mysteries*　I.e., secret rites or ceremonies.

10 For shade to shade will come too drowsily,
        And drown the wakeful anguish of the soul.

                          2
    But when the melancholy fit shall fall
        Sudden from heaven like a weeping cloud,
    That fosters the droop-headed flowers all,
        And hides the green hill in an April shroud;
15 Then glut thy sorrow on a morning rose,
        Or on the rainbow of the salt sand-wave,
            Or on the wealth of globed peonies;
    Or if thy mistress some rich anger shows,
        Emprison her soft hand, and let her rave,
20   And feed deep, deep upon her peerless eyes.

                          3
    She dwells with Beauty—Beauty that must die;
        And Joy, whose hand is ever at his lips
    Bidding adieu; and aching Pleasure nigh,
        Turning to poison while the bee-mouth sips:
25 Ay, in the very temple of Delight
        Veil'd Melancholy has her sovran° shrine,   *sovereign*
            Though seen of none save him whose
                strenuous tongue
    Can burst Joy's grape against his palate fine;°   *refined*
        His soul shall taste the sadness of her might,
30   And be among her cloudy trophies hung.
    —1820

Ode on Indolence [1]

"They toil not, neither do they spin."[2]

                          1
O   ne morn before me were three figures seen,
        With bowed necks, and joined hands, side-faced;
    And one behind the other stepp'd serene,
        In placid sandals, and in white robes graced;
5   They pass'd, like figures on a marble urn,

When shifted round to see the other side;
    They came again; as when the urn once more
Is shifted round, the first seen shades return;
    And they were strange to me, as may betide
10 With vases, to one deep in Phidian lore.[3]

                          2
How is it, shadows, that I knew ye not?
    How came ye muffled in so hush a masque?°   *play*
Was it a silent deep-disguised plot
    To steal away, and leave without a task
15 My idle days? Ripe was the drowsy hour;
    The blissful cloud of summer-indolence
        Benumb'd my eyes; my pulse grew less and less;
Pain had no sting, and pleasure's wreath no flower:
    O, why did ye not melt, and leave my sense
20   Unhaunted quite of all but—nothingness?

                          3
A third time pass'd they by, and, passing, turn'd
    Each one the face a moment whiles to me;
Then faded, and to follow them I burn'd
    And ached for wings because I knew the three;
25 The first was a fair Maid, and Love her name;
    The second was Ambition, pale of cheek,
        And ever watchful with fatigued eye;
The last, whom I love more, the more of blame
    Is heap'd upon her, maiden most unmeek,
30   I knew to be my demon Poesy.

                          4
They faded, and, forsooth! I wanted wings:
    O folly! What is Love! and where is it?
And for that poor Ambition! It springs
    From a man's little heart's short fever-fit;
35 For Poesy! No—she has not a joy—
    At least for me—so sweet as drowsy noons,
        And evenings steep'd in honeyed indolence;
O, for an age so shelter'd from annoy,°   *harm*
    That I may never know how change the moons,
40   Or hear the voice of busy common sense!

---

[1] *Ode on Indolence*   See the 1919 letter to George and Georgiana Keats, reprinted below, in which Keats describes the bout of indolence that is thought to have inspired this poem.

[2] *They toil ... spin*   From Matthew 6.28–89: "Consider the lilies of the field, how they grow; they toil not, neither do they spin: And yet I say unto you, That even Solomon in all his glory was not arrayed like one of these."

[3] *Phidian lore*   Lore concerning Phidias, the fifth-century Athenian sculptor of what were later named the Elgin Marbles, the marble sculptures that decorated the outside of the Parthenon and were brought to England by Lord Elgin.

A third time came they by—alas! wherefore?
  My sleep had been embroider'd with dim dreams;
My soul had been a lawn besprinkled o'er
  With flowers, and stirring shades, and baffled beams:
45 The morn was clouded, but no shower fell,
  Tho' in her lids hung the sweet tears of May;
    The open casement press'd a new-leav'd vine,
Let in the budding warmth and
    throstle's° lay;°   *thrush's / song*
  O shadows! 'twas a time to bid farewell!
50   Upon your skirts had fallen no tears of mine.

6

So, ye three ghosts, adieu! Ye cannot raise
  My head cool-bedded in the flowery grass;
For I would not be dieted with praise,
  A pet-lamb in a sentimental farce!
55 Fade softly from my eyes, and be once more
  In masque-like figures on the dreamy urn;
    Farewell! I yet have visions for the night,
And for the day faint visions there is store;
  Vanish, ye phantoms! from my idle spright,°   *spirit*
60   Into the clouds, and never more return!
—1848 (WRITTEN 1819)

To Autumn

1

Season of mists and mellow fruitfulness,
  Close bosom-friend of the maturing sun;
Conspiring with him how to load and bless
  With fruit the vines that round the thatch-eves run;
5 To bend with apples the moss'd cottage-trees,
  And fill all fruit with ripeness to the core;
    To swell the gourd, and plump the hazel shells
With a sweet kernel; to set budding more,
  And still more, later flowers for the bees,
10   Until they think warm days will never cease,
    For Summer has o'er-brimm'd their clammy cells.

2

Who hath not seen thee oft amid thy store?
  Sometimes whoever seeks abroad may find
Thee sitting careless on a granary floor,

15   Thy hair soft-lifted by the winnowing wind;
Or on a half-reap'd furrow sound asleep,
  Drows'd with the fume of poppies, while thy hook[1]
    Spares the next swath and all its twined flowers:
And sometimes like a gleaner[2] thou dost keep
20   Steady thy laden head across a brook;
  Or by a cider-press, with patient look,
    Thou watchest the last oozings hours by hours.

3

Where are the songs of Spring? Ay, where are they?
  Think not of them, thou hast thy music too—
25 While barred clouds bloom the soft-dying day,
  And touch the stubble-plains with rosy hue;
Then in a wailful choir the small gnats mourn
  Among the river sallows,° borne aloft   *willows*
    Or sinking as the light wind lives or dies;
30 And full-grown lambs loud bleat from hilly bourn;°   *realm*
  Hedge-crickets sing; and now with treble soft
  The red-breast whistles from a
    garden-croft;°   *enclosed garden*
  And gathering swallows twitter in the skies.
—1820

Lamia

Philostratus, in his fourth book *de Vita Apollonii*, hath a memorable instance in this kind, which I may not omit, of one Menippus Lycius, a young man of twenty-five years of age, that going betwixt Cenchreas and Corinth, met such a phantasm in the habit of a fair gentlewoman, which taking him by the hand, carried him home to her house, in the suburbs of Corinth, and told him she was a Phoenician by birth, and if he would tarry with her, he should hear her sing and play, and drink such wine as never any drank, and no man should molest him; but she, being fair and lovely, would live and die with him, that was fair and lovely to behold. The young man, a philosopher, otherwise staid and discreet, able to moderate his passions, though not this of love, tarried with her a while to his great content, and at last married her, to whose wedding, among other guests, came Apollonius; who, by some probable conjectures, found her out to be a serpent, a lamia; and that all her furniture was, like Tantalus' gold, described by Homer, no substance but

---

[1] *hook* I.e., a reaping-hook or scythe.

[2] *gleaner* One who gathers the grain left by the reaper.

mere illusions. When she saw herself descried, she wept, and desired Apollonius to be silent, but he would not be moved, and thereupon she, plate, house, and all that was in it, vanished in an instant: many thousand took notice of this fact, for it was done in the midst of Greece.[1]

PART I

Upon a time, before the faery broods
Drove Nymph and Satyr from the prosperous
    woods,
Before King Oberon's bright diadem,°   *crown*
Sceptre, and mantle, clasp'd with dewy gem,
5 Frighted away the Dryads and the Fauns
From rushes green, and brakes,° and cowslip'd   *ferns*
    lawns,[2]
The ever-smitten Hermes[3] empty left
His golden throne, bent warm on amorous theft:
From high Olympus had he stolen light,
10 On this side of Jove's clouds,[4] to escape the sight
Of his great summoner, and made retreat
Into a forest on the shores of Crete.[5]
For somewhere in that sacred island dwelt
A nymph, to whom all hoofed Satyrs knelt;
15 At whose white feet the languid Tritons[6] poured
Pearls, while on land they wither'd and adored.
Fast by the springs where she to bathe was wont,
And in those meads° where sometime she   *meadows*
    might haunt,

Were strewn rich gifts, unknown to any Muse,[7]
20 Though Fancy's casket were unlock'd to choose.
Ah, what a world of love was at her feet!
So Hermes thought, and a celestial heat
Burnt from his winged heels to either ear,
That from a whiteness, as the lily clear,
25 Blush'd into roses 'mid his golden hair,
Fallen in jealous curls about his shoulders bare.
From vale to vale, from wood to wood, he flew,
Breathing upon the flowers his passion new,
And wound with many a river to its head,
30 To find where this sweet nymph prepar'd her secret bed:
In vain; the sweet nymph might nowhere be found,
And so he rested, on the lonely ground,
Pensive, and full of painful jealousies
Of the Wood-Gods, and even the very trees.
35 There as he stood, he heard a mournful voice,
Such as once heard, in gentle heart, destroys
All pain but pity: thus the lone voice spake:
"When from this wreathed tomb shall I awake!
When move in a sweet body fit for life,
40 And love, and pleasure, and the ruddy strife
Of hearts and lips! Ah, miserable me!"
The God, dove-footed, glided silently
Round bush and tree, soft-brushing, in his speed,
The taller grasses and full-flowering weed,
45 Until he found a palpitating snake,
Bright, and cirque-couchant[8] in a dusky brake.

She was a gordian[9] shape of dazzling hue,
Vermilion°-spotted, golden, green, and blue;   *scarlet*
Striped like a zebra, freckled like a pard,°   *leopard*
50 Eyed like a peacock, and all crimson barr'd;
And full of silver moons, that, as she breathed,
Dissolv'd, or brighter shone, or interwreathed
Their lustres with the gloomier tapestries—
So rainbow-sided, touch'd with miseries,
55 She seem'd, at once, some penanced lady elf,
Some demon's mistress, or the demon's self.

---

[1] In a footnote originally placed at the end of *Lamia*, Keats provides the above quote from Robert Burton's *Anatomy of Melancholy* 3.2.1.1. (1621), his source for this narrative poem about a young man who falls in love with a lamia, a monster in the body of a woman.

[2] *before the ... lawns* In classical mythology, nymphs, dryads (wood nymphs), and satyrs and fauns (half-men, half-goats) were all minor deities. Oberon, in Shakespeare's *A Midsummer Night's Dream*, is king of the fairies, who were immortal beings of a later period.

[3] *Hermes* Wing-footed messenger of the gods (called Mercury in Roman mythology).

[4] *From high ... clouds* Jove is the King of the Roman gods, all of whom reside on Mt. Olympus.

[5] *Crete* Island in the Aegean Sea.

[6] *Tritons* Sea-gods, usually half-men and half-fish.

---

[7] *Muse* One of nine daughters of Zeus and Mnemosyne, each of whom presided over and provided inspiration for an aspect of learning or the arts.

[8] *cirque-couchant* French: lying in coils.

[9] *gordian* I.e., like the Gordian knot, tied by King Gordius of Phrygia and said to be impossible to untie. Alexander the Great eventually severed it with his sword.

Upon her crest she wore a wannish fire
Sprinkled with stars, like Ariadne's tiar:[1]
Her head was serpent, but ah, bitter-sweet!
60 She had a woman's mouth with all its pearls[2] complete:
And for her eyes: what could such eyes do there
But weep, and weep, that they were born so fair?
As Proserpine still weeps for her Sicilian air.[3]
Her throat was serpent, but the words she spake
65 Came, as through bubbling honey, for Love's sake,
And thus; while Hermes on his pinions° lay,   *wings*
Like a stoop'd[4] falcon ere he takes his prey.

    "Fair Hermes, crown'd with feathers, fluttering
        light,
I had a splendid dream of thee last night:
70 I saw thee sitting, on a throne of gold,
Among the Gods, upon Olympus old,
The only sad one; for thou didst not hear
The soft, lute-finger'd Muses chaunting clear,
Nor even Apollo when he sang alone,
75 Deaf to his throbbing throat's long, long melodious
        moan.
I dreamt I saw thee, robed in purple flakes,
Break amorous through the clouds, as morning breaks,
And, swiftly as a bright Phoebean dart,[5]
Strike for the Cretan isle; and here thou art!
80 Too gentle Hermes, hast thou found the maid?"
Whereat the star of Lethe[6] not delay'd
His rosy eloquence, and thus inquired:
"Thou smooth-lipp'd serpent, surely high inspired!
Thou beauteous wreath, with melancholy eyes,
85 Possess whatever bliss thou canst devise,
Telling me only where my nymph is fled—
Where she doth breathe!" "Bright planet, thou hast said,"
Return'd the snake, "but seal with oaths, fair God!"

"I swear," said Hermes, "by my serpent rod,[7]
90 And by thine eyes, and by thy starry crown!"
Light flew his earnest words, among the blossoms
        blown.
Then thus again the brilliance feminine:
"Too frail of heart! for this lost nymph of thine,
Free as the air, invisibly, she strays
95 About these thornless wilds; her pleasant days
She tastes unseen; unseen her nimble feet
Leave traces in the grass and flowers sweet;
From weary tendrils, and bow'd branches green,
She plucks the fruit unseen, she bathes unseen:
100 And by my power is her beauty veil'd
To keep it unaffronted, unassail'd
By the love-glances of unlovely eyes,
Of Satyrs, Fauns, and blear'd Silenus'[8] sighs.
Pale grew her immortality, for woe
105 Of all these lovers, and she grieved so
I took compassion on her, bade her steep
Her hair in weïrd° syrops, that would keep   *magical*
Her loveliness invisible, yet free
To wander as she loves, in liberty.
110 Thou shalt behold her, Hermes, thou alone,
If thou wilt, as thou swearest, grant my boon!"
Then, once again, the charmed God began
An oath, and through the serpent's ears it ran
Warm, tremulous, devout, psalterian.[9]
115 Ravish'd, she lifted her Circean head,[10]
Blush'd a live damask,[11] and swift-lisping said,
"I was a woman, let me have once more
A woman's shape, and charming as before.
I love a youth of Corinth—O the bliss!
120 Give me my woman's form, and place me where he is.
Stoop, Hermes, let me breathe upon thy brow,
And thou shalt see thy sweet nymph even now."
The God on half-shut feathers sank serene,
She breath'd upon his eyes, and swift was seen

---

[1] *Ariadne's tiar*   According to myth, after Ariadne married the god Bacchus she was converted into a constellation. In his painting of her, Italian painter Titian (c. 1488–1576) shows Ariadne wearing a crown of seven stars.

[2] *pearls*   I.e., teeth.

[3] *As Proserpine ... air*   Hades, god of the underworld, abducted Proserpine from her home in Sicily to be his queen.

[4] *stoop'd*   Swooping.

[5] *Phoeban dart*   Sunbeam, after Phoebus Apollo, god of the sun.

[6] *star of Lethe*   Hermes, who, like a star, guided the souls of the dead to the dark underworld (in which Lethe is a river).

---

[7] *my serpent rod*   On Hermes's wand, or a caduceus, two serpents were entwined.

[8] *Silenus*   Foster-father of Bacchus, god of wine, who is typically portrayed drunk.

[9] *psalterian*   Like the sound of a psaltery (a stringed instrument); or, possibly, like a psalm, which were printed in psalters.

[10] *Circean head*   Like that of Circe, the enchantress who turns men into beasts in Homer's *Odyssey*, Book 10.

[11] *damask*   Pink, like the color of a damask rose.

125　Of both the guarded nymph near-smiling on the green.
　　It was no dream; or say a dream it was,
　　Real are the dreams of Gods, and smoothly pass
　　Their pleasures in a long immortal dream.
　　One warm, flush'd moment, hovering, it might seem
130　Dash'd by the wood-nymph's beauty, so he burn'd;
　　Then, lighting on the printless verdure, turn'd
　　To the swoon'd serpent, and with languid arm,
　　Delicate, put to proof the lithe Caducean charm.
　　So done, upon the nymph his eyes he bent
135　Full of adoring tears and blandishment,
　　And towards her stept: she, like a moon in wane,
　　Faded before him, cower'd, nor could restrain
　　Her fearful sobs, self-folding like a flower
　　That faints into itself at evening hour:
140　But the God fostering her chilled hand,
　　She felt the warmth, her eyelids open'd bland,°   *soft*
　　And, like new flowers at morning song of bees,
　　Bloom'd, and gave up her honey to the lees.°   *dregs*
　　Into the green-recessed woods they flew;
145　Nor grew they pale, as mortal lovers do.

　　　　Left to herself, the serpent now began
　　To change; her elfin blood in madness ran,
　　Her mouth foam'd, and the grass, therewith
　　　　besprent,°   *besprinkled*
　　Wither'd at dew so sweet and virulent;
150　Her eyes in torture fix'd, and anguish drear,
　　Hot, glaz'd, and wide, with lid-lashes all sear,°   *withered*
　　Flash'd phosphor and sharp sparks, without one
　　　　cooling tear.
　　The colours all inflam'd throughout her train,°   *tail*
　　She writh'd about, convuls'd with scarlet pain:
155　A deep volcanian yellow took the place
　　Of all her milder-mooned[1] body's grace;
　　And, as the lava ravishes the mead,
　　Spoilt all her silver mail, and golden
　　　　brede;°   *interwoven pattern*
　　Made gloom of all her frecklings, streaks and bars,
160　Eclips'd her crescents, and lick'd up her stars:
　　So that, in moments few, she was undrest
　　Of all her sapphires, greens, and amethyst,
　　And rubious-argent:° of all these bereft,   *reddish-silver*
　　Nothing but pain and ugliness were left.
165　Still shone her crown; that vanish'd, also she

Melted and disappear'd as suddenly;
And in the air, her new voice luting soft,
Cried, "Lycius! gentle Lycius!" Borne aloft
With the bright mists about the mountains hoar°   *ancient*
170　These words dissolv'd: Crete's forests heard no more.

　　　　Whither fled Lamia, now a lady bright,
　　A full-born beauty new and exquisite?
　　She fled into that valley they pass o'er
　　Who go to Corinth from Cenchreas' shore;[2]
175　And rested at the foot of those wild hills,
　　The rugged founts of the Peraean rills,
　　And of that other ridge whose barren back
　　Stretches, with all its mist and cloudy rack,
　　South-westward to Cleone.[3] There she stood
180　About a young bird's flutter from a wood,
　　Fair, on a sloping green of mossy tread,
　　By a clear pool, wherein she passioned[4]
　　To see herself escap'd from so sore ills,
　　While her robes flaunted with the daffodils.

185　　　　Ah, happy Lycius!—for she was a maid
　　More beautiful than ever twisted braid,
　　Or sigh'd, or blush'd, or on spring-flowered lea°   *pasture*
　　Spread a green kirtle° to the minstrelsy: *gown*
　　A virgin purest lipp'd, yet in the lore
190　Of love deep learned to the red heart's core:
　　Not one hour old, yet of sciential° brain   *knowledgeable*
　　To unperplex° bliss from its neighbour pain;   *extricate*
　　Define their pettish° limits, and estrange   *uncertain*
　　Their points of contact, and swift counterchange;
195　Intrigue with the specious° chaos, and dispart°*seeming/cleave*
　　Its most ambiguous atoms with sure art;
　　As though in Cupid's[5] college she had spent
　　Sweet days a lovely graduate, still unshent,°   *unspoiled*
　　And kept his rosy terms in idle languishment.

200　　　　Why this fair creature chose so fairily
　　By the wayside to linger, we shall see;
　　But first 'tis fit to tell how she could muse
　　And dream, when in the serpent prison-house,

---

[2] *Cenchreas' shore* Shore of Cenchrea, the eastern harbor of Corinth, in southern Greece.

[3] *Cleone* Village between Corinth and Argos.

[4] *passioned* Was moved by intense passion.

[5] *Cupid* God of love.

---

[1] *milder-mooned* I.e., of a milder, silver-moon color.

Of all she list,° strange or magnificent: *desired*
205 How, ever, where she will'd, her spirit went;
Whether to faint Elysium,[1] or where
Down through tress-lifting waves the Nereids fair
Wind into Thetis' bower[2] by many a pearly stair;
Or where God Bacchus drains his cups divine,
210 Stretch'd out, at ease, beneath a glutinous pine;
Or where in Pluto's[3] gardens palatine°   *palatial*
Mulciber's columns gleam in far piazzian line.[4]
And sometimes into cities she would send
Her dream, with feast and rioting to blend;
215 And once, while among mortals dreaming thus,
She saw the young Corinthian Lycius
Charioting foremost in the envious race,
Like a young Jove with calm uneager face,
And fell into a swooning love of him.
220 Now on the moth-time of that evening dim
He would return that way, as well she knew,
To Corinth from the shore; for freshly blew
The eastern soft wind, and his galley now
Grated the quaystones with her brazen prow
225 In port Cenchreas, from Egina isle
Fresh anchor'd; whither he had been awhile
To sacrifice to Jove, whose temple there
Waits with high marble doors for blood and incense
      rare.
Jove heard his vows, and better'd his desire;
230 For by some freakful chance he made retire
From his companions, and set forth to walk,
Perhaps grown wearied of their Corinth talk:
Over the solitary hills he fared,
Thoughtless at first, but ere eve's star appeared
235 His phantasy was lost, where reason fades,
In the calm'd twilight of Platonic shades.°   *ghosts*
Lamia beheld him coming, near, more near—
Close to her passing, in indifference drear,
His silent sandals swept the mossy green;
240 So neighbour'd to him, and yet so unseen
She stood: he pass'd, shut up in mysteries,
His mind wrapp'd like his mantle, while her eyes

Follow'd his steps, and her neck regal white
Turn'd—syllabling thus, "Ah, Lycius bright,
245 And will you leave me on the hills alone?
Lycius, look back! and be some pity shown."
He did; not with cold wonder fearingly,
But Orpheus-like at an Eurydice;[5]
For so delicious were the words she sung,
250 It seem'd he had lov'd them a whole summer long:
And soon his eyes had drunk her beauty up,
Leaving no drop in the bewildering cup,
And still the cup was full—while he, afraid
Lest she should vanish ere his lip had paid
255 Due adoration, thus began to adore;
Her soft look growing coy, she saw his chain so sure:
"Leave thee alone! Look back! Ah, Goddess, see
Whether my eyes can ever turn from thee!
For pity do not this sad heart belie°—   *deceive*
260 Even as thou vanishest so I shall die.
Stay! though a Naiad° of the rivers, stay!   *water nymph*
To thy far wishes will thy streams obey:
Stay! though the greenest woods be thy domain,
Alone they can drink up the morning rain:
265 Though a descended Pleiad,[6] will not one
Of thine harmonious sisters keep in tune
Thy spheres, and as thy silver proxy shine?
So sweetly to these ravish'd ears of mine
Came thy sweet greeting, that if thou shouldst fade
270 Thy memory will waste me to a shade—
For pity do not melt!" "If I should stay,"
Said Lamia, "here, upon this floor of clay,
And pain my steps upon these flowers too rough,
What canst thou say or do of charm enough
275 To dull the nice remembrance of my home?
Thou canst not ask me with thee here to roam
Over these hills and vales, where no joy is—
Empty of immortality and bliss!
Thou art a scholar, Lycius, and must know
280 That finer spirits cannot breathe below
In human climes, and live: Alas! poor youth,
What taste of purer air hast thou to soothe

---

1. *Elysium* Paradise of the classical underworld.

2. *Nereids … bower* Thetis, the mother of Achilles, is a sea-nymph, or Nereid.

3. *Pluto* Another name for Hades, god of the underworld.

4. *Mulciber* Also called Vulcan, god of fire and metalworking; *piazzan line* Line of columns surrounding piazzas.

5. *But … Eurydice* The poet Orpheus won the right to lead his wife, Eurydice, back from the underworld on the condition that he not turn around to look at her on the journey back. When he could not resist doing so, she was forced to return to the underworld forever.

6. *Pleiad* One of the seven stars, daughters of the Titan Atlas, that comprise the constellation Pleiades.

My essence? What serener palaces,
Where I may all my many senses please,
285 And by mysterious sleights a hundred thirsts appease?
It cannot be—Adieu!" So said, she rose
Tiptoe with white arms spread. He, sick to lose
The amorous promise of her lone complain,°   *complaint*
Swoon'd, murmuring of love, and pale with pain.
290 The cruel lady, without any show
Of sorrow for her tender favourite's woe,
But rather, if her eyes could brighter be,
With brighter eyes and slow amenity,
Put her new lips to his, and gave afresh
295 The life she had so tangled in her mesh:
And as he from one trance was wakening
Into another, she began to sing,
Happy in beauty, life, and love, and every thing,
A song of love, too sweet for earthly lyres,
300 While, like held breath, the stars drew in their panting
     fires.
And then she whisper'd in such trembling tone,
As those who, safe together met alone
For the first time through many anguish'd days,
Use other speech than looks; bidding him raise
305 His drooping head, and clear his soul of doubt,
For that she was a woman, and without
Any more subtle fluid in her veins
Than throbbing blood, and that the self-same pains
Inhabited her frail-strung heart as his.
310 And next she wonder'd how his eyes could miss
Her face so long in Corinth, where, she said,
She dwelt but half retir'd, and there had led
Days happy as the gold coin could invent
Without the aid of love; yet in content
315 Till she saw him, as once she pass'd him by,
Where 'gainst a column he leant thoughtfully
At Venus'[1] temple porch, 'mid baskets heap'd
Of amorous herbs and flowers, newly reap'd
Late on that eve, as 'twas the night before
320 The Adonian feast;[2] whereof she saw no more,
But wept alone those days, for why should she adore?
Lycius from death awoke into amaze,
To see her still, and singing so sweet lays;
Then from amaze into delight he fell

325 To hear her whisper woman's lore so well;
And every word she spake entic'd him on
To unperplex'd° delight and pleasure known.   *certain*
Let the mad poets say whate'er they please
Of the sweets of Fairies, Peris,[3] Goddesses,
330 There is not such a treat among them all,
Haunters of cavern, lake, and waterfall,
As a real woman, lineal indeed
From Pyrrha's pebbles[4] or old Adam's seed.
Thus gentle Lamia judg'd, and judg'd aright,
335 That Lycius could not love in half a fright,
So threw the goddess off, and won his heart
More pleasantly by playing woman's part,
With no more awe than what her beauty gave,
That, while it smote, still guaranteed to save.
340 Lycius to all made eloquent reply,
Marrying to every word a twinborn sigh;
And last, pointing to Corinth, ask'd her sweet,
If 'twas too far that night for her soft feet.
The way was short, for Lamia's eagerness
345 Made, by a spell, the triple league decrease
To a few paces; not at all surmised
By blinded Lycius, so in her comprized.°   *absorbed*
They pass'd the city gates, he knew not how,
So noiseless, and he never thought to know.

350   As men talk in a dream, so Corinth all,
Throughout her palaces imperial,
And all her populous streets and temples lewd,[5]
Mutter'd, like tempest in the distance brew'd,
To the wide-spreaded night above her towers.
355 Men, women, rich and poor, in the cool hours,
Shuffled their sandals o'er the pavement white,
Companion'd or alone; while many a light
Flared, here and there, from wealthy festivals,
And threw their moving shadows on the walls,
360 Or found them cluster'd in the corniced shade
Of some arch'd temple door, or dusky colonnade.

---

[1] *Venus* Goddess of love.

[2] *Adonian feast* Festival in honor of Adonis, a beautiful young man who was loved by Venus and was killed when hunting a boar.

[3] *Peris* Beautiful women inhabiting the world of the Persian afterlife.

[4] *Pyrrha's pebbles* In classical myth, Jupiter exterminated humanity in a flood. Deucalion and his wife Pyrrha, the only two survivors, repopulated the earth by throwing pebbles, which turned into people.

[5] *temples lewd* Temples of Venus, goddess of love.

Muffling his face, of greeting friends in fear,
Her fingers he press'd hard, as one came near
With curl'd gray beard, sharp eyes, and smooth bald
    crown,
365 Slow-stepp'd, and robed in philosophic gown:
Lycius shrank closer, as they met and past,
Into his mantle, adding wings to haste,
While hurried Lamia trembled: "Ah," said he,
"Why do you shudder, love, so ruefully?
370 Why does your tender palm dissolve in dew?"
"I'm wearied," said fair Lamia: "tell me who
Is that old man? I cannot bring to mind
His features—Lycius! wherefore did you blind
Yourself from his quick eyes?" Lycius replied,
375 "'Tis Apollonius sage, my trusty guide
And good instructor; but to-night he seems
The ghost of folly haunting my sweet dreams."

While yet he spake they had arrived before
A pillar'd porch, with lofty portal door,
380 Where hung a silver lamp, whose phosphor glow
Reflected in the slabbed steps below,
Mild as a star in water; for so new,
And so unsullied was the marble hue,
So through the crystal polish, liquid fine,
385 Ran the dark veins, that none but feet divine
Could e'er have touch'd there. Sounds Æolian[1]
Breath'd from the hinges, as the ample span
Of the wide doors disclos'd a place unknown
Some time to any, but those two alone,
390 And a few Persian mutes, who that same year
Were seen about the markets: none knew where
They could inhabit; the most curious
Were foil'd, who watch'd to trace them to their house:
And but the flitter-winged verse must tell,
395 For truth's sake, what woe afterwards befell,
'Twould humour many a heart to leave them thus,
Shut from the busy world of more incredulous.

PART 2

Love in a hut, with water and a crust,
Is—Love, forgive us!—cinders, ashes, dust;
Love in a palace is perhaps at last
More grievous torment than a hermit's fast—
5 That is a doubtful tale from faery land,
Hard for the non-elect to understand.
Had Lycius liv'd to hand his story down,
He might have given the moral a fresh frown,
Or clench'd it quite: but too short was their bliss
10 To breed distrust and hate, that make the soft voice hiss.
Besides, there, nightly, with terrific glare,
Love, jealous grown of so complete a pair,
Hover'd and buzz'd his wings, with fearful roar,
Above the lintel[2] of their chamber door,
15 And down the passage cast a glow upon the floor.

For all this came a ruin: side by side
They were enthroned, in the even tide,
Upon a couch, near to a curtaining
Whose airy texture, from a golden string,
20 Floated into the room, and let appear
Unveil'd the summer heaven, blue and clear,
Betwixt two marble shafts—there they reposed,
Where use had made it sweet, with eyelids closed,
Saving a tithe[3] which love still open kept,
25 That they might see each other while they almost slept;
When from the slope side of a suburb hill,
Deafening the swallow's twitter, came a thrill
Of trumpets—Lycius started—the sounds fled,
But left a thought, a buzzing in his head.
30 For the first time, since first he harbour'd in
That purple-lined palace of sweet sin,
His spirit pass'd beyond its golden bourn°   *realm*
Into the noisy world almost forsworn.
The lady, ever watchful, penetrant,
35 Saw this with pain, so arguing a want
Of something more, more than her empery°   *empire*
Of joys; and she began to moan and sigh
Because he mused beyond her, knowing well
That but a moment's thought is passion's passing bell.[4]
40 "Why do you sigh, fair creature?" whisper'd he:
"Why do you think?" return'd she tenderly:
"You have deserted me;—where am I now?
Not in your heart while care weighs on your brow:
No, no, you have dismiss'd me; and I go

---

[1] *Sounds Aeolian* Sounds resembling those of an Aeolian harp, which produces music when exposed to currents of air. Aeolus was god of the winds.

[2] *lintel* Horizontal support beam.

[3] *tithe* I.e., a tenth, or very small part.

[4] *passing bell* Bell tolled following a death.

45 From your breast houseless: ay, it must be so."
He answer'd, bending to her open eyes,
Where he was mirror'd small in paradise,
"My silver planet, both of eve and morn![1]
Why will you plead yourself so sad forlorn,
50 While I am striving how to fill my heart
With deeper crimson, and a double smart?
How to entangle, trammel up and snare
Your soul in mine, and labyrinth you there
Like the hid scent in an unbudded rose?
55 Ay, a sweet kiss—you see your mighty woes.
My thoughts! shall I unveil them? Listen then!
What mortal hath a prize, that other men
May be confounded and abash'd withal,
But lets it sometimes pace abroad majestical,
60 And triumph, as in thee I should rejoice
Amid the hoarse alarm of Corinth's voice.
Let my foes choke, and my friends shout afar,
While through the thronged streets your bridal car
Wheels round its dazzling spokes." The lady's cheek
65 Trembled; she nothing said, but, pale and meek,
Arose and knelt before him, wept a rain
Of sorrows at his words; at last with pain
Beseeching him, the while his hand she wrung,
To change his purpose. He thereat was stung,
70 Perverse, with stronger fancy to reclaim
Her wild and timid nature to his aim:
Besides, for all his love, in self despite,
Against his better self, he took delight
Luxurious in her sorrows, soft and new.
75 His passion, cruel grown, took on a hue
Fierce and sanguineous as 'twas possible
In one whose brow had no dark veins to swell.
Fine was the mitigated fury, like
Apollo's presence when in act to strike
80 The serpent[2]—Ha, the serpent! certes,° she   *certainly*
Was none. She burnt, she lov'd the tyranny,
And, all subdued, consented to the hour
When to the bridal he should lead his paramour.
Whispering in midnight silence, said the youth,
85 "Sure some sweet name thou hast, though, by my truth,

I have not ask'd it, ever thinking thee
Not mortal, but of heavenly progeny,
As still I do. Hast any mortal name,
Fit appellation for this dazzling frame?
90 Or friends or kinsfolk on the citied earth,
To share our marriage feast and nuptial mirth?"
"I have no friends," said Lamia, "no, not one;
My presence in wide Corinth hardly known:
My parents' bones are in their dusty urns
95 Sepulchred, where no kindled incense burns,
Seeing all their luckless race are dead, save me,
And I neglect the holy rite for thee.
Even as you list° invite your many guests;   *desire to*
But if, as now it seems, your vision rests
100 With any pleasure on me, do not bid
Old Apollonius—from him keep me hid."
Lycius, perplex'd at words so blind and blank,
Made close inquiry; from whose touch she shrank,
Feigning a sleep; and he to the dull shade
105 Of deep sleep in a moment was betray'd.

It was the custom then to bring away
The bride from home at blushing shut of day,
Veiled, in a chariot, heralded along
By strewn flowers, torches, and a marriage song,
110 With other pageants: but this fair unknown
Had not a friend. So being left alone
(Lycius was gone to summon all his kin),
And knowing surely she could never win
His foolish heart from its mad pompousness,
115 She set herself, high-thoughted, how to dress
The misery in fit magnificence.
She did so, but 'tis doubtful how and whence
Came, and who were her subtle servitors.
About the halls, and to and from the doors,
120 There was a noise of wings, till in short space
The glowing banquet-room shone with wide-arched
     grace.
A haunting music, sole perhaps and lone
Supportress of the faery-roof, made moan
Throughout, as fearful the whole charm might fade.
125 Fresh carved cedar, mimicking a glade
Of palm and plantain, met from either side,
High in the midst, in honour of the bride:
Two palms and then two plantains, and so on,
From either side their stems branch'd one to one

---

[1] *My silver ... morn* I.e., my Venus (the planet that appears as both the morning and the evening star).

[2] *Apollo's ... serpent* Apollo killed a serpent, named Python, at Delphi; when his oracle was established there, the priestess was known as the Pythian.

130 All down the aisled place; and beneath all
There ran a stream of lamps straight on from wall to
    wall.
So canopied, lay an untasted feast
Teeming with odours. Lamia, regal drest,
Silently paced about, and as she went,
135 In pale contented sort of discontent,
Mission'd her viewless servants to enrich
The fretted[1] splendour of each nook and niche.
Between the tree-stems, marbled plain at first,
Came jasper panels; then, anon, there burst
140 Forth creeping imagery of slighter trees,
And with the larger wove in small intricacies.
Approving all, she faded at self-will,
And shut the chamber up, close, hush'd and still,
Complete and ready for the revels rude,
145 When dreadful guests would come to spoil her solitude.

The day appear'd, and all the gossip rout.
O senseless Lycius! Madman! wherefore flout
The silent-blessing fate, warm cloister'd hours,
And show to common eyes these secret bowers?
150 The herd approach'd; each guest, with busy brain,
Arriving at the portal, gaz'd amain,°   *intently*
And enter'd marveling: for they knew the sheet,
Remember'd it from childhood all complete
Without a gap, yet ne'er before had seen
155 That royal porch, that high-built fair demesne;°   *estate*
So in they hurried all, maz'd,° curious and keen: *bewildered*
Save one, who look'd thereon with eye severe,
And with calm-planted steps walk'd in austere;
'Twas Apollonius: something too he laugh'd,
160 As though some knotty problem, that had daft° *confounded*
His patient thought, had now begun to thaw,
And solve and melt— 'twas just as he foresaw.

He met within the murmurous vestibule
His young disciple. "'Tis no common rule,
165 Lycius," said he, "for uninvited guest
To force himself upon you, and infest
With an unbidden presence the bright throng
Of younger friends; yet must I do this wrong,
And you forgive me." Lycius blush'd, and led
170 The old man through the inner doors broad-spread;
With reconciling words and courteous mien°   *manner*

Turning into sweet milk the sophist's°   *philosopher's*
    spleen.°   *ill-humor*

Of wealthy lustre was the banquet-room,
Fill'd with pervading brilliance and perfume:
175 Before each lucid panel fuming stood
A censer[2] fed with myrrh and spiced wood,
Each by a sacred tripod held aloft,
Whose slender feet wide-swerv'd upon the soft
Wool-woofed° carpets: fifty wreaths of smoke   *woven*
180 From fifty censers their light voyage took
To the high roof, still mimick'd as they rose
Along the mirror'd walls by twin-clouds odorous.
Twelve sphered tables, by silk seats ensphered,° *encircled*
High as the level of a man's breast rear'd
185 On libbard's° paws, upheld the heavy gold   *leopard's*
Of cups and goblets, and the store thrice told
Of Ceres' horn,[3] and, in huge vessels, wine
Come from the gloomy° tun° with merry   *dark / cask*
    shine.
Thus loaded with a feast the tables stood,
190 Each shrining in the midst the image of a God.

When in an antechamber every guest
Had felt the cold full sponge to pleasure press'd,
By minist'ring slaves, upon his hands and feet,
And fragrant oils with ceremony meet
195 Pour'd on his hair, they all mov'd to the feast
In white robes, and themselves in order placed
Around the silken couches, wondering
Whence all this mighty cost and blaze of wealth could
    spring.

Soft went the music the soft air along,
200 While fluent Greek a vowel'd undersong
Kept up among the guests, discoursing low
At first, for scarcely was the wine at flow;
But when the happy vintage touchd' their brains,
Louder they talk, and louder come the strains
205 Of powerful instruments—the gorgeous dyes,
The space, the splendour of the draperies,
The roof of awful richness, nectarous cheer,
Beautiful slaves, and Lamia's self, appear,

---

[1] *fretted* Adorned with elaborate carved patterns.

[2] *censer* Vessel for burning incense.

[3] *Ceres' horn* Ceres, goddess of grain and agriculture, is sometimes depicted with a horn of plenty, overflowing with produce.

Now, when the wine has done its rosy deed,
210 And every soul from human trammels freed,
No more so strange; for merry wine, sweet wine,
Will make Elysian shades not too fair, too divine.
Soon was God Bacchus at meridian height;
Flush'd were their cheeks, and bright eyes double bright:
215 Garlands of every green, and every scent
From vales deflower'd, or forest-trees branch-rent,
In baskets of bright osier'd° gold were brought   *woven*
High as the handles heap'd, to suit the thought
Of every guest; that each, as he did please,
220 Might fancy-fit his brows, silk-pillow'd at his ease.

    What wreath for Lamia? What for Lycius?
What for the sage, old Apollonius?
Upon her aching forehead be there hung
The leaves of willow and of adder's tongue;[1]
225 And for the youth, quick, let us strip for him
The thyrsus,[2] that his watching eyes may swim
Into forgetfulness; and, for the sage,
Let spear-grass and the spiteful thistle wage
War on his temples. Do not all charms fly
230 At the mere touch of cold philosophy?[3]
There was an awful° rainbow once in heaven: *awe-inspiring*
We know her woof, her texture; she is given
In the dull catalogue of common things.
Philosophy will clip an angel's wings,
235 Conquer all mysteries by rule and line,
Empty the haunted air, and gnomed[4] mine—
Unweave a rainbow, as it erewhile made
The tender-person'd Lamia melt into a shade.

    By her glad Lycius sitting, in chief place,
240 Scarce saw in all the room another face,
Till, checking his love trance, a cup he took
Full brimm'd, and opposite sent forth a look
'Cross the broad table, to beseech a glance
From his old teacher's wrinkled countenance,
245 And pledge him. The bald-head philosopher
Had fix'd his eye, without a twinkle or stir
Full on the alarmed beauty of the bride,

Brow-beating her fair form, and troubling her sweet
    pride.
Lycius then press'd her hand, with devout touch,
250 As pale it lay upon the rosy couch:
'Twas icy, and the cold ran through his veins;
Then sudden it grew hot, and all the pains
Of an unnatural heat shot to his heart.
"Lamia, what means this? Wherefore dost thou start?
255 Know'st thou that man?" Poor Lamia answer'd not.
He gaz'd into her eyes, and not a jot
Own'd they the lovelorn piteous appeal:
More, more he gaz'd: his human senses reel:
Some hungry spell that loveliness absorbs;
260 There was no recognition in those orbs.
"Lamia!" he cried—and no soft-toned reply.
The many heard, and the loud revelry
Grew hush; the stately music no more breathes;
The myrtle sicken'd in a thousand wreaths.
265 By faint degrees, voice, lute, and pleasure ceased;
A deadly silence step by step increased,
Until it seem'd a horrid presence there,
And not a man but felt the terror in his hair.
"Lamia!" he shriek'd; and nothing but the shriek
270 With its sad echo did the silence break.
"Begone, foul dream!" he cried, gazing again
In the bride's face, where now no azure vein
Wander'd on fair-spaced temples; no soft bloom
Misted the cheek; no passion to illume
275 The deep-recessed vision—all was blight;
Lamia, no longer fair, there sat a deadly white.
"Shut, shut those juggling° eyes, thou   *beguiling*
    ruthless man!
Turn them aside, wretch! or the righteous ban
Of all the Gods, whose dreadful images
280 Here represent their shadowy presences,
May pierce them on the sudden with the thorn
Of painful blindness; leaving thee forlorn,
In trembling dotage to the feeblest fright
Of conscience, for their long offended might,
285 For all thine impious proud-heart sophistries,
Unlawful magic, and enticing lies.
Corinthians! look upon that gray-beard wretch!
Mark how, possess'd, his lashless eyelids stretch
Around his demon eyes! Corinthians, see!
290 My sweet bride withers at their potency."
"Fool!" said the sophist, in an undertone

---

[1] *adder's tongue* Fern that bears spikes resembling a snake's tongue.

[2] *thyrsus* Staff tipped with a pine cone and wreathed with vine leaves; carried by the followers of Bacchus.

[3] *philosophy* I.e., science.

[4] *gnomed* I.e., inhabited by gnomes.

Gruff with contempt; which a death-nighing moan
From Lycius answer'd, as heart-struck and lost,
He sank supine beside the aching ghost.
295 "Fool! Fool!" repeated he, while his eyes still
Relented not, nor mov'd; "from every ill
Of life have I preserv'd thee to this day,
And shall I see thee made a serpent's prey?"
Then Lamia breath'd death breath; the sophist's eye,
300 Like a sharp spear, went through her utterly,
Keen, cruel, perceant,° stinging: she, as well   *piercing*
As her weak hand could any meaning tell,
Motion'd him to be silent; vainly so,
He look'd and look'd again a level—No!
305 "A serpent!" echoed he; no sooner said,
Than with a frightful scream she vanished:
And Lycius' arms were empty of delight,
As were his limbs of life, from that same night.
On the high couch he lay! His friends came round—
310 Supported him—no pulse, or breath they found,
And, in its marriage robe, the heavy body wound.
—1820

This Living Hand [1]

This living hand, now warm and capable
Of earnest grasping, would, if it were cold
And in the icy silence of the tomb,
So haunt thy days and chill thy dreaming nights
5 That thou would wish thine own heart dry of blood
So in my veins red life might stream again,
and thou be conscience-calme'd—see here it is—
I hold it towards you—
—1898 (WRITTEN C. 1819)

Selected Letters

TO BENJAMIN BAILEY [2]
22 November 1817

My Dear Bailey,

… O I wish I was as certain of the end of all your troubles as that of your momentary start about the authenticity of the Imagination. I am certain of nothing but of the holiness of the Heart's affections and the truth of imagination—What the imagination seizes as Beauty must be truth—whether it existed before or not—for I have the same Idea of all our Passions as of Love they are all in their sublime, creative of essential Beauty—In a Word, you may know my favourite Speculation by my first Book and the little song I sent in my last [3]—which is a representation from the fancy of the probable mode of operating in these Matters—The Imagination may be compared to Adam's dream [4]—he awoke and found it truth. I am the more zealous in this affair, because I have never yet been able to perceive how any thing can be known for truth by consequitive [5] reasoning—and yet it must be—Can it be that even the greatest Philosopher ever arrived at his goal without putting aside numerous objections—However it may be, O for a Life of Sensations rather than of Thoughts! It is "a Vision in the form of Youth" a Shadow of reality to come—and this consideration has further convinced me for it has come as auxiliary to another favourite Speculation of mine, that we shall enjoy ourselves here after by having what we called happiness on Earth repeated in a finer tone and so repeated—And yet such a fate can only befall those who delight in sensation rather than hunger as you do after Truth—Adam's dream will do here and seems to be a conviction that Imagination and its empyreal [6] reflection is the same as

[1] *This Living Hand* A fragment whose context is unknown.

[2] *Benjamin Bailey* Undergraduate student in Divinity at Oxford University. Keats had stayed with him in September while he was working on *Endymion*.

[3] *my first book* I.e., the first book of *Endymion*; *little song … last* The first five stanzas of "Ode to Sorrow," from Book 4 of *Endymion*, which Keats had enclosed with his previous letter.

[4] *Adam's dream* See Milton, *Paradise Lost* 78.460–90, in which Adam dreams about Eve and wakes to find she has been created.

[5] *consequitive* Consecutive and consequent: a word of Keats's invention.

[6] *empyreal* Celestial; pertaining to the highest heavens.

human Life and its spiritual repetition. But as I was saying—the simple imaginative Mind may have its rewards in the repetition of its own silent Working coming continually on the spirit with a fine suddenness—to compare great things with small—have you never by being surprised with an old Melody—in a delicious place—by a delicious voice, felt over again your very speculations and surmises at the time it first operated on your soul—do you not remember forming to yourself the singer's face more beautiful [than] it was possible and yet with the elevation of the Moment you did not think so—even then you were mounted on the Wings of Imagination so high—that the Prototype must be here after—that delicious face you will see—What a time! I am continually running away from the subject—sure this cannot be exactly the case with a complex Mind—one that is imaginative and at the same time careful of its fruits—who would exist partly on sensation partly on thought—to whom it is necessary that years should bring the philosophic Mind[1]—such an one I consider yours and therefore it is necessary to your eternal Happiness that you not only have drink this old Wine of Heaven which I shall call the redigestion of our most ethereal Musings on Earth; but also increase in knowledge and know all things. I am glad to hear you are in a fair Way for Easter—you will soon get through your unpleasant reading and then!—but the world is full of troubles and I have not much reason to think myself pestered with many—I think Jane or Marianne has a better opinion of me than I deserve—for really and truly I do not think my Brother's illness connected with mine[2]—you know more of the real Cause than they do—nor have I any chance of being rack'd as you have been[3]—you perhaps at one time thought there was such a thing as Worldly Happiness to be arrived at, at certain periods of time marked out—you have of necessity from your disposition been thus led away—I scarcely remember counting upon any Happiness—I look not for it if it be not in the present hour—nothing startles me beyond the Moment. The setting sun will always set me to rights—or if a Sparrow come before my Window I take part in its existence and pick about the Gravel. The first thing that strikes me on hearing a Misfortune having befalled another is this. Well it cannot be helped.—he will have the pleasure of trying the resources of his spirit, and I beg now my dear Bailey that hereafter should you observe any thing cold in me not to [put] it to the account of heartlessness but abstraction—for I assure you I sometimes feel not the influence of a Passion or Affection during a whole week—and so long this sometimes continues I begin to suspect myself and the genuineness of my feelings at other times—thinking them a few barren Tragedy-tears—My Brother Tom is much improved—he is going to Devonshire—whither I shall follow him—at present I am just arrived at Dorking to change the Scene—change the Air and give me a spur to wind up my Poem, of which there are wanting 500 Lines. [...]

Your affectionate friend
John Keats—

I want to say much more to you—a few hints will set me going
Direct Burford Bridge near dorking

To George and Thomas Keats
21, 27 (?) December 1817
Hampstead Sunday

My Dear Brothers,
... I spent Friday evening with Wells[4] & went the next morning to see *Death on the Pale horse*. It is a wonderful picture, when West's[5] age is considered; But there is nothing to be intense upon; no women one feels mad to kiss; no face swelling into reality. the excellence of every Art is its intensity, capable of making all disagreeables evaporate, from their being in close relationship with Beauty & Truth—Examine *King Lear*[6] & you will find this exemplified throughout; but in this picture we have

---

[1] *philosophic Mind* Cf. Wordsworth, *Ode: Intimations of Immortality*, line 186.

[2] *Jane or ... mine* Jane and Marianne Reynolds, two friends of Keats, were afraid that his illness was a sign of tuberculosis, from which Keats's youngest brother, Tom, was suffering.

[3] *rack'd ... been* Bailey was upset over a love affair that had recently ended.

[4] *Wells* Charles Wells, a school friend of Tom Keats.

[5] *West* American painter Benjamin West (1738–1820), who moved to England and became President of the Royal Academy. The painting *Christ Rejected*, mentioned later in this letter, is West's.

[6] *King Lear* Painting by West that depicts the storm scene in Shakespeare's play.

Benjamin West, *King Lear* (1788).

unpleasantness without any momentous depth of speculation excited, in which to bury its repulsiveness—The picture is larger than *Christ rejected*—I dined with Haydon[1] the sunday after you left, & had a very pleasant day, I dined too (for I have been out too much lately) with Horace Smith[2] & met his two Brothers with Hill & Kingston & one Du Bois, they only served to convince me, how superior humour is to wit in respect to enjoyment—These men say things which make one start, without making one feel, they are all alike; their manners are alike; they all know fashionables; they have a mannerism in their very eating & drinking, in their mere handling a Decanter—They talked of Kean[3] & his low company—Would I were with that company instead of yours said I to myself! I know such like acquaintance will never do for me & yet I am going to Reynolds,[4] on Wednesday—Brown & Dilke[5] walked with me & back from the Christmas pantomime. I had not a dispute but a disquisition[6] with Dilke, on various subjects; several things dovetailed in my mind, & at once it struck me, what quality went to form a Man of Achievement especially in Literature & which Shakespeare possessed so enormously—I mean *Negative Capability*, that is when man is capable of being in uncertainties, Mysteries, doubts, without any irritable

---

[1] *Haydon* Painter Benjamin Haydon (1786–1846).

[2] *Horace Smith* Famous literary wit (1779–1849). The other men mentioned are all minor writers or literary critics.

[3] *Kean* Shakespearean actor Edmund Kean (1787–1833).

[4] *Reynolds* Lawyer and poet John Hamilton Reynolds (1796–1852).

[5] *Brown and Dilke* Writers Charles Wentworth Dilke (1789–1864) and Charles Armitage Brown (1786–1842), a close friend and housemate of Keats who cared for him after he first became ill and who later wrote his biography.

[6] *disquisition* Systematic investigation.

reaching after fact & reason—Coleridge, for instance, would let go by a fine isolated verisimilitude caught from the Penetralium[1] of mystery, from being incapable of remaining content with half knowledge. This pursued through Volumes would perhaps take us no further than this, that with a great poet the sense of Beauty overcomes every other consideration, or rather obliterates all consideration.

Shelley's poem[2] is out, & there are words about its being objected too, as much as Queen Mab was. Poor Shelley I think he has his Quota of good qualities, in sooth la!![3] Write soon to your most sincere friend & affectionate Brother.

John

To JOHN HAMILTON REYNOLDS
3 February 1818
Hampstead

My Dear Reynolds,

I thank you for your dish of Filberts[4]—Would I could get a basket of them by way of dessert every day for the sum of two pence—Would we were a sort of ethereal Pigs, & turn'd loose to feed upon spiritual Mast[5] & Acorns—which would be merely being a squirrel & feeding upon filberts. for what is a squirrel but an airy pig, or a filbert but a sort of archangelical acorn. About the nuts being worth cracking, all I can say is that where there are a throng of delightful Images ready drawn simplicity is the only thing. the first is the best on account of the first line, and the "arrow—foil'd of its antler'd food"[6]—and moreover (and this is the only word or two I find fault with, the more because I have had so much reason to shun it as a quicksand) the last

has "tender and true"—We must cut this, and not be rattle-snaked into any more of the like—It may be said that we ought to read our Contemporaries. that Wordsworth &c should have their due from us. but for the sake of a few fine imaginative or domestic passages, are we to be bullied into a certain Philosophy engendered in the whims of an Egotist—Every man has his speculations, but every man does not brood and peacock over them till he makes a false coinage and deceives himself—Many a man can travel to the very bourne[7] of Heaven, and yet want confidence to put down his halfseeing. Sancho[8] will invent a Journey heavenward as well as any body. We hate poetry that has a palpable design upon us—and if we do not agree, seems to put its hand in its breeches pocket.[9] Poetry should be great & unobtrusive, a thing which enters into one's soul, and does not startle it or amaze it with itself but with its subject.—How beautiful are the retired flowers! how would they lose their beauty were they to throng into the highway crying out, "admire me I am a violet! dote upon me I am a primrose!" Modern poets differ from the Elizabethans in this. Each of the moderns like an Elector of Hanover governs his petty state, & knows how many straws are swept daily from the Causeways in all his dominions & has a continual itching that all the Housewives should have their coppers well scoured: the antients were Emperors of vast Provinces, they had only heard of the remote ones and scarcely cared to visit them.—I will cut all this—I will have no more of Wordsworth or Hunt in particular—Why should we be of the tribe of Manasseh, when we can wander with Esau?[10] why should we kick against the Pricks, when we can walk on Roses? Why should we be owls, when we can be Eagles? Why be teased with "nice Eyed wagtails," when we have in sight "the Cherub Contemplation"?[11]—Why with Wordsworths "Matthew with a bough of wilding in his hand" when we can have

---

[1] *Penetralium* I.e., the innermost part. From the Latin *penetralia*, the innermost parts of a temple.

[2] *Shelley's poem* Shelley's *Laon and Cythna* (*The Revolt of Islam*), which he was forced to withdraw because readers objected to the poem's description of incestuous love between its hero and heroine.

[3] *in sooth la* In truth.

[4] *Filberts* Hazelnuts.

[5] *Mast* Fruit of certain woodland trees, such as beech, oak, and chestnut.

[6] *arrow ... food* Keats is commenting on Reynolds's "Sonnet on Robin Hood 1," which Reynolds had sent to Keats.

[7] *bourne* Realm.

[8] *Sancho* Sancho Panza, squire of the naive and idealistic Don Quixote in Miguel de Cervantes's *Don Quixote*.

[9] *put its ... pocket* I.e., refuse to fight (by putting one's fists away).

[10] *Why should ... Esau* In the Old Testament, the tribe of Manasseh lived according to the old way of life, while in Genesis 25 Esau sold his birthright and became an outlaw.

[11] *nice Eyed wagtails* From Leigh Hunt's *The Nymphs* 2.170; *the Cherub Contemplation* From Milton's *Il Penseroso* 54.

Jacques "under an oak &c"?[1]—The secret of the Bough of Wilding will run through your head faster than I can write it —Old Matthew spoke to him some years ago on some nothing, & because he happens in an Evening Walk to imagine the figure of the old man—he must stamp it down in black & white, and it is henceforth sacred—I don't mean to deny Wordsworth's grandeur & Hunt's merit, but I mean to say we need not be teazed with grandeur & merit—when we can have them uncontaminated & unobtrusive. Let us have the old Poets, & robin Hood Your letter and its sonnets gave me more pleasure than will the 4th Book of Childe Harold[2] & the whole of any body's life & opinions. In return for your dish of filberts, I have gathered a few Catkins, I hope they'll look pretty.[3]

Yr sincere friend and Coscribbler
John Keats

To John Taylor[4]
27 February 1818
Hampstead

My Dear Taylor,

Your alteration strikes me as being a great improvement —the page looks much better. And now I will attend to the Punctuations you speak of—the comma should be at *soberly,* and in the other passage the comma should follow *quiet.*[5] I am extremely indebted to you for this attention and also for your after admonitions—It is a sorry thing for me that any one should have to overcome Prejudices in reading my Verses—that affects me more than any hyper-criticism on any particular Passage. In *Endymion* I have most likely but moved into the Go-cart from the leading strings. In Poetry I have a few Axioms, and you will see how far I am from their Centre. 1st I think Poetry should surprise by a fine excess and not by Singularity—it should strike the Reader as a wording of his own highest thoughts, and appear almost a Remembrance—2nd Its touches of Beauty should never be half way thereby making the reader breathless instead of content: the rise, the progress, the setting of imagery should like the Sun come natural natural too him—shine over him and set soberly although in magnificence leaving him in the Luxury of twilight—but it is easier to think what Poetry should be than to write it—and this leads me on to another axiom. That if Poetry comes not as naturally as the Leaves to a tree it had better not come at all. However it may be with me I cannot help looking into new countries with "O for a Muse of fire to ascend!"[6]— If *Endymion* serves me as a Pioneer perhaps I ought to be content. I have great reason to be content, for thank God I can read and perhaps understand Shakespeare to his depths, and I have I am sure many friends, who, if I fail, will attribute any change in my Life and Temper to Humbleness rather than to Pride—to a cowering under the Wings of great Poets rather than to a Bitterness that I am not appreciated. I am anxious to get *Endymion* printed that I may forget it and proceed. I have copied the 3rd Book and have begun the 4th. On running my Eye over the Proofs—I saw one Mistake I will notice it presently and also any others if there be any—There should be no comma in "the raft branch down sweeping from a tall Ash top"[7]—I have besides made one or two alterations and also altered the 13 Line Page 32 to make sense of it as you will see. I will take care the Printer shall not trip up my Heels—There should be no dash after Dryope in this Line "Dryope's lone lulling of her Child."[8] Remember me to Percy Street.

Your sincere and oblig'd friend
John Keats—

P. S. You shall have a short *Preface* in good time—

[1] *Matthew … hand* From Wordsworth's *The Two April Mornings* 57–60; *under … etc* From Shakespeare's *As You Like It* 2.1.31.

[2] *4th … Harold* Canto 4 of Byron's *Childe Harold's Pilgrimage*, whose publication was eagerly anticipated at the time.

[3] *In return … pretty* In return for the sonnets on Robin Hood that Reynolds had sent, Keats enclosed two poems of his own, *Robin Hood* and *Lines on the Mermaid Tavern.*

[4] *John Taylor* Partner in the publishing firm of Taylor and Hessey, who were publishing Keats's poem *Endymion* at this time.

[5] *soberly … quiet* References to *Endymion* 1.149 and 1.247.

[6] *O for … ascend* Cf. Shakespeare, *Henry V* Prologue 1: "O for a Muse of fire, that would ascend / The brightest heaven of invention."

[7] *the raft … top* From *Endymion* 1.334–5.

[8] *Dryope's … Child* From *Endymion* lines 334–5.

To Benjamin Bailey
13 March 1818
Teignmouth

My dear Bailey,

... I have never had your Sermon[1] from Wordsworth but Mrs. Dilke lent it me—You know my ideas about Religion—I do not think myself more in the right than other people and that nothing in this world is proveable. I wish I could enter into all your feelings on the subject merely for one short 10 Minutes and give you a Page or two to your liking. I am sometimes so very sceptical as to think Poetry itself a mere Jack a lantern to amuse whoever may chance to be struck with its brilliance—As Tradesmen say every thing is worth what it will fetch, so probably every mental pursuit takes its reality and worth from the ardour of the pursuer—being in itself a nothing—Ethereal things may at least be thus real, divided under three heads—Things real—things semireal—and no things—Things real—such as existences of Sun Moon & Stars and passages of Shakespeare—Things semireal such as Love, the Clouds &c which require a greeting of the Spirit to make them wholly exist—and Nothings which are made Great and dignified by an ardent pursuit—Which by the by stamps the burgundy mark on the bottles of our Minds, insomuch as they are able to "*consecrate whate'er they look upon*"[2] I have written a Sonnet here of a somewhat collateral nature—so don't imagine it an a propos des bottes.[3]

[*The Human Seasons* is included here.]

Aye this may be carried—but what am I talking of—it is an old maxim of mine and of course must be well known that every point of thought is the centre of an intellectual world—the two uppermost thoughts in a Man's mind are the two poles of his World he revolves on them and every thing is southward or northward to him through their means—We take but three steps from feathers to iron. Now my dear fellow I must once for all tell you I have not one Idea of the truth of any of my speculations—I shall never be a Reasoner because I care not to be in the right, when retired from bickering and in a proper philosophical temper […] My Brother Tom desires to be remember'd to you—he has just this moment had a spitting of blood poor fellow —Remember me to [Gleig] and Whitehead—

Your affectionate friend
John Keats—

To Benjamin Bailey
18 July 1818

My dear Bailey,

... I am certain I have not a right feeling towards Women—at this moment I am striving to be just to them but I cannot—Is it because they fall so far beneath my Boyish imagination? When I was a Schoolboy I thought a fair Woman a pure Goddess, my mind was a soft nest in which some one of them slept though she knew it not—I have no right to expect more than their reality. I thought them ethereal above Men—I find them perhaps equal.... I do not like to think insults in a Lady's Company—I commit a Crime with her which absence would have not known—is it not extraordinary? When among Men I have no evil thoughts, no malice, no spleen[4]—I feel free to speak or to be silent—I can listen and from every one I can learn—my hands are in my pockets I am free from all suspicion and comfortable. When I am among Women I have evil thoughts, malice spleen—I cannot speak or be silent—I am full of Suspicions and therefore listen to no thing—I am in a hurry to be gone—You must be charitable and put all this perversity to my being disappointed since Boyhood—Yet with such feelings I am happier alone among Crowds of men, by myself or with a friend or two— With all this trust me Bailey I have not the least idea that Men of different feelings and inclinations are more short sighted than myself—I never rejoiced more than at my Brother's Marriage[5] and shall do so at that of any of my friends—. I must absolutely get over this—but how? The only way is to find the root of evil, and so

---

[1] *your Sermon*   Bailey, like many clergymen at the time, had written a memorial sermon for Princess Charlotte, who died in childbirth in 1817.

[2] *consecrate … upon*   From Percy Shelley's *Hymn to Intellectual Beauty* 13–14.

[3] *a propos des bottes*   French: on the subject of boots.

[4] *spleen*   Irritability; ill-humor; melancholy.

[5] *my Brother's Marriage*   Keats's brother George had recently married, as had Bailey.

cure it "with backward mutters of dissevering Power."[1] That is a difficult thing; for an obstinate Prejudice can seldom be produced but from a gordian complication[2] of feelings, which must take time to unravell and care to keep unravelled—I could say a good deal about this but I will leave it in hopes of better and more worthy dispositions—and also content that I am wronging no one, for after all I do think better of Womankind than to suppose they care whether Mister John Keats five feet high likes them or not....

Your affectionate friend
John Keats—

To Richard Woodhouse[3]

27 October 1818

My Dear Woodhouse,

Your Letter gave me a great satisfaction; more on account of its friendliness, than any relish of that matter in it which is accounted so acceptable in the "genus irritabile."[4] The best answer I can give you is in a clerklike manner to make some observations on two principle points, which seem to point like indices into the midst of the whole pro and con, about genius, and views and achievements and ambition and coetera.[5] 1st As to the poetical Character itself, (I mean that sort of which, if I am any thing, I am a Member; that sort distinguished from the wordsworthian or egotistical sublime; which is a thing per se and stands alone) it is not itself—it has no self—it is every thing and nothing—It has no character—it enjoys light and shade; it lives in gusto, be it foul or fair, high or low, rich or poor, mean or elevated—It has as much delight in

conceiving an Iago as an Imogen.[6] What shocks the virtuous philosopher delights the chameleon Poet. It does no harm from its relish of the dark side of things any more than from its taste for the bright one; because they both end in speculation. A Poet is the most unpoetical of any thing in existence; because he has no Identity—he is continually in for—and filling some other Body—The Sun, the Moon, the Sea and Men and Women who are creatures of impulse are poetical and have about them an unchangeable attribute—the poet has none; no identity—he is certainly the most unpoetical of all God's Creatures. If then he has no self, and if I am a Poet, where is the Wonder that I should say I would write no more? Might I not at that very instant [have] been cogitating on the Characters of saturn and Ops?[7] It is a. wretched thing to confess; but is a very fact that not one word I ever utter can be taken for granted as an opinion growing out of my identical nature—how can it, when I have no nature? When I am in a room with People if I ever am free from speculating on creations of my own brain, then not myself goes home to myself: but the identity of every one in the room begins [so] to press upon me that, I am in a very little time annihilated—not only among Men; it would be the same in a Nursery of children: I know not whether I make myself wholly understood: I hope enough so to let you see that no dependence is to be placed on what I said that day.[8]

In the second place I will speak of my views, and of the life I purpose to myself—I am ambitious of doing the world some good: if I should be spared that may be the work of maturer years—in the interval I will assay to reach to as high a summit in Poetry as the nerve bestowed upon me will suffer. The faint conceptions I have of Poems to come brings the blood frequently into my forehead—All I hope is that I may not lose all interest in human affairs—that the solitary indifference I feel for applause even from the finest Spirits, will not blunt any acuteness of vision I may have. I do not think

---

[1] with ... Power From Milton's Comus 816–17, in which the author describes the spells that will release a lady from the enchantment of Comus.

[2] gordian complication I.e., as difficult to undo as the intricate knot tied by King Gordias.

[3] Richard Woodhouse Young lawyer who worked with Keats's publishers. Woodhouse was struck by Keats's talent and preserved manuscript copies of many of his poems and letters.

[4] genus irritabile Latin: irritable tribe. The phrase, in reference to poets, was coined by the Roman poet Horace in his Epistles 2.2.102.

[5] coetera Latin: the following; the next.

[6] Iago Villain of Shakespeare's Othello; Imogen Heroine of Shakespeare's Cymbeline.

[7] saturn In Greek mythology, king of the Titan gods, who were overthrown by their children, the Olympians. The Titans figure prominently in Keats's Hyperion; Ops Titan goddess of the harvest.

[8] what I ... day Keats had told Woodhouse that he felt preempted by great poets of the past.

it will—I feel assured I should write from the mere yearning and fondness I have for the Beautiful even if my night's labours should be burnt every morning and no eye ever shine upon them. But even now I am perhaps not speaking from myself; but from some character in whose soul I now live. I am sure however that this next sentence is from myself. I feel your anxiety, good opinion and friendliness in the highest degree, and am

Yours most sincerely
John Keats

To George and Georgiana Keats[1]
14 February – 3 May 1819

My dear Brother & Sister—
… [19 March] Yesterday I got a black eye—the first time I took a Cricket bat—Brown who is always one's friend in a disaster applied a leech to the eyelid, and there is no inflammation this morning though the ball hit me directly on the sight—'t was a white ball—I am glad it was not a clout—This is the second black eye I have had since leaving school—during all my school days I never had one at all—we must eat a peck before we die[2]—This morning I am in a sort of temper indolent and supremely careless: I long after a stanza or two of Thomson's *Castle of indolence*[3]—My passions are all asleep from my having slumbered till nearly eleven and weakened the animal fibre all over me to a delightful sensation about three degrees on this side of faintness—if I had teeth of pearl and the breath of lilies I should call it langour—but as I am[4] I must call it Laziness—In this state of effeminacy the fibres of the brain are relaxed in common with the rest of the body, and to such a happy degree that pleasure has no show of enticement and pain no unbearable frown. Neither Poetry, nor Ambition, nor Love have any alertness of countenance as they pass by me: they seem rather like three figures on a greek vase—a Man and two women—whom no one but myself could distinguish in their disguisement. This is the only happiness; and is a rare instance of advantage in the body overpowering the Mind. I have this moment received a note from Haslam[5] in which he expects the death of his Father who has been for some time in a state of insensibility—his mother bears up he says very well—I shall go to [town] tomorrow to see him. This is the world—thus we cannot expect to give way many hours to pleasure—Circumstances are like Clouds continually gathering and bursting—While we are laughing the seed of some trouble is put into the wide arable land of events—while we are laughing it sprouts [it] grows and suddenly bears a poison fruit which we must pluck—Even so we have leisure to reason on the misfortunes of our friends; our own touch us too nearly for words. Very few men have ever arrived at a complete disinterestedness[6] of Mind: very few have been influenced by a pure desire of the benefit of others—in the greater part of the Benefactors of & to Humanity some meretricious motive has sullied their greatness—some melodramatic scenery has fascinated them—From the manner in which I feel Haslam's misfortune I perceive how far I am from any humble standard of disinterestedness—Yet this feeling ought to be carried to its highest pitch, as there is no fear of its ever injuring society—which it would do I fear pushed to an extremity—For in wild nature the Hawk would loose his Breakfast of Robins and the Robin his of Worms The Lion must starve as well as the swallow—The greater part of Men make their way with the same instinctiveness, the same unwandering eye from their purposes, the same animal eagerness as the Hawk—The Hawk wants a Mate, so does the Man—look at them both they set about it and procure one in the same manner—They want both a nest and they both set about one in the same manner—they get their food in the same manner—The noble animal Man for his amusement smokes his pipe—the Hawk balances about the Clouds—that is the only difference of their leisures. This it is that makes the Amusement of Life—to a speculative Mind. I go among

---

[1] *George and Georgiana Keats* Keats's brother and sister-in-law, who had emigrated to America. Keats would compose long letters to them, each of which spanned several months, and in which he would include transcriptions of his poems.

[2] *eat a peck … die* Proverbial: everyone must eat a peck of dirt before he or she dies.

[3] *Thomson … indolence* James Thomson's *The Castle of Indolence*, in which a wizard named Indolence puts a spell of indolence on tired travelers who are lured into his castle.

[4] [Keats's note] Especially as I have a black eye.

[5] *Haslam* Keats's friend William Haslam, a businessman.

[6] *disinterestedness* State unmotivated by self-interest.

the Fields and catch a glimpse of a stoat[1] or a fieldmouse peeping out of the withered grass—the creature hath a purpose and its eyes are bright with it—I go amongst the buildings of a city and I see a Man hurrying along—to what? The Creature has a purpose and his eyes are bright with it. But then as Wordsworth says, "we have all one human heart"[2]— there is an electric fire in human nature tending to purify—so that among these human creatures there is continually some birth of new heroism—The pity is that we must wonder at it: as we should at finding a pearl in rubbish—I have no doubt that thousands of people never heard of have had hearts completely disinterested: I can remember but two—Socrates and Jesus—their Histories evince it—What I heard a little time ago, Taylor observe with respect to Socrates, may be said of Jesus—That he was so great as man that though he transmitted no writing of his own to posterity, we have his Mind and his sayings and his greatness handed to us by others. It is to be lamented that the history of the latter was written and revised by Men interested in the pious frauds of Religion. Yet through all this I see his splendour. Even here though I myself am pursuing the same instinctive course as the veriest human animal you can think of—I am however young writing at random—straining at particles of light in the midst of a great darkness—without knowing the bearing of any one assertion of any one opinion. Yet may I not in this be free from sin? May there not be superior beings amused with any graceful, though instinctive attitude my mind my fall into, as I entertained with the alertness of a Stoat or the anxiety of a Deer? Though a quarrel in the streets is a thing to be hated, the energies displayed in it are fine; the commonest Man shows a grace in his quarrel—By a superior being our reasoning may take the same tone—though erroneous they may be fine—This is the very thing in which consists poetry; and if so it is not so fine a thing as philosophy—For the same reason that an eagle is not so fine a thing as a truth—Give me this credit—Do you not think I strive—to know myself? Give me this credit— and you will not think that on my own account I repeat Milton's lines

How charming is divine Philosophy

Not harsh and crabbed as dull fools suppose
But musical as is Apollo's lute—[3]

No—no for myself—feeling grateful as I do to have got into a state of mind to relish them properly—Nothing ever becomes real till it is experienced—Even a Proverb is no proverb to you till your Life has illustrated it— …

[21 April] I have been reading lately two very different books Robertson's *America* and Voltaire's *Siecle De Louis xiv* It is like walking arm and arm between Pizzarro and the great-little Monarch.[4] In How lamentable a case do we see the great body of the people in both instances: in the first, where Men might seem to inherit quiet of Mind from unsophisticated sense; from uncontamination of civilisation; and especially from their being as it were estranged from the mutual helps of Society and its mutual injuries—and thereby more immediately under the Protection of Providence—even there they had mortal pains to bear as bad; or even worse than Baliffs, Debts and Poverties of civilised Life—The whole appears to resolve into this—that Man is originally "a poor forked creature"[5] subject to the same mischances as the beasts of the forest, destined to hardships and disquietude of some kind or other. If he improves by degrees his bodily accommodations and comforts—at each stage, at each accent there are waiting for him a fresh set of annoyances—he is mortal and there is still a heaven with its Stars above his head. The most interesting question that can come before us is, How far by the persevering endeavours of a seldom appearing Socrates Mankind may be made happy—I can imagine such happiness carried to an extreme—but what must it end in?—Death—and who could in such a case bear with death—the whole troubles of life which are now frittered away in a series of years, would then be accumulated for the last days of a being who instead of hailing

---

[1] *stoat* Weasel-like creature.

[2] *we have … heart* From *The Old Cumberland Beggar* 152–53.

[3] *How charming … lute* Milton's *Comus* 475–77.

[4] *Robertson's … Monarch* William Robertson's *History of the Discovery and Settlement of America* (1777) describes the Spanish conquistadors, including Francisco Pizarro, who conquered the Incas in the sixteenth century. French philosopher Voltaire's *Le Siècle de Louis XIV* (1751) describes the rule of Louis XIV, who was often called "The Great Monarch."

[5] *a poor forked creature* From *King Lear* 3.4.112–13, in which Lear looks at "Poor Tom" and says "Unaccommodated man is no more but such a poor, bare, forked animal as though art."

its approach, would leave this world as Eve left Paradise—But in truth I do not at all believe in this sort of perfectibility—the nature of the world will not admit of it—the inhabitants of the world will correspond to itself—Let the fish philosophise the ice away from the Rivers in winter time and they shall be at continual play in the tepid delight of summer. Look at the Poles and at the sands of Africa, Whirlpools and volcanoes—Let men exterminate them and I will say that they may arrive at earthly Happiness—The point at which Man may arrive is as far as the parallel state in inanimate nature and no further—For instance suppose a rose to have sensation, it blooms on a beautiful morning it enjoys itself—but there comes a cold wind, a hot sun—it can not escape it, it cannot destroy its annoyances—they are as native to the world as itself: no more can man be happy in spite, the worldly elements will prey upon his nature—The common cognomen of this world among the misguided and superstitious is "a vale of tears" from which we are to be redeemed by a certain arbitrary interposition of God and taken to Heaven—What a little circumscribed straightened notion! Call the world if you Please "The vale of Soul-making" Then you will find out the use of the world (I am speaking now in the highest terms for human nature admitting it to be immortal which I will here take for granted for the purpose of showing a thought which has struck me concerning it) I say "*Soul making*" Soul as distinguished from an Intelligence—There may be intelligences or sparks of the divinity in millions—but they are not Souls till they acquire identities, till each one is personally itself. Intelligences are atoms of perception—they know and they see and they are pure, in short they are God—how then are Souls to be made? How then are these sparks which are God to have identity given them—so as ever to possess a bliss peculiar to each ones individual existence? How, but by the medium of a world like this? This point I sincerely wish to consider because I think it a grander system of salvation than the christian religion—or rather it is a system of Spirit-creation —This is effected by three grand materials acting the one upon the other for a series of years—These three Materials are the *Intelligence*—the *human heart* (as distinguished from intelligence or Mind) and the *World* or *Elemental space* suited for the proper action of *Mind and Heart* on each other for the purpose of forming the

Soul or Intelligence destined to possess the sense of Identity. I can scarcely express what I but dimly perceive—and yet I think I perceive it—that you may judge the more clearly I will put it in the most homely form possible—I will call the world a School instituted for the purpose of teaching little children to read—I will call the *human heart* the *horn Book*[1] used in that School—and I will call the *Child able to read, the Soul* made from that *school* and its *hornbook*. Do you not see how necessary a World of Pains and troubles is to school an Intelligence and make it a soul? A Place where the heart must feel and suffer in a thousand diverse ways! Not merely is the Heart a Hornbook, It is the Minds Bible, it is the Minds experience, it is the teat from which the Mind or intelligence sucks its identity—As various as the Lives of Men are—so various become their souls, and thus does God make individual beings, Souls, Identical Souls of the sparks of his own essence—This appears to me a faint sketch of a system of Salvation which does not affront our reason and humanity—I am convinced that many difficulties which christians labour under would vanish before it—there is one which even now Strikes me—the Salvation of Children—In them the Spark or intelligence returns to God without any identity—it having had no time to learn of, and be altered by, the heart—or seat of the human Passions—It is pretty generally suspected that the christian scheme has been copied from the ancient persian and greek Philosophers. Why may they not have made this simple thing even more simple for common apprehension by introducing Mediators and Personages in the same manner as in the heathen mythology abstractions are personified— Seriously I think it probable that this System of Soulmaking—may have been the Parent of all the more palpable and personal Schemes of Redemption, among the Zoroastrians the Christians and the Hindus. For as one part of the human species must have their carved Jupiter; so another part must have the palpable and named Mediatior and saviour, their Christ their Oromanes and their Vishnu[2]—If what I have said should not be plain enough, as I fear it may not be, I will but

---

[1] *horn Book* Child's primer, originally made of a sheet of paper mounted on wood and protected by a thin sheet of transparent horn.

[2] *Oromanes* Ahriman, the chief evil spirit in Zoroastrianism, who is locked in perpetual struggle with Ahura Mazda; *Vishnu* Hindu deity who protects and preserves the world.

[put] you in the place where I began in this series of thoughts—I mean, I began by seeing how man was formed by circumstances—and what are circumstances?—but touchstones of his heart?—and what are touchstones?—but provings of his heart? and what are provings of his heart but fortifiers or alterers of his nature? and what is his altered nature but his soul?—and what was his soul before it came into the world and had These provings and alterations and perfectionings?—An intelligence—without Identity—and how is this Identity to be made? Through the medium of the Heart? And how is the heart to become this Medium but in a world of Circumstances?—There now I think what with Poetry and Theology you may thank your Stars that my pen is not very long winded— …

… this is the 3ᵈ of May & every thing is in delightful forwardness; the violets are not withered, before the peeping of the first rose; You must let me know every thing, how parcels go &. come, what papers you have, &. what Newspapers you want, & other things—God bless you my dear Brother & Sister

Your ever Affectionate Brother
John Keats—

To Fanny Brawne[1]

25 July 1819
Sunday Night
Isle of Wight

My Sweet Girl,

I hope you did not blame me much for not obeying your request of a Letter on Saturday: we have had four in our small room playing at cards night and morning leaving me no undisturb'd opportunity to write. Now Rice and Martin are gone I am at liberty. Brown to my sorrow confirms the account you give of your ill health. You cannot conceive how I ache to be with you: how I would die for one hour—for what is in the world? I say you cannot conceive; it is impossible you should look with such eyes upon me as I have upon you: it cannot be. Forgive me if I wander a little this evening, for I have been all day employ'd in a very abstract Poem[2] and I am in deep love with you—two things which must excuse me. I have, believe me, not been an age in letting you take possession of me; the very first week I knew you I wrote myself your vassal; but burnt the Letter as the very next time I saw you I thought you manifested some dislike to me. If you should ever feel for Man at the first sight what I did for you, I am lost. Yet I should not quarrel with you, but hate myself if such a thing were to happen—only I should burst if the thing were not as fine as a Man as you are as a Woman. Perhaps I am too vehement, then fancy me on my knees, especially when I mention a part of your Letter which hurt me; you say speaking of Mr. Severn[3] "but you must be satisfied in knowing that I admired you much more than your friend." My dear love, I cannot believe there ever was or ever could be any thing to admire in me especially as far as sight goes—I cannot be admired, I am not a thing to be admired. You are, I love you; all I can bring you is a swooning admiration of your Beauty. I hold that place among Men which snubnos'd brunettes with meeting eyebrows do among women—they are trash to me—unless I should find one among them with a fire in her heart like the one that burns in mine. You absorb me in spite of myself—you alone: for I look not forward with any pleasure to what is call'd being settled in the world; I tremble at domestic cares—yet for you I would meet them, though if it would leave you the happier I would rather die than do so. I have two luxuries to brood over in my walks, your Loveliness and the hour of my death. O that I could have possession of them both in the same minute. I hate the world: it batters too much the wings of my self-will, and would I could take a sweet poison from your lips to send me out of it. From no others would I take it. I am indeed astonish'd to find myself so careless of all charms but yours—remembering as I do the time when even a bit of ribband was a matter of interest with me. What softer words can I find for you after this—what it is I will not read. Nor will I say more here, but in a Postscript answer any thing else you may

[1] *Fanny Brawne* Young woman whom Keats met in the summer of 1818, and to whom he was engaged by the end of the year (though the couple was waiting to marry until Keats felt he was financially secure). From October to May 1819 Keats stayed in his friend Charles Brown's apartment in Hampstead, which was next door to the Brawnes, who took care of him throughout the summer.

[2] *very abstract Poem* Most likely *The Fall of Hyperion*.

[3] *Mr. Severn* Joseph Severn, an artist and a friend of Keats. He cared for Keats during his final illness in Rome and was present when he died.

have mentioned in your Letter in so many words—for I am distracted with a thousand thoughts. I will imagine you Venus tonight and pray, pray, pray to your star like a Heathen.

Yours ever, fair Star,
John Keats

To PERCY BYSSHE SHELLEY [1]
16 August 1820
Hampstead

My Dear Shelley,

I am very much gratified that you, in a foreign country, and with a mind almost over occupied, should write to me in the strain of the Letter beside me. If I do not take advantage of your invitation it will be prevented by a circumstance I have very much at heart to prophesy—There is no doubt that an english winter would put an end to me, and do so in a lingering hateful manner, therefore I must either voyage or journey to Italy as a soldier marches up to a battery. My nerves at present are the worst part of me, yet they feel soothed when I think that come what extreme may, I shall not be destined to remain in one spot long enough to take a hatred of any four particular bedposts. I am glad you take any pleasure in my poor Poem;[2]—which I would willingly take the trouble to unwrite, if possible, did I care so much as I have done about Reputation. I received a copy of the Cenci,[3] as from yourself from Hunt. There is only one part of it I am judge of; the Poetry, and dramatic effect, which by many spirits now a days is considered the mammon.[4] A modern work it is said must have a purpose, which may be the God—*an artist* must serve Mammon—he must have "self concentration" selfishness perhaps. You I am sure will forgive me for sincerely remarking that you might curb your magnanimity and be more of an artist, and "load every

rift" of your subject with ore.[5] The thought of such discipline must fall like cold chains upon you, who perhaps never sat with your wings furl'd for six Months together. And is not this extraordinary talk for the writer of *Endymion*? whose mind was like a pack of scattered cards—I am pick'd up and sorted to a pip.[6] My Imagination is a Monastry and I am its Monk—you must explain my [metaphysics] to yourself. I am in expectation of *Prometheus*[7] every day. Could I have my own wish for its interest effected you would have it still in manuscript—or be but now putting an end to the second act. I remember you advising me not to publish my first-blights, on Hampstead heath—I am returning advice upon your hands. Most of the Poems in the volume I send you[8] have been written above two years, and would never have been publish'd but from a hope of gain; so you see I am inclined enough to take your advice now. I must express once more my deep sense of your kindness, adding my sincere thanks and respects for Mrs. Shelley. In the hope of soon seeing you I remain

most sincerely yours,
John Keats—

To CHARLES BROWN
30 November 1820
Rome

My Dear Brown,

'Tis the most difficult thing in the world to me to write a letter. My stomach continues so bad, that I feel it worse on opening any book,—yet I am much better than I was in Quarantine.[9] Then I am afraid to encounter the proing and conning of any thing interest-

---

[1] *To … Shelley* This letter is written in response to one from Shelley, in which he, having learned of Keats's serious illness, invites Keats to stay with him in Pisa for the winter.

[2] *my poor Poem* Keats's *Endymion*, which had received several negative reviews but which Shelley had praised in his letter.

[3] *Cenci* Shelley's blank-verse tragedy (1820).

[4] *mammon* Wealth and profit, regarded as a false god. Cf. Matthew 6.24, in which Jesus says, "Ye cannot serve God and Mammon."

[5] *load … ore* Reference to Spenser's *Faerie Queene* 2.7.28, in which he describes the Palace of Mammon: "Embost with massy gold of glorious gift, / And with rich metal loaded every rift."

[6] *sorted to a pip* Put in order. Pips are the markings on playing cards.

[7] *Prometheus* Shelley's *Prometheus Unbound* (1820), a copy of which he had promised to send to Keats.

[8] *the volume … you* Keats's 1820 volume, which Shelley had in his pocket when he drowned.

[9] *in Quarantine* Keats's ship was quarantined for ten days outside Naples, in extremely hot weather. Keats was writing this letter from Rome, where he was being cared for by Joseph Severn.

ing to me in England. I have an habitual feeling of my real life having past, and that I am leading a posthumous existence. God knows how it would have been—but it appears to me—however, I will not speak of that subject. I must have been at Bedhampton nearly at the time you were writing to me from Chichester—how unfortunate—and to pass on the river too! There was my star predominant! I cannot answer any thing in your letter, which followed me from Naples to Rome, because I am afraid to look it over again. I am so weak (in mind) that I cannot bear the sight of any hand writing of a friend I love so much as I do you. Yet I ride the little horse,[1]—and, at my worst, even in Quarantine, summoned up more puns, in a sort of desperation, in one week than in any year of my life. There is one thought enough to kill me—I have been well, healthy, alert &c, walking with her[2]—and now—the knowledge of contrast, feeling for light and shade, all that information (primitive sense) necessary for a poem are great enemies to the recovery of the stomach. There, you rogue, I put you to the torture,—but you must bring your philosophy to bear—as I do mine, really—or how should I be able to live? Dr Clarke is very attentive to me; he says, there is very little the matter with my lungs, but my stomach, he says, is very bad. I am well disappointed in hearing good news from George,—for it runs in my head we shall all die young. I have not written to * * * *[3] yet, which he must think very neglectful; being anxious to send him a good account of my health, I have delayed it from week to week. If I recover, I will do all in my power to correct the mistakes made during sickness; and if I should not, all my faults will be forgiven. I shall write to * * * * tomorrow, or next day. I will write to * * * * in the middle of next week. Severn is very well, though he leads so dull a life with me. Remember me to all friends, and tell * * * * I should not have left London without taking leave of him, but from being so low in body and mind. Write to George as soon as you receive this, and tell him how I am, as far as you can guess; and also a note to my sister—who walks about my imagination like a ghost—she is so like Tom.[4] I can scarcely bid you good bye even in a letter. I always made an awkward bow.

God bless you!

John Keats.

———————————

In Context

Politics, Poetry, and the "Cockney School Debate"

As literary journals and magazines of the time demonstrate, in the nineteenth century politics and literary theory were often inextricably intertwined. At the time, only a small minority of adult males had been granted the vote, and the political system was widely perceived to be corrupt. Leigh Hunt, John Keats, William Hazlitt, and Percy Bysshe Shelley were among those who pressed strongly for political reform. Leigh Hunt, with his brothers John and Robert, edited the *Examiner*, a liberal weekly journal that frequently riled the government. After offending the Prince of Wales, Leigh and John spent two years in prison (1813–15) for libel.

In August 1817 the *Edinburgh Review* began to refer to Wordsworth, Coleridge, and Robert Southey as "The Lake School"—all three had lived in and been inspired by England's Lake District. Those poets and some others—Lord Byron in particular—had been identified

---

[1] *Yet ... horse* Recommended by Keats's doctor for exercise.

[2] *her* Fanny Brawne.

[3] * * * * Brown, whose transcription of this letter is the only surviving copy, deleted the names of Keats's friends in order to conceal their identities.

[4] *my sister ... Tom* Keats's sister Fanny closely resembled his youngest brother Tom, who had died of tuberculosis in December 1818.

the previous year by Leigh Hunt as representative of a school of poets "who go directly to Nature for inspiration." Hunt had written his article "Young Poets" to bring to the attention of the public "three young writers [Shelley, Keats, and John Hamilton Reynolds] who appear to us to promise a considerable addition of strength to the new school." Hunt had not named himself as a member of this new group, but it was on him that John Gibson Lockhart focused in launching an attack on the group that was as much political as literary. Lockhart's series of articles on "The Cockney School of Poetry" appeared in *Blackwood's Edinburgh Magazine*, a conservative journal founded in response to the *Edinburgh Review*.

from Leigh Hunt, "Young Poets" (*Examiner*, 1 December 1816)

In sitting down to this subject, we happen to be restricted by time to a much shorter notice than we could wish: but we mean to take it up again shortly. Many of our readers however have perhaps observed for themselves, that there has been a new school of poetry rising of late, which promises to extinguish the French one that has prevailed among us since the time of Charles the 2d. It began with something excessive, like most revolutions, but this gradually wore away; and an evident aspiration after real nature and original fancy remained, which called to mind the finer times of the English Muse. In fact it is wrong to call it a new school, and still more so to represent it as one of innovation, its only object being to restore the same love of Nature, and of *thinking* instead of mere *talking*, which formerly rendered us real poets, and not merely versifying wits, and bead-rollers of couplets.

We were delighted to see the departure of the old school acknowledged in the number of the *Edinburgh Review* just published—a candour the more generous and spirited, inasmuch as that work has hitherto been the greatest surviving ornament of the same school in prose and criticism, as it is now destined, we trust, to be still the leader in the new.

We also felt the same delight at the third canto of Lord Byron's *Childe Harold*, in which, to our conceptions at least, he has fairly renounced a certain leaven of the French style, and taken his place where we always said he would be found—among the poets who have a real feeling for numbers,[1] and who go directly to Nature for inspiration. But more of this poem in our next.

The object of the present article is merely to notice three young writers, who appear to us to promise a considerable addition of strength to the new school. Of the first who came before us, we have, it is true, yet seen only one or two specimens, and these were no sooner sent us than we unfortunately mislaid them; but we shall procure what he has published, and if the rest answer to what we have seen, we shall have no hesitation in announcing him for a very striking and original thinker. His name is Percy Bysshe Shelley, and he is the author of a poetical work entitled *Alastor, or the Spirit of Solitude*.

The next with whose name we became acquainted was John Henry Reynolds, author of a tale called *Safie*, written, we believe, in imitation of Lord Byron, and more lately of a small set of poems published by Taylor and Hessey, the principal of which is called the *Naiad*. It opens thus:

> The gold sun went into the west,
> And soft airs sang him to his rest;
> And yellow leaves all loose and dry,
> Play'd on the branches listlessly:
> The sky wax'd palely blue, and high
> A cloud seem'd touch'd upon the sky—

---

[1]   *numbers*   I.e., metrical harmony, rhythm.

A spot of cloud—blue, thin, and still,
And silence bask'd on vale and hill. ...

We shall give another extract or two in a future number. The author's style is too artificial, though he is evidently an admirer of Mr. Wordsworth. Like all young poets too, properly so called, his love of detail is too overwrought and indiscriminate; but still he is a young poet, and only wants a still closer attention to things as opposed to the seduction of words, to realize all that he promises. His nature seems very true and amiable.

The last of these young aspirants who we have met with, and who promise to help the new school to revive Nature and

"To put a spirit of youth in every thing,"

is, we believe, the youngest of them all, and just of age. His name is John Keats. He has not yet published anything except in a newspaper; but a set of his manuscripts was handed us the other day, and fairly surprised us with the truth of their ambition, and ardent grappling with Nature. In the following sonnet there is one incorrect rhyme, which might be easily altered, but which shall serve in the mean time as a peace-offering to the rhyming critics. The rest of the composition, with the exception of a little vagueness in calling the regions of poetry "the realms of gold," we do not hesitate to pronounce excellent, especially the last six lines. The word *swims* is complete; and the whole conclusion is equally powerful and quiet

[Quotes "On First Looking Into Chapman's Homer"]

We have spoken with the less scruple of these poetical promises, because we really are not in the habit of lavishing praises and announcements, and because we have no fear of any pettier vanity on the part of young men who promise to understand human nature so well.

from John Lockhart ("Z."),"On the Cockney School of Poetry, No. 1" (*Blackwood's Edinburgh Magazine*, October 1817)

Our talk shall be (a theme we never tire on)
Of Chaucer, Spenser, Shakespeare, Milton, Byron,
(Our England's Dante)—Wordsworth—Hunt, and Keats,
The Muses' son of promise; and of what feats
He yet may do.
             —CORNELIUS WEBB

While the whole critical world is occupied with balancing the merits, whether in theory or in execution, of what is commonly called The Lake School, it is strange that no one seems to think it at all necessary to say a single word about another new school of poetry which has of late sprung up amongst us. This school has not, I believe, as yet received any name; but if I may be permitted to have the honour of christening it, it may henceforth be referred to by the designation of The Cockney School. Its chief Doctor and Professor is Mr. Leigh Hunt, a man certainly of some talents, of extravagant pretensions both in wit, poetry, and politics, and withal of exquisitely bad taste, and extremely vulgar modes of thinking and manners in all respects. He is a man of little education. He knows absolutely nothing of Greek, almost nothing of Latin, and his knowledge of Italian literature is confined to a few of the most popular of Petrarch's sonnets, and an imperfect acquaintance with Ariosto, through the medium of Mr. Hoole. As to the French poets, he dismisses them in the mass as a set of prim, precise, unnatural pretenders. The truth is, he is in a state of happy ignorance about them and all that they have done. …

With this stock of knowledge, Mr. Hunt presumes to become the founder of a new school of poetry, and throws away entirely the chance he might have had of gaining some true poetic fame, had he been less lofty in his pretensions. …

All the great poets of our country have been men of some rank in society, and there is no vulgarity in any of their writings; but Mr. Hunt cannot utter a dedication, or even a note, without betraying the *Shibboleth*[1] of low birth and low habits. He is the ideal of a Cockney Poet. He raves perpetually about "green fields," "jaunty streams," and "o'er-arching leafiness," exactly as a Cheapside shop-keeper does about the beauties of his box[2] on the Camberwell road. Mr. Hunt is altogether unacquainted with the face of nature in her magnificent scenes; he has never seen any mountain higher than Highgate-hill,[3] nor reclined by any stream more pastoral than the Serpentine River.[4] But he is determined to be a poet eminently rural, and he rings the changes—till one is sick of him, on the beauties of the different "high views" which he has taken of God and nature, in the course of some Sunday dinner parties, at which he has assisted in the neighbourhood of London. His books are indeed not known in the country; his fame as a poet (and I might almost say, as a politician too) is entirely confined to the young attorneys and embryo-barristers about town. In the opinion of these competent judges, London is the world—and Hunt is a Homer.

Mr. Hunt is not disqualified by his ignorance and vulgarity alone, for being the founder of a respectable sect in poetry. He labours under the burden of a sin more deadly than either of these. The two great elements of all dignified poetry, religious feeling and patriotic feeling, have no place in his writings. His religion is a poor tame dilution of the blasphemies of the *Encyclopaedie*[5]—his patriotism a crude, vague, ineffectual, and sour Jacobinism.[6] His works exhibit no reverence either for God or man; neither altar nor throne have any dignity in his eyes. He speaks well of nobody but two or three great dead poets, and in so speaking of them he does well; but alas! Mr. Hunt is no conjurer τεχνη ὅ λανθανει.[7] He pretends, indeed, to be an admirer of Spenser and Chaucer, but what he praises in them is never what is most deserving of praise—it is only that which he humbly conceives bears some resemblance to the more perfect productions of Mr. Leigh Hunt; and we can always discover in the midst of his most violent ravings about the Court of Elizabeth, and the days of Sir Philip Sidney, and the Fairy Queen, that the real objects of his admiration are the Coterie of Hampstead and the Editor of the Examiner. When he talks about chivalry and King Arthur, he is always thinking of himself, and "*a small party of friends, who meet once a week at a Round Table, to discuss the merits of a leg of mutton, and of the subjects upon which we are to write.*"[8]—Mr. Leigh Hunt's ideas concerning the sublime, and concerning his own powers, bear a considerable resemblance to those of his friend Bottom, the

---

[1]   *Shibboleth*   Word distinguishing a certain class or party.

[2]   *box*   Boxwood.

[3]   *Highgate-hill*   Hill (and district) in the north of London.

[4]   *Serpentine River*   Lake in Hyde Park, in the center of London.

[5]   *Encylopaedie*   Great manifesto of the French *philosophes*, prepared by Denis Diderot and Jean le Rond d'Alembert (1751).

[6]   *Jacobinism*   Extreme democratic principles; belief in complete equality (after the practice of the French political sect the Jacobins).

[7]   τεχνη ὅ λανθανει   Greek: his technique does not escape notice.

[8]   *a small … write*   From a feature in the *Examiner*, initiated by Leigh Hunt, called "The Round Table."

weaver, on the same subjects; "I will roar, that it shall do any man's heart good to hear me."—"I will roar you an 'twere any nightingale."[1]

The poetry of Mr. Hunt is such as might be expected from the personal character and habits of its author. As a vulgar man is perpetually labouring to be genteel—in like manner, the poetry of this man is always on the stretch to be grand. He has been allowed to look for a moment from the antechamber into the salon, and mistaken the waving of feathers and the painted floor for the *sine qua non*'s[2] of elegant society. He would fain be always tripping and waltzing, and is sorry that he cannot be allowed to walk about in the morning with yellow breeches and flesh-coloured silk-stockings. He sticks an artificial rosebud into his button hole in the midst of winter. ...

How such an indelicate writer as Mr. Hunt can pretend to be an admirer of Mr. Wordsworth, is to us a thing altogether inexplicable. One great charm of Wordsworth's noble compositions consists in the dignified purity of thought, and the patriarchal simplicity of feeling, with which they are throughout penetrated and imbued. We can conceive a vicious[3] man admiring with distant awe the spectacle of virtue and purity; but if he does so sincerely, he must also do so with the profoundest feeling of the error of his own ways, and the resolution to amend them. His admiration must be humble and silent, not pert and loquacious. Mr. Hunt praises the purity of Wordsworth as if he himself were pure, his dignity as if he also were dignified. ...

The founder of the Cockney School would fain claim poetical kindred with Lord Byron and Thomas Moore.[4] Such a connection would be as unsuitable for them as for William Wordsworth. The days of Mr. Moore's follies are long since over; and, as he is a thorough gentleman, he must necessarily entertain the greatest contempt for such an under-bred person as Mr. Leigh Hunt. But Lord Byron! ... We dare say Mr. Hunt has some fine dreams about the true nobility being the nobility of talent, and flatters himself, that with those who acknowledge only that sort of rank, he himself passes for being the *peer* of Byron. He is sadly mistaken. He is as completely a Plebeian[5] in his mind as he is in his rank and station in society. To that highest and unalienable nobility which the great Roman satirist styles "*sola atque unica*,"[6] we fear his pretensions would be equally unavailing.

The shallow and impotent pretensions, tenets, and attempts of this man—and the success with which his influence seems to be extending itself among a pretty numerous, though certainly a very paltry and pitiful, set of readers—have for the last two or three years been considered by us with the most sickening aversion. The very culpable manner in which his chief poem was reviewed in the *Edinburgh Review* (we believe it is no secret, at his own impatient and feverish request, by his partner in the Round Table[7]), was matter of concern to more readers than ourselves. The masterly pen which inflicted such signal chastisement on the early licentiousness of Moore, should not have been idle on that occasion. Mr. Jeffrey[8] does ill, when he delegates his important functions into such hands as those of Mr. Hazlitt. It was chiefly in consequence of that gentleman's allowing Leigh Hunt to pass unpunished through the scene of slaughter, which his execution might so highly have graced, that we

---

[1] *I will ... nightingale* From Shakespeare's *A Midsummer Night's Dream* 1.2, in which Bottom the weaver (who is later transformed into an ass) desires to play the lion's part in a play.

[2] *sine qua non* Latin: without which, not.

[3] *vicious* Immoral.

[4] *Thomas Moore* Irish poet (1779–1852).

[5] *Plebian* In ancient Rome, a commoner, a person of low birth or rank.

[6] *sola atque unique* Latin: alone and only. See Juvenal's *Satire* 8: "Virtue alone is the only true nobility."

[7] *partner ... Table* William Hazlitt, who contributed to both the *Examiner* and the *Edinburgh Review*. Hazlitt frequently wrote for the *Examiner* feature "The Round Table," and his first book-length collection of essays appeared in 1817 under that title.

[8] *Mr. Jeffrey* Francis Jeffrey (1773–1850), founder and editor of the *Edinburgh Review*.

came to the resolution of laying before our readers a series of essays on *the Cockney School*—of which here terminates the first.

from John Lockhart ("Z."), "On the Cockney School of Poetry, No. 4." (*Blackwood's Edinburgh Magazine*, August 1818)

———————— Of Keats,
The Muses' son of promise, and what feats
He yet may do, &c.
        —CORNELIUS WEBB

Of all the manias of this mad age, the most incurable, as well as the most common, seems to be no other than the *Metromanie*.[1] The just celebrity of Robert Burns and Miss Baillie[2] has had the melancholy effect of turning the heads of we know not how many farm-servants and unmarried ladies; our very footmen compose tragedies, and there is scarcely a superannuated governess in the island that does not leave a roll of lyrics behind her in her band-box. To witness the disease of any human understanding, however feeble, is distressing; but the spectacle of an able mind reduced to a state of insanity is of course ten times more afflicting. It is with such sorrow as this that we have contemplated the case of Mr. John Keats. This young man appears to have received from nature talents of an excellent, perhaps even of a superior order—talents which, devoted to the purpose of any useful profession, must have rendered him a respectable, if not an eminent citizen. His friends, we understand, destined him to the career of medicine, and he was bound apprentice some years ago to a worthy apothecary in town. But all has been undone by a sudden attack of the malady to which we have alluded. Whether Mr. John had been sent home with a diuretic or composing draught to some patient far gone in the poetical mania, we have not heard. This much is certain, that he has caught the infection, and that thoroughly. For some time we were in hopes that he might get off with a violent fit or two; but of late the symptoms are terrible. The frenzy of the "Poems"[3] was bad enough in its way; but it did not alarm us half so seriously as the calm, settled, imperturbable drivelling idiocy of "Endymion." We hope, however, that in so young a person, and with a constitution originally so good, even now the disease is not utterly incurable. Time, firm treatment, and rational restraint, do much for many apparently hopeless invalids; and if Mr. Keats should happen, at some interval of reason, to cast his eye upon our pages, he may perhaps be convinced of the existence of his malady, which in such cases is often all that is necessary to put the patient in a fair way of being cured. ...

[Keats's] Endymion is not a Greek shepherd, loved by a Grecian goddess;[4] he is merely a young Cockney rhymester, dreaming a fantastic dream at the full of the moon. Costume, were it worth while to notice such a trifle, is violated in every page of this goodly octavo. From his prototype Hunt, Keats has acquired a sort of vague idea that the Greeks were a most tasteful people, and that no mythology can be so finely adapted for the purposes of poetry as theirs. It is amusing to see what a hand the two Cockneys make of this mythology; the one confesses that he never read the Greek Tragedians, and

---

[1] *Metromanie*   Mania for writing poetry.

[2] *Miss Baillie*   Scottish poet and playwright Joanna Baillie (1762–1851).

[3] *Poems*   Keats's first volume of poetry, which was published in March 1817.

[4] *Endymion ... goddess*   "Endymion" retells the story of the goddess of the moon falling in love with a shepherd, as told by the Roman poet Ovid.

the other knows Homer only from Chapman;[1] and both of them write about Apollo, Pan, Nymphs, Muses, and Mysteries, as might be expected from persons of their education. We shall not, however, enlarge at present upon this subject, as we mean to dedicate an entire paper to the classical attainments and attempts of the Cockney poets. As for Mr. Keats' "Endymion," it has just as much to do with Greece as it has with "old Tartary the fierce;" no man whose mind has ever been imbued with the smallest knowledge or feeling of classical poetry or classical history could have stooped to profane and vulgarise every association in the manner which has been adopted by this "son of promise." Before giving any extracts, we must inform our readers that this romance is meant to be written in English heroic rhyme. To those who have read any of Hunt's poems, this hint might indeed be needless. Mr. Keats has adopted the loose, nerveless versification and Cockney rhymes of the poet of *Rimini*;[2] but, in fairness to that gentleman, we must add that the defects of the system are tenfold more conspicuous in his disciple's work than in his own. Mr. Hunt is a small poet, but he is a clever man. Mr. Keats is a still smaller poet, and he is only a boy of pretty abilities, which he has done every thing in his power to spoil.

---

[1] *Homer … Chapman* Keats knew very little Greek, and read it only in translation. George Chapman's edition of Homer's *Iliad* appeared in 1612, and his edition of the *Odyssey* in 1616.

[2] *Rimini* Hunt's long poem *The Story of Rimini* (1816).

MARY SHELLEY
1797 – 1851

A s Mary Wollstonecraft Shelley wrote in her introduction to the second edition of *Frankenstein*, readers constantly asked her "How I, then a young girl, came to think of, and to dilate upon, so hideous an idea." At the age of nineteen, Shelley created one of the most extraordinary and powerful horror stories in Western literature, one that continues to pervade our popular culture.

Frankenstein continues to overshadow all her other work, but Shelley has also come to be recognized as having produced a large body of fiction of vivid imaginative power that grapples in penetrating fashion with the political and social concerns of her day.

If Shelley's writing is extraordinary, nor is there anything of the ordinary in her famous parentage or her tumultuous life. She was born Mary Wollstonecraft Godwin in August of 1797. The only child of radical feminist Mary Wollstonecraft and the philosopher, author, and political journalist William Godwin, Shelley felt the weight of her parents' controversial reputations throughout her life. Her mother died just after giving birth, and Shelley came to know her only through her works—in particular the *Vindication of the Rights of Woman* (1792). Godwin, for whom Shelley later said she bore an "excess of attachment," raised Mary and her half-sister Fanny, educating them with the help of several friends and regular visitors—a group of supremely qualified teachers that included poet Samuel Taylor Coleridge, painter Thomas Lawrence, novelist Maria Edgeworth, and scientist Humphrey Davy.

After Godwin married Mary Jane Clairmont in 1801, Mary, who did not get along with her stepmother, spent extended periods of time with family friends in Scotland. On a visit home in 1814, she became acquainted with Percy Bysshe Shelley, a radical poet and admirer of Godwin's principles, who had become a regular visitor to the Godwin home. Although Percy was married at the time, within months the two declared their love for each other and eloped to France, taking Mary's stepsister Claire Clairmont with them. Godwin disowned his daughter upon her elopement and was only slightly mollified when the two married in 1816, following the suicide of Percy's first wife, Harriet.

The couple toured France, Switzerland, and Germany (a trip described in Shelley's first publication, *History of a Six Weeks' Tour*) before eventually settling in Italy near Lord Byron, with whom Claire was having an affair. The subsequent years in Italy were turbulent ones. Two of Shelley's children died in infancy, her three-year-old son William died in 1819, and Claire's daughter by Byron died in a convent in 1822. A life-threatening miscarriage that same year plunged Shelley into severe depression, and she and her husband became increasingly distant. When Percy drowned with his friend Edward Williams in July of 1822, her sorrow at his death was further augmented by her guilt at their estrangement.

Although she wrote some poetry and verse dramas, Shelley's only publication during these years was *Frankenstein, or The Modern Prometheus*, first published in 1818 and revised for a new edition in 1831. This novel about a motherless creature rejected by its father, cast out by society, and parented largely by books has clear points of connection with Shelley's own unusual upbringing and her anxiety concerning familial relationships, origins, and parental responsibility. But the enduring appeal of the novel lies in its narrative power and its ability to stimulate ideas in rich profusion. With its themes of repression and doubling it can be read as a psychodrama, and its unspoken preoccupation with incest allies it with other Gothic thrillers. As a reworking of both Milton's story of the fall of man in *Paradise Lost* and the Greek myth of Prometheus (who stole fire from the gods and gave it to humans, saving them from servility), Shelley's novel shows the consequences of using one's power over others without acknowledging the attendant responsibilities. *Frankenstein* can also be read as a moral tale, advising us to treat others in the way we would like to be treated; if we assume those who are unfamiliar or different are evil, we may ourselves create evil where none existed before. The novel also calls into question the Enlightenment celebration of scientific advancement and articulates a deep-seated fear of the consequences of interfering with the natural order.

As a result of the scandalous events in her past, the radicalism of her parents, and the unsavory reputation of her husband, Shelley felt exiled from society. After the death of Byron in 1824 she found herself without friendship or support. She had a small allowance from her father-in-law, Sir Timothy Shelley, but it was hardly enough to support her, and had been given on the stipulation that she not bring her husband's name before the public. Consequently, although Shelley was eager to see her husband's talent appreciated, his *Posthumous Poems* (1824) had to be withdrawn from circulation only a few months after its release.

Shelley had always felt that "as the daughter of two persons of distinguished literary celebrity" she should be a writer, so she turned to writing for income. She returned to London and began producing book reviews, essays, and short biographies while continuing to write novels. *The Last Man* (1826) presents a view of humanity in which a plague destroys the earth, leaving only one man, Lionel Verney. Shelley's novels *Valperga* (1823) and *The Fortunes of Perkin Warbeck: A Romance* (1830) experiment with the genre of historical fiction—a mode that had recently been made popular by Walter Scott—combining romance and fiction with historical and political analysis. In these novels, as well as in *The Last Man*, critics found evidence of the "unsavory politics" they expected from one of the Godwin circle. Critics and readers alike preferred Shelley's more traditional domestic fictions, such as *Lodore* (1835) and *Falkner* (1837).

In 1844 the concerns that had plagued Shelley since the death of her husband were relieved by the death of his father. Her son, Percy Florence, inherited Sir Thomas's title and estate, and Shelley was free to produce biographical work on her husband. In his final years Sir Thomas had allowed her to publish editions of Percy Shelley's work, and in 1839 she had released his four-volume *Poetical Works*, as well as his *Essays and Letters from Abroad, Translations and Fragments*. In writing about her husband, Shelley endeavored to rationalize his radical attitudes and behavior—particularly his atheism and sedition—in order to mediate his poetry for his audience and redeem his public image. Although she has been accused of altering his manuscripts and misrepresenting his politics, she succeeded in her goal of bringing his work to public notice.

Shelley spent her final years traveling with her son and helping him manage his estate. In 1848 he married Jane St. John, a widow and friend of Shelley. Jane nursed Shelley in the months before her death of a brain tumor in 1851.

⌘ ⌘ ⌘

The Last Man

Other than *Frankenstein*, Mary Shelley's 1824 novel *The Last Man* is the work that has excited the greatest critical interest and enjoyed the most attention from her readership over the past generation. In part this may relate to increased interest in apocalyptic visions around the turn of the millennium; it may also speak to humanity's perpetual fascination with the idea of its own extinction. Additional interest may stem from the parallels between the lives of Shelley and her companions and those of the characters in the novel—the circumstances of Percy Shelley's death are strikingly similar to those surrounding the drowning of Lionel Verney's companions. While Shelley's novel can be seen as a depiction of her own grief on a universal scale, her wistful look back at an idealized, but ultimately untenable, past may also be read as a political critique, and a disillusioned examination of Romanticism.

Shelley's protagonist, Lionel Verney, is the last man in the world, looking back on human history from 2100. During the final years of the twenty-first century the world has been devastated by plague. In its wake, humans have descended into brutality: American survivors have attacked Ireland; the Irish have invaded England; and, finally, small bands of English survivors have been wandering the now-ruined continent of Europe. Lionel Verney and his party suspect themselves to be the last of these groups of survivors. As the final two chapters open, Verney has two remaining companions, Adrian and Clara, the latter distraught after the death of her child. The party has been staying in an abandoned villa at Lake Como in the Alps.

---

from *The Last Man*

CHAPTER 29

Now—soft awhile—have I arrived so near the end? Yes! it is all over now—a step or two over those new-made graves, and the wearisome way is done. Can I accomplish my task? Can I streak my paper with words capacious of the grand conclusion? Arise, black Melancholy! quit thy Cimmerian solitude![1] Bring with thee murky fogs from hell, which may drink up the day; bring blight and pestiferous exhalations, which, entering the hollow caverns and breathing places of earth, may fill her stony veins with corruption, so that not only herbage may no longer flourish, the trees may rot, and the rivers run with gall—but the everlasting mountains be decomposed, and the mighty deep putrify, and the genial atmosphere which clips the globe, lose all powers of generation and sustenance. Do this, sad visaged power, while I write, while eyes read these pages.

And who will read them? Beware, tender offspring of the re-born world—beware, fair being, with human heart, yet untamed by care, and human brow, yet unploughed by time—beware, lest the cheerful current of thy blood be checked, thy golden locks turn grey, thy sweet dimpling smiles be changed to fixed, harsh wrinkles! Let not day look on these lines, lest garish day waste, turn pale, and die. Seek a cypress grove, whose moaning boughs will be harmony befitting; seek some cave, deep embowered in earth's dark entrails, where no light will penetrate, save that which struggles, red and flickering, through a single fissure, staining thy page with grimmest livery of death.

There is a painful confusion in my brain, which refuses to delineate distinctly succeeding events. Sometimes the irradiation of my friend's gentle smile comes before me; and methinks its light spans and fills eternity—then, again, I feel the gasping throes—

We quitted Como, and in compliance with Adrian's earnest desire, we took Venice in our way to Rome. There was something to the English peculiarly attractive in the idea of this wave-encircled, island-enthroned city.

---

[1] *Cimmerian solitude* Referring to the Cimmerians, mythical people of Homer's *Odyssey* who inhabit the dark, misty fringes of the world.

Adrian had never seen it. We went down the Po and the Brenta[1] in a boat; and, the days proving intolerably hot, we rested in the bordering palaces during the day, travelling through the night, when darkness made the bordering banks indistinct, and our solitude less remarkable; when the wandering moon lit the waves that divided before our prow, and the night-wind filled our sails, and the murmuring stream, waving trees, and swelling canvass, accorded in harmonious strain. Clara, long overcome by excessive grief, had to a great degree cast aside her timid, cold reserve, and received our attentions with grateful tenderness. While Adrian with poetic fervour discoursed of the glorious nations of the dead, of the beauteous earth and the fate of man, she crept near him, drinking in his speech with silent pleasure. We banished from our talk, and as much as possible from our thoughts, the knowledge of our desolation. And it would be incredible to an inhabitant of cities, to one among a busy throng to what extent we succeeded. It was as a man confined in a dungeon, whose small and grated rift at first renders the doubtful light more sensibly obscure, till, the visual orb having drunk in the beam, and adapted itself to its scantiness, he finds that clear noon inhabits his cell. So we, a simple triad on empty earth, were multiplied to each other, till we became all in all. We stood like trees, whose roots are loosened by the wind, which support one another, leaning and clinging with increased fervour while the wintry storms howl.

Thus we floated down the widening stream of the Po, sleeping when the cicale[2] sang, awake with the stars. We entered the narrower banks of the Brenta, and arrived at the shore of the Laguna[3] at sunrise on the sixth of September. The bright orb slowly rose from behind its cupolas and towers, and shed its penetrating light upon the glassy waters. Wrecks of gondolas, and some few uninjured ones, were strewed on the beach at Fusina.[4] We embarked in one of these for the widowed daughter of ocean,[5] who, abandoned and fallen, sat forlorn on her propping isles, looking towards the far mountains of Greece. We rowed lightly over the Laguna, and entered Canale Grande.[6] The tide ebbed sullenly from out the broken portals and violated halls of Venice: sea weed and sea monsters were left on the blackened marble, while the salt ooze defaced the matchless works of art that adorned their walls, and the sea gull flew out from the shattered window. In the midst of this appalling ruin of the monuments of man's power, nature asserted her ascendancy, and shone more beauteous from the contrast. The radiant waters hardly trembled, while the rippling waves made many sided mirrors to the sun; the blue immensity, seen beyond Lido,[7] stretched far, unspecked by boat, so tranquil, so lovely, that it seemed to invite us to quit the land strewn with ruins, and to seek refuge from sorrow and fear on its placid extent.

We saw the ruins of this hapless city from the height of the tower of San Marco, immediately under us, and turned with sickening hearts to the sea, which, though it be a grave, rears no monument, discloses no ruin. Evening had come apace. The sun set in calm majesty behind the misty summits of the Apennines, and its golden and roseate hues painted the mountains of the opposite shore. "That land," said Adrian, "tinged with the last glories of the day, is Greece." Greece! The sound had a responsive chord in the bosom of Clara. She vehemently reminded us that we had promised to take her once again to Greece, to the tomb of her parents. Why go to Rome? what should we do at Rome? We might take one of the many vessels to be found here, embark in it, and steer right for Albania.

I objected the dangers of ocean, and the distance of the mountains we saw, from Athens; a distance which, from the savage uncultivation of the country, was almost impassable. Adrian, who was delighted with Clara's proposal, obviated these objections. The season was favourable; the north-west that blew would take us transversely across the gulph; and then we might find, in

---

[1] *the Po and the Brenta* Both rivers flow from the Alps down into the Venetian plain.

[2] *cicale* Cicada.

[3] *the Laguna* The Laguna Veneta, which surrounds Venice.

[4] *Fusina* Located on the coast of the mainland, south of Venice.

[5] *widowed daughter of ocean* I.e., Venice. In an ancient ceremony, the ruler of Venice threw a ring into the sea each Ascension Day to symbolize the marriage of Venice and the ocean.

[6] *Canale Grande* Canal that runs through Venice.

[7] *Lido* Island that forms a breakwater between the sea and the Laguna Veneta.

some abandoned port, a light Greek caique,[1] adapted for such navigation, and run down the coast of the Morea, and, passing over the Isthmus of Corinth, without much land-travelling or fatigue, find ourselves at Athens. This appeared to me wild talk; but the sea, glowing with a thousand purple hues, looked so brilliant and safe; my beloved companions were so earnest, so determined, that, when Adrian said, "Well, though it is not exactly what you wish, yet consent, to please me"—I could no longer refuse. That evening we selected a vessel, whose size just seemed fitted for our enterprize; we bent the sails and put the rigging in order, and, reposing that night in one of the city's thousand palaces, agreed to embark at sunrise the following morning.

> When winds that move not its calm surface, sweep
> The azure sea, I love the land no more;
> The smiles of the serene and tranquil deep
> Tempt my unquiet mind—

Thus said Adrian, quoting a translation of Moschus's poem, as, in the clear morning light, we rowed over the Laguna, past Lido, into the open sea—I would have added in continuation,

> But, when the roar
> Of ocean's gray abyss resounds, and foam
> Gathers upon the sea, and vast waves burst—[2]

But my friends declared that such verses were evil augury; so in cheerful mood we left the shallow waters, and, when out at sea, unfurled our sails to catch the favourable breeze. The laughing morning air filled them while sun-light bathed earth, sky and ocean—the placid waves divided to receive our keel, and playfully kissed the dark sides of our little skiff, murmuring a welcome; as land receded, still the blue expanse, most waveless, twin sister to the azure empyrean, afforded smooth conduct to our bark.[3] As the air and waters were tranquil and balmy, so were our minds steeped in quiet. In comparison with the unstained deep, funeral earth appeared a grave, its high rocks and stately mountains

were but monuments, its trees the plumes of a hearse, the brooks and rivers brackish with tears for departed man. Farewell to desolate towns—to fields with their savage intermixture of corn and weeds—to ever multiplying relics of our lost species. Ocean, we commit ourselves to thee—even as the patriarch of old[4] floated above the drowned world, let us be saved, as thus we betake ourselves to thy perennial flood.

Adrian sat at the helm; I attended to the rigging, the breeze right aft filled our swelling canvas, and we ran before it over the untroubled deep. The wind died away at noon; its idle breath just permitted us to hold our course. As lazy, fair-weather sailors, careless of the coming hour, we talked gaily of our coasting voyage, of our arrival at Athens. We would make our home of one of the Cyclades,[5] and there in myrtle-groves, amidst perpetual spring, fanned by the wholesome sea-breezes — we would live long years in beatific union—Was there such a thing as death in the world?—

The sun passed its zenith and lingered down the stainless floor of heaven. Lying in the boat, my face turned up to the sky, I thought I saw on its blue white, marbled streaks, so slight, so immaterial, that now I said—"They are there"—and now, "It is a mere imagination." A sudden fear stung me while I gazed; and, starting up, and running to the prow—as I stood, my hair was gently lifted on my brow—a dark line of ripples appeared to the east, gaining rapidly on us—my breathless remark to Adrian was followed by the flapping of the canvas, as the adverse wind struck it, and our boat lurched—swift as speech, the web of the storm thickened overhead, the sun went down red, the dark sea was strewed with foam, and our skiff rose and fell in its increasing furrows.

Behold us now in our frail tenement, hemmed in by hungry, roaring waves, buffeted by winds. In the inky east two vast clouds, sailing contrary ways, met; the lightning leapt forth, and the hoarse thunder muttered. Again in the south, the clouds replied, and the forked stream of fire, running along the black sky, showed us the appalling piles of clouds, now met and obliterated by the heaving waves. Great God! And we alone—we three—alone—alone—sole dwellers on the sea and on the earth, we three must perish! The vast universe, its

---

[1] *caique* Small row-boat or sail-boat.

[2] *When winds ... burst* From Percy Shelley's sonnet "Translated from the Greek of Moschus" (1816), 2.1–6.

[3] *bark* Boat.

[4] *the patriarch of old* I.e., Noah.

[5] *Cyclades* Group of islands in the Aegean Sea.

myriad worlds, and the plains of boundless earth which we had left—the extent of shoreless sea around—contracted to my view—they and all that they contained, shrunk up to one point, even to our tossing bark, freighted with glorious humanity.

A convulsion of despair crossed the love-beaming face of Adrian, while with set teeth he murmured, "Yet they shall be saved!" Clara, visited by a human pang, pale and trembling, crept near him—he looked on her with an encouraging smile—"Do you fear, sweet girl? O, do not fear, we shall soon be on shore!"

The darkness prevented me from seeing the changes of her countenance; but her voice was clear and sweet, as she replied, "Why should I fear? Neither sea nor storm can harm us, if mighty destiny or the ruler of destiny does not permit. And then the stinging fear of surviving either of you is not here—one death will clasp us undivided."

Meanwhile we took in all our sails, save a jib;[1] and, as soon as we might without danger, changed our course, running with the wind for the Italian shore. Dark night mixed everything; we hardly discerned the white crests of the murderous surges, except when lightning made brief noon, and drank the darkness, showing us our danger, and restoring us to double night. We were all silent, except when Adrian, as steersman, made an encouraging observation. Our little shell obeyed the rudder miraculously well, and ran along on the top of the waves as if she had been an offspring of the sea, and the angry mother sheltered her endangered child.

I sat at the prow, watching our course; when suddenly I heard the waters break with redoubled fury. We were certainly near the shore—at the same time I cried, "About there!" and a broad lightning, filling the concave, showed us for one moment the level beach ahead, disclosing even the sands, and stunted, ooze-sprinkled beds of reeds, that grew at high water mark. Again it was dark, and we drew in our breath with such content as one may, who, while fragments of volcano-hurled rock darken the air, sees a vast mass plowing the ground immediately at his feet. What to do we knew not—the breakers here, there, everywhere, encompassed us—they roared, and dashed, and flung their hated spray in our faces. With considerable difficulty and danger we succeeded at length in altering our course, and stretched out from shore. I urged my companions to prepare for the wreck of our little skiff, and to bind themselves to some oar or spar which might suffice to float them. I was myself an excellent swimmer—the very sight of the sea was wont to raise in me such sensations as a huntsman experiences when he hears a pack of hounds in full cry; I loved to feel the waves wrap me and strive to overpower me; while I, lord of myself, moved this way or that, in spite of their angry bufferings. Adrian also could swim—but the weakness of his frame prevented him from feeling pleasure in the exercise, or acquiring any great expertness.

But what power could the strongest swimmer oppose to the overpowering violence of ocean in its fury? My efforts to prepare my companions were rendered nearly futile—for the roaring breakers prevented our hearing one another speak, and the waves that broke continually over our boat obliged me to exert all my strength in lading the water out, as fast as it came in. The while darkness, palpable and rayless, hemmed us round, dissipated only by the lightning; sometimes we beheld thunderbolts, fiery red, fall into the sea, and at intervals vast spouts stooped from the clouds, churning the wild ocean, which rose to meet them; while the fierce gale bore the rack[2] onwards, and they were lost in the chaotic mingling of sky and sea. Our gunwales had been torn away, our single sail had been rent to ribbands[3] and borne down the stream of the wind. We had cut away our mast, and lightened the boat of all she contained—Clara attempted to assist me in heaving the water from the hold, and, as she turned her eyes to look on the lightning, I could discern by that momentary gleam that resignation had conquered every fear. We have a power given us in any worst extremity, which props the else feeble mind of man, and enables us to endure the most savage tortures with a stillness of soul which in hours of happiness we could not have imagined. A calm, more dreadful in truth than the tempest, allayed the wild beatings of my heart—a calm like that of the gamester, the suicide, and the murderer, when the last die is on the point of being cast—while the poisoned cup is at the lips, as the death-blow is about to be given.

Hours passed thus—hours which might write old

---

[1] *jib* Triangular sail to the fore of a ship.

[2] *rack* Mass of clouds.

[3] *ribbands* I.e., ribbons.

age on the face of beardless youth, and grizzle the silky hair of infancy—hours, while the chaotic uproar continued, while each dread gust transcended in fury the one before, and our skiff hung on the breaking wave, and then rushed into the valley below, and trembled and spun between the watery precipices that seemed most to meet above her. For a moment the gale paused, and ocean sank to comparative silence—it was a breathless interval; the wind which, as a practised leaper, had gathered itself up before it sprung, now with terrific roar rushed over the sea, and the waves struck our stern. Adrian exclaimed that the rudder was gone—"We are lost," cried Clara, "Save yourselves—O save yourselves!" The lightning showed me the poor girl half buried in the water at the bottom of the boat; as she was sinking in it Adrian caught her up, and sustained her in his arms. We were without a rudder—we rushed prow foremost into the vast billows piled up ahead—they broke over and filled the tiny skiff; one scream I heard—one cry that we were gone, I uttered; I found myself in the waters; darkness was around. When the light of the tempest flashed, I saw the keel of our upset boat close to me—I clung to this, grasping it with clenched hand and nails, while I endeavoured during each flash to discover any appearance of my companions. I thought I saw Adrian at no great distance from me, clinging to an oar; I sprung from my hold, and with energy beyond my human strength, I dashed aside the waters as I strove to lay hold of him. As that hope failed, instinctive love of life animated me, and feelings of contention, as if a hostile will combated with mine. I breasted the surges, and flung them from me as I would the opposing front and sharpened claws of a lion about to enfang my bosom. When I had been beaten down by one wave, I rose on another, while I felt bitter pride curl my lip.

Ever since the storm had carried us near the shore, we had never attained any great distance from it. With every flash I saw the bordering coast; yet the progress I made was small, while each wave, as it receded, carried me back into ocean's far abysses. At one moment I felt my foot touch the sand, and then again I was in deep water; my arms began to lose their power of motion; my breath failed me under the influence of the strangling waters—a thousand wild and delirious thoughts crossed me: as well as I can now recall them, my chief feeling

was, how sweet it would be to lay my head on the quiet earth, where the surges would no longer strike my weakened frame, nor the sound of waters ring in my ears—to attain this repose, not to save my life, I made a last effort—the shelving shore suddenly presented a footing for me. I rose, and was again thrown down by the breakers—a point of rock, to which I was enabled to cling, gave me a moment's respite; and then, taking advantage of the ebbing of the waves, I ran forwards—gained the dry sands, and fell senseless on the oozy reeds that sprinkled them.

I must have lain long deprived of life; for when first, with a sickening feeling, I unclosed my eyes, the light of morning met them. Great change had taken place meanwhile: grey dawn dappled the flying clouds, which sped onwards, leaving visible at intervals vast lakes of pure ether. A fountain of light arose in an increasing stream from the east, behind the waves of the Adriatic, changing the grey to a roseate hue, and then flooding sky and sea with aerial gold.

A kind of stupor followed my fainting; my senses were alive, but memory was extinct. The blessed respite was short—a snake lurked near me to sting me into life. On the first retrospective emotion I would have started up, but my limbs refused to obey me; my knees trembled, the muscles had lost all power. I still believed that I might find one of my beloved companions cast like me, half alive, on the beach; and I strove in every way to restore my frame to the use of its animal functions. I wrung the brine from my hair; and the rays of the risen sun soon visited me with genial warmth. With the restoration of my bodily powers, my mind became in some degree aware of the universe of misery, henceforth to be its dwelling. I ran to the water's edge, calling on the beloved names. Ocean drank in and absorbed my feeble voice, replying with pitiless roar. I climbed a near tree: the level sands bounded by a pine forest, and the sea clipped round by the horizon, was all that I could discern. In vain I extended my researches along the beach; the mast we had thrown overboard, with tangled cordage, and remnants of a sail, was the sole relic land received of our wreck. Sometimes I stood still, and wrung my hands. I accused earth and sky—the universal machine and the Almighty power that misdirected it. Again I threw myself on the sands, and then the sighing wind, mimicking a human cry, roused me to bitter, fallacious hope. Assuredly if any little bark or smallest canoe had been near, I should have sought the savage plains of ocean, found the dear remains of my lost ones, and, clinging round them, have shared their grave.

The day passed thus; each moment contained eternity; although when hour after hour had gone by, I wondered at the quick flight of time. Yet even now I had not drunk the bitter potion to the dregs; I was not yet persuaded of my loss; I did not yet feel in every pulsation, in every nerve, in every thought, that I remained alone of my race—that I was the LAST MAN.

The day had clouded over, and a drizzling rain set in at sunset. Even the eternal skies weep, I thought; is there any shame then, that mortal man should spend himself in tears? I remembered the ancient fables, in which human beings are described as dissolving away through weeping into ever-gushing fountains. Ah! that so it were; and then my destiny would be in some sort akin to the watery death of Adrian and Clara. Oh! grief is fantastic; it weaves a web on which to trace the history of its woe from every form and change around; it incorporates itself with all living nature; it finds sustenance in every object; as light, it fills all things, and, like light, it gives its own colours to all.

I had wandered in my search to some distance from the spot on which I had been cast, and came to one of those watch-towers, which at stated distances line the Italian shore. I was glad of shelter, glad to find a work of human hands, after I had gazed so long on nature's drear barrenness; so I entered, and ascended the rough winding staircase into the guard-room. So far was fate kind, that no harrowing vestige remained of its former inhabitants; a few planks laid across two iron tressels, and strewed with the dried leaves of Indian corn, was the bed presented to me; and an open chest, containing some half mouldered biscuit, awakened an appetite, which perhaps existed before, but of which, until now, I was not aware. Thirst also, violent and parching, the result of the sea-water I had drank, and of the exhaustion of my frame, tormented me. Kind nature had gifted the supply of these wants with pleasurable sensations, so that I—even I!—was refreshed and calmed as I ate of this sorry fare, and drank a little of the sour wine which half filled a flask left in this abandoned dwelling. Then I stretched myself on the bed, not to be disdained by the victim of shipwreck. The earthy smell of the dried leaves

was balm to my sense after the hateful odour of sea-weed. I forgot my state of loneliness. I neither looked backward nor forward; my senses were hushed to repose; I fell asleep and dreamed of all dear inland scenes, of hay-makers, of the shepherd's whistle to his dog when he demanded his help to drive the flock to fold; of sights and sounds peculiar to my boyhood's mountain life, which I had long forgotten.

I awoke in a painful agony—for I fancied that ocean, breaking its bounds, carried away the fixed continent and deep rooted mountains, together with the streams I loved, the woods, and the flocks—it raged around, with that continued and dreadful roar which had accompanied the last wreck of surviving humanity. As my waking sense returned, the bare walls of the guard room closed round me, and the rain pattered against the single window. How dreadful it is to emerge from the oblivion of slumber and to receive as a good morrow the mute wailing of one's own hapless heart—to return from the land of deceptive dreams to the heavy knowledge of unchanged disaster!—Thus was it with me, now, and for ever! The sting of other griefs might be blunted by time; and even mine yielded sometimes during the day, to the pleasure inspired by the imagination or the senses; but I never look first upon the morning-light but with my fingers pressed tight on my bursting heart, and my soul deluged with the interminable flood of hopeless misery. Now I awoke for the first time in the dead world—I awoke alone—and the dull dirge of the sea, heard even amidst the rain, recalled me to the reflection of the wretch I had become. The sound came like a reproach, a scoff—like the sting of remorse in the soul—I gasped—the veins and muscles of my throat swelled, suffocating me. I put my fingers to my ears, I buried my head in the leaves of my couch, I would have dived to the centre to lose hearing of that hideous moan.

But another task must be mine—again I visited the detested beach, again I vainly looked far and wide, again I raised my unanswered cry, lifting up the only voice that could ever again force the mute air to syllable the human thought.

What a pitiable, forlorn, disconsolate being I was! My very aspect and garb told the tale of my despair. My hair was matted and wild, my limbs soiled with salt ooze; while at sea, I had thrown off those of my garments that encumbered me, and the rain drenched the thin summer-clothing I had retained—my feet were bare, and the stunted reeds and broken shells made them bleed—the while, I hurried to and fro, now looking earnestly on some distant rock which, islanded in the sands, bore for a moment a deceptive appearance—now with flashing eyes reproaching the murderous ocean for its unutterable cruelty.

For a moment I compared myself to that monarch of the waste—Robinson Crusoe.[1] We had been both thrown companionless—he on the shore of a desolate island: I on that of a desolate world. I was rich in the so-called goods of life. If I turned my steps from the near barren scene, and entered any of the earth's million cities, I should find their wealth stored up for my accommodation—clothes, food, books, and a choice of dwelling beyond the command of the princes of former times. Every climate was subject to my selection, while he was obliged to toil in the acquirement of every necessary, and was the inhabitant of a tropical island, against whose heats and storms he could obtain small shelter. Viewing the question thus, who would not have preferred the Sybarite[2] enjoyments I could command, the philosophic leisure, and ample intellectual resources, to his life of labour and peril? Yet he was far happier than I: for he could hope, nor hope in vain—the destined vessel at last arrived to bear him to countrymen and kindred, where the events of his solitude became a fire-side tale. To none could I ever relate the story of my adversity; no hope had I. He knew that, beyond the ocean which begirt his lonely island, thousands lived whom the sun enlightened when it shone also on him: beneath the meridian sun and visiting moon, I alone bore human features; I alone could give articulation to thought; and, when I slept, both day and night were unbeheld of any. He had fled from his fellows, and was transported with terror at the print of a human foot. I would have knelt down and worshipped the same. The wild and cruel Caribbee, the merciless Cannibal[3]—or worse than these, the uncouth, brute, and remorseless veteran in the vices of civilization, would have been to me a beloved companion, a treasure dearly prized. His nature would be kin to mine; his form cast in the same mould; human blood would flow in his veins; a human sympathy must link us for ever. It cannot be that I shall never behold a fellow being more!—never!—never!—not in the course of years!—Shall I wake, and speak to none, pass the interminable hours, my soul, islanded in the world, a solitary point, surrounded by vacuum? Will day follow day endlessly thus? No! no! a God rules the world—providence has not exchanged its golden sceptre for an aspic's[4] sting. Away! let me fly from the ocean-grave, let me depart from this barren nook, paled in,[5] as it is, from access by its own desolateness; let me tread once again the paved towns; step over the threshold of man's dwellings, and most certainly I shall find this thought a horrible vision—a maddening, but evanescent, dream.

I entered Ravenna[6] (the town nearest to the spot whereon I had been cast) before the second sun had set on the empty world; I saw many living creatures: oxen, and horses, and dogs, but there was no man among them. I entered a cottage, it was vacant; I ascended the marble stairs of a palace, the bats and the owls were nestled in the tapestry; I stepped softly, not to awaken the sleeping town. I rebuked a dog, that by yelping disturbed the sacred stillness; I would not believe that all was as it seemed—The world was not dead, but I was mad; I was deprived of sight, hearing, and sense of touch; I was labouring under the force of a spell, which permitted me to behold all sights of earth, except its human inhabitants; they were pursuing their ordinary labours. Every house had its inmate; but I could not perceive them. If I could have deluded myself into a belief of this kind, I should have been far more satisfied. But my brain, tenacious of its reason, refused to lend itself to such imaginations—and though I endeavoured to play the antic to myself, I knew that I, the offspring of man, during long years one among many—now remained sole survivor of my species.

The sun sank behind the western hills; I had fasted

---

[1] *Robinson Crusoe* Shipwrecked protagonist of Daniel Defoe's *The Life and Adventures of Robinson Crusoe* (1719).

[2] *Sybarite* Luxurious; from the Greek city of Sybaris, noted for its luxury.

[3] *Caribbee* Caribs, inhabitants of the southern West Indies; *Cannibal* Originally also a form of the word "Carib." The fierce inhabitants of this region were rumored to eat human flesh; thus the evolution of the word "cannibal" to its present meaning.

[4] *aspic* Asp, a poisonous snake.

[5] *paled in* Fenced in.

[6] *Ravenna* Town on the Adriatic Sea, approximately 80 miles south of Venice.

since the preceding evening, but, though faint and weary, I loathed food, nor ceased, while yet a ray of light remained, to pace the lonely streets. Night came on, and sent every living creature but me to the bosom of its mate. It was my solace to blunt my mental agony by personal hardship—of the thousand beds around, I would not seek the luxury of one; I lay down on the pavement—a cold marble step served me for a pillow—midnight came; and then, though not before, did my wearied lids shut out the sight of the twinkling stars, and their reflex on the pavement near. Thus I passed the second night of my desolation.

CHAPTER 30

I awoke in the morning, just as the higher windows of the lofty houses received the first beams of the rising sun. The birds were chirping, perched on the window sills and deserted thresholds of the doors. I awoke, and my first thought was, Adrian and Clara are dead. I no longer shall be hailed by their good-morrow, or pass the long day in their society. I shall never see them more. The ocean has robbed me of them—stolen their hearts of love from their breasts, and given over to corruption what was dearer to me than light, or life, or hope.

I was an untaught shepherd-boy when Adrian deigned to confer on me his friendship. The best years of my life had been passed with him. All I had possessed of this world's goods, of happiness, knowledge, or virtue, I owed to him. He had, in his person, his intellect, and rare qualities, given a glory to my life, which without him it had never known. Beyond all other beings he had taught me that goodness, pure and single, can be an attribute of man. It was a sight for angels to congregate to behold, to view him lead, govern, and solace the last days of the human race.

My lovely Clara also was lost to me—she who, last of the daughters of man, exhibited all those feminine and maiden virtues which poets, painters, and sculptors have in their various languages strove to express. Yet, as far as she was concerned, could I lament that she was removed in early youth from the certain advent of misery? Pure she was of soul, and all her intents were holy. But her heart was the throne of love, and the sensibility her lovely countenance expressed was the prophet of many woes, not the less deep and drear because she would have for ever concealed them.

These two wondrously endowed beings had been spared from the universal wreck to be my companions during the last year of solitude. I had felt, while they were with me, all their worth. I was conscious that every other sentiment, regret, or passion had by degrees merged into a yearning, clinging affection for them. I had not forgotten the sweet partner of my youth, mother of my children, my adored Idris; but I saw at least a part of her spirit alive again in her brother;[1] and after, that by Evelyn's[2] death I had lost what most dearly recalled her to me; I enshrined her memory in Adrian's form, and endeavoured to confound the two dear ideas. I sound the depths of my heart, and try in vain to draw thence the expressions that can typify my love for these remnants of my race. If regret and sorrow came athwart me, as well it might in our solitary and uncertain state, the clear tones of Adrian's voice, and his fervent look, dissipated the gloom; or I was cheered unaware by the mild content and sweet resignation Clara's cloudless brow and deep blue eyes expressed. They were all to me—the suns of my benighted soul, repose in my weariness, slumber in my sleepless woe. Ill, most ill, with disjointed words, bare and weak, have I expressed the feeling with which I clung to them. I would have wound myself like ivy inextricably round them, so that the same blow might destroy us. I would have entered and been a part of them—so that

If the dull substance of my flesh were thought,[3]

even now I had accompanied them to their new and incommunicable abode.

Never shall I see them more. I am bereft of their dear converse—bereft of sight of them. I am a tree rent by lightning; never will the bark close over the bared fibres—never will their quivering life, torn by the winds, receive the opiate of a moment's balm. I am alone in the world—but that expression as yet was less pregnant with misery than that Adrian and Clara are dead.

The tide of thought and feeling rolls on for ever the same, though the banks and shapes around, which

---

[1] *her brother* I.e., Adrian.

[2] *Evelyn* Lionel and Idris's youngest son.

[3] *If … thought* From Shakespeare's Sonnet 44, line 1.

govern its course, and the reflection in the wave, vary. Thus the sentiment of immediate loss in some sort decayed, while that of utter, irremediable loneliness grew on me with time. Three days I wandered through Ravenna—now thinking only of the beloved beings who slept in the oozy caves of ocean, now looking forward on the dread blank before me; shuddering to make an onward step, writhing at each change that marked the progress of the hours.

For three days I wandered to and fro in this melancholy town. I passed whole hours in going from house to house, listening whether I could detect some lurking sign of human existence. Sometimes I rang at a bell; it tinkled through the vaulted rooms, and silence succeeded to the sound. I called myself hopeless, yet still I hoped; and still disappointment ushered in the hours, intruding the cold, sharp steel, which first pierced me, into the aching festering wound. I fed like a wild beast, which seizes its food only when stung by intolerable hunger. I did not change my garb, or seek the shelter of a roof, during all those days. Burning heats, nervous irritation, a ceaseless but confused flow of thought, sleepless nights, and days instinct with a frenzy of agitation, possessed me during that time.

As the fever of my blood increased, a desire of wandering came upon me. I remember that the sun had set on the fifth day after my wreck when, without purpose or aim, I quitted the town of Ravenna. I must have been very ill. Had I been possessed by more or less of delirium, that night had surely been my last; for, as I continued to walk on the banks of the Mantone,[1] whose upward course I followed, I looked wistfully on the stream, acknowledging to myself that its pellucid waves could medicine my woes for ever, and was unable to account to myself for my tardiness in seeking their shelter from the poisoned arrows of thought that were piercing me through and through. I walked a considerable part of the night, and excessive weariness at length conquered my repugnance to the availing myself of the deserted habitations of my species. The waning moon, which had just risen, showed me a cottage, whose neat entrance and trim garden reminded me of my own England. I lifted up the latch of the door and entered. A kitchen first presented itself, where, guided by the moon beams, I found materials for striking a light.

Within this was a bed room; the couch was furnished with sheets of snowy whiteness; the wood piled on the hearth, and an array as for a meal might almost have deceived me into the dear belief that I had here found what I had so long sought—one survivor, a companion for my loneliness, a solace to my despair. I steeled myself against the delusion; the room itself was vacant: it was only prudent, I repeated to myself, to examine the rest of the house. I fancied that I was proof against the expectation; yet my heart beat audibly as I laid my hand on the lock of each door, and it sunk again, when I perceived in each the same vacancy. Dark and silent they were as vaults; so I returned to the first chamber, wondering what sightless host had spread the materials for my repast, and my repose. I drew a chair to the table and examined what the viands were of which I was to partake. In truth it was a death feast! The bread was blue and mouldy; the cheese lay a heap of dust. I did not dare examine the other dishes; a troop of ants passed in a double line across the table cloth; every utensil was covered with dust, with cobwebs, and myriads of dead flies. These were object each and all betokening the fallaciousness of my expectations. Tears rushed into my eyes; surely this was a wanton display of the power of the destroyer. What had I done, that each sensitive nerve was thus to be anatomized? Yet why complain more now than ever? This vacant cottage revealed no new sorrow—the world was empty; mankind was dead—I knew it well—why quarrel therefore with an acknowledged and stale truth? Yet, as I said, I had hoped in the very heart of despair, so that every new impression of the hard-cut reality on my soul brought with it a fresh pang, telling me the yet unstudied lesson, that neither change of place nor time could bring alleviation to my misery, but that, as I now was, I must continue, day after day, month after month, year after year, while I lived. I hardly dared conjecture what space of time that expression implied. It is true, I was no longer in the first blush of manhood; neither had I declined far in the vale of years—men have accounted mine the prime of life: I had just entered my thirty-seventh year; every limb was as well knit, every articulation as true, as when I had acted the shepherd on the hills of Cumberland; and with these advantages I was to commence the train of solitary life. Such were the reflections that ushered in my slumber on that night.

---

[1] *Mantone* River that flows through Ravenna and into the Adriatic.

The shelter, however, and less disturbed repose which I enjoyed, restored me the following morning to a greater portion of health and strength than I had experienced since my fatal shipwreck. Among the stores I had discovered on searching the cottage the preceding night, was a quantity of dried grapes; these refreshed me in the morning as I left my lodging and proceeded towards a town which I discerned at no great distance. As far as I could divine, it must have been Forli. I entered with pleasure its wide and grassy streets. All, it is true, pictured the excess of desolation; yet I loved to find myself in those spots which had been the abode of my fellow creatures. I delighted to traverse street after street, to look up at the tall houses, and repeat to myself, once they contained beings similar to myself—I was not always the wretch I am now. The wide square of Forli, the arcade around it, its light and pleasant aspect, cheered me. I was pleased with the idea, that, if the earth should be again peopled, we, the lost race, would, in the relics left behind, present no contemptible exhibition of our powers to the newcomers.

I entered one of the palaces and opened the door of a magnificent saloon. I started—I looked again with renewed wonder. What wild-looking, unkempt, half-naked savage was that before me? The surprise was momentary.

I perceived that it was I myself whom I beheld in a large mirror at the end of the hall. No wonder that the lover of the princely Idris should fail to recognize himself in the miserable object there portrayed. My tattered dress was that in which I had crawled half alive from the tempestuous sea. My long and tangled hair hung in elf locks on my brow; my dark eyes, now hollow and wild, gleamed from under them; my cheeks were discoloured by the jaundice, which (the effect of misery and neglect) suffused my skin, and were half hid by a beard of many days' growth.

Yet why should I not remain thus, I thought; the world is dead, and this squalid attire is a fitter mourning garb than the foppery of a black suit. And thus, methinks, I should have remained, had not hope, without which I do not believe man could exist, whispered to me that in such a plight I should be an object of fear and aversion to the being, preserved I knew not where, but, I fondly trusted, at length to be found by me. Will my readers scorn the vanity that made me attire myself with some care, for the sake of this visionary being? Or will they forgive the freaks of a half crazed imagination? I can easily forgive myself—for hope, however vague, was so dear to me, and a sentiment of pleasure of so rare occurrence, that I yielded readily to any idea that cherished the one, or promised any recurrence of the former to my sorrowing heart.

After such occupation, I visited every street, alley, and nook of Forli. These Italian towns presented an appearance of still greater desolation than those of England or France. Plague had appeared here earlier—it had finished its course and achieved its work much sooner than with us. Probably the last summer had found no human being alive in all the track included between the shores of Calabria and the northern Alps. My search was utterly vain, yet I did not despond. Reason methought was on my side; and the chances were by no means contemptible that there should exist in some part of Italy a survivor like myself—of a wasted, depopulate land. As therefore I rambled through the empty town, I formed my plan for future operations. I would continue to journey on towards Rome. After I should have satisfied myself, by a narrow search, that I left behind no human being in the towns through which I passed, I would write up in a conspicuous part of each, with white paint, in three languages, that "Verney, the last of the race of Englishmen, had taken up his abode in Rome."

In pursuance of this scheme, I entered a painter's shop and procured myself the paint. It is strange that so trivial an occupation should have consoled and even enlivened me. But grief renders one childish, despair fantastic. To this simple inscription, I merely added the adjuration, "Friend, come! I wait for thee!—*Deh, vieni! ti aspetto!*"

On the following morning, with something like hope for my companion, I quitted Forli on my way to Rome. Until now, agonizing retrospect and dreary prospects for the future had stung me when awake, and cradled me to my repose. Many times I had delivered myself up to the tyranny of anguish—many times I resolved a speedy end to my woes; and death by my own hands was a remedy whose practicability was even cheering to me. What could I fear in the other world? If there were a hell, and I were doomed to it, I should come an adept to the sufferance of its tortures—the act were easy, the speedy and certain end of my deplorable tragedy. But now these thoughts faded before the new-born expectation. I went on my way, not as before, feeling each hour, each minute, to be an age instinct with incalculable pain.

As I wandered along the plain, at the foot of the Appennines—through their valleys, and over their bleak summits—my path led me through a country which had been trodden by heroes, visited and admired by thousands. They had, as a tide, receded, leaving me blank and bare in the midst. But why complain? Did I not hope?—so I schooled myself, even after the enliven-ing spirit had really deserted me, and thus I was obliged to call up all the fortitude I could command, and that was not much, to prevent a recurrence of that chaotic and intolerable despair that had succeeded to the miserable shipwreck, that had consummated every fear, and dashed to annihilation every joy.

I rose each day with the morning sun, and left my desolate inn. As my feet strayed through the unpeopled country, my thoughts rambled through the universe, and I was least miserable when I could, absorbed in reverie, forget the passage of the hours. Each evening, in spite of weariness, I detested to enter any dwelling, there to take up my nightly abode—I have sat, hour after hour, at the door of the cottage I had selected, unable to lift the latch and meet face to face blank desertion within. Many nights, though autumnal mists were spread around, I passed under an ilex[1]—many times I have supped on arbutus berries and chestnuts, making a fire, gypsy-like, on the ground—because wild natural scenery reminded me less acutely of my hopeless state of loneliness. I counted the days, and bore with me a peeled willow-wand, on which, as well as I could remember, I had notched the days that had elapsed since my wreck, and each night I added another unit to the melancholy sum.

I had toiled up a hill which led to Spoleto. Around was spread a plain, encircled by the chestnut-covered Apennines. A dark ravine was on one side, spanned by an aqueduct, whose tall arches were rooted in the dell below and attested that man had once deigned to bestow labour and thought here, to adorn and civilize nature. Savage, ungrateful nature, which in wild sport defaced his remains, protruding her easily renewed and fragile growth of wild flowers and parasite plants around his eternal edifices. I sat on a fragment of rock and looked round. The sun had bathed in gold the western atmosphere, and in the east the clouds caught the radiance, and budded into transient loveliness. It set on a world that contained me alone for its inhabitant. I took out my wand—I counted the marks. Twenty-five were already traced—twenty-five days had already elapsed since human voice had gladdened my ears or human countenance met my gaze. Twenty-five long, weary days, succeeded by dark and lonesome nights, had mingled with foregone years and had become a part of the past—the never to be recalled—a real, undeniable portion of my life—twenty-five long, long days.

Why this was not a month!—Why talk of days—or weeks—or months—I must grasp years in my imagina-tion, if I would truly picture the future to my-self—three, five, ten, twenty, fifty anniversaries of that fatal epoch might elapse—every year containing twelve months, each of more numerous calculation in a diary, than the twenty-five days gone by—Can it be? Will it be?—We had been used to look forward to death tremulously—wherefore, but because its place was obscure? But more terrible, and far more obscure, was the unveiled course of my lone futurity. I broke my wand; I threw it from me. I needed no recorder of the inch and barley-corn growth of my life, while my unquiet thoughts created other divisions than those ruled over by the planets—and, in looking back on the age that had elapsed since I had been alone, I disdained to give the name of days and hours to the throes of agony which had in truth portioned it out.

I hid my face in my hands. The twitter of the young birds going to rest, and their rustling among the trees, disturbed the still evening-air—the crickets chirped, the aziolo cooed at intervals. My thoughts had been of death—these sounds spoke to me of life. I lifted up my eyes—a bat wheeled round—the sun had sunk behind the jagged line of mountains, and the paly[2] crescent moon was visible, silver white amidst the orange sunset, and accompanied by one bright star, prolonged thus the twilight. A herd of cattle passed along in the dell below, untended, towards their watering place—the grass was rustled by a gentle breeze, and the olive-woods, mel-lowed into soft masses by the moonlight, contrasted

1 *ilex* Evergreen oak.

2 *paly* Pale.

their sea-green with the dark chestnut foliage. Yes, this is the earth; there is no change, no ruin, no rent made in her verdurous expanse; she continues to wheel round and round, with alternate night and day, through the sky, though man is not her adorner or inhabitant. Why could I not forget myself like one of those animals, and no longer suffer the wild tumult of misery that I endure? Yet, ah! what a deadly breach yawns between their state and mine! Have not they companions? Have not they each their mate—their cherished young, their home, which, though unexpressed to us, is, I doubt not, endeared and enriched, even in their eyes, by the society which kind nature has created for them? It is I only that am alone—I, on this little hilltop, gazing on plain and mountain recess; on sky, and its starry population, listening to every sound of earth, and air, and murmuring wave—I only cannot express to any companion my many thoughts, nor lay my throbbing head on any loved bosom, nor drink from meeting eyes an intoxicating dew that transcends the fabulous nectar of the gods. Shall I not then complain? Shall I not curse the murderous engine which has mowed down the children of men, my brethren? Shall I not bestow a malediction on every other of nature's offspring, which dares live and enjoy, while I live and suffer?

Ah, no! I will discipline my sorrowing heart to sympathy in your joys; I will be happy, because ye are so. Live on, ye innocents, nature's selected darlings; I am not much unlike to you. Nerves, pulse, brain, joint, and flesh, of such am I composed, and ye are organized by the same laws. I have something beyond this, but I will call it a defect, not an endowment, if it leads me to misery, while ye are happy. Just then, there emerged from a near copse two goats and a little kid, by the mother's side; they began to browze[1] the herbage of the hill. I approached near to them without their perceiving me; I gathered a handful of fresh grass and held it out; the little one nestled close to its mother, while she timidly withdrew. The male stepped forward, fixing his eyes on me: I drew near, still holding out my lure, while he, depressing his head, rushed at me with his horns. I was a very fool; I knew it, yet I yielded to my rage. I snatched up a huge fragment of rock; it would have crushed my rash foe. I poised it—aimed it—then my heart failed me. I hurled it wide of the mark; it rolled clattering among the bushes into dell. My little visitants, all aghast, galloped back into the covert of the wood; while I, my very heart bleeding and torn, rushed down the hill, and by the violence of bodily exertion sought to escape from my miserable self.

No, no, I will not live among the wild scenes of nature, the enemy of all that lives. I will seek the towns—Rome, the capital of the world, the crown of man's achievements. Among its storied streets, hallowed ruins, and stupendous remains of human exertion, I shall not, as here, find every thing forgetful of man; trampling on his memory, defacing his works, proclaiming from hill to hill, and vale to vale—by the torrents freed from the boundaries which he imposed, by the vegetation liberated from the laws which he enforced, by his habitation abandoned to mildew and weeds—that his power is lost, his race annihilated for ever.

I hailed the Tiber, for that was, as it were, an unalienable possession of humanity. I hailed the wild Campagna,[2] for every rood[3] had been trod by man; and its savage uncultivation, of no recent date, only proclaimed more distinctly his power, since he had given an honourable name and sacred title to what else would have been a worthless, barren track. I entered Eternal Rome by the Porta del Popolo,[4] and saluted with awe its time-honoured space. The wide square, the churches near, the long extent of the Corso, the near eminence of Trinita de' Monti[5] appeared like fairy work, they were so silent, so peaceful, and so very fair. It was evening, and the population of animals which still existed in this mighty city had gone to rest; there was no sound, save the murmur of its many fountains, whose soft monotony was harmony to my soul. The knowledge that I was in Rome soothed me; that wondrous city, hardly more illustrious for its heroes and sages than for the power it exercised over the imaginations of men. I went to rest that night; the eternal burning of my heart quenched, my senses tranquil.

The next morning I eagerly began my rambles in

[1] *browze* Feed on.

[2] *Campagna* Plain to the north of Rome through which the Tiber River flows before entering the city.

[3] *rood* Measure of land, varying from six to eight yards.

[4] *Porta del Popolo* Italian: "Gate of the People."

[5] *Corso* Via del Corso, main street of central Rome; a fashionable promenade in Shelley's time; *Trinita de' Monti* Church located at the top of the Spanish Steps.

search of oblivion. I ascended the many terraces of the garden of the Colonna Palace,[1] under whose roof I had been sleeping; and, passing out from it at its summit, I found myself on Monte Cavallo. The fountain sparkled in the sun; the obelisk above pierced the clear dark-blue air. The statues on each side, the works, as they are inscribed, of Phidias and Praxiteles, stood in undiminished grandeur, representing Castor and Pollux,[2] who with majestic power tamed the rearing animal at their side. If those illustrious artists had in truth chiselled these forms, how many passing generations had their giant proportions outlived! and now they were viewed by the last of the species they were sculptured to represent and deify. I had shrunk into insignificance in my own eyes, as I considered the multitudinous beings these stone demigods had outlived, but this after-thought restored me to dignity in my own conception. The sight of the poetry eternized in these statues, took the sting from the thought, arraying it only in poetic ideality.

I repeated to myself—I am in Rome! I behold, and, as it were, familiarly converse with the wonder of the world, sovereign mistress of the imagination, majestic and eternal survivor of millions of generations of extinct men. I endeavoured to quiet the sorrows of my aching heart by even now taking an interest in what in my youth I had ardently longed to see. Every part of Rome is replete with relics of ancient times. The meanest streets are strewed with truncated columns, broken capitals—Corinthian and Ionic—and sparkling fragments of granite or porphyry. The walls of the most penurious dwellings enclose a fluted pillar or ponderous stone, which once made part of the palace of the Caesars; and the voice of dead time, in still vibrations, is breathed from these dumb things, animated and glorified as they were by man.

I embraced the vast columns of the temple of Jupiter Stator,[3] which survives in the open space that was the Forum, and leaning my burning cheek against its cold durability, I tried to lose the sense of present misery and present desertion by recalling to the haunted cell of my brain vivid memories of times gone by. I rejoiced at my success, as I figured Camillus, the Gracchi, Cato, and last the heroes of Tacitus,[4] which shine meteors of surpassing brightness during the murky night of the empire; as the verses of Horace and Virgil, or the glowing periods of Cicero,[5] thronged into the opened gates of my mind, I felt myself exalted by long forgotten enthusiasm. I was delighted to know that I beheld the scene which they beheld—the scene which their wives and mothers, and crowds of the unnamed, witnessed, while at the same time they honoured applauded, or wept for these matchless specimens of humanity. At length, then, I had found a consolation. I had not vainly sought the storied precincts of Rome—I had discovered a medicine for my many and vital wounds.

I sat at the foot of these vast columns. The Coliseum,[6] whose naked ruin is robed by nature in a verdurous and glowing veil, lay in the sunlight on my right. Not far off, to the left, was the Tower of the Capitol.[7] Triumphal arches, the falling walls of many temples, strewed the ground at my feet. I strove, I resolved, to force myself to see the Plebeian multitude and lofty Patrician forms congregated around; and, as the diorama of ages passed across my subdued fancy, they were replaced by the modern Roman: the Pope, in his white stole, distributing benedictions to the kneeling worshippers; the friar in his cowl; the dark-eyed girl, veiled by

---

[1] *Colonna Palace* Located on Monte Cavallo (also called Quirinal Hill), it contains an art gallery of sixteenth- and seventeeth- century paintings.

[2] *The statues ... Pollux* The statues of Castor and Pollux, the twin sons of Zeus and Leda, were then commonly (but incorrectly) ascribed to the fifth- and sixth-century BCE Greek sculptors Phidias and Praxiteles.

[3] *Jupiter Stator* Three large Corinthian columns remain of this temple, which is now thought to belong to Castor, rather than to Jupiter Stator (Jupiter the Stayer, or the Steadfast). The Forum, in

which these columns stand, was the location of the marketplace and the center for political, economic, and religious activities.

[4] *Camillus* Roman statesman and general of the fourth century BCE; *the Gracci* Brothers Tiberius and Caius Gracchus, second-century BCE supporters of the plebian cause; *Cato* Either Cato the Elder (234–149 BCE), a famous politician and orator, or Cato the Younger (95–46 BCE), a Roman statesman who committed suicide rather than submit to the tyranny of Octavius Caesar; *Tacitus* Roman historian (c. 55–115 CE) whose heroes include Alexander, Julius Caesar, Mithridates, and Seneca.

[5] *Horace ... Cicero* Horace and Virgil were two famous Roman poets of the first century BCE, famous for, respectively, *Odes* and *The Aeneid*. Cicero was a great orator, statesman, and prose writer who was assassinated by Caesar in 43 BCE.

[6] *Coliseum* Great amphitheater completed in 80 CE and used for gladiatorial combat.

[7] *Tower of the Capitol* Citadel located on Mons Capitolinus, one of the seven hills of Rome.

her mezzera;[1] the noisy, sun-burnt rustic, leading his herd of buffaloes and oxen to the Campo Vaccino.[2] The romance with which, dipping our pencils in the rainbow hues of sky and transcendent nature, we to a degree gratuitously endow the Italians, replaced the solemn grandeur of antiquity. I remembered the dark monk, and floating figures of "The Italian," and how my boyish blood had thrilled at the description.[3] I called to mind Corinna ascending the Capitol to be crowned,[4] and, passing from the heroine to the author, reflected how the Enchantress Spirit of Rome held sovereign sway over the minds of the imaginative, until it rested on me—sole remaining spectator of its wonders.

I was long wrapt by such ideas; but the soul wearies of a pauseless flight; and, stooping from its wheeling circuits round and round this spot, suddenly it fell ten thousand fathom deep, into the abyss of the present—into self-knowledge—into tenfold sadness. I roused myself—I cast off my waking dreams; and I, who just now could almost hear the shouts of the Roman throng, and was hustled by countless multitudes, now beheld the desert ruins of Rome sleeping under its own blue sky. The shadows lay tranquilly on the ground; sheep were grazing untended on the Palatine, and a buffalo stalked down the Sacred Way that led to the Capitol.[5] I was alone in the Forum; alone in Rome; alone in the world. Would not one living man—one companion in my weary solitude, be worth all the glory and remembered power of this time-honoured city? Double sorrow—sadness, bred in Cimmerian caves, robed my soul in a mourning garb. The generations I had conjured up to my fancy contrasted more strongly with the end of all—the single point in which, as a pyramid, the mighty fabric of society had ended, while I, on the giddy height, saw vacant space around me.

From such vague laments I turned to the contemplation of the minutiae of my situation. So far, I had not succeeded in the sole object of my desires, the finding a companion for my desolation. Yet I did not despair. It is true that my inscriptions were set up, for the most part, in insignificant towns and villages; yet, even without these memorials, it was possible that the person who, like me, should find himself alone in a depopulate land, should, like me, come to Rome. The more slender my expectation was, the more I chose to build on it, and to accommodate my actions to this vague possibility.

It became necessary, therefore, that for a time I should domesticate myself at Rome. It became necessary that I should look my disaster in the face—not playing the school-boy's part of obedience without submission; enduring life, and yet rebelling against the laws by which I lived.

Yet how could I resign myself? Without love, without sympathy, without communion with any, how could I meet the morning sun, and with it trace its oft repeated journey to the evening shades? Why did I continue to live—why not throw off the weary weight of time, and with my own hand let out the fluttering prisoner from my agonized breast? It was not cowardice that withheld me; for the true fortitude was to endure, and death had a soothing sound accompanying it that would easily entice me to enter its demesne. But this I would not do. I had, from the moment I had reasoned on the subject, instituted myself the subject to fate, and the servant of necessity, the visible laws of the invisible God—I believed that my obedience was the result of sound reasoning, pure feeling, and an exalted sense of the true excellence and nobility of my nature. Could I have seen in this empty earth, in the seasons and their change, the hand of a blind power only, most willingly would I have placed my head on the sod and closed my eyes on its loveliness for ever. But fate had administered life to me when the plague had already seized on its prey—she had dragged me by the hair from out the strangling waves. By such miracles she had bought me for her own; I admitted her authority, and bowed to her decrees. If, after mature consideration, such was my resolve, it was doubly necessary that I should not lose the end of life, the improvement of my faculties, and poison its flow by repinings without end. Yet how cease to repine, since there was no hand near to extract the

[1] *mezzera* Mesèro (Italian), a shawl worn by women over the head and shoulders.

[2] *Campo Vaccino* Italian: "Cattle Pasture," the original function of the Roman Forum.

[3] *I remember … description* References to the novel *The Italian* (1797), by Ann Radcliffe.

[4] *Corinna … crowned* Reference to the heroine of Anne-Louise-Germaine de Staël's novel *Corinne, ou l'Italie* (1807).

[5] *Palatine* Most important of the seven hills of Rome, it was the location of the earliest Roman settlement; *Sacred Way* Sacra Via (Latin), the oldest street in Rome.

barbed spear that had entered my heart of hearts? I stretched out my hand, and it touched none whose sensations were responsive to mine. I was girded, walled in, vaulted over, by seven-fold barriers of loneliness. Occupation alone, if I could deliver myself up to it, would be capable of affording an opiate to my sleepless sense of woe. Having determined to make Rome my abode, at least for some months, I made arrangements for my accommodation—I selected my home. The Colonna Palace was well adapted for my purpose. Its grandeur—its treasure of paintings, its magnificent halls were objects soothing and even exhilarating.

I found the granaries of Rome well stored with grain, and particularly with Indian corn; this product, requiring less art in its preparation for food, I selected as my principal support. I now found the hardships and lawlessness of my youth turn to account. A man cannot throw off the habits of sixteen years. Since that age, it is true, I had lived luxuriously, or at least surrounded by all the conveniences civilization afforded. But before that time, I had been "as uncouth a savage as the wolf-bred founder of old Rome"[1]—and now, in Rome itself, robber and shepherd propensities, similar to those of its founder, were of advantage to its sole inhabitant. I spent the morning riding and shooting in the Campagna; I passed long hours in the various galleries; I gazed at each statue, and lost myself in a reverie before many a fair Madonna or beauteous nymph. I haunted the Vatican, and stood surrounded by marble forms of divine beauty. Each stone deity was possessed by sacred gladness and the eternal fruition of love. They looked on me with unsympathizing complacency, and often in wild accents I reproached them for their supreme indifference—for they were human shapes, the human form divine was manifest in each fairest limb and lineament. The perfect moulding brought with it the idea of colour and motion; often, half in bitter mockery, half in self-delusion, I clasped their icy proportions, and, coming between Cupid and his Psyche's lips,[2] pressed the unconceiving marble.

I endeavoured to read. I visited the libraries of Rome. I selected a volume, and, choosing some seques-

tered, shady nook on the banks of the Tiber, or opposite the fair temple in the Borghese Gardens, or under the old pyramid of Cestius,[3] I endeavoured to conceal me from myself, and immerse myself in the subject traced on the pages before me. As if in the same soil you plant nightshade and a myrtle tree, they will each appropriate the mould, moisture, and air administered, for the fostering their several properties—so did my grief find sustenance, and power of existence, and growth, in what else had been divine manna, to feed radiant meditation. Ah! while I streak this paper with the tale of what my so-named occupations were—while I shape the skeleton of my days—my hand trembles, my heart pants, and my brain refuses to lend expression, or phrase, or idea, by which to image forth the veil of unutterable woe that clothed these bare realities. O worn and beating heart, may I dissect thy fibres, and tell how in each unmitigable misery, sadness dire, repinings, and despair, existed? May I record my many ravings—the wild curses I hurled at torturing nature, and how I have passed days shut out from light and food, from all except the burning hell alive in my own bosom?

I was presented, meantime, with one other occupation, the one best fitted to discipline my melancholy thoughts, which strayed backwards, over many a ruin, and through many a flowery glade, even to the mountain recess from which in early youth I had first emerged.

During one of my rambles through the habitations of Rome, I found writing materials on a table in an author's study. Parts of a manuscript lay scattered about. It contained a learned disquisition on the Italian language; one page an unfinished dedication to posterity, for whose profit the writer had sifted and selected the niceties of this harmonious language—to whose everlasting benefit he bequeathed his labours.

I also will write a book, I cried—for whom to read?—to whom dedicated? And then with silly flourish (what so capricious and childish as despair?) I wrote,

DEDICATION
TO THE ILLUSTRIOUS DEAD.
SHADOWS, ARISE, AND READ YOUR FALL!

---

[1] *as … Rome* Romulus, the founder of Rome, and his brother Remus were said to have been reared by a she-wolf. Lionel quotes a statement made earlier by himself, in Chapter 1.

[2] *Cupid … lips* Cupid, god of love, and his mortal lover, Psyche.

[3] *old … Cestius* Tomb of Praetor Gaius Cestius Epulo (d. 12 BCE), next to which is the Protestant cemetery in which Percy Shelley was buried.

BEHOLD THE HISTORY OF THE
LAST MAN.

Yet, will not this world be re-peopled, and the children of a saved pair of lovers, in some to me unknown and unattainable seclusion, wandering to these prodigious relics of the ante-pestilential race, seek to learn how beings so wondrous in their achievements, with imaginations infinite, and powers godlike, had departed from their home to an unknown country?

I will write and leave in this most ancient city, this "world's sole monument,"[1] a record of these things. I will leave a monument of the existence of Verney, the Last Man. At first I thought only to speak of plague, of death, and last, of desertion; but I lingered fondly on my early years, and recorded with sacred zeal the virtues of my companions. They have been with me during the fulfilment of my task. I have brought it to an end—I lift my eyes from my paper—again they are lost to me. Again I feel that I am alone.

A year has passed since I have been thus occupied. The seasons have made their wonted round, and decked this eternal city in a changeful robe of surpassing beauty. A year has passed; and I no longer *guess* at my state or my prospects—loneliness is my familiar, sorrow my inseparable companion. I have endeavoured to brave the storm—I have endeavoured to school myself to fortitude—I have sought to imbue myself with the lessons of wisdom. It will not do. My hair has become nearly grey—my voice, unused now to utter sound, comes strangely on my ears. My person, with its human powers and features, seem to me a monstrous excrescence of nature. How express in human language a woe human being until this hour never knew! How give intelligible expression to a pang none but I could ever understand!—No one has entered Rome. None will ever come. I smile bitterly at the delusion I have so long nourished, and still more when I reflect that I have exchanged it for another as delusive, as false, but to which I now cling with the same fond trust.

Winter has come again; and the gardens of Rome have lost their leaves—the sharp air comes over the Campagna, and has driven its brute inhabitants to take up their abode in the many dwellings of the deserted city. Frost has suspended the gushing fountains, and Trevi[2] has stilled her eternal music. I had made a rough calculation, aided by the stars, by which I endeavoured to ascertain the first day of the new year. In the old outworn age, the Sovereign Pontiff[3] was used to go in solemn pomp, and mark the renewal of the year by driving a nail in the gate of the temple of Janus.[4] On that day I ascended St. Peter's, and carved on its topmost stone the aera 2100, last year of the world!

My only companion was a dog, a shaggy fellow, half water- and half shepherd's-dog, whom I found tending sheep in the Campagna. His master was dead, but nevertheless he continued fulfilling his duties in expectation of his return. If a sheep strayed from the rest, he forced it to return to the flock, and sedulously kept off every intruder. Riding in the Campagna I had come upon his sheep-walk, and for some time observed his repetition of lessons learned from man, now useless, though unforgotten. His delight was excessive when he saw me. He sprung up to my knees; he capered round and round, wagging his tail, with the short, quick bark of pleasure: he left his fold to follow me, and from that day has never neglected to watch by and attend on me, showing boisterous gratitude whenever I caressed or talked to him. His pattering steps and mine alone were heard when we entered the magnificent extent of nave and aisle of St. Peter's.[5] We ascended the myriad steps together when on the summit I achieved my design, and in rough figures noted the date of the last year. I then turned to gaze on the country, and to take leave of Rome. I had long determined to quit it, and I now formed the plan I would adopt for my future career, after I had left this magnificent abode.

A solitary being is by instinct a wanderer, and that I would become. A hope of amelioration always attends on change of place, which would even lighten the burden of my life. I had been a fool to remain in Rome all this time: Rome noted for malaria, the famous caterer for death. But it was still possible, that, could I visit the

---

[1] *world's sole monument* From Edmund Spenser's *Ruins of Rome* (1591): "Rome living, was the world's sole ornament, / And dead, is now the world's sole monument" (lines 405-6).

[2] *Trevi* Fountain on the Quirinal Hill, built in 1762 by Nicola Salvi.

[3] *Sovereign Pontiff* I.e., the Pontifex Maximus, the Roman High Priest, a title later given to the pope.

[4] *Janus* Roman god of gates, of doorways, and of the new year.

[5] *nave* Main body of a church; *St Peter's* Basilica of the Vatican.

whole extent of earth, I should find in some part of the wide extent a survivor. Methought the sea-side was the most probable retreat to be chosen by such a one. If left alone in an inland district, still they could not continue in the spot where their last hopes had been extinguished; they would journey on, like me, in search of a partner for their solitude, till the watery barrier stopped their further progress.

To that water—cause of my woes—perhaps now to be their cure I would betake myself. Farewell, Italy!—farewell, thou ornament of the world, matchless Rome, the retreat of the solitary one during long months!—to civilized life—to the settled home and succession of monotonous days, farewell! Peril will now be mine; and I hail her as a friend—death will perpetually cross my path, and I will meet him as a benefactor; hardship, inclement weather, and dangerous tempests will be my sworn mates. Ye spirits of storm, receive me! ye powers of destruction, open wide your arms, and clasp me for ever! if a kinder power have not decreed another end, so that after long endurance I may reap my reward, and again feel my heart beat near the heart of another like to me.

Tiber, the road which is spread by nature's own hand, threading her continent, was at my feet, and many a boat was tethered to the banks. I would with a few books, provisions, and my dog, embark in one of these and float down the current of the stream into the sea; and then, keeping near land, I would coast the beauteous shores and sunny promontories of the blue Mediterranean, pass Naples, along Calabria,[1] and would dare the twin perils of Scylla and Charybdis;[2] then with fearless aim, (for what had I to lose?) skim ocean's surface towards Malta and the further Cyclades. I would avoid Constantinople, the sight of whose well-known towers and inlets belonged to another state of existence from my present one; I would coast Asia Minor, and Syria, and, passing the seven-mouthed Nile, steer northward again, till, losing sight of forgotten Carthage and deserted Lybia, I should reach the pillars of Hercu-les.[3] And then, no matter where—the oozy caves and soundless depths of ocean may be my dwelling before I accomplish this long-drawn voyage, or the arrow of disease find my heart as I float singly on the weltering Mediterranean; or, in some place I touch at, I may find what I seek—a companion; or, if this may not be, to endless time, decrepit and grey headed— youth already in the grave with those I love—the lone wanderer will still unfurl his sail, and clasp the tiller, and, still obeying the breezes of heaven, for ever round another and another promontory, anchoring in another and another bay, still ploughing seedless ocean, leaving behind the verdant land of native Europe, adown the tawny shore of Africa, having weathered the fierce seas of the Cape,[4] I may moor my worn skiff in a creek, shaded by spicy groves of the odorous islands of the far Indian ocean.

These are wild dreams. Yet since, now a week ago, they came on me, as I stood on the height of St. Peter's, they have ruled my imagination. I have chosen my boat, and laid in my scant stores. I have selected a few books; the principal are Homer and Shakespeare—but the libraries of the world are thrown open to me, and in any port I can renew my stock. I form no expectation of alteration for the better; but the monotonous present is intolerable to me. Neither hope nor joy are my pilots—restless despair and fierce desire of change lead me on. I long to grapple with danger, to be excited by fear, to have some task, however slight or voluntary, for each day's fulfilment. I shall witness all the variety of appearance that the elements can assume—I shall read fair augury in the rainbow, menace in the cloud, some lesson or record dear to my heart in everything. Thus around the shores of deserted earth, while the sun is high, and the moon waxes or wanes, angels, the spirits of the dead, and the ever-open eye of the Supreme, will behold the tiny bark, freighted with Verney—the LAST MAN.

THE END

—1826

---

1   *Calabria*   Region of southern Italy.

2   *Scylla and Charybdis*   From Greek mythology, a sea monster, later turned into rock cliffs, and a whirlpool, located in the Straits of Messina.

3   *the pillars of Hercules*   The Rock of Gibraltar and the Hill of Ceuta, two promontories flanking the eastern end to the Strait of Gibraltar, which were considered in ancient times to mark the ends of the earth.

4   *Cape*   Cape of Good Hope.

IN CONTEXT

The "Last Man" Theme in the Nineteenth Century

The theme of "the last man" was one that captured a great many imaginations in the 1820s and 1830s. Shelley's 1826 novel followed on the heels of Thomas Campbell's 1823 poem of the same name (to which, according to Campbell, Byron's poem "Darkness" owes its inspiration). Also in 1826 a number of magazine pieces were published on the same theme, including "The Last Man" (*Blackwoods*) and "The Death of the World" (*European Magazine*). That same year the painter John Martin, whose work often focused on apocalyptic visions, painted an initial study (now lost) of "The Last Man," a watercolor of which he completed in 1832, and an oil painting in 1849. The Campbell poem and the Martin painting are reproduced below; both envisage the end of the world occurring as a result of the sun's light being extinguished, rather than as a result of plague or other natural disaster.

Thomas Campbell, "The Last Man," *New Monthly Magazine* 8 (1823)

All worldly shapes shall melt in gloom,
The Sun himself must die,
Before this mortal shall assume
   Its Immortality!
5   I saw a vision in my sleep,
That gave my spirit strength to sweep
   Adown the gulf of Time!
I saw the last of human mould,
That shall Creation's death behold,
10   As Adam saw her prime!

The Sun's eye had a sickly glare,
   The Earth with age was wan,
The skeletons of nations were
   Around that lonely man!
15 Some had expir'd in fight—the brands
Still rusted in their bony hands;
   In plague and famine some!
Earth's cities had no sound nor tread;
And ships were drifting with the dead
20   To shores where all was dumb!

Yet, prophet like, that lone one stood,
   With dauntless words and high,
That shook the sere° leaves from the wood   *withered*
   As if a storm pass'd by,
25   Saying, we are twins in death, proud Sun,
Thy face is cold, thy race is run,
     'Tis Mercy bids thee go.
For thou ten thousand thousand years
Hast seen the tide of human tears,
30   That shall no longer flow.

What though beneath thee man put forth
   His pomp, his pride, his skill;
And arts that made fire, flood, and earth,
   The vassals of his will—
35   Yet mourn I not thy parted sway,
Thou dim discrownèd king of day:
     For all those trophied arts
And triumphs that beneath thee sprang,
Heal'd not a passion or a pang
40   Entail'd on human hearts.

Go, let oblivion's curtain fall
   Upon the stage of men,
Nor with thy rising beams recall
   Life's tragedy again.
45   Its piteous pageants bring not back,
Nor waken flesh, upon the rack
     Of pain anew to writhe;
Stretch'd in disease's shapes abhorr'd,
Or mown in battle by the sword,
50   Like grass beneath the scythe.

Ev'n I am weary in yon skies
   To watch thy fading fire;
Test of all sumless agonies,
   Behold not me expire.
55   My lips that speak thy dirge of death—
Their rounded gasp and gurgling breath
     To see thou shalt not boast.
The eclipse of Nature spreads my pall—
The majesty of Darkness shall
60   Receive my parting ghost!

This spirit shall return to Him
        That gave its heavenly spark;
Yet think not, Sun, it shall be dim
        When thou thyself art dark!
65   No! it shall live again, and shine
In bliss unknown to beams of thine,
        By Him recall'd to breath,
Who captive led captivity,
Who robb'd the grave of Victory—
70   And took the sting from Death!

Go, Sun, while Mercy holds me up
        On Nature's awful waste
To drink this last and bitter cup
        Of grief that man shall taste—
75   Go, tell the night that hides thy face,
Thou saw'st the last of Adam's race,
        On Earth's sepulchral clod,
The dark'ning universe defy
To quench his Immortality,
80   Or shake his trust in God!

from Thomas Campbell's letter to the editor of the *Edinburgh Review*, 28 February 1825

... You say that my poem, "The Last Man," seems to have been suggested by Lord Byron's poem "Darkness." Now the truth is, that fifteen, or it may be more, years ago, I called on Lord Byron, who at that time had lodgings near St. James's Street; and we had a long, and to me a very memorable, conversation, from which I have not a doubt that his Lordship imbibed those few ideas in the poem "Darkness" which have any resemblance to mine in "The Last Man." I remember my saying to him that I thought the idea of a being witnessing the extinction of his species and of the Creation, and of his looking, under the fading eye of nature, at desolate cities, ships floating at sea with the dead, would make a striking subject for a poem. I met those very ideas, many years afterwards, when I read Lord Byron's poem "Darkness."

John Martin, *The Last Man* (1849).

The Victorian Era

The word "Victorian" conjures up a series of images that both accurately describe and misrepresent the literature and culture of nineteenth-century Britain. Stiff collars and stiff upper lips, draped table legs, exceedingly long novels and gritty urban squalor have become the iconic images of Victorian Britain. But these images reveal only one dimension of what is a much more complex picture. While it is certainly the case that Victorians tended to place a high value on such qualities as honor, duty, moral seriousness and sexual propriety, it is a mistake to assume that most were humorless or repressed. And while many of the best known Victorian novels run to many hundreds of pages, we need to remember that Victorian audiences read them in weekly or monthly installments, or in shorter volumes. Although brutal factory conditions, pitiful wages, and crowded cities impoverished many millions of people, the Victorian period also saw the passage of progressive labor laws, unprecedented wealth creation for some, and the first public sewage systems in Britain.

It is fair to say that there was never a single "Victorian mindset" or "Victorian value system" but a range of them, and that they shifted throughout the century. Nor is there a consensus about when the Victorian era began and ended. Some point to the passage of the Reform Bill of 1832 as the dawn of a new era, or to the abolition of slavery in the British Empire, in 1833. Others argue for the unity of a longer period, beginning perhaps with the end of the Napoleonic Wars in 1815, perhaps even earlier (some see the seeds of "Victorianism" being planted as early as the late eighteenth century, with the re-emergence of Evangelicalism), and ending with the outbreak of World War I in 1914. The obvious choice is to date the period starting with Victoria's ascension to the throne in 1837 to her death in 1901, but there is good reason not to identify the period solely on the basis of her reign.

Franz Xavier Winterhalter, *Queen Victoria*, 1842.

Photographer unknown, *Her Majesty the Queen*, 21 June 1887.

Photographer unknown, *Queen Victoria*, c. 1897.
A picture of Albert is in the background.

Although a great deal of overlap can be found between the Romantic and Victorian periods, most agree that the 1830s was a pivotal decade, marked by the transition of the monarchy from William IV to Victoria and by the spread of a spirit of political and social reform that would characterize the next several decades. During the 1850s and 60s, Britain emerged from a depressed economy and experienced a level of political and social stability that made these decades the most prosperous of the century; the mid-Victorian period is now often regarded as a kind of high-water mark for Victorian culture. The 1870s and 1880s saw some decline in the strength of the economy and in Britain's imperial dominance abroad, despite its continued acquisition of colonial possessions. These decades were marked by the glimmerings of another wave of social change. The fin-de-siècle spirit of the 1890s saw many challenges to the values and conventions of the preceding decades in literature, politics, and everyday life.

A GROWING POWER

During Victoria's reign, Britain was the richest nation and the most powerful empire on the globe, with unchallenged military supremacy until the latter decades of the century and an imperial reach that covered one quarter of the earth's surface by 1897. As the world's first industrialized country, Britain experienced both the benefits and the horrors of enormous growth throughout the nineteenth century. The census of 1801 put the population of the country at eleven million people. At the end of the century that number had increased by almost three hundred percent to thirty-seven million. Just as striking was the movement of this population, from 75 percent rural distribution in the early decades to nearly the same percentage residing in urban districts by the end of the century. Northern industrial cities grew particularly fast: Manchester, a town of no more than 15,000 people in 1750, had grown to 75,000 by 1800, and to 125,000 by 1820; by 1850 its population was over 300,000. Between 1815 and 1914 more than 20 million people emigrated from Britain to other parts of the world, over half of them to the United States, but millions, too, to Australia and to Canada. (The writings of Susanna Moodie, excerpted in

Fleet Street, London, c. 1890.

Construction of the sewer beneath Fleet Street, London, early 1860s. By 1858 the stench of sewage from the Thames had become so overwhelming that the Houses of Parliament at Westminster found it impossible to meet; construction of a city-wide underground system of sewers, under the direction of Joseph Bazalgette, began the following year.

Building the Holborn Viaduct across the Fleet valley (*Illustrated Times*, 18 September 1869). The viaduct, carrying both road and rail traffic, was a vast project carried out by the Corporation of the City of London between 1863 and 1869.

this volume, provide a vivid sense of the immigrant experience in what was then the British colony of Upper Canada.)

The shift from an agrarian to an industrial wage economy meant an increase in income for many people, creating a sector of the population that was neither rich nor poor and was frequently coming to be termed "middle class." A spirit of entrepreneurship and market thinking dominated by upwardly mobile males was replacing an entrenched system of aristocratic patronage and paternalism in the world of business and trade. The Reform Bill of 1832 granted political representation in Parliament to certain sectors of the middle-class male population for the first time (although even with its passage, only one in six adult males could vote, and the suffrage was still linked to property ownership). Rail travel, the advent of the telegraph, daily newspapers, and the manufacture and import of goods via steamship from all over the globe collapsed time and space, and flooded the homes of the affluent with new luxuries and conveniences. The Great Exhibition of 1851, the first world's fair, showcased Britain's industrial dominance with exhibits of new consumer goods and remarkable technologies. The event symbolized Britain's reputation as the "workshop of the world." For many the overall mood was positive, and Thomas Macaulay's confident assertions on the nation's progress in his bestselling *History of England* rang true for much of his audience.

Alfred Morgan, *An Omnibus Ride to Piccadilly Circus—Mr. Gladstone Travelling with Ordinary Passengers*, 1885. The previous year Prime Minister William Gladstone's government had extended the franchise to working class males, through the Reform Bill of 1884.

GRINDING MILLS, GRINDING POVERTY

The paradox of the economic life of the time was summed up by Thomas Carlyle in 1843: "England is full of wealth," he wrote, "of multifarious produce, supply for human want in every kind; yet England is dying of inanition." For millions of people, low wages, unemployment, and fluctuations in trade created widespread misery in crowded industrial cities such as Manchester and Birmingham. According to one estimate, 70 percent of the population at mid-century

was considered poor. The new law divided and categorized the poor as either "deserving" (the elderly and the physically infirm) or "undeserving" (the able-bodied but unemployed). The poor were now eligible to receive public assistance only in the notorious workhouses, also known as the "Poor Law Bastilles" since they ended up punishing and stigmatizing the poor rather than relieving them. In addition, inadequate housing and slum conditions led to frequent outbreaks of illness and disease. Four cholera epidemics between 1831 and 1866 killed more than 140,000 people, inaugurating Britain's first wide-scale public health movement. Scores of statistical investigations, surveys, and government reports known as "Blue Books" on the condition of inner-city neighbourhoods culminated in the Public Health Acts of 1848 and the 1870s. Factories and mines producing iron, cotton, and coal were unregulated, employing men, women, and children in conditions that were often dirty and dangerous. A series of Factory Acts between 1802 and 1847 attempted to force employers to limit work hours (working fourteen hours a day was not uncommon) and prohibit the employment of children under the age of nine in certain industries.

In her poem, "The Cry of the Children," Elizabeth Barrett Browning drew attention to the problem of child labor, helping to create humanitarian awareness on the part of middle-class readers by asking "How long, O cruel nation, / Will you stand to move the world, on a child's heart." Thomas Hood's "The Song of the Shirt" focused on the plight of the genteel but impoverished female needleworker who toils alone in grim conditions for meager wages. Cast in the elevated and stylized "voices" of their victimized speakers, such poems were both wildly popular and highly sentimental, qualities that have until recently served to exclude them from serious study by scholars of English literature. Yet these poems did as much or more than government reports and statistical surveys to shed light on major social issues. So too did Carlyle's *Past and Present*, which called England to responsibility for the many starving workers in the land of "plenty":

> We have more riches than any Nation ever had before: we have less good of them than any Nation had before. ... We have forgotten everywhere that

Cash-payment is not the sole relation of human beings; we think, nothing doubting, that it absolves and liquidates all other engagements.

Such voices spoke up in support of the destitute and the working classes; increasingly, over the course of the century, the voices of working class people themselves were also heard. The 1828 publication of Robert Blincoe's *Memoir* of his appalling early life in the mills had a lasting impact; in addition to a direct effect on its readers, Blincoe's memoir provided much of the raw material for Frances Trollope's novel *Michael Armstrong: Factory Boy* (1840), and may also have inspired Dickens's *Oliver Twist*. Blincoe's memoir was followed by a number of other autobiographical narratives of working-class hardship (that of William Dodd notable among them). Ellen Johnson published a more wide-ranging memoir, *Autobiography of a Factory Girl* (1867), together with her poems and songs. Another prominent working-class poetic voice was that of Ebenezer Elliott, the "Corn-Law Rhymer" from Yorkshire who became an active force first in the Chartist movement and then in the struggle to repeal the Corn Laws (discussed below). In his *Corn-Law Rhymes* (1831) and in subsequent work Elliott attacked

> The deadly will that takes
> What labour ought to keep;
> It is the deadly power that makes
> Bread dear and labour cheap.

How best to respond to the force of this "deadly power"? If some emphasized the need to continually press for political reform, others appealed emotionally for hearts to change—and still others formulated new philosophical approaches to the underlying moral and socio-economic questions. Perhaps the most important of these was Utilitarianism, a broad-reaching philosophy that had first been developed in the late eighteenth century (primarily by Jeremy Bentham), and that was expounded in a more careful, subtle, and thoroughgoing fashion by John Stuart Mill in the nineteenth. Utilitarian thought began to shape governmental policy, including the New Poor Law, in the middle decades of the nineteenth century—and continues to be a shaping force in the social policy of most developed nations today. In its crude form Utilitarianism holds (in the

Thomas Iron Works, London, 1867.

words of Bentham's 1776 "A Fragment on Government") that "it is the greatest happiness of the greatest number that is the measure of right and wrong." In other words, the central guiding principle of social morality should be the pursuit of the what is good for all members of society, with no one person or group's interests given special weight. But how does one calculate "the greatest happiness of the greatest number"? Can social, legal, economic and political problems be resolved by a "moral arithmetic" that evaluates human pain and pleasure according to entirely rationalist principles? According to some crude versions of utilitarian philosophy (though certainly not that of Mill), the answer is yes; imagination, feeling, and individual desire are obsolete impediments to the operation of the "laws" of social improvement, which may be derived from empirical observation and calculation.

Hatting mill, Manchester, 1890s.

Writers such as Elizabeth Barrett Browning, Dickens, Carlyle, and John Ruskin were intensely critical of Utilitarianism, taking its crudest forms as representative and regarding it as a morally and spiritually bankrupt response to the human condition. Dickens, in particular, caricatured utilitarian thinking with telling directness in his portrayal of Thomas Gradgrind in *Hard*

Times. (It may perhaps be wondered, however, if the intensity of the opposition of such writers to Utilitarianism also related in part to a fear of the consequences if utilitarian notions were extended to their logical conclusion; certainly to Mill "the greatest number" included not only white people in poverty in England but also brown people and black people in poverty the world over, whereas Dickens, Carlyle and Ruskin, for all their sympathy for the British poor, looked at best with condescension and at worst with outright loathing on people of other races.) In any case, as the works of writers such as Dickens, Barrett Browning, and Elizabeth Gaskell amply demonstrated, opposition to the cruelties of poverty could be expressed as plausibly and at least as powerfully by means of emotional and aesthetic appeals through literature as it could by means of the philosophical arguments of the Utilitarians.

CORN LAWS, POTATO FAMINE

As the powerful and privileged attempted to confront the range of social crises facing a newly industrialized nation, economic depression, unemployment, political instability in Europe and a series of crop failures in the 1840s—a decade often dubbed the "Hungry Forties"—caused a disproportionate level of suffering for the poor. Artificial shortages of grain in the country inflated the price of bread beyond the reach of the working class, causing periodic bread riots and a discontented work force. These shortages were in part the result of the Corn Laws, which imposed heavy tariffs on imports of grain, and were intended to protect British agricultural interests and limit dependence on foreign supplies of cereal grains. The Corn Laws were repealed in 1846 under the pressure of the Anti-Corn-Law League, an alliance of free trade advocates and liberal, laissez-faire[1] trade reformers.

In the wake of the repeal of the Corn Laws, three successive crop failures in Ireland led to one of the worst humanitarian disasters of the century, the Irish potato

---

[1] The phrase "laissez-faire" (French, literally "allow to do") came to be used in the late eighteenth century as a shorthand for the belief that government is best advised to intervene as little as possible in the workings of the economy.

famine of 1845–47. Prime Minister Robert Peel's government attempted to alleviate the situation by importing emergency shipments of grain from the United States in 1845, but when Peel's government was replaced by Lord John Russell's Whig administration in 1846, Russell in effect put a stop to emergency aid; the laissez-faire interests of Russell and his supporters led to the transfer of responsibility for famine relief to the inadequate jurisdiction of the Irish Poor Law. By 1847 somewhere between 850,000 and 1,500,000 Irish— from ten to over fifteen per cent of the population—had died of starvation. English government policy toward Ireland, its nearest colonial possession, was in this instance one of neglect amounting to extraordinary cruelty.

Inevitably, hostility towards the English, and with it Irish nationalist sentiment, was greatly intensified by the potato famine. The seeds of the Irish independence movement had been effectively sown—and sown not only in Ireland but also in the United States, where hundreds of thousands of Irish emigrated during this period. As they prospered in America they provided more and more support for the Fenian movement that sprang up in the 1850s in support of Irish independence (and that launched attacks in the 1860s and 1870s not only in England but also against British possessions in New Brunswick, Upper Canada, and Manitoba), and for subsequent political groups with like aims. But the road to Irish independence was an extraordinarily rocky one: the Irish won the right to be represented in the British House of Commons, but their greatest Parliamentary spokesman, Charles Parnell, after surviving dozens of scurrilous attempts to discredit him, was finally brought down when his affair with a divorced woman became a public scandal; British Prime Minister William Gladstone became a convert to the cause of Home Rule for the Irish and passed a bill authorizing it through the House of Commons in 1886, only to have the measure killed in the House of Lords; a similar bill in 1893 suffered the same fate; another bill to enact Home Rule was put aside with the outbreak of the First World War in 1914; and in the end, independence was only achieved after the violent struggles of the 1916

Easter Uprising and the War of Independence of 1919–22. Even then, the British retained possession of a substantial area in northern Ireland.

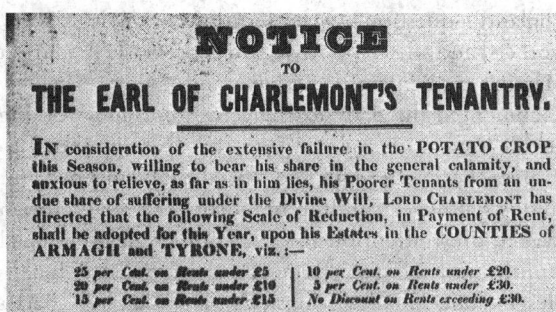

Notice of a rent abatement by an Irish landlord, 1846.

Evicted family, Glenbeigh, Ireland, 1888. In the 1880s an economic depression coincided with the election of a substantial number of Irish Home Rule Members of Parliament (under Charles Parnell's leadership), and with a campaign by the Land League to resist the practice of evicting impoverished tenant farmers unable to pay their rent.

"The Two Nations"

In the 1830s and 40s, the human costs of the industrial revolution—what became known as the "Condition of England" question—were scrutinized by legislators, workers, and writers. Carlyle, Dickens, Gaskell, Harriet Martineau, Benjamin Disraeli and Henry Mayhew documented the daily existence of poor and working people, and criticized the laws that were intended to address their suffering. The "social problem novel" or "industrial novel," an important subgenre of Victorian fiction, drew attention to class conflict and the social ramifications of laissez-faire economic policies. Examples include Charles Kingsley's *Alton Locke*, Charles Dickens's *Hard Times*, and Elizabeth Gaskell's *Mary Barton* and *North and South*. In his 1845 novel, *Sybil* future Prime Minister Benjamin Disraeli coined the phrase "the Two Nations" to describe the disparity in Britain between rich and poor. Novelists felt that their work could provoke social reform by exposing their middle-class audiences to the plight of the working classes, who were often portrayed as either vulnerable and victimized by forces beyond their control, or as a violent, angry "mass"; intervention by those of goodwill from other social classes is often implicitly recommended in such fiction as a way of ameliorating the situation. The middle-class narrator of Gaskell's 1848 novel *Mary Barton*, for example, adopts the role of mediator between Manchester's workers and their industrial "masters" in an attempt to foster understanding and prevent political insurrection.

Non-fiction writing such as Henry Mayhew's may have been as important as that of any novelist in nurturing the seeds of social change. Mayhew's interviews with working people and street folk for the *Morning Chronicle* newspaper opened a window for its readers onto the daily existence of an often voiceless underclass. They contained no overt political commentary or reform agenda, however. Friedrich Engels, by contrast, in his chronicle of urban squalor *The Condition of the Working Class in England in 1844*, not only described the extraordinary scale of the human suffering he witnessed, but also placed the blame squarely on the shoulders of

Jabez Hughes, *Benjamin Disraeli*, c. 1877. Disraeli, who led the Conservative Party from 1868 to 1880 (serving as Prime Minister briefly in 1868 and then again from 1874 to 1880), was seen as something of an exotic within the English establishment. His parents were Jewish, but he was baptized as an infant and remained a practicing Anglican throughout his life. Disraeli's prolific literary career, which began with the publication of his first novel, *Vivian Grey*, in 1826, made him a well-known man of letters. A fashionable figure, Disraeli was derided by his strait-laced rival, Liberal leader William Gladstone, as "Asiatic"—a word often used in Victorian times as a synonym for "indulgent and irresponsible." But Disraeli remained a popular figure with much of the general population as well as with much of the establishment—and with the Queen.

John Everett Millais, *Ophelia* (1851–52). The drowning of Ophelia (from Shakespeare's *Hamlet*) was a frequent subject in Victorian painting; the best known representation is that of Millais. As the scene is described in Act 4, Scene 7 of the play, the mentally-ill Ophelia comes to a stream "with fantastic garlands" of flowers. Distracted, she falls into the "weeping brook." For a while before she drowns "her clothes spread wide" hold her up.

Henry Wallis, *Chatterton* (1856). The suicide of Thomas Chatterton (1752–70), of arsenic poisoning after years of living close to starvation as a struggling poet, captured the Victorian imagination even more strongly than it had the Romantic one. Wallis's painting was widely praised when exhibited in 1856 at the Royal Academy; John Ruskin described it in his notes on the exhibit as "faultless and wonderful."

Thomas Jones Barker, *The Secret of England's Greatness* (detail), c. 1863. Barker's painting depicts the Queen presenting a Bible. The recipient and the specific occasion remain unidentified; in the background are Prince Alberta; Elizabeth, Duchess of Wellington (who served as Mistress of the Robes to the Queen); Lord Palmerston (then serving as Prime Minister); and Lord John Russell (then serving as Foreign Secretary). An engraving of the painting was published under the fuller title, *The Bible: the Secret of England's Greatness.*

Franz Xavier Winterhalter, *The Royal Family in 1846* (detail), 1846.

Ford Madox Brown, *Work*, c. 1852–c. 1865. This famous painting, which took over twelve years to complete, brings together Victorians from an extraordinary range of backgrounds. The central group of excavators was the painting's starting point—the inspiration coming from the artist observing work on the construction of the London sewers. Less well-off members of society include the flower seller to the left and the motherless children in the foreground, cared for by an older sibling. To the right are two "brain-workers" admired by the artist, Rev. F.D. Maurice (founder of the Working Man's College, where Brown was an art instructor) and Thomas Carlyle. In the background members of the gentry on horseback observe the scene.

George Clausen, *The Stone Pickers*, 1887.

William Holman Hunt, *The Awakening Conscience*, 1853–54. This canvas presents an elaborately coded story. In a letter to *The Times* of London, John Ruskin (signing himself as "The Author of *Modern Painters*") described the reaction of viewers—and elucidated the painting's intended significance: "… assuredly it is not understood. People gaze at it in a blank wonder, and leave it hopelessly; so that, although it is almost an insult to the painter to explain his thoughts in this instance, I cannot persuade myself to leave it thus misunderstood. The poor girl has been singing with her seducer; some chance words of the song "Oft in the stilly night" have struck upon the numbed places of her heart; she has started up in agony; he, not seeing her face, goes on singing, striking the keys carelessly with his gloved hand." As Ruskin discerned, the woman is evidently the mistress rather than the wife of the man; she wears a ring on every finger of her left hand except the fourth. The piece that has been played, "Oft in the stilly night," is a song in which a woman looks back to the innocence of her childhood. The doubling of the female figure through the use of the mirror suggests the possibility of a brighter future if she follows her awakened conscience and gives up the life of a "kept woman."

G.W. Joy, *General Gordon's Last Stand*, c. 1893. Gordon, who had held an administrative post in the Sudan in the 1870s (and played an important role during that period in ending the slave trade in the area) was sent again to the Sudan in 1884 on a mission to rescue garrisons of British troops that had been cut off after a rebellion by Mohammed Ahmad (known to the British as "the Mahdi"). Gordon's forces were besieged in Khartoum for ten months and finally overwhelmed, and he was killed during the battle (though almost certainly in the streets of the city, not as he is shown in Joy's iconic painting of the imagined scene). The incident became a *cause célèbre* in Britain, and there were many calls to avenge Gordon's death, but it was not until fourteen years later that the British under General Kitchener re-established British control of the Sudan.

Trade Emblem, Amalgamated Society of Engineers, Machinists, Millwrights, Smiths, and Pattern Makers, c. 1860.

Alfred Concanen, *Modern Advertising: A Railway Station in 1874*, 1874. This colored lithograph appeared as a fold-out frontispiece in the book *A History of Advertising from the Earliest Times*.

John O'Connor, *From Pentonville Road Looking West*, 1884. In the background is St. Pancras, one of the greatest of Victorian railway stations.

Advertisement, 1890s, "Cook's Tours in Scotland." Featured at lower left is the Firth of Forth Bridge (also known as the Forth Rail Bridge). The bridge, built in the wake of the collapse of the Firth of Tay Bridge, in which 75 lives had been lost, pioneered new techniques of cantilever construction; on its completion in 1890 it was by far the longest bridge in the world.

Benjamin Duterrau, *The Conciliation*, 1840. The painting shows a Methodist lay preacher instructing native Tasmanians.

Canadian election poster, 1891. The "Old Leader" was Sir John A. Macdonald, Canadian Prime Minister from 1867 to 1873 and again from 1878 to 1891. "The Old Policy" was Macdonald's National Policy, under the terms of which industries in the Dominion were protected by a tariff on imports from the United States, but "imperial preference" exempted goods from Britain and her possessions from any tariff.

a class system created by industrial capitalism: "Power lies in the hands of those who own, directly or indirectly, foodstuffs and the means of production. The poor, having no capital, inevitably bear the consequences of defeat in the struggle." (Engels's treatise, first published in Germany in 1845, was not translated into English until 1892.)

It was not only middle-class writers and observers who were bringing attention to the great divide between Britain's rich and poor. Chartism, a movement that initiated a series of political campaigns in the 1830s and 40s, was a concrete expression of the desire of working-class people to resist economic and social disparity and press for political reform. The People's Charter of 1838, from which the movement took its name, petitioned the government to adopt a range of key reforms, including annual elections, universal male suffrage, the abolition of property qualifications for Members of Parliament, and the secret ballot. The mouthpiece of the Chartist

The Matchgirl Strike Committee, 1888. A threatened strike by Bryant and May Match Company employees—most of them girls of no more than 15, earning starvation wages and exposed to hazardous phosphorous fumes—became a *cause célèbre* in 1888, and forced the company to change its practices. The action was led by Annie Besant (who had initially become famous during her 1877 trial for obscenity —the charge being based on the distribution of her pamphlet offering practical advice on contraception).

The Six Points
OF THE
PEOPLE'S
CHARTER.

1. A VOTE for every man twenty-one years of age, of sound mind, and not undergoing punishment for crime.

2. THE BALLOT.—To protect the elector in the exercise of his vote.

3. NO PROPERTY QUALIFICATION for Members of Parliament —thus enabling the constituencies to return the man of their choice, be he rich or poor.

4. PAYMENT OF MEMBERS, thus enabling an honest tradesman, working man, or other person, to serve a constituency, when taken from his business to attend to the interests of the country.

5. EQUAL CONSTITUENCIES, securing the same amount of representation for the same number of electors, instead of allowing small constituencies to swamp the votes of large ones.

6. ANNUAL PARLIAMENTS, thus presenting the most effectual check to bribery and intimidation, since though a constituency might be bought once in seven years (even with the ballot), no purse could buy a constituency (under a system of universal suffrage) in each ensuing twelvemonth; and since members, when elected for a year only, would not be able to defy and betray their constituents as now.

Chartist poster, 1838.

movement was the *Northern Star* newspaper, one of many working-class periodicals that flourished in the early decades of the nineteenth century. The Chartist petitions were signed by up to five million people and presented to Parliament by a coalition of workers in 1839, 1842, and 1848, but were rejected each time. A number of middle-class writers sympathetic to the claims of the working classes were nevertheless suspicious of the Chartist movement, particularly in light of the political revolutions taking place in continental Europe in the late 1840s. In his longing for the imagined social order of a feudal past, Carlyle denounced the "mad Chartisms" of the "anarchic multitude," comparing them to the events of the French Revolution and the

Reign of Terror. With the defeat of the third petition, Chartism collapsed, but it had helped instigate a new level of class consciousness among ordinary people, and is now considered to be the first independent working-class movement in Britain.

In the 1880s and 90s various socialist movements emerged, partly on the strength of Karl Marx's theories of capital, which he formulated under the dome of the British Library after moving to London in 1849. The Fabian Society was one of the most influential socialist organizations. Its membership was mainly drawn from the middle class, and included George Bernard Shaw, Sidney Webb and Beatrice Potter Webb, Edith Nesbit, and Annie Besant. The Fabians' tactics were reforming rather than revolutionary; they advocated public owner-ship of utilities, affordable housing, improved wages, and greater access to higher education for all. Trade unions and labor movements grew gradually in scope and strength throughout the century, with the Trade Union Act of 1871 granting legal status to unions for the first time. Newly mobilized workers in the 1880s organized to mount a series of strikes with varying degrees of success. Two of the most highly publicized of these were the matchgirls' strike in 1888 and the London dock workers' strike of 1889. Union membership doubled in these years, partly because of the success of these labor actions.

THE POLITICS OF GENDER

Gender consciousness was also central to Victorian England's political scene. At the beginning of the Victorian period, middle-class women were shut out of most remunerative employments and institutions of higher education, could not vote, and had few legal rights. By the end of the century the situation did not look radically different (universal female suffrage, for example, was not achieved in Britain until 1928), but several key developments heralded the changes to come in the twentieth century. The first major challenges by Victorian "strong-minded women" to patriarchal control were in the area of marriage law. The common law doctrine of coverture ensured that a woman's legal identity was subsumed in that of her husband upon marriage. In effect, the law of coverture regarded the husband and wife as "one person": the husband. This meant that upon marriage a husband had full control of his wife's personal property and any earnings she acquired during the marriage; he had absolute authority over their home and children; and he could legally use physical force to discipline the members of his family. If he deserted his wife, she could not sue for divorce and had no custody rights to their children. No viable legal mechanism was available to an average woman to contest her husband's decisions, since husband and wife were "one body" under the law. The essayist Frances Power Cobbe was among the most effective in pointing out the illogic of such arrangements, as well as the terrible toll they exacted. In contemplating, for example, the situation of "the poor woman whose husband has robbed her earnings, who leaves her and her children to starve, and then goes unpunished because the law can only recognize the relation of husband and wife as … one before the law," Cobbe observed in her provocative 1868 essay "Criminals, Idiots, Women, and Minors" that

> It is one of the numerous anomalies connected with women's affairs, that when they are under debate the same argument which would be held to determine other questions in one way is felt to settle theirs in another. If for instance it be proved of any other class of the community, that it is particularly liable to be injured, imposed upon, and tyrannized over (e.g., the children who work in factories), it is considered to follow as a matter of course that the law must step in for its protection. But it is the alleged *helplessness* of married women which, it is said, makes it indispensable to give all the support of the law, *not* to them, but to the stronger persons with whom they are unequally yoked.

Under pressure from organized networks of reformers, several key pieces of legislation were passed that challenged married women's legal disabilities. In addition, the Matrimonial Causes Act of 1878 accorded some legal protection to female victims of domestic violence, and the Infant Custody Acts of 1839 and 1886 granted a woman custodial rights to her children. Although full equality within marriage was not realized in law until the twentieth century, the passage of this legislation

TAXATION WITHOUT REPRESENTATION.

POLITICAL CANDIDATE: "As your husband is dead, madam, and women do not vote, it is no use my staying."

TAX COLLECTOR: "As your husband is dead, madam, and women have to pay taxes, you will have to pay the tax instead of him."

Cartoon from *Votes for Women III* (7 January 1910).

The movement to win the vote for women began in the 1850s, and articles and petitions on the issue appeared with increasing frequency thereafter. Many of the early arguments drew parallels with other efforts to extend the franchise; as Mary Margaret Dilke observed in an 1889 article, "it is really an interesting study to notice how every argument used to delay the enfranchisement of working men and farm labourers reappears to do duty against women. How often has the question been asked, 'What does Hodge know about finance and foreign policy, colonial affairs and commercial interests?'"

As the suffrage movement grew, differences of opinion developed over the appropriate level of militancy to adopt and over whether the movement should press for universal suffrage or only for certain categories of women to be allowed to vote. The granting of the vote eventually came in two stages, with certain classes of propertied women granted the right to vote in 1918 (the same year the vote was granted to all men of 21 years or more), and all women over the age of 21 finally being granted the franchise in 1928.

began to chip away at male patriarchal privilege, and challenged the legal and religious "justifications" for women's oppression within the family. In her 1851 essay "The Enfranchisement of Women" Harriet Taylor

Mill addressed those "justifications" one by one, and then cut to the heart of the matter: "The real question is, whether it is right and expedient that one half of the human race should pass through life in a state of forced subordination to the other half." *The Subjection of Women*, John Stuart Mill's famous extended essay on the topic,[1] grew out of Taylor Mill's essay (the two worked largely collaboratively); that work set out with utmost clarity the ideal that is still being striven for today: "the principle which regulates the existing social relations between the two sexes—the legal subordination of one sex to the other—is wrong in itself and now one of the chief hindrances to human improvement … it ought to be replaced by a principle of perfect equality, admitting no power or privilege on the one side, nor disability on the other."

The principles of which Cobbe and Mill and Taylor Mill spoke were, of course, not only matters of law and politics; they pervaded every aspect of British life, from employment, to educational access, to a variety of cultural matters. The principle of "perfect equality" was far from being realized in any of these areas even at century's end. But by 1900 some at least were beginning to feel that the slow movement towards acceptance of the principles of gender equality had become inexorable.

EMPIRE

Victorian Britain's internal politics, enormous wealth, and its sense of national and global identity cannot be adequately understood in isolation from its imperial rule abroad. In an address at Oxford in 1870, John Ruskin urged England to "found colonies as fast and as far as she is able, … seizing every piece of fruitful waste ground she can set her foot on, and there teaching these her colonists that their first aim is to be to advance the power of England by land and sea." And under Victoria's reign such power did indeed grow steadily, with eighteen major territories added to the British Empire (which included India, Canada, Australia, New Zealand, and much of East Africa and the Caribbean).

If the Empire arose largely from the desire to increase trade and maximize commercial interests, it also increasingly took hold of the political and cultural imagination. The often brutal effects of colonial domi-

nation were rationalized by a pseudo-science purporting to demonstrate the inferiority of dark-skinned peoples, by a felt sense of racial and cultural superiority over other peoples. A paternalistic sense of responsibility for the peoples of the "inferior races" became known as the "white man's burden" in Rudyard Kipling's famous phrasing. Or, as evolutionary theorist Alfred Russel Wallace put it, "the relation of a civilized to an uncivilized race, over which it rules, is exactly that of parent to child, or generally adults to infants." In missionary work, travel and exploration, scientific writing, advertising, visual art, and literature, the culture and logic of imperial rule were formulated as part of the everyday "common sense" of the age.

Not everyone was in complete agreement about Britain's imperial policies and practices. Impassioned public debates about the moral and economic injustice of slavery had culminated in the abolition of the slave trade in 1807 and of slavery in all British possessions in 1833. Britain continued to rely on cheap imports of raw materials from its Caribbean colonies, however, and conditions for free workers were sometimes little better than they had been for slaves. Attention to British rule in the "West Indies" was renewed in 1865 during the controversy that attended Governor Edward Eyre's actions, when black Jamaicans attempted to liberate a black prisoner from a courthouse. Violent clashes between the rebels and white authorities resulted in martial law and the execution of 600 black Jamaicans. The opinions of two of the century's most respected public intellectuals, Thomas Carlyle and John Stuart Mill, represented the opposing poles of the public's response, with Carlyle supporting Eyre's imposition of a harsh law and order regime, and Mill calling for Eyre to be tried for murder.

The "Indian Mutiny" of 1857–58 presented a major challenge to British rule in India, which until that point was still largely under the control of the East India Company. Sepoys (Indian men employed as soldiers by the British) staged a rebellion at Meerut early in 1857, killing British officers. The violence spread throughout

---

[1] *The Subjection of Women* was not published until 1869, though it had been completed many years earlier; Mill waited for a moment at which he felt the essay would exert a particularly strong effect on public opinion.

northern territories and to Delhi, with massacres of British men, women, and children taking place at Cawnpore and Lucknow. British reprisals were swift and bloody, and led to summary executions, looting, and massacres of Indian civilians. The Indian resistance was motivated by religious, cultural and political opposition to British policies, and had a lasting impact on British rule in India. Governance was transferred from the East India Company to the Crown in 1858. In England, the press was filled with lurid reports of the violence, resulting in greater public fascination with India than ever before. Countless eyewitness accounts, sermons, plays, novels, and poems—some still being written sixty years after the events—expressed moral outrage about the insurgency. There were also those, such as Benjamin Disraeli, who tried to contextualize the violence by criticizing Britain's exploitative attitudes and practices in India, but they remained very much a minority.

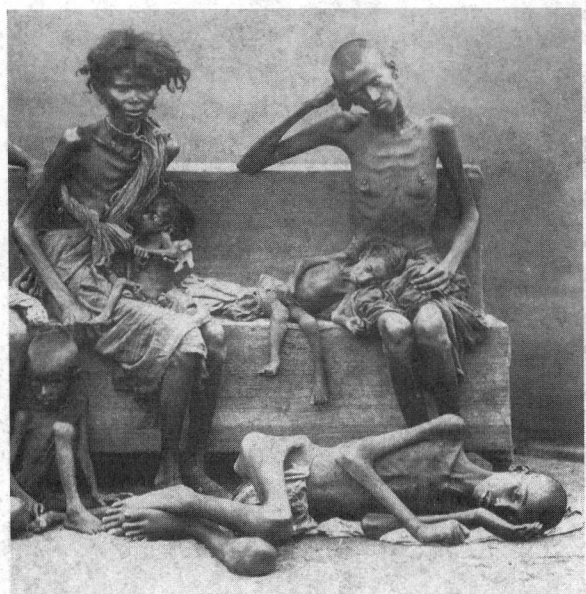

Famine Victims, Madras, c. 1877. Famine was a recurrent reality in India throughout the nineteenth century, but the famine of the 1870s was particularly harsh. It gave rise to considerable controversy in Britain, with some (such as Florence Nightingale) pressing for investment in health, sanitation, and irrigation as well as short-term relief measures; others (in sympathy with the harsh approach taken by the Viceroy, Edward Bulwer-Lytton), saw such measures as too expensive or too "lenient."

Britain participated in few major wars during Victoria's reign; when it did, the results were often less than heroic. In the Crimean War of 1854–56, Britain joined Turkey and France in fighting Russian encroachment into the Middle East, but the war did little to change the balance of power in Europe, and resulted in the deaths of 21,000 British troops, 16,000 of whom died of disease. (When the deplorable conditions of the military's hospitals became public knowledge through reports in the newspaper the *Times*, Florence Nightingale was despatched to the Crimea to superintend Britain's female nurses.) In the Anglo-Zulu War of 1878–79, the Zulus of southern Africa enjoyed considerable initial success against British forces before being subdued, and in the Anglo-Afghan War of 1878–80, the British suffered various reversals before achieving a

Edward Bulwer-Lytton, Viceroy of India, Calcutta, 1877.

Florence Nightingale in the Crimea, c. 1856.

Queen Victoria and her servant, Abdul Karim, 1893.

tenuous hold over Afghanistan. The Boer War of 1899–1902, in South Africa, was fought between the British and the Boers (white settlers of Dutch descent, also known as Afrikaners) over gold and diamond fields. For the Boers, the war was part of a larger struggle to prevent the influence of foreign powers on agricultural lands they had claimed. A guerilla war ensued, and Britain's image as the greatest military power in the world suffered when the army was unable to defeat the vastly outnumbered Boers.

In England, popular support for the Empire reached its zenith in the 1880s and 90s as Britain accelerated the pace of its drive to increase its imperial acquisitions to compete with European powers and with the United States. Queen Victoria's Golden and Diamond Jubilees, during which she celebrated the fiftieth and sixtieth anniversaries of her sovereignty, provided grand occasions for the expression of national pride. As the *Times* crowed, Britain was "the mightiest and most beneficial Empire ever known in the annals of mankind." Much popular reading in these decades was devoted to either a celebration of Empire or warnings of its imminent demise. Boys' adventure stories in such publications as

The Boy's Own Annual featured tales of manly prowess in the service of Empire and promoted the values of honor, courage, and duty to Queen and country. Travel and exploration narratives recounted the heroic journeys of Richard Burton and David Livingstone, among others, while travel journals by intrepid "lady explorers," including Mary Kingsley and Isabella Bird, unsettled conventional notions of Victorian femininity and satisfied the public taste for true stories with fictionalized elements.

Yet the Imperial romances of some authors were a symptom of the anxieties surrounding Britain's increasingly tenuous grip on its empire. Whereas early and mid-century Victorian fiction tends to imagine the Empire as a fairly static, unknown space to which characters can be exiled in the interests of narrative closure, late-century fiction often represents the Empire in darker, gothic terms. Incorporating supernatural and psychological elements in their work, writers such as H. Rider Haggard, Arthur Conan Doyle, Rudyard Kipling, and Robert Louis Stevenson used colonial settings to explore themes of racial degeneration and human "savagery." In his 1899 novella, *Heart of Darkness*, Joseph Conrad, a Polish émigré to England, drew on his experience in the merchant marine in his portrayal of imperial greed, exploitation, and corruption among ivory traders in the Congo. Even Kipling, called the "Laureate of Empire" for his energetic—and often jingoistic—portrayals of the glories of British imperialism, was not always unequivocal in his attitudes towards the Empire: in his 1897 poem "Recessional," he sounded a famous warning against Imperial hubris: "Far-called, our navies melt away; / On dune and headland sinks the fire: / Lo, all our pomp of yesterday / Is one with Nineveh and Tyre!"

Engraving by G. Durand, after a sketch by H. M. Stanley, "The Meeting of Livingstone and Stanley in Central Africa" (from *The Graphic*, 3 August 1872).

By 1869, it had been three years since the renowned missionary and explorer David Livingstone had embarked on an expedition in search of the source of the Nile River. American journalist Henry Morgan Stanley was commissioned in that year by a New York newspaper to find Livingstone; the story of the two finally meeting on the shores of Lake Tanganyika in 1871 became legendary. As Stanley described it, "I ... would have embraced him, only, he being an Englishman, I did not know how he would receive me; so I did what cowardice and false pride suggested was the best thing—walked deliberately to him, took off my hat, and said, 'Dr. Livingstone, I presume?'

'Yes,' said he, with a kind smile, lifting his cap slightly."

FAITH AND DOUBT

One of the most unsettling developments for average citizens during the Victorian period was the growing opposition to the authority of Christian faith and the established church. A rapidly changing social order, accompanied by the predominance of scientific rationalism and empiricist method, destabilized Christian certainty, creating a rising tide of secularism and religious skepticism. As critic J.A. Froude put it in 1841, "the very truths which have come forth have produced doubts ... this dazzle has too often ended in darkness." The poet Arthur Hugh Clough was a central figure in the expression of the religious doubt of the age; his verse conveys a strong sense of the passion that could accompany such feelings:

> My heart was hot within me; till at last
> My brain was lightened when my tongue had said—
> Christ is not risen!
> Christ is not risen, no—
> He lies and moulders low.

Biblical scholars in England and Europe in the early decades of the century had begun to question the Scriptures as a source of literal truth, and to present the figure of Jesus Christ as a mortal rather than a divine being. The German "higher critics" of the Bible, especially D.F. Strauss in his *Das Leben Jesu* (translated by George Eliot, 1844–46), were influential in this "scientific" discussion of Biblical texts. Influential Victorian thinkers such as Carlyle, Eliot, and Martineau wrote of personal religious crises, and wrestled publicly with doubts about the value and meaning of Christian belief. As Matthew Arnold wrote in 1880, "There is not a creed which is not shaken, nor an accredited dogma which is not shown to be questionable, not a received tradition which does not threaten to dissolve." In the climate of uncertainty as to whether the divine could be knowable, Carlyle's arrival, in *Sartor Resartus*, at an affirmation of "natural supernaturalism" offers a telling statement of the almost desperate determination to find the divine in both nature and other human beings.

Traditional religious belief received its greatest challenge in the Victorian period from the evidence of the fossil record and Darwinian explanations of the origins of the universe and human beings' place within it. Charles Darwin's theories of evolution and natural selection in *On the Origin of Species* (1859) and *The Descent of Man* (1871) rejected the Christian idea that human beings had been created in God's image, and were of a different order than the rest of the natural world. In *Descent*, Darwin provoked and challenged his audience by declaring, "He who is not content to look, like a savage, at the phenomena of nature as disconnected, cannot any longer believe that man is the work of a separate act of creation."

And religious controversy and doubt extended further still. Not only were the divinity of Christ, the literal truth of the Bible, and the processes of creation at issue; so too was the very existence of a creator or divine being. One of Darwin's strongest supporters, the scientist Thomas Henry Huxley, coined the term "agnostic" in 1869 at a party held in connection with the forming of the Metaphysical Society, a learned society which met regularly for over a decade to discuss theological issues, and whose members also included Tennyson, Ruskin, and Gladstone. The term agnostic named a person of a sort unimaginable in most earlier ages—one who neither believes nor disbelieves in the existence of God, holding instead that it is simply impossible for humans to possess knowledge of such matters. (Among Victorian authors George Eliot is perhaps the most prominent to have described herself as an agnostic.) It is to such beliefs—or the lack thereof— that Matthew Arnold refers when he writes in "Dover Beach" of the ebbing tide of the "Sea of Faith." Whereas in the twentieth century that ebbing tide was sometimes welcomed as representing a freeing of human potential, to Victorians it tended usually to be heard in the way that Arnold heard it, inextricably associated with an "eternal note of sadness."

The Established Church of England and Scotland (the Anglican denomination) remained a powerful entity throughout the Victorian era, but by century's end its power was more social than political. As had been the case since the time of Henry VIII's break with Rome in the 1530s, the Church was headed by the reigning monarch, the "Defender of the Faith." Until the late 1820s, only Anglicans could be admitted to

Parliament; until 1871, non-Anglicans were barred from taking degrees at Oxford and Cambridge. The Established Church was profoundly influenced by the gradual severance of church-state relations, and the increasing popularity of Evangelicalism, a broad-based movement comprising numerous Protestant denominations such as Methodism and Presbyterianism. These "Dissenting" or "nonconformist" faiths transformed religious practice in Britain, stressing the importance of an individual's personal relationship with God, of prudence and temperance, of conversion, of missionary work, and of humanitarian activism. In 1878, the Methodist minister William Booth founded the Salvation Army, which ministered to the poor in London's East End and became the center of social purity campaigns stressing chastity and public decency for both sexes. In general, Evangelical congregations were less hierarchical in organization than the traditional Anglican Church, were anti-Catholic in orientation, and attracted both middle- and working-class believers who felt that Anglicanism had lost its spiritual power and become a mere appendage of the state.

Henry Taunt, "Bible Stall at the St. Giles Fair, Oxford," 1880.

Evangelicalism—and the resistance to it—within the Church of England resulted in a split between Anglican Evangelicals (commonly referred to as Low Church), progressives (Broad Church, sometimes called Latitudinarians), and Anglo-Catholics (High Church). An important High Church reaction to Evangelicalism took place in the 1830s and 40s through the Oxford Movement, also called Tractarianism, led by Oxford theologians and intellectuals (chief among them John Henry Newman, John Keble, and Edward Pusey). Celebrating the mystical and aesthetic elements of worship, they advocated an increased emphasis on religious ritual and a strict observance of clerical hierarchy within the Anglican communion. Newman's conversion to Roman Catholicism in 1845 spelled the end of the Oxford Movement, and heralded a significant Catholic revival that saw many intellectuals rejecting Protestantism to embrace the Catholic faith and tradition. This was a significant religious as well as political development, since Catholics in England and especially in Ireland had for centuries been the objects of persecution. The Catholic Emancipation movement of the 1820s presaged the loosening of political and legal restrictions against members of the Catholic church, the majority of whom were barred from voting, holding office, running for Parliament, or attending the universities.

English Jews were also denied full rights of citizenship until a series of measures granted them access to Parliament, the military, the legal establishment, and institutions of higher learning. Anti-Semitic stereotypes were legion in Victorian novels such as *Oliver Twist*. In at least a few cases the writings of non-Jewish novelists challenged the stereotypes—sometimes tentatively—in ways that to some extent still participated in the culture of prejudice (as in Anthony Trollope's wide-ranging novel of capitalism, marriage, and religion, *The Way We Live Now*), sometimes more clearly and unequivocally (as in George Eliot's *Daniel Deronda*). And a significant body of Anglo-Jewish literature by writers such as Israel Zangwill and Amy Levy expressed a range of Jewish responses to social prejudice on the part of England's Christian majority.

Illustrations by George Cruikshank to Charles Dickens's *Oliver Twist* (1838). The captions identify the figures in the above illustrations as "Fagin and the boys" and as "Monks [another character in the novel] and the Jew." As presented by Dickens and Cruikshank, the character of Fagin is a caricature of evil—and of Jewishness. In passages such as the following Dickens's descriptions of Fagin give expression to some of the most extreme anti-Semitic stereotypes: "It seemed just the night when it befitted such a being as the Jew to be abroad. As he glided stealthily along, creeping beneath the shelter of the walls and doorways, the hideous old man seemed like some loathsome reptile, engendered in the slime and darkness through which he moved: crawling forth by night, in search of some rich offal for a meal." By repeatedly naming him as "the Jew" Dickens crudely implied that the characteristics of Fagin were also those of Jews in general. Dickens received complaints from readers on this score, and over time he altered his views. Beginning with the edition of 1867 he made revisions to *Oliver Twist*, changing to "Fagin" the previous references to "the Jew." The last novel Dickens completed, *Our Mutual Friend* (1864–65), is notable not least of all for the inclusion of a Jewish character (Riah) who is portrayed by Dickens in a distinctly positive light.

Although the religious establishment suffered many challenges to its power, it would be a mistake to assume that secularism, utilitarianism, and Darwinian theory stamped out religious faith or traditional religious practice: far from it. The Victorian period can be fairly characterized as an age of religious doubt that was also marked by intense religious feeling. As novels such as Anthony Trollope's *Barsetshire Chronicles* vividly convey, religious affiliation (irrespective of the strength of one's actual faith) shaped most people's sense of personal identity. And the quest for spiritual meaning was itself the driving force behind some of the most moving literary works of the age. Tennyson's elegy *In Memoriam* chronicles the spiritual crisis of one man in the aftermath of his friend's death. By the end of the poem, the speaker has reconciled his religious doubts and scientific skepticism to re-embrace a Christian vision of the afterlife. In the closing lines of the poem the speaker exalts "That God, which ever lives and loves, / One God, one law, one element, / And one far-off divine event, / To which the whole creation moves."

VICTORIAN DOMESTICITY

The center of British religious, cultural, and emotional life in the nineteenth century was the family. As industrialization transformed the household from a workspace into its "opposite," the home came to be regarded as an almost sacred space, to be shielded from the aggressive competitiveness of the public world of work. The family, especially among the rising middle class, was increasingly nuclear in structure; the extended networks of friends and relations that had formed strong household connections in pre-industrial society became more and more tenuous. Increasingly, the social arrangement perceived as ideal among the better-off social classes consisted of a male breadwinner, employed outside the home, and his female helpmeet, who nurtured the children, managed the servants, and served as a paragon of domestic virtue. One of the key signs of a man's professional success was his wife's "idleness" within the home. The separation of work and family life was reflected in city planning with the construction of the first modern suburbs, supported by public transportation systems. Middle-class domestic architecture en-

couraged the display of wealth and the division of sexual labor amongst family members by dividing houses into "public" and "private" spaces. The middle-class family model became the ideal for the working class as well, although economic necessity continued to force many working-class wives and children to contribute to household earnings through paid labor, both inside and outside the home.

The domestic ideal and the emphasis on the family circle was shaped and promoted within the most privileged sphere of society. Throughout her reign, Queen Victoria was a paragon of good manners, restraint, and

Illustration, *Wonders of a Toy-Shop*, c. 1852. Though it is sometimes claimed that children were treated as "little adults" in the nineteenth century, that was far less frequently the case than it had been a century or two earlier. In many respects, indeed, the nineteenth century marks the coming into prominence of "childhood" as a cultural entity. The changing attitudes towards children working in factories was one manifestation of change. Another was the evolution of "toy"—a word used before the nineteenth century to refer to a wide variety of trifles, but increasingly in the nineteenth century applied to playthings for children; toyshops specializing in such items became more and more widespread over the course of the Victorian period.

moral uprightness. In this she stood in contrast both to the escapades and excess that had surrounded the monarchies of her predecessors, George IV and William IV, and to the moral hypocrisy that characterized the reign of her son, Edward VII. In 1840, three years after her coronation, she married her first cousin, Prince Albert of Saxe-Coburg-Gotha. Together they had nine children, and Victoria became the nation's most revered icon of domestic femininity and maternal fecundity. She was a firm believer in separate spheres of influence and authority for men and women, and voiced a then-conventional feminine distaste for power: "I am every day more convinced," she at one point declared, "that we women, if we are to be good women, feminine and amiable and domestic, are not fitted to reign." The royal family exemplified an ideal of Victorian domesticity, with Albert exercising much influence over his wife's decisions, and Victoria displaying unwavering devotion to the practical, manly Albert. Yet for all her outwardly conventional feminine attitudes, Victoria privately expressed ambivalence towards childbirth and marriage; she once complained in a letter to her daughter that giving birth made her feel like "a dog or a cow." In 1853 she agreed to undergo anesthesia during the birth of her son Leopold. This was a controversial new medical procedure, not least of all because it challenged the curse laid upon Eve (and therefore all women) in Genesis 1: "In sorrow shalt thou bring forth children."

When Albert died of typhoid in 1861, the entire nation went into a state of mourning. Victoria was overwhelmed with grief, and for fifteen years after his death she was rarely seen in public, except at the unveiling of the many public monuments she arranged to have erected to his memory. Eventually many began to regard her seclusion as self-indulgent and excessive, and her popularity among her subjects suffered for several years. Yet Victoria's long widowhood was in many ways a sign of the times; it both reflected and influenced the Victorian vogue for elaborate mourning rituals and conventions governing the public observance of death.

Life expectancy during the Victorian period was almost certainly higher than it was in the late eighteenth century, and it did improve over the period, but for most of the century it was nevertheless extraordinarily low by the standards of the developed world today—

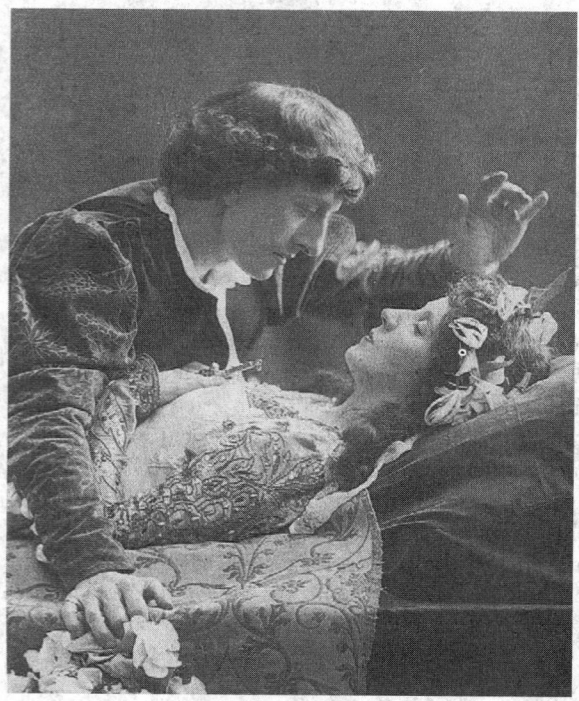

Romeo gazes at the dead Juliet: photograph of an 1895 production of Shakespeare's *Romeo and Juliet*, with Mrs. Patrick Campbell as Juliet.

probably no higher than forty years in many areas of the country. The death of relatively young people was far more common than it is today—not only deaths of children but also of young adults—of diseases such as "consumption" (tuberculosis), for example, and of cholera, and very commonly, mothers dying in childbirth. And it is no exaggeration to say that death became a commercial industry in the nineteenth century; funerals provided a public occasion to mourn the passing of a loved one as much as they offered an opportunity for rich and middle-income people to display wealth. Strict observance of funerary rituals in details of dress and deportment became a social necessity, and commemorative memorabilia, such as tea sets, photographs, and mourning jewelry (often made from the hair of the deceased) could be found in most homes. Many families were prepared to spend the bulk of their savings on the funerals of loved ones. For the poor, the story was of course much different. The indigent were buried with little or no ceremony in unmarked paupers' graves. Many working class families contributed to burial clubs, an early form of insurance that guaranteed that at least a modest amount of money would be set aside for a respectable funeral for family members.

Advertisement from *The Lady*, 4 October 1900.

The obsession with death in the Victorian period is reflected in much of the literature of the period; in Gaskell's novel *Mary Barton*, no fewer than thirteen deaths either take place or are recounted within the first ten chapters. Tennyson's elegy to his beloved friend Arthur Henry Hallam in *In Memoriam* is as much a celebration of death as it is a lament for the loss of a loved one. Countless Victorian novels feature prolonged death scenes, with grieving or greedy family members keeping vigil by the bedside of the dying. One of Dickens's most beloved characters, Little Nell (*The Old Curiosity Shop*) was modeled on his sister-in-law, Mary Hogarth, whose death had affected him deeply. Little Nell's death prompted an outpouring of grief from readers, many of whom wrote letters to Dickens in between installments of the novel imploring him to spare her. The beautiful, often eroticized corpse was a favorite image in both visual art and poetry. In Christina Rossetti's "After Death," a female speaker observes her lover's attitude towards her corpse, and realizes, "He did not love me living; but once dead / He pitied me; and very sweet it is / To know he still is warm tho' I am cold."

Though mortality rates, especially among infants, remained high throughout the century, there were significant medical advances in disease control and sanitation. Prominent among these was the verification of the bacterial theory of disease. Until late in the century most medical practitioners and lay people believed that disease was spread through miasma—the spread of harmful odors through the atmosphere. Susceptibility was routinely blamed on moral and social factors such as poverty, overcrowding, and sexual behaviors. During the cholera epidemics of the 1840s, researchers began to make links between incidents of the disease and water sources. Joseph Lister's work in the 1850s and 60s confirmed the existence of microorganisms, yet the miasma theory of disease was so entrenched that it was not until late in the century that bacterial theory was fully accepted. By 1890 the pathogens for several diseases, including tuberculosis, cholera, typhoid, rabies, and diphtheria, had been identified. Surgical practice was also transformed by Lister's work on antiseptic treatments and the adoption of anesthetics, particularly ether and chloroform.

CULTURAL TRENDS

When the Duke of Wellington died in 1852, a million and a half people lined the streets of London to pay their last respects to the military hero who had defeated Napoleon at Waterloo. The deaths of the eminent were marked by elaborate, theatrical state funerals that fed an increasing appetite for public spectacles, epitomized by the Great Exhibition of 1851. The culture of Victorian Britain was very much a visual one, with public amusements, popular shows, traveling exhibitions, circuses, sporting events, holiday resorts, and public gardens to cater to every stratum of a society that had a growing amount of both disposable income and leisure time. London's theaters drew thousands of spectators every night to witness ingenious visual effects created by London's theater impresarios; live animals, underwater sequences, mob scenes, flying machines, sumptuous interiors, and innovations in lighting stoked the public mania for stage realism. (Perhaps not by coincidence, this era of special-effects theatricality is now generally said to have marked a nadir in the history of English drama as a literary genre.) Music halls aimed at lower-middle- and working-class audiences featured a miscel-lany of comic songs, dance numbers, and magic shows by popular performers. Many public museums and galleries—which today draw thousands of visitors annually—were established in the Victorian period following the Great Exhibition, including the Victoria and Albert Museum, the National Portrait Gallery, and the Tate Gallery (founded by sugar magnate Henry Tate). Madame Tussaud's Wax Museum found a permanent home in London in 1835. From the 1870s and 80s onwards fashionable new shopping arcades and department stores filled with enticing consumer goods made shopping a respectable pastime for middle-class women.

"View of the Grand Entrance to the Great Exhibition, 1851" (from *The Official Illustrated and Descriptive Catalogue*, 1852). The idea for what became the Great Exhibition grew out of a proliferation of smaller exhibitions of the products of craft and industry in the 1840s, and out of an awareness that Paris was contemplating its own large-scale international exhibition. Organized largely by Henry Cole, with the strong support of Prince Albert, the "Great Exhibition of the Works of Industry of All Nations" was held in Hyde Park in 1851. The Crystal Palace, centerpiece of the Exhibition, was later dismantled and re-assembled at Sydenham in south London as a home for permanent exhibitions, where it stood until it was destroyed by fire in 1936.

Mass visual culture was inaugurated in the nineteenth century with the advent of a range of technologies including the kaleidoscope, the daguerreotype, the photograph, and the cinema. As on the stage, visual technologies exploited light and movement in an effort to create the illusion of reality and transport viewers across time and space. Panoramas and dioramas[1] featured foreign cities, battlefields, landscapes, and natural disasters, and anticipated the "moving pictures" of the cinema. Innovations in print technology and the explosion of illustrated print material from the 1830s onwards signaled the public's increasing demand for the pictorial representation of daily events. The popular *Illustrated London News*, established in 1842, was the world's first illustrated weekly paper to hit newsstands, and used increasingly sophisticated technologies—from woodcuts to steel engravings to photographs—in its pictorial coverage of events at home and abroad. Serial novels published in periodicals were accompanied by wood-engraved illustrations intended to heighten the reader's appreciation of the narrative; popular engraver-illustrators such as George Cruikshank and Hablot K. Browne ("Phiz"), both of whom illustrated for Dickens, were initially as celebrated as the author himself.

Victorian painters benefitted both from the emergence of a wealthy middle class able to purchase art for their homes and from the public's fascination with visual representation of contemporary life and historical drama. Scenes of everyday life with a narrative dimension and a moral message were especially popular with the viewing public. Like Victorian novelists and poets, many Victorian visual artists came to document the hardships of an industrial culture and landscape, depicting agricultural laborers, factory workers, and the unemployed in a highly realistic, yet often sentimental mode that has come to be known as social realism. Childhood innocence and scenes of domestic harmony were also common themes for many Victorian artists; new and inexpensive methods of art reproduction meant that such pictures could be sold cheaply to a wide audience that was interested in seeing the values of home and family reflected on its walls. Panoramic views of Victorian life in all its colorful variety were also popular: William Powell Frith's *Derby Day* (1858) and *Railway Station* (1877) portrayed scenes of ordinary Victorians in such realistic detail that they caused a great sensation when they were first exhibited at the Royal Academy. Founded in the eighteenth century under George III, the Royal Academy of Arts was institutionalized as the most important mediator of public taste in art in the Victorian period. It offered a free training school to many of the century's most significant artists, and its annual exhibitions of what it deemed the best works of the year drew thousands of spectators and buyers—as well as accusations of bias and preferential treatment on the part of those whose work had been excluded from the exhibitions or poorly hung.

The most influential movement in Victorian painting was the Pre-Raphaelite Brotherhood, composed of artists John Everett Millais, William Holman Hunt, Thomas Woolner, James Collinson, Frederick George Stephens, and the brothers of Christina Rossetti, artist and poet Dante Gabriel Rossetti, and critic William Michael Rossetti. At mid-century these artists began producing works that challenged the dominant taste for neoclassical style and subject matter by painting in the manner of medieval, pre-Renaissance artists. Close attention to natural detail, flattened perspective, vivid colors, an interest in literary subject matter, and erotically-charged images of spiritual and religious devotion were some of the hallmarks of the group. Their paintings of female figures as either ravishing "femmes fatales" or dreamy heroines in historical dress are today instantly recognizable (and are much reproduced). These paintings conveyed both women's power and vulnerability in nineteenth-century culture, and were sometimes twinned, in D.G. Rossetti's work especially, with a companion poem or with a quotation from a literary work. ("The Blessed Damozel" is one such example, in which the separation of two lovers by death in the poem is conveyed with two separate panels in the painting.) "Pre-Raphaelite," indeed, denotes a style of poetry as well as of painting; sensuous detail and a tendency to link earthly beauty to the divine are as characteristic of the poetry of Rossetti as they are of his paintings.

---

[1] In a diorama, spectators view a partially translucent painting in a specially designed building, with variations of light cast upon the image to simulate the movement of light in a daytime scene. The diorama was first exhibited in London in 1823.

William Powell Frith, *The Railway Station* (detail), 1862.
The painting depicts a scene at Paddington Station in London.

The Pre-Raphaelites should in part be considered alongside the Gothic Revival, a wave of interest in a Medieval and Gothic aesthetic that had begun in the Romantic period and influenced Victorian painting, architecture, design, literature, and religious practice. The idealization of the Middle Ages is exemplified in the writing of Thomas Carlyle, John Ruskin, William Morris, and Alfred Tennyson. Ruskin, an art critic who championed the work of the Pre-Raphaelites, argued in *The Stones of Venice* for the moral superiority of the Gothic style, in part because it was the product of artisan-workers who were free to use their creativity in their work, and so express their individual and spiritual nature. Ruskin urged his readers to re-examine the "ugly goblins" and "stern statues" of Gothic cathedrals, for "they are the signs of the life and liberty of every work-men who struck the stone; a freedom of thought, and rank in scale of being, such as no laws, no charters, no charities can secure." The Arts and Crafts Movement of the last few decades of the century, led by William Morris and influenced by Ruskin's ideas, was dedicated to the production of hand-crafted furniture, glassware, books, and art objects. Design firms such as Morris and Co. and the Century Guild revived the medieval guild system of production, rejecting the mass-produced manufactures of the assembly line in favor of the freedom and spontaneity of craft and its makers. In their critique of the ravages of industrial technology and the drudgery of mechanized labor, the practitioners of Gothic Revival imagined, and to some extent invented, the idea of the medieval past as a time of moral and religious stability, devotion to craft, and harmony with the rhythms of the natural world.

Arthur Hughes, *The Long Engagement* (detail). Hughes (1832–1915) was one of the most prominent of the second wave of Pre-Raphaelite painters.

The Palace of Westminster, home to both Houses of Parliament, was redesigned and rebuilt following the fire of 1834, in a vast project not completed until 1860. It is one of the most striking examples of the Gothic style applied to a secular construction.

TECHNOLOGY

The technological invention that typified the industrial age was the steam engine, a source and symbol of power both on land and at sea. Although the steam engine had been in use since the early eighteenth century, it was not until the nineteenth that steam technology helped transform an entire economy and a way of life. Steam engines were adapted for use in the production of coal, textiles, heavy metals, and printing presses, and were thus indispensable to Britain's industrial growth. Steamships powered the British Empire, with several major shipping lines established in the 1840s to serve routes to India, Africa, East Asia, and Australia. Railway steam locomotives epitomized the coming of the Victorian era, with the first local lines built in 1837 and 1838 as Victoria assumed the throne. In the "railway mania" of the 1840s, over eight thousand miles of new track were approved, and by 1900 over 900 million passengers were using Britain's rail system annually. London's underground rail system opened its first line in 1863 (horse-drawn transportation, however, continued to dominate the streetscape until the end of the century). The convenience and speed of rail travel caught on quickly with everyone from the Queen to the ordinary worker. Rail companies established excursions to special events, such as horse races or the seaside, inaugurating local and national tourism on a mass scale. From the 1850s onward railway stations became essential to the book trade and the spread of leisure reading; book stalls catering to thousands of daily commuters began to stock their shelves with newspapers, magazines, and cheap, popular fiction, which became known as "railway literature."

Robert Howlett, "Isambard Kingdom Brunel and the Launching Chains of the Great Eastern," 1857. The ship (designed largely by Brunel) remained the largest in the world throughout its 31 years on the seas. Brunel, the leading engineer of the age, also played an important role in designing such Victorian landmarks as the Crystal Palace, the new Houses of Parliament, Paddington Station, and the Clifton Suspension Bridge at Bristol.

CULTURAL IDENTITIES

The adoption of new technologies, the reorganization of employment, and the shift in power from the monarchy to the institutions of the modern liberal state revolutionized people's experience of work, family life, civic duty, and leisure time in the Victorian era. Such developments are almost always accompanied by shifts in the way people understand themselves as individuals in relation to their society. In the nineteenth century, the conditions and practices of one's class, gender, race, and sexuality began to take on new importance and to attract a new kind of attention. Changes in living conditions developed in connection with prescribed gender roles, which began to seem "natural" and

"innate" because they supported the logic of industrial capital and bourgeois family life. (This process did not begin in, but was rather extended and revised throughout, the Victorian period.) Victorians tended to think about identity in terms of oppositions: male and female, rich and poor, black and white, and, later in the century, homosexual and heterosexual. For example, the ideology of separate spheres for men and women proposed that gender and sexual identity were fixed categories, and that a "true womanhood" was the inherent opposite of a normative manliness. Yet in the literary works of the period, we see the line between these "opposites" constantly being crossed.

The "Angel in the House" (the phrase originated with a popular long poem by Coventry Patmore) became a common label for the Victorian ideal of respectable middle-class femininity. Quiet beauty, purity, devotion and selflessness were some of the essential features of the domestic wife and mother, who was described and exalted in advice literature and popular domestic novels aimed at women readers. "She must be enduringly, incorruptibly good," advised John Ruskin, "instinctively, infallibly wise—wise, not for self-development, but for self-renunciation; wise, not that she may set herself above her husband, but that she may never fall from his side." The absolute other to this paragon of virtue was the "fallen woman," a label that encompassed any form of female sexual experience deemed improper or immoral. Prostitutes, rape victims, unmarried mothers, adulteresses, homeless women, the insane, and any woman who displayed rebellious passions could be labeled "fallen." Yet the boundary between the domestic angel and the fallen woman was extraordinarily narrow; one false step and innocence became wickedness, followed by ostracism from society, poverty, and almost certain death for the transgressor, at least according to dominant narratives of fallenness. On the other hand, some fallen women were portrayed as penitent victims who embodied the feminine ideal even more fully than their uncorrupted female counterparts. Writers such as Elizabeth Gaskell, Christina Rossetti, George Eliot, Mary Elizabeth Braddon, Augusta Webster, and Thomas Hardy explored the tropes of purity and fallenness, bringing "pure" and "impure" women into each other's (and the reader's) proximity in order to probe the limits of the feminine ideal.

The male counterpart to the domestic angel was the Victorian gentleman, an heir of the chivalric ideal updated for the industrial age. In *The Idea of a University*, John Henry Newman characterized the gentleman as tender, merciful, prudent, patient, forbearing, resigned, and disciplined. Yet despite Newman's apparent confidence in this description, gentlemanliness was difficult to define: was it based on a man's mode of income or on his behavior? Was it a hereditary, professional, or moral category, or some combination? While eminent men were celebrated with great gusto in biography and prose works such as Carlyle's *On Heroes and Hero Worship*, men were also often regarded as morally inferior to women because of their greater contact with the competition and corruption of the public world. (On the other hand, women could just as easily be pressed into the role of evil temptress in accounting for a man's fall from grace.) Tennyson's dramatic monologue "Ulysses" wrestles with two competing versions of masculinity: the thwarted Romantic hero who longs for adventure and freedom from domestic encumbrance, and the reliable, managerial male who faithfully adheres to professional duty.

The concepts of the Victorian lady and gentlemen were also class categories, and served to both reinforce and blur distinctions between various socioeconomic groups. The boarding schools for the sons and daughters of the elite and the middle classes promulgated notions of proper female and male conduct in their curricula; increasingly, it was understood that one was not simply born a lady or a gentleman, but must learn to become one through rigorous training and constant self-scrutiny. As the terms "lady" and "gentleman" gradually lost their association with rank, socioeconomic boundaries became increasingly difficult to distinguish, and novelists began to focus on the gendered and class behaviors of individuals for their narrative content. In Charlotte Brontë's *Jane Eyre*, the moral awakening of the male hero, Edward Rochester, is achieved via the superior moral guidance of the "servant" governess, Jane Eyre, who, in avoiding becoming Rochester's mistress, teaches him the true nature of domestic love and Christian sacrifice, becoming his wife at his rebirth. In Dickens's novels, including *David Copperfield* and *Great Expectations*, the gentlemanly status of the male protagonists is achieved through diligence and perseverance rather than by birthright. The best-selling advice book for men, *Self Help* (1859) by Samuel Smiles, stressed thrift, hard work, and optimism as essential qualities of the "self-made man," who, no matter what his social status, could achieve respectability and success, in part by following the example of heroic men whose accomplishments Smiles recounted. Advice books, novels, and poems about the progress towards—or the fall from—"true" womanhood or manliness demonstrate that gendered and classed identities were cultural constructs that seemed "natural." The lady, the gentleman, the fallen woman, the hero—these gendered and class types, rationalized through the ideology of separate spheres, were cultural myths through which individuals made sense of their relationship to the social order.

As the century drew to a close, new styles of masculinity and femininity emerged to compete with the prevailing gender models of the previous decades. One of these new types was the "New Woman," a term that described a figure of greater sexual, economic, and social independence than the "Angel in the House." Although the term denoted a lifestyle and a literary category more than a political perspective, the figure of the New Woman was in part a product of the gains feminists had made by the 1880s and 90s in the areas of higher education, employment, political and legal rights, and civic visibility. The New Woman thus served as a flashpoint for opinion makers on either side of the "Woman Question." Smoking, swearing, riding a bicycle, debating in public, wearing men's clothes, and refusing marriage were some of the trademarks of the New Woman, who figured in novels, short stories, and popular journalism as someone either to emulate or to condemn. George Gissing, George Moore, and Thomas Hardy, among other male novelists, created memorable New Woman characters who grapple with the competing demands of personal autonomy and social expectation. The novels of Sarah Grand, such as *The Heavenly Twins* and the semi-autobiographical *The Beth Book*, present New Woman characters who triumph over social convention and the sexual double standard.

Advertisement for Swift Cycles, c. 1895.

against the Acts, led by the charismatic Josephine Butler, condemned the sexual double standard and the humiliation of poor and vulnerable women by police and doctors. Butler compared the compulsory medical examinations to "instrumental rape." The Acts were struck down in 1886 after much public controversy; the movement to repeal them, led mostly by middle-class women, marked the first instance in which women publicly debated the subject of sex on a broad scale. It was also one of the most visible of the many social purity campaigns of the 1870s, 80s, and 90s, in which moral reformers engaged in the rescue and "reformation" of prostitutes and other "fallen women," and urged men to take a vow of chastity. The mandate of the National Vigilance Association, for example, was to "create a universal ethic of chastity, for all men and women alike." In calling for a single standard of behavior, many of the social purity groups espoused moral coerciveness and interventionist policies, which often ended up stigmatizing and further repressing the women and girls they were attempting to help.

The preoccupations of the purity campaigners were part of a renewed cultural and scientific interest in human sexuality among Victorians from at least the early 1870s and the publication of Darwin's *Descent of Man.* In that book Darwin applied the theories from his *On the Origin of Species* to human evolution and behavior, positing that sexual selection among men and women accounted for their mental and physical differences. These "natural differences" were drawn straight from the catalogue of Victorian gender stereotypes, which held that men were inherently courageous, virile, and combative, and women intuitive, passive, and altruistic. The "complementarity" of these traits ensured the survival of the human "race," which evolutionists, anthropologists, and psychologists understood as a hierarchy: white European males at the top, followed by women, children, and the "primitive races." But, scientists wondered, how to explain the fact that some white males—seemingly nature's most civilized specimen—occasionally exhibited traits that resembled those of the women, children, primitives, and even the animals who were his biological and mental inferiors? Such questions were compounded by fears that Britain's empire was crumbling because the purity of the "white

For Grand and other feminist writers (such as Mona Caird and Olive Schreiner), the portrayal of the New Woman hinged on a critique of the male sexual privilege that had already come under fire in the 1870s and 80s during the social purity campaigns and the resistance to the Contagious Diseases Acts. This legislation, enacted in the 1860s, allowed for the forcible confinement and internal examination of prostitutes by doctors in order to prevent the spread of venereal disease, first among the military, and then within civilian communities. Underwriting these Acts was the assumption that because male sexual urges were "uncontrollable," prostitution was a necessary evil that should be regulated because it could not be eradicated. The campaign race" was being diluted through crossbreeding and racial mingling among English imperialists and the "savages" they ruled in the benighted labyrinths of the Empire. Closer to home, the poverty, crime and vice of England's urban districts was often racialized: "As there is a darkest Africa is there not also a darkest England?" asked William Booth, founder of the Salvation Army. "Civilisation, which can breed its own barbarians, does it not also breed its own pygmies? May we not find a parallel at our own doors, and discover within a stone's throw of our cathedrals and palaces similar horrors to those which Stanley has found existing in the great Equatorial forest?"

Social Darwinist theories of atavism (the reappearance of "primitive" characteristics in "advanced" populations) and degeneration (retrograde evolution) were formulated in the second half of the century to account for the "tendencies" of criminals, alcoholics, the poor, the mentally and physically disabled, and homosexuals. It was not until the 1880s that the term "homosexual" entered the English language; before that time homosexual acts among men were illegal (sodomy was punishable by death until 1861), but there was no concept of "the homosexual"—either male or female— as a distinct identity or way of being. With the emergence of a gay male subculture in London in the 1870s and 80s, homosexuals—also called "sexual inverts"—became subject to increased scientific and legal scrutiny.

The Criminal Law Amendment Act of 1885, which raised the age of sexual consent from thirteen to sixteen under pressure from the social purity campaigners, contained a clause—known as the Labouchère Amendment, after Member of Parliament Henry Labouchère, who had introduced it—that mandated imprisonment for any man found guilty of "gross indecency"— effectively, any sexual act[1]—with another man, even if the "indecency" were conducted entirely in private. Although "the lesbian" emerged as an identity in the 1890s, women were not subject to the same kinds of persecution as gay men, in part because of the belief that women were unmotivated by sexual desire, and that their passionate female "friendships" were innocent, temporary diversions from their true calling as wives and

mothers. The Labouchère Amendment served to demonize gay men as "degenerates" whose "unnatural" desires threatened the stability of marriage, the future of the race, and the strength of the Empire. Feminized male types—the dandy, the aesthete, the fop—surfaced in visual art and literature alongside the masculinized New Woman figure to characterize a climate of sexual and gender experimentation at the fin-de-siècle that was celebrated by a few and denounced by many. As the popular satirical magazine *Punch* joked, "A new fear my bosom vexes; / Tomorrow there may be no sexes!"

"Two Seated Sicilian Youths," photograph from c. 1893 (Victoria and Albert Museum).

In 1895 celebrity playwright Oscar Wilde, who had been making little attempt to hide his homosexuality, was brought to trial under the terms of the Labouchère Amendment and sentenced to two years in prison for

---

[1] Some such acts were already illegal: in particular, "buggery" (a British term for anal sex), whether between two males or between a man and a woman, had been illegal since the Buggery Act of 1553.

"gross indecency." The highly publicized Wilde trials brought the moral panic of the preceding two decades to a crisis point. Yet Wilde's trial testimony, his writing, and that of his contemporaries such as John Addington Symonds, Algernon Charles Swinburne, "Michael Field," Sarah Grand, Mona Caird, Vernon Lee, and Edward Carpenter signaled a new level of consciousness about sexual and gender identity. With remarkable candor the sexologist Havelock Ellis wrote, "we may not know exactly what sex is, ... we do know that it is mutable, with the possibility of one sex being changed into the other sex, that its frontiers are often mutable, and that there are many stages between a complete male and a complete female." Ellis broke new ground with his multi-volume *The Psychology of Sex* (1897–1910), an early volume of which, *Sexual Inversion* (1897), was particularly noteworthy for treating homosexuality in a purely descriptive fashion, rather than as a pathology. (In other volumes Ellis took a similar approach to many other topics, including "auto-erotism" [masturbation] and sado-masochism.) Sexuality and sexual practice had become topics of public conversation in a way that belies twentieth-century stereotypes of Victorian culture as sexually conservative or naïve. The apparent "repression" of sexual behaviors deemed improper or immoral only seemed to prohibit what was in fact an intense interest in the passions, proclivities, and practices of "other" Victorians.

REALISM

"Art is the nearest thing to life," wrote George Eliot in "The Natural History of German Life." "It is a mode of amplifying experience and extending our contact with our fellow-men beyond the bounds of our personal lot. All the more sacred is the task of the artist when he undertakes to paint the life of the People." Written in 1856, Eliot's essay anticipated the masterpieces of realist fiction she would begin writing in just a few years—*Adam Bede*, *The Mill on the Floss*, and *Middlemarch*

among them. For Eliot, as for many of her contemporaries, the true, even "sacred" purpose of art was to present an objective representation of real life that reflected the habits, desires, and aspirations of readers. For many novelists, realism seemed to be the form best suited to this purpose. In addition, Victorian poetry, especially at mid-century, was influenced by the predominance of realist fiction; long narrative poems such as Tennyson's *Idylls of the King* and Robert Browning's *The Ring and the Book* appropriated novelistic forms of storytelling, while combining trenchant social critique with formal experimentation. In Elizabeth Barrett Browning's "verse novel" and female Bildungsroman, *Aurora Leigh*, the speaker, Aurora Leigh herself, defines and defends her poetic practice of social engagement with the contemporary world, sounding very much like Eliot: "Nay, if there's room for poets in this world / A little overgrown (I think there is), / Their sole work is to represent the age, / Their age, not Charlemagne's ... / ... this is living art, / Which thus presents and thus records true life."

Much realist fiction of the Victorian period tends to center on the everyday experiences, moral progress, and inner struggles of an ordinary individual, while giving a sense of the connections between that individual and his or her broader social networks. Many realist novels, such as those by Anthony Trollope, William Thackeray, Dickens, and Eliot contain multiple plot lines and a range of characters across socio-economic strata, representing both the cohesiveness and the disintegration of various social communities in an industrialized, commercializing society. Detailed descriptions of landscapes, city streets, and domestic interiors and close attention to the emotionally complex motivations of characters— these too are characteristic of the realism of the Victorian novel. This broad vision is typically viewed from a single narrative perspective, whether that of the novel's protagonist or of an omniscient narrator.

Why did realism hold such appeal for Victorian novelists and their audiences? One explanation is that the revolutions of the nineteenth century created a climate in which people longed for a sense of verisimilitude in their literature in order to guide them through the changes and upheavals, both private and public, which they themselves faced. Many Victorian readers sought moral and ethical guidance from their authors, who assumed—or were thrust into—the role of "secular clerics" with varying degrees of confidence and authority. Realist fiction, along with other forms of writing such as biography, criticism, poetry, and history, was accepted as having a pedagogical function; such texts not only taught readers how to navigate the changes they were experiencing, but also how to imagine sympathetically the authenticity of others' experience. "We want to be taught to feel," wrote Eliot, "not for the heroic artisan or the sentimental peasant, but for the peasant in all his coarse apathy, and the artisan in all his suspicious selfishness."

In rejecting the heroic and the sentimental, Eliot positioned the realist novel in opposition to the heightened, "falsifying" sensibilities of the Romantic mode, as did many others. In 1785, Clara Reeve had observed that "the Novel is a picture of real life and manners, and of the times in which it was written. The Romance in lofty and elevated language, describes what never happened nor is likely to happen"; the same could be said of most Victorian fiction. Yet many of the best-known Victorian novels contain elements of the fantastic, the supernatural, or the mysterious: Dickens' *Oliver Twist* and, indeed, many of his novels set out to document the ravages of industrial poverty, but his plots depend on outrageous coincidence, and his stories are peopled with broadly-drawn character types befitting the romantic mode. His many orphans make this figure of the homeless child the Victorian rewriting of Wordsworth's child figures; Dickens's orphans inevitably confront the urban nightmares of Victorian life with well-nigh angelic purity (and, in Oliver's case, perfectly grammatical English). The novels of Charlotte and Emily Brontë memorably combine psychological realism

with gothic elements such as female imprisonment and suggestions of ghostly presences. The persistence of romantic elements in Victorian realist novels not only unsettles the confidence of our formal definitions, but also prompts us to consider just whose versions of "the real" were recognized as the most truthful.

Inevitably, realism's dominance in literature and in visual art came under attack. As early as the 1850s, but more widely in the 1880s and 90s, visual artists, writers, and critics began to question the moral imperatives of realist art in a series of movements that have come to be referred to under the umbrella term "aestheticism." In poetry, drama, criticism, and fiction, aestheticism stressed experimentation in form and composition, independence of imagination and expression, and freedom of content, however perverse, morbid, or tawdry. In rebelling against the harsh brutalities of British industrial culture, the Aesthetes sought a "pure" art and formal beauty dissociated from the concerns and surroundings of the everyday. The Aesthetes were not interested in instructing or edifying a mass readership; rather, they advocated aesthetic withdrawal in order to pursue the essential forms of art. "Art for art's sake," translated from the French by art critic Walter Pater, became the rallying cry of the Aesthetes. "Art never expresses anything but itself," declares one of Oscar Wilde's speakers. "It has an independent life, just as Thought has, and develops purely on its own lines. It is not necessarily realistic in an age of realism, nor spiritual in an age of faith. So far from being a creation of its own time, it is usually in direct opposition to it." By the 1890s, the Aesthetic Movement had been charged with elitism, hedonism, self-absorption, and homosexuality. Aestheticism by that time had shifted into Decadence, a term of either censure or praise, depending on who wielded it. The Decadents extended the precepts of aestheticism in their affirmation of the perversity, artificiality, and overindulgence of a culture and a century that was nearing its end.

Page of advertisements from the eighth number of the 1846 serial publication in ten numbers of Dickens's *Oliver Twist*. (Pages of advertisements appeared at the front and back of each number.)

THE VICTORIAN NOVEL

The dominant Victorian literary form was the novel. Although the genre of the novel emerged well in advance of the Victorian period, the literary legitimacy and cultural authority the novel wields today were solidified in the nineteenth century. The novel was a dynamic form, shifting according to popular taste and critical assessments of its potential value to readers, who were offered an ever-expanding list of authors and subgenres from which to choose. The early and mid-Victorian novels of Dickens, Thackeray, and Trollope were wildly successful, both with the critical establishment and the reading public. Women novelists, including the Brontës, Eliot, Braddon, Gaskell, Charlotte Yonge, and Ellen Price Wood were some of the most respected and prolific novelists of the century, and paved the way for legions of other women to enter the field of fiction writing. Although the profession of "novelist" achieved new respectability in the period for both men and women alike, the novel continued in some circles to be maligned as lightweight and "pernicious," associated with frivolous lady scribblers and their female readers. As George Henry Lewes, George Eliot's partner, observed, "Of all departments of literature, Fiction is the one to which, by nature and by circumstance, women are best adapted ... the very nature of fiction calls for that predominance of Sentiment which we have already attributed to the feminine mind."

The taste for particular subjects and approaches shifted regularly: the "silver fork" novels of the 1820s and 30s centered on the extravagances and corruptions of the rich and fashionable, while the "social problem" novels of the 1840s depicted the minute details of life at the very opposite end of the social scale. Domestic novels by both the famous and the obscure focused on the quotidian; George Eliot's *Middlemarch*, rich in psychological complexity and moral analysis, is one of the most outstanding examples of domestic fiction of the Victorian period. A heightened form of this domestic-centered fiction were the "sensation" novels which flourished in the 1860s and 1870s. Strong on dramatic incident and scandalous subject matter such as bigamy, murder, madness, and crime, sensation novels lifted the lid off the hidden corruptions and dirty secrets of the outwardly respectable middle class; Wilkie Collins, Braddon, and Wood were some of the leading practitioners of this wildly popular and much maligned sub-genre. The immense popular appeal of sensation novels helped inaugurate the concept of a "mass readership," much to the chagrin of the critical elite, who bemoaned the "degradation" of literature as the century drew to a close. In the latter decades of the century, mystery novels, detective fiction, horror, and adventure stories soared in popularity, partly on the strength of an expanding audience of lower-income readers, rising literacy rates, and cheaper methods of book production. The counterpart to these often lurid and shocking tales were the naturalistic novels of Thomas Hardy, George Gissing, and George Moore, whose late-century fiction offers bleak, social Darwinist portraits of urban class struggle, slum life, rural poverty, and sexual frustration.

Cover, *Famous Crimes*, Police Budget Edition, c. 1890. Sensationalized stories of crime and horror, priced at one penny each and known as "penny dreadfuls," became hugely popular in the late nineteenth century.

If the vogue for particular kinds of subject matter in novels shifted regularly, so too did their modes of publication, distribution, and consumption. One significant mode of publication was the three-volume edition, or "triple-decker." Readers who could not afford to buy the volumes themselves borrowed one volume at a time from lending libraries for a fee, generating huge profits for the most successful of these, Mudie's Select Library and W.H. Smith and Son. The triple-decker format was eventually supplanted by cheap single-volume editions that were sold in national book chains and at rail stations. Another mode of publication, and the one that made the novel a household word, was the monthly or weekly serial. Monthly installments of a few chapters, often accompanied by illustration and advertisements, were initially published and purchased in separate parts with paper wrappers, and generally appeared over a period of nineteen months. By the 1860s they were more often appearing in monthly or weekly literary magazines. Dickens's enormously successful *Pickwick Papers* appeared serially in 1836–37, launching the serial format as the most important publishing medium for Victorian fiction. (Long poems and works of non-fiction prose were also sometimes published serially; important examples include Robert Browning's *The Ring and the Book* and Matthew Arnold's *Culture and Anarchy*.) Serialization allowed readers with modest incomes to purchase new works when bound volumes were beyond their financial reach. Furthermore, the regular continuation of a novel over a period of months or years meant that novels and novel reading became woven into the fabric of daily life, mingling with news, opinion, and readers' personal experience.

POETRY

The novel's predominance and popularity have often meant that the significance of Victorian poetry is overlooked. Victorian poets throughout the century were greatly influenced by poets of the Romantic period, but key departures in form, content, and purpose set the Victorians apart from their predecessors. One of the most important of Victorian innovations was the development of the dramatic monologue, a lyric poem in the voice of a speaker who is not the poet, and who occasionally addresses a silent auditor. Although the Victorians did not invent the dramatic monologue, Robert Browning and Alfred Tennyson are typically credited with developing it into a form expressive of psychological complexity. Victorian psychologists were interested in exploring the boundary between sanity and madness, and the possibility of a lucid yet mentally unbalanced narrating persona appealed to Browning and Tennyson, who used the dramatic monologue to expose not only the unstable character of their speakers' passions, but also the social and cultural contexts that either produced or reflected their instability. Browning, in particular, chose a range of unstable, deluded, or even mentally deranged speakers whose self-perception is ironically distanced from the reader's, thus participating in pre-Freudian ideas about the divided self. The dramatic monologue was also employed by Elizabeth Barrett Browning, D.G. Rossetti, Augusta Webster, Thomas Hardy, Rudyard Kipling, and by many twentieth-century poets.

Many other poetic forms also flourished in the period. Epic poems are—perhaps surprisingly in an "age of realism"—a staple of the Victorian literary landscape, from Tennyson's *Idylls of the King* to George Eliot's *The Spanish Gypsy* and William Morris's *The Earthly Paradise*. Sonnet sequences too were a popular form, particularly among women poets; notable examples include George Eliot's *Brother and Sister Sonnets*, Christina Rossetti's *Monna Innominata*, Augusta Webster's *Mother and Daughter Sonnets*, and—most popular of all—Elizabeth Barrett Browning's *Sonnets from the Portuguese*. Through the work of these writers and a host of others—from Felicia Hemans and Letitia Landon at the beginning of the period to Charlotte Mew and Mathilde Blind at its end—the "poetess" became an accepted part of the literary landscape

The lyric introspection and self-exploration that is the hallmark of much Romantic verse was augmented in both form and content by a Victorian poetry of social engagement that strove to contextualize a speaker's moral and spiritual questions within the vicissitudes of contemporary life. In Tennyson's monologue *Maud*, the tormented speaker's mental deterioration and reawakening are represented as continuous with the effects of industrialization and England's entry into the Crimean War. In Augusta Webster's dramatic monologue *A Castaway* a high-class prostitute's self-scrutiny illustrates the relationship between political economy and the commodification of female identity, with "coin" as a central metaphor.

Not all poets accepted the view that poetry should speak to the issues and concerns of the present. In 1853, Matthew Arnold wrote that poets should respond to their world by mining "those elementary feelings which subsist permanently in the race, and are independent of time." In some of his later poetry Arnold turned to classical rather than contemporary subjects as a way of rejecting what he saw as the crass materialism and spiritual futility of modern life. Yet for all his melancholia, Arnold did not advocate artistic isolation; whereas many poets of the second half of the century called for the independence of art from the imperative to offer moral instruction, Arnold continued to feel that aesthetic endeavor also implied ethical responsibility.

In contrast, Swinburne's poetry of sensual experience, his carnal subject matter and verbal pyrotechnics revel in the corporeality of poetry, so much so that he was accused in one famous review of "fleshliness" to the exclusion of "meditation" and "thought." Swinburne's verse was important to the development of aestheticism, influencing later poets such as Wilde and Symonds, whose poetry tended to emphasize formal beauty, sonic effects, and the momentary over the timeless. Like the Spasmodic poets of the 1840s and 1850s, like Arthur Hugh Clough in the late 1850s and early 1860s, and, at the century's end, like Gerard Manley Hopkins, Swinburne also engaged in many challenging experiments with poetic form and meter, thereby anticipating some of the innovations and deliberate difficulties of modernist writing.

DRAMA

The Victorian period is not remembered for great stage dramas or for penetrating comedies, at least until the last decades of the century. Although Victorian audiences were avid theater-goers, they tended to prefer light-hearted entertainment to more serious fare. Comedies,

pantomimes, farces, and musicals attracted audiences from across the social spectrum, but it was the melodrama that became the most popular dramatic genre. For most literary critics, melodrama has little or no literary value, and is thus easy to dismiss as an aesthetically vacant genre. Yet popular texts can reveal much about a culture because they are so intimately connected with everyday assumptions and values. The melodrama of the Victorian period opens a window onto the nature of power relations within modern market culture and the patriarchal family; sometimes it seemed to support, and at other times to contest, these relations. With its sensational plots, stock characters, unadorned language, and a moral economy that unambiguously separates good from evil, melodrama exploited an audience's emotions, and invariably ended on a happy note. (We need look no further than the mass appeal of Hollywood films to begin to understand why stage melodrama was so popular.) Early in the century, melodramas often featured Gothic plots, settings, and characters, but the vogue for such subject matter gave way in the Victorian period to storylines centered on workaday conflicts in familiar settings, such as factories, cottages, and manor houses.

The most prolific and successful writer and adapter of melodramas was Dion Boucicault; his 1852 play *The Corsican Brothers* was such a hit with Queen Victoria that she saw it five times. Tom Taylor's popular *The Ticket-of-Leave Man* (1863) was set in recognizable London locations, and featured a sleuth named Jack Hawksure who became a prototype for later stage detectives. Many popular novels, including works by Dickens, Collins, and Braddon, were adapted or pirated for the stage soon after they had been published. Ellen Price Wood's *East Lynne*, a novel with a fallen woman theme, was adapted into several stage versions on the basis of its enormous success as one of the earliest sensation novels.

In 1881, theater impresario Richard D'Oyly Carte opened the Savoy Theatre in London for the express purpose of staging the comic operettas of W. S. Gilbert and Arthur Sullivan, whose collaboration had begun in 1875. Their most popular plays, such as *H.M.S. Pinafore*, *The Mikado*, and *Patience*, are still regularly staged today. Gilbert's storylines and lyrics combined frivolous romance with witty and genial mockery of certain contemporary values, as well as of the formulaic nature of most London stage fare; Sullivan's alternately lilting and bouncy melodies proved irresistible, and "Gilbert and Sullivan" rapidly became a popular phenomenon. The Savoy Operas, as they came to be known, anticipated the new directions in British theater of the 1890s, epitomized in the comic plays of Oscar Wilde and the "problem plays" of George Bernard Shaw; both Wilde and Shaw offered serious critiques of their society while dazzling their audiences with their audacious wit, brilliant dialogue, and shocking candor.

Prose Non-Fiction and Print Culture

Victorian writers of essays, criticism, history, and biography fully embraced the role of the public intellectual, whose particular mission was to instruct and edify readers on the day's key issues. Virtually no subject remained untouched: writers of non-fiction prose, also known as "sages," probed everything from the latest scientific developments, to religious controversies, to political and economic questions, to gender issues, to aesthetic developments, to social values and mores. In an age of growing religious skepticism, readers looked to their "sages" as latter-day prophets and interpreters who were uniquely qualified to offer an almost divinely-inspired wisdom. This role of the secular cleric emerged along with the rise of the professional writer, or "man of letters," who could earn a comfortable living by the pen and maintain a level of gentlemanly respectability. Carlyle, Arnold, Ruskin, Mill, Newman, Pater, and Wilde produced some of the most influential cultural criticism of the age, using a variety of rhetorical techniques, verbal styles, and literary forms. For women writers, the decision to offer social and cultural critique often came at a price, since women were discouraged from involvement in—and even knowledge of—political issues. Writers such as Frances Power Cobbe, Florence Nightingale, Harriet Martineau, Caroline Norton, George Eliot, and Harriet Taylor Mill exploited a variety of "voices"—some gendered "male"—in their critiques of the role of women in Victorian

"A Gaiety Girl," music hall poster, 1893.

society, and in their writing on a variety of other topics, from political commentary to literary criticism. What united most of these writers, male and female, was their simultaneous position as societal outsiders and insiders: in a range of rhetorical styles, from prophetic to disinterested, prose writers typically argued from a marginal position under the assumption that their particular viewpoint had been abandoned or would be resisted by their readers. Yet it was precisely this outsider perspective that guaranteed the sage's unique authority within a society hungry for moral guidance by a voice from "beyond."

The opening of the Manchester Free Library, 1852. In 1845, local governments were given the authority to raise tax revenues to support the establishment of public libraries and museums. Free public libraries were distinguished from fee-charging circulating libraries such as Mudie's and W.H. Smith's.

For every writer or sage celebrated by his or her reading public as a visionary, there were countless, often nameless "hack" writers who also contributed nonfiction prose, or, more properly, journalism, to newspapers and periodicals. Indeed, the periodical and newspaper press afforded both the sages and the hacks, novelists and poets a space to disseminate their work and reach ever-expanding audiences. In Wilkie Collins's words, it was "the age of periodicals." Early in the century, prominent literary journals such as the *Edinburgh Review*, *Blackwood's Magazine*, the *Quarterly Review*,

Fraser's Magazine and the *Athenaeum* attracted the most eminent writers. In the early Victorian era, writers in these journals generally published anonymously or under a pseudonym, however, no matter how distinguished they were; not until the latter half of the century did signature gradually begin to replace anonymity in many of the periodicals. Throughout the period, the number of periodicals steadily increased, until there was a magazine for every taste, every income level, every hobby group, every political and religious organization. Domestic magazines aimed at women readers, children's magazines, satirical or humor magazines, and monthly and quarterly miscellanies publishing fiction, poetry, criticism, and news all competed with each other for readers' interest, loyalty, and purchasing power in an increasingly diverse literary marketplace. Nearly all of the best-known literary writers across the genres saw their work published in magazines and newspapers: Barrett Browning's "The Cry of the Children" in *Blackwood's*, Dickens's *Oliver Twist* in *Bentley's Miscellany*, Arnold's *Culture and Anarchy* in the *Cornhill Magazine*, Yonge's *The Clever Woman of the Family* in the *Churchman's Family Magazine*. In addition, the periodical press was key to the development of modern literary criticism. Book reviews in influential periodicals such as the *Athenaeum* could make or break a writer's reputation; prominent literary reviewers (some of whom, such as Henry James, were also celebrated authors in their own right), both forged a professional identity for themselves as literary critics and formulated principles of literary analysis that are today's tools of the trade.

Victorians were, in general, fascinated with characterizing their "age": Carlyle's "Signs of the Times," Mill's "Spirit of the Age," and Eliza Lynn Linton's "Girl of the Period" became popular catchphrases that signaled a self-conscious awareness of a society in transition. It was "the age of steam," the "age of doubt," and, perhaps most notably for students of literature, the "age of reading." Reading, like many other social institutions and cultural practices, gradually became democratized during Victoria's reign. The 1870 Education Act instituted compulsory elementary education in England and Wales for the first time; adult literacy was nearly universal by century's end. Readers were everywhere: in pubs, on trains, around the family hearth, at gentlemen's clubs, and in reading rooms (these were private libraries where readers could pay an annual fee for access to current newspapers and the latest books and periodicals). The single reader—particularly the woman reader—was a common subject for Victorian painters. Reading aloud was also a popular pastime; it was common for middle-class fathers to gather together their dependents, including the servants, at the end of the day or week to read edifying family literature, such as sermons, tracts, and didactic fiction. Drawing on his background in the London theater, Dickens delivered public readings of his novels that attracted huge crowds and increased sales of his books. His performance of Little Nell's death scene left audiences weeping.

The explosion of reading and reading cultures in Victorian England went hand in hand with new print technologies, the removal of prohibitive taxes on reading material, the ease of distribution made possible through the rail system, the rise of cheap, mass-produced print, and those political, economic, and social reforms that affected people at all levels of their existence. At the beginning of the century, mass literacy was regarded as a recipe for political revolution. From at least the middle of the century onwards, some worried that reading was becoming too popular, that it was a kind of "mania" or "disease" that "consumed" people. Critics such as Matthew Arnold argued that the newly literate but untutored masses lacked the necessary skills to distinguish between the timeless and the trashy, signaling the demise of English Culture. Yet there were also those who argued that literacy was a human right, and it was ultimately this viewpoint that prevailed. In 1840, Carlyle wrote, "Books are written by martyr-men, not for rich men alone but for all men. If we consider it, every human being has, by the nature of the case, a *right* to hear what other wise human beings have spoken to him. It is one of the Rights of Men; a very cruel injustice if you deny it to a man." The history of reading—the history of what and how different people read, the expectations that existed about what women and men should read, both in their leisure time and professionally—is inseparable from the history of the Victorian period.

THE ENGLISH LANGUAGE IN THE VICTORIAN ERA

The vocabulary of English, of course, continued to expand throughout the period. New words entered the language to name aspects of the changing world of work (*trade-union* is recorded as first having entered the language in 1831, for example; *margin*, used with reference to profit to mean "amount of money available once certain costs are covered," in the 1850s). New words named aspects of human nature that were being seen in new ways or acknowledged for the first time (*personality*, used in the modern sense of "distinctive personal identity," in 1835; *sadism* in 1888; *homosexual* in 1892). New words were coined to name new religious movements (such as *evangelicanism*, *disestablishmentarianism*, and its famously long opposite *antidisestablishmentarianism*) and to name new developments in the culture of sports (*caddie* is first recorded in 1857). Less innocuously, new ways kept springing up to express old prejudices; *jew* is first recorded as being used derogatively as a transitive verb in 1845.

The Western Electric multiple telephone switchboard, the Royal Exchange, Manchester, 1888. The spread of English as the leading language of communication world-wide was aided by the invention of the telegraph in 1837, and of the telephone later in the century.

The coining of new words from Latin and Greek roots—especially new scientific terms—continued at a quickened pace, from *lithograph* and *locomotive*, to *photograph* and *phonograph*, to *telegraph*, *telephone* and *dictaphone*. Far fewer new words were entering English from French, however; the flow of new words from French into English, which had continued in the second half of the eighteenth century and the early years of the nineteenth at about the same pace as it had been a century earlier,[1] slowed to a trickle in the Victorian era; it was far more characteristic of the eighteenth-century English to turn to the French for *etiquette* (1750) than it was for Victorians to turn to the French for *élan* (1880).

The expansion of English in the nineteenth century was not restricted to new noun coinages. A lively feature of the growth of the language during this period was an expansion in the use of verb-adverb combinations (e.g., *bring up*, *hold up*, *let up*, *pass up*, *shut up*—to name only a few of those involving *up*). With the spread of such coinages (as well as of an ever-growing number of slang expressions) into the written language came a gradual reduction in the level of formality of standard English.

A reduction in dialect differences and in range of variation in English pronunciation had begun centuries earlier with the imposition of English authority over Wales, Scotland, and Ireland; no doubt it was influenced, too, by the inherently stabilizing effects of print culture following the introduction of the printing press to England in the late fifteenth century. This trend toward greater standardization of vocabulary and of pronunciation continued through the nineteenth century. The spread of standardized pronunciation in particular was assisted by the growing influence of the elite boarding schools (known as "public schools") as the preferred sites of education for the privileged classes and for those who aspired to join them. Increasingly in the late Victorian period, girls as well as boys were sent to such schools; the founding of boarding schools such as St. Andrews (1877) and Roedean (1885) were the first institutions for girls that were paralleled on centuries' old boys' schools such as Eton, Harrow, and Rugby.

Perhaps the greatest development relating to the history of the English language in the Victorian period was the initiation of a dictionary "on historical principles"—one that would record not only the various different meanings of words, but also how they had changed over time, and precisely when each meaning is first recorded in surviving written English. *The Oxford English Dictionary*, which was to be among the most ambitious of projects in an age of famously ambitious projects, had its origins in the work of the Philological Society, founded in 1842. In 1858, following the lead of a similar project initiated in Germany[2] and following years of discussion, the society issued a formal "Proposal for the Publication of a New Dictionary by the Philological Society." The society would invite volunteers to assist in sending in records they found of early or significant uses of words. (Eventually some six million slips with quotations written on them were submitted.) By 1879, the Philological Society concluded that the project was so vast that it would not be able to complete it on its own, and entered into an agreement with the Oxford University Press. Even with this assistance, it was not until 1884 that it proved possible to publish a volume covering one part of the letter *A*. By 1900 only four and one-half volumes had been published, and it was not until 1928 that a complete version of the full dictionary was available. (By then, of course, much of the early work was outdated; a second edition was published in 1989, and the *OED* is now continually being updated online.)

A less successful Victorian initiative was a multifaceted campaign to rationalize spelling—a campaign that extended in one form or another through almost the entire period; the prevalence of spellings that bear no relation to phonetic principles increasingly came to be criticised as antiquated and illogical.[3] In the early years

---

[1] The importation of French words into English, often thought of as beginning with the Norman conquest in 1066, in fact did not occur with any great frequency until roughly a century later; the flow reached its peak in the late fourteenth century.

[2] The *Deutsches Wöterbuch*, initiated by the classicist Franz Passow and the philologists (and compilers of fairy tales) Jacob and Wilhelm Grimm.

[3] As a late-Victorian spelling reformer pointed out, the ways in which English words are spelled often bear so little connection to pronunciation that it would be possible to spell *fish* as *ghoti*, with the *gh* pronounced as we do the *gh* in *cough*; the *o* pronounced as we do the *o* in *women*; and the *ti* pronounced as we do the *ti* in *nation*. This now-famous example is thought to have been first given common currency by Bernard Shaw (who later became a crusader for spelling reform).

of the Victorian era, interest in such matters was spurred by the introduction of Isaac Pitman's system of shorthand, with Pitman himself acting as a leading advocate for reform. By the 1850s, the Bible and a number of works were available in phonetic spelling versions, and by the end of the following decade, the Philological Society was taking an active role in airing all sides of the debate. Its American counterpart adopted a less impartial stance, calling in particular for the adoption of simplified phonetic spellings of words such as *tho*, *altho*, and *thruout*. Of their list only two—*program* and *catalog*—became generally adopted in the United States. In Britain resistance to such Americanisms carried the day—and in both countries, the campaign to rationalize spelling faltered by century's end in the face of a growing recognition of the degree to which English had become a written as well as a spoken language, with words comprehended very largely through the appearance on paper of the entire written word.

Resistance to Americanisms generally was felt not only in Britain herself, but also—indeed, perhaps even more strongly—in English Canada, in its unique position as staunchly British by history and by disposition but unavoidably "American" in the geographical sense. Complaints such as those of a contributor to the *Canadian Journal* in 1857 against words and expressions "imported by travellers, daily circulated by American newspapers, and eagerly incorporated into the language of our colour Provincial press," were far from uncommon. Words such as *travellers* (in its British spelling; *travelers* according to common practice in the United States) themselves became points of contention. As the American spellings of such words—introduced by Noah Webster in his dictionary in 1825—became entrenched in the United States, Canadians began to develop a hybrid somewhere in between British and American spellings.

Conventions for marking direct speech and quoted material finally stabilized in the Victorian period in something close to their current form (though with what are now established differences between American and British conventions of punctuation still unsettled). Quotation marks themselves are a relatively recent invention; they became widely used only in the eighteenth century. Even in the late eighteenth century a number of different indicators for quoted material were still being used, the most of common of which was to include quotation marks not only at the beginning of the quoted passage, but also at the beginning of each subsequent line for as long as the quotation extended. In the early Victorian period, it had become conventional to mark quotations with only an open quotation mark at the beginning of a passage and a closed quotation mark at the end—though it remained acceptable to use either single or double quotation marks.

The Victorian period also saw significant changes in the evolution of the paragraph as a primary means of signalling the shape of ideas in prose. The paragraph was originally simply a short horizontal marker added beneath a line in which a break in meaning occurred; in the sixteenth century it became conventional to mark such shifts by setting off blocks of text through indentation at the beginning of each block. Until the late eighteenth century, however, paragraphs of English prose were often extremely long by modern standards, and one paragraph of expository or argumentative prose might hold a large number of only loosely related ideas. Even in the Romantic era, a paragraph might often run to a page or more. Through the nineteenth century, however, paragraphs gradually but steadily became shorter, and the principle of restricting each paragraph to a set of closely related ideas became much more widely followed.

HISTORY OF THE LANGUAGE
AND OF PRINT CULTURE

In an effort to provide for readers a direct sense of the development of the language and of print culture, examples of texts in their original form (and of illustrations) have been provided for each period. A list of these within the Victorian Era appears below, arranged in chronological order. Overviews of "prose non-fiction and print culture" and of developments in the history of language during this period appear on pp. 533–37.

THOMAS CARLYLE
1795 – 1881

Reviewing a book of selections from Thomas Carlyle's writings in 1855, George Eliot evaluated Carlyle's influence on his contemporaries: "There is hardly a superior or active mind of this generation that has not been modified by Carlyle's writings; there has hardly been an English book written for the last ten or twelve years that would not have been different if Carlyle had not lived. The character of his influence is best seen in the fact that many of the men who have the least agreement with his opinions are those to whom the reading of *Sartor Resartus* was an epoch in the history of their minds."

This evaluation stands as essentially correct. Whether it was Charles Dickens or John Ruskin, Robert Browning or William Morris, Matthew Arnold or George Eliot herself, Carlyle's thought and work affected the thinking and perspectives of those around him as few other writers did. This Victorian "sage" who was to become fluent in seven languages and count Johann Wolfgang von Goethe, J.S. Mill, Ralph Waldo Emerson, Alfred Lord Tennyson, Dickens, and Browning among his friends, had very humble beginnings in the village of Ecclefechan, Scotland. Born in 1795, the eldest child of a poor, strict, Calvinist stonemason and a working class, uneducated mother, the young Carlyle showed early promise, and his parents were determined to give their son an education befitting his bright mind. At the age of 14, having attended local schools since he was five, Carlyle walked the nearly 100 miles from his home to enroll in a program at the University of Edinburgh, where he studied mathematics and prepared to enter the ministry. During his years at the University, however, his faith in God was challenged by his studies of skeptics such as David Hume, François-Marie Arouet de Voltaire, and Edward Gibbon. He left Edinburgh at age 19 without attaining a degree, and for some years he taught mathematics at Annan Academy.

He also continued what he began at Edinburgh, his life-long reading and study of German writers, whose work he was to introduce to English readers. In 1823 Carlyle completed a biography of the German poet Schiller, which was published serially in *The London Magazine*; his second publication was a translation of Goethe's *Wilhelm Meister* (1824). In 1827 he published an essay on Jean Paul Richter in the influential *Edinburgh Review*. This sign of recognition was repeated in 1829, when he published his "Signs of the Times" in the *Review*, the first of his essays that focused on the social problems of nineteenth-century England and its "Age of Machinery." With "Signs" and "Characteristics" (1831), the voice of the great social prophet of England emerged.

It is in this period, as well, that Carlyle met and married Jane Baillie Welsh, the brilliant, articulate, talented daughter of a prosperous surgeon. She was well-placed to select from amongst many suitors; why she chose a coarse man from a working class background was a mystery to her friends and a source of sorrow for her mother. Although their arguments were legendary, their union in 1826 was a true meeting of minds, Carlyle's creative genius and ambition matching Welsh's intellect and drive. In 1834, they moved to London, to a home in Cheyne Row in Chelsea, where Carlyle began the long career of writing that was to make him the voice of his contemporaries, and where Jane Carlyle continued writing the letters that are amongst the most brilliant of all portraits of nineteenth-century London life.

Carlyle's work shows clearly and urgently the writer's confrontation with the age's dual heritage of religion and Romanticism, of tradition and the "march of mind." Born in a Scottish-Calvinist home in the same year as Keats, Carlyle discovered early in his reading of Gibbon and the Germans that the "old theorem" by which his own father had lived had "passed away," its "immaterialism, mysterious, divine though invisible character" banished by Locke and the mechanic world of the eighteenth century. For Carlyle, claiming that the Bible was factual truth "flatly contradicted all human science and experience." Yet he also believed that the Romantics' response to the passing of the "old beliefs"—the effort he saw in the early Goethe to form "his world out of himself"—led to despair and solipsism. Carlyle's celebration of Goethe's spiritual progress from narcissistic self-focus to a capacious view of man's role in a larger world became one of the main themes of his early work. This estimation was to become one of Carlyle's signature lines: "Close thy Byron, Open thy Goethe," commands Diogenes Teufelsdröckh, the book's questing protagonist.

Sartor Resartus appeared serially in *Fraser's Magazine* (1833–34). This semi-autobiographical book, whose Latin title translates as "The Tailor Retailored," owes a debt for its clothing metaphor to Jonathan Swift's *Tale of a Tub.* Its quirky, densely allusive, and multi-faceted style derive from Laurence Sterne's *The Life and Opinions of Tristram Shandy* and from the German writers whom Carlyle loved. Diogenes Teufelsdröckh (literally, "God-born devil's dung") is a German "Professor of Things-in-General" at the University of Weissnichtwo (literally "Don't know where"). Professor Teufelsdröckh has a theory of clothing, or symbol, by which the visible is read as a pathway to the invisible. From this symbolic reading of the world, Carlyle develops his idea of "natural supernaturalism"; nature and man become the physical manifestation, the "clothing," of the divine, "in this poor, miserable, hampered, despicable Actual, wherein thou even now standest." In presenting the quest of his German protagonist to say "Yes" to existence (within an English Editor's meditations on the strangeness of that quest and its language), Carlyle charted what was to be the Victorian response to the Enlightenment and Romanticism, and to Industrialism and the perceived withdrawal of God. For Carlyle, "Here or no where is thy Ideal: work it out therefrom; and working, believe, live, be free." Thus, when in the third volume, Teufelsdröckh goes to London and sees the worlds of wealth and poverty that constitute the "two sects" of England that were to be Carlyle's focus in *The French Revolution*, "Chartism" (1839), and *Past and Present* (1841), the connection of philosophical thinking to the real world is made clear; social prophecy and national health comes out of spiritual progress. The gospel is not "Know thyself," thundered Carlyle's protagonist, "till it be translated into this partially possible one, *Know what thou canst work at.*"

Carlyle began to achieve great fame with the publication of *The French Revolution* in 1836. His style resembled that of no other historian: highly metaphoric language, sentences that seemed "barbarous" because of their German-inflected structures and jarring syntax, the use of the present tense, representations of men and women so vivid that they seemed like characters from a novel. Carlyle used this style to articulate a sweeping view of history as a continual mingling of past and present and as the unfolding of a divine will.

In *The French Revolution*, Carlyle sees Revolutionary France as a warning to England in the 1830s. He structures the drama of France's Revolution as he had the drama of Teufelsdröckh's life, around the questions forced upon individuals or nations when they lose sight of moral and social accountability. Carlyle sees in France's materialism and its leaders' sense of the life as a "Thespian stage" an emptying of meaning out of all symbols; in this world, proclaiming ideas of Brotherhood—of liberty equality, fraternity—"will the sooner and the more surely lead to Cannibalism" and a "Brotherhood of Cain."

This exploration of the "Brotherhood of Cain" and how it comes to be the belief of a nation governs Carlyle's greatest social writing, *Past and Present*. By juxtaposing the medieval past of England, with its monks and serfs living in an organic community focused around a monastery, and the industrialism and *laissez-faire* economics of England's present that had produced poverty and starvation, Carlyle created a remarkable picture of the desperate social crises of the hungry forties. The book begins in prison and ends with a vision of a "green flowery world." The landscape between these points is equally polarized: the "formed" world of Abbot Samson and the "enchanted," demonic, "inorganic" world of the industrial present where no one will be his brother's keeper—or his brother's brother—because all have become Cains. This latter-day England is populated by a group of vividly realized demons escaped out of Bunyan and the daily newspapers: Pandarus Dogdraught, Bobus of Houndsditch, Plugson of Undershot (a captain of industry), Sir Jabesh Windbag, the amphibious Pope, and the Dead Sea Apes (who believe that soul and stomach are synonymous). Carlyle does not idealize the medieval world of Abbot Samson; he exonerates his hero from what he sees as the "spiritual rubbish" that characterizes religious exercises then and in Carlyle's own time. In Samson's work, Carlyle finds genuine redemption: "*Laborare est Orare* ... true Work is Worship ... a making of Madness Sane." *Past and Present* constitutes one of the century's great denunciations of the "Gospel of Enlightened Selfishness" that Carlyle and others saw as reducing the connections between human beings to those of a "cash nexus."

In 1840 Carlyle gave, and then published, a series of lectures, *On Heroes and Hero-Worship*. Here again he sets out his religious ideas, finding value in the Norse god Odin and in Mahomet because they understood the divine will at work in the universe (as did Martin Luther, Robert Burns, Samuel Johnson, Oliver Cromwell, and Napoleon). Each man in this unlikely collection of heroes apprehends the workings of the divine and can lead humankind out of darkness—if human beings will listen.

For many readers, Carlyle's exaltation of authority has represented a danger. Certainly this strong-man theme became predominant in his later work, in which he turned towards conservativism and authoritarianism. *The Letters and Speeches of Oliver Cromwell* (1845) and *The History of Friedrich II of Prussia, Called Frederick the Great*, published between 1858 and 1865, furthered Carlyle's doctrine of hero-worship and his principles of order. He strongly opposed the enfranchisement of women and just as vehemently supported the enslavement of black people in the West Indies. (Carlyle's 1849 essay on this topic ended his friendship with Mill, who wrote a spirited reply.) His 1850 publication of *Latter-Day Pamphlet*s, with its corrosively satirical attacks on democracy and its representatives, is an extraordinarily splenetic outburst from a voice that had once challenged England to discover the godlike connections amongst all human beings.

Carlyle remained influential; Charles Dickens, John Ruskin, and Robert Browning all dedicated books to him. In 1874 he turned down a baronetcy offered by British Prime Minister Disraeli; he did, however, accept the Prussian Order of Merit in the same year. After his wife's death in 1866, he wrote little, though he did edit his wife's remarkable letters, *The Letters and Memorials of Jane Welsh Carlyle*, which were published after his death. Carlyle had earlier stated his aversion to the idea of being buried in Westminster Abbey; he was buried in 1881 beside his parents in Ecclefechan, Scotland. George Eliot's estimation of Carlyle is an apt epitaph: "When he is saying the opposite of what we think, he says it so finely, with so hearty conviction—he makes the object about which we differ stand out in such grand relief under the clear light of his strong and honest intellect—he appeals so constantly to our sense of the manly and the truthful—that we are obliged to say 'Hear! Hear!' to the writer before we can give the decorous 'Oh! Oh!' to his opinions."

⌘ ⌘ ⌘

from *Sartor Resartus*[1]

from BOOK 2
CHAPTER 6—SORROWS OF TEUFELSDRÖCKH

We have long felt that, with a man like our Professor, matters must often be expected to take a course of their own; that in so multiplex, intricate a nature, there might be channels, both for admitting and emitting, such as the Psychologist had seldom noted; in short, that on no grand occasion and convulsion, neither in the joy-storm nor in the woe-storm, could you predict his demeanour.

To our less philosophical readers, for example, it is now clear that the so passionate Teufelsdröckh, precipitated through "a shivered Universe" in this extraordinary way, has only one of three things which he can next do: Establish himself in Bedlam;[2] begin writing Satanic Poetry; or blow out his brains. In the progress towards any of which consummations, do not such readers anticipate extravagance enough: breast-beating, brow-beating (against walls), lion-bellowings of blasphemy and the like, stampings, smitings, breakages of furniture, if not arson itself?

Nowise so does Teufelsdröckh deport him. He quietly lifts his *Pilgerstab* (Pilgrim-staff), "old business being soon wound-up"; and begins a perambulation and circumambulation of the terraqueous[3] Globe! Curious it is, indeed, how with such vivacity of conception, such intensity of feeling, above all, with these unconscionable habits of Exaggeration in speech, he combines that wonderful stillness of his, that stoicism in external procedure. Thus, if his sudden bereavement, in this matter of the Flower-goddess[4] is talked of as a real Doomsday and Dissolution of Nature, in which light doubtless it partly appeared to himself, his own nature is nowise dissolved thereby, but rather is compressed closer. For once, as we might say, a Blumine by magic appliances has unlocked that shut heart of his, and its hidden things rush out tumultuous, boundless, like genii enfranchised from their glass phial; but no sooner are your magic appliances withdrawn, than the strange casket of a heart springs to again; and perhaps there is now no key extant that will open it, for a Teufelsdröckh, as we remarked, will not love a second time. Singular Diogenes! No sooner has that heartrending occurrence fairly taken place, than he affects to regard it as a thing natural, of which there is nothing more to be said. "One highest hope, seemingly legible in the eyes of an Angel, had recalled him as out of Death-shadows into celestial Life: but a gleam of Tophet[5] passed over the face of his Angel; he was rapt away in whirlwinds, and heard the laughter of Demons. It was a Calenture,"[6] adds he, "whereby the Youth saw green Paradise-groves in the waste Ocean-waters: a lying vision, yet not wholly a lie, for *he* saw it." But what things soever passed in him, when he ceased to see it; what ragings and despairings soever Teufelsdröckh's soul was the scene of, he has the goodness to conceal under a quite opaque cover of Silence. We know it well: the first mad paroxysm past, our brave Gneschen[7] collected his dismembered philosophies, and buttoned himself together; he was meek, silent, or spoke of the weather and the Journals; only by a transient knitting of those shaggy brows, by some deep flash of those eyes, glancing one knew not whether with tear-dew or with fierce fire, might you have guessed what a Gehenna was within, that a whole Satanic School were spouting, though inaudibly, there. To consume your own choler,[8] as some chimneys consume their own

---

[1] *Sartor Resartus* Latin: "The Tailor Retailored." Carlyle writes about the fictional German philosopher Diogenes Teufelsdröckh, the author of *Clothes: Their Origin and Influence*, whose name literally means "God-born devil's dung." Teufelsdröckh details his philosophy of clothes and clothing's relationship to Transcendentalist theories. Popular for a twenty-five year span within the Victorian period, Transcendentalism was a philosophical and literary movement that sought to integrate spirit and matter by integrating the natural and the supernatural worlds as "one great Unity." Teufelsdröckh also comments on clothing as an analogy for government and other institutions that "wear out" and need to be replaced every so often. In this chapter and others, a fictional English editor comments on the professor's theories.

[2] *Bedlam* Common name for the Hospital of St. Mary of Bethlehem, an overcrowded and frenetic asylum for the emotionally disturbed.

[3] *terraqueous* Composed of land and water.

[4] *Flower-goddess* Blumine, the woman Teufelsdröckh loves, but who marries his friend Towgood.

[5] *Tophet* Gehenna, or hell.

[6] *Calenture* Feverish disease once suffered by sailors in the tropics, characterized by a tendency to mistake the ocean for green fields, which tempted some to jump overboard.

[7] *Gneschen* The young Diogenes.

[8] *choler* Bile.

smoke; to keep a whole Satanic School spouting, if it must spout, inaudibly, is a negative yet no slight virtue, nor one of the commonest in these times.

Nevertheless, we will not take upon us to say, that in the strange measure he fell upon, there was not a touch of latent Insanity; whereof indeed the actual condition of these Documents in *Capricornus* and *Aquarius* is no bad emblem. His so unlimited Wanderings, toilsome enough, are without assigned or perhaps assignable aim; internal Unrest seems his sole guidance; he wanders, wanders, as if that curse of the Prophet had fallen on him, and he were "made like unto a wheel." Doubtless, too, the chaotic nature of these Paper-bags aggravates our obscurity. Quite without note of preparation, for example, we come upon the following slip: "A peculiar feeling it is that will rise in the Traveller, when turning some hill range in his desert road, he descries lying far below, embosomed among its groves and green natural bulwarks, and all diminished to a toybox, the fair Town, where so many souls, as it were seen and yet unseen, axe driving their multifarious traffic. Its white steeple is then truly a starward-pointing finger; the canopy of blue smoke seems like a sort of Life-breath, for always, of its own unity, the soul gives unity to whatsoever it looks on with love; thus does the little Dwellingplace of men, in itself a congeries[1] of houses and huts, become for us an individual, almost a person. But what thousand other thoughts unite thereto, if the place has to ourselves been the arena of joyous or mournful experiences; if perhaps the cradle we were rocked in still stands there, if our Loving ones still dwell there, if our Buried ones there slumber!" Does Teufelsdröckh, as the wounded eagle is said to make for its own eyrie, and indeed military deserters, and all hunted outcast creatures, turn as if by instinct in the direction of their birth-land, fly first, in this extremity, towards his native Entepfuhl; but reflecting that there no help awaits him, take only one wistful look from the distance, and then wend elsewhither?

Little happier seems to be his next flight: into the wilds of Nature, as if in her mother-bosom he would seek healing. So at least we incline to interpret the following Notice, separated from the former by some considerable space, wherein, however, is nothing noteworthy:

"Mountains were not new to him; but rarely are Mountains seen in such combined majesty and grace as here. The rocks are of that sort called Primitive by the mineralogists, which always arrange themselves in masses of a rugged, gigantic character; which ruggedness, however, is here tempered by a singular airiness of form, and softness of environment; in a climate favourable to vegetation, the gray cliff, itself covered with lichens, shoots up through a garment of foliage or verdure; and white, bright cottages, tree-shaded, cluster round the everlasting granite. In fine vicissitude, Beauty alternates with Grandeur; you ride through stony hollows, along strait passes, traversed by torrents, overhung by high walls of rock; now winding amid broken shaggy chasms, and huge fragments; now suddenly emerging into some emerald valley, where the streamlet collects itself into a Lake, and man has again found a fair dwelling, and it seems as if Peace had established herself in the bosom of Strength.

"To Peace, however, in this vortex of existence, can the Son of Time not pretend: still less if some Spectre haunt him from the Past; and the Future is wholly a Stygian[2] Darkness, spectrebearing. Reasonably might the Wanderer exclaim to himself: Are not the gates of this world's Happiness inexorably shut against thee; hast thou a hope that is not mad? Nevertheless, one may still murmur audibly, or in the original Greek if that suit thee better: 'Whoso can look on Death will start at no shadows.'

"From such meditations is the Wanderer's attention called outwards; for now the Valley closes in abruptly, intersected by a huge mountain mass, the stony waterworn ascent of which is not to be accomplished on horseback. Arrived aloft, he finds himself again lifted into the evening sunset light and cannot but pause, and gaze round him, some moments there. An upland irregular expanse of wold,[3] where valleys in complex branchings are suddenly or slowly arranging their descent towards every quarter of the sky. The mountain ranges are beneath your feet, and folded together; only the loftier summits look down here and there as on a second plain; lakes also lie clear and earnest in their solitude. No trace of man now visible, unless indeed it were he who fashioned that little visible link of High-

---

[1] *congeries* Collection.

[2] *Stygian* Like the river Styx, which runs across the entrance to Hades (or hell).

[3] *wold* Open country.

way, here, as would seem, scaling the inaccessible, to unite Province with Province. But sunwards, lo you! how it towers sheer up, a world of Mountains, the diadem[1] and centre of the mountain region! A hundred and a hundred savage peaks, in the last light of Day, all glowing, of gold and amethyst, like giant spirits of the wilderness; there in their silence, in their solitude, even as on the night when Noah's Deluge first dried! Beautiful, nay solemn, was the sudden aspect to our Wanderer. He gazed over those stupendous masses with wonder, almost with longing desire; never till this hour had he known Nature, that she was One, that she was his Mother and divine. And as the ruddy glow was fading into clearness in the sky, and the Sun had now departed, a murmur of Eternity and Immensity, of Death and of Life, stole through his soul; and he felt as if Death and Life were one, as if the Earth were not dead, as if the Spirit of the Earth had its throne in that splendour, and his own spirit were therewith holding communion.

"The spell was broken by a sound of carriage wheels. Emerging from the hidden Northward, to sink soon into the hidden Southward, came a gay Barouche-and-four;[2] it was open; servants and postillions[3] wore wedding favours; that happy pair, then, had found each other, it was their marriage evening! Few moments brought them near: *Du Himmel!*[4] It was Herr Towgood and—Blumine! With slight unrecognising salutation they passed me, plunged down amid the neighbouring thickets, onwards, to Heaven, and to England; and I, in my friend Richter's words, *I remained alone, behind them, with the Night.*"

Were it not cruel in these circumstances, here might be the place to insert an observation, gleaned long ago from the great *Clothes-Volume*, where it stands with quite other intent: "Some time before Smallpox was extirpated," says the Professor, "there came a new malady of the same spiritual sort on Europe: I mean the epidemic, now endemical, of View-hunting. Poets of old date, being privileged with Senses, had also enjoyed external Nature; but chiefly as we enjoy the crystal cup which holds good or bad liquor for us, that is to say, in silence, or with slight incidental commentary; never, as I compute, till after the *Sorrows of Werter*,[5] was there man found who would say: Come let us make a Description! Having drunk the liquor, come let us eat the glass! Of which endemic the Jenner[6] is unhappily still to seek." Too true!

We reckon it more important to remark that the Professor's Wanderings, so far as his stoical and cynical envelopment admits is to clear insight, here first take their permanent character, fatuous or not. That Basilisk-glance[7] of the Barouche-and-four seems to have withered up what little remnant of a purpose may have still lurked in him; Life has become wholly a dark labyrinth; wherein, through long years, our Friend, flying from spectres, has to stumble about at random, and naturally with more haste than progress.

Foolish were it in us to attempt following him, even from afar, in this extraordinary world-pilgrimage of his, the simplest record of which, were clear record possible, would fill volumes. Hopeless is the obscurity, unspeakable the confusion. He glides from country to country, from condition to condition, vanishing and reappearing, no man can calculate how or where. Through all quarters of the world he wanders, and apparently through all circles of society. If in any scene, perhaps difficult to fix geographically, he settles for a time, and forms connexions, be sure he will snap them abruptly asunder. Let him sink out of sight as Private Scholar (*Privatisirender*), living by the grace of God in some European capital, you may next find him as Hadjee[8] in the neighbourhood of Mecca. It is an inexplicable Phantasmagoria, capricious, quick-changing, as if our Traveller, instead of limbs and highways, had transported himself by some wishing-carpet, or Fortunatus' Hat.[9] The whole, too, imparted emblematically, in dim

---

1 *diadem* Crown.

2 *Barouche-and-four* Carriage for four passengers and driver.

3 *postillions* Messengers on horseback.

4 *Du Himmel!* German: Good heavens!

5 *Sorrows of Werter* *The Sorrows of Young Werther* (1774), a novel by German author Johann Wolfgang von Goethe about a young man who is rejected by his loved ones and who eventually decides to commit suicide.

6 *Jenner* Edward Jenner, the scientist who discovered the smallpox vaccine in 1796.

7 *Basilisk-glance* The glance of the basilisk, a serpent-like reptile, would kill.

8 *Hadjee* Muslim religious pilgrimage to Mecca.

9 *Fortunatus' Hat* Fortunatus was a hero of legend who was given an old hat that would transport him anywhere he wished to go.

multifarious tokens (as that collection of Street Advertisements), with only some touch of direct historical notice sparingly interspersed: little light-islets in the world of haze! So that, from this point, the Professor is more of an enigma than ever. In figurative language, we might say he becomes, not indeed a spirit, yet spiritualised, vaporised. Fact unparalleled in Biography: The river of his History, which we have traced from its tiniest fountains, and hoped to see flow onward, with increasing current, into the ocean, here dashes itself over that terrific Lover's Leap; and, as a mad-foaming cataract, flies wholly into tumultuous clouds of spray. Low down it indeed collects again into pools and plashes, yet only at a great distance, and with difficulty, if at all, into a general stream. To cast a glance into certain of those pools and plashes, and trace whither they run, must, for a chapter or two, form the limit of our endeavour.

For which end doubtless those direct historical Notices, where they can be met with, are the best. Nevertheless, of this sort too there occurs much, which, with our present light, it were questionable to emit. Teufelsdröckh, vibrating everywhere between the highest and the lowest levels, comes into contact with public History itself. For example, those conversations and relations with illustrious Persons, as Sultan Mahmoud, the Emperor Napoleon, and others, are they not as yet rather of a diplomatic character than of a biographic? The Editor, appreciating the sacredness of crowned heads, nay perhaps suspecting the possible trickeries of a Clothes-Philosopher, will eschew this province for the present; a new time may bring new insight and a different duty.

If we ask now, not indeed with what ulterior Purpose, for there was none, yet with what immediate outlooks, at all events, in what mood of mind, the Professor undertook and prosecuted this world pilgrimage, the answer is more distinct than favourable. "A nameless Unrest," says he, "urged me forward; to which the outward motion was some momentary lying solace. Whither should I go? My Loadstars were blotted out; in that canopy of grim fire shone no star. Yet forward must I; the ground burnt under me; there was no rest for the sole of my foot. I was alone, alone! Ever too the strong inward longing shaped Fantasms for itself; towards these, one after the other, must I fruitlessly wander. A feeling I had, that for my fever-thirst there was and must

be somewhere a healing Fountain. To many fondly imagined Fountains, the Saints' Wells of these days, did I pilgrim; to great Men, to great Cities, to great Events, but found there no healing. In strange countries, as in the well-known; in savage deserts, as in the press of corrupt civilisation, it was ever the same: how could your Wanderer escape from—*his own Shadow*? Nevertheless still Forward! I felt as if in great haste; to do I saw not what. From the depths of my own heart, it called to me, Forwards! The winds and the streams, and all Nature sounded to me, Forwards! *Ach Gott*,[1] I was even, once for all, a Son of Time."[2]

From which is it not clear that the internal Satanic School was till active enough? He says elsewhere: "The *Enchiridion of Epictetus*[3] I had ever with me, often as my sole rational companion, and regret to mention that the nourishment it yielded was trifling." Thou foolish Teufelsdröckh! How could it else? Hadst thou not Greek enough to understand thus much: *The end of Man is an Action, and not a Thought*, though it were the noblest? "How I lived?" writes he once: "Friend, hast thou considered the 'rugged all-nourishing Earth,' as Sophocles well names her; how she feeds the sparrow on the housetop, much more her darling, man? While thou stirrest and livest, thou hast a probability of victual. My breakfast of tea has been cooked by a Tartar[4] woman, with water of the Amur, who wiped her earthen kettle with a horse-tail. I have roasted wild eggs in the sand of Sahara; I have awakened in Paris *Estrapades* and Vienna *Malzleins*,[5] with no prospect of breakfast beyond elemental liquid. That I had my Living to seek saved me from Dying—by suicide. In our busy Europe, is there not an everlasting demand for Intellect, in the chemical, mechanical, political, religious, educational, commercial departments? In Pagan countries, cannot one write Fetishes? Living! Little knowest thou what alchemy[6] is

---

[1] *Ach Gott* German: Oh, God.

[2] *Son of Time* From Friedrich von Schiller's poem "The Artists" (1789).

[3] *Enchiridion of Epictetus* Handbook or manual for living, purportedly written in 135 BCE by Epictetus, a Greek Stoic philosopher.

[4] *Tartar* From the central Asian area formerly known as Tartary.

[5] *Paris Estrapades and Vienna Malzleins* Streets in Paris and Vienna.

[6] *alchemy* Here, magic power that transforms.

in an inventive Soul; how, as with its little finger, it can create provision enough for the body (of a Philosopher), and then, as with both hands, create quite other than provision, namely, spectres to torment itself withal."

Poor Teufelsdröckh! Flying with Hunger always parallel to him, and a whole Infernal Chase in his rear, so that the countenance of Hunger is comparatively a friend's! Thus must he, in the temper of ancient Cain,[1] or of the modern Wandering Jew, save only that he feels himself not guilty and but suffering the pains of guilt, wend to and fro with aimless speed. Thus must he, over the whole surface of the Earth (by foot-prints), write his *Sorrows of Teufelsdröckh,* even as the great Goethe, in passionate words, had to write his *Sorrows of Werter,* before the spirit freed herself, and he could become a Man. Vain truly is the hope of your swiftest Runner to escape "from his own Shadow"! Nevertheless, in these sick days, when the Born of Heaven first descries himself (about the age of twenty) in a world such as ours, richer than usual in two things, in Truths grown obsolete, and Trades grown obsolete—what can the fool think but that it is all a Den of Lies, wherein whoso will not speak Lies and act Lies, must stand idle and despair? Whereby it happens that, for your nobler minds, the publishing of some such Work of Art, in one or the other dialect, becomes almost a necessity. For what is it properly but an Altercation with the Devil, before you begin honestly Fighting him? Your Byron publishes his *Sorrows of Lord George,* in verse and in prose, and copiously otherwise; your Bonaparte represents his *Sorrows of Napoleon* Opera, in an all too stupendous style, with music of cannon volleys, and murder-shrieks of a world; his stage-lights are the fires of Conflagration; his rhyme and recitative are the tramp of embattled Hosts and the sound of falling Cities. Happier is he who, like our Clothes-Philosopher, can write such matter, since it must be written, on the insensible Earth, with his shoe-soles only, and also survive the writing thereof! ...

from BOOK 3
CHAPTER 8—NATURAL SUPERNATURALISM

It is in his stupendous Section, headed *Natural Supernaturalism,* that the Professor first becomes a Seer; and, after long effort, such as we have witnessed, finally subdues under his feet this refractory Clothes-Philosophy, and takes victorious possession thereof. Phantasms enough he has had to struggle with: "Cloth-webs and Cobwebs," of Imperial Mantles, Superannuated Symbols, and what not; yet still did he courageously pierce through. Nay, worst of all, two quite mysterious, world-embracing Phantasms, TIME and SPACE, have ever hovered round him, perplexing and bewildering; but with these also he now resolutely grapples, these also he victoriously rends asunder. In a word, he has looked fixedly on Existence, till, one after the other, its earthly hulls and garnitures[2] have all melted away; and now, to his rapt vision, the interior celestial Holy of Holies lies disclosed.

Here, therefore, properly it is that the Philosophy of Clothes attains to Transcendentalism;[3] this last leap, can we but clear it, takes us safe into the promised land, where *Palingenesis,*[4] in all senses, may be considered as beginning. "Courage, then!" may our Diogenes exclaim, with better right than Diogenes the First once did.[5] This stupendous Section we, after long painful meditation, have found not to be unintelligible, but, on the contrary, to grow clear, nay radiant, and all-illuminating. Let the reader, turning on it what utmost force of speculative intellect is in him, do his part, as we, by judicious selection and adjustment, shall study to do ours:

"Deep has been, and is, the significance of Miracles," thus quietly begins the Professor; "far deeper perhaps than we imagine. Meanwhile, the question of questions were: What specially is a Miracle? To that Dutch King of Siam, an icicle had been a miracle; whoso had carried

---

[1]   *Cain*   First son of Adam and Eve, who killed his brother Abel, and on whom God placed a mark of punishment (see Genesis 4).

[2]   *garnitures*   Ornaments.

[3]   *Transcendentalism*   In this case the professor refers to Transcendentalism's tendency to privilege the spiritual over the material. Nature, including human beings, has the powers, status, and authority traditionally attributed to an independent deity.

[4]   *Palingenesis*   Rebirth.

[5]   *"Courage, then!" ... once did*   Third-century philosopher Diogenes Laërtius once told his listeners to have faith that his dull lecture would soon be over.

with him an air-pump and vial of vitriolic ether, might have worked a miracle. To my Horse, again, who unhappily is still more unscientific, do not I work a miracle, and magical *Open sesame!*[1] every time I please to pay twopence and open for him an impassable *Schlagbaum*, or shut Turnpike?

"'But is not a real Miracle simply a violation of the Laws of Nature?' ask several. Whom I answer by this new question: What are the Laws of Nature? To me perhaps the rising of one from the dead were no violation of these Laws, but a confirmation, were some far deeper Law, now first penetrated into, and by Spiritual Force, even as the rest have all been, brought to bear on us with its Material Force.

"Here too may some inquire, not without astonishment: On what ground shall one, that can make Iron swim,[2] come and declare that therefore he can teach Religion? To us, truly, of the Nineteenth Century, such declaration were inept enough, which nevertheless to our fathers, of the First Century, was full of meaning.

"'But is it not the deepest Law of Nature that she be constant?' cries an illuminated class; 'Is not the Machine of the Universe fixed to move by unalterable rules?' Probable enough, good friends; nay I, too, must believe that the God, whom ancient inspired men assert to be 'without variableness or shadow of turning,'[3] does indeed never change; that Nature, that the Universe, which no one whom it so pleases can be prevented from calling a Machine, does move by the most unalterable rules. And now of you, too, I make the old inquiry: What those same unalterable rules, forming the complete Statute-Book of Nature, may possibly be?

"They stand written in our Works of Science, say you, in the accumulated records of Man's Experience?—Was Man with his Experience present at the Creation, then, to see how it all went on? Have any deepest scientific individuals yet dived down to the foundations of the Universe and gauged everything there? Did the Maker take them into His counsel; that they read His groundplan of the incomprehensible All; and can say, This stands marked therein, and no more

than this? Alas, not in anywise! These scientific individuals have been nowhere but where we also are, have seen some handbreadths deeper than we see into the Deep that is infinite, without bottom as without shore.

"Laplace's Book on the Stars,[4] wherein he exhibits that certain Planets, with their Satellites, gyrate round our worthy Sun, at a rate and in a course, which, by greatest good fortune, he and the like of him have succeeded in detecting, is to me as precious as to another. But is this what thou namest 'Mechanism of the Heavens,' and 'System of the World'; this, wherein Sirius[5] and the Pleiades, and all Herschel's[6] Fifteen-thousand Suns per minute, being left out, some paltry handful of Moons, and inert Balls, had been—looked at, nicknamed, and marked in the Zodiacal Way-bill,[7] so that we can now prate of their Whereabout; their How, their Why, their What, being hid from us, as in the signless Inane?

"System of Nature! To the wisest man, wide as is his vision, Nature remains of quite *infinite* depth, of quite infinite expansion; and all Experience thereof limits itself to some few computed centuries and measured square miles. The course of Nature's phases, on this our little fraction of a Planet, is partially known to us; but who knows what deeper courses these depend on; what infinitely larger Cycle (of causes) our little Epicycle[8] revolves on? To the Minnow every cranny and pebble, and quality and accident, of its little native Creek may have become familiar; but does the Minnow understand the Ocean Tides and periodic Currents, the Trade-winds, and Monsoons, and Moon's Eclipses, by all which the condition of its little Creek is regulated, and may, from time to time (*un*miraculously enough), be quite overset and reversed? Such a minnow is Man; his Creek this Planet Earth; his Ocean the immeasurable All; his Monsoons and periodic Currents the mysterious Course of Providence through Aeons of Aeons.

---

[1] *Open sesame!* Magical phrase used to open the cave in the story "Ali Baba and the Forty Thieves" in *The Arabian Nights*.

[2] *one ... Iron swim* From 2 Kings 6.6, in which Elisha causes an iron axe head to swim.

[3] *without ... turning* See James 1.17.

[4] *Laplace ... stars Celestial Mechanics* (1799–1825), by French astronomer Pierre Simon, Marquis de Laplace.

[5] *Sirius* The so-called "dog star," the brightest star in the constellation Canis Major (Latin: big dog).

[6] *Herschel* English astronomer Sir William Herschel (1738–1822).

[7] *Way-bill* Inventory of goods.

[8] *Epicycle* The Ptolemaic description of the evolution of a planet in a small circle, the center of which is orbiting in the circumference of a larger circle.

"We speak of the Volume of Nature, and truly a Volume it is—whose Author and Writer is God. To read it! Dost thou, does man, so much as well know the Alphabet thereof? With its Words, Sentences, and grand descriptive Pages, poetical and philosophical, spread out through Solar Systems, and Thousands of Years, we shall not try thee. It is a Volume written in celestial hieroglyphs, in the true Sacred-writing, of which even Prophets are happy that they can read here a line and there a line. As for your Institutes, and Academies of Science, they strive bravely; and, from amid the thick-crowded, inextricably intertwisted hieroglyphic writing, pick out, by dexterous combination, some Letters in the vulgar Character, and therefrom put together this and the other economic Recipe, of high avail in Practice. That Nature is more than some boundless Volume of such Recipes, or huge, well-nigh inexhaustible Domestic Cookery Book, of which the whole secret will in this manner one day evolve itself, the fewest dream.

"Custom," continues the Professor, "doth make dotards of us all.[1] Consider well, thou wilt find that Custom is the greatest of Weavers; and weaves air-raiment[2] for all the Spirits of the Universe; whereby indeed these dwell with us visibly, as ministering servants, in our houses and workshops; but their spiritual nature becomes, to the most, forever hidden. Philosophy complains that Custom has hoodwinked us, from the first; that we do everything by Custom, even Believe by it; that our very Axioms, let us boast of Free-thinking as we may, are oftenest simply such Beliefs as we have never heard questioned. Nay, what is Philosophy throughout but a continual battle against Custom; an ever-renewed effort to *transcend* the sphere of blind Custom, and so become Transcendental?

"Innumerable are the illusions and legerdemain-tricks[3] of Custom; but of all these, perhaps the cleverest is her knack of persuading us that the Miraculous, by simple repetition, ceases to be Miraculous. True, it is by this means we live, for man must work as well as wonder; and herein is Custom so far a kind nurse, guiding him to his true benefit. But she is a fond foolish nurse, or rather we are false foolish nurselings, when, in our resting and reflecting hours, we prolong the same deception. Am I to view the Stupendous with stupid indifference, because I have seen it twice, or two-hundred, or two-million times? There is no reason in Nature or in Art why I should; unless, indeed, I am a mere Work-Machine, for whom the divine gift of Thought were no other than the terrestrial gift of Steam is to the Steam-engine; a power whereby cotton might be spun, and money and money's worth realised.

"Notable enough too, here as elsewhere, wilt thou find the potency of Names, which indeed are but one kind of such custom-woven, wonder-hiding Garments. Witchcraft, and all manner of Spectre-work, and Demonology, we have now named Madness and Diseases of the Nerves. Seldom reflecting that still the new question comes upon us: What is Madness, what are Nerves? Ever, as before, does Madness remain a mysterious-terrific, altogether *infernal* boiling-up of the Nether Chaotic Deep, through this fair-painted Vision of Creation, which swims thereon, which we name the Real. Was Luther's Picture of the Devil[4] less a Reality, whether it were formed within the bodily eye, or without it? In even the wisest Soul lies a whole world of internal Madness, an authentic Demon-Empire, out of which, indeed, his world of Wisdom has been creatively built together, and now rests there, as on its dark foundations does a habitable flowery Earth-rind.

"But deepest of all illusory Appearances, for hiding Wonder, as for many other ends, are your two grand fundamental world-enveloping Appearances, SPACE and TIME. These, as spun and woven for us from before Birth itself, to clothe our celestial ME for dwelling here, and yet to blind it—lie all-embracing, as the universal canvas, or warp and woof, whereby all minor Illusions, in this Phantasm Existence, weave and paint themselves. In vain, while here on Earth, shall you endeavour to strip them off; you can, at best, but rend them asunder for moments, and look through.

"Fortunatus had a wishing Hat, which when he put on, and wished himself Anywhere, behold he was There. By this means had Fortunatus triumphed over Space, he had annihilated Space; for him there was no Where, but all was Here. Were a Hatter to establish himself, in the

---

1 *Custom ... us all* Cf. Shakespeare's *Hamlet* 3.1.91: "Thus conscience does make cowards of us all."

2 *raiment* Clothing.

3 *legerdemain tricks* Sleights of hand.

4 *Luther's Picture of the Devil* While he was translating the Psalms, German leader of the Protestant Reformation Martin Luther (1483–1546) threw his inkpot at an apparition of the devil.

Wahngasse of Weissnichtwo, and make felts of this sort for all mankind, what a world we should have of it! Still stranger, should, on the opposite side of the street, another Hatter establish himself, and, as his fellow-craftsman made Space-annihilating Hats, make Time-annihilating! Of both would I purchase, were it with my last groschen,[1] but chiefly of this latter. To clap-on your felt, and, simply by wishing that you were Any*where*, straightway to be *There*! Next to clap-on your other felt, and, simply by wishing that you were Any*when*, straightway to be *Then*! This were indeed the grander; shooting at will from the Fire-Creation of the World to its Fire-Consummation; here historically present in the First Century, conversing face to face with Paul and Seneca;[2] there prophetically in the Thirty-first, conversing also face to face with other Pauls and Senecas, who as yet stand hidden in the depth of that late Time!

"Or thinkest thou it were impossible, unimaginable? Is the Past annihilated, then, or only past; is the Future non-extant, or only future? Those mystic faculties of thine, Memory and Hope, already answer; already through those mystic avenues, thou the Earth-blinded summonest both Past and Future, and communest with them, though as yet darkly, and with mute beckonings. The curtains of Yesterday drop down, the curtains of Tomorrow roll up; but Yesterday and Tomorrow both *are*. Pierce through the Time-element, glance into the Eternal. Believe what thou findest written in the sanctuaries of Man's Soul, even as all Thinkers, in all ages, have devoutly read it there: that Time and Space are not God, but creations of God; that with God as it is a universal HERE, so is it an everlasting Now.

"And seest thou therein any glimpse of IMMORTAL-ITY?—O Heaven! Is the white Tomb of our Loved One, who died from our arms, and had to be left behind us there, which rises in the distance, like a pale, mournfully receding Milestone, to tell how many toilsome un-cheered miles we have journeyed on alone,—but a pale spectral Illusion! Is the lost Friend still mysteriously Here, even as we are Here mysteriously, with God!—Know of a truth that only the Time-shadows have perished, or are perishable; that the real Being of what-

ever was, and whatever is, and whatever will be, *is* even now and forever. This, should it unhappily seem new, thou mayest ponder at thy leisure, for the next twenty years, or the next twenty centuries; believe it thou must; understand it thou canst not.

"That the Thought-forms, Space and Time,[3] where-in, once for all, we are sent into this Earth to live, should condition and determine our whole Practical reasonings, conceptions, and imagings or imaginings, seems altogether fit, just, and unavoidable. But that they should, furthermore, usurp such sway over pure spiritual Meditation, and blind us to the wonder everywhere lying close on us, seems nowise so. Admit Space and Time to their due rank as Forms of Thought, nay even, if thou wilt, to their quite undue rank of Realities; and consider, then, with thyself how their thin disguises hide from us the brightest God-effulgences! Thus, were it not miraculous, could I stretch forth my hand and clutch the Sun? Yet thou seest me daily stretch forth my hand and therewith clutch many a thing, and swing it hither and thither. Art thou a grown baby, then, to fancy that the Miracle lies in miles of distance, or in pounds avoirdupois[4] of weight; and not to see that the true inexplicable God-revealing Miracle lies in this, that I can stretch forth my hand at all; that I have free Force to clutch aught therewith? Innumerable other of this sort are the deceptions, and wonder-hiding stupefactions, which Space practises, on us.

"Still worse is it with regard to Time. Your grand anti-magician, and universal wonder-hider, is this same lying Time. Had we but the Time-annihilating Hat, to put on for once only, we should see ourselves in a World of Miracles, wherein all fabled or authentic Thauma-turgy,[5] and feats of Magic, were outdone. But unhappily we have not such a Hat; and man, poor fool that he is, can seldom and scantily help himself without one.

---

[1] *groschen* German coin.

[2] *Paul and Seneca* Roman philosopher Seneca (3 BCE to 65 CE) was said to have met and exchanged thoughts with his contemporary the apostle St. Paul.

[3] *Thought-forms, Space and Time* Pertaining to philosopher Immanuel Kant's (1724–1804) view that space and time are not external realities, but rather what he called "categories," or modes of perception.

[4] *avoirdupois* System of measurement of weight; one stone is fourteen pounds avoirdupois.

[5] *Thaumaturgy* Working of miracles.

"Were it not wonderful, for instance, had Orpheus, or Amphion,[1] built the walls of Thebes by the mere sound of his Lyre? Yet tell me, Who built these walls of Weissnichtwo; summoning out all the sandstone rocks, to dance along from the *Steinbruch* (now a huge Troglodyte Chasm, with frightful green-mantled pools), and shape themselves into Doric and Ionic pillars, squared ashlar[2] houses and noble streets? Was it not the still higher Orpheus, or Orpheuses, who, in past centuries, by the divine Music of Wisdom, succeeded in civilising Man? Our highest Orpheus walked in Judea, eighteen-hundred years ago: his sphere-melody, flowing in wild native tones, took captive the ravished souls of men; and, being of a truth sphere-melody, still flows and sounds, though now with thousandfold accompaniments, and rich symphonies, through all our hearts; and modulates, and divinely leads them. Is that a wonder, which happens in two hours; and does it cease to be wonderful if happening in two million? Not only was Thebes built by the music of an Orpheus, but without the music of some inspired Orpheus was no city ever built, no work that man glories in ever done.

"Sweep away the Illusion of Time; glance, if thou have eyes, from the near moving-cause to its far-distant Mover. The stroke that came transmitted through a whole galaxy of elastic balls, was it less a stroke than if the last ball only had been struck, and sent flying? O, could I (with the Time-annihilating Hat) transport thee direct from the Beginnings to the Endings, how were thy eyesight unsealed, and thy heart set flaming in the Light-sea of celestial wonder! Then sawest thou that this fair Universe, were it in the meanest province thereof, is in very deed the star-domed City of God; that through every star, through every grass-blade, and most through every Living Soul, the glory of a present God still beams. But Nature, which is the Time-vesture of God, and reveals Him to the wise, hides Him from the foolish.

"Again, could anything be more miraculous than an actual authentic Ghost? The English Johnson longed, all his life, to see one, but could not, though he went to Cock Lane,[3] and thence to the church-vaults, and tapped on coffins. Foolish Doctor! Did he never, with the mind's eye as well as with the body's, look round him into that full tide of human Life he so loved; did he never so much as look into Himself? The good Doctor was a Ghost, as actual and authentic as heart could wish; well-nigh a million of Ghosts were travelling the streets by his side. Once more I say, sweep away the illusion of Time; compress the threescore years into three minutes; what else was he, what else are we? Are we not Spirits, that are shaped into a body, into an Appearance, and that fade away again into air and Invisibility? This is no metaphor, it is a simple scientific *fact*: we start out of Nothingness, take figure, and are Apparitions; round us, as round the veriest spectre, is Eternity; and to Eternity minutes are as years and aeons. Come there not tones of Love and Faith, as from celestial harp-strings, like the Song of beatified Souls? And again, do not we squeak and jibber (in our discordant, screech-owlish debatings and recriminatings); and glide bodeful, and feeble, and fearful; or uproar (*poltern*), and revel in our mad Dance of the Dead—till the scent of the morning air[4] summons us to our still Home; and dreamy Night becomes awake and Day? Where now is Alexander of Macedon; does the steel Host, that yelled in fierce battle-shouts at Issus and Arbela,[5] remain behind him; or have they all vanished utterly, even as perturbed Goblins must? Napoleon too, and his Moscow Retreats and Austerlitz Campaigns![6] Was it all other than the veriest Spectre-hunt, which has now, with its howling tumult that made Night hideous, flitted away?—Ghosts! There are nigh a thousand-million walking the Earth openly at noontide; some half-hundred have vanished from it, some half-hundred have arisen in it, ere thy watch ticks once.

"O Heaven, it is mysterious, it is awful to consider that we not only carry each a future Ghost within him, but are, in very deed, Ghosts! These Limbs, whence had we them; this stormy Force; this life-blood with its burning Passion? They are dust and shadow; a Shadow-

---

[1] *Orpheus or Amphion*   Musicians of Greek myth whose music had marvelous powers.

[2] *ashlar*   Stone block.

[3] *The English ... Cock Lane*   Samuel Johnson investigated a ghost sighting, which turned out to be a hoax, on Cock Lane in London.

[4] *scent of the morning air*   See Shakespeare's *Hamlet* 1.5.66.

[5] *Alexander ... Arbela*   Alexander the Great (356–323 BCE), King of Macedon, fought and won battles in Issus and Arbela in his quest to defeat the Persian Empire.

[6] *Napoleon ... Campaigns*   French Emperor Napoleon Bonaparte was successful in his Austerlitz campaign but was defeated when he invaded Russia.

system gathered round our ME, wherein, through some moments or years, the Divine Essence is to be revealed in the Flesh. That warrior on his strong war-horse, fire flashes through his eyes; force dwells in his arm and heart; but warrior and war-horse are a vision, a revealed Force, nothing more. Stately they tread the Earth, as if it were a firm substance; fool! the Earth is but a film; it cracks in twain, and warrior and war-horse sink beyond plummet's sounding.[1] Plummet's? Fantasy herself will not follow them. A little while ago, they were not; a little while, and they are not, their very ashes are not.

"So has it been from the beginning, so will it be to the end, Generation after generation takes to itself the Form of a Body; and forth-issuing from Cimmerian Night,[2] on Heaven's mission APPEARS. What Force and Fire is in each he expends; one grinding in the mill of Industry; one hunter-like climbing the giddy Alpine heights of Science; one madly dashed in pieces on the rocks of Strife, in war with his fellow—and then the Heaven-sent is recalled; his earthly Vesture falls away, and soon even to Sense becomes a vanished Shadow. Thus, like some wild-flaming, wild-thundering train of Heaven's Artillery, does this mysterious MANKIND thunder and flame, in long-drawn, quick-succeeding grandeur, through the unknown Deep. Thus, like a God-created, fire-breathing Spirit-host, we emerge from the Inane; haste stormfully across the astonished Earth; then plunge again into the Inane.[3] Earth's mountains are levelled, and her seas filled up, in our passage; can the Earth, which is but dead and a vision, resist Spirits which have reality and are alive? On the hardest adamant[4] some footprint of us is stamped in; the last Rear of the host will read traces of the earliest Van.[5] But whence?—O Heaven, whither? Sense knows not; Faith knows not; only that it is through Mystery to Mystery, from God and to God.

> We *are such stuff*
> As dreams are made of, and our little Life
> Is rounded with a sleep![6]

—1830–31

from *Past and Present*[7]

from BOOK 1
CHAPTER 1—MIDAS[8]

The condition of England, on which many pamphlets are now in the course of publication, and many thoughts unpublished are going on in every reflective head, is justly regarded as one of the most ominous, and withal one of the strangest, ever seen in this world. England is full of wealth, of multifarious produce, supply for human want in every kind; yet England is dying of inanition. With unabated bounty the land of England blooms and grows; waving with yellow harvests; thick-studded with workshops, industrial implements, with fifteen millions of workers, understood to be the strongest, the cunningest and the willingest our Earth ever had; these men are here; the work they have done, the fruit they have realised is here, abundant, exuberant on every hand of us: and behold, some baleful fiat as of Enchantment has gone forth, saying, "Touch it not, ye workers, ye master-workers, ye

---

[1] *plummet's sounding* See Shakespeare's *The Tempest* 5.1.61; a plummet is a plumb-bob, a line with a weight on the end, used to determine a straight vertical line.

[2] *Cimmerian Night* The Cimmerians of Homer's *Odyssey* (Book 11) lived in a land permanently enshrouded in darkness.

[3] *Inane* Here, void.

[4] *adamant* Hard rock or mineral.

[5] *Van* I.e., vanguard, the troops at the front of an army ("host").

[6] *We are … sleep!* From Shakespeare's *The Tempest* 4.1.156–58; the original reads "dreams are made on."

[7] *Past and Present* Carlyle wrote this treatise in seven weeks, in response to the lack of order and leadership that he felt was contributing to the widespread social and economic difficulties England was experiencing at that time. Carlyle blamed both the complacent aristocracy, which sought to maintain the status quo, and the spread of democracy, which he felt did little to provide heroic leaders. In 1837, industry in England entered into a depression that lasted several years. Many factories closed and others were forced to cut wages, which led to rioting in the manufacturing districts. By 1845, approximately one-twelfth of the population was unemployed, and many people ended up in overcrowded poorhouses. When the Chartists organized peaceful protests for social and economic reform, many British citizens began to fear a full-scale revolution.

[8] *Midas* Fabled king of Phrygia who, in one myth, was granted his wish that everything he touched would turn to gold. As a result, he was unable to eat. In another myth, he judges the music of the woodland god Pan to be superior to that of Apollo, god of music. Apollo, offended, changes Midas's ears to those of a donkey.

master-idlers; none of you can touch it, no man of you shall be the better for it; this is enchanted fruit!" On the poor workers such fiat[1] falls first, in its rudest shape; but on the rich master-workers too it falls; neither can the rich master-idlers, nor any richest or highest man escape, but all are like to be brought low with it, and made "poor" enough, in the money sense or a far fataler one.

Of these successful skilful workers some two millions, it is now counted, sit in Workhouses, Poor-law Prisons; or have "out-door relief"[2] flung over the wall to them—the workhouse Bastille[3] being filled to bursting, and the strong Poor-law broken asunder by a stronger. They sit there, these many months now; their hope of deliverance as yet small. In workhouses, pleasantly so-named, because work cannot be done in them. Twelve-hundred-thousand workers in England alone; their cunning right-hand lamed, lying idle in their sorrowful bosom; their hopes, outlooks, share of this fair world, shut-in by narrow walls. They sit there, pent up, as in a kind of horrid enchantment; glad to be imprisoned and enchanted, that they may not perish starved. The picturesque Tourist, in a sunny autumn day, through this bounteous realm of England, descries the Union Workhouse on his path. "Passing by the Workhouse of St. Ives in Huntingdonshire, on a bright day last autumn," says the picturesque Tourist, "I saw sitting on wooden benches, in front of their Bastille and within their ring-wall and its railings, some half-hundred or more of these men. Tall robust figures, young mostly or of middle age; of honest countenance, many of them thoughtful and even intelligent-looking men. They sat there, near by one another; but in a kind of torpor, especially in a silence, which was very striking. In silence: for, alas, what word was to be said? An Earth all lying round, crying, Come and till me, come and reap me—yet we here sit enchanted! In the eyes and brows of these men hung the gloomiest expression, not of anger, but of grief and shame and manifold inarticulate distress and weariness; they returned my glance with a glance that seemed to say, 'Do not look at us. We sit enchanted here, we know not why. The Sun shines and the Earth calls; and, by the governing Powers and Impotences of this England, we are forbidden to obey. It is impossible, they tell us!' There was something that reminded me of Dante's Hell[4] in the look of all this; and I rode swiftly away."

So many hundred thousands sit in workhouses, and other hundred thousands have not yet got even workhouses; and in thrifty Scotland itself, in Glasgow or Edinburgh City, in their dark lanes, hidden from all but the eye of God, and of rare Benevolence, the minister of God, there are scenes of woe and destitution and desolation, such as, one may hope, the Sun never saw before in the most barbarous regions where men dwelt. Competent witnesses, the brave and humane Dr. Alison,[5] who speaks what he knows, whose noble Healing Art in his charitable hands becomes once more a truly sacred one, report these things for us. These things are not of this year, or of last year, have no reference to our present state of commercial stagnation, but only to the common state. Not in sharp fever-fits, but in chronic gangrene of this kind is Scotland suffering. A Poor-law, any and every Poor-law, it may be observed, is but a temporary measure; an anodyne, not a remedy. Rich and Poor, when once the naked facts of their condition have come into collision, cannot long subsist together on a mere Poor-law. True enough—and yet, human beings cannot be left to die! Scotland too, till something better come, must have a Poor-law, if Scotland is not to be a byword among the nations. O what a waste is there; of noble and thrice-noble national virtues; peasant Stoicisms, Heroisms; valiant manful habits, soul of a Nation's worth, which all the metal of Potosi[6] cannot purchase back; to which the metal of Potosi, and all you can buy with *it*, is dross and dust!

Why dwell on this aspect of the matter? It is too

---

[1] *fiat* Order.

[2] *Workhouses* Established under the Poor Law Amendment Act of 1834 for the relief of the poor. They were designed to be as unpleasant as possible, in order to discourage people from entering them. Living conditions were poor, the work provided was equivalent to prison labor, and families were separated upon entering, with men and women lodged separately; *out-door relief* System, in place prior to the Poor Law Amendment Act, under which each parish would provide its poor with minimum allowances.

[3] *Bastille* Prison. (In reference to the Parisian prison of that name, the destruction of which by the mob in 1789 is commonly held to mark the beginning of the French Revolution.)

[4] *Dante's Hell* Reference to *The Divine Comedy* by thirteenth-century Italian poet Dante Alighieri.

[5] *Dr. Alison* Scottish physician and social reformer who wrote *Observations on the Management of the Poor in Scotland* (1840).

[6] *Potosi* Bolivian city fabled for its riches.

indisputable, not doubtful now to anyone. Descend where you will into the lower class, in Town or Country, by what avenue you will, by Factory Inquiries, Agricultural Inquiries, by Revenue Returns, by Mining-Labourer Committees, by opening your own eyes and looking, the same sorrowful result discloses itself: you have to admit that the working body of this rich English Nation has sunk or is fast sinking into a state, to which, all sides of it considered, there was literally never any parallel. At Stockport Assizes[1]—and this too has no reference to the present state of trade, being of date prior to that—a Mother and a Father are arraigned and found guilty of poisoning three of their children, to defraud a burial-society of some 3*l*.8*s*.[2] due on the death of each child. They are arraigned, found guilty; and the official authorities, it is whispered, hint that perhaps the case is not solitary, that perhaps you had better not probe farther into that department of things. This is in the autumn of 1841; the crime itself is of the previous year or season. "Brutal savages, degraded Irish,"[3] mutters the idle reader of Newspapers, hardly lingering on this incident. Yet it is an incident worth lingering on; the depravity, savagery, and degraded Irishism being never so well admitted. In the British land, a human Mother and Father, of white skin and professing the Christian religion, had done this thing; they, with their Irishism and necessity and savagery, had been driven to do it. Such instances are like the highest mountain apex emerged into view, under which lies a whole mountain region and land, not yet emerged. A human Mother and Father had said to themselves, What shall we do to escape starvation? We are deep sunk here, in our dark cellar; and help is far. Yes, in the Ugolino Hunger-tower[4] stern things happen; best-loved little Gaddo fallen dead on his Father's knees! The Stockport Mother

and Father think and hint: our poor little starveling Tom, who cries all day for victuals, who will see only evil and not good in this world; if he were out of misery at once; he well dead, and the rest of us perhaps kept alive? It is thought, and hinted; at last it is done. And now Tom being killed, and all spent and eaten, Is it poor little starveling Jack that must go, or poor little starveling Will? What a committee of ways and means!

In starved sieged cities, in the uttermost doomed ruin of old Jerusalem fallen under the wrath of God, it was prophesied and said, "The hands of the pitiful women have sodden their own children."[5] The stern Hebrew imagination could conceive no blacker gulf of wretchedness; that was the ultimatum of degraded god-punished man. And we here, in modern England, exuberant with supply of all kinds, besieged by nothing if it be not by invisible Enchantments, are we reaching that? How come these things? Wherefore are they, wherefore should they be?

Nor are they of the St. Ives workhouses, of the Glasgow lanes, and Stockport cellars, the only unblessed among us. This successful industry of England, with its plethoric wealth, has as yet made nobody rich; it is an enchanted wealth, and belongs yet to nobody. We might ask, Which of us has it enriched? We can spend thousands where we once spent hundreds, but can purchase nothing good with them. In Poor and Rich, instead of noble thrift and plenty, there is idle luxury alternating with mean scarcity and inability. We have sumptuous garnitures for our Life, but have forgotten to *live* in the middle of them. It is an enchanted wealth; no man of us can yet touch it. The class of men who feel that they are truly better off by means of it, let them give us their name!

Many men eat finer cookery, drink dearer liquors—with what advantage they can report, and their Doctors can; but in the heart of them, if we go out of the dyspeptic stomach, what increase of blessedness is there? Are they better, beautifuller, stronger, braver? Are they even what they call "happier"? Do they look with satisfaction on more things and human faces in this God's-Earth; do more things and human faces look with satisfaction on them? Not so. Human faces gloom discordantly, disloyally on one another. Things, if it be

---

[1] *Assizes* Court sessions held periodically in the various counties in England.

[2] *3l.8s.* Three pounds, eight shillings.

[3] *"Brutal ... Irish"* This passage reflects the prejudice of many Englishmen and women against the native people of Ireland.

[4] *Ugolino Hunger-tower* In the thirteenth century, Count Ugolino of Pisa and his children and nephews were imprisoned and starved to death when Ugolino betrayed his political allies. According to Dante's *Inferno*, Ugolino ate his children's bodies after they died, in order to stave off starvation. The tower in Pisa's central piazza in which Ugolino was imprisoned has since been called the Tower of Hunger.

[5] *The hands ... children* From Lamentations 4.10; *sodden* Boiled.

not mere cotton and iron things, are growing disobedient to man. The Master Worker is enchanted, for the present, like his Workhouse Workman; clamours, in vain hitherto, for a very simple sort of "Liberty"—the liberty "to buy where he finds it cheapest, to sell where he finds it dearest." With guineas jingling in every pocket, he was no whit richer; but now, the very guineas threatening to vanish, he feels that he is poor indeed. Poor Master Worker! And the Master Unworker,[1] is not he in a still fataler situation? Pausing amid his game-preserves, with awful eye—as he well may! Coercing fifty-pound tenants;[2] coercing, bribing, cajoling; "doing what he likes with his own." His mouth full of loud futilities, and arguments to prove the excellence of his Corn-law;[3] and in his heart the blackest misgiving, a desperate half-consciousness that his excellent Corn-law is *in*defensible, that his loud arguments for it are of a kind to strike men too literally *dumb*.

To whom, then, is this wealth of England wealth? Who is it that it blesses, makes happier, wiser, beautifuler, in any way better? Who has got hold of it, to make it fetch and carry for him, like a true servant, not like a false mock-servant, to do him any real service whatsoever? As yet no one. We have more riches than any Nation ever had before; we have less good of them than any Nation ever had before. Our successful industry is hitherto unsuccessful; a strange success, if we stop here! In the midst of plethoric plenty, the people perish; with gold walls, and full barns, no man feels himself safe or satisfied. Workers, Master Workers, Unworkers, all men, come to a pause; stand fixed, and cannot farther. Fatal paralysis spreading inwards, from the extremities, in St. Ives workhouses, in Stockport cellars, through all limbs, as if towards the heart itself. Have we actually got enchanted, then, accursed by some god?

Midas longed for gold, and insulted the Olympians. He got gold, so that whatsoever he touched became gold—and he, with his long ears, was little the better for it. Midas had misjudged the celestial music-tones; Midas

had insulted Apollo and the gods. The gods gave him his wish, and a pair of long ears, which also were a good appendage to it. What a truth in these old Fables! …

CHAPTER 6—HERO-WORSHIP

To the present Editor, not less than to Bobus,[4] a Government of the Wisest, what Bobus calls an Aristocracy of Talent, seems the one healing remedy; but he is not so sanguine as Bobus with respect to the means of realising it. He thinks that we have at once missed realising it, and come to need it so pressingly, by departing far from the inner eternal Laws, and taking-up with the temporary outer semblances of Laws. He thinks that "enlightened Egoism,"[5] never so luminous, is not the rule by which man's life can be led. That "Laissez-faire," "Supply-and-demand," "Cash-payment for the sole nexus,"[6] and so forth, were not, are not and will never be, a practicable Law of Union for a Society of Men. The Poor and Rich, that Governed and Governing, cannot long live together on any such Law of Union. Alas, he thinks that man has a soul in him, *different* from the stomach in any sense of this word; that if said soul be asphyxied, and lie quietly forgotten, the man and his affairs are in a bad way. He thinks that said soul will have to be resuscitated from its asphyxia; that if it prove irresuscitable, the man is not long for this world. In brief, that Midas-eared Mammonism, double-barrelled Dilettantism,[7] and their thousand adjuncts and corollaries, are *not* the Law by which God Almighty has appointed this his Universe to go; that, once for all, these are not the Law; and then, further, that we shall

---

[1] *Unworker* I.e., person who does not work.

[2] *fifty-pound tenants* Tenants who paid fifty pounds or more in rent. Under the Reform Bill of 1832, these tenants were allowed to vote.

[3] *Corn-law* One of a series of laws passed in 1815 to regulate the import of grain and keep the price of grain artificially high.

[4] *Bobus* Carlyle creates this fictional character, whom he earlier refers to as "Bobus Higgins, Sausage-maker on the great scale," as a caricature of members of the middle class who take a narrow-minded view of social reform.

[5] *enlightened Egoism* I.e., rational egoism, according to which it is beneficial for society if individuals act in their own best interests.

[6] *Laissez-faire* Theory of economics, holding that the government should not interfere with business or trade, and that the market will regulate itself; *Cash … nexus* I.e., cash is the only nexus (connection or bond) between people.

[7] *Mammonism* Worship of, or devotion to, Mammon, the personification of wealth. See Luke16.13:" "Ye cannot serve God and Mammon"; *Dilettantism* Pursuit of knowledge in an art or science as an idle pastime, without any serious interest or goal.

have to return to what *is* the Law—not by smooth flowery paths, it is like, and with "tremendous cheers" in our throat, but over steep untrodden places, through stormclad chasms, waste oceans, and the bosom of tornadoes; thank Heaven, if not through very Chaos and the Abyss! The resuscitating of a soul that has gone to asphyxia is no momentary or pleasant process, but a long and terrible one.

To the present Editor, Hero-worship, as he has elsewhere named it, means much more than an elected Parliament or stated Aristocracy of the Wisest; for in his dialect it is the summary, ultimate essence, and supreme practical perfection of all manner of worship, and true worthships and noblenesses whatsoever. Such blessed Parliament and, were it once in perfection, blessed Aristocracy of the Wisest, god-honoured and man-honoured, he does look for, more and more perfected—as the topmost blessed practical apex of a whole world reformed from sham-worship, informed anew with worship, with truth and blessedness! He thinks that Hero-worship, done differently in every different epoch of the world, is the soul of all social business among men; that the doing of it well, or the doing of it ill, measures accurately what degree of well-being or of ill-being there is in the world's affairs. He thinks that we, on the whole, do our Hero-worship worse than any Nation in this world ever did it before; that the Burns an Exciseman, the Byron a Literary Lion,[1] are intrinsically, all things considered, a baser and falser phenomenon than the Odin a God,[2] the Mahomet a Prophet of God. It is this Editor's clear opinion, accordingly, that we must learn to do our Hero-worship better; that to do it better and better means the awakening of the Nation's soul from its asphyxia, and the return of blessed life to us—Heaven's blessed life, not Mammon's galvanic[3] accursed one. To resuscitate the Asphyxied, apparently now moribund and in the last agony if not resuscitated, such and no other seems the consummation.

"Hero-worship," if you will—yes, friends; but, first of all, by being ourselves of heroic mind. A whole world of Heroes; a world not of Flunkies, where no Hero-King *can* reign: that is what we aim at! We, for our share, will put away all Flunkyism, Baseness, Unveracity from us; we shall then hope to have Noblenesses and Veracities set over us; never till then. Let Bobus and Company sneer, "That is your Reform!" Yes, Bobus, that is our Reform; and except in that, and what will follow out of that, we have no hope at all. Reform, like Charity, O Bobus, must begin at home. Once well at home, how will it radiate outwards, irrepressible, into all that we touch and handle, speak and work; kindling ever new light, by incalculable contagion, spreading in geometric ratio, far and wide—doing good only, wheresoever it spreads, and not evil.

By Reform Bills, Anti-Corn-Law Bills, and thousand other bills and methods, we will demand of our Governors, with emphasis, and for the first time not without effect, that they cease to be quacks, or else depart; that they set no quackeries and block-headisms anywhere to rule over us, that they utter or act no cant to us—it will be better if they do not. For we shall now know quacks when we see them; cant, when we hear it, shall be horrible to us! We will say, with the poor Frenchman at the Bar of the Convention, though in wiser style than he, and "for the space" not "of an hour" but of a lifetime: "*Je demands l'arrestation des coquins et des laches.*" "Arrestment of the knaves and dastards." Ah, we know what a work that is; how long it will be before *they* are all or mostly got "arrested"—but here is one; arrest him, in God's name; it is one fewer! We will, in all practicable ways, by word and silence, by act and refusal to act, energetically demand that arrestment—"*je demande cette arrestation-la!*"—and by degrees infallibly attain it. Infallibly, for light spreads; all human souls, never so bedarkened, love light; light once kindled spreads, till all is luminous, till the cry, "*Arrest* your knaves and dastards" rises imperative from millions of hearts, and rings and reigns from sea to sea. Nay, how many of them may we not "arrest" with our own hands, even now, we! Do not countenance them, thou there: turn away from their lacquered sumptuosities, their belauded sophistries, their serpent graciosities, their spoken and acted cant, with a

---

[1] *Burns* Poet Robert Burns (1759–96), who worked as an excise officer. Burns came to be regarded as Scotland's national poet; *Byron* Romantic poet George Gordon, Lord Byron (1788–1824).

[2] *Odin* Norse god of war, art, and culture.

[3] *galvanic* Applying electricity; having the effect of an electric shock.

sacred horror, with an *Apage Satanas*.[1] Bobus and Company, and all men, will gradually join us. We demand arrestment of the knaves and dastards, and begin by arresting our own poor selves out of that fraternity. There is no other reform conceivable. Thou and I, my friend, can, in the most flunky world, make, each of us, *one* non-flunky, one hero, if we like. That will be two heroes to begin with—Courage! even that is a whole world of heroes to end with, or what we poor Two can do in furtherance thereof!

Yes, friends: Hero-kings, and a whole world not unheroic—there lies the port and happy haven, towards which, through all these stormtost seas, French Revolutions, Chartisms, Manchester Insurrections,[2] that make the heart sick in these bad days, the Supreme Powers are driving us. On the whole, blessed be the Supreme Powers, stern as they are! Towards that haven will we, O friends; let all true men, with what of faculty is in them, bend valiantly, incessantly, with thousandfold endeavour, thither, thither! There, or else in the Ocean-abysses, it is very clear to me, we shall arrive.

Well, here truly is no answer to the Sphinx-question[3]—not the answer a disconsolate public, inquiring at the College of Health, was in hopes of! A total change of regimen, change of constitution and existence from the very centre of it; a new body to be got, with resuscitated soul—not without convulsive travail-throes, as all birth and new-birth presupposes travail! This is sad news to a disconsolate discerning Public, hoping to have got off by some Morrison's Pill,[4] some Saint-John's corrosive mixture and perhaps a little blistery friction on the back! We were prepared to part with our Corn-Law, with various Laws and Unlaws, but this, what is this?

Nor has the Editor forgotten how it fares with your ill-boding Cassandras in Sieges of Troy.[5] Imminent perdition is not usually driven away by words of warning. Didactic Destiny has other methods in store, or these would fail always. Such words should, nevertheless, be uttered, when they dwell truly in the soul of any man. Words are hard, are importunate; but how much harder the importunate events they foreshadow! Here and there a human soul may listen to the words—who knows how many human souls?—whereby the importunate events, if not diverted and prevented, will be rendered *less* hard. The present Editor's purpose is to himself full of hope.

For though fierce travails, though wide seas and roaring gulfs lie before us, is it not something if a Loadstar, in the eternal sky, do once more disclose itself; an everlasting light, shining through all cloud-tempests and roaring billows, ever as we emerge from the trough of the sea; the blessed beacon, far off on the edge of far horizons, towards which we are to steer incessantly for life? Is it not something, O Heavens, is it not all? There lies the Heroic Promised Land; under that Heaven's-light, my brethren, bloom the Happy Isles—there, O there! Thither will we;

"There dwells the great Achilles whom we knew."[6] There dwell all Heroes, and will dwell: thither, all ye heroic-minded! The Heaven's Loadstar once clearly in our eye, how will each true man stand truly to *his* work in the ship; how, with undying hope, will all things be fronted, all be conquered. Nay, with the ship's prow once turned in that direction, is not all, as it were, already well? Sick wasting misery has become noble manful effort with a goal in our eye. The choking Nightmare chokes us no longer, for we *stir* under it; the Nightmare has already fled.

Certainly, could the present Editor instruct men how to know Wisdom, Heroism, when they see it, that they might do reverence to *it* only, and loyally make it ruler over them, yes, he were the living epitome of all

---

[1]   *Apage Satanus*   Latin: Begone, Satan.

[2]   *Chartisms*   Movements by the Chartists, peaceful democratic reformers whose principles were set out in the "People's Charter," published in 1838; *Manchester Insurrections*   Rioting in Manchester in 1842 resulted from the reduction of wages in both the coal mines and the factories. Manchester was also the site of the famous 1819 Peterloo Massacre, at which cavalry charged on an outdoor political meeting, killing thirteen people and wounding several others.

[3]   *Sphinx-question*   Riddle, like those posed by the mythological sphinx, a winged half-woman, half-lion who would not allow travelers to pass unless they could correctly answer her riddle. If they answered incorrectly, they would be killed.

[4]   *Morrison's Pill*   I.e., a cure-all.

[5]   *Cassandras ... Troy*   Cassandra, daughter of the King of Troy, was given the gift of prophecy, but cursed so that nobody would believe her.

[6]   *There dwells ... knew*   Cf. lines 63–4 of Alfred Lord Tennyson's poem "Ulysses": "It may be we shall touch the Happy Isles, / And see the great Achilles, whom we knew." The Happy Isles were the Isles of the Blessed, supposedly (according to Greek myth) located in the Atlantic Ocean.

Editors, Teachers, Prophets, that now teach and prophesy; he were an *Apollo*-Morrison, a Trismegistus[1] and *effective* Cassandra! Let no Able Editor hope such things. It is to be expected the present laws of copyright, rate of reward per sheet, and other considerations will save him from that peril. Let no Editor hope such things; no—and yet let all Editors aim towards such things, and even towards such alone! One knows not what the meaning of editing and writing is, if even this be not it.

Enough, to the present Editor it has seemed possible some glimmering of light, for here and there a human soul might lie in these confused Paper-Masses now entrusted to him; wherefore he determines to edit the same. Out of old Books, new Writings, and much Meditation not of yesterday, he will endeavour to select a thing or two; and from the Past, in a circuitous way, illustrate the Present and the Future. The Past is a dim indubitable fact: the Future too is one, only dimmer; nay properly it is the *same* fact in new dress and development. For the Present holds it in both the whole Past and the whole Future—as the life-tree Igdrasil,[2] wide-waving, many-toned, has its roots down deep in the Death-kingdoms, among the oldest dead dust of men, and with its boughs reaches always beyond the stars, and in all times and places is one and the same Life-tree! ...

from BOOK 3

CHAPTER 2—GOSPEL OF MAMMONISM

Reader, even Christian Reader as thy title goes, hast thou any notion of Heaven and Hell? I rather apprehend, not. Often as the words are on our tongue, they have got a fabulous or semi-fabulous character for most of us, and pass on like a kind of transient similitude, like a sound signifying little.

Yet it is well worth while for us to know, once and always, that they are not a similitude, nor a fable nor semi-fable; that they are an everlasting highest fact! "No

Lake of Sicilian or other sulphur[3] burns now anywhere in these ages," sayest thou? Well, and if there did not! Believe that there does not; believe it if thou wilt; nay, hold by it as a real increase, a rise to higher stages, to wider horizons and empires. All this has vanished, or has not vanished; believe as thou wilt as to all this. But that an Infinite of Practical Importance, speaking with strict arithmetical exactness, an *Infinite*, has vanished or can vanish from the Life of any Man, this thou shalt not believe! O brother, the Infinite of Terror, of Hope, of Pity, did it not at any moment disclose itself to thee, indubitable, unnameable? Came it never, like the gleam of eternal Oceans, like the voice of old Eternities, far-sounding through thy heart of hearts? Never? Alas, it was not thy Liberalism, then; it was thy Animalism! The Infinite is more sure than any other fact. But only men can discern it; mere building beavers, spinning arachnes, much more the predatory vulturous and vulpine species, do not discern it well!

"The word Hell," says Sauerteig, "is still frequently in use among the English people, but I could not without difficulty ascertain what they meant by it. Hell generally signifies the Infinite Terror, the thing a man *is* infinitely afraid of, and shudders and shrinks from, struggling with his whole soul to escape from it. There is a Hell, therefore, if you will consider, which accompanies man in all stages of his history and religious or other development. But the Hells of men and Peoples differ notably. With Christians it is the infinite terror of being found guilty before the Just Judge. With old Romans, I conjecture, it was the terror not of Pluto,[4] for whom probably they cared little, but of doing unworthily, doing unvirtuously, which was their word for un*man*fully.[5] And now what is it, if you pierce through his Cants, his oft-repeated Hearsays, what he calls his Worships and so forth, what is it that the modern English soul does, in very truth, dread infinitely, and contemplate with entire despair? What *is* his Hell, after all these reputable, oft-repeated Hearsays, what is it? With hesitation, with astonishment, I pronounce it to

---

[1] *Apollo* Classical god of poetry, music, and prophecy; *Trismegistus* Greek: thrice great. This is an epithet of the classical god Hermes, the messenger and herald for the other gods.

[2] *Igdrasil* Great tree of Scandinavian mythology, the roots and branches of which stretched through the universe.

[3] *Lake ... sulphur* Sulphur, often found near volcanic rocks, was formerly known as "brimstone" (i.e., "burning stone") and was thought to feed the fires of hell. At this time, Sicily was the world's primary source of sulphur.

[4] *Pluto* Roman god of the underworld.

[5] *which was ... unmanfully* The Latin word for man is *vir*.

be the terror of "Not succeeding"; of not making money, fame, or some other figure in the world—chiefly of not making money! Is not that a somewhat singular Hell?"

Yes, O Sauerteig, it is very singular. If we do not "succeed," where is the use of us? We had better never have been born. "Tremble intensely," as our friend the Emperor of China says: *there* is the black Bottomless of Terror, what Sauerteig calls the "Hell of the English!" But indeed this Hell belongs naturally to the Gospel of Mammonism, which also has its corresponding Heaven. For there *is* one Reality among so many Phantasms; about one thing we are entirely in earnest: the making of money. Working Mammonism does divide the world with idle game-preserving Dilettantism—thank Heaven that there is even a Mammonism, *anything* we are in earnest about! Idleness is worst, Idleness alone is without hope: work earnestly at anything, you will by degrees learn to work at almost all things. There is endless hope in work, were it even work at making money.

True, it must be owned, we for the present, with our Mammon-Gospel, have come to strange conclusions. We call it a Society; and go about professing openly the totalest separation, isolation. Our life is not a mutual helpfulness; but rather, cloaked under due laws-of-war, named "fair competition" and so forth, it is a mutual hostility. We have profoundly forgotten everywhere that *Cash payment* is not the sole relation of human beings; we think, nothing doubting, that *it* absolves and liquidates all engagements of man. "My starving workers?" answers the rich mill-owner: "Did not I hire them fairly in the market? Did I not pay them, to the last sixpence, the sum covenanted for? What have I to do with them more?" Verily Mammon-worship is a melancholy creed. When Cain, for his own behoof, had killed Abel, and was questioned, "Where is thy brother?" he too made answer, "Am I my brother's keeper?" Did I not pay my brother *his* wages, the thing he had merited from me?[1]

O sumptuous Merchant Prince, illustrious game-preserving Duke, is there no way of "killing" thy brother but Cain's rude way! "A good man by the very look of him, by his very presence with us as a fellow wayfarer in this Life-pilgrimage, *promises* so much." Woe to him if he forget all such promises, if he never know that they were given! To a deadened soul, seared with the brute Idolatry of Sense, to whom going to Hell is equivalent to not making money, all "promises" and moral duties, that cannot be pleaded for in Courts of Requests,[2] address themselves in vain. Money he can be ordered to pay, but nothing more. I have not heard in all Past History, and expect not to hear in all Future History, of any Society anywhere under God's Heaven, supporting itself on such Philosophy. The Universe is not made so; it is made otherwise than so. The man or nation of men that thinks it is made so, marches forward nothing doubting, step after step, but marches—whither we know! In these last two centuries of Atheistic Government (near two centuries now, since the blessed restoration of his Sacred Majesty, and Defender of the Faith, Charles Second), I reckon that we have pretty well exhausted what of "firm earth" there was for us to march on—and are now, very ominously, shuddering, reeling, and let us hope trying to recoil, on the cliff's edge!

For out of this that we call Atheism come so many other *isms* and falsities, each falsity with its misery at its heels! A SOUL is not like wind (*spiritus*, or breath) contained within a capsule; the ALMIGHTY MAKER is not like a Clockmaker that once, in old immemorial ages, having *made* his Horologe of a Universe, sits ever since and sees it go! Not at all. Hence comes Atheism; come, as we say, many other *isms*, and, as the sum of all, comes Valetism,[3] the *reverse* of Heroism—sad root of all woes whatsoever. For indeed, as no man ever saw the above-said wind-element enclosed within its capsule, and finds it at bottom more deniable than conceivable; so too he finds, in spite of Bridgwater Bequests, your Clockmaker Almighty an entirely questionable affair, a deniable affair—and accordingly denies it, and along with it so much else. Alas, one knows not what and how much else! For the faith in an Invisible, Unnameable, Godlike, present everywhere in all that we see and work and suffer, is the essence of all faith whatsoever; and that once denied, or still worse, asserted with lips only, and out of bound prayerbooks only, what other thing remains believable? That Cant well-ordered is marketable Cant; that Heroism means gas-lighted

---

[1] *When Cain ... me* See Genesis 4.9.

[2] *Court of Requests* Court that examined the petitions of the poor.

[3] *Valetism* I.e., the character of a valet. Carlyle defines valetism in Book 2 as "cloth-worship and quack-worship."

Histrionism;[1] that seen with "clear eyes" (as they call Valet-eyes) no man is a Hero, or ever was a Hero, but all men are Valets and Varlets. The accursed practical quintessence of all sorts of Unbelief! For if there be now no Hero, and the Histrio himself begin to be seen into, what hope is there for the seed of Adam here below? We are the doomed everlasting prey of the Quack; who, now in this guise, now in that, is to filch us, to pluck and eat us, by such modes as are convenient for him. For the modes and guises I care little. The Quack once inevitable, let him come swiftly, let him pluck and eat me—swiftly, that I may at least have done with him, for in his Quack-world I can have no wish to linger. Though he slay me, yet will I *not* trust in him. Though he conquer nations, and have all the Flunkies of the Universe shouting at his heels, yet will I know well that *he* is an Inanity; that for him and his there is no continuance appointed, save only in Gehenna and the Pool.[2] Alas, the Atheist world, from its utmost summits of Heaven and Westminster Hall,[3] downwards through poor seven-feet Hats and "Unveracities fallen hungry," down to the lowest cellars and neglected hunger-dens of it, is very wretched.

One of Dr. Alison's Scotch facts struck us much. A poor Irish Widow, her husband having died in one of the Lanes of Edinburgh, went forth with her three children, bare of all resource, to solicit help from the Charitable Establishments of that City. At this Charitable Establishment and then at that she was refused, referred from one to the other, helped by none, till she had exhausted them all, till her strength and heart failed her. She sank down in typhus-fever, died, and infected her Lane with fever, so that "seventeen other persons" died of fever there in consequence. The humane Physician asks thereupon, as with a heart too full for speaking, Would it not have been *economy* to help this poor Widow? She took typhus-fever, and killed seventeen of you! Very curious. The forlorn Irish Widow applies to her fellow-creatures, as if saying, "Behold I am sinking, bare of help. Ye must help me! I am your sister, bone of your bone; one God made us. Ye must help me!" They answer, "No, impossible; thou art no sister of ours." But

she proves her sisterhood; her typhus-fever kills *them*. They actually were her brothers, though denying it! Had human creature ever to go lower for a proof?

For, as indeed was very natural in such case, all government of the Poor by the Rich has long ago been given over to Supply-and-demand, Laissez-faire and suchlike, and universally declared to be "impossible." "You are no sister of ours; what shadow of proof is there? Here are our parchments, our padlocks, proving indisputably our money-safes to be *ours*, and you to have no business with them. Depart! It is impossible!" Nay, what wouldst thou thyself have us do? cry indignant readers. Nothing, my friends—till you have got a soul for yourselves again. Till then all things are "impossible." Till then I cannot even bid you buy, as the old Spartans would have done, two-pence worth of powder and lead, and compendiously shoot to death this poor Irish Widow. Even that is "impossible" for you. Nothing is left but that she prove her sisterhood by dying, and infecting you with typhus. Seventeen of you lying dead will not deny such proof that she *was* flesh of your flesh; and perhaps some of the living may lay it to heart.

"Impossible": of a certain two-legged animal with feathers it is said, if you draw a distinct chalk-circle round him, he sits imprisoned, as if girt with the iron ring of Fate, and will die there, though within sight of victuals, or sit in sick misery there, and be fatted to death. The name of this poor two-legged animal is—Goose; and they make of him, when well fattened, *Pâté de foie gras,* much prized by some! ...

CHAPTER 13—DEMOCRACY

If the Serene Highnesses and Majesties do not take note of that,[4] then, as I perceive, *that* will take note of itself! The time for levity, insincerity, and idle babble and play-acting, in all kinds, is gone by; it is a serious, grave time. Old long-vexed questions, not yet solved in logical words or parliamentary laws, are fast solving themselves in facts, somewhat unblessed to behold! This largest of questions, this question of Work and Wages, which

---

[1] *Histrionism* Acting.

[2] *Gehenna and the Pool* I.e., Hell.

[3] *Westminster Hall* Location of the British Houses of Parliament.

[4] *that* At the end of the previous chapter, Carlyle urged that "the proper epic of this world" should be "Tools and the Man," rather than "Arms and the Man," a reference to the opening line of Virgil's *Aeneid*: "Arma virumque cano" (Latin: "Of arms and the man I sing").

ought, had we heeded Heaven's voice, to have begun two generations ago or more, cannot be delayed longer without hearing Earth's voice. "Labour" will verily need to be somewhat "organised," as they say—God knows with what difficulty. Man will actually need to have his debts and earnings a little better paid by man; which, let Parliaments speak of them or be silent of them, are eternally his due from man, and cannot, without penalty and at length not without death penalty,[1] be withheld. How much ought to cease among us straightway, how much ought to begin straightway, while the hours yet are!

Truly they are strange results to which this of leaving all to "Cash," of quietly shutting-up the God's Temple, and gradually opening wide-open the Mammon's Temple, with "Lassez-faire, and Every man for himself," have led us in these days! We have Upper, speaking Classes, who indeed do "speak" as never man spake before; the withered flimsiness, the godless baseness and barrenness of whose Speech might of itself indicate what kind of Doing and practical Governing went on under it! For Speech is the gaseous element out of which most kinds of Practice and Performance, especially all kinds of moral Performance, condense themselves, and take shape; as the one is, so will the other be. Descending, accordingly, into the Dumb Class in its Stockport Cellars and Poor-Law Bastilles, have we not to announce that they also are hitherto unexampled in the History of Adam's Posterity?

Life was never a May-game[2] for men. In all times the lot of the dumb millions born to toil was defaced with manifold sufferings, injustices, heavy burdens, avoidable and unavoidable—not play at all, but hard work that made the sinews sore and the heart sore. As bond-slaves, *villani, bordarii, sochemanni*,[3] nay indeed as dukes, earls, and kings, men were oftentimes made weary of their life, and had to say, in the sweat of their brow and of their soul, Behold, it is not sport, it is grim earnest, and our back can bear no more! Who knows not what massacrings and harryings there have been—grinding,

long-continuing, unbearable injustices—till the heart had to rise in madness, and some "*Eu Sachsen, nimith euer sachses*, You Saxons, out with your gully-knives,[4] then!" You Saxons, some "arrestment," partial "arrestment of the Knaves and Dastards" has become indispensable! The page of Dryasdust[5] is heavy with such details.

And yet I will venture to believe that in no time, since the beginnings of Society, was the lot of those same dumb millions of toilers so entirely unbearable as it is even in the days now passing over us. It is not to die, or even to die of hunger, that makes a man wretched; many men have died; all men must die—the last exit of us all is in a Fire-Chariot of Pain.[6] But it is to live miserable we know not why; to work sore and yet gain nothing; to be heart-worn, weary, yet isolated, unrelated, girt-in with a cold universal Laissez-faire: it is to die slowly all our life long, imprisoned in a deaf, dead, Infinite Injustice, as in the accursed iron belly of a Phalaris' Bull![7] This is and remains forever intolerable to all men whom God has made. Do we wonder at French Revolutions, Chartisms, Revolts of Three Days? The times, if we will consider them, are really unexampled.

Never before did I hear of an Irish Widow reduced to "prove" her sisterhood by dying of typhus-fever and infecting seventeen "persons," saying in such undeniable way, "You *see* I was your sister!" Sisterhood, brotherhood, was often forgotten; but not till the rise of these ultimate Mammon and Shotbelt Gospels[8] did I ever see it so expressly denied. If no pious Lord or *Law-ward* would remember it, always some pious Lady ("*Hlaf-dig*,"[9] Benefactress, "*Loaf-giveress*," they say she is—blessings on her beautiful heart!) was there, with mild mother-voice and hand, to remember it; some pious thoughtful *Elder*, what we now call "Prester," *Presbyter* or "Priest," was there to put all men in mind of it, in the

---

[1] *death penalty* Reference to the deaths caused by violent revolutions, such as the French Revolution.

[2] *May-game* Entertainment or performance (such as those traditionally making up part of the celebration on the first day of May).

[3] *villani … sochemanni* Classes of peasants in the feudal system.

[4] *gully-knives* Large household knives.

[5] *Dryasdust* Name given to a dull, pedantic historian, after the fictional antiquarian Dr. Jonas Dryasdust, to whom Walter Scott facetiously dedicated some of his novels.

[6] *last exit … Pain* See 2 Kings 2.11–12.

[7] *Phalaris' Bull* Phalaris, an ancient Sicilian tyrant, murdered wrong-doers by placing them in a brass bull that sat over a fire.

[8] *Shotbelt Gospels* I.e., principles of the landed aristocracy who sought to maintain their exclusive right to shoot game.

[9] *Hlaf-dig* I.e., loaf-giver.

name of the God who had made all.

Not even in Black Dahomey[1] was it ever, I think, forgotten to the typhus-fever length. Mungo Park,[2] resourceless, had sunk down to die under the Negro Village-Tree, a horrible White object in the eyes of all. But in the poor Black Woman, and her daughter who stood aghast at him, whose earthly wealth and funded capital consisted of one small calabash of rice, there lived a heart richer than *Laissez-faire*: they, with a royal munificence, boiled their rice for him; they sang all night to him, spinning assiduous on their cotton distaffs, as he lay to sleep: "Let us pity the poor white man; no mother has he to fetch him milk, no sister to grind him corn!" Thou poor black Noble One, thou *Lady* too. Did not a God make thee too; was there not in thee too something of a God!

Gurth, born thrall of Cedric the Saxon,[3] has been greatly pitied by Dryasdust and others. Gurth, with the brass collar round his neck, tending Cedric's pigs in the glades of the wood, is not what I call an exemplar of human felicity. But Gurth, with the sky above him, with the free air and tinted boscage and umbrage[4] round him, and in him at least the certainty of supper and social lodging when he came home, Gurth to me seems happy, in comparison with many a Lancashire and Buckinghamshire man of these days, not born thrall of anybody! Gurth's brass collar did not gall him; Cedric *deserved* to be his master. The pigs were Cedric's, but Gurth too would get his parings of them. Gurth had the inexpressible satisfaction of feeling himself related indissolubly, though in a rude brass-collar way, to his fellow-mortals in this Earth. He had superiors, inferiors, equals. Gurth is now "emancipated" long since, has what we call "Liberty." Liberty, I am told, is a divine thing. Liberty when it becomes the "Liberty to die by starvation" is not so divine!

Liberty? The true liberty of a man, you would say, consisted in his finding out, or being forced to find out, the right path, and to walk thereon. To learn, or to be taught, what work he actually was able for, and then by permission, persuasion, and even compulsion, to set about doing of the same! That is his true blessedness, honour, "liberty," and maximum of wellbeing: if liberty be not that, I for one have small care about liberty. You do not allow a palpable madman to leap over precipices; you violate his liberty, you that are wise, and keep him, were it in strait-waistcoats, away from the precipices! Every stupid, every cowardly and foolish man is but a less palpable madman: his true liberty were that a wiser man, that any and every wiser man, could, by brass collars, or in whatever milder or sharper way, lay hold of him when he was going wrong, and order and compel him to go a little righter. O, if thou really art my *Senior*, Seigneur, my *Elder*, Presbyter or Priest—if thou art in very deed my *Wiser*, may a beneficent instinct lead and impel thee to "conquer" me, to command me! If thou do know better than I what is good and right, I conjure thee in the name of God, force me to do it; were it by never such brass collars, whips and handcuffs, leave me not to walk over precipices! That I have been called, by all the Newspapers, a "free man" will avail me little, if my pilgrimage have ended in death and wreck. O that the Newspapers had called me slave, coward, fool, or what it pleased their *sweet* voices to name me, and I had attained not death, but life! Liberty requires new definitions.

A conscious abhorrence and intolerance of Folly, of Baseness, Stupidity, Poltroonery[5] and all that brood of things, dwells deep in some men; still deeper in others an *un*conscious abhorrence and intolerance, clotted moreover by the beneficent Supreme Powers in what stout appetites, energies, egoisms so-called, are suitable to it. These latter are your Conquerors, Romans, Normans, Russians, Indo-English; Founders of what we call Aristocracies. Which indeed have they not the most "divine right" to found—being themselves very truly Αριστοι[6] BRAVEST, BEST, and conquering generally a confused rabble of WORST, or at lowest, clearly enough, of WORSE? I think their divine right, tried, with affirmatory verdict, in the greatest Law-Court known to me,

---

[1] *Black Dahomey* Area of West Africa, formerly belonging to the French, in which human sacrifice and cannibalism were rumored to take place.

[2] *Mungo Park* Scottish explorer and author of *Travels in the Interior of Africa* (1799), who was killed by Africans in Bussa in 1806.

[3] *Gurth* In Walter Scott's *Ivanhoe* (1819), Gurth is a serf (thrall) of the wealthy farmer Cedric.

[4] *boscage and umbrage* Grove and shade.

[5] *Poltroonery* Cowardliness; mean-spiritedness.

[6] Αριστοι Greek: aristocrats.

was good! A class of men who are dreadfully exclaimed against by Dryasdust, of whom nevertheless beneficent Nature has oftentimes had need, and may, alas, again have need.

When, across the hundredfold poor scepticisms, trivialisms and constitutional cobwebberies of Dryasdust, you catch any glimpse of a William the Conqueror, a Tancred of Hauteville[1] or suchlike, do you not discern veritably some rude outline of a true God-made King, whom not the Champion of England cased in tin, but all Nature and the Universe were calling to the throne? It is absolutely necessary that he get thither. Nature does not mean her poor Saxon children to perish of obesity, stupor, or other malady, as yet. A stern Ruler and Line of Rulers therefore is called in—a stern but most beneficent *perpetual House-Surgeon* is by Nature herself called in, and even the appropriate *fees* are provided for him! Dryasdust talks lamentably about Hereward and the Fen Counties,[2] fate of Earl Waltheof,[3] Yorkshire and the North reduced to ashes—all which is undoubtedly lamentable. But even Dryasdust apprises me of one fact: "A child, in this William's reign, might have carried a purse of gold from end to end of England." My erudite friend, it is a fact which outweighs a thousand! Sweep away thy constitutional, sentimental, and other cobwebberies; look eye to eye, if thou still have any eye, in the face of this big burly William Bastard.[4] Thou wilt see a fellow of most flashing discernment, of most strong lion-heart, in whom, as it were, within a frame of oak and iron, the gods have planted the soul of "a man of genius"! Dost thou call that nothing? I call it an immense thing! Rage enough was in this Willelmus Conquaestor,[5] rage enough for his occasions—and yet the essential element

of him, as of all such men, is not scorching *fire*, but shining illuminative *light*. Fire and light are strangely interchangeable; nay, at bottom, I have found them different forms of the same most godlike "elementary substance" in our world—a thing worth stating in these days. The essential element of this Conquaestor is, first of all, the most sun-eyed perception of what *is* really what on this God's-Earth—which, thou wilt find, does mean at bottom "Justice," and "Virtues" not a few—*Conformity* to what the Maker has seen good to make; that, I suppose, will mean Justice and a Virtue or two?

Dost thou think Willelmus Conquaestor would have tolerated ten years' jargon, one hour's jargon, on the propriety of killing Cotton manufactures by partridge[6] Corn Laws? I fancy, this was not the man to knock out of his night's-rest with nothing but a noisy bedlamism[7] in your mouth! "Assist us still better to bush the partridges; strangle Plugson[8] who spins the shirts?"—"*Par la Splendeur de Dieu!*"[9]—Dost thou think Willelmus Conquaestor, in this new time, with Steamengine Captains of Industry on one hand of him, and Joe-Manton Captains of Idleness on the other, would have doubted which *was* really the BEST; which did deserve strangling, and which not?

I have a certain indestructible regard for Willelmus Conquaestor. A resident House-Surgeon, provided by Nature for her beloved English People, and even furnished with the requisite fees, as I said; for he by no means felt himself doing Nature's work, this Willelmus, but his own work exclusively! And his own work withal it was, informed "*par la Splendeur de Dieu!*" I say, it is necessary to get the work out of such a man, however harsh that be! When a world, not yet doomed for death, is rushing down to ever-deeper Baseness and Confusion, it is a dire necessity of Nature's to bring in her ARISTOCRACIES, her BEST, even by forcible methods. When their descendants or representatives cease entirely to be

---

[1] *William the Conqueror* King William I of England (who ruled from 1066 to 1087) was named "the Conqueror" after he won the throne from King Harold at the Battle of Hastings in 1066; *Tancred of Hauteville* Norman Crusader (1076–1112).

[2] *Hereward ... Counties* Anglo-Saxon who rebelled against William I and organized uprisings in Lincolnshire and its surrounding counties (known collectively as the "Fen Counties" because of their marshland).

[3] *Earl Waltheof* Anglo-Saxon who was executed for treason by William I, but was later believed innocent and regarded as a martyr.

[4] *William Bastard* William I was an illegitimate son of Robert I, Duke of Normandy.

[5] *Willelmus Conquaestor* Latin: William the Conqueror.

[6] *partridge* Reference to the aristocracy's attachment to hunting game.

[7] *bedlamism* Something characteristic of madness—specifically, of the Hospital of St. Mary of Bethlehem (referred to as "Bedlam"), an overcrowded and frenetic London asylum.

[8] *Plugson* Fictional industrial firm to which Carlyle refers several times throughout *Past and Present*.

[9] *Par la ... Dieu* French: By the splendor of God.

the Best, Nature's poor world will very soon rush down again to Baseness; and it becomes a dire necessity of Nature's to cast them out. Hence French Revolutions, Five-point Charters,[1] Democracies, and a mournful list of *Etceteras*, in these our afflicted times.

To what extent Democracy has now reached, how it advances irresistible with ominous, ever-increasing speed, he that will open his eyes on any province of human affairs may discern. Democracy is everywhere the inexorable demand of these ages, swiftly fulfilling itself. From the thunder of Napoleon battles, to the jabbering of Open-vestry in St. Mary Axe,[2] *all things announce Democracy.* A distinguished man, whom some of my readers will hear again with pleasure, thus writes to me what in these days he notes from the Wahngasse of Weissnichtwo,[3] where our London fashions seem to be in full vogue. Let us hear the Herr Teufelsdröckh[4] again, were it but the smallest word!

Democracy, which means despair of finding any Heroes to govern you, and contented putting-up with the want of them, alas, thou too, *mein Lieber*,[5] seest well how close it is of kin to *Atheism*, and other sad *Isms*: he who discovers no God whatever, how shall he discover Heroes, the visible Temples of God? Strange enough meanwhile it is to observe with what thoughtlessness, here in our rigidly Conservative Country, men rush into Democracy with full cry. Beyond doubt, his Excellenz the Titular Herr Ritter Kauderwalsch von Pferdefuss-Quacksalber,[6] he our distinguished Conservative Premier himself, and all but the thicker-headed of his Party discern Democracy to be inevitable as death, and are

even desperate of delaying it much!

"You cannot walk the streets without beholding Democracy announce itself. The very Tailor has become, if not properly Sansculottic, which to him would be ruinous, yet a Tailor unconsciously symbolising, and prophesying with his scissors, the reign of Equality. What now is our fashionable coat? A thing of superfinest texture, of deeply meditated cut, with Malines-lace[7] cuffs, quilted with gold; so that a man can carry, without difficulty, an estate of land on his back? *Keineswegs*, By no manner of means! The Sumptuary Laws[8] have fallen into such a state of desuetude[9] as was never before seen. Our fashionable coat is an amphibium between barn-sack and drayman's doublet. The cloth of it is studiously coarse; the colour, a speckled soot-black or rust-brown gray, the nearest approach to a Peasant's. And for shape—thou shouldst see it! The last consummation of the year now passing over us is definable as Three Bags: a big bag for the body, two small bags for the arms, and by way of collar a hem! The first Antique Cheruscan[10] who, of felt-cloth or bear's-hide, with bone or metal needle, set about making himself a coat, before Tailors had yet awakened out of Nothing, did not he make it even so? A loose wide poke for body, with two holes to let out the arms, this was his original coat—to which holes it was soon visible that two small loose pokes, or sleeves, easily appended, would be an improvement.

"Thus has the Tailor-art, so to speak, overset itself, like most other things, changed its centre-of-gravity, whirled suddenly over from zenith to nadir. Your Stulz,[11] with huge somerset,[12] vaults from his high shopboard down to the depths of primal savagery, carrying much along with him! For I will invite thee to reflect that the Tailor, as topmost ultimate froth of Human Society, is indeed swift-passing, evanescent, slippery to decipher, yet significant of much, nay of all. Topmost evanescent froth, he is churned-up from the very lees, and from all intermediate regions of the

[1] *Five-point Charters* The "People's Charter" (on which the Chartist movement was based) actually had six points, all concerning suffrage.

[2] *jabbering ... Axe* I.e., the bickering of the rate-paying parishioners, who were generally allowed to express their opinions on temporal affairs of the Church.

[3] *Wahngasse of Weissnichtwo* German: Delusion alley of I-know-not-where.

[4] *Herr Teufelsdröckh* Carlyle writes about this fictional German philosopher, Diogenes Teufelsdröckh, in *Sartor Resartus*. He is said to be the author of *Clothes: Their Origin and Influence*, and his name, in German, literally means "God-born devil's dung."

[5] *mein Lieber* German: my dear.

[6] *Excellenz ... Pferdefuss-Quacksalber* German: Mr. Knight Gibberish Horsefoot-Mountebank. A reference to Sir Robert Peel, the Conservative Prime Minister.

[7] *Malines-lace* Lace made in Malines, a town in Belgium.

[8] *Sumptuary Laws* Laws regulating expenditure on food, dress, etc.

[9] *desuetude* Disuse.

[10] *Cheruscan* Member of an ancient German tribe.

[11] *Stulz* I.e., name of a high-class tailor.

[12] *somerset* Somersault.

liquor. The general outcome he, visible to the eye, of what men aimed to do, and were obliged and enabled to do, in this one public department of symbolising themselves to each other by covering of their skins. A smack of all Human Life lies in the Tailor: its wild struggles towards beauty, dignity, freedom, victory; and how, hemmed-in by Sedan and Huddersfield,[1] by Nescience,[2] Dullness, Prurience,[3] and other sad necessities and laws of Nature, it has attained just to this: Gray savagery of Three Sacks with a hem!

"When the very Tailor verges towards Sansculottism, is it not ominous? The last Divinity of poor mankind dethroning himself, sinking *his* taper too, flame downmost, like the Genius of Sleep or of Death, admonitory that Tailor time shall be no more! For, little as one could advise Sumptuary Laws at the present epoch, yet nothing is clearer than that where ranks do actually exist, strict division of costumes will also be enforced; that if we ever have a new Hierarchy and Aristocracy, acknowledged veritably as such, for which I daily pray Heaven, the Tailor will reawaken, and be, by volunteering and appointment, consciously and unconsciously, a safeguard of that same." Certain farther observations, from the same invaluable pen, on our never-ending changes of mode, our perpetual nomadic and even ape-like appetite for change and mere change in all the equipments of our existence, and the "fatal revolutionary character" thereby manifested, we suppress for the present. It may be admitted that Democracy, in all meanings of the word, is in full career; irresistible by any Ritter Kauderwalsch or other Son of Adam, as times go. "Liberty" is a thing men are determined to have.

But truly, as I had to remark in the meanwhile, "the liberty of not being oppressed by your fellow man" is an indispensable, yet one of the most insignificant fractional, parts of Human Liberty. No man oppresses thee, can bid thee fetch or carry, come or go, without reason shown. True, from all men thou art emancipated; but from Thyself and from the Devil—? No man, wiser, unwiser, can make thee come or go; but thy own futilities, bewilderments, thy false appetites for Money,

Windsor Georges[4] and suchlike? No man oppresses thee, O free and independent Franchiser; but does not this stupid Porter-pot[5] oppress thee? No Son of Adam can bid thee come or go; but this absurd Pot of Heavy-wet,[6] this can and does! Thou art the thrall not of Cedric the Saxon, but of thy own brutal appetites and this scoured dish of liquor. And thou pratest of thy "liberty"? Thou entire blockhead!

Heavy-wet and gin; alas, these are not the only kinds of thraldom. Thou who walkest in a vain show, looking out with ornamental dilettante sniff and serene supremacy at all Life and all Death; and amblest jauntily, perking up thy poor talk into crotchets,[7] thy poor conduct into fatuous somnambulisms; and *art* as an "enchanted Ape" under God's sky, where thou mightest have been a man, had proper Schoolmasters and Conquerors, and Constables with cat-o'-nine tails,[8] been vouchsafed thee—dost thou call that "liberty"? Or your unreposing Mammon-worshipper again, driven, as if by Galvanisms,[9] by Devils and Fixed Ideas, who rises early and sits late, chasing the impossible, straining every faculty to "fill himself with the east wind"[10]—how merciful were it, could you, by mild persuasion, or by the severest tyranny so-called, check him in his mad path, and turn him into a wiser one! All painful tyranny, in that case again, were but mild "surgery," the pain of it cheap, as health and life, instead of galvanism and fixed-idea, are cheap at any price.

Sure enough, of all paths a man could strike into, there *is*, at any given moment, a *best path* for every man; a thing which, here and now, it were of all things *wisest* for him to do—which, could he be but led or driven to do, he were then doing "like a man," as we phrase it, all men and gods agreeing with him, the whole Universe virtually exclaiming Well-done to him! His success, in such case, were complete; his felicity a maximum. This

---

[1] *Sedan and Huddersfield*   Towns (the first French, the second English) where wool was woven.

[2] *Nescience*   Ignorance.

[3] *Prurience*   Tendency towards impure or lewd ideas.

[4] *Windsor Georges*   I.e., the pomp of royalty.

[5] *Porter-pot*   Vessel of porter, a dark beer.

[6] *Heavy-wet*   Malt liquor.

[7] *crotchets*   Odd notions; perverse conceits.

[8] *cat-o'-nine-tails*   Whip with nine lashes.

[9] *Galvanisms*   Applications of electricity.

[10] *east wind*   The east wind was proverbially harmful to one's health. In the Bible it is seen as destructive; the wind blowing from the east onto Palestine brings dry, hot air from the desert, and is harmful to crops.

path, to find this path and walk in it, is the one thing needful for him. Whatsoever forwards him in that, let it come to him even in the shape of blows and spurnings, is liberty; whatsoever hinders him, were it wardmotes,[1] open-vestries, pollbooths, tremendous cheers, rivers of heavy-wet, is slavery.

The notion that a man's liberty consists in giving his vote at election-hustings,[2] and saying, "Behold, now I too have my twenty-thousandth part of a Talker in our National Palaver;[3] will not all the gods be good to me?" is one of the pleasantest! Nature nevertheless is kind at present, and puts it into the heads of many, almost of all. The liberty especially which has to purchase itself by social isolation, and each man standing separate from the other, having no business with him but a cash-account, this is such a liberty as the Earth seldom saw—as the Earth will not long put up with, recommend it how you may. This liberty turns out, before it have long continued in action, with all men flinging up their caps round it, to be, for the Working Millions, a liberty to die by want of food; for the Idle Thousands and Units, alas, a still more fatal liberty to live in want of work, to have no earnest duty to do in this God's-World anymore. What becomes of a man in such predicament? Earth's Laws are silent, and Heaven's speak in a voice which is not heard. No work, and the ineradicable need of work, give rise to new very wondrous life-philosophies, new very wondrous life-practices! Dilettantism, Pococurantism, Beau-Brummelism,[4] with perhaps an occasional, half-mad, protesting burst of Byronism, establish themselves; at the end of a certain period, if you go back to "the Dead Sea," there is, say our Moslem friends, a very strange "Sabbath day" transacting itself there![5] Brethren, we know but imper-

fectly yet, after ages of Constitutional Government, what Liberty and Slavery are.

Democracy, the chase of Liberty in that direction shall go its full course, unrestrainable by him of Pferdefuss-Quacksalber, or any of *his* household. The Toiling Millions of Mankind, in most vital need and passionate instinctive desire of Guidance, shall cast away False-Guidance and hope, for an hour, that No-Guidance will suffice them; but it can be for an hour only. The smallest item of human Slavery is the oppression of man by his Mock Superiors; the palpablest, but I say at bottom the smallest. Let him shake off such oppression, trample it indignantly under his feet; I blame him not, I pity and commend him. But oppression by your Mock Superiors well shaken off, the grand problem yet remains to solve: that of finding government by your Real Superiors! Alas, how shall we ever learn the solution of that, benighted, bewildered, sniffing, sneering, god-forgetting unfortunates we are? It is a work for centuries, to be taught us by tribulations, confusions, insurrections, obstructions; who knows if not by conflagration and despair! It is a lesson inclusive of all other lessons; the hardest of all lessons to learn.

One thing I do know: those Apes, chattering on the branches by the Dead Sea, never got it learned, but chatter there to this day. To them no Moses need come a second time; a thousand Moseses would be but so many painted Phantasms, interesting Fellow-Apes of new strange aspect, whom they would "invite to dinner," be glad to meet with in lion-soirées. To them the voice of Prophecy, of heavenly monition, is quite ended. They chatter here, all Heaven shut to them, to the end of the world. The unfortunates! Oh, what is dying of hunger, with honest tools in your hand, with a manful purpose in your heart, and much real labour lying round you done, in comparison? You honestly quit your tools, quit a most muddy confused coil of sore work, short rations, of sorrow, dispiritments, and contradictions, having now honestly done with it all, and await, not entirely in a distracted manner, what the Supreme Powers, and the Silences and the Eternities may have to say to you.

A second thing I know: this lesson will have to be learned—under penalties! England will either learn it, or England also will cease to exist among Nations. England will either learn to reverence its Heroes, and discrimi-

---

[1] *wardmotes* Meetings of the citizens of a ward, or area of the city.

[2] *election-hustings* I.e., election proceedings. The husting was a temporary platform on which candidates for Parliament stood to address electors.

[3] *Palaver* Rigamarole, prolonged and tedious discussion.

[4] *Pococurantism* Attitude of indifference or unconcern, from an Italian expression describing an indifferent person; *Beau Brummelism* Obsession with fashion. George Bryan Brummel (known as "Beau Brummel") was a leader of fashion in Regency England.

[5] *there is … there* According to an Islamic myth, a tribe living on the banks of the Dead Sea were turned into apes after refusing to acknowledge Moses's prophecies.

nate them from its Sham-Heroes and Valets and gaslighted Histrios, and to prize them as the audible God's-voice, amid all inane jargons and temporary market-cries, and say to them with heart-loyalty, "Be ye King and Priest, and Gospel and Guidance for us," or else England will continue to worship new and ever-new forms of Quackhood—and so, with what resiliences and reboundings matters little, go down to the Father of Quacks! Can I dread such things of England? Wretched, thickeyed, gross-hearted mortals, why will ye worship lies, and "Stuffed Clothes-suits created by the ninth-parts[1] of men"! It is not your purses that suffer, your farm-rents, your commerces, your mill-revenues, loud as ye lament over these; no, it is not these alone, but a far deeper than these: it is your souls that lie dead, crushed down under despicable Nightmares, Atheisms, Brain-fumes, and are not souls at all, but mere succedanea[2] for *salt* to keep your bodies and their appetites from putre-fying! Your cotton-spinning and thrice-miraculous mechanism, what is this too, by itself, but a larger kind of Animalism? Spiders can spin, Beavers can build and show contrivance, the Ant lays-up accumulation of capital, and has, for aught I know, a Bank of Antland. If there is no soul in man higher than all that, did it reach to sailing on the cloud-rack and spinning sea-sand, then I say, man is but an animal, a more cunning kind of brute; he has no soul, but only a succedaneum for salt. Whereupon, seeing himself to be truly of the beasts that perish, he ought to admit it, I think—and also straight-way universally to kill himself, and so, in a manlike manner at least *end*, and wave these brute-worlds *his* dignified farewell! …

from BOOK 4
CHAPTER 4—CAPTAINS OF INDUSTRY

If I believed that Mammonism with its adjuncts was to continue henceforth the one serious principle of our existence, I should reckon it idle to solicit remedial measures from any Government, the disease being insusceptible of remedy. Government can do much, but

it can in no wise[3] do all. Government, as the most conspicuous object in Society, is called upon to give signal of what shall be done; and, in many ways, to preside over, further, and command the doing of it. But the Government cannot do, by all its signaling and commanding, what the Society is radically indisposed to do. In the long-run every Government is the exact symbol of its People, with their wisdom and unwisdom; we have to say, Like People like Government. The main substance of this immense Problem of Organising Labour, and first of all of Managing the Working Classes, will, it is very clear, have to be solved by those who stand practically in the middle of it, by those who themselves work and preside over work. Of all that can be enacted by any Parliament in regard to it, the germs must already lie potentially extant in those two Classes, who are to obey such enactment. A Human Chaos *in* which there is no light, you vainly attempt to irradiate by light shed *on* it; order never can arise there.

But it is my firm conviction that the "Hell of England" will *cease* to be that of "not making money," that we shall get a nobler Hell and a nobler Heaven! I anticipate light *in* the Human Chaos, glimmering, shining more and more, under manifold true signals from without That light shall shine. Our deity no longer being Mammon, O Heavens, each man will then say to himself, "Why such deadly haste to make money? I shall not go to Hell, even if I do not make money! There is another Hell, I am told!" Competition, at railway-speed, in all branches of commerce and work will then abate; good felt-hats for the head, in every sense, instead of seven-feet lath-and-plaster hats on wheels, will then be discoverable! Bubble-periods,[4] with their panics and commercial crises, will again become infrequent; steady modest industry will take the place of gambling specula-tion. To be a noble Master, among noble Workers, will again be the first ambition with some few; to be a rich Master only the second. How the Inventive Genius of England, with the whirr of its bobbins and billy-rollers[5] shoved somewhat into the backgrounds of the brain, will contrive and devise, not cheaper produce exclu-

---

[1] *the ninth-parts of men* I.e., worthless men.

[2] *succedanea* Substitutes.

[3] *wise* Way.

[4] *Bubble-periods* Violent fluctuations in the stock market.

[5] *bobbins* Wooden spools or cylinders on which cotton or thread is wound; *billy-rollers* Machines for preparing cotton or wool for spinning.

sively, but fairer distribution of the produce at its present cheapness! By degrees, we shall again have a Society with something of Heroism in it, something of Heaven's Blessing on it; we shall again have, as my German friend asserts, "instead of Mammon-Feudalism with unsold cotton-shirts and Preservation of the Game, noble just Industrialism and Government by the Wisest!"

It is with the hope of awakening here and there a British man to know himself for a man and divine soul, that a few words of parting admonition, to all persons to whom the Heavenly Powers have lent power of any kind in this land, may now be addressed. And first to those same Master-Workers, Leaders of Industry, who stand nearest and in fact powerfulest, though not most prominent, being as yet in too many senses a Virtuality rather than an Actuality.

The Leaders of Industry, if Industry is ever to be led, are virtually the Captains of the World; if there be no nobleness in them, there will never be an Aristocracy more. But let the Captains of Industry consider: once again, are they born of other clay than the old Captains of Slaughter, doomed forever to be no Chivalry, but a mere gold-plated *Doggery*—what the French well name *Canaille*, "Doggery" with more or less gold carrion at its disposal? Captains of Industry are the true Fighters, henceforth recognisable as the only true ones—Fighters against Chaos, Necessity, and the Devils and Jötuns[1]— and lead on Mankind in that great, and alone true and universal warfare; the stars in their courses fighting for them, and all Heaven and all Earth saying audibly, Well done! Let the Captains of Industry retire into their own hearts, and ask solemnly, If there is nothing but vulturous hunger for fine wines, valet reputation, and gilt carriages discoverable there? Of hearts made by the Almighty God I will not believe such a thing. Deephidden under wretchedest god-forgetting Cants, Epicurisms,[2] Dead-Sea Apisms, forgotten as under foulest fat Lethe[3] mud and weeds, there is yet, in all hearts born into this God's-World, a spark of the Godlike slumbering. Awake, O nightmare sleepers; awake, arise, or be forever fallen! This is not playhouse poetry, it is sober fact. Our England, our world, cannot live as it is. It will connect itself with a God again, or go down with nameless throes and fire-consummation to the Devils. Thou who feelest aught[4] of such a Godlike stirring in thee, any faintest intimation of it as through heavyladen dreams, follow *it*, I conjure thee. Arise, save thyself, be one of those that save thy country.

Buccaneers, Chactaw Indians,[5] whose supreme aim in fighting is that they may get the scalps, the money, that they may amass scalps and money—out of such came no Chivalry, and never will! Out of such came only gore and wreck, infernal rage and misery; desperation quenched in annihilation. Behold it, I bid thee; behold there, and consider! What is it that thou have a hundred thousand-pound bills laid-up in thy strongroom, a hundred scalps hung-up in thy wigwam? I value not them or thee. Thy scalps and thy thousand-pound bills are as yet nothing, if no nobleness from within irradiate them; if no Chivalry, in action, or in embryo ever struggling towards birth and action, be there.

Love of men cannot be bought by cash-payment, and without love men cannot endure to be together. You cannot lead a Fighting World without having it regimented, chivalried; the thing, in a day, becomes impossible. All men in it, the highest at first, the very lowest at last, discern consciously, or by a noble instinct, this necessity. And can you any more continue to lead a Working World unregimented, anarchic? I answer, and the Heavens and Earth are now answering, No! The thing becomes not "in a day" impossible; but in some two generations it does. Yes, when fathers and mothers, in Stockport hunger-cellars, begin to eat their children; and Irish widows have to prove their relationship by dying of typhus-fever; and amid Governing "Corporations of the Best and Bravest," busy to preserve their game by "bushing," dark millions of God's human creatures start up in mad Chartisms, impracticable

---

[1] *Jötuns* Members of a mythological Norse race of giants.

[2] *Epicurisms* Pursuits of sensual pleasures, luxury, and ease, so named after the philosophical system of third-century BCE Greek thinker Epicurus.

[3] *Lethe* River of forgetfulness in Hades, the classical underworld.

[4] *aught* Anything.

[5] *Chactaw Indians* The Choctaw, who formerly inhabited central and southern Mississippi and southwest Alabama, and who were known to take as trophies the scalps of enemies killed in battle. The tribe had a friendly relationship with the American settlers; secessions of their eastern land to the settlers allowed Mississippi to become a state. In exchange, they were granted land in present-day Oklahoma, to which they were removed between 1831 and 1903.

Sacred-Months, and Manchester Insurrections; and there is a virtual Industrial Aristocracy as yet only half-alive, spell-bound amid money-bags and ledgers; and an actual Idle Aristocracy seemingly near dead in somnolent delusions, in trespasses[1] and double-barrels, "sliding," as on inclined planes, which every new year they *soap* with new Hansard's-jargon[2] under God's sky, and so are "sliding," ever faster, towards a "scale" and balance-scale whereon is written *Thou art found Wanting*—in such days, after a generation or two, I say, it does become, even to the low and simple, very palpably impossible! No Working World, any more than a Fighting World, can be led on without a noble Chivalry of Work, and laws and fixed rules which follow out of that, far nobler than any Chivalry of Fighting was. As an anarchic multitude on mere Supply-and-demand, it is becoming inevitable that we dwindle in horrid suicidal convulsion and self-abrasion, frightful to the imagination, into *Chactaw* Workers. With wigwams and scalps, with palaces and thousand-pound bills, with savagery, depopulation, chaotic desolation! Good Heavens, will not one French Revolution and Reign of Terror suffice us, but must there be two? There will be two if needed; there will be twenty if needed; there will be precisely as many as are needed. The Laws of Nature will have themselves fulfilled. That is a thing certain to me.

Your gallant battle-hosts and work-hosts, as the others did, will need to be made loyally yours; they must and will be regulated, methodically secured in their just share of conquest under you—joined with you in veritable brotherhood, sonhood, by quite other and deeper ties than those of temporary day's wages! How would mere red-coated regiments, to say nothing of chivalries, fight for you, if you could discharge them on the evening of the battle, on payment of the stipulated shillings—and they discharge you on the morning of it! Chelsea Hospitals,[3] pensions, promotions, rigorous lasting covenant on the one side and on the other, are indispensable even for a hired fighter. The Feudal Baron, much more—how could he subsist with mere temporary mercenaries round him at sixpence a day, ready to go over to the other side, if sevenpence were offered? He could not have subsisted, and his noble instinct saved him from the necessity of even trying! The Feudal Baron had a Man's Soul in him, to which anarchy, mutiny, and the other fruits of temporary mercenaries were intolerable; he had never been a Baron otherwise, but had continued a Chactaw and Buccaneer. He felt it precious, and at last it became habitual, and his fruitful enlarged existence included it as a necessity, to have men round him who in heart loved him; whose life he watched over with rigour yet with love; who were prepared to give their life for him, if need came. It was beautiful; it was human! Man lives not otherwise, nor can live contented, anywhere or anywhen. Isolation is the sum-total of wretchedness to man. To be cut off, to be left solitary; to have a world alien, not your world, all a hostile camp for you, not a home at all, of hearts and faces who are yours, whose you are! It is the frightfulest enchantment, too truly a work of the Evil One. To have neither superior, nor inferior, nor equal, united manlike to you. Without father, without child, without brother. Man knows no sadder destiny. "How is each of us," exclaims Jean Paul,[4] "so lonely in the wide bosom of the All!" Encased each as in his transparent "ice-palace," our brother visible in his, making signals and gesticulations to us—visible, but forever unattainable; on his bosom we shall never rest, nor he on ours. It was not a God that did this; no!

Awake, ye noble Workers, warriors in the one true war; all this must be remedied. It is you who are already half-alive, whom I will welcome into life, whom I will conjure, in God's name, to shake off your enchanted sleep, and live wholly! Cease to count scalps, gold-purses; not in these lies your or our salvation. Even these, if you count only these, will not long be left. Let buccaneering be put far from you; alter, speedily abrogate all laws of the buccaneers, if you would gain any victory that shall endure. Let God's justice, let pity, nobleness and manly valour, with more gold-purses or with fewer, testify themselves in this your brief Life-transit to all the Eternities, the Gods and Silences. It is to you I call; for ye are not dead, ye are already half-alive; there is in you a sleepless dauntless energy, the

---

[1] *trespasses* I.e., fear of trespassers encroaching on their game preserves.

[2] *Hansard's-jargon* Parliamentary debate (the official report of which is known as "Hansard," after the printer Luke Hansard, who compiled it for many years).

[3] *Chelsea Hospitals* Homes such as the Chelsea Royal Hospital, for elderly or disabled veterans.

[4] *Jean Paul* German writer Jean Paul Richter (1763–1825).

prime-matter of all nobleness in man. Honour to you in your kind. It is to you I call; ye know at least this, That the mandate of God to His creature man is Work! The future Epic of the World rests not with those that are near dead, but with those that are alive, and those that are coming into life.

Look around you. Your world-hosts are all in mutiny, in confusion, destitution; on the eve of fiery wreck and madness! They will not march farther for you, on the sixpence a day and supply-and-demand principle; they will not, nor ought they, nor can they. Ye shall reduce them to order, begin reducing them. To order, to just subordination; noble loyalty in return for noble guidance. Their souls are driven nigh mad; let yours be sane and ever saner. Not as a bewildered bewildering mob, but as a firm regimented mass, with real captains over them, will these men march any more. All human interests, combined human endeavours, and social growths in this world, have, at a certain stage of their development, required organising; and Work, the grandest of human interests, does now require it.

God knows, the task will be hard; but no noble task was ever easy. This task will wear away your lives, and the lives of your sons and grandsons; but for what purpose, if not for tasks like this, were lives given to men? Ye shall cease to count your thousand-pound scalps; the noble of you shall cease! Nay, the very scalps, as I say, will not long be left if you count only these. Ye shall cease wholly to be barbarous vulturous Chactaws, and become noble European Nineteenth-Century Men. Ye shall know that Mammon, in never such gigs[1] and

flunky "respectabilities," is not the alone God, that of himself he is but a Devil, and even a Brute-god.

Difficult? Yes, it will be difficult. The short-fibre cotton, that too was difficult. The waste cotton-shrub, long useless, disobedient, as the thistle by the way-side—have ye not conquered it, made it into beautiful bandana webs, white woven shirts for men, bright-tinted air-garments wherein flit goddesses? Ye have shivered mountains asunder, made the hard iron pliant to you as soft putty; the Forest-giants, Marsh-jötuns bear sheaves of golden-grain; Aegir[2] the Sea-demon himself stretches his back for a sleek highway to you, and on Firehorses and Windhorses ye career. Ye are most strong. Thor[3] red-bearded, with his blue sun-eyes, with his cheery heart and strong thunder-hammer, he and you have prevailed. Ye are most strong, ye Sons of the icy North, of the far East—far marching from your rugged Eastern Wildernesses, hitherward from the gray Dawn of Time! Ye are Sons of the *Jötun-land*, the land of Difficulties Conquered. Difficult? You must try this thing. Once try it with the understanding that it will and shall have to be done. Try it as ye try the paltrier thing, making of money! I will bet on you once more, against all Jötuns, Tailor-gods, Double-barrelled Law-wards, and Denizens of Chaos whatsoever!

—1843

---

[1] *gigs* Two-wheeled carriages.

[2] *Aegir* Norse god of the sea.

[3] *Thor* Norse god of thunder and rain.

WORK AND POVERTY

CONTEXTS

The Industrial Revolution brought rapid, pervasive, and frequently disorienting change to Britain. Manufacturing changed the face of the nation, from its physical appearance to the structure of family life. The Industrial Revolution had begun in the eighteenth century with the invention of new technology for spinning and weaving, and with the invention of the steam engine to power these machines, manufacturers established factories (originally called "mills") for centralized production. Mill towns, such as Manchester boomed as workers crowded into cities seeking employment. There they lived in crowded, unsanitary conditions that bred disease—resulting in frequent epidemics of cholera or typhoid. The second wave of the Industrial Revolution came with the spread of the railway in the 1840s, which allowed the iron and coal industries to flourish. Before legislation began to be passed in the 1840s, workers, including small children, worked long hours in dangerous, unhealthy conditions, without job security, insurance, or benefits. When occasional economic depressions caused factories and mines to close or cut down hours of operation, these workers often starved.

When workers moved from the countryside to the growing cities, they adapted many of their rural traditions to their new surroundings, including those of the bawdy ballad, which laborers often sang while they worked. "The Steam Loom Weaver" is an example from the 1830s. The daily reality for most mill workers, however, was far from amusing, despite the contrary implications of this light-hearted ballad. The next selection is from the testimony of Elizabeth Bentley, one of the few women to speak before the 1832 Sadler Committee on the Labour of Children in Factories. Social reformer Michael Sadler had argued in Parliament for the passing of a Ten Hours Bill (limiting factory work to ten hours a day) and had detailed the suffering of child laborers in order to move his fellow members of Parliament to action. When the government asked for a committee of enquiry into the conditions of child laborers, Sadler chaired it, and the resulting testimony was published in Samuel Kydd's 1857 *History of the Factory Movement*. Bentley was one of thirty-eight workers (only three of whom were female) to be interviewed.

Andrew Ure's *The Philosophy of Manufacturers* was one of the best-known works arguing in favor of the factory system. Ure viewed the factory system as a self-regulating organism that should be beyond government regulation, and into which workers should be introduced at a very young age, when they could be easily disciplined. While Ure speaks of the national wealth and prosperity that the factory system created, William Dodd, a child laborer, gives evidence in the excerpt following of the human costs of such "prosperity." Dodd's narrative of his life, which he published to expose the falsities of "eye-witness" accounts such as Ure's, details the lifetime of suffering and physical deformity that resulted from his early introduction to factory life.

Around the 1840s, Victorians began to take a greater interest in issues of public health, particularly the living conditions of the poor. The very worst of these conditions were being documented in newspapers, books, magazines, and journals by those who sought to arouse public concern and effect change. For many modern readers, it is strange to see the correspondent in Joseph Adshead's *Distress in Manchester* (excerpted here) insisting that the conditions of the poor did not result from any moral failings of their own. At the time, however, such ideas were not readily accepted. Poverty and disease in slums was often assumed to result from moral failings among the poor, and it was somewhat radical to suggest that change could best be effected if reformers focused on improving the environmental, rather than the moral, conditions of the slums. Adshead's text, which combines personal testimony given by those working for the relief of the poor with economic facts about the status of the poor—their numbers, earnings, expenditures, living conditions, etc.—showed that most poor people were not poor out of any fault of their own, but were hapless victims of the Industrial Revolution. The reality for many working-class people was that they would work until they could work no more, at which point they would likely perish—a fate the woman in Thomas Hood's poem "Song of the Shirt" (reprinted below) seems to anticipate eagerly—or live the remainder of their days in a workhouse.

Friedrich Engels, author of *The Condition of the Working Class in England*, excerpted below, sought to expose not only the degrading conditions of the poor, but also the deliberate ways in which the middle classes shielded themselves from the realities of working-class people's suffering. Having come from Germany to study the cotton trade, Engels was struck by the conditions in England's urban centers. In this excerpt, he examines the living conditions of the working-class areas of Manchester (he also examines those of England's other "Great Towns," such as London) and the ways in which these areas are systematically hidden from the view of wealthier citizens. Engels went on to collaborate with Karl Marx on *The Communist Manifesto* (1848), and together the two men laid the foundation of modern Communism.

The excerpt following, from Elizabeth Gaskell's novel *Mary Barton: A Tale of Manchester Life*, shows the opposing effects of industrialism on the rich and the poor, and the ways in which the factory system resulted in further alienation between classes. Gaskell contrasts the home lives of the rich and poor and details the private suffering of the latter during the economic depression known as the "hungry forties." *Mary Barton* was part of a developing genre known as the "social problem novel," which focused on the rampant poverty, unemployment, and disease that pervaded the Industrial Revolution. In his slightly later novel *Hard Times*, Charles Dickens details the dehumanizing effects of the factory system and factory managers' lack of recognition of the shared humanity of their employees. The fictional "Coketown" (so called because of the soot that blackens the city), in which his novel is set, is based on Dickens's observations of northern industrial towns such as Manchester and Preston.

One of the era's most influential depictions of working class and poor people was author and social reformer Henry Mayhew's *London Labour and the London Poor*, excerpted below. Asked by *The Morning Chronicle* to document, as metropolitan correspondent, the lives of the urban poor, Mayhew produced eighty-two articles that he later expanded into a four-volume collection of testimony of the lives of the lower class. He painted the underworld of Victorian society in unprecedented detail, shedding light on the specificities of economic exchange and the economic order that governed the poor. Perhaps more importantly, his work provided Victorians with a personal glimpse into the lives of the poor that helped to shape Victorian social theories. The serial newspaper publications were so popular that they resulted in the establishment of a Labour and the Poor Fund. Mayhew had an ear for individual dialects, slang, and other oddities of speech, and composed each subject's narrative in language that, as closely as possible, imitated the speaker's own words. His characters were so compelling that Mayhew's narratives influenced the depiction of such characters in fiction, and writers such as Charles Dickens drew upon his representations of the poor to bring life to their own characters.

⌘ ⌘ ⌘

Anonymous, "The Steam Loom Weaver" (c. 1830)

Ohne morning in summer I did ramble,
   In the pleasant month of June,
The birds did sing the lambkins play,
Two lovers walking in their bloom,
5 The lassie was a steam loom weaver,
The lad an engine driver keen,
All their discourse was about weaving.
And the getting up of steam.

She said my loom is out of fettle,[1]
10 Can you right it yes or no,
You say you are an engine driver,
Which makes the steam so rapid flow;
My lambs and jacks[2] are out of order,
My laith[3] in motion has not been,
15 So work away without delay,
And quickly muster up the steam.

I said fair maid you seem determined,
No longer for to idle be,
Your healds[4] and laith I'll put in motion,
20 Then work you can without delay,
She said young man a pair of pickers,[5]
A shuttle too I want you ween,[6]
Without these three I cannot weave,
So useless would be the steam.

25 Dear lass these things I will provide,
But when to labour will you begin
As soon my lad as things are ready
My loom shop you can enter in.
A shuttle true and pickers too,
30 This young man did provide amain.[7]

And soon her loom was put in tune
So well it was supplied with steam.

Her loom worked well the shuttle flew,
His nickers[8] played the tune nick-nack,
35 Her laith did move with rapid motion,
Her temples, healds, long-lambs and jacks,
Her cloth beam rolled the cloth up tight,
The yarn beam emptied soon its seam,
The young man cried your loom works, light
40 And quickly then off shot the steam.

She said young man another web,
Upon the beam let's get don't strike,
But work away while yet it's day,
This steam loom weaving well I like.
45 He said good lass I cannot stay,
But if a fresh warp you will beam
If ready when I come this way,
I'd strive for to get up the steam.

from Elizabeth Bentley, *Testimony before the 1832 Committee on the Labour of Children in Factories* (1857)

"I am twenty-three years of age, and live at Leeds. I began to work at Mr. Busk's flax mill when I was six years old. I was then a little 'doffer.'[9] In that mill we worked from five in the morning till nine at night, when they were 'throng';[10] when they were not so 'throng,' the usual hours of labour were from six in the morning till seven at night. The time allowed for our meals was forty minutes at noon; not any time was allowed for breakfast or 'drinking': these we got as we could. When our work was bad, we had hardly any time to eat them at all: we were obliged to leave them or take them home. When we did not take our uneaten food home, the overlooker took it and gave it to his pigs. I consider 'doffing' to be a laborious employment. When the frames are full, the 'doffers' have to stop them, and

---

[1] *out of fettle* Out of order.

[2] *lambs and jacks* Lambs are foot pedals that operate the jacks, the oscillating levers that throw the yarn into two alternate sets.

[3] *laith* Loom; or (literally) the supporting stand of the loom.

[4] *healds* Small wires through which the warp passes.

[5] *pickers* Small instrument that moves back and forth in the shuttle-box, driving the shuttle through the warp (the threads that extend lengthwise in the loom).

[6] *ween* Consider; expect.

[7] *amain* At once.

---

[8] *nickers* Part of a center bit, which nicks a hole to be cut by a tool.

[9] *doffer* Worker who assists the spinner by removing the full spindles, or bobbins, from the carding machine (which combs the cotton or wool) and replacing them with empty ones.

[10] *throng* Busy.

take the 'flyers'[1] off, and take the full bobbins off, and carry them to the roller, and then put empty ones on, and set the frame going again. I was kept constantly on my feet; there were so many frames, and they run so quick, the labour was excessive, there was not time for anything. When the 'doffers' flagged[2] a little, or were too late, they were strapped. Those who were last in 'doffing' were constantly strapped—girls as well as boys. I have been strapped severely, and have been hurt by the strap excessively. The overlooker I was under was a very severe man. When I and others have been fatigued and worn out, and had not baskets enough to put the bobbins in, we used to put them in the window bottoms, and that broke the panes sometimes; and I broke one one time, and the overlooker strapped me on the arm, and it rose a blister, and I ran home to my mother. I worked at Mr. Busk's factory three or four years.

"When I left Mr. Busk's, I then went to Benyon's factory; I was about ten years of age, and was employed as a weigher in the card-room.[3] At Benyon's factory we worked from half-past five till eight at night; when they were 'throng,' until nine. The spinners at that mill were allowed forty minutes at noon for meals; no more time throughout the day was allowed. Those employed in the card-rooms had, in addition to the forty minutes at noon, a quarter of an hour allowed for their breakfast, and a quarter of an hour for their 'drinking.' The carding-room is more oppressive than the spinning department: those at work cannot see each other for dust. The 'cards' get so soon filled up with waste and dirt, they must be stopped or they would take fire: the stoppages are as much for the benefit of the employer as for the working people. The children at Benyon's factory were beat up to their labour with a strap…. The girls have many times had black marks upon their skins. Had the parents complained of this excessive ill-usage, the probable consequence would have been the loss of the employment of the child. Of this result the parents were afraid.

"I worked in the card-room; it was so dusty that the dust got upon my lungs, and the work was so hard. I was middling strong when I went there, but the work was so bad; I got so bad in health, that when I pulled the baskets down, I pulled my bones out of their places. The basket I pulled was a very large one; that was full of weights, upheaped, and pulling the basket, pulled my shoulder out of its place, and my ribs have grown over it. That hard work is generally done by women: it is not fit for children. There was no spinning for me, and I therefore did that work….

"I am considerably deformed in person in consequence of this labour. I was about thirteen years old when my deformity began to come on, and it has got worse since. It is five years since my mother died, and she was never able to get me a pair of good stays[4] to hold me up; and when my mother died I had to do for myself, and got me a pair. Before I worked at a mill I was as straight a little girl as ever went up and down town. I was straight until I was thirteen. I have been attended by a medical gentleman, Mr. Hare. He said it was owing to hard labour, and working in the factories. …

"I have had the misfortune, from being a straight and healthful girl, to become very much otherwise in person. I do not know of any other girls that have become weak and deformed in like manner. I have known others who have been similarly injured in health. I am deformed in the shoulders; it is very common indeed to have weak ankles and crooked knees, that is brought on by stopping the spindle.

"I have had experience in wet spinning—it is very uncomfortable. I have stood before the frames till I have been wet through to my skin; and in winter-time, when myself and others have gone home, our clothes have been frozen, and we have nearly caught our death from cold. We have stopped at home one or two days, just as we were situated in our health; had we stopped away any length of time we should have found it difficult to keep our situation.

"I am now in the poor-house at Hunslet. Not any of my former employers come to see me. When I was at home, Mr. Walker made me a present of 1s. or 2s.,[5] but since I left my work and have gone to the poor-house, no one has come nigh me. I was very willing to have

---

[1] *flyers*   Part of the spinning machine that twists the thread and winds it upon the bobbin.

[2] *flagged*   Slowed down.

[3] *card-room*   Room that held the carding machines, which combed and cleaned the wool or cotton in preparation for spinning.

[4] *stays*   Bodice stiffened with strips of whale-bone that gives support and shape to the figure; a corset.

[5] *s.*   Shilling.

worked as long as I was able, and to have supported my widowed mother. I am utterly incapable now of any exertion of that sort, and am supported by the parish."[1]

from Andrew Ure, *The Philosophy of Manufactures* (1835)

In its precise acceptation, the factory system is of recent origin, and may claim England for its birthplace. The mills for throwing silk, or making organzine,[2] which were mounted centuries ago in several of the Italian states, and furtively transferred to this country by Sir Thomas Lombe in 1718, contained indeed certain elements of a factory, and probably suggested some hints of those grander and more complex combinations of self-acting machines, which were first embodied half a century later in our cotton manufacture by Richard Arkwright, assisted by gentlemen of Derby, well acquainted with its celebrated silk establishment....

When the first water-frames for spinning cotton were erected at Cromford, in the romantic valley of the Derwent, about sixty years ago, mankind were little aware of the mighty revolution which the new system of labour was destined by Providence to achieve, not only in the structure of British society, but in the fortunes of the world at large. Arkwright alone had the sagacity to discern, and the boldness to predict in glowing language, how vastly productive human industry would become, when no longer proportioned in its results to muscular effort, which is by its nature fitful and capricious, but when made to consist in the task of guiding the work of mechanical fingers and arms, regularly impelled with great velocity by some indefatigable physical power. What his judgment so clearly led him to perceive, his energy of will enabled him to realize with such rapidity and success, as would have done honour to the most influential individuals, but were truly wonderful in that obscure and indigent artisan. The main difficulty did not, to my apprehension, lie so much in the invention of a proper self-acting mechanism for drawing out and twisting cotton into a continuous thread, as in the distribution

of the different members of the apparatus into one cooperative body, in impelling each organ with its appropriate delicacy and speed, and, above all, in training human beings to renounce their desultory[3] habits of work, and to identify themselves with the unvarying regularity of the complex automaton. To devise and administer a successful code of factory discipline, suited to the necessities of factory diligence, was the Herculean enterprise, the noble achievement of Arkwright. Even at the present day, when the system is perfectly organized, and its labour lightened to the utmost, it is found nearly impossible to convert persons past the age of puberty, whether drawn from rural or from handicraft occupations, into useful factory hands. After struggling for a while to conquer their listless or restive habits, they either renounce the employment spontaneously, or are dismissed by the overlookers on account of inattention....

It required, in fact, a man of a Napoleon nerve and ambition to subdue the refractory tempers of work-people accustomed to irregular paroxysms of diligence, and to urge on his multifarious and intricate constructions in the face of prejudice, passion, and envy. Such was Arkwright, who, suffering nothing to stay or turn aside his progress, arrived gloriously at the goal, and has for ever affixed his name to a great era in the annals of mankind, an era which has laid open unbounded prospects of wealth and comfort to the industrious, however much they may have been occasionally clouded by ignorance and folly.

... In my recent tour, continued during several months, through the manufacturing districts, I have seen tens of thousands of old, young, and middle-aged of both sexes, many of them too feeble to get their daily bread by any of the former modes of industry, earning abundant food, raiment, and domestic accommodation, without perspiring at a single pore, screened meanwhile from the summer's sun and the winter's frost, in apartments more airy and salubrious[4] than those of the metropolis, in which our legislative and fashionable aristocracies assemble. In those spacious halls the benignant power of steam summons around him his myriads of willing menials, and assigns to each the regulated task, substituting for painful muscular effort

---

[1]   *supported by the parish* I.e., with public funds.

[2]   *organzine* Silk yarn.

[3]   *desultory* Half-hearted, lacking enthusiasm.

[4]   *salubrious* Favorable to health.

on their part, the energies of his own gigantic arm, and demanding in return only attention and dexterity to correct such little aberrations as casually occur in his workmanship. The gentle docility of this moving force qualifies it for impelling the tiny bobbins of the lace-machine with a precision and speed inimitable by the most dexterous hands, directed by the sharpest eyes. Hence, under its auspices, and in obedience to Ark-wright's polity,[1] magnificent edifices, surpassing far in number, value, usefulness, and ingenuity of construction, the boasted monuments of Asiatic, Egyptian, and Roman despotism, have, within the short period of fifty years, risen up in this kingdom, to show to what extent capital, industry, and science may augment the resources of a state, while they meliorate the condition of its citizens. Such is the factory system, replete with prodigies in mechanics and political economy, which promises, in its future growth, to become the great minister of civilization to the terraqueous[2] globe, enabling this country, as its heart, to diffuse along with its commerce the life-blood of science and religion to myriads of people still lying "in the region and shadow of death."[3] ...

No master would wish to have any wayward children to work within the walls of his factory who do not mind their business without beating, and he therefore usually fines or turns away any spinners who are known to maltreat their assistants. Hence, ill-usage of any kind is a very rare occurrence. I have visited many factories, both in Manchester and in the surrounding districts, during a period of several months, entering the spinning rooms, unexpectedly, and often alone, at different times of the day, and I never saw a single instance of corporal chastisement inflicted on a child, nor indeed did I ever see children in ill-humour. They seemed to be always cheerful and alert, taking pleasure in the light play of their muscles—enjoying the mobility natural to their age. The scene of industry, so far from exciting sad emotions in my mind, was always exhilarating. It was delightful to observe the nimbleness with which they

pieced the broken ends, as the mule-carriage[4] began to recede from the fixed roller beam, and to see them at leisure, after a few seconds' exercise of their tiny fingers, to amuse themselves in any attitude they chose, till the stretch and winding-on were once more completed. The work of these lively elves seemed to resemble a sport, in which habit gave them a pleasing dexterity. Conscious of their skill, they were delighted to show it off to any stranger. As to exhaustion by the day's work, they evinced no trace of it on emerging from the mill in the evening; for they immediately began to skip about any neighbouring playground, and to commence their little amusements with the same alacrity as boys issuing from a school. It is moreover my firm conviction that if children are not ill-used by bad parents or guardians, but receive in food and raiment the full benefit of what they earn, they would thrive better when employed in our modern factories than if left at home in apartments too often ill-aired, damp, and cold.

from William Dodd, *A Narrative of the Experience and Sufferings of William Dodd, Factory Cripple, Written by Himself* (1841)

Dear Reader,— I wish it to be distinctly and clearly understood, that, in laying before you the following sheets, I am not actuated by any motive of ill-feeling to any party with whom I have formerly been connected; on the contrary, I have a personal respect for some of my former masters, and am convinced that, had they been in any other line of life, they would have shone forth as ornaments to the age in which they lived; but having witnessed the efforts of some writers (who can know nothing of the factories by experience) to mislead the minds of the public upon a subject of so much importance, I feel it to be my duty to give to the world a fair and impartial account of the working of the factory system, as I have found it in twenty-five years' experience.

---

[1] *polity* Mode of administration.

[2] *terraqueous* Consisting of land and water.

[3] *in the ... death* From Matthew 4.16.

[4] *broken ends* I.e., of thread. This was the job of the "piecer," who ensured that the process of spinning could continue uninterrupted; *mule-carriage* The movable part of the mule, a kind of spinning machine, invented in 1779, that could spin yarn of varying thicknesses.

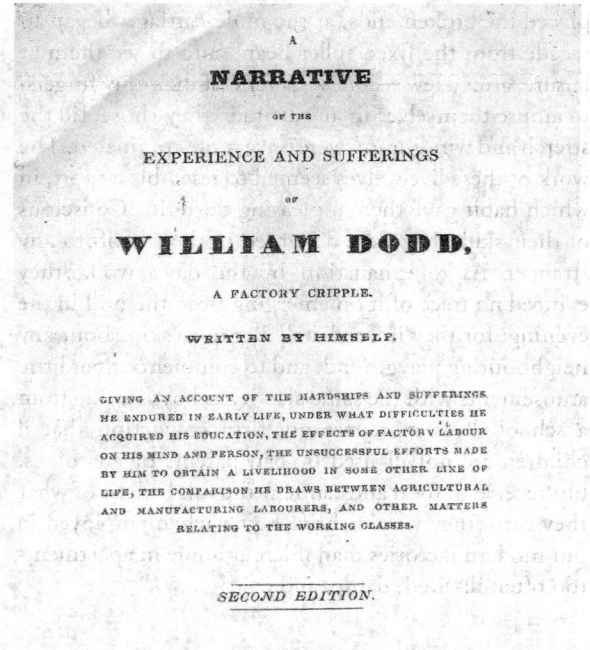

A

NARRATIVE

OF THE

EXPERIENCE AND SUFFERINGS

OF

WILLIAM DODD,

A FACTORY CRIPPLE.

WRITTEN BY HIMSELF.

GIVING AN ACCOUNT OF THE HARDSHIPS AND SUFFERINGS
HE ENDURED IN EARLY LIFE, UNDER WHAT DIFFICULTIES HE
ACQUIRED HIS EDUCATION, THE EFFECTS OF FACTORY LABOUR
ON HIS MIND AND PERSON, THE UNSUCCESSFUL EFFORTS MADE
BY HIM TO OBTAIN A LIVELIHOOD IN SOME OTHER LINE OF
LIFE, THE COMPARISON HE DRAWS BETWEEN AGRICULTURAL
AND MANUFACTURING LABOURERS, AND OTHER MATTERS
RELATING TO THE WORKING CLASSES.

SECOND EDITION.

LONDON:
PUBLISHED BY L. & G. SEELEY, 169, FLEET STREET,
AND HATCHARD & SON, 187, PICCADILLY.
1841.
PRICE ONE SHILLING.

Title page from William Dodd, *A Narrative of the Experience and Sufferings of William Dodd, Factory Cripple, Written by Himself* (1841).

..., Of four children in our family, I was the only boy; and we were all, at different periods, as we could meet with employers, sent to work in the factories. My eldest sister was ten years of age before she went; consequently, she was, in a manner, out of harm's way, her bones having become firmer and stronger than ours, and capable of withstanding the hardships to which she was exposed much better than we could.... I was born on the 18th of June, 1804; and in the latter part of 1809, being then turned of five years of age, I was put to work at card-making,[1] and about a year after I was sent, with my sisters, to the factories. I was then a fine, strong, healthy, hardy boy, straight in every limb, and remarkably stout and active....

From six to fourteen years of age, I went through a series of uninterrupted, unmitigated suffering, such as very rarely falls to the lot of mortals so early in life, except to those situated as I was, and such as I could not have withstood, had I not been strong, and of a good constitution.

My first place in the factories was that of piecer, or the lowest situation: but as the term conveys only a vague idea of the duties to be performed, it will be necessary here to give such explanation as may enable those unacquainted with the business to form a just conception of what those duties are, and to judge of the inadequacy of the remuneration or reward for their performance, and the cruelty of the punishments inflicted for the neglect of those duties....

The position in which the piecer stands to his work is with his right foot forward, and his right side facing the frame: the motion he makes in going along in front of the frame, for the purpose of piecing, is neither forwards nor backwards, but in a sidling direction, constantly keeping his right side towards the frame. In this position he continues during the day, with his hands, feet, and eyes constantly in motion. It will be easily seen, that the chief weight of his body rests upon his right knee, which is almost always the first joint to give way. The number of cripples with the right knee in, greatly exceed those with the left knee in; a great many have both knees in such as my own from this cause.

Another evil resulting from the position in which the piecer stands, is what is termed "splay-foot," which may be explained thus: in a well-formed foot, there is a finely formed arch of bones immediately under the instep and ankle joint. The continual pressure of the body on this arch, before it is sufficiently strong to bear such pressure (as in the case of boys and girls in the factories) causes it to give way: the bones fall gradually down, the foot then becomes broad and flat, and the owner drags it after him with the broad side first. A great many factory cripples are in this state; this is very often attended with weak ankle and knee joints. I have a brother-in-law exactly thus, who has tried everything likely to do him good, but without success.

---

[1] *card-making*   Cards combed and cleansed fibers in preparation for spinning.

A wood engraving of a child mine-worker included in the *Report of the Commission of the Employment of Children and Young Persons in the Mines* (1842).

The spinner and the piecer are intimately connected together:[1] the spinner works by the piece, being paid by the stone[2] for the yarn spun; the piecer is hired by the week, and paid according to his abilities. The piecers are the servants of the spinners, and both are under an overlooker; and liable to be dismissed at a week's notice. Being thus circumstanced, it is clearly the advantage of the spinner to have good able piecers, who ought, in return, to be well paid....

In order to induce the piecer to do his work quick and well, the spinner has recourse to many expedients, such as offering rewards of a penny or two-pence for a good week's work inducing them to sing, which, like the music in the army, has a very powerful effect, and keeps them awake and active longer than any other thing; and, as a last resource, when nothing else will do, he takes the strap, or the billy-roller,[3] which are laid on most unmercifully, accompanied by a round volley of oaths; and I pity the poor wretch who has to submit to the infliction of either.

On one occasion, I remember being thrashed with the billy-roller till my back, arms, and legs were covered with ridges as thick as my finger. This was more than I could bear, and, seeing a favourable opportunity, I slipped out and stole off home along some by-ways, so as not to be seen. Mother stripped me, and was shocked at my appearance. The spinner, not meeting with any other to suit him, had the assurance to come and beg that mother would let me go again, and promised not to strike me with the billy-roller any more. He kept his promise, but instead of using the roller, he used his fist.

... A piecer, it will be seen, is an important person in the factories, inasmuch as it is impossible to do without them. Formerly, boys and girls were sent to work in the factories as piecers at the early age of five or six years—as in my own case—but now, owing to the introduction of some wise laws for the regulation of factories,[4] they cannot employ any as piecers before they have attained the age of 9 years; at which age their bones are comparatively strong, generally speaking, and more able to endure the hardships to which they will be exposed.

---

[1] *The spinner ... together*   The spinner, who ran the "billy" (or "slubbing," the machine that spins yarn) was dependent on the piecer for the preparation of the wool.

[2] *stone*   Unit of measurement equal to 14 pounds.

[3] *billy-roller*   Uppermost of a series of wooden rollers through which the wool is moved to the spindles. It was very long and easily removed from the billy; as a result, it was a notorious instrument of punishment to factory children.

[4] *some wise ... factories*   The 1833 Factory Act, which prevented children under nine from working in any factories except silk mills. It also decreed that children under 11 (and, eventually, under 13) could not work more than 9 hours a day or 48 hours a week, and that all working children had to be provided with eduction at the expense of the factory owners.

They now enjoy many privileges that we had not, such as attending schools, limited hours of labour, &c.; but still it is far from being a desirable place for a child. Formerly, it was nothing but work till we could work no longer. I have frequently worked at the frame till I could scarcely get home, and in this state have been stopped by people in the streets who noticed me shuffling along, and advised me to work no more in the factories: but I was not my own master. Thus year after year passed away, my afflictions and deformities increasing. I could not associate with anybody; on the contrary, I sought every opportunity to rest myself, and to shrink into any corner to screen myself from the prying eye of the curious and scornful! During the day, I frequently counted the clock, and calculated how many hours I had still to remain at work; my evenings were spent in preparing for the following day—in rubbing my knees, ankles, elbows, and wrists with oil, &c., and wrapping them in warm flannel! (for everything was tried to benefit me, except the right one—that of taking me from the work) after which, with a look at, rather than eating my supper (the bad smells of the factory having generally taken my appetite away) I went to bed, to cry myself to sleep, and pray that the Lord would take me to Himself before morning.

… A great many are made cripples by over-exertion. Among those who have been brought up from infancy with me in the factories, and whom death has spared, few have escaped without some injury. My brother-in-law and myself have been crippled by this cause, but in different ways; my sister partly by over-exertion and partly by machinery. On going home to breakfast one morning, I was much surprised at seeing several of the neighbours and two doctors in our house. On inquiring the cause, I found that my second sister had nearly lost her hand in the machinery. She had been working all night, and, fatigued and sleepy, had not been so watchful as she otherwise would have been; and consequently, her right hand became entangled in the machine which she was attending. Four iron teeth of a wheel, three-quarters of an inch broad, and one-quarter of an inch thick, had been forced through her hand, from the back part, among the leaders, &c.; and the fifth iron tooth fell upon the thumb, and crushed it to atoms. It was thought, for some time, that she would lose her hand. But it was saved; and, as you may be sure, it is stiff and contracted, and is but a very feeble apology

for a hand. This accident might have been prevented, if the wheels above referred to had been boxed off,[1] which they might have been for a couple of shillings; and the very next week after this accident, a man had two fingers taken off his hand, by the very same wheels—and still they are not boxed off!

from Joseph Adshead, *Distress in Manchester. Evidence (Tabular and Otherwise) of the State of the Labouring Classes in 1840–42* (1842)

CHAPTER 3, NARRATIVES OF SUFFERING

The following painfully interesting report is furnished by a gentleman whose attention was directed to the social and moral condition of the labouring classes, with a view to its improvement. The inquiry was made in January last, and it will be seen that its details are, if possible, more harrowing than any yet given:

January, 1842.

Dear Sir,—An engagement I had made to oblige a friend rendered it necessary that I should visit the inhabitants of several streets in Ancoats and in the neighbourhood of Oldham Road. As this district is not selected as the most destitute, I believe a few cases I shall state will give a very faithful illustration of the condition of tens of thousands of the manufacturing poor.

Upon the first day of our visitation I called at a house occupied by a poor man, a widower with one child, a boy between seven and eight; they were in a state of extreme poverty; the man is about thirty-five years of age, and professed himself able and most anxious to work, but had not been able to obtain any employment for many months; both were living upon what the child could obtain by begging. Upon quitting this house the man called our attention to an adjoining cellar, occupied by a woman who had been deserted by

---

[1]   *the wheels … boxed off*   The Factory Act of 1844 decreed that fly-wheels connected to mechanical parts, such as shafts, had to be boxed off or fenced until the Factory Act of 1844. However, such a project would cost a few shillings per wheel, which would add up to a considerable expense, and would make it difficult for workers to clean the machinery. As a result, many factory owners ignored the law when it came into effect.

her husband. This cellar was both very dark and very damp, the roof not more than seven feet high, and the area of the floor not more than twelve square yards; its occupants were this woman and her child, a boy six years old, a widow, a lodger with three children, and a second widow with two children, sister of the woman who tenanted the cellar; these nine individuals are all crowded in a place so dark and contracted as to be unfit for the residence of any human being. It was in this abode of wretchedness that we witnessed a remarkable illustration of the sympathy and compassion of the poor for those who are still less favourably circumstanced. On the day previous to our visit one of these poor women had observed a poor houseless wanderer with two children, ready to sink with hunger and fatigue; this poor creature's husband had left her three months before to seek employment, which she was sure he had not been able to procure, or, as she said, he would soon have found her and let her know. Her poor hostess had no better accommodation to offer than a dark unpaved closet adjoining their cellar, and here, without bed or bedding beyond a handful of dirty shavings which she used as a pillow, the mother and her famishing children were thankful to take shelter: during the night the younger of the children, an infant eleven months old, died, doubtless from long exposure to cold and the want of that support which the breast of the poor, starved, and perishing mother had failed to supply. When we entered the cellar we saw this victim of want laid out upon a board suspended from the roof, and the other children (some of whom were so poorly provided with clothing as to be unfit to quit the cellar without indecent exposure) standing around; the poor mother had left her remaining child and gone out to beg assistance to inter her infant.

In the next house we entered we found two men, one twenty-seven, the other twenty-five, both weavers, and out of work; they both appeared in delicate health, one, however, much worse than the other; neither of them had been able to earn a shilling for several weeks. To our inquiry how they lived, they replied, "We do indeed *exist*, we cannot say we live." One of them produced a dish with potato peelings, which one of their wives had been successful in begging; this they assured us was the only food they had or expected to taste that day. These men were members of a temperance society,

Thomas Annan, *Close No. 193, High Street, Glasgow* (1868). Thomas Annan was hired by the Glasgow City Improvement Trust to photograph the city's slums before they were demolished. Many of his pictures show the open sewers and narrow passageways that were features of slum life. (See also Annan's photographs on p. 395.)

were both remarkably intelligent, and we inferred from the kind and patient manner in which they spoke of their poverty and its causes, which they appear perfectly to comprehend, that their minds were considerably under the influence of moral and religious principles. These men were not victims of intemperance, nor improvidence, nor idleness, nor disease, nor anything else which they could have foreseen or provided against; but, reduced and broken-hearted by the impossibility of obtaining work, they and their families are sinking in the midst of misery which they can neither remove nor flee from.

This is a spectacle more calculated than almost any other we can conceive to distress a rightly constituted mind. Men, with physical strength, mental cultivation, and moral principle in active exercise, after having spent their time, and strength, and money, it may be, in learning a trade, starving in the largest manufacturing town in the world for the want of employment! And why? Let the supporters of corn laws[1] answer. ...

Many were the families we visited who assured us they had not tasted food that day. Misery and want, hunger and nakedness, are not confined to particular localities: they are widely spread, and are spreading more widely. The number of the destitute is daily increasing. The universal testimony is, that there never was any distress equal to that which exists at present—that all other seasons of distress were trifling in comparison. The intemperate and the improvident, indeed, are the first to suffer in all seasons of distress; but it is long since distress has reached the sober, the industrious, the provident, and the respected among the labouring class.

Thomas Hood, "Song of the Shirt" (1843)

With fingers weary and worn,
   With eyelids heavy and red,
A woman sat, in unwomanly rags,
   Plying her needle and thread—
5 Stitch—stitch—stitch!
   In poverty, hunger, and dirt,
And still with a voice of dolorous pitch
   She sang the "Song of the Shirt."

   "Work—work—work
10 Till the brain begins to swim;
   Work—work—work
   Till the eyes are heavy and dim!
   Seam, and gusset,[2] and band,
   Band, and gusset, and seam;
15 Till over the buttons I fall asleep,
   And sew them on in a dream!

   "O! men, with sisters dear!
   O! men, with mothers and wives!
   It is not linen you're wearing out,
20 But human creatures' lives!

Stitch—stitch—stitch,
   In poverty, hunger, and dirt,
Sewing at once, with a double thread,
   A shroud[3] as well as a shirt.

25 "But why do I talk of Death?
   That phantom of grisly bone;
I hardly fear his terrible shape,
   It seems so like my own—
   It seems so like my own,
30 Because of the fasts I keep:
Oh! God! that bread should be so dear,
   And flesh and blood so cheap!

   "Work—work—work!
   My labour never flags;
35 And what are its wages? A bed of straw,
   A crust of bread and rags,
That shatter'd roof, and this naked floor
   A table—a broken chair—
   A wall so blank, my shadow I thank
40 For sometimes falling there!

   "Work—work—work!
   From weary chime to chime,
   Work—work—work
45 As prisoners work for crime!
   Band, and gusset, and seam,
   Seam, and gusset, and band,
Till the heart is sick, and the brain benumb'd,
   As well as the weary hand.

50 "Work—work—work,
   In the dull December light,
   And work—work—work,
When the weather is warm and bright—
   While underneath the eaves
55 The brooding swallows cling,
As if to show me their sunny backs
   And twit me with the spring.

   "Oh! but to breathe the breath
   Of the cowslip and primrose[4] sweet—

---

[1] *corn laws* Laws that kept the prices of grain artificially high to prevent an agricultural depression after the Napoleonic Wars (1803–15). Sir Robert Peel, the Prime Minister, repealed the laws in 1846.

[2] *gusset* Triangular piece of material inserted into a piece of clothing to strengthen or enlarge some part.

[3] *shroud* Sheet in which a corpse is wrapped for burial.

[4] *cowslip ... primrose* Wildflowers.

60 With the sky above my head,
And the grass beneath my feet,
For only one short hour
To feel as I used to feel,
Before I knew the woes of want
65 And the walk that costs a meal:

"Oh, but for one short hour!
A respite, however brief!
No blessed leisure for Love or Hope,
But only time for grief!
70 A little weeping would ease my heart,
But in their briny head
My tears must stop, for every drop
Hinders needle and thread!"

With fingers weary and worn,
75 With eyelids heavy and red,
A woman sat, in unwomanly rags,
Plying her needle and thread—
Stitch—stitch—stitch!
In poverty, hunger, and dirt,
80 And still with a voice of dolorous pitch,
Would that its tone could reach the rich!
She sang this "Song of the Shirt!"

from Friedrich Engels, *The Condition of the Working
Class in England in 1844* (1845; trans. Florence
Wischnewetzky, 1887)

CHAPTER 3, THE GREAT TOWNS

Manchester lies at the foot of the southern slope of
a range of hills, which stretch hither from Oldham, their last peak, Kersallmoor, being at once the
racecourse and the Mons Sacer[1] of Manchester. Manchester proper lies on the left bank of the Irwell, between that stream and the two smaller ones, the Irk and
the Medlock, which here empty into the Irwell. On the
right bank of the Irwell, bounded by a sharp curve of
the river, lies Salford, and farther westward Pendleton;
northward from the Irwell lie Upper and Lower Brough-

John Thomson's photograph of "The crawler"
(1877). This photograph is taken from Thomson's
famous project, *Street Life in London* (1877–78), one
of the era's most influential pieces of social
documentary. Thomson collaborated with Adolph
Smith to create text to accompany the photographs.
This picture, one of the best known, shows a
destitute woman who told Thomson that she spent
her nights on the steps of a workhouse and her days
looking after a friend's baby, in exchange for a cup
of tea and some bread.

ton; northward of the Irk, Cheetham Hill; south of the
Medlock lies Hulme; farther east Chorlton on Medlock;
still farther, pretty well to the east of Manchester,
Ardwick. The whole assemblage of buildings is commonly called Manchester, and contains about four

---

[1] *Mons Sacer* Latin: sacred mountain.

hundred thousand inhabitants, rather more than less. The town itself is peculiarly built, so that a person may live in it for years, and go in and out daily without coming into contact with a working people's quarter or even with workers, that is, so long as he confines himself to his business or to pleasure walks. This arises chiefly from the fact that by unconscious tacit agreement, as well as with outspoken conscious determination, the working people's quarters are sharply separated from the sections of the city reserved for the middle class; or, if this does not succeed, they are concealed with the cloak of charity. Manchester contains, at its heart, a rather extended commercial district, perhaps half a mile long and about as broad, and consisting almost wholly of offices and warehouses. Nearly the whole district is abandoned by dwellers, and is lonely and deserted at night; only watchmen and policemen traverse its narrow lanes with their dark lanterns. This district is cut through by certain main thoroughfares upon which the vast traffic concentrates, and in which the ground level is lined with brilliant shops. In these streets the upper floors are occupied, here and there, and there is a good deal of life upon them until late at night. With the exception of this commercial district, all Manchester proper, all Salford and Hulme, a great part of Pendleton and Chorlton, two-thirds of Ardwick, and single stretches of Cheetham Hill and Broughton are all unmixed working people's quarters, stretching like a girdle, averaging a mile and a half in breadth, around the commercial district. Outside, beyond this girdle, lives the upper and middle bourgeoisie, the middle bourgeoisie in regularly laid out streets in the vicinity of the working quarters, especially in Chorlton and the lower lying portions of Cheetham Hill; the upper bourgeoisie in remoter villas with gardens in Chorlton and Ardwick, or on the breezy heights of Cheetham Hill, Broughton, and Pendleton, in free, wholesome country air, in fine, comfortable homes, passed once every half or quarter hour by omnibuses going into the city. And the finest part of the arrangements is this, that the members of this money aristocracy can take the shortest road through the middle of all the labouring districts to their places of business, without ever seeing that they are in the midst of the grimy misery that lurks to the right and the left. For the thoroughfares leading from the Exchange in all directions out of the city are lined, on both sides, with an almost unbroken series of shops, and are so kept in the hands of the middle and lower bourgeoisie, which, out of self-interest, cares for a decent and cleanly external appearance and can *care* for it. True, these shops bear some relation to the districts which lie behind them, and are more elegant in the commercial and residential quarters than when they hide grimy working men's dwellings; but they suffice to conceal from the eyes of the wealthy men and women of strong stomachs and weak nerves the misery and grime which form the complement to their wealth. So, for instance, Deansgate, which leads from the Old Church directly southward, is lined first with mills and warehouses, then with second-rate shops and alehouses; farther south, when it leaves the commercial district, with less inviting shops, which grow dirtier and more interrupted by beer houses and gin palaces the farther one goes, until at the southern end the appearance of the shops leaves no doubt that workers and workers only are their customers. So Market Street running south-east from the Exchange; at first brilliant shops of the best sort, with counting-houses or warehouses above; in the continuation, Piccadilly, immense hotels and warehouses; in the farther continuation, London Road, in the neighbourhood of the Medlock, factories, beerhouses, shops for the humbler bourgeoisie and the working population; and from this point onward, large gardens and villas of the wealthier merchants and manufacturers. In this way anyone who knows Manchester can infer the adjoining districts, from the appearance of the thoroughfare, but one is seldom in a position to catch from the street a glimpse of the real labouring districts. I know very well that this hypocritical plan is more or less common to all great cities; I know, too, that the retail dealers are forced by the nature of their business to take possession of the great highways; I know that there are more good buildings than bad ones upon such streets everywhere, and that the value of land is greater near them than in remoter districts; but at the same time I have never seen so systematic a shutting out of the working class from the thoroughfares, so tender a concealment of everything which might affront the eye and the nerves of the bourgeoisie, as in Manchester. And yet, in other respects, Manchester is less built according to a plan, after official regulations, is more an outgrowth of accident, than any other city; and when I consider in this connection the eager assurances of the middle class that the working class is doing famously, I cannot help feeling that the liberal manufacturers, the "Big Wigs" of Manchester, are not so innocent after all, in the matter of this sensitive method of construction.

I may mention just here that the mills almost all adjoin the rivers or the different canals that ramify throughout the city, before I proceed at once to describe the labouring quarters. First of all, there is the Old Town of Manchester, which lies between the northern boundary of the commercial district and the Irk. Here the streets, even the better ones, are narrow and winding, like Todd Street, Long Millgate, Withy Grove, and Shude Hill, the houses dirty, old, and tumble-down, and the construction of the side streets utterly horrible. Going from the Old Church to Long Millgate, the stroller has at once a row of old-fashioned houses on the right, of which not one has kept its original level; these are remnants of the old pre-manufacturing Manchester, whose former inhabitants have removed with their descendants into better-built districts, and have left the houses, which were not good enough for them, to a working-class population strongly mixed with Irish blood. Here one is in an almost undisguised working men's quarter, for even the shops and beerhouses hardly take the trouble to exhibit a trifing degree of cleanliness. But all this is nothing in comparison with the courts and lanes which lie behind, to which access can be gained only through covered passages, in which no two human beings can pass at the same time. Of the irregular cramming together of dwellings in ways which defy all rational plan, of the tangle in which they are crowded literally one upon the other, it is impossible to convey an idea. And it is not the buildings surviving from the old times of Manchester which are to blame for this; the confusion has only recently reached its height when every scrap of space left by the old way of building has been filled up and patched over until not a foot of land is left to be further occupied....

The south bank of the Irk is here very steep and between fifteen and thirty feet high. On this abrupt slope there are planted three rows of houses, of which the lowest rise directly out of the river, while the front walls of the highest stand on the crest of the rise in Long Millgate. Among them are mills on the river; in short, the method of construction is as crowded and disorderly here as in the lower part of Long Millgate. Right and left a multitude of covered passages lead from the main street into numerous courts, and he who turns in thither gets into filth and disgusting grime, the equal of which is not to be found—especially in the courts which lead down to the Irk, and which contain unqualifiedly the most horrible dwellings which I have yet beheld. In one of these courts there stands directly at the entrance, at the end of the covered passage, a privy without a door, so dirty that the inhabitants can pass into and out of the court only by passing through foul pools of stagnant urine and excrement. This is the first court on the Irk above Ducie Bridge—in case anyone should care to look into it. Below it on the river there are several tanneries which fill the whole neighbourhood with the stench of animal putrefaction. Below Ducie Bridge the only entrance to most of the houses is by means of narrow, dirty stairs and over heaps of refuse and filth. The first court below Ducie Bridge, known as Allen's Court, was in such a state at the time of the cholera[1] that the sanitary police ordered it evacuated, swept, and disinfected with chloride of lime.... Since then, it seems to have been partially torn down and rebuilt; at least, looking down from Ducie Bridge, the passer-by sees several ruined walls and heaps of debris with some newer houses. The view from this bridge, mercifully concealed from mortals of small stature by a parapet as high as a man, is characteristic for the whole district. At the bottom flows, or rather stagnates, the Irk, a narrow, coal-black, foul-smelling stream, full of debris and

---

[1] *the time of cholera* I.e., 1832.

refuse, which it deposits on the lower right bank. In dry weather, a lone string of the most disgusting blackish-green slime pools are left standing on this bank, from the depths of which bubbles of miasmatic[1] gas constantly arise and give forth a stench unendurable even on the bridge forty or fifty feet above the surface of the stream. But besides this, the stream itself is checked every few paces by high weirs, behind which slime and refuse accumulate and rot in thick masses. Above the bridge are tanneries, bone mills, and gasworks, from which all drains and refuse find their way into the Irk, which receives further the contents of all the neighbouring sewers and privies. It may be easily imagined, therefore, what sort of residue the stream deposits. Below the bridge you look upon the piles of debris, the refuse, filth, and offal from the courts on the steep left bank; here each house is packed close behind its neighbour and a bit of each is visible, all black, smoky, crumbling, ancient, with broken panes and window-frames. The background is furnished by old barrack-like factory buildings. On the lower right bank stands a long row of houses and mills, the second row being a ruin without a roof, piled with debris; the third stands so low that the lowest floor is uninhabitable, and therefore without windows or doors. Here the background embraces the pauper burial-ground, the station of the Liverpool and Leeds railway, and, in the rear of this, the workhouse, the "Poor-Law Bastille"[2] of Manchester, which, like a citadel, looks threateningly down from behind its high walls and parapets on the hilltop, upon the working people's quarter below. ...

Such is the Old Town of Manchester, and, on re-reading my description, I am forced to admit that instead of being exaggerated, it is far from black enough to convey a true impression of the filth, ruin, and uninhabitableness, the defiance of all considerations of cleanliness, ventilation, and health which characterize the construction of this single district, containing at least twenty to thirty thousand inhabitants. And such a district exists in the heart of the second city of England,

the first manufacturing city of the world. If anyone wishes to see in how little space a human being can move, how little air—and *such* air—he can breathe, how little of civilization he may share and yet live, it is only necessary to travel hither. True, this is the *Old* Town, and the people of Manchester emphasize the fact whenever anyone mentions to them the frightful condition of this Hell upon Earth; but what does that prove? Everything which here arouses horror and indignation is of recent origin, belongs to the *industrial epoch*. The couple of hundred houses which belong to Old Manchester have been long since abandoned by their original inhabitants; the industrial epoch alone has crammed into them the swarms of workers whom they now shelter; the industrial epoch alone has built up every spot between these old houses to make a covering for the masses whom it has conjured hither from the agricultural districts and from Ireland; the industrial epoch alone enables the owners of these cattle sheds to rent them for high prices to human beings, to plunder the poverty of the workers, to undermine the health of thousands, in order that they only, the owners, may grow rich. In the industrial epoch alone has it become possible that the worker scarcely freed from feudal servitude can be used as mere material, a mere chattel; that he must let himself be crowded into a dwelling too bad for every other, which he for his hard-earned wages buys the right to let go utterly to ruin. This is what manufacture has achieved, and, without these workers and their poverty, this slavery would have been impossible. True, the original construction of this quarter was bad, little good could have been made out of it; but, have the land-owners, has the municipality done anything to improve it when rebuilding? On the contrary, wherever a nook or corner was free, a house has been run up; where a superfluous passage remained, it has been built on; the value of land rose with the blossoming out of manufacture, and the more it rose, the more madly was the work of building carried on, without reference to the health or comfort of the inhabitants, with sole reference to the highest possible profit, on the principle that *no hole is so bad but that some poor creature must take it who can pay for nothing better*. However, it is the Old Town, and with this reflection the bourgeoisie is comforted.

---

[1] *miasmatic* Consisting of noxious vapor.

[2] *Poor-Law Bastille* Because of the terrible conditions in the workhouses (established by the Poor Laws in the 1830s), including poor food, monotonous make-work, and the separation of families, workhouses were often compared to prisons such as the famous Bastille in Paris.

A cross-section of working-class low-lodgings. The crowded rooms and open sewer running beneath the building provide examples of the sort of deplorable living conditions described by Engels in his examination of Manchester.

from Elizabeth Gaskell, *Mary Barton* (1848), Chapter 6

John Barton was not far wrong in his idea that the Messrs. Carson would not be over-much grieved for the consequences of the fire in their mill. They were well insured; the machinery lacked the improvements of late years, and worked but poorly in comparison with that which might now be procured. Above all, trade was very slack; cottons could find no market, and goods lay packed and piled in many a warehouse. The mills were merely worked to keep the machinery, human and metal, in some kind of order and readiness for better times. So this was an excellent opportunity, Messrs. Carson thought, for refitting their factory with first-rate improvements, for which the insurance-money would amply pay. They were in no hurry about the business, however. The weekly drain of wages given for labour, useless in the present state of the market, was stopped. The partners had more leisure than they had known for years, and promised wives and daughters all manner of pleasant excursions, as soon as the weather should become more genial. It was a pleasant thing to be able to lounge over breakfast with a review or newspaper in hand; to have time for becoming acquainted with agreeable and accomplished daughters, on whose education no money had been spared, but whose fathers, shut up during a long day with calicoes[1] and accounts, had so seldom had leisure to enjoy their daughters' talents. There were happy family evenings, now that the men of business had time for domestic enjoyments. There is another side to the picture. There were homes over which Carsons' fire threw a deep, terrible gloom; the homes of those who would fain work, and no man gave unto them—the homes of those to whom leisure was a curse. There, the family music was angry wails, when week after week passed by, and there was no work to be had, and consequently no wages to pay for the bread the children cried aloud for in their young impatience of suffering. There was no breakfast to lounge over; their lounge was taken in bed, to try and keep warmth in them that bitter March weather, and, by being quiet, to deaden the gnawing wolf within. Many a penny that would have gone little way enough in oatmeal or potatoes bought opium to still the hungry little ones,[2] and make them forget their uneasiness in heavy troubled sleep. It was mother's mercy. The evil and the good of our nature came out strongly then. There were desperate fathers; there were bitter-tongued mothers (Oh God! what wonder!); there were reckless children; the very closest bonds of nature were snapped in that time of trial and distress. There was Faith such as the rich can never imagine on earth; there was "Love strong as death"; and, self-denial, among rude, coarse men, akin to that of Sir Philip Sidney's most glorious deed.[3] The vices of the poor sometimes astound us *here*; but when the secrets of all hearts shall be made known, their virtues will astound us in far greater degree. Of this I am certain.

As the cold, bleak spring came on (spring, in name alone), and consequently as trade continued dead, other mills shortened hours, turned off hands,[4] and finally stopped work altogether.

Barton worked short hours; Wilson, of course, being a hand in Carsons' factory, had no work at all. But his son, working at an engineer's, and a steady man, obtained wages enough to maintain all the family in a careful way. Still it preyed on Wilson's mind to be so long indebted to his son. He was out of spirits and depressed. Barton was morose, and soured towards mankind as a body, and the rich in particular. One evening, when the clear light at six o'clock contrasted strangely with the Christmas cold, and when the bitter wind piped down every entry, and through every cranny, Barton sat brooding over his stinted fire, and listening for Mary's step, in unacknowledged trust that her presence would cheer him. The door was opened, and Wilson came breathless in.

"You've not got a bit o' money by you, Barton?" asked he.

"Not I; who has now, I'd like to know. Whatten you want it for?"

"I donnot want it for mysel', tho' we've none to spare. But don[5] you know Ben Davenport as worked at Carsons'? He's down wi' the fever, and ne'er a stick o' fire nor a cowd[6] potato in the house."

"I han got no money, I tell ye," said Barton. Wilson looked disappointed. Barton tried not to be interested, but he could not help it in spite of his gruffness. He rose, and went to the cupboard (his wife's pride long ago). There lay the remains of his dinner, hastily put by ready for supper. Bread, and a slice of cold fat boiled bacon. He wrapped them in his handkerchief, put them in the crown of his hat and said—"Come, let's be going."

from Henry Mayhew, *London Labour and the London Poor*, "Boy Crossing-Sweepers and Tumblers" (written 1859–60, published 1861–65)

A remarkably intelligent lad, who, on being spoken to, at once consented to give all the information in his power, told me the following story of his life.

It will be seen from this boy's account, and the one or two following, that a kind of partnership exists among some of these young sweepers. They have

---

[1]   *calicoes* Cotton cloths.

[2]   *opium … hungry ones* The apparently common practice among working-class families of giving sick or hungry infants opium or laudanum to help them sleep was frequently discussed at the time.

[3]   *Sir Philip … deed* Poet and courtier Sir Philip Sidney (1554–86), who served in many diplomatic missions on the Continent, is said to have refused a glass of water offered to him when he lay dying on the battlefield at Zutphen, in the Netherlands. He instead gave the glass to a less seriously wounded soldier, saying "Thy necessity is greater than mine."

[4]   *turned off hands* I.e., laid off workers.

[5]   *don* Do.

[6]   *cowd* I.e., cold.

associated themselves together, appropriated several crossings to their use, and appointed a captain over them. They have their forms of trial, and "jury-house" for the settlement of disputes; laws have been framed, which govern their commercial proceedings, and a kind of language adopted by the society for its better protection from the arch-enemy, the policeman.

I found the lad who first gave me an insight into the proceedings of the associated crossing-sweepers crouched on the stone steps of a door in Adelaide Street, Strand; and when I spoke to him he was preparing to settle down in a corner and go to sleep—his legs and body being curled round almost as closely as those of a cat on a hearth. The moment he heard my voice he was upon his feet, asking me to "give a halfpenny to poor little Jack."

He was a good-looking lad, with a pair of large mild eyes, which he took good care to turn up with an expression of supplication as he moaned for a halfpenny.

A cap, or more properly a stuff bag, covered a crop of hair which had matted itself into the form of so many paint-brushes, while his face, from its roundness of feature and the complexion of dirt, had an almost Indian look about it; the colour of his hands, too, was such that you could imagine he had been shelling walnuts.

He ran before me, treading cautiously with his naked feet, until I reached a convenient spot to take down his statement, which was as follows:

"I've got no mother or father; mother has been dead for two years, and father's been gone for more than that—more nigh five years—he died at Ipswich, in Suffolk. He was a perfumer by trade, and used to make hair-dye, and scent, and pomatum,[1] and all kinds of scents. He didn't keep a shop himself, but he used to serve them as did; he didn't hawk his goods about, neether, but had regular customers, what used to send him a letter, and then he'd take them what they wanted. Yes, he used to serve some good shops: there was H——'s, of London Bridge, what's a large chemist's. He used to make a good deal of money, but he lost it betting; and so his brother, my uncle, did all his. . . .

"After mother died, sister still kept on making nets,[2] and I lived with her for some time. But she was keeping

The Boy Crossing Sweepers, from Henry Mayhew's *London Labour and the London Poor* (1851).

company with a young man, and one day they went out, and came back and said they'd been and got married. It was him as got rid of me.

"He was kind to me for the first two or three months, while he was keeping her company; but before he was married he got a little cross, and after he was married he begun to get more cross, and used to send me to play in the streets, and tell me not to come home again till night. One day he hit me, and I said I wouldn't be hit about by him, and then at tea that night sister gave me three shillings, and told me I must go and get my own living. So I bought a box and brushes (they cost me just the money) and went cleaning boots, and I done pretty well with them, till my box was stole from me by a boy where I was lodging. He's in prison now—got six calendar[3] for picking pockets. . . .

"I was fifteen the 24th of last May, sir, and I've been sweeping crossings now near upon two years. There's a party of six of us, and we have the crossings from St. Martin's Church as far as Pall Mall. I always go along with them as lodges in the same place as I do. In the daytime, if it's dry, we do anythink we can—open cabs, or anythink; but if it's wet, we separate, and I an' another gets a crossing—those who gets on it first, keeps it—and we stand on each side and take our chance.

"We do it this way: if I was to see two gentlemen coming, I should cry out, 'Two toffs!' and then they are mine; and whether they give me anythink or not they

[1] *pomatum* Scented ointment for the hair.

[2] *nets* Meshwork or network, used for various purposes.

[3] *six calendar* I.e., six months.

are mine, and my mate is bound not to follow them; for if he did he would get a hiding from the whole lot of us. If we both cry out together, then we share. If it's a lady and a gentleman, then we cries, 'A toff and a doll!' Sometimes we are caught out in this way. Perhaps it is a lady and gentleman and a child; and if I was to see them, and only say, 'A toff and a doll,' and leave out the child, then my mate can add the child; and as he is right and I wrong, then it's his party.

"If there's a policeman coming we musn't ask for money; but we are always on the look-out for policemen, and if we see one, then we calls out 'Phillup!' for that's our signal. One of the policemen at St. Martin's Church—Bandy, we calls him—knows what Phillup means, for he's up to us; so we had to change the word. (At the request of the young crossing-sweeper the present signal is omitted.)...

"When we see the rain we say together, 'Oh! there's a jolly good rain! we'll have a good day tomorrow.' If a shower comes on, and we are at our room, which we general are about three o'clock, to get somethink to eat—besides, we general go there to see how much each other's taken in the day—why, out we run with our brooms.

"At night-time we tumbles[1]—that is, if the policeman ain't nigh. We goes general to Waterloo Place when the opera's on. We sends on one of us ahead, as a looker-out, to look for the policeman, and then we follows. It's no good tumbling to gentlemen *going* to the opera; it's when they're coming back they gives us money. When they've got a young lady on their arm they laugh at us tumbling; some will give us a penny, others threepence, sometimes a sixpence or a shilling, and sometimes a halfpenny. We either do the cat'unwheel, or else we keep before the gentleman and lady, turning head-over-heels, putting our broom on the ground and then turning over it. ...

"When we are talking together we always talk in a kind of slang. Each policeman we gives a regular name— there's 'Bull's Head,' 'Bandy Shanks,' and 'Old Cherry Legs,' and 'Dot-and-carry-one'; they all knows their names as well as us. We never talks of crossings, but 'fakes.' We don't make no slang of our own, but uses the regular one."

---

[1] *tumbles* Perform leaps, somersaults, etc., like acrobats.

A group of homeless boys just after being admitted to a shelter. (Photograph by John Thomson, c. 1880.)

from Charles Dickens, *Hard Times* (1854)

CHAPTER 5, THE KEY-NOTE

Coketown, to which Messrs. Bounderby and Grad-grind now walked, was a triumph of fact; it had no greater taint of fancy in it than Mrs. Gradgrind herself. Let us strike the key-note, Coketown, before pursuing our tune.

It was a town of red brick, or of brick that would have been red if the smoke and ashes had allowed it; but as matters stood it was a town of unnatural red and black like the painted face of a savage. It was a town of machinery and tall chimneys, out of which interminable serpents of smoke trailed themselves forever and ever, and never got uncoiled. It had a black canal in it, and a river that ran purple with ill-smelling dye, and vast piles of building full of windows where there was a rattling and trembling all day long, and where the piston of the steam-engine worked monotonously up and down, like the head of an elephant in a state of melancholy madness. It contained several large streets all very like one another, and many small streets still more like one another, inhabited by people equally like one another, who all went in and out at the same hours, with the same sound upon the same pavements, to do the same work, and to whom every day was the same as yesterday and tomorrow, and every year the counterpart of the last and the next.

These attributes of Coketown were in the main inseparable from the work by which it was sustained; against them were to be set off, comforts of life which found their way all over the world, and elegancies of life which made, we will not ask how much of the fine lady, who could scarcely bear to hear the place mentioned. The rest of its features were voluntary, and they were these.

You saw nothing in Coketown but what was severely workful. If the members of a religious persuasion built a chapel there—as the members of eighteen religious persuasions had done—they made it a pious warehouse of red brick, with sometimes (but this is only in highly ornamental examples) a bell in a birdcage on the top of it. The solitary exception was the New Church; a stuccoed edifice with a square steeple over the door, terminating in four short pinnacles like florid wooden legs. All the public inscriptions in the town were painted alike, in severe characteristics of black and white. The jail might have been the infirmary, the infirmary might have been the jail, the town hall might have been either, or both, or anything else, for anything that appeared to the contrary in the graces of their construction. Fact, fact, fact, everywhere in the immaterial. The M'Choakumchild school was all fact, and the school of design was all fact, and the relations between master and man were all fact, and everything was fact between the lying-in hospital and the cemetery, and what you couldn't state in figures, or show to be purchaseable in the cheapest market and saleable in the dearest, was not, and never should be, world without end, Amen.[1]

A town so sacred to fact, and so triumphant in its assertion, of course got on well? Why no, not quite well. No? Dear me!

No. Coketown did not come out of its own furnaces, in all respects like gold that had stood the fire. First, the perplexing mystery of the place was, Who belonged to the eighteen denominations? Because, whoever did, the labouring people did not. It was very strange to walk through the streets on a Sunday morning, and note how few of *them* the barbarous jangling of bells that was driving the sick and nervous mad, called away from their own quarter, from their own close rooms, from the corners of their own streets, where they lounged listlessly, gazing at all the church and chapel going, as at a thing with which they had no manner of concern. Nor was it merely the stranger who noticed this, because there was a native organization in Coketown itself, whose members were to be heard of in the House of Commons every session, indignantly petitioning for Acts of Parliament that should make these people religious by main force.[2] Then came the Teetotal Society, who complained that these same people *would* get drunk, and showed their tabular statements that they did get drunk, and proved at tea parties that no inducement, human or divine (except a medal), would induce them to forego their custom of getting drunk. Then came the chemist and druggist, with other tabular statements, showing that when they didn't get drunk, they took opium. Then came the experienced chaplain of the jail, with more tabular statements, outdoing all the previous tabular statements, and showing that the same people *would* resort to low haunts, hidden from the public eye, where they heard low singing and saw low dancing, and mayhap joined in it; and where A. B., aged twenty-four next birthday, and committed for eighteen months' solitary, had himself said (not that he had ever shown himself particularly worthy of belief) his ruin began, as he was perfectly sure and confident that otherwise he would have been a tip-top moral specimen. Then came Mr. Gradgrind and Mr. Bounderby, the two gentlemen at this present

---

1 *never should be … Amen* From the Anglican Book of Common Prayer: "Glory be to the Father, and to the Son, and to the Holy Ghost; as it was in the beginning, is now, and ever shall be, world without end. Amen."

2 *members … main force* See Dickens's pamphlet *Sunday Under Three Heads* (written under the pseudonym "Timothy Sparks"), in which he vehemently opposes the "Sunday Observance Bill." Sir Andrew Agnew and his Evangelical group recommended to Parliament a series of moral reforms focusing on curtailing activities on Sunday, which Dickens contended would severely restrict the ability of the poor to enjoy their one day in the week that was free of labor.

moment walking through Coketown, and both
eminently practical, who could, on occasion, furnish
more tabular statements derived from their own
personal experience, and illustrated by cases they had
known and seen, from which it clearly appeared—in
short, it was the only clear thing in the case—that these
same people were a bad lot altogether, gentlemen; that
do what you would for them they were never thankful
for it, gentlemen; that they were restless, gentlemen;
that they never knew what they wanted; that they lived
upon the best, and bought fresh butter; and insisted on
Mocha coffee, and rejected all but prime parts of meat,
and yet were eternally dissatisfied and unmanageable. In
short, it was the moral of the old nursery fable:

There was an old woman, and what do you think
She lived upon nothing but victuals and drink;
Victuals and drink were the whole of her diet,
And yet this old woman would NEVER be quiet.

London Nomads by John Thomson,
from *Street Life in London* (1877).

JOHN STUART MILL
1806 — 1873

Philosopher, social reformer, economist, and politician, John Stuart Mill was one of the most influential of Victorian thinkers. His breadth of knowledge and interests was staggering, as was his ability to apply his intellect to a wide range of subjects, including women's rights, civil liberties, economic theories, logic, and poetics. Mill's *Utilitarianism* and *On Liberty* are both still regarded as central works in the fields of moral and social philosophy and political science.

Mill seemed destined from an early age to become a polymath—his childhood was practically a monument to over-achievement. He was born in London in 1806, the first child of Harriet Burrow and James Mill, a distinguished psychologist, philosopher, and historian. James was a disciple of Jeremy Bentham, who had founded the philosophical school of utilitarianism, an ethical doctrine whose main premise is that an action ought to be taken only if it produces happiness for all involved (later refined by J.S. Mill into the "greatest happiness principle," which suggests that people ought to act in ways that produce the greatest happiness for all involved). Participating in an experiment devised in part by Bentham, James decided that his eldest son would be a guinea pig for his educational theories, and at a very young age John began a rigorous education aimed at preparing him to become a future leader of the Benthamites.

In his autobiography, Mill described his formal instruction as beginning with Greek at age three; by the age of eight he could translate the works of Socrates and Plato. He then learned Latin well enough to translate such masters as Horace and Ovid, and also studied mathematics, the sciences, and English literature. Not being content to allow his son to learn simply by rote, James heavily emphasized rhetoric and debate, insisting that John make moral decisions about the principles he was learning. By the time he was 14, his father considered him to be ready for university study but felt that an institution would hold him back, and thus Mill began his career a full "quarter of a century before his contemporaries," as he would say in his autobiography.

James's experiment succeeded—John was a brilliant and erudite child, able to converse and debate with adults and to tutor all of his siblings from an early age. The daily ten-hour study regime, however, took a toll on him, and in his early twenties Mill experienced a period of deep depression that was relieved only when he discovered the poetry of William Wordsworth. During this time he pondered the virtues of Bentham's utilitarianism, which seemed to favor the good of the majority at the expense of the individual, who, Mill felt, is the best judge of his or her own happiness. Although he himself was an empiricist, he felt that Bentham's philosophy promoted the "science" of ethics at the expense of real life. Mill said of Bentham's utilitarianism: "It is wholly empirical and the empiricism of one who has had little experience." After reading the Romantic poets—Wordsworth in particular—Mill began to appreciate the therapeutic effects of poetry and the arts and the importance of an emotional life. The essay "What is Poetry?" (1833) speaks to his concerns about the necessity of individual pleasure.

After studying law for two years, Mill worked for decades in the East India Office, first as a clerk and then as head of his department, but he continued to be an outspoken advocate for individual rights and freedoms (he had been arrested as a teenager for disseminating literature in support of birth control). He published a modification of Bentham's philosophy, later reworked as *Utilitarianism* (1863); his most ambitious early work was *System of Logic*, published in 1843 and still highly regarded in philosophical circles today. The book that followed, *Principles of Political Economy* (1848), commands a similar level of respect in the field of economics. In 1859 Mill wrote another key work: *On Liberty*, a treatise that continued his theme of support for individual rights, deriding democratic majorities that conform to tradition and smother individuality.

In the planning and to some extent the writing of both these and subsequent works, Mill was assisted by Harriet Taylor, an aspiring author whom Mill had first met in 1831 and with whom he began to work closely. (The precise extent of Taylor's involvement remains the subject of debate among scholars.)

After serving as Member of Parliament from 1865 to 1868, Mill published *The Subjection of Women* (1869). He had worked on this book for years, and it had become a passionate subject for both Mill and Taylor. (The two were married in 1851 after her husband's death. Mill and Taylor never moved freely in society together, however; many of his friends, Carlyle and Tennyson included, viewed their relationship as inappropriate.) *The Subjection of Women* spoke to the rights of women, both legally and practically, arguing for government reforms of property and divorce laws, women's enfranchisement, and advocating the end of "slavery" in the home. Mill even argued in Parliament—well ahead of his time—for non-sexist language and the rewording of parliamentary bills to remove gender-specific terms.

Mill died in 1873 in Avignon, France, and was buried beside his wife, who had died prematurely in 1858. In his eloquent and insightful *Autobiography*, published shortly after his death, Mill wrote candidly about his childhood experiences with a demanding father and a thoroughly rational education; about his mental breakdown and his discovery of the value of works of the imagination; about his relationship with Harriet Taylor; and about his writing. The *Autobiography* is one of the great autobiographies in the English language.

⌘⌘⌘

from *The Subjection of Women*

CHAPTER I

If people are mostly so little aware how completely, during the greater part of the duration of our species, the law of force was the avowed rule of general conduct, any other being only a special and exceptional consequence of peculiar ties—and from how very recent a date it is that the affairs of society in general have been even pretended to be regulated according to any moral law; as little do people remember or consider, how institutions and customs which never had any ground but the law of force, last on into ages and states of general opinion which never would have permitted their first establishment. Less than forty years ago, Englishmen might still by law hold human beings in bondage as saleable property: within the present century they might kidnap them and carry them off, and work them literally to death. This absolutely extreme case of the law of force, condemned by those who can tolerate almost every other form of arbitrary power, and which, of all others, presents features the most revolting to the feelings of all who look at it from an impartial position, was the law of civilized and Christian England within the memory of persons now living: and in one half of Anglo-Saxon America three or four years ago, not only did slavery exist, but the slave trade, and the breeding of slaves expressly for it, was a general practice between slave states. Yet not only was there a greater strength of sentiment against it, but, in England at least, a less amount either of feeling or of interest in favour of it, than of any other of the customary abuses of force: for its motive was the love of gain, unmixed and undisguised; and those who profited by it were a very small numerical fraction of the country, while the natural feeling of all who were not personally interested in it, was unmitigated abhorrence. So extreme an instance makes it almost superfluous to refer to any other: but consider the long duration of absolute monarchy. In England at present it is the almost universal conviction that military despotism is a case of the law of force, having no other origin or justification. Yet in all the great nations of Europe except England it either still exists, or has only just ceased to exist, and has even now a strong party favourable to it in all ranks of the people, especially among persons of station and consequence. Such is the power of an established system, even when far from universal; when not only in almost every period of history there have been great and well-known examples of the contrary system, but these have almost invariably been afforded by the most illustrious and most prosperous communities. In this case, too, the possessor of the undue power, the person directly interested in it, is only one person, while those who are subject to it and suffer from it are literally all the rest. The yoke is naturally and necessarily humiliating to all persons, except the one who is on the throne, together with, at most, the one who expects to succeed to it. How different are these cases from that of the power of men over women! I am not now prejudging the question of its justifiableness. I am showing how vastly more permanent it could not but be, even if not justifiable, than these other dominations which have nevertheless lasted down to our own time. Whatever gratification of pride there is in the possession of power, and whatever personal interest in its exercise, is in this case not confined to a limited class, but common to the whole male sex. Instead of being, to most of its supporters, a thing desirable chiefly in the abstract, or, like the political ends usually contended for by factions, of little private importance to any but the leaders; it comes home to the person and hearth of every male head of a family, and of everyone who looks forward to being so. The clodhopper exercises, or is to exercise, his share of the power equally with the highest nobleman. And the case is that in which the desire of power is the strongest: for everyone who desires power, desires it most over those who are nearest to him, with whom his life is passed, with whom he has most concerns in common, and in whom any independence of his authority is oftenest likely to interfere with his individual prefer-

ences. If, in the other cases specified, powers manifestly grounded only on force, and having so much less to support them, are so slowly and with so much difficulty got rid of, much more must it be so with this, even if it rests on no better foundation than those. We must consider, too, that the possessors of the power have facilities in this case, greater than in any other, to prevent any uprising against it. Every one of the subjects lives under the very eye, and almost, it may be said, in the hands, of one of the masters—in closer intimacy with him than with any of her fellow-subjects; with no means of combining against him, no power of even locally overmastering him, and, on the other hand, with the strongest motives for seeking his favour and avoiding to give him offence. In struggles for political emancipation, everybody knows how often its champions are bought off by bribes, or daunted by terrors. In the case of women, each individual of the subject-class is in a chronic state of bribery and intimidation combined. In setting up the standard of resistance, a large number of the leaders, and still more of the followers, must make an almost complete sacrifice of the pleasures or the alleviations of their own individual lot. If ever any system of privilege and enforced subjection had its yoke tightly riveted on the necks of those who are kept down by it, this has. I have not yet shown that it is a wrong system: but everyone who is capable of thinking on the subject must see that even if it is, it was certain to outlast all other forms of unjust authority. And when some of the grossest of the other forms still exist in many civilized countries, and have only recently been got rid of in others, it would be strange if that which is so much the deepest rooted had yet been perceptibly shaken anywhere. There is more reason to wonder that the protests and testimonies against it should have been so numerous and so weighty as they are.

Some will object, that a comparison cannot fairly be made between the government of the male sex and the forms of unjust power which I have adduced in illustration of it, since these are arbitrary, and the effect of mere usurpation, while it on the contrary is natural. But was there ever any domination which did not appear natural to those who possessed it? There was a time when the division of mankind into two classes, a small one of masters and a numerous one of slaves, appeared, even to the most cultivated minds, to be a natural, and the only natural, condition of the human race. No less an intellect, and one which contributed no less to the progress of human thought, than Aristotle,[1] held this opinion without doubt or misgiving; and rested it on the same premises on which the same assertion in regard to the dominion of men over women is usually based, namely that there are different natures among mankind, free natures, and slave natures; that the Greeks were of a free nature, the barbarian races of Thracians[2] and Asiatics of a slave nature. But why need I go back to Aristotle? Did not the slaveowners of the Southern United States maintain the same doctrine, with all the fanaticism with which men cling to the theories that justify their passions and legitimate their personal interests? Did they not call heaven and earth to witness that the dominion of the white man over the black is natural, that the black race is by nature incapable of freedom, and marked out for slavery? some even going so far as to say that the freedom of manual labourers is an unnatural order of things anywhere. Again, the theorists of absolute monarchy have always affirmed it to be the only natural form of government; issuing from the patriarchal, which was the primitive and spontaneous form of society, framed on the model of the paternal, which is anterior to society itself, and, as they contend, the most natural authority of all. Nay, for that matter, the law of force itself, to those who could not plead any other, has always seemed the most natural of all grounds for the exercise of authority. Conquering races hold it to be Nature's own dictate that the conquered should obey the conquerors, or, as they euphoniously paraphrase it, that the feebler and more unwarlike races should submit to the braver and manlier. The smallest acquaintance with human life in the middle ages, shows how supremely natural the dominion of the feudal nobility over men of low condition appeared to the nobility themselves, and how unnatural the conception seemed, of a person of the inferior class claiming equality with them, or exercising authority over them. It hardly seemed less so to the class held in subjection. The emancipated serfs and burgesses, even in their most vigorous struggles, never made any pretension to a share of authority; they only demanded more or less of limitation to the power of tyrannizing over them. So true is it that unnatural generally means only uncustomary, and that everything which is usual appears natural. The subjection of women to men being a universal custom, any departure from it quite naturally appears unnatural. But how entirely, even in this case, the feeling is dependent on custom, appears by ample experience. Nothing so much astonishes the people of distant parts of the world, when they first learn anything about England, as to be told that it is under a queen: the thing seems to them so unnatural as to be almost incredible. To Englishmen this does not seem in the least degree unnatural, because they are used to it; but they do feel it unnatural that women should be soldiers or members of parliament. In the feudal ages, on the contrary, war and politics were not thought unnatural to women, because not unusual; it seemed natural that women of the privileged classes should be of manly character, inferior in nothing but bodily strength to their husbands and fathers. The independence of women seemed rather less unnatural to the Greeks than to other ancients, on account of the fabulous Amazons[3] (whom they believed to be historical), and the partial example afforded by the Spartan women; who, though no less subordinate by law than in other Greek states, were more free in fact, and being trained to bodily exercises in the same manner with men, gave ample proof that they were not naturally disqualified for them. There can be little doubt that Spartan experience suggested to Plato,[4] among many other of his doctrines, that of the social and political equality of the two sexes.

But, it will be said, the rule of men over women differs from all these others in not being a rule of force: it is accepted voluntarily; women make no complaint, and are consenting parties to it. In the first place, a great number of women do not accept it. Ever since there have been women able to make their sentiments known by their writings (the only mode of publicity which society permits to them), an increasing number of them have recorded protests against their present social condition: and recently many thousands of them, headed by the most eminent women known to the public, have petitioned parliament for their admission

---

[1]   *Aristotle*   See Aristotle's *Politics*.

[2]   *Thracians*   A warring group of tribes, the Thracians occupied the area north of Greece from 700 BCE to 4 CE.

[3]   *Amazons*   A race of women warriors.

[4]   *Plato*   See Plato's *The Republic*, 5.

to the Parliamentary Suffrage.[1] The claim of women to be educated as solidly, and in the same branches of knowledge, as men, is urged with growing intensity, and with a great prospect of success; while the demand for their admission into professions and occupations hitherto closed against them, becomes every year more urgent. Though there are not in this country, as there are in the United States, periodical Conventions and an organized party to agitate for the Rights of Women, there is a numerous and active Society organized and managed by women, for the more limited object of obtaining the political franchise. Nor is it only in our own country and in America that women are beginning to protest, more or less collectively, against the disabilities under which they labour. France, and Italy, and Switzerland, and Russia now afford examples of the same thing. How many more women there are who silently cherish similar aspirations, no one can possibly know; but there are abundant tokens how many *would* cherish them, were they not so strenuously taught to repress them as contrary to the proprieties of their sex. It must be remembered, also, that no enslaved class ever asked for complete liberty at once. When Simon de Montfort[2] called the deputies of the commons to sit for the first time in parliament, did any of them dream of demanding that an assembly, elected by their constituents, should make and destroy ministries, and dictate to the king in affairs of state? No such thought entered into the imagination of the most ambitious of them. The nobility had already these pretensions; the commons pretended to nothing but to be exempt from arbitrary taxation, and from the gross individual oppression of the king's officers. It is a political law of nature that those who are under any power of ancient origin, never begin by complaining of the power itself, but only of its oppressive exercise. There is never any want of women who complain of ill usage by their husbands. There would be infinitely more, if complaint were not the greatest of all provocatives to a repetition and increase of the ill usage. It is this which frustrates all attempts to maintain the power but protect the woman

against its abuses. In no other case (except that of a child) is the person who has been proved judicially to have suffered an injury, replaced under the physical power of the culprit who inflicted it. Accordingly wives, even in the most extreme and protracted cases of bodily ill usage, hardly ever dare avail themselves of the laws made for their protection: and if, in a moment of irrepressible indignation, or by the interference of neighbours, they are induced to do so, their whole effort afterwards is to disclose as little as they can, and to beg off their tyrant from his merited chastisement.

All causes, social and natural, combine to make it unlikely that women should be collectively rebellious to the power of men. They are so far in a position different from all other subject classes, that their masters require something more from them than actual service. Men do not want solely the obedience of women, they want their sentiments. All men, except the most brutish, desire to have, in the woman most nearly connected with them, not a forced slave but a willing one, not a slave merely, but a favourite. They have therefore put everything in practice to enslave their minds. The masters of all other slaves rely, for maintaining obedience, on fear; either fear of themselves, or religious fears. The masters of women wanted more than simple obedience, and they turned the whole force of education to effect their purpose. All women are brought up from the very earliest years in the belief that their ideal of character is the very opposite to that of men; not self-will, and government by self-control, but submission, and yielding to the control of others. All the moralities tell them that it is the duty of women, and all the current sentimentalities that it is their nature, to live for others; to make complete abnegation of themselves, and to have no life but in their affections. And by their affections are meant the only ones they are allowed to have—those to the men with whom they are connected, or to the children who constitute an additional and indefeasible tie between them and a man. When we put together three things—first, the natural attraction between opposite sexes; secondly, the wife's entire dependence on the husband, every privilege or pleasure she has being either his gift, or depending entirely on his will; and lastly, that the principal object of human pursuit, consideration, and all objects of social ambition, can in general be sought or obtained by her only

[1] *petitioned ... Parliamentary Suffrage* Mill himself also introduced such a petition to the House of Commons in 1866.

[2] *Simon de Montfort* The Earl of Leicester (c. 1208–65) led a baronial revolt against Henry III and subsequently established a newly representative Parliament.

through him, it would be a miracle if the object of being attractive to men had not become the polar star of feminine education and formation of character. And, this great means of influence over the minds of women having been acquired, an instinct of selfishness made men avail themselves of it to the utmost as a means of holding women in subjection, by representing to them meekness, submissiveness, and resignation of all individual will into the hands of a man, as an essential part of sexual attractiveness. Can it be doubted that any of the other yokes which mankind have succeeded in breaking, would have subsisted till now if the same means had existed, and had been so sedulously used, to bow down their minds to it? If it had been made the object of the life of every young plebeian to find personal favour in the eyes of some patrician, of every young serf with some seigneur;[1] if domestication with him, and a share of his personal affections, had been held out as the prize which they all should look out for, the most gifted and aspiring being able to reckon on the most desirable prizes; and if, when this prize had been obtained, they had been shut out by a wall of brass from all interests not centering in him, all feelings and desires but those which he shared or inculcated; would not serfs and seigneurs, plebeians and patricians, have been as broadly distinguished at this day as men and women are? and would not all but a thinker here and there, have believed the distinction to be a fundamental and unalterable fact in human nature?

The preceding considerations are amply sufficient to show that custom, however universal it may be, affords in this case no presumption, and ought not to create any prejudice, in favour of the arrangements which place women in social and political subjection to men. But I may go farther, and maintain that the course of history, and the tendencies of progressive human society, afford not only no presumption in favour of this system of inequality of rights, but a strong one against it; and that, so far as the whole course of human improvement up to this time, the whole stream of modern tendencies, warrants any inference on the subject, it is, that this relic of the past is discordant with the future, and must necessarily disappear.

For, what is the peculiar character of the modern world—the difference which chiefly distinguishes modern institutions, modern social ideas, modern life itself, from those of times long past? It is, that human beings are no longer born to their place in life, and chained down by an inexorable bond to the place they are born to, but are free to employ their faculties, and such favourable chances as offer, to achieve the lot which may appear to them most desirable. Human society of old was constituted on a very different principle. All were born to a fixed social position, and were mostly kept in it by law, or interdicted from any means by which they could emerge from it. As some men are born white and others black, so some were born slaves and others freemen and citizens; some were born patricians, others plebeians; some were born feudal nobles, others commoners and *roturiers*.[2] A slave or serf could never make himself free, nor, except by the will of his master, become so. In most European countries it was not till towards the close of the middle ages, and as a consequence of the growth of regal power, that commoners could be ennobled. Even among nobles, the eldest son was born the exclusive heir to the paternal possessions, and a long time elapsed before it was fully established that the father could disinherit him. Among the industrious classes, only those who were born members of a guild, or were admitted into it by its members, could lawfully practise their calling within its local limits; and nobody could practise any calling deemed important, in any but the legal manner—by processes authoritatively prescribed. Manufacturers have stood in the pillory[3] for presuming to carry on their business by new and improved methods. In modern Europe, and most in those parts of it which have participated most largely in all other modern improvements, diametrically opposite doctrines now prevail. Law and government do not undertake to prescribe by whom any social or industrial operation shall or shall not be conducted, or what modes of conducting them shall be lawful. These things are left to the unfettered choice of individuals. Even the laws which required that workmen should serve an apprenticeship, have in this country been repealed: there being ample assurance that in all cases in which an apprenticeship is necessary, its

---

[1] *plebeian* Commoner; *patrician* Aristocrat; *serf* Laborer in a condition of servitude; *seigneur* Feudal lord.

[2] *roturiers* Commoners who owned land in feudal times.

[3] *pillory* Wooden framework in which wrongdoers were locked and exposed to public derision.

necessity will suffice to enforce it. The old theory was, that the least possible should be left to the choice of the individual agent; that all he had to do should, as far as practicable, be laid down for him by superior wisdom. Left to himself he was sure to go wrong. The modern conviction, the fruit of a thousand years of experience, is, that things in which the individual is the person directly interested, never go right but as they are left to his own discretion; and that any regulation of them by authority, except to protect the rights of others, is sure to be mischievous. This conclusion, slowly arrived at, and not adopted until almost every possible application of the contrary theory had been made with disastrous result, now (in the industrial department) prevails universally in the most advanced countries, almost universally in all that have pretensions to any sort of advancement. It is not that all processes are supposed to be equally good, or all persons to be equally qualified for everything; but that freedom of individual choice is now known to be the only thing which procures the adoption of the best processes, and throws each operation into the hands of those who are best qualified for it. Nobody thinks it necessary to make a law that only a strong-armed man shall be a blacksmith. Freedom and competition suffice to make blacksmiths strong-armed men, because the weak-armed can earn more by engaging in occupations for which they are more fit. In consonance with this doctrine, it is felt to be an overstepping of the proper bounds of authority to fix beforehand, on some general presumption, that certain persons are not fit to do certain things. It is now thoroughly known and admitted that if some such presumptions exist, no such presumption is infallible. Even if it be well grounded in a majority of cases, which it is very likely not to be, there will be a minority of exceptional cases in which it does not hold: and in those it is both an injustice to the individuals, and a detriment to society, to place barriers in the way of their using their faculties for their own benefit and for that of others. In the cases, on the other hand, in which the unfitness is real, the ordinary motives of human conduct will on the whole suffice to prevent the incompetent person from making, or from persisting in, the attempt.

If this general principle of social and economical science is not true; if individuals, with such help as they can derive from the opinion of those who know them,

are not better judges than the law and the government, of their own capacities and vocation; the world cannot too soon abandon this principle, and return to the old system of regulations and disabilities. But if the principle is true, we ought to act as if we believed it, and not to ordain that to be born a girl instead of a boy, any more than to be born black instead of white, or a commoner instead of a nobleman, shall decide the person's position through all life—shall interdict people from all the more elevated social positions, and from all, except a few, respectable occupations. Even were we to admit the utmost that is ever pretended as to the superior fitness of men for all the functions now reserved to them, the same argument applies which forbids a legal qualification for members of parliament. If only once in a dozen years the conditions of eligibility exclude a fit person, there is a real loss, while the exclusion of thousands of unfit persons is no gain; for if the constitution of the electoral body disposes them to choose unfit persons, there are always plenty of such persons to choose from. In all things of any difficulty and importance, those who can do them well are fewer than the need, even with the most unrestricted latitude of choice: and any limitation of the field of selection deprives society of some chances of being served by the competent, without ever saving it from the incompetent.

At present, in the more improved countries, the disabilities of women are the only case, save one, in which laws and institutions take persons at their birth, and ordain that they shall never in all their lives be allowed to compete for certain things. The one exception is that of royalty. Persons still are born to the throne; no one, not of the reigning family, can ever occupy it, and no one even of that family can, by any means but the course of hereditary succession, attain it. All other dignities and social advantages are open to the whole male sex: many indeed are only attainable by wealth, but wealth may be striven for by anyone, and is actually obtained by many men of the very humblest origin. The difficulties, to the majority, are indeed insuperable without the aid of fortunate accidents; but no male human being is under any legal ban: neither law nor opinion superadd artificial obstacles to the natural ones. Royalty, as I have said, is excepted: but in this case everyone feels it to be an exception—an anomaly in the modern world, in marked opposition to its customs and principles, and to be justified only by extraordinary special expediencies, which, though individuals and nations differ in estimating their weight, unquestionably do in fact exist. But in this exceptional case, in which a high social function is, for important reasons, bestowed on birth instead of being put up to competition, all free nations contrive to adhere in substance to the principle from which they nominally derogate; for they circumscribe this high function by conditions avowedly intended to prevent the person to whom it ostensibly belongs from really performing it; while the person by whom it is performed, the responsible minister, does obtain the post by a competition from which no full-grown citizen of the male sex is legally excluded. The disabilities, therefore, to which women are subject from the mere fact of their birth, are the solitary examples of the kind in modern legislation. In no instance except this, which comprehends half the human race, are the higher social functions closed against anyone by a fatality of birth which no exertions, and no change of circumstances, can overcome; for even religious disabilities (besides that in England and in Europe they have practically almost ceased to exist) do not close any career to the disqualified person in case of conversion.

The social subordination of women thus stands out an isolated fact in modern social institutions; a solitary breach of what has become their fundamental law; a single relic of an old world of thought and practice exploded in everything else, but retained in the one thing of most universal interest; as if a gigantic dolmen,[1] or a vast temple of Jupiter Olympius, occupied the site of St. Paul's and received daily worship, while the surrounding Christian churches were only resorted to on fasts and festivals. This entire discrepancy between one social fact and all those which accompany it, and the radical opposition between its nature and the progressive movement which is the boast of the modern world, and which has successively swept away everything else of an analogous character, surely affords, to a conscientious observer of human tendencies, serious matter for reflection. It raises a *prima facie*[2] presumption on the unfavourable side, far outweighing any which custom and usage could in such circumstances create on

the favourable; and should at least suffice to make this, like the choice between republicanism and royalty, a balanced question.

The least that can be demanded is, that the question should not be considered as prejudged by existing fact and existing opinion, but open to discussion on its merits, as a question of justice and expediency: the decision on this, as on any of the other social arrangements of mankind, depending on what an enlightened estimate of tendencies and consequences may show to be most advantageous to humanity in general, without distinction of sex. And the discussion must be a real discussion, descending to foundations, and not resting satisfied with vague and general assertions. It will not do, for instance, to assert in general terms, that the experience of mankind has pronounced in favour of the existing system. Experience cannot possibly have decided between two courses, so long as there has only been experience of one. If it be said that the doctrine of the equality of the sexes rests only on theory, it must be remembered that the contrary doctrine also has only theory to rest upon. All that is proved in its favour by direct experience, is that mankind have been able to exist under it, and to attain the degree of improvement and prosperity which we now see; but whether that prosperity has been attained sooner, or is now greater, than it would have been under the other system, experience does not say. On the other hand, experience does say, that every step in improvement has been so invariably accompanied by a step made in raising the social position of women, that historians and philosophers have been led to adopt their elevation or debasement as on the whole the surest test and most correct measure of the civilization of a people or an age. Through all the progressive period of human history, the condition of women has been approaching nearer to equality with men. This does not of itself prove that the assimilation must go on to complete equality; but it assuredly affords some presumption that such is the case.

Neither does it avail anything to say that the *nature* of the two sexes adapts them to their present functions and position, and renders these appropriate to them. Standing on the ground of common sense and the constitution of the human mind, I deny that anyone knows, or can know, the nature of the two sexes, as long as they have only been seen in their present relation to

---

[1] *dolmen* Celtic monument associated with pagan rituals.

[2] *prima facie* Latin: arising at first sight.

one another. If men had ever been found in society without women, or women without men, or if there had been a society of men and women in which the women were not under the control of the men, something might have been positively known about the mental and moral differences which may be inherent in the nature of each. What is now called the nature of women is an eminently artificial thing—the result of forced repression in some directions, unnatural stimulation in others. It may be asserted without scruple, that no other class of dependents have had their character so entirely distorted from its natural proportions by their relation with their masters; for, if conquered and slave races have been, in some respects, more forcibly repressed, whatever in them has not been crushed down by an iron heel has generally been let alone, and if left with any liberty of development, it has developed itself according to its own laws; but in the case of women, a hot-house and stove cultivation has always been carried on of some of the capabilities of their nature, for the benefit and pleasure of their masters. Then, because certain products of the general vital force sprout luxuriantly and reach a great development in this heated atmosphere and under this active nurture and watering, while other shoots from the same root, which are left outside in the wintry air, with ice purposely heaped all round them, have a stunted growth, and some are burnt off with fire and disappear; men, with that inability to recognise their own work which distinguishes the unanalytic mind, indolently believe that the tree grows of itself in the way they have made it grow, and that it would die if one half of it were not kept in a vapour bath and the other half in the snow.

Of all difficulties which impede the progress of thought, and the formation of well-grounded opinions on life and social arrangements, the greatest is now the unspeakable ignorance and inattention of mankind in respect to the influences which form human character. Whatever any portion of the human species now are, or seem to be, such, it is supposed, they have a natural tendency to be: even when the most elementary knowledge of the circumstances in which they have been placed, clearly points out the causes that made them what they are. Because a cottier[1] deeply in arrears to his landlord is not industrious, there are people who think

that the Irish are naturally idle. Because constitutions can be overthrown when the authorities appointed to execute them turn their arms against them, there are people who think the French incapable of free government. Because the Greeks cheated the Turks, and the Turks only plundered the Greeks, there are persons who think that the Turks are naturally more sincere: and because women, as is often said, care nothing about politics except their personalities, it is supposed that the general good is naturally less interesting to women than to men. History, which is now so much better understood than formerly, teaches another lesson: if only by showing the extraordinary susceptibility of human nature to external influences, and the extreme variableness of those of its manifestations which are supposed to be most universal and uniform. But in history, as in travelling, men usually see only what they already had in their own minds; and few learn much from history, who do not bring much with them to its study.

Hence, in regard to that most difficult question, what are the natural differences between the two sexes—a subject on which it is impossible in the present state of society to obtain complete and correct knowledge—while almost everybody dogmatizes upon it, almost all neglect and make light of the only means by which any partial insight can be obtained into it. This is, an analytic study of the most important department of psychology, the laws of the influence of circumstances on character. For, however great and apparently ineradicable the moral and intellectual differences between men and women might be, the evidence of there being natural differences could only be negative. Those only could be inferred to be natural which could not possibly be artificial—the residuum, after deducting every characteristic of either sex which can admit of being explained from education or external circumstances. The profoundest knowledge of the laws of the formation of character is indispensable to entitle anyone to affirm even that there is any difference, much more what the difference is, between the two sexes considered as moral and rational beings; and since no one, as yet, has that knowledge (for there is hardly any subject which, in proportion to its importance, has been so little studied), no one is thus far entitled to any positive opinion on the subject. Conjectures are all that can at present be made; conjectures more or less probable,

[1] *cottier* Tenant who rents a cottage and often works for a landlord in return.

according as more or less authorized by such knowledge as we yet have of the laws of psychology, as applied to the formation of character.

Even the preliminary knowledge, what the differences between the sexes now are, apart from all question as to how they are made what they are, is still in the crudest and most incomplete state. Medical practitioners and physiologists have ascertained, to some extent, the differences in bodily constitution; and this is an important element to the psychologist: but hardly any medical practitioner is a psychologist. Respecting the mental characteristics of women; their observations are of no more worth than those of common men. It is a subject on which nothing final can be known, so long as those who alone can really know it, women themselves, have given but little testimony, and that little, mostly suborned. It is easy to know stupid women. Stupidity is much the same all the world over. A stupid person's notions and feelings may confidently be inferred from those which prevail in the circle by which the person is surrounded. Not so with those whose opinions and feelings are an emanation from their own nature and faculties. It is only a man here and there who has any tolerable knowledge of the character even of the women of his own family. I do not mean, of their capabilities; these nobody knows, not even themselves, because most of them have never been called out. I mean their actually existing thoughts and feelings. Many a man thinks he perfectly understands women, because he has had amatory relations with several, perhaps with many of them. If he is a good observer, and his experience extends to quality as well as quantity, he may have learnt something of one narrow department of their nature—an important department, no doubt. But of all the rest of it, few persons are generally more ignorant, because there are few from whom it is so carefully hidden. The most favourable case which a man can generally have for studying the character of a woman, is that of his own wife: for the opportunities are greater, and the cases of complete sympathy not so unspeakably rare. And in fact, this is the source from which any knowledge worth having on the subject has, I believe, generally come. But most men have not had the opportunity of studying in this way more than a single case: accordingly one can, to an almost laughable degree, infer what a man's wife is like, from his opinions about women in general. To make even this one case yield any result, the woman must be worth knowing, and the man not only a competent judge, but of a character so sympathetic in itself, and so well adapted to hers, that he can either read her mind by sympathetic intuition, or has nothing in himself which makes her shy of disclosing it. Hardly anything, I believe, can be more rare than this conjunction. It often happens that there is the most complete unity of feeling and community of interests as to all external things, yet the one has as little admission into the internal life of the other as if they were common acquaintance. Even with true affection, authority on the one side and subordination on the other prevent perfect confidence. Though nothing may be intentionally withheld, much is not shown. In the analogous relation of parent and child, the corresponding phenomenon must have been in the observation of everyone. As between father and son, how many are the cases in which the father, in spite of real affection on both sides, obviously to all the world does not know, nor suspect, parts of the son's character familiar to his companions and equals. The truth is, that the position of looking up to another is extremely unpropitious to complete sincerity and openness with him. The fear of losing ground in his opinion or in his feelings is so strong, that even in an upright character, there is an unconscious tendency to show only the best side, or the side which, though not the best, is that which he most likes to see: and it may be confidently said that thorough knowledge of one another hardly ever exists, but between persons who, besides being intimates, are equals. How much more true, then, must all this be, when the one is not only under the authority of the other, but has it inculcated on her as a duty to reckon everything else subordinate to his comfort and pleasure, and to let him neither see nor feel anything coming from her, except what is agreeable to him. All these difficulties stand in the way of a man's obtaining any thorough knowledge even of the one woman whom alone, in general, he has sufficient opportunity of studying. When we further consider that to understand one woman is not necessarily to understand any other woman; that even if he could study many women of one rank, or of one country, he would not thereby understand women of other ranks or countries; and even if he did, they are still only the women of a single period of history; we may safely assert that the knowledge which men can acquire of women, even as they have been and are, without reference to what they might be, is wretchedly imperfect and superficial, and always will be so, until women themselves have told all that they have to tell.

And this time has not come; nor will it come otherwise than gradually. It is but of yesterday that women have either been qualified by literary accomplishments or permitted by society, to tell anything to the general public. As yet very few of them dare tell anything, which men, on whom their literary success depends, are unwilling to hear. Let us remember in what manner, up to a very recent time, the expression, even by a male author, of uncustomary opinions, or what are deemed eccentric feelings, usually was, and in some degree still is, received; and we may form some faint conception under what impediments a woman, who is brought up to think custom and opinion her sovereign rule, attempts to express in books anything drawn from the depths of her own nature. The greatest woman who has left writings behind her sufficient to give her an eminent rank in the literature of her country, thought it necessary to prefix as a motto to her boldest work, "Un homme peut braver l'opinion; une femme doit s'y soumettre."[1] The greater part of what women write about women is mere sycophancy to men. In the case of unmarried women, much of it seems only intended to increase their chance of a husband. Many, both married and unmarried, overstep the mark, and inculcate a servility beyond what is desired or relished by any man, except the very vulgarest. But this is not so often the case as, even at a quite late period, it still was. Literary women are becoming more freespoken, and more willing to express their real sentiments. Unfortunately, in this country especially, they are themselves such artificial products, that their sentiments are compounded of a small element of individual observation and consciousness, and a very large one of acquired associations. This will be less and less the case, but it will remain true to a great extent, as long as social institutions do not admit the same free development of originality in women which is possible to men. When that time comes, and not before, we shall see, and not

merely hear, as much as it is necessary to know of the nature of women, and the adaptation of other things to it.

I have dwelt so much on the difficulties which at present obstruct any real knowledge by men of the true nature of women, because in this as in so many other things "opinio copiæ inter maximas causas inopiæ est;"[2] and there is little chance of reasonable thinking on the matter, while people flatter themselves that they perfectly understand a subject of which most men know absolutely nothing, and of which it is at present impossible that any man, or all men taken together, should have knowledge which can qualify them to lay down the law to women as to what is, or is not, their vocation. Happily, no such knowledge is necessary for any practical purpose connected with the position of women in relation to society and life. For, according to all the principles involved in modern society, the question rests with women themselves—to be decided by their own experience, and by the use of their own faculties. There are no means of finding what either one person or many can do, but by trying—and no means by which anyone else can discover for them what it is for their happiness to do or leave undone.

One thing we may be certain of—that what is contrary to women's nature to do, they never will be made to do by simply giving their nature free play. The anxiety of mankind to interfere in behalf of nature, for fear lest nature should not succeed in effecting its purpose, is an altogether unnecessary solicitude. What women by nature cannot do, it is quite superfluous to forbid them from doing. What they can do, but not so well as the men who are their competitors, competition suffices to exclude them from; since nobody asks for protective duties and bounties in favour of women; it is only asked that the present bounties and protective duties in favour of men should be recalled. If women have a greater natural inclination for some things than for others, there is no need of laws or social inculcation to make the majority of them do the former in preference to the latter. Whatever women's services are most wanted for, the free play of competition will hold out the strongest inducements to them to undertake. And, as the words imply, they are most wanted for the things

---

[1] [Mill's note] Title-page of Mme. de Staël's *Delphine*. [The French novelist's (1766–1817) words translate as: "A man can brave (public) opinion; a woman must submit to it."]

[2] *"opinio copiæ ... inopiæ est"* Latin: "The belief in sufficiency is one of the greatest causes of insufficiency."

for which they are most fit; by the apportionment of which to them, the collective faculties of the two sexes can be applied on the whole with the greatest sum of valuable result.

The general opinion of men is supposed to be, that the natural vocation of a woman is that of a wife and mother. I say, is supposed to be, because, judging from acts—from the whole of the present constitution of society—one might infer that their opinion was the direct contrary. They might be supposed to think that the alleged natural vocation of women was of all things the most repugnant to their nature; insomuch that if they are free to do anything else—if any other means of living, or occupation of their time and faculties, is open, which has any chance of appearing desirable to them— there will not be enough of them who will be willing to accept the condition said to be natural to them. If this is the real opinion of men in general, it would be well that it should be spoken out. I should like to hear somebody openly enunciating the doctrine (it is already implied in much that is written on the subject)—"It is necessary to society that women should marry and produce children. They will not do so unless they are compelled. Therefore it is necessary to compel them." The merits of the case would then be clearly defined. It would be exactly that of the slaveholders of South Carolina and Louisiana. "It is necessary that cotton and sugar should be grown. White men cannot produce them. Negroes will not, for any wages which we choose to give. *Ergo* they must be compelled." An illustration still closer to the point is that of impressment.[1] Sailors must absolutely be had to defend the country. It often happens that they will not voluntarily enlist. Therefore there must be the power of forcing them. How often has this logic been used! and, but for one flaw in it, without doubt it would have been successful up to this day. But it is open to the retort—First pay the sailors the honest value of their labour. When you have made it as well worth their while to serve you, as to work for other employers, you will have no more difficulty than others have in obtaining their services. To this there is no logical answer except "I will not:" and as people are now not only ashamed, but are not desirous, to rob the labourer of his hire, impressment is no longer advocated.

Those who attempt to force women into marriage by closing all other doors against them, lay themselves open to a similar retort. If they mean what they say, their opinion must evidently be, that men do not render the married condition so desirable to women, as to induce them to accept it for its own recommendations. It is not a sign of one's thinking the boon one offers very attractive, when one allows only Hobson's choice,[2] "that or none." And here, I believe, is the clue to the feelings of those men, who have a real antipathy to the equal freedom of women. I believe they are afraid, not lest women should be unwilling to marry, for I do not think that anyone in reality has that apprehension; but lest they should insist that marriage should be on equal conditions; lest all women of spirit and capacity should prefer doing almost anything else, not in their own eyes degrading, rather than marry, when marrying is giving themselves a master, and a master too of all their earthly possessions. And truly, if this consequence were necessarily incident to marriage, I think that the apprehension would be very well founded. I agree in thinking it probable that few women, capable of anything else, would, unless under an irresistible *entrainement*,[3] rendering them for the time insensible to anything but itself, choose such a lot, when any other means were open to them of filling a conventionally honourable place in life: and if men are determined that the law of marriage shall be a law of despotism, they are quite right, in point of mere policy, in leaving to women only Hobson's choice. But, in that case, all that has been done in the modern world to relax the chain on the minds of women, has been a mistake. They never should have been allowed to receive a literary education. Women who read, much more women who write, are, in the existing constitution of things, a contradiction and a disturbing element: and it was wrong to bring women up with any acquirements but those of an odalisque,[4] or of a domestic servant.

—1869

---

[1] *impressment* Policy that pressed men into public service, even against their will; this practice was discontinued after 1835.

[2] *Hobson's choice* Expression originating from a Cambridge-London carrier, Thomas Hobson (1544–1630), who refused, when hiring out his horses, to allow any to leave the stable out of turn.

[3] *entrainement* Enchantment or charm.

[4] *odalisque* Concubine.

THE PLACE OF WOMEN IN SOCIETY

CONTEXTS

Throughout the nineteenth century, there was much debate concerning the proper place of women and the proper characteristics of femininity. The traditional roles of wives, mothers, and daughters, the structure of the family, and the nature of marriage—these were all open for examination by both men and women. In a nation ruled by a female queen who supported education for women but not female suffrage, the lines between traditional masculine and feminine realms were often blurred, and many writers and thinkers voiced their opinions on how such tensions and inconsistencies should best be reconciled.

Sarah Stickney Ellis, the author of the first excerpt here, from *The Women of England*, ran a school for girls but did not support intellectual advancement for women. Instead, she educated her pupils to become capable managers of their homes, from which they could best facilitate the advancement of their husbands and sons. Her numerous guides to female conduct, including *The Daughters of England* (1842), *The Wives of England* (1843), and *The Mothers of England* (1845) were extremely popular.

As the next excerpt (from *Fraser's Magazine*) shows, the growing role of the governess in Victorian society posed problems for traditional conception of gender and class roles. The role of the governess grew in importance along with the increasing emphasis on female education and the growing prosperity of the middle classes. In Victorian social hierarchy, the governess was a "lady"; as a result, this was *socially* a desirable occupation for many women, especially those daughters of tradespeople who sought to better themselves. Nevertheless, as a paid employee, the governess was part of the work force and, therefore, of the public sphere (although she worked within the private realm of the home), two qualities that would normally disqualify a woman from being considered a "lady." Consequently, the status of the governess was rife with tensions that often resulted in difficult conditions (Charlotte Brontë complained of the "wretched bondage" of being a governess).

The female suffrage campaign, which began in the 1850s, heightened the debate over women's proper role in society. There were a variety of arguments used in the effort to justify the subordination of women to men; these included the scientific argument, which presented evidence for women's supposed intellectual and physical inferiority, and the "divine will" argument, which portrayed female inferiority as part of the natural order established by God in Genesis. In her argument for female suffrage in *The Enfranchisement of Women* (excerpted below), Harriet Taylor presents (and attacks) some additional arguments used to protest women's entrance into politics. In a slightly later article, "Criminals, Idiots, Women, and Children," Frances Power Cobbe criticizes similar arguments (which she refers to as those of "Justice," "Expediency," and "Sentiment") used to deprive women of the legal rights that even convicted felons were afforded.

Coventry Patmore's long poem *The Angel in the House*, which became a best-seller in both Britain and the United States, is a sentimental depiction of the ideal female as conceived by many Victorian men of the upper and middle classes. The poem, which celebrated Patmore's first wife (he remarried twice after her death) details their courtship and marriage and epitomizes the view of women held by many men at the time. In the twentieth century the poem became the object of attacks by many feminist critics, particularly Virginia Woolf, and the phrase "angel in the house" was commonly used as a sort of shorthand to refer to an oppressive Victorian attitude towards gender roles.

The traditional social order that Patmore idealizes and celebrates also came under attack in the course of debates over "the woman question" in the late nineteenth century. At the center of this "woman question" was the issue of female equality and suffrage. As the satirical *Punch* cartoon reproduced below demonstrates, female suffragettes were often viewed as the antithesis of the ideal woman, epitomizing instead traditionally "masculine" characteristics. In the excerpt following, Eliza Lynn Linton, perhaps the most vocal anti-feminist of the period, criticizes what she sees as the unnatural, masculine boldness of the "modern girl," whose unwillingness to serve and support her husband and nurture her children, Linton argues, makes her not only unsuitable for marriage, but a disgrace to England's national character. In a slightly later article excerpted below, "The New Aspect of the Woman Question," Sarah Grand portrays the modern woman in a very different light. Grand (whose real name was Frances Elizabeth Clarke McFall) was a novelist, lecturer, and women's rights advocate who coined the phrase "the new woman" in this *North American Review* essay to express the values—principally social, political, and educational equality with men, as well as economic independence—of many women of her generation.

Within Victorian society's complex network of genders and class distinction, many citizens relied upon printed material for guidance in matters of conduct and etiquette, as well as for more practical advice on household management and professional opportunities. *The Girl's Own Paper*, a weekly paper founded in 1880 as a companion to the very successful *Boy's Own Paper*, provided such information to many female readers, as the two articles excerpted here (giving advice on the proper treatment of servants and the opportunities for self-improvement between school and marriage) demonstrate. According to its editor, the paper, which was published by the Religious Tract Society, aimed to provide female readers with instruction "in the moral and domestic virtues, preparing them for the responsibility of womanhood and for a heavenly home."

As the debates concerning women's political rights, their education, and their need for economic independence grew more heated, many realized that "the Woman Question is the Marriage Question," as Sarah Grand comments in her essay. The final excerpt printed below is Mona Caird's somewhat humorous response to the *Daily Telegraph*'s question "Does Marriage Hinder a Woman's Self-Development?" Her hypothetical reversal of men's and women's roles demonstrates how arbitrary—and confining—definitions of "masculine" and "feminine" characteristics could be.

⌘ ⌘ ⌘

from Sarah Stickney Ellis, *The Daughters of England: Their Position in Society, Character and Responsibilities* (1842)

… The sphere upon which a young woman enters on first leaving school, or, to use a popular phrase, on "completing her education," is so entirely new to her, her mind is so often the subject of new impressions, and her attention so frequently absorbed by new motives for exertion, that, if at all accustomed to reflect, we cannot doubt but she will make these, or similar questions, the subject of serious inquiry—"What is my position in

society? What do I aim at? And what means do I intend to employ for the accomplishment of my purpose?" …

As women, then, the first thing of importance is to be content to be inferior to men—inferior in mental power, in the same proportion that you are inferior in bodily strength. Facility of movement, aptitude, and grace, the bodily frame of woman may possess in a higher degree than that of man; just as in the softer touches of mental and spiritual beauty her character may present a lovelier page than his. Yet, as the great attribute of power must still be wanting there, it becomes more immediately her business to inquire how this want may be supplied.

An able and eloquent writer on "Woman's Mission"[1] has justly observed that woman's strength is in her influence. And, in order to render this influence more complete, you will find on examination that you are by nature endowed with peculiar faculties—with a quickness of perception, facility of adaptation, and acuteness of feeling, which fit you especially for the part you have to act in life; and which, at the same time, render you, in a higher degree than men, susceptible both of pain and pleasure. ...

*   *   *

I have already stated that women, in their position in life, must be content to be inferior to men; but as their inferiority consists chiefly in their want of power, this deficiency is abundantly made up to them by their capability of exercising influence; it is made up to them also in other ways, incalculable in their number and extent; but in none so effectually as by that order of Divine Providence which places them, in a moral and religious point of view, on the same level with man; nor can it be a subject of regret to any right-minded woman that they are not only exempt from the most laborious occupations both of mind and body, but also from the necessity of engaging in those eager pecuniary speculations, and in that fierce conflict of worldly interests by which men are so deeply occupied as to be in a manner compelled to stifle their best feelings, until they become in reality the characters they at first only assumed. Can it be a subject of regret to any kind and feeling woman that her sphere of action is one adapted to the exercise of the affections, where she may love, and trust, and hope, and serve, to the utmost of her wishes? Can it be a subject of regret that she is not called upon, so much as man, to calculate, to compete, to struggle, but rather to occupy a sphere in which the elements of discord cannot with propriety be admitted—in which beauty and order are expected to denote her presence, and where the exercise of benevolence is the duty she is most frequently called upon to perform.

Women almost universally consider themselves, and wish to be considered by others, as extremely affectionate; scarcely can a more severe libel be pronounced upon a woman than to say that she is not so. Now the whole law of woman's life is a law of love. I propose, therefore, to treat the subject in this light—to try whether the neglect of their peculiar duties does not imply an absence of love, and whether the principle of love, thoroughly carried out, would not so influence their conduct and feelings as to render them all which their best friends could desire.

Let us, however, clearly understand each other at the outset. To love, is a very different thing from a desire to be beloved. To love, is woman's nature—to be beloved is the consequence of her having properly exercised and controlled that nature. To love, is a woman's duty—to be beloved, is her reward.

*   *   *

... There is yet another flight of female ambition, another course which the love of distinction is apt to make, more product of folly, and of disappointment, perhaps, than all the rest. It is the ambition of the female author who writes for fame. Could those young aspirants know how little real dignity there is connected with the *trade* of authorship, their harps would be exchanged for distaffs,[2] their rose-tinted paper would be converted into ashes, and their Parnassus[3] would dwindle to a molehill. ... The same want of sympathy which so often inspires the first effort of female authorship, might often find a sweet and abundant interchange of kindness in many a faithful heart beside the homely hearth. And after all, there is more true poetry in the fire-side affections of early life than in all those sympathetic associations with unknown and untried developments of mind which ever have existed either amongst the sons or the daughters of men.

Taking a more sober view of the case, there are, unquestionably, subjects of deep interest with which women have opportunities peculiar to themselves of becoming acquainted, and thus of benefiting their fellow creatures through the medium of their writings. But, after all, literature is not the natural channel for a woman's feelings; and pity, not envy, ought to be the

---

[1] *An able ... Mission* Sarah Lewis, whose *Woman's Mission*, a popular book on female conduct, was published in 1839.

[2] *distaff* Staff on which wool or flax was wound when spinning.

[3] *Parnassus* Mountain in Greece sacred to the Muses, the nine daughters of Zeus and Mnemosyne, each of whom presided over, and provided inspiration for, a different aspect of the arts and sciences.

meed[1] of her who writes for the public. How much of what with other women is reserved for the select and chosen intercourse of affection, with her must be laid bare to the coarse cavillings,[2] and coarser commendations, of amateur or professional critics. How much of what no woman loves to say, except to the listening ear of domestic affection, by her must be told—nay, blazoned—to the world. And then, in her season of depression, or of wounded feeling, when her spirit yearns to sit in solitude, or even in darkness, so that it may be still; to know and feel that the very essence of that spirit, now embodied in a palpable form, has become an article of sale and bargain, tossed over from the hands of one workman to another, free alike to the touch of the prince and the peasant, and no longer to be reclaimed at will by the original possessor, let the world receive it as it may.

Is such, I ask, an enviable distinction?

from Anonymous, "Hints on the Modern Governess System," *Fraser's Magazine,* November 1844

… To trace the growth of woman's desire after knowledge would be the task of a philosopher; for us, it suffices to see that it is, that is has been from all ages. The barter of Paradise for the means of knowledge is the first recorded act of woman's life; she tempted man to forego all tried blessings, for the untried boon of "knowing good and evil." Thenceforth, man wreaked his vengeance upon woman, for the loss of ease and plenty, by keeping her ignorant, and, consequently, helpless. But since the day that Christianity dawned on the world, an emancipation of the weak out of the power of the strong has been silently progressing. The faint cry, uplifted at intervals, swelled into a chorus; there was a sudden rush; all the world clamoured for a better education for women; no wonder, in such a struggle, that the greater number mistook chaff and husks[3] for bread. The movement was all too sudden. Education, in as far as it implies intellectual and moral growth, is the work of life; its operations are as secret and as self-derived as the gradual shooting of the green blade into the wheat-ear.

Now, when that cry of women after knowledge pierced the air, a thousand sprang up, mushroomwise, in a night, to answer it. Mothers who had only read their Bibles and receipt-books[4] found themselves unprepared for the emergency—we have so little patience, so little foresight. Then, teaching, that holy vocation of a woman, became a trade. An universal demand creates its own supply. Here was a tempting opening to all aspiring women, who were free to try a new field; the unmarried daughters of the gentry left with scanty portions had, till now, been content to eke out their small incomes in trade; many were the gentlewomen, in our great-grandmothers' days, who lived in honoured independence, though they kept small shops, to which their old friends resorted. They did not lose caste[5] because they sat for part of the day behind the counter. However, this refuge grew insecure from the outward pressure of public opinion in favour of refinement.… Many left their quiet homes for the school-rooms of halls and castles. As they mounted the stair, others came from a lower rank, and filled the vacant steps. The restless rage to push on had stirred all classes. Those who, disappointed in their new stand, looked wistfully back to the old, found that when they would return they could not. There was no place left for them but that which they had chosen. Like much else, it looked best from a distance. Here, then, was a whole class of women driven into a new line, for which they had received no fitting preparation.… The new generation, thirsting to be taught, found teachers at their mercy, hanging between two ranks. Do the weak desire to learn what they may expect from the strong? Let them ponder deeply the governess system of the present day. This was the watch-word, "Teach us on our own terms, or work, and cease to be gentlewomen." To the newly risen race of governesses, even such equivocal gentility was preferable to a second change, though it was to be gained at the price of isolation.…

---

[1]   *meed* Recompense; reward.

[2]   *cavillings* Unfair or petty fault-finding.

[3]   *chaff and husks* Material separated out from grains when threshing cereal crops.

[4]   *receipt-books* I.e., recipe books.

[5]   *lose caste* I.e., lose their position in society.

The policy of the world is to take advantage of want. It became apparent that a whole family of daughters might be taught by one of these single women, struggling for bread, for less than it formerly cost to send one girl to school. Where competition was so great, there was no difficulty in driving a bargain. The means of instruction might be had so cheaply that the grocer's daughters could be taught to read *Paul and Virginia* in the original tongue, and to strum *The Fall of Paris*.[1] In process of time, therefore, a governess became a necessary appanage[2] in every family.

Whether it be right or wrong, as a general rule, for mothers to delegate their most sacred trust to hired strangers, we are not here to discuss. The fact exists. Is the system carried out fairly for all parties? Is there any question astir as to its abuse? Philanthropic eyes are scanning many social evils. Is it yet considered how far a whole race of women are dragging out weary lives under a mass of trials, the detail of which would fill a "blue book"[3] by themselves? True, if the case were known, "a thousand voices" would be "uplifted."[4] The miseries of the governess may even swell that sickening clamour about the "rights of women," which would never have been raised had women been true to themselves. But that trite saying in this case has its point. The modern governess system is a case between woman and woman. Before one sex demands its due from the other, let it be just to itself.

Punch has ably pleaded in the cause of salaries and qualifications.[5] The statistics touching lunatic asylums give a frightful proportion of governesses in the list of the insane.[6] But has the whole life in home schoolrooms ever been investigated? We ask this with a real wish to be informed, with a hope of directing eyes to this unknown page of human life. Have kind, ladylike, cultivated women ever reflected on the relation which subsists between themselves and others of like minds, and, perhaps, formerly in similar circumstances? Have they ever tried to put themselves in the position of the young women devoting themselves to the education of their children, who yet live as strangers in the midst of homes? …

… When the lesson-books are closed, and the little ones have capered out of the school-room, what becomes of the teacher, who has not exchanged a thought or a word with any one of congenial mind all day? Hour after hour she has *bent down* her mind, and *raised* the children's to given points, which, however interesting, are exhausting. A young thing, perhaps, still herself, ready to spring up again at one kindly touch. Do not even fond mothers, who teach their own children, feel that after the labours of the day they need some interchange of *mind*? They have often felt refreshed when husband or friend has given them a new thought, or understood an articulated feeling, after the repression of the day, necessary in fulfilling the duty of teaching. Who is there that has not known the dryness of spending time with people of more limited capacities and interests than one's own? … Let mothers ask if they would not expect their own daughters to languish in spirits and energy, if they had no intercourse with older companions. Whilst the children are with their parents and their guests, the governess, quite as often as not, is expected to remain in the school-room, unless specially invited to join the circle. This is peculiarly the case in large establishments, where the school-room arrangements are distinct from the rest of the family. We believe that most young

---

[1] *Paul and Virginia*   The sentimental French novel *Paul et Virginie* (1787), by Jacques-Henri Bernadin de St. Pierre; *strum*   Play poorly on the piano; *The Fall of Paris*   Popular song of the period.

[2] *appanage*   Possession, perquisite.

[3] *blue book*   Parliamentary report.

[4] *a thousand … uplifted*   A reference to the epigraph of this article, from French novelist George Sand's collection of fictional letters, *Lettres à Marcie* (1837): "Society is full of abuses. Women complain of being brutally enslaved, badly brought up, badly educated, badly treated, and badly defended. All this is, unfortunately, true. These complaints are just, and do not doubt but that before long a thousand voices will be uplifted to remedy the evil."

[5] *Punch has … qualifications*   The satirical weekly magazine *Punch* had recently printed numerous articles advocating the improvement of conditions for governesses.

[6] *The statistics … insane*   During the early and mid nineteenth century it was a commonplace that governesses tended toward mental instability as a result of the stressful nature of their employment. While some statistics did show that there was a high percentage of governesses in asylums, this may have been due in part to the fact that private asylums sometimes provided the cheapest respectable accommodation for women without family or employment.

women of delicate perceptions would prefer their desolate apartment to feeling themselves clogs[1] upon the family party. But do people know what they are about when they leave young creatures alone, long evening after evening, following days of seclusion and exhaustion? Factory-girls, shop-women, teachers of accomplishments, return to their homes at night. The servants gather round the work-table or the hall-fire. Prisoners in gaol[2] may collect together in knots in their yards, look in each other's faces, hear the sound of human voices, tell their troubles and joys, and listen to their neighbours. Solitary confinement, even for felons, is reserved to punish some special offence. It is only the governess, and a certain class of private tutors, who must hear the echoes from the drawing-room and the offices, feeling that, in a house full of people, they dwell alone. Nervous irritability, dejection, loss of energy, are the inevitable results which follow a too solitary life in youth. Yet, without elasticity in her own frame, how can the governess be a fitting companion and teacher of such gay, volatile creatures as children—so easily cowed and spirit-broken by harshness or settled sadness in those who live with them? Would not querulous temper of depression of spirits in the governess be complained of by the parents? Do they consider, when they expect cheerfulness and an even composure of spirits from one fretted with children's restless waywardness, and chilled by the frosty indifference and neglect of the grown-up members of the family, that they ask an impossible thing?

from Harriet Taylor, *The Enfranchisement of Women* (1851)

When a prejudice, which has any hold on the feeling, finds itself reduced to the unpleasant necessity of assigning reasons, it thinks it has done enough when it has re-asserted the very point in the dispute, in phrases which appeal to the pre-existing feelings. Thus, many persons think they have sufficiently justified the restrictions on women's field of action when they have said that the pursuits from which women are excluded are *unfeminine*, and that the *proper sphere* of women is not politics or publicity, but private and domestic life.

We deny the right of any portion of the species to decide for another portion, or any individual for another individual, what is and what is not their "proper sphere." The proper sphere for all human beings is the largest and highest which they are able to attain to....

We shall follow the very proper convention, in not entering into the question of the alleged differences in physical or mental qualities between the sexes; not because we have nothing to say, but because we have too much.... But if those who assert that the "proper sphere" for women is the domestic, mean by this that they have not shown themselves qualified for any other, the assertion evinces great ignorance of life and of history. Women have shown fitness for the highest social functions, exactly in proportion as they have been admitted to them. By a curious anomaly, though ineligible to even the lowest offices of state, they are in some countries admitted to the highest of all, the regal; and if there is any one function for which they have shown a decided vocation, it is that of reigning....

Concerning the fitness, then, of women for politics, there can be no question: but the dispute is more likely to turn upon the fitness of politics for women. When the reasons alleged for excluding women from active life in all its higher departments are stripped of their garb of declamatory phrases, and reduced to the simple expression of a meaning, they seem to be mainly three: the incompatibility of active life with maternity and with the cares of a household; secondly, its alleged hardening effect on the character; and thirdly, the inexpediency of making an addition to the already excessive pressure of competition in every kind of professional or lucrative employment.

The first, the maternity argument, is usually laid most stress upon: although (it needs hardly be said) this reason, if it be one, can apply only to mothers. It is neither necessary nor just to make imperative on women that they shall be either mothers or nothing; or that if they have been mothers once, they shall be nothing else during the whole remainder of their lives. Neither women nor men need any law to exclude them from an

---

[1] *clogs* Encumbrances. Literally, blocks of wood attached to the leg or neck of a person or animal to prevent escape.

[2] *gaol* I.e., jail.

occupation if they have undertaken another which is incompatible with it. No one proposes to exclude the male sex from Parliament because a man may be a soldier or sailor in active service, or a merchant whose business requires all his time and energies. Nine-tenths of the occupations of men exclude them *de facto*[1] from public life, as effectually as if they were excluded by law; but that is no reason for making laws to exclude even the nine-tenths, much less the remaining tenth. The reason of the case is the same for women as for men. There is no need to make provision by law that a woman shall not carry on the active details of a household, or of the education of children, and at the same time practise a profession or be elected to Parliament. Where incompatibility is real, it will take care of itself: but there is gross injustice in making the incompatibility a pretence for the exclusion of those in whose case it does not exist. And these, if they were free to choose, would be a very large proportion. The maternity argument deserts its supporters in the case of single women, a large and increasing class of the population; a fact which, it is not irrelevant to remark, by tending to diminish the excessive competition of numbers, is calculated to assist greatly the prosperity of all. There is no inherent reason or necessity that all women should voluntarily choose to devote their lives to one animal function and its consequences. Numbers of women are wives and mothers only because there is no other career open to them, no other occupation for their feelings or their activities. Every improvement in their education, and enlargement of their faculties—everything which renders them more qualified for any other mode of life, increases the number of those to whom it is an injury and an oppression to be denied the choice. To say that women must be excluded from active life because maternity disqualifies them for it, is in fact to say that every other career should be forbidden them in order that maternity may be their only resource.

But secondly, it is urged that to give the same freedom of occupation to women as to men would be an injurious addition to the crowd of competitors, by whom the avenues to almost all kinds of employment are choked up, and its remuneration depressed. This argument, it is to be observed, does not reach the political question. It gives no excuse for withholding from women the rights of citizenship. The suffrage, the jury-box, admission to the legislature and to office, it does not touch. It bears only on the industrial branch of the subject. Allowing it, then, in an economical point of view, its full force; assuming that to lay open to women the employments now monopolized by men, would tend, like the breaking down of other monopolies, to lower the rate of remuneration in those employments; let us consider what is the amount of this evil consequence, and what the compensation for it. The worst ever asserted, much worse than is at all likely to be realized, is that if women competed with men, a man and a woman could not together earn more than is now earned by the man alone. Let us make this supposition, the most favourable supposition possible: the joint income of the two would be the same as before, while the woman would be raised from the position of a servant to that of a partner. Even if every woman, as matters now stand, had a claim on some man for support, how infinitely preferable is it that part of the income should be of the woman's earning, even if the aggregate sum were but little increased by it, rather than that she should be compelled to stand aside in order that men may be the sole earners, and the sole dispensers of what is earned. Even under the present laws respecting the property of women, a woman who contributes materially to the support of the family cannot be treated in the same contemptuously tyrannical manner as one who, however she may toil as a domestic drudge, is a dependent on the man for subsistence. As for the depression of wages by increase of competition, remedies will be found for it in time. Palliatives might be applied immediately; for instance, a more rigid exclusion of children from industrial employment, during the years in which they ought to be working only to strengthen their bodies and minds for after life. Children are necessarily dependent, and under the power of others; and their labour, being not for themselves but for the gain of their parents, is a proper subject for legislative regulation. With respect to the future, we neither believe that improvident multiplication, and the consequent excessive difficulty of gaining a subsistence, will always continue, nor that the division of mankind into capitalists and hired labourers, and the regulation

---

[1] *de facto* Latin: in reality; as a matter of fact.

of the reward of labourers mainly by demand and supply, will be for ever, or even much longer, the rule of the world. But so long as competition is the general law of human life, it is tyranny to shut out one half of the competitors. All who have attained the age of self-government have an equal claim to be permitted to sell whatever kind of useful labour they are capable of, for the price which it will bring.

The third objection to the admission of women to political or professional life, its alleged hardening tendency, belongs to an age now past, and is scarcely to be comprehended by people of the present time. There are still, however, persons who say that the world and its avocations render men selfish and unfeeling; that the struggles, rivalries, and collisions of business and of politics make them harsh and unamiable; that if half the species must unavoidably be given up to these things, it is the more necessary that the other half should be kept free from them; that to preserve women from the bad influences of the world is the only chance of preventing men from being wholly given up to them.

There would have been plausibility in this argument when the world was still in the age of violence; when life was full of physical conflict, and every man had to redress his injuries or those of others, by the sword or by the strength of his arm. Women, like priests, by being exempted from such responsibilities, and from some part of the accompanying dangers, may have been enabled to exercise a beneficial influence. But in the present condition of human life, we do not know where those hardening influences are to be found, to which men are subject and from which women are at present exempt. Individuals now-a-days are seldom called upon to fight hand to hand, even with peaceful weapons; personal enmities and rivalries count for little in worldly transactions; the general pressure of circumstances, not the adverse will of individuals, is the obstacle men now have to make head against. That pressure, when excessive, breaks the spirit, and cramps and sours the feelings, but not less of women than of men, since they suffer certainly not less from its evils. There are still quarrels and dislikes, but the sources of them are changed. The feudal chief once found his bitterest enemy in his powerful neighbour, the minister or courtier in his rival

for place: but opposition of interest in active life, as a cause of personal animosity, is out of date; the enmities of the present day arise not from great things but small, from what people say of one another, more than from what they do; and if there are hatred, malice, and all uncharitableness, they are to be found among women fully as much as among men. In the present state of civilization, the notion of guarding women from the hardening influences of the world could only be realized by secluding them from society altogether. The common duties of common life, as at present constituted, are incompatible with any other softness in women than weakness. Surely weak minds in weak bodies must ere long cease to be even supposed to be either attractive or amiable.

But, in truth, none of these arguments and considerations touch the foundations of the subject. The real question is, whether it is right and expedient that one half of the human race should pass through life in a state of forced subordination to the other half. If the best state of human society is that of being divided into two parts, one consisting of persons with a will and a substantive existence, the other of humble companions to these persons, attached, each of them to one, for the purpose of bringing up *his* children, and making *his* home pleasant to him; if this is the place assigned to women, it is but kindness to educate them for this; to make them believe that the greatest good fortune which can befall them is to be chosen by some man for this purpose; and that every other career which the world deems happy or honourable is closed to them by the law, not of social institutions, but of nature and destiny.

When, however, we ask why the existence of one-half the species should be merely ancillary to that of the other—why each woman should be a mere appendage to a man, allowed to have no interests of her own, that there may be nothing to compete in her mind with his interests and his pleasure; the only reason which can be given is, that men like it. It is agreeable to them that men should live for their own sake, women for the sake of men: and the qualities and conduct in subjects which are agreeable to rulers, they succeed for a long time in making the subjects themselves consider as their appropriate virtues.

from Coventry Patmore, *The Angel in the House*
(1854–56)

THE WIFE'S TRAGEDY

Man must be pleased; but him to please
    Is woman's pleasure; down the gulf
Of his condoled necessities
    She casts her best, she flings herself.
5 How often flings for nought! and yokes
    Her heart to an icicle or whim,
Whose each impatient word provokes
    Another, not from her, but him;
While she, too gentle even to force
10   His penitence by kind replies,
Waits by, expecting his remorse,
    With pardon in her pitying eyes;
And if he once, by shame oppressed,
    A comfortable word confers,
15 She leans and weeps against his breast,
    And seems to think the sin was hers;
And whilst his love has any life,
    Or any eye to see her charms,
At any time, she's still his wife,
20   Dearly devoted to his arms;
She loves with love that cannot tire;
    And when, ah woe, she loves alone,
Through passionate duty love flames higher,
    As grass grows taller round a stone....

THE FOREIGN LAND

A woman is a foreign land,
    Of which, though there he settle young
A man will ne'er quite understand
    The customs, politics, and tongue.
5 The foolish hie° them post-haste through,   *hasten*
    See fashions odd, and prospects fair,
Learn of the language, "How-d'ye do,"
    And go and brag that they've been there.
The most for leave to trade apply,
10   For once, at Empire's seat her heart,
Then get what knowledge ear and eye
    Glean chancewise in the life-long mart.°   *market*

And certain others few and fit,
    Attach them to the Court, and see
15 The country's best, its accent hit,
    And partly sound its polity.

from Eliza Lynn Linton, "The Girl of the Period,"
Saturday Review, March 1868

Time was when the stereotyped phrase "a fair young English girl" meant the ideal of womanhood, to us, at least, of home birth and breeding. It meant a creature generous, capable, and modest; something franker than a Frenchwoman, more to be trusted than an Italian, as brave as an American but more refined, as domestic as a German and more graceful. It meant a girl who could be trusted alone if need be, because of the innate purity and dignity of her nature, but who was neither bold in bearing nor masculine in mind; a girl who, when she married, would be her husband's friend and companion, but never his rival; one who would consider their interests identical, and not hold him as just so much fair game for spoil; who would make his house his true home and place of rest, not a mere passage-place for vanity and ostentation to go through; a tender mother, an industrious housekeeper, a judicious mistress. We prided ourselves as a nation on our women. We thought we had the pick of creation in this fair young English girl of ours, and envied no other men their own.... This was in the old time, and when English girls were content to be what God and nature had made them. Of late years we have changed the pattern, and have given to the world a race of women as utterly unlike the old insular ideal as if we had created another nation altogether. The girl of the period and the fair young English girl of the past have nothing in common save ancestry and their mother-tongue; and even of this last the modern version makes almost a new language, through the copious additions it has received from the current slang of the day.

    The girl of the period is a creature who dyes her hair and paints her face, as the first articles of her personal religion; whose sole idea of life is plenty of fun and luxury; and whose dress is the object of such thought

"THE ANGEL IN 'THE HOUSE;'" OR, THE RESULT OF FEMALE SUFFRAGE.
(A Troubled Dream of the Future.)

A satirical representation of the female suffragette, here having gained the vote and a position of political power, speaking in the House of Commons. She is knitting a "blue stocking," an allusion to the term "bluestocking," a derogatory term that began to be applied to free-thinking women in the eighteenth century.

and intellect as she possesses. Her main endeavour in this is to outvie her neighbours in the extravagance of fashion. No matter whether, as in the time of crinolines, she sacrificed decency, or, as now, in the time of trains, she sacrifices cleanliness; no matter either, whether she makes herself a nuisance and an inconvenience to every one she meets. The girl of the period has done away with such moral muffishness[1] as consideration for others, or regard for counsel and rebuke. It was all very well in old-fashioned times, when fathers and mothers had some authority and were treated with respect, to be tutored and made to obey, but she is far too fast and flourishing to be stopped in mid-career by these slow old morals; and as she dresses to please herself, she does not care if she displeases everyone else. Nothing is too extraordinary and nothing too exaggerated for her vitiated[2] taste; and things which in themselves would be useful reforms if let alone become monstrosities worse than those which they have displaced so soon as she begins to manipulate and improve. If a sensible fashion

---

[1]   *muffishness* Foolishness, often describing someone or something seen as old-fashioned.

[2]   *vitiated* Corrupted.

lifts the gown out of the mud, she raises hers midway to her knee. If the absurd structure of wire and buckram, once called a bonnet, is modified to something that shall protect the wearer's face without putting out the eyes of her companion, she cuts hers down to four straws and a rosebud, or a tag of lace and a bunch of glass beads! ... She has blunted the fine edges of feeling so much that she cannot understand why she should be condemned for an imitation of form which does not include imitation of fact; she cannot be made to see that modesty of appearance and virtue ought to be inseparable, and that no good girl can afford to appear bad, under penalty of receiving the contempt awarded to the bad.

This imitation of the *demi-monde*[1] in dress leads to something in manner and feeling, not quite so pronounced perhaps, but far too like to be honourable to herself or satisfactory to her friends. It leads to slang, bold talk, and fastness; to the love of pleasure and indifference to duty; to the desire of money before either love or happiness; to uselessness at home, dissatisfaction with the monotony of ordinary life, and horror of all useful work; in a word, to the worst forms of luxury and selfishness, to the most fatal effects arising from want of high principle and absence of tender feeling.... No one can say of the modern English girl that she is tender, loving, retiring, or domestic. The old fault so often found by keen-sighted Frenchwomen, that she was so fatally *romanesque*,[2] so prone to sacrifice appearances and social advantages for love, will never be set down to the girl of the period. Love indeed is the last thing she thinks of, and the least of the dangers besetting her. Love in a cottage, that seductive dream which used to vex the heart and disturb the calculations of prudent mothers, is now a myth of past ages. The legal barter of herself for so much money, representing so much dash, so much luxury and pleasure—that is her idea of marriage; the only idea worth entertaining. For all seriousness of thought respecting the duties or the consequences of marriage, she has not a trace. If children come, they find but a stepmother's cold welcome from her; and if her husband thinks that he has married

anything that is to belong to him—a *tacens et placens uxor*[3] pledged to make him happy—the sooner he wakes from his hallucination and understands that he has simply married someone who will condescend to spend his money on herself, and who will shelter her indiscretions behind the shield of his name, the less severe will be his disappointment. She has married his house, his carriage, his balance at the bankers, his title; and he himself is just the inevitable condition clogging the wheel of her fortune; at best an adjunct, to be tolerated with more or less patience as may chance. For it is only the old-fashioned sort, not girls of the period *pur sang*,[4] that marry for love, or put the husband before the banker. But she does not marry easily. Men are afraid of her; and with reason. They may amuse themselves with her of an evening, but they do not take her readily for life....

The marvel, in the present fashion of life among women, is how it holds its ground in spite of the disapprobation of men. It used to be an old-time notion that the sexes were made for each other, and that it was only natural for them to please each other, and to set themselves out for that end. But the girl of the period does not please men. She pleases them as little as she elevates them; and how little she does that, the class of women she has taken as her models of itself testifies. All men whose opinion is worth having prefer the simple and genuine girl of the past, with her tender little ways and pretty bashful modesties, to this loud and rampant modernization, with her false red hair and painted skin, talking slang as glibly as a man, and by preference leading the conversation to doubtful subjects. She thinks she is piquante[5] and exciting when she thus makes herself the bad copy of a worse original; and she will not see that though men laugh with her they do not respect her, though they flirt with her they do not marry her; she will not believe that she is not the kind of thing they want, and that she is acting against nature and her own interests when she disregards their advice and offends their taste. We do not see how she makes out her account, viewing her life from any side; but all we can

---

[1] *demi-monde* French: literally, "half world"; figuratively, the world existing below the level of respectable society. The term was often used to denote the world of the courtesan.

[2] *romanesque* French: romantic.

[3] *tacens ... uxor* Latin: silent and pleasing wife.

[4] *pur sang* French: pure-blooded.

[5] *piquante* Stimulating.

do is to wait patiently until the national madness has passed, and our women have come back again to the old English ideal, once the most beautiful, the most modest, the most essentially womanly in the world.

from Frances Power Cobbe, "Criminals, Idiots, Women, and Minors," *Fraser's Magazine*, December 1868

There was an allegory rather popular about thirty years ago, whose manifest purpose was to impress on the juvenile mind that tendency which Mr. Matthew Arnold has ingeniously designated "Hebraism."[1] The hero of the tale descends upon earth from some distant planet, and is conducted by a mundane cicerone[2] through one of our great cities, where he beholds the docks and arsenals, the streets and marts, the galleries of art, and the palaces of royalty. The visitor admires everything till he happens to pass a graveyard. "What is that gloomy spot?" he asks of his companion. "It is a cemetery," replies the guide.

"A—what did you say?" inquires the son of the star.

"A graveyard; a place of public interment; where we bury our dead," reiterates the cicerone.

The visitor, pale with awe and terror, learns at last that there is in this world such a thing as *Death*, and (as he is forbidden to return to his own planet) he resolves to dedicate every moment left to him to prepare himself for that fearful event and all that may follow it.

Had that visitor heard for the first time upon his arrival on earth of another incident of human existence—namely, *Marriage*, it may be surmised that his astonishment and awe would also have been considerable. To his eager inquiry whether men and women earnestly strove to prepare themselves for so momentous an occurrence, he would have received the puzzling reply that women frequently devoted themselves with perfectly Hebraistic singleness of aim to that special purpose; but that men, on the contrary, very rarely

included any preparation for the married state among the items of their widest Hellenistic culture. But this anomaly would be trifling compared to others which would be revealed to him. "Ah," we can hear him say to his guide as they pass into a village church. "What a pretty sight is this! What is happening to that sweet young woman in white who is giving her hand to the good-looking fellow beside her, all the company decked in holiday attire, and the joy-bells shaking the old tower overhead? She is receiving some great honour, is she not? The Prize of Virtue, perhaps?"

"Oh, yes," would reply the friend; "an honour certainly. She is being Married." After a little further explanation the visitor would pursue his inquiry:

"Of course, having entered this honourable state of matrimony, she has some privilege above the women who are not chosen by anybody? I notice her husband has just said, 'With all my worldly goods I thee endow.' Does that mean that she will henceforth have the control of his money altogether, or only that he takes her into partnership?"

"*Pas précisément*,[3] my dear sir. By our law it is *her* goods and earnings, present and future, which belong to him from this moment."

"You don't say so? But then, of course, his goods are hers also?"

"Oh dear, no! not at all. He is only bound to find her food; and truth to tell, not very strictly or efficaciously bound to do that."

"How! do I understand you? Is it possible that here in the most solemn religious act, which I perceive your prayer book calls 'The Solemnisation of Holy Matrimony,' every husband makes a generous promise, which promise is not only a mockery, but the actual reverse and parody of the real state of the case: the man who promises giving nothing, and the woman who is silent giving all?"

"Well, yes; I suppose that is something like it, as to the letter of the law. But then, of course, practically—"

"Practically, I suppose few men can really be so unmanly and selfish as the law warrants them in being. Yet some, I fear, may avail themselves of such authority. May I ask another question? As you subject women who enter the marriage state to such very severe penalties as

---

[1] *Hebraism* Originally denoting an attribute of the Hebrew people, the term was used by Arnold to describe a moral (rather than intellectual) theory of life. Arnold used the term "Hellenistic," in contrast, to denote the intellectual culture or way of life typified by the ancient Greeks.

[2] *cicerone* Guide.

[3] *Pas précisément* French: not exactly.

this, what worse have you in store for women who lead a dissolute life, to the moral injury of the community?"

"Oh, the law takes nothing from them. Whatever they earn or inherit is their own. They are able, also, to sue the fathers of their children for their maintenance, which a wife, of course, is not allowed to do on behalf of *her* little ones, because she and her husband are one in the eye of the law."

"One question still further—your criminals? Do they always forfeit their entire property on conviction?"

"Only for the most heinous crimes; felony and murder, for example."

"Pardon me; I must seem to you so stupid! Why is the property of the woman who commits Murder, and the property of the woman who commits Matrimony, dealt with alike by your law?"

Leaving our little allegory and in sober seriousness, we must all admit that the just and expedient treatment of women by men is one of the most obscure problems, alike of equity and of policy. Nor of women only, but of all classes and races of human beings whose condition is temporarily or permanently one of comparative weakness and dependence....

By the common law of England a married woman has no legal existence, so far as property is concerned, independently of her husband. The husband and wife are assumed to be one person, and that person is the husband. The wife can make no contract, and can neither sue nor be sued. Whatever she possess of personal property at the time of her marriage, or whatever she may afterwards earn or inherit, belongs to her husband, without control on her part.... If she possess real estate, so long as her husband lives he receives and spends the income derived from it, being only forbidden to sell it without her consent. From none of her property is he bound to reserve anything, or make any provision for her maintenance or that of her children. This is the law for all, but practically it affects only two classes of women, *viz.*[1] those who marry hurriedly or without proper advisers, and those whose property at the time of marriage is too small to permit of the expense of a settlement; in other words, the whole middle and lower ranks of women, and a certain portion of the upper ranks. Women of the richer class, with proper advisers, never come under the provisions of the Common Law, being carefully protected therefrom by an intricate system elaborated for the purpose by the courts of Equity, to which the victims of the Common Law have for years applied for redress. That system always involves considerable legal expenses, and an arrangement with trustees which is often extremely inconvenient and injurious to the interests of the married couple; nevertheless it is understood to be so great a boon that none who can afford to avail themselves of it fail to do so.

What then is the principle on which the Common Law mulcts[2] the poorer class of women of their property and earnings, and entails on the rich, if they wish to evade it, the costs and embarrassment of a marriage settlement? There is, of course, a principle in it, and one capable of clear statement. There are grounds for the law; first of Justice, then of Expediency, lastly (and as we believe) most influential of all, of Sentiment.

First, the grounds of Justice.

Man is the natural bread-winner. Woman lives by the bread which man has earned. Ergo, it is fit and right that the man who wins should have absolute disposal, not only of his winnings, but of every other small morsel or fraction of earning or property she may possess. It is a fair return to him for his labour in the joint interests of both.... The woman's case is that of a pauper who enters a workhouse. The ratepayers are bound to support him; but if he have any savings they must be given up to the board. HE cannot claim support and keep independent property.

Then for Expediency. "How can two walk together except they be agreed?" says the Bible. "How can they walk together except one of them have it all his own way?" says the voice of rough and ready practicality. Somebody must rule in a household, or everything will go to rack and ruin; and disputes will be endless. If somebody is to rule it can only be the husband, who is wiser, stronger, knows more of the world, and in any case has not the slightest intention of yielding his predominance. But to give a man such rule he must be allowed to keep the purse. Nothing but the power of the

---

[1] *viz.* Latin: namely; that is to say (an abbreviation of *videlicet*).

[2] *mulcts* Swindles.

purse—in default of the stick—can permanently and thoroughly secure authority....

Lastly, for the sentimental view. How painful is the notion of a wife holding back her money from him who is every day toiling for her support! How fair is the ideal picture of absolute concession on her part of all she possesses of this world's dross to the man to whom she gives her heart and life!... The young man and maiden, after years of affection, and carefully laying by of provision for the event, take each other at last, to be henceforth no more twain, but one flesh. Both have saved a little money, but it now belongs to the husband alone. He lays it out in the purchase of a cottage where they are henceforth to dwell. Day by day he goes forth to his labour, and weekly he brings home his earnings and places them in his wife's lap, bidding her spend them as she knows best for the supply of their homely board, their clothing which her deft fingers will make and many a time repair, and last for their common treasures, the little children who gather around them. Thus they grow old in unbroken peace and love, the man's will having never once been disputed, the wide yielding alike from choice and from necessity to his superior sense and his legal authority.

Surely this idea of life, for which the Common Law of England has done its utmost to provide, is well worth the pondering before we attempt to meddle with any of its safeguards? Who will suggest anything better in its room?

Alas, there are other scenes besides idylls of domestic peace and obedience promoted by the laws we are considering....

The existing Common Law is not *Just*, because it neither can secure nor actually even attempts to secure for the woman the equivalent support for whose sake she is forced to relinquish her property.

It is not *Expedient*, because while in happy marriages it is superfluous and useless, in unhappy ones it becomes highly injurious; often causing the final ruin of a family which the mother (if upheld by law) might have supported single-handed. It is also shown not to be considered expedient by the conduct of the entire upper class of the country, and even of the legislature itself in the system of the Court of Chancery. Where no one who can afford to evade the law fails to evade it, the pretence that it is believed to be generally expedient is absurd. Further, the classes which actually evade it, and the countries where it is non-existing, show in no degree less connubial harmony than those wherein it is enforced.

Lastly, it does not tend to fulfil, but to counteract, the *Sentiment* regarding the marriage union, to which it aims to add the pressure of force. Real unanimity is not produced between two parties by forbidding one of them to have any voice at all. The hard mechanical contrivance of the law for making husband and wife of one heart and mind is calculated to produce a precisely opposite result.

from "Between School and Marriage," *The Girl's Own Paper*, Vol. 7 (4 September 1886)

This time in a girl's life corresponds to that in a man's which is passed in a university, or in learning the work of his profession. Too many girls look on it as a *mauvais quart d'heure*,[1] which may be dawdled through in an irresponsible way until they have a house of their own. Marriage represents a home, a position; sometimes even less than that—a trousseau,[2] or a wedding tour. So they hasten through the years of adolescence as well as may be in order to reach the end of a wearisome task.

And yet if the girl is mother to the woman—that is to say, if the woman will be what the girl now is, this time, which is essentially one for settling habits, cannot be anything less than the most important in life. If the girl spend it in thoughtless idleness and discontented trifling, the result will be seen in the character of the woman. It is well for any of us when our work is cut out for us, so to speak, and we have not to look about for a profitable way of passing the time; but this last is the miserable condition of many girls belonging to daughter-full houses in easy circumstances. What can they do between school and marriage?

When the financial resources of her father are slender, a girl is quite right to seek for some employment by which she may earn her own living, and

---

[1]   *mauvais quart d'heure*   French: an unpleasant time (literally, an unpleasant quarter of an hour), from the French expression "*passer un mauvais quart d'heure*," meaning "to have a bad time of it."

[2]   *trousseau*   A bride's collection of clothing and linens.

The Girl's Own Paper, sold weekly for a penny, was mainly marketed to working- and middle-class women, but it was read by women from all classes and age groups and soon after its founding reached a circulation of over 250,000.

perhaps help her brothers and sisters; but when this is not the case, let no feeling of quixotic restlessness induce her to rashly leave home. It may be her plain duty to remain at home, and she may be independent and pay her way quite as much as one who earns and pays current coin. She can pay her way by filling in the little spaces in home life as only a dear daughter can, by lifting the weight of care from her mother, and by slipping in a soft word or a smile where it is like oil on the troubled waters of a father's spirit. What better remuneration can a father have for his expenditure upon his daughters than their laughter, good humour, and sympathy?...

from Emma Brewer, "Our Friends the Servants," *The Girl's Own Paper*, Vol. 14 (25 March 1893)

Among mistresses who earnestly desire the welfare of their servants there is no question which causes more trouble and anxiety than that of allowing visitors in the kitchen, men visitors especially. It is indeed a difficult question, and cannot be solved for every one alike.

I know several ladies who have thought it right that such of their maids as were engaged should be permitted to receive their sweethearts from time to time in the kitchen; but in every case where this has been granted that has come under my notice, the results have been so disastrous as to necessitate the withdrawal of the privilege. It was found utterly destructive of harmony in the kitchen, and gave no real pleasure to anyone. In some cases the fickle men forsook their old love in favour of some younger and more attractive of the fellow-servants, and it is not difficult to imagine the bitterness, anger, and sharp words which became the fashion after such faithlessness.

In others the sweethearts borrowed money of all the foolish girls in order to lay it upon horses in which they were interested; in others, where more stimulant had been taken than was good for them, they have boasted among other men of the beautiful silver, etc., in the houses where their young women lived, with what results may be guessed.

In simple fairness the privilege cannot be granted to one without extending it to all; this, in many houses, would fill the kitchens of an evening; for no maid would acknowledge that she had no young man, and would get one on the spot without considering his character, and such a one would scarcely add to the safety or morality of the kitchen....

There are a few things in the relationship between mistress and maid which distress me greatly, because I know they are utterly destructive of home-peace and comfort; one is a mistress reproving her servant in public, another is a maid answering her mistress rudely, and a third is a mistress finding fault with servants out of the room to one who is waiting in the room.

No good servant would endure the first nor be guilty of the second, but one and all are evil in their result, and it is easy to see that, let the fault be what it may, it cannot be remedied in this fashion.

Servants have feelings to be wounded and rights to be respected, and when these are ignored they feel that their occupation is compromising to their respectability and freedom.

We lose many good servants in this way, and get in their place large importations of very inferior ones from the Continent. It gives one a feeling of sadness that while the mother country stands in increased need of good and trustworthy servants, she cannot retain them or make friends of them, but has to look on while her colonies attract those she herself would so gladly keep.

I do not know if all are aware that every month ships leave England with a number of servants on board; indeed, as many as fourteen vessels go over to Queensland alone, carrying, on an average, two hundred servants on each ship. Any young woman with good health and good character can get a free passage to Queensland if she is under thirty-five years of age. This colony, even above others, values highly our friends the servants, whose success is undoubted. They try to live up to the high opinion formed of them, but it is grievous to see them leaving the old country which wants them even more than the colonies.

from Sarah Grand, "The New Aspect of the Woman Question," *North American Review* 158 (March 1894)

… What [the new woman] perceived at the outset was the sudden and violent upheaval of the suffering sex in all parts of the world. Women were awakening from their long apathy, and, as they woke, like healthy hungry children unable to articulate, they began to whimper for they knew not what. They might have been easily satisfied at that time had not society, like an ill-conditioned and ignorant nurse, instead of finding out what they lacked, shaken them and beaten them and stormed at them until what was once a little wail became convulsive shrieks and roused up the whole human household. Then man, disturbed by the uproar, came upstairs all anger and irritation, and, without waiting to learn what was the matter, added his own old theories to the din, but, finding they did not act rapidly, formed new ones, and made an intolerable nuisance of himself with his opinions and advice. He was in the state of one who cannot comprehend because he has no faculty to perceive the thing in question, and that is why he was so positive. The dimmest perception that you may be mistaken will save you from making an ass of yourself.

We must look upon man's mistakes, however, with some leniency, because we are not blameless in the matter ourselves. We have allowed him to arrange the whole social system and manage or mismanage it all these ages without ever seriously examining his work with a view to considering whether his abilities or motives were sufficiently good to qualify him for the task. We have listened without a smile to his preachments, about our place in life and all we are good for, on the text that "there is no understanding a woman." We have endured most poignant misery for his sins, and screened him when we should have exposed him and had him punished. We have allowed him to exact all things of us, and have been content to accept the little he grudgingly gave us in return. We have meekly bowed our heads when he called us bad names instead of demanding proofs of the superiority which alone would give him a right to do so. We have listened much edified to man's sermons on the subject of virtue, and have acquiesced uncomplainingly in the convenient arrangement by which this quality has come to be altogether practised for him by us vicariously. We have seen him set up Christ as an example for all men to follow, which argues his belief in the possibility of doing so, and have not only allowed his weakness and hypocrisy in the matter to pass without comment, but, until lately, have not even seen the humor of his pretensions when contrasted with his practices, nor held him up to that wholesome ridicule which is a stimulating corrective. Man deprived us of all proper education, and then jeered at us because we had no knowledge. He narrowed our outlook on life so that our view of it should be all distorted, and then declared that our mistaken impression of it proved us to be senseless creatures. He cramped our minds so that there was no room for reason in them, and then made merry at our want of logic. Our divine intuition was not to be controlled by him, but he did his best to damage it by sneering at it as an inferior feminine method of arriving at conclusions; and finally, after having had his own way until he lost his head completely, he set himself up as a sort of god and required us to worship him, and to our eternal shame be it said, we did so. The truth has all along been in us, but we have cared more for man than for truth, and so the whole human race has suffered. We have failed of our effect by neglecting our duty here, and have deserved much of the obloquy that was cast upon us. All that is over now, however, and while on the one hand man has shrunk to his true proportions in our estimation, we, on the other, have been expanding to our own; and now we come confidently forward to maintain, not that this or that was "intended," but that there are in ourselves, in both sexes, possibilities hitherto suppressed or abused, which, when properly developed, will supply to either what is lacking in the other.

The man of the future will be better, while the woman will be stronger and wiser. To bring this about is the whole aim and object of the present struggle, and with the discovery of the means lies the solution of the Woman Question. Man, having no conception of himself as imperfect from the woman's point of view, will find this difficult to understand, but we know his weakness, and will be patient with him, and help him with his lesson. It is the woman's place and pride and pleasure to teach the child, and man morally is in his infancy. There have been times when there was a doubt as to whether he was to be raised or woman was to be lowered, but we have turned that corner at last; and now woman holds out a strong hand to the child-man, and insists, but with infinite tenderness and pity, upon helping him up....

from Mona Caird, "Does Marriage Hinder A Woman's Self-Development?" *Lady's Realm*, March 1899

Perhaps it might throw some light on the question whether marriage interferes with a woman's self-development and career, if we were to ask ourselves honestly how a man would fare in the position, say, of his own wife.

We will take a mild case, so as to avoid all risk of exaggeration.

Our hero's wife is very kind to him. Many of his friends have far sadder tales to tell. Mrs. Brown is fond of her home and family. She pats the children on the head when they come down to dessert, and plies them with chocolate creams, much to the detriment of their health; but it amuses Mrs. Brown. Mr. Brown superintends the bilous[1] attacks, which the lady attributes to other causes. As she never finds fault with the children, and generally remonstrates with their father, in a good-natured way, when *he* does so, they are devoted to the indulgent parent, and are inclined to regard the other as second-rate....

John's faded cheeks, the hollow lines under the eyes, and hair out of curl, speak of the struggle for existence as it penetrates to the fireside. If Sophia but knew what it meant to keep going the multitudinous details and departments of a household!...

If incessant vigilance, tact, firmness, foresight, initiative, courage and judgment—in short, all the qualities required for governing a kingdom, and more—have made things go smoothly, the wife takes it as a matter of course; if they go wrong, she naturally lays the blame on the husband. In the same way, if the children are a credit to their parents, that is only as it should be. But if they are naughty, and fretful, and stupid, and untidy, is it not clear that there must be some serious flaw in the system which could produce such results in the offspring of Mrs. Brown? What word in the English language is too severe to describe the man who neglects to watch with sufficient vigilance over his children's health and moral training, who fails to see that his little boys' sailor-suits and knickerbockers are in good repair, that their bootlace ends do not fly out from their ankles at every step, that their hair is not like a hearth-brush, that they do not come down to dinner every day with dirty hands?

To every true man, the cares of fatherhood and home are sacred and all-sufficing. He realizes, as he looks around at his little ones, that they are his crown and recompense.

John often finds that *his* crown-and-recompense gives him a racking headache by war-whoops and

---

[1] *bilous* Angry, peevish.

stampedes of infinite variety, and there are moments when he wonders in dismay if he is really a true man! He has had the privilege of rearing and training five small crowns and recompenses, and he feels that he could face the future if further privilege, of this sort, were denied him. Not but that he is devoted to his family. Nobody who understands the sacrifices he has made for them could doubt that. Only, he feels that those parts of his nature which are said to distinguish the human from the animal kingdom are getting rather effaced.

He remembers the days before his marriage, when he was so bold, in his ignorant youth, as to cherish a passion for scientific research. He even went so far as to make a chemical laboratory of the family box-room, till attention was drawn to the circumstance by a series of terrific explosions, which shaved off his eyebrows, blackened his scientific countenance, and caused him to be turned out, neck and crop, with his crucibles, and a sermon on the duty that lay nearest him.... His own bent, however, has always been so painfully strong that he even yet tries to snatch spare moments for his researches; but the strain in so many directions has broken down his health. People always told him that a man's constitution was not fitted for severe brain-work. He supposes it is true....

John still hoped, after twenty years of experience, that presently, by some different arrangement, some better management on his part, he would achieve leisure and mental repose to do the work that his heart was in; but that time never came.

No doubt John was not infallible, and made mistakes in dealing with his various problems: do the best of us achieve consummate wisdom? No doubt, if he had followed the advice that we could all have supplied him with, in such large quantities, he might have done rather more than he did. But the question is: Did his marriage interfere with his self-development and career, and would many other Johns, in his circumstances, have succeeded much better?

Elizabeth Barrett Browning
1806 – 1861

Once considered for the position of poet laureate of England, Elizabeth Barrett Browning was a highly renowned poet in her day, admired by contemporaries such as Wordsworth and Dickinson, critics, and the general public alike. Her poetry fell out of fashion in the first half of the twentieth century, but Barrett Browning began to be lauded once again in the past generation, particularly for her long narrative poem *Aurora Leigh*. Best known among the general public for the romantic vision of her *Sonnets from the Portuguese* ("How do I love thee? Let me count the ways" from "Sonnet XLII" is one of the most famous lines in English literature), Barrett Browning also addressed significant moral and political issues in her work.

Elizabeth Barrett was the eldest of twelve children born to a wealthy plantation-owning family in Durham, England. Just prior to her birth her parents, Edward Barrett Moulton-Barrett and Mary Graham Clarke Moulton-Barrett, moved from their slave plantation in Jamaica to raise a family in England. The young Barrett grew up in the sheltered environment of a country manor called Hope End, learning languages and studying the classics, at a time when a young woman's education was typically restricted to the domestic sphere. An exceptional and intellectually voracious student, Barrett learned Latin, Greek, and French from her brothers' tutors and studied philosophical, historical, and religious works on her own. She had read Milton's *Paradise Lost* by the time she was 10 years old and, encouraged by her parents, anonymously published her first poem, an epic entitled *The Battle of Marathon*, a few years later. In 1826, she published *An Essay on Mind and Other Poems*. In 1833 she published her translation from the Greek of Aeschylus's *Prometheus Unbound*; she also included some of her own poems in the volume.

Due to the abolition of slavery, the Barretts' fortune began to wane, and in 1832 they were required to sell Hope End, eventually moving to Wimpole Street in London. Her father was overly protective of his children, however, and Barrett fell into semi-seclusion within the family home; her seclusion was compounded by illnesses that had begun to plague her when she was about 12 years old. Critics speculate as to the name of those illnesses, but there is evidence to suggest that Barrett may have suffered from tuberculosis and possibly from a spinal injury. Her maladies were no doubt exacerbated by the opiates prescribed by doctors and the depression that followed the accidental death of her beloved brother Edward, who had accompanied her while she recuperated in the south of England. This tragedy, and Barrett's subsequent feelings of anguish and guilt, inspired some of her best-known poems, including the elegiac sonnet "Grief."

Much has been written about Barrett's middle years, but the image of the bed-ridden recluse remains somewhat at odds with the prolific reader and writer who wrote poetry, essays, reviews, and criticism for magazines and journals and published *The Seraphim and Other Poems* in 1838. The two-volume collection of her *Poems* published in 1844 contains some of her most politically-charged poetry, including "The Cry of the Children," which condemned the employment of children in factories. During these years, Barrett kept up an active correspondence with many writers, critics, and artists and accepted occasional visitors in the confines of her family home. It was in this way that she met Robert Browning, who called upon her after the 1844 collection appeared. He visited her after first writing to express his admiration for work that had already made Barrett famous in England and was rapidly gaining recognition in the United States.

The subsequent exchange of 574 letters between Barrett and Browning, six years her junior, and their eventual elopement have received much attention, with some suggesting that Barrett Browning's best work was inspired by this passionate relationship. It is worth noting here that she had already begun to write love poetry, having translated Petrarch's sonnets and written her own before she met Browning. There is no doubt, however, that the force of their relationship inspired some of her most enduring work, notably her famous *Sonnets from the Portuguese*, written during her courtship with Browning and published in 1850. "My little Portuguese," an allusion to her dark skin, was Browning's pet name for his wife.

Her 1846 marriage to Browning and their ensuing life together in Italy were a boon to Barrett Browning's health and her work. Her beloved father, however, who had forbidden his children to marry, refused to speak to or see his daughter again, going so far as to return her letters unopened. In 1849 the Brownings' only child, Robert Wiedemann Barrett Browning (nicknamed "Pen"), was born in Casa Guidi, just outside Florence.

Not long after the publication of *Sonnets*, Barrett Browning published *Casa Guidi Windows*, which promoted the cause of *Risorgimento*, the Italian struggle for unification and independence from foreign domination (the subject also of many of the later *Poems before Congress*). In 1850, she published the abolition poem "The Runaway Slave at Pilgrim's Point," one of the great dramatic monologues and political-protest poems written in English in the nineteenth century. Barrett Browning's comment on Harriet Beecher Stowe's *Uncle Tom's Cabin* summarizes her consistent response to critics who questioned her choice of subjects: "… is it possible you think a woman has no business with questions like the question of slavery? Then she had better use a pen no more. She had better subside into slavery and concubinage herself, I think, as in the times of old, shut herself up with the Penelopes in the 'women's apartment,' and take no rank among thinkers and speakers." The 1856 work *Aurora Leigh* further cemented Barrett Browning's immense popularity, even though its subject matter was deemed scandalous by many at the time. Coventry Patmore, Victorian author of *The Angel in the House*, a book of poems lauding feminine domestic virtues, was among those who attacked Barrett Browning's candor and audacity in *Aurora Leigh*. An ambitious, epic poem, *Aurora Leigh* is narrated in nine books of blank verse and is the zenith of Barrett Browning's life work, encompassing her convictions on desire, power, art, love, romance, race, class structures, and the subjugation of women. The independent and progressive heroine of the books is named in part after Barrett Browning's idol, French writer Georges Sand (née Aurore Dupin), known for her liberal, feminist views and her penchant for wearing men's clothing. Like Sand, and also like Barrett Browning herself, Aurora Leigh is a writer, one who questions her identity as both artist and woman and struggles to achieve independence from subjugation by staid societal mores and manners and yet still preserve the ability to attain love and companionship.

Elizabeth Barrett Browning predeceased her husband by 28 years when she passed away in his arms in 1861; she is buried in the Protestant cemetery in Florence.

⌘ ⌘ ⌘

The Cry of the Children[1]

"Φεῦ, φεῦ, τί προσδέρκεσθέ μ' ὄμμασιν, τέκνα;" —Medea.[2]

1

Do ye hear the children weeping, O my brothers,
    Ere the sorrow comes with years?
They are leaning their young heads against their mothers,
    And *that* cannot stop their tears.
5 The young lambs are bleating in the meadows,
    The young birds are chirping in the nest,
The young fawns are playing with the shadows,
    The young flowers are blowing toward the west—
But the young, young children, O my brothers,
10   They are weeping bitterly!
They are weeping in the playtime of the others,
    In the country of the free.

2

Do you question the young children in the sorrow
    Why their tears are falling so?
15 The old man may weep for his tomorrow
    Which is lost in Long Ago;
The old tree is leafless in the forest,
    The old year is ending in the frost,
The old wound, if stricken, is the sorest,
20   The old hope is hardest to be lost.
But the young, young children, O my brothers,
    Do you ask them why they stand
Weeping sore before the bosoms of their mothers,
    In our happy Fatherland?

3

25 They look up with their pale and sunken faces,
    And their looks are sad to see,
For the man's hoary anguish draws and presses
    Down the cheeks of infancy.
"Your old earth," they say, "is very dreary;

30 Our young feet," they say, "are very weak!
Few paces have we taken, yet are weary—
    Our grave rest is very far to seek.
Ask the aged why they weep, and not the children;
    For the outside earth is cold;
35 And we young ones stand without, in our
        bewildering,
    And the graves are for the old."

4

"True," say the children, "it may happen
    That we die before our time;
Little Alice died last year—her grave is shapen
40   Like a snowball, in the rime.
We looked into the pit prepared to take her:
    Was no room for any work in the close clay!
From the sleep wherein she lieth none will wake her,
    Crying, 'Get up, little Alice! it is day.'
45 If you listen by that grave, in sun and shower,
    With your ear down, little Alice never cries;
Could we see her face, be sure we should not know her,
    For the smile has time for growing in her eyes:
And merry go her moments, lulled and stilled in
50   The shroud by the kirk° chime.   *church*
It is good when it happens," say the children,
    "That we die before our time."

5

Alas, alas, the children! they are seeking
    Death in life, as best to have;
55 They are binding up their hearts away from breaking,
    With a cerement° from the grave.   *shroud*
Go out, children, from the mine and from the city,
    Sing out, children, as the little thrushes do;
Pluck you handfuls of the meadow cowslips pretty,
60   Laugh aloud, to feel your fingers let them through!
But they answer, "Are your cowslips of the meadows
    Like our weeds anear the mine?
Leave us quiet in the dark of the coal shadows,
    From your pleasures fair and fine!

6

65 "For oh," say the children, "we are weary,
    And we cannot run or leap;

[1] *The Cry of the Children* This poem was written in response to Richard Henry Horne's 1843 "Report of the Children's Employment Commission" regarding child labor in the mining and manufacturing industries (see "In Context," below). Horne was the author of the epic poem *Orion* and the play *Cosmo de' Medici*, as well as *A New Spirit of the Age*, co-written with Elizabeth Barrett.

[2] Φεῦ ... τέκνα From Euripides's *Medea* (431 BCE) 1.1040, in which Medea says, upon killing her children: "Alas, why do you gaze at me thus, my children?"

If we cared for any meadows, it were merely
    To drop down in them and sleep.
Our knees tremble sorely in the stooping,
70   We fall upon our faces, trying to go;
And, underneath our heavy eyelids drooping,
    The reddest flower would look as pale as snow;
For, all day, we drag our burden tiring
    Through the coal dark, underground;
75 Or, all day, we drive the wheels of iron
    In the factories, round and round.

7

"For all day, the wheels are droning, turning,
    Their wind comes in our faces,
Till our hearts turn, our heads with pulses burning,
80   And the walls turn in their places:
Turns the sky in the high window blank and reeling,
    Turns the long light that drops adown the wall,
Turn the black flies that crawl along the ceiling,
    All are turning, all the day, and we with all.
85 And all day, the iron wheels are droning,
    And sometimes we could pray,
'O ye wheels,' (breaking out in a mad moaning)
    'Stop! be silent for today!'"

8

Aye, be silent! Let them hear each other breathing
90   For a moment, mouth to mouth!
Let them touch each other's hands, in a fresh wreathing
    Of their tender human youth!
Let them feel that this cold metallic motion
    Is not all the life God fashions or reveals:
95 Let them prove their living souls against the notion
    That they live in you, or under you, O wheels!
Still, all day, the iron wheels go onward,
    Grinding life down from its mark;
And the children's souls, which God is calling sunward,
100   Spin on blindly in the dark.

9

Now tell the poor young children, O my brothers,
    To look up to Him and pray;
So the blessed One who blesseth all the others,
    Will bless them another day.
105 They answer, "Who is God that He should hear us,

While the rushing of the iron wheels is stirred?
When we sob aloud, the human creatures near us
    Pass by, hearing not, or answer not a word.
And *we* hear not (for the wheels in their resounding)
110   Strangers speaking at the door:
Is it likely God, with angels singing round him,
    Hears our weeping any more?

10

"Two words, indeed, of praying we remember,
    And at midnight's hour of harm,
115 'Our Father,' looking upward in the chamber,
    We say softly for a charm.[1]
We know no other words except 'Our Father,'
    And we think that, in some pause of angels' song,
God may pluck them with the silence sweet to gather,
120   And hold both within His right hand which is strong.
'Our Father!' If He heard us, He would surely
    (For they call Him good and mild)
Answer, smiling down the steep world very purely,
    'Come and rest with me, my child.'"

11

125 "But no!" say the children, weeping faster,
    "He is speechless as a stone:
And they tell us, of His image is the master
    Who commands us to work on.
Go to!" say the children,—"up in heaven,
130   Dark, wheel-like, turning clouds are all we find.
Do not mock us; grief has made us unbelieving:
    We look up for God, but tears have made us blind."
Do you hear the children weeping and disproving,
    O my brothers, what ye preach?
135 For God's possible is taught by His world's loving,
    And the children doubt of each.

12

And well may the children weep before you!
    They are weary ere they run;
They have never seen the sunshine, nor the glory

---

[1] [Barrett Browning's note] A fact rendered pathetically historical by Mr. Horne's report of his commission. The name of the poet of *Orion* and *Cosmo de' Medici* has, however, a change of associations, and comes in time to remind me that we have some noble poetic heat of literature still, however open to the reproach of being somewhat gelid in our humanity. [*gelid* Cold.]

140   Which is brighter than the sun.
They know the grief of man, without its wisdom;
     They sink in man's despair, without its calm;
Are slaves, without the liberty in Christdom,
     Are martyrs, by the pang without the palm;
145 Are worn as if with age, yet unretrievingly
       The harvest of its memories cannot reap,—
Are orphans of the earthly love and heavenly.
       Let them weep! let them weep!

13

They look up with their pale and sunken faces,
150   And their look is dread to see,
For they mind you of their angels in high places,
      With eyes turned on Deity!
"How long," they say, "how long, O cruel nation,
     Will you stand, to move the world, on a child's
       heart,—
155 Stifle down with a mailed° heel its palpitation,   *armored*
     And tread onward to your throne amid the mart?
Our blood splashes upward, O gold-heaper,
      And your purple shows your path!
But the child's sob in the silence curses deeper
160   Than the strong man in his wrath."
—1844

To George Sand [1]
A Desire

Thou large-brained woman and large-hearted man,
   Self-called George Sand! whose soul, amid the lions
Of thy tumultuous senses, moans defiance
And answers roar for roar, as spirits can:
5 I would some mild miraculous thunder ran
Above the applauded circus, in appliance
Of thine own nobler nature's strength and science,
Drawing two pinions,° white as wings of swan,   *wings*
From thy strong shoulders, to amaze the place
10 With holier light! that thou to woman's claim

---

[1] *George Sand* Pseudonym of French author Amandine Aurore Lucie Dupin (1804–76), who was often condemned for her free-spirited ways, which included wearing men's clothing. For images of Sand see "In Context," below.

And man's, mightst join beside the angel's grace
Of a pure genius sanctified from blame,
Till child and maiden pressed to thine embrace
To kiss upon thy lips a stainless fame.
—1844

To George Sand
A Recognition

True genius, but true woman! dost deny
   The woman's nature with a manly scorn,
And break away the gauds° and armlets worn   *ornaments*
By weaker women in captivity?
5 Ah, vain denial! that revolted cry
Is sobbed in by a woman's voice forlorn,—
Thy woman's hair, my sister, all unshorn
Floats back dishevelled strength in agony,
Disproving thy man's name: and while before
10 The world thou burnest in a poet fire,
We see thy woman heart beat evermore
Through the large flame. Beat purer, heart, and higher,
Till God unsex thee on the heavenly shore
Where unincarnate spirits purely aspire!
—1844

A Year's Spinning

1

He listened at the porch that day,
   To hear the wheel go on, and on;
And then it stopped, ran back away,
    While through the door he brought the sun:
    But now my spinning is all done.

2

He sat beside me, with an oath
   That love ne'er ended, once begun;
I smiled—believing for us both,
    What was the truth for only one:
10   And now my spinning is all done.

3

My mother cursed me that I heard
    A young man's wooing as I spun:
Thanks, cruel mother, for that word—
    For I have, since, a harder known!
15   And now my spinning is all done.

4

I thought—O God!—my firstborn's cry
    Both voices to mine ear would drown:
I listened in mine agony—
    It was the *silence* made me groan!
20   And now my spinning is all done.

5

Bury me 'twixt my mother's grave,
    (Who cursed me on her deathbed lone)
And my dead baby's (God it save!)
    Who, not to bless me, would not moan.
25   And now my spinning is all done.

6

A stone upon my heart and head,
    But no name written on the stone!
Sweet neighbours, whisper low instead,
    "This sinner was a loving one—
30   And now her spinning is all done."

7

And let the door ajar remain,
    In case he should pass by anon;
And leave the wheel out very plain,—
    That HE, when passing in the sun,
35   May see the spinning is all done.
—1850

The Runaway Slave at Pilgrim's Point

1

I stand on the mark beside the shore
    Of the first white pilgrim's bended knee,
Where exile turned to ancestor,
    And God was thanked for liberty.
5   I have run through the night, my skin is as dark,

I bend my knee down on this mark:
    I look on the sky and the sea.

2

O pilgrim-souls, I speak to you!
    I see you come proud and slow
10   From the land of the spirits pale as dew
    And round me and round me ye go.
O pilgrims, I have gasped and run
All night long from the whips of one
    Who in your names works sin and woe!

3

15   And thus I thought that I would come
    And kneel here where you knelt before,
And feel your souls around me hum
    In undertone to the ocean's roar;
And lift my black face, my black hand,
20   Here, in your names, to curse this land
    Ye blessed in freedom's, evermore.

4

I am black, I am black,
    And yet God made me, they say:
But if He did so, smiling back
25   He must have cast His work away
Under the feet of His white creatures,
With a look of scorn, that the dusky features
    Might be trodden again to clay.

5

And yet He has made dark things
30   To be glad and merry as light:
There's a little dark bird sits and sings,
    There's a dark stream ripples out of sight,
And the dark frogs chant in the safe morass,
And the sweetest stars are made to pass
35   O'er the face of the darkest night.

6

But *we* who are dark, we are dark!
    Ah God, we have no stars!
About our souls in care and cark°   *troubles*
    Our blackness shuts like prison bars:
40   The poor souls crouch so far behind

That never a comfort can they find
    By reaching through the prison bars.

7

Indeed we live beneath the sky,
    That great smooth Hand of God stretched out
45 On all his children fatherly,
    To save them from the dread and doubt
Which would be if, from this low place,
All opened straight up to His face
    Into the grand eternity.

8

50 And still God's sunshine and His frost,
    They make us hot, they make us cold,
As if we were not black and lost;
    And the beasts and birds, in wood and fold,
Do fear and take us for very men:
55 Could the whippoorwill or the cat of the glen
    Look into my eyes and be bold?

9

I am black, I am black!
    But, once, I laughed in girlish glee,
For one of my colour stood in the track
60   Where the drivers drove, and looked at me,
And tender and full was the look he gave—
Could a slave look *so* at another slave?—
    I look at the sky and sea.

10

And from that hour our spirits grew
65   As free as if unsold, unbought:
Oh, strong enough, since we were two,
    To conquer the world, we thought.
The drivers drove us day by day;
We did not mind, we went one way,
70   And no better a freedom sought.

11

In the sunny ground between the canes,
    He said "I love you" as he passed;
When the shingle roof rang sharp with the rains,
    I heard how he vowed it fast:
75 While others shook he smiled in the hut,

As he carved me a bowl of the coconut
    Through the roar of the hurricanes.

12

I sang his name instead of a song,
    Over and over I sang his name,
80 Upward and downward I drew it along
    My various notes,—the same, the same!
I sang it low, that the slave girls near
Might never guess, from aught they could hear,
    It was only a name—a name.

13

85 I look on the sky and the sea.
    We were two to love, and two to pray:
Yes, two, O God, who cried to Thee,
    Though nothing didst Thou say!
Coldly Thou sat'st behind the sun:
90 And now I cry who am but one,
    Thou wilt not speak today.

14

We were black, we were black,
    We had no claim to love and bliss,
What marvel if each went to wrack?
    They wrung my cold hands out of his
95 They dragged him—where? I crawled to touch
His blood's mark in the dust … not much,
    Ye pilgrim-souls, though plain as this!

15

Wrong, followed by a deeper wrong!
100   Mere grief's too good for such as I:
So the white men brought the shame ere long
    To strangle the sob of my agony.
They would not leave me for my dull
Wet eyes!—it was too merciful
105   To let me weep pure tears and die.

16

I am black, I am black!
    I wore a child upon my breast,
An amulet that hung too slack,
    And, in my unrest, could not rest:
110 Thus we went moaning, child and mother,

One to another, one to another,
    Until all ended for the best.

17

For hark! I will tell you low, low,
    I am black, you see,—
115 And the babe who lay on my bosom so,
    Was far too white, too white for me;
As white as the ladies who scorned to pray
Beside me at church but yesterday,
    Though my tears had washed a place for my knee.

18

120 My own, own child! I could not bear
    To look in his face, it was so white;
I covered him up with a kerchief there,
    I covered his face in close and tight:
And he moaned and struggled, as well might be,
125 For the white child wanted his liberty—
    Ha, ha! he wanted the master right.

19

He moaned and beat with his head and feet,
    His little feet that never grew;
He struck them out, as it was meet,
130   Against my heart to break it through:
I might have sung and made him mild,
But I dared not sing to the white-faced child
    The only song I knew.

20

I pulled the kerchief very close:
135   He could not see the sun, I swear,
More, then, alive, than now he does
    From between the roots of the mango … where?
I know where. Close! A child and mother
Do wrong to look at one another
140   When one is black and one is fair.

21

Why, in that single glance I had
    Of my child's face, … I tell you all,
I saw a look that made me mad!
    The master's look, that used to fall
       like his lash … or worse!
       curse,

22

And he moaned and trembled from foot to head,
    He shivered from head to foot;
150 Till after a time, he lay instead
    Too suddenly still and mute.
I felt, beside, a stiffening cold:
I dared to lift up just a fold,
    As in lifting a leaf of the mango fruit.

23

155 But *my* fruit … ha, ha!—there, had been
    (I laugh to think on't at this hour!)
Your fine white angels (who have seen
    Nearest the secret of God's power)
And plucked my fruit to make them wine,
160 And sucked the soul of that child of mine
    As the hummingbird sucks the soul of the flower.

24

Ha, ha, the trick of the angels white!
    They freed the white child's spirit so.
I said not a word, but day and night
165   I carried the body to and fro,
And it lay on my heart like a stone, as chill.
—The sun may shine out as much as he will:
    I am cold, though it happened a month ago.

25

From the white man's house, and the black man's hut,
170   I carried the little body on;
The forest's arms did round us shut,
    And silence through the trees did run:
They asked no question as I went,
They stood too high for astonishment,
175   They could see God sit on His throne.

26

My little body, kerchiefed fast,
    I bore it on through the forest, on;
And when I felt it was tired at last,
    I scooped a hole beneath the moon:
180 Through the forest tops the angels far,
With a white sharp finger from every star,
    Did point and mock at what was done.

27

Yet when it was all done aright,—
    Earth, 'twixt me and my baby, strewed,—
185 All, changed to black earth,—nothing white,—
    A dark child in the dark!—ensued
Some comfort, and my heart grew young;
I sat down smiling there and sung
    The song I learnt in my maidenhood.

28

190 And thus we two were reconciled,
    The white child and black mother, thus;
For as I sang it soft and wild,
    The same song, more melodious,
Rose from the grave whereon I sat:
195 It was the dead child singing that,
    To join the souls of both of us.

29

I look on the sea and the sky.
    Where the pilgrims' ships first anchored lay
The free sun rideth gloriously,
200   But the pilgrim-ghosts have slid away
Through the earliest streaks of the morn:
My face is black, but it glares with a scorn
    Which they dare not meet by day.

30

Ha!—in their stead, their hunter sons!
205   Ha, ha! they are on me—they hunt in a ring!
Keep off! I brave you all at once,
    I throw off your eyes like snakes that sting!
You have killed the black eagle at nest, I think:
Did you ever stand still in your triumph, and shrink
210   From the stroke of her wounded wing?

31

(Man, drop that stone you dared to lift!—)
    I wish you who stand there five abreast,
Each, for his own wife's joy and gift,
    A little corpse as safely at rest
215 As mine in the mangoes! Yes, but she
May keep live babies on her knee,
    And sing the song she likes the best.

32

I am not mad: I am black.
    I see you staring in my face—
220 I know you staring, shrinking back,
    Ye are born of the Washington race,
And this land is the free America,
And this mark on my wrist—(I prove what I say)
    Ropes tied me up here to the flogging place.

33

225 You think I shrieked then? Not a sound!
    I hung, as a gourd hangs in the sun;
I only cursed them all around
    As softly as I might have done
My very own child: from these sands
230 Up to the mountains, lift your hands,
    O slaves, and end what I begun!

34

Whips, curses; these must answer those!
    For in this UNION you have set
Two kinds of men in adverse rows,
235   Each loathing each; and all forget
The seven wounds in Christ's body fair,
While HE sees gaping everywhere
    Our countless wounds that pay no debt.

35

Our wounds are different. Your white men
240   Are, after all, not gods indeed,
Nor able to make Christs again
    Do good with bleeding. We who bleed
(Stand off!) we help not in our loss!
We are too heavy for our cross,
245   And fall and crush you and your seed.

36

I fall, I swoon! I look at the sky.
    The clouds are breaking on my brain;
I am floated along, as if I should die
    Of liberty's exquisite pain.
250 In the name of the white child v
In the death dark where we m
White men, I leave you all
    In my broken heart'
—1850

from *Sonnets from the Portuguese*

1

I thought once how Theocritus[1] had sung
Of the sweet years, the dear and wished-for years,
Who each one in a gracious hand appears
To bear a gift for mortals, old or young:
5 And, as I mused it in his antique tongue,[2]
I saw, in gradual vision through my tears,
The sweet, sad years, the melancholy years,
Those of my own life, who by turns had flung
A shadow across me. Straightway I was 'ware,
10 So weeping, how a mystic Shape did move
Behind me, and drew me backward by the hair;
And a voice said in mastery, while I strove—
"Guess now who holds thee?"—"Death," I said. But,
      there,
The silver answer rang—"Not Death, but Love."

7

The face of all the world is changed, I think,
Since first I heard the footsteps of thy soul
Move still, oh, still, beside me, as they stole
Betwixt me and the dreadful outer brink
5 Of obvious death, where I, who thought to sink,
Was caught up into love, and taught the whole
Of life in a new rhythm. The cup of dole
God gave for baptism, I am fain to drink,
And praise its sweetness, Sweet, with thee anear.
10 The names of country, heaven, are changed away
For where thou art or shalt be, there or here;
And this ... this lute and song ... loved yesterday,
(The singing angels know) are only dear
Because thy name moves right in what they say.

13

And wilt thou have me fasten into speech
The love I bear thee, finding words enough,
And hold the torch out, while the winds are rough,
Between our faces, to cast light on each?—
5 I drop it at thy feet. I cannot teach

My hand to hold my spirit so far off
From myself—me—that I should bring thee proof
In words, of love hid in me out of reach.
Nay, let the silence of my womanhood
10 Commend my woman-love to thy belief—
Seeing that I stand unwon, however wooed,
And rend the garment of my life, in brief,
By a most dauntless, voiceless fortitude,
Lest one touch of this heart convey its grief.

21

Say over again, and yet once over again,
That thou dost love me. Though the word repeated
Should seem "a cuckoo-song," as thou dost treat it,
Remember, never to the hill or plain,
5 Valley and wood, without her cuckoo-strain
Comes the fresh Spring in all her green completed.
Belovèd, I, amid the darkness greeted
By a doubtful spirit-voice, in that doubt's pain
Cry, "Speak once more—thou lovest!" Who can fear
10 Too many stars, though each in heaven shall roll,
Too many flowers, though each shall crown the year?
Say thou dost love me, love me, love me—toll
The silver iterance![3]—only minding, Dear,
To love me also in silence with thy soul.

22

When our two souls stand up erect and strong,
Face to face, silent, drawing nigh and nigher,
Until the lengthening wings break into fire
At either curvèd point—what bitter wrong
5 Can the earth do to us, that we should not long
Be here contented? Think. In mounting higher,
The angels would press on us and aspire
To drop some golden orb of perfect song
Into our deep, dear silence. Let us stay
10 Rather on earth, Belovèd—where the unfit
Contrarious moods of men recoil away
And isolate pure spirits, and permit
A place to stand and love in for a day,
With darkness and the death hour rounding it.

Greek poet of the third century BCE who created the
      [obscured] (characterized by idyllic country life and love
      [obscured] pherdesses).

---

[3] *iterance* Repetition.

24

Let the world's sharpness, like a clasping knife,
Shut in upon itself and do no harm
In this close hand of Love, now soft and warm,
And let us hear no sound of human strife
5 After the click of the shutting. Life to life—
I lean upon thee, Dear, without alarm,
And feel as safe as guarded by a charm
Against the stab of worldlings, who if rife
Are weak to injure. Very whitely still
10 The lilies of our lives may reassure
Their blossoms from their roots, accessible
Alone to heavenly dews that drop not fewer,
Growing straight, out of man's reach, on the hill.
God only, who made us rich, can make us poor.

26

I lived with visions for my company
Instead of men and women, years ago,
And found them gentle mates, nor thought to know
A sweeter music than they played to me.
5 But soon their trailing purple was not free
Of this world's dust, their lutes did silent grow,
And I myself grew faint and blind below
Their vanishing eyes. Then *thou* didst come—to be,
Belovèd, what they seemed. Their shining fronts,
10 Their songs, their splendours (better, yet the same,
As river water hallowed into fonts),
Met in thee, and from out thee overcame
My soul with satisfaction of all wants:
Because God's gifts put man's best dreams to shame.

28

My letters! all dead paper, mute and white!
And yet they seem alive and quivering
Against my tremulous hands which loose the string
And let them drop down on my knee tonight.
5 This said—he wished to have me in his sight
Once, as a friend: this fixed a day in spring
To come and touch my hand … a simple thing,
Yet I wept for it!—this, … the paper's light …
Said, *Dear, I love thee;* and I sank and quailed
10 As if God's future thundered on my past.
This said, *I am thine*—and so its ink has paled
With lying at my heart that beat too fast.
And this … O Love, thy words have ill availed
If, what this said, I dared repeat at last!

43

How do I love thee? Let me count the ways.
I love thee to the depth and breadth and height
My soul can reach, when feeling out of sight
For the ends of Being and ideal Grace.
5 I love thee to the level of every day's
Most quiet need, by sun and candle-light.
I love thee freely, as men strive for Right;
I love thee purely, as they turn from Praise.
I love thee with the passion put to use
In my old griefs, and with my childhood's faith.
10 I love thee with a love I seemed to lose
With my lost saints—I love thee with the breath,
Smiles, tears, of all my life!—and, if God choose,
I shall but love thee better after death.
—1845–47

ALFRED, LORD TENNYSON
1809 – 1892

In 1850, the novelist and critic Charles Kingsley praised Tennyson's dramatic monologue, "Locksley Hall," as the poem that "has had most influence on the minds of the young men of our day." Throughout his long career, Tennyson's poems continued to resonate with Victorian audiences. The self-reflective grief of *In Memoriam* (1850) touched a chord of genuine sympathy in nineteenth-century readers, including Queen Victoria herself, much as Tennyson's re-telling of Arthurian legend in *Idylls of the King* (1859–85) echoed the nationalistic zeal of the later Victorian period. Britain's Poet Laureate from 1850 to his death in 1892, Tennyson was the quintessential poet of his age.

He was born in 1809 in Somersby, Lincolnshire, to a privileged family, and his poetic gifts became apparent early on. At age eight, Tennyson was composing pages of blank verse in the style of James Thomson; by ten or eleven he had graduated to studying the work of Alexander Pope, imitating hundreds of lines of Pope's translation of Homer's *Iliad*. At twelve, Tennyson set to work on his first epic, a six-thousand-line experiment that mimicked Walter Scott's octosyllabic extravaganzas of war and romance. "I wrote as much as seventy lines at one time," he later recalled, "and used to go shouting them about the fields in the dark." By age fourteen, with an Elizabethan-style drama entitled *The Devil and the Lady*, Tennyson's work was approaching the sonorous agility and understated pathos for which it would be known. His first publication, *Poems by Two Brothers* (1827), a collaborative effort by Tennyson and his two older brothers, Frederick and Charles, was completed just prior to Tennyson's entrance to Trinity College, Cambridge.

Tennyson distinguished himself at Cambridge, establishing his reputation as both a deep thinker and a poet. In June of 1829, he won the Chancellor's Gold Medal with a blank-verse poem, *Timbuctoo*. Some time in that year, Tennyson met Arthur Henry Hallam, who was to become the poet's closest friend and companion. It was also in 1829 that Tennyson joined the Cambridge Apostles, an undergraduate debating society of which Hallam and many of Tennyson's other Cambridge friends were a part. 1830 saw the publication of Tennyson's first important volume, *Poems, Chiefly Lyrical*, which Hallam reviewed for the *Englishman's Magazine* in an essay entitled "On Some of the Characteristics of Modern Poetry and on the Lyrical Poems of Alfred Tennyson." Hallam describes Tennyson as a poet of "sensation," one of a school of poets, including Shelley and Keats, whose "fine organs tremble into emotion at colors, and sounds, and movements" and who translate this physiological sensitivity into their verses. It was precisely such sensitivity that Christopher North (the pseudonym of John Wilson) later attacked in his 1832 *Blackwood's* review of the volume. Subsequently many critics have charted Tennyson's gradual movement away from a poetics of sensation and toward a more restrained poetic style.

The early 1830s were a difficult time for the young poet. Following the death of his father in 1831, Tennyson left Cambridge without taking his degree. Soon afterward, his brother Edward lost his sanity, succumbing to what was known as the "black blood" of the Tennyson family. Finally, and perhaps most devastatingly, Arthur Hallam died suddenly in 1833 of a hemorrhage to his brain. Having published one volume, *Poems*, in 1832, Tennyson would remain silent as a poet for the next ten years, refusing to publish his many works in progress until the *Poems* of 1842, the volume that brought him his reputation as both a remarkable poet and a great voice of his age. During the "ten years' silence," however, Tennyson composed much of what many consider his masterwork, *In Memoriam* (1850), in addition to the innovative dramatic monologues of the 1842 volume, including "Ulysses," "Locksley Hall," and "St. Simeon Stylites."

In 1847, Tennyson published *The Princess*, a poetic medley that explored, through a wildly improbable narrative, the relations between the sexes, and the viability of education for women. Interspersed throughout the work are many of Tennyson's best-known lyrics: "Sweet and Low," "The Splendour Falls," and "Tears, Idle Tears," among others. In 1850, Tennyson ascended to the Laureateship and married Emily Sellwood, to whom he had been engaged for fourteen years. That same year, Tennyson also published *In Memoriam*, the elegy on which he had been at work since Arthur Hallam's death. The first of many of Tennyson's books to sell in large numbers, *In Memoriam* went into three editions in its first year alone. Amid a rising swell of scientific discovery and industrial transformation, the poem captured the mood of the era, alternating between faith in science and faith in religion, and reflecting the hopes, doubts, and beliefs of the Victorians.

Tennyson's life changed notably as a result of both his marriage and his suddenly public role as Poet Laureate. The Tennysons had two sons within the next four years, the elder of whom was named Hallam after Tennyson's deceased friend. (After his father's death, Hallam Tennyson wrote a biography entitled *Alfred Lord Tennyson: A Memoir*, and he penned a second volume in 1911, *Tennyson and His Friends*. Alfred Tennyson's grandson Charles also wrote a biography in 1949.)

Many critics have argued that Tennyson's style changed after his appointment as Poet Laureate. Certainly it is true that he assumed a different voice in the occasional poems composed in his role as Poet Laureate, most notably the "Ode on the Death of the Duke of Wellington" (1852); likewise "The Charge of the Light Brigade" (1854) projects an explicit political stance largely absent in his earlier works. But Tennyson continued to evolve as a poet, publishing an experimental "monodrama," *Maud*, in 1855 and the first four segments of his epic, *Idylls of the King*, in 1859. *Maud* was in many ways Tennyson's most controversial publication. Critics complained of the poem's irregular rhythms and of the "screed of bombast" that seemed to some like "the rasping of a blacksmith's file." *Idylls of the King*, on the other hand, was largely—though not universally—hailed as a *magnum opus*. Tennyson had contemplated writing an epic from his childhood; the finished *Idylls* reflects the poet's mature thoughts about Victorian life, politics, and culture through the world of Camelot and King Arthur.

Tennyson's later publications include the plays *Queen Mary* (1875), *The Falcon* (1879), and *The Promise of May* (1882), all of which were produced on the Victorian stage, and numerous volumes of poetry, including *Enoch Arden* (1864), *Tiresias, and Other Poems* (1885), *Locksley Hall Sixty Years After* (1886), and *Demeter and Other Poems* (1889). In 1883, Tennyson accepted a baronetcy from the Queen and took a seat in the House of Lords. He died in 1892 at his second home, Aldworth, and is buried beside Robert Browning in the Poets' Corner of Westminster Abbey.

⌘ ⌘ ⌘

Julia Margaret Cameron, *Mariana*, 1875.

Mariana

Mariana in the moated grange
(Measure for Measure)[1]

With blackest moss the flower-plots
    Were thickly crusted, one and all:
The rusted nails fell from the knots
    That held the pear to the gable-wall.[2]
5 The broken sheds looked sad and strange:
    Unlifted was the clinking latch;
    Weeded and worn the ancient thatch
Upon the lonely moated grange.
      She only said, "My life is dreary,

10   He cometh not," she said;
      She said, "I am aweary, aweary,
      I would that I were dead!"

Her tears fell with the dews at even;°   *evening*
    Her tears fell ere° the dews were dried;   *before*
15 She could not look on the sweet heaven,
    Either at morn or eventide.
After the flitting of the bats,
    When thickest dark did trance° the sky,   *entrance*
    She drew her casement-curtain by,
20 And glanced athwart the glooming flats.[3]
      She only said, "The night is dreary,
      He cometh not," she said;
      She said, "I am aweary, aweary,
      I would that I were dead!"

25 Upon the middle of the night,
    Waking she heard the night-fowl crow:
The cock sung out an hour ere light:
    From the dark fen° the oxen's low   *lowlands*
Came to her: without hope of change,
30   In sleep she seemed to walk forlorn,
    Till cold winds woke the gray-eyed morn
About the lonely moated grange.
      She only said, "The day is dreary,
      He cometh not," she said;
35   She said, "I am aweary, aweary,
      I would that I were dead!"

About a stone-cast from the wall
    A sluice with blackened waters slept,
And o'er it many, round and small,
40   The clustered marish-mosses[4] crept.
Hard by a poplar shook alway,
    All silver-green with gnarlèd bark:
    For leagues no other tree did mark
The level waste, the rounding gray.
45   She only said, "My life is dreary,
      He cometh not," she said;
      She said, "I am aweary, aweary,
      I would that I were dead!"

---

[1] *Mariana … Measure* Tennyson's epigraph is adapted from the words of the Duke in Shakespeare's *Measure for Measure*, 3.1.277: "There, at the moated grange, lies this dejected Mariana." Earlier in the scene, the Duke has recounted how Mariana, having lost her dowry (and her brother) in a shipwreck, has been deserted by her betrothed; *moated grange* Cottage or small farmhouse surrounded by a moat, or water-filled ditch.

[2] *The rusted … wall* The pear has been espaliered, or trained to grow against a wall on a lattice or framework of stakes.

[3] *flats* Flatlands or lowlands.

[4] [Tennyson's note] *Marish-mosses*, the little marsh-moss lumps that float on the surface of the water.

And ever when the moon was low,
50 And the shrill winds were up and away,
In the white curtain, to and fro,
  She saw the gusty shadow sway.
But when the moon was very low,
  And wild winds bound within their cell,[1]
55   The shadow of the poplar fell
Upon her bed, across her brow.
    She only said, "The night is dreary,
     He cometh not," she said;
    She said, "I am aweary, aweary,
60   I would that I were dead!"

All day within the dreamy house,
  The doors upon their hinges creaked;
The blue fly° sung in the pane; the mouse   *bluebottle*
  Behind the mouldering wainscot shrieked,
65 Or from the crevice peered about.
  Old faces glimmered through the doors,
  Old footsteps trod the upper floors,
Old voices called her from without.
    She only said, "My life is dreary,
70   He cometh not," she said;
    She said, "I am aweary, aweary,
     I would that I were dead!"

The sparrow's chirrup on the roof,
  The slow clock ticking, and the sound
75 Which to the wooing wind aloof
  The poplar made, did all confound
Her sense; but most she loathed the hour
  When the thick-moted[2] sunbeam lay
Athwart the chambers, and the day
80 Was sloping toward his western bower.
    Then, said she, "I am very dreary,
     He will not come," she said;
    She wept, "I am aweary, aweary,
     Oh God, that I were dead!"
  —1830

The Palace of Art

I built my soul a lordly pleasure-house,
  Wherein at ease for aye° to dwell.   *ever*
I said, "O Soul, make merry and carouse,
  Dear soul, for all is well."

5 A huge crag-platform, smooth as burnished brass
  I chose. The rangèd ramparts bright
From level meadow-bases of deep grass
  Suddenly scaled the light.

Thereon I built it firm. Of ledge or shelf
10 The rock rose clear, or winding stair.
My soul would live alone unto herself
  In her high palace there.

And "while the world runs round and round," I said,
  "Reign thou apart, a quiet king,
15 Still as, while Saturn whirls, his steadfast shade
  Sleeps on his luminous ring."

To which my soul made answer readily:
  "Trust me, in bliss I shall abide
In this great mansion, that is built for me,
20 So royal-rich and wide."

Four courts I made, East, West and South and North,
  In each a squared lawn, wherefrom
The golden gorge of dragons spouted forth
  A flood of fountain-foam.

25 And round the cool green courts there ran a row
  Of cloisters, branched like mighty woods,
Echoing all night to that sonorous flow
  Of spouted fountain-floods.

And round the roofs a gilded gallery
30 That lent broad verge° to distant lands,   *view*
Far as the wild swan wings, to where the sky
  Dipped down to sea and sands.

---

1 *wild ... cell* A reference to Virgil's *Aeneid*, 1.52, in which Aeolus, god of winds, keeps the winds imprisoned in a cavern.

2 *thick-moted* I.e., thick with motes of dust.

From those four jets four currents in one swell
    Across the mountain streamed below
35 In misty folds, that floating as they fell
    Lit up a torrent-bow.[1]

And high on every peak a statue seemed
    To hang on tiptoe, tossing up
A cloud of incense of all odour steamed
40   From out a golden cup.

So that she thought, "And who shall gaze upon
    My palace with unblinded eyes,
While this great bow will waver in the sun,
    And that sweet incense rise?"

45 For that sweet incense rose and never failed,
    And, while day sank or mounted higher,
The light aerial gallery, golden-railed,
    Burnt like a fringe of fire.

Likewise the deep-set windows, stained and traced,
50   Would seem slow-flaming crimson fires
From shadowed grots° of arches interlaced,   *grottoes*
    And tipped with frost-like spires.

Full of long-sounding corridors it was,
    That over-vaulted grateful° gloom,   *pleasing*
55 Through which the livelong day my soul did pass,
    Well-pleased, from room to room.

Full of great rooms and small the palace stood,
    All various, each a perfect whole
From living Nature, fit for every mood
60   And change of my still soul.

For some were hung with arras° green and blue,   *tapestries*
    Showing a gaudy summer-morn,
Where with puffed cheek the belted hunter blew
    His wreathèd bugle-horn.

65 One seemed all dark and red—a tract of sand,
    And someone pacing there alone,
Who paced forever in a glimmering land,
    Lit with a low large moon.

One showed an iron coast and angry waves.
70   You seemed to hear them climb and fall
And roar rock-thwarted under bellowing caves,
    Beneath the windy wall.

And one, a full-fed river winding slow
    By herds upon an endless plain,
75 The ragged rims of thunder brooding low,
    With shadow-streaks of rain.

And one, the reapers at their sultry toil.
    In front they bound the sheaves. Behind
Were realms of upland, prodigal in oil,
80   And hoary to the wind.[2]

And one a foreground black with stones and slags,
    Beyond, a line of heights, and higher
All barred with long white cloud the scornful crags,
    And highest, snow and fire.

85 And one, an English home—gray twilight poured
    On dewy pastures, dewy trees,
Softer than sleep—all things in order stored,
    A haunt of ancient Peace.

Nor these alone, but every landscape fair,
90   As fit for every mood of mind,
Or gay, or grave, or sweet, or stern, was there
    Not less than truth designed.

Or the maid-mother by a crucifix,
    In tracts of pasture sunny-warm,
95 Beneath branch-work of costly sardonyx[3]
    Sat smiling, babe in arm.

Or in a clear-walled city on the sea,
    Near gilded organ-pipes, her hair
Wound with white roses, slept St. Cecily;[4]
100   An angel looked at her.

---

1 *torrent-bow* Rainbow formed in the spray of a torrent.

2 *hoary ... wind* The white underside of the olive leaves are exposed by the wind.

3 *sardonyx* Onyx striped with sard, a yellow or orange quartz.

4 *St. Cecily* St. Cecilia, patron saint of music.

Or thronging all one porch of Paradise
    A group of Houris[1] bowed to see
The dying Islamite, with hands and eyes
    That said, We wait for thee.

105 Or mythic Uther's deeply-wounded son[2]
    In some fair space of sloping greens
Lay, dozing in the vale of Avalon,
    And watched by weeping queens.

Or hollowing one hand against his ear,
110   To list° a foot-fall, ere he saw   *hear*
The wood-nymph, stayed the Ausonian king[3] to hear
    Of wisdom and of law.

Or over hills with peaky tops engrailed,°   *serrated*
    And many a tract of palm and rice.
115 The throne of Indian Cama[4] slowly sailed
    A summer fanned with spice.

Or sweet Europa's[5] mantle blew unclasped,
    From off her shoulder backward borne:
From one hand drooped a crocus: one hand grasped
120   The mild bull's golden horn.

Or else flushed Ganymede,[6] his rosy thigh
    Half-buried in the Eagle's down,
Sole as a flying star shot through the sky
    Above the pillared town.

125 Nor these alone: but every legend fair
    Which the supreme Caucasian mind
Carved out of Nature for itself, was there,
    Not less than life, designed.

Then in the towers I placed great bells that swung,
130   Moved of themselves, with silver sound;
And with choice paintings of wise men I hung
    The royal dais round.

For there was Milton like a seraph° strong,   *angel*
    Beside him Shakespeare bland and mild;
135 And there the world-worn Dante grasped his song,
    And somewhat grimly smiled.

And there the Ionian father[7] of the rest;
    A million wrinkles carved his skin;
A hundred winters snowed upon his breast,
140   From cheek and throat and chin.

Above, the fair hall-ceiling stately-set
    Many an arch high up did lift,
And angels rising and descending met
    With interchange of gift.

145 Below was all mosaic choicely planned
    With cycles of the human tale
Of this wide world, the times of every land
    So wrought, they will not fail.

The people here, a beast of burden slow,
150   Toiled onward, pricked with goads and stings;
Here played, a tiger, rolling to and fro
    The heads and crowns of kings;

Here rose, an athlete, strong to break or bind
    All force in bonds that might endure,
155 And here once more like some sick man declined,
    And trusted any cure.

But over these she trod: and those great bells
    Began to chime. She took her throne:
She sat betwixt the shining Oriels,°   *windows*
160   To sing her songs alone.

---

[1] *Houris* Nymphs of Muslim paradise.

[2] *Uther's ... son* King Arthur, son of Uther Pendragon, badly wounded in his last battle and carried to the mystic island of Avalon to heal.

[3] *Ausonian king* Numa, the legendary second king of Rome, who was said to have received the laws of the kingdom from the nymph Egeria; *Ausonia* was an ancient name for Italy often used by poets.

[4] [Tennyson's note] The Hindu God of young love, son of Brahma.

[5] *Europa* In Greek legend, the beautiful daughter of the king of Phoenicia. Zeus fell in love with her and assumed the shape of a bull in order to carry her off.

[6] *Ganymede* In Greek legend, a beautiful youth who was carried up to heaven at the command of Zeus, who made him cup-bearer to the gods.

---

[7] *Ionian father* Homer.

And through the topmost Oriels' coloured flame
  Two godlike faces gazed below;
Plato the wise, and large-browed Verulam,[1]
  The first of those who know.

165 And all those names, that in their motion were
  Full-welling fountainheads of change,
Betwixt the slender shafts were blazoned fair
  In diverse raiment° strange: *clothing*

Through which the lights, rose, amber, emerald, blue,
170 Flushed in her temples and her eyes,
And from her lips, as morn from Memnon, drew
  Rivers of melodies.[2]

No nightingale delighteth to prolong
  Her low preamble all alone,
175 More than my soul to hear her echoed song
  Throb through the ribbèd stone;

Singing and murmuring in her feastful mirth,
  Joying to feel herself alive,
Lord over Nature, Lord of the visible earth,
180 Lord of the senses five;

Communing with herself: "All these are mine,
  And let the world have peace or wars,
'Tis one to me." She—when young night divine
  Crowned dying day with stars,

185 Making sweet close of his delicious toils—
  Lit light in wreaths and anadems,° *garlands*
And pure quintessences of precious oils
  In hollowed moons of gems,

To mimic heaven; and clapped her hands and cried,
190 "I marvel if my still° delight   *constant*
In this great house so royal-rich, and wide,
  Be flattered to the height.

"O all things fair to sate my various eyes!
  O shapes and hues that please me well!
195 O silent faces of the Great and Wise,
  My Gods, with whom I dwell!

"O God-like isolation which art mine,
  I can but count thee perfect gain,
What time I watch the darkening droves of swine
200 That range on yonder plain.

"In filthy sloughs they roll a prurient skin,
  They graze and wallow, breed and sleep;
And oft some brainless devil enters in,
  And drives them to the deep."[3]

205 Then of the moral instinct would she prate
  And of the rising from the dead,
As hers by right of full-accomplished Fate;
  And at the last she said:

"I take possession of man's mind and deed.
210 I care not what the sects may brawl.
I sit as God holding no form of creed,
  But contemplating all."

Full oft the riddle of the painful earth
  Flashed through her as she sat alone,
215 Yet not the less held she her solemn mirth,
  And intellectual throne.

And so she throve and prospered: so three years
  She prospered: on the fourth she fell,
Like Herod, when the shout was in his ears,
220 Struck through with pangs of hell.[4]

Lest she should fail and perish utterly,
  God, before whom ever lie bare
The abysmal deeps of Personality,
  Plagued her with sore despair.

---

[1] *Oriels' ... Verulam* Recessed windows decorated with colored stained glass in images of Plato and Francis Bacon, one of whose titles was Baron Verulam.

[2] *Morn ... melodies* The statue of the legendary Ethiopian king Memnon at Thebes was said by the ancient Greeks to produce beautiful music when touched by the rays of the dawning sun.

[3] *oft ... deep* A reference to Matthew 8.28–32, in which Jesus casts devils out of two men and into a herd of swine, whereupon the herd stampedes off a cliff into the sea.

[4] *Herod ... hell* A reference to Acts 12.21–23, in which King Herod is struck dead as a crowd of his subjects shout that he is a god and not a man.

225 When she would think, where'er she turned her sight
    The airy hand confusion wrought,
Wrote, "Mene, mene,"[1] and divided quite
    The kingdom of her thought.

Deep dread and loathing of her solitude
230   Fell on her, from which mood was born
Scorn of herself; again, from out that mood
    Laughter at her self-scorn.

"What! is not this my place of strength," she said,
    "My spacious mansion built for me,
235 Whereof the strong foundation-stones were laid
    Since my first memory?"

But in dark corners of her palace stood
    Uncertain shapes; and unawares
On white-eyed phantasms weeping tears of blood,
240   And horrible nightmares,

And hollow shades enclosing hearts of flame,
    And, with dim fretted foreheads all,
On corpses three-months-old at noon she came,
    That stood against the wall.

245 A spot of dull stagnation, without light
    Or power of movement, seemed my soul,
'Mid onward-sloping motions infinite
    Making for one sure goal.

A still salt pool, locked in with bars of sand,
250   Left on the shore; that hears all night
The plunging seas draw backward from the land
    Their moon-led waters white.

A star that with the choral starry dance
    Joined not, but stood, and standing saw
255 The hollow orb of moving Circumstance
    Rolled round by one fixed law.

Back on herself her serpent pride had curled.
    "No voice," she shrieked in that lone hall,
"No voice breaks through the stillness of this world:
260   One deep, deep silence all!"

She, mouldering with the dull earth's mouldering sod,
    Inwrapt tenfold in slothful shame,
Lay there exilèd from eternal God,
    Lost to her place and name;

265 And death and life she hated equally,
    And nothing saw, for her despair,
But dreadful time, dreadful eternity,
    No comfort anywhere;

Remaining utterly confused with fears,
270   And ever worse with growing time,
And ever unrelieved by dismal tears,
    And all alone in crime:

Shut up as in a crumbling tomb, girt round
    With blackness as a solid wall,
275 Far off she seemed to hear the dully° sound   *faint*
    Of human footsteps fall.

As in strange lands a traveller walking slow,
    In doubt and great perplexity,
A little before moon-rise hears the low
280   Moan of an unknown sea;

And knows not if it be thunder, or a sound
    Of rocks thrown down, or one deep cry
Of great wild beasts; then thinketh, "I have found
    A new land, but I die."

285 She howled aloud, "I am on fire within.
    There comes no murmur of reply.
What is it that will take away my sin,
    And save me lest I die?"

So when four years were wholly finished,
290   She threw her royal robes away.
"Make me a cottage in the vale," she said,
    "Where I may mourn and pray.

---

1 *"Mene, mene"* The first of the words, seen by the Babylonian king Belshazzar, that are mysteriously written on the wall by a disembodied hand in Daniel 5.25–26. Daniel's interpretation of the words for the frightened king concludes with the phrase "Thy kingdom is divided."

"Yet pull not down my palace towers, that are
    So lightly, beautifully built:
295 Perchance I may return with others there
      When I have purged my guilt."
—1832 (REVISED 1842)

The Lady of Shalott [1]

PART 1

On either side the river lie
Long fields of barley and of rye,
That clothe the wold° and meet the sky;   *plain*
And through the field the road runs by
5   To many-towered Camelot;
And up and down the people go,
Gazing where the lilies blow
Round an island there below,
    The island of Shalott.

10 Willows whiten,[2] aspens quiver,
Little breezes dusk° and shiver   *darken*
Through the wave that runs for ever
By the island in the river
    Flowing down to Camelot.
15 Four gray walls, and four gray towers,
Overlook a space of flowers,
And the silent isle imbowers°   *encloses*
    The Lady of Shalott.

By the margin, willow-veiled,
20 Slide the heavy barges trailed
By slow horses; and unhailed
The shallop[3] flitteth silken-sailed
    Skimming down to Camelot:
But who hath seen her wave her hand?

25 Or at the casement seen her stand?
Or is she known in all the land,
    The Lady of Shalott?

Only reapers, reaping early
In among the bearded barley,
30 Hear a song that echoes cheerly
From the river winding clearly,
    Down to towered Camelot:
And by the moon the reaper weary,
Piling sheaves in uplands airy,
35 Listening, whispers "'Tis the fairy
    Lady of Shalott."

PART 2

There she weaves by night and day
A magic web with colours gay.
She has heard a whisper say,
40 A curse is on her if she stay
    To look down to Camelot.
She knows not what the curse may be,
And so she weaveth steadily,
And little other care hath she,
45   The Lady of Shalott.

And moving through a mirror clear
That hangs before her all the year,
Shadows of the world appear.
There she sees the highway near
50   Winding down to Camelot:
There the river eddy whirls,
And there the surly village-churls,
And the red cloaks of market girls,
    Pass onward from Shalott.

55 Sometimes a troop of damsels glad,
An abbot on an ambling pad,°   *horse*
Sometimes a curly shepherd-lad,
Or long-haired page in crimson clad,
    Goes by to towered Camelot;
60 And sometimes through the mirror blue
The knights come riding two and two:
She hath no loyal knight and true,
    The Lady of Shalott.

---

[1] *The Lady of Shalott* Elaine of the Arthurian romances, who dies of love for Lancelot; she is called "the lily maid of Astolat" in Malory's *Morte dArthur*. Tennyson first encountered the story, however, in a medieval Italian romance called "La Donna di Scalotta" and changed the name to Shalott for a softer sound.

[2] *Willows whiten* I.e., the wind exposes the white undersides of the leaves.

[3] *shallop* Light open boat for use in shallow water.

But in her web she still delights
65 To weave the mirror's magic sights,
For often through the silent nights
A funeral, with plumes and lights
    And music, went to Camelot:
Or when the moon was overhead,
70 Came two young lovers lately wed;
"I am half sick of shadows," said
    The Lady of Shalott.

PART 3

A bow-shot from her bower-eaves,
He rode between the barley-sheaves,
75 The sun came dazzling through the leaves,
And flamed upon the brazen greaves[1]
    Of bold Sir Lancelot.
A red-cross knight for ever kneeled
    To a lady in his shield,
80 That sparkled on the yellow field,
    Beside remote Shalott.

The gemmy° bridle glittered free,   *brilliant*
Like to some branch of stars we see
Hung in the golden Galaxy.
85 The bridle bells rang merrily
    As he rode down to Camelot:
And from his blazoned baldric° slung   *shoulder-strap*
A mighty silver bugle hung,
And as he rode his armour rung,
90   Beside remote Shalott.

All in the blue unclouded weather
Thick-jewelled shone the saddle-leather,
The helmet and the helmet-feather
Burned like one burning flame together,
95   As he rode down to Camelot.
As often through the purple night,
Below the starry clusters bright,
Some bearded meteor, trailing light,
    Moves over still Shalott.

100 His broad clear brow in sunlight glowed;
On burnished hooves his war-horse trode;
From underneath his helmet flowed
His coal-black curls as on he rode,
    As he rode down to Camelot.
105 From the bank and from the river
He flashed into the crystal mirror,
"Tirra lirra," by the river
    Sang Sir Lancelot.

She left the web, she left the loom,
110 She made three paces through the room,
She saw the water-lily bloom,
She saw the helmet and the plume,
    She looked down to Camelot.
Out flew the web and floated wide;
115 The mirror cracked from side to side;
"The curse is come upon me," cried
    The Lady of Shalott.

PART 4

In the stormy east-wind straining,
The pale yellow woods were waning,
120 The broad stream in his banks complaining,
Heavily the low sky raining
    Over towered Camelot;
Down she came and found a boat
Beneath a willow left afloat,
125 And round about the prow she wrote
    The Lady of Shalott.

And down the river's dim expanse
Like some bold seer in a trance,
Seeing all his own mischance—
130 With a glassy countenance
    Did she look to Camelot.
And at the closing of the day
She loosed the chain, and down she lay;
The broad stream bore her far away,
135   The Lady of Shalott.

---

[1] *greaves* Armor worn below the knee.

Lying, robed in snowy white
That loosely flew to left and right—
The leaves upon her falling light—
Through the noises of the night
140   She floated down to Camelot:
And as the boat-head wound along
The willowy hills and fields among,
They heard her singing her last song,
    The Lady of Shalott.

145   Heard a carol, mournful, holy,
Chanted loudly, chanted lowly,
Till her blood was frozen slowly,
And her eyes were darkened wholly,
    Turned to towered Camelot.
150   For ere she reached upon the tide
The first house by the water-side,
Singing in her song she died,
    The Lady of Shalott.

Under tower and balcony,
155   By garden-wall and gallery,
A gleaming shape she floated by,
Dead-pale between the houses high,
    Silent into Camelot.
Out upon the wharfs they came,
160   Knight and burgher, lord and dame,
And round the prow they read her name,
    The Lady of Shalott.

Who is this? and what is here?
And in the lighted palace near
165   Died the sound of royal cheer;
And they crossed themselves for fear,
    All the knights at Camelot:
But Lancelot mused a little space;
He said, "She has a lovely face;
170   God in his mercy lend her grace,
    The Lady of Shalott."

—1832 (REVISED 1842)

The Lotos-Eaters[1]

"Courage!" he said, and pointed toward the land,
    "This mounting wave will roll us shoreward
        soon."
In the afternoon they came unto a land
In which it seemed always afternoon.
5   All round the coast the languid air did swoon,
Breathing like one that hath a weary dream.
Full-faced above the valley stood the moon;
And like a downward smoke, the slender stream
Along the cliff to fall and pause and fall did seem.

10   A land of streams! some, like a downward smoke,
Slow-dropping veils of thinnest lawn,[2] did go;
And some through wavering lights and shadows broke,
Rolling a slumbrous sheet of foam below.
They saw the gleaming river seaward flow
15   From the inner land: far off, three mountain-tops,
Three silent pinnacles of agèd snow,
Stood sunset-flushed: and, dewed with showery drops,
Up-clomb the shadowy pine above the woven
        copse.°   *thicket*

The charmèd sunset lingered low adown
20   In the red West: through mountain clefts the dale
Was seen far inland, and the yellow down
Bordered with palm, and many a winding vale
And meadow, set with slender galingale;[3]
A land where all things always seemed the same!
25   And round about the keel with faces pale,
Dark faces pale against that rosy flame,
The mild-eyed melancholy Lotos-eaters came.

Branches they bore of that enchanted stem,
Laden with flower and fruit, whereof they gave
30   To each, but whoso did receive of them,

---

[1] *Lotos-Eaters* In Greek mythology, the Lotus Eaters (or Loto-phagi) were a race of people who inhabited an island near north Africa. They existed in peaceful apathy because of the narcotic effects of the lotus plants they ate. When Odysseus landed on the island, some of his men ate the lotus plants and wanted to stay on the island, rather than return home to their families. The incident is documented in Homer's *Odyssey* 9.2.

[2] *lawn* Fine fabric.

[3] *galingale* Species of sedge.

And taste, to him the gushing of the wave
Far far away did seem to mourn and rave
On alien shores; and if his fellow spake,
His voice was thin, as voices from the grave;
35 And deep-asleep he seemed, yet all awake,
And music in his ears his beating heart did make.

They sat them down upon the yellow sand,
Between the sun and moon upon the shore;
And sweet it was to dream of Fatherland,
40 Of child, and wife, and slave; but evermore
Most weary seemed the sea, weary the oar,
Weary the wandering fields of barren foam.
Then some one said, "We will return no more";
And all at once they sang, "Our island home
45 Is far beyond the wave; we will no longer roam."

CHORIC SONG[1]

1

There is sweet music here that softer falls
Than petals from blown roses on the grass,
Or night-dews on still waters between walls
Of shadowy granite, in a gleaming pass;
50 Music that gentlier on the spirit lies,
Than tired eyelids upon tired eyes;
Music that brings sweet sleep down from the blissful
    skies.
Here are cool mosses deep,
And through the moss the ivies creep,
55 And in the stream the long-leaved flowers weep,
And from the craggy ledge the poppy hangs in sleep.

2

Why are we weighed upon with heaviness,
And utterly consumed with sharp distress,
While all things else have rest from weariness?
60 All things have rest: why should we toil alone,
We only toil, who are the first of things,
And make perpetual moan,
Still from one sorrow to another thrown:
Nor ever fold our wings,
65 And cease from wanderings,
Nor steep our brows in slumber's holy balm;
Nor harken what the inner spirit sings,

"There is no joy but calm!"
Why should we only toil, the roof and crown of things?

3

70 Lo! in the middle of the wood,
The folded leaf is wooed from out the bud
With winds upon the branch, and there
Grows green and broad, and takes no care,
Sun-steeped at noon, and in the moon
75 Nightly dew-fed; and turning yellow
Falls, and floats adown the air.
Lo! sweetened with the summer light,
The full-juiced apple, waxing over-mellow,
Drops in a silent autumn night.
80 All its allotted length of days,
The flower ripens in its place,
Ripens and fades, and falls, and hath no toil,
Fast-rooted in the fruitful soil.

4

Hateful is the dark-blue sky,
85 Vaulted o'er the dark-blue sea.
Death is the end of life; ah, why
Should life all labour be?
Let us alone. Time driveth onward fast,
And in a little while our lips are dumb.
90 Let us alone. What is it that will last?
All things are taken from us, and become
Portions and parcels of the dreadful Past.
Let us alone. What pleasure can we have
To war with evil? Is there any peace
95 In ever climbing up the climbing wave?
All things have rest, and ripen toward the grave
In silence; ripen, fall and cease:
Give us long rest or death, dark death, or dreamful ease.

5

100 How sweet it were, hearing the downward stream,
With half-shut eyes ever to seem
Falling asleep in a half-dream!
To dream and dream, like yonder amber light,
Which will not leave the myrrh-bush on the height;
105 To hear each other's whispered speech;
Eating the Lotos day by day,
To watch the crisping ripples on the beach,

---

[1] *Choric Song* As performed by the Chorus in an ancient Greek play.

And tender curving lines of creamy spray;
To lend our hearts and spirits wholly
110 To the influence of mild-minded melancholy;
To muse and brood and live again in memory,
With those old faces of our infancy
Heaped over with a mound of grass,
Two handfuls of white dust,[1] shut in an urn of brass!

6

Dear is the memory of our wedded lives,
115 And dear the last embraces of our wives
And their warm tears: but all hath suffered change:
For surely now our household hearths are cold:
Our sons inherit us: our looks are strange:
And we should come like ghosts to trouble joy.
120 Or else the island princes over-bold
Have eat our substance, and the minstrel sings
Before them of the ten years' war in Troy,
And our great deeds, as half-forgotten things.
Is there confusion in the little isle?
125 Let what is broken so remain.
The Gods are hard to reconcile:
'Tis hard to settle order once again.
There *is* confusion worse than death,
Trouble on trouble, pain on pain,
130 Long labour unto agèd breath,
Sore task to hearts worn out by many wars
And eyes grown dim with gazing on the pilot-stars.

7

But, propped on beds of amaranth[2] and moly,[3]
How sweet (while warm airs lull us, blowing lowly)
135 With half-dropped eyelid still,
Beneath a heaven dark and holy,
To watch the long bright river drawing slowly
His waters from the purple hill—
To hear the dewy echoes calling
140 From cave to cave through the thick-twinèd vine—
To watch the emerald-coloured water falling
Through many a woven acanthus[4]-wreath divine!

Only to hear and see the far-off sparkling brine,
Only to hear were sweet, stretched out beneath the pine.

8

145 The Lotos blooms below the barren peak:
The Lotos blows by every winding creek:
All day the wind breathes low with mellower tone:
Through every hollow cave and alley lone
Round and round the spicy downs the yellow
      Lotos-dust is blown.
150 We have had enough of action, and of motion we,
Rolled to starboard, rolled to larboard,° when the   *port*
      surge was seething free,
Where the wallowing monster spouted his foam-
      fountains in the sea.
Let us swear an oath, and keep it with an equal mind,
In the hollow Lotos-land to live and lie reclined
155 On the hills like Gods together, careless of mankind.
For they lie beside their nectar, and the bolts are
      hurled
Far below them in the valleys, and the clouds are
      lightly curled
Round their golden houses, girdled with the gleaming
      world:
Where they smile in secret, looking over wasted lands,
160 Blight and famine, plague and earthquake, roaring
      deeps and fiery sands,
Clanging fights, and flaming towns, and sinking
      ships, and praying hands.
But they smile, they find a music centred in a doleful
      song
Steaming up, a lamentation and an ancient tale of
      wrong,
Like a tale of little meaning though the words are strong;
165 Chanted from an ill-used race of men that cleave the
      soil,
Sow the seed, and reap the harvest with enduring toil,
Storing yearly little dues of wheat, and wine and oil;
Till they perish and they suffer—some, 'tis whispered
      —down in hell
Suffer endless anguish, others in Elysian[5] valleys
      dwell,

---

[1] *white dust* I.e., cremated remains.

[2] *amaranth* Mythical flowers that never wilted.

[3] *moly* Herb with magical protective powers.

[4] *acanthus* Plant native to Mediterranean shores. The Greeks and
Romans esteemed the plant for the elegance of its leaves.

---

[5] *Elysian* Heavenly. According to the ancient Greeks, Elysium was
the dwelling place of the blessed after death.

170 Resting weary limbs at last on beds of asphodel.[1]
Surely, surely, slumber is more sweet than toil, the shore
Than labour in the deep mid-ocean, wind and wave
   and oar;
Oh rest ye, brother mariners, we will not wander more.
  —1832 (REVISED 1842)

Ulysses[2]

It little profits that an idle king,
  By this still hearth, among these barren crags,
Matched with an agèd wife, I mete and dole
Unequal laws unto a savage race,
5 That hoard, and sleep, and feed, and know not me.

I cannot rest from travel: I will drink
Life to the lees:° all times I have enjoyed   *dregs*
Greatly, have suffered greatly, both with those
That loved me, and alone; on shore, and when
10 Thro' scudding drifts the rainy Hyades[3]
Vexed the dim sea: I am become a name;
For always roaming with a hungry heart
Much have I seen and known; cities of men
And manners, climates, councils, governments,
15 Myself not least, but honoured of them all;
And drunk delight of battle with my peers,
Far on the ringing plains of windy Troy.
I am a part of all that I have met;
Yet all experience is an arch wherethrough
20 Gleams that untravelled world, whose margin°   *horizon*
   fades
For ever and for ever when I move.
How dull it is to pause, to make an end,
To rust unburnished, not to shine in use!
As though to breathe were life. Life piled on life
25 Were all too little, and of one to me
Little remains: but every hour is saved
From that eternal silence, something more,

A bringer of new things; and vile it were
For some three suns to store and hoard myself,
30 And this gray spirit yearning in desire
To follow knowledge like a sinking star,
Beyond the utmost bound of human thought.

This is my son, mine own Telemachus,
To whom I leave the sceptre and the isle—
35 Well-loved of me, discerning to fulfil
This labour, by slow prudence to make mild
A rugged people, and through soft degrees
Subdue them to the useful and the good.
Most blameless is he, centred in the sphere
40 Of common duties, decent not to fail
In offices of tenderness, and pay
Meet adoration to my household gods,
When I am gone. He works his work, I mine.

There lies the port; the vessel puffs her sail:
45 There gloom the dark broad seas. My mariners,
Souls that have toiled, and wrought, and thought
   with me—
That ever with a frolic welcome took
The thunder and the sunshine, and opposed
Free hearts, free foreheads—you and I are old;
50 Old age hath yet his honour and his toil;
Death closes all: but something ere the end,
Some work of noble note, may yet be done,
Not unbecoming men that strove with Gods.

The lights begin to twinkle from the rocks:
55 The long day wanes: the slow moon climbs: the deep
Moans round with many voices. Come, my friends,
'Tis not too late to seek a newer world.
Push off, and sitting well in order smite
The sounding furrows; for my purpose holds
60 To sail beyond the sunset, and the baths
Of all the western stars, until I die.
It may be that the gulfs will wash us down:
It may be we shall touch the Happy Isles,[4]
And see the great Achilles,[5] whom we knew.

---

[1] *asphodel* Plant said to cover the Elysian fields.

[2] *Ulysses* Latin name for Odysseus, the protagonist of Homer's *Odyssey*. Here, long after the adventures recounted in that book, the aged, yet restless, Ulysses prepares to embark on one last voyage of discovery.

[3] *Hyades* Group of stars near the constellation Taurus and associated with rainstorms.

[4] *Happy Isles* Elysium, or Isles of the Blessed, where heroes enjoyed the afterlife.

[5] *Achilles* Hero from Greek mythology, also the central character of Homer's *Iliad*.

65 Though much is taken, much abides; and though
We are not now that strength which in old days
Moved earth and heaven; that which we are, we are;
One equal temper of heroic hearts,
Made weak by time and fate, but strong in will
70 To strive, to seek, to find, and not to yield.
—1842 (WRITTEN 1833)

The Epic [Morte d'Arthur]

At Francis Allen's on the Christmas-eve,—
The game of forfeits done—the girls all kissed
Beneath the sacred bush[1] and past away—
The parson Holmes, the poet Everard Hall,
5 The host, and I sat round the wassail-bowl,[2]
Then half-way ebbed: and there we held a talk,
How all the old honour had from Christmas gone,
Or gone, or dwindled down to some odd games
In some odd nooks like this; till I, tired out
10 With cutting eights[3] that day upon the pond,
Where, three times slipping from the outer edge,
I bumped the ice into three several stars,
Fell in a doze; and half-awake I heard
The parson taking wide and wider sweeps,
15 Now harping on the church-commissioners,
Now hawking at Geology and schism;
Until I woke, and found him settled down
Upon the general decay of faith
Right through the world, "at home was little left,
20 And none abroad: there was no anchor, none,
To hold by." Francis, laughing, clapped his hand
On Everard's shoulder, with "I hold by him."
"And I," quoth Everard, "by the wassail-bowl."
"Why yes," I said, "we knew your gift that way
25 At college: but another which you had,
I mean of verse (for so we held it then),
What came of that?" "You know," said Frank, "he
        burnt
His epic, his King Arthur, some twelve books"—
And then to me demanding why? "Oh, sir,
30 He thought that nothing new was said, or else

Something so said 'twas nothing—that a truth
Looks freshest in the fashion of the day:
God knows: he has a mint of reasons: ask.
It pleased *me* well enough." "Nay, nay," said Hall,
35 "Why take the style of those heroic times?
For nature brings not back the Mastodon,
Nor we those times; and why should any man
Remodel models? these twelve books of mine
Were faint Homeric echoes, nothing-worth,
40 Mere chaff and draff,[4] much better burnt." "But I,"
Said Francis, "picked the eleventh from this hearth
And have it: keep a thing, its use will come.
I hoard it as a sugar-plum for Holmes."
He laughed, and I, though sleepy, like a horse
45 That hears the corn-bin open, pricked my ears;
For I remembered Everard's college fame
When we were freshmen: then at my request
He brought it; and the poet little urged,
But with some prelude of disparagement,
50 Read, mouthing out his hollow oes and aes,
Deep-chested music, and to this result.

Morte d'Arthur[5]

So all day long the noise of battle rolled
Among the mountains by the winter sea;
Until King Arthur's table, man by man,
Had fallen in Lyonnesse[6] about their Lord,
5 King Arthur: then, because his wound was deep,
The bold Sir Bedivere uplifted him,
Sir Bedivere, the last of all his knights,
And bore him to a chapel nigh the field,
A broken chancel[7] with a broken cross,
10 That stood on a dark strait of barren land.
On one side lay the ocean, and on one
Lay a great water, and the moon was full.

    Then spake King Arthur to Sir Bedivere:
"The sequel of today unsolders all

---

1   *sacred bush*   Mistletoe.

2   *wassail-bowl*   Punch bowl containing spiced ale.

3   *cutting eights*   Skating figure-eights.

4   *chaff and draff*   Here, refuse, material of little worth.

5   *Morte d'Arthur*   French: the death of [King] Arthur.

6   [Tennyson's note]   The country of legend that lay between Cornwall and the Scilly Islands.

7   *chancel*   Area around the altar.

15 The goodliest fellowship of famous knights
Whereof this world holds record. Such a sleep
They sleep—the men I loved. I think that we
Shall never more, at any future time,
Delight our souls with talk of knightly deeds,
20 Walking about the gardens and the halls
Of Camelot, as in the days that were.
I perish by this people which I made,—
Though Merlin sware that I should come again
To rule once more—but let what will be, be,
25 I am so deeply smitten through the helm
That without help I cannot last till morn.
Thou therefore take my brand° Excalibur,   *sword*
Which was my pride: for thou rememberest how
In those old days, one summer noon, an arm
30 Rose up from out the bosom of the lake,
Clothed in white samite,° mystic, wonderful,   *silk*
Holding the sword—and how I rowed across
And took it, and have worn it, like a king:
And, wheresoever I am sung or told
35 In aftertime, this also shall be known:
But now delay not: take Excalibur,
And fling him far into the middle mere:[1]
Watch what thou seest, and lightly bring me word."

To him replied the bold Sir Bedivere:
40 "It is not meet,° Sir King, to leave thee thus,   *appropriate*
Aidless, alone, and smitten through the helm.
A little thing may harm a wounded man.
Yet I thy hest° will all perform at full,   *command*
Watch what I see, and lightly bring thee word."

45 So saying, from the ruined shrine he stepped
And in the moon athwart the place of tombs,
Where lay the mighty bones of ancient men,
Old knights, and over them the sea-wind sang
Shrill, chill, with flakes of foam. He, stepping down
50 By zig-zag paths, and juts of pointed rock,
Came on the shining levels of the lake.

There drew he forth the brand Excalibur,
And o'er him, drawing it, the winter moon,
Brightening the skirts of a long cloud, ran forth
55 And sparkled keen with frost against the hilt:

For all the haft° twinkled with diamond sparks,   *handle*
Myriads of topaz-lights, and jacinth[2]-work
Of subtlest jewellery. He gazed so long
That both his eyes were dazzled, as he stood,
60 This way and that dividing the swift mind,
In act to throw: but at the last it seemed
Better to leave Excalibur concealed
There in the many-knotted waterflags,°   *iris*
That whistled stiff and dry about the marge.°   *shore*
65 So strode he back slow to the wounded King.

Then spake King Arthur to Sir Bedivere:
"Hast thou performed my mission which I gave?
What is it thou hast seen? or what hast heard?"

And answer made the bold Sir Bedivere:
70 "I heard the ripple washing in the reeds,
And the wild water lapping on the crag."

To whom replied King Arthur, faint and pale:
"Thou hast betrayed thy nature and thy name,
Not rendering true answer, as beseemed
75 Thy fealty,° nor like a noble knight: *sworn allegiance*
For surer sign had followed, either hand,
Or voice, or else a motion of the mere.
This is a shameful thing for men to lie.
Yet now, I charge thee, quickly go again
80 As thou art lief° and dear, and do the thing   *beloved*
I bad[3] thee, watch, and lightly bring me word."

Then went Sir Bedivere the second time
Across the ridge, and paced beside the mere,
Counting the dewy pebbles, fix'd in thought;
85 But when he saw the wonder of the hilt,
How curiously and strangely chased,° he smote   *engraved*
His palms together, and he cried aloud,

"And if indeed I cast the brand away,
Surely a precious thing, one worthy note,
90 Should thus be lost for ever from the earth,
Which might have pleased the eyes of many men.
What good should follow this, if this were done?
What harm, undone? deep harm to disobey,

---

[1] *middle mere* Middle of the lake.

[2] *jacinth* Reddish-orange gem.

[3] *bad* I.e., bade, commanded.

Seeing obedience is the bond of rule.
95   Were it well to obey then, if a king demand
An act unprofitable, against himself?
The King is sick, and knows not what he does.
What record, or what relic of my lord
Should be to aftertime, but empty breath
100   And rumours of a doubt? but were this kept,
Stored in some treasure-house of mighty kings,
Some one might show it at a joust of arms,
Saying, "King Arthur's sword, Excalibur,
Wrought by the lonely maiden of the Lake.
105   Nine years she wrought it, sitting in the deeps
Upon the hidden bases of the hills."
So might some old man speak in the aftertime
To all the people, winning reverence.
But now much honour and much fame were lost."

110   So spake he, clouded with his own conceit,
And hid Excalibur the second time,
And so strode back slow to the wounded King.

Then spoke King Arthur, breathing heavily:
"What is it thou hast seen? or what hast heard?"
115   And answer made the bold Sir Bedivere:
"I heard the water lapping on the crag,
And the long ripple washing in the reeds."

To whom replied King Arthur, much in wrath:
"Ah, miserable and unkind, untrue,
120   Unknightly, traitor-hearted! Woe is me!
Authority forgets a dying king,
Laid widowed of the power in his eye
That bowed the will. I see thee what thou art,
For thou, the latest-left of all my knights,
125   In whom should meet the offices of all,
Thou wouldst betray me for the precious hilt;
Either from lust of gold, or like a girl
Valuing the giddy pleasure of the eyes.
Yet, for a man may fail in duty twice,
30   And the third time may prosper, get thee hence:
But, if thou spare to fling Excalibur,
I will arise and slay thee with my hands."

Then quickly rose Sir Bedivere, and ran,
And, leaping down the ridges lightly, plunged

135   Among the bulrush-beds, and clutched the sword,
And strongly wheeled and threw it. The great brand
Made lightnings in the splendour of the moon,
And flashing round and round, and whirled in an arch,
Shot like a streamer of the northern morn,
140   Seen where the moving isles of winter shock
By night, with noises of the northern sea.
So flashed and fell the brand Excalibur:
But ere he dipped the surface, rose an arm
Clothed in white samite, mystic, wonderful,
145   And caught him by the hilt, and brandished him
Three times, and drew him under in the mere.
And lightly went the other to the King.

Then spoke King Arthur, drawing thicker breath:
"Now see I by thine eyes that this is done.
150   Speak out: what is it thou hast heard, or seen?"

And answer made the bold Sir Bedivere:
"Sir King, I closed mine eyelids, lest the gems
Should blind my purpose, for I never saw,
Nor shall see, here or elsewhere, till I die,
155   Not though I live three lives of mortal men,
So great a miracle as yonder hilt.
Then with both hands I flung him, wheeling him;
But when I looked again, behold an arm,
Clothed in white samite, mystic, wonderful,
160   That caught him by the hilt, and brandished him
Three times, and drew him under in the mere."

And answer made King Arthur, breathing hard:
"My end draws nigh; 'tis time that I were gone.
Make broad thy shoulders to receive my weight,
165   And bear me to the margin; yet I fear
My wound hath taken cold, and I shall die."

So saying, from the pavement he half rose,
Slowly, with pain, reclining on his arm,
And looking wistfully with wide blue eyes
170   As in a picture. Him Sir Bedivere
Remorsefully regarded through his tears,
And would have spoken, but he found not words,
Then took with care, and kneeling on one knee,
O'er both his shoulders drew the languid hands,
175   And rising bore him through the place of tombs.

But, as he walked, King Arthur panted hard,
Like one that feels a nightmare on his bed
When all the house is mute. So sighed the King,
Muttering and murmuring at his ear, "Quick, quick!
180 I fear it is too late, and I shall die."
But the other swiftly strode from ridge to ridge,
Clothed with his breath, and looking, as he walked,
Larger than human on the frozen hills.
He heard the deep behind him, and a cry
185 Before. His own thought drove him, like a goad.
Dry clashed his harness in the icy caves
And barren chasms, and all to left and right
The bare black cliff clanged round him, as he based
His feet on juts of slippery crag that rang
190 Sharp-smitten with the dint of armèd heels—
And on a sudden, lo! the level lake,
And the long glories of the winter moon.

Then saw they how there hove a dusky barge,
Dark as a funeral scarf from stem to stern,
195 Beneath them; and descending they were ware°   *aware*
That all the decks were dense with stately forms
Black-stoled, black-hooded, like a dream—by these
Three Queens with crowns of gold—and from them
     rose
A cry that shivered to the tingling stars,
200 And, as it were one voice, an agony
Of lamentation, like a wind, that shrills
All night in a waste land, where no one comes,
Or hath come, since the making of the world.

Then murmured Arthur, "Place me in the barge,"
205 And to the barge they came. There those three Queens
Put forth their hands, and took the King, and wept.
But she, that rose the tallest of them all
And fairest, laid his head upon her lap,
And loosed the shattered casque,° and chafed   *helmet*
     his hands,
210 And called him by his name, complaining loud,
And dropping bitter tears against his brow
Striped with dark blood: for all his face was white
And colourless, and like the withered moon
Smote by the fresh beam of the springing east;
215 And all his greaves and cuisses[1] dashed with drops
Of onset; and the light and lustrous curls—

That made his forehead like a rising sun
High from the dais-throne—were parched with dust;
Or, clotted into points and hanging loose,
220 Mix'd with the knightly growth that fringed his lips.
So like a shattered column lay the King;
Not like that Arthur who, with lance in rest,
From spur to plume a star of tournament,
Shot through the lists[2] at Camelot, and charged
225 Before the eyes of ladies and of kings.

Then loudly cried the bold Sir Bedivere,
"Ah! my Lord Arthur, whither shall I go?
Where shall I hide my forehead and my eyes?
For now I see the true old times are dead,
230 When every morning brought a noble chance,
And every chance brought out a noble knight.
Such times have been not since the light that led
The holy Elders with the gift of myrrh.
But now the whole Round Table is dissolved
235 Which was an image of the mighty world;
And I, the last, go forth companionless,
And the days darken round me, and the years,
Among new men, strange faces, other minds."

And slowly answered Arthur from the barge:
240 "The old order changeth, yielding place to new,
And God fulfils Himself in many ways,
Lest one good custom should corrupt the world.
Comfort thyself: what comfort is in me?
I have lived my life, and that which I have done
245 May He within Himself make pure! but thou,
If thou shouldst never see my face again,
Pray for my soul. More things are wrought by prayer
Than this world dreams of. Wherefore, let thy voice
Rise like a fountain for me night and day.
250 For what are men better than sheep or goats
That nourish a blind life within the brain,
If, knowing God, they lift not hands of prayer
Both for themselves and those who call them friend?
For so the whole round earth is every way
255 Bound by gold chains about the feet of God.
But now farewell. I am going a long way
With these thou seest—if indeed I go—
(For all my mind is clouded with a doubt)

---

[1] *greaves and cuisses* Armor for shins and thighs.

[2] *lists* Arenas in which jousting and tilting tournaments were held.

To the island-valley of Avilion;°   *i.e., Avalon*
260   Where falls not hail, or rain, or any snow,
Nor ever wind blows loudly; but it lies
Deep-meadowed, happy, fair with orchard-lawns
And bowery hollows crown'd with summer sea,
Where I will heal me of my grievous wound."

265   So said he, and the barge with oar and sail
Moved from the brink, like some full-breasted swan
That, fluting a wild carol ere her death,[1]
Ruffles her pure cold plume, and takes the flood
With swarthy webs.[2] Long stood Sir Bedivere
270   Revolving many memories, till the hull
Looked one black dot against the verge of dawn,
And on the mere the wailing died away.
                —1842 (WRITTEN 1833–34)

[Break, break, break]

Break, break, break,
    On thy cold gray stones, O Sea!
And I would that my tongue could utter
    The thoughts that arise in me.

5   O well for the fisherman's boy,
    That he shouts with his sister at play!
O well for the sailor lad,
    That he sings in his boat on the bay!

And the stately ships go on
10   To their haven under the hill;
But O for the touch of a vanished hand,
    And the sound of a voice that is still![3]

Break, break, break,
    At the foot of thy crags, O Sea!
15   But the tender grace of a day that is dead
    Will never come back to me.
                —1842 (WRITTEN 1834?)

---

[1] *swan ... death* Swans were said to sing only once, at their deaths.

[2] *webs* I.e., webbed feet.

[3] *But ... still* Probably a reference to Tennyson's closest friend, Arthur Hallam, who had died in 1833.

Locksley Hall

Comrades, leave me here a little, while as yet 'tis early morn:
Leave me here, and when you want me, sound upon the bugle-horn.

'Tis the place, and all around it, as of old, the curlews[4] call,
Dreary gleams about the moorland flying over Locksley Hall;

5   Locksley Hall, that in the distance overlooks the sandy tracts,
And the hollow ocean-ridges roaring into cataracts.

Many a night from yonder ivied casement, ere I went to rest,
Did I look on great Orion[5] sloping slowly to the West.

Many a night I saw the Pleiads,[6] rising through the mellow shade,
10   Glitter like a swarm of fire-flies tangled in a silver braid.

Here about the beach I wandered, nourishing a youth sublime
With the fairy tales of science, and the long result of Time;

When the centuries behind me like a fruitful land reposed;
When I clung to all the present for the promise that it closed:

15   When I dipped into the future far as human eye could see;

---

[4] *curlews* Species of shore-dwelling birds.

[5] *Orion* The constellation named after the hunter of Greek legend. It sets in November and so was associated with rains and storms.

[6] *Pleiads* The constellation commonly known as the Pleiades (named after the seven daughters of Atlas), which rises in May and sets in November.

Saw the Vision of the world, and all the wonder that
    would be.—

In the Spring a fuller crimson comes upon the robin's
    breast;
In the Spring the wanton lapwing gets himself
    another crest;

In the Spring a livelier iris changes on the burnished
    dove;
20 In the Spring a young man's fancy lightly turns to
    thoughts of love.

Then her cheek was pale and thinner than should be
    for one so young,
And her eyes on all my motions with a mute
    observance hung.

And I said, "My cousin Amy, speak, and speak the
    truth to me,
Trust me, cousin, all the current of my being sets to
    thee."

25 On her pallid cheek and forehead came a colour and a
    light,
As I have seen the rosy red flushing in the northern
    night.

And she turned—her bosom shaken with a sudden
    storm of sighs—
All the spirit deeply dawning in the dark of hazel eyes—

Saying, "I have hid my feelings, fearing they should
    do me wrong;"
30 Saying, "Dost thou love me, cousin?" weeping, "I
    have loved thee long."

Love took up the glass of Time,[1] and turned it in
    his glowing hands;
Every moment, lightly shaken, ran itself in golden
    sands.

Love took up the harp of Life, and smote on all the
    chords with might;

Smote the chord of Self, that, trembling, passed in
    music out of sight.

35 Many a morning on the moorland did we hear the
    copses ring,
And her whisper thronged my pulses with the fullness
    of the Spring.

Many an evening by the waters did we watch the
    stately ships,
And our spirits rushed together at the touching of
    the lips.

O my cousin, shallow-hearted! O my Amy, mine no
    more!
40 O the dreary, dreary moorland! O the barren, barren
    shore!

Falser than all fancy fathoms,° falser than all   *apprehends*
    songs have sung,
Puppet to a father's threat, and servile to a shrewish
    tongue!

Is it well to wish thee happy?—having known me—to
    decline
On a range of lower feelings and a narrower heart
    than mine!

45 Yet it shall be: thou shalt lower to his level day by day,
What is fine within thee growing coarse to sympathise
    with clay.

As the husband is, the wife is: thou art mated with a
    clown,[2]
And the grossness of his nature will have weight to
    drag thee down.

He will hold thee, when his passion shall have spent
    its novel force,
50 Something better than his dog, a little dearer than his
    horse.

What is this? his eyes are heavy: think not they are
    glazed with wine.

---

[1] *glass of Time* Hourglass.

[2] *Clown* Rustic, boorish fellow.

Go to him: it is thy duty: kiss him: take his hand in
    thine.

It may be my lord is weary, that his brain is
    overwrought:
Soothe him with thy finer fancies,° touch him with
    thy lighter thought.   *interests*

55 He will answer to the purpose, easy things to
    understand—
Better thou wert dead before me, though I slew thee
    with my hand!

Better thou and I were lying, hidden from the heart's
    disgrace,
Rolled in one another's arms, and silent in a last
    embrace.

Cursèd be the social wants that sin against the
    strength of youth!
60 Cursèd be the social lies that warp us from the
    living truth!

Cursèd be the sickly forms that err from honest
    Nature's rule!
Cursèd be the gold that gilds the straitened forehead
    of the fool![1]

Well—'tis well that I should bluster!—Hadst thou
    less unworthy proved—
Would to God—for I had loved thee more than ever
    wife was loved.

65 Am I mad, that I should cherish that which bears but
    bitter fruit?
I will pluck it from my bosom, though my heart be at
    the root.

Never, though my mortal summers to such length
    of years should come
As the many-wintered crow that leads the clanging
    rookery home.

Where is comfort? in division of the records of the
    mind?
70 Can I part her from herself, and love her, as I knew
    her, kind?

I remember one that perished: sweetly did she speak
    and move:
Such a one do I remember, whom to look at was to
    love.

Can I think of her as dead, and love her for the love
    she bore?
No—she never loved me truly: love is love for
    evermore.

75 Comfort? comfort scorned of devils! this is truth the
    poet sings,
That a sorrow's crown of sorrow is remembering
    happier things.[2]

Drug thy memories, lest thou learn it, lest thy heart be
    put to proof,
In the dead unhappy night, and when the rain is on
    the roof.

Like a dog, he hunts in dreams, and thou art staring at
    the wall,
80 Where the dying night-lamp flickers, and the
    shadows rise and fall.

Then a hand shall pass before thee, pointing to his
    drunken sleep,
To thy widowed[3] marriage-pillows, to the tears that
    thou wilt weep.

Thou shalt hear the "Never, never," whispered by the
    phantom years,
And a song from out the distance in the ringing of
    thine ears;

85 And an eye shall vex thee, looking ancient kindness on
    thy pain.

---

[1] *straitened … fool* Narrow or low foreheads were thought to
indicate stupidity.

[2] *this … things* Cf. Dante, *Inferno* v. 121–23: "No greater grief
than to remember joy, when misery is at hand."

[3] *widowed* In that she is no longer the poet's lover.

Turn thee, turn thee on thy pillow: get thee to thy
  rest again.

Nay, but Nature brings thee solace; for a tender
  voice will cry.
'Tis a purer life than thine; a lip to drain thy trouble dry.

Baby lips will laugh me down: my latest rival brings
  thee rest.
90 Baby fingers, waxen touches, press me from the
  mother's breast.

O, the child too clothes the father with a dearness not
  his due.
Half is thine and half is his: it will be worthy of the two.

O, I see thee old and formal, fitted to thy petty part,
With a little hoard of maxims preaching down a
  daughter's heart.

95 "They were dangerous guides the feelings—she[1]
  herself was not exempt—
Truly, she herself had suffered"—Perish in thy self-
  contempt!

Overlive it—lower yet—be happy! wherefore should I
  care?
I myself must mix with action, lest I wither by despair.

What is that which I should turn to, lighting upon
  days like these?
100 Every door is barred with gold, and opens but to
  golden keys.

Every gate is thronged with suitors, all the markets
  overflow.
I have but an angry fancy: what is that which I should
  do?

I had been content to perish, falling on the foeman's
  ground,
When the ranks are rolled in vapour, and the winds
  are laid with sound.

105 But the jingling of the guinea° helps the hurt   *coin*
  that Honour feels,
And the nations do but murmur, snarling at each
  other's heels.

Can I but relive in sadness? I will turn that earlier page.
Hide me from my deep emotion, O thou wondrous
  Mother-Age!

Make me feel the wild pulsation that I felt before the
  strife,
110 When I heard my days before me, and the tumult of
  my life;

Yearning for the large excitement that the coming
  years would yield,
Eager-hearted as a boy when first he leaves his father's
  field,

And at night along the dusky highway near and
  nearer drawn,
Sees in heaven the light of London flaring like a
  dreary dawn;

115 And his spirit leaps within him to be gone before him
  then,
Underneath the light he looks at, in among the
  throngs of men:

Men, my brothers, men the workers, ever reaping
  something new:
That which they have done but earnest of the things
  that they shall do:

For I dipped into the future, far as human eye could
  see,
120 Saw the Vision of the world, and all the wonder that
  would be;

Saw the heavens fill with commerce, argosies[2] of
  magic sails,
Pilots of the purple twilight, dropping down with
  costly bales;

---

1 *she* The poet's cousin, pictured in the future speaking in the
third person of herself to her daughter.

2 *argosies* Large merchant ships.

Heard the heavens fill with shouting, and there rained
  a ghastly dew
From the nations' airy navies grappling in the central
  blue;

125 Far along the world-wide whisper of the south-wind
  rushing warm,
With the standards of the peoples plunging through
  the thunder-storm;

Till the war-drum throbbed no longer, and the
  battle-flags were furled
In the Parliament of man, the Federation of the world.

There the common sense of most shall hold a fretful
  realm in awe,
130 And the kindly earth shall slumber, lapped in
  universal law.

So I triumphed ere my passion sweeping through me
  left me dry,
Left me with the palsied heart, and left me with the
  jaundiced eye;

Eye, to which all order festers, all things here are out
  of joint:
Science moves, but slowly slowly, creeping on from
  point to point:

135 Slowly comes a hungry people, as a lion creeping
  nigher,
Glares at one that nods and winks behind a slowly-
  dying fire.

Yet I doubt not through the ages one increasing
  purpose runs,
And the thoughts of men are widened with the
  process of the suns.

What is that to him that reaps not harvest of his
  youthful joys,
140 Though the deep heart of existence beat forever like a
  boy's?

Knowledge comes, but wisdom lingers, and I linger
  on the shore,
And the individual withers, and the world is more
  and more.

Knowledge comes, but wisdom lingers, and he bears a
  laden breast,
Full of sad experience, moving toward the stillness of
  his rest.

145 Hark, my merry comrades call me, sounding on the
  bugle-horn,
They to whom my foolish passion were a target for
  their scorn:

Shall it not be scorn to me to harp on such a
  mouldered string?
I am shamed through all my nature to have loved so
  slight a thing.

Weakness to be wroth° with weakness!   *angry*
  woman's pleasure, woman's pain—
150 Nature made them blinder motions bounded in a
  shallower brain:

Woman is the lesser man, and all thy passions,
  matched with mine,
Are as moonlight unto sunlight, and as water unto
  wine—

Here at least, where nature sickens, nothing. Ah, for
  some retreat
Deep in yonder shining Orient, where my life began
  to beat;

155 Where in wild Mahratta-battle[1] fell my father evil-
  starred;—[2]
I was left a trampled orphan, and a selfish uncle's
  ward.

Or to burst all links of habit—there to wander far away,
On from island unto island at the gateways of the day.

---

[1] *Mahratta-battle* Conflict between the British and the Mahratta
soldiers from Bombay in 1818.

[2] *evil-starred* Cursed with bad luck.

Larger constellations burning, mellow moons and
    happy skies,
160 Breadths of tropic shade and palms in cluster, knots of
    Paradise.

Never comes the trader, never floats an European flag,
Slides the bird o'er lustrous woodland, swings the
    trailer[1] from the crag;

Droops the heavy-blossomed bower, hangs the heavy-
    fruited tree—
Summer isles of Eden lying in dark-purple spheres
    of sea.

165 There methinks would be enjoyment more than in
    this march of mind,
In the steamship, in the railway, in the thoughts
    that shake mankind.

There the passions cramped no longer shall have
    scope and breathing space;
I will take some savage woman, she shall rear my
    dusky race.

Iron jointed, supple-sinewed, they shall dive, and they
    shall run,
170 Catch the wild goat by the hair, and hurl their lances
    in the sun;

Whistle back the parrot's call, and leap the rainbows
    of the brooks,
Not with blinded eyesight poring over miserable
    books—

Fool, again the dream, the fancy! but I *know* my
    words are wild,
But I count the gray barbarian lower than the
    Christian child.

175 I, to herd with narrow foreheads, vacant of our
    glorious gains,
Like a beast with lower pleasures, like a beast with
    lower pains!

Mated with a squalid savage—what to me were sun or
    clime?
I the heir of all the ages, in the foremost files[2] of
    time—

I that rather held it better men should perish one
    by one,
180 Than that earth should stand at gaze like Joshua's
    moon in Ajalon![3]

Not in vain the distance beacons. Forward,
    forward let us range,
Let the great world spin forever down the ringing
    grooves of change.

Through the shadow of the globe we sweep into
    the younger day:
Better fifty years of Europe than a cycle of
    Cathay.°   *China*

185 Mother-Age (for mine I knew not) help me as
    when life begun:
Rift° the hills, and roll the waters, flash the   *split open*
    lightnings, weigh the Sun.
O, I see the crescent promise of my spirit hath not set.
Ancient founts of inspiration well through all my
    fancy yet.

Howsoever these things be, a long farewell to Locksley
    Hall!
190 Now for me the woods may wither, now for me the
    roof-tree fall.

Comes a vapour from the margin, blackening over
    heath and holt,°   *wood*
Cramming all the blast before it, in its breast a
    thunderbolt.

Let it fall on Locksley Hall, with rain or hail, or fire or
    snow;
For the mighty wind arises, roaring seaward, and I go.
—1842

---

[1] *trailer* Vine or hanging branch.

[2] *files* The ages of time pictured as men marching in file.

[3] *Joshua's ... Ajalon* In Joshua 10.12–13, Joshua makes the moon and sun stand still during a battle in the valley of Ajalon.

from *The Princess*

[*Sweet and Low*]

Sweet and low, sweet and low,
   Wind of the western sea,
Low, low, breathe and blow,
   Wind of the western sea!
5 Over the rolling waters go,
Come from the dying moon, and blow,
   Blow him again to me;
While my little one, while my pretty one, sleeps.

Sleep and rest, sleep and rest,
10   Father will come to thee soon;
Rest, rest, on mother's breast,
    Father will come to thee soon;
Father will come to his babe in the nest,
Silver sails all out of the west
15   Under the silver moon:
Sleep, my little one, sleep, my pretty one, sleep.

[*The Splendour Falls*]

The splendour falls on castle walls
   And snowy summits old in story:
The long light shakes across the lakes,
   And the wild cataract° leaps in glory.   *waterfall*
5 Blow, bugle, blow, set the wild echoes flying,
Blow, bugle; answer, echoes, dying, dying, dying.

O hark, O hear! how thin and clear,
   And thinner, clearer, farther going!
O sweet and far from cliff and scar[1]
10   The horns of Elfland faintly blowing!
Blow, let us hear the purple glens replying:
Blow, bugle; answer, echoes, dying, dying, dying.

O love, they die in yon rich sky,
   They faint on hill or field or river:
Our echoes roll from soul to soul,
15

And grow for ever and for ever.
Blow, bugle, blow, set the wild echoes flying,
And answer, echoes, answer, dying, dying, dying.

[*Tears, Idle Tears*]

Tears, idle tears, I know not what they mean,
   Tears from the depth of some divine despair
Rise in the heart, and gather to the eyes,
In looking on the happy Autumn-fields,
5 And thinking of the days that are no more.

Fresh as the first beam glittering on a sail,
That brings our friends up from the underworld,
Sad as the last which reddens over one
That sinks with all we love below the verge;°   *horizon*
10 So sad, so fresh, the days that are no more.

Ah, sad and strange as in dark summer dawns
The earliest pipe of half-awakened birds
To dying ears, when unto dying eyes
The casement° slowly grows a glimmering *window frame*
   square;
15 So sad, so strange, the days that are no more.

Dear as remembered kisses after death,
And sweet as those by hopeless fancy feigned
On lips that are for others; deep as love,
Deep as first love, and wild with all regret;
20 O Death in Life, the days that are no more."

[*Now Sleeps the Crimson Petal*]

Now sleeps the crimson petal, now the white;
   Nor waves the cypress in the palace walk;
Nor winks the gold fin in the porphyry[2] font:
The fire-fly wakens: waken thou with me.

5 Now droops the milkwhite peacock like a ghost,
And like a ghost she glimmers on to me.

---

[1] *scar* Steep, craggy portion of mountainside.

[2] *porphyry* Beautiful, polished purple stone.

Now lies the Earth all Danaë[1] to the stars,
And all thy heart lies open unto me.

Now slides the silent meteor on, and leaves
10   A shining furrow, as thy thoughts in me.

Now folds the lily all her sweetness up,
And slips into the bosom of the lake:
So fold thyself, my dearest, thou, and slip
Into my bosom and be lost in me.

[Come Down, O Maid]

Come down, O maid, from yonder
   mountain height:
What pleasure lives in height (the shepherd sang)
In height and cold, the splendour of the hills?
But cease to move so near the Heavens, and cease
5   To glide a sunbeam by the blasted Pine,
To sit a star upon the sparkling spire;
And come, for Love is of the valley, come,
For Love is of the valley, come thou down
And find him; by the happy threshold, he,
10   Or hand in hand with Plenty in the maize,
Or red with spurted purple of the vats,
Or foxlike in the vine;[2] nor cares to walk
With Death and Morning on the silver horns,
Nor wilt thou snare him in the white ravine,
15   Nor find him dropped upon the firths° of ice,   *juttings*
That huddling slant in furrow-cloven falls
To roll the torrent out of dusky doors:
But follow; let the torrent dance thee down
To find him in the valley; let the wild
20   Lean-headed Eagles yelp alone, and leave
The monstrous ledges there to slope, and spill
Their thousand wreaths of dangling water-smoke,
That like a broken purpose waste in air:
So waste not thou; but come; for all the vales

25   Await thee; azure pillars of the hearth
Arise to thee; the children call, and I
Thy shepherd pipe, and sweet is every sound,
Sweeter thy voice, but every sound is sweet;
Myriads of rivulets hurrying through the lawn,
30   The moan of doves in immemorial elms,
And murmuring of innumerable bees.

[The Woman's Cause is Man's]

"Blame not thyself too much," I said, "nor blame
Too much the sons of men and barbarous laws;
These were the rough ways of the world till now.
Henceforth thou hast a helper, me, that know
5   The woman's cause is man's: they rise or sink
Together, dwarfed or godlike, bond or free:
For she that out of Lethe[3] scales with man
The shining steps of Nature, shares with man
His nights, his days, moves with him to one goal,
10   Stays° all the fair young planet in her hands—   *sustains*
If she be small, slight-natured, miserable,
How shall men grow? but work no more alone!
Our place is much: as far as in us lies
We two will serve them both in aiding her—
15   Will clear away the parasitic forms
That seem to keep her up but drag her down—
Will leave her space to burgeon out of all
Within her—let her make herself her own
To give or keep, to live and learn and be
20   All that not harms distinctive womanhood.
For woman is not undeveloped man,
But diverse: could we make her as the man,
Sweet Love were slain: his dearest bond is this,
Not like to like, but like in difference.
25   Yet in the long years liker must they grow;
The man be more of woman, she of man;
He gain in sweetness and in moral height,
Nor lose the wrestling thews° that throw   *muscles*
   the world;

---

1 *Danaë* In Greek mythology, a princess visited by Zeus in the form of a shower of gold.

2 *foxlike ... vine* See *Song of Solomon* 2.15: "Take us the foxes, the little foxes, that spoil the vines ...."

3 *Lethe* In Greek myth, one of the rivers of Hades. Drinking its waters caused the souls of the dead to forget their past lives.

She mental breadth, nor fail in childward care,
30   Nor lose the childlike in the larger mind;
Till at the last she set herself to man,
Like perfect music unto noble words;
And so these twain, upon the skirts° of Time,   *borders*
Sit side by side, full-summed in all their powers,
35   Dispensing harvest, sowing the To-be,
Self-reverent each and reverencing each,
Distinct in individualities,
But like each other even as those who love.
Then comes the statelier Eden back to men:
40   Then reign the world's great bridals, chaste and calm:
Then springs the crowning race of humankind.
May these things be!
        Sighing she spoke "I fear
They will not."
45   "Dear, but let us type them now
In our own lives, and this proud watchword rest
Of equal; seeing either sex alone
Is half itself, and in true marriage lies
Nor equal, nor unequal: each fulfils
50   Defect in each, and always thought in thought,
Purpose in purpose, will in will, they grow,
The single pure and perfect animal,
The two-celled heart beating, with one full stroke, Life."
        And again sighing she spoke: "A dream
55   That once was mine! what woman taught you this?"
—1847

In Memoriam A.H.H.[1]

[PROLOGUE]

Strong Son of God, immortal Love,
    Whom we, that have not seen Thy face,
        By faith, and faith alone, embrace,
Believing where we cannot prove;

5   Thine are these orbs of light and shade;
    Thou madest Life in man and brute;

Thou madest Death; and lo, Thy foot
Is on the skull which Thou hast made.

Thou wilt not leave us in the dust:
10   Thou madest man, he knows not why,
        He thinks he was not made to die;
And Thou hast made him: Thou art just.

Thou seemest human and divine,
        The highest, holiest manhood, Thou:
15   Our wills are ours, we know not how;
Our wills are ours, to make them Thine.

Our little systems have their day;
        They have their day and cease to be:
        They are but broken lights of Thee,
20   And Thou, O Lord, art more than they.

We have but faith: we cannot know;
        For knowledge is of things we see;
        And yet we trust it comes from Thee,
A beam in darkness: let it grow.

25   Let knowledge grow from more to more,
        But more of reverence in us dwell;
        That mind and soul, according well,
May make one music as before,[2]

But vaster. We are fools and slight;
30   We mock Thee when we do not fear:
        But help Thy foolish ones to bear;
Help Thy vain worlds to bear Thy light.

Forgive what seemed my sin in me;
        What seemed my worth since I began;
35   For merit lives from man to man,
And not from man, O Lord, to Thee.

Forgive my grief for one removed,
        Thy creature, whom I found so fair.
        I trust he lives in Thee, and there
40   I find him worthier to be loved.

---

[1] *In Memoriam* Latin: in memory of; *A.H.H.* Arthur Henry Hallam (1811–1833), English poet, and one of Tennyson's closest friends. Hallam died suddenly of a brain hemorrhage while on vacation in Vienna.

[2] [Tennyson's note]   As in the ages of faith.

Forgive these wild and wandering cries,
    Confusions of a wasted youth;
    Forgive them where they fail in truth,
And in Thy wisdom make me wise.
    —1849

1

I held it truth, with him who sings
    To one clear harp in divers tones,
    That men may rise on stepping-stones
Of their dead selves to higher things.[1]

5 But who shall so forecast the years
    And find in loss a gain to match?
    Or reach a hand through time to catch
The far-off interest of tears?

Let Love clasp Grief lest both be drowned,
10   Let darkness keep her raven gloss:
    Ah, sweeter to be drunk with loss,
To dance with death, to beat the ground,

Than that the victor Hours[2] should scorn
    The long result of love, and boast,
15   "Behold the man that loved and lost,
But all he was is overworn."

2

Old Yew,[3] which graspest at the stones
    That name the under-lying dead,
    Thy fibres net the dreamless head,
Thy roots are wrapped about the bones.

5 The seasons bring the flower again,
    And bring the firstling[4] to the flock;
    And in the dusk of thee, the clock
Beats out the little lives of men.

O not for thee the glow, the bloom,
10   Who changest not in any gale,
    Nor branding summer suns avail
To touch thy thousand years of gloom:

And gazing on thee, sullen tree,
    Sick[5] for thy stubborn hardihood,
15   I seem to fail from out my blood
And grow incorporate into thee.

3

O Sorrow, cruel fellowship,
    O Priestess in the vaults of Death,
    O sweet and bitter in a breath,
What whispers from thy lying lip?

5 "The stars," she whispers, "blindly run;
    A web is woven across the sky;
    From out waste places comes a cry,
And murmurs from the dying sun:

"And all the phantom, Nature, stands—
10   With all the music in her tone,
    A hollow echo of my own,—
A hollow form with empty hands."

And shall I take a thing so blind,
    Embrace her as my natural good;
15   Or crush her, like a vice of blood,
Upon the threshold of the mind?

4

To Sleep I give my powers away;
    My will is bondsman° to the dark;   *slave*
    I sit within a helmless bark,°   *ship*
And with my heart I muse and say:

5 O heart, how fares it with thee now,
    That thou should'st fail from thy desire,
    Who scarcely darest to inquire,
"What is it makes me beat so low?"

Something it is which thou hast lost,
10   Some pleasure from thine early years.

---

[1] *him ... things* The reference here is unclear. Tennyson said that he was alluding to a work by the German poet Goethe; however, the passage does not appear to correspond to any of Goethe's works.

[2] *Hours* Horai, Greek goddesses of time and of the changing of seasons.

[3] *Yew* Species of tree, often planted in graveyards and thus associated poetically with mourning.

[4] *firstling* Offspring born first in the season.

[5] *Sick* I.e., with envy.

Break, thou deep vase of chilling tears,
That grief hath shaken into frost!

Such clouds of nameless trouble cross
    All night below the darkened eyes;
15   With morning wakes the will, and cries,
"Thou shalt not be the fool of loss."

5

I sometimes hold it half a sin
    To put in words the grief I feel;
    For words, like Nature, half reveal
And half conceal the Soul within.

5 But, for the unquiet heart and brain,
    A use in measured language lies;
    The sad mechanic exercise,
Like dull narcotics, numbing pain.

In words, like weeds,[1] I'll wrap me o'er,
10   Like coarsest clothes against the cold:
    But that large grief which these enfold
Is given in outline and no more.

6

One writes, that "Other friends remain,"
    That "Loss is common to the race"—
    And common is the commonplace,
And vacant chaff well meant for grain.

5 That loss is common would not make
    My own less bitter, rather more:
    Too common! Never morning wore
To evening, but some heart did break.

O father, wheresoe'er thou be,
10   Who pledgest now thy gallant son;
    A shot, ere half thy draught be done,
Hath stilled the life that beat from thee.

O mother, praying God will save
    Thy sailor,—while thy head is bowed,

15 His heavy-shotted° hammock-shroud   *weighted*
Drops in his vast and wandering grave.

Ye know no more than I who wrought
    At that last hour to please him well;
    Who mused on all I had to tell,
20 And something written, something thought;

Expecting still his advent home;
    And ever met him on his way
    With wishes, thinking, "here today,"
Or "here tomorrow will he come."

25 O somewhere, meek, unconscious dove,[2]
    That sittest ranging° golden hair;   *arranging*
    And glad to find thyself so fair,
Poor child, that waitest for thy love!

For now her father's chimney glows
30   In expectation of a guest;
    And thinking "this will please him best,"
She takes a riband° or a rose;   *ribbon*

For he will see them on tonight;
    And with the thought her colour burns;
35   And, having left the glass, she turns
Once more to set a ringlet right;

And, even when she turned, the curse
    Had fallen, and her future Lord
    Was drowned in passing through the ford,
40 Or killed in falling from his horse.

O what to her shall be the end?
    And what to me remains of good?
    To her, perpetual maidenhood,
And unto me no second friend.

7

Dark house,[3] by which once more I stand
    Here in the long unlovely street,
    Doors, where my heart was used to beat
So quickly, waiting for a hand,

---

1 *weeds* Mourning clothes.

2 *dove* Here, pure young girl.

3 *Dark house* I.e., Hallam's house.

5 A hand that can be clasped no more—
      Behold me, for I cannot sleep,
      And like a guilty thing I creep
  At earliest morning to the door.

  He is not here; but far away
10   The noise of life begins again,
      And ghastly through the drizzling rain
  On the bald street breaks the blank day.

8

  A happy lover who has come
      To look on her that loves him well,
      Who 'lights[1] and rings the gateway bell,
  And learns her gone and far from home;

5 He saddens, all the magic light
      Dies off at once from bower and hall,
      And all the place is dark, and all
  The chambers emptied of delight:

  So find I every pleasant spot
10   In which we two were wont to meet,
      The field, the chamber and the street,
  For all is dark where thou art not.

  Yet as that other, wandering there
      In those deserted walks, may find
15   A flower beat with rain and wind,
  Which once she fostered up with care;

  So seems it in my deep regret,
      O my forsaken heart, with thee
      And this poor flower of poesy
20 Which little cared for fades not yet.

  But since it pleased a vanished eye,
      I go to plant it on his tomb,
      That if it can it there may bloom,
  Or dying, there at least may die.

9

  Fair ship, that from the Italian shore
      Sailest the placid ocean-plains

  With my lost Arthur's loved remains,
  Spread thy full wings, and waft him o'er.

5 So draw him home to those that mourn
      In vain; a favourable speed
      Ruffle thy mirrored mast, and lead
  Through prosperous floods his holy urn.

  All night no ruder° air perplex   *turbulent*
10   Thy sliding keel, till Phosphor,[2] bright
      As our pure love, through early light
  Shall glimmer on the dewy decks.

  Sphere all your lights around, above;
      Sleep, gentle heavens, before the prow;
15   Sleep, gentle winds, as he sleeps now,
  My friend, the brother of my love;

  My Arthur, whom I shall not see
      Till all my widowed race be run;
      Dear as the mother to the son,
20 More than my brothers are to me.

10

  I hear the noise about thy keel;
      I hear the bell struck in the night:
      I see the cabin-window bright;
  I see the sailor at the wheel.

5 Thou bring'st the sailor to his wife,
      And travelled men from foreign lands;
      And letters unto trembling hands;
  And, thy dark freight, a vanished life.

  So bring him: we have idle dreams:
10   This look of quiet flatters thus
      Our home-bred fancies: O to us,
  The fools of habit, sweeter seems

  To rest beneath the clover sod,
      That takes the sunshine and the rains,

---

1 *'lights* Alights from a horse.

2 *Phosphor* The planet Venus, also called the morning star.

15 Or where the kneeling hamlet[1] drains
    The chalice of the grapes of God;[2]

    Than if with thee the roaring wells
        Should gulf him fathom-deep in brine;
        And hands so often clasped in mine,
20 Should toss with tangle and with shells.

                    11

    Calm is the morn without a sound,
        Calm as to suit a calmer grief,
        And only through the faded leaf
    The chestnut pattering to the ground:

5   Calm and deep peace on this high wold,°   plain
        And on these dews that drench the furze,[3]
        And all the silvery gossamers°   cobwebs
    That twinkle into green and gold:

    Calm and still light on yon great plain
10   That sweeps with all its autumn bowers,
        And crowded farms and lessening towers,
    To mingle with the bounding main:

    Calm and deep peace in this wide air,
        These leaves that redden to the fall;
15   And in my heart, if calm at all,
    If any calm, a calm despair:

    Calm on the seas, and silver sleep,
        And waves that sway themselves in rest,
        And dead calm in that noble breast
20 Which heaves but with the heaving deep.

                    12

    Lo, as a dove when up she springs
        To bear through Heaven a tale of woe,
        Some dolorous message knit below
    The wild pulsation of her wings;

5   Like her I go; I cannot stay;
        I leave this mortal ark behind,

    A weight of nerves without a mind,
    And leave the cliffs, and haste away

    O'er ocean-mirrors rounded large,
10   And reach the glow of southern skies,
        And see the sails at distance rise,
    And linger weeping on the marge,°   shore

    And saying; "Comes he thus, my friend?
        Is this the end of all my care?"
15   And circle moaning in the air:
    "Is this the end? Is this the end?"

    And forward dart again, and play
        About the prow, and back return
        To where the body sits, and learn
20 That I have been an hour away.

                    13

    Tears of the widower, when he sees
        A late-lost form that sleep reveals,
        And moves his doubtful arms, and feels
    Her place is empty, fall like these;

5   Which weep a loss forever new,
        A void where heart on heart reposed;
        And, where warm hands have pressed and closed,
    Silence, till I be silent too.

    Which weep the comrade of my choice,
10   An awful thought, a life removed,
        The human-hearted man I loved,
    A Spirit, not a breathing voice.

    Come Time, and teach me, many years,
        I do not suffer in a dream;
15   For now so strange do these things seem,
    Mine eyes have leisure for their tears;

    My fancies time to rise on wing,
        And glance about the approaching sails,
        As though they brought but merchants' bales,[4]
20 And not the burden that they bring.

---

[1] *hamlet* I.e., the citizens of a hamlet.

[2] *drains ... God* I.e., partakes in communion.

[3] *furze* Evergreen shrubs.

[4] *bales* I.e., of cotton or other trade goods.

14

If one should bring me this report,
    That thou hadst touched the land today,
    And I went down unto the quay,
And found thee lying in the port;

5 And standing, muffled round with woe,
    Should see thy passengers in rank
    Come stepping lightly down the plank,
And beckoning unto those they know;

And if along with these should come
10   The man I held as half-divine;
    Should strike a sudden hand in mine,
And ask a thousand things of home;

And I should tell him all my pain,
    And how my life had drooped of late,
15   And he should sorrow o'er my state
And marvel what possessed my brain;

And I perceived no touch of change,
    No hint of death in all his frame,
    But found him all in all the same,
20 I should not feel it to be strange.

15

Tonight the winds begin to rise
    And roar from yonder dropping day:
    The last red leaf is whirled away,
The rooks° are blown about the skies;   *crows*

5 The forest cracked, the waters curled,
    The cattle huddled on the lea;°   *pasture*
    And wildly dashed on tower and tree
The sunbeam strikes along the world:

And but for fancies, which aver°   *declare*
10   That all thy motions gently pass
    Athwart a plane of molten glass,
I scarce could brook the strain and stir

That makes the barren branches loud;
    And but for fear it is not so,

15 The wild unrest that lives in woe
Would dote and pore on yonder cloud

That rises upward always higher,
    And onward drags a labouring breast,
    And topples round the dreary west,
20 A looming bastion° fringed with fire.   *fortress*

16

What words are these have fallen from me?
    Can calm despair and wild unrest
    Be tenants of a single breast,
Or sorrow such a changeling be?

5 Or doth she only seem to take
    The touch of change in calm or storm;
    But knows no more of transient form
In her deep self, than some dead lake

That holds the shadow of a lark
10   Hung in the shadow of a heaven?
    Or has the shock, so harshly given,
Confused me like the unhappy bark

That strikes by night a craggy shelf,
    And staggers blindly ere she sink?
15   And stunned me from my power to think
And all my knowledge of myself;

And made me that delirious man
    Whose fancy fuses old and new,
    And flashes into false and true,
20 And mingles all without a plan?

17

Thou comest, much wept for: such a breeze
    Compelled thy canvas, and my prayer
    Was as the whisper of an air
To breathe thee over lonely seas.

5 For I in spirit saw thee move
    Through circles of the bounding sky,
    Week after week: the days go by:
Come quick, thou bringest all I love.

Henceforth, wherever thou mayst roam,
10   My blessing, like a line of light,
      Is on the waters day and night,
And like a beacon guards thee home.

So may whatever tempest mars
      Mid-ocean, spare thee, sacred bark;
15   And balmy drops in summer dark
Slide from the bosom of the stars.

So kind an office hath been done,
      Such precious relics brought by thee;
      The dust of him I shall not see
20   Till all my widowed race be run.

18

'Tis well; 'Tis something; we may stand
      Where he in English earth is laid,
      And from his ashes may be made
The violet of his native land.

5   "'Tis little; but it looks in truth"
      As if the quiet bones were blest
      Among familiar names to rest
And in the places of his youth.

Come then, pure hands, and bear the head
10   That sleeps or wears the mask of sleep,
      And come, whatever loves to weep,
And hear the ritual of the dead.

Ah yet, even yet, if this might be,
      I, falling on his faithful heart,
15   Would breathing through his lips impart
The life that almost dies in me;

That dies not, but endures with pain,
      And slowly forms the firmer mind,
      Treasuring the look it cannot find,
20   The words that are not heard again.

19

The Danube[1] to the Severn[2] gave
      The darkened heart that beat no more;

They laid him by the pleasant shore,
And in the hearing of the wave.

5   There twice a day the Severn fills;
      The salt sea-water passes by,
      And hushes half the babbling Wye,[3]
And makes a silence in the hills.

The Wye is hushed nor moved along,
10   And hushed my deepest grief of all,
      When filled with tears that cannot fall,
I brim with sorrow drowning song.

The tide flows down, the wave again
      Is vocal in its wooded walls;
15   My deeper anguish also falls,
And I can speak a little then.

20

The lesser griefs that may be said,
      That breathe a thousand tender vows,
      Are but as servants in a house
Where lies the master newly dead;

5   Who speak their feeling as it is,
      And weep the fullness from the mind:
      "It will be hard," they say, "to find
Another service such as this."[4]

My lighter moods are like to these,
10   That out of words a comfort win;
      But there are other griefs within,
And tears that at their fountain freeze;

For by the hearth the children sit
      Cold in that atmosphere of Death,
15   And scarce endure to draw the breath,
Or like to noiseless phantoms flit:

But open converse is there none,
      So much the vital spirits sink

---

1   *Danube*   River that flows through Vienna.

2   *Severn*   River in England. Hallam is buried at Clevedon, in Somerset, overlooking the Severn estuary.

---

3   *Wye*   The River Wye forms part of the border between England and Wales.

4   *"It will ... this"*   I.e., it will be difficult to find employment with a master as good as this one.

To see the vacant chair, and think,
20   "How good! how kind! and he is gone."

21

I sing to him that rests below,
        And, since the grasses round me wave,
        I take the grasses of the grave,
And make them pipes whereon to blow.

5   The traveller hears me now and then,
        And sometimes harshly will he speak:
        "This fellow would make weakness weak,
And melt the waxen hearts of men."

Another answers, "Let him be,
10   He loves to make parade of pain,
        That with his piping he may gain
The praise that comes to constancy."

A third is wroth:° "Is this an hour   *indignant*
        For private sorrow's barren song,
15   When more and more the people throng°   *crowd*
The chairs and thrones of civil power?

"A time to sicken and to swoon,
        When Science reaches forth her arms
        To feel from world to world, and charms
20   Her secret from the latest moon?"

Behold, ye speak an idle thing:
        Ye never knew the sacred dust:
        I do but sing because I must,
And pipe but as the linnets[1] sing:

25   And one is glad; her note is gay,
        For now her little ones have ranged;
        And one is sad: her note is changed,
Because her brood is stolen away.

22

The path by which we twain did go,
        Which led by tracts that pleased us well,
        Through four sweet years arose and fell,
From flower to flower, from snow to snow:

5   And we with singing cheered the way,
        And, crowned with all the season lent,
        From April on to April went,
And glad at heart from May to May:

But where the path we walked began
10   To slant the fifth autumnal slope,[2]
        As we descended following Hope,
There sat the Shadow feared of man;

Who broke our fair companionship,
        And spread his mantle dark and cold,
15   And wrapped thee formless in the fold,
And dulled the murmur on thy lip,

And bore thee where I could not see
        Nor follow, though I walk in haste,
        And think, that somewhere in the waste
20   The Shadow sits and waits for me.

23

Now, sometimes in my sorrow shut,
        Or breaking into song by fits,
        Alone, alone, to where he sits,
The Shadow cloaked from head to foot,

5   Who keeps the keys of all the creeds,
        I wander, often falling lame,
        And looking back to whence I came,
Or on to where the pathway leads;

And crying, How changed from where it ran
10   Through lands where not a leaf was dumb;
        But all the lavish hills would hum
The murmur of a happy Pan:[3]

When each by turns was guide to each,
        And Fancy light from Fancy caught,
15   And Thought leapt out to wed with Thought
Ere Thought could wed itself with Speech;

---

[1] *linnets* Species of songbirds.

[2] *fifth ... slope* I.e., in the autumn of their fifth year of friendship.

[3] *Pan* Greek god of flocks and sheep, a common presence in English pastoral poetry. To the Romans, he was a universal god, the god of Nature.

And all we met was fair and good,
   And all was good that Time could bring,
   And all the secret of the Spring
20 Moved in the chambers of the blood;

And many an old philosophy
   On Argive° heights divinely sang,   *Greek*
   And round us all the thicket rang
To many a flute of Arcady.[1]

24

And was the day of my delight
   As pure and perfect as I say?
   The very source and fount of Day
Is dashed with wandering isles of night.[2]

5 If all was good and fair we met,
   This earth had been the Paradise
   It never looked to human eyes
Since our first Sun arose and set.

And is it that the haze of grief
10   Makes former gladness loom so great?
   The lowness of the present state,
That sets the past in this relief?

Or that the past will always win
   A glory from its being far;
15   And orb into the perfect star
We saw not, when we moved therein?

25

I know that this was Life,—the track
   Whereon with equal feet we fared;
   And then, as now, the day prepared
The daily burden for the back.

5 But this it was that made me move
   As light as carrier-birds in air;
   I loved the weight I had to bear,
Because it needed help of Love:

Nor could I weary, heart or limb,
10   When mighty Love would cleave in twain
   The lading° of a single pain,   *burden*
And part it, giving half to him.

26

Still onward winds the dreary way;
   I with it; for I long to prove
   No lapse of moons[3] can canker° Love,   *tarnish*
Whatever fickle tongues may say.

5 And if that eye which watches guilt
   And goodness, and hath power to see
   Within the green the mouldered tree,
And towers fallen as soon as built—

Oh, if indeed that eye foresee
10   Or see (in Him is no before)
   In more of life true life no more
And Love the indifference to be,

Then might I find, ere yet the morn
   Breaks hither over Indian seas,
15   That Shadow waiting with the keys,
To shroud me from my proper° scorn.   *own*

27

I envy not in any moods
   The captive void of noble rage,
   The linnet born within the cage,
That never knew the summer woods:

5 I envy not the beast that takes
   His license in the field of time,
   Unfettered by the sense of crime,
To whom a conscience never wakes;

Nor, what may count itself as blest,
10   The heart that never plighted troth[4]
   But stagnates in the weeds of sloth;
Nor any want-begotten rest.

---

1 *Arcady* Arcadia, a hilly area of central Greece, said to be the
home of Pan.

2 *source ... night* The Sun, dotted with sunspots.

---

3 *lapse ... moons* Span of time.

4 *plighted troth* Vowed faithfulness.

I hold it true, whate'er befall;
   I feel it, when I sorrow most;
15   'Tis better to have loved and lost
Than never to have loved at all.

28

The time draws near the birth of Christ:
   The moon is hid; the night is still;
   The Christmas bells from hill to hill
Answer each other in the mist.

5 Four voices of four hamlets round,
   From far and near, on mead° and moor,   *meadow*
   Swell out and fail, as if a door
Were shut between me and the sound:

Each voice four changes on the wind,
10   That now dilate, and now decrease,
   Peace and goodwill, goodwill and peace,
Peace and goodwill, to all mankind.

This year I slept and woke with pain,
   I almost wished no more to wake,
15   And that my hold on life would break
Before I heard those bells again:

But they my troubled spirit rule,
   For they controlled me when a boy;
   They bring me sorrow touched with joy,
20 The merry merry bells of Yule.

29

With such compelling cause to grieve
   As daily vexes household peace,
   And chains regret to his decease,
How dare we keep our Christmas-eve;

5 Which brings no more a welcome guest
   To enrich the threshold of the night
   With showered largess of delight
In dance and song and game and jest?

Yet go, and while the holly boughs
10   Entwine the cold baptismal font,

Make one wreath more for Use and Wont,[1]
That guard the portals of the house;

Old sisters of a day gone by,
   Gray nurses, loving nothing new;
15   Why should they miss their yearly due
Before their time? They too will die.

30

With trembling fingers did we weave
   The holly round the Christmas hearth;
   A rainy cloud possessed the earth,
And sadly fell our Christmas-eve.

5 At our old pastimes in the hall
   We gambolled,° making vain pretence   *danced*
   Of gladness, with an awful sense
Of one mute Shadow watching all.

We paused: the winds were in the beech:
10   We heard them sweep the winter land;
   And in a circle hand-in-hand
Sat silent, looking each at each.

Then echo-like our voices rang;
   We sung, though every eye was dim,
15   A merry song we sang with him
Last year: impetuously we sang:

We ceased: a gentler feeling crept
   Upon us: surely rest is meet:°   *appropriate*
   "They rest," we said, "their sleep is sweet,"
20 And silence followed, and we wept.

Our voices took a higher range;
   Once more we sang: "They do not die
   Nor lose their mortal sympathy,
Nor change to us, although they change;

25 "'Rapt from the fickle and the frail
   With gathered power, yet the same,

---

[1] *Use ... Wont* I.e., habit and custom.

Pierces the keen seraphic flame[1]
From orb to orb, from veil to veil."

Rise, happy morn, rise, holy morn,
30   Draw forth the cheerful day from night:
      O Father, touch the east, and light
The light that shone when Hope was born,

31

When Lazarus left his charnel-cave,
    And home to Mary's house returned,[2]
      Was this demanded—if he yearned
To hear her weeping by his grave?

5   "Where wert thou, brother, those four days?"
    There lives no record of reply,
      Which telling what it is to die
Had surely added praise to praise.

From every house the neighbours met,
10   The streets were filled with joyful sound,
      A solemn gladness even crowned
The purple brows of Olivet.[3]

Behold a man raised up by Christ!
    The rest remaineth unrevealed;
15   He told it not; or something sealed
The lips of that Evangelist.[4]

32

Her eyes are homes of silent prayer,
    Nor other thought her mind admits
      But, he was dead, and there he sits,
And He that brought him back is there.

5   Then one deep love doth supersede
    All other, when her ardent gaze

Roves from the living brother's face,
And rests upon the Life[5] indeed.

All subtle thought, all curious fears,
10   Borne down by gladness so complete,
      She bows, she bathes the Saviour's feet
With costly spikenard[6] and with tears.[7]

Thrice blest whose lives are faithful prayers,
    Whose loves in higher love endure;
15   What souls possess themselves so pure,
Or is there blessedness like theirs?

33

O thou that after toil and storm
    Mayst seem to have reached a purer air,
      Whose faith has centre everywhere,
Nor cares to fix itself to form,

5   Leave thou thy sister when she prays,
    Her early Heaven, her happy views;
      Nor thou with shadowed hint confuse
A life that leads melodious days.

Her faith through form is pure as thine,
10   Her hands are quicker unto good:
      Oh, sacred be the flesh and blood
To which she links a truth divine!

See thou, that countest reason ripe
    In holding by the law within,
15   Thou fail not in a world of sin,
And even for want of such a type.

34

My own dim life should teach me this,
    That life shall live for evermore,
      Else earth is darkness at the core,
And dust and ashes all that is;

---

[1] *seraphic flame* Intense, purifying fire, associated with the angel-like Seraphim.

[2] *Lazarus … returned* See John 11.1–44, in which Jesus raises Lazarus from the dead. The Biblical account does not include any mention of Lazarus returning home to his sister Mary.

[3] *Olivet* Mount of Olives, in Jerusalem.

[4] *Evangelist* John the Apostle, who recorded the event in his Gospel.

[5] *Life* I.e., Christ. See John 11.25: "I am the Resurrection and the Life."

[6] *spikenard* Expensive aromatic oil.

[7] *bathes … tears* See Luke 7.37–50. Unlike the Biblical passage, Tennyson appears to identify the woman as Mary, sister of the resurrected Lazarus.

5 This round of green, this orb of flame,[1]
  Fantastic beauty; such as lurks
  In some wild Poet, when he works
 Without a conscience or an aim.

 What then were God to such as I?
10 'Twere hardly worth my while to choose
  Of things all mortal, or to use
 A little patience ere I die;

 'Twere best at once to sink to peace,
  Like birds the charming serpent draws,
15 To drop head-foremost in the jaws
 Of vacant darkness and to cease.

35

 Yet if some voice that man could trust
  Should murmur from the narrow house,
  "The cheeks drop in; the body bows;
 Man dies: nor is there hope in dust:"

5 Might I not say? "Yet even here,
  But for one hour, O Love, I strive
  To keep so sweet a thing alive:"
 But I should turn mine ears and hear

 The moanings of the homeless sea,
10 The sound of streams that swift or slow
  Draw down Æonian° hills, and sow   *eternal*
 The dust of continents to be;

 And Love would answer with a sigh,
  "The sound of that forgetful shore
15 Will change my sweetness more and more,
 Half-dead to know that I shall die."

 O me, what profits it to put
  An idle case? If Death were seen
  At first as Death, Love had not been,
20 Or been in narrowest working shut,

 Mere fellowship of sluggish moods,
  Or in his coarsest Satyr-shape[2]

 Had bruised the herb and crushed the grape,
 And basked and battened° in the woods. *thrived*

36

Though truths in manhood darkly join,
 Deep-seated in our mystic frame,
 We yield all blessing to the name
Of Him that made them current coin;

5 For Wisdom dealt with mortal powers,
  Where truth in closest words shall fail,
  When truth embodied in a tale
Shall enter in at lowly doors.

 And so the Word had breath,[3] and wrought
10 With human hands the creed of creeds
  In loveliness of perfect deeds,
More strong than all poetic thought;

 Which he may read that binds the sheaf,
  Or builds the house, or digs the grave,
15 And those wild eyes that watch the wave
In roarings round the coral reef.

37

Urania[4] speaks with darkened brow:
 "Thou pratest° here where thou art least; *chatter*
 This faith has many a purer priest,
And many an abler voice than thou.

5 "Go down beside thy native rill,°   *stream*
  On thy Parnassus[5] set thy feet,
  And hear thy laurel whisper sweet
About the ledges of the hill."

 And my Melpomene[6] replies,
10 A touch of shame upon her cheek:
  "I am not worthy even to speak
Of thy prevailing mysteries;

---

[1] *round … flame* I.e., the earth and the sun.

[2] *Satyr-shape* In the shape of satyrs; half-human, half-beast. In Greek mythology, satyrs are a class of woodland gods.

[3] *Word … breath* See John 1.14: "The Word became flesh and dwelt among us."

[4] *Urania* Greek Muse of astronomy.

[5] *thy Parnassus* I.e., your home. Mount Parnassus was the home of the Muses.

[6] *Melpomene* Greek Muse of tragedy.

"For I am but an earthly Muse,
    And owning but a little art
15   To lull with song an aching heart,
And render human love his dues;

"But brooding on the dear one dead,
    And all he said of things divine,
    (And dear to me as sacred wine
20 To dying lips is all he said),

"I murmured, as I came along,
    Of comfort clasped in truth revealed;
    And loitered in the master's field,
And darkened sanctities with song."

38

With weary steps I loiter on,
    Though always under altered skies
    The purple from the distance dies,
My prospect and horizon gone.

5   No joy the blowing season gives,
    The herald melodies of spring,
    But in the songs I love to sing
A doubtful gleam of solace lives.

If any care for what is here
10   Survive in spirits rendered free,
    Then are these songs I sing of thee
Not all ungrateful to thine ear.

39

Old warder of these buried bones,
    And answering now my random stroke
    With fruitful cloud and living smoke,
Dark yew, that graspest at the stones

5   And dippest toward the dreamless head,
    To thee too comes the golden hour
    When flower is feeling after flower;
But Sorrow—fixed upon the dead,

And darkening the dark graves of men,—
10   What whispered from her lying lips?

Thy gloom is kindled at the tips,
And passes into gloom again.

40

Could we forget the widowed hour
    And look on Spirits breathed away,
    As on a maiden in the day
When first she wears her orange-flower![1]

5   When crowned with blessing she doth rise
    To take her latest leave of home,
    And hopes and light regrets that come
Make April of her tender eyes;

And doubtful joys the father move,
10   And tears are on the mother's face,
    As parting with a long embrace
She enters other realms of love;

Her office there to rear, to teach,
    Becoming as is meet and fit
15   A link among the days, to knit
The generations each with each;

And, doubtless, unto thee is given
    A life that bears immortal fruit
    In those great offices that suit
20 The full-grown energies of heaven.

Ay me, the difference I discern!
    How often shall her old fireside
    Be cheered with tidings of the bride,
How often she herself return,

25 And tell them all they would have told,
    And bring her babe, and make her boast,
    Till even those that missed her most
Shall count new things as dear as old:

But thou and I have shaken hands,
30   Till growing winters lay me low;

---

[1] *orange-flower* Brides often wore wreaths of orange-flowers in this period.

My paths are in the fields I know,
And thine in undiscovered lands.[1]

41

Thy spirit ere our fatal loss
    Did ever rise from high to higher;
    As mounts the heavenward altar-fire,
As flies the lighter through the gross.°   *heavier*

5 But thou art turned to something strange,
    And I have lost the links that bound
    Thy changes; here upon the ground,
No more partaker of thy change.

Deep folly! yet that this could be—
10   That I could wing my will with might
    To leap the grades of life and light,
And flash at once, my friend, to thee.

For though my nature rarely yields
    To that vague fear implied in death;
15   Nor shudders at the gulfs beneath,
The howlings from forgotten fields;

Yet oft when sundown skirts the moor
    An inner trouble I behold,
    A spectral° doubt which makes me cold,   *ghostly*
20 That I shall be thy mate no more,

Though following with an upward mind
    The wonders that have come to thee,
    Through all the secular to-be,
But evermore a life behind.

42

I vex my heart with fancies dim:
    He still outstripped me in the race;
    It was but unity of place
That made me dream I ranked with him.

5 And so may Place retain us still,
    And he the much-beloved again,

A lord of large experience, train
To riper growth the mind and will:

And what delights can equal those
10   That stir the spirit's inner deeps,
    When one that loves but knows not, reaps
A truth from one that loves and knows?

43

If Sleep and Death be truly one,
    And every spirit's folded bloom
    Through all its intervital[2] gloom
In some long trance should slumber on;

5 Unconscious of the sliding hour,
    Bare of the body, might it last,
    And silent traces of the past
Be all the colour of the flower:

So then were nothing lost to man;
10   So that still garden of the souls
    In many a figured leaf enrolls
The total world since life began;

And love will last as pure and whole
    As when he loved me here in Time,
15   And at the spiritual prime
Rewaken with the dawning soul.

44

How fares it with the happy dead?
    For here the man is more and more;
    But he forgets the days before
God shut the doorways of his head.

5 The days have vanished, tone and tint,
    And yet perhaps the hoarding sense
    Gives out at times (he knows not whence)
A little flash, a mystic hint;

And in the long harmonious years
10   (If Death so taste Lethean springs),[3]

---

1 *undiscovered lands* See *Hamlet* 3.1.79–80, in which death is "the undiscovered country, from whose bourne / No traveller returns."

2 *intervital* Between two stages of existence.

3 *Lethean springs* According to Greek mythology, drinking from the River Lethe in Hades caused the dead to forget their previous existences.

May some dim touch of earthly things
  Surprise thee ranging with thy peers.

If such a dreamy touch should fall,
  O turn thee round, resolve the doubt;
  My guardian angel will speak out
In that high place, and tell thee all.

15

45

The baby new to earth and sky,
  What time his tender palm is pressed
  Against the circle of the breast,
Has never thought that "this is I":

But as he grows he gathers much,
  And learns the use of "I," and "me,"
  And finds "I am not what I see,
And other than the things I touch."

So rounds he to a separate mind
  From whence clear memory may begin,
  As through the frame that binds him in
His isolation grows defined.

This use may lie in blood and breath,
  Which else were fruitless of their due,
  Had man to learn himself anew
Beyond the second birth of Death.

46

We ranging down this lower track,
  The path we came by, thorn and flower,
  Is shadowed by the growing hour,
Lest life should fail in looking back.

So be it: there no shade can last
  In that deep dawn behind the tomb,
  But clear from marge° to marge shall bloom   *shore*
The eternal landscape of the past;

A lifelong tract of time revealed;
  The fruitful hours of still increase;
  Days ordered in a wealthy peace,
And those five years its richest field.

O Love, thy province were not large,
  A bounded field, nor stretching far;
  Look also, Love, a brooding star,
A rosy warmth from marge to marge.

47

That each, who seems a separate whole,
  Should move his rounds, and fusing all
  The skirts of self again, should fall
Remerging in the general Soul,

Is faith as vague as all unsweet:
  Eternal form shall still divide
  The eternal soul from all beside;
And I shall know him when we meet:

And we shall sit at endless feast,
  Enjoying each the other's good:
  What vaster dream can hit the mood
Of Love on earth? He seeks at least

Upon the last and sharpest height,
  Before the spirits fade away,
  Some landing-place, to clasp and say,
"Farewell! We lose ourselves in light."

48

If these brief lays, of Sorrow born,
  Were taken to be such as closed
  Grave doubts and answers here proposed,
Then these were such as men might scorn:

Her care is not to part and prove;
  She takes, when harsher moods remit,
  What slender shade of doubt may flit,
And makes it vassal unto love:

And hence, indeed, she sports with words,
  But better serves a wholesome law,
  And holds it sin and shame to draw
The deepest measure from the chords:

Nor dare she trust a larger lay,°   *song*
  But rather loosens from the lip

15   Short swallow-flights of song, that dip
       Their wings in tears, and skim away.

49

From art, from nature, from the schools,
    Let random influences glance,
    Like light in many a shivered lance
That breaks about the dappled pools:

5   The lightest wave of thought shall lisp,
      The fancy's tenderest eddy wreathe,
      The slightest air of song shall breathe
To make the sullen surface crisp.

And look thy look, and go thy way,
10   But blame not thou the winds that make
      The seeming-wanton ripple break,
The tender-pencilled shadow play.

Beneath all fancied hopes and fears
    Ay me, the sorrow deepens down,
15   Whose muffled motions blindly drown
The bases of my life in tears.

50

Be near me when my light is low,
    When the blood creeps, and the nerves prick
    And tingle; and the heart is sick,
And all the wheels of Being slow.

5   Be near me when the sensuous frame
      Is racked with pangs that conquer trust;
      And Time, a maniac scattering dust,
And Life, a Fury slinging flame.

Be near me when my faith is dry,
10   And men the flies of latter spring,
      That lay their eggs, and sting and sing
And weave their petty cells and die.

Be near me when I fade away,
    To point the term of human strife,
15   And on the low dark verge of life
The twilight of eternal day.

51

Do we indeed desire the dead
    Should still be near us at our side?
    Is there no baseness we would hide?
No inner vileness that we dread?

5   Shall he for whose applause I strove,
      I had such reverence for his blame,
      See with clear eye some hidden shame
And I be lessened in his love?

I wrong the grave with fears untrue:
10   Shall love be blamed for want of faith?
      There must be wisdom with great Death:
The dead shall look me through and through.

Be near us when we climb or fall:
    Ye watch, like God, the rolling hours
15   With larger other eyes than ours,
To make allowance for us all.

52

I cannot love thee as I ought,
    For love reflects the thing beloved;
    My words are only words, and moved
Upon the topmost froth of thought.

5   "Yet blame not thou thy plaintive song,"
      The Spirit of true love replied;
      "Thou canst not move me from thy side,
Nor human frailty do me wrong.

"What keeps a spirit wholly true
10   To that ideal which he bears?
      What record? not the sinless years
That breathed beneath the Syrian blue:[1]

"So fret not, like an idle girl,
    That life is dashed with flecks of sin.
15   Abide: thy wealth is gathered in,
When Time hath sundered shell from pearl."

---

[1] *Syrian blue* Blue skies of Syria, commonly used as a term for the land in which Christ lived.

53

How many a father have I seen,
    A sober man, among his boys,
    Whose youth was full of foolish noise,
Who wears his manhood hale° and green: *robust*

5 And dare we to this fancy give,
    That had the wild oat not been sown,
    The soil, left barren, scarce had grown
The grain by which a man may live?

Or, if we held the doctrine sound
10   For life outliving heats of youth,
    Yet who would preach it as a truth
To those that eddy round and round?

Hold thou the good: define it well:
    For fear divine Philosophy
15   Should push beyond her mark, and be
Procuress to the Lords of Hell.

54

Oh yet we trust that somehow good
    Will be the final goal of ill,
    To pangs of nature, sins of will,
Defects of doubt, and taints of blood;

5 That nothing walks with aimless feet;
    That not one life shall be destroyed,
    Or cast as rubbish to the void,
When God hath made the pile complete;

That not a worm is cloven in vain;
10   That not a moth with vain desire
    Is shrivelled in a fruitless fire,
Or but subserves another's gain.

Behold, we know not anything;
    I can but trust that good shall fall
15   At last—far off—at last, to all,
And every winter change to spring.

So runs my dream: but what am I?
    An infant crying in the night:
An infant crying for the light:
20 And with no language but a cry.

55

The wish, that of the living whole
    No life may fail beyond the grave,
    Derives it not from what we have
The likest God within the soul?

5 Are God and Nature then at strife,
    That Nature lends such evil dreams?
    So careful of the type° she seems,   *species*
So careless of the single life;

That I, considering everywhere
10   Her secret meaning in her deeds,
    And finding that of fifty seeds
She often brings but one to bear,

I falter where I firmly trod,
    And falling with my weight of cares
15   Upon the great world's altar-stairs
That slope through darkness up to God,

I stretch lame hands of faith, and grope,
    And gather dust and chaff, and call
    To what I feel is Lord of all,
20 And faintly trust the larger hope.

56

"So careful of the type?" but no.
    From scarpèd[1] cliff and quarried stone
    She cries, "A thousand types are gone:
I care for nothing, all shall go.

5 "Thou makest thine appeal to me:
    I bring to life, I bring to death:
    The spirit does but mean the breath:
I know no more." And he, shall he,

Man, her last work, who seemed so fair,
10   Such splendid purpose in his eyes,
    Who rolled the psalm to wintry skies,
Who built him fanes° of fruitless prayer,   *temples*

---

[1] *scarpèd* Steeply cut.

Who trusted God was love indeed
    And love Creation's final law—
15   Though Nature, red in tooth and claw
With ravine,° shrieked against his creed—   *violence*

Who loved, who suffered countless ills,
    Who battled for the True, the Just,
    Be blown about the desert dust,
20 Or sealed within the iron hills?

No more? A monster then, a dream,
    A discord. Dragons° of the prime,   *dinosaurs*
    That tare° each other in their slime,   *tore*
Were mellow music matched with him.

25 O life as futile, then, as frail!
    O for thy voice to soothe and bless!
    What hope of answer, or redress?
Behind the veil, behind the veil.

57

Peace; come away: the song of woe
    Is after all an earthly song:
    Peace; come away: we do him wrong
To sing so wildly: let us go.

5 Come; let us go: your cheeks are pale;
    But half my life I leave behind:
    Methinks my friend is richly shrined;
But I shall pass; my work will fail.

Yet in these ears, till hearing dies,
10   One set slow bell will seem to toll
    The passing of the sweetest soul
That ever looked with human eyes.

I hear it now, and o'er and o'er,
    Eternal greetings to the dead;
15   And "Ave,° Ave, Ave," said,   *farewell*
"Adieu, adieu" for evermore.

58

In those sad words I took farewell:
    Like echoes in sepulchral halls,

As drop by drop the water falls
In vaults and catacombs, they fell;

5 And, falling, idly broke the peace
    Of hearts that beat from day to day,
    Half-conscious of their dying clay,
And those cold crypts where they shall cease.

The high Muse answered: "Wherefore grieve
10   Thy brethren with a fruitless tear?
    Abide a little longer here,
And thou shalt take a nobler leave."

59

O Sorrow, wilt thou live with me
    No casual mistress, but a wife,
    My bosom-friend and half of life;
As I confess it needs must be;

5 O Sorrow, wilt thou rule my blood,
    Be sometimes lovely like a bride,
    And put thy harsher moods aside,
If thou wilt have me wise and good.

My centred passion cannot move,
10   Nor will it lessen from today;
    But I'll have leave at times to play
As with the creature of my love;

And set thee forth, for thou art mine,
    With so much hope for years to come,
15   That, howsoe'er I know thee, some
Could hardly tell what name were thine.

60

He passed; a soul of nobler tone:
    My spirit loved and loves him yet,
    Like some poor girl whose heart is set
On one whose rank exceeds her own.

5 He mixing with his proper sphere,
    She finds the baseness of her lot,
    Half jealous of she knows not what,
And envying all that meet him there.

The little village looks forlorn;
 She sighs amid her narrow days,
 Moving about the household ways,
In that dark house where she was born.

The foolish neighbours come and go,
 And tease her till the day draws by:
 At night she weeps, "How vain am I!
How should he love a thing so low?"

61

If, in thy second state sublime,
 Thy ransomed reason change replies
 With all the circle of the wise,
The perfect flower of human time;

And if thou cast thine eyes below,
 How dimly charactered and slight,
 How dwarfed a growth of cold and night,
How blanched with darkness must I grow!

Yet turn thee to the doubtful shore,
 Where thy first form was made a man;
 I loved thee, Spirit, and love, nor can
The soul of Shakespeare love thee more.

62

Though if an eye that's downward cast
 Could make thee somewhat blench° or fail, *flinch*
 Then be my love an idle tale,
And fading legend of the past;

And thou, as one that once declined,
 When he was little more than boy,
 On some unworthy heart with joy,
But lives to wed an equal mind;

And breathes a novel world, the while
 His other passion wholly dies,
 Or in the light of deeper eyes
Is matter for a flying smile.

63

Yet pity for a horse o'er-driven,
 And love in which my hound has part,

Can hang no weight upon my heart
In its assumptions up to heaven;

And I am so much more than these,
 As thou, perchance, art more than I,
 And yet I spare them sympathy,
And I would set their pains at ease.

So mayst thou watch me where I weep,
 As, unto vaster motions bound,
 The circuits of thine orbit round
A higher height, a deeper deep.

64

Dost thou look back on what hath been,
 As some divinely gifted man,
 Whose life in low estate began
And on a simple village green;

Who breaks his birth's invidious° bar, *hated*
 And grasps the skirts of happy chance,
 And breasts the blows of circumstance,
And grapples with his evil star;

Who makes by force his merit known
 And lives to clutch the golden keys,
 To mould a mighty state's decrees,
And shape the whisper of the throne;

And moving up from high to higher,
 Becomes on Fortune's crowning slope
 The pillar of a people's hope,
The centre of a world's desire;

Yet feels, as in a pensive dream,
 When all his active powers are still,
 A distant dearness in the hill,
A secret sweetness in the stream,

The limit of his narrower fate,
 While yet beside its vocal springs
 He played at counsellors and kings,
With one that was his earliest mate;

25   Who ploughs with pain his native lea°   *land*
      And reaps the labour of his hands,
      Or in the furrow musing stands;
  "Does my old friend remember me?"

65

Sweet soul, do with me as thou wilt;
    I lull a fancy trouble-tossed
    With "Love's too precious to be lost,
A little grain shall not be spilt."

5   And in that solace can I sing,
    Till out of painful phases wrought
    There flutters up a happy thought,
Self-balanced on a lightsome wing:

Since we deserved the name of friends,
10   And thine effect so lives in me,
    A part of mine may live in thee
And move thee on to noble ends.

66

You thought my heart too far diseased;
    You wonder when my fancies play
    To find me gay among the gay,
Like one with any trifle pleased.

5   The shade by which my life was crossed,
    Which makes a desert in the mind,
    Has made me kindly with my kind,
And like to him whose sight is lost;

Whose feet are guided through the land,
10   Whose jest among his friends is free,
    Who takes the children on his knee,
And winds their curls about his hand:

He plays with threads, he beats his chair
    For pastime, dreaming of the sky;
15   His inner day can never die,
His night of loss is always there.

67

When on my bed the moonlight falls,
    I know that in thy place of rest

By that broad water of the west,[1]
  There comes a glory on the walls;

5   Thy marble bright in dark appears,
    As slowly steals a silver flame
    Along the letters of thy name,
And o'er the number of thy years.

The mystic glory swims away;
10   From off my bed the moonlight dies;
    And closing eaves of wearied eyes
I sleep till dusk is dipped in gray:

And then I know the mist is drawn
    A lucid veil from coast to coast,
15   And in the dark church like a ghost
Thy tablet glimmers to the dawn.

68

When in the down I sink my head,
    Sleep, Death's twin-brother, times my breath;
    Sleep, Death's twin-brother, knows not Death,
Nor can I dream of thee as dead:

5   I walk as ere I walked forlorn,
    When all our path was fresh with dew,
    And all the bugle breezes blew
Reveillée[2] to the breaking morn.

But what is this? I turn about,
10   I find a trouble in thine eye,
    Which makes me sad I know not why,
Nor can my dream resolve the doubt:

But ere the lark hath left the lea
    I wake, and I discern the truth;
15   It is the trouble of my youth
That foolish sleep transfers to thee.

69

I dreamed there would be Spring no more,
    That Nature's ancient power was lost:

---

1 *broad ... west*   I.e., the Severn Estuary.

2 *Reveillée*   Music played to awaken soldiers in the morning.

The streets were black with smoke and frost,
They chattered trifles at the door:

5 I wandered from the noisy town,
    I found a wood with thorny boughs:
    I took the thorns to bind my brows,
I wore them like a civic crown:[1]

I met with scoffs, I met with scorns
10   From youth and babe and hoary° hairs: *gray*
    They called me in the public squares
The fool that wears a crown of thorns:

They called me fool, they called me child:
    I found an angel of the night;
15   The voice was low, the look was bright;
He looked upon my crown and smiled:

He reached the glory of a hand,
    That seemed to touch it into leaf:
    The voice was not the voice of grief,
20 The words were hard to understand.

70

I cannot see the features right,
    When on the gloom I strive to paint
    The face I know; the hues are faint
And mix with hollow masks of night;

5 Cloud-towers by ghostly masons wrought,
    A gulf that ever shuts and gapes,
    A hand that points, and pallèd° shapes   *veiled*
In shadowy thoroughfares of thought;

And crowds that stream from yawning doors,
10   And shoals of puckered faces drive;
    Dark bulks that tumble half alive,
And lazy lengths on boundless shores;

Till all at once beyond the will
    I hear a wizard music roll,
15   And through a lattice on the soul
Looks thy fair face and makes it still.

71

Sleep, kinsman thou to death and trance
    And madness, thou hast forged at last
    A night-long Present of the Past
In which we went through summer France.[2]

5 Hadst thou such credit with the soul?
    Then bring an opiate trebly° strong,   *triply*
    Drug down the blindfold sense of wrong
That so my pleasure may be whole;

While now we talk as once we talked
10   Of men and minds, the dust of change,
    The days that grow to something strange,
In walking as of old we walked

Beside the river's wooded reach,
    The fortress, and the mountain ridge,
15   The cataract[3] flashing from the bridge,
The breaker breaking on the beach.

72

Risest thou thus, dim dawn, again,
    And howlest, issuing out of night,
    With blasts that blow the poplar white,[4]
And lash with storm the streaming pane?

5 Day, when my crowned estate begun
    To pine in that reverse of doom,
    Which sickened every living bloom,
And blurred the splendour of the sun;

Who usherest in the dolorous hour
10   With thy quick tears that make the rose
    Pull sideways, and the daisy close
Her crimson fringes to the shower;

Who might'st have heaved a windless flame
    Up the deep East, or, whispering, played
15   A chequer-work of beam and shade
Along the hills, yet looked the same,

---

[1] *civic crown* Highly prized garland of oak leaves and acorns,
bestowed upon one who has saved the life of another in war.

[2] *France* Tennyson and Hallam vacationed together in France in
1830.

[3] *cataract* Waterfall.

[4] *blow ... white* I.e., reveal the white underside of poplar leaves.

As wan,° as chill, as wild as now;   *pale*   5
    Day, marked as with some hideous crime,
    When the dark hand struck down through time,
20   And cancelled nature's best: but thou,

Lift as thou mayst thy burdened brows
    Through clouds that drench the morning star,[1]   10
    And whirl the ungarnered sheaf afar,
And sow the sky with flying boughs,

25   And up thy vault[2] with roaring sound
    Climb thy thick noon, disastrous day;
    Touch thy dull goal of joyless gray,
And hide thy shame beneath the ground.

73

So many worlds, so much to do,
    So little done, such things to be,
    How know I what had need of thee,
For thou wert strong as thou wert true?

5   The fame is quenched that I foresaw,
    The head hath missed an earthly wreath:
    I curse not nature, no, nor death;
For nothing is that errs from law.

We pass; the path that each man trod
10   Is dim, or will be dim, with weeds:
    What fame is left for human deeds
In endless age? It rests with God.

O hollow wraith of dying fame,
    Fade wholly, while the soul exults,
15   And self-infolds the large results
Of force that would have forged a name.

74

As sometimes in a dead man's face,
    To those that watch it more and more,
    A likeness, hardly seen before,
Comes out—to some one of his race:

So, dearest, now thy brows are cold,
    I see thee what thou art, and know
    Thy likeness to the wise below,
Thy kindred with the great of old.

But there is more than I can see,
    And what I see I leave unsaid,
    Nor speak it, knowing Death has made
His darkness beautiful with thee.

75

I leave thy praises unexpressed
    In verse that brings myself relief,
    And by the measure of my grief
I leave thy greatness to be guessed;

5   What practice howsoe'er expert
    In fitting aptest words to things,
    Or voice the richest-toned that sings,
Hath power to give thee as thou wert?

I care not in these fading days
10   To raise a cry that lasts not long,
    And round thee with the breeze of song
To stir a little dust of praise.

Thy leaf has perished in the green,
    And, while we breathe beneath the sun,
15   The world which credits what is done
Is cold to all that might have been.

So here shall silence guard thy fame;
    But somewhere, out of human view,
    Whate'er thy hands are set to do
20   Is wrought with tumult of acclaim.

76

Take wings of fancy, and ascend,
    And in a moment set thy face
    Where all the starry heavens of space
Are sharpened to a needle's end;

5   Take wings of foresight; lighten through
    The secular abyss to come,

---

1   *morning star*   The planet Venus.
2   *up thy vault*   Fill the sky.

And lo, thy deepest lays are dumb
  Before the mouldering of a yew;

And if the matin songs,[1] that woke
10   The darkness of our planet, last,
    Thine own shall wither in the vast,
  Ere half the lifetime of an oak.

Ere these have clothed their branchy bowers
    With fifty Mays, thy songs are vain;
15   And what are they when these remain
  The ruined shells of hollow towers?

77

What hope is here for modern rhyme
  To him, who turns a musing eye
  On songs, and deeds, and lives, that lie
Foreshortened in the tract of time?

5   These mortal lullabies of pain
    May bind a book, may line a box,
    May serve to curl a maiden's locks;[2]
  Or when a thousand moons shall wane

A man upon a stall may find,
10   And, passing, turn the page that tells
    A grief, then changed to something else,
  Sung by a long-forgotten mind.

But what of that? My darkened ways
    Shall ring with music all the same;
15   To breathe my loss is more than fame,
  To utter love more sweet than praise.

78

Again at Christmas did we weave
    The holly round the Christmas hearth;
    The silent snow possessed the earth,
  And calmly fell our Christmas-eve:

5   The yule-clog[3] sparkled keen with frost,
    No wing of wind the region swept,
    But over all things brooding slept
  The quiet sense of something lost.

As in the winters left behind,
10   Again our ancient games had place,
    The mimic picture's breathing grace,
  And dance and song and hoodman-blind.[4]

Who showed a token of distress?
    No single tear, no mark of pain:
15   O sorrow, then can sorrow wane?
  O grief, can grief be changed to less?

O last regret, regret can die!
    No—mixed with all this mystic frame,
    Her deep relations are the same,
20 But with long use her tears are dry.

79

"More than my brothers are to me,"—
    Let this not vex thee, noble heart!
    I know thee of what force thou art
  To hold the costliest love in fee.

5   But thou and I are one in kind,
    As moulded like in Nature's mint;
    And hill and wood and field did print
  The same sweet forms in either mind.

For us the same cold streamlet curled
10   Through all his eddying coves; the same
    All winds that roam the twilight came
  In whispers of the beauteous world.

At one dear knee we proffered vows,
    One lesson from one book we learned,
15   Ere childhood's flaxen ringlet turned
  To black and brown on kindred brows.

And so my wealth resembles thine,
    But he was rich where I was poor,

---

[1] *matin songs* Morning songs. Matins is the service that precedes the first Mass of the day.

[2] *curl ... locks* I.e., serve as scrap paper to protect a young woman's hair when it is being burned by hot tongs.

---

[3] *yule-clog* Large log of wood burnt at Christmas.

[4] *hoodman-blind* Blind-man's-bluff.

And he supplied my want the more
20   As his unlikeness fitted mine.

80

If any vague desire should rise,
  That holy Death ere Arthur died
  Had moved me kindly from his side,
And dropped the dust on tearless eyes;

5 Then fancy shapes, as fancy can,
  The grief my loss in him had wrought,
  A grief as deep as life or thought,
But stayed in peace with God and man.

I make a picture in the brain;
10   I hear the sentence that he speaks;
  He bears the burden of the weeks
But turns his burden into gain.

His credit thus shall set me free;
  And, influence-rich to soothe and save,
15   Unused example from the grave
Reach out dead hands to comfort me.

81

Could I have said while he was here,
  "My love shall now no further range;
  There cannot come a mellower change,
For now is love mature in ear."[1]

5 Love, then, had hope of richer store:
  What end is here to my complaint?
  This haunting whisper makes me faint,
"More years had made me love thee more."

But Death returns an answer sweet:
10   "My sudden frost was sudden gain,
  And gave all ripeness to the grain,
It might have drawn from after-heat."

82

I wage not any feud with Death
  For changes wrought on form and face;

No lower life that earth's embrace
May breed with him, can fright my faith.

5 Eternal process moving on,
  From state to state the spirit walks;
  And these are but the shattered stalks,
Or ruined chrysalis of one.

Nor blame I Death, because he bare
10   The use of virtue out of earth:
  I know transplanted human worth
Will bloom to profit, otherwhere.

For this alone on Death I wreak
  The wrath that garners in my heart;
15   He put our lives so far apart
We cannot hear each other speak.

83

Dip down upon the northern shore,
  O sweet new-year delaying long;
  Thou doest expectant nature wrong;
Delaying long, delay no more.

5 What stays thee from the clouded noons,
  Thy sweetness from its proper place?
  Can trouble live with April days,
Or sadness in the summer moons?

Bring orchis,° bring the foxglove spire,   *orchid*
10   The little speedwell's darling blue,
  Deep tulips dashed with fiery dew,
Laburnums,[2] dropping-wells of fire.

O thou, new-year, delaying long,
  Delayest the sorrow in my blood,
15   That longs to burst a frozen bud
And flood a fresher throat with song.

84

When I contemplate all alone
  The life that had been thine below,

---

1 *ear* I.e., of grain.

2 *Laburnums* Trees with hanging bunches of bright yellow flowers.

And fix my thoughts on all the glow
    To which thy crescent would have grown;

5   I see thee sitting crowned with good,
    A central warmth diffusing bliss
    In glance and smile, and clasp and kiss,
On all the branches of thy blood;

Thy blood, my friend, and partly mine;
10   For now the day was drawing on,
    When thou shouldst link thy life with one
Of mine own house, and boys of thine

Had babbled "Uncle" on my knee;
    But that remorseless iron hour
15   Made cypress[1] of her orange flower,
Despair of Hope, and earth of thee.

I seem to meet their least desire,
    To clap their cheeks, to call them mine.
    I see their unborn faces shine
20 Beside the never-lighted fire.

I see myself an honoured guest,
    Thy partner in the flowery walk
    Of letters, genial table-talk,
Or deep dispute, and graceful jest;

25 While now thy prosperous labour fills
    The lips of men with honest praise,
    And sun by sun the happy days
Descend below the golden hills

With promise of a morn as fair;
30   And all the train of bounteous hours
    Conduct by paths of growing powers,
To reverence and the silver hair;

Till slowly worn her earthly robe,
    Her lavish mission richly wrought,
35   Leaving great legacies of thought,
Thy spirit should fail from off the globe;

What time mine own might also flee,
    As linked with thine in love and fate,
    And, hovering o'er the dolorous strait
40 To the other shore, involved in thee,

Arrive at last the blessèd goal,
    And He that died in Holy Land[2]
    Would reach us out the shining hand,
And take us as a single soul.

45 What reed was that on which I leant?
    Ah, backward fancy, wherefore wake
    The old bitterness again, and break
The low beginnings of content.

85

This truth came borne with bier[3] and pall,[4]
    I felt it, when I sorrowed most,
    'Tis better to have loved and lost,
Than never to have loved at all—

5   O true in word, and tried in deed,
    Demanding, so to bring relief
    To this which is our common grief,
What kind of life is that I lead;

And whether trust in things above
10   Be dimmed of sorrow, or sustained;
    And whether love for him have drained
My capabilities of love;

Your words have virtue such as draws
    A faithful answer from the breast,
15   Through light reproaches, half expressed,
And loyal unto kindly laws.

My blood an even tenor kept,
    Till on mine ear this message falls,
    That in Vienna's fatal wall
20 God's ringer touched him, and he slept.

---

1 *cypress* Tree symbolic of mourning.

2 *He ... Land* I.e., Christ.

3 *bier* Moveable stand on which a corpse is carried to the grave.

4 *pall* Cloth that covers a corpse or a coffin.

The great Intelligences° fair   *angels*
    That range above our mortal state,
    In circle round the blessèd gate,
Received and gave him welcome there;   60

25 And led him through the blissful climes,
    And showed him in the fountain fresh
    All knowledge that the sons of flesh
Shall gather in the cycled times.

But I remained, whose hopes were dim,
30   Whose life, whose thoughts were little worth,
    To wander on a darkened earth,
Where all things round me breathed of him.

O friendship, equal-poised control,
    O heart, with kindliest motion warm,
35   O sacred essence, other form,
O solemn ghost, O crownèd soul!

Yet none could better know than I,
    How much of act at human hands
    The sense of human will demands
40 By which we dare to live or die.

Whatever way my days decline,
    I felt and feel, though left alone,
    His being working in mine own,
The footsteps of his life in mine;

45 A life that all the Muses decked
    With gifts of grace, that might express
    All-comprehensive tenderness,
All-subtilising° intellect: *elevating*

And so my passion hath not swerved
50   To works of weakness, but I find
    An image comforting the mind,
And in my grief a strength reserved.

Likewise the imaginative woe,
    That loved to handle spiritual strife,
55   Diffused the shock through all my life,
But in the present broke the blow.

My pulses therefore beat again
    For other friends that once I met;
    Nor can it suit me to forget
60 The mighty hopes that make us men.

I woo your love: I count it crime
    To mourn for any overmuch;
    I, the divided half of such
A friendship as had mastered Time;

65 Which masters Time indeed, and is
    Eternal, separate from fears:
    The all-assuming months and years
Can take no part away from this:

But Summer on the steaming floods,
70   And Spring that swells the narrow brooks,
    And Autumn, with a noise of rooks,
That gather in the waning woods,

And every pulse of wind and wave
    Recalls, in change of light or gloom,
75   My old affection of the tomb,
And my prime passion in the grave:

My old affection of the tomb,
    A part of stillness, yearns to speak:
    "Arise, and get thee forth and seek
80 A friendship for the years to come.

"I watch thee from the quiet shore;
    Thy spirit up to mine can reach;
    But in dear words of human speech
We two communicate no more."

85 And I, "Can clouds of nature stain
    The starry clearness of the free?
    How is it? Canst thou feel for me
Some painless sympathy with pain?"

And lightly does the whisper fall;
90   "'Tis hard for thee to fathom this;
    I triumph in conclusive bliss,
And that serene result of all."

So hold I commerce° with the dead;   *conversation*
   Or so methinks the dead would say;
95   Or so shall grief with symbols play
And pining life be fancy-fed.

Now looking to some settled end,
   That these things pass, and I shall prove
   A meeting somewhere, love with love,
100 I crave your pardon, O my friend;

If not so fresh, with love as true,
   I, clasping brother-hands, aver
   I could not, if I would, transfer
The whole I felt for him to you.

105 For which be they that hold apart
   The promise of the golden hours?
   First love, first friendship, equal powers,
That marry with the virgin heart.

Still mine, that cannot but deplore,
110 That beats within a lonely place,
   That yet remembers his embrace,
But at his footstep leaps no more,

My heart, though widowed, may not rest
   Quite in the love of what is gone,
115 But seeks to beat in time with one
That warms another living breast.

Ah, take the imperfect gift I bring,
   Knowing the primrose yet is dear,
   The primrose of the later year,
120 As not unlike to that of Spring.

86

Sweet after showers, ambrosial air,
   That rollest from the gorgeous gloom
   Of evening over brake° and bloom   *fern*
And meadow, slowly breathing bare

5 The round of space, and rapt below
   Through all the dewy-tasselled wood,
   And shadowing down the hornèd flood
In ripples, fan my brows and blow

The fever from my cheek, and sigh
10 The full new life that feeds thy breath
   Throughout my frame, till Doubt and Death,
Ill brethren, let the fancy fly

From belt to belt of crimson seas
   On leagues of odour streaming far,
15 To where in yonder orient star
A hundred spirits whisper "Peace."

87

I passed beside the reverend walls[1]
   In which of old I wore the gown;
   I roved at random through the town,
And saw the tumult of the halls;

5 And heard once more in college fanes°   *chapels*
   The storm their high-built organs make,
   And thunder-music, rolling, shake
The prophet blazoned on the panes;

And caught once more the distant shout,
10 The measured pulse of racing oars
   Among the willows; paced the shores
And many a bridge, and all about

The same gray flats again, and felt
   The same, but not the same; and last
15 Up that long walk of limes I passed
To see the rooms in which he dwelt.

Another name was on the door:
   I lingered; all within was noise
   Of songs, and clapping hands, and boys
20 That crashed the glass and beat the floor;

Where once we held debate, a band
   Of youthful friends, on mind and art,
   And labour, and the changing mart,°   *market*
And all the framework of the land;

25 When one would aim an arrow fair,
   But send it slackly from the string;

---

1 *reverend walls* Trinity College, Cambridge, where Tennyson and Hallam had been students, and where they first met.

And one would pierce an outer ring,
And one an inner, here and there;

And last the master-bowman, he,
30   Would cleave the mark. A willing ear
        We lent him. Who but hung to hear
The rapt oration flowing free

From point to point, with power and grace
        And music in the bounds of law,
35   To those conclusions when we saw
The God within him light his face,

And seem to lift the form, and glow
        In azure orbits heavenly-wise;
        And over those ethereal eyes
40 The bar[1] of Michael Angelo.

                    88

Wild bird, whose warble, liquid sweet,
        Rings Eden through the budded quicks,°   *hedgerows*
        O tell me where the senses mix,
O tell me where the passions meet,

5   Whence radiate: fierce extremes employ
        Thy spirits in the darkening leaf,
        And in the midmost heart of grief
Thy passion clasps a secret joy:

And I—my harp would prelude woe—
10   I cannot all command the strings;
        The glory of the sum of things
Will flash along the chords and go.

                    89

Witch-elms that counterchange° the floor   *checker*
        Of this flat lawn with dusk and bright;
        And thou, with all thy breadth and height
Of foliage, towering sycamore;

5   How often, hither wandering down,
        My Arthur found your shadows fair,

And shook to all the liberal air
The dust and din and steam of town:

He brought an eye for all he saw;
10   He mixed in all our simple sports;
        They pleased him, fresh from brawling courts
And dusty purlieus[2] of the law.

O joy to him in this retreat,
        Immantled in ambrosial dark,
15   To drink the cooler air, and mark
The landscape winking through the heat:

O sound to rout the brood of cares,
        The sweep of scythe in morning dew,
        The gust that round the garden flew,
20 And tumbled half the mellowing pears!

O bliss, when all in circle drawn
        About him, heart and ear were fed
        To hear him, as he lay and read
The Tuscan poets[3] on the lawn:

25 Or in the all-golden afternoon
        A guest, or happy sister, sung,
        Or here she brought the harp and flung
A ballad to the brightening moon:

Nor less it pleased in livelier moods,
30   Beyond the bounding hill to stray,
        And break the livelong summer day
With banquet in the distant woods;

Whereat we glanced from theme to theme,
        Discussed the books to love or hate,
35   Or touched the changes of the state,
Or threaded some Socratic[4] dream;

---

1 *bar* Forehead ridge. According to Tennyson's *Memoir* (1.38), Hallam once told Tennyson "Alfred, look over my eyes; surely I have the bar of Michael Angelo."

---

2 *purlieus* Physical bounds, limits.

3 *Tuscan poets* Renaissance poets Dante and Petrarch.

4 *Socratic* Relating to the Greek philosopher Socrates and/or his mode of philosophical inquiry through dialogue. Originally Tennyson wrote "Platonic"; he may have changed the word because "Platonic" was sometimes employed as a euphemism for "homosexual."

But if I praised the busy town,
    He loved to rail against it still,
    For "ground in yonder social mill
40 We rub each other's angles down,

"And merge," he said, "in form and gloss
    The picturesque of man and man."
    We talked: the stream beneath us ran,
The wine-flask lying couched in moss,

45 Or cooled within the glooming wave;
    And last, returning from afar,
    Before the crimson-circled star
Had fallen into her father's grave,

And brushing ankle-deep in flowers,
50   We heard behind the woodbine veil
    The milk that bubbled in the pail,
And buzzings of the honeyed hours.

90

He tasted love with half his mind,
    Nor ever drank the inviolate spring
    Where nighest heaven, who first could fling
This bitter seed among mankind;

5 That could the dead, whose dying eyes
    Were closed with wail, resume their life,
    They would but find in child and wife
An iron welcome when they rise:

'Twas well, indeed, when warm with wine,
10   To pledge them with a kindly tear,
    To talk them o'er, to wish them here,
To count their memories half divine;

But if they came who passed away,
    Behold their brides in other hands;
15   The hard heir strides about their lands,
And will not yield them for a day.

Yea, though their sons were none of these,
    Not less the yet-loved sire would make
    Confusion worse than death, and shake
20 The pillars of domestic peace.

Ah dear, but come thou back to me:
    Whatever change the years have wrought,
    I find not yet one lonely thought
That cries against my wish for thee.

91

When rosy plumelets tuft the larch,
    And rarely pipes the mounted thrush;
    Or underneath the barren bush
Flits by the sea-blue bird[1] of March;

5 Come, wear the form by which I know
    Thy spirit in time among thy peers;
    The hope of unaccomplished years
Be large and lucid round thy brow.

When summer's hourly-mellowing change
10   May breathe, with many roses sweet,
    Upon the thousand waves of wheat,
That ripple round the lonely grange;

Come: not in watches of the night,
    But where the sunbeam broodeth warm,
15   Come, beauteous in thine after form,
And like a finer light in light.

92

If any vision should reveal
    Thy likeness, I might count it vain
    As but the canker of the brain;
Yea, though it spake and made appeal

5 To chances where our lots were cast
    Together in the days behind,
    I might but say, I hear a wind
Of memory murmuring the past.

Yea, though it spake and bared to view
10   A fact within the coming year;
    And though the months, revolving near,
Should prove the phantom-warning true,

They might not seem thy prophecies,
    But spiritual presentiments,

---

[1] *sea-blue bird*   Kingfisher.

15   And such refraction of events
As often rises ere they rise.

93

I shall not see thee. Dare I say
    No spirit ever brake the band
    That stays him from the native land
Where first he walked when clasped in clay?

5 No visual shade of some one lost,
    But he, the Spirit himself, may come
    Where all the nerve of sense is numb;
Spirit to Spirit, Ghost to Ghost.

O, therefore from thy sightless range
10   With gods in unconjectured bliss,
    O, from the distance of the abyss
Of tenfold-complicated change,

Descend, and touch, and enter; hear
    The wish too strong for words to name;
15   That in this blindness of the frame
My Ghost may feel that thine is near.

94

How pure at heart and sound in head,
    With what divine affections bold
    Should be the man whose thought would hold
An hour's communion with the dead.

5 In vain shalt thou, or any, call
    The spirits from their golden day,
    Except, like them, thou too canst say,
My spirit is at peace with all.

They haunt the silence of the breast,
10   Imaginations calm and fair,
    The memory like a cloudless air,
The conscience as a sea at rest:

But when the heart is full of din,
    And doubt beside the portal waits,
15   They can but listen at the gates,
And hear the household jar° within.   *sound*

95

By night we lingered on the lawn,
    For underfoot the herb was dry;
    And genial warmth; and o'er the sky
The silvery haze of summer drawn;

5 And calm that let the tapers burn
    Unwavering; not a cricket chirred:
    The brook alone far-off was heard,
And on the board the fluttering urn:

And bats went round in fragrant skies,
10   And wheeled or lit the filmy shapes
    That haunt the dusk, with ermine capes
And woolly breasts and beaded eyes;

While now we sang old songs that pealed
    From knoll to knoll, where, couched at ease,
15   The white kine° glimmered, and the trees   *cattle*
Laid their dark arms about the field.

But when those others, one by one,
    Withdrew themselves from me and night,
    And in the house light after light
20 Went out, and I was all alone,

A hunger seized my heart; I read
    Of that glad year which once had been,
    In those fallen leaves which kept their green,
The noble letters of the dead:

25 And strangely on the silence broke
    The silent-speaking words, and strange
    Was love's dumb cry defying change
To test his worth; and strangely spoke

The faith, the vigour, bold to dwell
30   On doubts that drive the coward back,
    And keen through wordy snares to track
Suggestion to her inmost cell.

So word by word, and line by line,
    The dead man touched me from the past,
    And all at once it seemed at last
The living soul was flashed on mine,

And mine in this was wound, and whirled
    About empyreal° heights of thought,   *heavenly* 10
    And came on that which is, and caught
40 The deep pulsations of the world,

Æonian music measuring out
    The steps of Time—the shocks of Chance—
    The blows of Death. At length my trance
Was cancelled, stricken through with doubt.

45 Vague words! but ah, how hard to frame
    In matter-moulded forms of speech,
    Or even for intellect to reach
Through memory that which I became:

Till now the doubtful dusk revealed
50   The knolls once more where, couched at ease,
    The white kine glimmered, and the trees
Laid their dark arms about the field:

And sucked from out the distant gloom
    A breeze began to tremble o'er
55   The large leaves of the sycamore,
And fluctuate all the still perfume,

And gathering freshlier overhead,
    Rocked the full-foliaged elms, and swung
    The heavy-folded rose, and flung
60 The lilies to and fro, and said

"The dawn, the dawn," and died away;
    And East and West, without a breath,
    Mixed their dim lights, like life and death,
To broaden into boundless day.

96

You say, but with no touch of scorn,
    Sweet-hearted, you, whose light-blue eyes
    Are tender over drowning flies,
You tell me, doubt is Devil-born.

5 I know not: one indeed I knew
    In many a subtle question versed,
    Who touched a jarring lyre at first,
But ever strove to make it true:

Perplexed in faith, but pure in deeds,
    At last he beat his music out.
    There lives more faith in honest doubt,
Believe me, than in half the creeds.

He fought his doubts and gathered strength,
    He would not make his judgment blind,
15   He faced the spectres of the mind
And laid them: thus he came at length

To find a stronger faith his own;
    And Power was with him in the night,
    Which makes the darkness and the light,
20 And dwells not in the light alone,

But in the darkness and the cloud,
    As over Sinai's peaks of old,
    While Israel made their gods of gold,
Although the trumpet blew so loud.[1]

97

My love has talked with rocks and trees;
    He finds on misty mountain-ground
    His own vast shadow glory-crowned;
He sees himself in all he sees.

5 Two partners of a married life—
    I looked on these and thought of thee
    In vastness and in mystery,
And of my spirit as of a wife.

These two—they dwelt with eye on eye,
10   Their hearts of old have beat in tune,
    Their meetings made December June,
Their every parting was to die.

Their love has never passed away;
    The days she never can forget
15   Are earnest that he loves her yet,
Whate'er the faithless people say.

Her life is lone, he sits apart,
    He loves her yet, she will not weep,

---

1 *Sinai's ... loud* See Exodus 19.16–19, Exodus 32.1–5.

Though rapt in matters dark and deep
20   He seems to slight her simple heart.

He thrids° the labyrinth of the mind,   *threads*
    He reads the secret of the star,
    He seems so near and yet so far,
He looks so cold: she thinks him kind.

25   She keeps the gift of years before,
    A withered violet is her bliss:
    She knows not what his greatness is,
For that, for all, she loves him more.

For him she plays, to him she sings
30   Of early faith and plighted vows;
    She knows but matters of the house,
And he, he knows a thousand things.

Her faith is fixed and cannot move,
    She darkly feels him great and wise,
35   She dwells on him with faithful eyes,
"I cannot understand: I love."

98

You leave us: you will see the Rhine,
    And those fair hills I sailed below,
    When I was there with him; and go
By summer belts of wheat and vine

5   To where he breathed his latest breath,
    That City. All her splendour seems
    No livelier than the wisp that gleams
On Lethe in the eyes of Death.

Let her great Danube rolling fair
10   Enwind her isles, unmarked of me:
    I have not seen, I will not see
Vienna; rather dream that there,

A treble darkness, Evil haunts
    The birth, the bridal; friend from friend
15   Is oftener parted, fathers bend
Above more graves, a thousand wants

Gnarr° at the heels of men, and prey   *snarl*
    By each cold hearth, and sadness flings
    Her shadow on the blaze of kings:
20   And yet myself have heard him say,

That not in any mother town
    With statelier progress to and fro
    The double tides of chariots flow
By park and suburb under brown

25   Of lustier leaves; nor more content,
    He told me, lives in any crowd,
    When all is gay with lamps, and loud
With sport and song, in booth and tent,

Imperial halls, or open plain;
30   And wheels the circled dance, and breaks
    The rocket molten into flakes
Of crimson or in emerald rain.

99

Risest thou thus, dim dawn, again,
    So loud with voices of the birds,
    So thick with lowings of the herds,
Day, when I lost the flower of men;

5   Who tremblest through thy darkling red
    On yon swollen brook that bubbles fast
    By meadows breathing of the past,
And woodlands holy to the dead;

Who murmurest in the foliaged eaves
10   A song that slights the coming care,
    And Autumn laying here and there
A fiery finger on the leaves;

Who wakenest with thy balmy breath
    To myriads on the genial earth,
15   Memories of bridal, or of birth,
And unto myriads more, of death.

O wheresoever those may be,
    Betwixt the slumber of the poles,
    Today they count as kindred souls;
20   They know me not, but mourn with me.

100

I climb the hill: from end to end
   Of all the landscape underneath,
   I find no place that does not breathe
Some gracious memory of my friend;

5 No gray old grange, or lonely fold,
   Or low morass and whispering reed,
   Or simple stile from mead to mead,
Or sheepwalk up the windy wold;

Nor hoary knoll of ash and haw°   *hawthorn*
10   That hears the latest linnet trill,
   Nor quarry trenched along the hill
And haunted by the wrangling daw;°   *jackdaw*

Nor runlet tinkling from the rock;
   Nor pastoral rivulet that swerves
15   To left and right through meadowy curves,
That feed the mothers of the flock;

But each has pleased a kindred eye,
   And each reflects a kindlier day;
   And, leaving these, to pass away,
20 I think once more he seems to die.

101

Unwatched, the garden bough shall sway,
   The tender blossom flutter down,
   Unloved, that beech will gather brown,
This maple burn itself away;

5 Unloved, the sun-flower, shining fair,
   Ray round with flames her disk of seed,
   And many a rose-carnation feed
With summer spice the humming air;

Unloved, by many a sandy bar,
10   The brook shall babble down the plain,
   At noon or when the lesser wain[1]
Is twisting round the polar star;

Uncared for, gird the windy grove,
   And flood the haunts of hern° and crake;°   *heron / crow*
15   Or into silver arrows break
The sailing moon in creek and cove;

Till from the garden and the wild
   A fresh association blow,
   And year by year the landscape grow
20 Familiar to the stranger's child;

As year by year the labourer tills
   His wonted glebe,[2] or lops the glades;
   And year by year our memory fades
From all the circle of the hills.

102

We leave the well-belovèd place
   Where first we gazed upon the sky;
   The roofs, that heard our earliest cry,
Will shelter one of stranger race.

5 We go, but ere we go from home,
   As down the garden-walks I move,
   Two spirits of a diverse love
Contend for loving masterdom.

One whispers, "Here thy boyhood sung
10   Long since its matin song, and heard
   The low love-language of the bird
In native hazels tassel-hung."

The other answers, "Yea, but here
   Thy feet have strayed in after hours
15   With thy lost friend among the bowers,
And this hath made them trebly dear."

These two have striven half the day,
   And each prefers his separate claim,
   Poor rivals in a losing game,
20 That will not yield each other way.

I turn to go: my feet are set
   To leave the pleasant fields and farms;
   They mix in one another's arms
To one pure image of regret.

---

1 *lesser wain*   Constellation of Ursa Minor. Ursa Major and Ursa Minor (Latin: Great Bear and Little Bear) each contain seven stars. These are known as Charles's Wain and Lesser Wain. A wain is a wagon, with poles used for hitching a horse; the word "pole," or "plow" gives rise to the common names for the stars, "Great Plough" and "Little Plough."

2 *wonted glebe*   Customary field.

103

On that last night before we went
    From out the doors where I was bred,
    I dreamed a vision of the dead,
Which left my after-morn content.

5   Methought I dwelt within a hall,
    And maidens[1] with me: distant hills
    From hidden summits fed with rills
A river sliding by the wall.

The hall with harp and carol rang.
10   They sang of what is wise and good
    And graceful. In the centre stood
A statue veiled, to which they sang;

And which, though veiled, was known to me,
    The shape of him I loved, and love
15   Forever: then flew in a dove
And brought a summons from the sea:

And when they learnt that I must go
    They wept and wailed, but led the way
    To where a little shallop° lay   *dinghy*
20 At anchor in the flood below;

And on by many a level mead,
    And shadowing bluff that made the banks,
    We glided winding under ranks
Of iris, and the golden reed;

25 And still as vaster grew the shore
    And rolled the floods in grander space,
    The maidens gathered strength and grace
And presence, lordlier than before;

And I myself, who sat apart
30   And watched them, waxed in every limb;
    I felt the thews of Anakim,[2]
The pulses of a Titan's heart;

As one would sing the death of war,
    And one would chant the history
35   Of that great race, which is to be,
And one the shaping of a star;

Until the forward-creeping tides
    Began to foam, and we to draw
    From deep to deep, to where we saw
40 A great ship lift her shining sides.

The man we loved was there on deck,
    But thrice as large as man he bent
    To greet us. Up the side I went,
And fell in silence on his neck:

45 Whereat those maidens with one mind
    Bewailed their lot; I did them wrong:
    "We served thee here," they said, "so long,
And wilt thou leave us now behind?"

So rapt I was, they could not win
50   An answer from my lips, but he
    Replying, "Enter likewise ye
And go with us:" they entered in.

And while the wind began to sweep
    A music out of sheet and shroud,
55   We steered her toward a crimson cloud
That landlike slept along the deep.

104

The time draws near the birth of Christ;
    The moon is hid, the night is still;
    A single church below the hill
Is pealing, folded in the mist.

5   A single peal of bells below,
    That wakens at this hour of rest
    A single murmur in the breast,
That these are not the bells I know.

Like strangers' voices here they sound,
10   In lands where not a memory strays,
    Nor landmark breathes of other days,
But all is new unhallowed ground.

---

1 [Tennyson's note] They are the Muses, poetry, arts—all that made life beautiful here, which we hope will pass with us beyond the grave.

2 *Anakim* Race of giants mentioned in the Biblical books of Deuteronomy and Joshua.

105

Tonight ungathered let us leave
    This laurel, let this holly stand:
    We live within the stranger's land,
And strangely falls our Christmas-eve.

5   Our father's dust is left alone
    And silent under other snows:
    There in due time the woodbine blows,
The violet comes, but we are gone.

No more shall wayward grief abuse
10   The genial hour with mask and mime;
    For change of place, like growth of time,
Has broke the bond of dying use.

Let cares that petty shadows cast,
    By which our lives are chiefly proved,
15   A little spare the night I loved,
And hold it solemn to the past.

But let no footstep beat the floor,
    Nor bowl of wassail mantle warm;
    For who would keep an ancient form
20 Through which the spirit breathes no more?

Be neither song, nor game, nor feast;
    Nor harp be touched, nor flute be blown;
    No dance, no motion, save alone
What lightens in the lucid east

25 Of rising worlds by yonder wood.
    Long sleeps the summer in the seed;
    Run out your measured arcs, and lead
The closing cycle rich in good.

106

Ring out, wild bells, to the wild sky,
    The flying cloud, the frosty light:
    The year is dying in the night;
Ring out, wild bells, and let him die.

5   Ring out the old, ring in the new,
    Ring, happy bells, across the snow:

The year is going, let him go;
Ring out the false, ring in the true.

Ring out the grief that saps the mind,
10   For those that here we see no more;
    Ring out the feud of rich and poor,
Ring in redress to all mankind.

Ring out a slowly dying cause,
    And ancient forms of party strife;
15   Ring in the nobler modes of life,
With sweeter manners, purer laws.

Ring out the want, the care, the sin,
    The faithless coldness of the times;
    Ring out, ring out my mournful rhymes,
20 But ring the fuller minstrel in.

Ring out false pride in place and blood,
    The civic slander and the spite;
    Ring in the love of truth and right,
Ring in the common love of good.

25 Ring out old shapes of foul disease;
    Ring out the narrowing lust of gold;
    Ring out the thousand wars of old,
Ring in the thousand years of peace.

Ring in the valiant man and free,
30   The larger heart, the kindlier hand;
    Ring out the darkness of the land,
Ring in the Christ that is to be.

107

It is the day when he was born,
    A bitter day that early sank
    Behind a purple-frosty bank
Of vapour, leaving night forlorn.

5   The time admits not flowers or leaves
    To deck the banquet. Fiercely flies
    The blast of North and East, and ice
Makes daggers at the sharpened eaves,

And bristles all the brakes and thorns
10   To yon hard crescent, as she hangs
        Above the wood which grides° and clangs   *scrapes*
Its leafless ribs and iron horns

Together, in the drifts that pass
        To darken on the rolling brine
15   That breaks the coast. But fetch the wine,
Arrange the board and brim the glass;

Bring in great logs and let them lie,
        To make a solid core of heat;
        Be cheerful-minded, talk and treat
20 Of all things even as he were by;

We keep the day. With festal cheer,
        With books and music, surely we
        Will drink to him, whate'er he be,
And sing the songs he loved to hear.

108

I will not shut me from my kind,
        And, lest I stiffen into stone,
        I will not eat my heart alone,
Nor feed with sighs a passing wind:

5   What profit lies in barren faith,
        And vacant yearning, though with might
        To scale the heaven's highest height,
Or dive below the wells of Death?

What find I in the highest place,
10   But mine own phantom chanting hymns?
        And on the depths of death there swims
The reflex of a human face.

I'll rather take what fruit may be
        Of sorrow under human skies:
15   'Tis held that sorrow makes us wise,
Whatever wisdom sleep with thee.

109

Heart-affluence in discursive talk
        From household fountains never dry;

The critic clearness of an eye,
That saw through all the Muses' walk;

Seraphic intellect and force
5   To seize and throw the doubts of man;
        Impassioned logic, which outran
The hearer in its fiery course;

High nature amorous of the good,
10   But touched with no ascetic gloom;
        And passion pure in snowy bloom
Through all the years of April blood;

A love of freedom rarely felt,
        Of freedom in her regal seat
15   Of England; not the schoolboy heat,
The blind hysterics of the Celt;

And manhood fused with female grace
        In such a sort, the child would twine
        A trustful hand, unasked, in thine,
20 And find his comfort in thy face;

All these have been, and thee mine eyes
        Have looked on: if they looked in vain,
        My shame is greater who remain,
Nor let thy wisdom make me wise.

110

Thy converse drew us with delight,
        The men of rathe° and riper years: *counsel*
        The feeble soul, a haunt of fears,
Forgot his weakness in thy sight.

5   On thee the loyal-hearted hung,
        The proud was half disarmed of pride,
        Nor cared the serpent at thy side
To flicker with his double tongue.

The stern were mild when thou wert by,
10   The flippant put himself to school
        And heard thee, and the brazen fool
Was softened, and he knew not why;

While I, thy nearest, sat apart,
    And felt thy triumph was as mine;
15   And loved them more, that they were thine,
The graceful tact, the Christian art;

Nor mine the sweetness or the skill,
    But mine the love that will not tire,
    And, born of love, the vague desire
20 That spurs an imitative will.

III

The churl in spirit, up or down
    Along the scale of ranks, through all,
    To him who grasps a golden ball,[1]
By blood a king, at heart a clown;

5 The churl in spirit, howe'er he veil
    His want in forms for fashion's sake,
    Will let his coltish nature break
At seasons through the gilded pale:

For who can always act? but he,
10   To whom a thousand memories call,
    Not being less but more than all
The gentleness he seemed to be,

Best seemed the thing he was, and joined
    Each office of the social hour
15   To noble manners, as the flower
And native growth of noble mind;

Nor ever narrowness or spite,
    Or villain fancy fleeting by,
    Drew in the expression of an eye,
20 Where God and Nature met in light;

And thus he bore without abuse
    The grand old name of gentleman,
    Defamed by every charlatan,
And soiled with all ignoble use.

112

High wisdom holds my wisdom less,
    That I, who gaze with temperate eyes

On glorious insufficiencies,
Set light by narrower perfectness.

5 But thou, that fillest all the room
    Of all my love, art reason why
    I seem to cast a careless eye
On souls, the lesser lords of doom.

For what wert thou? some novel power
10   Sprang up forever at a touch,
    And hope could never hope too much,
In watching thee from hour to hour,

Large elements in order brought,
    And tracts of calm from tempest made,
15   And world-wide fluctuation swayed
In vassal tides that followed thought.

113

'Tis held that sorrow makes us wise;
    Yet how much wisdom sleeps with thee
    Which not alone had guided me,
But served the seasons that may rise;

5 For can I doubt, who knew thee keen
    In intellect, with force and skill
    To strive, to fashion, to fulfil—
I doubt not what thou wouldst have been:

A life in civic action warm,
10   A soul on highest mission sent,
    A potent voice of Parliament,
A pillar steadfast in the storm,

Should licensed boldness gather force,
    Becoming, when the time has birth,
15   A lever to uplift the earth
And roll it in another course,

With thousand shocks that come and go,
    With agonies, with energies,
    With overthrowings, and with cries,
20 And undulations to and fro.

---

[1] *golden ball* I.e., the orb of the monarch.

114

Who loves not Knowledge? Who shall rail
　　Against her beauty? May she mix
　　With men and prosper! Who shall fix
Her pillars? Let her work prevail.

5　But on her forehead sits a fire:
　　She sets her forward countenance
　　And leaps into the future chance,
Submitting all things to desire.

Half-grown as yet, a child, and vain—
10　She cannot fight the fear of death.
　　What is she, cut from love and faith,
But some wild Pallas[1] from the brain

Of Demons? fiery-hot to burst
　　All barriers in her onward race
15　For power. Let her know her place;
She is the second, not the first.

A higher hand must make her mild,
　　If all be not in vain; and guide
　　Her footsteps, moving side by side
20　With wisdom, like the younger child:

For she is earthly of the mind,
　　But Wisdom heavenly of the soul.
　　O, friend, who camest to thy goal
So early, leaving me behind,

25　I would the great world grew like thee,
　　Who grewest not alone in power
　　And knowledge, but by year and hour
In reverence and in charity.

115

Now fades the last long streak of snow,
　　Now burgeons every maze of quick°　　　　*vegetation*
　　About the flowering squares, and thick
By ashen roots the violets blow.

5　Now rings the woodland loud and long,
　　The distance takes a lovelier hue,
　　And drowned in yonder living blue
The lark becomes a sightless song.

Now dance the lights on lawn and lea,
10　The flocks are whiter down the vale,
　　And milkier every milky sail
On winding stream or distant sea;

Where now the seamew° pipes, or dives　　　*seagull*
　　In yonder greening gleam, and fly
15　The happy birds, that change their sky
To build and brood; that live their lives

From land to land; and in my breast
　　Spring wakens too; and my regret
　　Becomes an April violet,
20　And buds and blossoms like the rest.

116

Is it, then, regret for buried time
　　That keenlier in sweet April wakes,
　　And meets the year, and gives and takes
The colours of the crescent prime?

5　Not all: the songs, the stirring air,
　　The life re-orient out of dust,
　　Cry through the sense to hearten trust
In that which made the world so fair.

Not all regret: the face will shine
10　Upon me, while I muse alone;
　　And that dear voice, I once have known,
Still speak to me of me and mine:

Yet less of sorrow lives in me
　　For days of happy commune dead;
15　Less yearning for the friendship fled,
Than some strong bond which is to be.

117

O days and hours, your work is this
　　To hold me from my proper place,

---

[1] *Pallas* Pallas Athena, Greek goddess of wisdom, who was said to
have leapt out from the forehead of Zeus, rather than having been
born in the usual manner.

A little while from his embrace,
For fuller gain of after bliss:

5   That out of distance might ensue
Desire of nearness doubly sweet;
And unto meeting when we meet,
Delight a hundredfold accrue,

For every grain of sand that runs,
10   And every span of shade[1] that steals,
And every kiss of tothèd wheels,[2]
And all the courses of the suns.

118

Contemplate all this work of Time,
The giant labouring in his youth;
Nor dream of human love and truth,
As dying Nature's earth and lime;

5   But trust that those we call the dead
Are breathers of an ampler day
For ever nobler ends. They say,
The solid earth whereon we tread

In tracts of fluent heat began,
10   And grew to seeming-random forms,
The seeming prey of cyclic storms,
Till at the last arose the man;

Who throve and branched from clime to clime,
The herald of a higher race,
15   And of himself in higher place,
If so he type this work of time

Within himself, from more to more;
Or, crowned with attributes of woe
Like glories, move his course, and show
20   That life is not as idle ore,

But iron dug from central gloom,
And heated hot with burning fears,
And dipped in baths of hissing tears,
And battered with the shocks of doom

25   To shape and use. Arise and fly
The reeling Faun, the sensual feast;
Move upward, working out the beast,
And let the ape and tiger die.

119

Doors, where my heart was used to beat
So quickly, not as one that weeps
I come once more; the city sleeps;
I smell the meadow in the street;

5   I hear a chirp of birds; I see
Betwixt the black fronts long-withdrawn
A light-blue lane of early dawn,
And think of early days and thee,

And bless thee, for thy lips are bland,
10   And bright the friendship of thine eye;
And in my thoughts with scarce a sigh
I take the pressure of thine hand.

120

I trust I have not wasted breath:
I think we are not wholly brain,
Magnetic mockeries; not in vain,
Like Paul with beasts,[3] I fought with Death;

5   Not only cunning casts in clay:
Let Science prove we are, and then
What matters Science unto men,
At least to me? I would not stay.

Let him, the wiser man who springs
10   Hereafter, up from childhood shape
His action like the greater ape,
But I was *born* to other things.

121

Sad Hesper[4] o'er the buried sun
And ready, thou, to die with him,

---

1   [Tennyson's note]   The sun-dial.

2   *tothèd wheels*   Gears of a clock.

3   *Paul ... beasts*   See 1 Corinthians 15.32: "If I fought wild beasts in Ephesus for merely human reasons, what have I gained? If the dead are not raised, 'Let us eat and drink, for tomorrow we die.'"

4   *Hesper*   Hesperus, the evening star.

Thou watchest all things ever dim
And dimmer, and a glory done:

5   The team[1] is loosened from the wain,
The boat is drawn upon the shore;
Thou listenest to the closing door,
And life is darkened in the brain.

Bright Phosphor, fresher for the night,
10   By thee the world's great work is heard
Beginning, and the wakeful bird;
Behind thee comes the greater light:

The market boat is on the stream,
And voices hail it from the brink;
15   Thou hear'st the village hammer clink,
And see'st the moving of the team.

Sweet Hesper-Phosphor, double name
For what is one, the first, the last,
Thou, like my present and my past,
20   Thy place is changed; thou art the same.

122

Oh, wast thou with me, dearest, then,
While I rose up against my doom,
And yearned to burst the folded gloom,
To bare the eternal Heavens again,

5   To feel once more, in placid awe,
The strong imagination roll
A sphere of stars about my soul,
In all her motion one with law;

If thou wert with me, and the grave
10   Divide us not, be with me now,
And enter in at breast and brow,
Till all my blood, a fuller wave,

Be quickened with a livelier breath,
And like an inconsiderate boy,
15   As in the former flash of joy,
I slip the thoughts of life and death;

And all the breeze of Fancy blows,
And every dew-drop paints a bow,°   *rainbow*
The wizard lightnings[2] deeply glow,
20   And every thought breaks out a rose.

123

There rolls the deep where grew the tree.
O earth, what changes hast thou seen!
There where the long street roars, hath been
The stillness of the central sea.

5   The hills are shadows, and they flow
From form to form, and nothing stands;
They melt like mist, the solid lands,
Like clouds they shape themselves and go.

But in my spirit will I dwell,
10   And dream my dream, and hold it true;
For though my lips may breathe adieu,
I cannot think the thing farewell.

124

That which we dare invoke to bless;
Our dearest faith; our ghastliest doubt;
He, They, One, All; within, without;
The Power in darkness whom we guess;

5   I found Him not in world or sun,
Or eagle's wing, or insect's eye;
Nor through the questions men may try,
The petty cobwebs we have spun:

If e'er when faith had fallen asleep,
10   I heard a voice "believe no more"
And heard an ever-breaking shore
That tumbled in the Godless deep;

A warmth within the breast would melt
The freezing reason's colder part,
15   And like a man in wrath the heart
Stood up and answered "I have felt."

No, like a child in doubt and fear:
But that blind clamour made me wise;

---

[1] *team* I.e., of horses or oxen.

[2] *wizard lightnings* Northern lights, or aurora borealis.

Then was I as a child that cries,
20 But, crying, knows his father near;

And what I am beheld again
    What is, and no man understands;
    And out of darkness came the hands
That reach through nature, moulding men.

125

Whatever I have said or sung,
    Some bitter notes my harp would give,
    Yea, though there often seemed to live
A contradiction on the tongue,

5   Yet Hope had never lost her youth;
    She did but look through dimmer eyes;
    Or Love but played with gracious lies,
Because he felt so fixed in truth:

And if the song were full of care,
10   He breathed the spirit of the song;
    And if the words were sweet and strong
He set his royal signet there;

Abiding with me till I sail
    To seek thee on the mystic deeps,
15   And this electric force, that keeps
A thousand pulses dancing, fail.

126

Love is and was my Lord and King,
    And in his presence I attend
    To hear the tidings of my friend,
Which every hour his couriers bring.

5   Love is and was my King and Lord,
    And will be, though as yet I keep
    Within his court on earth, and sleep
Encompassed by his faithful guard,

And hear at times a sentinel
10   Who moves about from place to place,
    And whispers to the worlds of space,
In the deep night, that all is well.

127

And all is well, though faith and form
    Be sundered in the night of fear;
    Well roars the storm to those that hear
A deeper voice across the storm,

5   Proclaiming social truth shall spread,
    And justice, even though thrice again
    The red fool-fury of the Seine[1]
Should pile her barricades with dead.

But ill for him that wears a crown,
10   And him, the lazar,° in his rags: leper
    They tremble, the sustaining crags;
The spires of ice are toppled down,

And molten up, and roar in flood;
    The fortress crashes from on high,
15   The brute earth lightens to the sky,
And the great Æon° sinks in blood,   eon

And compassed by the fires of Hell;
    While thou, dear spirit, happy star,
    O'erlook'st the tumult from afar,
20 And smilest, knowing all is well.

128

The love that rose on stronger wings,
    Unpalsied when he met with Death,
    Is comrade of the lesser faith
That sees the course of human things.

5   No doubt vast eddies in the flood
    Of onward time shall yet be made,
    And thronèd races may degrade;
Yet O ye mysteries of good,

Wild Hours that fly with Hope and Fear,
10   If all your office had to do
    With old results that look like new;
If this were all your mission here,

---

1 *red ... Seine* I.e., the slaughter during the French Revolution.
The Seine is the river than runs through Paris.

To draw, to sheathe a useless sword,
    To fool the crowd with glorious lies,
15   To cleave a creed in sects and cries,
To change the bearing of a word,

To shift an arbitrary power,
    To cramp the student at his desk,
    To make old bareness picturesque
20 And tuft with grass a feudal tower;

Why then my scorn might well descend
    On you and yours. I see in part
    That all, as in some piece of art,
Is toil cöoperant to an end.

129

Dear friend, far off, my lost desire,
    So far, so near in woe and weal;
    O loved the most, when most I feel
There is a lower and a higher;

5 Known and unknown; human, divine;
    Sweet human hand and lips and eye;
    Dear heavenly friend that canst not die,
Mine, mine, for ever, ever mine;

Strange friend, past, present, and to be;
10   Loved deeplier, darklier understood;
    Behold, I dream a dream of good,
And mingle all the world with thee.

130

Thy voice is on the rolling air;
    I hear thee where the waters run;
    Thou standest in the rising sun,
And in the setting thou art fair.

5 What art thou then? I cannot guess;
    But though I seem in star and flower
    To feel thee some diffusive power,
I do not therefore love thee less:

My love involves the love before;
10   My love is vaster passion now;
    Though mixed with God and Nature thou,
I seem to love thee more and more.

Far off thou art, but ever nigh;
    I have thee still, and I rejoice;
15   I prosper, circled with thy voice;
I shall not lose thee though I die.

131

O living will that shalt endure
    When all that seems shall suffer shock,
    Rise in the spiritual rock,
Flow through our deeds and make them pure,

5 That we may lift from out of dust
    A voice as unto him that hears,
    A cry above the conquered years
To one that with us works, and trust,

With faith that comes of self-control,
10   The truths that never can be proved
    Until we close with all we loved,
And all we flow from, soul in soul.

[EPILOGUE]

O true and tried, so well and long,
    Demand not thou a marriage lay;
    In that it is thy marriage day
Is music more than any song.[1]

5 Nor have I felt so much of bliss
    Since first he told me that he loved
    A daughter of our house; nor proved
Since that dark day a day like this;

Though I since then have numbered o'er
10   Some thrice three years: they went and came,
    Remade the blood and changed the frame,
And yet is love not less, but more;

No longer caring to embalm
    In dying songs a dead regret,
15   But like a statue solid-set,
And moulded in colossal calm.

---

[1] *O true ... song* The Epilogue is a marriage song for Edmund Cushington and Tennyson's sister Cecilia.

Regret is dead, but love is more
    Than in the summers that are flown,
    For I myself with these have grown
20 To something greater than before;

Which makes appear the songs I made
    As echoes out of weaker times,
    As half but idle brawling rhymes,
The sport of random sun and shade.

25 But where is she, the bridal flower,
    That must be made a wife ere noon?
    She enters, glowing like the moon
Of Eden on its bridal bower:

On me she bends her blissful eyes
30   And then on thee; they meet thy look
    And brighten like the star that shook
Betwixt the palms of paradise.

O when her life was yet in bud,
    He too foretold the perfect rose.
35   For thee she grew, for thee she grows
Forever, and as fair as good.

And thou art worthy; full of power;
    As gentle; liberal-minded, great,
    Consistent; wearing all that weight
40 Of learning lightly like a flower.

But now set out: the noon is near,
    And I must give away the bride;
    She fears not, or with thee beside
And me behind her, will not fear.

45 For I that danced her on my knee,
    That watched her on her nurse's arm,
    That shielded all her life from harm
At last must part with her to thee;

Now waiting to be made a wife,
50   Her feet, my darling, on the dead;
    Their pensive tablets° round her head,   *gravestones*
And the most living words of life

Breathed in her ear. The ring is on;
    The "wilt thou" answered, and again
55   The "wilt thou" asked, till out of twain
Her sweet "I will" has made you one.

Now sign your names, which shall be read,
    Mute symbols of a joyful morn,
    By village eyes as yet unborn;
60 The names are signed, and overhead

Begins the clash and clang that tells
    The joy to every wandering breeze;
    The blind wall rocks, and on the trees
The dead leaf trembles to the bells.

65 O happy hour, and happier hours
    Await them. Many a merry face
    Salutes them—maidens of the place,
That pelt us in the porch with flowers.

O happy hour, behold the bride
70   With him to whom her hand I gave.
    They leave the porch, they pass the grave
That has today its sunny side.

Today the grave is bright for me,
    For them the light of life increased,
75   Who stay to share the morning feast,
Who rest tonight beside the sea.

Let all my genial spirits advance
    To meet and greet a whiter sun;
    My drooping memory will not shun
80 The foaming grape of eastern France.

It circles round, and fancy plays,
    And hearts are warmed and faces bloom,
    As drinking health to bride and groom
We wish them store of happy days.

85 Nor count me all to blame if I
    Conjecture of a stiller guest,
    Perchance, perchance, among the rest,
And, though in silence, wishing joy.

But they must go, the time draws on,
90   And those white-favoured horses wait;
They rise, but linger; it is late;
Farewell, we kiss, and they are gone.

A shade falls on us like the dark
        From little cloudlets on the grass,
95   But sweeps away as out we pass
To range the woods, to roam the park,

Discussing how their courtship grew,
        And talk of others that are wed,
        And how she looked, and what he said,
100   And back we come at fall of dew.

Again the feast, the speech, the glee,
        The shade of passing thought, the wealth
        Of words and wit, the double health,
The crowning cup, the three-times-three,[1]

105   And last the dance;—till I retire:
        Dumb is that tower which spake so loud,
        And high in heaven the streaming cloud,
And on the downs a rising fire:

And rise, O moon, from yonder down,
110   Till over down and over dale
        All night the shining vapour sail
And pass the silent-lighted town,

The white-faced halls, the glancing rills,
        And catch at every mountain head,
115   And o'er the friths[2] that branch and spread
Their sleeping silver through the hills;

And touch with shade the bridal doors,
        With tender gloom the roof, the wall;
        And breaking let the splendour fall
120   To spangle all the happy shores

By which they rest, and ocean sounds,
        And, star and system rolling past,

A soul shall draw from out the vast
And strike his being into bounds,

125   And, moved through life of lower phase
        Result in man, be born and think,
        And act and love, a closer link
Betwixt us and the crowning race

Of those that, eye to eye, shall look
130   On knowledge; under whose command
        Is Earth and Earth's, and in their hand
Is Nature like an open book;

No longer half-akin to brute,
        For all we thought and loved and did,
135   And hoped, and suffered, is but seed
Of what in them is flower and fruit;

Whereof the man, that with me trod
        This planet, was a noble type
        Appearing ere the times were ripe,
140   That friend of mine who lives in God,

That God, which ever lives and loves,
        One God, one law, one element,
        And one far-off divine event,
To which the whole creation moves.
—1850

The Eagle
[Fragment]

He clasps the crag with crooked hands;
Close to the sun in lonely lands,
Ringed with the azure world, he stands.

The wrinkled sea beneath him crawls;
5   He watches from his mountain walls,
And like a thunderbolt he falls.
—1851 (WRITTEN 1833?)

---

1   *three-times-three*   A toast: "Three-times-three cheers for the bride and groom!"

2   *friths*   Wooded areas.

The Charge of the Light Brigade[1]

1

Half a league,[2] half a league,
Half a league onward,
All in the valley of Death
    Rode the six hundred.[3]
5 "Forward, the Light Brigade!
Charge for the guns!" he said:
Into the valley of Death
    Rode the six hundred.

2

"Forward, the Light Brigade!"
10 Was there a man dismayed?
Not though the soldier knew
    Some one had blundered:
Their's not to make reply,
Their's not to reason why,
15 Their's but to do and die:
Into the valley of Death
    Rode the six hundred.

3

Cannon to right of them,
Cannon to left of them,
20 Cannon in front of them
    Volleyed and thundered;
Stormed at with shot and shell,
Boldly they rode and well,
Into the jaws of Death,
25 Into the mouth of Hell
    Rode the six hundred.

4

Flashed all their sabres bare,
Flashed as they turned in air

Sabring the gunners there,
30 Charging an army, while
    All the world wondered:
Plunged in the battery-smoke
Right through the line they broke;
Cossack and Russian
35 Reeled from the sabre-stroke
    Shattered and sundered.
Then they rode back, but not
    Not the six hundred.

5

Cannon to right of them,
40 Cannon to left of them,
Cannon behind them
    Volleyed and thundered;
Stormed at with shot and shell,
While horse and hero fell,
45 They that had fought so well
Came through the jaws of Death,
Back from the mouth of Hell,
All that was left of them,[4]
    Left of six hundred.

6

50 When can their glory fade?
O the wild charge they made!
    All the world wondered.
Honour the charge they made!
Honour the Light Brigade,
55   Noble six hundred!
—1854

[Flower in the Crannied Wall]

Flower in the crannied wall,
I pluck you out of the crannies,
I hold you here, root and all, in my hand,
Little flower—but if I could understand
5 What you are, root and all, and all in all,
I should know what God and man is.
—1869

---

[1] *The Charge … Brigade* Written some weeks after a disastrous engagement during the Crimean War. At the Battle of Balaclava on 25 October 1854, the 700 cavalrymen of the Light Brigade, acting on a misinterpreted order, directly charged the Russian artillery.

[2] *league* About three miles.

[3] *six hundred* The initial newspaper account read by Tennyson mentioned "607 sabres," and he retained the number even when the correct number was discovered to be considerably higher because "six is much better than seven hundred … metrically" (*Letters* ii.101).

[4] *All … them* Only 195 men survived the charge.

Vastness

1

Many a hearth upon our dark globe sighs after many
    a vanished face,
Many a planet by many a sun may roll with the dust
    of a vanished race.

2

Raving politics, never at rest—as this poor earth's
    pale history runs,—
What is it all but a trouble° of ants in the gleam   *agitation*
    of a million million of suns?

3

5 Lies upon this side, lies upon that side, truthless violence
    mourned by the Wise,
Thousands of voices drowning his own in a popular
    torrent of lies upon lies;

4

Stately purposes, valour in battle, glorious annals of army
    and fleet,
Death for the right cause, death for the wrong cause,
    trumpets of victory, groans of defeat;

5

Innocence seethed° in her mother's milk,[1] and   *boiled*
    Charity setting the martyr aflame;
10 Thraldom° who walks with the banner of   *bondage*
    Freedom, and recks not[2] to ruin a realm in her name.

6

Faith at her zenith, or all but lost in the gloom of doubts
    that darken the schools;
Craft with a bunch of all-heal[3] in her hand,
    followed up by her vassal° legion of fools;   *servile*

7

Trade flying over a thousand seas with her spice
    and her vintage, her silk and her corn;

Desolate offing,[4] sailorless harbours, famishing
    populace, wharves forlorn;

8

15 Star of the morning, Hope in the sunrise;
    gloom of the evening, Life at a close;
Pleasure who flaunts on her wide down-way
    with her flying robe and her poisoned rose;

9

Pain, that has crawled from the corpse of Pleasure,
    a worm which writhes all day, and at night
Stirs up again in the heart of the sleeper, and stings
    him back to the curse of the light;

10

Wealth with his wines and his wedded harlots;
    honest Poverty, bare to the bone;
20 Opulent Avarice, lean as Poverty; Flattery gilding
    the rift in a throne;

11

Fame blowing out from her golden trumpet
    a jubilant challenge to Time and to Fate;
Slander, her shadow, sowing the nettle on all the
    laurelled graves of the Great;

12

Love for the maiden, crowned with marriage,
    no regrets for aught that has been,
Household happinesss, gracious children,
    debtless competence, golden mean;

13

25 National hatreds of whole generations, and
    pigmy° spites of the village spire;   *trivial*
Vows that will last to the last death-ruckle,°   *death-rattle*
    and vows that are snapped in a moment of fire;

14

He that has lived for the lust of the minute,
    and died in the doing it, flesh without mind;

---

1 *Innocence ... milk* See *Exodus* 34.26: "Thou shalt not seethe a kid
in his mother's milk."

2 *recks not* Is not reluctant.

3 *all-heal* Name given to various plants believed to possess healing
properties.

4 *offing* Most distant part of the sea visible from shore.

He that has nailed all flesh to the Cross,
    till Self died out in the love of his kind;

15

Spring and Summer and Autumn and Winter,
    and all these old revolutions of earth;
30 All new-old revolutions of Empire—change of the
    tide—what is all of it worth?

16

What the philosophies, all the sciences, poesy,
    varying voices of prayer?
All that is noblest, all that is basest, all that is filthy
    with all that is fair?

17

What is it all, if we all of us end but in being our own
    corpse-coffins at last,
Swallowed in Vastness, lost in Silence, drowned
    in the deeps of a meaningless Past?

18

35 What but a murmur of gnats in the gloom,
    or a moment's anger of bees in their hive?—

*   *   *   *

Peace, let it be! for I loved him, and love him for ever:
    the dead are not dead but alive.
—1885; 1889

Crossing the Bar[1]

Sunset and evening star,
    And one clear call for me!
And may there be no moaning of the bar,
    When I put out to sea,

5 But such a tide as moving seems asleep,
    Too full for sound and foam,
When that which drew from out the boundless deep
    Turns again home.

Twilight and evening bell,
10   And after that the dark!
And may there be no sadness of farewell,
    When I embark;

For though from out our bourne° of Time and   *limit*
    Place
    The flood may bear me far,
15 I hope to see my Pilot face to face
    When I have crossed the bar.
—1889

---

1   *bar* Sandbank or shoal across the mouth of a harbor or estuary.

IN CONTEXT

Images of Tennyson

Particularly in his later years, Tennyson became an iconic figure in Victorian Britain. The best known photographic images of him are those taken by Julia Margaret Cameron, one of which is reproduced, below. (Another appears in the introduction to Tennyson, above.) Tennyson as a younger man is described below by Thomas Carlyle.

from Thomas Carlyle, Letter to Ralph Waldo Emerson, 5 August 1844

Alfred is one of the few British or Foreign Figures (a not increasing number I think!) who are and remain beautiful to me;—a true human soul, or some authentic approximation thereto, to whom your own soul can say, Brother!— However, I doubt he will not come; he often skips me, in these brief visits to Town; skips everybody indeed; being a man solitary and sad, as certain men are, dwelling in an element of gloom,—carrying a bit of Chaos about him, in short, which he is manufacturing into Cosmos!

Alfred is the son of a Lincolnshire Gentleman Farmer, I think; indeed, you see in his verses that he is a native of "moated granges," and green, fat pastures, not of mountains and their torrents and storms. He had his breeding at Cambridge, as if for the Law or Church; being master of a small annuity on his Father's decease, he preferred clubbing with his Mother and some Sisters, to live unpromoted and write Poems. In this way he lives still, now here, now there; the family always within reach of London, never in it; he himself making rare and brief visits, lodging in some old comrade's rooms. I think he must be under forty, not much under it. One of the finest-looking men in the world. A great shock of rough dusty-dark hair; bright-laughing hazel eyes; massive aquiline face, most massive yet most delicate; of sallow-brown complexion, almost Indian-looking; clothes cynically loose, free-and-easy;—smokes infinite tobacco. His voice is musical metallic,—fit for loud laughter and piercing wail, and all that may lie between; speech and speculation free and plenteous: I do not meet, in these late decades, such company over a pipe!—We shall see what he will grow to. He is often unwell; very chaotic,—his way is through Chaos and the Bottomless and Pathless; not handy for making out many miles upon.

Julia Margaret Cameron, *Alfred Tennyson*, 1865. Tennyson nicknamed this photograph "the dirty monk" and claimed that it was his favorite photograph of himself.

from Evert A. Duyckinck,
*Portrait Gallery of Eminent Men
and Women in Europe and America,*
1873. This portrait appears to be
from the 1850s.

IN CONTEXT

Victorian Images of Arthurian Legend

Arthurian romance was a frequent subject of Victorian painting and photography as well as Victorian literature; a sampling is reproduced below.

Julia Margaret Cameron, *The Parting of
Lancelot and Guinevere*, 1847.

Julia Margaret Cameron, *Vivien and
Merlin*, 1874.

John William Waterhouse, *The Lady of Shalott*, 1888.

William Holman Hunt, *The Lady of Shalott*, 1857.

IN CONTEXT

Crimea and the Camera

The Crimean War was the first to be photographed extensively—most notably by Roger Fenton, who spent three months in Crimea in 1855. Both the technology of the time and the demands of Victorian taste militated against shooting scenes of battle directly; unlike Matthew Brady and other photographers of the American Civil War a few years later, Fenton took no pictures of bloody and mangled corpses.

Fenton's most famous photograph of the war, *Valley of the Shadow of Death*, came to be closely associated with Tennyson's famous 1854 poem, "The Charge of the Light Brigade." The connection is not entirely a direct one, however. It was not the valley where the charge occurred that Fenton photographed but another valley in the vicinity—one that had begun to be referred to by soldiers as "the valley of the shadow of death" (in an echo both of Tennyson's poem and of the Bible) because of the frequency with which the Russians shelled it.

Roger Fenton,
*General Bosquet Giving Orders
to His Staff*, 1855.

Roger Fenton, *Captain Dames*, 1855.

Roger Fenton, *Group of Croat Chiefs*,
1855.

Roger Fenton, *Cookhouse of the 8ᵗʰ Hussars*, 1855.

Roger Fenton, *Valley of the Shadow of Death*, 1855.

ROBERT BROWNING
1812 — 1889

"The spirit of passionate and imaginative poetry is not dead among us," wrote an exultant R.H. Horne in 1844, while reviewing the poems of the young Robert Browning. But Browning, for all his passion and imagination, was not a popular poet for much of his lifetime. Indeed, until the 1860s, Browning was better known as the husband of Elizabeth Barrett. His own poetry, in the eyes of many of his contemporaries, was far too obscure, littered as it was with recondite historical and literary references and with dubious subject matter—husbands murdering their wives, artists frolicking with prostitutes. Fame did come, however, and scholars now credit Browning for having realized new

possibilities in the dramatic monologue, a form of poetry that, like a monologue in a dramatic production, showcases the speech of a character to an implied or imaginary audience. The poems are, in Browning's own words, "so many utterances of so many imaginary persons, not mine." As Browning's dramatic monologues unfold, their speakers reveal levels of psychological complexity that have inspired generations of poets, from the Pre-Raphaelites who were coming of age in the 1840s to Modernists such as Ezra Pound and T.S. Eliot.

Browning was the eldest of two children born in an upper middle-class suburb of London to a scholarly father and a devout, Protestant mother, Sarah Anna Wiedemann. An opponent of slavery, Robert Browning Sr. rejected employment on his family's plantation in St. Kitts in favor of less lucrative but more morally-acceptable work as a clerk for the Bank of England. Both parents helped to shape Browning's religious, social, and intellectual tastes and values, with Browning Sr. in particular feeding his son's voracious appetite for knowledge. The young Browning composed his first poem at the age of six. He attended Peckham School between the ages of ten and twelve and later some classes at University College in London. But the great majority of his schooling took place at home with tutors, and he spent many hours studying the books in his family's voluminous library. Despite his relative lack of formal schooling, then, Browning had an exceptionally bookish education—which may help to explain the intellectual cast of Browning's poetic vision.

Browning first arrived on the literary scene with the publication in 1833 of *Pauline: A Fragment of a Confession*, a long poem in the style of Shelley's *Alastor* (1816), which John Stuart Mill credited with "considerable poetic powers" that yet revealed "a more intense and morbid self-consciousness than I ever knew in any sane human being." The volume, published with family funds, apparently sold not even a single copy. It was followed in 1835 by *Paracelsus*, which, though similarly obscure, at least made Browning known to a few important critics and ultimately brought him into contact with Carlyle, Dickens, and Wordsworth, among others. With *Sordello* (1840), Browning secured his reputation for writing poetry of bewildering difficulty. Browning claimed that his "stress [in *Sordello*] lay on the incidents in the development of a soul: little else is worth study," and yet few could make sense of such incidents as Browning had chosen to portray them.

In 1842 Browning published a volume of shorter poems, *Dramatic Lyrics*, which marked an important break from his earlier productions. Included were many of the poems on which his reputation came to be based: "My Last Duchess," "Soliloquy of the Spanish Cloister," "Johannes Agricola in Meditation," and "Porphyria's Lover," the last two of which had been published in the

The Bishop Orders His Tomb at Saint Praxed's Church

Rome, 15—

Vanity, saith the preacher, vanity![1]
  Draw round my bed: is Anselm keeping back?
Nephews—sons mine … ah God, I know not! Well—
She, men would have to be your mother once,
5   Old Gandolf envied me, so fair she was!
What's done is done, and she is dead beside,
Dead long ago, and I am Bishop since,
And as she died so must we die ourselves,
And thence ye may perceive the world's a dream.
10 Life, how and what is it? As here I lie
In this state-chamber, dying by degrees,
Hours and long hours in the dead night, I ask
"Do I live, am I dead?" Peace, peace seems all.
Saint Praxed's ever was the church for peace;
15 And so, about this tomb of mine. I fought
With tooth and nail to save my niche, ye know:
—Old Gandolf cozened me,° despite my care;   *cheated*
Shrewd was that snatch from out the corner south
He graced his carrion with, God curse the same!
20 Yet still my niche is not so cramped but thence
One sees the pulpit o' the epistle side,[2]
And somewhat of the choir, those silent seats,
And up into the aery dome where live
The angels, and a sunbeam's sure to lurk:
25 And I shall fill my slab of basalt there,
And 'neath my tabernacle take my rest,
With those nine columns round me, two and two,
The odd one at my feet where Anselm stands:
Peach-blossom marble all, the rare, the ripe
30 As fresh-poured red wine of a mighty pulse.
—Old Gandolf with his paltry onion-stone,[3]
Put me where I may look at him! True peach,
Rosy and flawless: how I earned the prize!
Draw close: that conflagration of my church

35 —What then? So much was saved if aught were missed!
My sons, ye would not be my death? Go dig
The white-grape vineyard where the oil-press stood,
Drop water gently till the surface sink,
And if ye find … Ah God, I know not, I! …
40 Bedded in store of rotten fig leaves soft,
And corded up in a tight olive-frail,°   *basket*
Some lump, ah God, of *lapis lazuli*,[4]
Big as a Jew's head cut off at the nape,
Blue as a vein o'er the Madonna's breast …
45 Sons, all have I bequeathed you, villas, all,
That brave Frascati[5] villa with its bath,
So, let the blue lump poise between my knees,
Like God the Father's globe on both his hands
Ye worship in the Jesu Church[6] so gay,
50 For Gandolf shall not choose but see and burst!
Swift as a weaver's shuttle[7] fleet our years:
Man goeth to the grave, and where is he?[8]
Did I say basalt for my slab, sons? Black—
'Twas ever antique-black° I meant! How else   *black marble*
55 Shall ye contrast my frieze[9] to come beneath?
The bas-relief in bronze ye promised me,
Those Pans and Nymphs[10] ye wot of, and perchance
Some tripod, thyrsus,[11] with a vase or so,
The Saviour at his sermon on the mount,

---

[1] *Vanity, saith the preacher* From Ecclesiastes 1.2: "Vanity of vanities, saith the Preacher, vanity of vanities; all is vanity."

[2] *epistle side* Right-hand side, where the pulpit is and from which the epistles are read.

[3] *onion stone* Variety of less expensive marble that is named for its tendency to peel into layers.

[4] *lapis lazuli* Semi-precious blue stone; the altar-tomb of St. Ignatius at Il Gesù (Church of the Holy Name of Jesus) in Rome is decorated with huge columns made from lapis lazuli.

[5] *Frascati* Summer resort near Rome.

[6] *Jesu Church* Il Gesù.

[7] *Swift … years* From Job 7.6: "My days are swifter than a weaver's shuttle, and are spent without hope."

[8] *Man goeth … where is he?* From Job 7.9: "As the cloud is consumed and vanisheth away: so he that goeth down to the grave shall come up no more."

[9] *frieze* Painted or sculpted band on a wall or column.

[10] *bas-relief… Pans and Nymphs* Shallow carvings that depict Greek mythological figures alongside Biblical figures.

[11] *tripod* Vessel on which sat the Oracle at Delphi, where she delivered her prophecies; *thyrsus* Staff adorned with a pine cone and ivy, carried by Dionysus, the Greek god of wine, and his followers.

60 Saint Praxed[1] in a glory,° and one Pan[2]   *halo; lightbeam*
    Ready to twitch the Nymph's last garment off,
    And Moses with the tables°… but I know   *Ten Commandments*
    Ye mark me not! What do they whisper thee,
    Child of my bowels, Anselm? Ah, ye hope
65 To revel down my villas while I gasp
    Bricked o'er with beggar's mouldy travertine°   *limestone*
    Which Gandolf from his tomb top chuckles at!
    Nay, boys, ye love me—all of jasper,° then!   *precious stone*
    'Tis jasper ye stand pledged to, lest I grieve
70 My bath must needs be left behind, alas!
    One block, pure green as a pistachio nut,
    There's plenty jasper somewhere in the world—
    And have I not Saint Praxed's ear to pray
    Horses for ye, and brown Greek manuscripts,
75 And mistresses with great smooth marbly limbs?
    —That's if ye carve my epitaph aright,
    Choice Latin, picked phrase, Tully's[3] every word,
    No gaudy ware like Gandolf's second line—
    Tully, my masters? Ulpian[4] serves his need!
80 And then how I shall lie through centuries,
    And hear the blessed mutter of the mass,
    And see God made and eaten all day long,
    And feel the steady candle flame, and taste
    Good strong thick stupefying incense smoke!
85 For as I lie here, hours of the dead night,
    Dying in state and by such slow degrees,
    I fold my arms as if they clasped a crook,°   *bishop's staff*
    And stretch my feet forth straight as stone can point,
    And let the bedclothes, for a mortcloth,[5] drop
90 Into great laps and folds of sculptor's work:
    And as yon tapers dwindle, and strange thoughts
    Grow, with a certain humming in my ears,
    About the life before I lived this life,
    And this life too, popes, cardinals and priests,
95 Saint Praxed at his sermon on the mount,

    Your tall pale mother with her talking eyes,
    And newfound agate urns as fresh as day,
    And marble's language, Latin pure, discreet,
    —Aha, *ELUCESCEBAT*[6] quoth our friend?
100 No Tully, said I, Ulpian at the best!
    Evil and brief hath been my pilgrimage.[7]
    All *lapis*, all, sons! Else I give the Pope
    My villas! Will ye ever eat my heart?
    Ever your eyes were as a lizard's quick,
105 They glitter like your mother's for my soul,
    Or ye would heighten my impoverished frieze,
    Piece out its starved design, and fill my vase
    With grapes, and add a vizor and a Term,[8]
    And to the tripod ye would tie a lynx
110 That in his struggle throws the thyrsus down,
    To comfort me on my entablature°   *column*
    Whereon I am to lie till I must ask
    "Do I live, am I dead?" There, leave me, there!
    For ye have stabbed me with ingratitude
115 To death—ye wish it—God, ye wish it! Stone—
    Gritstone, a-crumble! Clammy squares which sweat
    As if the corpse they keep were oozing through—
    And no more lapis to delight the world!
    Well go! I bless ye. Fewer tapers° there,   *candles*
120 But in a row: and, going, turn your backs
    —Ay, like departing altar ministrants,
    And leave me in my church, the church for peace,
    That I may watch at leisure if he leers—
    Old Gandolf, at me, from his onion-stone,
125 As still he envied me, so fair she was!
    —1845

Meeting at Night

I

The grey sea and the long black land;
And the yellow half moon large and low;

---

1 *Saint Praxed*   Roman virgin of the second century who gave away all of her wealth to the poor.

2 *Pan*   Greek shepherd god of nature, who chased the nymph Syrinx until she turned herself into a bed of reeds.

3 *Tully*   Commonly known as Cicero, Roman orator, philosopher, and statesman of the first century BCE.

4 *Ulpian*   Roman jurist (?–228), whose writings were acknowledged to be of a lower standard than Cicero's.

5 *mortcloth*   Funeral cloth draped over the dead.

6 *ELUCESCEBAT*   Latin: "He was illustrious." *Elucescebat* is a later Latin verb form; Cicero would have written *elucebat*.

7 *Evil… pilgrimage*   Cf. Genesis 47.9: "Jacob said unto Pharaoh… few and evil have the days of the years of my life been, and have not attained unto the days of the years of the life of my fathers in the days of their pilgrimage."

8 *vizor*   Helmet piece represented in Roman sculpture; *Term* Statue of Terminus, Roman god of boundaries.

And the startled little waves that leap
In fiery ringlets from their sleep,
5   As I gain the cove with pushing prow,
And quench its speed i' the slushy sand.

2

Then a mile of warm sea-scented beach;
Three fields to cross till a farm appears;
A tap at the pane, the quick sharp scratch
10   And blue spurt of a lighted match,
And a voice less loud, thro' its joys and fears,
Than the two hearts beating each to each!
—1845

Parting at Morning

Round the cape of a sudden came the sea,
And the sun looked over the mountain's rim:
And straight was a path of gold for him,
And the need of a world of men for me.
—1845

How It Strikes a Contemporary

I only knew one poet in my life:
And this, or something like it, was his way.

You saw go up and down Valladolid,[1]
A man of mark, to know next time you saw.
5   His very serviceable suit of black
Was courtly once and conscientious still,
And many might have worn it, though none did:
The cloak, that somewhat shone and showed the
        threads,
Had purpose, and the ruff, significance.
10   He walked and tapped the pavement with his cane,
Scenting the world, looking it full in face,
An old dog, bald and blindish, at his heels.
They turned up, now, the alley by the church,
That leads nowhither; now, they breathed themselves
15   On the main promenade just at the wrong time:

You'd come upon his scrutinizing hat,
Making a peaked shade blacker than itself
Against the single window spared some house
Intact yet with its mouldered Moorish work—
20   Or else surprise the ferrel° of his stick   *metal cap*
Trying the mortar's temper 'tween the chinks
Of some new shop a-building, French and fine.
He stood and watched the cobbler at his trade,
The man who slices lemons into drink,
25   The coffee roaster's brazier, and the boys
That volunteer to help him turn its winch.
He glanced o'er books on stalls with half an eye,
And fly-leaf ballads on the vendor's string,
And broad-edge bold-print posters by the wall.
30   He took such cognizance of men and things,
If any beat a horse, you felt he saw;
If any cursed a woman, he took note;
Yet stared at nobody—you stared at him,
And found, less to your pleasure than surprise,
35   He seemed to know you and expect as much.
So, next time that a neighbour's tongue was loosed,
It marked the shameful and notorious fact,
We had among us, not so much a spy,
As a recording chief inquisitor,
40   The town's true master if the town but knew!
We merely kept a governor for form,
While this man walked about and took account
Of all thought, said and acted, then went home,
And wrote it fully to our Lord the King
45   Who has an itch to know things, he knows why,
And reads them in his bedroom of a night.
Oh, you might smile! there wanted not a touch,
A tang of ... well, it was not wholly ease
As back into your mind the man's look came.
50   Stricken in years a little—such a brow
His eyes had to live under!—clear as flint
On either side the formidable nose
Curved, cut and coloured like an eagle's claw.
Had he to do with A.'s surprising fate?
55   When altogether old B. disappeared
And young C. got his mistress—was't our friend,
His letter to the King, that did it all?
What paid the bloodless man for so much pains?
Our Lord the King has favourites manifold,
60   And shifts his ministry some once a month;

---

[1]   *Valladolid*   City in Spain north of Madrid.

Our city gets new governors at whiles—
But never word or sign, that I could hear,
Notified to this man about the streets
The King's approval of those letters conned°   *studied*
65 The last thing duly at the dead of night.
Did the man love his office? Frowned our Lord,
Exhorting when none heard—"Beseech me not!
Too far above my people—beneath me!
I set the watch—how should the people know?
70 Forget them, keep me all the more in mind!"
Was some such understanding 'twixt the two?

I found no truth in one report at least—
That if you tracked him to his home, down lanes
Beyond the Jewry,[1] and as clean to pace,
75 You found he ate his supper in a room
Blazing with lights, four Titians[2] on the wall,
And twenty naked girls to change his plate!
Poor man, he lived another kind of life
In that new stuccoed third house by the bridge,
80 Fresh-painted, rather smart than otherwise!
The whole street might o'erlook him as he sat,
Leg crossing leg, one foot on the dog's back,
Playing a decent cribbage with his maid
(Jacynth, you're sure her name was) o'er the cheese
85 And fruit, three red halves of starved winter pears,
Or treat of radishes in April. Nine,
Ten, struck the church clock, straight to bed went he.

My father, like the man of sense he was,
Would point him out to me a dozen times;
90 "'St—'St," he'd whisper, "the Corregidor!"°   *magistrate*
I had been used to think that personage
Was one with lacquered breeches, lustrous belt,
And feathers like a forest in his hat,
Who blew a trumpet and proclaimed the news,
95 Announced the bullfights, gave each church its turn,
And memorized the miracle in vogue!
He had a great observance from us boys;
We were in error; that was not the man.

I'd like now, yet had haply been afraid,
100 To have just looked, when this man came to die,

And seen who lined the clean gay garret sides
And stood about the neat low truckle-bed,[3]
With the heavenly manner of relieving guard.
Here had been, mark, the general-in-chief,
105 Thro' a whole campaign of the world's life and death,
Doing the King's work all the dim day long,
In his old coat and up to knees in mud,
Smoked like a herring, dining on a crust—
And, now the day was won, relieved at once!
110 No further show or need for that old coat,
You are sure, for one thing! Bless us, all the while
How sprucely we are dressed out, you and I!
A second, and the angels alter that.
Well, I could never write a verse—could you?
115 Let's to the Prado[4] and make the most of time.
—1855

Memorabilia[5]

1

Ah, did you once see Shelley plain,
    And did he stop and speak to you
And did you speak to him again?
    How strange it seems and new!

2

5 But you were living before that,
    And also you are living after;
And the memory I started at—
    My starting moves your laughter.

3

I crossed a moor, with a name of its own
10   And a certain use in the world no doubt,

---

[1] *Jewry* Area of the city in which Jews were required to live.

[2] *Titians* Paintings by the Venetian artist Titian (c. 1490–1576).

[3] *truckle-bed* Trundle bed (one that can be pushed under a bed of regular height).

[4] *Prado* Museum in Madrid.

[5] [Browning's note] I was one day in the bookshop of Hodgson, the well-known London bookseller, when a stranger came in, who, in the course of conversation with the bookseller, spoke of something that Shelley had once said to him. Suddenly, the stranger paused, and burst into laughter as he observed me staring at him with blanched face; and ... I still vividly remember how strangely the presence of a man who had seen and spoken with Shelley affected me.

Yet a hand's-breath of it shines alone
    'Mid the blank miles round about:

4

For there I picked up on the heather
    And there I put inside my breast
15 A moulted feather, an eagle feather!
    Well, I forget the rest.
—1855

Love Among the Ruins

1

Where the quiet-coloured end of evening smiles,
    Miles and miles
On the solitary pastures where our sheep
    Half-asleep
5 Tinkle homeward thro' the twilight, stray or stop
    As they crop—
Was the site once of a city great and gay,
    (So they say)
Of our country's very capital, its prince
10   Ages since
Held his court in, gathered councils, wielding far
    Peace or war.

2

Now—the country does not even boast a tree,
    As you see,
15 To distinguish slopes of verdure, certain rills°   *brooks*
    From the hills
Intersect and give a name to, (else they run
    Into one)
Where the domed and daring palace shot its spires
20   Up like fires
O'er the hundred-gated circuit of a wall
    Bounding all,
Made of marble, men might march on nor be pressed,
    Twelve abreast.

3

25 And such plenty and perfection, see, of grass
    Never was!

Such a carpet as, this summertime, o'erspreads
    And embeds
Every vestige of the city, guessed alone,
30   Stock or stone—
Where a multitude of men breathed joy and woe
    Long ago;
Lust of glory pricked their hearts up, dread of shame
    Struck them tame;
35 And that glory and that shame alike, the gold
    Bought and sold.

4

Now—the single little turret that remains
    On the plains,
By the caper° overrooted, by the gourd   *shrub*
40   Overscored,
While the patching houseleek's° head of blossom
    winks   *herb's*
    Through the chinks—
Marks the basement whence a tower in ancient time
    Sprang sublime,
45 And a burning ring, all round, the chariots traced
    As they raced,
And the monarch and his minions and his dames
    Viewed the games.

5

And I know, while thus the quiet-coloured eve
50   Smiles to leave
To their folding, all our many-tinkling fleece
    In such peace,
And the slopes and rills in undistinguished grey
    Melt away—
55 That a girl with eager eyes and yellow hair
    Waits me there
In the turret whence the charioteers caught soul
    For the goal,
When the king looked, where she looks now,
    breathless, dumb
60   Till I come.

6

But he looked upon the city, every side,
    Far and wide,

All the mountains topped with temples, all the glades'
      Colonnades,
65 All the causeys,° bridges, aqueducts—and then,   *embankments*
      All the men!
When I do come, she will speak not, she will stand,
      Either hand
On my shoulder, give her eyes the first embrace
70   Of my face,
Ere we rush, ere we extinguish sight and speech
      Each on each.

7

In one year they sent a million fighters forth
      South and north,
75 And they built their gods a brazen pillar high
      As the sky,
Yet reserved a thousand chariots in full force—
      Gold, of course.
Oh heart! oh blood that freezes, blood that burns!
80   Earth's returns
For whole centuries of folly, noise and sin!
      Shut them in,
With their triumphs and their glories and the rest!
      Love is best.

—1855

"Childe Roland to the Dark Tower Came"
(*See Edgar's song in* Lear)[1]

1

My first thought was, he lied in every word,
    That hoary°cripple, with malicious eye   *wizened*
      Askance to watch the working of his lie
On mine, and mouth scarce able to afford
5 Suppression of the glee, that pursed and scored
      Its edge, at one more victim gained thereby.

---

[1] *Edgar ... Lear* From Shakespeare's *King Lear* 3.4.130–32, in which the character Edgar, disguised as the beggar Poor Tom, sings about the French hero Rowland, nephew of Charlemagne: "Child Rowland to the dark tower came, / His word was still, Fie, foh, and fum, / I smell the blood of a British man." "Childe" refers to a youth born of noble stock, who would usually become a candidate for knighthood.

2

What else should he be set for, with his staff?
    What, save to waylay with his lies, ensnare
      All travellers who might find him posted there,
10 And ask the road? I guessed what skull-like laugh
Would break, what crutch 'gin° write my epitaph   *begin*
      For pastime in the dusty thoroughfare,

3

If at his counsel I should turn aside
    Into that ominous tract which, all agree,
15   Hides the Dark Tower. Yet acquiescingly
I did turn as he pointed: neither pride
Nor hope rekindling at the end descried,
      So much as gladness that some end might be.

4

For, what with my whole world-wide wandering,
20   What with my search drawn out thro' years, my
      hope
      Dwindled into a ghost not fit to cope
With that obstreperous joy success would bring—
I hardly tried now to rebuke the spring
      My heart made, finding failure in its scope.

5

25 As when a sick man very near to death
    Seems dead indeed, and feels begin and end
      The tears and takes the farewell of each friend,
And hears one bid the other go, draw breath
Freelier outside ("since all is o'er," he saith,
30   "And the blow fallen no grieving can amend");

6

While some discuss if near the other graves
    Be room enough for this, and when a day
      Suits best for carrying the corpse away,
With care about the banners, scarves and staves:
35 And still the man hears all, and only craves
      He may not shame such tender love and stay.

7

Thus, I had so long suffered in this quest,
    Heard failure prophesied so oft, been writ
      So many times among "The Band"—to wit,

40 The knights who to the Dark Tower's search addressed
    Their steps—that just to fail as they, seemed best,
        And all the doubt was now—should I be fit?

8

    So, quiet as despair, I turned from him,
        That hateful cripple, out of his highway
45   Into the path he pointed. All the day
    Had been a dreary one at best, and dim
    Was settling to its close, yet shot one grim
        Red leer to see the plain catch its estray.° *stray animal*

9

    For mark! no sooner was I fairly found
50   Pledged to the plain, after a pace or two,
        Than, pausing to throw backward a last view
    O'er the safe road, 'twas gone; grey plain all round:
    Nothing but plain to the horizon's bound.
        I might go on; nought else remained to do.

10

55 So, on I went. I think I never saw
        Such starved ignoble nature; nothing throve:
        For flowers—as well expect a cedar grove!
    But cockle, spurge,[1] according to their law
    Might propagate their kind, with none to awe,
60   You'd think; a burr had been a treasure trove.

11

    No! penury, inertness and grimace,
        In some strange sort, were the land's portion. "See
        Or shut your eyes," said Nature peevishly,
    "It nothing skills: I cannot help my case:
65 'Tis the Last Judgment's fire must cure this place,
        Calcine° its clods and set my prisoners
            free."   *burn completely*

12

    If there pushed any ragged thistle-stalk
        Above its mates, the head was chopped; the
            bents°   *reed-like grasses*
        Were jealous else. What made those holes and rents
70 In the dock's° harsh swarth leaves, bruised as to
        baulk   *weed's*

All hope of greenness? 'tis a brute must walk
    Pashing° their life out, with a brute's intents.   *smashing*

13

As for the grass, it grew as scant as hair
    In leprosy; thin dry blades pricked the mud
75   Which underneath looked kneaded up with blood.
One stiff blind horse, his every bone a-stare,
Stood stupefied, however he came there:
    Thrust out past service from the devil's stud!

14

Alive? he might be dead for aught I know,
80   With that red gaunt and colloped[2] neck a-strain,
        And shut eyes underneath the rusty mane;
Seldom went such grotesqueness with such woe;
I never saw a brute I hated so;
    He must be wicked to deserve such pain.

15

85 I shut my eyes and turned them on my heart.
        As a man calls for wine before he fights,
        I asked one draught of earlier, happier sights,
    Ere fitly I could hope to play my part.
    Think first, fight afterwards—the soldier's art:
90   One taste of the old time sets all to rights.

16

    Not it! I fancied Cuthbert's reddening face
        Beneath its garniture of curly gold,
        Dear fellow, till I almost felt him fold
    An arm in mine to fix me to the place,
95 That way he used. Alas, one night's disgrace!
        Out went my heart's new fire and left it cold.

17

    Giles then, the soul of honour—there he stands
        Frank as ten years ago when knighted first.
        What honest man should dare (he said) he durst.
100 Good—but the scene shifts—faugh! what hangman
        hands
    Pin to his breast a parchment? His own bands
        Read it. Poor traitor, spit upon and curst!

---

¹ *cockle, spurge* Types of weeds.

² *colloped* Having folds of fat.

18

Better this present than a past like that;
    Back therefore to my darkening path again!
105   No sound, no sight as far as eye could strain.
Will the night send a howlet° or a bat?   *owl*
I asked: when something on the dismal flat
    Came to arrest my thoughts and change their train.

19

A sudden little river crossed my path
110   As unexpected as a serpent comes.
    No sluggish tide congenial to the glooms;
This, as it frothed by, might have been a bath
For the fiend's glowing hoof—to see the wrath
    Of its black eddy bespate° with flakes and   *flooded*
        spumes.

20

115 So petty yet so spiteful! All along,
    Low scrubby alders kneeled down over it;
    Drenched willows flung them headlong in a fit
Of mute despair, a suicidal throng:
The river which had done them all the wrong,
120   Whate'er that was, rolled by, deterred no whit.

21

Which, while I forded—good saints, how I feared
    To set my foot upon a dead man's cheek,
    Each step, or feel the spear I thrust to seek
For hollows, tangled in his hair or beard!
125 —It may have been a water-rat I speared,
    But, ugh! it sounded like a baby's shriek.

22

Glad was I when I reached the other bank.
    Now for a better country. Vain presage!
    Who were the strugglers, what war did they wage,
130 Whose savage trample thus could pad the dank
Soil to a plash?° Toads in a poisoned tank,   *pool*
    Or wild cats in a red-hot iron cage—

23

The fight must so have seemed in that fell cirque.[1]
    What penned them there, with all the plain to
        choose?

---

[1] *fell cirque* Dreadful arena.

135 No footprint leading to that horrid mews,
None out of it. Mad brewage set to work
Their brains, no doubt, like galley slaves the Turk
    Pits for his pastime, Christians against Jews.

24

And more than that—a furlong on—why, there!
140   What bad use was that engine for, that wheel,
    Or brake, not wheel—that harrow fit to reel
Men's bodies out like silk? with all the air
Of Tophet's° tool, on earth left unaware,   *hell's*
    Or brought to sharpen its rusty teeth of steel.

25

145 Then came a bit of stubbed ground, once a wood,
    Next a marsh, it would seem, and now mere earth
    Desperate and done with; (so a fool finds mirth,
Makes a thing and then mars it, till his mood
Changes and off he goes!) within a rood°—   *quarter acre*
150   Bog, clay and rubble, sand and stark black dearth.

26

Now blotches rankling, coloured gay and grim,
    Now patches where some leanness of the soil's
    Broke into moss or substances like boils;
Then came some palsied oak, a cleft in him
155 Like a distorted mouth that splits its rim
    Gaping at death, and dies while it recoils.

27

And just as far as ever from the end!
    Nought in the distance but the evening, nought
    To point my footstep further! At the thought,
160 A great black bird, Apollyon's[2] bosom-friend,
Sailed past, nor beat his wide wing dragon-
        penned°   *winged*
    That brushed my cap—perchance the guide I sought.

28

For, looking up, aware I somehow grew,
    'Spite of the dusk, the plain had given place
165   All round to mountains—with such name to grace
Mere ugly heights and heaps now stolen in view.

---

[2] *Apollyon* Devil, or winged "angel of the bottomless pit," in Revelations 9.11.

How thus they had surprised me,—solve it, you!
    How to get from them was no clearer case.

29

170 Yet half I seemed to recognize some trick
    Of mischief happened to me, God knows when—
    In a bad dream perhaps. Here ended, then,
Progress this way. When, in the very nick
Of giving up, one time more, came a click
    As when a trap shuts—you're inside the den!

30

175 Burningly it came on me all at once,
    This was the place! those two hills on the right,
    Crouched like two bulls locked horn in horn in
        fight;
While to the left, a tall scalped mountain … Dunce,
Dotard, a-dozing at the very nonce,°   *moment*
180   After a life spent training for the sight!

31

What in the midst lay but the Tower itself?
    The round squat turret, blind as the fool's heart,
    Built of brown stone, without a counterpart
In the whole world. The tempest's mocking elf
185 Points to the shipman° thus the unseen shelf   *sailor*
    He strikes on, only when the timbers start.

32

Not see? because of night perhaps?—why, day
    Came back again for that! before it left,
    The dying sunset kindled through a cleft:
190 The hills, like giants at a hunting, lay,
Chin upon hand, to see the game at bay,—
    "Now stab and end the creature—to the
        heft!"°   *sword handle*

33

Not hear? when noise was everywhere! it tolled
    Increasing like a bell. Names in my ears
195   Of all the lost adventurers my peers—
How such a one was strong, and such was bold,
And such was fortunate, yet each of old
    Lost, lost! one moment knelled the woe of years.

34

There they stood, ranged along the hillsides, met
200   To view the last of me, a living frame
    For one more picture! in a sheet of flame
I saw them and I knew them all. And yet
Dauntless the slug-horn° to my lips I set,   *trumpet*
    And blew. "*Childe Roland to the Dark Tower came.*"
—1855

Fra Lippo Lippi [1]

I am poor brother Lippo, by your leave!
    You need not clap your torches to my face.
Zooks,[2] what's to blame? you think you see a monk!
What, 'tis past midnight, and you go the rounds,
5 And here you catch me at an alley's end
Where sportive ladies leave their doors ajar?
The Carmine's[3] my cloister: hunt it up,
Do—harry out, if you must show your zeal,
Whatever rat, there, haps on his wrong hole,
10 And nip each softling of a wee white mouse,
Weke, weke, that's crept to keep him company!
Aha, you know your betters! Then, you'll take
Your hand away that's fiddling on my throat,
And please to know me likewise. Who am I?
15 Why, one, sir, who is lodging with a friend
Three streets off—he's a certain … how d'ye call?
Master—a … Cosimo of the Medici,[4]
I' the house that caps the corner. Boh! you were best!
Remember and tell me, the day you're hanged,
20 How you affected such a gullet's-gripe!°   *stranglehold*
But you, sir, it concerns you that your knaves
Pick up a manner nor discredit you:

---

[1] *Fra Lippo Lippi* Browning extracted details of the life of Florentine painter and Carmelite monk Fra (Brother) Filippo Lippi
(1406–69) from Giorgio Vasari's *The Lives of the Painters* (1550);
the art theory Lippi propounds, however, is envisioned by Browning.

[2] *Zooks* Exclamation of surprise.

[3] *Carmine* Lippi was raised an orphan and eventually took his vows
in Santa Maria del Carmine, a Carmelite monastery.

[4] *Cosimo of the Medici* The wealthy Medici family, headed up by
Lippi's patron, Cosimo dé Medici (1389–1464), ruled Florence for
many years.

Zooks, are we pilchards,[1] that they sweep the streets
And count fair prize what comes into their net?
25 He's Judas to a tittle,[2] that man is!
Just such a face! Why, sir, you make amends.
Lord, I'm not angry! Bid your hangdogs go
Drink out this quarter-florin[3] to the health
Of the munificent House that harbours me
30 (And many more beside, lads! more beside!)
And all's come square again. I'd like his face—
His, elbowing on his comrade in the door
With the pike and lantern—for the slave that holds
John Baptist's head a-dangle by the hair
35 With one hand ("Look you, now," as who should say)
And his weapon in the other, yet unwiped!
It's not your chance to have a bit of chalk,
A wood-coal or the like? or you should see!
Yes, I'm the painter, since you style me so.
40 What, brother Lippo's doings, up and down,
You know them and they take you? like enough!
I saw the proper twinkle in your eye—
'Tell you, I liked your looks at very first.
Let's sit and set things straight now, hip to haunch.
45 Here's spring come, and the nights one makes up bands
To roam the town and sing out carnival,[4]
And I've been three weeks shut within my
    mew,°   *confined space*
A-painting for the great man, saints and saints
And saints again. I could not paint all night—
50 Ouf! I leaned out of window for fresh air.
There came a hurry of feet and little feet,
A sweep of lute strings, laughs, and whifts of song—
Flower o' the broom,
Take away love, and our earth is a tomb![5]
55 *Flower o' the quince,*
I let Lisa go, and what good in life since?
Flower o' the thyme—and so on. Round they went.
Scarce had they turned the corner when a titter

Like the skipping of rabbits by moonlight—three slim
    shapes,
60 And a face that looked up … zooks, sir, flesh and blood,
That's all I'm made of! Into shreds it went,
Curtain and counterpane and coverlet,
All the bed furniture—a dozen knots,
There was a ladder! Down I let myself,
65 Hands and feet, scrambling somehow, and so dropped,
And after them. I came up with the fun
Hard by Saint Laurence,[6] hail fellow, well met—
Flower o' the rose,
If I've been merry, what matter who knows?
70 And so as I was stealing back again
To get to bed and have a bit of sleep
Ere I rise up tomorrow and go work
On Jerome[7] knocking at his poor old breast
With his great round stone to subdue the flesh,
75 You snap me of the sudden. Ah, I see!
Though your eye twinkles still, you shake your head—
Mine's shaved—a monk, you say—the sting's in that!
If Master Cosimo announced himself,
Mum's the word naturally; but a monk!
80 Come, what am I a beast for? tell us, now!
I was a baby when my mother died
And father died and left me in the street.
I starved there, God knows how, a year or two
On fig skins, melon parings, rinds and shucks,
85 Refuse and rubbish. One fine frosty day,
My stomach being empty as your hat,
The wind doubled me up and down I went.
Old Aunt Lapaccia trussed me with one hand,
(Its fellow was a stinger as I knew)
90 And so along the wall, over the bridge,
By the straight cut to the convent. Six words there,
While I stood munching my first bread that month:
"So, boy, you're minded," quoth the good fat father
Wiping his own mouth, 'twas refection°-time—   *meal*
95 "To quit this very miserable world?
Will you renounce"… "the mouthful of bread?"
    thought I;
By no means! Brief, they made a monk of me;
I did renounce the world, its pride and greed,

---

[1] *pilchards* Herring-like fish.

[2] *to a tittle* Exactly (a "tittle" is a letter stroke or punctuation mark).

[3] *florin* Florentine currency.

[4] *carnival* Celebrations before Lent.

[5] *Flower … tomb* This song takes the form of a *stornelli*, a three-line Italian folk song about a flower.

---

[6] *Saint Laurence* Church of San Lorenzo in Florence.

[7] *Jerome* The ascetic St. Jerome, who lived many years as a hermit in the Syrian desert.

Palace, farm, villa, shop and banking-house,
100 Trash, such as these poor devils of Medici
Have given their hearts to—all at eight years old.
Well, sir, I found in time, you may be sure,
'Twas not for nothing—the good bellyful,
The warm serge and the rope that goes all round,[1]
105 And day-long blessed idleness beside!
"Let's see what the urchin's fit for"—that came next.
Not overmuch their way, I must confess.
Such a to-do! They tried me with their books:
Lord, they'd have taught me Latin in pure waste!
110 *Flower o' the clove,*
All the Latin I construe is, "amo," I love!
But, mind you, when a boy starves in the streets
Eight years together, as my fortune was,
Watching folk's faces to know who will fling
115 The bit of half-stripped grape bunch he desires,
And who will curse or kick him for his pains—
Which gentleman processional and fine,
Holding a candle to the Sacrament,
Will wink and let him lift a plate and catch
120 The droppings of the wax to sell again,
Or holla for the Eight[2] and have him whipped—
How say I?—nay, which dog bites, which lets drop
His bone from the heap of offal in the street—
Why, soul and sense of him grow sharp alike,
125 He learns the look of things, and none the less
For admonition from the hunger pinch.
I had a store of such remarks, be sure,
Which, after I found leisure, turned to use.
I drew men's faces on my copy books,
130 Scrawled them within the antiphonary's marge,[3]
Joined legs and arms to the long music notes,
Found eyes and nose and chin for A's and B's,
And made a string of pictures of the world
Betwixt the ins and outs of verb and noun,
135 On the wall, the bench, the door. The monks looked
    black.
"Nay," quoth the Prior, "turn him out, d'ye say?
In no wise. Lose a crow and catch a lark.

What if at last we get our man of parts,[4]
We Carmelites, like those Camaldolese
140 And Preaching Friars,[5] to do our church up fine
And put the front on it that ought to be!"
And hereupon he bade me daub away.
Thank you! my head being crammed, the walls a blank,
Never was such prompt disemburdening.
145 First, every sort of monk, the black and white,
I drew them, fat and lean: then, folk at church,
From good old gossips waiting to confess
Their cribs° of barrel droppings, candle ends— *pilferings*
To the breathless fellow at the altar foot,
150 Fresh from his murder, safe[6] and sitting there
With the little children round him in a row
Of admiration, half for his beard and half
For that white anger of his victim's son
Shaking a fist at him with one fierce arm,
155 Signing himself[7] with the other because of Christ
(Whose sad face on the cross sees only this
After the passion of a thousand years)
Till some poor girl, her apron o'er her head,
(Which the intense eyes looked through) came at eve
160 On tiptoe, said a word, dropped in a loaf,
Her pair of earrings and a bunch of flowers
(The brute took growling), prayed, and so was gone.
I painted all, then cried "'Tis ask and have;
Choose, for more's ready!"—laid the ladder flat,
165 And showed my covered bit of cloister wall.
The monks closed in a circle and praised loud
Till checked, taught what to see and not to see,
Being simple bodies—"That's the very man!
Look at the boy who stoops to pat the dog!
170 That woman's like the Prior's niece who comes
To care about his asthma: it's the life!"
But there my triumph's straw-fire flared and
    funked;°   *smoked*
Their betters took their turn to see and say:
The Prior and the learned pulled a face
175 And stopped all that in no time. "How? what's here?
Quite from the mark of painting, bless us all!

[1] *rope ... round* I.e., rope belt.
[2] *Eight* The eight magistrates who governed Florence.
[3] *antiphonary's marge* Margin of a book of choral—or antipho-
nal—music, normally sung in harmony by two choirs.
[4] *man of parts* Man of intellect, ability.
[5] *Preaching Friars* Dominican monks.
[6] *fellow ... safe* Safe from prosecution within the church.
[7] *Signing himself* Making the sign of the cross.

Faces, arms, legs and bodies like the true
As much as pea and pea! it's devil's game!
Your business is not to catch men with show,
180 With homage to the perishable clay,
But lift them over it, ignore it all,
Make them forget there's such a thing as flesh.
Your business is to paint the souls of men—
Man's soul, and it's a fire, smoke … no, it's not …
185 It's vapour done up like a newborn babe—
(In that shape when you die it leaves your mouth)
It's … well, what matters talking, it's the soul!
Give us no more of body than shows soul!
Here's Giotto,[1] with his Saint a-praising God,
190 That sets us praising—why not stop with him?
Why put all thoughts of praise out of our head
With wonder at lines, colours, and what not?
Paint the soul, never mind the legs and arms!
Rub all out, try at it a second time.
195 Oh, that white smallish female with the breasts,
She's just my niece … Herodias, I would say—
Who went and danced and got men's heads cut off![2]
Have it all out!' Now, is this sense, I ask?
A fine way to paint soul, by painting body
200 So ill, the eye can't stop there, must go further
And can't fare worse! Thus, yellow does for white
When what you put for yellow's simply black,
And any sort of meaning looks intense
When all beside itself means and looks nought.
205 Why can't a painter lift each foot in turn,
Left foot and right foot, go a double step,
Make his flesh liker and his soul more like,
Both in their order? Take the prettiest face,
The Prior's niece … patron saint—is it so pretty
210 You can't discover if it means hope, fear,
Sorrow or joy? won't beauty go with these?
Suppose I've made her eyes all right and blue,
Can't I take breath and try to add life's flash,
And then add soul and heighten them threefold?
215 Or say there's beauty with no soul at all—

(I never saw it—put the case the same—)
If you get simple beauty and nought else,
You get about the best thing God invents:
That's somewhat: and you'll find the soul you have
    missed,
220 Within yourself, when you return him thanks.
"Rub all out!" Well, well, there's my life, in short,
And so the thing has gone on ever since.
I'm grown a man no doubt, I've broken bounds:
You should not take a fellow eight years old
225 And make him swear to never kiss the girls.
I'm my own master, paint now as I please—
Having a friend, you see, in the Corner-house!
Lord, it's fast holding by the rings in front—
Those great rings serve more purposes than just
230 To plant a flag in, or tie up a horse!
And yet the old schooling sticks, the old grave eyes
Are peeping o'er my shoulder as I work,
The heads shake still—"It's art's decline, my son!
You're not of the true painters, great and old;
235 Brother Angelico's the man, you'll find;
Brother Lorenzo[3] stands his single peer:
Fag on at flesh, you'll never make the third!"
Flower o' the pine,
You keep your mistr … manners, and I'll stick to mine!
240 I'm not the third, then: bless us, they must know!
Don't you think they're the likeliest to know,
They with their Latin? So, I swallow my rage,
Clench my teeth, suck my lips in tight, and paint
To please them—sometimes do and sometimes don't;
245 For, doing most, there's pretty sure to come
A turn, some warm eve finds me at my saints—
A laugh, a cry, the business of the world—
(*Flower o' the peach,*
Death for us all, and his own life for each!)
250 And my whole soul revolves, the cup runs over,
The world and life's too big to pass for a dream,
And I do these wild things in sheer despite,
And play the fooleries you catch me at,
In pure rage! The old mill-horse, out at grass
255 After hard years, throws up his stiff heels so,
Although the miller does not preach to him

---

[1] *Giotto* Renowned Florentine artist (1267–1337), whose works consist mainly of religious paintings and frescoes.

[2] *Herodias … heads cut off* According to Matthew 14.6–10, King Herod's niece Salomé (the daughter of his sister Herodias) danced for the king and then requested that he bring her the head of John the Baptist, now the patron saint of Florence.

[3] *Brother Angelico … Brother Lorenzo* Italian Renaissance artists who painted in in the early 1400s in the conventional style, as opposed to Lippi's naturalist style.

The only good of grass is to make chaff.
What would men have? Do they like grass or no—
May they or mayn't they? all I want's the thing
260 Settled forever one way. As it is,
You tell too many lies and hurt yourself:
You don't like what you only like too much,
You do like what, if given you at your word,
You find abundantly detestable.
265 For me, I think I speak as I was taught;
I always see the garden and God there
A-making man's wife: and, my lesson learned,
The value and significance of flesh,
I can't unlearn ten minutes afterwards.

270   You understand me: I'm a beast, I know.
But see, now—why, I see as certainly
As that the morning star's about to shine,
What will hap some day. We've a youngster here
Comes to our convent, studies what I do,
275 Slouches and stares and lets no atom drop:
His name is Guidi[1]—he'll not mind the monks—
They call him Hulking Tom, he lets them talk—
He picks my practice up—he'll paint apace,
I hope so—though I never live so long,
280 I know what's sure to follow. You be judge!
You speak no Latin more than I, belike;
However, you're my man, you've seen the world
—The beauty and the wonder and the power,
The shapes of things, their colours, lights and shades,
285 Changes, surprises—and God made it all!
—For what? Do you feel thankful, ay or no,
For this fair town's face, yonder river's line,
The mountain round it and the sky above,
Much more the figures of man, woman, child,
290 These are the frame to? What's it all about?
To be passed over, despised? or dwelt upon,
Wondered at? oh, this last of course!—you say.
But why not do as well as say—paint these
Just as they are, careless what comes of it?
295 God's works—paint anyone, and count it crime
To let a truth slip. Don't object, "His works
Are here already; nature is complete:

Suppose you reproduce her—(which you can't)
There's no advantage! you must beat her, then."
300 For, don't you mark? we're made so that we love
First when we see them painted, things we have passed
Perhaps a hundred times nor cared to see;
And so they are better, painted—better to us,
Which is the same thing. Art was given for that;
305 God uses us to help each other so,
Lending our minds out. Have you noticed, now,
Your cullion's° hanging face? A bit of chalk,   *scoundrel's*
And trust me but you should, though! How much
    more,
If I drew higher things with the same truth!
310 That were to take the Prior's pulpit place,
Interpret God to all of you! Oh, oh,
It makes me mad to see what men shall do
And we in our graves! This world's no blot for us,
Nor blank; it means intensely, and means good:
315 To find its meaning is my meat and drink.
"Ay, but you don't so instigate to prayer!"
Strikes in the Prior: "when your meaning's plain
It does not say to folk—remember matins,[2]
Or, mind you fast next Friday!" Why, for this
320 What need of art at all? A skull and bones,
Two bits of stick nailed crosswise, or, what's best,
A bell to chime the hour with, does as well.
I painted a Saint Laurence[3] six months since
At Prato,[4] splashed the fresco in fine style:
325 "How looks my painting, now the scaffold's down?"
I ask a brother: "Hugely," he returns—
"Already not one phiz° of your three slaves   *face*
Who turn the Deacon off his toasted side,
But's scratched and prodded to our heart's content,
330 The pious people have so eased their own
With coming to say prayers there in a rage:
We get on fast to see the bricks beneath.
Expect another job this time next year,
For pity and religion grow i' the crowd—
335 Your painting serves its purpose!" Hang the fools!

---

[2]   *matins* Morning prayer services.

[3]   *Saint Laurence* Roman deacon (?–258) who was martyred by being burnt on a gridiron, an instrument of torture.

[4]   *Prato* Town west of Florence.

[1]   *Guidi* Tommaso Guidi (1401–28), who became known as Masaccio, was highly skilled at creating naturalistic portrayals of human figures; he was likely Lippi's teacher, not his student.

—That is—you'll not mistake an idle word
Spoke in a huff by a poor monk, God wot,
Tasting the air this spicy night which turns
The unaccustomed head like Chianti wine!
340 Oh, the church knows! don't misreport me, now!
It's natural a poor monk out of bounds
Should have his apt word to excuse himself:
And hearken how I plot to make amends.
I have bethought me: I shall paint a piece
345 … There's for you! Give me six months, then go, see
Something in Sant'Ambrogio's![1] Bless the nuns!
They want a cast o' my office. I shall paint
God in the midst, Madonna and her babe,
Ringed by a bowery flowery angel brood,
350 Lilies and vestments and white faces, sweet
As puff on puff of grated orris-root[2]
When ladies crowd to Church at midsummer.
And then i' the front, of course a saint or two—
Saint John, because he saves the Florentines,
355 Saint Ambrose, who puts down in black and white
The convent's friends and gives them a long day,
And Job, I must have him there past mistake,
The man of Uz[3] (and Us without the z,
Painters who need his patience). Well, all these
360 Secured at their devotion, up shall come
Out of a corner when you least expect,
As one by a dark stair into a great light,
Music and talking, who but Lippo! I!—
Mazed, motionless and moonstruck—I'm the man!
365 Back I shrink—what is this I see and hear?
I, caught up with my monk's things by mistake,
My old serge gown and rope that goes all round,
I, in this presence, this pure company!
Where's a hole, where's a corner for escape?
370 Then steps a sweet angelic slip of a thing
Forward, puts out a soft palm—"Not so fast!"
—Addresses the celestial presence, "nay—
He made you and devised you, after all,

Though he's none of you! Could Saint John there draw—
375 His camel hair[4] make up a painting brush?
We come to brother Lippo for all that,
Iste perfecit opus!"[5] So, all smile—
I shuffle sideways with my blushing face
Under the cover of a hundred wings
380 Thrown like a spread of kirtles° when you're gay   skirts
And play hot cockles,[6] all the doors being shut,
Till, wholly unexpected, in there pops
The hothead husband! Thus I scuttle off
To some safe bench behind, not letting go
385 The palm of her, the little lily thing
That spoke the good word for me in the nick,
Like the Prior's niece … Saint Lucy,[7] I would say.
And so all's saved for me, and for the church
A pretty picture gained. Go, six months hence!
390 Your hand, sir, and goodbye: no lights, no lights!
The street's hushed, and I know my own way back,
Don't fear me! There's the grey beginning. Zooks!
—1855

The Last Ride Together

I

I said—Then, dearest, since 'tis so,
Since now at length my fate I know,
Since nothing all my love avails,
Since all, my life seemed meant for, fails,
5   Since this was written and needs must be—
My whole heart rises up to bless
Your name in pride and thankfulness!
Take back the hope you gave—I claim
Only a memory of the same,
10 —And this beside, if you will not blame,
    Your leave for one more last ride with me.

---

1 *Sant' Ambrogio's* Lippi painted *Coronation of the Virgin* for the main altar of Florence's Sant' Ambrogio convent.

2 *orris-root* Roots of the iris flower, used as a fragrant cosmetic powder.

3 *man of Uz* See Job 1.1: Job was a righteous man who lost everything when God allowed Satan to challenge his faith.

4 *Saint John … camel hair* St. John the Baptist "was clothed in camel hair," according to Mark 1.6.

5 *Iste perfecit opus* Latin: he caused the work to be created; inscription on the *Coronation*, placed beside a portrait that Browning (following Vasari) mistakenly took to be Lippi's.

6 *hot cockles* Christmas game played blindfolded.

7 *Saint Lucy* Virgin martyr of Sicily (? –304?).

2

My mistress bent that brow of hers;
Those deep dark eyes where pride demurs
When pity would be softening through,
15 Fixed me a breathing-while or two
  With life or death in the balance: right!
The blood replenished me again;
My last thought was at least not vain:
I and my mistress, side by side
20 Shall be together, breathe and ride,
So, one day more am I deified.
  Who knows but the world may end tonight?

3

Hush! if you saw some western cloud
All billowy-bosomed, over-bowed
25 By many benedictions—sun's
And moon's and evening-star's at once—
  And so, you, looking and loving best,
Conscious grew, your passion drew
Cloud, sunset, moonrise, star-shine too,
30 Down on you, near and yet more near,
Till flesh must fade for heaven was here!—
Thus leant she and lingered—joy and fear!
  Thus lay she a moment on my breast.

4

Then we began to ride. My soul
35 Smoothed itself out, a long-cramped scroll
Freshening and fluttering in the wind.
Past hopes already lay behind.
  What need to strive with a life awry?
Had I said that, had I done this,
40 So might I gain, so might I miss.
Might she have loved me? just as well
She might have hated, who can tell!
Where had I been now if the worst befell?
  And here we are riding, she and I.

5

45 Fail I alone, in words and deeds?
Why, all men strive and who succeeds?
We rode; it seemed my spirit flew,
Saw other regions, cities new,
  As the world rushed by on either side.

50 I thought—All labour, yet no less
Bear up beneath their unsuccess.
Look at the end of work, contrast
The petty done, the undone vast,
This present of theirs with the hopeful past!
55   I hoped she would love me; here we ride.

6

What hand and brain went ever paired?
What heart alike conceived and dared?
What act proved all its thought had been?
What will but felt the fleshly screen?
60   We ride and I see her bosom heave.
There's many a crown for who can reach.
Ten lines, a statesman's life in each!
The flag stuck on a heap of bones,
A soldier's doing! what atones?
65 They scratch his name on the Abbey[1] stones.
  My riding is better, by their leave.

7

What does it all mean, poet? Well,
Your brains beat into rhythm, you tell
What we felt only; you expressed
70 You hold things beautiful the best,
  And pace them in rhyme so, side by side.
'Tis something, nay 'tis much: but then,
Have you yourself what's best for men?
Are you—poor, sick, old ere your time—
75 Nearer one whit your own sublime
Than we who never have turned a rhyme?
  Sing, riding's a joy! For me, I ride.

8

And you, great sculptor—so, you gave
A score of years to Art, her slave,
80 And that's your Venus,[2] whence we turn
To yonder girl that fords the burn!°   *stream*
  You acquiesce, and shall I repine?°   *complain*
What, man of music, you grown grey
With notes and nothing else to say,
85 Is this your sole praise from a friend,
"Greatly his opera's strains intend,

---

1 *Abbey* Westminster Abbey.

2 *Venus* Roman goddess of love.

But in music we know how fashions end!"
    I gave my youth; but we ride, *in fine*.[1]

9

Who knows what's fit for us? Had fate
90 Proposed bliss here should sublimate
My being—had I signed the bond—
Still one must lead some life beyond,
    Have a bliss to die with, dim-descried.
This foot once planted on the goal,
95 This glory-garland round my soul,
Could I descry such? Try and test!
I sink back shuddering from the quest.
Earth being so good, would heaven seem best?
    Now, heaven and she are beyond this ride.

10

100 And yet—she has not spoke so long!
What if heaven be that, fair and strong
At life's best, with our eyes upturned
Whither life's flower is first discerned,
    We, fixed so, ever should so abide?
105 What if we still ride on, we two
With life forever old yet new,
Changed not in kind but in degree,
The instant made eternity—
And heaven just prove that I and she
110   Ride, ride together, forever ride?
    —1855

Andrea del Sarto[2]
(Called "The Faultless Painter")

But do not let us quarrel any more,
No, my Lucrezia;[3] bear with me for once:
Sit down and all shall happen as you wish.
You turn your face, but does it bring your heart?

5 I'll work then for your friend's friend, never fear,
Treat his own subject after his own way,
Fix his own time, accept too his own price,
And shut the money into this small hand
When next it takes mine. Will it? tenderly?
10 Oh, I'll content him—but tomorrow, Love!
I often am much wearier than you think,
This evening more than usual, and it seems
As if—forgive now—should you let me sit
Here by the window with your hand in mine
15 And look a half-hour forth on Fiesole,[4]
Both of one mind, as married people use,
Quietly, quietly the evening through,
I might get up tomorrow to my work
Cheerful and fresh as ever. Let us try.
20 Tomorrow, how you shall be glad for this!
Your soft hand is a woman of itself,
And mine the man's bared breast she curls inside.
Don't count the time lost, neither; you must serve
For each of the five pictures we require:
25 It saves a model. So! keep looking so—
My serpentining beauty, rounds on rounds!
—How could you ever prick those perfect ears,
Even to put the pearl there! oh, so sweet—
My face, my moon, my everybody's moon,
30 Which everybody looks on and calls his,
And, I suppose, is looked on by in turn,
While she looks—no one's: very dear, no less.
You smile? why, there's my picture ready made,
There's what we painters call our harmony!
35 A common greyness silvers everything—
All in a twilight, you and I alike
—You, at the point of your first pride in me
(That's gone you know)—but I, at every point;
My youth, my hope, my art, being all toned down
40 To yonder sober pleasant Fiesole.
There's the bell clinking from the chapel top;
That length of convent wall across the way
Holds the trees safer, huddled more inside;
The last monk leaves the garden; days decrease,
45 And autumn grows, autumn in everything.
Eh? the whole seems to fall into a shape
As if I saw alike my work and self
And all that I was born to be and do,

---

[1] *in fine* In the end.

[2] *Andrea del Sarto* Browning's poem explores the life of the painter Andrea del Sarto (1486–1531), as narrated by Giorgio Vasari (once del Sarto's pupil) in *The Lives of the Painters*. In this biography, Vasari speculates as to why del Sarto (translated, this name means "son of a tailor") failed to fulfill the promise of his early paintings.

[3] *Lucrezia* Lucrezia del Fede, del Sarto's wife and model.

[4] *Fiesole* Hill town near Florence.

A twilight piece. Love, we are in God's hand.
50 How strange now, looks the life he makes us lead;
So free we seem, so fettered° fast we are!   *shackled*
I feel he laid the fetter: let it lie!
This chamber for example—turn your head—
All that's behind us! You don't understand
55 Nor care to understand about my art,
But you can hear at least when people speak:
And that cartoon,° the second from the door   *sketch*
—It is the thing, Love! so such things should be—
Behold Madonna!—I am bold to say.
60 I can do with my pencil what I know,
What I see, what at bottom of my heart
I wish for, if I ever wish so deep—
Do easily, too—when I say, perfectly,
I do not boast, perhaps: yourself are judge,
65 Who listened to the Legate's¹ talk last week,
And just as much they used to say in France.
At any rate 'tis easy, all of it!
No sketches first, no studies, that's long past:
I do what many dream of, all their lives,
70 —Dream? strive to do, and agonize to do,
And fail in doing. I could count twenty such
On twice your fingers, and not leave this town,
Who strive—you don't know how the others strive
To paint a little thing like that you smeared
75 Carelessly passing with your robes afloat—
Yet do much less, so much less, Someone says,
(I know his name, no matter)—so much less!
Well, less is more, Lucrezia: I am judged.
There burns a truer light of God in them,
80 In their vexed beating stuffed and stopped-up brain,
Heart, or whate'er else, than goes on to prompt
This low-pulsed forthright craftsman's hand of mine.
Their works drop groundward, but themselves, I know,
Reach many a time a heaven that's shut to me,
85 Enter and take their place there sure enough,
Though they come back and cannot tell the world.
My works are nearer heaven, but I sit here.
The sudden blood of these men! at a word—
Praise them, it boils, or blame them, it boils too.
90 I, painting from myself and to myself,
Know what I do, am unmoved by men's blame
Or their praise either. Somebody remarks

Morello's² outline there is wrongly traced,
His hue mistaken; what of that? or else,
95 Rightly traced and well ordered; what of that?
Speak as they please, what does the mountain care?
Ah, but a man's reach should exceed his grasp,
Or what's a heaven for? All is silver-grey
Placid and perfect with my art: the worse!
100 I know both what I want and what might gain,
And yet how profitless to know, to sigh
"Had I been two, another and myself,
Our head would have o'erlooked the world!" No doubt.
Yonder's a work now, of that famous youth
105 The Urbinate³ who died five years ago.
('Tis copied, George Vasari sent it me.)
Well, I can fancy how he did it all,
Pouring his soul, with kings and popes to see,
Reaching, that heaven might so replenish him,
110 Above and through his art—for it gives way;
That arm is wrongly put—and there again—
A fault to pardon in the drawing's lines,
Its body, so to speak: its soul is right,
He means right—that, a child may understand.
115 Still, what an arm! and I could alter it:
But all the play, the insight and the stretch—
Out of me, out of me! And wherefore out?
Had you enjoined them on me, given me soul,
We might have risen to Rafael, I and you!
120 Nay, Love, you did give all I asked, I think—
More than I merit, yes, by many times.
But had you—oh, with the same perfect brow,
And perfect eyes, and more than perfect mouth,
And the low voice my soul hears, as a bird
125 The fowler's pipe,⁴ and follows to the snare—
Had you, with these the same, but brought a mind!
Some women do so. Had the mouth there urged
"God and the glory! never care for gain.
The present by the future, what is that?
130 Live for fame, side by side with Agnolo!⁵
Rafael is waiting: up to God, all three!"

---

¹ *Legate*   Representative of the Pope.

² *Morello*   Monte Morello, a mountain near Florence.

³ *Urbinate*   The painter Raphael (1483–1520), who was born in Urbino.

⁴ *fowler's pipe*   Call used by hunters to lure fowl.

⁵ *Agnolo*   I.e., Michelangelo Buonarroti (1475–1564), sculptor and painter.

I might have done it for you. So it seems:
Perhaps not. All is as God over-rules.
Beside, incentives come from the soul's self;
135 The rest avail not. Why do I need you?
What wife had Rafael, or has Agnolo?
In this world, who can do a thing, will not;
And who would do it, cannot, I perceive:
Yet the will's somewhat—somewhat, too, the power—
140 And thus we half-men struggle. At the end,
God, I conclude, compensates, punishes.
'Tis safer for me, if the award be strict,
That I am something underrated here,
Poor this long while, despised, to speak the truth.
145 I dared not, do you know, leave home all day,
For fear of chancing on the Paris lords.[1]
The best is when they pass and look aside;
But they speak sometimes; I must bear it all.
Well may they speak! That Francis, that first time,
150 And that long festal year at Fontainebleau!
I surely then could sometimes leave the ground,
Put on the glory, Rafael's daily wear,
In that humane great monarch's golden look—
One finger in his beard or twisted curl
155 Over his mouth's good mark that made the smile,
One arm about my shoulder, round my neck,
The jingle of his gold chain in my ear,
I painting proudly with his breath on me,
All his court round him, seeing with his eyes,
160 Such frank French eyes, and such a fire of souls
Profuse, my hand kept plying by those hearts—
And, best of all, this, this, this face beyond,
This in the background, waiting on my work,
To crown the issue with a last reward!
165 A good time, was it not, my kingly days?
And had you not grown restless ... but I know—
'Tis done and past; 'twas right, my instinct said;
Too live the life grew, golden and not grey,
And I'm the weak-eyed bat no sun should tempt
170 Out of the grange whose four walls make his world.
How could it end in any other way?
You called me, and I came home to your heart.
The triumph was—to reach and stay there; since

I reached it ere the triumph, what is lost?
175 Let my hands frame your face in your hair's gold,
You beautiful Lucrezia that are mine!
"Rafael did this, Andrea painted that;
The Roman's is the better when you pray,
But still the other's Virgin was his wife—"
180 Men will excuse me. I am glad to judge
Both pictures in your presence; clearer grows
My better fortune, I resolve to think.
For, do you know, Lucrezia, as God lives,
Said one day Agnolo, his very self,
185 To Rafael ... I have known it all these years ...
(When the young man was flaming out his thoughts
Upon a palace wall for Rome to see,
Too lifted up in heart because of it)
"Friend, there's a certain sorry little scrub
190 Goes up and down our Florence, none cares how,
Who, were he set to plan and execute
As you are, pricked on by your popes and kings,
Would bring the sweat into that brow of yours!"
To Rafael's!—And indeed the arm is wrong.
195 I hardly dare ... yet, only you to see,
Give the chalk here—quick, thus the line should go!
Ay, but the soul! he's Rafael! rub it out!
Still, all I care for, if he spoke the truth,
(What he? why, who but Michel Agnolo?
200 Do you forget already words like those?)
If really there was such a chance, so lost—
Is, whether you're—not grateful—but more pleased.
Well, let me think so. And you smile indeed!
This hour has been an hour! Another smile?
205 If you would sit thus by me every night
I should work better, do you comprehend?
I mean that I should earn more, give you more.
See, it is settled dusk now; there's a star;
Morello's gone, the watch-lights show the wall,
210 The cue-owls[2] speak the name we call them by.
Come from the window, love—come in, at last,
Inside the melancholy little house
We built to be so gay with. God is just.
King Francis may forgive me: oft at nights
215 When I look up from painting, eyes tired out,
The walls become illumined, brick from brick

---

[1] *For fear ... lords* According to Vasari, del Sarto absconded with funds given to him at Fontainebleau by his patron, King Francis I of France.

[2] *cue-owls* Also known as scops-owls, whose cries sounds like "cue."

Distinct, instead of mortar, fierce bright gold,
That gold of his I did cement them with!
Let us but love each other. Must you go?
220 That cousin here again? he waits outside?
Must see you—you, and not with me? Those loans?
More gaming debts to pay? you smiled for that?
Well, let smiles buy me! have you more to spend?
While hand and eye and something of a heart
225 Are left me, work's my ware, and what's it worth?
I'll pay my fancy. Only let me sit
The grey remainder of the evening out,
Idle, you call it, and muse perfectly
How I could paint, were I but back in France,
230 One picture, just one more—the Virgin's face,
Not yours this time! I want you at my side
To hear them—that is, Michel Agnolo—
Judge all I do and tell you of its worth.
Will you? Tomorrow, satisfy your friend.
235 I take the subjects for his corridor,
Finish the portrait out of hand—there, there,
And throw him in another thing or two
If he demurs; the whole should prove enough
To pay for this same cousin's freak. Beside,
240 What's better and what's all I care about,
Get you the thirteen scudi° for the ruff!   *Italian currency*
Love, does that please you? Ah, but what does he,
The cousin! what does he to please you more?

    I am grown peaceful as old age tonight.
245 I regret little, I would change still less.
Since there my past life lies, why alter it?
The very wrong to Francis!—it is true
I took his coin, was tempted and complied,
And built this house and sinned, and all is said.
250 My father and my mother died of want.
Well, had I riches of my own? you see
How one gets rich! Let each one bear his lot.
They were born poor, lived poor, and poor they died:
And I have laboured somewhat in my time
255 And not been paid profusely. Some good son
Paint my two hundred pictures—let him try!
No doubt, there's something strikes a balance. Yes,
You loved me quite enough, it seems tonight.
This must suffice me here. What would one have?
260 In heaven, perhaps, new chances, one more chance—

Four great walls in the New Jerusalem,[1]
Meted on each side by the angel's reed,
For Leonard,[2] Rafael, Agnolo and me
To cover—the three first without a wife,
265 While I have mine! So—still they overcome
Because there's still Lucrezia—as I choose.

Again the cousin's whistle! Go, my Love.
—1855

A Woman's Last Word

1

Let's contend no more, Love,
    Strive nor weep:
All be as before, Love,
    —Only sleep!

2

5 What so wild as words are?
    I and thou
In debate, as birds are,
    Hawk on bough!

3

See the creature stalking
    While we speak!
10 Hush and hide the talking,
    Cheek on cheek!

4

What so false as truth is,
    False to thee?
15 Where the serpent's tooth is
    Shun the tree—

5

Where the apple reddens
    Never pry—
Lest we lose our Edens,
20   Eve and I.

6

Be a god and hold me
    With a charm!

---

[1] *Four ... Jerusalem* See Revelations 21.10.

[2] *Leonard* Artist Leonardo da Vinci (1452–1519).

Be a man and fold me
    With thine arm!

7

25 Teach me, only teach, Love!
    As I ought
I will speak thy speech, Love,
    Think thy thought—

8

Meet, if thou require it,
30   Both demands,
Laying flesh and spirit
    In thy hands.

9

That shall be tomorrow
    Not tonight:
35 I must bury sorrow
    Out of sight:

10

—Must a little weep, Love,
    (Foolish me!)
And so fall asleep, Love,
40   Loved by thee.
    —1855

CHARLES DICKENS
1812 — 1870

Few English novelists have attracted the huge audiences and lasting fame of Charles Dickens. People the world over are familiar with the moral transformation of *A Christmas Carol*'s Ebenezer Scrooge and the life of the orphan Oliver Twist, immortalized in his piteous request for a second bowl of water gruel: "Please, sir, I want some more." From Pickwick and Sam Weller in *The Pickwick Papers* to Mr. Micawber in *David Copperfield* to Pip in *Great Expectations*, from Mr. Guppy and Mrs. Jellyby in *Bleak House* to Mr. Gradgrind in *Hard Times* and Flora Finching in *Little Dorrit*, Dickens created a panoply of memorable characters. Combining his comic genius with astute criticisms of the laws, institutions, and the social order of Victorian society, he created novels that continue to command the attention of critics and the general public alike. His novels still stand as a testament to his stature both as a popular writer and as a social critic.

Dickens's early childhood was signally important as source material for the concerns and themes of his novels. His father worked as a naval office clerk in Portsmouth when Charles was born in 1812, the second of 10 children (two died in infancy). John and Elizabeth Dickens aspired to a middle-class life, but had unending difficulties controlling their spending and were always on the brink of penury. At one time, they served a four-month stint in the Marshalsea debtors' prison. Charles was able to attend school in Chatham, near London, after the family was transferred to the dockyards there, but in 1823 his education was halted, and he joined his parents in Camden Town, London. The young Dickens worked at odd jobs for his parents and was eventually sent off to work at Warren's Boot Blacking Factory at the age of 12. The psychological impact of this environment on Dickens was permanent. He never forgot the humiliation he had suffered or the dismay he had felt at the relatively harsh working conditions under which he and other children were forced to toil.

After the family came into a modest inheritance, Dickens returned to school, but in 1827, at just 15 years of age, he left school again because his father was unable to pay the fees. Working as a clerk in a law firm, he studied shorthand in his spare time, eventually becoming a parliamentary reporter. In 1833, *Monthly Magazine* published Dickens's first story, "Dinner at Poplar Walk." While working as a newspaper reporter the next year, he launched a highly popular series of articles that were eventually collected and published as *Sketches by Boz* (his journalistic pseudonym) in 1836. The success of this book allowed Dickens to marry Catherine Hogarth and to begin another series that cemented his fame and secured his financial stability. A monthly illustrated serial about the Pickwick Club was commissioned by publishers Chapman and Hall, and the absurd characters of Mr. Pickwick, Mr. Winkle, Mr. Tupman, Mr. Snodgrass, and Sam Weller soon had people all over England clamoring for the latest installment of *The Pickwick Papers*. Dickens consolidated this success by beginning *Oliver Twist* (1837–38) in *Bentley's Miscellany*, which he had begun editing, and then launching *Nicholas Nickleby* (1838–39) as a monthly serial.

In 1837, Dickens and his wife began to raise a family (they eventually had 10 children). In this same year, he lost his beloved sister-in-law, Mary Hogarth, who would become the inspiration for

Little Nell in *The Old Curiosity Shop* (1840–41) and for many of the childlike women that constitute the "good angels" of his novels. By the time this book was published, Dickens's fame had spread throughout North America; eager fans would line the piers in New York waiting for the latest installment of a Dickens story to arrive from England.

In 1842, Dickens journeyed to the United States to take advantage of his fame, but the trip turned out to be a disappointment. The hordes that crowded around him relentlessly, trying to speak to, touch, or even just glimpse the famous author were only part of the problem. He scorned, publicly and at any opportunity, the lack of international copyright laws, which meant that Americans could pirate editions of his books without any of the proceeds going to him. Dickens set out his disdain for American habits (such as chewing and spitting tobacco) and for American institutions, such as slavery, and what he thought was a ruthless prison system in a book about his travels, *American Notes* (1842), and made Americans the object of derision in his novel *Martin Chuzzlewit* (1843–44). Americans were incensed and reacted with an outpouring of vindictive editorials in the press. As it happened, *Martin Chuzzlewit* did not sell well on either side of the Atlantic. Americans began to forgive Dickens after the appearance of the overwhelmingly successful *A Christmas Carol* (1843), the first in his Christmas book series and a novel that is all about forgiveness and redemption.

Dickens was an astonishingly energetic and prolific writer, becoming the editor of *Household Words* in 1850, while writing and acting in theatrical works, traveling widely, and working in various social causes. Throughout the 1840s and 1850s, he published at an unprecedented rate: *Dombey and Son* (1846–48), *David Copperfield* (his most autobiographical work, 1849–50), *Bleak House* (1852–53), *Hard Times* (1854), *Little Dorrit* (1855–57), and *A Tale of Two Cities* (1859). Dickens published all of his novels in serial form. The episodic structure of his novels prompted Dickens to develop methods of characterizations that allowed immediate identification of characters by readers waiting for weekly or monthly installments. The Dickens "character" is invariably recognizable as a type that speaks in a marvelously individualized dialect and often more closely resembles a caricature from the popular press than a fully rounded character. (George Eliot complained that Dickens's characters had little psychology.) He also wove numerous peripheral stories and characters into the main plotlines, and used coincidence—in which, for example, characters discover long-lost parents and siblings by accident—with Victorian abandon. Yet for Dickens and his readers, coincidence did not undermine reality so much as suggest that divinity shapes our ends.

In 1858 Dickens separated from Catherine, an event complicated by his relationship with the actress Ellen Ternan and by the degree of publicity that (partly at Dickens's instigation) attended his change in marital status. In that same year, Dickens began an extensive tour of public readings, a most lucrative but exhausting enterprise that severely compromised his health. He continued touring throughout the 1860s while editing his new journal, *All the Year Round* (begun in 1859), in which he serialized both *A Tale of Two Cities* (1859) and *Great Expectations* (1860–61). During this decade Dickens completed only one other novel, *Our Mutual Friend* (1864–65). He was at work on *The Mystery of Edwin Drood* when he died in 1870 during a grueling schedule of readings. In his will Dickens requested an "unostentatious, and strictly private" burial attended only by a few close friends and family, but throngs gathered later around his grave in Westminster Abbey to mourn his death.

⌘⌘⌘

from *Sketches by Boz*

Dickens's *Sketches by Boz* was celebrated for its humor and wit, the vitality of its characters and the realism of its portrayals of London life. The following story from *Sketches by Boz*, published seven years before Dickens's widely successful *A Christmas Carol* (1843), contains elements of many of the themes and characters that he would later develop in that longer work. Several of the rituals of Christmas as it is now observed in Western societies were still to take shape during Dickens's time: the Christmas tree was introduced into England by Prince Albert in 1841, and the first Christmas card was designed in London in 1843. Christmas as an occasion of family get-togethers, mistletoe, and turkey dinners, however, was already well established, as the following piece illustrates.

CHAPTER 2: A CHRISTMAS DINNER

Christmas time! That man must be a misanthrope indeed, in whose breast something like a jovial feeling is not roused—in whose mind some pleasant associations are not awakened—by the recurrence of Christmas. There are people who will tell you that Christmas is not to them what it used to be; that each succeeding Christmas has found some cherished hope, or happy prospect, of the year before, dimmed or passed away; that the present only serves to remind them of reduced circumstances and straitened[1] incomes—of the feasts they once bestowed on hollow friends, and of the cold looks that meet them now, in adversity and misfortune. Never heed such dismal reminiscences. There are few men who have lived long enough in the world, who cannot call up such thoughts any day in the year. Then do not select the merriest of the three hundred and sixty-five for your doleful recollections, but draw your chair nearer the blazing fire—fill the glass and send round the song—and if your room be smaller than it was a dozen years ago, or if your glass be filled with reeking punch, instead of sparkling wine, put a good face on the matter, and empty it offhand, and fill

another, and troll off the old ditty you used to sing, and thank God it's no worse. Look on the merry faces of your children (if you have any) as they sit round the fire. One little seat may be empty; one slight form that gladdened the father's heart, and roused the mother's pride to look upon, may not be there. Dwell not upon the past; think not that one short year ago, the fair child now resolving into dust, sat before you, with the bloom of health upon its cheek and the gaiety of infancy in its joyous eye. Reflect upon your present blessings—of which every man has many—not your misfortunes, of which all men have some. Fill your glass again, with a merry face and contented heart. Our life on it, but your Christmas shall be merry, and your new year a happy one!

Who can be insensible to the outpourings of good feeling, and the honest interchange of affectionate attachment, which abound at this season of the year? A Christmas family party! We know nothing in nature more delightful! There seems a magic in the very name of Christmas. Petty jealousies and discords are forgotten; social feelings are awakened, in bosoms to which they have long been strangers; father and son, or brother and sister, who have met and passed with averted gaze, or a look of cold recognition, for months before, proffer and return the cordial embrace, and bury their past animosities in their present happiness. Kindly hearts that have yearned towards each other, but have been withheld by false notions of pride and self-dignity, are again re-united, and all is kindness and benevolence! Would that Christmas lasted the whole year through (as it ought), and that the prejudices and passions which deform our better nature were never called into action among those to whom they should ever be strangers!

The Christmas family party that we mean, is not a mere assemblage of relations got up at a week or two's notice, originating this year, having no family precedent in the last, and not likely to be repeated in the next. No. It is an annual gathering of all the accessible members of the family, young or old, rich or poor; and all the children look forward to it, for two months beforehand, in a fever of anticipation. Formerly it was held at grandpapa's; but grandpapa getting old, and grandmamma getting old too, and rather infirm, they have given up housekeeping, and domesticated themselves with Uncle

---

[1] *straitened* Insufficient.

George; so, the party always takes place at Uncle George's house, but grandmamma sends in most of the good things, and grandpapa always *will* toddle down, all the way to Newgate market, to buy the turkey, which he engages a porter to bring home behind him in triumph, always insisting on the man's being rewarded with a glass of spirits, over and above his hire, to drink "a merry Christmas and a happy new year" to Aunt George. As to grandmamma, she is very secret and mysterious for two or three days beforehand, but not sufficiently so to prevent rumours getting afloat that she has purchased a beautiful new cap with pink ribbons for each of the servants, together with sundry books, and pen-knives, and pencil-cases, for the younger branches; to say nothing of diverse secret additions to the order originally given by Aunt George at the pastry cook's, such as another dozen of mince pies for the dinner, and a large plum cake for the children.

On Christmas Eve, grandmamma is always in excellent spirits, and after employing all the children during the day, in stoning the plums, and all that, insists, regularly every year, on Uncle George coming down into the kitchen, taking off his coat, and stirring the pudding for half an hour or so, which Uncle George good humouredly does to the vociferous delight of the children and servants. The evening concludes with a glorious game of blindman's buff, in an early stage of which grandpapa takes great care to be caught, in order that he may have an opportunity of displaying his dexterity.

On the following morning, the old couple, with as many of the children as the pew will hold, go to church in great state: leaving Aunt George at home dusting decanters and filling castors, and Uncle George carrying bottles into the dining parlour, and calling for cork-screws, and getting into everybody's way.

When the church party return to lunch, grandpapa produces a small sprig of mistletoe from his pocket, and tempts the boys to kiss their little cousins under it—a proceeding which affords both the boys and the old gentleman unlimited satisfaction, but which rather outrages grandmamma's ideas of decorum, until grandpapa says that when he was just thirteen years and three months old *he* kissed grandmamma under a mistletoe too, on which the children clap their hands, and laugh very heartily, as do Aunt George and Uncle George; and grandmamma looks pleased, and says, with a benevolent smile, that grandpapa was an impudent young dog, on which the children laugh very heartily again, and grandpapa more heartily than any of them.

But all these diversions are nothing to the subsequent excitement when grandmamma in a high cap, and slate-coloured silk gown; and grandpapa with a beautifully plaited shirt frill, and white neckerchief; seat themselves on one side of the drawing room fire, with Uncle George's children and little cousins innumerable seated in the front, waiting the arrival of the expected visitors. Suddenly a hackney coach is heard to stop, and Uncle George, who has been looking out of the window, exclaims, "Here's Jane!" on which the children rush to the door, and helter skelter downstairs; and Uncle Robert and Aunt Jane, and the dear little baby, and the nurse, and the whole party, are ushered upstairs amidst tumultuous shouts of "Oh, my!" from the children, and frequently repeated warnings not to hurt baby from the nurse. And grandpapa takes the child, and grandmamma kisses her daughter, and the confusion of this first entry has scarcely subsided, when some other aunts and uncles with more cousins arrive, and the grown-up cousins flirt with each other, and so do the little cousins too, for that matter, and nothing is to be heard but a confused din of talking, laughing, and merriment.

A hesitating double knock at the street door, heard during a momentary pause in the conversation, excites a general inquiry of "Who's that?" and two or three children, who have been standing at the window, announce in a low voice, that it's "poor Aunt Margaret." Upon which, Aunt George leaves the room to welcome the newcomer; and grandmamma draws herself up, rather stiff and stately; for Margaret married a poor man without her consent, and poverty not being a sufficient weighty punishment for her offence, has been discarded by her friends, and debarred the society of her dearest relatives. But Christmas has come round, and the unkind feelings that have struggled against better dispositions during the year, have melted away before its genial influence, like half-formed ice beneath the morning sun. It is not difficult in a moment of angry feeling for a parent to denounce a disobedient child;

but, to banish her at a period of general good will and hilarity from the hearth, round which she has sat on so many anniversaries of the same day, expanding by slow degrees from infancy to girlhood, and then bursting, almost imperceptibly, into a woman, is widely different. The air of conscious rectitude, and cold forgiveness, which the old lady has assumed, sits ill upon her; and when the poor girl is led in by her sister, pale in looks and broken in hope—not from poverty, for that she could bear, but from the consciousness of undeserved neglect, and unmerited unkindness—it is easy to see how much of it is assumed. A momentary pause succeeds; the girl breaks suddenly from her sister and throws herself, sobbing, on her mother's neck. The father steps hastily forward, and takes her husband's hand. Friends crowd round to offer their hearty congratulations, and happiness and harmony again prevail.

As to the dinner, it's perfectly delightful—nothing goes wrong, and everybody is in the very best of spirits, and disposed to please and be pleased. Grandpapa relates a circumstantial account of the purchase of the turkey, with a slight digression relative to the purchase of previous turkeys, on former Christmas Days, which grandmamma corroborates in the minutest particular. Uncle George tells stories, and carves poultry, and takes wine, and jokes with the children at the side table, and winks at the cousins that are making love,[1] or being made love to, and exhilarates everybody with his good humour and hospitality; and when, at last, a stout servant staggers in with a gigantic pudding, with a sprig of holly in the top, there is such a laughing, and shouting, and clapping of little chubby hands, and kicking up of fat dumpy legs, as can only be equalled by the applause with which the astonishing feat of pouring lighted brandy into mince pies, is received by the younger visitors. Then the dessert!—and the wine!—and the fun! Such beautiful speeches, and *such* songs, from Aunt Margaret's husband, who turns out to be such a nice man, and *so* attentive to grandmamma! Even grandpapa not only sings his annual song with unprecedented vigour, but on being honoured with an unanimous *encore*, according to annual custom, actually comes out with a new one which nobody but grand-

mamma ever heard before; and a young scapegrace[2] of a cousin, who has been in some disgrace with the old people, for certain heinous sins of omission and commission—neglecting to call, and persisting in drinking Burton ale—astonishes everybody into convulsions of laughter by volunteering the most extraordinary comic songs that ever were heard. And thus the evening passes, in a strain of rational goodwill and cheerfulness, doing more to awaken the sympathies of every member of the party in behalf of his neighbour, and to perpetuate their good feeling, during the ensuing year, than half the homilies that have ever been written, by half the Divines that have ever lived.
—1836

A Walk in the Workhouse

The condition of the poor—and in particular the condition of poor children—was always of great concern to Dickens. Perhaps most notably among his previous work, *Oliver Twist* (1838) portrays the hardships for children of life in the workhouse. Dickens continued to write on the subject in later years; the following essay appeared in 1850 in Dickens's magazine *Household Words*.

On a certain Sunday I formed one of the congregation assembled in the chapel of a large metropolitan Workhouse. With the exception of the clergyman and clerk, and a very few officials, there were none but paupers present. The children sat in the galleries; the women in the body of the chapel, and in one of the side aisles; the men in the remaining aisle. The service was decorously performed, though the sermon might have been much better adapted to the comprehension and to the circumstances of the hearers. The usual supplications were offered, with more than the usual significancy in such a place, for the fatherless children and widows, for all sick persons and young children, for all that were desolate and oppressed, for the comforting and helping of the weak-hearted, for the raising up of them that had fallen; for all that were in danger, necessity, and tribulation. The prayers of the congregation were desired "for

---

[1]   *making love* Wooing; flirting.

[2]   *scapegrace* Rascal.

several persons in the various wards dangerously ill"; and others who were recovering returned their thanks to Heaven.

Among this congregation were some evil-looking young women, and beetle-browed young men; but not many—perhaps that kind of characters kept away. Generally, the faces (those of the children excepted) were depressed and subdued, and wanted colour. Aged people were there in every variety. Mumbling, blear-eyed, spectacled, stupid, deaf, lame; vacantly winking in the gleams of sun that now and then crept in through the open doors, from the paved yard; shading their listening ears, or blinking eyes, with their withered hands; poring over their books, leering at nothing, going to sleep, crouching and drooping in corners. There were weird old women, all skeleton within, all bonnet and cloak without, continually wiping their eyes with dirty dusters of pocket handkerchiefs; and there were ugly old crones, both male and female, with a ghastly kind of contentment upon them which was not at all comforting to see. Upon the whole, it was the dragon, Pauperism, in a very weak and impotent condition: toothless, fangless, drawing his breath heavily enough, and hardly worth chaining up.

When the service was over, I walked with the humane and conscientious gentleman whose duty it was to take that walk, that Sunday morning, through the little world of poverty enclosed within the workhouse walls. It was inhabited by a population of some fifteen hundred or two thousand paupers, ranging from the infant newly born or not yet come into the pauper world, to the old man dying on his bed.

In a room opening from a squalid yard, where a number of listless women were lounging to and fro, trying to get warm in the ineffectual sunshine of the tardy May morning—in the "Itch Ward," not to compromise the truth—a woman such as HOGARTH[1] has often drawn, was hurriedly getting on her gown before a dusty fire. She was the nurse, or wardswoman, of that insalubrious department—herself a pauper—flabby, raw-boned, untidy—unpromising and coarse of aspect as need be. But, on being spoken to

about the patients whom she had in charge, she turned round, with her shabby gown half on, half off, and fell a crying with all her might. Not for show, not querulously, not in any mawkish sentiment, but in the deep grief and affliction of her heart; turning away her dishevelled head: sobbing most bitterly, wringing her hands, and letting fall abundance of great tears, that choked her utterance. What was the matter with the nurse of the itch ward? Oh, "the dropped child" was dead! Oh, the child that was found in the street, and she had brought up ever since, had died an hour ago, and see where the little creature lay, beneath this cloth! The dear, the pretty dear!

The dropped child seemed too small and poor a thing for Death to be in earnest with, but Death had taken it; and already its diminutive form was neatly washed, composed, and stretched as if in sleep upon a box. I thought I heard a voice from Heaven saying, It shall be well for thee, O nurse of the itch ward, when some less gentle pauper does those offices to thy cold form, that such as the dropped child are the angels who behold my Father's face!

In another room were several ugly old women crouching, witch-like, round a hearth, and chattering and nodding, after the manner of the monkeys. "All well here? And enough to eat?" A general chattering and chuckling; at last an answer from a volunteer. "Oh yes, gentleman! Bless you, gentleman! Lord bless the Parish of St. So-and-So! It feed the hungry, sir, and give drink to the thusty, and it warm them which is cold, so it do, and good luck to the parish of St. So-and-So, and thankee, gentleman!" Elsewhere, a party of pauper nurses were at dinner. "How do YOU get on?" "Oh pretty well, sir! We works hard, and we lives hard—like the sodgers!"[2]

In another room, a kind of purgatory or place of transition, six or eight noisy madwomen were gathered together, under the superintendence of one sane attendant. Among them was a girl of two or three and twenty, very prettily dressed, of most respectable appearance and good manners, who had been brought in from the house where she had lived as domestic servant (having, I suppose, no friends), on account of being subject to epileptic fits, and requiring to be removed

---

[1]   *Hogarth*   Artist and printmaker William Hogarth (1697–1764), was greatly admired by Dickens for his satirical paintings and prints of eighteenth-century London life.

[2]   *sodgers*   I.e., soldiers.

under the influence of a very bad one. She was by no means of the same stuff, or the same breeding, or the same experience, or in the same state of mind, as those by whom she was surrounded; and she pathetically complained that the daily association and the nightly noise made her worse, and was driving her mad—which was perfectly evident. The case was noted for inquiry and redress, but she said she had already been there for some weeks.

If this girl had stolen her mistress's watch, I do not hesitate to say she would have been infinitely better off. We have come to this absurd, this dangerous, this monstrous pass, that the dishonest felon is, in respect of cleanliness, order, diet, and accommodation, better provided for, and taken care of, than the honest pauper.

And this conveys no special imputation on the workhouse of the parish of St. So-and-So, where, on the contrary, I saw many things to commend. It was very agreeable, recollecting that most infamous and atrocious enormity committed at Tooting[1]—an enormity which, a hundred years hence, will still be vividly remembered in the byways of English life, and which has done more to engender a gloomy discontent and suspicion among many thousands of the people than all the Chartist leaders[2] could have done in all their lives—to find the pauper children in this workhouse looking robust and well, and apparently the objects of very great care. In the Infant School—a large, light, airy room at the top of the building—the little creatures, being at dinner, and eating their potatoes heartily, were not cowed by the presence of strange visitors, but stretched out their small hands to be shaken, with a very pleasant confidence. And it was comfortable to see two mangy pauper rocking-horses rampant in a corner. In the girls' school, where the dinner was also in progress, everything bore a cheerful and healthy aspect. The meal was over in the boys' school by the time of our arrival there, and the room was not yet quite rearranged; but the boys were roaming unrestrained about a large and airy yard, as any other schoolboys might have done. Some of them had been drawing large ships upon the schoolroom wall; and if they had a mast with shrouds and stays set up for practice (as they have in the Middlesex House of Correction), it would be so much the better. At present, if a boy should feel a strong impulse upon him to learn the art of going aloft, he could only gratify it, I presume, as the men and women paupers gratify their aspirations after better board and lodging, by smashing as many workhouse windows as possible, and being promoted to prison.

In one place, the Newgate[3] of the workhouse, a company of boys and youths were locked up in a yard alone; their dayroom being a kind of kennel where the casual poor used formerly to be littered down at night. Diverse of them had been there some long time. "Are they never going away?" was the natural inquiry. "Most of them are crippled, in some form or other," said the wardsman, "and not fit for anything." They slunk about, like dispirited wolves or hyenas; and made a pounce at their food when it was served out, much as those animals do. The big-headed idiot shuffling his feet along the pavement, in the sunlight outside, was a more agreeable object everyway.

Groves of babies in arms; groves of mothers and other sick women in bed; groves of lunatics; jungles of men in stone-paved downstairs dayrooms, waiting for their dinners; longer and longer groves of old people, in upstairs infirmary wards, wearing out life, God knows how—this was the scenery through which the walk lay, for two hours. In some of these latter chambers, there were pictures stuck against the wall, and a neat display of crockery and pewter on a kind of sideboard; now and then it was a treat to see a plant or two; in almost every ward there was a cat.

In all of these long walks of aged and infirm, some old people were bedridden, and had been for a long time; some were sitting on their beds half naked; some dying in their beds; some out of bed, and sitting at a table near the fire. A sullen or lethargic indifference to what was asked, a blunted sensibility to everything but warmth and food, a moody absence of complaint as being of no use, a dogged silence and resentful desire to be left alone again, I thought were generally apparent.

---

[1] *Tooting* In 1849, after four half-starved children had died of cholera in a Tooting workhouse, the proprietor was found guilty of manslaughter.

[2] *Chartist leaders* The Chartist movement pressed for political (and by implication, social and economic) reform from 1836 onwards.

[3] *Newgate* Newgate was London's main prison.

On our walking into the midst of one of these dreary perspectives of old men, nearly the following little dialogue took place, the nurse not being immediately at hand:

"All well here?"

No answer. An old man in a Scotch cap[1] sitting among others on a form at the table, eating out of a tin porringer,[2] pushes back his cap a little to look at us, claps it down on his forehead again with the palm of his hand, and goes on eating.

"All well here?" (repeated).

No answer. Another old man sitting on his bed, paralytically peeling a boiled potato, lifts his head and stares.

"Enough to eat?"

No answer. Another old man, in bed, turns himself and coughs.

"How are YOU today?" To the last old man.

That old man says nothing; but another old man, a tall old man of very good address, speaking with perfect correctness, comes forward from somewhere, and volunteers an answer. The reply almost always proceeds from a volunteer, and not from the person looked at or spoken to.

"We are very old, sir," in a mild, distinct voice. "We can't expect to be well, most of us."

"Are you comfortable?"

"I have no complaint to make, sir." With a half shake of his head, a half shrug of his shoulders, and a kind of apologetic smile.

"Enough to eat?"

"Why, sir, I have but a poor appetite," with the same air as before; "and yet I get through my allowance very easily."

"But," showing a porringer with a Sunday dinner in it; "here is a portion of mutton, and three potatoes. You can't starve on that?"

"Oh dear no, sir," with the same apologetic air. "Not starve."

"What do you want?"

"We have very little bread, sir. It's an exceedingly small quantity of bread."

The nurse, who is now rubbing her hands at the questioner's elbow, interferes with, "It ain't much raly, sir. You see they've only six ounces a day, and when they've took their breakfast, there CAN only be a little left for night, sir." Another old man, hitherto invisible, rises out of his bedclothes, as out of a grave, and looks on.

"You have tea at night?" The questioner is still addressing the well-spoken old man.

"Yes, sir, we have tea at night."

"And you save what bread you can from the morning, to eat with it?"

"Yes, sir—if we can save any."

"And you want more to eat with it?"

"Yes, sir." With a very anxious face.

The questioner, in the kindness of his heart, appears a little discomposed, and changes the subject.

"What has become of the old man who used to lie in that bed in the corner?"

The nurse don't remember what old man is referred to. There has been such a many old men. The well-spoken old man is doubtful. The spectral old man who has come to life in bed says "Billy Stevens." Another old man who has previously had his head in the fireplace, pipes out, "Charley Walters."

Something like a feeble interest is awakened. I suppose Charley Walters had conversation in him.

"He's dead," says the piping old man.

Another old man, with one eye screwed up, hastily displaces the piping old man, and says.

"Yes! Charley Walters died in that bed, and—and—"

"Billy Stevens," persists the spectral old man.

"No, no! and Johnny Rogers died in that bed, and—and—they're both on 'em dead—and Sam'l Bowyer"; this seems very extraordinary to him; "he went out!"

With this he subsides, and all the old men (having had quite enough of it) subside, and the spectral old man goes into his grave again, and takes the shade of Billy Stevens with him.

As we turn to go out at the door, another previously invisible old man, a hoarse old man in a flannel gown, is standing there, as if he had just come up through the floor.

"I beg your pardon, sir, could I take the liberty of

---

[1]   *Scotch cap*   Woolen hat worn in the Highlands.

[2]   *porringer*   Bowl for porridge, soups, and other runny foods.

saying a word?"

"Yes, what is it?"

"I am greatly better in my health, sir; but what I want, to get me quite round," with his hand on his throat, "is a little fresh air, sir. It has always done my complaint so much good, sir. The regular leave for going out, comes round so seldom, that if the gentlemen, next Friday, would give me leave to go out walking, now and then—for only an hour or so, sir!—"

Who could wonder, looking through those weary vistas of bed and infirmity, that it should do him good to meet with some other scenes, and assure himself that there was something else on earth? Who could help wondering why the old men lived on as they did; what grasp they had on life; what crumbs of interest or occupation they could pick up from its bare board; whether Charley Walters had ever described to them the days when he kept company with some old pauper woman in the bud, or Billy Stevens ever told them of the time when he was a dweller in the far off foreign land called Home!

The morsel of burnt child, lying in another room, so patiently, in bed, wrapped in lint, and looking steadfastly at us with his bright quiet eyes when we spoke to him kindly, looked as if the knowledge of these things, and of all the tender things there are to think about, might have been in his mind as if he thought, with us, that there was a fellow-feeling in the pauper nurses which appeared to make them more kind to their charges than the race of common nurses in the hospitals—as if he mused upon the future of some older children lying around him in the same place, and thought it best, perhaps, all things considered, that he should die—as if he knew, without fear, of those many coffins, made and unmade, piled up in the store below—and of his unknown friend, "the dropped child," calm upon the box lid covered with a cloth. But there was something wistful and appealing, too, in his tiny face, as if, in the midst of all the hard necessities and incongruities he pondered on, he pleaded, in behalf of the helpless and the aged poor, for a little more liberty—and a little more bread.

—1850

Emily Brontë

1818 – 1848

It would seem that there were two Emily Brontës: one a shy, introverted, and unremarkable young woman, and the other the strong-willed, brilliant, and legendary woman who became almost a mythic figure after her death at the age of thirty. Both versions develop from the portrait her sister Charlotte gave of her in the second edition of *Wuthering Heights*, published shortly after her death. It is by this novel that most people now know her, although she also published a relatively small number of poems, often enigmatic and mystical in their tone. She was at work on a second, lost novel at the time of her death. While many Victorians were suspicious of *Wuthering Heights* on account of its expressions of passion and of violence, it became a classic text in the twentieth century. Its reputation has been enhanced by film adaptations, particularly by the 1939 version starring Laurence Olivier, which helped make it into a by-word for romantic tragedy.

Emily Brontë's literary talent flourished in a house of creative writers that included her sisters Charlotte (*Jane Eyre*) and Anne (*The Tenant of Wildfell Hall*). Emily was the fifth child of Patrick Brontë and Maria Branwell, born in 1818 into poor circumstances in Thornton, Yorkshire. Maria died just two years later, not long after Patrick, an Anglican clergyman, had taken a post in nearby Haworth, where he and the children remained for practically all their lives. The six children were cared for by Maria's sister, Elizabeth Branwell, and educated primarily by Patrick (who had graduated from Cambridge). For the most part the children had the run of the stone parsonage that sat next to a graveyard in the desolate West Yorkshire moors. At the same time, industrial Yorkshire was close at hand.

When she was just five years old, Emily followed her three elder sisters to a charity school for the daughters of poor clergy. The conditions there were wretched, and all the sisters returned home when the two eldest, Maria and Elizabeth, contracted tuberculosis; they died soon afterward. The remaining children were left mainly to their own devices, performing household chores, reading literary classics and current affairs periodicals, walking on the moors, and writing elaborate plays and stories together. The two oldest children, Charlotte and Branwell, created an imaginary kingdom called "Angria"; the two younger children, Emily and Anne, fashioned the island of "Gondal," inspired by their father's colorful descriptions of political and historical events. Although the children's transcripts of Gondal no longer exist, Brontë continued its themes in her later, published poems.

Brontë again went off to school when she was 16, to the harsh institution that Charlotte subsequently depicted in *Jane Eyre*; she returned home after only six months due to illness. Two years later she left home for another brief sojourn—this time to teach—but her homesickness and what she called her life of slavery brought her back again soon afterward. Her last stint away from home was in 1842, when she joined Charlotte at a teaching institution in Brussels. The two had planned to open their own school in Yorkshire, hoping they could turn around the family's desperate financial circumstances.

Charlotte eventually persuaded her sisters to publish a volume of their poems using pseudonyms. Unfortunately, *The Poems of Currer, Ellis, and Acton Bell* (1846), which was published with their own funds, sold only two copies and was ignored by most reviewers, although one did say that Ellis

(Emily) showed the most promise. Within a year, however, all three Brontë sisters had completed novels: Charlotte, *The Professor*; Emily, *Wuthering Heights*; and Anne, *Agnes Grey*. When Charlotte's subsequently published novel, *Jane Eyre*, became a bestseller, Emily's and Anne's books were also published together in three volumes (*Agnes Grey* being the third). All three sisters used their pseudonyms.

Wuthering Heights is a book so full of passion and violence that the Victorian public assumed it had been written by a man (some even speculated that Branwell Brontë penned it), and some conjectured that the author of *Jane Eyre* had written it. Its dark and brooding story is set against the wild and bleak landscape of the Yorkshire moors. Highly charged with sexuality and with powerful moral ambiguities, the novel broke many conventions of the time. The marriage plot is at once respected (the "good characters," Cathy Linton and Hareton Earnshaw, inherit their rightful property and a happy ending) and damned (the "lovers" Catherine and Heathcliff finally exist only in story, and in their graves, even if they are rumored to still roam the moors). The idea of love, so central to Victorian realism, exists in *Wuthering Heights* as at once "normal" and frightening. It is no wonder that some reviewers found the novel chaotically written, gloomy, too unrelenting in its violence, and morally suspect. Even Charlotte Brontë, who always championed the novel as a work of genius, questioned its meaning.

Much of Brontë's poetry shares the bleakness of *Wuthering Heights* and its preoccupation with passion, loss, and death. Many of the poems display a desire for transcendence reminiscent of Catherine and Heathcliff's yearnings and yet a tenderness that is not evident in them or in the narrators of the novel. There is often in the poems a view of an existence free of the restraints of everyday life, even though this existence is often realized only through the realm of the imagination—perspectives that connect Brontë to her Romantic predecessors much more than to her Victorian contemporaries.

In 1848 Emily Brontë caught a cold at the funeral of the only Brontë son, Branwell, a failed painter and writer and the sibling on whom the family had pinned its biggest hopes, who had died of complications from chronic alcohol and drug use. The cold soon afterward developed into tuberculosis, and, having refused all medical treatment, Emily Brontë died in December of 1848, only one year after the publication of *Wuthering Heights*.

⌘ ⌘ ⌘

Remembrance

Cold in the earth—and the deep snow piled above thee,
  Far, far removed, cold in the dreary grave!
Have I forgot, my only Love, to love thee,
  Severed at last by Time's all-severing wave?

5 Now, when alone, do my thoughts no longer hover
  Over the mountains, on that northern shore,
Resting their wings where heath and fern-leaves cover
  Thy noble heart for ever, ever more?

Cold in the earth—and fifteen wild Decembers,
10 From those brown hills, have melted into spring:
Faithful, indeed, is the spirit that remembers
  After such years of change and suffering!

Sweet Love of youth, forgive, if I forget thee,
  While the world's tide is bearing me along;
15 Other desires and other hopes beset me,
  Hopes which obscure, but cannot do thee wrong!

No later light has lightened up my heaven,
  No second morn has ever shone for me;

All my life's bliss from thy dear life was given,
20　　All my life's bliss is in the grave with thee.

But when the days of golden dreams had perished,
　　And even Despair was powerless to destroy;
Then did I learn how existence could be cherished,
　　Strengthened, and fed without the aid of joy.

25　Then did I check the tears of useless passion,
　　Weaned my young soul from yearning after thine;
Sternly denied its burning wish to hasten
　　Down to that tomb already more than mine.

And, even yet, I dare not let it languish,
30　　Dare not indulge in memory's rapturous pain;
Once drinking deep of that divinest anguish,
　　How could I seek the empty world again?
　　　—1846

Plead for Me

Oh, thy bright eyes must answer now,
　　When Reason, with a scornful brow,
Is mocking at my overthrow!
Oh, thy sweet tongue must plead for me
5　And tell, why I have chosen thee!

Stern Reason is to judgment come,
Arrayed in all her forms of gloom:
Wilt thou, my advocate, be dumb?
No, radiant angel, speak and say,
10　Why I did cast the world away.

Why I have persevered to shun
The common paths that others run,
And on a strange road journeyed on,
Heedless, alike, of wealth and power—
15　Of glory's wreath and pleasure's flower.

These, once, indeed, seemed Beings Divine;
And they, perchance, heard vows of mine,
And saw my offerings on their shrine;
But, careless gifts are seldom prized,
20　And mine were worthily despised.

So, with a ready heart I swore
To seek their altar-stone no more;
And gave my spirit to adore
Thee, ever-present, phantom thing;
25　My slave, my comrade, and my king,

A slave, because I rule thee still;
Incline thee to my changeful will,
And make thy influence good or ill:
A comrade, for by day and night
30　Thou art my intimate delight,—

My darling pain that wounds and sears
And wrings a blessing out from tears
By deadening me to earthly cares;
And yet, a king, though prudence well
35　Have taught thy subject to rebel.

And am I wrong to worship, where
Faith cannot doubt, nor hope despair,
Since my own soul can grant my prayer?
Speak, God of visions, plead for me,
40　And tell why I have chosen thee!
　　—1846

The Old Stoic

Riches I hold in light esteem;
　　And love I laugh to scorn;
And lust of fame was but a dream
　　That vanished with the morn:

5　And if I pray, the only prayer
　　That moves my lips for me
Is, "Leave the heart that now I bear,
　　And give me liberty!"[1]

Yes, as my swift days near their goal,
10　　'Tis all that I implore;

---

[1] *give me liberty!* Cf. Patrick Henry's 1775 speech, in which he recommended that his fellow Virginians rise in arms against British rule: "I know not what course others may take; but as for me, give me liberty or give me death!"

In life and death, a chainless soul,
   With courage to endure.
—1846 (WRITTEN 1841)

My Comforter

Well hast thou spoken, and yet, not taught
   A feeling strange or new;
Thou hast but roused a latent thought,
A cloud-closed beam of sunshine, brought
    To gleam in open view.

5

Deep down, concealed within my soul,
   That light lies hid from men;
Yet, glows unquenched—though shadows roll,
Its gentle ray cannot control,
    About the sullen den.

10

Was I not vexed, in these gloomy ways
   To walk alone so long?
Around me, wretches uttering praise,
Or howling o'er their hopeless days,
    And each with Frenzy's tongue;—

15

A brotherhood of misery,
   Their smiles as sad as sighs;
Whose madness daily maddened me,
Distorting into agony
    The bliss before my eyes!

20

So stood I, in Heaven's glorious sun,
   And in the glare of Hell;
My spirit drank a mingled tone,
Of seraph's° song, and demon's moan;   *angel's*
What my soul bore, my soul alone
    Within itself may tell!

25

Like a soft air, above a sea,
   Tossed by the tempest's stir;
A thaw-wind, melting quietly
The snow-drift, on some wintry lea;
No: what sweet thing resembles thee,
    My thoughtful Comforter?

30

And yet a little longer speak,
   Calm this resentful mood;
And while the savage heart grows meek,
For other token do not seek,
But let the tear upon my cheek
    Evince my gratitude!
—1846

35

[*Loud without the wind was roaring*]

Loud without the wind was roaring
   Through the waned autumnal sky,
Drenching wet, the cold rain pouring
    Spoke of stormy winters nigh.

All too like that dreary eve
   Sighed within repining grief—
Sighed at first—but sighed not long
Sweet—How softly sweet it came!
Wild words of an ancient song—
   Undefined, without a name—

5

10

"It was spring, for the skylark was singing."
Those words they awakened a spell—
They unlocked a deep fountain whose springing
Nor absence nor distance can quell.

In the gloom of a cloudy November
They uttered the music of May—
They kindled the perishing ember
Into fervour that could not decay

15

Awaken on all my dear moorlands
The wind in its glory and pride!
O call me from valleys and highlands
To walk by the hill-river's side!

20

It is swelled with the first snowy weather;
The rocks they are icy and hoar
And darker waves round the long heather
And the fern-leaves are sunny no more

25

There are no yellow-stars on the mountain,
The bluebells have long died away

From the brink of the moss-bedded fountain,
30   From the side of the wintery brae°—   *hillside*

But lovelier than cornfields all waving
In emerald and scarlet and gold
Are the slopes where the north wind is raving
And the glens where I wandered of old—

35   "It was morning; the bright sun was beaming."
How sweetly that brought back to me
The time when nor labour nor dreaming
Broke the sleep of the happy and free

But blithely we rose as the dusk heaven
40   Was melting to amber and blue—
And swift were the wings to our feet given
While we traversed the meadows of dew.

For the moors, for the moors where the short grass
Like velvet beneath us should lie!
45   For the moors, for the moors where each high pass
Rose sunny against the clear sky!

For the moors, where the linnet° was trilling   *songbird*
Its song on the old granite stone—
Where the lark—the wild skylark was filling
50   Every breast with delight like its own.

What language can utter the feeling
That rose when, in exile afar,
On the brow of a lonely hill kneeling
I saw the brown heath growing there.

55   It was scattered and stunted, and told me
That soon even that would be gone
It whispered, "The grim walls enfold me
I have bloomed in my last summer's sun."

But not the loved music whose waking
60   Makes the soul of the Swiss die away
Has a spell more adored and heartbreaking
Than in its half-blighted bells lay—

The spirit that bent 'neath its power
How it longed, how it burned to be free!

65   If I could have wept in that hour
Those tears had been heaven to me—

Well, well the sad minutes are moving
Though loaded with trouble and pain—
And sometime the loved and the loving
70   Shall meet on the mountains again—
—1850 (WRITTEN 1835)

[*A little while, a little while*]

A little while, a little while
The noisy crowd are barred away;
And I can sing and I can smile—
A little while I've holiday!

5   Where wilt thou go my harassed heart?
Full many a land invites thee now;
And places near, and far apart
Have rest for thee, my weary brow—

There is a spot 'mid barren hills
10   Where winter howls and driving rain
But if the dreary tempest chills
There is a light that warms again

The house is old, the trees are bare
And moonless bends the misty dome
15   But what on earth is half so dear—
So longed for as the hearth of home?

The mute bird sitting on the stone,
The dank moss dripping from the wall,
The garden-walk with weeds o'ergrown
20   I love them—how I love them all!

Shall I go there? Or shall I seek
Another clime, another sky.
Where tongues familiar music speak
In accents dear to memory?

25   Yes, as I mused, the naked room,
The flickering firelight died away

And from the midst of cheerless gloom
I passed to bright, unclouded day—

A little and a lone green lane
30 That opened on a common wide
A distant, dreamy, dim blue chain
Of mountains circling every side—

A heaven so clear, an earth so calm,
So sweet, so soft, so hushed an air
35 And, deepening still the dreamlike charm,
Wild moor-sheep feeding everywhere—

That was the scene—I knew it well
I knew the pathways far and near
That winding o'er each billowy swell
40 Marked out the tracks of wandering deer

Could I have lingered but an hour
It well had paid a week of toil
But truth has banished fancy's power
I hear my dungeon bars recoil—

45 Even as I stood with raptured eye
Absorbed in bliss so deep and dear
My hour of rest had fleeted by
And given me back to weary care—
—1850 (WRITTEN 1838)

[Shall Earth no more inspire thee]

Shall Earth no more inspire thee,
   Thou lonely dreamer now?
Since passion may not fire thee
Shall nature cease to bow?

5 Thy mind is ever moving
In regions dark to thee;
Recall its useless roving—
Come back and dwell with me.

I know my mountain breezes
10 Enchant and soothe thee still—

I know my sunshine pleases
Despite thy wayward will.

When day with evening blending
Sinks from the summer sky,
15 I've seen thy spirit bending
In fond idolatry.

I've watched thee every hour;
I know my mighty sway,
I know my magic power
20 To drive thy griefs away.

Few hearts to mortals given
On earth so wildly pine;
Yet none would ask a heaven
More like this earth than thine.

25 Then let my winds caress thee;
Thy comrade let me be—
Since nought beside can bless thee,
Return and dwell with me.
—1850 (WRITTEN 1841)

[No coward soul is mine] [1]

No coward soul is mine
   No trembler in the world's storm-troubled sphere
I see Heaven's glories shine
And Faith shines equal arming me from Fear

5 O God within my breast
Almighty ever-present Deity
Life, that in me hast rest
As I Undying Life, have power in Thee

Vain are the thousand creeds
10 That move men's hearts, unutterably vain,
Worthless as withered weeds
Or idlest froth amid the boundless main

original spelling

1 *No coward soul is mine*   Like much of Brontë's poetry, this poem
was not published until after her death. In preparing the poems for
publication in 1850, Charlotte Brontë made some alterations in
punctuation and syntax. The copy printed here is from the original
1846 manuscript, which is largely unpunctuated.

To waken doubt in one
Holding so fast by thy infinity
15 So surely anchored on
The steadfast rock of Immortality.

With wide-embracing love
Thy spirit animates eternal years
Pervades and broods above,
20 Changes, sustains, dissolves, creates and rears

Though Earth and moon were gone
And suns and universes ceased to be
And thou wert left alone
Every Existence would exist in thee

25 There is not room for Death
Nor atom that his might could render void
Since thou art Being and Breath
And what thou art may never be destroyed.
    —1850 (WRITTEN 1846)

original spelling

Stanzas[1]

Often rebuked, yet always back returning
    To those first feelings that were born with me,
And leaving busy chase of wealth and learning
    For idle dreams of things which cannot be:

5 Today, I will seek not the shadowy region;
    Its unsustaining vastness waxes drear;
And visions rising, legion after legion,
    Bring the unreal world too strangely near.

I'll walk, but not in old heroic traces,
10   And not in paths of high morality,
And not among the half-distinguished faces,
    The clouded forms of long-past history.

I'll walk where my own nature would be leading:
    It vexes me to choose another guide:

15 Where the gray flocks in ferny glens are feeding;
    Where the wild wind blows on the mountain side.

What have those lonely mountains worth revealing?
    More glory and more grief than I can tell:
The earth that wakes *one* human heart to feeling
20   Can centre both the worlds of heaven and hell.
    —1850[2]

[*The night is darkening round me*][3]

The night is darkening round me
    The wild winds coldly blow
But a tyrant spell has bound me
And I cannot cannot go

5 The giant trees are bending
Their bare boughs weighed with snow
And the storm is fast descending
And yet I cannot go

Clouds beyond clouds above me
10 Wastes beyond wastes below
But nothing drear can move me
I will not cannot go

_____

I'll come when thou art saddest
Laid alone in the darkened room
When the mad day's mirth has vanished
And the smile of joy is banished
5 From evening's chilly gloom

I'll come when the heart's real feeling
Has entire unbiased sway
And my influence o'er thee stealing

original spelling

_____

1 *Stanzas* This authorship of "Often rebuked" has been variously credited to Emily, Charlotte, and Anne Brontë; when the poem was first printed it was recorded as having been written by Emily.

2 *1850* Brontë did not record the date on which she composed this poem.

3 *The night … me* Sometimes considered three separate poems, "The Night" is unfinished. Brontë tended even in her published work to punctuate less heavily than most Victorian poets. As this poem demonstrates, the tendency was far more pronounced in her written drafts.

Grief deepening joy congealing
10 Shall bear thy soul away

Listen 'tis just the hour
The awful time for thee
Dost thou not feel upon thy soul
A flood of strange sensations roll
15 Forerunners of a sterner power
Heralds of me

_____

I would have touched the heavenly key
That spoke alike of bliss and thee
I would have woke the entrancing song
But its words died upon my tongue
5 And then I knew that entheal° strain   *hallowed*
Could never speak of joy again
And then I felt
—1902 (WRITTEN 1837)

original spelling (side)

[*I'm happiest when most away*]

I'm happiest when most away
I can bear my soul from its home of clay
On a windy night when the moon is bright
And the eye can wander through worlds of light—

5 When I am not and none beside—
Nor earth nor sea nor cloudless sky—
But only spirit wandering wide
Through infinite immensity.
—1910 (WRITTEN 1838)

[*If grief for grief can touch thee*]

If grief for grief can touch thee,
If answering woe for woe,
If any ruth° can melt thee   *compassion*
Come to me now!

5 I cannot be more lonely,
More drear I cannot be!
My worn heart throbs so wildly
'Twill break for thee—

And when the world despises—
10 When heaven repels my prayer—
Will not mine angel comfort?
Mine idol hear?

Yes by the tears I've poured,
By all my hours of pain
15 O I shall surely win thee
Beloved, again!
—1902 (WRITTEN 1840)

George Eliot
1819 – 1880

George Eliot chose her masculine pen name with good reason: she did not wish to be received by the public as a woman writer and judged by terms thought to be appropriate to women's work. Eliot was a writer who valued sympathy above all other qualities, and one who constructed memorable domestic and romantic scenes; hers was a notable intellectual and philosophical voice that produced perhaps the most remarkable novels of the Victorian period. She was hailed for the extraordinary writing and psychological acuity of such novels as *Adam Bede*, *The Mill on the Floss*, *Middlemarch*, and *Daniel Deronda*, as well as for important translations, criticism, and essays. She was also notorious in her time for her common-law relationship with the biographer, novelist, botanist, and literary and theatrical critic George Henry Lewes. Yet George Eliot's evocations of English provincial life and her acute and sympathetic perceptions of rural people remained immensely popular. As with many Victorians, George Eliot fell out of favor in the modernist period, but for many decades now readers have again been captivated by the portrayal of life in the English Midlands in such works as *The Mill on the Floss*, and by the intellectual and spiritual struggles of characters like Dorothea Brooke, the heroine from the provincial (and fictitious) town of Middlemarch, and Gewndolen Harleth and Daniel Deronda in her last great work.

Mary Anne Evans (she also used Mary Ann and later Marian) was born in rural Warwickshire, England, in 1819, the third child of Christiana Pearson and Robert Evans. This landscape was to figure in almost all her fiction. She was educated at various boarding schools where she distinguished herself as a studious, shy and introspective child. At one school, a compassionate teacher named Maria Lewis took her under her wing and molded her spiritual development, instilling evangelical beliefs that would persist into early adulthood. When her mother died in 1836, her formal education came to an end, but she continued to study theology, languages, philosophy, Romantic poetry, and German literature while caring for her father.

Her close relationship with her father was tested in 1842 when she announced her loss of faith in Christianity and organized religion, after falling under the influence of the freethinking, radical intellectuals Charles and Caroline Bray and Caroline's brother, Charles Hennell. Hennell urged her to translate *The Life of Jesus*, by the German "higher critic" David Friedrich Strauss,; the translation appeared in 1846. This study considered the Bible's texts not as factual histories ordained by God, but rather as myths, the products of people living in a specific historical period trying to find language to articulate their sense of the powers that ruled the universe; essentially, Strauss wrote as a cultural anthropologist of early Christianity. In 1854, she published her translation of Ludwig Feuerbach's *Essence of Christianity* (1854), her only publication to bear the name of Marian Evans on its title page. Here again she continued her radical work of introducing ideas that challenged traditional religious beliefs that were current on the continent to her English readers. Before this work, in 1851, she had become assistant editor of the radical *Westminster Review*, a position she held for two years, helping to restore the magazine to the high intellectual standards it had attained while under the editorship of the philosopher John Stuart Mill. Even after leaving her position at the *Review*, George Eliot continued to contribute many important essays to the magazine, among them "Silly Novels by Lady Novelists" and "The Natural History of German Life" (1856).

In 1851 she met George Henry Lewes, and in 1854 they began to live together (though he was married). The decision to live in a common-law "marriage," as they called it (indeed, George Eliot called herself and became known to many as "Mrs. Lewes"), came at great personal expense; the brother to whom she had once been very close persuaded the entire family to shun her, which they did for the duration of her quarter-century relationship with Lewes. The relationship also constricted her involvement in the literary and intellectual world of London, especially in the early years of her writing career.

George Eliot's novels and shorter fiction (three novellas were published in *Blackwood's Magazine* under her pseudonym and collected in *Scenes of Clerical Life* in 1858) mostly harken back to the early part of the century in pre-industrial England and concentrate on the lives of ordinary people at a time when great changes were on the horizon; indeed, she draws our attention to how tragedy, as well as sublime comedy, may form part of the lives of common people. In a passage in *The Mill on the Floss*, George Eliot explained the appeal of the Midland landscape and its Wordsworthian influence upon her imagination: "These familiar flowers, these well-remembered bird-notes, this sky, with its fitful brightness, these furrowed and grassy fields ... such things as these are the mother tongue of our imagination, the language that is laden with all the subtle inextricable associations the fleeting hours of our childhood left behind them. Our delight in the sunshine on the deep-bladed grass to-day, might be no more than the faint perception of wearied souls, if it were not for the sunshine and the grass in the far-off years which still live in us, and transform our perception into love." These scenes become the sources of the moral imagination, "with its deep immoveable roots in memory." They are also the sources of George Eliot's moral realism. As she wrote in Chapter 17 of *Adam Bede*, her focus was not heroes or sublimely beautiful women, but people who do "the rough work of the world" because human beings need to reverence "that other beauty ... which lies in no secret of proportion, but in the secret of deep human sympathy."

Even though George Eliot was almost forty when she began writing fiction, once she began she was prolific. *Adam Bede* appeared in 1859 to great critical acclaim (Queen Victoria was among its admirers); *The Mill on the Floss* was published in 1860 and *Silas Marner* in 1861; her Renaissance historical novel, *Romola*, in 1863; *Felix Holt, the Radical*, a book about the First Reform Bill, in 1866; a collection of poetry, *The Spanish Gypsy*, in 1868; *Middlemarch* in 1871–72; and another collection of poetry, *The Legend of Jubal and Other Poems*, in 1874. *Daniel Deronda* (1876) was George Eliot's final novel. Her interest in Judaism and in the Hebrew language informed this epic story, set in contemporary England, of a woman who is forced into an oppressive marriage with an aristocrat and of an idealistic young man, the eponymous Daniel, who discovers his Jewish roots and works toward a renewal of the Jewish nation. For the agnostic George Eliot, the appeal of Judaism lay in its role as the foundation of the images and texts that inform a morality divinely human; Judaism was the source of western culture's moral imagination. She may not have been a believer, but her fiction finds much of its life in the tropes and images of the religious imagination as she found them in the King James Bible, Milton, Bunyan, and the English hymns. This most intellectually sophisticated of all Victorian novelists was also one of its most deeply traditional.

In 1878, George Eliot's beloved "husband," as she called Lewes, died. In May of 1880, she married John Walter Cross, a man 20 years her junior. She died in December 1880, and was buried beside Lewes in Highgate Cemetery. Before her death she reconciled with her brother Isaac, who welcomed the "legitimacy" of her marriage to Cross. Five years after her death, Cross published a reverent biography of Mary Anne Evans, entitled *George Eliot's Life as Related in her Letters and Journals*.

⌘⌘⌘

O, May I Join the Choir Invisible

*Longum illud tempus, quum non ero, magis me movet, quam
hoc exiguum.*[1]

CICERO, ad Att., 12.18.

O, may I join the choir invisible
Of those immortal dead who live again
In minds made better by their presence: live
In pulses stirred to generosity,
5   In deeds of daring rectitude, in scorn
For miserable aims that end with self,
In thoughts sublime that pierce the night like stars,
And with their mild persistence urge man's search
To vaster issues.
10   So to live is heaven:
To make undying music in the world,
Breathing as beauteous order that controls
With growing sway the growing life of man.
So we inherit that sweet purity
15   For which we struggled, failed, and agonised
With widening retrospect that bred despair.
Rebellious flesh that would not be subdued,
A vicious parent shaming still its child,
Poor anxious penitence, is quick dissolved;
20   Its discords, quenched by meeting harmonies,
Die in the large and charitable air.
And all our rarer, better, truer self,
That sobbed religiously in yearning song,
That watched to ease the burthen of the world,
25   Laboriously tracing what must be,
And what may yet be better—saw within
A worthier image for the sanctuary,
And shaped it forth before the multitude
Divinely human, raising worship so
30   To higher reverence more mixed with love—
That better self shall live till human Time
Shall fold its eyelids, and the human sky

Be gathered like a scroll within the tomb
Unread forever.
35   This is life to come,
Which martyred men have made more glorious
For us who strive to follow. May I reach
That purest heaven, be to other souls
The cup of strength in some great agony,
40   Enkindle generous ardour, feed pure love,
Beget the smiles that have no cruelty—
Be the sweet presence of a good diffused,
And in diffusion ever more intense.
So shall I join the choir invisible,
45   Whose music is the gladness of the world.
—1867

from *Brother and Sister Sonnets*

SONNET II

School parted us; we never found again
That childish world where our two spirits mingled
Like scents from varying roses that remain
One sweetness, nor can evermore be singled.

5   Yet the twin habit of that early time
Lingered for long about the heart and tongue:
We had been natives of one happy clime,
And its dear accent to our utterance clung.

Till the dire years whose awful name is Change
10   Had grasped our souls still yearning in divorce,
And pitiless shaped them in two forms that range
Two elements which sever their life's course.

    But were another childhood world my share,
    I would be born a little sister there.
—1874

---

[1]   *Longum … exiguum* Latin: "And the great length of time after
I shall cease to be matters more to me than the short time I have
here."

from *Adam Bede*

CHAPTER 17: IN WHICH THE STORY PAUSES A LITTLE

"This Rector of Broxton is little better than a pagan!" I hear one of my readers exclaim. "How much more edifying it would have been if you had made him give Arthur some truly spiritual advice. You might have put into his mouth the most beautiful things—quite as good as reading a sermon."

Certainly I could, if I held it the highest vocation of the novelist to represent things as they never have been and never will be. Then, of course, I might refashion life and character entirely after my own liking; I might select the most unexceptionable type of clergyman, and put my own admirable opinions into his mouth on all occasions. But it happens, on the contrary, that my strongest effort is to avoid any such arbitrary picture, and to give a faithful account of men and things as they have mirrored themselves in my mind. The mirror is doubtless defective; the outlines will sometimes be disturbed, the reflection faint or confused; but I feel as much bound to tell you as precisely as I can what that reflection is, as if I were in the witness-box narrating my experience on oath.

Sixty years ago—it is a long time, so no wonder things have changed—all clergymen were not zealous; indeed there is reason to believe that the number of zealous clergymen was small, and it is probable that if one among the small minority had owned the livings of Broxton and Hayslope in the year 1799, you would have liked him no better than you like Mr. Irwine. Ten to one, you would have thought him a tasteless, indiscreet, methodistical[1] man. It is so very rarely that facts hit that nice medium required by our own enlightened opinions and refined taste! Perhaps you will say, "Do improve the facts a little, then; make them more accordant with those correct views which it is our privilege to possess. The world is just what we like; do touch it up with a tasteful pencil, and make believe it is not quite such a mixed entangled affair. Let all people who hold unexceptionable opinions act unexceptionably. Let your most faulty characters always be on the wrong side, and your virtuous ones on the right. Then we shall see at a glance whom we are to condemn, and whom we are to approve. Then we shall be able to admire, without the slightest disturbance of our prepossessions: we shall hate and despise with that true ruminant relish which belongs to undoubting confidence."

But, my good friend, what will you do then with your fellow parishioner who opposes your husband in the vestry?—with your newly-appointed vicar, whose style of preaching you find painfully below that of his regretted predecessor?—with the honest servant who worries your soul with her one failing?—with your neighbour, Mrs. Green, who was really kind to you in your last illness, but has said several ill-natured things about you since your convalescence?—nay, with your excellent husband himself, who has other irritating habits besides that of not wiping his shoes? These fellow mortals, every one, must be accepted as they are: you can neither straighten their noses, nor brighten their wit, nor rectify their dispositions; and it is these people—amongst whom your life is passed—that it is needful you should tolerate, pity, and love: it is these more or less ugly, stupid, inconsistent people, whose movements of goodness you should be able to admire—for whom you should cherish all possible hopes, all possible patience. And I would not, even if I had the choice, be the clever novelist who could create a world so much better than this, in which we get up in the morning to do our daily work, that you would be likely to turn a harder, colder eye on the dusty streets and the common green fields—on the real breathing men and women, who can be chilled by your indifference or injured by your prejudice, who can be cheered and helped onward by your fellow feeling, your forbearance, your outspoken, brave justice.

So I am content to tell my simple story, without trying to make things seem better than they were; dreading nothing, indeed, but falsity, which, in spite of one's best efforts, there is reason to dread. Falsehood is so easy, truth so difficult. The pencil is conscious of a delightful facility in drawing a griffin[2]—the longer the claws, and the larger the wings, the better; but that marvellous facility which we mistook for genius is apt to forsake us when we want to draw a real unexaggerated

---

[1]   *methodistical* Rigidly adhering to systems and methods.

[2]   *griffin* Mythological creature with features of both an eagle and a lion.

lion. Examine your words well, and you will find that even when you have no motive to be false, it is a very hard thing to say the exact truth, even about your own immediate feelings—much harder than to say something fine about them which is *not* the exact truth.

It is for this rare, precious quality of truthfulness that I delight in many Dutch paintings, which lofty-minded people despise. I find a source of delicious sympathy in these faithful pictures of a monotonous homely existence, which has been the fate of so many more among my fellow mortals than a life of pomp or of absolute indigence, of tragic suffering or of world-stirring actions. I turn, without shrinking, from cloud-borne angels, from prophets, sibyls, and heroic warriors, to an old woman bending over her flowerpot, or eating her solitary dinner, while the noonday light, softened perhaps by a screen of leaves, falls on her mob cap,[1] and just touches the rim of her spinning-wheel, and her stone jug, and all those cheap common things which are the precious necessaries of life to her—or I turn to that village wedding, kept between four brown walls, where an awkward bridegroom opens the dance with a high-shouldered, broad-faced bride, while elderly and middle-aged friends look on, with very irregular noses and lips, and probably with quart-pots in their hands, but with an expression of unmistakeable contentment and goodwill. "Foh!" says my idealistic friend, "what vulgar details! What good is there in taking all these pains to give an exact likeness of old women and clowns? What a low phase of life!—what clumsy, ugly people!"

But bless us, things may be lovable that are not altogether handsome, I hope? I am not at all sure that the majority of the human race have not been ugly, and even among those "lords of their kind," the British, squat figures, ill-shapen nostrils, and dingy complexions are not startling exceptions. Yet there is a great deal of family love amongst us. I have a friend or two whose class of features is such that the Apollo curl[2] on the summit of their brows would be decidedly trying; yet to my certain knowledge tender hearts have beaten for them, and their miniatures—flattering, but still not lovely—are kissed in secret by motherly lips. I have seen many an excellent matron, who could never in her best days have been handsome, and yet she had a packet of yellow love-letters in a private drawer, and sweet children showered kisses on her sallow cheeks. And I believe there have been plenty of young heroes, of middle stature and feeble beards, who have felt quite sure they could never love anything more insignificant than a Diana,[3] and yet have found themselves in middle life happily settled with a wife who waddles. Yes! thank God; human feeling is like the mighty rivers that bless the earth: it does not wait for beauty—it flows with resistless force and brings beauty with it.

All honour and reverence to the divine beauty of form! Let us cultivate it to the utmost in men, women, and children—in our gardens and in our houses. But let us love that other beauty too, which lies in no secret of proportion, but in the secret of deep human sympathy. Paint us an angel, if you can, with a floating violet robe, and a face paled by the celestial light; paint us yet oftener a Madonna, turning her mild face upward and opening her arms to welcome the divine glory; but do not impose on us any aesthetic rules which shall banish from the region of Art those old women scraping carrots with their work-worn hands, those heavy clowns taking holiday in a dingy pot-house,[4] those rounded backs and stupid weather-beaten faces that have bent over the spade and done the rough work of the world—those homes with their tin pans, their brown pitchers, their rough curs, and their clusters of onions. In this world there are so many of these common coarse people, who have no picturesque sentimental wretchedness! It is so needful we should remember their existence, else we may happen to leave them quite out of our religion and philosophy, and frame lofty theories which only fit a world of extremes. Therefore let Art always remind us of them; therefore let us always have men ready to give the loving pains of a life to the faithful representing of commonplace things—men who see beauty in these commonplace things, and delight in showing how kindly the light of heaven falls on them. There are few prophets in the world; few sublimely beautiful women; few heroes. I can't afford to give all my love and reverence to such rarities; I want a great deal of those

---

[1]   *mob cap*   Women's cotton bonnet with a ruffled edge that ties under the chin.

[2]   *Apollo curl*   I.e., curl like that of the Greek god Apollo.

[3]   *Diana*   Roman goddess of the hunt.

[4]   *pot-house*   Tavern.

feelings for my everyday fellow men, especially for the few in the foreground of the great multitude, whose faces I know, whose hands I touch, for whom I have to make way with kindly courtesy. Neither are picturesque lazzaroni[1] or romantic criminals half so frequent as your common labourer, who gets his own bread, and eats it vulgarly but creditably with his own pocketknife. It is more needful that I should have a fibre of sympathy connecting me with that vulgar citizen who weighs out my sugar in a vilely assorted cravat[2] and waistcoat, than with the handsomest rascal in red scarf and green feathers—more needful that my heart should swell with loving admiration at some trait of gentle goodness in the faulty people who sit at the same hearth with me, or in the clergyman of my own parish, who is perhaps rather too corpulent, and in other respects is not an Oberlin[3] or a Tillotson, than at the deeds of heroes whom I shall never know except by hearsay, or at the sublimest abstract of all clerical graces that was ever conceived by an able novelist.

And so I come back to Mr. Irwine, with whom I desire you to be in perfect charity, far as he may be from satisfying your demands on the clerical character. Perhaps you think he was not—as he ought to have been—a living demonstration of the benefits attached to a national church? But I am not sure of that; at least I know that the people in Broxton and Hayslope would have been very sorry to part with their clergyman, and that most faces brightened at his approach; and until it can be proved that hatred is a better thing for the soul than love, I must believe that Mr. Irwine's influence in his parish was a more wholesome one than that of the zealous Mr. Ryde, who came there twenty years afterwards, when Mr. Irwine had been gathered to his fathers. It is true, Mr. Ryde insisted strongly on the doctrines of the Reformation,[4] visited his flock a great

deal in their own homes, and was severe in rebuking the aberrations of the flesh—put a stop, indeed, to the Christmas rounds of the church singers, as promoting drunkenness, and too light a handling of sacred things. But I gathered from Adam Bede, to whom I talked of these matters in his old age, that few clergymen could be less successful in winning the hearts of their parishioners than Mr. Ryde. They learned a great many notions about doctrine from him, so that almost every churchgoer under fifty began to distinguish as well between the genuine gospel and what did not come precisely up to that standard, as if he had been born and bred a Dissenter;[5] and for some time after his arrival there seemed to be quite a religious movement in that quiet rural district. "But," said Adam, "I've seen pretty clear, ever since I was a young un, as religion's something else besides notions. It isn't notions sets people doing the right thing—it's feelings. It's the same with the notions in religion as it is with mathematics—a man may be able to work problems straight off in's head as he sits by the fire and smokes his pipe; but if he has to make a machine or a building, he must have a will and a resolution, and love something else better than his own ease. Somehow, the congregation began to fall off, and people began to speak light o' Mr. Ryde. I believe he meant right at bottom; but, you see, he was sourish-tempered, and was for beating down prices with the people as worked for him; and his preaching wouldn't go down well with that sauce. And he wanted to be like my lord judge i' the parish, punishing folks for doing wrong; and he scolded 'em from the pulpit as if he'd been a Ranter,[6] and yet he couldn't abide the Dissenters, and was a deal more set against 'em than Mr. Irwine was. And then he didn't keep within his income, for he seemed to think at first go-off that six hundred a year was to make him as big a man as Mr. Donnithorne; that's a sore mischief I've often seen with the poor curates jumping into a bit of a living all of a sudden. Mr. Ryde was a deal thought on at a distance, I believe, and he wrote books, but as for mathematics and the natur o' things, he was as ignorant as a woman. He was

---

1   *lazzaroni* Vagabonds or beggars.

2   *cravat* Neck scarf.

3   *Oberlin* German pastor J.F. Oberlin (1740–1826), who cared for Livonian author J.M.R. Lenz, and about whom Eliot might have read in Georg Büchner's novella *Lenz* (1850); *Tillotson* John Tillotson (1630–94), Archbishop of Canterbury.

4   *Reformation* Sixteenth-century religious movement that sought to reform the Catholic Church and eventually established the Protestant religion.

5   *Dissenter* Member of a Protestant sect that rebelled against and eventually broke with the Church of England.

6   *Ranter* Member of a religious sect called "Primitive Methodist," whose name arose from a tradition of singing in the streets.

very knowing about doctrines, and used to call 'em the bulwarks of the Reformation, but I've always mistrusted that sort o' learning as leaves folks foolish and unreasonable about business. Now Mester Irwine was as different as could be, as quick!—he understood what you meant in a minute; and he knew all about building, and could see when you'd made a good job. And he behaved as much like a gentleman to the farmers, and th' old women and the labourers, as he did to the gentry. You never saw *him* interfering and scolding, and trying to play th' emperor. Ah! he was a fine man as ever you set eyes on, and so kind to's mother and sisters. That poor sickly Miss Anne—he seemed to think more of her than of anybody else in the world. There wasn't a soul in the parish had a word to say against him; and his servants stayed with him till they were so old and pottering, he had to hire other folks to do their work."

"Well," I said, "that was an excellent way of preaching in the weekdays; but I daresay, if your old friend Mr. Irwine were to come to life again, and get into the pulpit next Sunday, you would be rather ashamed that he didn't preach better after all your praise of him."

"Nay, nay," said Adam, broadening his chest and throwing himself back in his chair, as if he were ready to meet all inferences, "nobody has ever heard me say Mr. Irwine was much of a preacher. He didn't go into deep speritial experience; and I know there's a deal in a man's inward life as you can't measure by the square, and say, 'Do this and that'll follow,' and, 'Do that and this'll follow.' There's things go on in the soul, and times when feelings come into you like a rushing mighty wind, as the Scripture says, and part your life in two a'most, so as you look back on yourself as if you was somebody else. Those are things as you can't bottle up in a 'do this' and 'do that'; and I'll go so far with the strongest Methodist ever you'll find. That shows me there's deep speritial things in religion. You can't make much out wi' talking about it, but you feel it. Mr. Irwine didn't go into those things; he preached short moral sermons, and that was all. But then he acted pretty much up to what he said; he didn't set up for being so different from other folks one day, and then be as like 'em as two peas the next. And he made folks love him and respect him, and that was better nor stirring up

their gall wi' being over busy. Mrs. Poyser used to say—you know she would have her word about everything—she said, Mr. Irwine was like a good meal o' victual, you were the better for him without thinking on it, and Mr. Ryde was like a dose o' physic, he gripped you and worreted[1] you, and after all he left you much the same."

"But didn't Mr. Ryde preach a great deal more about that spiritual part of religion that you talk of, Adam? Couldn't you get more out of his sermons than out of Mr. Irwine's?"

"Eh, I knowna. He preached a deal about doctrines. But I've seen pretty clear ever since I was a young un, as religion's something else besides doctrines and notions. I look at it as if the doctrines was like finding names for your feelings, so as you can talk of 'em when you've never known 'em, just as a man may talk o' tools when he knows their names, though he's never so much as seen 'em, still less handled 'em. I've heard a deal o' doctrine i' my time, for I used to go after the dissenting preachers along wi' Seth, when I was a lad o' seventeen, and got puzzling myself a deal about th' Arminians and the Calvinists. The Wesleyans,[2] you know, are strong Arminians; and Seth, who could never abide anything harsh, and was always for hoping the best, held fast by the Wesleyans from the very first; but I thought I could pick a hole or two in their notions, and I got disputing wi' one o' the class leaders down at Treddles'on, and harassed him so, first o' this side and then o' that, till at last he said, 'Young man, it's the devil making use o' your pride and conceit as a weapon to war against the simplicity o' the truth.' I couldn't help laughing then, but as I was going home, I thought the man wasn't far wrong. I began to see as all this weighing and sifting what this text means and that text means, and whether folks are saved all by God's grace, or whether there goes an ounce o' their own will to 't, was no part o' real religion at all. You may talk o' these things for hours on

---

[1]   *worreted*   Annoyed.

[2]   *Arminians*   Followers of Dutch Protestant theologian James Arminius (1560–1609), who opposed certain Calvinist doctrines, such as predestination, original sin, and the notion that God is the creator of both good and evil; *Calvinists*   Also called "Reformed Protestants"; Christian followers of John Calvin (1509–64); *Wesleyans*   Methodists; followers of John Wesley (1603–91), who embraced Arminian theology and founded Methodism.

end, and you'll only be all the more coxy[1] and conceited for 't. So I took to going nowhere but to church, and hearing nobody but Mr. Irwine, for he said nothing but what was good, and what you'd be the wiser for remembering. And I found it better for my soul to be humble before the mysteries o' God's dealings, and not be making a clatter about what I could never understand. And they're poor foolish questions after all; for what have we got either inside or outside of us but what comes from God? If we've got a resolution to do right, He gave it us, I reckon, first or last; but I see plain enough we shall never do it without a resolution, and that's enough for me."

Adam, you perceive, was a warm admirer, perhaps a partial judge, of Mr. Irwine, as, happily, some of us still are of the people we have known familiarly. Doubtless it will be despised as a weakness by that lofty order of minds who pant after the ideal, and are oppressed by a general sense that their emotions are of too exquisite a character to find fit objects among their everyday fellow men. I have often been favoured with the confidence of these select natures, and find them concur in the experience that great men are over-estimated and small men are insupportable; that if you would love a woman without ever looking back on your love as a folly, she must die while you are courting her; and if you would maintain the slightest belief in human heroism, you must never make a pilgrimage to see the hero. I confess I have often meanly shrunk from confessing to these accomplished and acute gentlemen what my own experience has been. I am afraid I have often smiled with hypocritical assent, and gratified them with an epigram on the fleeting nature of our illusions, which anyone moderately acquainted with French literature can command at a moment's notice. Human converse, I think some wise man has remarked, is not rigidly sincere. But I herewith discharge my conscience, and

declare that I have had quite enthusiastic movements of admiration towards old gentlemen who spoke the worst English, who were occasionally fretful in their temper, and who had never moved in a higher sphere of influence than that of parish overseer; and that the way in which I have come to the conclusion that human nature is lovable—the way I have learnt something of its deep pathos, its sublime mysteries—has been by living a great deal among people more or less commonplace and vulgar, of whom you would perhaps hear nothing very surprising if you were to inquire about them in the neighbourhoods where they dwelt. Ten to one most of the small shopkeepers in their vicinity saw nothing at all in them. For I have observed this remarkable coincidence, that the select natures who pant after the ideal, and find nothing in pantaloons or petticoats great enough to command their reverence and love, are curiously in unison with the narrowest and pettiest. For example, I have often heard Mr. Gedge, the landlord of the Royal Oak, who used to turn a bloodshot eye on his neighbours in the village of Shepperton, sum up his opinion of the people in his own parish—and they were all the people he knew—in these emphatic words: "Ay, sir, I've said if often, and I'll say it again, they're a poor lot i' this parish—a poor lot, sir, big and little." I think he had a dim idea that if he could migrate to a distant parish, he might find neighbours worthy of him; and indeed he did subsequently transfer himself to the Saracen's Head, which was doing a thriving business in the back street of a neighbouring market-town. But, oddly enough, he has found the people up that back street of precisely the same stamp as the inhabitants of Shepperton—"a poor lot, sir, big and little, and them as comes for a go o' gin are no better than them as comes for a pint o' twopenny[2]—a poor lot."

—1859

---

[1]   *coxy* cocky.

[2]   *twopenny* Ale.

JOHN RUSKIN

1819 – 1900

John Ruskin was a painter and a poet, author of dozens of books on the arts and sciences, and a dedicated believer in fundamental links between all disciplines. Famous as an art, cultural, and social critic, Ruskin synthesized subjects in fluid and poetic ways, and he exerted an enormous influence on the aesthetic, philosophical, and political sensibilities of his day. This influence bore heavily on the work of the Pre-Raphaelite painters, notably Dante Gabriel Rossetti, John Everett Millais, and William Holman Hunt. In addition, Ruskin's opposition to industrialization and his ideas about the sacredness of human work inspired William Morris and the Arts and Crafts Movement. Mahatma Gandhi, who translated Ruskin's *Unto the Last* into Gujarati, said about the work's effect on him: "I believe that I discovered some of my deepest convictions reflecting on this great book of Ruskin's, [... which] captured me and made me transform my life."

Ruskin was born in London in 1819 to Margaret Cox and John James Ruskin, a successful wine merchant. Possibly because the couple bore John in midlife and had no other children, the Evangelical Ruskins raised their child in an overprotective and cloistered manner, allowing him neither friends nor toys. The young John's schooling, administered by his mother, was strict and included hours of Bible study every day (the two would read the entire Bible and then resume from the beginning), while his father, also a stern Evangelical, procured tutors for the arts and languages. When Ruskin came of age, he attended Oxford (where he won the Newdigate Prize for poetry), but even then his mother accompanied him, living in rooms nearby, and his father joined the two every weekend.

Even though he had a talent for both poetry and painting, Ruskin realized after graduation that he did not wish to pursue either as a career. His admiration for the British painter J.M.W. Turner, however, led to his first work of art criticism, which evolved into the five-volume *Modern Painters*, published over a period of more than a decade. The first volume of *Modern Painters* was a defense of Turner's "fidelity" to his landscapes and his ability to see and express "truth" in nature. It was not only Ruskin's aesthetic analyses that attracted attention, however, but also his elegant and engaging prose style.

In 1848, Ruskin entered into a disastrous marriage with Euphemia ("Effie") Chalmers, which ended six years later in an annulment on the grounds that the marriage had never been consummated. The following year Effie married the painter John Everett Millais. Throughout his life, Ruskin's relationships with women were fraught, most notably his relationship with Rose La Touche, whom he met (and with whom he apparently fell in love) in 1858 when she was only nine years old. Ruskin proposed marriage to Rose in 1866, but because he had lost his religious faith (he said he had been "unconverted" while attending church in Turin) and she was a strict Evangelical, she ultimately rejected his offer. Not long after her death in 1875, Ruskin suffered an attack of madness, the first of many such episodes he experienced throughout his life.

Although there were times when Ruskin could not function due to mental illness, he was astonishingly prolific: his *Collected Works* fill thirty-nine volumes, and he wrote thousands of letters. His books on architecture, *The Seven Lamps of Architecture* (1849) and the three-volume *Stones of Venice* (1851–53), were so influential that they provoked a revival of Gothic architecture that in some ways ran counter to his philosophies. Ruskin felt that the hand of God was present in those who labored on the stone buildings of the Middle Ages, and that the magnificent Gothic architecture of Venice was a manifestation of a virtuous and honorable people. His writing inspired many to support the preservation and restoration of architectural treasures. Ruskin himself, however, promoted a social, rather than simply an architectural, restoration.

Ruskin's attacks on society became increasingly focused on the effects of modern production, and he became an outspoken challenger of the Industrial Age. His views on economic and social reform, radical at the time, have affected social thinking to this day. Ruskin was strongly opposed to *laissez faire* economics and advocated the organization of labor (the founders of the Labour Party in Britain attributed their ideas to Ruskin), cooperative business ventures, an old-age pension, a minimum wage, public libraries and art galleries, a national health service, equal education opportunities, and pollution control, among many other initiatives. In 1878, Ruskin founded the Guild of St. George, an organization that still exists today, in order to educate the public and to preserve and support small businesses and the production of local crafts.

After writing and lecturing throughout the 1860s, Ruskin was offered the first Slade Professorship of Fine Arts at Oxford, where he delivered (and subsequently published) many famous lectures and speeches to awestruck students, including the young Oscar Wilde. During this decade he also began a series of letters addressed to English laborers, published as *Fors Clavigera*. Ruskin was forced to resign his position at Oxford in 1880 due to mental illness, and although he resumed his professorship for a brief period and published two final books of lectures, *The Pleasures of England* and *The Art of England*, these years were not good to him. He managed to write many installments of his brilliant autobiography, *Praeterita*, but it remained unfinished. After a long illness he died in 1900. Although Westminster Abbey offered a resting place, Ruskin's last wishes were honored, and he was buried near his home in the Coniston graveyard. For the great Russian writer Leo Tolstoy, and for many others, Ruskin's legacy remained alive: "Ruskin was one of the most remarkable of men, not only of England and our time but of all countries and all times. He was one of those rare men who think with their hearts, and so he thought and said not only what he himself had seen and felt, but what everyone will think and say in the future."

⌘ ⌘ ⌘

from *Modern Painters*

A DEFINITION OF GREATNESS IN ART

Painting, or art generally, as such, with all its technicalities, difficulties, and particular ends, is nothing but a noble and expressive language, invaluable as the vehicle of thought, but by itself nothing. He who has learned what is commonly considered the whole art of painting, that is, the art of representing any natural object faithfully, has as yet only learned the language by which his thoughts are to be expressed. He has done just as much towards being that which we ought to respect as a great painter, as a man who has learned how to express himself grammatically and melodiously has towards being a great poet. The language is, indeed, more difficult of acquirement in the one case than in the other, and possesses more power of delighting the sense, while it speaks to the intellect; but it is, nevertheless, nothing more than language, and all those excellences which are peculiar to the painter as such, are merely what rhythm, melody, precision, and force are in the words of the orator and the poet, necessary to their greatness, but not the tests of their greatness. It is not by the mode of representing and saying, but by what is represented and said, that the respective greatness either of the painter or the writer is to be finally determined. . . .

So that, if I say that the greatest picture is that which conveys to the mind of the spectator the greatest number of the greatest ideas, I have a definition which will include as subjects of comparison every pleasure which art is capable of conveying. If I were to say, on the contrary, that the best picture was that which most closely imitated nature, I should assume that art could only please by imitating nature; and I should cast out of the pale of criticism those parts of works of art which are not imitative, that is to say, intrinsic beauties of colour and form, and those works of art wholly, which, like the Arabesques of Raffaelle[1] in the Loggias,[2] are not imitative at all. Now, I want a definition of art wide enough to include all its varieties of aim. I do not say, therefore, that the art is greatest which gives most pleasure, because perhaps there is some art whose end is to teach, and not to please. I do not say that the art is greatest which teaches us most, because perhaps there is some art whose end is to please, and not to teach. I do not say that the art is greatest which imitates best, because perhaps there is some art whose end is to create and not to imitate. But I say that the art is greatest which conveys to the mind of the spectator, by any means whatsoever, the greatest number of the greatest ideas; and I call an idea great in proportion as it is received by a higher faculty of the mind, and as it more fully occupies, and in occupying, exercises and exalts, the faculty by which it is received.

If this, then, be the definition of great art, that of a great artist naturally follows. He is the greatest artist who has embodied, in the sum of his works, the greatest number of the greatest ideas. . . .

---

[1]   *Raffaelle*   I.e., Raphael (1483–1520), Italian Renaissance painter.

[2]   *Loggias*   Open-air galleries.

I believe it is a result of the experience of all artists, that it is the easiest thing in the world to give a certain degree of depth and transparency to water; but that it is next to impossible, to give a full impression of surface. If no reflection be given, a ripple being supposed, the water looks like lead: if reflection be given, it, in nine cases out of ten, looks *morbidly* clear and deep, so that we always go down *into* it, even when the artist most wishes us to glide *over* it. Now, this difficulty arises from the very same circumstance which occasions the frequent failure in effect of the best-drawn foregrounds … the change, namely, of focus necessary in the eye in order to receive rays of light coming from different distances. Go to the edge of a pond in a perfectly calm day, at some place where there is duckweed floating on the surface, not thick, but a leaf here and there. Now, you may either see in the water the reflection of the sky, or you may see the duckweed; but you cannot, by any effort, see both together. If you look for the reflection, you will be sensible of a sudden change or effort in the eye, by which it adapts itself to the reception of the rays which have come all the way from the clouds, have struck on the water, and so been sent up again to the eye. The focus you adopt is one fit for great distance; and, accordingly, you will feel that you are looking down a great way under the water, while the leaves of the duckweed, though they lie upon the water at the very spot on which you are gazing so intently, are felt only as a vague uncertain interruption, causing a little confusion in the image below, but entirely undistinguishable as leaves, and even their colour unknown and unperceived. Unless you think of them, you will not even feel that anything interrupts your sight, so excessively slight is their effect. If, on the other hand, you make up your mind to look for the leaves of the duckweed, you will perceive an instantaneous change in the effort of the eye, by which it becomes adapted to receive near rays, those which have only come from the surface of the pond. You will then see the delicate leaves of the duckweed with perfect clearness, and in vivid green; but, while you do so, you will be able to perceive nothing of the reflections in the very water on which they float, nothing but a vague flashing and melting of light and dark hues, without form or meaning, which to investigate, or find out what they mean or are, you must quit your hold of the duckweed, and plunge down.

Hence it appears, that whenever we see plain reflections of comparatively distant objects, in near water, we cannot possibly see the surface, and *vice versa;* so that when in a painting we give the reflections with the same clearness with which they are visible in nature, we presuppose the effort of the eye to look under the surface, and, of course, destroy the surface, and induce an effect of clearness which, perhaps, the artist has not particularly wished to attain, but which he has found himself forced into, by his reflections, in spite of himself. And the reason of this effect of clearness appearing preternatural is, that people are not in the habit of looking at water with the distant focus adapted to the reflections, unless by particular effort. We invariably, under ordinary circumstances, use the surface focus; and, in consequence, receive nothing more than a vague and confused impression of the reflected colours and lines, however clearly, calmly, and vigorously all may be defined underneath, if we choose to look for them. We do not look for them, but glide along over the surface, catching only playing light and capricious colour for evidence of reflection, except where we come to images of objects close to the surface, which the surface focus is of course adapted to receive; and these we see clearly, as of the weeds on the shore, or of sticks rising out of the water, etc. Hence, the ordinary effect of water is only to be rendered by giving the reflections of the *margin* clear and distinct (so clear they usually are in nature, that it is impossible to tell where the water begins); but the moment we touch the reflection of distant objects, as of high trees or clouds, that instant we must become vague and uncertain in drawing, and, though vivid in colour and light as the object itself, quite indistinct in form and feature. If we take such a piece of water as that in the foreground of Turner's[1] Château of Prince Albert, the first impression from it is, "What a wide *surface!*" We glide over it a quarter of a mile into the picture before we know where we are, and yet the water is as calm and crystalline as a mirror; but we are not allowed to tumble into it, and gasp for breath as we go down, we are kept upon the surface, though

that surface is flashing and radiant with every hue of cloud, and sun, and sky, and foliage. But the secret is in the drawing of these reflections. We cannot tell, when we look *at* them and *for* them, what they mean. They have all character, and are evidently reflections of something definite and determined; but yet they are all uncertain and inexplicable; playing colour and palpitating shade, which, though we recognize them in an instant for images of something, and feel that the water is bright, and lovely, and calm, we cannot penetrate nor interpret; we are not allowed to go down to them, and we repose, as we should in nature, upon the lustre of the level surface. It is in this power of saying everything, and yet saying nothing too plainly, that the perfection of art here, as in all other cases, consists.

—1843

from *The Stones of Venice*

THE NATURE OF GOTHIC

… In the definition proposed, I shall only endeavour to analyze the idea which I suppose already to exist in the reader's mind. We all have some notion, most of us a very determined one, of the meaning of the term Gothic, but I know that many persons have this idea in their minds without being able to define it: that is to say, understanding generally that Westminster Abbey is Gothic, and St. Paul's is not, that Strasburg Cathedral is Gothic, and St. Peter's is not, they have, nevertheless, no clear notion of what it is that they recognize in the one or miss in the other, such as would enable them to say how far the work at Westminster or Strasburg is good and pure of its kind; still less to say of any nondescript building, like St. James's Palace or Windsor Castle, how much right Gothic element there is in it, and how much wanting. And I believe this inquiry to be a pleasant and profitable one; and that there will be found something more than usually interesting in tracing out this grey, shadowy, many-pinnacled image of the Gothic spirit within us; and discerning what fellowship there is between it and our Northern hearts. And if, at any point of the inquiry, I should interfere with any of the reader's

---

[1] *Turner* J.M.W. Turner (1775–1851), English landscape artist.

previously formed conceptions, and use the term Gothic in any sense which he would not willingly attach to it, I do not ask him to accept, but only to examine and understand, my interpretation, as necessary to the intelligibility of what follows in the rest of the work. …

I believe, then, that the characteristic or moral elements of Gothic are the following, placed in the order of their importance:

1. Savageness.
2. Changefulness.
3. Naturalism.
4. Grotesqueness.
5. Rigidity.
6. Redundance.

These characters are here expressed as belonging to the building; as belonging to the builder, they would be expressed thus: —1. Savageness or Rudeness. 2. Love of Change. 3. Love of Nature. 4. Disturbed Imagination. 5. Obstinacy. 6. Generosity. And I repeat, that the withdrawal of any one, or any two, will not at once destroy the Gothic character of a building, but the removal of a majority of them will. I shall proceed to examine them in their order.

(1.) Savageness. I am not sure when the word "Gothic" was first generically applied to the architecture of the North; but I presume that, whatever the date of its original usage, it was intended to imply reproach, and express the barbaric character of the nations among whom that architecture arose. It never implied that they were literally of Gothic lineage, far less that their architecture had been originally invented by the Goths themselves; but it did imply that they and their buildings together exhibited a degree of sternness and rudeness, which, in contradistinction to the character of Southern and Eastern nations, appeared like a perpetual reflection of the contrast between the Goth and the Roman in their first encounter. And when that fallen Roman, in the utmost impotence of his luxury, and insolence of his guilt, became the model for the imitation of civilized Europe, at the close of the so-called Dark ages, the word Gothic became a term of unmitigated contempt, not unmixed with aversion. From that contempt, by the exertion of the antiquaries

and architects of this century, Gothic architecture has been sufficiently vindicated; and perhaps some among us, in our admiration of the magnificent science of its structure, and sacredness of its expression, might desire that the term of ancient reproach should be withdrawn, and some other, of more apparent honourableness, adopted in its place. There is no chance, as there is no need, of such a substitution. As far as the epithet was used scornfully, it was used falsely; but there is no reproach in the word, rightly understood; on the contrary, there is a profound truth, which the instinct of mankind almost unconsciously recognizes. It is true, greatly and deeply true, that the architecture of the North is rude and wild; but it is not true, that, for this reason, we are to condemn it, or despise. Far otherwise: I believe it is in this very character that it deserves our profoundest reverence.

The charts of the world which have been drawn up by modern science have thrown into a narrow space the expression of a vast amount of knowledge, but I have never yet seen any one pictorial enough to enable the spectator to imagine the kind of contrast in physical character which exists between Northern and Southern countries. We know the differences in detail, but we have not that broad glance and grasp which would enable us to feel them in their fulness. We know that gentians[1] grow on the Alps, and olives on the Apennines; but we do not enough conceive for ourselves that variegated mosaic of the world's surface which a bird sees in its migration, that difference between the district of the gentian and of the olive which the stork and the swallow see far off, as they lean upon the sirocco wind.[2] Let us, for a moment, try to raise ourselves even above the level of their flight, and imagine the Mediterranean lying beneath us like an irregular lake, and all its ancient promontories sleeping in the sun: here and there an angry spot of thunder, a grey stain of storm, moving upon the burning field; and here and there a fixed wreath of white volcano smoke, surrounded by its circle of ashes; but for the most part a great peacefulness of light, Syria and Greece, Italy and Spain, laid like pieces of a golden pavement into the sea-blue, chased, as we stoop nearer to them, with bossy beaten work of

---

[1]   *gentians* Flowers.

[2]   *sirocco wind* Hot, moist wind from North Africa.

mountain chains, and glowing softly with terraced gardens, and flowers heavy with frankincense, mixed among masses of laurel, and orange, and plumy palm, that abate with their grey-green shadows the burning of the marble rocks, and of the ledges of porphyry[1] sloping under lucent sand. Then let us pass farther towards the north, until we see the orient colours change gradually into a vast belt of rainy green, where the pastures of Switzerland, and poplar valleys of France, and dark forests of the Danube and Carpathians stretch from the mouths of the Loire to those of the Volga, seen through clefts in grey swirls of rain-cloud and flaky veils of the mist of the brooks, spreading low along the pasture lands: and then, farther north still, to see the earth heave into mighty masses of leaden rock and heathy moor, bordering with a broad waste of gloomy purple that belt of field and wood, and splintering into irregular and grisly islands amidst the northern seas, beaten by storm, and chilled by ice-drift, and tormented by furious pulses of contending tide, until the roots of the last forests fail from among the hill ravines, and the hunger of the north wind bites their peaks into barrenness; and, at last, the wall of ice, durable like iron, sets, deathlike, its white teeth against us out of the polar twilight. And, having once traversed in thought this gradation of the zoned iris of the earth in all its material vastness, let us go down nearer to it, and watch the parallel change in the belt of animal life; the multitudes of swift and brilliant creatures that glance in the air and sea, or tread the sands of the southern zone; striped zebras and spotted leopards, glistening serpents, and birds arrayed in purple and scarlet. Let us contrast their delicacy and brilliancy of colour, and swiftness of motion, with the frost-cramped strength, and shaggy covering, and dusky plumage of the northern tribes; contrast the Arabian horse with the Shetland, the tiger and leopard with the wolf and bear, the antelope with the elk, the bird of paradise with the osprey; and then, submissively acknowledging the great laws by which the earth and all that it bears are ruled throughout their being, let us not condemn, but rejoice in the expression by man of his own rest in the statutes of the lands that gave him birth. Let us watch him with reverence as he sets side by side the burning gems, and smoothes with soft sculpture the

jasper pillars, that are to reflect a ceaseless sunshine, and rise into a cloudless sky: but not with less reverence let us stand by him, when, with rough strength and hurried stroke, he smites an uncouth animation out of the rocks which he has torn from among the moss of the moorland, and heaves into the darkened air the pile of iron buttress and rugged wall, instinct with work of an imagination as wild and wayward as the northern sea; creatures of ungainly shape and rigid limb, but full of wolfish life; fierce as the winds that beat, and changeful as the clouds that shade them. ...

In ... the first volume of this work, it was noticed that the systems of architectural ornament, properly so called, might be divided into three:—i. Servile ornament, in which the execution or power of the inferior workman is entirely subjected to the intellect of the higher;—2. Constitutional ornament, in which the executive inferior power is, to a certain point, emancipated and independent, having a will of its own, yet confessing its inferiority and rendering obedience to higher powers;—and 3. Revolutionary ornament, in which no executive inferiority is admitted at all. I must here explain the nature of these divisions at somewhat greater length.

Of Servile ornament, the principal schools are the Greek, Ninevite, and Egyptian; but their servility is of different kinds. The Greek master-workman was far advanced in knowledge and power above the Assyrian or Egyptian. Neither he nor those for whom he worked could endure the appearance of imperfection in anything; and, therefore, what ornament he appointed to be done by those beneath him was composed of mere geometrical forms—balls, ridges, and perfectly symmetrical foliage—which could be executed with absolute precision by line and rule, and were as perfect in their way, when completed, as his own figure sculpture. The Assyrian and Egyptian, on the contrary, less cognizant of accurate form in anything, were content to allow their figure sculpture to be executed by inferior workmen, but lowered the method of its treatment to a standard which every workman could reach, and then trained him by discipline so rigid, that there was no chance of his falling beneath the standard appointed. The Greek gave to the lower workman no subject which he could not perfectly execute. The

[1] *porphyry* Red crystalline rock.

Assyrian gave him subjects which he could only execute imperfectly, but fixed a legal standard for his imperfection. The workman was, in both systems, a slave.

——But in the mediaeval, or especially Christian, system of ornament, this slavery is done away with altogether; Christianity having recognized, in small things as well as great, the individual value of every soul. But it not only recognizes its value; it confesses its imperfection, in only bestowing dignity upon the acknowledgment of unworthiness. That admission of lost power and fallen nature, which the Greek or Ninevite felt to be intensely painful, and, as far as might be, altogether refused, the Christian makes daily and hourly, contemplating the fact of it without fear, as tending, in the end, to God's greater glory. Therefore, to every spirit which Christianity summons to her service, her exhortation is: Do what you can, and confess frankly what you are unable to do; neither let your effort be shortened for fear of failure, nor your confession silenced for fear of shame. And it is, perhaps, the principal admirableness of the Gothic schools of architecture, that they thus receive the results of the labour of inferior minds; and out of fragments full of imperfection, and betraying that imperfection in every touch, indulgently raise up a stately and unaccusable whole. . . .

And now, reader, look round this English room of yours, about which you have been proud so often, because the work of it was so good and strong, and the ornaments of it so finished. Examine again all those accurate mouldings, and perfect polishings, and unerring adjustments of the seasoned wood and tempered steel. Many a time you have exulted over them, and thought how great England was, because her slightest work was done so thoroughly. Alas! if read rightly, these perfectnesses are signs of a slavery in our England a thousand times more bitter and more degrading than that of the scourged African, or helot[1] Greek. Men may be beaten, chained, tormented, yoked like cattle, slaughtered like summer flies, and yet remain in one sense, and the best sense, free. But to smother their souls with them, to blight and hew into rotting pollards[2] the suckling branches of their human intelligence, to make the flesh and skin which, after the worm's work on it, is to see God, into leathern thongs to yoke machinery with—this is to be slave-masters indeed; and there might be more freedom in England, though her feudal lords' lightest words were worth men's lives, and though the blood of the vexed husbandman dropped in the furrows of her fields, than there is while the animation of her multitudes is sent like fuel to feed the factory smoke, and the strength of them is given daily to be wasted into the fineness of a web, or racked into the exactness of a line.

And, on the other hand, go forth again to gaze upon the old cathedral front, where you have smiled so often at the fantastic ignorance of the old sculptors: examine once more those ugly goblins, and formless monsters, and stern statues, anatomiless and rigid; but do not mock at them, for they are signs of the life and liberty of every workman who struck the stone; a freedom of thought, and rank in scale of being, such as no laws, no charters, no charities can secure; but which it must be the first aim of all Europe at this day to regain for her children. . . .

We have much studied and much perfected, of late, the great civilized invention of the division of labour; only we give it a false name. It is not, truly speaking, the labour that is divided; but the men: divided into mere segments of men—broken into small fragments and crumbs of life; so that all the little piece of intelligence that is left in a man is not enough to make a pin, or a nail, but exhausts itself in making the point of a pin or the head of a nail. Now it is a good and desirable thing, truly, to make many pins in a day; but if we could only see with what crystal sand their points were polished—sand of human soul, much to be magnified before it can be discerned for what it is—we should think there might be some loss in it also. And the great cry that rises from all our manufacturing cities, louder than their furnace blast, is all in very deed for this— that we manufacture everything there except men; we blanch cotton, and strengthen steel, and refine sugar, and shape pottery; but to brighten, to strengthen, to refine, or to form a single living spirit, never enters into

---

[1]   *helot* Of a class of serfs, falling between slave and citizen in the Spartan social hierarchy.

[2]   *pollards* Trees whose branches have been lopped off to shape them.

our estimate of advantages. And all the evil to which that cry is urging our myriads can be met only in one way: not by teaching nor preaching, for to teach them is but to show them their misery, and to preach to them, if we do nothing more than preach, is to mock at it. It can be met only by a right understanding, on the part of all classes, of what kinds of labour are good for men, raising them, and making them happy; by a determined sacrifice of such convenience, or beauty, or cheapness as is to be got only by the degradation of the workman; and by equally determined demand for the products and results of healthy and ennobling labour.

And how, it will be asked, are these products to be recognized, and this demand to be regulated? Easily: by the observance of three broad and simple rules:

1. Never encourage the manufacture of any article not absolutely necessary, in the production of which *Invention* has no share.

2. Never demand an exact finish for its own sake, but only for some practical or noble end.

3. Never encourage imitation or copying of any kind, except for the sake of preserving records of great works.

The second of these principles is the only one which directly rises out of the consideration of our immediate subject; but I shall briefly explain the meaning and extent of the first also, reserving the enforcement of the third for another place.

1. Never encourage the manufacture of anything not necessary, in the production of which invention has no share.

For instance. Glass beads are utterly unnecessary, and there is no design or thought employed in their manufacture. They are formed by first drawing out the glass into rods; these rods are chopped up into fragments of the size of beads by the human hand, and the fragments are then rounded in the furnace. The men who chop up the rods sit at their work all day, their hands vibrating with a perpetual and exquisitely timed palsy, and the beads dropping beneath their vibration like hail. Neither they, nor the men who draw out the rods or fuse the fragments, have the smallest occasion for the use of any single human faculty; and every young lady, therefore, who buys glass beads is engaged in the slave-trade, and in a much more cruel one than that

which we have so long been endeavouring to put down. . . .

[One example to] show the reader what I mean [comes] from the manufacture already alluded to, that of glass. Our modern glass is exquisitely clear in its substance, true in its form, accurate in its cutting. We are proud of this. We ought to be ashamed of it. The old Venice glass was muddy, inaccurate in all its forms, and clumsily cut, if at all. And the old Venetian was justly proud of it. For there is this difference between the English and Venetian workman, that the former thinks only of accurately matching his patterns, and getting his curves perfectly true and his edges perfectly sharp, and becomes a mere machine for rounding curves and sharpening edges; while the old Venetian cared not a whit whether his edges were sharp or not, but he invented a new design for every glass that he made, and never moulded a handle or a lip without a new fancy in it. And therefore, though some Venetian glass is ugly and clumsy enough when made by clumsy and uninventive workmen, other Venetian glass is so lovely in its forms that no price is too great for it; and we never see the same form in it twice. Now you cannot have the finish and the varied form too. If the workman is thinking about his edges, he cannot be thinking of his design; if of his design, he cannot think of his edges. Choose whether you will pay for the lovely form or the perfect finish, and choose at the same moment whether you will make the worker a man or a grindstone.

Nay, but the reader interrupts me—"If the workman can design beautifully, I would not have him kept at the furnace. Let him be taken away and made a gentleman, and have a studio, and design his glass there, and I will have it blown and cut for him by common workmen, and so I will have my design and my finish too."

All ideas of this kind are founded upon two mistaken suppositions: the first, that one man's thoughts can be, or ought to be, executed by another man's hands; the second, that manual labour is a degradation, when it is governed by intellect.

On a large scale, and in work determinable by line and rule, it is indeed both possible and necessary that the thoughts of one man should be carried out by the labour of others; in this sense I have already defined the best architecture to be the expression of the mind of manhood by the hands of childhood. But on a smaller scale, and in a design which cannot be mathematically defined, one man's thoughts can never be expressed by another; and the difference between the spirit of touch of the man who is inventing, and of the man who is obeying directions, is often all the difference between a great and a common work of art. How wide the separation is between original and second-hand execution, I shall endeavour to show elsewhere; it is not so much to our purpose here as to mark the other and more fatal error of despising manual labour when governed by intellect; for it is no less fatal an error to despise it when thus regulated by intellect, than to value it for its own sake. We are always in these days endeavouring to separate the two; we want one man to be always thinking, and another to be always working, and we call one a gentleman, and the other an operative; whereas the workman ought often to be thinking, and the thinker often to be working, and both should be gentlemen, in the best sense. As it is, we make both ungentle, the one envying, the other despising, his brother; and the mass of society is made up of morbid thinkers, and miserable workers. Now it is only by labour that thought can be made healthy, and only by thought that labour can be made happy, and the two cannot be separated with impunity. It would be well if all of us were good handicraftsmen in some kind, and the dishonour of manual labour done away with altogether; so that though there should still be a trenchant distinction of race between nobles and commoners, there should not, among the latter, be a trenchant distinction of employment, as between idle and working men, or between men of liberal and illiberal professions. All professions should be liberal, and there should be less pride felt in peculiarity of employment, and more in excellence of achievement. And yet more, in each several profession, no master should be too proud to do its hardest work. The painter should grind his own colours; the architect work in the mason's yard with his men. ... Hitherto I have used the words imperfect and perfect merely to distinguish between work grossly unskilful, and work executed with average precision and science; and I have been pleading that any degree of unskilfulness should be admitted, so only that the labourer's mind had room for expression.

But, accurately speaking, no good work whatever can be perfect, and *the demand for perfection is always a sign of a misunderstanding of the ends of art.*

This for two reasons, both based on everlasting laws. The first, that no great man ever stops working till he has reached his point of failure: that is to say, his mind is always far in advance of his powers of execution, and the latter will now and then give way in trying to follow it; ... And therefore, if we are to have great men working at all, or less men doing their best, the work will be imperfect, however beautiful. Of human work none but what is bad can be perfect, in its own bad way.

The second reason is, that imperfection is in some sort essential to all that we know of life. It is the sign of life in a mortal body, that is to say, of a state of progress and change. Nothing that lives is, or can be, rigidly perfect; part of it is decaying, part nascent. The foxglove blossom—a third part bud, a third part past, a third part in full bloom—is a type of the life of this world. And in all things that live there are certain irregularities and deficiencies which are not only signs of life, but sources of beauty. No human face is exactly the same in its lines on each side, no leaf perfect in its lobes, no branch in its symmetry. All admit irregularity as they imply change; and to banish imperfection is to destroy expression, to check exertion, to paralyze vitality. All things are literally better, lovelier, and more beloved for the imperfections which have been divinely appointed, that the law of human life may be Effort, and the law of human judgment, Mercy.

Accept this then for a universal law, that neither architecture nor any other noble work of man can be good unless it be imperfect; and let us be prepared for the otherwise strange fact, which we shall discern clearly as we approach the period of the Renaissance, that the first cause of the fall of the arts of Europe was a relentless requirement of perfection, incapable alike either of being silenced by veneration for greatness, or softened into forgiveness of simplicity.

Thus far then of the Rudeness or Savageness, which is the first mental element of Gothic architecture. It is an element in many other healthy architectures also, as the Byzantine and Romanesque; but true Gothic cannot exist without it.

The second mental element above named was

Changefulness, or Variety.

I have already enforced the allowing independent operation to the inferior workman, simply as a duty *to him*, and as ennobling the architecture by rendering it more Christian. We have now to consider what reward we obtain for the performance of this duty, namely, the perpetual variety of every feature of the building.

Wherever the workman is utterly enslaved, the parts of the building must of course be absolutely like each other; for the perfection of his execution can only be reached by exercising him in doing one thing, and giving him nothing else to do. The degree in which the workman is degraded may be thus known at a glance, by observing whether the several parts of the building are similar or not; and if, as in Greek work, all the capitals are alike, and all the mouldings unvaried, then the degradation is complete; if, as in Egyptian or Ninevite work, though the manner of executing certain figures is always the same, the order of design is perpetually varied, the degradation is less total; if, as in Gothic work, there is perpetual change both in design and execution, the workman must have been altogether set free.

How much the beholder gains from the liberty of the labourer may perhaps be questioned in England, where one of the strongest instincts in nearly every mind is that love of order which makes us desire that our house windows should pair like our carriage horses, and allows us to yield our faith unhesitatingly to architectural theories which fix a form for everything, and forbid variation from it. I would not impeach love of order: it is one of the most useful elements of the English mind; it helps us in our commerce and in all purely practical matters; and it is in many cases one of the foundation stones of morality. Only do not let us suppose that love of order is love of art. It is true that order, in its highest sense, is one of the necessities of art, just as time is a necessity of music; but love of order has no more to do with our right enjoyment of architecture or painting, than love of punctuality with the appreciation of an opera. ...

From these general uses of variety in the economy of the world, we may at once understand its use and abuse in architecture. The variety of the Gothic schools is the more healthy and beautiful, because in many cases it is entirely unstudied, and results, not from mere love of change, but from practical necessities. For in one point of view Gothic is not only the best, but the *only rational* architecture, as being that which can fit itself most easily to all services, vulgar or noble. Undefined in its slope of roof, height of shaft, breadth of arch, or disposition of ground plan, it can shrink into a turret, expand into a hall, coil into a staircase, or spring into a spire, with undegraded grace and unexhausted energy; and whenever it finds occasion for change in its form or purpose, it submits to it without the slightest sense of loss either to its unity or majesty,—subtle and flexible like a fiery serpent, but ever attentive to the voice of the charmer. And it is one of the chief virtues of the Gothic builders, that they never suffered ideas of outside symmetries and consistencies to interfere with the real use and value of what they did. If they wanted a window, they opened one; a room, they added one; a buttress, they built one; utterly regardless of any established conventionalities of external appearance, knowing (as indeed it always happened) that such daring interruptions of the formal plan would rather give additional interest to its symmetry than injure it. ...

The third constituent element of the Gothic mind was stated to be Naturalism; that is to say, the love of natural objects for their own sake, and the effort to represent them frankly, unconstrained by artistical laws.

This characteristic of the style partly follows in necessary connection with those named above. For, so soon as the workman is left free to represent what subjects he chooses, he must look to the nature that is round him for material, and will endeavour to represent it as he sees it, with more or less accuracy according to the skill he possesses, and with much play of fancy, but with small respect for law. There is, however, a marked distinction between the imaginations of the Western and Eastern races, even when both are left free; the Western, or Gothic, delighting most in the representation of facts, and the Eastern (Arabian, Persian, and Chinese) in the harmony of colours and forms. ...

Now the noblest art is an exact unison of the abstract value, with the imitative power, of forms and colours. It is the noblest composition, used to express the noblest facts. But the human mind cannot in general unite the two perfections: it either pursues the fact to the neglect of the composition, or pursues the composition to the neglect of the fact.

And it is intended by the Deity that it *should* do this: the best art is not always wanted. Facts are often wanted without art, as in a geological diagram; and art often without facts, as in a Turkey carpet. And most men have been made capable of giving either one or the other, but not both; only one or two, the very highest, can give both. ...

We have now, I believe, obtained a sufficiently accurate knowledge both of the spirit and form of Gothic architecture; but it may, perhaps, be useful to the general reader, if, in conclusion, I set down a few plain and practical rules for determining, in every instance, whether a given building be good Gothic or not, and, if not Gothic, whether its architecture is of a kind which will probably reward the pains of careful examination.

First, look if the roof rises in a steep gable, high above the walls. If it does not do this, there is something wrong: the building is not quite pure Gothic, or has been altered.

Secondly, look if the principal windows and doors have pointed arches with gables over them. If not pointed arches, the building is not Gothic; if they have not any gables over them, it is either not pure, or not first-rate.

If, however, it has the steep roof, the pointed arch, and gable all united, it is nearly certain to be a Gothic building of a very fine time. ...

... See if it looks as if it had been built by strong men; if it has the sort of roughness, and largeness, and nonchalance, mixed in places with the exquisite tenderness which seems always to be the sign-manual of the broad vision, and massy[1] power of men, who can see *past* the work they are doing, and betray here and there

The Ducal Palace—Bird's Eye View.

something like disdain for it. ...

Secondly, observe if it be irregular, its different parts fitting themselves to different purposes, no one caring what becomes of them, so that they do their work. If one part always answers accurately to another part, it is sure to be a bad building; and the greater and more conspicuous the irregularities, the greater the chances are that it is a good one. For instance, in the Ducal Palace,[2] of which a rough woodcut [appears here], the general idea is sternly symmetrical; but two windows are lower than the rest of the six; and if the reader will count the arches of the small arcade as far as to the great balcony, he will find it is not in the centre, but set to the right-hand side by the whole width of one of those arches. We may be pretty sure that the building is a good one; none but a master of his craft would have ventured to do this.

—1853

---

[1] *massy* Heavy.

[2] *Ducal Palace* Gothic palace in Venice.

MATTHEW ARNOLD
1822 – 1888

Nicknamed "the Emperor" by his friends and family, Matthew Arnold was an ardent and, in the view of some Victorians, arrogant critic of modernity. Arnold embodied both the idealist expectations and the apocalyptic anxieties of the approaching *fin-de-siécle* in his poetry and prose. In the face of an increasingly materialistic mass culture, dominated by the vacuity of what he called "the average man" or "Philistine" of the democratized middle classes, Arnold sought to revive culture in

the image of liberal humanism. Only an education in the ostensibly timeless and universal works of masters like Marcus Aurelius, Tolstoy, Homer and Wordsworth, Arnold believed, could cure the *malaise* of modern life.

"For the creation of a masterwork of literature, two powers must concur," Arnold wrote in 1865, "The power of the man and the power of the moment, and the man is not enough without the moment." Arnold believed that modern industrial life and the materialism it had made possible were radically indisposed towards artistic genius and indeed had created a climate of psychological and moral enervation that poetry was powerless to heal. The *Zeitgeist* (one of his terms for the powerful work of modern popular culture) was profoundly "unpoetical," and was best anatomized through prose. His own career shows symptoms of the fragmentation he analyzed. Arnold incisively broke with the often melancholic poetry of his early years in order to pursue prose criticism, for him the best possible literary work, he believed, in an era that he saw as spiritually bankrupt. Modern society was in no condition to produce great poets; the best that modern life could muster, according to Arnold, were powerful critics—*if* they stayed away from the politics of the passing moment.

The River Thames ran past the village of Laleham where Matthew Arnold was born in 1822. Arnold was the eldest son of Mary Penrose Arnold and Dr. Thomas Arnold. His father, a clergyman and headmaster of Rugby School, was celebrated for reforming the school's curriculum to foreground Christian values, classical languages, and competitive games. Ironically, Arnold, who in later life would come to resemble his father by valuing above all else great humanist texts and a classical education, was lazy, laconic and flippant as a student. Upon meeting the young dilettante, Charlotte Brontë wrote that "his manner displeases, from its seeming foppery." Yet, in spite of a flamboyant indifference to academia and a studied attempt to dissociate himself from all that his father represented, he amazed family and friends by winning a scholarship to Oxford's Balliol College in 1840, the prodigious Newdigate Prize for poetry in 1843, and a Fellowship at Oriel College in 1845.

Wordsworth, a friend of the family, was one of the most tangible influences on Arnold's poetry. When Wordsworth died, Arnold wondered sadly, "Who will teach us how to feel?" He frequently fled from classes to wander the countryside around the Lake District or to hike in the Alps, landscapes memorialized by Wordsworth and Coleridge. Many critics claim that Arnold was most accomplished as a poet of nature. The "simple joy the country yields," rendered in poems like "Thyrsis," reveals a surprising affinity with the quiet style of Thomas Gray; his "Resignation" speaks to Wordsworth's "Tintern Abbey." Arnold's personal manner, reminiscent of his idols Lord Byron and Goethe, did not cancel out a heartfelt relation to nature, whose unadorned expression modelled the "high seriousness" he admired in Sophocles and Aeschylus.

In 1847, Arnold obtained employment in London as a private secretary to the liberal politician Lord Lansdowne, a period during which he produced most of his poetry. 1849 saw the publication of *The Strayed Reveller, and Other Poems*, by "A," followed by *Empedocles on Etna, and Other Poems* (1852). The controversial preface to *Poems* (1853) provoked heated debate. Here Arnold focused on the ponderous force of the "unpoetical" nineteenth century writ large over his earlier work and damned the "dialogue of the mind with itself" that his *Empedocles on Etna* exhibited. Great poetry, Arnold claimed, must be distinguished from verse produced by a restless intellect fragmented by attempts to address the problems of contemporary life. Poetry should create works of beauty and unity that rise above the historical moment to "inspirit and rejoice" readers.

Letters to his best friend and fellow poet Arthur Hugh Clough, who did address the intellectual issues of the current moment, provide valuable insight into the demanding standards Arnold set for poetry. "I am glad you like the *Gypsy Scholar*," he wrote, "—but what does it *do* for you? Homer *animates*—Shakespeare *animates*— in its poor way I think *Sohrab and Rustum animates*—the *Gypsy Scholar* at best awakens a pleasing melancholy." Considered an often biting critic of the work of his contemporaries, including Clough, Arnold's harshest criticisms were first addressed to his own work. His poem "Dover Beach," probably written in 1851, but published in 1867, is one of English literature's profound expressions of modernity's disaffection with itself. Yet perceiving that his own poetry seemed passively ensnared in the "continual state of mental distress" that he took to task in the preface to *Poems*, he largely ceased writing poetry from the mid-1850s onward. After *New Poems* (1867), Arnold would refashion himself as a prose writer. According to Lionel Trilling, Arnold "perceived in himself the poetic power, but knew that his genius was not of the greatest, that the poetic force was not irresistible in him," not enough, at any rate, to act as a transformative agent in an age of disillusionment.

In 1851, Arnold married Frances Lucy Wightman and to support his family accepted a position as a public school inspector. Initially thinking the job would suffice "for the next three or four years," Arnold continued to be employed in the public service for thirty-five years. In contrast to writers like Tennyson or Carlyle, Arnold had to work for a living, writing only in his spare time. He believed that his inspections of schools in Britain and across Europe gave him first-hand experience to support his conviction that educating the public in a classical humanist tradition was key to "civilizing the next generation of the lower classes."

Arnold was elected Professor of Poetry at Oxford University in 1857, where he delivered public lectures for the following ten years. Though a proponent of an exacting standard of classical scholarship, Arnold was the first to lecture in English rather than Latin, altering an elitist institutional practice that acted as a barrier to the kind of education that the nineteenth century urgently needed, in his opinion. Arnold turned many of his lectures into essays and books, including *On Translating Homer* (1861) and *Friendship's Garland* (1871).

Though by his own standards of greatness Arnold could not *transform* society as a poet, as a critic he was determined to *reform* it. In his famous essay "The Function of Criticism at the Present Time," published in *Essays in Criticism* (1865), Arnold helped raise the value of criticism from its status as a "baneful and injurious employment" to a creative activity in its own right. Deftly juxtaposing snatches from tabloids alongside texts of high culture, Arnold's critical methodology foreshadowed the kind of work pursued in cultural studies today. While few have unanimously agreed with Arnold's pronouncements on literature and society, he has influenced almost every significant English-speaking critic since his time, including T.S. Eliot, F.R. Leavis, Lionel Trilling, and Raymond Williams.

In *Culture and Anarchy* (1869), arguably his most important work of social criticism, Arnold proposed that antagonistic factions of British society could learn to overcome their differences through an education in "disinterested" and universal human values. The differences allowed expression in democratic societies would disintegrate into anarchic disorder, thought Arnold, unless tethered to the "higher" ideals of the humanist tradition. His witty veneer and Apollonian appeal to transcendent virtues of "sweetness and light" sometimes enamored, and sometimes exasperated, a public whose prominent figures he often singled out by name for critical interrogation. Leslie Stephen, Virginia Woolf's father, remarked drily: "I often wished ... that I too had a little sweetness and light that I might be able to say such nasty things of my enemies."

During the 1870s, Arnold published a series of attacks on orthodox religion: *St. Paul and Protestantism* (1870), *Literature and Dogma* (1873) and *God and the Bible* (1875). Even in a period that witnessed the challenges to traditional religious belief posed by Darwin's theories, the work of geologists, and the "higher criticism" of the Bible that came from Germany and elsewhere, Arnold's religious critiques scandalized many Victorians. He recommended that Victorians exchange their faith in a religion founded on the assumption of the truth of the Bible for faith in a transcendent, secular humanism. When he returned to literary criticism in "The Study of Poetry" (1880), he claimed, as Thomas Carlyle had before him in the 1830s, that "most of what now passes for religion and philosophy will be replaced by poetry."

Like Dickens and Thackeray before him, Arnold embarked on a lecture tour of the United States, in 1883. Tired and burdened by debts, Arnold saw the trip as a money-making venture that would also allow him to visit a daughter who had married an American. He was loved in Washington but received with mixed success in other cities. He compiled his lectures in *Discourses in America* (1885), which contains his discussion of Emerson as well as the essay "Literature and Science." Here Arnold responds to Thomas Huxley's claim in "Science and Culture" (1881) that "for the purpose of attaining real culture, an exclusively scientific education is at least as effectual as an exclusively literary education." Especially in America, Arnold argued, where the democratic impulse to glorify "the average man" was particularly enthusiastic, education must safeguard the guiding ideals of the Western tradition, "the best that is known and thought."

Arnold died suddenly of a heart attack in 1888, leaving behind him a remarkable body of cultural criticism and a few poems familiar to all readers of English poetry. His statement about Oxford and modernity in *Culture and Anarchy* may well be taken as fitting epitaph: "We in Oxford ... have not failed to seize one truth,—the truth that beauty and sweetness are essential characters of a complete human perfection. ... We have not won our political battles, we have not carried our main points, we have not stopped our adversaries' advance, we have not marched victoriously with the modern world; but we have told silently upon the mind of the century, we have prepared currents of feeling which sap our adversaries' position when it seems gained, we have kept up our communications with the future."

⌘ ⌘ ⌘

The Forsaken Merman

Come, dear children, let us away;
    Down and away below!
Now my brothers call from the bay,
Now the great winds shoreward blow,
5   Now the salt tides seaward flow;

Now the wild white horses play,
Champ and chafe and toss in the spray.
Children dear, let us away!
This way, this way!

10 Call her once before you go—
Call once yet!

In a voice that she will know:
"Margaret! Margaret!"
Children's voices should be dear
15 (Call once more) to a mother's ear;
Children's voices, wild with pain—
Surely she will come again!
Call her once and come away;
This way, this way!
20 "Mother dear, we cannot stay!
The wild white horses foam and fret."
Margaret! Margaret!

Come, dear children, come away down;
Call no more!
25 One last look at the white-walled town,
And the little grey church on the windy shore,
Then come down!
She will not come though you call all day;
Come away, come away!

30 Children dear, was it yesterday
We heard the sweet bells over the bay?
In the caverns where we lay,
Through the surf and through the swell,
The far-off sound of a silver bell?
35 Sand-strewn caverns, cool and deep,
Where the winds are all asleep;
Where the spent lights quiver and gleam,
Where the salt weed sways in the stream,
Where the sea-beasts, ranged all round,
40 Feed in the ooze of their pasture-ground;
Where the sea-snakes coil and twine,
Dry their mail and bask in the brine;
Where great whales come sailing by,
Sail and sail, with unshut eye,
45 Round the world for ever and aye?
When did music come this way?
Children dear, was it yesterday?

Children dear, was it yesterday
(Call yet once) that she went away?
50 Once she sat with you and me,
On a red gold throne in the heart of the sea,

And the youngest sat on her knee.
She combed its bright hair, and she tended it well,
When down swung the sound of a far-off bell.
55 She sighed, she looked up through the clear green sea;
She said: "I must go, for my kinsfolk pray
In the little grey church on the shore today.
'Twill be Easter-time in the world—ah me!
And I lose my poor soul, Merman! here with thee." [1]
60 I said: "Go up, dear heart, through the waves;
Say thy prayer, and come back to the kind sea-caves!"
She smiled, she went up through the surf in the bay.
Children dear, was it yesterday?

Children dear, were we long alone?
65 The sea grows stormy, the little ones moan;
"Long prayers," I said, "in the world they say;
Come!" I said; and we rose through the surf in the bay.
We went up the beach, by the sandy down
Where the sea-stocks bloom, to the white-walled town;
70 Through the narrow paved streets, where all was still,
To the little grey church on the windy hill.
From the church came a murmur of folk at their
        prayers,
But we stood without in the cold blowing airs.
We climbed on the graves, on the stones worn with
        rains,
75 And we gazed up the aisle through the small leaded
        panes.
She sat by the pillar; we saw her clear:
"Margaret, hist! come quick, we are here!
Dear heart," I said, "we are long alone;
The sea grows stormy, the little ones moan."
80 But, ah, she gave me never a look,
For her eyes were seal'd to the holy book!
Loud prays the priest; shut stands the door.
Come away, children, call no more!
Come away, come down, call no more!

85   Down, down, down!
Down to the depths of the sea!
She sits at her wheel in the humming town,
Singing most joyfully.

---

[1] *I lose ... thee* According to popular folk belief, mermaids and
mermen had no souls, and humans who went to live with them
would lose theirs as well.

Hark what she sings: "O joy, O joy,
90   For the humming street, and the child with its toy!
For the priest, and the bell, and the holy well;
For the wheel where I spun,
And the blessed light of the sun!"
And so she sings her fill,
95   Singing most joyfully,
Till the spindle drops from her hand,
And the whizzing wheel stands still.
She steals to the window, and looks at the sand,
And over the sand at the sea;
100   And her eyes are set in a stare;
And anon there breaks a sigh,
And anon there drops a tear,
From a sorrow-clouded eye,
And a heart sorrow-laden,
105   A long, long sigh;
For the cold strange eyes of a little Mermaiden
And the gleam of her golden hair.

        Come away, away children;
Come children, come down!
110   The hoarse wind blows coldly;
Lights shine in the town.
She will start from her slumber
When gusts shake the door;
She will hear the winds howling,
115   Will hear the waves roar.
We shall see, while above us
The waves roar and whirl,
A ceiling of amber,
A pavement of pearl.
120   Singing: "Here came a mortal,
But faithless was she!
And alone dwell for ever
The kings of the sea."

        But, children, at midnight,
125   When soft the winds blow,
When clear falls the moonlight,
When spring-tides are low;

When sweet airs come seaward
From heaths starred with broom,[1]
130   And high rocks throw mildly
On the blanched sands a gloom;
Up the still, glistening beaches,
Up the creeks we will hie,°   *hasten*
Over banks of bright seaweed
135   The ebb-tide leaves dry.
We will gaze, from the sand-hills,
At the white, sleeping town;
At the church on the hill-side—
And then come back down.
140   Singing: "There dwells a loved one,
But cruel is she!
She left lonely for ever
The kings of the sea."
        —1849

Isolation. To Marguerite [2]

We were apart; yet, day by day,
    I bade my heart more constant be.
I bade it keep the world away,
And grow a home for only thee;
5   Nor feared but thy love likewise grew,
Like mine, each day, more tried, more true.

The fault was grave! I might have known,
What far too soon, alas! I learned—
The heart can bind itself alone,
10   And faith may oft be unreturned.
Self-swayed our feelings ebb and swell—
Thou lov'st no more—Farewell! Farewell!

Farewell!—and thou, thou lonely heart,
Which never yet without remorse
15   Even for a moment didst depart
From thy remote and sphered course

---

[1] *broom* Type of shrub bearing yellow flowers, common in England.

[2] *Marguerite* An unidentified woman, perhaps someone Arnold met in Switzerland in the 1840s, or Mary Claude, an Englishwoman Arnold knew during that same time.

To haunt the place where passions reign—
Back to thy solitude again!

Back! with the conscious thrill of shame
20   Which Luna felt, that summer-night,
Flash through her pure immortal frame,
When she forsook the starry height
To hang over Endymion's sleep
Upon the pine-grown Latmian steep.[1]

25   Yet she, chaste queen, had never proved
How vain a thing is mortal love,
Wandering in Heaven, far removed.
But thou hast long had place to prove
This truth—to prove, and make thine own:
30   "Thou hast been, shalt be, art, alone."

Or, if not quite alone, yet they
Which touch thee are unmating things—
Ocean and clouds and night and day;
Lorn autumns and triumphant springs;
35   And life, and others' joy and pain,
And love, if love, of happier men.

Of happier men—for they, at least,
Have *dream'd* two human hearts might blend
In one, and were through faith released
40   From isolation without end
Prolong'd; nor knew, although not less
Alone than thou, their loneliness.
—1857 (1849)

To Marguerite—Continued

Yes! in the sea of life enisled,
With echoing straits between us thrown,
Dotting the shoreless watery wild,
We mortal millions live *alone*.
5   The islands feel the enclasping flow,
And then their endless bounds they know.

But when the moon their hollows lights,
And they are swept by balms of spring,
And in their glens, on starry nights,
10   The nightingales divinely sing;
And lovely notes, from shore to shore,
Across the sounds and channels pour—

Oh! then a longing like despair
Is to their farthest caverns sent;
15   For surely once, they feel, we were
Parts of a single continent!
Now round us spreads the watery plain—
Oh might our marges° meet again!   *borders*

Who ordered, that their longing's fire
20   Should be, as soon as kindled, cooled?
Who renders vain their deep desire?—
A God, a God their severance ruled!
And bade betwixt their shores to be
The unplumbed, salt, estranging sea.
—1852 (1849)

The Buried Life

Light flows our war of mocking words, and yet,
Behold, with tears mine eyes are wet!
I feel a nameless sadness o'er me roll.
Yes, yes, we know that we can jest,
5   We know, we know that we can smile!
But there's a something in this breast,
To which thy light words bring no rest,
And thy gay smiles no anodyne.°   *remedy*
Give me thy hand, and hush awhile,
10   And turn those limpid eyes on mine,
And let me read there, love! thy inmost soul.

Alas! is even love too weak
To unlock the heart, and let it speak?
Are even lovers powerless to reveal
15   To one another what indeed they feel?
I knew the mass of men concealed
Their thoughts, for fear that if revealed
They would by other men be met
With blank indifference, or with blame reproved;

20 I knew they lived and moved
Tricked in disguises, alien to the rest
Of men, and alien to themselves—and yet
The same heart beats in every human breast!

But we, my love!—doth a like spell benumb
25 Our hearts, our voices?—must we too be dumb?

Ah! well for us, if even we,
Even for a moment, can get free
Our heart, and have our lips unchained;
For that which seals them hath been deep-ordained!
30 Fate, which foresaw
How frivolous a baby man would be—
By what distractions he would be possessed,
How he would pour himself in every strife,
And well-nigh change his own identity—
35 That it might keep from his capricious play
His genuine self, and force him to obey
Even in his own despite his being's law,
Bade through the deep recesses of our breast
The unregarded river of our life
40 Pursue with indiscernible flow its way;
And that we should not see
The buried stream, and seem to be
Eddying at large in blind uncertainty,
Though driving on with it eternally.

45 But often, in the world's most crowded streets,
But often, in the din of strife,
There rises an unspeakable desire
After the knowledge of our buried life;
A thirst to spend our fire and restless force
50 In tracking out our true, original course;
A longing to inquire
Into the mystery of this heart which beats
So wild, so deep in us—to know
Whence our lives come and where they go.
55 And many a man in his own breast then delves,
But deep enough, alas! none ever mines.
And we have been on many thousand lines,
And we have shown, on each, spirit and power;
But hardly have we, for one little hour,
60 Been on our own line, have we been ourselves—

Hardly had skill to utter one of all
The nameless feelings that course through our breast,
But they course on for ever unexpressed.
And long we try in vain to speak and act
65 Our hidden self, and what we say and do
Is eloquent, is well—but 'tis not true!
And then we will no more be racked
With inward striving, and demand
Of all the thousand nothings of the hour
70 Their stupefying power;
Ah yes, and they benumb us at our call!
Yet still, from time to time, vague and forlorn,
From the soul's subterranean depth upborne
As from an infinitely distant land,
75 Come airs, and floating echoes, and convey
A melancholy into all our day.

Only—but this is rare—
When a beloved hand is laid in ours,
When, jaded with the rush and glare
80 Of the interminable hours,
Our eyes can in another's eyes read clear,
When our world-deafened ear
Is by the tones of a loved voice caressed—
A bolt is shot back somewhere in our breast,
85 And a lost pulse of feeling stirs again.
The eye sinks inward, and the heart lies plain,
And what we mean, we say, and what we would, we
    know.
A man becomes aware of his life's flow,
And hears its winding murmur; and he sees
90 The meadows where it glides, the sun, the breeze.

And there arrives a lull in the hot race
Wherein he doth for ever chase
That flying and elusive shadow, rest.
An air of coolness plays upon his face,
95 And an unwonted calm pervades his breast.
And then he thinks he knows
The hills where his life rose,
And the sea where it goes.
—1852

The Scholar-Gipsy[1]

Go, for they call you, shepherd, from the hill;
　　Go, shepherd, and untie the wattled cotes![2]
　　　　No longer leave thy wistful flock unfed,
　　Nor let thy bawling fellows rack their throats,
5　　　　Nor the cropped herbage shoot another head.
　　　　　　But when the fields are still,
　　　　And the tired men and dogs all gone to rest,
　　　　And only the white sheep are sometimes seen
　　　　Cross and recross the strips of moon-blanched
　　　　　　green,
10　　Come, shepherd, and again begin the quest!

　　Here, where the reaper was at work of late—
　　　　In this high field's dark corner, where he leaves
　　　　　　His coat, his basket, and his earthen cruse,° *jug*
　　　　And in the sun all morning binds the sheaves,
15　　　　Then here, at noon, comes back his stores to
　　　　　　use—
　　　　　　Here will I sit and wait,
　　　　While to my ear from uplands far away
　　　　The bleating of the folded° flocks is borne, *enclosed*
　　　　With distant cries of reapers in the corn—
20　　All the live murmur of a summer's day.

Screened is this nook o'er the high, half-reaped field,
　　And here till sun-down, shepherd! will I be.
　　　　Through the thick corn the scarlet poppies peep,
　　And round green roots and yellowing stalks I see
25　　　　Pale pink convolvulus[3] in tendrils creep;
　　　　　　And air-swept lindens yield
　　　　Their scent, and rustle down their perfumed
　　　　　　showers
　　　　Of bloom on the bent grass where I am laid,
　　　　And bower me from the August sun with shade;
30　　And the eye travels down to Oxford's towers.

And near me on the grass lies Glanvil's book—
　　Come, let me read the oft-read tale again!
　　　　The story of the Oxford scholar poor,
　　Of pregnant[4] parts and quick inventive brain,
35　　　　Who, tired of knocking at preferment's door,
　　　　　　One summer-morn forsook
　　　　His friends, and went to learn the gipsy-lore,
　　　　And roamed the world with that wild
　　　　　　brotherhood,
　　　　And came, as most men deemed, to little good,
40　　But came to Oxford and his friends no more.

But once, years after, in the country-lanes,
　　Two scholars, whom at college erst he knew,
　　　　Met him, and of his way of life enquired;
　　Whereat he answered, that the gipsy-crew,
45　　　　His mates, had arts to rule as they desired
　　　　　　The workings of men's brains,
　　　　And they can bind them to what thoughts they
　　　　　　will.
　　　　"And I," he said, "the secret of their art,
　　　　When fully learned, will to the world impart;
50　　But it needs heaven-sent moments for this skill."

This said, he left them, and returned no more.
　　But rumours hung about the country-side,
　　　　That the lost Scholar long was seen to stray,
　　Seen by rare glimpses, pensive and tongue-tied,
55　　　　In hat of antique shape, and cloak of grey,
　　　　　　The same the gypsies wore.

---

[1]　*The Scholar-Gipsy*　Arnold said this poem was inspired by the following passage in Joseph Glanville's *Vanity of Dogmatizing* (1661): "There was very lately a lad in the University of Oxford, who was by his poverty forced to leave his studies there; and at last to join himself to a company of vagabond gypsies. Among these extravagant people, by the insinuating subtilty of his carriage, he quickly got so much of their love and esteem as that they discovered to him their mystery. After he had been a pretty while exercised in the trade, there chanced to ride by a couple of scholars, who had formerly been of his acquaintance. They quickly spied out their old friend among the gypsies; and he gave them an account of the necessity which drove him to that kind of life, and told them that the people he went with were not such imposters as they were taken for, but that they had a traditional kind of learning among them, and could do wonders by the power of imagination, their fancy binding that of others; that he himself had learned much of their art, and when he had compassed the whole secret, he intended, he said, to leave their company, and give the world an account of what he had learned." Arnold imagines this student still roaming the area surrounding Oxford, where Arnold spent "the freest and most delightful part, perhaps, of my life."

[2]　*wattled cotes*　Sheepfolds made of woven sticks.

[3]　*convolvulus*　Morning-glory.

[4]　*pregnant*　Full of ideas.

Shepherds had met him on the Hurst[1] in spring;
    At some lone alehouse in the Berkshire moors,
    On the warm ingle-bench,[2] the smock-frocked
        boors°   *rustics*
60 Had found him seated at their entering,

But, 'mid their drink and clatter, he would fly.
    And I myself seem half to know thy looks,
      And put the shepherds, wanderer! on thy trace;
    And boys who in lone wheatfields scare the rooks
65   I ask if thou hast passed their quiet place;
        Or in my boat I lie
Moored to the cool bank in the summer-heats,
    'Mid wide grass meadows which the sunshine
        fills,
    And watch the warm, green-muffled Cumner
        hills,
70 And wonder if thou haunt'st their shy retreats.

For most, I know, thou lov'st retired ground!
    Thee at the ferry Oxford riders blithe,
      Returning home on summer-nights, have met
    Crossing the stripling Thames at Bab-lock-hithe,
75   Trailing in the cool stream thy fingers wet,
        As the punt's[3] rope chops round;
    And leaning backward in a pensive dream,
      And fostering in thy lap a heap of flowers
      Plucked in shy fields and distant Wychwood
        bowers,
80 And thine eyes resting on the moonlit stream.

And then they land, and thou art seen no more!
    Maidens, who from the distant hamlets come
      To dance around the Fyfield elm in May,
    Oft through the darkening fields have seen thee
        roam,
85   Or cross a stile into the public way.
        Oft thou hast given them store
    Of flowers—the frail-leafed, white anemone,
      Dark bluebells drenched with dews of summer
        eves,

    And purple orchises with spotted leaves—
90 But none hath words she can report of thee.

And, above Godstow Bridge, when hay-time's here
    In June, and many a scythe in sunshine flames,
      Men who through those wide fields of breezy
        grass
    Where black-winged swallows haunt the glittering
        Thames,
95   To bathe in the abandoned lasher pass,[4]
        Have often passed thee near
Sitting upon the river bank o'ergrown;
    Marked thine outlandish garb, thy figure
        spare,
    Thy dark vague eyes, and soft abstracted air—
100 But, when they came from bathing, thou wast gone!

At some lone homestead in the Cumner hills,
    Where at her open door the housewife darns,
      Thou hast been seen, or hanging on a gate
    To watch the threshers in the mossy barns.
105   Children, who early range these slopes and late
        For cresses from the rills,
    Have known thee eyeing, all an April-day,
      The springing pastures and the feeding kine;° *cows*
    And marked thee, when the stars come out
        and shine,
110 Through the long dewy grass move slow away.

In autumn, on the skirts of Bagley Wood—
    Where most the gypsies by the turf-edged way
      Pitch their smoked tents, and every bush you
        see
    With scarlet patches tagged and shreds of grey,[5]
115   Above the forest-ground called Thessaly —
        The blackbird, picking food,
Sees thee, nor stops his meal, nor fears at all;
    So often has he known thee past him stray,
    Rapt, twirling in thy hand a withered spray,
120 And waiting for the spark from heaven to fall.

---

[1] *the Hurst* Hill outside Oxford. All the places mentioned in the stanzas following are located in the area surrounding Oxford.

[2] *ingle-bench* Fireside bench.

[3] *punt* Small, shallow boat propelled with a long pole pushed against the river bottom.

---

[4] *lasher pass* Place where water collects after spilling over a dam.

[5] *With scarlet ... grey* Reference to the clothes of the gypsies, which they hang on the bushes to dry.

And once, in winter, on the causeway chill
   Where home through flooded fields foot-travellers
      go,
      Have I not passed thee on the wooden bridge,
   Wrapt in thy cloak and battling with the snow,
125   Thy face toward Hinksey and its wintry ridge?
         And thou hast climbed the hill,
   And gained the white brow of the Cumner range;
      Turned once to watch, while thick the
         snowflakes fall,
      The line of festal light in Christ-Church hall[1]—
130 Then sought thy straw in some sequestered grange.

   But what—I dream! Two hundred years are flown
    Since first thy story ran through Oxford halls,
      And the grave Glanvil did the tale inscribe
   That thou wert wandered from the studious walls
135   To learn strange arts, and join a gipsy-tribe;
         And thou from earth art gone
   Long since, and in some quiet churchyard laid—
      Some country-nook, where o'er thy unknown
         grave
      Tall grasses and white flowering nettles wave,
140 Under a dark, red-fruited yew-tree's shade.

  —No, no, thou hast not felt the lapse of hours!
    For what wears out the life of mortal men?
      'Tis that from change to change their being
         rolls;
   'Tis that repeated shocks, again, again,
145   Exhaust the energy of strongest souls
         And numb the elastic powers.
   Till having used our nerves with bliss and
         teen,°   *vexation*
      And tired upon a thousand schemes our wit,
      To the just-pausing Genius[2] we remit
150 Our worn-out life, and are—what we have been.

   Thou hast not lived, why should'st thou perish, so?
    Thou hadst *one* aim, *one* business, *one* desire;

   Else wert thou long since numbered with the
      dead!
   Else hadst thou spent, like other men, thy fire!
155   The generations of thy peers are fled,
         And we ourselves shall go;
   But thou possessest an immortal lot,
      And we imagine thee exempt from age
      And living as thou liv'st on Glanvil's page,
160 Because thou hadst—what we, alas! have not.

   For early didst thou leave the world, with powers
    Fresh, undiverted to the world without,
      Firm to their mark, not spent on other things;
   Free from the sick fatigue, the languid doubt,
165   Which much to have tried, in much been
         baffled, brings.
         O life unlike to ours!
   Who fluctuate idly without term or scope,
      Of whom each strives, nor knows for what he
         strives,
      And each half lives a hundred different lives;
170 Who wait like thee, but not, like thee, in hope.

   Thou waitest for the spark from heaven! and we,
    Light half-believers of our casual creeds,
      Who never deeply felt, nor clearly willed,
   Whose insight never has borne fruit in deeds,
175   Whose vague resolves never have been fulfilled;
         For whom each year we see
   Breeds new beginnings, disappointments new;
      Who hesitate and falter life away,
      And lose tomorrow the ground won today—
180 Ah! do not we, wanderer! await it too?

   Yes, we await it!—but it still delays,
    And then we suffer! and amongst us one,
      Who most has suffered,[3] takes dejectedly
   His seat upon the intellectual throne;
185   And all his store of sad experience he
         Lays bare of wretched days;
   Tells us his misery's birth and growth and signs,

---

1 *Christ-Church hall* Dining hall of Christ Church, an Oxford College.

2 *Genius* Attendant spirit that accompanies a soul from birth to death and shapes his or her character.

3 *one ... suffered* Reference probably either to Tennyson—whose *In Memoriam* appeared in 1850, the year he succeeded Wordsworth as Poet Laureate—or to German philosopher Johann Wolfgang von Goethe (1749–1832).

And how the dying spark of hope was fed,
And how the breast was soothed, and how the
    head,
190   And all his hourly varied anodynes.

This for our wisest! and we others pine,
    And wish the long unhappy dream would end,
        And waive all claim to bliss, and try to bear;
    With close-lipped patience for our only friend,
195   Sad patience, too near neighbour to despair—
            But none has hope like thine!
Thou through the fields and through the woods
        dost stray,
        Roaming the country-side, a truant boy,
        Nursing thy project in unclouded joy,
200   And every doubt long blown by time away.

O born in days when wits were fresh and clear,
    And life ran gaily as the sparkling Thames;
        Before this strange disease of modern life,
    With its sick hurry, its divided aims,
205   Its heads o'ertaxed, its palsied hearts, was rife—
            Fly hence, our contact fear!
Still fly, plunge deeper in the bowering wood!
        Averse, as Dido did with gesture stern
        From her false friend's approach in Hades turn,[1]
210   Wave us away, and keep thy solitude!

Still nursing the unconquerable hope,
    Still clutching the inviolable shade,
        With a free, onward impulse brushing through,
    By night, the silvered branches of the glade—
215   Far on the forest-skirts, where none pursue.
           On some mild pastoral slope
Emerge, and resting on the moonlit pales
        Freshen thy flowers as in former years
        With dew, or listen with enchanted ears,
220   From the dark dingles,[2] to the nightingales!

But fly our paths, our feverish contact fly!
    For strong the infection of our mental strife,

Which, though it gives no bliss, yet spoils for rest;
    And we should win thee from thy own fair life,
225   Like us distracted, and like us unblest.
        Soon, soon thy cheer would die,
Thy hopes grow timorous, and unfixed thy powers,
        And thy clear aims be cross and shifting made;
    And then thy glad perennial youth would fade,
230   Fade, and grow old at last, and die like ours.

Then fly our greetings, fly our speech and smiles!
    —As some grave Tyrian[3] trader, from the sea,
        Descried at sunrise an emerging prow
Lifting the cool-haired creepers stealthily,
235   The fringes of a southward-facing brow
           Among the Aegean isles;
    And saw the merry Grecian coaster come,
        Freighted with amber grapes, and Chian wine,
        Green, bursting figs, and tunnies°   *tuna fish*
           steeped in brine—
240   And knew the intruders on his ancient home,

The young light-hearted masters of the waves—
    And snatched his rudder, and shook out more sail;
        And day and night held on indignantly
O'er the blue Midland waters with the gale,
245   Betwixt the Syrtes[4] and soft Sicily,
           To where the Atlantic raves
    Outside the western straits; and unbent sails
        There, where down cloudy cliffs, through
           sheets of foam,
    Shy traffickers, the dark Iberians[5] come;
250   And on the beach undid his corded bales.
—1853

---

[3] *Tyrian* From Tyre, ancient capital of Phoenicia.

[4] *Syrtes* Two treacherous gulfs off the coast of northern Africa.

[5] *dark Iberians* Inhabitants of Spain or Portugal. The story of these "shy traffickers" comes from fifth-century BCE Greek historian Herodotus's *History*, in which he explains that the Carthaginians would sail through the Strait of Gibraltar to trade with the West Africans. In a unique trading process, these Carthaginians would leave their goods on the beach, withdrawing to their ships. The Africans would come out of their hiding places and leave gold beside the goods they wished to purchase. After they had retreated, the Carthaginians would return and decide if this was adequate payment. The process would be repeated until the two sides reached an agreement.

---

[1] *as Dido ... turn* In Virgil's *Aeneid*, Dido, Queen of Carthage, commits suicide when her lover, Aeneas, deserts her. When he encounters her in Hades, she turns away from him.

[2] *dingles* Wooded dales.

Stanzas from The Grande Chartreuse[1]

Through Alpine meadows soft-suffused
     With rain, where thick the crocus blows,
Past the dark forges long disused,
The mule-track from Saint Laurent goes.
5   The bridge is crossed, and slow we ride,
Through forest, up the mountain-side.

The autumnal evening darkens round,
The wind is up, and drives the rain;
While, hark! far down, with strangled sound
10 Doth the Dead Guier's[2] stream complain,
Where that wet smoke, among the woods,
Over his boiling cauldron broods.

Swift rush the spectral vapours white
Past limestone scars with ragged pines,
15 Showing—then blotting from our sight!—
Halt—through the cloud-drift something shines!
High in the valley, wet and drear,
The huts of Courrerie appear.

Strike leftward! cries our guide; and higher
20 Mounts up the stony forest-way.
At last the encircling trees retire;
Look! through the showery twilight grey
What pointed roofs are these advance?
A palace of the Kings of France?

25 Approach, for what we seek is here!
Alight, and sparely sup, and wait
For rest in this outbuilding near;
Then cross the sward[3] and reach that gate.
Knock; pass the wicket! Thou art come
30 To the Carthusians' world-famed home.

The silent courts, where night and day
Into their stone-carved basins cold
The splashing icy fountains play—
The humid corridors behold!
35 Where, ghostlike in the deepening night,
Cowled forms brush by in gleaming white.

The chapel, where no organ's peal
Invests the stern and naked prayer—
With penitential cries they kneel
40 And wrestle; rising then, with bare
And white uplifted faces stand,
Passing the Host from hand to hand;

Each takes, and then his visage wan
Is buried in his cowl once more.
45 The cells!—the suffering Son of Man
Upon the wall—the knee-worn floor—
And where they sleep, that wooden bed,
Which shall their coffin be, when dead![4]

The library, where tract and tome
50 Not to feed priestly pride are there,
To hymn the conquering march of Rome,
Nor yet to amuse, as ours are!
They paint of souls the inner strife,
Their drops of blood, their death in life.

55 The garden, overgrown—yet mild,
See, fragrant herbs[5] are flowering there!
Strong children of the Alpine wild
Whose culture is the brethren's care;
Of human tasks their only one,
60 And cheerful works beneath the sun.

Those halls, too, destined to contain
Each its own pilgrim-host of old,
From England, Germany, or Spain—

---

[1] *Grande Chartreuse* Carthusian monastery in a nearly inaccessible valley in the French Alps, established by Saint Bruno in 1804. Arnold visited the monastery on his honeymoon in 1851. The Carthusians are known for their austerity, and devote their time to fasting, solitary contemplation, and prayer.

[2] *Dead Guier* Guiers Mort, a river that flows down past the monastery and into the Guiers Vif (French: "Living Guiers").

[3] *sward* Stretch of grass.

[4] *that wooden ... dead* Carthusians are buried on wooden planks. They are sometimes (incorrectly) thought to sleep in their coffins.

[5] *fragrant herbs* From which the Carthusians make the liqueur Chartreuse, the sales of which provide their primary source of income.

All are before me! I behold
65 The House, the Brotherhood austere!
—And what am I, that I am here?

For rigorous teachers seized my youth,
And purged its faith, and trimmed its fire,
Showed me the high, white star of Truth,
70 There bade me gaze, and there aspire.
Even now their whispers pierce the gloom:
What dost thou in this living tomb?

Forgive me, masters of the mind!
At whose behest I long ago
75 So much unlearnt, so much resigned—
I come not here to be your foe!
I seek these anchorites, not in ruth,°   remorse
To curse and to deny your truth;

Not as their friend, or child, I speak!
80 But as, on some far northern strand,
Thinking of his own Gods, a Greek
In pity and mournful awe might stand
Before some fallen Runic[1] stone—
For both were faiths, and both are gone.

85 Wandering between two worlds, one dead,
The other powerless to be born,
With nowhere yet to rest my head,
Like these, on earth I wait forlorn.
Their faith, my tears, the world deride—
90 I come to shed them at their side.

Oh, hide me in your gloom profound,
Ye solemn seats of holy pain!
Take me, cowled forms, and fence me round,
Till I possess my soul again;
95 Till free my thoughts before me roll,
Not chafed by hourly false control!

For the world cries your faith is now
But a dead time's exploded dream;
My melancholy, sciolists[2] say,
100 Is a passed mode, an outworn theme—

As if the world had ever had
A faith, or sciolists been sad!

Ah, if it *be* passed, take away,
At least, the restlessness, the pain;
105 Be man henceforth no more a prey
To these out-dated stings again!
The nobleness of grief is gone—
Ah, leave us not the fret alone!

But—if you cannot give us ease—
110 Last of the race of them who grieve
Here leave us to die out with these
Last of the people who believe!
Silent, while years engrave the brow;
Silent—the best are silent now.

115 Achilles[3] ponders in his tent,
The kings of modern thought are dumb;
Silent they are, though not content,
And wait to see the future come.
They have the grief men had of yore,
120 But they contend and cry no more.

Our fathers[4] watered with their tears
This sea of time whereon we sail,
Their voices were in all men's ears
Who passed within their puissant° hail.   powerful
125 Still the same ocean round us raves,
But we stand mute, and watch the waves.

For what availed it, all the noise
And outcry of the former men?
Say, have their sons achieved more joys,
130 Say, is life lighter now than then?
The sufferers died, they left their pain—
The pangs which tortured them remain.

What helps it now, that Byron bore,
With haughty scorn which mocked the smart,

---

[1] *Runic* Carved with runes (early Norse letters).

[2] *sciolists* Pretenders to knowledge.

[3] *Achilles* Greek warrior who, during the Trojan War, stayed in his tent, refusing to participate, until the death of his best friend, Patrocles, in battle, moved him to action.

[4] *Our fathers* I.e., the previous generation of writers.

135 Through Europe to the Aetolian shore[1]
     The pageant of his bleeding heart?
     That thousands counted every groan,
     And Europe made his woe her own?

     What boots it, Shelley! that the breeze
140 Carried thy lovely wail away,
     Musical through Italian trees
     Which fringe thy soft blue Spezzian bay?[2]
     Inheritors of thy distress
     Have restless hearts one throb the less?

145 Or are we easier, to have read,
     O Obermann![3] the sad, stern page,
     Which tells us how thou hidd'st thy head
     From the fierce tempest of thine age
     In the lone brakes of Fontainebleau,
150 Or chalets near the Alpine snow?

     Ye slumber in your silent grave!
     The world, which for an idle day
     Grace to your mood of sadness gave,
     Long since hath flung her weeds[4] away.
155 The eternal trifler breaks your spell;
     But we—we learnt your lore too well!

     Years hence, perhaps, may dawn an age,
     More fortunate, alas! than we,
     Which without hardness will be sage,
160 And gay without frivolity.
     Sons of the world, oh, speed those years;
     But, while we wait, allow our tears!

     Allow them! We admire with awe
     The exulting thunder of your race;
165 You give the universe your law,
     You triumph over time and space!

     Your pride of life, your tireless powers,
     We laud them, but they are not ours.

     We are like children reared in shade
170 Beneath some old-world abbey wall,
     Forgotten in a forest-glade,
     And secret from the eyes of all.
     Deep, deep the greenwood round them waves,
     Their abbey, and its close° of graves!   enclosure

175 But, where the road runs near the stream,
     Oft through the trees they catch a glance
     Of passing troops in the sun's beam—
     Pennon,[5] and plume, and flashing lance!
     Forth to the world those soldiers fare,
180 To life, to cities, and to war!

     And through the wood, another way,
     Faint bugle-notes from far are borne,
     Where hunters gather, staghounds bay,
     Round some fair forest-lodge at morn.
185 Gay dames are there, in sylvan green;
     Laughter and cries—those notes between!

     The banners flashing through the trees
     Make their blood dance and chain their eyes;
     That bugle-music on the breeze
190 Arrests them with a charmed surprise.
     Banner by turns and bugle woo:
     Ye shy recluses, follow too!

     O children, what do ye reply?
     "Action and pleasure, will ye roam
195 Through these secluded dells to cry
     And call us?—but too late ye come!
     Too late for us your call ye blow,
     Whose bent was taken long ago.

     "Long since we pace this shadowed nave;
200 We watch those yellow tapers shine,
     Emblems of hope over the grave,
     In the high altar's depth divine;

---

[1] *Aetolian shore* In Greece, where the English poet George
Gordon, Lord Byron, died.

[2] *Spezzian bay* Where English poet Percy Bysshe Shelley
drowned, in Italy.

[3] *Obermann* Protagonist of the 1804 novel of that name by
Etienne Pivert de Senancour (1770–1846).

[4] *weeds* Mourning garments.

---

[5] *Pennon* Narrow triangular flag, usually borne on the head of a
lance.

The organ carries to our ear
Its accents of another sphere.

205 "Fenced early in this cloistral round
Of reverie, of shade, of prayer,
How should we grow in other ground?
How should we flower in foreign air?
—Pass, banners, pass, and bugles, cease;
210 And leave our desert to its peace!"
—1855

Dover Beach

The sea is calm tonight.
The tide is full, the moon lies fair
Upon the straits—on the French coast the light
Gleams and is gone; the cliffs of England stand,
5   Glimmering and vast, out in the tranquil bay.
Come to the window, sweet is the night-air!
Only, from the long line of spray
Where the sea meets the moon-blanched land,
Listen! you hear the grating roar
10 Of pebbles which the waves draw back, and fling,
At their return, up the high strand,°   shore
Begin, and cease, and then again begin,
With tremulous cadence slow, and bring
The eternal note of sadness in.

15 Sophocles long ago
Heard it on the Aegean, and it brought
Into his mind the turbid ebb and flow
Of human misery;[1] we
Find also in the sound a thought,
20 Hearing it by this distant northern sea.

The Sea of Faith
Was once, too, at the full, and round earth's shore
Lay like the folds of a bright girdle furled.

But now I only hear
25 Its melancholy, long, withdrawing roar.
Retreating, to the breath
Of the night-wind, down the vast edges drear
And naked shingles[2] of the world.

Ah, love, let us be true
30 To one another! for the world, which seems
To lie before us like a land of dreams,
So various, so beautiful, so new,
Hath really neither joy, nor love, nor light,
Nor certitude, nor peace, nor help for pain;
35 And we are here as on a darkling plain
Swept with confused alarms of struggle and flight,
Where ignorant armies clash by night.[3]
—1867

East London[4]

'Twas August, and the fierce sun overhead
Smote on the squalid streets of Bethnal Green,
And the pale weaver, through his windows seen
In Spitalfields, looked thrice dispirited.

5   I met a preacher there I knew, and said:
"Ill and o'erworked, how fare you in this scene?"
"Bravely!" said he; "for I of late have been
Much cheered with thoughts of Christ, *the living
bread.*"

O human soul! as long as thou canst so
10 Set up a mark of everlasting light,
Above the howling senses' ebb and flow,

To cheer thee, and to right thee if thou roam—
Not with lost toil thou labourest through the night!
Thou mak'st the heaven thou hop'st indeed thy home.
—1867

---

[1] *Sophocles ... misery* Cf. Sophocles's *Antigone* 583–91: "Blest are those whose days have not tasted of evil. For when a house has once been shaken by the gods, no form of ruin is lacking, but it spreads over the bulk of the race, just as, when the surge is driven over the darkness of the deep by the fierce breath of Thracian sea-winds, it rolls up the black sand from the depths, and the wind-beaten headlands that front the blows of the storm give out a mournful roar."

[2] *shingles* Water-worn pebbles.

[3] *as on ... night* Reference to Thucydides's *History of the Peloponnesian War*, in which the invading Athenians became confused as night fell on the battle at Epipolae. Combatants could not tell friend from foe in the moonlight.

[4] *East London* Working-class area of the city. Bethnal Green and Spitalfields are districts in East London.

West London[1]

Crouched on the pavement, close by Belgrave
    Square,
A tramp I saw, ill, moody, and tongue-tied.
A babe was in her arms, and at her side
A girl; their clothes were rags, their feet were bare.

5 Some labouring men, whose work lay somewhere
    there,
Passed opposite ; she touched her girl, who hied°   *hastened*
Across, and begged, and came back satisfied.
The rich she had let pass with frozen stare.

Thought I: "Above her state this spirit towers;
10 She will not ask of aliens, but of friends,
Of sharers in a common human fate.

"She turns from that cold succour, which attends
The unknown little from the unknowing great,
And points us to a better time than ours."
—1867

from *The Function of Criticism at the Present Time*

Many objections have been made to a proposition which, in some remarks of mine on translating Homer,[2] I ventured to put forth; a proposition about criticism, and its importance at the present day. I said: "Of the literature of France and Germany, as of the intellect of Europe in general, the main effort, for now many years, has been a critical effort; the endeavour, in all branches of knowledge, theology, philosophy, history, art, science, to see the object as in itself it really is." I added, that owing to the operation in English literature of certain causes, "almost the last thing for which one would come to English literature is just that very thing which now Europe most desires—criticism"; and that the power and value of English literature was

thereby impaired. More than one rejoinder declared that the importance I here assigned to criticism was excessive, and asserted the inherent superiority of the creative effort of the human spirit over its critical effort. And the other day, having been led by a Mr. Shairp's excellent notice of Wordsworth[3] to turn again to his biography, I found, in the words of this great man, whom I, for one, must always listen to with the profoundest respect, a sentence passed on the critic's business, which seems to justify every possible disparagement of it. Wordsworth says in one of his letters:

> The writers in these publications [the reviews], while they prosecute their inglorious employment, can not be supposed to be in a state of mind very favourable for being affected by the finer influences of a thing so pure as genuine poetry.

And a trustworthy reporter of his conversation quotes a more elaborate judgement to the same effect:

> Wordsworth holds the critical power very low, infinitely lower than the inventive; and he said today that if the quantity of time consumed in writing critiques on the works of others were given to original composition, of whatever kind it might be, it would be much better employed; it would make a man find out sooner his own level, and it would do infinitely less mischief. A false or malicious criticism may do much injury to the minds of others, a stupid invention, either in prose or verse, is quite harmless.

It is almost too much to expect of poor human nature, that a man capable of producing some effect in one line of literature, should, for the greater good of society, voluntarily doom himself to impotence and

---

1 *West London* Wealthy end of the city. Belgrave Square was (and is) a particularly affluent district.

2 *in some ... Homer* In Arnold's *On Translating Homer* (1861).

3 [Arnold's note] I cannot help thinking that a practice, common in England during the last century, and still followed in France, of printing a notice of this kind—a notice by competent critics—to serve as an introduction to an eminent author's works, might be revived among us with advantage. To introduce all succeeding editions of Wordsworth, Mr. Shairp's notice might, it seems it me, excellently serve; it is written from the point of view of an admirer, nay, or a disciple, and that is right; but then the disciple must also be, as in this case he is, a critic, a man of letters, not, as too often happens, some relation or friend with no qualification for his task except affection for his author. [Arnold refers to J.C. Shairp's essay *Wordsworth: The Man and the Poet* (1864).]

obscurity in another. Still less is this to be expected from men addicted to the composition of the "false or malicious criticism" of which Wordsworth speaks. However, everybody would admit that a false or malicious criticism had better never been written. Everybody, too, would be willing to admit, as a general proposition, that the critical faculty is lower than the inventive. But is it true that criticism is really, in itself, a baneful and injurious employment; is it true that all time given to writing critiques on the works of others would be much better employed if it were given to original composition of whatever kind this may be? Is it true Johnson had better have gone on producing more *Irenes* instead of writing his *Lives of the Poets*;[1] nay, is it certain that Wordsworth himself was better employed in making his Ecclesiastical Sonnets than when he made his celebrated Preface,[2] so full of criticism, and criticism of the works of others? Wordsworth was himself a great critic, and it is to be sincerely regretted that he has not left us more criticism; Goethe[3] was one of the greatest of critics, and we may sincerely congratulate ourselves that he has left us so much criticism. Without wasting time over the exaggeration which Wordsworth's judgement on criticism clearly contains, or over an attempt to trace the causes—not difficult, I think, to be traced—which may have led Wordsworth to this exaggeration, a critic may with advantage seize an occasion for trying his own conscience, and for asking himself of what real service at any given moment the practice of criticism either is or may be made to his own mind and spirit, and to the minds and spirits of others.

The critical power is of lower rank than the creative. True; but in assenting to this proposition, one or two things are to be kept in mind. It is undeniable that the exercise of a creative power, that a free creative activity, is the highest function of man; it is proved to be so by man's finding in it his true happiness. But it is undeniable, also, that men may have the sense of exercising this free creative activity in other ways than in producing great words of literature or art; if it were not so, all but a very few men would be shut out from the true happiness of all men. They may have it in well-doing, they may have it in learning, they may have it even in criticising. This is one thing to be kept in mind. Another is, that the exercise of the creative power in the production of great works of literature or art, however high this exercise of it may rank, is not at all epochs and under all conditions possible; and that therefore labour may be vainly spent in attempting it, which might with more fruit be used in preparing for it, in rendering it possible. This creative power works with elements, with materials; what if it has not those materials, those elements, ready for its use? In that case it must surely wait till they are ready. Now in literature—I will limit myself to literature, for it is about literature that the question arises—the elements with which the creative power works are ideas; the best ideas, on every matter which literature touches, current at the time. At any rate we may lay it down as certain that in modern literature no manifestation of the creative power not working with these can be very important or fruitful. And I say current at the time, not merely accessible at the time; for creative literary genius does not principally show itself in discovering new ideas; that is rather the business of the philosopher. The grand work of literary genius is a work of synthesis and exposition, not of analysis and discovery; its gift lies in the faculty of being happily inspired by a certain intellectual and spiritual atmosphere, by a certain order of ideas, when it finds itself in them; of dealing divinely with these ideas, presenting them in the most effective and attractive combinations—making beautiful works with them, in short. But it must have the atmosphere, it must find itself amidst the order of ideas, in order to work freely; and these it is not so easy to command. This is why great creative epochs in literature are so rare, this is why there is so much that is unsatisfactory in the productions of many men of real genius; because, for the creation of a masterwork of literature two powers must concur, the power of the man and the power of the moment, and the man is not enough without the moment; the creative power has, for its happy exercise, appointed elements, and those

---

[1]   *Johnson ... Poets* Samuel Johnson is probably most celebrated today for his biographical and critical work *Lives of the English Poets* (1779–81), while his play *Irene* (1736) has never been highly regarded.

[2]   *Preface* To Wordsworth and Coleridge's *Lyrical Ballads* (1800). His *Ecclesiastical Sonnets* is not his best known work.

[3]   *Goethe* German poet and dramatist Johann Wolfgang von Goethe (1749–1832).

elements are not in its own control.

Nay, they are more within the control of the critical power. It is the business of the critical power, as I said in the words already quoted, "in all branches of knowledge, theology, philosophy, history, art, science, to see the object as in itself it really is." Thus it tends, at last, to make an intellectual situation of which the creative power can profitably avail itself. It tends to establish an order of ideas, if not absolutely true, yet true by comparison with that which it displaces; to make the best ideas prevail. Presently these new ideas reach society, the touch of truth is the touch of life, and there is a stir and growth everywhere; out of this stir and growth come the creative epochs of literature.

Or, to narrow our range, and quit these considerations of the general march of genius and of society—considerations which are apt to become too abstract and impalpable—every one can see that a poet, for instance, ought to know life and the world before dealing with them in poetry; and life and the world being in modern times very complex things, the creation of a modern poet, to be worth much, implies a great critical effort behind it; else it must be a comparatively poor, barren, and short-lived affair. This is why Byron's poetry had so little endurance in it, and Goethe's so much; both Byron and Goethe had a great productive power, but Goethe's was nourished by a great critical effort providing the true materials for it, and Byron's was not; Goethe knew life and the world, the poet's necessary subjects, much more comprehensively and thoroughly than Byron. He knew a great deal more of them, and he knew them much more as they really are.

It has long seemed to me that the burst of creative activity in our literature, through the first quarter of this century, had about it in fact something premature; and that from this cause its productions are doomed, most of them, in spite of the sanguine hopes which accompanied and do still accompany them, to prove hardly more lasting than the productions of far less splendid epochs. And this prematureness comes from its having proceeded without having its proper data, without sufficient materials to work with. In other words, the English poetry of the first quarter of this century, with plenty of energy, plenty of creative force, did not know

enough. This makes Byron so empty of matter, Shelley so incoherent, Wordsworth even, profound as he is, yet so wanting in completeness and variety. Wordsworth cared little for books, and disparaged Goethe. I admire Wordsworth, as he is, so much that I cannot wish him different; and it is vain, no doubt, to imagine such a man different from what he is, to suppose that he could have been different. But surely the one thing wanting to make Wordsworth an even greater poet than he is—his thought richer, and his influence of wider application—was that he should have read more books, among them, no doubt, those of that Goethe whom he disparaged without reading him.

But to speak of books and reading may easily lead to a misunderstanding here. It was not really books and reading that lacked to our poetry at this epoch; Shelley had plenty of reading, Coleridge had immense reading. Pindar[1] and Sophocles—as we all say so glibly, and often with so little discernment of the real import of what we are saying—had not many books; Shakespeare was no deep reader. True; but in the Greece of Pindar and Sophocles, in the England of Shakespeare, the poet lived in a current of ideas in the highest degree animating and nourishing to the creative power; society was, in the fullest measure, permeated by fresh thought, intelligent and alive. And this state of things is the true basis for the creative power's exercise, in this it finds its data, its materials, truly ready for its hand; all the books and reading in the world are only valuable as they are helps to this. Even when this does not actually exist, books and reading may enable a man to construct a kind of semblance of it in his own mind, a world of knowledge and intelligence in which he may live and work. This is by no means an equivalent to the artist for the nationally diffused life and thought of the epochs of Sophocles or Shakespeare; but, besides that it may be a means of preparation for such epochs, it does really constitute, if many share in it, a quickening and sustaining atmosphere of great value. Such an atmosphere the many-sided learning and the long and widely combined critical effort of Germany formed for Goethe, when he lived and worked. There was no national glow of life

---

[1]   *Pindar*   Greek lyric poet of the fifth century BCE.

and thought there, as in the Athens of Pericles[1] or the England of Elizabeth. That was the poet's weakness. But there was a sort of equivalent for it in the complete culture and unfettered thinking of a large body of Germans. That was his strength. In the England of the first quarter of this century there was neither a national glow of life and thought, such as we had in the age of Elizabeth, nor yet a culture and a force of learning and criticism such as were to be found in Germany. Therefore the creative power of poetry wanted, for success in the highest sense, materials and a basis; a thorough interpretation of the world was necessarily denied to it.

... The Englishman has been called a political animal, and he values what is political and practical so much that ideas easily become objects of dislike in his eyes, and thinkers "miscreants," because ideas and thinkers have rashly meddled with politics and practice. This would be all very well if the dislike and neglect confined themselves to ideas transported out of their own sphere, and meddling rashly with practice; but they are inevitably extended to ideas as such, and to the whole life of intelligence; practice is everything, a free play of the mind is nothing. The notion of the free play of the mind upon all subjects being a pleasure in itself, being an object of desire, being an essential provider of elements without which a nation's spirit, whatever compensations it may have for them, must, in the long run, die of inanition, hardly enters into an Englishman's thoughts. It is noticeable that the word *curiosity*, which in other languages is used in a good sense, to mean, as a high and fine quality of man's nature, just this disinterested love of a free play of the mind on all subjects, for its own sake—it is noticeable, I say, that this word has in our language no sense of the kind, no sense but a rather bad and disparaging one. But criticism, real criticism, is essentially the exercise of this very quality; it obeys an instinct prompting it to try to know the best that is known and thought in the world, irrespectively of practice, politics, and everything of the kind; and to value knowledge and thought as they approach this best, without the intrusion of any other considerations

whatever. This is an instinct for which there is, I think, little original sympathy in the practical English nature, and what there was of it has undergone a long benumbing period of blight and suppression in the epoch of concentration which followed the French Revolution.

But epochs of concentration cannot well endure for ever; epochs of expansion, in the due course of things, follow them. Such an epoch of expansion seems to be opening in this country. In the first place all danger of a hostile forcible pressure of foreign ideas upon our practice has long disappeared; like the traveller in the fable, therefore, we begin to wear our cloak a little more loosely.[2] Then, with a long peace, the ideas of Europe steal gradually and amicably in, and mingle, though in infinitesimally small quantities at a time, with our own notions. Then, too, in spite of all that is said about the absorbing and brutalising influence of our passionate material progress, it seems to me indisputable that this progress is likely, though not certain, to lead in the end to an apparition of intellectual life; and that man, after he has made himself perfectly comfortable and has now to determine what to do with himself next, may begin to remember that he has a mind, and that the mind may be made the source of great pleasure. I grant it is mainly the privilege of faith, at present, to discern this end to our railways, our business, and our fortune-making; but we shall see if, here as elsewhere, faith is not in the end the true prophet. Our ease, our travelling, and our unbounded liberty to hold just as hard and securely as we please to the practice to which our notions have given birth, all tend to beget an inclination to deal a little more freely with these notions themselves, to canvass them a little, to penetrate a little into their real nature. Flutterings of curiosity, in the foreign sense of the word, appear amongst us, and it is in these that criticism must look to find its account. Criticism first; a time of true creative activity, perhaps—which, as I have said, must inevitably be preceded amongst us by a time of criticism—hereafter, when criticism has done its work.

---

[1] *Athens of Pericles* Pericles was a leading Athenian statesman of the early fifth century BCE and was responsible for the construction of the Parthenon.

[2] *like the ... loosely* In one of Aesop's fables, the wind and the sun compete to see who is more powerful, betting on which of them can cause a traveler to take his cloak off first. The wind attempts to use force, but the fierce gusts only cause the traveler to clutch his cloak more tightly. When the sun shines on him, however, the traveler is persuaded to take off his cloak.

It is of the last importance that English criticism should clearly discern what rule for its course, in order to avail itself of the field now opening to it, and to produce fruit for the future, it ought to take. The rule may be summed up in one word—*disinterestedness*.[1] And how is criticism to show disinterestedness? By keeping aloof from what is called "the practical view of things"; by resolutely following the law of its own nature, which is to be a free play of the mind on all subjects which it touches. By steadily refusing to lend itself to any of those ulterior, political, practical considerations about ideas, which plenty of people will be sure to attach to them, which perhaps ought often to be attached to them, which in this country at any rate are certain to be attached to them quite sufficiently, but which criticism has really nothing to do with. Its business is, as I have said, simply to know the best that is known and thought in the world, and by in its turn making this known, to create a current of true and fresh ideas. Its business is to do this with inflexible honesty, with due ability; but its business is to do no more, and to leave alone all questions of practical consequences and applications, questions which will never fail to have due prominence given to them. Else criticism, besides being really false to its own nature, merely continues in the old rut which it has hitherto followed in this country, and will certainly miss the chance now given to it. For what is at present the bane of criticism in this country? It is that practical considerations cling to it and stifle it. It subserves interests not its own. Our organs of criticism are organs of men and parties having practical ends to serve, and with them those practical ends are the first thing and the play of the mind the second; so much play of mind as is compatible with the prosecution of those practical ends is all that is wanted. An organ like the *Revue des Deux Mondes*,[2] having for its main function to understand and utter the best that is known and thought in the world, existing, it may be said, as just an organ for a free play of the mind, we have not. But we have the *Edinburgh Review*, existing as an organ of the old Whigs, and for as much play of the mind as may suit its being that; we have the *Quarterly Review*, existing as an organ of the

Tories, and for as much play of mind as may suit its being that; we have the *British Quarterly Review*, existing as an organ of the political Dissenters, and for as much play of mind as may suit its being that; we have *The Times*, existing as an organ of the common, satisfied, well-to-do Englishman, and for as much play of mind as may suit its being that. And so on through all the various fractions, political and religious, of our society; every fraction has, as such, its organ of criticism, but the notion of combining all fractions in the common pleasure of a free disinterested play of mind meets with no favour. Directly this play of mind wants to have more scope, and to forget the pressure of practical considerations a little, it is checked, it is made to feel the chain. We saw this the other day in the extinction, so much to be regretted, of the *Home and Foreign Review*.[3] Perhaps in no organ of criticism in this country was there so much knowledge, so much play of mind; but these could not save it. The *Dublin Review* subordinates play of mind to the practical business of English and Irish Catholicism, and lives. It must needs be that men should act in sects and parties, that each of these sects and parties should have its organ, and should make this organ subserve the interests of its action; but it would be well, too, that there should be a criticism, not the minister of these interests, not their enemy, but absolutely and entirely independent of them. No other criticism will ever attain any real authority or make any real way towards its end—the creating a current of true and fresh ideas.

It is because criticism has so little kept in the pure intellectual sphere, has so little detached itself from practice, has been so directly polemical and controversial, that it has so ill accomplished, in this country, its best spiritual work; which is to keep man from a self-satisfaction which is retarding and vulgarizing, to lead him towards perfection, by making his mind dwell upon what is excellent in itself, and the absolute beauty and fitness of things. A polemical practical criticism makes men blind even to the ideal imperfection of their practice, makes them willingly assert its ideal perfection, in order the better to secure it against attack; and clearly this is narrowing and baneful for them. If they were

---

[1] *disinterestedness* I.e., objectivity.

[2] *Revue ... Mondes* International magazine founded in Paris in 1829.

[3] *Home ... Review* Liberal, predominantly Catholic periodical (1862–64).

reassured on the practical side, speculative considerations of ideal perfection they might be brought to
entertain, and their spiritual horizon would thus gradually widen. Sir Charles Adderley[1] says to the Warwickshire farmers—

> Talk of the improvement of breed! Why, the race we
> ourselves represent, the men and women, the old
> Anglo-Saxon race, are the best breed in the whole
> world...The absence of a too enervating climate, too
> unclouded skies, and a too luxurious nature, has
> produced so vigorous a race of people, and has
> rendered us so superior to all the world.

Mr. Roebuck says to the Sheffield cutlers—

> I look around me and ask what is the state of Eng-
> land? Is not property safe? Is not every man able to
> say what he likes? Can you not walk from one end
> of England to the other in perfect security? I ask you
> whether, the world over or in past history, there in
> anything like it? Nothing. I pray that our unrivaled
> happiness may last.

Now obviously there is a peril for poor human
nature in words and thoughts of such exuberant self-
satisfaction, until we find ourselves safe in the streets of
the Celestial City.

> Das wenige verschwindet leicht dem Blicke
> Der vorwärts sieht, wie viel noch übrig bleibt[2]—

says Goethe; "the little that is done seems nothing when
we look forward and see how much we have yet to do."
Clearly this is a better line of reflection for weak humanity, so long as it remains on this earthly field of labour
and trial.

But neither Sir Charles Adderley nor Mr. Roebuck
is by nature inaccessible to considerations of this sort.
They only lose sight of them owing to the controversial
life we all lead, and the practical from which all speculation takes with us. They have in view opponents whose
aim is not ideal, but practical; and in their zeal to
uphold their own practice against these innovators, they
go so far as even to attribute to this practice an ideal
perfection. Somebody has been wanting to introduce a
six-pound franchise, or to abolish church-rates, or to
collect agricultural statistics by force, or to diminish
local self-government. How natural, in reply to such
proposals, very likely improper or ill-timed, to go a little
beyond the mark and to say stoutly, "such a race of
people as we stand, so superior to all the world! The Old
Anglo-Saxon race, the best breed in the whole world! I
pray that our unrivaled happiness may last! I ask you
whether, the world over or in past history, there is
anything like it?" And so long as criticism answers this
dithyramb by insisting that the old Anglo-Saxon race
would be still more superior to all others if it had no
church-rates,[3] or that our unrivalled happiness would
last yet longer with a six-pound franchise, so long will
the strain, "The best breed in the whole world!" swell
louder and louder, everything ideal and refining will be
lost out of sight, and both the assailed and their critics
will remain in a sphere, to say the truth, perfectly
unvital, a sphere in which spiritual progression is
impossible. But let criticism leave church-rates and the
franchise alone, and in the most candid spirit, without
a single lurking thought of practical innovation, confront with our dithyramb this paragraph on which I
stumbled in a newspaper immediately after reading Mr.
Roebuck:

> A shocking child murder has just been committed at
> Nottingham. A girl named Wragg left the work-
> house there on Saturday morning with her young
> illegitimate child. The child was soon afterwards
> found dead on Mapperly Hills, having been stran-
> gled. Wragg is in custody.

Nothing but that; but, in juxtaposition with the
absolute eulogies of Sir Charles Adderley and Mr.
Roebuck, how eloquent, how suggestive are those few
lines! "Our old Anglo-Saxon breed, the best in the
whole world!"—how much that is harsh and ill-favoured
there is in this best! *Wragg*! If we are to talk of ideal

---

[1]   *Sir Charles Adderley*   Conservative member of Parliament and
landowner (1814–1905).

[2]   *Das wenige ... bleibt*   Goethe's *Iphigenie auf Tauris* 1.291–92.

[3]   *six-pound franchise*   Proposal to extend voting rights to anyone
whose property was worth six pounds or more annual rent—a radical
idea at the time; *church-rates*   Taxes paid to support the Church of
England.

perfection of "the best in the whole world," has any one reflected what a touch of grossness in our race, what an original shortcoming in the more delicate spiritual perceptions, is shown by the natural growth amongst us of such hideous names—Higginbottom, Stiggins, Bugg! In Ionia and Attica they were luckier in this respect than "the best race in the world"; by the Ilissus[1] there was no Wragg, poor thing! And "our unrivaled happiness"—what an element of grimness, bareness, and hideousness mixes with it and blurs it; the workhouse, the dismal Mapperly Hills[2]—how dismal those who have seen them will remember—the gloom, the smoke, the cold, the strangled illegitimate child! "I ask you whether, the world over or in past history, there is anything like it?" Perhaps not, one is inclined to answer; but at any rate, in that case, the world is very much to be pitied. And the final touch—short, bleak, and inhuman: *Wragg is in custody*. The sex lost in the confusion of our unrivalled happiness; or (shall I say?) the superfluous Christian name lopped off by the straightforward vigour of our old Anglo-Saxon breed! There is profit for the spirit in such contrasts as this; criticism serves the cause of perfection by establishing them. By eluding sterile conflict, by refusing to remain in the sphere where alone narrow and relative conceptions have any worth and validity, criticism may diminish its momentary importance, but only in this way has it a chance of gaining admittance for those wider and more perfect conceptions to which all its duty is really owed. Mr. Roebuck will have a poor opinion of an adversary who replies to his defiant songs of triumph only by murmuring under his breath, *Wragg is in custody*; but in no other way will these songs of triumph be induced gradually to moderate themselves, to get rid of what in them is excessive and offensive, and to fall into a softer and truer key.

It will be said that it is a very subtle and indirect action which I am thus prescribing for criticism, and that, by embracing in this manner the Indian virtue of detachment and abandoning the sphere of practical life, it condemns itself to a slow and obscure work. Slow and obscure it may be, but it is the only proper work of criticism. The mass of mankind will never have any ardent zeal for seeing things as they are; very inadequate ideas will always satisfy them. On these inadequate ideas reposes, and must repose, the general practice of the world. That is as much as saying that whoever sets himself to see things as they are will find himself one of a very small circle; but it is only by this small circle resolutely doing its own work that adequate ideas will ever get current at all. The rush and roar of practical life will always have a dizzying and attracting effect upon the most collected spectator, and tend to draw him into its vortex; most of all will this be the case where that life is so powerful as it is in England. But it is only by remaining collected, and refusing to lend himself to the point of view of the practical man, that the critic can do the practical man any service; and it is only by the greatest sincerity in pursuing his own course, and by at last convincing even the practical man of his sincerity, that he can escape misunderstandings which perpetually threaten him.

For the practical man is not apt for fine distinctions, and yet in these distinctions truth and the highest culture greatly find their account. But it is not easy to lead a practical man—unless you reassure him as to your practical intentions, you have no chance of leading him—to see a thing which he has always been used to look at from one side only, which he greatly values, and which, looked at from that side, quite deserves, perhaps, all the prizing and admiring which he bestows upon it—that this thing, looked at from another side, may appear much less beneficent and beautiful, and yet retain all its claims to our practical allegiance. Where shall we find language innocent enough, how shall we make the spotless purity of our intentions evident enough, to enable us to say to the political Englishman that the British Constitution itself, which, seen from the practical side, looks such a magnificent organ of progress and virtue, seen from the speculative side—with its compromises, its love of facts, its horror of theory, its studied avoidance of clear thoughts—that, seen from this side, our august Constitution sometimes looks—forgive me, shade of Lord Somers![3]—a colossal machine

---

[1]   *Ilisus*   River in Attica.

[2]   *Mapperly Hills*   Located near the coal-mining, industrial area of Nottingham.

[3]   *Lord Somers*   Statesman who presided over the creation of the Declaration of Rights (1689).

for the manufacture of Philistines?[1] How is Cobbett[2] to say this and not be misunderstood, blackened as he is with the smoke of a lifelong conflict in the field of political practice? How is Mr. Carlyle to say it and not be misunderstood, after his furious raid into this field with his *Latter-day Pamphlets*?[3] How is Mr. Ruskin, after his pugnacious political economy?[4] I say, the critic must keep out of the region of immediate practice in the political, social, humanitarian sphere, if he wants to make a beginning for that more free speculative treatment of things, which may perhaps one day make its benefits felt even in this sphere, but in a natural and thence irresistible manner. . . .

If I have insisted so much on the course which criticism must take where politics and religion are concerned, it is because, where these burning matters are in question, it is most likely to go astray. I have wished, above all, to insist on the attitude which criticism should adopt towards things in general; on its right tone and temper of mind. But then comes another question as to the subject-matter which literary criticism should most seek. Here, in general, its course is determined for it by the idea which is the law of its being; the idea of a disinterested endeavour to learn and propagate the best that is known and thought in the world, and thus to establish a current of fresh and true ideas. By the very nature of things, as England is not all the world, much of the best that is known and thought in the world cannot be of English growth, must be foreign; by the nature of things, again, it is just this that we are least likely to know, while English thought is streaming in upon us from all sides, and takes excellent care that we shall not be ignorant of its existence. The English critic of literature, therefore, must dwell much on foreign

thought, and with particular heed on any part of it, which, while significant and fruitful in itself, is for any reason specially likely to escape him. Again, judging is often spoken of as the critic's one business, and so in some sense it is; but the judgement which almost insensibly forms itself in a fair and clear mind, along with fresh knowledge, is the valuable one; and thus knowledge, and ever fresh knowledge, must be the critic's great concern for himself. And it is by communicating fresh knowledge, and letting his own judgement pass along with it—but insensibly, and in the second place, not the first, as a sort of companion and clue, not as an abstract lawgiver—that the critic will generally do most good to his readers. Sometimes, no doubt, for the sake of establishing an author's place in literature, and his relation to a central standard (and if this is not done, how are we to get at our best in the world?) criticism may have to deal with a subject-matter so familiar that fresh knowledge is out of the question, and then it must be all judgement; an enunciation and detailed application of principles. Here the great safeguard is never to let oneself become abstract, always to retain an intimate and lively consciousness of the truth of what one is saying, and, the moment this fails us, to be sure that something is wrong. Still, under all circumstances, this mere judgement and application of principles is, in itself, not the most satisfactory work to the critic; like mathematics, it is tautological, and cannot well give us, like fresh learning, the sense of creative activity.

But stop, someone will say; all this talk is of no practical use to us whatever; this criticism of yours is not what we have in our minds when we speak of criticism; when we speak of critics and criticism, we mean critics and criticism of the current English literature of the day; when you offer to tell criticism of its function, it is to this criticism that we expect you to address yourself. I am sorry for it, for I am afraid I must disappoint these expectations. I am bound by my own definition of criticism: a disinterested endeavour to learn and propagate the best that is known and thought in the world. How much of current English literature comes into this "best that is known and thought in the world"? Not very much, I fear; certainly less, at this moment, than of the current literature of France or Germany. Well, then, am I to alter my definition of criticism, in order to meet the

---

[1] *Philistines* Members of the Biblical tribe that fought against the Israelites. Here Arnold uses the term humorously to denote the unenlightened middle classes; "the enemy."

[2] *Cobbett* William Cobbett (1762–1835), farmer and radical political writer.

[3] *Latter-day Pamphlets* Satirical pamphlets, published in 1850, in which Thomas Carlyle expressed vehement anti-democratic views.

[4] *Mr. Ruskin ... economy* In his *Unto the Last* (1862), John Ruskin moved away from art criticism and attacked laissez-faire economics.

requirements of a number of practising English critics, who, after all, are free in their choice of a business? That would be making criticism lend itself just to one of those alien practical considerations, which, I have said, are so fatal to it. One may say, indeed, to those who have to deal with the mass—so much better disregarded—of current English literature, that they may at all events endeavour, in dealing with this, to try it, so far as they can, by the standard of the best that is known and thought in the world; one may say, that to get anywhere near this standard, every critic should try and possess one great literature, at least, besides his own; and the more unlike his own, the better. But, after all, the criticism I am really concerned with—the criticism which alone can much help us for the future, the criticism which, throughout Europe, is at the present day meant, when so much stress is laid on the importance of criticism and the critical spirit—is a criticism which regards Europe as being, for intellectual and spiritual purposes, one great confederation, bound to a joint action and working to a common result; and whose members have, for their proper outfit, a knowledge of Greek, Roman, and Eastern antiquity, and of one another. Special, local, and temporary advantages being put out of account, that modern nation will in the intellectual and spiritual sphere make most progress, which most thoroughly carries out this programme. And what is that but saying that we too, all of us, as individuals, the more thoroughly we carry it out, shall make the more progress?

There is so much inviting us!—what are we to take? what will nourish us in growth towards perfection? That is the question which, with the immense field of life and of literature lying before him, the critic has to answer; for himself first, and afterwards for others. In this idea of the critic's business the essays brought together in the following pages have had their origin; in this idea, widely different as are their subjects, they have, perhaps, their unity.

I conclude with what I said at the beginning: to have the sense of creative activity is the great happiness and the great proof of being alive, and it is not denied to criticism to have it; but then criticism must be sincere, simple, flexible, ardent, ever widening its knowledge. Then it may have, in no contemptible measure, a joyful sense of creative activity; a sense which a man of insight and conscience will prefer to what he might derive from a poor, starved, fragmentary, inadequate creation. And at some epochs no other creation is possible.

Still, in full measure, the sense of creative activity belongs only to genuine creation; in literature we must never forget that. But what true man of letters ever can forget it? It is no such common matter for a gifted nature to come into possession of a current of true and living ideas, and to produce amidst the inspiration of them, that we are likely to underrate it. The epochs of Aeschylus and Shakespeare make us feel their preeminence. In an epoch like those is, no doubt, the true life of literature; there is the promised land, towards which criticism can only beckon. That promised land it will not be ours to enter, and we shall die in the wilderness: but to have desired to enter it, to have saluted it from afar, is already, perhaps, the best distinction among contemporaries; it will certainly be the best title to esteem with posterity.

—1864

DANTE GABRIEL ROSSETTI
1828 – 1882

Dante Gabriel Rossetti's best work in both poetry and painting resembles a kind of illuminated manuscript glimpsed in "a fragment of Venetian glass." Walter Pater used these words to describe the Aesthetic arts whose efflorescence at the end of the nineteenth-century owed so much to Rossetti.

Stylized and radiant scenes of knights, maidens, and lovers—soon synonymous with Rossetti's name—found their original inspiration in works of early Italian, Christian, and medieval iconography. The subject of "The Blessed Damozel," one of Rossetti's finest poems, glows with the spiritually luminous effects associated with the religious poetry of Dante (Rossetti's namesake). Yet Rossetti also endowed his damsel with an earthly voluptuousness. Borrowing from Dantesque and Arthurian mythology, Rossetti created fantasies whose "stained glass" quality reflects both the literary outlines of religious allegory and the sensual strokes of an artist enraptured by the female figure. It was an artistic approach that ran the risk of causing offence at a time when soul and body, love and sex, were separate compartments of Victorian life, and Rossetti's work was frequently attacked in the later half of his career for trying to solder spiritual to "fleshly" desires.

Born in 1828 into an erudite family, Rossetti was the third of four children. He was a competitive yet fiercely fond older brother to his sister, the future poet Christina. His mother, Frances Polidori Rossetti, was Anglo-Italian; his father, Gabriele Rossetti, an exiled Italian patriot, was a Professor at King's College, London. The Rossetti's childhood home, with its assortment of orthodox and unorthodox books, was a meeting place where politicized ex-patriots spent many an evening debating the past and future of Italy. From the stream of sketches and literary compositions issuing from the temperamental imaginations of Dante Gabriel and Christina, it was apparent early on that the two youngest Rossettis were extraordinarily gifted. Their parents held high hopes that Dante Gabriel would become a great painter, even though his schooling in painting and his knowledge of European painting were not extensive.

Rossetti was a moody student at the Royal Academy art school in 1848 when he co-founded the Pre-Raphaelite Brotherhood with fellow painters William Holman Hunt, John Everett Millais, James Collinson, Frederic George Stephens, Thomas Woolner, and Dante Gabriel's brother, critic William Michael Rossetti. In a letter to his sister Christina, Rossetti spoke of it the group as a "Round Table" whose knights shared a mutual love of Keats. (They also adored Malory's *Morte Darthur*, the novels of Walter Scott, and the work of Blake, Dante, Tennyson, and Browning.) By referencing early Florentine and Sienese schools (dubbed "the Italian Primitives" because they predated the High Renaissance), the Pre-Raphaelites sought to reform what they saw as the florid emptiness of Victorian art and its lack of truth to nature. "Sincerity" as a quality of near-devotional feeling communicated through purity of line and color was more important to the Pre-Raphaelites than mere technical virtuosity. As one critic put it, the Pre-Raphaelites favored "primitive but vital imperfection, as opposed to lifeless perfection." A movement in both literature and painting, Pre-Raphaelitism was identified with a vivid palette, formal patterning, and symbolic details woven into exotic scenes of religious or romantic love whose settings evoked a sumptuous "elsewhere." In Pre-Raphaelite poetry and painting there was always a "definiteness of sensible imagery," as Pater said of "The Blessed Damozel."

When sixteen-year old Christina published *Verses* in 1847, Rossetti was compelled to try with meter what he was doing with color. "Colour and metre," Rossetti claimed, "are the true parents of nobility in painting and poetry." In 1850, the Pre-Raphaelite Brotherhood published a journal of poems and illustrations entitled *The Germ*, in which Rossetti's "The Blessed Damozel" first appeared. The publication gained Rossetti a small group of admirers that would steadily increase. Ruskin, who helped turn the tide in his favor by praising the art of the Pre-Raphaelites in *The Times* in 1851, became one of Rossetti's prominent patrons and closest friends. Rossetti cherished intellectual friendships with Robert Browning and William Morris, and socialized with the flamboyant Algernon Swinburne. He obtained stable employment teaching art at the Working Men's College. Stumbling across a book of William Blake's poems and paintings, Rossetti discovered another kindred spirit, albeit one who had died a year before he was born. Having secured his own reputation, Rossetti was able to rescue Blake from near oblivion, rediscovering him for a Victorian audience. In 1861, he also published *The Early Italian Poets*, which introduced, through his translations of the *Vita Nuova* and other poems by Dante and his predecessors and contemporaries, many poets whose work had been unknown in England.

Rossetti was also prone to what one biographer calls "rescue missions" of unknown beauties. Elizabeth Gaskell wrote that Rossetti was "hair-mad," with a penchant for the wavy tresses of women he and his friends called "stunners." On the one hand, Rossetti supported the equality and independence of working-class women like Elizabeth Siddal, whom he eventually married. On the other hand, his rescue of beautiful women from their class obscurity dramatized a sexual imbalance of power that was titillating; like many Victorian men, Rossetti enjoyed the license to "fall in love" with working class women without seriously compromising his reputation, a license prohibited women under the double standards of Victorian society.

Siddal, a model for the Pre-Raphaelites and an artist and poet in her own right, committed suicide in 1862, two years after her marriage to Rossetti. Invoking Dante's dead beloved, Beatrice, Rossetti memorialized Siddal in a painting entitled *Beata Beatrix* (c.1863). Seized with remorse at her funeral, he tucked a manuscript of poems into her coffin. He had them exhumed years later in order to publish his first collection of verse, *Poems* (1870). Though Rossetti afterwards lived with Fanny Cornforth, he fell in love with Jane Burden, the wife of William Morris. Both Fanny and "Janey" came from working class backgrounds and modeled for Rossetti, becoming sensuously stylized objects of desire in paintings such as *Proserpine* (1874).

Soon after the appearance of Rossetti's *The House of Life*, a sequence of 101 sonnets that appeared in his first volume of poetry, the poet Robert Buchanan denounced its "animalism" in a scalding critique entitled *The Fleshly School of Poetry* (1871). According to Buchanan, Rossetti's "house of life" was suggestive of a brothel and his sonnets bore the stamp of "the same sense of weary, wasting, yet exquisite sensuality." Rossetti counterattacked with *The Stealthy School of Criticism* (1872), but many readers since have felt that there was a germ of truth in Buchanan's criticisms: the spiritual impulse that strove to unite love and sexuality in Rossetti's art seems at times overshadowed by a carnal undergrowth verging upon the fetishistic.

Rossetti had always been temperamental, and Buchanan's attack temporarily deranged him. Though Yeats's youthful claim that he was "in all things Pre-Raphaelite" was proof of Rossetti's influence on the next generation of poets, Rossetti himself never fully recovered from being "stigmatized as a sensualist," in the words of one critic. He continued to paint and write, however, publishing *Ballads and Sonnets* in 1881. Bouts of nervous depression, made worse by the consumption of whiskey and narcotics, led to a decline in Rossetti's health; he died in 1882.

⌘ ⌘ ⌘

The Blessed Damozel [1]

The blessed damozel leaned out
    From the gold bar of Heaven;
Her eyes were deeper than the depth
    Of waters stilled at even;
5 She had three lilies in her hand,
    And the stars in her hair were seven.

Her robe, ungirt from clasp to hem,
    No wrought flowers did adorn,
But a white rose of Mary's gift,
10   For service meetly worn;
Her hair that lay along her back
    Was yellow like ripe corn.

Herseemed she scarce had been a day
    One of God's choristers;
15 The wonder was not yet quite gone
    From that still look of hers;
Albeit, to them she left, her day
    Had counted as ten years.

(To one, it is ten years of years.
20   ... Yet now, and in this place,
Surely she leaned o'er me—her hair
    Fell all about my face....
Nothing: the autumn-fall of leaves.
    The whole year sets apace.)

25 It was the rampart of God's house
    That she was standing on;
By God built over the sheer depth
    The which is Space begun;
So high, that looking downward thence
30   She scarce could see the sun.

Dante Gabriel Rossetti, *The Blessed Damozel* (1875–78).

It lies in Heaven, across the flood
    Of ether, as a bridge.
Beneath, the tides of day and night
    With flame and darkness ridge
35 The void, as low as where this earth
    Spins like a fretful midge. [2]

Around her, lovers, newly met
    'Mid deathless love's acclaims,
Spoke evermore among themselves
40   Their heart-remembered names;
And the souls mounting up to God
    Went by her like thin flames.

And still she bowed herself and stooped
    Out of the circling charm;

---

[1] *The Blessed Damozel* After the poem's publication, Rossetti told novelist Hall Caine that he had written it as something of a sequel to Edgar Allen Poe's poem "The Raven" (1845): "I saw that Poe had done the utmost it was possible to do with the grief of the lover on earth, and so determined to reverse the conditions, and give utterance to the yearning of the loved one in heaven." A "damozel" is a damsel, a young, unmarried woman.

---

[2] *midge* Small fly.

45 Until her bosom must have made
       The bar she leaned on warm,
   And the lilies lay as if asleep
       Along her bended arm.

   From the fixed place of Heaven she saw
50   Time like a pulse shake fierce
   Through all the worlds. Her gaze still strove
       Within the gulf to pierce
   Its path; and now she spoke as when
       The stars sang in their spheres.[1]

55 The sun was gone now; the curled moon
       Was like a little feather
   Fluttering far down the gulf; and now
       She spoke through the still weather.
   Her voice was like the voice the stars
60   Had when they sang together.

   (Ah sweet! Even now, in that bird's song,
       Strove not her accents there,
   Fain to be hearkened? When those bells
       Possessed the mid-day air,
65 Strove not her steps to reach my side
       Down all the echoing stair?)

   "I wish that he were come to me,
       For he will come," she said.
   "Have I not prayed in Heaven?—on earth,
70   Lord, Lord, has he not prayed?
   Are not two prayers a perfect strength?
       And shall I feel afraid?

   "When round his head the aureole° clings,   halo
       And he is clothed in white,
75 I'll take his hand and go with him
       To the deep wells of light;
   As unto a stream we will step down,
       And bathe there in God's sight.

   "We two will stand beside that shrine,
80   Occult,° withheld, untrod,   secret

Whose lamps are stirred continually
       With prayer sent up to God;
   And see our old prayers, granted, melt
       Each like a little cloud.

85 "We two will lie i'the shadow of
       That living mystic tree[2]
   Within whose secret growth the Dove[3]
       Is sometimes felt to be,
   While every leaf that His plumes touch
90   Saith His Name audibly.

   "And I myself will teach to him,
       I myself, lying so,
   The songs I sing here; which his voice
       Shall pause in, hushed and slow,
95 And find some knowledge at each pause,
       Or some new thing to know."

   (Alas! We two, we two, thou say'st!
       Yea, one wast thou with me
   That once of old. But shall God lift
100   To endless unity
   The soul whose likeness with thy soul
       Was but its love for thee?)

   "We two," she said, "will seek the groves
       Where the lady Mary is,
105 With her five handmaidens, whose names
       Are five sweet symphonies,
   Cecily, Gertrude, Magdalen,
       Margaret and Rosalys.

   "Circlewise sit they, with bound locks
110   And foreheads garlanded;
   Into the fine cloth white like flame
       Weaving the golden thread,
   To fashion the birth-robes for them
       Who are just born, being dead.

115 "He shall fear, haply,° and be dumb: perchance
       Then will I lay my cheek
   To his, and tell about our love,

---

[1] *as when ... spheres*   See Job 38.7, in which the morning stars sing on creation day. Rossetti probably also refers to the Pythagorean concept of the music of the spheres, inaudible to those on earth.

[2] *living mystic tree*   Tree of life (See Revelation 22.2).

[3] *Dove*   Holy Spirit.

Not once abashed or weak:
And the dear Mother will approve
120   My pride, and let me speak.

"Herself shall bring us, hand in hand,
    To him round whom all souls
Kneel, the clear-ranged unnumbered heads
    Bowed with their aureoles:°   haloes
125 And angels meeting us shall sing
    To their citherns and citoles.[1]

"There will I ask of Christ the Lord
    Thus much for him and me:
Only to live as once on earth
130   With Love—only to be,
As then awhile, for ever now
    Together, I and he."

She gazed and listened and then said,
    Less sad of speech than mild—
135 "All this is when he comes." She ceased.
    The light thrilled towards her, filled
With angels in strong level flight.
    Her eyes prayed, and she smiled.

(I saw her smile.) But soon their path
140   Was vague in distant spheres:
And then she cast her arms along
    The golden barriers,
And laid her face between her hands,
    And wept. (I heard her tears.)
—1850

The Woodspurge [2]

The wind flapped loose, the wind was still,
    Shaken out dead from tree and hill:

I had walked on at the wind's will—
I sat now, for the wind was still.

5 Between my knees my forehead was—
My lips, drawn in, said not Alas!
My hair was over in the grass,
My naked ears heard the day pass.

My eyes, wide open, had the run
10 Of some ten weeds to fix upon;
Among those few, out of the sun,
The woodspurge flowered, three cups in one.

From perfect grief there need not be
Wisdom or even memory:
15 One thing then learnt remains to me—
The woodspurge has a cup of three.
—1870

Jenny

"Vengeance of Jenny's case! Fie on her!
Never name her, child"
                                (Mrs. Quickly.)[3]

Lazy laughing languid Jenny,
    Fond of a kiss and fond of a guinea,[4]
Whose head upon my knee to-night
Rests for a while, as if grown light
5 With all our dances and the sound
To which the wild tunes spun you round:
Fair Jenny mine, the thoughtless queen
Of kisses which the blush between
Could hardly make much daintier;
10 Whose eyes are as blue skies, whose hair
Is countless gold incomparable;
Fresh flower, scarce touched with signs that tell
Of Love's exuberant hotbed—Nay,
Poor flower left torn since yesterday
15 Until to-morrow leave you bare;

---

[1] *citherns* Guitar-like instruments strung with wire and played with a quill, popular in the sixteenth and seventeenth centuries; *citoles* Stringed instruments common in the thirteenth to fifteenth centuries.

[2] *Woodspurge* Wildflower with cup-like, yellowish-green flowers that excrete a milky juice.

[3] *Vengeance ... Quickly* From Shakespeare's *The Merry Wives of Windsor* 1.1. The rest of Mistress Quickly's speech reads, "if she be a whore."

[4] *guinea* English gold coin.

Poor handful of bright spring-water
Flung in the whirlpool's shrieking face;
Poor shameful Jenny, full of grace
Thus with your head upon my knee—
20 Whose person or whose purse may be
The lodestar[1] of your reverie?

This room of yours, my Jenny, looks
A change from mine so full of books,
Whose serried[2] ranks hold fast, forsooth,
25 So many captive hours of youth—
The hours they thieve from day and night
To make one's cherished work come right,
And leave it wrong for all their theft,
Even as to-night my work was left:
30 Until I vowed that since my brain
And eyes of dancing seemed so fain,
My feet should have some dancing too—
And thus it was I met with you.
Well, I suppose 'twas hard to part,
35 For here I am. And now, sweetheart,
You seem too tired to get to bed.

It was a careless life I led
When rooms like this were scarce so strange
Not long ago. What breeds the change—
40 The many aims or the few years?
Because to-night it all appears
Something I do not know again.

The cloud's not danced out of my brain—
The cloud that made it turn and swim
45 While hour by hour the books grew dim.
Why, Jenny, as I watch you there,
For all your wealth of loosened hair,
Your silk ungirdled and unlaced
And warm sweets open to the waist,
50 All golden in the lamplight's gleam,
You know not what a book you seem,
Half-read by lightning in a dream!
How should you know, my Jenny? Nay,
And I should be ashamed to say—
55 Poor beauty, so well worth a kiss!

But while my thought runs on like this
With wasteful whims more than enough,
I wonder what you're thinking of.

If of myself you think at all,
60 What is the thought?—conjectural
On sorry matters best unsolved?—
Or inly° is each grace revolved   *inwardly*
To fit me with a lure?—or (sad
To think!) perhaps you're merely glad
65 That I'm not drunk or ruffianly
And let you rest upon my knee.

For sometimes, were the truth confessed,
You're thankful for a little rest—
Glad from the crush to rest within,
70 From the heart-sickness and the din
Where envy's voice at virtue's pitch
Mocks you because your gown is rich;
And from the pale girl's dumb rebuke,
Whose ill-clad grace and toil-worn look
75 Proclaim the strength that keeps her weak
And other nights than yours bespeak;
And from the wise unchildish elf,
To schoolmate lesser than himself
Pointing you out, what thing you are—
80 Yes, from the daily jeer and jar,
From shame and shame's outbraving too,
Is rest not sometimes sweet to you?
But most from the hatefulness of man
Who spares not to end what he began,
85 Whose acts are ill and his speech ill,
Who, having used you at his will,
Thrusts you aside, as when I dine
I serve the dishes and the wine.

Well, handsome Jenny mine, sit up,
90 I've filled our glasses, let us sup,
And do not let me think of you,
Lest shame of yours suffice for two.
What, still so tired? Well, well then, keep
Your head there, so you do not sleep;
95 But that the weariness may pass
And leave you merry, take this glass.
Ah! lazy lily hand, more blessed

---

[1]   *lodestar*   Pole star; i.e., guiding star.
[2]   *serried*   Pressed close together.

If ne'er in rings it had been dressed
Nor ever by a glove concealed!

100   Behold the lilies of the field,
They toil not neither do they spin;[1]
(So doth the ancient text begin—
Not of such rest as one of these
Can share.) Another rest and ease
105 Along each summer-sated path
From its new lord the garden hath,
Than that whose spring in blessings ran
Which praised the bounteous husbandman,
Ere yet, in days of hankering breath,
110 The lilies sickened unto death.

    What, Jenny, are your lilies dead?
Aye, and the snow-white leaves are spread
Like winter on the garden-bed.
But you had roses left in May—
115 They were not gone too. Jenny, nay,
But must your roses die, and those
Their purfled[2] buds that should unclose?
Even so; the leaves are curled apart,
Still red as from the broken heart,
120 And here's the naked stem of thorns.

    Nay, nay, mere words. Here nothing warns
As yet of winter. Sickness here
Or want alone could waken fear—
Nothing but passion wrings a tear.
125 Except when there may rise unsought
Haply° at times a passing thought   perchance
Of the old days which seem to be
Much older than any history
That is written in any book;
130 When she would lie in fields and look
Along the ground through the blown grass,
And wonder where the city was,
Far out of sight, whose broil° and bale°   tumult / woe
They told her then for a child's tale.

135 Jenny, you know the city now.
A child can tell the tale there, how
Some things which are not yet enrolled
In market-lists are bought and sold
Even till the early Sunday light,
140 When Saturday night is market-night
Everywhere, be it dry or wet,
And market-night in the Haymarket.
Our learned London children know,
Poor Jenny, all your pride and woe;
145 Have seen your lifted silken skirt
Advertise dainties through the dirt;
Have seen your coach-wheels splash rebuke
On virtue; and have learned your look
When, wealth and health slipped past, you stare
150 Along the streets alone, and there,
Round the long park, across the bridge,
The cold lamps at the pavement's edge
Wind on together and apart,
A fiery serpent for your heart.

155   Let the thoughts pass, an empty cloud!
Suppose I were to think aloud—
What if to her all this were said?
Why, as a volume seldom read
Being opened halfway shuts again,
160 So might the pages of her brain
Be parted at such words, and thence
Close back upon the dusty sense.
For is there hue or shape defined
In Jenny's desecrated mind,
165 Where all contagious currents meet,
A Lethe[3] of the middle street?
Nay, it reflects not any face,
Nor sound is in its sluggish pace,
But as they coil those eddies clot,
170 And night and day remember not.

    Why, Jenny, you're asleep at last!
Asleep, poor Jenny, hard and fast—
So young and soft and tired; so fair,
With chin thus nestled in your hair,

---

[1]   *Behold ... spin* Reference to Matthew 6.28: "And why take ye
thought for raiment? Consider the lilies of the field, how they grow;
they toil not, neither do they spin."

[2]   *purfled* Edged with another color.

---

[3]   *Lethe* River in Hades (the underworld of classical mythology)
whose waters bring forgetfulness to those who drink from them.

175　Mouth quiet, eyelids almost blue
　　As if some sky of dreams shone through!

　　　　Just as another woman sleeps!
　　Enough to throw one's thoughts in heaps
　　Of doubt and horror—what to say
180　Or think—this awful secret sway,
　　The potter's power over the clay!
　　Of the same lump (it has been said)
　　For honour and dishonour made,
　　Two sister vessels.[1] Here is one.

185　　　My cousin Nell is fond of fun,
　　And fond of dress, and change, and praise,
　　So mere a woman in her ways:
　　And if her sweet eyes rich in youth
　　Are like her lips that tell the truth,
190　My cousin Nell is fond of love.
　　And she's the girl I'm proudest of.
　　Who does not prize her, guard her well?
　　The love of change, in cousin Nell,
　　Shall find the best and hold it dear:
195　The unconquered mirth turn quieter
　　Not through her own, through others' woe:
　　The conscious pride of beauty glow
　　Beside another's pride in her,
　　One little part of all they share.
200　For Love himself shall ripen these
　　In a kind soil to just increase
　　Through years of fertilizing peace.

　　　　Of the same lump (as it is said)
　　For honour and dishonour made,
205　Two sister vessels. Here is one.

　　　　It makes a goblin of the sun.

　　　　So pure—so fallen! How dare to think
　　Of the first common kindred link?
　　Yet, Jenny, till the world shall burn
210　It seems that all things take their turn;
　　And who shall say but this fair tree

　　May need, in changes that may be,
　　Your children's children's charity?
　　Scorned then, no doubt, as you are scorned!
215　Shall no man hold his pride forewarned
　　Till in the end, the Day of Days,
　　At Judgment, one of his own race,
　　As frail and lost as you, shall rise—
　　His daughter, with his mother's eyes?

220　　　How Jenny's clock ticks on the shelf!
　　Might not the dial scorn itself
　　That has such hours to register?
　　Yet as to me, even so to her
　　Are golden sun and silver moon,
225　In daily largesse of earth's boon,
　　Counted for life-coins to one tune.
　　And if, as blindfold fates are tossed,
　　Through some one man this life be lost,
　　Shall soul not somehow pay for soul?

230　　　Fair shines the gilded aureole°　　　　　*halo*
　　In which our highest painters place
　　Some living woman's simple face.
　　And the stilled features thus descried
　　As Jenny's long throat droops aside—
235　The shadows where the cheeks are thin,
　　And pure wide curve from ear to chin—
　　With Raffael's, Leonardo's[2] hand
　　To show them to men's souls, might stand,
　　Whole ages long, the whole world through,
240　For preachings of what God can do.
　　What has man done here? How atone,
　　Great God, for this which man has done?
　　And for the body and soul which by
　　Man's pitiless doom must now comply
245　With lifelong hell, what lullaby
　　Of sweet forgetful second birth
　　Remains? All dark. No sign on earth
　　What measure of God's rest endows
　　The many mansions of his house.

250　　　If but a woman's heart might see
　　Such erring heart unerringly

---

[1]　*The potter's ... vessels*　Reference to Romans 9.21: "Hath not the
potter power over the clay, of the same lump to make one vessel
unto honor, and another unto dishonor?"

[2]　*Raffael's, Leonardo's*　I.e., Italian painters Raphael (1483–1520)
and Leonardo da Vinci (1452–1519).

For once! But that can never be.

    Like a rose shut in a book
In which pure women may not look,
255 For its base pages claim control
To crush the flower within the soul;
Where through each dead rose-leaf that clings,
Pale as transparent psyche-wings,
To the vile text, are traced such things
260 As might make lady's cheek indeed
More than a living rose to read;
So nought save foolish foulness may
Watch with hard eyes the sure decay;
And so the life-blood of this rose,
265 Puddled with shameful knowledge, flows
Through leaves no chaste hand may unclose:
Yet still it keeps such faded show
Of when 'twas gathered long ago,
That the crushed petals' lovely grain,
270 The sweetness of the sanguine stain,
Seen of a woman's eyes, must make
Her pitiful heart, so prone to ache,
Love roses better for its sake—
Only that this can never be:
275 Even so unto her sex is she.

    Yet, Jenny, looking long at you,
The woman almost fades from view.
A cipher of man's changeless sum
Of lust, past, present, and to come,
280 Is left. A riddle that one shrinks
To challenge from the scornful sphinx.[1]

    Like a toad within a stone
Seated while Time crumbles on;[2]

Which sits there since the earth was cursed
285 For Man's transgression at the first;
Which, living through all centuries,
Not once has seen the sun arise;
Whose life, to its cold circle charmed,
The earth's whole summers have not warmed;
290 Which always—whitherso the stone
Be flung—sits there, deaf, blind, alone;
Aye, and shall not be driven out
Till that which shuts him round about
Break at the very Master's stroke,
295 And the dust thereof vanish as smoke,
And the seed of Man vanish as dust—
Even so within this world is Lust.

    Come, come, what use in thoughts like this?
Poor little Jenny, good to kiss—
300 You'd not believe by what strange roads
Thought travels, when your beauty goads
A man to-night to think of toads!
Jenny, wake up … Why, there's the dawn!

    And there's an early wagon drawn
305 To market, and some sheep that jog
Bleating before a barking dog;
And the old streets come peering through
Another night that London knew;
And all as ghostlike as the lamps.

310   So on the wings of day decamps
My last night's frolic. Glooms begin
To shiver off as lights creep in
Past the gauze curtains half drawn-to,
And the lamp's doubled shade grows blue—
315 Your lamp, my Jenny, kept alight,
Like a wise virgin's, all one night!
And in the alcove coolly spread
Glimmers with dawn your empty bed;
And yonder your fair face I see
320 Reflected lying on my knee,
Where teems with first foreshadowings
Your pier-glass[3] scrawled with diamond rings:

---

[1] *sphinx* Winged creature of Greek mythology who killed those who could not answer its riddles.

[2] *Like a … on* The phenomenon of living toads, frogs, or other creatures trapped in stone or wood is one that has been occasionally reported. Once such instance occurred in 1865, when workers excavating in Hartlepool, England, split open a magnesium limestone rock found 25 feet underground to discover a living toad. The *Hartlepool Free Press* reported, "The cavity was no larger than its body, and presented the appearance of being cast for it." There was no evidence as to how the toad could have gotten into the stone or survived in it for any length of time. But, from its appearance and the age of the rock in which it was found, the toad was estimated to be over 6000 years old.

[3] *pier-glass* Large, tall mirror.

And on your bosom all night worn
Yesterday's rose now droops forlorn
325   But dies not yet this summer morn.

And now without, as if some word
Had called upon them that they heard,
The London sparrows far and nigh
Clamour together suddenly;
330   And Jenny's cage-bird grown awake
Here in their song his part must take,
Because here too the day doth break.

And somehow in myself the dawn
Among stirred clouds and veils withdrawn
335   Strikes greyly on her. Let her sleep.
But will it wake her if I heap
These cushions thus beneath her head
Where my knee was? No—there's your bed,
My Jenny, while you dream. And there
340   I lay among your golden hair
Perhaps the subject of your dreams,
These golden coins.

For still one deems
That Jenny's flattering sleep confers
345   New magic on the magic purse—
Grim web, how clogged with shrivelled flies!
Between the threads fine fumes arise
And shape their pictures in the brain.
There roll no streets in glare and rain,
350   Nor flagrant man-swine whets his tusk;
But delicately sighs in musk
The homage of the dim boudoir;
Or like a palpitating star
Thrilled into song, the opera-night
355   Breathes faint in the quick pulse of light;
Or at the carriage-window shine
Rich wares for choice; or, free to dine,
Whirls through its hour of health (divine
For her) the concourse of the Park.
360   And though in the discounted dark
Her functions there and here are one,
Beneath the lamps and in the sun
There reigns at least the acknowledged belle

Apparelled beyond parallel.
365   Ah Jenny, yes, we know your dreams.

For even the Paphian Venus[1] seems
A goddess o'er the realms of love,
When silver-shrined in shadowy grove:
Aye, or let offerings nicely placed
370   But hide Priapus[2] to the waist,
And whoso looks on him shall see
An eligible deity.

Why, Jenny, waking here alone
May help you to remember one,
375   Though all the memory's long outworn
Of many a double-pillowed morn.
I think I see you when you wake,
And rub your eyes for me, and shake
My gold, in rising, from your hair,
380   A Danaë[3] for a moment there.

Jenny, my love rang true! for still
Love at first sight is vague, until
That tinkling makes him audible.

And must I mock you to the last,
385   Ashamed of my own shame—aghast
Because some thoughts not born amiss
Rose at a poor fair face like this?
Well, of such thoughts so much I know:
In my life, as in hers, they show,
390   By a far gleam which I may near,
A dark path I can strive to clear.

Only one kiss. Goodbye, my dear.
—1870

---

[1]   *Paphian Venus* Venus, goddess of love, was said to have been born of sea-form, but emerged on the island of Paphos, Cypress.

[2]   *Priapus* God of procreation, and a personification of an erect phallus.

[3]   *Danaë* According to Greek mythology, Acrisius imprisoned his daughter Danaë in a room of bronze to ensure she would never conceive a son. Zeus, however, fell in love with Danaë and came to her through the ceiling as a shower of gold that fell in her lap.

My Sister's Sleep

She fell asleep on Christmas Eve:
    At length the long-ungranted shade
    Of weary eyelids overweighed
The pain nought else might yet relieve.

5   Our mother, who had leaned all day
    Over the bed from chime to chime,
    Then raised herself for the first time,
And as she sat her down, did pray.

Her little work-table was spread
10   With work to finish. For the glare
    Made by her candle, she had care
To work some distance from the bed.

Without, there was a cold moon up,
    Of winter radiance sheer and thin;
15   The hollow halo it was in
Was like an icy crystal cup.

Through the small room, with subtle sound
    Of flame, by vents the fireshine drove
    And reddened. In its dim alcove
20 The mirror shed a clearness round.

I had been sitting up some nights,
    And my tired mind felt weak and blank;
    Like a sharp strengthening wine it drank
The stillness and the broken lights.

25 Twelve struck. That sound, by dwindling years
    Heard in each hour, crept off; and then
    The ruffled silence spread again,
Like water that a pebble stirs.

Our mother rose from where she sat:
30   Her needles, as she laid them down,

Met lightly, and her silken gown
Settled: no other noise than that.

"Glory unto the Newly Born!"
    So, as said angels, she did say;
35   Because we were in Christmas Day,
Though it would still be long till morn.

Just then in the room over us
    There was a pushing back of chairs,
    As some who had sat unawares
40 So late, now heard the hour, and rose.

With anxious softly-stepping haste
    Our mother went where Margaret lay,
    Fearing the sounds o'erhead—should they
Have broken her long watched-for rest!

45 She stopped an instant, calm, and turned;
    But suddenly turned back again;
    And all her features seemed in pain
With woe, and her eyes gazed and yearned.

For my part, I but hid my face,
50   And held my breath, and spoke no word:
    There was none spoken; but I heard
The silence for a little space.

Our mother bowed herself and wept:
    And both my arms fell, and I said,
55   "God knows I knew that she was dead."
And there, all white, my sister slept.

Then kneeling, upon Christmas morn
    A little after twelve o'clock
    We said, ere the first quarter struck,
60 "Christ's blessing on the newly born!"
—1850

Dante Gabriel Rossetti, *Mary Magdalene at the Door of Simon the Pharisee* (1858).

Mary Magdalene at the Door of Simon the Pharisee [1] (For a Drawing) [2]

"Why wilt thou cast the roses from thine hair?
   Nay, be thou all a rose—wreath, lips, and
     cheek.
   Nay, not this house—that banquet-house we seek;
See how they kiss and enter; come thou there.

5 This delicate day of love we two will share
   Till at our ear love's whispering night shall speak.
   What, sweet one—hold'st thou still the foolish
     freak?°   *whim*
Nay, when I kiss thy feet they'll leave the stair."

"Oh loose me! See'st thou not my Bridegroom's face
10   That draws me to Him? For His feet my kiss,
    My hair, my tears He craves to-day—and oh!
What words can tell what other day and place
   Shall see me clasp those blood-stained feet of His?
    He needs me, calls me, loves me: let me go!"
—1870

from *The House of Life*

The Sonnet

A Sonnet is a moment's monument—
  Memorial from the Soul's eternity
  To one dead deathless hour. Look that it be,
Whether for lustral° rite or dire portent,   *purification*
5 Of its own arduous fulness reverent:
   Carve it in ivory or in ebony,
   As Day or Night may rule; and let Time see
Its flowering crest impearled and orient.

A Sonnet is a coin: its face reveals
10   The soul—its converse, to what Power 'tis due—
Whether for tribute to the august appeals
   Of Life, or dower in Love's high retinue,
It serve; or, 'mid the dark wharf's cavernous breath,
In Charon's [3] palm it pay the toll to Death.
—1881

---

[1] *Mary ... Pharisee* See Luke 7.36–50, which tells how an anonymous penitent, often assumed to be Mary Magdalene, burst into the house of Simon, a Pharisee, where Jesus was dining. She prostrated herself at his feet, which she then washed with her tears and dried with her hair.

[2] [Rossetti's note] In the drawing Mary has left a procession of revellers, and is ascending by a sudden impulse the steps of the house where she sees Christ. Her lover has followed her and is trying to turn her back.

[3] *Charon* In Greek mythology, ferryman of the river Styx who, for a fee, transports dead souls into Hades.

6a. Nuptial Sleep[1]

At length their long kiss severed, with sweet smart:
And as the last slow sudden drops are shed
From sparkling eaves when all the storm has fled,
So singly flagged the pulses of each heart.
5Their bosoms sundered, with the opening start
Of married flowers to either side outspread
From the knit stem; yet still their mouths, burnt red,
Fawned on each other where they lay apart.

Sleep sank them lower than the tide of dreams,
10And their dreams watched them sink, and slid away.
Slowly their souls swam up again, through gleams
Of watered light and dull drowned waifs of day;
Till from some wonder of new woods and streams
He woke, and wondered more: for there she lay.
—1870

10. The Portrait

O Lord of all compassionate control,
O Love! let this my lady's picture glow
Under my hand to praise her name, and show
Even of her inner self the perfect whole:
5That he who seeks her beauty's furthest goal,
Beyond the light that the sweet glances throw
And refluent wave of the sweet smile, may know
The very sky and sea-line of her soul.

Lo! it is done. Above the enthroning throat
10The mouth's mould testifies of voice and kiss,
The shadowed eyes remember and foresee.
Her face is made her shrine. Let all men note
That in all years (O Love, thy gift is this!)
They that would look on her must come to me.
—1870

Dante Gabriel Rossetti, *Sibylla Palmifera* (1868).

77. Soul's Beauty [2]

Under the arch of Life, where love and death,
Terror and mystery, guard her shrine, I saw
Beauty enthroned; and though her gaze struck awe,
I drew it in as simply as my breath.
5Hers are the eyes which, over and beneath,
The sky and sea bend on thee—which can draw,
By sea or sky or woman, to one law,
The allotted bondman of her palm and wreath.

This is that Lady Beauty, in whose praise
10Thy voice and hand shake still—long known to thee
By flying hair and fluttering hem—the beat
Following her daily of thy heart and feet,
How passionately and irretrievably,
In what fond flight, how many ways and days!
—1870

---

[1] *Nuptial Sleep* This sonnet was published in Rossetti's 1870 volume, *Poems*, but was omitted from the 1881 edition of *The House of Life* after Robert Buchanan, in his review *The Fleshly School of Poetry* (1871), attacked its depiction of "shameless nakedness."

[2] *Soul's Beauty* Originally titled "Sibylla Palmifera" ("palm-bearing sibyl"), this sonnet was composed to accompany the painting of that title, included above. The Sibyl (prophetess) of Cumae wrote her prophesies on palm leaves.

Dante Gabriel Rossetti, *Lady Lilith* (1868).

78. Body's Beauty[1]

O f Adam's first wife, Lilith, it is told
   (The witch he loved before the gift of Eve,)
     That, ere the snake's, her sweet tongue could deceive,
And her enchanted hair was the first gold.
5 And still she sits, young while the earth is old,
     And, subtly of herself contemplative,
     Draws men to watch the bright web she can weave,
Till heart and body and life are in its hold.

The rose and poppy are her flowers; for where
10   Is he not found, O Lilith, whom shed scent
And soft-shed kisses and soft sleep shall snare?
     Lo! as that youth's eyes burned at thine, so went
     Thy spell through him, and left his straight neck
       bent

---

1 *Body's Beauty* This sonnet, whose original title was "Lilith," was also composed to accompany a painting. Lilith was the first wife of Adam; according to Talmudic legend, she rejected Adam when she refused to accept a subservient position in sexual intercourse. She left the Garden of Eden and mated with various demons.

And round his heart one strangling golden hair.
—1870

97. A Superscription

L ook in my face; my name is Might-have-been;
   I am also called No-more, Too-late, Farewell;
     Unto thine ear I hold the dead-sea shell
Cast up thy Life's foam-fretted feet between;
5 Unto thine eyes the glass where that is seen
     Which had Life's form and Love's, but by my spell
     Is now a shaken shadow intolerable,
Of ultimate things unuttered the frail screen.

Mark me, how still I am! But should there dart
10   One moment through thy soul the soft surprise
     Of that winged Peace which lulls the breath of
       sighs—
Then shalt thou see me smile, and turn apart
Thy visage to mine ambush at thy heart
     Sleepless with cold commemorative eyes.
—1870

101. The One Hope

W hen vain desire at last and vain regret
   Go hand in hand to death, and all is vain,
     What shall assuage the unforgotten pain
And teach the unforgetful to forget?
5 Shall Peace be still a sunk stream long unmet—
     Or may the soul at once in a green plain
     Stoop through the spray of some sweet life- fountain
And cull the dew-drenched flowering amulet?[2]

Ah! when the wan soul in that golden air
10   Between the scriptured petals softly blown
     Peers breathless for the gift of grace unknown—
Ah! let none other alien spell soe'er
But only the one Hope's one name be there—
     Not less nor more, but even that word alone.
—1870

---

2 *amulet* Charm against evil, sickness, harm, etc.

ne of the most perfect poets
Swinburne claimed that
een less popular than
ding of sensuous
dmiration and
cism elicited
fresh and
setti's
al

ublic like." Rossetti nevertheless
n critics praised the volume for
both in theme and treatment."
Goblin Market" remains among
ael Rossetti's insistence that his
t many have found the precise

te *The Prince's Progress and Other*
, and *Verses* (1893). In *Sing-Song*
Monna Innominata," the "sonnet
d her own bold contribution to
nominata," Rossetti notes that
d the opportunity to speak for
"the portrait left us might have
devoted friend." According to
Elizabeth Barrett Browning do
her happy love-story, precluded
ast, speak of unfulfilled yearning
an's suffering such as Rossetti
e poem in biographical terms,
ductory prose-note … is a blind
on." But such readings, however

deep complexities of Rossetti's
work.

In 1871, Rossetti was stricken with exophthalmic bronchocele, or Graves's disease, a disease causing protrusion of the eyeballs, which led her to retreat even further into an already quiet life. Rossetti continued to live with and care for her mother and two aunts. She lived to see editions of her collected poems published in 1875 and then again in 1890, and in 1892 she was among those mentioned as a possible successor to Tennyson as England's Poet Laureate. She died in 1894 from cancer, having undergone surgery for breast cancer in 1892.

⌘ ⌘ ⌘

Goblin Market

Morning and evening
Maids heard the goblins cry:
"Come buy our orchard fruits,
Come buy, come buy:
5 Apples and quinces,
Lemons and oranges,
Plump unpecked cherries,
Melons and raspberries,
Bloom-down-cheeked peaches,
10 Swart°-headed mulberries,   dark

Wild free-born cranberries,
Crabapples, dewberries,
Pine-apples, blackberries,
Apricots, strawberries;—
15 All ripe together
In summer weather,—
Morns that pass by,
Fair eves that fly;
Come buy, come buy:
20 Our grapes fresh from the vine,
Pomegranates full and fine,
Dates and sharp bullaces,
Rare pears and greengages,

CHRISTINA ROSSETTI
1830 – 1894

To the late-Victorian critic Edmund Gosse, Christina Rossetti was "one of the most perfect poets of the age." Of her works, Rossetti's fellow-poet Algernon Charles Swinburne claimed that "nothing more glorious in poetry has ever been written." Rossetti may have been less popular than contemporaries such as Alfred Tennyson and Elizabeth Barrett Browning, melding of sensuous imagery and stringent form earned her the admiration and devotion of many nineteenth-century readers. Her lyricism elicited praise for being, as one critic wrote in 1862, "remarkably fresh and free," as well as "true and most genuine." The ease of Rossetti's lyric voice remains apparent in works as diverse as the sensual *Goblin Market* and the subtle religious hymns she penned throughout her career.

She was born in London in 1830, the youngest of four children. Her father, Gabriel Rossetti, was a scholar and an Italian exile, and her mother, Frances Polidori, was the English-Italian daughter of another Italian exile. Italian revolutionaries-in-exile frequented the Rossetti home, creating a provocative and unconventional environment for the Rossetti children. Other influences included their mother's devotion to Christianity and visits to their maternal grandfather's rural home. "If any one thing schooled me in the direction of poetry," Rossetti was later to write, "it was perhaps the delightful idle liberty to prowl all alone about my grandfather's cottage-grounds some thirty miles from London."

Rossetti's grandfather Polidori printed her first volume of poems, *Verses: Dedicated to Her Mother*, in 1847. Though immature in light of the works that would follow, the poems of the sixteen-year-old Rossetti already exhibited many of the qualities for which her work would later be known: directness of expression and simplicity of narrative colored with vivid and often sensuous detail. In 1850 several of her poems were published in *The Germ*, the journal of the Pre-Raphaelite Brotherhood founded in part by her two brothers, Dante Gabriel and William Michael. Although Rossetti was not formally a member of the Brotherhood, Rossetti's aesthetic sense—and especially her attention to color and detail—link her to the movement. Other Pre-Raphaelite values were also central to Rossetti's poetic vision, including a devotion to the faithful representation of nature and, at the same time, a penchant for symbolic representation.

The 1850s were a difficult time for Rossetti. Early in the decade she rejected, most likely on religious grounds, a suitor to whom she had been engaged for two years, the Pre-Raphaelite painter James Collinson. Collinson had converted to Anglicanism to please Rossetti, but he ultimately returned to his original faith, Catholicism. (In 1866 Rossetti appears to have rejected a second suitor, Charles Bagot Cayley, perhaps because he was an agnostic.) In 1854 Rossetti volunteered to join Florence Nightingale's nursing efforts in the Crimean War, but she was rejected for being too young. She volunteered instead at the Highgate Penitentiary for "fallen women." Throughout this period, she lived with her mother, sister, and brother William in the family home.

Rossetti first gained attention in the literary world with her 1862 publication of *Goblin Market and Other Poems*. Before publication of the volume, the eminent critic John Ruskin had declared the poems irregular in both their rhyme schemes and meters. Ruskin advised Rossetti to "exercise herself in the severest commonplace of metre until she [could] write as the public like." Rossetti nevertheless went ahead with publication, and the vast majority of her Victorian critics praised the volume for what one reviewer called its "very decided character and originality, both in theme and treatment." "Here," notes the *Eclectic Review*, "is a volume of really true poetry." "Goblin Market" remains among her most discussed works. Few readers have believed William Michael Rossetti's insistence that his sister "did not mean anything profound" by "Goblin Market," but many have found the precise nature of its deep suggestiveness elusive.

More volumes followed, among the most important of which were *The Prince's Progress and Other Poems* (1866), *Sing-Song* (1872), *A Pageant and Other Poems* (1881), and *Verses* (1893). In *Sing-Song* Rossetti proved herself a talented writer of children's verses. With "Monna Innominata," the "sonnet of sonnets" published in *A Pageant and Other Poems*, Rossetti offered her own bold contribution to the sonnet-sequence tradition. In the prose preface to "Monna Innominata," Rossetti notes that women such as Dante's Beatrice and Petrarch's Laura were denied the opportunity to speak for themselves. If either had spoken in her own voice, Rossetti writes, "the portrait left us might have appeared more tender, if less dignified, than any drawn even by a devoted friend." According to Rossetti, even the *Sonnets from the Portuguese* of the "Great Poetess" Elizabeth Barrett Browning do not offer us a voice "drawn from feeling": her circumstances, that is, her happy love-story, precluded her from giving her speaker such a voice. Rossetti's sonnets, in contrast, speak of unfulfilled yearning and painful loss, bringing to the sonnet form the voice of a woman's suffering such as Rossetti believed had never before been written. Critics have often read the poem in biographical terms, following from William Michael Rossetti's suggestion that the "introductory prose-note … is a blind … interposed to draw off attention from the writer in her proper person." But such readings, however tempting, limit interpretation of the poems and fail to account for the deep complexities of Rossetti's work.

In 1871, Rossetti was stricken with exophthalmic bronchocele, or Graves's disease, a disease causing protrusion of the eyeballs, which led her to retreat even further into an already quiet life. Rossetti continued to live with and care for her mother and two aunts. She lived to see editions of her collected poems published in 1875 and then again in 1890, and in 1892 she was among those mentioned as a possible successor to Tennyson as England's Poet Laureate. She died in 1894 from cancer, having undergone surgery for breast cancer in 1892.

⌘ ⌘ ⌘

Goblin Market

Morning and evening
Maids heard the goblins cry:
"Come buy our orchard fruits,
Come buy, come buy:
Apples and quinces,   5
Lemons and oranges,
Plump unpecked cherries,
Melons and raspberries,
Bloom-down-cheeked peaches,
Swart°-headed mulberries,   *dark*   10

Wild free-born cranberries,
Crabapples, dewberries,
Pine-apples, blackberries,
Apricots, strawberries;—
All ripe together   15
In summer weather,—
Morns that pass by,
Fair eves that fly;
Come buy, come buy:
Our grapes fresh from the vine,   20
Pomegranates full and fine,
Dates and sharp bullaces,
Rare pears and greengages,

Damsons[1] and bilberries
25 Taste them and try:
Currants and gooseberries,
Bright-fire-like barberries,
Figs to fill your mouth,
Citrons from the South,
30 Sweet to tongue and sound to eye;
Come buy, come buy."

Evening by evening
Among the brookside rushes,
Laura bowed her head to hear,
35 Lizzie veiled her blushes:
Crouching close together
In the cooling weather,
With clasping arms and cautioning lips,
With tingling cheeks and finger tips.
40 "Lie close," Laura said,
Pricking up her golden head:
"We must not look at goblin men,
We must not buy their fruits:
Who knows upon what soil they fed
45 Their hungry thirsty roots?"
"Come buy," call the goblins
Hobbling down the glen.
"Oh," cried Lizzie, "Laura, Laura,
You should not peep at goblin men."
50 Lizzie covered up her eyes,
Covered close lest they should look;
Laura reared her glossy head,
And whispered like the restless brook:
"Look, Lizzie, look, Lizzie,
55 Down the glen tramp little men.
One hauls a basket,
One bears a plate,
One lugs a golden dish
Of many pounds weight.
60 How fair the vine must grow
Whose grapes are so luscious;
How warm the wind must blow
Through those fruit bushes."
"No," said Lizzie: "No, no, no;
65 Their offers should not charm us,

Their evil gifts would harm us."
She thrust a dimpled finger
In each ear, shut eyes and ran:
Curious Laura chose to linger
70 Wondering at each merchant man.
One had a cat's face,
One whisked a tail,
One tramped at a rat's pace,
One crawled like a snail,
75 One like a wombat prowled obtuse and furry,
One like a ratel° tumbled hurry skurry.   *badger*
She heard a voice like voice of doves
Cooing all together:
They sounded kind and full of loves
80 In the pleasant weather.

sely she
Laura stretched her gleaming neck
smell Like a rush-imbedded swan,
Like a lily from the beck,°   *stream*
Like a moonlit poplar branch,
85 Like a vessel at the launch
When its last restraint is gone.

Backwards up the mossy glen
Turned and trooped the goblin men,
With their shrill repeated cry,
90 "Come buy, come buy."
When they reached where Laura was
They stood stock still upon the moss,
Leering at each other,
Brother with queer brother;
95 Signalling each other,
Brother with sly brother.
One set his basket down,
One reared his plate;
One began to weave a crown
100 Of tendrils, leaves, and rough nuts brown
(Men sell not such in any town);
One heaved the golden weight
Of dish and fruit to offer her:
"Come buy, come buy," was still their cry.
105 Laura stared but did not stir,
Longed but had no money:
The whisk-tailed merchant bade her taste
In tones as smooth as honey,

----

1 *bullaces ... Damsons* Bullaces, greengages, and damsons are all
varieties of plums.

The cat-faced purr'd,
110 The rat-paced spoke a word
Of welcome, and the snail-paced even was heard;
One parrot-voiced and jolly
Cried "Pretty Goblin" still for "Pretty Polly";—
One whistled like a bird.

115 But sweet-tooth Laura spoke in haste:
"Good Folk, I have no coin;
To take were to purloin:
I have no copper in my purse,
I have no silver either,
120 And all my gold is on the furze°   evergreen shrub
That shakes in windy weather
Above the rusty heather."
"You have much gold upon your head,"
They answered all together:
125 "Buy from us with a golden curl."
She clipped a precious golden lock,
She dropped a tear more rare than pearl,
Then sucked their fruit globes fair or red.
Sweeter than honey from the rock,[1]
130 Stronger than man-rejoicing wine,
Clearer than water flowed that juice;
She never tasted such before,
How should it cloy with length of use?
She sucked and sucked and sucked the more
135 Fruits which that unknown orchard bore;
She sucked until her lips were sore;
Then flung the emptied rinds away
But gathered up one kernel-stone,
And knew not was it night or day
140 As she turned home alone.

Lizzie met her at the gate
Full of wise upbraidings:
"Dear, you should not stay so late,
Twilight is not good for maidens;
145 Should not loiter in the glen
In the haunts of goblin men.
Do you not remember Jeanie,
How she met them in the moonlight,
Took their gifts both choice and many,
150 Ate their fruits and wore their flowers

Plucked from bowers
Where summer ripens at all hours?
But ever in the noonlight
She pined and pined away;
155 Sought them by night and day,
Found them no more but dwindled and grew grey;
Then fell with the first snow,
While to this day no grass will grow
Where she lies low:
160 I planted daisies there a year ago
That never blow.
You should not loiter so."
"Nay, hush," said Laura:
"Nay, hush, my sister:
165 I ate and ate my fill,
Yet my mouth waters still;
Tomorrow night I will
Buy more": and kissed her:
"Have done with sorrow;
170 I'll bring you plums tomorrow
Fresh on their mother twigs,
Cherries worth getting;
You cannot think what figs
My teeth have met in,
175 What melons icy cold
Piled on a dish of gold
Too huge for me to hold,
What peaches with a velvet nap,
Pellucid° grapes without one seed: translucent
180 Odorous indeed must be the mead
Whereon they grow, and pure the wave they drink
With lilies at the brink,
And sugar-sweet their sap."

Golden head by golden head,
185 Like two pigeons in one nest
Folded in each other's wings,
They lay down in their curtained bed:
Like two blossoms on one stem,
Like two flakes of new-fall'n snow,
190 Like two wands of ivory
Tipped with gold for awful° kings.   awe-inspiring
Moon and stars gazed in at them,
Wind sang to them lullaby,

---

[1]   *honey from the rock*   See Deuteronomy 32.13.

Lumbering owls forbore to fly,
195 Not a bat flapped to and fro
Round their rest:
Cheek to cheek and breast to breast
Locked together in one nest.

Early in the morning
200 When the first cock crowed his warning,
Neat like bees, as sweet and busy,
Laura rose with Lizzie:
Fetched in honey, milked the cows,
Aired and set to rights the house,
205 Kneaded cakes of whitest wheat,
Cakes for dainty mouths to eat,
Next churned butter, whipped up cream,
Fed their poultry, sat and sewed;
Talked as modest maidens should:
210 Lizzie with an open heart,
Laura in an absent dream,
One content, one sick in part;
One warbling for the mere bright day's delight,
One longing for the night.

215 At length slow evening came:
They went with pitchers to the reedy brooks;
Lizzie most placid in her look,
Laura most like a leaping flame.
They drew the gurgling water from its deep.
220 Lizzie plucked purple and rich golden flags,
Then turning homeward said: "The sunset flushes
Those furthest loftiest crags;
Come Laura, not another maiden lags.
No wilful squirrel wags,
225 The beasts and birds are fast asleep."
But Laura loitered still among the rushes,
And said the bank was steep.

And said the hour was early still,
The dew not fall'n, the wind not chill;
230 Listening ever, but not catching
The customary cry,
"Come buy, come buy,"
With its iterated jingle
Of sugar-baited words:
235 Not for all her watching

Once discerning even one goblin
Racing, whisking, tumbling, hobbling—
Let alone the herds
That used to tramp along the glen,
240 In groups or single,
Of brisk fruit-merchant men.
Till Lizzie urged, "O Laura, come;
I hear the fruit-call, but I dare not look:
You should not loiter longer at this brook:
245 Come with me home.
The stars rise, the moon bends her arc,
Each glowworm winks her spark,
Let us get home before the night grows dark:
For clouds may gather
250 Though this is summer weather,
Put out the lights and drench us thro';
Then if we lost our way what should we do?"

Laura turned cold as stone
To find her sister heard that cry alone,
255 That goblin cry,
"Come buy our fruits, come buy."
Must she then buy no more such dainty fruit?
Must she no more such succous° pasture find,   *juicy*
Gone deaf and blind?
260 Her tree of life drooped from the root:
She said not one word in her heart's sore ache;
But peering through the dimness, nought discerning,
Trudged home, her pitcher dripping all the way;
So crept to bed, and lay
265 Silent till Lizzie slept;
Then sat up in a passionate yearning,
And gnashed her teeth for baulked desire, and wept
As if her heart would break.

Day after day, night after night,
270 Laura kept watch in vain
In sullen silence of exceeding pain.
She never caught again the goblin cry,
"Come buy, come buy"—
She never spied the goblin men
275 Hawking their fruits along the glen:
But when the noon waxed bright
Her hair grew thin and grey;
She dwindled, as the fair full moon doth turn

To swift decay and burn
280 Her fire away.

One day remembering her kernel-stone
She set it by a wall that faced the south;
Dewed it with tears, hoped for a root,
Watched for a waxing shoot,
285 But there came none.
It never saw the sun,
It never felt the trickling moisture run:
While with sunk eyes and faded mouth
She dreamed of melons, as a traveller sees
290 False waves in desert drouth
With shade of leaf-crowned trees,
And burns the thirstier in the sandful breeze.

She no more swept the house,
Tended the fowl or cows,
295 Fetched honey, kneaded cakes of wheat,
Brought water from the brook:
But sat down listless in the chimney-nook
And would not eat.

Tender Lizzie could not bear
300 To watch her sister's cankerous care,
Yet not to share.
She night and morning
Caught the goblins' cry:
"Come buy our orchard fruits,
305 Come buy, come buy:"—
Beside the brook, along the glen,
She heard the tramp of goblin men,
The voice and stir
Poor Laura could not hear;
310 Longed to buy fruit to comfort her,
But feared to pay too dear.
She thought of Jeanie in her grave,
Who should have been a bride;
But who for joys brides hope to have
315 Fell sick and died
In her gay prime,
In earliest winter time,
With the first glazing rime,
With the first snow-fall of crisp Winter time.

320 Till Laura dwindling
Seemed knocking at Death's door.
Then Lizzie weighed no more
Better and worse;
But put a silver penny in her purse,
325 Kissed Laura, crossed the heath with clumps of furze
At twilight, halted by the brook:
And for the first time in her life
Began to listen and look.

Laughed every goblin
330 When they spied her peeping:
Came towards her hobbling,
Flying, running, leaping,
Puffing and blowing,
Chuckling, clapping, crowing.
335 Clucking and gobbling,
Mopping and mowing,
Full of airs and graces,
Pulling wry faces,
Demure grimaces,
340 Cat-like and rat-like,
Ratel- and wombat-like,
Snail-paced in a hurry,
Parrot-voiced and whistler,
Helter skelter, hurry skurry,
345 Chattering like magpies,
Fluttering like pigeons,
Gliding like fishes,—
Hugged her and kissed her:
Squeezed and caressed her:
350 Stretched up their dishes,
Panniers, and plates:
"Look at our apples
Russet and dun,
Bob at our cherries,
355 Bite at our peaches,
Citrons and dates,
Grapes for the asking,
Pears red with basking
Out in the sun,
360 Plums on their twigs;
Pluck them and suck them,—
Pomegranates, figs."

"Good folk," said Lizzie,
Mindful of Jeanie:
365   "Give me much and many"—
Held out her apron,
Tossed them her penny.
"Nay, take a seat with us,
Honour and eat with us,"
370   They answered grinning:
"Our feast is but beginning.
Night yet is early,
Warm and dew-pearly,
Wakeful and starry:
375   Such fruits as these
No man can carry;
Half their bloom would fly,
Half their dew would dry,
Half their flavour would pass by.
380   Sit down and feast with us,
Be welcome guest with us,
Cheer you and rest with us."—
"Thank you," said Lizzie: "But one waits
At home alone for me:
385   So without further parleying,°   *discussion*
If you will not sell me any
Of your fruits though much and many,
Give me back my silver penny
I tossed you for a fee."—
390   They began to scratch their pates,°   *heads*
No longer wagging, purring,
But visibly demurring,
Grunting and snarling.
One called her proud,
395   Cross-grained, uncivil;
Their tones waxed loud,
Their looks were evil.
Lashing their tails
They trod and hustled her,
400   Elbowed and jostled her,
Clawed with their nails,
Barking, mewing, hissing, mocking,
Tore her gown and soiled her stocking,
Twitched her hair out by the roots,
405   Stamped upon her tender feet,
Held her hands and squeezed their fruits
Against her mouth to make her eat.

White and golden Lizzie stood,
Like a lily in a flood,—
410   Like a rock of blue-veined stone
Lashed by tides obstreperously,—
Like a beacon left alone
In a hoary roaring sea,
Sending up a golden fire,—
415   Like a fruit-crowned orange tree
White with blossoms honey-sweet
Sore beset by wasp and bee,—
Like a royal virgin town
Topped with gilded dome and spire
420   Close beleaguered by a fleet
Mad to tug her standard down.

One may lead a horse to water,
Twenty cannot make him drink.
Though the goblins cuffed and caught her,
425   Coaxed and fought her,
Bullied and besought her,
Scratched her, pinched her black as ink,
Kicked and knocked her,
Mauled and mocked her,
430   Lizzie uttered not a word;
Would not open lip from lip
Lest they should cram a mouthful in:
But laughed in heart to feel the drip
Of juice that syruped all her face,
435   And lodged in dimples of her chin,
And streaked her neck which quaked like curd.
At last the evil people,
Worn out by her resistance,
Flung back her penny, kicked their fruit
440   Along whichever road they took,
Not leaving root or stone or shoot;
Some writhed into the ground,
Some dived into the brook
With ring and ripple,
445   Some scudded on the gale without a sound,
Some vanished in the distance.

In a smart, ache, tingle,
Lizzie went her way;
Knew not was it night or day;
450   Sprang up the bank, tore through the furze,

Threaded copse and dingle,°   dell
And heard her penny jingle
Bouncing in her purse,—
Its bounce was music to her ear.
455 She ran and ran
As if she feared some goblin man
Dogged her with gibe or curse
Or something worse:
But not one goblin skurried after,
460 Nor was she pricked by fear;
The kind heart made her windy-paced
That urged her home quite out of breath with haste
And inward laughter.

She cried, "Laura," up the garden,
465 "Did you miss me?
Come and kiss me.
Never mind my bruises,
Hug me, kiss me, suck my juices
Squeezed from goblin fruits for you,
470 Goblin pulp and goblin dew.
Eat me, drink me, love me;
Laura, make much of me;
For your sake I have braved the glen
And had to do with goblin merchant men."

475 Laura started from her chair,
Flung her arms up in the air,
Clutched her hair:
"Lizzie, Lizzie, have you tasted
For my sake the fruit forbidden?
480 Must your light like mine be hidden,
Your young life like mine be wasted,
Undone in mine undoing,
And ruined in my ruin,
Thirsty, cankered, goblin-ridden?"—
485 She clung about her sister,
Kissed and kissed and kissed her:
Tears once again
Refreshed her shrunken eyes,
Dropping like rain
490 After long sultry drouth;
Shaking with aguish[1] fear, and pain,
She kissed and kissed her with a hungry mouth.

Her lips began to scorch,
That juice was wormwood to her tongue,
495 She loathed the feast:
Writhing as one possessed she leaped and sung,
Rent all her robe, and wrung
Her hands in lamentable haste,
And beat her breast.
500 Her locks streamed like the torch
Borne by a racer at full speed,
Or like the mane of horses in their flight,
Or like an eagle when she stems the light
Straight toward the sun,
505 Or like a caged thing freed,
Or like a flying flag when armies run.

Swift fire spread through her veins, knocked at her
     heart,
Met the fire smouldering there
And overbore its lesser flame;
510 She gorged on bitterness without a name:
Ah! fool, to choose such part
Of soul-consuming care!
Sense failed in the mortal strife:
Like the watchtower of a town
515 Which an earthquake shatters down,
Like a lightning-stricken mast,
Like a wind-uprooted tree
Spun about,
Like a foam-topped waterspout
520 Cast down headlong in the sea,
She fell at last;
Pleasure past and anguish past,
Is it death or is it life?

Life out of death.
525 That night long Lizzie watched by her,
Counted her pulse's flagging stir,
Felt for her breath,
Held water to her lips, and cooled her face
With tears and fanning leaves.
530 But when the first birds chirped about their eaves,
And early reapers plodded to the place
Of golden sheaves,
And dew-wet grass
Bowed in the morning winds so brisk to pass,

---

[1] *aguish* Feverish.

535 And new buds with new day
Opened of cup-like lilies on the stream,
Laura awoke as from a dream,
Laughed in the innocent old way,
Hugged Lizzie but not twice or thrice;
540 Her gleaming locks showed not one thread of grey,
Her breath was sweet as May,
And light danced in her eyes.

Days, weeks, months, years
Afterwards, when both were wives
545 With children of their own;
Their mother-hearts beset with fears,
Their lives bound up in tender lives;
Laura would call the little ones
And tell them of her early prime,
550 Those pleasant days long gone
Of not-returning time:

Would talk about the haunted glen,
The wicked quaint fruit-merchant men,
Their fruits like honey to the throat
555 But poison in the blood;
(Men sell not such in any town):
Would tell them how her sister stood
In deadly peril to do her good,
And win the fiery antidote:
560 Then joining hands to little hands
Would bid them cling together,—
"For there is no friend like a sister
In calm or stormy weather;
To cheer one on the tedious way,
565 To fetch one if one goes astray,
To lift one if one totters down,
To strengthen whilst one stands."
—1862

In Context

Illustrating *Goblin Market*

The first edition of *Goblin Market* appeared in 1862 with a frontispiece by the author's brother, the Pre-Raphaelite painter and poet Dante Gabriel Rossetti. The round inset above the drawing of sisters Laura and Lizzie depicts the goblins carrying their fruits to market. Another notable edition was that of 1893, with art nouveau illustrations by artist and writer Laurence Housman (brother of poet A.E. Housman).

1862 Macmillan edition—illustration by
D.G. Rossetti.

Illustration by Laurence Housman from the 1893
Macmillan edition.

A Triad

Three sang of love together: one with lips
   Crimson, with cheeks and bosom in a glow,
Flushed to the yellow hair and finger tips;
   And one there sang who soft and smooth as snow
5   Bloomed like a tinted hyacinth at a show;

And one was blue with famine after love,
   Who like a harpstring snapped rang harsh and low
The burden of what those were singing of.
One shamed herself in love; one temperately
10   Grew gross in soulless love, a sluggish wife;
One famished died for love. Thus two of three
   Took death for love and won him after strife;
One droned in sweetness like a fattened bee:
   All on the threshold, yet all short of life.
—1862

Remember

Remember me when I am gone away,
   Gone far away into the silent land;
   When you can no more hold me by the hand,
Nor I half turn to go yet turning stay.
5 Remember me when no more day by day
   You tell me of our future that you planned:
   Only remember me; you understand
It will be late then to counsel or to pray.
Yet if you should forget me for a while
10   And afterwards remember, do not grieve:
   For if the darkness and corruption leave
A vestige of the thoughts that once I had,
Better by far you should forget and smile
   Than that you should remember and be sad.
—1862

A Birthday

My heart is like a singing bird
   Whose nest is in a watered shoot;
My heart is like an apple tree
   Whose boughs are bent with thickset fruit;
5 My heart is like a rainbow shell
   That paddles in a halcyon° sea;   *calm*
My heart is gladder than all these
   Because my love is come to me.

Raise me a dais of silk and down;
10   Hang it with vair° and purple dyes;   *squirrel fur*
Carve it in doves and pomegranates,

And peacocks with a hundred eyes;
Work it in gold and silver grapes,
    In leaves, and silver fleurs-de-lys;
15 Because the birthday of my life
    Is come, my love is come to me.
—1861

After Death

The curtains were half drawn, the floor was swept
    And strewn with rushes, rosemary and may
Lay thick upon the bed on which I lay,
Where thro' the lattice ivy-shadows crept.
5 He leaned above me, thinking that I slept
    And could not hear him; but I heard him say:
    "Poor child, poor child": and as he turned away
Came a deep silence, and I knew he wept.
He did not touch the shroud, or raise the fold
10   That hid my face, or take my hand in his,
    Or ruffle the smooth pillows for my head:
    He did not love me living; but once dead
He pitied me; and very sweet it is
To know he still is warm tho' I am cold.
—1862

An Apple-Gathering

I plucked pink blossoms from mine apple tree
    And wore them all that evening in my hair:
Then in due season when I went to see
    I found no apples there.

5 With dangling basket all along the grass
    As I had come I went the selfsame track:
My neighbours mocked me while they saw me pass
    So empty-handed back.

Lilian and Lilias smiled in trudging by,
10   Their heaped-up basket teazed me like a jeer;
Sweet-voiced they sang beneath the sunset sky,
    Their mother's home was near.

Plump Gertrude passed me with her basket full,
    A stronger hand than hers helped it along;
15 A voice talked with her thro' the shadows cool
    More sweet to me than song.

Ah Willie, Willie, was my love less worth
    Than apples with their green leaves piled above?
I counted rosiest apples on the earth
20   Of far less worth than love.

So once it was with me you stooped to talk
    Laughing and listening in this very lane;
To think that by this way we used to walk
    We shall not walk again!

25 I let my neighbours pass me, ones and twos
    And groups; the latest said the night grew chill,
And hastened: but I loitered, while the dews
    Fell fast I loitered still.
—1862

Echo

Come to me in the silence of the night;
    Come in the speaking silence of a dream;
Come with soft rounded cheeks and eyes as bright
    As sunlight on a stream;
5   Come back in tears,
O memory, hope, love of finished years.

O dream how sweet, too sweet, too bitter sweet,
    Whose wakening should have been in Paradise,
Where souls brimfull of love abide and meet;
10   Where thirsting longing eyes
    Watch the slow door
That opening, letting in, lets out no more.

Yet come to me in dreams, that I may live
    My very life again tho' cold in death:
15 Come back to me in dreams, that I may give
    Pulse for pulse, breath for breath:
    Speak low, lean low,
As long ago, my love, how long ago.
—1862

Winter: My Secret

I tell my secret? No indeed, not I:
　　Perhaps some day, who knows?
But not today; it froze, and blows, and snows,
And you're too curious: fie!
You want to hear it? well: 5
Only, my secret's mine, and I won't tell.

Or, after all, perhaps there's none:
Suppose there is no secret after all,
But only just my fun.
Today's a nipping day, a biting day;   10
In which one wants a shawl,
A veil, a cloak, and other wraps:
I cannot ope to every one who taps,
And let the draughts come whistling thro' my hall;
Come bounding and surrounding me,   15
Come buffeting, astounding me,
Nipping and clipping thro' my wraps and all.
I wear my mask for warmth: who ever shows
His nose to Russian snows
To be pecked at by every wind that blows?   20
You would not peck? I thank you for good will,
Believe, but leave that truth untested still.

Spring's an expansive time: yet I don't trust
March with its peck of dust,
Nor April with its rainbow-crowned brief showers,   25
Nor even May, whose flowers
One frost may wither thro' the sunless hours.

Perhaps some languid summer day,
When drowsy birds sing less and less,
And golden fruit is ripening to excess,   30
If there's not too much sun nor too much cloud,
And the warm wind is neither still nor loud,
Perhaps my secret I may say,
Or you may guess.
　—1862

"No, Thank You, John"

I never said I loved you, John:
　　Why will you teaze me day by day,
And wax a weariness to think upon
　　With always "do" and "pray"?

You know I never loved you, John;   5
　　No fault of mine made you my toast:[1]
Why will you haunt me with a face as wan
　　As shows an hour-old ghost?

I dare say Meg or Moll would take
　　Pity upon you, if you'd ask: 10
And pray don't remain single for my sake
　　Who can't perform that task.

I have no heart?—Perhaps I have not;
　　But then you're mad to take offence
That I don't give you what I have not got: 15
　　Use your own common sense.

Let bygones be bygones:
　　Don't call me false, who owed not to be true:
I'd rather answer "No" to fifty Johns
　　Than answer "Yes" to you.   20

Let's mar our pleasant days no more,
　　Songbirds of passage, days of youth:
Catch at today, forget the days before:
　　I'll wink at your untruth.

Let us strike hands as hearty friends;   25
　　No more, no less; and friendship's good:
Only don't keep in view ulterior ends,
　　And points not understood

In open treaty. Rise above
　　Quibbles and shuffling off and on: 30
Here's friendship for you if you like; but love,—
　　No, thank you, John.
　—1862

---

[1]   *your toast* I.e., the woman to whom John would raise a glass when toasting his lady.

A Pause Of Thought

I looked for that which is not, nor can be,
    And hope deferred made my heart sick in truth:
But years must pass before a hope of youth
    Is resigned utterly.

5 I watched and waited with a steadfast will:
    And though the object seemed to flee away
That I so longed for, ever day by day
    I watched and waited still.

Sometimes I said, "This thing shall be no more;
10   My expectation wearies and shall cease;
I will resign it now and be at peace:"
    Yet never gave it o'er.

Sometimes I said, "It is an empty name
    I long for; to a name why should I give
15 The peace of all the days I have to live?"—
    Yet gave it all the same.

Alas, thou foolish one! alike unfit
    For healthy joy and salutary pain:
Thou knowest the chase useless, and again
20   Turnest to follow it.
    —1848

Song

She sat and sang alway
    By the green margin of a stream,
Watching the fishes leap and play
    Beneath the glad sunbeam.

5 I sat and wept alway
    Beneath the moon's most shadowy beam,
Watching the blossoms of the May
    Weep leaves into the stream.

I wept for memory;
10   She sang for hope that is so fair:
My tears were swallowed by the sea;
    Her songs died on the air.
    —1862

Song

When I am dead, my dearest,
    Sing no sad songs for me;
Plant thou no roses at my head,
    Nor shady cypress tree.
5 Be the green grass above me
    With showers and dewdrops wet;
And if thou wilt, remember,
    And if thou wilt, forget.

I shall not see the shadows,
10   I shall not feel the rain;
I shall not hear the nightingale
    Sing on as if in pain.
And dreaming through the twilight
    That doth not rise nor set,
15 Haply° I may remember,   *by chance*
    And haply may forget.
    —1862

Dead Before Death

Ah! changed and cold, how changed and very cold!
    With stiffened smiling lips and cold calm eyes:
    Changed, yet the same; much knowing, little wise;
This was the promise of the days of old!
5 Grown hard and stubborn in the ancient mould,
    Grown rigid in the sham of lifelong lies:
    We hoped for better things as years would rise,
But it is over as a tale once told.
All fallen the blossom that no fruitage bore,
10   All lost the present and the future time,
All lost, all lost, the lapse that went before:
So lost till death shut-to the opened door,
    So lost from chime to everlasting chime,
So cold and lost for ever evermore.
    —1862

Monna Innominata [1]
A Sonnet of Sonnets

Beatrice, immortalized by "*altissimo poeta ... cotanto amante*";[2] Laura, celebrated by a great though an inferior bard[3]—have alike paid the exceptional penalty of exceptional honour, and have come down to us resplendent with charms, but (at least, to my apprehension) scant of attractiveness.

These heroines of worldwide fame were preceded by a bevy of unnamed ladies "*donne innominate*" sung by a school of less conspicuous poets; and in that land and that period which gave simultaneous birth to Catholics, to Albigenses, and to Troubadours,[4] one can imagine many a lady as sharing her lover's poetic aptitude, while the barrier between them might be one held sacred by both, yet not such as to render mutual love incompatible with mutual honour.

Had such a lady spoken for herself, the portrait left us might have appeared more tender, if less dignified, than any drawn even by a devoted friend. Or had the Great Poetess[5] of our own day and nation only been unhappy instead of happy, her circumstances would have invited her to bequeath to us, in lieu of the "Portuguese Sonnets," an inimitable "*donna innominata*" drawn not from fancy but from feeling, and worthy to occupy a niche beside Beatrice and Laura.

1

"Lo dì che han detto a' dolci amici addio."—DANTE
"Amor, con quanto sforzo oggi mi vinci!"—PETRARCA[6]

Come back to me, who wait and watch for you:—
⠀⠀Or come not yet, for it is over then,
⠀⠀⠀⠀And long it is before you come again,
So far between my pleasures are and few.

1⠀⠀*Monna Innominata*⠀⠀Italian: unnamed lady.

2⠀⠀*altissimo poeta ... cotanto amante*⠀⠀Italian: loftiest poet ... equally great lover (Italian). Rossetti refers to Italian poet Dante Alighieri (1265–1321), whose muse was Beatrice.

3⠀⠀*great ... bard*⠀⠀Italian poet Francesco Petrarca (1304–74) wrote many love songs to Laura.

4⠀⠀*Albigenses*⠀⠀Albigensians were members of a religious sect of the twelfth and thirteenth centuries; *Troubadours* Wandering lyric poets of the eleventh to thirteenth centuries.

5⠀⠀*Great Poetess*⠀⠀Elizabeth Barrett Browning.

6⠀⠀*Dante*⠀⠀From *Purgatorio* 8.3: "Who in the morn have bid sweet friends farewell"; *Petrarca* From *Canzone* 85.12: "Love, with what forces you conquer me now!"

5⠀While, when you come not, what I do I do
⠀⠀Thinking "Now when he comes," my sweetest "when":
⠀⠀For one man is my world of all the men
This wide world holds; O love, my world is you.
⠀⠀Howbeit, to meet you grows almost a pang
10⠀⠀⠀Because the pang of parting comes so soon;
⠀⠀⠀⠀My hope hangs waning, waxing, like a moon
⠀⠀⠀⠀⠀Between the heavenly days on which we meet:
Ah me, but where are now the songs I sang
⠀⠀When life was sweet because you called them sweet?

2

"Era già l'ora che volge il desio."—DANTE
"Ricorro al tempo ch' io vi vidi prima."—PETRARCA[7]

I wish I could remember that first day,
⠀⠀First hour, first moment of your meeting me,
⠀⠀If bright or dim the season, it might be
Summer or winter for aught I can say;
5⠀So unrecorded did it slip away,
⠀⠀So blind was I to see and to foresee,
⠀⠀So dull to mark the budding of my tree
That would not blossom yet for many a May.
If only I could recollect it, such
10⠀⠀A day of days! I let it come and go
⠀⠀⠀As traceless as a thaw of bygone snow;
It seemed to mean so little, meant so much;
If only now I could recall that touch,
⠀⠀First touch of hand in hand—Did one but know!

3

"O ombre vane, fuor che ne l'aspetto!"—DANTE
"Immaginata guida la conduce."—PETRARCA[8]

I dream of you to wake: would that I might
⠀⠀Dream of you and not wake but slumber on;
⠀⠀Nor find with dreams the dear companion gone,
As summer ended summer birds take flight.
5⠀In happy dreams I hold you full in sight,
⠀⠀I blush again who waking look so wan;

7⠀⠀*Dante*⠀⠀From *Purgatorio* 8.1: "Now was the hour that wakens fond desire"; *Petrarca* From Sonnet 20.3: "I remember when I saw you for the first time."

8⠀⠀*Dante*⠀⠀From *Purgatorio* 2.79: "Oh vain shadows, except in outward aspect"; *Petrarca* From *Canzone* 277.9: "An imagined guide leads her."

Brighter than sunniest day that ever shone,
In happy dreams your smile makes day of night.
Thus only in a dream we are at one,
10 Thus only in a dream we give and take
    The faith that maketh rich who take or give;
If thus to sleep is sweeter than to wake,
    To die were surely sweeter than to live,
Tho' there be nothing new beneath the sun.

4

"Poca favilla gran fiamma seconda."—DANTE
"Ogni altra cosa, ogni pensier va fore,
E sol ivi con voi rimansi amore."—PETRARCA[1]

I loved you first: but afterwards your love,
    Outsoaring mine, sang such a loftier song
As drowned the friendly cooings of my dove.
    Which owes the other most? My love was long,
5   And yours one moment seemed to wax more strong;
I loved and guessed at you, you construed me
And loved me for what might or might not be—
    Nay, weights and measures do us both a wrong.
For verily love knows not "mine" or "thine";
10   With separate "I" and "thou" free love has done,
    For one is both and both are one in love:
Rich love knows nought of "thine that is not mine";
    Both have the strength and both the length
        thereof,
    Both of us, of the love which makes us one.

5

"Amor che a nullo amato amar perdona."—DANTE
"Amor m'addusse in sì gioiosa spene."—PETRARCA[2]

O my heart's heart, and you who are to me
    More than myself myself, God be with you,
    Keep you in strong obedience leal° and true   *loyal*
To Him whose noble service setteth free;
5 Give you all good we see or can foresee,
    Make your joys many and your sorrows few,

Bless you in what you bear and what you do,
Yea, perfect you as He would have you be.
So much for you; but what for me, dear friend?
10   To love you without stint and all I can
Today, tomorrow, world without an end;
    To love you much and yet to love you more,
    As Jordan at his flood sweeps either shore;
Since woman is the helpmeet made for man.

6

"Or puoi la quantitate
Comprender de l'amor che a te mi scalda."—DANTE
"Non vo'che da tal nodo amor mi sciolglia."—PETRARCA[3]

Trust me, I have not earned your dear rebuke,
    I love, as you would have me, God the most;
    Would lose not Him, but you, must one be lost,
Nor with Lot's wife cast back a faithless look,[4]
5 Unready to forego what I forsook;
    This say I, having counted up the cost,
    This, tho' I be the feeblest of God's host,
The sorriest sheep Christ shepherds with His crook.
Yet while I love my God the most, I deem
10   That I can never love you overmuch;
    I love Him more, so let me love you too;
    Yea, as I apprehend it, love is such
I cannot love you if I love not Him,
    I cannot love Him if I love not you.

7

"Qui primavera sempre ed ogni frutto."—DANTE
"Ragionando con meco ed io con lui."—PETRARCA[5]

"Love me, for I love you"—and answer me,
    "Love me, for I love you": so shall we stand
    As happy equals in the flowering land
Of love, that knows not a dividing sea.
5 Love builds the house on rock and not on sand,
    Love laughs what while the winds rave desperately;

---

[1] *Dante* From *Paradiso* 1.34: "From a small spark a great flame rises"; *Petrarca* From *Canzone* 72.44–45: "All other hopes, all other thoughts are gone, and love with you remains there alone."

[2] *Dante* From *Inferno* 5.103: "Love, that denial takes from none beloved"; *Petrarca* From Sonnet 56.11: "Love urged me in this gladness to believe."

[3] *Dante* From *Purgatorio* 21.133–34: "Now has thou proved the force and ardor of the love I bear thee"; *Petrarca* From *Canzone* 59.17: "I do not wish love to release me from this knot."

[4] *Lot's wife … look* See Genesis 19.26: "[Lot's] wife looked back from behind him, and she became a pillar of salt."

[5] *Dante* From *Purgatorio* 28.143: "Perpetual spring and every fruit"; *Petrarca* From *Canzone* 35.14: "Speaking with me and I with him."

And who hath found love's citadel unmanned?
    And who hath held in bonds love's liberty?—
My heart's a coward tho' my words are brave—
    We meet so seldom, yet we surely part
    So often; there's a problem for your art!
Still I find comfort in his Book, who saith,
Tho' jealousy be cruel as the grave,
    And death be strong, yet love is strong as death.[1]

8

"Come dicesse a Dio, D'altro non calme." —DANTE
"Spero trovar pietà non che perdono."—PETRARCA[2]

"I, if I perish, perish"—Esther spake:[3]
    And bride of life or death she made her fair
    In all the lustre of her perfumed hair
And smiles that kindle longing but to slake.
She put on pomp of loveliness, to take
    Her husband through his eyes at unaware;
    She spread abroad her beauty for a snare,
Harmless as doves and subtle as a snake.
She trapped him with one mesh of silken hair,
    She vanquished him by wisdom of her wit,
        And built her people's house that it should
           stand:—
    If I might take my life so in my hand,
And for my love to Love put up my prayer,
    And for love's sake by Love be granted it!

9

"O dignitosa coscienza e netta!"—DANTE
"Spirto più acceso di virtuti ardenti."—PETRARCA[4]

Thinking of you, and all that was, and all
    That might have been and now can never be,
    I feel your honoured excellence, and see
Myself unworthy of the happier call:
For woe is me who walk so apt to fall,
    So apt to shrink afraid, so apt to flee,
    Apt to lie down and die (ah woe is me!)
Faithless and hopeless turning to the wall.
And yet not hopeless quite nor faithless quite,
    Because not loveless; love may toil all night,
        But take at morning; wrestle till the break
          Of day, but then wield power with God and
           man:—
        So take I heart of grace as best I can,
    Ready to spend and be spent for your sake.

10

"Con miglior corso e con migliore stella."—DANTE
"La vita fugge e non s'arresta un' ora."—Petrarca[5]

Time flies, hope flags, life plies a wearied wing;
    Death following hard on life gains ground apace;
    Faith runs with each and rears an eager face,
Outruns the rest, makes light of everything,
Spurns earth, and still finds breath to pray and sing;
    While love ahead of all uplifts his praise,
    Still asks for grace and still gives thanks for grace,
Content with all day brings and night will bring.
Life wanes; and when love folds his wings above
    Tired hope, and less we feel his conscious pulse,
        Let us go fall asleep, dear friend, in peace:
        A little while, and age and sorrow cease;
    A little while, and life reborn annuls
Loss and decay and death, and all is love.

---

[1] his Book … death See The Song of Solomon 6: "Set me as a seal upon your heart, as a seal upon your arm; for love is strong as death, passion fierce as the grave."

[2] *Dante* From *Purgatorio* 8.12: "As if telling God, "I care for nothing else""; *Petrarca* From *Canzone* 1.8: "I hope to find pity, not just forgiveness."

[3] *I … spake* From Esther 4.16, in which Queen Esther says to Mordecai, before donning beautiful robes and appealing to her husband to cease his mission to kill her people, the Jews: "Go, gather together all the Jews … and neither eat nor drink three days, night or day: I also and my maidens will fast likewise; and so will I go in unto the king, which is not according to the law: and if I perish, I perish."

[4] *Dante* From *Purgatorio* 3.8: "Oh conscience clear and upright!"; *Petrarca* From *Canzone* 283.3: "Spirit dazzling with blazing virtues."

[5] *Dante* From *Paradiso* 1.40: "In best course and in happiest constellation"; *Petrarca* From *Canzone* 272.1: "Life flies and doesn't stay for an hour."

11

"Vien dietro a me e lascia dir le genti."—DANTE
"Contando i casi della vita nostra."—PETRARCA[1]

Many in aftertimes will say of you
   "He loved her"—while of me what will they say?
   Not that I loved you more than just in play,
For fashion's sake as idle women do.
5 Even let them prate; who know not what we knew
   Of love and parting in exceeding pain,
   Of parting hopeless here to meet again,
Hopeless on earth, and heaven is out of view.
But by my heart of love laid bare to you,
10 My love that you can make not void nor vain,
Love that foregoes you but to claim anew
     Beyond this passage of the gate of death,
   I charge you at the Judgment make it plain
     My love of you was life and not a breath.

12

"Amor, che ne la mente mi ragiona."—DANTE
"Amor vien nel bel viso di costei."—PETRARCA[2]

If there be any one can take my place
   And make you happy whom I grieve to grieve,
   Think not that I can grudge it, but believe
I do commend you to that nobler grace,
5 That readier wit than mine, that sweeter face;
   Yea, since your riches make me rich, conceive
   I too am crowned, while bridal crowns I weave,
And thread the bridal dance with jocund° pace.   *merry*
For if I did not love you, it might be
10 That I should grudge you some one dear delight;
     But since the heart is yours that was mine own,
   Your pleasure is my pleasure, right my right,
Your honourable freedom makes me free,
     And you companioned I am not alone.

13

"E drizzeremo glí occhi al Primo Amore."—DANTE
"Ma trovo peso non de le mie braccia."—PETRARCA[3]

If I could trust mine own self with your fate,
   Shall I not rather trust it in God's hand?
   Without Whose Will one lily doth not stand,
Nor sparrow fall at His appointed date;
5 Who numbereth the innumerable sand,
Who weighs the wind and water with a weight,
To Whom the world is neither small nor great,
   Whose knowledge foreknew every plan we planned.
Searching my heart for all that touches you,
10 I find there only love and love's goodwill
Helpless to help and impotent to do,
     Of understanding dull, of sight most dim;
     And therefore I commend you back to Him
Whose love your love's capacity can fill.

14

"E la Sua Volontade è nostra pace."—DANTE
"Sol con questi pensier, con altre chiome."—PETRARCA[4]

Youth gone, and beauty gone if ever there
   Dwelt beauty in so poor a face as this;
   Youth gone and beauty, what remains of bliss?
I will not bind fresh roses in my hair,
5 To shame a cheek at best but little fair,—
   Leave youth his roses, who can bear a thorn,—
I will not seek for blossoms anywhere,
   Except such common flowers as blow with corn.[5]
Youth gone and beauty gone, what doth remain?
10 The longing of a heart pent up forlorn,
     A silent heart whose silence loves and longs;
     The silence of a heart which sang its songs
   While youth and beauty made a summer morn,
Silence of love that cannot sing again.
—1881

1 *Dante* From *Purgatorio* 5.13: "Come after me, and leave behind the people's babblings"; *Petrarca* From *Canzone* 285.12: "Telling of the changes in our lives."

2 *Dante* From *Purgatorio* 2.112: "Love that discourses in my thoughts"; *Petrarca* From *Canzone* 13.2: "Love appears in the beautiful face of this lady."

3 *Dante* From *Paradiso* 32.142: "And our eyes will turn unto the first Love"; *Petrarca* From Sonnet 20.5: "The burden I find too great a weight for my arms."

4 *Dante* From *Paradiso* 3.85: "And in his will is our tranquility"; *Petrarca* From *Canzone* 30.32: "Alone with these thoughts, with time-altered locks of hair."

5 *corn* Grain.

Cobwebs

It is a land with neither night nor day,
Nor heat nor cold, nor any wind, nor rain,
    Nor hills nor valleys; but one even plain
Stretches thro' long unbroken miles away:
While thro' the sluggish air a twilight grey   5
    Broodeth; no moons or seasons wax and wane,
    No ebb and flow are there along the main,
No bud-time no leaf-falling there for aye,°   *any*
No ripple on the sea, no shifting sand,
    No beat of wings to stir the stagnant space,   10
No pulse of life thro' all the loveless land:
And loveless sea; no trace of days before,
    No guarded home, no toil-won resting place
No future hope no fear for evermore.
—1896 (WRITTEN 1855)

In an Artist's Studio

One face[1] looks out from all his canvasses,
    One selfsame figure sits or walks or leans:
    We found her hidden just behind those screens,
That mirror gave back all her loveliness.
A queen in opal or in ruby dress,   5
    A nameless girl in freshest summer-greens,
    A saint, an angel;—every canvass means
The same one meaning, neither more nor less.
He feeds upon her face by day and night,
    And she with true kind eyes looks back on him,   10
Fair as the moon and joyful as the light:
    Not wan with waiting, nor with sorrow dim;
Not as she is, but was when hope shone bright;
    Not as she is, but as she fills his dream.
—1896

Dante Gabriel Rossetti's *Beata Beatrix* (1864–70).

Promises like Pie-crust [2]

Promise me no promises,
    So will I not promise you;
Keep we both our liberties,
    Never false and never true:
Let us hold the die uncast,   5
    Free to come as free to go;
For I cannot know your past,
    And of mine what can you know?

---

[1] *One face* I.e., Elizabeth (Lizzie) Siddal's. Siddal (1829–62) was D.G. Rossetti's model for *Beata Beatrix* and many other paintings; the two eventually married. She was a poet and artist in her own right.

[2] *Promises like Pie-crust* See Jonathan Swift's comment: "Promises and pie-crust are made to be broken."

You, so warm, may once have been
    Warmer towards another one;
10 I, so cold, may once have seen
    Sunlight, once have felt the sun:
Who shall show us if it was
    Thus indeed in time of old?
15 Fades the image from the glass
    And the fortune is not told.

If you promised, you might grieve
    For lost liberty again;
If I promised, I believe
20   I should fret to break the chain:
Let us be the friends we were,
    Nothing more but nothing less;
Many thrive on frugal fare
    Who would perish of excess.
    —1896 (WRITTEN 1861)

In Progress

Ten years ago it seemed impossible
    That she should ever grow so calm as this,
    With self-remembrance in her warmest kiss
And dim dried eyes like an exhausted well.
5 Slow-speaking when she has some fact to tell,
    Silent with long-unbroken silences,
    Centred in self yet not unpleased to please,

Gravely monotonous like a passing bell.
Mindful of drudging daily common things,
10   Patient at pastime, patient at her work,
Wearied perhaps but strenuous certainly.
Sometimes I fancy we may one day see
    Her head shoot forth seven stars from where they lurk
And her eyes lightnings and her shoulders wings.
    —1896

Sleeping at Last

Sleeping at last, the trouble & tumult over,
    Sleeping at last, the struggle & horror past,
Cold & white out of sight of friend & of lover
Sleeping at last.

5 No more a tired heart downcast or overcast,
No more pangs that wring or shifting fears that hover,
Sleeping at last in a dreamless sleep locked fast.

Fast asleep. Singing birds in their leafy cover
Cannot wake her, nor shake her gusty blast.
10 Under the purple thyme & the purple clover
Sleeping at last.
    —1896

LEWIS CARROLL
1832 – 1898

Lewis Carroll (the pseudonym of Charles Dodgson) created some of the most beloved and enduring literature for children ever written in English. *Alice's Adventures in Wonderland* and *Through the Looking-Glass* have remained perennially popular since their first publication. His famously frustrated protagonist, who engages in bewildering exchanges with such memorable characters as the Mad Hatter, the Cheshire Cat, the March Hare, and the Mock Turtle, is as familiar a figure as any character in nineteenth-century fiction.

Charles Lutwidge Dodgson was the third of eleven children born to Frances Jane Lutwidge and the Reverend Charles Dodgson, who was a mathematician and later a curate in Daresbury, Cheshire. Because they lived in a remote village, the Dodgson children were largely schooled at home and relied on one another for amusement; Charles contributed many stories and drawings to their various family magazines. He became a fine student when he later entered boarding school, winning many awards and scholarships.

Dodgson continued to excel at Oxford University, where he followed in his father's footsteps and took first place honors in mathematics. He thereafter spent almost his entire life as a lecturer in mathematics at Oxford, where he was given a lifetime fellowship, with the stipulation that he enter the ministry and refrain from marrying. During his early years there, he took up the then-new art of photography as a hobby and devoted himself to taking exquisite photographs—primarily of children, although he later also became known for his portraits of famous literary figures, Alfred, Lord Tennyson and Dante Gabriel Rossetti among them.

Dodgson eventually became acquainted with the family of Henry Liddell, who was then Dean of Christ Church College. As he had done with many other children, Dodgson endeared himself to the three Liddell daughters by weaving elaborate tales for their amusement. On one occasion, Dodgson and a friend took advantage of a beautiful summer's day to go boating down the Thames with the Liddell girls. During the outing Carroll began making up the story of Alice's adventures underground, wherein Alice goes down a rabbit hole and meets various characters that both fascinate and confound her. He later often looked back upon this day wistfully, as when he wrote of the "birth" of the Alice of his tales: "I can call it up almost as clearly as if it were yesterday—the cloudless blue above, the watery mirror below, the boat drifting idly on its way, the tinkle of the drops that fell from the oars … the three eager faces, hungry for news of fairy-land, and who would not be said 'nay' to: from whose lips 'Tell us a story, please,' had all the stern immutability of Fate!" The poet W.H. Auden later called July 4, the day of this 1862 outing, "as memorable a day in the history of literature as it is in American history."

After Dodgson had complied with Alice Liddell's request to write up the story for her, Henry Kingsley (brother of novelist Charles Kingsley) saw the manuscript and persuaded him to publish it. Having already published several books on mathematics under his own name, he took the name Lewis, which he anglicized from "Ludovicus," the Latin word for "Lutwidge," and Carroll from "Carolus," Latin for "Charles." *Alice's Adventures in Wonderland* appeared in 1865 with illustrations by *Punch* cartoonist John Tenniel. From that point on, Lewis Carroll's fame far surpassed that of

Charles Dodgson. In 1872 he published the sequel *Through the Looking-Glass and what Alice Found There*, which continued the tale of Alice as she passes through a mirror and finds herself engaged as a pawn in a topsy-turvy game of chess. (By this time, sadly, he was entirely estranged from the Liddells.)

Carroll later wrote three books of nonsense poems including *The Hunting of the Snark* (1876). He also published *Sylvie and Bruno* and *Sylvie and Bruno Concluded* (1889 and 1893), but the novel and its sequel never achieved the fame of the Alice series. The author died of bronchitis in 1898; he is buried in a cemetery near the home he bought for his family in Surrey.

⌘ ⌘ ⌘

Verses Recited by Humpty Dumpty[1]

In winter when the fields are white,
I sing this song for your delight.

In spring, when woods are getting green,
I'll try and tell you what I mean.

5   In summer, when the days are long,
Perhaps you'll understand the song.

In autumn, when the leaves are brown,
Take pen and ink and write it down.

I sent a message to the fish:
10   I told them "This is what I wish."

The little fishes of the sea,
They sent an answer back to me.

The little fishes' answer was
"We cannot do it, sir, because."

15   I sent to them again to say
"It will be better to obey."

The fishes answered with a grin,
"Why, what a temper you are in!"

I told them once, I told them twice;
20   They would not listen to advice.

I took a kettle large and new,
Fit for the deed I had to do.

My heart went hop, my heart went thump;
I filled the kettle at the pump.

25   Then someone came to me and said,
"The little fishes are in bed."

I said to him, I said it plain,
"Then you must wake them up again."

I said it very loud and clear;
30   I went and shouted in his ear.

But he was very stiff and proud;
He said, "You needn't shout so loud!"

And he was very proud and stiff;
He said, "I'd go and wake them, if ——"

35   I took a corkscrew from the shelf;
I went to wake them up myself.

And when I found the door was locked,
I pulled and pushed and kicked and knocked.

And when I found the door was shut,
40   I tried to turn the handle, but ——
("That's all," said Humpty Dumpty.)
   —1872

---

[1]   *Verses … Dumpty*   From *Through the Looking-Glass and What Alice Found There*, Ch. 6: "Humpty Dumpty."

Jabberwocky[1]

'Twas brillig and the slithy toves
 Did gyre and gimble in the wabe;
All mimsy were the borogroves,
 And the mome raths outgrabe.

5 "Beware the Jabberwock, my son!
 The jaws that bite, the claws that catch!
Beware the Jubjub bird, and shun
 The frumious Bandersnatch!"

He took his vorpal sword in hand:
10 Long time the manxome foe he sought—
So rested he by the Tumtum tree.
 And stood awhile in thought.

And as in uffish thought he stood,
 The Jabberwock, with eyes of flame,

15 Came whiffling through the tulgey wood,
 And burbled as it came!

One, two! One, two! And through and through
 The vorpal blade went snicker-snack!
He left it dead, and with its head
20 He went galumphing back.

"And hast thou slain the Jabberwock?
 Come to my arms, my beamish boy!
O frabjous day! Callooh! Callay!"
 He chortled in his joy.

25 'Twas brillig and the slithy toves
 Did gyre and gimble in the wabe;
All mimsy were the borogroves,
 And the mome raths outgrabe.
 —1872

IN CONTEXT

"Jabberwocky"

The poem "Jabberwocky" appears in the first chapter of *Through the Looking-Glass and What Alice Found There*. The first of the following excerpts provides the surrounding context in that chapter; the second is an excerpt from later in the book, when the poem is again discussed.

from *Through the Looking-Glass and What Alice Found There* (1872)

from CHAPTER I: LOOKING-GLASS HOUSE

There was a book lying near Alice on the table, and while she sat watching the White King (for she was still a little anxious about him, and had the ink all ready to throw over him, in case he fainted again), she turned over the leaves, to find some part that she could read, "—for it's all in some language I don't know," she said to herself.

It was like this.

YKCOWREBBAJ

'sevot yhtils eht dna ,gillirb sawT'
ebaw eht ni elbmig dna eryg diD
,sevorgorob eht erew ysmim llA

---

[1] *Jabberwocky* From *Through the Looking-Glass and What Alice Found There*, Ch. 1: "Looking-Glass House."

.ebargtuo shtar emom eht dnA

She puzzled over this for some time, but at last a bright thought struck her. "Why, it's a looking-glass book, of course! And if I hold it up to a glass, the words will all go the right way again."

This was the poem that Alice read.

[Here the poem appears.]

"It seems very pretty," she said when she had finished it, "but it's rather hard to understand." (You see she didn't like to confess, even to herself, that she couldn't make it out at all.) "Somehow it seems to fill my head with ideas—only I don't exactly know what they are! However, somebody killed something: that's clear, at any rate—."

from CHAPTER 6: HUMPTY DUMPTY

"You seem very clever at explaining words, sir," said Alice. "Would you kindly tell me the meaning of the poem called 'Jabberwocky'?"

"Let's hear it," said Humpty Dumpty. "I can explain all the poems that ever were invented—and a good many that haven't been invented just yet."

This sounded very hopeful, so Alice repeated the first verse:

" 'Twas brillig, and the slithy toves
    Did gyre and gimble in the wabe;
    All mimsy were the borogroves,
    And the mome raths outgrabe."

"That's enough to begin with," Humpty Dumpty interrupted: "there are plenty of hard words there. '*Brillig*' means four o'clock in the afternoon—the time when you begin *broiling* things for dinner."

"That'll do very well," said Alice: "and '*slithy*'?"

"Well, '*slithy*' means 'lithe and slimy.' 'Lithe' is the same as 'active.' You see it's like a portmanteau[1]— there are two meanings packed up into one word."

"I see it now," Alice remarked thoughtfully: "and what about '*toves*'?"

"Well, '*toves*' are something like badgers—they're something like lizards—and they're something like corkscrews."

"They must be very curious-looking creatures."

"They are that," said Humpty Dumpty: "also they made their nests under sundials—also they live on cheese."

"And what's to '*gyre*' and to '*gimble*'?"

"To '*gyre*' is to go round and round like a gyroscope. To '*gimble*' is to make holes like a gimlet.[2]"

"And 'the *wabe*' is the grass plot round a sundial, I suppose?" said Alice, surprised at her own ingenuity.

"Of course it is. It's called '*wabe*,' you know, because it goes a long way before it, and a long way behind it ——"

"And a long way beyond it on each side," Alice added.

"Exactly so. Well, then, '*mimsy*' is 'flimsy and miserable' (there's another portmanteau for you). And a '*borogrove*' is a thin, shabby-looking bird with its feathers sticking out all round—something like a live mop."

"And then '*mome raths*'?" said Alice. "If I'm not giving you too much trouble."

---

[1]   *portmanteau*   Leather carrying case; "portmanteau" has since entered the English language in the sense to which Humpty Dumpty refers, i.e., a blended word.

[2]   *gimlet*   Small tool used for boring holes.

"Well, a '*rath*' is a sort of green pig; but '*mome*' I'm not certain about. I think it's short for '*from home*'—meaning that they'd lost their way, you know."

"And what does '*outgrabe*' mean?"

"Well, '*outgribing*' is something between bellowing and whistling, with a kind of sneeze in the middle: however, you'll hear it done, maybe—down in the wood yonder—and when you've once heard it you'll be *quite* content. Who's been repeating all that hard stuff to you?"

"I read it in a book," said Alice.

IN CONTEXT

The Photographs of Lewis Carroll

Though as a photographer Carroll is best known for his images of children—and of Alice Liddell in particular—he was among the most accomplished of Victorian portrait photographers. Like many photographers of the time, he often portrayed his subjects in dramatic roles.

Alice, Lorina, Harry, and Edith Liddell, 1860.

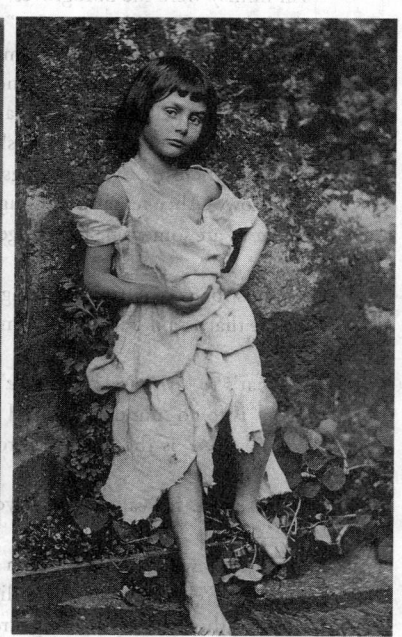

Alice Liddell as "The Beggar Maid," 1858.

Alexander Munro, the sculptor,
with his wife, Mary, 1863.

George Macdonald and his
daughter Lily, 1863.

Ella Chlora Monier-William, 1866.

"Andromeda," 1865.

"Captive Princess," 1875.

Augusta Webster
1837 – 1894

Augusta Webster is best known for bold poetic portraits that give dramatic voice to social issues in Victorian culture. Despite the considerable reputation she enjoyed when alive, for nearly a hundred years after her death she went missing from the English canon; the unstinting support of Victorian literary critic Theodore Watts-Gunn, who declared it "a monstrous thing that such a poet as Augusta Webster should be unknown," was not enough to prevent the politics of twentieth-century canon-formation from ignoring Webster. She lacked any powerful connections to secure her reputation, and the genres she favored—longer dramatic monologues and verse poems—do not lend themselves to anthologization. It was not until the 1980s and '90s that feminist scholarship rediscovered Webster.

Born in 1837 to Julia Hume Davies and Vice-Admiral George Davies of the British Navy in Poole, Dorset, Julia Augusta Davies spent her earliest years on board her father's ship, the *Griper*. It is said that Webster learned Greek at a young age to help her brother with his lessons; her mastery of a classical language traditionally reserved for male education may also have been motivated by literary ambitions, anticipating a career which included two translations of Greek plays. Webster attended the Cambridge School of Art and was admitted to the South Kensington Art School where, according to Ray Strachey, she "nearly dashed the prospects of women art students for ever by being expelled for whistling." In 1863 she married Thomas Webster, a fellow and law lecturer at Trinity College in Cambridge. Their only child, Margaret, is memorialized in one of Webster's finest works, the posthumously published sonnet sequence *Mother and Daughter*. While no personal documents exist to shed light on the Websters' marriage, the couple's decision to move to London suggests that it was not conventionally patriarchal; giving up a prestigious position in Cambridge, Webster's husband supported a move which would enable his wife to develop professionally in proximity to some of her literary models, such as Elizabeth Barrett Browning, Robert Browning, and Tennyson.

In London, Webster was poetry reviewer for the *Athenaeum* for a decade, and wrote regular columns for the *Examiner*. At a time when the dominant ideology of the British Medical Association warned against education for women on the grounds that it would sap the vital energy needed for reproduction, Webster campaigned on behalf of women's suffrage and education, becoming one of the first women to be elected to the London School Board.

Webster's writing is rich with social commentary. Her poem "A Castaway," praised by Robert Browning and called "her masterpiece" by Watts-Dunn, presents through the persona of a prostitute a powerful critique of the Victorian "economy of love" (to borrow the phrase of Webster scholar Christine Sutphin). "A Castaway," like "The Happiest Girl in the World" and "Jeanne D'Arc," is written in the poetic genre in which Webster excelled, the dramatic monologue. Two collections of monologues, *Dramatic Studies* (1866) and *Portraits* (1870), mark Webster's most lasting contribution to English poetry. In contrast to the psychological interiors dramatized by Robert Browning in monologues such as "Fra Lippo Lippi," Webster skillfully crafted the monologue to speak to external social circumstances. Webster was able to give voice to a sensual and political potency prohibited Victorian women by speaking through mythological surrogates in "Medea in Athens" and "Circe." While the implied, silent listener addressed within conventional dramatic monologues is often absent from Webster's treatments (leading the *London Review* to describe *Dramatic Studies* as "a set of soliloquies"), her monologues stage a voice whose message is a moving social performance.

The essays on love and marriage that Webster regularly contributed to the *Examiner* were, like most submissions to Victorian periodicals, anonymous. The editor of the *Examiner* held Webster's essay "A Translation and a Transcription" in high esteem, ranking it "the best article which ever appeared in its pages." Webster's first two books, *Blanche Lisle and Other Poems* (1860) and a narrative poem in blank verse entitled *Lilian Gray* (1864), were published under the pseudonym Cecil Home. All subsequent work, ranging from lyrics to verse dramas, appeared under Webster's own name. She even daringly attached her own name to her translations of *The Medea of Euripides* and *The Prometheus Bound of Aeschylus* at a time when scholarship in classical languages was considered to be strictly the province of "gentlemen."

Webster brought something of the unconventional to whatever genre she attempted. Whereas sonnet sequences had traditionally been vehicles for the expression of romantic love, her sonnet sequence *Mother and Daughter* (1894) took the love between a mother and a daughter as its subject.

When she died in 1894 Webster left behind no diaries or family letters, and only scanty evidence of correspondence with Christina Rossetti, Oliver Wendell Holmes, and a few other prominent writers of the day. Her poetic legacy, however, is increasingly regarded as being of very considerable substance.

⌘⌘⌘

A Castaway

Poor little diary, with its simple thoughts,
  Its good resolves, its "Studied French an hour,"
"Read Modern History," "Trimmed up my grey hat,"
"Darned stockings," "Tatted,"[1] "Practiced my new song,"
5 "Went to the daily service," "Took Bess soup,"
"Went out to tea." Poor simple diary!
And did *I* write it? Was I this good girl,
This budding colourless young rose of home?
Did I so live content in such a life,
10 Seeing no larger scope, nor asking it,
Than this small constant round—old clothes to mend,
New clothes to make, then go and say my prayers,
Or carry soup, or take a little walk
And pick the ragged-robins[2] in the hedge?
15 Then, for ambition, (was there ever life
That could forego that?) to improve my mind

And know French better and sing harder songs;
For gaiety, to go, in my best white
Well washed and starched and freshened with new bows,
20 And take tea out to meet the clergyman.
No wishes and no cares, almost no hopes,
Only the young girl's hazed and golden dreams
That veil the future from her.

                  So long since:
25 And now it seems a jest to talk of me
As if I could be one with her, of me
Who am ... me.

              And what is that? My looking-glass
Answers it passably; a woman sure,
30 No fiend, no slimy thing out of the pools,
A woman with a ripe and smiling lip
That has no venom in its touch I think,
With a white brow on which there is no ł
A woman none dare call not beautiful.
35 Not womanly in every woman's gra

---

[1] *Tatted* Made lace.

[2] *ragged-robin* Common English flower.

Aye, let me feed upon my beauty thus,
Be glad in it like painters when they see
At last the face they dreamed but could not find
Look from their canvas on them, triumph in it,
40   The dearest thing I have. Why, 'tis my all,
Let me make much of it: is it not this,
This beauty, my own curse at once and tool
To snare men's souls (I know what the good say
Of beauty in such creatures), is it not this
45   That makes me feel myself a woman still,
With still some little pride, some little—

Stop!
"Some little pride, some little"—Here's a jest!
What word will fit the sense but modesty?
50   A wanton I, but modest!

Modest, true;
I'm not drunk in the streets, ply not for hire
At infamous corners with my likenesses
Of the humbler kind; yes, modesty's my word—
55   'Twould shape my mouth well too, I think I'll try:
"Sir, Mr. What-you-will, Lord Who-knows-what,
My present lover or my next to come,
Value me at my worth, fill your purse full,
For I am modest; yes, and honour me
60   As though your schoolgirl sister or your wife
Could let her skirts brush mine or talk of me;
For I am modest."

Well, I flout myself:
But yet, but yet—

65   Fie, poor fantastic fool,
Why do I play the hypocrite alone,
Who am no hypocrite with others by?
Where should be my "But yet"? I am that thing
Called half a dozen dainty names, and none
0   Dainty enough to serve the turn and hide
The one coarse English worst that lurks beneath:
Just that, no worse, no better.

And, for me,
say let no one be above her trade;

75   I own my kindredship with any drab[1]
Who sells herself as I, although she crouch
In fetid garrets and I have a home
All velvet and marqueterie and pastilles,[2]
Although she hide her skeleton in rags
80   And I set fashions and wear cobweb lace:
The difference lies but in my choicer ware,
That I sell beauty and she ugliness;
Our traffic's one—I'm no sweet slaver-tongue
To gloze[3] upon it and explain myself
85   A sort of fractious angel misconceived—
Our traffic's one: I own it. And what then?
I know of worse that are called honourable.
Our lawyers, who with noble eloquence
And virtuous outbursts lie to hang a man,
90   Or lie to save him, which way goes the fee:
Our preachers, gloating on your future hell
For not believing what they doubt themselves:
Our doctors, who sort poisons out by chance
And wonder how they'll answer, and grow rich:
95   Our journalists, whose business is to fib
And juggle truths and falsehoods to and fro:
Our tradesmen, who must keep unspotted names
And cheat the least like stealing that they can:
Our —— all of them, the virtuous worthy men
100 Who feed on the world's follies, vices, wants,
And do their businesses of lies and shams
Honestly, reputably, while the world
Claps hands and cries "good luck," which of their
       trades,
Their honourable trades, barefaced like mine,
105 All secrets brazened out, would show more white?

And whom do I hurt more than they? as much?
The wives? Poor fools, what do I take from them
Worth crying for or keeping? If they knew
What their fine husbands look like seen by eyes
110 That may perceive there are more men than one!
But, if they can, let them just take the pains
To keep them: 'tis not such a mighty task
To pin an idiot to your apron-string;

---

[1]   *drab*   Common prostitute.

[2]   *marqueterie*   Inlaid mosaic work decorating furniture; *pastilles*
Aromatic pastes burnt as perfumes.

[3]   *gloze*   Interpret deceitfully or flatteringly.

And wives have an advantage over us,
115 (The good and blind ones have) the smile or pout
Leaves them no secret nausea at odd times.
Oh, they could keep their husbands if they cared,
But 'tis an easier life to let them go,
And whimper at it for morality.

120   Oh! those shrill carping virtues, safely housed
From reach of even a smile that should put red
On a decorous cheek, who rail at us
With such a spiteful scorn and rancorousness,
(Which maybe is half envy at the heart)
125 And boast themselves so measurelessly good
And us so measurelessly unlike them,
What is their wondrous merit that they stay
In comfortable homes whence not a soul
Has ever thought of tempting them, and wear
130 No kisses but a husband's upon lips
There is no other man desires to kiss—
Refrain in fact from sin impossible?
How dare they hate us so? what have they done,
What borne, to prove them other than we are?
135 What right have they to scorn us—glass-case saints,
Dianas[1] under lock and key—what right
More than the well-fed helpless barn-door fowl
To scorn the larcenous wild-birds?

                    Pshaw, let be!
140 Scorn or no scorn, what matter for their scorn?
I have outfaced my own—that's harder work.
Aye, let their virtuous malice dribble on—
Mock snowstorms on the stage—I'm proof long since:
I have looked coolly on my what and why,
145 And I accept myself.

                    Oh I'll endorse
The shamefullest revilings mouthed at me,
Cry "True! Oh perfect picture! Yes, that's I!"
And add a telling blackness here and there,
150 And then dare swear you, every nine of ten,
My judges and accusers, I'd not change
My conscience against yours, you who tread out
Your devil's pilgrimage along the roads
That take in church and chapel, and arrange

---

1 *Diana* Roman goddess of virginity.

155 A roundabout and decent way to hell.

    Well, mine's a short way and a merry one:
So says my pious hash of ohs and ahs,
Choice texts and choicer threats, appropriate names,
(Rahabs and Jezebels)[2] some fierce Tartuffe[3]
160 Hurled at me through the post. We had rare fun
Over that tract[4] digested with champagne.
Where is it? where's my rich repertory
Of insults Biblical?[5] *"I prey on souls"*—
Only my men have oftenest none I think:
165 *"I snare the simple ones"*—but in these days
There seem to be none simple and none snared
And most men have their favourite sinnings planned
To do them civilly and sensibly:
"I braid my hair"—but braids are out of date:
170 *"I paint my cheeks"*—I always wear them pale:
"I—"

    Pshaw! the trash is savourless today:
One cannot laugh alone. There, let it burn.
What, does the windy dullard think one needs
175 His wisdom dove-tailed on to Solomon's,[6]
His threats out-threatening God's, to teach the news
That those who need not sin have safer souls?
We know it, but we've bodies to save too;
And so we earn our living.

---

2 *Rahabs and Jezebels* I.e., harlots. Rahab was a Biblical harlot whose family was saved from the destruction of Jericho because she hid messengers that had been sent by Joshua to spy on the city. (See Joshua 6.17–25). Jezebel was a Phoenician princess who married Ahab, King of Israel. She refused to worship Yahweh, continuing to practice her country's traditional worship instead, and murdered Yahweh's prophets. Her name is often used to denote a cruel, sexually predatory woman. (See 1 Judges 16 and 18).

3 *Tartuffe* Hypocritical character who feigned virtue in Molière's 1664 play of that name.

4 *tract* Religious pamphlet.

5 *insults Biblical* See Ecclesiastes 7.26: "And I find more bitter than death the woman, whose heart is snares and nets, and her hand[s] as bands: whoso pleaseth God shall escape from her; but the s[inner] shall be taken by her," and 1 Timothy 2.9–10, which advises to "adorn themselves in modest apparel, with shamefac[ed] sobriety; not with braided hair, or gold, or pearls, or [ ] But (which becometh women professing godli[ness] works."

6 *Solomon* Biblical king of Israel who was

180 Well lit, tract!
At least you've made me a good leaping blaze.
Up, up, how the flame shoots! and now 'tis dead.
Oh proper finish, preaching to the last—
No such bad omen either; sudden end,
185 And no sad withering horrible old age.
How one would clutch at youth to hold it tight!
And then to know it gone, to see it gone,
Be taught its absence by harsh careless looks,
To live forgotten, solitary, old—
190 The cruellest word that ever woman learns.
Old—that's to be nothing, or to be at best
A blurred memorial that in better days
There was a woman once with such a name.
No, no, I could not bear it: death itself
195 Shows kinder promise ... even death itself,
Since it must come one day—

Oh this grey gloom!
This rain, rain, rain, what wretched thoughts it brings!
Death: I'll not think of it.

200 Will no one come?
'Tis dreary work alone.

Why did I read
That silly diary? Now, sing-song, ding-dong,
Come the old vexing echoes back again,
205 Church bells and nursery good-books, back again
Upon my shrinking ears that had forgotten—
I hate the useless memories: 'tis fools' work
Singing the hackneyed° dirge of "better days":   *stale*
Best take Now kindly, give the past good-bye,
210 Whether it were a better or a worse.

Yes, yes, I listened to the echoes once,
The echoes and the thoughts from the old days.
The worse for me: I lost my richest friend,
And that was all the difference. For the world,
5 I would not have that flight known. How they'd roar:
"What! Eulalie, when she refused us all,
'Ill' and 'away,' was doing Magdalene,[1]

Tears, ashes, and her Bible, and then off
To hide her in a Refuge[2] ... for a week!"

220 A wild whim that, to fancy I could change
My new self for my old because I wished!
Since then, when in my languid days there comes
That craving, like homesickness, to go back
To the good days, the dear old stupid days,
225 To the quiet and the innocence, I know
'Tis a sick fancy and try palliatives.

What is it? You go back to the old home,
And 'tis not *your* home, has no place for you,
And, if it had, you could not fit you in it.
230 And could I fit me to my former self?
If I had had the wit, like some of us,
To sow my wild-oats into three per cents,[3]
Could I not find me shelter in the peace
Of some far nook where none of them would come,
235 Nor whisper travel from this scurrilous world
(That gloats, and moralizes through its leers)
To blast me with my fashionable shame?
There I might—oh my castle in the clouds!
And where's its rent?—but there, were there a there,
240 I might again live the grave blameless life
Among such simple pleasures, simple cares:
But could they be my pleasures, be my cares?
The blameless life, but never the content—
Never. How could I henceforth be content
245 With any life but one that sets the brain
In a hot merry fever with its stir?
What would there be in quiet rustic days,
Each like the other, full of time to think,
To keep one bold enough to live at all?
250 Quiet is hell, I say—as if a woman
Could bear to sit alone, quiet all day,
And loathe herself and sicken on her thoughts.

They tried it at the Refuge, and I failed:
I could not bear it. Dreary hideous room,
255 Coarse pittance, prison rules, one might bear these

___

reform were known as "Magdalene houses."

[1] *doing Magdalene*   Becoming a reformed prostitute, so called after Mary Magdalene of the New Testament, one of Jesus's disciples. The ... ses in Victorian England to which prostitutes could come to

[2] *Refuge*   Shelter.

[3] *three per cents*   British government stocks, which returned three percent interest annually.

And keep one's purpose; but so much alone,
And then made faint and weak and fanciful
By change from pampering to half-famishing—
Good God, what thoughts come! Only one week more
260 And 'twould have ended: but in one day more
I must have killed myself. And I loathe death,
The dreadful foul corruption with who knows
What future after it.

               Well, I came back,
265 Back to my slough.[1] Who says I had my choice?
Could I stay there to die of some mad death?
And if I rambled out into the world
Sinless but penniless, what else were that
But slower death, slow pining shivering death
270 By misery and hunger? Choice! what choice
Of living well or ill? could I have that?
And who would give it me? I think indeed
If some kind hand, a woman's—I hate men—
Had stretched itself to help me to firm ground,
275 Taken a chance and risked my falling back,
I could have gone my way not falling back:
But, let her be all brave, all charitable,
How could she do it? Such a trifling boon—
A little work to live by, 'tis not much—
280 And I might have found will enough to last:
But where's the work? More seamstresses than shirts;
And defter hands at white work[2] than are mine
Drop starved at last: dressmakers, milliners,
Too many too they say; and then their trades
285 Need skill, apprenticeship. And who so bold
As hire me for their humblest drudgery?
Not even for scullery[3] slut; not even, I think,
For governess although they'd get me cheap.
And after all it would be something hard,
290 With the marts for decent women overfull,
If I could elbow in and snatch a chance
And oust some good girl so, who then perforce
Must come and snatch her chance among our crowd.

      Why, if the worthy men who think all's done
295 If we'll but come where we can hear them preach,

Could bring us all, or any half of us,
Into their fold, teach all us wandering sheep,
Or only half of us, to stand in rows
And baa them hymns and moral songs, good lack,[4]
300 What would they do with us? what could they do?
Just think! with were't but half of us on hand
To find work for ... or husbands. Would they try
To ship us to the colonies for wives?[5]

      Well, well, I know the wise ones talk and talk:
305 "Here's cause, here's cure": "No, here it is, and here":
And find society to blame, or law,
The Church, the men, the women, too few schools,
Too many schools, too much, too little taught:
Somewhere or somehow someone is to blame:
310 But I say all the fault's with God Himself
Who puts too many women in the world.
We ought to die off reasonably and leave
As many as the men want, none to waste.
Here's cause; the woman's superfluity:
315 And for the cure, why, if it were the law,
Say, every year, in due percentages,
Balancing them with males as the times need,
To kill off female infants, 'twould make room;
And some of us would not have lost too much,
320 Losing life ere we know what it *can* mean.

      The other day I saw a woman weep
Beside her dead child's bed: the little thing
Lay smiling, and the mother wailed half mad,
Shrieking to God to give it back again.
325 I could have laughed aloud: the little girl
Living had but her mother's life to live;
There she lay smiling, and her mother wept
To know her gone!

               My mother would have wept.

330   Oh, mother, mother, did you ever dream,
You good grave simple mother, you pure soul

---

1   *slough* State of moral degradation.

2   *white work* White-thread embroidery on white cloth.

3   *scullery* Room, adjoining the kitchen, in which dishes were washed.

4   *good lack* A polite exclamation.

5   *ship ... wives* Reference to Sir Sidney Herbert's proposal to send half a million "surplus" women, such as those driven to prostitution by a lack of employment, to the colonies, where there was a shortage of women from whom to choose for settlers who wished to marry.

No evil could come nigh, did you once dream
In all your dying cares for your lone girl
Left to fight out her fortune helplessly
335 That there would be *this* danger?—for *your* girl,
Taught by you, lapped in a sweet ignorance,
Scarcely more wise of what things sin could be
Than some young child a summer six months old,
Where in the north the summer makes a day,
340 Of what is darkness ... darkness that will come
Tomorrow suddenly. Thank God at least
For this much of my life, that when you died,
That when you kissed me dying, not a thought
Of this made sorrow for you, that I too
345 Was pure of even fear.

     Oh yes, I thought,
Still new in my insipid treadmill life,
(My father so late dead), and hopeful still,
There might be something pleasant somewhere in it,
350 Some sudden fairy come, no doubt, to turn
My pumpkin to a chariot, I thought then
That I might plod and plod and drum the sounds
Of useless facts into unwilling ears,
Tease children with dull questions half the day
355 Then con dull answers in my room at night
Ready for next day's questions, mend quill pens
And cut my fingers, add up sums done wrong
And never get them right; teach, teach, and teach—
What I half knew, or not at all—teach, teach
360 For years, a lifetime—*I*!

     And yet, who knows?
It might have been, for I was patient once,
And willing, and meant well; it might have been
Had I but still clung on in my first place—
365 A safe dull place, where mostly there were smiles
But never merry-makings; where all days
Jogged on sedately busy, with no haste;
Where all seemed measured out, but margins broad:
A dull home but a peaceful, where I felt
370 My pupils would be dear young sisters soon,
And felt their mother take me to her heart,
Motherly to all lonely harmless things.
But I must have a conscience, must blurt out
My great discovery of my ignorance!

375 And who required it of me? And who gained?
What did it matter for a more or less
The girls learnt in their schoolbooks, to forget
In their first season?[1] We did well together:
They loved me and I them: but I went off
380 To housemaid's pay, six crossgrained[2] brats to teach,
Wrangles and jangles, doubts, disgrace ... then this;
And they had a perfection found for them,
Who has all ladies' learning in her head
Abridged and scheduled, speaks five languages,
385 Knows botany and conchology[3] and globes,
Draws, paints, plays, sings, embroiders, teaches all
On a patent method never known to fail:
And now they're finished and, I hear, poor things,
Are the worst dancers and worst dressers out.[4]
390 And where's their profit of those prison years
All gone to make them wise in lesson-books?
Who wants his wife to know weeds' Latin names?
Who ever chose a girl for saying dates?
Or asked if she had learned to trace a map?

395   Well, well, the silly rules this silly world
Makes about women! This is one of them.
Why must there be pretence of teaching them
What no one ever cares that they should know,
What, grown out of the schoolroom, they cast off
400 Like the schoolroom pinafore,[5] no better fit
For any use of real grown-up life,
For any use to her who seeks or waits
The husband and the home, for any use,
For any shallowest pretence of use,
405 To her who has them? Do I not know this,
I, like my betters, that a woman's life,
Her natural life, her good life, her one life,
Is in her husband, God on earth to her,
And what she knows and what she can and is
410 Is only good as it brings good to him?

----

[1] *first season* The London social season, when Parliament is in session and everyone of social importance is in the city.

[2] *crossgrained* Difficult to manage.

[3] *conchology* The study of sea-shells.

[4] *out* I.e., appearing in society. Young girls did not attend public social functions, so it was said that they "came out" when they became old enough to do so.

[5] *pinafore* Garment worn by little girls.

Oh God, do I not know it? I the thing
Of shame and rottenness, the animal
That feeds men's lusts and preys on them, I, I,
Who should not dare to take the name of wife
415   On my polluted lips, who in the word
Hear but my own reviling, I know that.
I could have lived by that rule, how content:
My pleasure to make him some pleasure, pride
To be as he would have me, duty, care,
420   To fit all to his taste, rule my small sphere
To his intention; then to lean on him,
Be guided, tutored, loved—no not that word,
That *loved* which between men and women means
All selfishness, all cloying talk, all lust,
425   All vanity, all idiocy—not loved,
But cared for. I've been loved myself, I think,
Some once or twice since my poor mother died,
But *cared for*, never—that's a word for homes,
Kind homes, good homes, where simple children come
430   And ask their mother is this right or wrong,
Because they know she's perfect, cannot err;
Their father told them so, and he knows all,
Being so wise and good and wonderful,
Even enough to scold even her at times
435   And tell her everything she does not know.
Ah the sweet nursery logic!

                    Fool! thrice fool!
Do I hanker after that too? Fancy me
Infallible nursery saint, live code of law!
440   Me preaching! teaching innocence to be good!
A mother!

                Yet the baby thing that woke
And wailed an hour or two, and then was dead,
Was mine, and had he lived ... why then my name
445   Would have been mother. But 'twas well he died:
I could have been no mother, I, lost then
Beyond his saving. Had he come before
And lived, come to me in the doubtful days
When shame and boldness had not grown one sense,
450   For his sake, with the courage come of him,
I might have struggled back.

                    But how? But how?

His father would not then have let me go:
His time had not yet come to make an end
455   Of my "forever" with a hireling's fee
And civil light dismissal. None but him
To claim a bit of bread of if I went,
Child or no child: would he have given it me?
He! no; he had not done with me. No help,
460   No help, no help. Some ways can be trodden back,
But never our way, we who one wild day
Have given goodbye to what in our deep hearts
The lowest woman still holds best in life,
Good name—good name though given by the world
465   That mouths and garbles with its decent prate,
And wraps it in respectable grave shams,
And patches conscience partly by the rule
Of what one's neighbour thinks, but something more
By what his eyes are sharp enough to see.
470   How I could scorn it with its Pharisees,[1]
If it could not scorn me: but yet, but yet—
Oh God, if I could look it in the face!

        Oh I am wild, am ill, I think, tonight:
Will no one come and laugh with me? No feast,
475   No merriment tonight. So long alone!
Will no one come?

                At least there's a new dress
To try, and grumble at—they never fit
To one's ideal. Yes, a new rich dress,
480   With lace like this too, that's a soothing balm
For any fretting woman, cannot fail;
I've heard men say it ... and they know so well
What's in all women's hearts, especially
Women like me.

485   No help! no help! no help!
How could it be? It was too late long since—
Even at the first too late. Whose blame is that?
There are some kindly people in the world,
But what can *they* do? If one hurls oneself
490   Into a quicksand, what can be the end,
But that one sinks and sinks? Cry out for help?
Ah yes, and, if it came, who is so strong
To strain from the firm ground and lift one out?

---

[1] *Pharisees* I.e., hypocrites.

And how, so firmly clutching the stretched hand
495 As death's pursuing terror bids, even so,
How can one reach firm land, having to foot
The treacherous crumbling soil that slides and gives
And sucks one in again? Impossible path!
No, why waste struggles, I or anyone?
500 What is must be. What then? I where I am,
Sinking and sinking; let the wise pass by
And keep their wisdom for an apter use,
Let me sink merrily as I best may.

     Only, I think my brother—I forgot;
505 He stopped his brotherhood some years ago—
But if he had been just so much less good
As to remember mercy. Did he think
How once I was his sister, prizing him
As sisters do, content to learn for him
510 The lesson girls with brothers all must learn,
To do without?

          I have heard girls lament
That doing so without all things one would,
But I saw never aught to murmur at,
515 For men must be made ready for their work
And women all have more or less their chance
Of husbands to work for them, keep them safe
Like summer roses in soft greenhouse air
That never guess 'tis winter out of doors:
520 No, I saw never aught to murmur at,
Content with stinted fare and shabby clothes
And cloistered silent life to save expense,
Teaching myself out of my borrowed books,
While he for some one pastime (needful, true,
525 To keep him of his rank; 'twas not his fault)
Spent in a month what could have given me
My teachers for a year.

               'Twas no one's fault:
For could he be launched forth on the rude sea
Of this contentious world and left to find
530 Oars and the boatman's skill by some good chance?
'Twas no one's fault: yet still he might have thought
Of our so different youths and owned at least
'Tis pitiful when a mere nerveless girl
Untutored must put forth upon that sea,
535

Not in the woman's true place, the wife's place,
To trust a husband and be borne along,
But impotent blind pilot to herself.

     Merciless, merciless—like the prudent world
540 That will not have the flawed soul prank[1] itself
With a hoped second virtue, will not have
The woman fallen once lift up herself …
Lest she should fall again. Oh how his taunts,
His loathing fierce reproaches, scarred and seared
545 Like branding iron hissing in a wound!
And it was true—*that* killed me: and I felt
A hideous hopeless shame burn out my heart,
And knew myself forever that he said,
That which I was—Oh it was true, true, true.

550   No, not true then. I was not all that then.
Oh, I have drifted on before mad winds
And made ignoble shipwreck; not today
Could any breeze of heaven prosper me
Into the track again, nor any hand
555 Snatch me out of the whirlpool I have reached;
But then?

          Nay, he judged very well: he knew
Repentance was too dear a luxury
For a beggar's buying, knew it earns no bread—
560 And knew me a too base and nerveless thing
To bear my first fault's sequel and just die.
And how could he have helped me? Held my hand,
Owned me for his, fronted the angry world
Clothed with my ignominy? Or maybe
565 Taken me to his home to damn him worse?
What did I look for? for what less would serve
That he could do, a man without a purse?
He meant me well, he sent me that five pounds,
Much to him then; and, if he bade me work
570 And never vex him more with news of me,
We both knew him too poor for pensioners.
I see he did his best; I could wish now
Sending it back I had professed some thanks.

     But there! I was too wretched to be meek:
575 It seemed to me as if he, everyone,

---

[1]   *prank* Dress up, adorn.

The whole great world, were guilty of my guilt,
Abettors and avengers: in my heart
I gibed them back their gibings; I was wild.

I see clear now and know one has one's life
580 In hand at first to spend or spare or give
Like any other coin; spend it, or give,
Or drop it in the mire, can the world see
You get your value for it, or bar off
The hurrying of its marts to grope it up
585 And give it back to you for better use?
And if you spend or give, that is your choice;
And if you let it slip, that's your choice too,
You should have held it firmer. Yours the blame,
And not another's, not the indifferent world's
590 Which goes on steadily, statistically,
And count by censuses not separate souls—
And if it somehow needs to its worst use
So many lives of women, useless else,
It buys us of ourselves; we could hold back,
595 Free all of us to starve, and some of us,
(Those who have done no ill, and are in luck)
To slave their lives out and have food and clothes
Until they grow unserviceably old.

Oh, I blame no one—scarcely even myself.
600 It was to be: the very good in me
Has always turned to hurt; all I thought right
At the hot moment, judged of afterwards,
Shows reckless.

Why, look at it, had I taken
605 The pay my dead child's father offered me
For having been its mother, I could then
Have kept life in me—many have to do it,
That swarm in the back alleys, on no more,
Cold sometimes, mostly hungry, but they live—
610 I could have gained a respite trying it,
And maybe found at last some humble work
To eke the pittance out. Not I, forsooth,
I must have spirit, must have womanly pride,
Must dash back his contemptuous wages, I
615 Who had not scorned to earn them, dash them back
The fiercer that he dared to count our boy
In my appraising: and yet now I think

I might have taken it for my dead boy's sake;
It would have been *his* gift.

620   But I went forth
With my fine scorn, and whither did it lead?
Money's the root of evil do they say?
Money is virtue, strength: money to me
Would then have been repentance: could I live
625 Upon my idiot's pride?

                            Well, it fell soon.
I had prayed Clement might believe me dead,
And yet I begged of him—That's like me too,
Beg of him and then send him back his alms!
630 What if he gave as to a whining wretch
That holds her hand and lies? I am less to him
Than such a one; her rags do him no wrong,
But I, I wrong him merely that I live,
Being his sister. Could I not at least
635 Have still let him forget me? But 'tis past:
And naturally he may hope I am long dead.

Good God! to think that we were what we were
One to the other … and now!

                              He has done well;
640 Married a sort of heiress, I have heard,
A dapper little madam dimple cheeked
And dimple brained, who makes him a good wife—
No doubt she'd never own but just to him,
And in a whisper, she can even suspect
645 That we exist, we other women things:
What would she say if she could learn one day
She has a sister-in-law? So he and I
Must stand apart till doomsday.

                                But the jest,
650 To think how she would look! Her fright, poor thing!
The notion! I could laugh outright … or else,
For I feel near it, roll on the ground and sob.

Well, after all, there's not much difference
Between the two sometimes.

655   Was that the bell?

Someone at last, thank goodness. There's a voice,
And that's a pleasure. Whose though? Ah, I know.
Why did she come alone, the cackling goose?
Why not have brought her sister? She tells more
660   And titters less. No matter; half a loaf

Is better than no bread.

                    Oh, is it you?
Most welcome, dear: one gets so moped alone.
          —1870, 1893

ALGERNON CHARLES SWINBURNE
1837 – 1909

Victorian poet and critic Algernon Swinburne was physically slight, but he had a powerful personality, and he left behind a vast literary output. Much of his writing, however, on topics such as incest, cannibalism, sadomasochism, and necrophilia, was too outrageous for "respectable" Victorian tastes. Although he was born into a distinguished family of British aristocracy, Swinburne's opinions on politics, religion, and sexuality were offensive enough to have earned him the nickname "Swineborn" in *Punch* magazine. Swinburne's poetry, however, was also metrically innovative, musical, and often erudite. Oscar Wilde claimed him as his literary master but said of Swinburne's writing, "Words seem to dominate him. Alliteration tyrannizes over him. Mere sound often becomes his lord. He is so eloquent that whatever he touches becomes unreal." This "diffuseness" was, according to T.S. Eliot, one of his "glories." Although few have disputed the musicality of Swinburne's poetry, some critics have accused him of being vague and soporific.

Algernon Swinburne was born in 1837 into a highly respectable aristocratic family. His father, Admiral Charles Henry Swinburne, was the son of a baronet, and his mother, Lady Jane, was the daughter of an earl. Raised a devout Anglo-Catholic, Swinburne read profusely and acquired an intimate knowledge of the Bible, as well as a proficiency in French and Italian. His early years at Eton, however, were troubled ones; as a result of disciplinary problems, he was removed from the school before he graduated. After private tutoring, he entered Balliol College at Oxford in 1856. During his first two years there, Swinburne excelled in the Classics and won a scholarship for French and Italian; his unruliness got the better of him again, and he was forced to leave Balliol without a degree. He nevertheless made many important friends at Oxford, including Benjamin Jowett (then master of Balliol) and the Pre-Raphaelites Edward Burne-Jones, William Morris, and Dante Gabriel Rossetti (with whom he lived in London after Rossetti's wife, Elizabeth Siddall, died).

London saw the best and the worst of Swinburne. During the 1860s, he gained notoriety for his wild, drunken revelries and experiments with flagellation, as much as for the publication of two important works, *Atalanta in Calydon* (1865) and *Poems and Ballads* (1866). The classical Greek tragic form of the verse-play *Atalanta* and its concentration on fate and divine intervention belied the long poem's modern revolt against religious institutions and its sympathy, instead, with the "holy spirit of man." While Victorians might have been expected to rail against Swinburne's chastisement of religious orthodoxy, the lyrical and mellifluous tragedy held many in its sway, and won accolades from reviewers. John Ruskin said that it was the "grandest thing ever done by a youth—though he is a Demoniac youth," and Tennyson wrote to Swinburne praising the metrical creativity of *Atalanta*.

Poems and Ballads, on the other hand, had the public (Ruskin included) up in arms. In such poems as "The Triumph of Time," "Dolores, "The Leper," "Hymn to Prosperine," and "Laus Veneris," Swinburne explored themes of sexual perversion, paganism, and moral and spiritual decay. One reviewer said the author was an "unclean, fiery imp from the pit," while another, referring to

Swinburne's association with the Aesthetes, called him the "libidinous laureate of a pack of satyrs." Amid this outcry, the publishing house withdrew the book from publication, angering Swinburne and prompting his eloquent riposte in *Notes on Poems and Reviews*. *Poems and Ballads* was re-released shortly afterward by another publisher.

Swinburne's notoriety continued into the late 1860s and 1870s, as he cultivated his image as a "scandalous poet," to use his own words. He wrote at a feverish rate—even though his alcoholism was by then prompting seizures and blackouts—and produced such works as *A Song of Italy* (1867), a defense of Italian liberation; *Ave Atque Vale* (1878), an elegy to Baudelaire; the brilliant essay *William Blake* (1868); and *Songs Before Sunrise* (1871), which continued the theme of spiritual and political revolution. By the end of the 1870s, however, Swinburne was near death, his nerves destroyed by alcohol, and his body depleted from overwork. Luckily, in 1879, his friend Theodore Watts-Dunton took him to his house in Putney and helped nurse him back to health. There Swinburne lived in quiet solitude for the remaining 30 years of his life, writing and publishing prolifically, and finally succumbing to pneumonia in 1909.

In those final decades, Swinburne won the respect of many Victorians. Although the *Guardian* noted upon his death that his verse could be "careless, trivial, or inharmonious," the newspaper also acknowledged that "the greatest poet lately living is dead … and we cannot doubt that much of his poetry will live by virtue of its exquisite music."

⌘ ⌘ ⌘

Hymn to Proserpine[1]
(*After the Proclamation in Rome of the Christian Faith[2]*)

Vicisti, Galilæe[3]

I have lived long enough, having seen one thing, that
    love hath an end;
Goddess and maiden and queen, be near me now and
    befriend.
Thou art more than the day or the morrow, the
    seasons that laugh or that weep;

For these give joy and sorrow; but thou, Proserpina,
    sleep.
5   Sweet is the treading of wine, and sweet the feet of the
    dove;
But a goodlier gift is thine than foam of the grapes or
    love.
Yea, is not even Apollo,[4] with hair and harpstring of
    gold,
A bitter God to follow, a beautiful God to behold?
I am sick of singing: the bays burn deep and chafe: I
    am fain
10 To rest a little from praise and grievous pleasure and
    pain.
For the Gods we know not of, who give us our daily
    breath,
We know they are cruel as love or life, and lovely as
    death.
O Gods dethroned and deceased, cast forth, wiped
    out in a day!
From your wrath is the world released, redeemed from
    your chains, men say.

---

[1] *Proserpine* In Roman mythology, daughter of Jupiter and Ceres and wife of Pluto, King of the underworld, who stole her from her mother.

[2] *Proclamation … Faith* Roman Emperor Constantine the Great legalized the Christian faith when he proclaimed the Edict of Milan in 313 CE.

[3] *Vicisti, Galilæe* Latin: "Thou hast conquered, Galilee," said to be the dying words in 363 of Julian the Apostate, half-brother of Constantine the Great. Julian eventually became emperor after the deaths of Constantine I and II; he was a pagan who opposed instituting Christianity as the state religion (as it was eventually proclaimed by Emperor Theodosius in 380).

[4] *Apollo* Greek sun god; also god of the arts.

15 New Gods are crowned in the city; their flowers have broken your rods;

They are merciful, clothed with pity, the young compassionate Gods.

But for me their new device is barren, the days are bare;

Things long past over suffice, and men forgotten that were.

Time and the Gods are at strife; ye dwell in the midst thereof,

20 Draining a little life from the barren breasts of love.

I say to you, cease, take rest; yea, I say to you all, be at peace,

Till the bitter milk of her breast and the barren bosom shall cease.

Wilt thou yet take all, Galilean? but these thou shalt not take,

The laurel, the palms and the pæan,[1] the breast of the nymphs in the brake;[2]

25 Breasts more soft than a dove's that tremble with tenderer breath;

And all the wings of the Loves,[3] and all the joy before death;

All the feet of the hours that sound as a single lyre,

Dropped and deep in the flowers, with strings that flicker like fire.

More than these wilt thou give, things fairer than all these things?

30 Nay, for a little we live, and life hath mutable wings.

A little while and we die; shall life not thrive as it may?

For no man under the sky lives twice, outliving his day.

And grief is a grievous thing, and a man hath enough of his tears:

Why should he labour, and bring fresh grief to blacken his years?

35 Thou hast conquered, O pale Galilean; the world has grown grey from thy breath;

We have drunken of things Lethean,[4] and fed on the fullness of death.

Laurel is green for a season, and love is sweet for a day;

But love grows bitter with treason, and laurel outlives not May.

Sleep, shall we sleep after all? for the world is not sweet in the end;

40 For the old faiths loosen and fall, the new years ruin and rend.

Fate is a sea without shore, and the soul is a rock that abides;

But her ears are vexed with the roar and her face with the foam of the tides.

O lips that the live blood faints in, the leavings of racks and rods!

O ghastly glories of saints, dead limbs of gibbeted Gods!

45 Though all men abase them before you in spirit, and all knees bend,

I kneel not neither adore you, but standing, look to the end.

All delicate days and pleasant, all spirits and sorrows are cast

Far out with the foam of the present that sweeps to the surf of the past:

Where beyond the extreme sea-wall, and between the remote sea-gates,

50 Waste water washes, and tall ships founder, and deep death waits:

Where, mighty with deepening sides, clad about with the seas as with wings,

And impelled of invisible tides, and fulfilled of unspeakable things,

White-eyed and poisonous-finned, shark-toothed and serpentine-curled,

Rolls, under the whitening wind of the future, the wave of the world.

55 The depths stand naked in sunder behind it, the storms flee away;

In the hollow before it the thunder is taken and snared as a prey;

In its sides is the north-wind bound; and its salt is of all men's tears;

With light of ruin, and sound of changes, and pulse of years:

With travail of day after day, and with trouble of hour upon hour;

---

[1] *pæan* Hymn of praise.

[2] *brake* Ferns.

[3] *Loves* Cupids or other gods representing sexual love.

[4] *Lethean* Of the Greek mythological river Lethe in Hades (the underworld), the waters of which cause the dead to forget the past; also called the "River of Oblivion."

60   And bitter as blood is the spray; and the crests are as
    fangs that devour:
And its vapour and storm of its steam as the sighing of
    spirits to be;
And its noise as the noise in a dream; and its depth as
    the roots of the sea:
And the height of its heads as the height of the utmost
    stars of the air:
And the ends of the earth at the might thereof
    tremble, and time is made bare.
65   Will ye bridle the deep sea with reins, will ye chasten
    the high sea with rods?
Will ye take her to chain her with chains, who is older
    than all ye Gods?
All ye as a wind shall go by, as a fire shall ye pass and
    be past;
Ye are Gods, and behold, ye shall die, and the waves
    be upon you at last.
In the darkness of time, in the deeps of the years, in
    the changes of things,
70   Ye shall sleep as a slain man sleeps, and the world shall
    forget you for kings.
Though the feet of thine high priests tread where thy
    lords and our forefathers trod,
Though these that were Gods are dead, and thou
    being dead art a God,
Though before thee the throned Cytherean[1] be fallen,
    and hidden her head,
Yet thy kingdom shall pass, Galilean, thy dead shall go
    down to thee dead.
75   Of the maiden thy mother men sing as a goddess with
    grace clad around;
Thou art throned where another was king; where
    another was queen she is crowned.
Yea, once we had sight of another: but now she is
    queen, say these.
Not as thine, not as thine was our mother, a blossom
    of flowering seas,
Clothed round with the world's desire as with
    raiment, and fair as the foam,

80   And fleeter than kindled fire, and a goddess, and
    mother of Rome.
For thine came pale and a maiden, and sister to
    sorrow; but ours,
Her deep hair heavily laden with odour and colour of
    flowers,
White rose of the rose-white water, a silver splendour,
    a flame,
Bent down unto us that besought her, and earth grew
    sweet with her name.
85   For thine came weeping, a slave among slaves, and
    rejected; but she
Came flushed from the full-flushed wave, and
    imperial, her foot on the sea.
And the wonderful waters knew her, the winds and
    the viewless ways,
And the roses grew rosier, and bluer the sea-blue
    stream of the bays.
Ye are fallen, our lords, by what token? we wist[2] that
    ye should not fall.
90   Ye were all so fair that are broken; and one more fair
    than ye all.
But I turn to her still, having seen she shall surely
    abide in the end;
Goddess and maiden and queen, be near me now and
    befriend.
O daughter of earth, of my mother, her crown and
    blossom of birth,
I am also, I also, thy brother; I go as I came unto earth.
95   In the night where thine eyes are as moons are in
    heaven, the night where thou art,
Where the silence is more than all tunes, where sleep
    overflows from the heart,
Where the poppies[3] are sweet as the rose in our world,
    and the red rose is white,
And the wind falls faint as it blows with the fume of
    the flowers of the night.
And the murmur of spirits that sleep in the shadow of
    Gods from afar
100   Grows dim in thine ears and deep as the deep dim
    soul of a star,
In the sweet low light of thy face, under heavens
    untrod by the sun,

---

[1]   *throned Cytherean*   Venus, Roman goddess of love and beauty
(Aphrodite in Greek mythology), who was born of the foam of the
sea and, according to some accounts, came ashore on the Greek
island of Cythera.

[2]   *wist*   Know.

[3]   *poppies*   Flowers representing sleep, sacred to Proserpine.

Let my soul with their souls find place, and forget
    what is done and undone.
Thou art more than the Gods who number the days
    of our temporal breath;
For these give labour and slumber; but thou,
    Proserpina, death.
105 Therefore now at thy feet I abide for a season in
    silence. I know
I shall die as my fathers died, and sleep as they sleep;
    even so.
For the glass of the years is brittle wherein we gaze for
    a span;
A little soul for a little bears up this corpse which is
    man.[1]
So long I endure, no longer; and laugh not again,
    neither weep.
110 For there is no God found stronger than death; and
    death is a sleep.
    —1866

A Forsaken Garden

In a coign° of the cliff between lowland and   *wedge*
    highland,
    At the sea-down's edge between windward and lee,
Walled round with rocks as an inland island,
    The ghost of a garden fronts the sea.
5 A girdle of brushwood and thorn encloses
    The steep square slope of the blossomless bed
Where the weeds that grew green from the graves of
    its roses
    Now lie dead.

The fields fall southward, abrupt and broken,
10   To the low last edge of the long lone land.
If a step should sound or a word be spoken,
    Would a ghost not rise at the strange guest's hand?
So long have the grey bare walks lain guestless,
    Through branches and briars if a man make way,
15 He shall find no life but the sea-wind's, restless
    Night and day.

---

1 [Swinburne's note] ψυχάριον εἶ βαστάζον νεκρόν.—Epictetus
[Greek: "You are a little soul, carrying around a corpse."]

The dense hard passage is blind and stifled
    That crawls by a track none turn to climb
To the strait° waste place that the years have   *narrow*
    rifled
20   Of all but the thorns that are touched not of time.
The thorns he spares when the rose is taken;
    The rocks are left when he wastes the plain.
The wind that wanders, the weeds wind-shaken,
    These remain.

25 Not a flower to be pressed of the foot that falls not;
    As the heart of a dead man the seed-lots are dry;
From the thicket of thorns whence the nightingale
    calls not,
    Could she call, there were never a rose to reply.
Over the meadows that blossom and wither
30   Rings but the note of a sea-bird's song;
Only the sun and the rain come hither
    All year long.

The sun burns sere and the rain dishevels
    One gaunt bleak blossom of scentless breath.
35 Only the wind here hovers and revels
    In a round where life seems barren as death.
Here there was laughing of old, there was weeping,
    Haply, of lovers none ever will know,
Whose eyes went seaward a hundred sleeping
40   Years ago.

Heart handfast in heart as they stood, "Look thither,"
    Did he whisper? "look forth from the flowers to
    the sea;
For the foam-flowers endure when the rose-blossoms
    wither,
    And men that love lightly may die—but we?"
45 And the same wind sang and the same waves
    whitened,
    And or ever the garden's last petals were shed,
In the lips that had whispered, the eyes that had
    lightened,
    Love was dead.

Or they loved their life through, and then went whither?
50   And were one to the end—but what end who knows?
Love deep as the sea as a rose must wither,

As the rose-red seaweed that mocks the rose.
Shall the dead take thought for the dead to love them?
    What love was ever as deep as a grave?
55 They are loveless now as the grass above them
    Or the wave.

All are at one now, roses and lovers,
    Not known of the cliffs and the fields and the sea.
Not a breath of the time that has been hovers
60   In the air now soft with a summer to be.
Not a breath shall there sweeten the seasons hereafter
    Of the flowers or the lovers that laugh now or weep,
When as they that are free now of weeping and
        laughter
        We shall sleep.

65 Here death may deal not again forever;
    Here change may come not till all change end.
From the graves they have made they shall rise up
        never,

Who have left nought living to ravage and rend.
Earth, stones, and thorns of the wild ground growing,
70   While the sun and the rain live, these shall be;
Till a last wind's breath upon all these blowing
        Roll the sea.

Till the slow sea rise and the sheer cliff crumble,
    Till terrace and meadow the deep gulfs drink,
75 Till the strength of the waves of the high tides humble
    The fields that lessen, the rocks that shrink,
Here now in his triumph where all things falter,
    Stretched out on the spoils that his own hand
        spread,
As a god self-slain on his own strange altar,
80   Death lies dead.
—1876

THOMAS HARDY
1840 — 1928

Hardy was born in 1840 in Dorset, where much of his fiction was later set. A frail child, he did not attend the local school until the age of eight. However, his ill health fostered his love of reading. In his walks in the area, Hardy also came into contact with the local farmers and laborers, whose hardship and poverty deeply touched him. At the age of 15, he was apprenticed to a local architect, a career that would sustain him until he became established as a writer.

In 1862 Hardy moved to London to work with another architect. Always driven, he would rise at five in the morning to complete three or four hours of reading—in Homer, the Greek Testament,

the Renaissance poets—before going to the office. On his return from work, he would often stay up reading and writing until midnight. It was during this time that he began writing poetry and short stories. Although he submitted many pieces to various magazines and the editors often wrote that he showed promise, his work was consistently rejected. The hectic schedule that Hardy was following caused his health to deteriorate, and he was forced to return to the countryside in 1867 to recuperate. In Dorchester, he worked as an architect during the day and wrote in his spare time. It was in the course of his employment that he met his first wife, Emma Gifford. He had been sent to St. Juliot to draw plans for a church restoration, and Emma was the sister-in-law of the rector. The two struck up a close friendship and Emma was very support-ive of his writing. With Emma's encouragement, Hardy published his first novel *Desperate Remedies* (1871). The novel, which has much in common with sensation fiction, a popular sub-genre of the 1860s, met with mixed reviews, but he continued to write. *Under the Greenwood Tree*, published in 1872, brought him popular acclaim.

In his early novels, Hardy began to include real places from the Dorset area, renamed Wessex—and to be praised for his portrayal of the countryside and the people of the region. *A Pair of Blue Eyes* appeared in 1873, and mirrored his own courtship with Emma. The two were married in 1874. That year also saw the publication of *Far from the Madding Crowd*, the first of what are now regarded as his classic novels. It depicts the life and loves of Bathsheba Everdene, and provides a convincing portrait of rural life. The novel also includes one of Hardy's "fallen women"; the case of Fanny Robin, who is seduced and eventually dies in a workhouse, shocked many readers. Despite this, the novel was very popular, and allowed him to give up his architectural work and concentrate solely on writing.

The Return of the Native, published in 1878, was also very successful. All of Hardy's novels were by now appearing in serialized form in monthly family magazines—a development which affected both the way that he wrote and the content of his fiction. Like most serialized writers, Hardy incorporated a steady flow of incidents in his novels; he was catering to an audience that needed to be encouraged to keep reading and buy the next issue. The "family" nature of the magazines often led his editors (one of whom was Leslie Stephen, the father of Virginia Woolf) to caution him to tone down the racier scenes and rewrite large sections. Because of the strict morality that dominated editorial policy, for example, Hardy could not state explicitly that some of his characters might have been involved in extra-marital activities. Instead, such situations are written vaguely and readers are left to decide for themselves whether something illicit has taken place.

Serialization also affected the form of Hardy's next major novel, *The Mayor of Casterbridge* (1886), which appeared weekly rather than monthly; it is the most rapidly paced of all his novels. The novel exhibits Hardy's penchant for the tragic and macabre. Michael Henchard, a country laborer, sells his wife and daughter after a bout of drinking. He subsequently becomes wealthy and is elected mayor before his past catches up with him; he eventually dies impoverished on the outskirts of town. The fact that Hardy built the novel on a carefully allusive structure based on the story of Saul and David from the Hebrew scriptures to explore the passage of an older England into modernity indicates his life-long sense of life's ironies and of the wrenching changes in nineteenth-century English life.

Censure of Hardy's depiction of "immoral" subject matter reached its peak with the publication of his next two major novels, *Tess of the d'Urbervilles* (1891) and *Jude the Obscure* (1895). In the first of these, the aristocratic Alec d'Urberville forces himself upon Tess, who then bears his illegitimate child. Both the "seduction" itself and Tess's attempt to have the illegitimate child baptized shocked readers. Tess eventually marries Angel Clare but is forced back into a relationship with d'Urberville when Clare discovers the truth about her past and abandons her. Her husband eventually forgives her, but she kills d'Urberville and is hanged for it. Hardy rewrote many of the novel's explicit or controversial sections for serialization in *Longman's Magazine*, but when the novel was published as a complete volume, the controversial sections were restored.

Jude the Obscure depicts the thwarted life of Jude Fawley, a village mason who dreams of attending university but whose hopes are derailed by romantic entanglements—first with Arabella Dunn and later with Sue Bridehead—and by the deadening exclusions of class-conscious English society of the later nineteenth century. Some have seen Bridehead as a proto-feminist, respecting her intelligence and authority and her fear of and disdain for marriage. Hardy's own marriage was on shaky ground at the time, and his wife Emma attempted to halt the publication of the novel. Publication went forward, but criticism of the book was swift and cruel. The Bishop of Wakefield, for one, said he had "bought one of Mr. Hardy's novels, but was so disgusted with its insolence and indecency" that he "threw it into the fire." Unfavorable and uncomprehending responses to *Jude* encouraged Hardy to give up fiction; this was the last novel which he wrote.

Throughout his earlier writing life, Hardy also produced numerous stories. Like his novels, these are frequently rooted in the details of traditional rural and small town life, although they often touch on highly contemporary issues. Also like his novels, they often take in the broad sweep of his characters' lives, which are typically subject to remorseless twists of fate; the gods may haunt his texts, but no God is there. Ongoing tensions between the city and the countryside, the educated and the uneducated, and the rich and the poor frequently contribute to the tragedy that lies at the heart of the life of a typical Hardy character, although these material factors frequently combine with a more philosophically grounded pessimism.

From the mid-1890s, Hardy concentrated on composing poetry, continuing in *Wessex Poems* (1898) his portrayal of the region he had made famous in the novels. The long poem *The Dynasts* (1904–08) detailed the Napoleonic Wars. The death of Emma in 1912, and Hardy's subsequent remorse for what had become of their relationship, resulted in some of his finest poetry and love poems, which appeared in *Satires of Circumstance* (1914). Hardy remarried in 1914; his second wife, Florence, is listed as the author of a two-volume biography that appeared in 1928 and 1930, but it has since been established that Hardy wrote the work himself. Hardy was awarded the Order of Merit in 1910 and the Gold Medal of the Royal Society of Literature in 1912. When he died in 1928, his ashes were interred in Poets' Corner at Westminster Abbey, but his heart was buried with Emma in Stinsford, in southern England.

⌘ ⌘ ⌘

The Son's Veto

I

To the eyes of a man viewing it from behind, the nut-brown hair was a wonder and a mystery. Under the black beaver hat, surmounted by its tuft of black feathers, the long locks, braided and twisted and coiled like the rushes of a basket, composed a rare, if somewhat barbaric, example of ingenious art. One could understand such weavings and coiling being wrought to last intact for a year, or even a calendar month; but that they should be all demolished regularly at bedtime, after a single day of permanence, seemed a reckless waste of successful fabrication.

And she had done it all herself, poor thing. She had no maid, and it was almost the only accomplishment she could boast of. Hence the unstinted pains.

She was a young invalid lady—not so very much of an invalid—sitting in a wheeled chair, which had been pulled up in the front part of a green enclosure, close to a band-stand, where a concert was going on, during a warm June afternoon. It had place in one of the minor parks or private gardens that are to be found in the suburbs of London, and was the effort of a local association to raise money for some charity. There were worlds within worlds in the great city, and though nobody outside the immediate district had ever heard of the charity, or the band, or the garden, the enclosure was filled with an interested audience sufficiently informed of all these.

As the trains proceeded many of the listeners observed the chaired lady, whose back hair, by reason of her prominent position, so challenged inspection. Her face was not easily discernible, but the aforesaid cunning tress-weavings, the white ear and poll,[1] and the curve of a cheek which was neither flaccid nor sallow, were signals that led to the expectation of good beauty in front. Such expectations are not infrequently disappointed as soon as the disclosure comes; and in the present case, when the lady, by a turn of the head, at length revealed herself, she was not so handsome as the people behind her had supposed, and even hoped—they did not know why.

For one thing (alas! the commonness of this complaint), she was less young than they had fancied her to be. Yet attractive her face unquestionably was, and not at all sickly. The revelation of its details came each time she turned to talk to a boy of twelve or thirteen who stood beside her, and the shape of whose hat and jacket implied that he belonged to a well-known public school.[2] The immediate by-standers could hear that he called her "Mother."

When the end of the programme was reached, and the audience withdrew, many chose to find their way out by passing at her elbow. Almost all turned their heads to take a full and near look at the interesting woman, who remained stationary in the chair till the way should be clear enough for her to be wheeled out without obstruction. As if she expected their glances, and did not mind gratifying their curiosity, she met the eyes of several of her observers by lifting her own, showing these to be soft, brown, and affectionate orbs, a little plaintive in their regard.

She was conducted out of the garden, and passed along the pavement till she disappeared from view, the school-boy walking beside her. To inquiries made by some persons who watched her away, the answer came that she was the second wife of the incumbent of a neighbouring parish, and that she was lame. She was generally believed to be a woman with a story—an innocent one, but a story of some sort or other.

In conversing with her on their way home the boy who walked at her elbow said that he hoped his father had not missed them.

"He have been so comfortable these last few hours that I am sure he cannot have missed us," she replied.

"*Has,* dear mother—not *have*!" exclaimed the

---

[1] *poll* Nape of the neck.

[2] *public school* In England, private school.

public-school boy, with an impatient fastidiousness that was almost harsh. "Surely you know that by this time!"

His mother hastily adopted the correction, and did not resent his making it, or retaliate, as she might well have done, by bidding him to wipe that crumby mouth of his, whose condition had been caused by surreptitious attempts to eat a piece of cake without taking it out of the pocket wherein it lay concealed. After this the pretty woman and the boy went onward in silence.

That question of grammar bore upon her history, and she fell into reverie, of a somewhat sad kind to all appearance. It might have been assumed that she was wondering if she had done wisely in shaping her life as she had shaped it, to bring out such a result as this.

In a remote nook in North Wessex, forty miles from London, near the thriving county-town of Aldbrickham, there stood a pretty village with its church and parsonage, which she knew well enough, but her son had never seen. It was her native village, Gaymead, and the first event bearing upon her present situation had occurred at that place when she was only a girl of nineteen.

How well she remembered it, that first act in her little tragi-comedy, the death of her reverend husband's first wife. It happened on a spring evening, and she who now and for many years had filled that first wife's place was then parlor-maid in the parson's house.

When everything had been done that could be done, and the death was announced, she had gone out in the dusk to visit her parents, who were living in the same village, to tell them the sad news. As she opened the white swing-gate and looked towards the trees which rose westward, shutting out the pale light of the evening sky, she discerned, without much surprise, the figure of a man standing in the hedge, though she roguishly exclaimed, as a matter of form, "Oh Sam, how you frightened me!"

He was a young gardener of her acquaintance. She told him the particulars of the late event, and they stood silent, these two young people, in that elevated, calmly philosophic mind which is engendered when a tragedy has happened close at hand, and has not happened to the philosophers themselves. But it had its bearings upon their relations.

"And will you stay on now at the Vicarage, just the same?" asked he.

She had hardly thought of that. "Oh yes—I suppose," she said. "Everything will be just as usual, I imagine."

He walked beside her towards her mother's. Presently his arm stole round her waist. She gently removed it; but he placed it there again, and she yielded the point. "You see, dear Sophy, you don't know that you'll stay on; you may want a home; and I shall be ready to offer one some day, though I may not be ready just yet."

"Why, Sam, how can you be so fast? I've never even said I liked 'ee; and it is all your own doing, coming after me."

"Still, it is nonsense to say I am not to have a try at you, like the rest." He stooped to kiss her a farewell, for they had reached her mother's door.

"No, Sam; you sha'nt!" she cried, putting her hand over his mouth. "You ought to be more serious on such a night as this." And she bade him adieu without allowing him to kiss her or to come indoors.

The vicar just left a widower was at this time a man about forty years of age, of good family, and childless. He had led a secluded existence in this college living, partly because there were no resident landowners; and his loss now intensified his habit of withdrawal from outward observation. He was still less seen than heretofore, kept himself still less in time with the rhythm and racket of the movements called progress in the world without. For many months after his wife's decease the economy of his household remained as before; the cook, the house-maid, the parlor-maid, and the man out-of-doors performed their duties or left them undone, just as nature prompted them—the vicar knew not which. It was then represented to him that his servants seemed to have nothing to do in his small family of one. He was struck with the truth of this representation, and decided to cut down his establishment. But he was forestalled by Sophy, the parlor-maid, who said one evening that she wished to leave him.

"And why?" said the parson.

"Sam Hobson has asked me to marry him, sir."

"Well—do you want to marry?"

"Not much. But it would be a home for me. And we have heard that one of us will have to leave."

A day or two after she said: "I don't want to leave just yet, sir, if you don't wish it. Sam and I have quarreled."

He looked at her. He had hardly ever observed her before, though he had been frequently conscious of her soft presence in the room. What a kitten-like, flexuous, tender creature she was! She was the only one of the servants with whom he came into immediate and continuous relation. What should he do if Sophy were gone?

Sophy did not go, but one of the others did, and things proceeded quietly again.

When Mr. Twycott, the vicar, was ill, Sophy brought up his meals to him, and she had no sooner left the room one day than he heard a noise on the stairs. She had slipped down with the tray, and so twisted her foot that she could not stand. The village surgeon was called in; the vicar got better, but Sophy was incapacitated for a long time; and she was informed that she must never again walk much or engage in any occupation which required her to stand long on her feet. As soon as she was comparatively well she spoke to him alone. Since she was forbidden to walk and bustle about, and, indeed could not do so, it became her duty to leave. She could very well work at something sitting down, and she had an aunt, a seamstress.

The parson had been very greatly moved by what she had suffered on his account, and he exclaimed, "No, Sophy; lame or not lame, I cannot let you go. You must never leave me again."

He came close to her, and, though she could never exactly tell how it happened, she became conscious of his lips upon her cheek. He then asked her to marry him. Sophy did not exactly love him, but she had a respect for him which almost amounted to veneration. Even if she had wished to get away from him she hardly dared refuse a personage so reverend and august in her eyes, and she assented forthwith to be his wife.

Thus it happened that one fine morning, when the doors of the church were naturally open for ventilation, and the singing birds fluttered in and alighted on the tie-beams of the rood, there was a marriage-service at the communion rails which hardly a soul knew of. The parson and a neighbouring curate had entered at one door, and Sophy at another, followed by two necessary persons, whereupon in a short time there emerged a newly-made husband and wife.

Mr. Twycott knew perfectly well that he had committed social suicide by this step, despite Sophy's spotless character, and he had taken his measures accordingly. An exchange of livings had been arranged with an acquaintance who was incumbent of a church in the south of London, and as soon as possible the couple removed thither, abandoning their pretty country home with trees and shrubs and glebe[1] for a narrow, dusty house in a long, straight street, and their fine peal of bells for the wretchedest one-tongue clangor that ever tortured mortal ears. It was all on her account. They were, however, away from every one who had known her former position, and also under less observation from without than they would have had to put up with in any country parish.

Sophy the woman was as charming a partner as a man could possess, though Sophy the lady had her deficiencies. She showed a natural aptitude for little domestic refinements, so far as related to things and manners; but in what is called culture she was less intuitive. She had now been married more than fourteen years, and her husband had taken much trouble with her education; but she still held confused ideas on the use of "was" and "were", which did not beget a respect for her among the few acquaintances she made. Her great grief in this relation was that her only child, on whose education no expense had been or would be spared, was now old enough to perceive these deficiencies in his mother, and not only to see them but to feel irritated at their existence.

Thus she lived on in the city, and wasted hours in braiding her beautiful hair, till her once apple cheeks waned to pink of the very faintest. Her foot had never regained its natural strength after the accident, and she was mostly obliged to avoid walking altogether. Her husband had grown to like London for its freedom and its domestic privacy; but he was twenty years his Sophy's senior, and had latterly been seized with a serious illness. On this day, however, he had seemed to be well enough to justify her accompanying her son Randolph to the concert.

---

[1] *glebe* Land granted to clergyman.

2

The next time we get a glimpse of her is when she appears in the mournful attire of a widow.

Mr. Twycott had never rallied, and now lay in a well-packed cemetery to the south of the great city, where, if all the dead it contained had stood erect and alive, not one would have known him or recognized his name. The boy had dutifully followed him to the grave, and was now again at school.

Throughout these changes Sophy had been treated like the child she was in nature though not in years. She was left with no control over anything that had been her husband's beyond her modest personal income. In his anxiety lest her inexperience should be overreached he had safeguarded with trustees all he possibly could. The completion of the boy's course at the public school, to be followed in due time by Oxford and ordination, had been all provisioned and arranged, and she really had nothing to occupy her in the world but to eat and drink, and make a business of indolence, and go on weaving and coiling the nut-brown hair, merely keeping a home open for the son whenever he came to her during vacations.

Foreseeing his probable decease long years before her, her husband in his lifetime had purchased for her use a semi-detached villa in the same long, straight road whereon the church and parsonage faced, which was to be hers as long as she chose to live in it. Here she now resided, looking out upon the fragment of lawn in front, and through the railings at the ever-flowing traffic; or, bending forward over the window-sill on the first floor, stretching her eyes far up and down the vista of sooty trees, hazy air, and drab house façades, along which echoed the noises common to a suburban main thoroughfare.

Somehow, her boy, with his aristocratic school-knowledge, his grammar, and his aversions, was losing those wide infantile sympathies, extending as far as to the sun and moon themselves, with which he, like other children, had been born, and which his mother, a child of nature herself, had loved in him; he was reducing their compass to a population of a few thousand wealthy and titled people, the mere veneer of a thousand million or so of others who did not interest him at all. He drifted further and further away from her. Sophy's *milieu* being a suburb of minor tradesmen and under-clerks, and her almost only companions the two servants

of her own house, it was not surprising that after her husband's death she soon lost the little artificial tastes she had acquired from him, and became—in her son's eyes—a mother whose mistakes and origin it was his painful lot as a gentleman to blush for. As yet he was far from being man enough—if he ever would be—to rate these sins of hers at their true infinitesimal value beside the yearning fondness that welled up and remained penned in her heart till it should be more fully accepted by him, or by some other person or thing. If he had lived at home with her he would have had all of it; but he seemed to require so very little in present circum-stances, and it remained stored.

Her life became insupportably dreary; she could not take walks, and had no interest in going for drives, or, indeed, in traveling anywhere. Nearly two years passed without an event, and still she looked on that suburban road, thinking of the village in which she had been born, and whither she would have gone back—oh, how gladly!—even to work in the fields.

Taking no exercise, she often could not sleep, and would rise in the night or early morning and look out upon the then vacant thoroughfare, where the lamps stood like sentinels waiting for some procession to go by. An approximation to such a procession was indeed made every early morning about one o'clock, when the country vehicles passed up with loads of vegetables for Covent Garden market. She often saw them creeping along at this silent and dusky hour—wagon after wagon, bearing green bastions of cabbages nodding to their fall, yet never falling; walls of baskets enclosing masses of beans and pease; pyramids of snow-white turnips, swaying howdahs[1] of mixed produce—creeping along behind aged night-horses, who seemed ever patiently wondering between their hollow coughs why they had always to work at that still hour when all other sentient creatures were privileged to rest. Wrapped in a cloak, it was soothing to watch and sympathize with them when depression and nervousness hindered sleep, and to see how the fresh green-stuff brightened to life as it came opposite the lamp, and how the sweating animals steamed and shone with their miles of travel.

They had an interest, almost a charm, for Sophy, these semi-rural people and vehicles moving in an urban

---

[1]   *howdahs* Seats carried by elephants.

atmosphere, leading a life quite distinct from that of the daytime toilers on the same road. One morning a man who accompanied a wagon-load of potatoes gazed rather hard at the house fronts as he passed, and with a curious emotion she thought his form was familiar to her. She looked out for him again. His being an old-fashioned conveyance with a yellow front, it was easily recognizable, and on the third night after she saw it a second time. The man alongside was, as she had fancied, Sam Hobson, formerly gardener at Gaymead, who would at one time have married her.

She had occasionally thought of him, and wondered if life in a cottage with him would not have been a happier lot than the life she had accepted. She had not thought of him passionately, but her now dismal situation lent an interest to his resurrection—a tender interest which it is impossible to exaggerate. She went back to bed, and began thinking. When did these market-gardeners, who traveled up to town so regularly at one or two in the morning, come back? She dimly recollected seeing their empty wagons, hardly noticeable among the ordinary day-traffic, passing down at some hour before noon.

It was only April, but that morning, after breakfast, she had the window opened, and sat looking out, the feeble sun shining full upon her. She affected to sew, but her eyes never left the street. Between ten and eleven the desired wagon, now unladen, reappeared on its return journey. But Sam was not looking round him then, and drove on in a reverie.

"Sam!" cried she.

Turning with a start, his face lighted up. He called to him a little boy to hold the horse, alighted, and came and stood under her window.

"I can't come down easily, Sam, or I would!" she said. "Did you know I lived here?"

"Well, Mrs. Twycott, I knew you lived along here somewhere. I have often looked out for 'ee."

He briefly explained his own presence on the scene. He had long since given up his gardening in the village near Aldbrickham, and was now manager at a market-gardener's on the south side of London, it being part of his duty to go up to Covent Garden with wagon-loads of produce two or three times a week. In answer to her curious inquiry, he admitted that he had come to this particular district because he had seen in the Aldbrick-

Hobson came and stood under her window.[1]

ham paper a year or two before the announcement of the death in South London of the aforetime vicar of Gaymead, which had revived an interest in her dwelling-place that he could not extinguish, leading him to hover about the locality till his present post had been secured.

They spoke of their native village in dear old North Wessex, the spots in which they had played together as children. She tried to feel that she was a dignified personage now, that she must not be too confidential with Sam. But she could not keep it up, and the tears hanging in her eyes were indicated in her voice.

"You are not happy, Mrs. Twycott, I'm afraid," he said.

"Oh, of course not! I lost my husband only the year before last."

---

[1]   The illustrations that appear here and on page 860 accompanied "The Son's Veto" when it was first published in the *Illustrated London News*, 1 December 1891.

"Ah! I meant in another way. You'd like to be home again!"

"This is my home—for life. The house belongs to me. But I understand"—She let it out then.

"Yes, Sam. I long for home—*our* home! I *should* like to be there, and never leave it, and die there." But she remembered herself. "That's only a momentary feeling. I have a son, you know, a dear boy. He's at school now."

"Somewhere handy, I suppose? I see there's lots of 'em along this road."

"Oh no! Not in one of these wretched holes! At a public school—one of the most distinguished in England."

"Chok' it all! of course! I forgot, ma'am, that you've been a lady for so many years."

"No, I am not a lady," she said, sadly. "I never shall be. But he's a gentleman, and that—makes it—oh, how difficult for me!"

3

The acquaintance thus oddly reopened proceeded apace. She often looked out to get a few words with him by night or by day. Her sorrow was that she could not accompany her one old friend on foot a little way, and talk more freely than she could do while he paused before the house. One night, at the beginning of June, when she was again on the watch after an absence of some days from the window, he entered the gate and said, softly, "Now, wouldn't some air do you good? I've only half a load this morning. Why not ride up to Covent Garden with me? There's a nice seat on the cabbages, where I've spread a sack. You can be home again in a cab before anybody is up."

She refused at first, and then, trembling with excitement, hastily finished her dressing, and wrapped herself up in cloak and veil, afterwards sidling downstairs by the aid of the handrail, in a way she could adopt on an emergency. When she had opened the door she found Sam on the step, and he lifted her bodily on his strong arm across the little forecourt into his vehicle. Not a soul was visible or audible in the infinite length of the straight, flat highway, with its ever-waiting lamps converging to points in each direction. The air was fresh as country air at this hour, and the stars shone, except to the north-eastward, where there was a whitish light—

the dawn. Sam carefully placed her in the seat and drove on.

They talked as they had talked in old days, Sam pulling himself up now and then, when he thought himself too familiar. More than once she said with misgiving that she wondered if she ought to have indulged in the freak. "But I am so lonely in my house," she added, "and this makes me so happy!"

"You must come again, dear Mrs. Twycott. There is no time o' day for taking the air like this."

It grew lighter and lighter. The sparrows became busy in the streets, and the city waxed denser around them. When they approached the river it was day, and on the bridge they beheld the full blaze of morning sunlight in the direction of St. Paul's, the river glistening towards it, and not a craft stirring.

Near Covent Garden he put her into a cab, and they parted, looking into each other's faces like the very old friends they were. She reached home without adventure, limped to the door, and let herself in with her latch-key unseen.

The air and Sam's presence had revived her; her cheeks were quite pink—almost beautiful. She had something to live for in addition to her son. A woman of pure instincts, she knew there had been nothing really wrong in the journey, but supposed it conventionally to be very wrong indeed.

Soon, however, she gave way to the temptation of going with him again, and on this occasion their conversation was distinctly tender, and Sam said he never should forget her, notwithstanding that she had served him rather badly at one time. After much hesitation he told her of a plan it was in his power to carry out, and one he should like to take in hand, since he did not care for London work; it was to set up as a master gardener down at Aldbrickham, the county-town of their native place. He knew of an opening—a shop kept by aged people who wished to retire.

"And why don't you do it, then, Sam?" she asked, with a slight heart-sinking.

"Because I'm not sure if—you'd join me. I know you wouldn't—couldn't! Such a lady as ye've been so long, you couldn't be a wife to a man like me."

"I hardly suppose I could!" she assented, also frightened at the idea.

"If you could," he said, eagerly, "you'd on'y have to sit in the back parlor and look through the glass partition when I was away sometimes—just to keep an eye on things. The lameness wouldn't hinder that. I'd keep you as genteel as ever I could, dear Sophy—if I might think of it," he pleaded.

"Sam, I'll be frank," she said, putting her hand on his. "If it were only myself I would do it, and gladly, though everything I possess would be lost to me by marrying again."

"I don't mind that. It's more independent."

"That's good of you, dear, dear Sam. But there's something else. I have a son. I almost fancy when I am miserable sometimes that he is not really mine, but one I hold in trust for my late husband. He seems to belong so little to me personally, so entirely to his dead father. He is so much educated and I so little that I do not feel dignified enough to be his mother. Well, he would have to be told."

"Yes. Unquestionably." Sam saw her thought and her fear. "Still, you can do as you like, Sophy—Mrs. Twycott," he added. "It is not you who are the child, but he."

"Ah, you don't know! Sam, if I could, I would marry you, some day. But you must wait awhile, and let me think."

It was enough for him, and he was blithe at their parting. Not so she. To tell Randolph seemed impossible. She could wait till he had gone up to Oxford, when what she did would affect his life but little. But would he ever tolerate the idea? And if not, could she defy him?

She had not told him a word when the yearly cricket-match came on at Lord's[1] between the public schools, though Sam had already gone back to Aldbrickham. Mrs. Twycott felt stronger than usual. She went to the match with Randolph, and was able to leave her chair and walk about occasionally. The bright idea occurred to her that she could casually broach the subject while moving round among the spectators, when the boy's spirits were high with interest in the game, and he would weigh domestic matters as feathers in the scale

beside the day's victory. They promenaded under the lurid July sun, this pair, so wide apart, yet so near, and Sophy saw the large proportion of boys like her own, in their broad white collars and dwarf hats, and all around the rows of great coaches under which was jumbled the débris of luxurious luncheons—bones, pie-crusts, champagne-bottles, glasses, plates, napkins, and the family silver; while on the coaches sat the proud fathers and mothers; but never a poor mother like her. If Randolph had not appertained to these, had not centred all his interests in them, had not cared exclusively for the class they belonged to, how happy would things have been! A great huzza at some small performance with the bat burst from the multitude of relatives, and Randolph jumped wildly into the air to see what had happened. Sophy fetched up the sentence that had been already shaped; but she could not get it out. The occasion was, perhaps, an inopportune one. The contrast between her story and the display of fashion to which Randolph had grown to regard himself as akin would be fatal. She awaited a better time.

It was on an evening when they were alone in their plain suburban residence, where life was not blue but brown, that she ultimately broke silence, qualifying her announcement of a probable second marriage by assuring him that it would not take place for a long time to come, when he would be living quite independently of her.

The boy thought the idea a very reasonable one, and asked if she had chosen anybody. She hesitated; and he seemed to have a misgiving. He hoped his step-father would be a gentleman, he said.

"Not what you call a gentleman," she answered, timidly. "He'll be much as I was before I knew your father;" and by degrees she acquainted him with the whole. The youth's face remained fixed for a moment; then he flushed, leaned on the table, and burst into passionate tears.

His mother went up to him, kissed all of his face that she could get at, and patted his back as if he were still the baby he once had been, crying herself the while. When he had somewhat recovered from his paroxysm he went hastily to his own room and fastened the door. Parleyings were attempted through the key-hole, outside which she waited and listened. It was long

---

[1] *yearly cricket-match ... Lord's* Lord's cricket ground in London has been the site of an annual cricket match between two of the most prestigious public schools in England, Eton and Harrow, since 1805.

before he would reply, and when he did it was to say sternly at her from within: "I am ashamed of you! It will ruin me! A miserable boor! a churl! a clown! It will degrade me in the eyes of all the gentlemen of England!"

"Say no more—perhaps I am wrong! I will struggle against it!" she cried, miserably.

Before Randolph left her that summer a letter arrived from Sam to inform her that he had been unexpectedly fortunate in obtaining the shop. He was in possession; it was the largest in the town, combining fruit with vegetables, and he thought it would form a home worthy even of her some day. Might he not run up to town to see her?

She met him by stealth, and said he must still wait for her final answer. The autumn dragged on, and when Randolph was home at Christmas for the holidays she broached the matter again. But the young gentleman was inexorable.

It was dropped for months; renewed again; abandoned under his repugnance; again attempted, and thus the gentle creature reasoned and pleaded till four or five long years had passed. Then the faithful Sam revived his suit with some peremptoriness. Sophy's son, now an undergraduate, was down from Oxford one Easter, when she again opened the subject. As soon as he was ordained, she argued, he would have a home of his own, wherein she, with her bad grammar and her ignorance, would be an encumbrance to him. Better obliterate her as much as possible.

He showed a more manly anger now, but would not agree. She on her side was more persistent, and he had doubts whether she could be trusted in his absence. But by indignation and contempt for her taste he completely maintained his ascendancy; and finally taking her before a little cross and shrine that he had erected in his bedroom for his private devotions, there bade her kneel, and swear that she would not wed Samuel Hobson without his consent. "I owe this to my father!" he said.

The poor woman swore, thinking he would soften as soon as he was ordained and in full swing of clerical work. But he did not. His education had by this time sufficiently ousted his humanity to keep him quite firm; though his mother might have led an idyllic life with her faithful fruiterer and green-grocer, and nobody have been anything the worse in the world.

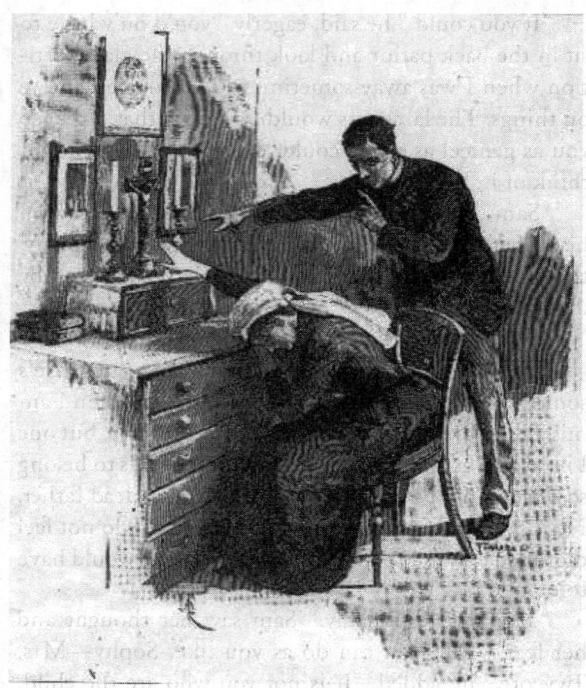

He made her swear before a little cross and shrine in his bed-room that she would not wed Samuel Hobson without his consent.

Her lameness became more confirmed as time went on, and she seldom or never left the house in the long southern thoroughfare, where she seemed to be pining her heart away. "Why mayn't I say to Sam that I'll marry him? Why mayn't I?" she would murmur plaintively to herself when nobody was near.

Some four years after this date a middle-aged man was standing at the door of the largest fruiterer's shop in Aldbrickham. He was the proprietor, but to-day, instead of his usual business attire, he wore a neat suit of black; and his window was partly shuttered. From the railway station a funeral procession was seen approaching; it passed his door and went out of the town towards the village of Gaymead. The man, whose eyes were wet, held his hat in his hand as the vehicles moved by; while from the mourning coach a young smooth-shaven priest in a high waistcoat looked black as a cloud at the shopkeeper standing there.

—DECEMBER 1891.

IN CONTEXT

Hardy's Notebooks and Memoranda

Hardy's notebooks and memoranda for the years during which "The Son's Veto" and other short stories were written contain an interesting mixture of observations on daily life, reflections on broader issues, and thoughts regarding the writing of fiction. The following entries, for example, give a vivid sense of aspects of Hardy's life in the autumn of 1892:

"*End of September*. In London. This is the time to realize London as an old city, all the pulsing excitements of May being absent."

"Drove home from dining with McIlvaine at the Café Royal, behind a horse who had no interest in me, was going a way he had no interest in going, and was whipped on by a man who had no interest in me, or the horse, or the way. Amid this string of compulsions reached home."

"*October*. At Great Fawley, Berks. Entered a ploughed vale which might be called the Valley of Brown Melancholy. The silence is remarkable .... Though I am alive with the living I can only see the dead here, and am scarcely conscious of the happy children at play."

"*October 7*. Tennyson died yesterday morning."

"*October 12*. Tennyson's funeral in Westminster Abbey. The music was sweet impressive, but as a funeral the scene was less penetrating than a plain country interment would have been."

Hardy's notations regarding specific stories are generally unrevealing (e.g., "January 13th. *The Fiddler of the Reels* posted to Messrs Scribner, New York," "December [no date]. Found and touched up a short story called 'An Imaginative Woman'.") They do include, however, several interesting comments about writing in general. On 24 October 1892, for example, Hardy reflected that "the best tragedy—highest tragedy in short—is that of the *worthy* encompassed by the *inevitable*. The tragedies of immoral and worthless people are not of the best." Three months later he made a note that is of particular relevance to his own fiction writing:

"*February 23*. A story must be exceptional enough to justify its telling. We tale-tellers are all Ancient Mariners, and none of us is warranted in stopping Wedding Guests (in other words, the hurrying public) unless he has something more unusual to relate than the ordinary experience of every average man and woman.

"The whole secret of fiction and the drama—in the constructional part—lies in the adjustment of things unusual to things eternal and universal. The writer who knows exactly how exceptional, and how non-exceptional, his events should be made, possesses the key to the art."

(The quotations from Hardy's notebooks and memoranda are as reproduced in Florence Hardy, *The Life of Thomas Hardy, Volume 2: The Later Years of Thomas Hardy, 1892–1928* [London: Macmillan, 1930] 13, 15, 26, 15–16.)

Hap° chance

If but some vengeful god would call to me
From up the sky, and laugh: "Thou suffering thing,
Know that thy sorrow is my ecstasy,
That thy love's loss is my hate's profiting!"

5   Then would I bear it, clench myself, and die,
Steeled by the sense of ire unmerited;
Half-eased in that a Powerfuller than I
Had willed and meted° me the tears I shed.   allotted

But not so. How arrives it joy lies slain,
10   And why unblooms the best hope ever sown?
—Crass Casualty obstructs the sun and rain,
And dicing Time for gladness casts a moan....
These purblind Doomsters[1] had as readily strown
Blisses about my pilgrimage as pain.
—1898 (WRITTEN 1866)

Neutral Tones

We stood by a pond that winter day,
And the sun was white, as though chidden of God,
And a few leaves lay on the starving sod;
—They had fallen from an ash, and were gray.

5   Your eyes on me were as eyes that rove
Over tedious riddles of years ago;
And some words played between us to and fro
On which lost the more by our love.

The smile on your mouth was the deadest thing
10   Alive enough to have strength to die;
And a grin of bitterness swept thereby
Like an ominous bird a-wing ...

Since then, keen° lessons that love deceives,   sharp
And wrings with wrong, have shaped to me
15   Your face, and the God-curst sun, and a tree,
And a pond edged with grayish leaves.
—1898 (WRITTEN 1867)

The Darkling° Thrush   in the dark

I leant upon a coppice gate[2]
When Frost was spectre-grey,
And Winter's dregs made desolate
The weakening eye of day.
5   The tangled bine[3]-stems scored the sky
Like strings of broken lyres,
And all mankind that haunted nigh
Had sought their household fires.

The land's sharp features seemed to be
10   The Century's corpse outleant,[4]
His crypt the cloudy canopy,
The wind his death-lament.
The ancient pulse of germ and birth
Was shrunken hard and dry,
15   And every spirit upon earth
Seemed fervorless as I.

At once a voice arose among
The bleak twigs overhead
In a full-hearted evensong
20   Of joy illimited;
An aged thrush, frail, gaunt, and small,
In blast-beruffled plume,[5]
Had chosen thus to fling his soul
Upon the growing gloom.

25   So little cause for carolings
Of such ecstatic sound
Was written on terrestrial things
Afar or nigh around,
That I could think there trembled through
30   His happy good-night air
Some blessed Hope, whereof he knew
And I was unaware.
—1901 (WRITTEN 31 DECEMBER 1900)

---

[1]   purblind Doomsters   Half-blind judges.

[2]   coppice gate   Gate leading to a thicket or small forest.

[3]   bine   Hop, a climbing plant.

[4]   The Century's corpse outleant   I.e., as if the century were leaning out of its coffin.

[5]   plume   I.e., feathers.

The Ruined Maid

"O 'Melia, my dear, this does everything crown!¹
   Who could have supposed I should meet you
      in Town?
And whence such fair garments, such prosperi-ty?"—
"O didn't you know I'd been ruined?" said she.

5 —"You left us in tatters, without shoes or socks,
Tired of digging potatoes, and spudding up docks;²
And now you've gay bracelets and bright feathers three!"—
"Yes: that's how we dress when we're ruined," said she.

  —"At home in the barton° you said 'thee' and 'thou,'   *barnyard*
10 And 'thik oon,' and 'theäs oon,' and 't'other'; but now
Your talking quite fits 'ee for high compa-ny!"—
"Some polish is gained with one's ruin," said she.

  —"Your hands were like paws then, your face blue
     and bleak
But now I'm bewitched by your delicate cheek,
15 And your little gloves fit as on any la-dy!"—
"We never do work when we're ruined," said she.

  —"You used to call home-life a hag-ridden dream,
And you'd sigh, and you'd sock;³ but at present you seem
To know not of megrims° or melancho-ly!"—   *depression*
20 "True. One's pretty lively when ruined," said she.

  —"I wish I had feathers, a fine sweeping gown,
And a delicate face, and could strut about Town!"—
"My dear—a raw country girl, such as you be,
Cannot quite expect that. You ain't ruined," said she.
   —1901 (WRITTEN 1866)

A Broken Appointment

You did not come.
And marching Time drew on, and wore me numb.—
Yet less for loss of your dear presence there

Than that I thus found lacking in your make
5 That high compassion which can overbear
Reluctance for pure lovingkindness' sake
Grieved I, when, as the hope-hour stroked its sum,
     You did not come.

    You love not me,
10 And love alone can lend you loyalty;
—I know and knew it. But, unto the store
Of human deeds divine in all but name,
Was it not worth a little hour or more
To add yet this: Once you, a woman, came
15 To soothe a time-torn man; even though it be
     You love not me?
   —1902

Shut out that Moon

Close up the casement, draw the blind,
   Shut out that stealing moon,
She wears too much the guise she wore
    Before our lutes were strewn
5 With years-deep dust, and names we read
    On a white stone were hewn.

Step not out on the dew-dashed lawn
    To view the Lady's Chair,
Immense Orion's glittering form,
10   The Less and Greater Bear:⁴
Stay in; to such sights we were drawn
    When faded ones were fair.

Brush not the bough for midnight scents
    That come forth lingeringly,
15 And wake the same sweet sentiments
    They breathed to you and me
When living seemed a laugh, and love
    All it was said to be.

Within the common lamp-lit room
20   Prison my eyes and thought;
Let dingy details crudely loom,

---

¹ *this does everything* This surpasses everything.
² *spudding up docks* Uprooting weeds.
³ *sock* Mouth your displeasure.

⁴ *Lady's Chair … Greater Bear* Constellations.

Mechanic° speech be wrought: *low, vulgar*
Too fragrant was Life's early bloom,
  Too tart the fruit it brought!
—1909

The Convergence of the Twain

(Lines on the Loss of the "Titanic")[1]

1

I n a solitude of the sea
  Deep from human vanity,
And the Pride of Life that planned her, stilly couches she.

2

  Steel chambers, late the pyres
   Of her salamandrine fires,[2]
5 Cold currents thrid,[3] and turn to rhythmic tidal lyres.

3

  Over the mirrors meant
   To glass the opulent
The sea-worm crawls—grotesque, slimed, dumb,
   indifferent.

4

10 Jewels in joy designed
   To ravish the sensuous mind
Lie lightless, all their sparkles bleared and black and blind.

5

  Dim moon-eyed fishes near
   Gaze at the gilded gear
15 And query: "What does this vaingloriousness down
   here?" …

6

  Well: while was fashioning
   This creature of cleaving wing,

The Immanent Will[4] that stirs and urges everything

7

  Prepared a sinister mate
   For her—so gaily great—
20 A Shape of Ice, for the time far and dissociate.

8

  And as the smart ship grew
   In stature, grace, and hue,
In shadowy silent distance grew the Iceberg too.

9

25 Alien they seemed to be:
   No mortal eye could see
The intimate welding of their later history,

10

  Or sign that they were bent
   By paths coincident
30 On being anon twin halves of one august event,

11

  Till the Spinner of the Years
   Said "Now!" And each one hears,
And consummation comes, and jars two hemispheres.
—1914

Channel Firing[5]

T hat night your great guns, unawares,
  Shook all our coffins as we lay,
And broke the chancel[6] window-squares,
We thought it was the Judgment-day

5 And sat upright. While drearisome
Arose the howl of wakened hounds:
The mouse let fall the altar-crumb,

---

1 *the "Titanic"*   At the time the largest ship ever built, the ocean liner *Titanic* had been described as unsinkable, but on its maiden voyage in 1912 it collided with an iceberg; over 1,400 people drowned when it sank.

2 *salamandrine fires*   According to mythology, salamanders are able to survive any heat.

3 *thrid*   Thread.

4 *The Immanent Will*   The force that pervades and determines human existence.

5 *Channel Firing*   In the months leading up to the First World War both the British and the German navies practised firing in the English Channel. (This poem was written in April 1914; the First World War began in August of the same year.)

6 *chancel*   Eastern part of a church, used by those who officiate at services.

The worms drew back into the mounds,

The glebe[1] cow drooled. Till God called, "No;
10   It's gunnery practice out at sea
Just as before you went below;
The world is as it used to be:

"All nations striving strong to make
Red war yet redder. Mad as hatters[2]
15   They do no more for Christés° sake   Christ's
Than you who are helpless in such matters.

"That this is not the judgment-hour
For some of them's a blessed thing,
For if it were they'd have to scour
20   Hell's floor for so much threatening. ...

"Ha, ha. It will be warmer when
I blow the trumpet (if indeed
I ever do; for you are men,
And rest eternal sorely need)."

25   So down we lay again. "I wonder,
Will the world ever saner be,"
Said one, "than when He sent us under
In our indifferent century!"

And many a skeleton shook his head.
30   "Instead of preaching forty year,"
My neighbour Parson Thirdly said,
"I wish I had stuck to pipes and beer."

Again the guns disturbed the hour,
Roaring their readiness to avenge,
35   As far inland as Stourton Tower,
And Camelot, and starlit Stonehenge.[3]
—1914

---

[1] glebe Field, especially a field belonging to a church.

[2] Mad as hatters Makers of felt hats in the late 18th and early 19th century frequently went insane as a result of breathing in mercury compounds used in the manufacture of the hats.

[3] Stourton Tower ... Stonehenge Stourton Tower was built to commemorate the victory of King Alfred over the Danes; Camelot was the site of King Arthur's court; Stonehenge is the famous prehistoric stone monument near Salisbury.

The Voice

Woman much missed, how you call to me, call to me,
    Saying that now you are not as you were
When you had changed from the one who was all to me,
    But as at first, when our day was fair.

5   Can it be you that I hear? Let me view you, then,
    Standing as when I drew near to the town
Where you would wait for me: yes, as I knew you then,
    Even to the original air-blue gown!

Or is it only the breeze, in its listlessness
10   Travelling across the wet mead° to me here,   meadow
    You being ever dissolved to wan wistlessness,
    Heard no more again far or near?

        Thus I; faltering forward,
        Leaves around me falling,
15   Wind oozing thin through the thorn from norward,
        And the woman calling.
—1914 (WRITTEN DECEMBER 1912)

Transformations

Portion of this yew[4]
    Is a man my grandsire knew,
Bosomed here at its foot:
This branch may be his wife,
5   A ruddy human life
Now turned to a green shoot.

These grasses must be made
Of her who often prayed,
Last century, for repose;
10   And the fair girl long ago
Whom I vainly tried to know
May be entering this rose.

So, they are not underground,
But as nerves and veins abound
15   In the growths of upper air,

---

[4] yew Traditionally, yew trees have been planted beside churches and near graveyards.

And they feel the sun and rain,
And the energy again
That made them what they were!
—1915

In Time of "The Breaking of Nations"[1]

1

Only a man harrowing clods
    In a slow silent walk
With an old horse that stumbles and nods
    Half asleep as they stalk.

2

5 Only thin smoke without flame
    From the heaps of couch-grass;
Yet this will go onward the same
    Though Dynasties pass.

3

Yonder a maid and her wight[2]
10   Come whispering by:
War's annals will fade into night
    Ere their story die.
—1916

The Photograph

The flame crept up the portrait line by line
    As it lay on the coals in the silence of night's profound,
        And over the arm's incline,
And along the marge of the silkwork superfine,
5 And gnawed at the delicate bosom's defenceless round.

Then I vented a cry of hurt, and averted my eyes;
The spectacle was one that I could not bear,
        To my deep and sad surprise;
But, compelled to heed, I again looked furtivewise
10 Till the flame had eaten her breasts, and mouth, and hair.

"Thank God, she is out of it now!" I said at last,
In a great relief of heart when the thing was done
        That had set my soul aghast,
And nothing was left of the picture unsheathed from
    the past
15 But the ashen ghost of the card it had figured on.

She was a woman long hid amid packs of years,
She might have been living or dead; she was lost to
    my sight,
        And the deed that had nigh drawn tears
Was done in a casual clearance of life's arrears;
20 But I felt as if I had put her to death that night! ...

—Well; she knew nothing thereof did she survive,
And suffered nothing if numbered among the dead;
        Yet—yet—if on earth alive
Did she feel a smart, and with vague strange anguish
    strive?
25 If in heaven, did she smile at me sadly and shake her
    head?
—1917

During Wind and Rain

They sing their dearest songs—
    He, she, all of them—yea,
Treble and tenor and bass,
    And one to play;
5 With the candles mooning each face....
    Ah, no; the years O!
How the sick leaves reel down in throngs!

They clear the creeping moss—
    Elders and juniors—aye,
10 Making the pathways neat
    And the garden gay;
And they build a shady seat....
    Ah, no; the years, the years;
See, the white storm-birds wing across.

15 They are blithely breakfasting all—
    Men and maidens—yea,
Under the summer tree,

---

1 *In Time of "The Breaking of Nations"* See Jeremiah 51.20: "Thou art my battleaxe and weapons of war: for with thee will I break in pieces the nations. ..."

2 *wight* I.e., man.

With a glimpse of the bay,
While pet fowl come to the knee....
20   Ah, no; the years O!
And the rotten rose is ript from the wall.

They change to a high new house,
He, she, all of them—aye,
Clocks and carpets and chairs
25   On the lawn all day,
And brightest things that are theirs....
          Ah, no; the years, the years;
Down their carved names the rain-drop ploughs.
—1917

The Oxen

Christmas Eve, and twelve of the clock.
    "Now they are all on their knees,"[1]
An elder said as we sat in a flock
    By the embers in hearthside ease.

5 We pictured the meek mild creatures where
        They dwelt in their strawy pen,
Nor did it occur to one of us there
        To doubt they were kneeling then.

So fair a fancy few would weave
10   In these years! Yet, I feel,
If someone said on Christmas Eve,
        "Come; see the oxen kneel,

"In the lonely barton° by yonder coomb°   *barnyard / valley*
        Our childhood used to know,"
15 I should go with him in the gloom,
        Hoping it might be so.
—1917

Going and Staying

1

The moving sun-shapes on the spray,
    The sparkles where the brook was flowing,
Pink faces, plightings, moonlit May—
These were the things we wished would stay;
5   But they were going.

2

Seasons of blankness as of snow,
The silent bleed of a world decaying,
The moan of multitudes in woe—
These were the things we wished would go;
10   But they were staying.

3

Then we looked closelier at Time,
And saw his ghostly arms revolving
To sweep off woeful things with prime,
Things sinister with things sublime
15   Alike dissolving.
—1920

---

[1] *Now they are all on their knees*   It was once widely believed that
oxen would kneel at the appointed time on Christmas every year in
imitation of the ox in the manger kneeling when Christ was born.

THOMAS HARDY

IN CONTEXT

Hardy's Reflections on the Writing of Poetry

The Life of Thomas Hardy, published under the name of his second wife, Florence Hardy, was later discovered to have been written by Hardy himself. When this third-person autobiography discusses Hardy's poetic career in relation to his fiction writing, the author reveals his sensitivity to suggestions that he had taken up poetry only as a result of the reaction against his later novels:

> In the early weeks of this year [1899] the poems were reviewed in the customary periodicals—mostly in a friendly tone, even in a tone of respect, and with praise for many pieces in the volume; though by some critics not without umbrage at Hardy's having taken the liberty to adopt another vehicle of expression than prose fiction without consulting them. ...
>
> Almost all the fault-finding was, in fact, based on the one great antecedent conclusion that an author who has published prose first, and that largely, must necessarily express himself badly in verse, no reservation being added to except cases in which he may have published prose for temporary or compulsory reasons, or prose of a poetical kind, or have written verse first of all, or for a long time intermediately. ... In the present case, although it was shown that many of the verses had been written before their author dreamt of novels, the critics' view was very little affected that he had "at the eleventh hour," as they untruly put it, taken up a hitherto uncared-for art.

A few pages on, the account is again at pains to emphasize the purity of Hardy's motives in abandoning prose fiction and devoting himself to poetry:

> When one considers how he might have made himself a man of affluence by taking the current of popularity as it served, writing "best sellers," and ringing changes upon the novels he had already written, his bias towards poetry must have been instinctive and disinterested.

Hardy includes few reflections on the nature of his own poetry, but he does take issue with Wordsworth's famous strictures against poetic diction, asserting that Wordsworth "should have put the matter somewhat like this: in works of *passion and sentiment* (not 'imagination and sentiment') the language of verse is the language of prose. In works of *fancy* (or *imagination*), 'poetic diction' (of the real kind) is proper, and even necessary." Here and there Hardy also makes interesting comments on the origin of particular poems. Here, for example, are his remarks concerning "In Time of 'The Breaking of Nations'":

> I believe it would be said by people who knew me well that I have a faculty (perhaps not uncommon) for burying an emotion in my heart or brain for forty years, and exhuming it at the end of that time as fresh as when interred. For instance, the poem entitled "The Breaking of Nations" contains a feeling that moved me in 1870, during the Franco-Prussian war, when I chanced to be looking at such an agricultural incident in Cornwall. But I did not write the verses till during the war with Germany of 1914, and onwards.

GERARD MANLEY HOPKINS
1844 – 1889

The Victorian priest and poet Gerard Manley Hopkins lived only 45 years, but his work spans three eras of literary history. A Romantic in his notions of the beauty and power of the natural world and of the importance of the imagination and the individual's connection with nature, Hopkins shared some affinities with Keats and other poets of the Romantic period. He also shared affinities with the Victorian Pre-Raphaelites, and like them was very influenced by the writings of John Ruskin. But because his poems and letters, in which he outlined his innovative poetic theories, were not published until 1918, some 30 years after his death, he is sometimes grouped with such Modernists as T.S. Eliot and Ezra Pound. Indeed these poets were influenced by Hopkins's experimental verse, with its unconventional syntax, dense alliteration, and "sprung rhythm" (the term Hopkins coined to describe his unique metric style).

Hopkins was born in Essex of affluent parents and showed promise as a scholar from an early age, but he was clearly also talented in music and the visual arts. His early schooling was at Highgate, where he studied under, and formed a lifelong friendship with, the Pre-Raphaelite poet R.W. Dixon. Hopkins went on to study classics at Oxford, where he became known as the "Star of Balliol [College]" and was educated by such luminaries as Benjamin Jowett and Walter Pater. While Pater's aestheticism was indeed an influence on Hopkins's artistic philosophies, no one at Oxford had a greater impact on him than did John Henry Newman. A convert to Roman Catholicism who later became a Cardinal, Newman was one of the leaders of the "Oxford Movement" of the 1830s and early 1840s, a Tractarian movement (because of the "Tracts for the Times" that Newman and others wrote) that called for the Church of England to recognize points of communion with the Roman Catholic Church.

Hopkins's conversion to Roman Catholicism in 1866 estranged him from his devout Anglican parents, who wrote "terrible" letters to try to dissuade him from his decision to become a Jesuit priest. He replied to his father's concerns by saying: "I am surprised you shd. say fancy and aesthetic tastes have led me to my present state of mind: these wd. be better satisfied in the Church of England, for bad taste is always meeting one in the accessories of Catholicism." Hopkins served the Catholic Church for the rest of his life, and for many of those years he renounced his own poetry, burning much of it in the belief that, with the exception of sermons, authorship was not becoming for a priest. It was obvious, however, that he did not cease thinking about the techniques of writing, as his journals and letters, many written to his Oxford friend and poet (later Poet Laureate) Robert Bridges, attest.

After a famous shipwreck in 1875, Hopkins's superiors encouraged him to write of the fate of five Franciscan nuns, exiled from Germany by the Falk Laws, who had drowned in the disaster. In the long ode *The Wreck of the Deutschland* he began experimenting with the rhythms he had been thinking about for so long. According to Hopkins, every object in the natural world has a unique and fluid identity, or "inscape," an essence that comprises its form and its meaning. Hopkins also coined the term "instress" to describe the way in which objects or people perceive "inscape." Instress is a powerful burst of energy that allows an observer to penetrate and experience the object's essence. Poetry, for Hopkins, is instress, and that which it seeks to penetrate is the divine.

In creating a poetic sound that would present the inscape of objects and of speech itself, Hopkins was inspired by the rhythms of Welsh nursery rhymes and Old English poetry. "Sprung rhythm" was the result, a syntactically disjunctive, highly alliterative, and densely rhyming style that reconfigured the nature of stresses and line length. The poems in this style that followed *Deutschland*—among them the famous "God's Grandeur"—often aimed to celebrate the spiritual and the divine. Notably, Hopkins added the dedication "*To Christ our Lord*" to "The Windhover."

Hopkins continued to write poetry, but his duties as a priest took priority. He served from 1877 to 1879 in various parishes in Sheffield, Oxford, and London, and then went on to fulfill demanding duties in the dreary slums of Manchester, Liverpool, and Glasgow. In 1881 he began teaching at Stonyhurst College in Lancashire, and in 1884 was appointed Professor of Greek and Latin at University College in Dublin. Hopkins disliked both his duties at this university and the city itself, which was still recovering from the Great Famine. Years of illness and depression followed, combined with doubts about his ability to give himself completely to God. During these years of angst, Hopkins composed what are now called his "terrible sonnets," among them "Carrion Comfort" and "No Worst, There is None," named for their themes of anguish and desolation.

Hopkins was not to live long in Ireland; he contracted typhoid fever and died in 1889 at the age of 45. Robert Bridges edited a volume of his poetry, *The Poems of Gerard Manley Hopkins*, and released it to the public thirty years after Hopkins's death, presumably waiting until the world was ready to hear the sound of the poet who acknowledged his "oddness" by saying: "The effect of studying masterpieces is to make me admire and do otherwise." Although his output was relatively small, the poet who "did otherwise" made an enormous impact on the literary world, and has influenced several generations of poets.

⌘ ⌘ ⌘

God's Grandeur

The world is charged with the grándeur of God.
    It will flame out, like shining from shook foil;[1]
It gathers to a greatness, like the ooze of oil
Crushed.[2] Why do men then now not reck°   *regard*   10
    his rod?
5 Génerátions have trod, have trod, have trod;
    And all is seared with trade; bleared, smeared, with
        toil;

And wears man's smudge and shares man's smell:
        the soil
Is bare now, nor can foot feel, being shod.

Ánd, for° all this, náture is never spent;   *despite*
    There lives the dearest freshness deep down things;
And though the last lights off the black West went
    Oh, morning, at the brown brink eastward,
        springs—
Because the Holy Ghost óver the bent
    World broods with warm breast and with ah!
        bright wings.
—1918 (WRITTEN 1877)

---

1 [Hopkins's note] I mean foil in its sense of leaf or tinsel....Shaken goldfoil gives off broad glares like sheet lightning and also, and this is true of nothing else, owing to its zigzag dints and creasings and network of small many cornered facets, a sort of fork lightning too.

2 *oil / Crushed* I.e., as olive oil.

The Wreck of the Deutschland [1]

December 6. 7.1875
To the happy memory of five Franciscan nuns, exiles by the Falck Laws,[2] drowned between midnight and morning of December 7

PART THE FIRST

1

Thou mastering me
God! giver of breath and bread;
Wórld's stránd,° swáy of the séa;   shore
Lord of living and dead;
5 Thou hast bóund bónes and véins in me, fástened me flésh,
And áfter it álmost únmade, what with dréad,
Thy doing: and dost thou touch me afresh?
Óver agáin I féel thy fínger and find thée.

2

I did say yes
10 O at líghtning and láshed ród;
Thou heardst me, truer than tongue, confess
Thy terror, O Christ, O God;
Thou knówest the wálls, áltar and hour and níght:
The swoon of a heart that the sweep and the hurl
of thee trod
15 Hárd dówn with a horror of height:
And the midriff astrain with leaning of, laced with fire
of stress.

3

The frown of his face
Before me, the hurtle of hell
Behind, where, where was a, where was a
place?—
20 I whirled out wings that spell

And fled with a fling of the heart to the heart of
the Host.—[3]
My heart, but you were dovewinged, I can tell,
Cárrier-wítted, I am bóld to bóast,
To flash from the flame to the flame then, tower from
the grace to the grace.

4

25 I am sóft síft
In an hourglass—at the wall
Fast, but mined with a motion, a drift,
And it crowds and it combs to the fall;
I stéady as a wáter in a wéll, to a póise, to a páne,
30 But roped with, always, all the way down from the
tall
Fells or flanks of the voel,[4] a vein
Of the góspel próffer, a préssure, a prínciple, Christ's
gíft.

5

I kiss my hand
To the stars, lovely-asunder
35 Starlight, wafting him out of it; and
Glow, glory in thunder;
Kiss my hand to the dappled-with-damson[5] west:
Since, thóugh he is únder the wórld's spléndour
and wónder,
His mýstery múst be instréssed,[6] stressed;
40 For I greet him the days I meet him, and bless when I
understand.

6

Not out of his bliss
Springs the stress felt
Nor first from heaven (and few know this)
Swings the stroke dealt—
45 Stroke and a stress that stars and storms deliver,

---

[1] *The Wreck of the Deutschland* The *Deutschland*, a German ship, ran aground on a shoal off the coast of England in December 1875. With the lifeboats of the ship stripped away by the storm, five nuns drowned in her hold. As they awaited death, their leader reportedly called out "O Christ, come quickly!"

[2] *Falck Laws* Anti-Catholic German legislation.

[3] *Host* The consecrated bread of the Holy Eucharist, which represents the Body of Christ.

[4] *Fells* Pastures; *voel* Mountain.

[5] *damson* Dark purple.

[6] *instréssed* The word, invented by Hopkins, means imbued with that force which sustains the uniqueness of an object, or the essential quality of a thing.

That guilt is hushed by, hearts are flushed by and
    melt—
    But it rídes tíme like ríding a ríver
(And here the faithful waver, the faithless fable and
    miss).

7

    It dates from day
      Of his going in Galilee;
   Warm-laid grave of a womb-life grey;
      Manger, maiden's knee;
The dense and the driven Passion, and frightful
    sweat:
Thence the discharge of it, there its swelling to be,
    Though félt befóre, though in high flood
      yét—
What none would have known of it, only the heart,
    being hard at bay,

8

    Is out with it! Oh,
      We lash with the best or worst
   Word last! How a lush-kept plush-capped sloe[1]
      Will, mouthed to flesh-burst,
Gush!—flush the man, the being with it, sour or
    sweet
Brim, in a flásh, fúll!—Híther then, lást or fírst,
    To hero of Calvary, Christ's feet—
Never ask if méaning it, wánting it, wárned of
    it—mén gó.

9

    Be adored among men,
      God, three-numberèd form;
   Wring thy rebel, dogged in den,
      Man's malice, with wrecking and storm.
Beyónd sáying swéet, past télling of tóngue,
Thou art lightning and love, I found it, a winter
    and warm;
   Father and fondler of heart thou hast wrung:
Hast thy dark descending and most art merciful then.

10

    With an anvil-ding

---

[1]   *sloe* Fruit of the blackthorn.

And with fire in him forge thy will
   Or rather, rather then, stealing as Spring
      Through him, melt him but master him
      still:
Whether át ónce, as ónce at a crásh Pául,
Or as Áustin,[2] a língering-óut swéet skíll,
   Make mercy in all of us, out of us all
Mástery, bút be adóred, bút be adóred King.

PART THE SECOND

11

    "Some find me a swórd; sóme
      The flánge° and the rául; fláme,   *rim*
   Fang, or flood" goes Death on drum,
      And stórms búgle his fáme.
But *wé* dréam we are róoted in éarth—Dúst!
Flesh falls within sight of us: we, though our
    flower the same,
   Wave with the meadow, forget that there must
The sóur scýthe crínge, and the bléar sháre cóme.

12

    —On Saturday sailed from Bremen,
      American-outward-bound,
   Take settler and seamen, tell men with
      women,
      Two hundred souls in the round—
O Father, not under thy feathers[3] nor ever as
    guessing
The goal was a shoal, of a fourth the doom to be
    drowned;
   Yet *did* the dark side of the bay of thy blessing
Not vault them, the million of rounds of thy mercy
    not reeve[4] even them in?

13

    Into the snows she sweeps,
      Hurling the Haven behind,

---

[2]   *Paul … Áustin* St. Paul, whose conversion in an instant on the
road to Damascus (Acts 9.1–19) was very different from the
conversion over many years of St. Augustine (354–430 CE).

[3]   *under thy feathers* Reference to Psalm 91.4: "He will cover you
with His feathers, and under His wings you will find refuge."

[4]   *reeve* Nautical term: to lace up with ropes.

The Deutschland, on Sunday; and so the sky
    keeps,
20   For the infinite air is unkind,
And the sea flint-flake, black-backed in the regular
    blow,
Sitting Eastnortheast, in cursed quarter, the wind;
    Wiry and white-fiery and whírlwind-swivellèd
       snów
Spins to the widow-making unchilding unfathering
    deeps.

14

25   She drove in the dark to leeward,
       She struck—not a reef or a rock
But the combs of a smother of sand: night
    drew her
       Dead to the Kentish Knock;[1]
And she beat the bank down with her bows and
    the ride of her keel;
30   The breakers rolled on her beam with ruinous
       shock;
       And, canvass and compass, the whorl and the
       wheel
Idle for ever to waft her or wind her with, these she
    endūred.

15

       Hope had grown grey hairs,
       Hope had mourning on,
35   Trénched with téars, cárved with cáres,
       Hope was twelve hours gone;
And frightful a nightfall folded rueful a day
Nor rescue, only rocket and lightship,[2] shone,
    And lives at last were washing away:
40   To the shrouds they took,—they shook in the hurling
    and horrible airs.

16

       One stirred from the rigging to save
       The wild woman-kind below,
With a rope's end round the man, handy and
    brave—
       He was pitched to his death at a blow,

45 For all his dreadnought° breast and braids   *fearless*
    of thew:°   *muscle*
    They could téll him for hóurs, dándled the tó and
       the fró
       Through the cobbled foam-fleece. What could
       he do
With the burl of the fóuntains of aír, búck and the
    flóod of the wave?

17

       They fought with God's cold—
50   And they could not, and fell to the deck
    (Crushed them) or water (and drowned them)
       or rolled
       With the searomp over the wreck.
Night roared, with the heartbreak hearing a
    heartbroke rabble,
The woman's wailing, the crying of child without
    check—
55   Till a líoness aróse bréasting the bábble,
A próphetess tówered in the túmult, a virginal tóngue
    tóld.

18

       Ah, touched in your bower of bone,
       Are you! turned, for an exquisite smart,
Have you! make words break from me here all
    alone,
60   Do you!—móther of béing in me, héart.
O unteachably after evil, but uttering truth,
Why, tears! is it? tears; such a melting, a
    madrigal° start!   *song*
       Never-eldering revel and river of youth,
What can it be, this glee? the good you have there of
    your own?

19

       Sister, a sister calling
       A master, her master and mine!—
       And the inboard seas run swirling and hawling;
65   The rash smart sloggering brine
Blinds her; but shé that wéather sees óne thing,
    óne;
70 Has óne fetch[3] ín her: she réars hersélf to divíne

---

[1] *Kentish Knock* Sandbank near the mouth of the Thames River.

[2] *lightship* Floating warning light.

[3] *fetch* Solution.

Éars, and the cáll of the táll nún
To the mén in the tóps and the táckle rode óver the
  stórm's brawling.

20

She was first of a five and came
  Of a coifèd sisterhood.[1]
75   (O Deutschland, double a desperate name!
    O wórld wíde of its góod!
But Gertrude, lily, and Luther,[2] are two of a town,
  Christ's líly, and béast of the wáste wóod:
    From life's dáwn it is dráwn dówn,
80 Ábel is Cáin's brother and bréasts they have súcked
  the sáme.)

21

Loathed for a love men knew in them,
  Banned by land of their birth,
Rhíne refúsed them, Thámes would rúin
    them;
  Surf, snow, river and earth
85 Gnashed: but thou art above, thou Orion of light;
Thy unchancelling poising palms were weighing
  the worth,
  Thou mártyr-máster: in thý síght
Storm flákes were scróll-leaved flówers, lily
  shówers—sweet héaven was astréw in them.

22

Five! the finding and sake
  And cipher of suffering Christ.
90 Márk, the márk is of mán's máke
  And the word of it Sacrificed,
But he scores it in scarlet himself on his own
  bespoken,
Before-time-taken, dearest prizèd and priced—
95   Stigma, signal, cinquefoil[3] token
For léttering of the lámb's fléece, rúddying of the
  róse-fláke.

1   *coifèd sisterhood*   Reference to the nuns' veils.

2   *Gertrude ... Luther*   Hopkins contrasts St. Gertrude the Great (1256–1301), the first nun's namesake, with Martin Luther (1483–1546) the Protestant reformer, whose doctrinal descendants enacted the laws that exiled the nuns. St. Gertrude is thought to have been born in the town of Eiselben, the birthplace of Luther.

3   *cinquefoil*   Five-leaved plant.

23

Joy fall to thee, father Francis,
  Drawn to the Life that died;
With the gnarls of the nails in thee, niche of
    the lance, his
100   Lovescape crucified
And seal of his seraph-arrival! and these thy
  daughters
And five-livèd and leavèd favour and pride,
  Are sísterly séaled in wíld wáters,
To bathe in his fall-gold mercies, to breathe in his all-
  fire glances.

24

105   Away in the loveable west,
    On a pastoral forehead of Wales,
I was under a roof here, I was at rest,
    And they the prey of the gales;
She to the black-about air, to the breaker, the
    thickly
110 Falling flakes, to the throng that catches and
    quails,
    Was calling "O Christ, Christ, come quickly":
The cross to her she calls Christ to her, christens her
  wild-worst Best.

25

The majesty! what did she mean?
  Breathe, arch and original Breath.
115 Is it lóve in her of the béing as her lóver had
    béen?
  Breathe, body of lovely Death.
They were élse-mínded then, áltogéther, the mén
Wóke thee with a *We are périshing* in the wéather
  of Gennésaréth.[4]
  Or ís it that she críed for the crówn thén,
120 The keener to come at the comfort for feeling the
  combating keen?

26

For how to the heart's cheering
  The down-dugged ground-hugged grey

4   *Gennésaréth*   Sea of Galilee. In Matthew 8.23–27, Jesus and his disciples are caught in a boat during a storm on the Sea of Galilee. His disciples cry out in fear, and Jesus calms the storm.

Hovers off, the jay-blue heavens appearing
    Of pied and peeled May!
125 Blue-beating and hoary-glow height; or night, still
    higher,
    With bélled fíre and the móth-soft Mílky Wáy.
      What bý your méasure is the héaven of desíre,
The tréasure never éyesight gót, nor was éver guessed
    whát for the héaring?

27

      Nó, but it was nót thése.
130   The jáding and the jár of the cárt,
    Time's tásking, it is fáthers that ásking for éase
    Of the sódden-with-its-sórrowing héart,
Not danger, electrical-horror; then, further, it finds
    The appéaling of the Pássion is ténderer in práyer
    apárt:
135   Other, I gather, in measure her mind's
    Búrden, in wínd's búrly and béat of endrágonèd séas.

28

      But how shall I ... Make me room there;
    Reach me a ... Fancy, come faster—
    Strike you the sight of it? look at it loom there,
140   Thing that she ... There then! the Master,
Ipse,° the ónly one, Chríst, Kíng, Héad: *Himself*
He was to cure the extremity where he had cast
    her;
    Do, deal, lord it with living and dead;
Let him ride, her pride, in his triumph, despatch and
    have done with his doom there.

29

145   Ah! thére was a héart right!
    There was single eye!
    Réad the unshápeable shóck níght
    And knew the who and the why;
Wording it how but by him that present and past,
150 Heaven and earth are word of, worded by?—
    The Símon-Péter of a sóul! to the blást
Tárpéïan-fast,[1] but a blówn béacon of líght.

30   Jésu, héart's líght,
    Jésu, máid's són,
155   Whát was the féast fóllowed the níght
    Thou hadst glóry of thís nún?—
Féast of the óne wóman withóut stáin.
For so conceivèd, so to conceive thee is done;
    But here was heart-throe, birth of a brain,
160 Wórd, that héard and képt thee and úttered thee
    óutríght.

31

      Well, shé has thée for the pain, for the
    Pátience; but píty of the rést of them!
    Heart, go and bleed at a bitterer vein for the
    Comfortless unconfessed of them—
165 No not uncomforted: lovely-felicitous Providence,
Finger of a ténder of, O of a féathery délicacy, the
    bréast of the
    Maiden could obey so, be a bell to, ring óf it,
    and
Stártle the poor shéep back! is the shópwrack then a
    hárvest, does témpest carry the gráin for thee?

32

      I admire thee, máster of the tídes,
170   Of the Yóre-flood,[2] of the yéar's fáll;
    The recúrb and the recóvery of the gúlf's sídes,
    The girth of it and the whárf of it and the
    wáll;
Stánching, quénching ócean of a mótionable mínd;
Gróund of béing and gránite of it: pást áll
175   Grásp Gód, thrónéd behínd
Déath, with a sóvereignty that héeds but hídes, bódes
    but abídes;

33

      With a mércy that oútrides
    The all of water, an ark
    For the lístener; for the língerer with a lóve
    glídes
180   Lówer than déath and the dárk;
A véin for the vísiting of the pást-prayer, pént in
    príson,

---

1 *Tárpéïan-fast* In the Roman Republic, convicted criminals were executed by being thrown off the Tarpeian Rock.

2 *Yóre-flood* Ancient flood (i.e., the Biblical flood).

The-last-breath penitent spirits—the uttermost
    mark
    Our passion-plungèd giant risen,
The Christ of the Father compassionate, fetched in
    the storm of his strides.

34

185   Now burn, new born to the world,
        Double-naturèd name,
    The heaven-flúng, heart-fléshed, máiden-fúrled
        Míracle-in-Máry-of-fláme,
    Mid-numberèd he in three of the thunder-throne!
190   Not a dóomsday dázzle in his cóming nor dárk as
        he cáme;
        Kind, but róyally recláiming his ówn;
A released shówer, let flásh to the shire, not a
    líghtning of fíre hard húrled.

35

        Dáme, at óur dóor
        Drówned, and among óur shóals,
195   Remémber us in the róads, the heaven-háven
        of the rewárd:
        Our kíng back, Oh, upon Énglish sóuls!
Let him éaster in us, be a dáyspring to the dímness
    of us, be a crímson-cresseted[1] east,
More bríghtening her, ráre-dear Britain, as his
    réign rólls,
Príde, rose, prínce, hero of us, hígh-príest,
200   Oür héart's charity's héarth's fíre, oür thóughts'
    chivalry's thróng's Lórd.
          —1918 (WRITTEN 1875–76)]

The Windhover:[2]
to Christ our Lord

I caught this morning morning's minion, king-
    dom of daylight's dauphin,[3] dapple-dáwn-drawn
    Falcon, in his riding

---

1   *cresseted* Lit by a cresset, a type of oil lamp.

2   *Windhover* Another name for a kestrel, a small falcon that appears to hover in the wind.

3   *dauphin* Title of the eldest son of the King of France—the heir.

Of the rólling level úndernéath him steady air, and
    striding
High there, how he rung upon the rein of a
    wimpling° wing   *rippling*
5 In his écstasy! then off, off forth on swing,
    As a skate's heel sweeps smooth on a bow-bend:
        the hurl and gliding
    Rebuffed the bíg wind. My heart in hiding
Stírred for a bird,—the achieve of, the mástery of the
    thing!

Brute beauty and valour and act, oh, air, pride, plúme,
    here
10   Buckle! AND the fire that breaks from thee then, a
    billion
Tímes told lovelier, more dangerous, O my
    chevalier!°   *horseman*

    No wónder of it: shéer plód makes plóugh down
    síllion°   *furrows*
Shíne, and blue-bleak embers, ah my dear,
    Fall, gáll themsélves, and gásh góld-vermílion.
          —1918 (WRITTEN 1877)

Pied[4] Beauty

Glóry be to God for dappled things—
    For skies of couple-colour as a brinded° cow; *spotted*
        For rose-moles all in stipple upon trout that
        swim;
Fresh-firecoal chestnut-fálls;[5] fínches' wings;
    Lándscape plotted and pieced—fold,° fallow, and
        plough;   *pasture*
        And áll trádes, their gear and tackle and
        trim.°   *equipment*

Áll things counter,° original, spáre,° stránge; *contrary / rare*
    Whatever is fickle, frecklèd (who knows how?)
        With swift, slów; sweet, soūr; adázzle, dím;
10 He fathers-forth whose beauty is pást chánge:
             Práise hím.

—1918 (WRITTEN 1877)

---

4   *Pied* Multicoloured.

5   *Fresh ... fálls* Freshly fallen, brightly coloured chestnuts.

Felix Randal

Félix Rándal the fárrier,[1] O is he déad then? my
    dúty all énded,
Who have watched his mould of man, big-bóned and
    hardy-handsome
Pining, pining, till time when reason rámbled in it
    and some
Fatal four disorders, fléshed thére, all contended?

Síckness bróke him. Impatient, he cursed at first, but
    mended
Being anointed[2] and all; though a heavenlier heart
    began some
Mónths éarlier, since I had our swéet repríeve and
    ránsom[3]
Téndered to him. Áh well, God rést him áll road
    éver[4] he offénded!

This séeing the síck endéars them tó us, us tóo it
    endéars.
My tongue had taught thee comfort, touch had
    quenched thy tears,
Thy tears that touched my heart, child, Félix, poor
    Felix Randal;

How far from then forethought of, all thy more
    boisterous years,
When thou at the random[5] grim fórge, pówerful
    amídst péers,
Didst fettle° for the great grey drayhorse[6] his bright
    and battering sandal!   *prepare*
—1918 (WRITTEN 1880)

1 *férrier* One who shoes horses.
2 *anointed* As in the sacrament of Extreme Unction, performed
for the dying.
3 *had our swéet repríeve and ránsom* I.e., had received Holy
Communion.
4 *all road éver* However.
5 *random* Roughly built.
6 *drayhorse* Powerful horse used for drawing a sled.

Spring and Fall: to a Young Child

Márgarét, áre you gríeving
Over Goldengrove unleaving?
Leáves, like the thíngs of mán, you
With your fresh thoughts care fór, can you?
Ah! ás the héart grows ólder
It will come to such sights colder
By and by, nor spare a sigh
Though worlds of wanwood leafmeal[7] lie;
And yet you *will* weep and know why.
Now no matter, child, the name:
Sórrow's spríngs áre the sáme.
Nor mouth had, no nor mind, expressed
What héart héard of, ghóst° guéssed: *spirit*
It ís the blíght mán was bórn for,
It is Margaret you mourn for.
—1918 (WRITTEN 1880)

[As kingfishers catch fire]

As kingfishers catch fire, dragonflies draw flame;
As tumbled over rim in roundy wells
    Stones ring; like each tucked° string tells, each
        hung bell's   *plucked*
Bow swung finds tongue to fling out broad its name;
Each mortal thing does one thing and the same:
    Deals out that being indoors each one dwells;
    Selves—goes its self; *myself* it speaks and spells,
Crying *What I do is me: for that I came.*

I say more: the just man justices;
    Keeps grace: that keeps all his goings graces;
Ácts in God's eye what in God's eye he is—

    Chríst. For Christ plays in ten thousand places,
Lovely in limbs, and lovely in eyes not his
    To the Father through the features of men's faces.
—1918 (WRITTEN 1879–82)

7 *wanwood leafmeal* Decaying wood and leaves.

[*No worst, there is none*]

No worst, there is none. Pitched past pitch of grief,
More pangs will, schooled at forepangs, wilder wring.
Comforter, where, where is your comforting?
Mary, mother of us, where is your relief?
5   My cries heave, herds-long; huddle in a main, a chief—
Woe, world-sorrow; on an áge-old ánvil wínce and
      síng—
Then lull, then leave off. Fury had shrieked "No ling-
Ering! Let me be fell:° force¹ I must be brief."   *fierce*
O the mind, mind has mountains; cliffs of fall
10 Frightful, sheer, no-man-fathomed. Hold them cheap
May who ne'er hung there. Nor does long our small
Durance deal with that steep or deep. Here! creep,
Wretch, under a comfort serves in a whirlwind: all
Life death does end and each day dies with sleep.
—1918 (WRITTEN 1884–85)

[*I wake and feel the fell² of dark, not day*]

I wake and feel the fell of dark, not day
What hours, O what black hours we have spent
This night! what sights you, heart, saw, ways you went!
And more must, in yet longer light's delay.

5   With witness I speak this. But where I say
Hours I mean years, mean life. And my lament
Is cries countless, cries like dead letters sent
To dearest him that lives alas! away.

I am gall, I am heartburn. God's most deep decree
10 Bitter would have me taste: my taste was me;
Bones built in me, flesh filled, blood brimmed the
      curse.

Selfyeast of spirit a dull dough sours. I see
The lost are like this, and their scourge to be
As I am mine, their sweating selves; but worse.
—1918

---

¹   *force* Perforce, or out of necessity.
²   *fell* Bitterness; also an animal hide, used as a covering.

[*Not, I'll not, carrion³ comfort*]

Not, I'll not, carrion comfort, Despair, not feast on
      thee;
Not untwist—slack they may be—these last strands of
      man
In me ór, most weary, cry *I can no more*. I can;
Can something, hope, wish day come, not choose not
      to be.

5   But ah, but O thou terrible, why wouldst thou rude
      on me⁴
Thy wring-world right foot rock? lay a lionlimb
      against me? scan
With darksome devouring eyes my bruisèd bones? and
      fan,
O in turns of tempest, me heaped there; me frantic to
      avoïd thee and flee?

Why? That my chaff might fly; my grain lie, sheer and
      clear.
10 Nay in all that toil, that coil,° since (seems) I kissed
      the rod,   *tumult*
Hand rather, my heart lo! lapped strength, stole joy,
      would laugh, cheer.
Cheer whóm though? The hero whose héaven-
      handling flúng me, fóot tród
Me? or mé that fóught him? O which one? is it éach
      one? That níght, that yéar
Of now done darkness I wretch lay wrestling with (my
      God!) my God.
—1918

That Nature is a Heraclitean Fire⁵ and of the Comfort of the Resurrection

Cloud-puffball, torn tufts, tossed pillows | flaunt
      forth, then chevy° on an air—   •   *race*

---

³   *carrion* Dead flesh.
⁴   *rude on me* Roughly against me.
⁵   *Heraclitean Fire* Heraclitus (c. 535–475 BCE), a Greek philosopher, taught that everything is derived from fire, and therefore in a
constant state of change.

Built thoroughfare: heaven-roysterers,[1] in gay-gangs |
    they throng; they glitter in marches.
Down roughcast,[2] down dazzling whitewash, |
    wherever an elm arches,
Shivelights[3] and shadowtackle[4] in long | lashes lace,
    lance, and pair.
5 Delightfully the bright wind boisterous | ropes,
    wrestles, beats earth bare
Of yestertempest's creases; in pool and rut peel
    parches
Squandering ooze to squeezed | dough, crúst, dust;   *reinforces*
    stánches,° stárches
Squadroned masks and manmarks | treadmire toil
    there
Fóotfretted in it. Million-fuelèd, | nature's bonfire
    burns on.
10 But quench her bonniest, dearest | to her, her
    clearest-selvèd spark
Mán, how fást his fíredint, | his mark on mind, is
    gone!
Bóth are in an únfáthomable, áll is in an enórmous
    dárk
Drowned. O pity and indig | nation! Manshape, that
    shone
Sheer off, disseveral,° a star, death blots black out; nor   *separate*
    mark
15   Is any of him at all so stark
But vastness blurs and time | beats level. Enough! the
    Resurrection,
A héart's-clarion! Awáy grief's gásping, | joyless days,
    dejection.
          Across my foundering deck shone
A beacon, an eternal beam. | Flesh fade, and mortal
    trash
20 Fáll to the residuary worm; | world's wildfire, leave
    but ash:

In a flash, at a trumpet crash,
I am all at once what Christ is, | since he was what I
    am, and
This Jack,° jóke, poor pótsherd,[5] | patch,[6]
matchwood,° immortal diamond,   *fellow / kindling*
    Is immortal diamond.
—1918 (WRITTEN 1888)

[*Thou art indeed just, Lord*]

Justus quidem tu es, Domine, si disputem tecum:
verumtamen justa loquar ad te: Quare via impiorum
prosperatur? etc.[7]

Thou art indeed just, Lord, if I contend
  With thee; but, sir, so what I plead is just.
  Why do sínners' ways prosper? and why must
Dísappóintment all I endeavour end?
  Wert thou my enemy, O thou my friend,
How wouldst thou worse, I wonder, than thou dost
Defeat, thwart me? Oh, the sots° and thralls   *drunkards*
  of lust
Do in spare hours more thrive than I that spend,
Sir, life upon thy cause. See, banks and brakes°   *thickets*
Now, leavèd how thick! lacèd they are again
With fretty chervil,[8] look, and fresh wind shakes
Them; birds build—but not I build; no, but strain,
Time's eunuch, and not breed one work that wakes.
Mine, O thou lord of life, send my roots rain.
—1918 (WRITTEN 1889)

---

[5] *potsherd* Piece of broken pottery.

[6] *patch* Simpleton.

[7] *Justus ... prosperatur* Latin: "You are always righteous, O Lord, when I bring a case before you. Yet I would speak with you about your justice: why does the way of the wicked prosper?" (Jeremiah 12.1).

[8] *fretty chervil* Interlaced leaves and stems of a garden herb.

---

[1] *roysterers* Noisy party-goers.

[2] *roughcast* Wall plastering made of lime and gravel.

[3] *Shivelights* Strips of light.

[4] *shadowtackle* Shadows which resemble a ship's rigging.

In Context

The Growth of "The Windhover"

Manuscript copies of Hopkins's poems open a remarkable window on his unique approach to poetic rhythm—and to poetic composition; "The Windhover" is a particularly interesting example.

The first page reproduced here (headed "Another version") is entirely in Hopkins's hand, and probably dates from 1877. The second dates from 1883; it is from an album of "fair copy" transcriptions of Hopkins's (often not very legible) manuscripts that was prepared by his friend and mentor, the poet Robert Bridges, and then corrected by Hopkins in 1884. According to Hopkins scholar Norman H. Mackenzie, the corrections and revisions here in Hopkins's handwriting include the addition of ": to Christ our Lord" to the title; the alteration of "o air" to "oh, air"; the replacement of the ampersand with the word "AND" in line 10; the addition of stress marks in lines two, 3, 12, and 14; the addition of a "slur" between "the" and "hurl" in line 6, and the addition of seven "outrides" (as Hopkins termed the curved marks below the line).

Adding marks to indicate particularly strong stresses and adding "slurs" and "outrides" were among the many ways Hopkins endeavored to direct the reading of his poems according to the principles of what he termed "sprung rhythm" (see the Glossary at the back of this volume for a definition). The meaning of the "slur" mark is fairly straightforward; it indicates where two syllables should be compressed together so as to be pronounced as one—much as in this case an apostrophe might be used to do (*th'hurl*). The "outride" denotes a much less familiar concept, and it may be best to quote Hopkins directly here. At one point he writes that "the outride under one or more syllables makes them extrametrical: a slight pause follows as if the voice were silently making its way back to the highroad of the verse." Elsewhere he describes syllables so marked as "hangers or outriders," meaning "one, two or three slack syllables added to a foot and not counted in the nominal scanning. They are so called because they seem to hang below the line or ride forward or backward from it in another dimension than the line itself, according to a principle needless to explain here."

When entering corrections and revisions in 1884 Hopkins also added at lower right the date and place of the poem's original composition. The marginal notes, however, were evidently added by Bridges when he transcribed them; "= A", for example, indicates that the hyphen Bridges has added to line 6 is taken from an early manuscript of the poem (referred to as manuscript A).

The Windhover (Another version) – to Christ our Lord.

I caught this morning morning's minion, king-
   dom Of daylight's dauphin, dapple-dawn-drawn Fal-
      con, in his riding   [and striding
Of the rolling level underneath him steady air,
High there
   O how he a rung upon the rein of a wimpling wing
In his ecstacy! then off, off forth on swing,
   As a skate's heel sweeps smooth on a bow-bend:
       the hurl and gliding
Rebuffed the big wind. my heart in hiding
Stirred for a bird — for the mastery of the thing!
     the achieve of

Brute beauty and valour and act; oh, air, pride, plume,
      here   [then, a billion
Buckle! and the fire that breaks from thee
Times told lovelier, more dangerous, O my
       chevalier!

No wonder of it: sheer; plod makes plough down
       sillion
Shine, and blue-bleak embers, ah my dear,
Fall, gall themselves, and gash: gold-vermilion.

⑧

The Windhover : to Christ our Lord

~

I caught this morning morning's minion, king-
dom of daylight's dauphin, dapple-dawn-drawn Falcon, in his riding
Of the rolling, level underneath him steady air, & striding
High there, how he rung upon the rein of a wimpling wing
In his ecstacy! then off, off forth on swing
As a skate's heel sweeps smooth on a bow-bend: the hurl & gliding   —A
Rebuffed the big wind. My heart in hiding
Stirred for a bird, — the achieve of, the mastery of the thing!   , A, A.

Brute beauty & valour & act, oh, air, pride, plume, here
Buckle! AND the fire that breaks from thee then, a billion
Times told lovelier, more dangerous, o my chevalier!
No wonder of it: sheer plod makes plough down sillion
Shine, & blue-bleak embers, ah my dear,
Fall, gall themselves, & gash gold-vermilion.

~   St. Beuno's. May 30 1877

from *Journal* 1870–1874

[*"Inscape" and "Instress"*]

[April 15] The white violets are broader and smell; the blue, scentless and finer made, have sharper whelking[1] and a more winged recoil in the leaves.

Take a *few* primroses in a glass and the instress[2] of—brilliancy, sort of starriness: I have not the right word—so simple a flower gives is remarkable. It is, I think, due to the strong swell given by the deeper yellow middle.

"The young lambs bound As to the tabour's sound."[3]

They toss and toss: it is as if it were the earth that flung them, not themselves. It is the pitch of graceful agility when we think that.

April 16—Sometimes they rest a little space on the hind legs and the fore-feet drop curling in on the breast, not so liquidly as we see it in the limbs of foals though.

Bright afternoon; clear distances; Pendle[4] dappled with tufted shadow; west wind; interesting clouding, flat and lying in the warp of the heaved but the pieces with rounded outline and dolphin-backs showing in places and all was at odds and at Z's, one piece with another. Later beautifully delicate crisping. Later rippling....

April 21—We have had other such afternoons, one today—the sky a beautiful grained blue, silky lingering clouds in flat-bottomed loaves, others a little browner in ropes or in burly-shouldered ridges swanny and lustrous, more in the Zenith[5] stray packs of a sort of violet paleness. White-rose cloud formed fast, not in the same density—some caked and swimming in a wan white-ness, the rest soaked with the blue and like the leaf of a flower held against the light and diapered out by the worm or veining of deeper blue between rosette and rosette. Later / moulding, which brought rain: in perspective it was vaulted in very regular ribs with fretting between: but these are not ribs; they are a "wracking" install made of these two realities—the frets, which are scarves of rotten cloud bellying upwards and drooping at their ends and shaded darkest at the brow or tropic where they double to the eye, and the whiter field of sky showing between: the illusion looking down the "wagon" is complete. These swaths of fretted cloud move in rank, not in file.

April 22—But such a lovely damasking in the sky as today I never felt before. The blue was charged with simple instress, the higher, zenith sky earnest and frowning, lower more light and sweet. High up again, breathing through woolly coats of cloud or on the quains[6] and branches of the flying pieces it was the true exchange of crimson, nearer the earth / against the sun / it was turquoise, and in the opposite south-western bay below the sun it was like clear oil but just as full of colour, shaken over with slanted flashing "travellers," all in flight, stepping one behind the other, their edges tossed with bright ravelling,[7] as if white napkins were thrown up in the sun but not quite at the same moment so that they were all in a scale down the air falling one after the other to the ground....

[May 9] This day and May 11 the bluebells in the little wood between the College[8] and the highroad and in one of the Hurst Green[9] cloughs.[10] In the little wood / opposite the light / they stood in blackish spreads or sheddings like the spots on a snake. The heads are then like thongs and solemn in grain and grape-colour. But in the clough / through the light / they came in falls of sky-colour washing the brows and slacks of the ground

---

[1] *whelking* Ridges.

[2] *instress* Hopkins's own term, meaning the force or energy which sustains an inscape, which is the individual or essential quality of a thing.

[3] *"The ... sound."* From William Wordsworth's *Ode: Intimations of Immortality*, line 20–21; *tabour's* Drum's.

[4] *Pendle* Pendle Hill in Lancashire, England.

[5] *Zenith* Point in the sky directly overhead.

[6] *quains* Angles (Hopkins's own term).

[7] *ravelling* Frayed edges.

[8] *College* Stonyhurst College, the seminary where Hopkins studied, in Lancashire, England.

[9] *Hurst Green* Village in Blackburn, Lancashire, England.

[10] *cloughs* Ravines.

with vein-blue, thickening at the double, vertical themselves and the young grass and brake fern combed vertical, but the brake struck the upright of all this with light winged transomes.[1] It was a lovely sight.—The bluebells in your hand baffle you with their inscape, made to every sense: if you draw your fingers through them they are lodged and struggle / with a shock of wet heads; the long stalks rub and click and flatten to a fan on one another like your fingers themselves would when you passed the palms hard across one another, making a brittle rub and jostle like the noise of a hurdle strained by leaning against; then there is the faint honey smell and in the mouth the sweet gum when you bite them. But this is easy, it is the eye they baffle. They give one a fancy of panpipes and of some wind instrument with stops—a trombone perhaps. The overhung necks—for growing they are little more than a staff with a simple crook but in water, where they stiffen, they take stronger turns, in the head like sheephooks[2] or, when more waved throughout, like the waves riding through a whip that is being smacked—what with these overhung necks and what with the crisped ruffled bells dropping mostly on one side and the gloss these have at their footstalks they have an air of the knights at chess. Then the knot or "knoop" of buds some shut, some just gaping, which makes the pencil of the whole spike, should be noticed: the inscape of the flower most finely carried out in the siding of the axes, each striking a greater and greater slant, is finished in these clustered buds, which for the most part are not straightened but rise to the end like a tongue and this and their tapering and a little flattening they have made them look like the heads of snakes.

[July 19, 1872] Stepped into a barn of ours, a great shadowy barn, where the hay had been stacked on either side, and looking at the great rudely arched timber-frames—principals(?) and tie-beams, which make them look like bold big *As* with the cross-bar high up—I thought how sadly beauty of inscape was unknown and buried away from simple people and yet how near at hand it was if they had eyes to see it and it could be called out everywhere again …

After the examinations we went for our holiday out to Douglas in the Isle of Man. Aug. 3—At this time I had first begun to get hold of the copy of Scotus[3] on the Sentences in the Baddely library and was flush with a new stroke of enthusiasm. It may come to nothing or it may be a mercy from God. But just then when I took in any inscape of the sky or sea I thought of Scotus …

Aug. 10—I was looking at high waves. The breakers always are parallel to the coast and shape themselves to it except where the curve is sharp however the wind blows. They are rolled out by the shallowing shore just as a piece of putty between the palms whatever its shape runs into a long roll. The slant ruck[4] or crease one sees in them shows the way of the wind. The regularity of the barrels surprised and charmed the eye; the edge behind the comb or crest was as smooth and bright as glass. It may be noticed to be green behind and silver white in front: the silver marks where the air begins, the pure white is foam, the green / solid water. Then looked at to the right or left they are scrolled over like mould-boards[5] or feathers or jibsails seen by the edge. It is pretty to see the hollow of the barrel disappearing as the white combs on each side run along the wave gaining ground till the two meet at a pitch and crush and overlap each other.

About all the turns of the scaping[6] from the break and flooding of wave to its run out again I have not yet satisfied myself. The shores are swimming and the eyes have before them a region of milky surf but it is hard for them to unpack the huddling and gnarls of the water and law out the shapes and the sequence of the running: I catch however the looped or forked wisp made by every big pebble the backwater runs over—if it were clear and smooth there would be a network from their overlapping, such as can in fact be seen on smooth sand after the tide is out; then I saw it run browner, the foam dwindling and twitched into long chains of suds, while

---

1   *transomes*   Crossbeams.

2   *sheephooks*   Shepherds' crooks.

3   *Scotus*   Duns Scotus (c. 1266–1308), Scottish-born theologian and philosopher. In his *Lectura*, he analyzes Thomas Lombard's *Sentences*.

4   *ruck*   Ridge.

5   *mouldboards*   Boards attached to plows, used to form furrows.

6   *scaping*   Hopkins's term for a reflection or impression of the individual quality of a thing or action.

the strength of the backdraught shrugged the stones together and clocked them one against another …

April 8 [1873]—The ashtree growing in the corner of the garden was felled. It was lopped first: I heard the sound and looking out and seeing it maimed there came at that moment a great pang and I wished to die and not to see the inscapes of the world destroyed any more. …

July 23—To Beaumont: it was the rector's day. It was a lovely day: shires-long of pearled cloud under cloud, with a grey stroke underneath marking each row; beautiful blushing yellow in the straw of the uncut rye fields, the wheat looking white and all the ears making a delicate and very true crisping along the top and with just enough air stirring for them to come and go gently; then there were fields reaping. All this I would have looked at again in returning but during dinner I talked too freely and unkindly and had to do penance going home. One field I saw from the balcony of the house behind an elmtree, which it threw up, like a square of pale goldleaf, as it might be, catching the light.

(WRITTEN 1871–73)

from *Letter to Robert Bridges*

St. Giles's, Oxford.
25 February 1879

… No doubt my poetry errs on the side of oddness. I hope in time to have a more balanced and Miltonic[1] style. But as air, melody, is what strikes me most of all in music and design in painting, so design, pattern or what I am in the habit of calling "inscape" is what I above all aim at in poetry. Now it is the virtue of design, pattern, or inscape to be distinctive and it is the virtue of distinctiveness to become queer. This vice I cannot have escaped …

(WRITTEN 1879)

---

[1] *Miltonic* In the manner of John Milton (1608–74), English poet.

Author's Preface[2]

The poems in this book are written some in Running Rhythm, the common rhythm in English use, some in Sprung Rhythm, and some in a mixture of the two. And those in the common rhythm are some counter-pointed,[3] some not.

Common English rhythm, called Running Rhythm above, is measured by feet[4] of either two or three syllables and (putting aside the imperfect feet at the beginning and end of lines and also some unusual measures in which feet seem to be paired together and double or composite feet to arise) never more or less.

Every foot has one principal stress or accent, and this or the syllable it falls on may be called the Stress of the foot and the other part, the one or two unaccented syllables, the Slack. Feet (and the rhythms made out of them) in which the stress comes first are called Falling Feet and Falling Rhythms, feet and rhythm in which the slack comes first are called Rising Feet and Rhythms, and if the stress is between two slacks there will be Rocking Feet and Rhythms. These distinctions are real and true to nature; but for purposes of scanning it is a great convenience to follow the example of music and take the stress always first, as the accent or the chief accent always comes first in a musical bar. If this is done there will be in common English verse only two possible feet—the so-called accentual Trochee[5] and Dactyl,[6] and correspondingly only two possible uniform rhythms, the so-called Trochaic and Dactylic. But they may be mixed and then what the Greeks called a Logaoedic Rhythm[7] arises. These are the facts and according to these the scanning of ordinary regularly-written English verse is very simple indeed and to bring in other principles is

---

[2] *Author's Preface* Prefatory to accompany Hopkins's manuscript poems.

[3] *counterpointed* Containing two types of rhythm in a line of verse.

[4] *feet* Metrical units.

[5] *Trochee* Metrical foot consisting of an accented syllable followed by an unaccented syllable.

[6] *Dactyl* Metrical foot consisting of an accented syllable followed by two unaccented syllables.

[7] *Logaoedic Rhythm* Rhythm in which dactyls are combined with trochees.

here unnecessary.

But because verse written strictly in these feet and by these principles will become same and tame the poets have brought in licences and departures from rule to give variety, and especially when the natural rhythm is rising, as in the common ten-syllable or five-foot verse, rhymed or blank. These irregularities are chiefly Reversed Feet and Reversed or Counterpoint Rhythm, which two things are two steps or degrees of licence in the same kind. By a reversed foot I mean the putting the stress where, to judge by the rest of the measure, the slack should be and the slack where the stress, and this is done freely at the beginning of a line and, in the course of a line, after a pause; only scarcely ever in the second foot or place and never in the last, unless when the poet designs some extraordinary effect; for these places are characteristic and sensitive and cannot well be touched. But the reversal of the first foot and of some middle foot after a strong pause is a thing so natural that our poets have generally done it, from Chaucer down, without remark and it commonly passes unnoticed and cannot be said to amount to a formal change of rhythm, but rather is that irregularity which all natural growth and motion shows. If however the reversal is repeated in two feet running, especially so as to include the sensitive second foot, it must be due either to great want of ear or else is a calculated effect, the super-inducing or *mounting* of a new rhythm upon the old; and since the new or mounted rhythm is actually heard and at the same time the mind naturally supplies the natural or standard foregoing rhythm, for we do not forget what the rhythm is that by rights we should be hearing, two rhythms are in some manner running at once and we have something answerable to counterpoint in music, which is two or more strains of tune going on together, and this is Counterpoint Rhythm. Of this kind of verse Milton is the great master and the choruses of *Samson Agonistes*[1] are written throughout in it—but with the disadvantage that he does not let the reader clearly know what the ground-rhythm is meant to be and so they have struck most readers as merely irregular. And in fact if you counterpoint throughout, since only one of the counter rhythms is actually heard, the other is really destroyed or

cannot come to exist, and what is written is one rhythm only and probably Sprung Rhythm, of which I now speak.

Sprung Rhythm, as used in this book, is measured by feet of from one to four syllables, regularly, and for particular effects any number of weak or slack syllables may be used. It has one stress, which falls on the only syllable, if there is only one, or, if there are more, then scanning as above, on the first, and so gives rise to four sorts of feet, a monosyllable and the so-called accentual Trochee, Dactyl, and the First Paeon.[2] And there will be four corresponding natural rhythms; but nominally the feet are mixed and any one may follow any other. And hence Sprung Rhythm differs from Running Rhythm in having or being only one nominal rhythm, a mixed or "logaoedic" one, instead of three, but on the other hand in having twice the flexibility of foot, so that any two stresses may either follow one another running or be divided by one, two, or three slack syllables. But strict Sprung Rhythm cannot be counterpointed. In Sprung Rhythm, as in logaoedic rhythm generally, the feet are assumed to be equally long or strong and their seeming inequality is made up by pause or stressing.

Remark also that it is natural in Sprung Rhythm for the lines to be *rove over*, that is for the scanning of each line immediately to take up that of the one before, so that if the first has one or more syllables at its end the other must have so many the less at its beginning; and in fact the scanning runs on without break from the beginning, say, of a stanza to the end and all the stanza is one long strain, though written in lines asunder.

Two licences are natural to Sprung Rhythm. The one is rests, as in music; but of this an example is scarcely to be found in this book, unless in the *Echos*, second line. The other is *hangers* or *outrides*, that is one, two, or three slack syllables added to a foot and not counting in the nominal scanning. They are so called because they seem to hang below the line or ride forward or backward from it in another dimension than the line itself, according to a principle needless to explain here. These outriding half feet or hangers are marked by a loop underneath them, and plenty of them will be found.

[1] *Samson Agonistes*   Dramatic poem published by Milton in 1671.

[2] *Paeon* Metrical foot consisting of one stressed and three unstressed syllables.

The other marks are easily understood, namely accents, where the reader might be in doubt which syllable should have the stress; slurs, that is loops *over* syllables, to tie them together into the time of one; little loops at the end of a line to show that the rhyme goes on to the first letter of the next line; what in music are called pauses ⌒, to show that the syllable should be dwelt on; and twirls ~, to mark reversed or counterpointed rhythm.

Note on the nature and history of Sprung Rhythm — Sprung Rhythm is the most natural of things. For (1) it is the rhythm of common speech and of written prose, when rhythm is perceived in them. (2) It is the rhythm of all but the most monotonously regular music, so that in the words of choruses and refrains and in songs written closely to music it arises. (3) It is found in nursery rhymes, weather saws, and so on; because, however these may have been once made in running rhythm, the terminations having dropped off by the change of language, the stresses come together and so

the rhythm is sprung. (4) It arises in common verse when reversed or counterpointed, for the same reason.

But nevertheless in spite of all this and though Greek and Latin lyric verse, which is well known, and the old English verse seen in "Pierce Ploughman"[1] are in sprung rhythm, it has in fact ceased to be used since the Elizabethan age, Greene[2] being the last writer who can be said to have recognized it. For perhaps there was not, down to our days, a single, even short, poem in English in which sprung rhythm is employed—not for single effects or in fixed places—but as the governing principle of the scansion. I say this because the contrary has been asserted: if it is otherwise the poem should be cited. . . .
—1883

[1] "Pierce Ploughman" I.e., *Piers Plowman*, by William Langland (written c. 1360–99).

[2] *Greene* Robert Greene (1558–92).

"MICHAEL FIELD"
KATHARINE BRADLEY AND EDITH COOPER
1848 – 1914   1862 – 1913

In May 1884, a volume of two plays by an unknown author, Michael Field, was published to critical acclaim. One reviewer wrote in *The Spectator*: "We know nothing of the author, but we have found a wealth of surprises in the strength, the simplicity, and the terseness of the imaginative feeling.… [The work] has the true poetic voice of fire in it. If this is the work of a young author, it is the work of the highest possible promise." The two authors who had taken the pen name "Michael Field," Katharine Bradley (her first name is spelled various ways, but she signed her name "Katharine") and Edith Cooper, had wished to receive the serious criticism accorded to male authors and also to conceal their relationship as lovers. The authors' identities did become widely known during their lifetimes, but "Michael" (Bradley) and "Field" (Cooper), as they called themselves, continued to collaborate on many books of plays and poetry, sometimes as "Michael Field," sometimes under other pseudonyms.

Bradley's father, a tobacco manufacturer, died in 1848, when she was two. Her mother educated her at home, and she later attended Newnham College, the new women's college at Cambridge. When her older sister, Emma, married James Cooper, the family stayed together with the married couple in Kenilworth, near Birmingham in central England. Bradley's mother died when she was twenty-two, and not long afterward Emma also passed away. Bradley stayed on to help raise her sister's children, Amy and Edith; Edith was then six years old. Katharine and her niece Edith shared a love of literature and writing, evident from the time Edith was young, and the two later attended Bristol University together.

Bradley wrote one volume of poetry on her own in 1875 (*The New Minnesinger*, published under the pseudonym Arran Leigh), but thereafter published only in collaboration with Cooper. A stanza from their poem "It was Deep April" describes their moment of decision: "The world was on us, pressing sore; / My love and I took hands and swore, / Against the world, to be / Poets and lovers evermore." The two eventually wrote some 30 plays and 11 volumes of poetry together in such a close collaboration that they later claimed in their journals that when they reviewed their work they could not distinguish who had written what. When their first collaborative work was published, the plays *Callirrhoë* and *Fair Rosamund*, they sent a copy to Robert Browning and revealed their true identities. Browning loved their work and became a close friend, but unfortunately he let slip to the public the authorship of the plays, a move that Bradley wrote back to tell him would "dwarf and enfeeble our work.… We cannot be stifled in drawing room conventionalities."

But even after their identities were exposed, Bradley and Cooper did not allow themselves to be stifled. They lived and traveled together and wrote poems about love between women; their first joint volume of poetry was inspired by Henry Wharton's translation of the ancient Greek Sappho's fragments of poetry, in which her love object was a woman. Their 1889 volume *Long Ago* was called by the journal *The Academy* "one of the most exquisite lyrical productions of the latter half of the nineteenth century."

For nearly half a century, Bradley and Cooper kept a journal that they called *Works and Days*, in which they described their daily lives and their abiding love for each other: "closer married" than the

Brownings, they said, because they also shared an artistic partnership. The younger Cooper was the first to die, of cancer, in 1913; eight months later Bradley died of the same disease.

⌘ ⌘ ⌘

The Magdalen

Timoteo Viti[1]

This tender sylph[2] of a maid
Is the Magdalen—this figure lone:
Her attitude is swayed
By the very breath she breathes,
5 The prayer of her being that takes no voice.
Boulders, the grass enwreathes,
Arch over her as a cave
That of old an earthquake clave
And filled with stagnant gloom:
10 Yet a woman has strength to choose it for her room.

Her long, fair hair is allowed
To wander in its thick simpleness;
The graceful tresses crowd
Unequal, yet close enough
15 To have woven about her neck and breast
A wimple of golden stuff.
Though the rock behind is rude,
The sweetness of solitude
Is on her face, the soft
20 Withdrawal that in wildflowers we have loved so oft.

Her mantle is scarlet red
In folds of severe resplendency;
Her hair beneath is spread
Full length; from its lower flakes
25 Her feet come forth in their naked charm:
A wind discreetly shakes
The scarlet raiment,° the hair.   dress

Her small hands, a tranquil pair,
Are laid together; her book
30 And cup of ointment furnish scantily her nook.

She is happy the livelong day,
Yet her thoughts are often with the past;
Her sins are done away,

---

[1] *The Magdalen / Timoteo Viti* Painting of the Biblical Mary Magdalene by Renaissance painter Timoteo Viti (reproduced here as an illustration).

[2] *sylph* Slight, graceful woman.

They can give her no annoy.
35 She is white—oh! infinitely clean
And her heart throbs with joy;
Besides, there is joy in heaven
That her sins are thus forgiven;
And she thinks till even-fall°   dusk
40 Of the grace, the strangeness, the wonder of it all.

She is shut from fellowship;
How she loved to mingle with her friends!
To give them eyes and lip;
She lived for their sake alone;
45 Not a braid of her hair, not a rose
Of her cheek was her own:
And she loved to minister
To any in want of her,
All service was so sweet:
50 Now she must stand all day on lithe, unsummoned feet.

Among the untrodden weeds
And moss she is glad to be remote;
She knows that when God needs
From the sinning world relief,
55 He will find her thus with the wild bees,
The doves and the plantain leaf,
Waiting in a perfect peace
For His kingdom's sure increase,
Waiting with a deeper glow
60 Of patience every day, because He tarrieth so.

By her side the box of nard[1]
Unbroken ... God is a great way off;
She loves Him: it is hard
That she may not now even spread
65 The burial spice, who would gladly keep
The tomb where He lay dead,
As it were her rocky cave;

And fold the linen and lave°   wash
The napkin that once bound
70 His head; no place for her pure arts is longer found.

And these are the things that hurt;
For the rest she gives herself no pain:
She wears no camel shirt,
She uses nor scourge, nor rod;
75 But bathes her fair body in the well
And keeps it pure for God:
The beauty, that He hath made
So bright, she guards in the shade,
For, as an angel's dress,
80 Spotless she must preserve her newborn loveliness.

Day by day and week by week,
She lives and muses and makes no sound;
She has no words to speak
The joy that her desert brings:
85 In her heart there is a song
And yet no song she sings.
Since the word Rabboni[2] came
Straightway at the call of her name
And the Master reproved,
90 It seems she has no choice—her lips have never moved.

She stole away when the pale
Light was trembling on the garden ground
And others told the tale,
Christ was risen; she roamed the wide,
95 Fearful countries of the wilderness
And many a riverside,
Till she found her destined grot,°   grotto
South, in France, a woody spot,
Where she is often glad,
100 Musing on those great days when she at first grew sad.
—1892

---

[1] *nard* Ointment made from the aromatic plant of the same name.

[2] *Rabboni* Hebrew: master, teacher.

La Gioconda[1]

Leonardo Da Vinci

Historic, sidelong, implicating eyes;
A smile of velvet's lustre on the cheek;
Calm lips the smile leads upward; hand that lies
Glowing and soft, the patience in its rest
5   Of cruelty that waits and doth not seek
For prey; a dusky forehead and a breast
Where twilight touches ripeness amorously:
Behind her, crystal rocks, a sea and skies
Of evanescent blue on cloud and creek;
10   Landscape that shines suppressive of its zest
For those vicissitudes by which men die.
—1892

---

[1]   *La Gioconda*   Da Vinci's painting, the *Mona Lisa*.

A girl

A girl,
Her soul a deep-wave pearl
Dim, lucent of all lovely mysteries;
A face flowered for heart's ease,
5   A brow's grace soft as seas
Seen through faint forest trees:
A mouth, the lips apart,
Like aspen leaflets trembling in the breeze
From her tempestuous heart.
10   Such: and our souls so knit,
I leave a page half-writ—
The work begun
Will be to heaven's conception done,
If she come to it.
—1893

It was deep April, and the morn

It was deep April, and the morn
Shakespeare was born;[2]
The world was on us, pressing sore;
My Love and I took hands and swore,
5   Against the world, to be
Poets and lovers evermore,
To laugh and dream on Lethe's[3] shore
To sing to Charon[4] in his boat,
Heartening the timid souls afloat;
10   Of judgment never to take heed,
But to those fast-locked souls to speed,
Who never from Apollo fled,
Who spent no hour among the dead;
Continually
15   With them to dwell,
Indifferent to heaven and hell.
—1893

---

[2]   *morn ... was born*   It is traditional to celebrate Shakespeare's birthday on 23 April, St. George's Day.

[3]   *Lethe*   In Greek mythology, a river in Hades (the underworld), the waters of which cause the dead to forget the past.

[4]   *Charon*   Greek mythological ferryman of the underworld who transports the souls of the dead across the River Styx.

To Christina Rossetti

Lady, we would behold thee moving bright
  As Beatrice or Matilda[1] mid the trees,
Alas! thy moan was as a moan for ease
And passage through cool shadows to the night:
5   Fleeing from love, hadst thou not poet's right
To slip into the universe? The seas
Are fathomless to rivers drowned in these,
And sorrow is secure in leafy light.
Ah, had this secret touched thee, in a tomb
10 Thou hadst not buried thy enchanting self,
As happy Syrinx[2] murmuring with the wind,
Or Daphne,[3] thrilled through all her mystic bloom,
From safe recess as genius or as elf,
Thou hadst breathed joy in earth and in thy kind.
—1896

---

1   *Beatrice* From Dante's *Divine Comedy*, Book 3, *Paradise*: a
woman who personifies love and acts as Dante's guide through
Paradise; *Matilda* From Book 2, *Purgatory*: a beautiful virgin who
meets Dante in the Garden of Eden and leads him to the river Lethe
to wash away his sins.

2   *Syrinx* In Greek mythology, the nymph Syrinx turned herself
into a bed of reeds in order to escape Pan's advances.

3   *Daphne* In Greek mythology, the nymph Daphne fled from the
god Apollo's advances and was transformed into a laurel tree in her
escape.

ROBERT LOUIS STEVENSON
1850 – 1894

Due in part to his belief in romance rather than realism and in part to the success of *Treasure Island* and *Kidnapped*, Robert Louis Stevenson was once considered primarily a writer of adventure fiction for children. His large body of work has been re-evaluated in the past half century, however. His most famous novel, the science-fiction thriller *The Strange Case of Dr. Jekyll and Mr.*

Hyde, has now taken a place among the canonical works of late Victorian literature. Stevenson's interest in the nature of good and evil lends this short novel a provocative moral complexity that has captivated the interest of a wide audience, with some readers viewing the book as a critique of Victorian double standards, others looking to the myth of the *doppelgänger*, or spiritual double, to explain the wicked Mr. Hyde, and still others adopting Freudian theories of the ego and the id to explain the two incarnations of Dr. Jekyll. Although he was long fascinated by the duality of the human psyche, in later years Stevenson turned to the concerns of his adopted country, Samoa, for subject matter, writing about the evils of imperialism and the damage done by foreign merchants. In all he wrote over 50 books in the course of his short life.

Stevenson's life was adventurous, but most of his travels were undertaken in search of respite from his ailments, which he wrote about in so much detail that he was once described as a "connoisseur of disease." He was an only child, born in Edinburgh in 1850 to Margaret Balfour, the daughter of a clergyman, and Thomas Stevenson, a well-known engineer for the Board of Northern Lighthouses. When he was young Stevenson contracted tuberculosis, and he remained frail ever after. He was put under the care of a nurse, who stimulated his interest in literature by reading to him everything from the Bible to serial adventure novels. Even as a child, he began spinning the raw material of these tales into stories of his own. In *Memories and Portraits* (1887), Stevenson said: "All through my boyhood and youth, I was known and pointed out for the pattern of an idler; and yet I was always busy on my own private end, which was to learn to write. I kept always two books in my pocket, one to read, one to write in. As I walked, my mind was busy fitting what I saw with appropriate words."

Stevenson continued writing in university, even though he was there initially to take an engineering degree and thereby continue the family tradition of his father and grandfather. He found himself uninterested in the profession, and switched to law, but after he had been called to the bar he decided to defy his father and pursue a career in writing. Stevenson began his legendary peregrinations soon after graduation; his first full-length published works, *An Inland Voyage* (1878) and *Travels with a Donkey in the Cévennes* (1879), record his travels through France. Both books found an enthusiastic audience. Two years later Stevenson published *Virginibus Puerisque*, a collection of essays previously published in *Macmillan's*, *Cornhill*, and *London* magazines. Many of these essays display the same gentle humor and wit that appears in the letters Stevenson wrote to his friends and family.

On one of his trips to France Stevenson met his future wife, Fanny Osbourne, an American who was then married, his elder by two years and the mother of two. He followed her to California, where she obtained a divorce, and the two were married in 1880. It was for his stepson Lloyd's pleasure that Stevenson created *Treasure Island* (1883), the "boy's story" of a man who procures a secret map and sets out alongside Long John Silver in a quest for hidden treasure. *Kidnapped* (1886) and its sequel *Catriona* (1893) were equally successful. 1886 also saw the publication of Stevenson's most enduring work of fiction, *The Strange Case of Dr. Jekyll and Mr. Hyde*, whose mystery concerns Dr. Jekyll's development of a drug that enables him to separate the good and bad parts of his nature. In these stories Stevenson was the romancer, eschewing the domestic realism that had defined the English novel as written by Dickens and George Eliot, with its complex focus on the home and the good woman who gives it moral definition. "This is a poison bad world for the romancer, this Anglo-Saxon world," he wrote; "I usually get out of it by not having any women in it at all." Later he would add: "Beware of realism; it is the devil."

Stevenson also enjoyed success as a poet and as a writer of short stories. The enormously popular *A Child's Garden of Verses* (1885) included many poems written in his Scottish dialect. His first collection of short stories, *New Arabian Nights* (1882), includes "The Pavilion on the Links," which Arthur Conan Doyle called "the very model of dramatic narrative." According to Doyle, the story is "the high-water mark of [Stevenson's] genius, ... enough in itself, without another line, to give a man a permanent place among the great storytellers of the race." *The Merry Men and Other Tales and Fables* was published in 1887, and *Island Nights' Entertainment* in 1893. The latter deals largely with the problems of imperialism in the South Sea islands; "The Beach of Falesà," for instance, concerns discord between colonial merchants and native islanders. Stevenson had come to live in Samoa after searching the South Seas for a more salubrious climate than that of his Scottish homeland. (He left Scotland in 1887 after his father's death, but he continued to express deep longing for it in his final years.)

Stevenson came to love Samoa profoundly. After his death from a cerebral hemorrhage in 1894, his many island friends carried his remains up Mt. Vaea to bury him as he had requested in his poem "Requiem," which also provided the epitaph engraved on his tombstone. Stevenson was in his prime at the time of his death, at work on *Weir of Hermiston* (1896)—a book that, although unfinished, is regarded by many as a masterpiece.

⌘ ⌘ ⌘

Requiem

Under the wide and starry sky
　Dig the grave and let me lie.
Glad did I live and gladly die,
　And I laid me down with a will.

5　This be the verse you 'grave for me:
　　Here he lies where he longed to be;
Home is the sailor, home from the sea,
　　And the hunter home from the hill.[1]
—1879

---

[1]　*Home ... hill*   These final two lines are engraved on Stevenson's tombstone.

from *A Child's Garden of Verses*

Whole Duty of Children

A child should always say what's true
　And speak when he is spoken to,
And behave mannerly at table;
　At least as far as he is able.

Looking Forward

When I am grown to man's estate
I shall be very proud and great,
And tell the other girls and boys
Not to meddle with my toys.

The Land of Nod

From breakfast on through all the day
At home among my friends I stay,
But every night I go abroad
Afar into the land of Nod.

5 All by myself I have to go,
With none to tell me what to do—
All alone beside the streams
And up the mountain-sides of dreams.

The strangest things are there for me,
10 Both things to eat and things to see,
And many frightening sights abroad
Till morning in the land of Nod.

Try as I like to find the way,
I never can get back by day,
15 Nor can remember plain and clear
The curious music that I hear.

Good and Bad Children

Children, you are very little,
And your bones are very brittle;
If you would grow great and stately,
You must try to walk sedately.

5 You must still be bright and quiet,
And content with simple diet;
And remain, through all bewild'ring,
Innocent and honest children.

Happy hearts and happy faces,
10 Happy play in grassy places—
That was how, in ancient ages,
Children grew to kings and sages.

But the unkind and the unruly,
And the sort who eat unduly,
15 They must never hope for glory—
Theirs is quite a different story!

Cruel children, crying babies,
All grew up as geese and gabies,
Hated, as their age increases,
20 By their nephews and their nieces.

Foreign Children

Little Indian, Sioux or Crow,
Little frosty Eskimo,
Little Turk or Japanee,
Oh! don't you wish that you were me?

5 You have seen the scarlet trees
And the lions over seas;
You have eaten ostrich eggs,
And turned the turtles off their legs.

Such a life is very fine,
10 But it's not so nice as mine:
You must often, as you trod,
Have wearied *not* to be abroad.

You have curious things to eat,
I am fed on proper meat;
15 You must dwell beyond the foam,
But I am safe and live at home.
Little Indian, Sioux or Crow,
Little frosty Eskimo,
Little Turk or Japanee,
20 Oh! don't you wish that you were me?
—1885

OSCAR WILDE
1854 – 1900

For his epigrammatic genius, his challenges to bourgeois sensibilities, and his dazzling essays, dramas, and other writings, Oscar Wilde has been both reverenced and reviled for more than a century. Notorious for his flamboyance and wit before he had ever published a word, Wilde established himself in the literary world with his sole novel, *The Picture of Dorian Gray*, and even more with such sparkling social comedies as *An Ideal Husband* and *The Importance of Being Earnest*. He was a vocal advocate of aestheticism; Wilde saw in art the possibility for a life beyond the day-to-day monotony of ordinary existence. The "aesthetic movement," he writes, "produced certain colours, subtle in their loveliness and fascinating in their almost mystical tone. They were, and are, our reaction against the crude primaries of a doubtless more respectable but certainly less cultivated age."

Wilde began his life as Oscar Fingal O'Flahertie Wills Wilde. His parents, themselves no strangers to controversy, were Lady Jane Francesca Elgee and Dr. (later Sir) William Wilde. Both were accomplished writers. William, an ear and eye surgeon, wrote a book on medical and literary institutions in Austria and another about his voyage to North Africa and the Middle East. He achieved fame for his work on the Irish Census, for which he conducted a groundbreaking demographic study of the Great Famine, earning a knighthood in 1864. His reputation was somewhat tainted, however, by his womanizing; he fathered three children out of wedlock. Lady Wilde was also a prominent figure. Born Jane Frances Agnes Elgee, she adopted the more Italian-sounding "Francesca" to reinforce the family's claim that they were descended from Dante Alighieri (truth never stood in the way of a good Wilde family story). Lady Wilde took yet another name, "Speranza," when she published poems in *The Nation*, a weekly Dublin newspaper published by an anti-British revolutionary group called the Young Irelanders.

Wilde grew up in the colorful environment of his mother's famous salon, where she hosted leading Dublin artists and writers. Once when Wilde returned from college, he invited a friend to Lady Wilde's weekly "conversazione," saying: "I want to introduce you to my mother. We have founded a society for the suppression of virtue." Wilde was a brilliant student at Trinity College, graduating in 1874 with the Berkeley Gold Medal for Classics and receiving a scholarship to study at Oxford. Before long, he was celebrated at Oxford's Magdalen College for his wit, decadence, and ostentatious appearance. He was most influenced in his academic years by two rivals at Oxford, John Ruskin and Walter Pater. From Ruskin, perhaps the most influential art critic of the century, Wilde took counsel on what the older scholar believed to be the spiritual, ethical, and moral nature of art. From Pater, who was already infamous following the publication of his *Studies in the History of the Renaissance* (1873), Wilde picked up elements of aestheticism he would eventually transform into his own theories of art. Wilde would later describe Pater's *Renaissance* as "the holy writ of beauty."

After winning the Newdigate prize for poetry and graduating with first class honors, Wilde moved to London and began his career as a divisive public figure. He was known, for example, for a formal jacket, called his "cello coat," that he wore to the opening of the Grosvenor Gallery in 1877, and for being more generally a poster-boy of the emerging aesthetic movement. By the time he published a book of poems in 1881, he had already become the butt of many caricatures in *Punch* magazine; he had taken to modeling his look on the character of Bunthorne in Gilbert and Sullivan's satirical comic opera *Patience*. For the next few years Wilde delivered lectures in the United States and Great Britain about the aesthetic movement, for which he had ambitious plans: "I want to make this artistic movement the basis for a new civilization." In Boston he voiced some of the ideas about art and life for which he would best be known: "The supreme object of life is to live. Few people live. It is true life only to realize one's own perfection, to make one's every dream a reality. Even this is possible."

In 1884 Wilde married Constance Lloyd, with whom he would have two sons, Cyril and Vyvyan. From 1887 to 1889 he edited *Woman's World*, a popular magazine. Through the late 1880s, Wilde wrote reviews of many of his most famous contemporaries, including the painter James Whistler and the poets D.G. Rossetti, William Morris, Algernon Swinburne, and others. He was also at work on the volume that would ultimately constitute the most thorough account of his aesthetic philosophy, *Intentions* (1891), which included the essays "The Decay of Lying" and "The Critic as Artist." The essays argue for the paramount importance of art in human life: "[Art's] are ... the great archetypes of which things that have existence are but unfinished copies." Rather than artists copying from the world about them, writes Wilde, we as individuals interpret the world *through art*, through the "archetypes" presented to us by works of art. Hence "[T]here may have been fogs for centuries in London," but "no one saw them .... till Art had invented them." The early 1890s also saw the publication of Wilde's novel, *The Picture of Dorian Gray*, which both puts forward Wilde's aesthetic beliefs and suggests some of the dangers of a life given over to aesthetic consumption.

Wilde was clearly at his very best in the early 1890s. In addition to *Intentions* and *Dorian Gray*, Wilde penned a string of brilliant social comedies, including *Lady Windermere's Fan* (1892), *A Woman of No Importance* (1893), and *An Ideal Husband* (1895). His final comedy was his masterpiece of farce, *The Importance of Being Earnest*; it first played in 1895 to wildly enthusiastic crowds at the St. James Theatre in London. Success came to an end only through Wilde's ill-fated affair with a young aristocrat, Lord Alfred Douglas ("Bosie"). Douglas's father, the mentally-unstable Marquis of Queensbury, was infuriated by the relationship, and in 1895 he publicly accused Wilde of sodomy. Convinced he had to defend his own and Douglas's honor, Wilde sued the Marquis for libel. After Wilde failed in his suit against Queensbury, the government used evidence from the trial to launch a criminal investigation against Wilde because homosexuality was a criminal offence. Wilde was found guilty of "gross indecency" and sentenced to two years of imprisonment with hard labor.

Prison left Wilde financially and emotionally broken. The horrid conditions of late-Victorian prison life—including a poor diet, enforced silence, and physically-taxing labor—were especially difficult to handle. From prison Wilde wrote a moving autobiographical letter to Bosie, later entitled *De Profundis*, that accuses the younger man of heartless and selfish behavior. (Bosie had treated Wilde poorly all along, and he abandoned Wilde during his imprisonment.) Even from his cell, however, Wilde wrote of seeing "new developments in Art and Life." Upon his release he composed "The Ballad of Reading Gaol" (1898), a heartfelt indictment of the prison system and capital punishment, as well as a meditation on the universal characteristics of human nature.

Wilde's last years were spent in Italy and France. He seems never to have recovered fully from his prison experience, and by late in 1900 he was quite ill. He died and was buried in Paris before the year ended; the immediate cause of his death has never been conclusively established. In 1995 a window in the Poets' Corner of Westminster Abbey was dedicated in his honor.

⌘⌘⌘

Impression du Matin[1]

The Thames nocturne of blue and gold[2]
  Changed to a harmony in gray:
    A barge with ochre-coloured hay
Dropped from the wharf: and chill and cold

5 The yellow fog came creeping down
    The bridges, till the houses' walls
      Seemed changed to shadows and St. Paul's
Loomed like a bubble o'er the town.

Then suddenly arose the clang
10   Of waking life; the streets were stirred
      With country wagons: and a bird
Flew to the glistening roofs and sang.

But one pale woman all alone,
    The daylight kissing her wan hair,
15   Loitered beneath gas lamps' flare,
With lips of flame and heart of stone.
  —1881

E Tenebris[3]

Come down, O Christ, and help me! Reach thy hand,
  For I am drowning in a stormier sea
    Than Simon on thy lake of Galilee:[4]
The wine of life is spilt upon the sand,
5 My heart is as some famine-murdered land
  Whence all good things have perished utterly,
    And well I know my soul in Hell must lie
If I this night before God's throne should stand.
"He sleeps perchance, or rideth to the chase,
10   Like Baal, when his prophets howled that name
    From morn to noon on Carmel's smitten height."[5]
Nay, peace, I shall behold, before the night,
  The feet of brass,[6] the robe more white than flame,
The wounded hands, the weary human face.
  —1881

To Milton

Milton! I think thy spirit hath passed away
  From these white cliffs and high-embattled
    towers;
This gorgeous fiery-coloured world of ours
Seems fallen into ashes dull and grey,
5 And the age changed unto a mimic play
Wherein we waste our else too-crowded hours:
For all our pomp and pageantry and powers
We are but fit to delve the common clay,
Seeing this little isle on which we stand,
10 This England, this sea-lion of the sea,
By ignorant demagogues is held in fee,

---

1 *Impression du Matin* French: impression of the morning.

2 *gold* Cf. James McNeill Whistler's series of paintings, the "Nocturnes." Two of the most famous of these are "Nocturne in Blue and Gold: Old Battersea Bridge" and "Nocturne in Black and Gold: the Falling Rocket," both of which were painted in the 1870s. These and other similar paintings were important precursors of the movement that came to be known as Impressionism; painters such as Claude Monet and Edgar Degas, like Whistler, strove to capture the transitory effects of light both on the landscape and on human figures. Much as Wilde was moved to write his own "impressions" in verse (this is one of several Wilde poems that include the word "impression" in their title), he did not respond positively to Whistler's radical experiments with impressions on canvas. His response to "Nocturne in Black and Gold: the Falling Rocket" on seeing it exhibited at the Grosvenor Gallery in 1877 was to call it "worth looking at for about as long as one looks at a real rocket, that is, for something less than a quarter of a minute." This judgement concurred with that of the famous art critic John Ruskin (who had been a teacher of Wilde's at Oxford). Ruskin criticized Whistler for "flinging a pot of paint in the public's face" with works such as "Nocturne in Black and Gold: the Falling Rocket"—an insult for which Whistler sued him in a famous trial. (Whistler won the case, but was awarded only one farthing in damages and had to pay the costs of the trial, which contributed to his eventual bankruptcy.)

3 *E Tenebris* Latin: out of the darkness.

4 *Simon ... Galilee* In Matthew 14.24–31, Simon Peter, one of the twelve apostles, nearly drowns in a storm at sea when Christ bids him to walk across the water to him. Christ reaches out his hand and saves him, saying "O thou of little faith, wherefore didst thou doubt?"

5 *"He sleeps ... height"* In 1 Kings 18.19–40, Elijah mocks the priests of Baal (who had called upon their God all day in vain) by saying, "either he is talking, or he is pursuing, or he is in a journey, or peradventure he sleepeth, and must be awaked." Here the speaker imagines a similar voice taunting him.

6 *feet of brass* Revelation 1.13–16 describes a vision of the Son of man in which his feet are "like unto fine brass."

Who love her not: Dear God! is this the land
Which bare a triple empire in her hand
When Cromwell spake the word "Democracy!"
—1881

from *The Critic as Artist* [1]

ERNEST.   … [S]urely, the higher you place the creative artist, the lower must the critic rank.

GILBERT.   Why so?

ERNEST.   Because the best that he can give us will be but an echo of rich music, a dim shadow of clear-outlined form. It may, indeed, be that life is chaos, as you tell me that it is; that its martyrdoms are mean and its heroisms ignoble; and that it is the function of Literature to create, from the rough material of actual existence, a new world that will be more marvellous, more enduring, and more true than the world that common eyes look upon, and through which common natures seek to realize their perfection. But surely, if this new world has been made by the spirit and touch of a great artist, it will be a thing so complete and perfect that there will be nothing left for the critic to do. I quite understand now, and indeed admit most readily, that it is far more difficult to talk about a thing than to do it. But it seems to me that this sound and sensible maxim, which is really extremely soothing to one's feelings, and should be adopted as its motto by every Academy of Literature all over the world, applies only to the relations that exist between Art and Life, and not to any relations that there may be between Art and Criticism.

GILBERT.   But, surely, Criticism is itself an art. And just as artistic creation implies the working of the critical faculty, and, indeed, without it cannot be said to exist at all, so Criticism is really creative in the highest sense of the word. Criticism is, in fact, both creative and independent.

ERNEST.   Independent?

GILBERT.   Yes; independent. Criticism is no more to be judged by any low standard of imitation or resemblance than is the work of poet or sculptor. The critic occupies the same relation to the work of art that he criticizes as the artist does to the visible world of form and colour, or the unseen world of passion and of thought. He does not even require for the perfection of his art the finest materials. Anything will serve his purpose. And just as out of the sordid and sentimental amours of the silly wife of a small country doctor in the squalid village of Yonville-l'Abbaye, near Rouen, Gustave Flaubert was able to create a classic and make a masterpiece of style,[2] so, from subjects of little or no importance, such as the pictures in this year's Royal Academy, or in any year's Royal Academy for that matter, Mr. Lewis Morris's poems, M. Ohnet's novels, or the plays of Mr. Henry Arthur Jones,[3] the true critic can, if it be his pleasure so to direct or waste his faculty of contemplation, produce work that will be flawless in beauty and instinct with intellectual subtlety. Why not? Dullness is always an irresistible temptation for brilliancy, and stupidity is the permanent *Bestia Trionfans*[4] that calls wisdom from its cave. To an artist so creative as the critic, what does subject matter signify? No more and no less than it does to the novelist and the painter. Like them, he can find his motives everywhere. Treatment is the test. There is nothing that has not in it suggestion or challenge.

ERNEST.   But is Criticism really a creative art?

GILBERT.   Why should it not be? It works with materials, and puts them into a form that is at once new and delightful. What more can one say of poetry? Indeed, I would call criticism a creation within a creation. For just as the great artists, from Homer and Aeschylus down to

---

[1]   *The Critic as Artist*   In this dialogue, the two men debate the merits of art criticism. Earlier, Ernest had questioned the usefulness of criticism, asking, "Why should the artist be troubled by the shrill clamour of criticism? Why should those who cannot create take it upon themselves to estimate the value of creative work?" In response, Gilbert argued that criticism is itself an art, that "there is no fine art without self-consciousness, and self-consciousness and the critical spirit are one," and, furthermore, that it is "very much more difficult to talk about a thing than to do it."

[2]   *masterpiece of style*   I.e., Flaubert's *Madame Bovary*.

[3]   *Mr. Lewis Morris*   Popular Anglo-Welsh poet; *M. Ohnet* Georges Ohnet, nineteenth-century French novelist, many of whose works were successfully dramatized; *Mr. Henry Arthur Jones* Innovative playwright of the late nineteenth century.

[4]   *Bestia Trionfans*   Latin: triumphant beast. From the title of sixteenth-century philosopher Giordano Bruno's allegory *Spacio della Bestia Trionfante* (*Expulsion of the Triumphant Beast*).

Shakespeare and Keats,[1] did not go directly to life for their subject-matter, but sought for it in myth, and legend, and ancient tale, so the critic deals with materials that others have, as it were, purified for him, and to which imaginative form and colour have been already added. Nay, more, I would say that the highest Criticism, being the purest form of personal impression, is in its way more creative than creation, as it has least reference to any standard external to itself, and is, in fact, its own reason for existing, and, as the Greeks would put it, in itself, and to itself, an end. Certainly, it is never trammelled by any shackles of verisimilitude. No ignoble considerations of probability, that cowardly concession to the tedious repetitions of domestic or public life, affect it ever. One may appeal from fiction unto fact. But from the soul there is no appeal.

ERNEST.   From the soul?

GILBERT.   Yes, from the soul. That is what the highest criticism really is, the record of one's own soul. It is more fascinating than history, as it is concerned simply with oneself. It is more delightful than philosophy, as its subject is concrete and not abstract, real and not vague. It is the only civilized form of autobiography, as it deals not with the events, but with the thoughts of one's life; not with life's physical accidents of deed or circumstance, but with the spiritual moods and imaginative passions of the mind. I am always amused by the silly vanity of those writers and artists of our day who seem to imagine that the primary function of the critic is to chatter about their second-rate work. The best that one can say of most modern creative art is that it is just a little less vulgar than reality, and so the critic, with his fine sense of distinction and sure instinct of delicate refinement, will prefer to look into the silver mirror or through the woven veil, and will turn his eyes away from the chaos and clamour of actual existence, though the mirror be tarnished and the veil be torn. His sole aim is to chronicle his own impressions. It is for him that pictures are painted, books written, and marble hewn into form.

ERNEST.   I seem to have heard another theory of Criticism.

GILBERT.   Yes: it has been said by one whose gracious memory we all revere, and the music of whose pipe once lured Proserpina from her Sicilian fields, and made those white feet stir, and not in vain, the Cumnor cowslips, that the proper aim of Criticism is to see the object as in itself it really is.[2] But this is a very serious error, and takes no cognizance of Criticism's most perfect form, which is in its essence purely subjective, and seeks to reveal its own secret and not the secret of another. For the highest Criticism deals with art not as expressive but as impressive purely.

ERNEST.   But is that really so?

GILBERT.   Of course it is. Who cares whether Mr. Ruskin's views on Turner[3] are sound or not? What does it matter? That mighty and majestic prose of his, so fervid and so fiery-coloured in its noble eloquence, so rich in its elaborate symphonic music, so sure and certain, at its best, in subtle choice of word and epithet, is at least as great a work of art as any of those wonderful sunsets that bleach or rot on their corrupted canvases in England's Gallery;[4] greater indeed, one is apt to think at times, not merely because its equal beauty is more enduring, but on account of the fuller variety of its appeal, soul speaking to soul in those long-cadenced lines, not through form and colour alone, though through these, indeed, completely and without loss, but with intellectual and emotional utterance, with lofty passion and with loftier thought, with imaginative insight, and with poetic aim; greater, I always think, even as Literature is the greater art.

—1890

---

1   *Homer*   Greek poet to whom the authorship of *The Iliad* and *The Odyssey* is attributed (?850 BCE); *Shakespeare*   William Shakespeare, English poet and playwright (1564–1616); *Keats*   John Keats, English poet (1795–1821).

2   *it has . . . really is*   Matthew Arnold, whose poem *Thyrsis* attempts to summon the goddess Proserpine from the pastoral landscape of Sicily to the Cumnor hills of England. Arnold discusses the aim of criticism in his essay *The Function of Criticism at the Present Time.*

3   *Turner*   English landscape painter Joseph Mallord William Turner. Cf. John Ruskin's *Modern Painters.*

4   *England's Gallery*   The Tate Gallery in London, upon which a major bequest of Turner's paintings was bestowed in 1856.

from *The Decay of Lying*[1]

CYRIL. ... [I]n order to avoid making any error I want you to tell me briefly the doctrines of the new aesthetics.

VIVIAN. Briefly, then, they are these. Art never expresses anything but itself. It has an independent life, just as Thought has, and develops purely on its own lines. It is not necessarily realistic in an age of realism, nor spiritual in an age of faith. So far from being the creation of its time, it is usually in direct opposition to it, and the only history that it preserves for us is the history of its own progress. Sometimes it returns upon its footsteps, and revives some antique form, as happened in the archaistic movement of late Greek Art, and in the Pre-Raphaelite movement of our own day. At other times it entirely anticipates its age, and produces in one century work that it takes another century to understand, to appreciate, and to enjoy. In no case does it reproduce its age. To pass from the art of a time to the time itself is the great mistake that all historians commit.

The second doctrine is this. All bad art comes from returning to Life and Nature and elevating them into ideals. Life and Nature may sometimes be used as part of Art's rough material, but before they are of any real service to art they must be translated into artistic conventions. The moment Art surrenders its imaginative medium it surrenders everything. As a method Realism is a complete failure, and the two things that every artist should avoid are modernity of form and modernity of subject matter. To us, who live in the nineteenth century, any century is a suitable subject for art except our own. The only beautiful things are the things that do not concern us. It is, to have the pleasure of quoting myself, exactly because Hecuba is nothing to us that her sorrows are so suitable a motive for a tragedy.[2] Besides, it is only the modern that ever becomes old-fashioned. M. Zola[3] sits down to give us a picture of the Second Empire. Who cares for the Second Empire now? It is out of date. Life goes faster than Realism, but Romanticism is always in front of Life.

The third doctrine is that Life imitates Art far more than Art imitates Life. This results not merely from Life's imitative instinct, but from the fact that the self-conscious aim of Life is to find expression, and that Art offers it certain beautiful forms through which it may realize that energy. It is a theory that has never been put forward before, but it is extremely fruitful, and throws an entirely new light upon the history of Art.

It follows, as a corollary from this, that external Nature also imitates Art. The only effects that she can show us are effects that we have already seen through poetry, or in paintings. This is the secret of Nature's charm, as well as the explanation of Nature's weakness.

The final revelation is that Lying, the telling of beautiful untrue things, is the proper aim of Art. But of this I think I have spoken at sufficient length. And now let us go out on the terrace, where "droops the milk-white peacock like a ghost,"[4] while the evening star "washes the dusk with silver."[5] At twilight nature becomes a wonderfully suggestive effect, and is not without loveliness, though perhaps its chief use is to illustrate quotations from the poets. Come! We have talked long enough.

—1889

---

[1] *"The Decay of Lying"* In this Platonic dialogue, Wilde sets out a new theory of aesthetics through the conversation of two characters, Vivian and Cyril (named after Wilde's two sons). Vivian, prompted by Cyril's questioning, has been reading from his essay in progress, called "The Decay of Lying," which explores and confirms Plato's claim in *The Republic* that art is falsehood, yet challenges his assertion that art is a mere imitation of life, and that the lies of art are morally repugnant. On the contrary, Vivian celebrates the lies of art, declaring, "if something cannot be done to check, or at least modify, our monstrous worship of facts, Art will become sterile and Beauty will pass from the land." At the heart of this work is a challenge to the Victorian adherence to realism and advocacy of faithful imitation of nature.

[2] *Hecuba ... tragedy* Hecuba, Queen of Troy when that city was conquered by the Greeks, saw her husband and her sons murdered. In Shakespeare's *Hamlet*, one of the players performing for Hamlet recites an emotional monologue on the terrible fate of Hecuba, prompting Hamlet to wonder, "What's Hecuba to him, or he to Hecuba, / That he should weep for her?" (2.2.)

[3] *M. Zola* (Monsieur) Émile Zola, French novelist (1840–1902).

[4] *"droops ... ghost"* From "The Princess" by Alfred Lord Tennyson.

[5] *"washes ... silver"* From "To the Evening Star" by William Blake.

Preface to *The Picture of Dorian Gray*[1]

The artist is the creator of beautiful things.
To reveal art and conceal the artist is art's aim.
The critic is he who can translate into another medium or a new material his impression of beautiful things.

The highest as the lowest form of criticism is a mode of autobiography.

Those who find ugly meanings in beautiful things are corrupt without being charming. This is a fault.

Those who find beautiful meanings in beautiful things are cultivated. For these there is hope.

They are the elect to whom beautiful things mean only beauty.

There is no such thing as a moral or an immoral book. Books are well written, or badly written. That is all.

The nineteenth century dislike of Realism is the rage of Caliban[2] seeing his own face in a glass.

The nineteenth century dislike of Romanticism is the rage of Caliban not seeing his own face in a glass.

The moral life of man forms part of the subject matter of the artist, but the morality of art consists in the perfect use of an imperfect medium.

No artist desires to prove anything. Even things that are true can be proved.

No artist has ethical sympathies. An ethical sympathy in an artist is an unpardonable mannerism of style.

No artist is ever morbid. The artist can express everything.

Thought and language are to the artist instruments of an art.

Vice and virtue are to the artist materials for an art.

From the point of view of form, the type of all the arts is the art of the musician.

From the point of view of feeling, the actor's craft is the type.

All art is at once surface and symbol.

Those who go beneath the surface do so at their peril.

Those who read the symbol do so at their peril.

It is the spectator, and not life, that art really mirrors.

Diversity of opinion about a work of art shows that the work is new, complex, and vital.

When critics disagree the artist is in accord with himself.

We can forgive a man for making a useful thing as long as he does not admire it. The only excuse for making a useless thing is that one admires it intensely.

All art is quite useless.

—1891

The Importance of Being Earnest
A Trivial Comedy for Serious People

THE PERSONS IN THE PLAY

John Worthing, J.P.[3]
Algernon Moncrieff
Rev. Canon Chasuble, D.D.[4]
Merriman, *Butler*
Lane, *Manservant*
Lady Bracknell
Hon.[5] Gwendolen Fairfax
Cecily Cardew
Miss Prism, *Governess*

THE SCENES IN THE PLAY

ACT 1. Algernon Moncrieff's Flat in Half-Moon Street,[6] W.
ACT 2. The Garden at the Manor House, Woolton.[7]
ACT 3. Drawing-Room at the Manor House, Woolton.

TIME: The Present.

---

[1] *Preface* Published in 1891, the year after the novel's first appearance, this preface was a response to the charges of immorality leveled at the novel by numerous critics.

[2] *Caliban* The "monster" of Shakespeare's *The Tempest*, Caliban is a native of the island and has been enslaved by Prospero.

[3] *J.P.* Justice of the Peace.

[4] *D.D.* Doctor of Divinity.

[5] *Hon.* I.e., The Honorable. The honorific in this case designates the daughter of a peer below the rank of Earl.

[6] *Half-Moon Street* Street located in a fashionable area of London.

[7] *Woolton* A fictional location.

ACT 1

SCENE

(*Morning-room in Algernon's flat in Half-Moon Street. The room is luxuriously and artistically furnished. The sound of a piano is heard in the adjoining room.*)

(*Lane is arranging afternoon tea on the table, and after the music has ceased, Algernon enters.*)

ALGERNON. Did you hear what I was playing, Lane?

LANE. I didn't think it polite to listen, sir.

ALGERNON. I'm sorry for that, for your sake. I don't play accurately—any one can play accurately—but I play with wonderful expression. As far as the piano is concerned, sentiment is my forte. I keep science for Life.

LANE. Yes, sir.

ALGERNON. And, speaking of the science of Life, have you got the cucumber sandwiches[1] cut for Lady Bracknell?

LANE. Yes, sir. (*Hands them on a salver.[2]*)

ALGERNON. (*Inspects them, takes two, and sits down on the sofa.*) Oh! … by the way, Lane, I see from your book that on Thursday night, when Lord Shoreman and Mr. Worthing were dining with me, eight bottles of champagne are entered as having been consumed.

LANE. Yes, sir; eight bottles and a pint.

ALGERNON. Why is it that at a bachelor's establishment the servants invariably drink the champagne? I ask merely for information.

LANE. I attribute it to the superior quality of the wine, sir. I have often observed that in married households the champagne is rarely of a first-rate brand.

ALGERNON. Good heavens! Is marriage so demoralising as that?

LANE. I believe it is a very pleasant state, sir. I have had very little experience of it myself up to the present. I have only been married once. That was in consequence of a misunderstanding between myself and a young person.

ALGERNON. (*Languidly.*) I don't know that I am much interested in your family life, Lane.

LANE. No, sir; it is not a very interesting subject. I never think of it myself.

ALGERNON. Very natural, I am sure. That will do, Lane, thank you.

LANE. Thank you, sir. (*Lane goes out.*)

ALGERNON. Lane's views on marriage seem somewhat lax. Really, if the lower orders don't set us a good example, what on earth is the use of them? They seem, as a class, to have absolutely no sense of moral responsibility.

(*Enter Lane.*)

LANE. Mr. Ernest Worthing.

(*Enter Jack. Lane goes out.*)

ALGERNON. How are you, my dear Ernest? What brings you up to town?

JACK. Oh, pleasure, pleasure! What else should bring one anywhere? Eating as usual, I see, Algy!

ALGERNON. (*Stiffly.*) I believe it is customary in good society to take some slight refreshment at five o'clock. Where have you been since last Thursday?

JACK. (*Sitting down on the sofa.*) In the country.

ALGERNON. What on earth do you do there?

JACK. (*Pulling off his gloves.*) When one is in town[3] one amuses oneself. When one is in the country one amuses other people. It is excessively boring.

ALGERNON. And who are the people you amuse?

JACK. (*Airily.*) Oh, neighbours, neighbours.

ALGERNON. Got nice neighbours in your part of Shropshire?

JACK. Perfectly horrid! Never speak to one of them.

ALGERNON. How immensely you must amuse them! (*Goes over and takes sandwich.*) By the way, Shropshire is your county, is it not?

JACK. Eh? Shropshire? Yes, of course. Hallo! Why all these cups? Why cucumber sandwiches? Why such reckless extravagance in one so young? Who is coming to tea?

---

[1] *cucumber sandwiches* Small sandwiches of cucumber on thinly-sliced bread, a staple of afternoon tea in polite English society.

[2] *salver* Serving tray, typically silver.

[3] *in town* In London.

ALGERNON.   Oh! merely Aunt Augusta and Gwendolen.

JACK.   How perfectly delightful!

70 ALGERNON.   Yes, that is all very well; but I am afraid Aunt Augusta won't quite approve of your being here.

JACK.   May I ask why?

ALGERNON.   My dear fellow, the way you flirt with Gwendolen is perfectly disgraceful. It is almost as bad as

75 the way Gwendolen flirts with you.

JACK.   I am in love with Gwendolen. I have come up to town expressly to propose to her.

ALGERNON.   I thought you had come up for pleasure? … I call that business.

80 JACK.   How utterly unromantic you are!

ALGERNON.   I really don't see anything romantic in proposing. It is very romantic to be in love. But there is nothing romantic about a definite proposal. Why, one may be accepted. One usually is, I believe. Then the

85 excitement is all over. The very essence of romance is uncertainty. If ever I get married, I'll certainly try to forget the fact.

JACK.   I have no doubt about that, dear Algy. The Divorce Court was specially invented for people whose

90 memories are so curiously constituted.

ALGERNON.   Oh! there is no use speculating on that subject. Divorces are made in Heaven—(*Jack puts out his hand to take a sandwich. Algernon at once interferes.*) Please don't touch the cucumber sandwiches. They are

95 ordered specially for Aunt Augusta. (*Takes one and eats it.*)

JACK.   Well, you have been eating them all the time.

ALGERNON.   That is quite a different matter. She is my aunt. (*Takes plate from below.*) Have some bread and

100 butter. The bread and butter is for Gwendolen. Gwendolen is devoted to bread and butter.

JACK.   (*Advancing to table and helping himself.*) And very good bread and butter it is too.

ALGERNON.   Well, my dear fellow, you need not eat as if

105 you were going to eat it all. You behave as if you were married to her already. You are not married to her already, and I don't think you ever will be.

JACK.   Why on earth do you say that?

ALGERNON.   Well, in the first place girls never marry the

110 men they flirt with. Girls don't think it right.

JACK.   Oh, that is nonsense!

ALGERNON.   It isn't. It is a great truth. It accounts for the extraordinary number of bachelors that one sees all over the place. In the second place, I don't give my consent.

115 JACK.   Your consent!

ALGERNON.   My dear fellow, Gwendolen is my first cousin. And before I allow you to marry her, you will have to clear up the whole question of Cecily. (*Rings bell.*)

120 JACK.   Cecily! What on earth do you mean? What do you mean, Algy, by Cecily! I don't know any one of the name of Cecily.

(*Enter Lane.*)

ALGERNON.   Bring me that cigarette case Mr. Worthing left in the smoking-room the last time he dined here.

125 LANE.   Yes, sir.

(*Lane goes out.*)

JACK.   Do you mean to say you have had my cigarette case all this time? I wish to goodness you had let me know. I have been writing frantic letters to Scotland Yard about it. I was very nearly offering a large reward.

130 ALGERNON.   Well, I wish you would offer one. I happen to be more than usually hard up.

JACK.   There is no good offering a large reward now that the thing is found.

(*Enter Lane with the cigarette case on a salver. Algernon takes it at once. Lane goes out.*)

ALGERNON.   I think that is rather mean of you, Ernest,

135 I must say. (*Opens case and examines it.*) However, it makes no matter, for, now that I look at the inscription inside, I find that the thing isn't yours after all.

JACK.   Of course it's mine. (*Moving to him.*) You have seen me with it a hundred times, and you have no right

140 whatsoever to read what is written inside. It is a very ungentlemanly thing to read a private cigarette case.

ALGERNON.   Oh! it is absurd to have a hard and fast rule about what one should read and what one shouldn't. More than half of modern culture depends on what one

145 shouldn't read.

JACK. I am quite aware of the fact, and I don't propose to discuss modern culture. It isn't the sort of thing one should talk of in private. I simply want my cigarette case back.

150 ALGERNON. Yes; but this isn't your cigarette case. This cigarette case is a present from some one of the name of Cecily, and you said you didn't know any one of that name.

JACK. Well, if you want to know, Cecily happens to be 155 my aunt.

ALGERNON. Your aunt!

JACK. Yes. Charming old lady she is, too. Lives at Tunbridge Wells. Just give it back to me, Algy.

ALGERNON. (*Retreating to back of sofa.*) But why does 160 she call herself little Cecily if she is your aunt and lives at Tunbridge Wells? (*Reading.*) "From little Cecily with her fondest love."

JACK. (*Moving to sofa and kneeling upon it.*) My dear fellow, what on earth is there in that? Some aunts are 165 tall, some aunts are not tall. That is a matter that surely an aunt may be allowed to decide for herself. You seem to think that every aunt should be exactly like your aunt! That is absurd! For Heaven's sake give me back my cigarette case. (*Follows Algernon round the room.*)

170 ALGERNON. Yes. But why does your aunt call you her uncle? "From little Cecily, with her fondest love to her dear Uncle Jack." There is no objection, I admit, to an aunt being a small aunt, but why an aunt, no matter what her size may be, should call her own nephew her 175 uncle, I can't quite make out. Besides, your name isn't Jack at all; it is Ernest.

JACK. It isn't Ernest; it's Jack.

ALGERNON. You have always told me it was Ernest. I have introduced you to every one as Ernest. You answer 180 to the name of Ernest. You look as if your name was Ernest. You are the most earnest-looking person I ever saw in my life. It is perfectly absurd your saying that your name isn't Ernest. It's on your cards. Here is one of them. (*Taking it from case.*) "Mr. Ernest Worthing, B. 185 4, The Albany." I'll keep this as a proof that your name is Ernest if ever you attempt to deny it to me, or to Gwendolen, or to any one else. (*Puts the card in his pocket.*)

JACK. Well, my name is Ernest in town and Jack in the 190 country, and the cigarette case was given to me in the country.

ALGERNON. Yes, but that does not account for the fact that your small Aunt Cecily, who lives at Tunbridge Wells, calls you her dear uncle. Come, old boy, you had 195 much better have the thing out at once.

JACK. My dear Algy, you talk exactly as if you were a dentist. It is very vulgar to talk like a dentist when one isn't a dentist. It produces a false impression.

ALGERNON. Well, that is exactly what dentists always 200 do. Now, go on! Tell me the whole thing. I may mention that I have always suspected you of being a confirmed and secret Bunburyist; and I am quite sure of it now.

JACK. Bunburyist? What on earth do you mean by a 205 Bunburyist?

ALGERNON. I'll reveal to you the meaning of that incomparable expression as soon as you are kind enough to inform me why you are Ernest in town and Jack in the country.

210 JACK. Well, produce my cigarette case first.

ALGERNON. Here it is. (*Hands cigarette case.*) Now produce your explanation, and pray make it improbable. (*Sits on sofa.*)

JACK. My dear fellow, there is nothing improbable about 215 my explanation at all. In fact it's perfectly ordinary. Old Mr. Thomas Cardew, who adopted me when I was a little boy, made me in his will guardian to his granddaughter, Miss Cecily Cardew. Cecily, who addresses me as her uncle from motives of respect that you could 220 not possibly appreciate, lives at my place in the country under the charge of her admirable governess, Miss Prism.

ALGERNON. Where in that place in the country, by the way?

225 JACK. That is nothing to you, dear boy. You are not going to be invited ... I may tell you candidly that the place is not in Shropshire.

ALGERNON. I suspected that, my dear fellow! I have Bunburyed all over Shropshire on two separate occa-230 sions. Now, go on. Why are you Ernest in town and Jack in the country?

JACK. My dear Algy, I don't know whether you will be able to understand my real motives. You are hardly serious enough. When one is placed in the position of guardian, one has to adopt a very high moral tone on all subjects. It's one's duty to do so. And as a high moral tone can hardly be said to conduce very much to either one's health or one's happiness, in order to get up to town I have always pretended to have a younger brother of the name of Ernest, who lives in the Albany, and gets into the most dreadful scrapes. That, my dear Algy, is the whole truth pure and simple.

ALGERNON.   The truth is rarely pure and never simple. Modern life would be very tedious if it were either, and modern literature a complete impossibility!

JACK.   That wouldn't be at all a bad thing.

ALGERNON.   Literary criticism is not your forte, my dear fellow. Don't try it. You should leave that to people who haven't been at a University. They do it so well in the daily papers. What you really are is a Bunburyist. I was quite right in saying you were a Bunburyist. You are one of the most advanced Bunburyists I know.

JACK.   What on earth do you mean?

ALGERNON.   You have invented a very useful younger brother called Ernest, in order that you may be able to come up to town as often as you like. I have invented an invaluable permanent invalid called Bunbury, in order that I may be able to go down into the country whenever I choose. Bunbury is perfectly invaluable. If it wasn't for Bunbury's extraordinary bad health, for instance, I wouldn't be able to dine with you at Willis's to-night, for I have been really engaged to Aunt Augusta for more than a week.

JACK.   I haven't asked you to dine with me anywhere to-night.

ALGERNON.   I know. You are absurdly careless about sending out invitations. It is very foolish of you. Nothing annoys people so much as not receiving invitations.

JACK.   You had much better dine with your Aunt Augusta.

ALGERNON.   I haven't the smallest intention of doing anything of the kind. To begin with, I dined there on Monday, and once a week is quite enough to dine with one's own relations. In the second place, whenever I do dine there I am always treated as a member of the family, and sent down[1] with either no woman at all, or two. In the third place, I know perfectly well whom she will place me next to, to-night. She will place me next Mary Farquhar, who always flirts with her own husband across the dinner-table. That is not very pleasant. Indeed, it is not even decent … and that sort of thing is enormously on the increase. The amount of women in London who flirt with their own husbands is perfectly scandalous. It looks so bad. It is simply washing one's clean linen in public. Besides, now that I know you to be a confirmed Bunburyist I naturally want to talk to you about Bunburying. I want to tell you the rules.

JACK.   I'm not a Bunburyist at all. If Gwendolen accepts me, I am going to kill my brother, indeed I think I'll kill him in any case. Cecily is a little too much interested in him. It is rather a bore. So I am going to get rid of Ernest. And I strongly advise you to do the same with Mr. … with your invalid friend who has the absurd name.

ALGERNON.   Nothing will induce me to part with Bunbury, and if you ever get married, which seems to me extremely problematic, you will be very glad to know Bunbury. A man who marries without knowing Bunbury has a very tedious time of it.

JACK.   That is nonsense. If I marry a charming girl like Gwendolen, and she is the only girl I ever saw in my life that I would marry, I certainly won't want to know Bunbury.

ALGERNON.   Then your wife will. You don't seem to realise, that in married life three is company and two is none.

JACK.   (Sententiously.) That, my dear young friend, is the theory that the corrupt French Drama has been propounding for the last fifty years.

ALGERNON.   Yes; and that the happy English home has proved in half the time.

JACK.   For heaven's sake, don't try to be cynical. It's perfectly easy to be cynical.

ALGERNON.   My dear fellow, it isn't easy to be anything nowadays. There's such a lot of beastly competition about. (The sound of an electric bell is heard.) Ah! that must be Aunt Augusta. Only relatives, or creditors, ever ring in that Wagnerian[2] manner. Now, if I get her out

---

[1]   *sent down* I.e., sent from the drawing-room (typically upstairs) down to the dining-room (typically on a lower floor).

[2]   *Wagnerian* Suggesting the music of German composer Richard Wagner (1813–83), known for dramatic, stirring compositions such as *Tannhäuser, Lohergrin,* and *Der Ring des Nibelungen.*

of the way for ten minutes, so that you can have an
320 opportunity for proposing to Gwendolen, may I dine
with you to-night at Willis's?

JACK.   I suppose so, if you want to.

ALGERNON.   Yes, but you must be serious about it. I hate
people who are not serious about meals. It is so shallow
325 of them.

(*Enter Lane.*)

Lady Bracknell and Miss Fairfax.

(*Algernon goes forward to meet them. Enter Lady Bracknell
and Gwendolen.*)

LADY BRACKNELL.   Good afternoon, dear Algernon, I
hope you are behaving very well.

ALGERNON.   I'm feeling very well, Aunt Augusta.

330 LADY BRACKNELL.   That's not quite the same thing. In
fact the two things rarely go together. (*Sees Jack and
bows to him with icy coldness.*)

ALGERNON.   (*To Gwendolen.*) Dear me, you are smart!

GWENDOLEN.   I am always smart! Am I not, Mr. Wor-
335 thing?

JACK.   You're quite perfect, Miss Fairfax.

GWENDOLEN.   Oh! I hope I am not that. It would leave
no room for developments, and I intend to develop in
many directions.

(*Gwendolen and Jack sit down together in the corner.*)

340 LADY BRACKNELL.   I'm sorry if we are a little late,
Algernon, but I was obliged to call on dear Lady Harbury. I hadn't been there since her poor husband's
death. I never saw a woman so altered; she looks quite
twenty years younger. And now I'll have a cup of tea,
345 and one of those nice cucumber sandwiches you promised me.

ALGERNON.   Certainly, Aunt Augusta. (*Goes over to teatable.*)

LADY BRACKNELL.   Won't you come and sit here,
350 Gwendolen?

GWENDOLEN.   Thanks, mamma, I'm quite comfortable
where I am.

ALGERNON.   (*Picking up empty plate in horror.*) Good
heavens! Lane! Why are there no cucumber sandwiches?
355 I ordered them specially.

LANE.   (*Gravely.*) There were no cucumbers in the
market this morning, sir. I went down twice.

ALGERNON.   No cucumbers!

LANE.   No, sir. Not even for ready money.

360 ALGERNON.   That will do, Lane, thank you.

LANE.   Thank you, sir. (*Goes out.*)

ALGERNON.   I am greatly distressed, Aunt Augusta,
about there being no cucumbers, not even for ready
money.

365 LADY BRACKNELL.   It really makes no matter, Algernon.
I had some crumpets with Lady Harbury, who seems to
me to be living entirely for pleasure now.

ALGERNON.   I hear her hair has turned quite gold from
grief.

370 LADY BRACKNELL.   It certainly has changed its colour.
From what cause I, of course, cannot say. (*Algernon
crosses and hands tea.*) Thank you. I've quite a treat for
you to-night, Algernon. I am going to send you down
with Mary Farquhar. She is such a nice woman, and so
375 attentive to her husband. It's delightful to watch them.

ALGERNON.   I am afraid, Aunt Augusta, I shall have to
give up the pleasure of dining with you to-night after
all.

LADY BRACKNELL.   (*Frowning.*) I hope not, Algernon. It
380 would put my table completely out. Your uncle would
have to dine upstairs. Fortunately he is accustomed to
that.

ALGERNON.   It is a great bore, and, I need hardly say, a
terrible disappointment to me, but the fact is I have just
385 had a telegram to say that my poor friend Bunbury is
very ill again. (*Exchanges glances with Jack.*) They seem
to think I should be with him.

LADY BRACKNELL.   It is very strange. This Mr. Bunbury
seems to suffer from curiously bad health.

390 ALGERNON.   Yes; poor Bunbury is a dreadful invalid.

LADY BRACKNELL.   Well, I must say, Algernon, that I
think it is high time that Mr. Bunbury made up his
mind whether he was going to live or to die. This shilly-
shallying with the question is absurd. Nor do I in any
395 way approve of the modern sympathy with invalids. I
consider it morbid. Illness of any kind is hardly a thing
to be encouraged in others. Health is the primary duty
of life. I am always telling that to your poor uncle, but

he never seems to take much notice ... as far as any
400 improvement in his ailment goes. I should be much
obliged if you would ask Mr. Bunbury, from me, to be
kind enough not to have a relapse on Saturday, for I rely
on you to arrange my music for me. It is my last reception, and one wants something that will encourage
405 conversation, particularly at the end of the season when
every one has practically said whatever they had to say,
which, in most cases, was probably not much.

ALGERNON. I'll speak to Bunbury, Aunt Augusta, if he
is still conscious, and I think I can promise you he'll be
410 all right by Saturday. Of course the music is a great
difficulty. You see, if one plays good music, people don't
listen, and if one plays bad music people don't talk. But
I'll run over the programme I've drawn out, if you will
kindly come into the next room for a moment.

415 LADY BRACKNELL. Thank you, Algernon. It is very
thoughtful of you. (*Rising, and following Algernon.*) I'm
sure the programme will be delightful, after a few
expurgations. French songs I cannot possibly allow.
People always seem to think that they are improper, and
420 either look shocked, which is vulgar, or laugh, which is
worse. But German sounds a thoroughly respectable
language, and indeed, I believe is so. Gwendolen, you
will accompany me.

GWENDOLEN. Certainly, mamma.

(*Lady Bracknell and Algernon go into the music-room,
Gwendolen remains behind.*)

425 JACK. Charming day it has been, Miss Fairfax.

GWENDOLEN. Pray don't talk to me about the weather,
Mr. Worthing. Whenever people talk to me about the
weather, I always feel quite certain that they mean
something else. And that makes me so nervous.

430 JACK. I do mean something else.

GWENDOLEN. I thought so. In fact, I am never wrong.

JACK. And I would like to be allowed to take advantage
of Lady Bracknell's temporary absence ...

GWENDOLEN. I would certainly advise you to do so.
435 Mamma has a way of coming back suddenly into a
room that I have often had to speak to her about.

JACK. (*Nervously.*) Miss Fairfax, ever since I met you I
have admired you more than any girl ... I have ever met
since ... I met you.

440 GWENDOLEN. Yes, I am quite well aware of the fact.
And I often wish that in public, at any rate, you had
been more demonstrative. For me you have always had
an irresistible fascination. Even before I met you I was
far from indifferent to you. (*Jack looks at her in amaze-*
445 *ment.*) We live, as I hope you know, Mr. Worthing, in
an age of ideals. The fact is constantly mentioned in the
more expensive monthly magazines, and has reached the
provincial[1] pulpits, I am told; and my ideal has always
been to love some one of the name of Ernest. There is
450 something in that name that inspires absolute confidence. The moment Algernon first mentioned to me
that he had a friend called Ernest, I knew I was destined
to love you.

JACK. You really love me, Gwendolen?

455 GWENDOLEN. Passionately!

JACK. Darling! You don't know how happy you've made
me.

GWENDOLEN. My own Ernest!

JACK. But you don't really mean to say that you couldn't
460 love me if my name wasn't Ernest?

GWENDOLEN. But your name is Ernest.

JACK. Yes, I know it is. But supposing it was something
else? Do you mean to say you couldn't love me then?

GWENDOLEN. (*Glibly.*) Ah! that is clearly a metaphysical
465 speculation, and like most metaphysical speculations has
very little reference at all to the actual facts of real life, as
we know them.

JACK. Personally, darling, to speak quite candidly, I
don't much care about the name of Ernest ... I don't
470 think the name suits me at all.

GWENDOLEN. It suits you perfectly. It is a divine name.
It has a music of its own. It produces vibrations.

JACK. Well, really, Gwendolen, I must say that I think
there are lots of other much nicer names. I think Jack,
475 for instance, a charming name.

GWENDOLEN. Jack? ... No, there is very little music in
the name Jack, if any at all, indeed. It does not thrill. It
produces absolutely no vibrations ... I have known
several Jacks, and they all, without exception, were more
480 than usually plain. Besides, Jack is a notorious domesticity for John! And I pity any woman who is married to a

---

[1] *provincial* "Province" does not indicate a formal British
jurisdiction; "the provinces" is a colloquial term for all areas of the
country that are some distance from London.

man called John. She would probably never be allowed to know the entrancing pleasure of a single moment's solitude. The only really safe name is Ernest.

485 JACK. Gwendolen, I must get christened at once—I mean we must get married at once. There is no time to be lost.

GWENDOLEN. Married, Mr. Worthing?

JACK. (*Astounded.*) Well … surely. You know that I love
490 you, and you led me to believe, Miss Fairfax, that you were not absolutely indifferent to me.

GWENDOLEN. I adore you. But you haven't proposed to me yet. Nothing has been said at all about marriage. The subject has not even been touched on.

495 JACK. Well … may I propose to you now?

GWENDOLEN. I think it would be an admirable opportunity. And to spare you any possible disappointment, Mr. Worthing, I think it only fair to tell you quite frankly before-hand that I am fully determined to accept
500 you.

JACK. Gwendolen!

GWENDOLEN. Yes, Mr. Worthing, what have you got to say to me?

JACK. You know what I have got to say to you.

505 GWENDOLEN. Yes, but you don't say it.

JACK. Gwendolen, will you marry me? (*Goes on his knees.*)

GWENDOLEN. Of course I will, darling. How long you have been about it! I am afraid you have had very little
510 experience in how to propose.

JACK. My own one, I have never loved any one in the world but you.

GWENDOLEN. Yes, but men often propose for practice. I know my brother Gerald does. All my girl-friends tell
515 me so. What wonderfully blue eyes you have, Ernest! They are quite, quite, blue. I hope you will always look at me just like that, especially when there are other people present. (*Enter Lady Bracknell.*)

LADY BRACKNELL. Mr. Worthing! Rise, sir, from this
520 semi-recumbent posture. It is most indecorous.

GWENDOLEN. Mamma! (*He tries to rise; she restrains him.*) I must beg you to retire. This is no place for you. Besides, Mr. Worthing has not quite finished yet.

LADY BRACKNELL. Finished what, may I ask?

525 GWENDOLEN. I am engaged to Mr. Worthing, mamma.

(*They rise together.*)

LADY BRACKNELL. Pardon me, you are not engaged to any one. When you do become engaged to some one, I, or your father, should his health permit him, will inform you of the fact. An engagement should come on a young
530 girl as a surprise, pleasant or unpleasant, as the case may be. It is hardly a matter that she could be allowed to arrange for herself … And now I have a few questions to put to you, Mr. Worthing. While I am making these inquiries, you, Gwendolen, will wait for me below in
535 the carriage.

GWENDOLEN. (*Reproachfully.*) Mamma!

LADY BRACKNELL. In the carriage, Gwendolen!

(*Gwendolen goes to the door. She and Jack blow kisses to each other behind Lady Bracknell's back. Lady Bracknell looks vaguely about as if she could not understand what the noise was. Finally turns round.*)

Gwendolen, the carriage!

GWENDOLEN. Yes, mamma. (*Goes out, looking back at
540 Jack.*)

LADY BRACKNELL. (*Sitting down.*) You can take a seat, Mr. Worthing. (*Looks in her pocket for note-book and pencil.*)

JACK. Thank you, Lady Bracknell, I prefer standing.

545 LADY BRACKNELL. (*Pencil and note-book in hand.*) I feel bound to tell you that you are not down on my list of eligible young men, although I have the same list as the dear Duchess of Bolton has. We work together, in fact. However, I am quite ready to enter your name, should
550 your answers be what a really affectionate mother requires. Do you smoke?

JACK. Well, yes, I must admit I smoke.

LADY BRACKNELL. I am glad to hear it. A man should always have an occupation of some kind. There are far
555 too many idle men in London as it is. How old are you?

JACK. Twenty-nine.

LADY BRACKNELL. A very good age to be married at. I have always been of opinion that a man who desires to get married should know either everything or nothing.
560 Which do you know?

JACK. (*After some hesitation.*) I know nothing, Lady Bracknell.

LADY BRACKNELL.   I am pleased to hear it. I do not approve of anything that tampers with natural igno-
565 rance. Ignorance is like a delicate exotic fruit; touch it and the bloom is gone. The whole theory of modern education is radically unsound. Fortunately in England, at any rate, education produces no effect whatsoever. If it did, it would prove a serious danger to the upper
570 classes, and probably lead to acts of violence in Gros-venor Square.[1] What is your income?

JACK.   Between seven and eight thousand a year.

LADY BRACKNELL.   (*Makes a note in her book.*) In land, or in investments?

575 JACK.   In investments, chiefly.

LADY BRACKNELL.   That is satisfactory. What between the duties[2] expected of one during one's lifetime, and the duties exacted from one after one's death, land has ceased to be either a profit or a pleasure. It gives one
580 position, and prevents one from keeping it up. That's all that can be said about land.

JACK.   I have a country house with some land, of course, attached to it, about fifteen hundred acres, I believe; but I don't depend on that for my real income. In fact, as far
585 as I can make out, the poachers are the only people who make anything out of it.

LADY BRACKNELL.   A country house! How many bed-rooms? Well, that point can be cleared up afterwards. You have a town house, I hope? A girl with a simple,
590 unspoiled nature, like Gwendolen, could hardly be expected to reside in the country.

JACK.   Well, I own a house in Belgrave Square, but it is let by the year to Lady Bloxham. Of course, I can get it back whenever I like, at six months' notice.

595 LADY BRACKNELL.   Lady Bloxham? I don't know her.

JACK.   Oh, she goes about very little. She is a lady consid-erably advanced in years.

LADY BRACKNELL.   Ah, nowadays that is no guarantee of respectability of character. What number in Belgrave
600 Square?

JACK.   149.

LADY BRACKNELL.   (*Shaking her head.*) The unfashion-able side. I thought there was something. However, that could easily be altered.

605 JACK.   Do you mean the fashion, or the side?

LADY BRACKNELL.   (*Sternly.*) Both, if necessary, I pre-sume. What are your politics?

JACK.   Well, I am afraid I really have none. I am a Liberal Unionist.[3]

610 LADY BRACKNELL.   Oh, they count as Tories. They dine with us. Or come in the evening, at any rate. Now to minor matters. Are your parents living?

JACK.   I have lost both my parents.

LADY BRACKNELL.   To lose one parent, Mr. Worthing,
615 may be regarded as a misfortune; to lose both looks like carelessness. Who was your father? He was evidently a man of some wealth. Was he born in what the Radical papers call the purple of commerce,[4] or did he rise from the ranks of the aristocracy?

620 JACK.   I am afraid I really don't know. The fact is, Lady Bracknell, I said I had lost my parents. It would be nearer the truth to say that my parents seem to have lost me … I don't actually know who I am by birth. I was … well, I was found.

625 LADY BRACKNELL.   Found!

JACK.   The late Mr. Thomas Cardew, an old gentleman of a very charitable and kindly disposition, found me, and gave me the name of Worthing, because he hap-pened to have a first-class ticket for Worthing in his
630 pocket at the time. Worthing is a place in Sussex. It is a seaside resort.

LADY BRACKNELL.   Where did the charitable gentleman who had a first-class ticket for this seaside resort find you?

635 JACK.   (*Gravely.*) In a hand-bag.

LADY BRACKNELL.   A hand-bag?

JACK.   (*Very seriously.*) Yes, Lady Bracknell. I was in a hand-bag—a somewhat large, black leather hand-bag, with handles to it—an ordinary hand-bag in fact.

640 LADY BRACKNELL.   In what locality did this Mr. James, or Thomas, Cardew come across this ordinary hand-bag?

JACK.   In the cloak-room at Victoria Station. It was given

---

1 *Grosvenor Square* Located in a fashionable part of central London.

2 *duties* Taxes.

3 *Liberal Unionist* The Liberal Unionists, who in 1886 had broken away from the Liberal party in reaction to Prime Minister William Gladstone's support for Irish Home Rule, occupied the political center between the two large parties, the Liberals and the Conservatives.

4 *Was he born … the purple of commerce* I.e., was he born into a wealthy merchant or trading family. (The color purple is tradition-ally associated with royalty.)

to him in mistake for his own.

LADY BRACKNELL. The cloak-room at Victoria Station?

645 JACK. Yes. The Brighton line.

LADY BRACKNELL. The line is immaterial. Mr. Worthing, I confess I feel somewhat bewildered by what you have just told me. To be born, or at any rate bred, in a hand-bag, whether it had handles or not, seems to me to 650 display a contempt for the ordinary decencies of family life that reminds one of the worst excesses of the French Revolution. And I presume you know what that unfortunate movement led to? As for the particular locality in which the hand-bag was found, a cloak-room at a 655 railway station might serve to conceal a social indiscretion— has probably, indeed, been used for that purpose before now—but it could hardly be regarded as an assured basis for a recognised position in good society.

JACK. May I ask you then what you would advise me to 660 do? I need hardly say I would do anything in the world to ensure Gwendolen's happiness.

LADY BRACKNELL. I would strongly advise you, Mr. Worthing, to try and acquire some relations as soon as possible, and to make a definite effort to produce at any 665 rate one parent, of either sex, before the season[1] is quite over.

JACK. Well, I don't see how I could possibly manage to do that. I can produce the hand-bag at any moment. It is in my dressing-room at home. I really think that 670 should satisfy you, Lady Bracknell.

LADY BRACKNELL. Me, sir! What has it to do with me? You can hardly imagine that I and Lord Bracknell would dream of allowing our only daughter—a girl brought up with the utmost care—to marry into a 675 cloak-room, and form an alliance with a parcel? Good morning, Mr. Worthing!

(*Lady Bracknell sweeps out in majestic indignation.*)

JACK. Good morning! (*Algernon, from the other room, strikes up the Wedding March. Jack looks perfectly furious,* 680 *and goes to the door.*) For goodness' sake don't play that ghastly tune, Algy. How idiotic you are!

(*The music stops and Algernon enters cheerily.*)

ALGERNON. Didn't it go off all right, old boy? You don't mean to say Gwendolen refused you? I know it is a way she has. She is always refusing people. I think it is 685 most ill-natured of her.

JACK. Oh, Gwendolen is as right as a trivet.[2] As far as she is concerned, we are engaged. Her mother is perfectly unbearable. Never met such a Gorgon[3] ... I don't really know what a Gorgon is like, but I am quite sure that 690 Lady Bracknell is one. In any case, she is a monster, without being a myth, which is rather unfair ... I beg your pardon, Algy, I suppose I shouldn't talk about your own aunt in that way before you.

ALGERNON. My dear boy, I love hearing my relations 695 abused. It is the only thing that makes me put up with them at all. Relations are simply a tedious pack of people, who haven't got the remotest knowledge of how to live, nor the smallest instinct about when to die.

JACK. Oh, that is nonsense!

700 ALGERNON. It isn't!

JACK. Well, I won't argue about the matter. You always want to argue about things.

ALGERNON. That is exactly what things were originally made for.

705 JACK. Upon my word, if I thought that, I'd shoot myself ... (*A pause.*) You don't think there is any chance of Gwendolen becoming like her mother in about a hundred and fifty years, do you, Algy?

ALGERNON. All women become like their mothers. That 710 is their tragedy. No man does. That's his.

JACK. Is that clever?

ALGERNON. It is perfectly phrased! and quite as true as any observation in civilized life should be.

JACK. I am sick to death of cleverness. Everybody is 715 clever nowadays. You can't go anywhere without meeting clever people. The thing has become an absolute public nuisance. I wish to goodness we had a few fools left.

ALGERNON. We have.

1   *the season* The London social season, which ran while Parliament was sitting. Many wealthy families spent the rest of the year at their country homes.

2   *as right as a trivet* Proverbial expression indicating stability (a trivet is a three-footed stand or support).

3   *Gorgon* In Greek mythology the three Gorgons are sisters who have repulsive features (including snakes growing out of their heads instead of hair); anyone who looks at them turns into stone.

JACK. I should extremely like to meet them. What do they talk about?

ALGERNON. The fools? Oh! about the clever people, of course.

JACK. What fools!

ALGERNON. By the way, did you tell Gwendolen the truth about your being Ernest in town, and Jack in the country?

JACK. (*In a very patronising manner.*) My dear fellow, the truth isn't quite the sort of thing one tells to a nice, sweet, refined girl. What extraordinary ideas you have about the way to behave to a woman!

ALGERNON. The only way to behave to a woman is to make love to her, if she is pretty, and to some one else, if she is plain.

JACK. Oh, that is nonsense.

ALGERNON. What about your brother? What about the profligate Ernest?

JACK. Oh, before the end of the week I shall have got rid of him. I'll say he died in Paris of apoplexy.[1] Lots of people die of apoplexy, quite suddenly, don't they?

ALGERNON. Yes, but it's hereditary, my dear fellow. It's a sort of thing that runs in families. You had much better say a severe chill.

JACK. You are sure a severe chill isn't hereditary, or anything of that kind?

ALGERNON. Of course it isn't!

JACK. Very well, then. My poor brother Ernest is carried off suddenly, in Paris, by a severe chill. That gets rid of him.

ALGERNON. But I thought you said that … Miss Cardew was a little too much interested in your poor brother Ernest? Won't she feel his loss a good deal?

JACK. Oh, that is all right. Cecily is not a silly romantic girl, I am glad to say. She has got a capital appetite, goes on long walks, and pays no attention at all to her lessons.

ALGERNON. I would rather like to see Cecily.

JACK. I will take very good care you never do. She is excessively pretty, and she is only just eighteen.

ALGERNON. Have you told Gwendolen yet that you have an excessively pretty ward who is only just eighteen?

JACK. Oh! one doesn't blurt these things out to people. Cecily and Gwendolen are perfectly certain to be extremely great friends. I'll bet you anything you like that half an hour after they have met, they will be calling each other sister.

ALGERNON. Women only do that when they have called each other a lot of other things first. Now, my dear boy, if we want to get a good table at Willis's, we really must go and dress. Do you know it is nearly seven?

JACK. (*Irritably.*) Oh! It always is nearly seven.

ALGERNON. Well, I'm hungry.

JACK. I never knew you when you weren't …

ALGERNON. What shall we do after dinner? Go to a theatre?

JACK. Oh no! I loathe listening.

ALGERNON. Well, let us go to the Club?

JACK. Oh, no! I hate talking.

ALGERNON. Well, we might trot round to the Empire[2] at ten?

JACK. Oh, no! I can't bear looking at things. It is so silly.

ALGERNON. Well, what shall we do?

JACK. Nothing!

ALGERNON. It is awfully hard work doing nothing. However, I don't mind hard work where there is no definite object of any kind.

(*Enter Lane.*)

LANE. Miss Fairfax.

(*Enter Gwendolen. Lane goes out.*)

ALGERNON. Gwendolen, upon my word!

GWENDOLEN. Algy, kindly turn your back. I have something very particular to say to Mr. Worthing.

ALGERNON. Really, Gwendolen, I don't think I can allow this at all.

GWENDOLEN. Algy, you always adopt a strictly immoral attitude towards life. You are not quite old enough to do that. (*Algernon retires to the fireplace.*)

JACK. My own darling!

GWENDOLEN. Ernest, we may never be married. From the expression on mamma's face I fear we never shall. Few parents nowadays pay any regard to what their children say to them. The old-fashioned respect for the young is fast dying out. Whatever influence I ever had

---

[1]   *apoplexy* Stroke.

[2]   *the Empire* Theater that often featured risqué variety shows.

over mamma, I lost at the age of three. But although she may prevent us from becoming man and wife, and I may marry some one else, and marry often, nothing that she can possibly do can alter my eternal devotion to you.

805

JACK. Dear Gwendolen!

GWENDOLEN. The story of your romantic origin, as related to me by mamma, with unpleasing comments, has naturally stirred the deeper fibres of my nature. Your Christian name has an irresistible fascination. The simplicity of your character makes you exquisitely incomprehensible to me. Your town address at the Albany[1] I have. What is your address in the country?

810

JACK. The Manor House, Woolton, Hertfordshire.

(Algernon, who has been carefully listening, smiles to himself, and writes the address on his shirt-cuff. Then picks up the Railway Guide.)

815

GWENDOLEN. There is a good postal service, I suppose? It may be necessary to do something desperate. That of course will require serious consideration. I will communicate with you daily.

JACK. My own one!

820

GWENDOLEN. How long do you remain in town?

JACK. Till Monday.

GWENDOLEN. Good! Algy, you may turn round now.

ALGERNON. Thanks, I've turned round already.

GWENDOLEN. You may also ring the bell.

825

JACK. You will let me see you to your carriage, my own darling?

GWENDOLEN. Certainly.

JACK. *(To Lane, who now enters.)* I will see Miss Fairfax out.

830

LANE. Yes, sir. *(Jack and Gwendolen go off.)*

(Lane presents several letters on a salver to Algernon. It is to be surmised that they are bills, as Algernon, after looking at the envelopes, tears them up.)

ALGERNON. A glass of sherry, Lane.

LANE. Yes, sir.

ALGERNON. To-morrow, Lane, I'm going Bunburying.

LANE. Yes, sir.

835

ALGERNON. I shall probably not be back till Monday.

You can put up my dress clothes, my smoking jacket, and all the Bunbury suits …

LANE. Yes, sir. *(Handing sherry.)*

ALGERNON. I hope to-morrow will be a fine day, Lane.

840

LANE. It never is, sir.

ALGERNON. Lane, you're a perfect pessimist.

LANE. I do my best to give satisfaction, sir.

(Enter Jack. Lane goes off.)

JACK. There's a sensible, intellectual girl! the only girl I ever cared for in my life. *(Algernon is laughing immoder-*

845

ately.) What on earth are you so amused at?

ALGERNON. Oh, I'm a little anxious about poor Bunbury, that is all.

JACK. If you don't take care, your friend Bunbury will get you into a serious scrape some day.

850

ALGERNON. I love scrapes. They are the only things that are never serious.

JACK. Oh, that's nonsense, Algy. You never talk anything but nonsense.

ALGERNON. Nobody ever does.

(Jack looks indignantly at him, and leaves the room. Algernon lights a cigarette, reads his shirt-cuff, and smiles.)

ACT DROP

ACT 2

SCENE

(Garden at the Manor House. A flight of grey stone steps leads up to the house. The garden, an old-fashioned one, full of roses. Time of year, July. Basket chairs, and a table covered with books, are set under a large yew-tree. Miss Prism discovered seated at the table. Cecily is at the back watering flowers.)

MISS PRISM. *(Calling.)* Cecily, Cecily! Surely such a utilitarian occupation as the watering of flowers is rather Moulton's duty than yours? Especially at a moment when intellectual pleasures await you. Your German grammar is on the table. Pray open it at page fifteen. We

5

will repeat yesterday's lesson.

CECILY. *(Coming over very slowly.)* But I don't like

---

1   the Albany Fashionable men's club in London.

German. It isn't at all a becoming language. I know perfectly well that I look quite plain after my German lesson.

MISS PRISM.   Child, you know how anxious your guardian is that you should improve yourself in every way. He laid particular stress on your German, as he was leaving for town yesterday. Indeed, he always lays stress on your German when he is leaving for town.

CECILY.   Dear Uncle Jack is so very serious! Sometimes he is so serious that I think he cannot be quite well.

MISS PRISM.   (*Drawing herself up.*) Your guardian enjoys the best of health, and his gravity of demeanour is especially to be commended in one so comparatively young as he is. I know no one who has a higher sense of duty and responsibility.

CECILY.   I suppose that is why he often looks a little bored when we three are together.

MISS PRISM.   Cecily! I am surprised at you. Mr. Worthing has many troubles in his life. Idle merriment and triviality would be out of place in his conversation. You must remember his constant anxiety about that unfortunate young man his brother.

CECILY.   I wish Uncle Jack would allow that unfortunate young man, his brother, to come down here sometimes. We might have a good influence over him, Miss Prism. I am sure you certainly would. You know German, and geology, and things of that kind influence a man very much. (*Cecily begins to write in her diary.*)

MISS PRISM.   (*Shaking her head.*) I do not think that even I could produce any effect on a character that according to his own brother's admission is irretrievably weak and vacillating. Indeed I am not sure that I would desire to reclaim him. I am not in favour of this modern mania for turning bad people into good people at a moment's notice. As a man sows so let him reap.[1] You must put away your diary, Cecily. I really don't see why you should keep a diary at all.

CECILY.   I keep a diary in order to enter the wonderful secrets of my life. If I didn't write them down, I should probably forget all about them.

MISS PRISM.   Memory, my dear Cecily, is the diary that we all carry about with us.

CECILY.   Yes, but it usually chronicles the things that have never happened, and couldn't possibly have happened. I believe that Memory is responsible for nearly all the three-volume novels that Mudie sends us.[2]

MISS PRISM.   Do not speak slightingly of the three-volume novel, Cecily. I wrote one myself in earlier days.

CECILY.   Did you really, Miss Prism? How wonderfully clever you are! I hope it did not end happily? I don't like novels that end happily. They depress me so much.

MISS PRISM.   The good ended happily, and the bad unhappily. That is what Fiction means.

CECILY.   I suppose so. But it seems very unfair. And was your novel ever published?

MISS PRISM.   Alas! no. The manuscript unfortunately was abandoned. (*Cecily starts.*) I use the word in the sense of lost or mislaid. To your work, child, these speculations are profitless.

CECILY.   (*Smiling.*) But I see dear Dr. Chasuble coming up through the garden.

MISS PRISM.   (*Rising and advancing.*) Dr. Chasuble! This is indeed a pleasure.

(*Enter Canon Chasuble.*)

CHASUBLE.   And how are we this morning? Miss Prism, you are, I trust, well?

CECILY.   Miss Prism has just been complaining of a slight headache. I think it would do her so much good to have a short stroll with you in the Park, Dr. Chasuble.

MISS PRISM.   Cecily, I have not mentioned anything about a headache.

CECILY.   No, dear Miss Prism, I know that, but I felt instinctively that you had a headache. Indeed I was thinking about that, and not about my German lesson, when the Rector came in.

CHASUBLE.   I hope, Cecily, you are not inattentive.

CECILY.   Oh, I am afraid I am.

CHASUBLE.   That is strange. Were I fortunate enough to be Miss Prism's pupil, I would hang upon her lips. (*Miss Prism glares.*) I spoke metaphorically.—My metaphor was drawn from bees. Ahem! Mr. Worthing, I suppose, has not returned from town yet?

---

1   *As a man sows so let him reap*   Galatians 6.7: "whatsoever a man soweth, that shall he also reap."

2   *nearly all ... Mudie sends us*   Commercial lending libraries of the time, such as Mudie's, specialized in lending novels that were published in three volumes.

MISS PRISM. We do not expect him till Monday after-
90   noon.

CHASUBLE. Ah yes, he usually likes to spend his Sunday in London. He is not one of those whose sole aim is enjoyment, as, by all accounts, that unfortunate young man his brother seems to be. But I must not disturb
95   Egeria and her pupil any longer.

MISS PRISM. Egeria? My name is Lætitia, Doctor.

CHASUBLE. (*Bowing.*) A classical allusion merely, drawn from the Pagan authors.[1] I shall see you both no doubt at Evensong?[2]

100 MISS PRISM. I think, dear Doctor, I will have a stroll with you. I find I have a headache after all, and a walk might do it good.

CHASUBLE. With pleasure, Miss Prism, with pleasure. We might go as far as the schools and back.

105 MISS PRISM. That would be delightful. Cecily, you will read your Political Economy in my absence. The chapter on the Fall of the Rupee you may omit. It is somewhat too sensational. Even these metallic problems have their melodramatic side.[3]

(*Goes down the garden with Dr. Chasuble.*)

110 CECILY. (*Picks up books and throws them back on table.*) Horrid Political Economy! Horrid Geography! Horrid, horrid German!

(*Enter Merriman with a card on a salver.*)

MERRIMAN. Mr. Ernest Worthing has just driven over from the station. He has brought his luggage with him.

115 CECILY. (*Takes the card and reads it.*) "Mr. Ernest Worthing, B. 4, The Albany, W." Uncle Jack's brother! Did you tell him Mr. Worthing was in town?

MERRIMAN. Yes, Miss. He seemed very much disappointed. I mentioned that you and Miss Prism were in

120 the garden. He said he was anxious to speak to you privately for a moment.

CECILY. Ask Mr. Ernest Worthing to come here. I suppose you had better talk to the housekeeper about a room for him.

125 MERRIMAN. Yes, Miss.

(*Merriman goes off.*)

CECILY. I have never met any really wicked person before. I feel rather frightened. I am so afraid he will look just like every one else. (*Enter Algernon, very gay and debonair.*) He does!

130 ALGERNON. (*Raising his hat.*) You are my little cousin Cecily, I'm sure.

CECILY. You are under some strange mistake. I am not little. In fact, I believe I am more than usually tall for my age. (*Algernon is rather taken aback.*) But I am your
135   cousin Cecily. You, I see from your card, are Uncle Jack's brother, my cousin Ernest, my wicked cousin Ernest.

ALGERNON. Oh! I am not really wicked at all, cousin Cecily. You mustn't think that I am wicked.

140 CECILY. If you are not, then you have certainly been deceiving us all in a very inexcusable manner. I hope you have not been leading a double life, pretending to be wicked and being really good all the time. That would be hypocrisy.

145 ALGERNON. (*Looks at her in amazement.*) Oh! Of course I have been rather reckless.

CECILY. I am glad to hear it.

ALGERNON. In fact, now you mention the subject, I have been very bad in my own small way.

150 CECILY. I don't think you should be so proud of that, though I am sure it must have been very pleasant.

ALGERNON. It is much pleasanter being here with you.

CECILY. I can't understand how you are here at all. Uncle Jack won't be back till Monday afternoon.

155 ALGERNON. That is a great disappointment. I am obliged to go up by the first train on Monday morning. I have a business appointment that I am anxious ... to miss!

CECILY. Couldn't you miss it anywhere but in London?

160 ALGERNON. No: the appointment is in London.

---

1   *A classical allusion ... pagan authors* In Roman mythology, the nymph Egeria taught Numa, the second King of Rome, the lessons of wisdom and law which he then used to found the institutions of Rome.

2   *Evensong* The evening service in the Anglican church (and various other Christian denominations).

3   *The chapter ... melodramatic side* The rupee (India's currency) declined dramatically in the early 1890s as a result of a variety of disasters, including an outbreak of plague.

CECILY.   Well, I know, of course, how important it is not
to keep a business engagement, if one wants to retain
any sense of the beauty of life, but still I think you had
better wait till Uncle Jack arrives. I know he wants to
165 speak to you about your emigrating.

ALGERNON.   About my what?

CECILY.   Your emigrating. He has gone up to buy your
outfit.

ALGERNON.   I certainly wouldn't let Jack buy my outfit.
170 He has no taste in neckties at all.

CECILY.   I don't think you will require neckties. Uncle
Jack is sending you to Australia.[1]

ALGERNON.   Australia! I'd sooner die.

CECILY.   Well, he said at dinner on Wednesday night,
175 that you would have to choose between this world, the
next world, and Australia.

ALGERNON.   Oh, well! The accounts I have received of
Australia and the next world are not particularly encouraging. This world is good enough for me, cousin Cecily.

180 CECILY.   Yes, but are you good enough for it?

ALGERNON.   I'm afraid I'm not that. That is why I want
you to reform me. You might make that your mission,
if you don't mind, cousin Cecily.

CECILY.   I'm afraid I've no time, this afternoon.

185 ALGERNON.   Well, would you mind my reforming
myself this afternoon?

CECILY.   It is rather Quixotic of you. But I think you
should try.

ALGERNON.   I will. I feel better already.

190 CECILY.   You are looking a little worse.

ALGERNON.   That is because I am hungry.

CECILY.   How thoughtless of me. I should have remembered that when one is going to lead an entirely new life,
one requires regular and wholesome meals. Won't you
195 come in?

ALGERNON.   Thank you. Might I have a buttonhole[2]
first? I never have any appetite unless I have a buttonhole first.

CECILY.   A Maréchal Niel?[3] (Picks up scissors.)

200 ALGERNON.   No, I'd sooner have a pink rose.

CECILY.   Why? (Cuts a flower.)

ALGERNON.   Because you are like a pink rose, Cousin
Cecily.

CECILY.   I don't think it can be right for you to talk to
205 me like that. Miss Prism never says such things to me.

ALGERNON.   Then Miss Prism is a short-sighted old lady.
(Cecily puts the rose in his buttonhole.) You are the
prettiest girl I ever saw.

CECILY.   Miss Prism says that all good looks are a snare.

210 ALGERNON.   They are a snare that every sensible man
would like to be caught in.

CECILY.   Oh, I don't think I would care to catch a
sensible man. I shouldn't know what to talk to him
about.

(They pass into the house. Miss Prism and Dr. Chasuble
return.)

215 MISS PRISM.   You are too much alone, dear Dr. Chasuble. You should get married. A misanthrope I can
understand—a womanthrope,[4] never!

CHASUBLE.   (With a scholar's shudder.) Believe me, I do
not deserve so neologistic a phrase. The precept as well
220 as the practice of the Primitive Church[5] was distinctly
against matrimony.

MISS PRISM.   (Sententiously.) That is obviously the reason
why the Primitive Church has not lasted up to the
present day. And you do not seem to realize, dear
225 Doctor, that by persistently remaining single, a man
converts himself into a permanent public temptation.
Men should be more careful; this very celibacy leads
weaker vessels astray.

CHASUBLE.   But is a man not equally attractive when
230 married?

MISS PRISM.   No married man is ever attractive except to
his wife.

CHASUBLE.   And often, I've been told, not even to her.

MISS PRISM.   That depends on the intellectual sympa-
235 thies of the woman. Maturity can always be depended
on. Ripeness can be trusted. Young women are green.
(Dr. Chasuble starts.) I spoke horticulturally. My metaphor was drawn from fruits. But where is Cecily?

---

[1]   Australia   A former penal colony, at the time still considered to
be largely composed of wilderness.

[2]   buttonhole   Boutonniere, flower for one's lapel.

[3]   Maréchal Niel   Variety of yellow rose.

[4]   misanthrope … womanthrope   The correct word for someone
who hates women is a "misogynist"; a "misanthrope" is someone
who hates all humanity.

[5]   Primitive Church   Early Christian church.

CHASUBLE. Perhaps she followed us to the schools.

(*Enter Jack slowly from the back of the garden. He is dressed in the deepest mourning, with crepe hatband and black gloves.*)

240 MISS PRISM. Mr. Worthing!

CHASUBLE. Mr. Worthing?

MISS PRISM. This is indeed a surprise. We did not look for you till Monday afternoon.

JACK. (*Shakes Miss Prism's hand in a tragic manner.*) I
245 have returned sooner than I expected. Dr. Chasuble, I hope you are well?

CHASUBLE. Dear Mr. Worthing, I trust this garb of woe does not betoken some terrible calamity?

JACK. My brother.

250 MISS PRISM. More shameful debts and extravagance?

CHASUBLE. Still leading his life of pleasure?

JACK. (*Shaking his head.*) Dead!

CHASUBLE. Your brother Ernest dead?

JACK. Quite dead.

255 MISS PRISM. What a lesson for him! I trust he will profit by it.

CHASUBLE. Mr. Worthing, I offer you my sincere condolence. You have at least the consolation of knowing that you were always the most generous and forgiv-
260 ing of brothers.

JACK. Poor Ernest! He had many faults, but it is a sad, sad blow.

CHASUBLE. Very sad indeed. Were you with him at the end?

265 JACK. No. He died abroad; in Paris, in fact. I had a telegram last night from the manager of the Grand Hotel.

CHASUBLE. Was the cause of death mentioned?

JACK. A severe chill, it seems.

270 MISS PRISM. As a man sows, so shall he reap.

CHASUBLE. (*Raising his hand.*) Charity, dear Miss Prism, charity! None of us are perfect. I myself am peculiarly susceptible to draughts. Will the interment take place here?

275 JACK. No. He seems to have expressed a desire to be buried in Paris.

CHASUBLE. In Paris! (*Shakes his head.*) I fear that hardly points to any very serious state of mind at the last. You

would no doubt wish me to make some slight allusion
280 to this tragic domestic affliction next Sunday. (*Jack presses his hand convulsively.*) My sermon on the meaning of the manna in the wilderness[1] can be adapted to almost any occasion, joyful, or, as in the present case, distressing. (*All sigh.*) I have preached it at harvest
285 celebrations, christenings, confirmations,[2] on days of humiliation and festal days. The last time I delivered it was in the Cathedral, as a charity sermon on behalf of the Society for the Prevention of Discontent among the Upper Orders. The Bishop, who was present, was much
290 struck by some of the analogies I drew.

JACK. Ah! that reminds me, you mentioned christenings I think, Dr. Chasuble? I suppose you know how to christen all right? (*Dr. Chasuble looks astounded.*) I mean, of course, you are continually christening, aren't you?

295 MISS PRISM. It is, I regret to say, one of the Rector's most constant duties in this parish. I have often spoken to the poorer classes on the subject. But they don't seem to know what thrift is.

CHASUBLE. But is there any particular infant in whom
300 you are interested, Mr. Worthing? Your brother was, I believe, unmarried, was he not?

JACK. Oh yes.

MISS PRISM. (*Bitterly.*) People who live entirely for pleasure usually are.

305 JACK. But it is not for any child, dear Doctor. I am very fond of children. No! the fact is, I would like to be christened myself, this afternoon, if you have nothing better to do.

CHASUBLE. But surely, Mr. Worthing, you have been
310 christened already?

JACK. I don't remember anything about it.

CHASUBLE. But have you any grave doubts on the subject?

JACK. I certainly intend to have. Of course I don't know
315 if the thing would bother you in any way, or if you think I am a little too old now.

CHASUBLE. Not at all. The sprinkling, and, indeed, the

---

[1] *manna in the wilderness* See Exodus 16.

[2] *christenings, confirmations* Whereas a christening formally admits a person to the Christian church through baptism (usually as an infant), in many Christian denominations a person's standing as a full member of the church must be confirmed at a later ceremony (typically as a young adult).

immersion of adults is a perfectly canonical practice.

JACK. Immersion!

320 CHASUBLE. You need have no apprehensions. Sprinkling is all that is necessary, or indeed I think advisable. Our weather is so changeable. At what hour would you wish the ceremony performed?

JACK. Oh, I might trot round about five if that would

325 suit you.

CHASUBLE. Perfectly, perfectly! In fact I have two similar ceremonies to perform at that time. A case of twins that occurred recently in one of the outlying cottages on your own estate. Poor Jenkins the carter,[1] a

330 most hard-working man.

JACK. Oh! I don't see much fun in being christened along with other babies. It would be childish. Would half-past five do?

CHASUBLE. Admirably! Admirably! (*Takes out watch.*)

335 And now, dear Mr. Worthing, I will not intrude any longer into a house of sorrow. I would merely beg you not to be too much bowed down by grief. What seem to us bitter trials are often blessings in disguise.

MISS PRISM. This seems to me a blessing of an extremely

340 obvious kind.

(*Enter Cecily from the house.*)

CECILY. Uncle Jack! Oh, I am pleased to see you back. But what horrid clothes you have got on! Do go and change them.

345 MISS PRISM. Cecily!

CHASUBLE. My child! my child!

(*Cecily goes towards Jack; he kisses her brow in a melancholy manner.*)

CECILY. What is the matter, Uncle Jack? Do look happy! You look as if you had toothache, and I have got such a surprise for you. Who do you think is in the dining-

350 room? Your brother!

JACK. Who?

CECILY. Your brother Ernest. He arrived about half an hour ago.

JACK. What nonsense! I haven't got a brother.

355 CECILY. Oh, don't say that. However badly he may have

behaved to you in the past he is still your brother. You couldn't be so heartless as to disown him. I'll tell him to come out. And you will shake hands with him, won't you, Uncle Jack? (*Runs back into the house.*)

360 CHASUBLE. These are very joyful tidings.

MISS PRISM. After we had all been resigned to his loss, his sudden return seems to me peculiarly distressing.

JACK. My brother is in the dining-room? I don't know what it all means. I think it is perfectly absurd.

(*Enter Algernon and Cecily hand in hand. They come slowly up to Jack.*)

365 JACK. Good heavens! (*Motions Algernon away.*)

ALGERNON. Brother John, I have come down from town to tell you that I am very sorry for all the trouble I have given you, and that I intend to lead a better life in the future. (*Jack glares at him and does not take his*

370 *hand.*)

CECILY. Uncle Jack, you are not going to refuse your own brother's hand?

JACK. Nothing will induce me to take his hand. I think his coming down here disgraceful. He knows perfectly

375 well why.

CECILY. Uncle Jack, do be nice. There is some good in every one. Ernest has just been telling me about his poor invalid friend Mr. Bunbury whom he goes to visit so often. And surely there must be much good in one who

380 is kind to an invalid, and leaves the pleasures of London to sit by a bed of pain.

JACK. Oh! he has been talking about Bunbury, has he?

CECILY. Yes, he has told me all about poor Mr. Bunbury, and his terrible state of health.

385 JACK. Bunbury! Well, I won't have him talk to you about Bunbury or about anything else. It is enough to drive one perfectly frantic.

ALGERNON. Of course I admit that the faults were all on my side. But I must say that I think that Brother John's

390 coldness to me is peculiarly painful. I expected a more enthusiastic welcome, especially considering it is the first time I have come here.

CECILY. Uncle Jack, if you don't shake hands with Ernest I will never forgive you.

395 JACK. Never forgive me?

CECILY. Never, never, never!

---

[1] *carter* Cart driver.

JACK. Well, this is the last time I shall ever do it. (*Shakes hands with Algernon and glares.*)

CHASUBLE. It's pleasant, is it not, to see so perfect a
400 reconciliation? I think we might leave the two brothers
together.

MISS PRISM. Cecily, you will come with us.

CECILY. Certainly, Miss Prism. My little task of reconciliation is over.

405 CHASUBLE. You have done a beautiful action to-day,
dear child.

MISS PRISM. We must not be premature in our judgments.

CECILY. I feel very happy.

(*They all go off except Jack and Algernon.*)

410 JACK. You young scoundrel, Algy, you must get out of
this place as soon as possible. I don't allow any
Bunburying here.

(*Enter Merriman.*)

MERRIMAN. I have put Mr. Ernest's things in the room
next to yours, sir. I suppose that is all right?

415 JACK. What?

MERRIMAN. Mr. Ernest's luggage, sir. I have unpacked
it and put it in the room next to your own.

JACK. His luggage?

MERRIMAN. Yes, sir. Three portmanteaus, a dressing-
420 case, two hat-boxes, and a large luncheon-basket.

ALGERNON. I am afraid I can't stay more than a week
this time.

JACK. Merriman, order the dog-cart[1] at once. Mr. Ernest
has been suddenly called back to town.

425 MERRIMAN. Yes, sir. (*Goes back into the house.*)

ALGERNON. What a fearful liar you are, Jack. I have not
been called back to town at all.

JACK. Yes, you have.

ALGERNON. I haven't heard any one call me.

430 JACK. Your duty as a gentleman calls you back.

ALGERNON. My duty as a gentleman has never interfered with my pleasures in the smallest degree.

---

[1] *dog-cart* Small horse-drawn carriage in which the occupants
would sit back-to-back; a box for conveying hunting dogs was also
typically part of the contraption.

JACK. I can quite understand that.

ALGERNON. Well, Cecily is a darling.

435 JACK. You are not to talk of Miss Cardew like that. I
don't like it.

ALGERNON. Well, I don't like your clothes. You look
perfectly ridiculous in them. Why on earth don't you go
up and change? It is perfectly childish to be in deep
440 mourning for a man who is actually staying for a whole
week with you in your house as a guest. I call it grotesque.

JACK. You are certainly not staying with me for a whole
week as a guest or anything else. You have got to leave
445 … by the four-five train.

ALGERNON. I certainly won't leave you so long as you
are in mourning. It would be most unfriendly. If I were
in mourning you would stay with me, I suppose. I
should think it very unkind if you didn't.

450 JACK. Well, will you go if I change my clothes?

ALGERNON. Yes, if you are not too long. I never saw
anybody take so long to dress, and with such little result.

JACK. Well, at any rate, that is better than being always
over-dressed as you are.

455 ALGERNON. If I am occasionally a little over-dressed, I
make up for it by being always immensely over-edu-
cated.

JACK. Your vanity is ridiculous, your conduct an outrage, and your presence in my garden utterly absurd.
460 However, you have got to catch the four-five, and I
hope you will have a pleasant journey back to town.
This Bunburying, as you call it, has not been a great
success for you. (*Goes into the house.*)

ALGERNON. I think it has been a great success. I'm in
465 love with Cecily, and that is everything.

(*Enter Cecily at the back of the garden. She picks up the
can and begins to water the flowers.*)

But I must see her before I go, and make arrangements
for another Bunbury. Ah, there she is.

CECILY. Oh, I merely came back to water the roses. I
thought you were with Uncle Jack.

470 ALGERNON. He's gone to order the dog-cart for me.

CECILY. Oh, is he going to take you for a nice drive?

ALGERNON. He's going to send me away.

CECILY. Then have we got to part?

ALGERNON.   I am afraid so. It's a very painful parting.

475 CECILY.   It is always painful to part from people whom one has known for a very brief space of time. The absence of old friends one can endure with equanimity. But even a momentary separation from anyone to whom one has just been introduced is almost unbear-
480 able.

ALGERNON.   Thank you.

(*Enter Merriman.*)

MERRIMAN.   The dog-cart is at the door, sir.

(*Algernon looks appealingly at Cecily.*)

CECILY.   It can wait, Merriman for … five minutes.

MERRIMAN.   Yes, Miss.

(*Exit Merriman.*)

ALGERNON.   I hope, Cecily, I shall not offend you if I
485 state quite frankly and openly that you seem to me to be in every way the visible personification of absolute perfection.

CECILY.   I think your frankness does you great credit, Ernest. If you will allow me, I will copy your remarks
490 into my diary. (*Goes over to table and begins writing in diary.*)

ALGERNON.   Do you really keep a diary? I'd give anything to look at it. May I?

CECILY.   Oh no. (*Puts her hand over it.*) You see, it is
495 simply a very young girl's record of her own thoughts and impressions, and consequently meant for publication. When it appears in volume form I hope you will order a copy. But pray, Ernest, don't stop. I delight in taking down from dictation. I have reached "absolute
500 perfection." You can go on. I am quite ready for more.

ALGERNON.   (*Somewhat taken aback.*) Ahem! Ahem!

CECILY.   Oh, don't cough, Ernest. When one is dictating one should speak fluently and not cough. Besides, I don't know how to spell a cough. (*Writes as Algernon
505 speaks.*)

ALGERNON.   (*Speaking very rapidly.*) Cecily, ever since I first looked upon your wonderful and incomparable beauty, I have dared to love you wildly, passionately,

devotedly, hopelessly.

510 CECILY.   I don't think that you should tell me that you love me wildly, passionately, devotedly, hopelessly. Hopelessly doesn't seem to make much sense, does it?

ALGERNON.   Cecily!

(*Enter Merriman.*)

MERRIMAN.   The dog-cart is waiting, sir.
515 ALGERNON.   Tell it to come round next week, at the same hour.

MERRIMAN.   (*Looks at Cecily, who makes no sign.*) Yes, sir.

(*Merriman retires.*)

CECILY.   Uncle Jack would be very much annoyed if he knew you were staying on till next week, at the same
520 hour.

ALGERNON.   Oh, I don't care about Jack. I don't care for anybody in the whole world but you. I love you, Cecily. You will marry me, won't you?

CECILY.   You silly boy! Of course. Why, we have been
525 engaged for the last three months.

ALGERNON.   For the last three months?

CECILY.   Yes, it will be exactly three months on Thursday.

ALGERNON.   But how did we become engaged?
530 CECILY.   Well, ever since dear Uncle Jack first confessed to us that he had a younger brother who was very wicked and bad, you of course have formed the chief topic of conversation between myself and Miss Prism. And of course a man who is much talked about is always
535 very attractive. One feels there must be something in him, after all. I daresay it was foolish of me, but I fell in love with you, Ernest.

ALGERNON.   Darling! And when was the engagement actually settled?
540 CECILY.   On the 14th of February last. Worn out by your entire ignorance of my existence, I determined to end the matter one way or the other, and after a long struggle with myself I accepted you under this dear old tree here. The next day I bought this little ring in your
545 name, and this is the little bangle with the true lover's knot I promised you always to wear.

ALGERNON.   Did I give you this? It's very pretty, isn't it?

CECILY. Yes, you've wonderfully good taste, Ernest. It's the excuse I've always given for your leading such a bad life. And this is the box in which I keep all your dear letters. (*Kneels at table, opens box, and produces letters tied up with blue ribbon.*)

ALGERNON. My letters! But, my own sweet Cecily, I have never written you any letters.

CECILY. You need hardly remind me of that, Ernest. I remember only too well that I was forced to write your letters for you. I wrote always three times a week, and sometimes oftener.

ALGERNON. Oh, do let me read them, Cecily?

CECILY. Oh, I couldn't possibly. They would make you far too conceited. (*Replaces box.*) The three you wrote me after I had broken off the engagement are so beautiful, and so badly spelled, that even now I can hardly read them without crying a little.

ALGERNON. But was our engagement ever broken off?

CECILY. Of course it was. On the 22nd of last March. You can see the entry if you like. (*Shows diary.*) "To-day I broke off my engagement with Ernest. I feel it is better to do so. The weather still continues charming."

ALGERNON. But why on earth did you break it off? What had I done? I had done nothing at all. Cecily, I am very much hurt indeed to hear you broke it off. Particularly when the weather was so charming.

CECILY. It would hardly have been a really serious engagement if it hadn't been broken off at least once. But I forgave you before the week was out.

ALGERNON. (*Crossing to her, and kneeling.*) What a perfect angel you are, Cecily.

CECILY. You dear romantic boy. (*He kisses her, she puts her fingers through his hair.*) I hope your hair curls naturally, does it?

ALGERNON. Yes, darling, with a little help from others.

CECILY. I am so glad.

ALGERNON. You'll never break off our engagement again, Cecily?

CECILY. I don't think I could break it off now that I have actually met you. Besides, of course, there is the question of your name.

ALGERNON. Yes, of course. (*Nervously.*)

CECILY. You must not laugh at me, darling, but it had always been a girlish dream of mine to love some one whose name was Ernest. (*Algernon rises, Cecily also.*) There is something in that name that seems to inspire absolute confidence. I pity any poor married woman whose husband is not called Ernest.

ALGERNON. But, my dear child, do you mean to say you could not love me if I had some other name?

CECILY. But what name?

ALGERNON. Oh, any name you like—Algernon—for instance …

CECILY. But I don't like the name of Algernon.

ALGERNON. Well, my own dear, sweet, loving little darling, I really can't see why you should object to the name of Algernon. It is not at all a bad name. In fact, it is rather an aristocratic name. Half of the chaps who get into the Bankruptcy Court are called Algernon. But seriously, Cecily … (*Moving to her*) … if my name was Algy, couldn't you love me?

CECILY. (*Rising.*) I might respect you, Ernest, I might admire your character, but I fear that I should not be able to give you my undivided attention.

ALGERNON. Ahem! Cecily! (*Picking up hat.*) Your Rector here is, I suppose, thoroughly experienced in the practice of all the rites and ceremonials of the Church?

CECILY. Oh, yes. Dr. Chasuble is a most learned man. He has never written a single book, so you can imagine how much he knows.

ALGERNON. I must see him at once on a most important christening—I mean on most important business.

CECILY. Oh!

ALGERNON. I shan't be away more than half an hour.

CECILY. Considering that we have been engaged since February the 14th, and that I only met you to-day for the first time, I think it is rather hard that you should leave me for so long a period as half an hour. Couldn't you make it twenty minutes?

ALGERNON. I'll be back in no time.

(*Kisses her and rushes down the garden.*)

CECILY. What an impetuous boy he is! I like his hair so much. I must enter his proposal in my diary.

(*Enter Merriman.*)

MERRIMAN. A Miss Fairfax has just called to see Mr. Worthing. On very important business, Miss Fairfax states.

CECILY. Isn't Mr. Worthing in his library?

MERRIMAN.   Mr. Worthing went over in the direction of
635   the Rectory some time ago.

CECILY.   Pray ask the lady to come out here; Mr. Worthing is sure to be back soon. And you can bring tea.

MERRIMAN. Yes, Miss. (*Goes out.*)

CECILY.   Miss Fairfax! I suppose one of the many good
640   elderly women who are associated with Uncle Jack in
some of his philanthropic work in London. I don't quite
like women who are interested in philanthropic work. I
think it is so forward of them.

(*Enter Merriman.*)

MERRIMAN.   Miss Fairfax.

(*Enter Gwendolen. Exit Merriman.*)

645   CECILY.   (*Advancing to meet her.*) Pray let me introduce
myself to you. My name is Cecily Cardew.

GWENDOLEN.   Cecily Cardew? (*Moving to her and
shaking hands.*) What a very sweet name! Something tells
me that we are going to be great friends. I like you
650   already more than I can say. My first impressions of
people are never wrong.

CECILY.   How nice of you to like me so much after we
have known each other such a comparatively short time.
Pray sit down.

655   GWENDOLEN.   (*Still standing up.*) I may call you Cecily,
may I not?

CECILY.   With pleasure!

GWENDOLEN.   And you will always call me Gwendolen,
won't you?

660   CECILY.   If you wish.

GWENDOLEN.   Then that is all quite settled, is it not?

CECILY.   I hope so. (*A pause. They both sit down together.*)

GWENDOLEN.   Perhaps this might be a favourable
opportunity for my mentioning who I am. My father is
665   Lord Bracknell. You have never heard of Papa, I suppose?

CECILY.   I don't think so.

GWENDOLEN.   Outside the family circle, Papa, I am glad
to say, is entirely unknown. I think that is quite as it
670   should be. The home seems to me to be the proper

sphere for the man. And certainly once a man begins to
neglect his domestic duties he becomes painfully effeminate, does he not? And I don't like that. It makes men
so very attractive. Cecily, Mamma, whose views on
675   education are remarkably strict, has brought me up to be
extremely short-sighted; it is part of her system; so do
you mind my looking at you through my glasses?

CECILY.   Oh! not at all, Gwendolen. I am very fond of
being looked at.

680   GWENDOLEN.   (*After examining Cecily carefully through
a lorgnette.*) You are here on a short visit, I suppose.

CECILY.   Oh no! I live here.

GWENDOLEN.   (*Severely.*) Really? Your mother, no
doubt, or some female relative of advanced years, resides
685   here also?

CECILY.   Oh no! I have no mother, nor, in fact, any
relations.

GWENDOLEN.   Indeed?

CECILY.   My dear guardian, with the assistance of Miss
690   Prism, has the arduous task of looking after me.

GWENDOLEN.   Your guardian?

CECILY.   Yes, I am Mr. Worthing's ward.

GWENDOLEN.   Oh! It is strange he never mentioned to
me that he had a ward. How secretive of him! He grows
695   more interesting hourly. I am not sure, however, that
the news inspires me with feelings of unmixed delight.
(*Rising and going to her.*) I am very fond of you, Cecily;
I have liked you ever since I met you! But I am bound
to state that now that I know that you are Mr. Worth-
700   ing's ward, I cannot help expressing a wish you were—
well, just a little older than you seem to be—and not
quite so very alluring in appearance. In fact, if I may
speak candidly—

CECILY.   Pray do! I think that whenever one has anything
705   unpleasant to say, one should always be quite candid.

GWENDOLEN.   Well, to speak with perfect candour,
Cecily, I wish that you were fully forty-two, and more
than usually plain for your age. Ernest has a strong
upright nature. He is the very soul of truth and honour.
710   Disloyalty would be as impossible to him as deception.
But even men of the noblest possible moral character are
extremely susceptible to the influence of the physical
charms of others. Modern, no less than Ancient History,
supplies us with many most painful examples of what I
715   refer to. If it were not so, indeed, History would be

quite unreadable.

CECILY. I beg your pardon, Gwendolen, did you say Ernest?

GWENDOLEN. Yes.

720 CECILY. Oh, but it is not Mr. Ernest Worthing who is my guardian. It is his brother—his elder brother.

GWENDOLEN. (*Sitting down again.*) Ernest never mentioned to me that he had a brother.

CECILY. I am sorry to say they have not been on good 725 terms for a long time.

GWENDOLEN. Ah! that accounts for it. And now that I think of it I have never heard any man mention his brother. The subject seems distasteful to most men. Cecily, you have lifted a load from my mind. I was 730 growing almost anxious. It would have been terrible if any cloud had come across a friendship like ours, would it not? Of course you are quite, quite sure that it is not Mr. Ernest Worthing who is your guardian?

CECILY. Quite sure. (*A pause.*) In fact, I am going to be 735 his.

GWENDOLEN. (*Inquiringly.*) I beg your pardon?

CECILY. (*Rather shy and confidingly.*) Dearest Gwendolen, there is no reason why I should make a secret of it to you. Our little county newspaper is sure to chronicle 740 the fact next week. Mr. Ernest Worthing and I are engaged to be married.

GWENDOLEN. (*Quite politely, rising.*) My darling Cecily, I think there must be some slight error. Mr. Ernest Worthing is engaged to me. The announcement will 745 appear in the *Morning Post* on Saturday at the latest.

CECILY. (*Very politely, rising.*) I am afraid you must be under some misconception. Ernest proposed to me exactly ten minutes ago. (*Shows diary.*)

GWENDOLEN. (*Examines diary through her lorgnettte* 750 *carefully.*) It is certainly very curious, for he asked me to be his wife yesterday afternoon at 5.30. If you would care to verify the incident, pray do so. (*Produces diary of her own.*) I never travel without my diary. One should always have something sensational to read in the train. 755 I am so sorry, dear Cecily, if it is any disappointment to you, but I am afraid I have the prior claim.

CECILY. It would distress me more than I can tell you, dear Gwendolen, if it caused you any mental or physical anguish, but I feel bound to point out that since Ernest 760 proposed to you he clearly has changed his mind.

GWENDOLEN. (*Meditatively.*) If the poor fellow has been entrapped into any foolish promise I shall consider it my duty to rescue him at once, and with a firm hand.

CECILY. (*Thoughtfully and sadly.*) Whatever unfortunate 765 entanglement my dear boy may have got into, I will never reproach him with it after we are married.

GWENDOLEN. Do you allude to me, Miss Cardew, as an entanglement? You are presumptuous. On an occasion of this kind it becomes more than a moral duty to speak 770 one's mind. It becomes a pleasure.

CECILY. Do you suggest, Miss Fairfax, that I entrapped Ernest into an engagement? How dare you? This is no time for wearing the shallow mask of manners. When I see a spade I call it a spade.

775 GWENDOLEN. (*Satirically.*) I am glad to say that I have never seen a spade. It is obvious that our social spheres have been widely different.

(*Enter Merriman, followed by the footman. He carries a salver, table cloth, and plate stand. Cecily is about to retort. The presence of the servants exercises a restraining influence, under which both girls chafe.*)

MERRIMAN. Shall I lay tea here as usual, Miss?

CECILY. (*Sternly, in a calm voice.*) Yes, as usual.

(*Merriman begins to clear table and lay cloth. A long pause. Cecily and Gwendolen glare at each other.*)

780 GWENDOLEN. Are there many interesting walks in the vicinity, Miss Cardew?

CECILY. Oh! yes! a great many. From the top of one of the hills quite close one can see five counties.

GWENDOLEN. Five counties! I don't think I should like 785 that; I hate crowds.

CECILY. (*Sweetly.*) I suppose that is why you live in town?

(*Gwendolen bites her lip, and beats her foot nervously with her parasol.*)

GWENDOLEN. (*Looking round.*) Quite a well-kept garden this is, Miss Cardew.

790 CECILY. So glad you like it, Miss Fairfax.

GWENDOLEN. I had no idea there were any flowers in

the country.

CECILY. Oh, flowers are as common here, Miss Fairfax, as people are in London.

795 GWENDOLEN. Personally I cannot understand how anybody manages to exist in the country, if anybody who is anybody does. The country always bores me to death.

CECILY. Ah! This is what the newspapers call agricultural
800 depression,[1] is it not? I believe the aristocracy are suffering very much from it just at present. It is almost an epidemic amongst them, I have been told. May I offer you some tea, Miss Fairfax?

GWENDOLEN. (*With elaborate politeness.*) Thank you.
805 (*Aside.*) Detestable girl! But I require tea!

CECILY. (*Sweetly.*) Sugar?

GWENDOLEN. (*Superciliously.*) No, thank you. Sugar is not fashionable any more. (*Cecily looks angrily at her, takes up the tongs and puts four lumps of sugar into the*
810 *cup.*)

CECILY. (*Severely.*) Cake or bread and butter?

GWENDOLEN. (*In a bored manner.*) Bread and butter, please. Cake is rarely seen at the best houses nowadays.

CECILY. (*Cuts a very large slice of cake, and puts it on the*
815 *tray.*) Hand that to Miss Fairfax.

(*Merriman does so, and goes out with footman. Gwendolen drinks the tea and makes a grimace. Puts down cup at once, reaches out her hand to the bread and butter, looks at it, and finds it is cake. Rises in indignation.*)

GWENDOLEN. You have filled my tea with lumps of sugar, and though I asked most distinctly for bread and butter, you have given me cake. I am known for the gentleness of my disposition, and the extraordinary
820 sweetness of my nature, but I warn you, Miss Cardew, you may go too far.

CECILY. (*Rising.*) To save my poor, innocent, trusting boy from the machinations of any other girl there are no lengths to which I would not go.

825 GWENDOLEN. From the moment I saw you I distrusted you. I felt that you were false and deceitful. I am never deceived in such matters. My first impressions of people are invariably right.

---

[1] *agricultural depression* The British economy in general was in depression from 1873 until the mid-1890s; the agricultural sector was depressed from 1875 until the mid-1890s.

CECILY. It seems to me, Miss Fairfax, that I am trespass-
830 ing on your valuable time. No doubt you have many other calls of a similar character to make in the neighbourhood.

(*Enter Jack.*)

GWENDOLEN. (*Catching sight of him.*) Ernest! My own Ernest!

835 JACK. Gwendolen! Darling! (*Offers to kiss her.*)

GWENDOLEN. (*Draws back.*) A moment! May I ask if you are engaged to be married to this young lady? (*Points to Cecily.*)

JACK. (*Laughing.*) To dear little Cecily! Of course not!
840 What could have put such an idea into your pretty little head?

GWENDOLEN. Thank you. You may! (*Offers her cheek.*)

CECILY. (*Very sweetly.*) I knew there must be some misunderstanding, Miss Fairfax. The gentleman whose
845 arm is at present round your waist is my guardian, Mr. John Worthing.

GWENDOLEN. I beg your pardon?

CECILY. This is Uncle Jack.

GWENDOLEN. (*Receding.*) Jack! Oh!

(*Enter Algernon.*)

850 CECILY. Here is Ernest.

ALGERNON. (*Goes straight over to Cecily without noticing any one else.*) My own love! (*Offers to kiss her.*)

CECILY. (*Drawing back.*) A moment, Ernest! May I ask you—are you engaged to be married to this young lady?

855 ALGERNON. (*Looking round.*) To what young lady? Good heavens! Gwendolen!

CECILY. Yes! to good heavens, Gwendolen, I mean to Gwendolen.

ALGERNON. (*Laughing.*) Of course not! What could
860 have put such an idea into your pretty little head?

CECILY. Thank you. (*Presenting her cheek to be kissed.*) You may.

(*Algernon kisses her.*)

GWENDOLEN. I felt there was some slight error, Miss Cardew. The gentleman who is now embracing you is

865 my cousin, Mr. Algernon Moncrieff.

CECILY. (*Breaking away from Algernon.*) Algernon Moncrieff! Oh!

(*The two girls move towards each other and put their arms round each other's waists as if for protection.*)

CECILY. Are you called Algernon?

ALGERNON. I cannot deny it.

870 CECILY. Oh!

GWENDOLEN. Is your name really John?

JACK. (*Standing rather proudly.*) I could deny it if I liked. I could deny anything if I liked. But my name certainly is John. It has been John for years.

875 CECILY. (*To Gwendolen.*) A gross deception has been practised on both of us.

GWENDOLEN. My poor wounded Cecily!

CECILY. My sweet wronged Gwendolen!

GWENDOLEN. (*Slowly and seriously.*) You will call me

880 sister, will you not? (*They embrace. Jack and Algernon groan and walk up and down.*)

CECILY. (*Rather brightly.*) There is just one question I would like to be allowed to ask my guardian.

GWENDOLEN. An admirable idea! Mr. Worthing, there

885 is just one question I would like to be permitted to put to you. Where is your brother Ernest? We are both engaged to be married to your brother Ernest, so it is a matter of some importance to us to know where your brother Ernest is at present.

890 JACK. (*Slowly and hesitatingly.*) Gwendolen—Cecily— it is very painful for me to be forced to speak the truth. It is the first time in my life that I have ever been reduced to such a painful position, and I am really quite inexperienced in doing anything of the kind. However, I will

895 tell you quite frankly that I have no brother Ernest. I have no brother at all. I never had a brother in my life, and I certainly have not the smallest intention of ever having one in the future.

CECILY. (*Surprised.*) No brother at all?

900 JACK. (*Cheerily.*) None!

GWENDOLEN. (*Severely.*) Had you never a brother of any kind?

JACK. (*Pleasantly.*) Never. Not even of an kind.

GWENDOLEN. I am afraid it is quite clear, Cecily, that

905 neither of us is engaged to be married to any one.

CECILY. It is not a very pleasant position for a young girl suddenly to find herself in. Is it?

GWENDOLEN. Let us go into the house. They will hardly venture to come after us there.

910 CECILY. No, men are so cowardly, aren't they?

(*They retire into the house with scornful looks.*)

JACK. This ghastly state of things is what you call Bunburying, I suppose?

ALGERNON. Yes, and a perfectly wonderful Bunbury it is. The most wonderful Bunbury I have ever had in my

915 life.

JACK. Well, you've no right whatsoever to Bunbury here.

ALGERNON. That is absurd. One has a right to Bunbury anywhere one chooses. Every serious Bunburyist knows that.

920 JACK. Serious Bunburyist! Good heavens!

ALGERNON. Well, one must be serious about something, if one wants to have any amusement in life. I happen to be serious about Bunburying. What on earth you are serious about I haven't got the remotest idea. About

925 everything, I should fancy. You have such an absolutely trivial nature.

JACK. Well, the only small satisfaction I have in the whole of this wretched business is that your friend Bunbury is quite exploded. You won't be able to run

930 down to the country quite so often as you used to do, dear Algy. And a very good thing too.

ALGERNON. Your brother is a little off colour, isn't he, dear Jack? You won't be able to disappear to London quite so frequently as your wicked custom was. And not

935 a bad thing either.

JACK. As for your conduct towards Miss Cardew, I must say that your taking in a sweet, simple, innocent girl like that is quite inexcusable. To say nothing of the fact that she is my ward.

940 ALGERNON. I can see no possible defence at all for your deceiving a brilliant, clever, thoroughly experienced young lady like Miss Fairfax. To say nothing of the fact that she is my cousin.

JACK. I wanted to be engaged to Gwendolen, that is all.

945 I love her.

ALGERNON. Well, I simply wanted to be engaged to Cecily. I adore her.

JACK. There is certainly no chance of your marrying Miss Cardew.

950 ALGERNON. I don't think there is much likelihood, Jack, of you and Miss Fairfax being united.

JACK. Well, that is no business of yours.

ALGERNON. If it was my business, I wouldn't talk about it. (*Begins to eat muffins.*) It is very vulgar to talk about 955 one's business. Only people like stock-brokers do that, and then merely at dinner parties.

JACK. How can you sit there, calmly eating muffins when we are in this horrible trouble, I can't make out. You seem to me to be perfectly heartless.

960 ALGERNON. Well, I can't eat muffins in an agitated manner. The butter would probably get on my cuffs. One should always eat muffins quite calmly. It is the only way to eat them.

JACK. I say it's perfectly heartless your eating muffins at 965 all, under the circumstances.

ALGERNON. When I am in trouble, eating is the only thing that consoles me. Indeed, when I am in really great trouble, as any one who knows me intimately will tell you, I refuse everything except food and drink. At 970 the present moment I am eating muffins because I am unhappy. Besides, I am particularly fond of muffins. (*Rising.*)

JACK. (*Rising.*) Well, that is no reason why you should eat them all in that greedy way. (*Takes muffins from* 975 *Algernon.*)

ALGERNON. (*Offering tea-cake.*) I wish you would have tea-cake instead. I don't like tea-cake.

JACK. Good heavens! I suppose a man may eat his own muffins in his own garden.

980 ALGERNON. But you have just said it was perfectly heartless to eat muffins.

JACK. I said it was perfectly heartless of you, under the circumstances. That is a very different thing.

ALGERNON. That may be. But the muffins are the same.

(*He seizes the muffin-dish from Jack.*)

985 JACK. Algy, I wish to goodness you would go.

ALGERNON. You can't possibly ask me to go without having some dinner. It's absurd. I never go without my dinner. No one ever does, except vegetarians and people like that. Besides I have just made arrangements with

990 Dr. Chasuble to be christened at a quarter to six under the name of Ernest.

JACK. My dear fellow, the sooner you give up that nonsense the better. I made arrangements this morning with Dr. Chasuble to be christened myself at 5:30, and 995 I naturally will take the name of Ernest. Gwendolen would wish it. We can't both be christened Ernest. It's absurd. Besides, I have a perfect right to be christened if I like. There is no evidence at all that I have ever been christened by anybody. I should think it extremely 1000 probable I never was, and so does Dr. Chasuble. It is entirely different in your case. You have been christened already.

ALGERNON. Yes, but I have not been christened for years.

1005 JACK. Yes, but you have been christened. That is the important thing.

ALGERNON. Quite so. So I know my constitution can stand it. If you are not quite sure about your ever having been christened, I must say I think it rather dangerous 1010 your venturing on it now. It might make you very unwell. You can hardly have forgotten that some one very closely connected with you was very nearly carried off this week in Paris by a severe chill.

JACK. Yes, but you said yourself that a severe chill was 1015 not hereditary.

ALGERNON. It usen't to be, I know—but I daresay it is now. Science is always making wonderful improvements in things.

JACK. (*Picking up the muffin-dish.*) Oh, that is nonsense; 1020 you are always talking nonsense.

ALGERNON. Jack, you are at the muffins again! I wish you wouldn't. There are only two left. (*Takes them.*) I told you I was particularly fond of muffins.

JACK. But I hate tea-cake.

1025 ALGERNON. Why on earth then do you allow tea-cake to be served up for your guests? What ideas you have of hospitality!

JACK. Algernon! I have already told you to go. I don't want you here. Why don't you go!

1030 ALGERNON. I haven't quite finished my tea yet! and there is still one muffin left. (*Jack groans, and sinks into a chair. Algernon still continues eating.*)

ACT DROP

ACT 3

SCENE

(*Morning-room at the Manor House. Gwendolen and Cecily are at the window, looking out into the garden.*)

GWENDOLEN. The fact that they did not follow us at once into the house, as any one else would have done, seems to me to show that they have some sense of shame left.

5 CECILY. They have been eating muffins. That looks like repentance.

GWENDOLEN. (*After a pause.*) They don't seem to notice us at all. Couldn't you cough?

CECILY. But I haven't got a cough.

10 GWENDOLEN. They're looking at us. What effrontery!

CECILY. They're approaching. That's very forward of them.

GWENDOLEN. Let us preserve a dignified silence.

CECILY. Certainly. It's the only thing to do now.

(*Enter Jack followed by Algernon. They whistle some dreadful popular air from a British Opera.*)

15 GWENDOLEN. This dignified silence seems to produce an unpleasant effect.

CECILY. A most distasteful one.

GWENDOLEN. But we will not be the first to speak.

CECILY. Certainly not.

20 GWENDOLEN. Mr. Worthing, I have something very particular to ask you. Much depends on your reply.

CECILY. Gwendolen, your common sense is invaluable. Mr. Moncrieff, kindly answer me the following question. Why did you pretend to be my guardian's brother?

25 ALGERNON. In order that I might have an opportunity of meeting you.

CECILY. (*To Gwendolen.*) That certainly seems a satisfactory explanation, does it not?

GWENDOLEN. Yes, dear, if you can believe him.

30 CECILY. I don't. But that does not affect the wonderful beauty of his answer.

GWENDOLEN. True. In matters of grave importance, style, not sincerity is the vital thing. Mr. Worthing, what explanation can you offer to me for pretending to

35 have a brother? Was it in order that you might have an opportunity of coming up to town to see me as often as possible?

JACK. Can you doubt it, Miss Fairfax?

GWENDOLEN. I have the gravest doubts upon the

40 subject. But I intend to crush them. This is not the moment for German scepticism.[1] (*Moving to Cecily.*) Their explanations appear to be quite satisfactory, especially Mr. Worthing's. That seems to me to have the stamp of truth upon it.

45 CECILY. I am more than content with what Mr. Moncrieff said. His voice alone inspires one with absolute credulity.

GWENDOLEN. Then you think we should forgive them?

CECILY. Yes. I mean no.

50 GWENDOLEN. True! I had forgotten. There are principles at stake that one cannot surrender. Which of us should tell them? The task is not a pleasant one.

CECILY. Could we not both speak at the same time?

GWENDOLEN. An excellent idea! I nearly always speak at

55 the same time as other people. Will you take the time from me?

CECILY. Certainly.

(*Gwendolen beats time with uplifted finger.*)

GWENDOLEN and CECILY (*Speaking together.*) Your Christian names are still an insuperable barrier. That is

60 all!

JACK and ALGERNON (*Speaking together.*) Our Christian names! Is that all? But we are going to be christened this afternoon.

GWENDOLEN. (*To Jack.*) For my sake you are prepared

65 to do this terrible thing?

JACK. I am.

CECILY. (*To Algernon.*) To please me you are ready to face this fearful ordeal?

ALGERNON. I am!

70 GWENDOLEN. How absurd to talk of the equality of the sexes! Where questions of self-sacrifice are concerned, men are infinitely beyond us.

JACK. We are. (*Clasps hands with Algernon.*)

CECILY. They have moments of physical courage of

75 which we women know absolutely nothing.

---

[1] *German scepticism* According to the school of philosophy deriving from Immanuel Kant, we do not always perceive the true state of things-in-themselves.

GWENDOLEN.   (*To Jack.*) Darling!

ALGERNON.   (*To Cecily.*) Darling! (*They fall into each other's arms.*)

(*Enter Merriman. When he enters he coughs loudly, seeing the situation.*)

MERRIMAN.   Ahem! Ahem! Lady Bracknell!

80 JACK.   Good heavens!

(*Enter Lady Bracknell. The couples separate in alarm. Exit Merriman.*)

LADY BRACKNELL.   Gwendolen! What does this mean?

GWENDOLEN.   Merely that I am engaged to be married to Mr. Worthing, Mamma.

LADY BRACKNELL.   Come here. Sit down. Sit down
85 immediately. Hesitation of any kind is a sign of mental decay in the young, of physical weakness in the old. (*Turns to Jack.*) Apprised, sir, of my daughter's sudden flight by her trusty maid, whose confidence I purchased by means of a small coin, I followed her at once by a
90 luggage train. Her unhappy father is, I am glad to say, under the impression that she is attending a more than usually lengthy lecture by the University Extension Scheme on the Influence of a permanent income on Thought. I do not propose to undeceive him. Indeed I
95 have never undeceived him on any question. I would consider it wrong. But of course, you will clearly understand that all communication between yourself and my daughter must cease immediately from this moment. On this point, as indeed on all points, I am firm.

100 JACK.   I am engaged to be married to Gwendolen, Lady Bracknell!

LADY BRACKNELL.   You are nothing of the kind, sir. And now, as regards Algernon! ... Algernon!

ALGERNON.   Yes, Aunt Augusta.

105 LADY BRACKNELL.   May I ask if it is in this house that your invalid friend Mr. Bunbury resides?

ALGERNON.   (*Stammering.*) Oh! No! Bunbury doesn't live here. Bunbury is somewhere else at present. In fact, Bunbury is dead.

110 LADY BRACKNELL.   Dead! When did Mr. Bunbury die? His death must have been extremely sudden.

ALGERNON.   (*Airily.*) Oh! I killed Bunbury this after-noon. I mean poor Bunbury died this afternoon.

LADY BRACKNELL.   What did he die of?

115 ALGERNON.   Bunbury? Oh, he was quite exploded.

LADY BRACKNELL.   Exploded! Was he the victim of a revolutionary outrage? I was not aware that Mr. Bunbury was interested in social legislation. If so, he is well punished for his morbidity.

120 ALGERNON.   My dear Aunt Augusta, I mean he was found out! The doctors found out that Bunbury could not live, that is what I mean—so Bunbury died.

LADY BRACKNELL.   He seems to have had great confidence in the opinion of his physicians. I am glad,
125 however, that he made up his mind at the last to some definite course of action, and acted under proper medical advice. And now that we have finally got rid of this Mr. Bunbury, may I ask, Mr. Worthing, who is that young person whose hand my nephew Algernon is now
130 holding in what seems to me a peculiarly unnecessary manner?

JACK.   That lady is Miss Cecily Cardew, my ward.

(*Lady Bracknell bows coldly to Cecily.*)

ALGERNON.   I am engaged to be married to Cecily, Aunt Augusta.

135 LADY BRACKNELL.   I beg your pardon?

CECILY.   Mr. Moncrieff and I are engaged to be married, Lady Bracknell.

LADY BRACKNELL.   (*With a shiver, crossing to the sofa and sitting down.*) I do not know whether there is anything
140 peculiarly exciting in the air of this particular part of Hertfordshire, but the number of engagements that go on seems to me considerably above the proper average that statistics have laid down for our guidance. I think some preliminary inquiry on my part would not be out
145 of place. Mr. Worthing, is Miss Cardew at all connected with any of the larger railway stations in London? I merely desire information. Until yesterday I had no idea that there were any families or persons whose origin was a Terminus.

(*Jack looks perfectly furious, but restrains himself.*)

150 JACK.   (*In a clear, cold voice.*) Miss Cardew is the grand-daughter of the late Mr. Thomas Cardew of 149 Bel-

grave Square, S.W.; Gervase Park, Dorking, Surrey; and the Sporran, Fifeshire, N.B.

LADY BRACKNELL. That sounds not unsatisfactory. Three addresses always inspire confidence, even in tradesmen. But what proof have I of their authenticity?

JACK. I have carefully preserved the Court Guides[1] of the period. They are open to your inspection, Lady Bracknell.

LADY BRACKNELL. (*Grimly.*) I have known strange errors in that publication.

JACK. Miss Cardew's family solicitors are Messrs. Markby, Markby, and Markby.

LADY BRACKNELL. Markby, Markby, and Markby? A firm of the very highest position in their profession. Indeed I am told that one of the Mr. Markbys is occasionally to be seen at dinner parties. So far I am satisfied.

JACK. (*Very irritably.*) How extremely kind of you, Lady Bracknell! I have also in my possession, you will be pleased to hear, certificates of Miss Cardew's birth, baptism, whooping cough, registration, vaccination, confirmation, and the measles; both the German and the English variety.

LADY BRACKNELL. Ah! A life crowded with incident, I see; though perhaps somewhat too exciting for a young girl. I am not myself in favour of premature experiences. (*Rises, looks at her watch.*) Gwendolen! the time approaches for our departure. We have not a moment to lose. As a matter of form, Mr. Worthing, I had better ask you if Miss Cardew has any little fortune?

JACK. Oh! about a hundred and thirty thousand pounds in the Funds. That is all. Goodbye, Lady Bracknell. So pleased to have seen you.

LADY BRACKNELL. (*Sitting down again.*) A moment, Mr. Worthing. A hundred and thirty thousand pounds! And in the Funds! Miss Cardew seems to me a most attractive young lady, now that I look at her. Few girls of the present day have any really solid qualities, any of the qualities that last, and improve with time. We live, I regret to say, in an age of surfaces. (*To Cecily.*) Come over here, dear. (*Cecily goes across.*) Pretty child! your dress is sadly simple, and your hair seems almost as Nature might have left it. But we can soon alter all that.

A thoroughly experienced French maid produces a really marvellous result in a very brief space of time. I remember recommending one to young Lady Lancing, and after three months her own husband did not know her.

JACK. And after six months nobody knew her.

LADY BRACKNELL. (*Glares at Jack for a few moments. Then bends, with a practised smile, to Cecily.*) Kindly turn round, sweet child. (*Cecily turns completely round.*) No, the side view is what I want. (*Cecily presents her profile.*) Yes, quite as I expected. There are distinct social possibilities in your profile. The two weak points in our age are its want of principle and its want of profile. The chin a little higher, dear. Style largely depends on the way the chin is worn. They are worn very high, just at present. Algernon!

ALGERNON. Yes, Aunt Augusta!

LADY BRACKNELL. There are distinct social possibilities in Miss Cardew's profile.

ALGERNON. Cecily is the sweetest, dearest, prettiest girl in the whole world. And I don't care twopence about social possibilities.

LADY BRACKNELL. Never speak disrespectfully of Society, Algernon. Only people who can't get into it do that. (*To Cecily.*) Dear child, of course you know that Algernon has nothing but his debts to depend upon. But I do not approve of mercenary marriages. When I married Lord Bracknell I had no fortune of any kind. But I never dreamed for a moment of allowing that to stand in my way. Well, I suppose I must give my consent.

ALGERNON. Thank you, Aunt Augusta.

LADY BRACKNELL. Cecily, you may kiss me!

CECILY. (*Kisses her.*) Thank you, Lady Bracknell.

LADY BRACKNELL. You may also address me as Aunt Augusta for the future.

CECILY. Thank you, Aunt Augusta.

LADY BRACKNELL. The marriage, I think, had better take place quite soon.

ALGERNON. Thank you, Aunt Augusta.

CECILY. Thank you, Aunt Augusta.

LADY BRACKNELL. To speak frankly, I am not in favour of long engagements. They give people the opportunity of finding out each other's character before marriage, which I think is never advisable.

JACK. I beg your pardon for interrupting you, Lady

---

1 *Court Guides* Directory of names and addresses of those members of the nobility, gentry, and society who have been presented at court.

Bracknell, but this engagement is quite out of the
question. I am Miss Cardew's guardian, and she cannot
marry without my consent until she comes of age. That
consent I absolutely decline to give.

LADY BRACKNELL. Upon what grounds may I ask?
Algernon is an extremely, I may almost say an ostentatiously, eligible young man. He has nothing, but he
looks everything. What more can one desire?

JACK. It pains me very much to have to speak frankly to
you, Lady Bracknell, about your nephew, but the fact is
that I do not approve at all of his moral character. I
suspect him of being untruthful.

(*Algernon and Cecily look at him in indignant amazement.*)

LADY BRACKNELL. Untruthful! My nephew Algernon?
Impossible! He is an Oxonian.[1]

JACK. I fear there can be no possible doubt about the
matter. This afternoon during my temporary absence in
London on an important question of romance, he
obtained admission to my house by means of the false
pretence of being my brother. Under an assumed name
he drank, I've just been informed by my butler, an
entire pint bottle of my Perrier-Jouet, Brut, '89; wine I
was specially reserving for myself. Continuing his
disgraceful deception, he succeeded in the course of the
afternoon in alienating the affections of my only ward.
He subsequently stayed to tea, and devoured every
single muffin. And what makes his conduct all the more
heartless is, that he was perfectly well aware from the
first that I have no brother, that I never had a brother,
and that I don't intend to have a brother, not even of
any kind. I distinctly told him so myself yesterday
afternoon.

LADY BRACKNELL. Ahem! Mr. Worthing, after careful
consideration I have decided entirely to overlook my
nephew's conduct to you.

JACK. That is very generous of you, Lady Bracknell. My
own decision, however, is unalterable. I decline to give
my consent.

LADY BRACKNELL. (*To Cecily.*) Come here, sweet child.
(*Cecily goes over.*) How old are you, dear?

CECILY. Well, I am really only eighteen, but I always
admit to twenty when I go to evening parties.

LADY BRACKNELL. You are perfectly right in making
some slight alteration. Indeed, no woman should ever be
quite accurate about her age. It looks so calculating …
(*In a meditative manner.*) Eighteen, but admitting to
twenty at evening parties. Well, it will not be very long
before you are of age and free from the restraints of
tutelage. So I don't think your guardian's consent is,
after all, a matter of any importance.

JACK. Pray excuse me, Lady Bracknell, for interrupting
you again, but it is only fair to tell you that according to
the terms of her grandfather's will Miss Cardew does not
come legally of age till she is thirty-five.

LADY BRACKNELL. That does not seem to me to be a
grave objection. Thirty-five is a very attractive age.
London society is full of women of the very highest
birth who have, of their own free choice, remained
thirty-five for years. Lady Dumbleton is an instance in
point. To my own knowledge she has been thirty-five
ever since she arrived at the age of forty, which was
many years ago now. I see no reason why our dear
Cecily should not be even still more attractive at the age
you mention than she is at present. There will be a large
accumulation of property.

CECILY. Algy, could you wait for me till I was thirty-
five?

ALGERNON. Of course I could, Cecily. You know I
could.

CECILY. Yes, I felt it instinctively, but I couldn't wait all
that time. I hate waiting even five minutes for anybody.
It always makes me rather cross. I am not punctual
myself, I know, but I do like punctuality in others, and
waiting, even to be married, is quite out of the question.

ALGERNON. Then what is to be done, Cecily?

CECILY. I don't know, Mr. Moncrieff.

LADY BRACKNELL. My dear Mr. Worthing, as Miss
Cardew states positively that she cannot wait till she is
thirty-five—a remark which I am bound to say seems to
me to show a somewhat impatient nature— I would beg
of you to reconsider your decision.

JACK. But my dear Lady Bracknell, the matter is entirely
in your own hands. The moment you consent to my
marriage with Gwendolen, I will most gladly allow your
nephew to form an alliance with my ward.

LADY BRACKNELL. (*Rising and drawing herself up.*) You

---

[1] *Oxonian* One who has attended Oxford University.

must be quite aware that what you propose is out of the
325   question.
JACK.   Then a passionate celibacy is all that any of us can
look forward to.
LADY BRACKNELL.   That is not the destiny I propose for
Gwendolen. Algernon, of course, can choose for him-
330   self. (*Pulls out her watch.*) Come, dear, (*Gwendolen rises*)
we have already missed five, if not six, trains. To miss
any more might expose us to comment on the platform.

(*Enter Dr. Chasuble.*)

CHASUBLE.   Everything is quite ready for the christenings.
335   LADY BRACKNELL.   The christenings, sir! Is not that
somewhat premature?
CHASUBLE.   (*Looking rather puzzled, and pointing to Jack
and Algernon.*) Both these gentlemen have expressed a
desire for immediate baptism.
340   LADY BRACKNELL.   At their age? The idea is grotesque
and irreligious! Algernon, I forbid you to be baptized. I
will not hear of such excesses. Lord Bracknell would be
highly displeased if he learned that that was the way in
which you wasted your time and money.
345   CHASUBLE.   Am I to understand then that there are to be
no christenings at all this afternoon?
JACK.   I don't think that, as things are now, it would be
of much practical value to either of us, Dr. Chasuble.
CHASUBLE.   I am grieved to hear such sentiments from
350   you, Mr. Worthing. They savour of the heretical views
of the Anabaptists,[1] views that I have completely
refuted in four of my unpublished sermons. However,
as your present mood seems to be one peculiarly
secular, I will return to the church at once. Indeed, I
355   have just been informed by the pew-opener[2] that for
the last hour and a half, Miss Prism has been waiting
for me in the vestry.
LADY BRACKNELL.   (*Starting.*) Miss Prism! Did I hear

you mention a Miss Prism?
360   CHASUBLE.   Yes, Lady Bracknell. I am on my way to join
her.
LADY BRACKNELL.   Pray allow me to detain you for a
moment. This matter may prove to be one of vital
importance to Lord Bracknell and myself. Is this Miss
365   Prism a female of repellent aspect, remotely connected
with education?
CHASUBLE.   (*Somewhat indignantly.*) She is the most
cultivated of ladies, and the very picture of respectability.
370   LADY BRACKNELL.   It is obviously the same person. May
I ask what position she holds in your household?
CHASUBLE.   (*Severely.*) I am a celibate, madam.
JACK.   (*Interposing.*) Miss Prism, Lady Bracknell, has
been for the last three years Miss Cardew's esteemed
375   governess and valued companion.
LADY BRACKNELL.   In spite of what I hear of her, I must
see her at once. Let her be sent for.
CHASUBLE.   (*Looking off.*) She approaches; she is nigh.

(*Enter Miss Prism hurriedly.*)

MISS PRISM.   I was told you expected me in the vestry,
380   dear Canon. I have been waiting for you there for an
hour and three-quarters.

(*Catches sight of Lady Bracknell, who has fixed her with a
stony glare. Miss Prism grows pale and quails. She looks
anxiously round as if desirous to escape.*)

LADY BRACKNELL.   (*In a severe, judicial voice.*) Prism!
(*Miss Prism bows her head in shame.*) Come here, Prism!
(*Miss Prism approaches in a humble manner.*) Prism!
385   Where is that baby? (*General consternation. The Canon
starts back in horror. Algernon and Jack pretend to be
anxious to shield Cecily and Gwendolen from hearing the
details of a terrible public scandal.*) Twenty-eight years
ago, Prism, you left Lord Bracknell's house, Number
390   104, Upper Grosvenor Street, in charge of a perambulator that contained a baby of the male sex. You never
returned. A few weeks later, through the elaborate
investigations of the Metropolitan police, the perambulator was discovered at midnight, standing by itself in a
395   remote corner of Bayswater. It contained the manuscript

---

[1]   *heretical views ... Anabaptists* Although Anabaptists, members
of a Protestant sect that rejects Anglican doctrine, believe in
baptism, they reject the Anglican custom of baptizing infants. Dr.
Chasuble is suggesting that Jack is heretical in denying the value of
baptism in the Anglican church.

[2]   *pew-opener* One assigned to open the doors of pews for
privileged churchgoers.

of a three-volume novel of more than usually revolting sentimentality. (*Miss Prism starts in involuntary indignation.*) But the baby was not there! (*Every one looks at Miss Prism.*) Prism! Where is that baby? (*A pause.*)

400 MISS PRISM.   Lady Bracknell, I admit with shame that I do not know. I only wish I did. The plain facts of the case are these. On the morning of the day you mention, a day that is for ever branded on my memory, I prepared as usual to take the baby out in its perambulator. I had
405 also with me a somewhat old, but capacious hand-bag in which I had intended to place the manuscript of a work of fiction that I had written during my few unoccupied hours. In a moment of mental abstraction, for which I never can forgive myself, I deposited the manuscript in
410 the bassinette, and placed the baby in the hand-bag.

JACK.   (*Who has been listening attentively.*) But where did you deposit the hand-bag?

MISS PRISM.   Do not ask me, Mr. Worthing.

JACK.   Miss Prism, this is a matter of no small impor-
415 tance to me. I insist on knowing where you deposited the hand-bag that contained that infant.

MISS PRISM.   I left it in the cloak-room of one of the larger railway stations in London.

JACK.   What railway station?

420 MISS PRISM.   (*Quite crushed.*) Victoria. The Brighton line. (*Sinks into a chair.*)

JACK.   I must retire to my room for a moment. Gwendolen, wait here for me.

GWENDOLEN.   If you are not too long, I will wait here
425 for you all my life.

(*Exit Jack in great excitement.*)

CHASUBLE.   What do you think this means, Lady Bracknell?

LADY BRACKNELL.   I dare not even suspect, Dr. Chasuble. I need hardly tell you that in families of high
430 position strange coincidences are not supposed to occur. They are hardly considered the thing.

(*Noises heard overhead as if some one was throwing trunks about. Every one looks up.*)

CECILY.   Uncle Jack seems strangely agitated.

CHASUBLE.   Your guardian has a very emotional nature.

LADY BRACKNELL.   This noise is extremely unpleasant.
435 It sounds as if he was having an argument. I dislike arguments of any kind. They are always vulgar, and often convincing.

CHASUBLE.   (*Looking up.*) It has stopped now. (*The noise is redoubled.*)

440 LADY BRACKNELL.   I wish he would arrive at some conclusion.

GWENDOLEN.   This suspense is terrible. I hope it will last.

(*Enter Jack with a hand-bag of black leather in his hand.*)

JACK.   (*Rushing over to Miss Prism.*) Is this the handbag,
445 Miss Prism? Examine it carefully before you speak. The happiness of more than one life depends on your answer.

MISS PRISM.   (*Calmly.*) It seems to be mine. Yes, here is the injury it received through the upsetting of a Gower
450 Street omnibus[1] in younger and happier days. Here is the stain on the lining caused by the explosion of a temperance beverage,[2] an incident that occurred at Leamington. And here, on the lock, are my initials. I had forgotten that in an extravagant mood I had had
455 them placed there. The bag is undoubtedly mine. I am delighted to have it so unexpectedly restored to me. It has been a great inconvenience being without it all these years.

JACK.   (*In a pathetic voice.*) Miss Prism, more is restored
460 to you than this hand-bag. I was the baby you placed in it.

MISS PRISM.   (*Amazed.*) You?

JACK.   (*Embracing her.*) Yes ... mother!

MISS PRISM.   (*Recoiling in indignant astonishment.*) Mr.
465 Worthing! I am unmarried!

JACK.   Unmarried! I do not deny that is a serious blow. But after all, who has the right to cast a stone against one who has suffered? Cannot repentance wipe out an act of folly? Why should there be one law for men, and
470 another for women? Mother, I forgive you. (*Tries to embrace her again.*)

---

[1]   *Gower Street omnibus*   Public horse-drawn bus on a route in central London.

[2]   *temperance beverage*   Non-alcoholic drink. (The temperance movement aimed to prohibit all alcoholic beverages.)

MISS PRISM.   (*Still more indignant.*) Mr. Worthing, there is some error. (*Pointing to Lady Bracknell.*) There is the lady who can tell you who you really are.

475 JACK.   (*After a pause.*) Lady Bracknell, I hate to seem inquisitive, but would you kindly inform me who I am?

LADY BRACKNELL.   I am afraid that the news I have to give you will not altogether please you. You are the son of my poor sister, Mrs. Moncrieff, and consequently

480 Algernon's elder brother.

JACK.   Algy's elder brother! Then I have a brother after all. I knew I had a brother! I always said I had a brother! Cecily,—how could you have ever doubted that I had a brother? (*Seizes hold of Algernon.*) Dr. Chasuble, my

485 unfortunate brother. Miss Prism, my unfortunate brother. Gwendolen, my unfortunate brother. Algy, you young scoundrel, you will have to treat me with more respect in the future. You have never behaved to me like a brother in all your life.

490 ALGERNON.   Well, not till to-day, old boy, I admit. I did my best, however, though I was out of practice. (*Shakes hands.*)

GWENDOLEN.   (*To Jack.*) My own! But what own are you? What is your Christian name, now that you have

495 become some one else?

JACK.   Good heavens! … I had quite forgotten that point. Your decision on the subject of my name is irrevocable, I suppose?

GWENDOLEN.   I never change, except in my affections.

500 CECILY.   What a noble nature you have, Gwendolen!

JACK.   Then the question had better be cleared up at once. Aunt Augusta, a moment. At the time when Miss Prism left me in the hand-bag, had I been christened already?

505 LADY BRACKNELL.   Every luxury that money could buy, including christening, had been lavished on you by your fond and doting parents.

JACK.   Then I was christened! That is settled. Now, what name was I given? Let me know the worst.

510 LADY BRACKNELL.   Being the eldest son you were naturally christened after your father.

JACK.   (*Irritably.*) Yes, but what was my father's Christian name?

LADY BRACKNELL.   (*Meditatively.*) I cannot at the present

515 moment recall what the General's Christian name was. But I have no doubt he had one. He was eccentric, I admit. But only in later years. And that was the result of the Indian climate, and marriage, and indigestion, and other things of that kind.

520 JACK.   Algy! Can't you recollect what our father's Christian name was?

ALGERNON.   My dear boy, we were never even on speaking terms. He died before I was a year old.

JACK.   His name would appear in the Army Lists[1] of the

525 period, I suppose, Aunt Augusta?

LADY BRACKNELL.   The General was essentially a man of peace, except in his domestic life. But I have no doubt his name would appear in any military directory.

JACK.   The Army Lists of the last forty years are here.

530 These delightful records should have been my constant study. (*Rushes to bookcase and tears the books out.*) M. Generals … Mallam, Maxbohm, Magley, what ghastly names they have—Markby, Migsby, Mobbs, Moncrieff! Lieutenant 1840, Captain, Lieutenant-Colonel, Colo-

535 nel, General 1869, Christian names, Ernest John. (*Puts book very quietly down and speaks quite calmly.*) I always told you, Gwendolen, my name was Ernest, didn't I? Well, it is Ernest after all. I mean it naturally is Ernest.

LADY BRACKNELL.   Yes, I remember now that the

540 General was called Ernest, I knew I had some particular reason for disliking the name.

GWENDOLEN.   Ernest! My own Ernest! I felt from the first that you could have no other name!

JACK.   Gwendolen, it is a terrible thing for a man to find

545 out suddenly that all his life he has been speaking nothing but the truth. Can you forgive me?

GWENDOLEN.   I can. For I feel that you are sure to change.

JACK.   My own one!

550 CHASUBLE.   (*To Miss Prism.*) Laetitia! (*Embraces her.*)

MISS PRISM.   (*Enthusiastically.*) Frederick! At last!

ALGERNON.   Cecily! (*Embraces her.*)   At last!

JACK.   Gwendolen! (*Embraces her.*)   At last!

LADY BRACKNELL.   My nephew, you seem to be display-

555 ing signs of triviality.

JACK.   On the contrary, Aunt Augusta, I've now realized for the first time in my life the vital Importance of Being Earnest.

TABLEAU

—1895

---

1   *Army Lists*   Directories of officers.

IN CONTEXT

Wilde and "The Public"

Interview with Oscar Wilde, *St. James Gazette*, January 1895

I found Mr. Oscar Wilde (writes a Representative) making ready to depart on a short visit to Algiers, and reading—of course, nothing so obvious as a time-table, but a French newspaper which contained an account of the first night of *The Ideal Husband*[1] and its author's appearance after the play.

"How well the French appreciate these brilliant willful moments in an artist's life," remarked Mr. Wilde, handing me the article as if he considered the interview already at an end.

"Does it give you any pleasure," I inquired, "to appear before the curtain after the production of your plays?"

"None whatsoever. No artist finds any interest in seeing the public. The public is very much interested in seeing an artist. Personally, I prefer the French custom, according to which the name of the dramatist is announced to the public by the oldest actor in the piece."

"Would you advocate," I asked, "this custom in England?"

"Certainly. The more the public is interested in artists, the less it is interested in art. The personality of the artist is not a thing the public should know anything about. It is too accidental." Then, after a pause—

"It might be more interesting if the name of the author were announced by the *youngest* actor present."

"It is only in deference, then, to the imperious mandate of the public that you have appeared before the curtain?"

"Yes; I have always been very good-natured about that. The public has always been so appreciative of my work I felt it would be a pity to spoil its evening."

"I notice some people have found fault with the character of your speeches."

"Yes, the old-fashioned idea was that the dramatist should appear and merely thank his kind friends for their patronage and presence. I am glad to say I have altered all that. The artist cannot be degraded into the servant of the public. While I have always recognized the cultured appreciation that actors and audience have shown for my work, I have equally recognized that humility is for the hypocrite, modesty for the incompetent. Assertion is at once the duty and privilege of the artist."

"To what do you attribute, Mr. Wilde, the fact that so few men of letters besides yourself have written plays for public presentation?"

"Primarily the existence of an irresponsible censorship. The fact that my *Salomé* cannot be performed is sufficient to show the folly of such an institution. If painters were obliged to show their pictures to clerks at Somerset House, those who think in form and colour would adopt some other mode of expression. If every novel had to be submitted to a police magistrate, those whose passion is fiction would seek some new mode of realization. No art ever survived censorship; no art ever will."

"And secondly?"

"Secondly to the rumour persistently spread abroad by journalists for the last thirty years, that the duty of the dramatist was to please the public. The aim of art is no more to give pleasure than to give

---

[1]   *The Ideal Husband*   I.e., Wilde's play *An Ideal Husband*. The play, which had opened on 3 January 1895, was currently enjoying a very successful run at the Haymarket Theatre.

pain. The aim of art is to be art. As I said once before, the work of art is to dominate the spectator—the spectator is not to dominate art."

"You admit no exceptions?"

"Yes. Circuses where it seems the wishes of the public might be reasonably carried out."

"Do you think," I inquired, "that French dramatic criticism is superior to our own?"

"It would be unfair to confuse French dramatic criticism with English theatrical criticism. The French dramatic critic is always a man of culture and generally a man of letters. In France poets like Gautier[1] have been dramatic critics. In England they are drawn from a less distinguished class. They have neither the same capacities nor the same opportunities. They have all the moral qualities, but none of the artistic qualifications. For the criticism of such a complex mode of art as the drama the highest culture is necessary. No one can criticize drama who is not capable of receiving impressions from the other arts also."

"You admit they are sincere?"

"Yes; but their sincerity is little more than stereotyped stupidity. The critic of the drama should be versatile as the actor. He should be able to change his mood at will and should catch the colour of the moment."

"At least they are honest?"

"Absolutely. I don't believe there is a single dramatic critic in London who would deliberately set himself to misrepresent the work of any dramatist—unless, of course, he personally disliked the dramatist, or had some play of his own he wished to produce at the same theatre, or had an old friend among the actors, or some natural reasons of that kind. I am speaking, however, of London dramatic critics. In the provinces both audience and critics are cultured. In London it is only the audience who are cultured."

"I fear you do not rate our dramatic critics very highly, Mr. Wilde; but, at all events, they are incorruptible?"

"In a market where there are no bidders."

"Still their memories stand them in good stead," I pleaded.

"The old talk of having seen Macready[;][2] that must be a very painful memory. The middle-aged boast that they can recall Diplomacy;[3] hardly a pleasant reminiscence."

"You deny them, then, even a creditable past?"

"They have no past and no future, and are incapable of realizing the colour of the moment that finds them at the play."

"What do you propose should be done?"

"They should be pensioned off, and only allowed to write on politics or theology or bimetallism, or some subject easier than art."

"In fact," I said, carried away by Mr. Wilde's aphorisms, "they should be seen and not heard."

"The old should neither be seen nor heard," said Mr. Wilde with some emphasis.

"You said the other day there were only two dramatic critics in London. May I ask—"

"They must have been greatly gratified by such an admission from me; but I am bound to say that since last week I have struck one of them from the list."

"Whom have you left in?"

"I think I had better not mention his name. It might make him too conceited. Conceit is the privilege of the creative."

"How would you define ideal dramatic criticism?"

---

[1]   *Gautier*   Théophile Gautier (1811–72), French poet, novelist, and dramatist.

[2]   *Macready*   William Charles Macready (1793–1873), English actor and theater manager.

[3]   *Diplomacy*   An English adaptation of the French play *Dora* (1878), by Victorien Sardou (1831–1908).

"As far as my work is concerned[,] unqualified appreciation."

"And whom have you omitted?"

"Mr. William Archer, of the *World*."[1]

"What do you chiefly object to in his article?"

"I object to nothing in the article, but I grieve at everything in it. It is bad taste in him to write of me by my Christian name, and he need not have stolen his vulgarisms from the *National Observer* in its most impudent and impotent days."

"Mr. Archer asked whether[,] if it was agreeable to you to be hailed by your Christian name when the enthusiastic spectators called you before the curtain."

"To be so addressed by enthusiastic spectators is as great a compliment as to be written of by one's Christian name is in a journalist bad manners. Bad manners make a journalist."

"Do you think French actors, like French criticism, superior to our own?"

"The English actors act quite as well; but they act best between the lines. They lack the superb elocution of the French—so clear, so cadenced, and so musical. A long sustained speech seems to exhaust them. At the Théâtre Français we go to listen, to an English theatre we go to look. There are, of course, exceptions. Mr. George Alexander, Mr. Lewis Waller, Mr. Forbes Robertson, and others I might mention, have superb voices and know how to use them. I wish I could say the same of the critics; but in the case of the literary drama in England there is too much of what is technically known as 'business.' Yet there is more than one of our English actors who is capable of producing a wonderful dramatic effect by aid of a monosyllable and two cigarettes."

For a moment Mr. Wilde was silent, and then added, "Perhaps, after all, that is acting."

"But are you satisfied with the interpreters of *The Ideal Husband*?"

"I am charmed with all of them. Perhaps they are a little too fascinating. The stage is the refuge of the too fascinating."

"Have you heard it said that all the characters in your play talk as you do?"

"Rumours of that kind have reached me from time to time," said Mr. Wilde, lighting a cigarette, "and I should fancy that some such criticism has been made. The fact is that it is only in the last few years that the dramatic critic has had the opportunity of seeing plays written by anyone who has a mastery of style. In the case of a dramatist, also an artist, it is impossible not to feel that the work of art, to be a work of art, must be dominated by the artist. Every play of Shakespeare is dominated by Shakespeare. Ibsen and Dumas[2] dominate their works. My works are dominated by myself."

"Have you ever been influenced by any of your predecessors?"

"It is enough for me to state definitely, and I hope once for all, that not a single dramatist in this century has ever in the smallest degree influenced me. Only two have interested me."

"And they are?"

"Victor Hugo and Maeterlinck"[3]

"Other writers surely have influenced your other works?"

[1]   *Mr. William ... World*   For Archer's criticism of Wilde, see *"An Ideal Husband," The World*, 9 January 1895, 26–27.

[2]   *Ibsen*   Norwegian playwright Henrik Ibsen (1828–1906); *Dumas*   French author and playwright Alexandre Dumas *fils* (1824–95).

[3]   *Maeterlinck*   Maurice Maeterlinck (1862–1949), Belgian poet and playwright who was awarded the Nobel Prize for Literature in 1911.

"Setting aside the prose and poetry of Greek and Latin authors, the only writers who have influenced me are Keats, Flaubert, and Walter Pater;[1] and before I came across them I had already gone more than halfway to meet them. Style must be in one's soul before one can recognize it in others."

"And do you consider *The Ideal Husband* the best of your plays?"

A charming smile crossed Mr. Wilde's face.

"Have you forgotten my classical expression—that only mediocrities improve? My three plays are to each other, as a wonderful young poet has beautifully said,

as one white rose
On one green stalk to another one.

They form a perfect cycle, and in their delicate sphere complete both life and art."

"Do you think that the critics will understand your new play,[2] which Mr. George Alexander has secured?"

"I hope not."

"I dare not ask, I suppose, if it will please the public?"

"When a play that is a work of art is produced on the stage, what is being tested is not the play, but the stage; when a play that is *not* a work of art is produced on the stage, what is being tested is not the play, but the public."

"What sort of play are we to expect?"

"It is exquisitely trivial, a delicate bubble of fancy, and it has its philosophy."

"Its philosophy!"

"That we should treat all the trivial things of life very seriously, and all the serious things of life with sincere and studied triviality."[3]

"You have no leanings towards realism?"

"None whatever. Realism is only a background; it cannot form an artistic motive for a play that is to be a work of art."

"Still I have heard you congratulated on your pictures of London society."

"If Robert Chiltern, the Ideal Husband, were a common clerk, the humanity of his tragedy would be none the less poignant. I have placed him in the higher ranks of life merely because that is the side of social life with which I am best acquainted. In a play dealing with actualities to write with ease one must write with knowledge."

"Then you see nothing suggestive of treatment in the tragedies of everyday existence?"

"If a journalist is run over by a four-wheeler in the Strand, an incident I regret to say I have never witnessed, it suggests nothing to me from a dramatic point of view. Perhaps I am wrong; but the artist must have his limitations."

"Well," I said, rising to go, "I have enjoyed myself immensely."

"I was sure you would," said Mr. Wilde. "But tell me how you manage your interviews."

---

[1]   *Keats ... Pater   Keats*   John Keats, English poet (1795–1821); *Flaubert*   French novelist Gustave Flaubert (1821–80), celebrated author of *Madame Bovary* (1867); *Walter Pater*   English critic and scholar; he had reviewed some of Wilde's works.

[2]   *new play   The Importance of Being Earnest*, which opened on 14 February 1895.

[3]   *It is ... philosophy*   The full title of the play is *The Importance of Being Earnest: A Trivial Comedy For Serious People*.

"Oh, Pitman," I said carelessly.

"Is that your name? It's not a very *nice* name."

Then I left.

IN CONTEXT

The First Wilde Trial (1895)

Portrait of Oscar Wilde at the time of his trial, by Henri de Toulouse-Lautrec.

The following is an excerpt from the transcripts of the cross examination of Wilde by Edward Carson, the attorney defending the Marquess of Queensberry in the libel action[1] Wilde had brought against him.

---

from *The Transcripts of the Trial*

CARSON.   You stated that your age was thirty-nine. I think you are over forty. You were born on 16th October 1854?

WILDE.   I have no wish to pose as being young. I am thirty-nine or forty. You have my certificate and that settles the matter.

CARSON.   But being born in 1854 makes you more than forty?

WILDE.   Ah! Very well.

CARSON.   What age is Lord Alfred Douglas?

WILDE.   Lord Alfred Douglas is about twenty-four, and was between twenty and twenty-one years of age when I first knew him. Down to the time of the interview in Tite Street, Lord Queensberry was friendly. I did not receive a letter on 3rd April in which Lord Queensberry desired that my acquaintance with his son should cease. After the interview I had no doubt that such was Lord Queensberry's desire. Notwithstanding Lord Queensberry's protest, my intimacy with Lord Alfred Douglas has continued down to the present moment.

CARSON.   You have stayed with him at many places?

WILDE.   Yes.

CARSON.   At Oxford? Brighton on several occasions? Worthing?

WILDE.   Yes.

CARSON.   You never took rooms for him?

WILDE.   No.

CARSON.   Were you at other places with him?

WILDE.   Yes; at Cromer and at Torquay.

CARSON.   And in various hotels in London?

WILDE.   Yes; at one in Albemarle Street, and in Dover Street, and at the Savoy.

CARSON.   Did you ever take rooms yourself in addition to your house in Tite Street?

WILDE.   Yes; at 10 and 11 St. James's Place. I kept the rooms from the month of October 1893 to the end of March 1894. Lord Alfred Douglas has stayed in those chambers, which are not far from Piccadilly. I have been abroad with him several times and even lately to Monte Carlo. With reference to the writings which have been mentioned, it was not at Brighton, in 20 King's Road, that I wrote my article for *The Chameleon*.[1] I observed that there were also contributions from Lord Alfred Douglas, but these were not written at Brighton. I have seen them. I thought them exceedingly beautiful poems. One was "In Praise of Shame" and the other "Two Loves."

CARSON.   These loves. They were two boys?

WILDE.   Yes.

CARSON.   One boy calls his love "true love," and the other boy calls his love "shame"?

WILDE.   Yes.

CARSON.   Did you think that made any improper suggestion?

WILDE.   No, none whatever.

CARSON.   You read "The Priest and the Acolyte"?

WILDE.   Yes.

CARSON.   You have no doubt whatever that that was an improper story?

WILDE.   From the literary point of view it was highly improper. It is impossible for a man of

---

[1]   *The Chameleon* Oxford undergraduate magazine, of which there was only one issue, that of December 1894 to which Wilde refers. In this issue Wilde's "Phrases and Philosophies for the Use of the Young" appeared, as well as an anonymous story about male homosexuality (actually written not by Wilde but by the editor), called "The Priest and the Acolyte." Though Wilde was not the author, the mere fact that a piece signed by him appeared juxtaposed to this story proved damaging to his reputation.

literature to judge it otherwise; by literature, meaning treatment, selection of subject, and the like. I thought the treatment rotten and the subject rotten.

CARSON.   You are of opinion, I believe, that there is no such thing as an immoral book?

WILDE.   Yes.

CARSON.   May I take it that you think "The Priest and the Acolyte" was not immoral?

WILDE.   It was worse; it was badly written.

CARSON.   Was not the story that of a priest who fell in love with a boy who served him at the altar, and was discovered by the rector in the priest's room, and a scandal arose?

WILDE.   I have read it only once, in last November, and nothing will induce me to read it again. I don't care for it. It doesn't interest me.

CARSON.   Do you think the story blasphemous?

WILDE.   I think it violated every artistic canon of beauty.

CARSON.   That is not an answer?

WILDE.   It is the only one I can give.

CARSON.   I want to see the position you pose in?

WILDE.   I do not think you should say that.

CARSON.   I have said nothing out of the way. I wish to know whether you thought the story blasphemous?

WILDE.   The story filled me with disgust. The end was wrong.

CARSON.   Answer the question, sir. Did you or did you not consider the story blasphemous?

WILDE.   I thought it disgusting.

CARSON.   I am satisfied with that. You know that when the priest in the story administers poison to the boy, he uses the words of the sacrament of the Church of England?

WILDE.   That I entirely forgot.

CARSON.   Do you consider that blasphemous?

WILDE.   I think it is horrible. "Blasphemous" is not a word of mine.

[*Carson then read the following passage from "The Priest and the Acolyte."*]:

> Just before the consecration the priest took a tiny phial from the pocket of his cassock, blessed it, and poured the contents into the chalice.
>
> When the time came for him to receive from the chalice, he raised it to his lips, but did not taste of it.
>
> He administered the sacred wafer to the child, and then he took his hand; he turned towards him; but when he saw the light in the beautiful face he turned again to the crucifix with a low moan. For one instant his courage failed him; then he turned to the little fellow again, and held the chalice to his lips:
>
> "The Blood of our Lord Jesus Christ, which was shed for thee, preserve thy body and soul unto everlasting life."

CARSON.   Do you approve of those words?

WILDE.   I think them disgusting, perfect twaddle.

CARSON.   I think you will admit that anyone who would approve of such an article would pose as guilty of improper practices?

WILDE.   I do not think so in the person of another contributor to the magazine. It would show very bad literary taste. I strongly objected to the whole story. I took no steps to express disapproval of *The Chameleon* because I think it would have been beneath my dignity as a man of letters to associate myself with an Oxford undergraduate's productions. I am aware that the magazine may have been circulated among the undergraduates of Oxford. I do not believe that any book or work of art ever had any effect whatever on morality.

CARSON. Am I right in saying that you do not consider the effect in creating morality or immorality?

WILDE. Certainly, I do not.

CARSON. So far as your works are concerned, you pose as not being concerned about morality or immorality?

WILDE. I do not know whether you use the word "pose" in any particular sense.

CARSON. It is a favorite word of your own?

WILDE. Is it? I have no pose in this matter. In writing a play or a book, I am concerned entirely with literature—that is, with art. I aim not at doing good or evil, but in trying to make a thing that will have some quality of beauty.

CARSON. Listen, sir. Here is one of the "Phrases and Philosophies for the Use of the Young" which you contributed: "Wickedness is a myth invented by good people to account for the curious attractiveness of others." You think that true?

WILDE. I rarely think that anything I write is true.

CARSON. Did you say "rarely"?

WILDE. I said "rarely." I might have said "never"—not true in the actual sense of the word.

CARSON. "Religions die when they are proved to be true." Is that true?

WILDE. Yes; I hold that. It is a suggestion towards a philosophy of the absorption of religions by science, but it is too big a question to go into now.

CARSON. Do you think that was a safe axiom to put forward for the philosophy of the young?

WILDE. Most stimulating.

CARSON. "If one tells the truth, one is sure, sooner or later, to be found out"?

WILDE. That is a pleasing paradox, but I do not set very high store on it as an axiom.

CARSON. Is it good for the young?

WILDE. Anything is good that stimulates thought in whatever age.

CARSON. Whether moral or immoral?

WILDE. There is no such thing as morality or immorality in thought. There is immoral emotion.

CARSON. "Pleasure is the only thing one should live for"?

WILDE. I think that the realization of oneself is the prime aim of life, and to realize oneself through pleasure is finer than to do so through pain. I am, on that point, entirely on the side of the ancients—the Greeks. It is a pagan idea.

CARSON. "A truth ceases to be true when more than one person believes in it"?

WILDE. Perfectly. That would be my metaphysical definition of truth; something so personal that the same truth could never be appreciated by two minds.

CARSON. "The condition of perfection is idleness: the aim of perfection is youth"?

WILDE. Oh, yes; I think so. Half of it is true. The life of contemplation is the highest life, and so recognized by the philosopher.

CARSON. "There is something tragic about the enormous number of young men there are in England at the present moment who start life with perfect profiles, and end by adopting some useful profession"?

WILDE. I should think that the young have enough sense of humour.

CARSON. You think that is humourous?

WILDE. I think it is an amusing paradox, an amusing play on words.

CARSON. What would anyone say would be the effect of "Phrases and Philosophies" taken in connection with such an article as "The Priest and the Acolyte"?

WILDE.   Undoubtedly it was the idea that might be formed that made me object so strongly to the story. I saw at once that maxims that were perfectly nonsensical, paradoxical, or anything you like, might be read in conjunction with it.

CARSON.   After the criticisms that were passed on *Dorian Gray*, was it modified a good deal?

WILDE.   No. Additions were made. In one case it was pointed out to me—not in a newspaper or anything of that sort, but by the only critic of the century whose opinion I set high, Mr. Walter Pater—that a certain passage was liable to misconstruction, and I made an addition.

CARSON.   This is in your introduction to *Dorian Gray*: "There is no such thing as a moral or an immoral book. Books are well written, or badly written." That expresses your view?

WILDE.   My view on art, yes.

CARSON.   Then I take it that no matter how immoral a book may be, if it is well written, it is, in your opinion, a good book?

WILDE.   Yes, if it were well written so as to produce a sense of beauty, which is the highest sense of which a human being can be capable. If it were badly written, it would produce a sense of disgust.

CARSON.   Then a well-written book putting forward perverted moral views may be a good book?

WILDE.   No work of art ever puts forward views. Views belong to people who are not artists.

CARSON.   A perverted novel might be a good book?

WILDE.   I don't know what you mean by a "perverted" novel.

CARSON.   Then I will suggest *Dorian Gray* as open to the interpretation of being such a novel?

WILDE.   That could only be to brutes and illiterates. The views of Philistines on art are incalculably stupid.

CARSON.   An illiterate person reading *Dorian Gray* might consider it such a novel?

WILDE.   The views of illiterates on art are unaccountable. I am concerned only with my view of art. I don't care twopence what other people think of it.

CARSON.   The majority of persons would come under your definition of Philistines and illiterates?

WILDE.   I have found wonderful exceptions.

CARSON.   Do you think that the majority of people live up to the position you are giving us?

WILDE.   I am afraid they are not cultivated enough.

CARSON.   Not cultivated enough to draw the distinction between a good book and a bad book?

WILDE.   Certainly not.

CARSON.   The affection and love of the artist of *Dorian Gray* might lead an ordinary individual to believe that it might have a certain tendency?

WILDE.   I have no knowledge of the views of ordinary individuals.

CARSON.   You did not prevent the ordinary individual from buying your book?

WILDE.   I have never discouraged him.

[*Carson then read a long passage from Chapter 1 of* The Picture of Dorian Gray *(from "The story is simply this …" to "I must see Dorian Gray".)*]

CARSON.   Now I ask you, Mr. Wilde, do you consider that that description of the feeling of one man towards a youth just grown up was a proper or an improper feeling?

WILDE.   I think it is the most perfect description of what an artist would feel on meeting a beautiful personality that was in some way necessary to his art and life.

CARSON.   You think that is a feeling a young man should have towards another?

WILDE.   Yes, as an artist.

[*Carson then read a long passage from Chapter 9 of* The Picture of Dorian Gray *(from "Let us sit down, Dorian" to "You are made to be worshipped").*]

CARSON. Do you mean to say that that passage describes the natural feeling of one man towards another?

WILDE. It would be the influence produced by a beautiful personality.

CARSON. A beautiful person?

WILDE. I said a "beautiful personality." You can describe it as you like. Dorian Gray's was a most remarkable personality.

CARSON. May I take it that you, as an artist, have never known the feeling described here?

WILDE. I have never allowed any personality to dominate my art.

CARSON. Then you have never known the feeling you described?

WILDE. No. It is a work of fiction.

CARSON. So far as you are concerned you have no experience as to its being a natural feeling?

WILDE. I think it is perfectly natural for any artist to admire intensely and love a young man. It is an incident in the life of almost every artist.

CARSON. But let us go over it phrase by phrase. "I quite admit that I adored you madly." What do you say to that? Have you ever adored a young man madly?

WILDE. No, not madly; I prefer love—that is a higher form.

CARSON. Never mind about that. Let us keep down to the level we are at now?

WILDE. I have never given adoration to anybody except myself. (*Loud laughter.*)

CARSON. I suppose you think that a very smart thing?

WILDE. Not at all.

CARSON. Then you have never had that feeling?

WILDE. No. The whole idea was borrowed from Shakespeare, I regret to say—yes, from Shakespeare's sonnets.

CARSON. I believe you have written an article to show that Shakespeare's sonnets were suggestive of unnatural vice?

WILDE. On the contrary I have written an article to show that they are not.[1] I objected to such a perversion being put upon Shakespeare.

CARSON. "I have adored you extravagantly"?

WILDE. Do you mean financially?

CARSON. Oh, yes, financially! Do you think we are talking about finance?

WILDE. I don't know what you are talking about.

CARSON. Don't you? Well, I hope I shall make myself very plain before I have done. "I was jealous of everyone to whom you spoke." Have you ever been jealous of a young man?

WILDE. Never in my life.

CARSON. "I wanted to have you all to myself." Did you ever have that feeling?

WILDE. No; I should consider it an intense nuisance, an intense bore.

CARSON. "I grew afraid that the world would know of my idolatry." Why should he grow afraid that the world should know of it?

WILDE. Because there are people in the world who cannot understand the intense devotion, affection, and admiration that an artist can feel for a wonderful and beautiful personality. These are the conditions under which we live. I regret them.

CARSON. These unfortunate people, that have not the high understanding that you have, might put it down to something wrong?

WILDE. Undoubtedly; to any point they chose. I am not concerned with the ignorance of others.

CARSON. In another passage Dorian Gray receives a book. Was the book to which you refer a moral book?

---

[1]   *an article ... not* Cf. "The Portrait of Mr. W.H." first published in *Blackwood's Edinburgh Magazine*, 146.885 (July 1889), and then again in a limited edition in 1921.

WILDE.   Not well written, but it gave me an idea.

CARSON.   Was not the book you have in mind of a certain tendency?

WILDE.   I decline to be cross-examined upon the work of another artist. It is an impertinence and a vulgarity.

[*Wilde then stated the book Carson referred to was* A Rebours, *by J.K. Huysmans; and, following an appeal by Sir Edward Clarke, Wilde's attorney, the judge ruled against further reference to it. Carson then read a long passage from Chapter 12 of* The Picture of Dorian Gray *(from "... I think it right that you should know the most dreadful things are being said about you in London" to "Dorian, your reputation is infamous ... ").*]

CARSON.   Does not this passage suggest a charge of unnatural vice?

WILDE.   It describes Dorian Gray as a man of very corrupt influence, though there is no statement as to the nature of the influence. But as a matter of fact I do not think that one person influences another, nor do I think there is any bad influence in the world.

CARSON.   A man never corrupts a youth?

WILDE.   I think not.

CARSON.   Nothing could corrupt him?

WILDE.   If you are talking of separate ages.

CARSON.   No, sir, I am talking common sense.

WILDE.   I do not think one person influences another.

CARSON.   You don't think that flattering a young man, making love[1] to him, in fact, would be likely to corrupt him?

WILDE.   No.

CARSON.   Where was Lord Alfred Douglas staying when you wrote that letter to him?

WILDE.   At the Savoy; and I was at Babbacombe, near Torquay.

CARSON.   It was a letter in answer to something he had sent you?

WILDE.   Yes, a poem.

CARSON.   Why should a man of your age address a boy nearly twenty years younger as "My own boy"?

WILDE.   I was fond of him. I have always been fond of him.

CARSON.   Do you adore him?

WILDE.   No, but I have always liked him. I think it is a beautiful letter. It is a poem. I was not writing an ordinary letter. You might as well cross-examine me as to whether *King Lear* or a sonnet of Shakespeare was proper.

CARSON.   Apart from art, Mr. Wilde?

WILDE.   I cannot answer apart from art.

CARSON.   Suppose a man who was not an artist had written this letter, would you say it was a proper letter?

WILDE.   A man who was not an artist could not have written that letter.

Carson.   Why?

WILDE.   Because nobody but an artist could write it. He certainly could not write the language unless he were a man of letters.

CARSON.   I can suggest, for the sake of your reputation, that there is nothing very wonderful in this "red rose-leaf lips of yours"?

---

[1]   *making love*   Until the 1960s this expression was generally used to refer to the process of wooing or courtship, not to any physical act of lovemaking.

WILDE. A great deal depends on the way it is read.

CARSON. "Your slim gilt soul walks between passion and poetry." Is that a beautiful phrase?

WILDE. Not as you read it, Mr. Carson. You read it very badly.

CARSON. I do not profess to be an artist; and when I hear you give evidence, I am glad I am not—

SIR EDWARD CLARKE. I don't think my friend should talk like that. (*To witness*) Pray, do not criticize my friend's reading again.

CARSON. Is that not an exceptional letter?

WILDE. It is unique, I should say.

CARSON. Was that the ordinary way in which you carried on your correspondence?

WILDE. No; but I have often written to Lord Alfred Douglas, though I never wrote to another young man in the same way.

CARSON. Have you often written letters in the same style as this?

WILDE. I don't repeat myself in style.

CARSON. Here is another letter which I believe you also wrote to Lord Alfred Douglas. Will you read it?

WILDE. No; I decline. I don't see why I should.

CARSON. Then I will.

> Savoy Hotel,
> Victoria Embankment, London.
> Dearest of all Boys,
> Your letter was delightful, red and yellow wine to me; but I am sad and out of sorts. Bosie,[1] you must not make scenes with me. They kill me, they wreck the loveliness of life. I cannot see you, so Greek and gracious, distorted with passion. I cannot listen to your curved lips saying hideous things to me. I would sooner——than have you bitter, unjust, hating.... I must see you soon. You are the divine thing I want, the thing of grace and beauty; but I don't know how to do it. Shall I come to Salisbury? My bill here is £49 for a week. I have also got a new sitting-room.... Why are you not here, my dear, my wonderful boy? I fear I must leave—no money, no credit, and a heart of lead.
> Your own Oscar. ...

Is that an ordinary letter?

WILDE. Everything I write is extraordinary. I do not pose as being ordinary, great heavens! Ask me any question you like about it.

CARSON. Is it the kind of letter a man writes to another?

WILDE. It was a tender expression of my great admiration for Lord Alfred Douglas. It was not, like the other, a prose poem.

---

[1]   *Bosie* Lord Alfred Douglas's nickname.

VERNON LEE
1856 – 1935

Vernon Lee was the author of some fifty books of fiction, philosophical and intellectual criticism, and art history, but her reputation now rests mainly on her stories of the fantastic and her first novel, *Miss Brown*. Walter Pater once called her one of "the very few best critical writers of all time"; among her other admirers were Robert Browning, Henry James, and George Bernard Shaw, all of whom recognized her intellectual prowess.

Violet Paget (Vernon Lee was her pen name) was born in Boulogne, France, in 1856. Her father, Henry Ferguson Paget, was a former Polish soldier who fled to Paris during the 1848 Warsaw uprising. He worked as a tutor, eventually marrying the mother of one of his students, and soon afterward the couple had their own child, Violet. They moved frequently, settling briefly in Germany, Switzerland, and Italy, so the children received schooling in many different languages. In Nice, France, when she was ten, Lee forged a friendship with an American child, John Singer Sargent, and the two prophesied correctly that he would become a famous painter and she a writer.

Lee's parents recognized that their daughter was intellectually gifted, and they encouraged her scholarship. Her first article was published when she was just thirteen. At the age of twenty-four she published her first book, *Studies of the Eighteenth Century in Italy* (1880), a scholarly monograph that received considerable acclaim. On her move from Florence to London after its publication, she joined a literary and intellectual circle that included Browning and Pater. Although initially very supportive of her writing, Pater cooled somewhat for a time after Lee published *Miss Brown* in 1884. The novel was viewed by many as a thinly-veiled *roman à clef* in which Lee satirized the Pre-Raphaelites (such as Dante Gabriel Rossetti) and Aesthetes (Oscar Wilde). Even Henry James, who was a fan of her writing, said to Lee, "You have impregnated all those people too much with the sexual, the basely erotic preoccupation: your hand was too violent, the touch of life is lighter."

Lee wrote prolifically during the following two decades. Chief among her publications was *Euphorion: Being Studies of the Antique and the Medieval in the Renaissance* (1884), a study of Italian art and culture that the American journal *The Nation* called "clever with the cleverness of precocious and presumptuous youth, lively and amusing even in its pretentiousness." Lee furthered her aesthetic theories in her work with her close friend, artist Clementina (Kit) Anstruther-Thomson. The two collaborated on *Beauty and Ugliness and other Studies in Psychological Aesthetics* (1912), which Lee followed with *The Beautiful: An Introduction to Psychological Aesthetics* (1913). On her own Lee also published *The Handling of Words and other Studies in Literary Psychology* (1923), an analytical study that anticipated a number of later twentieth-century trends in theory and criticism.

Lee's interest in and knowledge of other cultures yielded seven volumes of travel essays, including *The Enchanted Woods, and Other Essays on the Genius of Place* (1905), a book she described as a "pilgrimage through the open and hidden ways where, without any noisy calling, the *Genus Loci* [spirit of the place]" met her. Her travel writing was much admired by Aldous Huxley and Edith Wharton, and by a member of the Bloomsbury group, Desmond MacCarthy, who would declare that there was "no doubt [that] Vernon Lee will be read by posterity, for her work is a rare combination of intellectual curiosity and imaginative sensibility." Lee also wrote popular works of fiction, including the short story collections *Hauntings: Fantastic Stories* (1890) and *Pope Jacynth and Other Fantastic Tales* (1904), and the play *Ariadne in Mantua: A Romance in Five Acts* (1903). A later satirical play, *The Ballet of the Nations: A Present-day Morality* (1915), was disparaged by many who objected to its anti-war position.

Lee's popularity and influence were already waning when she died in Florence in 1935. That same year she had complained to a friend that she felt like "an alien, having no ties, either of nation, blood, class or profession." In a biography (1964), Peter Gunn described her as "a shadowy figure, at the most perhaps only a vaguely remembered name; a name, however, which recalls to an older generation a literary craftsman and polemicist of undoubted importance in her day ... one of the most brilliant and gifted women of her time ... a writer and a talker who both stimulated and irritated her contemporaries." Recently there has been a marked revival of critical interest in her work.

⌘ ⌘ ⌘

The Virgin of the Seven Daggers

I

In a grass-grown square of the city of Grenada,[1] with the snows of the Sierra[2] staring down on it all winter, and the sunshine glaring on its coloured tiles all summer, stands the yellow free-stone Church of Our Lady of the Seven Daggers. Huge garlands of pears and melons hang, carved in stone, about the cupolas and windows; and monstrous heads with laurel wreaths and epaulets burst forth from all the arches. The roof shines barbarically, green, white, and brown, above the tawny stone; and on each of the two balconied and staircased belfries, pricked up like ears above the building's monstrous front, there sways a weathervane, figuring a heart transfixed with seven long-hilted daggers. Inside, the church presents a superb example of the pompous, pedantic, and contorted Spanish architecture of the reign of Philip IV.[3]

On colonnade is hoisted colonnade, pilasters climb upon pilasters, bases and capitals jut out, double and threefold, from the ground, in midair and near the ceiling; jagged lines everywhere as of spikes for exhibit-

ing the heads of traitors; dizzy ledges as of mountain precipices for dashing to bits Morisco rebels;[4] line warring with line and curve with curve; a place in which the mind staggers bruised and half-stunned. But the grandeur of the church is not merely terrific—it is also gallant and ceremonious: everything on which labor can be wasted is labored, everything on which gold can be lavished is gilded; columns and architraves curl like the curls of a peruke;[5] walls and vaultings are flowered with precious marbles and fretted with carving and gilding like a gala dress; stone and wood are woven like lace; stucco is whipped and clotted like pastry cooks' cream and crust; everything is crammed with flourishes like a tirade by Calderon, or a sonnet by Gongora.[6] A golden retablo closes the church at the end; a black and white rood screen, of jasper[7] and alabaster, fences it in the middle; while along each aisle hang chandeliers as for a ball; and paper flowers are stacked on every altar.

Amidst all this gloomy yet festive magnificence, and surrounded, in each minor chapel, by a train of waxen

---

[1] *Granada* City in Spain, location of the palace-citadel of the Alhambra, constructed by the founder of the Nasrid kingdom, Mohammed ibn Yusaf ben Nasr, in the mid-thirteenth century.

[2] *Sierra* I.e., the Sierra Nevada mountain range in Andalusia, Spain.

[3] *Philip IV* King of Spain and Portugal (1605–65).

[4] *Morisco rebels* Muslim freedom fighters of the Morisco Rebellion (1568–71), a revolt against the Christian suppression of Islamic religion, culture, and trade.

[5] *peruke* Wig.

[6] *Calderon* Pedro Calderón de la Barca, prolific Spanish playwright of the seventeenth century (called Spain's Golden Age); *Gongora* Luis de Góngora y Argote, poet of the same era.

[7] *retablo* Frame enclosing a religious painting above the altar of a church; *rood* Here, large wooden crucifix; *jasper* Opaque quartz.

Christs with bloody wounds and spangled loincloths, and madonnas of lesser fame weeping beady tears and carrying bewigged infants, thrones the great Madonna of the Seven Daggers.

Is she seated or standing? 'Tis impossible to decide. She seems, beneath the gilded canopy and between the twisted columns of jasper, to be slowly rising, or slowly sinking, in a solemn court curtsy, buoyed up by her vast farthingale.[1] Her skirts bulge out in melon-shaped folds, all damasked with minute heart's-ease,[2] and brocaded with silver roses; the reddish shimmer of the gold wire, the bluish shimmer of the silver floss, blending into a strange melancholy hue without a definite name. Her body is cased like a knife in its sheath, the mysterious russet and violet of the silk made less definable still by the network of seed pearl, and the veils of delicate lace which fall from head to waist. Her face, surmounting rows upon rows of pearls, is made of wax, white with black glass eyes and a tiny coral mouth; she stares steadfastly forth with a sad and ceremonious smile. Her head is crowned with a great jeweled crown; her slippered feet rest on a crescent moon, and in her right hand she holds a lace pocket-handkerchief. In her bodice, a little clearing is made among the brocade and the seed pearl, and into this are stuck seven gold-hilted knives.

Such is Our Lady of the Seven Daggers; and such her church.

One winter afternoon, more than two hundred years ago, Charles the Melancholy being King of Spain and the New World, there chanced to be kneeling in that church, already empty and dim save for the votive lamps, and more precisely on the steps before the Virgin of the Seven Daggers, a cavalier[3] of very great birth, fortune, magnificence, and wickedness, Don[4] Juan Gusman del Pulgar, Count of Miramor. "O great Madonna, star of the sea, tower of ivory, ungathered flower, cedar of Lebanon, Empress of Heaven"—thus prayed that devout man of quality—"look down benignly on thy knight and servant, accounted judiciously

one of the greatest men of this kingdom, in wealth and honours, fearing neither the vengeance of foes, nor the rigour of laws, yet content to stand foremost among thy slaves. Consider that I have committed every crime without faltering, both murder, perjury, blasphemy, and sacrilege, yet have I always respected thy name, nor suffered any man to give greater praise to other Madonnas, neither her of Good Counsel, nor her of Swift Help, nor our Lady of Mount Carmel, nor our Lady of St. Luke of Bologna in Italy, nor our Lady of the Slipper of Famagosta, in Cyprus, nor our Lady of the Pillar of Saragossa, great Madonnas every one, and revered throughout the world for their powers, and by most men preferred to thee; yet has thy servant, Juan Gusman del Pulgar, ever asserted, with words and blows, their infinite inferiority to thee.

"Give me, therefore, O Great Madonna of the Seven Daggers, Snow Peak untrodden of the Sierras, O Sea unnavigated of the tropics, O Gold Ore unhandled by the Spaniard, O New Minted Doubloon[5] unpocketed by the Jew,[6] give unto me therefore, pray thee, the promise that thou wilt save me ever from the clutches of Satan, as thou hast wrested me ever on earth from the King, Alguazils[7] and the Holy Office's[8] delatours,[9] and let me never burn in eternal fire in punishment of my sins. Neither think that I ask too much, for I swear to be provided always with absolution[10] in all rules, whether by employing my own private chaplain or using violence thereunto to any monk, priest, canon, dean, bishop, cardinal, or even the Holy Father[11] himself.

"Grant me this boon, O Burning Water and Cooling Fire, O Sun that shineth at midnight, and Galaxy

---

[1]   *farthingale*   Hooped petticoat.

[2]   *heart's-ease*   Pansy.

[3]   *cavalier*   Knight.

[4]   *Don*   Title for a Spanish noblemen.

[5]   *Doubloon*   Gold coin.

[6]   *unpocketed by the Jew*   Remarks such as this, which we now consider racist and offensive, were casually made at this time. Jews were frequently associated with the lending of money (for centuries one of the few occupations they were not restricted from entering) and thus with pressing to be paid amounts owed.

[7]   *Alguazils*   Government officials.

[8]   *Holy Office*   At this time, the Spanish Inquisition, a legally constituted court founded for the suppression of heresy.

[9]   *delatours*   Informers.

[10]   *absolution*   Forgiveness of sins through the sacrament of Confession.

[11]   *Holy Father*   The Pope.

that resplendeth at noon—grant me this boon, and I will assert always with my tongue and my sword, in the face of His Majesty and at the feet of my latest love, that although I have been beloved of all the fairest women of the world, high and low, both Spanish, Italian, German, French, Dutch, Flemish, Jewish, Saracen,[1] and Gypsy, to the number of many hundreds, and by seven ladies, Dolores, Fatma, Catalina, Elvira, Violante, Azahar, and Sister Seraphita, for each of whom I broke a commandment and took several lives (the last, moreover, being a cloistered nun, and therefore a case of inexpiable sacrilege), despite all this I will maintain before all men and all the Gods of Olympus that no lady was ever so fair as our Lady of the Seven Daggers of Grenada."

The church was filled with ineffable fragrance, exquisite music, among which Don Juan seemed to recognize the voice of Syphax, His Majesty's own soprano singer, murmured amongst the cupolas, and the Virgin of the Seven Daggers, slowly dipped in her lace and silver brocade hoop, rising as slowly again to her full height, and inclined her white face imperceptibly towards her jeweled bosom.

The Count of Miramor clasped his hands in ecstasy to his breast; then he rose, walked quickly down the aisle, dipped his fingers in the black marble holy water stoop, threw a sequin[2] to the beggar who pushed open the leathern curtain, put his black hat covered with black feathers on his head, dismissed a company of bravos and guitar players who awaited him in the square, and, gathering his black cloak about him, went forth, his sword tucked under his arm, in search of Baruch, the converted Jew of the Albaycin.[3]

Don Juan Gusman del Pulgar, Count of Miramor, Grandee of the First Class, Knight of Calatrava, and of the Golden Fleece, and Prince of the Holy Roman Empire, was thirty-two and a great sinner. This cavalier was tall, of large bone, his forehead low and cheekbones high, chin somewhat receding, aquiline nose, white complexion, and black hair; he wore no beard, but mustachios cut short over the lip and curled upwards at the corners leaving the mouth bare; and his hair flat,

parted through the middle and falling nearly to his shoulders. His clothes, when bent on business or pleasure, were most often of black satin, slashed with black. His portrait has been painted by Domingo Zurbaran of Seville.[4]

2

All the steeples of Grenada seemed agog with bell-ringing; the big bell on the Tower of the Sail[5] clanging irregularly into the more professional tinklings and roarings, under the vigorous but flurried pulls of the elderly damsels, duly accompanied by their well-ruffed duennas,[6] who were ringing themselves a husband or the newly begun year, according to the traditions of the city. Green garlands decorated the white glazed balconies, and banners with the arms of Castile and Aragon,[7] and the pomegranate of Grenada, waved or drooped alongside the hallowed palm branches over the carved escutcheons[8] on the doors. From the barracks arose a practising of fifes and bugles; and from the little wine shops on the outskirts of the town a sound of guitar strumming and castanets. The coming day was a very solemn feast for the city, being the anniversary of its liberation from the rule of the Infidels.[9]

But although all Grenada felt festive, in anticipation of the grand bullfight of the morrow, and the grand burning of heretics and relapses in the square of Bibrambla,[10] Don Juan Gusman del Pulgar, Count of Miramor, was fevered with intolerable impatience, not for the following day but for the coming and tediously lagging night.

---

[1] *Saracen* Muslim.

[2] *sequin* Turkish coin.

[3] *Albaycin* Neighborhood of Granada that encompasses the Alhambra.

[4] *Domingo Zurbaran of Seville* Perhaps a reference to painter Francisco de Zurbarán of Seville (1598–1664).

[5] *Tower of the Sail* The Torre de la Vela, or Tower of the Sail, at the Alhambra.

[6] *duennas* Chaperones.

[7] *Castile and Aragon* Spanish kingdoms.

[8] *escutcheons* Shields bearing coats of arms.

[9] *Infidels* The Moors, who ruled southern Spain until 1492. In the Spanish Inquisition of 1480–1834, the Roman Catholic majority in Spain conducted a violent campaign to root out "unbelievers," in the course of which they expelled or killed large numbers of Spanish Muslims and Jews.

[10] *Bibrambla* Large open square where hundreds of people visit and congregate in central Granada.

Not, however, for the reason which had made him a thousand times before upbraid the Sun God, in true poetic style, for showing so little of the proper anxiety to hasten the happiness of one of the greatest cavaliers of Spain. The delicious heart-beating with which he had waited, sword under his cloak, for the desired rope to be lowered from a mysterious window, or the muffled figure to loom from round a corner; the fierce joy of awaiting, with a band of gallant murderers, some inconvenient father, or brother, or husband on his evening stroll; the rapture even, spiced with awful sacrilege, of stealing in amongst the lemon trees of that cloistered court, after throwing the Sister Portress[1] to tell-tale in the convent well—all, and even this, seemed to him trumpery and mawkish.

Don Juan sprang from the great bed, covered and curtained with dull, blood-coloured damask, on which he had been lying dressed, vainly courting sleep, beneath a painted hermit, black and white in his lantern-jawed-ness, fondling a handsome skull. He went to the balcony, and looked out of one of its glazed windows. Below a marble goddess shimmered among the myrtle hedges and the cypresses of the tiled garden, and the pet dwarf of the house played at cards with the chaplain, the chief bravo, and a threadbare poet who was kept to make the odes and sonnets required in the course of his master's daily courtships.

"Get out of my sight, you lazy scoundrels, all of you!" cried Don Juan, with a threat and an oath alike terrible to repeat, which sent the party, bowing and scraping as they went, scattering their cards, and pursued by his lordship's jack-boots, guitar, and missal.[2]

Don Juan stood at the window rapt in contemplation of the towers of the Alhambra, their tips still reddened by the departing sun, their bases already lost in the encroaching mists, on the hill yon side of the river.

He could just barely see it, that Tower of the Cypresses, where the magic hand held the key engraven on the doorway, about which, as a child, his nurse from the Morisco village of Andarax had told such marvellous stories of hidden treasures and slumbering infantas.[3] He stood long at the window, his lean, white hands clasped on the rail as on the handle of his sword, gazing out with knit brows and clenched teeth, and that look which made men hug the wall and drop aside on his path.

Ah, how different from any of his other loves! The only one, decidedly, at all worthy of lineage as great as his, and a character as magnanimous. Catalina, indeed, had been exquisite when she danced, and Elvira was magnificent at a banquet, and each had long possessed his heart, and had cost him, one many thousands of doubloons for a husband, and the other the death of a favourite fencing master, killed in a fray with her relations. Violante had been a Venetian worthy of Titian,[4] for whose sake he had been imprisoned beneath the ducal palace, escaping only by the massacre of three jailers; for Fatma, the Sultana of the King of Fez, he had well nigh been impaled, and for shooting the husband of Dolores he had very nearly been broken on the wheel; Azahar, who was called so because of her cheeks like white jessamine, he had carried off at a church door, out of the arms of her bridegroom—without counting that he had cut down her old father, a Grandee of the First Class; and as to Sister Seraphita—ah! she had seemed worthy of him, and Seraphita had nearly come up to his idea of an angel.

But oh, what had any of these ladies cost him compared with what he was about to risk tonight? Letting alone the chance of being roasted by the Holy Office (after all, he had already run that, and the risk of more serious burning hereafter also, in the case of Sister Seraphita), what if the business proved a swindle of that Jewish hound, Baruch?—Don Juan put his hand on his dagger and his black mustachios bristled up at the bare thought—letting alone the possibility of imposture (though who could be so bold as to venture to impose upon him?) the adventure was full of dreadful things. It was terrible, after all, to have to blaspheme the Holy Catholic Apostolic Church, and all her saints, and inconceivably odious to have to be civil to that dog of a

---

[1]   *Sister Portress*   Nun who keeps the convent gates; the door-keeper.

[2]   *jack-boots*   Above-the-knee boots worn by the cavalry; *missal* Book that contains the service of the Mass.

[3]   *infantas*   Daughters of the king and queen; princesses.

[4]   *Titian*   Renaissance Venetian painter Tiziano Vecellio (c. 1490–1576), commonly known as Titian.

Mahomet[1] of theirs; also, he had not much enjoyed a previous experience of calling up devils, who had smelled most vilely of brimstone and asafœtida,[2] besides using most impolite language; and he really could not stomach that Jew Baruch, whose trade among others consisted in procuring for the archbishop a batch of renegade Moors, who were solemnly dressed in white and baptized afresh every year. It was odious that this fellow should even dream of obtaining the treasure buried under the Tower of the Cypresses.

Then there were the traditions of his family, descended in direct line from the Cid,[3] and from that Fernan del Pulgar[4] who had nailed the Ave Maria[5] to the Mosque; and half his other ancestors were painted with their foot on a Moor's discollated[6] head, much resembling a hairdresser's block, and their very title, Miramor, was derived from a castle which had been built in full Moorish territory to stare the Moor out of countenance.

But, after all, this only made it more magnificent, more delicious, more worthy of so magnanimous and high-born a cavalier.... "Ah, princess ... more exquisite than Venus, more noble than Juno, and infinitely more agreeable than Minerva ..."[7] sighed Don Juan at his window. The sun had long since set, making a trail of blood along the distant river reach, among the sere spider-like poplars, turning the snows of Mulhacen[8] a livid, bluish blood-red, and leaving all along the lower slopes of the Sierra wicked russet stains, as of the rust of blood upon marble. Darkness had come over the world, save where some illuminated courtyard or window suggested preparations for next day's revelry; the air was piercingly cold, as if filled with minute snowflakes from the mountains. The joyful singing had ceased; and from a neighbouring church there came only a casual death toll, executed on a cracked and lugubrious bell. A shudder ran through Don Juan. "Holy Virgin of the Seven Daggers, take me under thy benign protection," he murmured mechanically.

A discreet knock aroused him.

"The Jew Baruch—I mean his worship, Senor Don Bonaventura," announced the page.

3

The Tower of the Cypresses, destroyed in our times by the explosion of a powder magazine, formed part of the inner defenses of the Alhambra. In the middle of its horseshoe arch was engraved a huge hand holding a flag-shaped key, which was said to be that of the subterranean and enchanted palace; and the two great cypress trees, uniting their shadows into one tapering cone of black, were said to point, under a given position of the moon, to the exact spot where the wise King Yahya, of Cordova, had judiciously buried his jewels, his plate, and his favourite daughter many hundred years ago.

At the foot of this tower, and in the shade of the cypresses, Don Juan ordered his companion to spread out his magic paraphernalia. From a neatly packed basket, beneath which he had staggered up the steep hillside in the moonlight, the learned Jew produced a book, a variety of lamps, some packets of frankincense, a pound of dead man's fat, the bones of a stillborn child who had been boiled by the witches, a live cock that had never crowed, a very ancient toad, and sundry other rarities, all of which he proceeded to dispose in the latest necromantic[9] fashion, while the Count of Miramor mounted guard, sword in hand. But when the fire was laid, the lamps lit, and the first layer of ingredients had already been placed in the cauldron; nay, when he had even borrowed Don Juan's embroidered pocket-handkerchief to envelop the cock that had never crowed, Baruch the Jew suddenly flung himself down before his

---

[1] *Mahomet* The prophet Mohammed, who founded Islam. Don Juan's characterization of Mohammed is highly offensive to modern ears; Lee clearly intends this speech to add to the reader's understanding of the viciousness of Don Juan's character.

[2] *asafœtida* Plant gum used as a medicine and spice.

[3] *the Cid* Rodrigo Diaz, otherwise known as "El Cid" (the chief), Spanish knight who fought against the Moors in the 11th century.

[4] *Fernan del Pulgar* Spanish historian and author (c. 1430–92).

[5] *Ave Maria* Roman Catholic prayer to Mary, the mother of Jesus Christ.

[6] *discollated* Cut off.

[7] *Venus* Roman goddess of love; *Juno* Queen of the Roman gods; *Minerva* Roman goddess of war. The three goddesses, in their Greek identities of Aphrodite, Hera and Athena, famously competed for the title of the most beautiful goddess, setting in motion the train of events that would culminate in the Trojan War.

[8] *Mulhacen* Mulhacén, the highest mountain in Continental Spain.

[9] *necromantic* Using sorcery.

patron and implored him to desist from the terrible enterprise for which they had come.

"I have come hither," wailed the Jew, "lest your lordship should possibly entertain doubts of my obligingness. I have run the risk of being burned alive in the Square of Bibrambla tomorrow morning before the bullfight; I have imperiled my eternal soul and laid out large sums of money in the purchase of the necessary ingredients, all of which are abomination in the eyes of a true Jew—I mean of a good Christian;[1] but now I implore your lordship to desist. You will see things so terrible that to mention them is impossible; you will be suffocated by the vilest stenches, and shaken by earthquakes and whirlwinds, besides having to listen to imprecations of the most horrid sort; you will have to blaspheme our Holy Mother Church and invoke Mahomet—may he roast everlastingly in hell; you will infallibly go to hell yourself in due course; and all this for the sake of a paltry treasure of which it will be most difficult to dispose to the pawnbrokers; and of a lady, about whom, thanks to my former medical position in the harem of the Emperor of Tetuan, I may assert with confidence that she is fat, ill-favoured, stained with henna, and most disagreeably redolent of camphor...."

"Peace, villain!" cried Don Juan, snatching him by the throat and pulling him violently onto his feet. "Prepare thy messes and thy stinks, begin thy antics, and never dream of offering advice to a cavalier like me. And remember, one other word against her royal highness, my bride, against the princess whom her own father has been keeping three hundred years for my benefit, and by the Virgin of the Seven Daggers, thou shalt be hurled into yonder precipice; which, by the way, will be a very good move, in any case, when thy services are no longer required." So saying, he snatched from Baruch's hand the paper of responses, which the necromancer had copied out from his book of magic; and began to study it by the light of a supernumerary[2] lamp.

"Begin!" he cried. "I am ready, and thou, great Virgin of the Seven Daggers, guard me!"

"Jab, jam, jam—Credo in Grilgoth, Astaroth et Rappatun; trish, trash, trum," began Baruch in faltering

tones, as he poked a flame-tipped reed under the cauldron.

"Patapol, Valde Patapol," answered Don Juan from his paper of responses.

The flame of the cauldron leaped up with a tremendous smell of brimstone. The moon was veiled, the place was lit up crimson, and a legion of devils with the bodies of apes, the talons of eagles, and the snouts of pigs suddenly appeared in the battlements all round.

"Credo," again began Baruch; but the blasphemies he gabbled out, and which Don Juan indignantly echoed, were such as cannot possibly be recorded. A hot wind rose, whirling a desertful of burning sand that stung like gnats; the bushes were on fire, each flame turned into a demon like a huge locust or scorpion, who uttered piercing shrieks and vanished, leaving a choking atmosphere of melted tallow.

"Fal lal Polychronicon Nebuzaradon," continued Baruch. "Leviathan! Esto nobis!" answered Don Juan. The earth shook, the sound of millions of gongs filled the air, and a snowstorm enveloped everything like a shuddering cloud. A legion of demons, in the shape of white elephants, but with snakes for their trunks and tails, and the bosoms of fair women, executed a frantic dance round the cauldron, and, holding hands, balanced on their hind legs.

At this moment the Jew uncovered the Black Cock who had never crowed before.

"Osiris! Apollo! Balshazar!" he cried, and flung the cock with superb aim into the boiling cauldron. The cock disappeared; then rose again, shaking his wings, and clawing the air, and giving a fearful piercing crow.

"O Sultan Yahya, Sultan Yahya," answered a terrible voice from the bowels of the earth.

Again the earth shook; streams of lava bubbled from beneath the cauldron, and a flame, like a sheet of green lightning, leaped up from the fire. As it did so a colossal shadow appeared on the high palace wall, and the great hand, shaped like a glover's sign, engraven on the outer arch of the tower gateway, extended its candle-shaped fingers, projected a wrist, an arm to the elbow, and turned slowly in a secret lock the flag-shaped key engraven on the inside vault of the portal.

The two necromancers fell on their faces, utterly stunned.

---

[1] *true... Christian* This speech is meant to imply that Baruch is not truly converted to Christianity.

[2] *supernumerary* Extra.

The first to revive was Don Juan, who roughly brought the Jew back to his senses. The moon made serene daylight. There was no trace of earthquake, volcano, or simoon;[1] and the devils had disappeared without traces; only the circle of lamps was broken through, and the cauldron upset among the embers. But the great horseshoe portals of the tower stood open; and, at the bottom of a dark corridor, there shone a speck of dim light.

"My lord," cried Baruch, suddenly grown bold, and plucking Don Juan by the cloak, "we must now, if you please, settle a trifling business matter. Remember that the treasure was to be mine provided the Infanta were yours. Remember also, that the smallest indiscretion on your part, such as may happen to a gay young cavalier, will result in our being burned, with the batch of heretics and relapses, in Bibrambla tomorrow, immediately after high Mass and just before people go to early dinner, on account of the bullfight."

"Business! Discretion! Bibrambla! Early dinner!" exclaimed the Count of Miramor. "Thinkest thou I shall ever go back to Grenada and its frumpish women once I am married to my Infanta, or let thee handle my late father-in-law, King Yahya's treasure! Execrable renegade, take the reward of thy blasphemies." And having rapidly run him through the body, he pushed Baruch into the precipice hard by. Then, covering his left arm with his cloak, and swinging his bare sword horizontally in his right hand, he advanced into the darkness of the tower.

4

Don Juan Gusman del Pulgar plunged down a narrow corridor, as black as the shaft of a mine, following the little speck of reddish light which seemed to advance before him. The air was icy damp and heavy with a vague choking mustiness, which Don Juan imagined to be the smell of dead bats. Hundreds of these creatures fluttered all round; and hundreds more, apparently hanging head downwards from the low roof, grazed his face with their claws, their damp furry coats, and clammy leathern wings. Underfoot, the ground was slippery with innumerable little snakes, who, instead of being crushed, just wriggled under the thread. The

corridor was rendered even more gruesome by the fact that it was a strongly inclined plane, and that one seemed to be walking straight into a pit.

Suddenly a sound mingled itself with that of his footsteps, and of the drip-drop of water from the roof, or, rather, detached itself as a whisper from it.

"Don Juan, Don Juan," it murmured.

"Don Juan, Don Juan," murmured the walls and roof a few yards farther—a different voice this time.

"Don Juan Gusman del Pulgar!" a third voice took up, clearer and more plaintive than the others.

The magnanimous cavalier's blood began to run cold, and icy perspiration to clot his hair. He walked on nevertheless.

"Don Juan," repeated a fourth voice, a little buzz close to his ear.

But the bats set up a dreadful shrieking which drowned it.

He shivered as he went; it seemed to him he had recognized the voice of the jasmine-cheeked Azahar, as she called on him from her deathbed.

The reddish speck had meanwhile grown large at the bottom of the shaft, and he had understood that it was not a flame but the light of some place beyond. Might it be hell? he thought. But he strode on nevertheless, grasping his sword and brushing away the bats with his cloak.

"Don Juan! Don Juan!" cried the voices issuing faintly from the darkness. He began to understand that they tried to detain him; and he thought he recognized the voices of Dolores and Fatma, his dead mistresses.

"Silence, you sluts!" he cried. But his knees were shaking, and great drops of sweat fell from his hair on to his cheek.

The speck of light had now become quite large, and turned from red to white. He understood that it represented the exit from the gallery. But he could not understand why, as he advanced, the light, instead of being brighter, seemed filmed over and fainter.

"Juan, Juan," wailed a new voice at his ear. He stood still half a second; a sudden faintness came over him.

"Seraphita," he murmured—"it is my little nun Seraphita." But he felt that she was trying to call him back.

---

[1] *simoon* Extremely hot desert wind.

"Abominable witch!" he cried. "Avaunt!"[1]

The passage had grown narrower and narrower; so narrow that now he could barely squeeze along beneath the clammy walls, and had to bend his head lest he should hit the ceiling with its stalactites of bats.

Suddenly there was a great rustle of wings, and a long shriek. A night bird had been startled by his tread and had whirled on before him, tearing through the veil of vagueness that dimmed the outer light. As the bird tore open its way, a stream of dazzling light entered the corridor: it was as if a curtain had suddenly been drawn.

"Too-hoo! Too-hoo!" shrieked the bird, and Don Juan, following its flight, brushed his way through the cobwebs of four centuries and issued, blind and dizzy, into the outer world.

5

For a long while the Count of Miramor stood dazed and dazzled, unable to see anything save the whirling flight of the owl, which circled in what seemed a field of waving, burning red. He closed his eyes; but through the singed lids he still saw that waving red atmosphere, and the black creature whirling about him.

Then, gradually, he began to perceive and comprehend: lines and curves arose shadowy before him, and the faint plash of waters cooled his ringing ears.

He found that he was standing in a lofty colonnade, with a deep tank at his feet, surrounded by high hedges of flowering myrtles, whose jade-coloured water held the reflection of Moorish porticos, shining orange in the sunlight, of high walls covered with shimmering blue and green tiles, and of a great red tower, raising its battlements into the cloudless blue. From the tower waved two flags, a white one and one of purple with a gold pomegranate. As he stood there, a sudden breath of air shuddered through the myrtles, wafting their fragrance towards him; the fountain began to bubble; and the reflection of the porticos and hedges and tower to vacillate in the jade-green water, furling and unfurling like the pieces of a fan; and, above, the two banners unfolded themselves slowly, and little by little began to stream in the wind.

Don Juan advanced. At the farther end of the tank a peacock was standing by the myrtle hedge, immovable

as if made of precious enamels; but as Don Juan went by, the short blue-green feathers of his neck began to ruffle; he moved his tail, and, swelling himself out, he slowly unfolded it in a dazzling wheel. As he did so, some blackbirds and thrushes in gilt cages hanging within an archway, began to twitter and to sing.

From the court of the tank, Don Juan entered another and smaller court, passing through a narrow archway. On its marble steps lay three warriors, clad in long embroidered surcoats[2] of silk, beneath which gleamed their armour, and wearing on their heads strange helmets of steel mail,[3] which hung loose on to their gorgets[4] and were surmounted by gilded caps; beneath them— for they had seemingly leaned on them in their slumbers—lay round targes or shields, and battle-axes of Damascus work. As he passed they began to stir and breathe heavily. He strode quickly by, and at the entrance of the smaller court, from which issued a delicious scent of full-blown Persian roses, another sentinel was leaning against a column, his hands clasped round his lance, his head bent on his breast. As Don Juan passed he slowly raised his head, and opened one eye, then the other. Don Juan rushed past, a cold sweat on his brow.

Low beams of sunlight lay upon the little inner court, in whose midst, surrounded by rose hedges, stood a great basin of alabaster, borne on four thickset pillars; a skin, as of ice, filmed over the basin; but, as if someone should have thrown a stone onto a frozen surface, the water began to move and to trickle slowly into the other basin below.

"The waters are flowing, the nightingales singing," murmured a figure which lay by the fountain, grasping, like one just awakened, a lute that lay by his side. From the little court Don Juan entered a series of arched and domed chambers, whose roofs were hung as with icicles of gold and silver, or encrusted with mother-of-pearl constellations that twinkled in the darkness, while the walls shone with patterns that seemed carved of ivory and pearl and beryl and amethyst where the sunbeam grazed them, or imitated some strange sea caves, filled

---

[1] *Avaunt!* Go away!

[2] *surcoats* Richly decorated coats.

[3] *mail* Rings or plates.

[4] *gorgets* Armored collars.

with flitting colours, where the shadow rose fuller and higher. In these chambers Don Juan found a number of sleepers, soldiers and slaves, black and white, all of whom sprang to their feet and rubbed their eyes and made obeisance as he went. Then he entered a long passage, lined on either side by a row of sleeping eunuchs, dressed in robes of honour, each leaning, sword in hand, against the wall, and of slave girls with stuff of striped silver about their loins, and sequins at the end of their long hair, and drums and timbrels[1] in their hands.

At regular intervals stood great golden cressets,[2] in which burned sweet-smelling wood, casting a reddish light over the sleeping faces. But as Don Juan approached, the slaves inclined their bodies to the ground, touching it with their turbans, and the girls thumped on their drums and jingled the brass bells of their timbrels. Thus he passed on from chamber to chamber till he came to a great door formed of stars of cedar and ivory studded with gold nails, and bolted by a huge gold bolt, on which ran mystic inscriptions. Don Juan stopped. But, as he did so, the bolt slowly moved in its socket, retreating gradually, and the immense portals swung slowly back, each into its carved hinge column.

Behind them was disclosed a vast circular hall, so vast that you could not possibly see where it ended, and filled with a profusion of lights, wax candles held by rows and rows of white maidens, and torches held by rows and rows of white-robed eunuchs, and cressets burning upon lofty stands, and lamps dangling from the distant vault, through which here and there entered, blending strangely with the rest, great beams of white daylight. Don Juan stopped short, blinded by this magnificence, and as he did so the fountain in the midst of the hall arose and shivered its cypress-like crest against the topmost vault, and innumerable voices of exquisite sweetness burst forth in strange, wistful chants, and instruments of all kinds, both such as are blown and such as are twanged and rubbed with a bow, and such as are shaken and thumped, united with the voices and filled the hall with sound, as it was already filled with light.

Don Juan grasped his sword and advanced. At the extremity of the hall a flight of alabaster steps led up to a dais or raised recess, overhung by an archway whose stalactites shone like beaten gold, and whose tiled walls glistened like precious stones. And on the dais, on a throne of sandalwood and ivory, encrusted with gems and carpeted with the product of the Chinese loom,[3] sat the Moorish Infanta, fast asleep.

To the right and the left, but on a step beneath the princess, stood her two most intimate attendants, the Chief Duenna and the Chief Eunuch, to whom the prudent King Yahya had entrusted his only child during her sleep of four hundred years. The Chief Duenna was habited in a suit of sad-coloured violet weeds,[4] with many modest swathings of white muslin round her yellow and wrinkled countenance. The Chief Eunuch was a portly negro, of a fine purple hue, with cheeks like an allegorical wind,[5] and a complexion as shiny as a well-worn door-knocker: he was enveloped from top to toe in marigold-coloured robes, and on his head he wore a towering turban of embroidered cashmere.

Both these great personages held, beside their especial insignia of office, namely, a Mecca rosary in the hand of the Duenna, and a silver wand in the hand of the Eunuch, great fans of white peacock's tails wherewith to chase away from their royal charge any ill-advised fly. But at this moment all the flies in the place were fast asleep, and the Duenna and the Eunuch also. And between them, canopied by a parasol of white silk on which were embroidered, in figures which moved like those in dreams, the histories of Jusuf and Zuleika,[6] of Solomon and the Queen of Sheba, and of many other famous lovers, sat the Infanta, erect, but veiled in gold-starred gauzes, as an unfinished statue is veiled in the roughness of the marble.

Don Juan walked quickly between the rows of prostrate slaves, and the singing dancing girls, and those holding tapers and torches; and stopped only at the very foot of the throne steps.

"Awake!" he cried. "My princess, my bride, awake!"

A faint stir arose in the veils of the muffled form; and Don Juan felt his temples throb, and, at the same

---

1   *timbrels*   Tambourines.

2   *cressets*   Vessels that hold combustible materials, for light.

3   *product … loom*   I.e., silk.

4   *weeds*   Clothes.

5   *cheeks … wind*   I.e., puffed out, as if ready to blow.

6   *Jusuf and Zuleika*   Subjects of a love story written by Sufi author Jami (c. 1490).

time, a deathly coldness steal over him.

"Awake!" he repeated boldly. But instead of the Infanta, it was the venerable Duenna who raised her withered countenance and looked round with a startled jerk, awakened not so much by the voices and instruments as by the tread of a masculine boot. The Chief Eunuch also awoke suddenly; but with the grace of one grown old in the antechamber of kings he quickly suppressed a yawn, and, laying his hand on his embroidered vest, made a profound obeisance.

"Verily," he remarked, "Allah (who alone possesses the secrets of the universe) is remarkably great, since he not only—"

"Awake, awake, princess!" interrupted Don Juan ardently, his foot on the lowest step of the throne.

But the Chief Eunuch waved him back with his wand, continuing his speech—"since he not only gave unto his servant King Yahya (may his shadow never be less!) power and riches far exceeding that of any of the kings of the earth or even of Solomon the son of David—"

"Cease, fellow!" cried Don Juan, and pushing aside the wand and the negro's dimpled chocolate hand, he rushed up the steps and flung himself at the foot of the veiled Infanta, his rapier clanging strangely as he did so.

"Unveil, my beloved, more beautiful than Oriana, for whom Amadis wept in the Black Mountain, than Gradasilia whom Felixmarte sought on the winged dragon, than Helen of Sparta who fired the towers of Troy, than Calixto whom Jove was obliged to change into a female bear, than Venus herself on whom Paris bestowed the fatal apple. Unveil and arise, like the rosy Aurora from old Tithonus'[1] couch, and welcome the knight who has confronted every peril for thee, Juan Gusman del Pulgar, Count of Miramor, who is ready, for thee, to confront every other peril of the world or of hell; and to fix upon thee alone his affections, more roving hitherto than those of Prince Galaor or of the many-shaped god Proteus!"

A shiver ran through the veiled princess. The Chief Eunuch gave a significant nod, and waved his white wand thrice. Immediately a concert of voices and instruments, as numerous as those of the forces of the air when mustered before King Solomon, filled the vast hall. The dancing girls raised their tambourines over their heads and poised themselves on tiptoe. A wave of fragrant essences passed through the air filled with the spray of innumerable fountains. And the Duenna, slowly advancing to the side of the throne, took in her withered fingers the topmost fold of shimmering gauze, and, slowly gathering it backwards, displayed the Infanta unveiled before Don Juan's gaze.

The breast of the princess heaved deeply; her lips opened with a little sigh, and she languidly raised her long-fringed lids, then cast down her eyes on the ground and resumed the rigidity of a statue. She was most marvellously fair. She sat on the cushions of the throne with modestly crossed legs; her hands, with nails tinged violet with henna, demurely folded in her lap. Through the thinness of her embroidered muslins shone the magnificence of purple and orange vests, stiff with gold and gems, and all subdued into a wondrous opalescent radiance. From her head there descended on either side of her person a diaphanous veil of shimmering colours, powdered over with minute glittering spangles. Her breast was covered with rows and rows of the largest pearls, a perfect network reaching from her slender throat to her waist, among which flashed diamonds embroidered in her vest.

Her face was oval, with the silver pallor of the young moon; her mouth, most subtly carmined,[2] looked like a pomegranate flower among tuberoses, for her cheeks were painted white, and the orbits of her great long-fringed eyes were stained violet. In the middle of each cheek, however, was a delicate spot of pink, in which an exquisite art had painted a small pattern of pyramid shape, so naturally that you might have thought that a real piece of embroidered stuff was decorating the maiden's countenance. On her head she wore a high tiara of jewels, the ransom of many kings, which sparkled and blazed like a lit-up altar. The eyes of the princess were decorously fixed on the ground.

Don Juan stood silent in ravishment.

"Princess!" he at length began.

But the Chief Eunuch laid his wand gently on his shoulder.

---

[1] *Oriana … Tithonus* Don Juan alludes to numerous love stories from romance, epic and myth.

[2] *carmined* Rubbed with crimson pigment.

"My Lord," he whispered, "it is not etiquette that your Magnificence should address her Highness in any direct fashion; let alone the fact that her Highness does not understand the Castilian tongue, nor your Magnificence the Arabic. But through the mediumship of this most respectable lady, her Discretion the Principal Duenna, and my unworthy self, a conversation can be carried on equally delicious and instructive to both parties."

"A plague upon the old brute!" thought Don Juan; but he reflected upon what had never struck him before, that they had indeed been conversing, or attempting to converse, in Spanish, and that the Castilian spoken by the Chief Eunuch was, although correct, quite obsolete, being that of the sainted King Ferdinand. There was a whispered consultation between the two great dignitaries; and the Duenna approached her lips to the Infanta's ear. The princess moved her pomegranate lips in a faint smile, but without raising her eyelids, and murmured something which the ancient lady whispered to the Chief Eunuch, who bowed thrice in answer. Then turning to Don Juan with most mellifluous tones, "Her Highness the Princess," he said, bowing thrice as he mentioned her name, "is, like all princesses, but to an even more remarkable extent, endowed with the most exquisite modesty. She is curious, therefore, despite the superiority of her charms—so conspicuous even to those born blind—to know whether your Magnificence does not consider her the most beautiful thing you have ever beheld."

Don Juan laid his hand upon his heart with an affirmative gesture more eloquent than any words.

Again an almost invisible smile hovered about the pomegranate mouth, and there was a murmur and a whispering consultation.

"Her Highness," pursued the Chief Eunuch blandly, "has been informed by the judicious instructors of her tender youth, that cavaliers are frequently fickle, and that your Lordship in particular has assured many ladies in succession that each was the most beautiful creature you had ever beheld. Without admitting for an instant the possibility of a parallel, she begs your Magnificence to satisfy her curiosity on the point. Does your Lordship consider her as infinitely more beautiful than the Lady Catalina?"

Now Catalina was one of the famous seven for whom Don Juan had committed a deadly crime.

He was taken aback by the exactness of the Infanta's information; he was rather sorry they should have told her about Catalina.

"Of course," he answered hastily; "pray do not mention such a name in her Highness's presence."

The princess bowed imperceptibly.

"Her Highness," pursued the Chief Eunuch, "still actuated by the curiosity due to her high birth and tender youth, is desirous of knowing whether your Lordship considers her far more beautiful than the Lady Violante?"

Don Juan made an impatient gesture. "Slave! Never speak of Violante in my princess's presence!" he exclaimed, fixing his eyes upon the tuberose cheeks and the pomegranate mouth which bloomed among that shimmer of precious stones.

"Good. And may the same be said to apply to the ladies Dolores and Elvira?"

"Dolores and Elvira and Fatma and Azahar," answered Don Juan, greatly provoked at the Chief Eunuch's want of tact, "and all the rest of womankind."

"And shall we add also, than Sister Seraphita of the Convent of Santa Isabel la Real?"

"Yes," cried Don Juan, "than Sister Seraphita, for whom I committed the greatest sin which can be committed by living man."

As he said these words, Don Juan was about to fling his arms about the princess and cut short this rather too elaborate courtship.

But again he was waved back by the white wand.

"One question more, only one, my dear Lord," whispered the Chief Eunuch. "I am most concerned at your impatience, but the laws of etiquette and the caprices of young princesses *must* go before everything, as you will readily admit. Stand back, I pray you."

Don Juan felt sorely inclined to thrust his sword through the yellow bolster of the great personage's vest; but he choked his rage, and stood quietly on the throne steps, one hand on his heart, the other on his sword-hilt, the boldest cavalier in all the kingdom of Spain.

"Speak, speak!" he begged.

The princess, without moving a muscle of her exquisite face, or unclosing her flower-like mouth, murmured some words to the Duenna, who whispered them mysteriously to the Chief Eunuch.

At this moment also the Infanta raised her heavy eyelids, stained violet with henna, and fixed upon the cavalier a glance long, dark, and deep, like that of the wild antelope.

"Her Highness," resumed the Chief Eunuch, with a sweet smile, "is extremely gratified with your Lordship's answers, although, of course, they could not possibly have been at all different. But there remains yet another lady—"

Don Juan shook his head impatiently.

"Another lady concerning whom the Infanta desires some information. Does your Lordship consider her more beautiful also than the Virgin of the Seven Daggers?"

The place seemed to swim about Don Juan. Before his eyes rose the throne, all vacillating in its splendour, and on the throne the Moorish Infanta with the triangular patterns painted on her tuberose cheeks, and the long look in her henna'd eyes; and the image of her was blurred, and imperceptibly it seemed to turn into the effigy, black and white in her stiff puce frock and seed-pearl stomacher,[1] of the Virgin of the Seven Daggers staring blankly into space.

"My Lord," remarked the Chief Eunuch, "methinks that love has made you somewhat inattentive, a great blemish in a cavalier, when answering the questions of a lovely princess. I therefore venture to repeat: do you consider her more beautiful than the Virgin of the Seven Daggers?"

"Do you consider her more beautiful than the Virgin of the Seven Daggers?" repeated the Duenna, glaring at Don Juan.

"Do you consider me more beautiful than the Virgin of the Seven Daggers?" asked the princess, speaking suddenly in Spanish, or, at least, in language perfectly intelligible to Don Juan. And, as she spoke the words, all the slave-girls and eunuchs and singers and players, the whole vast hallful, seemed to echo the same question.

The Count of Miramor stood silent for an instant; then raising his hand and looking around him with quiet decision, he answered in a loud voice:

"No!"

"In that case," said the Chief Eunuch, with the politeness of a man desirous of cutting short an embarrassing silence, "in that case I am very sorry it should be my painful duty to intimate to your Lordship that you must undergo the punishment usually allotted to cavaliers who are disobliging to young and tender princesses."

So saying, he clapped his black hands, and, as if by magic, there arose at the foot of the steps a gigantic Berber of the Rif,[2] his brawny sunburned limbs left bare by a scanty striped shirt fastened round his waist by a wisp of rope, his head shaven blue except in the middle, where, encircled by a coronet of worsted rag, there flamed a topknot of dreadful orange hair.

"Decapitate that gentleman," ordered the Chief Eunuch in his most obliging tones. Don Juan felt himself collared, dragged down the steps, and forced into a kneeling posture on the lowest landing, all in the twinkling of an eye.

From beneath the bronzed left arm of the ruffian he could see the milk white of the alabaster steps, the gleam of an immense scimitar,[3] the mingled blue and yellow of the cressets and tapers, the daylight filtering through the constellations in the dark cedar vault, the glitter of the Infanta's diamonds, and, of a sudden, the twinkle of the Chief Eunuch's eye.

Then all was black, and Don Juan felt himself, that is to say, his own head, rebound three times like a ball upon the alabaster steps.

6

It had evidently all been a dream—perhaps a delusion induced by the vile fumigations of that filthy ruffian of a renegade Jew. The infidel dogs had certain abominable drugs which gave them visions of paradise and hell when smoked or chewed—nasty brutes that they were—and this was some of their devilry. But he should pay for it, the cursed old graybeard, the Holy Office should keep him warm, or a Miramor was not a Miramor. For Don Juan forgot, or disbelieved, not only that he himself had been beheaded by a Rif Berber the evening before, but that he had previously run poor Baruch through the

---

[1]   *stomacher*   Jeweled chest covering.

[2]   *Berber*   Member of a tribe of North Africa, in this case from the Rif district in Morocco.

[3]   *scimitar*   Curved sword.

body and hurled him down the rocks near the Tower of the Cypresses.

This confusion of mind was excusable on the part of the cavalier. For, on opening his eyes, he had found himself lying in a most unlikely resting place, considering the time and season, namely, a heap of old bricks and rubbish, half-hidden in withered reeds and sprouting weeds, on a ledge of the precipitous hillside that descends into the River Darro. Above him rose the dizzy red-brick straightness of the tallest tower of the Alhambra, pierced at its very top by an arched and pillared window, and scantily overgrown with the roots of a dead ivy tree. Below, at the bottom of the precipice, dashed the little Darro, brown and swollen with melted snows, between its rows of leafless poplars; beyond it, the roofs and balconies and orange trees of the older part of Grenada; and above that, with the morning sunshine and mists fighting among its hovels, its square belfries and great masses of prickly pear and aloe, the Albaycin, whose highest convent tower stood out already against a sky of winter blue. The Albaycin—that was the quarter of that villain Baruch, who dared to play practical jokes on grandees of Spain of the very first class.

This thought caused Don Juan to spring up, and, grasping his sword, to scramble through the sprouting elder-bushes and the heaps of broken masonry, down to the bridge over the river.

It was a beautiful winter morning, sunny, blue, and crisp through the white mists; and Don Juan sped along as with wings to his feet, for having remembered that it was the anniversary of the Liberation, and that he, as descendant of Fernan Perez del Pulgar, would be expected to carry the banner of the city at High Mass in the Cathedral, he had determined that his absence from the ceremony should raise no suspicions of his ridiculous adventure. For ridiculous it had been—and the sense of its being ridiculous filled the generous breast of the Count of Miramor with a longing to murder every man, woman, or child he encountered as he sped through the streets. "Look at his Excellency the Count of Miramor; look at Don Juan Gusman del Pulgar! He's been made a fool of by old Baruch the renegade Jew!" he imagined everybody to be thinking.

But, on the contrary, no one took the smallest notice of him. The muleteers, driving along their beasts laden with heather and myrtle for the bakehouse ovens, allowed their loads to brush him as if he had been the merest errand-boy; the stout black housewives, going to market with their brass braziers tucked under their cloaks, never once turned round as he pushed them rudely on the cobbles; nay, the very beggars, armless and legless and shameless, who were alighting from their go-carts and taking up their station at the church doors, did not even extend a hand towards the passing cavalier. Before a popular barber's some citizens were waiting to have their topknots plaited into tidy tails, discussing the while the olive harvest, the price of spart-grass[1] and the chances of the bull-ring. This, Don Juan expected, would be a fatal spot, for from the barber's shop the news must go about that Don Juan del Pulgar, hatless and covered with mud, was hurrying home with a discomfited countenance, ill-befitting the hero of so many nocturnal adventures. But, although Don Juan had to make his way right in front of the barber's, not one of the clients did so much as turn his head, perhaps out of fear of displeasing so great a cavalier. Suddenly, as Don Juan hurried along, he noticed for the first time, among the cobbles and the dry mud of the street, large drops of blood, growing larger as they went, becoming an almost uninterrupted line, then, in the puddles, a little red stream. Such were by no means uncommon vestiges in those days of duels and town broils;[2] besides, some butcher or early sportsman, a wild boar on his horse, might have been passing.

But somehow or other this track of blood exerted an odd attraction over Don Juan; and unconsciously to himself, instead of taking the shortcut to his palace, he followed it along some of the chief streets of Grenada. The bloodstains, as was natural, led in the direction of the great hospital, founded by St. John of God, to which it was customary to carry the victims of accidents and street fights. Before the monumental gateway, where St. John of God knelt in effigy before the Madonna, a large crowd was collected, above whose heads oscillated the black-and-white banners of a mortuary confraternity, and the flame and smoke of their torches. The street was blocked with carts, and with riders rising in their stirrups to look over the crowd, and even by gaily

---

[1]   *spart-grass*   Spanish broom, or rushes.
[2]   *broils*   Battles.

trapped mules and gilded coaches, in which veiled ladies were anxiously questioning their lackeys and outriders. The throng of idle and curious citizens, of monks and brothers of mercy, reached up the steps and right into the cloistered court of the hospital.

"Who is it?" asked Don Juan, with his usual masterful manner pushing his way into the crowd. The man whom he addressed, a stalwart peasant with a long tail pinned under his hat, turned round vaguely, but did not answer.

"Who is it?" repeated Don Juan louder.

But no one answered, although he accompanied the question with a good push, and even a thrust with his sheathed sword.

"Cursed idiots! Are you all deaf and dumb that you cannot answer a cavalier?" he cried angrily, and taking a portly priest by the collar he shook him roughly.

"Jesus Maria Joseph!" exclaimed the priest; but turning round he took no notice of Don Juan, and merely rubbed his collar, muttering, "Well, if the demons are to be allowed to take respectable canons by the collar, it *is* time that we should have a good witch-burning."

Don Juan took no heed of his words, but thrust onward, upsetting, as he did so, a young woman who was lifting her child to let it see the show. The crowd parted as the woman fell, and people ran to pick her up, but no one took any notice of Don Juan. Indeed, he himself was struck by the way in which he passed through its midst, encountering no opposition from the phalanx of robust shoulders and hips.

"Who is it?" asked Don Juan again.

He had got into a clearing of the crowd. On the lowest step of the hospital gate stood a little knot of black penitents, their black linen cowls flung back on their shoulders, and of priests and monks muttering together. Some of them were beating back the crowd, others snuffing their torches against the paving-stones, and letting the wax drip off their tapers. In the midst of them, with a standard of the Virgin at its head, was a light wooden bier, set down by its bearers. It was covered with coarse black serge, on which were embroidered in yellow braid a skull and crossbones, and the monogram I.H.S.[1] Under the bier was a little red pool.

"Who is it?" asked Don Juan one last time; but instead of waiting for an answer, he stepped forward, sword in hand, and rudely pulled aside the rusty black pall.

On the bier was stretched a corpse dressed in black velvet, with lace cuffs and collar, loose boots, buff gloves, and a blood-clotted dark matted head, lying loose half an inch above the mangled throat.

Don Juan Gusman del Pulgar stared fixedly.

It was himself.

The church into which Don Juan had fled was that of the Virgin of the Seven Daggers. It was deserted, as usual, and filled with chill morning light, in which glittered the gilded cornices and altars, and gleamed, like pools of water, the many precious marbles. A sort of mist seemed to hang about it all and dim the splendour of the high altar.

Don Juan del Pulgar sank down in the midst of the nave; not on his knees, for (O horror!) he felt that he had no longer any knees, nor indeed any back, any arms, or limbs of any kind, and he dared not ask himself whether he was still in possession of a head: his only sensations were such as might be experienced by a slowly trickling pool, or a snow-wreath in process of melting, or a cloud fitting itself on to a flat surface of rock.

He was disembodied. He now understood why no one had noticed him in the crowd, why he had been able to penetrate through its thickness, and why, when he struck people and pulled them by the collar and knocked them down, they had taken no more notice of him than of a blast of wind. He was a ghost. He was dead. This was the afterlife; and he was infallibly within a few minutes of hell.

"O Virgin, Virgin of the Seven Daggers," he cried with hopeless bitterness, "is this the way you recompense my faithfulness? I have died unshriven,[2] in the midst of mortal sin, merely because I would not say you were less beautiful than the Moorish Infanta; and is this all my reward?"

But even as he spoke these words an extraordinary miracle took place. The white winter light broke into wondrous iridescences; the white mist collected into

---

[1]   *I.H.S.*   Represents the Greek abbreviation of the word Jesus.

[2]   *unshriven*   Without the sacrament of Confession and the accompanying forgiveness of sins.

shoals of dim palm-bearing angels; the cloud of stale incense, still hanging over the high altar, gathered into fleecy balls, which became the heads and backs of well-to-do cherubs; and Don Juan, reeling and fainting, felt himself rise, higher and higher, as if borne up on clusters of soap bubbles. The cupola began to rise and expand; the painted clouds to move and blush a deeper pink; the painted sky to recede and turn into deep holes of real blue. As he was borne upwards, the allegorical virtues in the lunettes began to move and brandish their attributes; the colossal stucco angels on the cornices to pelt him with flowers no longer of plaster of Paris; the place was filled with delicious fragrance of incense, and with sounds of exquisitely played lutes and viols, and of voices, among which he distinctly recognized Syphax, His Majesty's chief soprano. And, as Don Juan floated upwards through the cupola of the church, his heart suddenly filled with a consciousness of extraordinary virtue; the gold transparency at the top of the dome expanded; its rays grew redder and more golden, and there burst from it at last a golden moon crescent, on which stood, in her farthingale of puce and her

stomacher of seed-pearl, her big black eyes fixed mildly upon him, the Virgin of the Seven Daggers.

"Your story of the late noble Count of Miramor, Don Juan Gusman del Pulgar," wrote Don Pedro Calderon de la Barca, in March 1666, to his friend, the Archpriest Morales, at Grenada, "so veraciously revealed in a vision to the holy prior of St. Nicholas, is indeed such as must touch the heart of the most stubborn. Were it presented in the shape of a play, adorned with graces of style and with flowers of rhetoric, it would be indeed (with the blessing of heaven) well calculated to spread the glory of our holy church. But alas, my dear friend, the snows of age are as thick on my head as the snows of winter upon your Mulhacen; and who knows whether I shall ever be able to write again?"

The forecast of the illustrious dramatic poet proved, indeed, too true; and hence it is that unworthy modern hands have sought to frame the veracious and moral history of Don Juan and the Virgin of the Seven Daggers.
—1889

RUDYARD KIPLING
1865 – 1936

The name "Rudyard Kipling" evokes images of the Raj in India, a time when Britannia ruled the waves and the sun never set on the British Empire. Indeed his life spanned most of the duration of British Colonial Office rule in India (1858–1947). Kipling, for many years considered England's unofficial poet laureate, was a strong proponent of imperialism; he believed it was Britain's duty to govern and civilize colonized lands. Though he was also capable of offering serious critiques of empire—and though he acknowledged that colonized people were "captives"— Kipling gave frequent voice to his belief that the British were in India to serve the native people. His famous 1899 poem, "The White Man's Burden," published in *McClure's Magazine*, aroused a storm of controversy, coming out at a time when many people were beginning to question the right of imperialist powers to subjugate foreigners. Nevertheless, for more than a half century Kipling's poems, short stories, and novels were wildly popular in India, Great Britain, and the United States, and in 1907 the Nobel Foundation honored him "in consideration of the power of observation, originality of imagination, virility of ideas and remarkable talent for narration which characterize the creations of this world-famous author." Thus Kipling became the first British writer to be awarded the Nobel Prize for Literature.

Kipling was named after Rudyard Lake in England, but he was born in Bombay (now Mumbai), India. Both his father, John Lockwood Kipling, professor of architectural sculpture at the University of Bombay, and his mother, Alice Macdonald, were children of Methodist ministers. Macdonald and her sisters were all associated with distinguished people—one sister married the neoclassical painter Sir Edward Poynter; another was the mother of Stanley Baldwin, who became Prime Minister of England in 1923; and another was the wife of the Pre-Raphaelite painter Sir Edward Burne-Jones. Kipling spent his first six years with his parents, learning the languages of his Indian friends and imbibing the cultural wealth of India. Of his school years, however, Kipling would say in his autobiography that his only happy moments were spent at the Burne-Jones home. Like many children of expatriates, he and his sister were sent to England for their education, where they spent five miserable years with severe, Calvinist foster parents in a home that Kipling would later call the House of Desolation. In 1878 he transferred to a boarding school in Devon (depicted in *Stalky and Co.*), which was also brutal at times, but where he acquired his schoolboy ethos (the sense of loyalty to and camaraderie with his peers so evident in his work) and began to write in earnest.

Upon graduation, Kipling moved back to India, working first as a newspaper journalist for the *Civil and Military Gazette* in Lahore (now part of Pakistan) and then as an editor of *Pioneer* in Allahabad. Many of the poems and stories he wrote during that time were collected in *Departmental Ditties* (1886) and *Plain Tales from the Hills* (1888), in which Kipling wrote about the moral and psychological difficulties of integrating Indian and British cultures. The Indian Railway Library also published some of Kipling's stories, such as *The Phantom Rickshaw* and *Wee Willie Winkie* (1888), in booklet form. By the time he returned to England in 1889, Kipling was a well-established author in India and had become very popular in Britain as well. The English public loved his "tales of the exotic," which took them to worlds they could scarcely imagine and introduced them to cultures they would likely never experience first-hand.

Kipling published several collections of short stories and poems in the early 1890s; the volume *Barrack-Room Ballads and Other Verses* (1892), which included such well-known poems as "Mandalay" and "Gunga Din," went into more than 50 editions in the 30 years following. Two early novels, *The Light that Failed* (1891) and *The Naulahka* (1892), did not fare as well. Nevertheless, in this period Kipling acquired a reputation as a spokesman for the people. With lyrics often inspired by street ballads and music hall ditties, he wrote using everyday language and expressed the thoughts of soldiers and other working people.

In 1892 Kipling married an American, Caroline Balestier, and the couple settled in Vermont. Although Kipling was unhappy in the United States, he wrote some of his most esteemed works during his five-year stay there, including *The Jungle Book* (1894), *The Second Jungle Book* (1895), and *Captains Courageous* (1897). On a return trip to the United States in 1899, Josephine, one of the three Kipling children, died. Another child, John, died in action in World War I; Kipling dealt with his grief by writing a history of his son's regiment, *The Irish Guards in the Great War*, published in 1923.

The family eventually settled in Sussex, England, but Kipling continued to travel the world as a newspaper correspondent. He covered the Boer War in South Africa in 1899 and returned to the region annually thereafter, staying in a house given to him by Cecil Rhodes, the famous British imperialist and business magnate. Kipling's own imperialist political sentiments were disseminated widely at the turn of the century, most notably in the London *Times*, which published "Recessional," composed in honor of Queen Victoria's Diamond Jubilee, and "The White Man's Burden." The latter poem was soon afterward countered in the London magazine *Truth* with a poem by Henry Labouchère, which changed Kipling's opening refrain from "Take up the white man's burden," to "Pile on the brown man's burden." Amid the controversy that ensued, a letter to the editor was published that read: "There is something almost sickening in this 'imperial' talk of assuming and bearing burdens for the good of others. They are never assumed or held where they are not found to be of material advantage or ministering to honor or glory." Kipling himself suggested that his poem offered neither a noble call to arms nor a justification for colonization, but rather a warning of the costs involved on both sides of imperialist missions abroad.

Kipling's least controversial and best-loved novel appeared in 1901. *Kim* is a picaresque adventure tale of a British beggar boy, the orphaned son of an Irish soldier. Raised in Lahore by an opium-addicted, half-caste woman, Kim O'Hare comes to believe he is destined for greatness and eventually travels through India with a holy man in search of his glorious future. In 1907, the Nobel committee said that in *Kim* "there is an elevated diction as well as a tenderness and charm.... In sketching a personality he makes clear, almost in his first words, the peculiar traits of that person's character and temper.... [Kipling is] capable of reproducing with astounding accuracy the minutest detail from real life."

In the decades following his Nobel Prize, Kipling's literary output dwindled somewhat amid controversy over his politics and grief over the loss of two of his three children. Even former admirers, such as W.B. Yeats and T.S. Eliot, began to be critical of Kipling's unwavering allegiance to British imperialism. Nevertheless, the last half century has seen a resurgence of interest in his work.

Sir Ian Hamilton said that Kipling's death in January 1936 (two days before the death of Kipling's friend, King George V) placed "a full stop to the period when war was a romance and the expansion of our Empire a duty." When his ashes were interred in Poets' Corner of Westminster Abbey, Kipling's pallbearers included the then-prime minister of England, a field marshal, and the admiral of the fleet; the poem "Recessional" was sung as a hymn. Kipling's unfinished autobiography, *Something of Myself*, was published posthumously a year after his death.

⌘ ⌘ ⌘

Gunga Din

You may talk o' gin and beer
When you're quartered safe out 'ere,
An' you're sent to penny-fights° an' Aldershot[1] it;   skirmishes
But when it comes to slaughter
5 You will do your work on water,
An' you'll lick the bloomin' boots of 'im that's got it.
Now in Injia's sunny clime,
Where I used to spend my time
A-servin' of 'Er Majesty the Queen,
10 Of all them blackfaced crew
The finest man I knew
Was our regimental bhisti,° Gunga Din.   water carrier
        He was "Din! Din! Din!
    "You limpin' lump o' brick-dust, Gunga Din!
15   "Hi! Slippy hitherao![2]
        "Water, get it! Panee lao,[3]
    "You squidgy-nosed old idol, Gunga Din."

The uniform 'e wore
Was nothin' much before,
20 An' rather less than 'arf o' that be'ind,
For a piece o' twisty rag
An' a goatskin water bag
Was all the field equipment 'e could find.
When the sweatin' troop train lay
25 In a sidin' through the day,
Where the 'eat would make your bloomin' eyebrows crawl,
We shouted "Harry By!"[4]
Till our throats were bricky-dry,
Then we wopped 'im 'cause 'e couldn't serve us all.
30   It was "Din! Din! Din!
    "You 'eathen, where the mischief 'ave you been?
        "You put some juldee[5] in it

"Or I'll marrow[6] you this minute
    "If you don't fill up my helmet, Gunga Din!"
35 'E would dot an' carry one[7]
Till the longest day was done;
An' 'e didn't seem to know the use o' fear.
If we charged or broke or cut,
You could bet your bloomin' nut,
40 'E'd be waitin' fifty paces right flank rear.
With 'is mussick° on 'is back,   waterbag
'E would skip with our attack,
An' watch us till the bugles made "Retire,"
An' for all 'is dirty 'ide
45 'E was white, clear white, inside
When 'e went to tend the wounded under fire!
        It was "Din! Din! Din!"
    With the bullets kickin' dust spots on the green.
        When the cartridges ran out,
50   You could hear the front ranks shout,
    "Hi! ammunition mules an' Gunga Din!"

I shan't forgit the night
When I dropped be'ind the fight
With a bullet where my belt plate should 'a' been.
55 I was chokin' mad with thirst,
An' the man that spied me first
Was our good old grinnin,' gruntin' Gunga Din.
'E lifted up my 'ead,
An' he plugged me where I bled,
60 An' 'e guv me 'arf-a-pint o' water green.
It was crawlin' and it stunk,
But of all the drinks I've drunk,
I'm gratefullest to one from Gunga Din.
        It was "Din! Din! Din!
65 "'Ere's a beggar with a bullet through 'is spleen;
    "'E's chawin' up the ground,
        "An' 'e's kickin' all around:
    "For Gawd's sake git the water, Gunga Din!"

---

1 *Aldershot*   Town southwest of London, site of a military training center.

2 *Slippy hitherao*   I.e., *idhar ao*. Urdu: Come here!

3 *Panee lao*   Urdu: Bring water.

4 *Harry By*   I.e., *arré bhai!* Urdu: in this context, Hey, you!

5 *julee*   I.e., *juldee karo*. Urdu: Hurry!

6 *marrow*   I.e., *maro*. Urdu: hit.

7 *dot an' carry one*   From mathematics: calculate.

'E carried me away
70 To where a dooli° lay,   *stretcher*
An' a bullet come an' drilled the beggar clean.
'E put me safe inside,
An' just before 'e died,
"I 'ope you liked your drink," sez Gunga Din.
75 So I'll meet 'im later on
At the place where 'e is gone—
Where it's always double drill and no canteen.
'E'll be squattin' on the coals
Givin' drink to poor damned souls,
80 An' I'll get a swig in hell from Gunga Din!
    Yes, Din! Din! Din!
  You Lazarushian[1]-leather Gunga Din!
    Though I've belted you and flayed you,
    By the livin' Gawd that made you,
85   You're a better man than I am, Gunga Din!
—1890

The Widow at Windsor[2]

'Ave you 'eard o' the Widow at Windsor
  With a hairy gold crown on 'er 'ead?
She 'as ships on the foam—she 'as millions at 'ome,
  An' she pays us poor beggars in red.[3]
5   (Ow, poor beggars in red!)
There's 'er nick[4] on the cavalry 'orses,
  There's 'er mark[5] on the medical stores—
An' 'er troopers° you'll find with a fair wind be'ind   *troop-ships*
  That takes us to various wars.
10   (Poor beggars!—barbarious wars!)
    Then 'ere's to the Widow at Windsor,
      An 'ere's to the stores an' the guns,
    The men an' the 'orses what makes up the
      forces
      O' Missis Victorier's sons.
15   (Poor beggars! Victorier's sons!)

Walk wide o' the Widow at Windsor,
  For 'alf o' Creation she owns:
We 'ave bought 'er the same with the sword an' the flame,
  An' we've salted it down with our bones.
20   (Poor beggars!—it's blue with our bones!)
Hands off o' the sons o' the Widow,
  Hands off o' the goods in 'er shop,
For the kings must come down an' the emperors frown
  When the Widow at Windsor says "Stop!"
25   (Poor beggars!—we're sent to say "Stop!")
    Then 'ere's to the lodge o' the Widow,
      From the pole to the tropics it runs—
    To the lodge that we tile with the rank an' the file,
      An' open in form with the guns.
30   (Poor beggars!—it's always they guns!)

We 'ave 'eard o' the Widow at Windsor,
  It's safest to leave 'er alone:
For 'er sentries we stand by the sea an' the land
  Wherever the bugles are blown.
35   (Poor beggars!—an' don't we get blown!)
Take 'old o' the Wings o' the Mornin',[6]
  An' flop round the earth till you're dead;
But you won't get away from the tune that they play
  To the bloomin' old rag over'ead.
40   (Poor beggars!—it's 'ot over'ead!)
    Then 'ere's to the sons o' the Widow,
      Wherever, 'owever they roam.
    'Ere's all they desire, an' if they require
      A speedy return to their 'ome.
45   (Poor beggars! they'll never see 'ome!)
—1890

---

[1] *Lazarushian* Cf. Luke 16; the good Lazarus was a leper/beggar.

[2] *The Widow at Windsor* Queen Victoria, who, upon losing her husband in 1861, went into permanent mourning. (See the "In Context" section below for more information.)

[3] *red* Red coats of British soldiers.

[4] *'er nick* Mark distinguishing animals as belonging to the queen.

[5] *'er mark* "V.R.I.," the Queen's identification mark.

[6] *Wings of the Mornin'* From Psalm 139.9–10: "If I take the wings of the morning, and dwell in the uttermost parts of the sea; / Even there shall thy hand lead me, and thy right hand shall hold me."

Recessional[1]

God of our fathers, known of old,
    Lord of our far-flung battle-line,
Beneath whose awful Hand we hold
    Dominion over palm and pine—
5   Lord God of Hosts, be with us yet,
Lest we forget[2]—lest we forget!

The tumult and the shouting dies;
    The captains and the kings depart:
Still stands Thine ancient sacrifice,
10   An humble and a contrite heart.[3]
Lord God of Hosts, be with us yet,
Lest we forget—lest we forget!

Far-called, our navies melt away;
    On dune and headland sinks the fire:
15 Lo, all our pomp of yesterday
    Is one with Nineveh and Tyre![4]
Judge of the nations, spare us yet,
Lest we forget—lest we forget!

If, drunk with sight of power, we loose
20   Wild tongues that have not Thee in awe,
Such boastings as the Gentiles use,
    Or lesser breeds without the law[5]—
Lord God of Hosts, be with us yet,
Lest we forget—lest we forget!

25 For heathen heart that puts her trust
    In reeking tube and iron shard,

All valiant dust that builds on dust,
    And guarding, calls not Thee to guard,
For frantic boast and foolish word—
30 Thy mercy on Thy people, Lord!
    —1897

The White Man's Burden

THE UNITED STATES AND THE PHILIPPINE ISLANDS[6]

Take up the White Man's burden—
    Send forth the best ye breed—
Go bind your sons to exile
    To serve your captives' need;
5   To wait in heavy harness
    On fluttered folk and wild—
Your new-caught, sullen peoples,
    Half devil and half child.

Take up the White Man's burden—
10   In patience to abide,
To veil the threat of terror
    And check the show of pride;
By open speech and simple,
    An hundred times made plain.
15 To seek another's profit,
    And work another's gain.

Take up the White Man's burden—
    The savage wars of peace—
Fill full the mouth of Famine
20   And bid the sickness cease;
And when your goal is nearest
    The end for others sought,
Watch Sloth and heathen Folly
    Bring all your hope to nought.

---

[1] *Recessional*   Hymn written for Queen Victoria's sixtieth anniversary Jubilee.

[2] *Lest we forget*   Cf. Deuteronomy 4.9: "[T]ake heed to thyself, and keep thy soul diligently, lest thou forget the things which thine eyes have seen, and lest they depart from thy heart all the days of thy life: but teach them thy sons, and thy sons' sons."

[3] *contrite heart*   Cf. Psalms 51.17: "The sacrifices of God are a broken spirit: a broken and a contrite heart."

[4] *Nineveh and Tyre*   Ruined cities that were once capitals of empires.

[5] *Gentiles … law*   Cf. Romans 2.14: "For when the Gentiles, which have not the law, do by nature the things contained in the law, these, having not the law, are a law unto themselves."

---

[6] *United States and the Philippine Islands*   Response to the American takeover of the Philippines after the Spanish American War of 1898. (See the "In Context" section below for more information.)

Take up the White Man's burden—
    No tawdry rule of kings,
But toil of serf and sweeper—
    The tale of common things.
The ports ye shall not enter,
    The roads ye shall not tread,
Go make them with your living,
    And mark them with your dead!

Take up the White Man's burden—
    And reap his old reward:
The blame of those ye better,
    The hate of those ye guard—
The cry of hosts ye humour
    (Ah, slowly!) toward the light:—
"Why brought ye us from bondage,
    "Our loved Egyptian night?"

Take up the White Man's burden—
    Ye dare not stoop to less—
Nor call too loud on Freedom
    To cloak your weariness;
By all ye cry or whisper,
    By all ye leave or do,
The silent, sullen peoples
    Shall weigh your gods and you.

Take up the White Man's burden—
    Have done with childish days—
The lightly proffered laurel,[1]
    The easy, ungrudged praise.
Comes now, to search your manhood
    Through all the thankless years,
Cold-edged with dear-bought wisdom,
    The judgment of your peers!
    —1899

If—[2]

If you can keep your head when all about you
    Are losing theirs and blaming it on you,
If you can trust yourself when all men doubt you,
    But make allowance for their doubting too;
If you can wait and not be tired by waiting,
    Or being lied about, don't deal in lies,
Or being hated, don't give way to hating,
    And yet don't look too good, nor talk too wise:

If you can dream—and not make dreams your master;
    If you can think—and not make thoughts your aim;
If you can meet with Triumph and Disaster
    And treat those two impostors just the same;
If you can bear to hear the truth you've spoken
    Twisted by knaves to make a trap for fools,
Or watch the things you gave your life to, broken,
    And stoop and build 'em up with worn out tools:

If you can make one heap of all your winnings
    And risk it on one turn of pitch-and-toss,[3]
And lose, and start again at your beginnings
    And never breathe a word about your loss;
If you can force your heart and nerve and sinew
    To serve your turn long after they are gone,
And so hold on when there is nothing in you
    Except the Will which says to them: "Hold on!"

If you can talk with crowds and keep your virtue,
    Or walk with kings—nor lose the common touch,
If neither foes nor loving friends can hurt you,
    If all men count with you, but none too much;
If you can fill the unforgiving minute
    With sixty seconds' worth of distance run,
Yours is the earth and everything that's in it,
    And—which is more—you'll be a man, my son!
    —1910

[2] *If* Among other possibilities, this poem may have been written in celebration of Dr. Leander Starr Jameson. Jameson launched the failed Jameson Raid of British troops against the Boers in South Africa in 1895, which ultimately led to the Boer War (1899–1902). Jameson went on to serve as Premier of the Cape Colony from 1904–08.

[3] *pitch-and-toss* Coin tossing game.

[1] *laurel* Leaves of the bay laurel tree are a symbol of victory.

IN CONTEXT

Victoria and Albert

Queen Victoria was widowed when Prince Albert died on 14 December 1861. His partnership with the Queen had been an extraordinarily successful one—as a professional partnership as well as in family life. For many years after his death the Queen was a recluse, so much so that the public began to lose patience with and sympathy for Victoria in her mourning. It was not until the early 1870s that the Queen began to re-emerge. As she did so she gradually regained public favor, and by the time Kipling's "The Widow at Windsor" was published in 1890 she was widely revered. Her 60th Anniversary Jubilee in 1897—for which Kipling composed "Recessional"—was a massive national celebration.

Frederick Shuckard's painting of an idealized 18-year-old Princess Victoria receiving news of her accession to the throne in 1837.

Queen Victoria and Prince Albert in the early
1850s. (Photograph by Roger Fenton.)

Queen Victoria in mourning, 1867.

Queen Victoria with John Brown, a servant who
had been personal ghillie (the term applied to
the attendant to a Highland Chief) to Prince
Albert and who later served Queen Victoria;
Brown is credited with helping to bring the
Queen out from seclusion.
(Photo by W & D Downy.)

The Queen with Princess Beatrice, Princess
Victoria, and great-grand-daughter Alice, 1867.
(Photographer unknown.)

Queen Victoria in the Golden Jubilee procession,
1897.

Victoria holding the future Edward VIII on the occasion of his baptism;
her sons Edward (later Edward VII) and George (later George V) are in the background.

In Context

The "White Man's Burden" in the Philippines

The Philippine Islands had long been a Spanish colony, but Spain's defeat in 1898 at the hands of American Admiral George Dewey during the Spanish-American War was followed by an agreement ceding the islands to the United States for $20 million. Local forces (under Emilio Agninaldo) had been rebelling against the Spanish, and, expecting the American victory to lead to liberation, declared a republic. The Americans, however, deciding that the natives were not ready for independence, ruthlessly suppressed the insurrection of Agninaldo's forces (which continued until 1905). Not until 1946 was the Republic of the Philippines granted full independence. The American annexation of the islands in 1899 was widely popular in the United States, but a significant minority loudly protested the expression of American imperialism that was the occasion for Kipling's famous poem. Following are excerpts from the platform adopted by one American organization at their founding meeting in Chicago, 17 October 1899.

Platform of the American Anti-Imperialist League

We hold that the policy known as imperialism is hostile to liberty and tends toward militarism, an evil from which it has been our glory to be free. We regret that it has become necessary in the land of Washington and Lincoln to reaffirm that all men, of whatever race or color, are entitled to life, liberty, and the pursuit of happiness. We maintain that governments derive their just powers from the consent of the governed. We insist that the subjugation of any people is "criminal aggression" and open disloyalty to the distinctive principles of our government.

We earnestly condemn the policy of the present national administration in the Philippines. It seeks to extinguish the spirit of 1776 in those islands. We deplore the sacrifice of our soldiers and sailors, whose bravery deserves admiration even in an unjust war. We denounce the slaughter of the Filipinos as a needless horror. We protest against the extension of American sovereignty by Spanish methods.

We demand the immediate cessation of the war against liberty, begun by Spain and continued by us. We urge that Congress be promptly convened to announce to the Filipinos our purpose to concede to them the independence for which they have so long fought and which of right is theirs.

The United States have always protested against the doctrine of international law which permits the subjugation of the weak by the strong. A self-governing state cannot accept sovereignty over an unwilling people. The United States cannot act upon the ancient heresy that might makes right.

Imperialists assume that with the destruction of self-government in the Philippines by American hands, all opposition here will cease. This is a grievous error. Much as we abhor the war of "criminal aggression" in the Philippines, greatly as we regret that the blood of the Filipinos is on American hands, we more deeply resent the betrayal of American institutions at home. The real firing line is not in the suburbs of Manila. The foe is of our own household. The attempt of 1861 was to divide the country. That of 1899 is to destroy its fundamental principles and noblest ideals.

Whether the ruthless slaughter of the Filipinos shall end next month or next year is but an incident in a contest that must go on until the Declaration of Independence and the Constitution of the United States are rescued from the hands of their betrayers. Those who dispute about standards of value while the Republic is undermined will be listened to as little as there who would wrangle about the small economies of the household while the house is on fire. The training of a great people for a century, the aspiration for liberty of a vast immigration are forces that will hurl aside those who in the delirium of conquest seek to destroy the character of our institutions.

We deny that the obligation of all citizens to support their Government in times of grave national peril applies to the present situation. If an administration may with impunity ignore the issues upon which it was chosen, deliberately create a condition of war anywhere on the face of the globe, debauch the civil service for spoils to promote the adventure, organize a truth suppressing censorship and demand of all citizens a suspension of judgement and their unanimous support while it chooses to continue the fighting, representative government itself is imperiled.

We propose to contribute to the defeat of any person or party that stands for the forcible subjugation of any people. We shall oppose for reelection all who in the White House or in Congress betray American liberty in pursuit of un-American gains. We still hope that both of our great political parties will support and defend the Declaration of Independence in the closing campaign of the century.

We hold, with Abraham Lincoln, that "no man is good enough to govern another man without that other's consent. When the white man governs himself, that is self-government, but when he governs himself and also governs another man, that is more than self-government—that is despotism." "Our reliance is in the love of liberty which God has planted in us. Our defense is in the spirit which prizes liberty as the heritage of all men in all lands. Those who deny freedom to others deserve it not for themselves, and under a just God cannot long retain it."

We cordially invite the co-operation of all men and women who remain loyal to the Declaration of Independence and the Constitution of the United States.

Race, Empire, and A Wider World
CONTEXTS

In the Victorian era colonies in the British Empire were divided into two broad categories. In one category were crown colonies ruled by governments with no direct responsibility to the people they ruled, but only to the Foreign Office and the home country as a whole. The vast majority of the populace in such colonies did not share in the history, religion, or traditions of England or other European cultures, and were brown or black in color; in this category were the bulk of British possessions in Africa, Asia, and the Caribbean. In areas of the Empire where emigration from Britain and other European nations had created a majority or a substantial minority of a population sharing the cultural and racial makeup of "the old country," on the other hand, responsible government became the norm. Under the terms of Imperial arrangements in the latter category, administration was still overseen by British authority, but governments with a substantial degree of real power were elected by and responsible to the local populace, and were composed of local leaders rather than temporary appointees from abroad. Canada, the Australian colonies, and New Zealand were prominent in this second category.

India was in many ways a special case, with local hereditary rulers in some cases maintaining considerable authority under an umbrella of British rule over the subcontinent, and with Imperial rule complicated both by the existence of the India Office as a separate government department in Britain, and by the authority wielded (until 1858) by the East India Company. The latter was the last such entity to hold substantial power in a British colony. In the seventeenth century, the East India Company, the Hudson's Bay Company, and the Royal Africa Company were among the commercial entities given royal charters, empowering them not only to trade commercially in particular parts of the globe but also to exercise political authority over the local people. Beginning in the eighteenth century, such authority began to be transferred to government of a more conventional sort.

Throughout the history of the British Empire various notions of "Empire" competed with one another. Perhaps the least complicated was the notion that Empire should be based purely on the commercial interests of the Imperial power. It was this notion that was foremost in the minds of many commercial adventurers staking out an Imperial claim—but also in the minds of many "little Englanders" in the nineteenth century who did not necessarily have any desire to abandon the Empire as a whole, but felt it would be expedient and appropriate to "cut loose" colonies that were perceived to represent a net drain on Britain's resources, financial and otherwise. For others, though, the Empire was a vital symbol of the nation's importance in the world—and of its "greatness" (a word in which power and morality came to be inextricably entangled). Finally, there were those whose notions of Empire were shaped by a hope and a confidence that Britain would improve the lot of her subject peoples—improve their economic conditions, certainly, but also bring to them literacy and an appropriate level of education, what were perceived to be the benefits of Christianity, and a broader set of cultural benefits, as well. It is easy to be cynical about this last set of ideas, and there was surely much in these "enlightened" notions of Empire that was hypocritical, patronizing, and racist. That there was also frequently some kernel of altruism in the "enlightened imperialism" of the likes of William Gladstone or David Livingstone, however, is difficult to doubt, even as it must now be plain to all how horrifically misguided such impulses often were.

There was no pretense made that the greatest of horrors endured by subject peoples under British imperialism was a civilizing mission. After a long struggle, outright slavery had been abolished in all British possessions in 1833, but in certain British colonies in the Caribbean, practices tantamount to slavery continued for decades thereafter—prompting incidents such as the uprising against British Governor Edward Eyre in Jamaica in 1865. Nor was there anything civilizing in the unspeakable atrocities meted out during the suppression of the Indian mutiny in 1857–58, or the brutal treatment accorded the aboriginal peoples of Australia, New Zealand, and (to a somewhat lesser extent) Canada; all these represented Imperialism stripped of any veneer of civilization.

The feelings of cultural and racial superiority on which rationalizations of the subjugation of other peoples were founded took a variety of forms. The sort of anthropological theorizing that Adam Smith and other eighteenth-century thinkers had engaged in was comparatively benign, and remained popular throughout the nineteenth century. According to this way of thinking, other peoples were not inherently inferior; they were simply at a less fully advanced stage of social and economic organization than were European peoples. An anthropological "stages of development" approach often led to an assumption by the British and other Europeans of a "childish" mentality among peoples elsewhere in the globe, but it also left room for the moral anthropology of Rousseau and others that ascribed to the "noble savage" the attribute of an innocence largely lost to "higher" stages of civilization. (It is this view with which Charles Dickens takes vehement issue in the essay from *Household Words* excerpted in this section.)

Although this approach was widely held throughout the Victorian era, pseudo-scientific claims of a biological sort were increasingly made. According to many making such claims, other peoples were not at a lower stage of development (from which they could, with assistance, be raised over the course of time to the level of Europeans); rather they were inherently, biologically inferior, and it would thus always be appropriate to treat them as creatures of a lower order.

Through most of the twentieth century little direct attention was paid to the attitudes of leading Victorian literary figures towards these issues, and it came to be widely assumed that writers who had deplored, for example, the brutality of conditions for workers in industry in England would also have deplored oppression and brutality overseas. As Edward Said and others were instrumental in demonstrating, in the late twentieth-century, however, this was simply not the case. While John Stuart Mill and some others did indeed hold what we now acknowledge to be relatively enlightened views on the subject of race and culture, the list of those espousing views which today can only be described as racist (tellingly, neither the word "racialist" or the word "racist" is recorded as having been used before the twentieth century) is a long one, and includes such major figures as Thomas Carlyle, William Thackeray, John Ruskin, and Walter Bagehot. It is difficult to read the pronouncements of many of these figures on such matters without feeling a sense of revulsion. Again, though, we should be wary of presuming ourselves to be at a moral pinnacle; it may well be that in another 150 years we will look back on the views that predominate in our own time—our willingness to ignore genocide so long as it is happening in faraway lands, for example—with as much revulsion as we feel toward the racism of many of the great Victorians.

⌘ ⌘ ⌘

from Frances Trollope, *Domestic Manners of the Americans* (1832)

The novelist Frances Trollope's account of her visit
to the United States features a number of reflections
on the direction taken by the American character in
the decades since America became independent from
Britain.

from Chapter 1: Entrance of the Mississippi

On the 4th of November, 1827, I sailed from
London, accompanied by my son and two daughters; and after a favourable, though somewhat tedious
voyage, arrived on Christmas-day at the mouth of the
Mississippi.

The first indication of our approach to land was the
appearance of this mighty river pouring forth its muddy
mass of waters, and mingling with the deep blue of the
Mexican Gulf. The shores of this river are so utterly flat,
that no object upon them is perceptible at sea, and we
gazed with pleasure on the muddy ocean that met us,
for it told us we were arrived, and seven weeks of sailing
had wearied us; yet it was not without a feeling like
regret that we passed from the bright blue waves, whose
varying aspect had so long furnished our chief amusement, into the murky stream which now received us.

Large flights of pelicans were seen standing upon the
long masses of mud which rose above the surface of the
waters, and a pilot came to guide us over the bar, long
before any other indication of land was visible.

I never beheld a scene so utterly desolate as this
entrance of the Mississippi. Had Dante seen it, he might
have drawn images of another Bolgia[1] from its horrors.
One only object rears itself above the eddying waters;
this is the mast of a vessel long since wrecked in attempting to cross the bar, and it still stands, a dismal
witness of the destruction that has been, and a boding
prophet of that which is to come.

By degrees bulrushes of enormous growth become
visible, and a few more miles of mud brought us within
sight of a cluster of huts called the Balize, by far the
most miserable station that I ever saw made the dwelling
of man, but I was told that many families of pilots and
fishermen lived there.

For several miles above its mouth, the Mississippi
presents no objects more interesting than mud banks,
monstrous bulrushes, and now and then a huge crocodile luxuriating in the slime. Another circumstance that
gives to this dreary scene an aspect of desolation, is the
incessant appearance of vast quantities of drift wood,
which is ever finding its way to the different mouths of
the Mississippi. Trees of enormous length, sometimes
still bearing their branches, and still oftener their uptorn
roots entire, the victims of the frequent hurricane, come
floating down the stream. Sometimes several of these,
entangled together, collect among their boughs a
quantity of floating rubbish, that gives the mass the
appearance of a moving island, bearing a forest, with its
roots mocking the heavens; while the dishonoured
branches lash the tide in idle vengeance: this, as it
approaches the vessel, and glides swiftly past, looks like
the fragment of a world in ruins.

from Chapter 3: Company on Board the Steam Boat

The weather was warm and bright, and we found the
guard of the boat, as they call the gallery that runs round
the cabins, a very agreeable station; here we all sat as
long as light lasted, and sometimes wrapped in our
shawls, we enjoyed the clear bright beauty of American
moonlight long after every passenger but ourselves had
retired. We had a full complement of passengers on
board. The deck, as is usual, was occupied by the
Kentucky flat-boat men, returning from New Orleans,
after having disposed of the boat and cargo which they
had conveyed thither, with no other labour than that of
steering her, the current bringing her down at the rate
of four miles an hour. We had about two hundred of
these men on board, but the part of the vessel occupied
by them is so distinct from the cabins, that we never saw
them, except when we stopped to take in wood; and
then they ran, or rather sprung and vaulted over each
other's heads to the shore, whence they all assisted in
carrying wood to supply the steam engine; the performance of this duty being a stipulated part of the pay-

---

[1] *Dante* Italian poet Dante Alighieri (1265–1321), author of the
epic poem *The Divine Comedy*, composed of three sections describing Heaven (*Paradiso*), Purgatory (*Purgatorio*), and Hell (*Inferno*);
Bolgia Level of Hell in Dante's *Inferno*.

ment of their passage.

From the account given by a man servant we had on board, who shared their quarters, they are a most disorderly set of persons, constantly gambling and wrangling, very seldom sober, and never suffering a night to pass without giving practical proof of the respect in which they hold the doctrines of equality, and community of property. The clerk of the vessel was kind enough to take our man under his protection, and assigned him a berth in his own little nook; but as this was not inaccessible, he told him by no means to detach his watch or money from his person during the night. Whatever their moral characteristics may be, these Kentuckians are a very noble-looking race of men; their average height considerably exceeds that of Europeans, and their countenances, excepting when disfigured by red hair, which is not unfrequent, extremely handsome.

The gentlemen in the cabin (we had no ladies) would certainly neither, from their language, manners, nor appearance, have received that designation in Europe; but we soon found their claim to it rested on more substantial ground, for we heard them nearly all addressed by the titles of general, colonel, and major. On mentioning these military dignities to an English friend some time afterwards, he told me that he too had made the voyage with the same description of company, but remarking that there was not a single captain among them; he made the observation to a fellow-passenger, and asked how he accounted for it. "Oh, sir, the captains are all on deck," was the reply.

… I know it is equally easy and invidious[1] to ridicule the peculiarities of appearance and manner in people of a different nation from ourselves; we may, too, at the same moment, be undergoing the same ordeal in their estimation; and, moreover, I am by no means disposed to consider whatever is new to me as therefore objectionable; but, nevertheless, it was impossible not to feel repugnance to many of the novelties that now surrounded me.

The total want of all the usual courtesies of the table, the voracious rapidity with which the viands[2] were seized and devoured, the strange uncouth phrases and pronunciation; the loathsome spitting, from the contamination of which it was absolutely impossible to protect our dresses; the frightful manner of feeding with their knives, till the whole blade seemed to enter into the mouth; and the still more frightful manner of cleaning the teeth afterwards with a pocket knife, soon forced us to feel that we were not surrounded by the generals, colonels, and majors of the old world; and that the dinner hour was to be any thing rather than an hour of enjoyment.

The little conversation that went forward while we remained in the room, was entirely political, and the respective claims of Adams and Jackson[3] to the presidency were argued with more oaths and more vehemence than it had ever been my lot to hear. Once a colonel appeared on the verge of assaulting a major, when a huge seven-foot Kentuckian gentleman horse-dealer, asked of the heavens to confound them both, and bade them sit still and be d——d. We too thought we should share this sentence; at least sitting still in the cabin seemed very nearly to include the rest of it, and we never tarried[4] there a moment longer than was absolutely necessary to eat.

from CHAPTER 34: RETURN TO NEW YORK—CONCLUSION

… Nothing could be more beautiful than our passage down the Hudson on the following day, as I thought of some of my friends in England, dear lovers of the picturesque; … not even a moving panoramic view, gliding before their eyes for an hour together, in all the scenic splendour of Drury Lane, or Covent Garden,[5] could give them an idea of it. They could only see one side at a time. The change, the contrast, the ceaseless variety of beauty, as you skim from side to side, the liquid smoothness of the broad mirror that reflects the scene, and most of all, the clear bright air through which

---

[1] *invidious* Tending to incite ill-feeling or unpopularity against others.

[2] *viands* Food.

[3] *Adams* John Quincy Adams (1767–1848) won a controversial majority in the American election of 1824 by joining forces with third candidate Henry Clay, whom he later named Secretary of State; *Jackson* Andrew Jackson (1767–1845) contested Adams's government and went on to win the 1829 election.

[4] *tarried* Delayed, prolonged.

[5] *Drury Lane* Street in London, England, location of the famous theater of that name; *Covent Garden* Theater and entertainment district in central London, England.

you look at it; all this can only be seen and believed by crossing the Atlantic.

As we approached New York the burning heat of the day relaxed, and the long shadows of evening fell coolly on the beautiful villas we passed. I really can conceive nothing more exquisitely lovely than this approach to the city. The magnificent boldness of the Jersey shore on the one side, and the luxurious softness of the shady lawns on the other, with the vast silvery stream that flows between them, altogether form a picture which may well excuse a traveller for saying, once and again, that the Hudson River can be surpassed in beauty by none on the outside of Paradise.

It was nearly dark when we reached the city, and it was with great satisfaction that we found our comfortable apartments in Hudson Street unoccupied; and our pretty, kind (Irish) hostess willing to receive us again. We passed another fortnight there; and again we enjoyed the elegant hospitality of New York, though now it was offered from beneath the shade of their beautiful villas. In truth, were all America like this fair city, and all, no, only a small proportion of its population like the friends we left there, I should say, that the land was the fairest in the world.

It is a matter of historical notoriety that the original stock of the white population now inhabiting the United States, were persons who had banished themselves, or were banished from the mother country. The land they found was favourable to their increase and prosperity; the colony grew and flourished. Years rolled on, and the children, the grand-children, and the great grand-children of the first settlers, replenished the land, and found it flowing with milk and honey. That they should wish to keep this milk and honey to themselves, is not very surprising. What did the mother country do for them? She sent them out gay and gallant officers to guard their frontier; the which they thought they could guard as well themselves; and then she taxed their tea. Now, this was disagreeable; and to atone for it, the distant colony had no great share in her mother's grace and glory. It was not from among them that her high and mighty were chosen; the rays which emanated from that bright sun of honour, the British throne, reached them but feebly. They knew not, they cared not, for her

kings nor her heroes; their thriftiest trader was their noblest man; the holy seats of learning were but the cradles of superstition; the splendour of the aristocracy, but a leech that drew their "golden blood." The wealth, the learning, the glory of Britain, was to them nothing; the having their own way every thing. Can any blame their wish to obtain it? Can any lament that they succeeded?…

As long as their governments are at peace with each other, the individuals of every nation in Europe make it a matter of pride, as well as of pleasure, to meet each other frequently, to discuss, compare, and reason upon their national varieties, and to vote it a mark of fashion and good taste to imitate each other in all the external embellishments of life.

The consequence of this is most pleasantly perceptible at the present time, in every capital of Europe. The long peace has given time for each to catch from each what was best in customs and manners, and the rapid advance of refinement and general information has been the result.

To those who have been accustomed to this state of things, the contrast upon crossing to the new world is inconceivably annoying; and it cannot be doubted that this is one great cause of the general feeling of irksomeness, and fatigue of spirits, which hangs upon the memory while recalling the hours passed in American society.

A single word indicative of doubt, that any thing, or every thing, in that country is not the very best in the world, produces an effect which must be seen and felt to be understood. If the citizens of the United States were indeed the devoted patriots they call themselves, they would surely not thus encrust themselves in the hard, dry, stubborn persuasion, that they are the first and best of the human race, that nothing is to be learnt, but what they are able to teach, and that nothing is worth having, which they do not possess.

The art of man could hardly discover a more effectual antidote to improvement, than this persuasion; and yet I never listened to any public oration, or read any work, professedly addressed to the country, in which they did not labour to impress it on the minds of the people.

from Thomas Babington Macaulay, "Minute on Indian Education" (1835)

> In this 1835 speech, Macaulay, then a member of the Council of India, argued that the sum set aside by the British Parliament for the education of Indian citizens should be used to teach the English language and the scientific and cultural advancements of Britain, rather than to promote the study of India's native cultures and languages. In the paragraphs immediately preceding this excerpt, Macaulay put forward the claim that the people of India should not be taught in any of their native languages, as the various dialects are "poor and rude," and "contain neither literary nor scientific information." In addition, he asserted, the historical, philosophical, and literary achievements of works written in European languages far surpassed their Sanskrit and Arabic equivalents.

from "Minute on Indian Education"

… How, then, stands the case? We have to educate a people who cannot at present be educated by means of their mother-tongue. We must teach them some foreign language. The claims of our own language it is hardly necessary to recapitulate. It stands pre-eminent even among the languages of the west. It abounds with works of imagination not inferior to the noblest which Greece has bequeathed to us; with models of every species of eloquence; with historical compositions, which, considered merely as narratives, have seldom been surpassed, and which, considered as vehicles of ethical and political instruction, have never been equalled; with just and lively representations of human life and human nature; with the most profound speculations on metaphysics, morals, government, jurisprudence,[1] and trade; with full and correct information respecting every experimental science which tends to preserve the health, to increase the comfort, or to expand the intellect of man. Whoever knows that language has ready access to all the vast intellectual wealth which all the wisest nations of the earth have created and hoarded in the course of ninety generations. It may safely be said that the literature now extant in that language is of far greater value than all the literature which three hundred years ago was extant in all the languages of the world together. Nor is this all. In India, English is the language spoken by the ruling class. It is spoken by the higher class of natives at the seats of government. It is likely to become the language of commerce throughout the seas of the East. It is the language of two great European communities which are rising, the one in the south of Africa, the other in Australasia; communities which are every year becoming more important, and more closely connected with our Indian Empire. Whether we look at the intrinsic value of our literature, or at the particular situation of this country, we shall see the strongest reason to think that, of all foreign tongues, the English tongue is that which would be the most useful to our native subjects.

The question now before us is simply whether, when it is in our power to teach this language, we shall teach languages in which, by universal confession, there are no books on any subject which deserve to be compared to our own; whether, when we can teach European science, we shall teach systems which, by universal confession, whenever they differ from those of Europe, differ for the worse; and whether, when we can patronize sound philosophy and true history, we shall countenance, at the public expense, medical doctrines which would disgrace an English farrier,[2] astronomy which would move laughter in girls at an English boarding-school, history abounding with kings thirty feet high, and reigns thirty thousand years long, and geography made up of seas of treacle and seas of butter.

We are not without experience to guide us. History furnishes several analogous cases, and they all teach the same lesson. There are in modern times, to go no further, two memorable instances of a great impulse given to the mind of a whole society—of prejudices overthrown, of knowledge diffused, of taste purified, of arts and sciences planted in countries which had recently been ignorant and barbarous.

The first instance to which I refer is the great revival of letters among the western nations at the close of the fifteenth, and the beginning of the sixteenth, century. At that time almost everything that was worth reading was contained in the writings of the ancient Greeks and Romans. Had our ancestors acted as the Committee of

---

[1] *jurisprudence* Law.

[2] *farrier* One who shoes or cares for horses.

Public Instruction has hitherto acted;[1] had they neglected the language of Cicero and Tacitus;[2] had they confined their attention to the old dialects of our own island; had they printed nothing, and taught nothing at the universities, but chronicles in Anglo-Saxon, and romances in Norman-French, would England have been what she now is? What the Greek and Latin were to the contemporaries of More and Ascham,[3] our tongue is to the people of India. The literature of England is now more valuable than that of classical antiquity. I doubt whether the Sanskrit literature be as valuable as that of our Saxon and Norman progenitors. In some departments—in history, for example—I am certain that it is much less so.

Another instance may be said to be still before our eyes. Within the last hundred and twenty years, a nation which had previously been in a state as barbarous as that in which our ancestors were before the crusades, has gradually emerged from the ignorance in which it was sunk, and has taken its place among civilized communities—I speak of Russia. There is now in that country a large educated class, abounding with persons fit to serve the state in the highest functions, and in no wise inferior to the most accomplished men who adorn the best circles of Paris and London. There is reason to hope that this vast empire, which in the time of our grandfathers was probably behind the Punjab, may, in the time of our grandchildren, be pressing close on France and Britain in the career of improvement. And how was this change effected? Not by flattering national prejudices; not by feeding the mind of the young Muscovite[4] with old women's stories which his rude fathers had believed; not by filling his head with lying legends about St.

Nicholas;[5] not by encouraging him to study the great question, whether the world was or was not created on the 13th of September; not by calling him "a learned native," when he has mastered all these points of knowledge: but by teaching him those foreign languages in which the greatest mass of information had been laid up, and thus putting all that information within his reach. The languages of Western Europe civilized Russia. I cannot doubt that they will do for the Hindu what they have done for the Tartar.[6] ...

It is impossible for us, with our limited means, to attempt to educate the body of the people. We must at present do our best to form a class who may be interpreters between us and the millions whom we govern; a class of persons, Indian in blood and colour, but English in taste, in opinions, in morals, and in intellect. To that class we may leave it to refine the vernacular dialects of the country, to enrich those dialects with terms of science borrowed from the Western nomenclature, and to render them by degrees fit vehicles for conveying knowledge to the great mass of the population.

from Report of a Speech by William Charles Wentworth, Australian Legislative Council (1844)

In 1844 the aboriginal populace in Australia probably still outnumbered that of the whites. Official policy called for "amity and kindness" and forbade "any unnecessary interruption" of aboriginal existence, but, as the excerpt below suggests, attitudes towards native peoples that prevailed were often brutally harsh.

He could not see if the whites in this colony were to go out into the land and possess it, that the Government had much to do with them. No doubt there would be battles between the settlers and the border tribes; but they might be settled without the aid of the Government. The civilized people had come in and the savage must go back. They must go on progressing until their dominancy was established, and therefore he could

---

[1] *Committee ... acted* The Committee of Public Instruction had hitherto used the allocated funds solely for promoting the study of Arabic and Sanskrit literature and for encouraging those "learned natives" who studied the science, religions, and histories of their native cultures.

[2] *Cicero* Roman orator of the first century BCE; *Tacitus* First-century CE author of two works of Roman history, *Histories* and *Annals*.

[3] *More* Sir Thomas More (1478–1535), English politician and humanist scholar, author of *Utopia*; *Ascham* Roger Ascham (1515–68), Latin Secretary to Edward VI, Mary I, and Elizabeth I.

[4] *Muscovite* Resident of Moscow.

[5] *St. Nicholas* Patron saint of sailors, revered in Christian Orthodox tradition.

[6] *Tartar* Here, Russian.

think that no measure was wise or merciful to the blacks which clothed them with a degree of seeming protection, which their position would not allow them to maintain.... It was not the policy of a wise Government to attempt the perpetuation of the aboriginal race of New South Wales.... They must give way before the arms, aye! even the diseases of civilized nations—they must give way before they attain the power of those nations.

from William H. Smith, *Smith's Canadian Gazetteer* (1846)

Smith states in his preface that he was "induced to undertake the task" of writing his gazetteer by the "great ignorance" which he found to exist respecting the province of Canada West (now Ontario), "not only amongst persons in Great Britain, or newly arrived emigrants, but even amongst many of those who had been for years resident in the country." The gazetteer includes information on all towns and geographical areas in the province. The following excerpts are taken from the section of general reflections with which the work concludes.

It is most extraordinary, so long as Canada has been settled, that its great natural advantages should still be so little known; that so many persons who are either compelled by necessity to emigrate, or who do so from choice, should continue to pass it by and go on to the west of the United States, or otherwise emigrate to the more distant colonies of the Cape, New South Wales, or New Zealand and yet such is the case....

In what respects will the advocates of emigration to the United States pretend to say that any portion of that country is superior to Canada. Is it in the climate? A tree may be judged of by its fruits, and very many of the native Canadians, in point of robust appearance and complexion, might be taken for English emigrants. Will any one venture to make the same assertion respecting a native of Ohio, Indiana, Illinois, or Missouri? And of what avail is it that the climate will grow cotton and tobacco, if the settler neither has the strength to cultivate them, nor a market in which to dispose of them, when grown? In the winter and spring of 1841–2, pork (a staple article of the State) was selling in Illinois, at from a dollar to a dollar and a half per 100 lbs.; and at that price it was almost impossible to obtain cash for it; wheat at a quarter dollar, and Indian corn from five to ten cents per bushel; butter, fifteen and sixteen pounds for a dollar; fowls, half a dollar per dozen; and other farming produce in proportion. At such prices farming could not be very profitable. A man certainly might live cheaply, and cram himself with bacon and corn bread till he brought on bilious fever;[1] but he could *make nothing* of what he raised. And a farmer having a fat ox, has even been known after killing it, to take from it the hide and tallow, and drag the carcass into the woods to be devoured by the wolves; finding from the small price the beef would fetch, that it was more profitable to do so than to sell the whole animal!

Is it from the nature of the government, that the States are so much more desirable as a place of residence—where the only law is mob law, and the bowie knife is the constant companion of the citizens, and is used even in the halls of legislature themselves? Or is New Zealand much to be preferred, where the settler in taking his morning ramble, to acquire an appetite for his breakfast, frequently receives a "settler" himself, and instead of returning to his morning's meal, is roasted for the breakfast of some native chief, and his interesting family. Canada, on the contrary, suffers under none of these disadvantages and annoyances. The government and constitution of the country are English; the laws English; the climate is fine and healthy; the Indians are tolerably civilized, none of them at any rate are cannibals, and few of them are even thieves; and bowie knives are not "the fashion." The settler, unless he has been guilty of the folly of planting himself down beyond the bounds of civilization and of roads, may always command a fair price and cash for whatever he can raise—he need never be beyond the reach of medical attendance, churches, and schools—he can obtain as much land as he need wish to purchase, at a fair and moderate rate—he knows that whatever property he acquires is as secure as if he had it in England—his landed property, if he possesses any, is gradually increasing in value—and if he is only moderately careful and industrious, he need have no anxiety for the future—his sons, growing up in and with the country, and as they grow, acquiring a

---

[1] *bilious fever* Over-secretion of bile, causing indigestion.

knowledge of the country and its customs, and the various modes of doing business in it, if steady, will have no difficulty in succeeding in any business they may select, or may be qualified for.

Much has been written on the subject of emigration, and many speculations entered into as to *who* are the proper persons to emigrate? The only answer that can be given to this question is—*those who are obliged to do so.* Let no person who is doing *well* at home, no matter what may be his profession or occupation, emigrate with the expectation of doing *better*,—let him not leave his home and travel over the world, in search of advantages which he may not find elsewhere. But those who are *not* doing well, who find it difficult to struggle against increasing competition, who fear the loss in business of what little property they possess, or who find it difficult with an increasing family to keep up appearances as they have been accustomed to do, and find it necessary to make a change—all these may safely emigrate, with a fair prospect of improving their condition. Persons of small, independent incomes may live cheaply in Canada, particularly in the country, and enjoy many comforts, and even luxuries, that were not within their reach at home. Retired military men do not generally make good settlers. They usually, when they leave the army, sell out, instead of retiring on half pay; and when they emigrate they are apt to squander their property in purchasing land and in building, till at length they come to a stand for want of the means to proceed, frequently with their buildings half-finished, from being planned on too large a scale; although, if they had been asked in the commencement how they intended to *live* when the ready money was expended, they would have been unable to give an intelligible answer. If they succeed in getting some government office, the emoluments[1] of which are sufficient for their support, they will manage to get along very well; otherwise they will sink gradually lower and lower, and their children are apt to get into idle and dissipated habits. The idle and inactive life to which they have been accustomed while in the army, particularly during these "piping times of peace,"[2]

totally incapacitates them for making good settlers in the backwoods. *A lounger, unless independent, has no business in Canada.* Naval officers, on the contrary, make settlers of a very different character. They have been accustomed, when on service, to a life of activity; and if they have been long on service, they have generally seen a great deal of the world—they have their half-pay to fall back on, which fortunately for them they cannot sell—and they generally make very excellent settlers. Lawyers are not wanted: Canada swarms with them; and they multiply in the province so fast, that the demand is not by any means equal to the supply. Medical men may find many openings in the country, where they will have no difficulty in making a tolerable living; but they will have to work hard for it, having frequently to ride fifteen, twenty-five, or even thirty miles to see a patient! And in the towns, the competition is as great as in England....

Carlyle, Mill, and "The Negro Question"

In the wake of the abolition of slavery in all British possessions in 1837, and of the ending of the preferential tariff on sugar in 1846, plantation owners in the British West Indies complained vociferously about their situation, arguing that they were placed in the unfair position of having to compete against sugar produced in countries such as Brazil where slavery was still permitted. Amongst the many in Britain who supported their arguments was Thomas Carlyle, who sets out his position in the essay excerpted below. Shortly thereafter, John Stuart Mill delivered a stinging reply, also excerpted below. Carlyle reprinted a revised version of the essay in 1853 under the more incendiary title "Occasional Discourse on the Nigger Question."[3] In the 1860s the two also disagreed publicly over the Eyre rebel-

---

[1] *emoluments* Salary, remuneration.

[2] *piping ... peace* See William Shakespeare's *Richard III* 1.1.24: "Why, I, in this weak piping time of peace, / Have no delight to pass away the time."

[3] *more incendiary ... Nigger Question* From the late sixteenth century into the eighteenth, the term "nigger" was generally used in a more or less neutral fashion, and rarely in a way that directly expressed hostility towards blacks. In the late eighteenth and early nineteenth centuries the word began to be used more and more frequently to express contempt. An example from the same period at which Carlyle was writing is Hartley Coleridge's 1849 complaint against turning Othello "into a rank wooly-pated, thick-lipped nigger."

lion (an uprising in Jamaica against the oppressive conditions under which black Jamaicans were forced to work, which became a *cause célèbre* in England when the rebellion was suppressed, with extraordinary brutality, by Governor Edward John Eyre).

from Thomas Carlyle, "Occasional Discourse on the Negro Question," *Fraser's Magazine* (1849)

West Indian affairs, as we all know, and some of us know to our cost, are in a rather troublous condition this good while. In regard to West Indian affairs, however, Lord John Russell[1] is able to comfort us with one fact, indisputable where so many are dubious, that the negroes are all very happy and doing well. A fact very comfortable indeed. West Indian whites, it is admitted, are far enough from happy; West Indian colonies not unlike sinking wholly into ruin; at home, too, the British whites are rather badly off—several millions of them hanging on the verge of continual famine—and, in single towns, many thousands of them very sore put to it, at this time … to live at all—these, again, are uncomfortable facts; and they are extremely extensive and important ones. But … how pleasant to have always this fact to fall back upon; our beautiful black darlings are at last happy; with little labor except to the teeth, *which*, surely, in those excellent horse-jaws of theirs, will not fail!

Exeter Hall,[2] my philanthropic friends, has had its way in this matter. The twenty millions, a mere trifle, despatched with a single dash of the pen, are paid; and, far over the sea, we have a few black persons rendered extremely "free" indeed. Sitting yonder, with their beautiful muzzles up to the ears in pumpkins, imbibing sweet pulps and juices; the grinder and incisor teeth ready for every new work, and the pumpkins cheap as grass in those rich climates; while the sugar crops rot round them, uncut, because labor cannot be hired. … A state of matters lovely to contemplate, in these emancipated epochs of the human mind, which has earned us, not only the praises of Exeter Hall, and loud, long-eared hallelujahs of laudatory psalmody[3] from the friends of freedom everywhere, but lasting favor (it is hoped) from the heavenly powers themselves; which may, at least, justly appeal to the heavenly powers, and ask them, if ever, in terrestrial procedure, they saw the match of it! Certainly, in the past history of the human species, it has no parallel; nor, one hopes, will it have in the future. …

Truly, my philanthropic friends, Exeter Hall philanthropy is wonderful; and the social science … which finds the secret of this universe in "supply and demand," and reduces the duty of human governors to that of letting men alone, is also wonderful. A dreary, desolate and, indeed, quite abject and distressing one; what we might call, by way of eminence, the *dismal science*.[4] These two, Exeter Hall philanthropy and the Dismal Science, led by any sacred cause of black emancipation, or the like, to fall in love and make a wedding of it—will give birth to progenies and prodigies: dark extensive moon-calves, unnameable abortions, wide-coiled monstrosities, such as the world has not seen hitherto!…

My philanthropic friends, can you discern no fixed headlands in this wide-weltering[5] deluge of benevolent twaddle and revolutionary grapeshot that has burst forth on us—no sure bearings at all? Fact and nature, it seems to me, say a few words to us, if, happily, we have still an ear for fact and nature. Let us listen a little, and try. And first, with regard to the West Indies, it may be laid down as a principle, which no eloquence in Exeter Hall, or Westminster Hall,[6] or elsewhere, can invalidate or hide, except for a short time only, that no black man, who will not work according to what ability the gods

---

[1]   *Lord John Russell*   Russell (1792–1878) was British Prime Minister from 1846 to 1852 and from 1865 to 1866.

[2]   *Exeter Hall*   Exeter Hall, on the Strand, in London, was built in 1830 to serve as a meeting place for a variety of religious groups, benevolent associations, and other charitable institutions.

[3]   *psalmody*   Singing of psalms.

[4]   *dismal science*   This famous phrase describing the science now known as economics has often been cited as first used by Carlyle in his "Latter Day Pamphlet" (1850), rather than in the present essay.

[5]   *wide-weltering*   State of turmoil, often used to describe the sea.

[6]   *Westminster Hall*   Location of British Parliament.

have given him for working, has the smallest right to eat pumpkin, or to any fraction of land that will grow pumpkin, however plentiful such land may be, but has an indisputable and perpetual *right* to be compelled, by the real proprietors of said land, to do competent work for his living. This is the everlasting duty of all men, black or white, who are born into this world. To do competent work, to labor honestly according to the ability given them; for that, and for no other purpose, was each one of us sent into this world; and woe is to every man who by friend or by foe, is prevented from fulfilling this, the end of his being....

The idle black man in the West Indies had, not long since, the right, and will again, under better form, if it please Heaven, have the right (actually the first "right of man" for an indolent person) to be *compelled* to work as he was fit, and to *do* the Maker's will, who had constructed him with such and such prefigurements of capability....

And now observe, my friends, it was not Black Quashee,[1] or those he represents, that made those West India islands what they are, or can, by any hypothesis, be considered to have the right of growing pumpkins there. For countless ages, since they first mounted oozy on the back of earthquakes, from their dark bed in the ocean deeps, and reeking, saluted the tropical sun, and ever onward, till the European white man first saw them, some three short centuries ago, those islands had produced mere jungle, savagery, poison reptiles and swamp malaria till the white European first saw them, they were, as if not yet created; their noble elements of cinnamon—sugar, coffee, pepper, black and gray, lying all asleep, waiting the white Enchanter, who should say to them, awake! Till the end of human history, and the sounding of the trump of doom, they might have lain so, had Quashee, and the like of him, been the only artists in the game. Swamps, fever-jungles, man-eating caribs, rattle-snakes, and reeking waste and putrefaction: this had been the produce of them under the incompetent caribal[2] (what we call cannibal) possessors till that time; and Quashee knows, himself, whether ever he

could have introduced an improvement. Him, had he, by a miraculous chance, been wafted thither, the caribals would have eaten, rolling him as a fat morsel under their tongue—for him, till the sounding of the trump of doom, the rattlesnakes and savageries would have held on their way. It was not he, then—it was another than he! ... Quashee, if he will not help in bringing out the spices, will get himself made a slave again (which state will be a little less ugly than his present one), and with beneficent whip, since other methods avail not, will be compelled to work. ... The gods are long-suffering; but the law, from the beginning, was, He that will not work shall perish from the earth—and the patience of the gods has limits!

Before the West Indies could grow a pumpkin for any negro, how much European heroism had to spend itself in obscure battle; to sink, in mortal agony, before the jungles, the putrescences and waste savageries could become arable, and the devils be, in some measure, chained there! The West Indies grow pineapples, and sweet fruits, and spices; we hope they will, one day, grow beautiful, heroic human lives too, which is surely the ultimate object they were made for; beautiful souls and brave; sages, poets, what not—making the earth nobler round them, as their kindred from of old have been doing; ... heroic white men, worthy to be called old Saxons, browned with a mahogany tint in those new climates and conditions. But under the soil of Jamaica, before it could even produce spices, or any pumpkin, the bones of many thousand British men had to be laid....

Already one hears of black *Adscripti glebae*,[3] which seems a promising arrangement, one of the first to suggest itself in such a complicacy. It appears the Dutch blacks, in Java, are already a kind of *Adscripts*, after the manner of the old European serfs; bound by royal authority, to give so many days of work a year. Is not this something like a real approximation; the first step toward all manner of such? Wherever, in British territory, there exists a black man, and needful work to the just extent is not to be got out of him, such a law, in defect of better, should be brought to bear upon said black man!...

---

[1] *Quashee* African first name, used by some eighteenth- and nineteenth-century writers to stand for all black people.

[2] *caribal* Insulting combination of "Carib," indigenous person of the West Indies, and "cannibal."

[3] *Adscripti glebae* Latin: permanently tied to the land; serf.

from John Stuart Mill, "The Negro Question,"
Fraser's Magazine (1850)

TO THE EDITOR OF *Fraser's Magazine*

Sir:

Your last month's number contains a speech against the "rights of Negroes," the doctrines and spirit of which ought not to pass without remonstrance. The author issues his opinions, or rather ordinances, under imposing auspices no less than those of the "immortal gods." "The Powers," "the Destinies," announce, through him, not only what *will* be, but what *shall* be done; what they "have decided upon, passed their eternal act of Parliament for." This is speaking "as one having authority"; but authority from whom? If by the quality of the message we may judge of those who sent it, not from any powers to whom just or good men acknowledge allegiance. This so-called "eternal act of Parliament" is no new law, but the old law of the strongest—a law against which the great teachers of mankind have in all ages protested—it is the law of force and cunning; the law that whoever is more power-ful than an other, is "born lord" of that other, the other being born his "servant," who must be "compelled to work" for him by "beneficent whip," if "other methods avail not." I see nothing divine in this injunction. If "the gods" will this, it is the first duty of human beings to resist such gods. Omnipotent these "gods" are *not*, for powers which demand *human* tyranny and injustice cannot accomplish their purpose unless human beings cooperate. The history of human improvement is the record of a struggle by which inch after inch of ground has been wrung from these maleficent[1] powers, and more and more of human life rescued from the iniqui-tous[2] dominion of the law of might. Much, very much of this work still remains to do; but the progress made in it is the best and greatest achievement yet performed by mankind, and it was hardly to be expected at this period of the world that we should be enjoined, by way of a great reform in human affair, to begin *un*doing it.

... I must first set my anti-philanthropic opponent right on a matter of fact. He entirely misunderstands the great national revolt of the conscience of this country against slavery and the slave-trade if he supposes it to have been an affair of sentiment. It depended no more on humane feelings than any cause which so irresistibly appealed to them must necessarily do: Its first victories were gained while the lash yet ruled uncontested in the barrack-yard, and the rod in schools, and while men were still hanged by dozens for stealing to the value of forty shillings. It triumphed because it was the cause of justice; and, in the estimation of the great majority of its supporters, of religion. Its originators and leaders were persons of a stern sense of moral obligation, who, in the spirit of the religion of their time, seldom spoke much of benevolence and philanthropy, but often of duty, crime, and sin. For nearly two centuries had negroes, many thousands annually, been seized by force or treachery and carried off to the West Indies to be worked to death, literally to death; for it was the re-ceived maxim, the acknowledged dictate of good economy, to wear them out quickly and import more. In this fact every other possible cruelty, tyranny, and wanton oppression was by implication included. And the motive on the part of the slave-owners was the love of gold; or, to speak more truly, of vulgar and puerile ostentation. I have yet to learn that anything more detestable than this has been done by human beings towards human beings in any part of the earth....

After fifty years of toil and sacrifice, the object was accomplished, and the negroes, freed from the despo-tism of their fellow-beings, were left to themselves, and to the chances which the arrangements of existing society provide for these who have no resource but their labour. These chances proved favorable to them, and, for the last ten years, they afford the unusual spectacle of a labouring class whose labour bears so high a price that they can exist in comfort on the wages of a compar-atively small quantity of work. This, to the ex-slave-owners, is an inconvenience; but I have not yet heard that any of them has been reduced to beg his bread, or even to dig for it, as the negro, however scandalously he enjoys himself, still must.... If the [plantation owners] cannot continue to realize their large incomes without more labourers, let them find them, and bring them from where they can best be procured, only not by force. Not so, thinks your anti-philanthropic contribu-

---

[1] *maleficent* Harmful, evil.

[2] *iniquitous* Unjust, unrighteous.

tor. That negroes should exist, and enjoy existence, on so little work, is a scandal, in his eyes, worse than their former slavery. It must be put a stop to at any price. He does not "wish to see" them slaves again "if it can be avoided"; but "decidedly" they "will have to be servants," "servants to the whites," "compelled to labour," and "not to go idle another minute." "Black Quashee," "up to the ears in pumpkins," and "working about half an hour a day," is to him the abomination of abominations.

… To give it a rational meaning, it must first be known what he means by work. Does work mean everything which people *do*? No; or he would not reproach people with doing no work. Does it mean laborious exertion? No; for many a day spent in killing game, includes more muscular fatigue than a day's ploughing. Does it mean *useful* exertion? But your contributor always scoffs at the idea of utility. Does he mean that all persons ought to earn their living? But some earn their living by doing nothing, and some by doing mischief; and the negroes, whom he despises, still do earn by labour the "pumpkins" they consume and the finery they wear.

Work, I imagine, is not a good in itself. There is nothing laudable in work for work's sake. To work voluntarily for a worthy object is laudable; but what constitutes a worthy object? On this matter, the oracle of which your contributor is the prophet[1] has never yet been prevailed on to declare itself. He revolves in an eternal circle round the idea of work, as if turning up the earth, or driving a shuttle or a quill, were ends in themselves, and the ends of human existence. Yet, even in the case of the most sublime service to humanity, it is not because it is work that it is worthy; the worth lies in the service itself, and in the will to render it—the noble feelings of which it is the fruit; and if the nobleness of will is proved by other evidence than work, as for instance by danger or sacrifice, there is the same worthiness. While we talk only of work, and not of its object, we are far from the root of the matter; or, if it may be called the root, it is a root without flower or fruit.

In the present case, it seems, a noble object means "spices."——"The gods wish, besides pumpkins, that spices and valuable products be grown in their West Indies"——the "noble elements of cinnamon, sugar, coffee, pepper black and gray," "things far nobler than pumpkins." Why so? Is what supports life inferior in dignity to what merely gratifies the sense of taste? Is it the verdict of the "immortal gods" that pepper is noble, freedom (even freedom from the lash) contemptible? But spices lead "towards commerces, arts, polities, and social developments." Perhaps so; but of what sort? When they must be produced by slaves, the "polities and social developments" they lead to are such as the world, I hope, will not choose to be cursed with much longer.

The worth of work does not surely consist in its leading to other work, and so on to work upon work without end. On the contrary, the multiplication of work, for purposes not worth caring about, is one of the evils of our present condition. When justice and reason shall be the rule of human affairs, one of the first things to which we may expect them to be applied is the question. How many of the so-called luxuries, conveniences, refinements, and ornaments of life, are *worth* the labour which must be undergone as the condition of producing them? The beautifying of existence is as worthy and useful an object as the sustaining of it; but only a vitiated[2] taste can see any such result in those fopperies[3] of so-called civilization, which myriads of hands are now occupied and lives wasted in providing. In opposition to the "gospel of work," I would assert the gospel of leisure, and maintain that human beings *cannot* rise to the finer attributes of their nature compatibly with a life filled with labour. I do not include under the name labour such work, if work it be called, as is done by writers and afforders of "guidance," an occupation which, let alone the vanity of the thing, cannot be called by the same name with the real labour, the exhausting, stiffening, stupefying toil of many kinds of agricultural and manufacturing labourers. To reduce very greatly the quantity of work required to carry on existence is as needful as to distribute it more equally; and the progress of science, and the increasing ascendency of justice and good sense, tend to this result.

[1] *prophet* With the publication of *Past and Present* in 1843, Carlyle began to be considered a visionary, even a prophetic voice, of social and cultural commentary in England.

[2] *vitiated* Corrupted.

[3] *fopperies* Here, useless consumer goods.

There is a portion of work rendered necessary by the fact of each person's existence: no one could exist unless work, to a certain amount, were done either by or for him. Of this each person is bound, in justice, to perform his share; and society has an incontestable right to declare to every one, that if he work not, at this work of necessity, neither shall he eat. Society has not enforced this right, having in so far postponed the rule of justice to other considerations. But there is an ever-growing demand that it be enforced, so soon as any endurable plan can be devised for the purpose. If this experiment is to be tried in the West Indies, let it be tried impartially; and let the whole produce belong to those who do the work which produces it. We would not have black labourers compelled to grow spices which they do not want, and white proprietors who do not work at all exchanging the spices for houses in Belgrave Square.[1] We would not withold from the whites, any more than from the blacks, the "divine right" of being compelled to labour. Let them have exactly the same share in the produce that they have in the work. If they do not like this, let them remain as they are, so long as they are permitted, and make the best of supply and demand.

Your contributor's notions of justice and proprietary right are of another kind than these. According to him, the whole West Indies belong to the whites: the negroes have no claim there, to either land or food, but by their sufferance. "It was not Black Quashee, or those he represents, that made those West India islands what they are." I submit, that those who furnished the thews[2] and sinews really had something to do with the matter.

But the great ethical doctrine of the discourse, … than which a doctrine more damnable, I should think, never was propounded by a professed moral reformer, is, that one kind of human beings are born servants to another kind. "You will have to be servants," he tells the negroes, "to those that are born wiser than you, that are born lords of you—servants to the whites, if they are (as what mortal can doubt that they are?) born wiser than you." I do not hold him to the absurd letter of his dictum; it belongs to the mannerism in which he is enthralled like a child in swaddling clothes. By "born wiser," I will suppose him to mean, born more capable

of wisdom; a proposition which, he says, no mortal can doubt, but which, I will make bold to say, that a full moiety[3] of all thinking persons, who have attended to the subject, either doubt or positively deny.

Among the things for which your contributor professes entire disrespect, is the analytical examination of human nature. It is by analytical examination that we have learned whatever we know of the laws of external nature; and if he had not disdained to apply the same mode of investigation to the laws of the formation of character, he would have escaped the vulgar error of imputing every difference which he finds among human beings to an original difference of nature. As well might it be said, that of two trees, sprung from the same stock one cannot be taller than another but from greater vigor in the original seedling. Is nothing to be attributed to soil, nothing to climate, nothing to difference of exposure—has no storm swept over the one and not the other, no lightning scathed it, no beast browsed on it, no insects preyed on it, no passing stranger stripped off its leaves or its bark? If the trees grew near together, may not the one which, by whatever accident, grew up first, have retarded the other's development by its shade? Human beings are subject to an infinitely greater variety of accidents and external influences than trees, and have infinitely more operation in impairing the growth of one another; since those who begin by being strongest, have almost always hitherto used their strength to keep the others weak. What the original differences are among human beings, I know no more than your contributor, and no less; it is one of the questions not yet satisfactorily answered in the natural history of the species. This, however, is well known—that spontaneous improvement, beyond a very low grade—improvement by internal development, without aid from other individuals or peoples—is one of the rarest phenomena in history; and whenever known to have occurred, was the result of an extraordinary combination of advantages; in addition doubtless to many accidents of which all trace is now lost. No argument against the capacity of negroes for improvement, could be drawn from their not being one of these rare exceptions. It is curious, withal, that the earliest known civilization was, we have the strongest reason to believe, a negro civilization. The

---

[1] *Belgrave Square* Fashionable area of London.

[2] *thews* Muscles.

[3] *moiety* Half.

original Egyptians are inferred, from the evidence of their sculptures, to have been a negro race: it was from negroes, therefore, that the Greeks learnt their first lessons in civilization; ... but I again renounce all advantage from facts: [even if it *were* true that] whites [were] born ever so superior in intelligence to the blacks, and competent by nature to instruct and advise them, it would not be the less monstrous to assert that they had therefore a right either to subdue them by force, or circumvent them by superior skill; to throw upon them the toils and hardships of life, reserving for themselves, under the misapplied name of work, its agreeable excitements....

Though we cannot extirpate[1] all pain, we can, if we are sufficiently determined upon it, abolish all tyranny; one of the greatest victories yet gained over that enemy is slave-emancipation and all Europe is struggling, with various success, towards further conquests over it. If, in the pursuit of this, we lose sight of any object equally important; if we forget that freedom is not the only thing necessary for human beings, let us be thankful to any one who points out what is wanting; but let us not consent to turn back. That this country should turn back, in the matter of negro slavery, I have not the smallest apprehension.

There is, however, another place where that tyranny still flourishes, but now for the first time finds itself seriously in danger. At this crisis of American slavery, when the decisive conflict between right and iniquity seems about to commence, your contributor steps in, and flings this missile, loaded with the weight of his reputation, into the abolitionist camp. The words of English writers of celebrity are words of power on the other side of the ocean; and the owners of human flesh, who probably thought they had not an honest man on their side between the Atlantic and the Vistula,[2] will welcome such an auxiliary. Circulated as his dissertation will probably be, by those whose interests profit by it, from one end of the American Union to the other, I hardly know of an act by which one person could have done so much mischief as this may possibly do; and I hold that by thus acting, he has made himself an instru-

ment of what an able writer in the *Inquirer* justly calls "a true work of the devil."[3]

from Henry Mayhew, *London Labour and the London Poor* (1851)

> Mayhew's work is known primarily for the sympathetic attention it drew to the plight of poor Londoners. When the poor were not of "English stock," however, Mayhew was decidedly less sympathetic—as the following excerpt from his section on "Hindo Beggars" illustrates.

HINDO BEGGARS

[These] are those spare, snake-eyed Asiatics who walk the streets, coolly dressed in Manchester cottons, or chintz of a pattern commonly used for bed-furniture, to which the resemblance is carried out by the dark, polished colour of the thin limbs which it envelopes. They very often affect to be converts to the Christian religion, and give away tracts; with the intention of entrapping the sympathy of elderly ladies. They assert that they have been high-caste Brahmins,[4] but as untruth, even when not acting professionally, is habitual to them, there is not the slightest dependence to be placed on what they say. Sometimes, in the winter, they "do shallow," that is, stand on the kerb-stone of the pavement, in their thin, ragged clothes, and shiver as with cold and hunger, or crouch against a wall and whine like a whipped animal; at others they turn out with a small, barrel-shaped drum, on which they make a monotonous noise with their fingers, to which music they sing and dance. Or they will "stand pad with a fakement," i.e., wear a placard upon their breasts, that describes them as natives of Madagascar, in distress, converts to Christianity, anxious to get to a seaport where they can work their passage back. This is a favourite artifice with Lascars[5]—

---

[1] *extirpate* To remove, literally pull out roots.

[2] *between the Atlantic and the Vistula* I.e., in Britain or in Continental Europe. (The Vistula is a river in Poland.)

[3] *writer ... devil* From an article responding to Carlyle in *London Inquirer*: "It is a true work of the Devil, the fostering of a tyrannical prejudice."

[4] *Brahmins* Members of the highest Hindu class or caste.

[5] *Lascars* East Indian sailors.

or they will sell lucifers,[1] or sweep a crossing, or do anything where their picturesque appearance, of which they are proud and conscious, can be effectively displayed. They are as cunning as they look, and can detect a sympathetic face among a crowd. They never beg of soldiers, or sailors, to whom they always give a wide berth as they pass them in the streets....

Dickens and Thackeray on the Race Question

Charles Dickens and William Makepeace Thackeray, widely regarded as the two greatest novelists of the age, were also great friends. And, as the excerpts below show, they held similar views on the question of race.

from Charles Dickens, "The Noble Savage," Household Words (1853)

To come to the point at once, I beg to say that I have not the least belief in the Noble Savage.[2] I consider him a prodigious nuisance, and an enormous superstition. His calling rum firewater, and me a pale face, wholly fail to reconcile me to him. I don't care what he calls me. I call him a savage, and I call a savage a something highly desirable to be civilised off the face of the earth. I think a mere gent (which I take to be the lowest form of civilisation) better than a howling, whistling, clucking, stamping, jumping, tearing savage. It is all one to me, whether he sticks a fish-bone through his visage, or bits of trees through the lobes of his ears, or bird's feathers in his head; whether he flattens his hair between two boards, or spreads his nose over the breadth of his face, or drags his lower lip down by great weights, or blackens his teeth, or knocks them out, or paints one cheek red and the other blue, or tattoos himself, or oils himself, or rubs his body with fat, or crimps it with knives. Yielding to whichsoever of these agreeable

eccentricities, he is a savage cruel, false, thievish, murderous; addicted more or less to grease, entrails, and beastly customs; a wild animal with the questionable gift of boasting; a conceited, tiresome, bloodthirsty, monotonous humbug.

Yet it is extraordinary to observe how some people will talk about him, as they talk about the good old times; how they will regret his disappearance, in the course of this world's development, from such and such lands where his absence is a blessed relief and an indispensable preparation for the sowing of the very first seeds of any influence that can exalt humanity; how, even with the evidence of himself before them, they will either be determined to believe, or will suffer themselves to be persuaded into believing, that he is something which their five senses tell them he is not.

There was Mr. Catlin,[3] some few years ago, with his Ojibbeway Indians. Mr. Catlin was an energetic, earnest man, who had lived among more tribes of Indians than I need reckon up here, and who had written a picturesque and glowing book about them. With his party of Indians squatting and spitting on the table before him, or dancing their miserable jigs after their own dreary manner, he called, in all good faith, upon his civilised audience to take notice of their symmetry and grace, their perfect limbs, and the exquisite expression of their pantomime; and his civilised audience, in all good faith, complied and admired. Whereas, as mere animals, they were wretched creatures, very low in the scale and very poorly formed; and as men and women possessing any power of truthful dramatic expression by means of action, they were no better than the chorus at an Italian Opera in England—and would have been worse if such a thing were possible.

Mine are no new views of the noble savage. The greatest writers on natural history found him out long ago. Buffon[4] knew what he was, and showed why he is the sulky tyrant that he is to his women, and how it happens (Heaven be praised!) that his race is spare in numbers. For evidence of the quality of his moral

---

[1] *lucifers* Cheap matches sold by street peddlers.

[2] *Noble Savage* The notion of the "noble savage" is associated with the ideas of the French philosopher Jean-Jacques Rousseau (1712–78), who held that human beings are naturally innocent and good, but become corrupted by civilized society. According to this way of thinking, indigenous peoples were seen as inherently nobler because they were closer to a "state of nature."

[3] *Mr. Catlin* George Catlin (1796–1872), pioneered the Wild West Show, which brought indigenous peoples and cultures from the American West to the American east coast and to Europe.

[4] *Buffon* George-Louis Leclerc, Comte de Buffon (1707–88), French naturalist and mathematician.

nature, pass himself for a moment and refer to his "faithful dog." Has he ever improved a dog, or attached a dog, since his nobility first ran wild in woods, and was brought down (at a very long shot) by Pope?[1] Or does the animal that is the friend of man, always degenerate in his low society?

It is not the miserable nature of the noble savage that is the new thing; it is the whimpering over him with maudlin admiration, and the affecting to regret him, and the drawing of any comparison of advantage between the blemishes of civilisation and the tenor of his swinish life. There may have been a change now and then in those diseased absurdities, but there is none in him.

Think of the Bushmen.[2] Think of the two men and the two women who have been exhibited about England for some years. Are the majority of persons—who remember the horrid little leader of that party in his festering bundle of hides, with his filth and his antipathy to water, and his straddled legs, and his odious eyes shaded by his brutal hand, and his cry of "Qu-u-u-u-aaa!" (Bosjesman[3] for something desperately insulting I have no doubt)—conscious of an affectionate yearning towards that noble savage, or is it idiosyncratic in me to abhor, detest, abominate, and abjure him? I have no reserve on this subject, and will frankly state that, setting aside that stage of the entertainment when he counterfeited the death of some creature he had shot, by laying his head on his hand and shaking his left leg—at which time I think it would have been justifiable homicide to slay him—I have never seen that group sleeping, smoking, and expectorating round their brazier, but I have sincerely desired that something might happen to the charcoal smouldering therein, which would cause the immediate suffocation of the whole of the noble strangers.

There is at present a party of Zulu Kaffirs[4] exhibiting at the St. George's Gallery, Hyde Park Corner, London. These noble savages are represented in a most agreeable manner; they are seen in an elegant theatre, fitted with appropriate scenery of great beauty, and they are described in a very sensible and unpretending lecture, delivered with a modesty which is quite a pattern to all similar exponents. Though extremely ugly, they are much better shaped than such of their predecessors as I have referred to; and they are rather picturesque to the eye, though far from odoriferous to the nose. What a visitor left to his own interpretings and imaginings might suppose these noblemen to be about, when they give vent to that pantomimic expression which is quite settled to be the natural gift of the noble savage, I cannot possibly conceive; for it is so much too luminous for my personal civilisation that it conveys no idea to my mind beyond a general stamping, ramping, and raving, remarkable (as everything in savage life is) for its dire uniformity. But let us—with the interpreter's assistance, of which I for one stand so much in need—see what the noble savage does in Zulu Kaffirland.

The noble savage sets a king to reign over him, to whom he submits his life and limbs without a murmur or question, and whose whole life is passed chin deep in a lake of blood; but who, after killing incessantly, is in his turn killed by his relations and friends, the moment a grey hair appears on his head. All the noble savage's wars with his fellow-savages (and he takes no pleasure in anything else) are wars of extermination—which is the best thing I know of him, and the most comfortable to my mind when I look at him. He has no moral feelings of any kind, sort, or description; and his "mission" may be summed up as simply diabolical.

The ceremonies with which he faintly diversifies his life are, of course, of a kindred nature. If he wants a wife he appears before the kennel of the gentleman whom he has selected for his father-in-law, attended by a party of male friends of a very strong flavour, who screech and whistle and stamp an offer of so many cows for the young lady's hand. The chosen father-in-law—also supported by a high-flavoured party of male friends—screeches, whistles, and yells (being seated on the ground, he can't stamp) that there never was such a daughter in the market as his daughter, and that he must have six more cows. The son-in-law and his select circle of backers screech, whistle, stamp, and yell in reply, that they will give three more cows. The father-in-law (an old deluder, overpaid at the beginning) accepts

---

[1] *Pope* Alexander Pope (1688–1744), British poet.

[2] *Bushmen* European name for peoples of the Kalahari desert.

[3] *Bosjesman* Language of the "Bushmen."

[4] *Kaffirs* Derogatory term for Africans.

four, and rises to bind the bargain. The whole party, the young lady included, then falling into epileptic convulsions, and screeching, whistling, stamping, and yelling together—and nobody taking any notice of the young lady (whose charms are not to be thought of without a shudder)—the noble savage is considered married, and his friends make demoniacal leaps at him by way of congratulation.

When the noble savage finds himself a little unwell, and mentions the circumstance to his friends, it is immediately perceived that he is under the influence of witchcraft. A learned personage, called an Imyanger or Witch Doctor, is immediately sent for to Nooker the Umtargartie, or smell out the witch. The male inhabitants of the kraal[1] being seated on the ground, the learned doctor, got up like a grizzly bear, appears, and administers a dance of a most terrific nature, during the exhibition of which remedy he incessantly gnashes his teeth, and howls:—"I am the original physician to Nooker the Umtargartie. Yow yow yow! No connexion with any other establishment. Till till till! All other Umtargarties are feigned Umtargarties, Boroo Boroo! but I perceive here a genuine and real Umtargartie, Hoosh Hoosh Hoosh! in whose blood I, the original Imyanger and Nookerer, Blizzerum Boo! will wash these bear's claws of mine. O yow yow yow!" All this time the learned physician is looking out among the attentive faces for some unfortunate man who owes him a cow, or who has given him any small offence, or against whom, without offence, he has conceived a spite. Him he never fails to Nooker as the Umtargartie, and he is instantly killed. In the absence of such an individual, the usual practice is to Nooker the quietest and most gentlemanly person in company. But the nookering is invariably followed on the spot by the butchering.

Some of the noble savages in whom Mr. Catlin was so strongly interested, and the diminution of whose numbers, by rum and smallpox, greatly affected him, had a custom not unlike this, though much more appalling and disgusting in its odious details.

The women being at work in the fields, hoeing the Indian corn, and the noble savage being asleep in the shade, the chief has sometimes the condescension to come forth, and lighten the labour by looking at it. On these occasions, he seats himself in his own savage chair, and is attended by his shield-bearer: who holds over his head a shield of cowhide—in shape like an immense mussel shell fearfully and wonderfully, after the manner of a theatrical supernumerary. But lest the great man should forget his greatness in the contemplation of the humble works of agriculture, there suddenly rushes in a poet, retained for the purpose, called a Praiser. This literary gentleman wears a leopard's head over his own, and a dress of tigers' tails; he has the appearance of having come express on his hind legs from the Zoological Gardens; and he incontinently strikes up the chief's praises, plunging and tearing all the while. There is a frantic wickedness in this brute's manner of worrying the air, and gnashing out, "O what a delightful chief he is! O what a delicious quantity of blood he sheds! O how majestically he laps it up! O how charmingly cruel he is! O how he tears the flesh of his enemies and crunches the bones! O how like the tiger and the leopard and the wolf and the bear he is! O, row row row row, how fond I am of him!" which might tempt the Society of Friends to charge at a hand-gallop into the Swartz-Kop location and exterminate the whole kraal.

When war is afoot among the noble savages—which is always—the chief holds a council to ascertain whether it is the opinion of his brothers and friends in general that the enemy shall be exterminated. On this occasion, after the performance of an Umsebeuza, or war song,— which is exactly like all the other songs, the chief makes a speech to his brothers and friends, arranged in single file. No particular order is observed during the delivery of this address, but every gentleman who finds himself excited by the subject, instead of crying "Hear, hear!" as is the custom with us, darts from the rank and tramples out the life, or crushes the skull, or mashes the face, or scoops out the eyes, or breaks the limbs, or performs a whirlwind of atrocities on the body, of an imaginary enemy. Several gentlemen becoming thus excited at once, and pounding away without the least regard to the orator, that illustrious person is rather in the position of an orator in an Irish House of Commons. But, several of these scenes of savage life bear a strong generic resemblance to an Irish election, and I think would be

---

[1] *kraal* A community of indigenous people in southern or central Africa, typically dwelling in huts surrounded by a stockade.

extremely well received and understood at Cork.[1]

In all these ceremonies the noble savage holds forth to the utmost possible extent about himself; from which (to turn him to some civilised account) we may learn, I think, that as egotism is one of the most offensive and contemptible littlenesses a civilised man can exhibit, so it is really incompatible with the interchange of ideas; inasmuch as if we all talked about ourselves we should soon have no listeners, and must be all yelling and screeching at once on our own separate accounts: making society hideous. It is my opinion that if we retained in us anything of the noble savage, we could not get rid of it too soon. But the fact is clearly otherwise. Upon the wife and dowry question, substituting coin for cows, we have assuredly nothing of the Zulu Kaffir left. The endurance of despotism is one great distinguishing mark of a savage always. The improving world has quite got the better of that too. In like manner, Paris is a civilised city, and the Théâtre Français a highly civilised theatre; and we shall never hear, and never have heard in these later days (of course) of the Praiser THERE. No, no, civilised poets have better work to do. As to Nookering Umtargarties, there are no pretended Umtargarties in Europe, and no European powers to Nooker them; that would be mere spydom, subordination, small malice, superstition, and false pretence. And as to private Umtargarties, are we not in the year eighteen hundred and fifty-three, with spirits rapping at our doors?

To conclude as I began. My position is, that if we have anything to learn from the Noble Savage, it is what to avoid. His virtues are a fable; his happiness is a delusion; his nobility, nonsense.

We have no greater justification for being cruel to the miserable object, than for being cruel to a WILLIAM SHAKESPEARE or an ISAAC NEWTON; but he passes away before an immeasurably better and higher power than ever ran wild in any earthly woods, and the world will be all the better when his place knows him no more.

from William Makepeace Thackeray, Letters to Mrs. Carmichael-Smyth

To Mrs. Carmichael-Smyth, 26 January 1853

… I don't believe Blacky *is* my man and my brother, though God forbid I should own him or flog him, or part him from his wife and children. But the question is a much longer [one than] is set forth in Mrs. Stowe's philosophy:[2] and I shan't speak about it, till I know it, or till it's my business, or I think I can do good.

To Mrs. Carmichael-Smyth, 13 February 1853

… They are not my men and brethren,[3] these strange people with retreating foreheads, with great obtruding lips and jaws: with capacities for thought, pleasure, endurance quite different to mine. They are not suffering as you are impassioning yourself for their wrongs as you read Mrs. Stowe, they are grinning and joking in the sun; roaring with laughter as they stand about the streets in squads; very civil, kind and gentle, even winning in their manner when you accost them at gentlemen's houses, where they do all the service. But they don't seem to me to be the same as white men, any more than asses are the same animals as horses; I don't mean this disrespectfully, but simply that there is such a difference of colour, habits, conformation of brains, that we must acknowledge it, and can't by any rhetorical phrase get it over; Sambo[4] is not my man and my brother; the very aspect of his face is grotesque and inferior. … As soon as the cheap substitute is found, depend on it the Planter, who stoutly pleads humanity now as the one of the reasons why he can't liberate his people, will get rid of them quickly enough; & the price of the slave-goods will fall so that owners won't care to hold such an unprofitable & costly stock.

[2] *Mrs. Stowe's philosophy* Reference to Harriet Beecher Stowe's anti-slavery novel, *Uncle Tom's Cabin* (1852).

[3] *They are … brethren* Reference to abolitionist materials that featured a slave in chains accompanied by the caption "Am I not a man and your brother?"

[4] *Sambo* Common slave name which became a derogatory term for any black person.

[1] *Several gentlemen … Cork* Dickens is displaying his prejudice against the Irish, who had historically been held, by many Englishmen and women, to have been "savages."

Conservatives, Liberals, and Empire

The following excerpts from speeches by Liberal Prime Minister William Gladstone, Conservative Prime Minister Benjamin Disraeli, and businessman, mining magnate, politician, and colonizer Cecil Rhodes provide three different perspectives on the attitudes taken by Britain's two main political parties towards issues of Empire in the second half of the nineteenth century.

from William Gladstone, "Our Colonies" (1855)

But an idea far more important and effective to a far greater extent has been the idea that the colonies ought to be maintained for the purpose of establishing an exclusive trade, the whole profit of which should be confined to the mother country, and should be enjoyed by the mother country. This was in fact the basis of the modern colonial system of Europe. I do not speak now of the political system, but it was the basis of the commercial laws of the countries which had colonies: that the industry of the colonists, instead of having a fair field and equal favour given to it, was attempted to be made entirely subservient to the interests and the profit of the mother country. It was placed in an unfair position. People were told in fact that they might go to the colonies, but that whatever they produced in the colonies must be sent to the British market—nay, that it must be sent in British vessels to the British market—nay, that whatever was produced must be sent to the British market in British vessels and in the state of raw produce, because if sent in other vessels, although it were sent better and cheaper, it would not be for the interest of the British shipowner, and if sent in a manufactured state it would not be for the interest of the British manufacturer....

Now, as I repudiate any and all of these reasons for desiring the possession of colonies, it is but fair that I should endeavour to state why I think colonies are desirable for a country circumstanced as England is. I have stated, that I do not think them desirable simply to puff up our reputation, apart from the basis and substance on which it rests. It is plain that they are not to be desired for revenue, because they do not yield it. It is plain that they are not to be desired for trading monopoly, because that we have entirely abandoned. It is plain they are not to be desired for patronage, properly so called, within their limits, because they will not allow us to exercise patronage, and I am bound to say, I do not think the public men of this country have any desire so to exercise it. With respect to territory, it is perfectly plain that mere extension of territory is not a legitimate object of ambition, unless you can show that you are qualified to make use of that territory for the purposes for which God gave the earth to man. Why then are colonies desirable? In my opinion, and I submit it to you with great respect, they are desirable both for the material and for the moral and social results which a wise system of colonisation is calculated to produce. As to the first, the effect of colonisation undoubtedly is to increase the trade and employment of the mother country. Take the case of the emigrant going across the Atlantic. Why does he go across the Atlantic? Because he expects—and in general he is the best judge of his own interests—to get better wages across the Atlantic than he can get at home. If he goes across the Atlantic to get better wages, he leaves in the labour market at home fewer persons than before, and consequently raises the rate of wages at home by carrying himself away from the competition with his fellows. By going to the colony and supplying it with labour he likewise creates a demand for capital there, and by this means he creates a trade between the colony and the mother country. The capital and labour thus employed in the colony raise and export productions, for which commodities are wanted in return....

But I do not concede that the material benefit of colonies is the only consideration which we are able to plead. Their moral and social advantage is a very great one. If we are asked why, on these grounds, it is desirable that colonies should be founded and possessed, I answer by asking another question—Why is it desirable that your population at home should increase? Why is it that you rejoice, always presuming that the increase of population goes hand in hand with equally favourable or more favourable conditions of existence for the mass of the people—why is it that you rejoice in an increase of population at home? Because an increase of population is an increase of power, an increase of strength and stability to the state, and because it multiplies the number of people who, as we hope, are living under good laws, and belong to a country to which it is an honour and an advantage to belong. That is the great moral benefit that attends the foundation of British colonies. We think that our country is a country blessed with laws and a constitution that are eminently beneficial to mankind, and if so, what can be more to be desired than that we should have the means of reproducing in different portions of the globe something as like as may be to that country which we honour and revere? I think it is in a work by Mr. Roebuck that the expression is used, "that the object of colonisation is the creation of so many happy Englands." It is the reproduction of the image and likeness of England—the reproduction of a country in which liberty is reconciled with order, in which ancient institutions stand in harmony with popular freedom, and a full recognition of popular rights, and in which religion and law have found one of their most favoured homes....

from Benjamin Disraeli, "Conservative and Liberal Principles" (1872)

Gentlemen, there is another and second great object of the Tory party. If the first is to maintain the institutions of the country, the second is, in my opinion, to uphold the Empire of England. If you look to the history of this country since the advent of Liberalism—forty years ago—you will find that there has been no effort so continuous, so subtle, supported by so much energy, and carried on with so much ability and acumen, as the attempts of Liberalism to effect the disintegration of the Empire of England.

And, gentlemen, of all its efforts, this is the one which has been the nearest to success. Statesmen of the highest character, writers of the most distinguished ability, the most organised and efficient means, have been employed in this endeavour. It has been proved to all of us that we have lost money by our colonies. It has been shown with precise, with mathematical demonstra-

tion, that there never was a jewel in the Crown of England that was so truly costly as the possession of India. How often has it been suggested that we should at once emancipate ourselves from this incubus.[1] Well, that result was nearly accomplished. When those subtle views were adopted by the country under the plausible plea of granting self-government to the colonies, I confess that I myself thought that the tie was broken. Not that I for one object to self-government. I cannot conceive how our distant colonies can have their affairs administered except by self-government. But self-government, in my opinion, when it was conceded, ought to have been conceded as part of a great policy of Imperial consolidation. It ought to have been accompanied by an Imperial tariff, by securities for the people of England for the enjoyment of the unappropriated lands which belonged to the Sovereign as their trustee, and by a military code which should have precisely defined the means and the responsibilities by which the colonies should be defended, and by which, if necessary, this country should call for aid from the colonies themselves. It ought, further, to have been accompanied by the institution of some representative council in the metropolis, which would have brought the colonies into constant and continuous relations with the Home Government. All this, however, was omitted because those who advised that policy—and I believe their convictions were sincere—looked upon the colonies of England, looked even upon our connection with India, as a burden upon this country, viewing everything in a financial aspect, and totally passing by those moral and political considerations which make nations great, and by the influence of which alone men are distinguished from animals.

Well, what has been the result of this attempt during the reign of Liberalism for the disintegration of the Empire? It has entirely failed. But how has it failed? Through the sympathy of the colonies with the Mother Country. They have decided that the Empire shall not be destroyed, and in my opinion no minister in this country will do his duty who neglects any opportunity

---

[1] *incubus* Mythical demon said to rape sleeping women, and in so doing to drain their life force to sustain itself. Figuratively, an evil that drains vital energy.

THE RHODES COLOSSUS
STRIDING FROM CAPE TOWN TO CAIRO.

Cecil Rhodes (1858–1902), nowadays best known for having endowed the Rhodes Scholarships for study at Oxford University, was the leading Briton in Southern Africa in the late nineteenth century—and a leading backer of the extension of British commercial and political interests in Africa as a whole. (The statue of the Colossus in the ancient city of Rhodes to which this cartoon alludes is said to have straddled the entrance to the harbor.)

of reconstructing as much as possible our Colonial Empire, and of responding to those distant sympathies which may become the source of incalculable strength and happiness to this land....

from Cecil Rhodes, Speech Delivered in Cape Town, 18 July 1899

And, sir, my people have changed. I speak of the English people, with their marvellous common sense, coupled with their powers of imagination—all thoughts of a Little England are over. They are tumbling over each other, Liberals and Conservatives, to show which side are the greatest and most enthusiastic Imperialists. The people have changed, and so do all the parties, just like the Punch and Judy show[1] at a country fair. The people have found out that England is small, and her trade is large, and they have also found out that other people are taking their share of the world, and enforcing hostile tariffs. The people of England are finding out that "trade follows the flag,"[2] and they have all become Imperialists. They are not going to part with any territory. And the bygone ideas of nebulous republics are over. The English people intend to retain every inch of land they have got, and perhaps, sir, they intend to secure a few more inches. ...

from David Livingstone, "Cambridge Lecture Number 1" (1858)

The following excerpts are from a speech delivered at Cambridge University by the famous missionary; it was received with extended cheering.

When I went to Africa about seventeen years ago I resolved to acquire an accurate knowledge of the native tongues; and as I continued, while there, to speak generally in the African languages, the result is that I am not now very fluent in my own; but if you will excuse

my imperfections under that head, I will endeavour to give you as clear an idea of Africa as I can....

My object in going into the country south of the desert was to instruct the natives in a knowledge of Christianity, but many circumstances prevented my living amongst them more than seven years, amongst which were considerations arising out of the slave system carried on by the Dutch Boers. I resolved to go into the country beyond, and soon found that, for the purposes of commerce, it was necessary to have a path to the sea. I might have gone on instructing the natives in religion, but as civilization and Christianity must go on together, I was obliged to find a path to the sea, in order that I should not sink to the level of the natives. The chief was overjoyed at the suggestion, and furnished me with twenty-seven men, and canoes, and provisions, and presents for the tribes through whose country we had to pass. We might have taken a shorter path to the sea than that to the north, and then to the west, by which we went; but along the country by the shorter route, there is an insect called the tsetse, whose bite is fatal to horses, oxen, and dogs, but not to men or donkeys. You seem to think there is a connexion between the two. The habitat of that insect is along the shorter route to the sea. The bite of it is fatal to domestic animals, not immediately, but certainly in the course of two or three months; the animal grows leaner and leaner, and gradually dies of emaciation: a horse belonging to Gordon Cumming died of a bite five or six months after it was bitten.

On account of this insect, I resolved to go to the north, and then westwards to the Portuguese settlement of Loanda. Along the course of the river which we passed, game was so abundant that there was no difficulty in supplying the wants of my whole party: antelopes were so tame that they might be shot from the canoe. But beyond 14 degrees of south latitude the natives had guns, and had themselves destroyed the game, so that I and my party had to live on charity. The people, however, in that central region were friendly and hospitable: but they had nothing but vegetable productions: the most abundant was the cassava, which, however nice when made into tapioca pudding, resembles in its more primitive condition nothing so much as a mess of laundress's starch. There was a desire in the

---

[1] *Punch and Judy show* Puppet show involving Mr. Punch and his wife Judy.

[2] *trade ... flag* Popular dictum of the period, meant to encourage colonization.

various villages through which we passed to have intercourse with us, and kindness and hospitality were shown us; but when we got near the Portuguese settlement of Angola the case was changed, and payment was demanded for every thing. But I had nothing to pay with. Now the people had been in the habit of trading with the slavers, and so they said I might give one of my men in payment for what I wanted. When I shewed them that I could not do this, they looked upon me as an interloper, and I was sometimes in danger of being murdered.

As we neared the coast, the name of England was recognized, and we got on with ease. Upon one occasion, when I was passing through the parts visited by slave-traders, a chief who wished to shew me some kindness offered me a slave-girl: upon explaining that I had a little girl of my own, whom I should not like my own chief to give to a black man, the chief thought I was displeased with the size of the girl, and sent me one a head taller. By this and other means I convinced my men of my opposition to the principle of slavery; and when we arrived at Loanda I took them on board a British vessel, where I took a pride in showing them that those countrymen of mine and those guns were there for the purpose of putting down the slave-trade. They were convinced from what they saw of the honesty of Englishmen's intentions; and the hearty reception they met with from the sailors made them say to me, "We see they are your countrymen, for they have hearts like you." On the journey, the men had always looked forward to reaching the coast: they had seen Manchester prints and other articles imported therefrom, and they could not believe they were made by mortal hands. On reaching the sea, they thought that they had come to the end of the world. They said, "We marched along with our father, thinking the world was a large plain without limit; but all at once the land said 'I am finished, there is no more of me'"; and they called themselves the true old men—the true ancients—having gone to the end of the world. On reaching Loanda, they commenced trading in firewood, and also engaged themselves at sixpence a day in unloading coals, brought by a steamer for the supply of the cruiser lying there to watch the slave-vessels. On their return, they told their people "we worked for a whole moon, carrying away the stones that burn." By the time they were ready to go back to their own country, each had secured a large bundle of goods. On the way back, however, fever detained them, and their goods were all gone, leaving them on their return home, as poor as when they started....

A prospect is now before us of opening Africa for commerce and the Gospel. Providence has been preparing the way, for even before I proceeded to the Central basin it had been conquered and rendered safe by a chief named Sebituane, and the language of the Bechuanas made the fashionable tongue, and that was one of the languages into which Mr. Moffat had translated the Scriptures. Sebituane also discovered Lake Ngami some time previous to my explorations in that part. In going back to that country my object is to open up traffic along the banks of the Zambesi, and also to preach the Gospel. The natives of Central Africa are very desirous of trading, but their only traffic is at present in slaves, of which the poorer people have an unmitigated horror; it is therefore most desirable to encourage the former principle, and thus open a way for the consumption of free productions, and the introduction of Christianity and commerce. By encouraging the native propensity for trade, the advantages that might be derived in a commercial point of view are incalculable; nor should we lose sight of the inestimable blessings it is in our power to bestow upon the unenlightened African, by giving him the light of Christianity. Those two pioneers of civilization—Christianity and commerce—should ever be inseparable; and Englishmen should be warned by the fruits of neglecting that principle as exemplified in the result of the management of Indian affairs. By trading with Africa, also, we should at length be independent of slave labour, and thus discountenance practices so obnoxious to every Englishman.

Though the natives are not absolutely anxious to receive the Gospel, they are open to Christian influences. Among the Bechuanas the Gospel was well received. These people think it a crime to shed a tear, but I have seen some of them weep at the recollection of their sins when God had opened their hearts to Christianity and repentance....

I beg to direct your attention to Africa; I know that in a few years I shall be cut off in that country, which is now open; do not let it be shut again! I go back to Africa to try to make an open path for commerce and Christianity; do you carry out the work which I have begun. I LEAVE IT WITH YOU!

Eliza M., "Account of Cape Town," *King William's Town Gazette* (1863)

The following account (brought to light by M.J. Daymond et al. and the Women Writing Africa Project[1]) is one of the most remarkable literary descriptions we have of the world of nineteenth-century British colonialism from the point of view of one of the colonized. King William's Town was a small town some 500 miles east of Cape Town, and Eliza M., as she was identified in the *King William's Town Gazette*, had attended school at St. Matthews Mission in the area. As Daymond et al. suggest, such a piece as this would in all likelihood have "been written as a school exercise." It would have been published, they speculate, "partly because its naiveté was amusing to the whites, but also because it was proof of the civilizing policies of the missionaries. It was translated from Xhosa into English by an unknown translator." What may have seemed "amusing naiveté" to nineteenth-century settlers is more likely to strike the modern reader as a style of elemental freshness.

We left East London on the Sunday, while it was raining; the sea was fighting very much, and there were soldiers going to England and their wives. On the Tuesday we arrived at Algoa Bay, and boats came to fetch the people who were going there, and other people came in. The ship went off the same day. A great wind blew, and I thought myself that if it had been another ship, it would not have been able to go on, but in its going, it kept twisting about, it did not go straight, but it went well on the day of our arrival, for the wind was good. We arrived on the Friday. While I was in the ship, I forgot I was on the water, it was like a house inside, but outside it was not like a house. There is everything that is kept at home; there were fowls and sheep and pigs, and slaughtering every day. I kept looking at the thing which makes the ship go. There are two horses inside, made of iron, which make it go; and when I looked inside, it was very frightful. There are many bedrooms inside. The ship we were in is named the *Norman*, it is a steamer. It was unpleasant when nothing appeared, but when we left the Bay, we saw the mountains till we got to the Cape. One mountain is called the Lion's Head, and another is called Green Point, and I myself saw those mountains. That which is called the Lion's Head, is like a lion asleep. And another mountain above the town is that called Table Mountain; nevertheless it is not like a table, still that name is proper for it.

Before I came into the town, my heart said, "this place is not large," but when I entered it, I wondered, and was afraid. Oh, we slept that day. I have forgotten to relate something I saw the day I arrived. I saw black people, and I thought they were our kind, but they are not; they are Slams, called in English, Malays. Also, I was astonished at their large hats, pointed at the top, and large below. I saw some making baskets of reeds, and I wished I knew how to do it. On the Saturday evening, we went to a shop to buy butter and bread. At night lights were hung up throughout the whole town. I had thought we were going to walk in the darkness. I have not yet seen houses built with grass, like those we live in, they are high beautiful houses. The roads where people walk, are very fine. I have not yet seen a dirty, muddy place in the whole town. On the Sunday, bells sounded; there is one big one, and other small ones; we went to service in the great church.

Early on the Monday, wagons came about to sell things. Really people here get these things for nothing from their owners. A person can get men's trousers for three shilling each, yet in other places a person can never get them for that money. You can get three pairs of stockings for a shilling, a child's cap for a penny; you can get a width of a dress for threepence, if it is five widths, it is a shilling and threepence. There are little wagons, the man who drives the horses sits behind, the proprietor does nothing, he sits so.

Another thing. The shoes of the Malays astonished me. There is a heel, and yonder on before a piece of wood sticks out, and they put it between their toes, and so make a clattering like the Germans. As things are to

---

[1] *Women Writing Africa Project* M.J. Daymond et al., eds., *Women Writing Africa: The Southern Region* (New York: The Feminist Press, 2003), 98–104.

be got for such little money, how cheap must they be in England!

On Friday I saw a man riding in a wagon, there was a barrel inside and a cross-bar, and the water came out there. I don't know how it came out. It watered the new road, which is being made. And on Tuesday I saw people working at slates, taking off their ends—it was a great heap; the people who were at work were four. On the day of our arrival, a house was burnt, the people escaped, but I don't know whether the goods escaped. There are carts which go every day, carrying earth to throw on the road which is being mended, drawn by one horse.

There is a house where there are all kinds of beasts, and there are figures of black people, as if they were alive; their blackness is very ugly; also the bones of a man when he is dead, and birds and elephants, and lions, and tigers and sea-shells. I was afraid of those people, and the skeleton. There is also an ape holding Indian Corn, and there are monkeys.

In the evening we went out again, we went to the houses of the Malays; we went to see their decorations, for they were rejoicing because their days of fasting were ended. They were very beautiful; they had made flowers of paper, you would never think they were made of paper. We went for the sole purpose of seeing these works. They made a great noise, singing as they walked; you would laugh to see the children dancing outside and clapping their hands.

There are also wagons there for the sale of fish. The proprietors sound a thing like a horn to announce that he who wishes to buy let him buy. There are others for collecting dust-heaps, they ring a bell. There are vehicles to convey two people, he who drives the horses, and he who sits inside. In some there are windows and lights lit at night: those windows are two.

There are not many trees in the town; in some places there are not many at all, but in one place it is like the bush; it is pleasant underneath the trees; there are stools to sit on when a person is tired. That path is very long; I saw two Newfoundland dogs. I did not know that I should ever come to see them when I heard them spoken of. They are dogs with large heads and great long ears; the hair is like sheep's wool, and they have great claws; they are suited to assist people. It seemed as if

they could swallow me without chewing; I was very much afraid, but one was not very big, it was about the size of the dogs of black people, when it barks, it says so with a great voice. Also, I saw sheep rather unlike others, in the tail here it was very large, the head was small, and the body was large and fat.

I have forgotten to mention something which I ought to have said before; when I came out of the ship and walked on land the earth seemed to move, and when I entered a house, it seemed to imitate the sailing of a ship, and when I lay down it seemed to move.

I saw an ox-wagon here, but I had not imagined that I should see a wagon.

We go to a very large beautiful Church; I don't forget the people who sing, the English; the prayers are said with thin voices as if it were singing; but the chief thing done is singing frequently, all the while there is continually singing, and then sitting. There is a Kafir school here; I went one day, they were reading; they can read well; there are also carpenters &c.

There is another place besides that which I said is like the bush, and in that place there are trees and flowers, and two fountains; a thing is stuck in, and the water comes out above. I saw the date-tree when it is young; it is one leaf, yet when it is grown, it is a very large tree. In that place there are wild birds, doves are there, and those birds which the English call canaries, and a very beautiful bird, its tail is long, its bill is red.

Yesterday the soldiers had sports, the music-band played, and when they finished playing they fired. They were many, and they fired together. And as we were walking, they fired; I was very much startled and afraid. And to-day they are playing the music. It seems to-day it exceeds in sweetness, I mean its sound.

There came a person here who is a Kafir. I rejoiced very much when I heard that he too was one. He asked me what I had come to do here; I said "I am only travelling." He asked whether I was a prisoner, and I said "No." He said he was very glad, he had thought I was a prisoner. I told him that I was going away again, and he said "May you go in peace, the Lord preserve you well till you arrive whence you came." I never saw a person like him of such kindness; he said he had come here to learn, he came from where I did; but I should not have known him to be a Kafir, and he did not know that I was one.

There are creatures which are eaten; they come from the sea, their name is called crawfish, they are frightful in appearance, yet their flesh is very fine and white.

The person of this house is a dyer of clothes, the white he makes red, and the red green, and the brown he makes black. I saw the wood with which they dye. Soap is cut in pieces, and put in water, and heated and boiled well, and continually stirred. This thing—dyeing clothes, is a great work. Water is even in the house; I don't know where it comes from, a person turns a thing, and fresh water comes out as if it were of a river.

There are also carts for selling meat, and for selling bread. I saw the fire-wagon, I did nothing but wonder. I did not know that it was such a big thing. It is long, with many wheels, they are not so large as those of an ox-wagon; people sit in places inside. The wheels run on metal; I say I could do nothing but wonder very much. I had not thought that it was such a great thing. And when it is about to proceed it says "Sh!" I don't know whether it is the boiling of the water; it hastens exceedingly, a person would be unable to notice it well, yet now some people say that this is a small one which I have seen. If it treads on anything, it must smash it, it is a very great thing. I shall never forget it. Where I saw it, the place was fenced on both sides, and I beheld it from the outside. I entered it another week after I had seen it; we went to Somerset West and slept one night. In the morning we returned by it: when I was inside, the earth seemed to move; it is pleasant to ride inside. I end now although this is not all the news about it. When I was in it, I saw a sugar plant; it is not a large plant, it is short with red flowers. I saw other trees at Somerset West which I had never seen before.

One day I saw people going to a burial, the carriages were black, but that people should wear black clothes is done also among the natives where a person has died; there were stuck up black feathers, and on the graves were placed stones with writing; the name of the person was written, and the years of his age, and the year in which he died.

I have seen to-day another thing which I did not know of, that thing which is said to be always done by white people in this month of May. They make themselves black people, they smear themselves with some-thing black, with red patches on the cheeks; a thing is made with evergreens, and a man is put inside, and two people carry it, and another man carries a pan, and goes begging for money.

Another thing which I saw during the past month, was people going to the Governor's house—little chiefs, and chiefs of the soldiers, some had hats with red and white feathers, and silver coats, and gold swords, and the bishop went too. I heard it said that they were going to hear the things which were about to be spoken by people who had come from Graham's Town, King William's Town, Beaufort, and other places; it was said that these people were going to speak of the state of those towns and the doings of the people who live there. I do not say that those coats were really of gold, I say there was gold on some parts of them, on the arms and the back.

Also I have seen the fruit of the tree which the English call the chestnut; I did not see what the tree is like, the fruit is nice, the outside of it is hard; when you eat it it is sweet and edible like the potato, you can roast it or boil it. There is another fruit called Banana in English, it also is a nice fruit; it is not boiled or roasted, it is eaten like other fruits. There is a great white sweet potato, it is called Sweet Potato; those potatoes are very large, I had never seen them before, they are nearly all long: I do not know whether they are the potatoes named "Medicine" by the Fingoes.

I am puzzled to know how to begin to relate what was done yesterday, but I will try. Yesterday was said to be the wedding-day of the Great Son of Victoria, but it was not really the day of his marriage, for he has been married some time. The thing first done was arranging the children of the schools and I was there too. All walked in threes, going from one street to another. When we left the school-house we took up our station on an open piece of ground, other people climbed on the houses, and others looked on from below. On one house where we were standing there was the figure of a man like a king, a red cloth was put as if it were held by him, it is called in English a flag. Amongst all of us there were flags of different beautiful kinds; we stood there a great while, till we saw a multitude of soldiers and their officers and little chiefs and different sorts of people: one set wore clothes all alike, another had different clothes and ancient hats which were worn by the people of that time. All these now went in front, a very long line, then followed the ranks of another school, and we came after them. When we had finished going through many streets, we went to stand in another open spot of ground. All the time we were walking we were singing the song of Victoria. And there we saw the Governor and his wife; we all saluted. Although it seems that I have written a great deal I have not yet wondered at the things done at night, but let me finish those of the day. We were given food. We saw boats going along with people inside and boys wearing red clothes; there followed one with an old man, his hairs were long and white. There was a woman at his side wearing short clothes. Other boats followed with people in them, all the time they were appearing the drum and trumpets were sounded. I don't know how I shall make myself understood. I never saw such a beautiful thing; some of the men wore short dresses and short coats, and others wore short trousers like those of the French. All these things were red. When we had finished walking we went to stand in an open piece of ground, then we all went home. I do not know if any other things were done.

We went out again in the evening to see the fireworks. First we went into the gardens, where there were what I shall call candles; but nevertheless they are not called so in English. They were lights put inside little red and green glasses—When I was at a distance I thought they were little round things, all these were hung up and fastened in the trees,—there were some large ones and there were others not put in glasses.

We walked and went to a great crowd of people, we could not tell what we should do to see that which we came to see. There we saw a tall man with a high hat, I did not understand how it was made, and another man wearing women's clothes continually playing with that tall man. All these things have their names in English, some were called *Punch & Judy, Spectre, Father of the Doomed Arm-chair,* or the *Maid, the Murderer and the Midnight Avenger,*[1] and many other plays besides these.

We passed on from that woman and man and went to see white people smeared with soot, they went into a house made of a tent where there were stools, and two came out and spoke to the people saying, "Ladies and gentlemen, come in and see what we have got here inside." Some went in and others did not, afterwards they opened that the people might see; there were black people sitting on chairs and singing. So we left; at the entrance of the garden there was written in letters of fire, "GOD bless Albert and Alexandra." In another place there were other things of fire, that place is called in English the Parade, where there was a thing like a light-house, on all sides there were candles. Some people sent up fire from Table Mountain, others from Green Point, others sent up fire in the midst of the town, it went up and came down again.

Besides these things there was another thing done, an ox was baked whole, the legs were not removed, only the inside and the hoofs. Many tables were set underneath the trees; that ox was intended for the poor people.

I am going to end now; I am very glad that I was brought here to see things which I never thought I should see.

There is another thing which has lately taken place, the birthday of Queen Victoria. Two balloons were made, no one went in them, there were only lights. That sort is called fire-balloons. The first was sent up; it rose very high till it was like a star: I did not see it again where it went. The other reappeared, it did not rise high like the first, it burnt, and fire came down like two stars.

I saw where newspapers are printed; four people were at work. I do not know what I shall say to tell about it. There is a thing which folds the papers and another thing which continually receives them. It made us sleepy.

E.M.
Translator unknown

---

[1] *Spectre ... Avenger*   Popular plays of the period.

from Agnes Macdonald, "By Car and Cowcatcher,"
Murray's Magazine (1887)

> The essay from which the passages below are ex-
> cerpted describes Macdonald's trip across Canada by
> train with her husband, Canadian Prime Minister
> Sir John A. Macdonald.

… The description of a cow-catcher is less easy. To
begin with, it is misnamed, for it catches no cows at all.
Sometimes, I understand, it throws up on the buffer-
beam whatever maimed or mangled animal it has struck,
but in most cases it clears the line by shoving forward,
or tossing aside, any removable obstruction. It is best
described as a sort of barred iron beak, about six feet
long, projecting close over the track in a V shape, and
attached to the buffer-beam by very strong bolts. It is
sometimes sheathed with thin iron plates in winter, and
acts then as a small snow-plough.

Behold me now, enthroned on the candle-box, with
a soft felt hat well over my eyes, and a linen carriage-
cover tucked round me from waist to foot. Mr. E.[1] had
seated himself on the other side of the headlight. He
had succumbed to the inevitable, ceased further expos-
tulation, disclaimed all responsibility, and, like the jewel
of a Superintendent he was, had decided on sharing my
peril! I turn to him, peeping round the headlight, with
my best smile. "This is *lovely*," I triumphantly announce, seeing that a word of comfort is necessary,
"*quite lovely*; I shall travel on this cowcatcher from
summit to sea!"

Mr. Superintendent, in his turn, peeps round the
headlight and surveys me with solemn and resigned
surprise. "I—suppose—you—will," he says slowly, and
I see that he is hoping, at any rate, that I shall live to do
it!

With a mighty snort, a terribly big throb, and
shrieking whistle, No. 374 moves slowly forward. The
very small population of Laggan have all come out to
see. They stand in the hot sunshine, and shade their eyes
as the stately engine moves on. "It is an awful thing to
do!" I hear a voice say, as the little group lean forward;
and for a moment I feel a thrill that is very like fear; but

it is gone at once, and I can think of nothing but the
novelty, the excitement, and the fun of this mad ride in
glorious sunshine and intoxicating air, with magnificent
mountains before and around me, their lofty peaks
smiling down on us, and never a frown on their grand
faces!

The pace quickens gradually, surely, swiftly, and
then we are rushing up to the summit. We soon stand
on the "Great Divide"—5300 feet above sea-level—
between the two great oceans. As we pass, Mr. E. by a
gesture, points out a small river (called Bath Creek, I
think) which, issuing from a lake on the narrow
summit-level, winds near the track. I look, and lo! the
water, flowing *eastward* towards the Atlantic side, turns
in a moment as the Divide is passed, and pours *westward*
down the Pacific slope!

Another moment and a strange silence has fallen
round us. With steam shut off and brakes down, the 60-
ton engine, by its own weight and impetus alone, glides
into the pass of the Kicking Horse River, and begins a
descent of 2800 feet in twelve miles. We rush onward
through the vast valley stretching before us, bristling
with lofty forests, dark and deep, that, clinging to the
mountain side, are reared up into the sky. The river,
widening, grows white with dashing foam, and rushes
downwards with tremendous force. Sunlight flashes on
glaciers, into gorges, and athwart[2] huge, towering masses
of rock crowned with magnificent tree crests that rise all
round us of every size and shape. Breathless—almost
awe-stricken—but with a wild triumph in my heart, I
look from farthest mountain peak, lifted high before
me, to the shining pebbles at my feet! Warm wind
rushes past; a thousand sunshine colours dance in the
air. With a firm right hand grasping the iron stanchion,
and my feet planted on the buffer beam, there was not
a yard of that descent in which I faltered for a moment.
If I had, then assuredly in the wild valley of the Kicking
Horse River, on the western slope of the Rocky Mountains, a life had gone out that day! I did not think of
danger, or remember what a giddy post I had. I could
only gaze at the glaciers that the mountains held so
closely, 5000 feet above us, at the trace of snow ava-
lanches which had left a space a hundred feet wide
massed with torn and prostrate trees; on the shadows

---

[1] *Mr. E.* John M. Egan, general superintendent of the western
division of the Canadian Pacific Railroad at the time.

[2] *athwart* Run across in oblique direction.

that played over the distant peaks; and on a hundred rainbows made by the foaming, dashing river, which swirls with tremendous rapidity down the gorge on its way to the Columbia in the valley below. ...

Halted at Palliser. The Chief and his friends walked up to the cow-catcher to make a morning call. I felt a little "superior" and was rather condescending. Somewhat flushed with excitement, but still anxious to be polite, I asked "would the Chief step up and take a drive?" To the horror of the bystanders he carelessly consented, and in another moment had taken the place of Mr. E., the latter seating himself at our feet on the buffer-beam. There was a general consternation among our little group of friends and the few inhabitants of Palliser—the Chief rushing through the flats of the Columbia on a cow-catcher! and, worse still, possibly even among the wild Selkirk Mountains—those mountains of which scarcely three years before, in his charming book, "From Old Westminster to New," my friend Mr. Sandford Fleming[1] had said, "no one had been through the western slope of the Selkirks"! Every one is horrified. It is a comfort to the other occupant of the buffer to find some one else wilful, and as we steamed away towards Donald, at the eastern base of the Selkirks, I felt not so bad after all! ...

---

[1] *Sanford Fleming* Canadian engineer and inventor (1827–1915).

The Early Twentieth Century: From 1900 to Mid-Century

The first half of the twentieth century saw a fracturing of almost every aspect of British life. At the beginning of the century, Queen Victoria, monarch for 63 years, still reigned over a nation that had become the world's greatest economic and political power. Over the course of the nineteenth century, the industrial revolution had transformed the economy and Great Britain had become "factory to the world." Despite a high level of religious anxiety among the educated classes of the late Victorian period, the established church retained its authority over a God-fearing society. The working class was not always contented with its lot—and with reason—but the class hierarchy remained extraordinarily stable. So, too, did gender roles; a small minority of women was pressing to be given the vote, but they were regarded as extremists by the vast majority of the population. Expressions of sexuality were tightly circumscribed, and the possibility of having an orientation other than heterosexual was unmentioned (except for occasional veiled references to difficulties or scandals "of the Oscar Wilde sort.") And the British Empire had reached its zenith. The vast dominions of Canada and Australia had become semi-autonomous (in 1867 and 1901 respectively), but overwhelmingly their people were proud to call themselves British subjects. Despite a lively debate in the latter half of the nineteenth century as to whether Britain's imperial ambitions were truly benefitting either the colonizers or the colonized, the majority of British citizens were not "little Englanders" looking to reduce Britain's overseas commitments; they were pleased that British rule extended over all of India, a very large part of Africa, and a considerable amount of the rest of the world. England was seen by the English, in the words of the popular poet W.E. Henley, as the "Chosen daughter of the Lord." Britain had certainly not been immune to change in the second half the nineteenth century—indeed, many of the lines along which twentieth-century society would fracture were in place in the late Victorian era. Political and ideological strains that would shake class structure were already forming; categories of gender and sexuality were already becoming far less stable than they had been a decade or two earlier; and the "Aesthetes" had begun in the 1890s to break free of characteristically Victorian patterns of anxiety over the religious, the moral, and the aesthetic. But for most British people the world in 1900 seemed recognizably the same world as that of 1850, and Britain held a central place within it.

By 1950 that world had been distinctly altered. The four years of World War I had resulted in the deaths of millions and had had a catastrophic effect on the nation's spirit; the great economic depression of the 1930s had bred poverty and despair; the seven years of World War II had threatened Britain's survival and left the nation exhausted, even in victory; and immediately in its wake, with Britain still physically and emotionally devastated, had begun a new war, a "Cold War" against the Soviet Union. Exhausted by these struggles, Britain in 1950 had lost its place as the world's leading power to the United States. Daily life had been radically altered by the radio, the telephone, and the automobile. Church-going was in decline, and the nation was well on its way to becoming a secular society. Though Britain remained more class-conscious than North America or Australia, the class structure itself had seen great change; only the wealthy had servants, and all social classes partook of the same culture to an unprecedented extent. The Labour Party government of Clement Attlee, elected in 1945 in a clean break from Winston Churchill and the glorious but conservative path that he represented, had for five years been building a welfare state; this was Britain's first avowedly socialist government. "Votes for women"—to most minds a far-fetched notion in 1900—had in 1950 been a reality for over 30 years; women had done "men's work" during two long world wars, and were starting to wonder if winning the vote might represent the beginning rather than the end of the struggle for gender equality. Much

King Edward VII.

The streets of London decorated for the Coronation of Edward VII, 1902.

of Britain was as repressed sexually as it had been in 1900—but more and more people were starting to see the awkwardness that surrounded sexual matters as an obstacle to be overcome rather than as the expression of a necessary and appropriate sense of modesty. And the sun was rapidly setting on the British Empire. The dominions were now fully independent and beginning to drift away from the mother country culturally; India had been partitioned in 1947 into two independent nations; and in Britain's African and Caribbean possessions the stirrings of unrest that would lead to independence had already begun. In literature Britain had in the years between 1900 and 1950 undergone the Modernist revolution.[1] The sometimes fractured, some-

times free-flowing approaches to form that the poetry of T.S. Eliot, the plays of Samuel Beckett, and the prose fiction of James Joyce and Virginia Woolf represented had not been taken up by the majority of writers. Yet many serious writers in 1950 were aware of the expanded possibilities of literary form that modernism had revealed—and many wrote with a sense that the world was not the ordered and coherent whole that it had been widely assumed to be at the dawn of the twentieth century.

THE EDWARDIAN PERIOD

If it is true to say that the first half of the twentieth century may be characterized as a period in which the old Britain and the old world broke apart, it is also true that much of that fracturing did not begin to be readily visible until the years after 1910. 1910 was marked by the death of Edward VII, but more significantly this was the time of the first explosions of Modernism—Cubism in painting, Imagism in poetry, in music such ground-breaking works as Stravinsky's *The Rite of Spring* (1913). With these began the fracturing of form that would become a dominant theme in the cultural history of much of the rest of the century. With 1914 came the

---

[1] "Modernist" and "Modernism" are commonly used as umbrella terms to describe a wide range of inter-connected intellectual and aesthetic developments of the first half of the twentieth century that occurred in France, Italy, the United States and other areas as well as in Britain. A connecting thread is that expressions of Modernism tend to shun the linear, the decorative, and the sentimental. They tend too towards the presentation of reality fractured into its component pieces—and conversely, towards a rejection of aesthetic traditions through which reality is represented through the construction of conventionally unified wholes, through a single point of view, or through a single, unbroken narrative. Modernism is discussed more fully both later in this introduction and in a separate "Contexts" section elsewhere in this volume.

outbreak of World War I, and with 1915 and 1916—the years of the gruesomely drawn-out battles of Ypres and of the Somme—came a more visceral sense of fracturing as the full horror of the war's unprecedented carnage began to sink home.

The deaths of Victoria in 1901 and of her son Edward nine years later have often been seen as defining moments in the change from the Victorian to the modern world. Edwardian Britain liked to see itself as highly distinct from its Victorian predecessor. And certainly there were some changes; architectural style became rather less ornate, for example, and social style rather less formal. But at its core the Edwardian era was as much a continuation from the Victorian one as a break with it. Established religion, a hierarchy of social class, a largely inflexible set of attitudes towards gender roles, a complacent confidence in Britain's dominant position in the world—all these remained largely unchanged.

In some respects a "Victorian" sense of Empire carried on into the 1920s and 1930s. Here Queen Mary (wife of George V) is shown visiting the Burma pavilion at the British Empire Exhibition, London, 1924. Though some complained that the Exhibition's strongly patriotic flavor was excessively self-congratulatory, it was highly popular with most Londoners.

A sternwheel steamer and trading canoes at Okopedi on the Eyong River, Nigeria, 1909. Nigeria was among the last British possessions to be governed through a trading company; in 1900, control was transferred from the Royal Niger Company to the government, and the territory became the Protectorate of Southern Nigeria. The Niger Company continued as the leading trading entity in the region.

In the literary world Victorian traditions were being carried forward by novelists such as George Moore and Arnold Bennett, dramatists such as Arthur Wing Pinero, and poets such as Robert Bridges and W.E. Henley, the immensely popular author of "Invictus" and "Pro Rege Nostro" ("England, My England"). And even much of the literature that we now think of as recognizably modern may as readily be seen as connecting with that of the late Victorian era as anticipating the later literature of the century. The prose fiction of Joseph Conrad, for example, with its laying bare of the dark corners of the human soul (and of the dark realities of colonialism), touches the nerves of the reader in ways that we think of as distinctively modern. Indeed, the cry "that was no more than a breath" of the dying ivory agent

Kurtz in Conrad's *Heart of Darkness* (1899, 1902)— "The horror! The horror!"—is often regarded as a defining expression of the anguish that came to be felt as characteristic of the twentieth century. And some of Conrad's narrative techniques break ground that would become heavily tilled in the twentieth century; through layering of viewpoints (stories within stories, multiple narrators) Conrad found ways to create a narrative density that at once intensifies and destabilizes the reader's experience of the events being recounted. But Conrad was an extraordinary innovator, not a revolutionary; however original, the threads of most of his fiction are still woven through a storytelling art that draws on the conventions of fiction writing that held sway through the nineteenth century—conventions of realism through which implausible coincidences or exotic adventures could be made believable to the reader. As a *New York Times* reviewer put it in 1903, "the adventures he describes are little short of miraculous and are laid among scenes wholly alien to commonplace life, [but] they are wrought into a tissue of truth so firm and so tough as to resist the keenest scepticism.... Not even his Kurtz, the man of impenetrable darkness of soul, is either a bloodless or an incredible figure."

The novelist E.M. Forster is recognizably an author of the twentieth century in his treatment not only of the sexual (see below for a discussion of his novel *Maurice*) but also of the spiritual; his approach to the spiritual realities that transcend everyday life connects to the work of later twentieth-century writers such as Elizabeth Bowen, Graham Greene, and Kazuo Ishiguro. And in some stylistic respects (notably, the shifting, ironic narrative voice of *A Passage to India* [1924]), his fiction has affinities with modernism. But the texture of his work—most notably of the novels *A Room With a View* (1908) and *Howard's End* (1910)—is woven of nuances of social interaction and of subtle modulations of feeling, and relates at least as strongly to the conventions of Victorian realism as it does to those of Modernism. Forster is above all a social novelist, whose work recognizably connects with the traditions of his nineteenth-century predecessors.

Much of H.G. Wells's fiction was forward-looking in a more precise sense. Beginning in 1895 with the publication of *The Time Machine*, and continuing with *The Island of Dr. Moreau* (1896), *The Invisible Man* (1897), and *The War of the Worlds* (1898), Wells had founded the genre of science fiction as we still know it today. He continued in this vein in the new century with such works as *The First Men in Moon* (1901) and *The War in the Air* (1908). But in the style of his fiction Wells, too, was a traditional storyteller. And, though he is remembered today primarily for his science fiction, he wrote in a vein of social comedy with at least as much frequency, and with even greater success in his own lifetime. *Love and Mr. Lewisham* (1900), *Kipps: The Story of a Simple Soul* (1905), and *The History of Mr. Polly* (1910) are comic novels that draw on Wells's own struggles in painting an entertaining but strongly critical picture of the English social class system.

Like many writers of the time—playwright George Bernard Shaw perhaps most prominent among them—Wells became a committed socialist in the early years of the twentieth century. The chief vehicle of socialist response in Britain at the time was the Fabian society, founded in 1884 to promote *evolutionary* socialism (thus disavowing violent class struggle). The Fabian Society, led by Shaw, Sidney Webb, and Beatrice Potter Webb, was instrumental in forming the Labour Representation Committee in 1900; that committee, with substantial input as well from the Trades Union Congress, transformed itself into a political party in 1906, and over the course of the next generation the Labour Party managed to displace the Liberal Party as the main political alternative to Britain's Conservative Party. *Mrs Warren's Profession* is among the earliest of a long series of plays that give dramatic life to Shaw's progressive views; among its most memorable successors are *Major Barbara* (1905) and *Pygmalion* (1913). Shaw continued to write for the stage well into the 1920s (and lived until 1950), but he too expressed a powerful sense of change more in the content of his work than in its form. And other writers of the Edwardian era—including novelists and dramatists of thoroughly modern views such as Sarah Grand, Ella Hepworth Dixon, and Cicely Hamilton (all of whom expressed their strong feminist views through their work), for the most part structured their texts in traditional ways.

Members of a slum-dwelling family in London, c. 1913. Though Britain was the world's wealthiest nation, the poor often lived in appalling conditions of hardship.

David Lloyd George, 1906. Lloyd George was a leading advocate of the interests of the working class in the early years of the century. As Chancellor of the Exchequer, he introduced the "Peoples' Budget" of 1909, calling for new taxes on the better-off to pay for measures to improve the lot of the poor, including an old age pension. The Old Age Pensions Act was resisted so strongly by the House of Lords that the Liberal Government acted to reduce the power of the House; both that Act and the Parliament Act, which established the supremacy of the House of Commons, became law in 1911. Lloyd George was also responsible for the National Insurance Act (1911), which provided some protection for workers who lost earnings through illness or unemployment.

Workers share a paper to read the news during the General Strike of 1926. The condition of the working class had improved somewhat by the 1920s, but in some sectors—notably coal mining—efforts were being made to roll back improvements in wages and working conditions. The 1926 General Strike in support of the coal miners lasted nine days.

THE WORLD WARS

As Lord Earl Grey, the British Foreign Secretary, watched the streetlights being lit from his office window one evening just before the outbreak of war in August 1914, he is famously reported to have remarked to a friend, "The lamps are going out all over Europe; we shall not see them lit again in our lifetime." At the time such thinking went against the grain; at the outset of the "Great War," many in England firmly expected their soldiers to be home before Christmas. But over the next thirty years many came to believe that the moment at which the First World War broke out had heralded nothing less than the collapse of civilization as it had long been known. At the outset of the Second World War in 1940, George Orwell adopted this vein of apocalyptic pessimism in his long essay "Inside the Whale":

The war of 1914–1918 was only a heightened moment in an almost continuous crisis. At this date it hardly needs a war to bring home to us the disintegration of our society and the increasingly helplessness of all decent people. ... While I have been writing this book another European war has broken out. It will either last several years and tear western civilization to pieces, or it will end inconclusively and prepare the way for yet another war that will do the job once and for all.

Western civilization has proved to be rather more resilient than Orwell had feared, but his view of the period beginning in 1914 as "an almost continuous crisis" is now widely shared by historians; increasingly the two world wars of the twentieth century are being seen as part of a continuum. From more than one angle this makes sense. In both wars, Britain and her Empire/Commonwealth allies, joined belatedly by the United States, were fighting against a militaristic and expansionist Germany. In both wars much of the rest of the world was drawn in to the conflict, though there was no parallel in World War I to the crucial importance of the Pacific theater and the struggle between the Allies and Japan in World War II.

The two wars are also linked through a chain of causation. Though all authorities agree that both wars had multiple causes, it is also universally agreed that one vitally important cause of the Second World War was the decision by the allies after World War I to demand reparations—a decision that had the effect in the short term of crippling Germany economically—and that had the even more pernicious effect over the longer term of so embittering the German people as to make a majority highly receptive to Hitler's appeals to nationalism, expansionism, anti-Semitism, and hate. The British economist John Maynard Keynes had been among those prescient enough to foresee the problem early on. In his chapter on "Europe after the Treaty" in *The Economic Consequences of the Peace* (1919), he summarized the matter with blunt eloquence:

This chapter must be one of pessimism. The treaty includes no provisions for the economic rehabilitation of Europe—nothing to make the defeated ... into good neighbours, nothing to

Wyndham Lewis, *Workshop*, c. 1915. The Canadian-born writer and artist Wyndham Lewis (1882–1957) lived largely in England from 1908 onwards. In the period 1912–15 he was a leader among those painters variously described as Futurist, Cubist, and "Vorticist"—the last of these a term that Lewis himself coined. (See the Contexts section on "Modernism" in this volume for more on this topic.) Though his writing—like that of Pound and others in their circle—is tainted by anti-Semitism, misogyny, and, in Lewis's case, venomous portrayals of homosexuals, Lewis is unquestionably a figure central to British Modernism. *Workshop* is one of the works that extend furthest his vision of harsh lines and fragmented shapes conveying a sense of the modern city, and of modernity itself.

World War I recruiting poster used in Ireland, c. 1915.

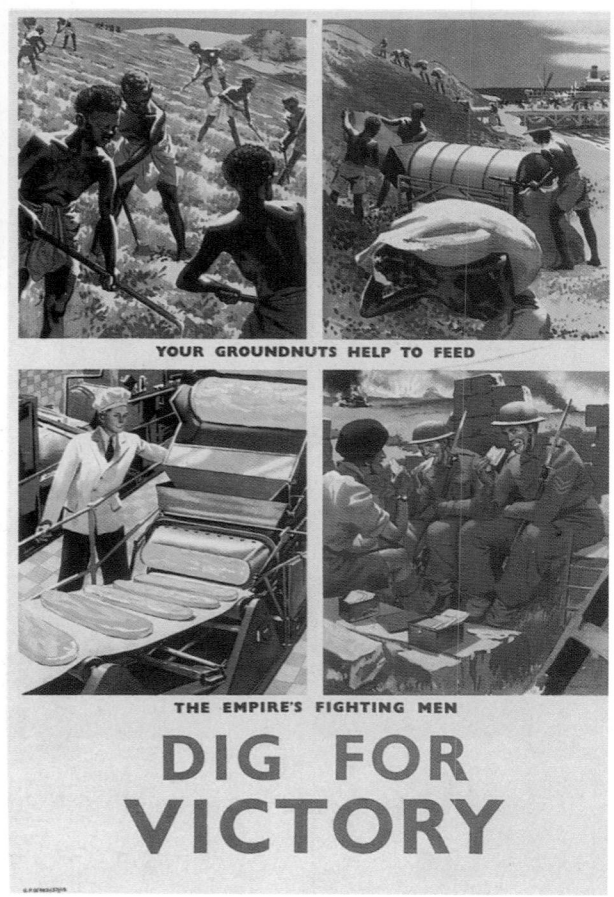

"Dig for Victory" poster,
distributed in Britain's West African colonies, 1940.

A bombed street in London, 1940. The photographer is unknown.

Sirkka-Liisa Konttinen, *Kendal Street, 1969*. A member of the Amber collective, between 1969 and 1983 Finnish-born Konttinen documented the life and eventual demolition of Byker, a terraced community in Newcastle upon Tyne in northern England. In 2003 she and Amber returned to document the Byker Wall Estate that replaced it.

Bill Brandt, *The Lambeth Walk*, 1936. This photo, originally published in the illustrated weekly magazine *Picture Post*, was taken in the Bethnal Green area of London. The girl performs a dance popular at the time.

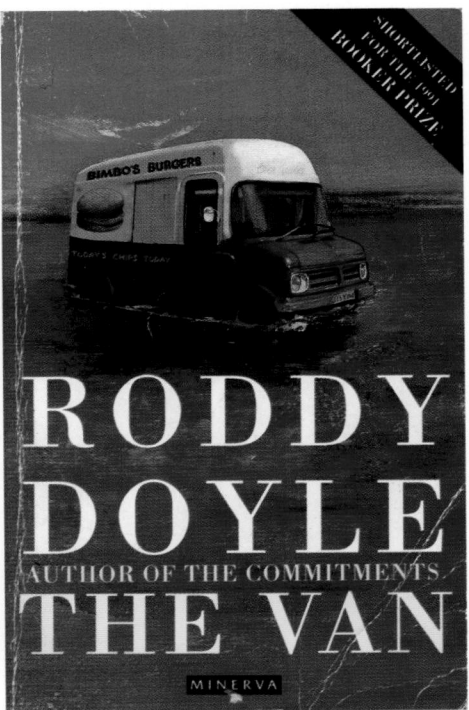

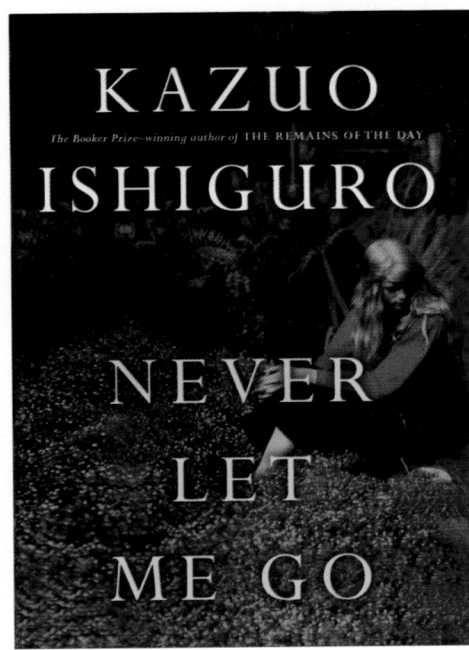

A sampling of book covers: Graham Greene's *Journey Without Maps* (1936; Pan paperback edition, 1948), Roddy Doyle's *The Van* (1991; Minerva paperback edition, 1992), and Kazuo Ishiguro's *Never Let Me Go* (2005). The image on the Ishiguro cover is "Christina," from a famous 1912–13 series of photographs by Lieutenant-Colonel Mervyn O'Gorman of his daughters, whom he photographed both in autochrome color and in black and white, sometimes on a beach near their Dorset home, sometimes (as here) in a garden setting.

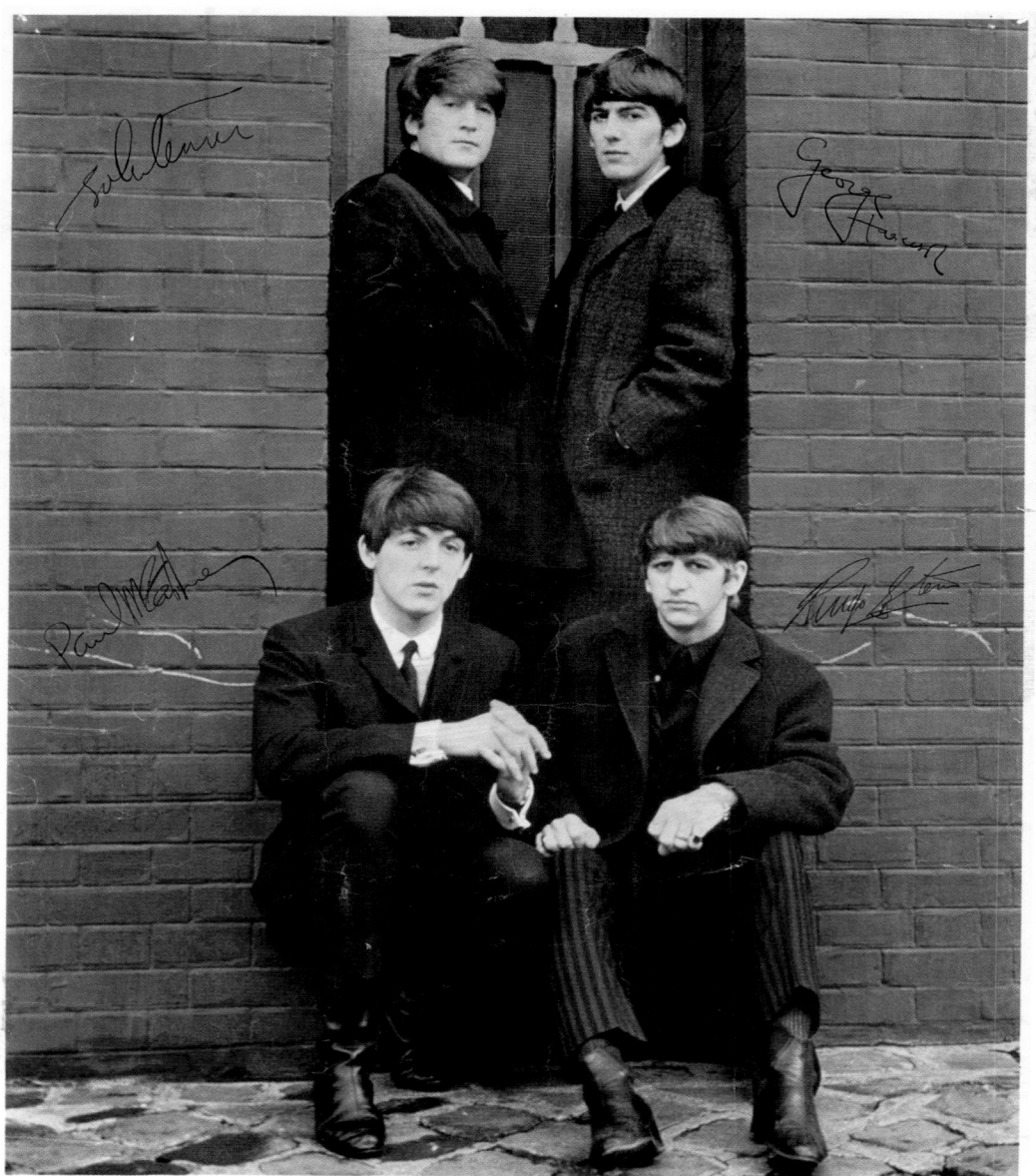

THE **BEATLES**.. LONDON PALLADIUM
ROYAL COMMAND PERFORMANCE. 1963

ORIGINAL MADE IN GREAT BRITAIN.   Litho by Louis F. Dow Co., U.S.A.   © 1964 NEMS ENTERPRISES LTD.

Poster, The Beatles London Palladium Royal Command Performance, 1963. The Royal Variety Performance (also known as the Royal Command Performance) is a gala variety show held every year, the proceeds of which go to charity. When The Beatles performed at the show on 4 November 1963, the audience included the Queen Mother, Princess Margaret, and Lord Snowdon, but not the Queen. As the group was about to play their hit song "Twist and Shout," John Lennon made a request: "Will the people in the cheaper seats clap their hands? And the rest of you, if you'll just rattle your jewelry."

David Hockney, *My Mother, Bolton Abbey, Yorkshire*, 1982. Painter and photographer David Hockney (b. 1937) has long maintained his reputation as one of Britain's leading visual artists. Hockney initially created controversy with his open homosexuality, and in recent years he has incited debate with his views on art history, arguing strenuously that the old Masters employed camera-like techniques in order to achieve realistic effects. A native of Bradford, Hockney has lived largely in California since the 1970s.

Peel Square, Bradford, c. 1995. From the 1950s onwards many immigrants from Asia have settled in Bradford.

Notting Hill Carnival, Notting Hill, London, 1979. The Carnival was started in 1964 to celebrate Caribbean culture within Britain.

stabilise the new states of Europe; ... Nor does it promote in any way a compact of economic solidarity amongst the Allies themselves ... It is an extraordinary fact that the fundamental economic problem of a Europe starving and disintegrating before their eyes, was the one question in which it was impossible to arouse the interest of the Four [powers that imposed the peace treaty].

Hitler's eventual rise to power, then, was partly fueled by the hardships imposed on the Germans by the Allies at the conclusion of World War I.

The Western Front in World War I, 1915.

Londoners sleeping in the Elephant and Castle underground station during the bombing raids of 1940. These raids, popularly referred to as "the Blitz," were intended by the Nazis to "soften up" the English in preparation for a German invasion. Though much of London (and of other cities) was destroyed, the efforts of the British Air Force against superior numbers in what came to be known as the "Battle of Britain" were highly successful, and Hitler eventually decided against attempting an invasion of the British Isles; only the two Channel Islands fell to the Nazi forces. The Battle of Britain during the Blitz subsequently became a defining event in the British national consciousness.

If there are similarities and connections between the two world wars, there are also important differences. There are differences in the way the wars were fought, to start with—the trench warfare, stagnation and machine gun carnage of World War I contrasts with the tanks, submarines, airplanes, and bombs of World War II. There is usually also agreed to be a substantial difference in the moral context in which the two wars were fought. Many have suggested that ethically there was little to choose between the two sides in World War I—that the essential nature of the conflict was simply a power struggle between Britain and Germany as co-aggressors. And it has often (and rightly) been suggested that the tangle of old world alliances that existed prior to the First World War did much to facilitate the sort of stumbling into war that occurred in the wake of the assassination of Archduke Franz Ferdinand of Austria on 28 June 1914. In fact there probably was to some degree a legitimate moral case to be made on the side of Britain at the outset of World War I—much as the jingoism of the time on all sides may now strike us as repulsive. There is no question, though, that the moral imperative that lay behind the Allies' decision to go to war with Germany in 1939 was far stronger than it was at any time during World War I. Nazi atrocities against the Jews had in 1939 not yet reached their full extent, but already Hitler had shown that he was a dictator willing to persecute minorities ruthlessly and to invade neighboring countries on the flimsiest of pretexts.

This image of the 1940 Battle of Britain was taken from the cockpit of a German fighter plane. It shows a British Hurricane fighter with its left wing torn off; the wing is visible in the top right of the photo, and the pilot, parachuting to safety, is seen in the top left.

World War II, then, was driven far more persuasively than was the first by a moral imperative, and there was thus much less of a disconnect than there had been in World War I between idealistic calls for sacrifice and the reality as it was sensed by the ordinary soldier; few looked at Nazi Germany in the autumn of 1939 with the detached tone that the poet W.H. Auden famously adopted in "September 1, 1939" in seeking to explain the phenomenon of Hitler, the "psychopathic god": "Those to whom evil is done / Do evil in return." To most it seemed clear that both in the case of Hitler as an individual and in the case of the people of Nazi Germany as a whole, the evil that was being done was far disproportionate to whatever evil had been committed against them. (Even today, many who admire Auden's poem as an affirmation of the humane in the face of the more basely human and in the face of war as a general proposition find the feelings the poem expresses odd or inappropriate in the moral context of World War II.)

A crucial difference between the experience of World War I and II was that in World War II the horrors of war had less shock value. Paul Fussell, whose *The Great War and Modern Memory* is a landmark study of the connections between wartime experience and literature, was a soldier himself in World War II; by the time of World War II, as he put it, "we didn't need to be told by people like Remarqué [author of *All Quiet on the Western Front*] and Siegfried Sassoon how nasty war was. We knew that already, and we just had to pursue it in a sort of controlled despair. It didn't have the ironic shock value of the Great War." It should perhaps not surprise us, then, that the body of serious literature that arose *directly* from the experience of World War II turned out to be slighter than the body of such literature that emerged during and after World War I. Certainly works such as Robert Graves's *Goodbye to All That*, Siegfried Sassoon's *Memoirs of an Infantry Officer*, David Jones's *In Parenthesis*, and the poetry of Wilfred Owen, Isaac Rosenberg and others all seem to have secured a place in the canon of British literature, whereas few if any works emerging directly out of the combat experience of World War II have staked such a claim. Indeed, Auden's "September 1, 1939" and Virginia Woolf's *Between the Acts* are among the few works still widely read from that time on themes that relate to the experience of the war even tangentially.

Two aspects of the 1939–45 conflict have come to be seen as defining elements of twentieth-century experience. The first of these was the planned extermination of an entire people—the event that resulted in the murder of approximately six million Jews (as well as significant numbers of other groups deemed "undesirables" by the Nazis, notably homosexuals and Roma), and that has come to be known as "The Holocaust." The second is the use of the atomic bomb against Japan by the United States in 1945—and the consequent dawning among the world's population of an awareness that humans now had the capacity to destroy the entire human race. From those most horrific aspects of World War II has emerged a literature that will surely be lasting (including the works of Primo Levi, the diaries of Anne Frank, John Hersey's *Hiroshima*)—but few if any of its most important works are by British writers.

Brighton Rock (1938), Graham Greene's "entertainment" about the lives of young British gangsters, was first issued in a Penguin paperback in 1943. The price of 2 shillings is equivalent to a little over £3 in 2006 UK currency.

THIS IS A WARTIME BOOK

THIS POCKET BOOK INCLUDES EVERY WORD CONTAINED IN THE ORIGINAL, HIGHER-PRICED EDITION. IT IS PRINTED FROM BRAND-NEW PLATES MADE FROM COMPLETELY RESET, LARGE, CLEAR, EASY-TO-READ TYPE, AND IS PRODUCED IN FULL COMPLIANCE WITH THE GOVERNMENT'S REGULATIONS FOR CONSERVING PAPER AND OTHER ESSENTIAL MATERIALS.

F-1

Printed in Canada

Notice from copyright page of a 1945 printing of the paperback edition of Mazo de la Roche's *Jalna*, one volume of the family saga that has remained extraordinarily popular from its publication in 1927.

As in World War I, however, there was a rich body of literary work produced in Britain during World War II that was not directly *about* the war. Works of this sort in the years 1914–18 includes T.S. Eliot's *Prufrock and Other Observations* (1917) and James Joyce's *Portrait of an Artist as a Young Man* (1916).[1] In the years 1939–45, the list of such works is both long and remarkably diverse, and include the exuberant verse of Dylan Thomas's *The Map of Love* (1939); Eliot's *Four Quartets* (which he regarded as his finest work); many of Auden's finest lyrics, including "Lay Your Sleeping Head, My Love," "Musee des Beaux Arts," and "Song (As I Walked Out One Evening)" (all first published in 1940); the bubbling hilarity of Noel Coward's play about the afterlife, *Blithe Spirit* (1942); the memorably self-deprecating and socially observant light comedy of Monica Dickens's memoir *One Pair of Hands* (1939); now-classic memoirs by Vera Brittain (*Testament of Friendship*, 1940) and Flora Thompson (*Lark Rise to Candleford*, 1940); Joyce Cary's novel of the memorable artist and outsider Gulley Jimson, *The Horse's Mouth* (1944); Graham Greene's tragic novel of a disillusioned

---

[1] See below under "Modernism" for a discussion of these authors.

"whisky priest" in revolutionary Mexico, *The Power and the Glory* (1940); and two very different but equally devastating fictional treatments of the horrors of totalitarian communism, Arthur Koestler's grim novel of the suffering endured by a "deviationist," *Darkness at Noon* (1940), and Orwell's fable of a collectivist society that comes to be based on the principle that "all animals are equal, but some are more equal than others," *Animal Farm* (1945). In writing the following comments in 1940 about the literature of World War I, Orwell clearly also had World War II in mind:

> In 1917 there was nothing a thinking and sensitive person could do, except remain human, if possible. … By simply staying aloof and keeping in touch with pre-war emotions, Eliot [in publishing *Prufrock* in 1917] was carrying on the human heritage.… So different from bayonet drill! After the bombs and the food queues and the recruiting posters, a human voice! What a relief!

MARX, EINSTEIN, FREUD, AND MODERNISM

Several towering figures in the intellectual and cultural life of the twentieth century played a key part in shaping the world view according to which human life was subject to forces over which, individually, humans could have little control, and of which they would often be entirely unaware. The first of these figures—Karl Marx—died 17 years before the end of the nineteenth century. But his vision of economic forces and class struggles saturated with historical inevitability continued to shape political and social attitudes (as well as a good many literary ones) throughout the twentieth century. An intellectual underpinning derived from Marx is, to a large extent, what differentiates the attitudes of social realist writers such as Shaw, Wells, and George Gissing from those of predecessors such as Charles Dickens and Elizabeth Gaskell. Much as Dickens and Gaskell had deplored the conditions of inequality that beset Victorian Britain, they believed that the actions and the goodwill of individual human beings could ameliorate social problems. The approach of 1890s and early twentieth-century socially progressive writers, in contrast, derived largely from the Marxist view that individuals are typically caught in a web of large social and economic forces over which they have no control; that class oppression is a systemic matter; and that mass struggle and political action (rather than appeals to the higher natures of the ruling classes) are the appropriate means of bringing about a better world. Thus for Shaw, for example, the "fundamental condition of the existence" of prostitution was that "a large class of women are more highly paid and better treated as prostitutes than they would be as respectable women." The activist writer and publisher Nancy Cunard was equally alert to the interactions of class, gender, money—and race. Author of some of a number of important essays on colonialism (and publisher of such key modernist works as Samuel Beckett's *Whoroscope* and Pound's *Cantos*), Cunard spoke of the British Empire in unvarnished terms of class and race as few had before: when writing in *Negro* of the system of British rule in Jamaica, for example, she understood it clearly as having been purposefully structured as "white at the top, mulatto in the centre and back at the bottom of the economic and social scale" so as to rule by dividing "the peoples of African and semi-African descent."[1]

If the socially progressive literature of the early twentieth century had intellectual underpinnings derived largely from Marx, the intellectual underpinnings of twentieth-century modernist literature are intimately connected with the ideas of physicist Albert Einstein, of philosophers of language such as Bertrand Russell, and of the psychoanalyst Sigmund Freud. Einstein's paper, "The Electrodynamics of Moving Bodies" (1905), later to become known as his Special Theory of Relativity, posited that both time and motion are not absolute but rather relative to the observer. In the same year he completed his thesis on "A New Determination of Molecular Dimension," a major step forward in the development of quantum theory in which he postulated (among other things) that light was both waves and tiny particles of light quanta, or photons. Much as they may have been imperfectly under-

---

[1] Cunard was greatly assisted in these endeavors by George Padmore (1902–59), a Trinidadian-born writer and activist who later lived in the United States and in Britain and who played an important role in various progressive causes in the 1930s. A strong pan-Africanist, Padmore eventually became personal advisor to Kwame Nkrumah, Ghana's first President.

stood, the broad outlines of Einstein's theories became widely disseminated in subsequent years, and clearly contributed to a growing sense of a world that was being discovered to be in a far less stable form that it had been thought.

New language-based trends in analytic philosophy were also undermining certainties. The ideas developed by Gottleib Frege, Bertrand Russell, and Ludwig Wittgenstein in the late nineteenth and early twentieth century had the effect of destabilizing what had been thought of as largely fixed relationships between words and meanings. The focus of these philosophers was on analysing the content of what we mean when we make statements, whether they be statements referring to objects in the "real" world or statements involving claims of a more abstract sort. They endeavored to design symbolic systems that could convey meaning more reliably than words, for their work suggested that relationships between a word and a presumed referent were exceedingly complex and inherently unstable; Wittgenstein's work, in particular, suggested that it was in the nature of language for words to float largely free of fixed referents in any world of "objective truth." Indeed, Wittgenstein suggested in his groundbreaking 1921 work *Tractatus Logico-Philosophicus* that "Language disguises thought. So much so, that from the outward form of the clothing it is impossible to infer the form of the thought beneath it, because the outward form of the clothing is not designed to reveal the form of the body, but for entirely different purposes."

The perceived unreliability and instability of language and of meaning affected the realm of ethics as much as it did those of metaphysics and epistemology, and from about 1910 onward, moral relativism was a subject of lively debate. (G.E. Moore's *Ethics*, an influential attempt to hold such relativism at bay, was published in 1912; T.S. Eliot read a paper on "The Relativity of the Moral Judgement" in the Cambridge rooms of his friend Bertrand Russell in 1915.) Russell became famous as a result of his pacifism (for which he was jailed in 1918), his efforts to undermine the authority of Christianity over Western society, and his challenge to societal constrictions on sexual behavior. But the changes that he helped to bring about to the foundations of analytic philosophy may have been even more

revolutionary—and more influential in the literary realm—than his shocking views on social issues.

Just as important as the work of Marx, Einstein, or the philosophers of language to the intellectual shape of the twentieth century was that of several explorers of the human psyche. Of these, pride of place is traditionally accorded to Sigmund Freud, an Austrian psychiatrist who advanced revolutionary notions of the importance and complexity of sexuality in the human psyche, and of the importance of the unconscious in human thought and behavior. Both notions had an enormous effect on twentieth-century intellectual life in general and on imaginative literature in particular, as writers sought ways to represent sexuality as a much more central element of human experience than had been the habit of the Victorians, and sought ways in which to represent the richness of the human unconscious.[1]

Another key pioneer in the study of the human mind was the American William James (brother of novelist Henry James). Among James's most important contributions was his conceptualization of the fluidity of consciousness. James entitled a chapter in his *Principles of Psychology* (1892) "The Stream of Consciousness," beginning by observing that "within each personal consciousness states are always changing" and that "each personal consciousness is sensibly continuous." The connections between the ideas of James and twentieth-century literary developments are not difficult to discern. Most obviously, the "stream of consciousness" technique of prose fiction that features so prominently in core Modernist texts such as Dorothy Richardson's *Pilgrimage* (1915–67), Virginia Woolf's *Mrs. Dalloway* (1925), and James Joyce's *Ulysses* (1922) represents a new form of realism that is psychological rather than

---

[1] Though Freud's important work began in the 1890s, he began to become well-known in the English-speaking world only after 1910, with the publication of a series of lectures he had given at Clark University in the United States on *The Origin and Development of Psychoanalysis*. Of his most important works, *The Interpretation of Dreams* (1900) was translated in 1913, *The Psychopathology of Everyday Life* (1901) in 1914; soon after his work came to the attention of the Bloomsbury Group in England, and both Leonard Woolf and Lytton Strachey wrote reviews of or commentaries on Freud's work. (In the 1920s the Woolfs' Hogarth Press became for a time the leading publisher of English translations of Freud's work.)

social in character. These writers aim at an increased awareness of the ways in which the mind associates freely, in which "irrelevant" thoughts may connect with repressed impulses or emotions that are central to the psyche, and in which unpredictable but meaningful details are constantly jostling together with the quotidian.

A similar apparent disconnectedness is also an obvious feature of Modernist poetry—most obviously in the disjunctions that characterize many of the poems of Ezra Pound and T.S. Eliot. To be sure, many have argued persuasively that a unity both of thought and of feeling emerges from the extended allusive density of poems such as *The Waste Land*. But it is abundantly clear that any such unity is very different in character from the unity that emerges, say, from a defining long poem of the Victorian period such as Tennyson's *In Memoriam*, just as whatever unity emerges from Joyce's *Ulysses* is very different in character from that of the classic realism of Victorian novels such as George Eliot's *Middlemarch* or Anthony Trollope's *The Way We Live Now*.

Less frequently discussed is the modernity of Eliot's later poetry—most notably, *The Four Quartets* (1935–43), an extended poetic expression of the search for meaning and truth in a context of instability. Much as the poem is infused with the Anglo-Catholicism to which Eliot had converted in 1927, it is also deeply colored by the sorts of destabilizing awareness that were so central to the habits of thought that came to the fore in the first half of the twentieth century. The poet continually struggles to conceptualize the movements of time, but finds that

> Words strain,
> Crack, and sometimes break, under the burden,
> Under the tension, slip, slide, perish,
> Decay with imprecision, will not stay in place,
> Will not stay still.

Samuel Beckett, one of the first to appreciate that most disconnected of all Joyce's works, *Finnegan's Wake* (1939), became the last great figure of Modernist literature. It was Beckett, above all, who pioneered the expression in action of the psychological insights of Modernism and the despair that so often accompanied them. It is perhaps the case that "action" should here be put in quotation marks, however, for Beckett's plays—perhaps most notably *Waiting For Godot* (1952), *Krapp's Last Tape* (1958), and *Endgame* (1957)—are informed by an unprecedented awareness of the degree to which a *lack* of action may be as expressive as action, just as silences may be as expressive as words. Beckett extended the Modernist project in his prose fiction as well as in his plays—and in French as well as in English through to the 1970s; it is perhaps due more to his influence than that of any of the other great figures of Modernism that ripples from the Modernist tradition have continued to radiate in British literature even into the twenty-first century.

A common tendency is to assume that what is aesthetically revolutionary will substantially overlap with what is politically revolutionary (or at least with what is progressive). In fact there is no necessary connection between the two—and, indeed, a striking feature of twentieth-century Modernism is that many of its key figures were politically conservative or even reactionary.[1] During his lifetime, T.S. Eliot was probably almost as influential for his political, religious, and cultural conservatism as he was for his revolutionary aesthetic. Writer and artist Wyndham Lewis, whose concept of Vorticism was for a time central to the intellectual currents of Modernism, embraced political views that could fairly be characterized as reactionary rather than conservative. Ezra Pound, for his part, who was even more revolutionary than Eliot in his Modernist aesthetic, ended even further to the right politically—notoriously lending his support to the fascist cause, and calling for the extermination of Jews during World War II. Eliot and Pound were also far from progressive in their attitudes on gender and sex; many have suggested that a dark sense of sexuality is a fundamental aspect of Eliot's world view—and almost as many have suggested that a disturbing element of misogyny lurks not far below the surface of much of his writing (his early writing in particular).

---

[1] The roots of this conservatism are in part in various nineteenth-century political and ideological developments—especially a strain of ultra-conservatism in France that developed in the second half of the century and that connects both with Pound and the Symbolists and with twentieth-century fascisms.

Leading modernist women writers, by contrast, more often combined the freedom of modernist forms with progressive, unconventional, or even revolutionary political and social views. The futurist poet Mina Loy, for example, was a strong feminist and decidedly left of center politically; Nancy Cunard was a pioneer of left-of-center class analysis as well as of modernist publishing; and Virginia Woolf, though she rarely shared the unqualified sense of political conviction that came to motivate her husband Leonard (who ran for Parliament as a Labour Party candidate in 1920), was herself not only a powerful voice for feminism but also a Labour Party member and a supporter of a variety of socialist and progressive causes.

It was Woolf who famously assigned a specific point in time to the great change that Modernism represented: "on or about December 1910," she commented in a 1924 essay (excerpted in the "Modernism" Contexts section in this volume), "human character changed." She was, of course, exaggerating for effect; few in her era were more acutely aware of how erratically change may occur, and of the ways in which the characteristics of one era may extend into the next. In that connection it is worth reminding ourselves that, much as the Modernism of Eliot, Joyce, and Woolf has come to take on the character of the defining spirit of British literature in the 1910s and 1920s, its centrality was far from obvious at the time. For every admirer of the Cubist paintings of Picasso and Braque, there were many who reacted with contempt or ridicule. For every gallery-goer who was stirred by the modernist sculptures of Jacob Epstein (such as the young colonial P.K. Page, as recounted in her poem "Ecce Homo"), there were many chuckling over the way in which such sculpture was lampooned in the pages of the satirical magazine *Punch*. And for every dedicated reader of *The Waste Land* or *To the Lighthouse* there were dozens of readers of the ballads of Robert Service, and of the traditionally structured novels of Arnold Bennett and John Galsworthy. Not until 1948 and 1969 respectively were T.S. Eliot and Samuel Beckett awarded the Nobel Prize for literature; the only British writers to receive the award before 1940 were Rudyard Kipling (1907), W.B. Yeats (1923), George Bernard Shaw (1925), and Galsworthy (1932).

Illustration by Ernest H. Shepard from the chapter "The Further Adventures of Toad" in Kenneth Grahame's *The Wind in the Willows* (1908). The early decades of the twentieth century are remembered for the dawn of Modernism, but they were also something of a golden age for children's literature; in addition to Grahame's work, Sir J.M. Barrie's *Peter Pan* (1906), Lucy Maud Montgomery's *Anne of Green Gables* (1908), and A.A. Milne's *Winnie the Pooh* (1926) and *The House at Pooh Corner* (1928) all remain popular classics.

THE PLACE OF WOMEN

As well as being a central figure of Modernism in the British literary tradition, Woolf is central to what is arguably the most important historical development of the twentieth century, the attempt to free women from the dense network of social, economic, and legal restrictions that had always ensured male dominance and control. If *To the Lighthouse* (1927) and *Mrs. Dalloway* (1925), with their psychological realism, are key documents of Modernism, *A Room of One's Own* (1929) is a key document of the struggle by women in the twentieth century for full equality. Woolf's call for change, and also her evocation of personal experience in a male-dominated social and literary milieu, continue to resonate with readers in the present century.

Illustration accompanying the article "Presentation Day at London University," by "A Lady Graduate" in *The Girl's Own Paper*, July 1898. The University of London had begun to admit women as full degree students at the undergraduate level in 1878, but it was not until the 1920s that Oxford and Cambridge followed suit, even at the undergraduate level.

As the twentieth century opened women were still second-class citizens in almost every respect—unable to vote, subject to a variety of employment limitations, restricted for the most part from higher education, and restricted too in myriad intangible ways by social nuance and convention. Oppression in the workplace in the context of the industrial revolution has long been widely acknowledged; at least as pervasive in the late nineteenth and early twentieth centuries was the exploitation of retail workers, as the Report of the Royal Commission on Labour detailed:

> The maximum salary in addition to board and lodging ever paid to women in the shop working 70 3/4 hours was stated at 35 to 40 shillings [equivalent

to roughly £200 in 2006]; in the other shops 30 shillings was stated as the maximum salary ever given. The girls declared that they had nothing to complain of, except the long hours of work and the short time allowed for meals, which had seriously affected their health. No one closed earlier than 11:00 p.m. on Saturdays, 9:30 on Fridays, and 9:00 on Mondays, Tuesdays, and Wednesdays, beginning in each case at 8:30 a.m.

For decades, those in the suffrage movement and other women's groups struggled to bring change. In 1903, Emmeline Pankhurst, together with others frustrated with the pace of change and with the "lady-like" tone of the protests by other women's groups, formed The Women's Social and Political Union, taking as their motto "Deeds Not Words." As Pankhurst recalled in 1914,

> From the very first, in those early London days, when … we were few in numbers and very poor in purse, we made the public aware of the woman suffrage movement as it had never been before. We adopted Salvation Army methods and went out into the highways and byways after converts.

Real change finally began to take effect just before the end of the war in 1918, with the Representation of the People Act granting the vote to all men over the age of 21 and to women over the age of 30 who also met one or more of several restrictive criteria regarding marital status and property.[1] (Not until 1928 were all such restrictions lifted and all women over 21 granted the franchise.) The London *Times* provided a (doubtless oversimplified) summary of the effect of the war on the suffrage movement in an article on the occasion of the 1930 commemoration by Prime Minister Stanley Baldwin of a statue of Pankhurst:

> The World War came. In the twinkling of an eye …
> the militant suffragettes laid aside their banners.

---

[1] Two "Contexts" sections elsewhere in this volume ("War and Revolution" and "Gender and Sexual Orientation") document the events of World War I and the ways in which they hastened the move towards equality.

They put on their overalls and went into the factory and into the field; they were nursing, they made munitions, and they endured sacrifices with the men, and the effective opposition to the movement melted in the furnace of the War.

The success of the suffrage movement and the change in the role women played in the workplace were the most dramatic gender-related changes during this period, but there were many other important developments; as a "Contexts" section elsewhere in this volume discusses, the era was also characterized by changing notions regarding gender and education, contraception and reproductive technology, and the nature of masculinity.

The arrest of Emmeline Pankhurst during a suffragette demonstration near Buckingham Palace, 1914.

Sylvia Pankhurst (daughter of suffragette leader Emmeline Pankhurst) painting the slogan "Votes for Women" on the front of the Women's Social Defence League offices in London, 1912.

Women's contingent to the 1930 "Hunger March," a demonstration in London's Hyde Park.

AVANT-GARDE AND MASS CULTURE

The concept of the avant-garde, of a tiny minority far in advance of the popular taste in culture (or of the majority view politically) came into its own in the twentieth century. No doubt it may have resonated with particular force simply because of the degree to which cultural activity was being extended to "the masses"; with primary education having been made compulsory in Britain through the Education Act of 1870, the twentieth century was the first in which the vast majority of British people were fully literate. The expansion of libraries had helped to spread the habit of reading through the nineteenth century, and with the publishing industry's shift in the 1890s away from "triple deckers" intended for purchase by libraries and toward one-volume novels of modest length aimed at individual buyers, the habit of book-buying began to spread at a comparable rate. In the early years of the century, publishers introduced series of relatively affordable hardcover editions of literary classics, aimed at a broad popular market (chief among them the Everyman's Library series from Dent and the World's Classics series from Oxford University Press).

The British film industry was competitive with that of the United States in the 1920s and early 1930s. In this 1920s photograph a scene from the (now lost) film *The Thrill* is being shot on a beach near Brighton.

THE PUBLISHERS OF *EVERYMAN'S LIBRARY* WILL BE PLEASED TO SEND FREELY TO ALL APPLICANTS A LIST OF THE PUBLISHED AND PROJECTED VOLUMES TO BE COMPRISED UNDER THE FOLLOWING THIRTEEN HEADINGS:

TRAVEL ❧ SCIENCE ❧ FICTION
THEOLOGY & PHILOSOPHY
HISTORY ❧ CLASSICAL
FOR YOUNG PEOPLE
ESSAYS ❧ ORATORY
POETRY & DRAMA
BIOGRAPHY
REFERENCE
ROMANCE

IN FOUR STYLES OF BINDING: CLOTH, FLAT BACK, COLOURED TOP; LEATHER, ROUND CORNERS, GILT TOP; LIBRARY BINDING IN CLOTH, & QUARTER PIGSKIN

LONDON: J. M. DENT & SONS, LTD.
NEW YORK: E. P. DUTTON & CO.

Preliminary advertising page from *Captain Cook's Voyages of Discovery*, one of the Everyman's Library volumes published in 1906, the year the series was founded. Eventually its list grew to include over 1,000 titles.

An even more revolutionary step came in 1936, with the introduction of Penguin Books' series of affordable paperback editions. "The Penguin books are splendid value for sixpence," wrote George Orwell in reviewing Penguin's third batch of ten titles, "so splendid that if the other publishers had any sense they could combine against them and suppress them. [If instead] the other publishers follow suit, the result may be a flood of cheap reprints which will cripple the lending libraries … and check the output of new novels." Within a few years the paperback novel had indeed become ubiquitous in British society, but with none of the disastrous effects Orwell had feared; the size of the market for books had been expanded sufficiently by the arrival of the paperback to more than compensate authors and publishers for the lower revenue per copy sold.

Along with the spread of a mass literary culture—and the spread as well of the cinema and of radio—came huge social and cultural changes. If Modernism was a cultural movement concentrated in a small elite, modernity swept through every corner of society in the 1920s and 1930s. The social and cultural attitudes of the late Victorian age may have persisted through to the end of the Edwardian era, but within 10

World War I and the years that followed brought huge changes in women's fashion, with shorter skirts and dresses and more freedom of movement. This photograph, from the 1920s, shows two London models.

years "Victorian" had become a synonym for "stuffy and old fashioned." The book that set the tone more than any other was Lytton Strachey's *Eminent Victorians* (1918), a series of biographical essays on four leading members of Victorian society (Henry Edward Cardinal Manning, Florence Nightingale, Matthew Arnold, and General Charges George Gordon). Strachey's work is often characterized as "satirical," but "irreverent" is perhaps a better adjective. He writes in a breezy, brilliant, style, but he is interested in the depths of human emotion as well as the surfaces. He pokes fun at his subjects, to be sure, but he is more interested in exploring the workings of what he sees as pretension, hypocrisy, ambition, and self-deception than he is in ridiculing them. Here is how Strachey begins his essay on Florence Nightingale:

> Everyone knows the popular conception of Florence Nightingale. The saintly, self-sacrificing woman, the delicate maiden of high degree who threw aside the pleasures of a life of ease to succour the afflicted, the Lady with the Lamp, gliding through the horrors of the hospital at Scutari, and consecrating with the radiance of her goodness the dying soldier's couch—the vision is familiar to all. But the truth was different. The Miss Nightingale of fact was not as facile fancy painted her. She worked in another fashion, and towards another end; she moved under the stress of an impetus which finds no place in the popular imagination. A Demon possessed her. Now demons, whatever else they may be, are full of interest. And so it happens that in the real Miss Nightingale there was more that was interesting than in the legendary one; there was also less that was agreeable.

The deft touch of Strachey's satire became simplified and coarsened in the ridicule popularly directed at Victorian styles—and, in particular, at Victorian attitudes towards sexuality—as an emerging mass society sought to define itself against the backdrop of supposed Victorian narrowness and prudery. The reaction may have been overdone, and certainly the characterization of the Victorians was simplistic, but there could be no doubt that the short skirts, jazz music, and sexual attitudes of the 1920s and 1930s were as far removed from those of only fifteen or twenty years before as those of 1905 or 1910 had been from the attitudes and styles of a full century earlier. Virginia Woolf's recollections of a Bloomsbury scene from the 1920s in which Woolf, her sister Vanessa Bell, and her husband Clive Bell are together in the drawing room at 46 Gordon Square give something of the flavor of the time:

> Suddenly the door opened and the long and sinister figure of Mr. Lytton Strachey stood on the threshold. He pointed a finger at a stain on Vanessa's white dress.
>   "Semen?" he said.

Can one really say it? I thought and we burst out laughing. With that one word all barriers of reticence and reserve went down. ... So there was now nothing that one could not say, nothing that one could not do, at 46 Gordon Square.

A larger excerpt from Woolf's recollections of this and related incidents appears in the "Contexts" section "Gender and Sexuality" elsewhere in this volume. As that section also makes clear, few places in Britain in the 1920s and 1930s had left Victorian conventions of respectability so firmly behind as had 46 Gordon Square; few others had travelled so far in the same direction, or so fast, as had the "bohemians" of the Bloomsbury Group.

Indeed, the literary portrayal even of heterosexual love (let alone of homosexuality) remained largely off limits through to the 1960s. A litmus test was D.H. Lawrence's *Lady Chatterley's Lover*, which was published in 1928, but with certain passages, which were considered objectionable on account of their sexual content, removed. Not until 1960, after a high profile court case, was the unexpurgated text of the novel (by today's standards still far from explicit in its portrayal of sexuality) finally published. Despite such strictures, however, change was occurring throughout society, and "Victorian" attitudes seemed to many to be part of the distant past.

Two women, outside a London bookshop, holding copies of the newly-published paperback edition of *Lady Chatterley's Lover* (1960).

A commuter chooses *Lady Chatterley's Lover* over *The Times*, London, 1960.

SEXUAL ORIENTATION

The number of leading writers in the first half of the twentieth century who acknowledged a same-sex sexual orientation, at least among their circle of friends, was probably greater than it had been in any previous era of British history—certainly greater than at any time since the early years of the seventeenth century. The list of writers and intellectuals who are now known to have been gay, lesbian, or bisexual includes not only W.H. Auden and Christopher Isherwood, but also A.E. Housman, Nancy Cunard, E.M. Forster, Radclyffe Hall, John Maynard Keynes, Lytton Strachey, Sylvia Townsend-Warner, and a number of others.

It should be emphasized here that sexual identities are far from being stable, trans-historical categories. As a "Contexts" section elsewhere in this volume details, notions of and attitudes towards same-sex orientation were in flux throughout the late nineteenth and early twentieth centuries. Until well into the second half of the twentieth century, however (interestingly, at about the time that the word gay began to be used to identify those with a same-sex sexual orientation), there was little or no tolerance of same-sex sexuality in most sectors of society. As Auden and his friend and sometime literary collaborator Isherwood tacitly recognized when they moved to the United States, Britain in the 1920s and 1930s was even less ready than was America to openly acknowledge the legitimacy of same-sex relationships. Famously, the novelist and playwright Oscar Wilde had been tried and imprisoned in 1895 for "acts of gross indecency," and homosexuality continued to be widely regarded (in a somewhat contradictory fashion) both as a sin and as a disease throughout the first half of the century. E.M. Forster's novel on the theme of homosexual love, *Maurice*, which was not published until after his death in 1971, but which he had completed in 1914, gives a strong sense of the reality. When Maurice, having realized that "he loved men and had always loved them," confesses to his doctor that he is "an unspeakable of the Oscar Wilde sort," he is met with disgust and denial:

> "Rubbish, rubbish!...Now listen to me, Maurice, never let that evil hallucination, that temptation from the devil, occur to you again."
>
> The voice impressed him; was not science speaking?
>
> "Who put that lie into your head? You whom I see and know to be a decent fellow! We'll never mention it again. No—I'll not discuss. I'll not discuss. The worst thing I could do for you is to discuss it."

Maurice eventually does accept his sexual identity, but not before a further consultation, this one with a Mr. Lasker-Jones, who claims a fifty-per cent rate of "cure" by means of hypnotism for what he terms "congenital homosexuality."

If male homosexuality remained "unspeakable" through much of this period, female homosexuality remained for many unimaginable. In 1921 the British Parliament debated adding "acts of gross indecency between women" to the list of acts prohibited in the criminal statutes, but elected not to do so for fear of advertising homosexuality to "innocent" women. A few years later Hall's novel *The Well of Loneliness* was the occasion for the greatest literary storm of the era, over its alleged "obscenity." The novel recounts the story of a young woman named Stephen (whose parents had hoped for and expected a boy, and gone forward with the planned name regardless when the baby turned out to be a girl), and the romantic relationships she forms

with other women. That the book could have been deemed obscene is astonishing to many readers today. In many ways the book is striking for the sense of normalcy it evokes as to the quotidian aspects of love:

> And now for the first time the old house was home. Mary went quickly from room to room humming a little tune as she did so, feeling that she saw with a new understanding the intimate objects that filled those rooms—were they not Stephen's? Every now and again she must pause to touch them because they were Stephen's.

Even when the novel's prose becomes effusive over the physical and spiritual aspects of the union, the most specific suggestions of the expression of sexual love between two women are passages such as the following: "Stephen bent down and kissed Mary's hands very humbly, for now she could find no words any more ... and that night they were not divided."

Such effusive attestations of the rapturous purity of unions at once physical and spiritual as one finds in

Radclyffe Hall, c. 1920.

Maurice and *The Well of Loneliness* may seem unexceptionable today, and even at the time many people were supportive; *The Well of Loneliness* was published to a generally favorable reception in the press. In the view of *The Sunday Times*, Hall's novel was written "with distinction, with a lively sense of characterization, and with a feeling for the background of her subject which makes her work delightful reading. And, first and last, she has courage and honesty." *The Daily Herald* asserted that there was "nothing pornographic" in the book:

> The evil minded will seek in vain in these pages for any stimulant to sexual excitement. The lustful [figures] of popular fiction may continue their sadistic course unchecked in those pornographic novels which are sold by the million, but Miss Radclyffe Hall has entirely ignored these crude and violent figures of sexual melodrama. She has given to English literature a profound and moving study of a profound and moving problem.

The Daily Express was the lone dissenter; a 19 August 1928 article headed "A Book That Must Be Suppressed" accused the novel of "devastating young souls" with its story of "sexual inversion and perversion." It seems probable that the *Express* represented popular feeling at the time more accurately than did the *Sunday Times* or the *Daily Herald*; soon after the *Express* article appeared, the Home Office advised the publishers to discontinue publication, and the police then charged the publishers under the 1857 Obscene Publications Act. Despite the support of dozens of high-profile authors and intellectuals, the magistrate Sir Charles Biron ruled against *The Well of Loneliness*:

> Unfortunately these women exist, and the book asks that their existence and vices should be recognised and tolerated, and not treated with condemnation, as they are at present by all decent people. This being the tenor of the book I have no hesitation in saying it is an ... offence against public decency, and an obscene libel, and I shall order it to be destroyed.

The inevitable focus of history on landmark cases such as those of Oscar Wilde and *The Well of Loneliness* has to a considerable degree sensationalized and darkened our sense of late nineteenth- and early twentieth-century life outside the heterosexual mainstream. That it could be a dark and depressing existence there can be no doubt—the pessimism that Forster expressed even as late as 1960 ("police prosecutions will continue ...") is surely understandable. But, as documents such as the letters exchanged between Strachey and Keynes attest, it could also be one of self-assured candour, zestful comedy, and a wholehearted enjoyment of life. "Our time will come," declared Strachey, speaking confidently in an 8 April 1906 letter to Keynes of the situation of homosexuals in Britain, "about a hundred years hence." A hundred years later it is beginning to seem that Strachey's optimism may have been at least as well founded as Forster's more pessimistic view.

A young boy sings nationalist songs to a crowd outside Mountjoy Prison, Dublin, where an Irish Republican Army prisoner is about to be executed (1921).

IRELAND

If a remarkable amount of memorable literature emerged in Britain from the years of turmoil between the two World Wars in the first half of the twentieth century, the same statement could be made of Ireland, as the Irish endured the state of turmoil that remained a constant throughout the first half of the century. The fiction of James Joyce and the plays of Samuel Beckett have already been mentioned as central to the evolution of Modernist literature. The other important Irish literary work of the period includes J.M. Synge's vivid portrayals of the elemental life of the Aran Islanders on the coast of western Ireland in plays such as *Riders of the Sea* (1904) and *The Playboy of the Western World* (1907); the plays of Lady Augusta Gregory; the sweeping expressiveness of Sean O'Casey's great dramas *Juno and the Paycock* (1924) and *The Plough and the Stars* (1926); and the extraordinary range of the poetry of William Butler Yeats from the 1890s through the 1930s—lyrical, Romantic, Symbolist, mystical, political, Existential, and perhaps above all, passionate.

To this list should be added the plays of George Bernard Shaw, who was born in Dublin and lived there for the first twenty years of his life. Shaw has often been called the most important dramatist in English after Shakespeare; he was a socially committed writer who understood, as he puts it in the "Preface" to his 1905 play *Major Barbara*, that "it is difficult to make people realise that an evil is an evil." Shaw *was* able to make people realize such things, not only through effective polemic but also (and more memorably) through the sparkling wit of his plays. Shaw's important work extends from brilliantly biting works of the 1890s and early 1900s such as *Mrs. Warren's Profession*, *Arms and the Man*, and *Major Barbara* (on the topics of prostitution, militaristic attitudes, and religion and social reform, respectively); to *Pygmalion* (1912), a satire of attitudes toward social class and its expression through language, on which the 1950s musical *My Fair Lady* was based; to the epic historical drama *Saint Joan* (1923).

Cover, *Major Barbara: A Screen Version*, Penguin, 1945. This early "film tie-in" publication (number 500 in the Penguin series) was still in the standard early Penguin format; not until the 1960s did it become common for book publishers to employ a different cover design in such situations.

If the Irish Shaw is arguably the greatest "British" dramatist of the twentieth century, one of the greatest "British" writers of the 1890s, Oscar Wilde, had also been born and raised in Ireland before moving to London. Indeed, many have judged the literary outpouring from Irish writers during the period 1890–1960 to amount to a more important body of work than the entire literature of Britain over the same period—despite the fact that the combined population of England, Scotland, and Wales, at almost 50 million, was more than ten times that of Ireland.

But how are Britain and Ireland to be defined? Here matters become tangled, for during this period Ireland, for centuries a predominantly Catholic (and mostly unwilling) component of the United Kingdom, finally achieved the status of an independent republic. In the process, however, it became geographically split, with several largely Protestant counties of Northern Ireland remaining a political unit of the United Kingdom.

The Irish had been treated as second-class citizens throughout the centuries of English rule over Ireland. But the hardships they endured in the nineteenth century were particularly severe; the potato famine of 1845–51 alone is estimated to have killed almost a million Irish—almost 10 per cent of the population. By the 1880s and 1890s political pressure in Ireland for radical change had become extremely powerful. And there was pressure for cultural change too; the Celtic Revival (also known as the Irish Literary revival), begun in 1896 by Irishmen and women such as Yeats and Lady Augusta Gregory, was remarkably successful both in increasing appreciation for the traditions of Irish culture and in encouraging the creation of new works in those traditions.

In the late nineteenth century, too, many in England became more sympathetic to Irish aspirations. In an effort to end the long history of oppression and resistance in British-controlled Ireland, Liberal governments twice introduced bills providing for one form or another of "Home Rule" (the term used to refer to limited Irish self-government) in the British House of Commons. The second of these was passed by the House of Commons but defeated in the Conservative-dominated House of Lords. In 1912, another Home Rule Bill was passed, and again the House of Lords rejected it. But now the rules had been changed; as a result of the previous year's Parliament Act, a veto by the House of Lords retained force for only three years. As the date in 1914 approached when the veto was due to expire and Home Rule would thus come into effect, tension rose to such a pitch that many felt civil war to be a real possibility. Substantial areas of the north of Ireland that had been forcibly settled by the English in earlier eras were now staunchly Protestant and vowed resistance to any government order to allow an Ireland dominated by "Papists" to become independent of Britain. And since Protestants from Ulster, in the north of Ireland, were heavily represented in the British army's

contingent of troops stationed in Ireland, the military could not be relied on to carry out orders. With the onset of World War I, however, the implementation of the Home Rule Bill was postponed until after the war—and in a fateful move, Prime Minister Herbert Asquith promised that the British government would never force Ulster Protestants to accept Home Rule involuntarily.

Given the long history of vetoes and postponements—and given that the promised self-government in any case was to bring only a limited independence from Britain—it is unsurprising that Irish nationalists were impatient. On Easter Monday, 1916, rebels stormed public buildings in Dublin and proclaimed a republic. In the struggle, as Yeats famously wrote in "Easter, 1916," the Irish were "transformed utterly" and "a terrible beauty" was born. The uprising was brutally suppressed, but the nationalist Sinn Fein continued to wage a guerrilla opposition to British rule. Yet another Home Rule Bill was passed in 1920, providing for six counties of Ulster to be partitioned at independence, and the remainder of the island to remain a part of the British Empire but to be granted Dominion status (parallel to that of Canada, Australia, New Zealand, and South Africa) as the Irish Free State. That limited form of independence came into effect in 1922, but many Irish Republicans refused to accept any form of subservience to the British Crown, and the Irish Republican Army continued a clandestine struggle. In 1937 a new constitution changed the status of the country to that of a sovereign state within the British Commonwealth—a status sufficiently independent of Britain that Ireland was able to remain neutral in World War II—and in 1949 an Irish Republic was finally proclaimed, with the nation withdrawing from the Commonwealth. But the long struggle was still not fully over; tensions within Northern Ireland would continue to haunt Britain into the twenty-first century.

An understanding of the politics and religion of Ireland is essential background for an understanding of Irish history—and Irish literary history—during this period. But it gives little sense of the daily reality of Catholics and Protestants who lived largely in isolation from each other, Catholics overwhelmingly the majority in Ireland, Protestants forming the majority in Northern

Ireland. The novelist Elizabeth Bowen, who was raised mainly in Dublin in an Irish Protestant family (she "was taught to say 'Church of Ireland,' not 'Protestant'") later described her experiences in *Seven Winters: Memories of a Dublin Childhood* (1943):

> It was not until the end of those seven winters that I understood that we Protestants were a minority, and that the unquestioned rules of our being came, in fact, from the closeness of a minority world. .... I took the existence of Roman Catholics for granted but met few and was not interested in them. They were, simply, "the others," whose world lay along-side ours but never touched. As to the difference between the two religions, I was too discreet to ask questions—if I wanted to know. This appeared to share a delicate, awkward aura with those two other differences—of sex, of class. So quickly in a child's mind does prudery seed itself and make growth that I remember, even, an almost sexual shyness on the subject of Roman Catholics. I walked with hurried steps and averted cheek past porticos of churches that were "not ours," uncomfortably registering in my nostrils the pungent, unlikely smell [of incense] that came round curtains, through swinging doors.

IDEOLOGY AND ECONOMICS IN THE 1930s AND 1940s

How do ideologies differ from ideas? In part they are simply sets of ideas, but the question goes beyond that: an ideology is a systematic set of beliefs that is shared widely, and that prescribes a program of political action in association with those beliefs. In the twentieth century, such ideologies as communism, socialism, fascism, and liberalism all exerted enormous power. The central concepts of liberal democracy took shape in the nineteenth century, and by the end of the twentieth century had spread to much of the world. But for much of the twentieth century they were powerfully chal-lenged by those of other ideologies: socialism (and its relative, communism) and fascism.

Fascism is identified as an ideology of the far right and it has indeed often co-existed with capitalist eco-nomic structures. But the strength of its appeal is—like that of communism—collectivist in nature. As the official name of the Nazi party in Germany (the Na-tional Socialist Party) suggests, fascism is "socialist" in its appeal to the egalitarian instincts of the populace. But whereas socialism and communism are (in theory at least) internationalist, appealing to the fellow-feeling of humans *as humans*, fascism appeals strongly to national-ist feeling—to the instinct of the population to pull together *as a nation*. More broadly, the egalitarian ideals of fascist societies are never inclusive; the nation defines itself not only against other nations, but typically also against a backdrop of a perceived "other" within its midst. Whether the "other" be immigrants, those of a different skin color, those of a different religion, or a group such as the Jews that is defined by race, culture, and religion, the otherness is typically used as a focal point for the defining the nation's identity, and for lending intensity to the ideological allegiance of the fascist core.

Nazi authorities affix a poster to a shop as part of their campaign of persecution, 1935. The sign reads "Buy nothing from Jews!"

If fascism weirdly approaches socialism from one direction, communism departs from socialist ideals in another. Socialist ideals are above all those of fairness and equality in a society in which government is prepared to intervene consistently on behalf of the greater good—to control capitalism, in socialism's weaker version (social democracy), or to replace it with a system of government ownership of the means of production on behalf of the entire population, in the full-fledged socialist model. Such ideals are built on foundations very similar to those of communist ideology, but the differences turn out in practice to be crucial. Perhaps the most important difference is that communist ideology—especially as it attained full force in the twentieth century—embodied the paradoxical notion that an elite could act as the "vanguard" for the masses, and that a "dictatorship of the proletariat" could reasonably act on behalf of all the people, without the people in practice having a direct say in who was to govern, or how. With the benefit of hindsight, it seems obvious that such an ideology was likely to result in almost as much oppression and cruelty as was the ideology of fascism. But in a Russia that had been laboring under the inequalities of a semi-feudal system, or indeed in Depression-era North America or Great Britain, when the engines of capitalism seemed to be merciless and unrestrained by government, to many communism seemed the only realistic path toward a society that would be both more free and more fair for all citizens.

The greatest ideological struggles of the first half the century were unquestionably those that unfolded in Russia in 1917 and in Germany and Italy in the 1930s, but an ideologically charged climate was a worldwide reality. In some ways, the twentieth-century ideological tapestry may be seen in sharpest focus in the context of the Spanish Civil War (1936-39). Under the banner of those fighting for the Republican cause were liberals, socialists, communists, and anarchists—all ranged against the fascist forces of Generalissimo Francisco Franco. As George Orwell details in his account of the ideological and physical battles of the war, *Homage to Catalonia* (1938), the Spanish Civil War became a battleground not only between democracy and fascism, but also between the various factions on the Republican side, with idealism all too often being trumped by self-interest or by the dictates of outside governments lending support. In the end, the Communist government of the Soviet Union was as reluctant as were the capitalist governments of Britain or the United States to stand in the way of the anticipated "stable" government that the fascist General Franco represented.

The Spanish Civil War is often regarded as central to 1930s intellectual currents, and certainly the degree to which intellectuals from Britain (and indeed, from throughout the western world) rallied to the Republican side was remarkable. Sylvia Townsend Warner was among the leading British writers in Spain during the war; as she reported in a 1937 magazine article, the conflict was extraordinary not least of all for the bond that grew up between intellectuals and common citizens: "It is unusual for writers to hear words such as 'Here come the Intellectuals' spoken by working-class people and common soldiers in tones of kindliness and enthusiasm."

Others spoke out not only against fascism but against all forms of militarism—and against war itself. Notably, Virginia Woolf's polemic *Three Guineas* (1938) inquired into the role that women could play in the prevention of war, concluding that war is not merely a public issue—that, rather, "the public and the private worlds are inseparably connected; that the tyrannies and servilities of the one are the tyrannies and servilities of the other."

Even before the Spanish Civil War became a focal point for literature and politics, literature in the 1930s had become more highly political than that of the 1920s. Writers such as Auden (in his early work), Christopher Isherwood, C. Day Lewis, Louis MacNeice, Stephen Spender, and Edward Upward were all, in the view of MacNeice in his *Modern Poetry* (1932), "unlike Yeats and Eliot … emotionally partisan":

> Yeats [in the 1930s] proposed to turn his back on desire and hatred; Eliot sat back and watched other people's emotions with ennui and ironical self-pity. … The whole poetry, on the other hand, of Auden, Spender, and Day Lewis implies that they have desires and hatreds of their own and, further, that they think some things *ought* to be desired and others hated.

Many of these writers joined or were sympathetic to the Communist Party through much of the 1930s. In the later twentieth century it would have been unimaginable for most of the important writers of a generation to be sympathetic to "the Party," as it came to be called, but in the early 1930s the brutality of Soviet communism under Stalin was not yet public knowledge—and the mainstream parties in Britain (Labour as well as the Conservatives) were dealing timorously and ineffectively with an economic downturn of unprecedented severity.

A young woman takes aim during target practice,
Spain, 1936.

The Great Depression that began late in 1929 and lasted until the outbreak of war ten years later was a worldwide phenomenon—and one exacerbated in Britain (as in North America) by the determination of governments not to go into debt in order to provide support for the unemployed and otherwise impoverished, or to invest in getting the economy moving. Individuals, too, reacted with fear, and strove to increase their savings, thereby contributing to what British economist John Maynard Keynes termed "the paradox of thrift": when people saved rather than spending what little they had, they further reduced the demand for goods, which in turn led to further reductions in production, more unemployment, lower wages for those still working—and so the cycle continued. By the end of 1930, some 20% of the British workforce was unemployed, and by the mid-1930s it was estimated that a quarter of the population had been reduced to a subsistence diet.

Keynes—an important figure in the Bloomsbury Group, and something of a cultural icon as well as one of the most important twentieth-century economists—broke new ground with his arguments for government intervention in the economy—recommending both that governments intervene to control inflation and that they act to "even out" the imbalances of the economic cycle by spending more during downturns. Conservatives argued that such imbalances would right themselves in the long run in any case, and should not be tampered with; Keynes's response was that "the long run is a misleading guide to current affairs. In the long run we are all dead." It was not until after World War II, though, that governments in Britain and elsewhere adopted Keynes's prescriptions for smoothing out the business cycle; although economic conditions improved somewhat in the south of Britain in the late 1930s, it was not until the war that economic growth resumed throughout the country.

A turn toward the political left is to be expected during any severe and prolonged economic downturn; given that the Great Depression was more severe and prolonged a downturn than any in the twentieth century, it is unsurprising that writers and intellectuals moved further to the left politically during the 1930s than at any other time during the century. But why did they embrace, in such large numbers, the relatively rigid doctrines of the Communist Party? As Orwell looked back in 1940, he took the view that the ideological coloring of the intellectual life of the 1930s had been as broadly connected to cultural as it had been to economic trends:

> By 1930 ... the debunking of western civilization had reached its climax.... How many of the values by which our grandfathers lived could now be taken seriously? Patriotism, religion, the Empire, the family, the sanctity of marriage, the Old School Tie, birth, breeding, honour, discipline—anyone of ordinary education could turn the whole lot of them inside out in three minutes. But what do you achieve, after all, by getting rid of such primal things as patriotism and religion? You have not necessarily gotten rid of the need for something to believe in.... It is significant that [those intellectuals who did embrace religion in these years] went almost invariably to the Roman Church.... They went, that is, to the church with a world-wide organization, the one with a rigid discipline, the one with power and

prestige behind it. ... I do not think one need look farther than this for the reason the young writers of the thirties flocked into or towards the Communist Party. It was simply something to believe in. Here was a church, an army, an orthodoxy, a discipline.

With World War II, however, another form of discipline inevitably took hold; even though Britain and the United States became allies, the ties between the British and American intellectual communities and the Soviet Communist Party steadily loosened. With the beginning of the "Cold War" between the West and the USSR immediately following the end of World War II (and a new sense of purpose in the Labour Party under Clement Attlee), the link between British intellectuals and the Communist Party had for the most part come to an end.

THE LITERATURE OF THE 1930S AND 1940S

George Orwell may be seen as one of the writers who most fully expresses the ideological conflicts over socialism, communism, fascism, and liberal democracy that were at the heart of so much of twentieth-century life. His earlier works detail the appalling toll that capitalism was exacting on the working class. In *Down and Out in Paris and London* (1933), he recounts from personal experience the reality of the life of a vagrant, and of the life of the lowest of workers in the Paris hotel and restaurant industry. In *The Road to Wigan Pier* (1937), Orwell details the hardships of miners in the north of England, and of the working class population throughout the country. Orwell was an avowed socialist; ironically enough, however, the two works for which he remains best known have often been portrayed as attacks on socialism; they are both novels in which he attacks the corruption of socialist ideals under Soviet-style communism. *Animal Farm* is a fable that shows the ways in which power may readily be seized by the most powerful and unprincipled in a "collectivist" system; *1984* is a futurist view of a society in which "Big Brother" controls people's minds as much as their actions.

Another writer of central importance to twentieth-century literature who was initially defined against a backdrop of ideology is the poet W.H. Auden. Auden

Like Orwell's *1984*, Aldous Huxley's *Brave New World* (1932) is a dystopia in which the State effectively controls the minds of its citizens, who are convinced that they are expressing human potential to its fullest.

first became famous as a political poet, particularly with his memorable call to arms against fascism in "Spain, 1937": "But today the struggle." Auden quickly became disenchanted with political polemic, however, not least of all his own. He became disillusioned with the Republican side in the Spanish Civil War after witnessing the persecution of Catholic priests by members of the Republican army, and after traveling through China in the wake of the 1937–38 Nanking Massacre he became convinced that violence is a disease that lurks within every human heart. "The act of taking sides," he became convinced, "spelled out the death of free culture and the triumph ... of its enemies." Auden's poetic response to the outbreak of World War II, "September 1, 1939," was famously equivocal, the emphasis being placed on the expiration of the 1930s—dubbed by Auden "a low, dishonest decade"—rather than on the imminence of the fascist threat to freedom.

"Spain, 1937" and "September 1, 1939" were among those poems that Auden refused to allow to be printed in later volumes of his poetry. Even in the 1930s, his work was extraordinarily diverse, and more and more as the years went by his name became paired with that of T.S. Eliot; after the death of Yeats in 1939, Eliot and Auden were almost universally regarded as the leading poets of the day. But the two may in more than one respect be seen as polar opposites. Whereas Eliot had moved permanently from the United States to England as a young man, Auden moved permanently from Britain to New York to 1939. Eliot's first marriage had failed in the face of the mental illness of his wife, Vivienne; she was eventually confined in a mental institution, and Eliot embraced the stiff collar traditions of Church and of respectable society with ever-greater conviction. Auden's marriage to novelist Thomas Mann's daughter Erica also ended, but it could hardly have been said to have "failed," since it had been entered into only to protect Erica from persecution at the hands of the Nazis. Auden made no secret of his same-sex sexual orientation (at a time when it took considerable courage to do so), and felt stifled by the society of which Eliot was a pillar; he moved in 1939 to New York, where he soon entered into a lifelong relationship with the poet Chester Kallman, and where his rumpled figure became a quiet fixture on the literary scene. If Eliot was a central figure of Modernism, Auden's connections to the forms of Modernism were more tenuous. His skill with poetic forms was extraordinarily wide ranging, but unlike Eliot he kept returning to accentual-syllabic meters, and to the use of rhyme.

The explosive sexuality of D.H. Lawrence's fiction has been touched on above. If sexual love was one of the great themes of his work, the other was surely the corrosive effect that the British class system exerted on human relationships. In the 1930s that became a theme more and more widely taken up by novelists, in works such as Henry Green's *Living* (1929), Walter Greenwood's *Love on the Dole* (1933), and J.B. Priestley's *Angel Pavement* (1930). With the notable exception of the novels and stories of Edward Upward, however, expressions of outrage against the capitalist order of things tended to be fewer in number and milder in tone in the prose fiction of the time than they were in its poetry.

Somerset Maugham's *The Razor's Edge* (1944), a novel of romance and spirituality, became one of the twentieth century's bestselling novels both in Britain and in North America. It was issued in paperback editions on both sides of the Atlantic in 1946. Pocket Books, which had followed Penguin's lead and introduced mass market paperbacks into the United States in 1941, published the American paperback edition (shown here).

At least as numerous and at least as popular in Britain during this era were fiction writers of a more conservative political stripe, including Somerset Maugham, with his tightly crafted novels and short stories; Evelyn Waugh, with his bitingly satirical novels; and P.G. Wodehouse, with his more light-hearted brand of satirical fiction. Many have seen an inherent conservatism, too, in what was then a new genre of popular fiction, the detective novel. The genre saw few if any worthy successors to Sir Arthur Conan Doyle's nineteenth-century creation, Sherlock Holmes, until Agatha Christie introduced her detective Hercule Poirot and the equally astute Jane Marple to readers in the late 1920s and 1930s. Together with the Father Brown novels of the Catholic conservative G. K. Chesterton,

Christie's works founded an enduring tradition of English mystery novels.

The revolutionary experiments of Modernism that are so central to the literary history of the 1910s and 1920s were for the most part not extended in the following decades. To this generalization, David Jones's *In Parenthesis* (1937) is a notable exception; written partly in prose, partly in free verse, Jones's epic of World War I bears the unmistakable stamp of Modernism. And some other authors continued to experiment with literary form. Henry Green's *Living*, for example, is written with an economy of expression that mirrors the economies of the working-class life it depicts, with articles and nouns frequently omitted from the normal syntactical flow. But most fiction writers of the period adopted a traditional approach to narrative, and even T. S. Eliot seemed to be backing away from Modernism with his ritualized play *Murder in the Cathedral* (1935)—and, following World War II, with a series of drawing room comedies.

From the late 1930s well into the 1970s one of the leading figures of British literature was unquestionably Graham Greene. Greene exploded onto the literary scene in 1938 with the publication of *Brighton Rock,* a tautly written exploration of the seediness and cruelty that lurked not far below the surface of much of British life. In subsequent novels, perhaps most notable among them *The Power and the Glory* (1940) and *The Heart of the Matter* (1948), Greene went on to explore the same qualities in human life generally. The setting of Greene's novels might be colonial Africa, rural Mexico, or war-torn London, but it is always recognizably "Greeneland"; always in the background is a sense of anguished Catholicism tinged with a bleak sense of despair.

LITERATURE AND EMPIRE

No matter how widely Greene's geographical imagination ranged, the human souls he was interested in exploring were mostly those of white males from the Western world. Other British writers of the time, however, were beginning to reach for an understanding of the world that would take fuller account of the lives and the souls of those who lived under British rule in Africa, India, and much of the rest of the world. The essays of Nancy Cunard, along with those of Orwell, expressed a wide-ranging understanding of the mechanisms of Imperial rule, and of the reality of life for many who suffered under it. In fiction, the novelist Joyce Cary broke new ground with his *Mr. Johnson* (1939), a comic novel with a Nigerian clerk as its protagonist. The novel represents the Nigerian in ways that are bound to make today's reader wince. Yet it also gives expression to a specifically Nigerian sense of humor, and conveys a genuinely sympathetic understanding of the situation both of Johnson and of Nigerians generally under British rule. *Mr. Johnson* is a long way from the literature of the last few decades of the twentieth century in its approach to colonial and multi-cultural realities (let alone the debates of the late twentieth century over "appropriation of voice"). Yet in a very real sense it marks a step forward for British literature in the possibilities it demonstrates for the British imagination of connecting with the rest of the world. In a very direct sense there is also a connection between *Mr. Johnson* and the explosion of African literature later in the century (in the first half of the century exceedingly few African writers were published). As Chinua Achebe later recalled, reading the Cary novel was one of the things that led him to become a writer; "in spite of [Cary's] ability, in spite of his sympathy and understanding, he could not get under the skin of his African. They just did not communicate. And I felt if a good [English white] writer could make this mess perhaps we ought to try our hand."

The twentieth century had begun for Britain with a war in South Africa that had ended with a Pyrrhic victory. In a struggle against white colonists of Dutch background (Afrikaaners, or "Boers") that came to involve the Zulus and other native populations, the superior firepower of the British prevailed—but not without the adoption of a variety of brutally oppressive measures as the British struggled to control a guerrilla campaign by the Afrikaaners. At the time, the war seemed an extension of the British struggle against the Afrikaaners that had been continuing on and off for more than fifty years—and, as with previous conflicts, this one resulted in an expansion of the size of the British Empire. The war aroused objections to the

Imperial project to an unprecedented degree, however; more than a century later, it is difficult not to see in it a foreshadowing of the loss of Empire. The brutalities in which the British allowed themselves to engage as they struggled to assert control seem a foretaste of the struggles against the Independence Movement in India in the 1930s and 1940s that would end with the independence of India in 1947, and of the struggles in Kenya and elsewhere in Africa in the 1950s could be resolved only through the independence of those colonies. In one of his most famous speeches during the dark days of the Battle of Britain in 1940, Prime Minister Winston Churchill alluded to the possibility of the British Empire lasting for "a thousand years." Even then its foundations had crumbled, and within another 20 years the edifice of Empire would be almost entirely dismantled.

THE ENGLISH LANGUAGE IN THE EARLY TWENTIETH CENTURY

Many trends in the development of the English language that had begun in the nineteenth century or earlier continued through the first half of the twentieth. Punctuation became simpler: whereas, for example, it remained common in Britain through to the end of the nineteenth century and into the twentieth to precede a dash with a comma, by mid-century the norm was always to use one or the other, never both. Long periodic sentences had been on the decline through most of the nineteenth century, and this trend continued into the twentieth; on both sides of the Atlantic, sentences became shorter. Paragraphs also became shorter. To these generalizations, however, there were significant exceptions. With the growth of universities and the expansion of business, government, and political bureaucracies came an increase in academic, administrative, and political jargon of the sort of which Orwell complained in his famous essay "Politics and the English Language" (1946). While the majority of people (including most writers of fiction) were using shorter sentences, in other quarters writers were, in Orwell's words, "gumming together long strips of words which have already been set in order by someone else, and making the results presentable by sheer humbug."

In the twentieth century spelling was largely stable on both sides of the Atlantic; though shortened forms of some of the more archaic spellings in standard English became common in down-market forms of advertising, particularly in the United States (*thru, donut*), even there few of these came close to displacing the longer traditional forms. Conventions for marking direct speech also stabilized on both sides of the Atlantic, with the British using single quotation marks and the Canadians adopting the American convention of using double quotation marks.

Vocabulary, of course, continued to expand, with many new coinages entering the language as the result of new developments in science and technology. Interestingly, Britain and the United States developed largely separate terminologies regarding that most influential of twentieth century developments in technology, the automobile; in Britain cars run on *petrol*, the engine is under the *bonnet*, the luggage goes in the *boot*, and you drive on the *motorway*—without much noise unless there is a hole in your *silencer*. In numerous other areas in which new coinages were necessary, British usage developed as quite distinct from that in the United States—from television *presenters* (hosts); to *breeze block* construction (concrete block), to battery-powered *torches* (flashlights), to *Wellingtons* (rubber boots), to *hire purchase plans* (instalment plans), British English remained distinct from American English. (Former British possessions such as Canada and Australia partook of both in forming their own national patterns.)

Perhaps the greatest structural shift in English in the first half of the twentieth century was the simplification or elimination of forms marking the subjunctive mood. In constructions such as "If I were to travel through time I would…," for example, the old subjunctive form came to be largely replaced by the simple past form of the verb ("If I traveled through time I would …").

Throughout the nineteenth century, the spread of literacy and of mass transportation led to a steady decrease in the distinctiveness of the various dialects of English spoken in Britain, and in the distinctiveness of regional accents. That movement toward standardization continued in the twentieth century, with radio and television as its new vehicles. In 1922, the government set up the BBC (at first the initials stood for British

Broadcasting Company, but the name was soon changed to British Broadcasting Corporation), and it remained the dominant force in British radio—and, from the 1950s on, British television—for most of the century. In 1926, John Reith, the BBC's managing director, created an Advisory Committee on Spoken English, chaired by Robert Bridges, then the Poet Laureate, with the task of making recommendations to facilitate a standard of pronunciation over the air. Reith specifically asked that the committee seek a "style or quality of English that would not be laughed at in any part of the country." In practice, the standardized pronunciations recommended by the committee—which remained largely mandatory for announcers until 1989—were broadly similar to the pronunciations taught in the nation's elite "public" schools (see the glossary at the back of this volume for a discussion of this term) in southern England. Indeed, the three terms "public school pronunciation," "BBC pronunciation," and "Received Standard Pronunciation" (a term introduced by Henry Cecil Wyld in the early twentieth century to denote "the form which ... is heard with practically no variation among speakers of the better class all over the country") are all roughly synonymous. Despite the ongoing trend towards standardization of speech in the twentieth century, however, the varieties of British English remained extraordinarily diverse throughout the century—so much so that someone from London could at century's end still have great difficulty understanding the accent of a Glaswegian or a "Geordie" (a native of the Newcastle area).

HISTORY OF THE LANGUAGE AND OF PRINT CULTURE

In an effort to provide for readers a direct sense of the development of the language and of print culture, examples of texts in their original form (and of illustrations) have been provided for each period. A list of these within the present volume, arranged chronologically, appears below. An overview of developments in the history of language during the first half of the century appears on pp. 1031–32, and material on developments in the history of language since World War II appears on pp. 1404, 1411–12, and 1414–16.

Advertising page from a volume in Everyman's Library, p. 1018.

John Macrae, autograph copy of "In Flanders Fields," p. 1123.

A Soldier's Own Diary, pages for November 4–10, 1917, p. 1130.

Cover of Penguin edition of Graham Greene's *Brighton Rock*, p. 1011.

Cover of Pan edition of Graham Greene's *Journey Without Maps*, color insert pages.

"Wartime Book" notice from the copyright page of a 1945 printing of Mazo de la Roche's *Jalna*, p. 1011.

Cover of Penguin edition of Bernard Shaw's *Major Barbara: A Screen Version*, p. 1023.

Cover of Pocket Book edition of Somerset Maugham's *The Razor's Edge*, p. 1029.

Photographs of readers of the 1960 Penguin edition of D.H. Lawrence's *Lady Chatterley's Lover*, soon after publication, p. 1020.

Cover of Minerva paperback edition of Roddy Doyle's *The Van*, color insert pages.

Cover of Kazuo Ishiguro's *Never Let Me Go*, color insert pages.

Cover of *Political Spider: Stories from Black Orpheus*, p. 1404.

Cover of the Broadview edition of Wilkie Collins's *The Evil Genius*, p. 1408.

BERNARD SHAW

1856 – 1950

Considered by many to be the greatest dramatist of his age, George Bernard Shaw was at times revered by, at times alienated from, the London society he criticized through his plays. A committed socialist, Shaw often used his plays to expound his views on the rights of women, on numerous social injustices, or on the deleterious effects of capitalism. In some cases he treated topics (such as prostitution and religion) in ways that caused his plays to be banned in England for many years, but Shaw himself always remained in the public eye. In the end he wrote more than 50 plays, and was awarded the Nobel Prize for Literature, the prize money for which he directed be used for the translation of Swedish works into English. He is the only Nobel laureate to have won an Academy Award (for his screenplay *Pygmalion*). The adjective "Shavian" was coined to describe his witty dialogue and epigrams.

Shaw was born into somewhat shabby gentility in Dublin in 1856, the son of a failing corn merchant and alcoholic father and a music teacher and singer mother. Shaw spent a great deal of time with the servants, one of whom exposed him to the realities of working-class life in Dublin when she was supposed to be taking him for air. The poverty and hardship he saw, and the ragtag characters with whom he came into contact, stayed with him for life and greatly influenced his later work. He and his two older sisters had a governess for their early education, but neither parent showed a particular interest in their children's formal education. As a result, Shaw flitted from school to school, attending irregularly; he finally gave it all up at age 15 to work as a clerk in a land surveyor's office. One of his duties was to collect rent from poor tenants. Shaw hated his work, but it provided fodder for his plays, the first of which, *Widowers' Houses* (1892), dealt with slum landlords. It was also during this time that Shaw dropped the "George" from his name, and became known as Bernard Shaw.

In 1876 Shaw moved to London to join his mother, who had moved there in 1873 with her music teacher. For the next nine years, Shaw honed his writing skills, building a successful career as a music and art critic. It was also during this time that he began to develop his creative writing. From 1879 to 1883 Shaw wrote five novels, none of which was published at the time. (Shaw eventually gave up writing novels; he said he had come to dislike the form, and called it clumsy and unreal.) From 1891 onward, Shaw dedicated himself to work as a playwright. His family background—a music-filled home, a mother who had been a performer—had helped foster a love of the stage, and he had become particularly interested in theater while still in Dublin, where he had frequented the Theatre Royal.

From 1891 to 1903 Shaw wrote 12 plays, some of which had very short runs in London, while others premiered in America (e.g., *The Devil's Disciple*) or Germany (*Caesar and Cleopatra*). By 1898 he was earning enough in royalties from his plays to be financially secure; it was also in that year that he married Charlotte Payne Townshend, a marriage that brought still greater financial stability.

Shaw created several categories for his plays: his *Plays Unpleasant* engage with various social issues. In addition to *Widowers' Houses*, these include *The Philanderer* (1905) and *Mrs. Warren's Profession*

(1902), which explored the topic of prostitution and was banned from public performance in England for 30 years. His next set of plays, *Plays Pleasant*, received better reviews and gave him his first commercial successes. These plays include *Candida*, *Arms and the Man*, *The Man of Destiny*, and *You Never Can Tell*. He termed various of his other plays "Comedies," "Chronicles," and "Political Extravaganzas." During Shaw's lifetime his most highly acclaimed plays included *Man and Superman* (1905), *Major Barbara* (1905), *Pygmalion* (1913), *Heartbreak House* (1920), and *Saint Joan* (1923). Throughout his long career Shaw remained very involved in the production of his plays, often arranging the casting, direction, and staging.

In awarding Shaw the Nobel Prize for 1925, the selection committee commended him for his "work which is marked by both idealism and humanity, its stimulating satire often being infused with a singular poetic beauty." He was offered a knighthood in 1926, but declined it, as he did many other honors. Shaw died in 1950, after falling from a tree he had been pruning. Throughout his life he had remained an eccentric, distinguished not only by his literary reputation but also by his vegetarianism, his discordant political views (he opposed Britain's involvement in World War I), and odd clothing (he wore an unbleached wool suit through much of his life for its perceived health benefits). In almost every way Shaw was an original.

⌘ ⌘ ⌘

Mrs. Warren's Profession

A Note on the Text of *Mrs. Warren's Profession*

Mrs. Warren's Profession was first published in 1898 in volume 1 (*Plays Unpleasant*) of *Plays Pleasant and Unpleasant*, in London by Grant Richards, and in Chicago and New York by Herbert S. Stone. The other plays in *Plays Unpleasant* were *Widowers' Houses* and *The Philanderer*. The first separate edition of *Mrs. Warren's Profession* was published in London by Grant Richards in 1902 in an identical text, but with a new preface by Shaw and photographs of the Stage Society production of 5–6 January 1902. Shaw revised *Mrs. Warren's Profession* for the *Plays Unpleasant* volume (1930) of *The Works of Bernard Shaw: Collected Edition*, published in London by Constable between 1930 and 1938. This was the text of *Mrs. Warren's Profession* used for *Bernard Shaw: Collected Plays with Their Prefaces* published in seven volumes by Max Reinhardt between 1970 and 1974 under the editorial supervision of Dan H. Laurence, and subsequently by Penguin Books, again under the editorial supervision of Dan H. Laurence. The definitive Penguin text is the copytext for the Broadview edition on which the text printed here is based.

Shaw made numerous revisions in the 1898 text for the 1930 edition. Many are relatively minor, but those that suggest significant changes in Shaw's thinking about a character or situation are recorded here in footnotes in this edition.

Shaw had strong opinions on matters of spelling, punctuation, and typography. He retained some archaic spellings (e.g. *shew* for *show*), and dropped the "u" in "our" spellings such as *honor*, *labor*, and *neighbor*. He preferred to reserve the use of italics for stage directions and descriptions of settings and characters (which are detailed and elaborate for the benefit of readers who might never have the opportunity of seeing his plays), electing to indicate emphasis of a word by spacing the letters (e.g., d e a r for *dear*, v e r y for *very*). He had no choice but to use italics for stressing *I*, and he sometimes chose to use small capital letters for stressing some words (e.g., ME for *me*).

Shaw disliked the apostrophe, believing it to be redundant (and ugly) in most instances. He eliminated it whenever he could (e.g., in *Ive, youve, thats, werent, dont, wont*), though it was necessary to retain it where its omission might cause confusion (e.g. *I'll, it's, he'll*).

For some readers Shaw's rationale for these practices is unconvincing, and the idiosyncrasies are irritating. They are, however, Shaw's clear preferences, and serve if nothing else as a frequent reminder of his nonconformity—the essence of the man and his work—and have, therefore, been retained in this anthology.

⌘ ⌘ ⌘

Mrs. Warren's Profession [1]

ACT 1

(*Summer afternoon in a cottage garden on the eastern slope of a hill a little south of Haslemere[2] in Surrey. Looking up the hill, the cottage is seen in the left hand corner of the garden, with its thatched roof and porch, and a large lattice[3] window to the left of the porch. A paling[4] completely shuts in the garden, except for a gate on the right. The common rises uphill beyond the paling to the sky line. Some folded canvas garden chairs are leaning against the side bench in the porch. A lady's bicycle is propped against the wall, under the window. A little to the right of the porch a hammock is slung from two posts. A big canvas umbrella, stuck in the ground, keeps the sun off the hammock, in which a young lady lies reading and making notes, her head towards the cottage and her feet towards the gate. In front of the hammock, and within reach of her hand, is a common kitchen chair, with a pile of serious-looking books and a supply of writing paper on it.*

A gentleman walking on the common comes into sight from behind the cottage. He is hardly past middle age, with something of the artist about him, unconventionally but carefully dressed and clean-shaven except for a moustache, with an eager susceptible face and very amiable and considerate manners. He has silky black hair, with waves of

grey and white in it. His eyebrows are white, his moustache black. He seems not certain of his way. He looks over the paling; takes stock of the place; and sees the young lady.*)

THE GENTLEMAN. (*Taking off his hat.*) I beg your pardon. Can you direct me to Hindhead View—Mrs Alison's?

THE YOUNG LADY. (*Glancing up from her book.*) This is 5 Mrs Alison's. (*She resumes her work.*)

THE GENTLEMAN. Indeed! Perhaps—may I ask are you Miss Vivie Warren?

THE YOUNG LADY. (*Sharply, as she turns on her elbow to get a good look at him.*) Yes.

THE GENTLEMAN. (*Daunted and conciliatory.*) I'm 10 afraid I appear intrusive. My name is Praed.[5] (*Vivie at once throws her books upon the chair, and gets out of the hammock.*) Oh, pray dont[6] let me disturb you.

VIVIE. (*Striding to the gate and opening it for him.*) Come in, Mr. Praed. (*He comes in.*) Glad to see you. (*She* 15 *proffers her hand and takes his with a resolute and hearty grip. She is an attractive specimen of the sensible, able, highly-educated young middle-class Englishwoman. Age 22. Prompt, strong, confident, self-possessed. Plain business-like dress, but not dowdy. She wears a chatelaine[7] at her belt,* 20 *with a fountain pen and a paper knife among its pendants.*)

---

[1] *Mrs. Warren's Profession* Shaw took the name of Mrs. Warren from Warren Street, near one of his early London homes in Fitzroy Square, Bloomsbury. Mrs. Warren's profession—prostitution—is never explicitly identified in the play.

[2] *Haslemere* Market town about 40 miles southwest of London.

[3] *lattice* Divided by strips into square or diamond-shaped sections.

[4] *paling* Fence.

[5] *Praed* Praed's name is perhaps an allusion to Winthrop Mackworth Praed (1802–39), a Cambridge-educated politician and poet. His portrait hung in the National Gallery in London. Praed St. is just north of Hyde Park in west-central London.

[6] *dont* Shaw often omits the apostrophe in contractions such as "dont," "Ive," and "doesnt." See above, "A Note on the Text."

[7] *chatelaine* Set of short chains attached to a woman's belt used for carrying small items (such as Vivie's fountain pen and paper knife).

PRAED. Very kind of you indeed, Miss Warren. (*She shuts the gate with a vigorous slam. He passes in to the middle of the garden, exercising his fingers, which are slightly numbed by her greeting.*) Has your mother arrived?

VIVIE. (*Quickly, evidently scenting aggression.*) Is she coming?

PRAED. (*Surprised.*) Didnt you expect us?

VIVIE. No.

PRAED. Now, goodness me, I hope Ive not mistaken the day. That would be just like me, you know. Your mother arranged that she was to come down from London and that I was to come over from Horsham[1] to be introduced to you.

VIVIE. (*Not at all pleased.*) Did she? Hm! My mother has rather a trick of taking me by surprise—to see how I behave myself when she's away, I suppose. I fancy I shall take my mother very much by surprise one of these days, if she makes arrangements that concern me without consulting me beforehand. She hasnt come.

PRAED. (*Embarrassed.*) I'm really very sorry.

VIVIE. (*Throwing off her displeasure.*) It's not your fault, Mr Praed, is it? And I'm very glad youve come. You are the only one of my mother's friends I have ever asked her to bring to see me.

PRAED. (*Relieved and delighted.*) Oh, now this is really very good of you, Miss Warren!

VIVIE. Will you come indoors; or would you rather sit out here and talk?

PRAED. It will be nicer out here, dont you think?

VIVIE. Then I'll go and get you a chair. (*She goes to the porch for a garden chair.*)

PRAED. (*Following her.*) Oh, pray, pray! Allow me. (*He lays hands on the chair.*)

VIVIE. (*Letting him take it.*) Take care of your fingers, theyre rather dodgy things, those chairs. (*She goes across to the chair with the books on it; pitches them into the hammock; and brings the chair forward with one swing.*)

PRAED. (*Who has just unfolded his chair.*) Oh, now do let me take that hard chair. I like hard chairs.

VIVIE. So do I. Sit down, Mr Praed. (*This invitation she gives with genial peremptoriness, his anxiety to please her*

clearly striking her as a sign of weakness of character on his part. But he does not immediately obey.*)

PRAED. By the way, though, hadnt we better go to the station to meet your mother?

VIVIE. (*Coolly.*) Why? She knows the way.

PRAED. (*Disconcerted.*) Er—I suppose she does. (*He sits down.*)

VIVIE. Do you know, you are just like what I expected. I hope you are disposed to be friends with me.

PRAED. (*Again beaming.*) Thank you, my d e a r[2] Miss Warren: thank you. Dear me! I'm so glad your mother hasnt spoilt you!

VIVIE. How?

PRAED. Well, in making you too conventional. You know, my dear Miss Warren, I am a born anarchist. I hate authority. It spoils the relations between parent and child: even between mother and daughter. Now I was always afraid that your mother would strain her authority to make you very conventional. It's such a relief to find that she hasnt.

VIVIE. Oh! have I been behaving unconventionally?

PRAED. Oh no: oh dear no. At least not conventionally unconventionally, you understand. (*She nods and sits down. He goes on, with a cordial outburst.*) But it was so charming of you to say that you were disposed to be friends with me! You modern young ladies are splendid: perfectly splendid!

VIVIE. (*Dubiously.*) Eh? (*Watching him with dawning disappointment as to the quality of his brains and character.*)

PRAED. When I was your age, young men and women were afraid of each other: there was no good fellowship. Nothing real. Only gallantry copied out of novels, and as vulgar and affected as it could be. Maidenly reserve! gentlemanly chivalry! always saying no when you meant yes! simple purgatory[3] for shy and sincere souls.

VIVIE. Yes, I imagine there must have been a frightful waste of time. Especially women's time.

PRAED. Oh, waste of life, waste of everything. But things are improving. Do you know, I have been in a positive state of excitement about meeting you ever

---

[1] *Horsham* Market town about 38 miles southwest of London (about 15 miles east of Haslemere).

[2] *d e a r* The spacing between letters is Shaw's way of indicating an emphasis on the word. See above, "A Note on the Text."

[3] *purgatory* In Catholic doctrine, a place for spiritual cleansing of the dead before entry to heaven.

since your magnificent achievements at Cambridge: a thing unheard of in my day. It was perfectly splendid, your tieing with the third wrangler.[1] Just the right place, you know. The first wrangler is always a dreamy, morbid fellow, in whom the thing is pushed to the length of a disease.

VIVIE.   It doesnt pay. I wouldnt do it again for the same money!

PRAED.   (*Aghast.*) The same money!

VIVIE.   I did it for £50.[2]

PRAED.   Fifty pounds!

VIVIE.   Yes. Fifty pounds. Perhaps you dont know how it was. Mrs Latham, my tutor at Newnham,[3] told my mother that I could distinguish myself in the mathematical tripos[4] if I went in for it in earnest. The papers were full just then of Phillipa Summers[5] beating the senior wrangler. You remember about it, of course.

PRAED.   (*Shakes his head energetically*) !!!

VIVIE.   Well anyhow she did: and nothing would please my mother but that I should do the same thing. I said flatly it was not worth my while to face the grind since I was not going in for teaching; but I offered to try for fourth wrangler or thereabouts for £50. She closed with me at that, after a little grumbling; and I was better than my bargain. But I wouldnt do it again for that. £200 would have been better near the mark.

PRAED.   (*Much damped.*) Lord bless me! Thats a very practical way of looking at it.

VIVIE.   Did you expect to find me an unpractical person?

PRAED.   But surely its practical to consider not only the work these honors cost, but also the culture they bring.

VIVIE.   Culture! My dear Mr Praed: do you know what the mathematical tripos means? It means grind, grind, grind for six to eight hours a day at mathematics, and nothing but mathematics. I'm supposed to know something about science; but I know nothing except the mathematics it involves. I can make calculations for engineers, electricians, insurance companies, and so on; but I know next to nothing about engineering or electricity or insurance. I dont even know arithmetic well. Outside mathematics, lawn-tennis, eating, sleeping, cycling, and walking, I'm a more ignorant barbarian than any woman could possibly be who hadnt gone in for the tripos.

PRAED.   (*Revolted.*) What a monstrous, wicked, rascally system! I knew it! I felt at once that it meant destroying all that makes womanhood beautiful.

VIVIE.   I dont object to it on that score in the least. I shall turn it to very good account, I assure you.

PRAED.   Pooh! in what way?

VIVIE.   I shall set up chambers[6] in the City, and work at actuarial calculations and conveyancing.[7] Under cover of that I shall do some law, with one eye on the Stock Exchange all the time. Ive come down here by myself to read law: not for a holiday, as my mother imagines. I hate holidays.

PRAED.   You make my blood run cold. Are you to have no romance, no beauty in your life?

VIVIE.   I dont care for either, I assure you.

PRAED.   You cant mean that.

VIVIE.   Oh yes I do. I like working and getting paid for it. When I'm tired of working, I like a comfortable chair, a cigar, a little whisky, and a novel with a good detective story in it.

PRAED.   (*Rising in a frenzy of repudiation.*) I dont believe it. I am an artist; and I cant believe it: I refuse to believe

---

[1]   *wrangler*   Wranglers were those who achieved a first-class honors degree in mathematics at Cambridge. Vivie had placed equal third among the wranglers in her year. The top student was designated senior wrangler.

[2]   *£50*   It would have taken most working-class women in England at this time two years to earn this amount.

[3]   *Newnham*   Newnham College was founded as a women's college of Cambridge University in 1871. The first Cambridge college for women, Girton, was founded in 1869. All other colleges of the University admitted men only.

[4]   *tripos*   The Tripos was (and is) the honors course at Cambridge, so-called because of the medieval tradition of the candidate sitting on a three-legged stool.

[5]   *Phillipa Summers*   Allusion to Philippa Fawcett, daughter of Henry Fawcett (1833–84), Professor of Political Economy at Cambridge and Liberal Member of Parliament, and Millicent Fawcett (1847–1929), leader of the women's suffrage movement and strong proponent of women's education at Cambridge. Philippa Fawcett gained the highest mark in the mathematical tripos in June 1890 (*The Times*, 9 June 1890), the first woman to do so.

[6]   *chambers*   Law office.

[7]   *conveyancing*   Vivie will specialize as an actuary (compiling and analyzing statistics to calculate insurance risks and premiums) and a conveyancer (transferring ownership of property).

it. It's only that you havnt discovered yet what a wonderful world art can open up to you.

VIVIE.   Yes I have. Last May I spent six weeks in London with Honoria Fraser. Mamma thought we were doing a round of sightseeing together; but I was really at Honoria's chambers in Chancery Lane[1] every day, working away at actuarial calculations for her, and helping her as well as a greenhorn could. In the evenings we smoked and talked, and never dreamt of going out except for exercise. And I never enjoyed myself more in my life. I cleared all my expenses, and got initiated into the business without a fee into the bargain.

PRAED.   But bless my heart and soul, Miss Warren, do you call that discovering art?

VIVIE.   Wait a bit. That wasnt the beginning. I went up to town on an invitation from some artistic people in Fitzjohn's Avenue:[2] one of the girls was a Newnham chum. They took me to the National Gallery —[3]

PRAED.   (Approving.) Ah!! (He sits down, much relieved.)

VIVIE.   (Continuing.) —to the Opera—

PRAED.   (Still more pleased.) Good!

VIVIE.   —and to a concert where the band played all the evening: Beethoven and Wagner[4] and so on. I wouldnt go through that experience again for anything you could offer me. I held out for civility's sake until the third day; and then I said, plump out, that I couldnt stand anymore of it, and went off to Chancery Lane. Now you know the sort of perfectly splendid modern young lady I am. How do you think I shall get on with my mother?

PRAED.   (Startled.) Well, I hope—er—

VIVIE.   It's not so much what you hope as what you believe, that I want to know.

PRAED.   Well, frankly, I am afraid your mother will be a little disappointed. Not from any shortcoming on your part, you know: I dont mean that. But you are so different from her ideal.

VIVIE.   Her what?!

PRAED.   Her ideal.

VIVIE.   Do you mean her ideal of ME?

PRAED.   Yes.

VIVIE.   What on Earth is it like?

PRAED.   Well, you must have observed, Miss Warren, that people who are dissatisfied with their own bringing-up generally think that the world would be all right if everybody were to be brought up quite differently. Now your mother's life has been—er—I suppose you know—

VIVIE.   Dont suppose anything, Mr Praed. I hardly know my mother. Since I was a child I have lived in England, at school or college, or with people paid to take charge of me. I have been boarded out all my life. My mother has lived in Brussels or Vienna and never let me go to her. I only see her when she visits England for a few days. I dont complain: it's been very pleasant; for people have been very good to me; and there has always been plenty of money to make things smooth. But dont imagine I know anything about my mother. I know far less than you do.

PRAED.   (Very ill at ease.) In that case—(He stops, quite at a loss. Then, with a forced attempt at gaiety.) But what nonsense we are talking! Of course you and your mother will get on capitally. (He rises, and looks abroad at the view.) What a charming little place you have here!

VIVIE.   (Unmoved.) Rather a violent change of subject, Mr Praed. Why wont my mother's life bear being talked about?

PRAED.   Oh, you really musnt say that. Isnt it natural that I should have a certain delicacy in talking to my old friend's daughter about her behind her back? You and she will have plenty of opportunity of talking about it when she comes.

VIVIE.   No: s h e wont talk about it either. (Rising.) However, I daresay you have good reasons for telling me nothing. Only, mind this, Mr Praed. I expect there will be a battle royal when my mother hears of my Chancery Lane project.

PRAED.   (Ruefully.) I'm afraid there will.

VIVIE.   Well, I shall win because I want nothing but my fare to London to start there to-morrow earning my

---

[1] *Chancery Lane*   Street in west-central London, the location of many legal offices and related businesses.

[2] *Fitzjohn's Avenue*   Street in the fashionable district of Hampstead, northwest of central London.

[3] *National Gallery*   Founded in 1824, the National Gallery moved to its current location on the north side of Trafalgar Square in 1838. The Gallery holds one of the world's finest collections of European paintings. Shaw was a frequent visitor.

[4] *Beethoven and Wagner*   German composers Ludwig van Beethoven (1770–1827) and Wilhelm Richard Wagner (1813–83) were Shaw's favorite composers.

own living by devilling[1] for Honoria. Besides, I have no mysteries to keep up; and it seems she has. I shall use that advantage over her if necessary.

PRAED. (*Greatly shocked.*) Oh no! No, pray. Youd not do such a thing.

VIVIE. Then tell me why not.

PRAED. I really cannot. I appeal to your good feeling. (*She smiles at his sentimentality.*) Besides, you may be too bold. Your mother is not to be trifled with when she's angry.

VIVIE. You can't frighten me, Mr Praed. In that month at Chancery Lane I had opportunities of taking the measure of one or two women v e r y like my mother. You may back me to win. But if I hit harder in my ignorance than I need, remember that it is you who refuse to enlighten me. Now, let us drop the subject. (*She takes her chair and replaces it near the hammock with the same vigorous swing as before.*)

PRAED. (*Taking a desperate resolution.*) One word, Miss Warren. I had better tell you. It's very difficult; but –

(*Mrs Warren and Sir George Crofts arrive at the gate. Mrs Warren is between* 40 *and* 50, *formerly pretty, showily dressed in a brilliant hat and a gay blouse fitting tightly over her bust and flanked by fashionable sleeves. Rather spoilt and domineering, and decidedly vulgar, but, on the whole, a genial and fairly presentable old blackguard[2] of a woman.*

Crofts is a tall powerfully-built man of about 50, *fashionably dressed in the style of a young man. Nasal voice, reedier than might be expected from his strong frame. Clean-shaven bulldog jaws, large flat ears, and thick neck: gentlemanly combination of the most brutal types of city man, sporting man, and man about town.*)

VIVIE. Here they are. (*Coming to them as they enter the garden.*) How do, mater?[3] Mr Praed's been here this half hour waiting for you.

MRS WARREN. Well, if youve been waiting, Praddy, it's your own fault: I thought youd have had the gumption[4] to know I was coming by the 3:10 train. Vivie: put your hat on, dear: youll get sunburnt. Oh, I forgot to introduce you. Sir George Crofts: my little Vivie.

(*Crofts advances to Vivie with his most courtly manner. She nods, but makes no motion to shake hands.*)

CROFTS. May I shake hands with a young lady whom I have known by reputation very long as the daughter of one of my oldest friends?

VIVIE. (*Who has been looking him up and down sharply.*) If you like. (*She takes his tenderly proffered hand and gives it a squeeze that makes him open his eyes; then turns away and says to her mother*) Will you come in, or shall I get a couple more chairs? (*She goes into the porch for the chairs.*)

MRS WARREN. Well, George, what do you think of her?

CROFTS. (*Ruefully.*) She has a powerful fist. Did you shake hands with her, Praed?

PRAED. Yes: it will pass off presently.

CROFTS. I hope so. (*Vivie reappears with two more chairs. He hurries to her assistance.*) Allow me.

MRS WARREN. (*Patronizingly.*) Let Sir George help you with the chairs, dear.

VIVIE. (*Pitching them into his arms.*) Here you are. (*She dusts her hands and turns to Mrs Warren.*) Youd like some tea, wouldnt you?

MRS WARREN. (*Sitting in Praed's chair and fanning herself.*) I'm dying for a drop to drink.

VIVIE. I'll see about it. (*She goes into the cottage.*)

(*Sir George has by this time managed to unfold a chair and plant it beside Mrs Warren, on her left. He throws the other on the grass and sits down, looking dejected and rather foolish, with the handle of his stick in his mouth. Praed, still very uneasy, fidgets about the garden on their right.*)

MRS WARREN. (*To Praed, looking at Crofts.*) Just look at him, Praddy: he looks cheerful, dont he? He's been worrying my life out these three years to have that little

---

[1] *devilling* Serve as a barrister's (i.e., lawyer's) junior assistant.

[2] *blackguard* Person characterized by dishonorable behavior; here used by Shaw more as a term of endearment. In the 1898 text Mrs. Warren is still "good-looking" (not just "formerly pretty"), and she is not described as "decidedly vulgar."

[3] *mater* Latin: mother. University slang.

[4] *gumption* Common sense.

girl of mine shewn to him; and now that Ive done it, he's quite out of countenance. (*Briskly.*) Come! Sit up, George; and take your stick out of your mouth. (*Crofts. sulkily obeys.*)

310 PRAED. I think, you know—if you dont mind my saying so—that we had better get out of the habit of thinking of her as a little girl. You see she has really distinguished herself; and I'm not sure, from what I have seen of her, that she is not older than any of us.

315 MRS WARREN. (*Greatly amused.*) Only listen to him, George! Older than any of us! Well, she h a s been stuffing you nicely with her importance.

PRAED. But young people are particularly sensitive about being treated in that way.

320 MRS WARREN. Yes; and young people have to get all that nonsense taken out of them, and a good deal more besides. Dont you interfere, Praddy: I know how to treat my own child as well as you do. (*Praed, with a grave shake of his head, walks up the garden with his hands*

325 *behind his back. Mrs Warren pretends to laugh, but looks after him with perceptible concern. Then she whispers to Crofts.*) Whats the matter with him? What does he take it like that for?

CROFTS. (*Morosely.*) Youre afraid of Praed.

330 MRS WARREN. What! Me! Afraid of dear old Praddy! Why, a fly wouldnt be afraid of him.

CROFTS. Youre afraid of him.

MRS WARREN. (*Angry.*) I'll trouble you to mind your own business, and not try any of your sulks on me. I'm

335 not afraid of y o u, anyhow. If you cant make yourself agreeable, youd better go home. (*She gets up, and, turning her back on him, finds herself face to face with Praed.*) Come, Praddy, I know it was only your tender-heartedness. Youre afraid I'll bully her.

340 PRAED. My dear Kitty: you think I'm offended. Dont imagine that: pray dont. But you know I often notice things that escape you; and though you never take my advice, you sometimes admit afterwards that you ought to have taken it.

345 MRS WARREN. Well, what do you notice now?

PRAED. Only that Vivie is a grown woman. Pray, Kitty, treat her with every respect.

MRS WARREN. (*With genuine amazement.*) Respect! Treat my own daughter with respect! What next, pray!

350 VIVIE. (*Appearing at the cottage door and calling to Mrs Warren.*) Mother: will you come to my room before tea?

MRS WARREN. Yes, dearie. (*She laughs indulgently at Praed's gravity, and pats him on the cheek as she passes him on her way to the porch.*) Dont be cross, Praddy. (*She*

355 *follows Vivie in to the cottage.*)

CROFTS. (*Furtively.*) I say, Praed.

PRAED. Yes.

CROFTS. I want to ask you a rather particular question.

PRAED. Certainly. (*He takes Mrs Warren's chair and sits*

360 *close to Crofts.*)

CROFTS. Thats right: they might hear us from the window. Look here: did Kitty ever tell you who that girl's father is?

PRAED. Never.

365 CROFTS. Have you any suspicion of who it might be?

PRAED. None.

CROFTS. (*Not believing him.*) I know, of course, that you perhaps might feel bound not to tell if she had said anything to you. But it's very awkward to be uncertain

370 about it now that we shall be meeting the girl every day. We wont exactly know how we ought to feel towards her.

PRAED. What difference can that make? We take her on her own merits. What does it matter who her father

375 was?

CROFTS. (*Suspiciously.*) Then you know who he was?

PRAED. (*With a touch of temper.*) I said no just now. Did you not hear me?

CROFTS. Look here, Praed. I ask you as a particular

380 favor. If you d o know (*Movement of protest from Praed.*)—I only say, if you know, you might at least set my mind at rest about her. The fact is, I feel attracted.

PRAED. (*Sternly.*) What do you mean?

CROFTS. Oh, dont be alarmed: it's quite an innocent

385 feeling. Thats what puzzles me about it. Why, for all I know *I* might be her father.

PRAED. You! Impossible!

CROFTS. (*Catching him up cunningly.*) You know for certain that I'm not?

390 PRAED. I know nothing about it, I tell you, anymore than you. But really, Crofts—oh no, it's out of the question. Theres not the least resemblance.

CROFTS.   As to that, theres no resemblance between her and her mother that I can see. I suppose she's not y o u r daughter, is she?

PRAED.   (*Rising indignantly.*) Really, Crofts—!

CROFTS.   No offence, Praed. Quite allowable as between two men of the world.

PRAED.   (*Recovering himself with an effort and speaking gently and gravely.*) Now listen to me, my dear Crofts. (*He sits down again.*) I have nothing to do with that side of Mrs Warren's life, and never had. She has never spoken to me about it; and of course I have never spoken to her about it. Your delicacy will tell you that a handsome woman needs some friends who are not—well, not on that footing with her. The effect of her own beauty would become a torment to her if she could not escape from it occasionally. You are probably on much more confidential terms with Kitty than I am. Surely you can ask her the question yourself.

CROFTS.   I h a v e asked her, often enough. But she's so determined to keep the child all to herself that she would deny that it ever had a father if she could. (*Rising.*) I'm thoroughly uncomfortable about it, Praed.

PRAED.   (*Rising also.*) Well, as you are, at all events, old enough to be her father, I dont mind agreeing that we both regard Miss Vivie in a parental way, as a young girl whom we are bound to protect and help. What do you say?

CROFTS.   (*Aggressively.*) I'm no older than you, if you come to that.

PRAED.   Yes you are, my dear fellow: you were born old. I was born a boy: Ive never been able to feel the assurance of a grown-up man in my life. (*He folds his chair and carries it to the porch.*)

MRS WARREN.   (*Calling from within the cottage.*) Prad-dee! George! Tea-ea-ea-ea!

CROFTS.   (*Hastily.*) She's calling us. (*He hurries in.*)

(*Praed shakes his head bodingly, and is following Crofts when he is hailed by a young gentleman who has just appeared on the common, and is making for the gate. He is pleasant, pretty, smartly dressed, cleverly good-for-nothing, not long turned 20, with a charming voice and agreeably disrespectful manners. He carries a light sporting magazine rifle.[1]*)

THE YOUNG GENTLEMAN.   Hallo! Praed!

PRAED.   Why, Frank Gardner! (*Frank comes in and shakes hands cordially.*) What on earth are you doing here?

FRANK.   Staying with my father.

PRAED.   The Roman father?[2]

FRANK.   He's rector here. I'm living with my people this autumn for the sake of economy. Things came to a crisis in July: the Roman father had to pay my debts. He's stony broke in consequence; and so am I. What are you up to in these parts? Do you know the people here?

PRAED.   Yes: I'm spending the day with a Miss Warren.

FRANK.   (*Enthusiastically.*) What! Do you know Vivie? Isnt she a jolly girl? I'm teaching her to shoot with this (*putting down the rifle*). I'm so glad she knows you: youre just the sort of fellow she ought to know. (*He smiles, and raises the charming voice almost to a singing tone as he exclaims.*) It's e v e r so jolly to find you here, Praed.

PRAED.   I'm an old friend of her mother. Mrs Warren brought me over to make her daughter's acquaintance.

FRANK.   The mother! Is s h e here?

PRAED.   Yes: inside, at tea.

MRS WARREN.   (*Calling from within.*) Prad-dee-ee-ee-eee! The tea-cake'll be cold.

PRAED.   (*Calling.*) Yes, Mrs Warren. In a moment. Ive just met a friend here.

MRS WARREN.   A what?

PRAED.   (*Louder.*) A friend.

MRS WARREN.   Bring him in.

PRAED.   (*To Frank.*) Will you accept the invitation?

FRANK.   (*Incredulous, but immensely amused.*) Is that Vivie's mother?

PRAED.   Yes.

FRANK.   By Jove! What a lark! Do you think she'll like me?

PRAED.   Ive no doubt youll make yourself popular as usual. Come in and try. (*Moving toward the house.*)

FRANK.   Stop a bit. (*Seriously.*) I want to take you into my confidence.

---

[1]   *magazine rifle*   Automatic rifle.

[2]   *Roman father*   This might be thought to suggest that Frank's father is a Catholic priest, but he is in fact a clergyman of the Church of England. It is more likely an ironic reference to supposed "Roman" qualities of strictness and integrity.

PRAED. Pray dont. It's only some fresh folly, like the barmaid at Redhill.[1]

FRANK. Its ever so much more serious than that. You say youve only just met Vivie for the first time?

PRAED. Yes.

FRANK. (*Rhapsodically.*) Then you can have no idea what a girl she is. Such character! Such sense! And her cleverness! Oh, my eye, Praed, but I can tell you she is clever! And—need I add?—she loves me.

CROFTS. (*Putting his head out of the window.*) I say, Praed: what are you about? Do come along. (*He disappears.*)

FRANK. Hallo! Sort of chap that would take a prize at a dog show, aint he? Who's he?

PRAED. Sir George Crofts, an old friend of Mrs Warren's. I think we had better come in.

(*On their way to the porch they are interrupted by a call from the gate. Turning, they see an elderly clergyman looking over it.*)

THE CLERGYMAN. (*Calling.*) Frank!

FRANK. Hallo! (*To Praed.*) The Roman father. (*To The Clergyman.*) Yes, gov'nor: all right: presently. (*To Praed.*) Look here, Praed: youd better go in to tea. I'll join you directly.

PRAED. Very good. (*He goes into the cottage.*)

(*The Clergyman remains outside the gate, with his hands on the top of it. The Rev. Samuel Gardner, a beneficed[2] clergyman of the Established Church,[3] is over 50. Externally he is pretentious, booming, noisy, important. Really he is that obsolescent social phenomenon the fool of the family dumped on the Church by his father the patron, clamorously asserting himself as father and clergyman without being able to command respect in either capacity.*)

REV. S. Well, sir. Who are your friends here, if I may ask?

FRANK. Oh, it's all right, gov'nor! Come in.

REV. S. No, sir; not until I know whose garden I am entering.

FRANK. It's all right. It's Miss Warren's.

REV. S. I have not seen her at church since she came.

FRANK. Of course not: she's a third wrangler. Ever so intellectual. Took a higher degree than you did; so why should she go to hear you preach?

REV. S. Dont be disrespectful, sir.

FRANK. Oh, it dont matter: nobody hears us. Come in. (*He opens the gate, unceremoniously pulling his father with it into the garden.*) I want to introduce you to her. Do you remember the advice you gave me last July, gov'nor?

REV. S. (*Severely.*) Yes. I advised you to conquer your idleness and flippancy, and to work your way into an honorable profession and live on it and not upon me.

FRANK. No: thats what you thought of afterwards. What you actually said was that since I had neither brains nor money, I'd better turn my good looks to account by marrying somebody with both. Well, look here, Miss Warren has brains: you cant deny that.

REV. S. Brains are not everything.

FRANK. No, of course not: theres the money—

REV. S. (*Interrupting him austerely.*) I was not thinking of money sir. I was speaking of higher things. Social position, for instance.

FRANK. I dont care a rap about that.

REV. S. But I do, sir.

FRANK. Well, nobody wants y o u to marry her. Anyhow, she has what amounts to a high Cambridge degree;[4] and she seems to have as much money as she wants.

REV. S. (*Sinking into a feeble vein of humor.*) I greatly doubt whether she has as much money as you will want.

FRANK. Oh, come: I havnt been so very extravagant. I live ever so quietly; I dont drink; I dont bet much; and I never go regularly on the razzle-dazzle as you did when you were my age.

REV. S. (*Booming hollowly.*) Silence, sir.

FRANK. Well, you told me yourself, when I was making ever such an ass of myself about the barmaid at Redhill,

---

[1] *Redhill* Small town about 25 miles south of London. Frank's "folly" with the barmaid is not further explained, but it hints at the nature of his pre-Vivie relationships.

[2] *beneficed* Supported by the church (with house and salary).

[3] *Established Church* Church of England.

[4] *Cambridge degree* Vivie has not actually been awarded a degree by Cambridge, only, as Frank says, "what amounts to one." Although women were allowed to attend lectures and sit examinations at Cambridge in the nineteenth century, they were not awarded degrees until 1921.

that you once offered a woman £50 for the letters you wrote to her when—

REV. S. (*Terrified*.) Sh-sh-sh, Frank, for Heaven's sake! (*He looks around apprehensively. Seeing no one within earshot he plucks up courage to boom again, but more subduedly.*) You are taking an ungentlemanly advantage of what I confided to you for your own good, to save you from an error you would have repented all your life long. Take warning by your father's follies, sir; and dont make them an excuse for your own.

FRANK. Did you ever hear the story of the Duke of Wellington and his letters?

REV. S. No, sir; and I dont want to hear it.

FRANK. The old Iron Duke didnt throw away £50: not he. He just wrote: "Dear Jenny: publish and be damned! Yours affectionately, Wellington." Thats what you should have done.[1]

REV. S. (*Piteously*.) Frank, my boy: when I wrote those letters I put myself into that woman's power. When I told you about them I put myself, to some extent, I am sorry to say, in your power. She refused my money with these words, which I shall never forget. "Knowledge is power," she said; "and I never sell power." Thats more than twenty years ago; and she has never made use of her power or caused me a moment's uneasiness. You are behaving worse to me than she did, Frank.

FRANK. Oh yes I dare say! Did you ever preach at her the way you preach at me every day?

REV. S. (*Wounded almost to tears.*) I leave you, sir. You are incorrigible. (*He turns toward the gate.*)

FRANK. (*Utterly unmoved.*) Tell them I shant be home to tea, will you, gov'nor, like a good fellow? (*He moves towards the cottage door and is met by Praed and Vivie coming out.*)

VIVIE. (*To Frank.*) Is that your father, Frank? I do so want to meet him.

FRANK. Certainly. (*Calling after his father.*) Gov'nor. Youre wanted. (*The parson turns at the gate, fumbling nervously at his hat. Praed crosses the garden to the opposite side, beaming in anticipation of civilities.*) My father: Miss Warren.

VIVIE. (*Going to The Clergyman. and shaking his hand.*) Very glad to see you here, Mr Gardner. (*Calling to the cottage.*) Mother: come along: youre wanted.

(*Mrs Warren appears on the threshold, and is immediately transfixed recognizing The Clergyman.*)

VIVIE. (*Continuing.*) Let me introduce —

MRS WARREN. (*Swooping on the Reverend Samuel.*) Why, it's Sam Gardner, gone into the church! Well, I never! Dont you know us, Sam? This is George Crofts, as large as life and twice as natural. Dont you remember me?

REV. S. (*Very red.*) I really—er—

MRS WARREN. Of course you do. Why, I have a whole album of your letters still: I came across them only the other day.

REV. S. (*Miserably confused.*) Miss Vavasour,[2] I believe.

MRS WARREN. (*Correcting him quickly in a loud whisper.*) Tch! Nonsense! Mrs Warren: Don't you see my daughter there?

ACT 2

(*Inside the cottage after nightfall. Looking eastward from within instead of westward from without, the latticed window, with its curtains drawn, is now seen in the middle of the front wall of the cottage, with the porch door to the left of it. In the left-hand side wall is the door leading to the kitchen. Farther back against the same wall is a dresser with a candle and matches on it, and Frank's rifle standing beside them, with the barrel resting in the plate-rack. In the centre a table stands with a lighted lamp on it. Vivie's books and writing materials are on a table to the right of the window, against the wall. The fireplace is on the right with a settle:[3] there is no fire. Two of the chairs are set right and left of the table.*)

---

1. *Thats what you should have done* Arthur Wellesley, 1st Duke of Wellington (1769–1852), defeated Napoleon at Waterloo in 1815. He later served as Prime Minister, 1828–30. His comment "Publish and be damned" was in response to a blackmail letter concerning a London courtesan well-known to Wellington. Wellington's iron-fisted discipline in military matters caused him to be known as the Iron Duke.

2. *Miss Vavasour* Name used by Mrs Warren at the time the Reverend Samuel knew her. A vavasour was a medieval vassal owing allegiance to a great lord.

3. *settle* A wooden bench with high back and arms, and a box or draw under the seat.

The cottage door opens, shewing a fine starlit night without; and Mrs Warren, her shoulders wrapped in a shawl borrowed from Vivie, enters, followed by Frank, who throws his cap on the window seat. She has had enough of walking, and gives a gasp of relief as she unpins her hat; takes it off; sticks the pin through the crown; and puts it on the table.)

MRS WARREN.   O Lord! I dont know which is the worst of the country, the walking or the sitting at home with nothing to do. I could do with a whisky and soda now very well, if only they had such a thing in this place.

⁵ FRANK.   Perhaps Vivie's got some.

MRS WARREN.   Nonsense! What would a young girl like her be doing with such things! Never mind: it dont matter. I wonder how she passes her time here! I'd a good deal rather be in Vienna.

¹⁰ FRANK.   Let me take you there. (*He helps her to take off her shawl, gallantly giving her shoulders a very perceptible squeeze¹ as he does so.*)

MRS WARREN.   Ah! would you? I'm beginning to think youre a chip of the old block.²

¹⁵ FRANK.   Like the gov'nor, eh? (*He hangs the shawl on the nearest chair and sits down.*)

MRS WARREN.   Never you mind. What do you know about such things? Youre only a boy. (*She goes to the hearth, to be farther from temptation.*)

²⁰ FRANK.   Do come to Vienna with me. It'd be ever such larks.

MRS WARREN.   No, thank you. Vienna is no place for you—at least not until youre a little older. (*She nods at him to emphasize this piece of advice. He makes a mock-²⁵ piteous face, belied by his laughing eyes. She looks at him; then comes back to him.*) Now, look here, little boy. (*Taking his face in her hands and turning it up to her.*) I know you through and through by your likeness to your father, better than you know yourself. Dont you go ³⁰ taking any silly ideas into your head about me. Do you hear?

FRANK.   (*Gallantly wooing her with his voice.*) Cant help it, my dear Mrs Warren: it runs in the family.

(*She pretends to box his ears; then looks at the pretty laughing upturned face for a moment, tempted. At last she kisses him, and immediately turns away, out of patience with herself.*)

³⁵ MRS WARREN.   There! I shouldnt have done that. I a m wicked. Never mind, my dear: it's only a motherly kiss. Go and make love to Vivie.

FRANK.   So I have.

MRS WARREN.   (*Turning on him with a sharp note of ⁴⁰ alarm in her voice.*) What!

FRANK.   Vivie and I are ever such chums.

MRS WARREN.   What do you mean? Now see here: I wont have any young scamp tampering with my little girl. Do you hear? I wont have it.

⁴⁵ FRANK.   (*Quite unabashed.*) My dear Mrs Warren: dont you be alarmed. My intentions are honorable: ever so honorable; and your little girl is jolly well able to take care of herself. She dont need looking after half so much as her mother. She aint so handsome, you know.

⁵⁰ MRS WARREN.   (*Taken aback by his assurance.*) Well, you have got a nice healthy two inches thick of cheek all over you. I dont know where you got it. Not from your father, anyhow.

CROFTS.   (*In the garden.*) The gipsies, I suppose?

⁵⁵ REV. S.   (*Replying.*) The broomsquires³ are far worse.

MRS WARREN.   (*To Frank.*) Sh-sh! Remember! youve had your warning.

(*Crofts and the Reverend Samuel come in from the garden, the Clergyman continuing his conversation as he enters.*)

REV. S.   The perjury at the Winchester assizes is deplorable.⁴

⁶⁰ MRS WARREN.   Well? what became of you two? And wheres Praddy and Vivie?

CROFTS.   (*Putting his hat on the settle and his stick in the chimney corner.*) They went up the hill. We went to the

---

¹ *squeeze*   In the 1898 text Frank's "*very perceptible squeeze*" is "*the most delicate possible little caress.*"

² *chip of the old block*   "Chip *off* the old block" is relatively recent usage. "Chip *of* the old block" was standard in Shaw's time.

³ *broomsquires*   Itinerant makers and vendors of brooms made from a bunch of heather or twigs.

⁴ *Winchester assizes*   Courts of law held periodically in Winchester, as in other counties in England, for the administering of civil and criminal justice. Shaw may have had a particular case in mind, but it has not been traced. The line does not appear in the 1898 text.

village. I wanted a drink. (*He sits down on the settle, putting his legs up along the seat.*)

MRS WARREN.   We she oughtnt go off like that without telling me. (*To Frank.*) Get your father a chair, Frank: where are your manners? (*Frank springs up and gracefully offers his father his chair; then takes another from the wall and sits down at the table, in the middle, with his father on his right and Mrs Warren on his left.*) George: where are you going to stay tonight? You cant stay here. And whats Praddy going to do?

CROFTS.   Gardner'll put me up.

MRS WARREN.   Oh, no doubt youve taken care of yourself! But what about Praddy?

CROFTS.   Dont know. I suppose he can sleep at the inn.

MRS WARREN.   Havnt you room for him, Sam?

REV. S.   Well—er—you see, as rector here, I am not free to do as I like. Er—what is Mr Praed's social position?

MRS WARREN.   Oh, he's all right: he's an architect. What an old stick-in-the-mud you are, Sam!

FRANK.   Yes, it's all right, gov'nor. He built that place down in Wales for the Duke. Caernarvon Castle they call it. You must have heard of it. (*He winks with lightning smartness at Mrs Warren, and regards his father blandly.*)

REV. S.   Oh, in that case, of course we shall only be too happy. I suppose he knows the Duke personally.

FRANK.   Oh, ever so intimately! We can stick him in Georgina's old room.

MRS WARREN.   Well, thats settled. Now if only those two would only come in and let us have supper. Theyve no right to stay out after dark like this.

CROFTS.   (*Aggressively.*) What harm are they doing you?

MRS WARREN.   Well, harm or not, I dont like it.

FRANK.   Better not wait for them, Mrs Warren. Praed will stay out as long as possible. He has never known before what it is to stray over the heath on a summer night with my Vivie.

CROFTS.   (*Sitting up in some consternation.*) I say, you know! Come!

REV. S.   (*Rising, startled out of his professional manner into real force and sincerity.*) Frank, once for all, it's out of the question. Mrs Warren will tell you that it's not to be thought of.

CROFTS.   Of course not.

FRANK.   (*With enchanting placidity.*) Is that so, Mrs Warren?

MRS WARREN.   (*Reflectively.*) Well, Sam, I dont know. If the girl wants to get married, no good can come of keeping her unmarried.

REV. S.   (*Astounded.*) But married to h i m!—your daughter to my son! Only think: it's impossible.

CROFTS.   Of course it's impossible. Dont be a fool, Kitty.

MRS WARREN.   (*Nettled.*) Why not? Isnt my daughter good enough for your son?

REV. S.   But surely, my dear Mrs Warren, you know the reasons—

MRS WARREN.   (*Defiantly.*) I know no reasons. If you know any, you can tell them to the lad, or to the girl, or to your congregation, if you like.

REV. S.   (*Collapsing helplessly into his chair.*) You know very well that I couldnt tell anyone the reasons. But my boy will believe me when I tell him there a r e reasons.

FRANK.   Quite right, Dad: he will. But has your boy's conduct ever been influenced by your reasons?

CROFTS.   You cant marry her; and thats all about it. (*He gets up and stands on the hearth, with his back to the fireplace, frowning determinedly.*)

MRS WARREN.   (*Turning on him sharply.*) What have you got to do with it, pray?

FRANK.   (*With his prettiest lyrical cadence.*) Precisely what I was going to ask myself, in my own graceful fashion.

CROFTS.   (*To Mrs Warren.*) I suppose you dont want to marry the girl to a man younger than herself and without either a profession or twopence to keep her on. Ask Sam, if you dont believe me. (*To the parson.*) How much more money are you going to give him?

REV. S.   Not another penny. He has had his patrimony and he spent the last of it in July. (*Mrs Warren's face falls.*)

CROFTS.   (*Watching her.*) There! I told you. (*He resumes his place on the settle and puts his legs on the seat again, as if the matter were finally disposed of.*)

FRANK.   (*Plaintively.*) This is ever so mercenary. Do you suppose Miss Warren's going to marry for money? If we love one another—

MRS WARREN.   Thank you. Your love's a pretty cheap commodity, my lad. If you have no means of keeping a wife, that settles it: you cant have Vivie.

FRANK. (*Much amused.*) What do y o u say, gov'nor, eh?

REV. S. I agree with Mrs Warren.

155 FRANK. And good old Crofts has already expressed his opinion.

CROFTS. (*Turning angrily on his elbow.*) Look here: I want none of y o u r cheek.

FRANK. (*Pointedly.*) I'm e v e r so sorry to surprise you, Crofts, but you allowed yourself the liberty of speaking to me like a father a moment ago. One father is enough, thank you.

CROFTS. (*Contemptuously.*) Yah! (*He turns away again.*)

FRANK. (*Rising.*) Mrs Warren: I cannot give my Vivie 165 up, even for your sake.

MRS WARREN. (*Muttering.*) Young scamp!

FRANK. (*Continuing.*) And as you no doubt intend to hold out other prospects to her, I shall lose no time in placing my case before her. (*They stare at him, and he 170 begins to declaim gracefully*)

He either fears his fate too much,
Or his deserts are small,
That dares not put it to the touch
To gain or lose it all.[1]

(*The cottage door opens whilst he is reciting; and Vivie and Praed come in. He breaks off. Praed puts his hat on the dresser. There is an immediate improvement in the company's behavior. Crofts takes down his legs from the settle and pulls himself together as Praed joins him at the fireplace. Mrs Warren loses her ease of manner and takes refuge in querulousness.*)[2]

175 MRS WARREN. Wherever have you been, Vivie?

VIVIE. (*Taking off her hat and throwing it carelessly on the table.*) On the hill.

MRS WARREN. Well, you shouldnt go off like that without letting me know. How could I tell what had 180 become of you? And night coming on too!

VIVIE. (*Going to the door of the kitchen and opening it, ignoring her mother.*) Now, about supper? (*All rise except Mrs Warren.*) We shall be rather crowded in here, I'm afraid.

185 MRS WARREN. Did you hear what I said, Vivie?

VIVIE. (*Quietly.*) Yes, mother. (*Reverting to the supper difficulty.*) How many are we? (*Counting.*) One, two, three, four, five, six. Well, two will have to wait until the rest are done: Mrs Alison has only plates and knives 190 for four.

PRAED. Oh, it doesnt matter about me. I—

VIVIE. You have had a long walk and are hungry, Mr Praed: you shall have your supper at once. I can wait myself. I want one person to wait with me. Frank: are 195 you hungry?

FRANK. Not the least in the world. Completely off my peck,[3] in fact.

MRS WARREN. (*To Crofts.*) Neither are you, George. You can wait.

200 CROFTS. Oh, hang it, Ive eaten nothing since tea-time. Cant Sam do it?

FRANK. Would you starve my poor father?

REV. S. (*Testily.*) Allow me to speak for myself, sir. I am perfectly willing to wait.

205 VIVIE. (*Decisively.*) Theres no need. Only two are wanted. (*She opens the door of the kitchen.*) Will you take my mother in, Mr Gardner. (*The parson takes Mrs Warren; and they pass into the kitchen. Praed and Crofts follow. All except Praed clearly disapprove of the 210 arrangement, but do not know how to resist it. Vivie stands at the door looking in at them.*) Can you squeeze past to that corner, Mr Praed: it's a rather tight fit. Take care of your coat against the white-wash: thats right. Now, are you all comfortable?

215 PRAED. (*Within.*) Quite, thank you.

MRS WARREN. (*Within.*) Leave the door open, dearie. (*Vivie frowns; but Frank checks her with a gesture, and steals to the cottage door, which he softly sets wide open.*) Oh Lor, what a draught! Youd better shut it, dear.

(*Vivie shuts it with a slam,[4] and then, noting with disgust that her mother's hat and shawl are lying about, takes them tidily to the window seat, whilst Frank noiselessly shuts the cottage door.*)

---

[1] *He either ... all* From "My Dear and Only Love," a poem by the Scottish soldier and writer James Graham, Marquess of Montrose (1612–50). Frank slightly misquotes. "He either fears his fate too much, / Or his deserts are small, / That puts it not unto the touch / To win or lose it all."

[2] *querulousness* Petulance.

[3] *off my peck* Not hungry.

[4] *with a slam* In the 1898 text Vivie merely shuts the door "*promptly.*"

FRANK. (*Exulting.*) Aha! Got rid of em. Well, Vivvums: what do you think of my governor?

VIVIE. (*Preoccupied and serious.*) Ive hardly spoken to him. He doesnt strike me as being a particularly able person.

FRANK. Well, you know, the old man is not altogether such a fool as he looks. You see, he was shoved into the church rather; and in trying to live up to it he makes a much bigger ass of himself than he really is. I dont dislike him as much as you might expect. He means well. How do you think youll get on with him?

VIVIE. (*Rather grimly.*) I dont think my future life will be much concerned with him, or with any of that old circle of my mother's, except perhaps Praed. (*She sits down on the settle.*) What do you think of my mother?

FRANK. Really and truly?

VIVIE. Yes, really and truly.

FRANK. Well, she's ever so jolly. But she's rather a caution,[1] isnt she? And Crofts! oh, my eye, Crofts! (*He sits beside her.*)

VIVIE. What a lot, Frank!

FRANK. What a crew!

VIVIE. (*With intense contempt for them.*) If I thought that *I* was like that—that I was going to be a waster, shifting along from one meal to another with no purpose, and no character, and no grit in me, I'd open an artery and bleed to death without one moment's hesitation.

FRANK. Oh no, you wouldnt. Why should they take any grind when they can afford not to? I wish I had their luck. No: what I object to is their form. It isnt the thing: it's slovenly, ever so slovenly.

VIVIE. Do you think your form will be any better when youre as old as Crofts, if you dont work?

FRANK. Of course I do. Ever so much better. Vivvums musnt lecture: her little boy is incorrigible. (*He attempts to take her face caressingly in his hands.*)

VIVIE. (*Striking his hands down sharply.*) Off with you: Vivvums is not in a humor for petting her little boy this evening. (*She rises and comes forward to the other side of the room.*)

FRANK. (*Following her.*) How unkind!

VIVIE. (*Stamping at him.*) Be serious. I'm serious.

FRANK. Good. Let us talk learnedly. Miss Warren: do you know that all the most advanced thinkers are agreed that half the diseases of modern civilization are due to starvation of the affections in the young. Now, I—

VIVIE. (*Cutting him short.*) You are very tiresome. (*She opens the inner door.*) Have you room for Frank there? He's complaining of starvation.

MRS WARREN. (*Within.*) Of course there is (*Clatter of knives and glasses as she moves the things on the table.*) Here! theres room now beside me. Come along, Mr Frank.

FRANK. Her little boy will be ever so even with his Vivvums for this. (*He passes into the kitchen.*)

MRS WARREN. (*Within.*) Here, Vivie: come on you too, child. You must be famished. (*She enters, followed by Crofts, who holds the door open for Vivie with marked deference. She goes out without looking at him; and shuts the door after her.*) Why, George, you cant be done: youve eaten nothing. Is there anything wrong with you?

CROFTS. Oh, all I wanted was a drink. (*He thrusts his hands in his pockets, and begins prowling around the room, restless and sulky.*)

MRS WARREN. Well, I like enough to eat. But a little of that cold beef and cheese and lettuce goes a long way. (*With a sigh of only half repletion she sits down lazily on the settle.*)

CROFTS. What do you go encouraging that young pup for?

MRS WARREN. (*On the alert at once.*) Now see here, George: what are you up to about that girl? Ive been watching your way of looking at her. Remember: I know you and what your looks mean.

CROFTS. Theres no harm in looking at her, is there?

MRS WARREN. I'd put you out and pack you back to London pretty soon if I saw any of your nonsense. My girl's little finger is more to me than any of your body and soul. (*Crofts receives this with a sneering grin. Mrs Warren, flushing a little at her failure to impose on him in the character of a theatrically devoted mother, adds in a lower key.*) Make your mind easy: the young pup has no more chance than you have.

CROFTS. Maynt a man take an interest in a girl?

MRS WARREN. Not a man like you.

CROFTS. How old is she?

MRS WARREN. Never you mind how old she is.

CROFTS. Why do you make such a secret of it?

MRS WARREN. Because I choose.

---

[1] *a caution* Eccentric person; a "bit of a character."

CROFTS.   Well, I'm not fifty yet; and my property is as
good as ever it was—

MRS WARREN.   (*Interrupting him.*) Yes, because youre as
stingy as youre vicious.

CROFTS.   (*Continuing.*) And a baronet[1] isnt to be picked
up every day. No other man in my position would put
up with you for a mother-in-law. Why shouldnt she
marry me?

MRS WARREN.   You!

CROFTS.   We three could live together quite comfortably: I'd die before her and leave her a bouncing widow
with plenty of money. Why not? It's been growing in
my mind all the time Ive been walking with that fool
inside there.

MRS WARREN.   (*Revolted.*) Yes: it's the sort of thing that
w o u l d grow in your mind.

(*He halts in his prowling; and the two look at one another,
she steadfastly, with a sort of awe behind her contemptuous
disgust: he stealthily, with a carnal gleam in his eye and a
loose grin.*)

CROFTS.   (*Suddenly becoming anxious and urgent as he sees
no sign of sympathy in her.*) Look here, Kitty: youre a
sensible woman: you neednt put on any moral airs. I'll
ask no more questions; and you need answer none. I'll
settle the whole property on her; and if you want a
cheque for yourself on the wedding day, you can name
any figure you like—in reason.

MRS WARREN.   So it's come to that with you, George,
like all the other worn-out old creatures!

CROFTS.   (*Savagely.*) Damn you!

(*Before she can retort[2] the door of the kitchen is opened;
and the voices of the others are heard returning. Crofts,
unable to recover his presence of mind, hurries out of the
cottage. The Clergyman appears at the kitchen door.*)

REV. S.   (*Looking around.*) Where is Sir George?

MRS WARREN. Gone out to have a pipe. (*The
Clergyman takes his hat from the table, and joins Mrs
Warren at the fireside. Meanwhile Vivie comes in, followed
by Frank, who collapses into the nearest chair with an air
of extreme exhaustion. Mrs Warren looks round at Vivie
and says, with her affectation of maternal patronage ever
more forced than usual.*) Well, dearie, have you had a
good supper?

VIVIE.   You know what Mrs Alison's suppers are. (*She
turns to Frank and pets him.*) Poor Frank! was all the beef
gone? did it get nothing but bread and cheese and
ginger beer? (*Seriously, as if she had done quite enough
trifling for one evening.*) Her butter is really awful. I must
get some down from the stores.

FRANK.   Do, in Heaven's name!

(*Vivie goes to the writing-table and makes a memorandum
to order the butter. Praed comes in from the kitchen,
putting up his handkerchief, which he has been using as a
napkin.*)

REV. S.   Frank, my boy: it is time for us to be thinking of
home. Your mother does not know yet that we have
visitors.

PRAED.   I'm afraid we're giving trouble.

FRANK.   (*Rising.*) Not the least in the world: my mother
will be delighted to see you. She's a genuinely
intellectual artistic woman; and she sees nobody here
from one year's end to another except the gov'nor; so
you can imagine how jolly dull it pans out for her. (*To
his father.*) Y o u r e not intellectual or artistic: are you
pater? So take Praed home at once; and I'll stay here and
entertain Mrs Warren. Youll pick up Crofts in the
garden. He'll be excellent company for the bull-pup.[3]

PRAED.   (*Taking his hat from the dresser, and coming close
to Frank.*) Come with us, Frank. Mrs Warren has not
seen Miss Vivie for a long time; and we have prevented
them from having a moment together yet.

FRANK.   (*Quite softened and looking at Praed with
romantic admiration.*) Of course. I forgot. Ever so
thanks for reminding me. Perfect gentleman, Praddy.
Always were. My ideal through life. (*He rises to go, but
pauses a moment between the two older men, and puts his
hand on Praed's shoulder.*) Ah, if you had only been my

---

1   *baronet* The lowest of Britain's hereditary titles, established in 1611. It confers a knighthood, however: hence, *Sir* George Crofts. His wife would be titled *Lady* Crofts.

2   *Before she can retort* In the 1898 text Mrs Warren is given more time: "*She rises and turns fiercely on him.*"

3   *bull-pup* Sarcastic reference to Praed. He's not a bull-*dog*.

father instead of this unworthy old man! (*He puts his other hand on his father's shoulder.*)

REV. S.   (*Blustering.*) Silence, sir, silence: you are profane.

MRS WARREN.   (*Laughing heartily.*) You should keep him in better order, Sam. Goodnight. Here: take George his hat and stick with my compliments.

REV. S.   (*Taking them.*) Goodnight. (*They shake hands. As he passes Vivie he shakes hands with her also and bids her goodnight. Then, in booming command, to Frank.*) Come along, sir, at once. (*He goes out.*)

MRS WARREN.   Byebye, Praddy.

PRAED.   Byebye, Kitty.

(*They shake hands affectionately and go out together, she accompanying him to the garden gate.*)

FRANK.   (*To Vivie.*) Kissums?

VIVIE.   (*Fiercely.*) No. I hate you.[1] (*She takes a couple of books and some paper from the writing-table, and sits down with them at the middle table, at the end next the fireplace.*)

FRANK.   (*Grimacing.*) Sorry. (*He goes for his cap and rifle. Mrs Warren returns. He takes her hand.*) Goodnight, d e a r Mrs Warren. (*He kisses her hand.[2] She snatches it away, her lips tightening, and looks more than half disposed to box his ears. He laughs mischievously and runs off, clapping-to[3] the door behind him.*)

MRS WARREN.   (*Resigning herself to an evening of boredom now that the men are gone.*) Did you ever in your life hear anyone rattle on so? Isnt he a tease? (*She sits at the table.*) Now that I think of it, dearie, dont you go encouraging him. I'm sure he's a regular good-for-nothing.

VIVIE.   (*Rising to fetch more books.*) I'm afraid so. Poor Frank! I shall have to get rid of him; but I shall feel sorry for him, though he's not worth it. That man Crofts does not seem to me to be good for much either: is he? (*She throws the books on the table rather roughly.*)

MRS WARREN.   (*Galled by Vivie's indifference.*)[4] What do you know of men, child, to talk that way about them? Youll have to make up your mind to see a good deal of Sir George Crofts, as he's a friend of mine.

VIVIE.   (*Quite unmoved.*) Why? (*She sits down and opens a book.*) Do you expect that we shall be much together? You and I, I mean?

MRS WARREN.   (*Staring at her.*) Of course: until youre married. Youre not going back to college again.

VIVIE.   Do you think my way of life would suit you? I doubt it.

MRS WARREN.   Y o u r way of life! What do you mean?

VIVIE.   (*Cutting a page[5] of her book with the paper knife on her chatelaine.*) Has it really never occurred to you, mother, that I have a way of life like other people?

MRS WARREN.   What nonsense is this youre trying to talk? Do you want to shew your independence, now that youre a great little person at school? Dont be a fool, child.

VIVIE.   (*Indulgently.*) Thats all you have to say on the subject, is it, mother?

MRS WARREN.   (*Puzzled, then angry.*) Dont you keep on asking me questions like that. (*Violently.*) Hold your tongue. (*Vivie works on, losing no time, and saying nothing.*) You and your way of life, indeed! What next? (*She looks at Vivie again. No reply.*) Your way of life will be what I please, so it will. (*Another pause.*) Ive been noticing these airs in you ever since you got that tripos or whatever you call it. If you think I'm going to put up with them youre mistaken; and the sooner you find it out, the better. (*Muttering.*) All I have to say on the subject, indeed! (*Again rising her voice angrily.*) Do you know who youre speaking to, Miss?

VIVIE.   (*Looking across at her without raising her head from her book.*) No. Who are you? What are you?

MRS WARREN.   (*Rising breathless.*) You young imp!

VIVIE.   Everybody knows my reputation, my social standing, and the profession I intend to pursue. I know nothing about you. What is that way of life which you invite me to share with you and Sir George Crofts, pray?

MRS WARREN.   Take care. I shall do something I'll be sorry for after, and you too.

---

[1] *I hate you* In the 1898 text Frank "*silently begs a kiss*," and receives in return from Vivie "*a stern glance*," rather than her fierce comment.

[2] *kisses her hand* In the 1898 text Frank "*squeezes*" Mrs. Warren's hand.

[3] *clapping-to* Slamming.

---

[4] *Vivie's indifference* In the 1898 text Mrs. Warren is galled by Vivie's "*cool tone*," rather than her indifference.

[5] *Cutting a page* Books were sold with their pages uncut, that is, as folded by the binder.

VIVIE. (*Putting aside her books with cool decision.*) Well, let us drop the subject until you are better able to face it. (*Looking critically at her mother.*) You want some good walks and a little lawn tennis to set you up. You are shockingly out of condition: you were not able to manage twenty yards uphill today without stopping to pant; and your wrists are mere rolls of fat. Look at mine. (*She holds out her wrists.*)

MRS WARREN. (*After looking at her helplessly, begins to whimper.*) Vivie—

VIVIE. (*Springing up sharply.*) Now pray dont begin to cry. Anything but that. I really cannot stand whimpering. I will go out of the room if you do.

MRS WARREN. (*Piteously.*) Oh, my darling, how can you be so hard on me? Have I no rights over you as your mother?

VIVIE. A r e you my mother?

MRS WARREN. (*Appalled.*) A m I your mother! Oh, Vivie!

VIVIE. Then where are our relatives? my father? our family friends? You claim the rights of a mother: the right to call me fool and child; to speak to me as no woman in authority over me at college dare speak to me; to dictate my way of life; and to force on me the acquaintance of a brute whom any one can see to be the most vicious sort of London man about town. Before I give myself the trouble to resist such claims, I may as well find out whether they have any real existence.

MRS WARREN. (*Distracted, throwing herself on her knees.*) Oh no, no. Stop, stop. I a m your mother, I swear it. Oh, you cant mean to turn on me—my own child! it's not natural. You believe me, dont you? Say you believe me.

VIVIE. Who was my father?

MRS WARREN. You dont know what youre asking. I cant tell you.

VIVIE. (*Determinedly.*) Oh yes you can, if you like. I have a right to know; and you know very well that I have that right. You can refuse to tell me, if you please; but if you do you will see the last of me tomorrow morning.

MRS WARREN. Oh, it's too horrible to hear you talk like that. You wouldnt—you c o u l d n t leave me.

VIVIE. (*Ruthlessly.*) Yes, without a moment's hesitation, if you trifle with me about this. (*Shivering with disgust.*)

How can I feel sure that I may not have the contaminated blood of that brutal waster in my veins?

MRS WARREN. No, no. On my oath it's not he, nor any of the rest that you have ever met. I'm certain of that, at least.

(*Vivie's eyes fasten sternly on her mother as the significance of this flashes on her.*)

VIVIE. (*Slowly.*) You are certain of that, at l e a s t. Ah! You mean that that is all you are certain of. (*Thoughtfully.*) I see. (*Mrs Warren buries her face in her hands.*) Dont do that, mother: you know you dont feel it a bit. (*Mrs Warren takes down her hands and looks up deplorably at Vivie, who takes out her watch and says*) Well, that is enough for tonight. At what hour would you like breakfast? Is half-past eight too early for you?

MRS WARREN. (*Wildly.*) My God, what sort of woman are you?

VIVIE. (*Coolly.*) The sort the world is mostly made of, I should hope. Otherwise I dont understand how it gets its business done. Come (*taking her mother by the wrist, and pulling her up pretty resolutely*): pull yourself together. Thats right.

MRS WARREN. (*Querulously.*) Youre very rough with me, Vivie.

VIVIE. Nonsense. What about bed? It's past ten.

MRS WARREN. (*Passionately.*) Whats the use of my going to bed? Do you think I could sleep?

VIVIE. Why not? I shall.

MRS WARREN. You! youve no heart. (*She suddenly breaks out vehemently in her natural tongue—the dialect of a woman of the people—with all her affectations of maternal authority and conventional manners gone, and an overwhelming inspiration of true conviction and scorn in her.*) Oh, I wont bear it: I wont put up with the injustice of it. What right have you to set yourself up above m e like this? You boast of what you are to me—to me, who gave you the chance of being what you are. What chance had I? Shame on you for a bad daughter and a stuck-up prude!

VIVIE. (*Sitting down with a shrug,[1] no longer confident; for her replies, which have sounded sensible and strong to her*)

---

[1] *with a shrug* In the 1898 text Vivie is still "*cool and determined*" at this point.

so far, now begin to ring rather woodenly and even priggishly against the new tone of her mother.) Dont think for a moment I set myself up against you in any way. You attacked me with the conventional authority of a mother: I defended myself with the conventional superiority of a respectable woman. Frankly, I am not going to stand any of your nonsense; and when you drop it I shall not expect you to stand any of mine. I shall always respect your right to your own opinions and your own way of life.

MRS WARREN. My own opinions and my own way of life! Listen to her talking! Do you think I was brought up like you? able to pick and choose my own way of life? Do you think I did what I did because I liked it, or thought it right, or wouldnt rather have gone to college and been a lady if I'd had the chance?

VIVIE. Everybody has some choice, mother. The poorest girl alive may not be able to choose between being Queen of England or Principal of Newnham; but she can choose between ragpicking and flowerselling, according to her taste. People are always blaming their circumstances for what they are. I dont believe in circumstances. The people who get on this world are the people who get up and look for the circumstances they want, and, if they cant find them, make them.

MRS WARREN. Oh, it's easy to talk, very easy, isnt it? Here! would you like to know what m y circumstances were?

VIVIE. Yes: you had better tell me. Wont you sit down?

MRS WARREN. Oh, I'll sit down: dont you be afraid. (*She plants her chair farther forward with brazen energy, and sits down. Vivie is impressed in spite of herself.*) D'you know what your gran'mother was?

VIVIE. No.

MRS WARREN. No, you dont. I do. She called herself a widow and had a fried-fish shop down by the Mint,[1] and kept herself and four daughters out of it. Two of us were sisters: that was me and Liz; and we were both good-looking and well made. I suppose our father was a well-fed man: mother pretended he was a gentleman; but I dont know. The other two were only half sisters: undersized, ugly, starved looking, hard working, honest poor creatures: Liz and I would have half-murdered them if mother hadnt half-murdered u s to keep our hands off them. They were the respectable ones. Well, what did they get by their respectability? I'll tell you. One of them worked in a whitelead factory[2] twelve hours a day for nine shillings a week until she died of lead poisoning. She only expected to get her hands a little paralyzed; but she died. The other was always held up to us as a model because she married a Government laborer in the Deptford victualling yard,[3] and kept his room and the three children neat and tidy on eighteen shillings a week—until he took to drink. That was worth being respectable for, wasnt it?

VIVIE. (*Now thoughtfully attentive.*) Did you and your sister think so?

MRS WARREN. Liz didnt, I can tell you: she had more spirit. We both went to a church school—that was part of the ladylike airs we gave ourselves to be superior to the children that knew nothing and went nowhere—and we stayed there until Liz went out one night and never came back. I know the schoolmistress thought I'd soon follow her example; for the clergyman was always warning me that Lizzie'd end by jumping off Waterloo Bridge.[4] Poor fool: that was all he knew about it! But I was more afraid of the whitelead factory than I was of the river; and so would you have been in my place. That clergyman got me a situation as scullery[5] maid in a temperance restaurant[6] where they sent out for anything you liked. Then I was waitress; and then I went to the bar at Waterloo station:[7] fourteen hours a day serving drinks and washing glasses for four shillings a week and

---

[1] *the Mint* The Royal Mint is the official manufacturer of British coinage. In Shaw's time it was located in working-class East End London. It moved in 1968 to its present location in Llantrisant, South Wales.

[2] *whitelead factory* Whitelead is a mixture of lead carbonate and hydrated lead oxide used as a white pigment in paint.

[3] *Deptford victualling yard* The Royal Victualling Yard—for providing supplies and provisions for the Royal Navy—was established at Deptford (on the River Thames) in 1742.

[4] *Waterloo Bridge* Waterloo Bridge connects Victoria Embankment with Waterloo on the south bank of the Thames in London. The original bridge (built in 1817) was demolished in 1936 and replaced with the present structure.

[5] *scullery* Small room adjacent to the kitchen used mainly for washing dishes.

[6] *temperance restaurant* Restaurant that does not serve alcohol.

[7] *Waterloo station* Then, and now, one of London's principal railway stations.

my board. That was considered a great promotion for
me. Well, one cold, wretched night, when I was so tired
I could hardly keep myself awake, who should come up
for a half of scotch[1] but Lizzie, in a long fur cloak,
elegant and comfortable, with a lot of sovereigns[2] in her
purse.

VIVIE. (*Grimly.*) My aunt Lizzie!

MRS WARREN. Yes; and a very good aunt to have, too.
She's living down at Winchester[3] now, close to the
cathedral, one of the most respectable ladies there.
Chaperones girls at the county ball, if you please. No
river for Liz, thank you! You remind me of Liz a little:
she was a first-rate business woman—saved money from
the beginning—never let herself look too like what she
was—never lost her head or threw away a chance. When
she saw I'd grown up good-looking she said to me across
the bar "What are you doing there, you little fool?
wearing out your health and your appearance for other
people's profit!" Liz was saving money then to take a
house for herself in Brussels; and she thought we two
could save faster than one. So she lent me some money
and gave me a start; and I saved steadily and first paid
her back, and then went into business with her as her
partner. Why shouldnt I have done it? The house in
Brussels was real high class: a much better place for a
woman to be in than the factory where Anne Jane got
poisoned. None of our girls were ever treated as I was
treated in the scullery of that temperance place, or at the
Waterloo bar, or at home. Would you have had me stay
in them and become a worn-out old drudge before I was
forty?

VIVIE. (*Intensely interested by this time.*) No, but why did
you choose that business? Saving money and good
management will succeed in any business.

MRS WARREN. Yes, saving money. But where can a
woman get the money to save in any other business?
Could you save out of four shillings a week and keep
yourself dressed as well? Not you. Of course, if youre a
plain woman and cant earn anything more; or if you
have a turn for music, or the stage, or newspaper-
writing: thats different. But neither Liz nor I had any
turn for such things: all we had was our appearance and

our turn for pleasing men. Do you think we were such
fools as to let other people trade in our good looks by
employing us as shopgirls, or barmaids, or waitresses,
when we could trade in them ourselves and get all the
profits instead of starvation wages? Not likely.

VIVIE. You were certainly quite justified—from the
business point of view.

MRS WARREN. Yes; or any other point of view. What is
any respectable girl brought up to do but to catch some
rich man's fancy and get the benefit of his money by
marrying him?—as if a marriage ceremony could make
any difference in the right or wrong of the thing! Oh,
the hypocrisy of the world makes me sick! Liz and I had
to work and save and calculate just like other people;
elseways[4] we should be as poor as any good-for-nothing
drunken waster of a woman that thinks her luck will last
forever. (*With great energy.*) I despise such people: theyve
no character; and if theres a thing I hate in a woman, it's
want of character.

VIVIE. Come now, mother: Frankly! Isn't it part of what
you call character in a woman that she should greatly
dislike such a way of making money?

MRS WARREN. Why, of course. Everybody dislikes
having to work and make money; but they have to do it
all the same. I'm sure Ive often pitied a poor girl, tired
out and in low spirits, having to try to please some man
that she doesnt care two straws for—some half-drunken
fool that thinks he's making himself agreeable when he's
teasing and worrying and disgusting a woman so that
hardly any money could pay her for putting up with it.
But she has to bear with disagreeables and take the
rough with the smooth, just like a nurse in a hospital or
anyone else. It's not work that any woman would do for
pleasure, goodness knows; though to hear the pious
people talk you would suppose it was a bed of roses.

VIVIE. Still, you consider it worth while. It pays.

MRS WARREN. Of course it's worth while to a poor girl,
if she can resist temptation and is good-looking and well
conducted and sensible. It's far better than any other
employment open to her. I always thought that oughtnt
to be. It c a n t be right, Vivie, that there shouldnt be
better opportunities for women. I stick to that: it's
wrong. But it's so, right or wrong; and a girl must make
the best of it. But of course it's not worth while for a

---

[1] *half of scotch*   Large glass of Scotch whisky.

[2] *sovereigns*   Gold coins worth £1.

[3] *Winchester*   City about 65 miles southwest of London.

[4] *elseways*   Otherwise.

lady. If you took to it youd be a fool; but I should have been a fool if I'd taken to anything else.

695 VIVIE. (*More and more deeply moved.*) Mother: suppose we were both as poor as you were in those wretched old days, are you quite sure that you wouldnt advise me to try the Waterloo bar, or marry a laborer, or even go into the factory?

700 MRS WARREN. (*Indignantly.*) Of course not. What sort of mother do you take me for! How could you keep your self-respect in such starvation and slavery? And whats a woman worth? whats life worth? without self-respect! Why am I independent and able to give my

705 daughter a first-rate education, when other women that had just as good opportunities are in the gutter? Because I always knew how to respect myself and control myself. Why is Liz looked up to in a cathedral town? The same reason. Where would we be now if we'd minded the

710 clergyman's foolishness? Scrubbing floors for one and sixpence a day and nothing to look forward to but the workhouse infirmary.[1] Dont you be led astray by people who dont know the world, my girl. The only way for a woman to provide for herself decently is for her to be

715 good to some man that can afford to be good to her. If she's in his own station of life, let her make him marry her; but if she's far beneath him she cant expect it: why should she? it wouldnt be for her own happiness. Ask any lady in London society that has daughters; and she'll

720 tell you the same, except that I tell you straight and she'll tell you crooked. Thats all the difference.

VIVIE. (*Fascinated, gazing at her.*) My dear mother: you are a wonderful woman: you are stronger than all England. And are you really and truly not one wee bit

725 doubtful—or—or—ashamed?

MRS WARREN. Well, of course, dearie, it's only good manners to be ashamed of it: it's expected from a woman. Women have to pretend to feel a great deal that they dont feel. Liz used to be angry with me for

730 plumping out the truth about it. She used to say that when every woman could learn enough from what was

going on in the world before her eyes, there was no need to talk about it to her. But then Liz was such a perfect lady! She had the true instinct of it; while I was always

735 a bit of a vulgarian. I used to be so pleased when you sent me your photos to see that you were growing up like Liz: youve just her ladylike, determined way. But I cant stand saying one thing when everyone knows I mean another. Whats the use in such hypocrisy? If

740 people arrange the world that way for women, there's no good pretending it's arranged the other way. No: I never was a bit ashamed really. I consider I had a right to be proud of how we managed everything so respectably, and never had a word against us, and how the girls were

745 so well taken care of. Some of them did very well: one of them married an ambassador. But of course now I darent talk about such things: whatever would they think of us! (*She yawns.*) Oh dear! I do believe I'm getting sleepy after all. (*She stretches herself lazily,*

750 *thoroughly relieved by her explosion, and placidly ready for her night's rest.*)

VIVIE. I believe it is I who will not be able to sleep now. (*She goes to the dresser and lights the candle. Then she extinguishes the lamp, darkening the room a good deal.*)

755 Better let in some fresh air before locking up. (*She opens the cottage door, and finds that it is a broad moonlight.*) What a beautiful night! Look! (*She draws aside the curtains of the window. The landscape is seen bathed in the radiance of the harvest moon rising over Blackdown.[2]*)

760 MRS WARREN. (*With a perfunctory glance of the scene.*) Yes, dear; but take care you dont catch your death of cold from the night air.

VIVIE. (*Contemptuously.*) Nonsense.

MRS WARREN. (*Querulously.*) Oh yes: everything I say

765 is nonsense, according to you.

VIVIE. (*Turning to her quickly.*) No: really that is not so, mother. You have got completely the better of me tonight, though I intended it to be the other way. Let us be good friends now.

770 MRS WARREN. (*Shaking her head a little ruefully.*) So it has been the other way. But I suppose I must give in to it. I always got the worst of it from Liz; and now I suppose it'll be the same with you.

VIVIE. Well, never mind. Come: goodnight, dear old

775 mother. (*She takes her mother in her arms.*)

---

[1] *workhouse infirmary* Workhouses, which supported the sick and the indigent, had existed in England since the early seventeenth century. The Poor Law Amendment Act of 1834 limited assistance to the able-bodied poor and made conditions as uncomfortable as possible. Most workhouses had their own infirmaries where rudimentary medical help was provided. Workhouses were phased out in England by about 1930.

[2] *Blackdown* Prominent hill about three miles south of Haslemere.

MRS WARREN. (*Fondly.*) I brought you up well, didnt I, dearie?

VIVIE. You did.

MRS WARREN. And youll be good to your poor old mother for it, wont you?

VIVIE. I will, dear. (*Kissing her.*) Goodnight.

MRS WARREN. (*With unction.*) Blessings on my own dearie darling! a mother's blessing!

(*She embraces her daughter protectingly, instinctively looking upward for divine sanction.*)

ACT 3

(*In the Rectory garden next morning, with the sun shining from a cloudless sky. The garden wall has a five-barred wooden gate, wide enough to admit a carriage, in the middle. Beside the gate hangs a bell on a coiled spring, communicating with a pull outside. The carriage drive comes down the middle of the garden and then swerves to its left, where it ends in a little gravelled circus[1] opposite the Rectory porch. Beyond the gate is seen the dusty high road, parallel with the wall, bounded on the farther side by a strip of turf and an unfenced pine wood. On the lawn, between the house and the drive, is a clipped yew tree, with a garden bench in its shade. On the opposite side the garden is shut in by a box hedge; and there is a sundial on the turf, with an iron chair near it. A little path leads off through the box hedge, behind the sundial.*

Frank, seated on the chair near the sundial, on which he has placed the morning papers, is reading The Standard.[2] His father comes from the house, red-eyed and shivery, and meets Frank's eye with misgiving.)

FRANK. (*Looking at his watch.*) Half-past eleven. Nice hour for a rector to come down to breakfast!

REV. S. Dont mock, Frank: dont mock. I am a little—er—(*Shivering.*)—

FRANK. Off color?

REV. S. (*Repudiating the expression.*) No, sir: u n w e l l this morning. Wheres your mother?

FRANK. Dont be alarmed: she's not here. Gone to town by the 11.13 with Bessie. She left several messages for you. Do you feel equal to receiving them now, or shall I wait til you have breakfasted?

REV. S. I h a v e breakfasted, sir. I am surprised at your mother going to town when we have people staying with us. Theyll think it very strange.

FRANK. Possibly she has considered that. At all events, if Crofts is going to stay here, and you are going to sit up every night with him until four, recalling the incidents of your fiery youth, it is clearly my mother's duty, as a prudent housekeeper, to go up to the stores and order a barrel of whisky and a few hundred siphons.[3]

REV. S. I did not observe that Sir George drank excessively.

FRANK. You were not in a condition to, gov'nor.

REV. S. Do you mean to say that *I*—?

FRANK. (*Calmly.*) I never saw a beneficed clergyman less sober. The anecdotes you told about your past career were so awful that I really dont think Praed would have passed the night under your roof if it hadnt been for the way my mother and he took to one another.

REV. S. Nonsense, sir. I am Sir George Crofts' host. I must talk to him about something; and he has only one subject. Where is Mr Praed now?

FRANK. He is driving my mother and Bessie to the station.

REV. S. Is Crofts up yet?

FRANK. Oh, long ago. He hasnt turned a hair: he's in much better practice than you. He has kept it up ever since, probably. He's taken himself off somewhere to smoke.

(*Frank resumes his paper. The parson turns disconsolately towards the gate; then comes back irresolutely.*)

REV. S. Er—Frank.

FRANK. Yes.

REV. S. Do you think the Warrens will expect to be asked here after yesterday afternoon?

FRANK. Theyve been asked already.

REV. S. (*Appalled.*) What!!

FRANK. Crofts informed us at breakfast that you told

---

[1] *circus* Circular driveway.

[2] *The Standard* A leading London daily newspaper, first published in 1827.

[3] *siphons* Bottles of soda (to mix with the whisky).

him to bring Mrs Warren and Vivie over here today, and to invite them to make this house their home. My
50 mother then found she must go to town by the 11.13 train.

REV. S.   (*With despairing vehemence.*) I never gave any such invitation. I never thought of such a thing.

FRANK.   (*Compassionately.*) How do you know, gov'nor,
55 what you said and thought last night?

PRAED.   (*Coming in through the hedge.*) Good morning.

REV. S.   Good morning. I must apologize for not having met you at breakfast. I have a touch of—of—

FRANK.   Clergyman's sore throat, Praed. Fortunately
60 not chronic.

PRAED.   (*Changing the subject.*) Well, I must say your house is in a charming spot here. Really most charming.

REV. S.   Yes: it is indeed. Frank will take you for a walk, Mr Praed, if you like. I'll ask you to excuse me: I must
65 take the opportunity to write my sermon while Mrs Gardner is away and you are all amusing yourself. You wont mind, will you?

PRAED.   Certainly not. Dont stand on the slightest ceremony with me.

70 REV. S.   Thank you. I'll—er—er—(*He stammers his way to the porch and vanishes into the house.*)

PRAED.   Curious thing it must be writing a sermon every week.

FRANK.   Ever so curious, if he did it. He buys em. He's
75 gone for some soda water.

PRAED.   My dear boy: I wish you would be more respectful to your father. You know you can be so nice when you like.

FRANK.   My dear Praddy: you forget that I have to live
80 with the governor. When two people live together—it dont matter whether theyre father and son or husband and wife or brother and sister—they cant keep up the polite humbug thats so easy for ten minutes on an afternoon call. Now the governor, who unites to many
85 admirable domestic qualities the irresoluteness of a sheep and the pompousness and aggressiveness of a jackass—

PRAED.   No, pray, pray, my dear Frank, remember! He is your father.

90 FRANK.   I give him due credit for that. (*Rising and flinging down his paper.*) But just imagine his telling Crofts to bring the Warrens over here! He must have

been ever so drunk. You know, my dear Praddy, my mother wouldnt stand Mrs Warren for a moment. Vivie
95 mustnt come here until she has gone back to town.

PRAED.   But your mother doesnt know anything about Mrs Warren, does she? (*He picks up the paper and sits down to read it.*)

FRANK.   I dont know. Her journey to town looks as if
100 she did. Not that my mother would mind in the ordinary way: she has stuck like a brick to lots of women who had got into trouble. But they were all nice women. Thats what makes the real difference. Mrs Warren, no doubt, has her merits; but she's ever so rowdy; and my
105 mother simply wouldnt put up with her. So—hallo! (*This exclamation is provoked by the reappearance of the clergyman, who comes out of the house in haste and dismay.*)

REV. S.   Frank: Mrs Warren and her daughter are
110 coming across the heath with Crofts: I saw them from the study windows. What am I to say about your mother?

FRANK.   Stick on your hat and go out and say how delighted you are to see them; and that Frank's in the
115 garden; and that mother and Bessie have been called to the bedside of a sick relative, and were ever so sorry that they couldnt stop; and that you hope Mrs Warren slept well; and—and—say any blessed thing except the truth, and leave the rest to Providence.

120 REV. S.   But how are we to get rid of them afterwards?

FRANK.   Theres no time to think of that now. Here! (*He bounds into the house.*)

REV. S.   He's so impetuous. I dont know what to do with him, Mr Praed.

125 FRANK.   (*Returning with a clerical felt hat, which he claps on his father's head.*) Now: off with you. (*Rushing him through the gate.*) Praed and I'll wait here, to give the thing an unpremeditated air. (*The clergyman, dazed but obedient, hurries off.*)

130 FRANK.   We must get the old girl back to town somehow, Praed. Come! Honestly, dear Praddy, do you like seeing them together?

PRAED.   Oh, why not?

FRANK.   (*His teeth on edge.*) Dont it make your flesh
135 creep ever so little? that wicked old devil, up to every villainy under the sun, I'll swear, and Vivie—ugh!

PRAED.   Hush, pray. Theyre coming.

(*The clergyman and Crofts are seen coming along the road, followed by Mrs Warren and Vivie walking affectionately together.*)

FRANK.   Look: she actually has her arm round the old
140   woman's waist. It's her right arm: she began it. She's
gone sentimental, by God! Ugh! ugh! Now do you feel
the creeps? (*The clergyman opens the gate; and Mrs
Warren and Vivie pass him and stand in the middle of the
garden looking at the house. Frank, in an ecstasy of*
145   *dissimulation, turns gaily to Mrs Warren, exclaiming*) Ever
so delighted to see you, Mrs Warren. This quiet old
rectory garden becomes you perfectly.

MRS WARREN.   Well, I never! Did you hear that,
George? He says I look well in a quiet old rectory
150   garden.

REV. S.   (*Still holding the gate for Crofts who loafs through
it, heavily bored.*) You look well everywhere, Mrs
Warren.

FRANK.   Bravo, gov'nor! Now look here: lets have a treat
155   before lunch. First lets see the church. Everyone has to
do that. It's a regular old thirteenth century church, you
know: the gov'nor's ever so fond of it, because he got up
a restoration fund and had it completely rebuilt six years
ago. Praed will be able to shew its points.

160   PRAED.   (*Rising.*) Certainly, if the restoration has left any
to shew.

REV. S.   (*Mooning[1] hospitably at them.*) I shall be pleased,
I'm sure, if Sir George and Mrs Warren really care about
it.

165   MRS WARREN.   Oh, come along and get it over.

CROFTS.   (*Turning back towards the gate.*) Ive no
objection.

REV. S.   Not that way. We go through the fields, if you
dont mind. Round here. (*He leads the way by the little*
170   *path through the box hedge.*)

CROFTS.   Oh, all right. (*He goes with the parson.*)

(*Praed follows with Mrs Warren. Vivie does not stir: she
watches them until they have gone, with all the lines of
purpose in her face marking it strongly.*)

FRANK.   Aint you coming?

VIVIE.   No. I want to give you a warning, Frank. You
175   were making fun of my mother just now when you said
that about the rectory garden. That is barred in the
future. Please treat my mother with as much respect as
you treat your own.

FRANK.   My dear Viv: she wouldnt appreciate it: the two
180   cases require different treatment. But what on earth has
happened to you? Last night we were perfectly agreed as
to your mother and her set. This morning I find you
attitudinizing sentimentally with your arm round your
parent's waist.

VIVIE.   (*Flushing.*) Attitudinizing!

185   FRANK.   That was how it struck me. First time I ever saw
you do a second-rate thing.

VIVIE.   (*Controlling herself.*) Yes, Frank: there has been a
change; but I dont think it a change for the worse.
Yesterday I was a little prig.

190   FRANK.   And today?

VIVIE.   (*Wincing; then looking at him steadily.*) Today I
know my mother better than you do.

FRANK.   Heaven forbid!

VIVIE.   What do you mean?

195   FRANK.   Viv: theres a freemasonry among thoroughly
immoral people that you know nothing of. Youve too
much character. T h a t s the bond between your
mother and me: thats why I know her better than youll
ever know her.

200   VIVIE.   You are wrong: you know nothing about her. If
you knew the circumstances against which my mother
had to struggle—

FRANK.   (*Adroitly finishing the sentence for her.*) I should
know why she is what she is, shouldnt I? What
205   difference would that make? Circumstances or no
circumstances, Viv, you wont be able to stand your
mother.

VIVIE.   (*Very angrily.*) Why not?

FRANK.   Because she's an old wretch, Viv. If you ever
210   put your arm round her waist in my presence again, I'll
shoot myself there and then as a protest against an
exhibition which revolts me.

VIVIE.   Must I choose between dropping your acquaintance and dropping my mother's?

215   FRANK.   (*Gracefully.*) That would put the old lady at ever
such a disadvantage. No, Viv; your infatuated little boy
will have to stick to you in any case. But he's all the
more anxious that you shouldnt make mistakes. It's no

---

[1]   *mooning*   Listlessly, without energy (he has a hangover).

use, Viv: your mother's impossible. She may be a good
sort; but she's a bad lot, a very bad lot.

VIVIE.   (*Hotly.*) Frank—! (*He stands his ground. She turns away and sits down on the bench under the yew tree, struggling to recover her self-command. Then she says*) Is she to be deserted by all the world because she's what you call a bad lot? Has she no right to live?

FRANK.   No fear of that, Viv: she wont ever be deserted. (*He sits on the bench beside her.*)

VIVIE.   But I am to desert her, I suppose.

FRANK.   (*Babyishly, lulling her and making love to her with his voice.*) Musnt go live with her. Little family group of mother and daughter wouldnt be a success. Spoil o u r little group.

VIVIE.   (*Falling under the spell.*) What little group?

FRANK.   The babes in the wood: Vivie and little Frank. (*He nestles against her like a weary child.*) Lets go and get covered up with leaves.

VIVIE.   (*Rhythmically, rocking him like a nurse.*) Fast asleep, hand in hand, under the trees.

FRANK.   The wise little girl with her silly little boy.

VIVIE.   The dear little boy with his dowdy little girl.

FRANK.   Ever so peaceful, and relieved from the imbecility of the little boy's father and the questionableness of the little girl's—

VIVIE.   (*Smothering the word against her breast.*) Sh-sh-sh-sh! little girl wants to forget all about her mother. (*They are silent for some moments, rocking one another. Then Vivie wakes up with a shock, exclaiming*) What a pair of fools we are! Come: sit up. Gracious! your hair. (*She smooths it.*) I wonder do all grown up people play in that childish way when nobody is looking. I never did it when I was a child.

FRANK.   Neither did I. You are my first playmate. (*He catches her hand to kiss it, but checks himself to look round first. Very unexpectedly, he sees Crofts emerging from the box hedge.*) Oh damn!

VIVIE.   Why damn, dear?

FRANK.   (*Whispering.*) Sh! Heres this brute Crofts. (*He sits farther away from her with an unconcerned air.*)[1]

CROFTS.   Could I have a few words with you, Miss Vivie?

VIVIE.   Certainly.

CROFTS.   (*To Frank.*) Youll excuse me, Gardner. Theyre waiting for you in the church, if you dont mind.

FRANK.   (*Rising.*) Anything to oblige you, Crofts— except church. If you should happen to want me, Vivvums, ring the gate bell. (*He goes into the house with unruffled suavity.*)

CROFTS.   (*Watching him with a crafty air as he disappears, and speaking to Vivie with an assumption of being on privileged terms with her.*) Pleasant young fellow that, Miss Vivie. Pity he has no money, isnt it?

VIVIE.   Do you think so?

CROFTS.   Well, whats he to do? No profession. No property. Whats he good for?

VIVIE.   I realize his disadvantages, Sir George.

CROFTS.   (*A little taken aback at being so precisely interpreted.*) Oh, it's not that. But while we're in this world, we're in it; and money's money. (*Vivie does not answer.*) Nice day, isnt it?

VIVIE.   (*With scarcely veiled contempt for this effort at conversation.*) Very.

CROFTS.   (*With brutal good humor, as if he liked her pluck.*) Well, thats not what I came to say. (*Sitting down beside her.*) Now listen, Miss Vivie I'm quite aware that I'm not a young lady's man.

VIVIE.   Indeed, Sir George?

CROFTS.   No; and to tell you the honest truth I dont want to be either. But when I say a thing I mean it; when I feel a sentiment I feel it in earnest; and what I value I pay hard money for. Thats the sort of man I am.

VIVIE.   It does you great credit, I'm sure.

CROFTS.   Oh, I dont mean to praise myself. I have my faults, Heaven knows: no man is more sensible of[2] that than I am. I know I'm not perfect; thats one of the advantages of being a middle-aged man; for I'm not a young man, and I know it. But my code is a simple one, and, I think, a good one. Honor between man and man; fidelity between man and woman; and no cant about this religion or that religion, but an honest belief that things are making for good on the whole.

VIVIE.   (*With biting irony.*) "A power, not ourselves, that

---

[1] At this point in the 1898 text Vivie says: "Dont be rude to him, Frank. I particularly want to be polite to him. It will please my mother."

[2] *sensible of* Aware of.

makes for righteousness,"[1] eh?

CROFTS. (*Taking her seriously.*) Oh certainly. Not ourselves, of course. You understand what I mean. Well, now as to practical matters. You may have an idea that I have flung my money about; but I havnt: I'm richer today than when I first came into the property. Ive used my knowledge of the world to invest my money in ways that other men have overlooked; and whatever else I may be, I'm a safe man from the money point of view.

VIVIE. It's very kind of you to tell me all this.

CROFTS. Oh well, come, Miss Vivie: you neednt pretend you dont see what I'm driving at. I want to settle down with a Lady Crofts. I suppose you think me very blunt, eh?

VIVIE. Not at all: I am much obliged to you for being so definite and business-like. I quite appreciate the offer: the money, the position, L a d y C r o f t s and so on. But I think I will say no, if you dont mind. I'd rather not. (*She rises, and strolls across to the sundial to get out of his immediate neighborhood.*)

CROFTS. (*Not at all discouraged, and taking advantage of the additional room left him on the seat to spread himself comfortably, as if a few preliminary refusals were part of the inevitable routine of courtship.*) I'm in no hurry. It was only just to let you know in case young Gardner should try to trap you. Leave the question open.

VIVIE. (*Sharply.*) My no is final. I wont go back from it.

(*Crofts is not impressed. He grins; leans forward with his elbows on his knees to prod with his stick at some unfortunate insect in the grass; and looks cunningly at her. She turns away impatiently.*)

CROFTS. I'm a good deal older than you. Twenty-five years: quarter of a century. I shant live forever; and I'll take care that you shall be well off when I'm gone.

VIVIE. I am proof against even that inducement, Sir George. Dont you think youd better take your answer? There is not the slightest chance of my altering it.

CROFTS. (*Rising, after a final slash at a daisy, and coming nearer to her.*) Well, no matter. I could tell you some things that would change your mind fast enough; but I

wont, because I'd rather win you by honest affection. I was a good friend to your mother: ask her whether I wasnt. She'd never have made the money that paid for your education if it hadnt been for my advice and help, not to mention the money I advanced her. There are not many men who would have stood by her as I have. I put not less than £40,000 into it, from first to last.

VIVIE. (*Staring at him.*) Do you mean to say you were my mother's business partner?

CROFTS. Yes. Now just think of all the trouble and the explanations it would save if we were to keep the whole thing in the family, so to speak. Ask your mother whether she'd like to have to explain all her affairs to a perfect stranger.

VIVIE. I see no difficulty, since I understand that the business is wound up, and the money invested.

CROFTS. (*Stopping short, amazed.*) Wound up! Wind up a business thats paying 35 per cent in the worst years! Not likely. Who told you that?

VIVIE. (*Her color quite gone.*) Do you mean that it is still—? (*She stops abruptly, and puts her hand on the sundial to support herself. Then she gets quickly to the iron chair and sits down.*) What business are you talking about?

CROFTS. Well, the fact is it's not what would be considered exactly a high-class business in my set—the county set, you know—o u r set it will be if you think better of my offer. Not that theres any mystery about it: dont think that. Of course you know by your mother's being in it that it's perfectly straight and honest. Ive known her for many years; and I can say of her that she'd cut off her hands sooner than touch anything that was not what it ought to be. I'll tell you all about it if you like. I dont know whether youve found in travelling how hard it is to find a really comfortable private hotel.

VIVIE. (*Sickened, averting her face.*) Yes: go on.

CROFTS. Well, thats all it is. Your mother has a genius for managing such things. Weve got two in Brussels, one in Ostend, one in Vienna and two in Budapest.[2] Of course there are others besides ourselves in it: but we hold most of the capital; and your mother's indispensable as managing director. Youve noticed, I dare say, that she travels a good deal. But you see you

---

[1] *A power … righteousness* Matthew Arnold, *Literature and Dogma* (1873), chapter 8: "The eternal *not ourselves* that makes for righteousness."

[2] In the 1898 text the count of brothels is slightly different: two in Brussels, one in Berlin, one in Vienna, and two in Budapest.

cant mention such things in society. Once let out the word hotel and everybody says you keep a public-house. You wouldnt like people to say that of your mother, would you? Thats why we're so reserved about it. By the way, youll keep it to yourself, wont you? Since its been a secret so long, it had better remain so.

VIVIE.   And this is the business you invite me to join you in?

CROFTS.   Oh, no. My wife shant be troubled with business. Youll not be in it more than youve always been.

VIVIE.   *I* always been! What do you mean?

CROFTS.   Only that youve always lived on it. It paid for your education and the dress you have on your back. Dont turn up your nose at business, Miss Vivie; where would your Newnhams and Girtons be without it?

VIVIE.   (*Rising, almost beside herself.*) Take care. I know what this business is.

CROFTS.   (*Starting, with a suppressed oath.*) Who told you?

VIVIE.   Your partner. My mother.

CROFTS.   (*Black with rage.*) The old—

VIVIE.   Just so.

(*He swallows the epithet and stands for a moment swearing and raging foully to himself. But he knows that his cue is to be sympathetic. He takes refuge in generous indignation.*)

CROFTS.   She ought to have had more consideration for you. *I*'d never have told you.

VIVIE.   I think you would probably have told me when we were married: it would have been a convenient weapon to break me in with.

CROFTS.   (*Quite sincerely.*) I never intended that. On my word as a gentleman I didnt.

(*Vivie wonders at him. Her sense of the irony of his protest cools and braces her. She replies with contemptuous self-possession.*)

VIVIE.   It does not matter. I suppose you understand that when we leave here today our acquaintance ceases.

CROFTS.   Why? Is it for helping your mother?

VIVIE.   My mother was a very poor woman who had no reasonable choice but to do as she did. You were a rich gentleman; and you did the same for the sake of 35 per

cent. You are a pretty common sort of scoundrel, I think. That is my opinion of you.

CROFTS.   (*After a stare: not at all displeased, and much more at his ease on these frank terms than on their former ceremonious ones.*) Ha! ha! ha! ha! Go it, little missie, go it; it doesnt hurt me and it amuses you. Why the devil shouldnt I invest my money that way? I take the interest on my capital like other people: I hope you dont think I dirty my own hands with the work. Come! you wouldnt refuse the acquaintance of my mother's cousin the Duke of Belgravia[1] because some of the rents he gets are earned in queer ways. You wouldnt cut the Archbishop of Canterbury,[2] I suppose, because the Ecclesiastical Commissioners[3] have a few publicans and sinners among their tenants. Do you remember your Crofts scholarship at Newnham? Well, that was founded by my brother the M.P. He gets his 22 per cent out of a factory with 600 girls in it, and not one of them getting wages enough to live on. How d'ye suppose they manage when they have no family to fall back on? Ask your mother. And do you expect me to turn my back on 35 per cent when all the rest are pocketing what they can, like sensible men? No such fool! If youre going to pick and choose your acquaintances on moral principles, youd better clear out of this country, unless you want to cut yourself out of all decent society.

VIVIE.   (*Conscience stricken.*) You might go on to point out that I myself never asked where the money I spent came from. I believe I am just as bad as you.

CROFTS.   (*Greatly reassured.*) Of course you are; and a very good thing too! What harm does it do after all? (*Rallying her jocularly.*) So you dont think me such a scoundrel now you come to think it over. Eh?

VIVIE.   I have shared profits with you; and I admitted you just now to the familiarity of knowing what I think

---

[1] *Belgravia* Belgravia was (and is) a fashionable and expensive residential area of London. The title "Duke of Belgravia" is fictitious.

[2] *Archbishop of Canterbury* The Archbishop of Canterbury in office at the time that Shaw was writing *Mrs. Warren's Profession* was Edward White Benson (1829–96), Archbishop from 1882 to his death.

[3] *Ecclesiastical Commissioners* A body established in 1836 to buy, sell, and manage land and property and oversee other business operations for the Church of England. It consisted of leading ecclesiastics, politicians, and judges.

of you.

CROFTS. (*With serious friendliness.*) To be sure you did. You wont find me a bad sort: I dont go in for being superfine intellectually: but Ive plenty of honest human feeling; and the old Crofts breed comes out in a sort of instinctive hatred of anything low, in which I'm sure youll sympathize with me. Believe me, Miss Vivie, the world isnt such a bad place as the croakers[1] make out. As long as you dont fly openly in the face of society, society doesnt ask any inconvenient questions; and it makes precious short work of the cads who do. There are no secrets better kept than the secrets everybody guesses. In the class of people I can introduce you to, no lady or gentleman would so far forget themselves as to discuss my business affairs or your mother's. No man can offer you a safer position.

VIVIE. (*Studying him curiously.*) I suppose you really think youre getting on famously with me.

CROFTS. Well, I hope I may flatter myself that you think better of me than you did at first.

VIVIE. (*Quietly.*)[2] I hardly find you worth thinking about at all now. When I think of the society that tolerates you, and the laws that protect you! when I think of how helpless nine out of ten young girls would be in the hands of you and my mother! the unmentionable woman and her capitalist bully—

CROFTS. (*Livid.*) Damn you!

VIVIE. You need not. I feel among the damned already.

(*She raises the latch of the gate to open it and go out. He follows her and puts his hand heavily on the top bar to prevent its opening.*)

CROFTS. (*Panting with fury.*) Do you think I'll put up with this from you, you young devil?

VIVIE. (*Unmoved.*) Be quiet. Some one will answer the bell. (*Without flinching a step she strikes the bell with the back of her hand. It clangs harshly; and he starts back involuntarily. Almost immediately Frank appears at the porch with his rifle.*)

FRANK. (*With cheerful politeness.*) Will you have the rifle, Viv; or shall I operate?

---

[1] *croakers* Those who speaks dismally, forebodingly.

[2] *quietly* The 1898 text specifies that Vivie speaks to Crofts "*almost gently, but with intense conviction.*"

VIVIE. Frank: have you been listening?

FRANK. (*Coming down into the garden.*) Only for the bell, I assure you; so that you shouldnt have to wait. I think I shewed great insight into your character, Crofts..

CROFTS. For two pins I'd take that gun from you and break it across your head.

FRANK. (*Stalking him cautiously.*) Pray dont. I'm ever so careless in handling firearms. Sure to be a fatal accident, with a reprimand from the coroner's jury for my negligence.

VIVIE. Put the rifle away, Frank; it's quite unnecessary.

FRANK. Quite right, Viv. Much more sportsmanlike to catch him in a trap. (*Crofts, understanding the insult, makes a threatening movement.*) Crofts: there are fifteen cartridges in the magazine here; and I am a dead shot at the present distance and at an object of your size.

CROFTS. Oh, you neednt be afraid. I'm not going to touch you.

FRANK. Ever so magnanimous of you under the circumstances! Thank you!

CROFTS. I'll just tell you this before I go. It may interest you, since youre so fond of one another. Allow me, Mr Frank, to introduce you to your half-sister, the eldest daughter of the Reverend Samuel Gardner. Miss Vivie: your half-brother. Good morning. (*He goes out through the gate along the road.*)

FRANK. (*After a pause of stupefaction, raising the rifle.*) Youll testify before the coroner that its an accident, Viv. (*He takes aim at the retreating figure of Crofts. Vivie seizes the muzzle and pulls it round against her breast.*)

VIVIE. Fire now. You may.

FRANK. (*Dropping his end of the rifle hastily.*) Stop! take care. (*She lets it go. It falls on the turf.*) Oh, youve given your little boy such a turn. Suppose it had gone off! ugh! (*He sinks on the garden seat overcome.*)

VIVIE. Suppose it had: do you think it would not have been a relief to have some sharp physical pain tearing through me?

FRANK. (*Coaxingly.*) Take it ever so easy, dear Viv. Remember: even if the rifle scared that fellow into telling the truth for the first time in his life, that only makes us the babes in the wood in earnest. (*He holds out his arms to her.*) Come and be covered up with leaves again.

VIVIE.   (*With a cry of disgust.*) Ah, not that, not that. You make all my flesh creep.

535 FRANK.   Why, whats the matter?

VIVIE.   Goodbye. (*She makes for the gate.*)

FRANK.   (*Jumping up.*) Hallo! Stop! Viv! Viv! (*She turns in the gateway.*) Where are you going to? Where shall we find you?

540 VIVIE.   At Honoria Fraser's chambers, 67 Chancery Lane, for the rest of my life. (*She goes off quickly in the opposite direction to that taken by Crofts.*)

FRANK.   But I say—wait dash it! (*He runs after her.*)

ACT 4

(*Honoria Fraser's chambers in Chancery Lane. An office at the top of New Stone Buildings, with a plate-glass window, distempered[1] walls, electric light, and a patent stove.[2] Saturday afternoon. The chimneys of Lincoln's Inn[3] and the western sky beyond are seen through the window. There is a double writing table in the middle of the room, with a cigar box, ash pans,[4] and a portable electric reading lamp almost snowed up in heaps of papers and books. This table has knee holes and chairs right and left and is very untidy. The clerk's desk, closed and tidy, with its high stool, is against the wall, near a door communicating with the inner rooms. In the opposite wall is the door leading to the public corridor. Its upper panel is of opaque glass, lettered in black on the outside, Fraser and Warren. A baize screen hides the corner between this door and the window.*)

Frank, in a fashionable light-colored coaching suit, with his stick, gloves, and white hat in his hands, is pacing up and down the office. Somebody tries the door with a key.)

FRANK.   (*Calling.*) Come in. It's not locked.

---

[1] *distempered*   Painted.

[2] *patent stove*   Open stove.

[3] *Lincoln's Inn*   One of four (Lincoln's Inn, Gray's Inn, Inner Temple, Middle Temple) institutions, all located in London, that have exercised the exclusive right since the Middle Ages of admitting barristers (lawyers) to the bar (i.e., to practise law). Lincoln's Inn is located just off Chancery Lane, near to Honoria Fraser's chambers.

[4] *ash pans*   I.e., ashtrays.

(*Vivie comes in, in her hat and jacket. She stops and stares at him.*)

VIVIE.   (*Sternly.*) What are you doing here?

FRANK.   Waiting to see you. Ive been here for hours. Is this the way you attend to your business? (*He puts his hat and stick on the table, and perches himself with a vault on the clerk's stool looking at her with every appearance of being in a specially restless, teasing, flippant mood.*)

VIVIE.   Ive been away exactly twenty minutes for a cup of tea. (*She takes off her hat and jacket and hangs them up behind the screen.*) How did you get in?

FRANK.   The staff had not left when I arrived. He's gone to play cricket on Primrose Hill.[5] Why dont you employ a woman, and give your sex a chance?

VIVIE.   What have you come for?

15 FRANK.   (*Springing off the stool and coming close to her.*) Viv: lets go and enjoy the Saturday half-holiday somewhere, like the staff. What do you say to Richmond,[6] and then a music hall,[7] and a jolly supper?

VIVIE.   Cant afford it. I shall put in another six hours work before I go to bed.

FRANK.   Cant afford it, cant we? Aha! Look here. (*He takes out a handful of sovereigns and makes them chink.*) Gold, Viv: gold!

VIVIE.   Where did you get it?

25 FRANK.   Gambling, Viv: gambling. Poker.

VIVIE.   Pah! It's meaner than stealing it. No: I'm not coming. (*She sits down to work at the table, with her back to the glass door, and begins turning over the papers.*)

FRANK.   (*Remonstrating piteously.*) But, my dear Viv, I want to talk to you ever so seriously.

VIVIE.   Very well: sit down in Honoria's chair and talk here. I like ten minutes chat after tea. (*He murmurs.*) No use groaning: I'm inexorable. (*He takes the opposite seat disconsolately.*) Pass that cigar box, will you?

35 FRANK.   (*Pushing the cigar box across.*) Nasty womanly habit. Nice men dont do it any longer.

---

[5] *Primrose Hill*   Parkland area northwest of central London, frequently visited by Shaw.

[6] *Richmond*   Town on the Thames, a few miles southwest of central London.

[7] *music hall*   Music halls were popular places of entertainment in Victorian England, featuring songs, comedy, dances, and novelty acts.

VIVIE.   Yes: they object to the smell in the office; and weve had to take to cigarets. See! (*She opens the box and takes out a cigaret, which she lights. She offers him one; but he shakes his head with a wry face. She settles herself comfortably in her chair, smoking.*) Go ahead.

FRANK.   Well, I want to know what youve done—what arrangements youve made.

VIVIE.   Everything was settled twenty minutes after I arrived here. Honoria has found the business too much for her this year; and she was on the point of sending for me and proposing partnership when I walked in and told her I hadnt a farthing[1] in the world. So I installed myself and packed her off for a fortnight's holiday. What happened at Haslemere when I left?

FRANK.   Nothing at all. I said you had gone to town on particular business.

VIVIE.   Well?

FRANK.   Well, either they were too flabbergasted to say anything, or else Crofts had prepared your mother. Anyhow, she didnt say anything; and Crofts didnt say anything; and Praddy only stared. After tea they got up and went; and Ive not seen them since.

VIVIE.   (*Nodding placidly with one eye on a wreath of smoke.*) Thats all right.

FRANK.   (*Looking round disparagingly.*) Do you intend to stick in this confounded place?

VIVIE.   (*Blowing the wreath decisively away, and sitting straight up.*) Yes. These two days have given me back all my strength and self-possession. I will never take a holiday again as long as I live.

FRANK.   (*With a very wry face.*) Mps! You look quite happy. And as hard as nails.

VIVIE.   (*Grimly.*) Well for me that I am!

FRANK.   (*Rising.*) Look here, Viv: we must have an explanation. We parted the other day under a complete misunderstanding. (*He sits on the table, close to her.*)

VIVIE.   (*Putting away the cigaret.*) Well: clear it up.

FRANK.   You remember what Crofts said?

VIVIE.   Yes.

FRANK.   That revelation was supposed to bring about a complete change in the nature of our feeling for one another. It placed us on the footing of brother and sister.

VIVIE.   Yes.

FRANK.   Have you ever had a brother?

VIVIE.   No.

FRANK.   Then you dont know what being brother and sister feels like? Now I have lots of sisters; and the fraternal feeling is quite familiar to me. I assure you my feeling for you is not the least in the world like it. The girls will go their way; I will go mine; and we shant care if we never see one another again. Thats brother and sister. But as to you, I cant be easy if I have to pass a week without seeing you. Thats not brother and sister. It's exactly what I felt an hour before Crofts made his revelation. In short, dear Viv, it's love's young dream.

VIVIE.   (*Bitingly.*) The same feeling, Frank, that brought your father to my mother's feet. Is that it?

FRANK.   (*So revolted that he slips off the table for a moment.*) I very strongly object, Viv, to have my feelings compared to any which the Reverend Samuel is capable of harboring; and I object still more to a comparison of you to your mother. (*Resuming his perch.*) Besides, I dont believe the story. I have taxed my father with it, and obtained from him what I consider tantamount to a denial.

VIVIE.   What did he say?

FRANK.   He said he was sure there must be some mistake.

VIVIE.   Do you believe him?

FRANK.   I am prepared to take his word as against Crofts'.

VIVIE.   Does it make any difference? I mean in your imagination or conscience; for of course it makes no real difference.

FRANK.   (*Shaking his head.*) None whatever to m e.

VIVIE.   Nor to me.

FRANK.   (*Staring.*) But this is ever so surprising! (*He goes back to his chair.*) I thought our whole relations were altered in your imagination and conscience, as you put it, the moment those words were out of that brute's muzzle.

VIVIE.   No: it was not that. I didnt believe him. I only wish I could.

Frank.   Eh?

VIVIE.   I think brother and sister would be a very suitable relation for us.

---

[1] *farthing* A bronze coin, the smallest denomination of British currency (one quarter of a penny). The farthing was withdrawn from circulation in 1961.

FRANK.   You really mean that?

125 VIVIE.   Yes. It's the only relation I care for, even if we could afford any other. I mean that.

FRANK.   (*Raising his eyebrows like one on whom a new light has dawned, and rising with quite an effusion of chivalrous sentiment.*) My dear Viv: why didnt you say so

130 before? I am ever so sorry for persecuting you. I understand, of course.

VIVIE.   (*Puzzled.*) Understand what?

FRANK.   Oh, I'm not a fool in the ordinary sense: only in the Scriptural sense of doing all the things the wise man

135 declared to be folly, after trying them himself on the most extensive scale.[1] I see I am no longer Vivvum's little boy. Dont be alarmed: I shall never call you Vivvums again—at least unless you get tired of your new little boy, whoever he may be.

140 VIVIE.   My new little boy!

FRANK.   (*With conviction.*) Must be a new little boy. Always happens that way. No other way, in fact.

VIVIE.   None that you know of, fortunately for you.

(*Someone knocks at the door.*)

FRANK.   My curse upon yon caller, whoe'er he be!

145 VIVIE.   It's Praed. He's going to Italy and wants to say goodbye. I asked him to call this afternoon. Go and let him in.

FRANK.   We can continue our conversation after his departure for Italy. I'll stay him out. (*He goes to the door*

150 *and opens it.*) How are you, Praddy? Delighted to see you. Come in.

(*Praed, dressed for travelling, comes in, in high spirits.*)

PRAED.   How do you do, Miss Warren? (*She presses his hand cordially, though a certain sentimentality in his high spirits jars on her.*) I start in an hour from the Holborn

155 Viaduct.[2] I wish I could persuade you to try Italy.

VIVIE.   What for?

PRAED.   Why, to saturate yourself with beauty and romance, of course.

---

[1] *extensive scale* Perhaps a reference to Solomon's comments on folly throughout the Book of Proverbs.

[2] *Holborn Viaduct* The Holborn Viaduct opened in London in 1869 as a route for trains over the valley of the Fleet River (which had been covered over since the middle of the eighteenth century).

(*Vivie, with a shudder, turns her chair to the table, as if the work waiting for her there were a support to her. Praed sits opposite to her. Frank places a chair near Vivie, and drops lazily and carelessly into it, talking at her over his shoulder.*)

FRANK.   No use, Praddy. Viv is a little Philistine.[3] She is

160 indifferent to my romance, and insensible to my beauty.

VIVIE.   Mr Praed: once for all, there is no beauty and no romance in life for me. Life is what it is; and I am prepared to take it as it is.

PRAED.   (*Enthusiastically.*) You will not say that if you

165 come with me to Verona and on to Venice. You will cry with delight at living in such a beautiful world.

FRANK.   This is most eloquent, Praddy. Keep it up.

PRAED.   Oh, I assure you *I* have cried—I shall cry again, I hope—at fifty! At your age, Miss Warren, you would

170 not need to go so far as Verona. Your spirits would absolutely fly up at the mere sight of Ostend. You would be charmed with the gaiety, the vivacity, the happy air of Brussels.

VIVIE.   (*Springing up with an exclamation of loathing.*)

175 Agh!

PRAED.   (*Rising.*) Whats the matter?

FRANK.   (*Rising.*) Hallo, Viv!

VIVIE.   (*To Praed, with deep reproach.*) Can you find no better example of your beauty and romance than

180 Brussels to talk to me about?

PRAED.   (*Puzzled.*) Of course it's very different from Verona. I dont suggest for a moment that—

VIVIE.   (*Bitterly.*) Probably the beauty and romance come to much the same in both places.

185 PRAED.   (*Completely sobered and much concerned.*) My dear Miss Warren: I—(*Looking inquiringly at Frank.*) Is anything the matter?

FRANK.   She thinks your enthusiasm frivolous, Praddy. She's had ever such a serious call.[4]

190 VIVIE.   (*Sharply.*) Hold your tongue, Frank. Dont be silly.

FRANK.   (*Sitting down.*) Do you call this good manners, Praed?

---

[3] *Philistine* From the historical Philistines, enemies of the Israelites; the modern sense of the word denotes someone hostile or indifferent to culture and the arts.

[4] *call* I.e., divine prompting to service.

PRAED. (*Anxious and considerate.*) Shall I take him away, Miss Warren? I feel sure we have disturbed you at your work.

VIVIE. Sit down: I'm not ready to go back to work yet. (*Praed sits.*) You both think I have an attack of nerves. Not a bit of it. But there are two subjects I want dropped, if you dont mind. One of them (*To Frank.*) is love's young dream in any shape or form: the other (*To Praed.*) is the romance and beauty of life, especially Ostend and the gaiety of Brussels. You are welcome to any illusions you have left on these subjects: I have none. If we three are to remain friends, I must be treated as a woman of business, permanently single (*To Frank.*) and permanently unromantic (*To Praed.*).

FRANK. I shall also remain permanently single until you change your mind. Praddy: change the subject. Be eloquent about something else.

PRAED. (*Diffidently.*) I'm afraid theres nothing else in the world I c a n talk about. The Gospel of Art is the only one I can preach. I know Miss Warren is a great devotee of the Gospel of Getting On; but we cant discuss that without hurting your feelings, Frank, since you are determined not to get on.

FRANK. Oh, dont mind my feelings. Give me some improving advice by all means: it does me ever so much good. Have another try to make a successful man of me, Viv. Come: lets have it all: energy, thrift, foresight, self-respect, character. Dont you hate people who have no character, Viv?

VIVIE. (*Wincing.*) Oh, stop, stop: let us have no more of that horrible cant. Mr Praed: if there are really only those two gospels in the world, we had better all kill ourselves; for the same taint is in both, through and through.

FRANK. (*Looking critically at her.*) There is a touch of poetry about you today, Viv, which has hitherto been lacking.

PRAED. (*Remonstrating.*) My dear Frank: arnt you a little unsympathetic?

VIVIE. (*Merciless to herself.*) No: it's good for me. It keeps me from being sentimental.

FRANK. (*Bantering her.*) Checks your strong natural propensity that way, dont it?

VIVIE. (*Almost hysterically.*) Oh yes: go on: dont spare me. I was sentimental for one moment in my life—beautifully sentimental—by moonlight; and now—

FRANK. (*Quickly.*) I say, Viv: take care. Dont give yourself away.

VIVIE. Oh, do you think Mr Praed does not know all about my mother? (*Turning on Praed.*) You had better have told me that morning, Mr Praed. You are very old fashioned in your delicacies, after all.

PRAED. Surely it is you who are a little old fashioned in your prejudices, Miss Warren. I feel bound to tell you, speaking as an artist, and believing that the most intimate human relationships are far beyond and above the scope of the law, that though I know that your mother is an unmarried woman, I do not respect her the less on that account. I respect her more.

FRANK. (*Airily.*) Hear! Hear!

VIVIE. (*Staring at him.*) Is that a l l you know?

PRAED. Certainly that is all.

VIVIE. Then you neither of you know anything. Your guesses are innocence itself compared to the truth.

PRAED. (*Rising, startled and indignant, and preserving his politeness with an effort.*) I hope not. (*More empathetically.*) I hope not, Miss Warren.

FRANK. (*Whistles.*) Whew!

VIVIE. You are not making it easy for me to tell you, Mr Praed.

PRAED. (*His chivalry drooping before their conviction.*) If there i s anything worse—that is, anything else—are you sure you are right to tell us, Miss Warren?

VIVIE. I am sure that if I had the courage I should spend the rest of my life in telling everybody—stamping and branding it into them until they all felt their part in its abomination as I feel mine. There is nothing I despise more than the wicked convention that protects these things by forbidding a woman to mention them. And yet I cant tell you. The two infamous words[1] that describe what my mother is are ringing in my ears and struggling on my tongue; but I cant utter them: the shame of them is too horrible for me. (*She buries her face in her hands. The two men, astonished, stare at one another and then at her. She raises her head again desperately and snatches a sheet of paper and a pen.*) Here:

---

[1] *two infamous words* Having read the page proofs of *Mrs Warren's Profession* in July 1897, actress Ellen Terry asked Shaw what the "two infamous words" were. Shaw replied, "Prostitute and Procuress."

let me draft you a prospectus.

FRANK.   Oh, she's mad. Do you hear, Viv? mad. Come! pull yourself together.

VIVIE.   You shall see. (*She writes.*) "Paid up capital: not less than £40,000 standing in the name of Sir George Crofts, Baronet, the chief shareholder. Premises at Brussels, Ostend, Vienna and Budapest. Managing director: Mrs Warren"; and now dont let us forget her qualifications: the two words. (*She writes the words and pushes the paper to them.*) There! Oh no: dont read it: dont! (*She snatches it back and tears it to pieces; then seizes her head in her hands and hides her face on the table.*)

(*Frank, who has watched the writing over her shoulder, and opened his eyes very widely at it, takes a card from his pocket; scribbles the two words on it; and silently hands it to Praed, who reads it with amazement, and hides it hastily in his pocket.*)

FRANK.   (*Whispering tenderly.*) Viv, dear: thats all right. I read what you wrote: so did Praddy. We understand. And we remain, as this leaves us at present, yours ever so devotedly.

PRAED.   We do indeed, Miss Warren. I declare you are the most splendidly courageous woman I ever met.

(*This sentimental compliment braces Vivie. She throws it away from her with an impatient shake, and forces herself to stand up, though not without some support from the table.*)

FRANK.   Dont stir, Viv, if you dont want to. Take it easy.

VIVIE.   Thank you. You can always depend on me for two things: not to cry and not to faint. (*She moves a few steps toward the door of the inner room, and stops close to Praed to say*) I shall need much more courage than that when I tell my mother that we have come to the parting of the ways. Now I must go into the next room for a moment to make myself neat again, if you dont mind.

PRAED.   Shall we go away?

VIVIE.   No: I'll be back presently. Only for a moment. (*She goes into the other room, Praed opening the door for her.*)

PRAED.   What an amazing revelation! I'm extremely disappointed in Crofts: I am indeed.

FRANK.   I'm not in the least. I feel he's perfectly accounted for at last. But what a facer[1] for me, Praddy! I cant marry her now.

PRAED.   (*Sternly.*) Frank! (*The two look at one another, Frank unruffled, Praed deeply indignant.*) Let me tell you, Gardner, that if you desert her now you will behave very despicably.

FRANK.   Good old Praddy! Ever chivalrous! But you mistake: it's not the moral aspect of the case: it's the money aspect. I really cant bring myself to touch the old woman's money now.

PRAED.   And was that what you were going to marry on?

FRANK.   What else? *I* havnt any money, nor the smallest turn for making it. If I married Viv now she would have to support me; and I should cost her more than I am worth.

PRAED.   But surely a clever bright fellow like you can make something by your own brains.

FRANK.   Oh yes, a little. (*He takes out his money again.*) I made all that yesterday in an hour and a half. But I made it in a highly speculative business. No, dear Praddy: even if Bessie and Georgina[2] marry millionaires and the governor dies after cutting them off with a shilling,[3] I shall have only four hundred a year. And he wont die until he's three score and ten.[4] He hasnt originality enough. I shall be on short allowance for the next twenty years. No short allowance for Viv, if I can help it. I withdraw gracefully and leave the field to the guilded youth of England. So thats settled. I shant worry her about it: I'll just send her a little note after we're gone. She'll understand.

PRAED.   (*Grasping his hand.*) Good fellow, Frank! I heartily beg your pardon. But must you never see her again?

FRANK.   Never see her again! Hang it all, be reasonable. I shall come along as often as possible, and be her brother. I c a n n o t understand the absurd consequences you romantic people expect from the most ordinary

---

[1]   *facer* A blow in the face (figuratively); a sudden difficulty.

[2]   *Bessie and Georgina* Frank's sisters. In the 1898 text Bessie is Jessie, and Frank has other (unnamed) sisters.

[3]   *shilling* A shilling was one-twentieth part of £1 in the British currency system prior to decimilization in 1971.

[4]   *three score and ten* From Psalms 90.10: "The days of our years are three-score years and ten ..." I.e., the number of years traditionally allotted to human beings.

350 transactions. (*A knock at the door.*) I wonder who this is. Would you mind opening the door? If it's a client it will look more respectable than if I appeared.

PRAED.   Certainly. (*He goes to the door, and opens it. Frank sits down in Vivie's chair to scribble a note.*) My
355 dear Kitty: come in: come in.

(*Mrs Warren comes in, looking apprehensively round for Vivie. She has done her best to make herself matronly and dignified. The brilliant hat is replaced by a sober bonnet, and the gay blouse covered by a costly black silk mantle. She is pitiably anxious and ill at ease: evidently panic-stricken.*)

MRS WARREN.   (*To Frank.*) What! Y o u r e here, are you?

FRANK.   (*Turning in his chair from his writing, but not*
360 *rising.*) Here, and charmed to see you. You come like a breath of spring.

MRS WARREN.   Oh, get out with your nonsense. (*In a low voice.*) Wheres Vivie?

(*Frank points expressively to the door of the inner room, but says nothing.*)

MRS WARREN.   (*Sitting down suddenly and almost*
365 *beginning to cry.*) Praddy: wont she see me, dont you think?

PRAED.   My dear Kitty: dont distress yourself. Why should she not?

MRS WARREN.   Oh, you never can see why not: youre
370 too innocent.[1] Mr Frank: did she say anything to you?

FRANK.   (*Folding his note.*) She m u s t see you, if (*very expressively*) you wait til she comes in.

MRS WARREN.   (*Frightened.*) Why shouldnt I wait?

(*Frank looks quizzically at her; puts his note carefully on the ink bottle, so that Vivie cannot fail to find it when next she dips her pen; then rises and devotes his attention to her.*)

FRANK.   My dear Mrs Warren: suppose you were a
375 sparrow—ever so tiny and pretty a sparrow hopping in the roadway—and you saw a steam roller coming in your direction, would you wait for it?

MRS WARREN.   Oh, dont bother me with your sparrows.

---

[1] *too innocent* In the 1898 text Praed is "too amiable."

What did she run away from the Haslemere like that
380 for?

FRANK.   I'm afraid she'll tell you if you rashly await her return.

MRS WARREN.   Do you want me to go away?

FRANK.   No: I always want you to stay. But I a d v i s e
385 you to go away.

MRS WARREN.   What! And never see her again!

FRANK.   Precisely.

MRS WARREN.   (*Crying again.*) Praddy: dont let him be cruel to me. (*She hastily checks her tears and wipes her*
390 *eyes.*) She'll be so angry if she sees Ive been crying.

FRANK.   (*With a touch of real compassion in his airy tenderness.*) You know that Praddy is the soul of kindness, Mrs Warren. Praddy: what do y o u say? Go or stay?

395 PRAED.   (*To Mrs Warren.*) I really should be very sorry to cause you unnecessary pain; but I think perhaps you had better not wait. The fact is—(*Vivie is heard at the inner door.*)

FRANK.   Sh! Too late. She's coming.

400 MRS WARREN.   Dont tell her I was crying. (*Vivie comes in. She stops gravely on seeing Mrs Warren, who greets her with hysterical cheerfulness.*) Well, dearie. So here you are at last.

VIVIE.   I am glad you have come. I want to speak to you.
405 You said you were going, Frank, I think.

FRANK.   Yes. Will you come with me, Mrs Warren? What do you say to a trip to Richmond, and the theatre in the evening? There is safety in Richmond. No steam roller there.

410 VIVIE.   Nonsense, Frank. My mother will stay here.

MRS WARREN.   (*Scared.*) I dont know: perhaps I'd better go. We're disturbing you at your work.

VIVIE.   (*With quiet decision.*) Mr Praed: please take Frank away. Sit down, mother. (*Mrs Warren obeys helplessly.*)

415 PRAED.   Come, Frank. Goodbye, Miss Vivie.

VIVIE.   (*Shaking hands.*) Goodbye. A pleasant trip.

PRAED.   Thank you: thank you. I hope so.

FRANK.   (*To Mrs Warren.*) Goodbye: youd ever so much better have taken my advice. (*He shakes hands with her.*
420 *Then airily to Vivie.*) Byebye, Viv.

VIVIE.   Goodbye. (*He goes out gaily without shaking hands with her.*)

PRAED.   (*Sadly.*) Goodbye, Kitty.

MRS WARREN.   (*Snivelling.*) —oobye!

(*Praed goes. Vivie, composed and extremely grave, sits down in Honoria's chair, and waits for her mother to speak. Mrs Warren, dreading a pause, loses no time in beginning.*)

425 MRS WARREN.   Well, Vivie, what did you go away like that for without saying a word to me? How could you do such a thing! And what have you done to poor George? I wanted him to come with me; but he shuffled out of it. I could see that he was quite afraid of you.
430 Only fancy: he wanted me not to come. As if (*Trembling.*) I should be afraid of you, dearie. (*Vivie's gravity deepens.*) But of course I told him it was all settled and comfortable between us, and that we were on the best of terms. (*She breaks down.*) Vivie: whats the meaning of
435 this? (*She produces a commercial envelope, and fumbles at the enclosure with trembling fingers.*) I got it from the bank this morning.
VIVIE.   It is my month's allowance. They sent it to me as usual the other day. I simply sent it back to be placed to
440 your credit, and asked them to send you the lodgment receipt.[1] In future I shall support myself.
MRS WARREN.   (*Not daring to understand.*) Wasnt it enough? Why didnt you tell me? (*With a cunning gleam in her eye.*) I'll double it: I was intending to double it.
445 Only let me know how much you want.
VIVIE.   You know very well that that has nothing to do with it. From this time I go my own way in my own business and among my own friends. And you will go yours. (*She rises.*) Goodbye.
450 MRS WARREN.   (*Rising, appalled.*) Goodbye?
VIVIE.   Yes: Goodbye. Come: dont let us make a useless scene: you understand perfectly well. Sir George Crofts has told me the whole business.
MRS WARREN.   (*Angrily.*) Silly old—(*She swallows an
455 epithet, and turns white at the narrowness of her escape from uttering it.*)
VIVIE.   Just so.
MRS WARREN.   He ought to have his tongue cut out. But I thought it was ended: you said you didnt mind.
460 VIVIE.   (*Steadfastly.*) Excuse me: I d o mind.
MRS WARREN. But I explained—
VIVIE.   You explained how it came about. You did not

tell me that it is still going on. (*She sits.*)

(*Mrs Warren, silenced for a moment, looks forlornly at Vivie, who waits, secretly hoping that the combat is over. But the cunning expression comes back into Mrs Warren's face; and she bends across the table, sly and urgent, half whispering.*)

MRS WARREN.   Vivie: do you know how rich I am?
465 VIVIE.   I have no doubt you are very rich.
MRS WARREN.   But you dont know all that that means: youre too young. It means a new dress every day; it means theatres and balls every night; it means having the pick of all the gentlemen in Europe at your feet; it
470 means a lovely house and plenty of servants; it means the choicest of eating and drinking; it means everything you like, everything you want, everything you can think of. And what are you here? A mere drudge, toiling and moiling[2] early and late for your bare living and two
475 cheap dresses a year. Think over it. (*Soothingly.*) Youre shocked, I know. I can enter into your feelings; and I think they do you credit; but trust me, nobody will blame you: you may take my word for that. I know what young girls are; and I know youll think better of it when
480 youve turned it over in your mind.
VIVIE.   So thats how it's done, is it? You must have said all that to many a woman, mother, to have it so pat.
MRS WARREN.   (*Passionately.*) What harm am I asking you to do? (*Vivie turns away contemptuously. Mrs Warren
485 continues desperately.*) Vivie: listen to me: you dont understand: youve been taught wrong on purpose: you dont know what the world is really like.
VIVIE.   (*Arrested.*) Taught wrong on purpose! What do you mean?
490 MRS WARREN.   I mean that youre throwing away all your chances for nothing. You think that people are what they pretend to be: that the way you were taught at school and college to think right and proper is the way things really are. But it's not: it's all only a pretence,
495 to keep the cowardly slavish common run of people quiet. Do you want to find that out, like other women, at forty when youve thrown yourself away and lost your chances; or wont you take it in good time now from your own mother, that loves you and swears to you that

---

[1] *lodgment receipt* Deposit receipt.

[2] *toiling and moiling* Working extremely hard.

it's truth: gospel truth? (*Urgently.*) Vivie: the big people, the clever people, the managing people, all know it. They do as I do, and think what I think. I know plenty of them. I know them to speak to, to introduce you to, to make friends of for you. I dont mean anything wrong: thats what you dont understand: your head is full of ignorant ideas about me. What do the people that taught you know about life or about people like me? When did they ever meet me, or speak to me, or let anyone tell them about me? the fools! Would they ever have done anything for you if I hadnt paid them? Havnt I told you that I want you to be respectable? Havnt I brought you up to be respectable? And how can you keep it up without my money and my influence and Lizzie's friends? Cant you see that youre cutting your own throat as well as breaking my heart in turning your back on me?

VIVIE. I recognize the Crofts philosophy of life, mother. I heard it all from him that day at the Gardners'.

MRS WARREN. You think I want to force that played-out old sot on you! I dont, Vivie: on my oath I dont.

VIVIE. It would not matter if you did: you would not succeed. (*Mrs Warren winces, deeply hurt by the implied indifference towards her affectionate intention. Vivie, neither understanding this nor concerning herself about it, goes on calmly.*) Mother: you dont at all know the sort of person I am. I dont object to Crofts more than to any other coarsely built man of his class. To tell you the truth, I rather admire him for being strongminded enough to enjoy himself in his own way and make plenty of money instead of living the usual shooting, hunting, dining-out, tailoring, loafing life of his set merely because all the rest do it. And I'm perfectly aware that if I'd been in the same circumstances as my aunt Liz, I'd have done exactly what she did. I dont think I'm more prejudiced or straightlaced than you: I think I'm less. I'm certain I'm less sentimental. I know very well that fashionable morality is all a pretence, and that if I took your money and devoted the rest of my life to spending it fashionably, I might be as worthless and vicious and the silliest woman could possibly want to be without having a word said to me about it. But I dont want to be worthless. I shouldnt enjoy trotting about the park to advertise my dressmaker and carriage builder, or being bored at the opera to shew off a shopwindowful of diamonds.

MRS WARREN. (*Bewildered.*) But—

VIVIE. Wait a moment. Ive not done. Tell me why you continue your business now that you are independent of it. Your sister, you told me, has left all that behind her. Why dont you do the same?

MRS WARREN. Oh, it's all very easy for Liz: she likes good society, and has the air of being a lady. Imagine m e in a cathedral town! Why, the very rooks in the trees would find me out even if I could stand the dulness of it. I must have work and excitement, or I should go melancholy mad. And what else is there for me to do? The life suits me: I'm fit for it and not for anything else. If I didnt do it, somebody else would; so I dont do any real harm by it. And then it brings in money; and I like making money. No: it's no use: I cant give it up—not for anybody. But what need you know about it? I'll never mention it. I'll keep Crofts away. I'll not trouble you much: you see I have to be constantly running about from one place to another. Youll be quit of me altogether when I die.

VIVIE. No: I am my mother's daughter. I am like you: I must have work, and must make more money than I spend. But my work is not your work, and my way not your way. We must part. It will not make much difference to us: instead of meeting one another for perhaps a few months in twenty years, we shall never meet: thats all.

MRS WARREN. (*Her voice stifled in tears.*) Vivie: I meant to have been more with you: I did indeed.

VIVIE. It's no use, mother: I am not to be changed by a few cheap tears and entreaties any more than you are, I daresay.

MRS WARREN. (*Wildly.*) Oh, you call a mother's tears cheap.

VIVIE. They cost you nothing; and you ask me to give you the peace and quietness of my whole life in exchange for them. What use would my company be to you if you could get it? What have we two in common that could make either of us happy together?

MRS WARREN. (*Lapsing recklessly into her dialect.*) We're mother and daughter. I want my daughter. Ive a right to you. Who is to care for me when I'm old? Plenty of girls have taken to me like daughters and cried at leaving me; but I let them all go because I had you to look forward

590 to. I kept myself lonely for you. Youve no right to turn on me now and refuse to do your duty as daughter.

VIVIE. (*Jarred and antagonized by the echo of the slums in her mother's voice.*) My duty as a daughter! I thought we should come to that presently. Now once for all, 595 mother, you want a daughter and Frank wants a wife. I dont want a mother; and I dont want a husband. I have spared neither Frank nor myself in sending him about his business. Do you think I will spare y o u?

MRS WARREN. (*Violently.*) Oh, I know the sort you are: 600 no mercy for yourself or anyone else. *I* know. My experience has done that for me anyhow: I can tell the pious, canting, hard, selfish woman when I meet her. Well, keep yourself to yourself: *I* dont want you. But listen to this. Do you now what I would do with you if 605 you were a baby again? aye, as sure as theres a Heaven above us.

VIVIE. Strangle me, perhaps.

MRS WARREN. No: I'd bring you up to be a real daughter to me, and not what you are now, with your 610 pride and your prejudices and the college education you stole from me: yes, stole: deny it if you can: what was it but stealing? I'd bring you up in my own house, I would.

VIVIE. (*Quietly.*) In one of your own houses.

615 MRS WARREN. (*Screaming.*) Listen to her! listen to how she spits on her mother's grey hairs! Oh, may you live to have your own daughter tear and trample on you as you have trampled on me. And you will: you will. No woman ever had luck with a mother's curse on her.

620 VIVIE. I wish you wouldnt rant, mother. It only hardens me. Come: I suppose I am the only young woman you ever had in your power that you did good to. Dont spoil it all now.

MRS WARREN. Yes, Heaven forgive me, it's true; and 625 you are the only one that ever turned on me. Oh, the injustice of it! the injustice! the injustice! I always wanted to be a good woman. I tried honest work; and I was slave-driven until I cursed the day I ever heard of honest work. I was a good mother; and because I made

630 my daughter a good woman she turns me out as if I was a leper. Oh, if I only had my life to live over again! I'd talk to that lying clergyman in the school. From this time forth, so help me Heaven in my last hour, I'll do wrong and nothing but wrong. And I'll prosper on it.

635 VIVIE. Yes: it's better to choose your line and go through with it. If I had been you, mother, I might have done as you did: but I should not have lived one life and believed in another. You are a conventional woman at heart. That is why I am bidding you goodbye now. I am 640 right, am I not?

MRS WARREN. (*Taken aback.*) Right to throw away all my money?

VIVIE. No: right to get rid of you! I should be a fool not to. Isnt that so?

645 MRS WARREN. (*Sulkily.*) Oh well, yes, if you come to that, I suppose you are. But Lord help the world if everybody took to doing the right thing! And now I'd better go than stay where I'm not wanted. (*She turns to the door.*)

650 VIVIE. (*Kindly.*) Wont you shake hands?

MRS WARREN. (*After looking at her fiercely for a moment with a savage impulse to strike her.*) No, thank you. Goodbye.

VIVIE. (*Matter-of-factly.*) Goodbye. (*Mrs Warren goes* 655 *out, slamming the door behind her. The strain on Vivie's face relaxes; her grave expression breaks up into one of joyous content; her breath goes out in a half sob, half laugh of intense relief. She goes buoyantly to her place at the writing-table; pushes the electric lamp out of the way; pulls* 660 *over a great sheaf of papers; and is in the act of dipping her pen in the ink when she finds Frank's note. She opens it unconcernedly and reads it quickly, giving a little laugh at some quaint turn of expression in it.*) And goodbye, Frank. (*She tears the note up and tosses the pieces into the* 665 *waste paper basket without a second thought. Then she goes at her work with a plunge, and soon becomes absorbed in its figures.*)

—1898, 1930

Joseph Conrad

1857 – 1924

Joseph Conrad has long been recognized as one of the twentieth century's greatest writers of fiction in English—an extraordinary fact given that English was his third language, and that a significant portion of his early adult life was spent in nautical, rather than literary, pursuits. He did not become a British citizen until he was almost 30 years old, and did not begin his career as an author until he was almost 40. Yet in spite of his status as an outsider to the vibrant literary circles of late nineteenth-century British society, Conrad soon established himself as one of the finest literary craftsmen of his

age. Initially many regarded him as an able seaman who simply turned his colorful experiences into material for his novels; it soon became evident that Joseph Conrad was an exceptional writer whose work demonstrated a careful and deliberate attention to political, psychological, and social nuances.

Joseph Conrad was born Jozef Teodor Konrad Nalecz Korzeniowski on 3 December 1857, in Poland (then under Russian rule). His parents, Apollo and Evalina, were members of the educated, landed gentry who opposed Czarist Russian control in Poland. Apollo was arrested for revolutionary conspiracy, and, in 1862, the family was exiled to Vologda in northern Russia and forced to endure years of hardship and illness; Conrad's mother died in 1865 and his father in 1868.

Following the death of his parents, Conrad came under the guardianship of his maternal uncle in Kraków, Poland; he spent much of the next few years reading translations of Shakespeare, Dickens, and Victor Hugo. Yet Conrad seemed to dislike school life; he was bored and restless. At the age of fifteen, he expressed his desire to go to sea. He spent the next two years pressing his family for permission against strong opposition. His pleas were eventually heard, and in 1874, nearing his seventeenth birthday, Conrad traveled to Marseilles and joined the French merchant navy.

From 1874 to 1877, Conrad made a number of voyages to Martinique and the West Indies aboard French ships, where he quickly acquired great skill as a sailor. During these years he spent time engaged in illicit gunrunning on behalf of the Carlist Royalists in Spain. In 1878, due to huge debts acquired through smuggling and gambling, Conrad shot himself in the chest. He long claimed that this injury was the result of a duel, rather than what seems to have been a suicide attempt. Whatever the case, Conrad recovered from his injury and escaped his creditors by joining the British merchant navy. Knowing just a few words in English, Conrad began to learn the language in voyages between the ports of Lowescroft and Newcastle, aboard a coal schooner.

Over the next sixteen years, Conrad traveled to Australia, South America, India, Borneo, and the South Pacific in the service of the British merchant navy. In 1886, he achieved several important milestones: he received his certificate as a master mariner, became a British citizen, and changed his name to Joseph Conrad. In 1888, Conrad was given his only sea command as captain of the *Otago*; he spent the next 15 months journeying from Bangkok to Singapore, about the Malay Archipelago, and to Australia and Mauritius. Conrad would later use his experiences aboard the *Otago* as inspiration for *The Secret Sharer*. In 1890 he took a steamboat up the Congo River to take command of a

Belgian steamer—a journey that was an unmitigated disaster and yet would form the template for his best known work, *Heart of Darkness*. It was also while in the Congo that Conrad contracted malaria, the effects of which would plague him for years. In ill health and with his interest in writing increasing steadily, Conrad retired from seafaring and settled permanently in England in 1894; his first published novel was *Almayer's Folly* in 1895. He would dedicate the rest of his life to literary pursuits, writing prolifically until his death of a heart attack, near Canterbury, in 1924.

Conrad wrote 13 novels, two volumes of memoirs, and 28 short stories, but suffered from persistent doubts as to the quality of his creative output and from constant financial pressure. His experiences at sea form the background for many of his stories; his major interest is the profound moral and psychological ambiguities of the human experience. In *Lord Jim* (1900) he explores the concept of personal honor by presenting the hero's history as a life spent in atonement for an act of cowardice as a young marine officer. In *The Nigger of the "Narcissus"* (1897), Conrad shows how a single black seaman's plight affects the morale of an entire ship's crew. In *Heart of Darkness* (1902), Conrad revisits his own terrifying journey to the Congo as he explores the extent of human corruptibility.

In his later works, Conrad shifted his attention away from the sea and toward the complexities of politics. With *Nostromo* (1904), he explored the effects of politics and "material interests" on human relationships and the futility of human attempts at change. *The Secret Agent* (1906) concerns an anarchist bomb plot in London, and *Under Western Eyes* (1911) presents a story of betrayal and a search for redemption amidst antigovernment violence in Czarist Russia.

Conrad has long been considered a master of English prose—an extraordinary feat for a man who was twenty-one years of age before he began speaking a word of English. In part, however, his distanced relationship with the language may have helped free him to make English prose do new things. Words are carefully chosen for their evocative and symbolic functions and his often poetic prose style seems to float free of local idiosyncrasies.

Like much of Conrad's work, *The Secret Sharer* (1912) reflects his own personal experience—in this case, his experience as a new captain aboard the *Otago,* when he felt like an interloper aboard his own ship. The story features a *doppelgänger,* in the character of Leggatt; in addition to being a real character and contributor to the events of the story, Leggatt functions as the Captain's second self or alter ego. The work may be best viewed in the context of the late nineteenth- and early twentieth-century preoccupation with the unconscious and "true self." Like much of Conrad's work, it displays a tendency to regard society and the individual in terms of dualisms: good and evil, savagery and civilization, emotion and intellect. But whereas for many others of the time such dualisms fostered simplistic habits of thought, in Conrad's work they give rise to complexity and ambiguity.

In the "Preface" to *The Nigger of the "Narcissus,"* Conrad outlined his aims as an artist. The "Preface" was written a few months after finishing the work itself, and first appeared in the 1898 version of the book, at a time when Conrad had fully dedicated himself to his writing and found himself (in his own words) "done with the sea."

⌘ ⌘ ⌘

An Outpost of Progress

I

There were two white men in charge of the trading station. Kayerts, the chief, was short and fat; Carlier, the assistant, was tall, with a large head and a very broad trunk perched upon a long pair of thin legs. The third man on the staff was a Sierra Leone nigger,[1] who maintained that his name was Henry Price. However, for some reason or other, the natives down the river had given him the name of Makola, and it stuck to him through all his wanderings about the country. He spoke English and French with a warbling accent, wrote a beautiful hand, understood bookkeeping, and cherished in his innermost heart the worship of evil spirits. His wife was a negress from Loanda,[2] very large and very noisy. Three children rolled about in sunshine before the door of his low, shed-like dwelling. Makola, taciturn and impenetrable, despised the two white men. He had charge of a small clay storehouse with a dried-grass roof, and pretended to keep a correct account of beads, cotton cloth, red kerchiefs, brass wire, and other trade goods it contained. Besides the storehouse and Makola's hut, there was only one large building in the cleared ground of the station. It was built neatly of reeds, with a verandah on all the four sides. There were three rooms in it. The one in the middle was the living-room, and had two rough tables and a few stools in it. The other two were the bedrooms for the white men. Each had a bedstead and a mosquito net for all furniture. The plank floor was littered with the belongings of the white men; open half-empty boxes, torn wearing apparel, old boots; all the things dirty, and all the things broken, that accumulate mysteriously round untidy men. There was also another dwelling-place some distance away from the buildings. In it, under a tall cross much out of the perpendicular, slept the man who had seen the beginning of all this; who had planned and had watched the construction of this outpost of progress. He had been, at home, an unsuccessful painter who, weary of pursuing fame on an empty stomach, had gone out there through high protections. He had been the first chief of

that station. Makola had watched the energetic artist die of fever in the just finished house with his usual kind of "I told you so" indifference. Then, for a time, he dwelt alone with his family, his account books, and the Evil Spirit that rules the lands under the equator. He got on very well with his god. Perhaps he had propitiated him by a promise of more white men to play with, by and by. At any rate the director of the Great Trading Company, coming up in a steamer that resembled an enormous sardine box with a flat-roofed shed erected on it, found the station in good order, and Makola as usual quietly diligent. The director had the cross put up over the first agent's grave, and appointed Kayerts to the post. Carlier was told off as second in charge. The director was a man ruthless and efficient, who at times, but very imperceptibly, indulged in grim humour. He made a speech to Kayerts and Carlier, pointing out to them the promising aspect of their station. The nearest trading-post was about three hundred miles away. It was an exceptional opportunity for them to distinguish themselves and to earn percentages on the trade. This appointment was a favour done to beginners. Kayerts was moved almost to tears by his director's kindness. He would, he said, by doing his best, try to justify the flattering confidence, &c., &c. Kayerts had been in the Administration of the Telegraphs, and knew how to express himself correctly. Carlier, an ex-non-commissioned officer of cavalry in an army guaranteed from harm by several European Powers, was less impressed. If there were commissions to get, so much the better; and, trailing a sulky glance over the river, the forests, the impenetrable bush that seemed to cut off the station from the rest of the world, he muttered between his teeth, "We shall see, very soon."

Next day, some bales of cotton goods and a few cases of provisions having been thrown on shore, the sardine-box steamer went off, not to return for another six months. On the deck the director touched his cap to the two agents, who stood on the bank waving their hats, and turning to an old servant of the Company on his passage to headquarters, said, "Look at those two imbeciles. They must be mad at home to send me such specimens. I told those fellows to plant a vegetable garden, build new storehouses and fences, and construct a landing-stage. I bet nothing will be done! They won't

---

[1] *nigger*   The use of derogatory racial terms in literature remained common until the 1930s.

[2] *Loanda*   Capital of Angola (also Luanda).

know how to begin. I always thought the station on this river useless, and they just fit the station!"

"They will form themselves there," said the old stager with a quiet smile.

"At any rate, I am rid of them for six months," retorted the director.

The two men watched the steamer round the bend, then, ascending arm in arm the slope of the bank, returned to the station. They had been in this vast and dark country only a very short time, and as yet always in the midst of other white men, under the eye and guidance of their superiors. And now, dull as they were to the subtle influences of surroundings, they felt themselves very much alone, when suddenly left unassisted to face the wilderness; a wilderness rendered more strange, more incomprehensible by the mysterious glimpses of the vigorous life it contained. They were two perfectly insignificant and incapable individuals, whose existence is only rendered possible through the high organization of civilized crowds. Few men realize that their life, the very essence of their character, their capabilities and their audacities, are only the expression of their belief in the safety of their surroundings. The courage, the composure, the confidence; the emotions and principles; every great and every insignificant thought belongs not to the individual but to the crowd: to the crowd that believes blindly in the irresistible force of its institutions and of its morals, in the power of its police and of its opinion. But the contact with pure unmitigated savagery, with primitive nature and primitive man, brings sudden and profound trouble into the heart. To the sentiment of being alone of one's kind, to the clear perception of the loneliness of one's thoughts, of one's sensations—to the negation of the habitual, which is safe, there is added the affirmation of the unusual, which is dangerous; a suggestion of things vague, uncontrollable, and repulsive, whose discomposing intrusion excites the imagination and tries the civilized nerves of the foolish and the wise alike.

Kayerts and Carlier walked arm in arm, drawing close to one another as children do in the dark; and they had the same, not altogether unpleasant, sense of danger which one half suspects to be imaginary. They chatted persistently in familiar tones. "Our station is prettily situated," said one. The other assented with enthusiasm, enlarging volubly on the beauties of the situation. Then they passed near the grave. "Poor devil!" said Kayerts. "He died of fever, didn't he?" muttered Carlier, stopping short. "Why," retorted Kayerts, with indignation, "I've been told that the fellow exposed himself recklessly to the sun. The climate here, everybody says, is not at all worse than at home, as long as you keep out of the sun. Do you hear that, Carlier? I am chief here, and my orders are that you should not expose yourself to the sun!" He assumed his superiority jocularly, but his meaning was serious. The idea that he would, perhaps, have to bury Carlier and remain alone, gave him an inward shiver. He felt suddenly that this Carlier was more precious to him here, in the centre of Africa, than a brother could be anywhere else. Carlier, entering into the spirit of the thing, made a military salute and answered in a brisk tone, "Your orders shall be attended to, chief!" Then he burst out laughing, slapped Kayerts on the back and shouted, "We shall let life run easily here! Just sit still and gather in the ivory those savages will bring. This country has its good points, after all!" They both laughed loudly while Carlier thought: That poor Kayerts; he is so fat and unhealthy. It would be awful if I had to bury him here. He is a man I respect." … Before they reached the verandah of their house they called one another "my dear fellow."

The first day they were very active, pottering about with hammers and nails and red calico, to put up curtains, make their house habitable and pretty; resolved to settle down comfortably to their new life. For them an impossible task. To grapple effectually with even purely material problems requires more serenity of mind and more lofty courage than people generally imagine. No two beings could have been more unfitted for such a struggle. Society, not from any tenderness, but because of its strange needs, had taken care of those two men, forbidding them all independent thought, all initiative, all departure from routine; and forbidding it under pain of death. They could only live on condition of being machines. And now, released from the fostering care of men with pens behind the ears, or of men with gold lace on the sleeves, they were like those lifelong prisoners who, liberated after many years, do not know what use to make of their freedom. They did not know what use to make of their faculties, being both, through want of practice, incapable of independent thought.

At the end of two months Kayerts often would say, "If it was not for my Melie, you wouldn't catch me here." Melie was his daughter. He had thrown up his post in the Administration of the Telegraphs, though he had been for seventeen years perfectly happy there, to earn a dowry for his girl. His wife was dead, and the child was being brought up by his sisters. He regretted the streets, the pavements, the cafés, his friends of many years; all the things he used to see, day after day; all the thoughts suggested by familiar things—the thoughts effortless, monotonous, and soothing of a Government clerk; he regretted all the gossip, the small enmities, the mild venom, and the little jokes of Government offices. "If I had had a decent brother-in-law," Carlier would remark, "a fellow with a heart, I would not be here." He had left the army and had made himself so obnoxious to his family by his laziness and impudence, that an exasperated brother-in-law had made superhuman efforts to procure him an appointment in the Company as a second-class agent. Having not a penny in the world he was compelled to accept this means of livelihood as soon as it became quite clear to him that there was nothing more to squeeze out of his relations. He, like Kayerts, regretted his old life. He regretted the clink of sabre and spurs on a fine afternoon, the barrack-room witticisms, the girls of garrison towns; but, besides, he had also a sense of grievance. He was evidently a much ill-used man. This made him moody, at times. But the two men got on well together in the fellowship of their stupidity and laziness. Together they did nothing, absolutely nothing, and enjoyed the sense of idleness for which they were paid. And in time they came to feel something resembling affection for one another.

They lived like blind men in a large room, aware only of what came in contact with them (and of that only imperfectly), but unable to see the general aspect of things. The river, the forest, all the great land throbbing with life, were like a great emptiness. Even the brilliant sunshine disclosed nothing intelligible. Things appeared and disappeared before their eyes in an unconnected and aimless kind of way. The river seemed to come from nowhere and flow nowhither. It flowed through a void. Out of that void, at times, came canoes, and men with spears in their hands would suddenly crowd the yard of the station. They were naked, glossy black, ornamented with snowy shells and glistening brass wire, perfect of limb. They made an uncouth babbling noise when they spoke, moved in a stately manner, and sent quick, wild glances out of their startled, never-resting eyes. Those warriors would squat in long rows, four or more deep, before the verandah, while their chiefs bargained for hours with Makola over an elephant tusk. Kayerts sat on his chair and looked down on the proceedings, understanding nothing. He stared at them with his round blue eyes, called out to Carlier, "Here, look! look at that fellow there—and that other one, to the left. Did you ever see such a face? Oh, the funny brute!"

Carlier, smoking native tobacco in a short wooden pipe, would swagger up twirling his moustaches, and surveying the warriors with haughty indulgence, would say—

"Fine animals. Brought any bone? Yes? It's not any too soon. Look at the muscles of that fellow—third from the end. I wouldn't care to get a punch on the nose from him. Fine arms, but legs no good below the knee. Couldn't make cavalry men of them." And after glancing down complacently at his own shanks, he always concluded: "Pah! Don't they stink! You, Makola! Take that herd over to the fetish" (the storehouse was in every station called the fetish, perhaps because of the spirit of civilization it contained) "and give them up some of the rubbish you keep there. I'd rather see it full of bone than full of rags."

Kayerts approved.

"Yes, yes! Go and finish that palaver[1] over there, Mr. Makola. I will come round when you are ready, to weigh the tusk. We must be careful." Then turning to his companion: "This is the tribe that lives down the river; they are rather aromatic. I remember, they had been once before here. D'ye hear that row? What a fellow has got to put up with in this dog of a country! My head is split."

Such profitable visits were rare. For days the two pioneers of trade and progress would look on their empty courtyard in the vibrating brilliance of vertical sunshine. Below the high bank, the silent river flowed on glittering and steady. On the sands in the middle of the stream, hippos and alligators sunned themselves side

---

[1] *palaver* Discussion (particularly one concerning matters of trade).

by side. And stretching away in all directions, surrounding the insignificant cleared spot of the trading post, immense forests, hiding fateful complications of fantastic life, lay in the eloquent silence of mute greatness. The two men understood nothing, cared for nothing but for the passage of days that separated them from the steamer's return. Their predecessor had left some torn books. They took up these wrecks of novels, and, as they had never read anything of the kind before, they were surprised and amused. Then during long days there were interminable and silly discussions about plots and personages. In the centre of Africa they made acquaintance of Richelieu and of d'Artagnan, of Hawk's Eye and of Father Goriot,[1] and of many other people. All these imaginary personages became subjects for gossip as if they had been living friends. They discounted their virtues, suspected their motives, decried their successes; were scandalized at their duplicity or were doubtful about their courage. The accounts of crimes filled them with indignation, while tender or pathetic passages moved them deeply. Carlier cleared his throat and said in a soldierly voice, "What nonsense!" Kayerts, his round eyes suffused with tears, his fat cheeks quivering, rubbed his bald head, and declared, "This is a splendid book. I had no idea there were such clever fellows in the world." They also found some old copies of a home paper. That print discussed what it was pleased to call "Our Colonial Expansion" in high-flown language. It spoke much of the rights and duties of civilization, of the sacredness of the civilizing work, and extolled the merits of those who went about bringing light, and faith and commerce to the dark places of the earth. Carlier and Kayerts read, wondered, and began to think better of themselves. Carlier said one evening, waving his hand about, "In a hundred years, there will be perhaps a town here. Quays, and warehouses, and barracks, and—and—billiard-rooms. Civilization, my boy, and virtue—and all. And then, chaps will read that two good fellows, Kayerts and Carlier, were the first civilized men to live in this very spot!" Kayerts nodded, "Yes, it is a consolation to think of that." They seemed to forget their dead

[1]. of ... Goriot Cardinal Richelieu and d'Artagnan appear as characters in Alexandre Dumas' *The Three Musketeers* (1844); Hawkeye is a character in James Fenimore Cooper's "Leatherstocking Novels" (1823–41); Father Goriot is the protagonist in Honoré de Balzac's 1834 novel *Père Goriot*.

predecessor; but, early one day, Carlier went out and replanted the cross firmly. "It used to make me squint whenever I walked that way," he explained to Kayerts over the morning coffee. "It made me squint, leaning over so much. So I just planted it upright. And solid, I promise you! I suspended myself with both hands to the cross-piece. Not a move. Oh, I did that properly."

At times Gobila came to see them. Gobila was the chief of the neighbouring villages. He was a gray-headed savage, thin and black, with a white cloth round his loins and a mangy panther skin hanging over his back. He came up with long strides of his skeleton legs, swinging a staff as tall as himself, and, entering the common room of the station, would squat on his heels to the left of the door. There he sat, watching Kayerts, and now and then making a speech which the other did not understand. Kayerts, without interrupting his occupation, would from time to time say in a friendly manner: "How goes it, you old image?" and they would smile at one another. The two whites had a liking for that old and incomprehensible creature, and called him Father Gobila. Gobila's manner was paternal, and he seemed really to love all white men. They all appeared to him very young, indistinguishably alike (except for stature), and he knew that they were all brothers, and also immortal. The death of the artist, who was the first white man whom he knew intimately, did not disturb this belief, because he was firmly convinced that the white stranger had pretended to die and got himself buried for some mysterious purpose of his own, into which it was useless to inquire. Perhaps it was his way of going home to his own country? At any rate, these were his brothers, and he transferred his absurd affection to them. They returned it in a way. Carlier slapped him on the back, and recklessly struck off matches for his amusement. Kayerts was always ready to let him have a sniff at the ammonia bottle. In short, they behaved just like that other white creature that had hidden itself in a hole in the ground. Gobila considered them attentively. Perhaps they were the same being with the other—or one of them was. He couldn't decide—clear up that mystery; but he remained always very friendly. In consequence of that friendship the women of Gobila's village walked in single file through the reedy grass, bringing every morning to the station, fowls, and sweet potatoes, and palm wine, and sometimes a goat. The Company never provisions the stations fully, and the agents required those local supplies to live. They had them through the good-will of Gobila, and lived well. Now and then one of them had a bout of fever, and the other nursed him with gentle devotion. They did not think much of it. It left them weaker, and their appearance changed for the worse. Carlier was hollow-eyed and irritable. Kayerts showed a drawn, flabby face above the rotundity of his stomach, which gave him a weird aspect. But being constantly together, they did not notice the change that took place gradually in their appearance, and also in their dispositions. Five months passed in that way.

Then, one morning, as Kayerts and Carlier, lounging in their chairs under the verandah, talked about the approaching visit of the steamer, a knot of armed men came out of the forest and advanced towards the station. They were strangers to that part of the country. They were tall, slight, draped classically from neck to heel in blue fringed cloths, and carried percussion muskets over their bare right shoulders. Makola showed signs of excitement, and ran out of the storehouse (where he spent all his days) to meet these visitors. They came into the courtyard and looked about them with steady, scornful glances. Their leader, a powerful and determined-looking negro with bloodshot eyes, stood in front of the verandah and made a long speech. He gesticulated much, and ceased very suddenly.

There was something in his intonation, in the sounds of the long sentences he used, that startled the two whites. It was like a reminiscence of something not exactly familiar, and yet resembling the speech of civilized men. It sounded like one of those impossible languages which sometimes we hear in our dreams.

"What lingo is that?" said the amazed Carlier. "In the first moment I fancied the fellow was going to speak French. Anyway, it is a different kind of gibberish to what we ever heard."

"Yes," replied Kayerts. "Hey, Makola, what does he say? Where do they come from? Who are they?"

But Makola, who seemed to be standing on hot bricks, answered hurriedly, "I don't know. They come from very far. Perhaps Mrs. Price will understand. They are perhaps bad men."

The leader, after waiting for a while, said something sharply to Makola, who shook his head. Then the man, after looking round, noticed Makola's hut and walked over there. The next moment Mrs. Makola was heard speaking with great volubility. The other strangers—they were six in all—strolled about with an air of ease, put their heads through the door of the storeroom, congregated round the grave, pointed understandingly at the cross, and generally made themselves at home.

"I don't like those chaps—and, I say, Kayerts, they must be from the coast; they've got firearms," observed the sagacious Carlier.

Kayerts also did not like those chaps. They both, for the first time, became aware that they lived in conditions where the unusual may be dangerous, and that there was no power on earth outside of themselves to stand between them and the unusual. They became uneasy, went in and loaded their revolvers. Kayerts said, "We must order Makola to tell them to go away before dark."

The strangers left in the afternoon, after eating a meal prepared for them by Mrs. Makola. The immense woman was excited, and talked much with the visitors. She rattled away shrilly, pointing here and there at the forests and at the river. Makola sat apart and watched. At times he got up and whispered to his wife. He accompanied the strangers across the ravine at the back of the station-ground, and returned slowly looking very thoughtful. When questioned by the white men he was very strange, seemed not to understand, seemed to have forgotten French—seemed to have forgotten how to speak altogether. Kayerts and Carlier agreed that the nigger had had too much palm wine.

There was some talk about keeping a watch in turn, but in the evening everything seemed so quiet and peaceful that they retired as usual. All night they were disturbed by a lot of drumming in the villages. A deep, rapid roll near by would be followed by another far off—then all ceased. Soon short appeals would rattle out here and there, then all mingle together, increase, become vigorous and sustained, would spread out over the forest, roll through the night, unbroken and ceaseless, near and far, as if the whole land had been one immense drum booming out steadily an appeal to heaven. And through the deep and tremendous noise sudden yells that resembled snatches of songs from a madhouse darted shrill and high in discordant jets of sound which seemed to rush far above the earth and drive all peace from under the stars.

Carlier and Kayerts slept badly. They both thought they had heard shots fired during the night—but they could not agree as to the direction. In the morning Makola was gone somewhere. He returned about noon with one of yesterday's strangers, and eluded all Kayerts' attempts to close with him: had become deaf apparently. Kayerts wondered. Carlier, who had been fishing off the bank, came back and remarked while he showed his catch, "The niggers seem to be in a deuce of a stir; I wonder what's up. I saw about fifteen canoes cross the river during the two hours I was there fishing." Kayerts, worried, said, "Isn't this Makola very queer today?" Carlier advised, "Keep all our men together in case of some trouble."

2

There were ten station men who had been left by the Director. Those fellows, having engaged themselves to the Company for six months (without having any idea of a month in particular and only a very faint notion of time in general), had been serving the cause of progress for upwards of two years. Belonging to a tribe from a very distant part of the land of darkness and sorrow, they did not run away, naturally supposing that as wandering strangers they would be killed by the inhabitants of the country; in which they were right. They lived in straw huts on the slope of a ravine overgrown with reedy grass, just behind the station buildings. They were not happy, regretting the festive incantations, the sorceries, the human sacrifices of their own land; where they also had parents, brothers, sisters, admired chiefs, respected magicians, loved friends, and other ties supposed generally to be human. Besides, the rice rations served out by the Company did not agree with them, being a food unknown to their land, and to which they could not get used. Consequently they were unhealthy and miserable. Had they been of any other tribe they would have made up their minds to die—for nothing is easier to certain savages than suicide—and so have escaped from the puzzling difficulties of existence. But belonging, as they did, to a warlike tribe with filed

teeth, they had more grit, and went on stupidly living through disease and sorrow. They did very little work, and had lost their splendid physique. Carlier and Kayerts doctored them assiduously without being able to bring them back into condition again. They were mustered every morning and told off to different tasks—grass-cutting, fence-building, tree-felling, &c, &c, which no power on earth could induce them to execute efficiently. The two whites had practically very little control over them.

In the afternoon Makola came over to the big house and found Kayerts watching three heavy columns of smoke rising above the forests. "What is that?" asked Kayerts. "Some villages burn," answered Makola, who seemed to have regained his wits. Then he said abruptly: "We have got very little ivory; bad six months' trading. Do you like get a little more ivory?"

"Yes," said Kayerts, eagerly. He thought of percentages which were low.

"Those men who came yesterday are traders from Loanda who have got more ivory than they can carry home. Shall I buy? I know their camp."

"Certainly," said Kayerts. "What are those traders?"

"Bad fellows," said Makola, indifferently. "They fight with people, and catch women and children. They are bad men, and got guns. There is a great disturbance in the country. Do you want ivory?"

"Yes," said Kayerts. Makola said nothing for a while. Then: "Those workmen of ours are no good at all," he muttered, looking round. "Station in very bad order, sir. Director will growl. Better get a fine lot of ivory, then he say nothing."

"I can't help it; the men won't work," said Kayerts. "When will you get that ivory?"

"Very soon," said Makola. "Perhaps tonight. You leave it to me, and keep indoors, sir. I think you had better give some palm wine to our men to make a dance this evening. Enjoy themselves. Work better tomorrow. There's plenty palm wine—gone a little sour."

Kayerts said "yes," and Makola, with his own hands, carried big calabashes to the door of his hut. They stood there till the evening, and Mrs. Makola looked into every one. The men got them at sunset. When Kayerts and Carlier retired, a big bonfire was flaring before the men's huts. They could hear their shouts and drumming. Some men from Gobila's village had joined the station hands, and the entertainment was a great success.

In the middle of the night, Carlier waking suddenly, heard a man shout loudly; then a shot was fired. Only one. Carlier ran out and met Kayerts on the verandah. They were both startled. As they went across the yard to call Makola, they saw shadows moving in the night. One of them cried, "Don't shoot! It's me, Price." Then Makola appeared close to them. "Go back, go back, please," he urged, "you spoil all." "There are strange men about," said Carlier. "Never mind; I know," said Makola. Then he whispered, "All right. Bring ivory. Say nothing! I know my business." The two white men reluctantly went back to the house, but did not sleep. They heard footsteps, whispers, some groans. It seemed as if a lot of men came in, dumped heavy things on the ground, squabbled a long time, then went away. They lay on their hard beds and thought: "This Makola is invaluable." In the morning Carlier came out, very sleepy, and pulled at the cord of the big bell. The station hands mustered every morning to the sound of the bell. That morning nobody came. Kayerts turned out also, yawning. Across the yard they saw Makola come out of his hut, a tin basin of soapy water in his hand. Makola, a civilized nigger, was very neat in his person. He threw the soapsuds skilfully over a wretched little yellow cur he had, then turning his face to the agent's house, he shouted from the distance, "All the men gone last night!"

They heard him plainly, but in their surprise they both yelled out together: "What!" Then they stared at one another. "We are in a proper fix now," growled Carlier. "It's incredible!" muttered Kayerts. "I will go to the huts and see," said Carlier, striding off. Makola coming up found Kayerts standing alone.

"I can hardly believe it," said Kayerts, tearfully. "We took care of them as if they had been our children."

"They went with the coast people," said Makola after a moment of hesitation.

"What do I care with whom they went—the ungrateful brutes!" exclaimed the other. Then with sudden suspicion, and looking hard at Makola, he added: "What do you know about it?"

Makola moved his shoulders, looking down on the ground. "What do I know? I think only. Will you come and look at the ivory I've got there? It is a fine lot. You never saw such."

He moved towards the store. Kayerts followed him mechanically, thinking about the incredible desertion of the men. On the ground before the door of the fetish lay six splendid tusks.

"What did you give for it?" asked Kayerts, after surveying the lot with satisfaction.

"No regular trade," said Makola. "They brought the ivory and gave it to me. I told them to take what they most wanted in the station. It is a beautiful lot. No station can show such tusks. Those traders wanted carriers badly, and our men were no good here. No trade, no entry in books; all correct."

Kayerts nearly burst with indignation. "Why!" he shouted, "I believe you have sold our men for these tusks!" Makola stood impassive and silent. "I—I—will—I," stuttered Kayerts. "You fiend!" he yelled out.

"I did the best for you and the Company," said Makola, imperturbably. "Why you shout so much? Look at this tusk."

"I dismiss you! I will report you—I won't look at the tusk. I forbid you to touch them. I order you to throw them into the river. You—you!"

"You very red, Mr. Kayerts. If you are so irritable in the sun, you will get fever and die—like the first chief!" pronounced Makola impressively.

They stood still, contemplating one another with intense eyes, as if they had been looking with effort across immense distances. Kayerts shivered. Makola had meant no more than he said, but his words seemed to Kayerts full of ominous menace! He turned sharply and went away to the house. Makola retired into the bosom of his family; and the tusks, left lying before the store, looked very large and valuable in the sunshine.

Carlier came back on the verandah. "They're all gone, hey?" asked Kayerts from the far end of the common room in a muffled voice. "You did not find anybody?"

"Oh, yes," said Carlier, "I found one of Gobila's people lying dead before the huts—shot through the body. We heard that shot last night."

Kayerts came out quickly. He found his companion staring grimly over the yard at the tusks, away by the store. They both sat in silence for a while. Then Kayerts related his conversation with Makola. Carlier said nothing. At the midday meal they ate very little. They hardly exchanged a word that day. A great silence seemed to lie heavily over the station and press on their lips. Makola did not open the store; he spent the day playing with his children. He lay full-length on a mat outside his door, and the youngsters sat on his chest and clambered all over him. It was a touching picture. Mrs. Makola was busy cooking all day as usual. The white men made a somewhat better meal in the evening. Afterwards, Carlier smoking his pipe strolled over to the store; he stood for a long time over the tusks, touched one or two with his foot, even tried to lift the largest one by its small end. He came back to his chief, who had not stirred from the verandah, threw himself in the chair and said—

"I can see it! They were pounced upon while they slept heavily after drinking all that palm wine you've allowed Makola to give them. A put-up job! See? The worst is, some of Gobila's people were there, and got carried off too, no doubt. The least drunk woke up, and got shot for his sobriety. This is a funny country. What will you do now?"

"We can't touch it, of course," said Kayerts.

"Of course not," assented Carlier.

"Slavery is an awful thing," stammered out Kayerts in an unsteady voice.

"Frightful—the sufferings," grunted Carlier with conviction.

They believed their words. Everybody shows a respectful deference to certain sounds that he and his fellows can make. But about feelings people really know nothing. We talk with indignation or enthusiasm; we talk about oppression, cruelty, crime, devotion, self-sacrifice, virtue, and we know nothing real beyond the words. Nobody knows what suffering or sacrifice mean—except, perhaps the victims of the mysterious purpose of these illusions.

Next morning they saw Makola very busy setting up in the yard the big scales used for weighing ivory. By and by Carlier said: "What's that filthy scoundrel up to?" and lounged out into the yard. Kayerts followed. They stood watching. Makola took no notice. When the balance was swung true, he tried to lift a tusk into the

scale. It was too heavy. He looked up helplessly without a word, and for a minute they stood round that balance as mute and still as three statues. Suddenly Carlier said: "Catch hold of the other end, Makola—you beast!" and together they swung the tusk up. Kayerts trembled in every limb. He muttered, "I say! O! I say!" and putting his hand in his pocket found there a dirty bit of paper and the stump of a pencil. He turned his back on the others, as if about to do something tricky, and noted stealthily the weights which Carlier shouted out to him with unnecessary loudness. When all was over Makola whispered to himself: "The sun's very strong here for the tusks." Carlier said to Kayerts in a careless tone: "I say, chief, I might just as well give him a lift with this lot into the store."

As they were going back to the house Kayerts observed with a sigh: "It had to be done." And Carlier said: "It's deplorable, but, the men being Company's men the ivory is Company's ivory. We must look after it." "I will report to the Director, of course," said Kayerts. "Of course; let him decide," approved Carlier.

At midday they made a hearty meal. Kayerts sighed from time to time. Whenever they mentioned Makola's name they always added to it an opprobrious epithet. It eased their conscience. Makola gave himself a half-holiday, and bathed his children in the river. No one from Gobila's villages came near the station that day. No one came the next day, and the next, nor for a whole week. Gobila's people might have been dead and buried for any sign of life they gave. But they were only mourning for those they had lost by the witchcraft of white men, who had brought wicked people into their country. The wicked people were gone, but fear remained. Fear always remains. A man may destroy everything within himself, love and hate and belief, and even doubt; but as long as he clings to life he cannot destroy fear: the fear, subtle, indestructible, and terrible, that pervades his being; that tinges his thoughts; that lurks in his heart; that watches on his lips the struggle of his last breath. In his fear, the mild old Gobila offered extra human sacrifices to all the Evil Spirits that had taken possession of his white friends. His heart was heavy. Some warriors spoke about burning and killing, but the cautious old savage dissuaded them. Who could foresee the woe those mysterious creatures, if irritated, might bring? They should be left alone. Perhaps in time they would disappear into the earth as the first one had disappeared. His people must keep away from them, and hope for the best.

Kayerts and Carlier did not disappear, but remained above on this earth, that, somehow, they fancied had become bigger and very empty. It was not the absolute and dumb solitude of the post that impressed them so much as an inarticulate feeling that something from within them was gone, something that worked for their safety, and had kept the wilderness from interfering with their hearts. The images of home; the memory of people like them, of men that thought and felt as they used to think and feel, receded into distances made indistinct by the glare of unclouded sunshine. And out of the great silence of the surrounding wilderness, its very hopelessness and savagery seemed to approach them nearer, to draw them gently, to look upon them, to envelop them with a solicitude irresistible, familiar, and disgusting.

Days lengthened into weeks, then into months. Gobila's people drummed and yelled to every new moon, as of yore, but kept away from the station. Makola and Carlier tried once in a canoe to open communications, but were received with a shower of arrows, and had to fly back to the station for dear life. That attempt set the country up and down the river into an uproar that could be very distinctly heard for days. The steamer was late. At first they spoke of delay jauntily, then anxiously, then gloomily. The matter was becoming serious. Stores were running short. Carlier cast his lines off the bank, but the river was low, and the fish kept out in the stream. They dared not stroll far away from the station to shoot. Moreover, there was no game in the impenetrable forest. Once Carlier shot a hippo in the river. They had no boat to secure it, and it sank. When it floated up it drifted away, and Gobila's people secured the carcass. It was the occasion for a national holiday, but Carlier had a fit of rage over it and talked about the necessity of exterminating all the niggers before the country could be made habitable. Kayerts mooned about silently; spent hours looking at the portrait of his Melie. It represented a little girl with long bleached tresses and a rather sour face. His legs were much swollen, and he could hardly walk. Carlier, undermined by fever, could not swagger any more, but kept tottering about, still with a devil-may-care air, as became a man who remembered his crack regiment. He had become hoarse, sarcastic, and inclined to say unpleasant things. He called it "being frank with you." They had long ago reckoned their percentages on trade, including in them that last deal of "this infamous Makola." They had also concluded not to say anything about it. Kayerts hesitated at first—was afraid of the Director.

"He has seen worse things done on the quiet," maintained Carlier, with a hoarse laugh. "Trust him! He won't thank you if you blab. He is no better than you or me. Who will talk if we hold our tongues? There is nobody here."

That was the root of the trouble! There was nobody there; and being left there alone with their weakness, they became daily more like a pair of accomplices than like a couple of devoted friends. They had heard nothing from home for eight months. Every evening they said, "Tomorrow we shall see the steamer." But one of the Company's steamers had been wrecked, and the Director was busy with the other, relieving very distant and important stations on the main river. He thought that the useless station, and the useless men, could wait. Meantime Kayerts and Carlier lived on rice boiled without salt, and cursed the Company, all Africa, and the day they were born. One must have lived on such diet to discover what ghastly trouble the necessity of swallowing one's food may become. There was literally nothing else in the station but rice and coffee; they drank the coffee without sugar. The last fifteen lumps Kayerts had solemnly locked away in his box, together with a half-bottle of Cognac, "in case of sickness," he explained. Carlier approved. "When one is sick," he said, "any little extra like that is cheering."

They waited. Rank grass began to sprout over the courtyard. The bell never rang now. Days passed, silent, exasperating, and slow. When the two men spoke, they snarled; and their silences were bitter, as if tinged by the bitterness of their thoughts.

One day after a lunch of boiled rice, Carlier put down his cup untasted, and said: "Hang it all! Let's have a decent cup of coffee for once. Bring out that sugar, Kayerts!"

"For the sick," muttered Kayerts, without looking

up.

"For the sick," mocked Carlier. "Bosh! … Well! I am sick."

"You are no more sick than I am, and I go without," said Kayerts in a peaceful tone.

"Come! out with that sugar, you stingy old slave-dealer."

Kayerts looked up quickly. Carlier was smiling with marked insolence. And suddenly it seemed to Kayerts that he had never seen that man before. Who was he? He knew nothing about him. What was he capable of? There was a surprising flash of violent emotion within him, as if in the presence of something undreamt-of, dangerous, and final. But he managed to pronounce with composure—

"That joke is in very bad taste. Don't repeat it."

"Joke!" said Carlier, hitching himself forward on his seat. "I am hungry—I am sick—I don't joke! I hate hypocrites. You are a hypocrite. You are a slave-dealer. I am a slave-dealer. There's nothing but slave-dealers in this cursed country. I mean to have sugar in my coffee today, anyhow!"

"I forbid you to speak to me in that way," said Kayerts with a fair show of resolution.

"You!—What?" shouted Carlier, jumping up.

Kayerts stood up also. "I am your chief," he began, trying to master the shakiness of his voice.

"What?" yelled the other. "Who's chief? There's no chief here. There's nothing here: there's nothing but you and I. Fetch the sugar—you pot-bellied ass."

"Hold your tongue. Go out of this room," screamed Kayerts. "I dismiss you—you scoundrel!"

Carlier swung a stool. All at once he looked dangerously in earnest. "You flabby, good-for-nothing civilian—take that!" he howled.

Kayerts dropped under the table, and the stool struck the grass inner wall of the room. Then, as Carlier was trying to upset the table, Kayerts in desperation made a blind rush, head low, like a cornered pig would do, and over-turning his friend, bolted along the verandah, and into his room. He locked the door, snatched his revolver, and stood panting. In less than a minute Carlier was kicking at the door furiously, howling, "If you don't bring out that sugar, I will shoot you at sight, like a dog. Now then—one—two—three. You won't?

I will show you who's the master."

Kayerts thought the door would fall in, and scrambled through the square hole that served for a window in his room. There was then the whole breadth of the house between them. But the other was apparently not strong enough to break in the door, and Kayerts heard him running round. Then he also began to run laboriously on his swollen legs. He ran as quickly as he could, grasping the revolver, and unable yet to understand what was happening to him. He saw in succession Makola's house, the store, the river, the ravine, and the low bushes; and he saw all those things again as he ran for the second time round the house. Then again they flashed past him. That morning he could not have walked a yard without a groan.

And now he ran. He ran fast enough to keep out of sight of the other man.

Then as, weak and desperate, he thought, "Before I finish the next round I shall die," he heard the other man stumble heavily, then stop. He stopped also. He had the back and Carlier the front of the house, as before. He heard him drop into a chair cursing, and suddenly his own legs gave way, and he slid down into a sitting posture with his back to the wall. His mouth was as dry as a cinder, and his face was wet with perspiration—and tears. What was it all about? He thought it must be a horrible illusion; he thought he was dreaming; he thought he was going mad! After a while he collected his senses. What did they quarrel about? That sugar! How absurd! He would give it to him—didn't want it himself. And he began scrambling to his feet with a sudden feeling of security. But before he had fairly stood upright, a common-sense reflection occurred to him and drove him back into despair. He thought: If I give way now to that brute of a soldier, he will begin this horror again tomorrow—and the day after—every day—raise other pretensions, trample on me, torture me, make me his slave—and I will be lost! Lost! The steamer may not come for days—may never come. He shook so that he had to sit down on the floor again. He shivered forlornly. He felt he could not, would not move any more. He was completely distracted by the sudden perception that the position was without issue—that death and life had in a moment become equally difficult and terrible.

All at once he heard the other push his chair back; and he leaped to his feet with extreme facility. He listened and got confused. Must run again! Right or left? He heard footsteps. He darted to the left, grasping his revolver, and at the very same instant, as it seemed to him, they came into violent collision. Both shouted with surprise. A loud explosion took place between them; a roar of red fire, thick smoke; and Kayerts, deafened and blinded, rushed back thinking: I am hit—it's all over. He expected the other to come round—to gloat over his agony. He caught hold of an upright of the roof—"All over!" Then he heard a crashing fall on the other side of the house, as if somebody had tumbled headlong over a chair—then silence. Nothing more happened. He did not die. Only his shoulder felt as if it had been badly wrenched, and he had lost his revolver. He was disarmed and helpless! He waited for his fate. The other man made no sound. It was a stratagem. He was stalking him now! Along what side? Perhaps he was taking aim this very minute!

After a few moments of an agony frightful and absurd, he decided to go and meet his doom. He was prepared for every surrender. He turned the corner, steadying himself with one hand on the wall; made a few paces, and nearly swooned. He had seen on the floor, protruding past the other corner, a pair of turned-up feet. A pair of white naked feet in red slippers. He felt deadly sick, and stood for a time in profound darkness. Then Makola appeared before him, saying quietly: "Come along, Mr. Kayerts. He is dead." He burst into tears of gratitude; a loud, sobbing fit of crying. After a time he found himself sitting in a chair and looking at Carlier, who lay stretched on his back. Makola was kneeling over the body.

"Is this your revolver?" asked Makola, getting up.

"Yes," said Kayerts; then he added very quickly, "He ran after me to shoot me—you saw!"

"Yes, I saw," said Makola. "There is only one revolver; where's his?"

"Don't know," whispered Kayerts in a voice that had become suddenly very faint.

"I will go and look for it," said the other, gently. He made the round along the verandah, while Kayerts sat still and looked at the corpse. Makola came back empty-handed, stood in deep thought, then stepped quietly

into the dead man's room, and came out directly with a revolver, which he held up before Kayerts. Kayerts shut his eyes. Everything was going round. He found life more terrible and difficult than death. He had shot an unarmed man.

After meditating for a while, Makola said softly, pointing at the dead man who lay there with his right eye blown out—

"He died of fever." Kayerts looked at him with a stony stare. "Yes," repeated Makola, thoughtfully, stepping over the corpse, "I think he died of fever. Bury him tomorrow."

And he went away slowly to his expectant wife, leaving the two white men alone on the verandah.

Night came, and Kayerts sat unmoving on his chair. He sat quiet as if he had taken a dose of opium. The violence of the emotions he had passed through produced a feeling of exhausted serenity. He had plumbed in one short afternoon the depths of horror and despair, and now found repose in the conviction that life had no more secrets for him: neither had death! He sat by the corpse thinking; thinking very actively, thinking very new thoughts. He seemed to have broken loose from himself altogether. His old thoughts, convictions, likes and dislikes, things he respected and things he abhorred, appeared in their true light at last! Appeared contemptible and childish, false and ridiculous. He revelled in his new wisdom while he sat by the man he had killed. He argued with himself about all things under heaven with that kind of wrong-headed lucidity which may be observed in some lunatics. Incidentally he reflected that the fellow dead there had been a noxious beast anyway; that men died every day in thousands; perhaps in hundreds of thousands—who could tell?—and that in the number, that one death could not possibly make any difference; couldn't have any importance, at least to a thinking creature. He, Kayerts, was a thinking creature. He had been all his life, till that moment, a believer in a lot of nonsense like the rest of mankind—who are fools; but now he thought! He knew! He was at peace; he was familiar with the highest wisdom! Then he tried to imagine himself dead, and Carlier sitting in his chair watching him; and his attempt met with such unexpected success, that in a very few moments he became not at all sure who was dead and who was alive. This extraordinary achievement of his fancy startled him, however, and by a clever and timely effort of mind he saved himself just in time from becoming Carlier. His heart thumped, and he felt hot all over at the thought of that danger. Carlier! What a beastly thing! To compose his now disturbed nerves—and no wonder!—he tried to whistle a little. Then, suddenly, he fell asleep, or thought he had slept; but at any rate there was a fog, and somebody had whistled in the fog.

He stood up. The day had come, and a heavy mist had descended upon the land: the mist penetrating, enveloping, and silent; the morning mist of tropical lands; the mist that clings and kills; the mist white and deadly, immaculate and poisonous. He stood up, saw the body, and threw his arms above his head with a cry like that of a man who, waking from a trance, finds himself immured forever in a tomb. "*Help! ... My God!*"

A shriek inhuman, vibrating and sudden, pierced like a sharp dart the white shroud of that land of sorrow. Three short, impatient screeches followed, and then, for a time, the fog-wreaths rolled on, undisturbed, through a formidable silence. Then many more shrieks, rapid and piercing, like the yells of some exasperated and ruthless creature, rent the air. Progress was calling to Kayerts from the river. Progress and civilization and all the virtues. Society was calling to its accomplished child to come, to be taken care of, to be instructed, to be judged, to be condemned; it called him to return to that rubbish heap from which he had wandered away, so that justice could be done.

Kayerts heard and understood. He stumbled out of the verandah, leaving the other man quite alone for the first time since they had been thrown there together. He groped his way through the fog, calling in his ignorance upon the invisible heaven to undo its work. Makola flitted by in the mist, shouting as he ran—

"Steamer! Steamer! They can't see. They whistle for the station. I go ring the bell. Go down to the landing, sir. I ring."

He disappeared. Kayerts stood still. He looked upwards; the fog rolled low over his head. He looked round like a man who has lost his way, and he saw a dark smudge, a cross-shaped stain, upon the shifting purity of the mist. As he began to stumble towards it, the station bell rang in a tumultuous peal its answer to the impatient clamour of the steamer.

The Managing Director of the Great Civilizing Company (since we know that civilization follows trade) landed first, and incontinently lost sight of the steamer. The fog down by the river was exceedingly dense; above, at the station, the bell rang unceasing and brazen.

The Director shouted loudly to the steamer:

"There is nobody down to meet us; there may be something wrong, though they are ringing. You had better come, too!"

And he began to toil up the steep bank. The captain and the engine-driver of the boat followed behind. As they scrambled up the fog thinned, and they could see their Director a good way ahead. Suddenly they saw him start forward, calling to them over his shoulder: "Run! Run to the house! I've found one of them. Run, look for the other!"

He had found one of them! And even he, the man of varied and startling experience, was somewhat discomposed by the manner of this finding. He stood and fumbled in his pockets (for a knife) while he faced Kayerts, who was hanging by a leather strap from the cross! He had evidently climbed the grave, which was high and narrow, and after tying the end of the strap to the arm, had swung himself off. His toes were only a couple of inches above the ground; his arms hung stiffly down; he seemed to be standing rigidly at attention, but with one purple cheek playfully posed on the shoulder. And, irreverently, he was putting out a swollen tongue at his Managing Director.

—1897

The Preface to *The Nigger of the "Narcissus"*[1]
[The Task of the Artist]

A work that aspires, however humbly, to the condition of art should carry its justification in every line. And art itself may be defined as a single-minded attempt to render the highest kind of justice to the visible universe, by bringing to light the truth, manifold and one, underlying its every aspect. It is an attempt to find in its forms, in its colours, in its light, in its shadows, in the aspects of matter and in the facts of life, what of each is fundamental, what is enduring and essential—their one illuminating and convincing quality—the very truth of their existence. The artist, then, like the thinker or the scientist, seeks the truth and makes his appeal. Impressed by the aspect of the world the thinker plunges into ideas, the scientist into facts—whence, presently, emerging they make their appeal to those qualities of our being that fit us best for the hazardous enterprise of living. They speak authoritatively to our common-sense, to our intelligence, to our desire of peace or to our desire of unrest; not seldom to our prejudices, sometimes to our fears, often to our egoism—but always to our credulity. And their words are heard with reverence, for their concern is with weighty matters: with the cultivation of our minds and the proper care of our bodies; with the attainment of our ambitions; with the perfection of the means and the glorification of our precious aims.

It is otherwise with the artist.

Confronted by the same enigmatical spectacle the artist descends within himself, and in that lonely region of stress and strife, if he be deserving and fortunate, he finds the terms of his appeal. His appeal is made to our less obvious capacities: to that part of our nature which, because of the warlike conditions of existence, is necessarily kept out of sight within the more resisting and hard qualities—like the vulnerable body within the steel armour. His appeal is less loud, more profound, less distinct, more stirring—and sooner forgotten. Yet its effect endures for ever. The changing wisdom of successive generations discards ideas, questions facts, demolishes theories. But the artist appeals to that part of our being which is not dependent on wisdom: to that in us which is a gift and not an acquisition—and, therefore, more permanently enduring. He speaks to our capacity for delight and wonder, to the sense of mystery surrounding our lives; to our sense of pity, and beauty, and pain; to the latent feeling of fellowship with all creation—and to the subtle but invincible, conviction of solidarity that knits together the loneliness of innumerable hearts: to the solidarity in dreams, in joy, in sorrow, in aspirations, in illusions, in hope, in fear, which binds men to each other, which binds together all humanity—the dead to the living and the living to the unborn.

It is only some such train of thought, or rather of feeling, that can in a measure explain the aim of the attempt, made in the tale which follows, to present an unrestful episode in the obscure lives of a few individuals out of all the disregarded multitude of the bewildered, the simple and the voiceless. For, if there is any part of truth in the belief confessed above, it becomes evident that there is not a place of splendour or a dark corner of the earth that does not deserve, if only a passing glance of wonder and pity. The motive, then, may be held to justify the matter of the work; but this preface, which is simply an avowal of endeavour, cannot end here—for the avowal is not yet complete.

Fiction—if it at all aspires to be art—appeals to temperament. And in truth it must be, like painting, like music, like all art, the appeal of one temperament to all the other innumerable temperaments whose subtle and resistless power endows passing events with their true meaning, and creates the moral, the emotional atmosphere of the place and time. Such an appeal, to be

---

[1] *Preface … Narcissus* Conrad's novella *The Nigger of the "Narcissus"* was first published in *The New Review* in 1897. Conrad added the preface when it came out in book form in 1898. The novella deals with the death of a black seaman aboard a merchant ship called the *Narcissus*. Conrad had served as first mate on a ship bearing that name in 1883. It was not until after World War II that the racist term "nigger" came to be regarded as unacceptable usage. In Britain, the term continued to appear in book titles until the late 1930s; Agatha Christie's *Ten Little Niggers* (later *Ten Little Indians*) was published in 1939. In the US, however, Conrad was pressured by the American publisher (Dodd Mead & Co.) into changing the title of this work to *The Children of the Sea* for the 1897 American edition— not so much out of a fear that some readers might object to any implied racism as out of a conviction that most readers would assume any book that promised to focus on a "nigger" to be uninteresting and/or repugnant.

effective, must be an impression conveyed through the senses; and, in fact, it cannot be made in any other way, because temperament, whether individual or collective, is not amenable to persuasion. All art, therefore, appeals primarily to the senses, and the artistic aim when expressing itself in written words must also make its appeal through the senses, if its high desire is to reach the secret spring of responsive emotions. It must strenuously aspire to the plasticity of sculpture, to the colour of painting, and to the magic suggestiveness of music—which is the art of arts. And it is only through complete, unswerving devotion to the perfect blending of form and substance; it is only through an unremitting, never-discouraged care for the shape and ring of sentences that an approach can be made to plasticity, to colour; and the light of magic suggestiveness may be brought to play for an evanescent instant over the commonplace surface of words: of the old, old words, worn thin, defaced by ages of careless usage.

The sincere endeavour to accomplish that creative task, to go as far on that road as his strength will carry him, to go undeterred by faltering, weariness or reproach, is the only valid justification for the worker in prose. And if his conscience is clear, his answer to those who, in the fulness of a wisdom which looks for immediate profit, demand specifically to be edified, consoled, amused; who demand to be promptly improved, or encouraged, or frightened, or shocked, or charmed, must run thus:—My task which I am trying to achieve is, by the power of the written word, to make you hear, to make you feel—it is, before all, to make you *see*. That—and no more, and it is everything. If I succeed, you shall find there according to your deserts: encouragement, consolation, fear, charm—all you demand; and, perhaps, also that glimpse of truth for which you have forgotten to ask.

To snatch in a moment of courage, from the remorseless rush of time, a sapping phase of life is only the beginning of the task. The task approached in tenderness and faith is to hold up unquestioningly, without choice and without fear, the rescued fragment before all eyes and in the light of a sincere mood. It is to show its vibration, its colour, its form; and through its movement, its form, and its colour, reveal the substance of its truth—disclose its inspiring secret: the stress and passion within the core of each convincing moment. In a single-minded attempt of that kind, if one be deserving and fortunate, one may perchance attain to such clearness of sincerity that at last the presented vision of regret or pity, of terror or mirth, shall awaken in the hearts of the beholders that feeling of unavoidable solidarity; of the solidarity in mysterious origin, in toil, in joy, in hope, in uncertain fate, which binds men to each other and all mankind to the visible world.

It is evident that he who, rightly or wrongly, holds by the convictions expressed above cannot be faithful to any one of the temporary formulas of his craft. The enduring part of them—the truth which each only imperfectly veils—should abide with him as the most precious of his possessions, but they all: Realism, Romanticism, Naturalism, even the unofficial sentimentalism (which, like the poor, is exceedingly difficult to get rid of);[1] all these gods must, after a short period of fellowship, abandon him—even on the very threshold of the temple—to the stammerings of his conscience and to the outspoken consciousness of the difficulties of his work. In that uneasy solitude the supreme cry of Art for Art, even, loses the exciting ring of its apparent immorality. It sounds far off. It has ceased to be a cry, and is heard only as a whisper, often incomprehensible, but at times, and faintly, encouraging.

Sometimes, stretched at ease in the shade of a roadside tree, we watch the motions of a labourer in a distant field, and after a time, begin to wonder languidly as to what the fellow may be at. We watch the movements of his body, the waving of his arms, we see him bend down, stand up, hesitate, begin again. It may add to the charm of an idle hour to be told the purpose of his exertions. If we know he is trying to lift a stone, to dig a ditch, to uproot a stump, we look with a more real interest at his efforts; we are disposed to condone the jar of his agitation upon the restfulness of the landscape; and even, if in a brotherly frame of mind, we may bring ourselves to forgive his failure. We understood his object, and, after all, the fellow has tried, and perhaps he had not the strength, and perhaps he had not the knowledge. We forgive, go on our way—and forget.

---

[1] *like the poor ... get rid of* The reference is to John 12.8: "for the poor always you have with you."

And so it is with the workman of art. Art is long and life is short,[1] and success is very far off. And thus, doubtful of strength to travel so far, we talk a little about the aim—the aim of art, which, like life itself, is inspiring, difficult—obscured by mists. It is not in the clear logic of a triumphant conclusion; it is not in the unveiling of one of those heartless secrets which are called the Laws of Nature. It is not less great, but only more difficult.

To arrest, for the space of a breath, the hands busy about the work of the earth, and compel men entranced by the sight of distant goals to glance for a moment at the surrounding vision of form and colour, of sunshine and shadows; to make them pause for a look, for a sigh, for a smile—such is the aim, difficult and evanescent, and reserved only for a very few to achieve. But sometimes, by the deserving and the fortunate, even that task is accomplished. And when it is accomplished—behold! —all the truth of life is there: a moment of vision, a sigh, a smile—and the return to an eternal rest.
—1898

The Secret Sharer

I

On my right hand there were lines of fishing stakes resembling a mysterious system of half-submerged bamboo fences, incomprehensible in its division of the domain of tropical fishes, and crazy of aspect as if abandoned forever by some nomad tribe of fishermen now gone to the other end of the ocean; for there was no sign of human habitation as far as the eye could reach. To the left a group of barren islets, suggesting ruins of stone walls, towers, and blockhouses, had its foundations set in a blue sea that itself looked solid, so still and stable did it lie below my feet; even the track of light from the westering sun shone smoothly, without that animated glitter which tells of an imperceptible ripple. And when I turned my head to take a parting glance at the tug which had just left us anchored outside the bar, I saw the straight line of the flat shore joined to the stable sea, edge to edge, with a perfect and un-

marked closeness, in one leveled floor half brown, half blue under the enormous dome of the sky. Corresponding in their insignificance to the islets of the sea, two small clumps of trees, one on each side of the only fault in the impeccable joint, marked the mouth of the river Meinam[2] we had just left on the first preparatory stage of our homeward journey; and, far back on the inland level, a larger and loftier mass, the grove surrounding the great Paknam pagoda,[3] was the only thing on which the eye could rest from the vain task of exploring the monotonous sweep of the horizon. Here and there gleams as of a few scattered pieces of silver marked the windings of the great river; and on the nearest of them, just within the bar, the tug steaming right into the land became lost to my sight, hull and funnel and masts, as though the impassive earth had swallowed her up without an effort, without a tremor. My eye followed the light cloud of her smoke, now here, now there, above the plain, according to the devious curves of the stream, but always fainter and farther away, till I lost it at last behind the miter-shaded hill of the great pagoda. And then I was left alone with my ship, anchored at the head of the Gulf of Siam.[4]

She floated at the starting point of a long journey, very still in an immense stillness, the shadows of her spars[5] flung far to the eastward by the setting sun. At that moment I was alone on her decks. There was not a sound in her—and around us nothing moved, nothing lived, not a canoe on the water, not a bird in the air, not a cloud in the sky. In this breathless pause at the threshold of a long passage we seemed to be measuring our fitness for a long and arduous enterprise, the appointed task of both our existences to be carried out, far from all human eyes, with only sky and sea for spectators and for judges.

---

[1] *Art is long and life is short* The Latin proverb *ars longa, vita brevis* derives from a saying of the Greek physician Hippocrates.

[2] *the river Meinam* Conrad may have been referring to the Chao Phraya river in the city of Samut Prakan, Thailand. Located just south of Bangkok, Samut Prakan is a port city on the Gulf of Thailand.

[3] *Paknam pagoda* Located in Samut Prakan, the Phra Samut Chedi pagoda was originally built in the middle of the river. Today it adjoins the west bank due to silt accumulation.

[4] *Siam* Thailand.

[5] *spars* Mast attachments securing the sail; also called booms or gaffs.

There must have been some glare in the air to interfere with one's sight, because it was only just before the sun left us that my roaming eyes made out beyond the highest ridges of the principal islet of the group something which did away with the solemnity of perfect solitude. The tide of darkness flowed on swiftly; and with tropical suddenness a swarm of stars came out above the shadowy earth, while I lingered yet, my hand resting lightly on my ship's rail as if on the shoulder of a trusted friend. But, with all that multitude of celestial bodies staring down at one, the comfort of quiet communion with her was gone for good. And there were also disturbing sounds by this time—voices, footsteps forward; the steward flitted along the main-deck, a busily ministering spirit; a hand bell tinkled urgently under the poop deck[1]…

I found my two officers waiting for me near the supper table, in the lighted cuddy.[2] We sat down at once, and as I helped the chief mate, I said:

"Are you aware that there is a ship anchored inside the islands? I saw her mastheads above the ridge as the sun went down."

He raised sharply his simple face, overcharged by a terrible growth of whisker, and emitted his usual ejaculations: "Bless my soul, sir! You don't say so!"

My second mate was a round-cheeked, silent young man, grave beyond his years, I thought; but as our eyes happened to meet I detected a slight quiver on his lips. I looked down at once. It was not my part to encourage sneering on board my ship. It must be said, too, that I knew very little of my officers. In consequence of certain events of no particular significance, except to myself, I had been appointed to the command only a fortnight before. Neither did I know much of the hands forward. All these people had been together for eighteen months or so, and my position was that of the only stranger on board. I mention this because it has some bearing on what is to follow. But what I felt most was my being a stranger to the ship; and if all the truth must be told, I was somewhat of a stranger to myself. The youngest man on board (barring the second mate), and untried as yet by a position of the fullest responsibility, I was willing to take the adequacy of the others for granted. They had simply to be equal to their tasks; but I wondered how far I should turn out faithful to that ideal conception of one's own personality every man sets up for himself secretly.

Meantime the chief mate, with an almost visible effect of collaboration on the part of his round eyes and frightful whiskers, was trying to evolve a theory of the anchored ship. His dominant trait was to take all things into earnest consideration. He was of a painstaking turn of mind. As he used to say, he "liked to account to himself" for practically everything that came in his way, down to a miserable scorpion he had found in his cabin a week before. The why and the wherefore of that scorpion—how it got on board and came to select his room rather than the pantry (which was a dark place and more what a scorpion would be partial to), and how on earth it managed to drown itself in the inkwell of his writing desk—had exercised him infinitely. The ship within the islands was much more easily accounted for; and just as we were about to rise from table he made his pronouncement. She was, he doubted not, a ship from home lately arrived. Probably she drew too much water to cross the bar except at the top of spring tides. Therefore she went into that natural harbour to wait for a few days in preference to remaining in an open roadstead.

"That's so," confirmed the second mate, suddenly, in his slightly hoarse voice. "She draws over twenty feet. She's the Liverpool ship *Sephora* with a cargo of coal. Hundred and twenty-three days from Cardiff."

We looked at him in surprise.

"The tugboat skipper told me when he came on board for your letters, sir," explained the young man. "He expects to take her up the river the day after tomorrow."

After thus overwhelming us with the extent of his information he slipped out of the cabin. The mate observed regretfully that he "could not account for that young fellow's whims." What prevented him telling us all about it at once, he wanted to know.

I detained him as he was making a move. For the last two days the crew had had plenty of hard work, and the night before they had very little sleep. I felt painfully that I—a stranger—was doing something unusual when I directed him to let all hands turn in without setting an

---

[1] *poop deck* Highest and aftermost deck on a ship.

[2] *cuddy* Small ship-board cabin.

anchor watch. I proposed to keep on deck myself till one o'clock or thereabouts. I would get the second mate to relieve me at that hour.

"He will turn out the cook and the steward at four," I concluded, "and then give you a call. Of course at the slightest sign of any sort of wind we'll have the hands up and make a start at once."

He concealed his astonishment. "Very well, sir." Outside the cuddy he put his head in the second mate's door to inform him of my unheard-of caprice to take a five hours' anchor watch on myself. I heard the other raise his voice incredulously—"What? The Captain himself?" Then a few more murmurs, a door closed, then another. A few moments later I went on deck.

My strangeness, which had made me sleepless, had prompted that unconventional arrangement, as if I had expected in those solitary hours of the night to get on terms with the ship of which I knew nothing, manned by men of whom I knew very little more. Fast alongside a wharf, littered like any ship in port with a tangle of unrelated things, invaded by unrelated shore people, I had hardly seen her yet properly. Now, as she lay cleared for sea, the stretch of her main-deck seemed to me very find under the stars. Very fine, very roomy for her size, and very inviting. I descended the poop and paced the waist, my mind picturing to myself the coming passage through the Malay Archipelago, down the Indian Ocean, and up the Atlantic. All its phases were familiar enough to me, every characteristic, all the alternatives which were likely to face me on the high seas—everything!… except the novel responsibility of command. But I took heart from the reasonable thought that the ship was like other ships, the men like other men, and that the sea was not likely to keep any special surprises expressly for my discomfiture.

Arrived at that comforting conclusion, I bethought myself of a cigar and went below to get it. All was still down there. Everybody at the after end of the ship was sleeping profoundly. I came out again on the quarter-deck, agreeably at ease in my sleeping suit on that warm breathless night, barefooted, a glowing cigar in my teeth, and, going forward, I was met by the profound silence of the fore end of the ship. Only as I passed the door of the forecastle, I heard a deep, quiet, trustful sigh of some sleeper inside. And suddenly I rejoiced in the great security of the sea as compared with the unrest of the land, in my choice of that untempted life presenting no disquieting problems, invested with an elementary moral beauty by the absolute straightforwardness of its appeal and by the singleness of its purpose.

The riding light in the forerigging burned with a clear, untroubled, as if symbolic, flame, confident and bright in the mysterious shades of the night. Passing on my way aft along the other side of the ship, I observed that the rope side ladder, put over, no doubt, for the master of the tug when he came to fetch away our letters, had not been hauled in as it should have been. I became annoyed at this, for exactitude in some small matters is the very soul of discipline. Then I reflected that I had myself peremptorily dismissed my officers from duty, and by my own act had prevented the anchor watch being formally set and things properly attended to. I asked myself whether it was wise ever to interfere with the established routine of duties even from the kindest of motives. My action might have made me appear eccentric. Goodness only knew how that absurdly whiskered mate would "account" for my conduct, and what the whole ship thought of that informality of their new captain. I was vexed with myself.

Not from compunction certainly, but, as it were mechanically, I proceeded to get the ladder in myself. Now a side ladder of that sort is a light affair and comes in easily, yet my vigorous tug, which should have brought it flying on board, merely recoiled upon my body in a totally unexpected jerk. What the devil!… I was so astounded by the immovableness of that ladder that I remained stockstill, trying to account for it to myself like that imbecile mate of mine. In the end, of course, I put my head over the rail.

The side of the ship made an opaque belt of shadow on the darkling glassy shimmer of the sea. But I saw at once something elongated and pale floating very close to the ladder. Before I could form a guess a faint flash of phosphorescent light, which seemed to issue suddenly from the naked body of a man, flickered in the sleeping water with the elusive, silent play of summer lightning in a night sky. With a gasp I saw revealed to my stare a pair of feet, the long legs, a broad livid back immersed right up to the neck in a greenish cadaverous glow. One hand, awash, clutched the bottom rung of the ladder.

He was complete but for the head. A headless corpse! The cigar dropped out of my gaping mouth with a tiny plop and a short hiss quite audible in the absolute stillness of all things under heaven. At that I suppose he raised up his face, a dimly pale oval in the shadow of the ship's side. But even then I could only barely make out down there the shape of his black-haired head. However, it was enough for the horrid, frost-bound sensation which had gripped me about the chest to pass off. The moment of vain exclamations was past, too. I only climbed on the spare spar and leaned over the rail as far as I could, to bring my eyes nearer to that mystery floating alongside.

As he hung by the ladder, like a resting swimmer, the sea lightning played about his limbs at every stir; and he appeared in it ghastly, silvery, fishlike. He remained as mute as a fish, too. He made no motion to get out of the water, either. It was inconceivable that he should not attempt to come on board, and strangely troubling to suspect that perhaps he did not want to. And my first words were prompted by just that troubled incertitude.

"What's the matter?" I asked in my ordinary tone, speaking down to the face upturned exactly under mine.

"Cramp," it answered, no louder. Then slightly anxious, "I say, no need to call anyone."

"I was not going to," I said.

"Are you alone on deck?"

"Yes."

I had somehow the impression that he was on the point of letting go the ladder to swim away beyond my ken—mysterious as he came. But, for the moment, this being appearing as if he had risen from the bottom of the sea (it was certainly the nearest land to the ship) wanted only to know the time. I told him. And he, down there, tentatively:

"I suppose your captain's turned in?"

"I am sure he isn't," I said.

He seemed to struggle with himself, for I heard something like the low, bitter murmur of doubt. "What's the good?" His next words came out with a hesitating effort.

"Look here, my man. Could you call him out quietly?"

I thought the time had come to declare myself.

"I am the captain."

I heard a "By Jove!" whispered at the level of the water. The phosphorescence flashed in the swirl of the water all about his limbs, his other hand seized the ladder.

"My name's Leggatt."

The voice was calm and resolute. A good voice. The self-possession of that man had somehow induced a corresponding state in myself. It was very quietly that I remarked:

"You must be a good swimmer."

"Yes. I've been in the water practically since nine o'clock. The question for me now is whether I am to let go this ladder and go on swimming till I sink from exhaustion, or—to come on board here."

I felt this was no mere formula of desperate speech, but a real alternative in the view of a strong soul. I should have gathered from this that he was young; indeed, it is only the young who are ever confronted by such clear issues. But at the time it was pure intuition on my part. A mysterious communication was established already between us two—in the face of that silent, darkened tropical sea. I was young, too; young enough to make no comment. The man in the water began suddenly to climb up the ladder, and I hastened away from the rail to fetch some clothes.

Before entering the cabin I stood still, listening in the lobby at the foot of the stairs. A faint snore came through the closed door of the chief mate's room. The second mate's door was on the hook, but the darkness in there was absolutely soundless. He, too, was young and could sleep like a stone. Remained the steward, but he was not likely to wake up before he was called. I got a sleeping suit out of my room and, coming back on deck, saw the naked man from the sea sitting on the main hatch, glimmering white in the darkness, his elbows on his knees and his head in his hands. In a moment he had concealed his damp body in a sleeping suit of the same gray-stripe pattern as the one I was wearing and followed me like my double on the poop. Together we moved right aft, barefooted, silent.

"What is it?" I asked in a deadened voice, taking the lighted lamp out of the binnacle,[1] and raising it to his face.

"An ugly business."

---

[1] *binnacle* Box, or stand, containing a compass and lantern.

He had rather regular features; a good mouth; light eyes under somewhat heavy, dark eyebrows; a smooth, square forehead; no growth on his cheeks; a small, brown mustache, and a well-shaped, round chin. His expression was concentrated, meditative, under the inspecting light of the lamp I held up to his face; such as a man thinking hard in solitude might wear. My sleeping suit was just right for his size. A well-knit young fellow of twenty-five at most. He caught his lower lip with the edge of white, even teeth.

"Yes," I said, replacing the lamp in the binnacle. The warm, heavy tropical night closed upon his head again.

"There's a ship over there," he murmured.

"Yes, I know. The *Sephora*. Did you know of us?"

"Hadn't the slightest idea. I am the mate of her—" He paused and corrected himself. "I should say I *WAS*."

"Aha! Something wrong?"

"Yes. Very wrong indeed. I've killed a man."

"What do you mean? Just now?"

"No, on the passage. Weeks ago. Thirty-nine south. When I say a man—"

"Fit of temper," I suggested, confidently.

The shadowy, dark head, like mine, seemed to nod imperceptibly above the ghostly gray of my sleeping suit. It was, in the night, as though I had been faced by my own reflection in the depths of a somber and immense mirror.

"A pretty thing to have to own up to for a Conway boy," murmured my double, distinctly.

"You're a Conway boy?"

"I am," he said, as if startled. Then, slowly… "Perhaps you too—"

It was so; but being a couple of years older I had left before he joined. After a quick interchange of dates a silence fell; and I thought suddenly of my absurd mate with his terrific whiskers and the "Bless my soul—you don't say so" type of intellect. My double gave me an inkling of his thoughts by saying: "My father's a parson in Norfolk. Do you see me before a judge and jury on that charge? For myself I can't see the necessity. There are fellows that an angel from heaven—And I am not that. He was one of those creatures that are just simmering all the time with a silly sort of wickedness. Miserable devils that have no business to live at all. He wouldn't do his duty and wouldn't let anybody else do theirs. But

what's the good of talking! You know well enough the sort of ill-conditioned snarling cur—"

He appealed to me as if our experiences had been as identical as our clothes. And I knew well enough the pestiferous danger of such a character where there are no means of legal repression. And I knew well enough also that my double there was no homicidal ruffian. I did not think of asking him for details, and he told me the story roughly in brusque, disconnected sentences. I needed no more. I saw it all going on as though I were myself inside that other sleeping suit.

"It happened while we were setting a reefed foresail,[1] at dusk. Reefed foresail! You understand the sort of weather. The only sail we had left to keep the ship running; so you may guess what it had been like for days. Anxious sort of job, that. He gave me some of his cursed insolence at the sheet. I tell you I was overdone with this terrific weather that seemed to have no end to it. Terrific, I tell you—and a deep ship. I believe the fellow himself was half crazed with funk. It was no time for gentlemanly reproof, so I turned round and felled him like an ox. He up and at me. We closed just as an awful sea made for the ship. All hands saw it coming and took to the rigging, but I had him by the throat, and went on shaking him like a rat, the men above us yelling, 'Look out! look out!' Then a crash as if the sky had fallen on my head. They say that for over ten minutes hardly anything was to be seen of the ship—just the three masts and a bit of the forecastle head and of the poop all awash driving along in a smother of foam. It was a miracle that they found us, jammed together behind the forebitts. It's clear that I meant business, because I was holding him by the throat still when they picked us up. He was black in the face. It was too much for them. It seems they rushed us aft together, gripped as we were, screaming 'Murder!' like a lot of lunatics, and broke into the cuddy. And the ship running for her life, touch and go all the time, any minute her last in a sea fit to turn your hair gray only a-looking at it. I understand that the skipper, too, started raving like the rest of them. The man had been deprived of sleep for more than a week, and to have this sprung on him at the height of a furious gale nearly drove him out

---

[1] *reefed fore sail* The sail set furthest forward; also known as the jib. A reefed sail has been tied back to reduce the sail area.

of his mind. I wonder they didn't fling me overboard after getting the carcass of their precious shipmate out of my fingers. They had rather a job to separate us, I've been told. A sufficiently fierce story to make an old judge and a respectable jury sit up a bit. The first thing I heard when I came to myself was the maddening howling of that endless gale, and on that the voice of the old man. He was hanging on to my bunk, staring into my face out of his sou'wester.[1]

"'Mr. Leggatt, you have killed a man. You can act no longer as chief mate of this ship.'"

His care to subdue his voice made it sound monotonous. He rested a hand on the end of the skylight to steady himself with, and all that time did not stir a limb, so far as I could see. "Nice little tale for a quiet tea party," he concluded in the same tone.

One of my hands, too, rested on the end of the skylight; neither did I stir a limb, so far as I knew. We stood less than a foot from each other. It occurred to me that if old "Bless my soul—you don't say so" were to put his head up the companion and catch sight of us, he would think he was seeing double, or imagine himself come upon a scene of weird witchcraft; the strange captain having a quiet confabulation by the wheel with his own gray ghost. I became very much concerned to prevent anything of the sort. I heard the other's soothing undertone.

"My father's a parson in Norfolk," it said. Evidently he had forgotten he had told me this important fact before. Truly a nice little tale.

"You had better slip down into my stateroom now," I said, moving off stealthily. My double followed my movements; our bare feet made no sound; I let him in, closed the door with care, and, after giving a call to the second mate, returned on deck for my relief.

"Not much sign of any wind yet," I remarked when he approached.

"No, sir. Not much," he assented, sleepily, in his hoarse voice, with just enough deference, no more, and barely suppressing a yawn.

"Well, that's all you have to look out for. You have got your orders."

"Yes, sir."

I paced a turn or two on the poop and saw him take up his position face forward with his elbow in the ratlines of the mizzen[2] rigging before I went below. The mate's faint snoring was still going on peacefully. The cuddy lamp was burning over the table on which stood a vase with flowers, a polite attention from the ship's provision merchant—the last flowers we should see for the next three months at the very least. Two bunches of bananas hung from the beam symmetrically, one on each side of the rudder casing. Everything was as before in the ship—except that two of her captain's sleeping suits were simultaneously in use, one motionless in the cuddy, the other keeping very still in the captain's stateroom.

It must be explained here that my cabin had the form of the capital letter L, the door being within the angle and opening into the short part of the letter. A couch was to the left, the bed place to the right; my writing desk and the chronometers' table faced the door. But anyone opening it, unless he stepped right inside, had no view of what I call the long (or vertical) part of the letter. It contained some lockers surmounted by a bookcase; and a few clothes, a thick jacket or two, caps, oilskin coat, and such like, hung on hooks. There was at the bottom of that part a door opening into my bathroom, which could be entered also directly from the saloon. But that way was never used.

The mysterious arrival had discovered the advantage of this particular shape. Entering my room, lighted strongly by a big bulkhead lamp swung on gimbals above my writing desk, I did not see him anywhere till he stepped out quietly from behind the coats hung in the recessed part.

"I heard somebody moving about, and went in there at once," he whispered.

I, too, spoke under my breath.

"Nobody is likely to come in here without knocking and getting permission."

He nodded. His face was thin and the sunburn faded, as though he had been ill. And no wonder. He had been, I heard presently, kept under arrest in his cabin for nearly seven weeks. But there was nothing sickly in his eyes or in his expression. He was not a bit

[1] sou'wester Waterproof, often oilskin, hat with a wide slanting brim that is longer in back than in front.

[2] mizzen The shorter mast behind the main mast aboard a ketch or yawl.

like me, really; yet, as we stood leaning over my bed place, whispering side by side, with our dark heads together and our backs to the door, anybody bold enough to open it stealthily would have been treated to the uncanny sight of a double captain busy talking in whispers with his other self.

"But all this doesn't tell me how you came to hang on to our side ladder," I inquired, in the hardly audible murmurs we used, after he had told me something more of the proceedings on board the *Sephora* once the bad weather was over.

"When we sighted Java Head I had had time to think all those matters out several times over. I had six weeks of doing nothing else, and with only an hour or so every evening for a tramp on the quarter-deck."

He whispered, his arms folded on the side of my bed place, staring through the open port. And I could imagine perfectly the manner of this thinking out—a stubborn if not a steadfast operation; something of which I should have been perfectly incapable.

"I reckoned it would be dark before we closed with the land," he continued, so low that I had to strain my hearing near as we were to each other, shoulder touching shoulder almost. "So I asked to speak to the old man. He always seemed very sick when he came to see me—as if he could not look me in the face. You know, that foresail saved the ship. She was too deep to have run long under bare poles. And it was I that managed to set it for him. Anyway, he came. When I had him in my cabin—he stood by the door looking at me as if I had the halter round my neck already—I asked him right away to leave my cabin door unlocked at night while the ship was going through Sunda Straits.[1] There would be the Java coast within two or three miles, off Angier Point. I wanted nothing more. I've had a prize for swimming my second year in the Conway."

"I can believe it," I breathed out.

"God only knows why they locked me in every night. To see some of their faces you'd have thought they were afraid I'd go about at night strangling people. Am I a murdering brute? Do I look it? By Jove! If I had been he wouldn't have trusted himself like that into my room. You'll say I might have chucked him aside and

bolted out, there and then—it was dark already. Well, no. And for the same reason I wouldn't think of trying to smash the door. There would have been a rush to stop me at the noise, and I did not mean to get into a confounded scrimmage. Somebody else might have got killed—for I would not have broken out only to get chucked back, and I did not want any more of that work. He refused, looking more sick than ever. He was afraid of the men, and also of that old second mate of his who had been sailing with him for years—a gray-headed old humbug; and his steward, too, had been with him devil knows how long—seventeen years or more—a dogmatic sort of loafer who hated me like poison, just because I was the chief mate. No chief mate ever made more than one voyage in the *Sephora*, you know. Those two old chaps ran the ship. Devil only knows what the skipper wasn't afraid of (all his nerve went to pieces altogether in that hellish spell of bad weather we had)—of what the law would do to him—of his wife, perhaps. Oh, yes! she's on board. Though I don't think she would have meddled. She would have been only too glad to have me out of the ship in any way. The 'brand of Cain' business, don't you see. That's all right. I was ready enough to go off wandering on the face of the earth—and that was price enough to pay for an Abel of that sort. Anyhow, he wouldn't listen to me. 'This thing must take its course. I represent the law here.' He was shaking like a leaf. 'So you won't?' 'No!' 'Then I hope you will be able to sleep on that,' I said, and turned my back on him. 'I wonder that *you* can,' cries he, and locks the door.

"Well after that, I couldn't. Not very well. That was three weeks ago. We have had a slow passage through the Java Sea; drifted about Carimata for ten days. When we anchored here they thought, I suppose, it was all right. The nearest land (and that's five miles) is the ship's destination; the consul would soon set about catching me; and there would have been no object in bolting to these islets there. I don't suppose there's a drop of water on them. I don't know how it was, but tonight that steward, after bringing me my supper, went out to let me eat it, and left the door unlocked. And I ate it—all there was, too. After I had finished I strolled out on the quarter-deck. I don't know that I meant to do anything. A breath of fresh air was all I wanted, I believe. Then a sudden temptation came over me. I kicked off my slippers and was in the water before I had made up my mind fairly. Somebody heard the splash and they raised an awful hullabaloo. 'He's gone! Lower the boats! He's committed suicide! No, he's swimming.' Certainly I was swimming. It's not so easy for a swimmer like me to commit suicide by drowning. I landed on the nearest islet before the boat left the ship's side. I heard them pulling about in the dark, hailing, and so on, but after a bit they gave up. Everything quieted down and the anchorage became still as death. I sat down on a stone and began to think. I felt certain they would start searching for me at daylight. There was no place to hide on those stony things—and if there had been, what would have been the good? But now I was clear of that ship, I was not going back. So after a while I took off all my clothes, tied them up in a bundle with a stone inside, and dropped them in the deep water on the outer side of that islet. That was suicide enough for me. Let them think what they liked, but I didn't mean to drown myself. I meant to swim till I sank—but that's not the same thing. I struck out for another of these little islands, and it was from that one that I first saw your riding light. Something to swim for. I went on easily, and on the way I came upon a flat rock a foot or two above water. In the daytime, I dare say, you might make it out with a glass from your poop. I scrambled up on it and rested myself for a bit. Then I made another start. That last spell must have been over a mile."

His whisper was getting fainter and fainter, and all the time he stared straight out through the porthole, in which there was not even a star to be seen. I had not interrupted him. There was something that made comment impossible in his narrative, or perhaps in himself; a sort of feeling, a quality, which I can't find a name for. And when he ceased, all I found was a futile whisper: "So you swam for our light?"

"Yes—straight for it. It was something to swim for. I couldn't see any stars low down because the coast was in the way, and I couldn't see the land, either. The water was like glass. One might have been swimming in a confounded thousand-feet deep cistern with no place for scrambling out anywhere; but what I didn't like was the notion of swimming round and round like a crazed bullock before I gave out; and as I didn't mean to go

back…No. Do you see me being hauled back, stark naked, off one of these little islands by the scruff of the neck and fighting like a wild beast? Somebody would have got killed for certain, and I did not want any of that. So I went on. Then your ladder—"

"Why didn't you hail the ship?" I asked, a little louder.

He touched my shoulder lightly. Lazy footsteps came right over our heads and stopped. The second mate had crossed from the other side of the poop and might have been hanging over the rail for all we knew.

"He couldn't hear us talking—could he?" My double breathed into my very ear, anxiously.

His anxiety was in answer, a sufficient answer, to the question I had put to him. An answer containing all the difficulty of that situation. I closed the porthole quietly, to make sure. A louder word might have been overheard.

"Who's that?" he whispered then.

"My second mate. But I don't know much more of the fellow than you do."

And I told him a little about myself. I had been appointed to take charge while I least expected anything of the sort, not quite a fortnight ago. I didn't know either the ship or the people. Hadn't had the time in port to look about me or size anybody up. And as to the crew, all they knew was that I was appointed to take the ship home. For the rest, I was almost as much of a stranger on board as himself, I said. And at the moment I felt it most acutely. I felt that it would take very little to make me a suspect person in the eyes of the ship's company.

He had turned about meantime; and we, the two strangers in the ship, faced each other in identical attitudes.

"Your ladder——" he murmured, after a silence. "Who'd have thought of finding a ladder hanging over at night in a ship anchored out here! I felt just then a very unpleasant faintness. After the life I've been leading for nine weeks, anybody would have got out of condition. I wasn't capable of swimming round as far as your rudder chains. And, lo and behold! there was a ladder to get hold of. After I gripped it I said to myself, 'What's the good?' When I saw a man's head looking over I thought I would swim away presently and leave him shouting—in whatever language it was. I didn't mind being looked at. I—I liked it. And then you speaking to me so quietly—as if you had expected me—made me hold on a little longer. It had been a confounded lonely time—I don't mean while swimming. I was glad to talk a little to somebody that didn't belong to the *Sephora*. As to asking for the captain, that was a mere impulse. It could have been no use, with all the ship knowing about me and the other people pretty certain to be round here in the morning. I don't know—I wanted to be seen, to talk with somebody, before I went on. I don't know what I would have said.... 'Fine night, isn't it?' or something of the sort."

"Do you think they will be round here presently?" I asked with some incredulity.

"Quite likely," he said, faintly.

He looked extremely haggard all of a sudden. His head rolled on his shoulders.

"H'm. We shall see then. Meantime get into that bed," I whispered. "Want help? There."

It was a rather high bed place with a set of drawers underneath. This amazing swimmer really needed the lift I gave him by seizing his leg. He tumbled in, rolled over on his back, and flung one arm across his eyes. And then, with his face nearly hidden, he must have looked exactly as I used to look in that bed. I gazed upon my other self for a while before drawing across carefully the two green serge curtains which ran on a brass rod. I thought for a moment of pinning them together for greater safety, but I sat down on the couch, and once there I felt unwilling to rise and hunt for a pin. I would do it in a moment. I was extremely tired, in a peculiarly intimate way, by the strain of stealthiness, by the effort of whispering and the general secrecy of this excitement. It was three o'clock by now and I had been on my feet since nine, but I was not sleepy; I could not have gone to sleep. I sat there, fagged out, looking at the curtains, trying to clear my mind of the confused sensation of being in two places at once, and greatly bothered by an exasperating knocking in my head. It was a relief to discover suddenly that it was not in my head at all, but on the outside of the door. Before I could collect myself the words "Come in" were out of my mouth, and the steward entered with a tray, bringing in my morning coffee. I had slept, after all, and I was so frightened that

I shouted, "This way! I am here, steward," as though he had been miles away. He put down the tray on the table next the couch and only then said, very quietly, "I can see you are here, sir." I felt him give me a keen look, but I dared not meet his eyes just then. He must have wondered why I had drawn the curtains of my bed before going to sleep on the couch. He went out, hooking the door open as usual.

I heard the crew washing decks above me. I knew I would have been told at once if there had been any wind. Calm, I thought, and I was doubly vexed. Indeed, I felt dual more than ever. The steward reappeared suddenly in the doorway. I jumped up from the couch so quickly that he gave a start.

"What do you want here?"

"Close your port, sir—they are washing decks."

"It is closed," I said, reddening.

"Very well, sir." But he did not move from the doorway and returned my stare in an extraordinary, equivocal manner for a time. Then his eyes wavered, all his expression changed, and in a voice unusually gentle, almost coaxingly:

"May I come in to take the empty cup away, sir?"

"Of course!" I turned my back on him while he popped in and out. Then I unhooked and closed the door and even pushed the bolt. This sort of thing could not go on very long. The cabin was as hot as an oven, too. I took a peep at my double, and discovered that he had not moved, his arm was still over his eyes; but his chest heaved; his hair was wet; his chin glistened with perspiration. I reached over him and opened the port.

"I must show myself on deck," I reflected.

Of course, theoretically, I could do what I liked, with no one to say nay to me within the whole circle of the horizon; but to lock my cabin door and take the key away I did not dare. Directly I put my head out of the companion I saw the group of my two officers, the second mate barefooted, the chief mate in long India-rubber boots, near the break of the poop, and the steward halfway down the poop ladder talking to them eagerly. He happened to catch sight of me and dived, the second ran down on the main-deck shouting some order or other, and the chief mate came to meet me, touching his cap.

There was a sort of curiosity in his eye that I did not

like. I don't know whether the steward had told them that I was "queer" only, or downright drunk, but I know the man meant to have a good look at me. I watched him coming with a smile which, as he got into point-blank range, took effect and froze his very whiskers. I did not give him time to open his lips.

"Square the yards by lifts and braces before the hands go to breakfast."

It was the first particular order I had given on board that ship; and I stayed on deck to see it executed, too. I had felt the need of asserting myself without loss of time. That sneering young cub got taken down a peg or two on that occasion, and I also seized the opportunity of having a good look at the face of every foremast man as they filed past me to go to the after braces. At breakfast time, eating nothing myself, I presided with such frigid dignity that the two mates were only too glad to escape from the cabin as soon as decency permitted; and all the time the dual working of my mind distracted me almost to the point of insanity. I was constantly watching myself, my secret self, as dependent on my actions as my own personality, sleeping in that bed, behind that door which faced me as I sat at the head of the table. It was very much like being mad, only it was worse because one was aware of it.

I had to shake him for a solid minute, but when at last he opened his eyes it was in the full possession of his senses, with an inquiring look.

"All's well so far," I whispered. "Now you must vanish into the bathroom."

He did so, as noiseless as a ghost, and then I rang for the steward, and facing him boldly, directed him to tidy up my stateroom while I was having my bath—"and be quick about it." As my tone admitted of no excuses, he said, "Yes, sir," and ran off to fetch his dustpan and brushes. I took a bath and did most of my dressing, splashing, and whistling softly for the steward's edification, while the secret sharer of my life stood drawn up bolt upright in that little space, his face looking very sunken in daylight, his eyelids lowered under the stern, dark line of his eyebrows drawn together by a slight frown.

When I left him there to go back to my room the steward was finishing dusting. I sent for the mate and engaged him in some insignificant conversation. It was,

as it were, trifling with the terrific character of his whiskers; but my object was to give him an opportunity for a good look at my cabin. And then I could at last shut, with a clear conscience, the door of my stateroom and get my double back into the recessed part. There was nothing else for it. He had to sit still on a small folding stool, half smothered by the heavy coats hanging there. We listened to the steward going into the bathroom out of the saloon, filling the water bottles there, scrubbing the bath, setting things to rights, whisk, bang, clatter—out again into the saloon—turn the key—click. Such was my scheme for keeping my second self invisible. Nothing better could be contrived under the circumstances. And there we sat; I at my writing desk ready to appear busy with some papers, he behind me out of sight of the door. It would not have been prudent to talk in daytime; and I could not have stood the excitement of that queer sense of whispering to myself. Now and then, glancing over my shoulder, I saw him far back there, sitting rigidly on the low stool, his bare feet close together, his arms folded, his head hanging on his breast—and perfectly still. Anybody would have taken him for me.

I was fascinated by it myself. Every moment I had to glance over my shoulder. I was looking at him when a voice outside the door said:

"Beg pardon, sir."

"Well!"… I kept my eyes on him, and so when the voice outside the door announced, "There's a ship's boat coming our way, sir," I saw him give a start—the first movement he had made for hours. But he did not raise his bowed head.

"All right. Get the ladder over."

I hesitated. Should I whisper something to him? But what? His immobility seemed to have been never disturbed. What could I tell him he did not know already?… Finally I went on deck.

2

The skipper of the *Sephora* had a thin red whisker all round his face, and the sort of complexion that goes with hair of that colour; also the particular, rather smeary shade of blue in the eyes. He was not exactly a showy figure; his shoulders were high, his stature but middling—one leg slightly more bandy than the other.

He shook hands, looking vaguely around. A spiritless tenacity was his main characteristic, I judged. I behaved with a politeness which seemed to disconcert him. Perhaps he was shy. He mumbled to me as if he were ashamed of what he was saying; gave his name (it was something like Archbold—but at this distance of years I hardly am sure), his ship's name, and a few other particulars of that sort, in the manner of a criminal making a reluctant and doleful confession. He had had terrible weather on the passage out—terrible—terrible —wife aboard, too.

By this time we were seated in the cabin and the steward brought in a tray with a bottle and glasses. "Thanks! No." Never took liquor. Would have some water, though. He drank two tumblerfuls. Terrible thirsty work. Ever since daylight had been exploring the islands round his ship.

"What was that for—fun?" I asked, with an appearance of polite interest.

"No!" He sighed. "Painful duty."

As he persisted in his mumbling and I wanted my double to hear every word, I hit upon the notion of informing him that I regretted to say I was hard of hearing.

"Such a young man, too!" he nodded, keeping his smeary blue, unintelligent eyes fastened upon me. "What was the cause of it—some disease?" he inquired, without the least sympathy and as if he thought that, if so, I'd got no more than I deserved.

"Yes; disease," I admitted in a cheerful tone which seemed to shock him. But my point was gained, because he had to raise his voice to give me his tale. It is not worth while to record his version. It was just over two months since all this had happened, and he had thought so much about it that he seemed completely muddled as to its bearings, but still immensely impressed.

"What would you think of such a thing happening on board your own ship? I've had the *Sephora* for these fifteen years. I am a well-known shipmaster."

He was densely distressed—and perhaps I should have sympathized with him if I had been able to detach my mental vision from the unsuspected sharer of my cabin as though he were my second self. There he was on the other side of the bulkhead, four or five feet from us, no more, as we sat in the saloon. I looked politely at Captain Archbold (if that was his name), but it was the other I saw, in a gray sleeping suit, seated on a low stool, his bare feet close together, his arms folded, and every word said between us falling into the ears of his dark head bowed on his chest.

"I have been at sea now, man and boy, for seven-and-thirty years, and I've never heard of such a thing happening in an English ship. And that it should be my ship. Wife on board, too."

I was hardly listening to him.

"Don't you think," I said, "that the heavy sea which, you told me, came aboard just then might have killed the man? I have seen the sheer weight of a sea kill a man very neatly, by simply breaking his neck."

"Good God!" he uttered, impressively, fixing his smeary blue eyes on me. "The sea! No man killed by the sea ever looked like that." He seemed positively scandalized at my suggestion. And as I gazed at him certainly not prepared for anything original on his part, he advanced his head close to mine and thrust his tongue out at me so suddenly that I couldn't help starting back.

After scoring over my calmness in this graphic way he nodded wisely. If I had seen the sight, he assured me, I would never forget it as long as I lived. The weather was too bad to give the corpse a proper sea burial. So next day at dawn they took it up on the poop, covering its face with a bit of bunting; he read a short prayer, and then, just as it was, in its oilskins and long boots, they launched it amongst those mountainous seas that seemed ready every moment to swallow up the ship herself and the terrified lives on board of her.

"That reefed foresail saved you," I threw in.

"Under God—it did," he exclaimed fervently. "It was by a special mercy, I firmly believe, that it stood some of those hurricane squalls."

"It was the setting of that sail which—" I began.

"God's own hand in it," he interrupted me. "Nothing less could have done it. I don't mind telling you that I hardly dared give the order. It seemed impossible that we could touch anything without losing it, and then our last hope would have been gone."

The terror of that gale was on him yet. I let him go on for a bit, then said, casually—as if returning to a minor subject:

"You were very anxious to give up your mate to the

shore people, I believe?"

He was. To the law. His obscure tenacity on that point had in it something incomprehensible and a little awful; something, as it were, mystical, quite apart from his anxiety that he should not be suspected of "countenancing any doings of that sort." Seven-and-thirty virtuous years at sea, of which over twenty of immaculate command, and the last fifteen in the Sephora, seemed to have laid him under some pitiless obligation.

"And you know," he went on, groping shamefacedly amongst his feelings, "I did not engage that young fellow. His people had some interest with my owners. I was in a way forced to take him on. He looked very smart, very gentlemanly, and all that. But do you know—I never liked him, somehow. I am a plain man. You see, he wasn't exactly the sort for the chief mate of a ship like the *Sephora*."

I had become so connected in thoughts and impressions with the secret sharer of my cabin that I felt as if I, personally, were being given to understand that I, too, was not the sort that would have done for the chief mate of a ship like the *Sephora*. I had no doubt of it in my mind.

"Not at all the style of man. You understand," he insisted, superfluously, looking hard at me.

I smiled urbanely. He seemed at a loss for a while.

"I suppose I must report a suicide."

"Beg pardon?"

"Suicide! That's what I'll have to write to my owners directly I get in."

"Unless you manage to recover him before tomorrow," I assented, dispassionately… "I mean, alive."

He mumbled something which I really did not catch, and I turned my ear to him in a puzzled manner. He fairly bawled:

"The land—I say, the mainland is at least seven miles off my anchorage."

"About that."

My lack of excitement, of curiosity, of surprise, of any sort of pronounced interest, began to arouse his distrust. But except for the felicitous pretense of deafness I had not tried to pretend anything. I had felt utterly incapable of playing the part of ignorance properly, and therefore was afraid to try. It is also certain that he had brought some ready-made suspicions with

him, and that he viewed my politeness as a strange and unnatural phenomenon. And yet how else could I have received him? Not heartily! That was impossible for psychological reasons, which I need not state here. My only object was to keep off his inquiries. Surlily? Yes, but surliness might have provoked a point-blank question. From its novelty to him and from its nature, punctilious courtesy was the manner best calculated to restrain the man. But there was the danger of his breaking through my defense bluntly. I could not, I think, have met him by a direct lie, also for psychological (not moral) reasons. If he had only known how afraid I was of his putting my feeling of identity with the other to the test! But, strangely enough—(I thought of it only afterwards)—I believe that he was not a little disconcerted by the reverse side of that weird situation, by something in me that reminded him of the man he was seeking—suggested a mysterious similitude to the young fellow he had distrusted and disliked from the first.

However that might have been, the silence was not very prolonged. He took another oblique step.

"I reckon I had no more than a two-mile pull to your ship. Not a bit more."

"And quite enough, too, in this awful heat," I said.

Another pause full of mistrust followed. Necessity, they say, is mother of invention, but fear, too, is not barren of ingenious suggestions. And I was afraid he would ask me point-blank for news of my other self.

"Nice little saloon, isn't it?" I remarked, as if noticing for the first time the way his eyes roamed from one closed door to the other. "And very well fitted out, too. Here, for instance," I continued, reaching over the back of my seat negligently and flinging the door open, "is my bathroom."

He made an eager movement, but hardly gave it a glance. I got up, shut the door of the bathroom, and invited him to have a look round, as if I were very proud of my accommodation. He had to rise and be shown round, but he went through the business without any raptures whatever.

"And now we'll have a look at my stateroom," I declared, in a voice as loud as I dared to make it, crossing the cabin to the starboard side with purposely heavy steps.

He followed me in and gazed around. My intelligent double had vanished. I played my part.

"Very convenient—isn't it?"

"Very nice. Very comf … " He didn't finish and went out brusquely as if to escape from some unrighteous wiles of mine. But it was not to be. I had been too frightened not to feel vengeful; I felt I had him on the run, and I meant to keep him on the run. My polite insistence must have had something menacing in it, because he gave in suddenly. And I did not let him off a single item; mate's room, pantry, storerooms, the very sail locker which was also under the poop—he had to look into them all. When at last I showed him out on the quarter-deck he drew a long, spiritless sigh, and mumbled dismally that he must really be going back to his ship now. I desired my mate, who had joined us, to see to the captain's boat.

The man of whiskers gave a blast on the whistle which he used to wear hanging round his neck, and yelled, "*Sephora's* away!" My double down there in my cabin must have heard, and certainly could not feel more relieved than I. Four fellows came running out from somewhere forward and went over the side, while my own men, appearing on deck too, lined the rail. I escorted my visitor to the gangway ceremoniously, and nearly overdid it. He was a tenacious beast. On the very ladder he lingered, and in that unique, guiltily conscientious manner of sticking to the point:

"I say … you … you don't think that—"

I covered his voice loudly:

"Certainly not … I am delighted. Good-by."

I had an idea of what he meant to say, and just saved myself by the privilege of defective hearing. He was too shaken generally to insist, but my mate, close witness of that parting, looked mystified and his face took on a thoughtful cast. As I did not want to appear as if I wished to avoid all communication with my officers, he had the opportunity to address me.

"Seems a very nice man. His boat's crew told our chaps a very extraordinary story, if what I am told by the steward is true. I suppose you had it from the captain, sir?"

"Yes. I had a story from the captain."

"A very horrible affair—isn't it, sir?"

"It is."

"Beats all these tales we hear about murders in Yankee ships."

"I don't think it beats them. I don't think it resembles them in the least."

"Bless my soul—you don't say so! But of course I've no acquaintance whatever with American ships, not I so I couldn't go against your knowledge. It's horrible enough for me…. But the queerest part is that those fellows seemed to have some idea the man was hidden aboard here. They had really. Did you ever hear of such a thing?"

"Preposterous—isn't it?"

We were walking to and fro athwart the quarter-deck. No one of the crew forward could be seen (the day was Sunday), and the mate pursued:

"There was some little dispute about it. Our chaps took offense. 'As if we would harbour a thing like that,' they said. 'Wouldn't you like to look for him in our coal-hole?' Quite a tiff. But they made it up in the end. I suppose he did drown himself. Don't you, sir?"

"I don't suppose anything."

"You have no doubt in the matter, sir?"

"None whatever."

I left him suddenly. I felt I was producing a bad impression, but with my double down there it was most trying to be on deck. And it was almost as trying to be below. Altogether a nerve-trying situation. But on the whole I felt less torn in two when I was with him. There was no one in the whole ship whom I dared take into my confidence. Since the hands had got to know his story, it would have been impossible to pass him off for anyone else, and an accidental discovery was to be dreaded now more than ever….

The steward being engaged in laying the table for dinner, we could talk only with our eyes when I first went down. Later in the afternoon we had a cautious try at whispering. The Sunday quietness of the ship was against us; the stillness of air and water around her was against us; the elements, the men were against us—everything was against us in our secret partnership; time itself—for this could not go on forever. The very trust in Providence was, I suppose, denied to his guilt. Shall I confess that this thought cast me down very much? And as to the chapter of accidents which counts for so much in the book of success, I could only hope that it was closed. For what favourable accident could be expected?

"Did you hear everything?" were my first words as soon as we took up our position side by side, leaning over my bed place.

He had. And the proof of it was his earnest whisper, "The man told you he hardly dared to give the order."

I understood the reference to be to that saving foresail.

"Yes. He was afraid of it being lost in the setting."

"I assure you he never gave the order. He may think he did, but he never gave it. He stood there with me on the break of the poop after the main topsail blew away, and whimpered about our last hope—positively whimpered about it and nothing else—and the night coming on! To hear one's skipper go on like that in such weather was enough to drive any fellow out of his mind. It worked me up into a sort of desperation. I just took it into my own hands and went away from him, boiling, and—But what's the use telling you? YOU know!… Do you think that if I had not been pretty fierce with them I should have got the men to do anything? Not it! The bo's'n[1] perhaps? Perhaps! It wasn't a heavy sea—it was a sea gone mad! I suppose the end of the world will be something like that; and a man may have the heart to see it coming once and be done with it— but to have to face it day after day—I don't blame anybody. I was precious little better than the rest. Only—I was an officer of that old coal wagon, anyhow—"

"I quite understand," I conveyed that sincere assurance into his ear. He was out of breath with whispering; I could hear him pant slightly. It was all very simple. The same strung-up force which had given twenty-four men a chance, at least, for their lives, had, in a sort of recoil, crushed an unworthy mutinous existence.

But I had no leisure to weigh the merits of the matter—footsteps in the saloon, a heavy knock. "There's enough wind to get under way with, sir." Here was the call of a new claim upon my thoughts and even upon my feelings.

"Turn the hands up," I cried through the door. "I'll be on deck directly."

I was going out to make the acquaintance of my ship. Before I left the cabin our eyes met—the eyes of the only two strangers on board. I pointed to the recessed part where the little campstool awaited him and laid my finger on my lips. He made a gesture—somewhat vague—a little mysterious, accompanied by a faint smile, as if of regret.

This is not the place to enlarge upon the sensations of a man who feels for the first time a ship move under his feet to his own independent word. In my case they were not unalloyed. I was not wholly alone with my command; for there was that stranger in my cabin. Or rather, I was not completely and wholly with her. Part of me was absent. That mental feeling of being in two places at once affected me physically as if the mood of secrecy had penetrated my very soul. Before an hour had elapsed since the ship had begun to move, having occasion to ask the mate (he stood by my side) to take a compass bearing of the pagoda, I caught myself reaching up to his ear in whispers. I say I caught myself, but enough had escaped to startle the man. I can't describe it otherwise than by saying that he shied. A grave, preoccupied manner, as though he were in possession of some perplexing intelligence, did not leave him henceforth. A little later I moved away from the rail to look at the compass with such a stealthy gait that the helmsman noticed it—and I could not help noticing the unusual roundness of his eyes. These are trifling instances, though it's to no commander's advantage to be suspected of ludicrous eccentricities. But I was also more seriously affected. There are to a seaman certain words, gestures, that should in given conditions come as naturally, as instinctively as the winking of a menaced eye. A certain order should spring on to his lips without thinking; a certain sign should get itself made, so to speak, without reflection. But all unconscious alertness had abandoned me. I had to make an effort of will to recall myself back (from the cabin) to the conditions of the moment. I felt that I was appearing an irresolute commander to those people who were watching me more or less critically.

And, besides, there were the scares. On the second day out, for instance, coming off the deck in the afternoon (I had straw slippers on my bare feet) I stopped at the open pantry door and spoke to the steward. He was doing something there with his back to me. At the

---

[1] *bo's'n* Boatswain (petty officer in charge of ship's rigging, sails, anchors, and deck crew).

sound of my voice he nearly jumped out of his skin, as the saying is, and incidentally broke a cup.

"What on earth's the matter with you?" I asked, astonished.

He was extremely confused. "Beg your pardon, sir. I made sure you were in your cabin."

"You see I wasn't."

"No, sir. I could have sworn I had heard you moving in there not a moment ago. It's most extraordinary … very sorry, sir."

I passed on with an inward shudder. I was so identified with my secret double that I did not even mention the fact in those scanty, fearful whispers we exchanged. I suppose he had made some slight noise of some kind or other. It would have been miraculous if he hadn't at one time or another. And yet, haggard as he appeared, he looked always perfectly self-controlled, more than calm—almost invulnerable. On my suggestion he remained almost entirely in the bathroom, which, upon the whole, was the safest place. There could be really no shadow of an excuse for anyone ever wanting to go in there, once the steward had done with it. It was a very tiny place. Sometimes he reclined on the floor, his legs bent, his head sustained on one elbow. At others I would find him on the campstool, sitting in his gray sleeping suit and with his cropped dark hair like a patient, unmoved convict. At night I would smuggle him into my bed place, and we would whisper together, with the regular footfalls of the officer of the watch passing and repassing over our heads. It was an infinitely miserable time. It was lucky that some tins of fine preserves were stowed in a locker in my stateroom; hard bread I could always get hold of; and so he lived on stewed chicken, *paté de foie gras*, asparagus, cooked oysters, sardines—on all sorts of abominable sham delicacies out of tins. My early-morning coffee he always drank; and it was all I dared do for him in that respect.

Every day there was the horrible maneuvering to go through so that my room and then the bathroom should be done in the usual way. I came to hate the sight of the steward, to abhor the voice of that harmless man. I felt that it was he who would bring on the disaster of discovery. It hung like a sword over our heads.

The fourth day out, I think (we were then working down the east side of the Gulf of Siam, tack for tack, in light winds and smooth water)—the fourth day, I say, of this miserable juggling with the unavoidable, as we sat at our evening meal, that man, whose slightest movement I dreaded, after putting down the dishes ran up on deck busily. This could not be dangerous. Presently he came down again; and then it appeared that he had remembered a coat of mine which I had thrown over a rail to dry after having been wetted in a shower which had passed over the ship in the afternoon. Sitting stolidly at the head of the table I became terrified at the sight of the garment on his arm. Of course he made for my door. There was no time to lose.

"Steward," I thundered. My nerves were so shaken that I could not govern my voice and conceal my agitation. This was the sort of thing that made my terrifically whiskered mate tap his forehead with his forefinger. I had detected him using that gesture while talking on deck with a confidential air to the carpenter. It was too far to hear a word, but I had no doubt that this pantomime could only refer to the strange new captain.

"Yes, sir," the pale-faced steward turned resignedly to me. It was this maddening course of being shouted at, checked without rhyme or reason, arbitrarily chased out of my cabin, suddenly called into it, sent flying out of his pantry on incomprehensible errands, that accounted for the growing wretchedness of his expression.

"Where are you going with that coat?"

"To your room, sir."

"Is there another shower coming?"

"I'm sure I don't know, sir. Shall I go up again and see, sir?"

"No! never mind."

My object was attained, as of course my other self in there would have heard everything that passed. During this interlude my two officers never raised their eyes off their respective plates; but the lip of that confounded cub, the second mate, quivered visibly.

I expected the steward to hook my coat on and come out at once. He was very slow about it; but I dominated my nervousness sufficiently not to shout after him. Suddenly I became aware (it could be heard plainly enough) that the fellow for some reason or other was opening the door of the bathroom. It was the end. The place was literally not big enough to swing a cat in. My voice died in my throat and I went stony all over. I expected to hear a yell of surprise and terror, and made a movement, but had not the strength to get on my legs. Everything remained still. Had my second self taken the poor wretch by the throat? I don't know what I could have done next moment if I had not seen the steward come out of my room, close the door, and then stand quietly by the sideboard.

"Saved," I thought. "But, no! Lost! Gone! He was gone!"

I laid my knife and fork down and leaned back in my chair. My head swam. After a while, when sufficiently recovered to speak in a steady voice, I instructed my mate to put the ship round at eight o'clock himself.

"I won't come on deck," I went on. "I think I'll turn in, and unless the wind shifts I don't want to be disturbed before midnight. I feel a bit seedy."

"You did look middling bad a little while ago," the chief mate remarked without showing any great concern.

They both went out, and I stared at the steward clearing the table. There was nothing to be read on that wretched man's face. But why did he avoid my eyes, I asked myself. Then I thought I should like to hear the sound of his voice.

"Steward!"

"Sir!" Startled as usual.

"Where did you hang up that coat?"

"In the bathroom, sir." The usual anxious tone. "It's not quite dry yet, sir."

For some time longer I sat in the cuddy. Had my double vanished as he had come? But of his coming there was an explanation, whereas his disappearance would be inexplicable … I went slowly into my dark room, shut the door, lighted the lamp, and for a time dared not turn round. When at last I did I saw him standing bolt-upright in the narrow recessed part. It would not be true to say I had a shock, but an irresistible doubt of his bodily existence flitted through my mind. Can it be, I asked myself, that he is not visible to other eyes than mine? It was like being haunted. Motionless, with a grave face, he raised his hands slightly at me in a gesture which meant clearly, "Heavens! what a narrow escape!" Narrow indeed. I think I had come creeping quietly as near insanity as any man who has not

actually gone over the border. That gesture restrained me, so to speak.

The mate with the terrific whiskers was now putting the ship on the other tack. In the moment of profound silence which follows upon the hands going to their stations I heard on the poop his raised voice: "Hard alee!"[1] and the distant shout of the order repeated on the main-deck. The sails, in that light breeze, made but a faint fluttering noise. It ceased. The ship was coming round slowly: I held my breath in the renewed stillness of expectation; one wouldn't have thought that there was a single living soul on her decks. A sudden brisk shout, "Mainsail haul!" broke the spell, and in the noisy cries and rush overhead of the men running away with the main brace we two, down in my cabin, came together in our usual position by the bed place.

He did not wait for my question. "I heard him fumbling here and just managed to squat myself down in the bath," he whispered to me. "The fellow only opened the door and put his arm in to hang the coat up. All the same—"

"I never thought of that," I whispered back, even more appalled than before at the closeness of the shave, and marveling at that something unyielding in his character which was carrying him through so finely. There was no agitation in his whisper. Whoever was being driven distracted, it was not he. He was sane. And the proof of his sanity was continued when he took up the whispering again.

"It would never do for me to come to life again."

It was something that a ghost might have said. But what he was alluding to was his old captain's reluctant admission of the theory of suicide. It would obviously serve his turn—if I had understood at all the view which seemed to govern the unalterable purpose of his action.

"You must maroon me as soon as ever you can get amongst these islands off the Cambodge[2] shore," he went on.

"Maroon you! We are not living in a boy's adventure tale," I protested. His scornful whispering took me up.

"We aren't indeed! There's nothing of a boy's tale in this. But there's nothing else for it. I want no more. You

---

[1] *Hard alee* "Hard a lee" (meaning "hard towards the leeward side") is the command given when a ship comes about.

[2] *Cambodge* Cambodia.

don't suppose I am afraid of what can be done to me? Prison or gallows or whatever they may please. But you don't see me coming back to explain such things to an old fellow in a wig and twelve respectable tradesmen, do you? What can they know whether I am guilty or not— or of *what* I am guilty, either? That's my affair. What does the Bible say? 'Driven off the face of the earth.' Very well, I am off the face of the earth now. As I came at night so I shall go."

"Impossible!" I murmured. "You can't."

"Can't? ... Not naked like a soul on the Day of Judgment. I shall freeze on to this sleeping suit. The Last Day is not yet—and ... you have understood thoroughly. Didn't you?"

I felt suddenly ashamed of myself. I may say truly that I understood—and my hesitation in letting that man swim away from my ship's side had been a mere sham sentiment, a sort of cowardice.

"It can't be done now till next night," I breathed out. "The ship is on the off-shore tack and the wind may fail us."

"As long as I know that you understand," he whispered. "But of course you do. It's a great satisfaction to have got somebody to understand. You seem to have been there on purpose." And in the same whisper, as if we two whenever we talked had to say things to each other which were not fit for the world to hear, he added, "It's very wonderful."

We remained side by side talking in our secret way—but sometimes silent or just exchanging a whispered word or two at long intervals. And as usual he stared through the port. A breath of wind came now and again into our faces. The ship might have been moored in dock, so gently and on an even keel she slipped through the water, that did not murmur even at our passage, shadowy and silent like a phantom sea.

At midnight I went on deck, and to my mate's great surprise put the ship round on the other tack. His terrible whiskers flitted round me in silent criticism. I certainly should not have done it if it had been only a question of getting out of that sleepy gulf as quickly as possible. I believe he told the second mate, who relieved him, that it was a great want of judgment. The other only yawned. That intolerable cub shuffled about so sleepily and lolled against the rails in such a slack,

improper fashion that I came down on him sharply.

"Aren't you properly awake yet?"

"Yes, sir! I am awake."

"Well, then, be good enough to hold yourself as if you were. And keep a lookout. If there's any current we'll be closing with some islands before daylight."

The east side of the gulf is fringed with islands, some solitary, others in groups. On the blue background of the high coast they seem to float on silvery patches of calm water, arid and gray, or dark green and rounded like clumps of evergreen bushes, with the larger ones, a mile or two long, showing the outlines of ridges, ribs of gray rock under the dark mantle of matted leafage. Unknown to trade, to travel, almost to geography, the manner of life they harbour is an unsolved secret. There must be villages—settlements of fishermen at least—on the largest of them, and some communication with the world is probably kept up by native craft. But all that forenoon, as we headed for them, fanned along by the faintest of breezes, I saw no sign of man or canoe in the field of the telescope I kept on pointing at the scattered group.

At noon I have no orders for a change of course, and the mate's whiskers became much concerned and seemed to be offering themselves unduly to my notice. At last I said:

"I am going to stand right in. Quite in—as far as I can take her."

The stare of extreme surprise imparted an air of ferocity also to his eyes, and he looked truly terrific for a moment.

"We're not doing well in the middle of the gulf," I continued, casually. "I am going to look for the land breezes tonight."

"Bless my soul! Do you mean, sir, in the dark amongst the lot of all them islands and reefs and shoals?"

"Well—if there are any regular land breezes at all on this coast one must get close inshore to find them, mustn't one?"

"Bless my soul!" he exclaimed again under his breath. All that afternoon he wore a dreamy, contemplative appearance which in him was a mark of perplexity. After dinner I went into my stateroom as if I meant to take some rest. There we two bent our dark heads over a half-unrolled chart lying on my bed.

"There," I said. "It's got to be Koh-ring. I've been looking at it ever since sunrise. It has got two hills and a low point. It must be inhabited. And on the coast opposite there is what looks like the mouth of a biggish river—with some towns, no doubt, not far up. It's the best chance for you that I can see."

"Anything. Koh-ring let it be."

He looked thoughtfully at the chart as if surveying chances and distances from a lofty height—and following with his eyes his own figure wandering on the blank land of Cochin-China, and then passing off that piece of paper clean out of sight into uncharted regions. And it was as if the ship had two captains to plan her course for her. I had been so worried and restless running up and down that I had not had the patience to dress that day. I had remained in my sleeping suit, with straw slippers and a soft floppy hat. The closeness of the heat in the gulf had been most oppressive, and the crew were used to seeing me wandering in that airy attire.

"She will clear the south point as she heads now," I whispered into his ear. "Goodness only knows when, though, but certainly after dark. I'll edge her in to half a mile, as far as I may be able to judge in the dark—"

"Be careful," he murmured, warningly—and I realized suddenly that all my future, the only future for which I was fit, would perhaps go irretrievably to pieces in any mishap to my first command.

I could not stop a moment longer in the room. I motioned him to get out of sight and made my way on the poop. That unplayful cub had the watch. I walked up and down for a while thinking things out, then beckoned him over.

"Send a couple of hands to open the two quarter-deck ports," I said, mildly.

He actually had the impudence, or else so forgot himself in his wonder at such an incomprehensible order, as to repeat:

"Open the quarter-deck ports! What for, sir?"

"The only reason you need concern yourself about is because I tell you to do so. Have them open wide and fastened properly."

He reddened and went off, but I believe made some jeering remark to the carpenter as to the sensible practice of ventilating a ship's quarter-deck. I know he

popped into the mate's cabin to impart the fact to him because the whiskers came on deck, as it were by chance, and stole glances at me from below—for signs of lunacy or drunkenness, I suppose.

A little before supper, feeling more restless than ever, I rejoined, for a moment, my second self. And to find him sitting so quietly was surprising, like something against nature, inhuman.

I developed my plan in a hurried whisper.

"I shall stand in as close as I dare and then put her round. I will presently find means to smuggle you out of here into the sail locker, which communicates with the lobby. But there is an opening, a sort of square for hauling the sails out, which gives straight on the quarter-deck and which is never closed in fine weather, so as to give air to the sails. When the ship's way is deadened in stays and all the hands are aft at the main braces you will have a clear road to slip out and get overboard through the open quarter-deck port. I've had them both fastened up. Use a rope's end to lower yourself into the water so as to avoid a splash—you know. It could be heard and cause some beastly complication."

He kept silent for a while, then whispered, "I understand."

"I won't be there to see you go," I began with an effort. "The rest … I only hope I have understood, too."

"You have. From first to last"—and for the first time there seemed to be a faltering, something strained in his whisper. He caught hold of my arm, but the ringing of the supper bell made me start. He didn't though; he only released his grip.

After supper I didn't come below again till well past eight o'clock. The faint, steady breeze was loaded with dew; and the wet, darkened sails held all there was of propelling power in it. The night, clear and starry, sparkled darkly, and the opaque, lightless patches shifting slowly against the low stars were the drifting islets. On the port bow there was a big one more distant and shadowily imposing by the great space of sky it eclipsed.

On opening the door I had a back view of my very own self looking at a chart. He had come out of the recess and was standing near the table.

"Quite dark enough," I whispered.

He stepped back and leaned against my bed with a level, quiet glance. I sat on the couch. We had nothing to say to each other. Over our heads the officer of the watch moved here and there. Then I heard him move quickly. I knew what that meant. He was making for the companion; and presently his voice was outside my door.

"We are drawing in pretty fast, sir. Land looks rather close."

"Very well," I answered. "I am coming on deck directly."

I waited till he was gone out of the cuddy, then rose. My double moved too. The time had come to exchange our last whispers, for neither of us was ever to hear each other's natural voice.

"Look here!" I opened a drawer and took out three sovereigns. "Take this anyhow. I've got six and I'd give you the lot, only I must keep a little money to buy some fruit and vegetables for the crew from native boats as we go through Sunda Straits."

He shook his head.

"Take it," I urged him, whispering desperately. "No one can tell what—"

He smiled and slapped meaningly the only pocket of the sleeping jacket. It was not safe, certainly. But I produced a large old silk handkerchief of mine, and tying the three pieces of gold in a corner, pressed it on him. He was touched, I supposed, because he took it at last and tied it quickly round his waist under the jacket, on his bare skin.

Our eyes met; several seconds elapsed, till, our glances still mingled, I extended my hand and turned the lamp out. Then I passed through the cuddy, leaving the door of my room wide open…"Steward!"

He was still lingering in the pantry in the greatness of his zeal, giving a rub-up to a plated cruet stand the last thing before going to bed. Being careful not to wake up the mate, whose room was opposite, I spoke in an undertone.

He looked round anxiously. "Sir!"

"Can you get me a little hot water from the galley?"

"I am afraid, sir, the galley fire's been out for some time now."

"Go and see."

He flew up the stairs.

"Now," I whispered, loudly, into the saloon—too loudly, perhaps, but I was afraid I couldn't make a sound. He was by my side in an instant—the double captain slipped past the stairs—through a tiny dark passage…a sliding door. We were in the sail locker, scrambling on our knees over the sails. A sudden thought struck me. I saw myself wandering barefooted, bareheaded, the sun beating on my dark poll. I snatched off my floppy hat and tried hurriedly in the dark to ram it on my other self. He dodged and fended off silently. I wonder what he thought had come to me before he understood and suddenly desisted. Our hands met gropingly, lingered united in a steady, motionless clasp for a second…No word was breathed by either of us when they separated.

I was standing quietly by the pantry door when the steward returned.

"Sorry, sir. Kettle barely warm. Shall I light the spirit lamp?"

"Never mind."

I came out on deck slowly. It was now a matter of conscience to shave the land as close as possible—for now he must go overboard whenever the ship was put in stays. Must! There could be no going back for him. After a moment I walked over to leeward and my heart flew into my mouth at the nearness of the land on the bow. Under any other circumstances I would not have held on a minute longer. The second mate had followed me anxiously.

I looked on till I felt I could command my voice.

"She will weather," I said then in a quiet tone.

"Are you going to try that, sir?" he stammered out incredulously.

I took no notice of him and raised my tone just enough to be heard by the helmsman.

"Keep her good full."

"Good full, sir."

The wind fanned my cheek, the sails slept, the world was silent. The strain of watching the dark loom of the land grow bigger and denser was too much for me. I had shut my eyes—because the ship must go closer. She must! The stillness was intolerable. Were we standing still?

When I opened my eyes the second view started my heart with a thump. The black southern hill of Koh-ring seemed to hang right over the ship like a towering fragment of everlasting night. On that enormous mass of blackness there was not a gleam to be seen, not a sound to be heard. It was gliding irresistibly towards us and yet seemed already within reach of the hand. I saw the vague figures of the watch grouped in the waist, gazing in awed silence.

"Are you going on, sir?" inquired an unsteady voice at my elbow.

I ignored it. I had to go on.

"Keep her full. Don't check her way. That won't do now," I said warningly.

"I can't see the sails very well," the helmsman answered me, in strange, quavering tones.

Was she close enough? Already she was, I won't say in the shadow of the land, but in the very blackness of it, already swallowed up as it were, gone too close to be recalled, gone from me altogether.

"Give the mate a call," I said to the young man who stood at my elbow as still as death. "And turn all hands up."

My tone had a borrowed loudness reverberated from the height of the land. Several voices cried out together: "We are all on deck, sir."

Then stillness again, with the great shadow gliding closer, towering higher, without a light, without a sound. Such a hush had fallen on the ship that she might have been a bark of the dead floating in slowly under the very gate of Erebus.[1]

"My God! Where are we?"

It was the mate moaning at my elbow. He was thunderstruck, and as it were deprived of the moral support of his whiskers. He clapped his hands and absolutely cried out, "Lost!"

"Be quiet," I said, sternly.

He lowered his tone, but I saw the shadowy gesture of his despair. "What are we doing here?"

"Looking for the land wind."

He made as if to tear his hair, and addressed me recklessly.

"She will never get out. You have done it, sir. I knew it'd end in something like this. She will never weather, and you are too close now to stay. She'll drift ashore before she's round. O my God!"

I caught his arm as he was raising it to batter his poor devoted head, and shook it violently.

"She's ashore already," he wailed, trying to tear himself away.

"Is she? … Keep good full there!"

"Good full, sir," cried the helmsman in a frightened, thin, childlike voice.

I hadn't let go the mate's arm and went on shaking it. "Ready about, do you hear? You go forward"—shake—"and stop there"—shake—"and hold your noise"—shake—"and see these head-sheets properly overhauled"—shake, shake—shake.

And all the time I dared not look towards the land lest my heart should fail me. I released my grip at last and he ran forward as if fleeing for dear life.

I wondered what my double there in the sail locker thought of this commotion. He was able to hear everything—and perhaps he was able to understand why, on my conscience, it had to be thus close—no less. My first order "Hard alee!" re-echoed ominously under the towering shadow of Koh-ring as if I had shouted in a mountain gorge. And then I watched the land intently. In that smooth water and light wind it was impossible to feel the ship coming-to. No! I could not feel her. And my second self was making now ready to ship out and lower himself overboard. Perhaps he was gone already…?

The great black mass brooding over our very mast-heads began to pivot away from the ship's side silently. And now I forgot the secret stranger ready to depart, and remembered only that I was a total stranger to the ship. I did not know her. Would she do it? How was she to be handled?

I swung the mainyard and waited helplessly. She was perhaps stopped, and her very fate hung in the balance, with the black mass of Koh-ring like the gate of the everlasting night towering over her taffrail.[2] What would she do now? Had she way on her yet? I stepped to the side swiftly, and on the shadowy water I could see nothing except a faint phosphorescent flash revealing the glassy smoothness of the sleeping surface. It was impossible to tell—and I had not learned yet the feel of my ship. Was she moving? What I needed was something easily seen, a piece of paper, which I could throw overboard and watch. I had nothing on me. To run

[1]　*Erebus*　In classical myth, a place of darkness between earth and Hades, the underworld.

[2]　*taffrail*　Stern rail.

down for it I didn't dare. There was no time. All at once my strained, yearning stare distinguished a white object floating within a yard of the ship's side. White on the black water. A phosphorescent flash passed under it. What was that thing?… I recognized my own floppy hat. It must have fallen off his head … and he didn't bother. Now I had what I wanted—the saving mark for my eyes. But I hardly thought of my other self, now gone from the ship, to be hidden forever from all friendly faces, to be a fugitive and a vagabond on the earth, with no brand of the curse on his sane forehead to stay a slaying hand … too proud to explain.

And I watched the hat—the expression of my sudden pity for his mere flesh. It had been meant to save his homeless head from the dangers of the sun. And now—behold—it was saving the ship, by serving me for a mark to help out the ignorance of my strangeness. Ha! It was drifting forward, warning me just in time that the ship had gathered sternaway.

"Shift the helm," I said in a low voice to the seaman standing still like a statue.

The man's eyes glistened wildly in the binnacle light as he jumped round to the other side and spun round the wheel.

I walked to the break of the poop. On the over-shadowed deck all hands stood by the forebraces waiting for my order. The stars ahead seemed to be gliding from right to left. And all was so still in the world that I heard the quiet remark, "She's round," passed in a tone of intense relief between two seamen.

"Let go and haul."

The foreyards ran round with a great noise, amidst cheery cries. And now the frightful whiskers made themselves heard giving various orders. Already the ship was drawing ahead. And I was alone with her. Nothing! no one in the world should stand now between us, throwing a shadow on the way of silent knowledge and mute affection, the perfect communion of a seaman with his first command.

Walking to the taffrail, I was in time to make out, on the very edge of a darkness thrown by a towering black mass like the very gateway of Erebus—yes, I was in time to catch an evanescent glimpse of my white hat left behind to mark the spot where the secret sharer of my cabin and of my thoughts, as though he were my second self, had lowered himself into the water to take his punishment: a free man, a proud swimmer striking out for a new destiny.

—1912

A.E. HOUSMAN
1859 – 1936

During his lifetime, A.E. Housman published only two slim volumes of poetry, *A Shropshire Lad* and *Last Poems*. Yet his poems were widely read by both popular and academic audiences, and these two books continue to receive substantial critical attention. In 1996, as part of the festivities commemorating the centenary of the publication of *A Shropshire Lad*, a window in the Poets' Corner of Westminster Abbey was dedicated to Housman. Tom Stoppard's play about Housman, *The Invention of Love*, was produced at the National Theatre, London, in 1997, and debuted in the United States in the winter of 1999–2000.

Although Housman is now known primarily for his poetry, he considered his life's work to be classical scholarship. By the time he was appointed Professor of Latin at Cambridge, Housman had published 99 classical papers, the first volume of his edition of Manilius, an edition of Juvenal, and an edition of Ovid's *Ibis*. In a testimony to Housman's scholarly writings, T.S. Eliot commented in 1933 that Housman "is one of the few living masters of English prose."

The eldest of seven children, Alfred Edward Housman was born on 26 March 1859 to Sarah Jane Williams, a clergyman's daughter, and Edward Housman, a lawyer. As a young child, Housman took great pleasure in words, and was writing verse by the age of eight. He frequently directed the younger children in playacting and wrote out a family magazine that he circulated among friends and relatives. His happy childhood at the family home in Bromsgrove, Worcestershire was dramatically interrupted by the news, in 1869, that his mother had breast cancer. In a sad coincidence, she died on 26 March 1871, on Housman's twelfth birthday. During his wife's illness, Edward Housman began to drink heavily; the family maintained respectable appearances but his drinking worsened, as did their financial situation.

In 1870, a scholarship enabled Housman to enter Bromsgrove School as a day-boy. He was serious and quiet, nicknamed "Mouse" by his classmates, but also a gifted student, winning prizes for English verse, freehand drawing, French, and Latin and Greek verse. These successes resulted in a scholarship to study Classics at St. John's College, Oxford, in 1877 where Housman initially excelled, passing the required second-year examinations with First Class Honours. During this time, his poetry began to be published by *Waifs and Strays*, an Oxford magazine. In 1880, Housman moved out of the college buildings to share a residence with A.W. Pollard and Moses Jackson. Some biographers have argued that Jackson was the love of Housman's life; if so, however, his feelings were apparently never reciprocated. Housman's Oxford career ended in disappointment when, in May 1881, he failed the final set of examinations required of undergraduates. Housman returned to Oxford in 1882 so that he could take another exam and receive the lesser "pass" degree.

With his father's health in decline and the family finances in a shambles, Housman passed the Civil Service exam in June 1882 in order to qualify himself for employment. Shortly after, he accepted a position as clerk in the Patent Office in London, where Moses Jackson also worked. Housman toiled for ten years in the Patent Office, all the while continuing his study of Classics by reading in the evenings at the British Museum. His first scholarly article appeared in 1882 in the *Journal of Philology*; during his time at the Patent Office he would publish 25 essays, although many of his colleagues were unaware of his scholarly pursuits. By 1892, when Housman applied for the position of Professor of Latin at University College, London, he was a well-respected classical scholar with an international reputation.

Housman's first book of poetry, *A Shropshire Lad*, has never been out of print. The manuscript was originally rejected by the Macmillan publishing company, as well as several others, and Housman published it at his own expense with the firm of Kegan Paul in 1896. Housman composed most of the poems in *A Shropshire Lad* in the wake of two deaths—that of his friend Adalbert Jackson in 1892, and that of his father in 1894. Coincidentally, the period of the poems' composition was also the period of Oscar Wilde's trial and conviction under the Labouchere Amendment that outlawed homosexuality in England. Housman carefully guarded his own sexuality in his life and his work, no doubt aware that he would have risked prison and exile if he had chosen to express himself openly. Several modern critics have pointed to the ways in which Housman expresses same-sex love through various poetic codes, and certainly he left ample scope for a broader public to read his poems as expressing a love that was entirely conventional. In form, Housman tends to choose straightforward iambic rhythms and simple rhymes, and in its subject matter his poetry returns again and again to themes of loss, of pastoral beauty, of idealized (and often unrequited) love, and of patriotism. Much as Housman was an intellectual in his approach to classical literature—meticulous in his scholarship, and scathing in his criticism of those less careful or competent—he was fundamentally a Romantic in his own poetry; he argued in his essay *The Name and Nature of Poetry* (1933) that poetry should appeal more to the emotions than to the intellect, and his own work embodies that belief. It was an approach that went against the grain of the intellectual currents of modernism, but that was entirely in line with early twentieth-century popular sentiment.

A Shropshire Lad was followed, in 1922, by the publication of *Last Poems*. As with Housman's first book of poetry, this new collection immediately found a wide audience. In 1921, after nineteen years as Professor of Latin at University College, Housman was appointed Professor of Latin at Trinity College, Cambridge, and for the next 25 years he occupied the Kennedy Chair in Latin. On 24 April 1936, Housman gave his last lecture at Cambridge, and six days later he died. After Housman's death, his brother Laurence produced *More Poems* from the finished poems contained within Housman's notebooks. Many of these pieces, as well as *Additional Poems*, published in Laurence's biography of his brother, contain explicitly homosexual material that Housman dared not publish within his lifetime. (The propriety of publishing poems that Housman had, in his will, instructed his brother to destroy has been extensively debated by biographers and scholars.)

⌘ ⌘ ⌘

Loveliest of Trees

Loveliest of trees, the cherry now
  Is hung with bloom along the bough,
And stands about the woodland ride
Wearing white for Eastertide.

5 Now, of my threescore years and ten,
Twenty will not come again,

And take from seventy springs a score,
It only leaves me fifty more.

And since to look at things in bloom
10 Fifty springs are little room,
About the woodlands I will go
To see the cherry hung with snow.
    —1896

To an Athlete Dying Young

The time you won your town the race
We chaired you through the market-place;
Man and boy stood cheering by,
And home we brought you shoulder-high.

5   Today, the road all runners come,
Shoulder-high we bring you home,
And set you at your threshold down,
Townsman of a stiller town.

Smart lad, to slip betimes away
10   From fields where glory does not stay,
And early though the laurel[1] grows
It withers quicker than the rose.

Eyes the shady night has shut
Cannot see the record cut,°   broken
15   And silence sounds no worse than cheers
After earth has stopped the ears:

Now you will not swell the rout°   group
Of lads that wore their honours out,
Runners whom renown outran
20   And the name died before the man.

So set, before its echoes fade,
The fleet foot on the sill of shade,
And hold to the low lintel[2] up
The still-defended challenge-cup.

25   And round that early laurelled head
Will flock to gaze the strengthless dead
And find unwithered on its curls
The garland briefer than a girl's.
                              —1896

---

[1]   *laurel*   Evergreen bush or tree whose branches were used to crown victorious athletes in ancient Greece.

[2]   *lintel*   Horizontal support beam, often running across a doorway or window.

Terence, This Is Stupid Stuff

"Terence,[3] this is stupid stuff:
You eat your victuals fast enough;
There can't be much amiss, 'tis clear,
To see the rate you drink your beer.
5   But oh, good Lord, the verse you make,
It gives a chap the belly-ache.
The cow, the old cow, she is dead;
It sleeps well, the hornèd head:
We poor lads, 'tis our turn now
10   To hear such tunes as killed the cow.
Pretty friendship 'tis to rhyme
Your friends to death before their time
Moping melancholy mad:
Come, pipe a tune to dance to, lad."

15   Why, if 'tis dancing you would be,
There's brisker pipes than poetry.
Say, for what were hop-yards[4] meant,
Or why was Burton built on Trent?[5]
Oh many a peer[6] of England brews
20   Livelier liquor than the Muse,[7]
And malt does more than Milton can
To justify God's ways to man.[8]
Ale, man, ale's the stuff to drink
For fellows whom it hurts to think:
25   Look into the pewter pot°   mug
To see the world as the world's not.
And faith, 'tis pleasant till 'tis past:
The mischief is that 'twill not last.

---

[3]   *Terence*   This poem is from Housman's *The Shropshire Lad* (originally titled *The Poems of Terence Hearsay*), a series of poems that tell the story of a central character, Terence Hearsay, who leaves his hometown and moves to London.

[4]   *hop-yards*   Or hop-gardens: areas of land upon which hops are grown.

[5]   *Burton … Trent*   Burton-on-Trent, a town in East Staffordshire, is the historical center of the British brewing industry. Brewing was first begun there by Benedictine monks in the eleventh century.

[6]   *peer*   Member of the British nobility. Brewers were among those raised to the peerage, and were thus referred to as "beer barons."

[7]   *Muse*   One of nine Greek goddesses of arts and learning; here, the source of poetic inspiration.

[8]   *Milton … man*   Cf. John Milton's *Paradise Lost* (1667), Book 1.26.

Oh I have been to Ludlow[1] fair
30 And left my necktie God knows where,
And carried half-way home, or near,
Pints and quarts of Ludlow beer:
Then the world seemed none so bad,
And I myself a sterling lad;
35 And down in lovely muck I've lain,
Happy till I woke again.
Then I saw the morning sky:
Heigho, the tale was all a lie;
The world, it was the old world yet,
40 I was I, my things were wet,
And nothing now remained to do
But begin the game anew.

　　Therefore, since the world has still
Much good, but much less good than ill,
45 And while the sun and moon endure
Luck's a chance, but trouble's sure,
I'd face it as a wise man would,
And train for ill and not for good.
'Tis true the stuff I bring for sale
50 Is not so brisk a brew as ale:
Out of a stem that scored the hand
I wrung it in a weary land.
But take it: if the smack is sour,
The better for the embittered hour;
55 It should do good to heart and head
When your soul is in my soul's stead;
And I will friend you, if I may,
In the dark and cloudy day.

　　There was a king reigned in the East:
60 There, when kings will sit to feast,
They get their fill before they think
With poisoned meat and poisoned drink.
He gathered all that springs to birth
From the many-venomed earth;
65 First a little, thence to more,
He sampled all her killing store;
And easy, smiling, seasoned sound,

Sate the king when healths went round.
They put arsenic in his meat
70 And stared aghast to watch him eat;
They poured strychnine in his cup
And shook to see him drink it up:
They shook, they stared as white's their shirt:
Them it was their poison hurt.
75 —I tell the tale that I heard told.
Mithridates, he died old.[2]
—1896

The Chestnut Casts His Flambeaux[3]

The chestnut casts his flambeaux, and the flowers
　　Stream from the hawthorn in the wind away,
The doors clap to, the pane is blind with showers.
　　Pass me the can,[4] lad; there's an end of May.

5 There's one spoilt spring to scant° our mortal lot,   *reduce*
　　One season ruined of our little store.
May will be fine next year as like as not:
　　Oh ay, but then we shall be twenty-four.

We for a certainty are not the first
10 　　Have sat in taverns while the tempest hurled
Their hopeful plans to emptiness, and cursed
　　Whatever brute and blackguard[5] made the world.

It is in truth iniquity on high
15 　　To cheat our sentenced souls of aught they crave,
And mar the merriment as you and I
　　Fare on our long fool's-errand to the grave.

Iniquity it is; but pass the can.
　　My lad, no pair of kings our mothers bore;

---

[2] *There was ... died old* According to Pliny's *Natural History*, Mithridates, king of Pontus from approximately 114 to 63 BCE, gradually built up a tolerance to all known poisons by ingesting a small amount of each daily, starting in childhood.

[3] *Flambeaux* French: torch or candlestick. The horse chestnut is known for its long, upright clusters (or "candles") of flowers, usually white in color with a reddish tinge.

[4] *can* I.e., of beer; mug or tankard.

[5] *blackguard* Scoundrel.

---

[1] *Ludlow* Market town in Shropshire.

20   Our only portion is the estate of man:
            We want the moon, but we shall get no more.

        If here today the cloud of thunder lours[1]
            Tomorrow it will hie° on far behests;°   *hasten / commands*
        The flesh will grieve on other bones than ours
25   Soon, and the soul will mourn in other breasts.

        The troubles of our proud and angry dust
            Are from eternity, and shall not fail.
        Bear them we can, and if we can we must.
            Shoulder the sky, my lad, and drink your ale.
        —1922

Epitaph on an Army of Mercenaries[2]

These, in the day when heaven was falling,
    The hour when earth's foundations fled,
Followed their mercenary calling
    And took their wages and are dead.

5   Their shoulders held the sky suspended;
        They stood, and earth's foundations stay;
    What God abandoned, these defended,
        And saved the sum of things for pay.
    —1922

---

[1] *lours* Looks dark and ominous.

[2] *Epitaph … Mercenaries* Housman published this poem in *The Times* on 31 October 1917, the third anniversary of the First Battle of Ypres, in order to honor the bravery of the professional soldiers who fought and died in the battle.

Siegfried Sassoon
1886 – 1967

Siegfried Sassoon gained his reputation during and after World War I as a poet who stridently protested the war. Shocked by the realities of the front, he transformed his horror and disgust into accusatory, didactic verse meant to confront those at home with the atrocities of war.

Sassoon was born into a wealthy merchant family, and his privileged upbringing that included horseback riding, fox hunting, a Cambridge education, and London socializing left him little prepared for war. Having decided to become a poet, however, he found that because he was without ambition or direction in life his poetry lacked passion. On the morning that war was declared, he enlisted.

When Sassoon was first commissioned into the Royal Welch Fusiliers, his poetry was neither satirical nor disillusioned; like many young poets of the day, he gave voice to patriotic sentiments. His perception changed dramatically after surviving the Battle of the Somme on 1 July 1916—the day on which 19,000 British men were killed and 38,000 wounded. Sassoon distinguished himself with his fierce courage in this battle—earning himself a Military Cross (which he later threw away) and the nickname "Mad Jack"—but the experience purged him of any romantic notions as to the glory of war.

In a new, starkly realistic voice, Sassoon attacked commanding officers, Church and State, and all those back home who were ignorant of or indifferent to the conditions of war. His compressed, intense verses use graphic descriptions, colloquial language, and explosive direct speech to convey the brutalities of war. They often also rely on simple oppositions—such as between innocent and guilty, home and front, men and women—to achieve ironic effect.

In April 1917, Sassoon was sent home to recover from a sniper wound. There he drafted his famous public protest, published in *The Times* on 31 July 1917, in which he declared that the war had become a mere matter of "aggression and conquest" and that it was being deliberately prolonged. Sassoon was saved from prison only by the intervention of his friend Robert Graves, a fellow poet and Welch Fusilier, who testified that Sassoon was shell-shocked. Eager to avoid making a martyr of Sassoon, a medical board sent him to Edinburgh's Craiglockhart War Hospital instead.

While at Craiglockhart (where he met Wilfred Owen, another poet), Sassoon began to experiment with longer, dramatic-narrative poems that evoked the physical details of the trench. He was declared fit for active duty in 1918, but was on the front lines only a month before he received a shot in the head that sent him back to England for good. His war poems were published—to little critical acclaim—in *The Old Huntsman* (1917) and *Counter-Attack and Other Poems* (1918). After the war, Sassoon continued to launch vociferous poetic salvos, now directed against the Allies' vindictive treatment of Germany and the British government's neglect of returned soldiers. Gradually, however, anger subsided into disillusionment with and alienation from a world he could not change.

Sassoon retreated into his own memories, beginning a six-volume autobiography that took nearly twenty years to complete. The first three volumes, *Memoirs of a Fox-Hunting Man* (1928), *Memoirs of an Infantry Officer* (1930), and *Sherston's Progress* (1936), revisit the past under the guise of a fictional persona, George Sherston, while the second three, *The Old Century and Seven More Years* (1938), *The Weald of Youth* (1942), and *Siegfried's Journey: 1916–1920* (1945) are autobiography. In all six of these volumes, however, Sassoon noticeably distanced himself from his most traumatic experiences as he attempted to deal with the war and its after-effects. Sassoon's posthumously published diaries make clear exactly how much he had omitted, including the turbulent events surrounding his marriage in 1933, the birth of his son George in 1936, the dissolution of his marriage in 1941, and a long period of anguish over his homosexuality.

Sassoon continued to write, but he published most of his later poetry collections privately. He felt his work was frequently misunderstood, particularly as his religious faith increased and he became a self-proclaimed "religious poet" in the years preceding his conversion to Roman Catholicism in 1957. After this point Sassoon wrote very little poetry, and he spent the remainder of his life in relative seclusion at his home in Wiltshire, where he died in 1967.

⌘⌘⌘

They

The Bishop tells us: "When the boys come back
    They will not be the same; for they'll have fought
In a just cause: they lead the last attack
On Anti-Christ; their comrades' blood has bought
5 New right to breed an honourable race,
They have challenged Death and dared him face to face."
"We're none of us the same!" the boys reply.
"For George lost both his legs; and Bill's stone blind;
Poor Jim's shot through the lungs and like to die;
10 And Bert's gone syphilitic: you'll not find
A chap who's served that hasn't found *some* change."
And the Bishop said: "The ways of God are strange!"
    —1917 (WRITTEN 31 OCTOBER 1916)

Glory of Women

You love us when we're heroes, home on leave,
    Or wounded in a mentionable place.
You worship decorations; you believe
That chivalry redeems the war's disgrace.
5 You make us shells. You listen with delight,
By tales of dirt and danger fondly thrilled.
You crown our distant ardours while we fight,

And mourn our laurelled memories when we're killed.
You can't believe that British troops "retire"
10 When hell's last horror breaks them, and they run,
Trampling the terrible corpses—blind with blood.
O German mother dreaming by the fire,
While you are knitting socks to send your son
His face is trodden deeper in the mud.
    —1918 (WRITTEN 1917)

Everyone Sang

Everyone suddenly burst out singing;
    And I was filled with such delight
As prisoned birds must find in freedom,
Winging wildly across the white
5 Orchards and dark-green fields; on—on—and out of
        sight.

Everyone's voice was suddenly lifted;
And beauty came like the setting sun:
My heart was shaken with tears; and horror
Drifted away ... O, but Everyone
10 Was a bird; and the song was wordless; the singing
        will never be done.
    —1919

from *Memoirs of an Infantry Officer*[1]

On July the first, the weather, after an early morning mist, was of the kind commonly called heavenly. Down in our frowsty[2] cellar we breakfasted at six, unwashed and apprehensive. Our table, appropriately enough, was an empty ammunition box. At six-forty-five the final bombardment began, and there was nothing for us to do except sit round our candle until the tornado ended. For more than forty minutes the air vibrated and the earth rocked and shuddered. Through the sustained uproar the tap and rattle of machine-guns could be identified; but except for the whistle of bullets no retaliation came our way until a few 5.9 shells[3] shook the roof of our dugout. Barton and I sat speechless, deafened and stupefied by the seismic state of affairs, and when he lit a cigarette the match flame staggered crazily. Afterwards I asked him what he had been thinking about. His reply was "Carpet slippers and Kettle-holders." My own mind had been working in much the same style, for during that cannonading cataclysm the following refrain was running in my head:

> They come as a boon and a blessing to men,
> The Something, the Owl, and the Waverley Pen.[4]

For the life of me I couldn't remember what the first one was called. Was it the Shakespeare? Was it the Dickens? Anyhow it was an advertisement which I'd often seen in smoky railway stations. Then the bombardment lifted and lessened, our vertigo abated, and we looked at one another in dazed relief. Two brigades of our division were now going over the top on our right. Our brigade was to attack "when the main assault had reached its final objective." In our fortunate role of privileged spectators Barton and I went up the stairs to see what we could from Kingston Road Trench. We left

Jenkins crouching in a corner, where he remained most of the day. His haggard blinking face haunts my memory. He was an example of the paralysing effect which such an experience could produce on a nervous system sensitive to noise, for he was a good officer both before and afterwards. I felt no sympathy for him at the time, but I do now. From the support-trench, which Barton called "our opera box," I observed as much of the battle as the formation of the country allowed, the rising ground on the right making it impossible to see anything of the attack towards Mametz. A small shiny black notebook contains my pencilled particulars, and nothing will be gained by embroidering them with afterthoughts. I cannot turn my field-glasses on to the past....

7.45. The barrage is now working to the right of Fricourt and beyond. I can see the 21st Division advancing about three-quarters of a mile away on the left and a few Germans coming to meet them, apparently surrendering. Our men in small parties (not extended in line) go steadily on to the German front-line. Brilliant sunshine and a haze of smoke drifting along the landscape. Some Yorkshires[5] a little way below on the left, watching the show and cheering as if at a football match. The noise almost as bad as ever.

9.30. Came back to dug-out and had a shave. 21st Division still going across the open, apparently without casualties. The sunlight flashes on bayonets as the tiny figures move quietly forward and disappear beyond mounds of trench debris. A few runners come back and ammunition parties go across. Trench-mortars[6] are knocking hell out of Sunken Road Trench and the ground where the Manchesters will attack soon. Noise not so bad now and very little retaliation.

9.50. Fricourt half-hidden by clouds of drifting smoke, blue, pinkish and grey. Shrapnel bursting in small bluish-white puffs with tiny flashes. The birds seem bewildered; a lark begins to go up and then flies feebly along, thinking better of it. Others flutter above the trench with querulous cries, weak on the wing. I can

---

[1] *from ... Officer* The following excerpt, which describes the beginning of the Battle of the Somme in 1916, is taken from Section 4, Chapter 2, entitled "Battle."

[2] *frowsty* Musty; stale or unpleasant smelling.

[3] *5.9 shells* 5.9-caliber shells.

[4] *They come ... Pen* This then-popular slogan of MacNiven and Cameron, Ltd. (a producer of pen nibs) advertises three types of nibs: the Pickwick (the missing term) the Owl, and the Waverley.

[5] *Yorkshires* I.e., men belonging to one of the battalions of the Yorkshire Regiment that fought at the Battle of the Somme.

[6] *Trench-mortars* Small mortars used to propel bombs into enemy trenches.

see seven of our balloons,[1] on the right. On the left our men still filing across in twenties and thirties. Another huge explosion in Fricourt and a cloud of brown-pink smoke. Some bursts are yellowish.

10.5. I can see the Manchesters down in New Trench, getting ready to go over. Figures filing down the trench. Two of them have gone out to look at our wire gaps![2] Have just eaten my last orange.... I am staring at a sunlit picture of Hell, and still the breeze shakes the yellow weeds, and the poppies glow under Crawley Ridge where some shells fell a few minutes ago. Manchesters are sending forward some scouts. A bayonet glitters. A runner comes back across the open to their Battalion Headquarters, close here on the right. 21st Division still trotting along the sky line toward La Boisselle. Barrage going strong to the right of Contalmaison Ridge. Heavy shelling toward Mametz.

12.15. Quieter the last two hours. Manchesters still waiting. Germans putting over a few shrapnel shells. Silly if I got hit! Weather cloudless and hot. A lark singing confidently overhead.

1.30. Manchesters attack at 2.30. Mametz and Montauban reported taken. Mametz consolidated.

2.30. Manchesters left New Trench and apparently took Sunken Road Trench, bearing rather to the right. Could see about 400. Many walked casually across with sloped arms. There were about forty casualties on the left (from machine-gun in Fricourt). Through my glasses I could see one man moving his left arm up and down as he lay on his side; his face was a crimson patch. Others lay still in the sunlight while the swarm of figures disappeared over the hill. Fricourt was a cloud of pinkish smoke. Lively machine-gun fire on the far side of the hill. At 2.50 no one to be seen in No Man's Land except the casualties (about half-way across). Our dug-out shelled again since 2.30.

5.0. I saw about thirty of our A Company crawl across to Sunken Road from New Trench. Germans put a few big shells on the cemetery and traversed Kingston Road with machine-gun. Manchester wounded still out

there. Remainder of A Company went across—about 100 altogether. Manchesters reported held up in Bois Français Support. Their Colonel went across and was killed.

8.0. Staff Captain of our brigade has been along. Told Barton that Seventh Division has reached its objectives with some difficulty, except on this brigade front. Manchesters are in trouble, and Fricourt attack has failed. Several hundred prisoners brought in on our sector.

9.30. Our A Company holds Rectangle and Sunken Road. Jenkins gone off in charge of a carrying-party.[3] Seemed all right again. C Company now reduced to six runners, two stretcher-bearers, Company-Sergeant-Major, signallers, and Barton's servant. Flook away on carrying-party. Sky cloudy westward. Red sunset. Heavy gunfire on the left.

2.30. (Next afternoon.) Adjutant[4] has just been up here, excited, optimistic, and unshaven. He went across last night to ginger up A Company who did very well, thanks to the bombers. About 40 casualties; only 4 killed. Fricourt and Rose Trench occupied this morning without resistance. I am now lying out in front of our trench in the long grass, basking in sunshine where yesterday there were bullets. Our new front-line on the hill is being shelled. Fricourt is full of troops wandering about in search of souvenirs. The village was a ruin and is now a dust heap. A gunner (Forward Observation Officer) has just been along here with a German helmet in his hand. Said Fricourt is full of dead; he saw one officer lying across a smashed machine-gun with his head bashed in—"a fine looking chap," he said, with some emotion, which rather surprised me.

8.15. Queer feeling, seeing people moving about freely between here and Fricourt. Dumps being made. Shacks and shelters being put up under skeleton trees and all sorts of transport arriving at Cemetery Cross Roads. We stay here till to-morrow morning. Feel a bit of a fraud.

—1930 (WRITTEN 1916)

---

[1] *balloons* As a defense against hostile aircrafts, troops set up a series of connected balloons attached to long wire cables.

[2] *wire gaps* Holes made in the protective barbed wire by enemy shells.

[3] *carrying-party* Party sent to deliver supplies.

[4] *Adjutant* Military officer whose role is to communicate the orders of superior officers.

WILFRED OWEN
1893 – 1918

Wilfred Owen's humane responses to World War I, his compassionate depictions of the suffering that war engendered, and his critique of nationalism challenged the imperialist rhetoric of honor, glory, and patriotic duty, prompting Dylan Thomas later to declare him "a poet of all times, all places, and all wars."

Owen was the first-born son and of Thomas Owen and Susan Shaw of Shropshire, and the favorite of his mother, who hoped to see him become a clergyman. When Owen left school in 1911 he took a post as lay assistant to the Vicar of Dunsden, who would help him prepare for his university entrance exam in exchange for parish work. Owen, however, became increasingly critical of the Church's response to the suffering of the poor, and found his passion for poetry eclipsed his religious faith. He left the vicarage and, having failed to win a university scholarship, departed for France to work as a private tutor.

Though Owen had little intention of joining up when war broke out, pressure to do so increased as the fighting continued. In 1915 he returned to England, enlisted in the Artists' Rifles, and was commissioned lieutenant in the Manchester Regiment. Owen crossed the channel in December of 1916 to join his men on the Somme, where he began recording his impressions in letters and poems immediately. His use of a pastoral mode owed much to the influence of Keats, but his powerful descriptions of death, wounded bodies, and the weapons of war, which coupled startling images and shifting angles of vision, subverted the traditional pastoral. Owen also developed his own approach to rhyme, in which half rhymes (pararhymes) and assonance featured prominently. This gave his poetry a discordant, mournful quality that echoed his pessimistic warnings of further suffering to come, and helped create haunting elegies for the generation he shows being slaughtered like cattle in "Anthem for Doomed Youth" (1920).

Owen had been at the front only four months when a shell exploded a few feet from his head, resulting in his nearly being buried alive. A few weeks later he was removed to Craiglockhart War Hospital, outside Edinburgh, and treated for shell shock. There he met Siegfried Sassoon, another war poet whose stridently satirical poetry Owen greatly admired. It was during this time, while recovering from his trauma, that Owen wrote most of his poems. The influence of Sassoon is evident in his more didactic work, such as "Dulce et Decorum Est" (1920), which uses graphic descriptions of the battlefield and powerful direct speech to attack the classic dictum that it is sweet and fitting to die for one's country.

In his expressions of pity for his fellow soldiers, Owen occasionally fell into the trap of romanticizing death and sacrifice for which he criticized both Church and State, at times portraying soldiers as Christ-figures crucified by those in charge. The men of his poems, regardless of nationality, are usually victims passively laying down their lives, never killing. Several of Owen's strongest poems—such as "Strange Meeting" (1920)—attempt to confront and explore these contradictions.

Owen faced a similar incongruity in his own attitude towards war. Though he opposed the fighting in principle, he was glad to be able to return to the front in August 1918 and to resume serving with his men in battle. He was, he said, "a conscientious objector with a very seared conscience." Owen was killed less than three months after returning to his regiment—only a week before the war's end—while leading an offensive on the banks of the Sambre Canal.

⌘ ⌘ ⌘

Arms and the Boy

Let the boy try along this bayonet-blade
How cold steel is, and keen with hunger of blood;
Blue with all malice, like a madman's flash;
And thinly drawn with famishing for flesh.

5 Lend him to stroke these blind, blunt bullet-heads
Which long to nuzzle in the hearts of lads,
Or give him cartridges of fine zinc teeth,
Sharp with the sharpness of grief and death.

For his teeth seem for laughing round an apple.
10 There lurk no claws behind his fingers supple;
And God will grow no talons at his heels,
Nor antlers through the thickness of his curls.
                                                    —1920

Dulce et Decorum Est[1]

Bent double, like old beggars under sacks,
Knock-kneed, coughing like hags, we cursed
        through sludge,
Till on the haunting flares we turned our backs,
And towards our distant rest began to trudge.
5 Men marched asleep. Many had lost their boots,
But limped on, blood-shod. All went lame, all blind;
Drunk with fatigue; deaf even to the hoots
Of gas-shells dropping softly behind.

Gas! GAS! Quick, boys!—An ecstasy of fumbling,
10 Fitting the clumsy helmets just in time,
But someone still was yelling out and stumbling
And flound'ring like a man in fire or lime—
Dim, through the misty panes[2] and thick green light,
As under a green sea, I saw him drowning.

15 In all my dreams before my helpless sight
He plunges at me, guttering, choking, drowning.

If in some smothering dreams, you too could pace
Behind the wagon that we flung him in,
And watch the white eyes writhing in his face,
20 His hanging face, like a devil's sick of sin;
If you could hear, at every jolt, the blood
Come gargling from the froth-corrupted lungs,
Bitter as the cud
Of vile, incurable sores on innocent tongues,—
25 My friend, you would not tell with such high zest
To children ardent for some desperate glory,
The old Lie: Dulce et decorum est
Pro patria mori.
                                                    —1920

Anthem for Doomed Youth

What passing-bells for these who die as cattle?
    Only the monstrous anger of the guns.
Only the stuttering rifles' rapid rattle
Can patter out their hasty orisons.°   prayers
5 No mockeries for them from prayers or bells,
Nor any voice of mourning save the choirs,—

---

1 *Dulce et Decorum Est*   Owen's poem takes its title from a famous line from the Roman poet Horace's *Odes* (3.2): "Dulce et decorum est pro patria mori" (Latin: "Sweet and fitting it is to die for one's country").

---

2 *panes*   Visors of the gas masks.

The shrill, demented choirs of wailing shells;
And bugles calling for them from sad shires.

What candles may be held to speed them all?
10 Not in the hands of boys, but in their eyes
Shall shine the holy glimmers of good-byes.
The pallor of girls' brows shall be their pall;[1]
Their flowers the tenderness of silent minds,
And each slow dusk a drawing-down of blinds.
—1920

Strange Meeting

It seemed that out of battle I escaped
Down some profound dull tunnel, long since
    scooped
Through granites which titanic wars had groined.
Yet also there encumbered sleepers groaned,
5 Too fast in thought or death to be bestirred.
Then, as I probed them, one sprang up, and stared
With piteous recognition in fixed eyes,
Lifting distressful hands as if to bless.
And by his smile, I knew that sullen hall,
10 By his dead smile I knew we stood in Hell.
With a thousand pains that vision's face was grained;
Yet no blood reached there from the upper ground,
And no guns thumped, or down the flues made moan.
"Strange friend," I said, "here is no cause to mourn."
15 "None," said the other, "save the undone years,
The hopelessness. Whatever hope is yours,
Was my life also; I went hunting wild
After the wildest beauty in the world,
Which lies not calm in eyes, or braided hair,
20 But mocks the steady running of the hour,
And if it grieves, grieves richlier than here.
For of my glee might many men have laughed,
And of my weeping something had been left,
Which must die now. I mean the truth untold,
25 The pity of war, the pity war distilled.
Now men will go content with what we spoiled.

Or, discontent, boil bloody, and be spilled.
They will be swift with swiftness of the tigress,
None will break ranks, though nations trek from progress.
30 Courage was mine, and I had mystery,
Wisdom was mine, and I had mastery;
To miss the march of this retreating world
Into vain citadels that are not walled.
Then, when much blood had clogged their chariot-
    wheels,
35 I would go up and wash them from sweet wells,
Even with truths that lie too deep for taint.
I would have poured my spirit without stint
But not through wounds; not on the cess° of war.   bog
Foreheads of men have bled where no wounds were.
40 I am the enemy you killed, my friend.
I knew you in this dark; for so you frowned
Yesterday through me as you jabbed and killed.
I parried; but my hands were loath and cold.
Let us sleep now. ..."
—1920

Futility

Move him into the sun—
Gently its touch awoke him once,
At home, whispering of fields half-sown.
Always it woke him, even in France,
5 Until this morning and this snow.
If anything might rouse him now
The kind old sun will know.

Think how it wakes the seeds—
Woke once the clays of a cold star.
10 Are limbs, so dear achieved, are sides
Full-nerved, still warm, too hard to stir?
Was it for this the clay grew tall?
—O what made fatuous sunbeams toil
To break earth's sleep at all?
—1920

---

1 *pall* Cloth spread over a coffin, hearse, or tomb.

WAR AND REVOLUTION
CONTEXTS

Britain declared war on Germany on 4 August 1914, and nearly every family in England had lost someone before the Armistice on 11 November 1918. Roughly nine million soldiers died—nearly one in every eight who enlisted. Eighteen million more were wounded. While soldiers and civilians alike began the war filled with idealism, there was little room for glory in the trench warfare that became the dominant mode of conflict during the war. The battle line on the Western Front remained virtually unmoved for three years, with both sides making attempted advancements at great loss of life. The German use of poison gas at the second battle of Ypres (1915), the British landing at Gallipoli (1915), and the British introduction of tanks at the Somme (1916) were all launched in the hope they would lead to a victorious breakthrough–and all ended horrifically. Indeed, the "Great War," as it was called at the time, was characterized from first to last by extreme disillusionment, from the misplaced hope at its outset that the fighting would end by Christmas 1914, to the confidence voiced by Woodrow Wilson (the American President who brought the United States into the war in 1917) that the conflict would lead nations to come together in a new League of Nations that would make this "a war to end all wars." After the war the British people would never again recapture the idealism and firm faith in technology, progress, and traditional values that had been prevalent earlier in the century. In stark contrast to Wilson's optimism, many were persuaded by the war's end that technological progress and failed humanity were driving civilization towards a perpetual state of war. Subsequent years were filled with unrest as the British people struggled to make sense of the sweeping changes war had brought.

The war was certainly unprecedented in its technology—airplanes as well as tanks were used for the first time in warfare, and machine guns facilitated new levels of mass slaughter. And the industrial nature of the war meant that civilians were relied upon nearly as much as soldiers for military success. Morale was thus important almost as much at home as on the front, and artists, photographers, poets, actors and performers became important participants in the manufacture of patriotism. This section opens with a testament to the importance of patriotic poetry during wartime, and a sampling of popular poems and songs. There was little that was heroic or romantic about the daily life of soldiers in the trenches, but through songs such as "I Learned to Wash in Shell-holes" and "It's a Lovely War" soldiers might keep up morale by viewing their deplorable living conditions with humor. ("It's a Lovely War," by J.P. Long and Maurice Scott, became once again widely known after the 1960s stage production *Oh, What a Lovely War!* and the film that took its title from the play's.)

The war was unprecedented too in its geographic scope; the fighting extended into Africa and the Middle East as well as across Europe and into Asia. The British Empire fought as one, with troops from all areas serving under imperial command. Canadian troops were particularly influential at Vimy Ridge, where in April 1917 they forced German troops to retreat from their dominant position on the northern front. Soldiers from Australia and New Zealand were vitally important in offensives at the Somme and Gallipoli, where they sustained heavy losses.

War transformed everyday life and affected every aspect of society. Everyone was at risk, and everyone had a part to play in the war effort. While Victorian society had been characterized by rigid boundaries—between public and private space, between masculine and feminine realms and duties, and between classes—the war forced a sudden breakdown of these categories. After the war they were partially restored, but society was forever transformed. In her essay "The Cordite Makers," Rebecca West (the pen name of Cicily Fairfield) highlights the parallels between the daily lives of soldiers on the home front and that of many women working in the arms industry—particularly in terms of the personal sacrifices that they made and the dangers that they faced.

Ivor Gurney's poem "To His Love" and Vince Palmer's "The Farmer Remembers the Somme," both of which appear below, provide a grim sense of how firm a grip the memory of horror and of loss took upon those who had experienced the fighting at first hand. Less focused on the horror of battle is the excerpt below from poet Robert Graves's *Goodbye to All That*. Graves's description of his war years as an officer in the Royal Welch Fusiliers, is among the most vivid and detailed prose accounts of life on the front. The passage excerpted here gives among other things a clear sense of the stark differences between civilians' and soldiers' perceptions of the war.

If the Great War revolutionized the way in which British people saw the world, it also helped to bring full-scale revolution to Britain's largest ally. The Russian Revolution was the product of many causes, but not the least of these was the hardship and desperation brought on by the war itself. Ultimately, the Revolution proved to be one of the central events of the twentieth century; over the course of the next two generations, the ideological models of Marx and Lenin and the institutional models of Lenin and Stalin would spread through much of the world. The excerpt included in these pages highlights the conflict between communist idealism and totalitarian realism that came to a head almost immediately following the Bolshevik "October Revolution" of 1917.

⌘⌘⌘

from Anonymous, Introduction to *Songs and Sonnets for England in War Time* (1914)

The *Songs and Sonnets for England in War Time* anthology was the first of a genre that became common in World War I, the popular anthology of war poetry. The introduction provides a straightforward statement of the rationale for such volumes.

In the stress of a nation's peril, the poet at last comes into his own again, and with clarion call he rouses the sleeping soul of the Empire. Prophet he is, champion and consoler.

If in these later times the poet has been neglected, now in our infinite need, in our pride and our sorrow, he is here to strengthen, comfort and inspire. The poet is vindicated.

What can so nobly uplift the hearts of a people facing war with its unspeakable agony as music and poetry? The sound of martial music steels men's hearts before battle. The sound of martial words inspires human souls to do and to endure. God, His poetry, and His music are the Holy Trinity of war.

… The greatest songs [have not always been those] that have sent men on to victory. Sometimes it has been a modest verse that has found refuge in the heart of the soldier ready for the ultimate sacrifice, cheered on his way by the lilt of a humble song. Who else, indeed, can take the place of a poet?

Recruitment poster for South Australia, 1914.

Recruitment poster for Canada, 1914.

"In Flanders Fields": The Poem and Some Responses

Canadian physician John McCrae's "In Flanders Fields," scribbled in twenty minutes while he was sitting on the back of an ambulance just north of the field of Ypres, remains the most widely recited poem of the war. McCrae, not satisfied with the poem, would have thrown it away, but a fellow officer sent it to London, where it was published by *Punch* (after being rejected by *The Spectator*). The responses to the poem reproduced below are only three of many—a testimony to the strength of emotion the poem evoked in readers. Elizabeth Daryush's more personal description of loss provides a sharp contrast to the two more patriotic poems by Mitchell and Armstrong.

John McCrae, "In Flanders Fields" (1915)

In Flanders Fields the poppies blow
Between the crosses, row on row,
That mark our place; and in the sky
The larks, still bravely singing, fly
Scarce heard amid the guns below.   5

We are the Dead. Short days ago
We lived, felt dawn, saw sunset glow,
Loved and were loved, and now we lie
In Flanders Fields.

Take up our quarrel with the foe: 10
To you from failing hands we throw
The torch; be yours to hold it high.

In Flanders Fields

—

In Flanders fields the poppies grow
Between the crosses, row on row
That mark our place : and in the sky
The larks still bravely singing, fly
Scarce heard amid the guns below.

We are the Dead . Short days ago
We lived, felt dawn, saw sunset glow,
Loved, and were loved, and now we lie
In Flanders fields.

Take up our quarrel with the foe :
To you from failing hands we throw
The torch : be yours to hold it high !
If ye break faith with us who die
We shall not sleep, though poppies grow
In Flanders fields.

John McCrae

An autograph copy of McCrae's famous poem.
Note that in this version he has replaced "blow" with "grow" in the first line.

If ye break faith with us who die
We shall not sleep, though poppies grow
15   In Flanders Fields.

John Mitchell, "Reply to 'In Flanders Fields'" (1916)

Oh! sleep in peace where poppies grow;
The torch your falling hands let go
Was caught by us, again held high,
A beacon light in Flanders sky
5   That dims the stars to those below.
You are our dead, you held the foe,
And ere the poppies cease to blow,
We'll prove our faith in you who lie
In Flanders Fields.

10   Oh! rest in peace, we quickly go
To you who bravely died, and know
In other fields was heard the cry,
For freedom's cause, of you who lie,
So still asleep where poppies grow,
15   In Flanders Fields.

As in rumbling sound, to and fro,
The lightning flashes, sky aglow,
The mighty hosts appear, and high
Above the din of battle cry,
20   Scarce heard amidst the guns below,
Are fearless hearts who fight the foe,
And guard the place where poppies grow.
Oh! sleep in peace, all you who lie
In Flanders Fields.

25   And still the poppies gently blow,
Between the crosses, row on row.
The larks, still bravely soaring high,
Are singing now their lullaby
To you who sleep where poppies grow
30   In Flanders Fields.

German troops in a trench on
the Western Front, 1918.

J.A. Armstrong, "Another Reply to 'In Flanders
Fields'" (1916)

In Flanders Fields the cannons boom,
And fitful flashes light the gloom;
While up above, like eagles, fly
The fierce destroyers of the sky;
5   With stains the earth wherein you lie
Is redder than the poppy bloom,
In Flanders Fields.
Sleep on, ye brave! The shrieking shell,
The quaking trench, the startling yell,
10   The fury of the battle hell
Shall wake you not, for all is well;
Sleep peacefully, for all is well.
Your flaming torch aloft we bear,
With burning heart and oath we swear
15   To keep the faith, to fight it through,
To crush the foe, or sleep with you,
In Flanders Fields.

Elizabeth Daryush, "Flanders Fields" (1916)

Here the scented daisy glows
Glorious as the carmined° rose;   reddened
Here the hill-top's verdure mean
Fair is with unfading green;
5 Here, where sorrow still must tread,
All her graves are garlanded.

And still, O glad passer-by
Of the fields of agony,
Lower laughter's voice, and bare
10 Thy head in the valley where
Poppies bright and rustling wheat
Are a desert to love's feet.

Shells inscribed by soldiers.
(Imperial War Museum, London.)

Anonymous, "I Learned to Wash in Shell-Holes"

I learned to wash in shell-holes and to shave myself in
   tea,
While the fragments of a mirror did a balance on my knee;
I learned to dodge the whizzbangs[1] and the flying lumps
   of lead,
And to keep a foot of earth between the snipers and my
   head.

5 I learned to keep my haversack[2] well filled with
   buckshee[3] food,
To take my army issue and to pinch what else I could;
I learned to cook Maconochie[4] with candle ends and
   string,
With four-by-two[5] and sardine oil and any old darn
   thing.

I learned to use my bayonet according, as you please,
10 For a bread-knife or a chopper or a prong for toasting
   cheese;

I learned to gather souvenirs that home I hoped to send,
And hump them round for months and months and
   dump them in the end.

I never used to grumble after breakfast in the line
That the eggs were cooked too lightly or the bacon cut
   too fine;
15 I never told the sergeant just exactly what I thought;
I never did a pack-drill[6] for I never quite got caught.
I never stopped a whizzbang though I've stopped a lot
   of mud,
But the one that Fritz[7] sent over with my name on was
   a dud.

J.P Long and Maurice Scott, "Oh! It's a Lovely War" (1917)

Up to your waist in water, up to your eyes in slush,
  Using the kind of language that makes the sergeant
   blush,
Who wouldn't join the army? That's what we all
   enquire.
Don't we pity the poor civilians sitting beside the fire.

---

[1] *whizzbangs* Shells fired by small-caliber, high-velocity German guns.

[2] *haversack* Stout canvas bag for carrying daily rations.

[3] *buckshee* Extra, spare.

[4] *Maconochie* Tinned vegetable stew (named after its inventor).

[5] *four-by-two* Rag for cleaning the barrel of a rifle.

---

[6] *pack-drill* Form of drill used as punishment, in which soldiers had to march in full uniform while carrying a heavy pack.

[7] *Fritz* Nickname for a German soldier.

(Chorus)
5   *Oh, oh, oh it's a lovely war.*
Who wouldn't be a soldier, eh? Oh it's a shame to take the
*   pay.*
As soon as reveille[1] has gone we feel just as heavy as lead,
But we never get up till the sergeant brings our breakfast up
*   to bed.*
Oh, oh, oh it's a lovely war.
10   *What do we want with eggs and ham when we've got plum*
*   and apple jam?*
Form fours. Right turn. How shall we spend the money we
*   earn?*
Oh, oh, oh it's a lovely war.

When does a soldier grumble? When does he make a
    fuss?
No one is more contented in all the world than us.
15   Oh it's a cushy life, boys, really we love it so:
Once a fellow was sent on leave and simply refused to
    go.

Come to the cookhouse door, boys, sniff at the lovely
    stew.
Who is it says the colonel gets better grub than you?
Any complaints this morning? Do we complain? Not
    we.
20   What's the matter with lumps of onion floating around
    the tea?

from Rebecca West, "The Cordite Makers" (1916)

The world was polished to brightness by an east wind
    when I visited the cordite[2] factory, and shone with
hard colours like a German toy-landscape. The marshes
were very green and the scattered waters very blue, and
little white clouds roamed one by one across the sky like
grazing sheep on a meadow. On the hills around stood
elms, and grey churches and red farms and yellow ricks,[3]
painted bright by the sharp sunshine. And very distinct
on the marshes there lay the village which is always full

A ship full of Australian and New Zealand troops on
their way to the Turkish peninsula of Gallipoli in the
summer of 1915. The Gallipoli offensive was disastrous. Winston Churchill (then First Lord of the
Admiralty) had hoped Gallipoli would provide an
alternative to the trench warfare of the sort endured in
Flanders, but the offensive was doomed by poor
planning, insufficient knowledge of the terrain, and an
underestimation of the enemy's strength. (Imperial War
Museum, London.)

of people, and yet is the home of nothing except death.

In the glare it showed that like so many institutions
of the war it has the disordered and fantastic quality of
a dream. It consists of a number of huts, some like the
government-built cottages for Irish labourers, and some
like the open-air shelters in a sanatorium, scattered over
five hundred acres; they are connected by raised wooden
gangways and interspersed with green mounds and rush
ponds. It is of such vital importance to the State that it
is ringed with barbed-wire entanglements and patrolled
by sentries, and its products must have sent tens of
thousands of our enemies to their death. And it is
inhabited chiefly by pretty young girls clad in a Red-
Riding-Hood fancy dress of khaki and scarlet.

Every morning at six, when the night mist still hangs
over the marshes, 250 of these girls are fetched by a light
railway from their barracks on a hill two miles away.
When I visited the works they had already been at work
for nine hours, and would work for three more. This
twelve-hour shift is longer than one would wish, but it
is not possible to introduce three shifts, since the girls

---

[1]   *reveille*   Morning drum beat or bugle call to wake the soldiers.

[2]   *cordite*   Type of smokeless explosive.

[3]   *ricks*   Haystacks.

would find an eight-hour day too light and would complain of being debarred from the opportunity of making more money; and it is not so bad as it sounds, for in these airy and isolated huts there is neither the orchestra of rattling machines nor the sense of a confined area crowded with tired people which make the ordinary factory such a fatiguing place. Indeed, these girls, working in teams of six or seven in those clean and tidy rooms, look as if they were practising a neat domestic craft rather than a deadly domestic process. …

But how deceptive this semblance of normal life is; what extraordinary work this is for women and how extraordinarily they are doing it, is made manifest in a certain row of huts where the cordite is being pressed through wire mesh. This, in all the world, must be the place where war and grace are closest linked. Without, a strip of garden runs beside the huts, gay with shrubs and formal with a sundial. Within there is a group of girls that composes into so beautiful a picture that one remembers that the most glorious painting in the world, Velasquez's[1] *The Weavers*, shows women working just like this.

One girl stands high on a platform against the wall, filling the cordite paste into one of the two great iron presses, and when she has finished with that she swings round the other one on a swivel with a fine free gesture. The other girls stand round the table laying out the golden cords in graduated sizes from the thickness of rope to the thinness of macaroni, the clear khaki and scarlet of their dresses shining back from the wet floor in a perpetually changing pattern as they move quickly about their work. They look very young in their pretty, childish dresses, and one thinks them good children for working so diligently. And it occurs to one as something incredible that they are now doing the last three hours of a twelve-hour shift.

If one asks the manager whether this zeal can possibly be normal, whether it is not perhaps the result of his presence, one is confronted by the awful phenomenon, beside which a waterspout or a volcano in eruption would be a little thing, of a manager talking about his employees with reverence. It seems that the girls work all day with a fury which mounts to a climax

in the last three hours before the other 250 girls step into their places for the twelve-hour night shift. In these hours spies are sent out to walk along the verandah to see how the teams in the other huts are getting on, and their reports set the girls on to an orgy of competitive industry. Here again it was said that for attention, enthusiasm and discipline, there could not be better workmen than these girls.

There is matter connected with these huts, too, that showed the khaki and scarlet hoods to be no fancy dress, but a military uniform. They are a sign, for they have been dipped in a solution that makes them fireproof, that the girls are ready to face an emergency, which had arisen in those huts only a few days ago. There had been one of those incalculable happenings of which high explosives are so liable, an inflammatory mixture of air with acetone, and the cordite was ignited. Two huts were instantly gutted, and the girls had to walk out through the flame. In spite of the uniform one girl lost a hand. These, of course, are the everyday dangers of the high-explosives factory. There is very little to be feared by our enemies by land, and it is the sentries' grief and despair that their total bag for the eighteen months of their patrol of the marshes consists of one cow.

Surely, never before in modern history can women have lived a life so completely parallel to that of the regular Army. The girls who take up this work sacrifice almost as much as men who enlist; for although they make on an average 30s[2] a week they are working much harder than most of them, particularly the large number who were formerly domestic servants, would ever have dreamed of working in peacetime. And, although their colony of wooden huts has been well planned by their employers, and is pleasantly administered by the Young Women's Christian Association, it is, so far as severance of home-ties goes, barrack life. For although they are allowed to go home for Sunday, travelling is difficult from this remote village, and the girls are so tired that most of them spend the day in bed.

And there are two things about the cordite village which the State ought never to forget, and which ought to be impressed upon the public mind by the bestowal of military rank upon the girls. First of all there is the

---

[1] *Velasquez* Spanish painter Diego Velásquez (1599–1660).

[2] *s* Shillings.

cold fact that they face more danger every day than any soldier on home defence has seen since the beginning of the war. And secondly, there is the fact—and one wishes it could be expressed in terms of the saving of English and the losing of German life—that it is because of this army of cheerful and disciplined workers that this cordite factory has been able to increase its output since the beginning of the war by something over 1,500 per cent. It was all very well for the Army to demand high explosives, and for Mr. Lloyd George[1] to transmit the demand to industry; in the last resort the matter lay in the hands of the girls in the khaki and scarlet hoods, and the State owes them a very great debt for the way in which they have handled it.

from Francis Marion Beynon, *Aleta Day* (1919)

The following excerpt is from Francis Marion Beynon's autobiographical novel *Aleta Day*, which recounts the heroine's childhood in a small town in Manitoba, Canada, and her subsequent love for a man who enlists when World War I begins. Beynon herself was a journalist known for her feminist views and her pacifism—a stance that lost her her job in 1917. This excerpt, however, expresses the idealism that permeated the nation in the months after the declaration of war, before the realities of trench warfare were realized.

from CHAPTER 24: WAR

Then the war came. It burst like a cloud upon our holidaying world, and set us all a-tremble and a-thrill. Germany had broken the peace of the world and plunged us into night. Very well, we would collect a few Canadians and send them over and they would settle the matter in a few months and come home, and we would give them a banquet, and allow them to die in the poorhouse, as had been done to the heroes of other wars.

What days those were! An extra[2] every half-hour! War maps in every hand! A half mile towards Paris—

---

[1] *Mr. Lloyd George* David Lloyd George (1863–1945), British Prime Minister.

[2] *extra* Additional issue of a newspaper.

Female workers at a Birmingham airplane factory in September 1918. (Imperial War Museum, London.)

gloom for two days! A great ship sunk—gloom for a week! Our hearts were sensitive to suffering then and the death of a hundred thousand men meant something to us. The blood reeked in our nostrils.

Yet for all that we [were] women, old men and cripples, how we did shout our patriotism from the housetops, so that nobody should miss our voice in the great songs.

What days those were!

The even tramp of troops along the streets! The morning call of the bugle! The thrill of an hourly excitement! The awful torment of soul as one read of rivers full of dead bodies. Human bodies! It broke our hearts to read of men with their legs and arms blown off; with their faces shattered to pieces; men who would go on living under the most horrible physical limitations. That was early in the war before we had grown callous to the pain of other human beings.

And yet, mixed with our horror, there was a thrill, a feeling that something had really happened in our time.

What days those were!

Ivor Gurney, "To his Love" (1919)

Ivor Gurney (1890–1937) fought on the Western front from May 1916 to October 1917 (when he was poisoned by gas). He published two collections of war poems, as well as other work, but was increasingly affected by severe mental illness, and in 1922 was certified as insane.

He's gone, and all our plans
Are useless indeed.
We'll walk no more on Cotswold[1]
    Where the sheep feed
5   Quietly and take no heed.

His body that was so quick
    Is not as you
Knew it, on Severn River
    Under the blue
10   Driving our small boat through.
You would not know him now....
    But still he died
Nobly, so cover him over
    With violets of pride
15   Purple from Severn side.
Cover him, cover him soon!

    And with thick-set
Masses of memoried flowers
    Hide that red wet
20   Thing I must somehow forget.

---

[1] *Cotswold*   Range of hills in western England.

Vance Palmer, "The Farmer Remembers the Somme" (1920)

Both Vance Palmer (1885–1959), who was better known as a writer of fiction than as a poet, and his wife, Nettie Palmer, a leading critic as well as a poet, played central roles in Australian cultural life from the 1920s through to the 1950s. Vance Palmer joined the Australian Army in 1918, but never saw active service.

Will they never fade or pass!
    The mud, and the misty figures endlessly coming
In file through the foul morass,°   *marsh*
And the grey flood-water lipping the reeds and grass,
5 And the steel wings drumming.

The hills are bright in the sun:
There's nothing changed or marred in the well-known
    places;
When work for the day is done
There's talk, and quiet laughter, and gleams of fun
10 On the old folks' faces.

I have returned to these:
The farm, and the kindly Bush, and the young calves
    lowing;
But all that my mind sees
Is a quaking bog in a mist—stark, snapped trees,
15 and the dark Somme flowing.

11th Month NOVEMBER 1917	1917 NOVEMBER 30 Days
4 Sun—22nd after Trinity	
5 Mon	8 Th
6 Tues—(Last Quarter, 5.8 9.85)	9 Fri
7 Wed	10 Sat—s. R. 7.10, 5. 5. 4.13

NEWLY-DUG TRENCHES. Apart from uniforms, there are times when soldiers have no chance of disguising their whereabouts from an enemy. A hastily-prepared trench may indicate your position more clearly than the brightest accoutrements.

Suppose, as in the sketch on opposite page, you have only just had time to throw up an entrenchment, the newly-turned earth, AA, will stand up in the shape of a very distinct wall against a green background, and so your enemy will quickly "spot" you.

A page from the *Soldier's Own Diary*, copies of which were widely distributed to troops during the war.

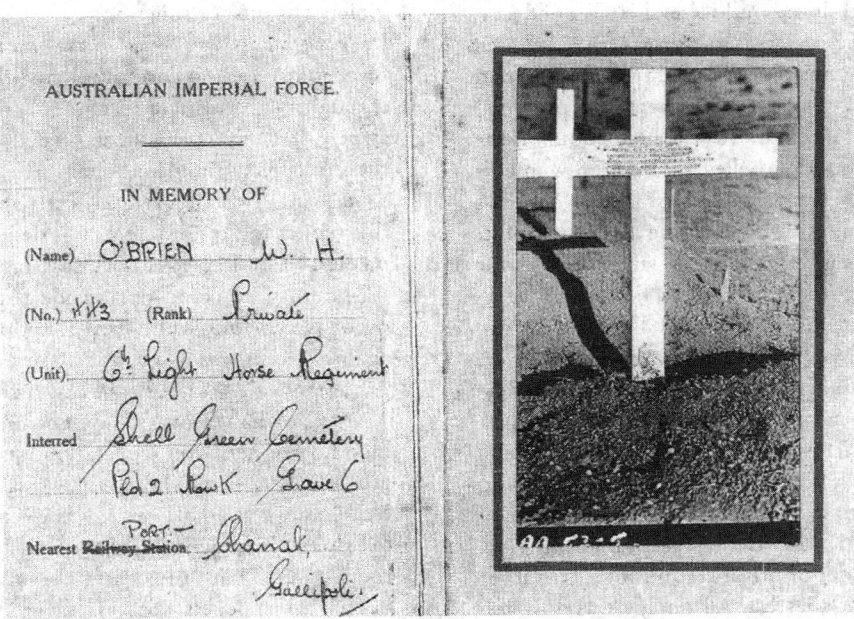

AUSTRALIAN IMPERIAL FORCE.

IN MEMORY OF

(Name) O'BRIEN   W. H.

(No.) ××3   (Rank) Private

(Unit) 6th Light Horse Regiment

Interred   Shell Green Cemetery
Ped 2 Row K Grave 6

Nearest Railway Station   Port— Anzac,
Gallipoli.

Memorial card for an Australian soldier killed and buried at Gallipoli. After the war, when the process of gathering the remains of soldiers and of constructing cemeteries began, Gallipoli became the final resting place for many New Zealand and Australian soldiers. Because most families could not arrange a visit to their loved one's grave, pictures were supplied to these families upon request.

from Robert Graves, *Good-Bye to All That* (1929, revised 1957)

from CHAPTER 17

We[1] once discussed which were the cleanest troops in trenches, taken by nationalities. We agreed on a descending-order list like this: English and German Protestants; Northern Irish, Welsh and Canadians; Irish and German Catholics; Scots, with certain higher-ranking exceptions; Mohammedan Indians; Algerians; Portuguese; Belgians; French. We put the Belgians and French there for spite; they could not have been dirtier than the Algerians and the Portuguese.

Propaganda reports of atrocities were, it was agreed, ridiculous. We remembered that while the Germans *could* commit atrocities against enemy civilians, Ger-

many itself, except for an early Russian cavalry raid, had never had the enemy on her soil. We no longer believed the highly-coloured accounts of German atrocities in Belgium; knowing the Belgians now at first-hand. By atrocities we meant, specifically, rape, mutilation and torture—not summary shootings of suspected spies, harbourers of spies, *francs-tireurs*,[2] or disobedient local officials. If the atrocity-list had to include the accidental-on-purpose bombing or machine-gunning of civilians from the air, the Allies were now committing as many atrocities as the Germans. French and Belgian civilians had often tried to win our sympathy by exhibiting mutilations of children—stumps of hands and feet, for instance—representing them as deliberate, fiendish atrocities when, as likely as not, they were merely the result of shell-fire. We did not believe rape to be any more common on the German side of the line than on

[1] *We* Graves, who was an officer in the Royal Welch Fusiliers, is here recounting his discussions with other British officers.

[2] *francs-tireurs* French: sharp-shooters.

the Allied side. And since a bully-beef diet, fear of death, and absence of wives made ample provision of women necessary in the occupied areas, no doubt the German Army authorities provided brothels in the principal French towns behind the line, as the French did on the Allied side. We did not believe stories of women's forcible enlistment in these establishments. "What's wrong with the voluntary system?" we asked cynically.

As for atrocities against soldiers—where should one draw the line? The British soldier, at first, regarded as atrocious the use of bowie-knives[1] by German patrols. After a time, he learned to use them himself; they were cleaner killing weapons than revolvers or bombs. The Germans regarded as equally atrocious the British Mark VII rifle-bullet, which was more apt to turn on striking than the German bullet. For true atrocities, meaning personal rather than military violations of the code of war, few opportunities occurred—except in the interval between the surrender of prisoners and their arrival (or non-arrival) at Headquarters. Advantage was only too often taken of this opportunity. Nearly every instructor in the Mess could quote specific instances of prisoners having been murdered on the way back. The commonest motives were, it seems, revenge for the death of friends or relatives, jealousy of the prisoner's trip to a comfortable prison camp in England, military enthusiasm, fear of being suddenly overpowered by the prisoners or, more simply, impatience with the escorting job. In any of these cases the conductors would report on arrival at Headquarters that a German shell had killed the prisoners; and no questions would be asked. We had every reason to believe that the same thing happened on the German side, where prisoners, as useless mouths to feed in a country already short of rations, would be even less welcome. None of us had heard of German prisoners being more than threatened at Headquarters to get military information from them. The sort that they could give was not of sufficient importance to make torture worth while; and anyhow, it had been found that, when treated kindly, prisoners were anxious in gratitude to tell as much as they knew. German intelligence officers had probably discovered that too.

The troops with the worst reputation for acts of

violence against prisoners were the Canadians (and later the Australians). The Canadians' motive was said to be revenge for a Canadian found crucified with bayonets through his hands and feet in a German trench. This atrocity had never been substantiated; nor did we believe the story, freely circulated, that the Canadians crucified a German officer in revenge shortly afterwards. How far this reputation for atrocities was deserved, and how far it could be ascribed to the overseas habit of bragging and leg-pulling, we could not decide. At all events, most overseas men, and some British troops, made atrocities against prisoners a boast, not a confession.

Later in the War, I heard two first-hand accounts.

A Canadian-Scot: "They sent me back with three bloody prisoners, you see, and one started limping and groaning, so I had to keep on kicking the sod down the trench. He was an officer. It was getting dark and I felt fed up, so I thought: 'I'll have a bit of a game.' I had them covered with the officer's revolver and made 'em open their pockets without turning round. Then I dropped a Mills bomb[2] in each, with the pin out, and ducked behind a traverse. Bang, bang, bang! No more bloody prisoners. No good Fritzes[3] but dead 'uns."

An Australian: "Well, the biggest lark I had was at Morlancourt, when we took it the first time. There were a lot of Jerries[4] in a cellar, and I said to 'em: 'Come out, you Camarades!' So out they came, a dozen of 'em, with their hands up. 'Turn out your pockets,' I told 'em. They turned 'em out. Watches, and gold and stuff, all dinkum.[5] Then I said: 'Now back to your cellar, you sons of bitches!' For I couldn't be bothered with 'em. When they were all safely down I threw half a dozen Mills bombs in after 'em. I'd got the stuff all right, and we weren't taking prisoners that day."

An old woman at Cardonette on the Somme gave me my first-hand account of large-scale atrocities. I was billeted with her in July 1916. Close to her home, a battalion of French Turcos[6] overtook the rear-guard of

[1] bowie-knives Curved, double-edged knives of about 15 inches in length.

[2] Mills bomb Type of hand grenade made to form shrapnel on explosion.

[3] Fritzes Nickname for German soldiers.

[4] Jerries Nickname for German soldiers.

[5] dinkum Australian slang: genuine, authentic.

[6] French Turcos Algerians serving in the French infantry.

a German division retreating from the Marne in September 1914. The Turcos surprised the dead-weary Germans while still marching in column. The old woman went, with gestures, through the pantomime of slaughter, and ended: "*Et enfin, ces animaux leur ont arraché les oreilles et les ont mis à la poche!*"[1] ...

We discussed the continuity of regimental morale. A captain in a Line battalion of a Surrey regiment said: "Our battalion has never recovered from the first Battle of Ypres. What's wrong is that we have a rotten depot. The drafts are bad, and so we get a constant re-infection." He told me one night in our sleeping hut: "In both the last two shows I had to shoot a man of my company to get the rest out of the trench. It was so bloody awful, I couldn't stand it. That's why I applied to be sent down here." This was the truth, not the usual loose talk that one heard at the base. I felt sorrier for him than for any other man I met in France. He deserved a better regiment.

The boast of every good battalion was that it had never lost a trench; both our Line battalions made it—meaning, that they had never been forced out of a trench without recapturing it before the action ended. Capturing a German trench and being unable to hold it for lack of reinforcements did not count; nor did retirement by order from Headquarters, or when the battalion next door had broken and left a flank in the air. And, towards the end of the War, trenches could be honourably abandoned as being wholly obliterated by bombardment, or because not really trenches at all, but a line of selected shell-craters.

We all agreed on the value of arms-drill as a factor in morale. "Arms-drill as it should be done," someone said, "is beautiful, especially when the company feels itself as a single being, and each movement is not a synchronized movement of every man together, but the single movement of one large creature." I used to get big bunches of Canadians to drill: four or five hundred at a time. Spokesmen stepped forward once and asked what sense there was in sloping and ordering arms, and fixing and unfixing bayonets. They said they had come across to fight, and not to guard Buckingham Palace. I told them that in every division of the four in which I had

served—the First, Second, Seventh and Eighth—there had been three different kinds of troops. Those that had guts but were no good at drill; those that were good at drill but had no guts; and those that had guts and were good at drill. These last, for some reason or other, fought by far the best when it came to a show—I didn't know why, and I didn't care. I told them that when they were better at fighting than the Guards they could perhaps afford to neglect their arms-drill.

We often theorized in the Mess about drill. I held that the best drill never resulted from being bawled at by a sergeant-major: that there must be perfect respect between the man who gives the order and the men who carry it out. The test of drill came, I said, when the officer gave an incorrect word of command. If his company could, without hesitation, carry out the order intended or, if the order happened to be impossible, could stand absolutely still, or continue marching, without confusion in the ranks, that was good drill. Some instructors regarded the corporate spirit that resulted from drilling together as leading to loss of initiative in the men drilled.

Others argued that it acted just the other way round: "Suppose a section of men with rifles get isolated from the rest of the company, without an N.C.O.[2] in charge, and meet a machine-gun. Under the stress of danger this section will have that all-one-body feeling of drill, and obey an imaginary word of command. There may be no communication between its members, but there will be a drill movement, with two men naturally opening fire on the machine-gun while the remainder work round, part on the left flank and part on the right; and the final rush will be simultaneous. Leadership is supposed to be the perfection for which drill has been instituted. That's wrong. Leadership is only the first stage. Perfection of drill is communal action. Though drill may seem to be antiquated parade-ground stuff, it's the foundation of tactics and musketry. Parade-ground musketry won all the battles in our regimental histories; this War, which is unlikely to open out, and must end with the collapse, by 'attrition,' of one side or the other, will be won by parade-ground tactics—by the simple drill tactics of small units fighting in limited spaces, and in noise and

---

[1] *Et enfin ... poche* French: And finally, these animals tore off their ears [i.e., the ears of their prisoners] and put them in their pockets.

[2] *N.C.O.* Non-commissioned officer.

confusion so great that leadership is quite impossible." Despite variance on this point we all agreed that regimental pride remained the strongest moral force that kept a battalion going as an effective fighting unit; contrasting it particularly with patriotism and religion.

Patriotism, in the trenches, was too remote a sentiment, and at once rejected as fit only for civilians, or prisoners. A new arrival who talked patriotism would soon be told to cut it out. As "Blighty,"[1] a geographical concept, Great Britain was a quiet, easy place for getting back to out of the present foreign misery; but as a nation it included not only the trench-soldiers themselves and those who had gone home wounded, but the staff, Army Service Corps, lines-of-communication troops, base units, home-service units, and all civilians down to the detested grades of journalists, profiteers, "starred" men exempted from enlistment, conscientious objectors, and members of the Government. The trench-soldier, with this carefully graded caste-system of honour, never considered that the Germans opposite might have built up exactly the same system themselves. He thought of Germany as a nation in arms, a unified nation inspired with the sort of patriotism that he himself despised. He believed most newspaper reports on conditions and sentiments in Germany, though believing little or nothing of what he read about similar conditions and sentiments in England. Yet he never under-rated the German as a soldier. Newspaper libels on Fritz's courage and efficiency were resented by all trench-soldiers of experience.

Hardly one soldier in a hundred was inspired by religious feeling of even the crudest kind. It would have been difficult to remain religious in the trenches even if one had survived the irreligion of the training battalion at home. A regular sergeant at Montagne, a Second Battalion man, had recently told me that he did not hold with religion in time of war. He said that the "niggers" (meaning the Indians) were right in officially relaxing their religious rules while fighting. "And all this damn nonsense, Sir—excuse me, Sir—that we read in the papers, Sir, about how miraculous it is that the wayside crucifixes are always getting shot at, but the figure of our Lord Jesus somehow don't get hurt, it fairly makes me sick, Sir." This was his explanation why,

when giving practice fire-orders from the hill-top, he had shouted, unaware that I stood behind him: "Seven hundred, half left, bloke on cross, five rounds, concentrate, FIRE!" And why, for "concentrate," he had humorously substituted "consecrate." His platoon, including the two unusual "Bible-wallahs" whose letters home always began in the same formal way: "Dear Sister in Christ," or "Dear Brother in Christ," blazed away.

Women celebrating on V-day, London, 1918.

from May Wedderburn Cannan, *Grey Ghosts and Voices* (1976)

The following is taken from the autobiography of May Wedderburn Cannan, daughter of the head of the Oxford University Press. During the war Cannan worked at the Press and as a volunteer nurse, participating in the mobilization of the Red Cross. She also went to France to volunteer in a soldiers' canteen in Rouen, an experience she describes in the excerpt below. Cannan gives a sense of the change of attitude—from optimism to cynicism—among both poets and the general public as the war progressed when she explains the popular expression at the time, "Went to the war with Rupert Brooke and came home with Siegfried Sassoon." While Brooke was an idealistic poet whose verse celebrated his country and its cause, Sassoon's verse painted in grim detail the horrors of a war the senseless atrocities of which could not be idealized. After years of trench warfare, the poems of Brooke seemed naive and simplistic to many.

---

[1] *Blighty* England; home.

I suppose it is difficult for anyone to realise now what "France" meant to us. In the Second War I met a young man of the Left who assured me that Rupert Brooke's[1] verse was of no account, phoney, because it was "impossible that anyone should have thought like that." I turned and rent him, saying that he was entitled to his own opinion of Rupert Brooke's verse, but not entitled to say that no one could have thought like that. How could he know how we had thought?—All our hopes and all our loves, and God knew, all our fears, were in France; to get to France, if only to stand on her soil, was something; to share, in however small a way, in what was done there was Heart's Desire.

I asked my Father could I take all my holidays in one and go for four weeks to France—I did not want holidays, I said, but I did want France. It was dark and we were walking home through the confines of Little Clarendon Street; my voice, I knew, shook; he took his pipe out of his mouth, halted his step for a moment and looked down at me. "Ah! France" he said, "France, yes, I think you should go. We'll manage." I stammered thanks and we walked home in silence, understanding each other.

The Canteen was started at Rouen because Lord Brassey's yacht *The Sunbeam* had made two or three journeys there during the shortage of hospital ships bringing wounded home. Lady Mabelle Egerton, his daughter, looking round the desolate railway yards beyond the quays asked the R.T.O.[2] if there was anything that could be done for the troops; drafts going up the line to Railhead, who had to spend a long day there, and sometimes a long night.

He said that the men brought their rations, including tea, but that there was no means of making hot water. (It was long before the days of another war when motorised infantry "brewed up" with their petrol cans) —Could she find some philanthropic person to take on the job? She could find no one—and decided to do it herself, and so the Canteen, later known affectionately

to thousands of the B.E.F. and the New Armies[3] as "the Coffee Shop," was born....

Along the length of railway line ran a row of sheds with huge sliding doors. In the first, and smaller one, was established a boiler room where enormous vats of hot water forever boiled. Beyond, steps led to a room where we ate our own meals when there was time and kept books for anyone who asked for something to read going up the Line. And across the whole of the great sheds ran heavy tables, ours with shelves under which at night held guttering candles and trays for change. Behind were the steaming cauldrons where we washed, (when a draft had left), the unbelievably pink French bowls in which we served coffee.

Coffee had proved more possible to get than tea and to it was added ham sandwiches. We had hundreds of someone's "Handy Hams" enclosed in a kind of scaly protection. In cold weather when we could not peel them we flung them with violence onto the stone floor to crack them; then endlessly we cut slices of ham.

I remember at the end of a long cutting session my left hand could not close itself; it had held the ham steady against the knife for so long, but we did have two machines for cutting bread. Butter in the cold weather was hard and stiff to spread, and when it was hot it dripped.

We were wanted because there had been an epidemic of measles among the staff; one girl had died of pneumonia, and another was home on sick leave—we were gapfillers only, but we were wanted —they needed us. ...

When the big trains were due in we opened the sliding doors of the sheds, the train doors banged and banged down the long line of the corridors and some 2,000 men would surge in. Barricaded behind our heavy table, and thankful for it when the pressure was heavy or a draft had somehow got hold of some drink, we handed out bowls of coffee and sandwiches, washed dirty bowls till the water in the tall vats was chocolate brown, and served again.

Someone would play the piano; Annie Laurie; Loch Lomond. Blurred lanterns lit the scene as best they might when it rained and our candles in the tills under

[1] *Rupert Brooke* Poet (1887–1915) known for his patriotic, idealistic verse. Brooke died of blood poisoning on the way to Gallipoli in 1915.

[2] *R.T.O.* Railroad Transportation Officer.

[3] *B.E.F.* British Expeditionary Force; *New Armies* Forces assembled from the 1914 volunteer recruitment campaign of the Earl of Kitchener, Secretary of State for War.

the tables guttered in the wind. One was hot or horrid cold, harried, dirty, and one's feet ached with the stone floors. When the smaller drafts came one could distinguish faces, and regimental badges; have a word or two. Two men told me with impressment that they were "the New Army, Kitchener's!" I said yes, and we had been expecting them, and thought of the old Army and the T.A.[1] Worried young officers asked one to change a pound note and frowned over getting "25 shillings" (francs) to the pound. Twice I came on an old friend but there was no time save for a brief greeting and a "good bye and good luck."

When the whistle blew they stood to save the King[2] and the roof came off the sheds. Two thousand men, maybe, singing—it was the most moving thing I knew. Then there'd be the thunder of seats pushed back, the stamp of army boots on the pave, and as the train went out they sang Tipperary[3]—

No one seemed to know how the song, written and first sung at Stalybridge in 1912, had become the song of the B.E.F. My brother-in-law, a Mons man,[4] said they did not sing it till they read in the papers that they were—then they learned it! …

That spring I collected such verse as I thought "possible," got my Father to "cast an eye over it," and set forth to see Mr. Blackwell.[5] He had a small office up an uncarpeted stair at the back of the famous bookshop in the Broad.[6] At the last moment my Father said he would come with me. I think that he wanted to make sure that I was not published in any series or involved in any clique.

Mr. Blackwell was, I remember, very kind, but as I was practically blind and deaf with nerves I have a blurred recollection of what happened. We walked up the Broad together afterwards, and, suddenly realising that his ridiculous daughter was struggling with tears, he stopped dead. "Why are you crying?" "I'm not," I said, using the old formula; "It's all right only I did think he might take it." "But he has!" "Has he?" I asked astounded. "Yes, of course" said my Father, and continuing up the street; "The trouble with you and that young man is that you have both got the Oxford manner so badly you can't understand each other." He seemed amused. As I have never been able to discover what the Oxford manner is I have never known what he meant. …

I was lucky for after the Somme there was a change of heart among poets. Siegfried Sassoon wrote to the Press from France saying that the war was now a war of conquest and without justification,[7] and declared himself to be a conscientious objector. He was rescued from trouble by Robert Graves and his friends who claimed a breakdown. C.E. Montague wrote *Disenchantment* and Wilfred Owen was much influenced by him.[8] A saying went round, "Went to the war with Rupert Brooke and came home with Siegfried Sassoon."

I had much admired some of Sassoon's verse but I was not coming home with him. Someone must go on writing for those who were still convinced of the right of the cause for which they had taken up arms.

The conscription tribunals were often ruthless and sometimes, rather horrible; but by no means always (after all the army did not want unwilling, and therefore bad, soldiers), and, testifying their conscientious objections, persistent defenders of culture and antiwar writers were excused active service and able to do other work. There was a colony of them at Garsington near Oxford where Philip and Lady Ottoline Morrell[9] had their

---

[1]   *T.A.*   Territorial Army.

[2]   *to save the King*   I.e., they stood to sing the national anthem, "God Save the King."

[3]   *Tipperary*   The song "It's a Long Way to Tipperary."

[4]   *Mons man*   I.e., a man who had fought at the Battle of Mons, in Belgium, the first battle of World War I (23 August 1914).

[5]   *Blackwell*   The publisher Basil Blackwell (1889–1984).

[6]   *bookshop in the Broad*   I.e., Blackwell's, Broad Street, Oxford.

[7]   *Siegfried Sassoon … justification*   Sassoon's letter, in which he condemned the war as a mere matter of "aggression and conquest," was published in *The Times* on 31 July 1917. After his friend and fellow poet Robert Graves testified that Sassoon was suffering from shell-shock, a medical board sent Sassoon to Craiglockhart War Hospital, Edinburgh, rather than to prison.

[8]   *C.E. Montague*   Journalist and novelist Charles Edward Montague (1867–1928), whose *Disenchantment* comprised a series of articles he had published in the *Manchester Guardian* in 1920 and 1921 on the impact of the war; *Wilfred Owen*   War poet (1893–1918).

[9]   *Philip and Lady Ottoline Morrell*   Solicitor and politician Philip Morrell (1870–1943) and his wife Ottoline (1873–1938), a well-known literary hostess. Both were pacifists, and their Oxford home, Garsington Manor, provided a refuge for conscientious objectors during the war.

home and entertained such people as Middleton Murry, Katherine Mansfield, Lawrence, Bertrand Russell,[1] my cousin Gilbert Cannan and others of the intellectual élite who stayed there talking of art and verse and genius and pure intellect....

from "Proceedings" of the All-Russian Central Executive Committee of Soviets of Workers', Soldiers', and Peasants' Deputies[2] (17 November 1917)

In March of 1917 (February according to the old Julian calendar, which the Russians used until 1918, when they adopted the Gregorian calendar), with Russia suffering from extreme poverty and in the midst of the war against Germany, the autocratic regime of Czar Nicholas II crumbled as troops refused orders to suppress workers' risings in Moscow and St. Petersburg. The Czar was replaced by a provisional government led by Alexander Kerensky, a democratic socialist. In November (October, according to the Julian calendar), a second revolution occurred when the more radical Bolsheviks, led by V.I. Lenin, seized power. Between June 1917 and January of the following year, representatives of councils of workers (or "soviets") met in Petrograd (St. Petersburg). The discussions shed interesting light on the connections between the revolution and World War I and touch on vitally important issues such as the degree to which the new government would tolerate free speech and the ways in which it contemplated interacting with the rest of the world. The way in which many of the issues discussed here were handled by the Communist government would shape a great deal of twentieth-century history.

The speakers in the excerpts below are V.A. Avanesov, soon to become Secretary of the Central Executive Committee of the new government; A. L. Kalegayev and V. A. Karelin, leaders of the Socialist-Revolutionary Party; Soviet representative S.M. Zaks; Vladimir Lenin, leader of the Bolshevik Party (forerunner of the Communist Party, which dominated the country from 1917 until the collapse of the USSR in 1989–91); and Leon Trotsky, Lenin's second-in-command. (Trotsky later broke with Communist Party authorities after Joseph Stalin came to power; he was murdered while living in exile in Mexico.)

AVANESOV. The question of press freedom must be seen in the context of the current political situation in the country as a whole. It seems that no one objects to closure of bourgeois newspapers during an insurrection, when fighting is in progress. If this is so, [we must ask ourselves] whether the struggle is indeed over and the moment has come when we can pass on to a normal mode of life. Having silenced the bourgeois press, [the revolutionary authorities] would be very naive if they were to let slip from their hands such a powerful means of influencing the ideals of all workers, soldiers, and peasants. All these measures are designed to facilitate the creation of a new regime, free from capitalist oppression, in which a socialist press will ensure freedom of speech for all citizens and for all tendencies of thought.

We defend freedom of the press [in principle], but this concept must be divorced from old petty-bourgeois or bourgeois notions of liberty. If the new government has had the strength to abolish private landed property, thereby infringing the rights of the landlords, it would be ridiculous for Soviet power to stand up for antiquated notions about liberty of the press. First the newspapers must be freed from capitalist oppression, just as we have freed the land from the landlords, and then we can promulgate new socialist laws and norms enshrining a liberty that will serve the whole toiling people, and not just capital....

KALEGAYEV. ... [T]here is a profound disagreement between our position and that of the Bolsheviks. [The latter argue:] previously we defended all civil liberties, but now we are prepared to muzzle our opponents. However, one cannot emancipate society from the fetters of capitalism by taking repressive measures against newspapers. Nor is it possible to carve up freedom of the press like a loaf of bread, allocating so much freedom to each group according to the influence exerted by its ideas. When the Bolsheviks talk of poisoning the people's consciousness by the printed word, they

---

[1] *Middleton Murry* Writer and editor John Middleton Murry (1889–1957), husband of author Katherine Mansfield (1888–1923); *Lawrence* Writer D.H. Lawrence (1885–1930); *Bertrand Russell* Philosopher and journalist (1872–1970).

[2] *Proceedings ... Deputies* Translated by H.L. Keep.

are adopting the viewpoint of [the editors of] *Zemshchina*.[1]

TROTSKY. One should distinguish between the situation during a civil war and the situation once victory is complete. To demand that all repressive measures should be abandoned during a civil war is equivalent to demanding that the war itself should cease. Such a demand could come only from adversaries of the proletariat. Our opponents are not offering us peace. No one can provide a guarantee against [a victory of] the Komilovites.[2] During a civil war it is legitimate to suppress newspapers that support the other side. But when we are finally victorious our attitude toward the press will be analogous to that on freedom of trade. Then we shall naturally move on to a [regular] regime in press matters. In our party press we have for a long time been accustomed to take a non-proprietorial view of press freedom. Measures taken against [suspect] individuals should also be taken against press organs. We should confiscate and socialize printing-presses and stocks of newsprint … (*Shouts from the floor:* "And Bolshevik ones too?") Yes, all these stocks should be transferred to public ownership. Any group of [workers,] soldiers, or peasants will be able to submit an application for [access to supplies of] newsprint and to a printing-press.…

KARELIN. It is a Hottentot[3] morality which holds that it's bad if someone steals my wife but good if I steal someone else's. I say this because Trotsky has been critical of our party. It is surprising that we should hear [such arguments] from a party which itself now enjoys freedom of the press. We cannot have double standards of morality.

But I would rather discuss this question in terms of political expediency. Is it expedient to muzzle the expression of any trend of opinion? History teaches that whenever this is done it only makes such opinions more attractive. Forbidden fruit is sweet. I agree with Trotsky that we have to eliminate capitalist oppression in regard to the press. But the measures [he proposes] are risky. One can attain this objective without muzzling opinion, simply by undertaking a wide range of protective actions in the distribution of material. The [Bolshevik] resolution proposes that parties and groups should have [the right to publish] newspapers in proportion to the number of their supporters, but such calculations will scarcely be practicable. It would be absurd to distribute [opportunities to publish] in proportion to [the strength of various currents of] opinion; this would be like socializing thought itself.

I should make it clear that in advocating freedom of opinion we do not seek to extend it to the weakest sector [in terms of popular support]. Trotsky alleges that we are arguing from the standpoint of capital. I say that whoever puts the question in such terms is arguing from the standpoint of his own ministerial portfolio. Genuine representatives of the people should not be afraid of minority opinions. Such fear betrays an awareness that one's own opinions are weak. "Who wants press freedom?" Trotsky asks. The answer is: everyone who cherishes the [revolutionary] movement of our people.…

ZAKS. [I]f we burn our bridges will we not be entirely isolated? After all, we have won precious little support so far. Western Europe is shamefully silent. One can't build socialism by decree and by relying solely upon a single party.

LENIN. The phrase "the west is shamefully silent" is impermissible from the lips of an internationalist.[4] One would have to be blind not to notice the ferment that has gripped the working classes of Germany and the west [in general]. The leaders of the German proletariat, the socialist intelligentsia, consist in main of defensists, as they do everywhere else, but their proletarian followers are prepared to desert them and to respond to our call. The savage discipline that prevails in the German army and navy has not prevented elements opposed [to the war] from taking action. The revolutionary sailors in the German navy, knowing that their enterprise was

---

[1] *Zemshchina* Russian newspaper whose title translates as "lands of the state," i.e., lands where the workers live (as opposed to the *oprichnina*, which was the personal domain of the Tsar).

[2] *Kornilovites* Supporters of General Kornilov, who attempted to replace Kerensky with a military government.

[3] *Hottentot* I.e., ignorant; inferior. (A derogatory term deriving from the name then given to members of a Southwest African people.)

[4] *internationalist* Socialists who supported an international workers' rebellion, and who thought such a movement should take precedence over the war.

doomed to fail, went to meet their fate heroically, in the hope that their sacrifice would awaken the spirit of insurrection among the people. ...

We believe in a revolution in the west. We know that this is inevitable, but of course we can't bring it about to order. Did we know last December what was to happen in February? Did we know for sure in September that next month Russian revolutionary democracy would bring off the greatest overturn in world [history]? We knew that the old government was sitting on a volcano and we could guess from many signs that beneath the surface a great change was occurring in people's ideas. We could feel the electricity in the air, we knew that it would inevitably discharge itself in a purifying storm. But we could not predict the day and hour when the storm would break. It is exactly the same now in the case of Germany. There too the people's sullen discontent is growing and is bound to erupt in the form of a broad mass movement. We cannot decree the revolution, but we can at least help it along. We shall organize fraternization in the trenches and help the western peoples to launch the invincible socialist revolution.

Revolutionary soldiers during the March 1917 uprising in Petrograd.

Vladimir Lenin and Leon Trotsky, c. 1917.

William Butler Yeats
1865 – 1939

In *On Poetry and Poets* (1957), fellow poet and contemporary T.S. Eliot wrote of William Butler Yeats: "Born into a world in which the doctrine of "Art for Art's Sake" was generally accepted, and living on into one in which art has been asked to be instrumental to social purposes, he held firmly to the right view which is between these, though not in any way a compromise between them, and showed that an artist, by serving his art with entire integrity, is at the same time rendering the greatest service he can to his own nation and to the whole world." In truth, few poets of the twentieth century have contributed as much to the cultural, political, and social framework of their own country, and to English literature in general. An analysis of Yeats's poetry, however, is impossible without understanding the deeply personal and biographical nature of his writing, and Yeats's own endeavor to shape his entire canon of work into a unified body of art.

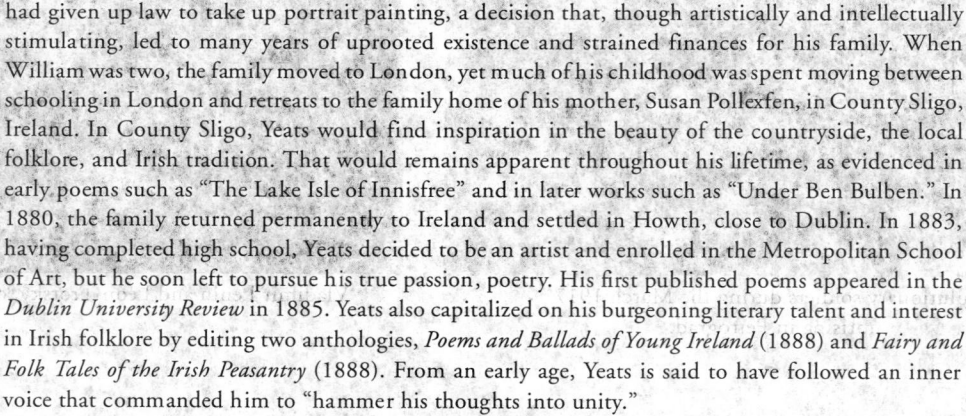

William Butler Yeats was born in the Dublin suburb of Sandymount on 13 June 1865. His father, John Butler Yeats, had given up law to take up portrait painting, a decision that, though artistically and intellectually stimulating, led to many years of uprooted existence and strained finances for his family. When William was two, the family moved to London, yet much of his childhood was spent moving between schooling in London and retreats to the family home of his mother, Susan Pollexfen, in County Sligo, Ireland. In County Sligo, Yeats would find inspiration in the beauty of the countryside, the local folklore, and Irish tradition. That would remains apparent throughout his lifetime, as evidenced in early poems such as "The Lake Isle of Innisfree" and in later works such as "Under Ben Bulben." In 1880, the family returned permanently to Ireland and settled in Howth, close to Dublin. In 1883, having completed high school, Yeats decided to be an artist and enrolled in the Metropolitan School of Art, but he soon left to pursue his true passion, poetry. His first published poems appeared in the *Dublin University Review* in 1885. Yeats also capitalized on his burgeoning literary talent and interest in Irish folklore by editing two anthologies, *Poems and Ballads of Young Ireland* (1888) and *Fairy and Folk Tales of the Irish Peasantry* (1888). From an early age, Yeats is said to have followed an inner voice that commanded him to "hammer his thoughts into unity."

Also at an early age, influenced by his father's religious skepticism, Yeats developed a strong interest in occultism, folklore, and theosophism, a system of philosophical thought based on the direct and immediate experience of the divine. In 1885 he joined with friends to form the Dublin Hermetic Society, a group devoted to discussion of occult sciences and pseudo-sciences of the day. This group was predominantly influenced by a more famous mystical society, The Theosophical Society, founded in New York by Madame Helena Blavatsky. In 1887, Yeats met with Madame Blavatsky and later joined the Esoteric section of the London chapter of the Theosophical Society. In 1890, Yeats left the Society to join the Hermetic Order of the Golden Dawn, an occult society that drew upon astrology, tarot, kabbala, and Eastern mysticism for its teachings. Throughout his life and career, Yeats would turn to mythology and the occult as tools for developing his own vision of history and imagination.

In his poetry, this vision is evident in an elaborate system of images and symbols that Yeats would continually investigate and refine.

In 1889 Yeats's first collection, *The Wanderings of Oisin and Other Poems*, was published. The collection was well received, but the attention of one reader in particular would be responsible for what Yeats would term "the troubling of my life." The beautiful actress and Irish nationalist Maud Gonne was introduced to Yeats by a mutual friend, John O'Leary, shortly after the collection was published. The meeting marked a fateful moment in the life of Yeats, as Gonne would become his obsession for the next quarter-century, and his poetry would resonate with his love and despair for her in poems such as "Adam's Curse" (1904), "No Second Troy" (1910), and "A Prayer for My Daughter" (1921). Despite remaining intimate with Yeats for many years, Maud Gonne persistently refused to marry him, and added to his turmoil with her marriage to an Irish soldier, John MacBride, in 1903. Yet in spite of the heartache Yeats endured through his relationship with Gonne, she helped inspire him in two new cultural endeavors: the establishment of an Irish national theatre and the development of a public voice for the Irish nationalist movement for independence.

For several years after the publication of *The Wanderings of Oisin and Other Poems*, Yeats continued to gain literary prominence with further collections of poetry and studies of Irish folklore and fairy tales. In 1896 Yeats met Lady Augusta Gregory, a fellow writer and promoter of Irish literature, who invited him to stay in her country house at Coole Park. Through her influence, Yeats became involved in the founding of the Irish National Theatre in 1899. In writing for the theater, Yeats found a new voice for his interest in mythology, mysticism, Irish nationalism, and Maud Gonne. In 1902, Gonne played the title role in Yeats's nationalist play *Cathleen Ni Houlihan*. In 1904, the Irish National Theatre's permanent home, The Abbey Theatre, opened with Yeats's play *On Baile's Strand*. As the Abbey's director and dramatist, Yeats helped develop it into one of the world's leading theaters and, perhaps more importantly to him, into the center of the Irish literary renaissance.

In 1908, eight volumes of Yeats's *Collected Works* were published. Although Yeats was most interested in the Abbey Theatre during this period, this publication by no means heralded the slowdown of his poetic career. On the contrary, as he was becoming a figure of national importance, Yeats began to develop a more public voice in his poetry. Abandoning the more lyrical and self-conscious mode of his earlier poems, Yeats began to trace the growing political upheaval of the period. The publication of *The Green Helmet and Other Poems* in 1910 marks Yeats's transition into the second phase of his poetic career. Where his early poems often offered romantic melancholy and idyllic meditations on pagan themes, the poetry of this second phase became more direct in its analysis of the events and attitudes of the period. As Yeats became embittered by the small-minded nationalism of The Abbey's middle-class audiences, and as he watched with horror the growing violence in the struggle for Irish independence, poems such as "Easter 1916," "Meditations In Time of Civil War," and "Nineteen Hundred and Nineteen" began to reflect his distrust of popular judgement and concern for the future of his country.

At the same time, Yeats continued to develop his complex system of symbolism and esoteric theories regarding the movement of history and human intellect. In 1917, having exhausted his proposals to Maud Gonne and suffered another humiliating refusal by Gonne's daughter Iseult, Yeats married Georgie Hyde-Lees, whom he had met in 1911. On their honeymoon, Hyde-Lees delighted Yeats with her gift for automatic writing (believed by Yeats to be dictated by spirits), and for several years her writings inspired Yeats to refine his symbolic system, as described in his book *A Vision* (1925). Although Yeats's poetry is by no means unintelligible without an understanding of *A Vision*, many of his poems refer directly to the patterns and imagery examined within its pages. According to Yeats, the progress of art and thought is directly interwoven through the spirals, or gyres, of human history, represented in *A Vision* by two interpenetrating cones that make up antithetical cycles of 2000 years. These ideas became increasingly evident in his poetic works, particularly later poems such as "Byzantium" and "Sailing to Byzantium."

In 1922 Yeats was elected Senator of the Irish Free State; a year later, he was awarded the Nobel Prize for Literature, becoming the first Irish writer to receive the award. Yeats continued to produce major poetry well into his later years. As his health began to decline, his poetry took on a defiant tone, reflecting an awareness of his own mortality. Poems of this period, such as "Lapis Lazuli," "The Circus Animals' Desertion," and "Under Ben Bulben," rage against old age while reflecting on his life and body of work. Poems published in *The Tower* (1928), *The Winding Stair* (1933), and *Last Poems* (1939) are thought by many critics to be among his finest.

Following a long period of heart trouble, Yeats died on 28 January 1939, and was buried in Roquebrune, France, where he had been spending the winter. In 1948, his remains were reinterred, as he had wished, in Drumcliff, County Sligo. Also according to his wishes, his epitaph is taken from "Under Ben Bulben": "Cast a cold eye / On life, on death. / Horseman, pass by!"

⌘ ⌘ ⌘

The Lake Isle of Innisfree [1]

I will arise and go now, and go to Innisfree,
And a small cabin build there, of clay and wattles made;[2]
Nine bean-rows will I have there, a hive for the honey bee,
And live alone in the bee-loud glade.

5 And I shall have some peace there, for peace comes dropping slow,
Dropping from the veils of the morning to where the cricket sings;
There midnight's all a glimmer, and noon a purple glow,
And evening full of the linnet's° wings.   *small songbird's*

I will arise and go now, for always night and day
10 I hear lake water lapping with low sounds by the shore;
While I stand on the roadway, or on the pavements grey,
I hear it in the deep heart's core.
—1890

When You Are Old [3]

When you are old and gray and full of sleep,
And nodding by the fire, take down this book,
And slowly read, and dream of the soft look
Your eyes had once, and of their shadows deep;

5 How many loved your moments of glad grace,
And loved your beauty with love false or true,
But one man loved the pilgrim soul in you,
And loved the sorrows of your changing face;

And bending down beside the glowing bars,
10 Murmur, a little sadly, how Love fled
And paced upon the mountains overhead
And hid his face amid a crowd of stars.
—1892

---

[1] *Lake Isle of Innisfree* A small island in Lough Gill, County Sligo; Innisfree (*Inis Fraoigh* in Gaelic) means "Heather Island."

[2] *wattles* Poles and reeds interwoven to create a thatched wall or roof.

[3] *When You Are Old* Based on one of Pierre de Ronsard's (1524–85) *Sonnets pour Hélène*, "*Quand vous serez bien vieille, au soir, à la chandelle,*" which translates to: "When you very old, sitting by the candlelight at night."

Who Goes with Fergus?[1]

Who will go drive with Fergus now,
    And pierce the deep wood's woven shade,
And dance upon the level shore?
Young man, lift up your russet brow,
5 And lift your tender eyelids, maid,
And brood on hopes and fear no more.

And no more turn aside and brood
Upon love's bitter mystery;
For Fergus rules the brazen cars,
10 And rules the shadows of the wood,
And the white breast of the dim sea
And all dishevelled wandering stars.
—1893

Adam's Curse [2]

We sat together at one summer's end,
    That beautiful mild woman,[3] your close friend,
And you[4] and I, and talked of poetry.
I said, "A line will take us hours maybe;
5 Yet if it does not seem a moment's thought,
Our stitching and unstitching has been naught.
Better go down upon your marrow-bones
And scrub a kitchen pavement, or break stones
Like an old pauper, in all kinds of weather;
10 For to articulate sweet sounds together
Is to work harder than all these, and yet
Be thought an idler by the noisy set
Of bankers, schoolmasters, and clergymen
The martyrs call the world."

15   And thereupon
That beautiful mild woman for whose sake

There's many a one shall find out all heartache
On finding that her voice is sweet and low
Replied, "To be born woman is to know —
20 Although they do not talk of it at school —
That we must labour to be beautiful."

I said, "It's certain there is no fine thing
Since Adam's fall but needs much labouring.
There have been lovers who thought love should be
25 So much compounded of high courtesy
That they would sigh and quote with learned looks
Precedents out of beautiful old books;
Yet now it seems an idle trade enough."

We sat grown quiet at the name of love;
30 We saw the last embers of daylight die,
And in the trembling blue-green of the sky
A moon, worn as if it had been a shell
Washed by time's waters as they rose and fell
About the stars and broke in days and years.

35 I had a thought for no one's but your ears:
That you were beautiful, and that I strove
To love you in the old high way of love;
That it had all seemed happy, and yet we'd grown
As weary-hearted as that hollow moon.
—1904

No Second Troy [5]

Why should I blame her[6] that she filled my days
    With misery, or that she would of late[7]
Have taught to ignorant men most violent ways,
Or hurled the little streets upon the great,
5 Had they but courage equal to desire?
What could have made her peaceful with a mind
That nobleness made simple as a fire,
With beauty like a tightened bow, a kind
That is not natural in an age like this,

---

[1] *Fergus* Ancient Irish king who gave up his throne in order to spend more time fighting, feasting, and hunting.

[2] *Adam's Curse* Cf. Genesis 3.17–19: Adam was banished from the Garden of Eden for disobeying God and was thereafter cursed to live a life of hard work.

[3] *That beautiful mild woman* The sister of Maud Gonne, prominent Irish activist, Kathleen Pilcher.

[4] *you* Maud Gonne.

[5] *Troy* During the Trojan War, the Greeks besieged and destroyed the city of Troy in an effort to retrieve Helen, who had been abducted by the Trojan, Paris, from her husband, the Greek Menelaus.

[6] *her* Maud Gonne.

[7] *of late* Gonne ceased her political work in 1905.

10 Being high and solitary and most stern?
     Why, what could she have done being what she is?
     Was there another Troy for her to burn?

—1910

Easter 1916[1]

I have met them at close of day
     Coming with vivid faces
From counter or desk among grey
Eighteenth-century houses.
5   I have passed with a nod of the head
     Or polite meaningless words,
     Or have lingered awhile and said
     Polite meaningless words,
     And thought before I had done
10 Of a mocking tale or a gibe
     To please a companion
     Around the fire at the club,
     Being certain that they and I
     But lived where motley° is worn: *jester's costume*
15 All changed, changed utterly:
     A terrible beauty is born.

That woman's days were spent
     In ignorant good-will,
     Her nights in argument
20 Until her voice grew shrill.[2]
     What voice more sweet than hers
     When, young and beautiful,
     She rode to harriers?
     This man had kept a school

25 And rode our wingèd horse;[3]
     This other his helper and friend[4]
     Was coming into his force;
     He might have won fame in the end,
     So sensitive his nature seemed,
30 So daring and sweet his thought.
     This other man I had dreamed
     A drunken, vainglorious lout.[5]
     He had done most bitter wrong
     To some who are near my heart,
35 Yet I number him in the song;
     He, too, has resigned his part
     In the casual comedy;
     He, too, has been changed in his turn,
     Transformed utterly:
40 A terrible beauty is born.

Hearts with one purpose alone
     Through summer and winter seem
     Enchanted to a stone
     To trouble the living stream.
45 The horse that comes from the road,
     The rider, the birds that range
     From cloud to tumbling cloud,
     Minute by minute they change;
     A shadow of cloud on the stream
50 Changes minute by minute;
     A horse-hoof slides on the brim,
     And a horse plashes within it;
     The long-legged moor-hens dive,
     And hens to moor-cocks call;
55 Minute by minute they live:
     The stone's in the midst of all.

Too long a sacrifice
     Can make a stone of the heart.
     O when may it suffice?

---

1 *Easter 1916* On Easter Monday, 24 April 1916, Irish nationalists instigated an unsuccessful rebellion against the British government (which was then at war with Germany); the Easter rebellion lasted until 29 April. Many of the Irish nationalist leaders were executed that May.

2 *That woman's … shrill* Countess Markiewicz, née Constance Gore-Booth (1868–1927), played a central role in the Easter Rebellion; she was arrested and sentenced to death (though the death sentence was later commuted). Yeats later wrote a poem about her and her Irish-nationalist sister, "In Memory of Eva Gore-Booth and Con Markiewicz" (1929).

3 *This man … wingèd horse* Pádraic Pearse (1879–1916) founded St. Enda's School near Dublin. He was a leader in the effort to revive the Gaelic language, and wrote both Irish and English poetry; the "wingèd horse" refers to Pegasus, the horse of the Muses.

4 *This other his helper and friend* Thomas MacDonagh (1878–1916), an Irish poet and playwright who also taught school.

5 *vainglorious lout* Major John MacBride (1865–1916), estranged husband of Irish nationalist Maud Gonne; their separation just two years after marriage was due in part to his drinking bouts.

60 That is Heaven's part, our part
To murmur name upon name,
As a mother names her child
When sleep at last has come
On limbs that had run wild.
65 What is it but nightfall?
No, no, not night but death;
Was it needless death after all?
For England may keep faith
For all that is done and said.[1]
70 We know their dream; enough
To know they dreamed and are dead;
And what if excess of love
Bewildered them till they died?
I write it out in a verse—
75 MacDonagh and MacBride
And Connolly[2] and Pearse[3]
Now and in time to be,
Wherever green is worn,
Are changed, changed utterly:
80 A terrible beauty is born.
                    —1916

The Wild Swans at Coole [4]

The trees are in their autumn beauty,
    The woodland paths are dry,
Under the October twilight the water
Mirrors a still sky;
5 Upon the brimming water among the stones
Are nine-and-fifty swans.

The nineteenth autumn[5] has come upon me
Since I first made my count;

I saw, before I had well finished,
10 All suddenly mount
And scatter wheeling in great broken rings
Upon their clamorous wings.

I have looked upon those brilliant creatures,
And now my heart is sore.
15 All's changed since I, hearing at twilight,
The first time on this shore,
The bell-beat of their wings above my head,
Trod with a lighter tread.

Unwearied still, lover by lover,
20 They paddle in the cold
Companionable streams or climb the air;
Their hearts have not grown old;
Passion or conquest, wander where they will,
Attend upon them still.

25 But now they drift on the still water,
Mysterious, beautiful;
Among what rushes will they build,
By what lake's edge or pool
Delight men's eyes, when I awake some day
30 To find they have flown away?
                    —1917

In Memory of Major Robert Gregory [6]

I

Now that we're almost settled in our house[7]
    I'll name the friends that cannot sup with us
Beside a fire of turf[8] in th' ancient tower,
And having talked to some late hour
5 Climb up the narrow winding stair to bed:
Discoverers of forgotten truth

---

[1] *For England ... said* England had originally granted Ireland Home Rule in 1913, but then postponed it due to World War I, promising to institute it after the war.

[2] *Connolly* James Connolly (1868–1916), Irish Socialist.

[3] *MacDonagh ... Pearse* All four men were executed for their involvement in the Easter Uprising of 1916.

[4] *Coole* Coole Park, County Galway estate of Lady Gregory, friend and patron of Yeats.

[5] *nineteenth autumn* Yeats first visited Coole Park in 1897, nineteen years before he wrote this poem.

[6] [Yeats's note] Major Robert Gregory [Lady Gregory's only son (1881–1918)], R.F.C. [Royal Flying Corps], M.C. [Military Cross], Legion of Honour, was killed in action on the Italian Front, January 23, 1918.

[7] *our house* Yeats had bought a section of Lady Gregory's estate at Coole Park; Thoor Ballylee, an ancient Norman tower situated there, became his home.

[8] *turf* Dried peat used for fuel.

Or mere companions of my youth,
All, all are in my thoughts tonight being dead.

2

Always we'd have the new friend meet the old
10   And we are hurt if either friend seem cold,
And there is salt to lengthen out the smart
In the affections of our heart,
And quarrels are blown up upon that head;
But not a friend that I would bring
15   This night can set us quarrelling,
For all that come into my mind are dead.

3

Lionel Johnson[1] comes the first to mind,
That loved his learning better than mankind,
Though courteous to the worst; much falling he
20   Brooded upon sanctity
Till all his Greek and Latin learning seemed
A long blast upon the horn that brought
A little nearer to his thought
A measureless consummation that he dreamed.

4

25   And that enquiring man John Synge[2] comes next,
That dying chose the living world for text
And never could have rested in the tomb
But that, for long travelling, he had come
Towards nightfall upon certain set apart
30   In a most desolate stony place,[3]
Towards nightfall upon a race
Passionate and simple like his heart.

5

And then I think of old George Pollexfen,[4]
In muscular youth well known to Mayo[5] men
35   For horsemanship at meets or at racecourses,
That could have shown how pure-bred horses

And solid men, for all their passion, live
But as the outrageous stars incline
By opposition, square and trine;[6]
40   Having grown sluggish and contemplative.

6

They were my close companions many a year,
A portion of my mind and life, as it were,
And now their breathless faces seem to look
Out of some old picture-book;
45   I am accustomed to their lack of breath,
But not that my dear friend's dear son,
Our Sidney[7] and our perfect man,
Could share in that discourtesy of death.

7

For all things the delighted eye now sees
50   Were loved by him; the old storm-broken trees
That cast their shadows upon road and bridge;
The tower set on the stream's edge;
The ford where drinking cattle make a stir
Nightly, and startled by that sound
55   The water-hen must change her ground;
He might have been your heartiest welcomer.

8

When with the Galway foxhounds he would ride
From Castle Taylor to the Roxborough side
Or Esserkelly plain, few kept his pace;
60   At Mooneen he had leaped a place[8]
So perilous that half the astonished meet
Had shut their eyes; and where was it
He rode a race without a bit?
And yet his mind outran the horses' feet.

---

[1] *Lionel Johnson*   English poet and scholar (1867–1902).

[2] *John Synge*   Irish playwright (1871–1909), co-director, along with Yeats and Lady Gregory, of the Abbey Theatre.

[3] *set apart … place*   Synge had set some of his plays in the Aran Islands, off the west coast of Ireland.

[4] *George Pollexfen*   Yeats's maternal uncle, an astrologer.

[5] *Mayo*   County north of Galway.

[6] *opposition, square and trine*   Astrological terms used to describe angles between heavenly bodies.

[7] *Sidney*   Elizabethan poet Sir Philip Sidney (1554–86), who, like Gregory, was an artist, scholar, and statesman who died young in battle.

[8] *Castle … Mooneen*   Country manors in the County of Galway: Roxborough was Lady Gregory's childhood home; Mooneen is beside Esserkelly, which is near Ardrahan in County Galway.

9

65 We dreamed that a great painter had been born
To cold Clare[1] rock and Galway rock and thorn,
To that stern colour and that delicate line
That are our secret discipline
Wherein the gazing heart doubles her might.
70 Soldier, scholar, horseman, he,
And yet he had the intensity
To have published all to be a world's delight.

10

What other could so well have counselled us
In all lovely intricacies of a house
75 As he that practised or that understood
All work in metal or in wood,
In moulded plaster or in carven stone?
Soldier, scholar, horseman, he,
And all he did done perfectly
80 As though he had but that one trade alone.

11

Some burn faggots,° others may consume   *bundles of twigs*
The entire combustible world in one small room
As though dried straw, and if we turn about
The bare chimney is gone black out
85 Because the work had finished in that flare.
Soldier, scholar, horseman, he,
As 'twere all life's epitome,
What made us dream that he could comb grey hair?

12

I had thought, seeing how bitter is that wind
90 That shakes the shutter, to have brought to mind
All those that manhood tried, or childhood loved
Or boyish intellect approved,
With some appropriate commentary on each;
Until imagination brought
95 A fitter welcome; but a thought
Of that late death took all my heart for speech.
—1918

---

1 *Clare* County to the south of Galway.

Nineteen Hundred and Nineteen[2]

I

Many ingenious lovely things are gone
That seemed sheer miracle to the multitude,
Protected from the circle of the moon
That pitches common things about. There stood
5 Amid the ornamental bronze and stone
An ancient image made of olive wood —[3]
And gone are Phidias' famous ivories[4]
And all the golden grasshoppers and bees.[5]

We too had many pretty toys when young;
10 A law indifferent to blame or praise,
To bribe or threat; habits that made old wrong
Melt down, as it were wax in the sun's rays;
Public opinion ripening for so long
We thought it would outlive all future days.
15 O what fine thought we had because we thought
That the worst rogues and rascals had died out.

All teeth were drawn, all ancient tricks unlearned,
And a great army but a showy thing;
What matter that no cannon had been turned
20 Into a ploughshare?[6] Parliament and king
Thought that unless a little powder burned
The trumpeters might burst with trumpeting
And yet it lack all glory; and perchance
The guardsmen's drowsy chargers would not prance.

---

2 *Nineteen Hundred and Nineteen* 1919 was a year of increasing armed confrontation between the Irish Republican Army and the Irish government, which was controlled by Britain.

3 *ancient ... wood* Statue of Athena, patron goddess of Athens, was carved out of the wood of the sacred olive tree and stood on the Acropolis; the statue was later destroyed in a fire.

4 *Phidias's famous ivories* Phidias (sometimes spelled "Pheidias" or "Phideas," c. 500–c. 432 BCE) was a celebrated Greek sculptor who created an ivory- and gold-encrusted statue of Athena (since destroyed) in the Parthenon.

5 *golden grasshoppers and bees* Offerings to the gods in the form of golden trinkets; Thucydides wrote of the Athenian custom of tying up a lock of hair with a golden grasshopper.

6 *no cannon ... ploughshare* Cf. Isaiah 2.4: "They shall beat their swords into plowshares ... nation shall not lift up sword against nation, neither shall they learn war anymore."

25 Now days are dragon-ridden, the nightmare
    Rides upon sleep: a drunken soldiery
    Can leave the mother, murdered at her door,
    To crawl in her own blood, and go scot-free;
    The night can sweat with terror as before
30 We pieced our thoughts into philosophy,
    And planned to bring the world under a rule,
    Who are but weasels fighting in a hole.

    He who can read the signs nor sink unmanned
    Into the half-deceit of some intoxicant
35 From shallow wits; who knows no work can stand,
    Whether health, wealth or peace of mind were spent
    On master-work of intellect or hand,
    No honour leave its mighty monument,
    Has but one comfort left: all triumph would
40 But break upon his ghostly solitude.

    But is there any comfort to be found?
    Man is in love and loves what vanishes,
    What more is there to say? That country round
    None dared admit, if such a thought were his,
45 Incendiary or bigot could be found
    To burn that stump on the Acropolis,
    Or break in bits the famous ivories
    Or traffic in the grasshoppers or bees.

2

50 When Loie Fuller's[1] Chinese dancers enwound
    A shining web, a floating ribbon of cloth,
    It seemed that a dragon of air
    Had fallen among dancers, had whirled them round
    Or hurried them off on its own furious path;
55 So the Platonic Year[2]
    Whirls out new right and wrong,
    Whirls in the old instead;
    All men are dancers and their tread
    Goes to the barbarous clangour of a gong.

[1] *Loie Fuller* An American dancer and choreographer (1862–
1928); her dancers were Japanese, not Chinese.
[2] *Platonic Year* Full revolution of the constellations in relation to
the equinoxes, approximately 26,000 years.

3

60 Some moralist or mythological poet
    Compares the solitary soul to a swan;
    I am satisfied with that,
    Satisfied if a troubled mirror show it,
    Before that brief gleam of its life be gone,
65 An image of its state;
    The wings half spread for flight,
    The breast thrust out in pride
    Whether to play, or to ride
    Those winds that clamour of approaching night.

70 A man in his own secret meditation
    Is lost amid the labyrinth that he has made
    In art or politics;
    Some Platonist affirms that in the station
    Where we should cast off body and trade
75 The ancient habit sticks,
    And that if our works could
    But vanish with our breath
    That were a lucky death,
    For triumph can but mar our solitude.

80 The swan has leaped into the desolate heaven:
    That image can bring wildness, bring a rage
    To end all things, to end
    What my laborious life imagined, even
    The half-imagined, the half-written page;
85 O but we dreamed to mend
    Whatever mischief seemed
    To afflict mankind, but now
    That winds of winter blow
    Learn that we were crack-pated when we dreamed.

4

90 We, who seven years ago
    Talked of honour and of truth,
    Shriek with pleasure if we show
    The weasel's twist, the weasel's tooth.

5

    Come let us mock at the great
95 That had such burdens on the mind
    And toiled so hard and late

To leave some monument behind,
Nor thought of the levelling wind.

Come let us mock at the wise;
100 With all those calendars whereon
They fixed old aching eyes,
They never saw how seasons run,
And now but gape at the sun.

Come let us mock at the good
105 That fancied goodness might be gay,
And sick of solitude
Might proclaim a holiday:
Wind shrieked—and where are they?

Mock mockers after that
110 That would not lift a hand maybe
To help good, wise or great
To bar that foul storm out, for we
Traffic in mockery.

6

Violence upon the roads: violence of horses;
115 Some few have handsome riders, are garlanded
On delicate sensitive ear or tossing mane,
But wearied running round and round in their courses
All break and vanish, and evil gathers head:
Herodias' daughters have returned again,[1]
120 A sudden blast of dusty wind and after
Thunder of feet, tumult of images,
Their purpose in the labyrinth of the wind;
And should some crazy hand dare touch a daughter
All turn with amorous cries, or angry cries,
125 According to the wind, for all are blind.
But now wind drops, dust settles; thereupon
There lurches past, his great eyes without thought
Under the shadow of stupid straw-pale locks,
That insolent fiend Robert Artisson[2]

130 To whom the love-lorn Lady Kyteler brought
Bronzed peacock feathers, red combs of her cocks.[3]
—1919

A Prayer for my Daughter [4]

Once more the storm is howling, and half hid
Under this cradle-hood and coverlid
My child sleeps on. There is no obstacle
But Gregory's wood[5] and one bare hill
5 Whereby the haystack- and roof-levelling wind,
Bred on the Atlantic, can be stayed;
And for an hour I have walked and prayed
Because of the great gloom that is in my mind.

I have walked and prayed for this young child an hour
10 And heard the sea-wind scream upon the tower,[6]
And under the arches of the bridge, and scream
In the elms above the flooded stream;
Imagining in excited reverie
That the future years had come,
15 Dancing to a frenzied drum,
Out of the murderous innocence of the sea.

May she be granted beauty and yet not
Beauty to make a stranger's eye distraught,
Or hers before a looking-glass, for such,
20 Being made beautiful overmuch,
Consider beauty a sufficient end,
Lose natural kindness and maybe
The heart-revealing intimacy
That chooses right, and never find a friend.

[3] *To whom ... cocks* It was said that Artisson seduced Lady Kyteler, who supposedly sacrificed cocks and peacocks to him and was accused of poisoning her husbands; *combs* Pronounced ridges on cocks' crowns.

[4] *My Daughter* Anne Butler Yeats, born 26 February 1919.

[5] *Gregory's wood* Lady Gregory's wood at Coole Park, her estate in western Ireland.

[6] *tower* Thoor Ballylee, the ancient Norman tower on the land Yeats bought from Lady Gregory in June 1917.

[1] *Herodias' ... again* The reference here is not to the Biblical character (whose daughter was Salomé) but rather to the eponymous witch-goddess of Germanic mythology. Her daughters are associated with violently whirling winds.

[2] [Yeats's note] My last symbol, Robert Artisson, was an evil spirit much run after in Kilkenny at the start of the fourteenth century.

25 Helen[1] being chosen found life flat and dull
And later had much trouble from a fool,
While that great Queen, that rose out of the spray,[2]
Being fatherless could have her way
Yet chose a bandy-leggèd smith[3] for man.
30 It's certain that fine women eat
A crazy salad with their meat
Whereby the Horn of Plenty is undone.

In courtesy I'd have her chiefly learned;
Hearts are not had as a gift but hearts are earned
35 By those that are not entirely beautiful;
Yet many, that have played the fool
For beauty's very self, has charm made wise,
And many a poor man that has roved,
Loved and thought himself beloved,
40 From a glad kindness cannot take his eyes.

May she become a flourishing hidden tree
That all her thoughts may like the linnet be,
And have no business but dispensing round
Their magnanimities of sound,
45 Nor but in merriment begin a chase,
Nor but in merriment a quarrel.
O may she live like some green laurel
Rooted in one dear perpetual place.

My mind, because the minds that I have loved,
50 The sort of beauty that I have approved,
Prosper but little, has dried up of late,
Yet knows that to be choked with hate
May well be of all evil chances chief.
If there's no hatred in a mind
55 Assault and battery of the wind
Can never tear the linnet from the leaf.

An intellectual hatred is the worst,
So let her think opinions are accursed.

---

[1] *Helen* Wife of Menelaus. She was abducted by Paris, the son of the king of Troy; the Greeks besieged the city for ten years to save her, finally bringing her back to her husband.

[2] *that great Queen … spray* Aphrodite, the Greek goddess of love, beauty, and fecundity, rose out of the sea at birth.

[3] *bandy-leggèd smith* Hephaestus, god of fire and husband of Aphrodite, was born lame.

Have I not seen the loveliest woman[4] born
60 Out of the mouth of Plenty's horn,
Because of her opinionated mind
Barter that horn and every good
By quiet natures understood
For an old bellows full of angry wind?

65 Considering that, all hatred driven hence,
The soul recovers radical innocence
And learns at last that it is self-delighting,
Self-appeasing, self-affrighting,
And that its own sweet will is Heaven's will;
70 She can, though every face should scowl
And every windy quarter howl
Or every bellows burst, be happy still.

And may her bridegroom bring her to a house
Where all's accustomed, ceremonious;
75 For arrogance and hatred are the wares
Peddled in the thoroughfares.
How but in custom and in ceremony
Are innocence and beauty born?
Ceremony's a name for the rich horn,
80 And custom for the spreading laurel tree.
—1919

An Irish Airman Foresees his Death

I know that I shall meet my fate
Somewhere among the clouds above;
Those that I fight I do not hate
Those that I guard I do not love;
5 My country is Kiltartan Cross,[5]
My countrymen Kiltartan's poor,
No likely end could bring them loss
Or leave them happier than before.
Nor law, nor duty bade me fight,
10 Nor public man, nor cheering crowds,
A lonely impulse of delight
Drove to this tumult in the clouds;

---

[4] *loveliest woman* Maud Gonne, whom Yeats had loved, was an important Irish liberation activist; she married Major John MacBride in 1903.

[5] *Kiltartan Cross* In County Galway, Ireland.

I balanced all, brought all to mind,
The years to come seemed waste of breath,
15 A waste of breath the years behind
In balance with this life, this death.
—1919

The Second Coming [1]

Turning and turning in the widening gyre[2]
The falcon cannot hear the falconer;
Things fall apart; the centre cannot hold;
Mere anarchy is loosed upon the world,
5 The blood-dimmed tide is loosed, and everywhere
The ceremony of innocence is drowned;
The best lack all conviction, while the worst
Are full of passionate intensity.

Surely some revelation is at hand;
10 Surely the Second Coming is at hand.
The Second Coming! Hardly are those words out
When a vast image out of *Spiritus Mundi*[3]
Troubles my sight: somewhere in sands of the desert
A shape with lion body and the head of a man,[4]
15 A gaze blank and pitiless as the sun,
Is moving its slow thighs, while all about it
Reel shadows of the indignant desert birds.
The darkness drops again; but now I know
That twenty centuries of stony sleep
20 Were vexed to nightmare by a rocking cradle,[5]
And what rough beast, its hour come round at last,
Slouches towards Bethlehem to be born?
—1920

---

[1] *The Second Coming* The return of Christ, as predicted in the New Testament. See Revelation 1.7: "Behold, he cometh with clouds; and every eye shall see him."

[2] *gyre* Spiral formed from concentric circles.

[3] *Spiritus Mundi* Universal spirit that houses the images of civilization's past memories and provides divine inspiration for the poet; the human race is a connected whole in the *spiritus mundi*.

[4] *shape ... man* The Egyptian Sphinx.

[5] *rocking cradle* Cradle of the Christ Child.

Meditations in Time of Civil War

I
Ancestral Houses

Surely among a rich man's flowering lawns,
Amid the rustle of his planted hills,
Life overflows without ambitious pains;
And rains down life until the basin spills,
5 And mounts more dizzy high the more it rains
As though to choose whatever shape it wills
And never stoop to a mechanical
Or servile shape, at others' beck and call.

Mere dreams, mere dreams! Yet Homer had not sung
10 Had he not found it certain beyond dreams
That out of life's own self-delight had sprung
The abounding glittering jet;[6] though now it seems
As if some marvellous empty sea-shell flung
Out of the obscure dark of the rich streams,
15 And not a fountain, were the symbol which
Shadows the inherited glory of the rich.

Some violent bitter man, some powerful man
Called architect and artist in, that they,
Bitter and violent men, might rear in stone
20 The sweetness that all longed for night and day,
The gentleness none there had ever known;
But when the master's buried mice can play,
And maybe the great-grandson of that house,
For all its bronze and marble, 's but a mouse.

25 O what if gardens where the peacock strays
With delicate feet upon old terraces,
Or else all Juno[7] from an urn displays
Before the indifferent garden deities;
O what if levelled lawns and gravelled ways
30 Where slippered Contemplation finds his ease
And Childhood a delight for every sense,
But take our greatness with our violence?
What if the glory of escutcheoned doors,
And buildings that a haughtier age designed,

---

[6] *jet* Stream of liquid emerging from a fountain.

[7] *Juno* Roman goddess of marriage and protector of women.

35 The pacing to and fro on polished floors
   Amid great chambers and long galleries, lined
   With famous portraits of our ancestors;
   What if those things the greatest of mankind
   Consider most to magnify, or to bless,
40 But take our greatness with our bitterness?

2
My House

   An ancient bridge, and a more ancient tower,
   A farmhouse that is sheltered by its wall,
   An acre of stony ground,
   Where the symbolic rose can break in flower,
45 Old ragged elms, old thorns innumerable,
   The sound of the rain or sound
   Of every wind that blows;
   The stilted water-hen
   Crossing stream again
50 Scared by the splashing of a dozen cows;

   A winding stair, a chamber arched with stone,
   A grey stone fireplace with an open hearth,
   A candle written page.
   Il Penseroso's Platonist[1] toiled on
55 In some like chamber, shadowing forth
   How the daemonic rage
   Imagined everything.
   Benighted travellers
   From markets and from fairs
60 Have seen his midnight candle glimmering.

   Two men have founded here. A man-at-arms
   Gathered a score of horse and spent his days
   In this tumultuous spot,
   Where through long wars and sudden night alarms
65 His dwindling score and he seemed castaways
   Forgetting and forgot;
   And I, that after me
   My bodily heirs may find,
   To exalt a lonely mind,
70 Befitting emblems of adversity.

3
My Table

   Two heavy trestles, and a board
   Where Sato's gift, a changeless sword,[2]
   By pen and paper lies,
   That it may moralise
75 My days out of their aimlessness.
   A bit of an embroidered dress
   Covers its wooden sheath.
   Chaucer had not drawn breath
   When it was forged. In Sato's house,
80 Curved like new moon, moon-luminous,
   It lay five hundred years.
   Yet if no change appears
   No moon; only an aching heart
   Conceives a changeless work of art.
85 Our learned men have urged
   That when and where 'twas forged
   A marvellous accomplishment,
   In painting or in pottery, went
   From father unto son
90 And through the centuries ran
   And seemed unchanging like the sword.
   Soul's beauty being most adored,
   Men and their business took
   The soul's unchanging look;
95 For the most rich inheritor,
   Knowing that none could pass Heaven's door
   That loved inferior art,
   Had such an aching heart
   That he, although a country's talk
100 For silken clothes and stately walk,
   Had waking wits; it seemed
   Juno's peacock screamed.[3]

4
My Descendants

Having inherited a vigorous mind

---

[1] *Il Penseroso's Platonist* Hermes Trismegistus, a semi-mythical character in Milton's poem, purported to be the author of thousands of Neo-Platonic texts.

[2] *Sato's gift, a changeless sword* Japanese sword given to Yeats by his friend Junzo Sato in 1920.

[3] *Juno's peacock screamed* Peacocks are sacred to Juno, Roman queen of the gods and goddess of childbirth. The peacock was once said to complain to Juno that although he was beautiful, his cry was shrill.

From my old fathers, I must nourish dreams
105 And leave a woman and a man[1] behind
As vigorous of mind, and yet it seems
Life scarce can cast a fragrance on the wind,
Scarce spread a glory to the morning beams,
But the torn petals strew the garden plot;
110 And there's but common greenness after that.

And what if my descendants lose the flower
Through natural declension of the soul,
Through too much business with the passing hour,
Through too much play, or marriage with a fool?
115 May this laborious stair and this stark tower
Become a roofless ruin that the owl
May build in the cracked masonry and cry
Her desolation to the desolate sky.

The Primum Mobile[2] that fashioned us
120 Has made the very owls in circles move;
And I, that count myself most prosperous,
Seeing that love and friendship are enough,
For an old neighbour's[3] friendship chose the house
And decked and altered it for a girl's[4] love,
125 And know whatever flourish and decline
These stones remain their monument and mine.

5
The Road at My Door

An affable Irregular,[5]
A heavily-built Falstaffian[6] man,
Comes cracking jokes of civil war
130 As though to die by gunshot were
The finest play under the sun.

A brown Lieutenant[7] and his men,
Half dressed in national uniform,
Stand at my door, and I complain
135 Of the foul weather, hail and rain,
A pear tree broken by the storm.

I count those feathered balls of soot
The moor-hen guides upon the stream,
To silence the envy in my thought;
140 And turn towards my chamber, caught
In the cold snows of a dream.

6
The Stare's Nest by My Window[8]

The bees build in the crevices
Of loosening masonry, and there
The mother birds bring grubs and flies.
145 My wall is loosening; honey-bees,
Come build in the empty house of the stare.

We are closed in, and the key is turned
On our uncertainty; somewhere
A man is killed, or a house burned,
150 Yet no clear fact to be discerned:
Come build in the empty house of the stare.

A barricade of stone or of wood;
Some fourteen days of civil war;
Last night they trundled down the road
155 That dead young soldier in his blood:
Come build in the empty house of the stare.

We had fed the heart on fantasies,
The heart's grown brutal from the fare;
More substance in our enmities
160 Than in our love; O honey-bees,
Come build in the empty house of the stare.

---

[1] *a woman and a man* Anne and Michael Butler Yeats, Yeats's daughter and son.

[2] *Primum Mobile* Cause of all things; "the first mover."

[3] *an old neighbour* Lady Augusta Gregory.

[4] *a girl's* Georgie Yeats's.

[5] *Irregular* Member of the Irish Republican Army.

[6] *Falstaffian* Resembling the Shakespearean character Sir John Falstaff, known for his girth, roguish joviality, lustfulness, brashness, and fondness for alcohol.

[7] *brown Lieutenant* Member of the National Army of England.

[8] [Yeats's note] In the west of Ireland we call a starling a stare, and during the civil war one built a hole in the masonry by my bedroom window.

7
I See Phantoms of Hatred and of the Heart's Fullness and of the Coming Emptiness

I climb to the tower-top and lean upon broken stone,
A mist that is like blown snow is sweeping over all,
Valley, river, and elms, under the light of a moon
165 That seems unlike itself, that seems unchangeable,
A glittering sword out of the east. A puff of wind
And those white glimmering fragments of the mist
    sweep by.
Frenzies bewilder, reveries perturb the mind;
Monstrous familiar images swim to the mind's eye.

170 "Vengeance upon the murderers,"[1] the cry goes up,
"Vengeance for Jacques Molay."[2] In cloud-pale rags,
    or in lace,
The rage-driven, rage-tormented, and rage-hungry
    troop,
Trooper belabouring trooper, biting at arm or at face,
Plunges towards nothing, arms and fingers spreading
    wide
175 For the embrace of nothing; and I, my wits astray
Because of all that senseless tumult, all but cried
For vengeance on the murderers of Jacques Molay.

Their legs long, delicate and slender, aquamarine their
    eyes,
Magical unicorns bear ladies on their backs.[3]
180 The ladies close their musing eyes. No prophecies,
Remembered out of Babylonian almanacs,
Have closed the ladies' eyes, their minds are but a pool
Where even longing drowns under its own excess;
Nothing but stillness can remain when hearts are full
185 Of their own sweetness, bodies of their loveliness.

The cloud-pale unicorns, the eyes of aquamarine,
The quivering half-closed eyelids, the rags of cloud or
    of lace,
Or eyes that rage has brightened, arms it has made lean,
Give place to an indifferent multitude, give place
190 To brazen hawks.[4] Nor self-delighting reverie,
Nor hate of what's to come, nor pity for what's gone,
Nothing but grip of claw, and the eye's complacency,
The innumerable clanging wings that have put out
    the moon.

I turn away and shut the door, and on the stair
195 Wonder how many times I could have proved my
    worth
In something that all others understand or share;
But O! ambitious heart, had such a proof drawn forth
A company of friends, a conscience set at ease,
It had but made us pine the more. The abstract joy,
200 The half-read wisdom of daemonic images,
Suffice the ageing man as once the growing boy.
—1923

Leda and the Swan[5]

A sudden blow: the great wings beating still
Above the staggering girl, her thighs caressed
By the dark webs, her nape caught in his bill,
He holds her helpless breast upon his breast.

5 How can those terrified vague fingers push
The feathered glory from her loosening thighs?
And how can body, laid in that white rush,
But feel the strange heart beating where it lies?

A shudder in the loins engenders there
10 The broken wall, the burning roof and tower

---

1 [Yeats's note] A cry for vengeance because of the murder of the Grand Master of the Templars seems to me fit symbol for those who labour for hatred, and so for sterility in various kinds. It is said to have been incorporated in the ritual of certain Masonic societies of the eighteenth century, and to have fed class-hatred.

2 *Jacques Molay* Jacques de Molay, Grand Master of the Order of Knights Templar, was tortured and burned at the stake in 1314 after refusing to confess to heresy.

3 *Magical unicorns … backs* In Gustave Moreau's painting *Ladies and Unicorns*.

4 [Yeats's note] I suppose that I must have put hawks in the fourth stanza because I have a ring with a hawk and a butterfly upon it, to symbolize the straight road of logic, and so of mechanism, and the crooked road of intuition: "For wisdom is a butterfly and not a gloomy bird of prey."

5 *Leda and the Swan* Zeus came to Leda in the form of a swan and raped her; she then gave birth to Helen of Troy (whose abduction from her husband, King Menelaus, by Paris, initiated the Trojan War) and the twins, Castor and Pollux.

And Agamemnon[1] dead.

              Being so caught up,
So mastered by the brute blood of the air,
Did she put on his knowledge with his power
Before the indifferent beak could let her drop?

—1924

Among School Children

1

I walk through the long schoolroom questioning;
A kind old nun in a white hood replies;
The children learn to cipher and to sing,
To study reading-books and history,
5 To cut and sew, be neat in everything
In the best modern way—the children's eyes
In momentary wonder stare upon
A sixty-year-old smiling public man.

2

I dream of a Ledaean[2] body, bent
10 Above a sinking fire, a tale that she
Told of a harsh reproof, or trivial event
That changed some childish day to tragedy—
Told, and it seemed that our two natures blent
Into a sphere from youthful sympathy,
15 Or else, to alter Plato's parable,
Into the yolk and white of the one shell.[3]

3

And thinking of that fit of grief or rage
I look upon one child or t'other there
And wonder if she stood so at that age—
20 For even daughters of the swan[4] can share
Something of every paddler's heritage—
And had that colour upon cheek or hair,

And thereupon my heart is driven wild:
She stands before me as a living child.

4

25 Her present image floats into the mind—
Did Quattrocento finger[5] fashion it
Hollow of cheek as though it drank the wind
And took a mess of shadows for its meat?
And I though never of Ledaean kind
30 Had pretty plumage once—enough of that,
Better to smile on all that smile, and show
There is a comfortable kind of old scarecrow.

5

What youthful mother, a shape upon her lap
Honey of generation[6] had betrayed,
35 And that must sleep, shriek, struggle to escape
As recollection or the drug decide,
Would think her son, did she but see that shape
With sixty or more winters on its head,
A compensation for the pang of his birth,
40 Or the uncertainty of his setting forth?

6

Plato thought nature but a spume that plays
Upon a ghostly paradigm of things;[7]
Solider Aristotle played the taws
Upon the bottom of a king of kings;[8]
45 World-famous golden-thighed Pythagoras

---

[1] broken wall ... Agamemnon dead   Events of the Trojan War.

[2] Ledaean   Like that of Leda (see note on Leda below).

[3] Plato's parable ... shell   A speaker in Plato's Symposium explains that man was originally both male and female in one form, but was then divided into two; love was the reunion of man with his other half.

[4] daughters of the swan   Leda, raped by Zeus in the form of a swan, gave birth to Helen of Troy.

[5] Quattrocento finger   Skillful hand of a fifteenth-century Italian artist.

[6] [Yeats's note] I have taken the "honey of generation" from Porphyry's essay on "The Cave of the Nymphs," but find no warrant in Porphyry for considering it the "drug" that destroys the "recollection" of prenatal freedom. [The Neoplatonic philosopher Porphyry (233–c. 304) stated that the pleasure of sexual intercourse, like the sweetness of honey, drugs infants, thereby causing them to forget prenatal bliss before being born into this mortal world.]

[7] Plato ... things   Plato argued that the appearance of nature was merely an imitation of the real world; therefore, nature itself was unreal, but provided a "ghostly" image of the real "paradigm of things."

[8] Solider ... kings   Unlike Plato, Aristotle believed that reality took form in the image of nature; therefore, nature was reality itself. Aristotle tutored Alexander the Great, the son of King Philip of Macedonia; taws Leather whip.

Fingered upon a fiddle-stick or strings[1]
What a star sang and careless Muses heard:
Old clothes upon old sticks to scare a bird.

7

Both nuns and mothers worship images,
50 But those the candles light are not as those
That animate a mother's reveries,
But keep a marble or a bronze repose.
And yet they too break hearts—O Presences
That passion, piety or affection knows,
55 And that all heavenly glory symbolise—
O self-born mockers of man's enterprise;

8

Labour is blossoming or dancing where
The body is not bruised to pleasure soul,
Nor beauty born out of its own despair,
60 Nor blear-eyed wisdom out of midnight oil.
O chestnut tree, great-rooted blossomer,
Are you the leaf, the blossom, or the bole?°   trunk
O body swayed to music, O brightening glance,
How can we know the dancer from the dance?
—1927

Sailing to Byzantium [2]

I

That is no country for old men. The young
In one another's arms, birds in the trees
— Those dying generations — at their song,
The salmon-falls, the mackerel-crowded seas,
5 Fish, flesh, or fowl, commend all summer long
Whatever is begotten, born, and dies.
Caught in that sensual music all neglect
Monuments of unageing intellect.

2

An aged man is but a paltry thing,
10 A tattered coat upon a stick, unless
Soul clap its hands and sing, and louder sing
For every tatter in its mortal dress,
Nor is there singing school but studying
Monuments of its own magnificence;
15 And therefore I have sailed the seas and come
To the holy city of Byzantium.

3

O sages standing in God's holy fire
As in the gold mosaic of a wall,
Come from the holy fire, perne in a gyre,[3]
20 And be the singing-masters of my soul.
Consume my heart away; sick with desire
And fastened to a dying animal
It knows not what it is; and gather me
Into the artifice of eternity.

4

25 Once out of nature I shall never take
My bodily form from any natural thing,
But such a form as Grecian goldsmiths make
Of hammered gold and gold enamelling
To keep a drowsy Emperor awake;
30 Or set upon a golden bough to sing[4]
To lords and ladies of Byzantium
Of what is past, or passing, or to come.
—1927

---

[1] *golden-thighed … strings* Pythagoras, a Greek philosopher of the sixth century BCE, developed a theory of the mathematical regularity of the universe and the mathematical origins of musical harmony. He was said to have a golden thigh.

[2] *Byzantium* Ancient city eventually renamed Constantinople (now Istanbul), capital of the Eastern Roman Empire. In *A Vision*, Yeats envisioned Byzantium as a center for artists: "The painter, the mosaic worker, the worker in gold and silver, the illuminator of sacred books were almost impersonal, almost perhaps without the consciousness of individual design, absorbed in their subject matter and that the vision of a whole people."

[3] *perne in a gyre* Rotate in a spiral; the literal definition of "perne" is bobbin.

[4] [Yeats's note] I have read somewhere that in the Emperor's palace at Byzantium was a tree made of gold and silver, and artificial birds that sang.

The Tower [1]

1

What shall I do with this absurdity—
O heart, O troubled heart—this caricature,
Decrepit age that has been tied to me
As to a dog's tail?
5   Never had I more
Excited, passionate, fantastical
Imagination, nor an ear and eye
That more expected the impossible—
No, not in boyhood when with rod and fly,
10 Or the humbler worm, I climbed Ben Bulben's [2] back
And had the livelong summer day to spend.
It seems that I must bid the Muse go pack,
Choose Plato and Plotinus [3] for a friend
Until imagination, ear and eye,
15 Can be content with argument and deal
In abstract things; or be derided by
A sort of battered kettle at the heel.

2

I pace upon the battlements and stare
On the foundations of a house, or where
20 Tree, like a sooty finger, starts from the earth;
And send imagination forth
Under the day's declining beam, and call
Images and memories
From ruin or from ancient trees,
25 For I would ask a question of them all.

Beyond that ridge lived Mrs. French, and once
When every silver candlestick or sconce
Lit up the dark mahogany and the wine,
A serving-man, that could divine
30 That most respected lady's every wish,
Ran and with the garden shears
Clipped an insolent farmer's ears
And brought them in a little covered dish. [4]

Some few remembered still when I was young
35 A peasant girl commended by a song,
Who'd lived somewhere upon that rocky place,
And praised the colour of her face,
And had the greater joy in praising her,
Remembering that, if walked she there,
40 Farmers jostled at the fair
So great a glory did the song confer.

And certain men, being maddened by those rhymes,
Or else by toasting her a score of times,
Rose from the table and declared it right
45 To test their fancy by their sight;
But they mistook the brightness of the moon
For the prosaic light of day—
Music had driven their wits astray—
And one was drowned in the great bog of Cloone. [5]

50 Strange, but the man who made the song was blind;
Yet, now I have considered it, I find
That nothing strange; the tragedy began
With Homer that was a blind man,
And Helen has all living hearts betrayed. [6]
55 O may the moon and sunlight seem
One inextricable beam,
For if I triumph I must make men mad.

And I myself created Hanrahan [7]
And drove him drunk or sober through the dawn

---

[1] [Yeats's note] The persons mentioned are associated by legend, story and tradition with the neighbourhood of Thoor Ballylee or Ballylee Castle [the "tower" in which Yeats lived], where the poem was written.

[2] *Ben Bulben* Mountain in County Sligo; Yeats is buried within sight of the mountain at Drumcliff Churchyard.

[3] [Yeats's note] When I wrote the lines about Plato and Plotinus I forgot that it is something in our own eyes that makes us see them as all transcendence.

[4] [Yeats's note] Mrs. French lived at Peterswell in the eighteenth century and was related to Sir Jonah Barrington, who described the incident of the ears and the trouble that came of it. [Jonah Barrington's description appears in his book of local history, *Personal Sketches of His Own Time*.]

[5] [Yeats's note] The peasant beauty and the blind poet are Mary Hynes and [Anthony] Raftery, and the incident of the man drowned in Cloone Bog [County Galway] is recorded in my *Celtic Twilight*.

[6] *Homer ... betrayed* Helen of Troy was the gorgeous daughter of the Greek god Zeus and his mortal lover Leda; the ten-year Trojan War was fought over her. The story of the Trojan war is told in Homer's *Iliad*.

[7] *Hanrahan* Red Hanrahan, a character in Yeats's prose and poetry.

60 From somewhere in the neighbouring cottages.
Caught by an old man's juggleries
He stumbled, tumbled, fumbled to and fro
And had but broken knees for hire
And horrible splendour of desire;
65 I thought it all out twenty years ago:[1]

Good fellows shuffled cards in an old bawn;° *fortified pasture*
And when that ancient ruffian's turn was on
He so bewitched the cards under his thumb
That all but the one card became
70 A pack of hounds and not a pack of cards,
And that he changed into a hare.
Hanrahan rose in frenzy there
And followed up those baying creatures towards—

O towards I have forgotten what—enough!
75 I must recall a man that neither love
Nor music nor an enemy's clipped ear
Could, he was so harried, cheer;
A figure that has grown so fabulous
There's not a neighbour left to say
80 When he finished his dog's day:
An ancient bankrupt master of this house.

Before that ruin came, for centuries,
Rough men-at-arms, cross-gartered to the knees
Or shod in iron, climbed the narrow stairs,
85 And certain men-at-arms there were
Whose images, in the Great Memory stored,
Come with loud cry and panting breast
To break upon a sleeper's rest
While their great wooden dice beat on the board.[2]

90 As I would question all, come all who can;
Come old, necessitous, half-mounted man;
And bring beauty's blind rambling celebrant;
The red man the juggler sent
Through God-forsaken meadows; Mrs. French,

95 Gifted with so fine an ear;
The man drowned in a bog's mire,
When mocking Muses chose the country wench.

Did all old men and women, rich and poor,
Who trod upon these rocks or passed this door,
100 Whether in public or in secret rage
As I do now against old age?
But I have found an answer in those eyes
That are impatient to be gone;
Go therefore; but leave Hanrahan,
105 For I need all his mighty memories.

Old lecher with a love on every wind,
Bring up out of that deep considering mind
All that you have discovered in the grave,
For it is certain that you have
110 Reckoned up every unforeknown, unseeing
Plunge, lured by a softening eye,
Or by a touch or a sigh,
Into the labyrinth of another's being;

Does the imagination dwell the most
115 Upon a woman won or woman lost?
If on the lost, admit you turned aside
From a great labyrinth out of pride,
Cowardice, some silly over-subtle thought
Or anything called conscience once;
120 And that if memory recur, the sun's
Under eclipse and the day blotted out.

3
It is time that I wrote my will;
I choose upstanding men
That climb the streams until
125 The fountain leap, and at dawn
Drop their cast at the side
Of dripping stone; I declare
They shall inherit my pride,
The pride of people that were
130 Bound neither to Cause nor to State,
Neither to slaves that were spat on,
Nor to the tyrants that spat,

[1] [Yeats's note] Hanrahan's pursuit of the phantom hare and hounds is from my *Stories of Red Hanrahan*.

[2] [Yeats's note] The ghosts have been seen at their game of dice in what is now my bedroom, and the old bankrupt man lived about a hundred years ago. According to one legend he could only leave the Castle upon a Sunday because of his creditors, and according to another he hid in the secret passage.

The people of Burke and of Grattan[1]
That gave, though free to refuse—
135 Pride, like that of the morn,
When the headlong light is loose,
Or that of the fabulous horn,[2]
Or that of the sudden shower
When all streams are dry,
140 Or that of the hour
When the swan must fix his eye
Upon a fading gleam,
Float out upon a long
Last reach of glittering stream
145 And there sing his last song.[3]
And I declare my faith:
I mock Plotinus' thought
And cry in Plato's teeth,
Death and life were not
150 Till man made up the whole,
Made lock, stock and barrel
Out of his bitter soul,
Aye, sun and moon and star, all,
And further add to that
155 That, being dead, we rise,
Dream and so create
Translunar Paradise.
I have prepared my peace
With learned Italian things
160 And the proud stones of Greece,
Poet's imaginings
And memories of love,
Memories of the words of women,
All those things whereof
165 Man makes a superhuman
Mirror-resembling dream.

As at the loophole there

The daws° chatter and scream,   *crows*
And drop twigs layer upon layer.
170 When they have mounted up,
The mother bird will rest
On their hollow top,
And so warm her wild nest.

I leave both faith and pride
175 To young upstanding men
Climbing the mountain-side,
That under bursting dawn
They may drop a fly;
Being of that metal made
180 Till it was broken by
This sedentary trade.

Now shall I make my soul,
Compelling it to study
In a learned school
185 Till the wreck of body,
Slow decay of blood,
Testy delirium
Or dull decrepitude,
Or what worse evil come—
190 The death of friends, or death
Of every brilliant eye
That made a catch in the breath—
Seem but the clouds of the sky
When the horizon fades;
195 Or a bird's sleepy cry
Among the deepening shades.
—1927

---

1 *Burke* Edmund Burke (1729–97), political writer and statesman; *Grattan* Henry Grattan (1746–1820), Protestant Member of the Irish House of Commons, who opposed efforts to unite Ireland with Great Britain. Both men supported Catholic relief and emancipation.

2 *fabulous horn* Horn of Plenty.

3 [Yeats's note] I have unconsciously echoed one of the loveliest lyrics of our time—Mr. Sturge Moore's "Dying Swan." I often recited it during an American lecturing tour, which explains the theft.

A Dialogue of Self and Soul

I

My Soul. I summon to the winding ancient stair;
Set all your mind upon the steep ascent,
Upon the broken, crumbling battlement,
Upon the breathless starlit air,
5 Upon the star that marks the hidden pole;
Fix every wandering thought upon
That quarter where all thought is done:
Who can distinguish darkness from the soul?

My Self. The consecrated blade upon my knees
10   Is Sato's ancient blade,[1] still as it was,
Still razor-keen, still like a looking-glass
Unspotted by the centuries;
That flowering, silken, old embroidery, torn
From some court-lady's dress and round
15   The wooden scabbard bound and wound
Can, tattered, still protect, faded adorn.

My Soul. Why should the imagination of a man
Long past his prime remember things that are
Emblematical of love and war?
20   Think of ancestral night that can,
If but imagination scorn the earth
And intellect is wandering
To this and that and t'other thing,
Deliver from the crime of death and birth.

25   *My Self.* Montashigi,[2] third of his family, fashioned it
Five hundred years ago, about it lie
Flowers from I know not what embroidery—
Heart's purple—and all these I set
For emblems of the day against the tower
30   Emblematical of the night,
And claim as by a soldier's right
A charter to commit the crime once more.

My Soul. Such fullness in that quarter overflows
And falls into the basin of the mind
35   That man is stricken deaf and dumb and blind,
For intellect no longer knows
Is from the *Ought,* or *Knower* from the *Known*—
That is to say, ascends to Heaven;
Only the dead can be forgiven;
40   But when I think of that my tongue's a stone.

2

My Self. A living man is blind and drinks his drop.
What matter if the ditches are impure?
What matter if I live it all once more?
Endure that toil of growing up;
45   The ignominy of boyhood; the distress

Of boyhood changing into man;
The unfinished man and his pain
Brought face to face with his own clumsiness;

The finished man among his enemies?—
50   How in the name of Heaven can he escape
That defiling and disfigured shape
The mirror of malicious eyes
Casts upon his eyes until at last
He thinks that shape must be his shape?
55   And what's the good of an escape
If honour find him in the wintry blast?

I am content to live it all again
And yet again, if it be life to pitch
Into the frog-spawn of a blind man's ditch,
60   A blind man battering blind men;
Or into that most fecund ditch of all,
The folly that man does
Or must suffer, if he woos
A proud woman not kindred of his soul.

65   I am content to follow to its source
Every event in action or in thought;
Measure the lot; forgive myself the lot!
When such as I cast out remorse
So great a sweetness flows into the breast
70   We must laugh and we must sing,
We are blest by everything,
Everything we look upon is blest.
—1929

Byzantium[3]

The unpurged images of day recede;
   The Emperor's drunken soldiery are abed;
Night resonance recedes, night walkers'[4] song

---

1   *Sato's ancient blade*   Japanese sword given to Yeats in 1920 by his friend Junzo Sato.

2   *Montashigi*   Swordmaker.

3   *Byzantium*   Constantinople (today, Istanbul); Yeats recorded "the subject for a poem" in his diary of 1930: "Describe Byzantium as it is in the system towards the end of the first Christian millennium… Flames at the street corners where the soul is purified, birds of hammered gold singing in the golden trees, in the harbour [dolphins] offering their backs to the wailing dead that they may carry them to Paradise."

4   *night walkers*   Prostitutes.

After great cathedral gong;[1]
5 A starlit or a moonlit dome disdains
All that man is,
All mere complexities,
The fury and the mire of human veins.

Before me floats an image, man or shade,
10 Shade more than man, more image than a shade;
For Hades'[2] bobbin° bound in mummy-cloth   *spool*
May unwind the winding path;
A mouth that has no moisture and no breath
Breathless mouths may summon;
15 I hail the superhuman;
I call it death-in-life and life-in-death.[3]

Miracle, bird or golden handiwork,
More miracle than bird or handiwork,
Planted on the star-lit golden bough,
20 Can like the cocks of Hades crow,[4]
Or, by the moon embittered, scorn aloud
In glory of changeless metal
Common bird or petal
And all complexities of mire or blood.

25 At midnight on the Emperor's pavement flit
Flames that no faggot feeds, nor steel has lit,
Nor storm disturbs, flames begotten of flame,
Where blood-begotten spirits come
And all complexities of fury leave,
30 Dying into a dance,
An agony of trance,
An agony of flame that cannot singe a sleeve.

Astraddle on the dolphin's mire and blood,[5]
Spirit after spirit! The smithies break the flood,
35 The golden smithies of the Emperor!
Marbles of the dancing floor
Break bitter furies of complexity,
Those images that yet
Fresh images beget,
40 That dolphin-torn, that gong-tormented sea.
—1930

For Anne Gregory [6]

"Never shall a young man,
Thrown into despair
By those great honey-coloured
Ramparts at your ear,
5 Love you for yourself alone
And not your yellow hair."

"But I can get a hair-dye
And set such colour there,
Brown, or black, or carrot,
10 That young men in despair
May love me for myself alone
And not my yellow hair."

"I heard an old religious man
But yesternight declare
15 That he had found a text to prove
That only God, my dear,
Could love you for yourself alone
And not your yellow hair."
—1932

[1] *great cathedral* Church of St. Sophia, built in Byzantium by the emperor Justinian I in 532–37.

[2] *Hades* Greek god of the underworld.

[3] *death-in-life and life-in-death* Cf. Tennyson's "Tears, Idle Tears," 20: "O Death in Life" and Coleridge's *The Rime of the Ancient Mariner* 3.193: "The Nightmare LIFE-IN-DEATH was she."

[4] *the cocks of Hades crow* Because cocks symbolized rebirth and resurrection, they appeared on Roman tombstones as a sign of the continuation of human life.

[5] *Astraddle ... blood* According to Neoplatonism, dolphins symbolize the soul in transition, as they transport the recently departed to the Islands of the Blest.

[6] *Anne Gregory* Granddaughter of Lady Gregory, well-known figure of the Irish literary revival and close friend of Yeats.

Crazy Jane Talks with the Bishop

I met the Bishop on the road
And much said he and I.
"Those breasts are flat and fallen now,
Those veins must soon be dry;
5   Live in a heavenly mansion,
Not in some foul sty."

"Fair and foul are near of kin,
And fair needs foul," I cried.
"My friends are gone, but that's a truth
10 Nor grave nor bed denied,
Learned in bodily lowliness
And in the heart's pride.

"A woman can be proud and stiff
When on love intent;
15 But Love has pitched his mansion in
The place of excrement;
For nothing can be sole or whole
That has not been rent."
        —1933

Lapis Lazuli [1]
(For Harry Clifton) [2]

I have heard that hysterical women say
They are sick of the palette and fiddle-bow,
Of poets that are always gay,
For everybody knows or else should know
5   That if nothing drastic is done
Aeroplane and Zeppelin [3] will come out,

Pitch like King Billy bomb-balls [4] in
Until the town lie beaten flat.

All perform their tragic play,
10 There struts Hamlet, there is Lear,
That's Ophelia, that Cordelia; [5]
Yet they, should the last scene be there,
The great stage curtain about to drop,
If worthy their prominent part in the play,
15 Do not break up their lines to weep.
They know that Hamlet and Lear are gay;
Gaiety transfiguring all that dread.
All men have aimed at, found and lost;
Black out; Heaven blazing into the head:
20 Tragedy wrought to its uttermost.
Though Hamlet rambles and Lear rages,
And all the drop-scenes drop at once
Upon a hundred thousand stages,
It cannot grow by an inch or an ounce.

25 On their own feet they came, or on shipboard,
Camel-back, horse-back, ass-back, mule-back,
Old civilisations put to the sword.
Then they and their wisdom went to rack:
No handiwork of Callimachus, [6]
30 Who handled marble as if it were bronze,
Made draperies that seemed to rise
When sea-wind swept the corner, stands;
His long lamp-chimney shaped like the stem
Of a slender palm, stood but a day;
35 All things fall and are built again,
And those that build them again are gay.

---

[1] *Lapis Lazuli* Yeats received a carving made of lapis lazuli (semiprecious blue stone) on his birthday, 13 June 1935. Yeats described the stone in a letter to Dorothy Wellesley (English poet and friend): "Ascetic, pupil, hard stone, eternal theme of the sensual east. The heroic cry in the midst of despair. But no, I am wrong, the east has its solutions always and therefore knows nothing of tragedy. It is we, not the east, that must raise the heroic cry."

[2] *Harry Clifton* Yeats's apprentice, who gave the elder poet a gift made of lapis lazuli for his seventieth birthday.

[3] *Zeppelin* German airship used to bomb London during World War I; in 1938 another war with Germany seemed imminent.

[4] *King Billy bomb-balls* King William III (William of Orange) overcame the soldiers of the deposed king James II at the Battle of the Boyne in Ireland, 1690. An anonymous ballad describes the fight: "King William he threw his bomb-balls in, / And set them on fire." Also a nickname for Kaiser Wilhelm, German emperor and king of Prussia during World War I.

[5] *There struts ... Cordelia* References to tragedies by Shakespeare: *Hamlet* tells the story of the death of Ophelia, beloved of Prince Hamlet, and then of Hamlet himself; *King Lear* tells of the death first of Lear's daughter Cordelia, then of Lear himself.

[6] *Callimachus* Greek sculptor of the fifth century BCE.

Two Chinamen, behind them a third,
Are carved in lapis lazuli,
Over them flies a long-legged bird,
40 A symbol of longevity;
The third, doubtless a serving-man,
Carries a musical instrument.

Every discoloration of the stone,
Every accidental crack or dent,
45 Seems a water-course or an avalanche,
Or lofty slope where it still snows
Though doubtless plum or cherry-branch
Sweetens the little half-way house
Those Chinamen climb towards, and I
50 Delight to imagine them seated there;
There, on the mountain and the sky,
On all the tragic scene they stare.
One asks for mournful melodies;
Accomplished fingers begin to play.
55 Their eyes mid many wrinkles, their eyes,
Their ancient, glittering eyes, are gay.
—1938

The Circus Animals' Desertion

1

I sought a theme and sought for it in vain,
I sought it daily for six weeks or so.
Maybe at last, being but a broken man,
I must be satisfied with my heart, although
5 Winter and summer till old age began
My circus animals were all on show,
Those stilted boys, that burnished chariot,[1]
Lion and woman and the Lord knows what.

2

What can I but enumerate old themes?
10 First that sea-rider Oisín[2] led by the nose

Through three enchanted islands, allegorical dreams,
Vain gaiety, vain battle, vain repose,
Themes of the embittered heart, or so it seems,
That might adorn old songs or courtly shows;
15 But what cared I that set him on to ride,
I, starved for the bosom of his faery bride?

And then a counter-truth filled out its play,
The Countess Cathleen[3] was the name I gave it;
She, pity-crazed, had given her soul away,
20 But masterful Heaven had intervened to save it.
I thought my dear must her own soul destroy,
So did fanaticism and hate enslave it,
And this brought forth a dream and soon enough
This dream itself had all my thought and love.

25 And when the Fool and Blind Man stole the bread
Cuchulain fought the ungovernable sea;[4]
Heart-mysteries there, and yet when all is said
It was the dream itself enchanted me:
Character isolated by a deed
30 To engross the present and dominate memory.
Players and painted stage took all my love,
And not those things that they were emblems of.

3

Those masterful images because complete
Grew in pure mind, but out of what began?
35 A mound of refuse or the sweepings of a street,
Old kettles, old bottles, and a broken can,
Old iron, old bones, old rags, that raving slut[5]
Who keeps the till. Now that my ladder's gone,

---

returns to Ireland 150 years later he finds his friends dead and his country converted to Christianity.

[3] *The Countess Cathleen* Play written by Yeats in 1892; an Irish countess, modeled on the Irish activist Maud Gonne, sells her soul to the devil to save the starving peasantry, but in the end is saved by God for her magnanimous motives.

[4] *And when ... sea* In Yeats's play *On Baile's Strand* (1904), Cuchulain goes mad after he discovers that he has killed his own son. He runs out to the sea to fight the waves; meanwhile, the fool and the blind man steal bread from the ovens of the townspeople watching Cuchulain's sea-battle.

[5] *slut* Foul or unkempt woman. (Here the word has no connotation of sexual looseness.)

[1] *Those stilted ... chariot* Yeats may be alluding to the ancient Irish heroes of his first works; the chariot may refer to the carriage built on the stage of his play, *The Unicorn from the Stars* (1908).

[2] *Oisín* Irish warrior of Yeats's *The Wanderings of Oisín* (1889); Oisín is led by the fairy, Niamh, to three islands—called Delight, Many Fears, Forgetfulness—purported to be paradisiacal. When he

I must lie down where all the ladders start,
40 In the foul rag-and-bone shop of the heart.
—1939

Under Ben Bulben[1]

Swear by what the sages spoke
Round the Mareotic Lake[2]
That the Witch of Atlas[3] knew,
Spoke and set the cocks a-crow.
5 Swear by those horsemen, by those women
Complexion and form prove superhuman,
That pale, long-visaged company
That air an immortality
Completeness of their passions won;
10 Now they ride the wintry dawn[4]
Where Ben Bulben sets the scene.
Here's the gist of what they mean.

2

Many times man lives and dies
Between his two eternities,
15 That of race and that of soul,
And ancient Ireland knew it all.
Whether man die in his bed
Or the rifle knocks him dead,
A brief parting from those dear
20 Is the worst man has to fear.
Though grave-diggers' toil is long,
Sharp their spades, their muscles strong,
They but thrust their buried men
Back in the human mind again.

3

25 You that Mitchel's prayer have heard,
"Send war in our time, O Lord!"[5]
Know that when all words are said
And a man is fighting mad,
Something drops from eyes long blind,
30 He completes his partial mind,
For an instant stands at ease,
Laughs aloud, his heart at peace.
Even the wisest man grows tense
With some sort of violence
35 Before he can accomplish fate,
Know his work or choose his mate.

4

Poet and sculptor, do the work,
Nor let the modish painter shirk
What his great forefathers did.
40 Bring the soul of man to God,
Make him fill the cradles right.
Measurement began our might:
Forms a stark Egyptian thought,[6]
Forms that gentler Phidias[7] wrought.
45 Michelangelo[8] left a proof
On the Sistine Chapel roof,
Where but half-awakened Adam
Can disturb globe-trotting Madam
Till her bowels are in heat,
50 Proof that there's a purpose set
Before the secret working mind:
Profane perfection of mankind.
Quattrocento[9] put in paint

---

[1] *Ben Bulben*   Mountain in County Sligo; Yeats is buried within sight of the mountain at Drumcliff Churchyard.

[2] *Mareotic Lake*   Lake Mareotis, south of Alexandria in Egypt, was associated with the Christian Neoplatonists and the rise of Christian monasticism.

[3] *the Witch of Atlas*   Cf. Percy Bysshe Shelley's poem "The Witch of Atlas": "By Moeris and the Mareotid lakes / ... / The shadows of the massy temples lie, / And never are erased—but tremble ever" (505–15).

[4] *those horsemen ... wintry dawn*   The Sidhe, the fairy people of ancient Irish mythology, who were said to ride through the country on the wind.

[5] *Mitchel's prayer ... O Lord*   John Mitchel (1815–75) was an Irish nationalist imprisoned for his activism; in *Jail Journal* he wrote: "Give us war in our time, O Lord!," a play on the Book of Common Prayer's "Give us peace in our time, O Lord."

[6] *stark Egyptian thought*   Possibly that of Plotinus, Egyptian philosopher of the third century BCE who founded Neoplatonism.

[7] *Phidias*   Greek sculptor of the fifth century BCE.

[8] *Michelangelo*   Michelangelo Buonarroti (1475–1564), Italian Renaissance artist.

[9] *Quattrocentro*   Fifteenth century; by extension, the Italian Renaissance art for which the century is famous.

On backgrounds for a God or Saint
55 Gardens where a soul's at ease;
Where everything that meets the eye,
Flowers and grass and cloudless sky,
Resemble forms that are or seem
When sleepers wake and yet still dream,
60 And when it's vanished still declare,
With only bed and bedstead there,
That heavens had opened.
    Gyres[1] run on;
When that greater dream had gone
65 Calvert and Wilson, Blake and Claude,[2]
Prepared a rest for the people of God,[3]
Palmer's phrase,[4] but after that
Confusion fell upon our thought.

5

Irish poets, learn your trade,
70 Sing whatever is well made,
Scorn the sort now growing up
All out of shape from toe to top,

Their unremembering hearts and heads
Base-born products of base beds.
75 Sing the peasantry, and then
Hard-riding country gentlemen,
The holiness of monks, and after
Porter-drinkers' randy laughter;
Sing the lords and ladies gay
80 That were beaten into the clay
Through seven heroic centuries;
Cast your mind on other days
That we in coming days may be
Still the indomitable Irishry.

6

85 Under bare Ben Bulben's head
In Drumcliff churchyard Yeats is laid.
An ancestor[5] was rector there
Long years ago, a church stands near,
By the road an ancient cross.
90 No marble, no conventional phrase;
On limestone quarried near the spot
By his command these words are cut:
    Cast a cold eye
    On life, on death.
95   *Horseman, pass by!*[6]
    —1939

[1] *Gyres* Spirals formed from concentric circles.

[2] *Calvert* Edward Calvert (1799–1883), English wood-engraver and painter, a follower of William Blake; *Wilson* Richard Wilson (1714–82), English landscape painter; *Blake* William Blake (1757–1827), English poet and artist; *Claude* Claude Lorrain (1600–82), French landscape artist.

[3] *a rest ... God* From Hebrews 4.9: "There remaineth therefore a rest to the people of God."

[4] *Palmer's phrase* Samuel Palmer (1805–81), an English artist, used the phrase from Hebrews to describe Blake's illustrations as "a drawing aside of the fleshly curtain, and the glimpse which all the most holy, studious saints and sages have enjoyed, of the rest which remains to the people of God."

[5] *An ancestor* Yeats's great-grandfather, the Reverend John Yeats (1774–1846).

[6] *Cast ... pass by* Initially buried in France, where he died, Yeats was reinterred at Drumcliff Churchyard in 1948; on his tombstone are engraved these final lines.

IN CONTEXT

The Struggle for Irish Independence

The leaders of the Easter Rebellion, the failed Irish nationalist uprising of 1916, issued the following document, written and read by Pádraic Pearse, upon their occupation of the Dublin General Post Office. (For an overview of historical developments, see the Introduction to this volume, pp. LV–LVII.)

Poblacht na h-Eireann[1] / *Proclamation of the Irish Republic* (Easter 1916)

THE PROVISIONAL GOVERNMENT OF THE IRISH REPUBLIC TO THE PEOPLE OF IRELAND

Irishmen and Irishwomen:

In the name of God and of the dead generations from which she receives her old tradition of nationhood, Ireland, through us, summons her children to her flag and strikes for her freedom. Having organised and trained her manhood through her secret revolutionary organisation, the Irish Republican Brotherhood, and through her open military organisations, the Irish Volunteers and the Irish Citizen Army, having patiently perfected her discipline, having resolutely waited for the right moment to reveal itself, she now seizes that moment, and, supported by her exiled children in America and by gallant allies in Europe, but relying in the first on her own strength, she strikes in full confidence of victory.

We declare the right of the people of Ireland to the ownership of Ireland, and to the unfettered control of Irish destinies, to be sovereign and indefeasible. The long usurpation of that right by a foreign people and government has not extinguished the right, nor can it ever be extinguished except by the destruction of the Irish people. In every generation the Irish have asserted their right to national freedom and sovereignty; six times during the past three hundred years they have asserted it in arms. Standing on that fundamental right and again asserting it in arms in the face of the world, we hereby proclaim the Irish Republic as a Sovereign Independent State, and we pledge our lives and the lives of our comrades-in-arms to the cause of its freedom, of its welfare, and of its exaltation among the nations.

The Irish Republic is entitled to, and hereby claims, the allegiance of every Irishman and Irishwoman. The Republic guarantees religious and civil liberty, equal rights and equal opportunities to all its citizens, and declares its resolve to pursue the happiness and prosperity of the whole nation and of all its parts, cherishing all the children of the nation equally, and oblivious of the differences carefully fostered by an alien government, which have divided a minority from the majority in the past.

Until our arms have brought the opportune moment for the establishment of a permanent National Government, representative of the whole people of Ireland and elected by the suffrages of all her men and women, the Provisional Government, hereby constituted, will administer the civil and military affairs of the Republic in trust for the people.

We place the cause of the Irish Republic under the protection of the Most High God, Whose blessing we invoke upon our arms, and we pray that no one who serves that cause will dishonor it by

---

[1] *Poblacht na h-Eireann* Irish Republic.

cowardice, inhumanity, or rapine.[1] In this supreme hour the Irish nation must, by its valour and discipline and by the readiness of its children to sacrifice themselves for the common good, prove itself worthy of the august destiny to which it is called.

Signed on Behalf of the Provisional Government,

Thomas J. Clarke,
Sean MacDiarmada,
Thomas MacDonagh,
P.H. Pearse,
Eamonn Ceannt,
James Connolly,
Joseph Plunkett.

Pádraic Pearse, Statement (1916)

Pádraic Pearse (1879–1916) was a poet and politician who fought for Irish independence. He was one of the leaders of the failed Easter Rebellion of 1916, in which Irish nationalists took arms against British rule. Pearse was taken prisoner during the uprising and was executed by a firing squad soon after delivering this statement.

The following is the substance of what I said when asked today by the President of the Court-Martial at Richmond Barracks whether I had anything to say in my defence:

I desire, in the first place, to repeat what I have already said in letters to General Maxwell and Brigadier General Lowe. My object in agreeing to an unconditional surrender was to prevent the further slaughter of the civil population of Dublin and to save the lives of our gallant fellows, who, having made for six days a stand unparalleled in military history, were now surrounded, and in the case of those under the immediate command of H.Q., without food. I fully understand now, as then, that my own life is forfeit to British law, and I shall die very cheerfully if I can think that the British Government, as it has already shown itself strong, will now show itself magnanimous enough to accept my single life in forfeiture and to give a general amnesty to the brave men and boys who have fought at my bidding.

In the second place, I wish it to be understood that any admissions I make here are to be taken as involving myself alone. They do not involve and must not be used against anyone who acted with me, not even those who may have set their names to documents with me. (The Court assented to this.)

I admit that I was Commandant-General Commanding-in-Chief of the forces of the Irish Republic which have been acting against you for the past week, and that I was President of the Provisional Government. I stand over all my acts and words done or spoken, in these capacities. When I was a child of ten I went on my bare knees by my bedside one night and promised God that I should devote my life to an effort to free my country. I have kept the promise. I have helped to organize, to arm, to train, and to discipline my fellow countrymen to the sole end that, when the time came, they might fight for Irish freedom. The time, as it seemed to me, did come, and we went into the fight. I am glad we did, we seem to have lost, but we have not lost. To refuse to fight would have been to lose, to fight is to win; we have kept faith with the past, and handed on a tradition to the future. I repudiate the assertion of the prosecutor that I sought to aid and abet England's enemy.

---

[1] *rapine* Robbery.

Germany is no more to me than England is. I asked and accepted German aid in the shape of arms and an expeditionary force; we neither asked for nor accepted German gold, nor had any traffic with Germany but what I state. My object was to win Irish freedom. We struck the first blow ourselves, but I should have been glad of an ally's aid.

I assume that I am speaking to Englishmen who value their freedom and who profess to be fighting for the freedom of Belgium and Serbia; believe that we too love freedom and desire it. To us it is more desirable than anything in the world. If you strike us down now we shall rise again and renew the fight; you cannot conquer Ireland, you cannot extinguish the Irish passion for freedom; if our deed has not been sufficient to win freedom, then our children will win it by a better deed.

VIRGINIA WOOLF
1882 – 1941

A towering figure in the history of twentieth-century feminist thought, Virginia Woolf also occupies a central place in the development of the twentieth-century novel. Woolf, along with contemporaries such as James Joyce and Dorothy Richardson, rejected the traditional conventions of fiction, which included narrative coherence, omniscient narration, and emphasis on external settings and events. Instead, she explored the everyday, internal lives of her characters in a style—often called stream-of-consciousness—that mimics the flow of her characters' thoughts. In her fiction and essays alike, she examined the ways in which social roles and values are constructed and the effects these have on the lives and interactions of individuals.

Virginia Woolf was born Adeline Virginia Stephen, the third child of an illustrious, upper-middle-class London family. Her father, Leslie Stephen, a philosopher and literary critic, was primarily known as editor of the *Dictionary of National Biography* and President of the London Library. Her mother, born Julia Jackson, had been married into the Duckworth publishing family, and then married Stephen some time after the death of her first husband. Deeply connected to Victorian literary circles, the Stephen family included among its friends Henry James, Matthew Arnold, and George Eliot. From childhood, Woolf was drown to a literary career, and her father in particular encouraged her, as she says, "to read what one liked because one liked it, never to pretend to admire what one did not. … To write in the fewest possible words, as clearly as possible, exactly what one meant."

Surrounded by her father's impressive library, Woolf immersed herself in the study of languages and literary classics. While her brothers Thoby and Adrian went to public schools and eventually to university at Cambridge, Woolf and her sister Vanessa were educated at home by their father and private tutors. The lack of formal education for women would become a pervasive issue in Woolf's novels and later essays such as *A Room of One's Own* (1929) and *Three Guineas* (1938). A frequent exploration into the emotional effects of death in her later writing would also stem from Woolf's youthful experience. In 1895, her mother died of influenza; a few months later, at the age of thirteen, Woolf suffered a mental breakdown, symptoms of which included hearing voices, avoiding food, and experiencing extreme anxiety. Her mother's death was followed by that of her beloved half-sister and maternal substitute, Stella Duckworth, in childbirth, and then by that of her father, from cancer, in 1904. A second breakdown resulted. These breakdowns were harbingers of Woolf's lifelong struggle with manic and depressive episodes, which were generally brought about by stress—such as the emotional and mental anxiety that accompanied the completion of a book.

Despite Woolf's emotional turmoil in the year following her father's death, the event freed her from her family's inhibiting influence and facilitated her emergence amongst London's intelligentsia. With an unsigned review, she received her first publication in *The Guardian*, and against her extended family's attempts to introduce her into polite society, Woolf and several of her siblings moved to the Bloomsbury area of London. There they began associating with her brother Thoby's Cambridge friends, and what began as a social gathering of casual friends for drinks and conversation eventually came to be known as the Bloomsbury Group, a cultural circle bound together by an intense interest in current literary, philosophical, artistic, sexual, and political issues. Its members included novelist E.M. Forster, biographer and essayist Lytton Strachey, painter Duncan Grant, art critics Roger Fry and Clive Bell (the future husband of Woolf's sister Vanessa), economist John Maynard Keynes, and political theorist Leonard Woolf. Although Thoby Stephen died of typhoid in 1906, the group continued to meet throughout Woolf's lifetime. It attracted a certain amount of controversy as a result of the new ideas (particularly concerning sexuality) and frank artistic expression it fostered, and also because of the class snobbery it was perceived to exhibit (to the extent that the word *Bloomsbury* later became widely used to connote an insular and patronizing aestheticism).

In 1912, Virginia Stephen married Leonard Woolf, who throughout her life provided her with the time, encouragement, and emotional support necessary for her to continue writing as she alternated between periods of stability and intense productivity and episodes of immobilizing emotional collapse. In 1915, *The Voyage Out*, Woolf's first major novel, was published, introducing her readers for the first time to the character of Clarissa Dalloway, whom Woolf would make central to her later novel *Mrs. Dalloway* (1925). *The Voyage Out* and its successor, *Night and Day* (1919), are Woolf's most conventional works.

In 1917, Woolf and her husband Leonard bought a hand press and established Hogarth Press at their London home, intending to publish their own works and those of their friends. The Hogarth Press soon became a highly successful enterprise, publishing the early works of authors such as E.M. Forster, Katherine Mansfield, and T.S. Eliot, as well as English translations of the works of Sigmund Freud.

Woolf's 1922 novel, *Jacob's Room*, based on the life and death of Woolf's brother Thoby, represented a stylistic breakthrough for her. In this novel, she tried an entirely different approach, ignoring much of the framework of external events and descriptions present in her earlier work. In this novel, she said, there was "no scaffolding; scarcely a brick to be seen; all crepuscular." By 1925, Woolf had completed *Mrs. Dalloway*, the culmination of many years' experimentation with narrative technique. Originally titled *The House*, *Mrs. Dalloway* takes place in a twenty-four hour period in London, and explores the subjectivities of characters who never meet, but whose observations, experiences, and memories reveal a curious kinship between them. Describing her new method of characterization, Woolf said, "I dig out beautiful caves behind my characters.... The idea is that the caves shall connect and each come to daylight at the present moment."

In Woolf's next novel, *To the Lighthouse* (1927), Woolf further developed her stream-of-consciousness style, relying heavily on imagery and rich symbolism to convey meaning. Divided into three distinct parts that take place against the backdrop of ordinary domestic events, the novel experiments with the passage of time through the consciousness of its various characters. By alternating between various viewpoints, Woolf demonstrates how rare, tenuous, and fleeting the moments of real connection between people are.

In 1929, Woolf's best-known work of non-fiction was published. Originally constructed as lecture notes for talks to be given at Newnham and Girton Colleges at Cambridge, the work was expanded and published as *A Room of One's Own*. The essay, which has become a foundational text of literary feminism, explores the traditional barriers and prejudices faced by women writers. At the core of Woolf's argument is her conclusion that a woman must have financial independence and privacy (a room of her own) if she is to write fiction successfully. In presenting the concept of the androgynous mind, Woolf also provides insight into her own literary process. As defined by Woolf, the successful author of whatever sex must possess the ability to draw creative forces from all facets of his or her emotional and intellectual being—regardless of whether these facets are traditionally classified as "masculine" or "feminine." To do so, the author must move beyond any awareness of his or her own gender role as dictated by social customs; as Woolf says, "It is fatal for anyone who writes to think of their sex." In her novel of the previous year, *Orlando*, Woolf had celebrated what she saw as the androgynous creative mind of her friend Vita Sackville-West. Subtitled *A Biography*, *Orlando* plays overtly with the form of genre as Woolf follows her main character—who is able to change sex as the times and his or her desires demanded—across several hundred years of British history.

For the next twelve years, Woolf continued to pursue more radical experiments with form while developing her ideas about writing, genre, and gender roles in numerous essays (most of which are collected in two volumes of her *Common Readers*). Woolf's next novel, *The Waves* (1931), is a poem-novel written "to a rhythm and not to a plot" that focuses on the mutability of life. In 1938, Woolf extended the feminist critique of male privilege begun in *A Room of One's Own* with *Three Guineas*, which implicitly links the values of patriarchal society with those of fascism. Less popular at the time than its predecessor, *Three Guineas*, and the pacifism is advocates, have found a more receptive audience in the later twentieth and early twenty-first centuries.

Just as *The Waves* sought to combine poetry and the novel, Woolf described her 1937 work, *The Years*, as an "essay-novel," and her final novel, *Between the Acts* (1941), is something of a drama-novel, focusing on the audience reception of an amateur pageant that takes place as the threat of war is imminent. Woolf herself, discouraged by the progress of World War II and its implications for herself and her Jewish husband, and dreading the critical reception this work would receive, faced another emotional breakdown. Before she could complete the revisions of *Between the Acts*, she began to feel mental illness engulf her. She composed a note to her husband explaining that she felt that this time she would not recover, filled her pockets with stones, and drowned herself in the River Ouse near her home.

Throughout her lifetime, Woolf was offered numerous honors, all of which she refused because of her avowed contempt for patriarchal society. After declining an honorary degree from Manchester University, she wrote in her diary, "It is an utterly corrupt society …, and I will take nothing that it can give me." She did not want to be condescended to or used as a "token woman." Nevertheless, the honors continued to be offered, and, after her death, the loss of her unique vision and style were greatly mourned. She has since been hailed as a pioneer of the modernist novel, a central early figure in the development of feminist theory, and a central figure in the twentieth-century world of letters. Her personal diaries and letters, published posthumously in several volumes, provide unique insight into her aims as an artist and her intellectual development in a remarkable literary and artistic milieu.

⌘ ⌘ ⌘

The Mark on the Wall

Perhaps it was the middle of January in the present year that I first looked up and saw the mark on the wall. In order to fix a date it is necessary to remember what one saw. So now I think of the fire; the steady film of yellow light upon the page of my book; the three chrysanthemums in the round glass bowl on the mantelpiece. Yes, it must have been the winter time, and we had just finished our tea, for I remember that I was smoking a cigarette when I looked up and saw the mark on the wall for the first time. I looked up through the smoke of my cigarette and my eye lodged for a moment upon the burning coals, and that old fancy of the crimson flag flapping from the castle tower came into my mind, and I thought of the cavalcade of red knights riding up the side of the black rock. Rather to my relief the sight of the mark interrupted the fancy, for it is an old fancy, an automatic fancy, made as a child perhaps. The mark was a small round mark, black upon the white wall, about six or seven inches above the mantelpiece.

How readily our thoughts swarm upon a new object, lifting it a little way, as ants carry a blade of straw so feverishly, and then leave it…. If that mark was made by a nail, it can't have been for a picture, it must have been for a miniature—the miniature of a lady with white powdered curls, powder-dusted cheeks, and lips like red carnations. A fraud of course, for the people who had this house before us would have chosen pictures in that way—an old picture for an old room. That is the sort of people they were—very interesting people, and I think of them so often, in such queer places, because one will never see them again, never know what happened next. They wanted to leave this house because they wanted to change their style of furniture, so he said, and he was in process of saying that in his opinion art should have ideas behind it when we were torn asunder, as one is torn from the old lady about to pour out tea and the young man about to hit the tennis ball in the back garden of the suburban villa as one rushes past in the train.

But as for that mark, I'm not sure about it; I don't believe it was made by a nail after all; it's too big, too round, for that. I might get up, but if I got up and looked at it, ten to one I shouldn't be able to say for certain; because once a thing's done, no one ever knows how it happened. Oh! dear me, the mystery of life! The inaccuracy of thought! The ignorance of humanity! To show how very little control of our possessions we have—what an accidental affair this living is after all our civilization—let me just count over a few of the things lost in our lifetime, beginning, for that seems always the most mysterious of losses—what cat would gnaw, what rat would nibble—three pale blue canisters of book-binding tools? Then there were the bird cages, the iron hoops, the steel skates, the Queen Anne coal-scuttle, the bagatelle board,[1] the hand organ—all gone, and jewels too. Opals and emeralds, they lie about the roots of turnips. What a scraping paring affair it is to be sure! The wonder is that I've any clothes on my back, that I sit surrounded by solid furniture at this moment. Why, if one wants to compare life to anything, one must liken it to being blown through the Tube[2] at fifty miles an hour—landing at the other end without a single hairpin in one's hair! Shot out at the feet of God entirely naked!

Tumbling head over heels in the asphodel[3] meadows like brown paper parcels pitched down a shoot in the post office! With one's hair flying back like the tail of a racehorse. Yes, that seems to express the rapidity of life, the perpetual waste and repair; all so casual, all so haphazard.…

But after life. The slow pulling down of thick green stalks so that the cup of the flower, as it turns over, deluges one with purple and red light. Why, after all, should one not be born there as one is born here, helpless, speechless, unable to focus one's eyesight, groping at the roots of the grass, at the toes of the Giants? As for saying which are trees, and which are men and women, or whether there are such things, that one won't be in a condition to do for fifty years or so. There will be nothing but spaces of light and dark, intersected by thick stalks, and rather higher up perhaps, rose-shaped blots of an indistinct colour—dim pinks and blues—which will, as time goes on, become more definite, become—I don't know what.…

And yet the mark on the wall is not a hole at all. It may even be caused by some round black substance, such as a small rose leaf, left over from the summer, and I, not being a very vigilant housekeeper—look at the dust on the mantelpiece, for example, the dust which, so they say, buried Troy three times over, only fragments of pots utterly refusing annihilation, as one can believe.

The tree outside the window taps very gently on the pane … I want to think quietly, calmly, spaciously, never to be interrupted, never to have to rise from my chair, to slip easily from one thing to another, without any sense of hostility, or obstacle. I want to sink deeper and deeper, away from the surface, with its hard separate facts. To steady myself, let me catch hold of the first idea that passes … Shakespeare … Well, he will do as well as another. A man who sat himself solidly in an arm-chair, and looked into the fire, so—A shower of ideas fell perpetually from some very high Heaven down through his mind. He leant his forehead on his hand, and people, looking in through the open door—for this scene is supposed to take place on a summer's evening—But how dull this is, this historical fiction! It

---

1   *bagatelle board*   Playing surface for a game similar to billiards.

2   *Tube*   Nickname for the London Underground, the system of subway lines that underlies the city of London.

3   *asphodel*   Genus of liliaceous flowers; said to cover the Elysian fields, the paradise where (according to Greek mythology) the blessed would reside after death.

doesn't interest me at all. I wish I could hit upon a pleasant track of thought, a track indirectly reflecting credit upon myself, for those are the pleasantest thoughts, and very frequent even in the minds of modest mouse-coloured people, who believe genuinely that they dislike to hear their own praises. They are not thoughts directly praising oneself; that is the beauty of them; they are thoughts like this:

"And then I came into the room. They were discussing botany. I said how I'd seen a flower growing on a dust heap on the site of an old house in Kingsway. The seed, I said, must have been sown in the reign of Charles the First. What flowers grew in the reign of Charles the First?" I asked—(but I don't remember the answer). Tall flowers with purple tassels to them perhaps. And so it goes on. All the time I'm dressing up the figure of myself in my own mind, lovingly, stealthily, not openly adoring it, for if I did that, I should catch myself out, and stretch my hand at once for a book in self-protection. Indeed, it is curious how instinctively one protects the image of oneself from idolatry or any other handling that could make it ridiculous, or too unlike the original to be believed in any longer. Or is it not so very curious after all? It is a matter of great importance. Suppose the looking-glass smashes, the image disappears, and the romantic figure with the green of forest depths all about it is there no longer, but only that shell of a person which is seen by other people—what an airless, shallow, bald, prominent world it becomes! A world not to be lived in. As we face each other in omnibuses and underground railways we are looking into the mirror; that accounts for the vagueness, the gleam of glassiness, in our eyes. And the novelists in future will realise more and more the importance of these reflections, for of course there is not one reflection but an almost infinite number; those are the depths they will explore, those the phantoms they will pursue, leaving the description of reality more and more out of their stories, taking a knowledge of it for granted, as the Greeks did and Shakespeare perhaps—but these generalisations are very worthless. The military sound of the word is enough. It recalls leading articles, cabinet ministers—a whole class of things indeed which as a child one thought the thing itself, the standard thing, the real thing, from which one could not depart save at the risk of nameless damnation.

Generalisations bring back somehow Sunday in London, Sunday afternoon walks, Sunday luncheons, and also ways of speaking of the dead, clothes, and habits—like the habit of sitting all together in one room until a certain hour, although nobody liked it. There was a rule for everything. The rule for tablecloths at that particular period was that they should be made of tapestry with little yellow compartments marked upon them, such as you may see in photographs of the carpets in the corridors of the royal palaces. Tablecloths of a different kind were not real tablecloths. How shocking, and yet how wonderful it was to discover that these real things, Sunday luncheons, Sunday walks, country houses, and tablecloths were not entirely real, were indeed half phantoms, and the damnation which visited the disbeliever in them was only a sense of illegitimate freedom. What now takes the place of those things I wonder, those real standard things? Men perhaps, should you be a woman; the masculine point of view which governs our lives, which sets the standard, which establishes Whitaker's Table of Precedency,[1] which has become, I suppose, since the war half a phantom to many men and women, which soon, one may hope, will be laughed into the dustbin where the phantoms go, the mahogany sideboards and the Landseer prints,[2] Gods and Devils, Hell and so forth, leaving us all with an intoxicating sense of illegitimate freedom—if freedom exists. . . .

In certain lights that mark on the wall seems actually to project from the wall. Nor is it entirely circular. I cannot be sure, but it seems to cast a perceptible shadow, suggesting that if I ran my finger down that strip of the wall it would, at a certain point, mount and descend a small tumulus, a smooth tumulus like those barrows on the South Downs[3] which are, they say, either tombs or camps. Of the two I should prefer them to be tombs, desiring melancholy like most English people, and finding it natural at the end of a walk to think of the bones stretched beneath the turf . . . There must be

---

[1] *Table of Precedency* Table in *Whitaker's Almanac* that illustrates the hierarchy of the various ranks of the British social order.

[2] *Landseer prints* Edwin Henry Landseer (1802–73) produced paintings and engravings of animals.

[3] *South Downs* Range of chalk hills in southeastern England; *barrows* Mounds of earth or stone.

some book about it. Some antiquary[1] must have dug up those bones and given them a name … What sort of a man is an antiquary, I wonder? Retired Colonels for the most part, I daresay, leading parties of aged labourers to the top here, examining clods of earth and stone, and getting into correspondence with the neighbouring clergy, which, being opened at breakfast time, gives them a feeling of importance, and the comparison of arrowheads necessitates cross-country journeys to the country towns, an agreeable necessity both to them and to their elderly wives, who wish to make plum jam or to clean out the study, and have every reason for keeping that great question of the camp or the tomb in perpetual suspension, while the Colonel himself feels agreeably philosophic in accumulating evidence on both sides of the question. It is true that he does finally incline to believe in the camp; and, being opposed, indites a pamphlet which he is about to read at the quarterly meeting of the local society when a stroke lays him low, and his last conscious thoughts are not of wife or child, but of the camp and that arrowhead there, which is now in the case at the local museum, together with the foot of a Chinese murderess, a handful of Elizabethan nails, a great many Tudor clay pipes, a piece of Roman pottery, and the wine-glass that Nelson drank out of—proving I really don't know what.

No, no, nothing is proved, nothing is known. And if I were to get up at this very moment and ascertain that the mark on the wall is really—what shall I say?—the head of a gigantic old nail, driven in two hundred years ago, which has now, owing to the patient attrition of many generations of housemaids, revealed its head above the coat of paint, and is taking its first view of modern life in the sight of a white-walled fire-lit room, what should I gain? Knowledge? Matter for further speculation? I can think sitting still as well as standing up. And what is knowledge? What are our learned men save the descendants of witches and hermits who crouched in caves and in woods brewing herbs, interrogating shrew-mice and writing down the language of the stars? And the less we honour them as our superstitions dwindle and our respect for beauty and health of mind increases … Yes, one could imagine a very pleasant world. A quiet spacious world, with the flowers so red and blue in the open fields. A world without professors or specialists or house-keepers with the profiles of policemen, a world which one could slice with one's thought as a fish slices the water with his fin, grazing the stems of the water-lilies, hanging suspended over nests of white sea eggs…. How peaceful it is down here, rooted in the centre of the world and gazing up through the grey waters, with their sudden gleams of light, and their reflections—if it were not for Whitaker's Almanack—if it were not for the Table of Precedency!

I must jump up and see for myself what that mark on the wall really is—a nail, a rose-leaf, a crack in the wood?

Here is Nature once more at her old game of self-preservation. This train of thought, she perceives, is threatening mere waste of energy, even some collision with reality, for who will ever be able to lift a finger against Whitaker's Table of Precedency? The Archbishop of Canterbury is followed by the Lord High Chancellor; the Lord High Chancellor is followed by the Archbishop of York. Everybody follows somebody, such is the philosophy of Whitaker; and the great thing is to know who follows whom. Whitaker knows, and let that, so Nature counsels, comfort you, instead of enraging you; and if you can't be comforted, if you must shatter this hour of peace, think of the mark on the wall.

I understand Nature's game—her prompting to take action as a way of ending any thought that threatens to excite or to pain. Hence, I suppose, comes our slight contempt for men of action—men, we assume, who don't think. Still, there's no harm in putting a full stop to one's disagreeable thoughts by looking at a mark on the wall.

Indeed, now that I have fixed my eyes upon it, I feel that I have grasped a plank in the sea; I feel a satisfying sense of reality which at once turns the two Archbishops and the Lord High Chancellor to the shadows of shades. Here is something definite, something real. Thus, waking from a midnight dream of horror, one hastily turns on the light and lies quiescent, worshipping the chest of drawers, worshipping solidity, worshipping reality, worshipping the impersonal world which is proof of some existence other than ours. That is what one wants to be sure of…. Wood is a pleasant thing to think about. It comes from a tree; and trees grow, and we don't know how they grow. For years and years they

---

[1] *antiquary* Collector of antiquities, usually a non-professional.

grow, without paying any attention to us, in meadows, in forests, and by the side of rivers—all things one likes to think about. The cows swish their tails beneath them on hot afternoons; they paint rivers so green that when a moorhen dives one expects to see its feathers all green when it comes up again. I like to think of the fish balanced against the stream like flags blown out; and of water-beetles slowly raising domes of mud upon the bed of the river. I like to think of the tree itself: first the close dry sensation of being wood; then the grinding of the storm; then the slow, delicious ooze of sap. I like to think of it, too, on winter's nights standing in the empty field with all leaves close-furled, nothing tender exposed to the iron bullets of the moon, a naked mast upon an earth that goes tumbling, tumbling all night long. The song of birds must sound very loud and strange in June; and how cold the feet of insects must feel upon it, as they make laborious progresses up the creases of the bark, or sun themselves upon the thin green awning of the leaves, and look straight in front of them with diamond-cut red eyes…. One by one the fibres snap beneath the immense cold pressure of the earth, then the last storm comes and, falling, the highest branches drive deep into the ground again. Even so, life isn't done with; there are a million patient, watchful lives still for a tree, all over the world, in bedrooms, in ships, on the pavement, lining rooms, where men and women sit after tea, smoking cigarettes. It is full of peaceful thoughts, happy thoughts, this tree. I should like to take each one separately—but something is getting in the way…. Where was I? What has it all been about? A tree? A river? The Downs? Whitaker's Almanack? The fields of asphodel? I can't remember a thing. Everything's moving, falling, slipping, vanishing…. There is a vast upheaval of matter. Someone is standing over me and saying—

"I'm going out to buy a newspaper."

"Yes?"

"Though it's no good buying newspapers…. Nothing ever happens. Curse this war; God damn this war! … All the same, I don't see why we should have a snail on our wall."

Ah, the mark on the wall! It was a snail.

—1921

Blue & Green

GREEN

The pointed fingers of glass hang downwards. The light slides down the glass, and drops a pool of green. All day long the ten fingers of the lustre drop green upon the marble. The feathers of parakeets—their harsh cries—sharp blades of palm trees—green, too; green needles glittering in the sun. But the hard glass drips on to the marble; the pools hover above the desert sand; the camels lurch through them; the pools settle on the marble; rushes edge them; weeds clog them; here and there a white blossom; the frog flops over; at night the stars are set there unbroken. Evening comes, and the shadow sweeps the green over the mantelpiece; the ruffled surface of ocean. No ships come; the aimless waves sway beneath the empty sky. It's night; the needles drip blots of blue. The green's out.

BLUE

The snub-nosed monster rises to the surface and spouts through his blunt nostrils two columns of water, which, fiery-white in the centre, spray off into a fringe of blue beads. Strokes of blue line the black tarpaulin of his hide. Slushing the water through mouth and nostrils he sinks, heavy with water, and the blue closes over him dowsing the polished pebbles of his eyes. Thrown upon the beach he lies, blunt, obtuse, shedding dry blue scales. Their metallic blue stains the rusty iron on the beach. Blue are the ribs of the wrecked rowing boat. A wave rolls beneath the blue bells. But the cathedral's different, cold, incense laden, faint blue with the veils of madonnas.

—1921

Kew Gardens

From the oval-shaped flower-bed there rose perhaps a hundred stalks spreading into heart-shaped or tongue-shaped leaves half way up and unfurling at the tip red or blue or yellow petals marked with spots of colour raised upon the surface; and from the red, blue or yellow gloom of the throat emerged a straight bar, rough with gold dust and slightly clubbed at the end. The petals were voluminous enough to be stirred by the summer breeze, and when they moved, the red, blue, and yellow lights passed one over the other, staining an inch of the brown earth beneath with a spot of the most intricate colour. The light fell either upon the smooth grey back of a pebble, or the shell of a snail with its brown circular veins, or, falling into a raindrop, it expanded with such intensity of red, blue, and yellow the thin walls of water that one expected them to burst and disappear. Instead, the drop was left in a second silver grey once more, and the light now settled upon the flesh of a leaf, revealing the branching thread of fibre beneath the surface, and again it moved on and spread its illumination in the vast green spaces beneath the dome of the heart-shaped and tongue-shaped leaves. Then the breeze stirred rather more briskly overhead and the colour was flashed into the air above, into the eyes of the men and women who walk in Kew Gardens in July.

The figures of these men and women straggled past the flower-bed with a curiously irregular movement not unlike that of the white and blue butterflies who crossed the turf in zig-zag flights from bed to bed. The man was about six inches in front of the woman, strolling care-lessly, while she bore on with greater purpose, only turning her head now and then to see that the children were not too far behind. The man kept this distance in front of the woman purposely, though perhaps uncon-sciously, for he wanted to go on with his thoughts.

"Fifteen years ago I came here with Lily," he thought. "We sat somewhere over there by a lake, and I begged her to marry me all through the hot afternoon. How the dragon-fly kept circling round us: how clearly I see the dragon-fly and her shoe with the square silver buckle at the toe. All the time I spoke I saw her shoe and when it moved impatiently I knew without looking up what she was going to say: the whole of her seemed to be in her shoe. And my love, my desire, were in the dragon-fly; for some reason I thought that if it settled there, on that leaf, the broad one with the red flower in the middle of it, if the dragonfly settled on the leaf she would say 'Yes' at once. But the dragon-fly went round and round: it never settled anywhere—of course not, happily not, or I shouldn't be walking here with Eleanor and the children —Tell me, Eleanor, d'you ever think

of the past?"

"Why do you ask, Simon?"

"Because I've been thinking of the past. I've been thinking of Lily, the woman I might have married … Well, why are you silent? Do you mind my thinking of the past?"

"Why should I mind, Simon? Doesn't one always think of the past, in a garden with men and women lying under the trees? Aren't they one's past, all that remains of it, those men and women, those ghosts lying under the trees … one's happiness, one's reality?"

"For me, a square silver shoe-buckle and a dragon-fly—"

"For me, a kiss. Imagine six little girls sitting before their easels twenty years ago, down by the side of a lake, painting the water-lilies, the first red water-lilies I'd ever seen. And suddenly a kiss, there on the back of my neck. And my hand shook all the afternoon so that I couldn't paint. I took out my watch and marked the hour when I would allow myself to think of the kiss for five minutes only—it was so precious—the kiss of an old grey-haired woman with a wart on her nose, the mother of all my kisses all my life. Come Caroline, come Hubert."

They walked on past the flower-bed, now walking four abreast, and soon diminished in size among the trees and looked half transparent as the sunlight and shade swam over their backs in large trembling irregular patches.

In the oval flower-bed the snail, whose shell had been stained red, blue and yellow for the space of two minutes or so, now appeared to be moving very slightly in its shell, and next began to labour over the crumbs of loose earth which broke away and rolled down as it passed over them. It appeared to have a definite goal in front of it, differing in this respect from the singular high-stepping angular green insect who attempted to cross in front of it, and waited for a second with its antennae trembling as if in deliberation, and then stepped off as rapidly and strangely in the opposite direction. Brown cliffs with deep green lakes in the hollows, flat blade-like trees that waved from root to tip, round boulders of grey stone, vast crumpled surfaces of a thin crackling texture—all these objects lay across the snail's progress between one stalk and another to his goal. Before he had decided whether to circumvent the arched tent of a dead leaf or to breast it there came past the bed the feet of other human beings.

This time they were both men. The younger of the two wore an expression of perhaps unnatural calm; he raised his eyes and fixed them very steadily in front of him while his companion spoke, and directly his companion had done speaking he looked on the ground again and sometimes opened his lips only after a long pause and sometimes did not open them at all. The elder man had a curiously uneven and shaky method of walking, jerking his hand forward and throwing up his head abruptly, rather in the manner of an impatient carriage horse tired of waiting outside a house; but in the man these gestures were irresolute and pointless. He talked almost incessantly; he smiled to himself and again began to talk, as if the smile had been an answer. He was talking about spirits—the spirits of the dead, who, according to him, were even now telling him all sorts of odd things about their experiences in Heaven.

"Heaven was known to the ancients as Thessaly, William, and now, with this war, the spirit matter is rolling between the hills like thunder." He paused, seemed to listen, smiled, jerked his head and continued:—

"You have a small electric battery and a piece of rubber to insulate the wire—isolate?—insulate?—well, we'll skip the details, no good going into details that wouldn't be understood—and in short the little machine stands in any convenient position by the head of the bed, we will say, on a neat mahogany stand. All arrangements being properly fixed by workmen under my direction, the widow applies her ear and summons the spirit by sign as agreed. Women! Widows! Women in black—"

Here he seemed to have caught sight of a woman's dress in the distance, which in the shade looked a purple black. He took off his hat, placed his hand upon his heart, and hurried towards her muttering and gesticulating feverishly. But William caught him by the sleeve and touched a flower with the tip of his walking-stick in order to divert the old man's attention. After looking at it for a moment in some confusion the old man bent his ear to it and seemed to answer a voice speaking from it, for he began talking about the forests of Uruguay which he had visited hundreds of years ago in company with

the most beautiful young woman in Europe. He could be heard murmuring about forests of Uruguay blanketed with the wax petals of tropical roses, nightingales, sea beaches, mermaids and women drowned at sea, as he suffered himself to be moved on by William, upon whose face the look of stoical patience grew slowly deeper and deeper.

Following his steps so closely as to be slightly puzzled by his gestures came two elderly women of the lower middle class, one stout and ponderous, the other rosy-cheeked and nimble. Like most people of their station[1] they were frankly fascinated by any signs of eccentricity betokening a disordered brain, especially in the well-to-do; but they were too far off to be certain whether the gestures were merely eccentric or genuinely mad. After they had scrutinised the old man's back in silence for a moment and given each other a queer, sly look, they went on energetically piecing together their very complicated dialogue:

"Nell, Bert, Lot, Cess, Phil, Pa, he says, I says, she says, I says, I says, I says—"

"My Bert, Sis, Bill, Grandad, the old man, sugar,
    Sugar, flour, kippers, greens
    Sugar, sugar, sugar."

The ponderous woman looked through the pattern of falling words at the flowers standing cool, firm and upright in the earth, with a curious expression. She saw them as a sleeper waking from a heavy sleep sees a brass candlestick reflecting the light in an unfamiliar way, and closes his eyes and opens them, and seeing the brass candlestick again, finally starts broad awake and stares at the candlestick with all his powers. So the heavy woman came to a standstill opposite the oval-shaped flower-bed, and ceased even to pretend to listen to what the other woman was saying. She stood there letting the words fall over her, swaying the top part of her body slowly backwards and forwards, looking at the flowers. Then she suggested that they should find a seat and have their tea.

The snail had now considered every possible method of reaching his goal without going round the dead leaf or climbing over it. Let alone the effort needed for climbing a leaf, he was doubtful whether the thin

---

[1] *their station* I.e., their position in English society.

texture which vibrated with such an alarming crackle when touched even by the tip of his horns would bear his weight; and this determined him finally to creep beneath it, for there was a point where the leaf curved high enough from the ground to admit him. He had just inserted his head in the opening and was taking stock of the high brown roof and was getting used to the cool brown light when two other people came past outside on the turf. This time they were both young, a young man and a young woman. They were both in the prime of youth, or even in that season which precedes the prime of youth, the season before the smooth pink folds of the flower have burst their gummy case, when the wings of the butterfly, though fully grown, are motionless in the sun.

"Lucky it isn't Friday," he observed.

"Why? D'you believe in luck?"

"They make you pay sixpence on Friday."

"What's sixpence anyway? Isn't it worth sixpence?"

"What's 'it'—what do you mean by 'it'?"

"O anything—I mean—you know what I mean."

Long pauses came between each of these remarks: they were uttered in toneless and monotonous voices. The couple stood still on the edge of the flower-bed, and together pressed the end of her parasol deep down into the soft earth. The action and the fact that his hand rested on the top of hers expressed their feelings in a strange way, as these short insignificant words also expressed something, words with short wings for their heavy body of meaning, inadequate to carry them far and thus alighting awkwardly upon the very common objects that surrounded them and were to their inexperienced touch so massive: but who knows (so they thought as they pressed the parasol into the earth) what precipices aren't concealed in them, or what slopes of ice don't shine in the sun on the other side? Who knows? Who has ever seen this before? Even when she wondered what sort of tea they gave you at Kew, he felt that something loomed up behind her words, and stood vast and solid behind them; and the mist very slowly rose and uncovered—O Heavens,—what were those shapes?—little white tables, and waitresses who looked first at her and then at him; and there was a bill that he would pay with a real two shilling piece, and it was real, all real, he assured himself, fingering the coin in his pocket, real to everyone except to him and to her; even to him it began to seem real; and then—but it was too exciting to stand and think any longer, and he pulled the parasol out of the earth with a jerk and was impatient to find the place where one had tea with other people, like other people.

"Come along, Trissie; it's time we had our tea."

"Wherever does one have one's tea?" she asked with the oddest thrill of excitement in her voice, looking vaguely round and letting herself be drawn on down the grass path, trailing her parasol, turning her head this way and that way, forgetting her tea, wishing to go down there and then down there, remembering orchids and cranes among wild flowers, a Chinese pagoda and a crimson-crested bird; but he bore her on.

Thus one couple after another with much the same irregular and aimless movement passed the flower-bed and were enveloped in layer after layer of green-blue vapour, in which at first their bodies had substance and a dash of colour, but later both substance and colour dissolved in the green-blue atmosphere. How hot it was! So hot that even the thrush chose to hop, like a mechanical bird, in the shadow of the flowers, with long pauses between one movement and the next; instead of rambling vaguely the white butterflies danced one above another, making with their white shifting flakes the outline of a shattered marble column above the tallest flowers; the glass roofs of the palm house shone as if a whole market full of shiny green umbrellas had opened in the sun; and in the drone of the aeroplane the voice of the summer sky murmured its fierce soul. Yellow and black, pink and snow white, shapes of all these colours, men, women, and children, were spotted for a second upon the horizon, and then, seeing the breadth of yellow that lay upon the grass, they wavered and sought shade beneath the trees, dissolving like drops of water in the yellow and green atmosphere, staining it faintly with red and blue. It seemed as if all gross and heavy bodies had sunk down in the heat motionless and lay huddled upon the ground, but their voices went wavering from them as if they were flames lolling from the thick waxen bodies of candles. Voices, yes, voices, wordless voices, breaking the silence suddenly with such depth of contentment, such passion of desire, or, in the voices of children, such freshness of surprise; breaking the silence?

But there was no silence; all the time the motor omni-buses were turning their wheels and changing their gear; like a vast nest of Chinese boxes all of wrought steel turning ceaselessly one within another the city murmured; on the top of which the voices cried aloud and the petals of myriads of flowers flashed their colours into the air.

—1921

Mrs. Dalloway in Bond Street

Mrs. Dalloway said she would buy the gloves herself. Big Ben was striking as she stepped out into the street. It was eleven o'clock and the unused hour was fresh as if issued to children on a beach. But there was something solemn in the deliberate swing of the repeated strokes; something stirring in the murmur of wheels and the shuffle of footsteps.

No doubt they were not all bound on errands of happiness. There is much more to be said about us than that we walk the streets of Westminster. Big Ben too is nothing but steel rods consumed by rust were it not for the care of H.M.'s Office of Works. Only for Mrs. Dalloway the moment was complete; for Mrs. Dalloway June was fresh. A happy childhood—and it was not to his daughters only that Justin Parry had seemed a fine fellow (weak of course on the Bench); flowers at evening, smoke rising; the caw of rooks falling from ever so high, down down through the October air—there is nothing to take the place of childhood. A leaf of mint brings it back: or a cup with a blue ring.

Poor little wretches, she sighed, and pressed forward. Oh, right under the horses' noses, you little demon! and there she was left on the kerb stretching her hand out, while Jimmy Dawes grinned on the further side.

A charming woman, poised, eager, strangely white-haired for her pink cheeks, so Scope Purvis, C. B.,[1] saw her as he hurried to his office. She stiffened a little, waiting for Durtnall's van to pass. Big Ben struck the tenth; struck the eleventh stroke. The leaden circles dissolved in the air. Pride held her erect, inheriting,

handing on, acquainted with discipline and with suffering. How people suffered, how they suffered, she thought, thinking of Mrs. Foxcroft at the Embassy last night decked with jewels, eating her heart out, because that nice boy was dead, and now the old Manor House (Durtnall's van passed) must go to a cousin.

"Good morning to you!" said Hugh Whitbread raising his hat rather extravagantly by the china shop, for they had known each other as children. "Where are you off to?"

"I love walking in London," said Mrs. Dalloway. "Really it's better than walking in the country!"

"We've just come up," said Hugh Whitbread. "Unfortunately to see doctors."

"Milly?" said Mrs. Dalloway, instantly compassionate.

"Out of sorts," said Hugh Whitbread. "That sort of thing. Dick all right?"

"First rate!" said Clarissa.

Of course, she thought, walking on, Milly is about my age—fifty—fifty-two. So it is probably that, Hugh's manner had said so, said it perfectly—dear old Hugh, thought Mrs. Dalloway, remembering with amusement, with gratitude, with emotion, how shy, like a brother—one would rather die than speak to one's brother—Hugh had always been, when he was at Oxford, and came over, and perhaps one of them (drat the thing!) couldn't ride. How then could women sit in Parliament? How could they do things with men? For there is this extraordinarily deep instinct, something inside one; you can't get over it; it's no use trying; and men like Hugh respect it without our saying it, which is what one loves, thought Clarissa, in dear old Hugh.

She had passed through the Admiralty Arch and saw at the end of the empty road with its thin trees Victoria's white mound,[2] Victoria's billowing motherliness, amplitude and homeliness, always ridiculous, yet how sublime, thought Mrs. Dalloway, remembering Kensington Gardens and the old lady in horn spectacles and being told by Nanny to stop dead still and bow to the Queen. The flag flew above the Palace. The King and Queen were back then. Dick had met her at lunch the other day—a thoroughly nice woman. It matters so

[1]   *C.B.*   Companion of the Bath. The Order of the Bath is an order of chivalry conferred by the sovereign of England.

[2]   *Victoria's white mound*   Monument to Queen Victoria at the entrance to Buckingham Palace.

much to the poor, thought Clarissa, and to the soldiers. A man in bronze stood heroically on a pedestal with a gun on her left hand side—the South African war. It matters, thought Mrs. Dalloway walking towards Buckingham Palace. There it stood four-square, in the broad sunshine, uncompromising, plain. But it was character, she thought; something inborn in the race; what Indians respected. The Queen went to hospitals, opened bazaars—the Queen of England, thought Clarissa, looking at the Palace. Already at this hour a motor car passed out at the gates; soldiers saluted; the gates were shut. And Clarissa, crossing the road, entered the Park,[1] holding herself upright.

June had drawn out every leaf on the trees. The mothers of Westminster with mottled breasts gave suck to their young. Quite respectable girls lay stretched on the grass. An elderly man, stooping very stiffly, picked up a crumpled paper, spread it out flat and flung it away. How horrible! Last night at the Embassy Sir Dighton had said, "If I want a fellow to hold my horse, I have only to put up my hand." But the religious question is far more serious than the economic, Sir Dighton had said, which she thought extraordinarily interesting, from a man like Sir Dighton. "Oh, the country will never know what it has lost," he had said, talking of his own accord, about dear Jack Stewart.

She mounted the little hill lightly. The air stirred with energy. Messages were passing from the Fleet to the Admiralty. Piccadilly and Arlington Street and the Mall[2] seemed to chafe the very air in the Park and lift its leaves hotly, brilliantly, upon waves of that divine vitality which Clarissa loved. To ride; to dance; she had adored all that. Or going long walks in the country, talking, about books, what to do with one's life, for young people were amazingly priggish—oh, the things one had said! But one had conviction. Middle age is the devil. People like Jack'll never know that, she thought; for he never once thought of death, never, they said, knew he was dying. And now can never mourn—how did it go?—a head grown grey ... From the contagion

of the world's slow stain[3] ... have drunk their cup a round or two before.[4] ... From the contagion of the world's slow stain! She held herself upright.

But how Jack would have shouted! Quoting Shelley, in Piccadilly! "You want a pin," he would have said. He hated frumps. "My God Clarissa! My God Clarissa!"— she could hear him now at the Devonshire House[5] party, about poor Sylvia Hunt in her amber necklace and that dowdy old silk. Clarissa held herself upright for she had spoken aloud and now she was in Piccadilly, passing the house with the slender green columns, and the balconies; passing club windows full of newspapers; passing old Lady Burdett-Coutts's house where the glazed white parrot used to hang; and Devonshire House, without its gilt leopards; and Claridge's,[6] where she must remember Dick wanted her to leave a card on Mrs. Jepson or she would be gone. Rich Americans can be very charming. There was St. James's Palace; like a child's game with bricks; and now—she had passed Bond Street—she was by Hatchard's book shop. The stream was endless—endless—endless. Lords, Ascot, Hurlingham—what was it? What a duck, she thought, looking at the frontispiece of some book of memoirs spread wide in the bow window, Sir Joshua perhaps or Romney;[7] arch, bright, demure; the sort of girl—like her own Elizabeth—the only real sort of girl. And there was that absurd book, Soapy Sponge,[8] which Jim used to quote by the yard; and Shakespeare's Sonnets. She knew them by heart. Phil and she had argued all day about the Dark Lady, and Dick had said straight out at dinner that night that he had never heard of her. Really, she had

1 *the Park* St. James's Park, London.
2 *the Mall* Walk bordered by trees in St. James's Park.

3 *how did it ... stain* See Percy Shelley's "Adonais" (1821): "From the contagion of the world's slow stain / He is secure, and now can never mourn. / A heart grown cold, a head grown grey in vain" (lines 356–58).
4 *have drunk ... before* See Edward Fitzgerald's *The Rubáiyát of Omar Khayyám* (1859): "Lo! some we loved, the loveliest and best / That Time and Fate of all their Vintage prest / Have drunk their Cup a Round or two before / And one by one crept silently to Rest."
5 *Devonshire House* London home of the Duke of Devonshire.
6 *Claridge's* Claridge's Hotel.
7 *Sir Joshua ... Romney* Sir Joshua Reynolds (1723–92) and George Romney (1734–1802), English painters.
8 *Soapy Sponge* The nickname of the protagonist of R.S. Surtees's novel *Mr. Sponge's Sporting Tour* (1853).

married him for that! He had never read Shakespeare! There must be some little cheap book she could buy for Milly—*Cranford*[1] of course! Was there ever anything so enchanting as the cow in petticoats? If only people had that sort of humour, that sort of self-respect now, thought Clarissa, for she remembered the broad pages; the sentences ending; the characters—how one talked about them as if they were real. For all the great things one must go to the past, she thought. From the contagion of the world's slow stain ... Fear no more the heat o' the sun.[2] ... And now can never mourn, can never mourn, she repeated, her eyes straying over the window; for it ran in her head; the test of great poetry; the moderns had never written anything one wanted to read about death, she thought; and turned.

Omnibuses joined motor cars; motor cars vans; vans taxicabs, taxicabs motor cars—here was an open motor car with a girl, alone. Up till four, her feet tingling, I know, thought Clarissa, for the girl looked washed out, half asleep, in the corner of the car after the dance. And another car came; and another. No! No! No! Clarissa smiled good-naturedly. The fat lady had taken every sort of trouble, but diamonds! orchids! at this hour of the morning! No! No! No! The excellent policeman would, when the time came, hold up his hand. Another motor car passed. How utterly unattractive! Why should a girl of that age paint black round her eyes? And a young man, with a girl, at this hour, when the country—The admirable policeman raised his hand and Clarissa acknowledging his sway, taking her time, crossed, walked towards Bond Street; saw the narrow crooked street, the yellow banners; the thick notched telegraph wires stretched across the sky.

A hundred years ago her great-great-grandfather, Seymour Parry, who ran away with Conway's daughter, had walked down Bond Street. Down Bond Street the Parrys had walked for a hundred years, and might have met the Dalloways (Leighs on the mother's side) going

up. Her father got his clothes from Hill's. There was a roll of cloth in the window, and here just one jar on a black table, incredibly expensive; like the thick pink salmon on the ice block at the fishmonger's. The jewels were exquisite—pink and orange stars, paste, Spanish, she thought, and chains of old gold; starry buckles, little brooches which had been worn on sea-green satin by ladies with high head-dresses. But no good looking! One must economise. She must go on past the picture dealer's where one of the odd French pictures hung, as if people had thrown confetti—pink and blue—for a joke. If you had lived with pictures (and it's the same with books and music) thought Clarissa, passing the Aeolian Hall, you can't be taken in by a joke.

The river of Bond Street was clogged. There, like a Queen at a tournament, raised, regal, was Lady Bexborough. She sat in her carriage, upright, alone, looking through her glasses. The white glove was loose at her wrist. She was in black, quite shabby, yet, thought Clarissa, how extraordinarily it tells, breeding, self-respect, never saying a word too much or letting people gossip; an astonishing friend; no one can pick a hole in her after all these years, and now, there she is, thought Clarissa, passing the Countess who waited powdered, perfectly still, and Clarissa would have given anything to be like that, the mistress of Clarefield, talking politics, like a man. But she never goes anywhere, thought Clarissa, and it's quite useless to ask her, and the carriage went on and Lady Bexborough was borne past like a Queen at a tournament, though she had nothing to live for and the old man is failing and they say she is sick of it all, thought Clarissa and the tears actually rose to her eyes as she entered the shop.

"Good morning," said Clarissa in her charming voice. "Gloves," she said with her exquisite friendliness and putting her bag on the counter began, very slowly, to undo the buttons. "White gloves," she said. "Above the elbow," and she looked straight into the shop-woman's face—but this was not the girl she remembered? She looked quite old. "These really don't fit," said Clarissa. The shop-girl looked at them. "Madame wears bracelets?" Clarissa spread out her fingers. "Perhaps it's my rings." And the girl took the grey gloves with her to the end of the counter.

Yes, thought Clarissa, if it's the girl I remember,

---

[1] *Cranford*   Novel by Elizabeth Gaskell (1853). In the book, Miss Betsy Barker dresses her cow in grey flannel after a fall into a lime pit removes all its hair.

[2] *Fear ... sun*   From Shakespeare's *Cymbeline*, 4.2: "Fear no more the heat o' the sun / Nor the furious winter's rages / Thou thy worldly task hast done / Home art gone, and ta'en thy wages / Golden lads and girls all must / As chimney-sweepers, come to dust."

she's twenty years older .... There was only one other customer, sitting sideways at the counter, her elbow poised, her bare hand drooping, vacant; like a figure on a Japanese fan, thought Clarissa, too vacant perhaps, yet some men would adore her. The lady shook her head sadly. Again the gloves were too large. She turned round the glass. "Above the wrist," she reproached the grey-headed woman; who looked and agreed.

They waited; a clock ticked; Bond Street hummed, dulled, distant; the woman went away holding gloves. "Above the wrist," said the lady, mournfully, raising her voice. And she would have to order chairs, ices, flowers, and cloak-room tickets, thought Clarissa. The people she didn't want would come; the others wouldn't. She would stand by the door. They sold stockings—silk stockings. A lady is known by her gloves and her shoes, old Uncle William used to say. And through the hanging silk stockings quivering silver she looked at the lady, sloping shouldered, her hand drooping, her bag slipping, her eyes vacantly on the floor. It would be intolerable if dowdy women came to her party! Would one have liked Keats[1] if he had worn red socks? Oh, at last—she drew into the counter and it flashed into her mind:

"Do you remember before the war you had gloves with pearl buttons?"

"French gloves, Madame?"

"Yes, they were French," said Clarissa. The other lady rose very sadly and took her bag, and looked at the gloves on the counter. But they were all too large—always too large at the wrist.

"With pearl buttons," said the shop-girl, who looked ever so much older. She split the lengths of tissue paper apart on the counter. With pearl buttons, thought Clarissa, perfectly simple—how French!

"Madame's hands are so slender," said the shop-girl, drawing the glove firmly, smoothly, down over her rings. And Clarissa looked at her arm in the looking-glass. The glove hardly came to the elbow. Were there others half an inch longer? Still it seemed tiresome to bother her—perhaps the one day in the month, thought Clarissa, when it's an agony to stand. "Oh, don't bother," she said. But the gloves were brought.

"Don't you get fearfully tired," she said in her charming voice, "standing? When d'you get your holiday?"

"In September, Madame, when we're not so busy."

When we're in the country thought Clarissa. Or shooting. She has a fortnight at Brighton. In some stuffy lodging. The landlady takes the sugar. Nothing would be easier than to send her to Mrs. Lumley's right in the country (and it was on the tip of her tongue). But then she remembered how on their honeymoon Dick had shown her the folly of giving impulsively. It was much more important, he said, to get trade with China. Of course he was right. And she could feel the girl wouldn't like to be given things. There she was in her place. So was Dick. Selling gloves was her job. She had her own sorrows quite separate, "and now can never mourn, can never mourn," the words ran in her head. "From the contagion of the world's slow stain," thought Clarissa holding her arm stiff, for there are moments when it seems utterly futile (the glove was drawn off leaving her arm flecked with powder)—simply one doesn't believe, thought Clarissa, any more in God.

The traffic suddenly roared; the silk stockings brightened. A customer came in.

"White gloves," she said, with some ring in her voice that Clarissa remembered.

It used, thought Clarissa, to be so simple. Down down through the air came the caw of the rooks. When Sylvia died, hundreds of years ago, the yew hedges looked so lovely with the diamond webs in the mist before early church. But if Dick were to die tomorrow, as for believing in God—no, she would let the children choose, but for herself, like Lady Bexborough, who opened the bazaar, they say, with the telegram in her hand—Roden, her favourite, killed—she would go on. But why, if one doesn't believe? For the sake of others, she thought, taking the glove in her hand. The girl would be much more unhappy if she didn't believe.

"Thirty shillings," said the shop-woman. "No, pardon me Madame, thirty-five. The French gloves are more."

For one doesn't live for oneself, thought Clarissa.

And then the other customer took a glove, tugged it, and it split.

"There!" she exclaimed.

"A fault of the skin," said the grey-headed woman hurriedly. "Sometimes a drop of acid in tanning. Try

---

[1] *Keats*　John Keats (1795–1821), English Romantic poet.

this pair, Madame."

"But it's an awful swindle to ask two pound ten!"

Clarissa looked at the lady; the lady looked at Clarissa.

"Gloves have never been quite so reliable since the war," said the shop-girl, apologising, to Clarissa.

But where had she seen the other lady?—elderly, with a frill under her chin; wearing a black ribbon for gold eyeglasses; sensual, clever, like a Sargent[1] drawing. How one can tell from a voice when people are in the habit, thought Clarissa, of making other people—"It's a shade too tight," she said—obey. The shop-woman went off again. Clarissa was left waiting. Fear no more she repeated, playing her finger on the counter. Fear no more the heat o' the sun. Fear no more she repeated. There were little brown spots on her arm. And the girl crawled like a snail. Thou thy worldly task hast done. Thousands of young men had died that things might go on. At last! Half an inch above the elbow; pearl buttons; five and a quarter. My dear slow coach, thought Clarissa, do you think I can sit here the whole morning? Now you'll take twenty-five minutes to bring me my change!

There was a violent explosion in the street outside. The shop-women cowered behind the counters. But Clarissa, sitting very upright, smiled at the other lady. "Miss Anstruther!" she exclaimed.

—1923

Modern Fiction

In making any survey, even the freest and loosest, of modern fiction, it is difficult not to take it for granted that the modern practice of the art is somehow an improvement upon the old. With their simple tools and primitive materials, it might be said, Fielding did well and Jane Austen even better,[2] but compare their opportunities with ours! Their masterpieces certainly have a strange air of simplicity. And yet the analogy between literature and the process, to choose an example, of making motor cars scarcely holds good beyond the first glance. It is doubtful whether in the course of the centuries, though we have learnt much about making machines, we have learnt anything about making literature. We do not come to write better; all that we can be said to do is to keep moving, now a little in this direction, now in that, but with a circular tendency should the whole course of the track be viewed from a sufficiently lofty pinnacle. It need scarcely be said that we make no claim to stand, even momentarily, upon that vantage ground. On the flat, in the crowd, half blind with dust, we look back with envy to those happier warriors, whose battle is won and whose achievements wear so serene an air of accomplishment that we can scarcely refrain from whispering that the fight was not so fierce for them as for us. It is for the historian of literature to decide; for him to say if we are now beginning or ending or standing in the middle of a great period of prose fiction, for down in the plain little is visible. We only know that certain gratitudes and hostilities inspire us; that certain paths seem to lead to fertile land, others to the dust and the desert; and of this perhaps it may be worth while to attempt some account.

Our quarrel, then, is not with the classics, and if we speak of quarrelling with Mr. Wells, Mr. Bennett, and Mr. Galsworthy,[3] it is partly that by the mere fact of their existence in the flesh their work has a living, breathing, everyday imperfection which bids us take what liberties with it we choose. But it is also true that, while we thank them for a thousand gifts, we reserve our unconditional gratitude for Mr. Hardy, for Mr. Conrad, and in a much lesser degree for the Mr. Hudson of *The Purple Land, Green Mansions,* and *Far Away and Long Ago.*[4] Mr. Wells, Mr. Bennett, and Mr. Galsworthy have excited so many hopes and disappointed them so persistently that our gratitude largely takes the form of

---

[1] *Sargent painting* John Singer Sargent (1856–1925), the celebrated American artist, was (and is) known for his portraits of women of fashion.

[2] *Fielding ... better* Henry Fielding (1707–54) and Jane Austen (1775–1817), British novelists.

[3] *Mr. Wells ... Galsworthy* H.G. Wells (1866–1946), Arnold Bennett (1867–1931), and John Galsworthy (1867–1933), three popular novelists at the time.

[4] *Mr. Hardy ... Ago* Thomas Hardy (1840–1928), author of *Tess of the D'Urbervilles* and *Jude the Obscure*; Joseph Conrad (1857–1924), author of *Heart of Darkness*; William Henry Hudson (1841–1922), Argentinean author and naturalist who lived in London. *The Purple Land* and *Green Mansions* are romances set in Argentina, and *Far Away and Long Ago* is an account of Hudson's early life in Argentina.

thanking them for having shown us what they might have done but have not done; what we certainly could not do, but as certainly, perhaps, do not wish to do. No single phrase will sum up the charge or grievance which we have to bring against a mass of work so large in its volume and embodying so many qualities, both admirable and the reverse. If we tried to formulate our meaning in one word we should say that these three writers are materialists. It is because they are concerned not with the spirit but with the body that they have disappointed us, and left us with the feeling that the sooner English fiction turns its back upon them, as politely as may be, and marches, if only into the desert, the better for its soul. Naturally, no single word reaches the centre of three separate targets. In the case of Mr. Wells it falls notably wide of the mark. And yet even with him it indicates to our thinking the fatal alloy in his genius, the great clod of clay that has got itself mixed up with the purity of his inspiration. But Mr. Bennett is perhaps the worst culprit of the three, inasmuch as he is by far the best workman. He can make a book so well constructed and solid in its craftsmanship that it is difficult for the most exacting of critics to see through what chink or crevice decay can creep in. There is not so much as a draught between the frames of the windows, or a crack in the boards. And yet—if life should refuse to live there? That is a risk which the creator of *The Old Wives' Tale*, George Cannon, Edwin Clayhanger,[1] and hosts of other figures, may well claim to have surmounted. His characters live abundantly, even unexpectedly, but it remains to ask how do they live, and what do they live for? More and more they seem to us, deserting even the well-built villa in the Five Towns,[2] to spend their time in some softly padded first-class railway carriage, pressing bells and buttons innumerable; and the destiny to which they travel so luxuriously becomes more and more unquestionably an eternity of bliss spent in the very best hotel in Brighton. It can scarcely be said of Mr. Wells that he is a materialist in the sense that he takes too much delight in the solidity of his fabric. His mind

is too generous in its sympathies to allow him to spend much time in making things shipshape and substantial. He is a materialist from sheer goodness of heart, taking upon his shoulders the work that ought to have been discharged by Government officials, and in the plethora of his ideas and facts scarcely having leisure to realise, or forgetting to think important, the crudity and coarseness of his human beings. Yet what more damaging criticism can there be both of his earth and of his Heaven than that they are to be inhabited here and hereafter by his Joans and his Peters? Does not the inferiority of their natures tarnish whatever institutions and ideals may be provided for them by the generosity of their creator? Nor, profoundly though we respect the integrity and humanity of Mr. Galsworthy, shall we find what we seek in his pages.

If we fasten, then, one label on all these books, on which is one word materialists, we mean by it that they write of unimportant things; that they spend immense skill and immense industry making the trivial and the transitory appear the true and the enduring.

We have to admit that we are exacting, and, further, that we find it difficult to justify our discontent by explaining what it is that we exact. We frame our question differently at different times. But it reappears most persistently as we drop the finished novel on the crest of a sigh—Is it worth while? What is the point of it all? Can it be that, owing to one of those little deviations which the human spirit seems to make from time to time, Mr. Bennett has come down with his magnificent apparatus for catching life just an inch or two on the wrong side? Life escapes; and perhaps without life nothing else is worth while. It is a confession of vagueness to have to make use of such a figure as this, but we scarcely better the matter by speaking, as critics are prone to do, of reality. Admitting the vagueness which afflicts all criticism of novels, let us hazard the opinion that for us at this moment the form of fiction most in vogue more often misses than secures the thing we seek. Whether we call it life or spirit, truth or reality, this, the essential thing, has moved off, or on, and refuses to be contained any longer in such ill-fitting vestments as we provide. Nevertheless, we go on perseveringly, conscientiously, constructing our two and thirty chapters after a design which more and more ceases to resemble the

---

[1] *Geroge … Clayhanger*   Characters from Bennett's novels *The Roll-Call* and *Clayhanger*.

[2] *the Five Towns*   Five towns in Staffordshire that comprise the center of England's pottery industry and that provide the setting for many of Bennett's novels.

vision in our minds. So much of the enormous labour of proving the solidity, the likeness to life, of the story is not merely labour thrown away but labour misplaced to the extent of obscuring and blotting out the light of the conception. The writer seems constrained, not by his own free will but by some powerful and unscrupulous tyrant who has him in thrall, to provide a plot, to provide comedy, tragedy, love interest, and an air of probability embalming the whole so impeccable that if all his figures were to come to life they would find themselves dressed down to the last button of their coats in the fashion of the hour. The tyrant is obeyed; the novel is done to a turn. But sometimes, more and more often as time goes by, we suspect a momentary doubt, a spasm of rebellion, as the pages fill themselves in the customary way. Is life like this? Must novels be like this?

Look within and life, it seems, is very far from being "like this." Examine for a moment an ordinary mind on an ordinary day. The mind receives a myriad impressions—trivial, fantastic, evanescent, or engraved with the sharpness of steel. From all sides they come, an incessant shower of innumerable atoms; and as they fall, as they shape themselves into the life of Monday or Tuesday, the accent falls differently from of old; the moment of importance came not here but there; so that, if a writer were a free man and not a slave, if he could write what he chose, not what he must, if he could base his work upon his own feeling and not upon convention, there would be no plot, no comedy, no tragedy, no love interest or catastrophe in the accepted style, and perhaps not a single button sewn on as the Bond Street tailors would have it. Life is not a series of gig lamps symmetrically arranged; life is a luminous halo, a semitransparent envelope surrounding us from the beginning of consciousness to the end. Is it not the task of the novelist to convey this varying, this unknown and uncircumscribed spirit, whatever aberration or complexity it may display, with as little mixture of the alien and external as possible? We are not pleading merely for courage and sincerity; we are suggesting that the proper stuff of fiction is a little other than custom would have us believe it.

It is, at any rate, in some such fashion as this that we seek to define the quality which distinguishes the work of several young writers, among whom Mr. James Joyce[1] is the most notable, from that of their predecessors. They attempt to come closer to life, and to preserve more sincerely and exactly what interests and moves them, even if to do so they must discard most of the conventions which are commonly observed by the novelist. Let us record the atoms as they fall upon the mind in the order in which they fall, let us trace the pattern, however disconnected and incoherent in appearance, which each sight or incident scores upon the consciousness. Let us not take it for granted that life exists more fully in what is commonly thought big than in what is commonly thought small. Any one who has read *The Portrait of the Artist as a Young Man* or, what promises to be a far more interesting work, *Ulysses*,[2] now appearing in the *Little Review*, will have hazarded some theory of this nature as to Mr. Joyce's intention. On our part, with such a fragment before us, it is hazarded rather than affirmed; but whatever the intention of the whole, there can be no question but that it is of the utmost sincerity and that the result, difficult or unpleasant as we may judge it, is undeniably important. In contrast with those whom we have called materialists, Mr. Joyce is spiritual; he is concerned at all costs to reveal the flickerings of that innermost flame which flashes its messages through the brain, and in order to preserve it he disregards with complete courage whatever seems to him adventitious, whether it be probability, or coherence, or any other of these signposts which for generations have served to support the imagination of a reader when called upon to imagine what he can neither touch nor see. The scene in the cemetery,[3] for instance, with its brilliancy, its sordidity, its incoherence, its sudden lightning flashes of significance, does undoubtedly come so close to the quick of the mind that, on a first reading at any rate, it is difficult not to acclaim a masterpiece. If we want life itself, here surely we have it. Indeed, we find ourselves fumbling rather awkwardly if we try to say what else we wish, and for what reason a work of such originality yet fails to compare, for we must take high examples, with *Youth* or *The Mayor of*

---

[1] *Mr. James Joyce* James Joyce (1882–1941), Irish novelist.

[2] [Woolf's note] Written in April, 1919.

[3] *The scene … cemetery* In the "Hades" section of *Ulysses*.

Casterbridge.[1] It fails because of the comparative poverty of the writer's mind, we might say simply and have done with it. But it is possible to press a little further and wonder whether we may not refer our sense of being in a bright yet narrow room, confined and shut in, rather than enlarged and set free, to some limitation imposed by the method as well as by the mind. Is it the method that inhibits the creative power? Is it due to the method that we feel neither jovial nor magnanimous, but centred in a self which, in spite of its tremor of susceptibility, never embraces or creates what is outside itself and beyond? Does the emphasis laid, perhaps didactically, upon indecency, contribute to the effect of something angular and isolated? Or is it merely that in any effort of such originality it is much easier, for contemporaries especially, to feel what it lacks than to name what it gives? In any case it is a mistake to stand outside examining "methods." Any method is right, every method is right, that expresses what we wish to express, if we are writers; that brings us closer to the novelist's intention if we are readers. This method has the merit of bringing us closer to what we were prepared to call life itself; did not the reading of *Ulysses* suggest how much of life is excluded or ignored, and did it not come with a shock to open *Tristram Shandy* or even *Pendennis*[2] and be by them convinced that there are not only other aspects of life, but more important ones into the bargain.

However this may be, the problem before the novelist at present, as we suppose it to have been in the past, is to contrive means of being free to set down what he chooses. He has to have the courage to say that what interests him is no longer "this" but "that": out of "that" alone must he construct his work. For the moderns "that," the point of interest, lies very likely in the dark places of psychology. At once, therefore, the accent falls a little differently; the emphasis is upon something hitherto ignored; at once a different outline of form becomes necessary, difficult for us to grasp, incomprehensible to our predecessors. No one but a modern, no one perhaps but a Russian, would have felt the interest

of the situation which Tchekov[3] has made into the short story which he calls "Gusev."[4] Some Russian soldiers lie ill on board a ship which is taking them back to Russia. We are given a few scraps of their talk and some of their thoughts; then one of them dies and is carried away; the talk goes on among the others for a time, until Gusev himself dies, and looking "like a carrot or a radish" is thrown overboard. The emphasis is laid upon such unexpected places that at first it seems as if there were no emphasis at all; and then, as the eyes accustom themselves to twilight and discern the shapes of things in a room we see how complete the story is, how profound, and how truly in obedience to his vision Tchekov has chosen this, that, and the other, and placed them together to compose something new. But it is impossible to say "this is comic," or "that is tragic," nor are we certain, since short stories, we have been taught, should be brief and conclusive, whether this, which is vague and inconclusive, should be called a short story at all.

The most elementary remarks upon modern English fiction can hardly avoid some mention of the Russian influence, and if the Russians are mentioned one runs the risk of feeling that to write of any fiction save theirs is waste of time. If we want understanding of the soul and heart where else shall we find it of comparable profundity? If we are sick of our own materialism the least considerable of their novelists has by right of birth a natural reverence for the human spirit. "Learn to make yourself akin to people .... But let this sympathy be not with the mind—for it is easy with the mind—but with the heart, with love towards them." In every great Russian writer we seem to discern the features of a saint, if sympathy for the sufferings of others, love towards them, endeavour to reach some goal worthy of the most exacting demands of the spirit constitute saintliness. It is the saint in them which confounds us with a feeling of our own irreligious triviality, and turns so many of our famous novels to tinsel and trickery. The conclusions of the Russian mind, thus comprehensive and compassionate, are inevitably, perhaps, of the utmost sadness. More accurately indeed we might speak of the

[1] *Youth ... Casterbridge* By Joseph Conrad and Thomas Hardy, respectively.

[2] *Tristram ... Pendennis* Novels by Laurence Sterne (1713–68) and William Makepeace Thackeray (1811–68), respectively.

[3] *Tchekov* Russian playwright and short story writer Anton Chekhov (1860–1904).

[4] *"Gusev"* Published in 1890.

inconclusive-ness of the Russian mind. It is the sense that there is no answer, that if honestly examined life presents question after question which must be left to sound on and on after the story is over in hopeless interrogation that fills us with a deep, and finally it may be with a resentful, despair. They are right perhaps; unquestionably they see further than we do and without our gross impediments of vision. But perhaps we see something that escapes them, or why should this voice of protest mix itself with our gloom? The voice of protest is the voice of another and an ancient civilisation which seems to have bred in us the instinct to enjoy and fight rather than to suffer and understand. English fiction from Sterne to Meredith[1] bears witness to our natural delight in humour and comedy, in the beauty of earth, in the activities of the intellect, and in the splendour of the body. But any deductions that we may draw from the comparison of two fictions so immeasurably far apart are futile save indeed as they flood us with a view of the infinite possibilities of the art and remind us that there is no limit to the horizon, and that nothing—no "method," no experiment, even of the wildest—is forbidden, but only falsity and pretence. "The proper stuff of fiction" does not exist; everything is the proper stuff of fiction, every feeling, every thought; every quality of brain and spirit is drawn upon; no perception comes amiss. And if we can imagine the art of fiction come alive and standing in our midst, she would undoubtedly bid us break her and bully her, as well as honour and love her, for so her youth is renewed and her sovereignty assured.

—1925

---

from *A Room of One's Own*[2]

CHAPTER I

But, you may say, we asked you to speak about women and fiction—what has that got to do with a room of one's own? I will try to explain. When you asked me to speak about women and fiction I sat down on the banks of a river and began to wonder what the words meant. They might mean simply a few remarks about Fanny Burney; a few more about Jane Austen; a tribute to the Brontës and a sketch of Haworth Parsonage under snow; some witticisms if possible about Miss Mitford; a respectful allusion to George Eliot; a reference to Mrs. Gaskell and one would have done.[3] But at second sight the words seemed not so simple. The title women and fiction might mean, and you may have meant it to mean, women and what they are like; or it might mean women and the fiction that they write; or it might mean women and the fiction that is written about them; or it might mean that somehow all three are inextricably mixed together and you want me to consider them in that light. But when I began to consider the subject in this last way, which seemed the most interesting, I soon saw that it had one fatal drawback. I should never be able to come to a conclusion. I should never be able to fulfil what is, I understand, the first duty of a lecturer—to hand you after an hour's discourse a nugget of pure truth to wrap up between the pages of your notebooks and keep on the mantel-piece for ever. All I could do was to offer you an opinion upon one minor point—a woman must have money and a room

---

[1] *Meredith*   George Meredith, novelist and poet (1828–1909).

[2] [Woolf's note]   This essay is based upon two papers read to the Arts Society at Newnham and the Odtaa at Girton in October 1928. The papers were too long to be read in full, and have since been altered and expanded. [Newnham and Girton are women's colleges at Cambridge University, and Odtaa (an acronym for "One Damn Thing After Another") was a literary society whose name was taken from John Masefield's 1926 novel of that title.]

[3] *Fanny Burney* (1752–1840) Novelist, diarist, and dramatist; *Haworth Parsonage* The family home of novelists Charlotte (1816–55), Emily (1818–48), and Anne (1820–49) Brontë; *Miss Mitford* Mary Russell Mitford (1787–1855), poet; *George Eliot* Pseudonym of Marian Evans (1810–65), author of many novels, including *The Mill on the Floss* (1860) and *Adam Bede* (1959); *Elizabeth Gaskell* Novelist (1810–65), author of *Cranford* and *Mary Barton*.

of her own if she is to write fiction; and that, as you will see, leaves the great problem of the true nature of woman and the true nature of fiction unsolved. I have shirked the duty of coming to a conclusion upon these two questions—women and fiction remain, so far as I am concerned, unsolved problems. But in order to make some amends I am going to do what I can to show you how I arrived at this opinion about the room and the money. I am going to develop in your presence as fully and freely as I can the train of thought which led me to think this. Perhaps if I lay bare the ideas, the prejudices, that lie behind this statement you will find that they have some bearing upon women and some upon fiction. At any rate, when a subject is highly controversial—and any question about sex is that—one cannot hope to tell the truth. One can only show how one came to hold whatever opinion one does hold. One can only give one's audience the chance of drawing their own conclusions as they observe the limitations, the prejudices, the idiosyncrasies of the speaker. Fiction here is likely to contain more truth than fact. Therefore I propose, making use of all the liberties and licences of a novelist, to tell you the story of the two days that preceded my coming here—how, bowed down by the weight of the subject which you have laid upon my shoulders, I pondered it, and made it work in and out of my daily life. I need not say that what I am about to describe has no existence; Oxbridge is an invention; so is Fernham;[1] "I" is only a convenient term for somebody who has no real being. Lies will flow from my lips, but there may perhaps be some truth mixed up with them; it is for you to seek out this truth and to decide whether any part of it is worth keeping. If not, you will of course throw the whole of it into the wastepaper basket and forget all about it.

Here then was I (call me Mary Beton, Mary Seton, Mary Carmichael[2] or by any name you please—it is not a matter of any importance) sitting on the banks of a river a week or two ago in fine October weather, lost in thought. That collar I have spoken of, women and fiction, the need of coming to some conclusion on a subject that raises all sorts of prejudices and passions, bowed my head to the ground. To the right and left bushes of some sort, golden and crimson, glowed with the colour, even it seemed burnt with the heat, of fire. On the further bank the willows wept in perpetual lamentation, their hair about their shoulders. The river reflected whatever it chose of sky and bridge and burning tree, and when the undergraduate had oared his boat through the reflections they closed again, completely, as if he had never been. There one might have sat the clock round lost in thought. Thought—to call it by a prouder name than it deserved—had let its line down into the stream. It swayed, minute after minute, hither and thither among the reflections and the weeds, letting the water lift it and sink it, until—you know the little tug—the sudden conglomeration of an idea at the end of one's line: and then the cautious hauling of it in, and the careful laying of it out? Alas, laid on the grass how small, how insignificant this thought of mine looked; the sort of fish that a good fisherman puts back into the water so that it may grow fatter and be one day worth cooking and eating. I will not trouble you with that thought now, though if you look carefully you may find it for yourselves in the course of what I am going to say.

But however small it was, it had, nevertheless, the mysterious property of its kind—put back into the mind, it became at once very exciting, and important; and as it darted and sank, and flashed hither and thither, set up such a wash and tumult of ideas that it was impossible to sit still. It was thus that I found myself walking with extreme rapidity across a grass plot. Instantly a man's figure rose to intercept me. Nor did I at first understand that the gesticulations of a curious-looking object, in a cut-away coat and evening shirt, were aimed at me. His face expressed horror and indignation. Instinct rather than reason came to my help; he was a Beadle;[3] I was a woman. This was the turf; there was the path. Only the Fellows and Scholars are allowed here; the gravel is the place for me. Such thoughts were the work of a moment. As I regained the path the arms of the Beadle sank, his face assumed its usual repose, and

---

1   *Oxbridge* Amalgamation of the names of the Universities of Oxford and Cambridge, a term used to describe the two collectively; *Fernham* Woolf combines characteristics of Newnham and Girton in her description of this fictional college.

2   *Mary Beton … Carmichael* See the "Ballad of Mary Hamilton," in which the companions of Mary, Queen of Scots were "Mary Beton and Mary Seton, / Mary Carmichael and me."

3   *Beadle* Minor church or college official.

though turf is better walking than gravel, no very great harm was done. The only charge I could bring against the Fellows and Scholars of whatever the college might happen to be was that in protection of their turf, which has been rolled for 300 years in succession, they had sent my little fish into hiding.

What idea it had been that had sent me so audaciously trespassing I could not now remember. The spirit of peace descended like a cloud from heaven, for if the spirit of peace dwells anywhere, it is in the courts and quadrangles of Oxbridge on a fine October morning. Strolling through those colleges past those ancient halls the roughness of the present seemed smoothed away; the body seemed contained in a miraculous glass cabinet through which no sound could penetrate, and the mind, freed from any contact with facts (unless one trespassed on the turf again), was at liberty to settle down upon whatever meditation was in harmony with the moment. As chance would have it, some stray memory of some old essay about revisiting Oxbridge in the long vacation brought Charles Lamb[1] to mind—Saint Charles, said Thackeray,[2] putting a letter of Lamb's to his forehead. Indeed, among all the dead (I give you my thoughts as they came to me), Lamb is one of the most congenial; one to whom one would have liked to say, Tell me then how you wrote your essays? For his essays are superior even to Max Beerbohm's,[3] I thought, with all their perfection, because of that wild flash of imagination, that lightning crack of genius in the middle of them which leaves them flawed and imperfect, but starred with poetry. Lamb then came to Oxbridge perhaps a hundred years ago. Certainly he wrote an essay—the name escapes me—about the manuscript of one of Milton's poems which he saw here. It was *Lycidas* perhaps, and Lamb wrote how it shocked him to think it possible that any word in *Lycidas* could have been different from what it is. To think of Milton changing the words in that poem seemed to him a sort of sacrilege. This led me to remem-

ber what I could of *Lycidas* and to amuse myself with guessing which word it could have been that Milton had altered, and why. It then occurred to me that the very manuscript itself which Lamb had looked at was only a few hundred yards away, so that one could follow Lamb's footsteps across the quadrangle to that famous library[4] where the treasure is kept. Moreover, I recollected, as I put this plan into execution, it is in this famous library that the manuscript of Thackeray's *Esmond* is also preserved. The critics often say that *Esmond* is Thackeray's most perfect novel. But the affectation of the style, with its imitation of the eighteenth century, hampers one, so far as I remember; unless indeed the eighteenth-century style was natural to Thackeray—a fact that one might prove by looking at the manuscript and seeing whether the alterations were for the benefit of the style or of the sense. But then one would have to decide what is style and what is meaning, a question which—but here I was actually at the door which leads into the library itself. I must have opened it, for instantly there issued, like a guardian angel barring the way with a flutter of black gown instead of white wings, a deprecating, silvery, kindly gentleman, who regretted in a low voice as he waved me back that ladies are only admitted to the library if accompanied by a Fellow of the College or furnished with a letter of introduction.

That a famous library has been cursed by a woman is a matter of complete indifference to a famous library. Venerable and calm, with all its treasures safe locked within its breast, it sleeps complacently and will, so far as I am concerned, so sleep for ever. Never will I wake those echoes, never will I ask for that hospitality again, I vowed as I descended the steps in anger. Still an hour remained before luncheon, and what was one to do? Stroll on the meadows? Sit by the river? Certainly it was a lovely autumn morning; the leaves were fluttering red to the ground; there was no great hardship in doing either. But the sound of music reached my ear. Some service or celebration was going forward. The organ complained magnificently as I passed the chapel door. Even the sorrow of Christianity sounded in that serene air more like the recollection of sorrow than sorrow

[1] *Charles Lamb* English essayist (1775–1834). The essay referred to later in this paragraph is "Oxford in the Vacation" (1820).

[2] *Thackeray* William Makepeace Thackeray, English novelist (1811–1863).

[3] *Max Beerbohm* English parodist, essayist, and cartoonist (1872–1956).

[4] *that famous library* The manuscript of Milton's *Lycidas* held by the library of Trinity College, Cambridge.

itself; even the groanings of the ancient organ seemed lapped in peace. I had no wish to enter had I the right, and this time the verger[1] might have stopped me, demanding perhaps my baptismal certificate, or a letter of introduction from the Dean. But the outside of these magnificent buildings is often as beautiful as the inside. Moreover, it was amusing enough to watch the congregation assembling, coming in and going out again, busying themselves at the door of the chapel like bees at the mouth of a hive. Many were in cap and gown; some had tufts of fur on their shoulders; others were wheeled in bath-chairs;[2] others, though not past middle age, seemed creased and crushed into shapes so singular that one was reminded of those giant crabs and crayfish who heave with difficulty across the sand of an aquarium. As I leant against the wall the University indeed seemed a sanctuary in which are preserved rare types which would soon be obsolete if left to fight for existence on the pavement of the Strand.[3] Old stories of old deans and old dons came back to mind, but before I had summoned up courage to whistle—it used to be said that at the sound of a whistle old Professor —— instantly broke into a gallop—the venerable congregation had gone inside. The outside of the chapel remained. As you know, its high domes and pinnacles can be seen, like a sailing-ship always voyaging never arriving, lit up at night and visible for miles, far away across the hills.[4] Once, presumably, this quadrangle with its smooth lawns, its massive buildings, and the chapel itself was marsh too, where the grasses waved and the swine rootled.[5] Teams of horses and oxen, I thought, must have hauled the stone in wagons from far countries, and then with infinite labour the grey blocks in whose shade I was now standing were poised in order one on top of another, and then the painters brought their glass for the windows, and the masons were busy for centuries up on that roof with putty and cement, spade and trowel.

Every Saturday somebody must have poured gold and silver out of a leathern purse into their ancient fists, for they had their beer and skittles[6] presumably of an evening. An unending stream of gold and silver, I thought, must have flowed into this court perpetually to keep the stones coming and the masons working; to level, to ditch, to dig and to drain. But it was then the age of faith, and money was poured liberally to set these stones on a deep foundation, and when the stones were raised, still more money was poured in from the coffers of kings and queens and great nobles to ensure that hymns should be sung here and scholars taught. Lands were granted; tithes were paid. And when the age of faith was over and the age of reason had come, still the same flow of gold and silver went on; fellowships were founded; lectureships endowed; only the gold and silver flowed now, not from the coffers of the king, but from the chests of merchants and manufacturers, from the purses of men who had made, say, a fortune from industry, and returned, in their wills, a bounteous share of it to endow more chairs, more lectureships, more fellowships in the university where they had learnt their craft. Hence the libraries and laboratories; the observatories; the splendid equipment of costly and delicate instruments which now stands on glass shelves, where centuries ago the grasses waved and the swine rootled. Certainly, as I strolled round the court, the foundation of gold and silver seemed deep enough; the pavement laid solidly over the wild grasses. Men with trays on their heads went busily from staircase to staircase. Gaudy blossoms flowered in window-boxes. The strains of the gramophone blared out from the rooms within. It was impossible not to reflect—the reflection whatever it may have been was cut short. The clock struck. It was time to find one's way to luncheon.

It is a curious fact that novelists have a way of making us believe that luncheon parties are invariably memorable for something very witty that was said, or for something very wise that was done. But they seldom spare a word for what was eaten. It is part of the novelist's convention not to mention soup and salmon and ducklings, as if soup and salmon and ducklings were of no importance whatsoever, as if nobody ever smoked a

---

[1] *verger*   Church attendant.

[2] *bath-chairs*   Large chairs on wheels for invalids, so named for Bath, an English spa city, and retreat for ill and elderly people.

[3] *the Strand*   Busy street in London that runs parallel to the northern bank of the Thames.

[4] *As you ... hills*   Description of the chapel of King's College, Cambridge, which was built from 1446 to 1547.

[5] *rootled*   Rooted about.

[6] *skittles*   Game resembling bowling. The expression "all beer and skittles" denotes pure enjoyment.

cigar or drank a glass of wine. Here, however, I shall take the liberty to defy that convention and to tell you that the lunch on this occasion began with soles, sunk in a deep dish, over which the college cook had spread a counterpane of the whitest cream, save that it was branded here and there with brown spots like the spots on the flanks of a doe. After that came the partridges, but if this suggests a couple of bald, brown birds on a plate you are mistaken. The partridges, many and various, came with all their retinue of sauces and salads, the sharp and the sweet, each in its order; their potatoes, thin as coins but not so hard; their sprouts, foliated as rosebuds but more succulent. And no sooner had the roast and its retinue been done with than the silent serving-man, the Beadle himself perhaps in a milder manifestation, set before us, wreathed in napkins, a confection which rose all sugar from the waves. To call it pudding and so relate it to rice and tapioca would be an insult. Meanwhile the wineglasses had flushed yellow and flushed crimson; had been emptied; had been filled. And thus by degrees was lit, halfway down the spine, which is the seat of the soul, not that hard little electric light which we call brilliance, as it pops in and out upon our lips, but the more profound, subtle and subterranean glow, which is the rich yellow flame of rational intercourse. No need to hurry. No need to sparkle. No need to be anybody but oneself. We are all going to heaven and Vandyck is of the company[1]—in other words, how good life seemed, how sweet its rewards, how trivial this grudge or that grievance, how admirable friendship and the society of one's kind, as, lighting a good cigarette, one sunk among the cushions in the window-seat.

If by good luck there had been an ashtray handy, if one had not knocked the ash out of the window in default, if things had been a little different from what they were, one would not have seen, presumably, a cat without a tail. The sight of that abrupt and truncated animal padding softly across the quadrangle changed by some fluke of the subconscious intelligence the emotional light for me. It was as if some one had let fall a

shade. Perhaps the excellent hock[2] was relinquishing its hold. Certainly, as I watched the Manx cat pause in the middle of the lawn as if it too questioned the universe, something seemed lacking, something seemed different. But what was lacking, what was different, I asked myself, listening to the talk. And to answer that question I had to think myself out of the room, back into the past, before the war indeed, and to set before my eyes the model of another luncheon party held in rooms not very far distant from these; but different. Everything was different. Meanwhile the talk went on among the guests, who were many and young, some of this sex, some of that; it went on swimmingly, it went on agreeably, freely, amusingly. And as it went on I set it against the background of that other talk, and as I matched the two together I had no doubt that one was the descendant, the legitimate heir of the other. Nothing was changed; nothing was different save only—here I listened with all my ears not entirely to what was being said, but to the murmur or current behind it. Yes, that was it—the change was there. Before the war at a luncheon party like this people would have said precisely the same things but they would have sounded different, because in those days they were accompanied by a sort of humming noise, not articulate, but musical, exciting, which changed the value of the words themselves. Could one set that humming noise to words? Perhaps with the help of the poets one could. A book lay beside me and, opening it, I turned casually enough to Tennyson. And here I found Tennyson was singing:

There has fallen a splendid tear
    From the passion-flower at the gate.
She is coming, my dove, my dear;
    She is coming, my life, my fate;
The red rose cries, "She is near, she is near;"
    And the white rose weeps, "She is late;"
The larkspur listens, "I hear, I hear;"
    And the lily whispers, "I wait."[3]

Was that what men hummed at luncheon parties before the war? And the women?

---

[1] We are all ... company These were said to be the last words of English portrait and landscape painter Thomas Gainsborough (1727–88); Vandyck Sir Anthony Van Dyck (1599–1641), portrait artist.

[2] hock I.e., Hochheimer, a German white wine.

[3] There has ... wait from Alfred, Lord Tennyson's "Maud" (1855), 1.22.10.

> *My heart is like a singing bird*
>   *Whose nest is in a water'd shoot;*
> *My heart is like an apple tree*
>   *Whose boughs are bent with thick-set fruit—*
> *My heart is like a rainbow shell*
>   *That paddles in a halycon sea;*
> *My heart is gladder than all these*
>   *Because my love is come to me.*[1]

Was that what women hummed at luncheon parties before the war?

There was something so ludicrous in thinking of people humming such things even under their breath at luncheon parties before the war that I burst out laughing, and had to explain my laughter by pointing at the Manx cat, who did look a little absurd, poor beast, without a tail, in the middle of the lawn. Was he really born so, or had he lost his tail in an accident? The tailless cat, though some are said to exist in the Isle of Man, is rarer than one thinks. It is a queer animal, quaint rather than beautiful. It is strange what a difference a tail makes—you know the sort of things one says as a lunch party breaks up and people are finding their coats and hats.

This one, thanks to the hospitality of the host, had lasted far into the afternoon. The beautiful October day was fading and the leaves were falling from the trees in the avenue as I walked through it. Gate after gate seemed to close with gentle finality behind me. Innumerable beadles were fitting innumerable keys into well-oiled locks; the treasure-house was being made secure for another night. After the avenue one comes out upon a road—I forget its name—which leads you, if you take the right turning, along to Fernham. But there was plenty of time. Dinner was not till half-past seven. One could almost do without dinner after such a luncheon. It is strange how a scrap of poetry works in the mind and makes the legs move in time to it along the road. Those words—

> *There has fallen a splendid tear*
> *From the passion-flower at the gate.*
> *She is coming, my dove, my dear—*

sang in my blood as I stepped quickly along towards Headingley. And then, switching off into the other measure, I sang, where the waters are churned up by the weir:

> *My heart is like a singing bird*
>   *Whose nest is in a water'd shoot;*
> *My heart is like an apple tree ....*

What poets, I cried aloud, as one does in the dusk, what poets they were!

In a sort of jealousy, I suppose, for our own age, silly and absurd though these comparisons are, I went on to wonder if honestly one could name two living poets now as great as Tennyson and Christina Rossetti were then. Obviously it is impossible, I thought, looking into those foaming waters, to compare them. The very reason why the poetry excites one to such abandonment, such rapture, is that it celebrates some feeling that one used to have (at luncheon parties before the war perhaps), so that one responds easily, familiarly, without troubling to check the feeling, or to compare it with any that one has now. But the living poets express a feeling that is actually being made and torn out of us at the moment. One does not recognize it in the first place; often for some reason one fears it; one watches it with keenness and compares it jealously and suspiciously with the old feeling that one knew. Hence the difficulty of modern poetry; and it is because of this difficulty that one cannot remember more than two consecutive lines of any good modern poet. For this reason—that my memory failed me—the argument flagged for want of material. But why, I continued, moving on towards Headingley, have we stopped humming under our breath at luncheon parties? Why has Alfred ceased to sing

> *She is coming, my dove, my dear?*

Why has Christina ceased to respond

> *My heart is gladder than all these*
> *Because my love is come to me?*

Shall we lay the blame on the war? When the guns fired in August 1914, did the faces of men and women show so plain in each other's eyes that romance was killed? Certainly it was a shock (to women in particular with

---

[1] *My heart ... me* The opening stanza of Christina Rossetti's "A Birthday" (1861).

their illusions about education, and so on) to see the faces of our rulers in the light of the shell-fire. So ugly they looked—German, English, French—so stupid. But lay the blame where one will, on whom one will, the illusion which inspired Tennyson and Christina Rossetti to sing so passionately about the coming of their loves is far rarer now than then. One has only to read, to look, to listen, to remember. But why say "blame"? Why, if it was an illusion, not praise the catastrophe, whatever it was, that destroyed illusion and put truth in its place? For truth … those dots mark the spot where, in search of truth, I missed the turning up to Fernham. Yes indeed, which was truth and which was illusion, I asked myself. What was the truth about these houses, for example, dim and festive now with their red windows in the dusk, but raw and red and squalid, with their sweets and their boot-laces, at nine o'clock in the morning? And the willows and the river and the gardens that run down to the river, vague now with the mist stealing over them, but gold and red in the sunlight—which was the truth, which was the illusion about them? I spare you the twists and turns of my cogitations, for no conclusion was found on the road to Headingley, and I ask you to suppose that I soon found out my mistake about the turning and retraced my steps to Fernham.

As I have said already that it was an October day, I dare not forfeit your respect and imperil the fair name of fiction by changing the season and describing lilacs hanging over garden walls, crocuses, tulips and other flowers of spring. Fiction must stick to facts, and the truer the facts the better the fiction—so we are told. Therefore it was still autumn and the leaves were still yellow and falling, if anything, a little faster than before, because it was now evening (seven twenty-three to be precise) and a breeze (from the southwest to be exact) had risen. But for all that there was something odd at work:

> My heart is like a singing bird
> Whose nest is in a water'd shoot;
> My heart is like an apple tree
> Whose boughs are bent with thick-set fruit—

perhaps the words of Christina Rossetti were partly responsible for the folly of the fancy—it was nothing of course but a fancy—that the lilac was shaking its flowers over the garden walls, and the brimstone butterflies were

scudding hither and thither, and the dust of the pollen was in the air. A wind blew, from what quarter I know not, but it lifted the half-grown leaves so that there was a flash of silver grey in the air. It was the time between the lights when colours undergo their intensification and purples and golds burn in window-panes like the beat of an excitable heart; when for some reason the beauty of the world revealed and yet soon to perish (here I pushed into the garden, for, unwisely, the door was left open and no beadles seemed about), the beauty of the world which is so soon to perish, has two edges, one of laughter, one of anguish, cutting the heart asunder. The gardens of Fernham lay before me in the spring twilight, wild and open, and in the long grass, sprinkled and carelessly flung, were daffodils and bluebells, not orderly perhaps at the best of times, and now wind-blown and waving as they tugged at their roots. The windows of the building, curved like ships' windows among generous waves of red brick, changed from lemon to silver under the flight of the quick spring clouds. Somebody was in a hammock, somebody, but in this light they were phantoms only, half guessed, half seen, raced across the grass—would no one stop her?—and then on the terrace, as if popping out to breathe the air, to glance at the garden, came a bent figure, formidable yet humble, with her great forehead and her shabby dress—could it be the famous scholar, could it be J —— H ——[1] herself? All was dim, yet intense too, as if the scarf which the dusk had flung over the garden were torn asunder by star or sword—the flash of some terrible reality leaping, as its way is, out of the heart of the spring. For youth—

Here was my soup. Dinner was being served in the great dining-hall. Far from being spring it was in fact an evening in October. Everybody was assembled in the big dining-room. Dinner was ready. Here was the soup. It was a plain gravy soup. There was nothing to stir the fancy in that. One could have seen through the transparent liquid any pattern that there might have been on the plate itself. But there was no pattern. The plate was plain. Next came beef with its attendant greens and potatoes—a homely trinity, suggesting the rumps of cattle in a muddy market, and sprouts curled and yellowed at the edge, and bargaining and cheapening,

[1] J —— H —— Jane Harrison (1850–1928), cultural anthropologist and archaeologist who was a Fellow at Newnham College.

and women with string bags on Monday morning. There was no reason to complain of human nature's daily food, seeing that the supply was sufficient and coal-miners doubtless were sitting down to less. Prunes and custard followed. And if any one complains that prunes, even when mitigated by custard, are an uncharitable vegetable (fruit they are not), stringy as a miser's heart and exuding a fluid such as might run in misers' veins who have denied themselves wine and warmth for eighty years and yet not given to the poor, he should reflect that there are people whose charity embraces even the prune. Biscuits and cheese came next, and here the water-jug was liberally passed round, for it is the nature of biscuits to be dry, and these were biscuits to the core. That was all. The meal was over. Everybody scraped their chairs back; the swing-doors swung violently to and fro; soon the hall was emptied of every sign of food and made ready no doubt for breakfast next morning. Down corridors and up staircases the youth of England went banging and singing. And was it for a guest, a stranger (for I had no more right here in Fernham than in Trinity or Somerville or Girton or Newnham or Christchurch[1]), to say, "The dinner was not good," or to say (we were now, Mary Seton and I, in her sitting-room), "Could we not have dined up here alone?" for if I had said anything of the kind I should have been prying and searching into the secret economies of a house which to the stranger wears so fine a front of gaiety and courage. No, one could say nothing of the sort. Indeed, conversation for a moment flagged. The human frame being what it is, heart, body and brain all mixed together, and not contained in separate compartments as they will be no doubt in another million years, a good dinner is of great importance to good talk. One cannot think well, love well, sleep well, if one has not dined well. The lamp in the spine does not light on beef and prunes. We are all *probably* going to heaven, and Vandyck is, we *hope*, to meet us round the next corner—that is the dubious and qualifying state of mind that beef and prunes at the end of the day's work breed between them. Happily my friend, who taught science, had a cupboard where there was a squat bottle and little

glasses—(but there should have been sole and partridge to begin with)—so that we were able to draw up to the fire and repair some of the damages of the day's living. In a minute or so we were slipping freely in and out among all those objects of curiosity and interest which form in the mind in the absence of a particular person, and are naturally to be discussed on coming together again—how somebody has married, another has not; one thinks this, another that; one has improved out of all knowledge, the other most amazingly gone to the bad—with all those speculations upon human nature and the character of the amazing world we live in which spring naturally from such beginnings. While these things were being said, however, I became shamefacedly aware of a current setting in of its own accord and carrying everything forward to an end of its own. One might be talking of Spain or Portugal, or book or racehorse, but the real interest of whatever was said was none of those things, but a scene of masons on a high roof some five centuries ago. Kings and nobles brought treasure in huge sacks and poured it under the earth. This scene was for ever coming alive in my mind and placing itself by another of lean cows and a muddy market and withered greens and the stringy hearts of old men—these two pictures, disjointed and disconnected and nonsensical as they were, were for ever coming together and combating each other and had me entirely at their mercy. The best course, unless the whole talk was to be distorted, was to expose what was in my mind to the air, when with good luck it would fade and crumble like the head of the dead king when they opened the coffin at Windsor. Briefly, then, I told Miss Seton about the masons who had been all those years on the roof of the chapel, and about the kings and queens and nobles bearing sacks of gold and silver on their shoulders, which they shovelled into the earth; and then how the great financial magnates of our own time came and laid cheques and bonds, I suppose, where the others had laid ingots and rough lumps of gold. All that lies beneath the colleges down there, I said; but this college, where we are now sitting, what lies beneath its gallant red brick and the wild unkempt grasses of the garden? What force is behind the plain china off which we dined, and (here it popped out of my mouth before I could stop it) the beef, the custard and the prunes?

---

[1] *Trinity … Christchurch* Somerville and Christchurch are colleges at Oxford, while Trinity, Girton, and Newnham are Cambridge colleges.

Well, said Mary Seton, about the year 1860—Oh, but you know the story, she said, bored, I suppose, by the recital. And she told me—rooms were hired. Committees met. Envelopes were addressed. Circulars were drawn up. Meetings were held; letters were read out; so-and-so has promised so much; on the contrary, Mr. —— won't give a penny. The *Saturday Review* has been very rude. How can we raise a fund to pay for offices? Shall we hold a bazaar? Can't we find a pretty girl to sit in the front row? Let us look up what John Stuart Mill[1] said on the subject. Can any one persuade the editor of the —— to print a letter? Can we get Lady —— to sign it? Lady —— is out of town. That was the way it was done, presumably, sixty years ago, and it was a prodigious effort, and a great deal of time was spent on it. And it was only after a long struggle and with the utmost difficulty that they got thirty thousand pounds together.[2] So obviously we cannot have wine and partridges and servants carrying tin dishes on their heads, she said. We cannot have sofas and separate rooms. "The amenities," she said, quoting from some book or other, "will have to wait."[3]

At the thought of all those women working year after year and finding it hard to get two thousand pounds together, and as much as they could do to get thirty thousand pounds, we burst out in scorn at the reprehensible poverty of our sex. What had our mothers been doing then that they had no wealth to leave us? Powdering their noses? Looking in at shop windows? Flaunting in the sun at Monte Carlo? There were some photographs on the mantel-piece. Mary's mother—if that was her picture—may have been a wastrel[4] in her spare time (she had thirteen children by a minister of the church), but if so her gay and dissipated life had left

too few traces of its pleasures on her face. She was a homely body; an old lady in a plaid shawl which was fastened by a large cameo; and she sat in a basket-chair, encouraging a spaniel to look at the camera, with the amused, yet strained expression of one who is sure that the dog will move directly the bulb is pressed. Now if she had gone into business; had become a manufacturer of artificial silk or a magnate on the Stock Exchange; if she had left two or three hundred thousand pounds to Fernham, we could have been sitting at our ease tonight and the subject of our talk might have been archaeology, botany, anthropology, physics, the nature of the atom, mathematics, astronomy, relativity, geography. If only Mrs. Seton and her mother and her mother before her had learnt the great art of making money and had left their money, like their fathers and their grandfathers before them, to found fellowships and lectureships and prizes and scholarships appropriated to the use of their own sex, we might have dined very tolerably up here alone off a bird and a bottle of wine; we might have looked forward without undue confidence to a pleasant and honourable lifetime spent in the shelter of one of the liberally endowed professions. We might have been exploring or writing; mooning about the venerable places of the earth; sitting contemplative on the steps of the Parthenon, or going at ten to an office and coming home comfortably at half-past four to write a little poetry. Only, if Mrs. Seton and her like had gone into business at the age of fifteen, there would have been— that was the snag in the argument—no Mary. What, I asked, did Mary think of that? There between the curtains was the October night, calm and lovely, with a star or two caught in the yellowing trees. Was she ready to resign her share of it and her memories (for they had been a happy family, though a large one) of games and quarrels up in Scotland, which she is never tired of praising for the fineness of its air and the quality of its cakes, in order that Fernham might have been endowed with fifty thousand pounds or so by a stroke of the pen? For, to endow a college would necessitate the suppression of families altogether. Making a fortune and bearing thirteen children—no human being could stand it. Consider the facts, we said. First there are nine months before the baby is born. Then the baby is born. Then there are three or four months spent in feeding

1. *John Stuart Mill* English philosopher and economist (1806–73) who was interested in the status and treatment of women; author of *The Subjection of Women.*

2. [Woolf's note] "We are told that we ought to ask for 30,000 at least.... It is not a large sum, considering that there is to be but one college of this sort for Great Britain, Ireland, and the Colonies, and considering how easy it is to raise immense sums for boys' schools. But considering how few people really wish women to be educated, it is a good deal."—Lady Stephen, *Life of Miss Emily Davies.*

3. [Woolf's note] "Every penny which could be scraped together was set aside for building, and the amenities had to be postponed." –R. Strachey, *The Cause.*

4. *wastrel* Spendthrift.

the baby. After the baby is fed there are certainly five years spent in playing with the baby. You cannot, it seems, let children run about the streets. People who have seen them running wild in Russia say that the sight is not a pleasant one. People say, too, that human nature takes its shape in the years between one and five. If Mrs. Seton, I said, had been making money, what sort of memories would you have had of games and quarrels? What would you have known of Scotland, and its fine air and cakes and all the rest of it? But it is useless to ask these questions, because you would never have come into existence at all. Moreover, it is equally useless to ask what might have happened if Mrs. Seton and her mother and her mother before her had amassed great wealth and laid it under the foundations of college and library, because, in the first place, to earn money was impossible for them, and in the second, had it been possible, the law denied them the right to possess what money they earned. It is only for the last forty-eight years that Mrs. Seton has had a penny of her own.[1] For all the centuries before that it would have been her husband's property—a thought which, perhaps, may have had its share in keeping Mrs. Seton and her mothers off the Stock Exchange. Every penny I earn, they may have said, will be taken from me and disposed of according to my husband's wisdom—perhaps to found a scholarship or to endow a fellowship in Balliol or Kings,[2] so that to earn money, even if I could earn money, is not a matter that interests me very greatly. I had better leave it to my husband.

At any rate, whether or not the blame rested on the old lady who was looking at the spaniel, there could be no doubt that for some reason or other our mothers had mismanaged their affairs very gravely. Not a penny could be spared for "amenities"; for partridges and wine, beadles and turf, books and cigars, libraries and leisure. To raise bare walls out of the bare earth was the utmost they could do.

So we talked standing at the window and looking, as so many thousands look every night, down on the domes and towers of the famous city beneath us. It was very beautiful, very mysterious in the autumn moonlight. The old stone looked very white and venerable. One thought of all the books that were assembled down there; of the pictures of old prelates and worthies hanging in the panelled rooms; of the painted windows that would be throwing strange globes and crescents on the pavement; of the tablets and memorials and inscriptions; of the fountains and the grass; of the quiet rooms looking across the quiet quadrangles. And (pardon me the thought) I thought, too, of the admirable smoke and drink and the deep armchairs and the pleasant carpets: of the urbanity, the geniality, the dignity which are the offspring of luxury and privacy and space. Certainly our mothers had not provided us with anything comparable to all this—our mothers who found it difficult to scrape together thirty thousand pounds, our mothers who bore thirteen children to ministers of religion at St. Andrews.

So I went back to my inn, and as I walked through the dark streets I pondered this and that, as one does at the end of the day's work. I pondered why it was that Mrs. Seton had no money to leave us; and what effect poverty has on the mind; and what effect wealth has on the mind; and I thought of the queer old gentlemen I had seen that morning with tufts of fur upon their shoulders; and I remembered how if one whistled one of them ran; and I thought of the organ booming in the chapel and of the shut doors of the library; and I thought how unpleasant it is to be locked out; and I thought how it is worse perhaps to be locked in; and, thinking of the safety and prosperity of the one sex and of the poverty and insecurity of the other and of the effect of tradition and of the lack of tradition upon the mind of a writer, I thought at last that it was time to roll up the crumpled skin of the day, with its arguments and its impressions and its anger and its laughter, and cast it into the hedge. A thousand stars were flashing across the blue wastes of the sky. One seemed alone with an inscrutable society. All human beings were laid asleep—prone, horizontal, dumb. Nobody seemed stirring in the streets of Oxbridge. Even the door of the hotel sprang open at the touch of an invisible hand—not a boots[3] was sitting up to light me to bed, it was so late.

---

1. *It is ... own*   Reference to the Married Women's Property Acts of 1870 and 1882, which allowed married women the same rights to their property that single women enjoyed.

2. *Balliol or Kings*   Two colleges, the first at Oxford and the second at Cambridge.

3. *boots*   I.e., hotel servant, because one of a servant's chores was to clean the guests' boots.

CHAPTER 2

The scene, if I may ask you to follow me, was now changed. The leaves were still falling, but in London now, not Oxbridge; and I must ask you to imagine a room, like many thousands, with a window looking across people's hats and vans and motor-cars to other windows, and on the table inside the room a blank sheet of paper on which was written in large letters WOMEN AND FICTION, but no more. The inevitable sequel to lunching and dining at Oxbridge seemed, unfortunately, to be a visit to the British Museum. One must strain off what was personal and accidental in all these impressions and so reach the pure fluid, the essential oil of truth. For that visit to Oxbridge and the luncheon and the dinner had started a swarm of questions. Why did men drink wine and women water? Why was one sex so prosperous and the other so poor? What effect has poverty on fiction? What conditions are necessary for the creation of works of art?—a thousand questions at once suggested themselves. But one needed answers, not questions; and an answer was only to be had by consulting the learned and the unprejudiced, who have removed themselves above the strife of tongue and the confusion of body and issued the result of their reasoning and research in books which are to be found in the British Museum. If truth is not to be found on the shelves of the British Museum, where, I asked myself, picking up a notebook and a pencil, is truth?

Thus provided, thus confident and enquiring, I set out in the pursuit of truth. The day, though not actually wet, was dismal, and the streets in the neighbourhood of the Museum were full of open coal-holes, down which sacks were showering; four-wheeled cabs were drawing up and depositing on the pavement corded boxes containing, presumably, the entire wardrobe of some Swiss or Italian family seeking fortune or refuge or some other desirable commodity which is to be found in the boarding-houses of Bloomsbury[1] in the winter. The usual hoarse-voiced men paraded the streets with plants on barrows. Some shouted; others sang. London was like a workshop. London was like a machine. We were all

being shot backwards and forwards on this plain foundation to make some pattern. The British Museum was another department of the factory. The swing-doors swung open; and there one stood under the vast dome, as if one were a thought in the huge bald forehead which is so splendidly encircled by a band of famous names. One went to the counter; one took a slip of paper; one opened a volume of the catalogue, and .... the five dots here indicate five separate minutes of stupefaction, wonder, and bewilderment. Have you any notion of how many books are written about women in the course of one year? Have you any notion how many are written by men? Are you aware that you are, perhaps, the most discussed animal in the universe? Here had I come with a notebook and pencil proposing to spend a morning reading, supposing that at the end of the morning I should have transferred the truth to my notebook. But I should need to be a herd of elephants, I thought, and a wilderness of spiders, desperately referring to the animals that are reputed longest lived and most multitudinously eyed, to cope with all this. I should need claws of steel and beak of brass even to penetrate the husk. How shall I ever find the grains of truth embedded in all this mass of paper, I asked myself, and in despair began running my eye up and down the long list of titles. Even the names of the books gave me food for thought. Sex and its nature might well attract doctors and biologists; but what was surprising and difficult of explanation was the fact that sex—woman, that is to say—also attracts agreeable essayists, light-fingered novelists, young men who have taken the M.A. degree; men who have taken no degree; men who have no apparent qualification save that they are not women. Some of these books were, on the face of it, frivolous and facetious; but many, on the other hand, were serious and prophetic, moral and hortatory. Merely to read the titles suggested innumerable schoolmasters, innumerable clergymen mounting their platforms and pulpits and holding forth with a loquacity which far exceeded the hour usually allotted to such discourse on this one subject. It was a most strange phenomenon; and apparently—here I consulted the letter M—one confined to male sex. Women do not write books about men—a fact that I could not help welcoming with relief, for if I had first to read all that men have written

---

[1] *Bloomsbury* Area of London in which the British Museum is located and in which many of Woolf's circle (known collectively as "The Bloomsbury Group") lived.

about women, then all that women have written about men, the aloe that flowers once in a hundred years would flower twice before I could set pen to paper. So, making a perfectly arbitrary choice of a dozen volumes or so, I sent my slips of paper to lie in the wire tray, and waited in my stall, among the other seekers for the essential oil of truth.

What could be the reason, then, of this curious disparity, I wondered, drawing cart-wheels on the slips of paper provided by the British taxpayer for other purposes. Why are women, judging from this catalogue, so much more interesting to men than men are to women? A very curious fact it seemed, and my mind wandered to picture the lives of men who spend their time in writing books about women; whether they were old or young, married or unmarried, red-nosed or humpbacked—anyhow, it was flattering, vaguely, to feel oneself the object of such attention, provided that it was not entirely bestowed by the crippled and the infirm—so I pondered until all such frivolous thoughts were ended by an avalanche of books sliding down on to the desk in front of me. Now the trouble began. The student who has been trained in research at Oxbridge has no doubt some method of shepherding his question past all distractions till it runs into its answer as a sheep runs into its pen. The student by my side, for instance, who was copying assiduously from a scientific manual was, I felt sure, extracting pure nuggets of the essential ore every ten minutes or so. His little grunts of satisfaction indicated so much. But if, unfortunately, one has had no training in a university, the question far from being shepherded into its pen flies like a frightened flock hither and thither, helter-skelter, pursued by a whole pack of hounds. Professors, schoolmasters, sociologists, clergymen, novelists, essayists, journalists, men who had no qualification save that they were not women, chased my simple and single question—Why are women poor?—until it became fifty questions; until the fifty questions leapt frantically into mid-stream and were carried away. Every page in my notebook was scribbled over with notes. To show the state of mind I was in, I will read you a few of them, explaining that the page was headed quite simply, WOMEN AND POVERTY, in block letters; but what followed was something like this:

Condition in Middle Ages of,
Habits in the Fiji Islands of,
Worshipped as goddesses by,
Weaker in moral sense than,
Idealism of,
Greater conscientiousness of,
South Sea Islanders, age of puberty among,
Attractiveness of,
Offered as sacrifice to,
Small size of brain of,
Profounder sub-consciousness of,
Less hair on the body of,
Mental, moral and physical inferiority of,
Love of children of,
Greater length of life of,
Weaker muscles of,
Strength of affections of,
Vanity of,
Higher education of,
Shakespeare's opinion of,
Lord Birkenhead's[1] opinion of,
Dean Inge's[2] opinion of,
La Bruyère's[3] opinion of,
Dr. Johnson's[4] opinion of,
Mr. Oscar Browning's[5] opinion of, …

Here I drew breath and added, indeed, in the margin, Why does Samuel Butler[6] say, "Wise men never say what they think of women?" Wise men never say anything else apparently. But, I continued, leaning back in my chair and looking at the vast dome in which I was a single but by now somewhat harassed thought, what is so unfortunate is that wise men never think the same thing about women. Here is Pope:

---

[1] *Lord Birkenhead* Frederick Elwin Smith, Earl of Birkenhead, who was Lord Chancellor from 1919 to 1922 and an opponent of women's suffrage.

[2] *Dean Inge* William Ralph Inge, Dean of St. Paul's Cathedral from 1911 to 1934.

[3] *La Bruyère* Jean de La Bruyère, French essayist and moralist (1645–1696).

[4] *Dr. Johnson* Samuel Johnson (1709–84), British lexicographer, critic, poet, and essayist.

[5] *Mr. Oscar Browning* History lecturer at King's College, Cambridge (1837–1923).

[6] *Samuel Butler* Nineteenth-century English author (1835–1902).

Most women have no character at all.[1]

And here is La Bruyère:

*Les femmes sont extrêmes; elles sont meilleures ou
pires que les hommes—*[2]

a direct contradiction by keen observers who were contemporary. Are they capable of education or incapable? Napoleon thought them incapable. Dr. Johnson thought the opposite.[3] Have they souls or have they not souls? Some savages say they have none. Others, on the contrary, maintain that women are half divine and worship them on that account.[4] Some sages hold that they are shallower in the brain; others that they are deeper in the consciousness. Goethe[5] honoured them; Mussolini[6] despises them. Wherever one looked men thought about women and thought differently. It was impossible to make head or tail of it all, I decided, glancing with envy at the reader next door who was making the neatest abstracts, headed often with an A or a B or a C, while my own notebook rioted with the wildest scribble of contradictory jottings. It was distressing, it was bewildering, it was humiliating. Truth had run through my fingers. Every drop had escaped.

I could not possibly go home, I reflected, and add as a serious contribution to the study of women and fiction that women have less hair on their bodies than men, or that the age of puberty among the South Sea Islanders is nine—or is it ninety?—even the handwriting had become in its distraction indecipherable. It was disgraceful to have nothing more weighty or respectable to show after a whole morning's work. And if I could not grasp the truth about W. (as for brevity's sake I had come to call her) in the past, why bother about W. in the future? It seemed pure waste of time to consult all those gentlemen who specialise in woman and her effect on whatever it may be—politics, children, wages, morality—numerous and learned as they are. One might as well leave their books unopened.

But while I pondered I had unconsciously, in my listlessness, in my desperation, been drawing a picture where I should, like my neighbour, have been writing a conclusion. I had been drawing a face, a figure. It was the face and the figure of Professor von X. engaged in writing his monumental work entitled *The Mental, Moral, and Physical Inferiority of the Female Sex.* He was not in my picture a man attractive to women. He was heavily built; he had a great jowl; to balance that he had very small eyes; he was very red in the face. His expression suggested that he was labouring under some emotion that made him jab his pen on the paper as if he were killing some noxious insect as he wrote, but even when he had killed it that did not satisfy him; he must go on killing it; and even so, some cause for anger and irritation remained. Could it be his wife, I asked, looking at my picture. Was she in love with a cavalry officer? Was the cavalry officer slim and elegant and dressed in astrachan?[7] Had he been laughed at, to adopt the Freudian theory, in his cradle by a pretty girl? For even in his cradle the professor, I thought, could not have been an attractive child. Whatever the reason, the professor was made to look very angry and very ugly in my sketch, as he wrote his great book upon the mental, moral and physical inferiority of women. Drawing pictures was an idle way of finishing an unprofitable morning's work. Yet it is in our idleness, in our dreams, that the submerged truth sometimes comes to the top. A very elementary exercise in psychology, not to be dignified by the name of psycho-analysis, showed me,

---

[1] *Most ... all* From the opening of English poet and satirist Alexander Pope's Epistle 2, "To a Lady" from his *Moral Essays*: "Nothing so true as what you once let fall, / 'Most women have no character at all.'"

[2] *Les ... hommes* "Women are extreme: they are better or worse than men." From La Bruyère's *Les Caractères* (1688).

[3] [Woolf's note] "'Men know that women are an overmatch for them, and therefore they choose the weakest or the most ignorant. If they did not think so, they never would be afraid of women knowing as much as themselves.' ... In justice to the sex, I think it but candid to acknowledge that, in a subsequent conversation, he told me that he was serious in what he said."—Boswell, *The Journal of a Tour to the Hebrides.*

[4] [Woolf's note] "The ancient Germans believed that there was something holy in women, and accordingly consulted them as oracles."—Frazer, *Golden Bough.*

[5] *Goethe* German writer Johann Wolfgang van Goethe (1749–1832).

[6] *Mussolini* Benito Mussolini (1833–1945), Italian Fascist dictator.

[7] *astrachan* I.e., astrakhan, wool of very young lambs.

on looking at my notebook, that the sketch of the angry professor had been made in anger. Anger had snatched my pencil while I dreamt. But what was anger doing there? Interest, confusion, amusement, boredom—all these emotions I could trace and name as they succeeded each other throughout the morning. Had anger, the black snake, been lurking among them? Yes, said the sketch, anger had. It referred me unmistakably to the one book, to the one phrase, which had roused the demon; it was the professor's statement about the mental, moral and physical inferiority of women. My heart had leapt. My cheeks had burnt. I had flushed with anger. There was nothing specially remarkable, however foolish, in that. One does not like to be told that one is naturally the inferior of a little man—I looked at the student next me—who breathes hard, wears a ready-made tie, and has not shaved this fortnight. One has certain foolish vanities. It is only human nature, I reflected, and began drawing cart-wheels and circles over the angry professor's face till he looked like a burning bush or a flaming comet—anyhow, an apparition without human semblance or significance. The professor was nothing now but a faggot[1] burning on the top of Hampstead Heath.[2] Soon my own anger was explained and done with; but curiosity remained. How explain the anger of the professors? Why were they angry? For when it came to analysing the impression left by these books there was always an element of heat. This heat took many forms; it showed itself in satire, in sentiment, in curiosity, in reprobation. But there was another element which was often present and could not immediately be identified. Anger, I called it. But it was anger that had gone underground and mixed itself with all kinds of other emotions. To judge from its odd effects, it was anger disguised and complex, not anger simple and open.

Whatever the reason, all these books, I thought, surveying the pile on the desk, are worthless for my purposes. They were worthless scientifically, that is to say, though humanly they were full of instruction, interest, boredom, and very queer facts about the habits of the Fiji Islanders. They had been written in the red light of emotion and not in the white light of truth. Therefore they must be returned to the central desk and restored each to his own cell in the enormous honeycomb. All that I had retrieved from that morning's work had been the one fact of anger. The professors—I lumped them together thus—were angry. But why, I asked myself, having returned the books, why, I repeated, standing under the colonnade among the pigeons and the prehistoric canoes, why are they angry? And, asking myself this question, I strolled off to find a place for luncheon. What is the real nature of what I call for the moment their anger? I asked. Here was a puzzle that would last all the time that it takes to be served with food in a small restaurant somewhere near the British Museum. Some previous luncher had left the lunch edition of the evening paper on a chair, and, waiting to be served, I began idly reading the headlines. A ribbon of very large letters ran across the page. Somebody had made a big score in South Africa. Lesser ribbons announced that Sir Austen Chamberlain was at Geneva.[3] A meat axe with human hair on it had been found in a cellar. Mr. Justice —— commented in the Divorce Courts upon the Shamelessness of Women. Sprinkled about the paper were other pieces of news. A film actress had been lowered from a peak in California and hung suspended in mid-air. The weather was going to be foggy. The most transient visitor to this planet, I thought, who picked up this paper could not fail to be aware, even from this scattered testimony, that England is under the rule of a patriarchy. Nobody in their senses could fail to detect the dominance of the professor. His was the power and the money and the influence. He was the proprietor of the paper and its editor and sub-editor. He was the Foreign Secretary and the Judge. He was the cricketer; he owned the race-horses and the yachts. He was the director of the company that pays two hundred per cent to its shareholders. He left millions to charities and colleges that were ruled by himself. He suspended the film actress in mid-air. He will decide if the hair on the meat axe is human; he it is who will acquit or convict the murderer, and hang him, or let him go free. With the exception of the fog he seemed to control

---

[1] *faggot*   Bundle of sticks for fuel.
[2] *Hampstead Heath*   Natural area in north London and the highest point in the city.

[3] *Sir Austin Chamberlain*   Statesman, member of the British House of Commons and Secretary of State of Foreign Affairs from 1924 to 1929; *Geneva*   Location of the League of Nations headquarters.

everything. Yet he was angry. I knew that he was angry by this token. When I read what he wrote about women I thought, not of what he was saying, but of himself. When an arguer argues dispassionately he thinks only of the argument; and the reader cannot help thinking of the argument too. If he had written dispassionately about women, had used indisputable proofs to establish his argument and had shown no trace of wishing that the result should be one thing rather than another, one would not have been angry either. One would have accepted the fact, as one accepts the fact that a pea is green or a canary yellow. So be it, I should have said. But I had been angry because he was angry. Yet it seemed absurd, I thought, turning over the evening paper, that a man with all this power should be angry. Or is anger, I wondered, somehow, the familiar, the attendant sprite on power? Rich people, for example, are often angry because they suspect that the poor want to seize their wealth. The professors, or patriarchs, as it might be more accurate to call them, might be angry for that reason partly, but partly for one that lies a little less obviously on the surface. Possibly they were not "angry" at all; often, indeed, they were admiring, devoted, exemplary in the relations of private life. Possibly when the professor insisted a little too emphatically upon the inferiority of women, he was concerned not with their inferiority, but with his own superiority. That was what he was protecting rather hot-headedly and with too much emphasis, because it was a jewel to him of the rarest price. Life for both sexes—and I looked at them, shouldering their way along the pavement—is arduous, difficult, a perpetual struggle. It calls for gigantic courage and strength. More than anything, perhaps, creatures of illusion as we are, it calls for confidence in oneself. Without self-confidence we are as babes in the cradle. And how can we generate this imponderable quality, which is yet so invaluable, most quickly? By thinking that other people are inferior to oneself. By feeling that one has some innate superiority—it may be wealth, or rank, a straight nose, or the portrait of a grandfather by Romney[1]—for there is no end to the pathetic devices of the human imagination—over other people. Hence the enormous importance to a patriarch

who has to conquer, who has to rule, of feeling that great numbers of people, half the human race indeed, are by nature inferior to himself. It must indeed be one of the chief sources of his power. But let me turn the light of this observation on to real life, I thought. Does it help to explain some of those psychological puzzles that one notes in the margin of daily life? Does it explain my astonishment the other day when Z, most humane, most modest of men, taking up some book by Rebecca West[2] and reading a passage in it, exclaimed, "The arrant feminist! She says that men are snobs!" The exclamation, to me so surprising—for why was Miss West an arrant feminist for making a possibly true if uncomplimentary statement about the other sex?—was not merely the cry of wounded vanity; it was a protest against some infringement of his power to believe in himself. Women have served all these centuries as looking-glasses possessing the magic and delicious power of reflecting the figure of man at twice its natural size. Without that power probably the earth would still be swamp and jungle. The glories of all our wars would be unknown. We should still be scratching the outlines of deer on the remains of mutton bones and bartering flints for sheepskins or whatever simple ornament took our unsophisticated taste. Supermen and Fingers of Destiny would never have existed. The Czar and the Kaiser would never have worn their crowns or lost them. Whatever may be their use in civilised societies, mirrors are essential to all violent and heroic action. That is why Napoleon and Mussolini both insist so emphatically upon the inferiority of women, for if they were not inferior, they would cease to enlarge. That serves to explain in part the necessity that women so often are to men. And it serves to explain how restless they are under her criticism; how impossible it is for her to say to them this book is bad, this picture is feeble, or whatever it may be, without giving far more pain and rousing far more anger than a man would do who gave the same criticism. For if she begins to tell the truth, the figure in the looking-glass shrinks; his fitness for life is diminished. How is he to go on giving judgement, civilising natives, making laws, writing books, dressing up and speechifying at banquets, unless he can see himself at

---

[1] *Romney*   George Romney, eighteenth-century British painter and portraitist.

[2] *Rebecca West*   Assumed name of Cecily Isabel Andrews (1892–1983), English novelist, critic, and journalist.

breakfast and at dinner at least twice the size he really is? So I reflected, crumbling my bread and stirring my coffee and now and again looking at the people in the street. The looking-glass vision is of supreme importance because it charges the vitality; it stimulates the nervous system. Take it away and man may die, like the drug fiend deprived of his cocaine. Under the spell of that illusion, I thought, looking out of the window, half the people on the pavement are striding to work. They put on their hats and coats in the morning under its agreeable rays. They start the day confident, braced, believing themselves desired at Miss Smith's tea party; they say to themselves as they go into the room, I am the superior of half the people here, and it is thus that they speak with that self-confidence, that self-assurance, which have had such profound consequences in public life and lead to such curious notes in the margin of the private mind.

But these contributions to the dangerous and fascinating subject of the psychology of the other sex—it is one, I hope, that you will investigate when you have five hundred a year of your own—were interrupted by the necessity of paying the bill. It came to five shillings and ninepence. I gave the waiter a ten-shilling note and he went to bring me change. There was another ten-shilling note in my purse; I noticed it, because it is a fact that still takes my breath away—the power of my purse to breed ten-shilling notes automatically. I open it and there they are. Society gives me chicken and coffee, bed and lodging, in return for a certain number of pieces of paper which were left me by an aunt, for no other reason than that I share her name.

My aunt, Mary Beton, I must tell you, died by a fall from her horse when she was riding out to take the air in Bombay. The news of my legacy reached me one night about the same time that the act was passed that gave votes to women. A solicitor's letter fell into the post-box and when I opened it I found that she had left me five hundred pounds a year for ever. Of the two—the vote and the money—the money, I own, seemed infinitely the more important. Before that I had made my living by cadging odd jobs from newspapers, by reporting a donkey show here or a wedding there; I had earned a few pounds by addressing envelopes, reading to old ladies, making artificial flowers, teaching the alphabet to small children in a kindergarten. Such were the chief occupations that were open to women before 1918. I need not, I am afraid, describe in any detail the hardness of the work, for you know perhaps women who have done it; nor the difficulty of living on the money when it was earned, for you may have tried. But what still remains with me as a worse infliction than either was the poison of fear and bitterness which those days bred in me. To begin with, always to be doing work that one did not wish to do, and to do it like a slave, flattering and fawning, not always necessarily perhaps, but it seemed necessary and the stakes were too great to run risks; and then the thought of that one gift which it was death to hide—a small one but dear to the possessor—perishing and with it myself, my soul—all this became like a rust eating away the bloom of the spring, destroying the tree at its heart. However, as I say, my aunt died; and whenever I change a ten-shilling note a little of that rust and corrosion is rubbed off; fear and bitterness go. Indeed, I thought, slipping the silver into my purse, it is remarkable, remembering the bitterness of those days, what a change of temper a fixed income will bring about. No force in the world can take from me my five hundred pounds. Food, house, and clothing are mine for ever. Therefore not merely do effort and labour cease, but also hatred and bitterness. I need not hate any man; he cannot hurt me. I need not flatter any man; he has nothing to give me. So imperceptibly I found myself adopting a new attitude towards the other half of the human race. It was absurd to blame any class or any sex, as a whole. Great bodies of people are never responsible for what they do. They are driven by instincts which are not within their control. They too, the patriarchs, the professors, had endless difficulties, terrible drawbacks to contend with. Their education had been in some ways as faulty as my own. It had bred in them defects as great. True, they had money and power, but only at the cost of harbouring in their breasts an eagle, a vulture, for ever tearing the liver out and plucking at the lungs—the instinct for possession, the rage for acquisition which drives them to desire other people's fields and goods perpetually; to make frontiers and flags; battleships and poison gas; to offer up their own lives and their children's lives. Walk through the

Admiralty Arch[1] (I had reached that monument), or any other avenue given up to trophies and cannon, and reflect upon the kind of glory celebrated there. Or watch in the spring sunshine the stockbroker and the great barrister going indoors to make money and more money and more money when it is a fact that five hundred pounds a year will keep one alive in the sunshine. These are unpleasant instincts to harbour, I reflected. They are bred of the conditions of life; of the lack of civilisation, I thought, looking at the statue of the Duke of Cambridge, and in particular at the feathers in his cocked hat, with a fixity that they have scarcely ever received before. And, as I realised these drawbacks, by degrees fear and bitterness modified themselves into pity and toleration; and then in a year or two, pity and toleration went, and the greatest release of all came, which is freedom to think of things in themselves. That building, for example, do I like it or not? Is that picture beautiful or not? Is that in my opinion a good book or a bad? Indeed my aunt's legacy unveiled the sky to me, and substituted for the large and imposing figure of a gentleman, which Milton recommended for my perpetual adoration,[2] a view of the open sky.

So thinking, so speculating, I found my way back to my house by the river. Lamps were being lit and an indescribable change had come over London since the morning hour. It was as if the great machine after labouring all day had made with our help a few yards of something very exciting and beautiful—a fiery fabric flashing with red eyes, a tawny monster roaring with hot breath. Even the wind seemed flung like a flag as it lashed the houses and rattled the hoardings.

In my little street, however, domesticity prevailed. The house painter was descending his ladder; the nursemaid was wheeling the perambulator carefully in and out back to nursery tea; the coal-heaver was folding his empty sacks on top of each other; the woman who keeps the green-grocer's shop was adding up the day's takings with her hands in red mittens. But so engrossed was I with the problem you have laid upon my shoulders that I could not see even these usual sights without referring them to one centre. I thought how much harder it is now than it must have been even a century ago to say which of these employments is the higher, the more necessary. Is it better to be a coal-heaver or a nursemaid; is the charwoman[3] who has brought up eight children of less value to the world than the barrister who has made a hundred thousand pounds? It is useless to ask such questions; for nobody can answer them. Not only do the comparative values of charwomen and lawyers rise and fall from decade to decade, but we have no rods with which to measure them even as they are at the moment. I had been foolish to ask my professor to furnish me with "indisputable proofs" of this or that in his argument about women. Even if one could state the value of any one gift at the moment, those values will change; in a century's time very possibly they will have changed completely. Moreover, in a hundred years, I thought, reaching my own doorstep, women will have ceased to be the protected sex. Logically they will take part in all the activities and exertions that were once denied them. The nursemaid will heave coal. The shopwoman will drive an engine. All assumptions founded on the facts observed when women were the protected sex will have disappeared—as, for example (here a squad of soldiers marched down the street), that women and clergymen and gardeners live longer than other people. Remove that protection, expose them to the same exertions and activities, make them soldiers and sailors and engine-drivers and dock labourers, and will not women die off so much younger, so much quicker, than men that one will say, "I saw a woman today," as one used to say, "I saw an aeroplane." Anything may happen when womanhood has ceased to be a protected occupation, I thought, opening the door. But what bearing has all this upon the subject of my paper, Women and Fiction? I asked, going indoors.

CHAPTER 3

It was disappointing not to have brought back in the evening some important statement, some authentic fact. Women are poorer than men because—this or that.

---

[1] *Admiralty Arch*   Triple arch leading from Trafalgar Square into the Mall in London, forming part of the ceremonial approach to Buckingham Palace.

[2] *gentleman ... adoration*   In *Paradise Lost* (1667), Milton suggests that man (Adam) was formed "for God only" and woman (Eve) "for God in him" (4.299).

[3] *charwoman*   Cleaning woman.

Perhaps now it would be better to give up seeking for the truth, and receiving on one's head an avalanche of opinion hot as lava, discoloured as dish-water. It would be better to draw the curtains; to shut out distractions; to light the lamp; to narrow the enquiry and to ask the historian, who records not opinions but facts, to describe under what conditions women lived, not throughout the ages, but in England, say in the time of Elizabeth.

For it is a perennial puzzle why no woman wrote a word of that extraordinary literature when every other man, it seemed, was capable of song or sonnet. What were the conditions in which women lived, I asked myself; for fiction, imaginative work that is, is not dropped like a pebble upon the ground, as science may be; fiction is like a spider's web, attached ever so lightly perhaps, but still attached to life at all four corners. Often the attachment is scarcely perceptible; Shakespeare's plays, for instance, seem to hang there complete by themselves. But when the web is pulled askew, hooked up at the edge, torn in the middle, one remembers that these webs are not spun in mid-air by incorporeal creatures, but are the work of suffering human beings, and are attached to grossly material things, like health and money and the houses we live in.

I went, therefore, to the shelf where the histories stand and took down one of the latest, Professor Trevelyan's *History of England*.[1] Once more I looked up Women, found "position of," and turned to the pages indicated. "Wife-beating," I read, "was a recognised right of man, and was practised without shame by high as well as low.... Similarly," the historian goes on, "the daughter who refused to marry the gentleman of her parents' choice was liable to be locked up, beaten and flung about the room, without any shock being inflicted on public opinion. Marriage was not an affair of personal affection, but of family avarice, particularly in the 'chivalrous' upper classes.... Betrothal often took place while one or both of the parties was in the cradle, and marriage when they were scarcely out of the nurses' charge." That was about 1470, soon after Chaucer's time. The next reference to the position of women is some two hundred years later, in the time of the Stuarts.

"It was still the exception for women of the upper and middle class to choose their own husbands, and when the husband had been assigned, he was lord and master, so far at least as law and custom could make him. Yet even so," Professor Trevelyan concludes, "neither Shakespeare's women nor those of authentic seventeenth-century memoirs, like the Verneys and the Hutchinsons,[2] seem wanting in personality and character." Certainly, if we consider it, Cleopatra must have had a way with her; Lady Macbeth, one would suppose, had a will of her own; Rosalind, one might conclude, was an attractive girl.[3] Professor Trevelyan is speaking no more than the truth when he remarks that Shakespeare's women do not seem wanting in personality and character. Not being a historian, one might go even further and say that women have burnt like beacons in all the works of all the poets from the beginning of time—Clytemnestra, Antigone, Cleopatra, Lady Macbeth, Phedre, Cressida, Rosalind, Desdemona, the Duchess of Malfi, among the dramatists;[4] then among the prose writers: Millamant, Clarissa, Becky Sharp, Anna Karenina, Emma Bovary, Madame de Guermantes[5]—the names flock to mind, nor do they recall women "lacking in personality and character." Indeed, if woman had no existence save in the fiction written by men, one would imagine her a person of the utmost importance; very various; heroic and mean; splendid and sordid; infinitely beautiful and hideous in the extreme;

[1] *Professor ... England* George Macaulay Trevelyan's *History of England* (1929).

[2] *Verneys* The *Memoirs of the Verney Family* (published 1892) is a family history that records, as one of its authors boasted, "an ordinary gentleman's family of the higher class" consisting of "good average specimens of hundreds of men or women of their age." *Hutchinsons* Lucy Hutchinson's *Memoirs of the Life of Colonel Hutchinson* (published 1806) detailed the life of her husband, John Hutchinson, and his experiences in the civil war.

[3] *Cleopatra ... girl* Cleopatra, Lady Macbeth, and Rosalind are the heroines of Shakespeare's *Antony and Cleopatra*, *Macbeth*, and *As You Like It*, respectively.

[4] *Clytemnestra ... dramatists* Heroines from Aeschylus's *Agamemnon*; Sophocles's *Antigone*; Shakespeare's *Antony and Cleopatra* and *Macbeth*; Racine's *Phèdre*; Shakespeare's *Troilus and Cressida*, *As You Like It*, and *Othello*; and Webster's *The Duchess of Malfi*.

[5] *then ... Guermantes* Characters from, respectively, Congreve's *Way of the World*; Richardson's *Clarissa*; Thackeray's *Vanity Fair*; Tolstoy's *Anna Karenina*; Flaubert's *Madame Bovary*; and Proust's *À la recherche du temps perdu*.

as great as a man, some think even greater.[1] But this is woman in fiction. In fact, as Professor Trevelyan points out, she was locked up, beaten and flung about the room.

A very queer, composite being thus emerges. Imaginatively she is of the highest importance; practically she is completely insignificant. She pervades poetry from cover to cover; she is all but absent from history. She dominates the lives of kings and conquerors in fiction; in fact she was the slave of any boy whose parents forced a ring upon her finger. Some of the most inspired words, some of the most profound thoughts in literature fall from her lips; in real life she could hardly read, could scarcely spell, and was the property of her husband.

It was certainly an odd monster that one made up by reading the historians first and the poets afterwards—a worm winged like an eagle; the spirit of life and beauty in a kitchen chopping up suet. But these monsters, however amusing to the imagination, have no existence in fact. What one must do to bring her to life was to think poetically and prosaically at one and the same moment, thus keeping in touch with fact—that she is Mrs. Martin, aged thirty-six, dressed in blue, wearing a black hat and brown shoes; but not losing sight of fiction either—that she is a vessel in which all sorts of spirits and forces are coursing and flashing perpetually. The moment, however, that one tries this method with the Elizabethan woman, one branch of illumination fails; one is held up by the scarcity of facts. One knows

nothing detailed, nothing perfectly true and substantial about her. History scarcely mentions her. And I turned to Professor Trevelyan again to see what history meant to him. I found by looking at his chapter headings that it meant—"The Manor Court and the Methods of Open-field Agriculture ... The Cistercians and Sheep-farming ... The Crusades ... The University ... The House of Commons ... The Hundred Years' War ... The War of the Roses ... The Renaissance Scholars ... The Dissolution of the Monasteries ... Agrarian and Religious Strife ... The Origin of English Sea-power ... The Armada ..." and so on. Occasionally an individual woman is mentioned, an Elizabeth, or a Mary; a queen or a great lady. But by no possible means could middle-class women with nothing but brains and character at their command have taken part in any one of the great movements which, brought together, constitute the historian's view of the past. Nor shall we find her in any collection of anecdotes. Aubrey[2] hardly mentions her. She never writes her own life and scarcely keeps a diary; there are only a handful of her letters in existence. She left no plays or poems by which we can judge her. What one wants, I thought—and why does not some brilliant student at Newnham or Girton supply it?—is a mass of information; at what age did she marry; how many children had she as a rule; what was her house like; had she a room to herself; did she do the cooking; would she be likely to have a servant? All these facts lie somewhere, presumably, in parish registers and account books; the life of the average Elizabethan woman must be scattered about somewhere, could one collect it and make a book of it. It would be ambitious beyond my daring, I thought, looking about the shelves for books that were not there, to suggest to the students of those famous colleges that they should re-write history, though I own that it often seems a little queer as it is, unreal, lop-sided; but why should they not add a supplement to history? calling it, of course, by some inconspicuous name so that women might figure there without impropriety? For one often catches a glimpse of them in the lives of the great, whisking away into the background, concealing, I sometimes think, a wink, a laugh, perhaps a tear. And, after all, we have lives enough of Jane

[1] [Woolf's note] "It remains a strange and almost inexplicable fact that in Athena's city, where women were kept in almost Oriental suppression as odalisques or drudges, the stage should yet have produced figures like Clytemnestra and Cassandra, Atossa and Antigone, Phèdra and Medea, and all the other heroines who dominate play after play of the 'misogynist' Euripides. But the paradox of this world where in real life a respectable woman could hardly show her face alone in the street, and yet on the stage woman equals or surpasses man, has never been satisfactorily explained. In modern tragedy the same predominance exists. At all events, a very cursory survey of Shakespeare's work (similarly with Webster, though not with Marlowe or Jonson) suffices to reveal how this dominance, this initiative of women, persists from Rosalind to Lady Macbeth. So too in Racine; six of his tragedies bear their heroines' names; and what male characters of his shall we set against Hermione and Andromaque, Bérénice and Roxane, Phèdre and Athalie? So again with Ibsen; what men shall we match with Solveig and Nora, Hedda and Hilda Wangel and Rebecca West?"—F.L. Lucas, *Tragedy*, pp. 114–15.

[2] *Aubrey* John Aubrey (1626–97), writer and antiquary known for his *Brief Lives*, a collection of short, informal biographies.

Austen; it scarcely seems necessary to consider again the influence of the tragedies of Joanna Baillie[1] upon the poetry of Edgar Allen Poe; as for myself, I should not mind if the homes and haunts of Mary Russell Mitford[2] were closed to the public for a century at least. But what I find deplorable, I continued, looking about the bookshelves again, is that nothing is known about women before the eighteenth century. I have no model in my mind to turn about this way and that. Here I am asking why women did not write poetry in the Elizabethan age, and I am not sure how they were educated; whether they were taught to write; whether they had sitting-rooms to themselves; how many women had children before they were twenty-one; what, in short, they did from eight in the morning till eight at night. They had no money evidently; according to Professor Trevelyan they were married whether they liked it or not before they were out of the nursery, at fifteen or sixteen very likely. It would have been extremely odd, even upon this showing, had one of them suddenly written the plays of Shakespeare, I concluded, and I thought of that old gentleman, who is dead now, but was a bishop, I think, who declared that it was impossible for any woman, past, present, or to come, to have the genius of Shakespeare. He wrote to the papers about it. He also told a lady who applied to him for information that cats do not as a matter of fact go to heaven, though they have, he added, souls of a sort. How much thinking those old gentlemen used to save one! How the borders of ignorance shrank back at their approach! Cats do not go to heaven. Women cannot write the plays of Shakespeare.

Be that as it may, I could not help thinking, as I looked at the works of Shakespeare on the shelf, that the bishop was right at least in this; it would have been impossible, completely and entirely, for any woman to have written the plays of Shakespeare in the age of Shakespeare. Let me imagine, since facts are so hard to come by, what would have happened had Shakespeare had a wonderfully gifted sister, called Judith, let us say. Shakespeare himself went, very probably—his mother was an heiress—to the grammar school, where he may have learnt Latin—Ovid, Virgil, and Horace—and the elements of grammar and logic. He was, it is well known, a wild boy who poached rabbits, perhaps shot a deer, and had, rather sooner than he should have done, to marry a woman in the neighbourhood, who bore him a child rather quicker than was right. That escapade sent him to seek his fortune in London. He had, it seemed, a taste for the theatre; he began by holding horses at the stage door. Very soon he got work in the theatre, became a successful actor, and lived at the hub of the universe, meeting everybody, knowing everybody, practising his art on the boards, exercising his wits in the streets, and even getting access to the palace of the queen. Meanwhile his extraordinarily gifted sister, let us suppose, remained at home. She was as adventurous, as imaginative, as agog to see the world as he was. But she was not sent to school. She had no chance of learning grammar and logic, let alone of reading Horace and Virgil. She picked up a book now and then, one of her brother's perhaps, and read a few pages. But then her parents came in and told her to mend the stockings or mind the stew and not moon about with books and papers. They would have spoken sharply but kindly, for they were substantial people who knew the conditions of life for a woman and loved their daughter—indeed, more likely than not she was the apple of her father's eye. Perhaps she scribbled some pages up in an apple loft on the sly, but was careful to hide them or set fire to them. Soon, however, before she was out of her teens, she was to be betrothed to the son of a neighbouring wool-stapler.[3] She cried out that marriage was hateful to her, and for that she was severely beaten by her father. Then he ceased to scold her. He begged her instead not to hurt him, not to shame him in this matter of her marriage. He would give her a chain of beads or a fine petticoat, he said; and there were tears in his eyes. How could she disobey him? How could she break his heart? The force of her own gift alone drove her to it. She made up a small parcel of her belongings, let herself down by a rope one summer's night and took the road to London. She was not seventeen. The birds that sang

---

[1] *Joanna Baillie* Romantic English poet and dramatist (1787–1865).

[2] *Mary Russell Mitford* Poet, novelist, and playwright whose correspondence with notable authors, including Elizabeth Barrett Browning, Charles Lamb, and Harriet Martineau, provides insight into the literary world of the early nineteenth century.

[3] *wool-stapler* Dealer in wool.

in the hedge were not more musical than she was. She had the quickest fancy, a gift like her brother's, for the tune of words. Like him, she had a taste for the theatre. She stood at the stage door; she wanted to act, she said. Men laughed in her face. The manager—a fat, loose-lipped man—guffawed. He bellowed something about poodles dancing and women acting[1]—no woman, he said, could possibly be an actress. He hinted—you can imagine what. She could get no training in her craft. Could she even seek her dinner in a tavern or roam the streets at midnight? Yet her genius was for fiction and lusted to feed abundantly upon the lives of men and women and the study of their ways. At last—for she was very young, oddly like Shakespeare the poet in her face, with the same grey eyes and rounded brows—at last Nick Greene the actor-manager took pity on her; she found herself with child by that gentleman and so—who shall measure the heat and violence of the poet's heart when caught and tangled in a woman's body?—killed herself one winter's night and lies buried at some cross-roads where the omnibuses now stop outside the Elephant and Castle.[2]

That, more or less, is how the story would run, I think, if a woman in Shakespeare's day had had Shakespeare's genius. But for my part, I agree with the deceased bishop, if such he was—it is unthinkable that any woman in Shakespeare's day should have had Shakespeare's genius. For genius like Shakespeare's is not born among labouring, uneducated, servile people. It was not born in England among the Saxons and the Britons. It is not born today among the working classes. How, then, could it have been born among women whose work began, according to Professor Trevelyan, almost before they were out of the nursery, who were forced to it by their parents and held to it by all the power of law and custom? Yet genius of a sort must have existed among women as it must have existed among the working classes. Now and again an Emily Brontë or a Robert Burns blazes out and proves its presence. But certainly it never got itself on to paper. When, however, one reads of a witch being ducked, of a woman possessed by devils, of a wise woman selling herbs, or even of a very remarkable man who had a mother, then I think we are on the track of a lost novelist, a suppressed poet, of some mute and inglorious Jane Austen,[3] some Emily Brontë who dashed her brains out on the moor or mopped and mowed about the highways crazed with the torture that her gift had put her to. Indeed, I would venture to guess that Anon, who wrote so many poems without signing them, was often a woman. It was a woman Edward Fitzgerald,[4] I think, suggested who made the ballads and the folk-songs, crooning them to her children, beguiling her spinning with them, or the length of the winter's night.

This may be true or it may be false—who can say?—but what is true in it, so it seemed to me, reviewing the story of Shakespeare's sister as I had made it, is that any woman born with a great gift in the sixteenth century would certainly have gone crazed, shot herself, or ended her days in some lonely cottage outside the village, half witch, half wizard, feared and mocked at. For it needs little skill in psychology to be sure that a highly gifted girl who had tried to use her gift for poetry would have been so thwarted and hindered by other people, so tortured and pulled asunder by her own contrary instincts, that she must have lost her health and sanity to a certainty. No girl could have walked to London and stood at a stage door and forced her way into the presence of actor-managers without doing herself a violence and suffering an anguish which may have been irrational—for chastity may be a fetish invented by certain societies for unknown reasons—but were none the less inevitable. Chastity had then, it has even now, a religious importance in a woman's life, and has so wrapped itself round with nerves and instincts that to cut it free and bring it to the light of day demands courage of the rarest. To have lived a free life in

---

[1] *He ... acting* Reference to Samuel Johnson's infamous statement, recorded by Boswell, that "a woman's preaching is like a dog's walking on its hinder legs. It is not done well; but you are surprised to find it done at all" (James Boswell, *Life of Samuel Johnson*, 31 July 1763).

[2] *lies buried ... Castle* It was common practice to bury victims of suicide at crossroads. The Elephant and Castle was a pub located south of the Thames.

[3] *some ... Austen* See Thomas Gray, "Elegy Written in a Country Church-Yard" (1751): "Some mute and inglorious Milton here may rest" (line 59).

[4] *Edward Fitzgerald* Author of *The Rubáiyát of Omar Khayyám* (1859).

London in the sixteenth century would have meant for a woman who was poet and playwright a nervous stress and dilemma which might well have killed her. Had she survived, whatever she had written would have been twisted and deformed, issuing from a strained and morbid imagination. And undoubtedly, I thought, looking at the shelf where there are no plays by women, her work would have gone unsigned. That refuge she would have sought certainly. It was the relic of the sense of chastity that dictated anonymity to women even so late as the nineteenth century. Currer Bell, George Eliot, George Sand,[1] all the victims of inner strife as their writings prove, sought ineffectively to veil themselves by using the name of a man. Thus they did homage to the convention, which if not implanted by the other sex was liberally encouraged by them (the chief glory of a woman is not to be talked of, said Pericles,[2] himself a much-talked-of man), that publicity in women is detestable. Anonymity runs in their blood. The desire to be veiled still possesses them. They are not even now as concerned about the health of their fame as men are, and, speaking generally, will pass a tombstone or a signpost without feeling an irresistible desire to cut their names on it, as Alf, Bert, or Chas. must do in obedience to their instinct, which murmurs if it sees a fine woman go by, or even a dog, Ce chien est à moi.[3] And, of course, it may not be a dog, I thought, remembering Parliament Square, the Sièges Allée[4] and other avenues; it may be a piece of land or a man with curly black hair. It is one of the great advantages of being a woman that one can pass even a very fine negress without wishing to make an Englishwoman of her.

That woman, then, who was born with a gift of poetry in the sixteenth century, was an unhappy woman, a woman at strife against herself. All the conditions of her life, all her own instincts, were hostile to the state of mind which is needed to set free whatever is in the brain. But what is the state of mind that is most propitious to the act of creation, I asked. Can one come by any notion of the state that furthers and makes possible that strange activity? Here I opened the volume containing the Tragedies of Shakespeare. What was Shakespeare's state of mind, for instance, when he wrote *Lear* and *Antony and Cleopatra?* It was certainly the state of mind most favourable to poetry that there has ever existed. But Shakespeare himself said nothing about it. We only know casually and by chance that he "never blotted a line."[5] Nothing indeed was ever said by the artist himself about his state of mind until the eighteenth century perhaps. Rousseau[6] perhaps began it. At any rate, by the nineteenth century self-consciousness had developed so far that it was the habit for men of letters to describe their minds in confessions and autobiographies. Their lives also were written, and their letters were printed after their deaths. Thus, though we do not know what Shakespeare went through when he wrote *Lear*, we do know what Carlyle went through when he wrote the *French Revolution*; what Flaubert went through when he wrote *Madame Bovary*; what Keats was going through when he tried to write poetry against the coming of death and the indifference of the world.[7]

And one gathers from this enormous modern literature of confession and self-analysis that to write a work of genius is almost always a feat of prodigious difficulty. Everything is against the likelihood that it will come from the writer's mind whole and entire. Generally material circumstances are against it. Dogs will bark; people will interrupt; money must be made; health will break down. Further, accentuating all these difficulties and making them harder to bear is the world's notorious indifference. It does not ask people to write poems and novels and histories; it does not need them. It does not care whether Flaubert finds the right word or whether Carlyle scrupulously verifies this or that fact. Naturally, it will not pay for what it does not want. And so the

---

[1] *Currer ... Sand* Male pseudonyms under which female authors Charlotte Brontë, Mary Anne Evans, and Amandine Dupin published.

[2] *Pericles* Athenian statesman (d. 429 BCE).

[3] *Ce ... moi* French: this dog is mine.

[4] *Sièges Allée* Victory Avenue, in Berlin.

[5] *never ... line* Ben Jonson, *Timber*: "I remember, the players have often mentioned it as an honour to Shakespeare that in his writing (whatsoever he penned) he never blotted out a line."

[6] *Rousseau* French philosopher Jean-Jacques Rousseau (1712–87).

[7] *we do ... world* Philosopher Thomas Carlyle provided this autobiographical information in his *Reminiscences* (1881), while French novelist Gustave Flaubert and English Romantic poet John Keats wrote extensively about their writing experiences in their letters.

writer, Keats, Flaubert, Carlyle, suffers, especially in the creative years of youth, every form of distraction and discouragement. A curse, a cry of agony, rises from those books of analysis and confession. "Mighty poets in their misery dead"[1]—that is the burden of their song. If anything comes through in spite of all this, it is a miracle, and probably no book is born entire and uncrippled as it was conceived.

But for women, I thought, looking at the empty shelves, these difficulties were infinitely more formidable. In the first place, to have a room of her own, let alone a quiet room or a sound-proof room, was out of the question, unless her parents were exceptionally rich or very noble, even up to the beginning of the nineteenth century. Since her pin money, which depended on the good will of her father, was only enough to keep her clothed, she was debarred from such alleviations as came even to Keats or Tennyson or Carlyle, all poor men, from a walking tour, a little journey to France, from the separate lodging which, even if it were miserable enough, sheltered them from the claims and tyrannies of their families. Such material difficulties were formidable; but much worse were the immaterial. The indifference of the world which Keats and Flaubert and other men of genius have found so hard to bear was in her case not indifference but hostility. The world did not say to her as it said to them, Write if you choose; it makes no difference to me. The world said with a guffaw, Write? What's the good of your writing? Here the psychologists of Newnham and Girton might come to our help, I thought, looking again at the blank spaces on the shelves. For surely it is time that the effect of discouragement upon the mind of the artist should be measured, as I have seen a dairy company measure the effect of ordinary milk and Grade A milk upon the body of the rat. They set two rats in cages side by side, and of the two one was furtive, timid, and small, and the other was glossy, bold, and big. Now what food do we feed women as artists upon? I asked, remembering, I suppose, that dinner of prunes and custard. To answer that question I had only to open the evening paper and to read that Lord Birkenhead[2] is of opinion—but really I am not going to trouble to copy out Lord Birkenhead's opinion upon the writing of women. What Dean Inge[3] says I will leave in peace. The Harley Street[4] specialist may be allowed to rouse the echoes of Harley Street with his vociferations without raising a hair on my head. I will quote, however, Mr. Oscar Browning, because Mr. Oscar Browning was a great figure in Cambridge at one time, and used to examine the students at Girton and Newnham. Mr. Oscar Browning was wont to declare "that the impression left on his mind, after looking over any set of examination papers, was that, irrespective of the marks he might give, the best woman was intellectually the inferior of the worst man." After saying that Mr. Browning went back to his rooms—and it is this sequel that endears him and makes him a human figure of some bulk and majesty—he went back to his rooms and found a stable-boy lying on the sofa—"a mere skeleton, his cheeks were cavernous and sallow, his teeth were black, and he did not appear to have the full use of his limbs. ... 'That's Arthur' [said Mr. Browning]. 'He's a dear boy really and most high-minded.'"[5] The two pictures always seem to me to complete each other. And happily in this age of biography the two pictures often do complete each other, so that we are able to interpret the opinions of great men not only by what they say, but by what they do.

But though this is possible now, such opinions coming from the lips of important people must have been formidable enough even fifty years ago. Let us suppose that a father from the highest motives did not wish his daughter to leave home and become writer, painter or scholar. "See what Mr. Oscar Browning says," he would say; and there was not only Mr. Oscar Browning; there was the *Saturday Review*; there was Mr. Greg—the "essentials of a woman's being," said Mr. Greg[6] emphatically, "are that *they are supported by, and they minister to, men*"—there was an enormous body of masculine opinion to the effect that nothing could be

---

1. *Mighty ... dead*   William Wordsworth, *Resolution and Independence* (1807).

2. *Lord Birkenhead*   Lord Chancellor from 1919 to 1922.

3. *Dean Inge*   Dean of St. Paul's Cathedral, London.

4. *Harley Street*   Street upon which many of the most highly regarded or fashionable medical practices were located.

5. *Mr. Oscar Browning ... high-minded*   Oscar Browning (1837–1923), history lecturer at King's College, Cambridge.

6. *Mr. Greg*   Probably W.H. Greg, a well-known journalist of the era.

expected of women intellectually. Even if her father did
not read out loud these opinions, any girl could read
them for herself; and the reading, even in the nineteenth
century, must have lowered her vitality, and told profoundly upon her work. There would always have been
that assertion—you cannot do this, you are incapable of
doing that—to protest against, to overcome. Probably
for a novelist this germ is no longer of much effect; for
there have been women novelists of merit. But for
painters it must still have some sting in it; and for
musicians, I imagine, is even now active and poisonous
in the extreme. The woman composer stands where the
actress stood in the time of Shakespeare. Nick Greene,
I thought, remembering the story I had made about
Shakespeare's sister, said that a woman acting put him
in mind of a dog dancing. Johnson repeated the phrase
two hundred years later of women preaching. And here,
I said, opening a book about music, we have the very
words used again in this year of grace, 1928, of women
who try to write music. "Of Mlle. Germaine Tailleferre
one can only repeat Dr. Johnson's dictum concerning a
woman preacher, transposed into terms of music. 'Sir,
a woman's composing is like a dog's walking on his hind
legs. It is not done well, but you are surprised to find it
done at all.'"[1] So accurately does history repeat itself.

Thus, I concluded, shutting Mr. Oscar Browning's
life and pushing away the rest, it is fairly evident that
even in the nineteenth century a woman was not
encouraged to be an artist. On the contrary, she was
snubbed, slapped, lectured, and exhorted. Her mind
must have been strained and her vitality lowered by the
need of opposing this, of disproving that. For here again
we come within range of that very interesting and
obscure masculine complex which has had so much
influence upon the woman's movement; that the deep-
seated desire, not so much that *she* shall be inferior as
that *he* shall be superior, which plants him wherever one
looks, not only in front of the arts, but barring the way
to politics too, even when the risk to himself seems
infinitesimal and the suppliant humble and devoted.

Even Lady Bessborough,[2] I remembered, with all her
passion for politics, must humbly bow herself and write
to Lord Granville Leveson-Gower: " … notwithstanding
all my violence in politics and talking so much on that
subject, I perfectly agree with you that no woman has
any business to meddle with that or any other serious
business, farther than giving her opinion (if she is
ask'd)." And so she goes on to spend her enthusiasm
where it meets with no obstacle whatsoever upon that
immensely important subject, Lord Granville's maiden
speech in the House of Commons. The spectacle is
certainly a strange one, I thought. The history of men's
opposition to women's emancipation is more interesting
perhaps than the story of that emancipation itself. An
amusing book might be made of it if some young
student at Girton or Newnham would collect examples
and deduce a theory—but she would need thick gloves
on her hands, and bars to protect her of solid gold.

But what is amusing now, I recollected, shutting
Lady Bessborough, had to be taken in desperate earnest
once. Opinions that one now pastes in a book labelled
cock-a-doodle-dum and keeps for reading to select
audiences on summer nights once drew tears, I can
assure you. Among your grandmothers and great-
grandmothers there were many that wept their eyes out.
Florence Nightingale shrieked aloud in her agony.[3]
Moreover, it is all very well for you, who have got
yourselves to college and enjoy sitting-rooms—or is it
only bed-sitting-rooms?—of your own to say that genius
should disregard such opinions; that genius should be
above caring what is said of it. Unfortunately, it is
precisely the men or women of genius who mind most
what is said of them. Remember Keats. Remember the
words he had cut on his tombstone.[4] Think of Tennyson; think—but I need hardly multiply instances of the
undeniable, if very unfortunate, fact that it is the nature
of the artist to mind excessively what is said about him.
Literature is strewn with the wreckage of men who have

[1] [Woolf's note] *A Survey of Contemporary Music*, Cecil Gray,
p.246.

[2] *Lady Bessborough* Henrietta Elizabeth, daughter of the first Earl
Spencer, later Lady Bessborough (1761–1821). Lady Bessborough
had an affair with Lord Granville.

[3] [Woolf's note] *See Cassandra*, by Florence Nightingale, printed
in *The Cause*, by R. Strachey.

[4] *Remember … tombstone* "Here lies one whose name was writ in
water."

minded beyond reason the opinions of others.

And this susceptibility of theirs is doubly unfortunate, I thought, returning again to my original enquiry into what state of mind is most propitious for creative work, because the mind of an artist, in order to achieve the prodigious effort of freeing whole and entire the work that is in him, must be incandescent, like Shakespeare's mind, I conjectured, looking at the book which lay open at *Antony and Cleopatra*. There must be no obstacle in it, no foreign matter unconsumed.

For though we say that we know nothing about Shakespeare's state of mind, even as we say that, we are saying something about Shakespeare's state of mind. The reason perhaps why we know so little of Shakespeare—compared with Donne or Ben Jonson or Milton—is that his grudges and spites and antipathies are hidden from us. We are not held up by some "revelation" which reminds us of the writer. All desire to protest, to preach, to proclaim an injury, to pay off a score, to make the world the witness of some hardship or grievance was fired out of him and consumed. Therefore his poetry flows from him free and unimpeded. If ever a human being got his work expressed completely, it was Shakespeare. If ever a mind was incandescent, unimpeded, I thought, turning again to the bookcase, it was Shakespeare's mind.

—1929

from *A Sketch of the Past* [1]

—I begin: the first memory.

This was of red and purple flowers on a black ground—my mother's dress; and she was sitting either in a train or in an omnibus, and I was on her lap. I therefore saw the flowers she was wearing very close; and can still see purple and red and blue, I think, against the black; they must have been anemones, I suppose. Perhaps we were going to St. Ives;[2] more probably, for from the light it must have been evening, we were coming back to London. But it is more convenient

artistically to suppose that we were going to St. Ives, for that will lead to my other memory, which also seems to be my first memory, and in fact it is the most important of all my memories. If life has a base that it stands upon, if it is a bowl that one fills and fills and fills—then my bowl without a doubt stands upon this memory. It is of lying half asleep, half awake, in bed in the nursery at St. Ives. It is of hearing the waves breaking, one, two, one, two, and sending a splash of water over the beach; and then breaking, one, two, one, two, behind a yellow blind. It is of hearing the blind draw its little acorn[3] across the floor as the wind blew the blind out. It is of lying and hearing this splash and seeing this light, and feeling, it is almost impossible that I should be here; of feeling the purest ecstasy I can conceive.

I could spend hours trying to write that as it should be written, in order to give the feeling which is even at this moment very strong in me. But I should fail (unless I had some wonderful luck); I dare say I should only succeed in having the luck if I had begun by describing Virginia herself.

Here I come to one of the memoir writer's difficulties—one of the reasons why, though I read so many, so many are failures. They leave out the person to whom things happened. The reason is that it is so difficult to describe any human being. So they say. "This is what happened"; but they do not say what the person was like to whom it happened. And the events mean very little unless we know first to whom they happened. Who was I then? Adeline Virginia Stephen, the second daughter of Leslie and Julia Prinsep Stephen, born on 25th January 1882, descended from a great many people, some famous, others obscure; born into a large connection, born not of rich parents, but of well-to-do parents, born into a very communicative, literate, letter writing, visiting, articulate, late nineteenth century world; so that I could if I liked to take the trouble, write a great deal here not only about my mother and father but about uncles and aunts, cousins, and friends. But I do not know how much of this, or what part of this, made me feel what I felt in the nursery at St. Ives. I do not know how far I differ from other people. That is another memoir writer's difficulty. Yet to describe oneself truly

---

[1] *A Sketch of the Past* An essay that was published as part of *Moments of Being* (1976), a collection of Woolf's autobiographical writings the title of which has its origins in this excerpt.

[2] *St. Ives* Town in Cornwall at which Woolf's family spent holidays. It is the setting of Woolf's novel *To The Lighthouse*.

[3] *acorn* I.e., acorn-shaped bead on the end of a curtain pull.

one must have some standard of comparison; was I clever, stupid, good looking, ugly, passionate, cold—? Owing partly to the fact that I was never at school, never competed in any way with children of my own age, I have never been able to compare my gifts and defects with other people's. But of course there was one external reason for the intensity of this first impression: the impression of the waves and the acorn on the blind; the feeling, as I describe it sometimes to myself, of lying in a grape and seeing through a film of semi-transparent yellow—it was due partly to the many months we spent in London. The change of nursery was a great change. And there was the long train journey; and the excitement. I remember the dark; the lights; the stir of the going up to bed.

But to fix my mind upon the nursery—it had a balcony; there was a partition, but it joined the balcony of my father's and mother's bedroom. My mother would come out onto her balcony in a white dressing gown. There were passion flowers growing on the wall; they were great starry blossoms, with purple streaks, and large green buds, part empty, part full.

If I were a painter I should paint these first impressions in pale yellow, silver, and green. There was the pale yellow blind; the green sea; and the silver of the passion flowers. I should make a picture that was globular; semi-transparent. I should make a picture of curved petals; of shells; of things that were semi-transparent; I should make curved shapes, showing the light through, but not giving a clear outline. Everything would be large and dim; and what was seen would at the same time be heard; sounds would come through this petal or leaf—sounds indistinguishable from sights. Sound and sight seem to make equal parts of these first impressions. When I think of the early morning in bed I also hear the caw of rooks falling from a great height. The sound seems to fall through an elastic, gummy air; which holds it up; which prevents it from being sharp and distinct.... The rooks cawing is part of the waves breaking—one, two, one, two—and the splash as the wave drew back and then it gathered again, and I lay there half awake, half asleep, drawing in such ecstasy as I cannot describe.

The next memory—all these colour-and-sound memories hang together at St. Ives—was much more

robust; it was highly sensual. It was later. It still makes me feel warm; as if everything were ripe; humming; sunny; smelling so many smells at once; and all making a whole that even now makes me stop—as I stopped then going down to the beach; I stopped at the top to look down at the gardens. They were sunk beneath the road. The apples were on a level with one's head. The gardens gave off a murmur of bees; the apples were red and gold; there were also pink flowers; and grey and silver leaves. The buzz, the croon, the smell, all seemed to press voluptuously against some membrane; not to burst it; but to hum round one such a complete rapture of pleasure that I stopped, smelt; looked. But again I cannot describe that rapture. It was rapture rather than ecstasy....

But the peculiarity of these two strong memories is that each was very simple. I am hardly aware of myself, but only of the sensation. I am only the container of the feeling of ecstasy, of the feeling of rapture. Perhaps this is characteristic of all childhood memories; perhaps it accounts for their strength. Later we add to feelings much that makes them more complex; and therefore less strong; or if not less strong, less isolated, less complete. But instead of analysing this, here is an instance of what I mean—my feeling about the looking-glass in the hall.

There was a small looking-glass in the hall at Talland House.[1] It had, I remember, a ledge with a brush on it. By standing on tiptoe I could see my face in the glass. When I was six or seven perhaps, I got into the habit of looking at my face in the glass. But I only did this if I was sure that I was alone. I was ashamed of it. A strong feeling of guilt seemed naturally attached to it. But why was this so? One obvious reason occurs to me—Vanessa[2] and I were both what was called tomboys; that is, we played cricket, scrambled over rocks, climbed trees, were said not to care for clothes and so on. Perhaps therefore to have been found looking in the glass would have been against our tomboy code. But I think that my feeling of shame went a great deal deeper. I am almost inclined to drag in my grandfather—Sir James, who once smoked a cigar, liked it, and so threw away his cigar and never smoked another. I am almost inclined to think that I

---

1 *Talland House*   Name of the Stephens's summer house.
2 *Vanessa*   Woolf's older sister; later Vanessa Bell.

inherited a streak of the puritan, of the Clapham Sect.[1] At any rate, the looking-glass shame has lasted all my life, long after the tomboy phase was over. I cannot now powder my nose in public. Everything to do with dress—to be fitted, to come into a room wearing a new dress—still frightens me; at least makes me shy, self-conscious, uncomfortable. "Oh to be able to run, like Julian Morrell, all over the garden in a new dress," I thought not many years ago at Garsington;[2] when Julian undid a parcel and put on a new dress and scampered round and round like a hare. Yet femininity was very strong in our family. We were famous for our beauty—my mother's beauty, Stella's[3] beauty, gave me as early as I can remember, pride and pleasure. What then gave me this feeling of shame, unless it were that I inherited some opposite instinct? My father was spartan, ascetic, puritanical. He had I think no feeling for pictures; no ear for music; no sense of the sound of words. This leads me to think that my—I would say "our" if I knew enough about Vanessa, Thoby and Adrian[4]—but how little we know even about brothers and sisters—this leads me to think that my natural love for beauty was checked by some ancestral dread. Yet this did not prevent me from feeling ecstasies and raptures spontaneously and intensely and without any shame or the least sense of guilt, so long as they were disconnected with my own body. I thus detect another element in the shame which I had in being caught looking at myself in the glass in the hall. I must have been ashamed or afraid of my own body. Another memory, also of the hall, may help to explain this. There was a slab outside the dining room door for standing dishes upon. Once when I was very small Gerald Duckworth lifted me onto this, and as I sat there he began to explore my body. I can remember

the feel of his hand going under my clothes; going firmly and steadily lower and lower. I remember how I hoped that he would stop; how I stiffened and wriggled as his hand approached my private parts. But it did not stop. His hand explored my private parts too. I remember resenting, disliking it—what is the word for so dumb and mixed a feeling? It must have been strong, since I still recall it. This seems to show that a feeling about certain parts of the body; how they must not be touched; how it is wrong to allow them to be touched; must be instinctive. It proves that Virginia Stephen was not born on the 25th January 1882, but was born many thousands of years ago; and had from the very first to encounter instincts already acquired by thousands of ancestresses in the past.

And this throws light not merely on my own case, but upon the problem that I touched on the first page; why it is so difficult to give any account of the person to whom things happen. The person is evidently immensely complicated. Witness the incident of the looking-glass. Though I have done my best to explain why I was ashamed of looking at my own face I have only been able to discover some possible reasons; there may be others; I do not suppose that I have got at the truth; yet this is a simple incident; and it happened to me personally; and I have no motive for lying about it. In spite of all this, people write what they call "lives" of other people; that is, they collect a number of events, and leave the person to whom it happened unknown. Let me add a dream; for it may refer to the incident of the looking-glass. I dreamt that I was looking in a glass when a horrible face—the face of an animal—suddenly showed over my shoulder. I cannot be sure if this was a dream, or if it happened. Was I looking in the glass one day when something in the background moved, and seemed to me alive? I cannot be sure. But I have always remembered the other face in the glass, whether it was a dream or a fact, and that it frightened me.

These then are some of my first memories. But of course as an account of my life they are misleading, because the things one does not remember are as important; perhaps they are more important. If I could remember one whole day I should be able to describe, superficially at least, what life was like as a child. Unfortunately, one only remembers what is exceptional. And

---

[1] *Clapham Sect* Group of wealthy English social reformers based in the town of Clapham. Its members, mostly evangelical Anglicans, devoted their time and money to worthy Christian causes, primarily the abolition of slavery. Woolf's grandfather, James Stephen, married Jane Catherine Venn, whose father and grandfather, John and Henry Venn, were the rector and curate of Clapham.

[2] *Julian Morrell* The daughter of Philip Morrell, a member of Parliament, and Ottoline Morrell, prominent member of literary society; *Garsington* Morrell family home.

[3] *Stella* Stella Duckworth, Woolf's half-sister. Stella's brother Gerald is mentioned later in this paragraph.

[4] *Thoby and Adrian* Woolf's brothers.

there seems to be no reason why one thing is exceptional and another not. Why have I forgotten so many things that must have been, one would have thought, more memorable than what I do remember? Why remember the hum of bees in the garden going down to the beach, and forget completely being thrown naked by father into the sea? (Mrs. Swanwick says she saw that happen.)[1]

This leads to a digression, which perhaps may explain a little of my own psychology; even of other people's. Often when I have been writing one of my so-called novels I have been baffled by this same problem; that is, how to describe what I call in my private shorthand—"non-being." Every day includes much more non-being than being. Yesterday for example, Tuesday the 18th of April, was it happened a good day; above the average in "being." It was fine; I enjoyed writing these first pages; my head was relieved of the pressure of writing about Roger;[2] I walked over Mount Misery[3] and along the river; and save that the tide was out, the country, which I notice very closely always, was coloured and shaded as I like—there were the willows, I remember, all plumy and soft green and purple against the blue. I also read Chaucer with pleasure; and began a book—the memoirs of Madame de la Fayette—which interested me. These separate moments of being were however embedded in many more moments of non-being. I have already forgotten what Leonard and I talked about at lunch; and at tea; although it was a good day the goodness was embedded in a kind of nonde-script cotton wool. This is always so. A great part of every day is not lived consciously. One walks, eats, sees things, deals with what has to be done; the broken vacuum cleaner; ordering dinner; writing orders to Mabel;[4] washing; cooking dinner; bookbinding. When it is a bad day the proportion of non-being is much

larger. I had a slight temperature last week; almost the whole day was non-being. The real novelist can some-how convey both sorts of being. I think Jane Austen can; and Trollope; perhaps Thackeray and Dickens and Tolstoy. I have never been able to do both. I tried—in *Night and Day*; and in *The Years*. But I will leave the literary side alone for the moment.

As a child then, my days, just as they do now, contained a large proportion of this cotton wool, this non-being. Week after week passed at St. Ives and nothing made any dint upon me. Then, for no reason that I know about, there was a sudden violent shock; something happened so violently that I have remem-bered it all my life. I will give a few instances. The first: I was fighting with Thoby on the lawn. We were pommelling each other with our fists. Just as I raised my fist to hit him, I felt: why hurt another person? I dropped my hand instantly, and stood there, and let him beat me. I remember the feeling. It was a feeling of hopeless sadness. It was as if I became aware of some-thing terrible; and of my own powerlessness. I slunk off alone, feeling horribly depressed. The second instance was also in the garden at St. Ives. I was looking at the flower bed by the front door; "That is the whole," I said. I was looking at a plant with a spread of leaves; and it seemed suddenly plain that the flower itself was a part of the earth; that a ring enclosed what was the flower; and that was the real flower; part earth; part flower. It was a thought I put away as being likely to be very useful to me later. The third case was also at St. Ives. Some people called Valpy had been staying at St. Ives, and had left. We were waiting at dinner one night, when some-how I overheard my father or my mother say that Mr. Valpy had killed himself. The next thing I remember is being in the garden at night and walking on the path by the apple tree. It seemed to me that the apple tree was connected with the horror of Mr. Valpy's suicide. I could not pass it. I stood there looking at the grey-green creases of the bark—it was a moonlit night—in a trance of horror. I seemed to be dragged down, hopelessly, into some pit of absolute despair from which I could not escape. My body seemed paralysed.

These are three instances of exceptional moments. I often tell them over, or rather they come to the surface unexpectedly. But now that for the first time I have

---

[1] *Mrs. Swanwick ... happen* In her autobiography, *I Have Been Young* (1935), Helena Sickert Swanwick, who became acquainted with Leslie Stephen at St. Ives, remembers watching "with delight his naked babies running around the beach or being towed into the sea between his legs."

[2] *Roger* Woolf was working on *Roger Fry: A Biography*, which was published in 1940.

[3] *Mount Misery* The nickname given to two cottages located between Piddinghow and Southease in the Ouse River valley.

[4] *Mabel* The Woolfs's maid.

written them down, I realise something that I have never realised before. Two of these moments ended in a state of despair. The other ended, on the contrary, in a state of satisfaction. When I said about the flower "That is the whole," I felt that I had made a discovery. I felt that I had put away in my mind something that I should go back, to turn over and explore. It strikes me now that this was a profound difference. It was the difference in the first place between despair and satisfaction. This difference I think arose from the fact that I was quite unable to deal with the pain of discovering that people hurt each other; that a man I had seen had killed himself. The sense of horror held me powerless. But in the case of the flower I found a reason; and was thus able to deal with the sensation. I was not powerless. I was conscious—if only at a distance—that I should in time explain it. I do not know if I was older when I saw the flower than I was when I had the other two experiences. I only know that many of these exceptional moments brought with them a peculiar horror and a physical collapse; they seemed dominant; myself passive. This suggests that as one gets older one has a greater power through reason to provide an explanation; and that this explanation blunts the sledge-hammer force of the blow. I think this is true, because though I still have the peculiarity that I receive these sudden shocks, they are now always welcome; after the first surprise, I always feel instantly that they are particularly valuable. And so I go on to suppose that the shock-receiving capacity is what makes me a writer. I hazard the explanation that a shock is at once in my case followed by the desire to explain it. I feel that I have had a blow; but it is not, as I thought as a child, simply a blow from an enemy hidden behind the cotton wool of daily life; it is or will become a revelation of some order; it is a token of some real thing behind appearances; and I make it real by putting it into words. It is only by putting it into words that I make it whole; this wholeness means that it has lost its power to hurt me; it gives me, perhaps because by doing so I take away the pain, a great delight to put the severed parts together. Perhaps this is the strongest pleasure known to me. It is the rapture I get when in writing I seem to be discovering what belongs to what; making a scene come right; making a character come together. From this I reach what I might call a philosophy; at any rate it is a constant idea of mine; that behind the cotton wool is hidden a pattern; that we—I mean all human beings—are connected with this; that the whole world is a work of art; that we are parts of the work of art. *Hamlet* or a Beethoven quartet is the truth about this vast mass that we call the world. But there is no Shakespeare, there is no Beethoven; certainly and emphatically there is no God; we are the words; we are the music; we are the thing itself. And I see this when I have a shock.

This intuition of mine—it is so instinctive that it seems given to me, not made by me—has certainly given its scale to my life ever since I saw the flower in the bed by the front door at St. Ives. . . .

—1979 (WRITTEN 1939–40)

IN CONTEXT

Woolf and Bloomsbury[1]

Virginia Woolf was a central figure in a group of talented and influential friends that came to be known as the "Bloomsbury Group" after the part of London in which many of them lived. In addition to Woolf and her husband Leonard, the group included Woolf's sister Vanessa Bell, historian and intellectual Lytton Strachey, economist John Maynard Keynes, artist Duncan Grant, art critic Roger Fry, and novelist E.M. Forster. On the fringes of the group were such other leading figures as T.S. Eliot; since many of the group's central figures were widely connected, the social circle that revolved around Bloomsbury was a large one. As Eliot put it after she died, Woolf "was the center not merely of an esoteric group, but of the literary life of London....With the death of Virginia Woolf, a whole pattern of culture is broken."[2]

Vanessa Bell, *Virginia Woolf*, 1912.

The Woolfs were publishers as well as writers; small though it was, Hogarth Press published several of the most important books of the era, including Eliot's *Poems*, Katherine Mansfield's *Prelude*, and the first English edition of several of Sigmund Freud's works, as well as Woolf's own fiction. One of their friends, John Lehman, has given a good sense of the press's physical operations:

> The Hogarth Press was named after Hogarth house in Richmond where [the Woolfs] were living when they began printing and publishing. In 1924 they moved to No. 52 Tavistock

---

[1]   *Woolf and Bloomsbury*   Unless otherwise specified, all quotes are from *Recollections of Virginia Woolf*, edited by Joan Russell Noble (1972).

[2]   *was the ... broken*   From T.S. Eliot's obituary of Woolf in *Horizon*, May 1941, 313–16.

Square in Bloomsbury. Leonard and Virginia lived upstairs, and the activities of the Press were concentrated in the basement—a rather ramshackle basement, as was the case with any of the old Bloomsbury houses. The front room, looking on to the square, was the general office, in which there were as a rule not more than two or three girls at work, whose business it was to deal with the order, make out the invoices, pack up the books and handle the general correspondence. Leading out of the basement front room was a longish, dark corridor, piled with binders' packets of recently published books. On one side was the former scullery, in which Leonard had installed the treadle[1] printing press, still used for occasional small and special books.

Of Woolf herself, many have left vivid recollections—many of them touching on the strong sense of *joie de vivre* that she often radiated. In the context of the frequent depression that she experienced this may seem surprising, but the accounts are too numerous to be doubted. For Clive Bell, a sense of fun is the most lasting impression left by Woolf:[2]

> Writing was her passion and her joy and her poison. Yet, I repeat, hers was a happy nature. … My children, from the time they were old enough to enjoy anything beyond their animal satisfactions, enjoyed beyond anything a visit from Virginia: "Virginia's coming, what fun we shall have." That is what they said and felt when they were children and went on saying and feeling to the end. And so said all of us. So said everyone who knew her. … She might be divinely witty or outrageously fanciful; she might retail village gossip or tell stories of her London friends; always she was indescribably entertaining.

Bell also speaks of how Woolf sometimes "grew angry and lashed out" when she suspected she was being condescended to. She often felt resentful of "the way in which men, as she thought, patronized women, especially women who were attempting to create works of art or succeed in what were once considered manly professions. Assuredly Virginia did not wish to be a man, or to be treated as a man: she wished to be treated as an equal—just possibly as a superior."

Others describe a similar mixture in Woolf's personality. According to the novelist Elizabeth Bowen, Woolf could be "awfully naughty," even "fiendish." "She could say things about people, all in a flash, which remained with one. Fleetingly malicious, rather than outright cruel." Bowen also recalled a streak of superciliousness: "I was reminded sometimes of 'The Lord thy God is a jealous God: Thou shalt have no other God but me.' There was a touch of that about her." But, like Bell, Bowen recalls more strongly her exuberant and joyful spirit: "I was aware, one could not but be aware, of an undertow often of sadness, of melancholy, of great fear. But the main impression was of a creature of laughter and movement. … And her laughter was entrancing, it was outrageous laughter, almost like a child's laughter." Bowen has also likened Woolf's inquisitiveness to that of a child:

> She wanted to know all the details of people's lives. … She would say to anybody, to me, or anyone to whom she was talking, "Now what did you do, *exactly* what did you do? … You say you went to a party, where was it, who was there, what were they wearing?" Or, "You walked down the street, now *why* did you walk down the street? Who were you with? What did you see? Did you see a cat, did you see a dog?" It was that sort of inquisitiveness—almost childish. I never knew her to probe *deeply* into anything, and I don't know whether she really took much interest in people's affairs of the heart or not. … Past a point, her own imagination took over.

---

[1] *treadle* Lever worked by the foot.

[2] *Clive Bell … Woolf* All Clive Bell's recollections are from his *Old Friends: Personal Recollections* (1956).

Bowen is one of many to have remarked on Woolf's intensity as a writer; another is E.M. Forster. As he put it when comparing her to many of her contemporaries, "she liked writing with an intensity which few writers have attained or desired":

> Most of them write with half an eye on their royalties, half an eye on their critics, and a third half eye on improving the world, which leaves them with only half an eye for the task on which she concentrated her entire vision. She would not look elsewhere, and her circumstances combined with her temperament to focus her. Money she had not to consider, because she possessed a private income, and though financial independence is not always a safeguard against commercialism, it was in her case.

Even those who were not always sympathetic to Woolf or to Bloomsbury recognized that her approach both to those around her and to the craft of writing was in many respects extraordinary. The poet Stephen Spender was among those who sniped at Bloomsbury, calling it a "clique" rather than a group, and suggesting that Woolf "moved in a very limited social world." Yet even he felt obliged to remark on the "undiluted purity of one of those uncorrupted natures which seem set aside from the world for a special task by a strange conjunction of fortune and misfortune."[1] With Woolf, he ventured, "style, form, and material are indivisible."

Anonymous, *Virginia Woolf and T.S. Eliot*, 1920s.

---

[1] *undiluted ... misfortune* This and the following quote are from Stephen Spender's obituary of Woolf in the *Listener*, 10 April 1941, 533.

JAMES JOYCE
1882 – 1941

Irish novelist James Joyce's prose style and subject matter were so innovative and influential that fellow writer T.S. Eliot was prompted to declare that Joyce had helped to make "the modern world possible for art" by discovering "a way of controlling, or ordering, of giving a shape and a significance to the panorama of futility and anarchy which is contemporary history." Joyce's works as a whole redefined realism as they sought to access reality as perceived by the mind—whether awake or dreaming. Although throughout his life Joyce battled publishers, critics, and readers who objected to his frank treatment of the more "vulgar" aspects of his characters' thoughts and actions, Joyce became a literary figure of the first magnitude during his lifetime, and has remained so since.

James Augustus Aloysius Joyce was born in the middle-class Dublin suburb of Rathgar and was the first surviving son in a family of twelve siblings. Through his father's fecklessness, Joyce's family situation would eventually devolve into poverty. John Joyce's increasing dependence on alcohol created strains both on the family's finances and on its morale. On the other hand, Joyce's mother, Mary Jane Joyce, exposed the young Joyce to the arts and to religion, as she was both accomplished in music and devout in her Catholicism. The former he would embrace with as much fervor as he rejected the latter.

At the age of 6, Joyce started his studies under the tutorship of the Jesuits. During the course of his schooling, however, he became increasingly cynical about the Church. His intellectual and spiritual rebelliousness grew so that by the time he entered university he had begun to believe that religion, family, and nation were all traps of conventionality that the true artist must avoid.

While at University College, Joyce attempted to write poetry and enjoyed writing articles parodying various literary styles. A penchant for experimentation with form stayed with him, from the economy of voice exhibited in *Dubliners*, to the variety of narrative expressions created for *A Portrait of the Artist as a Young Man* and *Ulysses*, to the radical linguistic experimentation of *Finnegan's Wake*. In political matters, he rejected the single-minded nationalism of his peers and wrote outspoken articles that were published privately after the school advisory board barred publication in the school newspaper. Meanwhile, he was very successful in his chosen field of study—modern languages.

Joyce originally moved to Paris in 1902 to study medicine, but it was not until about 1904 that he took up his artistic mission in earnest and decided to leave Ireland. Apart from some brief periods, Joyce remained an exile from the country about which he would spend his life writing. For Joyce, exile was a prerequisite for artistic objectivity and freedom; he believed that his self-imposed exile allowed him to see the truth of Ireland and Irishness with clarity, precision, and detachment.

In June 1904, Joyce was invited by the paper *The Irish Homestead* to submit a short story. In the end he wrote a series of fifteen stories that were published in 1914 under the title *Dubliners*. Along the way Joyce had a series of arguments with publishers that would also dog and delay the publication of *A Portrait of the Artist as a Young Man,* as editors objected to what they saw as the inappropriate subject matter and language of his work. In 1909, he wrote to London publisher Grant Richards, with whom he was in negotiations for *Dubliners,* "I seriously believe that you will retard the course of civilization in Ireland by preventing the Irish people from having one good look at themselves in my nicely polished looking-glass." Richards, however, was in no financial position to advance the course of Irish civilization, and the book was rejected, not to be published until 1914.

Joyce described *Dubliners* as "a chapter of the moral history of my country." The book is divided—according to a letter Joyce wrote to his publisher—into four sections, representing childhood, adolescence, maturity, and public life. The fifteenth story, "The Dead," was not part of Joyce's original manuscript. This story, the longest in the collection, became the showpiece of the book upon its publication. Thematically, each of the stories in *Dubliners* deals with the lives of ordinary people, many of whom suffer from a sort of emotional paralysis—as a result of internal or external forces or moral decay—that makes them unable to move forward.

Many of these stories have as their focus a moment of self-recognition on the part of a character, a moment Joyce referred to as an "epiphany." The triggers to an epiphany are often accidental, "little errors and gestures—mere straws in the wind," as Joyce described them in a letter to his brother Stanislaus. The sharp focus allowed by a sudden flash of clarity is fleeting but allows characters a moment in which to see above their particular circumstances.

1904 was also the year Joyce met the woman who would be his lifelong partner. As legend has it, it was on 16 June, or "Bloomsday" (the day on which the events in *Ulysses* take place), that James Joyce first went out walking with Nora Barnacle, a chambermaid from Galway. Uninterested in literature, but with a fresh charm and wit and, like Joyce, an interest in music, she followed Joyce to the city of Pola, in the Austro-Hungarian Empire, four months after their meeting. They lived there a short time, without the sanction of marriage, and later moved to Trieste, Italy, where Joyce continued to write and eked out a meager living teaching English. The couple produced two children, Lucia and Georgio, and ultimately married, in 1931.

During their time in Trieste, in the fall of 1907, Joyce started editing, cutting, and reshaping the almost 1,000 pages of *Stephen Hero,* a novel he had begun in 1904. The result would be *A Portrait of the Artist as a Young Man*, on which Joyce continued to work intermittently for the next nine years. The novel-in-progress began to be published serially in *The Egoist* in 1914. It was not published as a volume until 1916, by the New York publisher B.W. Huebsch. It had been rejected by every London publisher to whom Joyce had sent it, despite the support of some major literary figures of the day, including W.B. Yeats, H.G. Wells, and Ezra Pound.

The hero of *Portrait*, Stephen Dedalus, bears a striking similarity to Joyce himself. The novel details the artistic growth of a writer, from childhood to the age of twenty, and outlines Joyce's artistic mission in life: to "record … with extreme care" epiphanic moments of sublime self-awareness; it also extends Joyce's experiments with style. The voice of the implied narrator changes and develops in correspondence with the development of the central character.

Ulysses details a day in Dublin life. Events in the novel follow the comings and goings of Stephen Dedalus, continuing the artistic journey on which Joyce set him in *A Portrait of the Artist as a Young Man*, and Leo Bloom, the Jewish-Irish Everyman who is the hero of the novel. *Ulysses* takes as its model Homer's *Odyssey*; an everyday journey through the neighborhoods of Dublin becomes highly symbolic as Leo Bloom follows a path that parallels that of Homer's hero. Meanwhile, Stephen Dedalus plays the role of Homer's Telemachus; Joyce imagines him an artist and visionary cut off from society. Joyce believed that Odysseus was perhaps the most well-rounded character in Western literature, embodying the best and the worst in human behavior: he was both brave and cowardly, a liar and an intellectual. Joyce's endeavors to portray these traits in his hero make Leo Bloom one of the most warmly compelling characters in all of twentieth-century literature.

In form, each chapter is an ironic rewriting of a chapter from Homer's *Odyssey*, and is written in a broadly different literary style from the one that precedes it. The novel adopts a stream-of-consciousness approach that makes little or no distinction between what is happening externally and what takes place in a character's mind. Perspectives move fluidly from internal to external dialogue, from character to character, and from event to event, with little to indicate the change. The novel's central themes are those that recur in Joyce's work: the inner life of Dublin in all its beauty and hollowness, and the outsider status of Leo Bloom (because of his Jewishness) and Stephen Dedalus (because of his artistic mission). This shared experience of Leo and Stephen, and Stephen's figurative search for an absent father, link the two thematically throughout the story.

Ulysses began to be published serially in the *Little Review* beginning in 1918, but in 1920 publication ceased in the face of obscenity charges. Not until 1922 was *Ulysses* published, and even then it was printed in Paris, not Britain. An American edition was published in 1934, after a landmark court case decided the book was not pornography. The weary judge at the time acquiesced to the view that the book was a work of art, even if many readers would not understand it. A British edition of *Ulysses* finally appeared in 1937.

It was not until about 1920 that the Joyce family began to attain a modest level of financial security, largely the result of the support and patronage of a number of people who had as much faith in Joyce's genius as he himself did. The family moved from Trieste to Zurich in 1914, then to Paris in 1920, then back to Zurich in 1940, where Joyce died of a perforated ulcer, just after seeing the publication of his final—and perhaps least understood—novel, *Finnegan's Wake* (1939). In stylistic terms, the novel goes beyond the playful, self-conscious mode of *Ulysses* and enters a far more obscure territory. The title refers to a common folk song in which a laborer, Finnegan, falls and hits his head. His friends assume he is dead and hold a wake for him; he finally awakens after having whiskey spilled on him. *Finnegan's Wake* is ostensibly the dream of Finnegan's successor, a Dublin Everyman with the initials H.C.E. (which stand for a variety of names, including Humphrey Chimpden Earwicker and Here Comes Everybody), and also features H.C.E.'s wife, A.L.P. (Anna Livia Plurabelle, Amnis Limina Permanent) and their twin sons, Shem and Shaun. Everything that occurs, and all the characters present, belong at least partially to the realm of dream. The novel's form relies on the cyclical view of history set out by Italian philosopher Giambattista Vico (detailed in Samuel Beckett's essay "Dante … Bruno. Vico … Joyce," included here). The narrative is largely composed of multi-leveled puns that are fraught with symbolic meaning. Joyce used elements of English and seven other languages to create the texture of the novel, reinventing not just the form of the novel but the structure of language itself in order to escape the stifling traditions in which he felt conventional language was steeped.

During his lifetime Joyce promised his writing would "keep the professors busy," and in this he has succeeded, and continues to succeed, to an extent that even he might not have expected. For many years scholars were occupied with historical, cultural, and anthropological research into the background of Joyce's Dublin. While this research continues, developments in critical theory (such as postcolonialism) have also opened up many new ways to interpret Joyce's texts. During his lifetime much of his work was, as one of Joyce's friends said, "outside of literature"; "literature" has since shifted to accommodate Joyce.

⌘ ⌘ ⌘

Eveline

She sat at the window watching the evening invade the avenue. Her head was leaned against the window curtains and in her nostrils was the odour of dusty cretonne.[1] She was tired.

Few people passed. The man out of the last house passed on his way home; she heard his footsteps clacking along the concrete pavement and afterwards crunching on the cinder path before the new red houses. One time there used to be a field there in which they used to play every evening with other people's children. Then a man from Belfast bought the field and built houses in it—not like their little brown houses but bright brick houses with shining roofs. The children of the avenue used to play together in that field—the Devines, the Waters, the Dunns, little Keogh the cripple, she and her brothers and sisters. Ernest, however, never played: he was too grown up. Her father used often to hunt them in out of the field with his blackthorn stick but usually little Keogh used to keep nix[2] and call out when he saw her father coming. Still they seemed to have been rather happy then. Her father was not so bad then, and besides her mother was alive. That was a long time ago; she and her brothers and sisters were all grown up; her mother was dead. Tizzie Dunn was dead, too, and the Waters had gone back to England. Everything changes. Now she was going to go away like the others, to leave her home.

Home! She looked round the room reviewing all its familiar objects which she had dusted once a week for so many years, wondering where on earth all the dust came from. Perhaps she would never see again those familiar objects from which she had never dreamed of being divided. And yet during all those years she had never found out the name of the priest whose yellowing photograph hung on the wall above the broken harmonium[3] beside the coloured print of the promises made to Blessed Margaret Mary Alacoque.[4] He had been a school friend of her father's. Whenever he showed the photograph to a visitor her father used to pass it with a casual word:

—He is in Melbourne now.

She had consented to go away, to leave her home. Was that wise? She tried to weigh each side of the question. In her home anyway she had shelter and food; she had those whom she had known all her life about her. Of course she had to work hard both in the house and at business. What would they say of her in the stores when they found out that she had run away with a fellow? Say she was a fool, perhaps; and her place would be filled up by advertisement. Miss Gavan would be glad. She had always had an edge on her, especially whenever there were people listening.

—Miss Hill, don't you see these ladies are waiting?

—Look lively, Miss Hill, please.

She would not cry many tears at leaving the stores.

But in her new home, in a distant unknown country, it would not be like that. Then she would be married—she, Eveline. People would treat her with respect then. She would not be treated as her mother had been. Even now, though she was over nineteen, she sometimes felt herself in danger of her father's violence. She knew it was that that had given her the palpitations. When they were growing up he had never gone for her, like he used to go for Harry and Ernest, because she was a girl; but latterly he had begun to threaten her and say what he would do to her only for her dead mother's sake. And now she had nobody to protect her. Ernest was dead and Harry, who was in the church decorating business, was nearly always down somewhere in the country. Besides, the invariable squabble for money on Saturday nights had begun to weary her unspeakably. She always gave her entire wages—seven shillings—and Harry always sent up what he could but the trouble was to get any money from her father. He said she used to

---

[1] *cretonne*   Thick, unglazed, cotton fabric often used for chair covers and curtains.

[2] *keep nix*   Keep watch.

[3] *harmonium*   Type of reed organ.

[4] *Blessed Margaret Mary Alacoque*   Seventeenth-century French nun whose devotion led her to perform extreme acts of penance, such as drinking water in which laundry had been washed and carving the name of Jesus into her chest.

squander the money, that she had no head, that he wasn't going to give her his hard earned money to throw about the streets and much more for he was usually fairly bad of a Saturday night. In the end he would give her the money and ask her had she any intention of buying Sunday's dinner. Then she had to rush out as quickly as she could and do her marketing, holding her black leather purse tightly in her hand as she elbowed her way through the crowds and returning home late under her load of provisions. She had hard work to keep the house together and to see that the two young children who had been left to her charge went to school regularly and got their meals regularly. It was hard work—a hard life—but now that she was about to leave it she did not find it a wholly undesirable life.

She was about to explore another life with Frank. Frank was very kind, manly, openhearted. She was to go away with him by the night boat to be his wife and to live with him in Buenos Ayres where he had a home waiting for her. How well she remembered the first time she had seen him; he was lodging in a house on the main road where she used to visit. It seemed a few weeks ago. He was standing at the gate, his peaked cap pushed back on his head and his hair tumbled forward over a face of bronze. Then they had come to know each other. He used to meet her outside the stores every evening and see her home. He took her to see the *Bohemian Girl*[1] and she felt elated as she sat in an unaccustomed part of the theatre with him. He was awfully fond of music and sang a little. People knew that they were courting and when he sang about the lass that loves a sailor she always felt pleasantly confused. He used to call her Poppens out of fun. First of all it had been an excitement for her to have a fellow and then she had begun to like him. He had tales of distant countries. He had started as a deck boy at a pound a month on a ship of the Allan line[2] going out to Canada. He told her the names of the ships he had been on and the names of the different services. He had sailed through the Straits of

Magellan and he told her stories of the terrible Patagonians.[3] He had fallen on his feet in Buenos Ayres, he said, and had come over to the old country just for a holiday. Of course, her father had found out the affair and had forbidden her to have anything to say to him:

—I know these sailor chaps, he said.

One day he had quarrelled with Frank and after that she had to meet her lover secretly.

The evening deepened in the avenue. The white of two letters in her lap grew indistinct. One was to Harry, the other was to her father. Ernest had been her favourite but she liked Harry too. Her father was becoming old lately, she noticed; he would miss her. Sometimes he could be very nice. Not long before, when she had been laid up for a day, he had read her out a ghost story and made toast for her at the fire. Another day, when their mother was alive, they had all gone for a picnic to the Hill of Howth.[4] She remembered her father putting on her mother's bonnet to make the children laugh.

Her time was running out but she continued to sit by the window, leaning her head against the window curtain, inhaling the odour of dusty cretonne. Down far in the avenue she could hear a street organ playing. She knew the air. Strange that it should come that very night to remind her of the promise to her mother, her promise to keep the home together as long as she could. She remembered the last night of her mother's illness; she was again in the close dark room at the other side of the hall and outside she heard a melancholy air of Italy. The organ player had been ordered to go away and given sixpence. She remembered her father strutting back into the sickroom saying:

—Damned Italians! coming over here!

As she mused the pitiful vision of her mother's life laid its spell on the very quick of her being—that life of commonplace sacrifices closing in final craziness. She trembled as she heard again her mother's voice saying constantly with foolish insistence:

---

[1] *Bohemian Girl*   1843 opera by Dubliner Michael Balfe (1808–70).

[2] *the Allan line*   The Allan Steamship Company, founded in 1852 by Sir Hugh Allan, made weekly departures from Liverpool to the Western coast of Canada (with stops along the way, including at Cape Horn and Buenos Aires).

[3] *the terrible Patagonians*   The tall stature of these South American natives was greatly exaggerated in the seventeenth and eighteenth centuries, and they were rumored to be fierce giants.

[4] *Hill of Howth*   Located northeast of Dublin, on the Howth peninsula.

—Derevaun Seraun! Derevaun Seraun![1]

She stood up in a sudden impulse of terror. Escape! She must escape! Frank would save her. He would give her life, perhaps love too. But she wanted to live. Why should she be unhappy? She had a right to happiness. Frank would take her in his arms, fold her in his arms. He would save her.

She stood among the swaying crowd in the station at the North Wall. He held her hand and she knew that he was speaking to her, saying something about the passage over and over again. The station was full of soldiers with brown baggages. Through the wide doors of the sheds she caught a glimpse of the black mass of the boat lying in beside the quay wall, with illumined portholes. She answered nothing. She felt her cheek pale and cold and out of a maze of distress she prayed to God to direct her, to show her what was her duty. The boat blew a long mournful whistle into the mist. If she went, tomorrow she would be on the sea with Frank, steaming towards Buenos Ayres. Their passage had been booked. Could she still draw back after all he had done for her? Her distress awoke a nausea in her body and she kept moving her lips in silent fervent prayer.

A bell clanged upon her heart. She felt him seize her hand:

—Come!

All the seas of the world tumbled about her heart. He was drawing her into them: he would drown her. She gripped with both hands at the iron railing.

—Come!

No! No! No! It was impossible. Her hands clutched the iron in frenzy. Amid the seas she sent a cry of anguish.

—Eveline! Evvy!

He rushed beyond the barrier and called to her to follow. He was shouted at to go on but he still called to her. She set her white face to him, passive, like a helpless animal. Her eyes gave him no sign of love or farewell or recognition.

—1914

Araby[2]

North Richmond Street, being blind,[3] was a quiet street except at the hour when the Christian Brothers' School set the boys free. An uninhabited house of two storeys stood at the blind end, detached from its neighbours in a square ground. The other houses of the street, conscious of decent lives within them, gazed at one another with brown imperturbable faces.

The former tenant of our house, a priest, had died in the back drawingroom. Air, musty from having been long enclosed, hung in all the rooms and the waste room behind the kitchen was littered with old useless papers. Among these I found a few papercovered books, the pages of which were curled and damp: *The Abbot* by Walter Scott, *The Devout Communicant* and *The Memoirs of Vidocq*.[4] I liked the last best because its leaves were yellow. The wild garden behind the house contained a central apple tree and a few straggling bushes under one of which I found the late tenant's rusty bicycle pump. He had been a very charitable priest; in his will he had left all his money to institutions and the furniture of his house to his sister.

When the short days of winter came dusk fell before we had well eaten our dinners. When we met in the street the houses had grown sombre. The space of sky above us was the colour of everchanging violet and towards it the lamps of the street lifted their feeble lanterns. The cold air stung us and we played till our bodies glowed. Our shouts echoed in the silent street. The career of our play brought us through the dark muddy lanes behind the houses where we ran the gantlet of the rough tribes from the cottages, to the back doors of the dark dripping gardens where odours arose from the ashpits, to the dark odorous stables where a coachman smoothed and combed the horse or shook music from the buckled harness. When we returned to the street light from the kitchen windows had filled the

---

[1] *Derevaun Seraun* The meaning of this phrase, if there is one, is uncertain. While some scholars believe it to be garbled Irish, others assert it is gibberish.

[2] *Araby* Charity bazaar held in Dublin in 1894.

[3] *blind* A dead end.

[4] *The Devout Communicant* Catholic religious manual published in 1831; *The Memoirs of Viducq* Written by François-Eugène Vidocq (1775–1857), a career criminal who was appointed chief of a French detective force.

areas.[1] If my uncle was seen turning the corner we hid in the shadow until we had seen him safely housed. Or if Mangan's sister came out on the doorstep to call her brother in to his tea we watched her from our shadow peer up and down the street. We waited to see whether she would remain or go in and if she remained we left our shadow and walked up to Mangan's steps resignedly. She was waiting for us, her figure defined by the light from the half-opened door. Her brother always teased her before he obeyed and I stood by the railings looking at her. Her dress swung as she moved her body and the soft rope of her hair tossed from side to side.

Every morning I lay on the floor in the front parlour watching her door. The blind was pulled down to within an inch of the sash so that I could not be seen. When she came out on the doorstep my heart leaped. I ran to the hall, seized my books and followed her. I kept her brown figure always in my eye and when we came near the point at which our ways diverged I quickened my pace and passed her. This happened morning after morning. I had never spoken to her except for a few casual words and yet her name was like a summons to all my foolish blood.

Her image accompanied me even in places the most hostile to romance. On Saturday evenings when my aunt went marketing I had to go to carry some of the parcels. We walked through the flaring streets, jostled by drunken men and bargaining women, amid the curses of labourers, the shrill litanies of shop boys who stood on guard by the barrels of pigs' cheeks, the nasal chanting of street singers who sang a come-all-you about O'Donovan Rossa[2] or a ballad about the troubles in our native land. These noises converged in a single sensation of life for me: I imagined that I bore my chalice safely through a throng of foes. Her name sprang to my lips at moments in strange prayers and praises which I myself did not understand. My eyes were often full of tears (I could not tell why) and at times a flood from my heart seemed to pour itself out into my bosom. I thought little

of the future. I did not know whether I would ever speak to her or not or, if I spoke to her, how I could tell her of my confused adoration. But my body was like a harp and her words and gestures were like fingers running upon the wires.

One evening I went into the back drawingroom in which the priest had died. It was a dark rainy evening and there was no sound in the house. Through one of the broken panes I heard the rain impinge upon the earth, the fine incessant needles of water playing in the sodden beds. Some distant lamp or lighted window gleamed below me. I was thankful that I could see so little. All my senses seemed to desire to veil themselves and, feeling that I was about to slip from them, I pressed the palms of my hands together until they trembled, murmuring: *O love! O love!* many times.

At last she spoke to me. When she addressed the first words to me I was so confused that I did not know what to answer. She asked me was I going to *Araby*. I forget whether I answered yes or no. It would be a splendid bazaar, she said; she would love to go.

—And why can't you? I asked.

While she spoke she turned a silver bracelet round and round her wrist. She could not go, she said, because there would be a retreat that week in her convent.[3] Her brother and two other boys were fighting for their caps and I was alone at the railings. She held one of the spikes, bowing her head towards me. The light from the lamp opposite our door caught the white curve of her neck, lit up the hair that rested there and, falling, lit up the hand upon the railing. It fell over one side of her dress and caught the white border of a petticoat, just visible as she stood at ease.

—It's well for you, she said.

—If I go, I said, I will bring you something.

What innumerable follies laid waste my waking and sleeping thoughts after that evening! I wished to annihilate the tedious intervening days. I chafed against the work of school. At night in my bedroom and by day in the classroom her image came between me and the page I strove to read. The syllables of the word *Araby* were called to me through the silence in which my soul luxuriated and cast an eastern enchantment over me. I

---

[1] *areas* Spaces between the railings and the fronts of houses, below street level.

[2] *come-all-you* Ballad (so called because many ballads started with this phrase); *O'Donovan Rossa* Jeremiah Donovan, Irish nationalist who was sentenced to a lifetime of penal servitude but was granted amnesty and departed for America.

[3] *convent* I.e., convent school.

asked for leave to go to the bazaar on Saturday night. My aunt was surprised and hoped it was not some freemason affair.[1] I answered few questions in class. I watched my master's face pass from amiability to sternness; he hoped I was not beginning to idle. I could not call my wandering thoughts together. I had hardly any patience with the serious work of life which, now that it stood between me and my desire, seemed to me child's play, ugly monotonous child's play.

On Saturday morning I reminded my uncle that I wished to go to the bazaar in the evening. He was fussing at the hallstand, looking for the hatbrush, and answered me curtly:

—Yes, boy, I know.

As he was in the hall I could not go into the front parlour and lie at the window. I left the house in bad humour and walked slowly towards the school. The air was pitilessly raw and already my heart misgave me.

When I came home to dinner my uncle had not yet been home. Still it was early. I sat staring at the clock for some time and when its ticking began to irritate me I left the room. I mounted the staircase and gained the upper part of the house. The high cold empty gloomy rooms liberated me and I went from room to room singing. From the front window I saw my companions playing below in the street. Their cries reached me weakened and indistinct and, leaning my forehead against the cool glass, I looked over at the dark house where she lived. I may have stood there for an hour seeing nothing but the brownclad figure cast by my imagination, touched discreetly by the lamplight at the curved neck, at the hand upon the railings and at the border below the dress.

When I came downstairs again I found Mrs. Mercer sitting at the fire. She was an old garrulous woman, a pawnbroker's widow who collected used stamps for some pious purpose. I had to endure the gossip of the teatable. The meal was prolonged beyond an hour and still my uncle did not come. Mrs. Mercer stood up to go: she was sorry she couldn't wait any longer but it was

after eight o'clock and she did not like to be out late as the night air was bad for her. When she had gone I began to walk up and down the room, clenching my fists. My aunt said:

—I'm afraid you may put off your bazaar for this night of Our Lord.

At nine o'clock I heard my uncle's latchkey in the halldoor. I heard him talking to himself and heard the hallstand rocking when it had received the weight of his overcoat. I could interpret these signs. When he was midway through his dinner I asked him to give me the money to go to the bazaar. He had forgotten.

—The people are in bed and after their first sleep now, he said.

I did not smile. My aunt said to him energetically:

—Can't you give him the money and let him go? You've kept him late enough as it is.

My uncle said he was very sorry he had forgotten. He said he believed in the old saying: *All work and no play makes Jack a dull boy*. He asked me where I was going and when I had told him a second time he asked me did I know *The Arab's Farewell to his Steed*.[2] When I left the kitchen he was about to recite the opening lines of the piece to my aunt.

I held a florin tightly in my hand as I strode down Buckingham Street towards the station. The sight of the streets thronged with buyers and glaring with gas recalled to me the purpose of my journey. I took my seat in a third class carriage of a deserted train. After an intolerable delay the train moved out of the station slowly. It crept onward among ruinous houses and over the twinkling river. At Westland Row Station a crowd of people pressed at the carriage doors; but the porters moved them back, saying that it was a special train for the bazaar. I remained alone in the bare carriage. In a few minutes the train drew up beside an improvised wooden platform. I passed out on to the road and saw by the lighted dial of a clock that it was ten minutes to ten. In front of me was a large building which displayed the magical name.

I could not find any sixpenny entrance and, fearing that the bazaar would be closed, I passed in quickly through a turnstile, handing a shilling to a wearylooking

---

[1] *freemason affair* Affiliated with the Freemasons, a secret society originally made up of skilled stone-workers. The society was said to be anti-Catholic, and the Archbishop of Dublin had decreed that any Catholics caught at a freemason bazaar could be excommunicated.

[2] *The Arab's ... Steed* Popular romantic poem by Caroline Norton (1808–77).

man. I found myself in a big hall girdled at half its height by a gallery. Nearly all the stalls were closed and the greater part of the hall was in darkness. I recognised a silence like that which pervades a church after a service. I walked into the centre of the bazaar timidly. A few people were gathered about the stalls which were still open. Before a curtain over which the words *Café Chantant*[1] were written in coloured lamps two men were counting money on a salver. I listened to the fall of the coins.

Remembering with difficulty why I had come I went over to one of the stalls and examined porcelain vases and flowered teasets. At the door of the stall a young lady was talking and laughing with two young gentlemen. I remarked their English accents and listened vaguely to their conversation.

—O, I never said such a thing!

—O, but you did!

—O, but I didn't!

—Didn't she say that?

—She did. I heard her.

—O, there's a … fib!

Observing me the young lady came over and asked me did I wish to buy anything. The tone of her voice was not encouraging: she seemed to have spoken to me out of a sense of duty. I looked humbly at the great jars that stood like eastern guards at either side of the dark entrance to her stall and murmured:

—No, thank you.

The young lady changed the position of one of the vases and went back to the two young men. They began to talk of the same subject. Once or twice the young lady glanced at me over her shoulder.

I lingered before her stall, though I knew my stay was useless, to make my interest in her wares seem the more real. Then I turned away slowly and walked down the middle of the bazaar. I allowed the two pennies to fall against the sixpence in my pocket. I heard a voice call from one end of the gallery that the light was out. The upper part of the hall was now completely dark.

Gazing up into the darkness I saw myself as a creature driven and derided by vanity: and my eyes burned with anguish and anger.

—1914

---

1 *Café Chantant*   Café that provides musical entertainment.

The Dead

Lily, the caretaker's daughter, was literally run off her feet. Hardly had she brought one gentleman into the little pantry behind the office on the ground floor and helped him off with his overcoat when the wheezy hall-door bell clanged again and she had to scamper along the bare hallway to let in another guest. It was well for her she had not to attend to the ladies also. But Miss Kate and Miss Julia had thought of that and had converted the bathroom upstairs into a ladies' dressing-room. Miss Kate and Miss Julia were there, gossiping and laughing and fussing, walking after each other to the head of the stairs, peering down over the banisters and calling down to Lily to ask her who had come.

It was always a great affair, the Misses Morkan's annual dance. Everybody who knew them came to it, members of the family, old friends of the family, the members of Julia's choir, any of Kate's pupils that were grown up enough and even some of Mary Jane's pupils too. Never once had it fallen flat. For years and years it had gone off in splendid style as long as anyone could remember, ever since Kate and Julia, after the death of their brother Pat, had left the house in Stony Batter and taken Mary Jane, their only niece, to live with them in the dark gaunt house on Usher's Island, the upper part of which they had rented from Mr. Fullam, the corn factor[2] on the ground floor. That was a good thirty years ago if it was a day. Mary Jane, who was then a little girl in short clothes, was now the main prop of the household for she had the organ in Haddington Road. She had been through the academy[3] and gave a pupils' concert every year in the upper room of the Antient Concert Rooms. Many of her pupils belonged to better class families on the Kingstown and Dalkey line. Old as they were, her aunts also did their share. Julia, though she was quite grey, was still the leading soprano in Adam and Eve's[4] and Kate, being too feeble to go about much, gave music lessons to beginners on the old square piano in the back room. Lily, the caretaker's daughter, did housemaid work for them. Though their life was modest

---

2 *corn factor*   Grain merchant.

3 *the academy*   Royal Irish Academy of Music.

4 *Adam and Eve's*   Roman Catholic church in Dublin.

they believed in eating well, the best of everything: diamond bone sirloins, three shilling tea and the best bottled stout. But Lily seldom made a mistake in the orders so that she got on well with her three mistresses. They were fussy, that was all. But the only thing they would not stand was back answers.[1]

Of course they had good reason to be fussy on such a night. And then it was long after ten o'clock and yet there was no sign of Gabriel and his wife. Besides they were dreadfully afraid that Freddy Malins might turn up screwed.[2] They would not wish for worlds that any of Mary Jane's pupils should see him under the influence: and when he was like that it was sometimes very hard to manage him. Freddy Malins always came late but they wondered what could be keeping Gabriel: and that was what brought them every two minutes to the banisters to ask Lily had Gabriel or Freddy come.

—O, Mr. Conroy, said Lily to Gabriel when she opened the door for him, Miss Kate and Miss Julia thought you were never coming. Good night, Mrs. Conroy.

—I'll engage they did, said Gabriel, but they forget that my wife here takes three mortal hours to dress herself.

He stood on the mat, scraping the snow from his goloshes, while Lily led his wife to the foot of the stairs and called out:

—Miss Kate, here's Mrs. Conroy.

Kate and Julia came toddling down the dark stairs at once. Both of them kissed Gabriel's wife, said she must be perished alive and asked was Gabriel with her.

—Here I am as right as the mail, Aunt Kate! Go on up. I'll follow, called out Gabriel from the dark.

He continued scraping his feet vigorously while the three women went upstairs, laughing, to the ladies' dressingroom. A light fringe of snow lay like a cape on the shoulders of his overcoat and like toecaps on the toes of his goloshes; and, as the buttons of his overcoat slipped with a squeaking noise through the snow-stiffened frieze,[3] a cold fragrant air from out of doors escaped from crevices and folds.

—Is it snowing again, Mr. Conroy? asked Lily.

She had preceded him into the pantry to help him off with his overcoat. Gabriel smiled at the three syllables she had given his surname and glanced at her. She was a slim growing girl, pale in complexion and with haycoloured hair. The gas in the pantry made her look still paler. Gabriel had known her when she was a child and used to sit on the lowest step nursing[4] a rag doll.

—Yes, Lily, he answered, and I think we're in for a night of it. He looked up at the pantry ceiling which was shaking with the stamping and shuffling of feet on the floor above, listened for a moment to the piano and then glanced at the girl who was folding his overcoat carefully at the end of a shelf.

—Tell me, Lily, he said in a friendly tone, do you still go to school?

—O no, sir, she answered, I'm done schooling this year and more.

—O then, said Gabriel gaily, I suppose we'll be going to your wedding one of these fine days with your young man—eh?

The girl glanced back at him over her shoulder and said with great bitterness:

—The men that is now is only all palaver[5] and what they can get out of you.

Gabriel coloured as if he felt he had made a mistake and, without looking at her, kicked off his goloshes and flicked actively with his muffler at his patent leather shoes.

He was a stout tallish young man. The high colour of his cheeks pushed upwards even to his forehead where it scattered itself in a few formless patches of pale red; and on his hairless face there scintillated restlessly the polished lenses and bright gilt rims of the glasses which screened his delicate and restless eyes. His glossy black hair was parted in the middle and brushed in a long curve behind his ears where it curled slightly beneath the groove left by his hat.

When he had flicked lustre into his shoes he stood up and pulled his waistcoat down more tightly on his plump body. Then he took a coin rapidly from his pocket.

---

[1] *back answers* Rudeness; back-talk.

[2] *screwed* Drunk.

[3] *frieze* Coarse woolen cloth.

[4] *nursing* Here, taking care of.

[5] *palaver* Flattering talk.

—O Lily, he said, thrusting it into her hand, it's Christmas time, isn't it? Just … here's a little …

He walked rapidly towards the door.

—O no, sir! cried the girl, following him. Really, sir, I wouldn't take it.

—Christmas time! Christmas time! said Gabriel, almost trotting to the stairs and waving his hand to her in deprecation.

The girl, seeing that he had gained the stairs, called out after him:

—Well, thank you, sir.

He waited outside the drawingroom door until the waltz should finish, listening to the skirts that swept against it and to the shuffling of feet. He was still discomposed by the girl's bitter and sudden retort. It had cast a gloom over him which he tried to dispel by arranging his cuffs and the bows of his tie. Then he took from his waistcoat pocket a little paper and glanced at the headings he had made for his speech. He was undecided about the lines from Robert Browning[1] for he feared they would be above the heads of his hearers. Some quotation that they could recognise from Shakespeare or from the Melodies[2] would be better. The indelicate clacking of the men's heels and the shuffling of their soles reminded him that their grade of culture differed from his. He would only make himself ridiculous by quoting poetry to them which they could not understand. They would think that he was airing his superior education. He would fail with them just as he had failed with the girl in the pantry. He had taken up a wrong tone. His whole speech was a mistake from first to last, an utter failure.

Just then his aunts and his wife came out of the ladies' dressingroom. His aunts were two small plainly dressed old women. Aunt Julia was an inch or so the taller. Her hair, drawn low over the tops of her ears, was grey; and grey also, with darker shadows, was her large flaccid face. Though she was stout in build and stood erect her slow eyes and parted lips gave her the appearance of a woman who did not know where she was or where she was going. Aunt Kate was more vivacious. Her face, healthier than her sister's, was all puckers and

creases like a shrivelled red apple and her hair, braided in the same oldfashioned way, had not lost its ripe nut colour.

They both kissed Gabriel frankly. He was their favourite nephew, the son of their dead elder sister Ellen who had married T. J. Conroy of the Port and Docks.[3]

—Gretta tells me you're not going to take a cab back to Monkstown tonight, Gabriel, said Aunt Kate.

—No, said Gabriel, turning to his wife, we had quite enough of that last year, hadn't we? Don't you remember, Aunt Kate, what a cold Gretta got out of it? Cab windows rattling all the way and the east wind blowing in after we passed Merrion. Very jolly it was. Gretta caught a dreadful cold.

Aunt Kate frowned severely and nodded her head at every word.

—Quite right, Gabriel, quite right, she said. You can't be too careful.

—But as for Gretta there, said Gabriel, she'd walk home in the snow if she were let.

Mrs. Conroy laughed.

—Don't mind him, Aunt Kate, she said. He's really an awful bother, what with green shades for Tom's eyes at night and making him do the dumbbells and forcing Lottie to eat the stirabout.[4] The poor child! And she simply hates the sight of it! … O, but you'll never guess what he makes me wear now!

She broke out into a peal of laughter and glanced at her husband whose admiring and happy eyes had been wandering from her dress to her face and hair. The two aunts laughed heartily too for Gabriel's solicitude was a standing joke with them.

—Goloshes! said Mrs. Conroy. That's the latest. Whenever it's wet underfoot I must put on my goloshes. Tonight even he wanted me to put them on but I wouldn't. The next thing he'll buy me will be a diving suit.

Gabriel laughed nervously and patted his tie reassuringly while Aunt Kate nearly doubled herself so heartily did she enjoy the joke. The smile soon faded from Aunt Julia's face and her mirthless eyes were directed towards her nephew's face. After a pause she asked:

—And what are goloshes, Gabriel?

---

[1] *Robert Browning*   English poet (1812–89).

[2] *Melodies*   Thomas Moore's collection of poetry and songs, *Irish Melodies*.

[3] *Port and Docks*   Dublin Port and Docks Board, an essential part of Dublin's commercial life.

[4] *stirabout*   Porridge.

—Goloshes, Julia! exclaimed her sister. Goodness me, don't you know what goloshes are? You wear them over your ... over your boots, Gretta, isn't it?

—Yes, said Mrs. Conroy. Guttapercha[1] things. We both have a pair now. Gabriel says everyone wears them on the continent.[2]

—O, on the continent, murmured Aunt Julia, nodding her head slowly.

Gabriel knitted his brows and said, as if he were slightly angered:

—It's nothing very wonderful but Gretta thinks it very funny because she says the word reminds her of christy minstrels.[3]

—But tell me, Gabriel, said Aunt Kate with brisk tact. Of course you've seen about the room. Gretta was saying ...

—O, the room is all right, replied Gabriel. I've taken one in the Gresham.[4]

—To be sure, said Aunt Kate, by far the best thing to do. And the children, Gretta, you're not anxious about them?

—O, for one night, said Mrs. Conroy. Besides Bessie will look after them.

—To be sure, said Aunt Kate again. What a comfort it is to have a girl like that, one you can depend on! There's that Lily, I'm sure I don't know what has come over her lately. She's not the girl she was at all.

Gabriel was about to ask his aunt some questions on this point but she broke off suddenly to gaze after her sister who had wandered down the stairs and was craning her neck over the banisters.

—Now, I ask you, she said almost testily, where is Julia going. Julia! Julia! Where are you going?

Julia who had gone half way down one flight came back and announced blandly:

—Here's Freddy!

At the same moment a clapping of hands and a final flourish of the pianist told that the waltz had ended. The drawingroom door was opened from within and some couples came out. Aunt Kate drew Gabriel aside hurriedly and whispered into his ear:

—Slip down, Gabriel, like a good fellow and see if he's all right and don't let him up if he's screwed. I'm sure he's screwed. I'm sure he is.

Gabriel went to the stairs and listened over the banisters. He could hear two persons talking in the pantry. Then he recognised Freddy Malins' laugh. He went down the stairs noisily.

—It's such a relief, said Aunt Kate to Mrs. Conroy, that Gabriel is here. I always feel easier in my mind when he's here ...

—Julia, there's Miss Daly and Miss Power will take some refreshment. Thanks for your beautiful waltz, Miss Daly. It made lovely time.

A tall wizenfaced man with a stiff grizzled moustache and swarthy skin who was passing out with his partner said:

—And may we have some refreshment too, Miss Morkan?

—Julia, said Aunt Kate summarily, and here's Mr. Browne and Miss Furlong. Take them in, Julia, with Miss Daly and Miss Power.

—I'm the man for the ladies, said Mr. Browne, pursing his lips until his moustache bristled and smiling in all his wrinkles. You know, Miss Morkan, the reason they are so fond of me is ...

He did not finish his sentence but, seeing that Aunt Kate was out of earshot, at once led the three young ladies into the back room. The middle of the room was occupied by two square tables placed end to end and on these Aunt Julia and the caretaker were straightening and smoothing a large cloth. On the sideboard were arrayed dishes and plates and glasses and bundles of knives and forks and spoons. The top of the closed square piano served also as a sideboard for viands and sweets. At a smaller sideboard in one corner two young men were standing, drinking hop bitters.[5]

Mr. Browne led his charges thither and invited them all, in jest, to some ladies' punch, hot, strong and sweet. As they said they never took anything strong he opened three bottles of lemonade for them. Then he asked one of the young men to move aside and, taking hold of the decanter, filled out for himself a goodly measure of

---

[1] *Guttapercha* Substance similar to rubber and used for waterproofing.

[2] *continent* I.e., Europe.

[3] *christy minstrels* Minstrel show. From the nineteenth-century minstrel show founded by George Christy.

[4] *Gresham* One of Dublin's top hotels.

[5] *hop bitters* Unfermented liquor flavored with hops.

whisky. The young men eyed him respectfully while he took a trial sip.

—God help me, he said smiling, it's the doctor's orders.

His wizened face broke into a broader smile and the three young ladies laughed in musical echo to his pleasantry, swaying their bodies to and fro, with nervous jerks of their shoulders. The boldest said:

—O, now, Mr. Browne, I'm sure the doctor never ordered anything of the kind.

Mr. Browne took another sip of his whisky and said, with sidling mimicry:

—Well, you see, I'm like the famous Mrs. Cassidy who is reported to have said: *Now, Mary Grimes, if I don't take it make me take it for I feel I want it.*

His hot face had leaned forward a little too confidentially and he had assumed a very low Dublin accent so that the young ladies, with one instinct, received his speech in silence. Miss Furlong, who was one of Mary Jane's pupils, asked Miss Daly what was the name of the pretty waltz she had played; and Mr. Browne, seeing that he was ignored, turned promptly to the two young men who were more appreciative.

A redfaced young woman, dressed in pansy, came into the room, excitedly clapping her hands and crying:

—Quadrilles!¹ Quadrilles!

Close on her heels came Aunt Kate, crying:

—Two gentlemen and three ladies, Mary Jane!

—O, here's Mr. Bergin and Mr. Kerrigan, said Mary Jane. Mr. Kerrigan, will you take Miss Power. Miss Furlong, may I get you a partner, Mr. Bergin. O, that'll just do now.

—Three ladies, Mary Jane, said Aunt Kate.

The two young gentlemen asked the ladies if they might have the pleasure and Mary Jane turned to Miss Daly.

—O, Miss Daly, you're really awfully good after playing for the last two dances but really we're so short of ladies tonight.

—I don't mind in the least, Miss Morkan.

—But I've a nice partner for you, Mr. Bartell D'Arcy, the tenor. I'll get him to sing later on. All Dublin is raving about him.

—Lovely voice, lovely voice! said Aunt Kate.

As the piano had twice begun the prelude to the first figure Mary Jane led her recruits quickly from the room. They had hardly gone when Aunt Julia wandered slowly into the room, looking behind her at something.

—What is the matter, Julia? asked Aunt Kate anxiously. Who is it?

Julia, who was carrying in a column of table-napkins, turned to her sister and said simply, as if the question had surprised her:

—It's only Freddy, Kate, and Gabriel with him.

In fact right behind her Gabriel could be seen piloting Freddy Malins across the landing. The latter, a young man of about forty, was of Gabriel's size and build with very round shoulders. His face was fleshy and pallid, touched with colour only at the thick hanging lobes of his ears and at the wide wings of his nose. He had coarse features, a blunt nose, a convex and receding brow, tumid and protruded lips. His heavylidded eyes and the disorder of his scanty hair made him look sleepy. He was laughing heartily in a high key at a story which he had been telling Gabriel on the stairs and at the same time rubbing the knuckles of his left fist backwards and forwards into his left eye.

—Good evening, Freddy, said Aunt Julia.

Freddy Malins bade the Misses Morkan good evening in what seemed an offhand fashion by reason of the habitual catch in his voice and then, seeing that Mr. Browne was grinning at him from the sideboard, crossed the room on rather shaky legs and began to repeat in an undertone the story he had just told to Gabriel.

—He's not so bad, is he? said Aunt Kate to Gabriel.

Gabriel's brows were dark but he raised them quickly and answered:

—O no, hardly noticeable.

—Now, isn't he a terrible fellow! she said. And his poor mother made him take the pledge² on New Year's Eve. But come on, Gabriel, into the drawingroom.

Before leaving the room with Gabriel she signalled to Mr. Browne by frowning and shaking her forefinger in warning to and fro. Mr. Browne nodded in answer and, when she had gone, said to Freddy Malins:

—Now then, Teddy, I'm going to fill you out a good glass of lemonade just to buck you up.

---

¹ *Quadrilles* Type of square dance.

² *take the pledge* I.e., pledge to abstain from alcoholic beverages.

Freddy Malins, who was nearing the climax of his story, waved the offer aside impatiently but Mr. Browne, having first called Freddy Malins' attention to a disarray in his dress, filled out and handed him a full glass of lemonade. Freddy Malins' left hand accepted the glass mechanically, his right hand being engaged in the mechanical readjustment of his dress. Mr. Browne, whose face was once more wrinkling with mirth, poured out for himself a glass of whisky while Freddy Malins exploded, before he had well reached the climax of his story, in a kink of highpitched bronchitic laughter and, setting down his untasted and overflowing glass, began to rub the knuckles of his left fist backwards and forwards into his left eye, repeating words of his last phrase as well as his fit of laughter would allow him.

Gabriel could not listen while Mary Jane was playing her academy piece, full of runs and difficult passages, to the hushed drawingroom. He liked music but the piece she was playing had no melody for him and he doubted whether it had any melody for the other listeners though they had begged Mary Jane to play something. Four young men, who had come from the refreshment room to stand in the doorway at the sound of the piano, had gone away quietly in couples after a few minutes. The only persons who seemed to follow the music were Mary Jane herself, her hands racing along the keyboard or lifted from it at the pauses like those of a priestess in momentary imprecation, and Aunt Kate standing at her elbow to turn the page.

Gabriel's eyes, irritated by the floor which glittered with beeswax under the heavy chandelier, wandered to the wall above the piano. A picture of the balcony scene in *Romeo and Juliet* hung there and beside it was a picture of the two murdered princes in the tower[1] which Aunt Julia had worked[2] in red, blue and brown wools when she was a girl. Probably in the school they had gone to as girls that kind of work had been taught, for one year his mother had worked for him as a birthday present a waistcoat of purple tabinet[3] with little foxes'

heads upon it, lined with brown satin and having round mulberry buttons. It was strange that his mother had had no musical talent though Aunt Kate used to call her the brainscarrier of the Morkan family. Both she and Julia had always seemed a little proud of their serious and matronly sister. Her photograph stood before the pierglass.[4] She held an open book on her knees and was pointing out something in it to Constantine who, dressed in a man-o'-war suit,[5] lay at her feet. It was she who had chosen the names for her sons for she was very sensible of the dignity of family life. Thanks to her, Constantine was now senior curate in Balbriggan and, thanks to her, Gabriel himself had taken his degree in the Royal University. A shadow passed over his face as he remembered her sullen opposition to his marriage. Some slighting phrases she had used still rankled in his memory. She had once spoken of Gretta as being country cute and that was not true of Gretta at all. It was Gretta who had nursed her all during her last long illness in their house at Monkstown.

He knew that Mary Jane must be near the end of her piece for she was playing again the opening melody with runs of scales after every bar and while he waited for the end the resentment died down in his heart. The piece ended with a trill of octaves in the treble and a final deep octave in the bass. Great applause greeted Mary Jane as, blushing and rolling up her music nervously, she escaped from the room. The most vigorous clapping came from the four young men in the doorway who had gone away to the refreshment room at the beginning of the piece but had come back when the piano had stopped.

Lancers[6] were arranged. Gabriel found himself partnered with Miss Ivors. She was a frankmannered talkative young lady with a freckled face and prominent brown eyes. She did not wear a lowcut bodice and the large brooch which was fixed in the front of her collar bore on it an Irish device.

When they had taken their places she said abruptly:

—I have a crow to pluck with you.

—With me? said Gabriel.

---

[1] *the two ... tower* Edward IV's two sons were murdered in the Tower of London in about 1483–84, allegedly at the instigation of their uncle, the future Richard III.

[2] *worked* I.e., wrought; made.

[3] *tabinet* Fabric made of silk and wool, similar to poplin.

[4] *pierglass* Tall mirror.

[5] *man-o'-war suit* Sailor suit, frequently worn by children.

[6] *Lancers* Type of quadrille.

She nodded her head gravely.

—What is it? asked Gabriel, smiling at her solemn manner.

—Who is G.C.? answered Miss Ivors turning her eyes upon him.

Gabriel coloured and was about to knit his brows as if he did not understand when she said bluntly:

—O, innocent Amy! I have found out that you write for the *Daily Express*. Now aren't you ashamed of yourself?

—Why should I be ashamed of myself? asked Gabriel blinking his eyes and trying to smile.

—Well, I'm ashamed of you, said Miss Ivors frankly. To say you'd write for a rag like that. I didn't think you were a west Briton.[1]

A look of perplexity appeared on Gabriel's face. It was true that he wrote a literary column every Wednesday in the *Daily Express* for which he was paid fifteen shillings. But that did not make him a west Briton surely. The books he received for review were almost more welcome than the paltry cheque. He loved to feel the covers and turn over the pages of newly printed books. Nearly every day when his teaching in the college was ended he used to wander down the quays to the secondhand booksellers, to Hickey's on Bachelor's Walk, to Webb's or Massey's on Aston's Quay or to Clohissey's in the bystreet. He did not know how to meet her charge. He wanted to say that literature was above politics. But they were friends of many years' standing and their careers had been parallel, first at the university and then as teachers: he could not risk a grandiose phrase with her. He continued blinking his eyes and trying to smile and murmured lamely that he saw nothing political in writing reviews of books.

When their turn to cross had come he was still perplexed and inattentive. Miss Ivors promptly took his hand in a warm grasp and said in a soft friendly tone:

—Of course, I was only joking. Come, we cross now. When they were together again she spoke of the university question[2] and Gabriel felt more at ease. A

friend of hers had shown her his review of Browning's poems. That was how she had found out the secret: but she liked the review immensely. Then she said suddenly:

—O, Mr. Conroy, will you come for an excursion to the Aran Isles[3] this summer? We're going to stay there a whole month. It will be splendid out in the Atlantic. You ought to come. Mr. Clancy is coming and Mr. Kilkelly and Kathleen Kearney. It would be splendid for Gretta too if she'd come. She's from Connacht,[4] isn't she?

—Her people are, said Gabriel shortly.

—But you will come, won't you? said Miss Ivors, laying her warm hand eagerly on his arm.

—The fact is, said Gabriel, I have already arranged to go …

—Go where? asked Miss Ivors.

—Well, you know, every year I go for a cycling tour with some fellows and so …

—But where? asked Miss Ivors.

—Well, we usually go to France or Belgium or perhaps Germany, said Gabriel awkwardly.

—And why do you go to France and Belgium, said Miss Ivors, instead of visiting your own land?

—Well, said Gabriel, it's partly to keep in touch with the languages and partly for a change.

—And haven't you your own language to keep in touch with, Irish? asked Miss Ivors.

—Well, said Gabriel, if it comes to that, you know, Irish is not my language.

Their neighbours had turned to listen to the cross-examination. Gabriel glanced right and left nervously and tried to keep his good humour under the ordeal which was making a blush invade his forehead.

—And haven't you your own land to visit, continued Miss Ivors, that you know nothing of, your own people and your own country?

—O, to tell you the truth, retorted Gabriel suddenly, I'm sick of my own country, sick of it!

—Why? asked Miss Ivors.

Gabriel did not answer for his retort had heated him.

1 *west Briton* Colloquial term for an Irish person who sees Ireland as the western part of Great Britain, rather than as a separate nation.

2 *university question* Concerning the establishment of an Irish national university, the representation of "Irish" values in universities, and the provision of equal access to education for Catholics

(Trinity College was open only to Protestants).

3 *Aran Isles* Three islands off the coast of Country Galway, on Ireland's west coast.

4 *Connacht* Connaught, in west Ireland.

—Why? repeated Miss Ivors.

They had to go visiting[1] together and, as he had not answered her, Miss Ivors said warmly:

—Of course, you've no answer.

Gabriel tried to cover his agitation by taking part in the dance with great energy. He avoided her eyes for he had seen a sour expression on her face. But when they met in the long chain he was surprised to feel his hand firmly pressed. She looked at him from under her brows for a moment quizzically until he smiled. Then, just as the chain was about to start again, she stood on tiptoe and whispered into his ear:

—West Briton!

When the lancers were over Gabriel went away to a remote corner of the room where Freddy Malins' mother was sitting. She was a stout feeble old woman with white hair. Her voice had a catch in it like her son's and she stuttered slightly. She had been told that Freddy had come and that he was nearly all right. Gabriel asked her whether she had had a good crossing. She lived with her married daughter in Glasgow and came to Dublin on a visit once a year. She answered placidly that she had had a beautiful crossing and that the captain had been most attentive to her. She spoke also of the beautiful house her daughter kept in Glasgow and of the nice friends they had there. While her tongue rambled on Gabriel tried to banish from his mind all memory of the unpleasant incident with Miss Ivors. Of course the girl or woman or whatever she was was an enthusiast but there was a time for all things. Perhaps he ought not to have answered her like that. But she had no right to call him a west Briton before people, even in joke. She had tried to make him ridiculous before people, heckling him and staring at him with her rabbit's eyes.

He saw his wife making her way towards him through the waltzing couples. When she reached him she said into his ear:

—Gabriel, Aunt Kate wants to know won't you carve the goose as usual. Miss Daly will carve the ham and I'll do the pudding.

—All right, said Gabriel.

—She's sending in the younger ones first as soon as this waltz is over so that we'll have the table to ourselves.

—Were you dancing? asked Gabriel.

—Of course I was. Didn't you see me? What words had you with Molly Ivors?

—No words. Why! Did she say so?

—Something like that. I'm trying to get that Mr. D'Arcy to sing. He's full of conceit, I think.

—There were no words, said Gabriel moodily, only she wanted me to go for a trip to the west of Ireland and I said I wouldn't.

His wife clasped her hands excitedly and gave a little jump.

—O, do go, Gabriel, she cried. I'd love to see Galway again.

—You can go if you like, said Gabriel coldly.

She looked at him for a moment, then turned to Mrs. Malins and said:

—There's a nice husband for you, Mrs. Malins.

While she was threading her way back across the room Mrs. Malins, without adverting to the interruption, went on to tell Gabriel what beautiful places there were in Scotland and beautiful scenery. Her son-in-law brought them every year to the lakes and they used to go fishing. Her son-in-law was a splendid fisher. One day he caught a fish, a beautiful big big fish: and the man in the hotel boiled it for their dinner.

Gabriel hardly heard what she said. Now that supper was coming near he began to think again about his speech and about the quotation. When he saw Freddy Malins coming across the room to visit his mother Gabriel left the chair free for him and retired into the embrasure of the window. The room had already cleared and from the back room came the clatter of plates and knives. Those who still remained in the drawingroom seemed tired of dancing and were conversing quietly in little groups. Gabriel's warm trembling fingers tapped the cold pane of the window. How cool it must be outside! How pleasant it would be to walk out alone, first along by the river and then through the park! The snow would be lying on the branches of the trees and forming a bright cap on the top of the Wellington monument.[2] How much more pleasant it would be there than at the supper table!

He ran over the headings of his speech: Irish hospi-

---

[1] *go visiting* Reference to the part of the dance in which the partners cross the floor together and meet another couple.

[2] *Wellington monument* Monument to the Duke of Wellington, an English military hero born in Ireland.

tality, sad memories, the Three Graces, Paris,[1] the quotation from Browning. He repeated to himself a phrase he had written in his review: *One feels that one is listening to a thought-tormented music.* Miss Ivors had praised the review. Was she sincere? Had she really any life of her own behind all her propagandism? There had never been any ill feeling between them until that night. It unnerved him to think that she would be at the supper table, looking up at him while he spoke with her critical quizzing eyes. Perhaps she would not be sorry to see him fail in his speech. An idea came into his mind and gave him courage. He would say, alluding to Aunt Kate and Aunt Julia: *Ladies and gentlemen, the generation which is now on the wane among us may have had its faults but for my part I think it had certain qualities of hospitality, of humour, of humanity, which the new and very serious and hypereducated generation that is growing up around us seems to me to lack.* Very good: that was one for Miss Ivors. What did he care that his aunts were only two ignorant old women?

A murmur in the room attracted his attention. Mr. Browne was advancing from the door, gallantly escorting Aunt Julia who leaned upon his arm, smiling and hanging her head. An irregular musketry of applause escorted her also as far as the piano and then, as Mary Jane seated herself on the stool and Aunt Julia, no longer smiling, half turned so as to pitch her voice fairly into the room, gradually ceased. Gabriel recognised the prelude. It was that of an old song of Aunt Julia's, *Arrayed for the Bridal.*[2] Her voice strong and clear in tone attacked with great spirit the runs which embellish the air and, though she sang very rapidly, she did not miss even the smallest of the grace notes. To follow the voice, without looking at the singer's face, was to feel and share the excitement of swift and secure flight.

Gabriel applauded loudly with all the others at the close of the song and loud applause was borne in from the invisible supper table. It sounded so genuine that a little colour struggled into Aunt Julia's face as she bent to replace in the music stand the old leatherbound song-book that had her initials on the cover. Freddy Malins, who had listened with his head perched sideways to hear the better, was still applauding when everyone else had ceased and talking animatedly to his mother who nodded her head gravely and slowly in acquiescence. At last, when he could clap no more, he stood up suddenly and hurried across the room to Aunt Julia, whose hand he seized and held in both his hands, shaking it when words failed him or the catch in his voice proved too much for him.

—I was just telling my mother, he said, I never heard you sing so well, never. No, I never heard your voice so good as it is tonight. Now! Would you believe that now? That's the truth. Upon my word and honour that's the truth. I never heard your voice sound so fresh and so ... so clear and fresh, never.

Aunt Julia smiled broadly and murmured something about compliments as she released her hand from his grasp. Mr. Browne extended his open hand towards her and said to those who were near him in the manner of a showman introducing a prodigy to an audience:

—Miss Julia Morkan, my latest discovery!

He was laughing very heartily at this himself when Freddy Malins turned to him and said:

—Well, Browne, if you're serious you might make a worse discovery. All I can say is I never heard her sing half so well as long as I am coming here. And that's the honest truth.

—Neither did I, said Mr. Browne. I think her voice has greatly improved.

Aunt Julia shrugged her shoulders and said with meek pride:

—Thirty years ago I hadn't a bad voice as voices go.

—I often told Julia, said Aunt Kate emphatically, that she was simply thrown away in that choir. But she never would be said by[3] me.

She turned as if to appeal to the good sense of the others against a refractory child while Aunt Julia gazed

---

[1] *Three Graces* In Greek mythology, the three daughters of Zeus and Eurynome who embodied the qualities of beauty and charm; *Paris* In Greek mythology, Paris was asked by the gods to judge a beauty contest between Hera, Athena, and Aphrodite. All three goddesses offered Paris a bribe. When he chose Aphrodite, she rewarded him by granting him the most beautiful woman in the world, who was Helen of Troy. Paris's abduction of Helen from her husband, Menelaus, is the putative cause of the Trojan War.

[2] *Arrayed ... Bridal* Popular and challenging song from Bellini's opera *I Puritani* (1835) that begins with the words "Arrayed for the bridal, in beauty behold her."

[3] *be said by* Be ruled by; submit to.

in front of her, a vague smile of reminiscence playing on her face.

—No, continued Aunt Kate, she wouldn't be said or led by anyone, slaving there in that choir night and day, night and day. Six o'clock on Christmas morning! And all for what?

—Well, isn't it for the honour of God, Aunt Kate? asked Mary Jane twisting round on the piano stool and smiling.

Aunt Kate turned fiercely on her niece and said:

—I know all about the honour of God, Mary Jane, but I think it's not at all honourable for the pope to turn out the women out of the choirs that have slaved there all their lives and put little whippersnappers of boys over their heads. I suppose it is for the good of the church if the pope does it. But it's not just, Mary Jane, and it's not right.[1]

She had worked herself into a passion and would have continued in defence of her sister for it was a sore subject with her but Mary Jane, seeing that all the dancers had come back, intervened pacifically:

—Now, Aunt Kate, you're giving scandal to Mr. Browne who is of the other persuasion.[2]

Aunt Kate turned to Mr. Browne, who was grinning at this allusion to his religion, and said hastily:

—O, I don't question the pope's being right. I'm only a stupid old woman and I wouldn't presume to do such a thing. But there's such a thing as common everyday politeness and gratitude. And if I were in Julia's place I'd tell that Father Healy straight up to his face …

—And besides, Aunt Kate, said Mary Jane, we really are all hungry and when we are hungry we are all very quarrelsome.

—And when we are thirsty we are also quarrelsome, added Mr. Browne.

—So that we had better go to supper, said Mary Jane, and finish the discussion afterwards.

On the landing outside the drawingroom Gabriel

found his wife and Mary Jane trying to persuade Miss Ivors to stay for supper. But Miss Ivors, who had put on her hat and was buttoning her cloak, would not stay. She did not feel in the least hungry and she had already overstayed her time.

—But only for ten minutes, Molly, said Mrs. Conroy. That won't delay you.

—To take a pick itself,[3] said Mary Jane, after all your dancing.

—I really couldn't, said Miss Ivors.

—I am afraid you didn't enjoy yourself at all, said Mary Jane hopelessly.

—Ever so much, I assure you, said Miss Ivors, but you really must let me run off now.

—But how can you get home? asked Mrs. Conroy.

—O, it's only two steps up the quay. Gabriel hesitated a moment and said:

—If you will allow me, Miss Ivors, I'll see you home if you really are obliged to go.

But Miss Ivors broke away from them.

—I won't hear of it, she cried. For goodness' sake go in to your suppers and don't mind me. I'm quite well able to take care of myself.

—Well, you're the comical girl, Molly, said Mrs. Conroy frankly.

—*Beannacht libh*,[4] cried Miss Ivors with a laugh as she ran down the staircase.

Mary Jane gazed after her, a moody puzzled expression on her face, while Mrs. Conroy leaned over the banisters to listen for the hall door. Gabriel asked himself was he the cause of her abrupt departure. But she did not seem to be in ill humour: she had gone away laughing. He stared blankly down the staircase.

At that moment Aunt Kate came toddling out of the supper room, almost wringing her hands in despair.

—Where is Gabriel? she cried. Where on earth is Gabriel? There's everyone waiting in there, stage to let, and nobody to carve the goose!

—Here I am, Aunt Kate! cried Gabriel with sudden animation, ready to carve a flock of geese, if necessary.

A fat brown goose lay at one end of the table and at the other end, on a bed of creased paper strewn with sprigs of parsley, lay a great ham, stripped of its outer

[1] *I know … right* On 22 November 1903, Pope Pius X issued a papal bull, in which he announced that the singing of Church music constituted a liturgical function for which women were ineligible and that, henceforth, soprano and alto voices would be produced by young boys.

[2] *of the other persuasion* I.e., a Protestant.

[3] *a pick itself* I.e., a little bit.

[4] *Beannacht libh* Gaelic: blessing to you; goodbye.

skin and peppered over with crust crumbs, a neat paper frill round its shin, and beside this was a round of spiced beef. Between these rival ends ran parallel lines of side dishes: two little minsters of jelly, red and yellow, a shallow dish full of blocks of blancmange[1] and red jam, a large green leafshaped dish with a stalkshaped handle on which lay bunches of purple raisins and peeled almonds, a companion dish on which lay a solid rectangle of Smyrna figs, a dish of custard topped with grated nutmeg, a small bowl full of chocolates and sweets wrapped in gold and silver papers and a glass vase in which stood some tall celery stalks. In the centre of the table there stood, as sentries to a fruit stand which upheld a pyramid of oranges and American apples, two squat oldfashioned decanters of cut glass, one containing port and the other dark sherry. On the closed square piano a pudding in a huge yellow dish lay in waiting and behind it were three squads of bottles of stout and ale and minerals drawn up according to the colours of their uniforms, the first two black with brown and red labels, the third and smallest squad white, with transverse green sashes.

Gabriel took his seat boldly at the head of the table and, having looked to the edge of the carver, plunged his fork firmly into the goose. He felt quite at ease now for he was an expert carver and liked nothing better than to find himself at the head of a well laden table.

—Miss Furlong, what shall I send you? he asked. A wing or a slice of the breast?

—Just a small slice of the breast.

—Miss Higgins, what for you?

—O, anything at all, Mr. Conroy.

While Gabriel and Miss Daly exchanged plates of goose and plates of ham and spiced beef Lily went from guest to guest with a dish of hot floury potatoes wrapped in a white napkin. This was Mary Jane's idea and she had also suggested apple sauce for the goose but Aunt Kate had said that plain roast goose without any apple sauce had always been good enough for her and she hoped she might never eat worse. Mary Jane waited on her pupils and saw that they got the best slices and Aunt Kate and Aunt Julia opened and carried across from the piano bottles of stout and ale for the gentlemen and bottles of minerals for the ladies. There was a

great deal of confusion and laughter and noise, the noise of orders and counterorders, of knives and forks, of corks and glass stoppers. Gabriel began to carve second helpings as soon as he had finished the first round without serving himself. Everyone protested loudly so that he compromised by taking a long draught of stout for he had found the carving hot work. Mary Jane settled down quietly to her supper but Aunt Kate and Aunt Julia were still toddling round the table, walking on each other's heels, getting in each other's way and giving each other unheeded orders. Mr. Browne begged of them to sit down and eat their supper and so did Gabriel but they said they were time enough so that, at last, Freddy Malins stood up and, capturing Aunt Kate, plumped her down on her chair amid general laughter.

When everyone had been well served Gabriel said smiling:

—Now if anyone wants a little more of what vulgar people call stuffing let him or her speak.

A chorus of voices invited him to begin his own supper and Lily came forward with three potatoes which she had reserved for him.

—Very well, said Gabriel amiably as he took another preparatory draught, kindly forget my existence, ladies and gentlemen, for a few minutes.

He set to his supper and took no part in the conversation with which the table covered Lily's removal of the plates. The subject of talk was the opera company which was then at the Theatre Royal. Mr. Bartell D'Arcy, the tenor, a dark-complexioned young man with a smart moustache, praised very highly the leading contralto of the company but Miss Furlong thought she had a rather vulgar style of production. Freddy Malins said there was a negro chieftain singing in the second part of the Gaiety pantomime who had one of the finest tenor voices he had ever heard.

—Have you heard him? he asked Mr. Bartell D'Arcy across the table.

—No, answered Mr. Bartell D'Arcy carelessly.

—Because, Freddy Malins explained, now I'd be curious to hear your opinion of him. I think he has a grand voice.

—It takes Teddy to find out the really good things, said Mr. Browne familiarly to the table.

---

[1] *blancmange* Milk jelly.

—And why couldn't he have a voice too? asked Freddy Malins sharply. Is it because he's only a black?

Nobody answered this question and Mary Jane led the table back to the legitimate opera. One of her pupils had given her a pass for *Mignon*.[1] Of course, it was very fine, she said, but it made her think of poor Georgina Burns.[2] Mr. Browne could go back farther still to the old Italian companies that used to come to Dublin, Tietjens, Trebelli, Ilma de Murzka, Campanini, the great Giuglini, Ravelli, Aramburo. Those were the days, he said, when there was something like singing to be heard in Dublin. He told too of how the top gallery of the old Royal used to be packed night after night, of how one night an Italian tenor had sung five encores to *Let Me Like a Soldier Fall*, introducing a high C every time, and of how the gallery boys would sometimes in their enthusiasm unyoke the horses from the carriage of some great *prima donna* and pull her themselves through the streets to her hotel. Why did they never play the grand old operas now, he asked. *Dinorah*, *Lucrezia Borgia*?[3] Because they could not get the voices to sing them: that was why.

—O, well, said Mr. Bartell D'Arcy, I presume there are as good singers today as there were then.

—Where are they? asked Mr. Browne defiantly.

—In London, Paris, Milan, said Mr. Bartell D'Arcy warmly. I suppose Caruso,[4] for example, is quite as good, if not better than any of the men you have mentioned.

—Maybe so, said Mr. Browne. But I may tell you I doubt it strongly.

—O, I'd give anything to hear Caruso sing, said Mary Jane.

—For me, said Aunt Kate, who had been picking a bone, there was only one tenor. To please me, I mean. But I suppose none of you ever heard of him.

—Who was he, Miss Morkan? asked Mr. Bartell D'Arcy politely.

—His name, said Aunt Kate, was Parkinson. I heard him when he was in his prime and I think he had then the purest tenor voice that was ever put into a man's throat.

—Strange, said Mr. Bartell D'Arcy. I never even heard of him.

—Yes, yes, Miss Morkan is right, said Mr. Browne. I remember hearing of old Parkinson but he's too far back for me.

—A beautiful pure sweet mellow English tenor, said Aunt Kate with enthusiasm.

Gabriel having finished, the huge pudding was transferred to the table. The clatter of forks and spoons began again. Gabriel's wife served out spoonfuls of the pudding and passed the plates down the table. Midway down they were held up by Mary Jane who replenished them with raspberry or orange jelly or with blancmange and jam. The pudding was of Aunt Julia's making and she received praises for it from all quarters. She herself said that it was not quite brown enough.

—Well, I hope, Miss Morkan, said Mr. Browne, that I'm brown enough for you because, you know, I'm all brown.

All the gentlemen, except Gabriel, ate some of the pudding out of compliment to Aunt Julia. As Gabriel never ate sweets the celery had been left for him. Freddy Malins also took a stalk of celery and ate it with his pudding. He had been told that celery was a capital thing for the blood and he was just then under doctor's care. Mrs. Malins, who had been silent all through the supper, said that her son was going down to Mount Melleray[5] in a week or so. The table then spoke of Mount Melleray, how bracing the air was down there, how hospitable the monks were and how they never asked for a penny-piece from their guests.

—And do you mean to say, asked Mr. Browne incredulously, that a chap can go down there and put up there as if it were a hotel and live on the fat of the land and then come away without paying a farthing?

—O, most people give some donation to the monastery when they leave, said Mary Jane.

—I wish we had an institution like that in our church, said Mr. Browne candidly.

---

1. *Mignon*   1866 opera by Ambroise Thomas.

2. *Georgina Burns*   Famous soprano who made her Dublin début in 1878.

3. *Dinorah*   1859 comic opera by Giacomo Meyerbeer; *Lucrezia Borgia*   1833 opera by Gaetano Donizetti.

4. *Caruso*   Tenor Enrico Caruso (1874–1921).

5. *Mount Melleray*   Site of the Abbey of St. Bernard de Trappe, founded in 1831 by the Cistercian monks.

He was astonished to hear that the monks never spoke, got up at two in the morning and slept in their coffins.[1] He asked what they did it for.

—That's the rule of the order, said Aunt Kate firmly.

—Yes, but why? asked Mr. Browne.

Aunt Kate repeated that it was the rule, that was all. Mr. Browne still seemed not to understand. Freddy Malins explained to him, as best he could, that the monks were trying to make up for the sins committed by all the sinners in the outside world. The explanation was not very clear for Mr. Browne grinned and said:

—I like that idea very much but wouldn't a comfortable spring bed do them as well as a coffin?

—The coffin, said Mary Jane, is to remind them of their last end.

As the subject had grown lugubrious it was buried in a silence of the table during which Mrs. Malins could be heard saying to her neighbour in an indistinct undertone:

—They are very good men, the monks, very pious men.

The raisins and almonds and figs and apples and oranges and chocolates and sweets were now passed about the table and Aunt Julia invited all the guests to have either port or sherry. At first Mr. Bartell D'Arcy refused to take either but one of his neighbours nudged him and whispered something to him upon which he allowed his glass to be filled. Gradually as the last glasses were being filled the conversation ceased. A pause followed, broken only by the noise of the wine and by unsettlings of chairs. The Misses Morkan, all three, looked down at the tablecloth. Someone coughed once or twice and then a few gentlemen patted the table gently as a signal for silence. The silence came and Gabriel pushed back his chair and stood up.

The patting at once grew louder in encouragement and then ceased altogether. Gabriel leaned his ten trembling fingers on the tablecloth and smiled nervously at the company. Meeting a row of upturned faces he raised his eyes to the chandelier. The piano was playing a waltz tune and he could hear the skirts sweeping against the drawingroom door. People perhaps were standing in the snow on the quay outside, gazing up at the lighted windows and listening to the waltz music. The air was pure there. In the distance lay the park where the trees were weighted with snow. The Wellington monument wore a gleaming cap of snow that flashed westward over the white field of Fifteen Acres.

He began:

—Ladies and gentlemen.

It has fallen to my lot this evening as in years past to perform a very pleasing task, but a task for which I am afraid my poor powers as a speaker are all too inadequate.

—No, no, said Mr. Browne.

—But, however that may be, I can only ask you tonight to take the will for the deed and to lend me your attention for a few moments while I endeavour to express to you in words what my feelings are on this occasion.

—Ladies and gentlemen. It is not the first time that we have gathered together under this hospitable roof, around this hospitable board. It is not the first time that we have been the recipients—or, perhaps I had better say, the victims—of the hospitality of certain good ladies.

He made a circle in the air with his arm and paused. Everyone laughed or smiled at Aunt Kate and Aunt Julia and Mary Jane who all turned crimson with pleasure. Gabriel went on more boldly:

—I feel more strongly with every recurring year that our country has no tradition which does it so much honour and which it should guard so jealously as that of its hospitality. It is a tradition that is unique so far as my experience goes (and I have visited not a few places abroad) among the modern nations. Some would say, perhaps, that with us it is rather a failing than anything to be boasted of. But granted even that, it is, to my mind, a princely failing and one that I trust will long be cultivated among us. Of one thing, at least, I am sure. As long as this one roof shelters the good ladies aforesaid—and I wish from my heart it may do so for many and many a long year to come—the tradition of genuine warmhearted courteous Irish hospitality, which our forefathers have handed down to us and which we in turn must hand down to our descendants, is still alive among us.

---

[1] *slept in their coffins*   Though commonly believed, this is not a real custom of the Cistercians.

A hearty murmur of assent ran round the table. It shot through Gabriel's mind that Miss Ivors was not there and that she had gone away discourteously: and he said with confidence in himself:

—Ladies and gentlemen.

A new generation is growing up in our midst, a generation actuated by new ideas and new principles. It is serious and enthusiastic for these new ideas and its enthusiasm, even when it is misdirected, is, I believe, in the main sincere. But we are living in a sceptical and, if I may use the phrase, a thought-tormented age: and sometimes I fear that this new generation, educated or hypereducated as it is, will lack those qualities of humanity, of hospitality, of kindly humour which belonged to an older day. Listening tonight to the names of all those great singers of the past it seemed to me, I must confess, that we were living in a less spacious age. Those days might without exaggeration be called spacious days: and if they are gone beyond recall let us hope, at least, that in gatherings such as this we shall still speak of them with pride and affection, still cherish in our hearts the memory of those dead and gone great ones whose fame the world will not willingly let die.

—Hear! hear! said Mr. Browne loudly.

—But yet, continued Gabriel, his voice falling into a softer inflection, there are always in gatherings such as this sadder thoughts that will recur to our minds: thoughts of the past, of youth, of changes, of absent faces that we miss here tonight. Our path through life is strewn with many such sad memories: and were we to brood upon them always we could not find the heart to go on bravely with our work among the living. We have all of us living duties and living affections which claim, and rightly claim, our strenuous endeavours.

Therefore I will not linger on the past. I will not let any gloomy moralising intrude upon us here tonight. Here we are gathered together for a brief moment from the bustle and rush of our everyday routine. We are met here as friends, in the spirit of good fellowship, as colleagues also, to a certain extent, in the true spirit of camaraderie, and as the guests of—what shall I call them?—the three Graces of the Dublin musical world.

The table burst into applause and laughter at this sally. Aunt Julia vainly asked each of her neighbours in turn to tell her what Gabriel had said.

—He says we are the three Graces, Aunt Julia, said Mary Jane. Aunt Julia did not understand but she looked up, smiling, at Gabriel who continued in the same vein:

—Ladies and gentlemen.

I will not attempt to play tonight the part that Paris played on another occasion. I will not attempt to choose between them. The task would be an invidious one and one beyond my poor powers. For when I view them in turn, whether it be our chief hostess herself, whose good heart, whose too good heart, has become a byword with all who know her, or her sister, who seems to be gifted with perennial youth and whose singing must have been a surprise and a revelation to us all tonight, or, last but not least, when I consider our youngest hostess, talented, cheerful, hard-working and the best of nieces, I confess, ladies and gentlemen, that I do not know to which of them I should award the prize.

Gabriel glanced down at his aunts and, seeing the large smile on Aunt Julia's face and the tears which had risen to Aunt Kate's eyes, hastened to his close. He raised his glass of port gallantly while every member of the company fingered a glass expectantly and said loudly:

—Let us toast them all three together. Let us drink to their health, wealth, long life, happiness and prosperity and may they long continue to hold the proud and self-won position which they hold in their profession and the position of honour and affection which they hold in our hearts.

All the guests stood up, glass in hand and, turning towards the three seated ladies, sang in unison with Mr. Browne as leader:

—For they are jolly gay fellows,
For they are jolly gay fellows,
For they are jolly gay fellows,
Which nobody can deny.

Aunt Kate was making frank use of her handkerchief and even Aunt Julia seemed moved. Freddy Malins beat time with his pudding fork and the singers turned towards one another as if in melodious conference, while they sang with emphasis:

—Unless he tells a lie,
Unless he tells a lie.

Then turning once more towards their hostesses they sang:

—For they are jolly gay fellows,
For they are jolly gay fellows,
For they are jolly gay fellows
Which nobody can deny.

The acclamation which followed was taken up beyond the door of the supper room by many of the other guests and renewed time after time, Freddy Malins acting as officer with his fork on high.

The piercing morning air came into the hall where they were standing so that Aunt Kate said:

—Close the door, somebody. Mrs. Malins will get her death of cold.

—Browne is out there, Aunt Kate, said Mary Jane.

—Browne is everywhere, said Aunt Kate lowering her voice.

Mary Jane laughed at her tone.

—Really, she said archly, he is very attentive.

—He has been laid on here like the gas, said Aunt Kate in the same tone, all during the Christmas.

She laughed herself this time good-humouredly and then added quickly:

—But tell him to come in, Mary Jane, and close the door. I hope to goodness he didn't hear me.

At that moment the hall door was opened and Mr. Browne came in from the doorstep, laughing as if his heart would break. He was dressed in a long green overcoat with mock astrakhan[1] cuffs and collar and wore on his head an oval fur cap. He pointed down the snowcovered quay whence the sound of shrill prolonged whistling was borne in.

—Teddy will have all the cabs in Dublin out, he said. Gabriel advanced from the little pantry behind the office, struggling into his overcoat and, looking round the hall, said:

—Gretta not down yet?

—She's getting on her things, Gabriel, said Aunt Kate.

—Who's playing up there? asked Gabriel.

—Nobody. They're all gone.

—O no, Aunt Kate, said Mary Jane. Bartell D'Arcy and Miss O'Callaghan aren't gone yet.

—Someone is strumming at the piano, anyhow, said Gabriel. Mary Jane glanced at Gabriel and Mr. Browne and said with a shiver:

—It makes me feel cold to look at you two gentlemen muffled up like that. I wouldn't like to face your journey home at this hour.

—I'd like nothing better this minute, said Mr. Browne stoutly, than a rattling fine walk in the country or a fast drive with a good spanking goer between the shafts.

—We used to have a very good horse and trap[2] at home, said Aunt Julia sadly.

—The never-to-be-forgotten Johnny, said Mary Jane laughing. Aunt Kate and Gabriel laughed too.

—Why, what was wonderful about Johnny? asked Mr. Browne.

—The late lamented Patrick Morkan, our grandfather that is, explained Gabriel, commonly known in his later years as the old gentleman, was a glue boiler.

—O now, Gabriel, said aunt Kate laughing, he had a starch mill.

—Well, glue or starch, said Gabriel, the old gentleman had a horse by the name of Johnny. And Johnny used to work in the old gentleman's mill walking round and round in order to drive the mill. That was all very well; but now comes the tragic part about Johnny. One fine day the old gentleman thought he'd like to drive out with the quality to a military review in the park.

—The Lord have mercy on his soul, said Aunt Kate compassionately.

—Amen, said Gabriel. So the old gentleman, as I said, harnessed Johnny and put on his very best tall hat and his very best stock collar and drove out in grand style from his ancestral mansion somewhere near Back Lane, I think.

Everyone laughed, even Mrs. Malins, at Gabriel's manner and Aunt Kate said:

---

[1] *astrakhan* Lambskin.

[2] *trap* Small, two-wheeled carriage on springs.

—O now, Gabriel, he didn't live in Back Lane really. Only the mill was there.

—Out from the mansion of his forefathers, continued Gabriel, he drove with Johnny. And everything went on beautifully until Johnny came in sight of King Billy's[1] statue: and whether he fell in love with the horse King Billy sits on or whether he thought he was back again in the mill, anyhow he began to walk round the statue.

Gabriel paced in a circle round the hall in his goloshes amid the laughter of the others.

—Round and round he went, said Gabriel, and the old gentleman, who was a very pompous old gentleman, was highly indignant. *Go on, sir! What do you mean, sir? Johnny! Johnny! Most extraordinary conduct! Can't understand the horse!*

The peals of laughter which followed Gabriel's imitation of the incident were interrupted by a resounding knock at the hall door. Mary Jane ran to open it and let in Freddy Malins. Freddy Malins, with his hat well back on his head and his shoulders humped with cold, was puffing and steaming after his exertions.

—I could only get one cab, he said.

—O, we'll find another along the quay, said Gabriel.

—Yes, said Aunt Kate. Better not keep Mrs. Malins standing in the draught.

Mrs. Malins was helped down the front steps by her son and Mr. Browne and, after many manoeuvres, hoisted into the cab. Freddy Malins clambered in after her and spent a long time settling her on the seat, Mr. Browne helping him with advice. At last she was settled comfortably and Freddy Malins invited Mr. Browne into the cab. There was a good deal of confused talk, then Mr. Browne got into the cab. The cabman settled his rug over his knees and bent down for the address. The confusion grew greater and the cabman was directed differently by Freddy Malins and Mr. Browne, each of whom had his head out through a window of the cab. The difficulty was to know where to drop Mr. Browne along the route and Aunt Kate, Aunt Julia and Mary Jane helped the discussion from the doorstep with cross-directions and contradictions and abundance of laughter. As for Freddy Malins he was speechless with

laughter. He popped his head in and out of the window every moment, to the great danger of his hat, and told his mother how the discussion was progressing till at last Mr. Browne shouted to the bewildered cabman above the din of everybody's laughter:

—Do you know Trinity College?

—Yes, sir, said the cabman.

—Well, drive bang up against Trinity College gates, said Mr. Browne, and then we'll tell you where to go. You understand now?

—Yes, sir, said the cabman.

—Make like a bird for Trinity College.

—Right, sir, cried the cabman.

The horse was whipped up and the cab rattled off along the quay amid a chorus of laughter and adieus.

Gabriel had not gone to the door with the others. He was in a dark part of the hall gazing up the staircase. A woman was standing near the top of the first flight in the shadow also. He could not see her face but he could see the terracotta and salmonpink panels of her skirt which the shadow made appear black and white. It was his wife. She was leaning on the banisters listening to something. Gabriel was surprised at her stillness and strained his ear to listen also. But he could hear little save the noise of laughter and dispute on the front steps, a few chords struck on the piano and a few notes of a man's voice singing.

He stood still in the gloom of the hall, trying to catch the air that the voice was singing and gazing up at his wife. There was grace and mystery in her attitude as if she were a symbol of something. He asked himself what is a woman standing on the stairs in the shadow, listening to distant music, a symbol of. If he were a painter he would paint her in that attitude. Her blue felt hat would show off the bronze of her hair against the darkness and the dark panels of her skirt would show off the light ones. *Distant Music* he would call the picture if he were a painter.

The hall door was closed and Aunt Kate, Aunt Julia and Mary Jane came down the hall, still laughing.

—Well, isn't Freddy terrible? said Mary Jane. He's really terrible.

Gabriel said nothing but pointed up the stairs towards where his wife was standing. Now that the hall door was closed the voice and the piano could be heard

---

[1] *King Billy* King William III (William of Orange), who took the British throne in the Glorious Revolution of 1688.

more clearly. Gabriel held up his hand for them to be silent. The song seemed to be in the old Irish tonality and the singer seemed uncertain both of his words and of his voice. The voice made plaintive by the distance and by the singer's hoarseness faintly illuminated the cadence of the air with words expressing grief:

—*O, the rain falls on my heavy locks*
And the dew wets my shin,
My babe lies cold …

—O, exclaimed Mary Jane. It's Bartell D'Arcy singing and he wouldn't sing all the night. O, I'll get him to sing a song before he goes.

—O do, Mary Jane, said Aunt Kate.

Mary Jane brushed past the others and ran to the staircase but before she reached it the singing stopped and the piano was closed abruptly.

—O, what a pity! she cried. Is he coming down, Gretta? Gabriel heard his wife answer yes and saw her come down towards them. A few steps behind her were Mr. Bartell D'Arcy and Miss O'Callaghan.

—O, Mr. D'Arcy, cried Mary Jane, it's downright mean of you to break off like that when we were all in raptures listening to you.

—I have been at him all the evening, said Miss O'Callaghan, and Mrs. Conroy too, and he told us he had a dreadful cold and couldn't sing.

—O, Mr. D'Arcy, said Aunt Kate, now that was a great fib to tell.

—Can't you see that I'm as hoarse as a crow? said Mr. D'Arcy roughly.

He went into the pantry hastily and put on his overcoat. The others, taken aback by his rude speech, could find nothing to say. Aunt Kate wrinkled her brows and made signs to the others to drop the subject. Mr. D'Arcy stood swathing his neck carefully and frowning.

—It's the weather, said Aunt Julia after a pause.

—Yes, everybody has colds, said Aunt Kate readily, everybody.

—They say, said Mary Jane, we haven't had snow like it for thirty years: and I read this morning in the newspaper that the snow is general all over Ireland.

—I love the look of snow, said Aunt Julia sadly.

—So do I, said Miss O'Callaghan. I think Christmas is never really Christmas unless we have the snow on the ground.

—But poor Mr. D'Arcy doesn't like the snow, said Aunt Kate smiling.

Mr. D'Arcy came from the pantry, fully swathed and buttoned, and in a repentant tone told them the history of his cold. Everyone gave him advice and said it was a great pity and urged him to be very careful of his throat in the night air. Gabriel watched his wife who did not join in the conversation. She was standing right under the dusty fanlight and the flame of the gas lit up the rich bronze of her hair which he had seen her drying at the fire a few days before. She was in the same attitude and seemed unaware of the talk about her. At last she turned towards them and Gabriel saw that there was colour on her cheeks and that her eyes were shining. A sudden tide of joy went leaping out of his heart.

—Mr. D'Arcy, she said, what is the name of that song you were singing?

—It's called *The Lass of Aughrim*,[1] said Mr. D'Arcy, but I couldn't remember it properly. Why? Do you know it?

—*The Lass of Aughrim*, she repeated. I couldn't think of the name.

—It's a very nice air, said Mary Jane. I'm sorry you were not in voice tonight.

—Now, Mary Jane, said Aunt Kate, don't annoy Mr. D'Arcy. I won't have him annoyed.

Seeing that all were ready to start she shepherded them to the door where goodnight was said:

—Well, goodnight Aunt Kate, and thanks for the pleasant evening.

—Goodnight, Gabriel. Goodnight, Gretta!

—Goodnight, Aunt Kate, and thanks ever so much. Goodnight, Aunt Julia.

—O, goodnight, Gretta, I didn't see you.

—Goodnight, Mr. D'Arcy. Goodnight, Miss O'Callaghan.

—Goodnight, Miss Morkan.

—Goodnight again.

—Goodnight all. Safe home.

—Goodnight. Goodnight.

[1] *The Lass of Aughrim* Irish ballad about a peasant girl who commits suicide when her noble seducer refuses to recognize her when she arrives at his door pregnant with his child.

The morning was still dark. A dull yellow light brooded over the houses and the river and the sky seemed to be descending. It was slushy underfoot and only streaks and patches of snow lay on the roofs, on the parapets of the quay and on the area railings. The lamps were still burning redly in the murky air and, across the river, the palace of the Four Courts[1] stood out menacingly against the heavy sky.

She was walking on before him with Mr. Bartell D'Arcy, her shoes in a brown parcel tucked under one arm and her hands holding her skirt up from the slush. She had no longer any grace of attitude but Gabriel's eyes were still bright with happiness. The blood went bounding along his veins and the thoughts went rioting through his brain, proud, joyful, tender, valorous.

She was walking on before him so lightly and so erect that he longed to run after her noiselessly, catch her by the shoulders and say something foolish and affectionate into her ear. She seemed to him so frail that he longed to defend her against something and then to be alone with her. Moments of their secret life together burst like stars upon his memory. A heliotrope envelope was lying beside his breakfast cup and he was caressing it with his hand. Birds were twittering in the ivy and the sunny web of the curtain was shimmering along the floor: he could not eat for happiness. They were standing on the crowded platform and he was placing a ticket inside the warm palm of her glove. He was standing with her in the cold, looking in through a grated window at a man making bottles in a roaring furnace. It was very cold. Her face, fragrant in the cold air, was quite close to his and suddenly she called out to the man at the furnace:

—Is the fire hot, sir?

But the man could not hear her with the noise of the furnace. It was just as well. He might have answered rudely.

A wave of yet more tender joy escaped from his heart and went coursing in warm flood along his arteries. Like the tender fire of stars moments of their life together, that no one knew of or would ever know of, broke upon and illumined his memory. He longed to recall to her those moments, to make her forget the years of their dull existence together and remember only their moments of ecstasy. For the years, he felt, had not quenched his soul or hers. Their children, his writing, her household cares had not quenched all their souls' tender fire. In one letter that he had written to her then he had said: *Why is it that words like these seem to me so dull and cold? Is it because there is no word tender enough to be your name?*

Like distant music these words that he had written years before were borne towards him from the past. He longed to be alone with her. When the others had gone away, when he and she were in their room in the hotel, then they would be alone together. He would call her softly:

—Gretta!

Perhaps she would not hear at once: she would be undressing. Then something in his voice would strike her. She would turn and look at him ...

At the corner of Winetavern Street they met a cab. He was glad of its rattling noise as it saved him from conversation. She was looking out of the window and seemed tired. The others spoke only a few words, pointing out some building or street. The horse galloped along wearily under the murky morning sky, dragging his old rattling box after his heels, and Gabriel was again in a cab with her galloping to catch the boat, galloping to their honeymoon.

As the cab drove across O'Connell bridge Miss O'Callaghan said:

—They say you never cross O'Connell bridge without seeing a white horse.

—I see a white man this time, said Gabriel.

—Where? asked Mr. Bartell D'Arcy.

Gabriel pointed to the statue[2] on which lay patches of snow. Then he nodded familiarly to it and waved his hand.

—Goodnight, Dan, he said gaily.

When the cab drew up before the hotel Gabriel jumped out and, in spite of Mr. Bartell D'Arcy's protest, paid the driver. He gave the man a shilling over his fare. The man saluted and said:

—A prosperous new year to you, sir.

—The same to you, said Gabriel cordially.

---

[1] *palace ... Courts* Judicial building; home of the four traditional divisions of the judicial system in Ireland.

[2] *the statue* The O'Connell Memorial, commemorating Irish nationalist Daniel O'Connell (1775–1847).

She leaned for a moment on his arm in getting out of the cab and while standing at the kerbstone bidding the others goodnight. She leaned lightly on his arm, as lightly as when she had danced with him a few hours before. He had felt proud and happy then, happy that she was his, proud of her grace and wifely carriage. But now after the kindling again of so many memories, the first touch of her body, musical and strange and perfumed, sent through him a keen pang of lust. Under cover of her silence he pressed her arm closely to his side: and, as they stood at the hotel door, he felt that they had escaped from their lives and duties, escaped from home and friends and run away together with wild and radiant hearts to a new adventure.

An old man was dozing in a great hooded chair in the hall. He lit a candle in the office and went before them to the stairs. They followed him in silence, their feet falling in soft thuds on the thickly carpeted stairs. She mounted the stairs behind the porter, her head bowed in the ascent, her frail shoulders curved as with a burden, her skirt girt tightly about her. He could have flung his arms about her hips and held her still for his arms were trembling with desire to seize her and only the stress of his nails against the palms of his hands held the wild impulse of his body in check. The porter halted on the stairs to settle his guttering candle. They halted too on the steps below him. In the silence Gabriel could hear the falling of the molten wax into the tray and the thumping of his own heart against his ribs.

The porter led them along a corridor and opened a door. Then he set his unstable candle down on a toilet table and asked at what hour they were to be called in the morning.

—Eight, said Gabriel.

The porter pointed to the tap of the electric light and began a muttered apology but Gabriel cut him short.

—We don't want any light. We have light enough from the street. And, I say, he added pointing to the candle, you might remove that handsome article, like a good man.

The porter took up his candle again, but slowly, for he was surprised by such a novel idea. Then he mumbled goodnight and went out. Gabriel shot the lock to.

A ghostly light from the street lamp lay in a long shaft from one window to the door. Gabriel threw his overcoat and hat on a couch and crossed the room towards the window. He looked down into the street in order that his emotion might calm a little. Then he turned and leaned against a chest of drawers with his back to the light. She had taken off her hat and cloak and was standing before a large swinging mirror, unhooking her waist. Gabriel paused for a few moments, watching her, and then said:

—Gretta!

She turned away from the mirror slowly and walked along the shaft of light towards him. Her face looked so serious and weary that the words would not pass Gabriel's lips. No, it was not the moment yet.

—You look tired, he said.

—I am a little, she answered.

—You don't feel ill or weak?

—No, tired: that's all.

She went on to the window and stood there, looking out. Gabriel waited again and then, fearing that diffidence was about to conquer him, he said abruptly:

—By the way, Gretta!

—What is it?

—You know that poor fellow Malins? he said quickly.

—Yes, what about him?

—Well, poor fellow, he's a decent sort of chap after all, continued Gabriel in a false voice. He gave me back that sovereign I lent him and I didn't expect it really. It's a pity he wouldn't keep away from that Browne because he's not a bad fellow at heart.

He was trembling now with annoyance. Why did she seem so abstracted? He did not know how he could begin. Was she annoyed too about something? If she would only turn to him or come to him of her own accord! To take her as she was would be brutal. No, he must see some ardour in her eyes first. He longed to be master of her strange mood.

—When did you lend him the pound? she asked after a pause. Gabriel strove to restrain himself from breaking out into brutal language about the sottish Malins and his pound. He longed to cry to her from his soul, to crush her body against his, to overmaster her. But he said:

—O, at Christmas, when he opened that little Christmas card shop in Henry Street.

He was in such a fever of rage and desire that he did

not hear her come from the window. She stood before him for an instant looking at him strangely. Then, suddenly raising herself on tiptoe and resting her hands lightly on his shoulders, she kissed him.

—You are a very generous person, Gabriel, she said.

—Gabriel, trembling with delight at her sudden kiss and at the quaintness of her phrase, put his hands on her hair and began smoothing it back, scarcely touching it with his fingers. The washing had made it fine and brilliant. His heart was brimming over with happiness. Just when he was wishing for it she had come to him of her own accord. Perhaps her thoughts had been running with his. Perhaps she had felt the impetuous desire that was in him and then the yielding mood had come upon her. Now that she had fallen to him so easily he wondered why he had been so diffident.

He stood, holding her head between his hands. Then, slipping one arm swiftly about her body and drawing her towards him, he said softly:

—Gretta dear, what are you thinking about?

She did not answer nor yield wholly to his arm. He said again softly:

—Tell me what it is, Gretta. I think I know what is the matter. Do I know?

She did not answer at once. Then she said in an outburst of tears:

—O, I am thinking about that song, *The Lass of Aughrim*.

She broke loose from him and ran to the bed and, throwing her arms across the bedrail, hid her face. Gabriel stood stockstill for a moment in astonishment and then followed her. As he passed in the way of the cheval glass he caught sight of himself in full length, his broad, wellfilled shirtfront, the face whose expression always puzzled him when he saw it in a mirror and his glimmering gilt-rimmed eyeglasses. He halted a few paces from her and said:

—What about the song? Why does that make you cry?

She raised her head from her arms and dried her eyes with the back of her hand like a child. A kinder note than he had intended went into his voice.

—Why, Gretta? he asked.

—I am thinking about a person long ago who used to sing that song.

—And who was the person long ago? asked Gabriel smiling.

—It was a person I used to know in Galway when I was living with my grandmother, she said.

The smile passed away from Gabriel's face. A dull anger began to gather again at the back of his mind and the dull fires of his lust began to glow angrily in his veins.

—Someone you were in love with? he asked ironically.

—It was a young boy I used to know, she answered, named Michael Furey. He used to sing that song, *The Lass of Aughrim*. He was very delicate.

Gabriel was silent. He did not wish her to think that he was interested in this delicate boy.

—I can see him so plainly, she said after a moment. Such eyes as he had, big dark eyes! And such an expression in them—an expression! …

—O, then you were in love with him? said Gabriel.

—I used to go out walking with him, she said, when I was in Galway.

A thought flew across Gabriel's mind.

—Perhaps that was why you wanted to go to Galway with that Ivors girl? he said coldly.

She looked at him and asked in surprise:

—What for?

Her eyes made Gabriel feel awkward. He shrugged his shoulders and said:

—How do I know? To see him, perhaps.

She looked away from him along the shaft of light towards the window in silence.

—He is dead, she said at length. He died when he was only seventeen. Isn't it a terrible thing to die so young as that?

—What was he? asked Gabriel, still ironically.

—He was in the gasworks, she said.

Gabriel felt humiliated by the failure of his irony and by the evocation of this figure from the dead, a boy in the gasworks. While he had been full of memories of their secret life together, full of tenderness and joy and desire, she had been comparing him in her mind with another. A shameful consciousness of his own person assailed him. He saw himself as a ludicrous figure, acting as a pennyboy for his aunts, a nervous wellmeaning sentimentalist, orating to vulgarians and idealising his own clownish lusts, the pitiable fatuous fellow he had caught a glimpse of in the mirror. Instinctively he turned his back more to the light lest she might see the shame that burned upon his forehead.

He tried to keep up his tone of cold interrogation but his voice when he spoke was humble and indifferent.

—I suppose you were in love with this Michael Furey, Gretta, he said.

—I was great with him at that time, she said.

Her voice was veiled and sad. Gabriel, feeling now how vain it would be to try to lead her whither he had purposed, caressed one of her hands and said also sadly:

—And what did he die of so young, Gretta? Consumption, was it?

—I think he died for me, she answered.

A vague terror seized Gabriel at this answer as if, at that hour when he had hoped to triumph, some impalpable and vindictive being was coming against him, gathering forces against him in its vague world. But he shook himself free of it with an effort of reason and continued to caress her hand. He did not question her again for he felt that she would tell him of herself. Her hand was warm and moist: it did not respond to his touch but he continued to caress it just as he had caressed her first letter to him that spring morning.

—It was in the winter, she said, about the beginning of the winter when I was going to leave my grandmother's and come up here to the convent. And he was ill at the time in his lodgings in Galway and wouldn't be let out and his people in Oughterard were written to. He was in decline, they said, or something like that. I never knew rightly.

She paused for a moment and sighed.

—Poor fellow, she said, he was very fond of me and he was such a gentle boy. We used to go out together walking, you know, Gabriel, like the way they do in the country. He was going to study singing only for his health. He had a very good voice, poor Michael Furey.

—Well, and then? asked Gabriel.

—And then when it came to the time for me to leave Galway and come up to the convent he was much worse and I wouldn't be let see him so I wrote him a letter saying I was going up to Dublin and would be back in the summer and hoping he would be better then.

She paused for a moment to get her voice under control and then went on:

—Then the night before I left I was in my grandmother's house in Nun's Island, packing up, and I heard gravel thrown up against the window. The window was so wet I couldn't see so I ran downstairs as I was and slipped out the back into the garden and there was the poor fellow at the end of the garden shivering.

—And did you not tell him to go back? asked Gabriel.

—I implored of him to go home at once and told him he would get his death in the rain. But he said he did not want to live. I can see his eyes as well as well![1] He was standing at the end of the wall where there was a tree.

—And did he go home? asked Gabriel.

—Yes, he went home. And when I was only a week in the convent he died and he was buried in Oughterard where his people came from. O, the day I heard that, that he was dead! …

She stopped, choking with sobs and, overcome by emotion, flung herself face downward on the bed, sobbing in the quilt. Gabriel held her hand for a moment longer, irresolutely, and then, shy of intruding on her grief, let it fall gently and walked quietly to the window. She was fast asleep.

Gabriel, leaning on his elbow, looked for a few moments unresentfully at her tangled hair and half open mouth, listening to her deep drawn breath. So she had had that romance in her life: a man had died for her sake. It hardly pained him now to think how poor a part he, her husband, had played in her life. He watched her while she slept as though he and she had never lived together as man and wife. His curious eyes rested long upon her face and on her hair: and as he thought of what she must have been then, in that time of her first girlish beauty, a strange friendly pity for her entered his soul. He did not like to say even to himself that her face was no longer beautiful but he knew that it was no longer the face for which Michael Furey had braved death.

Perhaps she had not told him all the story. His eyes moved to the chair over which she had thrown some of her clothes. A petticoat string dangled to the floor. One boot stood upright, its limp upper fallen down: the

---

[1] *as well as well* I.e., as well as well can be.

fellow of it lay upon its side. He wondered at his riot of emotions of an hour before. From what had it proceeded? From his aunts' supper, from his own foolish speech, from the wine and dancing, the merrymaking when saying goodnight in the hall, the pleasure of the walk along the river in the snow. Poor Aunt Julia! She too would soon be a shade[1] with the shade of Patrick Morkan and his horse. He had caught that haggard look upon her face for a moment when she was singing *Arrayed for the Bridal*. Soon perhaps he would be sitting in that same drawingroom, dressed in black, his silk hat on his knees. The blinds would be drawn down and Aunt Kate would be sitting beside him, crying and blowing her nose and telling him how Julia had died. He would cast about in his mind for some words that might console her and would find only lame and useless ones. Yes, yes: that would happen very soon.

The air of the room chilled his shoulders. He stretched himself cautiously along under the sheets and lay down beside his wife. One by one they were all becoming shades. Better pass boldly into that other world, in the full glory of some passion, than fade and wither dismally with age. He thought of how she who lay beside him had locked in her heart for so many years that image of her lover's eyes when he had told her that he did not wish to live.

Generous tears filled Gabriel's eyes. He had never felt like that himself towards any woman but he knew that such a feeling must be love. The tears gathered more thickly in his eyes and in the partial darkness he imagined he saw the form of a young man standing under a dripping tree. Other forms were near. His soul had approached that region where dwell the vast hosts of the dead. He was conscious of, but could not apprehend, their wayward and flickering existence. His own identity was fading out into a grey impalpable world: the solid world itself which these dead had one time reared and lived in was dissolving and dwindling.

A few light taps upon the pane made him turn to the window. It had begun to snow again. He watched sleepily the flakes, silver and dark, falling obliquely against the lamplight. The time had come for him to set out on his journey westward. Yes, the newspapers were

right: snow was general all over Ireland. It was falling on every part of the dark central plain, on the treeless hills, falling softly upon the Bog of Allen and, farther westward, softly falling into the dark mutinous Shannon waves. It was falling, too, upon every part of the lonely churchyard on the hill where Michael Furey lay buried. It lay thickly drifted on the crooked crosses and headstones, on the spears of the little gate, on the barren thorns. His soul swooned slowly as he heard the snow falling faintly through the universe and faintly falling, like the descent of their last end, upon all the living and the dead.

—1914

Ulysses

The chapter of *Ulysses* reprinted here follows Book 5 of Homer's *Odyssey*, in which Odysseus is beached on the land of the Phaeacians, where he hides in a thicket to sleep. He is awakened by Princess Nausicaa and her ladies-in-waiting, who have come to do their washing on the beach and are playing a ball game. He reveals himself and begs for their help in returning home to his wife, Penelope. In Joyce's version, Leopold Bloom is loitering on the beach, avoiding returning home to his unfaithful Penelope, Molly Bloom. In this episode it is not Bloom but Gerty (the Nausicaa figure) who reveals herself.

from *Ulysses*

CHAPTER 13 [NAUSICAA]

The summer evening had begun to fold the world in its mysterious embrace. Far away in the west the sun was setting and the last glow of all too fleeting day lingered lovingly on sea and strand,[2] on the proud promontory of dear old Howth[3] guarding as ever the waters of the bay, on the weedgrown rocks along Sandymount shore and, last but not least, on the quiet church whence there streamed forth at times upon the stillness

---

[1] *shade* Ghost.

[2] *strand* Shore.

[3] *Howth* Fishing port on the northeast headland of Dublin Bay. Howth Head overlooks Sandymount, on the shore of Dublin Bay.

the voice of prayer to her who is in her pure radiance a beacon ever to the stormtossed heart of man, Mary, star of the sea.[1]

The three girl friends were seated on the rocks, enjoying the evening scene and the air which was fresh but not too chilly. Many a time and oft were they wont to come there to that favourite nook to have a cosy chat beside the sparkling waves and discuss matters feminine, Cissy Caffrey and Edy Boardman with the baby in the push-car and Tommy and Jacky Caffrey, two little curlyheaded boys, dressed in sailor suits with caps to match and the name H.M.S. Belleisle printed on both. For Tommy and Jacky Caffrey were twins, scarce four years old and very noisy and spoiled twins sometimes but for all that darling little fellows with bright merry faces and endearing ways about them. They were dabbling in the sand with their spades and buckets, building castles as children do, or playing with their big coloured ball, happy as the day was long. And Edy Boardman was rocking the chubby baby to and fro in the pushcar while that young gentleman fairly chuckled with delight. He was but eleven months and nine days old and, though still a tiny toddler, was just beginning to lisp his first babyish words. Cissy Caffrey bent over him to tease his fat little plucks[2] and the dainty dimple in his chin.

—Now, baby, Cissy Caffrey said. Say out big, big. I want a drink of water.

And baby prattled after her:

—A jink a jink a jawbo.

Cissy Caffrey cuddled the wee chap for she was awfully fond of children, so patient with little sufferers and Tommy Caffrey could never be got to take his castor oil unless it was Cissy Caffrey that held his nose and promised him the scatty[3] heel of the loaf or brown bread with golden syrup on. What a persuasive power that girl had! But to be sure baby was as good as gold, a perfect little dote in his new fancy bib. None of your

spoilt beauties, Flora Mac Flimsy[4] sort, was Cissy Caffrey. A truerhearted lass never drew the breath of life, always with a laugh in her gipsylike eyes and a frolicsome word on her cherryripe red lips, a girl lovable in the extreme. And Edy Boardman laughed too at the quaint language of little brother.

But just then there was a slight altercation between Master Tommy and Master Jacky. Boys will be boys and our two twins were no exception to this golden rule. The apple of discord[5] was a certain castle of sand which Master Jacky had built and Master Tommy would have it right go wrong that it was to be architecturally improved by a frontdoor like the Martello tower[6] had. But if Master Tommy was headstrong Master Jacky was selfwilled too and, true to the maxim that every little Irishman's house is his castle, he fell upon his hated rival and to such purpose that the wouldbe assailant came to grief and (alas to relate!) the coveted castle too. Needless to say the cries of discomfited Master Tommy drew the attention of the girl friends.

—Come here, Tommy, his sister called imperatively, at once! And you, Jacky, for shame to throw poor Tommy in the dirty sand. Wait till I catch you for that.

His eyes misty with unshed tears Master Tommy came at her call for their big sister's word was law with the twins. And in a sad plight he was after his misadventure. His little man-o'-war[7] top and unmentionables[8] were full of sand but Cissy was a past mistress in the art of smoothing over life's tiny troubles and and very quickly not one speck of sand was to be seen on his smart little suit. Still the blue eyes were glistening with

---

[1] *Mary ... sea* The Roman Catholic Church of Mary, Star of the Sea, is located near Sandymount beach. *Stella Maris* is an attribute of the Virgin Mary.

[2] *plucks* Cheeks.

[3] *scatty* Crumbled.

[4] *Flora Mac Flimsy* Miss Flora MacFlimsey of Madison Square, a character in American poet William Allen Butler's "Nothing to Wear" (1857) who is mocked for her obsession with fashionable clothing.

[5] *apple of discord* Reference to the Greek myth in which Eris (goddess of discord) threw a golden apple into the midst of a wedding banquet and said that it belonged to the fairest goddess present. The subsequent argument between Athena, Aphrodite, and Hera as to its rightful owner and the resolution of the argument is the putative cause of the Trojan War.

[6] *Martello tower* Round, fortified tower near Sandymount, one of a series of such structures built by the British in the nineteenth century to deter a sea invasion.

[7] *man-o'-war* Sailor suit, frequently worn by children.

[8] *unmentionables* Underwear.

hot tears that would well up so she kissed away the hurtness and shook her hand at Master Jacky the culprit and said if she was near him she wouldn't be far from him, her eyes dancing in admonition.

—Nasty bold Jacky! she cried.

She put an arm round the little mariner and coaxed winningly:

—What's your name? Butter and cream?[1]

—Tell us who is your sweetheart, spoke Edy Boardman. Is Cissy your sweetheart?

—Nao, tearful Tommy said.

—Is Edy Boardman your sweetheart? Cissy queried.

—Nao, Tommy said.

—I know, Edy Boardman said none too amiably with an arch glance from her shortsighted eyes. I know who is Tommy's sweetheart, Gerty is Tommy's sweetheart.

—Nao, Tommy said on the verge of tears.

Cissy's quick motherwit guessed what was amiss and she whispered to Edy Boardman to take him there behind the pushcar where the gentlemen couldn't see and to mind he didn't wet his new tan shoes.

But who was Gerty?

Gerty MacDowell who was seated near her companions, lost in thought, gazing far away into the distance was in very truth as fair a specimen of winsome Irish girlhood as one could wish to see. She was pronounced beautiful by all who knew her though, as folks often said, she was more a Giltrap than a MacDowell. Her figure was slight and graceful, inclining even to fragility but those iron jelloids[2] she had been taking of late had done her a world of good much better than the Widow Welch's female pills[3] and she was much better of those discharges she used to get and that tired feeling. The waxen pallor of her face was almost spiritual in its ivorylike purity though her rosebud mouth was a genuine Cupid's bow, Greekly perfect. Her hands were of finely veined alabaster with tapering fingers and as white as lemon juice and queen of ointments could make them though it was not true that she used to wear kid gloves in bed or take a milk footbath either. Bertha Supple told that once to Edy Boardman, a deliberate lie, when she was black out at daggers drawn with Gerty (the girl chums had of course their little tiffs from time to time like the rest of mortals) and she told her to not let on whatever she did that it was her that told her or she'd never speak to her again. No. Honour where honour is due. There was an innate refinement, a languid queenly *hauteur*[4] about Gerty which was unmistakably evidenced in her delicate hands and higharched instep. Had kind fate but willed her to be born a gentlewoman of high degree in her own right and had she only received the benefit of a good education Gerty MacDowell might easily have held her own beside any lady in the land and have seen herself exquisitely gowned with jewels on her brow and patrician suitors at her feet vying with one another to pay their devoirs[5] to her. Mayhap it was this, the love that might have been, that lent to her softlyfeatured face at whiles a look, tense with suppressed meaning, that imparted a strange yearning tendency to the beautiful eyes, a charm few could resist. Why have women such eyes of witchery? Gerty's were of the bluest Irish blue, set off by lustrous lashes and dark expressive brows. Time was when those brows were not so silkily seductive. It was Madame Vera Verity, directress of the Woman Beautiful page of the Princess novelette,[6] who had first advised her to try eyebrowleine which gave that haunting expression to the eyes, so becoming in leaders of fashion, and she had never regretted it. Then there was blushing scientifically cured and how to be tall increase your height and you have a beautiful face but your nose? That would suit Mrs. Dignam because she had a button one. But Gerty's crowning glory was her wealth of wonderful hair. It was dark brown with a natural wave in it. She had cut it that very morning on account of the new moon[7] and it nestled about her pretty head in a profusion of luxuriant

---

1 *What's your ... cream* From a popular rhyme: "What's your name? / Butter an' crame / All the way from / Dirty Lane."

2 *iron jelloids* Gelatine lozenges containing iron and sold as a cure for anemia.

3 *Widow ... pills* Brand of medicine advertised as a remedy for gynecological problems.

4 *hauteur* Haughtiness, elevation of manner.

5 *devoirs* Dues; respects.

6 *Princess novelette* Weekly London magazine *The Princess Novelettes.*

7 *She had ... moon* According to popular superstition, it was best to cut one's hair during a new moon.

clusters and pared her nails too, Thursday for wealth.[1] And just now at Edy's words as a telltale flush, delicate as the faintest rosebloom, crept into her cheeks she looked so lovely in her sweet girlish shyness that of a surety God's fair land of Ireland did not hold her equal.

For an instant she was silent with rather sad downcast eyes. She was about to retort but something checked the words on her tongue. Inclination prompted her to speak out: dignity told her to be silent. The pretty lips pouted a while but then she glanced up and broke out into a joyous little laugh which had in it all the freshness of a young May morning. She knew right well, no-one better, what made squinty Edy say that because of him cooling in his attentions when it was simply a lover's quarrel. As per usual somebody's nose was out of joint about the boy that had the bicycle always riding up and down in front of her window. Only now his father kept him in the evenings studying hard to get an exhibition in the intermediate[2] that was on and he was going to Trinity college to study for a doctor when he left the high school like his brother W. E. Wylie who was racing in the bicycle races in Trinity college university. Little recked[3] he perhaps for what she felt, that dull aching void in her heart sometimes, piercing to the core. Yet he was young and perchance he might learn to love her in time. They were protestants in his family and of course Gerty knew Who came first and after Him the blessed Virgin and then Saint Joseph.[4] But he was undeniably handsome with an exquisite nose and he was what he looked, every inch a gentleman, the shape of his head too at the back without his cap on that she would know anywhere something off the common and the way he turned the bicycle at the lamp with his hands off the bars and also the nice perfume of those good cigarettes and besides they were both of a size and that was why Edy Boardman thought she was so frightfully clever because he didn't go and ride up and down in front of

her bit of a garden.

Gerty was dressed simply but with the instinctive taste of a votary of Dame Fashion for she felt that there was just a might that he might be out. A neat blouse of electric blue, selftinted by dolly dyes[5] (because it was expected in the *Lady's Pictorial* that electric blue would be worn), with a smart vee opening down to the division and kerchief pocket (in which she always kept a piece of cottonwool scented with her favourite perfume because the handkerchief spoiled the sit) and a navy threequarter skirt cut to the stride showed off her slim graceful figure to perfection. She wore a coquettish little love of a hat of wideleaved nigger straw contrast trimmed with an underbrim of eggblue chenille and at the side a butterfly bow to tone. All Tuesday week[6] afternoon she was hunting to match that chenille but at last she found what she wanted at Clery's[7] summer sales, the very it, slightly shopsoiled but you would never notice, seven fingers two and a penny. She did it up all by herself and what joy was hers when she tried it on then, smiling at the lovely reflection which the mirror gave back to her! And when she put it on the waterjug to keep the shape she knew that that would take the shine out of some people she knew. Her shoes were the newest thing in footwear (Edy Boardman prided herself that she was very *petite* but she never had a foot like Gerty MacDowell, a five, and never would ash, oak or elm[8]) with patent toecaps and just one smart buckle at her higharched instep. Her well-turned ankle displayed its perfect proportions beneath her skirt and just the proper amount and no more of her shapely limbs encased in finespun hose with highspliced heels and wide garter tops. As for undies they were Gerty's chief care and who that knows the fluttering hopes and fears of sweet seventeen (though Gerty would never see seventeen again) can find it in his heart to blame her? She had four dinky sets, with awfully pretty stitchery, three garments and nighties extra, and each set slotted with different coloured ribbons, rosepink, pale blue, mauve and

---

[1] *Thursday for wealth*   According to astrologers, Thursday (the day sacred to Jupiter) is a good day on which to transact business and to be courageous.

[2] *exhibition in the intermediate*   Exams given at the end of the school year to determine the winners of various cash prizes.

[3] *recked*   Cared or knew.

[4] *Who came … Joseph*   More polite version of the oath "Jesus, Mary and Joseph."

[5] *dolly dyes*   Brand of dye.

[6] *Tuesday week*   I.e., a week ago last Tuesday.

[7] *Clery's*   Major Dublin department store.

[8] *ash, oak or elm*   I.e., for the rest of time.

peagreen and she aired them herself and blued[1] them when they came home from the wash and ironed them and she had a brickbat[2] to keep the iron on because she wouldn't trust those washerwomen as far as she'd see them scorching the things. She was wearing the blue for luck, hoping against hope, her own colour and the lucky colour too for a bride to have a bit of blue somewhere on her because the green she wore that day week brought grief because his father brought him in to study for the intermediate exhibition and because she thought perhaps he might be out because when she was dressing that morning she nearly slipped up the old pair on her inside out and that was for luck and lovers' meetings if you put those things on inside out so long as it wasn't of a Friday.

And yet and yet! That strained look on her face! A gnawing sorrow is there all the time. Her very soul is in her eyes and she would give worlds to be in the privacy of her own familiar chamber where, giving way to tears, she could have a good cry and relieve her pentup feelings. Though not too much because she knew how to cry nicely before the mirror. You are lovely, Gerty, it said. The paly light of evening falls upon a face infinitely sad and wistful. Gerty MacDowell yearns in vain. Yes, she had known from the first that her daydream of a marriage has been arranged and the weddingbells ringing for Mrs. Reggy Wylie T.C.D.[3] (because the one who married the elder brother would be Mrs. Wylie) and in the fashionable intelligence[4] Mrs. Gertrude Wylie was wearing a sumptuous confection of grey trimmed with expensive blue fox was not to be. He was too young to understand. He would not believe in love, a woman's birthright. The night of the party long ago in Stoers' (he was still in short trousers) when they were alone and he stole an arm round her waist she went white to the very lips. He called her little one in a strangely husky voice and snatched a half kiss (the first!) but it was only the end of her nose and then he hastened from the room with a remark about refreshments. Impetuous fellow! Strength of character had never been

Reggy Wylie's strong point and he who would woo and win Gerty MacDowell must be a man among men. But waiting, always waiting to be asked and it was leap year[5] too and would soon be over. No prince charming is her beau ideal to lay a rare and wondrous love at her feet but rather a manly man with a strong quiet face who had not found his ideal, perhaps his hair slightly flecked with grey, and who would understand, take her in his sheltering arms, strain her to him in all the strength of his deep passionate nature and comfort her with a long long kiss. It would be like heaven. For such a one she yearns this balmy summer eve. With all the heart of her she longs to be his only, his affianced bride for riches for poor, in sickness in health, till death us two part, from this to this day forward.

And while Edy Boardman was with little Tommy behind the pushcar she was just thinking would the day ever come when she could call herself his little wife to be. Then they could talk about her till they went blue in the face, Bertha Supple too, and Edy, the spitfire, because she would be twenty-two in November. She would care for him with creature comforts too for Gerty was womanly wise and knew that a mere man liked that feeling of hominess. Her griddlecakes done to a golden-brown hue and queen Ann's pudding of delightful creaminess had won golden opinions from all because she had a lucky hand also for lighting a fire, dredge in the fine selfraising flour and always stir in the same direction then cream the milk and sugar and whisk well the white of eggs though she didn't like the eating part when there were any people that made her shy and often she wondered why you couldn't eat something poetical like violets or roses and they would have a beautifully appointed drawingroom with pictures and engravings and the photograph of grandpapa Giltrap's lovely dog Garryowen that almost talked, it was so human, and chintz covers for the chairs and that silver toastrack in Clery's summer jumble sales like they have in rich houses. He would be tall with broad shoulders (she had always admired tall men for a husband) with glistening white teeth under his carefully trimmed sweeping moustache and they would go on the continent[6] for

---

[1] *blued*   Treated with bluing, a cleaning agent that helps keep colors bright.

[2] *brickbat*   Piece of brick.

[3] *T.C.D.*   Trinity College, Dublin.

[4] *fashionable intelligence*   I.e., society columns.

[5] *a leap year*   The only time, according to traditional belief, when it was permissible for a woman to propose to a man.

[6] *continent*   I.e., Europe.

their honeymoon (three wonderful weeks!) and then, when they settled down in a nice snug and cosy little homely house, every morning they would both have brekky,[1] simple but perfectly served, for their own two selves and before he went out to business he would give his dear little wifey a good hearty hug and gaze for a moment deep down into her eyes.

Edy Boardman asked Tommy Caffrey was he done and he said yes, so then she buttoned up his little knickerbockers for him and told him to run off and play with Jacky and to be good now and not to fight. But Tommy said he wanted the ball and Edy told him no that baby was playing with the ball and if he took it there'd be wigs on the green[2] but Tommy said it was his ball and he wanted his ball and he pranced on the ground, if you please. The temper of him! O, he was a man already was little Tommy Caffrey since he was out of pinnies.[3] Edy told him no, no and to be off now with him and she told Cissy Caffrey not to give in to him.

—You're not my sister, naughty Tommy said. It's my ball.

But Cissy Caffrey told baby Boardman to look up, look up high at her finger and she snatched the ball quickly and threw it along the sand and Tommy after it in full career, having won the day.

—Anything for a quiet life, laughed Ciss.

And she tickled tiny tot's two cheeks to make him forget and played here's the lord mayor, here's his two horses, here's his gingerbread carriage and here he walks in, chinchopper, chinchopper, chinchopper chin. But Edy got as cross as two sticks about him getting his own way like that from everyone always petting him.

—I'd like to give him something, she said, so I would, where I won't say.

—On the beeoteetom, laughed Cissy merrily.

Gerty MacDowell bent down her head and crimsoned at the idea of Cissy saying an unladylike thing like that out loud she'd be ashamed of her life to say, flushing a deep rosy red, and Edy Boardman said she was sure the gentleman opposite heard what she said. But not a pin cared Ciss.

—Let him! she said with a pert toss of her head and

a piquant tilt of her nose. Give it to him too on the same place as quick as I'd look at him.

Madcap Ciss with her golliwog[4] curls. You had to laugh at her sometimes. For instance when she asked you would you have some more Chinese tea and jaspberry ram and when she drew the jugs too and the men's faces on her nails with red ink make you split your sides or when she wanted to go where you know she said she wanted to run and pay a visit to the Miss White. That was just like Cissycums. O, and will you ever forget the evening she dressed up in her father's suit and hat and the burned cork moustache and walked down Tritonville road, smoking a cigarette. There was none to come up to her for fun. But she was sincerity itself, one of the bravest and truest hearts heaven ever made, not one of your twofaced things, too sweet to be wholesome.

And then there came out upon the air the sound of voices and the pealing anthem of the organ. It was the men's temperance retreat conducted by the missioner, the reverend John Hughes S.J.[5] rosary, sermon and benediction of the Most Blessed Sacrament. They were there gathered together without distinction of social class (and a most edifying spectacle it was to see) in that simple fane[6] beside the waves, after the storms of this weary world, kneeling before the feet of the immaculate, reciting the litany of Our Lady of Loreto, beseeching her to intercede for them, the old familiar words, holy Mary, holy virgin of virgins. How sad to poor Gerty's ears! Had her father only avoided the clutches of the demon drink, by taking the pledge or those powders the drink habit cured in Pearson's Weekly, she might now be rolling in her carriage, second to none. Over and over had she told herself that as she mused by the dying embers in a brown study[7] without the lamp because she hated two lights or oftentimes gazing out of the window dreamily by the hour at the rain falling on the rusty bucket, thinking. But that vile decoction which has ruined so many hearths and homes had cast its shadow over her childhood days. Nay, she had even witnessed in the home circle deeds of violence caused by intemperance and had seen her own father, a prey to the fumes of

---

[1] *brekky* Breakfast.

[2] *wigs on the green* I.e., a brawl (Irish slang).

[3] *pinnies* Pinafores (babies' clothing).

[4] *golliwog* Black-faced male doll with frizzy hair.

[5] *S.J.* Society of Jesus (the Jesuits).

[6] *fane* Temple.

[7] *in a brown study* Expression meaning lost in thought.

intoxication, forget himself completely for if there was one thing of all things that Gerty knew it was the man who lifts his hand to a woman save in the way of kindness deserves to be branded as the lowest of the low.

And still the voices sang in supplication to the Virgin most powerful, Virgin most merciful. And Gerty, rapt in thought, scarce saw or heard her companions or the twins at their boyish gambols[1] or the gentleman off Sandymount green that Cissy Caffrey called the man that was so like himself passing along the strand taking a short walk. You never saw him anyway screwed[2] but still and for all that she would not like him for a father because he was too old or something or on account of his face (it was a palpable case of doctor Fell)[3] or his carbuncly nose with the pimples on it and his sandy moustache a bit white under his nose. Poor father! With all his faults she loved him still when he sang *Tell me, Mary, how to woo thee* or *My love and cottage near Rochelle* and they had stewed cockles and lettuce with Lazenby's salad dressing for supper and when he sang *The moon hath raised* with Mr. Dignam that died suddenly and was buried, God have mercy on him, from a stroke. Her mother's birthday that was and Charley was home on his holidays and Tom and Mr. Dignam and Mrs. and Patsy and Freddy Dignam and they were to have had a group[4] taken. No-one would have thought the end was so near. Now he was laid to rest. And her mother said to him to let that be a warning to him for the rest of his days and he couldn't even go to the funeral on account of the gout and she had to go into town to bring him the letters and samples from his office about Catesby's cork lino,[5] artistic standard designs, fit for a palace, gives tiptop wear and always bright and cheery in the home.

A sterling good daughter was Gerty just like a second mother in the house, a ministering angel too with a little

heart worth its weight in gold. And when her mother had those raging splitting headaches who was it rubbed on the menthol cone[6] on her forehead but Gerty though she didn't like her mother taking pinches of snuff and that was the only single thing they ever had words about, taking snuff. Everyone thought the world of her for her gentle ways. It was Gerty who turned off the gas at the main every night and it was Gerty who tacked up on the wall of that place where she never forgot every fortnight the chlorate of lime[7] Mr. Tunney the grocer's christmas almanac the picture of halcyon days where a young gentleman in the costume they used to wear then with a threecornered hat was offering a bunch of flowers to his ladylove with oldtime chivalry through her lattice window. You could see there was a story behind it. The colours were done something lovely. She was in a soft clinging white in a studied attitude and the gentleman was in chocolate and he looked a thorough aristocrat. She often looked at them dreamily when she went there for a certain purpose and felt her own arms that were white and soft just like hers with the sleeves back and thought about those times because she had found out in Walker's pronouncing dictionary that belonged to grandpapa Giltrap about the halcyon days[8] what they meant.

The twins were now playing in the most approved brotherly fashion, till at last Master Jacky who was really as bold as brass there was no getting behind that deliberately kicked the ball as hard as ever he could down towards the seaweedy rocks. Needless to say poor Tommy was not slow to voice his dismay but luckily the gentleman in black who was sitting there by himself came gallantly to the rescue and intercepted the ball. Our two champions claimed their plaything with lusty cries and to avoid trouble Cissy Caffrey called to the gentleman to throw it to her please. The gentleman aimed the ball once or twice and then threw it up the strand towards Cissy Caffrey but it rolled down the slope and stopped right under Gerty's skirt near the little pool by the rock. The twins clamoured again for it and Cissy told her to kick it away and let them fight for it so Gerty drew back her foot but she wished their

---

1 *gambols* Merrymaking.

2 *screwed* Drunk.

3 *doctor Fell* John Fell was Dean of Christ Church, Oxford. When he supposedly threatened satirist Thomas Brown with expulsion from the college, Brown is said to have responded poetically: "I do not love thee, Dr. Fell / The reason why I cannot tell; / But this alone I know full well, / I do not love thee, Dr. Fell."

4 *group* I.e., group photo.

5 *lino* Linoleum.

6 *menthol cone* Menthol, with its cooling effects, was a common home remedy for headaches.

7 *chlorate of lime* Used to disinfect and deodorize outdoor toilets.

8 *halcyon days* Calm, peaceful days.

stupid ball hadn't come rolling down to her and she gave a kick but she missed and Edy and Cissy laughed.

—If you fail try again, Edy Boardman said.

Gerty smiled assent and bit her lip. A delicate pink crept into her pretty cheek but she was determined to let them see so she just lifted her skirt a little but just enough and took good aim and gave the ball a jolly good kick and it went ever so far and the two twins after it down towards the shingle.[1] Pure jealousy of course it was nothing else to draw attention on account of the gentleman opposite looking. She felt the warm flush, a danger signal always with Gerty MacDowell, surging and flaming into her cheeks. Till then they had only exchanged glances of the most casual but now under the brim of her new hat she ventured a look at him and the face that met her gaze there in the twilight, wan and strangely drawn, seemed to her the saddest she had ever seen.

Through the open window of the church the fragrant incense was wafted and with it the fragrant names of her who was conceived without stain of original sin, spiritual vessel, pray for us, honourable vessel, pray for us, vessel of singular devotion, pray for us, mystical rose. And careworn hearts were there and toilers for their daily bread and many who had erred and wandered, their eyes wet with contrition but for all that bright with hope for the reverend father Hughes had told them what the great saint Bernard said in his famous prayer of Mary,[2] the most pious Virgin's intercessory power that it was not recorded in any age that those who implored her powerful protection were ever abandoned by her.

The twins were now playing again right merrily for the troubles of childhood are but as fleeting summer showers. Cissy played with baby Boardman till he crowed with glee, clapping baby hands in air. Peep she cried behind the hood of the pushcar and Edy asked where was Cissy gone and then Cissy popped up her head and cried ah! and, my word, didn't the little chap enjoy that! And then she told him to say papa.

—Say papa, baby. Say pa pa pa pa pa pa pa.

And baby did his level best to say it for he was very intelligent for eleven months everyone said and big for his age and the picture of health, a perfect little bunch of love, and he would certainly turn out to be something great, they said.

—Haja ja ja haja.

Cissy wiped his little mouth with the dribbling bib and wanted him to sit up properly and say pa pa pa but when she undid the strap she cried out, holy saint Denis, that he was possing wet and to double the half blanket the other way under him. Of course his infant majesty was most obstreperous at such toilet formalities and he let everyone know it:

—Habaa baaaahabaaa baaaa.

And two great big lovely big tears coursing down his cheeks. It was all no use soothering him with no, nono, baby, no and telling him about the geegee and where was the puffpuff but Ciss, always, readywitted, gave him in his mouth the teat of the suckingbottle and the young heathen was quickly appeased.

Gerty wished to goodness they would take their squalling baby home out of that and not get on her nerves no hour to be out and the little brats of twins. She gazed out towards the distant sea. It was like the paintings that man used to do on the pavement with all the coloured chalks and such a pity too leaving them there to be all blotted out, the evening and the clouds coming out and the Bailey light on Howth[3] and to hear the music like that and the perfume of those incense they burned in the church like a kind of waft. And while she gazed her heart went pitapat. Yes, it was her he was looking at and there was meaning in his look. His eyes burned into her as though they would search her through and through, read her very soul. Wonderful eyes they were, superbly expressive, but could you trust them? People were so queer. She could see at once by his dark eyes and his pale intellectual face that he was a foreigner the image of the photo she had of Martin Harvey, the matinee idol, only for the moustache which she preferred because she wasn't stagestruck like Winny Rippingham that wanted they two to always dress the same on account of a play but she could not see whether he had an aquiline nose or a slightly *retroussé*[4] from

---

[1] *shingle* Pebbly beach.

[2] *his famous … Mary* Reference to the "Memorare," a prayer frequently used by Saint Bernard of Clairvaux but not actually composed by him.

[3] *Bailey … Howth* Lighthouse on Howth Head.

[4] *retroussé* Turned up.

where he was sitting. He was in deep mourning,[1] she could see that, and the story of a haunting sorrow was written on his face. She would have given worlds to know what it was. He was looking up so intently, so still and he saw her kick the ball and perhaps he could see the bright steel buckles of her shoes if she swung them like that thoughtfully with the toes down. She was glad that something told her to put on the transparent stockings thinking Reggy Wylie might be out but that was far away. Here was that of which she had so often dreamed. It was he who mattered and there was joy on her face because she wanted him because she felt instinctively that he was like no-one else. The very heart of the girlwoman went out to him, her dreamhusband, because she knew on the instant it was him. If he had suffered, more sinned against than sinning, or even, even, if he had been himself a sinner, a wicked man, she cared not. Even if he was a protestant or methodist she could convert him easily if he truly loved her. There were wounds that wanted healing with heartbalm. She was a womanly woman not like other flighty girls, unfeminine, he had known, those cyclists showing off what they hadn't got and she just yearned to know all, to forgive all if she could make him fall in love with her, make him forget the memory of the past. Then mayhap he would embrace her gently, like a real man, crushing her soft body to him, and love her, his ownest girlie, for herself alone.

Refuge of sinners. Comfortress of the afflicted. *Ora pro nobis.*[2] Well has it been said that whosoever prays to her with faith and constancy can never be lost or cast away: and fitly is she too a haven of refuge for the afflicted because of the seven dolours which transpierced her own heart. Gerty could picture the whole scene in the church, the stained glass windows lighted up, the candles, the flowers and the blue banners of the blessed Virgin's sodality[3] and Father Conroy was helping Canon O'Hanlon at the altar, carrying things in and out with his eyes cast down. He looked almost a saint and his confessionbox was so quiet and clean and dark and his hands were just like white wax and if ever she became a

Dominican nun in their white habit perhaps he might come to the convent for the novena of Saint Dominic. He told her that time when she told him about that in confession crimsoning up to the roots of her hair for fear he could see, not to be troubled because that was only the voice of nature and we were all subject to nature's laws, he said, in this life and that that was no sin because that came from the nature of woman instituted by God, he said, and that Our Blessed Lady herself said to the archangel Gabriel be it done unto me according to Thy Word. He was so kind and holy and often and often she thought and thought could she work a ruched teacosy with embroidered floral design for him as a present or a clock but they had a clock she noticed on the mantelpiece white and gold with a canary bird that came out of a little house to tell the time the day she went there about the flowers for the forty hours' adoration[4] because it was hard to know what sort of a present to give or perhaps an album of illuminated views of Dublin or some place.

The exasperating little brats of twins began to quarrel again and Jacky threw the ball out towards the sea and they both ran after it. Little monkeys common as ditch-water. Someone ought to take them and give them a good hiding for themselves to keep them in their places, the both of them. And Cissy and Edy shouted after them to come back because they were afraid the tide might come in on them and be drowned.

—Jacky! Tommy!

Not they! What a great notion they had! So Cissy said it was the very last time she'd ever bring them out. She jumped up and called them and she ran down the slope past him, tossing her hair behind her which had a good enough colour if there had been more of it but with all the thingamerry she was always rubbing into it she couldn't get it to grow long because it wasn't natural so she could just go and throw her hat at it.[5] She ran with long gandery strides it was a wonder she didn't rip up her skirt at the side that was too tight on her because there was a lot of the tomboy about Cissy Caffrey and

---

[1] *in deep mourning* I.e., dressed in black, out of respect for a recently deceased friend or family member.

[2] *Ora pro nobis* Latin: pray for us.

[3] *sodality* Religious guild or society.

[4] *forty hours' adoration* Forty hours' prayer in memory of the time during which Jesus lay in His tomb before the Resurrection.

[5] *throw her … it* When a woman could not attract a man's attention any other way (i.e., by her appearance), it was said that she might as well "throw her hat at him."

she was a forward piece[1] whenever she thought she had a good opportunity to show off and just because she was a good runner she ran like that so that he could see all the end of her petticoat running and her skinny shanks up as far as possible. It would have served her just right if she had tripped up over something accidentally on purpose with her high crooked French heels on her to make her look tall and got a fine tumble. *Tableau!*[2] That would have been a very charming exposé for a gentleman like that to witness.

Queen of angels, queen of patriarchs, queen of prophets, of all saints, they prayed, queen of the most holy rosary and then Father Conroy handed the thurible[3] to Canon O' Hanlon and he put in the incense and censed the Blessed Sacrament and Cissy Caffrey caught the two twins and she was itching to give them a ringing good clip on the ear but she didn't because she thought he might be watching but she never made a bigger mistake in all her life because Gerty could see without looking that he never took his eyes off of her and then Canon O'Hanlon handed the thurible back to Father Conroy and knelt down looking up at the Blessed Sacrament and the choir began to sing *Tantum ergo*[4] and she just swung her foot in and out in time as the music rose and fell to the *Tantumer gosa cramen turn*. Three and eleven she paid for those stockings in Sparrow's of George's street on the Tuesday, no the Monday before Easter and there wasn't a brack[5] on them and that was what he was looking at, transparent, and not at her insignificant ones that had neither shape nor form (the cheek of her!) because he had eyes in his head to see the difference for himself.

Cissy came up along the strand with the two twins and their ball with her hat anyhow on her to one side after her run and she did look a streel[6] tugging the two

kids along with the flimsy blouse she bought only a fortnight before like a rag on her back and a bit of her petticoat hanging like a caricature. Gerty just took off her hat for a moment to settle her hair and a prettier, a daintier head of nutbrown tresses was never seen on a girl's shoulders, a radiant little vision, in sooth, almost maddening in its sweetness. You would have to travel many a long mile before you found a head of hair the like of that. She could almost see the swift answering flush of admiration in his eyes that set her tingling in every nerve. She put on her hat so that she could see from underneath the brim and swung her buckled shoe faster for her breath caught as she caught the expression in his eyes. He was eyeing her as a snake eyes its prey. Her woman's instinct told her that she had raised the devil in him and at the thought a burning scarlet swept from throat to brow till the lovely colour of her face became a glorious rose.

Edy Boardman was noticing it too because she was squinting at Gerty, half smiling, with her specs, like an old maid, pretending to nurse the baby. Irritable little gnat she was and always would be and that was why no-one could get on with her, poking her nose into what was no concern of hers. And she said to Gerty:

—A penny for your thoughts.

—What? replied Gerty with a smile reinforced by the whitest of teeth. I was only wondering was it late.

Because she wished to goodness they'd take the snottynosed twins and their baby home to the mischief out of that so that was why she just gave a gentle hint about its being late. And when Cissy came up Edy asked her the time and Miss Cissy, as glib as you like, said it was half past kissing time, time to kiss again. But Edy wanted to know because they were told to be in early.

—Wait, said Cissy, I'll ask my uncle Peter over there what's the time by his conundrum.

So over she went and when he saw her coming she could see him take his hand out of his pocket, getting nervous, and beginning to play with his watchchain, looking at the church. Passionate nature though he was Gerty could see that he had enormous control over himself. One moment he had been there, fascinated by a loveliness that made him gaze and the next moment it was the quiet gravefaced gentleman, selfcontrol expressed in every line of his distinguishedlooking figure.

---

[1] *piece* Slang: attractive woman.

[2] *Tableau* French: picture. Name of a popular parlor game in which participants would strike poses to convey a particular scene, announcing "tableau!" to indicate their pose was ready to be interpreted.

[3] *thurible* Vessel for burning and disseminating incense.

[4] *Tantum ergo* Hymn beginning *Tantum ergo Sacramentum* (Latin: so great a sacrament).

[5] *brack* Flaw.

[6] *streel* Disreputable woman.

Cissy said to excuse her would he mind telling her what was the right time and Gerty could see him taking out his watch, listening to it and looking up and clearing his throat and he said he was very sorry his watch was stopped but he thought it must be after eight because the sun was set. His voice had a cultured ring in it and though he spoke in measured accents there was a suspicion of a quiver in the mellow tones. Cissy said thanks and came back with her tongue out and said uncle said his waterworks were out of order.

Then they sang the second verse of the *Tantum ergo* and Canon O'Hanlon got up again and censed the Blessed Sacrament and knelt down and he told Father Conroy that one of the candles was just going to set fire to the flowers and Father Conroy got up and settled it all right and she could see the gentleman winding his watch and listening to the works and she swung her leg more in and out in time. It was getting darker but he could see and he was looking all the time that he was winding the watch or whatever he was doing to it and then he put it back and put his hands back into his pockets. She felt a kind of a sensation rushing all over her and she knew by the feel of her scalp and that irritation against her stays that that thing must be coming on because the last time too was when she clipped her hair on account of the moon. His dark eyes fixed themselves on her again drinking in her every contour, literally worshipping at her shrine. If ever there was undisguised admiration in a man's passionate gaze it was there plain to be seen on that man's face. It is for you, Gertrude MacDowell, and you know it.

Edy began to get ready to go and it was high time for her and Gerty noticed that that little hint she gave had the desired effect because it was a long way along the strand to where there was the place to push up the pushcar and Cissy took off the twins' caps and tidied their hair to make herself attractive of course and Canon O'Hanlon stood up with his cope[1] poking up at his neck and Father Conroy handed him the card to read off and he read out *Panem de coelo praestitisti eis*[2] and Edy and Cissy were talking about the time all the time and asking her but Gerty could pay them back in their own coin and she just answered with scathing politeness

when Edy asked her was she heartbroken about her best boy throwing her over. Gerty winced sharply. A brief cold blaze shone from her eyes that spoke volumes of scorn immeasurable. It hurt. O yes, it cut deep because Edy had her own quiet way of saying things like that she knew would wound like the confounded little cat she was. Gerty's lips parted swiftly to frame the word but she fought back the sob that rose to her throat, so slim, so flawless, so beautifully moulded it seemed one an artist might have dreamed of. She had loved him better than he knew. Lighthearted deceiver and fickle like all his sex he would never understand what he had meant to her and for an instant there was in the blue eyes a quick stinging of tears. Their eyes were probing her mercilessly but with a brave effort she sparkled back in sympathy as she glanced at her new conquest for them to see.

—O, responded Gerty, quick as lightning, laughing, and the proud head flashed up. I can throw my cap at who I like because it's leap year.

Her words rang out crystalclear, more musical than the cooing of the ringdove but they cut the silence icily. There was that in her young voice that told that she was not a one to be lightly trifled with. As for Mr. Reggy with his swank and his bit of money she could just chuck him aside as if he was so much filth and never again would she cast as much as a second thought on him and tear his silly postcard into a dozen pieces. And if ever after he dared to presume she could give him one look of measured scorn that would make him shrivel up on the spot. Miss puny little Edy's countenance fell to no slight extent and Gerty could see by her looking as black as thunder that she was simply in a towering rage though she hid it, the little kinnatt,[3] because that shaft had struck home for her petty jealousy and they both knew that she was something aloof, apart in another sphere, that she was not of them and there was somebody else too that knew it and saw it so they could put that in their pipe and smoke it.

Edy straightened up baby Boardman to get ready to go and Cissy tucked in the ball and the spades and buckets and it was high time too because the sandman was on his way for Master Boardman junior and Cissy told him too that Billy Winks was coming and that baby was to go deedaw and baby looked just too ducky,

---

1   *cope* Cloak-like ecclesiastical vestment.

2   *Panem ... eis* Latin: You have given them bread from Heaven.

3   *kinnatt* Impudent puppy.

laughing up out of his gleeful eyes, and Cissy poked him like that out of fun in his wee fat tummy and baby, without as much as by your leave, sent up his compliments on to his brand-new dribbling bib.

—O my! Puddeny pie! protested Ciss. He has his bib destroyed.

The slight *contretemps*[1] claimed her attention but in two twos she set that little matter to rights.

Gerty stifled a smothered exclamation and gave a nervous cough and Edy asked what and she was just going to tell her to catch it while it was flying but she was ever ladylike in her deportment so she simply passed it off with consummate tact by saying that that was the benediction because just then the bell rang out from the steeple over the quiet seashore because Canon O'Hanlon was up on the altar with the veil that Father Conroy put round him round his shoulders giving the benediction with the Blessed Sacrament in his hands.

How moving the scene there in the gathering twilight, the last glimpse of Erin,[2] the touching chime of those evening bells and at the same time a bat flew forth from the ivied belfry through the dusk, hither, thither, with a tiny lost cry. And she could see far away the lights of the lighthouses so picturesque she would have loved to do with a box of paints because it was easier than to make a man and soon the lamplighter would be going his rounds past the presbyterian church grounds and along by shady Tritonville avenue where the couples walked and lighting the lamp near her window where Reggy Wylie used to turn his freewheel like she read in that book *The Lamplighter*[3] by Miss Cummins, author of *Mabel Vaughan* and other tales. For Gerty had her dreams that no-one knew of. She loved to read poetry and when she got a keepsake from Bertha Supple of that lovely confession album with the coralpink cover to write her thoughts in she laid it in the drawer of her toilettable which, though it did not err on the side of luxury, was scrupulously neat and clean. It was there she kept her girlish treasures trove, the tortoiseshell combs, her child of Mary badge, the whiterose scent, the eyebrowleine, her alabaster pouncetbox and the ribbons to change when her things came home from the wash and there were some beautiful thoughts written in it in violet ink that she bought in Hely's of Dame Street for she felt that she too could write poetry if she could only express herself like that poem that appealed to her so deeply that she had copied out of the newspaper she found one evening round the potherbs. *Art thou real, my ideal?* it was called by Louis J. Walsh, Magherafelt,[4] and after there was something about twilight, *wilt thou ever?* and ofttimes the beauty of poetry, so sad in its transient loveliness, had misted her eyes with silent tears that the years were slipping by for her, one by one, and but for that one shortcoming she knew she need fear no competition and that was an accident coming down Dalkey hill and she always tried to conceal it. But it must end, she felt. If she saw that magic lure in his eyes there would be no holding back for her. Love laughs at locksmiths.[5] She would make the great sacrifice. Her every effort would be to share his thoughts. Dearer than the whole world would she be to him and gild his days with happiness. There was the allimportant question and she was dying to know was he a married man or a widower who had lost his wife or some tragedy like the nobleman with the foreign name from the land of song had to have her put into a madhouse, cruel only to be kind. But even if—what then? Would it make a very great difference? From everything in the least indelicate her finebred nature instinctively recoiled. She loathed that sort of person, the fallen women off the accommodation walk beside the Dodder[6] that went with the soldiers and coarse men, with no respect for a girl's honour, degrading the sex and being taken up to the police station. No, no: not that. They would be just good friends like a big brother and sister without all that other in spite of the conventions of Society with a big ess. Perhaps it was an old flame he was in mourning for from the days beyond recall. She thought she understood. She would try to understand him because men were so different. The old love was waiting, waiting with little white hands stretched out, with blue appealing

---

[1] *contretemps* Mishap.

[2] *Erin* Ireland.

[3] *The Lamplighter* Title of 1854 novel by American novelist Maria Cummins. Gerty is also the name of Cummins's protagonist.

[4] *Louis J. Walsh* Orator and versifier (1880–1942); *Magherafelt* Parish in northeastern Ireland.

[5] *Love ... locksmiths* Title of an 1803 play by George Colman that then became a proverbial phrase.

[6] *Dodder* River in Ireland.

eyes. Heart of mine! She would follow her dream of love, the dictates of her heart that told her he was her all in all, the only man in all the world for her for love was the master guide. Nothing else mattered. Come what might she would be wild, untrammelled, free.

Canon O'Hanlon put the Blessed Sacrament back into the tabernacle[1] and the choir sang *Laudate Dominum omnes gentes*[2] and then he locked the tabernacle door because the benediction was over and Father Conroy handed him his hat to put on and crosscat Edy asked wasn't she coming but Jacky Caffrey called out:

—O, look, Cissy!

And they all looked was it sheet lightning but Tommy saw it too over the trees beside the church, blue and then green and purple.

—It's fireworks, Cissy Caffrey said.

And they all ran down the strand to see over the houses and the church, helterskelter, Edy with the pushcar with baby Boardman in it and Cissy holding Tommy and Jacky by the hand so they wouldn't fall running.

—Come on, Gerty, Cissy called. It's the bazaar fireworks.

But Gerty was adamant. She had no intention of being at their beck and call. If they could run like rossies[3] she could sit so she said she could see from where she was. The eyes that were fastened upon her set her pulses tingling. She looked at him a moment, meeting his glance, and a light broke in upon her. Whitehot passion was in that face, passion silent as the grave and it had made her his. At last they were left alone without the others to pry and pass remarks and she knew he could be trusted to the death, steadfast, a sterling man, a man of inflexible honour to his fingertips. His hands and face were working and a tremor went over her. She leaned back far to look up where the fireworks were and she caught her knee in her hands so as not to fall back looking up and there was no-one to see only him and her when she revealed all her graceful beautifully shaped legs like that, supply soft and delicately rounded, and she seemed to hear the panting of his heart, his hoarse breathing, because she knew about the passion of men like that, hotblooded, because Bertha Supple told her once in dead secret and made her swear she'd never about the gentleman lodger that was staying with them out of the Congested Districts Board[4] that had pictures cut out of papers of those skirtdancers and highkickers and she said he used to do something not very nice that you could imagine sometimes in the bed. But this was altogether different from a thing like that because there was all the difference because she could almost feel him draw her face to his and the first quick hot touch of his handsome lips. Besides there was absolution so long as you didn't do the other thing before being married and there ought to be women priests that would understand without your telling out and Cissy Caffrey too sometimes had that dreamy kind of dreamy look in her eyes so that she too, my dear, and Winny Rippingham so mad about actors' photographs and besides it was on account of that other thing coming on the way it did.

And Jacky Caffrey shouted to look, there was another and she leaned back and the garters were blue to match on account of the transparent and they all saw it and shouted to look, look there it was and she leaned back ever so far to see the fireworks and something queer was flying about through the air, a soft thing to and fro, dark. And she saw a long Roman candle going up over the trees up, up, and, in the tense hush, they were all breathless with excitement as it went higher and higher and she had to lean back more and more to look up after it, high, high, almost out of sight, and her face was suffused with a divine, an entrancing blush from straining back and he could see her other things too, nainsook knickers, the fabric that caresses the skin, better than those other pettiwidth,[5] the green, four and eleven, on account of being white and she let him and she saw that he saw and then it went so high it went out of sight a moment and she was trembling in every limb from being bent so far back that he had a full view high up above her knee where no-one ever not even on the swing or wading and she wasn't ashamed and he wasn't either to look in that immodest way like that because he couldn't resist the sight of the wondrous revealment half

---

[1] *tabernacle* Receptacle for the consecrated Host.

[2] *Laudate … gentes* Latin: Give praise to the Lord, O ye nations.

[3] *rossies* Unchaste women.

[4] *Congested Districts Board* Established in 1891 to deal with the perceived problems of overpopulation in poor rural areas.

[5] *pettiwidth* Name of a brand of underwear.

offered like those skirtdancers behaving so immodest before gentlemen looking and he kept on looking, looking. She would fain have cried to him chokingly, held out her snowy slender arms to him to come, to feel his lips laid on her white brow, the cry of a young girl's love, a little strangled cry, wrung from her, that cry that has rung through the ages. And then a rocket sprang and bang shot blind blank and O! then the Roman candle burst and it was like a sigh of O! and everyone cried O! O! in raptures and it gushed out of it a stream of rain gold hair threads and they shed and ah! they were all greeny dewy stars falling with golden, O so lovely! O so soft, sweet, soft!

Then all melted away dewily in the grey air: all was silent. Ah! She glanced at him as she bent forward quickly, a pathetic little glance of piteous protest, of shy reproach under which he coloured like a girl. He was leaning back against the rock behind. Leopold Bloom (for it is he) stands silent, with bowed head before those young guileless eyes. What a brute he had been! At it again? A fair unsullied soul had called to him and, wretch that he was, how had he answered? An utter cad he had been. He of all men! But there was an infinite store of mercy in those eyes, for him too a word of pardon even though he had erred and sinned and wandered. Should a girl tell? No, a thousand times no. That was their secret, only theirs, alone in the hiding twilight and there was none to know or tell save the little bat that flew so softly through the evening to and fro and little bats don't tell.

Cissy Caffrey whistled, imitating the boys in the football field to show what a great person she was: and then she cried:

—Gerty! Gerty! We're going. Come on. We can see from farther up.

Gerty had an idea, one of love's little ruses. She slipped a hand into her kerchief pocket and took out the wadding and waved in reply of course without letting him and then slipped it back. Wonder if he's too far to. She rose. Was it goodbye? No. She had to go but they would meet again, there, and she would dream of that till then, tomorrow, of her dream of yester eve. She drew herself up to her full height. Their souls met in a last lingering glance and the eyes that reached her heart, full of a strange shining, hung enraptured on her sweet flowerlike face. She half smiled at him wanly, a sweet forgiving smile, a smile that verged on tears, and then they parted.

Slowly without looking back she went down the uneven strand to Cissy, to Edy, to Jacky and Tommy Caffrey, to little baby Boardman. It was darker now and there were stones and bits of wood on the strand and slippy seaweed. She walked with a certain quiet dignity characteristic of her but with care and very slowly because, because Gerty MacDowell was …

Tight boots? No. She's lame! O!

Mr. Bloom watched her as she limped away. Poor girl! That's why she's left on the shelf and the others did a sprint. Thought something was wrong by the cut of her jib.[1] Jilted beauty. A defect is ten times worse in a woman. But makes them polite. Glad I didn't know it when she was on show. Hot little devil all the same. Wouldn't mind. Curiosity like a nun or a negress or a girl with glasses. That squinty one is delicate. Near her monthlies, I expect, makes them feel ticklish. I have such a bad headache today.[2] Where did I put the letter? Yes, all right. All kinds of crazy longings. Licking pennies. Girl in Tranquilla convent that nun told me liked to smell rock oil. Virgins go mad in the end I suppose. Sister? How many women in Dublin have it today? Martha, she. Something in the air. That's the moon. But then why don't all women menstruate at the same time with same moon, I mean? Depends on the time they were born, I suppose. Or all start scratch then get out of step. Sometimes Molly and Milly[3] together. Anyhow I got the best of that. Damned glad I didn't do it in the bath this morning over her silly I will punish you letter. Made up for that tramdriver this morning. That gouger M'Coy stopping me to say nothing. And his wife engagement in the country valise, voice like a pickaxe. Thankful for small mercies. Cheap too. Yours for the asking. Because they want it themselves. Their natural craving. Shoals of them every evening poured

---

[1] *cut of her jib* Originally a nautical term, referring to the configuration of a boat's sails. It was also commonly used to refer to a person's look or style.

[2] *I have … today* This sentence is from a letter Bloom received from his secret correspondent, Martha Clifford, earlier that morning.

[3] *Molly and Milly* Bloom's wife (Molly is short for Marion) and daughter.

out of offices. Reserve better. Don't want it they throw it at you. Catch em alive, O. Pity they can't see themselves. A dream of wellfilled hose. Where was that? Ah, yes. Mutoscope[1] pictures in Capel street: for men only. Peeping Tom. Willy's hat and what the girls did with it. Do they snapshot those girls or is it all a fake. *Lingerie* does it. Felt for the curves inside her *deshabillé*.[2] Excites them also when they're. I'm all clean come and dirty me. And they like dressing one another for the sacrifice. Milly delighted with Molly's new blouse. At first. Put them all on to take them all off. Molly. Why I bought her the violet garters. Us too: the tie he[3] wore, his lovely socks and turnedup trousers. He wore a pair of gaiters the night that first we met. His lovely shirt was shining beneath his what? of jet. Say a woman loses a charm with every pin she takes out. Pinned together. O Mairy lost the pin of her. Dressed up to the nines for somebody. Fashion part of their charm. Just changes when you're on the track of the secret. Except the east: Mary, Martha:[4] now as then. No reasonable offer refused. She wasn't in a hurry either. Always off to a fellow when they are. They never forget an appointment. Out on spec probably. They believe in chance because like themselves. And the others inclined to give her an odd dig. Girl friends at school, arms round each other's necks or with ten fingers locked, kissing and whispering secrets about nothing in the convent garden. Nuns with whitewashed faces, cool coif and their rosaries going up and down, vindictive too for what they can't get. Barbed wire.[5] Be sure now and write to me. And I'll write to you. Now won't you? Molly and Josie Powell. Till Mr. Right comes along, then meet once in a blue moon. *Tableau!* O, look who it is for the love of God! How are you at all? What have you been doing with yourself? Kiss and delighted to, kiss, to see you. Picking holes in each other's appearance. You're looking splendid. Sister souls showing their teeth at one another. How many have you left? Wouldn't lend each other a pinch of salt. Ah!

Devils they are when that's coming on them. Dark devilish appearance. Molly often told me feel things a ton weight. Scratch the sole of my foot. O that way! O, that's exquisite! Feel it myself too. Good to rest once in a way. Wonder if it's bad to go with them then. Safe in one way. Turns milk, makes fiddlestrings snap. Something about withering plants I read in a garden. Besides they say if the flower withers she wears she's a flirt. All are. Daresay she felt I. When you feel like that you often meet what you feel. Liked me or what? Dress they look at. Always know a fellow courting: collars and cuffs. Well cocks and lions do the same and stags. Same time might prefer a tie undone or something. Trousers? Suppose I when I was? No. Gently does it. Dislike rough and tumble. Kiss in the dark and never tell. Saw something in me. Wonder what. Sooner have me as I am than some poet chap with bearsgrease plastery hair, lovelock over his dexter optic.[6] To aid gentleman in literary. Ought to attend to my appearance my age. Didn't let her see me in profile. Still, you never know. Pretty girls and ugly men marrying. Beauty and the beast. Besides I can't be so if Molly. Took off her hat to show her hair. Wide brim bought to hide her face, meeting someone might know her, bend down or carry a bunch of flowers to smell. Hair strong in rut.[7] Ten bob I got for Molly's combings when we were on the rocks in Holies street. Why not? Suppose he gave her money. Why not? All a prejudice. She's worth ten, fifteen, more a pound. What? I think so. All that for nothing. Bold hand. Mrs. Marion.[8] Did I forget to write address on that letter like the postcard I sent to Flynn. And the day I went to Drimmie's[9] without a necktie. Wrangle with Molly it was put me off. No, I remember.

---

1. *Mutoscope* Device for viewing, in quick succession, a series of pictures of objects in motion.

2. *deshabillé* Revealing undergarment. Here Bloom is remembering phrases from the pornographic book, *Sweets of Sin*, that he bought earlier that day.

3. *he* Dublin singer Hugh "Blazes" Boylan, with whom Molly Bloom is having an affair.

4. *Mary, Martha* Biblical sisters of Lazarus. See Luke 10.38–42.

5. *Barbed wire* Reference to the fictitious belief that barbed wire was invented by nuns.

6. *lovelock* Curl of particular shape or style; *dexter optic* Latin: right eye.

7. *Hair … rut* During mating season, the odor of an animal's skin changes. Here Bloom imagines similar changes occurring in women.

8. *Mrs. Marion* Reference to the letter Blazes Boylan wrote to Marion Bloom.

9. *Drimmie's* David Drimmie and Sons, the law office where Bloom used to work.

Richie Goulding. He's another. Weighs on his mind. Funny my watch stopped at half past four. Dust. Shark liver oil[1] they use to clean could do it myself. Save. Was that just when he, she?

O, he did. Into her. She did. Done.

Ah!

Mr. Bloom with careful hand recomposed his wet shirt. O Lord, that little limping devil. Begins to feel cold and clammy. After effect not pleasant. Still you have to get rid of it someway. They don't care. Complimented perhaps. Go home to nicey bread and milky and say night prayers with the kiddies. Well, aren't they. See her as she is spoil all. Must have the stage setting, the rouge, costume, position, music. The name too. Amours[2] of actresses. Nell Gwynn, Mrs. Bracegirdle, Maud Branscombe.[3] Curtain up. Moonlight silver effulgence. Maiden discovered with pensive bosom. Little sweetheart come and kiss me. Still I feel. The strength it gives a man. That's the secret of it. Good job I let off there behind coming out of Dignam's. Cider that was. Otherwise I couldn't have. Makes you want to sing after. Lacaus esant taratara.[4] Suppose I spoke to her. What about? Bad plan however of you don't know how to end the conversation. Ask them a question they ask you another. Good idea if you're in a cart. Wonderful of course if you say: good evening, and you see she's on for it: good evening. O but the dark evening in the Appian way[5] I nearly spoke to Mrs. Clinch O thinking she was. Whew! Girl in Meath street that night. All the dirty things I made her say all wrong of course. My arks she called it. It's so hard to find one who. Aho! If you don't answer when they solicit must be horrible for them till they harden. And kissed my hand when I gave her the extra two shillings. Parrots. Press the button and the bird will squeak. Wish she hadn't called me sir. O, her mouth in the dark! And you a married man with a single girl! That's what they enjoy. Taking a man from another woman. Or even hear of it. Different with me. Glad to get away from other chap's wife. Eating off his cold plate. Chap in the Burton today spitting back gum-chewed gristle. French letter[6] still in my pocketbook. Cause of half the trouble. But might happen sometime, I don't think. Come in. All is prepared. I dreamt. What? Worst is beginning. How they change the venue when it's not what they like. Ask you do you like mushrooms because she once knew a gentleman who. Or ask you what someone was going to say when he changed his mind and stopped. Yet if I went the whole hog, say: I want to, something like that. Because I did. She too. Offend her. Then make it up. Pretend to want something awfully, then cry off for her sake. Flatters them. She must have been thinking of someone else all the time. What harm? Must since she came to the use of reason, he, he and he. First kiss does the trick. The propitious moment. Something inside them goes pop. Mushy like, tell by their eye, on the sly. First thoughts are best. Remember that till their dying day. Molly, lieutenant Mulvey that kissed her under the Moorish wall[7] beside the gardens. Fifteen she told me. But her breasts were developed. Fell asleep then. After Glencree dinner that was when we drove home the featherbed mountain. Gnashing her teeth in sleep. Lord mayor had his eye on her too. Val Dillon. Apoplectic.

There she is with them down there for the fireworks. My fireworks. Up like a rocket, down like a stick. And the children, twins they must be, waiting for something to happen. Want to be grownups. Dressing in mother's clothes. Time enough, understand all the ways of the world. And the dark one with the mop head and the nigger mouth. I knew she could whistle. Mouth made for that. Like Molly. Why that high class whore in Jammet's wore her veil only to her nose. Would you mind, please, telling me the right time? I'll tell you the right time up a dark lane. Say prunes and prisms forty times every morning, cure for fat lips.[8] Caressing the little boy too. Onlookers see most of the game. Of course they understand birds, animals, babies. In their line.

---

[1] Shark liver oil   Used to lubricate machinery.

[2] Amours   Love affairs.

[3] Nell ... Branscombe   Famous English actresses of the seventeenth, eighteenth, and nineteenth centuries, respectively.

[4] Lacaus esant taratara   Bloom's rendition of a quote from Giacomo Meyerbeer's opera Les Huguenots (1836): La causa è santa (Italian: The cause is sacred).

[5] Appian way   Street on the southern edge of Dublin.

[6] French letter   Slang: condom.

[7] Moorish wall   In Gibraltar, where Molly was raised.

[8] Say prunes ... lips   See Dickens's Little Dorrit (1857): "Papa, potatoes, poultry, prunes, and prism are all very good words for the lips: especially prunes and prism."

Didn't look back when she was going down the strand. Wouldn't give that satisfaction. Those girls, those girls, those lovely seaside girls. Fine eyes she had, clear. It's the white of the eye brings that out not so much the pupil. Did she know what I? Course. Like a cat sitting beyond a dog's jump. Women never meet one like that Wilkins in the high school drawing a picture of Venus with all his belongings on show. Call that innocence? Poor idiot! His wife has her work cut out for her. Never see them sit on a bench marked *Wet Paint*. Eyes all over them. Look under the bed for what's not there. Longing to get the fright of their lives. Sharp as needles they are. When I said to Molly the man at the corner of Cuffe street was goodlooking, thought she might like, twigged at once he had a false arm. Had too. Where do they get that? Typist going up Roger Greene's stairs two at a time to show her understandings. Handed down from father to mother to daughter, I mean. Bred in the bone. Milly for example drying her handkerchief on the mirror to save the ironing. Best place for an ad to catch a woman's eye on a mirror.[1] And when I sent her for Molly's Paisley shawl to Presscott's, by the way that ad I must, carrying home the change in her stocking. Clever little minx! I never told her. Neat way she carries parcels too. Attract men, small thing like that. Holding up her hand, shaking it, to let the blood flow back when it was red. Who did you learn that from? Nobody. Something the nurse taught me. O, don't they know? Three years old she was in front of Molly's dressingtable just before we left Lombard street west. Me have a nice pace. Mullingar. Who knows? Ways of the world. Young student. Straight on her pins anyway not like the other. Still she was game. Lord, I am wet. Devil you are. Swell of her calf. Transparent stockings, stretched to breaking point. Not like that frump today. A.E.[2] Rumpled stockings. Or the one in Grafton street. White. Wow! Beef to the heel.[3]

A monkey puzzle rocket burst, spluttering in darting crackles. Zrads and zrads, zrads, zrads. And Cissy and

Tommy ran out to see and Edy after with the pushcar and then Gerty beyond the curve of the rocks. Will she? Watch! Watch! See! Looked round. She smelt an onion.[4] Darling, I saw your. I saw all.

Lord!

Did me good all the same. Off colour after Kiernan's, Dignam's. For this relief much thanks. In *Hamlet*,[5] that is. Lord! It was all things combined. Excitement. When she leaned back felt an ache at the butt of my tongue. Your head it simply swirls. He's right. Might have made a worse fool of myself however. Instead of talking about nothing. Then I will tell you all. Still it was a kind of language between us. It couldn't be? No, Gerty they called her. Might be false name however like my and the address Dolphin's barn a blind.

Her maiden name was Jemima Brown
And she lived with her mother in Irishtown.[6]

Place made me think of that I suppose. All tarred with the same brush. Wiping pens in their stockings. But the ball rolled down to her as if it understood. Every bullet has its billet.[7] Course I never could throw anything straight at school. Crooked as a ram's horn. Sad however because it lasts only a few years till they settle down to pot-walloping and papa's pants will soon fit Willy and fullers' earth[8] for the baby when they hold him out to do ah ah. No soft job. Saves them. Keeps them out of harm's way. Nature. Washing child, washing corpse.[9] Dignam. Children's hands always round them. Cocoanut skulls, monkeys, not even closed at first, sour milk in their swaddles and tainted curds. Oughtn't to have given that child an empty teat to suck. Fill it up with wind. Mrs. Beaufoy, Purefoy. Must call

---

[1] *Best place … mirror* Bloom is in the advertising industry; he sells ad space in newspapers.

[2] *A.E.* Pen name of Irish writer and artist George Russell (1865–1935).

[3] *Beef to the heel* Said of women whose legs are very thick, right down to their feet.

[4] *smelt an onion* Reference to a popular joke in which a man eats a raw onion whenever he will be around a woman so that she will not tempt him to become entangled in an affair. His plan is foiled when he meets a woman who finds the onion smell attractive.

[5] *In Hamlet* See *Hamlet* 1.1.8, in which one of the guards thanks another for relieving him.

[6] *Her maiden … Irishtown* From an Irish street ballad.

[7] *Every bullet … billet* Expression meaning everything has its place.

[8] *fullers' earth* Used for cleaning grease from clothing.

[9] *washing corpse* It was traditionally the women's job to prepare a body for burial.

to the hospital.[1] Wonder is nurse Callan there still. She used to look over some nights when Molly was in the Coffee Palace. That young doctor O'Hare I noticed her brushing his coat. And Mrs. Breen and Mrs. Dignam once like that too, marriageable. Worst of all at night Mrs. Duggan told me in the City Arms. Husband rolling in drunk, stink of pub off him like a polecat. Have that in your nose in the dark, whiff of stale boose. Then ask in the morning: was I drunk last night? Bad policy however to fault the husband. Chickens come home to roost. They stick by one another like glue. Maybe the women's fault also. That's where Molly can knock spots off them.[2] It is the blood of the south. Moorish. Also the form, the figure. Hands felt for the opulent. Just compare for instance those others. Wife locked up at home, skeleton in the cupboard. Allow me to introduce my. Then they trot you out some kind of a nondescript, wouldn't know what to call her. Always see a fellow's weak point in his wife. Still there's destiny in it, falling in love. Have their own secrets between them. Chaps that would go to the dogs if some woman didn't take them in hand. Then little chits of girls, height of a shilling in coppers,[3] with little hubbies. As God made them He matched them. Sometimes children turn out well enough. Twice nought makes one. Or old rich chap of seventy and blushing bride. Marry in May and repent in December. This wet is very unpleasant. Stuck. Well the foreskin is not back. Better detach.

Ow!

Other hand a sixfooter with a wifey up to his watchpocket. Long and the short of it. Big he and little she. Very strange about my watch. Wristwatches are always going wrong. Wonder is there any magnetic influence between the person because that was about the time he. Yes, I suppose at once. Cat's away the mice will play. I remember looking in Pill lane. Also that now is magnetism. Back of everything magnetism. Earth for instance pulling this and being pulled. That causes movement. And time? Well that's the time the movement takes. Then if one thing stopped the whole ghesabo[4] would stop bit by

bit. Because it's all arranged. Magnetic needle tells you what's going on in the sun, the stars. Little piece of steel iron. When you hold out the fork. Come. Come. Tip. Woman and man that is. Fork and steel. Molly, he. Dress up and look and suggest and let you see and see more and defy you if you're a man to see that and, like a sneeze coming, legs, look, look and if you have any guts in you. Tip. Have to let fly.

Wonder how is she feeling in that region. Shame all put on before third person. More put out about a hole in her stocking. Molly, her underjaw stuck out, head back, about the farmer in the ridingboots and spurs at the horse show. And when the painters were in Lombard street west. Fine voice that fellow had. How Giuglini[5] began. Smell that I did, like flowers. It was too. Violets. Came from the turpentine probably in the paint. Make their own use of everything. Same time doing it scraped her slipper on the floor so they wouldn't hear. But lots of them can't kick the beam,[6] I think. Keep that thing up for hours. Kind of a general all round over me and half down my back.

Wait. Hm. Hm. Yes. That's her perfume. Why she waved her hand. I leave you this to think of me when I'm far away on the pillow. What is it? Heliotrope? No, Hyacinth? Hm. Roses, I think. She'd like scent of that kind. Sweet and cheap: soon sour. Why Molly likes opoponax. Suits her with a little jessamine mixed. Her high notes and her low notes. At the dance night she met him, dance of the hours.[7] Heat brought it out. She was wearing her black and it had the perfume of the time before. Good conductor, is it? Or bad? Light too. Suppose there's some connection. For instance if you go into a cellar where it's dark. Mysterious thing too. Why did I smell it only now? Took its time in coming like herself, slow but sure. Suppose it's ever so many millions of tiny grains blown across. Yes, it is. Because those spice islands, Cinghalese this morning, smell them leagues off. Tell you what it is. It's like a fine fine veil or web they have all over the skin, fine like what do you call it gossamer and they're always spinning it out of them, fine as anything, rainbow colours without knowing it.

---

[1] *Must call ... hospital* The Blooms's family friend, Mina Purefoy, is in labor.

[2] *knock spots off them* Beat them; be much better than they are.

[3] *shilling ... coppers* Equal to twelve pennies ("coppers").

[4] *whole ghesabo* I.e., whole show.

[5] *Giuglini* Italian tenor Antonio Giuglini (1827–65).

[6] *kick the beam* Experience orgasm.

[7] *dance of the hours* Ballet from Amilcare Ponchiellei's *La Gioconda*.

Clings to everything she takes off. Vamp of her stockings. Warm shoe. Stays. Drawers: little kick, taking them off. Byby till next time. Also the cat likes to sniff in her shift on the bed. Know her smell in a thousand. Bathwater too. Reminds me of strawberries and cream. Wonder where it is really. There or the armpits or under the neck. Because you get it out of all holes and corners. Hyacinth perfume made of oil or ether or something. Muskrat. Bag under their tails one grain pour off odour for years. Dogs at each other behind. Good evening. Evening, How do you sniff? Hm. Hm. Very well, thank you. Animals go by that. Yes now, look at it that way. We're the same. Some women for instance warn you off when they have their period. Come near. Then get a hogo[1] you could hang your hat on. Like what? Potted herrings gone stale or. Boof! Please keep off the grass.

Perhaps they get a man smell off us. What though? Cigary gloves Long John had on his desk the other. Breath? What you eat and drink gives that. No. Mansmell, I mean. Must be connected with that because priests that are supposed to be are different. Women buzz round it like flies round treacle. Railed off the altar get on to it at any cost. The tree of forbidden priest. O father, will you? Let me be the first to. That diffuses itself all through the body, permeates. Source of life and it's extremely curious the smell. Celery sauce. Let me.

Mr. Bloom inserted his nose. Hm. Into the. Hm. Opening of his waistcoat. Almonds or. No. Lemons it is. Ah no, that's the soap.[2]

O by the by that lotion. I knew there was something on my mind. Never went back and the soap not paid. Dislike carrying bottles like that hag this morning. Hynes might have paid me that three shillings. I could mention Meagher's[3] just to remind him. Still if he works that paragraph. Two and nine. Bad opinion of me he'll have. Call tomorrow. How much do I owe you? Three and nine? Two and nine, sir. Ah. Might stop him giving credit another time. Lose your customers that way. Pubs do. Fellows run up a bill on the slate and then slinking around the back streets into somewhere else.

Here's this nobleman passed before. Blown in from the bay. Just went as far as turn back. Always at home at dinnertime. Looks mangled out: had a good tuck in.[4] Enjoying nature now. Grace after meals. After supper walk a mile. Sure he has a small bank balance somewhere, government sit.[5] Walk after him now make him awkward like those newsboys me today. Still you learn something. See ourselves as others see us. So long as women don't mock what matter? That's the way to find out. Ask yourself who is he now. *The Mystery Man on the Beach*, prize titbit story by Mr. Leopold Bloom. Payment at the rate of one guinea per column. And that fellow today at the graveside in the brown macintosh. Corns on his kismet[6] however. Healthy perhaps absorb all the. Whistle brings rain they say. Must be some somewhere. Salt in the Ormond damp. The body feels the atmosphere. Old Betty's joints are on the rack. Mother Shipton's prophecy that is about ships around they fly in the twinkling.[7] No. Signs of rain it is. The royal reader.[8] And distant hills seem coming nigh.

Howth. Bailey light. Two, four, six, eight, nine. See. Has to change or they might think it a house. Wreckers. Grace darling.[9] People afraid of the dark. Also glowworms, cyclists: lightingup time. Jewels diamonds flash better. Light is a kind of reassuring. Not going to hurt you. Better now of course than long ago. Country roads. Run you through the small guts for nothing. Still two types there are you bob against. Scowl or smile. Pardon! Not at all. Best time to spray plants too in the shade after the sun. Some light still. Red rays are longest.

---

1 *hogo* Scent.

2 *the soap* Bloom bought lemon soap earlier, and is carrying it in his pocket. He has also ordered the hand lotion that he mentions in the following paragraph.

3 *Meagher's* A pub.

4 *tuck in* Meal.

5 *sit* Position.

6 *Corns on his kismet* I.e., he is having bad luck.

7 *Mother Shipton's … twinkling* Mother Shipton was a famous prophetess of Tudor England. Here Bloom confuses two quotations from Charles Hindley's 1862 fictional work *The Wonderful History and Surprising Prophecies of Mother Shipton*. The first is a prediction of the telegraph ("Around the world thoughts shall fly / In the twinkling of an eye"), and the second is a prediction of steam locomotion ("Water shall yet more wonders do, / Now strange, yet shall be true").

8 *royal reader* School textbook.

9 *Grace darling* Grace Darling and her father, William, were lighthouse keepers who became national heroes after they braved dangerous waters to rescue the victims of a shipwreck in 1838.

Roygbiv Vance taught us: red, orange, yellow, green, blue, indigo, violet. A star I see. Venus? Can't tell yet. Two, when three it's night. Were those nightclouds there all the time? Looks like a phantom ship. No. Wait. Trees are they? An optical illusion. Mirage. Land of the setting sun this. Homerule sun setting in the southeast. My native land, goodnight.

Dew falling. Bad for you, dear, to sit on that stone. Brings on white fluxions. Never have little baby then less he was big strong fight his way up through. Might get piles myself. Sticks too like a summer cold, sore on the mouth. Cut with grass or paper worst. Friction of the position. Like to be that rock she sat on. O sweet little, you don't know how nice you looked. I begin to like them at that age. Green apples. Grab at all that offer. Suppose it's the only time we cross legs, seated. Also the library today: those girl graduates. Happy chairs under them. But it's the evening influence. They feel all that. Open like flowers, know their hours, sunflowers, Jerusalem artichokes, in ballrooms, chandeliers, avenues under the lamps. Nightstock in Mat Dillon's garden where I kissed her shoulder. Wish I had a full length oilpainting of her then. June that was too I wooed. The year returns. History repeats itself. Ye crags and peaks I'm with you once again. Life, love, voyage round your own little world. And now? Sad about her lame of course but must be on your guard not to feel too much pity. They take advantage.

All quiet on Howth now. The distant hills seem. Where we.[1] The rhododendrons. I am a fool perhaps. He gets the plums and I the plumstones. Where I come in. All that old hill has seen. Names change: that's all. Lovers: yum yum.

Tired I feel now. Will I get up? O wait. Drained all the manhood out of me, little wretch. She kissed me. My youth. Never again. Only once it comes. Or hers. Take the train there tomorrow. No. Returning not the same. Like kids your second visit to a house. The new I want. Nothing new under the sun. Care of P.O. Dolphin's barn. Are you not happy in your? Naughty darling. At Dolphin's barn charades in Luke Doyle's house. Mat Dillon and his bevy of daughters: Tiny, Atty, Floey, Maimy, Louy, Hetty. Molly too. Eighty-

seven that was. Year before we. And the old major partial to his drop of spirits. Curious she an only child, I an only child. So it returns. Think you're escaping and run into yourself. Longest way round is the shortest way home. And just when he and she. Circus horse walking in a ring. Rip van Winkle we played. Rip: tear in Henny Doyle's overcoat. Van: breadvan delivering. Winkle: cockles and periwinkles. Then I did Rip van Winkle coming back. She leaned on the sideboard watching. Moorish eyes. Twenty years asleep in Sleepy Hollow. All changed. Forgotten. The young are old. His gun rusty from the dew.

Ba. What is that flying about? Swallow? Bat probably. Thinks I'm a tree, so blind. Have birds no smell? Metempsychosis.[2] They believed you could be changed into a tree from grief. Weeping willow. Ba. There he goes. Funny little beggar. Wonder where he lives. Belfry up there. Very likely. Hanging by his heels in the odour of sanctity. Bell scared him out, I suppose. Mass seems to be over. Could hear them all at it. Pray for us. And pray for us. And pray for us. Good idea the repetition. Same thing with ads. Buy from us. And buy from us. Yes, there's the light in the priest's house. Their frugal meal. Remember about the mistake in the valuation when I was in Thom's. Twentyeight it is.[3] Two houses they have. Gabriel Conroy's brother is curate. Ba. Again. Wonder why they come out at night like mice. They're a mixed breed. Birds are like hopping mice. What frightens them, light or noise? Better sit still. All instinct like the bird in drouth got water out of the end of a jar by throwing in pebbles.[4] Like a little man in a cloak he is with tiny hands. Weeny bones. Almost see them shimmering, kind of a bluey white. Colours depend on the light you see. Stare the sun for example like the eagle[5] then look at a shoe see a blotch blob yellowish. Wants to stamp his trademark on everything. Instance, that cat this morning on the staircase. Colour of brown

---

[1] *Where we* Where Leopold courted Molly.

[2] *Metempsychosis* Belief that after death the soul moves into another body.

[3] *Remember about ... it is* Bloom seems to be referring to a mistake that was made while he was working for Thom's, in which the priest's house was evaluated at 28 pounds.

[4] *like the ... pebbles* One of Aesop's Fables.

[5] *like the eagle* According to myth, eagles could stare at the sun, and by flying up toward the sun would rejuvenate their eyes.

turf. Say you never see them with three colours. Not true. That half tabbywhite tortoiseshell in the *City Arms* with the letter em on her forehead. Body fifty different colours. Howth a while ago amethyst. Glass flashing. That's how that wise man what's his name with the burning glass.[1] Then the heather goes on fire. It can't be tourists' matches. What? Perhaps the sticks dry rub together in the wind and light. Or broken bottles in the furze act as a burning glass in the sun. Archimedes. I have it! My memory's not so bad.

Ba. Who knows what they're always flying for. Insects? That bee last week got into the room playing with his shadow on the ceiling. Might be the one bit me, come back to see. Birds too never find out what they say. Like our small talk. And says she and says he. Nerve they have to fly over the ocean and back. Lots must be killed in storms, telegraph wires. Dreadful life sailors have too. Big brutes of oceangoing steamers floundering along in the dark, lowing out like seacows. *Faugh a ballagh.*[2] Out of that, bloody curse to you. Others in vessels, bit of a handkerchief sail, pitched about like snuff at a wake when the stormy winds do blow. Married too. Sometimes away for years at the ends of the earth somewhere. No ends really because it's round. Wife in every port they say. She has a good job if she minds it till Johnny comes marching home again. If ever he does. Smelling the tail end of ports. How can they like the sea? Yet they do. The anchor's weighed. Off he sails with a scapular or a medal on him for luck. Well? And the tephilim[3] no what's this they call it poor papa's father had on his door to touch. That brought us out of the land of Egypt and into the house of bondage. Something in all those superstitions because when you go out never know what dangers. Hanging on to a plank or astride of a beam for grim life, lifebelt round round him, gulping salt water, and that's the last of his nibs till the sharks catch hold of him. Do fish ever get seasick?

Then you have a beautiful calm without a cloud, smooth sea, placid, crew and cargo in smithereens, Davy Jones' locker.[4] Moon looking down. Not my fault, old cockalorum.[5]

A lost long candle wandered up the sky from Mirus bazaar in search of funds for Mercer's hospital and broke, drooping, and shed a cluster of violet but one white stars. They floated, fell: they faded. The shepherd's hour: the hour of folding: hour of tryst. From house to house, giving his everwelcome double knock, went the nine o'clock postman, the glowworm's lamp at his belt gleaming here and there through the laurel hedges. And among the five young trees a hoisted lintstock[6] lit the lamp at Leahy's terrace. By screens of lighted windows, by equal gardens a shrill voice went crying, wailing: *Evening Telegraph, stop press edition! Result of the Gold Cup races!* and from the door of Dignam's house a boy ran out and called. Twittering the bat flew here, flew there. Far out over the sands the coming surf crept, grey. Howth settled for slumber tired of long days, of yumyum rhododendrons (he was old) and felt gladly the night breeze lift, ruffle his fell of ferns. He lay but opened a red eye unsleeping, deep and slowly breathing, slumberous but awake. And far on Kish bank the anchored lightship twinkled, winked at Mr. Bloom.

Life those chaps out there must have, stuck in the same spot. Irish Lights board.[7] Penance for their sins. Coastguards too. Rocket and breeches buoy and lifeboat. Day we went out for the pleasure cruise in the Erin's King,[8] throwing them the sack of old papers. Bears in the zoo. Filthy trip. Drunkards out to shake up their livers. Puking overboard to feed the herrings. Nausea. And the women, fear of God in their faces. Milly, no sign of funk. Her blue scarf loose, laughing. Don't know what death is at that age. And then their stomachs clean. But being lost they fear. When we hid behind the tree at Crumlin. I didn't want to. Mamma!

---

[1] *wise man ... glass* Greek mathematician Archimedes was said to have set the Roman fleet on fire by concentrating the sun's rays with mirrors.

[2] *Faugh a ballagh* Irish battle cry: clear the way.

[3] *tephilim* Jewish phyllactery. The words Bloom is thinking of is the Hebrew word "mezuzah," a piece of parchment containing Biblical passages that is placed in a case on the doorpost.

[4] *Davy Jones' locker* According to sailors' folklore, this locker at the bottom of the ocean was where all things lost at sea were stored.

[5] *cockalorum* Self-important person.

[6] *lintstock* Long staff with a forked head to hold a match.

[7] *Irish Lights board* Board that maintained lighthouses and lightships.

[8] *Erin's King* Ship that took tourists around Dublin Bay.

Mamma! Babes in the wood. Frightening them with masks too. Throwing them up in the air to catch them. I'll murder you. Is it only half fun? Or children playing battle. Whole earnest. How can people aim guns at each other. Sometimes they go off. Poor kids. Only troubles wildfire and nettlerash. Calomel purge[1] I got her for that. After getting better asleep with Molly. Very same teeth she has. What do they love? Another themselves? But the morning she chased her with the umbrella. Perhaps so as not to hurt. I felt her pulse. Ticking. Little hand it was: now big. Dearest Papli.[2] All that the hand says when you touch. Loved to count my waistcoat buttons. Her first stays I remember. Made me laugh to see. Little paps to begin with. Left one is more sensitive, I think.[3] Mine too. Nearer the heart. Padding themselves out if fat is in fashion. Her growing pains at night, calling, wakening me. Frightened she was when her nature came on her first. Poor child! Strange moment for the mother too. Brings back her girlhood. Gibraltar. Looking from Buena Vista. O'Hara's tower. The seabirds screaming. Old Barbary ape that gobbled all his family. Sundown, gunfire for the men to cross the lines. Looking out over the sea she told me. Evening like this, but clear, no clouds. I always thought I'd marry a lord or a gentleman with a private yacht. *Buenas noches, señorita. El hombre ama la muchaha hermosa.*[4] Why me? Because you were so foreign from the others.

Better not stick here all night like a limpet. This weather makes you dull. Must be getting on for nine by the light. Go home. Too late for *Leah, Lily of Killarney.*[5] No. Might be still up. Call to the hospital to see. Hope she's over. Long day I've had. Martha, the bath, funeral, house of keys, museum with those goddesses, Dedalus' song. Then that bawler in Barney Kiernan's. Got my own back there. Drunken ranters. What I said about his God made him wince. Mistake to hit back. Or? No.

Ought to go home and laugh at themselves. Always want to be swilling in company. Afraid to be alone like a child of two. Suppose he hit me. Look at it other way round. Not so bad then. Perhaps not to hurt he meant. Three cheers for Israel. Three cheers for the sister-in-law he hawked about, three fangs in her mouth. Same style of beauty. Particularly nice old party for a cup of tea. The sister of the wife of the wild man of Borneo has just come to town. Imagine that in the early morning at close range. Everyone to his taste as Morris said when he kissed the cow. But Dignam's put the boots on it.[6] Houses of mourning so depressing because you never know. Anyhow she wants the money. Must call to those Scottish widows[7] as I promised. Strange name. Takes it for granted we're going to pop off first. That widow on Monday was is outside Cramer's that looked at me. Buried the poor husband but progressing favourably on the premium. Her widow's mite. Well? What do you expect her to do? Must wheedle her way along. Widower I hate to see. Looks so forlorn. Poor man O'Connor wife and five children poisoned by mussels here. The sewage. Hopeless. Some good matronly woman in a porkpie hat to mother him. Take him in tow, platter face and a large apron. Ladies' grey flannelette bloomers, three shillings a pair, astonishing bargain. Plain and loved, loved for ever, they say. Ugly: no woman thinks she is. Love, lie and be handsome for tomorrow we die. See him sometimes walking about trying to find out who played the trick. U. p: up. Fate that is. He, not me. Also a shop often noticed. Curse seems to dog it. Dreamt last night? Wait. Something confused. She had red slippers on. Turkish. Wore the breeches. Suppose she does. Would I like her in pyjamas? Damned hard to answer. Nannetti's gone. Mailboat. Near Holyhead by now. Must nail that ad of Keyes's. Work Hynes and Crawford. Petticoats for Molly. She has something to put in them. What's that? Might be money.

Mr. Bloom stooped and turned over a piece of paper on the strand. He brought it near his eyes and peered. Letter? No. Can't read. Better go. Better. I'm tired to move. Page of an old copybook. All those holes and

---

[1] *Calomel purge* Calomel is used to relieve skin irritations.

[2] *Dearest Papli* The opening of Milly's letter to her father, which he received that morning.

[3] *paps* Breasts; *Left one ... think* A common belief, because the left breast is nearer to the heart.

[4] *Buenas ... hermosa* Spanish: Good evening, Miss. The man loves the beautiful young girl.

[5] *Leah ... Killarney* *Leah*, a popular play, and *Lily of Killarney*, an opera.

[6] *put the ... it* I.e., brought things to a head.

[7] *Scottish widows* Name of a life insurance company.

pebbles. Who could count them? Never know what you find. Bottle with story of a treasure in it thrown from a wreck. Parcels post. Children always want to throw things in the sea. Trust? Bread cast on the waters.[1] What's this? Bit of stick.

O! Exhausted that female has me. Not so young now. Will she come here tomorrow? Wait for her somewhere for ever. Must come back. Murderers do.[2] Will I?

Mr. Bloom with his stick gently vexed the thick sand at his foot. Write a message for her. Might remain. What?

I.

Some flatfoot tramp on it in the morning. Useless. Washed away. Tide comes here a pool near her foot. Bend, see my face there, dark mirror, breathe on it, stirs. All these rocks with lines and scars and letters. O, those transparent! Besides they don't know. What is the meaning of that other world. I called you naughty boy because I do not like.[3]

AM. A.

No room. Let it go.

Mr. Bloom effaced the letters with his slow boot. Hopeless thing sand. Nothing grows in it. All fades. No fear of big vessels coming up here. Except Guinness's barges. Round the Kish[4] in eighty days. Done half by design.

He flung his wooden pen away. The stick fell in silted sand, stuck. Now if you were trying to do that for a week on end you couldn't. Chance. We'll never meet again. But it was lovely. Goodbye, dear. Thanks. Made me feel so young.

Short snooze now if I had. Must be near nine. Liverpool boat long gone. Not even the smoke. And she can do the other. Did too. And Belfast.[5] I won't go. Race there,

race back to Ennis.[6] Let him. Just close my eyes a moment. Won't sleep though. Half dream. It never comes the same. Bat again. No harm in him. Just a few.

O sweety all your little girlwhite up I saw dirty bracegirdle made me do love sticky we two naughty Grace darling she him half past the bed met him pike hoses frillies for Raoul to perfume your wife black hair heave under embon *señorita* young eyes Mulvey plump years dreams return tail end Agendath swoony lovey showed me her next year in drawers return next in her next her next.

A bat flew. Here. There. Here. Far in the grey a bell chimed. Mr. Bloom with open mouth, his left boot sanded sideways, leaned, breathed. Just for a few

Cuckoo
Cuckoo
Cuckoo.

The clock on the mantelpiece in the priest's house cooed where Canon O'Hanlon and Father Conroy and the reverend John Hughes S.J. were taking tea and sodabread and butter and fried mutton chops with catsup and talking about

Cuckoo
Cuckoo
Cuckoo.

Because it was a little canarybird bird that came out of its little house to tell the time that Gerty MacDowell noticed the time she was there because she was as quick as anything about a thing like that, was Gerty Mac-Dowell, and she noticed at once that that foreign gentleman that was sitting on the rocks looking was

Cuckoo
Cuckoo
Cuckoo.

—1922

---

[1] *Bread ... waters* See Ecclesiastes 11.1: "Cast thy bread upon the waters: for thou shalt find it after many days."

[2] *Must come ... do* Reference to the old adage that murderers always return to the scene of the crime.

[3] *What is ... like* From Martha Clifford's letter.

[4] *Kish* Southeast of Dublin Bay.

[5] *Belfast* Bloom is thinking of the concert tour on which Molly will be embarking with Blazes Boylan.

[6] *Ennis* Where Bloom's father committed suicide, and where Bloom will be returning for the anniversary of his father's death—June 27.

D.H. LAWRENCE
1885 – 1930

D.H. Lawrence declared that "one sheds one's sicknesses in books." That claim suggests not only the sufferings of a man whose fierce desire to live was helplessly incarcerated in a body wasting away from tuberculosis, but also the broader afflictions associated with British modernization: the rise of machine culture, the devastating loss of life in World War I, and the outmoded moral values governing relations between the sexes and the classes. A prolific writer, Lawrence "shed" a staggering array of novels, short stories, essays and poems that relentlessly—and usually scandalously—broke cultural prohibitions to pioneer a new language of sexual and social possibility.

Some critics claim that Lawrence's only lasting allegiance was to his mother, an omnipresent figure who haunted his thoughts long after her death from cancer when he was twenty-five. David Herbert Lawrence, the fourth of five children born in the English mining town of Eastwood, Nottinghamshire, was his mother's favorite. Lawrence's parents were miserably mismatched. Lydia Lawrence felt she had married beneath herself, and struggled to cultivate more than working-class sensibilities in her children. Arthur Lawrence, the miner father, felt belittled by his own family. Marital tensions remembered from childhood percolate through Lawrence's works. If at first he villainized his father in the guise of various literary characters, Lawrence slowly gained sympathy for his father's awkward role in the family and for his earthy vitality. Scenes of an educated woman being sexually liberated through a liaison with a virile working-class man—most controversially explicit in *Lady Chatterley's Lover* (1928)—are seen throughout the works of Lawrence. His early novel *Sons and Lovers* (1913), while often interpreted as an Oedipal tale of mother-love, has also been read as a story of matricide.

Feminist critics have noted how his texts encode both adoration and dread of the primal power Lawrence imagined that the female held over the male.

Lawrence worked as a clerk and an elementary-school teacher to pay for his studies at Nottingham University College, and obtained his teacher's certificate in 1908. He secured a good teaching position at the Davidson Road School in Croydon, one of England's spacious new turn-of-the-century state schools. But two severe attacks of pneumonia, at ages sixteen and twenty-six, nearly killed Lawrence and led him to give up his teaching career. His close encounters with death left him, in the words of one critic, "with a heightened awareness of the physical world and a messianic tendency to preach." A suspected if not yet confirmed consumptive, Lawrence broke off an uninspired engagement to Louie Burrows on the grounds that his doctor advised against marriage.

Ford Madox Ford, editor of *The English Review* when the prestigious journal published Lawrence's first poems in 1909, introduced Lawrence to literati who were fascinated by the idea of meeting a young working-class genius in the flesh. A "primitivism" that at the time was prompting writers and artists to seek a remedy for European modernity in non-European cultures also supported fantasies about the curative raw talent of the working class. (Lawrence, romanticized for his class background, would himself exoticize Mexican culture in his 1926 novel, *The Plumed Serpent*.)

Though Lawrence castigated homosexual desire throughout his life (most sharply in his introduction to Maurice Magnus's steamy *Memoirs of the Foreign Legion*, 1924), a homoerotic element in his work makes its appearance in the first of his novels, *The White Peacock* (1910). The figure of "Cyril" in the novel, based upon his childhood friend Alan Chambers, may have represented one of the loves of Lawrence's life. Soon after his second illness, however, Lawrence was to have a fateful encounter with Frieda von Richthofen at the home of Ernest Weekley, one of Lawrence's favorite professors from college. Lawrence was by now rebelling against the universe of Christian guilt and glorifying an animal instinct in its place; he quickly came to worship the sensuality of Weekley's wife, a German baroness (and cousin of the WWI German flying ace Manfred von Richthofen, the "Red Baron"). Though Frieda left her husband and three children to be with Lawrence, she had little intention of re-marrying; it was Lawrence who pressured Frieda into marriage and cut her off from her young children, fearful that he could not compete with the force of maternal love which he himself knew so well.

Before meeting Lawrence, Frieda had been the lover of Otto Gross, a Freudian disciple who believed in sexually revolutionizing society to a degree never endorsed by Freud, and the indomitable Frieda continued to have countless lovers after marrying Lawrence. Lawrence's commitment to monogamy was in conflict with his goal of transcending sexual possessiveness. The Lawrences' many arguments were recorded by many visitors, yet the two remained together until Lawrence's death. To an acquaintance who asked what his ultimate message was, Lawrence wrote, "You shall love your wife completely and implicitly and in entire nakedness of body and spirit." Yet as one biographer dryly noted, "Lawrence's complete love included throttling her and covering her with bruises."

Lawrence's second major work of fiction, *The Rainbow*, was published in 1915, but its descriptions of sex and its coarse language led not only to its suppression, but also to legal difficulties for Lawrence. Persecuted, as well, during the war years, on account of his German wife and his provocative views, Lawrence felt exiled. Embracing a tramp-like lifestyle with Frieda, Lawrence set up house successively in Italy, Australia, the United States, Mexico, and France. World War I bred in Lawrence a fierce desire to form a community of the like-minded in tune with archetypal life forces, and the Lawrences' nomadic lifestyle was largely fueled by his restless utopian desires.

If Lawrence's sexual frankness created controversy, his radical dissolution of conventional narrative voice also disturbed many contemporaries. By the time he published *Women in Love* (1921), a story of two sisters who leave the countryside in pursuit of modern careers and sexual freedom, Lawrence no longer put any stock in individual subjectivity. His fiction strove to capture poetically the impersonal forces of nature that work through individuals but are in themselves vast and impersonal. To many minds, *Women in Love* succeeds magnificently in conveying a sense of individuals caught in the struggle with larger forces.

The publication of *Lady Chatterley's Lover* (1928) further scandalized the British public. The novel graphically depicts the primal sexuality awakened in Constance Chatterley by her working-class lover, Mellors. An anonymous critic who reviewed the novel in *John Bull* famously called it "a cesspool, the most obscene book in the English language." The publication of the book provoked censorship debates in the British Parliament in 1929, and the novel's label of "obscene" was not officially lifted until 1960.

Both Lawrence and his wife refused to admit that he was dying of tuberculosis until the disease was too advanced to deny. He died in 1930 at the age of 45 in the south of France.

⌘⌘⌘

Tortoise Shout

I thought he was dumb,
  I said he was dumb,
Yet I've heard him cry.

First faint scream,
5 Out of life's unfathomable dawn,
Far off, so far, like a madness, under the horizon's
    dawning rim,
Far, far off, far scream.

Tortoise *in extremis*.[1]

Why were we crucified into sex?
10 Why were we not left rounded off, and finished in
    ourselves,
As we began,
As he certainly began, so perfectly alone?

A far, was-it-audible scream,
Or did it sound on the plasm direct?

15 Worse than the cry of the new-born,
A scream,
A yell,
A shout,
A paean,
20 A death-agony,
A birth-cry,
A submission,
All tiny, tiny, far away, reptile under the first dawn.

War-cry, triumph, acute-delight, death-scream
    reptilian,
25 Why was the veil torn?[2]
The silken shriek of the soul's torn membrane?
The male soul's membrane
Torn with a shriek half music, half horror.

Crucifixion.
30 Male tortoise, cleaving behind the hovel-wall of that
    dense female,
Mounted and tense, spread-eagle, out-reaching out of
    the shell
In tortoise-nakedness,
Long neck, and long vulnerable limbs extruded,
    spread-eagle over her house-roof,
And the deep, secret, all-penetrating tail curved
    beneath her walls,
35 Reaching and gripping tense, more reaching anguish
    in uttermost tension
Till suddenly, in the spasm of coition, tupping°   *copulating*
    like a jerking leap, and oh!
Opening its clenched face from his outstretched neck
And giving that fragile yell, that scream,
Super-audible,
40 From his pink, cleft, old-man's mouth,
Giving up the ghost,
Or screaming in Pentecost,[3] receiving the ghost.

His scream, and his moment's subsidence,
The moment of eternal silence,
45 Yet unreleased, and after the moment, the sudden,
    startling jerk of coition, and at once
The inexpressible faint yell—
And so on, till the last plasm of my body was melted
    back
To the primeval rudiments of life, and the secret.

So he tups, and screams
50 Time after time that frail, torn scream
After each jerk, the longish interval,
The tortoise eternity,
Age-long, reptilian persistence,
Heart-throb, slow heart-throb, persistent for the next
    spasm.

55 I remember, when I was a boy,
I heard the scream of a frog, which was caught with
    his foot in the mouth of an up-starting snake;

---

[1] *in extremis* Latin: at the point of death.

[2] *Why ... torn* See Matthew 27.50–51: "Jesus, when he had cried
again with a loud voice, yielded up the ghost. And, behold, the veil
of the temple was rent in twain, from the top to the bottom; and the
earth did quake, and the rocks rent."

[3] *Pentecost* Feast day commemorating the day on which the Holy
Spirit descended on the twelve disciples and granted them the gift of
speaking many languages.

I remember when I first heard bull-frogs break into
     sound in the spring;
I remember hearing a wild goose out of the throat of night
Cry loudly, beyond the lake of waters;
60   I remember the first time, out of a bush in the
     darkness, a nightingale's piercing cries and
     gurgles startled the depths of my soul;
I remember the scream of a rabbit as I went through a
     wood at midnight;
I remember the heifer in her heat, blorting and
     blorting through the hours, persistent and
     irrepressible;
I remember my first terror hearing the howl of weird,
     amorous cats;
I remember the scream of a terrified, injured horse,
     the sheet-lightning,
65   And running away from the sound of a woman in
     labour, something like an owl whooing,
And listening inwardly to the first bleat of a lamb,
The first wail of an infant,
And my mother singing to herself,
And the first tenor singing of the passionate throat of
     a young collier,[1] who has long since drunk
     himself to death,
70   The first elements of foreign speech
On wild dark lips.

And more than all these,
And less than all these,
This last,
75   Strange, faint coition yell
Of the male tortoise at extremity,
Tiny from under the very edge of the farthest far-off
     horizon of life.

The cross,
The wheel on which our silence first is broken,
80   Sex, which breaks up our integrity, our single
     inviolability, our deep silence,
Tearing a cry from us.

Sex, which breaks us into voice, sets us calling across
     the deeps, calling, calling for the complement,

Singing, and calling, and singing again, being
     answered, having found.

Torn, to become whole again, after long seeking for
     what is lost,
85   The same cry from the tortoise as from Christ, the
     Osiris[2]-cry of abandonment,
That which is whole, torn asunder,
That which is in part, finding its whole again
     throughout the universe.
—1921

Snake

A Snake came to my water-trough
     On a hot, hot day, and I in pyjamas for the heat,
To drink there.

In the deep, strange-scented shade of the great dark
     carob-tree
5   I came down the steps with my pitcher
And must wait, must stand and wait, for there he was
     at the trough before me.

He reached down from a fissure in the earth-wall in
     the gloom
And trailed his yellow-brown slackness soft-bellied
     down, over the edge of the stone trough
And rested his throat upon the stone bottom,
10   And where the water had dripped from the tap, in a
     small clearness,
He sipped with his straight mouth,
Softly drank through his straight gums, into his slack
     long body,
Silently.

Someone was before me at my water-trough,
15   And I, like a second comer, waiting.

He lifted his head from his drinking, as cattle do,
And looked at me vaguely, as drinking cattle do,
And flickered his two-forked tongue from his lips, and
     mused a moment,

---

[1] *collier* Coal miner.

[2] *Osiris* Egyptian king, murdered by his brother Set, who scattered pieces of his body throughout the country. Osiris was then resurrected as god of the underworld.

And stooped and drank a little more,
20 Being earth-brown, earth-golden from the burning
        bowels of the earth
On the day of Sicilian July, with Etna[1] smoking.

The voice of my education said to me
He must be killed,
For in Sicily the black, black snakes are innocent, the
        gold are venomous.

25 And voices in me said, If you were a man
You would take a stick and break him now, and finish
        him off.

But must I confess how I liked him,
How glad I was he had come like a guest in quiet, to
        drink at my water-trough
And depart peaceful, pacified, and thankless,
30 Into the burning bowels of this earth?

Was it cowardice, that I dared not kill him?
Was it perversity, that I longed to talk to him?
Was it humility, to feel so honoured?
I felt so honoured.

35 And yet those voices:
If you were not afraid, you would kill him!

And truly I was afraid, I was most afraid,
But even so, honoured still more
That he should seek my hospitality
40 From out the dark door of the secret earth.

He drank enough
And lifted his head, dreamily, as one who has
        drunken,
And flickered his tongue like a forked night on the
        air, so black,
Seeming to lick his lips,
45 And looked around like a god, unseeing, into the air,
And slowly turned his head,
And slowly, very slowly, as if thrice adream,
Proceeded to draw his slow length curving round
And climb again the broken bank of my wall-face.

50 And as he put his head into that dreadful hole,
And as he slowly drew up, snake-easing his shoulders,
        and entered farther,
A sort of horror, a sort of protest against his
        withdrawing into that horrid black hole,
Deliberately going into the blackness, and slowly
        drawing himself after,
Overcame me now his back was turned.

55 I looked round, I put down my pitcher,
I picked up a clumsy log
And threw it at the water-trough with a clatter.

I think it did not hit him,
But suddenly that part of him that was left behind
        convulsed in undignified haste,
60 Writhed like lightning, and was gone
Into the black hole, the earth-lipped fissure in the
        wall-front,
At which, in the intense still noon, I stared with
        fascination.

And immediately I regretted it.
I thought how paltry, how vulgar, what a mean act!
65 I despised myself and the voices of my accursed
        human education.

And I thought of the albatross,[2]
And I wished he would come back, my snake.

For he seemed to me again like a king,
Like a king in exile, uncrowned in the underworld,
70 Now due to be crowned again.

And so, I missed my chance with one of the lords
Of life.
And I have something to expiate;
A pettiness.
—1923

---

[1] *Etna* Volcano in Sicily.

[2] *albatross* Reference to Samuel Taylor Coleridge's *Rime of the Ancient Mariner* (1798), in which a sailor needlessly and thoughtlessly kills an albatross.

Bavarian Gentians

Not every man has gentians[1] in his house
in soft September, at slow, sad Michaelmas.[2]

Bavarian gentians, big and dark, only dark
darkening the day-time, torch-like with the smoking
    blueness of Pluto's[3] gloom,
5 ribbed and torch-like, with their blaze of darkness
    spread blue
down flattening into points, flattened under the sweep
    of white day
torch-flower of the blue-smoking darkness, Pluto's
    dark-blue daze,
black lamps from the halls of Dis, burning dark blue,
giving off darkness, blue darkness, as Demeter's pale
    lamps give off light,
10 lead me then, lead the way.

Reach me a gentian, give me a torch!
let me guide myself with the blue, forked torch of this
    flower
down the darker and darker stairs, where blue is
    darkened on blueness
even where Persephone goes, just now, from the
    frosted September
15 to the sightless realm where darkness is awake upon
    the dark
and Persephone herself is but a voice
or a darkness invisible enfolded in the deeper dark
of the arms Plutonic, and pierced with the passion of
    dense gloom,
among the splendour of torches of darkness, shedding
    darkness on the lost bride and her groom.[4]

—1933

[1] *gentians* Herb that bears blue flowers.

[2] *Michaelmas* Feast of St. Michael the Archangel, on September 29.

[3] *Pluto* Greek God of the underworld (Roman Dis). He abducted Persephone, daughter of Demeter (the goddess of agriculture), and brought her to Hades to be his queen. Her mother grieved for her loss, putting the earth into an eternal winter. Finally she was allowed to return to earth for half the year (the reason for spring and summer) if she returned to Hades for the other half (the reason for fall and winter).

[4] *among … groom* In another, longer version of the poem (thought to be an earlier version), the following three lines follow: "Give me a flower on a tall stem, and three dark flames, / for I will go to the wedding, and be wedding-guest / at the marriage of the living dark."

The Prussian[5] Officer

I

They had marched more than thirty kilometres since dawn, along the white, hot road where occasional thickets of trees threw a moment of shade, then out into the glare again. On either hand, the valley, wide and shallow, glittered with heat; dark green patches of rye, pale young corn, fallow and meadow and black pine woods spread in a dull, hot diagram under a glistening sky. But right in front the mountains ranged across, pale blue and very still, snow gleaming gently out of the deep atmosphere. And towards the mountains, on and on, the regiment marched between the rye fields and the meadows, between the scraggy fruit trees set regularly on either side the high road. The burnished, dark green rye threw off a suffocating heat, the mountains drew gradually nearer and more distinct. While the feet of the soldiers grew hotter, sweat ran through their hair under their helmets, and their knapsacks could burn no more in contact with their shoulders, but seemed instead to give off a cold, prickly sensation.

He walked on and on in silence, staring at the mountains ahead, that rose sheer out of the land, and stood fold behind fold, half earth, half heaven, the heaven, the barrier with slits of soft snow, in the pale, bluish peaks.

He could now walk almost without pain. At the start, he had determined not to limp. It had made him sick to take the first steps, and during the first mile or so, he had compressed his breath, and the cold drops of sweat had stood on his forehead. But he had walked it off. What were they after all but bruises! He had looked at them, as he was getting up: deep bruises on the backs of his thighs. And since he had made his first step in the morning, he had been conscious of them, till now he had a tight, hot place in his chest, with suppressing the pain, and holding himself in. There seemed no air when he breathed. But he walked almost lightly.

The Captain's hand had trembled at taking his coffee at dawn: his orderly[6] saw it again. And he saw the fine figure of the Captain wheeling on horseback at the

[5] *Prussian* Inhabitant of Prussia, a duchy or kingdom that was divided between East and West Germany, Poland, and the Soviet Union in 1947.

[6] *orderly* Soldier who acts as a servant for a superior officer.

farm-house ahead, a handsome figure in pale blue uniform with facings of scarlet, and the metal gleaming on the black helmet and the sword-scabbard, and dark streaks of sweat coming on the silky bay horse. The orderly felt he was connected with that figure moving so suddenly on horseback: he followed it like a shadow, mute and inevitable and damned by it. And the officer was always aware of the tramp of the company behind, the march of his orderly among the men.

The Captain was a tall man of about forty, grey at the temples. He had a handsome, finely knit figure, and was one of the best horsemen in the West. His orderly, having to rub him down, admired the amazing riding-muscles of his loins.

For the rest, the orderly scarcely noticed the officer any more than he noticed himself. It was rarely he saw his master's face: he did not look at it. The Captain had reddish-brown, stiff hair, that he wore short upon his skull. His moustache was also cut short and bristly over a full, brutal mouth. His face was rather rugged, the cheeks thin. Perhaps the man was the more handsome for the deep lines in his face, the irritable tension of his brow, which gave him the look of a man who fights with life. His fair eyebrows stood bushy over light blue eyes that were always flashing with cold fire.

He was a Prussian aristocrat, haughty and overbear-ing. But his mother had been a Polish Countess. Having made too many gambling debts when he was young, he had ruined his prospects in the Army, and remained an infantry captain. He had never married: his position did not allow of it, and no woman had ever moved him to it. His time he spent riding—occasionally he rode one of his own horses at the races—and at the officers' club. Now and then he took himself a mistress. But after such an event, he returned to duty with his brow still more tense, his eyes still more hostile and irritable. With the men, however, he was merely impersonal, though a devil when roused; so that, on the whole, they feared him, but had no great aversion from him. They accepted him as the inevitable.

To his orderly he was at first cold and just and indif-ferent: he did not fuss over trifles. So that his servant knew practically nothing about him, except just what orders he would give, and how he wanted them obeyed. That was quite simple. Then the change gradually came.

The orderly was a youth of about twenty-two, of medium height, and well built. He had strong, heavy limbs, was swarthy, with a soft, black, young moustache. There was something altogether warm and young about him. He had firmly marked eyebrows over dark, expres-sionless eyes, that seemed never to have thought, only to have received life direct through his senses, and acted straight from instinct.

Gradually the officer had become aware of his servant's young, vigorous, unconscious presence about him. He could not get away from the sense of the youth's person, while he was in attendance. It was like a warm flame upon the older man's tense, rigid body, that had become almost unliving, fixed. There was something so free and self-contained about him, and something in the young fellow's movement, that made the officer aware of him. And this irritated the Prussian. He did not choose to be touched into life by his servant. He might easily have changed his man; but he did not. He now very rarely looked direct at his orderly, but kept his face averted, as if to avoid seeing him. And yet as the young soldier moved unthinking about the apartment, the elder watched him, and would notice the movement of his strong young shoulders under the blue cloth, the bend of his neck. And it irritated him. To see the soldier's young, brown, shapely peasant's hand grasp the loaf or the wine-bottle sent a flash of hate or of anger through the elder man's blood. It was not that the youth was clumsy: it was rather the blind, instinctive sureness of movement of an unhampered young animal that irritated the officer to such a degree.

Once, when a bottle of wine had gone over, and the red gushed out on to the tablecloth, the officer had started up with an oath, and his eyes, bluey like fire, had held those of the confused youth for a moment. It was a shock for the young soldier. He felt something sink deeper, deeper into his soul, where nothing had ever gone before. It left him rather blank and wondering. Some of his natural completeness in himself was gone, a little uneasiness took its place. And from that time an undiscovered feeling had held between the two men.

Henceforward the orderly was afraid of really meeting his master. His subconsciousness remembered those steely blue eyes and the harsh brows, and did not intend to meet them again. So he always stared past his master, and avoided him. Also, in a little anxiety, he waited for the three months to have gone, when his time would be up. He began to feel a constraint in the Captain's presence, and the soldier even more than the officer wanted to be left alone, in his neutrality as servant.

He had served the Captain for more than a year, and knew his duty. This he performed easily, as if it were natural to him. The officer and his commands he took for granted, as he took the sun and the rain, and he served as a matter of course. It did not implicate him personally.

But now if he were going to be forced into a personal interchange with his master he would be like a wild thing caught, he felt he must get away.

But the influence of the young soldier's being had penetrated through the officer's stiffened discipline, and perturbed the man in him. He, however, was a gentleman, with long, fine hands and cultivated movements, and was not going to allow such a thing as the stirring of his innate self. He was a man of passionate temper, who had always kept himself suppressed. Occasionally there had been a duel, an outburst before the soldiers. He knew himself to be always on the point of breaking out. But he kept himself hard to the idea of the Service. Whereas the young soldier seemed to live out his warm, full nature, to give it off in his very movements, which had a certain zest, such as wild animals have in free movement. And this irritated the officer more and more.

In spite of himself, the Captain could not regain his neutrality of feeling towards his orderly. Nor could he leave the man alone. In spite of himself, he watched him, gave him sharp orders, tried to take up as much of his time as possible. Sometimes he flew into a rage with the young soldier, and bullied him. Then the orderly shut himself off, as it were out of earshot, and waited, with sullen, flushed face, for the end of the noise. The words never pierced to his intelligence, he made himself, protectively, impervious to the feelings of his master.

He had a scar on his left thumb, a deep seam going across the knuckle. The officer had long suffered from it, and wanted to do something to it. Still it was there, ugly and brutal on the young, brown hand. At last the Captain's reserve gave way. One day, as the orderly was smoothing out the tablecloth, the officer pinned down his thumb with a pencil, asking:

"How did you come by that?"

The young man winced and drew back at attention. "A wood axe, Herr Hauptmann," he answered.

The officer waited for further explanation. None came. The orderly went about his duties. The elder man was sullenly angry. His servant avoided him. And the next day he had to use all his will-power to avoid seeing the scarred thumb. He wanted to get hold of it and—A hot flame ran in his blood.

He knew his servant would soon be free, and would be glad. As yet, the soldier had held himself off from the elder man. The Captain grew madly irritable. He could not rest when the soldier was away, and when he was present, he glared at him with tormented eyes. He hated those fine, black brows over the unmeaning, dark eyes, he was infuriated by the free movement of the handsome limbs, which no military discipline could make stiff. And he became harsh and cruelly bullying, using contempt and satire. The young soldier only grew more mute and expressionless.

"What cattle were you bred by, that you can't keep straight eyes? Look me in the eyes when I speak to you."

And the soldier turned his dark eyes to the other's face, but there was no sight in them: he stared with the slightest possible cast, holding back his sight, perceiving the blue of his master's eyes, but receiving no look from them. And the elder man went pale, and his reddish eyebrows twitched. He gave his order, barrenly.

Once he flung a heavy military glove into the young soldier's face. Then he had the satisfaction of seeing the black eyes flare up into his own, like a blaze when straw is thrown on a fire. And he had laughed with a little tremor and a sneer.

But there were only two months more. The youth instinctively tried to keep himself intact: he tried to serve the officer as if the latter were an abstract authority and not a man. All his instinct was to avoid personal contact, even definite hate. But in spite of himself the hate grew, responsive to the officer's passion. However, he put it in the background. When he had left the Army he could dare acknowledge it. By nature he was active, and had many friends. He thought what amazing good fellows they were. But, without knowing it, he was alone. Now this solitariness was intensified. It would carry him through his term. But the officer seemed to be going irritably insane, and the youth was deeply frightened.

The soldier had a sweetheart, a girl from the mountains, independent and primitive. The two walked together, rather silently. He went with her, not to talk, but to have his arm round her, and for the physical contact. This eased him, made it easier for him to ignore the Captain; for he could rest with her held fast against his chest. And she, in some unspoken fashion, was there for him. They loved each other.

The Captain perceived it, and was mad with irritation. He kept the young man engaged all the evenings long, and took pleasure in the dark look that came on his face. Occasionally, the eyes of the two men met, those of the younger sullen and dark, doggedly unalterable, those of the elder sneering with restless contempt.

The officer tried hard not to admit the passion that had got hold of him. He would not know that his feeling for his orderly was anything but that of a man incensed by his stupid, perverse servant. So, keeping quite justified and conventional in his consciousness, he let the other thing run on. His nerves, however, were suffering. At last he slung the end of a belt in his servant's face. When he saw the youth start back, the pain-tears in his eyes and the blood on his mouth, he had felt at once a thrill of deep pleasure and of shame.

But this, he acknowledged to himself, was a thing he had never done before. The fellow was too exasperating. His own nerves must be going to pieces. He went away for some days with a woman.

It was a mockery of pleasure. He simply did not want the woman. But he stayed on for his time. At the end of it, he came back in an agony of irritation, torment, and misery. He rode all the evening, then came straight in to supper. His orderly was out. The officer sat with his long, fine hands lying on the table, perfectly still, and all his blood seemed to be corroding.

At last his servant entered. He watched the strong, easy young figure, the fine eyebrows, the thick black hair. In a week's time the youth had got back his old well-being. The hands of the officer twitched and seemed to be full of mad flame. The young man stood at attention, unmoving, shut off.

The meal went in silence. But the orderly seemed eager. He made a clatter with the dishes.

"Are you in a hurry?" asked the officer, watching the intent, warm face of his servant. The other did not reply.

"Will you answer my question?" said the Captain.

"Yes, sir," replied the orderly, standing with his pile of deep Army-plates. The Captain waited, looked at him, then asked again:

"Are you in a hurry?"

"Yes, sir," came the answer, that sent a flash through the listener.

"For what?"

"I was going out, sir."

"I want you this evening."

There was a moment's hesitation. The officer had a curious stiffness of countenance.

"Yes, sir," replied the servant, in his throat.

"I want you tomorrow evening also—in fact, you may consider your evenings occupied, unless I give you leave."

The mouth with the young moustache set close.

"Yes, sir," answered the orderly, loosening his lips for a moment.

He again turned to the door.

"And why have you a piece of pencil in your ear?"

The orderly hesitated, then continued on his way without answering. He set the plates in a pile outside the door, took the stump of pencil from his ear, and put it in his pocket. He had been copying a verse for his sweetheart's birthday card. He returned to finish clearing the table. The officer's eyes were dancing, he had a little, eager smile.

"Why have you a piece of pencil in your ear?" he asked. The orderly took his hands full of dishes. His master was standing near the great green stove, a little smile on his face, his chin thrust forward. When the young soldier saw him his heart suddenly ran hot. He felt blind. Instead of answering, he turned dazedly to the door. As he was crouching to set down the dishes, he was pitched forward by a kick from behind. The pots went in a stream down the stairs, he clung to the pillar of the banisters. And as he was rising he was kicked heavily again, and again, so that he clung sickly to the post for some moments. His master had gone swiftly into the room and closed the door. The maid-servant downstairs looked up the staircase and made a mocking face at the crockery disaster.

The officer's heart was plunging. He poured himself a glass of wine, part of which he spilled on the floor, and gulped the remainder, leaning against the cool, green stove. He heard his man collecting the dishes from the stairs. Pale, as if intoxicated, he waited. The servant entered again. The Captain's heart gave a pang, as of pleasure, seeing the young fellow bewildered and uncertain on his feet, with pain.

"Schöner!" he said.

The soldier was a little slower in coming to attention.

"Yes, sir!"

The youth stood before him, with pathetic young moustache, and fine eyebrows very distinct on his forehead of dark marble.

"I asked you a question."

"Yes, sir."

The officer's tone bit like acid.

"Why had you a pencil in your ear?"

Again the servant's heart ran hot, and he could not breathe. With dark, strained eyes, he looked at the officer, as if fascinated. And he stood there sturdily planted, unconscious. The withering smile came into the Captain's eyes, and he lifted his foot.

"I—I forgot it—sir," panted the soldier, his dark eyes fixed on the other man's dancing blue ones.

"What was it doing there?"

He saw the young man's breast heaving as he made an effort for words.

"I had been writing."

"Writing what?"

Again the soldier looked up and down. The officer could hear him panting. The smile came into the blue eyes. The soldier worked his dry throat, but could not speak. Suddenly the smile lit like a flame on the officer's face, and a kick came heavily against the orderly's thigh. The youth moved a pace sideways. His face went dead, with two black, staring eyes.

"Well?" said the officer.

The orderly's mouth had gone dry, and his tongue rubbed in it as on dry brown-paper. He worked his throat. The officer raised his foot. The servant went stiff.

"Some poetry, sir," came the crackling, unrecognizable sound of his voice.

"Poetry, what poetry?" asked the Captain, with a sickly smile.

Again there was the working in the throat. The Captain's heart had suddenly gone down heavily, and he stood sick and tired.

"For my girl, sir," he heard the dry, inhuman sound.

"Oh!" he said, turning away. "Clear the table."

"Click!" went the soldier's throat; then again, "click!" and then the half-articulate:

"Yes, sir."

The young soldier was gone, looking old, and walking heavily.

The officer, left alone, held himself rigid, to prevent himself from thinking. His instinct warned him that he must not think. Deep inside him was the intense gratification of his passion, still working powerfully. Then there was a counter-action, a horrible breaking down of something inside him, a whole agony of reaction. He stood there for an hour motionless, a chaos of sensations, but rigid with a will to keep blank his consciousness, to prevent his mind grasping. And he held himself so until the worst of the stress had passed, when he began to drink, drank himself to an intoxication, till he slept obliterated. When he woke in the morning he was shaken to the base of his nature. But he had fought off the realization of what he had done. He had prevented his mind from taking it in, had suppressed it along with his instincts, and the conscious man had nothing to do with it. He felt only as after a bout of intoxication, weak, but the affair itself all dim and not to be recovered. Of the drunkenness of his passion he successfully refused remembrance. And when his orderly appeared with coffee, the officer assumed the same self he had had the morning before. He refused the event of the past night—denied it had ever been—and was successful in his denial. He had not done any such thing—not he himself. Whatever there might be lay at the door of a stupid, insubordinate servant.

The orderly had gone about in a stupor all the evening. He drank some beer because he was parched, but not much, the alcohol made his feeling come back, and he could not bear it. He was dulled, as if nine-tenths of the ordinary man in him were inert. He crawled about disfigured. Still, when he thought of the kicks, he went sick, and when he thought of the threat of more kicking, in the room afterwards, his heart went hot and faint, and he panted, remembering the one that had come. He had been forced to say, "For my girl." He was much too done even to want to cry. His mouth hung slightly open, like an idiot's. He felt vacant, and wasted. So, he wandered at his work, painfully, and very slowly and clumsily, fumbling blindly with the brushes, and finding it difficult, when he sat down, to summon the energy to move again. His limbs, his jaw, were slack and nerveless. But he was very tired. He got to bed at last, and slept inert, relaxed, in a sleep that was rather stupor than slumber, a dead night of stupefaction shot through with gleams of anguish.

In the morning were the manoeuvres. But he woke even before the bugle sounded. The painful ache in his chest, the dryness of his throat, the awful steady feeling of misery made his eyes come awake and dreary at once. He knew, without thinking, what had happened. And he knew that the day had come again, when he must go on with his round. The last bit of darkness was being pushed out of the room. He would have to move his inert body and go on. He was so young, and had known so little trouble, that he was bewildered. He only wished it would stay night, so that he could lie still, covered up by the darkness. And yet nothing would prevent the day from coming, nothing would save him from having to get up and saddle the Captain's horse, and make the Captain's coffee. It was there, inevitable. And then, he thought, it was impossible. Yet they would not leave him free. He must go and take the coffee to the Captain. He was too stunned to understand it. He only knew it was inevitable—inevitable, however long he lay inert.

At last, after heaving at himself, for he seemed to be a mass of inertia, he got up. But he had to force every one of his movements from behind, with his will. He felt lost, and dazed, and helpless. Then he clutched hold of the bed, the pain was so keen. And looking at his thighs, he saw the darker bruises on his swarthy flesh and he knew that, if he pressed one of his fingers on one of the bruises, he should faint. But he did not want to faint—he did not want anybody to know. No one should ever know. It was between him and the Captain. There were only the two people in the world now—himself and the Captain.

Slowly, economically, he got dressed and forced himself to walk. Everything was obscure, except just what he had his hands on. But he managed to get through his work. The very pain revived his dull senses. The worst remained yet. He took the tray and went up to the Captain's room. The officer, pale and heavy, sat at the table. The orderly, as he saluted, felt himself put out of existence. He stood still for a moment submitting

to his own nullification—then he gathered himself, seemed to regain himself, and then the Captain began to grow vague, unreal, and the younger soldier's heart beat up. He clung to this situation—that the Captain did not exist—so that he himself might live. But when he saw his officer's hand tremble as he took the coffee, he felt everything falling shattered. And he went away, feeling as if he himself were coming to pieces, disintegrated. And when the Captain was there on horseback, giving orders, while he himself stood, with rifle and knapsack, sick with pain, he felt as if he must shut his eyes—as if he must shut his eyes on everything. It was only the long agony of marching with a parched throat that filled him with one single, sleep-heavy intention: to save himself.

2

He was getting used even to his parched throat. That the snowy peaks were radiant among the sky, that the whitey-green glacier-river twisted through its pale shoals, in the valley below, seemed almost supernatural. But he was going mad with fever and thirst. He plodded on uncomplaining. He did not want to speak, not to anybody. There were two gulls, like flakes of water and snow, over the river. The scent of green rye soaked in sunshine came like a sickness. And the march continued, monotonously, almost like a bad sleep.

At the next farm-house, which stood low and broad near the high road, tubs of water had been put out. The soldiers clustered round to drink. They took off their helmets, and the steam mounted from their wet hair. The Captain sat on horseback, watching. He needed to see his orderly. His helmet threw a dark shadow over his light, fierce eyes, but his moustache and mouth and chin were distinct in the sunshine. The orderly must move under the presence of the figure of the horseman. It was not that he was afraid, or cowed. It was as if he was disembowelled, made empty, like an empty shell. He felt himself as nothing, a shadow creeping under the sunshine. And, thirsty as he was, he could scarcely drink, feeling the Captain near him. He would not take off his helmet to wipe his wet hair. He wanted to stay in shadow, not to be forced into consciousness. Starting, he saw the light heel of the officer prick the belly of the horse; the Captain cantered away, and he himself could relapse into vacancy.

Nothing, however, could give him back his living

place in the hot, bright morning. He felt like a gap among it all. Whereas the Captain was prouder, overriding. A hot flash went through the young servant's body. The Captain was firmer and prouder with life, he himself was empty as a shadow. Again the flash went through him, dazing him out. But his heart ran a little firmer.

The company turned up the hill, to make a loop for the return. Below, from among the trees, the farm-bell clanged. He saw the labourers, mowing barefoot at the thick grass, leave off their work and go downhill, their scythes hanging over their shoulders, like long, bright claws curving down behind them. They seemed like dream-people, as if they had no relation to himself. He felt as in a blackish dream: as if all the other things were there and had form, but he himself was only a consciousness, a gap that could think and perceive. The soldiers were tramping silently up the glaring hillside. Gradually his head began to revolve, slowly, rhythmically. Sometimes it was dark before his eyes, as if he saw this world through a smoked glass, frail shadows and unreal. It gave him a pain in his head to walk.

The air was too scented, it gave no breath. All the lush greenstuff seemed to be issuing its sap, till the air was deathly, sickly with the smell of greenness. There was the perfume of clover, like pure honey and bees. Then there grew a faint acrid tang—they were near the beeches; and then a queer clattering noise, and a suffocating, hideous smell; they were passing a flock of sheep, a shepherd in a black smock, holding his crook. Why should the sheep huddle together under this fierce sun? He felt that the shepherd would not see him, though he could see the shepherd.

At last there was the halt. They stacked rifles in a conical stack, put down their kit in a scattered circle around it, and dispersed a little, sitting on a small knoll high on the hillside. The chatter began. The soldiers were steaming with heat, but were lively. He sat still, seeing the blue mountains rising upon the land, twenty kilometers away. There was a blue fold in the ranges, then out of that, at the foot, the broad, pale bed of the river, stretches of whitey-green water between pinkish-grey shoals among the dark pine woods. There it was, spread out a long way off. And it seemed to come downhill, the river. There was a raft being steered, a mile away. It was a strange country. Nearer, a red-roofed,

broad farm with white base and square dots of windows crouched beside the wall of beech foliage on the wood's edge. There were long strips of rye and clover and pale green corn. And just at his feet, below the knoll, was a darkish bog, where globe flowers stood breathless still on their slim stalks. And some of the pale gold bubbles were burst, and a broken fragment hung in the air. He thought he was going to sleep.

Suddenly something moved into this coloured mirage before his eyes. The Captain, a small, light-blue and scarlet figure, was trotting evenly between the strips of corn, along the level brow of the hill. And the man making flag-signals was coming on. Proud and sure moved the horseman's figure, the quick, bright thing, in which was concentrated all the light of this morning, which for the rest lay a fragile, shining shadow. Submissive, apathetic, the young soldier sat and stared. But as the horse slowed to a walk, coming up the last steep path, the great flash flared over the body and soul of the orderly. He sat waiting. The back of his head felt as if it were weighted with a heavy piece of fire. He did not want to eat. His hands trembled slightly as he moved them. Meanwhile the officer on horseback was approaching slowly and proudly. The tension grew in the orderly's soul. Then again, seeing the Captain ease himself on the saddle, the flash blazed through him.

The Captain looked at the patch of light blue and scarlet, and dark heads, scattered closely on the hillside. It pleased him. The command pleased him. And he was feeling proud. His orderly was among them in common subjection. The officer rose a little on his stirrups to look. The young soldier sat with averted, dumb face. The Captain relaxed on his seat. His slim-legged, beautiful horse, brown as a beech nut, walked proudly uphill. The Captain passed into the zone of the company's atmosphere: a hot smell of men, of sweat, of leather. He knew it very well. After a word with the lieutenant, he went a few paces higher, and sat there, a dominant figure, his sweat-marked horse swishing its tail, while he looked down on his men, on his orderly, a nonentity among the crowd.

The young soldier's heart was like fire in his chest, and he breathed with difficulty. The officer, looking downhill, saw three of the young soldiers, two pails of water between them, staggering across a sunny green field. A table had been set up under a tree, and there the slim lieutenant stood, importantly busy. Then the Captain summoned himself to an act of courage. He called his orderly.

The flame leapt into the young soldier's throat as he heard the command, and he rose blindly, stifled. He saluted, standing below the officer. He did not look up. But there was the flicker in the Captain's voice.

"Go to the inn and fetch me …" the officer gave his commands. "Quick!" he added.

At the last word, the heart of the servant leapt with a flash, and he felt the strength come over his body. But he turned in mechanical obedience, and set off at a heavy run downhill, looking almost like a bear, his trousers bagging over his military boots. And the officer watched this blind, plunging run all the way.

But it was only the outside of the orderly's body that was obeying so humbly and mechanically. Inside had gradually accumulated a core into which all the energy of that young life was compact and concentrated. He executed his commission, and plodded quickly back uphill. There was a pain in his head, as he walked, that made him twist his features unknowingly. But hard there in the centre of his chest was himself, himself, firm, and not to be plucked to pieces.

The Captain had gone up into the wood. The orderly plodded through the hot, powerfully smelling zone of the company's atmosphere. He had a curious mass of energy inside him now. The Captain was less real than himself. He approached the green entrance to the wood. There, in the half-shade, he saw the horse standing, the sunshine and the flickering shadow of leaves dancing over his brown body. There was a clearing where timber had lately been felled. Here, in the gold-green shade beside the brilliant cup of sunshine, stood two figures, blue and pink, the bits of pink showing out plainly. The Captain was talking to his lieutenant.

The orderly stood on the edge of the bright clearing, where great trunks of trees, stripped and glistening, lay stretched like naked, brown-skinned bodies. Chips of wood littered the trampled floor, like splashed light, and the bases of the felled trees stood here and there, with their raw, level tops. Beyond was the brilliant, sunlit green of a beech.

"Then I will ride forward," the orderly heard his Captain say. The lieutenant saluted and strode away. He himself went forward. A hot flash passed through his belly, as he tramped towards his officer.

The Captain watched the rather heavy figure of the young soldier stumble forward, and his veins, too, ran hot. This was to be man to man between them. He yielded before the solid, stumbling figure with bent head. The orderly stooped and put the food on a level-sawn tree-base. The Captain watched the glistening, sun-inflamed, naked hands. He wanted to speak to the young soldier, but could not. The servant propped a bottle against his thigh, pressed open the cork, and poured out the beer into the mug. He kept his head bent. The Captain accepted the mug.

"Hot!" he said, as if amiably.

The flame sprang out of the orderly's heart, nearly suffocating him.

"Yes, sir," he replied, between shut teeth.

And he heard the sound of the Captain's drinking, and he clenched his fists, such a strong torment came into his wrists. Then came the faint clang of the closing pot-lid. He looked up. The Captain was watching him. He glanced swiftly away. Then he saw the officer stoop and take a piece of bread from the tree-base. Again the flash of flame went through the young soldier, seeing the stiff body stoop beneath him, and his hands jerked. He looked away. He could feel the officer was nervous. The bread fell as it was being broken. The officer ate the other piece. The two men stood tense and still, the master laboriously chewing his bread, the servant staring with averted face, his fist clenched.

Then the young soldier started. The officer had pressed open the lid of the mug again. The orderly watched the lid of the mug, and the white hand that clenched the handle, as if he were fascinated. It was raised. The youth followed it with his eyes. And then he saw the thin, strong throat of the elder man moving up and down as he drank, the strong jaw working. And the instinct which had been jerking at the young man's wrists suddenly jerked free. He jumped, feeling as if it were rent in two by a strong flame.

The spur of the officer caught in a tree-root, he went down backwards with a crash, the middle of his back thudding sickeningly against a sharp-edged tree-base, the pot flying away. And in a second the orderly, with serious, earnest young face, and underlip between his teeth, had got his knee in the officer's chest and was pressing the chin backward over the farther edge of the tree-stump, pressing, with all his heart behind in a passion of relief, the tension of his wrists exquisite with relief. And with the base of his palms he shoved at the chin, with all his might. And it was pleasant, too, to have that chin, that hard jaw already slightly rough with beard, in his hands. He did not relax one hair's breadth, but, all the force of all his blood exulting in his thrust, he shoved back the head of the other man, till there was a little "cluck" and a crunching sensation. Then he felt as if his head went to vapour. Heavy convulsions shook the body of the officer, frightening and horrifying the young soldier. Yet it pleased him, too, to repress them. It pleased him to keep his hands pressing back the chin, to feel the chest of the other man yield in expiration to the weight of his strong, young knees, to feel the hard twitchings of the prostrate body jerking his own whole frame, which was pressed down on it.

But it went still. He could look into the nostrils of the other man, the eyes he could scarcely see. How curiously the mouth was pushed out, exaggerating the full lips, and the moustache bristling up from them. Then, with a start, he noticed the nostrils gradually filled with blood. The red brimmed, hesitated, ran over, and went in a thin trickle down the face to the eyes.

It shocked and distressed him. Slowly, he got up. The body twitched and sprawled there, inert. He stood and looked at it in silence. It was a pity it was broken. It represented more than the thing which had kicked and bullied him. He was afraid to look at the eyes. They were hideous now, only the whites showing, and the blood running to them. The face of the orderly was drawn with horror at the sight. Well, it was so. In his heart he was satisfied. He had hated the face of the Captain. It was extinguished now. There was a heavy relief in the orderly's soul. That was as it should be. But he could not bear to see the long, military body lying broken over the tree-base, the fine fingers crisped. He wanted to hide it away.

Quickly, busily, he gathered it up and pushed it under the felled tree-trunks, which rested their beautiful, smooth length either end on logs. The face was horrible with blood. He covered it with the helmet. Then he pushed the limbs straight and decent, and brushed the dead leaves off the fine cloth of the uniform. So, it lay quite still in the shadow under there. A little strip of sunshine ran along the breast, from a chink between the logs. The orderly sat by it for a few moments. Here his own life also ended.

Then, through his daze, he heard the lieutenant, in a loud voice, explaining to the men outside the wood, that they were to suppose the bridge on the river below was held by the enemy. Now they were to march to the attack in such and such a manner. The lieutenant had no gift of expression. The orderly, listening from habit, got muddled. And when the lieutenant began it all again he ceased to hear.

He knew he must go. He stood up. It surprised him that the leaves were glittering in the sun, and the chips of wood reflecting white from the ground. For him a change had come over the world. But for the rest it had not—all seemed the same. Only he had left it. And he could not go back. It was his duty to return with the beer-pot and the bottle. He could not. He had left all that. The lieutenant was still hoarsely explaining. He must go, or they would overtake him. And he could not bear contact with anyone now.

He drew his fingers over his eyes, trying to find out where he was. Then he turned away. He saw the horse standing in the path. He went up to it and mounted. It hurt him to sit in the saddle. The pain of keeping his seat occupied him as they cantered through the wood. He would not have minded anything, but he could not get away from the sense of being divided from the others. The path led out of the trees. On the edge of the wood he pulled up and stood watching. There in the spacious sunshine of the valley soldiers were moving in a little swarm. Every now and then, a man harrowing on a strip of fallow shouted to his oxen, at the turn. The village and the white-towered church was small in the sunshine. And he no longer belonged to it—he sat there, beyond, like a man outside in the dark. He had gone out from everyday life into the unknown, and he could not, he even did not want to go back.

Turning from the sun-blazing valley, he rode deep into the wood. Tree-trunks, like people standing grey and still, took no notice as he went. A doe, herself a moving bit of sunshine and shadow, went running through the flecked shade. There were bright green rents in the foliage. Then it was all pine wood, dark and cool. And he was sick with pain, he had an intolerable great pulse in his head, and he was sick. He had never been ill in his life. He felt lost, quite dazed with all this.

Trying to get down from the horse, he fell, astonished at the pain and his lack of balance. The horse shifted uneasily. He jerked its bridle and sent it cantering jerkily away. It was his last connection with the rest of things.

But he only wanted to lie down and not be disturbed. Stumbling through the trees, he came on a quiet place where beeches and pine trees grew on a slope. Immediately he had lain down and closed his eyes, his consciousness went racing on without him. A big pulse of sickness beat in him as if it throbbed through the whole earth. He was burning with dry heat. But he was too busy, too tearingly active in the incoherent race of delirium to observe.

3

He came to with a start. His mouth was dry and hard, his heart beat heavily, but he had not the energy to get up. His heart beat heavily. Where was he?—the barracks—at home? There was something knocking. And, making an effort, he looked round—trees, and litter of greenery, and reddish, bright, still pieces of sunshine on the floor. He did not believe he was himself, he did not believe what he saw. Something was knocking. He made a struggle towards consciousness, but relapsed. Then he struggled again. And gradually his surroundings fell into relationship with himself. He knew, and a great pang of fear went through his heart. Somebody was knocking. He could see the heavy, black rags of a fir tree overhead. Then everything went black. Yet he did not believe he had closed his eyes. He had not. Out of the blackness sight slowly emerged again. And someone was knocking. Quickly, he saw the blood-disfigured face of his Captain, which he hated. And he held himself still with horror. Yet, deep inside him, he knew that it was so, the Captain should be dead. But the physical delirium got hold of him. Someone was knocking. He lay perfectly still, as if dead, with fear. And he went unconscious.

When he opened his eyes again, he started, seeing something creeping swiftly up a tree-trunk. It was a little bird. And the bird was whistling overhead. Tap-tap-tap—it was the small, quick bird rapping the tree-trunk with its beak, as if its head were a little round hammer. He watched it curiously. It shifted sharply, in its creeping fashion. Then, like a mouse, it slid down the bare trunk. Its swift creeping sent a flash of revulsion through him. He raised his head. It felt a great weight. Then, the little bird ran out of the shadow across a still patch of sunshine, its little head bobbing swiftly, its white legs twinkling brightly for a moment. How neat it was in its build, so compact, with pieces of white on its wings. There were several of them. They were so pretty—but they crept like swift, erratic mice, running here and there among the beech-mast.

He lay down again exhausted, and his consciousness lapsed. He had a horror of the little creeping birds. All his blood seemed to be darting and creeping in his head. And yet he could not move.

He came to with a further ache of exhaustion. There was the pain in his head, and the horrible sickness, and his inability to move. He had never been ill in his life. He did not know where he was or what he was. Probably he had got sunstroke. Or what else?—he had silenced the Captain for ever—some time ago—oh, a long time ago. There had been blood on his face, and his eyes had turned upwards. It was all right, somehow. It was peace. But now he had got beyond himself. He had never been here before. Was it life, or not life? He was by himself. They were in a big, bright place, those others, and he was outside. The town, all the country, a big bright place of light: and he was outside, here, in the darkened open beyond, where each thing existed alone. But they would all have to come out there sometime, those others. Little, and left behind him, they all were. There had been father and mother and sweetheart. What did they all matter? This was the open land.

He sat up. Something scuffled. It was a little, brown squirrel running in lovely, undulating bounds over the floor, its red tail completing the undulation of its body—and then, as it sat up, furling and unfurling. He watched it, pleased. It ran on again, friskily, enjoying itself. It flew wildly at another squirrel, and they were chasing each other, and making little scolding, chattering noises. The soldier wanted to speak to them. But only a hoarse sound came out of his throat. The squirrels burst away—they flew up the trees. And then he saw the one peeping round at him, half-way up a tree-trunk. A start of fear went through him, though, in so far as he was conscious, he was amused. It still stayed, its little, keen face staring at him halfway up the tree-trunk, its little ears pricked up, its clawey little hands clinging to the bark, its white breast reared. He started from it in panic.

Struggling to his feet, he lurched away. He went on walking, walking, looking for something—for a drink. His brain felt hot and inflamed for want of water. He stumbled on. Then he did not know anything. He went unconscious as he walked. Yet he stumbled on, his mouth open.

When, to his dumb wonder, he opened his eyes on the world again, he no longer tried to remember what it was. There was thick, golden light behind golden-green glitterings, and tall, grey-purple shafts, and darknesses further off, surrounding him, growing deeper. He was conscious of a sense of arrival. He was amid the reality, on the real, dark bottom. But there was the thirst burning in his brain. He felt lighter, not so heavy. He supposed it was newness. The air was muttering with thunder. He thought he was walking wonderfully swiftly and was coming straight to relief—or was it to water?

Suddenly he stood still with fear. There was a tremendous flare of gold, immense—just a few dark trunks like bars between him and it. All the young level wheat was burnished gold glaring on its silky green. A woman, full-skirted, a black cloth on her head for head-dress, was passing like a block of shadow through the glistening, green corn, into the full glare. There was a farm, too, pale blue in shadow, and the timber black. And there was a church spire, nearly fused away in the gold. The woman moved on, away from him. He had no language with which to speak to her. She was the bright, solid unreality. She would make a noise of words that would confuse him, and her eyes would look at him without seeing him. She was crossing there to the other side. He stood against a tree.

When at last he turned, looking down the long, bare grove whose flat bed was already filling dark, he saw the mountains in a wonder-light, not far away, and radiant. Behind the soft, grey ridge of the nearest range the further mountains stood golden and pale grey, the snow all radiant like pure, soft gold. So still, gleaming in the sky, fashioned pure out of the ore of the sky, they shone in their silence. He stood and looked at them, his face illuminated. And like the golden, lustrous gleaming of the snow he felt his own thirst bright in him. He stood

and gazed, leaning against a tree. And then everything slid away into space.

During the night the lightning fluttered perpetually, making the whole sky white. He must have walked again. The world hung livid round him for moments, fields a level sheen of grey-green light, trees in dark bulk, and the range of clouds black across a white sky. Then the darkness fell like a shutter, and the night was whole. A faint flutter of a half-revealed world, that could not quite leap out of the darkness!—Then there again stood a sweep of pallor for the land, dark shapes looming, a range of clouds hanging overhead. The world was a ghostly shadow, thrown for a moment upon the pure darkness, which returned ever whole and complete.

And the mere delirium of sickness and fever went on inside him—his brain opening and shutting like the night—then sometimes convulsions of terror from something with great eyes that stared round a tree—then the long agony of the march, and the sun decomposing his blood—then the pang of hate for the Captain, followed by a pang of tenderness and ease. But everything was distorted, born of an ache and resolving into an ache.

In the morning he came definitely awake. Then his brain flamed with the sole horror of thirstiness! The sun was on his face, the dew was steaming from his wet clothes. Like one possessed, he got up. There, straight in front of him, blue and cool and tender, the mountains ranged across the pale edge of the morning sky. He wanted them—he wanted them alone—he wanted to leave himself and be identified with them. They did not move, they were still soft, with white, gentle markings of snow. He stood still, mad with suffering, his hands crisping and clutching. Then he was twisting in a paroxysm on the grass.

He lay still, in a kind of dream of anguish. His thirst seemed to have separated itself from him, and to stand apart, a single demand. Then the pain he felt was another single self. Then there was the clog of his body, another separate thing. He was divided among all kinds of separate beings. There was some strange, agonized connection between them, but they were drawing further apart. Then they would all split. The sun, drilling down on him, was drilling through the bond. Then they would all fall, fall through the everlasting lapse of space. Then again, his consciousness reasserted itself. He roused on to his elbow and stared at the gleaming mountains. There they ranked, all still and wonderful between earth and heaven. He stared till his eyes went black, and the mountains, as they stood in their beauty, so clean and cool, seemed to have it, that which was lost in him.

4

When the soldiers found him, three hours later, he was lying with his face over his arm, his black hair giving off heat under the sun. But he was still alive. Seeing the open, black mouth the young soldiers dropped him in horror.

He died in the hospital at night, without having seen again.

The doctors saw the bruises on his legs, behind, and were silent.

The bodies of the two men lay together, side by side, in the mortuary, the one white and slender, but laid rigidly at rest, the other looking as if every moment it must rouse into life again, so young and unused, from a slumber.

—1914

Odour of Chrysanthemums

1

The small locomotive engine, Number 4, came clanking, stumbling down from Selston with seven full wagons. It appeared round the corner with loud threats of speed, but the colt that it startled from among the gorse,[1] which still flickered indistinctly in the raw afternoon, out-distanced it at a canter. A woman, walking up the railway line to Underwood, drew back into the hedge, held her basket aside, and watched the footplate of the engine advancing. The trucks thumped heavily past, one by one, with slow inevitable movement, as she stood insignificantly trapped between the jolting black wagons and the hedge; then they curved away towards the coppice[2] where the withered oak leaves dropped noiselessly, while the birds, pulling at the scarlet hips beside the track, made off into the dusk that

had already crept into the spinney.[3] In the open, the smoke from the engine sank and cleaved to the rough grass. The fields were dreary and forsaken, and in the marshy strip that led to the whimsey,[4] a reedy pit-pond, the fowls had already abandoned their run among the alders, to roost in the tarred fowl-house. The pit-bank loomed up beyond the pond, flames like red sores licking its ashy sides, in the afternoon's stagnant light. Just beyond rose the tapering chimneys and the clumsy black headstocks of Brinsley Colliery.[5] The two wheels were spinning fast up against the sky, and the winding engine rapped out its little spasms. The miners were being turned up.

The engine whistled as it came into the wide bay of railway lines beside the colliery, where rows of trucks stood in harbour.

Miners, single, trailing and in groups, passed like shadows diverging home. At the edge of the ribbed level of sidings squat a low cottage, three steps down from the cinder track. A large bony vine clutched at the house, as if to claw down the tiled roof. Round the bricked yard grew a few wintry primroses. Beyond, the long garden sloped down to a bush-covered brook course. There were some twiggy apple trees, winter-crack trees, and ragged cabbages. Beside the path hung dishevelled pink chrysanthemums, like pink cloths hung on bushes. A woman came stooping out of the felt-covered fowl-house, halfway down the garden. She closed and padlocked the door, then drew herself erect, having brushed some bits from her white apron.

She was a tall woman of imperious mien,[6] handsome, with definite black eyebrows. Her smooth black hair was parted exactly. For a few moments she stood steadily watching the miners as they passed along the railway: then she turned towards the brook course. Her face was calm and set, her mouth was closed with disillusionment. After a moment she called:

"John!" There was no answer. She waited, and then said distinctly:

"Where are you?"

---

[1] *gorse*   Prickly shrub.

[2] *coppice*   Thicket of small trees.

[3] *spinney*   Small copse.

[4] *whimsey*   Machine used to raise water or ore from a mine.

[5] *headstocks*   Supports of revolving machine parts; *Colliery*   Coal mine.

[6] *mien*   Bearing.

"Here!" replied a child's sulky voice from among the bushes. The woman looked piercingly through the dusk.

"Are you at that brook?" she asked sternly.

For answer the child showed himself before the raspberry-canes that rose like whips. He was a small, sturdy boy of five. He stood quite still, defiantly.

"Oh!" said the mother, conciliated. "I thought you were down at that wet brook—and you remember what I told you—"

The boy did not move or answer.

"Come, come on in," she said more gently, "it's getting dark. There's your grandfather's engine coming down the line!"

The lad advanced slowly, with resentful, taciturn movement. He was dressed in trousers and waistcoat of cloth that was too thick and hard for the size of the garments. They were evidently cut down from a man's clothes.

As they went slowly towards the house he tore at the ragged wisps of chrysanthemums and dropped the petals in handfuls among the path.

"Don't do that—it does look nasty," said his mother. He refrained, and she, suddenly pitiful, broke off a twig with three or four wan flowers and held them against her face. When mother and son reached the yard her hand hesitated, and instead of laying the flower aside, she pushed it in her apron-band. The mother and son stood at the foot of the three steps looking across the bay of lines at the passing home of the miners. The trundle of the small train was imminent. Suddenly the engine loomed past the house and came to a stop opposite the gate.

The engine-driver, a short man with round grey beard, leaned out of the cab high above the woman.

"Have you got a cup of tea?" he said in a cheery, hearty fashion.

It was her father. She went in, saying she would mash.[1] Directly, she returned.

"I didn't come to see you on Sunday," began the little grey-bearded man.

"I didn't expect you," said his daughter.

The engine-driver winced; then, reassuming his cheery, airy manner, he said:

"Oh, have you heard then? Well, and what do you think—?"

"I think it is soon enough," she replied.

At her brief censure the little man made an impatient gesture, and said coaxingly, yet with dangerous coldness:

"Well, what's a man to do? It's no sort of life for a man of my years, to sit at my own hearth like a stranger. And if I'm going to marry again it may as well be soon as late—what does it matter to anybody?"

The woman did not reply, but turned and went into the house. The man in the engine-cab stood assertive, till she returned with a cup of tea and a piece of bread and butter on a plate. She went up the steps and stood near the footplate of the hissing engine.

"You needn't 'a' brought me bread an' butter," said her father. "But a cup of tea"—he sipped appreciatively—"it's very nice." He sipped for a moment or two, then: "I hear as Walter's got another bout[2] on," he said.

"When hasn't he?" said the woman bitterly.

"I heerd tell of him in the 'Lord Nelson'[3] braggin' as he was going to spend that b—— afore he went: half a sovereign[4] that was."

"When?" asked the woman.

"A' Sat'day night—I know that's true."

"Very likely," she laughed bitterly. "He gives me twenty-three shillings."

"Aye, it's a nice thing, when a man can do nothing with his money but make a beast of himself!" said the grey-whiskered man. The woman turned her head away. Her father swallowed the last of his tea and handed her the cup.

"Aye," he sighed, wiping his mouth. "It's a settler,[5] it is—"

He put his hand on the lever. The little engine strained and groaned, and the train rumbled towards the crossing. The woman again looked across the metals. Darkness was settling over the spaces of the railway and trucks: the miners, in grey sombre groups, were still passing home. The winding engine pulsed hurriedly, with brief pauses. Elizabeth Bates looked at the dreary flow of men, then she went indoors. Her husband did not come.

The kitchen was small and full of firelight; red coals piled glowing up the chimney mouth. All the life of the

---

1   *mash*   Brew tea.

2   *bout*   I.e., of drinking.

3   *'Lord Nelson'*   I.e., the pub.

4   *sovereign*   Coin worth twenty shillings.

5   *settler*   Finishing or deciding blow.

room seemed in the white, warm hearth and the steel fender reflecting the red fire. The cloth was laid for tea; cups glinted in the shadows. At the back, where the lowest stairs protruded into the room, the boy sat struggling with a knife and a piece of white wood. He was almost hidden in the shadow. It was half-past four. They had but to await the father's coming to begin tea. As the mother watched her son's sullen little struggle with the wood, she saw herself in his silence and pertinacity; she saw the father in her child's indifference to all but himself. She seemed to be occupied by her husband. He had probably gone past his home, slunk past his own door, to drink before he came in, while his dinner spoiled and wasted in waiting. She glanced at the clock, then took the potatoes to strain them in the yard. The garden and fields beyond the brook were closed in uncertain darkness. When she rose with the saucepan, leaving the drain steaming into the night behind her, she saw the yellow lamps were lit along the high road that went up the hill away beyond the space of the railway lines and the field.

Then again she watched the men trooping home, fewer now and fewer.

Indoors the fire was sinking and the room was dark red. The woman put her saucepan on the hob, and set a batter-pudding near the mouth of the oven. Then she stood unmoving. Directly, gratefully, came quick young steps to the door. Someone hung on the latch a moment, then a little girl entered and began pulling off her outdoor things, dragging a mass of curls, just ripening from gold to brown, over her eyes with her hat.

Her mother chid her for coming late from school, and said she would have to keep her at home the dark winter days.

"Why, mother, it's hardly a bit dark yet. The lamp's not lighted, and my father's not home."

"No, he isn't. But it's a quarter to five! Did you see anything of him?"

The child became serious. She looked at her mother with large, wistful blue eyes.

"No, mother, I've never seen him. Why? Has he come up an' gone past, to Old Brinsley? He hasn't, mother, 'cos I never saw him."

"He'd watch that," said the mother bitterly, "he'd take care as you didn't see him. But you may depend upon it, he's seated in the 'Prince o' Wales.' He would-

n't be this late."

The girl looked at her mother piteously.

"Let's have our teas, mother, should we?" said she.

The mother called John to table. She opened the door once more and looked out across the darkness of the lines. All was deserted: she could not hear the winding-engines.

"Perhaps," she said to herself, "he's stopped to get some ripping[1] done."

They sat down to tea. John, at the end of the table near the door, was almost lost in the darkness. Their faces were hidden from each other. The girl crouched against the fender slowly moving a thick piece of bread before the fire. The lad, his face a dusky mark on the shadow, sat watching her who was transfigured in the red glow.

"I do think it's beautiful to look in the fire," said the child.

"Do you?" said her mother. "Why?"

"It's so red, and full of little caves—and it feels so nice, and you can fair smell it."

"It'll want mending directly," replied her mother, "and then if your father comes he'll carry on and say there never is a fire when a man comes home sweating from the pit. A public-house is always warm enough."

There was silence till the boy said complainingly: "Make haste, our Annie."

"Well, I am doing! I can't make the fire do it no faster, can I?"

"She keeps wafflin' it about so's to make 'er slow," grumbled the boy.

"Don't have such an evil imagination, child," replied the mother.

Soon the room was busy in the darkness with the crisp sound of crunching. The mother ate very little. She drank her tea determinedly, and sat thinking. When she rose her anger was evident in the stern unbending of her head. She looked at the pudding in the fender, and broke out:

"It is a scandalous thing as a man can't even come home to his dinner! If it's crozzled[2] up to a cinder I don't see why I should care. Past his very door he goes to get to a public-house, and here I sit with his dinner

---

[1] *ripping*   Cutting away coal.
[2] *crozzled*   Curled; burnt.

waiting for him—"

She went out. As she dropped piece after piece of coal on the red fire, the shadows fell on the walls, till the room was almost in total darkness.

"I canna see," grumbled the invisible John. In spite of herself, the mother laughed.

"You know the way to your mouth," she said. She set the dust-pan outside the door. When she came again like a shadow on the hearth, the lad repeated, complaining sulkily:

"I canna see."

"Good gracious!" cried the mother irritably, "you're as bad as your father if it's a bit dusk!"

Nevertheless, she took a paper spill[1] from a sheaf on the mantelpiece and proceeded to light the lamp that hung from the ceiling in the middle of the room. As she reached up, her figure displayed itself just rounding with maternity.

"Oh, mother—!" exclaimed the girl.

"What?" said the woman, suspended in the act of putting the lamp-glass over the flame. The copper reflector shone handsomely on her, as she stood with uplifted arm, turning to face her daughter.

"You've got a flower in your apron!" said the child, in a little rapture at this unusual event.

"Goodness me!" exclaimed the woman, relieved. "One would think the house was afire." She replaced the glass and waited a moment before turning up the wick. A pale shadow was seen floating vaguely on the floor.

"Let me smell!" said the child, still rapturously, coming forward and putting her face to her mother's waist.

"Go along, silly!" said the mother, turning up the lamp. The light revealed their suspense so that the woman felt it almost unbearable. Annie was still bending at her waist. Irritably, the mother took the flowers out from her apron-band.

"Oh, mother—don't take them out!" Annie cried, catching her hand and trying to replace the sprig.

"Such nonsense!" said the mother, turning away. The child put the pale chrysanthemums to her lips, murmuring:

"Don't they smell beautiful!"

Her mother gave a short laugh.

"No," she said, "not to me. It was chrysanthemums when I married him, and chrysanthemums when you were born, and the first time they ever brought him home drunk, he'd got brown chrysanthemums in his button-hole."

She looked at the children. Their eyes and their parted lips were wondering. The mother sat rocking in silence for some time. Then she looked at the clock.

"Twenty minutes to six!" In a tone of fine bitter carelessness she continued: "Eh, he'll not come now till they bring him. There he'll stick! But he needn't come rolling in here in his pit-dirt, for I won't wash him. He can lie on the floor—Eh, what a fool I've been, what a fool! And this is what I came here for, to this dirty hole, rats and all, for him to slink past his very door. Twice last week—he's begun now—"

She silenced herself, and rose to clear the table. While for an hour or more the children played, subduedly intent, fertile of imagination, united in fear of the mother's wrath, and in dread of their father's home-coming, Mrs. Bates sat in her rocking-chair making a "singlet"[2] of thick cream-coloured flannel, which gave a dull wounded sound as she tore off the grey edge. She worked at her sewing with energy, listening to the children, and her anger wearied itself, lay down to rest, opening its eyes from time to time and steadily watching, its ears raised to listen. Sometimes even her anger quailed and shrank, and the mother suspended her sewing, tracing the footsteps that thudded along the sleepers outside; she would lift her head sharply to bid the children "hush," but she recovered herself in time, and the footsteps went past the gate, and the children were not flung out of their play-world.

But at last Annie sighed, and gave in. She glanced at her wagon of slippers, and loathed the game. She turned plaintively to her mother.

"Mother!"—but she was inarticulate.

John crept out like a frog from under the sofa. His mother glanced up.

"Yes," she said, "just look at those shirt-sleeves!"

The boy held them out to survey them, saying nothing. Then somebody called in a hoarse voice away down the line, and suspense bristled in the room, till two people had gone by outside, talking.

"It is time for bed," said the mother.

"My father hasn't come," wailed Annie plaintively.

[1] *paper spill* Folded or twisted paper used for lighting candle, fire, lamp, etc.

[2] *singlet* Undershirt.

But her mother was primed with courage.

"Never mind. They'll bring him when he does come—like a log." She meant there would be no scene. "And he may sleep on the floor till he wakes himself. I know he'll not go to work tomorrow after this!"

The children had their hands and faces wiped with a flannel. They were very quiet. When they had put on their nightdresses, they said their prayers, the boy mumbling. The mother looked down at them, at the brown silken bush of intertwining curls in the nape of the girl's neck, at the little black head of the lad, and her heart burst with anger at their father, who caused all three such distress. The children hid their faces in her skirts for comfort.

When Mrs. Bates came down, the room was strangely empty, with a tension of expectancy. She took up her sewing and stitched for some time without raising her head. Meantime her anger was tinged with fear.

2

The clock struck eight and she rose suddenly, dropping her sewing on her chair. She went to the stair-foot door, opened it, listening. Then she went out, locking the door behind her.

Something scuffled in the yard, and she started, though she knew it was only the rats with which the place was over-run. The night was very dark. In the great bay of railway lines, bulked with trucks, there was no trace of light, only away back she could see a few yellow lamps at the pit-top, and the red smear of the burning pit-bank on the night. She hurried along the edge of the track, then, crossing the converging lines, came to the stile by the white gates, whence she emerged on the road. Then the fear which had led her shrank. People were walking up to New Brinsley; she saw the lights in the houses; twenty yards farther on were the broad windows of the "Prince of Wales," very warm and bright, and the loud voices of men could be heard distinctly. What a fool she had been to imagine that anything had happened to him! He was merely drinking over there at the "Prince of Wales." She faltered. She had never yet been to fetch him, and she never would go. So she continued her walk towards the long straggling line of houses, standing back on the highway. She entered a passage between the dwellings.

"Mr. Rigley?—Yes! Did you want him? No, he's not in at this minute."

The raw-boned woman leaned forward from her dark scullery and peered at the other, upon whom fell a dim light through the blind of the kitchen window.

"Is it Mrs. Bates?" she asked in a tone tinged with respect.

"Yes. I wondered if your Master was at home. Mine hasn't come yet."

"'Asn't 'e! Oh, Jack's been 'ome an' 'ad 'is dinner an' gone out. 'E's just gone for 'alf an hour afore bed-time. Did you call at the 'Prince of Wales'?"

"No—"

"No, you didn't like—! It's not very nice." The other woman was indulgent. There was an awkward pause. "Jack never said nothink about—about your Master," she said.

"No!—I expect he's stuck in there!"

Elizabeth Bates said this bitterly, and with recklessness. She knew that the woman across the yard was standing at her door listening, but she did not care. As she turned:

"Stop a minute! I'll just go an' ask Jack if 'e knows anythink," said Mrs. Rigley.

"Oh no—I wouldn't like to put——!"

"Yes, I will, if you'll just step inside an' see as th' childer doesn't come downstairs and set theirselves afire."

Elizabeth Bates, murmuring a remonstrance, stepped inside. The other woman apologised for the state of the room.

The kitchen needed apology. There were little frocks and trousers and childish undergarments on the squab[1] and on the floor, and a litter of playthings everywhere. On the black American cloth[2] of the table were pieces of bread and cake, crusts, slops, and a teapot with cold tea.

"Eh, ours is just as bad," said Elizabeth Bates, looking at the woman, not at the house. Mrs. Rigley put a shawl over her head and hurried out, saying:

"I shanna be a minute."

The other sat, noting with faint disapproval the general untidiness of the room. Then she fell to counting the shoes of various sizes scattered over the floor. There were twelve. She sighed and said to herself: "No wonder!"—glancing at the litter. There came the scratching of two pairs of feet on the yard, and the Rigleys entered. Elizabeth Bates rose. Rigley was a big

---

[1] *squab* Sofa.

[2] *American cloth* Flexible enameled cloth used for covering furniture.

man, with very large bones. His head looked particularly bony. Across his temple was a blue scar, caused by a wound got in the pit, a wound in which the coal-dust remained blue like tattooing.

"'Asna 'e come whoam yit?" asked the man, without any form of greeting, but with deference and sympathy. "I couldna say wheer he is—'e's non ower theer!"—he jerked his head to signify the "Prince of Wales."

"'E's 'appen gone up to th' 'Yew,'" said Mrs. Rigley. There was another pause. Rigley had evidently something to get off his mind:

"Ah left 'im finishin' a stint," he began. "Loose-all[1] 'ad bin gone about ten minutes when we com'n away, an' I shouted: 'Are ter comin', Walt?' an' 'e said: 'Go on, Ah shanna be but a'ef a minnit,' so we com'n ter th' bottom, me an' Bowers, thinkin' as 'e wor just behint, an' 'ud come up i' th' next bantle[2]—"

He stood perplexed, as if answering a charge of deserting his mate. Elizabeth Bates, now again certain of disaster, hastened to reassure him:

"I expect 'e's gone up to th' 'Yew Tree,' as you say. It's not the first time. I've fretted myself into a fever before now. He'll come home when they carry him."

"Ay, isn't it too bad!" deplored the other woman.

"I'll just step up to Dick's an' see if 'e is theer," offered the man, afraid of appearing alarmed, afraid of taking liberties.

"Oh, I wouldn't think of bothering you that far," said Elizabeth Bates, with emphasis, but he knew she was glad of his offer.

As they stumbled up the entry, Elizabeth Bates heard Rigley's wife run across the yard and open her neighbour's door. At this, suddenly all the blood in her body seemed to switch away from her heart.

"Mind!" warned Rigley. "Ah've said many a time as Ah'd fill up them ruts in this entry, sumb'dy 'll be breakin' their legs yit."

She recovered herself and walked quickly along with the miner.

"I don't like leaving the children in bed, and nobody in the house," she said.

"No, you dunna!" he replied courteously. They were soon at the gate of the cottage.

"Well, I shanna be many minnits. Dunna you be

frettin' now, 'e'll be all right," said the butty.[3]

"Thank you very much, Mr. Rigley," she replied.

"You're welcome!" he stammered, moving away. "I shanna be many minnits."

The house was quiet. Elizabeth Bates took off her hat and shawl, and rolled back the rug. When she had finished, she sat down. It was a few minutes past nine. She was startled by the rapid chuff of the winding-engine at the pit, and the sharp whirr of the brakes on the rope as it descended. Again she felt the painful sweep of her blood, and she put her hand to her side, saying aloud: "Good gracious!—it's only the nine o'clock deputy going down," rebuking herself.

She sat still, listening. Half an hour of this, and she was wearied out.

"What am I working myself up like this for?" she said pitiably to herself, "I s'll only be doing myself some damage."

She took out her sewing again.

At a quarter to ten there were footsteps. One person! She watched for the door to open. It was an elderly woman, in a black bonnet and a black woollen shawl—his mother. She was about sixty years old, pale, with blue eyes, and her face all wrinkled and lamentable. She shut the door and turned to her daughter-in-law peevishly.

"Eh, Lizzie, whatever shall we do, whatever shall we do!" she cried.

Elizabeth drew back a little, sharply.

"What is it, mother?" she said.

The elder woman seated herself on the sofa.

"I don't know, child, I can't tell you!"—she shook her head slowly. Elizabeth sat watching her, anxious and vexed.

"I don't know," replied the grandmother, sighing very deeply. "There's no end to my troubles, there isn't. The things I've gone through, I'm sure it's enough—!" She wept without wiping her eyes, the tears running.

"But, mother," interrupted Elizabeth, "what do you mean? What is it?"

The grandmother slowly wiped her eyes. The fountains of her tears were stopped by Elizabeth's directness. She wiped her eyes slowly.

"Poor child! Eh, you poor thing!" she moaned. "I don't know what we're going to do, I don't—and you as you are—it's a thing, it is indeed!"

---

[1] *Loose-all* Signal to finish working in the pits.

[2] *bantle* Group.

[3] *butty* Buddy; workmate.

Elizabeth waited.

"Is he dead?" she asked, and at the words her heart swung violently, though she felt a slight flush of shame at the ultimate extravagance of the question. Her words sufficiently frightened the old lady, almost brought her to herself.

"Don't say so, Elizabeth! We'll hope it's not as bad as that; no, may the Lord spare us that, Elizabeth. Jack Rigley came just as I was sittin' down to a glass afore going to bed, an' 'e said: ''Appen you'll go down th' line, Mrs. Bates. Walt's had an accident. 'Appen you'll go an' sit wi' 'er till we can get him home.' I hadn't time to ask him a word afore he was gone. An' I put my bonnet on an' come straight down, Lizzie. I thought to myself: 'Eh, that poor blessed child, if anybody should come an' tell her of a sudden, there's no knowin' what'll 'appen to 'er.' You mustn't let it upset you, Lizzie—or you know what to expect. How long is it, six months—or is it five, Lizzie? Ay!"—the old woman shook her head—"time slips on, it slips on! Ay!"

Elizabeth's thoughts were busy elsewhere. If he was killed—would she be able to manage on the little pension and what she could earn?—she counted up rapidly. If he was hurt—they wouldn't take him to the hospital—how tiresome he would be to nurse!—but perhaps she'd be able to get him away from the drink and his hateful ways. She would—while he was ill. The tears offered to come to her eyes at the picture. But what sentimental luxury was this she was beginning? She turned to consider the children. At any rate she was absolutely necessary for them. They were her business.

"Ay!" repeated the old woman, "it seems but a week or two since he brought me his first wages. Ay—he was a good lad, Elizabeth, he was, in his way. I don't know why he got to be such a trouble, I don't. He was a happy lad at home, only full of spirits. But there's no mistake he's been a handful of trouble, he has! I hope the Lord'll spare him to mend his ways. I hope so, I hope so. You've had a sight o' trouble with him, Elizabeth, you have indeed. But he was a jolly enough lad wi' me, he was, I can assure you. I don't know how it is. ..."

The old woman continued to muse aloud, a monotonous irritating sound, while Elizabeth thought concentratedly, startled once, when she heard the winding-engine chuff quickly, and the brakes skirr with a shriek. Then she heard the engine more slowly, and the brakes made no sound. The old woman did not notice. Elizabeth waited in suspense. The mother-in-law talked, with lapses into silence.

"But he wasn't your son, Lizzie, an' it makes a difference. Whatever he was, I remember him when he was little, an' I learned to understand him and to make allowances. You've got to make allowances for them—"

It was half-past ten, and the old woman was saying: "But it's trouble from beginning to end; you're never too old for trouble, never too old for that—" when the gate banged back, and there were heavy feet on the steps.

"I'll go, Lizzie, let me go," cried the old woman, rising. But Elizabeth was at the door. It was a man in pit-clothes.

"They're bringin' 'im, Missis," he said. Elizabeth's heart halted a moment. Then it surged on again, almost suffocating her.

"Is he—is it bad?" she asked.

The man turned away, looking at the darkness:

"The doctor says 'e'd been dead hours. 'E saw 'im i' th' lamp-cabin."

The old woman, who stood just behind Elizabeth, dropped into a chair, and folded her hands, crying: "Oh, my boy, my boy!"

"Hush!" said Elizabeth, with a sharp twitch of a frown. "Be still, mother, don't waken th' children: I wouldn't have them down for anything!"

The old woman moaned softly, rocking herself. The man was drawing away. Elizabeth took a step forward.

"How was it?" she asked.

"Well, I couldn't say for sure," the man replied, very ill at ease. "'E wor finishin' a stint an' th' butties 'ad gone, an' a lot o' stuff come down atop 'n 'im."

"And crushed him?" cried the widow, with a shudder.

"No," said the man, "it fell at th' back of 'im. 'E wor under th' face, an' it niver touched 'im. It shut 'im in. It seems 'e wor smothered."

Elizabeth shrank back. She heard the old woman behind her cry:

"What?—what did 'e say it was?"

The man replied, more loudly: "'E wor smothered!"

Then the old woman wailed aloud, and this relieved Elizabeth.

"Oh, mother," she said, putting her hand on the old woman, "don't waken th' children, don't waken th' children."

She wept a little, unknowing, while the old mother rocked herself and moaned. Elizabeth remembered that they were bringing him home, and she must be ready. "They'll lay him in the parlour," she said to herself, standing a moment pale and perplexed.

Then she lighted a candle and went into the tiny room. The air was cold and damp, but she could not make a fire, there was no fireplace. She set down the candle and looked round. The candlelight glittered on the lustre-glasses, on the two vases that held some of the pink chrysanthemums, and on the dark mahogany. There was a cold, deathly smell of chrysanthemums in the room. Elizabeth stood looking at the flowers. She turned away, and calculated whether there would be room to lay him on the floor, between the couch and the chiffonier. She pushed the chairs aside. There would be room to lay him down and to step round him. Then she fetched the old red tablecloth, and another old cloth, spreading them down to save her bit of carpet. She shivered on leaving the parlour; so, from the dresser drawer she took a clean shirt and put it at the fire to air. All the time her mother-in-law was rocking herself in the chair and moaning.

"You'll have to move from there, mother," said Elizabeth. "They'll be bringing him in. Come in the rocker."

The old mother rose mechanically, and seated herself by the fire, continuing to lament. Elizabeth went into the pantry for another candle, and there, in the little pent-house[1] under the naked tiles, she heard them coming. She stood still in the pantry doorway, listening. She heard them pass the end of the house, and come awkwardly down the three steps, a jumble of shuffling footsteps and muttering voices. The old woman was silent. The men were in the yard.

Then Elizabeth heard Matthews, the manager of the pit, say: "You go in first, Jim. Mind!"

The door came open, and the two women saw a collier[2] backing into the room, holding one end of a stretcher, on which they could see the nailed pit-boots of the dead man. The two carriers halted, the man at the head stooping to the lintel[3] of the door.

"Wheer will you have him?" asked the manager, a short, white-bearded man.

Elizabeth roused herself and came from the pantry carrying the unlighted candle.

"In the parlour," she said.

"In there, Jim!" pointed the manager, and the carriers backed round into the tiny room. The coat with which they had covered the body fell off as they awkwardly turned through the two doorways, and the women saw their man, naked to the waist, lying stripped for work. The old woman began to moan in a low voice of horror.

"Lay th' stretcher at th' side," snapped the manager, "an' put 'im on th' cloths. Mind now, mind! Look you now—!"

One of the men had knocked off a vase of chrysanthemums. He stared awkwardly, then they set down the stretcher. Elizabeth did not look at her husband. As soon as she could get in the room, she went and picked up the broken vase and the flowers.

"Wait a minute!" she said.

The three men waited in silence while she mopped up the water with a duster.

"Eh, what a job, what a job, to be sure!" the manager was saying, rubbing his brow with trouble and perplexity. "Never knew such a thing in my life, never! He'd no business to ha' been left. I never knew such a thing in my life! Fell over him clean as a whistle, an' shut him in. Not four foot of space, there wasn't—yet it scarce bruised him."

He looked down at the dead man, lying prone, half naked, all grimed with coal-dust.

"'Sphyxiated,' the doctor said. It *is* the most terrible job I've ever known. Seems as if it was done o' purpose. Clean over him, an' shut 'im in, like a mouse-trap"—he made a sharp, descending gesture with his hand.

The colliers standing by jerked aside their heads in hopeless comment.

The horror of the thing bristled upon them all.

Then they heard the girl's voice upstairs calling shrilly:

"Mother, mother—who is it? Mother, who is it?"

Elizabeth hurried to the foot of the stairs and opened the door:

---

[1] *pent-house* Subsidiary structure with a sloping roof, attached to the wall of the main building.

[2] *collier* Coal miner.

[3] *lintel* Horizontal support beam.

"Go to sleep!" she commanded sharply. "What are you shouting about? Go to sleep at once—there's nothing—"

Then she began to mount the stairs. They could hear her on the boards, and on the plaster floor of the little bedroom. They could hear her distinctly:

"What's the matter now?—what's the matter with you, silly thing?"—her voice was much agitated, with an unreal gentleness.

"I thought it was some men come," said the plaintive voice of the child. "Has he come?"

"Yes, they've brought him. There's nothing to make a fuss about. Go to sleep now, like a good child."

They could hear her voice in the bedroom, they waited whilst she covered the children under the bed-clothes.

"Is he drunk?" asked the girl, timidly, faintly.

"No! No—he's not! He—he's asleep."

"Is he asleep downstairs?"

"Yes—and don't make a noise."

There was silence for a moment, then the men heard the frightened child again:

"What's that noise?"

"It's nothing, I tell you, what are you bothering for?"

The noise was the grandmother moaning. She was oblivious of everything, sitting on her chair rocking and moaning. The manager put his hand on her arm and bade her "Sh—sh!!"

The old woman opened her eyes and looked at him. She was shocked by this interruption, and seemed to wonder.

"What time is it?" the plaintive thin voice of the child, sinking back unhappily into sleep, asked this last question.

"Ten o'clock," answered the mother more softly. Then she must have bent down and kissed the children.

Matthews beckoned to the men to come away. They put on their caps and took up the stretcher. Stepping over the body, they tiptoed out of the house. None of them spoke till they were far from the wakeful children.

When Elizabeth came down she found her mother alone on the parlour floor, leaning over the dead man, the tears dropping on him.

"We must lay him out," the wife said. She put on the kettle, then returning knelt at the feet, and began to unfasten the knotted leather laces. The room was clammy and dim with only one candle, so that she had to bend her face almost to the floor. At last she got off the heavy boots and put them away.

"You must help me now," she whispered to the old woman. Together they stripped the man.

When they arose, saw him lying in the naïve dignity of death, the woman stood arrested in fear and respect. For a few moments they remained still, looking down, the old mother whimpering. Elizabeth felt countermanded. She saw him, how utterly inviolable he lay in himself. She had nothing to do with him. She could not accept it. Stooping, she laid her hand on him, in claim. He was still warm, for the mine was hot where he had died. His mother had his face between her hands, and was murmuring incoherently. The old tears fell in succession as drops from wet leaves; the mother was not weeping, merely her tears flowed. Elizabeth embraced the body of her husband, with cheek and lips. She seemed to be listening, inquiring, trying to get some connection. But she could not. She was driven away. He was impregnable.

She rose, went into the kitchen, where she poured warm water into a bowl, brought soap and flannel and a soft towel.

"I must wash him," she said.

Then the old mother rose stiffly, and watched Elizabeth as she carefully washed his face, carefully brushing the big blond moustache from his mouth with the flannel. She was afraid with a bottomless fear, so she ministered to him. The old woman, jealous, said:

"Let me wipe him!"—and she kneeled on the other side drying slowly as Elizabeth washed, her big black bonnet sometimes brushing the dark head of her daughter-in-law. They worked thus in silence for a long time. They never forgot it was death, and the touch of the man's dead body gave them strange emotions, different in each of the women; a great dread possessed them both, the mother felt the lie was given to her womb, she was denied; the wife felt the utter isolation of the human soul, the child within her was a weight apart from her.

At last it was finished. He was a man of handsome body, and his face showed no traces of drink. He was blond, full-fleshed, with fine limbs. But he was dead.

"Bless him," whispered his mother, looking always at his face, and speaking out of sheer terror. "Dear lad—bless him!" She spoke in a faint, sibilant ecstasy of fear and mother love.

Elizabeth sank down again to the floor, and put her face against his neck, and trembled and shuddered. But she had to draw away again. He was dead, and her living flesh had no place against his. A great dread and weariness held her: she was so unavailing. Her life was gone like this.

"White as milk he is, clear as a twelve-month baby, bless him, the darling!" the old mother murmured to herself. "Not a mark on him, clear and clean and white, beautiful as ever a child was made," she murmured with pride. Elizabeth kept her face hidden.

"He went peaceful, Lizzie—peaceful as sleep. Isn't he beautiful, the lamb? Ay—he must ha' made his peace, Lizzie. 'Appen he made it all right, Lizzie, shut in there. He'd have time. He wouldn't look like this if he hadn't made his peace. The lamb, the dear lamb. Eh, but he had a hearty laugh. I loved to hear it. He had the heartiest laugh, Lizzie, as a lad—"

Elizabeth looked up. The man's mouth was fallen back, slightly open under the cover of the moustache. The eyes, half shut, did not show glazed in the obscurity. Life with its smoky burning gone from him, had left him apart and utterly alien to her. And she knew what a stranger he was to her. In her womb was ice of fear, because of this separate stranger with whom she had been living as one flesh. Was this what it all meant—utter, intact separateness, obscured by heat of living? In dread she turned her face away. The fact was too deadly. There had been nothing between them, and yet they had come together, exchanging their nakedness repeatedly. Each time he had taken her, they had been two isolated beings, far apart as now. He was no more responsible than she. The child was like ice in her womb. For as she looked at the dead man, her mind, cold and detached, said clearly: "Who am I? What have I been doing? I have been fighting a husband who did not exist. *He* existed all the time. What wrong have I done? What was that I have been living with? There lies the reality, this man." And her soul died in her for fear: she knew she had never seen him, he had never seen her, they had met in the dark and had fought in the dark, not knowing whom they met nor whom they fought. And now she saw, and turned silent in seeing. For she had been wrong. She had said he was something he was

not; she had felt familiar with him. Whereas he was apart all the while, living as she never lived, feeling as she never felt.

In fear and shame she looked at his naked body, that she had known falsely. And he was the father of her children. Her soul was torn from her body and stood apart. She looked at his naked body and was ashamed, as if she had denied it. After all, it was itself. It seemed awful to her. She looked at his face, and she turned her own face to the wall. For his look was other than hers, his way was not her way. She had denied him what he was—she saw it now. She had refused him as himself. And this had been her life, and his life. She was grateful to death, which restored the truth. And she knew she was not dead.

And all the while her heart was bursting with grief and pity for him. What had he suffered? What stretch of horror for this helpless man! She was rigid with agony. She had not been able to help him. He had been cruelly injured, this naked man, this other being, and she could make no reparation. There were the children—but the children belonged to life. This dead man had nothing to do with them. He and she were only channels through which life had flowed to issue in the children. She was a mother—but how awful she knew it now to have been a wife. And he, dead now, how awful he must have felt it to be a husband. She felt that in the next world he would be a stranger to her. If they met there, in the beyond, they would only be ashamed of what had been before. The children had come, for some mysterious reason, out of both of them. But the children did not unite them. Now he was dead, she knew how eternally he was apart from her, how eternally he had nothing more to do with her. She saw this episode of her life closed. They had denied each other in life. Now he had withdrawn. An anguish came over her. It was finished then: it had become hopeless between them long before he died. Yet he had been her husband. But how little!

"Have you got his shirt, 'Lizabeth?"

Elizabeth turned without answering, though she strove to weep and behave as her mother-in-law expected. But she could not, she was silenced. She went into the kitchen and returned with the garment.

"It is aired," she said, grasping the cotton shirt here and there to try. She was almost ashamed to handle him; what right had she or anyone to lay hands on him; but her touch was humble on his body. It was hard work to clothe him. He was so heavy and inert. A terrible dread gripped her all the while: that he could be so heavy and utterly inert, unresponsive, apart. The horror of the distance between them was almost too much for her—it was so infinite a gap she must look across.

At last it was finished. They covered him with a sheet and left him lying, with his face bound. And she fastened the door of the little parlour, lest the children should see what was lying there. Then, with peace sunk heavy on her heart, she went about making tidy the kitchen. She knew she submitted to life, which was her immediate master. But from death, her ultimate master, she winced with fear and shame.

—1914

KATHERINE MANSFIELD
1888 – 1923

In her short life, Katherine Mansfield managed to secure a reputation as one of the world's most gifted writers of short fiction. Her later stories in particular are important for their experimentation with style and atmosphere. Instead of a conventional storyline, these stories present a series of loosely linked moments, portraying the small details of human life as a means of illuminating a specific character at a specific point of crisis or epiphany. Among Mansfield's favorite devices are internal monologues, daydreams, the flexible manipulation of time and tense, and the use of rhythm and sound to convey mood and meaning. Her stories also often feature a variety of viewpoints, with language and syntax specific to each. Mansfield also experimented with the short story cycle, linking character and/or setting and utilizing repeating images and motifs. In "The Garden Party," for instance, the Sheridan family maintains the ongoing family chronicle Mansfield created in her earlier works (using the name "Burnell").

Kathleen Mansfield Beauchamp was born in Wellington, New Zealand, the third of six children of Harold Beauchamp and Annie Burnell Dyer Beauchamp. Her father was of working-class origins, but became a successful industrialist and later chairman of the Bank of New Zealand; his rise in the financial and commercial world was rewarded with a knighthood in the year of Mansfield's death. Dyer Beauchamp was a genteel woman of delicate persuasion, for whom the regimens of household management and child rearing seemed both too taxing and beneath her social ambitions. As a result, Mansfield's memories of her mother were more frequently detached than affectionate.

Mansfield's school years were divided between the country village of Karori and the capital, Wellington, where the family moved to a mansion at Tinakori Road (the setting for "The Garden Party"). In 1903, she and her sisters entered Queen's College in London. She immersed herself in French and German while contemplating a career as a cellist. Mansfield also advanced her literary career as she became a contributor to and editor of the College's magazine. It was at Queen's College that she developed a close relationship with Ida Baker (to whom she referred as Leslie Moore)—a relationship Mansfield would depend upon for the rest of her life. By this time, the young author and musician Kathleen Beauchamp had decided to adopt the professional name of "Katherine Mansfield."

At the conclusion of her studies in London, Mansfield returned unwillingly to Wellington. Having flourished artistically in the cosmopolitan environment of London, she despised the provincial lifestyle of her home, and for nearly two years she exhausted her parents with constant pleas to return to England. In 1908, with the support of Baker, she was given leave to return to London and never saw New Zealand again.

Within weeks of returning, Mansfield fell in love with a fellow musician, Garnett Trowell. When their relationship collapsed within a few months, she impulsively married G.C. Bowden, a singing teacher whose name she bore for the next nine years, despite having left him on their wedding night. She returned to Trowell and traveled with his opera company until she became pregnant and was sent by her mother to an unfashionable Bavarian spa for the duration of her pregnancy, which ended in miscarriage. During her stay in Germany, she wrote a series of satirical sketches of German characters that were published individually in *The New Age*; they were later collected and published as *In a German Pension* (1911). On her return to London Mansfield was diagnosed with rheumatic fever; it was later discovered to be gonorrhea, a condition that contributed to her failing health for the rest of her life.

By late 1911, Mansfield had begun contributing to *Rhythm*, an avant-garde quarterly edited by John Middleton Murry. A year later she became *Rhythm*'s editor and began a lifelong, tumultuous love affair with Murry. The "Two Tigers," as they were known, cultivated several close relationships within literary circles, most notably with D.H. Lawrence (a friendship that would end bitterly in 1920), Virginia Woolf, and Aldous Huxley. In 1913, *Rhythm* became *The Blue Review* after the publisher absconded, leaving Mansfield and Murry with considerable debts. *The Blue Review* folded after only three months, despite an impressive list of contributors including Lawrence, H.G. Wells, Hugh Walpole, and T.S. Eliot.

In 1915, Mansfield's youngest brother Leslie was killed in France. Her profound grief sent her into self-imposed exile in that country, where in an effort to console herself she began writing stories about her childhood in New Zealand; thus began her most productive and successful period as a writer. That same year Mansfield finally divorced G.C. Bowden and married John Murry. Later in the year she was diagnosed with tuberculosis; for the remaining years of her life she traveled between London, Switzerland, and the French Riviera in search of modern treatments and salubrious climates.

In 1919 Mansfield began reviewing novels for the *Athenaeum*, the editor of which was Murry, and a year later she published *Bliss, and Other Stories*. In the next two years she wrote many of her most notable works, several of which are included in *The Garden Party and Other Stories* (1922). In October of that year she entered the Gurdjieff Institute in France for controversial therapy under the guidance of mystic George Ivanovich Gurdjieff. In early 1923, overexcited by a visit from her husband, Mansfield suffered a severe lung hemorrhage upon rapidly climbing the steps to her room; she died later that evening. Although Mansfield had requested in her will that Murry publish as little of her work as possible, two further collections of her stories were published, as well as a collection of poetry and other works.

The stories included here are representative of Mansfield's favorite themes: the evolution of the self, the terrors of childhood, the solitude of the outsider, and the reality of death. Malcolm Cowley, a contemporary of Mansfield, wrote that her stories "have a thesis: namely, that life is a very wonderful spectacle, but disagreeable for the actors."

⌘⌘⌘

Bliss

Although Bertha Young was thirty she still had moments like this when she wanted to run instead of walk, to take dancing steps on and off the pavement, to bowl a hoop, to throw something up in the air and catch it again, or to stand still and laugh at—nothing—at nothing, simply.

What can you do if you are thirty and, turning the corner of your own street, you are overcome, suddenly, by a feeling of bliss—absolute bliss!—as though you'd suddenly swallowed a bright piece of that late afternoon sun and it burned in your bosom, sending out a little shower of sparks into every particle, into every finger and toe?…

Oh, is there no way you can express it without being "drunk and disorderly"? How idiotic civilisation is! Why be given a body if you have to keep it shut up in a case like a rare, rare fiddle?

"No, that about the fiddle is not quite what I mean," she thought, running up the steps and feeling in her bag for the key—she'd forgotten it, as usual—and rattling the letterbox. "It's not what I mean, because—Thank you, Mary"—she went into the hall. "Is nurse back?"

"Yes, M'm."

"And has the fruit come?"

"Yes, M'm. Everything's come."

"Bring the fruit up to the dining room, will you? I'll arrange it before I go upstairs."

It was dusky in the dining room and quite chilly. But all the same Bertha threw off her coat; she could not bear the tight clasp of it another moment, and the cold air fell on her arms.

But in her bosom there was still that bright glowing place—that shower of little sparks coming from it. It was almost unbearable. She hardly dared to breathe for fear of fanning it higher, and yet she breathed deeply, deeply. She hardly dared to look into the cold mirror—but she did look, and it gave her back a woman, radiant, with smiling, trembling lips, with big, dark eyes and an air of listening, waiting for something … divine to happen … that she knew must happen … infallibly.

Mary brought in the fruit on a tray and with it a glass bowl, and a blue dish, very lovely, with a strange sheen on it as though it had been dipped in milk.

"Shall I turn on the light, M'm?"

"No, thank you. I can see quite well."

There were tangerines and apples stained with strawberry pink. Some yellow pears, smooth as silk, some white grapes covered with a silver bloom and a big cluster of purple ones. These last she had bought to tone in with the new dining room carpet. Yes, that did sound rather farfetched and absurd, but it was really why she had bought them. She had thought in the shop: "I must have some purple ones to bring the carpet up to the table." And it had seemed quite sense at the time.

When she had finished with them and had made two pyramids of these bright round shapes, she stood away from the table to get the effect—and it really was most curious. For the dark table seemed to melt into the dusky light and the glass dish and the blue bowl to float in the air. This, of course, in her present mood, was so incredibly beautiful. … She began to laugh.

"No, no. I'm getting hysterical." And she seized her bag and coat and ran upstairs to the nursery.

Nurse sat at a low table giving Little B her supper after her bath. The baby had on a white flannel gown and a blue woollen jacket, and her dark, fine hair was brushed up into a funny little peak. She looked up when she saw her mother and began to jump.

"Now, my lovey, eat it up like a good girl," said nurse, setting her lips in a way that Bertha knew, and that meant she had come into the nursery at another wrong moment.

"Has she been good, Nanny?"

"She's been a little sweet all the afternoon," whispered Nanny. "We went to the park and I sat down on a chair and took her out of the pram and a big dog came along and put its head on my knee and she clutched its ear, tugged it. Oh, you should have seen her."

Bertha wanted to ask if it wasn't rather dangerous to let her clutch at a strange dog's ear. But she did not dare to. She stood watching them, her hands by her side, like the poor little girl in front of the rich little girl with the doll.

The baby looked up at her again, stared, and then smiled so charmingly that Bertha couldn't help crying:

"Oh, Nanny, do let me finish giving her her supper while you put the bath things away."

"Well, M'm, she oughtn't to be changed hands while she's eating," said Nanny, still whispering. "It unsettles her; it's very likely to upset her."

How absurd it was. Why have a baby if it has to be kept—not in a case like a rare, rare fiddle—but in another woman's arms?

"Oh, I must!" said she.

Very offended, Nanny handed her over.

"Now, don't excite her after her supper. You know you do, M'm. And I have such a time with her after!"

Thank heaven! Nanny went out of the room with the bath towels.

"Now I've got you to myself, my little precious," said Bertha, as the baby leaned against her.

She ate delightfully, holding up her lips for the spoon and then waving her hands. Sometimes she wouldn't let the spoon go; and sometimes, just as Bertha had filled it, she waved it away to the four winds.

When the soup was finished Bertha turned round to the fire.

"You're nice—you're very nice!" said she, kissing her warm baby. "I'm fond of you. I like you."

And, indeed, she loved Little B so much—her neck as she bent forward, her exquisite toes as they shone transparent in the firelight—that all her feeling of bliss came back again, and again she didn't know how to express it—what to do with it.

"You're wanted on the telephone," said Nanny, coming back in triumph and seizing *her* Little B.

Down she flew. It was Harry.

"Oh, is that you, Ber? Look here. I'll be late. I'll take a taxi and come along as quickly as I can, but get dinner put back ten minutes—will you? Alright?"

"Yes, perfectly. Oh, Harry!"

"Yes?"

What had she to say? She'd nothing to say. She only wanted to get in touch with him for a moment. She couldn't absurdly cry: "Hasn't it been a divine day!"

"What is it?" rapped out the little voice.

"Nothing. *Entendu*"[1] said Bertha, and hung up the receiver, thinking how much more than idiotic civilisation was.

They had people coming to dinner. The Norman Knights—a very sound couple—he was about to start a theatre, and she was awfully keen on interior decoration, a young man, Eddie Warren, who had just published a little book of poems and whom everybody was asking to dine, and a "find" of Bertha's called Pearl Fulton. What Miss Fulton did, Bertha didn't know. They had met at the club and Bertha had fallen in love with her, as she always did fall in love with beautiful women who had something strange about them.

The provoking thing was that, though they had been about together and met a number of times and really talked, Bertha couldn't make her out. Up to a certain point Miss Fulton was rarely, wonderfully frank, but the certain point was there, and beyond that she would not go.

Was there anything beyond it? Harry said "No." Voted her dullish, and "cold like all blonde women, with a touch, perhaps, of anæmia of the brain." But Bertha wouldn't agree with him; not yet, at any rate.

"No, the way she has of sitting with her head a little on one side, and smiling, has something behind it, Harry, and I must find out what that something is."

"Most likely it's a good stomach," answered Harry.

He made a point of catching Bertha's heels with replies of that kind … "liver frozen, my dear girl," or "pure flatulence," or "kidney disease," … and so on. For some strange reason Bertha liked this, and almost admired it in him very much.

She went into the drawing room and lighted the fire; then, picking up the cushions, one by one, that Mary had disposed so carefully, she threw them back onto the chairs and the couches. That made all the difference; the room came alive at once. As she was about to throw the last one she surprised herself by suddenly hugging it to her, passionately, passionately. But it did not put out the fire in her bosom. Oh, on the contrary!

The windows of the drawing room opened onto a balcony overlooking the garden. At the far end, against the wall, there was a tall, slender pear tree in fullest, richest bloom; it stood perfect, as though becalmed against the jade green sky. Bertha couldn't help feeling, even from this distance, that it had not a single bud or a faded petal. Down below, in the garden beds, the red and yellow tulips, heavy with flowers, seemed to lean upon the dusk. A grey cat, dragging its belly, crept across the lawn, and a black one, its shadow, trailed after. The sight of them, so intent and so quick, gave Bertha a curious shiver.

"What creepy things cats are!" she stammered, and she turned away from the window and began walking up and down. . . .

How strong the jonquils[2] smelled in the warm room. Too strong? Oh, no. And yet, as though overcome, she flung down on a couch and pressed her hands to her eyes.

"I'm too happy—too happy!" she murmured.

And she seemed to see on her eyelids the lovely pear tree with its wide open blossoms as a symbol of her own life.

Really—really—she had everything. She was young. Harry and she were as much in love as ever, and they

---

[1] *Entendu* Heard; understood.

[2] *jonquils* Daffodils.

got on together splendidly and were really good pals. She had an adorable baby. They didn't have to worry about money. They had this absolutely satisfactory house and garden. And friends—modern, thrilling friends, writers and painters and poets or people keen on social questions—just the kind of friends they wanted. And then there were books, and there was music, and she had found a wonderful little dressmaker, and they were going abroad in the summer, and their new cook made the most superb omelettes. ...

"I'm absurd. Absurd!" She sat up; but she felt quite dizzy, quite drunk. It must have been the spring.

Yes, it was the spring. Now she was so tired she could not drag herself upstairs to dress.

A white dress, a string of jade beads, green shoes and stockings. It wasn't intentional. She had thought of this scheme hours before she stood at the drawing room window.

Her petals rustled softly into the hall, and she kissed Mrs. Norman Knight, who was taking off the most amusing orange coat with a procession of black monkeys round the hem and up the fronts.

"... Why! Why! Why is the middle-class so stodgy — so utterly without a sense of humour! My dear, it's only by a fluke that I am here at all—Norman being the protective fluke. For my darling monkeys so upset the train that it rose to a man and simply ate me with its eyes. Didn't laugh—wasn't amused—that I should have loved. No, just stared—and bored me through and through."

"But the cream of it was," said Norman, pressing a large tortoiseshell-rimmed monocle into his eye, "you don't mind me telling this, Face, do you?" (In their home and among their friends they called each other Face and Mug.) "The cream of it was when she, being full fed, turned to the woman beside her and said: 'Haven't you ever seen a monkey before?'"

"Oh yes!" Mrs. Norman Knight joined in the laughter. "Wasn't that too absolutely creamy?"

And a funnier thing still was that now her coat was off she did look like a very intelligent monkey—who had even made that yellow silk dress out of scraped banana skins. And her amber earrings: they were like little dangling nuts.

"This is a sad, sad fall!" said Mug, pausing in front of Little B's perambulator. "When the perambulator comes into the hall—"[1] and he waved the rest of the quotation away.

The bell rang. It was lean, pale Eddie Warren (as usual) in a state of acute distress.

"It *is* the right house, *isn't* it?" he pleaded.

"Oh, I think so—I hope so," said Bertha brightly.

"I have had such a *dreadful* experience with a taxi man; he was *most* sinister. I couldn't get him to *stop*. The *more* I knocked and called *the faster* he went. And *in* the moonlight this *bizarre* figure with the *flattened* head *crouching* over the *lit-tle* wheel ..."

He shuddered, taking off an immense white silk scarf. Bertha noticed that his socks were white, too—most charming.

"But how dreadful!" she cried.

"Yes, it really was," said Eddie, following her into the drawing room. "I saw myself *driving* through Eternity in a *timeless* taxi."

He knew the Norman Knights. In fact, he was going to write a play for N.K. when the theatre scheme came off.

"Well, Warren, how's the play?" said Norman Knight, dropping his monocle and giving his eye a moment in which to rise to the surface before it was screwed down again.

And Mrs. Norman Knight: "Oh, Mr. Warren, what happy socks?"

"I *am* so glad you like them," said he, staring at his feet. "They seem to have got so *much* whiter since the moon rose." And he turned his lean sorrowful young face to Bertha. "There *is* a moon, you know."

She wanted to cry: "I am sure there is—often— often!"

He really was a most attractive person. But so was Face, crouched before the fire in her banana skins, and so was Mug, smoking a cigarette and saying as he flicked the ash: "Why doth the bridegroom tarry?"

"There he is, now."

Bang went the front door open and shut. Harry shouted: "Hullo, you people. Down in five minutes." And they heard him swarm up the stairs. Bertha couldn't help smiling; she knew how he loved doing

---

[1] *This is ... hall* Quotation unidentified.

things at high pressure. What, after all, did an extra five minutes matter? But he would pretend to himself that they mattered beyond measure. And then he would make a great point of coming into the drawing room, extravagantly cool and collected.

Harry had such a zest for life. Oh, how she appreciated it in him. And his passion for fighting—for seeking in everything that came up against him another test of his power and of his courage—that, too, she understood. Even when it made him just occasionally, to other people, who didn't know him well, a little ridiculous perhaps.... For there were moments when he rushed into battle where no battle was.... She talked and laughed and positively forgot until he had come in (just as she had imagined) that Pearl Fulton had not turned up.

"I wonder if Miss Fulton has forgotten?"

"I expect so," said Harry. "Is she on the phone?"

"Ah! There's a taxi now." And Bertha smiled with that little air of proprietorship that she always assumed while her women finds were new and mysterious. "She lives in taxis."

"She'll run to fat if she does," said Harry coolly, ringing the bell for dinner. "Frightful danger for blonde women."

"Harry—don't," warned Bertha, laughing up at him.

Came another tiny moment, while they waited, laughing and talking, just a trifle too much at their ease, a trifle too unaware. And then Miss Fulton, all in silver, with a silver fillet binding her pale blonde hair, came in smiling, her head a little on one side.

"Am I late?"

"No, not at all," said Bertha. "Come along." And she took her arm and they moved into the dining room.

What was there in the touch of that cool arm that could fan—fan—start blazing—blazing—the fire of bliss that Bertha did not know what to do with?

Miss Fulton did not look at her; but then she seldom did look at people directly. Her heavy eyelids lay upon her eyes and the strange half-smile came and went upon her lips as though she lived by listening rather than seeing. But Bertha knew, suddenly, as if the longest, most intimate look had passed between them—as if they had said to each other: "You, too?"— that Pearl Fulton, stirring the beautiful red soup in the grey plate, was feeling just what she was feeling.

And the others? Face and Mug, Eddie and Harry, their spoons rising and falling—dabbing their lips with their napkins, crumbling bread, fiddling with the forks and glasses and talking.

"I met her at the Alpha show—the weirdest little person. She'd not only cut off her hair, but she seemed to have taken a dreadfully good snip off her legs and arms and her neck and her poor little nose as well."

"Isn't she very *liée* with[1] Michael Oat?"

"The man who wrote *Love in False Teeth*?"

"He wants to write a play for me. One act. One man. Decides to commit suicide. Gives all the reasons why he should and why he shouldn't. And just as he has made up his mind either to do it or not to do it— curtain. Not half a bad idea."

"What's he going to call it—'Stomach Trouble'?"

"I *think* I've come across the *same* idea in a lit-tle French review, *quite* unknown in England."

No, they didn't share it. They were dears—dears — and she loved having them there, at her table, and giving them delicious food and wine. In fact, she longed to tell them how delightful they were, and what a decorative group they made, how they seemed to set one another off and how they reminded her of a play by Chekhov![2]

Harry was enjoying his dinner. It was part of his—well, not his nature, exactly, and certainly not his pose—his—something or other—to talk about food and to glory in his "shameless passion for the white flesh of the lobster" and "the green of pistachio ices—green and cold like the eyelids of Egyptian dancers."

When he looked up at her and said: "Bertha, this is a very admirable *soufflé*!" she almost could have wept with childlike pleasure.

Oh, why did she feel so tender towards the whole world tonight? Everything was good—was right. All that happened seemed to fill again her brimming cup of bliss.

And still, in the back of her mind, there was the pear tree. It would be silver now, in the light of poor dear Eddie's moon, silver as Miss Fulton, who sat there

---

[1] *very liée with*   Bound to, close to.

[2] *Chekhov*   Anton Chekhov (1860–1904), Russian playwright and short story writer.

turning a tangerine in her slender fingers that were so pale a light seemed to come from them.

What she simply couldn't make out—what was miraculous—was how she should have guessed Miss Fulton's mood so exactly and so instantly. For she never doubted for a moment that she was right, and yet what had she to go on? Less than nothing.

"I believe this does happen very, very rarely between women. Never between men," thought Bertha. "But while I am making the coffee in the drawing room perhaps she will 'give a sign.'"

What she meant by that she did not know, and what would happen after that she could not imagine.

While she thought like this she saw herself talking and laughing. She had to talk because of her desire to laugh.

"I must laugh or die."

But when she noticed Face's funny little habit of tucking something down the front of her bodice—as if she kept a tiny, secret hoard of nuts there, too— Bertha had to dig her nails into her hands—so as not to laugh too much.

It was over at last. And: "Come and see my new coffee machine," said Bertha.

"We only have a new coffee machine once a fort-night," said Harry. Face took her arm this time; Miss Fulton bent her head and followed after.

The fire had died down in the drawing room to a red, flickering "nest of baby phoenixes," said Face.

"Don't turn up the light for a moment. It is so lovely."

And down she crouched by the fire again. She was always cold … "without her little red flannel jacket, of course," thought Bertha.

At that moment Miss Fulton "gave the sign."

"Have you a garden?" said the cool, sleepy voice.

This was so exquisite on her part that all Bertha could do was to obey. She crossed the room, pulled the curtains apart, and opened those long windows.

"There!" she breathed.

And the two women stood side by side looking at the slender, flowering tree. Although it was so still it seemed, like the flame of a candle, to stretch up, to point, to quiver in the bright air, to grow taller and taller as they gazed—almost to touch the rim of the round, silver moon.

How long did they stand there? Both, as it were, caught in that circle of unearthly light, understanding each other perfectly, creatures of another world, and wondering what they were to do in this one with all this blissful treasure that burned in their bosoms and dropped, in silver flowers, from their hair and hands?

For ever—for a moment? And did Miss Fulton murmur:

"Yes. Just *that*." Or did Bertha dream it?

Then the light was snapped on and Face made the coffee and Harry said: "My dear Mrs. Knight, don't ask me about my baby. I never see her. I shan't feel the slightest interest in her until she has a lover," and Mug took his eye out of the conservatory for a moment and then put it under glass again and Eddie Warren drank his coffee and set down the cup with a face of anguish as though he had drunk and seen the spider.

"What I want to do is to give the young men a show. I believe London is simply teeming with first-chop,[1] unwritten plays. What I want to say to 'em is: 'Here's the theatre. Fire ahead.'"

"You know, my dear, I am going to decorate a room for the Jacob Nathans. Oh, I am so tempted to do a fried fish scheme, with the backs of the chairs shaped like frying pans and lovely chip potatoes embroidered all over the curtains."

"The trouble with our young writing men is that they are still too romantic. You can't put out to sea without being seasick and wanting a basin. Well, why won't they have the courage of those basins?"

"A *dreadful* poem about a *girl* who was *violated* by a beggar *without* a nose in a lit-tle wood. …"

Miss Fulton sank into the lowest, deepest chair and Harry handed round the cigarettes.

From the way he stood in front of her shaking the silver box and saying abruptly: "Egyptian? Turkish? Virginian? They're all mixed up," Bertha realised that she not only bored him; he really disliked her. And she decided from the way Miss Fulton said: "No, thank you, I won't smoke," that she felt it, too, and was hurt.

"Oh, Harry, don't dislike her. You are quite wrong about her. She's wonderful, wonderful. And, besides,

---

[1] *first-chop* First-class.

how can you feel so differently about someone who means so much to me. I shall try to tell you when we are in bed tonight what has been happening. What she and I have shared."

At those last words something strange and almost terrifying darted into Bertha's mind. And this something blind and smiling whispered to her: "Soon these people will go. The house will be quiet—quiet. The lights will be out. And you and he will be alone together in the dark room—the warm bed...."

She jumped up from her chair and ran over to the piano.

"What a pity someone does not play!" she cried. "What a pity somebody does not play."

For the first time in her life Bertha Young desired her husband.

Oh, she'd loved him—she'd been in love with him, of course, in every other way, but just not in that way. And equally, of course, she'd understood that he was different. They'd discussed it so often. It had worried her dreadfully at first to find that she was so cold, but after a time it had not seemed to matter. They were so frank with each other—such good pals. That was the best of being modern.

But now—ardently! ardently! The word ached in her ardent body! Was this what that feeling of bliss had been leading up to? But then, then—

"My dear," said Mrs. Norman Knight, "you know our shame. We are the victims of time and train. We live in Hampstead. It's been so nice."

"I'll come with you into the hall," said Bertha. "I loved having you. But you must not miss the last train. That's so awful, isn't it?"

"Have a whisky, Knight, before you go?" called Harry.

"No, thanks, old chap."

Bertha squeezed his hand for that as she shook it.

"Good night, goodbye," she cried from the top step, feeling that this self of hers was taking leave of them forever.

When she got back into the drawing room the others were on the move.

"... Then you can come part of the way in my taxi."

"I shall be *so* thankful *not* to have to face *another* drive *alone* after my *dreadful* experience."

"You can get a taxi at the rank just at the end of the street. You won't have to walk more than a few yards."

"That's a comfort. I'll go and put on my coat."

Miss Fulton moved towards the hall and Bertha was following when Harry almost pushed past.

"Let me help you."

Bertha knew that he was repenting his rudeness—she let him go. What a boy he was in some ways—so impulsive—so—simple.

And Eddie and she were left by the fire.

"I *wonder* if you have seen Bilks' *new* poem called *Table d'Hôte*,"[1] said Eddie softly. "It's *so* wonderful. In the last anthology. Have you got a copy? I'd *so* like to *show* it to you. It begins with an *incredibly* beautiful line: 'Why Must it Always be Tomato Soup?'"

"Yes," said Bertha. And she moved noiselessly to a table opposite the drawing room door and Eddie glided noiselessly after her. She picked up the little book and gave it to him; they had not made a sound.

While he looked it up she turned her head towards the hall. And she saw ... Harry with Miss Fulton's coat in his arms and Miss Fulton with her back turned to him and her head bent. He tossed the coat away, put his hands on her shoulders and turned her violently to him. His lips said: "I adore you," and Miss Fulton laid her moonbeam fingers on his cheeks and smiled her sleepy smile. Harry's nostrils quivered; his lips curled back in a hideous grin while he whispered: "Tomorrow," and with her eyelids Miss Fulton said: "Yes."

"Here it is," said Eddie. "'Why Must it Always be Tomato Soup?' It's *so deeply* true, don't you feel? Tomato soup is so *dreadfully* eternal."

"If you prefer," said Harry's voice, very loud, from the hall, "I can phone you a cab to come to the door."

"Oh, no. It's not necessary," said Miss Fulton, and she came up to Bertha and gave her the slender fingers to hold.

"Goodbye. Thank you so much."

"Goodbye," said Bertha.

Miss Fulton held her hand a moment longer.

"Your lovely pear tree!" she murmured.

---

[1] *Table d'Hôte*   Set meal.

And then she was gone, with Eddie following, like the black cat following the grey cat.

"I'll shut up shop," said Harry, extravagantly cool and collected.

"Your lovely pear tree—pear tree—pear tree!"

Bertha simply ran over to the long windows.

"Oh, what is going to happen now?" she cried.

But the pear tree was as lovely as ever and as full of flower and as still.

—1920

The Garden Party

And after all the weather was ideal. They could not have had a more perfect day for a garden party if they had ordered it. Windless, warm, the sky without a cloud. Only the blue was veiled with a haze of light gold, as it is sometimes in early summer. The gardener had been up since dawn, mowing the lawns and sweeping them, until the grass and the dark flat rosettes where the daisy plants had been seemed to shine. As for the roses, you could not help feeling they understood that roses are the only flowers that impress people at garden parties, the only flowers that everybody is certain of knowing. Hundreds, yes, literally hundreds, had come out in a single night; the green bushes bowed down as though they had been visited by archangels.

Breakfast was not yet over before the men came to put up the marquee.

"Where do you want the marquee put, mother?"

"My dear child, it's no use asking me. I'm determined to leave everything to you children this year. Forget I am your mother. Treat me as an honoured guest."

But Meg could not possibly go and supervise the men. She had washed her hair before breakfast, and she sat drinking her coffee in a green turban, with a dark wet curl stamped on each cheek. Jose, the butterfly, always came down in a silk petticoat and a kimono jacket.

"You'll have to go, Laura; you're the artistic one."

Away Laura flew, still holding her piece of bread and butter. It's so delicious to have an excuse for eating out of doors and, besides, she loved having to arrange things; she always felt she could do it so much better than anybody else.

Four men in their shirt sleeves stood grouped together on the garden path. They carried staves[1] covered with rolls of canvas and they had big toolbags slung on their backs. They looked impressive. Laura wished now that she was not holding that piece of bread and butter, but there was nowhere to put it and she couldn't possibly throw it away. She blushed and tried to look severe and even a little bit shortsighted as she came up to them.

"Good morning," she said, copying her mother's voice. But that sounded so fearfully affected that she was ashamed, and stammered like a little girl, "Oh—er—have you come—is it about the marquee?"

"That's right, miss," said the tallest of the men, a lanky, freckled fellow, and he shifted his tool bag, knocked back his straw hat and smiled down at her. "That's about it."

His smile was so easy, so friendly, that Laura recovered. What nice eyes he had, small, but such a dark blue! And now she looked at the others, they were smiling too. "Cheer up, we won't bite," their smile seemed to say. How very nice workmen were! And what a beautiful morning! She mustn't mention the morning; she must be businesslike. The marquee.

"Well, what about the lily lawn? Would that do?"

And she pointed to the lily lawn with the hand that didn't hold the bread and butter. They turned, they stared in the direction. A little fat chap thrust out his underlip and the tall fellow frowned.

"I don't fancy it," said he. "Not conspicuous enough. You see, with a thing like a marquee"—and he turned to Laura in his easy way—"you want to put it somewhere where it'll give you a bang slap in the eye, if you follow me."

Laura's upbringing made her wonder for a moment whether it was quite respectful of a workman to talk to her of bangs slap in the eye. But she did quite follow him.

"A corner of the tennis court," she suggested. "But the band's going to be in one corner."

"H'm, going to have a band, are you?" said another of the workmen. He was pale. He had a haggard look as

---

[1] *staves* Rods.

his dark eyes scanned the tennis court. What was he thinking?

"Only a very small band," said Laura gently. Perhaps he wouldn't mind so much if the band was quite small. But the tall fellow interrupted.

"Look here, miss, that's the place. Against those trees. Over there. That'll do fine."

Against the karakas. Then the karaka trees would be hidden. And they were so lovely, with their broad, gleaming leaves, and their clusters of yellow fruit. They were like trees you imagined growing on a desert island, proud, solitary, lifting their leaves and fruits to the sun in a kind of silent splendour. Must they be hidden by a marquee?

They must. Already the men had shouldered their staves and were making for the place. Only the tall fellow was left. He bent down, pinched a sprig of lavender, put his thumb and forefinger to his nose and snuffed up the smell. When Laura saw that gesture she forgot all about the karakas in her wonder at him caring for things like that—caring for the smell of lavender. How many men that she knew would have done such a thing. Oh, how extraordinarily nice workmen were, she thought. Why couldn't she have workmen for friends rather than the silly boys she danced with and who came to Sunday night supper? She would get on much better with men like these.

It's all the fault, she decided, as the tall fellow drew something on the back of an envelope, something that was to be looped up or left to hang, of these absurd class distinctions. Well, for her part, she didn't feel them. Not a bit, not an atom.... And now there came the chock-chock of wooden hammers. Someone whistled, someone sang out, "Are you right there, matey?" "Matey!" The friendliness of it, the—the— Just to prove how happy she was, just to show the tall fellow how at home she felt, and how she despised stupid conventions, Laura took a big bite of her bread and butter as she stared at the little drawing. She felt just like a work girl.

"Laura, Laura, where are you? Telephone, Laura!" a voice cried from the house.

"Coming!" Away she skimmed, over the lawn, up the path, up the steps, across the veranda and into the porch. In the hall her father and Laurie were brushing their hats ready to go to the office.

"I say, Laura," said Laurie very fast, "you might just give a squiz[1] at my coat before this afternoon. See if it wants pressing."

"I will," said she. Suddenly she couldn't stop herself. She ran at Laurie and gave him a small, quick squeeze. "Oh, I do love parties, don't you?" gasped Laura.

"Ra—ther," said Laurie's warm, boyish voice, and he squeezed his sister too and gave her a gentle push. "Dash off to the telephone, old girl."

The telephone. "Yes, yes; oh yes. Kitty? Good morning, dear. Come to lunch? Do, dear. Delighted, of course. It will only be a very scratch[2] meal—just the sandwich crusts and broken meringue shells and what's left over. Yes, isn't it a perfect morning? Your white? Oh, I certainly should. One moment—hold the line. Mother's calling." And Laura sat back. "What, mother? Can't hear."

Mrs. Sheridan's voice floated down the stairs. "Tell her to wear that sweet hat she had on last Sunday."

"Mother says you're to wear that sweet hat you had on last Sunday. Good. One o'clock. Bye-bye."

Laura put back the receiver, flung her arms over her head, took a deep breath, stretched and let them fall. "Huh," she sighed, and the moment after the sigh she sat up quickly. She was still, listening. All the doors in the house seemed to be open. The house was alive with soft, quick steps and running voices. The green baize door[3] that led to the kitchen regions swung open and shut with a muffled thud. And now there came a long, chuckling absurd sound. It was the heavy piano being moved on its stiff castors. But the air! If you stopped to notice, was the air always like this? Little faint winds were playing chase in at the tops of the windows, out at the doors. And there were two tiny spots of sun, one on the inkpot, one on a silver photograph frame, playing too. Darling little spots. Especially the one on the inkpot lid. It was quite warm. A warm little silver star. She could have kissed it.

---

[1] *squiz* Glance.

[2] *scratch* Quickly thrown together.

[3] *baize door* Door, covered with a green felt-like material, that separates the kitchen from the rest of the house in large English homes.

The front door bell pealed and there sounded the rustle of Sadie's print skirt on the stairs. A man's voice murmured; Sadie answered, careless, "I'm sure I don't know. Wait. I'll ask Mrs. Sheridan."

"What is it, Sadie?" Laura came into the hall.

"It's the florist, Miss Laura."

It was, indeed. There, just inside the door, stood a wide, shallow tray full of pots of pink lilies. No other kind. Nothing but lilies—canna lilies, big pink flowers, wide open, radiant, almost frighteningly alive on bright crimson stems.

"O—oh, Sadie!" said Laura, and the sound was like a little moan. She crouched down as if to warm herself at that blaze of lilies; she felt they were in her fingers, on her lips, growing in her breast.

"It's some mistake," she said faintly. "Nobody ever ordered so many. Sadie, go and find mother."

But at that moment Mrs. Sheridan joined them.

"It's quite right," she said calmly. "Yes, I ordered them. Aren't they lovely?" She pressed Laura's arm. "I was passing the shop yesterday, and I saw them in the window. And I suddenly thought for once in my life I shall have enough canna lilies. The garden party will be a good excuse."

"But I thought you said you didn't mean to interfere," said Laura. Sadie had gone. The florist's man was still outside at his van. She put her arm round her mother's neck and gently, very gently, she bit her mother's ear.

"My darling child, you wouldn't like a logical mother, would you? Don't do that. Here's the man."

He carried more lilies still, another whole tray.

"Bank them up, just inside the door, on both sides of the porch, please," said Mrs. Sheridan. "Don't you agree, Laura?"

"Oh, I do, mother."

In the drawing room Meg, Jose and good little Hans had at last succeeded in moving the piano.

"Now, if we put this chesterfield against the wall and move everything out of the room except the chairs, don't you think?"

"Quite."

"Hans, move these tables into the smoking room, and bring a sweeper to take these marks off the carpet and—one moment, Hans—" Jose loved giving orders to the servants and they loved obeying her. She always made them feel they were taking part in some drama. "Tell mother and Miss Laura to come here at once."

"Very good, Miss Jose."

She turned to Meg. "I want to hear what the piano sounds like, just in case I'm asked to sing this afternoon. Let's try over 'This Life is Weary.'"

Pom! Ta-ta-ta *Tee*-ta! The piano burst out so passionately that Jose's face changed. She clasped her hands. She looked mournfully and enigmatically at her mother and Laura as they came in.

This Life is *Wee*-ary,
A Tear—a Sigh.
A Love that *Chan*-ges,
This Life is *Wee*-ary,
A Tear—a Sigh.
A Love that *Chan*-ges,
And then … Goodbye!

But at the word "Goodbye," and although the piano sounded more desperate than ever, her face broke into a brilliant, dreadfully unsympathetic smile.

"Aren't I in good voice, mummy?" she beamed.

This Life is *Wee*-ary,
Hope comes to Die.
A Dream—a *Wa*-kening.

But now Sadie interrupted them. "What is it, Sadie?"

"If you please, m'm, cook says have you got the flags for the sandwiches?"

"The flags for the sandwiches, Sadie?" echoed Mrs. Sheridan dreamily. And the children knew by her face that she hadn't got them. "Let me see." And she said to Sadie firmly, "Tell cook I'll let her have them in ten minutes."

Sadie went.

"Now, Laura," said her mother quickly, "come with me into the smoking room. I've got the names somewhere on the back of an envelope. You'll have to write them out for me. Meg, go upstairs this minute and take that wet thing off your head. Jose, run and finish dressing this instant. Do you hear me, children, or shall I have to tell your father when he comes home tonight?

And—and, Jose, pacify cook if you do go into the kitchen, will you? I'm terrified of her this morning."

The envelope was found at last behind the dining room clock, though how it had got there Mrs. Sheridan could not imagine.

"One of you children must have stolen it out of my bag, because I remember vividly—cream cheese and lemon curd. Have you done that?"

"Yes."

"Egg and—" Mrs. Sheridan held the envelope away from her. "It looks like mice. It can't be mice, can it?"

"Olive, pet," said Laura, looking over her shoulder.

"Yes, of course, olive. What a horrible combination it sounds. Egg and olive."

They were finished at last, and Laura took them off to the kitchen. She found Jose there pacifying the cook, who did not look at all terrifying.

"I have never seen such exquisite sandwiches," said Jose's rapturous voice. "How many kinds did you say there were, cook? Fifteen?"

"Fifteen, Miss Jose."

"Well, cook, I congratulate you."

Cook swept up crusts with the long sandwich knife, and smiled broadly.

"Godber's has come," announced Sadie, issuing out of the pantry. She had seen the man pass the window.

That meant the cream puffs had come. Godber's were famous for their cream puffs. Nobody ever thought of making them at home.

"Bring them in and put them on the table, my girl," ordered cook.

Sadie brought them in and went back to the door. Of course Laura and Jose were far too grown up to really care about such things. All the same, they couldn't help agreeing that the puffs looked very attractive. Very. Cook began arranging them, shaking off the extra icing sugar.

"Don't they carry one back to all one's parties?" said Laura.

"I suppose they do," said practical Jose, who never liked to be carried back. "They look beautifully light and feathery, I must say."

"Have one each, my dears," said cook in her comfortable voice. "Yer ma won't know."

Oh, impossible. Fancy cream puffs so soon after breakfast. The very idea made one shudder. All the same, two minutes later Jose and Laura were licking their fingers with that absorbed inward look that only comes from whipped cream.

"Let's go into the garden, out by the back way," suggested Laura. "I want to see how the men are getting on with the marquee. They're such awfully nice men."

But the back door was blocked by cook, Sadie, Godber's man and Hans.

Something had happened.

"Tuk-tuk-tuk," clucked cook like an agitated hen. Sadie had her hand clapped to her cheek as though she had toothache. Han's face was screwed up in the effort to understand. Only Godber's man seemed to be enjoying himself; it was his story.

"What's the matter? What's happened?"

"There's been a horrible accident," said cook. "A man killed."

"A man killed! Where? How? When?"

But Godber's man wasn't going to have his story snatched from under his very nose.

"Know those little cottages just below here, miss?" Know them? Of course she knew them. "Well, there's a young chap living there, name of Scott, a carter. His horse shied at a traction engine, corner of Hawke Street this morning, and he was thrown out on the back of his head. Killed."

"Dead!" Laura stared at Godber's man.

"Dead when they picked him up," said Godber's man with relish. "They were taking the body home as I come up here." And he said to the cook, "He's left a wife and five little ones."

"Jose, come here." Laura caught hold of her sister's sleeve and dragged her through the kitchen to the other side of the green baize door. There she paused and leaned against it. "Jose!" she said, horrified, "however are we going to stop everything?"

"Stop everything, Laura!" cried Jose in astonishment. "What do you mean?"

"Stop the garden party, of course." Why did Jose pretend?

But Jose was still more amazed. "Stop the garden party? My dear Laura, don't be so absurd. Of course we can't do anything of the kind. Nobody expects us to. Don't be so extravagant."

"But we can't possibly have a garden party with a man dead just outside the front gate."

That really was extravagant, for the little cottages were in a lane to themselves at the very bottom of a steep rise that led up to the house. A broad road ran between. True, they were far too near. They were the greatest possible eyesore and they had no right to be in that neighbourhood at all. They were little mean dwellings painted a chocolate brown. In the garden patches there was nothing but cabbage stalks, sick hens and tomato cans. The very smoke coming out of their chimneys was poverty stricken. Little rags and shreds of smoke, so unlike the great silvery plumes that uncurled from the Sheridans' chimneys. Washerwomen lived in the lane and sweeps and a cobbler and a man whose house front was studded all over with minute birdcages. Children swarmed. When the Sheridans were little they were forbidden to set foot there because of the revolting language and of what they might catch. But since they were grown up Laura and Laurie on their prowls sometimes walked through. It was disgusting and sordid. They came out with a shudder. But still one must go everywhere; one must see everything. So through they went.

"And just think of what the band would sound like to that poor woman," said Laura.

"Oh, Laura!" Jose began to be seriously annoyed. "If you're going to stop a band playing every time someone has an accident, you'll lead a very strenuous life. I'm every bit as sorry about it as you. I feel just as sympathetic." Her eyes hardened. She looked at her sister just as she used to when they were little and fighting together. "You won't bring a drunken workman back to life by being sentimental," she said softly.

"Drunk! Who said he was drunk?" Laura turned furiously on Jose. She said just as they had used to say on those occasions, "I'm going straight up to tell mother."

"Do, dear," cooed Jose.

"Mother, can I come into your room?" Laura turned the big glass doorknob.

"Of course, child. Why, what's the matter? What's given you such a colour?" And Mrs. Sheridan turned round from her dressing table. She was trying on a new hat.

"Mother, a man's been killed," began Laura.

"*Not* in the garden?" interrupted her mother.

"No, no!"

"Oh, what a fright you gave me!" Mrs. Sheridan sighed with relief and took off the big hat and held it on her knees.

"But listen, mother," said Laura. Breathless, half choking, she told the dreadful story. "Of course, we can't have our party, can we?" she pleaded. "The band and everybody arriving. They'd hear us, mother; they're nearly neighbours!"

To Laura's astonishment her mother behaved just like Jose; it was harder to bear because she seemed amused. She refused to take Laura seriously.

"But, my dear child, use your common sense. It's only by accident we've heard of it. If someone had died there normally—and I can't understand how they keep alive in those poky little holes—we should still be having our party, shouldn't we?"

Laura had to say "yes" to that, but she felt it was all wrong. She sat down on her mother's sofa and pinched the cushion frill.

"Mother, isn't it really terribly heartless of us?" she asked.

"Darling!" Mrs. Sheridan got up and came over to her, carrying the hat. Before Laura could stop her she had popped it on. "My child!" said her mother, "the hat is yours. It's made for you. It's much too young for me. I have never seen you look such a picture. Look at yourself!" And she held up her hand-mirror.

"But, mother," Laura began again. She couldn't look at herself; she turned aside.

This time Mrs. Sheridan lost patience just as Jose had done.

"You are being very absurd, Laura," she said coldly. "People like that don't expect sacrifices from us. And it's not very sympathetic to spoil everybody's enjoyment as you're doing now."

"I don't understand," said Laura, and she walked quickly out of the room into her own bedroom. There, quite by chance, the first thing she saw was this charming girl in the mirror, in her black hat trimmed with gold daisies and a long black velvet ribbon. Never had she imagined she could look like that. Is mother right? she thought. And now she hoped her mother was right. Am I being extravagant? Perhaps it was extravagant. Just for a moment she had another glimpse of that poor woman and those little children and the body being carried into the house. But it all seemed blurred, unreal, like a picture in the newspaper. I'll remember it again after the party's over, she decided. And somehow that seemed quite the best plan. . . .

Lunch was over by half-past one. By half-past two they were all ready for the fray. The green-coated band had arrived and was established in a corner of the tennis court.

"My dear!" trilled Kitty Maitland, "aren't they too like frogs for words? You ought to have arranged them round the pond with the conductor in the middle on a leaf."

Laurie arrived and hailed them on his way to dress. At the sight of him Laura remembered the accident again. She wanted to tell him. If Laurie agreed with the others, then it was bound to be all right. And she followed him into the hall.

"Laurie!"

"Hallo!" He was halfway upstairs, but when he turned round and saw Laura he suddenly puffed out his cheeks and goggled his eyes at her. "My word, Laura! You do look stunning," said Laurie. "What an absolutely topping hat!"

Laura said faintly "Is it?" and smiled up at Laurie and didn't tell him after all.

Soon after that people began coming in streams. The band struck up; the hired waiters ran from the house to the marquee. Wherever you looked there were couples strolling, bending to the flowers, greeting, moving on over the lawn. They were like bright birds that had alighted in the Sheridans' garden for this one afternoon, on their way to—where? Ah, what happiness it is to be with people who all are happy, to press hands, press cheeks, smile into eyes.

"Darling Laura, how well you look!"

"What a becoming hat, child!"

"Laura, you look quite Spanish. I've never seen you look so striking."

And Laura, glowing, answered softly, "Have you had tea? Won't you have an ice? The passion fruit ices really are rather special." She ran to her father and begged him: "Daddy darling, can't the band have something to drink?"

And the perfect afternoon slowly ripened, slowly faded, slowly its petals closed.

"Never a more delightful garden party …" "The greatest success …" "Quite the most …"

Laura helped her mother with the goodbyes. They stood side by side in the porch till it was all over.

"All over, all over, thank heaven," said Mrs. Sheridan. "Round up the others, Laura. Let's go and have some fresh coffee. I'm exhausted. Yes, it's been very successful. But oh, these parties, these parties! Why will you children insist on giving parties!" And they all of them sat down in the deserted marquee.

"Have a sandwich, daddy dear. I wrote the flag."

"Thanks." Mr. Sheridan took a bite and the sandwich was gone. He took another. "I suppose you didn't hear of a beastly accident that happened today?" he said.

"My dear," said Mrs. Sheridan, holding up her hand, "we did. It nearly ruined the party. Laura insisted we should put it off."

"Oh, mother!" Laura didn't want to be teased about it.

"It was a horrible affair all the same," said Mr. Sheridan. "The chap was married too. Lived just below in the lane, and leaves a wife and half a dozen kiddies, so they say."

An awkward little silence fell. Mrs. Sheridan fidgeted with her cup. Really, it was very tactless of father. . . .

Suddenly she looked up. There on the table were all those sandwiches, cakes, puffs, all uneaten, all going to be wasted. She had one of her brilliant ideas.

"I know," she said. "Let's make up a basket. Let's send that poor creature some of this perfectly good food. At any rate, it will be the greatest treat for the children. Don't you agree? And she's sure to have neighbours calling in and so on. What a point to have it all ready prepared. Laura!" She jumped up. "Get me the big basket out of the stairs cupboard."

"But, mother, do you really think it's a good idea?" said Laura.

Again, how curious, she seemed to be different from them all. To take scraps from their party. Would the poor woman really like that?

"Of course! What's the matter with you today? An hour or two ago you were insisting on us being sympathetic."

Oh well! Laura ran for the basket. It was filled, it was now heaped by her mother.

"Take it yourself, darling," said she. "Run down just as you are. No, wait, take the arum lilies too. People of that class are so impressed by arum lilies."

"The stems will ruin her lace frock," said practical Jose.

So they would. Just in time. "Only the basket, then. And, Laura!"—her mother followed her out of the marquee—"don't on any account——"

"What, mother?"

No, better not put such ideas into the child's head! "Nothing! Run along."

It was just growing dusky as Laura shut their garden gates. A big dog ran by like a shadow. The road gleamed white, and down below in the hollow the little cottages were in deep shade. How quiet it seemed after the afternoon. Here she was going down the hill to somewhere where a man lay dead, and she couldn't realise it. Why couldn't she? She stopped a minute. And it seemed to her that kisses, voices, tinkling spoons, laughter, the smell of crushed grass were somehow inside her. She had no room for anything else. How strange! She looked up at the pale sky, and all she thought was, "Yes, it was the most successful party."

Now the broad road was crossed. The lane began, smoky and dark. Women in shawls and men's tweed caps hurried by. Men hung over the palings; the children played in the doorways. A low hum came from the mean little cottages. In some of them there was a flicker of light, and a shadow, crab-like, moved across the window. Laura bent her head and hurried on. She wished now she had put on a coat. How her frock shone! And the big hat with the velvet streamer—if only it was another hat! Were the people looking at her? They must be. It was a mistake to have come; she knew all along it was a mistake. Should she go back even now?

No, too late. This was the house. It must be. A dark knot of people stood outside. Beside the gate an old, old woman with a crutch sat in a chair, watching. She had her feet on a newspaper. The voices stopped as Laura drew near. The group parted. It was as though she was expected, as though they had known she was coming here.

Laura was terribly nervous. Tossing the velvet ribbon over her shoulder, she said to a woman standing by, "Is this Mrs. Scott's house?" and the woman, smiling queerly, said, "It is, my lass."

Oh, to be away from this! She actually said, "Help me, God," as she walked up the tiny path and knocked. To be away from those staring eyes, or to be covered up in anything, one of those women's shawls even. I'll just leave the basket and go, she decided. I shan't even wait for it to be emptied.

Then the door opened. A little woman in black showed in the gloom.

Laura said, "Are you Mrs. Scott?" But to her horror the woman answered, "Walk in, please, miss," and she was shut in the passage.

"No," said Laura, "I don't want to come in. I only want to leave this basket. Mother sent——"

The little woman in the gloomy passage seemed not to have heard her. "Step this way, please, miss," she said in an oily voice, and Laura followed her.

She found herself in a wretched little low kitchen, lighted by a smoky lamp. There was a woman sitting before the fire.

"Em," said the little creature who had let her in. "Em! It's a young lady." She turned to Laura. She said meaningly, "I'm 'er sister, miss. You'll excuse 'er, won't you?"

"Oh, but of course!" said Laura. "Please, please don't disturb her. I—I only want to leave——"

But at that moment the woman at the fire turned round. Her face, puffed up, red, with swollen eyes and swollen lips, looked terrible. She seemed as though she couldn't understand why Laura was there. What did it mean? Why was this stranger standing in the kitchen with a basket? What was it all about? And the poor face puckered up again.

"All right, my dear," said the other. "I'll thenk the young lady."

And again she began, "You'll excuse her, miss, I'm sure," and her face, swollen too, tried an oily smile.

Laura only wanted to get out, to get away. She was back in the passage. The door opened. She walked straight through into the bedroom, where the dead man was lying.

"You'd like a look at 'im, wouldn't you?" said Em's sister, and she brushed past Laura over to the bed. "Don't be afraid, my lass"—and now her voice sounded fond and sly, and fondly she drew down the sheet—"'e looks a picture. There's nothing to show. Come along, my dear."

Laura came.

There lay a young man, fast asleep—sleeping so soundly, so deeply, that he was far, far away from them both. Oh, so remote, so peaceful. He was dreaming. Never wake him up again. His head was sunk in the pillow, his eyes were closed; they were blind under the closed eyelids. He was given up to his dream. What did garden parties and baskets and lace frocks matter to him? He was far from all those things. He was wonderful, beautiful. While they were laughing and while the band was playing, this marvel had come to the lane. Happy … happy…. All is well, said that sleeping face. This is just as it should be. I am content.

But all the same you had to cry, and she couldn't go out of the room without saying something to him. Laura gave a loud childish sob.

"Forgive my hat," she said.

And this time she didn't wait for Em's sister. She found her way out of the door, down the path past all those dark people. At the corner of the lane she met Laurie.

He stepped out of the shadow. "Is that you, Laura?"

"Yes."

"Mother was getting anxious. Was it all right?"

"Yes, quite, Oh, Laurie!" She took his arm, she pressed up against him.

"I say, you're not crying, are you?" asked her brother.

Laura shook her head. She was.

Laurie put his arm round her shoulder. "Don't cry," he said in his warm, loving voice. "Was it awful?"

"No," sobbed Laura. "It was simply marvellous. But, Laurie—" She stopped, she looked at her brother. "Isn't life," she stammered, "isn't life—" But what life was she couldn't explain. No matter. He quite understood.

"*Isn't* it, darling?" said Laurie.

—1922

T.S. ELIOT
1888 – 1965

The poetry and prose of T.S. Eliot probably did more than that of any other writer to transform the face of twentieth-century English writing. His Modernist poems of the 1910s and 1920s (*The Waste Land* chief among them) were revolutionary both in their form and in their content—yet Eliot himself, the most unlikely of revolutionaries, became an icon of the literary establishment. He voiced in unique fashion the bleakness and despair that was characteristically felt by many in the early twentieth century—yet he became a leading voice of traditional Christianity. He embraced difficulty as the literary strategy most consonant with the character of his era—yet he also wrote a succession of highly accessible plays for the popular stage. He strove for Christian virtue, but has been strongly criticized for alleged hostility towards women and towards Jews. In short, he is a central figure of the twentieth century not only because his works are central documents of its literature, but also because they embody many of the paradoxes of the age.

Thomas Stearns Eliot was born in St. Louis, Missouri, in 1888, the youngest son in a distinguished New England family that traced its roots back to the first Puritan settlers of

Massachusetts. Eliot followed his older brother to Harvard in 1906, where he joined the board of Harvard's literary magazine and started a lifelong friendship with Conrad Aiken, a fellow board member. In 1909, the year before he completed his M.A., Eliot began drafting the poems that would become "The Love Song of J. Alfred Prufrock," "Preludes," "Portrait of a Lady," and "Rhapsody on a Windy Night." He spent a postgraduate year at the Sorbonne in Paris and then began doctoral studies in philosophy at Harvard. His dissertation was on the ideas of the then-influential French philosopher Henri Bergson, whose emphasis on the intuitive and subjective aspects of reality and on the importance of change may have influenced Eliot's poetic explorations of the human psyche. Certainly a strong awareness of the subjectivity of perception, of the importance of the unconscious, and of alienation and social claustrophobia in an unpredictably changing world are all powerful elements in Eliot's early poetry.

While both Eliot and Aiken were in London in 1914, Aiken showed the manuscript of "Prufrock" to American poet and critic Ezra Pound (then living abroad), who immediately recognized it as extraordinary work. The alliance of Pound and Eliot marked the beginning not only of Eliot's career as a poet (Pound and his wife financed the 1917 publication of *Prufrock and Other Observations*), but of a literary collaboration that profoundly influenced the development of modern literature.

"The Love Song of J. Alfred Prufrock," as critic James F. Knapp said, changed "our conception of what kind of shape a poem might take." With little connecting or transitional material, the poem juxtaposes disparate thoughts and scenes and combines classical literary references with images of urban, industrial twentieth-century life. Eliot was heavily influenced by French Symbolist poets Charles Baudelaire and Jules Laforgue. Their powerful, disconnected imagery, their ironic, detached tones, and their themes of alienation helped Eliot discover his own poetic voice. With strong rhythms that blend formal and informal speech and striking metaphors, Eliot creates an ironic love song in the frustrated inner voice of "Prufrock"'s central figure, who, in the face of his bleak physical and spiritual life, is unable to act on his love.

Inspired by what he referred to as "the mind of Europe," and with some persuasion by Pound, Eliot chose England as his permanent home. His decision was solidified by an impulsive decision in 1915 to marry Vivien Haigh-Wood, an Englishwoman whom he had met that spring. In England, Eliot balanced writing and editorial work for the avant-garde magazine *The Egoist* with more reliable employment as a schoolteacher and then as a bank clerk at Lloyd's Bank in London.

Eliot's first book of criticism, *The Sacred Wood* (1920), established him as a discerning and erudite literary critic and introduced a new set of critical precepts that would become highly influential. Eliot placed a high value on "impersonality" in poetry, and on the idea of an "objective correlative" as a means of expressing emotion through a set of objects, circumstances, or chain of events. Eliot's introduction of these ideas to the literary world helped pave the way for the critical approach known as "New Criticism." In the writings of I.A. Richards and others of this school, the focus was on the work itself as an artefact independent of authorial intention. Eliot's essays also examined his sense of the necessary difficulty of modern writing, which he believed had the nearly impossible task of synthesizing the seemingly unrelated, chaotic experiences of modern citizens.

By 1921, affected by the strain of overwork and the increasing pressure of his wife's failing physical and mental health, Eliot had a nervous breakdown. During a three-month-long rest cure, he was finally able to complete *The Waste Land*, a project he had begun in 1914. Originally composed as a series of narrative poems, *The Waste Land* was considerably longer in its original version; Pound helped Eliot pare down and fuse the diverse materials into a rhythmically coherent whole. Published in 1922, *The Waste Land* deviated far more decisively than had "Prufrock" from accepted notions of what constituted poetry. Written in fragmented form, this poem of complex imagery, multiple voices, jazz rhythms, and dense literary and mythological allusions jumps between perspectives and scenes without connective or transitional passages. With its radical break from established conventions in structure, theme, and expression, and its blending of western and of non-western ideologies, *The Waste Land* can be disorienting for readers—so much so, in fact, that when the poem first appeared some writers and critics wondered if the poem was a hoax orchestrated by Eliot and his literary friends.

Much as *The Waste Land* was derided in some quarters, in others it established Eliot as a groundbreaking writer. Meanwhile, his critical writing in the international literary journal *The Criterion* (which Eliot founded in 1922) helped to round out his reputation as one of London's leading literary figures. In 1925, Eliot was recruited by the publishing firm Faber and Gwyer (later Faber and Faber) as a literary editor and board member. The position, which he held for many years, further extended Eliot's influence, as he was able to cultivate young writers—such as W.H. Auden—whose work he found promising.

Eliot's next long poem, *The Hollow Men* (1925), in some ways extends *The Waste Land*'s articulation of alienation and despair, but it also deals with more transcendent themes of what Eliot called "the salvation of the soul." Eliot's Christian faith continued to strengthen, and in 1927, the same year he was naturalized as a British citizen, Eliot was baptized into the Church of England. Religion thereafter became the focus of his life, and in 1933 he moved to Glenville Place presbytery, where he served as a church warden for seven years. There he wrote a series of poetic meditations on religious themes and scenarios, including *Journey of the Magi* (1927) and *Marina* (1930). Steeped in Eliot's studies of Shakespeare and Dante, these works meditate on spiritual growth while experimenting with more traditional dramatic forms. The dramatic monologue form in which *Journey of the Magi* is constructed, for example, is reminiscent of Robert Browning's work.

Much of Eliot's later career focused on dramatic writing. For many years he worked on *Sweeney Agonistes*, an unfinished experimental play of modern life, written in rhythmic prose accented by drum beats. He then published two ecclesiastical dramas, one of which was *Murder in the Cathedral* (1935), a ritual drama based on the murder of Thomas à Becket, before turning to clever West End social dramas like *The Cocktail Party* (1950). Though innovative in their attempts to reconcile classical drama with modern themes, these plays have not been successfully revived in recent decades. Ironically, however, a book of playful children's verse that Eliot wrote for his godchildren, *Old Possum's Book of Practical Cats* (1939), has been much more successful on the stage than any of Eliot's plays; it was adapted by British composer Andrew Lloyd Webber into the hit musical *Cats* (1980).

Despite a busy lecturing schedule and a marriage that was increasingly taxing (Vivien was institutionalized in 1938), Eliot produced four long poems in the late 1930s and early 1940s that together, published as *Four Quartets* (1943), he considered his crowning achievement. Comprising "Burnt Norton," "The Dry Salvages," "East Coker," and "Little Gidding," *Four Quartets* was in part inspired by the later string quartets of Beethoven. With its powerfully suggestive imagery and elaborate patterns of sound, it is among Eliot's most complex and technically masterful works. It also gives voice to Eliot's conviction that, in a world otherwise devoid of meaning, submission to God is essential. *Four Quartets* for a time took pride of place over *The Waste Land* as Eliot's most celebrated work.

The late years of Eliot's life were filled with personal happiness and public recognition of his contribution to modern literature. He was awarded eighteen honorary degrees, and in 1948 he was awarded both a Nobel Prize for Literature and the British Order of Merit. Vivien having died in 1947, in 1957 Elliot married Valerie Fletcher and enjoyed what he described as the only happy period of his life since childhood. He died in London in 1965 and was buried, according to his wishes, in his ancestors' parish church at East Coker. The plaque on the church wall bears his chosen epitaph, from *Four Quartets*: "In my beginning is my end, in my end is my beginning."

Near the end of his life Eliot commented, with sly irony, that he would "perhaps have a certain historical place in the literary history of our period." And indeed, he was lauded on his death as a unique literary figure; his obituary in *Life* magazine declared that "our age beyond any doubt has been, and will continue to be, the Age of Eliot." In subsequent decades the praise has been less effusive, and in two respects Eliot's work has been sharply criticized: most critics now acknowledge elements of misogyny and of anti-Semitism in his writing. But the impact of his poetic innovation is lasting, and a sense of the centrality of Eliot's work to the literary history of the twentieth century has remained constant. As Northrop Frye observed, "Whether he is liked or disliked is of no importance, but he must be read."

⌘⌘⌘

The Love Song of J. Alfred Prufrock[1]

S'io credesse che mia risposta fosse
A persona che mai tornasse al mondo,
Questa fiamma staria senza piu scosse.
Ma perciocche giammai di questo fondo
Non torno viva alcun, s'i'odo il vero,
Senza tema d'infamia ti rispondo.[2]

Let us go then, you and I,
When the evening is spread out against the sky

[1] *J. Alfred Prufrock* The name is likely taken from the The Prufrock-Littau Company, a furniture dealer located in St. Louis, Eliot's birthplace.

[2] *S'io credesse ... ti rispondo* Italian: "If I thought that my reply were given to anyone who might return to the world, this flame would stand forever still; but since never from this deep place has anyone ever returned alive, if what I hear is true, without fear of infamy I answer thee," Dante's *Inferno* 27.61–66; Guido da Montefeltro's speech as he burns in Hell.

Like a patient etherized upon a table;
Let us go, through certain half-deserted streets,
5   The muttering retreats
Of restless nights in one-night cheap hotels
And sawdust restaurants with oyster-shells:
Streets that follow like a tedious argument
Of insidious intent
10   To lead you to an overwhelming question …
Oh, do not ask, "What is it?"
Let us go and make our visit.

In the room the women come and go
Talking of Michelangelo.

15   The yellow fog that rubs its back upon the
          window-panes,
The yellow smoke that rubs its muzzle on the
          window-panes
Licked its tongue into the corners of the evening,
Lingered upon the pools that stand in drains,
Let fall upon its back the soot that falls from chimneys,
20   Slipped by the terrace, made a sudden leap,
And seeing that it was a soft October night,
Curled once about the house, and fell asleep.

And indeed there will be time
For the yellow smoke that slides along the street,
25   Rubbing its back upon the window panes;
There will be time, there will be time[1]
To prepare a face to meet the faces that you meet
There will be time to murder and create,
And time for all the works and days[2] of hands
30   That lift and drop a question on your plate;
Time for you and time for me,
And time yet for a hundred indecisions,
And for a hundred visions and revisions,
Before the taking of a toast and tea.

35   In the room the women come and go
Talking of Michelangelo.

And indeed there will be time
To wonder, "Do I dare?" and, "Do I dare?"
Time to turn back and descend the stair,
40   With a bald spot in the middle of my hair—
(They will say: "How his hair is growing thin!")
My morning coat,[3] my collar mounting firmly to the
          chin,
My necktie rich and modest, but asserted by a simple
          pin—
(They will say: "But how his arms and legs are thin!")
45   Do I dare
Disturb the universe?
In a minute there is time
For decisions and revisions which a minute will reverse.

For I have known them all already, known them
          all—
50   Have known the evenings, mornings, afternoons,
I have measured out my life with coffee spoons;
I know the voices dying with a dying fall[4]
Beneath the music from a farther room.
          So how should I presume?

55   And I have known the eyes already, known them
          all—
The eyes that fix you in a formulated phrase,
And when I am formulated, sprawling on a pin,
When I am pinned and wriggling on the wall,
Then how should I begin
60   To spit out all the butt-ends of my days and ways?
          And how should I presume?

And I have known the arms already, known them
          all—
Arms that are braceleted and white and bare
(But in the lamplight, downed with light brown hair!)
65   Is it perfume from a dress
That makes me so digress?
Arms that lie along a table, or wrap about a shawl.

---

[1] *there will be time*   See Ecclesiastes 3.1–8. "To everything there is a season, and a time to every purpose under heaven: A time to be born, and a time to die; a time to plant, and a time to pluck up that which is planted; a time to kill, and a time to heal …"

[2] *works and days*   Title of a poem by eighth-century BCE Greek poet Hesiod.

[3] *morning coat*   A formal coat with tails.

[4] *with a dying fall*   In Shakespeare's *Twelfth Night* 1.1.1–15. Duke Orsino commands, "That strain again, it had a dying fall."

And should I then presume?
And how should I begin?

*   *   *

70 Shall I say, I have gone at dusk through narrow streets
And watched the smoke that rises from the pipes
Of lonely men in shirt-sleeves, leaning out of
    windows? ...[1]

    I should have been a pair of ragged claws
Scuttling across the floors of silent seas.[2]

*   *   *

75 And the afternoon, the evening, sleeps so peacefully!
Smoothed by long fingers,
Asleep ... tired ... or it malingers,
Stretched on the floor, here beside you and me.
Should I, after tea and cakes and ices,
80 Have the strength to force the moment to its crisis?
But though I have wept and fasted, wept and prayed,
Though I have seen my head (grown slightly bald)
    brought in upon a platter,[3]
I am no prophet[4]—and here's no great matter;
I have seen the moment of my greatness flicker,
85 And I have seen the eternal Footman hold my coat,
    and snicker,
And in short, I was afraid.

    And would it have been worth it, after all,
After the cups, the marmalade, the tea,
Among the porcelain, among some talk of you and me,

90 Would it have been worth while,
To have bitten off the matter with a smile,
To have squeezed the universe into a ball[5]
To roll it toward some overwhelming question,
To say: "I am Lazarus,[6] come from the dead,
95 Come back to tell you all, I shall tell you all"—
If one, settling a pillow by her head,
    Should say: "That is not what I meant at all;
    That is not it, at all."

    And would it have been worth it, after all,
100 Would it have been worth while,
After the sunsets and the dooryards and the sprinkled
    streets,[7]
After the novels, after the teacups, after the skirts that
    trail along the floor—
And this, and so much more?—
It is impossible to say just what I mean!
105 But as if a magic lantern[8] threw the nerves in patterns
    on a screen:
Would it have been worth while
If one, settling a pillow or throwing off a shawl,
And turning toward the window, should say:
    "That is not it at all,
110   That is not what I meant, at all."

*   *   *

No! I am not Prince Hamlet, nor was meant to be;
Am an attendant lord, one that will do
To swell a progress,[9] start a scene or two,
Advise the prince; no doubt, an easy tool,
115 Deferential, glad to be of use,
Politic, cautious, and meticulous;
Full of high sentence,[10] but a bit obtuse;

---

[1] ...   The ellipsis here makes note of a 38 line insertion written by Eliot, entitled *Prufrock's Pervigilium*. The subtitle and 33 of the lines were later removed.

[2] *I should ... seas* See Shakespeare's *Hamlet* 2.2, in which Hamlet tells Polonius, "for you yourself, sir, should be old as I am, if like a crab you could go backwards."

[3] *brought in upon a platter* Reference to Matthew 14.1–12, in which the prophet John the Baptist is beheaded at the command of Herod, and his head presented to Salomé upon a platter.

[4] *I am no prophet* See Amos 7.14. When commanded by King Amiziah not to prophesy, the Judean Amos answered; "I was no prophet, neither was I a prophet's son; but I was a herdsman, and a farmer of sycamore fruit."

[5] *Squeezed ... ball* See Andrew Marvell's "To His Coy Mistress" 41–2: "Let us roll our strength and all / Our sweetness up into one ball."

[6] *Lazarus* Raised from the dead by Jesus in John 11.1–44.

[7] *sprinkled streets* Streets sprayed with water to keep dust down.

[8] *magic lantern* In Victorian times, a device used to project images painted on glass onto a blank screen or wall.

[9] *progress* Journey made by royalty through the country.

[10] *high sentence* Serious, elevated sentiments or opinions.

At times, indeed, almost ridiculous—
Almost, at times, the Fool.

120   I grow old ... I grow old ...
I shall wear the bottoms of my trousers rolled.

Shall I part my hair behind? Do I dare to eat a
peach?
I shall wear white flannel trousers, and walk upon the
beach.
I have heard the mermaids singing,[1] each to each.

125   I do not think that they will sing to me.

I have seen them riding seaward on the waves
Combing the white hair of the waves blown back
When the wind blows the water white and black.

We have lingered in the chambers of the sea
130   By sea-girls wreathed with seaweed red and brown
Till human voices wake us, and we drown.
—1915, 1917

Preludes [2]

1

The winter evening settles down
With smell of steaks in passageways.
Six o'clock.
The burnt-out ends of smoky days.
5   And now a gusty shower wraps
The grimy scraps
Of withered leaves about your feet
And newspapers from vacant lots;
The showers beat
10   On broken blinds and chimney-pots,
And at the corner of the street
A lonely cab-horse steams and stamps.
And then the lighting of the lamps.

2

The morning comes to consciousness
15   Of faint stale smells of beer
From the sawdust-trampled[3] street
With all its muddy feet that press
To early coffee-stands.
With the other masquerades
20   That time resumes,
One thinks of all the hands
That are raising dingy shades
In a thousand furnished rooms.

3

You tossed a blanket from the bed,
25   You lay upon your back, and waited;
You dozed, and watched the night revealing
The thousand sordid images
Of which your soul was constituted;
They flickered against the ceiling.
30   And when all the world came back
And the light crept up between the shutters,
And you heard the sparrows in the gutters,
You had such a vision of the street
As the street hardly understands;
35   Sitting along the bed's edge, where
You curled the papers from your hair,[4]
Or clasped the yellow soles of feet
In the palms of both soiled hands.

4

His soul stretched tight across the skies
40   That fade behind a city block,
Or trampled by insistent feet
At four and five and six o'clock;
And short square fingers stuffing pipes,
And evening newspapers, and eyes
45   Assured of certain certainties,
The conscience of a blackened street
Impatient to assume the world.

I am moved by fancies that are curled
Around these images, and cling:

[1] *I have ... singing* See John Donne's "Song": "Teach me to hear the mermaids singing."

[2] *Preludes* In Parts 3 and 4 of this poem, many of the images and details of setting are taken from Charles-Louis Philippe's novel *Bubu-de-Montparnasse* (1898).

[3] *sawdust-trampled* Sawdust was placed on the floors of bars and restaurants to absorb dirt.

[4] *papers ... hair* I.e., "curl papers," used to curl hair.

50 The notion of some infinitely gentle
Infinitely suffering thing.

    Wipe your hand across your mouth, and laugh;
The worlds revolve like ancient women
Gathering fuel in vacant lots.
    —1915

Burbank with a Baedeker: Bleistein with a Cigar [1]

Tra-la- la- la- la- la-laire—nil nisi divinum stabile est; caetera fumus [2]—the gondola stopped, the old palace was there, how charming its grey and pink [3]—goats and monkeys, with such hair too! [4]—so the countess passed on until she came through the little park, where Niobe presented her with a cabinet, and so departed. [5]

Burbank crossed a little bridge
    Descending at a small hotel;
Princess Volupine arrived,
    They were together, and he fell. [6]

5 Defunctive° music under sea   *dying*
    Passed seaward with the passing bell

Slowly: the God Hercules
    Had left him, that had loved him well. [7]

The horses, under the axletree
10   Beat up the dawn from Istria [8]
With even feet. Her shuttered barge
    Burned on the water all the day.

But this or such was Bleistein's way:
    A saggy bending of the knees
15 And elbows, with the palms turned out,
    Chicago Semite Viennese.

A lustreless protrusive eye
    Stares from the protozoic slime
At a perspective of Canaletto. [9]
20   The smoky candle end of time

Declines. On the Rialto [10] once.
    The rats are underneath the piles.
The jew is underneath the lot. [11]
    Money in furs. [12] The boatman smiles,

25 Princess Volupine extends
    A meagre, blue-nailed, phthisic° hand   *consumptive*
To climb the waterstair. Lights, lights,
    She entertains Sir Ferdinand

---

[1] *Baedeker* Popular line of guide-books; *Bleistein* Jewish-German name literally meaning "Leadstone."

[2] *nil ... fumus* Latin: Nothing but the divine endures; all the rest is smoke.

[3] *the gondola ... pink* From Henry James's *Aspern Papers* (1888), Chapter 1. The passage is narrated by an American woman living in Venice who is giving her visiting friend a tour of the city: "The gondola stopped, the old palace was there.... 'How charming! It's grey and pink!' my companion exclaimed."

[4] *goats and monkeys* An exclamation made by Othello in Shakespeare's *Othello* 4.1 (set in Venice) when he becomes convinced his wife is having an affair; *with such hair too* From Robert Browning's "A Toccata of Galuppi's," about the eighteenth-century Venetian composer Baldassare Galuppi (1706–85).

[5] *so the ... departed* From the stage directions of *Entertainment of Alice, Dowager Countess of Derby* by John Marston (c.1575–1634); *Niobe* Mother in Greek myth who boasted that her children were better than those of Zeus.

[6] *They were ... fell* From Alfred Tennyson's "The Sisters" (Eliot has changed the pronoun from "she" to "he").

[7] *Defunctive music ... well* See Shakespeare's *Antony and Cleopatra* 4.3, in which Cleopatra's soldiers hear music just before they are defeated by Caesar's army. "'Tis the god Hercules, whom Antony lov'd, / Now leaves him," one soldier says.

[8] *Horses ... dawn* In classical myth, the sun is a chariot pulled across the sky; *Istria* Peninsula that juts into the northeast Adriatic.

[9] *Canaletto* Italian painter Antonio Canale (1697–1768), famous for his paintings of Venice and London.

[10] *Rialto* Island in Venice, containing the old mercantile quarter of the medieval city.

[11] *The jew ... lot* For a discussion of the controversy over Eliot's attitudes towards Jewish people, see the "In Context" section on "Eliot and Anti-Semitism" later in this volume.

[12] *Money in furs* Venice was a center for fur trade from the Black Sea.

Klein. Who clipped the lion's wings[1]
30   And flea'd his rump and pared his claws?
Thought Burbank, meditating on
      Time's ruins, and the seven laws.[2]
—1919

Gerontion[3]

Thou hast nor youth nor age
But as it were an after dinner sleep
Dreaming of both.[4]

Here I am, an old man in a dry month,
    Being read to by a boy, waiting for rain.[5]
I was neither at the hot gates[6]
Nor fought in the warm rain
5   Nor knee deep in the salt marsh, heaving a cutlass,
Bitten by flies, fought.
My house is a decayed house,
And the jew squats on the window sill, the owner,
Spawned in some estaminet[7] of Antwerp,
10 Blistered in Brussels, patched and peeled in London.[8]

The goat coughs at night in the field overhead;
Rocks, moss, stonecrop, iron, merds.[9]
The woman keeps the kitchen, makes tea,
Sneezes at evening, poking the peevish gutter.[10]
15   I an old man,
A dull head among windy spaces.

    Signs are taken for wonders. "We would see a sign!"
The word within a word, unable to speak a word,
Swaddled with darkness.[11] In the juvescence°   *youth*
    of the year
20 Came Christ the tiger

    In depraved May, dogwood and chestnut,
      flowering judas,[12]
To be eaten, to be divided, to be drunk
Among whispers; by Mr. Silvero
With caressing hands, at Limoges[13]
25 Who walked all night in the next room;

    By Hakagawa, bowing among the Titians;[14]
By Madame de Tornquist, in the dark room
Shifting the candles; Fraulein von Kulp
Who turned in the hall, one hand on the door.
30   Vacant shuttles
Weave the wind. I have no ghosts,
An old man in a draughty house
Under a windy knob.[15]

---

[1] *lion's wings* The winged lion was a symbol of the Venetian Republic.

[2] *seven laws* Either the seven laws of architecture that John Ruskin outlined in his *Seven Lamps of Architecture* (1849), which describes Venice's Gothic style as the ideal, or the Noachian Laws, the Seven Commandments of the Sons of Noah from the Jewish Talmud.

[3] *Gerontion* Greek: little old man. Eliot originally planned to print this poem as a prelude to *The Waste Land*, but when Ezra Pound advised against this he published it separately.

[4] *Thou hast ... both* From Shakespeare's *Measure for Measure* 3.1.32–34.

[5] *Here I ... rain* These two lines are based on a sentence in A.C. Benson's biography *Edward Fitzgerald* (1905), in which the poet is described as sitting "in a dry month, old and blind, being read to by a country boy, longing for rain."

[6] *hot gates* Literal translation of the Greek *Thermopylae*, a pass between northern and central Greece and the location of several historical battles, including that between the Greeks and the Persians in 480 BCE.

[7] *stonecrop* Herb with yellow flowers that grows on rocks or old walls; *estaminet* French: café.

[8] *the jew ... London* The association of Jews with images of squalor, decay, and disgusting physicality was one of the many ways in which anti-Semitism was expressed in British literary tradition. For more on the controversy over such elements as they appear in

Eliot's verse see the "In Context" section below.

[9] *merds* Feces.

[10] *gutter* Sputtering fire.

[11] *Signs are ... darkness* Reference to two Biblical passages. The first is Matthew 12.39: "An evil and adulterous generation seeketh after a sign; and there shall no sign be given to it, but the sign of the prophet Jonas," and the second is John 1.1: "In the beginning was the Word, and the Word was with God, and the Word was God." Both of these passages were sources for a Christmas sermon given by Anglican preacher Lancelot Andrewes in 1618.

[12] *judas* Purple-flowered tree of southern Europe named after Judas, who was said to have hanged himself from a tree of this type after betraying Jesus.

[13] *Limoges* French town known for its china of the same name.

[14] *Titians* Paintings by Venetian painter Titian (1485–1576).

[15] *Vacant shuttles ... knob* See Job 7.6–7: "My days are swifter than a weaver's shuttle, and are spent without hope. O remember that my life is wind: mine eye shall no more see good"; *knob* Knoll.

After such knowledge, what forgiveness? Think now
35   History has many cunning passages, contrived
      corridors
  And issues, deceives with whispering ambitions,
  Guides us by vanities. Think now
  She gives when our attention is distracted
  And what she gives, gives with such supple confusions
40   That the giving famishes the craving. Gives too late
  What's not believed in, or if still believed,
  In memory only, reconsidered passion. Gives too soon
  Into weak hands,[1] what's thought can be dispensed with
  Till the refusal propagates a fear. Think
45   Neither fear nor courage saves us. Unnatural vices
  Are fathered by our heroism. Virtues
  Are forced upon us by our impudent crimes.
  These tears are shaken from the wrath-bearing tree.

    The tiger springs in the new year. Us he devours.
      Think at last
50   We have not reached conclusion, when I
  Stiffen in a rented house. Think at last
  I have not made this show purposelessly
  And it is not by any concitation°   *stirring up*
  Of the backward devils.[2]
55   I would meet you upon this honestly.
  I that was near your heart was removed therefrom
  To lose beauty in terror, terror in inquisition.
  I have lost my passion: why should I need to keep it
  Since what is kept must be adulterated?
60   I have lost my sight, smell, hearing, taste and touch:
  How should I use them for your closer contact?

    These with a thousand small deliberations
  Protract the profit of their chilled delirium,
  Excite the membrane, when the sense has cooled,
65   With pungent sauces, multiply variety
  In a wilderness of mirrors. What will the spider do,
  Suspend its operations, will the weevil
  Delay? De Bailhache, Fresca, Mrs. Cammel, whirled
  Beyond the circuit of the shuddering Bear[3]

70   In fractured atoms. Gull against the wind, in the
      windy straits
  Of Belle Isle, or running on the Horn,[4]
  White feathers in the snow, the Gulf[5] claims,
  And an old man driven by the Trades[6]
  To a sleepy corner.

75   Tenants of the house,
  Thoughts of a dry brain in a dry season.
  —1920

The Waste Land

The title and plan of Eliot's groundbreaking poem *The Waste Land* were substantially influenced by Jessie Weston's *From Ritual to Romance* (1920), which details the various legends of the Holy Grail and explores the influence of pre-Christian religions on these legends. According to most accounts of the Grail, the sacred vessel lies in the heart of a (formerly fertile) Waste Land that is now stricken with drought and presided over by a Fisher King who is cursed with impotence. The land and its king can only be saved from permanent sterility by a knight who is able to pass several tests and attain the Grail, thus bringing about regeneration. Overlaying this myth with a modern setting and numerous cultural references, Eliot shows that a similar sterility plagues a contemporary society characterized by casual sexuality, blatant materialism, and industrial exploitation of nature.

With its disparate images, ever-shifting narrative events, and seemingly random structure, *The Waste Land* embraces the fragmented present while looking back to a more coherent past. Allusions to seventeenth-century poets, to Chaucer, to Shakespeare, to Dante, to pre-Socratic philosophers, and to works of history and anthropology, such as James Frazer's

---

[1] *too soon ... hands* See Percy Shelley's *Adonais* (1821), in which he describes Keats's death: "Too soon, and with weak hands."

[2] *backward devils* In Dante's *Inferno*, tellers of the future were punished by being forced to walk backwards.

[3] *Bear* Constellation Ursa Major (the Great Bear).

[4] *Belle Isle* Channel between Labrador and Newfoundland at the entrance to the Gulf of St. Lawrence; *the Horn* Cape Horn, the southernmost tip of South America.

[5] *Gulf* Gulf stream, a warm ocean current in the North Atlantic.

[6] *Trades* Trade winds, which blow, almost constantly, towards the equator.

twelve-volume anthropological study *The Golden Bough* (1890–1915), gesture towards the presence of a recurring order beneath contemporary history and indicate the possibility of regeneration. The poem's disconnected and highly allusive character (which gives it a sense of difficulty more often heightened than alleviated by Eliot's copious notes) provoked charges of intentional obscurity upon the poem's publication, but Eliot maintained that any poetry developed out of such a complex and various society must itself be various and complex.

By its very nature, *The Waste Land* seems to resist order and any cohesive account of meaning; its complexity and ambiguity make possible a variety of interpretations. Even the identity of its narrator is unclear: are all the disparate voices filtered through any single voice? And, if so, is the voice that of the blind prophet Tiresias, or some other nameless narrator, or is the speaker Eliot himself? This very complexity may in large part be responsible for the continued vitality of the poem, however. Eliot's friend Conrad Aiken maintained that the poem was important primarily for its private "emotional value," and that readers should rely as much on their first responses to the diverse elements of the poem as on the copious and ever-expanding body of scholarship surrounding it. As much as *The Waste Land* has taken its place as a central document of the modernist movement, it retains as well the ability to speak directly to readers.

The Waste Land [1]

"Nam Sibyllam quidem Cumis ego ipse oculis meis vidi in ampulla pendere, et cum illi pueri dicerent: Σίβυλλα τί

θέλεις; respondebat illa: ἀποθανεῖν θέλω."[2]

For Ezra Pound
il miglior fabbro.[3]

1. THE BURIAL OF THE DEAD[4]

April is the cruellest month, breeding
Lilacs out of the dead land, mixing
Memory and desire, stirring
Dull roots with spring rain.
5 Winter kept us warm, covering
Earth in forgetful snow, feeding
A little life with dried tubers.
Summer surprised us, coming over the Starnbergersee[5]
With a shower of rain; we stopped in the colonnade,
10 And went on in sunlight, into the Hofgarten,[6]
And drank coffee, and talked for an hour.
Bin gar keine Russin, stamm' aus Litauen, echt deutsch.[7]
And when we were children, staying at the archduke's,
My cousin's, he took me out on a sled,
15 And I was frightened. He said, Marie,
Marie, hold on tight. And down we went.
In the mountains, there you feel free.
I read, much of the night, and go south in the winter.

What are the roots that clutch, what branches
    grow

---

[1] [Eliot's note] Not only the title, but the plan and a good deal of the incidental symbolism of the poem were suggested by Miss Jessie L. Weston's book on the Grail legend: *From Ritual to Romance* (Cambridge). Indeed, so deeply am I indebted, Miss Weston's book will elucidate the difficulties of the poem much better than my notes can do; and I recommend it (apart from the great interest of the book itself) to any who think such elucidation of the poem worth the trouble. To another work of anthropology I am indebted in general, one which has influenced our generation profoundly; I mean [Sir James Frazer's 1890 to 1915 twelve-volume] *The Golden Bough*; I have used especially the two volumes *Adonis, Attis, Osiris*. Anyone who is acquainted with these works will immediately recognise in the poem certain references to vegetation ceremonies.

[2] *Nam … θέλω* Latin and Greek: "For once I saw with my own eyes the Sybil at Cumae hanging in a cage, and when the boys asked her, 'Sybil, what do you want?' she responded, 'I want to die.'" From the *Satyricon* of Petronius Arbiter (first-century CE Roman writer). The most famous of the prophetic Sibyls of Greek mythology, the Cumaean Sibyl received immortality from the god Apollo, but neglected to ask him for eternal youth.

[3] *il miglior fabbro* Italian: the better craftsman. This compliment was originally paid by Dante, in his *Purgatorio* (26.117), to the Provençal poet, Arnaut Daniel. Eliot adopts it for his dedication to fellow expatriate and Modernist American poet, Ezra Pound (1885–1972), who played a key editorial role in the poem's production.

[4] *The Burial of the Dead* Reference to the Anglican Order for the Burial of the Dead.

[5] *Starnbergersee* Lake near Munich, Germany.

[6] *Hofgarten* Public park in Munich.

[7] *Bin … deutsch* German: I'm not Russian at all, I come from Lithuania, a pure German.

20 Out of this stony rubbish? Son of man,[1]
You cannot say, or guess, for you know only
A heap of broken images, where the sun beats,
And the dead tree gives no shelter, the cricket no
 relief,[2]
And the dry stone no sound of water. Only
25 There is shadow under this red rock,[3]
(Come in under the shadow of this red rock),
And I will show you something different from either
Your shadow at morning striding behind you
Or your shadow at evening rising to meet you;
30 I will show you fear in a handful of dust.
   Frisch weht der Wind
   Der Heimat zu
   Mein Irisch Kind,
   Wo weilest du?[4]
35 "You gave me hyacinths first a year ago;
They called me the hyacinth girl."
—Yet when we came back, late, from the Hyacinth
 garden,
Your arms full, and your hair wet, I could not
Speak, and my eyes failed, I was neither
40 Living nor dead, and I knew nothing,
Looking into the heart of light, the silence.
Oed' und leer das Meer.[5]

Madame Sosostris,[6] famous clairvoyante,
Had a bad cold, nevertheless
45 Is known to be the wisest woman in Europe,
With a wicked pack of cards.[7] Here, said she,
Is your card, the drowned Phoenician Sailor,
(Those are pearls that were his eyes.[8] Look!)
Here is Belladonna, the Lady of the Rocks,[9]
50 The lady of situations.
Here is the man with three staves, and here the Wheel,[10]
And here is the one-eyed merchant, and this card,
Which is blank, is something he carries on his back,
Which I am forbidden to see. I do not find
55 The Hanged Man.[11] Fear death by water.
I see crowds of people, walking round in a ring.
Thank you. If you see dear Mrs. Equitone,
Tell her I bring the horoscope myself:
One must be so careful these days.

---

[1] *Son of man* Eliot's note cites Ezekiel 2.1, in which God addresses Ezekiel, whose mission will be to preach the coming of the Messiah to unbelievers, saying, "Son of man, stand upon thy feet, and I will speak unto thee."

[2] *cricket no relief* Eliot's note cites Ecclesiastes 12.5, in which the preacher speaks of the fearful deprivations of old age: "Also *when* they shall be afraid of *that which is* high, and fears *shall be* in the way, and the almond tree shall flourish, and the grasshopper shall be a burden, and desire shall fail: because man goeth to his long home, and the mourners go about the streets …"

[3] *There is shadow … rock* See Isaiah 32.2, in which the blessings of Christ's kingdom are described: "And a man shall be as an hiding place from the wind, and a covert from the tempest; as rivers of water in a dry place, as the shadow of a great rock in a weary land."

[4] *Frisch … du?* German: "Fresh blows the wind to the homeland—my Irish child, where do you tarry?" From Richard Wagner's opera *Tristan und Isolde* (1865), 1.5–8, this is a sailor's lament for the girl he has left behind in Ireland.

[5] *Oed' … Meer* German: "Desolate and empty is the sea." Eliot's note cites *Tristan und Isolde* 3.24, in which Tristan lies dying, waiting for his beloved, Isolde, to come to him, but there is no sign of her ship on the sea.

[6] *Madame Sosostris* This name is often thought to have been "unconsciously" borrowed by Eliot from the name of the fortune-teller Madame Sesostris in Aldous Huxley's novel *Crome Yellow* (1921). It may more plausibly have derived from the Greek word for saviour, *soteros*.

[7] [Eliot's note] I am not familiar with the exact constitution of the Tarot pack of cards, from which I have obviously departed to suit my own convenience. The Hanged Man, a member of the traditional pack, fits my purpose in two ways: because he is associated in my mind with the Hanged God of Frazer, and because I associate him with the hooded figure in the passage of the disciples to Emmaus in Part V. The Phoenician Sailor and the Merchant appear later; also the "crowds of people," and Death by Water is executed in Part IV. The Man with Three Staves (an authentic member of the Tarot pack) I associate, quite arbitrarily, with the Fisher King himself. [The Tarot pack, generally used for fortune-telling, consists of 78 cards in four suits—cups, wands, swords, and pentangles. It originated in France and Italy in the fourteenth century.]

[8] *Those are … eyes* From Ariel's song in Shakespeare's *The Tempest* 1.2.397-403: "Full fathom five thy father lies; / Of his bones are coral made; / Those are pearls that were his eyes; / Nothing of him that doth fade / But doth suffer a sea-change / Into something rich and strange: / Sea nymphs hourly ring his knell: / *Burden*. Ding-dong. / Hark! Now I hear them—ding-dong bell."

[9] *Belladonna* Italian: beautiful woman. Also another name for the poisonous plant deadly nightshade, once used for cosmetic purposes by Italian women; *Lady of the Rocks* Possible ironic reference to Leonardo da Vinci's painting *Madonna of the Rocks*.

[10] *Wheel* Wheel of Fortune.

[11] *Hanged Man* This man's self-sacrifice in the role of fertility god is necessary for the annual rejuvenation of the land.

60   Unreal City,[1]
     Under the brown fog of a winter dawn,
     A crowd flowed over London Bridge, so many,
     I had not thought death had undone so many.[2]
     Sighs, short and infrequent, were exhaled,
65   And each man fixed his eyes before his feet.
     Flowed up the hill and down King William Street,
     To where Saint Mary Woolnoth[3] kept the hours
     With a dead sound on the final stroke of nine.[4]
     There I saw one I knew, and stopped him, crying
       "Stetson![5]
70   You who were with me in the ships at Mylae![6]
     That corpse you planted last year in your garden,
     Has it begun to sprout? Will it bloom this year?
     Or has the sudden frost disturbed its bed?
     Oh keep the Dog far hence, that's friend to men,
75   Or with his nails he'll dig it up again![7]
     You! hypocrite lecteur!—mon semblable,—mon frère!"[8]

---

[1] *Unreal City*   Eliot's note cites the following lines from the 1859
poem "Les sept vieillards" by poet Charles Baudelaire: "Fourmillante
cité, cité pleine de rêves, / Où le spectre en plein jour raccroche le
passant." (French: "Swarming city, city full of dreams, / Where the
daylight spectre intercepts the passerby.") "The City" is the name for
London's financial district, located north of London Bridge.

[2] *so many ... so many*   Eliot's note cites Dante's *Inferno* 3.55–57:
"such a long stream / of people, that I would not have thought / that
death had undone so many." This is spoken by Dante soon after he
has entered the Gates of Hell in the company of Virgil, his guide
through the underworld.

[3] *Saint Mary Woolnoth*   Church in King William Street. Eliot
joined a campaign to have this church, and others like it that were
slated for demolition, preserved.

[4] [Eliot's note]   A phenomenon which I have often noticed.

[5] *Stetson*   Eliot, when questioned, maintained this was a reference
to the average City clerk, and not, as some had suggested, to Ezra
Pound, whose nickname was "Buffalo Bill."

[6] *Mylae*   The Battle of Mylae (260 BCE) took place in the trade-
based First Punic War between the Romans and the Carthaginians.

[7] *O keep ... men*   Eliot's note cites the dirge in John Webster's play
The White Devil (1612) 5.4: "But keep the wolf far thence, that's foe
to men, / For with his nails he'll dig them up again." Sirius, the Dog
Star, heralded the annual flooding of the Nile in Egyptian mythology.

[8] *hypocrite ... mon frère*   French: "Hypocrite reader—my double—my brother!" Eliot's note cites the preface of Baudelaire's *Fleurs
du Mal*.

---

2. A GAME OF CHESS [9]

     The Chair she sat in, like a burnished throne,[10]
     Glowed on the marble, where the glass
     Held up by standards wrought with fruited vines
80   From which a golden Cupidon peeped out
     (Another hid his eyes behind his wing)
     Doubled the flames of sevenbranched candelabra
     Reflecting light upon the table as
     The glitter of her jewels rose to meet it,
85   From satin cases poured in rich profusion;
     In vials of ivory and coloured glass
     Unstoppered, lurked her strange synthetic perfumes,
     Unguent, powdered, or liquid—troubled, confused
     And drowned the sense in odours; stirred by the air
90   That freshened from the window, these ascended
     In fattening the prolonged candle-flames,
     Flung their smoke into the laquearia,[11]
     Stirring the pattern on the coffered ceiling.
     Huge sea-wood fed with copper
95   Burned green and orange, framed by the coloured
       stone,
     In which sad light a carved dolphin swam.
     Above the antique mantel was displayed
     As though a window gave upon the sylvan scene[12]
     The change of Philomel, by the barbarous king
100 So rudely forced;[13] yet there the nightingale
     Filled all the desert with inviolable voice
     And still she cried, and still the world pursues,

---

[9] *A Game of Chess*   Title of Thomas Middleton's 1624 satirical
political drama. In Middleton's play *Women Beware Women*, a game
of chess distracts a mother-in-law, preventing her from noticing that
her daughter-in-law is being seduced upstairs. Each move in the
chess game mirrors a move in the seduction.

[10] [Eliot's note]   Cf. Antony and Cleopatra, 2.2.190. [This is the
beginning of Enorbarbus's description of the first meeting of Antony
and Cleopatra: "The barge she sat in, like a burnished throne, /
Burned on the water."]

[11] *laquearia*   Latin: paneled ceiling. Eliot's note cites Virgil's *Aeneid*
1.726, describing a banquet given by Queen Dido of Carthage for
her soon-to-be lover, Aeneas: "Burning lamps hang from the gold-
paneled ceiling, and torches dispel the night with their flames."

[12] *sylvan scene*   Eliot's note cites Milton's *Paradise Lost* 4.140, which
describes the Garden of Eden seen through Satan's eyes.

[13] *The change ... forced*   Eliot's notes for this passage cite Greek poet
Ovid's *Metamorphoses* 6, which tells the Greek myth of Philomela,
who was raped by King Tereus of Thrace (her sister's husband) and
had her tongue cut out before being changed into a nightingale.

"Jug Jug"[1] to dirty ears.
And other withered stumps of time
105 Were told upon the walls; staring forms
Leaned out, leaning, hushing the room enclosed.
Footsteps shuffled on the stair.
Under the firelight, under the brush, her hair
Spread out in fiery points
110 Glowed into words, then would be savagely still.

     "My nerves are bad to-night. Yes, bad. Stay with me.
Speak to me. Why do you never speak. Speak.
     What are you thinking of? What thinking? What?
I never know what you are thinking. Think."

115   I think we are in rats' alley[2]
Where the dead men lost their bones.

     "What is that noise?"
               The wind under the door.[3]
     "What is that noise now? What is the wind doing?"
120   Nothing again nothing.
                         "Do
You know nothing? Do you see nothing? Do you
    remember
Nothing?"

     I remember
125 Those are pearls that were his eyes.
"Are you alive, or not? Is there nothing in your head?"
                                 But

O O O O that Shakespeherian Rag[4]—
It's so elegant
130 So intelligent
"What shall I do now? What shall I do?"
"I shall rush out as I am, and walk the street
With my hair down, so. What shall we do to-morrow?

What shall we ever do?"
135   The hot water at ten.
And if it rains, a closed car at four.
And we shall play a game of chess,
Pressing lidless eyes and waiting for a knock upon the
    door.[5]

When Lil's husband got demobbed,[6] I said—
140 I didn't mince my words, I said to her myself,
HURRY UP PLEASE ITS TIME[7]
Now Albert's coming back, make yourself a bit smart.
He'll want to know what you done with that money he
    gave you
To get yourself some teeth. He did, I was there.
145 You have them all out, Lil, and get a nice set,
He said, I swear, I can't bear to look at you.
And no more can't I, I said, and think of poor Albert,
He's been in the army four years, he wants a good time,
And if you don't give it him, there's others will, I said.
150 Oh is there, she said. Something o' that, I said.
Then I'll know who to thank, she said, and give me a
    straight look.
HURRY UP PLEASE ITS TIME
If you don't like it you can get on with it, I said.
Others can pick and choose if you can't.
155 But if Albert makes off, it won't be for lack of telling.
You ought to be ashamed, I said, to look so antique.
(And her only thirty-one.)
I can't help it, she said, pulling a long face,
It's them pills I took, to bring it off, she said.
160 (She's had five already, and nearly died of young
    George.)
The chemist° said it would be alright, but I've never
    been the same.   *pharmacist*
You are a proper fool, I said.
Well, if Albert won't leave you alone, there it is, I said,
What you get married for if you don't want children?
165 HURRY UP PLEASE ITS TIME
Well, that Sunday Albert was home, they had a hot
    gammon,°   *smoked ham*

---

[1] *Jug Jug* In Elizabethan poetry, a conventional representation of a nightingale's song. Also, a crude reference to sexual intercourse.

[2] [Eliot's note] Cf. part 3, line 195 [of *Metamorphoses* 6].

[3] *The wind ... door* Eliot's note cites a line from John Webster's *The Devil's Law Case* (3.2.162). A patient who is believed to have been stabbed to death groans in pain, prompting the surgeon ask, "Is the wind in that door still?"

[4] *O ... Rag* Reference to a popular American ragtime song performed in Ziegfield's Follies in 1912.

[5] [Eliot's note] Cf. the game of chess in Middleton's *Women Beware Women*.

[6] *demobbed* Demobilized; released from military service.

[7] *HURRY ... TIME* Expression used by bartenders in Britain to announce closing time.

And they asked me in to dinner, to get the beauty of it
    hot—
HURRY UP PLEASE ITS TIME
HURRY UP PLEASE ITS TIME
170 Goonight Bill. Goonight Lou. Goonight May. Goonight.
Ta ta. Goonight. Goonight.
Good night, ladies, good night, sweet ladies, good night,
    good night.[1]

3. THE FIRE SERMON [2]

The river's tent is broken: the last fingers of leaf
Clutch and sink into the wet bank. The wind
175 Crosses the brown land, unheard. The nymphs are
    departed.
Sweet Thames, run softly, till I end my song.[3]
The river bears no empty bottles, sandwich papers,
Silk handkerchiefs, cardboard boxes, cigarette ends
Or other testimony of summer nights. The nymphs
    are departed.
180 And their friends, the loitering heirs of city directors;
Departed, have left no addresses.
By the waters of Leman I sat down and wept ...[4]
Sweet Thames, run softly till I end my song,
Sweet Thames, run softly, for I speak not loud or long.
185 But at my back in a cold blast I hear
The rattle of the bones, and chuckle spread from ear
    to ear.[5]

A rat crept softly through the vegetation
Dragging its slimy belly on the bank
While I was fishing in the dull canal
190 On a winter evening round behind the gashouse
Musing upon the king my brother's wreck
And on the king my father's death before him.[6]
White bodies naked on the low damp ground
And bones cast in a little low dry garret,
195 Rattled by the rat's foot only, year to year.
But at my back from time to time I hear
The sound of horns and motors, which shall bring[7]
Sweeney[8] to Mrs. Porter in the spring.
O the moon shone bright on Mrs. Porter
200 And on her daughter
They wash their feet in soda water[9]
Et O ces voix d'enfants, chantant dans la coupole![10]

    Twit twit twit
Jug jug jug jug jug jug

---

[1] *Good night ... night* Ophelia's last words in Shakespeare's *Hamlet* (4.5.72–3) before she drowns herself. These words are taken by her father as evidence that she had been driven insane by Hamlet's seeming indifference to her.

[2] *The Fire Sermon* Sermon preached by the Buddha against passions (such as lust, anger, and envy) that consume people and prevent their regeneration.

[3] *Sweet Thames ... song* Eliot's note cites the refrain of Edmund Spenser's *Prothalamion* (1596), a poem that celebrates the ideals of marriage, written to commemorate the joint marriages of the two daughters of the Earl of Worcester.

[4] *By the ... wept* Reference to Psalm 137, in which the Hebrews lament their exile in Babylon and their lost homeland of Jerusalem: "By the rivers of Babylon, there sat we down, yea, we wept, when we remembered Zion." For Babylon Eliot substitutes "Leman," the French name for Lake Geneva. "Leman" is also a medieval word meaning sweetheart.

[5] *But at ... ear* Eliot's note cites Andrew Marvell's "To His Coy Mistress": "But at my back I always hear / Time's wingèd chariot hurrying near" (lines 21–22).

[6] *And on ... him* Eliot's note cites Shakespeare's *The Tempest* 1.2.388–93, in which Ferdinand, shipwrecked on the shore, is prompted by Ariel's music to ponder the supposed drowning of his father, King Alonso: "Sitting on a bank, / Weeping again the king my father's wrack / This music crept by me upon the waters, / Allaying both their fury and my passion / With its sweet air." Eliot also quotes from this passage on line 257.

[7] [Eliot's note] Cf. [John] Day, *Parliament of Bees*: "When of the sudden, listening, you shall hear, / A noise of horns and hunting, which shall bring / Actaeon to Diana in the spring, / Where all shall see her naked skin..." [According to classical myth, when the hunter Actaeon saw Diana, goddess of chastity and the hunt, bathing naked with her nymphs, she changed him into a stag and set his dogs upon him.]

[8] *Sweeney* Character in two earlier poems by Eliot, "Sweeney Erect" and "Sweeney Among the Nightingales."

[9] [Eliot's note] I do not know the origin of the ballad from which these are taken: it was reported to me from Sydney, Australia. [One version of this ballad, which was sung by Australian soldiers in World War I, is as follows: "O the moon shone bright on Mrs. Porter / And on the daughter / Of Mrs. Porter / They wash their feet in soda water / And so they oughter / To keep them clean."]

[10] *Et O ... coupole* French: "And O those children's voices singing under the cupola." Eliot's note indicates that this is the last line of French poet Paul Verlaine's sonnet "Parsifal" (1886). Verlaine refers to the opera *Parsifal* (1882) by Richard Wagner, in which a choir of children sings while the innocent knight Parsifal has his feet washed before entering the Castle of the Grail.

205 So rudely forc'd.
Tereu[1]

   Unreal City
Under the brown fog of a winter noon
Mr. Eugenides, the Smyrna[2] merchant
210 Unshaven, with a pocket full of currants
C.i.f. London: documents at sight,[3]
Asked me in demotic[4] French
To luncheon at the Cannon Street Hotel[5]
Followed by a weekend at the Metropole.[6]

215   At the violet hour, when the eyes and back
Turn upward from the desk, when the human engine
   waits
Like a taxi throbbing waiting,
I Tiresias,[7] though blind, throbbing between two lives,

Old man with wrinkled female breasts, can see
220 At the violet hour, the evening hour that strives
Homeward, and brings the sailor home from sea,[8]
The typist home at teatime, clears her breakfast, lights
Her stove, and lays out food in tins.
Out of the window perilously spread
225 Her drying combinations[9] touched by the sun's last
   rays,
On the divan are piled (at night her bed)
Stockings, slippers, camisoles, and stays.°   *corset*
I Tiresias, old man with wrinkled dugs°   *breasts*
Perceived the scene, and foretold the rest—
230 I too awaited the expected guest.
He, the young man carbuncular,° arrives,   *pimply*
A small house agent's clerk, with one bold stare,
One of the low on whom assurance sits
As a silk hat on a Bradford[10] millionaire.
235 The time is now propitious, as he guesses,
The meal is ended, she is bored and tired,
Endeavours to engage her in caresses
Which still are unreproved, if undesired.
Flushed and decided, he assaults at once;
240 Exploring hands encounter no defence;
His vanity requires no response,
And makes a welcome of indifference.
(And I Tiresias have foresuffered all
Enacted on this same divan or bed;
245 I who have sat by Thebes below the wall
And walked among the lowest of the dead.)[11]

---

1 *Tereu* Latin vocative form of Tereus, who raped Philomela.

2 *Smyrna* Port city in western Turkey.

3 *C.i.f. ... sight* Eliot's note explains that "C.i.f." means that the price includes "cost, insurance, freight to London," and that "documents on sight" indicates that "the Bill of Lading, etc., were to be handed to the buyer upon payment of the sight draft."

4 *demotic* Popular; vulgar.

5 *Cannon Street Hotel* Hotel near the Cannon Street train station, a terminus for travelers to and from the continent.

6 *Metropole* Large hotel on the seashore at Brighton.

7 [Eliot's note] Tiresias, although a mere spectator and not indeed a "character," is yet the most important personage in the poem, uniting all the rest. Just as the one-eyed merchant, seller of currants, melts into the Phoenician Sailor, and the latter is not wholly distinct from Ferdinand Prince of Naples, so all the women are one woman, and the two sexes meet in Tiresias. What Tiresias sees, in fact, is the substance of the poem. The whole passage from Ovid is of great anthropological interest. [Eliot then quotes in Latin the passage from *Metamorphoses* that describes Tiresias's sex change. Jove, who had drunk a great deal, "jested with Juno. He said, 'Your pleasure in love is really greater than that enjoyed by men.' She denied it; so they decided to seek the opinion of the wise Tiresias, for he knew both aspects of love. For once, with a blow of his staff, he had committed violence on two huge snakes as they copulated in the green forest; and—wonderful to tell—was turned into a woman and thus spent seven years. In the eighth year he saw the same snakes again and said: 'If a blow struck at you is so powerful that it changes the sex of the giver, I will now strike at you again.' With these words she struck the snakes, and again became a man. So he was appointed arbiter in the playful quarrel, and supported Jove's statement. It is said that Saturnia [Juno] was quite disproportionately upset, and condemned the arbiter to perpetual blindness. But the almighty father (for no god may undo what has been done by another god), in return for the

sight that was taken away, gave him the power to know the future and so lightened the penalty paid by the honor."]

8 [Eliot's note] This may not appear as exact as Sappho's lines but I had in mind the "longshore" or "dory" fisherman, who returns at nightfall. [Eliot refers to seventh-century BCE Greek poet Sappho's poem, known as Fragment 149, in which Hesperus, the evening star, brings home "all things the bright dawn disperses," including "the sheep, the goat, the child to its mother."]

9 *combinations* Undergarments that combined the chemise and panties.

10 *Bradford* Textile center in industrial Yorkshire, many of whose residents became extremely wealthy during the textile boom that accompanied World War I.

11 *I who ... dead* In *Oedipus Rex*, by fifth-century BCE Greek dramatist Sophocles, Tiresias perceives that the curse of infertility that plagues the people and land of Thebes has been brought upon them by the unwitting marriage of Oedipus to his mother, Queen Jocasta. In book 9 of Homer's *Odyssey*, Odysseus journeys to the underworld, where he consults Tiresias.

Bestows one final patronising kiss,
And gropes his way, finding the stairs unlit …

  She turns and looks a moment in the glass,
250 Hardly aware of her departed lover;
Her brain allows one half-formed thought to pass:
"Well now that's done: and I'm glad it's over."
When lovely woman stoops to folly and[1]
Paces about her room again, alone,
255 She smoothes her hair with automatic hand,
And puts a record on the gramophone.

  "This music crept by me upon the waters"[2]
And along the Strand, up Queen Victoria Street.
O City city, I can sometimes hear
260 Beside a public bar in Lower Thames Street,
The pleasant whining of a mandoline
And a clatter and a chatter from within
Where fishmen lounge at noon: where the walls
Of Magnus Martyr[3] hold
265 Inexplicable splendour of Ionian white and gold.[4]

    The river sweats[5]
    Oil and tar
    The barges drift
    With the turning tide
270   Red sails

Wide
To leeward, swing on the heavy spar.
The barges wash
Drifting logs
275 Down Greenwich reach
Past the Isle of Dogs.[6]
    Weialala leia
    Wallala leialala[7]

  Elizabeth and Leicester[8]
280 Beating oars
The stern was formed
A gilded shell
Red and gold
The brisk swell
285 Rippled both shores
Southwest wind
Carried down stream
The peal of bells
White towers
290   Weialala leia
    Wallala leialala

"Trams and dusty trees.
Highbury bore me. Richmond and Kew
Undid me. By Richmond I raised my knees
295 Supine on the floor of a narrow canoe."[9]

---

[1] *When … and* Eliot's note cites Oliver Goldsmith's novel *The Vicar of Wakefield* (1762), in which Olivia, returning to the place where she was seduced, sings: "When lovely woman stoops to folly / And finds to late that men betray / What charm can soothe her melancholy, / What art can wash her guilt away? / The only art her guilt to cover, / To hide her shame from every eye, / To give repentance to her lover, / And wring his bosom—is to die."

[2] [Eliot's note] V. [I.e., "see," from the Latin *vide*.] *The Tempest*, as above.

[3] [Eliot's note] The interior of St. Magnus Martyr is to my mind one of the finest among [Sir Christopher] Wren's interiors. See *The Proposed Demolition of Nineteen City Churches* (P.S. King & Son, Ltd.).

[4] *Inexplicable … gold* Reference to the slender Ionic columns inside the church.

[5] [Eliot's note] The Song of the (three) Thames-daughters begins here. From line 292 to 306 inclusive they speak in turn. V. *Gotterdammerung*, 3.1: the Rhine-daughters. [Eliot refers to Wagner's opera *The Twilight of the Gods*, in which the Rhine maidens lament the theft of the Rhine's gold, which has also robbed the river of its beauty.]

[6] *Isle of Dogs* Peninsula formed by a bend in the river Thames. Opposite this peninsula, on the south side of the Thames, lies the London borough of Greenwich.

[7] *Weialala … leialala* In Wagner's opera, this is the ecstatic cry repeated by the maidens as they guard the lump of gold in the river.

[8] [Eliot's note] V. Froude, *Elizabeth*, Vol. 1, ch. 4, letter of De Quadra to Philip of Spain:
"In the afternoon we were in a barge, watching the games on the river. (The queen) was alone with Lord Robert and myself on the poop, when they began to talk nonsense, and went so far that Lord Robert at last said, as I was on the spot there was no reason why they should not be married if the queen pleased." [Eliot refers to *History of England from the Fall of Wolsey to the Death of Elizabeth* (1856–70), by James Anthony Froude. Froude quotes from a letter by Alvarez de Quadra, Bishop of Aquila and Spanish Ambassador to Queen Elizabeth's court. De Quadra believed the young queen would marry Lord Dudley.]

[9] *Trams and … canoe* Eliot's note cites the lines from Dante's *Purgatorio* (5.130–136) that he parodies: "Remember me, who am La Pia [Piety]; / Sienna made me and the Maremma undid me"; *Highbury* Middle-class suburb in north London; *Richmond and Kew* Areas of London located on the Thames in southwest London.

"My feet are at Moorgate,[1] and my heart
Under my feet. After the event
He wept. He promised 'a new start.'
I made no comment. What should I resent?"

300   "On Margate Sands.[2]
I can connect
Nothing with nothing.
The broken fingernails of dirty hands.
My people humble people who expect
305   Nothing."
　　　　　la la

To Carthage then I came[3]

Burning burning burning burning[4]
O Lord Thou pluckest me out[5]
310   O Lord Thou pluckest

burning

4. DEATH BY WATER

Phlebas the Phoenician, a fortnight dead,
Forgot the cry of gulls, and the deep sea swell
And the profit and loss.
315   　　　　　A current under sea
Picked his bones in whispers. As he rose and fell
He passed the stages of his age and youth

Between them lies Kew Gardens.

[1] *Moorgate*   Area in the east of the City.

[2] *Margate Sands*   Primary beach in the Kent seaside resort of Margate.

[3] *To Carthage ... came*   Eliot's note cites the opening of Book 3 of *The Confessions of Saint Augustine*: "To Carthage then I came, where a cauldron of unholy loves sang all about mine ears."

[4] [Eliot's note]   The complete text of the Buddha's Fire Sermon (which corresponds in importance to the Sermon on the Mount) from which these words are taken, will be found translated in the late Henry Clarke Warren's *Buddhism in Translation* (Harvard Oriental Series). Mr. Warren was one of the great pioneers of Buddhist studies in the Occident.

[5] [Eliot's note]   From St. Augustine's *Confessions* again. The collocation of these two representatives of eastern and western asceticism, as the culmination of this part of the poem, is not an accident. [Eliot refers to 10.237–38 of the Confessions: "I entangle my steps with these outward beauties, but thou pluckest me out, O Lord, thou pluckest me out."]

Entering the whirlpool.
　　　　　　　　Gentile or Jew
320   O you who turn the wheel and look to windward,
Consider Phlebas, who was once handsome and tall as
　　you.

5. WHAT THE THUNDER SAID [6]

After the torchlight red on sweaty faces
After the frosty silence in the gardens
After the agony in stony places
325   The shouting and the crying
Prison and palace and reverberation
Of thunder of spring over distant mountains
He who was living is now dead[7]
We who were living are now dying
330   With a little patience

Here is no water but only rock
Rock and no water and the sandy road
The road winding above among the mountains
Which are mountains of rock without water
335   If there were water we should stop and drink
Amongst the rock one cannot stop or think
Sweat is dry and feet are in the sand
If there were only water amongst the rock
Dead mountain mouth of carious[8] teeth that cannot spit
340   Here one can neither stand nor lie nor sit
There is not even silence in the mountains
But dry sterile thunder without rain
There is not even solitude in the mountains
But red sullen faces sneer and snarl
345   From doors of mudcracked houses
　　　　　　　　　　If there were water

　　And no rock
　　If there were rock

---

[6] [Eliot's note]   In the first part of Part 5 three themes are employed: the journey to Emmaus, the approach to the Chapel Perilous (see Miss Weston's book), and the present decay of eastern Europe. [*journey to Emmaus* See Luke 24.13–31, in which Jesus, after being resurrected, joins two of his disciples on the road to Emmaus, but they do not recognize him; *Chapel Perilous* The final stage of the Grail quest.]

[7] *After the torchlight ... dead* References to the events from the betrayal of Christ to His death.

[8] *carious* Decayed.

And also water
350 And water
A spring
A pool among the rock
If there were the sound of water only
Not the cicada[1]
355 And dry grass singing
But sound of water over a rock
Where the hermit-thrush sings in the pine trees[2]
Drip drop drip drop drop drop drop
But there is no water

360 Who is the third who walks always beside you?[3]
When I count, there are only you and I together
But when I look ahead up the white road
There is always another one walking beside you
Gliding wrapt in a brown mantle, hooded
365 I do not know whether a man or a woman
—But who is that on the other side of you?

What is that sound high in the air
Murmur of maternal lamentation
Who are those hooded hordes swarming
370 Over endless plains, stumbling in cracked earth
Ringed by the flat horizon only
What is the city over the mountains
Cracks and reforms and bursts in the violet air
Falling towers

375 Jerusalem Athens Alexandria
Vienna London
Unreal[4]

A woman drew her long black hair out tight
And fiddled whisper music on those strings
380 And bats with baby faces in the violet light
Whistled, and beat their wings
And crawled head downward down a blackened wall
And upside down in air were towers
Tolling reminiscent bells, that kept the hours
385 And voices singing out of empty cisterns and exhausted
    wells.

In this decayed hole among the mountains
In the faint moonlight, the grass is singing
Over the tumbled graves, about the chapel
There is the empty chapel, only the wind's home.[5]
390 It has no windows, and the door swings,
Dry bones can harm no one.
Only a cock stood on the rooftree
Co co rico co co rico[6]
In a flash of lightning. Then a damp gust
395 Bringing rain

Ganga[7] was sunken, and the limp leaves
Waited for rain, while the black clouds

---

1 *cicada* Grasshopper. See Ecclesiastes 12.4: "Also when they shall be afraid of that which is high, and fears shall be in the way, and the almond tree shall flourish, and the grasshopper shall be a burden, and desire shall fail: because man goeth to his long home, and the mourners go about the streets."

2 [Eliot's note] This is *Turdus aonalaschkae pallasii*, the hermit-thrush which I have heard in Quebec Province. Chapman says (*Handbook of Birds of Eastern North America*) "it is most at home in secluded woodland and thickety retreats. … Its notes are not remarkable for variety or volume, but in purity and sweetness of tone and exquisite modulation they are unequalled." Its "water-dripping song" is justly celebrated.

3 [Eliot's note] The following lines were stimulated by the account of one of the Antarctic expeditions (I forget which, but I think one of Shackleton's): it was related that the party of explorers, at the extremity of their strength, had the constant delusion that there was *one more member* than could actually be counted. [Eliot refers to Sir Ernest Shakleton's third journey to the Antarctic (1914–17), during which he and his men attempted to cross the Antarctic ice cap on foot. See *South: The Story of Shackleton's Last Expedition, 1914-1917* (1919).]

4 *What is that … unreal* Eliot's note for these lines quotes in German Herman Hesse, *Blick ins Chaos: Drei Aufsätze* (*A Glimpse into Chaos: Three Essays*). "Already half of Europe, already at least half of Eastern Europe, on the way to chaos, drives drunk in sacred infatuation along the edge of the precipice, singing drunkenly, as though singing hymns, as Dmitri Karamazov sang. The offended bourgeois laughs at the songs; the saint and the seer hear them with tears." Dmitri Karamazov is a character in Fyodor Dostoevsky's *The Brothers Karamazov* (1879–80).

5 *There is … home* The Chapel Perilous appeared to be surrounded by death and decay; these nightmare visions were meant to induce despair in the questing knight. Once inside the Chapel, the knight's courage would be tested with further horrors.

6 *Only a … rico* The crowing of the cock signals the coming of the morning and the departure of ghosts and evil spirits, as in *Hamlet* 1.1, when Hamlet's father's ghost disappears with its call. Also, in the Gospels Peter repents his repudiation of Christ after the cock crows.

7 *Ganga* The Ganges, a sacred river in India.

Gathered far distant, over Himavant.[1]
The jungle crouched, humped in silence.
400 Then spoke the thunder
DA[2]
Datta: what have we given?
My friend, blood shaking my heart
The awful daring of a moment's surrender
405 Which an age of prudence can never retract
By this, and this only, we have existed
Which is not to be found in our obituaries
Or in memories draped by the beneficent spider[3]
Or under seals broken by the lean solicitor
410 In our empty rooms
DA
Dayadhvam: I have heard the key[4]
Turn in the door once and turn once only
We think of the key, each in his prison
415 Thinking of the key, each confirms a prison
Only at nightfall, aetherial rumours

Revive for a moment a broken Coriolanus[5]
DA
Damyata: The boat responded
420 Gaily, to the hand expert with sail and oar
The sea was calm, your heart would have responded
Gaily, when invited, beating obedient
To controlling hands

                 I sat upon the shore
425 Fishing, with the arid plain behind me[6]
Shall I at least set my lands in order?[7]
London Bridge is falling down falling down falling
      down
Poi s'ascose nel foco che gli affina[8]
Quando fiam ceu chelidon[9]—O swallow swallow
430 *Le Prince d'Aquitaine a la tour abolie*[10]
These fragments I have shored against my ruins

---

[1] *Himavant* Sanskrit: snowy. Adjective used to describe the Himalayas.

[2] [Eliot's note] "Datta, dayadhvam, damyata" (Give, sympathise, control). The fable of the meaning of the Thunder is found in the *Brihadaranyaka—Upanishad*, 5, 1. A translation is found in Deussen's *Sechzig Upanishads des Veda*, p. 489. [Eliot refers to the Hindu fable in which gods, men, and demons, each, in turn, ask the Lord of Creation, Prajapati, "Please instruct us, Sir." To each he utters the syllable "Da," and each group interprets the answer differently: "Damyata," practice self-control; "Datta," give alms; "Dayadhvam," have compassion. According to the fable, "This very thing is repeated even today by the heavenly voice, in the form of thunder, as 'Da,' 'Da,' 'Da,' which means: 'Control yourselves,' 'Give,' and 'Have compassion.'"]

[3] [Eliot's note] Cf. [John] Webster, *The White Devil*, 5, 6: "... they'll remarry / Ere the worm pierce your winding-sheet, ere the spider / Make a thin curtain for your epitaphs." [In this excerpt from the play, the villain Flamineo urges men never to trust their wives.]

[4] *I have ... key* Eliot's note cites the passage in Dante's *Inferno* 33.46, in which Ugolino della Gherardesca remembers being locked up with his children in the tower, where they all starved to death. Eliot also quotes philosopher Francis Herbert Bradley's *Appearance and Reality: A Metaphysical Essay* (1893), p. 346: "My external sensations are no less private to myself than are my thoughts or my feelings. In either case my experience falls within my own circle, a circle closed on the outside; and, with all its elements alike, every sphere is opaque to the others which surround it.... In brief, regarded as an existence which appears in a soul, the whole world for each is peculiar and private to that soul."

[5] *Coriolanus* Roman general of Shakespeare's play of that name. A character who is motivated by pride rather than duty, Coriolanus leads the enemy against Rome, the city from which he has been exiled.

[6] *Fishing ... me* Eliot's note refers readers to Weston's *From Ritual to Romance*, chapter 9, "The Fisher King." In this chapter, Weston comments upon the Fisher King's intimate relation with his people and his land, "a relation mainly dependent upon the identification of the King with the Divine principle of Life and Fertility." Weston also argues that "the Fish is a Life symbol of immemorial antiquity, and that the title of Fisher has, from the earliest ages, been associated with Deities who were held to be specially connected with the origin and preservation of life."

[7] *Shall I ... order* See Isaiah 38.1, in which the prophet Isaiah counsels the sickly King Hezekiah, whose kingdom has been destroyed by the conquering Assyrians, "Thus saith the Lord, Set thine house in order: for thou shalt die, and not live."

[8] *Poi ... affina* Italian: "Then he vanished into the fire that refines them" (Dante's *Purgatorio* 26.148). Eliot's note quotes, in Italian, the three lines of the *Purgatorio* immediately preceding, in which the poet Arnaut Daniel, who is in Purgatory for lust, says to Dante "Now I pray you, by the goodness that guides you to the top of the staircase [of purgatory], be mindful in time of my suffering."

[9] *Quando ... chelidon* Latin: "When shall I be as the swallow?" Eliot's note cites an anonymous Latin poem about Venus and the spring, "The Vigil of Venus," as well as the story of Philomela, whose sister Procne (the wife of Tereus) was turned into a swallow. "The Vigil of Venus" refers to Philomela and Procne in its closing lines.

[10] *Le Prince ... abolie* French: "The Prince of Aquitaine in the ruined tower." Eliot's note cites French poet Gerard de Nerval's sonnet "El Desdichado" (1853). One of the Tarot cards shows a tower struck by lightning.

Why then Ile fit you. Hieronymo's mad againe.[1]
Datta. Dayadhvam. Damyata.
     Shantih   shantih   shantih[2]
—1922

Journey of the Magi [3]

"A cold coming we had of it,
    Just the worst time of the year
For a journey, and such a long journey:
The ways deep and the weather sharp,
5 The very dead of winter."[4]
And the camels galled, sore-footed, refractory,
Lying down in the melting snow.
There were times we regretted
The summer palaces on slopes, the terraces,
10 And the silken girls bringing sherbet.
Then the camel men cursing and grumbling
And running away, and wanting their liquor and
    women,
And the night-fires going out, and the lack of shelters,
And the cities hostile and the towns unfriendly
15 And the villages dirty and charging high prices:
A hard time we had of it.
At the end we preferred to travel all night,
Sleeping in snatches,
With the voices singing in our ears, saying
20 That this was all folly.

Then at dawn we came down to a temperate valley,
Wet, below the snow line, smelling of vegetation;
With a running stream and a water-mill beating the
    darkness,
And three trees[5] on the low sky,
25 And an old white horse[6] galloped away in the meadow.
Then we came to a tavern with vine-leaves over the
    lintel,[7]
Six hands at an open door dicing for pieces of silver,[8]
And feet kicking the empty wine-skins.
But there was no information, and so we continued
30 And arrived at evening, not a moment too soon
Finding the place; it was (you may say) satisfactory.

All this was a long time ago, I remember,
And I would do it again, but set down
This set down
35 This: were we led all that way for
Birth or Death? There was a Birth, certainly,
We had evidence and no doubt. I had seen birth and
    death,
But had thought they were different; this Birth was
Hard and bitter agony for us, like Death, our death.
40 We returned to our places, these Kingdoms,
But no longer at ease here, in the old dispensation,
With an alien people clutching their gods.
I should be glad of another death.
—1927

---

[1] *Why then ... againe* Eliot's note cites Thomas Kyd's *The Spanish Tragedy: Hieronymo Is Mad Againe* (1592). In the play, Hieronymo, whose son has been murdered, is asked to write a play for the court. He responds "Why then Ile fit you (i.e., "I'll accommodate you," or "I'll give you your due"). He writes the play and persuades the murderers to act in it. During the course of the play, his son's murder is avenged.

[2] [Eliot's note] Shantih. Repeated as here, a formal ending to an Upanishad. "The Peace which passeth understanding" is our equivalent to this word. [The Upanishads are poetic dialogues that comment on the Vedas, the ancient Hindu Scriptures. Eliot's phrasing derives from Paul's letter to the early Christians in Philippians 4.7: "And the peace of God, which passeth all understanding, shall keep your hearts and minds through Jesus Christ."]

[3] *Magi* Three wise men who journeyed to Bethlehem to honor Jesus at His birth (see Matthew 2.1–12).

[4] *A cold ... winter* Adapted from a sermon given by Anglican preacher Lancelot Andrews on Christmas Day, 1622.

[5] *three trees* Suggests the three crosses on Calvary, on which Christ and two criminals were crucified (see Luke 23.32–43).

[6] *white horse* Ridden by Christ in Revelation 6.2 and 19.11–14.

[7] *lintel* Doorframe.

[8] *dicing ... silver* Allusion to Judas's betrayal of Jesus for thirty pieces of silver, and to the soldiers who dice for the robes of Christ at His crucifixion (Matthew 26.14 and 27.35).

Marina [1]

Quis hic locus, quae regio, quae mundi plaga? [2]

What seas what shores what grey rocks and what
     islands
What water lapping the bow
And scent of pine and the woodthrush singing
     through the fog
What images return
5 O my daughter.

Those who sharpen the tooth of the dog, meaning
Death
Those who glitter with the glory of the humming-
     bird, meaning
Death
10 Those who sit in the stye of contentment, meaning
Death
Those who suffer the ecstasy of the animals, meaning
Death

Are become unsubstantial, reduced by a wind,
15 A breath of pine, and the woodsong fog
By this grace dissolved in place

What is this face, less clear and clearer
The pulse in the arm, less strong and stronger—
Given or lent? more distant than stars and nearer than
     the eye

20 Whispers and small laughter between leaves and
     hurrying feet
Under sleep, where all the waters meet.

Bowsprit [3] cracked with ice and paint cracked
     with heat.
I made this, I have forgotten
And remember.
25 The rigging weak and the canvas rotten
Between one June and another September.
Made this unknowing, half conscious, unknown, my
     own.
The garboard strake [4] leaks, the seams need caulking.
This form, this face, this life
30 Living to live in a world of time beyond me; let me
Resign my life for this life, my speech for that
     unspoken,
The awakened, lips parted, the hope, the new ships.

What seas what shores what granite islands
     towards my timbers
And woodthrush calling through the fog
My daughter.
—1930

Burnt Norton

τοῦ λόλου δ᾽ ἐόντος ξυνοῦ ζώουσιν οἱ πολλοί
ὡς ἰδίαν ἔχοντες φρόνησιν.

1. p. 77. Fr. 2

ὁδὸς ἄνω κάτω μία καὶ ὡυτή.

1. p. 89. Fr. 60

Diels: *Die Fragmente der der Vorsokratiker (Herakleitos).* [5]

---

[1] *Marina* In Shakespeare's *Pericles*, the daughter of the title character. She is born during a storm at sea and her mother dies giving birth to her. Pericles gives her to the governor of Tarsus and his wife to raise. Through a series of plot twists, Marina is believed, by age sixteen, to have died. Pericles, maddened by grief, becomes a wanderer. During his travels he finds Marina and they are restored to one another.

[2] *Quis hic ... plaga* Latin: "What place is this, what region, what corner of the world?" Spoken by Hercules in Seneca's *Hercules Furens* (*The Mad Hercules*) after he regains his senses following a period of madness during which he murders his children and wife.

[3] *Bowsprit* Large spar projecting from the front of a boat.

[4] *garboard strake* Thick wooden plank forming a ridge along the keel of a boat.

[5] *Burnt Norton* Name of a large country house in Gloucestershire, England, that was built on the site of an earlier home that had burned down in the seventeenth century. Eliot visited the home in 1934. This poem was first published in 1935, and then republished in 1943 as one of the *Four Quartets*. Eliot modeled the structure of this long poem on one of Beethoven's final quartets, particularly the A Minor Quartet (Beethoven's last), which Eliot found "quite inexhaustible to study. There is some sort of heavenly or at least more than human gaiety about some of his later things which one imagines must come to oneself as the fruit of reconciliation and relief after immense suffering; I should like to get something of that into verse before I die." The epigraphs are from the writings of sixth-century BCE philosopher Heraclites: τοῦ ... φρόνησιν Greek: "Although the Word governs all things, most people live as though they had wisdom of their own." ὁδὸς ... ὡυτή Greek: "The way up and the way down are the same."

1

Time present and time past
Are both perhaps present in time future,
And time future contained in time past.
If all time is eternally present
5 All time is unredeemable.
What might have been is an abstraction
Remaining a perpetual possibility
Only in a world of speculation.
What might have been and what has been
10 Point to one end, which is always present.
Footfalls echo in the memory
Down the passage which we did not take
Towards the door we never opened
Into the rose-garden. My words echo
15 Thus, in your mind.
                          But to what purpose
Disturbing the dust on a bowl of rose-leaves
I do not know.
                     Other echoes
20 Inhabit the garden. Shall we follow?
Quick, said the bird, find them, find them,
Round the corner. Through the first gate,
Into our first world, shall we follow
The deception of the thrush? Into our first world.
25 There they were, dignified, invisible,
Moving without pressure, over the dead leaves,
In the autumn heat, through the vibrant air,
And the bird called, in response to
The unheard music hidden in the shrubbery,
30 And the unseen eyebeam crossed, for the roses
Had the look of flowers that are looked at.
There they were as our guests, accepted and accepting.
So we moved, and they, in a formal pattern,
Along the empty alley, into the box circle,
35 To look down into the drained pool.
Dry the pool, dry concrete, brown edged,
And the pool was filled with water out of sunlight,
And the lotos[1] rose, quietly, quietly,
The surface glittered out of heart of light,
40 And they were behind us, reflected in the pool.
Then a cloud passed, and the pool was empty.
Go, said the bird, for the leaves were full of children,
Hidden excitedly, containing laughter.

Go, go, go, said the bird: human kind
45 Cannot bear very much reality.
Time past and time future
What might have been and what has been
Point to one end, which is always present.

2

Garlic and sapphires in the mud
50 Clot the bedded axle-tree.
The trilling wire in the blood
Sings below inveterate scars
And reconciles forgotten wars.
The dance along the artery
55 The circulation of the lymph
Are figured in the drift of stars
Ascend to summer in the tree
We move above the moving tree
In light upon the figured leaf
60 And hear upon the sodden floor
Below, the boarhound and the boar
Pursue their pattern as before
But reconciled among the stars.

At the still point of the turning world. Neither
    flesh nor fleshless;
65 Neither from nor towards; at the still point, there the
    dance is,
But neither arrest nor movement. And do not call it
    fixity,
Where past and future are gathered. Neither
    movement from nor towards,
Neither ascent nor decline. Except for the point, the
    still point,
There would be no dance, and there is only the dance.
70 I can only say, *there* we have been: but I cannot say where.
And I cannot say, how long, for that is to place it in time.

The inner freedom from the practical desire,
The release from action and suffering, release from the
    inner
And the outer compulsion, yet surrounded
75 By a grace of sense, a white light still and moving,
Erhebung[2] without motion, concentration

---

[1] *lotos* Plant whose flowers, according to Greek myth, produced dreamy forgetfulness in those who ate them.

[2] *Erhebung* German: lifting up. Term used by the German philosopher Georg Wilhelm Friedrich Hegel (1770–1831) to denote a new level of understanding.

Without elimination, both a new world
And the old made explicit, understood
In the completion of its partial ecstasy,
80 The resolution of its partial horror.
Yet the enchainment of past and future
Woven in the weakness of the changing body,
Protects mankind from heaven and damnation
Which flesh cannot endure.
85   Time past and time future
Allow but a little consciousness.
To be conscious is not to be in time
But only in time can the moment in the rose-garden,
The moment in the arbour where the rain beat,
90 The moment in the draughty church at smokefall
Be remembered; involved with past and future.
Only through time time is conquered.

                        3
Here is a place of disaffection
Time before and time after
95 In a dim light: neither daylight
Investing form with lucid stillness
Turning shadow into transient beauty
With slow rotation suggesting permanence
Nor darkness to purify the soul
100 Emptying the sensual with deprivation
Cleansing affection from the temporal.
Neither plenitude nor vacancy. Only a flicker
Over the strained time-ridden faces
Distracted from distraction by distraction
105 Filled with fancies and empty of meaning
Tumid apathy with no concentration
Men and bits of paper, whirled by the cold wind
That blows before and after time,
Wind in and out of unwholesome lungs
110 Time before and time after.
Eructation° of unhealthy souls   *belching*
Into the faded air, the torpid
Driven on the wind that sweeps the gloomy hills of
     London,
Hampstead and Clerkenwell, Campden and Putney,
115 Highgate, Primrose and Ludgate. Not here
Not here the darkness, in this twittering world.

     Descend lower, descend only
Into the world of perpetual solitude,
World not world, but that which is not world,

120 Internal darkness, deprivation
And destitution of all property,
Desiccation of the world of sense,
Evacuation of the world of fancy,
Inoperancy of the world of spirit;
125 This is the one way, and the other
Is the same, not in movement
But abstention from movement; while the world moves
In appetency,[1] on its metalled ways
Of time past and time future.

                        4
130 Time and the bell have buried the day,
The black cloud carries the sun away.
Will the sunflower turn to us, will the clematis[2]
Stray down, bend to us; tendril and spray
Clutch and cling?
135 Chill
Fingers of yew be curled
Down on us? After the kingfisher's wing
Has answered light to light, and is silent, the light is still
At the still point of the turning world.

                        5
140 Words move, music moves
Only in time; but that which is only living
Can only die. Words, after speech, reach
Into the silence. Only by the form, the pattern,
Can words or music reach
145 The stillness, as a Chinese jar still
Moves perpetually in its stillness.
Not the stillness of the violin, while the note lasts,
Not that only, but the co-existence,
Or say that the end precedes the beginning,
150 And the end and the beginning were always there
Before the beginning and after the end.
And all is always now. Words strain,
Crack and sometimes break, under the burden,
Under the tension, slip, slide, perish,
155 Decay with imprecision, will not stay in place,
Will not stay still. Shrieking voices
Scolding, mocking, or merely chattering,
Always assail them. The Word in the desert
Is most attacked by voices of temptation,

---

[1] *appetency* Instinctive inclination.
[2] *clematis* Type of twining shrub.

160 The crying shadow in the funeral dance,
The loud lament of the disconsolate chimera.[1]

The detail of the pattern is movement,
As in the figure of the ten stairs.[2]
Desire itself is movement
165 Not in itself desirable;
Love is itself unmoving,
Only the cause and end of movement,
Timeless, and undesiring
Except in the aspect of time
170 Caught in the form of limitation
Between un-being and being.
Sudden in a shaft of sunlight
Even while the dust moves
There rises the hidden laughter
175 Of children in the foliage
Quick now, here, now, always—
Ridiculous the waste sad time
Stretching before and after.
—1935, 1943

Tradition and the Individual Talent

I

In English writing we seldom speak of tradition, though we occasionally apply its name in deploring its absence. We cannot refer to "the tradition" or to "a tradition"; at most, we employ the adjective in saying that the poetry of So-and-so is "traditional" or even "too traditional." Seldom, perhaps, does the word appear except in a phrase of censure. If otherwise, it is vaguely approbative, with the implication, as to the work approved, of some pleasing archaeological reconstruction. You can hardly make the word agreeable to English ears without this comfortable reference to the reassuring science of archaeology.

Certainly the word is not likely to appear in our appreciations of living or dead writers. Every nation, every race, has not only its own creative, but its own critical turn of mind; and is even more oblivious of the shortcomings and limitations of its critical habits than of those of its creative genius. We know, or think we know, from the enormous mass of critical writing that has appeared in the French language, the critical method or habit of the French; we only conclude (we are such unconscious people) that the French are "more critical than we," and sometimes even plume ourselves a little with the fact, as if the French were the less spontaneous. Perhaps they are; but we might remind ourselves that criticism is as inevitable as breathing, and that we should be none the worse for articulating what passes in our minds when we read a book and feel an emotion about it, for criticizing our own minds in their work of criticism. One of the facts that might come to light in this process is our tendency to insist, when we praise a poet, upon those aspects of his work in which he least resembles anyone else. In these aspects or parts of his work we pretend to find what is individual, what is the peculiar essence of the man. We dwell with satisfaction upon the poet's difference from his predecessors, especially his immediate predecessors; we endeavour to find something that can be isolated in order to be enjoyed. Whereas if we approach a poet without this prejudice we shall often find that not only the best, but the most individual parts of his work may be those in which the dead poets, his ancestors, assert their immortality most vigorously. And I do not mean the impressionable period of adolescence, but the period of full maturity.

Yet if the only form of tradition, of handing down, consisted in following the ways of the immediate generation before us in a blind or timid adherence to its successes, "tradition" should positively be discouraged. We have seen many such simple currents soon lost in the sand; and novelty is better than repetition. Tradition is a matter of much wider significance. It cannot be inherited, and if you want it you must obtain it by great labour. It involves, in the first place, the historical sense, which we may call nearly indispensable to anyone who would continue to be a poet beyond his twenty-fifth year; and the historical sense involves a perception, not only of the pastness of the past, but of its presence; the historical sense compels a man to write not merely with his own generation in his bones, but with a feeling that

---

[1] *chimera* Fire-breathing monster of Greek mythology that was usually represented as part goat, part lion, and part serpent. Hence, any fantastic monster of disparate parts or fanciful illusion.

[2] *ten stairsi* According to Spanish poet and mystic St. John of the Cross (1542–91), there are ten steps on the mystical ladder of divine love.

the whole of the literature of Europe from Homer[1] and within it the whole of the literature of his own country has a simultaneous existence and composes a simultaneous order. This historical sense, which is a sense of the timeless as well as of the temporal and of the timeless and of the temporal together, is what makes a writer traditional. And it is at the same time what makes a writer most acutely conscious of his place in time, of his own contemporaneity.

No poet, no artist of any art, has his complete meaning alone. His significance, his appreciation is the appreciation of his relation to the dead poets and artists. You cannot value him alone; you must set him, for contrast and comparison, among the dead. I mean this as a principle of aesthetic, not merely historical, criticism. The necessity that he shall conform, that he shall cohere, is not one-sided; what happens when a new work of art is created is something that happens simultaneously to all the works of art which preceded it. The existing monuments form an ideal order among themselves, which is modified by the introduction of the new (the really new) work of art among them. The existing order is complete before the new work arrives; for order to persist after the supervention of novelty, the *whole* existing order must be, if ever so slightly, altered; and so the relations, proportions, values of each work of art toward the whole are readjusted; and this is conformity between the old and the new. Whoever has approved this idea of order, of the form of European, of English literature will not find it preposterous that the past should be altered by the present as much as the present is directed by the past. And the poet who is aware of this will be aware of great difficulties and responsibilities.

In a peculiar sense he will be aware also that he must inevitably be judged by the standards of the past. I say judged, not amputated, by them; not judged to be as good as, or worse or better than, the dead; and certainly not judged by the canons of dead critics. It is a judgement, a comparison, in which two things are measured by each other. To conform merely would be for the new work not really to conform at all; it would not be new, and would therefore not be a work of art. And we do not quite say that the new is more valuable because it fits in; but its fitting in is a test of its value—a test, it is

true, which can only be slowly and cautiously applied, for we are none of us infallible judges of conformity. We say: it appears to conform, and is perhaps individual, or it appears individual, and may conform; but we are hardly likely to find that it is one and not the other.

To proceed to a more intelligible exposition of the relation of the poet to the past: he can neither take the past as a lump, an indiscriminate bolus,[2] nor can he form himself wholly on one or two private admirations, nor can he form himself wholly upon one preferred period. The first course is inadmissible, the second is an important experience of youth, and the third is a pleasant and highly desirable supplement. The poet must be very conscious of the main current, which does not at all flow invariably through the most distinguished reputations. He must be quite aware of the obvious fact that art never improves, but that the material of art is never quite the same. He must be aware that the mind of Europe—the mind of his own country—a mind which he learns in time to be much more important than his own private mind—is a mind which changes, and that this change is a development which abandons nothing *en route*, which does not superannuate either Shakespeare, or Homer, or the rock drawing of the Magdalenian draughtsmen.[3] That this development, refinement perhaps, complication certainly, is not, from the point of view of the artist, any improvement. Perhaps not even an improvement from the point of view of the psychologist or not to the extent which we imagine; perhaps only in the end based upon a complication in economics and machinery. But the difference between the present and the past is that the conscious present is an awareness of the past in a way and to an extent which the past's awareness of itself cannot show.

Someone said: "The dead writers are remote from us because we *know* so much more than they did." Precisely, and they are that which we know.

I am alive to a usual objection to what is clearly part of my programme for the *métier* of poetry. The objection is that the doctrine requires a ridiculous amount of erudition (pedantry), a claim which can be rejected by appeal to the lives of poets in any pantheon. It will even be affirmed that much learning deadens or perverts

---

[1] *Homer* Greek poet (c. 700 BCE), author of the *Iliad* and the *Odyssey*.

[2] *bolus* Round mass.

[3] *Magdalenian draughtsmen* Magdalenian cave paintings of the Paleolithic period are among the first known works of art.

poetic sensibility. While, however, we persist in believing that a poet ought to know as much as will not encroach upon his necessary receptivity and necessary laziness, it is not desirable to confine knowledge to whatever can be put into a useful shape for examinations, drawing rooms, or the still more pretentious modes of publicity. Some can absorb knowledge, the more tardy must sweat for it. Shakespeare acquired more essential history from Plutarch[1] than most men could from the whole British Museum. What is to be insisted upon is that the poet must develop or procure the consciousness of the past and that he should continue to develop this consciousness throughout his career.

What happens is a continual surrender of himself as he is at the moment to something which is more valuable. The progress of an artist is a continual self-sacrifice, a continual extinction of personality.

There remains to define this process of depersonalization and its relation to the sense of tradition. It is in this depersonalization that art may be said to approach the condition of science. I therefore invite you to consider, as a suggestive analogy, the action which takes place when a bit of finely filiated[2] platinum is introduced into a chamber containing oxygen and sulphur dioxide.

2

Honest criticism and sensitive appreciation is directed not upon the poet but upon the poetry. If we attend to the confused cries of the newspaper critics and the susurrus[3] of popular repetition that follows, we shall hear the names of poets in great numbers; if we seek not Blue-book[4] knowledge but the enjoyment of poetry, and ask for a poem, we shall seldom find it. I have tried to point out the importance of the relation of the poem to other poems by other authors, and suggested the conception of poetry as a living whole of all the poetry that has ever been written. The other aspect of this Impersonal theory of poetry is the relation of the poem to its author. And I hinted, by an analogy, that the mind of the mature poet differs from that of the immature one not precisely in any valuation of "personality," not being necessarily more interesting, or having "more to say," but rather by being a more finely perfected medium in which special, or very varied, feelings are at liberty to enter into new combinations.

The analogy was that of the catalyst. When the two gases previously mentioned are mixed in the presence of a filament of platinum, they form sulphurous acid. This combination takes place only if the platinum is present; nevertheless, the newly formed acid contains no trace of platinum, and the platinum itself is apparently unaffected: has remained inert, neutral, and unchanged. The mind of the poet is the shred of platinum. It may partly or exclusively operate upon the experience of the man himself; but, the more perfect the artist, the more completely separate in him will be the man who suffers and the mind which creates; the more perfectly will the mind digest and transmute the passions which are its material.

The experience, you will notice, the elements which enter the presence of the transforming catalyst, are of two kinds: emotions and feelings. The effect of a work of art upon the person who enjoys it is an experience different in kind from any experience not of art. It may be formed out of one emotion, or may be a combination of several; and various feelings, inhering for the writer in particular words or phrases or images, may be added to compose the final result. Or great poetry may be made without the direct use of any emotion whatever: composed out of feelings solely. Canto XV of the *Inferno*[5] (Brunetto Latini) is a working up of the emotion evident in the situation; but the effect, though single as that of any work of art, is obtained by considerable complexity of detail. The last quatrain gives an image, a feeling attaching to an image, which "came," which did not develop simply out of what precedes, but which was probably in suspension in the poet's mind until the proper combination arrived for it to add itself to. The poet's mind is in fact a receptacle for seizing and storing up numberless feelings, phrases, images, which remain there until all the particles which can unite to form a new compound are present together.

---

[1] *Plutarch* Greek biographer of the first century CE who a strong influence on English literature; Shakespeare drew some of his characters in plays such as *Coriolanus, Antony and Cleopatra,* and *Julius Caesar* from Plutarch's biographies.

[2] *filiated* Made into filament, or fine thread.

[3] *susurrus* Whispering or muttering.

[4] *Blue-book* Official reports of the British Government.

[5] *Canto XV of the Inferno* In this canto, Dante meets an old acquaintance, Brunetto Latini, who is in Hell for being a Sodomite.

If you compare several representative passages of the greatest poetry you see how great is the variety of types of combination, and also how completely any semi-ethical criterion of "sublimity" misses the mark. For it is not the "greatness," the intensity, of the emotions, the components, but the intensity of the artistic process, the pressure, so to speak, under which the fusion takes place, that counts. The episode of Paolo and Francesca[1] employs a definite emotion, but the intensity of the poetry is something quite different from whatever intensity in the supposed experience it may give the impression of. It is no more intense, furthermore, than Canto XXVI, the voyage of Ulysses, which has not the direct dependence upon an emotion. Great variety is possible in the process of transmutation of emotion: the murder of Agamemnon,[2] or the agony of Othello,[3] gives an artistic effect apparently closer to a possible original than the scenes from Dante. In the *Agamemnon,* the artistic emotion approximates to the emotion of an actual spectator; in *Othello* to the emotion of the protagonist himself. But the difference between art and the event is always absolute; the combination which is the murder of Agamemnon is probably as complex as that which is the voyage of Ulysses. In either case there has been a fusion of elements. The ode of Keats contains a number of feelings which have nothing particular to do with the nightingale, but which the nightingale, partly perhaps because of its attractive name, and partly because of its reputation, served to bring together.

The point of view which I am struggling to attack is perhaps related to the metaphysical theory of the substantial unity of the soul: for my meaning is, that the poet has, not a "personality" to express, but a particular medium, which is only a medium and not a personality, in which impressions and experiences combine in peculiar and unexpected ways. Impressions and experiences which are important for the man may take no place in the poetry, and those which become important

in the poetry may play quite a negligible part in the man, the personality.

I will quote a passage which is unfamiliar enough to be regarded with fresh attention in the light—or darkness—of these observations:

And now methinks I could e'en chide myself
For doting on her beauty, though her death
Shall be revenged after no common action.
Does the silkworm expend her yellow labours
For thee? For thee does she undo herself?
Are lordships sold to maintain ladyships
For the poor benefit of a bewildering minute?
Why does yon fellow falsify highways,
And put his life between the judge's lips,
To refine such a thing—keeps horse and men
To beat their valours for her?...[4]

In this passage (as is evident if it is taken in its context) there is a combination of positive and negative emotions: an intensely strong attraction toward beauty and an equally intense fascination by the ugliness which is contrasted with it and which destroys it. This balance of contrasted emotion is in the dramatic situation to which the speech is pertinent, but that situation alone is inadequate to it. This is, so to speak, the structural emotion, provided by the drama. But the whole effect, the dominant tone, is due to the fact that a number of floating feelings, having an affinity to this emotion by no means superficially evident, have combined with it to give us a new art emotion.

It is not in his personal emotions, the emotions provoked by particular events in his life, that the poet is in anyway remarkable or interesting. His particular emotions may be simple, or crude, or flat. The emotion in his poetry will be a very complex thing, but not with the complexity of the emotions of people who have very complex or unusual emotions in life. One error, in fact, of eccentricity in poetry is to seek for new human emotions to express; and in this search for novelty in the wrong place it discovers the perverse. The business of the poet is not to find new emotions, but to use the ordinary ones and, in working them up into poetry, to express feelings which are not in actual emotions at all.

[1] *episode of Paolo and Francesca* Two illicit lovers (Paolo is Francesca's husband's brother).

[2] *murder of Agamemnon* In Aeschylus's play, Clytemnestra kills her husband Agamemnon after he sacrifices their daughter to the god Artemis.

[3] *agony of Othello* In the play by Shakespeare, Othello mistakenly thinks that his wife is unfaithful, kills her, and then, upon learning the truth, commits suicide.

[4] *And now ... for her* From *The Revenger's Tragedy* (1607), a play variously ascribed to Cyril Tourneur and to Thomas Middleton.

And emotions which he has never experienced will serve his turn as well as those familiar to him. Consequently, we must believe that "emotion recollected in tranquillity"[1] is an inexact formula. For it is neither emotion, nor recollection, nor, without distortion of meaning, tranquillity. It is a concentration, and a new thing resulting from the concentration, of a very great number of experiences which to the practical and active person would not seem to be experiences at all; it is a concentration which does not happen consciously or of deliberation. These experiences are not "recollected," and they finally unite in an atmosphere which is "tranquil" only in that it is a passive attending upon the event. Of course this is not quite the whole story. There is a great deal, in the writing of poetry, which must be conscious and deliberate. In fact, the bad poet is usually unconscious where he ought to be conscious, and conscious where he ought to be unconscious. Both errors tend to make him "personal." Poetry is not a turning loose of emotion, but an escape from emotion; it is not the expression of personality, but an escape from personality. But, of course, only those who have personality and emotions know what it means to want to escape from these things.

3

ὁ δὲ νοῦς ἴσως θειότερόν τι καὶ ἀπαθές ἐστιν[2]

This essay proposes to halt at the frontier of metaphysics or mysticism, and confine itself to such practical conclusions as can be applied by the responsible person interested in poetry. To divert interest from the poet to the poetry is a laudable aim: for it would conduce to a juster estimation of actual poetry, good and bad. There are many people who appreciate the expression of sincere emotion in verse, and there is a smaller number of people who can appreciate technical excellence. But very

few know when there is an expression of *significant* emotion, emotion which has its life in the poem and not in the history of the poet. The emotion of art is impersonal. And the poet cannot reach this impersonality without surrendering himself wholly to the work to be done. And he is not likely to know what is to be done unless he lives in what is not merely the present, but the present moment of the past, unless he is conscious, not of what is dead, but of what is already living.

—1919

The Metaphysical Poets[3]

By collecting these poems from the work of a generation more often named than read, and more often read than profitably studied, Professor Grierson has rendered a service of some importance. Certainly the reader will meet with many poems already preserved in other anthologies, at the same time that he discovers poems such as those of Aurelian Townshend or Lord Herbert of Cherbury here included. But the function of such an anthology as this is neither that of Professor Saintsbury's admirable edition of Caroline poets nor that of *The Oxford Book of English Verse*. Mr. Grierson's book is in itself a piece of criticism, and a provocation of criticism; and we think that he was right in including so many poems of Donne, elsewhere (though not in many editions) accessible, as documents in the case of "metaphysical poetry." The phrase has long done duty as a term of abuse, or as the label of a quaint and pleasant taste. The question is to what extent the so-called metaphysicals formed a school (in our own time we should say a "movement"), and how far this so-called school or movement is a digression from the main current.

Not only is it extremely difficult to define metaphysical poetry, but difficult to decide what poets practise it and in which of their verses. The poetry of Donne (to whom Marvell and Bishop King are sometimes nearer than any of the other authors) is late Elizabethan, its feeling often very close to that of Chapman. The "courtly" poetry is derivative from Jonson, who bor-

---

[1] *"emotion ... tranquillity"* From William Wordsworth's Preface to *Lyrical Ballads* (1800): "Poetry is the spontaneous overflow of powerful feelings: it takes its origin from emotion recollected in tranquillity: the emotion is contemplated till by a species of reaction the tranquillity gradually disappears, and an emotion, kindred to that which was before the subject of contemplation, is gradually produced, and does itself actually exist in the mind."

[2] ὁ δὲ ... ἐστιν   Greek: "The mind is doubtless something more divine and unaffected." From Aristotle's *De Anima* (Latin: On the Soul) 1.4.

[3] *The Metaphysical Poets*   Originally published in the *Times Literary Supplement* as a review of the Clarendon Press volume *Metaphysical Lyrics and Poems of the Seventeenth Century: Donne to Butler* (1921), edited by Herbert J.C. Grierson.

rowed liberally from the Latin; it expires in the next century with the sentiment and witticism of Prior. There is finally the devotional verse of Herbert, Vaughan, and Crashaw (echoed long after by Christina Rossetti and Francis Thompson); Crashaw, sometimes more profound and less sectarian than the others, has a quality which returns through the Elizabethan period to the early Italians. It is difficult to find any precise use of metaphor, simile, or other conceit, which is common to all the poets and at the same time important enough as an element of style to isolate these poets as a group. Donne, and often Cowley, employ a device which is sometimes considered characteristically "metaphysical"; the elaboration (contrasted with the condensation) of a figure of speech to the furthest stage to which ingenuity can carry it. Thus Cowley develops the commonplace comparison of the world to a chess-board through long stanzas ("To Destiny"),[1] and Donne, with more grace, in "A Valediction,"[2] the comparison of two lovers to a pair of compasses. But elsewhere we find, instead of the mere explication of the content of a comparison, a development by rapid association of thought which requires considerable agility on the part of the reader.

> On a round ball
> A workeman that hath copies by, can lay
> An Europe, Afrique, and an Asia,
> And quickly make that, which was nothing, All,
> So doth each teare,
> Which thee doth weare,
> A globe, yea world by that impression grow,
> Till thy tears mixt with mine doe overflow
> This world, by waters sent from thee, my heaven
> dissolved so.[3]

Here we find at least two connexions which are not implicit in the first figure, but are forced upon it by the poet: from the geographer's globe to the tear, and the tear to the deluge. On the other hand, some of Donne's most successful and characteristic effects are secured by brief words and sudden contrasts:

> A bracelet of bright hair about the bone,[4]

where the most powerful effect is produced by the sudden contrast of associations of "bright hair" and of "bone." This telescoping of images and multiplied associations is characteristic of the phrase of some of the dramatists of the period which Donne knew: not to mention Shakespeare, it is frequent in Middleton, Webster, and Tourneur, and is one of the sources of the vitality of their language.

Johnson, who employed the term "metaphysical poets," apparently having Donne, Cleveland, and Cowley chiefly in mind, remarks of them that "the most heterogeneous ideas are yoked by violence together."[5] The force of this impeachment lies in the failure of the conjunction, the fact that often the ideas are yoked but not united; and if we are to judge of styles of poetry by their abuse, enough examples may be found in Cleveland to justify Johnson's condemnation. But a degree of heterogeneity of material compelled into unity by the operation of the poet's mind is omnipresent in poetry. We need not select for illustration such a line as

> Notre ame est un trois-mats cherchant son Icarie;[6]

we may find it in some of the best lines of Johnson himself (The Vanity of Human Wishes):

> His fate was destined to a barren strand,
> A petty fortress, and a dubious hand;
> He left a name at which the world grew pale,
> To point a moral, or adorn a tale—

where the effect is due to a contrast of ideas, different in degree but the same in principle, as that which Johnson mildly reprehended. And in one of the finest poems of the age (a poem which could not have been written in any other age), the Exequy of Bishop King, the extended comparison is used with perfect success: the idea and the simile become one, in the passage in which the Bishop illustrates his impatience to see his dead wife, under the figure of a journey:

---

[1] "To Destiny" Abraham Cowley's "Destiny" (1656).

[2] "A Valediction" Donne's poem "A Valediction: Forbidding Mourning" (1633).

[3] On a round ... dissolved so From Donne's "A Valediction: Of Weeping," 10–18.

[4] A bracelet ... bone From "The Relic" (1633), 6.

[5] "the most ... together" Samuel Johnson in his "Life of Cowley" (1779).

[6] Notre ... Icarie French: "Our soul is a three-masted ship seeking its Icarie." From Charles Baudelaire's Le Voyage.

Stay for me there; I will not faile
To meet thee in that hollow Vale.
And think not much of my delay;
I am already on the way,
And follow thee with all the speed
Desire can make, or sorrows breed.
Each minute is a short degree,
And ev'ry houre a step towards thee.
At night when I betake to rest,
Next morn I rise nearer my West
Of life, almost by eight houres sail,
Than when sleep breath'd his drowsy gale. . . .
But heark! My Pulse, like a soft Drum
Beats my approach, tells Thee *I come;*
And slow howere my marches be,
I shall at last sit down by Thee.

(In the last few lines there is that effect of terror which is several times attained by one of Bishop King's admirers, Edgar Poe.) Again, we may justly take these quatrains from Lord Herbert's "Ode,"[1] stanzas which would, we think, be immediately pronounced to be of the metaphysical school:

So when from hence we shall be gone,
And be no more, nor you, nor I,
As one another's mystery,
Each shall be both, yet both but one.

This said, in her up-lifted face,
Her eyes, which did that beauty crown,
Were like two starrs, that having faln down,
Look up again to find their place:

While such a moveless silent peace
Did seize on their becalmed sense,
One would have thought some influence
Their ravished spirits did possess.

There is nothing in these lines (with the possible exception of the stars, a simile not at once grasped, but lovely and justified) which fits Johnson's general observations on the metaphysical poets in his essay on Cowley. A good deal resides in the richness of association which is at the same time borrowed from and given to the word

"becalmed"; but the meaning is clear, the language simple and elegant. It is to be observed that the language of these poets is as a rule simple and pure; in the verse of George Herbert this simplicity is carried as far as it can go—a simplicity emulated without success by numerous modern poets. The *structure* of the sentences, on the other hand, is sometimes far from simple, but this is not a vice; it is a fidelity to thought and feeling. The effect, at its best, is far less artificial than that of an ode by Gray. And as this fidelity induces variety of thought and feeling, so it induces variety of music. We doubt whether, in the eighteenth century, could be found two poems in nominally the same metre, so dissimilar as Marvell's "Coy Mistress" and Crashaw's "Saint Teresa"; the one producing an effect of great speed by the use of short syllables, and the other an ecclesiastical solemnity by the use of long ones:

Love, thou art absolute sole lord
Of life and death.

If so shrewd and sensitive (though so limited) a critic as Johnson failed to define metaphysical poetry by its faults, it is worthwhile to inquire whether we may not have more success by adopting the opposite method: by assuming that the poets of the seventeenth century (up to the Revolution)[2] were the direct and normal development of the precedent age; and, without prejudicing their case by the adjective "metaphysical," consider whether their virtue was not something permanently valuable, which subsequently disappeared, but ought not to have disappeared. Johnson has hit, perhaps by accident, on one of their peculiarities, when he observes that "their attempts were always analytic"; he would not agree that, after the dissociation, they put the material together again in a new unity.

It is certain that the dramatic verse of the later Elizabethan and early Jacobean poets expresses a degree of development of sensibility which is not found in any of the prose, good as it often is. If we except Marlowe, a man of prodigious intelligence, these dramatists were directly or indirectly (it is at least a tenable theory) affected by Montaigne. Even if we except also Jonson and Chapman, these two were notably erudite, and were notably men who incorporated their erudition into their

---

[1] *Lord Herbert's "Ode"* Edward Herbert, Lord Cherbury's "An Ode Upon a Question Moved, Whether Love Should Continue Forever?" (1664).

[2] *Revolution* I.e., the English Revolution, 1640–60.

sensibility: their mode of feeling was directly and freshly altered by their reading and thought. In Chapman especially there is a direct sensuous apprehension of thought, or a re-creation of thought into feeling, which is exactly what we find in Donne:

> in this one thing, all the discipline
> Of manners and of manhood is contained;
> A man to join himself with th' Universe
> In his main sway, and make in all things fit
> One with that All, and go on, round as it;
> Not plucking from the whole his wretched part,
> And into straits, or into nought revert,
> Wishing the complete Universe might be
> Subject to such a rag of it as he;
> But to consider great Necessity.[1]

We compare this with some modern passage:

> No, when the fight begins within himself,
> A man's worth something. God stoops o'er his head
> Satan looks up between his feet—both tug—
> He's left, himself, i' the middle; the soul wakes
> And grows. Prolong that battle through his life![2]

It is perhaps somewhat less fair, though very tempting (as both poets are concerned with the perpetuation of love by offspring), to compare with the stanzas already quoted from Lord Herbert's "Ode" the following from Tennyson:

> One walked between his wife and child,
> With measured footfall firm and mild,
> And now and then he gravely smiled.
>
> The prudent partner of his blood
> Leaned on him, faithful, gentle,
> Wearing the rose of womanhood.
>
> And in their double love secure,
> The little maiden walked demure,
> Pacing with downward eyelids pure.
>
> These three made unity so sweet,

> My frozen heart began to beat,
> Remembering its ancient beat.[3]

The difference is not a simple difference of degree between poets. It is something which had happened to the mind of England between the time of Donne or Lord Herbert of Cherbury and the time of Tennyson and Browning; it is the difference between the intellectual poet and the reflective poet. Tennyson and Browning are poets, and they think; but they do not feel their thought as immediately as the odour of a rose. A thought to Donne was an experience; it modified his sensibility. When a poet's mind is perfectly equipped for its work, it is constantly amalgamating disparate experience; the ordinary man's experience is chaotic, irregular, fragmentary. The latter falls in love, or reads Spinoza, and these two experiences have nothing to do with each other, or with the noise of the typewriter or the smell of cooking; in the mind of the poet these experiences are always forming new wholes.

We may express the difference by the following theory: The poets of the seventeenth century, the successors of the dramatists of the sixteenth, possessed a mechanism of sensibility which could devour any kind of experience. They are simple, artificial, difficult, or fantastic, as their predecessors were; no less nor more than Dante, Guido Cavalcanti, Guinicelli, or Cino. In the seventeenth century a dissociation of sensibility set in, from which we have never recovered; and this dissociation, as is natural, was aggravated by the influence of the two most powerful poets of the century, Milton and Dryden. Each of these men performed certain poetic functions so magnificently well that the magnitude of the effect concealed the absence of others. The language went on and in some respects improved; the best verse of Collins, Gray, Johnson, and even Goldsmith satisfies some of our fastidious demands better than that of Donne or Marvell or King. But while the language became more refined, the feeling became more crude. The feeling, the sensibility, expressed in the "Country Churchyard"[4] (to say nothing of Tennyson and

---

[1] *in this one ... Necessity* From *The Revenge of Bussy d'Ambois* (1613), 4.1.

[2] *No ... life* From Robert Browning's "Bishop Blougram's Apology" (1855), 693–97.

[3] *One walked ... beat* From "The Two Voices" (1833,) 412–33.

[4] *"Country Churchyard"* "Elegy Written in a Country Church-Yard," by Thomas Gray (1716–71).

Browning) is cruder than that in the "Coy Mistress."[1]

The second effect of the influence of Milton and Dryden followed from the first, and was therefore slow in manifestation. The sentimental age began early in the eighteenth century, and continued. The poets revolted against the ratiocinative, the descriptive; they thought and felt by fits, unbalanced; they reflected. In one or two passages of Shelley's "Triumph of Life," in the second *Hyperion*,[2] there are traces of a struggle toward unification of sensibility. But Keats and Shelley died, and Tennyson and Browning ruminated.

After this brief exposition of a theory—too brief, perhaps, to carry conviction—we may ask, what would have been the fate of the "metaphysical" had the current of poetry descended in a direct line from them, as it descended in a direct line to them? They would not, certainly, be classified as metaphysical. The possible interests of a poet are unlimited; the more intelligent he is the better; the more intelligent he is the more likely that he will have interests: our only condition is that he turn them into poetry, and not merely meditate on them poetically. A philosophical theory which has entered into poetry is established, for its truth or falsity in one sense ceases to matter, and its truth in another sense is proved. The poets in question have, like other poets, various faults. But they were, at best, engaged in the task of trying to find the verbal equivalent for states of mind and feeling. And this means both that they are more mature, and that they wear better, than later poets of certainly not less literary ability.

It is not a permanent necessity that poets should be interested in philosophy, or in any other subject. We can only say that it appears likely that poets in our civilization, as it exists at present, must be *difficult*. Our civilization comprehends great variety and complexity, and this variety and complexity, playing upon a refined sensibility, must produce various and complex results. The poet must become more and more comprehensive, more allusive, more indirect, in order to force, to dislocate if necessary, language into his meaning. (A brilliant and extreme statement of this view, with which it is not requisite to associate oneself, is that of M. Jean

Epstein,[3] *La Poésie d'aujourd'hui*.) Hence we get something which looks very much like the conceit—we get, in fact, a method curiously similar to that of the "metaphysical poets," similar also in its use of obscure words and of simple phrasing.

> *O géraniums diaphanes, guerroyeurs sortilèges,*
> *Sacrilèges monomanes!*
> *Emballages, dévergondages, douches! O pressoirs*
> *Des vendanges des grands soirs!*
> *Layettes aux abois,*
> *Thyrses au fond des bois!*
> *Transfusions, représailles,*
> *Relevailles, compresses et l'éternel potion,*
> *Angélus! n'en pouvoir plus*
> *De débâcles nuptiales! de débâcles nuptiales!*[4]

The same poet could write also simply:

> *Elle est bien loin, elle pleure,*
> *Le grand vent se lamente aussi …*[5]

Jules Laforgue, and Tristan Corbière in many of his poems, are nearer to the "school of Donne" than any modern English poet. But poets more classical than they have the same essential quality of transmuting ideas into sensations, of transforming an observation into a state of mind.

> *Pour l'enfant, amoureux de cartes et d'estampes,*
> *L'univers est égal à son vaste appétit.*
> *Ah, que le monde est grand à la clarté des lampes!*
> *Aux yeux du souvenir que le monde est petit!*[6]

---

[1] *"Coy Mistress"* "To His Coy Mistress," by Andrew Marvell (1621–78).

[2] *Hyperion* John Keats began his epic fragment in 1818; in 1819 he revised the poem and wrote *The Fall of Hyperion, A Dream*.

[3] *M. Jean Epstein* French intellectual (1897–1953).

[4] *O géraniums … nuptiales* French: "O diaphanous geraniums, warrior magic spells, / Monomaniacal sacrileges! / Packing materials, licentiousness, showers! O presses / Of the great evening grape harvests! / Pressed baby clothes, / Thyrsis deep in the woods! / Transfusions, reprisals, / Reawakenings, compresses, and the eternal potion, / Angelus! No longer able / Marriage debacles! Marriage debacles!" From Jules Laforgue's *Derniers vers* (1890).

[5] *Elle est bien … aussi* French: "She is far away, she cries, / The high wind also laments." From *Derniers vers*.

[6] *Pour l'enfant … est petit* French: "For the child, loving maps and stamps, / The universe is his vast appetite. / Ah, how large the world is by the clear light of the lamps! / To eyes remembering that the world is small." From Baudelaire's *Le Voyage*.

In French literature the great master of the seventeenth century—Racine—and the great master of the nineteenth—Baudelaire—are in some ways more like each other than they are like anyone else. The greatest two masters of diction are also the greatest two psychologists, the most curious explorers of the soul. It is interesting to speculate whether it is not a misfortune that two of the greatest masters of diction in our language, Milton and Dryden, triumph with a dazzling disregard of the soul. If we continued to produce Miltons and Drydens it might not so much matter, but as things are it is a pity that English poetry has remained so incomplete. Those who object to the "artificiality" of Milton or Dryden sometimes tell us to "look into our hearts and write." But that is not looking deep enough; Racine or Donne looked into a good deal more than the heart. One must look into the cerebral cortex, the nervous system, and the digestive tracts.

May we not conclude, then, that Donne, Crashaw, Vaughan, Herbert and Lord Herbert, Marvell, King, Cowley at his best, are in the direct current of English poetry, and that their faults should be reprimanded by this standard rather than coddled by antiquarian affection? They have been enough praised in terms which are implicit limitations because they are "metaphysical" or "witty," "quaint" or "obscure," though at their best they have not these attributes more than other serious poets. On the other hand, we must not reject the criticism of Johnson (a dangerous person to disagree with) without having mastered it, without having assimilated the Johnsonian canons of taste. In reading the celebrated passage in his essay on Cowley we must remember that by wit he clearly means something more serious than we usually mean today; in his criticism of their versification we must remember in what a narrow discipline he was trained, but also how well trained; we must remember that Johnson tortures chiefly the chief offenders, Cowley and Cleveland. It would be a fruitful work, and one requiring a substantial book, to break up the classification of Johnson and exhibit these poets in all their difference of kind and of degree, from the massive music of Donne to the faint, pleasing tinkle of Aurelian Townshend.

—1921

IN CONTEXT

T.S. Eliot and Anti-Semitism

Considerable controversy occurred in the latter years of the twentieth century over the issue of T.S. Eliot and anti-Semitism. The issue had been raised here and there during Eliot's lifetime: J.V. Healy raised the matter in correspondence with Eliot in 1940; a letter of George Orwell's in 1948 reveals that some were then suggesting in conversation that Eliot was anti-Semitic, and so on. Orwell no doubt gave voice to a then-common view in dismissing the suggestion:

> It is nonsense what Fyvel said about Eliot being anti-Semitic. Of course you can find what would now be called antisemitic remarks in his early work, but who didn't say such things at that time? (Letter to Julian Symons, 29 October 1948)

That anti-Semitism was widespread in the 1910s and 1920s in both the USA and Britain is unquestionable, and to some extent Eliot's views on the question were no doubt those of the majority at the time. But few published literary works displayed the consistency of association that one finds in Eliot's early poetry between what is Jewish and what is squalid and distasteful. Still, leading critics and scholars did not begin to air the matter publicly until 1971, when the issue of anti-Semitism in Eliot's works was raised by a leading critic, George Steiner, in a letter to *The Listener*:

The obstinate puzzle is Eliot's uglier touches tend to occur at the heart of very good poetry (which is *not* the case with Pound). One thinks of the notorious "the Jew squats on the window-sill ... Spawned in some estaminet of Antwerp" in "Geron-tion"; of

> The rats are underneath the piles.
> The Jew is underneath the lot.

In "Burbank with a Baedeker: Bleistein with a Cigar"; of

> Rachel nee Rabinovich
>
> tears at the grapes with murderous paws

in "Sweeney among the Nightingales." (*The Listener*, 29 April 1971)

The question Steiner raised as to how the uglier touches in Eliot's work connected with the aesthetic quality of the whole is one that has continued to interest scholars and critics. In an important 1988 book, another leading scholar, Christopher Ricks, put forward an extended analysis of the ways in which various forms of prejudice may have animated both Eliot's work itself and responses to it. Ricks begins his study with a look at prejudice against women; he notes how the critics had picked up on the latent element of misogyny in two famous lines from "The Love Song of J. Alfred Prufrock":

> John Crowe Ransom [puts a] rhetorical question: "How could they ['the women'] have had any inkling of that glory which Michaelangelo had put into his marbles and his paintings?"
>   Helen Gardner does not as a woman have any different sense of the women: "The absurdity of discussing his giant art, in high-pitched feminine voices, drifting through a drawing room, adds merely extra irony to the underlying sense of the lines."
>   [T]he critics miss ... one of the things that is salutory in the lines
>
> > In the room the women come and go
> > Talking of Michaelangelo.
>
> What none of the critics will own is how much their sense of the lines is incited by prejudice.... Grover Smith [writes that] "the women meanwhile are talking, no doubt tediously and ignorantly, of Michaelangelo." For all we know, as against suspect (perhaps justifiably, but still), the women could be talking as invaluably as [renowned art historian] Kenneth Clark (*T.S. Eliot and Prejudice*, 10–11).

Ricks analyzes at length and with considerable subtlety the "uglier touches" in Eliot's poetry, noting how these are associative rather than unequivocally prejudicial or inciteful. A line such as "The Jew is underneath the lot," he comments, does not "come clean, since the effect of the article 'The Jew' is to disparage all Jews ... while nevertheless leaving open a bolt-hole for the disingenuous reply that a particular Jew only is meant" (35).

As Ricks pointed out, some of Eliot's other writings are at least as disturbing as the published poems. Particularly troubling are an unpublished poem, "Dirge," that was part of an early draft of *The Waste Land*, and a passage from *After Strange Gods*, a series of lectures given by Eliot in Virginia in 1933, and published in book form a year later. (Eliot never allowed the book to be reprinted.) In the passage Eliot is describing what he feels is to be striven for in a society that properly values tradition:

The population should be homogenous.... What is still more important is unity of religious background; and reasons of race and religion combine to make any large number of free-thinking Jews undesirable. There must be a proper balance between urban and rural, industrial and agricultural development. And a spirit of excessive tolerance is to be deprecated (*After Strange Gods*, 20).

If Ricks's focus was primarily a literary one, that of Anthony Julius in his *T.S. Eliot, Anti-Semitism, and Literary Form* (1995) was more broadly social—and more clearly provocative. With his searing indictment both of the anti-Semitism of Eliot's age and its memorable expressions in Eliot's verse, Julius touched a raw nerve. Whereas Ricks's criticisms are often elliptical, and his tone generally reserved, Julius is direct and unrelenting:

"Women," "jews," and "negroes" are not interchangeable "aliens" in Eliot's work. They are, respectively, intimidating, sightless, and transparent; their deaths are respectively longed for, delighted in, and noted without emotion. ...
... However, this does not amount to an argument for suppression. I censure; I do not wish to censor. ... Eliot's anti-Semitic poems are integral to his oeuvre, an oeuvre which is to be valued and preserved. ... One can teach anti-Semitism from such texts; one can also teach poetry. One reads them, appalled, and impressed.

Like Steiner a generation earlier, Julius concludes that Eliot is "able to place his anti-Semitism at the service of his art." A storm of controversy followed the publication of Julius's book, with many defending Julius but many others continuing to argue either that Eliot was not anti-Semitic or that anti-Semitism was irrelevant to his work. A further camp held that anti-Semitism was in fact a significant presence, but that the poetry succeeds despite such "uglier touches" rather than in any way because of them. Today there remains no consensus on these issues, but there can be no doubt that the controversy has left a mark; it is unlikely that extended discussion of Eliot's poetry will again be able to take place without any reference to this troubling issue.

JEAN RHYS
1890 – 1979

Jean Rhys, born Ella Gwendolyn Rees Williams, was a West Indies-born writer whose works are strongly marked by her cultural background and by her experience of life as a white Creole woman in the heavily colonized Caribbean and later in metropolitan London. Although she published four novels early in her career, she was not recognized as a major literary figure until the publication of *Wide Sargasso Sea* (1966), which won the prestigious WH Smith Literary Award and became one of the most widely-read novels of the late twentieth century. The novel is a "prequel" to Charlotte

Brontë's *Jane Eyre* (1847), in which Rhys gives a voice to Rochester's insane and confined wife, Bertha Mason. Rhys made no secret of her motive for writing the book; as she remarked in an interview, "I was convinced Charlotte Brontë must have had something against the West Indies, and I was angry about it." She was thus led to explore the conflict of cultures between colonizer and colonized as she cast in a different light the central motif of *Jane Eyre*—that of a helpless female outsider, powerless and victimized, who relies on older European men for protection. In doing so, Rhys anticipated by a decade or more many of the insights of postcolonialism, the literary movement examining the repercussions of imperialism on subject nations and their citizens that became prevalent in the 1990s. She was one of the first to explicitly connect the marginalization of women with issues of race and class.

Rhys was born in 1890 in Roseau, Dominica, in the West Indies. Her father was a Welsh doctor, and her mother a Dominican Creole of Scottish lineage. She began her education in Roseau, in a convent school. As a white Creole in a predominantly black area, she often felt socially isolated, despite identifying with the black community from an early age. At sixteen she traveled to England, attending the prestigious Perse Prepatory girls' school in Cambridge. While there, Rhys excelled academically, taking first prize in Roman literature in the exams for Cambridge and Oxford. She attended one term at the Royal Academy of Dramatic Art in London in 1909, though she never made it to university; her father died in 1910, leaving Rhys in severely reduced circumstances. Alone and destitute in England, Rhys lived a drifter's life, taking on a variety of jobs: chorus girl (under the stage name Vivian Gray), actress, volunteer cook during World War I, secretary, and ghostwriter of a book about furniture.

In 1919 Rhys married the first of her three husbands. The pair had two children—a son who died as an infant and a daughter—and lived a largely itinerant existence, residing sporadically in Vienna, Budapest, and Paris. During this period she acquainted herself with works of modern art and literature, and began to suffer from the alcoholism that would plague her for the rest of her life. In Paris in 1922, she met Modernist novelist Ford Madox Ford (1873–1939) under whose patronage she began to write. She published her first short story, "Vienne," in Ford's magazine *The Transatlantic Review* in 1924, and followed this with her first collection, *The Left Bank and Other Stories*, in 1927. She continued to publish steadily during the 1930s. Her first novel, *Postures* (1928; *Quartet*, 1929, in the United States), further developed the typical Rhys heroine: sexually alluring, sensitive, and dependent. She followed this with a trio of critically acclaimed semi-autobiographical novels, *After*

Leaving Mr. Mackenzie (1930), *Voyage in the Dark* (1934), and *Good Morning, Midnight* (1939). For some time these publications allowed her to enjoy moderate literary recognition and financial security, but the late 1940s and 50s were marked for Rhys by near-poverty, continuing alcoholism, and trouble with the authorities. Her second husband was jailed in the 1950s for financial misdoing, and she herself spent time in London's Holloway Prison in 1949 after an altercation with neighbors. Rhys brings this period to vivid life in her story of the displaced black drifter, Selina, "Let Them Call It Jazz."

Rhys fell into relative obscurity during the 1940s and 50s, but interest in her work revived with the radio production of *Good Morning, Midnight* in 1958. She followed this with her 1966 masterpiece, *Wide Sargasso Sea*, which she had begun to write over twenty years earlier. The rest of her career was devoted to her memoirs, *Smile Please* (published posthumously in 1979), and her collections *Tigers are Better-Looking* (1968) and *Sleep It Off, Lady* (1976). Rhys died in Devonshire, England, in 1979, at the age of 88.

⌘ ⌘ ⌘

Let Them Call It Jazz

One bright Sunday morning in July I have trouble with my Notting Hill[1] landlord because he ask for a month's rent in advance. He tell me this after I live there since winter, settling up[2] every week without fail. I have no job at the time, and if I give the money he want there's not much left. So I refuse. The man drunk already at that early hour, and he abuse me—all talk, he can't frighten me. But his wife is a bad one—now she walk in my room and say she must have cash. When I tell her no, she give my suitcase one kick and it burst open. My best dress fall out, then she laugh and give another kick. She say month in advance is usual, and if I can't pay find somewhere else.

Don't talk to me about London. Plenty people there have heart like stone. Any complaint—the answer is "prove it." But if nobody see and bear witness for me, how to prove anything? So I pack up and leave, I think better not have dealings with that woman. She too cunning, and Satan don't lie worse.

I walk about till a place nearby is open where I can have coffee and a sandwich. There I start talking to a man at my table. He talk to me already, I know him, but I don't know his name. After a while he ask, "What's the matter? Anything wrong?" and when I tell

him my trouble he say I can use an empty flat[3] he own till I have time to look around.

This man is not at all like most English people. He see very quick, and he decide very quick. English people take long time to decide—you three-quarter dead before they make up their mind about you. Too besides, he speak very matter of fact, as if it's nothing. He speak as if he realize well what it is to live like I do—that's why I accept and go.

He tell me somebody occupy the flat till last week, so I find everything all right, and he tell me how to get there—three-quarters of an hour from Victoria Station,[4] up a steep hill, turn left, and I can't mistake the house. He give me the keys and an envelope with a telephone number on the back. Underneath is written "After 6 p.m. ask for Mr. Sims."

In the train that evening I think myself lucky, for to walk about London on a Sunday with nowhere to go—that take the heart out of you.

I find the place and the bedroom of the downstairs flat is nicely furnished—two looking glass, wardrobe, chest of drawers, sheets, everything. It smell of jasmine scent, but it smell strong of damp too.

I open the door opposite and there's a table, a couple chairs, a gas stove and a cupboard, but this room so big it look empty. When I pull the blind up I notice the

---

[1] *Notting Hill*   At this time, an unfashionable and relatively cheap district in London.

[2] *settling up*   Paying.

[3] *flat*   Apartment.

[4] *Victoria Station*   Major railway station in London.

paper peeling off and mushrooms growing on the walls—you never see such a thing.

The bathroom the same, all the taps rusty. I leave the two other rooms and make up the bed. Then I listen, but I can't hear one sound. Nobody come in, nobody go out of that house. I lie awake for a long time, then I decide not to stay and in the morning I start to get ready quickly before I change my mind. I want to wear my best dress, but it's a funny thing—when I take up that dress and remember how my landlady kick it I cry. I cry and I can't stop. When I stop I feel tired to my bones, tired like old woman. I don't want to move again—I have to force myself. But in the end I get out in the passage and there's a postcard for me. "Stay as long as you like. I'll be seeing you soon—Friday probably. Not to worry." It isn't signed, but I don't feel so sad and I think, "All right, I wait here till he come. Perhaps he know of a job for me."

Nobody else live in the house but a couple on the top floor—quiet people and they don't trouble me. I have no word to say against them.

First time I meet the lady she's opening the front door and she give me a very inquisitive look. But next time she smile a bit and I smile back—once she talk to me. She tell me the house very old, hundred and fifty year old, and she and her husband live there since long time. "Valuable property," she says, "it could have been saved, but nothing done of course." Then she tells me that as to the present owner—if he is the owner—well he have to deal with local authorities and she believe they make difficulties. "These people are determined to pull down all the lovely old houses—it's shameful."

So I agree that many things shameful. But what to do? What to do? I say it have an elegant shape, it make the other houses in the street look cheap trash, and she seem pleased. That's true too. The house sad and out of place, especially at night. But it have style. The second floor shut up, and as for my flat, I go in the two empty rooms once, but never again.

Underneath was the cellar, full of old boards and broken-up furniture—I see a big rat there one day. It was no place to be alone in I tell you, and I get the habit of buying a bottle of wine most evenings, for I don't like whisky and the rum here no good. It don't even *taste* like rum. You wonder what they do to it.

After I drink a glass or two I can sing and when I sing all the misery goes from my heart. Sometimes I make up songs but next morning I forget them, so other times I sing the old ones like *Tantalizin'* or *Don't Trouble Me Now.*

I think I go but I don't go. Instead I wait for the evening and the wine and that's all. Everywhere else I live—well, it doesn't matter to me, but this house is different—empty and no noise and full of shadows, so that sometimes you ask yourself what make all those shadows in an empty room.

I eat in the kitchen, then I clean up everything nice and have a bath for coolness. Afterwards I lean my elbows on the windowsill and look at the garden. Red and blue flowers mix up with the weeds and there are five-six apple trees. But the fruit drop and lie in the grass, so sour nobody want it. At the back, near the wall, is a bigger tree—this garden certainly take up a lot of room, perhaps that's why they want to pull the place down.

Not much rain all the summer, but not much sunshine either. More of a glare. The grass get brown and dry, the weeds grow tall, the leaves on the trees hang down. Only the red flowers—the poppies—stand up to that light, everything else look weary.

I don't trouble about money, but what with wine and shillings for the slot-meters,[1] it go quickly; so I don't waste much on food. In the evening I walk outside—not by the apple trees but near the street—it's not so lonely.

There's no wall here and I can see the woman next door looking at me over the hedge. At first I say good evening, but she turn away her head, so afterwards I don't speak. A man is often with her, he wear a straw hat with a black ribbon and goldrim spectacles. His suit hang on him like it's too big. He's the husband it seems and he stare at me worse than his wife—he stare as if I'm wild animal let loose. Once I laugh in his face because why these people have to be like that? I don't bother them. In the end I get that I don't even give them one single glance. I have plenty other things to worry about.

---

[1] *shillings* Coins used in the United Kingdom prior to 1971, each worth 1/20th of a pound; *slot-meters* Meters, here for hot water, operated by inserting a coin into a slot, often used to provide gas heating.

To show you how I felt. I don't remember exactly. But I believe it's the second Saturday after I come that when I'm at the window just before I go for my wine I feel somebody's hand on my shoulder and it's Mr Sims. He must walk very quiet because I don't know a thing till he touch me.

He says hullo, then he tells me I've got terrible thin, do I ever eat. I say of course I eat but he goes on that it doesn't suit me at all to be so thin and he'll buy some food in the village. (That's the way he talk. There's no village here. You don't get away from London so quick.)

It don't seem to me he look very well himself, but I just say bring a drink instead, as I am not hungry.

He come back with three bottles—vermouth, gin and red wine. Then he ask if the little devil who was here last smash all the glasses and I tell him she smash some, I find the pieces. But not all. "You fight with her, eh?"

He laugh, and he don't answer. He pour out the drinks then he says, "Now, you eat up those sandwiches."

Some men when they are there you don't worry so much. These sort of men you do all they tell you blindfold because they can take the trouble from your heart and make you think you're safe. It's nothing they say or do. It's a feeling they can give you. So I don't talk with him seriously—I don't want to spoil that evening. But I ask about the house and why it's so empty and he says:

"Has the old trout upstairs been gossiping?"

I tell him, "She suppose they make difficulties for you."

"It was a damn bad buy," he says and talks about selling the lease or something. I don't listen much.

We were standing by the window then and the sun low. No more glare. He puts his hand over my eyes. "Too big—much too big for your face," he says and kisses me like you kiss a baby. When he takes his hand away I see he's looking out at the garden and he says this—"It gets you. My God it does."

I know very well it's not me he means, so I ask him, "Why sell it then? If you like it, keep it."

"Sell what?" he says. "I'm not talking about this damned house."

I ask what he's talking about. "Money," he says. "Money. That's what I'm talking about. Ways of making it."

"I don't think so much of money. It don't like me and what do I care?" I was joking, but he turns around, his face quite pale and he tells me I'm a fool. He tells me I'll get push around all my life and die like a dog, only worse because they'd finish off a dog, but they'll let me live till I'm a caricature of myself. That's what he say, "Caricature of yourself." He say I'll curse the day I was born and everything and everybody in this bloody world before I'm done.

I tell him, "No I'll never feel like that," and he smiles, if you can call it a smile, and says he's glad I'm content with my lot. "I'm disappointed in you, Selina. I thought you had more spirit."

"If I contented that's all right," I answer him, "I don't see very many looking contented over here." We're standing staring at each other when the door bell rings. "That's a friend of mine," he says. "I'll let him in."

As to the friend, he's all dressed up in stripe pants and a black jacket and he's carrying a brief-case. Very ordinary looking but with a soft kind of voice.

"Maurice, this is Selina Davis," says Mr. Sims, and Maurice smiles very kind but it don't mean much, then he looks at his watch and says they ought to be getting along.

At the door Mr. Sims tells me he'll see me next week and I answer straight out, "I won't be here next week because I want a job and I won't get one in this place."

"Just what I'm going to talk about. Give it a week longer, Selina."

I say, "Perhaps I stay a few more days. Then I go. Perhaps I go before."

"Oh no you won't go," he says.

They walk to the gates quickly and drive off in a yellow car. Then I feel eyes on me and it's the woman and her husband in the next door garden watching. The man make some remark and she look at me so hateful, so hating I shut the front door quick.

I don't want more wine. I want to go to bed early because I must think. I must think about money. It's true I don't care for it. Even when somebody steal my savings—this happen soon after I get to the Notting Hill house—I forget it soon. About thirty pounds they steal. I keep it roll up in a pair of stockings, but I go to the drawer one day, and no money. In the end I have to tell the police. They ask me exact sum and I say I don't count it lately, about thirty pounds. "You don't know how much?" they say. "When did you count it last? Do you remember? Was it before you move or after?"

I get confuse, and I keep saying, "I don't remember," though I remember well I see it two days before. They don't believe me and when a policeman come to the house I hear the landlady tell him, "She certainly had no money when she came here. She wasn't able to pay a month's rent in advance for her room though it's a rule in this house." "These people terrible liars," she say and I think "it's you a terrible liar, because when I come you tell me weekly or monthly as you like." It's from that time she don't speak to me and perhaps it's she take it. All I know is I never see one penny of my savings again, all I know is they pretend I never have any, but as it's gone, no use to cry about it. Then my mind goes to my father, for my father is a white man and I think a lot about him. If I could see him only once, for I too small to remember when he was there. My mother is fair coloured woman, fairer than I am they say, and she don't stay long with me either. She have a chance to go to Venezuela when I three-four year old and she never come back. She send money instead. It's my grandmother take care of me. She's quite dark and what we call "country-cookie" but she's the best I know.

She save up all the money my mother send, she don't keep one penny for herself—that's how I get to England. I was a bit late in going to school regular, getting on for twelve years, but I can sew very beautiful, excellent—so I think I get a good job—in London perhaps.

However here they tell me all this fine handsewing take too long. Waste of time—too slow. They want somebody to work quick and to hell with the small stitches. Altogether it don't look so good for me, I must say, and I wish I could see my father. I have his name—Davis. But my grandmother tell me, "Every word that come out of that man's mouth a damn lie. He is certainly first class liar, though no class otherwise." So perhaps I have not even his real name.

Last thing I see before I put the light out is the postcard on the dressing table. "Not to worry."

Not to worry! Next day is Sunday, and it's on the Monday the people next door complain about me to the police. That evening the woman is by the hedge, and

when I pass her she says in very sweet quiet voice, "*Must you stay? Can't you go?*" I don't answer. I walk out in the street to get rid of her. But she run inside her house to the window, she can still see me. Then I start to sing, so she can understand I'm not afraid of her. The husband call out: "If you don't stop that noise I'll send for the police." I answer them quite short. I say, "You go to hell and take your wife with you." And I sing louder.

The police come pretty quick—two of them. Maybe they just round the corner. All I can say about police, and how they behave is I think it all depend who they dealing with. Of my own free will I don't want to mix up with police. No.

One man says, you can't cause this disturbance here. But the other asks a lot of questions. What is my name? Am I tenant of a flat in No. 17? How long have I lived there? Last address and so on. I get vexed the way he speak and I tell him, "I come here because somebody steal my savings. Why you don't look for my money instead of bawling at me? I work hard for my money. All-you don't do one single thing to find it."

"What's she talking about?" the first one says, and the other one tells me, "You can't make that noise here. Get along home. You've been drinking."

I see that woman looking at me and smiling, and other people at their windows, and I'm so angry I bawl at them too. I say, "I have absolute and perfect right to be in the street same as anybody else, and I have absolute and perfect right to ask the police why they don't even look for my money when it disappear. It's because a dam' English thief take it you don't look," I say. The end of all this is that I have to go before a magistrate, and he fine me five pounds for drunk and disorderly, and he give me two weeks to pay.

When I get back from the court I walk up and down the kitchen, up and down, waiting for six o'clock because I have no five pounds left, and I don't know what to do. I telephone at six and a woman answers me very short and sharp, then Mr. Sims comes along and he don't sound too pleased either when I tell him what happen. "Oh Lord!" he says, and I say I'm sorry. "Well don't panic," he says, "I'll pay the fine. But look, I don't think …" Then he breaks off and talk to some other person in the room. He goes on, "Perhaps better not stay at No. 17. I think I can arrange something else. I'll call for you Wednesday—Saturday latest. Now behave till then." And he hang up before I can answer that I don't want to wait till Wednesday, much less Saturday. I want to get out of that house double quick and with no delay. First I think I ring back, then I think better not as he sound so vex.

I get ready, but Wednesday he don't come, and Saturday he don't come. All the week I stay in the flat. Only once I go out and arrange for bread, milk and eggs to be left at the door, and seems to me I meet up with a lot of policemen. They don't look at me, but they see me all right. I don't want to drink—I'm all the time listening, listening and thinking, how can I leave before I know if my fine is paid? I tell myself the police let me know, that's certain. But I don't trust them. What they care? The answer is Nothing. Nobody care. One afternoon I knock at the old lady's flat upstairs, because I get the idea she give me good advice. I can hear her moving about and talking, but she don't answer and I never try again.

Nearly two weeks pass like that, then I telephone. It's the woman speaking and she say, "Mr. Sims is not in London at present." I ask, "When will he be back—it's urgent," and she hang up. I'm not surprised. Not at all. I knew that would happen. All the same I feel heavy like lead. Near the phone box is a chemist's shop, so I ask him for something to make me sleep, the day is bad enough, but to lie awake all night—Ah no! He gives me a little bottle marked "*One or two tablets only*" and I take three when I go to bed because more and more I think that sleeping is better than no matter what else. However, I lie there, eyes wide open as usual, so I take three more. Next thing I know the room is full of sunlight, so it must be late afternoon, but the lamp is still on. My head turn around and I can't think well at all. At first I ask myself how I get to the place. Then it comes to me, but in pictures—like the landlady kicking my dress, and when I take my ticket at Victoria Station, and Mr. Sims telling me to eat the sandwiches, but I can't remember everything clear, and I feel very giddy and sick. I take in the milk and eggs at the door, go in the kitchen, and try to eat but the food hard to swallow.

It's when I'm putting the things away that I see the bottles—pushed back on the lowest shelf in the cupboard.

There's a lot of drink left, and I'm glad I tell you. Because I can't bear the way I feel. Not any more. I mix a gin and vermouth and I drink it quick, then I mix another and drink it slow by the window. The garden looks different, like I never see it before. I know quite well what I must do, but it's late now—tomorrow. I have one more drink, of wine this time, and then a song come in my head, I sing it and I dance it, and more I sing, more I am sure this is the best tune that has ever come to me in all my life.

The sunset light from the window is gold colour. My shoes sound loud on the boards. So I take them off, my stockings too and go on dancing but the room feel shut in, I can't breathe, and I go outside still singing. Maybe I dance a bit too. I forget all about that woman till I hear her saying, "Henry, look at this." I turn around and I see her at the window. "Oh yes, I wanted to speak with you," I say, "Why bring the police and get me in bad trouble? Tell me that."

"And you tell *me* what you're doing here at all," she says. "This is a respectable neighbourhood."

Then the man come along. "Now young woman, take yourself off. You ought to be ashamed of this behaviour."

"It's disgraceful," he says, talking to his wife, but loud so I can hear, and she speaks loud too—for once. "At least the other tarts[1] that crook installed here were *white* girls," she says.

"You a dam' fouti[2] liar," I say. "Plenty of those girls in your country already. Numberless as the sands on the shore. You don't need me for that."

"You're not a howling success at it certainly." Her voice sweet sugar again. "And you won't be seeing much more of your friend Mr. Sims. He's in trouble too. Try somewhere else. Find somebody else. If you can, of course." When she say that my arm moves of itself. I pick up a stone and bam! through the window. Not the one they are standing at but the next, which is of coloured glass, green and purple and yellow.

I never see a woman look so surprise. Her mouth fall open she so full of surprise. I start to laugh, louder and louder—I laugh like my grandmother, with my hands on my hips and my head back. (When she laugh like that you can hear her to the end of our street.) At last I say, "Well, I'm sorry. An accident. I get it fixed tomorrow early." "That glass is irreplaceable," the man

---

[1]   *tarts*   Women considered sexually promiscuous.

[2]   *fouti*   Crazy.

says. "Irreplaceable." "Good thing," I say, "those colours look like they sea-sick to me. I buy you a better window-glass."

He shake his fist at me. "You won't be let off with a fine this time," he says. Then they draw the curtains. I call out at them. "You run away. Always you run away. Ever since I come here you hunt me down because I don't answer back. It's you shameless." I try to sing "Don't trouble me now."

> Don't trouble me now
> You without honour.
> Don't walk in my footstep
> You without shame.

But my voice don't sound right, so I get back indoors and drink one more glass of wine—still wanting to laugh, and still thinking of my grandmother for that is one of her songs.

It's about a man whose doudou[1] give him the go-by when she find somebody rich and he sail away to Panama. Plenty people die there of fever when they make that Panama canal so long ago. But he don't die. He come back with dollars and the girl meet him on the jetty, all dressed up and smiling. Then he sing to her, "You without honour, you without shame." It sound good in Martinique patois[2] too: "Sans honte."

Afterwards I ask myself, "Why I do that? It's not like me. But if they treat you wrong over and over again the hour strike when you burst out that's what."

Too besides, Mr. Sims can't tell me now I have no spirit. I don't care, I sleep quickly and I'm glad I break the woman's ugly window. But as to my own song it go *right* away and it never come back. A pity.

Next morning the doorbell ringing wake me up. The people upstairs don't come down, and the bell keeps on like fury self. So I go to look, and there is a policeman and a policewoman outside. As soon as I open the door the woman put her foot in it. She wear sandals and thick stockings and I never see a foot so big or so bad. It look like it want to mash up the whole world. Then she come in after the foot, and her face not so pretty either. The policeman tell me my fine is not

paid and people make serious complaints about me, so they're taking me back to the magistrate. He show me a paper and I look at it, but I don't read it. The woman push me in the bedroom, and tell me to get dress quickly, but I just stare at her, because I think perhaps I wake up soon. Then I ask her what I must wear. She say she suppose I had some clothes on yesterday. Or not? "What's it matter, wear anything," she says. But I find clean underclothes and stockings and my shoes with high heels and I comb my hair. I start to file my nails, because I think they too long for magistrate's court but she get angry. "Are you coming quietly or aren't you?" she says. So I go with them and we get in a car outside.

I wait for a long time in a room full of policemen. They come in, they go out, they telephone, they talk in low voices. Then it's my turn, and first thing I notice in the court room is a man with frowning black eyebrows. He sit below the magistrate, he dressed in black and he so handsome I can't take my eyes off him. When he see that he frown worse than before.

First comes a policeman to testify I cause disturbance, and then comes the old gentleman from next door. He repeat that bit about nothing but the truth so help me God. Then he says I make dreadful noise at night and use abominable language, and dance in obscene fashion. He says when they try to shut the curtains because his wife so terrify of me, I throw stones and break a valuable stain-glass window. He say his wife get serious injury if she'd been hit, and as it is she in terrible nervous condition and the doctor is with her. I think, "Believe me, if I aim at your wife I hit your wife—that's certain." "There was no provocation," he says. "None at all." Then another lady from across the street says this is true. She heard no provocation whatsoever, and she swear that they shut the curtains but I go on insulting them and using filthy language and she saw all this and heard it.

The magistrate is a little gentleman with a quiet voice, but I'm very suspicious of these quiet voices now. He ask me why I don't pay my fine, and I say because I haven't the money. I get the idea they want to find out all about Mr. Sims—they listen so very attentive. But they'll find out nothing from me. He ask how long I have the flat and I say I don't remember. I know they want to trip me up like they trip me up about my

---

[1] *doudou* Sweetheart.

[2] *Martinique* West Indian island colonized by the French; *patois* Regional dialect, in this case the Creole dialect of Martinique.

savings so I won't answer. At last he ask if I have anything to say as I can't be allowed to go on being a nuisance. I think, "I'm nuisance to you because I have no money that's all." I want to speak up and tell him how they steal all my savings, so when my landlord asks for month's rent I haven't got it to give. I want to tell him the woman next door provoke me since long time and call me bad names but she have a soft sugar voice and nobody hear—that's why I broke her window, but I'm ready to buy another after all. I want to say all I do is sing in that old garden, and I want to say this in decent quiet voice. But I hear myself talking loud and I see my hands wave in the air. Too besides it's no use, they won't believe me, so I don't finish. I stop, and I feel the tears on my face. "Prove it." That's all they will say. They whisper, they whisper. They nod, they nod.

Next thing I'm in a car again with a different policewoman, dressed very smart. Not in uniform. I ask her where she's taking me and she says "Holloway"[1] just that "Holloway."

I catch hold of her hand because I'm afraid. But she takes it away. Cold and smooth her hand slide away and her face is china face—smooth like a doll and I think, "This is the last time I ask anything from anybody. So help me God."

The car come up to a black castle and little mean streets are all round it. A lorry[2] was blocking up the castle gates. When it get by we pass through and I am in jail. First I stand in a line with others who are waiting to give up handbags and all belongings to a woman behind bars like in a post office. The girl in front bring out a nice compact, look like gold to me, lipstick to match and a wallet full of notes. The woman keep the money, but she give back the powder and lipstick and she half-smile. I have two pounds seven shillings and sixpence in pennies. She take my purse, then she throw me my compact (which is cheap) my comb and my handkerchief like everything in my bag is dirty. So I think, "Here too, here too." But I tell myself, "Girl, what you expect, eh? They all like that. All."

Some of what happen afterwards I forget, or perhaps better not remember. Seems to me they start by trying to frighten you. But they don't succeed with me for I don't care for nothing now, it's as if my heart hard like a rock and I can't feel.

Then I'm standing at the top of a staircase with a lot of women and girls. As we are going down I notice the railing very low on one side, very easy to jump, and a long way below there's the grey stone passage like it's waiting for you.

As I'm thinking this a uniform woman step up alongside quick and grab my arm. She say, "Oh no you don't."

I was just noticing the railing very low that's all—but what's the use of saying so.

Another long line waits for the doctor. It move forward slowly and my legs terrible tired. The girl in front is very young and she cry and cry. "I'm scared," she keeps saying. She's lucky in a way—as for me I never will cry again. It all dry up and hard in me now. That, and a lot besides. In the end I tell her to stop, because she doing just what these people want her to do.

She stop crying and start a long story, but while she is speaking her voice get very far away, and I find I can't see her face clear at all.

Then I'm in a chair, and one of those uniform women is pushing my head down between my knees, but let her push—everything go away from me just the same.

They put me in the hospital because the doctor say I'm sick. I have cell by myself and it's all right except I don't sleep. The things they say you mind I don't mind.

When they clang the door on me I think, "You shut me in, but you shut all those other dam' devils *out*. They can't reach me now."

At first it bothers me when they keep on looking at me all through the night. They open a little window in the doorway to do this. But I get used to it and get used to the night chemise[3] they give me. It very thick, and to my mind it not very clean either—but what's that matter to me? Only the food I can't swallow—especially the porridge. The woman ask me sarcastic, "Hunger striking?" But afterwards I can leave most of it, and she don't say nothing.

One day a nice girl comes around with books and she give me two, but I don't want to read so much. Beside one is about a murder, and the other is about a ghost and I don't think it's at all like those books tell you.

---

[1] *Holloway*   Notorious women's prison in London.

[2] *lorry*   Truck.

[3] *night chemise*   Nightgown.

There is nothing I want now. It's no use. If they leave me in peace and quiet that's all I ask. The window is barred but not small, so I can see a little thin tree through the bars, and I like watching it.

After a week they tell me I'm better and I can go out with the others for exercise. We walk round and round one of the yards in that castle—it is fine weather and the sky is a kind of pale blue, but the yard is a terrible sad place. The sunlight fall down and die there. I get tired walking in high heels and I'm glad when that's over.

We can talk, and one day an old woman come up and ask me for dog-ends. I don't understand, and she start muttering at me like she very vexed. Another woman tell me she mean cigarette ends, so I say I don't smoke. But the old woman still look angry, and when we're going in she give me one push and I nearly fall down. I'm glad to get away from these people, and hear the door clang and take my shoes off.

Sometimes I think, "I'm here because I wanted to sing" and I have to laugh. But there's a small looking glass in my cell and I see myself and I'm like somebody else. Like some strange new person. Mr. Sims tell me I too thin, but what he say now to this person in the looking glass? So I don't laugh again.

Usually I don't think at all. Everything and everybody seem small and far away, that is the only trouble.

Twice the doctor come to see me. He don't say much and I don't say anything, because a uniform woman is always there. She look like she thinking, "Now the lies start." So I prefer not to speak. Then I'm sure they can't trip me up. Perhaps I there still, or in a worse place. But one day this happen.

We were walking round and round in the yard and I hear a woman singing—the voice come from high up, from one of the small barred windows. At first I don't believe it. Why should anybody sing here? Nobody want to sing in jail, nobody want to do anything. There's no reason, and you have no hope. I think I must be asleep, dreaming, but I'm awake all right and I see all the others are listening too. A nurse is with us that afternoon, not a policewoman. She stop and look up at the window.

It's a smoky kind of voice, and a bit rough sometimes, as if those old dark walls theyselves are complaining, because they see too much misery—too much. But it don't fall down and die in the courtyard;

seems to me it could jump the gates of the jail easy and travel far, and nobody could stop it. I don't hear the words—only the music. She sing one verse and she begin another, then she break off sudden. Everybody starts walking again, and nobody say one word. But as we go in I ask the woman in front who was singing. "That's the Holloway song," she says. "Don't you know it yet? She was singing from the punishment cells, and she tell the girls cheerio and never say die." Then I have to go one way to the hospital block and she goes another so we don't speak again.

When I'm back in my cell I can't just wait for bed. I walk up and down and I think. "One day I hear that song on trumpets and these walls will fall and rest."[1] I want to get out so bad I could hammer on the door, for I know now that anything can happen, and I don't want to stay lock up here and miss it.

Then I'm hungry. I eat everything they bring and in the morning I'm still so hungry I eat the porridge. Next time the doctor come he tells me I seem much better. Then I say a little of what really happen in that house. Not much. Very careful.

He look at me hard and kind of surprised. At the door he shake his finger and says, "Now don't let me see you here again."

That evening the woman tells me I'm going, but she's so upset about it I don't ask questions. Very early, before it's light she bangs the door open and shouts at me to hurry up. As we're going along the passages I see the girl who gave me the books. She's in a row with others doing exercises. Up Down, Up Down, Up. We pass quite close and I notice she's looking very pale and tired. It's crazy, it's all crazy. This up down business and everything else too. When they give me my money I remember I leave my compact in the cell, so I ask if I can go back for it. You should see that policewoman's face as she shoo me on.

There's no car, there's a van and you can't see through the windows. The third time it stop I get out with one other, a young girl, and it's the same magistrates' court as before.

The two of us wait in a small room, nobody else there, and after a while the girl say, "What the hell are they doing? I don't want to spend all day here." She go

---

[1] *One day ... rest* Cf. Joshua 6, in which the sound of trumpets brings down the walls of Jericho.

to the bell and she keep her finger press on it. When I look at her she say, "Well, what are they *for?*" That girl's face is hard like a board—she could change faces with many and you wouldn't know the difference. But she get results certainly. A policeman come in, all smiling, and we go in the court. The same magistrate, the same frowning man sits below, and when I hear my fine is paid I want to ask who paid it, but he yells at me. "Silence."

I think I will never understand the half of what happen, but they tell me I can go, and I understand that. The magistrate ask if I'm leaving the neighbourhood and I say yes, then I'm out in the streets again, and it's the same fine weather, same feeling I'm dreaming.

When I get to the house I see two men talking in the garden. The front door and the door of the flat are both open. I go in, and the bedroom is empty, nothing but the glare streaming inside because they take the Venetian blinds away. As I'm wondering where my suitcase is, and the clothes I leave in the wardrobe, there's a knock and it's the old lady from upstairs carrying my case packed, and my coat is over her arm. She says she sees me come in. "I kept your things for you." I start to thank her but she turn her back and walk away. They like that here, and better not expect too much. Too besides, I bet they tell her I'm terrible person.

I go in the kitchen, but when I see they are cutting down the big tree at the back I don't stay to watch.

At the station I'm waiting for the train and a woman asks if I feel well. "You look so tired," she says. "Have you come a long way?" I want to answer, "I come so far I lose myself on that journey." But I tell her, "Yes, I am quite well. But I can't stand the heat." She says she can't stand it either, and we talk about the weather till the train come in.

I'm not frightened of them any more—after all what else can they do ? I know what to say and everything go like a clock works.

I get a room near Victoria where the landlady accept one pound in advance, and next day I find a job in the kitchen of a private hotel close by. But I don't stay there long. I hear of another job going in a big store—altering ladies' dresses and I get that. I lie and tell them I work in very expensive New York shop. I speak bold and smooth faced, and they never check up on me. I make a friend there—Clarice—very light coloured, very smart, she have a lot to do with the customers and she laugh at some of them behind their backs. But I say it's not their fault if the dress don't fit. Special dress for one person only—that's very expensive in London. So it's take in, or let out all the time. Clarice have two rooms not far from the store. She furnish them herself gradual and she gives parties sometimes Saturday nights. It's there I start whistling the Holloway Song. A man comes up to me and says, "Let's hear that again." So I whistle it again (I never sing now) and he tells me "Not bad." Clarice have an old piano somebody give her to store and he plays the tune, jazzing it up. I say, "No, not like that," but everybody else say the way he do it is first class. Well I think no more of this till I get a letter from him telling me he has sold the song and as I was quite a help he encloses five pounds with thanks.

I read the letter and I could cry. For after all, that song was all I had. I don't belong nowhere really, and I haven't money to buy my way to belonging. I don't want to either.

But when that girl sing, she sing to me, and she sing for me. I was there because I was *meant* to be there. It was *meant* I should hear it—this I *know.*

Now I've let them play it wrong, and it will go from me like all the other songs—like everything. Nothing left for me at all.

But then I tell myself all this is foolishness. Even if they played it on trumpets, even if they played it just right, like I wanted—no walls would fall so soon. "So let them call it jazz," I think, and let them play it wrong. That won't make no difference to the song I heard.

I buy myself a dusty pink dress with the money.

—1962

GEORGE ORWELL
1903 – 1950

George Orwell struggled throughout his life to live his convictions as well as to write from them. His most famous novels, *Animal Farm* (1945) and *1984* (1949), have been translated into more than sixty languages and have sold over forty million copies. While his writerly craftsmanship and strongly articulated views on the importance of linguistic integrity (most directly expressed in his 1946 essay "Politics and the English Language") are admired and respected, he is recognized even more widely for his moral integrity, independence of mind, and scope of vision.

Born Eric Arthur Blair in Motihari, India on 25 June 1903, Orwell came from a family with strong colonial ties on both sides. His father, Richard Blair, worked as an opium agent for the British Imperial government; his mother, Ida Limouzin, grew up in Burma surrounded by a large staff of native servants, taking work as a governess in India when her father lost his wealth. Although the baby Eric returned to England with his mother and older sister in 1904, his sense of identity was moulded by the colonial experience. He was also strongly marked by his experiences as an economically poor but culturally middle-class student in English boarding schools, first at St. Cyprian's School (an experience later immortalized in his 1953 *Such, Such Were the Joys*) and then as a scholarship student at Eton.

Despite his evident abilities as a scholar, Eric did not apply himself while at Eton and was ultimately discouraged from pursuing university-level studies; in fact, he was himself more interested in returning to his colonial roots and pursuing a more adventurous career. After sitting eight days of qualifying examinations, he was selected to travel to Burma to join the Imperial Police. He served there from 1922 to 1927 in an array of posts around the country before deciding that the work was not suited to his character or his ideals; it had also taken its toll physically. His experiences left him feeling profoundly ambivalent about the colonial presence of the British, and about the nature of imperialist authority in general. He resigned his assignment upon his return to England, filled with a profound sense of guilt.

Although he was at this point determined to become a writer, he had not written much of anything while in Burma, nor published any adult work. Nevertheless, he decided that living in poverty, first in the East End of London, then in Paris, taking various low-paying jobs here and there, would help provide him with suitable material and would also condition his mind for the task of writing. He spent the years 1928–29 in Paris, taking menial jobs in restaurants and hotels and contracting pneumonia in the process, and then returned to England where he spent some time living as a tramp. His first book, *Down and Out in Paris and London*, appeared in 1933 under the pseudonym of George Orwell, chosen to protect his family and to distance himself from them and from his own earlier life.

Orwell spent nine months in 1934 living with his parents while he finished his second book, the novel *A Clergyman's Daughter* (1935). He then moved out, took work in a bookshop, and continued to write; his *Burmese Days*, which drew on his experiences in Burma and expressed his sense of indignation about imperialism, appeared in 1934. *A Clergyman's Daughter* was published the following year; in it Orwell attempted to use his tramping experiences as material for fiction, but was himself dissatisfied with the results. In later years he did his best to keep this and his next autobiographical novel, *Keep the Aspidistra Flying* (1936), out of view, preventing their reissues; the latter did not appear in the United States until 1956.

In 1936, emboldened by an advance for his next, nonfictional project, Orwell married Eileen O'Shaughnessy. Eileen abandoned her graduate studies in Educational Psychology at University College in London to move with Orwell into a tiny, isolated, and primitive cottage in Wallington, Hertfordshire, where they kept a garden, goats, and chickens, and managed a small shop, and where Orwell continued to write. His study of the dismal lives of the poor and unemployed in the industrial towns of the north of England took him tramping once again; *The Road to Wigan Pier* (1937) gave voice to his socialist views and established his reputation as a political writer.

Orwell's political idealism was severely tested when he fought for the Republicans in the Spanish Civil War. He witnessed first-hand the intense in-fighting amongst the various factions of the Left, and he became an intense critic of all political orthodoxies as a result. His next book, *Homage to Catalonia*, combined personal recollection with biting political analysis; it was as critical of the Soviet-influenced Communist faction in Spain as it was of Franco's Fascists. It received a mixed reception when it appeared in 1938. Today, however, it is recognized as an eloquent illustration of Orwell's passionate intellectual and political independence of mind.

World War II broke out three months after the publication of Orwell's next novel, *Coming Up for Air* (1939); unable to join the army due to his poor health, Orwell worked for two years for the BBC's Eastern Service, in addition to writing various essays and reviews. In 1944, Orwell and his wife adopted a son, Richard Horatio Blair, to whom they were both deeply devoted. But in 1945, Orwell's life changed: Eileen died (and her death devastated Orwell), and *Animal Farm* was published and brought overnight literary and financial success. This short novel is a fable that satirizes the corruption of socialist ideals that had by then occurred in the Soviet Union under Joseph Stalin; everyone was supposedly equal but "some animals are more equal than others," in Orwell's famous phrase.

Orwell spent most of the last years of his life in an isolated cottage on the island of Jura, off the coast of Scotland, with Richard, a nanny, and his sister Avril for company. As he gradually succumbed to tuberculosis, he wrote *1984*, widely considered his most ambitious and important work. This dark novel imagines a totalitarian future in which absolute conformity is rigidly enforced; "Big Brother is watching you" is the catchword of a society in which privacy and individual freedom have all but disappeared. In 1949 that book was published, and Orwell entered a sanatorium in England. Three months before his death on 21 January 1950, he married Sonia Brownell.

⌘ ⌘ ⌘

from *Homage to Catalonia*

It must have been three days after the Barcelona fighting[1] ended that we returned to the front. After

the fighting—more particularly after the slanging-match in the newspapers—it was difficult to think about this war in quite the same naively idealistic manner as before. I suppose there is no one who spent more than a few weeks in Spain without being in some degree

---

[1] *the Barcelona fighting* The Spanish Civil War officially broke out in 1936, after a period of turmoil following the collapse of the monarchy in 1931. A leftist Popular Front government, elected in February of 1936, promised substantial land reforms to a nation made up of large agricultural estates on which peasants worked for little money. A conservative military uprising, led by Francisco Franco, attempted to thwart the Popular Front, but the Spanish people united and initially defeated these forces. Franco then

appealed to other fascist leaders for support. Troops from Italy, Germany, and Portugal arrived. Meanwhile, as the war continued, volunteers from all over Europe and North America formed International Brigades and came to Spain to fight against fascism. Orwell, a committed socialist, was among them. The "Barcelona fighting" referred to here occurred from May 3 to 7, 1937—five days referred to as the "May Days."

disillusioned. My mind went back to the newspaper correspondent whom I had met my first day in Barcelona, and who said to me: "This war is a racket the same as any other." The remark had shocked me deeply, and at that time (December) I do not believe it was true; it was not true even now, in May; but it was becoming truer. The fact is that every war suffers a kind of progressive degradation with every month that it continues, because such things as individual liberty and a truthful press are simply not compatible with military efficiency.

One could begin now to make some kind of guess at what was likely to happen. It was easy to see that the Caballero Government[1] would fall and be replaced by a more Right-wing Government with a stronger Communist influence (this happened a week or two later), which would set itself to break the power of the trade unions once and for all. And afterwards, when Franco was beaten—and putting aside the huge problems raised by the reorganization of Spain—the prospect was not rosy. As for the newspaper talk about this being a "war for democracy," it was plain eyewash. No one in his senses supposed that there was any hope of democracy, even as we understand it in England or France, in a country so divided and exhausted as Spain would be when the war was over. It would have to be a dictatorship, and it was clear that the chance of a working-class dictatorship had passed. That meant that the general movement would be in the direction of some kind of Fascism. Fascism called, no doubt, by some politer name, and—because this was Spain—more human and less efficient than the German or Italian varieties. The only alternatives were an infinitely worse dictatorship by Franco, or (always a possibility) that the war would end with Spain divided up, either by actual frontiers or into economic zones.

Whichever way you took it it was a depressing outlook. But it did not follow that the Government was not worth fighting for as against the more naked and developed Fascism of Franco and Hitler. Whatever faults the post-war Government might have, Franco's regime would certainly be worse. To the workers—the town proletariat—it might in the end make very little

difference who won, but Spain is primarily an agricultural country and the peasants would almost certainly benefit by a Government victory. Some at least of the seized lands would remain in their possession, in which case there would also be a distribution of land in the territory that had been Franco's, and the virtual serfdom that had existed in some parts of Spain was not likely to be restored. The Government in control at the end of the war would at any rate be anti-clerical and anti-feudal. It would keep the Church in check, at least for the time being, and would modernize the country—build roads, for instance, and promote education and public health; a certain amount had been done in this direction even during the war. Franco, on the other hand, in so far as he was not merely the puppet of Italy and Germany, was tied to the big feudal landlords and stood for a stuffy clerico-military reaction.

The Popular Front might be a swindle, but Franco was an anachronism. Only millionaires or romantics could want him to win....

There was not much happening at the front. The battle round the Jaca road had died away and did not begin again till mid-June. In our position the chief trouble was the snipers. The Fascist trenches were more than a hundred and fifty yards away, but they were on higher ground and were on two sides of us, our line forming a right-angle salient. The corner of the salient was a dangerous spot; there had always been a toll of sniper casualties there. From time to time the Fascists let fly at us with a rifle-grenade or some similar weapon. It made a ghastly crash—unnerving, because you could not hear it coming in time to dodge—but was not really dangerous; the hole it blew in the ground was no bigger than a wash-tub. The nights were pleasantly warm, the days blazing hot, the mosquitoes were becoming a nuisance, and in spite of the clean clothes we had brought from Barcelona we were almost immediately lousy. Out in the deserted orchards in no man's land the cherries were whitening on the trees. For two days there were torrential rains, the dugouts flooded and the parapet sank a foot; after that there were more days of digging out the sticky clay with the wretched Spanish spades which have no handles and bend like tin spoons.

They had promised us a trench-mortar for the company; I was looking forward to it greatly. At nights

[1] *Caballero Government*   The Republican government was led by Largo Caballero from 4 September 1936 to 17 May 1937, when a new government was formed under Dr. Juan Negrin, a Socialist with Communist sympathies.

we patrolled as usual—more dangerous than it used to be, because the Fascist trenches were better manned and they had grown more alert; they had scattered tin cans just outside their wire and used to open up with the machine-guns when they heard a clank. In the daytime we sniped from no man's land. By crawling a hundred yards you could get to a ditch, hidden by tall grasses, which commanded a gap in the Fascist parapet. We had set up a rifle-rest in the ditch. If you waited long enough you generally saw a khaki-clad figure slip hurriedly across the gap. I had several shots. I don't know whether I hit anyone—it is most unlikely; I am a very poor shot with a rifle. But it was rather fun, the Fascists did not know where the shots were coming from, and I made sure I would get one of them sooner or later. However, the dog it was that died[1]—a Fascist sniper got me instead. I had been about ten days at the front when it happened. The whole experience of being hit by a bullet is very interesting and I think it is worth describing in detail.

It was at the corner of the parapet, at five o'clock in the morning. This was always a dangerous time, because we had the dawn at our backs, and if you stuck your head above the parapet it was clearly outlined against the sky. I was talking to the sentries preparatory to changing the guard. Suddenly, in the very middle of saying something, I felt—it is very hard to describe what I felt, though I remember it with the utmost vividness.

Roughly speaking it was the sensation of being at the centre of an explosion. There seemed to be a loud bang and a blinding flash of light all round me, and I felt a tremendous shock—no pain, only a violent shock, such as you get from an electric terminal; with it a sense of utter weakness, a feeling of being stricken and shrivelled up to nothing. The sand-bags in front of me receded into immense distance. I fancy you would feel much the same if you were struck by lightning. I knew immediately that I was hit, but because of the seeming bang and flash I thought it was a rifle nearby that had gone off accidentally and shot me. All this happened in a space of time much less than a second. The next moment my knees crumpled up and I was falling, my head hitting

the ground with a violent bang which, to my relief, did not hurt. I had a numb, dazed feeling, a consciousness of being very badly hurt, but no pain in the ordinary sense.

The American sentry I had been talking to had started forward. "Gosh! Are you hit?" People gathered round. There was the usual fuss—"Lift him up! Where's he hit? Get his shirt open!" etc., etc. The American called for a knife to cut my shirt open. I knew that there was one in my pocket and tried to get it out, but discovered that my right arm was paralysed. Not being in pain, I felt a vague satisfaction. This ought to please my wife, I thought; she had always wanted me to be wounded, which would save me from being killed when the great battle came. It was only now that it occurred to me to wonder where I was hit, and how badly; I could feel nothing, but I was conscious that the bullet had struck me somewhere in the front of the body. When I tried to speak I found that I had no voice, only a faint squeak, but at the second attempt I managed to ask where I was hit. In the throat, they said. Harry Webb, our stretcher-bearer, had brought a bandage and one of the little bottles of alcohol they gave us for field-dressings. As they lifted me up a lot of blood poured out of my mouth, and I heard a Spaniard behind me say that the bullet had gone clean through my neck. I felt the alcohol, which at ordinary times would sting like the devil, splash on to the wound as a pleasant coolness.

They laid me down again while somebody fetched a stretcher. As soon as I knew that the bullet had gone clean through my neck I took it for granted that I was done for. I had never heard of a man or an animal getting a bullet through the middle of the neck and surviving it. The blood was dribbling out of the corner of my mouth. "The artery's gone," I thought. I wondered how long you last when your carotid artery is cut; not many minutes, presumably. Everything was very blurry. There must have been about two minutes during which I assumed that I was killed. And that too was interesting—I mean it is interesting to know what your thoughts would be at such a time. My first thought, conventionally enough, was for my wife. My second was a violent resentment at having to leave this world which, when all is said and done, suits me so well. I had time to feel this very vividly. The stupid mischance infuriated me. The meaninglessness of it! To be bumped off, not

---

[1] *the dog . . . died*   Reference to Oliver Goldsmith's poem "An Elegy on the Death of a Mad Dog" (1766), in which a mad dog bites a man, who is expected to die from the wound. However, "the man recovered of the bite, / the dog it was that died" (21–22).

even in battle, but in this stale corner of the trenches, thanks to a moment's carelessness! I thought, too, of the man who had shot me—wondered what he was like, whether he was a Spaniard or a foreigner, whether he knew he had got me, and so forth. I could not feel any resentment against him. I reflected that as he was a Fascist I would have killed him if I could, but that if he had been taken prisoner and brought before me at this moment I would merely have congratulated him on his good shooting. It may be, though, that if you were really dying your thoughts would be quite different.

They had just got me on to the stretcher when my paralysed right arm came to life and began hurting damnably. At the time I imagined that I must have broken it in falling; but the pain reassured me, for I knew that your sensations do not become more acute when you are dying. I began to feel more normal and to be sorry for the four poor devils who were sweating and slithering with the stretcher on their shoulders. It was a mile and a half to the ambulance, and vile going, over lumpy, slippery tracks. I knew what a sweat it was, having helped to carry a wounded man down a day or two earlier. The leaves of the silver poplars which, in places, fringed our trenches brushed against my face; I thought what a good thing it was to be alive in a world where silver poplars grow. But all the while the pain in my arm was diabolical, making me swear and then try not to swear, because every time I breathed too hard the blood bubbled out of my mouth.

The doctor re-bandaged the wound, gave me a shot of morphia, and sent me off to Sietamo.[1] The hospitals at Sietamo were hurriedly constructed wooden huts where the wounded were, as a rule, only kept for a few hours before being sent on to Barbastro or Lerida.[2] I was dopey from morphia but still in great pain, practically unable to move and swallowing blood constantly. It was typical of Spanish hospital methods that while I was in this state the untrained nurse tried to force the regulation hospital meal—a huge meal of soup, eggs, greasy stew and so forth—down my throat and seemed surprised when I would not take it. I asked for a cigarette, but this was one of the periods of tobacco famine and there was not a cigarette in the place. Presently two comrades who had got permission to leave the line for a few hours appeared at my bedside.

"Hullo! You're alive, are you? Good. We want your watch and your revolver and your electric torch. And your knife, if you've got one."

They made off with all my portable possessions. This always happened when a man was wounded—everything he possessed was promptly divided up; quite rightly, for watches, revolvers, and so forth were precious at the front and if they went down the line in a wounded man's kit they were certain to be stolen somewhere on the way.

By the evening enough sick and wounded had trickled in to make up a few ambulance-loads, and they sent us on to Barbastro. What a journey! It used to be said that in this war you got well if you were wounded in the extremities, but always died of a wound in the abdomen. I now realized why. No one who was liable to bleed internally could have survived those miles of jolting over metal roads that had been smashed to pieces by heavy lorries and never repaired since the war began. Bang, bump, wallop! It took me back to my early childhood and a dreadful thing called the Wiggle-Woggle at the White City[3] Exhibition. They had forgotten to tie us into the stretchers. I had enough strength in my left arm to hang on, but one poor wretch was spilt on to the floor and suffered God knows what agonies. Another, a walking case who was sitting in the corner of the ambulance, vomited all over the place. The hospital in Barbastro was very crowded, the beds so close together that they were almost touching. Next morning they loaded a number of us on to the hospital train and sent us down to Lerida.

I was five or six days in Lerida. It was a big hospital, with sick, wounded, and ordinary civilian patients more or less jumbled up together. Some of the men in my ward had frightful wounds. In the next bed to me there was a youth with black hair who was suffering from some disease or other and was being given medicine that made his urine as green as emerald. His bed-bottle was one of the sights of the ward. An English-speaking Dutch Communist, having heard that there was an Englishman in the hospital, befriended me and brought me English newspapers. He had been terribly wounded in the October fighting, and had somehow managed to

---

[1] *Sietamo* Town in the Huesca region, in the province of Aragón.

[2] *Barbastro or Lerida* Two larger towns south of Sietamo.

[3] *White City* Area of greater London, site of a Franco-British Exhibition and the Olympic Games in 1908.

settle down at Lerida hospital and had married one of the nurses. Thanks to his wound, one of his legs had shrivelled till it was no thicker than my arm. Two militiamen on leave, whom I had met my first week at the front, came in to see a wounded friend and recognized me. They were kids of about eighteen. They stood awkwardly beside my bed, trying to think of something to say, and then, as a way of demonstrating that they were sorry I was wounded, suddenly took all the tobacco out of their pockets, gave it to me, and fled before I could give it back. How typically Spanish! I discovered afterwards that you could not buy tobacco anywhere in the town and what they had given me was a week's ration.

After a few days I was able to get up and walk about with my arm in a sling. For some reason it hurt much more when it hung down. I also had, for the time being, a good deal of internal pain from the damage I had done myself in falling, and my voice had disappeared almost completely, but I never had a moment's pain from the bullet wound itself. It seems this is usually the case. The tremendous shock of a bullet prevents sensation locally; a splinter of shell or bomb, which is jagged and usually hits you less hard, would probably hurt like the devil. There was a pleasant garden in the hospital grounds, and in it was a pool with gold-fishes and some small dark grey fish—bleak, I think. I used to sit watching them for hours. The way things were done at Lerida gave me an insight into the hospital system on the Aragon front—whether it was the same on other fronts I do not know. In some ways the hospitals were very good. The doctors were able men and there seemed to be no shortage of drugs and equipment. But there were two bad faults on account of which, I have no doubt, hundreds or thousands of men have died who might have been saved.

One was the fact that all the hospitals anywhere near the front line were used more or less as casualty clearing-stations. The result was that you got no treatment there unless you were too badly wounded to be moved. In theory most of the wounded were sent straight to Barcelona or Tarragona, but owing to the lack of transport they were often a week or ten days in getting there. They were kept hanging about at Sietamo, Barbastro, Monzon, Lerida, and other places, and meanwhile they were getting no treatment except an occasional clean bandage, sometimes not even that. Men with dreadful shell wounds, smashed bones and so forth, were swathed in a sort of casing made of bandages and plaster of Paris; a description of the wound was written in pencil on the outside, and as a rule the casing was not removed till the man reached Barcelona or Tarragona ten days later. It was almost impossible to get one's wound examined on the way; the few doctors could not cope with the work, and they simply walked hurriedly past your bed, saying: "Yes, yes, they'll attend to you at Barcelona." There were always rumours that the hospital train was leaving for Barcelona *mañana*.[1] The other fault was the lack of competent nurses. Apparently there was no supply of trained nurses in Spain, perhaps because before the war this work was done chiefly by nuns. I have no complaint against the Spanish nurses, they always treated me with the greatest kindness, but there is no doubt that they were terribly ignorant. All of them knew how to take a temperature, and some of them knew how to tie a bandage, but that was about all. The result was that men who were too ill to fend for themselves were often shamefully neglected. The nurses would let a man remain constipated for a week on end, and they seldom washed those who were too weak to wash themselves. I remember one poor devil with a smashed arm telling me that he had been three weeks without having his face washed. Even beds were left unmade for days together. The food in all the hospitals was very good—too good, indeed. Even more in Spain than elsewhere it seemed to be the tradition to stuff sick people with heavy food. At Lerida the meals were terrific. Breakfast, at about six in the morning, consisted of soup, an omelette, stew, bread, white wine, and coffee, and lunch was even larger—this at a time when most of the civil population was seriously underfed. Spaniards seem not to recognize such a thing as a light diet. They give the same food to sick people as to well ones—always the same rich, greasy cookery, with everything sodden in olive oil.

One morning it was announced that the men in my ward were to be sent down to Barcelona today. I managed to send a wire to my wife, telling her that I was coming, and presently they packed us into buses and took us down to the station. It was only when the train was actually starting that the hospital orderly who

---

[1]   *mañana* Spanish: tomorrow.

travelled with us casually let fall that we were not going to Barcelona after all, but to Tarragona. I suppose the engine-driver had changed his mind. "Just like Spain!" I thought. But it was very Spanish, too, that they agreed to hold up the train while I sent another wire, and more Spanish still that the wire never got there.

They had put us into ordinary third-class carriages with wooden seats, and many of the men were badly wounded and had only got out of bed for the first time that morning. Before long, what with the heat and the jolting, half of them were in a state of collapse and several vomited on the floor. The hospital orderly threaded his way among the corpse-like forms that sprawled everywhere, carrying a large goat-skin bottle full of water which he squirted into this mouth or that. It was beastly water; I remember the taste of it still. We got into Tarragona as the sun was getting low. The line runs along the shore a stone's throw from the sea. As our train drew into the station a troop-train full of men from the International Column was drawing out, and a knot of people on the bridge were waving to them. It was a very long train, packed to bursting-point with men, with field-guns lashed on the open trucks and more men clustering round the guns. I remember with peculiar vividness the spectacle of that train passing in the yellow evening light; window after window full of dark, smiling faces, the long tilted barrels of the guns, the scarlet scarves fluttering—all this gliding slowly past us against a turquoise-coloured sea.

"Estranjeros—foreigners," said someone. "They're Italians."

Obviously they were Italians. No other people could have grouped themselves so picturesquely or returned the salutes of the crowd with so much grace—a grace that was none the less because about half the men on the train were drinking out of up-ended wine bottles. We heard afterwards that these were some of the troops who won the great victory at Guadalajara in March; they had been on leave and were being transferred to the Aragon front. Most of them, I am afraid, were killed at Huesca only a few weeks later. The men who were well enough to stand had moved across the carriage to cheer the Italians as they went past. A crutch waved out of the window; bandaged forearms made the Red Salute. It was like an allegorical picture of war; the trainload of fresh men gliding proudly up the line, the maimed men sliding slowly down, and all the while the guns on the open trucks making one's heart leap as guns always do, and reviving that pernicious feeling, so difficult to get rid of, that war *is* glorious after all.

The hospital at Tarragona was a very big one and full of wounded from all fronts. What wounds one saw there! They had a way of treating certain wounds which I suppose was in accordance with the latest medical practice, but which was peculiarly horrible to look at. This was to leave the wound completely open and unbandaged, but protected from flies by a net of butter-muslin, stretched over wires. Under the muslin you would see the red jelly of a half-healed wound. There was one man wounded in the face and throat who had his head inside a sort of spherical helmet of butter-muslin; his mouth was closed up and he breathed through a little tube that was fixed between his lips. Poor devil, he looked so lonely, wandering to and fro, looking at you through his muslin cage and unable to speak. I was three or four days at Tarragona. My strength was coming back, and one day, by going slowly, I managed to walk down as far as the beach. It was queer to see the seaside life going on almost as usual; the smart cafes along the promenade and the plump local bourgeoisie bathing and sunning themselves in deck-chairs as though there had not been a war within a thousand miles. Nevertheless, as it happened, I saw a bather drowned, which one would have thought impossible in that shallow and tepid sea.

Finally, eight or nine days after leaving the front, I had my wound examined. In the surgery where newly-arrived cases were examined, doctors with huge pairs of shears were hacking away the breast-plates of plaster in which men with smashed ribs, collar-bones and so forth had been cased at the dressing-stations behind the line; out of the neck-hole of the huge clumsy breastplate you would see protruding an anxious, dirty face, scrubby with a week's beard. The doctor, a brisk, handsome man of about thirty, sat me down in a chair, grasped my tongue with a piece of rough gauze, pulled it out as far as it would go, thrust a dentist's mirror down my throat and told me to say "Eh!" After doing this till my tongue was bleeding and my eyes running with water, he told me that one vocal cord was paralysed.

"When shall I get my voice back?" I said.

"Your voice? Oh, you'll never get your voice back,"

he said cheerfully.

However, he was wrong, as it turned out. For about two months I could not speak much above a whisper, but after that my voice became normal rather suddenly, the other vocal cord having "compensated." The pain in my arm was due to the bullet having pierced a bunch of nerves at the back of the neck. It was a shooting pain like neuralgia, and it went on hurting continuously for about a month, especially at night, so that I did not get much sleep. The fingers of my right hand were also semi-paralysed. Even now, five months afterwards, my forefinger is still numb—a queer effect for a neck wound to have.

The wound was a curiosity in a small way and various doctors examined it with much clicking of tongues and "Que suerte! Que suerte!"[1] One of them told me with an air of authority that the bullet had missed the artery by "about a millimetre." I don't know how he knew. No one I met at this time—doctors, nurses, *practicantes*,[2] or fellow-patients—failed to assure me that a man who is hit through the neck and survives it is the luckiest creature alive. I could not help thinking that it would be even luckier not to be hit at all.

—1938

Politics and the English Language

Most people who bother with the matter at all would admit that the English language is in a bad way, but it is generally assumed that we cannot by conscious action do anything about it. Our civilization is decadent and our language—so the argument runs—must inevitably share in the general collapse. It follows that any struggle against the abuse of language is a sentimental archaism, like preferring candles to electric light or hansom cabs to aeroplanes. Underneath this lies the half-conscious belief that language is a natural growth and not an instrument which we shape for our own purposes.

Now, it is clear that the decline of a language must ultimately have political and economic causes: it is not due simply to the bad influence of this or that individ-ual writer. But an effect can become a cause, reinforcing the original cause and producing the same effect in an intensified form, and so on indefinitely. A man may take to drink because he feels himself to be a failure, and then fail all the more completely because he drinks. It is rather the same thing that is happening to the English language. It becomes ugly and inaccurate because our thoughts are foolish, but the slovenliness of our language makes it easier for us to have foolish thoughts. The point is that the process is reversible. Modern English, especially written English, is full of bad habits which spread by imitation and which can be avoided if one is willing to take the necessary trouble. If one gets rid of these habits one can think more clearly, and to think clearly is a necessary first step towards political regeneration: so that the fight against bad English is not frivolous and is not the exclusive concern of professional writers. I will come back to this presently, and I hope that by that time the meaning of what I have said here will have become clearer. Meanwhile, here are five specimens of the English language as it is now habitually written.

These five passages have not been picked out because they are especially bad—I could have quoted far worse if I had chosen—but because they illustrate various of the mental vices from which we now suffer. They are a little below the average, but are fairly representative samples. I number them so that I can refer back to them when necessary:

1. I am not, indeed, sure whether it is not true to say that the Milton who once seemed not unlike a seventeenth-century Shelley had not become, out of an experience ever more bitter in each year, more alien (*sic*) to the founder of that Jesuit sect which nothing could induce him to tolerate.
   Professor Harold Laski
        (Essay in *Freedom of Expression*).

2. Above all, we cannot play ducks and drakes with a native battery of idioms which prescribes such egregious collocations of vocables as the Basic *put up with* for *tolerate* or *put at a loss* for *bewilder*.
   Professor Lancelot Hogben (*Interglossa*).

3. On the one side we have the free personality: by definition it is not neurotic, for it has neither

---

[1] *Que suerte* Spanish: What luck!

[2] *practicantes* Spanish: practitioners.

conflict nor dream. Its desires, such as they are, are transparent, for they are just what institutional approval keeps in the forefront of consciousness; another institutional pattern would alter their number and intensity; there is little in them that is natural, irreducible, or culturally dangerous. But *on the other side*, the social bond itself is nothing but the mutual reflection of these self-secure integrities. Recall the definition of love. Is not this the very picture of a small academic? Where is there a place in this hall of mirrors for either personality or fraternity?

Essay on psychology in *Politics* (New York).

4. All the "best people" from the gentlemen's clubs, and all the frantic Fascist captains, united in common hatred of Socialism and bestial horror of the rising tide of the mass revolutionary movement, have turned to acts of provocation, to foul incendiarism, to medieval legends of poisoned wells, to legalise their own destruction to proletarian organisations, and rouse the agitated petty-bourgeoisie to chauvinistic fervour on behalf of the fight against the revolutionary way out of the crisis.

Communist pamphlet.

5. If a new spirit *is* to be infused into this old country, there is one thorny and contentious reform which must be tackled, and that is the humanisation and galvanisation of the BBC.[1] Timidity here will bespeak canker and atrophy of the soul. The heart of Britain may be sound and of strong beat, for instance, but the British lion's roar at present is like that of Bottom in Shakespeare's *Midsummer Night's Dream*—as gentle as any sucking dove. A virile new Britain cannot continue indefinitely to be traduced in the eyes, or rather ears, of the world by the effete languors of Langham Place,[2] brazenly masquerading as "standard English." When the Voice of Britain is heard at nine o'clock, better far and infinitely less ludicrous to hear aitches honestly dropped than the present priggish, inflated, inhibited, school-ma'amish arch braying of blameless bashful mewing maidens!

Letter in *Tribune*.

Each of these passages has faults of its own, but, quite apart from avoidable ugliness, two qualities are common to all of them. The first is staleness of imagery: the other is lack of precision. The writer either has a meaning and cannot express it, or he inadvertently says something else, or he is almost indifferent as to whether his words mean anything or not. This mixture of vagueness and sheer incompetence is the most marked characteristic of modern English prose, and especially of any kind of political writing. As soon as certain topics are raised, the concrete melts into the abstract and no one seems able to think of turns of speech that are not hackneyed: prose consists less and less of *words* chosen for the sake of their meaning, and more of *phrases* tacked together like the sections of a prefabricated hen-house. I list below, with notes and examples, various of the tricks by means of which the work of prose construction is habitually dodged:

Dying metaphors. A newly invented metaphor assists thought by evoking a visual image, while on the other hand a metaphor which is technically "dead" (e.g., *iron resolution*) has in effect reverted to being an ordinary word and can generally be used without loss of vividness. But in between these two classes there is a huge dump of worn-out metaphors which have lost all evocative power and are merely used because they save people the trouble of inventing phrases for themselves. Examples are: *Ring the changes on, take up the cudgels for, toe the line, ride roughshod over, stand shoulder to shoulder with, play into the hands of, no axe to grind, grist to the mill, fishing in troubled waters, rift within the lute, on the order of the day, Achilles' heel, swan song, hotbed*. Many of these are used without knowledge of their meaning (What is a "rift," for instance?), and incompatible metaphors are frequently mixed, a sure sign that the writer is not interested in what he is saying. Some metaphors now current have been twisted out of their original meaning without those who use them even being aware of the fact. For example, *toe the line* is sometimes written *tow the line*. Another example is *the hammer and the anvil*, now always used with the implication that the anvil gets the worst of it. In real life it is always the anvil that breaks the hammer, never the other way about: a writer who stopped to think what he was

---

[1] *BBC* British Broadcasting Corporation.

[2] *Langham Place* Location of the main office of the BBC.

saying would be aware of this, and would avoid pervert-
ing the original phrase.

Operators, or *verbal false limbs*. These save the trouble of
picking out appropriate verbs and nouns, and at the
same time pad each sentence with extra syllables which
give it an appearance of symmetry. Characteristic
phrases are: *render inoperative, militate against, prove
unacceptable, make contact with, be subjected to, give rise
to, give grounds for, have the effect of, play a leading part
(role) in, make itself felt, take effect, exhibit a tendency to,
serve the purpose of*, etc etc. The keynote is the elimination of simple verbs. Instead of being a single word, such
as *break, stop, spoil, mend, kill*, a verb becomes a *phrase*,
made up of a noun or adjective tacked on to some
general-purposes verb such as *prove, serve, form, play,
render*. In addition, the passive voice is wherever possible
used in preference to the active, and noun constructions
are used instead of gerunds (*by examination of* instead of
by examining). The range of verbs is further cut down by
means of the *-ise* and *de-* formations, and banal statements are given an appearance of profundity by means
of the *not un-* formation. Simple conjunctions and
prepositions are replaced by such phrases as *with respect
to, having regard to, the fact that, by dint of, in view of, in
the interests of, on the hypothesis that;* and the ends of
sentences are saved from anticlimax by such resounding
commonplaces as *greatly to be desired, cannot be left out
of account, a development to be expected in the near future,
deserving of serious consideration, brought to a satisfactory
conclusion*, and so on and so forth.

Pretentious diction. Words like *phenomenon, element,
individual* (as noun), *objective, categorical, effective,
virtual, basic, primary, promote, constitute, exhibit,
exploit, utilise, eliminate, liquidate*, are used to dress up
simple statements and give an air of scientific impartial-
ity to biassed judgements. Adjectives like *epoch-making,
epic, historic, unforgettable, triumphant, age-old, inevitable, inexorable, veritable*, are used to dignify the sordid
processes of international politics, while writing that
aims at glorifying war usually takes on an archaic colour,
its characteristic words being: *realm, throne, chariot,
mailed fist, trident, sword, shield, buckler, banner, jackboot, clarion*. Foreign words and expressions such as *cul
de sac, ancien régime, deus ex machina, mutatis mutandis,*

status quo, Gleichschaltung, Weltanschauung,[1] are used to
give an air of culture and elegance. Except for the useful
abbreviation *i.e., e.g.*, and *etc.*, there is no real need for
any of the hundreds of foreign phrases now current in
English. Bad writers, and especially scientific, political,
and sociological writers, are nearly always haunted by
the notion that Latin or Greek words are grander than
Saxon ones, and unnecessary words like *expedite, ameliorate, predict, extraneous, deracinated, clandestine, sub-
aqueous* and hundreds of others constantly gain ground
from their Anglo-Saxon opposite numbers.[2] The jargon
peculiar to Marxist writing (*hyena, hangman, cannibal,
petty bourgeois, these gentry, lacquey, flunkey, mad dog,
White Guard*, etc.) consists largely of words and phrases
translated from Russian, German, or French; but the
normal way of coining a new word is to use a Latin or
Greek root with the appropriate affix and, where
necessary, the *-ise* formation. It is often easier to make
up words of this kind (*deregionalise, impermissible,
extramarital, non-fragmentatory* and so forth) than to
think up the English words that will cover one's meaning. The result, in general, is an increase in slovenliness
and vagueness.

Meaningless words. In certain kinds of writing, particularly in art criticism and literary criticism, it is normal to
come across long passages which are almost completely
lacking in meaning.[3] Words like *romantic, plastic, values,
human, dead, sentimental, natural, vitality*, as used in art

---

[1]   *ancien ... Weltanschauung* Phrases meaning, respectively, old
system of government (French), god from the machine (Latin), the
necessary changes being made (Latin), the state of things (Latin),
enforced political conformity (German), philosophy of life (German).

[2]   [Orwell's note]   An interesting illustration of this is the way in
which the English flower names which were in use till very recently
are being ousted by Greek ones, *snapdragon* becoming *atirrhinum,
forget-me-not* becoming *myosotis*, etc. It is hard to see any practical
reason for this change in fashion: it is probably due to an instinctive
turning-away from the more homely word and a vague feeling that
the Greek word is scientific.

[3]   [Orwell's note]   Example: "Comfort's catholicity of perception
and image, strangely Whitmanesque in range, continues to evoke
that trembling atmospheric accumulative hinting at a cruel, an
inexorably serene timelessness … Wrey Gardiner scores by aiming at
simple bullseyes with precision. Only they are not so simple, and
through this contented sadness runs more than the surface bitter-
sweet of resignation" (*Poetry Quarterly*).

criticism, are strictly meaningless, in the sense that they not only do not point to any discoverable object, but are hardly even expected to do so by the reader.

When one critic writes, "The outstanding features of Mr. X's work is its living quality," while another writes, "The immediately striking thing about Mr. X's work is its peculiar deadness," the reader accepts this as a simple difference of opinion. If words like *black* and *white* were involved, instead of the jargon words *dead* and *living*, he would see at once that language was being used in an improper way. Many political words are similarly abused. The word *Fascism* has now no meaning except in so far as it signifies "something not desirable." The words *democracy, socialism, freedom patriotic, realistic, justice*, have each of them several different meanings which cannot be reconciled with one another. In the case of a word like *democracy*, not only is there no agreed definition, but the attempt to make one is resisted from all sides. It is almost universally felt that when we call a country democratic we are praising it: consequently the defenders of every kind of regime claim that it is a democracy, and fear that they might have to stop using the word if it were tied down to any one meaning. Words of this kind are often used in a consciously dishonest way. That is, the person who uses them has his own private definition, but allows his hearer to think he means something quite different. Statements like *Marshal Pétain*[1] *was a true patriot, The Soviet press is the freest in the world, The Catholic Church is opposed to persecution*, are almost always made with intent to deceive. Other words used in variable meanings, in most cases more or less dishonestly, are: *class, totalitarian, science, progressive, reactionary, bourgeois, equality*.

Now that I have made this catalogue of swindles and perversions, let me give another example of the kind of writing that they lead to. This time it must of its nature be an imaginary one. I am going to translate a passage of good English into modern English of the worst sort. Here is a well-known verse from *Ecclesiastes*:

> I returned and saw under the sun, that the race is not to the swift, nor the battle to the strong, neither yet bread to the wise, nor yet riches to men of

understanding, nor yet favour to men of skill; but time and chance happeneth to them all.

Here it is in modern English:

> Objective considerations of contemporary phenomena compels the conclusion that success or failure in competitive activities exhibits no tendency to be commensurate with innate capacity, but that a considerable element of the unpredictable must invariably be taken into account.

This is a parody, but not a very gross one. Exhibit 3, above, for instance, contains several patches of the same kind in English. It will be seen that I have not made a full translation. The beginning and ending of the sentence follow the original meaning fairly closely, but in the middle the concrete illustrations— race, battle, bread—dissolve into the vague phrase "success or failure in competitive activities." This had to be so, because no modern writer of the kind I am discussing—no one capable of using phrases like "objective consideration of contemporary phenomena"—would ever tabulate his thoughts in that precise and detailed way. The whole tendency of modern prose is away from concreteness. Now analyse these two sentences a little more closely. The first contains forty-nine words but only sixty syllables, and all its words are those of everyday life. The second contains thirty-eight words of ninety syllables: eighteen of its words are from Latin roots, and one from Greek. The first sentence contains six vivid images, and only one phrase ("time and chance") that could be called vague. The second contains not a single fresh, arresting phrase, and in spite of its ninety syllables it gives only a shortened version of the meaning contained in the first. Yet without a doubt it is the second kind of sentence that is gaining ground in modern English. I do not want to exaggerate. This kind of writing is not yet universal, and outcrops of simplicity will occur here and there in the worst-written page. Still, if you or I were told to write a few lines on the uncertainty of human fortunes, we should probably come much nearer to my imaginary sentence than to the one from *Ecclesiastes*.

As I have tried to show, modern writing at its worst does not consist in picking out words for the sake of their meaning and inventing images in order to make the meaning clearer. It consists in gumming together

---

[1] *Marshal Pétain*   French general (1856–1951) who was appointed head of the Vichy government, which ruled Occupied France during World War II in collaboration with the Nazis.

long strips of words which have already been set in order by someone else, and making the results presentable by sheer humbug. The attraction of this way of writing is that it is easy. It is easier—even quicker, once you have the habit—to say *In my opinion it is a not unjustifiable assumption that* than to say *I think*. If you use ready-made phrases, you not only don't have to hunt about for words; you also don't have to bother with the rhythms of your sentences, since these phrases are generally so arranged as to be more or less euphonious. When you are composing in a hurry—when you are dictating to a stenographer, for instance, or making a public speech—it is natural to fall into a pretentious, Latinized style. Tags like *a consideration which we should do well to bear in mind* or *a conclusion to which all of us would readily assent* will save many a sentence from coming down with a bump. By using stale metaphors, similes, and idioms, you save much mental effort, at the cost of leaving your meaning vague, not only for your reader but for yourself. This is the significance of mixed metaphors. The sole aim of a metaphor is to call up a visual image. When these images clash—as in *The Fascist octopus has sung its swan song, the jackboot is thrown into the melting pot*—it can be taken as certain that the writer is not seeing a mental image of the objects he is naming; in other words he is not really thinking.

Look again at the examples I gave at the beginning of this essay. Professor Laski (1) uses five negatives in 53 words. One of these is superfluous, making nonsense of the whole passage, and in addition there is the slip *alien* for akin, making further nonsense, and several avoidable pieces of clumsiness which increase the general vagueness. Professor Hogben (2) plays ducks and drakes with a battery which is able to write prescriptions, and, while disapproving of the everyday phrase *put up with*, is unwilling to look *egregious* up in the dictionary and see what it means. (3), if one takes an uncharitable attitude towards it, is simply meaningless: probably one could work out its intended meaning by reading the whole of the article in which it occurs. In (4) the writer knows more or less what he wants to say, but an accumulation of stale phrases chokes him like tea-leaves blocking a sink. In (5) words and meaning have almost parted company. People who write in this manner usually have a general emotional meaning—they dislike one thing and want to express solidarity with another—but they

are not interested in the detail of what they are saying. A scrupulous writer, in every sentence that he writes, will ask himself at least four questions, thus: What am I trying to say? What words will express it? What image or idiom will make it clearer? Is this image fresh enough to have an effect? And he will probably ask himself two more: Could I put it more shortly? Have I said anything that is avoidably ugly? But you are not obliged to go to all this trouble. You can shirk it by simply throwing your mind open and letting the ready-made phrases come crowding in. They will construct your sentences for you—even think your thoughts for you, to a certain extent—and at need they will perform the important service of partially concealing your meaning even from yourself. It is at this point that the special connection between politics and the debasement of language becomes clear.

In our time it is broadly true that political writing is bad writing. Where it is not true, it will generally be found that the writer is some kind of rebel, expressing his private opinions, and not a "party line." Orthodoxy, of whatever colour, seems to demand a lifeless, imitative style. The political dialects to be found in pamphlets, leading articles, manifestos, White Papers,[1] and the speeches of Under-Secretaries do, of course, vary from party to party, but they are all alike in that one almost never finds in them a fresh, vivid, homemade turn of speech. When one watches some tired hack on the platform mechanically repeating the familiar phrases— *bestial atrocities, iron heel, blood-stained tyranny, free peoples of the world, stand shoulder to shoulder*—one often has a curious feeling that one is not watching a live human being but some kind of dummy: a feeling which suddenly becomes stronger at moments when the light catches the speaker's spectacles and turns them into blank discs which seem to have no eyes behind them. And this is not altogether fanciful. A speaker who uses that kind of phraseology has gone some distance towards turning himself into a machine. The appropriate noises are coming out of his larynx, but his brain is not involved as it would be if he were choosing his words for himself. If the speech he is making is one that he is accustomed to make over and over again, he may be almost unconscious of what he is saying, as one is when one utters the responses in church. And this reduced

---

[1]   *White Papers*   Parliamentary documents.

state of consciousness, if not indispensable, is at any rate favourable to political conformity.

In our time, political speech and writing are largely the defence of the indefensible. Things like the continuance of British rule in India, the Russian purges and deportations, the dropping of the atom bombs on Japan, can indeed be defended, but only by arguments which are too brutal for most people to face, and which do not square with the professed aims of political parties. Thus political language has to consist largely of euphemism, question-begging and sheer cloudy vagueness. Defenceless villages are bombarded from the air, the inhabitants driven out into the countryside, the cattle machinegunned, the huts set on fire with incendiary bullets: this is called *pacification*. Millions of peasants are robbed of their farms and sent trudging along the roads with no more than they can carry: this is called *transfer of population* or *rectification of frontiers*. People are imprisoned for years without trial, or shot in the back of the neck, or sent to die of scurvy in Arctic lumber camps: this is called *elimination of unreliable elements*. Such phraseology is needed if one wants to name things without calling up mental pictures of them. Consider for instance some comfortable English professor defending Russian totalitarianism. He cannot say outright, "I believe in killing off your opponents when you can get good results by doing so." Probably, therefore, he will say something like this:

> While freely conceding that the Soviet regime exhibits certain features which the humanitarian may be inclined to deplore, we must, I think, agree that a certain curtailment of the right to political opposition is an unavoidable concomitant of transitional periods, and that the rigours which the Russian people have been called upon to undergo have been amply justified in the sphere of concrete achievement.

The inflated style is itself a kind of euphemism. A mass of Latin words falls upon the facts like soft snow, blurring the outlines and covering up all the details. The great enemy of clear language is insincerity. When there is a gap between one's real and one's declared aims, one turns as it were instinctively to long words and exhausted idioms, like a cuttlefish[1] squirting out ink. In our age there is no such thing as "keeping out of politics." All issues are political issues, and politics itself is a mass of lies, evasions, folly, hatred and schizophrenia. When the general atmosphere is bad, language must suffer. I should expect to find—this is a guess which I have not sufficient knowledge to verify—that the German, Russian, and Italian languages have all deteriorated in the last ten or fifteen years, as a result of dictatorship.

But if thought corrupts language, language can also corrupt thought. A bad usage can spread by tradition and imitation, even among people who should and do know better. The debased language that I have been discussing is in some ways very convenient. Phrases like *a not unjustifiable assumption, leaves much to be desired, would serve no good purpose, a consideration which we should do well to bear in mind*, are a continuous temptation, a packet of aspirins always at one's elbow. Look back through this essay, and for certain you will find that I have again and again committed the very faults I am protesting against. By this morning's post I have received a pamphlet dealing with conditions in Germany. The author tells me that he "felt impelled" to write it. I open it at random, and here is almost the first sentence that I see: "(The Allies) have an opportunity not only of achieving a radical transformation of Germany's social and political structure in such a way as to avoid a nationalistic reaction in Germany itself, but at the same time of laying the foundations of a co-operative and unified Europe." You see, he "feels impelled" to write—feels, presumably, that he has something new to say—and yet his words, like cavalry horses answering the bugle, group themselves automatically into the familiar dreary pattern. This invasion of one's mind by readymade phrases (*lay the foundations, achieve a radical transformation*) can only be prevented if one is constantly on guard against them, and every such phrase anaesthetises a portion of one's brain.

I said earlier that the decadence of our language is probably curable. Those who deny this would argue, if they produced an argument at all, that language merely reflects existing social conditions, and that we cannot influence its development by any direct tinkering with words and constructions. So far as the general tone or spirit of a language goes, this may be true, but it is not true in detail. Silly words and expressions have often

---

[1] *cuttleefish* Octopus.

disappeared, not through any evolutionary process but owing to the conscious action of a minority. Two recent examples were *explore every avenue* and *leave no stone unturned*, which were killed by the jeers of a few journalists. There is a long list of flyblown metaphors which could similarly be got rid of if enough people would interest themselves in the job; and it should also be possible to laugh the *not un-* formation out of existence,[1] to reduce the amount of Latin and Greek in the average sentence, to drive out foreign phrases and strayed scientific words, and, in general, to make pretentiousness unfashionable. But all these are minor points. The defence of the English language implies more than this, and perhaps it is best to start by saying what it does *not* imply.

To begin with it has nothing to do with archaism, with the salvaging of obsolete words and turns of speech, or with the setting up of a "standard English" which must never be departed from. On the contrary, it is especially concerned with the scrapping of every word or idiom which has outworn its usefulness. It has nothing to do with correct grammar and syntax, which are of no importance so long as one makes one's meaning clear, or with the avoidance of Americanisms, or with having what is called a "good prose style." On the other hand it is not concerned with fake simplicity and the attempt to make written English colloquial. Nor does it even imply in every case preferring the Saxon word to the Latin one, though it does imply using the fewest and shortest words that will cover one's meaning. What is above all needed is to let the meaning choose the word, and not the other way about. In prose, the worst thing one can do with words is to surrender to them. When you think of a concrete object, you think wordlessly, and then, if you want to describe the thing you have been visualizing you probably hunt about till you find the exact words that seem to fit it. When you think of something abstract you are more inclined to use words from the start, and unless you make a conscious effort to prevent it, the existing dialect will come rushing in and do the job for you, at the expense of blurring or even changing your meaning. Probably it is better to put off using words as long as possible and get

one's meaning as clear as one can through pictures or sensations. Afterwards one can choose—not simply accept—the phrases that will best cover the meaning, and then switch round and decide what impression one's words are likely to make on another person. This last effort of the mind cuts out all stale or mixed images, all prefabricated phrases, needless repetitions, and humbug and vagueness generally. But one can often be in doubt about the effect of a word or a phrase, and one needs rules that one can rely on when instinct fails. I think the following rules will cover most cases:

(i) Never use a metaphor, simile, or other figure of speech which you are used to seeing in print.

(ii) Never use a long word where a short one will do.

(iii) If it is possible to cut a word out, always cut it out.

(iv) Never use the passive where you can use the active.

(v) Never use a foreign phrase, a scientific word, or a jargon word if you can think of an everyday English equivalent.

(vi) Break any of these rules sooner than say anything outright barbarous.

These rules sound elementary, and so they are, but they demand a deep change of attitude in anyone who has grown used to writing in the style now fashionable. One could keep all of them and still write bad English, but one could not write the kind of stuff that I quoted in those five specimens at the beginning of this article.

I have not here been considering the literary use of language, but merely language as an instrument for expressing and not for concealing or preventing thought. Stuart Chase and others have come near to claiming that all abstract words are meaningless, and have used this as a pretext for advocating a kind of political quietism. Since you don't know what Fascism is, how can you struggle against Fascism? One need not swallow such absurdities as this, but one ought to recognise that the present political chaos is connected with the decay of language, and that one can probably bring about some improvement by starting at the verbal end. If you simplify your English, you are freed from the worst follies of orthodoxy. You cannot speak any of the necessary dialects, and when you make a stupid remark

---

[1] [Orwell's note] One can cure oneself of the *not un-* formation by memorizing this sentence: *A not unblack dog was chasing a not unsmall rabbit across a not ungreen field.*

its stupidity will be obvious, even to yourself. Political language—and with variations this is true of all political parties, from Conservatives to Anarchists—is designed to make lies sound truthful and murder respectable, and to give an appearance of solidity to pure wind. One cannot change this all in a moment, but one can at least change one's own habits, and from time to time one can even, if one jeers loudly enough, send some worn-out and useless phrase—some *jackboot, Achilles' heel, hotbed, melting pot, acid test, veritable inferno* or other lump of verbal refuse—into the dustbin where it belongs.

—1946

Shooting an Elephant

In Moulmein, in Lower Burma, I was hated by large numbers of people—the only time in my life that I have been important enough for this to happen to me. I was sub-divisional police officer of the town, and in an aimless, petty kind of way anti-European feeling was very bitter. No one had the guts to raise a riot, but if a European woman went through the bazaars alone somebody would probably spit betel juice over her dress. As a police officer I was an obvious target and was baited whenever it seemed safe to do so. When a nimble Burman tripped me up on the football field and the referee (another Burman) looked the other way, the crowd yelled with hideous laughter. This happened more than once. In the end the sneering yellow faces of young men that met me everywhere, the insults hooted after me when I was at a safe distance, got badly on my nerves. The young Buddhist priests were the worst of all. There were several thousands of them in the town and none of them seemed to have anything to do except stand on street corners and jeer at Europeans.

All this was perplexing and upsetting. For at that time I had already made up my mind that imperialism was an evil thing and the sooner I chucked up my job and got out of it the better. Theoretically—and secretly, of course—I was all for the Burmese and all against their oppressors, the British. As for the job I was doing, I hated it more bitterly than I can perhaps make clear. In a job like that you see the dirty work of Empire at close quarters. The wretched prisoners huddling in the stinking cages of the lock-ups, the grey, cowed faces of the long-term convicts, the scarred buttocks of the men who had been flogged with bamboos—all these oppressed me with an intolerable sense of guilt. But I could get nothing into perspective. I was young and ill-educated and I had had to think out my problems in the utter silence that is imposed on every Englishman in the East. I did not even know that the British Empire is dying, still less did I know that it is a great deal better than the younger empires that are going to supplant it. All I knew was that I was stuck between my hatred of the empire I served and my rage against the evil-spirited little beasts who tried to make my job impossible. With one part of my mind I thought of the British Raj as an unbreakable tyranny, as something clamped down, *in saecula saeculorum,*[1] upon the will of prostrate peoples; with another part I thought that the greatest joy in the world would be to drive a bayonet into a Buddhist priest's guts. Feelings like these are the normal by-products of imperialism; ask any Anglo-Indian official, if you can catch him off duty.

One day something happened which in a round-about way was enlightening. It was a tiny incident in itself, but it gave me a better glimpse than I had had before of the real nature of imperialism—the real motives for which despotic governments act. Early one morning the sub-inspector at a police station the other end of the town rang me up on the 'phone and said that an elephant was ravaging the bazaar. Would I please come and do something about it? I did not know what I could do, but I wanted to see what was happening and I got on to a pony and started out. I took my rifle, an old .44 Winchester and much too small to kill an elephant, but I thought the noise might be useful *in terrorem.*[2] Various Burmans stopped me on the way and told me about the elephant's doings. It was not, of course, a wild elephant, but a tame one which had gone "must."[3] It had been chained up, as tame elephants always are when their attack of "must" is due, but on the previous night it had broken its chain and escaped. Its mahout,[4] the only person who could manage it when it was in that state, had set out in pursuit, but had taken

---

[1]   *in saecula saeculorum*   Latin: for centuries upon centuries; forever.

[2]   *terrorem*   Latin: in fright, terror, or alarm.

[3]   *"must"*   I.e., condition characterized by aggressive behavior brought on by a surge in testosterone.

[4]   *mahout*   Elephant trainer or keeper.

the wrong direction and was now twelve hours' journey away, and in the morning the elephant had suddenly reappeared in the town. The Burmese population had no weapons and were quite helpless against it. It had already destroyed somebody's bamboo hut, killed a cow, and raided some fruit-stalls and devoured the stock; also it had met the municipal rubbish van, and, when the driver jumped out and took to his heels, had turned the van over and inflicted violences upon it.

The Burmese sub-inspector and some Indian constables were waiting for me in the quarter where the elephant had been seen. It was a very poor quarter, a labyrinth of squalid bamboo huts, thatched with palm-leaf, winding all over a steep hillside. I remember that it was a cloudy, stuffy morning at the beginning of the rains. We began questioning the people as to where the elephant had gone, and, as usual, failed to get any definite information. That is invariably the case in the East; a story always sounds clear enough at a distance, but the nearer you get to the scene of events the vaguer it becomes. Some of the people said that the elephant had gone in one direction, some said that he had gone in another, some professed not even to have heard of any elephant. I had almost made up my mind that the whole story was a pack of lies, when we heard yells a little distance away. There was a loud, scandalized cry of "Go away, child! Go away this instant!" and an old woman with a switch in her hand came round the corner of a hut, violently shooing away a crowd of naked children. Some more women followed, clicking their tongues and exclaiming; evidently there was something that the children ought not to have seen. I rounded the hut and saw a man's dead body sprawling in the mud. He was an Indian, a black Dravidian coolie, almost naked, and he could not have been dead many minutes. The people said that the elephant had come suddenly upon him round the corner of the hut, caught him with its trunk, put its foot on his back and ground him into the earth. This was the rainy season and the ground was soft, and his face had scored a trench a foot deep and a couple of yards long. He was lying on his belly with arms crucified and head sharply twisted to one side. His face was coated with mud, the eyes wide open, the teeth bared and grinning with an expression of unendurable agony. (Never tell me, by the way, that the dead look peaceful. Most of the corpses I have seen looked devil-

ish.) The friction of the great beast's foot had stripped the skin from his back as neatly as one skins a rabbit. As soon as I saw the dead man I sent an orderly to a friend's house nearby to borrow an elephant rifle. I had already sent back the pony, not wanting it to go mad with fright and throw me if it smelt the elephant.

The orderly came back in a few minutes with a rifle and five cartridges, and meanwhile some Burmans had arrived and told us that the elephant was in the paddy fields below, only a few hundred yards away. As I started forward practically the whole population of the quarter flocked out of the houses and followed me. They had seen the rifle and were all shouting excitedly that I was going to shoot the elephant. They had not shown much interest in the elephant when he was merely ravaging their homes, but it was different now that he was going to be shot. It was a bit of fun to them, as it would be to an English crowd; besides they wanted the meat. It made me vaguely uneasy. I had no intention of shooting the elephant—I had merely sent for the rifle to defend myself if necessary—and it is always unnerving to have a crowd following you. I marched down the hill, looking and feeling a fool, with the rifle over my shoulder and an ever-growing army of people jostling at my heels. At the bottom, when you got away from the huts, there was a metalled road and beyond that a miry waste of paddy fields a thousand yards across, not yet ploughed but soggy from the first rains and dotted with coarse grass. The elephant was standing eight yards from the road, his left side towards us. He took not the slightest notice of the crowd's approach. He was tearing up bunches of grass, beating them against his knees to clean them and stuffing them into his mouth.

I had halted on the road. As soon as I saw the elephant I knew with perfect certainty that I ought not to shoot him. It is a serious matter to shoot a working elephant—it is comparable to destroying a huge and costly piece of machinery—and obviously one ought not to do it if it can possibly be avoided. And at that distance, peacefully eating, the elephant looked no more dangerous than a cow. I thought then and I think now that his attack of "must" was already passing off; in which case he would merely wander harmlessly about until the mahout came back and caught him. Moreover, I did not in the least want to shoot him. I decided that I would watch him for a little while to make sure that he did not turn savage again, and then go home.

But at that moment I glanced round at the crowd that had followed me. It was an immense crowd, two thousand at the least and growing every minute. It blocked the road for a long distance on either side. I looked at the sea of yellow faces above the garish clothes—faces all happy and excited over this bit of fun, all certain that the elephant was going to be shot. They were watching me as they would watch a conjurer about to perform a trick. They did not like me, but with the magical rifle in my hands I was momentarily worth watching. And suddenly I realized that I should have to shoot the elephant after all. The people expected it of me and I had got to do it; I could feel their two thousand wills pressing me forward, irresistibly. And it was at this moment, as I stood there with the rifle in my hands, that I first grasped the hollowness, the futility of the white man's dominion in the East. Here was I, the white man with his gun, standing in front of the unarmed native crowd—seemingly the leading actor of the piece; but in reality I was only an absurd puppet pushed to and fro by the will of those yellow faces behind. I perceived in this moment that when the white man turns tyrant it is his own freedom that he destroys. He becomes a sort of hollow, posing dummy, the conventionalized figure of a sahib. For it is the condition of his rule that he shall spend his life in trying to impress the "natives," and so in every crisis he has got to do what the "natives" expect of him. He wears a mask, and his face grows to fit it. I had got to shoot the elephant. I had committed myself to doing it when I sent for the rifle. A sahib has got to act like a sahib; he has got to appear resolute, to know his own mind and do definite things. To come all that way, rifle in hand, with two thousand people marching at my heels, and then to trail feebly away, having done nothing—no, that was impossible. The crowd would laugh at me. And my whole life, every white man's life in the East, was one long struggle not to be laughed at.

But I did not want to shoot the elephant. I watched him beating his bunch of grass against his knees, with that preoccupied grandmotherly air that elephants have. It seemed to me that it would be murder to shoot him. At that age I was not squeamish about killing animals, but I had never shot an elephant and never wanted to. (Somehow it always seems worse to kill a *large* animal.)

Besides, there was the beast's owner to be considered. Alive, the elephant was worth at least a hundred pounds; dead, he would only be worth the value of his tusks, five pounds, possibly. But I had got to act quickly. I turned to some experienced-looking Burmans who had been there when we arrived, and asked them how the elephant had been behaving. They all said the same thing: he took no notice of you if you left him alone, but he might charge if you went too close to him.

It was perfectly clear to me what I ought to do. I ought to walk up to within, say, twenty-five yards of the elephant and test his behaviour. If he charged I could shoot, if he took no notice of me it would be safe to leave him until the mahout came back. But also I knew that I was going to do no such thing. I was a poor shot with a rifle and the ground was soft mud into which one would sink at every step. If the elephant charged and I missed him, I should have about as much chance as a toad under a steam-roller. But even then I was not thinking particularly of my own skin, only of the watchful yellow faces behind. For at that moment, with the crowd watching me, I was not afraid in the ordinary sense, as I would have been if I had been alone. A white man mustn't be frightened in front of "natives"; and so, in general, he isn't frightened. The sole thought in my mind was that if anything went wrong those two thousand Burmans would see me pursued, caught, trampled on and reduced to a grinning corpse like that Indian up the hill. And if that happened it was quite probable that some of them would laugh. That would never do. There was only one alternative. I shoved the cartridges into the magazine and lay down on the road to get a better aim.

The crowd grew very still, and a deep, low, happy sigh, as of people who see the theatre curtain go up at last, breathed from innumerable throats. They were going to have their bit of fun after all. The rifle was a beautiful German thing with cross-hair sights. I did not then know that in shooting an elephant one would shoot to cut an imaginary bar running from ear-hole to ear-hole. I ought, therefore, as the elephant was sideways on, to have aimed straight at his ear-hole; actually I aimed several inches in front of this, thinking the brain would be further forward.

When I pulled the trigger I did not hear the bang or feel the kick—one never does when a shot goes home

—but I heard the devilish roar of glee that went up from the crowd. In that instant, in too short a time, one would have thought, even for the bullet to get there, a mysterious, terrible change had come over the elephant. He neither stirred nor fell, but every line of his body had altered. He looked suddenly stricken, shrunken, immensely old, as though the frightful impact of the bullet had paralysed him without knocking him down. At last, after what seemed a long time—it might have been five seconds, I dare say—he sagged flabbily to his knees. His mouth slobbered. An enormous senility seemed to have settled upon him. One could have imagined him thousands of years old. I fired again into the same spot. At the second shot he did not collapse but climbed with desperate slowness to his feet and stood weakly upright, with legs sagging and head drooping. I fired a third time. That was the shot that did for him. You could see the agony of it jolt his whole body and knock the last remnant of strength from his legs. But in falling he seemed for a moment to rise, for as his hind legs collapsed beneath him he seemed to tower upwards like a huge rock toppling, his trunk reaching skywards like a tree. He trumpeted, for the first and only time. And then down he came, his belly towards me, with a crash that seemed to shake the ground even where I lay.

I got up. The Burmans were already racing past me across the mud. It was obvious that the elephant would never rise again, but he was not dead. He was breathing very rhythmically with long rattling gasps, his great mound of a side painfully rising and falling. His mouth was wide open—I could see far down into caverns of pale pink throat. I waited a long time for him to die, but his breathing did not weaken. Finally I fired my two remaining shots into the spot where I thought his heart must be. The thick blood welled out of him like red velvet, but still he did not die. His body did not even jerk when the shots hit him, the tortured breathing continued without a pause. He was dying, very slowly and in great agony, but in some world remote from me where not even a bullet could damage him further. I felt that I had got to put an end to that dreadful noise. It seemed dreadful to see the great beast lying there, powerless to move and yet powerless to die, and not even to be able to finish him. I sent back for my small rifle and poured shot after shot into his heart and down his throat. They seemed to make no impression. The tortured gasps continued as steadily as the ticking of a clock.

In the end I could not stand it any longer and went away. I heard later that it took him half an hour to die. Burmans were bringing dahs[1] and baskets even before I left, and I was told they had stripped his body almost to the bones by the afternoon.

Afterwards, of course, there were endless discussions about the shooting of the elephant. The owner was furious, but he was only an Indian and could do nothing. Besides, legally I had done the right thing, for a mad elephant has to be killed, like a mad dog, if its owner fails to control it. Among the Europeans opinion was divided. The older men said I was right, the younger men said it was a damn shame to shoot an elephant for killing a coolie, because an elephant was worth more than any damn Coringhee coolie. And afterwards I was very glad that the coolie had been killed; it put me legally in the right and it gave me a sufficient pretext for shooting the elephant. I often wondered whether any of the others grasped that I had done it solely to avoid looking a fool.

—1950

---

[1] *dahs* Short swords or knives.

IN CONTEXT

Elephants in Asia

There are two types of elephant: the African elephant is by definition a wild animal, but the smaller Asian (or Indian) elephant may be tamed. The latter has long been employed as a beast of burden in many parts of Asia, used for transport, logging, and various other tasks—including hunting, as in the photograph below, of a royal expedition to India in 1912, illustrates.

SAMUEL BECKETT
1906 – 1989

Though Samuel Beckett was a prolific writer of poetry, prose fiction, and criticism, he remains best known for two of his plays, *Waiting for Godot* and *Endgame*, which are credited with having revolutionized theater, and which continue to be performed worldwide today. Fragmented, filled with absences and silences, and sparing of plot, characterization, and setting, Beckett's work is broadly innovative; it attempts to dispense with elements previously thought to be essential to dramatic productions. By paring down his writing to the bare necessities, Beckett created new possibilities of form and produced works whose brevity and lack of structure leaves them open to a variety of critical interpretations.

Beckett was born on 13 April 1906 in Foxrock, an upper-class, Protestant suburb of Dublin. He attended a boarding school in Northern Ireland and from there continued on (in 1923) to Trinity College, Dublin, where he studied French and Italian. Upon graduation, having excelled academically, Beckett was offered a two-year position as an exchange lecturer in Paris, and it was there that his writing career began. Within months of arriving in Paris he had been introduced to fellow Dublin writer James Joyce, whose writing Beckett greatly admired. Beckett established himself as part of Joyce's circle of literary friends in Paris, and in 1928 was commissioned to write an essay on Joyce's *Finnegan's Wake*, which was still a work in progress at the time. That essay (excerpts from which are included in this anthology as contextual material relating to Joyce's work) and a short story of Beckett's were published simultaneously in the Paris literary magazine *transition*. Shortly thereafter his first poem, *Whoroscope* (1930), was published by Nancy Cunard's Hours Press. Beckett had been encouraged by a friend to submit a poem to Cunard's competition for the best short poem on the subject of time. Using existing notes, he composed the prize-winning poem about French philosopher René Descartes in one night.

After living in Paris for two years, Beckett was loath to return to Ireland. He found the atmosphere and literary community in Paris far more conducive to his writing, but largely as a result of financial pressures, he spent the following seven years (1930–37) in Ireland, moving between his family home in Foxtrot and Dublin, where he taught at Trinity College for two years immediately following his departure from Paris. Beckett also spent some time in London undergoing therapy for recurring panic attacks and bouts of depression. During these seven years he worked on several projects, including his first novel, *Dream of Fair to Middling Women*; the series of short stories *More Pricks than Kicks* (1970); the novel *Murphy*; and a small collection of poems. This early work was not well received: his collection of poetry barely sold, *Dream* (1992) was not published during his lifetime, *More Pricks* received mixed reviews, and *Murphy* was rejected dozens of times before finally being accepted in 1938, two years after its completion.

In October 1937 Beckett returned to Paris, intending to settle there permanently and devote himself to his writing. This writer's life, however, was not without incident. Walking home late one night in January 1938, Beckett was stabbed in the chest and spent months recovering in hospital. There he was visited by Suzanne Deschevaux-Dumesnil, the woman who eventually became his wife.

(Though the two were living together less than a year later, they did not marry until 1961.) Beckett and Deschevaux-Dumesnil were forced to leave Paris twice during World War II. The first time, in 1940, they escaped the city days before it fell to German forces. Upon returning to Paris a few months later, Beckett began working for the French Resistance (for which service he was decorated by the French government after the war). In 1942 the two had to flee Paris again when Beckett's Resistance cell was betrayed. They escaped their apartment only hours before the Gestapo arrived.

Though Beckett was able to do some writing while in hiding in the south of France, his most prolific period occurred after his return to his Paris flat in 1945. Between 1946 and 1950 he underwent what he referred to as "the siege in the room," composing four novellas, two plays, and four novels. Three of these novels—*Molloy* (1951), *Malone Dies* (*Malone meurt*, 1951), and *The Unnamable* (*L'innommable*, 1953)—comprise a trilogy and are perhaps his most highly regarded prose works. All the prose from this period departs from his earlier work in several ways. First, Beckett had decided to write entirely in French, translating his work back into English once it was completed. This helped him to avoid lyricism and enhanced the distinctive sparseness of his writing style. He also abandoned the omniscient narration of his earlier novels in favor of a first-person point of view. Frequently, as in *Texts for Nothing* (*Textes pour rien*, 1955) these narratives are more like fragmented meditations or monologues than stories. In fact, Beckett's prose, like his plays, tended towards monologue as his writing career progressed, to the point where the distinction between the two sometimes becomes blurred; many of his later works of short prose, such as *Imagination Dead Imagine* (*Imagination morte imaginez*, 1965), have been given stage performances.

To take a break from his trilogy, Beckett began working on *Waiting for Godot* (*En attendant Godot*, 1952), the two-act play in which, as Irish critic Vivian Mercier famously said, "Nothing happens, twice." The lack of progression in this play about two men waiting for someone called Godot (who never arrives) is characteristic of the majority of Beckett's drama. Set on practically bare stages, lacking significant character development, and consisting of plots with neither climax nor resolution, Beckett's plays have been referred to as more "anti-theater" than theater. The spareness of the setting of *Godot* ("A country road. A tree.") is exceeded by that of the setting of *Endgame* (*Fin de partie*, 1957)—a nearly empty room. In *Endgame*, which Beckett called "more inhuman than *Godot*," the characters are also waiting, though for nothing in particular, except the inevitable end. The frequently nonsensical dialogue of this play, like that of Beckett's others, often doubles back on itself and is interrupted by long silences; Beckett believed the role of theater was not to give "meaning" but to provide an "experience" from which audience members could generate their own meaning if they so desired.

Beckett's characters are largely of a piece. They tend to be aging, homeless, in mental and physical pain, and isolated from those around them yet desperately trying to maintain a sense of connection. Their bodies are sources of anguish, and they are constantly plagued by some difficulty or other. Their sense of disconnection from the outside world and from one another is a source of anxiety, as is the seemingly tenuous nature of their sterile existence. They attempt to alleviate this anxiety and give meaning to their existence through action, but to little avail. The dialogue, movements, and choices of these characters are rarely shown to have logic or consequence, and the result is by turns painful and funny to watch. Beckett's plays, like those of Eugène Ionesco and Jean Genet, are central texts to any discussion of absurdist theater—they present the absurdity and futility of the human condition as a given. Though often bleak, absurdist drama can also be highly comic; as Nell says in *Endgame*, "Nothing is funnier than unhappiness."

At no point in his career did Beckett demonstrate any concern for audience expectations, or feel the need to write in any currently popular style. Perhaps as a result, his work pushed the limits of what was thought possible. His willingness to experiment with new ideas, new media, and new technology resulted in a remarkably rich and diverse body of work. In 1958, shortly after reel-to-reel tape recorders were invented, Beckett incorporated one into a ground-breaking short play, *Krapp's Last*

Tape (*La dernière bande*, 1958), in which a man conducts a "conversation" with a recording of his own voice from years before. In 1964 Beckett forayed into the world of film, writing a script for a film (titled simply *Film*) and travelling to New York to assist in making it.

As he aged, Beckett increasingly despaired of the ability of language to express anything meaningful about the nature of human existence. His 1969 play *Breath* is the most extreme manifestation of such feelings; it lasts less than one minute and includes sounds but no articulated words.

The extraordinary importance of Beckett's work was acknowledged in 1969 when he was awarded the Nobel Prize for Literature. He continued to direct many of his plays and to assist in their production for television up until only a few years before his death in 1989.

⌘ ⌘ ⌘

Krapp's Last Tape

A late evening in the future.

Krapp's den.

Front centre a small table, the two drawers of which open towards audience.

Sitting at the table, facing front, i.e. across from the drawers, a wearish old man: Krapp.

Rusty black narrow trousers too short for him. Rusty black sleeveless waistcoat, four capacious pockets. Heavy silver watch and chain. Grimy white shirt open at neck, no collar. Surprising pair of dirty white boots, size ten at least, very narrow and pointed.

White face. Purple nose. Disordered grey hair. Unshaven.

Very near-sighted (but unspectacled). Hard of hearing.

Cracked voice. Distinctive intonation.

Laborious walk.

On the table a tape-recorder with microphone and a number of cardboard boxes containing reels of recorded tapes.

Table and immediately adjacent area in strong white light. Rest of stage in darkness.

Krapp remains a moment motionless, heaves a great sigh, looks at his watch, fumbles in his pockets, takes out an envelope, puts it back, fumbles, takes out a small bunch of keys, raises it to his eyes, chooses a key, gets up and moves to front of table. He stoops, unlocks first drawer, peers into it, feels about inside it, takes out a reel of tape, peers at it, puts it back, locks drawer, unlocks second drawer, peers into it, feels about inside it, takes out a large banana, peers at it, locks drawer, puts keys back in his pocket. He turns, advances to edge of stage, halts, strokes banana, peels it, drops skin at his feet, puts end of banana in his mouth and remains motionless, staring vacuously before him. Finally he bites off the end, turns aside and begins pacing to and fro at edge of stage, in the light, i.e. not more than four or five paces either way, meditatively eating banana. He treads on skin, slips, nearly falls, recovers himself, stoops and peers at skin and finally pushes it, still stooping, with his foot over the edge of stage into pit. He resumes his pacing, finishes banana, returns to table, sits down, remains a moment motionless, heaves a great sigh, takes keys from his pockets, raises them to his eyes, chooses key, gets up and moves to front of table, unlocks second drawer, takes out a second large banana, peers at it, locks drawer, puts back keys in his pocket, turns, advances to edge of stage, halts, strokes banana, peels it, tosses skin into pit, puts end of banana in his mouth and remains motionless, staring vacuously before him. Finally he has an idea, puts banana in his waistcoat pocket, the end emerging, and goes with all the speed he can muster backstage into darkness. Ten seconds. Loud pop of cork. Fifteen seconds. He comes back into light carrying an old ledger and sits down at table. He lays ledger on table, wipes his mouth, wipes his hands on the front of his waistcoat, brings them smartly together and rubs them.

KRAPP. (*Briskly.*) Ah! (*He bends over ledger, turns the pages, finds the entry he wants, reads.*) Box … thrree … spool … five. (*He raises his head and stares front. With relish.*) Spool! (*Pause.*) Spooool! (*Happy smile. Pause. He bends over table, starts peering and poking at the boxes.*) Box … thrree … thrree … four … two … (*With surprise.*) nine! good God! … seven … ah! the little rascal! (*He takes up box, peers at it.*) Box thrree. (*He lays it on table, opens it and peers at spools inside.*) Spool … (*He peers at ledger.*) … five … (*He peers at spools.*) … five … five … ah! the little scoundrel! (*He takes out a spool, peers at it.*) Spool five. (*He lays it on table, closes box three, puts it back with the others, takes up the spool.*) Box thrree, spool five. (*He bends over the machine, looks up. With relish.*) Spooool! (*Happy smile. He bends, loads spool on machine, rubs his hands.*) Ah! (*He peers at ledger, reads entry at foot of page.*) Mother at rest at last … Hm … The black ball … (*He raises his head, stares blankly front. Puzzled.*) Black ball? … (*He peers again at ledger, reads.*) The dark nurse … (*He raises his head, broods, peers again at ledger, reads.*) Slight improvement in bowel condition … Hm … Memorable … what? (*He peers closer.*) Equinox, memorable equinox. (*He raises his head, stares blankly front. Puzzled.*) Memorable equinox? … (*Pause. He shrugs his shoulders, peers again at ledger, reads.*) Farewell to—(*He turns the page.*—) love.

(*He raises his head, broods, bends over machine, switches on and assumes listening posture, i.e. leaning forward, elbows on table, hand cupping ear towards machine, face front.*)

TAPE. (*Strong voice, rather pompous, clearly Krapp's at a much earlier time.*) Thirty-nine today, sound as a—(*Settling himself more comfortably he knocks one of the boxes off the table, curses, switches off, sweeps boxes and ledger violently to the ground, winds tape back to beginning, switches on, resumes posture.*) Thirty-nine today, sound as a bell, apart from my old weakness, and intellectually I have now every reason to suspect at the … (*Hesitates.*) … crest of the wave—or thereabouts. Celebrated the awful occasion, as in recent years, quietly at the Wine-house. Not a soul. Sat before the fire with closed eyes, separating the grain from the husks. Jotted down a few notes, on the back of an envelope. Good to be back in my den, in my old rags. Have just eaten I regret to say three bananas and only with difficulty refrained from a fourth. Fatal things for a man with my condition. (*Vehemently.*) Cut 'em out! (*Pause.*) The new light above my table is a great improvement. With all this darkness round me I feel less alone. (*Pause.*) In a way. (*Pause.*) I love to get up and move about in it, then back here to … (*Hesitates.*) … me. (*Pause.*) Krapp.

(*Pause.*)

The grain, now what I wonder do I mean by that, I mean … (*Hesitates.*) … I suppose I mean those things worth having when all the dust has—when all *my* dust has settled. I close my eyes and try and imagine them.

(*Pause. Krapp closes his eyes briefly.*)

Extraordinary silence this evening, I strain my ears and do not hear a sound. Old Miss McGlome always sings at this hour. But not tonight. Songs of her girlhood, she says. Hard to think of her as a girl. Wonderful woman though. Connaught,[1] I fancy. (*Pause.*) Shall I sing when I am her age, if I ever am? No. (*Pause.*) Did I sing as a boy? No. (*Pause.*) Did I ever sing? No.

(*Pause.*)

Just been listening to an old year, passages at random. I did not check in the book, but it must be at least ten or twelve years ago. At that time I think I was still living on and off with Bianca in Kedar Street. Well out of that, Jesus yes! Hopeless business. (*Pause.*) Not much about her, apart from a tribute to her eyes. Very warm. I suddenly saw them again. (*Pause.*) Incomparable! (*Pause.*) Ah well … (*Pause.*) These old P.M.s are gruesome, but I often find them—(*Krapp switches off, broods, switches on.*) —a help before embarking on a new … (*Hesitates.*) … retrospect. Hard to believe I was ever that young whelp. The voice! Jesus! And the aspirations! (*Brief laugh in which Krapp joins.*) And the resolutions! (*Brief laugh in which Krapp joins.*) To drink less, in

---

[1] *Connaught* Western province of Ireland.

particular. (*Brief laugh of Krapp alone.*) Statistics. Seventeen hundred hours, out of the preceding eight thousand odd, consumed on licensed premises alone. More than 20%, say 40% of his waking life. (*Pause.*) Plans for a less … (*Hesitates.*) … engrossing sexual life. Last illness of his father. Flagging pursuit of happiness. Unattainable laxation.[1] Sneers at what he calls his youth and thanks to God that it's over. (*Pause.*) False ring there. (*Pause.*) Shadows of the opus … magnum. Closing with a—(*Brief laugh.*)—yelp to Providence. (*Prolonged laugh in which Krapp joins.*) What remains of all that misery? A girl in a shabby green coat, on a railway-station platform? No?

(*Pause.*)

When I look—

(*Krapp switches off, broods, looks at his watch, gets up, goes backstage into darkness. Ten seconds. Pop of cork. Ten seconds. Second cork. Ten seconds. Third cork. Ten seconds. Brief burst of quavering song.*)

KRAPP.   (*Sings.*)   Now the day is over,
Night is drawing nigh-igh,
Shadows—[2]

(*Fit of coughing. He comes back into light, sits down, wipes his mouth, switches on, resumes his listening posture.*)

TAPE.   —back on the year that is gone, with what I hope is perhaps a glint of the old eye to come, there is of course the house on the canal where mother lay a-dying, in the late autumn, after her long viduity (*Krapp gives a start.*), and the—(*Krapp switches off, winds back tape a little, bends his ear closer to machine, switches on.*) —a-dying, after her long viduity, and the—

(*Krapp switches off, raises his head, stares blankly before him. His lips move in the syllables of "viduity." No sound. He gets up, goes backstage into darkness, comes back with an enormous dictionary, lays it on table, sits down and looks up the word.*)

KRAPP.   (*Reading from dictionary.*) State—or condition of being—or remaining—a widow—or widower. (*Looks up. Puzzled.*) Being—or remaining? … (*Pause. He peers again at dictionary. Reading.*) "Deep weeds of viduity" … Also of an animal, especially a bird … the vidua or weaver-bird … Black plumage of male … (*He looks up. With relish.*) The vidua-bird!

(*Pause. He closes dictionary, switches on, resumes listening posture.*)

TAPE.   —bench by the weir from where I could see her window. There I sat, in the biting wind, wishing she were gone. (*Pause.*) Hardly a soul, just a few regulars, nursemaids, infants, old men, dogs. I got to know them quite well—oh by appearance of course I mean! One dark young beauty I recollect particularly, all white and starch, incomparable bosom, with a big black hooded perambulator, most funereal thing. Whenever I looked in her direction she had her eyes on me. And yet when I was bold enough to speak to her—not having been introduced—she threatened to call a policeman. As if I had designs on her virtue! (*Laugh. Pause.*) The face she had! The eyes! Like … (*Hesitates.*) … chrysolite![3] (*Pause.*) Ah well … (*Pause.*) I was there when—(*Krapp switches off, broods, switches on again.*) —the blind went down, one of those dirty brown roller affairs, throwing a ball for a little white dog, as chance would have it. I happened to look up and there it was. All over and done with, at last. I sat on for a few moments with the ball in my hand and the dog yelping and pawing at me. (*Pause.*) Moments. Her moments, my moments. (*Pause.*) The dog's moments. (*Pause.*) In the end I held it out to him and he took it in his mouth, gently, gently. A small, old, black, hard, solid rubber ball. (*Pause.*) I shall feel it, in my hand, until my dying day. (*Pause.*) I might have kept it. (*Pause.*) But I gave it to the dog.

(*Pause.*)

Ah well …

(*Pause.*)

---

[1] *laxation* Relaxed state.

[2] *Now … Shadows* From an old hymn, words by Sabine Baring-Gould (1865).

[3] *chrysolite* Green gem.

Spiritually a year of profound gloom and indigence until that memorable night in March, at the end of the jetty, in the howling wind, never to be forgotten, when suddenly I saw the whole thing. The vision, at last. This I fancy is what I have chiefly to record this evening, against the day when my work will be done and perhaps no place left in my memory, warm or cold, for the miracle that ... (*Hesitates.*) ... for the fire that set it alight. What I suddenly saw then was this, that the belief I had been going on all my life, namely—(*Krapp switches off impatiently, winds tape forward, switches on again.*)—great granite rocks the foam flying up in the light of the lighthouse and the wind-gauge spinning like a propeller, clear to me at last that the dark I have always struggled to keep under is in reality my most— (*Krapp curses, switches off, winds tape forward, switches on again.*)—unshatterable association until my dissolution of storm and night with the light of the understanding and the fire—(*Krapp curses louder, switches off, winds tape forward, switches on again.*) —my face in her breasts and my hand on her. We lay there without moving. But under us all moved, and moved us, gently, up and down, and from side to side.

(*Pause.*)

Past midnight. Never knew such silence. The earth might be uninhabited.

(*Pause.*)

Here I end—

(*Krapp switches off, winds tape back, switches on again.*)

—upper lake, with the punt,[1] bathed off the bank, then pushed out into the stream and drifted. She lay stretched out on the floorboards with her hands under her head and her eyes closed. Sun blazing down, bit of a breeze, water nice and lively. I noticed a scratch on her thigh and asked her how she came by it. Picking gooseberries, she said. I said again I thought it was hopeless and no good going on, and she agreed, without opening her eyes. (*Pause.*) I asked her to look at me and after a few moments—(*Pause.*)—after a few moments

she did, but the eyes just slits, because of the glare. I bent over her to get them in the shadow and they opened. (*Pause. Low.*) Let me in. (*Pause.*) We drifted in among the flags[2] and stuck. The way they went down, sighing, before the stem! (*Pause.*) I lay down across her with my face in her breasts and my hand on her. We lay there without moving. But under us all moved, and moved us, gently, up and down, and from side to side.

(*Pause.*)

Past midnight. Never knew—

(*Krapp switches off, broods. Finally he fumbles in his pockets, encounters the banana, takes it out, peers at it, puts it back, fumbles, brings out the envelope, fumbles, puts back envelope, looks at his watch, gets up and goes backstage into darkness. Ten seconds. Sound of bottle against glass, then brief siphon. Ten seconds. Bottle against glass alone. Ten seconds. He comes back a little unsteadily into light, goes to front of table, takes out keys, raises them to his eyes, chooses key, unlocks first drawer, peers into it, feels about inside, takes out reel, peers at it, locks drawer, puts keys back in his pocket, goes and sits down, takes reel off machine, lays it on dictionary, loads virgin reel on machine, takes envelope from his pocket, consults back of it, lays it on table, switches on, clears his throat and begins to record.*)

KRAPP. Just been listening to that stupid bastard I took myself for thirty years ago, hard to believe I was ever as bad as that. Thank God that's all done with anyway. (*Pause.*) The eyes she had! (*Broods, realizes he is recording silence, switches off, broods. Finally.*) Everything there, everything, all the—(*Realizes this is not being recorded, switches on.*) Everything there, everything on this old muckball, all the light and dark and famine and feasting of ... (*Hesitates.*) ... the ages! (*In a shout.*) Yes! (*Pause.*) Let that go! Jesus! Take his mind off his homework! Jesus! (*Pause. Weary.*) Ah well, maybe he was right. (*Pause.*) Maybe he was right. (*Broods. Realizes. Switches off. Consults envelope.*) Pah! (*Crumples it and throws it away. Broods. Switches on.*) Nothing to say, not a squeak. What's a year now? The sour cud and the iron stool. (*Pause.*) Revelled in the word spool. (*With relish.*)

---

[1] *punt* Shallow, flat-bottomed boat.

[2] *flags* Irises.

Spooool! Happiest moment of the past half million. (*Pause.*) Seventeen copies sold, of which eleven at trade price to free circulating libraries beyond the seas. Getting known. (*Pause.*) One pound six and something, eight I have little doubt. (*Pause.*) Crawled out once or twice, before the summer was cold. Sat shivering in the park, drowned in dreams and burning to be gone. Not a soul. (*Pause.*) Last fancies. (*Vehemently.*) Keep 'em under! (*Pause.*) Scalded the eyes out of me reading *Effie*[1] again, a page a day, with tears again. Effie … (*Pause.*) Could have been happy with her, up there on the Baltic, and the pines, and the dunes. (*Pause.*) Could I? (*Pause.*) And she? (*Pause.*) Pah! (*Pause.*) Fanny came in a couple of times. Bony old ghost of a whore. Couldn't do much, but I suppose better than a kick in the crutch. The last time wasn't so bad. How do you manage it, she said, at your age? I told her I'd been saving up for her all my life. (*Pause.*) Went to Vespers[2] once, like when I was in short trousers. (*Pause. Sings.*)

> Now the day is over,
> Night is drawing nigh-igh,
> Shadows—(*Coughing, then almost* inaudible.) —of
>   the evening
> Steal across the sky.

(*Gasping.*) Went to sleep and fell off the pew. (*Pause.*) Sometimes wondered in the night if a last effort mightn't—(*Pause.*) Ah finish your booze now and get to your bed. Go on with this drivel in the morning. Or leave it at that. (*Pause.*) Leave it at that. (*Pause.*) Lie propped up in the dark—and wander. Be again in the dingle[3] on a Christmas Eve, gathering holly, the red-berried. (*Pause.*) Be again on Croghan[4] on a Sunday morning, in the haze, with the bitch, stop and listen to the bells. (*Pause.*) And so on. (*Pause.*) Be again, be again.

(*Pause.*) All that old misery. (*Pause.*) Once wasn't enough for you. (*Pause.*) Lie down across her.

(*Long pause. He suddenly bends over machine, switches off, wrenches off tape, throws it away, puts on the other, winds it forward to the passage he wants, switches on, listens staring front.*)

TAPE.   —gooseberries, she said. I said again I thought it was hopeless and no good going on, and she agreed, without opening her eyes. (*Pause.*) I asked her to look at me and after a few moments—(*Pause.*) —after a few moments she did, but the eyes just slits, because of the glare. I bent over her to get them in the shadow and they opened. (*Pause. Low.*) Let me in. (*Pause.*) We drifted in among the flags and stuck. The way they went down, sighing, before the stem! (*Pause.*) I lay down across her with my face in her breasts and my hand on her. We lay there without moving. But under us all moved, and moved us, gently, up and down, and from side to side.

(*Pause. Krapp's lips move. No sound.*)

Past midnight. Never knew such silence. The earth might be uninhabited.

(*Pause.*)

Here I end this reel. Box—(*Pause.*)—three, spool—(*Pause.*)—five. (*Pause.*) Perhaps my best years are gone. When there was a chance of happiness. But I wouldn't want them back. Not with the fire in me now. No, I wouldn't want them back.

(*Krapp motionless staring before him. The tape runs on in silence.*)

CURTAIN
—1958

---

[1] *Effie   Effi Briest* (1895), a sentimental novel by Theodor Fontane about a failed love affair.

[2] *Vespers*   Evening prayer service.

[3] *dingle*   Valley.

[4] *Croghan*   Croghan Hill in County Wicklow, Ireland.

W.H. Auden
1907 – 1973

W.H. Auden's poetry documents the changing political, social, and psychological landscape of his time, using language firmly rooted in the world around him. In describing the physical and spiritual ills of society and seeking order and clarity in human existence, he developed a poetry that couples contemporary speech with more traditional, structured verse forms. "Auden was an epoch-making poet on public themes," Seamus Heaney said, "the register of a new sensibility."

Born in York, England, in 1907, Wystan Hugh Auden was the youngest of three sons. His chief childhood interests were scientific: he was fascinated by engineering, mineralogy, and geology, and won a scholarship to study natural science at Oxford. A developing passion for poetry, however, led him to transfer to English, although his interest in science—and his experiences growing up in industrial England (he spent his childhood in Birmingham)—remain evident in the themes that permeate his poetry. He became a central member of a group of writers known as the "Oxford Group," which included Cecil Day Lewis, Stephen Spender, and Louis MacNeice. Auden published numerous poems in undergraduate magazines, and when he had assembled a first volume, he sent it to T.S. Eliot at the publishing house of Faber and Gwyer (later Faber and Faber). The volume was rejected, and Auden had it printed privately on Spender's handpress. Eliot had expressed interest in Auden's work, however, and in 1930 he published Auden's *Poems*. Heavily colored by a sense of political commitment, *Poems* addresses concrete social problems, such as the poverty in depressed areas of industrial England. Many poems are experiments with tone and form—for example, Auden melded Anglo-Saxon sound patterns with modern subject matter.

After graduating from Oxford, Auden spent a year in Germany with a university friend, Christopher Isherwood, and was influenced by German music, literature, and theater—particularly the leftist political theater of Bertolt Brecht and Kurt Weill. When he returned to England, Auden worked variously as a schoolmaster, a university lecturer, a writer of experimental drama, and a verse commentator on documentary films. In this last position he worked with composer Benjamin Britten, who became a close friend and artistic collaborator. Collaborative work appealed to Auden, who went on to co-write three plays with Isherwood: *The Dog Beneath the Skin* (1935), *The Ascent of F6* (1936), and *On the Frontier* (1938). A trip to Iceland with MacNeice, funded by Auden's publishers, resulted in the collaborative travel book *Letters from Iceland* (1937), an unconventional collection of essays, poems, letters, and notes on everything from touring the country to contemporary politics.

Although Auden was openly homosexual, he agreed in 1935 to marry German novelist Thomas Mann's daughter Erika, whose passport was about to be revoked by the Nazis. When the Spanish Civil War began a year later, he volunteered for the Spanish Republic as a medical worker, but the authorities instead gave him work in the censor's office, writing government propaganda. He was disturbed by the extent to which Stalin's government controlled the Republic and also by the fact that the government had forced the churches to close. Although Auden had abandoned his religious beliefs after childhood, the experience caused him to reconsider the importance of spirituality.

Auden later traveled with Isherwood to China and Japan to observe the Sino-Japanese war. There they wrote *Journey to a War* (1939), largely about the complexity of political writing. In his poems of this period Auden developed his characteristically sparse, terse, and often fragmented style, relying on concrete images and colloquial language to create a sense of immediacy and intensity. His explicitly political poems of this period, such as "Spain, 1937," had helped to establish his reputation as a poet, but in 1939, the year he moved to New York, he decided he would never again write anything that resembled propaganda, regardless of cause. In fact, in later years he often rewrote and even suppressed his earlier, more left-wing poems.

In New York, where Auden settled for most of his later life, he devoted himself to his poetry with renewed energy. He became involved in a serious relationship with Chester Kallman, a nineteen-year-old student who would become his lifelong companion and an important literary collaborator. The 1940 volume *Another Time* signals his desire to move on to explore new subjects and modes of expression. *Another Time* meticulously measures the social pulse of the thirties—which Auden characterized as "the age of anxiety"—and includes some of his best-known works, including "Musée des Beaux Arts," "September 1, 1939" (his response to the declaration of war), and elegies to poets Matthew Arnold, A.E. Housman, and W.B. Yeats, all of whom had been significant influences on his poetic development.

From then on, Auden's poetry began to take on more intimate and subjective overtones, often with religious themes. In 1941 he began attending the Anglican church regularly and experienced a renewal of religious faith. While his earlier poetry examined concrete social ills, his later poetry developed a more complex worldview, often focusing on spiritual aspects of society and casting social problems in terms of personal responsibility. His next major collection, *For the Time Being* (1944), includes the Christmas Oratorio "For the Time Being" and "The Sea and the Mirror," a poetic commentary on Shakespeare's *The Tempest* that explored Auden's ideas of poetry in the light of Christianity. With *The Collected Poetry* (1945), Auden began revising and retitling his earlier work, a task he would continue, almost compulsively, throughout his life.

In 1948, Auden was awarded the Pulitzer Prize for *The Age of Anxiety* (1947), a verse dialogue between four people in a New York bar. *The Shield of Achilles* (1955), which won the National Book Award, displays the influence of Anglo-Catholic theology and rituals, which Auden increasingly explored in verse. During these years he also wrote a considerable body of criticism and taught at various universities. In 1956 he became a Professor of Poetry at Oxford, where he gave three lectures per year for five years. These lectures, together with numerous reviews and essays, were collected in *The Dyer's Hand* (1962).

In his later years, with volumes such as *About the House* (1965) and *City Without Walls* (1969), Auden cemented his reputation as one of the leading poets of his day. After awarding him the National Medal for Literature in 1967, the National Book Committee declared that Auden's poetry "has illuminated our lives and times with grace, wit, and vitality. His work, branded by the moral and ideological fires of our age, breathes with eloquence, perception, and intellectual power." In 1972, seeking to return to a small community in which he could live peacefully as a writer, Auden accepted an honorary studentship at Christ Church, Oxford, his alma mater. He died there the following year. A final volume of poetry, *Thank You, Fog,* was published posthumously in 1974. Auden's careful attention to poetic form and meter, his sensitivity to language and to the music of words, and his concern with eternal questions of spirituality, love, and humanity's place in the world have all served to secure his current standing as one of the twentieth century's most significant poetic voices.

⌘ ⌘ ⌘

[O what is that sound]

O what is that sound which so thrills the ear
    Down in the valley drumming, drumming?
Only the scarlet soldiers, dear,
    The soldiers coming.

5 O what is that light I see flashing so clear
    Over the distance brightly, brightly?
Only the sun on their weapons, dear,
    As they step lightly.

O what are they doing with all that gear,
10   What are they doing this morning, this morning?
Only their usual manoeuvres, dear,
    Or perhaps a warning.

O why have they left the road down there,
    Why are they suddenly wheeling, wheeling?
15 Perhaps a change in their orders, dear.
    Why are you kneeling?

O haven't they stopped for the doctor's care,
    Haven't they reined their horses, their horses?
Why, they are none of them wounded, dear,
20   None of these forces.

O is it the parson they want, with white hair,
    Is it the parson, is it, is it?
No, they are passing his gateway, dear,
    Without a visit.

25 O it must be the farmer who lives so near.
    It must be the farmer so cunning, so cunning?
They have passed the farmyard already, dear,
    And now they are running.

O where are you going? Stay with me here!
30   Were the vows you swore deceiving, deceiving?
No, I promised to love you, dear,
    But I must be leaving.

O it's broken the lock and splintered the door,
    O it's the gate where they're turning, turning;
35 Their boots are heavy on the floor
    And their eyes are burning.
         —1934, 1945

[At last the secret is out]

At last the secret is out, as it always must come in
    the end,
The delicious story is ripe to tell to the intimate friend;
Over the tea-cups and into the square the tongue has
    its desire;
Still waters run deep, my dear, there's never smoke
    without fire.

5 Behind the corpse in the reservoir, behind the ghost
    on the links,[1]
Behind the lady who dances and the man who madly
    drinks,
Under the look of fatigue the attack of migraine and
    the sigh
There is always another story, there is more than
    meets the eye.

For the clear voice suddenly singing, high up in the
    convent wall,
10 The scent of the elder bushes, the sporting prints in
    the hall,
The croquet matches in summer, the handshake, the
    cough, the kiss,
There is always a wicked secret, a private reason for this.
         —1936

[Funeral Blues][2]

Stop all the clocks, cut off the telephone,
    Prevent the dog from barking with a juicy bone,
Silence the pianos and with muffled drum
Bring out the coffin, let the mourners come.

---

[1] *links* Undulating, sandy ground near a shore.

[2] [*Funeral Blues*] This poem first appeared, along with "At last the secret is out," in *The Ascent of F6*, a play co-written by Auden and Christopher Isherwood. It then appeared, in a revised version and with this present title, in Auden's 1940 collection *Another Time*.

5   Let aeroplanes circle moaning overhead
     Scribbling on the sky the message He Is Dead,
     Put crêpe bows[1] round the white necks of the public
          doves,
     Let the traffic policemen wear black cotton gloves.

     He was my North, my South, my East and West,
10   My working week and my Sunday rest,
     My noon, my midnight, my talk, my song;
     I thought that love would last for ever: I was wrong.

     The stars are not wanted now: put out every one;
     Pack up the moon and dismantle the sun;
15   Pour away the ocean and sweep up the wood;
     For nothing now can ever come to any good.
     —1936, 1940

Spain 1937[2]

Yesterday all the past. The language of size
Spreading to China along the trade-routes; the
     diffusion

Of the counting-frame and the cromlech;[3]
Yesterday the shadow-reckoning in the sunny climates.

5   Yesterday the assessment of insurance by cards,
     The divination of water; yesterday the invention
          Of cart-wheels and clocks, the taming of
     Horses; yesterday the bustling world of the navigators.

     Yesterday the abolition of fairies and giants;
10   The fortress like a motionless eagle eyeing the valley,
          The chapel built in the forest;
     Yesterday the carving of angels and of frightening
          gargoyles.

     The trial of heretics among the columns of stone;
     Yesterday the theological feuds in the taverns
15   And the miraculous cure at the fountain;
     Yesterday the Sabbath of Witches.[4] But today the
          struggle.

     Yesterday the installation of dynamos[5] and turbines;
     The construction of railways in the colonial desert;
          Yesterday the classic lecture
20   On the origin of Mankind. But today the struggle.

     Yesterday the belief in the absolute value of Greek;
     The fall of the curtain upon the death of a hero;
          Yesterday the prayer to the sunset,
     And the adoration of madmen. But today the struggle.

25   As the poet whispers, startled among the pines
     Or, where the loose waterfall sings, compact, or upright
          On the crag by the leaning tower:
     "O my vision. O send me the luck of the sailor."

     And the investigator peers through his instruments
30   At the inhuman provinces, the virile bacillus
          Or enormous Jupiter finished:
     "But the lives of my friends. I inquire, I inquire."

---

[1] *crêpe bows*   Black crepe, a woven fabric with a wrinkled surface, is the traditional fabric of mourning clothes.

[2] *Spain, 1937*   In the 1930s, Spain was a nation in which wealthy landowners and a conservative Roman Catholic Church hierarchy controlled much of society, and much inequality existed. The election of a left-of-center government in 1936 signaled a break with the past; the new government promised to enact a substantial program of land reform and a variety of other progressive changes. Almost immediately following the government's election, conservative forces began to plan its overthrow. An attempted coup was launched by army factions on 18 July 1936, but faced stiff resistance. This was the beginning of the Spanish Civil War, which ended with the victory of Francisco Franco's Nationalists—a Fascist party—and the installation of Franco as commander-in-chief and Head of State. Progressives, liberal democrats, communists, and anarchists from around the world were drawn to the Republican cause, and many came to Spain to fight with the forces loyal to the democratically elected government. On the other side the fascist dictatorships of Hitler in Germany, Mussolini in Italy, and Salazar in Portugal all provided support for Franco's army. Sympathetic to the Republicans, Auden went to Spain in January 1937 with a medical unit. He wrote this poem in March 1937, after he had returned to Britain, and had it printed as a separate pamphlet, the proceeds of which went to aid Spanish medical work.

[3] *cromlech*   Ancient Celtic stone structure.

[4] *Sabbath of Witches*   Nocturnal gathering of witches believed by medieval Christians to be a demonic orgy or a heretical parody of the Mass.

[5] *dynamos*   Machines that rotate copper wire coils in a magnetic field to convert mechanical into electrical energy.

And the poor in their fireless lodgings dropping the
    sheets
Of the evening paper: "Our day is our loss. O show us
35   History the operator, the
Organiser, Time the refreshing river."

And the nations combine each cry, invoking the life
That shapes the individual belly and orders
       The private nocturnal terror:
40 "Did you not found once the city state of the sponge,

"Raise the vast military empires of the shark
And the tiger, establish the robin's plucky
       canton?°   *territory*
       Intervene. O descend as a dove or
A furious papa or a mild engineer: but descend."

45 And the life, if it answers at all, replies from the heart
And the eyes and the lungs, from the shops and
       squares of the city:
       "O no, I am not the Mover,
Not today, not to you. To you I'm the

"Yes-man, the bar-companion, the easily-duped:
50 I am whatever you do; I am your vow to be
       Good, your humorous story;
I am your business voice; I am your marriage.

"What's your proposal? To build the Just City?[1] I will.
I agree. Or is it the suicide pact, the romantic
55   Death? Very well, I accept, for
I am your choice, your decision: yes, I am Spain."

Many have heard it on remote peninsulas,
On sleepy plains, in the aberrant fishermen's islands,
       In the corrupt heart of the city;
60 Have heard and migrated like gulls or the seeds of a
       flower.

They clung like burrs to the long expresses that lurch
Through the unjust lands, through the night, through
       the alpine tunnel;

       They floated over the oceans;
They walked the passes: they came to present their lives.

65 On that arid square, that fragment nipped off from hot
Africa, soldered so crudely to inventive Europe,
       On that tableland scored by rivers,
Our fever's menacing shapes are precise and alive.

To-morrow, perhaps, the future: the research on fatigue
70 And the movements of packers; the gradual exploring
       of all the
       Octaves of radiation;
To-morrow the enlarging of consciousness by diet and
       breathing.

To-morrow the rediscovery of romantic love;
The photographing of ravens; all the fun under
75   Liberty's masterful shadow;
To-morrow the hour of the pageant-master and the
       musician.

To-morrow, for the young, the poets exploding like
       bombs,
The walks by the lake, the winter of perfect communion;
       To-morrow the bicycle races
80 Through the suburbs on summer evenings: but today
       the struggle.

To-day the inevitable increase in the chances of death;
The conscious acceptance of guilt in the fact of murder;
       To-day the expending of powers
On the flat ephemeral pamphlet and the boring meeting.

85 To-day the makeshift consolations; the shared cigarette;
The cards in the candle-lit barn and the scraping concert,
       The masculine jokes; today the
Fumbled and unsatisfactory embrace before hurting.

The stars are dead; the animals will not look:
90 We are left alone with our day, and the time is short and
       History to the defeated
May say Alas but cannot help or pardon.
    —1937

---

[1] *the Just City* In Plato's *Republic*, Socrates discusses what is required to make a just city, and recommends rule by a "philosopher-king."

[*Lullaby*]

Lay your sleeping head, my love,
  Human on my faithless arm;
Time and fevers burn away
Individual beauty from
5 Thoughtful children, and the grave
Proves the child ephemeral:
But in my arms till break of day
Let the living creature lie,
Mortal, guilty, but to me
10 The entirely beautiful.

Soul and body have no bounds:
To lovers as they lie upon
Her tolerant enchanted slope
In their ordinary swoon,
15 Grave the vision Venus[1] sends
Of supernatural sympathy,
Universal love and hope;
While an abstract insight wakes
Among the glaciers and the rocks
20 The hermit's carnal ecstasy.

Certainty, fidelity
On the stroke of midnight pass
Like vibrations of a bell,
And fashionable madmen raise
25 Their pedantic boring cry:
Every farthing of the cost,
All the dreaded cards foretell,
Shall be paid, but from this night
Not a whisper, not a thought,
30 Not a kiss nor look be lost.

Beauty, midnight, vision dies:
Let the winds of dawn that blow
Softly round your dreaming head
Such a day of sweetness show
5 Eye and knocking heart may bless,
Find the mortal world enough;
Noons of dryness see you fed
By the involuntary powers,
Nights of insult let you pass

40 Watched by every human love.
—1937

[*As I walked out one evening*]

As I walked out one evening,
  Walking down Bristol Street,
The crowds upon the pavement
  Were fields of harvest wheat.

5 And down by the brimming river
  I heard a lover sing
Under an arch of the railway:
  "Love has no ending.

"I'll love you, dear, I'll love you
10 Till China and Africa meet,
And the river jumps over the mountain
  And the salmon sing in the street,

"I'll love you till the ocean
  Is folded and hung up to dry
15 And the seven stars[2] go squawking
  Like geese about the sky.

"The years shall run like rabbits,
  For in my arms I hold
The Flower of the Ages,
20 And the first love of the world."

But all the clocks in the city
  Began to whirr and chime:
"O let not Time deceive you,
  You cannot conquer Time.

25 "In the burrows of the Nightmare
  Where Justice naked is,
Time watches from the shadow
  And coughs when you would kiss.

"In headaches and in worry
30 Vaguely life leaks away,

---

1 *Venus* Roman goddess of beauty and love, mother of Cupid.

2 *seven stars* Pleiades, seven daughters of Atlas who, according to Greek mythology, were transformed into stars by Zeus.

And Time will have his fancy
    To-morrow or to-day.

"Into many a green valley
    Drifts the appalling snow;
35 Time breaks the threaded dances
    And the diver's brilliant bow.

"O plunge your hands in water,
    Plunge them in up to the wrist;
Stare, stare in the basin
40   And wonder what you've missed.

"The glacier knocks in the cupboard,
    The desert sighs in the bed,
And the crack in the tea-cup opens
    A lane to the land of the dead.

45 "Where the beggars raffle the banknotes
    And the Giant is enchanting to Jack,[1]
And the Lily-white Boy is a Roarer,[2]
    And Jill goes down on her back.

"O look, look in the mirror,
50   O look in your distress:
Life remains a blessing
    Although you cannot bless.

"O stand, stand at the window
    As the tears scald and start;
55 You shall love your crooked neighbour
    With your crooked heart."

It was late, late in the evening,
    The lovers they were gone;
The clocks had ceased their chiming,
60   And the deep river ran on.
      —1938

---

[1] *Giant ... Jack* Auden alters the story of Jack and the Beanstalk.

[2] *Lily-white ... Roarer* Allusion to the English folk song, "Green Grow the Rushes, O": "Two, two lily-white boys / Clothed all in green, O." A "roarer" is a riotous or disorderly person.

Musée des Beaux Arts[3]

About suffering they were never wrong,
  The Old Masters: how well they understood
Its human position; how it takes place
While someone else is eating or opening a window or
    just walking dully along;
5 How, when the aged are reverently, passionately waiting
For the miraculous birth, there always must be
Children who did not specially want it to happen,
    skating
On a pond at the edge of the wood:
They never forgot
10 That even the dreadful martyrdom must run its course
Anyhow in a corner, some untidy spot
Where the dogs go on with their doggy life and the
    torturer's horse
Scratches its innocent behind on a tree.

In Brueghel's *Icarus*, for instance: how everything
    turns away
15 Quite leisurely from the disaster;[4] the ploughman may
Have heard the splash, the forsaken cry,
But for him it was not an important failure; the sun
    shone
As it had to on the white legs disappearing into the
    green
Water; and the expensive delicate ship that must have
    seen
20 Something amazing, a boy falling out of the sky,
Had somewhere to get to and sailed calmly on.
    —1939, 1940

---

[3] *Musée des Beaux Arts* The Royal Museum of Fine Arts in Brussels owns several paintings by Flemish painter Pieter Brueghel (1525–69), including *Landscape with the Fall of Icarus*. According to Greek myth, Icarus and his father, Daedalus, escaped from the island of Crete, where they were imprisoned, by constructing wings with feathers and wax. Icarus flew too close to the sun, however, and the wax of his wings melted, causing him to plummet into the sea.

[4] *how everything ... disaster* In Brueghel's painting, a shepherd, a farmer, and a fisher carry on with their respective jobs, ignoring Icarus's legs disappearing into the water in the picture's lower right corner.

In Memory of W. B. Yeats[1]
(d. Jan. 1939)

1

He disappeared in the dead of winter:
The brooks were frozen, the airports almost
    deserted,
And snow disfigured the public statues;
The mercury sank in the mouth of the dying day.
5 O all the instruments agree[2]
The day of his death was a dark cold day.

Far from his illness
The wolves ran on through the evergreen forests,
The peasant river was untempted by the fashionable
    quays;
10 By mourning tongues
The death of the poet was kept from his poems.

But for him it was his last afternoon as himself,
An afternoon of nurses and rumours;
The provinces of his body revolted,
15 The squares of his mind were empty,
Silence invaded the suburbs,
The current of his feeling failed: he became his
    admirers.

Now he is scattered among a hundred cities
And wholly given over to unfamiliar affections;
20 To find his happiness in another kind of wood
And be punished under a foreign code of conscience.
The words of a dead man
Are modified in the guts of the living.

But in the importance and noise of to-morrow
25 When the brokers are roaring like beasts on the floor
    of the Bourse,[3]
And the poor have the sufferings to which they are
    fairly accustomed,
And each in the cell of himself is almost convinced of
    his freedom;

A few thousand will think of this day
As one thinks of a day when one did something
    slightly unusual.
30 O all the instruments agree
The day of his death was a dark cold day.

2

You were silly like us: your gift survived it all;
The parish of rich women, physical decay,
Yourself. Mad Ireland hurt you into poetry.
35 Now Ireland has her madness and her weather still,
For poetry makes nothing happen: it survives
In the valley of its saying where executives
Would never want to tamper, flows on south
From ranches of isolation and the busy griefs,
40 Raw towns that we believe and die in; it survives,
A way of happening, a mouth.

3

Earth, receive an honoured guest;
William Yeats is laid to rest:
Let the Irish vessel lie
45 Emptied of its poetry.

Time that is intolerant
Of the brave and innocent,
And indifferent in a week
To a beautiful physique,

50 Worships language and forgives
Everyone by whom it lives;
Pardons cowardice, conceit,
Lays its honours at their feet.

Time that with this strange excuse
55 Pardoned Kipling and his views,[4]
And will pardon Paul Claudel,[5]
Pardons him for writing well.

In the nightmare of the dark
All the dogs of Europe bark,

---

1 *W.B. Yeats* Irish poet William Butler Yeats (1865–1939).

2 *O all … agree* Auden later changed this line to read "What instruments we have agree."

3 *Bourse* Paris Stock Exchange.

4 *Kipling … views* Rudyard Kipling (1865–1936) was an Indian-born English writer whose work often celebrated imperialism.

5 *Paul Claudel* French-Catholic poet, playwright, and diplomat (1868–1955) who was widely criticized for supporting Franco's fascist insurgency in the Spanish Civil War.

60 And the living nations wait,
Each sequestered in its hate;

Intellectual disgrace
Stares from every human face,
And the seas of pity lie
65 Locked and frozen in each eye.

Follow, poet, follow right
To the bottom of the night,
With your unconstraining voice
Still persuade us to rejoice;

70 With the farming of a verse
Make a vineyard of the curse,
Sing of human unsuccess
In a rapture of distress;

In the deserts of the heart
75 Let the healing fountain start,
In the prison of his days
Teach the free man how to praise.

—1939

September 1, 1939[1]

I sit in one of the dives
On Fifty-Second Street
Uncertain and afraid
As the clever hopes expire
5 Of a low dishonest decade:
Waves of anger and fear
Circulate over the bright
And darkened lands of the earth,
Obsessing our private lives;
10 The unmentionable odour of death
Offends the September night.

Accurate scholarship can
Unearth the whole offence
From Luther[2] until now

15 That has driven a culture mad,
Find what occurred at Linz,[3]
What huge imago[4] made
A psychopathic god:
I and the public know
20 What all schoolchildren learn,
Those to whom evil is done
Do evil in return.

Exiled Thucydides[5] knew
All that a speech can say
25 About Democracy,
And what dictators do,
The elderly rubbish they talk
To an apathetic grave;
Analysed all in his book,
30 The enlightenment driven away,
The habit-forming pain,
Mismanagement and grief:
We must suffer them all again.

Into this neutral air
35 Where blind skyscrapers use
Their full height to proclaim
The strength of Collective Man,
Each language pours its vain
Competitive excuse:
40 But who can live for long
In an euphoric dream;
Out of the mirror they stare,
Imperialism's face
And the international wrong.

markedly more anti-Semitic as he aged; in *Mein Kampf,* Hitler ranks Martin Luther as one of three great German cultural heroes, along with Frederick the Great and Richard Wagner.

[3] *Linz* Town in Austria in which Hitler grew up; he returned in 1938 to announce Germany's annexation of Austria.

[4] *imago* According to psychiatrist and founder of analytical psychology C.G. Jung (1875–1961), an idealized image of a person formed in childhood.

[5] *Thucydides* Greek historian and general (c. 460–c. 400 BCE) and author of *The History of the Peloponnesian War* who was exiled at the war's end for failing to prevent the surrender of Amphipolis to the Spartans. One of the speeches in Thucydides's *History,* Pericles's funeral oration for the dead Athenian soldiers, outlines the dangers and benefits of democracy. Elected 16 times to the position of general, Pericles instituted many democratic reforms while retaining a significant degree of personal power.

[1] *September 1, 1939* Date of Hitler's invasion of Poland; Britain and France declared war on Germany two days later. Auden had moved to New York in January 1939.

[2] *Luther* Martin Luther (1483–1546), German monk whose attempts to reform the Catholic Church were instrumental in bringing about the Protestant Reformation. Luther's writings grew

45 Faces along the bar
Cling to their average day:
The lights must never go out,
The music must always play,
All the conventions conspire
50 To make this fort assume
The furniture of home;
Lest we should see where we are,
Lost in a haunted wood,
Children afraid of the night
55 Who have never been happy or good.

The windiest militant trash
Important Persons shout
Is not so crude as our wish:
What mad Nijinsky wrote
60 About Diaghilev[1]
Is true of the normal heart;
For the error bred in the bone
Of each woman and each man
Craves what it cannot have,
65 Not universal love
But to be loved alone.

From the conservative dark
Into the ethical life
The dense commuters come,
70 Repeating their morning vow,
"I *will* be true to the wife,
I'll concentrate more on my work,"
And helpless governors wake
To resume their compulsory game:
75 Who can release them now,
Who can reach the deaf,
Who can speak for the dumb?

All I have is a voice
To undo the folded lie,
80 The romantic lie in the brain
Of the sensual man-in-the-street

And the lie of Authority
Whose buildings grope the sky:
There is no such thing as the State
85 And no one exists alone;
Hunger allows no choice
To the citizen of the police;
We must love one another or die.[2]

Defenceless under the night
90 Our world in stupor lies;
Yet, dotted everywhere,
Ironic points of light
Flash out wherever the Just
Exchange their messages:
95 May I, composed like them
Of Eros[3] and of dust,
Beleaguered by the same
Negation and despair,
Show an affirming flame.
—1939

from *The Sea and the Mirror*

[Song of the Master and Boatswain][4]

At Dirty Dick's and Sloppy Joe's
We drank our liquor straight,
Some went upstairs with Margery,
And some, alas, with Kate;

---

[1] *Nijinsky … Diaghilev* Vaslav Nijinsky (1890–1950), Russian ballet dancer and choreographer who was diagnosed with schizophrenia in 1919. In 1936, Nijinsky's wife published a heavily edited version of her husband's 1919 diary, in which he said of his former lover, founder of the Ballets Russes Sergei Pavlovich Diaghilev, "Some politicians are hypocrites like Diaghilev, who does not want universal love, but to be loved alone."

[2] *All I have … die* In a revised edition of this poem, printed in *The Collected Poetry of W.H. Auden* (1945), this stanza is removed.

[3] *Eros* In contrast to The New Testament *agape*, or Christian love, *eros* represents earthly, or sexual love. In Greek myth, the winged Eros, son of Aphrodite, is the god of love.

[4] *Song … Boatswain* Auden's *The Sea and the Mirror* is a poetic response to Shakespeare's *The Tempest*. "The Master and Boatswain" refers to the prostitutes mentioned by a drunken Stephano in 2.2.46–54:
The master, the swabber, the boatswain, and I,
The gunner and his mate,
Loved Mall, Meg, and Marian, and Margery,
But none of us cared for Kate;
For she had a tongue with a tang,
Would cry to a sailor, "Go hang!"
She loved not the savour of tar nor of pitch,
Yet a tailor might scratch her where e'er she did itch.
Then to sea, boys, and let her go hang!

5 And two by two like cat and mouse
The homeless played at keeping house.

There Wealthy Meg, the Sailor's Friend,
   And Marion, cow-eyed,
Opened their arms to me but I
10   Refused to step inside;
I was not looking for a cage
In which to mope in my old age.

The nightingales[1] are sobbing in
   The orchards of our mothers,
15 And hearts that we broke long ago
   Have long been breaking others;
Tears are round, the sea is deep:
Roll them overboard and sleep.

—1944

The Shield of Achilles[2]

S he looked over his shoulder
   For vines and olive trees,
Marble well-governed cities
   And ships upon untamed seas,
5 But there on the shining metal
   His hands had put instead
An artificial wilderness
   And a sky like lead.

A plain without a feature, bare and brown,
10   No blade of grass, no sign of neighborhood,
Nothing to eat and nowhere to sit down,

Yet, congregated on its blankness, stood
   An unintelligible multitude,
A million eyes, a million boots in line,
15 Without expression, waiting for a sign.

Out of the air a voice without a face
   Proved by statistics that some cause was just
In tones as dry and level as the place:
   No one was cheered and nothing was discussed;
20   Column by column in a cloud of dust
They marched away enduring a belief
Whose logic brought them, somewhere else, to grief.

She looked over his shoulder
   For ritual pieties,
25 White flower-garlanded heifers,
   Libation and sacrifice,[3]
But there on the shining metal
   Where the altar should have been,
She saw by his flickering forge-light
30   Quite another scene.

Barbed wire enclosed an arbitrary spot
   Where bored officials lounged (one cracked a joke)
And sentries sweated for the day was hot:
   A crowd of ordinary decent folk
35   Watched from without and neither moved nor spoke
As three pale figures were led forth and bound
To three posts driven upright in the ground.

The mass and majesty of this world, all
   That carries weight and always weighs the same
40 Lay in the hands of others; they were small
   And could not hope for help and no help came:
   What their foes liked to do was done, their shame
Was all the worst could wish; they lost their pride
And died as men before their bodies died.

45 She looked over his shoulder
   For athletes at their games,
Men and women in a dance
   Moving their sweet limbs

---

[1] *nightingales* In Greek myth, Philomela, the daughter of the king of Athens, was transformed into a nightingale after being raped by her brother-in-law, Tereus, King of Thrace, who had cut out her tongue to prevent her from talking. A "nightingale" is also a slang term for a prostitute.

[2] *The Shield of Achilles* Achilles, a Greek hero in Homer's *Iliad*, was a fierce warrior who chose the glory of an honourable death at Troy instead of a long and comfortable life. Book 18 of the Iliad recounts the story of Achilles's shield, wrought by Hephaestus, the lame god of fire and metals, at the request of Achilles's sea-nymph mother, Thetis. Achilles had lost his armor after lending it to Patroclus, who was later killed by the Trojan commander, Hector. Achilles's new shield depicted the earth, heavens, sun, moon, and stars, as well as scenes of agriculture, a bountiful harvest, and two cities, all encircled by the ocean.

[3] *She looked … sacrifice* See John Keats's "Ode on a Grecian Urn" 31-4: "Who are these coming to the sacrifice? / To what green altar, o mysterious priest, / Lead'st thou that heifer lowing at the skies, / And all her silken flanks with garlands drest?"

Quick, quick, to music,
50   But there on the shining shield
His hands had set no dancing-floor
            But a weed-choked field.

A ragged urchin, aimless and alone,
        Loitered about that vacancy; a bird
55 Flew up to safety from his well-aimed stone:
        That girls are raped, that two boys knife a third,
        Were axioms to him, who'd never heard
Of any world where promises were kept,
Or one could weep because another wept.

60   The thin-lipped armourer,
                Hephaestos, hobbled away,
            Thetis of the shining breasts
                Cried out in dismay
            At what the god had wrought
65   To please her son, the strong
            Iron-hearted man-slaying Achilles
                Who would not live long.

—1952

"The Truest Poetry is the Most Feigning"
(for Edgar Wind)[1]

By all means sing of love but, if you do,
    Please make a rare old proper hullabaloo:
When ladies ask *How much do you love me?*
The Christian answer is *così-così*;[2]
5 But poets are not celibate divines:
Had Dante[3] said so, who would read his lines?
Be subtle, various, ornamental, clever,
And do not listen to those critics ever
Whose crude provincial gullets crave in books
10 Plain cooking made still plainer by plain cooks,[4]

As though the Muse[5] preferred her half-wit sons;
Good poets have a weakness for bad puns.

Suppose your Beatrice be, as usual, late,
And you would tell us how it feels to wait,
15 You're free to think, what may be even true,
You're so in love that one hour seems like two,
But write—*As I sat waiting for her call,*
Each second longer darker seemed than all
(Something like this but more elaborate still)
20 *Those raining centuries it took to fill*
That quarry whence Endymion's[6] *Love was torn*;
From such ingenious fibs are poems born.
Then, should she leave you for some other guy,
Or ruin you with debts, or go and die,
25 No metaphor, remember, can express
A real historical unhappiness;
Your tears have value if they make us gay;
O Happy Grief! is all sad verse can say.

The living girl's your business (some odd sorts
30 Have been an inspiration to men's thoughts):
Yours may be old enough to be your mother,
Or have one leg that's shorter than the other,
Or play Lacrosse or do the Modern Dance,
To you that's destiny, to us it's chance;
35 We cannot love your love till she take on,
Through you, the wonders of a paragon.
Sing her triumphant passage to our land,
The sun her footstool, the moon in her right hand,
And seven planets blazing in her hair,
40 Queen of the Night and Empress of the Air;
Tell how her fleet by nine king swans is led,
Wild geese write magic letters overhead
And hippocampi[7] follow in her wake

---

1 *The Truest … Feigning* Touchstone's words to Audrey in Shakespeare's *As You Like It*, 3.3.19–20; *Edgar Wind* Renaissance scholar and friend of Auden's.

2 *così-così* Italian: so-so.

3 *Dante* Dante Alighieri (1265–1321), Italian poet famed in part for the depth of his devotion to his muse, Beatrice.

4 *Plain cooking … cooks* Auden reworks a quotation by the well-known British cookery writer of the 1930s and 1940s, Countess Morphy: "Plain cooking cannot be entrusted to plain cooks."

5 *Muse* One of nine daughters of Zeus and Mnemosyne, each of whom presided over and provided inspiration for an aspect of the arts and sciences.

6 *Endymion* Beautiful shepherd youth who attracted the attention of the moon goddess, Selene; she begged Zeus to grant her lover one wish. Endymion chose eternal sleep, by which he would remain forever youthful. Endymion is the subject of Keats's long poem *Endymion: A Poetic Romance* (1818).

7 *hippocampi* Fish-tailed horses of the ocean who carried the sea gods.

With Amphisboene,[1] gentle for her sake;
45 Sing her descent on the exulting shore
To bless the vines and put an end to war.

If half-way through such praises of your dear,
Riot and shooting fill the streets with fear,
And overnight as in some terror dream
50 Poets are suspect with the New Regime,
Stick at your desk and hold your panic in,
What you are writing may still save your skin:
Re-sex the pronouns, add a few details,
And, lo, a panegyric ode which hails
55 (How is the Censor, bless his heart, to know?)
The new pot-bellied Generalissimo.
Some epithets, of course, like *lily-breasted*
Need modifying to, say, *lion-chested*,
A title *Goddess of wry-necks*[2] *and wrens*
60 To *Great Reticulator*[3] of the fens,
But in an hour your poem qualifies
For a State pension or His annual prize,

And you will die in bed (which He will not:
That public nuisance will be hanged or shot).
65 Though honest Iagos,[4] true to form, will write
Shame! in your margins, *Toady! Hypocrite!*
True hearts, clear heads will hear the note of glory
And put inverted commas round the story.
Thinking—*Old Sly-boots! We shall never know*
70 *Her name or nature. Well, it's better so.*

For given Man, by birth, by education,
Imago Dei[5] who forgot his station,
The self-made creature who himself unmakes,
The only creature ever made who fakes,
75 With no more nature in his loving smile
Than in his theories of a natural style,
What but tall tales, the luck of verbal playing,
Can trick his lying nature into saying
That love, or truth in any serious sense,
80 Like orthodoxy, is a reticence?
—1954

---

[1] *Amphisboene* Winged Greek serpents with two legs, glowing eyes, and heads on either ends of their bodies, who were known for swiftness and cunning.

[2] *wry-necks* Members of the woodpecker family.

[3] *Reticulator* One who divides or marks in such a way as to render a network.

[4] *honest Iagos* In Shakespeare's *Othello* the spiteful and jealous "honest Iago" convinces Othello that his innocent wife, Desdemona, is having an affair.

[5] *Imago Dei* Latin: image of God.

―――――――――

In Context

Auden on the Nature and Craft of Poetry

Auden's writings about poetry—many of which are collected in *The Dyer's Hand and Other Essays*—offer a remarkable range of insights into the nature of poetry as well as into his own work. The following passages are excerpted from one of the most wide-ranging of those essays.

from "Writing" (1962)

... The intellect of man is forced to choose
Perfection of the life or of the work. (YEATS)

This is untrue; perfection is possible in neither. All one can say is that a writer who, like all men, has his personal weaknesses and limitations, should be aware of them and try his best to keep them out of his work. For every writer, there are certain subjects which, because of defects in his character and his talent, he should never touch.

What makes it difficult for a poet not to tell lies is that, in poetry, all facts and all beliefs cease to be true or false and become interesting possibilities. The reader does not have to share the beliefs expressed in a poem in order to enjoy it. Knowing this, a poet is constantly tempted to make use of an idea or a belief, not because he believes it to be true, but because he sees it has interesting poetic possibilities. It may not, perhaps, be absolutely necessary that he *believe* it, but it is certainly necessary that his emotions be deeply involved, and this they can never be unless, as a man, he takes it more seriously than as a mere poetic convenience.

The integrity of a writer is more threatened by appeals to his social conscience, his political or religious convictions, than by appeals to his cupidity.[1] It is morally less confusing to be goosed by a traveling salesman than by a bishop. Some writers confuse authenticity, which they ought always to aim at, with originality, which they should never bother about. There is a certain kind of person who is so dominated by the desire to be loved for himself alone that he has constantly to test those around him by tiresome behavior; what he says and does must be admired, not because it is intrinsically admirable, but because it is *his* remark, *his* act. Does not this explain a good deal of avant-garde art?

... Rhymes, meters, stanza forms, etc., are like servants. If the master is fair enough to win their affection and firm enough to command their respect, the result is an orderly happy household. If he is too tyrannical, they give notice; if he lacks authority, they become slovenly, impertinent, drunk and dishonest.

The poet who writes "free" verse is like Robinson Crusoe on his desert island: he must do all his cooking, laundry, and darning for himself. In a few exceptional cases, this manly independence produces something original and impressive, but more often the result is squalor—dirty sheets on the unmade bed and empty bottles on the unswept floor.

There are some poets, Kipling[2] for example, whose relation to language reminds one of a drill sergeant: the words are taught to wash behind their ears, stand properly at attention and execute complicated maneuvers, but at the cost of never being allowed to think for themselves. There are

―――――――――

[1] *cupidity*　Desire for wealth.

[2] *Kipling*　English author Rudyard Kipling (1865–1936).

others, Swinburne, for example, who remind one more of Svengali:[1] under their hypnotic suggestion, an extraordinary performance is put on, not by raw recruits, but by feeble-minded schoolchildren. ...

The difference between verse and prose is self-evident but it is a sheer waste of time to look for a definition of the difference between poetry and prose. Frost's[2] definition of poetry as the untranslatable element in language looks plausible at first sight but, on closer examination, will not quite do. In the first place, even in the most rarefied poetry, there are some elements which are translatable. The sound of the words, their rhythmical relations, and all meanings and association of meanings which depend upon sound, like rhymes and puns, are, of course, untranslatable, but poetry is not, like music, pure sound. Any elements in a poem which are not based on verbal experience are, to some degree, translatable into another tongue, for example, images, similes, and metaphors which are drawn from sensory experience. ...

Poetry is not magic. In so far as poetry, or any other of the arts, can be said to have an ulterior purpose, it is, by telling the truth, to disenchant and disintoxicate.

"The unacknowledged legislators of the world"[3] describes the secret police, not the poets.

Catharsis is properly effected, not by works of art, but by religious rites. It is also effected, usually improperly, by bullfights, professional football matches, bad movies, military bands, and monster rallies at which ten thousand Girl Guides form themselves into a model of the national flag.

The condition of mankind is, and always has been, so miserable and depraved that, if anyone were to say to the poet: "For God's sake stop singing and do something useful like putting on the kettle or fetching bandages," what just reason could he give for refusing? But nobody says this. The self-appointed unqualified nurse says: "You are to sing the patient a song which will make him believe that I, and I alone, can cure him. If you can't or won't, I shall confiscate your passport and send you to the mines." And the poor patient in his delirium cries: "Please sing me a song which will give me sweet dreams instead of nightmares. If you succeed, I will give you a penthouse in New York or a ranch in Arizona."

---

[1] *Swinburne* Victorian poet Algernon Charles Swinburne (1837–1909); *Svengali* Notorious hypnotist in George Du Maurier's novel *Trilby* (1894).

[2] *Frost* American poet Robert Frost (1874–1963).

[3] *The unacknowledged ... world* From Percy Shelley's description of poets in his *Defense of Poetry* (1820).

The Late Twentieth Century and Beyond: 1945 to the Twenty-First Century

The End of the War and the Coming of the Welfare State

Winston Churchill had inspired the nation—many said saved the nation—in the dark days of 1940, and remained over the following five years, by all accounts, one of the greatest war leaders in British history. Yet in 1945, the electorate unceremoniously dumped him and the Conservative party from office, and installed the Labour Party under Clement Attlee in its place. Much as people were grateful to Churchill for his leadership in the war effort, he was seen very much as war leader and a figure of the past at a time at which people felt strongly that they had fought not so much to preserve the world of the past as for their right to make a better world.[1] All too clearly, voters had seen that Churchill's fondest wish at the end of the war was to return to the peacetime Britain of earlier days—a Britain with a vast Empire abroad and a rigid class system at home. Unlike the Prime Minister, at war's end the British people were increasingly seeing Imperial possessions as a drain on the nation's scarce resources, and the class system as an impediment to prosperity and an affront to notions of equality. With remarkably little fanfare, the old British world of masters and servants had already largely disappeared, but its husk still gave shape to many social attitudes; it remained almost impossibly difficult to "get ahead" if one came from a working-class background and had the "wrong accent," one could never be fully accepted in many social milieus if one's background was "in trade," and so on.

Quite aside from the issue of increasingly anachronistic social attitudes, the working class and the lower middle class continued to face great obstacles simply in their daily physical existence. For many, conditions at the end of World War II were little better than they had been at the end of World War I; with its calls to redistribute wealth and to engage the forces of government throughout the economy on behalf of general good, Labour represented a real change. And unquestionably, the various measures enacted by the Attlee government (many of them following on the recommendations of the 1942 and 1944 Reports to Parliament of William Beveridge) made Britain a much fairer society than she had been at any time previously in her history. The new initiatives included the establishment of the National Health Service and the National Insurance Act, which provided a measure of protection against poverty resulting from unemployment—or indeed from any other source.

If British life became more egalitarian during the Attlee years, however, much of what was being shared was still hardship. In a fifty-years-on retrospective, Doug Saunders memorably summarized the situation in postwar Britain:

> Food rationing during the war was bad. After the war it was terrible. Posters were put up reading "Eat Less Bread: Eat Potatoes Instead." Then, in the spring of 1946, those posters went down: there was no bread at all. ... Coal supplies were cut back to almost nil, so that in the winter of 1947, the coldest in British history, people were ordered not to heat their homes. ... If the economies and buildings and cities were fractured, even worse damage was done to families. About four million children had been shipped away from their parents to unknown locations and with almost no contact, for years. Children and parents alike returned from the war to find things utterly different. ... Susan Goodman, who was ten years old at the end of the war, had

---

[1] Churchill might still have been elected had it not been for his veer to the extreme ideological right during the course of the campaign. Apparently strongly influenced by having read F.A. Hayek's polemic against socialism, in his speech on 4 June 1945 Churchill likened Britain's Labour Party to Hitler's secret police, suggesting that no Labour government "could afford to allow free expression of public discontent.... They would have to fall back on some sort of Gestapo." That speech is excerpted in a "Contexts" section elsewhere in this volume.

lived in the countryside, with her mother in London and her father in the armed forces. She recalls the moment when "this man got off the train—he was very tall and very yellow. He came up and said, 'Hello Sue, I'm Daddy,' and I put out my hand and said 'How do you do.' It was not auspicious."

Even into the 1950s, food and fuel shortages persisted—and as the hardships continued, people grew as tired of Attlee and Labour as they had been of Churchill and the Conservatives in 1945. With the 1950 election Churchill was returned to office, and he presided over a period of relative calm from 1950 to 1955. In terms of the ideological direction of the nation, however, it was the election of 1945 that had represented the great turning point. From the late 1940s through to the late 1970s, periods of Labour rule (first under Attlee, later under Prime Ministers Harold Wilson and James Callaghan) alternated with periods of Conservative rule (first under Churchill again, later under Prime Ministers Harold Macmillan and Edward Heath). Under Labour, the growth of what came to be known as the "welfare state" was fostered, while under the Conservatives, the social activism of Labour was eschewed—but even while the Conservatives were in power, little attempt was made to dismantle the structures through which Labour was attempting to reshape British society; for thirty years the domestic agenda for Britain remained one of building a more egalitarian society.

If the political shape of the 1950s, 1960s, and 1970s in Britain has something of a unity to it, the same cannot be said for the shape of its economic and cultural life over that period. Britain recovered far more slowly economically after World War II than did North America and many other parts of the world. The 1950s in North America are thought of as years of contentment in the midst of robust economic growth. Not so in Britain; for many, through much of that decade British life remained dreary and unsatisfying. The major literary movement of the era—the writings of the so-called "angry young men"—represented a reaction against the dreariness and lack of opportunity that characterized so much of British life. John Osborne's play *Look Back in Anger* (1956), which depicted the struggles of the rebellious Jimmy Porter,

Wartime rationing in Montreal, 1942. Unlike in Britain, hardships on the home front ended soon after the war in countries such as Canada and Australia.

The "London fog" for which the city became famous in the nineteenth and twentieth centuries was primarily created by air pollution. From December 1953 to March 1954, conditions became worse than ever, and there were more than 12,000 smog-related deaths. Since the 1950s air (and water) quality in London has improved dramatically as a result of anti-pollution measures.

became the touchstone in discussions of the movement, but works of prose fiction such as John Braine's *Room at the Top* (1957) and Alan Sillitoe's *Saturday Night and Sunday Morning* (1958) and *The Loneliness of the Long Distance Runner* (1959), which also dealt with the conflicts and resentments of young working-class or lower middle-class males struggling to get on in society, had almost as great an impact.

Two other writers—Kingsley Amis and Philip Larkin—were initially often mentioned in the same breath as Osborne and Sillitoe, but even in the 1950s these two were on quite different literary paths, and in the 1960s and 1970s, their work diverged even further both from that of angry young men and from each other's (though the two remained lifelong friends). With *Lucky Jim* (1954), a social satire about class distinctions, romantic bungling, and university life, Amis achieved literary celebrity at an early age. His subsequent novels were written in a similar vein—social satire bordering on farce—but as the years went on, the humor was tinged more with bitterness than with insight, and was discolored by misogyny. Larkin, too, tried his hand early on in his career with social satire— *A Girl in Winter* (1947) being the more notable of his two novels—but with Larkin, the satire was more gentle, and did not sit entirely at ease with his evident aim of achieving a high degree of psychological realism. It was as a poet that Larkin made a lasting mark; poetry turned out to be the perfect medium for his unique variety of psychological understanding, his sometimes wry biting wit, and his bleak honesty about old age and death. Like Amis, Larkin had his share of bitter and misogynist feelings (as his posthumously-published letters revealed), but these are far less obtrusive in his work than they are in that of Amis, and where Amis's work became more coarse and superficial over the years, Larkin's became more varied, more resonant, and more memorable. In its subject matter but also in its form, Larkin's poetry was quite out of step with the vast majority of British poetry published in the second half of the twentieth century; almost all his poems are built on a foundation of accentual syllabic meter, and most have a regular rhyme scheme. Yet they found a remarkably large audience; his final book, *High Windows*, made some British best seller lists in 1974.

Increasingly, critics and literary historians are coming to regard Larkin as the most important British poet of the second half of the twentieth century.

Another quite different group of writers might with equal appropriateness be described as "angry young men": those who emigrated to Britain from her overseas possessions. Particularly prominent were immigrants from the Caribbean; large numbers were recruited from Jamaica, Trinidad, and other Caribbean islands in the decade following World War II to help rebuild Britain's bombed-out cities. Though they made a real contribution to that rebuilding, they were often treated as second-class citizens, discriminated against in virtually every public sphere; the reaction was a series of race riots, beginning in the late 1950s.

The Caribbean-led wave of immigration in the postwar years was the beginning of a movement that would transform Britain demographically and culturally. Amongst their number were many of the founding voices of what would become known as post-colonial literature, including Samuel Selvon, George Lamming, and Derek Walcott. From the beginning, they wrote largely in opposition to (rather than within) British literary traditions; this was the beginning of the literary movement that Salman Rushdie memorably characterized a few decades later with the phrase, "The Empire writes back."

The important women writers from this period were far less angry in their work than their male counterparts —though doubtless they had at least as much cause to be. The novels of Iris Murdoch, of Muriel Spark, and of Doris Lessing work with vastly different settings and story materials, ranging from the story of the life of a school mistress at a girls' boarding school in Spark's *The Prime of Miss Jean Brodie* to a philosophically tinged exploration of faith and moral imagination in Iris Murdoch's *The Bell* (1958) to an evocation of the gritty edges of colonial existence in Southern Rhodesia in Lessing's *The Grass is Singing* (1950). Almost all are written in the vein of social or psychological realism— and most have something of an ethos of stoicism in the face of adversity. As a character in Murdoch's *Under the Net* (1954) puts it, "one must just blunder on. Truth lies in blundering on."

THE END OF EMPIRE

If in the generation following World War II, the Conservatives came to accept many of the egalitarian social principles in which Labour believed, they also came to accept that the old approach to Empire was no longer workable. Britain's stature as a world power suffered serious damage during the Suez crisis of 1956, when it attempted unsuccessfully to block the nationalization by Egypt of the Suez Canal, and it suffered as well in the face of increasing resistance to Imperial rule in British colonies. (Perhaps most notably, the Mau Mau rebellion in East Africa of 1952–56 showed to what extent a relatively small uprising could destabilize colonial rule, inspiring brutal reprisals and widespread fear). By the early 1960s the die was cast; as a "Contexts" section on "The End of Empire" elsewhere in this anthology documents, Harold Macmillan's 1960 "Wind of Change" speech signaled Britain's intention to grant independence to virtually all of its remaining colonies, in Asia and the Caribbean as well as in Africa.

The HMS *Antelope* under attack during the Falklands War, 1982. One case in which the British forcibly resisted efforts to wrest a colonial possession from their control was that of the Falkland Islands off the coast of Argentina, to which Argentina also laid claim. When the Argentinian Armed Forces invaded in April 1982, Margaret Thatcher's government declared war. By early June, the British had retaken the Islands, and on June 14, Argentina surrendered. Before the war Thatcher had been deeply unpopular; in its wake her popularity soared, and in 1983 she was re-elected in a landslide.

Independence in a significant number of these nations also meant majority rule by blacks, which was anathema to many white settlers. In some new nations, independence was followed by an exodus of whites, while in Rhodesia, the government of Ian Smith unilaterally declared independence from Britain in order to maintain the white minority's privileged position and prevent majority rule. Most nations joined Britain in refusing to recognize Smith's regime and imposing sanctions against it, but it was not until 1980, after a ten-year guerrilla war, that the people of Rhodesia—renamed Zimbabwe—established a state based on the principles of majority rule. By 1980, then, all of Britain's former colonial possessions in Africa were independent, as were most in Asia and the Caribbean; the only remnants of the British Empire were a scattering of small territories such as Hong Kong, Gibraltar, the Falkland Islands off the coast of Argentina, and several Caribbean islands.

Doris Lessing was one of many post-war writers to focus in their fiction on the failings of colonialism. A few years before her novels and stories of southern Africa began to appear, Alan Paton's *Cry the Beloved Country* (1948), a simple and emotionally powerful tale of the hardships suffered by black South Africans under white rule, had achieved enormous success. At first such hardships were recounted for a wide audience only in novels by white writers. In the 1960s and 1970s, however, a new generation of writers of color emerged, and were rapidly accorded a place in the first rank of writing in English. Among the most important of these are V.S. Naipaul, whose major works include novels set in India (*A House for Mr. Biswas*, 1962), in Africa (*A Bend in the River*, 1979), and in his native Trinidad (*Miguel Street*, 1959); the Nigerian playwright Wole Soyinka, awarded the Nobel Prize for Literature in 1986; the Nigerian novelist Chinua Achebe, whose novels of struggle, corruption and loss in the post-colonial era (*Things Fall Apart* [1958] most notable among them) have taken on iconic status; the Trinidadian poet Derek Walcott; and the Kenyan novelist Ngũgĩ wa Thiong'o.

One of the most important vehicles with which African writing was brought to the attention of the rest of the world was the African Writers Series, launched by the UK publisher Heinemann in 1962 at the instigation of Alan Hill and initially under the general editorship of Chinua Achebe. By the end of 1969, the year that *Political Spider: Stories from Black Orpheus* was published, the series had grown to 82 titles, including Achebe's *Things Fall Apart* and *Arrow of God*; *Weep Not Child* and *A Grain of Wheat* by "James Ngugi" (Ngũgĩ wa Thiong'o); and Wole Soyinka's *The Interpreters*.

All of these authors deal pointedly with issues of colonialism and post-colonialism in their work. It is Ngugi, however, who has raised most pointedly the issue of the ways in which politics and literature connect also with language. Ngugi's early novels—including *A River Between* (1965), a novel about young people grappling with the conventions of tribal life in a world in which almost no one speaks English—were written in English, and Ngugi established a worldwide reputation as an English novelist. In midlife, he decided both for personal and political reasons to write instead in his first language, Kikuyu; he argues persuasively in *Decolonizing the Mind* (1986) that English is inherently tainted by the culture of the colonizer: "language has a dual character; it is both a means of communication and a carrier of culture." The debate over this issue involved many of the leading writers in Britain's former colonies; Achebe and Soyinka were among those who decided to write some works in English, others in their first language. Even those who chose to write in English, however, no longer felt obliged to adopt the "correct" English of the English themselves; whether through the use of idioms, of non-standard syntax, or of local dialects and rhythms of speech, they have extended the linguistic range of literature in English.

While the 1960s and '70s saw an explosion of literature in English in nations newly independent from Britain, these decades also ushered in a new vibrancy and maturity in the literatures of Canada and Australia, which had long been formally independent from Britain but had retained into the 1950s a pervasive sense of Great Britain as "the mother country." By the 60s and 70s both nations were beginning to define themselves as much in terms with their relationship with the United States (and, in the case of Australia, with Asian countries) as they did in connection with their old relationship towards Britain. Here and there the work of important Canadian and Australian authors such as Margaret Atwood, P.K. Page, and Judith Wright illuminated the old connections with Britain, but just as often the work of these writers—like that of other major Australian and Canadian authors such as Patrick White (winner of the Nobel Prize in 1973), Les Murray, Peter Carey, Alice Munro, Carol Shields, and Michael Ondaatje—bears few traces of a British connection. Increasingly, indeed, literature in English had started to become more broadly international. Ondaatje, for example, has shown himself to be as comfortable writing about Italy and North Africa in World War II (in his Booker Prize-winning novel *The English Patient*) as he has writing about his native Sri Lanka and Canada.

Rohinton Mistry has lived in Canada since he was 23, but he continues to set his major works—most notably his novel *A Fine Balance* (1996)—in his native India.

FROM THE 1960S TO CENTURY'S END

Within Britain, the 1960s and '70s were also a time of cultural explosion—though here literature may be said to have shared the stage with other forms of cultural expression, most notably popular music. The music of The Beatles and The Rolling Stones played a central part in defining "the swinging '60s," but these groups were part of a much broader movement as a large generation of young people sought—through long hair, the lively clothing styles of Carnaby Street, and a new-found sexual freedom—to reject the values of their parents' generation.

Ironically, the most lasting literary reflections of this memorable cultural moment may not be in any literary expression of exuberance from the 1960s, but in detached and faintly critical after-the-fact poems on the subject by Larkin, such as "Annus Mirabilis":

> Sexual intercourse began
> In nineteen sixty-three
> (which was rather late for me)—
> Between the end of the *Chatterley* ban
> And the Beatles' first LP.

The comic novels of Amis and of David Lodge (notably *Changing Places*, 1975) also give some sense of the cultural moment. But several of the most important figures of British literature of these years maintained a considerable distance between their own work and the cultural ferment of the times. Lawrence Durrell com-

In a controversial award, the Beatles were appointed MBEs (Members of the British Empire) in 1965. Even more controversially, John Lennon commented in March of the following year that the group was "more popular than Jesus."

Lord of the Flies has sold exceptionally well ever since its publication in 1954—including to high schools. This still from Peter Brook's 1963 film version of *Lord of the Flies* was also used as a cover image for the "educational edition" of the book the same year.

pleted the last of his series of evocative novels of the Anglo-Egyptian world, *The Alexandria Quartet*, in 1960; Anthony Powell continued to publish novels in his unique sequence *A Dance to the Music of Time*; and William Golding, who had burst onto the literary scene in 1954 with *Lord of the Flies*, a horrific depiction of young boys forced to create a society for themselves, continued to publish novelistic explorations of the psyche and of ethical questions.

One of the most important poetic voices to emerge in Britain in the 1960s and '70s also maintained a certain distance from the cultural mainstream; the focus of Ted Hughes's work remained largely on the natural world, and on the ways in which humans might connect to that world on a primal level. Doris Lessing, however, with the publication of her novel *The Golden Notebook* (1962), most certainly did connect with the mainstream of social and cultural change. Along with the non-fiction work *The Female Eunuch* by the Australian Germaine Greer, *The Golden Notebook* became a touchstone for women as they realized the extent to which they had been suppressed by the patriarchal structures and attitudes of society.

Committed as politicians had been to egalitarianism from the 1940s through to the 1970s, they had been largely unable to loosen the control that the British upper-class and upper middle-class continued to exert over key elements of British society. Perhaps the most egregious expression of this control was the connection that continued to exist between the best jobs and the old established universities. In almost all professions, preference continued to be given to graduates of Oxford and Cambridge. Though the Education Act of 1944 had put forward measures to increase the number of working-class students at British universities, many of the old attitudes persisted.

Ironically, it may have been a Conservative rather than a Labour government that challenged the old ethos most successfully. Margaret Thatcher (Prime Minister from 1979 to 1990), represented a very different brand of Conservatism from that of Winston Churchill and earlier Conservatives, much as she admired him and shared some of the old notions of Britain as a power in

world affairs. A grocer's daughter, she stood in her own way as firmly against the restrictions of a hierarchical class structure as did her political opponents. But whereas Labour had sought to achieve equity by creating a welfare state, Thatcher aimed to do so by bringing the universities to heel, creating a sense of empowerment among the working-class and lower middle-class—and dismantling much of the welfare state in order to lower taxes. Thatcher succeeded in changing a great many British attitudes over the eleven years she held power, but in the course of doing so she fiercely divided the nation.

The 18 years of Conservative party government in Britain from 1979 to 1997—for the most part under Thatcher as Prime Minister—was a period in which government support for culture was cut back. In a series of moves that paralleled developments in the United States under Ronald Reagan, Thatcher attacked the foundations of the welfare state and conveyed a sense that Britain's cultural identity was to be expressed through fiercely defending the last remnants of Empire (she led a war against Argentina over the Falkland Islands in 1982) and in resisting integration with continental Europe rather than in fostering cultural expression through literature, music, and the visual arts. Ironically, this period saw perhaps the greatest flowering of British literature since the first decades of the twentieth century. Novelists were especially prominent, with Margaret Drabble, A.S. Byatt, Ian McEwan, Martin Amis, Graham Swift, and Jeannette Winterson all creating impressive bodies of work. Ironically, too, literature in Britain experienced a cultural broadening that stands in direct contrast to the narrowness of Thatcher's cultural focus. Britain itself was increasingly becoming a multi-cultural society with the continuing influx of immigrants from former British possessions; more and more, that diversity began to shape the British literary scene. Among the major figures of British literature during this period are Salman Rushdie, a novelist with a Pakistani family background whose works—from *Midnight's Children* (1980) and *Shame* (1983) to *Shalimar's Clown* (2005)—explore the cultures of India and Pakistan as much as they do that of Britain; Vikram Seth, another novelist whose major works (most notable among them *A Suitable Boy*, 1993) are set in India; Zadie Smith, who burst onto the literary scene in 2000 with a wide-ranging novel of post-colonial communities in England, *White Teeth*; and Nagasaki-born Kazuo Ishiguro, whose Japanese heritage informs much of his work but who has lived in Britain since the age of six.

Ishiguro's best known work, *The Remains of the Day* (1989), recounts the story of a British butler in a country house where collaborators with the Nazi regime are holding secret meetings; the novel has been widely acclaimed as among the most fully rounded fictional expressions of life under the old British class system, and of the stifling of human feeling under the sense of reserve that formed an integral part of that system. Much of Ishiguro's other work is set in the world of post-war Japan (*A Pale View of Hills*, 1982) and/or in dreamlike worlds that resist identification with fixed geographical or temporal locations (*The Unconsoled*, 1995). In his acclaimed novel *Never Let Me Go* (2005), young people are prepared for a mysterious fate at a boarding school in an English countryside where the precise geographical setting remains vague, and the temporal setting in an unspecified future even more so.

Like the literatures of Canada and Australia, that of Britain in the late twentieth and early twenty-first centuries was often more difficult to place. The diversity of British writing also came to be expressed during this period through an unrestricted openness regarding sexual orientation. Whereas leading writers such as W.H. Auden in the 1930s and Tom Gunn in the 1950s had left Britain for America in large part because American cities such as New York and San Francisco were then far more accepting of homosexuality than was London (let alone any other part of the British Isles), in the 1980s and 1990s gay and lesbian writers such as Hanif Kureishi and Jeannette Winterson remained in Britain and became central figures of London's literary culture. And in the twenty-first century, Carol Ann Duffy came to be acknowledged as a leading poetic voice in Britain.

Diversity of form and style also became increasingly characteristic of British literature in the 1980s and 1990s. Poets such as Geoffrey Hill carried on something akin to the Modernist tradition, while poets such as Tony Harrison infused their work with powerful political content; poets such as Alice Oswald revived and extended traditions of English nature poetry; and a range of other poets (including Grace Nichols, Moniza Alvi, and Linton Kwesi Johnson) gave full expression to the new Britain. Women poets came to the fore as never before, in Ireland as well as in Britain, with Eavan Boland and Maedbh McGuckian particularly highly regarded. (A fuller discussion of these and other developments of the period appears elsewhere in this volume as an introduction to "Directions in Late Twentieth- and Early Twenty-First Century Poetry.")

The 1980s and 1990s may in some respects be characterized as the era of postmodernism in British literary culture; *postmodern* is a notoriously slippery term, however, and one worth pausing over. The most fruitful avenue of approach may be to look at Modernism and postmodernism side by side. In some ways postmodernism represents a reaction to Modernism, in others an extension of it—and in many ways the history of the one parallels that of the other. As Modernism had been the leading artistic and intellectual movement of the second and third decades of the twentieth century, so was postmodernism during the century's final two decades—at least in literature and the visual arts. Both Modernism and postmodernism may be said to have begun in France—Modernism with poets such as Arthur Rimbaud and Stephane Mallarmé and the Post-Impressionist and Cubist painters, postmodernism with philosophers such as Jacques Derrida and Michel Foucault. Modernism had at its core a rejection of traditional artistic forms and a tendency towards fragmentation of meaning as well as of form. The breaking down of the image in poetry and in painting was accompanied by extensive theorizing—by Mallarmé and the French Symbolists, by Ezra Pound and the Imagists, by the Italian Futurists, and by various others. Postmodernism was even more deeply colored by theory; indeed, it may be said to have begun at the "meta" level of theorizing rather than at the level of practice. It is notoriously resistant to definition—indeed, resistance to fixed definitions is itself a characteristic of postmodernism. Like Modernism, postmodernism embraces difficulty and distrusts the simple and straightforward. More broadly, postmodernism is characterized by a rejection of absolute truth or value, of closed systems, of grand unified narratives. As the French social philosopher Jean Baudrillard put it in 1987, "truth is what we should rid ourselves of as fast as possible and pass it on to somebody else. As with illnesses, it's the only way to be cured of it. He who hangs on to truth has lost."

Graham Law's edition of Wilkie Collins's *The Evil Genius*, one of the series-launching batch of four Broadview Literary Texts published in 1994. Even as English Studies focused to an unprecedented degree in the 1980s and '90s on literary theory, the discipline was also becoming increasingly aware of the importance of historicizing literary works—understanding them first of all in the cultural context out of which they emerged. An important related publishing venture was the launch of the Broadview series (later renamed Broadview Editions), which includes within each volume appendices of relevant historical and cultural documents.

As a style of discourse rather than a philosophical system, postmodernist theory dominated the academic study of literature in British and North American universities through much of the 1980s and 1990s. Postmodernism never came to dominate literature itself during that period to anything like the same degree, but the 1980s and 1990s fictions of Rushdie, Byatt, Ishiguro, Winterson, and Will Self, among others, often played with reality and illusion in ways that could be broadly characterized as postmodern. Works such as Byatt's novel *Possession* (1990) and Winterson's *Written on the Body* (1992), for example, display a willingness to combine different styles or forms in a single work—just as in architecture the postmodernist spirit embodies a willingness to borrow from seemingly disparate styles in designing a single structure.

One of the main thrusts of Modernism had been to apprehend consciousness directly in its often-chaotic progression. The main thrust of postmodernism, by contrast, was one of analysis more than of direct apprehension; the characteristic spirit of postmodernism is one of *self*-consciousness, of a highly attuned awareness to the problematized state of the writer, artist, or theorist as observer. Often that awareness encompasses a playfulness with regard to time—as famously expressed, for example, in the opening lines of Rushdie's Booker Prize-winning novel *Midnight's Children* (1980): "I was born in the city of Bombay ... once upon a time. No, that won't do, there's no getting away from the date."

British drama, which was influenced both by Modernism and by postmodernism, experienced great success throughout most of the second half of the twentieth century, and the beginning of the twenty-first. Major figures such as Harold Pinter and Tom Stoppard followed on from the work of Samuel Beckett in the attention that they paid to life's absurdity. In his most important plays, Pinter's focus was on personal and family relationships, whereas Stoppard's was on surprising conjunctions of circumstance and large ideas. In the groundbreaking *Rosencrantz and Guildenstern Are Dead* (1967), for example, he rewrote Shakespeare's *Hamlet* from the point of view of two of its most minor characters; in *Arcadia* (1993), which takes place both in the present and in the early years of the nineteenth century, he brought together ideas about eighteenth-century formal gardens, the science of Isaac Newton, and the life of Byron. Other leading dramatists of the period extended the frontiers of British drama in a variety of other directions. David Hare combined elements of realism with an often larger-than-life framework in plays such as *Plenty* (1978); Caryl Churchill experimented broadly with form in plays such as *Cloud Nine* (1979) and *Top Girls* (1982)—the latter informed both by an ear for dialogue closely attuned to the realities of contemporary Britain and by Churchill's strong feminist convictions; Alan Ayckbourn displayed a talent for farce in the extraordinary tour-de-force *The Norman Conquests*, and a deep sense, as well, of the ways in which the apparently meaningless surface details of life relate to its sad undertones; and Michael Frayn created works ranging from farce as broad as that of Ayckbourn (as in *Noises Off*, 1982) to large scale dramas of ideas (such as *Copenhagen*, 1998) as ambitious as those of Stoppard.

As British literature underwent these changes in the last few decades of the twentieth century, so too did it expand to embrace a range of new modes of expression. In the 1940s and 1950s, Graham Greene had been a rarity among major British writers in his willingness to write screenplays for films based on his works. By the end of the century, however, "crossover" writing of this sort had become common with Harold Pinter, Tom Stoppard, Hanif Kureishi, Neil Jordan, and Irvine Welsh among those who had written screenplays based on their novels or plays. Many also wrote for television; indeed, some of the finest drama of the era—including Stoppard's remarkable comedy *Professional Foul* (1977) on the conjunction of language philosophy and football (i.e., British soccer)—was written for the BBC. Some regularly scheduled British television programs may also lay claim to being among the more important works of the second half of the twentieth century. The comedy sketches of *Monty Python's Flying Circus* invented a new form of absurdist comedy in the early 1970s; the twelve episodes of *Fawlty Towers* (1975) set what some argued to be entirely new standards of farce; and the many episodes of *Yes, Minister* and its sequel *Yes, Prime Minister* introduced a new brand of cynical and yet warmly human comedy about the workings of British politics. Arguably, more recent television programs such

as *The Office* (2001–02) have reached an equally high standard of comedy.

IRELAND, SCOTLAND, WALES

The establishment of the Republic of Ireland in 1949 did not bring enduring peace to the island. With the six Ulster counties of Northern Ireland remaining a part of the United Kingdom of Great Britain and Northern Ireland, there was ongoing tension and, beginning in the late 1960s, almost recurrent violence over the status of Northern Ireland. The conflict came to be referred to as "The Troubles." A cycle of violence and repression continued, into the 1990s, as the Irish Republican Army (IRA) launched attacks on targets in England as well as in Northern Ireland, and the police and the British army launched repeated crackdowns, often involving considerable brutality. Staunchly Protestant Northern Irish politicians (the Reverend Ian Paisley most prominent among them) vowed "no surrender" to those who sought a compromise solution with Ireland and the Catholic minority in Northern Ireland.

In the late 1970s and early 1980s, a series of hunger strikes by IRA prisoners under British internment heightened tensions still further, and even after an Anglo-Irish agreement in 1985, periodic ceasefires brought only temporary cessations of conflict. In 1997, however, the IRA was persuaded to declare a ceasefire that showed promise of holding, and its political arm, Sinn Fein, joined in the multilateral Stormont talks aimed at finding a lasting solution. On 10 April 1998, an agreement was finally signed by the British and Irish governments. The Belfast Agreement (or "Good Friday Agreement") was endorsed by the major political parties of Ireland and of Northern Ireland, and in separate referendums by the electorates of both Ireland and Northern Ireland. Among the key provisions of the agreement were a commitment by all involved to an exclusively peaceful and democratic approach to change; abandonment by the Republic of its territorial claim to Northern Ireland; acceptance of the principle that the citizens of Northern Ireland had the right to determine by majority vote their constitutional future (in other words, partition was formally accepted, but so was the possibility that the Northern Irish could one day vote to

A gaping hole in front of the Grand Hotel in Brighton, site of the Conservative Party's conference in October 1980, was the result of an IRA bomb. Five were killed and many others injured; Prime Minister Thatcher was in her suite at the hotel when the explosion occurred, but was unharmed. An IRA statement acknowledged that Thatcher had been a target; "Today we were unlucky, but remember—we only have to be lucky once: you will have to be lucky always."

join the Republic); and provision for a Northern Ireland Assembly to which additional power would devolve from the British government (still leaving Northern Ireland as part of the United Kingdom). Troubles of one sort or another remained in both Ireland and

Northern Ireland, but "The Troubles" ended with the 1998 agreement; leaders on both sides were awarded the Nobel Peace Prize for their efforts.

Perhaps as important to the evolution of late twentieth- and early twenty-first-century Ireland as the coming of peace have been a precipitous decline of religious authority over Irish life and an extraordinary economic boom that has transformed the economy, particularly of the Irish Republic. Ireland has been slower than other Roman-Catholic-dominated societies of Europe (such as France, Italy, and Spain) to distance itself from the more socially conservative pronouncements of the papacy; not until 1995 was divorce permitted under Irish law, and it remains illegal to obtain an abortion in Ireland. But over the past generation, Ireland has steadily become a more secular society. Over the course of a remarkably brief period in the 1980s and 1990s it also went from being one of the poorest countries in Europe to one of the wealthiest and most dynamic. Changed attitudes, a highly educated workforce, and programs to encourage particular sectors of high-tech industry wrought an extraordinary economic transformation.

Perhaps not surprisingly, given these circumstances, one of the most engaging literary treatments in all of English literature of the transformative effects of capitalism on the human psyche emerged from this period of economic and cultural change in Ireland. Dublin novelist Roddy Doyle's *The Van* (1991) deals with a variety of business start-up—a fish-and-chip van—that is at the opposite end of the economic spectrum from the high-tech businesses that were the well-publicized stars of Ireland's economic transformation. But in the tragicomic microcosm that Doyle creates, he captures with deep understanding the ways in which energy, imagination, and heartlessness fuse together in the heated environment in which businesses grow. (Doyle's distinguished body of work includes two trilogies, among them the Barrytown trilogy of which *The Van* forms a part, as well as his 1993 Booker Prize-winning novel of childhood, *Paddy Clarke Ha Ha Ha*.)

The Irish contribution to the literature of the English-speaking world was scarcely less in the late twentieth century than it had been in the extraordinary period 1890–1960—the period of Oscar Wilde, George Bernard Shaw, J.M. Synge, W.B. Yeats, James Joyce, and Samuel Beckett. Interestingly, a disproportionate number of the important Irish writers of the late twentieth and early twenty-first centuries are poets of Northern Irish background—among them Seamus Heaney, Derek Mahon, Medbh McGuckian, Paul Muldoon, and Tom Paulin. (It is important to note here that Heaney and others on this list self-identify as Irish, not as Northern Irish.) The list of important Irish writers in this period, however, includes writers in all genres and regions, from the short story writer William Trevor, whose early years in a Protestant family in County Cork provided him with a unique perspective; to the acclaimed poet and Dubliner Eavan Boland; to the fiction-writer and film-maker Neil Jordan, a native of County Sligo in the northwest of Ireland, whose *The Crying Game* (1992) remains among the most memorable depictions of "The Troubles"; to the novelist Edna O'Brien, whose reaction against her childhood in what she later described as the "enclosed, fervid, and bigoted" atmosphere of the 1930s in a small village in County Clare colored much of her later fiction; to the novelist and Belfast native (in later life, Canadian citizen) Brian Moore; to the novelist, journalist, and Wexford native John Banville, whose *The Sea* (2005) was awarded the Booker Prize; and to Dublin dramatist and film-maker Conor McPherson, whose plays *The Weir* (1997) and *Shining City* (2004) explore the worlds of the living and the dead, and the ways in which Ireland continues to be possessed by its past.

Discontent with the dominant role played by England within Great Britain was a constant throughout the twentieth century in both Wales and Scotland, though in neither case was there a history of violence. In 1997 Tony Blair's Labour Party included in its election platform a commitment to devolution—a granting of power by the central government to proposed regional governments in Scotland and Wales. (Unlike the allocation of powers in a federal system, the granting of power under a system of devolution may be reversed; ultimate authority continues to reside with the central government.) Labour was elected with a solid majority, and devolution was approved in Scottish and Welsh referendums in the autumn of 1997; elections for the new Scottish Parliament and Welsh National assembly were held in May 1999, and since then the two regional governments have assumed a variety of responsibilities in such areas as health, housing, education, and culture.

A number of important British writers in the second half of the twentieth century were either Scottish or Welsh, including the Scottish novelist Muriel Spark, the Scottish poet Edwin Muir, and the Welsh poets Dylan Thomas and Gwyneth Lewis. Concern over the preservation of local language has been a constant both in Scotland and in Wales. The language known as Gaelic in Scotland, where it is the traditional language of the Highlands, is in its Irish variant referred to simply as Irish; on both sides of the Irish Sea it was long under pressure from English, but it was substantially revived in both Scotland and Ireland over the course of the twentieth century. In Ireland, both Irish and English are official languages, and approximately 100,000 are able to speak and 300,000 able to read Irish; in Scotland, there were in the late twentieth century approximately 80,000 able to speak Gaelic. Lowland Scots, on the other hand, is a variant of English—a very substantially different dialect from that spoken by most in England, but still a related tongue. It, too, was considered to be threatened by "Standard English," but determined efforts were made in the twentieth century to maintain its vitality. In the early twentieth century, the poet and political activist Hugh MacDiarmid (1892-1978) played a leading role in such efforts. A founder in 1928 of the National Party of Scotland, MacDiarmid worked to revive many of the words he found in John Jamieson's 1808 *Etymological Dictionary of the Scottish Language*, and enjoyed considerable success in reviving Scots as a language of poetry. And in the late twentieth and early twenty-first centuries, Lowland Scots has remained very much alive, in literature as well as in speech. Such is the case, for example, with the Edinburgh dialect that is reproduced by the novelist and film-maker Irvine Welsh in *Trainspotting* (novel 1993; film screenplay 1996): "Johnny wis a junky as well as a dealer. Ye hud tae go a wee bit further up the ladder before ye found a dealer whae didnae use."

Like Gaelic/Irish, Welsh is a language quite distinct from English. From the time of Henry VIII until the second half of the twentieth century, the Welsh language had been in more or less steady decline. Henry VIII had united England and Wales and forbidden the use of Welsh for official purposes with the 1536 Statute of Wales and the 1542 Acts of Union. In 1962, however, as a central element in the budding Welsh nationalist movement, a Welsh Language Society (Cymdeithas yr Iaith Gymraeg) was formed, and in 1967 its protests prompted the British Government to pass the Welsh Language Act, assigning equal status within Wales to Welsh and English—and declaring Wales to be no longer an official part of England. Since then the teaching of Welsh has been made an integral part of the educational system, and public agencies are obliged to offer bilingual service. It is now estimated that over 500,000 people in Wales are bilingual in Welsh and English, with the percentage of the population speaking the language increasing for the first time in over a century. In 2005 Gwyneth Lewis, who writes both in English and in Welsh, was named Wales's first Poet Laureate.

THE NEW MILLENNIUM

Through the era of Conservative government under Thatcher and John Major, Britain remained deeply divided politically—over cultural politics and issues such as immigration policy; over to what extent Britain should be a free market economy or a social democratic one; and over foreign affairs. With the coming to power of Tony Blair and "New Labour," as the Labour Party began to style itself in 1994, a new era dawned in British politics. Blair had blunted the power of the unions within his own party, and the party now blended its long-standing commitment to social justice with a commitment to economic enterprise and to modernity that had been sorely lacking in the Labour Party for the previous generation or more. At century's end, long-divisive issues such as the racial composition of Britain and the conflict in Northern Ireland seemed well on the way to being resolved. Constitutional reforms had included not only the devolution of considerable power to new assemblies in Scotland and Wales but also a phasing-out of the hereditary peerage; no longer would one be able to inherit a seat in the House of Lords. Class divisions had receded, and Britons expressed a fresh confidence and a fresh sense of unity. The British seemed to have finally come to terms with their place in the world—a position of far less importance than that which they had held a century earlier, but one that no longer forced them to carry the economic and moral baggage of imperialism. It was also a position of surprising strength economically—particularly in the south of England, with London consolidating its position as one of the great financial centers of the world. Britain seemed to be in the forefront culturally, too. In the visual arts and in fashion, London held a central place, with publicity generating an annual furor over the awarding of the Turner Prize for best work by a British artist under the age of 50, and with brashly controversial artists such as Damien Hirst, Chris Ofili, and Gillian Wearing and celebrity collectors such as advertising mogul Charles Saatchi driving a culture of "Sensation" (to echo the name of the highly controversial 1997 and 2000 exhibitions from the Saatchi Collection in London and Brooklyn, respectively). London also laid claim to be the literary center of the world. "Rule, Britannia" had been Britain's defining song at its Imperial zenith; "Cool Britannia" was the term now coined to define Britain. During the millennium celebrations of 2000, Britain was as confident, as united, and as prosperous as she had been at any time since the great celebrations over the Diamond Jubilee of Queen Victoria, 100 years before Tony Blair, New Labour, and "Cool Britannia."

The sky over Britain at the millennium was far from cloudless, however, and in the early years of the twenty-first century many have perceived Britain's problems as standing out in bolder relief than her triumphs. In the first few years of the twentieth century the British people—the *English* people, especially—were stereo-typically thought of as a people of civility and self-restraint, adherence to religion and religious propriety, and modesty that verged on prudery. In the first few years of the twenty-first century the stereotype of the British—again, the *English*, especially—included the behavior of the "lager louts" that went on nightly rampages in city centers; the lowest rates of church attendance in Europe; drunken hooliganism among soccer fans, displayed since the 1970s at matches across Europe as well as at home; and poverty-stricken and largely racially defined ghettos in post-industrial towns such as Leeds—areas which, as the suicide bombings on the London transport system in 2005 made painfully clear, could become breeding grounds for terrorism. According to social critics such as Theodore Dalrymple in works such as *Life at the Bottom* (2002), the lack of civility commonly associated with an alienated under-class was becoming more and more pervasive throughout all Britain, fueled by a "radical egotism" that had taken root in the new cultural freedom of the 1960s and that had become more and more strongly tainted during the late 1970s and the Thatcher years by materialism and uncaring individualism.

Grafted onto concern over these domestic issues was a broad concern over the place of a new Britain in a changed world. Was Britain's appropriate role that of aggressive ally of an increasingly bellicose United States? Could intervention in other nations' affairs, on either humanitarian or strategic grounds, be readily justified in a world in which concerns about terrorism, about human rights, and about the potential for a world-wide clash of cultures were coming to the fore? The participation by Prime Minister Tony Blair's govern-ment in the early twentieth-century wars in Afghanistan and Iraq provided powerful fuel for these debates.

These troubled aspects of British life are memorably represented in the literature of the late twentieth and early twenty-first centuries. The hooliganism that began to plague England in the late 1960s and 1970s was foreshadowed in Anthony Burgess's novel *A Clockwork Orange* (1962), in which the protagonist, fifteen-year old Alex DeLarge, leads a gang that commits a variety of violent crimes purely for the "kick" it gives them. The early fiction of Ian McEwan—perhaps most notably his first novel, *The Cement Garden* (1978)—depicts the grim plight of young people fending for themselves in the bleakness of a post-industrial landscape. The occasion for Tony Harrison's wide-ranging long poem *v* (1985) was the graffiti left on gravestones by Leeds United soccer hooligans; in a cemetery above the ground where "Leeds United play but disappoint their fans week after week," the fans "spray words on tombstones, pissed on beer":

Subsidence makes the obelisks all list.
One leaning left's marked FUCK, one right's
     marked SHIT
sprayed by some peeved supporter who was pissed. ...

In some cases the graffiti is football-related as well as foul-mouthed:

Or, more expansively, there's LEEDS v.
the opponent of last week, this week, or next,
and a repertoire of blunt four-letter curses
on the team or race that makes the sprayer vexed.

And, Harrison suggests, there is a wider resonance to these oppositions:

These Vs are all the versuses of life
From LEEDS v. DERBY, Black/White
and (as I've known to my cost) man v. wife,
Communist v. Fascist, Left v. Right,

Class v. class as bitter as before,
the unending violence of US and THEM ...

Hanif Kureishi's *My Son the Fanatic* (both a short story and a screenplay for a film, 1997) depicts the violent radicalization in Britain of Islamic youth as a reaction to what they see as the hypocrisy and decadence of their fathers' assimilated Britishness. Caryl Churchill's work—notably her short apocalyptic play *Far Away* (2000)—presents a world in which individuals abandon responsibility for one another, and in which the possibility of wider and wider conflict (not only nations or civilizations at war with one another, but also the human at war with the non-human environment) is beginning to seem increasingly real. And Ian MacEwan's celebrated novel *Saturday* (2005) captures much of the ambivalence towards violence that at the time was coming to seem a part of British life—violence both on the streets of Britain and overseas. That novel, which concerns a surgeon who becomes terrorized by violent criminals and is provoked to violent response, is set against a backdrop of looming military conflict in Iraq. Asked if he is "for the war," the beleaguered surgeon Henry Perowne replies, "I'm not for any war. But this one could be the lesser evil. In five years' time we'll know."

In a the space of a few hours in 2005 Britain experi-enced the extremes of jubilation and anguish as four coordinated terrorist attacks by suicide bombers (three of them British born) shook the London Transport system less than 24 hours after London had been announced as the surprise winner in the competition to host the 2012

Summer Olympics. Those experiences may perhaps be set beside each other as symbolic of the powerful grounds for both optimism and pessimism in Britain. Will the lively spirit that animated Britain culturally and economically at the beginning of the millennium continue to flourish and expand, with the 2012 London Olympics as a centerpiece? Or will the shadows that have been cast across modern Britain lengthen and darken? On the future of Britain itself and of its role in the world, the jury is surely still out—and it is far from certain that "in five years' time we'll know." But there can be no doubt of the continuing vitality of British literature as we move further into the twenty-first century.

THE HISTORY OF THE ENGLISH LANGUAGE

Perhaps the most extraordinary feature of English language in the late twentieth and early twenty-first century has been the pace of its growth—growth in its size and communicative capacity, but also in the extent to which it is spoken around the world. The two phenomena are now closely linked. Linguist Paul Payack of Global Language Monitor has estimated that English likely passed the one million word mark in 2006. (By comparison, the number of words in Old English was less than 60,000.) As in the first half of the twentieth century, much of that growth comes from new scientific coinages. But much of it is now also coming from "Chinglish" (Chinese-English) or "Hinglish" (Hindi-English) words, or other dual-language coinages. "Torunbusiness," for example, draws both on English and on the Mandarin word meaning *operating*; it means *open*, with reference to a business during opening hours.

In the twenty-year period 1947–67, almost all of Britain's former colonies became independent. Recognising the importance of English as a world-wide means of communication, most retained some official status for the English language. When India became independent in 1947, Hindi was declared the official language, English an "associate official language." In many new nations, English was accorded equal status with one or more other languages; thus in Malawi English and Chichewa are the official languages, in Swaziland, English and Swazi. In former colonies such as Nigeria and Zambia, where many local languages are spoken in different areas of the country, English was declared the *only* official language.

The speaking of English acquired a different coloring as it became the world's lingua franca, not only in the proliferation of accents but also in the timing of speech, and in the use of pitch rather than stress to mark "strong" syllables. English as it is spoken in Britain, the United States, Canada, Australia, and New Zealand remains a strongly inflected, stress-timed language; in other words, speakers typically stress certain syllables much more strongly than others, and vary the speed of speech in order to make the elapsed time between stresses more nearly equal. In other regions, however, where most people's first language is syllable- rather than stress-timed, and where pitch rather than stress marks "accented" syllables, those habits tend to be carried over into local habits of English pronunciation.

Inevitably, very substantial differences have arisen as well in the conventions of grammar and usage in different areas of the world. In the most extreme cases—as in Jamaica and several other Caribbean nations, pidgin and Creole forms of English that have become independent languages are more widely spoken than English itself. Elsewhere, conventions of spoken and of written English very different from those of "Standard English" have come to be broadly received as acceptable variants. In India "He is working here, isn't it?" or "I am not very much pleased" are generally regarded as entirely acceptable local usage. Indian Prime Minister Manmohan Singh put the matter clearly in a 2005 speech at Oxford University (excerpted in the "Contexts" section on "The End of Empire" elsewhere in this volume):

> Of course, people here may not recognise the language we speak, but let me assure you that it *is* English! In indigenising English, as so many people have done in so many nations across the world, we have made the language our own. Our choice of prepositions may not always be the Queen's English; we might occasionally split the infinitive; and we may drop an article here and add an extra one there. I am sure everyone will agree, however, that English has been enriched by Indian creativity. ...

Some of the most important changes in the English language in the second half of the twentieth century stemmed from the growing realization that the language had a systemic bias towards the male. In a landmark case referred to Britain by the Canadian courts, the Privy Council ruled in 1929 that the word *person* could not legally be taken to refer only to men. But could the word *man* be taken in an unbiased fashion to mean *human being*? To many, such usages seemed unproblematic—until they started to be brought up short by usages such as "the gestation period of the elephant is eleven months; that of man is nine months." From the 1970s onward it came to be more and more widely understood that *man* and *mankind* would always carry with them a whiff of malenesss, and thus could never fully and fairly represent all of humanity. Similarly the use of *he* to stand for both males and females has come to be widely criticised—and widely replaced, whether by "he or she" or simply by the use of plural constructions ("students … they" rather than "a student … he"); gender-specific nouns have largely been superceded by gender-neutral alternatives (*police officer* for *policeman*, *server* for *waitress*); and patronizing gender terms ("the girls in the office") have largely fallen into disuse. Such change did not occur without a struggle, however. For many decades, those who ventured to suggest gender-neutral alternatives to the general practice were subjected to the sort of ridicule that H.W. Fowler and F.G. Fowler (authors of *Modern English Usage* and for most of the twentieth century considered the leading arbiters of proper English usage) aimed at one S. Ferrier in *The King's English* (1906, 1931; issued without further revision in paperback, 1962). Existing habit or convention was in such cases often the only "argument" advanced against principles of fairness:

> *He*, *his*, *him* may generally be allowed to stand for the common gender; the particular aversion to them shown by Miss Ferrier in the examples [quoted by the Fowlers] may be referred to her sex; and, ungallant as it may seem, we shall probably persist in refusing women their due here as stubbornly as Englishmen continue to offend the Scots by saying *England* instead of *Britain*.

One of the visible manifestations of changes in attitudes in the late twentieth century was the radical shift in the meaning of certain words and expressions relating to sexual behavior and sexual orientation. At mid-century *queer* was both an adjective meaning strange and a "descriptive" term with derogatory implications, used casually and openly by heterosexuals to denote homosexuals; in the 1970s it had come to be acknowledged as an offensive word that should be avoided; in the 1980s and 1990s it was claimed by the gay and lesbian community, many of whom began to self-identify as queer. In the academic community queer theory grew up as a sub-discipline of literary theory and criticism. *Gay*, which until mid-century had meant *merry* or *given to merriment*, began in the 1970s to replace *queer* as a colloquial designator—but one that carried positive rather than negative connotations. (Towards the end of the century, however, those positive associations began to be eroded somewhat, as heterosexual youth began to use *gay* in a derogatory fashion.)

Terms relating to heterosexual relationships were often also unstable. A noteworthy example is *making love*, which until the 1950s referred to the process of courting, emphatically not including the act of sexual intercourse. In the early 1960s, the meaning of the phrase quickly shifted, so that by the 1970s, the *only* commonly used denotation of *to make love* was *to have sex*. That was one of many examples of an increasingly overt sexualization of the language. In the case of a number of words that in the early twentieth century could carry either a sexual or a non-sexual meaning (e.g., *intercourse*, *ejaculate*), the sexual meaning had completely crowded out the non-sexual one by the end of the 1960s.

The twentieth century also saw a great change in the use of obscenities. In 1914, the utterance on stage of the phrase "not bloody likely" caused an uproar during the first English performance of Bernard Shaw's *Pygmalion*. Over the first half of the century, other swear words gradually made their way into print ("d— it all," for example, eventually gave way to "damn it all"). As the Christian religion held less and less sway over Britain in the second half of the century, so the sharp shock of swear words with religious referents was rubbed smooth, and stronger and stronger sexual terms came to replace them. In the world of literary publishing the publication of Philip Larkin's "This Be The Verse" in 1974 ("They fuck you up, your mum and dad") was something of a watershed. For some time after that, most reputable newspapers and magazines resisted the appearance of "the f-word" in their pages, but in last few years of the twentieth century and the early twenty-first that, too, has changed. In 2006, even the eminently respectable British newsmagazine *The Economist* found it acceptable to use such language in the course of quoting others; here is how their report in their 25–31 March 2006 issue on the state of Iraq three years after the 2003 invasion by American and British troops concluded: "On a toilet-wall in an American airbase in Western Iraq an American soldier has scrawled his own summary analysis: 'We came, we wasted a year of our lives. At least we got the fuckers to vote.'" In 1903—even in 1953 or 1963—such language in a respectable publication would have been entirely unimaginable.

London's Millennium Bridge (above). The Bridge, the first new river crossing since the Tower Bridge opened in 1894, was designed jointly by Foster and Partners and Sir Anthony Caro. It opened on 10 June 2000 but had to be closed three days later due to unexpectedly strong swaying. Since its re-opening on 22 February 2002 it has proved enormously popular. To the north is St. Paul's Cathedral, to the south the Tate Modern gallery. The Tate Modern opened on 12 May 2000 in a building that had previously served as the Battersea Power Station. It now houses the Tate's collection of twentieth- and twenty-first century art; the original Tate Gallery in Chelsea, now renamed Tate Britain, houses the gallery's main collection.

The 41-storey tower universally known as "The Gherkin," which houses offices of the insurance company Swiss Re, has quickly become one of London's most recognizable structures. Designed by the prominent British architect Sir Norman Foster, it officially opened on 27 April 2004. The previous day Foster chanced to discover that Sir Christopher Wren, designer of St. Paul's Cathedral, had sketched plans for a similar structure more than 300 years earlier.

DYLAN THOMAS
1914 – 1953

The fiery career of Dylan Thomas left a burning after-image on the poetic retina of the English-speaking world in the mid-twentieth century. Thomas was a rollicking, even raucous, fixture in the taverns of London's Soho-Fitzrovia district, but he also haunted the rural hills and seashores of

Wales, where he sought to articulate, through the tumbling power of his words, his sense that life and death were rolled together in nature's driving "green fuse."

Born in Swansea, Wales, Dylan Thomas grew up speaking English; his mother, Florence Hannah Williams, and his father, D.J. Thomas, chose the Anglicized urban world of Swansea over their Welsh roots. Thomas's father was a schoolteacher at Swansea Grammar School, which Dylan Thomas attended and where he proved to be far from a prize pupil. However, from an early age Dylan Thomas was writing poems whose images, rhythms and rhymes would soon be romanticized as "dark-rooted" and "atavistic" by critics who located his passionate verse in Celtic tradition. Yet if Thomas tapped into Welsh imagery, by the age of 15 he was more consciously modeling himself after the French symbolist poet Arthur Rimbaud, even calling himself "the Rimbaud of Cwmdonkin Drive." What attracted Thomas to poets such as Rimbaud and Keats was not only their iconoclasm, but also the fact that they had died young. Thomas regularly cut classes to pore over his own poetry, and launched into a habit of boisterous drinking that was destined to make his career as tragically brief as those of his idols.

In 1933, when Thomas was only 18 years old, the *New English Weekly* published an astonishing poem, his "And Death Shall Have No Dominion." When Thomas's *18 Poems* was published the following year, the strange and disturbing power of his verse woke up London's literary establishment. The cool, controlled style of T.S. Eliot, which conditioned poetic attitudes well into the 1950s, appeared subdued next to the chaotic heat generated by what one critic calls Thomas's "belligerent syntax." For a time, Thomas was labeled a Surrealist and a Dadaist, labels that framed his poetry as a jumble of random signs and erotic images startled out of a Freudian unconscious. Thomas initially exploited the cultural mileage that these early associations gave him, but when his reputation grew sturdier he was careful to distinguish his work from the Surrealists', and to avow that Freud had never been a direct influence. *18 Poems* won Thomas many admirers, including Edith Sitwell, a tireless champion of the curly-haired, Anglo-Welsh "cherub" who churned out formidable verse. "And Death Shall Have No Dominion" was included in his next volume, *25 Poems* (1936), which was also well received. *The Map of Love* (1939) failed to excite much critical acclaim, but with the postwar publication of *Deaths and Entrances* (1946) Thomas won over both the literati and the general public with the lilting rhythms and fresh imagery of poems such as "Fern Hill."

By this time, Thomas had become notorious as an indefatigable carouser, constantly appealing to friends for money and adored by women who wanted to "save" him from his excesses. In 1937, he met Caitlin Macnamara and entered into a stormy marriage that somehow survived an endless stream of creditors, mad bouts of drinking, and mutual infidelities. Caitlin bore Thomas three children.

During the Second World War, Thomas avoided military service on the grounds of poor health, instead finding employment writing film and radio scripts for Strand Films and the BBC. While Thomas remains best known for his early poetry, some critics contend that he was a better playwright and prose writer than poet. The autobiographical stories compiled in *Portrait of the Artist as a Young Dog* (1940) and the posthumously published *Adventures in the Skin Trade* (1955) feature prose that is by turns humorous, raw, and risqué. In his 1945 BBC broadcast "Quite Early One Morning," Thomas's love of place, his fine ear for dialogue, his comic wit and his unforgettable voice fused in a narrative of everyday life in New Quay which endeared him to radio audiences. Around the same time in America, Thomas's poetry was inspiring an almost devotional following with the publications of *The World I Breathe* (1939), *New Poems* (1943), and *Selected Writings* (1946).

For Thomas, the meaning of a word was by no means fixed. As with "Wales," which he savoured as if it were a "gobstopper of magical properties, ringing the word like a bell, making it rise and fall, whisper and thunder like the Welsh sea," Thomas was fascinated by the earthy taste, cadence, and physical horseplay inspired by language. He held that poetry was quintessentially the spoken word, and was meant to be read out loud. In a booming voice that detonated the energy stored in language, Thomas performed radio broadcasts and poetry readings throughout the 1940s and the early 50s – performances that were hugely popular both in Europe and in North America. In 1950 he traveled to New York, where the poet John Malcolm Brinnin had arranged a taxing, but lucrative, schedule of public readings and talks. (The lucre, as usual, quickly evaporated.) Whether reciting his own poetry or favorite poems by Auden, Hardy, and Sitwell, Thomas retained the ability to enthrall a crowd with his magnetic voice and his wildboy antics. His reputation preceded him across the American midwest, and on to San Francisco and Vancouver.

Some critics hold that in the last years of his life Thomas was running on empty, producing only strained works that tried to simulate the tremendous effect captured in his earliest poetry. Others see his writing mature in later works such as "Poem in October" (1945) and the radio drama *Under Milk Wood* (1954). Only a few years before Thomas's final, fatal trip to the United States, he and his family moved into The Boat House in Laugharne, Wales. His stay at The Boat House was to prove the last time Thomas would immerse himself in the landscape of the Welsh shoreline, where he had so often glimpsed the cycle that seemed to him to turn living and dying into almost indistinguishable forces. The respite was short-lived: on a third trip to New York in 1953, Thomas set out on a punishing drinking spree and died, as he had always imagined he would, before reaching the age of 40.

⌘ ⌘ ⌘

The Force That Through the Green Fuse Drives the Flower

The force that through the green fuse drives the
    flower
Drives my green age; that blasts the roots of trees
Is my destroyer.
And I am dumb to tell the crooked rose
5 My youth is bent by the same wintry fever.

The force that drives the water through the rocks
Drives my red blood; that dries the mouthing streams
Turns mine to wax.
And I am dumb to mouth unto my veins
10 How at the mountain spring the same mouth sucks.

The hand that whirls the water in the pool[1]
Stirs the quicksand; that ropes the blowing wind
Hauls my shroud sail.

---

[1] *hand … pool* See John 5.4.

And I am dumb to tell the hanging man
15 How of my clay is made the hangman's lime.[1]

The lips of time leech to the fountain head;
Love drips and gathers, but the fallen blood
Shall calm her sores.
And I am dumb to tell a weather's wind
20 How time has ticked a heaven round the stars.

And I am dumb to tell the lover's tomb
How at my sheet goes the same crooked worm.
—1933

Fern Hill

Now as I was young and easy under the apple boughs
About the lilting house and happy as the grass was
green,
The night above the dingle[2] starry,
Time let me hail and climb
5 Golden in the heydays of his eyes,
And honoured among wagons I was prince of the
apple towns
And once below a time I lordly had the trees and leaves
Trail with daisies and barley
Down the rivers of the windfall light.

10 And as I was green and carefree, famous among the barns
About the happy yard and singing as the farm was home,
In the sun that is young once only,
Time let me play and be
Golden in the mercy of his means,
15 And green and golden I was huntsman and herdsman,
the calves
Sang to my horn, the foxes on the hills barked clear
and cold,
And the sabbath rang slowly
In the pebbles of the holy streams.

All the sun long it was running, it was lovely, the hay
20 Fields high as the house, the tunes from the chimneys,
it was air

And playing, lovely and watery
And fire green as grass.
And nightly under the simple stars
As I rode to sleep the owls were bearing the farm away,
25 All the moon long I heard, blessed among stables, the
nightjars[3]
Flying with the ricks,° and the horses   *haystacks*
Flashing into the dark.

And then to awake, and the farm, like a wanderer white
With the dew, come back, the cock on his shoulder:
it was all
30 Shining, it was Adam and maiden,
The sky gathered again
And the sun grew round that very day.
So it must have been after the birth of the simple light
In the first, spinning place, the spellbound horses
walking warm
35 Out of the whinnying green stable
On to the fields of praise.

And honoured among foxes and pheasants by the gay
house
Under the new made clouds and happy as the heart
was long,
In the sun born over and over,
40 I ran my heedless ways,
My wishes raced through the house high hay
And nothing I cared, at my sky blue trades,[4] that time
allows
In all his tuneful turning so few and such morning songs
Before the children green and golden
45 Follow him out of grace,

Nothing I cared, in the lamb white days, that time
would take me
Up to the swallow thronged loft by the shadow of my
hand,
In the moon that is always rising,
Nor that riding to sleep
50 I should hear him fly with the high fields
And wake to the farm forever fled from the childless land.
Oh as I was young and easy in the mercy of his means,

---

[1] *lime* Mineral used to speed up decomposition.

[2] *dingle* Wooded dell.

[3] *nightjars* Nocturnal birds.

[4] *trades* Occupations.

Time held me green and dying
Though I sang in my chains like the sea.
—1946

Do Not Go Gentle Into That Good Night

Do not go gentle into that good night,
Old age should burn and rave at close of day;
Rage, rage against the dying of the light.

Though wise men at their end know dark is right,
5   Because their words had forked no lightning they
Do not go gentle into that good night.

Good men, the last wave by, crying how bright
Their frail deeds might have danced in a green bay,
Rage, rage against the dying of the light.

10   Wild men who caught and sang the sun in flight,
And learn, too late, they grieved it on its way,
Do not go gentle into that good night.

Grave men, near death, who see with blinding sight
Blind eyes could blaze like meteors and be gay,
15   Rage, rage against the dying of the light.

And you, my father, there on the sad height,
Curse, bless, me now with your fierce tears, I pray.
Do not go gentle into that good night.
Rage, rage against the dying of the light.
—1951

A Refusal To Mourn The Death, By Fire, Of A Child In London

Never until the mankind making
Bird beast and flower
Fathering and all humbling darkness
Tells with silence the last light breaking
5   And the still hour
Is come of the sea tumbling in harness

And I must enter again the round
Zion[1] of the water bead
And the synagogue of the ear of corn
10   Shall I let pray the shadow of a sound
Or sow my salt seed
In the least valley of sackcloth to mourn

The majesty and burning of the child's death.
I shall not murder
15   The mankind of her going with a grave truth
Nor blaspheme down the stations of the breath
With any further
Elegy of innocence and youth.

Deep with the first dead lies London's daughter,
20   Robed in the long friends,
The grains beyond age, the dark veins of her mother,
Secret by the unmourning water
Of the riding Thames.[2]
After the first death, there is no other.
—1946

---

1 *Zion* Hill in Jerusalem, previous center of Jewish worship; by extension, the house of God.

2 *Thames* River in London.

Philip Larkin

1922 – 1985

Although Philip Larkin published two novels in his lifetime as well as several other nonfiction works, his reputation as one of the most important figures in twentieth-century British literature rests on his poetry. His accessible style and straightforward language; the commentary he provided on Britain's changing post-war status; and above all the extraordinary skill with which he crafted poetic expressions of emotions widely shared (if not always expressed) made him one of the most popular poets of his time. Though often described as anti-social, Larkin was a witty conversationalist, and he maintained several relationships that spanned most of his adult life. His work is often (and

rightly) described as bleakly pessimistic, and frequently touches on themes of solitude and mortality. Yet his poems are also often funny—Larkin is equally capable of dry wit and broad humor.

Larkin was born in Coventry in the West Midlands of England in 1922 to Sydney and Eva Larkin. He was their second child and only son. Although he describes his childhood as "dull, pot-bound, and slightly mad," he appears to have had a comfortable upbringing. His father was the city treasurer and the family led a typical middle-class existence. Larkin describes his parents as "awkward" and "shy"; it seems likely that the sterility of their relationship influenced his own views towards marriage. The family home may have been emotionless, but his father kept a well-stocked library, where Larkin was first introduced to the classics. Between 1930 and 1940 Larkin attended King Henry VIII School, where he described himself as having been unhappy, an "unsuccessful schoolboy." His unhappiness may have been caused by his stammer, a condition from which he continued to suffer until he was well into his thirties. Whether despite or because of his unhappiness, Larkin did begin writing during this period; his first poem was published in the school paper, *The Coventrian*, in 1934, when he was 12.

In 1940, Larkin sent one of his poems to the literary magazine *The Listener*, which accepted and published "Ultimatum" in November of that year. In the same year he entered Oxford to study English, and the experience of university turned out to be a great stimulus for him in terms both of writing and of personal friendships. It was while he was at Oxford that he met Kingsley Amis, some years later to become famous as a novelist; the two remained fast friends for life. (Although they often showed each other their work in its early stages, it was a love of jazz above all that first drew them together.) Larkin developed in these years a distrust of the Modernist notion that twentieth-century literature should express the difficulties of twentieth-century life, and gained an appreciation for a plainer style of writing. He greatly admired W.H. Auden and W.B. Yeats, and tried for years to mimic Yeats's writing in particular.

Larkin graduated in 1943 and returned to his parents' house in Coventry that year, his poor eyesight making him ineligible to fight in World War II. After failing the civil service exam twice, Larkin answered an advertisement in the paper for a librarian in Wellington, Shropshire. He remained in the profession for the rest of his life, stating that "librarianship suits me." The solitude of the work as well as the regular hours gave him sufficient time to pursue his writing; during this period he produced his first volume of poetry, *The North Ship*, published at his own expense in 1945. It went largely unnoticed. The following two years produced Larkin's only novels, *Jill* in 1946 and *A Girl in Winter* in 1947. Larkin later described the novels as "over-sized poems"; their lack of success encouraged him to give up the form, and from that point onwards he concentrated on poetry. While in Shropshire Larkin also qualified professionally as a librarian; from 1955 until his death he worked as a librarian at the University of Hull.

In the 1950s Larkin began to be associated with a literary group known simply as "The Movement." Its members included Amis as well as Bruce Montgomery, Thom Gunn, and Donald Davie. They were all representatives of a new style of British writing that was anti-romantic, sardonic, and concerned with everyday British life. In Larkin's case, it was *The Less Deceived* (1955), and the poem "Church Going" in particular, that solidified his poetic reputation as an anti-romantic poet. With this volume Larkin shook off the influence of Yeats and established his own style and voice. Spare in their imagery, and typically with a strong but unobtrusive framework of rhythm and rhyme, the poems often chronicle the place of choice or fate in a person's life. Loneliness, misunderstanding, and deception are central themes in Larkin's work, and the aesthetic act often seemed his only bulwark against despair. "People say I'm very negative and I suppose I am," he admitted, "but the impulse for producing a poem is never negative; the most negative poem in the world is a very positive thing to have done."

The Less Deceived was followed by *The Whitsun Weddings* and *High Windows* in 1964 and 1974 respectively; the poems in these later collections are largely in the same vein as Larkin's earlier work but are less frequently ironic, more often directly revealing of emotion. Larkin also occasionally adopted a different voice in which the presence of rhyme is more obtrusive, the thoughts bluntly pointed, and the tone loudly sardonic. Two of the poems from *High Windows* written in this tone —"This Be The Verse" and "Annus Mirabilis"—caused something of a sensation on the book's publication, and have remained among the most often quoted of Larkin's poems.

In addition to his poetry, Larkin was engaged with other literary pursuits. From 1961 to 1971 he published a regular jazz column in *The Daily Telegraph*. Some of these columns were later reproduced in *All What Jazz*, published in 1970. He was editor of the *Oxford Book of Twentieth-Century Verse* (1973), and his nonfiction writing was collected in *Required Writing* (1983). Larkin won the Queen's Gold Medal for Poetry in 1965, was appointed a Companion of the British Empire in 1975, and received seven honorary doctorates. He was offered the position of British Poet Laureate in 1984, but turned it down because he did not want the media attention with which it was associated. Although Larkin had a number of romantic relationships, he never married, and once said that "two can live as stupidly as one." (The publication in 1992 of Larkin's *Selected Letters*, which contains derogatory language about women, as well as slurs against socialists and various racial groups, led many to attribute Larkin's views on marriage as much to his tendency towards misogyny as to his innate pessimism with regard to the human condition.) Larkin's poetic output was much reduced in the 1980s; his last major poem, "Aubade," was published in the *Times Literary Supplement* in 1977. Larkin was admitted to hospital in 1985, suffering from cancer, and had his esophagus removed. He died later that year.

⌘ ⌘ ⌘

Days

What are days for?
Days are where we live.
They come, they wake us
Time and time over.
5   They are to be happy in:
Where can we live but days?

Ah, solving that question
Brings the priest and the doctor
In their long coats
10   Running over the fields.
—1953

Church Going

Once I am sure there's nothing going on
I step inside, letting the door thud shut.
Another church: matting, seats, and stone,
And little books; sprawlings of flowers, cut
5   For Sunday, brownish now; some brass and stuff
Up at the holy end; the small neat organ;
And a tense, musty, unignorable silence,
Brewed God knows how long. Hatless, I take off
My cycle-clips in awkward reverence,

10   Move forward, run my hand around the font.[1]
From where I stand, the roof looks almost new—
Cleaned, or restored? Someone would know: I don't.
Mounting the lectern, I peruse a few
Hectoring large-scale verses, and pronounce
15   "Here endeth" much more loudly than I'd meant.
The echoes snigger briefly. Back at the door
I sign the book, donate an Irish sixpence,
Reflect the place was not worth stopping for.

Yet stop I did: in fact I often do,
20   And always end much at a loss like this,
Wondering what to look for; wondering, too,
When churches fall completely out of use
What we shall turn them into, if we shall keep
A few cathedrals chronically on show,

25   Their parchment, plate and pyx[2] in locked cases,
And let the rest rent-free to rain and sheep.
Shall we avoid them as unlucky places?

Or, after dark, will dubious women come
To make their children touch a particular stone;
30   Pick simples° for a cancer; or on some   *medicinal herbs*
Advised night see walking a dead one?
Power of some sort or other will go on
In games, in riddles, seemingly at random;
But superstition, like belief, must die,
35   And what remains when disbelief has gone?
Grass, weedy pavement, brambles, buttress, sky,

A shape less recognisable each week,
A purpose more obscure. I wonder who
Will be the last, the very last, to seek
40   This place for what it was; one of the crew
That tap and jot and know what rood-lofts° were? *church galleries*
Some ruin-bibber, randy for antique,
Or Christmas-addict, counting on a whiff
Of gown-and-bands and organ-pipes and myrrh?
45   Or will he be my representative,

Bored, uninformed, knowing the ghostly silt
Dispersed, yet tending to this cross of ground
Through suburb scrub because it held unspilt
So long and equally what since is found
50   Only in separation—marriage, and birth,
And death, and thoughts of these—for which was built
This special shell? For, though I've no idea
What this accoutred frowsty° barn is worth,   *stuffy*
It pleases me to stand in silence here;

55   A serious house on serious earth it is,
In whose blent air all our compulsions meet,
Are recognised, and robed as destinies.
And that much never can be obsolete,
Since someone will forever be surprising
60   A hunger in himself to be more serious,
And gravitating with it to this ground,
Which, he once heard, was proper to grow wise in,
If only that so many dead lie round.
—1954

[1] *font* Baptismal receptacle.

[2] *pyx* Vessel in which the bread of the Eucharist is kept.

Talking in Bed

Talking in bed ought to be easiest,
  Lying together there goes back so far,
An emblem of two people being honest.

Yet more and more time passes silently.
5 Outside, the wind's incomplete unrest
Builds and disperses clouds about the sky,

And dark towns heap up on the horizon.
None of this cares for us. Nothing shows why
At this unique distance from isolation

10 It becomes still more difficult to find
Words at once true and kind,
Or not untrue and not unkind.
—1960

Dockery and Son

"Dockery was junior to you,
  Wasn't he?" said the Dean. "His son's here now."
Death-suited, visitant, I nod. "And do
You keep in touch with—" Or remember how
5 Black-gowned, unbreakfasted, and still half-tight
We used to stand before that desk, to give
"Our version" of "these incidents last night"?
I try the door of where I used to live:

Locked. The lawn spreads dazzlingly wide.
10 A known bell chimes. I catch my train, ignored.
Canal and clouds and colleges subside
Slowly from view. But Dockery, good Lord,
Anyone up[1] today must have been born
In '43, when I was twenty-one.
15 If he was younger, did he get this son
At nineteen, twenty? Was he that withdrawn

High-collared public[2]-schoolboy, sharing rooms
With Cartwright who was killed? Well, it just shows
How much … How little … Yawning, I suppose
20 I fell asleep, waking at the fumes
And furnace-glares of Sheffield, where I changed,[3]
And ate an awful pie, and walked along
The platform to its end to see the ranged
Joining and parting lines reflect a strong

25 Unhindered moon. To have no son, no wife,
No house or land still seemed quite natural.
Only a numbness registered the shock
Of finding out how much had gone of life,
How widely from the others. Dockery, now:
30 Only nineteen, he must have taken stock
Of what he wanted, and been capable
Of … No, that's not the difference: rather, how

Convinced he was he should be added to!
Why did he think adding meant increase?
35 To me it was dilution. Where do these
Innate assumptions come from? Not from what
We think truest, or most want to do:
Those warp tight-shut, like doors. They're more a style
Our lives bring with them: habit for a while,
40 Suddenly they harden into all we've got

And how we got it; looked back on, they rear
Like sand-clouds, thick and close, embodying
For Dockery a son, for me nothing,
Nothing with all a son's harsh patronage.
45 Life is first boredom, then fear.
Whether or not we use it, it goes,
And leaves what something hidden from us chose,
And age, and then the only end of age.
—1963

---

[1] *Anyone up* To refer to being "up" at Oxford or Cambridge was a common colloquialism for attending university in those towns. Both of these ancient universities are composed of many colleges.

[2] *public* In Britain the term "public school" came into use in the late sixteenth century to distinguish grammar schools operated by private individuals or church authorities from those open to a broader public. Such schools were (and are) fee-charging institutions attended overwhelmingly by privileged students; they are thus similar to *private* schools in such countries as the United States and Canada.

[3] *Sheffield, where I changed* Larkin, who attended Oxford University, was for most of his adult life a librarian at the University of Hull. When traveling between Oxford and Hull by train one would normally change trains at Sheffield.

Annus Mirabilis[1]

Sexual intercourse began
In nineteen sixty-three
(Which was rather late for me)—
Between the end of the *Chatterley* ban[2]
5   And the Beatles' first LP.

Up till then there'd only been
A sort of bargaining,
A wrangle for a ring,
A shame that started at sixteen
10 And spread to everything.

Then all at once the quarrel sank:
Everyone felt the same,
And every life became
A brilliant breaking of the bank,
15 A quite unlosable game.

So life was never better than
In nineteen sixty-three (Though just too late for me)—
Between the end of the *Chatterley* ban
And the Beatles' first LP.
—1967

High Windows

When I see a couple of kids
And guess he's fucking her and she's
Taking pills or wearing a diaphragm,
I know this is paradise

5   Everyone old has dreamed of all their lives—
Bonds and gestures pushed to one side

Like an outdated combine harvester,
And everyone young going down the long slide

To happiness, endlessly. I wonder if
10 Anyone looked at me, forty years back,
And thought, *That'll be the life;*
No God any more, or sweating in the dark

About hell and that, or having to hide
What you think of the priest. He
15 *And his lot will all go down the long slide*
Like free bloody birds. And immediately

Rather than words comes the thought of high windows:
The sun-comprehending glass,
And beyond it, the deep blue air, that shows
20 Nothing, and is nowhere, and is endless.
—1967

This Be The Verse

They fuck you up, your mum and dad.
    They may not mean to, but they do.
They fill you with the faults they had
    And add some extra, just for you.

5   But they were fucked up in their turn
    By fools in old-style hats and coats,
Who half the time were soppy-stern
    And half at one another's throats.

Man hands on misery to man.
10   It deepens like a coastal shelf.
Get out as early as you can,
    And don't have any kids yourself.
—1971

---

1   *Annus Mirabilis*   Latin: wondrous year.
2   *the Chatterley ban*   D.H. Lawrence's novel *Lady Chatterley's Lover* was banned in both the UK and USA on the grounds of obscenity; it contained four-letter words and descriptions of sexual activity that were, for the time, quite explicit. On 2 November 1960, Penguin Books won an obscenity trial over the issue, and the ban was lifted in the UK.

Vers de Société[1]

My wife and I have asked a crowd of craps
    To come and waste their time and ours; perhaps
You'd care to join us? In a pig's arse, friend.
Day comes to an end.
5   The gas fire breathes, the trees are darkly swayed.
And so *Dear Warlock-Williams*: I'm afraid—

Funny how hard it is to be alone.
I could spend half my evenings, if I wanted,
Holding a glass of washing sherry, canted°   *obliquely pushed*
10 Over to catch the drivel of some bitch
Who's read nothing but *Which*;[2]
Just think of all the spare time that has flown

Straight into nothingness by being filled
With forks and faces, rather than repaid
15 Under a lamp, hearing the noise of wind,
And looking out to see the moon thinned
To an air-sharpened blade.
A life, and yet how sternly it's instilled

All solitude is selfish. No one now
20 Believes the hermit with his gown and dish[3]
Talking to God (who's gone too); the big wish
Is to have people nice to you, which means
Doing it back somehow.
Virtue is social. Are, then, these routines

25 Playing at goodness, like going to church?
Something that bores us, something we don't do well
(Asking that ass about his fool research)
But try to feel, because, however crudely,
It shows us what should be?
30 Too subtle, that. Too decent, too. Oh hell,

Only the young can be alone freely.
The time is shorter now for company,
And sitting by a lamp more often brings

Not peace, but other things.
35 Beyond the light stand failure and remorse
Whispering *Dear Warlock-Williams: Why, of course*—
                                            —1971

The Old Fools

*W*hat do they think has happened, the old fools,
    To make them like this? Do they somehow suppose
It's more grown-up when your mouth hangs open and
        drools
And you keep on pissing yourself, and can't remember
5   Who called this morning? Or that, if they only chose,
They could alter things back to when they danced all night,
Or went to their wedding, or sloped arms some September?
Or do they fancy there's really been no change,
And they've always behaved as if they were crippled or
        tight,
10 Or sat through days of thin continuous dreaming
Watching light move? If they don't (and they can't),
        it's strange;
                    Why aren't they screaming?

At death, you break up: the bits that were you
Start speeding away from each other for ever
15 With no one to see. It's only oblivion, true:
We had it before, but then it was going to end,
And was all the time merging with a unique endeavour
To bring to bloom the million-petalled flower
Of being here. Next time you can't pretend
20 There'll be anything else. And these are the first signs:
Not knowing how, not hearing who, the power
Of choosing gone. Their looks show that they're for it:
Ash hair, toad hands, prune face dried into lines—
                    How can they ignore it?

25 Perhaps being old is having lighted rooms
Inside your head, and people in them, acting.
People you know, yet can't quite name; each looms
Like a deep loss restored, from known doors turning,
Setting down a lamp, smiling from a stair, extracting
30 A known book from the shelves; or sometimes only
The rooms themselves, chairs and a fire burning,
The blown bush at the window, or the sun's
Faint friendliness on the wall some lonely

---

[1] *Vers de Société* Poem about social life.

[2] *Which* British consumer product testing magazine.

[3] Followers of an important strain of hermitic Christianity in medieval Europe who wore gowns of sackcloth or rough material (intended to be uncomfortable) and held out their dishes to solicit alms from other Christians.

Rain-ceased midsummer evening. That is where they
    live:
35 Not here and now, but where all happened once.
        This is why they give

An air of baffled absence, trying to be there
Yet being here. For the rooms grow farther, leaving
Incompetent cold, the constant wear and tear
40 Of taken breath, and them crouching below
Extinction's alp, the old fools, never perceiving
How near it is. This must be what keeps them quiet:
The peak that stays in view wherever we go
For them is rising ground. Can they never tell
45 What is dragging them back, and how it will end?
Not at night? Not when the strangers come? Never,
    throughout
The whole hideous inverted childhood? Well,
        We shall find out.

—1973

Aubade [1]

I work all day, and get half-drunk at night.
Waking at four to soundless dark, I stare.
In time the curtain-edges will grow light.
Till then I see what's really always there:
5 Unresting death, a whole day nearer now,
Making all thought impossible but how
And where and when I shall myself die.
Arid interrogation: yet the dread
Of dying, and being dead,
10 Flashes afresh to hold and horrify.

The mind blanks at the glare. Not in remorse
—The good not done, the love not given, time
Torn off unused—nor wretchedly because
An only life can take so long to climb
15 Clear of its wrong beginnings, and may never;

But at the total emptiness for ever,
The sure extinction that we travel to
And shall be lost in always. Not to be here,
Not to be anywhere,
20 And soon; nothing more terrible, nothing more true.

This is a special way of being afraid
No trick dispels. Religion used to try,
That vast moth-eaten musical brocade
Created to pretend we never die,
25 And specious° stuff that says *No rational being*   misleading
Can fear a thing it will not feel, not seeing
That this is what we fear—no sight, no sound,
No touch or taste or smell, nothing to think with,
Nothing to love or link with,
30 The anaesthetic from which none come round.

And so it stays just on the edge of vision,
A small unfocused blur, a standing chill
That slows each impulse down to indecision.
Most things may never happen: this one will,
35 And realisation of it rages out
In furnace-fear when we are caught without
People or drink. Courage is no good:
It means not scaring others. Being brave
Lets no one off the grave.
40 Death is no different whined at than withstood.

Slowly light strengthens, and the room takes shape.
It stands plain as a wardrobe, what we know,
Have always known, know that we can't escape,
Yet can't accept. One side will have to go.
45 Meanwhile telephones crouch, getting ready to ring
In locked-up offices, and all the uncaring
Intricate rented world begins to rouse.
The sky is white as clay, with no sun.
Work has to be done.
50 Postmen like doctors go from house to house.

—1977

[1] *aubade* From the Old French "alba," an early morning song or poem, the motif of which is usually a call for lovers to wake before parting.

TED HUGHES
1930 — 1998

When Ted Hughes was chosen to succeed Sir John Betjeman as England's Poet Laureate in 1984, a reporter in *The Times* described the selection as "a bit like appointing a grim young cow to replace a cuddly old teddy bear." Coming on the British literary scene in the 1950s, Hughes startled readers with his poetic voice. With bold metaphors and forceful rhythms, his poems paint grim, often violent, visions of human existence. At the same time, he celebrates the power of nature and attempts to reunite humanity with the natural world, using myth and folklore to explore alternative possibilities of spirituality.

Edward James Hughes was born in Mytholmroyd, a county in West Yorkshire, the landscape of which—with its valleys, cliffs, and surrounding moors—pervades much of his poetry. Hughes studied English literature for two years at Cambridge before switching to archaeology and anthropology in his final year of study—seeking to escape what he called "the terrible, suffocating, maternal octopus" of the English poetic tradition. In 1956 after graduating, Hughes met and married Sylvia Plath, an American student studying at Cambridge on a Fulbright Fellowship. The following year, having published some individual poems, Hughes released his first collection, *The Hawk in the Rain* (1957). The poems of this début—including "The Thought-Fox" and "Pike"—depict animals participating in a natural world from which humans are isolated by their intellect.

After teaching briefly in the United States, Hughes and Plath returned to England, where their two children were born and where Hughes published his second collection, *Lupercal* (1960). Hughes also began writing children's books and radio plays during this period. After Plath committed suicide in 1963, following the couple's separation, Hughes put his own poetry on hold to focus on editing and publishing his wife's poems and journals.

Hughes's return to poetry, *Wodwo* (1967), signaled a change in direction from his earlier work. An interest in anthropology began to color his work, as did a marked interest in occult, mythic, and folktale sources. The collection often features characters looking for meaning or identity through various belief systems—such as the mysterious wodwo figure in the collection's title poem, who seeks to know, "What am I?" The volume following, *Crow: From the Life and Songs of the Crow* (1970), created in collaboration with artist Leonard Baskin, presents a series of poems informed by Hughes's own mythology. These poems, which follow a crow from the genesis of the world until nuclear apocalypse, lay bare the brutality in nature, though with more humor than was present in his earlier work. Hughes said his goal in the Crow poems was to achieve a certain style consisting of "a super-simple and a super-ugly language which would in a way shed everything except just what he [Crow] wanted to say." Perhaps not surprisingly, this carrion-eating, graceless, self-serving protagonist (who became the main character of several subsequent works) brought charges of misanthropy and crudeness upon Hughes.

With *Crow* Hughes discovered his penchant for collaborative ventures, and more followed, including *Cave Birds* (1978), also with Leonard Baskin; *Remains of Elmet* (1979), in which he explores, with photographer Fay Godwin, the history of his native region from ancient to industrial times; and *River* (1983), which, accompanied by photographs by Peter Keen, provides a composite view of a river over the course of a year. Another of his later collections, *Moortown* (1979), documents his experiences dairy farming with Jack Orchard, the father of his second wife, Carol.

Though Hughes continued to publish volumes of new and collected poems, in his later years he devoted himself increasingly to judging competitions and performing readings—particularly for children—and became an active supporter of environmental and ecological causes. Hughes also turned to writing prose and to translating, publishing *Tales from Ovid* (1997), a collection of essays entitled *Winter Pollen* (1994), and his critical work on Shakespeare, *Shakespeare and the Goddess of Complete Being* (1992), which united his interest in the author with his passion for mythology.

In 1998 Hughes broke his thirty-year silence concerning his marriage with Plath and published *Birthday Letters*, a series of poems addressed to his dead wife. During the years following her death, Hughes had frequently been accused by some of Plath's admirers of "murdering" the female poet, and his surname was repeatedly defaced on her gravestone. Hughes's last collection had the effect of silencing, rather than reigniting, the expected opposition, and sales for the book have remained high since its publication.

Hughes was diagnosed with colon cancer in 1997 and died in 1998, two weeks after receiving the Order of Merit from Queen Elizabeth II. Hughes's unique vision of the natural world—and of humanity's place in it—has endured after his death, and his poetry remains widely read and studied. Of his continued popularity, British poet and critic Dick Davis explains, "He brings back to our suburban, centrally-heated and, above all, *safe* lives reports from an authentic frontier of reality and the imagination. His poems speak to us of a world that is constantly true in a way that we know our temporary comforts cannot be."

⌘ ⌘ ⌘

The Thought-Fox

I imagine this midnight moment's forest:
Something else is alive
Beside the clock's loneliness
And this blank page where my fingers move.

5 Through the window I see no star:
Something more near
Though deeper within darkness
Is entering the loneliness:

Cold, delicately as the dark snow
10 A fox's nose touches twig, leaf;
Two eyes serve a movement, that now
And again now, and now, and now

15 Sets neat prints into the snow
Between trees, and warily a lame
Shadow lags by stump and in hollow
Of a body that is bold to come

Across clearings, an eye,
A widening deepening greenness,
Brilliantly, concentratedly,
20 Coming about its own business

Till, with a sudden sharp hot stink of fox,
It enters the dark hole of the head.
The window is starless still; the clock ticks,
The page is printed.

—1957

Pike

Pike, three inches long, perfect
Pike in all parts, green tigering the gold.
Killers from the egg: the malevolent aged grin.
They dance on the surface among the flies.

5 Or move, stunned by their own grandeur,
Over a bed of emerald, silhouette
Of submarine delicacy and horror.
A hundred feet long in their world.

In ponds, under the heat-struck lily pads—
10 Gloom of their stillness:
Logged on last year's black leaves, watching upwards.
Or hung in an amber cavern of weeds

The jaws' hooked clamp and fangs
Not to be changed at this date;
15 A life subdued to its instrument;
The gills kneading quietly, and the pectorals.

Three we kept behind glass,
Jungled in weed: three inches, four,
And four and a half: fed fry to them—
20 Suddenly there were two. Finally one.

With a sag belly and the grin it was born with.
And indeed they spare nobody.
Two, six pounds each, over two feet long,
High and dry and dead in the willow-herb—

25 One jammed past its gills down the other's gullet:
The outside eye stared: as a vice locks—
The same iron in this eye
Though its film shrank in death.

A pond I fished, fifty yards across,
30 Whose lilies and muscular tench[1]
Had outlasted every visible stone
Of the monastery that planted them—

Stilled legendary depth:
It was as deep as England. It held
35 Pike too immense to stir, so immense and old
That past nightfall I dared not cast

But silently cast and fished
With the hair frozen on my head
For what might move, for what eye might move.
40 The still splashes on the dark pond,

Owls hushing the floating woods
Frail on my ear against the dream
Darkness beneath night's darkness had freed,
That rose slowly towards me, watching.
—1959

Wodwo[2]

What am I? Nosing here, turning leaves over
Following a faint stain on the air to the river's edge
I enter water. What am I to split
The glassy grain of water looking upward I see the bed
5 Of the river above me upside down very clear
What am I doing here in mid-air? Why do I find
this frog so interesting as I inspect its most secret
interior and make it my own? Do these weeds
know me and name me to each other have they
10 seen me before, do I fit in their world? I seem
separate from the ground and not rooted but dropped
out of nothing casually I've no threads
fastening me to anything I can go anywhere
I seem to have been given the freedom
15 of this place what am I then? And picking
bits of bark off this rotten stump gives me
no pleasure and it's no use so why do I do it
me and doing that have coincided very queerly
But what shall I be called am I the first
20 have I an owner what shape am I what
shape am I am I huge if I go
to the end on this way past these trees and past these trees

---

[1] *tench* Fish, like a carp.

[2] *Wodwo* Middle English word, taken from *Sir Gawain and the Green Knight*, that means "an enemy in the forest," "a wild man of the woods," or (Hughes's own definition) "some sort of goblin creature."

till I get tired that's touching one wall of me
for the moment if I sit still how everything
25 stops to watch me I suppose I am the exact centre
but there's all this what is it roots
roots roots roots and here's the water
again very queer but I'll go on looking
—1967

Theology

No, the serpent did not
Seduce Eve to the apple.
All that's simply
Corruption of the facts.

5   Adam ate the apple.
Eve ate Adam.
The serpent ate Eve.
This is the dark intestine.

The serpent, meanwhile,
10 Sleeps his meal off in Paradise—
Smiling to hear
God's querulous calling.
—1967

A Childish Prank

Man's and woman's bodies lay without souls,
Dully gaping, foolishly staring, inert
On the flowers of Eden.
God pondered.

5   The problem was so great, it dragged him asleep.

Crow laughed.
He bit the Worm, God's only son,
Into two writhing halves.

He stuffed into man the tail half
10 With the wounded end hanging out.

He stuffed the head half headfirst into woman
And it crept in deeper and up
To peer out through her eyes
Calling its tail-half to join up quickly, quickly
15 Because O it was painful.

Man awoke being dragged across the grass.
Woman awoke to see him coming.
Neither knew what had happened.

God went on sleeping.

20 Crow went on laughing.
—1972

The Seven Sorrows

The first sorrow of autumn
Is the slow goodbye
Of the garden who stands so long in the evening—

A brown poppy head,
5   The stalk of a lily,
And still cannot go.

The second sorrow
Is the empty feet
Of the pheasant who hangs from a hook with his
        brothers.
10 The woodland of gold
Is folded in feathers
With its head in a bag.

And the third sorrow
Is the slow goodbye
15 Of the sun who has gathered the birds and who gathers
The minutes of evening,
The golden and holy
Ground of the picture.

The fourth sorrow
20 Is the pond gone black

Ruined and sunken the city of water—
The beetle's palace,
The catacombs
Of the dragonfly.

25 And the fifth sorrow
Is the slow goodbye
Of the woodland that quietly breaks up its camp.
One day it's gone. It has left only litter—
Firewood, tentpoles.

30 And the sixth sorrow
Is the fox's sorrow
The joy of the huntsman, the joy of the hounds,
The hooves that pound
Till earth closes her ear
35 To the fox's prayer.

And the seventh sorrow
Is the slow goodbye
Of the face with its wrinkles that looks through the
        window
As the year packs up
40 Like a tatty fairground
That came for the children.
                                          —1975

Heptonstall Old Church.

Heptonstall Old Church[1]

A great bird landed here.

Its song drew men out of rock,
Living men out of bog and heather.

Its song put a light in the valleys
5   And harness on the long moors.

Its song brought a crystal from space
And set it in men's heads.

Then the bird died.

Its giant bones
10 Blackened and became a mystery.

The crystal in men's heads
Blackened and fell to pieces.

The valleys went out.
The moorland broke loose.
                                          —1979

---

[1] *Heptonstall Old Church*   The town of Heptonstall was three miles
from Hughes's childhood home of Mytholmroyd, in West Yorkshire. The ruins of the "old church" (dating from the thirteenth
century) stand beside the present church, constructed in 1854. The
bodies of Sylvia Plath and of Hughes's parents are buried in its
churchyard.

You Hated Spain[1]

Spain frightened you. Spain
Where I felt at home. The blood-raw light,
The oiled anchovy faces, the African
Black edges to everything, frightened you.
5 Your schooling had somehow neglected Spain.
The wrought-iron grille, death and the Arab drum.
You did not know the language, your soul was empty
Of the signs, and the welding light
Made your blood shrivel. Bosch[2]
10 Held out a spidery hand and you took it
Timidly, a bobby-sox[3] American.
You saw right down to the Goya[4] funeral grin
And recognized it, and recoiled
As your poems winced into chill, as your panic
15 Clutched back towards college America.
So we sat as tourists at the bullfight
Watching bewildered bulls awkwardly butchered,
Seeing the grey-faced matador, at the barrier
Just below us, straightening his bent sword
20 And vomiting with fear. And the horn
That hid itself inside the blowfly belly
Of the toppled picador punctured
What was waiting for you. Spain
Was the land of your dreams: the dust-red cadaver
25 You dared not wake with, the puckering amputations
No literature course had glamorized.
The juju[5] land behind your African lips.
Spain was what you tried to wake up from
And could not. I see you, in moonlight,
30 Walking the empty wharf at Alicante[6]
Like a soul waiting for the ferry,

A new soul, still not understanding,
Thinking it is still your honeymoon
In the happy world, with your whole life waiting,
35 Happy, and all your poems still to be found.
—1998

Daffodils

Remember how we[7] picked the daffodils?
Nobody else remembers, but I remember.
Your daughter came with her armfuls, eager and happy,
Helping the harvest. She has forgotten.
5 She cannot even remember you. And we sold them.
It sounds like sacrilege, but we sold them.
Were we so poor? Old Stoneman, the grocer,
Boss-eyed, his blood-pressure purpling to beetroot
(It was his last chance,
10 He would die in the same great freeze as you),
He persuaded us. Every Spring
He always bought them, sevenpence a dozen,
"A custom of the house."

Besides, we still weren't sure we wanted to own
15 Anything. Mainly we were hungry
To convert everything to profit.
Still nomads—still strangers
To our whole possession. The daffodils
Were incidental gilding of the deeds,
20 Treasure trove. They simply came,
And they kept on coming.
As if not from the sod but falling from heaven.
Our lives were still a raid on our own good luck.
We knew we'd live for ever. We had not learned
25 What a fleeting glance of the everlasting
Daffodils are. Never identified
The nuptial flight of the rarest ephemera—
Our own days!
              We thought they were a windfall.
30 Never guessed they were a last blessing.
So we sold them. We worked at selling them
As if employed on somebody else's
Flower-farm. You bent at it
In the rain of that April—your last April.

---

1 *You Hated Spain* Both this poem and "Daffodils" are from Hughes's collection *Birthday Letters*, the poems in which are all addressed to Sylvia Plath.

2 *Bosch* Dutch painter Hieronymus Bosch (c. 1450–1516), whose works often depicted figures that were part human, part monster.

3 *bobby-sox* I.e., adolescent. "Bobby-socks" were short socks, reaching just above the ankle, often worn by girls in their early teens in the 1950s and early 1960s.

4 *Goya* Spanish painter Françisco de Goya (1746–1828), known for his grotesques.

5 *juju* Possessing supernatural or magical powers.

6 *Alicante* Port and tourist center in southeastern Spain.

7 *we* I.e., Hughes and Sylvia Plath.

35   We bent there together, among the soft shrieks
      Of their jostled stems, the wet shocks shaken
      Of their girlish dance-frocks—
      Fresh-opened dragonflies, wet and flimsy,
      Opened too early.

40   We piled their frailty lights on a carpenter's bench,
      Distributed leaves among the dozens—
      Buckling blade-leaves, limber, groping for air, zinc-
           silvered—
      Propped their raw butts in bucket water,
      Their oval, meaty butts,
45   And sold them, sevenpence a bunch—

      Wind-wounds, spasms from the dark earth,
      With their odourless metals,
      A flamy purification of the deep grave's stony cold
      As if ice had a breath—

50   We sold them, to wither.
      The crop thickened faster than we could thin it.
      Finally, we were overwhelmed
      And we lost our wedding-present scissors.

      Every March since they have lifted again
55   Out of the same bulbs, the same
      Baby-cries from the thaw,
      Ballerinas too early for music, shiverers
      In the draughty wings of the year.
      On that same groundswell of memory, fluttering
60   They return to forget you stooping there
      Behind the rainy curtains of a dark April,
      Snipping their stems.

      But somewhere your scissors remember.
      Wherever they are.
65   Here somewhere, blades wide open,
      April by April
      Sinking deeper
      Through the sod—an anchor, a cross of rust.
      —1998

CHINUA ACHEBE
b. 1930

Chinua Achebe gained international attention with the publication of his first novel, *Things Fall Apart* (1958); it has since attained the status of a modern classic, and has sold over ten million copies. *Things Fall Apart*, together with Achebe's subsequent novels, follows the course of Nigerian history from just before colonial rule until immediately after independence. Written from the perspective of the colonized Nigerians, these works record the trauma that resulted from Africa's experience with European rule and—without idealizing Nigerians—demonstrate the value, dignity, and beauty of a culture that was all but lost during colonial rule. Though Achebe's writing, whether short story, novel, or political essay, often focuses explicitly on his native country, he argues against a narrowly nationalistic approach and seeks what he calls "universal communication across racial and cultural boundaries as a means of fostering respect for all people."

Achebe was born Albert Chinualumoga Achebe in 1930 in eastern Nigeria. Both Achebe's parents were Christian converts, and his father was employed as a catechist for the Church Missionary Society. Achebe attended the prestigious Government College at Umuahia before enrolling in University College, Ibadan, a newly constituent college of the University of London. There Achebe decided to study literature, following a curriculum that mirrored that of the College's British parent school—with the sole addition of some writers thought relevant to African students, such as Joseph Conrad, H. Rider Haggard, and colonial administrators such as Joyce Cary (whose novel *Mister Johnson* had a profound influence on Achebe). The work of these writers, which frequently features stereotypical and racist depictions of African people, helped to persuade Achebe to write, and also determined his choice to write in English. Unlike many other African writers (such as Kenyan writer Ngūgī wa Thiongo) who choose to use their native language rather than that of their colonizers, Achebe feels that by writing in English he can more directly take issue with these colonial writers by replacing their portraits of the African with his own.

While in university, Achebe contributed several stories to the *University Herald*. These stories, published much later in *Girls at War and Other Stories* (1972), foreground the ways in which conflicts between modern and traditional values have been exacerbated by colonial contact. The traditional balance between material and spiritual aspects of society, and between a concern for self and for community, is typically disrupted, robbing subjects of a strong culture on which to rely. Achebe, himself educated in a system that favored all elements of the new, colonial order—whether cultural, religious, or academic—over those of traditional Biafran society, had to learn for himself much of the history of his people.

After graduating from university, Achebe married, started a family, and embarked on a twelve-year career as a producer for the Nigerian Broadcasting Corporation. Encouraged by literary critic Gilbert Phelps, one of his teachers at the BBC staff school, Achebe published *Things Fall Apart* in 1958. Much of what struck readers of this first novel was Achebe's ability to adapt the English language to his own goals in writing about Nigeria. He relies heavily on Ibo proverbs—which often highlight the themes of his works or help further characterization—and vernacular speech patterns, as well as on native imagery and folklore. In this way his English manages to convey the flavor of Nigerian experience, belief, and culture. In Achebe's view, "the price a world language must be prepared to pay is submission to many different kinds of use. The African writer should aim to use English in a way that brings out his message best. ... He should aim at fashioning out an English which is at once universal and able to carry his peculiar experience."

No Longer at Ease (1960), *Arrow of God* (1964), *A Man of the People* (1966), and *Anthills of the Savannah* (1987), Achebe's other novels, have also been highly acclaimed. Achebe's prescience has often been noted in his examinations of Nigeria's political situation. *A Man of the People*, for example, expressed Achebe's concern over what he identified as Nigeria's lack of strong leadership—a lack that led to Nigeria's first military coup in January 1966, the month of the novel's publication.

During the civil war that followed, Achebe traveled and spoke extensively on behalf of his people, who briefly formed the independent state of Biafra in 1967. Following the conclusion of civil war in 1970, Achebe continued his political activities while accepting various teaching posts at American schools. The poetry and essays written during this period are more overtly political than his earlier work. *Morning Yet on Creation Day* (1974) contains both literary and political essays; many of these have been reprinted in the collection *Hopes and Impediments* (1988), which opens with Achebe's controversial essay on Joseph Conrad's *Heart of Darkness*.

Achebe returned to work at the University of Nigeria in 1976, but after a serious car accident in 1990 he moved to the United States to recuperate, accepting a post at Bard College, New York. There he published a new collection of poems and essays, *Another Africa* (1997), and a memoir in the form of three essays, entitled *Home and Exile* (2000).

Throughout his career Achebe has insisted that his political actions and his literary pursuits are not two separate activities, but two ways of attempting to achieve the same end. He firmly believes that storytelling, far from being an idle pursuit, is a socially relevant form of political engagement. "Literature, whether handed down by word of mouth or in print, gives us a second handle on reality; enabling us to encounter in the safe manageable dimensions of make-believe the very same threats to integrity that may assail the psyche in real life; and at the same time providing through the self-discovery which it imparts, a veritable weapon for coping with these threats."

⌘ ⌘ ⌘

The Sacrificial Egg

Julius Obi sat gazing at his typewriter. The fat Chief Clerk, his boss, was snoring at his table. Outside, the gatekeeper in his green uniform was sleeping at his post. You couldn't blame him; no customer had passed through the gate for nearly a week. There was an empty basket on the giant weighing machine. A few palm-kernels lay desolately in the dust around the machine. Only the flies remained in strength.

Julius went to the window that overlooked the great market on the bank of the River Niger. This market, though still called Nkwo, had long spilled over into Eke, Oye, and Afo with the coming of civilization and the growth of the town into the big palm-oil port. In spite of this encroachment, however, it was still busiest on its original Nkwo day, because the deity who had presided over it from antiquity still cast her spell only on her own day—let men in their greed spill over themselves. It was said that she appeared in the form of an old woman in the centre of the market just before cock-crow and waved her magic fan in the four directions of the earth—in front of her, behind her, to the right, and to the left—to draw to the market men and women from distant places. And they came bringing the produce of their lands—palm-oil and kernels, cola nuts, cassava, mats, baskets and earthenware pots; and took home many-coloured cloths, smoked fish, iron pots and plates. These were the forest peoples. The other half of the world who lived by the great rivers came down also—by canoe, bringing yams and fish. Sometimes it was a big canoe with a dozen or more people in it; sometimes it was a lone fisherman and his wife in a small vessel from the swift-flowing Anambara.[1] They moored their canoe on the bank and sold their fish, after much haggling. The woman then walked up the steep banks of the river to the heart of the market to buy salt and oil and, if the sales had been very good, even a length of cloth. And for her children at home she bought bean cakes and mai-mai[2] which the Igara women cooked. As evening approached, they took up their paddles again and paddled away, the water shimmering in the sunset and their canoe becoming smaller and smaller in the distance until it was just a dark crescent on the water's face and two dark bodies swaying forwards and backwards in it. Umuru then was the meeting place of the forest people who were called Igbo and the alien river folk whom the Igbo called Olu and beyond whom the world stretched in indefiniteness.

Julius Obi was not a native of Umuru. He had come like countless others from some bush village inland. Having passed his Standard Six in a mission school he had come to Umuru to work as a clerk in the offices of the all-powerful European trading company which bought palm-kernels at its own price and cloth and metalware, also at its own price. The offices were situated beside the famous market so that in his first two or three weeks Julius had to learn to work within its huge enveloping hum. Sometimes when the Chief Clerk was away he walked to the window and looked down on the vast anthill activity. Most of these people were not here yesterday, he thought, and yet the market had been just as full. There must be many, many people in the world to be able to fill the market day after day like this. Of course they say not all who came to the great market were real people. Janet's mother, Ma, had said so.

"Some of the beautiful young women you see squeezing through the crowds are not people like you or me but mammy-wota[3] who have their town in the depths of the river," she said. "You can always tell them, because they are beautiful with a beauty that is too perfect and too cold. You catch a glimpse of her with the tail of your eye, then you blink and look properly, but she has already vanished in the crowd."

Julius thought about these things as he now stood at the window looking down on the silent, empty market. Who would have believed that the great boisterous market could ever be quenched like this? But such was the strength of Kitikpa, the incarnate power of smallpox. Only he could drive away all those people and leave the market to the flies.

When Umuru was a little village, there was an agegrade[4] who swept its market-square every Nkwo day. But progress had turned it into a busy, sprawling, crowded and dirty river port, a no-man's-land where strangers outnumbered by far the sons of the soil, who could do nothing about it except shake their heads at this gross perversion of their prayer. For indeed they had prayed—who will blame them—for their town to grow and prosper. And it had grown. But there is good growth and there is bad growth. The belly does not bulge out only with food and drink; it might be the abominable disease which would end by sending its sufferer out of the house even before he was fully dead.

The strangers who came to Umuru came for trade and money, not in search of duties to perform, for they had those in plenty back home in their village which was real home.

And as if this did not suffice, the young sons and daughters of Umuru soil, encouraged by schools and churches were behaving no better than the strangers. They neglected all their old tasks and kept only the revelries.

Such was the state of the town when Kitikpa came to see it and to demand the sacrifice the inhabitants owed the gods of the soil. He came in confident knowledge of the terror he held over the people. He was an evil deity, and boasted it. Lest he be offended those he

---

[1] *Anambara* Anambara River, a south-flowing tributary of the River Niger.

[2] *mai-mai* Cakes made of beans, eggs, and chilies.

[3] *mammy-wota* River deities; legendary seductresses who bring wealth but no children.

[4] *agegrade* Member of a specific age set, a group of young men of similar ages who occupy different social roles, or perform different duties, at each stage of maturation.

killed were not killed but decorated, and no one dared weep for them. He put an end to the coming and going between neighbours and between villages. They said, "Kitikpa is in that village," and immediately it was cut off by its neighbours.

Julius was sad and worried because it was almost a week since he had seen Janet, the girl he was going to marry. Ma had explained to him very gently that he should no longer go to see them "until this thing is over, by the power of Jehovah." (Ma was a very devout Christian convert and one reason why she approved of Julius for her only daughter was that he sang in the choir of the CMS church.)

"You must keep to your rooms," she had said in hushed tones, for Kitikpa strictly forbade any noise or boisterousness. "You never know whom you might meet on the streets. That family has got it." She lowered her voice even more and pointed surreptitiously at the house across the road whose doorway was barred with a yellow palm-frond. "He has decorated one of them already and the rest were moved away today in a big government lorry."

Janet walked a short way with Julius and stopped; so he stopped too. They seemed to have nothing to say to each other yet they lingered on. Then she said goodnight and he said goodnight. And they shook hands, which was very odd, as though parting for the night were something new and grave.

He did not go straight home, because he wanted desperately to cling, even alone, to this strange parting. Being educated he was not afraid of whom he might meet, so he went to the bank of the river and just walked up and down it. He must have been there a long time because he was still there when the wooden gong of the night-mask sounded. He immediately set out for home, half-walking and half-running, for night-masks were not a matter of superstition; they were real. They chose the night for their revelry because like the bat's their ugliness was great.

In his hurry he stepped on something that broke with a slight liquid explosion. He stopped and peeped down at the footpath. The moon was not up yet but there was a faint light in the sky which showed that it would not be long delayed. In this half-light he saw that

he had stepped on an egg offered in sacrifice. Someone oppressed by misfortune had brought the offering to the crossroads in the dusk. And he had stepped on it. There were the usual young palm-fronds around it. But Julius saw it differently as a house where the terrible artist was at work. He wiped the sole of his foot on the sandy path and hurried away, carrying another vague worry in his mind. But hurrying was no use now; the fleet-footed mask was already abroad. Perhaps it was impelled to hurry by the threatening imminence of the moon. Its voice rose high and clear in the still night air like a flaming sword. It was yet a long way away, but Julius knew that distances vanished before it. So he made straight for the cocoyam farm beside the road and threw himself on his belly, in the shelter of the broad leaves. He had hardly done this when he heard the rattling staff of the spirit and a thundering stream of esoteric speech. He shook all over. The sounds came bearing down on him, almost pressing his face into the moist earth. And now he could hear the footsteps. It was as if twenty evil men were running together. Panic sweat broke all over him and he was nearly impelled to get up and run. Fortunately he kept a firm hold on himself … In no time at all the commotion in the air and on the earth—the thunder and torrential rain, the earthquake and flood—passed and disappeared in the distance on the other side of the road.

The next morning at the office, the Chief Clerk, a son of the soil spoke bitterly about last night's provocation of Kitikpa by the headstrong youngsters who had launched the noisy fleet-footed mask in defiance of their elders, who knew that Kitikpa would be enraged, and then …

The trouble was that the disobedient youths had never yet experienced the power of Kitikpa themselves; they had only heard of it. But soon they would learn.

As Julius stood at the window looking out on the emptied market he lived through the terror of that night again. It was barely a week ago but already it seemed like another life, separated from the present by a vast emptiness. This emptiness deepened with every passing day. On this side of it stood Julius, and on the other Ma and Janet whom the dread artist decorated.

—1959, 1972

from *An Image of Africa:*
Racism in Conrad's Heart of Darkness

In the fall of 1974 I was walking one day from the English Department at the University of Massachusetts to a parking lot. It was a fine autumn morning such as encouraged friendliness to passing strangers. Brisk youngsters were hurrying in all directions, many of them obviously freshmen in their first flush of enthusiasm. An older man going the same way as I turned and remarked to me how very young they came these days. I agreed. Then he asked me if I was a student too. I said no, I was a teacher. What did I teach? African literature. Now that was funny, he said, because he knew a fellow who taught the same thing, or perhaps it was African history, in a certain community college not far from here. It always surprised him, he went on to say, because he never had thought of Africa as having that kind of stuff, you know. By this time I was walking much faster. "Oh well," I heard him say finally, behind me: "I guess I have to take your course to find out."

A few weeks later, I received two very touching letters from high school children in Yonkers, New York, who—bless their teacher—had just read *Things Fall Apart*. One of them was particularly happy to learn about the customs and superstitions of an African tribe.

I propose to draw from these rather trivial encounters rather heavy conclusions which at first sight might seem somewhat out of proportion to them. But only, I hope, at first sight.

The young fellow from Yonkers, perhaps partly on account of his age, but I believe also for much deeper and more serious reasons, is obviously unaware that the life of his own tribesmen in Yonkers, New York, is full of odd customs and superstitions and, like everybody else in his culture, imagines that he needs a trip to Africa to encounter those things.

The other person being fully my own age could not be excused on the grounds of his years. Ignorance might be a more likely reason; but here again I believe that something more willful than a mere lack of information was at work. For did not that erudite British historian and Regius Professor at Oxford, Hugh Trevor-Roper,[1]

also pronounce that African history did not exist?

If there is something in these utterances more than youthful inexperience, more than a lack of factual knowledge, what is it? Quite simply it is the desire—one might indeed say the need—in Western psychology to set Africa up as a foil to Europe, as a place of negations at once remote and vaguely familiar, in comparison with which Europe's own state of spiritual grace will be manifest.

This need is not new; which should relieve us all of considerable responsibility and perhaps make us even willing to look at this phenomenon dispassionately. I have neither the wish nor the competence to embark on the exercise with the tools of the social and biological sciences but do so more simply in the manner of a novelist responding to one famous book of European fiction: Joseph Conrad's *Heart of Darkness*, which better than any other work that I know displays that Western desire and need which I have just referred to. Of course there are whole libraries of books devoted to the same purpose, but most of them are so obvious and so crude that few people worry about them today. Conrad, on the other hand, is undoubtedly one of the great stylists of modern fiction and a good storyteller into the bargain. His contribution therefore falls automatically into a different class—permanent literature—read and taught and constantly evaluated by serious academics. *Heart of Darkness* is indeed so secure today that a leading Conrad scholar has numbered it "among the half-dozen greatest short novels in the English language."[2] I will return to this critical opinion in due course, because it may seriously modify my earlier suppositions about who may or may not be guilty in some of the matters I will now raise.

Heart of Darkness projects the image of Africa as "the other world," the antithesis of Europe and therefore of civilization, a place where man's vaunted intelligence and refinement are finally mocked by triumphant bestiality. The book opens on the River Thames, tranquil, resting peacefully "at the decline of day after ages of good service done to the race that peopled its banks." But the actual story will take place on the River

---

[1] *British ... Trevor-Roper* In 1963, Trevor-Roper made the comment, "Perhaps in the future there will be some African history to teach. But at the present there is none; there is only the history of Europeans in Africa. The rest is darkness, and darkness is not the subject of history."

[2] *among the ... language* From Albert J. Guerard's introduction to *Heart of Darkness*, 1950.

666674 CHINUA ACHEBE

Congo, the very antithesis of the Thames. The River Congo is quite decidedly not a River Emeritus. It has rendered no service and enjoys no old-age pension. We are told that "going up that river was like travelling back to the earliest beginning of the world."

Is Conrad saying then that these two rivers are very different, one good, the other bad? Yes, but that is not the real point. It is not the differentness that worries Conrad but the lurking hint of kinship, of common ancestry. For the Thames too "has been one of the dark places of the earth." It conquered its darkness, of course, and is now in daylight and at peace. But if it were to visit its primordial relative, the Congo, it would run the terrible risk of hearing grotesque echoes of its own forgotten darkness, and falling victim to an avenging recrudescence of the mindless frenzy of the first beginnings. These suggestive echoes comprise Conrad's famed evocation of the African atmosphere in *Heart of Darkness*. In the final consideration his method amounts to no more than a steady, ponderous, fake-ritualistic repetition of two antithetical sentences, one about silence and the other about frenzy. We can inspect samples of this on pages 103 and 105 of the New American Library edition:[1] (a) "It was the stillness of an implacable force brooding over an inscrutable intention" and (b) "The steamer toiled along slowly on the edge of a black and incomprehensible frenzy." Of course there is a judicious change of adjective from time to time, so that instead of "inscrutable," for example, you might have "unspeakable," even plain "mysterious," etc., etc.

The eagle-eyed English critic F.R. Leavis drew attention long ago to Conrad's "adjectival insistence upon inexpressible and incomprehensible mystery."[2] That insistence must not be dismissed lightly, as many Conrad critics have tended to do, as a mere stylistic flaw; for it raises serious questions of artistic good faith. When a writer while pretending to record scenes, incidents, and their impact is in reality engaged in inducing hypnotic stupor in his readers through a bombardment of emotive words and other forms of

trickery, much more has to be at stake than stylistic felicity. Generally normal readers are well armed to detect and resist such underhand activity. But Conrad chose his subject well—one which was guaranteed not to put him in conflict with the psychological predisposition of his readers or raise the need for him to contend with their resistance. He chose the role of purveyor of comforting myths.

The most interesting and revealing passages in *Heart of Darkness* are, however, about people. I must crave the indulgence of my reader to quote almost a whole page from about the middle of the story when representatives of Europe in a steamer going down the Congo encounter the denizens of Africa:

We were wanderers on a prehistoric earth, on an earth that wore the aspect of an unknown planet. We could have fancied ourselves the first of men taking possession of an accursed inheritance, to be subdued at the cost of profound anguish and of excessive toil. But suddenly, as we struggled round a bend, there would be a glimpse of rush walls, of peaked grass-roofs, a burst of yells, a whirl of black limbs, a mass of hands clapping, of feet stamping, of bodies swaying, of eyes rolling, under the droop of heavy and motionless foliage. The steamer toiled along slowly on the edge of the black and incomprehensible frenzy. The prehistoric man was cursing us, praying to us, welcoming us—who could tell? We were cut off from the comprehension of our surroundings; we glided past like phantoms, wondering and secretly appalled, as sane men would be before an enthusiastic outbreak in a madhouse. We could not understand because we were too far and could not remember because we were travelling in the night of first ages, of those ages that are gone, leaving hardly a sign—and no memories.

The earth seemed unearthly. We are accustomed to look upon the shackled form of a conquered monster, but there—there you could look at a thing monstrous and free. It was unearthly, and the men were—No, they were not inhuman. Well, you know, that was the worst of it—this suspicion of their not being inhuman. It would come slowly to one. They howled and leaped, and spun, and made horrid faces; but what thrilled you was just the thought of their humanity—like yours—the thought of your remote kinship with this wild and

___

[1] *pages ... edition* Pages 105 and 107 of the Broadview edition (D.C.R.A. Goonetilleke, ed., 2nd edition, 1999). From this point on, all page numbers, provided in square brackets, are those of the Broadview edition.

[2] *adjectival ... mystery* From F.R. Leavis, *The Great Tradition* (1950).

passionate uproar. Ugly. Yes, it was ugly enough; but if you were man enough you would admit to yourself that there was in you just the faintest trace of a response to the terrible frankness of that noise, a dim suspicion of there being a meaning in it which you—you so remote from the night of first ages—could comprehend. [107–08]

Herein lies the meaning of *Heart of Darkness* and the fascination it holds over the Western mind: "What thrilled you was just the thought of their humanity—like yours ... Ugly."

Having shown us Africa in the mass, Conrad then zeros in, half a page later, on a specific example, giving us one of his rare descriptions of an African who is not just limbs or rolling eyes:

And between whiles I had to look after the savage who was fireman. He was an improved specimen; he could fire up a vertical boiler. He was there below me, and, upon my word, to look at him was as edifying as seeing a dog in a parody of breeches and a feather hat, walking on his hind legs. A few months of training had done for that really fine chap. He squinted at the steam gauge and at the water gauge with an evident effort of intrepidity—and he had filed his teeth, too, the poor devil, and the wool of his pate shaved into queer patterns, and three ornamental scars on each of his cheeks. He ought to have been clapping his hands and stamping his feet on the bank, instead of which he was hard at work, a thrall to strange witchcraft, full of improving knowledge. [108]

As everybody knows, Conrad is a romantic on the side. He might not exactly admire savages clapping their hands and stamping their feet but they have at least the merit of being in their place, unlike this dog in a parody of breeches. For Conrad things being in their place is of the utmost importance. "Fine fellows—cannibals—in their place," he tells us pointedly. Tragedy begins when things leave their accustomed place, like Europe leaving its safe stronghold between the policeman and the baker to take a peep into the heart of darkness.

Before the story takes us into the Congo basin proper we are given this nice little vignette as an example of things in their place:

Now and then a boat from the shore gave one a momentary contact with reality. It was paddled by black fellows. You could see from afar the white of their eyeballs glistening. They shouted, sang; their bodies streamed with perspiration; they had faces like grotesque masks—these chaps; but they had bone, muscle, a wild vitality, an intense energy of movement, that was as natural and true as the surf along their coast. They wanted no excuse for being there. They were a great comfort to look at. [80]

Towards the end of the story Conrad lavishes a whole page quite unexpectedly on an African woman who has obviously been some kind of mistress to Mr. Kurtz and now presides (if I may be permitted a little liberty) like a formidable mystery over the inexorable imminence of his departure:

She was savage and superb, wild-eyed and magnificent ... She stood looking at us without a stir and like the wilderness itself, with an air of brooding over an inscrutable purpose. [137–38]

This Amazon is drawn in considerable detail, albeit of a predictable nature, for two reasons. First, she is in her place and so can win Conrad's special brand of approval; and second, she fulfils a structural requirement of the story: a savage counterpart to the refined, European woman who will step forth to end the story:

She came forward, all in black with a pale head, floating toward me in the dusk. She was in mourning ... She took both my hands in hers and murmured, "I had heard you were coming" ... She had a mature capacity for fidelity, for belief, for suffering. [154]

The difference in the attitude of the novelist to these two women is conveyed in too many direct and subtle ways to need elaboration. But perhaps the most significant difference is the one implied in the author's bestowal of human expression to the one and the withholding of it from the other. It is clearly not part of Conrad's purpose to confer language on the "rudimentary souls" of Africa. In place of speech they made "a violent babble of uncouth sounds." They "exchanged short grunting phrases" even among themselves. But most of the time they were too busy with their frenzy. There are two occasions in the book, however, when Conrad departs somewhat from his practice and confers speech, even English speech, on the savages. The first occurs when cannibalism gets the better of them:

> "Catch 'im," he snapped, with a bloodshot widening of his eyes and a flash of sharp white teeth—"catch 'im. Give 'im to us." "To you, eh?" I asked; "what would you do with them?" "Eat 'im!" he said curtly. [113]

The other occasion was the famous announcement:

> "Mistah Kurtz—he dead" [148].

At first sight these instances might be mistaken for unexpected acts of generosity from Conrad. In reality they constitute some of his best assaults. In the case of the cannibals the incomprehensible grunts that had thus far served them for speech suddenly proved inadequate for Conrad's purpose of letting the European glimpse the unspeakable craving in their hearts. Weighing the necessity for consistency in the portrayal of the dumb brutes against the sensational advantages of securing their conviction by clear, unambiguous evidence issuing out of their own mouths, Conrad chose the latter. As for the announcement of Mr. Kurtz's death by the "insolent black head in the doorway," what better or more appropriate *finis* could be written to the horror story of that wayward child of civilization who wilfully had given his soul to the powers of darkness and "taken a high seat amongst the devils of the land" than the proclamation of his physical death by the forces he had joined?

It might be contended, of course, that the attitude to the African in *Heart of Darkness* is not Conrad's but that of his fictional narrator, Marlow, and that far from endorsing it Conrad might indeed be holding it up to irony and criticism. Certainly, Conrad appears to go to considerable pains to set up layers of insulation between himself and the moral universe of his story. He has, for example, a narrator behind a narrator. The primary narrator is Marlow, but his account is given to us through the filter of a second, shadowy person. But if Conrad's intention is to draw a *cordon sanitaire*[1] be-

tween himself and the moral and psychological *malaise* of his narrator, his care seems to me totally wasted because he neglects to hint, clearly and adequately, at an alternative frame of reference by which we may judge the actions and opinions of his characters. It would not have been beyond Conrad's power to make that provision if he had thought it necessary. Conrad seems to me to approve of Marlow, with only minor reservations—a fact reinforced by the similarities between their two careers.

Marlow comes through to us not only as a witness of truth, but one holding those advanced and humane views appropriate to the English liberal tradition which required all Englishmen of decency to be deeply shocked by atrocities in Bulgaria or the Congo of King Leopold of the Belgians or wherever.

Thus Marlow is able to toss out such bleeding-heart sentiments as these:

> They were all dying slowly—it was very clear. They were not enemies, they were not criminals, they were nothing earthly now—nothing but black shadows of disease and starvation, lying confusedly in the greenish gloom. Brought from all the recesses of the coast in all the legality of time contracts, lost in uncongenial surroundings, fed on unfamiliar food, they sickened, became inefficient, and were then allowed to crawl away and rest. [84]

The kind of liberalism espoused here by Marlow/Conrad touched all the best minds of the age in England, Europe, and America. It took different forms in the minds of different people but almost always managed to sidestep the ultimate question of equality between white people and black people. That extraordinary missionary Albert Schweitzer,[2] who sacrificed brilliant careers in music and theology in Europe for a life of service to Africans in much the same area as Conrad writes about, epitomizes the ambivalence. In a comment which has often been quoted Schweitzer says: "The African is indeed my brother but my junior brother." And so he proceeded to build a hospital appropriate to the needs of junior brothers with standards of hygiene reminiscent of medical practice in the

---

1 *cordon sanitaire*   French: quarantine line.

2 *Albert Schweitzer*   M.D., humanitarian, and winner of the Nobel Peace Prize (1875–1965).

days before the germ theory of disease came into being. Naturally he became a sensation in Europe and America. Pilgrims flocked, and I believe still flock even after he has passed on, to witness the prodigious miracle in Lambéréné,[1] on the edge of the primeval forest.

Conrad's liberalism would not take him quite as far as Schweitzer's, though. He would not use the word "brother" however qualified; the farthest he would go was "kinship." When Marlow's African helmsman falls down with a spear in his heart he gives his white master one final disquieting look:

> And the intimate profundity of that look he gave me when he received his hurt remains to this day in my memory—like a claim of distant kinship affirmed in a supreme moment. [125–26]

It is important to note that Conrad, careful as ever with his words, is concerned not so much about "distant kinship" as about someone *laying a claim* on it. The black man lays a claim on the white man which is well-nigh intolerable. It is the laying of this claim which frightens and at the same time fascinates Conrad, "the thought of their humanity—like yours ... Ugly."

The point of my observations should be quite clear by now, namely that Joseph Conrad was a thoroughgoing racist. That this simple truth is glossed over in criticisms of his work is due to the fact that white racism against Africa is such a normal way of thinking that its

manifestations go completely unremarked. Students of *Heart of Darkness* will often tell you that Conrad is concerned not so much with Africa as with the deterioration of one European mind caused by solitude and sickness. They will point out to you that Conrad is, if anything, less charitable to the Europeans in the story than he is to the natives, that the point of the story is to ridicule Europe's civilizing mission in Africa. A Conrad student informed me in Scotland that Africa is merely a setting for the disintegration of the mind of Mr. Kurtz.

Which is partly the point. Africa as setting and backdrop which eliminates the African as human factor. Africa as a metaphysical battlefield devoid of all recognizable humanity, into which the wandering European enters at his peril. Can nobody see the preposterous and perverse arrogance in thus reducing Africa to the role of props for the break-up of one petty European mind? But that is not even the point. The real question is the dehumanization of Africa and Africans which this age-long attitude has fostered and continues to foster in the world. And the question is whether a novel which celebrates this dehumanization, which depersonalizes a portion of the human race, can be called a great work of art. My answer is: No, it cannot.

—1977

---

[1] *miracle in Lambéréné* Hospital built in 1913 by Schweitzer and his wife, Helene Bresslau, in what is now Gabon.

SEAMUS HEANEY
b. 1939

The American poet Robert Lowell once referred to Seamus Heaney as "the best Irish poet since Yeats." Since winning the Nobel Prize for literature in 1995, Heaney has been one of the most popular poets writing in English. Often praised for its lyricism, Heaney's work reflects his rural upbringing, with a focus on the soil, the past, and lost friends. Many of his poems also deal with the troubles in his native Northern Ireland, and some have criticized him for an alleged ambivalence about the political conflict.

Heaney grew up in a Roman Catholic household in the predominantly Protestant north. The eldest of nine children, he was not marked in childhood by the strife that would later affect the region. Instead, he experienced a community that lived in harmony, regardless of religious affiliation. Heaney's parents were farmers in County Derry, just outside Belfast. He grew up with an appreciation for country life, for those who work the land, and for the importance of close-knit community. It was the radio that taught him the "thrill of story" and introduced him to a wider world beyond his county. His poetry is often filled with images from this period of his life.

Heaney's career as a published poet began while he was completing a teacher's certificate at St. Joseph's College in Belfast. Writing under the pseudonym "Incertus," he had just finished his Bachelor of Arts in English Language and Literature at Queen's University when he joined a poetry workshop. Known as "The Belfast Group," this forum allowed new poets to showcase their work and have it critiqued by their peers. The Group introduced him to other young poets, including his future wife, and was also a forum for the discussion of the political issues of the day. Many of Heaney's early poems were first read and discussed at Group meetings.

The publication in 1966 of Heaney's first book of poems, *Death of a Naturalist*, began what would be a career filled with awards and accolades. This volume won the Somerset Maugham Award, among others. While establishing his career as a poet, Heaney was working as a lecturer in English at various colleges in Ireland and the United States to support his growing family, which would eventually include two sons and a daughter. His move south to the Republic of Ireland in 1972 was in many respects a positive one, but moving away from the political controversies of Northern Ireland to the relative stability of the south was seen by some as a betrayal. Establishing a home just outside Dublin did not, however, lead Heaney to forget the political turmoil of his birthplace. It was during this time that he wrote some of his most political works: *North* (1975) and *Field Work* (1979). He did not want to be seen solely as a political poet, though, and felt he needed distance from the conflicts of the north to provide scope for objectivity.

Heaney's rising international fame led to his appointment as Boylston Professor of Rhetoric and Oratory at Harvard in 1984. This position allowed him to teach one semester at Harvard in the spring and spend the remaining eight months of the year at his home in Dublin. The death of Heaney's mother, also in 1984, was the occasion for some of his most touching poetry, published in *Haw Lantern* (1987). When questioned about his memorializing of lost friends and family, Heaney responded: "The elegiac Heaney? There's nothing else." Heaney uses this fascination with the past to comment indirectly on the present. In one of his "bog poems," "Punishment," Heaney compares a first-century girl who was drowned as punishment for adultery to women in Northern Ireland today. In other poems he uses the details of rural life, such as digging potatoes, churning milk, and eating wild fruit, to comment on universal issues.

In 1995 Heaney was awarded the Nobel Prize for literature. In making the award, the committee cited his "works of lyrical beauty and ethical depth, which exalt everyday miracles and the living past." In his Nobel acceptance speech he wrote that the "form of the poem ... is crucial to poetry's power to do the thing which always is and always will be to poetry's credit: the power to persuade that vulnerable part of our consciousness of its rightness in spite of the evidence of wrongness all around it."

In 1999, Heaney published a translation of *Beowulf*, which won the Whitbread Book of the Year Award in 2000. When asked why he writes poetry, he responded that the "excitement of something coming out right ... that is indeed its own reward."

⌘ ⌘ ⌘

Digging

Between my finger and my thumb
The squat pen rests; snug as a gun.

Under my window, a clean rasping sound
When the spade sinks into gravelly ground:
5 My father, digging. I look down

Till his straining rump among the flowerbeds
Bends low, comes up twenty years away
Stooping in rhythm through potato drills[1]
Where he was digging.

10 The coarse boot nestled on the lug, the shaft
Against the inside knee was levered firmly.
He rooted out tall tops, buried the bright edge deep
To scatter new potatoes that we picked
Loving their cool hardness in our hands.

15 By God, the old man could handle a spade.
Just like his old man.

My grandfather cut more turf[2] in a day
Than any other man on Toner's bog.
Once I carried him milk in a bottle

20 Corked sloppily with paper. He straightened up
To drink it, then fell to right away
Nicking and slicing neatly, heaving sods
Over his shoulder, going down and down
For the good turf. Digging.

25 The cold smell of potato mould, the squelch and slap
Of soggy peat, the curt cuts of an edge
Through living roots awaken in my head.
But I've no spade to follow men like them.

Between my finger and my thumb
30 The squat pen rests.
I'll dig with it.
—1966

___
[1] *potato drills*   Row of sown potatoes.
[2] *turf*   Slabs of peat.

Thatcher

Bespoke for weeks, he turned up some morning
Unexpectedly, his bicycle slung
With a light ladder and a bag of knives.
He eyed the old rigging, poked at the eaves,

5 Opened and handled sheaves of lashed wheat-straw.
Next, the bundled rods: hazel and willow
Were flicked for weight, twisted in case they'd snap.
It seemed he spent the morning warming up:

Then fixed the ladder, laid out well-honed blades
10 And snipped at straw and sharpened ends of rods
That, bent in two, made a white-pronged staple
For pinning down his world, handful by handful.

Couchant° for days on sods above the rafters,   *lying*
He shaved and flushed the butts,[1] stitched all together
15 Into a sloped honeycomb, a stubble patch,
And left them gaping at his Midas touch.[2]
    —1969

The Wife's Tale

When I had spread it all on linen cloth
    Under the hedge, I called them over.
The hum and gulp of the thresher ran down
And the big belt slewed to a standstill, straw
5 Hanging undelivered in the jaws.
There was such quiet that I heard their boots
Crunching the stubble twenty yards away.

He lay down and said, "Give these fellows theirs,
I'm in no hurry," plucking grass in handfuls
10 And tossing it in the air. "That looks well."
(He nodded at my white cloth on the grass.)
"I declare a woman could lay out a field
Though boys like us have little call for cloths."
He winked, then watched me as I poured a cup
15 And buttered the thick slices that he likes.
"It's threshing better than I thought, and mind
It's good clean seed. Away over there and look."
Always this inspection has to be made
Even when I don't know what to look for.

20 But I ran my hand in the half-filled bags
Hooked to the slots. It was hard as shot,
Innumerable and cool. The bags gaped
Where the chutes ran back to the stilled drum
And forks were stuck at angles in the ground
25 As javelins might mark lost battlefields.
I moved between them back across the stubble.

---

1 *butts* Branch tips.

2 *Midas touch* Reference to the Greek myth of King Midas, whose touch turned everything to gold.

They lay in the ring of their own crusts and dregs,
Smoking and saying nothing. "There's good yield,
Isn't there?"—as proud as if he were the land itself—
30 "Enough for crushing and for sowing both."
And that was it. I'd come and he had shown me,
So I belonged no further to the work.
I gathered cups and folded up the cloth
And went. But they still kept their ease,
35 Spread out, unbuttoned, grateful, under the trees.
    —1969

The Grauballe Man[3]

As if he had been poured
    in tar, he lies
on a pillow of turf
and seems to weep

5 the black river of himself
The grain of his wrists
is like bog oak,[4]
the ball of his heel

like a basalt egg.
10 His instep has shrunk
cold as a swan's foot
or a wet swamp root.

His hips are the ridge
and purse of a mussel,
15 his spine an eel arrested
under a glisten of mud.

The head lifts,
the chin is a visor
raised above the vent
20 of his slashed throat

that has tanned and toughened.
The cured wound
opens inwards to a dark
elderberry place.

---

3 *Grauballe Man* Man from the first century BCE whose preserved remains were found in 1952, in a peat bog near the village of Grauballe, Denmark.

4 *bog oak* Wood of an oak tree preserved in peat-bog.

25   Who will say "corpse"
     to his vivid cast?
     Who will say "body"
     to his opaque repose?

     And his rusted hair,
30   a mat unlikely
     as a foetus's.
     I first saw his twisted face

     in a photograph,
     a head and shoulder
35   out of the peat,
     bruised like a forceps baby,

     but now he lies
     perfected in my memory,
     down to the red horn
40   of his nails,

     hung in the scales
     with beauty and atrocity:
     with the Dying Gaul
     too strictly compassed

45   on his shield,
     with the actual weight
     of each hooded victim,
     slashed and dumped.
     —1975

Punishment[1]

I can feel the tug
of the halter at the nape
of her neck, the wind
on her naked front.

5   It blows her nipples
     to amber beads,
     it shakes the frail rigging
     of her ribs.

     I can see her drowned
10   body in the bog,
     the weighing stone,
     the floating rods and boughs.

     Under which at first
     she was a barked sapling
15   that is dug up
     oak-bone, brain-firkin:[2]

     her shaved head
     like a stubble of black corn,
     her blindfold a soiled bandage,
20   her noose a ring

     to store
     the memories of love.
     Little adulteress,
     before they punished you

25   you were flaxen-haired,
     undernourished, and your
     tar-black face was beautiful.
     My poor scapegoat,

     I almost love you
30   but would have cast, I know,
     the stones of silence.
     I am the artful voyeur

     of your brain's exposed
     and darkened combs,
35   your muscles' webbing
     and all your numbered bones:

     I who have stood dumb
     when your betraying sisters,
     cauled° in tar,   *capped*
40   wept by the railings,[3]

---

[1] *Punishment* In 1951 the body of a fourteen-year-old girl from the first century BCE was discovered in a German bog. The left side of her head had been shaved, her eyes bandaged shut, and a collar tied around her neck. Her body had been weighed down with tree branches and a stone. Germanic people often punished adulterous women by shaving their hair and either killing them or expelling them from the village. After the girl's body was found, the brain was removed and examined.

[2] *firkin* Small cask or barrel.

[3] *your betraying … railings* In Belfast, women who kept company with British soldiers were sometimes shaved, stripped, tarred, and handcuffed to railings by the IRA as punishment.

who would connive
in civilized outrage
yet understand the exact
and tribal, intimate revenge.
—1975

Casualty

1

He would drink by himself
And raise a weathered thumb
Towards the high shelf,
Calling another rum
5   And blackcurrant, without
Having to raise his voice,
Or order a quick stout
By a lifting of the eyes
And a discreet dumb-show
10   Of pulling off the top;
At closing time would go
In waders and peaked cap
Into the showery dark,
A dole-kept breadwinner
15   But a natural for work.
I loved his whole manner,
Sure-footed but too sly,
His deadpan sidling tact,
His fisherman's quick eye
20   And turned observant back.

Incomprehensible
To him, my other life.
Sometimes, on his high stool,
Too busy with his knife
25   At a tobacco plug
And not meeting my eye,
In the pause after a slug
He mentioned poetry.
We would be on our own
30   And, always politic
And shy of condescension,

I would manage by some trick
To switch the talk to eels
Or lore of the horse and cart
35   Or the Provisionals.[1]

But my tentative art
His turned back watches too:
He was blown to bits
Out drinking in a curfew
40   Others obeyed, three nights
After they shot dead
The thirteen men in Derry.
PARAS THIRTEEN, the walls said,
BOGSIDE NIL.[2] That Wednesday
45   Everybody held
His breath and trembled.

2

It was a day of cold
Raw silence, wind-blown
Surplice and soutane:[3]
50   Rained-on, flower-laden
Coffin after coffin
Seemed to float from the door
Of the packed cathedral
Like blossoms on slow water.
55   The common funeral
Unrolled its swaddling band,
Lapping, tightening
Till we were braced and bound
Like brothers in a ring.

60   But he would not be held
At home by his own crowd
Whatever threats were phoned,
Whatever black flags waved.
I see him as he turned
65   In that bombed offending place,
Remorse fused with terror

---

[1] *Provisionals* Members of the Provisional Branch of the IRA.

[2] *PARAS ... NIL* I.e., the British Army's Parachute Regiment had killed thirteen people, while the Roman Catholic people of the Bogside district, in Londonderry, had killed none.

[3] *Surplice and soutane* Vestments worn by the Roman Catholic clergy.

In his still knowable face,
His cornered outfaced stare
Blinding in the flash.

70   He had gone miles away
For he drank like a fish
Nightly, naturally
Swimming towards the lure
Of warm lit-up places,
75   The blurred mesh and murmur
Drifting among glasses
In the gregarious smoke.
How culpable was he
That last night when he broke
80   Our tribe's complicity?
"Now you're supposed to be
An educated man,"
I hear him say. "Puzzle me
The right answer to that one."

3

85   I missed his funeral,
Those quiet walkers
And sideways talkers
Shoaling out of his lane
To the respectable
90   Purring of the hearse …
They move in equal pace
With the habitual
Slow consolation
Of a dawdling engine,
95   The line lifted, hand
Over fist, cold sunshine
On the water, the land
Banked under fog: that morning
I was taken in his boat,
100   The screw° purling, turning   *propeller*
Indolent fathoms white,
I tasted freedom with him.
To get out early, haul
Steadily off the bottom,
105   Dispraise the catch, and smile
As you find a rhythm
Working you, slow mile by mile,

Into your proper haunt
Somewhere, well out, beyond …

110   Dawn-sniffing revenant,[1]
Plodder through midnight rain,
Question me again.
        —1979

Seeing Things

1

Inishbofin[2] on a Sunday morning.
Sunlight, turfsmoke,[3] seagulls, boatslip,° diesel.   *deck*
One by one we were being handed down
Into a boat that dipped and shilly-shallied
5   Scaresomely every time. We sat tight
On short cross-benches, in nervous twos and threes,
Obedient, newly close, nobody speaking
Except the boatmen, as the gunwales sank
And seemed they might ship water any minute.
10   The sea was very calm but even so,
When the engine kicked and our ferryman
Swayed for balance, reaching for the tiller,
I panicked at the shiftiness and heft
Of the craft itself. What guaranteed us—
15   That quick response and buoyancy and swim—
Kept me in agony. All the time
As we went sailing evenly across
The deep, still, seeable-down-into water,
It was as if I looked from another boat
20   Sailing through air, far up, and could see
How riskily we fared into the morning,
And loved in vain our bare, bowed, numbered heads.

2

Claritas.[4] The dry-eyed Latin word
Is perfect for the carved stone of the water
25   Where Jesus stands up to his unwet knees
And John the Baptist pours out more water
Over his head: all this in bright sunlight

---

[1] *revenant* One who returns to life from the dead.

[2] *Inishbofin* Small island west of Ireland.

[3] *turfsmoke* Smoke from burning slabs of peat ("turf"), which was
used as fuel.

[4] *Claritas* Latin: clarity.

On the façade of a cathedral. Lines
Hard and thin and sinuous represent
30 The flowing river. Down between the lines
Little antic fish are all go. Nothing else.
And yet in that utter visibility
The stone's alive with what's invisible:
Waterweed, stirred sand-grains hurrying off,
35 The shadowy, unshadowed stream itself.
All afternoon, heat wavered on the steps
And the air we stood up to our eyes in wavered
Like the zigzag hieroglyph for life itself.

3

Once upon a time my undrowned father
40 Walked into our yard. He had gone to spray
Potatoes in a field on the riverbank
And wouldn't bring me with him. The horse-sprayer
Was too big and newfangled, bluestone°   copper sulphate
      might
Burn me in the eyes, the horse was fresh, I
45 Might scare the horse, and so on. I threw stones
At a bird on the shed roof, as much for
The clatter of the stones as anything,
But when he came back, I was inside the house
And saw him out the window, scatter-eyed
50 And daunted, strange without his hat,
His step unguided, his ghosthood immanent.
When he was turning on the riverbank,
The horse had rusted and reared up and pitched
Cart and sprayer and everything off balance,
55 So the whole rig went over into a deep
Whirlpool, hoofs, chains, shafts, cartwheels, barrel
And tackle, all tumbling off the world,
And the hat already merrily swept along
The quieter reaches. That afternoon
60 I saw him face to face, he came to me
With his damp footprints out of the river,
And there was nothing between us there
That might not still be happily ever after.
—1991

Englands of the Mind[1]

One of the most precise and suggestive of T.S. Eliot's critical formulations was his notion of what he called "the auditory imagination," "the feeling for syllable and rhythm, penetrating far below the conscious levels of thought and feeling, invigorating every word; sinking to the most primitive and forgotten, returning to the origin and bringing something back," fusing "the most ancient and the most civilized mentality."[2] I presume Eliot was thinking here about the cultural depth-charges latent in certain words and rhythms, that binding secret between words in poetry that delights not just the ear but the whole backward and abysm of mind and body; thinking of the energies beating in and between words that the poet brings into half-deliberate play; thinking of the relationship between the word as pure vocable, as articulate noise, and the word as etymological occurrence, as symptom of human history, memory and attachments.

It is in the context of this auditory imagination that I wish to discuss the language of Ted Hughes, Geoffrey Hill, and Philip Larkin.[3] All of them return to an origin and bring something back, all three live off the hump of the English poetic achievement, all three, here and now, in England, imply a continuity with another England, there and then. All three are hoarders and shorers of what they take to be the real England. All three treat England as a region—or rather treat their region as England—in different and complementary ways. I believe they are afflicted with a sense of history that was once the peculiar affliction of the poets of other nations who were not themselves natives of England but who spoke the English language. The poets of the mother culture, I feel, are now possessed of that defensive love of their territory which was once shared only by those poets whom we might call colonial—Yeats, MacDiarmid, Carlos Williams.[4] They are aware of their

---

[1] *Englands of the Mind* Beckman Lecture given by Heaney at the University of California, Berkeley, May 1976.

[2] *the auditory ... mentality* From T.S. Eliot, *The Use of Poetry and the Use of Criticism* (1933).

[3] *Ted Hughes ... Larkin* Three British poets of the twentieth century.

[4] *Yeats* Irish poet William Butler Yeats (1865–1939); *MacDiarmid* Hugh MacDiarmid, pen name of Scottish poet Christopher Murray Grieve (1892–1978); *Carlos Williams* American poet William Carlos Williams (1883–1963).

Englishness as deposits in the descending storeys of the literary and historical past. Their very terrain is becoming consciously precious. A desire to preserve indigenous traditions, to keep open the imagination's supply lines to the past, to receive from the stations of Anglo-Saxon confirmations of ancestry, to perceive in the rituals of show Saturdays and race-meetings and seaside outings, of church-going and marriages at Whitsun,[1] and in the necessities that crave expression after the ritual of church-going has passed away, to perceive in these a continuity of communal ways, and a confirmation of an identity which is threatened—all this is signified by their language.

When we examine that language, we find that their three separate voices are guaranteed by three separate foundations which, when combined, represent almost the total resources of the English language itself. Hughes relies on the northern deposits, the pagan Anglo-Saxon and Norse elements, and he draws energy also from a related constellation of primitive myths and world views. The life of his language is a persistence of the stark outline and vitality of Anglo-Saxon that became the Middle English alliterative tradition and then went underground to sustain the folk poetry, the ballads, and the ebullience of Shakespeare and the Elizabethans. Hill is also sustained by the Anglo-Saxon base, but his proper guarantor is that language as modified and amplified by the vocabularies and values of the Mediterranean, by the early medieval Latin influence; his is to a certain extent a scholastic imagination founded on an England that we might describe as Anglo-Romanesque, touched by the polysyllabic light of Christianity but possessed by darker energies which might be acknowledged as barbaric. Larkin then completes the picture, because his proper hinterland is the English language Frenchified and turned humanist by the Norman conquest and the Renaissance, made nimble, melodious, and plangent by Chaucer and Spenser, and besomed[2] clean of its inkhornisms[3] and its irrational magics by the eighteenth century.

And their Englands of the mind might be correspondingly characterized. Hughes's is a primeval landscape where stones cry out and horizons endure, where the elements inhabit the mind with a religious force, where the pebble dreams "it is the foetus of God," "where the staring angels go through," "where all the stars bow down," where, with appropriately pre-Socratic[4] force, water lies "at the bottom of all things / utterly worn out utterly clear." It is England as King Lear's heath which now becomes a Yorkshire moor where sheep and foxes and hawks persuade "unaccommodated man" that he is a poor bare forked thing, kinned not in a chain but on a plane of being with the animals themselves. There monoliths and lintels.[5] The air is menaced by God's voice in the wind, by demonic protean crow-shapes; and the poet is a wanderer among the ruins, cut off by catastrophe from consolation and philosophy. Hill's England, on the other hand, is more hospitable to the human presence. The monoliths make way for the keeps[6] and chantries[7] if also for the beheading block. The heath's loneliness is kept at bay by the natural magic of the grove and the intellectual force of the scholar's cell. The poet is not a wanderer but a clerk or perhaps an illuminator or one of a guild of masters: he is in possession of a history rather than a mythology; he has a learned rather than an oral tradition. There are wars, but there are also dynasties, ideas of inheritance and order, possibilities for the "true governaunce of England." His elegies are not laments for the irrevocable dispersal of the comitatus[8] and the ring-giver in the hall, but solemn requiems for Plantagenet kings[9] whose murderous wars are set in a great pattern, to be understood only when "the sea / Across daubed rocks evacuates its dead." And Larkin's England similarly reflects features from the period that his language is hived off. His trees and flowers and grasses are neither animistic, nor hallowed by half-remembered druidic lore; they are emblems of mutabilitie. Behind them lies the sensibility of troubadour and courtier. "Cut grass lies frail; / Brief is the breath / Mown stalks exhale"; his landscape is dominated neither by the

[1] whitsun   I.e., at Whit Sunday or Whitsuntide, the Pentecost.
[2] besomed   Swept.
[3] inkhornisms   Pedantic words or expressions.
[4] pre-Socratic   Characteristic of the period before the philosopher Socrates (i.e., before the sixth century BCE) and his system of inquiry into the causes of things.
[5] lintels   Horizontal support beams over doors and windows.
[6] keeps   Medieval strongholds, towers.
[7] chantries   Chapels in which priests sing daily mass for the founders.
[8] comitatus   Latin: escort; imperial retinue.
[9] Plantagenet kings   English dynasty that ruled 1154–1485 (Henry II to Richard III).

untamed heath nor the totemistic architectures of spire and battlement but by the civic prospects, by roofs and gardens and prospects where urban and pastoral visions interact as "postal districts packed like squares of wheat." The poet is no longer a bardic remnant nor an initiate in curious learning nor a jealous master of the secrets of a craft; he is a humane and civilized member of the customs service or the civil service or, indeed, the library service. The moon is no longer his white goddess but his poetic property, to be image rather than icon: "high and preposterous and separate," she watches over unfenced existence, over fulfilment's desolate attic, over an England of department stores, canals and floatings of industrial froth, explosions in mines, effigies in churches, secretaries in offices; and she hauls tides of life where only one ship is worth celebration, not a Golden Hind or a Victory,[1] but "black- / Sailed unfamiliar, towing at her back / A huge and birdless silence."

Hughes's sensibility is pagan in the original sense: he is a haunter of the *pagus*,[2] a heath-dweller, a heathen; he moves by instinct in the thickets beyond the *urbs*;[3] he is neither urban nor urbane. His poetry is as redolent of the lair as it is of the library. The very titles of his books are casts made into the outback of our animal recognitions. *Lupercal*, a word infested with wolfish stinks yet returning to an origin in Shakespeare's *Julius Caesar*: "You all did see that on the Lupercal / I thrice presented him a kingly crown." Yet the word passes back through Shakespeare into the Lupercal, a cave below the western corner of the Palatine Hill in Rome; and the Lupercal was also the festival held on 15 February when, after the sacrifice of goats and a dog, youths dressed only in girdles made from the skins of these victims ran about the bounds of the Palatine city, striking those whom they met, especially women, with strips of goatskin. It was a fertility rite, and it was also a ritual beating of the bounds of the city, and in a way Hughes's language is just this also. Its sensuous fetch, its redolence of blood and gland and grass and water, recalled English poetry in the fifties from a too suburban aversion of the attention from the elemental; and the poems beat the bounds

of a hidden England in streams and trees, on moors and in byres.[4] Hughes appeared like Poor Tom on the heath, a civilized man tasting and testing the primitive facts; he appeared as *Wodwo*, a nosing wild man of the woods. The volume *Wodwo* appeared in 1967 and carried as its epigraph a quotation from *Gawain and the Green Knight*, and that deliberate affiliation is instructive. Like the art of Gawain, Hughes's art is one of clear outline and inner richness. His diction is consonantal, and it snicks through the air like an efficient blade, marking and carving out fast definite shapes; but within those shapes, mysteries and rituals are hinted at. They are circles within which he conjures up presences.

Hughes's vigour has much to do with this matter of consonants that take the measure of his vowels like calipers, or stud the line like rivets. "Everything is inheriting everything," as he says in one of his poems, and what he has inherited through Shakespeare and John Webster and Hopkins and Lawrence[5] is something of that primary life of stress which is the quick of the English poetic matter. His consonants are the Norsemen, the Normans, the Roundheads[6] in the world of his vocables, hacking and hedging and hammering down the abundance and luxury and possible lasciviousness of the vowels. "I imagine this midnight moment's forest"—the first line of the well-known "The Thought Fox"—is hushed, but it is a hush achieved by the quelling, battening-down action of the m's and d's and t's: I iMagine this MiDnighT MoMenT's foresT. Hughes's aspiration in these early poems is to command all the elements, to bring them within the jurisdiction of his authoritarian voice. And in "The Thought Fox" the thing at the beginning of the poem which lives beyond his jurisdiction is characteristically fluid and vowelling and sibilant: "Something else is alive" whispers of a presence not yet accounted for, a presence that is granted its full vowel music as its epiphany—"Something more near / Though deeper within darkness / Is entering the loneliness." It is granted this dilation of its mystery before it is conjured into the possession of the

---

[1] *Golden Hind*   Ship captained by Sir Francis Drake that circumnavigated the globe (1577–80); *Victory*   Flagship of Admiral Lord Nelson in the Battle of Trafalgar (1805).

[2] *pagus*   Latin: countryside.

[3] *urbs*   Latin: city.

[4] *byres*   Cow-houses.

[5] *John Webster*   Jacobean dramatist John Webster (1580–1625); *Hopkins*   Poet Gerard Manley Hopkins (1844–89); *Lawrence* Novelist D.H. Lawrence (1885–1930).

[6] *Roundheads*   Members or supporters of the seventeenth-century Parliamentary Party before and during the Civil War; i.e., Puritans.

poet-warden, the vowel-keeper; and its final emergence in the fully sounded i's and e's of "an eye, / A widening deepening greenness," is gradually mastered by the braking action of "brilliantly, concentratedly," and by the shooting of the monosyllabic consonantal bolts in the last stanza:

> Till, with a sudden sharp hot stink of fox
> It enters the dark hole of the head.
> The window is starless still; the clock ticks,
> The page is printed.

Next a poem whose subject might be expected to woo the tender pious vowels from a poet rather than the disciplining consonants. About a "Fern":

> Here is the fern's frond, unfurling a gesture,

The first line is an Anglo-Saxon line, four stresses, three of them picked out by alliteration; and although the frosty grip of those f's thaws out, the fern is still subsumed into images of control and discipline and regal authority:

> And, among them, the fern
> Dances gravely, like the plume
> Of a warrior returning, under the low hills,
>
> Into his own kingdom.

But of course we recognize that Hughes's "Thistles" are vegetation more kindred to his spirit than the pliant fern. And when he turns his attention to them, they become reincarnations of the Norsemen in a poem entitled "The Warriors of the North":

> Bringing their frozen swords, their salt-bleached eyes, their salt-bleached hair,
> The snow's stupefied anvils in rows,
> Bringing their envy,
> The slow ships feelered Southward, snails over the steep sheen of the water-globe

and he imagines them resurrected in all their arctic mail "into the iron arteries of Calvin," and into "Thistles." The thistles are emblems of the Hughes voice as I see it, born of an original vigour, fighting back over the same

ground; and it is not insignificant that in this poem Hughes himself imagines the thistles as images of a fundamental speech, uttering itself in gutturals from behind the sloped arms of consonants:

> Every one a revengeful burst
> Of resurrection, a grasped fistful
> Of splintered weapons and Icelandic frost thrust up
>
> From the underground stain of a decayed Viking.
> They are like pale hair and the gutturals of dialects.
> Every one manages a plume of blood.
>
> Then they grow grey, like men.
> Mown down, it is a feud. Their sons appear,
> Stiff with weapons, fighting back over the same ground.

The gutturals of dialects, which Hughes here connects with the Nordic stratum of English speech, he pronounces in another place to be the germinal secret of his own voice. In an interview published in the *London Magazine* in January 1971 he said:

> I grew up in West Yorkshire. They have a very distinctive dialect there. Whatever other speech you grow into, presumably your dialect stays alive in a sort of inner freedom ... it's your childhood self there inside the dialect and that is possibly your real self or the core of it. ... Without it, I doubt if I would ever have written verse. And in the case of the West Yorkshire dialect, of course, it connects you directly and in your most intimate self to Middle English poetry.

In other words he finds that the original grain of his speech is a chip off the old block and that his work need not be a new planting but a new bud on an old bough. What other poet would have the boldness to entitle a collection *Wodwo*? Yet *Gawain and the Green Knight*, with its beautiful alliterating and illuminated form, its interlacing and trellising of natural life and mythic life, is probably closer in spirit to Hughes's poetry than Hughes's poetry is to that of his English contemporaries. Everything inherits everything—and Hughes is the rightful heir to this alliterative tradition, and to the cleaving simplicity of the Border ballad, which he elevates to the status of touchstone later in that same interview. He says that he started writing again in 1955:

> The poems that set me off were odd pieces by Shapiro, Lowell, Merwin, Wilbur and Crowe Ransom.[1] Crowe Ransom was the one who gave me a model I felt I could use. He helped me get my words into focus. ... But this whole business of influences is mysterious. ... And after all the campaigns to make it new you're stuck with the fact that some of the Scots Border ballads still cut a deeper groove than anything written in the last forty years. Influences just seem to make it more and more unlikely that a poet will write what he alone could write.

What Hughes alone could write depended for its release on the discovery of a way to undam the energies of the dialect, to get a stomping ground for that inner freedom, to get that childhood self a disguise to roam at large in. Freedom and naturalness and homeliness are positives in Hughes's critical vocabulary, and they are linked with both the authenticity of individual poets and the genius of the language itself. Speaking of Keith Douglas[2] in 1964, Hughes could have been speaking of himself; of the way his language and his imagination alerted themselves when the hunt for the poem in the adult world became synonymous with the hunt for the animal in the world of childhood, the world of dialect:

> The impression is of a sudden mobilizing of the poet's will, a clearing of his vision, as if from sitting considering possibilities and impossibilities he stood up to act. Pictures of things no longer interest him much: he wants their substance, their nature and their consequences in life. At once, and quite suddenly, his mind is whole. ... He is a renovator of language. It is not that he uses words in jolting combinations, or with titanic extravagance, or curious precision. His triumph is in the way he renews the simplicity of ordinary talk. ... The music that goes along with this ... is the natural path of such confident, candid thinking. ... A utility general purpose style that combines a colloquial prose readiness with poetic breadth, a ritual intensity of music with clear direct feeling, and yet in the end is nothing but casual speech.

This combination of ritual intensity, prose readiness, direct feeling, and casual speech can be discovered likewise in the best poems of *Lupercal*, because in *Hawk in the Rain* and indeed in much of *Wodwo* and *Crow*, we are often in the presence of that titanic extravagance Hughes mentions, speech not so much mobilizing and standing up to act as flexing and straining until it verges on the grotesque. But in poems like "Pike," "Hawk Roosting," "The Bull Moses," and "An Otter" we get this confident, speedy, hammer-and-tongs proficiency. And in this poem from *Wodwo*, called "Pibroch," a poem uniquely Hughesian in its very title, fetching energy and ancestry from what is beyond the Pale[3] and beneath the surface, we have the elements of the Scottish piper's *ceol mor*,[4] the high style, implicit in words like "dead," "heaven," "universe," "aeon," "angels," and in phrases like "the foetus of God," "the stars bow down"—a phrase which cunningly makes its cast and raises Blake in the pool of the ear. We have elements of this high style, ritual intensity, whatever you want to call it; and we have also the "prose readiness," the "casual speech" of "bored," "hangs on," "lets up," "tryout," and the workaday cadences of "Over the stone rushes the wind," and "her mind's gone completely." The landscape of the poem is one that the Anglo-Saxon wanderer or seafarer would be completely at home in:

> The sea cries with its meaningless voice
> Treating alike its dead and its living,
> Probably bored with the appearance of heaven
> After so many millions of nights without sleep,
> Without purpose, without self-deception.
>
> Stone likewise. A pebble is imprisoned
> Like nothing in the Universe.
> Created for black sleep. Or growing
> Conscious of the sun's red spot occasionally,
> Then dreaming it is the foetus of God.
>
> Over the stone rushes the wind
> Able to mingle with nothing,

---

1. *Shapiro ... Ransom* Karl Shapiro, Robert Lowell, W.S. Merwin, Richard Wilbur, and John Crowe Ransom—all twentieth-century American poets.

2. *Keith Douglas* British poet (1920–44).

3. *beyond the Pale* I.e., outside the bounds of acceptable behavior.

4. *ceol mor* Gaelic: the great music. Classical Scottish music played exclusively on the great highland bagpipe.

Like the hearing of the blind stone itself.
Or turns, as if the stone's mind came feeling
A fantasy of directions.

Drinking the sea and eating the rock
A tree struggles to make leaves—
An old woman fallen from space
Unprepared for these conditions.
She hangs on, because her mind's gone completely.

Minute after minute, aeon after aeon,
Nothing lets up or develops.
And this is neither a bad variant nor a tryout.
This is where the staring angels go through.
This is where all the stars bow down.

Hughes attempts to make vocal the inner life, the simple being-thereness, "the substance, nature and consequences in life" of sea, stone, wind and tree. Blake's pebble and tiger[1] are shadowy presences in the background, as are the landscapes of Anglo-Saxon poetry. And the whole thing is founded on rock, that rock which Hughes presented in his autobiographical essay as his birthstone, holding his emergence in place just as his headstone will hold his decease:

> This was the *memento mundi*[2] over my birth: my spiritual midwife at the time and my godfather ever since—or one of my godfathers. From my first day it watched. If it couldn't see me direct, a towering gloom over my pram, it watched me through a species of periscope: that is, by infiltrating the very light of my room with its particular shadow. From my home near the bottom of the south-facing slope of the valley, the cliff was both the curtain and backdrop to existence.

I quote this piece because it links the childhood core with the adult opus, because that rock is the equivalent in his poetic landscape of dialect in his poetic speech. The rock persists, survives, sustains, endures and informs his imagination, just as it is the bedrock of the language upon which Hughes founds his version of survival and endurance. ...

Finally, to come to Larkin, where what accrues in the language is not "a golden and stinking blaze," not the rank and fermenting composts of philology and history, but the bright senses of words worn clean in literate conversation. In Larkin's language as in his vision of water, "any angled light ... congregate[s] endlessly." There is a gap in Larkin between the perceiver and the thing perceived, a refusal to melt through long perspectives, an obstinate insistence that the poet is neither a race memory nor a myth-kitty nor a mason, but a real man in a real place. The cadences and vocabulary of his poems are tuned to a rational music. It would seem that he has deliberately curtailed his gift for evocation, for resonance, for symbolist *frissons*. He turned from Yeats to Hardy as his master. He never followed the Laurentian success of his early poem "Wedding Wind" which ends with a kind of biblical swoon, an image of fulfilled lovers "kneeling like cattle by all generous waters." He rebukes romantic aspiration and afflatus with a scrupulous meanness. If he sees the moon, he sees it while groping back to bed after a piss. If he is forced to cry out "O wolves of memory, immensements," he is also forced to recognize that he is past all that swaddling of sentiment, even if it is "for others, undiminished, somewhere." "Undiminished"—the word, with its hovering balance between attenuated possibilities and the possibility of amplitude, is typical. And Christopher Ricks[3] has pointed out how often negatives operate in Larkin's best lines. Lovers talking in bed, for example, discover it ever more difficult

> to find
> Words at once true and kind,
> Or not untrue and not unkind.

His tongue moves hesitantly, precisely, honestly, among ironies and negatives. He is the poet of rational light, a light that has its own luminous beauty but which has also the effect of exposing clearly the truths which it touches. Larkin speaks neither a dialect nor a pulpit language; there are no "hectoring large scale verses" in his three books, nor is there the stubbly intimacy of "oath-edged talk and pipe-smoke" which he nostalgically annotates among the miners. His language would

---

[1] *Blake's ... tiger* See William Blake's "The Clod & the Pebble" and "The Tyger," from *Songs of Innocence and Experience* (1789).

[2] *memento mundi* Latin: reminder of the world.

[3] *Christopher Ricks* Renowned British scholar and literary critic (b. 1933).

have pleased those Tudor and Augustan guardians who wanted to polish and beautify their speech, to smooth it for art. What we hear is a stripped standard English voice, a voice indeed with a unique break and remorseful tone, but a voice that leads back neither to the thumping beat of Anglo-Saxon nor to the Gregorian chant of the Middle Ages. Its ancestry begins, in fact, when the Middle Ages are turning secular, and plays begin to take their place beside the Mass as a form of communal telling and knowing. In the first few lines of Larkin's poem "Money," for example, I think I hear the cadences of *Everyman*,[1] the querulous tones of Riches reproaching the hero:

> Quarterly, is it, money reproaches me:
>   "Why do you let me lie here wastefully?
> I am all you never had of goods and sex.
>   You could get them still just by writing a few cheques."

Those endstopped lines, sliding down to rhymed conclusions, suggest the beginning of that period out of which Larkin's style arises. After *Everyman*, there is Skelton,[2] a common-sensical wobble of rhyme, a humorous wisdom, a practical lyricism:

> Oh, no one can deny
> That Arnold is less selfish than I.
> He married a wife to stop her getting away
> Now she's there all day, ...

There is as well the Cavalier[3] Larkin, the maker of songs, where the conversational note and the dainty disciplines of a metrical form are in beautiful equilibrium:

> Yet still the unresting castles thresh
> In fullgrown thickness every May.
> Last year is dead, they seem to say.
> Begin afresh, afresh, afresh.

Even in that short space, by the way, one can see the

peculiar Larkin fusion of parsimony and abundance—the gorgeousness of "unresting castles," the poignant sweetness of "afresh, afresh" are held in check by the quotidian "last year is dead." Yet it is by refusing to pull out the full stops, or by almost refusing, that Larkin gains his own brand of negative capability.

As well as the Cavalier Larkin, there is a late Augustan[4] Larkin, the poet of decorous melancholy moods, of twilit propriety and shadowy melody. His poem about superannuated racehorses, for example, entitled "At Grass," could well be subtitled, "An Elegy in a Country Paddock." Behind the trees where the horses shelter there could well rise the spire of Stoke Poges church;[5] and behind the smooth numbers of wind distressing the tails and manes, there is the donnish exactitude of tresses being *dis*tressed:

> The eye can hardly pick them out
> From the cold shade they shelter in
> Till wind distresses tail and mane ...

And when, at the conclusion of the poem, "the groom and the groom's boy / With bridles in the evening come," their footsteps surely echo the ploughman homeward plodding his weary way. There is, moreover, a Tennysonian Larkin and a Hardy-esque Larkin. There is even, powerfully, an Imagist Larkin:

> There is an evening coming in
> Across the fields, one never seen before,
> That lights no lamps.
>
> Silken it seems at a distance, yet
> When it is drawn up over the knees and breast
> It brings no comfort.
>
> Where has the tree gone, that locked
> Earth to the sky? What is under my hands,
> That I cannot feel?
>
> What loads my hands down?

Then there is Larkin, the coiner of compounds—which

---

[1] *Everyman*   Fifteenth-century morality play.

[2] *Skelton*   I.e., Skeltonesque; resembling the work of John Skelton (c. 1460–1529).

[3] *Cavalier*   Cavaliers were supporters of the Stuart monarchy during the political unrest of the mid-seventeenth century; i.e., a courtly poet.

[4] *Augustan*   I.e., characteristic of an eighteenth-century poet.

[5] *Stoke Poges church*   Church of Stoke Poges, Buckinghamshire, the churchyard of which is believed to be the setting of Thomas Gray's famous poem "Elegy Written in a Country Churchyard" (1751).

we may choose to call Hopkinsian or even perhaps, briefly, Shakespearean—who writes of "some lonely rain-ceased midsummer evening," of "light unanswerable and tall and wide," of "the million-petalled flower of being here," of "thin continuous dreaming," and "wasteful, weak, propitiatory flowers."

And to go from the sublime to the ridiculous, there is the seaside-postcard Larkin, as true to the streak of vulgarity in the civilization as he is sensitive to its most delicious refinements: "Get stewed: / Books are a load of crap." Or get this disfigurement of a poster of a bathing beauty:

> Huge tits and a fissured crotch
> Were scored well in, and the space
> Between her legs held scrawls
> That set her fairly astride
> A tuberous cock and balls.

And then, elsewhere,

> They fuck you up, your mum and dad.
> They may not mean to but they do.
> They fill you with the faults they had
> And add some extra, just for you.

And again, in "Sad Steps":

> Groping back to bed after a piss
> I part thick curtains, and am startled by
> The rapid clouds, the moon's cleanliness.

But despite the piss, and the snigger of the demotic in all of these places, that title, "Sad Steps," reminds us that Larkin is solicitous for his Sidney[1] also. He too returns to origins and brings something back, although he does not return to "roots." He puts inverted commas round his "roots," in fact. His childhood, he says, was a forgotten boredom. He sees England from train windows, fleeting past and away. He is urban modern man, the insular Englishman, responding to the tones of his own clan, ill at ease when out of his environment. He is a poet, indeed, of composed and tempered English nationalism, and his voice is the not untrue, not unkind voice of post-war England, where the cloth cap and the

royal crown have both lost some of their potent symbolism, and the categorical, socially defining functions of the working-class accent and the aristocratic drawl have almost been eroded. Larkin's tones are mannerly but not exquisite, well-bred but not mealy-mouthed. If his England and his English are not as deep as Hughes's or as solemn as Hill's, they are nevertheless dearly beloved, and during his sojourn in Belfast in the late fifties, he gave thanks, by implication, for the nurture that he receives by living among his own. The speech, the customs, the institutions of England are, in the words of another English poet, domiciled in Ireland, "wife to his creating thought." That was Hopkins in Dublin in the 1880s, sensing that his individual talent was being divorced from his tradition. Here is Larkin remembering the domicile in Belfast in the 1950s:

> Lonely in Ireland, since it was not home,
> Strangeness made sense. The salt rebuff of speech,
> Insisting so on difference, made me welcome:
> Once that was recognised, we were in touch.
>
> Their draughty streets, end-on to hills, the faint
> Archaic smell of dockland, like a stable,
> The herring-hawker's cry, dwindling, went
> To prove me separate, not unworkable.
>
> Living in England has no such excuse:
> These are my customs and establishments
> It would be much more serious to refuse.
> Here no elsewhere underwrites my existence.

Larkin's England of the mind is in many ways continuous with the England of Rupert Brooke's "Grantchester" and Edward Thomas's "Adlestrop," an England of customs and institutions, industrial and domestic, but also an England whose pastoral hinterland is threatened by the very success of those institutions. Houses and roads and factories mean that a certain England is "Going, Going":

> It seems, just now,
> To be happening so very fast;
> Despite all the land left free
> For the first time I feel somehow
> That it isn't going to last,

---

[1] *Sidney* Poet Sir Philip Sidney (1154–86).

That before I snuff it, the whole
Boiling will be bricked in
Except for the tourist parts—
First slum of Europe: a role
It won't be so hard to win,
With a cast of crooks and tarts.

And that will be England gone,
The shadows, the meadows, the lanes,
The guildhalls, the carved choirs.
There'll be books; it will linger on
In galleries; but all that remains
For us will be concrete and tyres.

I think that sense of an ending has driven all three of these writers into a kind of piety towards their local origins, has made them look in, rather than up, to England. The loss of imperial power, the failure of economic nerve, the diminished influence of Britain inside Europe, all this has led to a new sense of the shires, a new valuing of the native English experience. Donald Davie, for example, has published a book of poems, with that very title, *The Shires*, which attempts to annex to his imagination by personal memory or historical meditation or literary connections, each shire of England. It is a book at once intimate and exclusive, a topography of love and impatience, and it is yet another symptom that English poets are being forced to explore not just the matter of England, but what is the matter with England. I have simply presumed to share in that exploration through the medium which England has, for better or worse, impressed upon us all, the English language itself.

—1980

ALICE MUNRO
b. 1931

Alice Munro's reputation as a writer of short fiction has grown steadily since the publication of her first volume of stories in 1968; upon the publication of her most recent collection Jonathan Franzen suggested in *The New York Review of Books* that Munro "has a strong claim to being the best fiction writer now working in North America," and the *Atlantic Monthly*'s reviewer described her as "the living writer most likely to be read in a hundred years."

Alice Munro was born into a farming community in Wingham, Huron County, Ontario. The landscape of southwestern Ontario would later appear as the setting in many of her short stories. Her father's fox fur business was unsuccessful and the family found itself in an awkward position: they were not rich enough to belong to the elite of the town, but because of their education, they did not quite fit elsewhere. Munro has described the characters with whom she came into social contact as "a community of outcasts," saying that she "was always an outsider, and you just couldn't ask for a better beginning for a writer."

After graduating from high school, Munro won a partial scholarship to attend the University of Western Ontario where she completed two years towards a degree in English. It was while she was there that she had her first story published in the university magazine. Due to strained finances, she was not able to complete her degree. She married and moved with her husband to Vancouver, British Columbia in 1951, where the couple would eventually have three daughters. Munro has often commented that the genre of the short story was well-suited to a working mother who could only snatch moments of time in which to write while taking care of her family. During the 1950s and 1960s she published stories at the rate of one or two a year, in publications such as *Chatelaine* and *The Tamarack Review*. Munro lived for some time during these years in Victoria—of all Canadian cities the most English in character—where, in addition to raising a family, she and her husband also operated a bookstore, Munro's Books. These years in British Columbia have continued to provide raw material for some of Munro's best fiction, perhaps most notably in the linked stories "Chance," "Soon," and "Silence" (2004).

In 1968, Munro's growing reputation as a short story writer led Ryerson Press to request that she gather some of her stories for a collection; this was the genesis of *Dance of the Happy Shades*, for which she would win her first Governor General's Award. In 1971, she published *The Lives of Girls and Women*, a collection of interlinked stories. The collection charts the development of the young Del Jordan as she grows up in the constricting atmosphere of the small town of Jubilee; Munro later commented that the novel "is autobiographical in form but not in fact."

Munro moved back to southwestern Ontario in 1973 after the dissolution of her marriage. She taught at York University, and later at the University of Western Ontario. She continued to write and publish, and began a longstanding connection with the *The New Yorker*, which would eventually publish many of her stories. The publication of the collection *Who Do You Think You Are?* would result in Munro's second Governor General's Award; the book was also shortlisted for the Booker Prize in 1978. Munro won her third Governor General's Award in 1986 for *The Progress of Love*. Her more recent works include *Friend of My Youth* (1990), *The Love of a Good Woman* (1998), and *Hateship, Friendship, Courtship, Loveship, Marriage* (2001), and *Runaway* (2005). Munro's later stories are often longer and more complex than her earlier works—her 2005 story "The View from

Castle Rock," which explores the immigrant experience, is a case in point—but she has retained a keen eye for detail and a fine sense of emotional nuance. Among her many awards are the W.H. Smith Literary Award in Britain, the National Book Critics Circle Award in the United States, and two Giller Prizes in Canada.

⌘ ⌘ ⌘

The View from Castle Rock

On a visit to Edinburgh with his father when he is nine or ten years old, Andrew finds himself climbing the damp, uneven stone steps of the Castle. His father is in front of him, some other men behind—it's a wonder how many friends his father has found, standing in cubbyholes where there are bottles set on planks, in the High Street—until at last they crawl out on a shelf of rock, from which the land falls steeply away. It has just stopped raining, the sun is shining on a silvery stretch of water far ahead of them, and beyond that is a pale green and grayish-blue land, a land as light as mist, sucked into the sky.

"America," his father tells them, and one of the men says that you would never have known it was so near.

"It is the effect of the height we are on," another says.

"There is where every man is sitting in the midst of his own properties and even the beggars is riding around in carriages," Andrew's father says, paying no attention to them. "So there you are, my lad"—he turns to Andrew—"and God grant that one day you will see it closer, and I will myself, if I live."

Andrew has an idea that there is something wrong with what his father is saying, but he is not well enough acquainted with geography to know that they are looking at Fife. He does not know if the men are mocking his father or if his father is playing a trick on them. Or if it is a trick at all.

Some years later, in the harbor of Leith,[1] on the fourth of June, 1818, Andrew and his father—whom I must call Old James, because there is a James in every generation—and Andrew's pregnant wife, Agnes, his brother Walter, his sister Mary, and also his son James, who is not yet two years old, set foot on board a ship for the first time in their lives.

Old James makes this fact known to the ship's officer who is checking off the names.

"The first time, serra, in all my long life. We are men of the Ettrick.[2] It is a landlocked part of the world."

The officer says a word which is unintelligible to them but plain in meaning. *Move along.* He has run a line through their names. They move along or are pushed along, Young James riding on Mary's hip.

"What is this?" Old James says, regarding the crowd of people on deck. "Where are we to sleep? Where have all these rabble come from? Look at the faces on them—are they the blackamoors?"[3]

"Black Highlanders, more like," Walter says. This is a joke, muttered so that his father cannot hear, Highlanders being one of the sorts the old man despises.

"There are too many people," his father continues. "The ship will sink."

"No," Walter says, speaking up now. "Ships do not often sink because of too many people. That's what the fellow was there for, to count the people."

Barely on board the vessel and this seventeen-year-old whelp has taken on knowing airs; he has taken to contradicting his father. Fatigue, astonishment, and the weight of the greatcoat he is wearing prevent Old James from cuffing him.

The business of life aboard ship has already been explained to the family. In fact, it has been explained by the old man himself. He was the one who knew all about provisions, accommodations, and the kinds of people you would find on board. All Scotsmen and all decent folk. No Highlanders, no Irish.

But now he cries out that it is like the swarm of bees in the carcass of the lion.

---

[1] *Leith* Harbor town adjoining Edinburgh.

[2] *Ettrick* Located in the Scottish borderlands.

[3] *blackamoors* Appellation formerly used to describe any black African person.

"An evil lot, an evil lot. Oh, that ever we left our native land."

"We have not left yet," Andrew says. "We are still looking at Leith. We would do best to go below and find ourselves a place."

More lamentation. The bunks are narrow planks with horsehair pallets that are both hard and prickly.

"Better than nothing," Andrew says.

"Oh, that ever I was enticed to bring us here, onto this floating sepulchre."

Will nobody shut him up? Agnes thinks. This is the way he will go on and on, like a preacher or a lunatic, when the fit takes him. She cannot abide it. She is in more agony herself than he is ever likely to know.

"Well, are we going to settle here or are we not?" she says.

Some people have hung up their plaids[1] or shawls to make a half-private space for their families. She goes ahead and takes off her outer wrappings to do the same.

The child is turning somersaults in her belly. Her face is hot as a coal, her legs throb, and the swollen flesh in between them—the lips the child must soon part to get out—is a scalding sack of pain.

Her mother would have known what to do about that. She would have known which leaves to mash to make a soothing poultice. At the thought of her mother such misery overcomes her that she wants to kick somebody.

Why does Andrew not speak plainly to his father, reminding him of whose idea it was, who harangued and borrowed and begged to get them just where they are now? Andrew will not do it, Walter will only joke, and as for Mary she can hardly get her voice out of her throat in her father's presence.

Agnes comes from a large Hawick family of weavers, who work in the mills now but worked for generations at home. Working there they learned the art of cutting one another down to size, of squabbling and surviving in close quarters. She is still surprised by the rigid manners, the deference and silences in her husband's family. She thought from the beginning that they were a queer sort and she thinks so still. They are as poor as her own folk but they have such a great notion of themselves. And what have they got to back it up?

Mary has taken Young James back up to the deck. She could tell that he was frightened down there in the half-dark. He does not have to whimper or complain—she knows his feelings by the way he digs his little knees into her.

The sails are furled tight. "Look up there, look up there," Mary says, and points to a sailor who is busy high up in the rigging. The boy on her hip makes his sound for bird—"peep." "Sailor-peep, sailor-peep," she says. She and he communicate in a half-and-half language—half her teaching and half his invention. She believes that he is one of the cleverest children ever born into the world. Being the eldest of her family, and the only girl, she has tended to all her brothers, and been proud of them all at one time, but she has never known a child like this. Nobody else has any idea how original and independent he is. Men have no interest in children so young, and Agnes, his mother, has no patience with him.

"Talk like folk," Agnes tells him, and if he doesn't she gives him a clout. "What are you?" she says. "Are you a folk or an elfit?"

Mary fears Agnes's temper, but in a way she doesn't blame her. She thinks that women like Agnes—men's women, mother women—lead an appalling life. First with what the men do to them—even as good a man as Andrew—and then with what the children do, coming out. She will never forget the way her own mother lay in bed, out of her mind with a fever, not knowing anyone, till she died, three days after Walter was born. She screamed at the black pot hanging over the fire, thinking it was full of devils.

Mary—her brothers call her "poor Mary"—is under five feet tall and has a tight little face with a lump of protruding chin, and skin that is subject to fiery eruptions that take a long time to fade. When she is spoken to, her mouth twitches as if the words were all mixed up with her spittle and her crooked teeth, and the response she manages is a dribble of speech so faint and scrambled that it is hard for people not to think her dim-witted. She has great difficulty looking anybody in the eyes—even the members of her own family. It is only when she gets the boy hitched onto the narrow shelf of her hip that she is capable of some coherent and decisive speech—and then it is mostly to him.

[1] *plaids* Woolen scarves used as cloaks.

She hears the cow bawling before she can see it. Then she looks up and sees the brown beast dangling in the air, all caged in ropes and kicking and roaring frantically. It is held by a hook on a crane, which now hauls it out of sight. People around her are hooting and clapping their hands. A child cries out, wanting to know if the cow will be dropped into the sea. A man tells him no—she will go along with them on the ship.

"Will they milk her, then?"

"Aye. Keep still. They'll milk her," the man says reprovingly. And another man's voice climbs boisterously over his.

"They'll milk her till they take the hammer to her, and then ye'll have the blood pudding for yer dinner."

Now follow the hens, swung through the air in crates, all squawking and fluttering in their confinement and pecking one another when they can, so that some feathers escape and float down through the air. And after them a pig trussed up like the cow, squealing with a human note in its distress and shifting wildly in midair, so that howls of both delight and outrage rise below, depending on whether they come from those who are hit or those who see others hit.

James is laughing, too. He recognizes shite, and cries out his own word for it, which is "gruggin."

Someday he may remember this, Mary thinks. *I saw a cow and a pig fly through the air.* Then he may wonder if it was a dream. And nobody will be there—she certainly won't—to tell him that it was not, that it happened on this ship. It's possible that he will never see a ship like this again in all his waking life. She has no idea where they will go when they reach the other shore, but she imagines that it will be someplace inland, among the hills, someplace like the Ettrick.

She does not think that she will live long, wherever they go. She coughs in the summer as well as the winter, and when she coughs her chest aches. She suffers from sties, and cramps in the stomach, and her bleeding comes rarely but may last a month when it does. She hopes, though, that she will not die while James is still in need of her, which he will be for a while yet. She knows that the time will come when he will turn away, as her brothers did, when he will become ashamed of the connection with her. At least, that is what she tells herself will happen, but like anybody in love she cannot believe it.

On a trip to Peebles, Walter bought himself a notebook to write in, but for several days he has found too much to pay attention to and too little space or quiet on the deck even to open it. Finally, after some investigating, he has discovered a favorable spot, near the cabins on the upper deck.

We came on board on the 4th day of June and lay the 5th, 6th, 7th, and 8th in the Leith roads getting the ship to a place where we could set sail, which was on the 9th. We passed the corner of Fifeshire all well nothing occurring worth mentioning till this day the 13th in the morning when we were awakened by a cry, John o'Groat's House. We could see it plain and had a fine sail across the Pentland Firth having both wind and tide in our favour and it was in no way dangerous as we had heard tell. There was a child had died, the name of Ormiston and its body was thrown overboard sewed up in a piece of canvas with a large lump of coal at its feet.

He pauses in his writing to think of the weighted sack falling down through the water. Would the piece of coal do its job, would the sack fall straight down to the very bottom of the sea? Or would the current of the sea be strong enough to keep lifting it up and letting it fall, pushing it sideways, taking it as far as Greenland or south to the tropical waters full of rank weeds, the Sargasso Sea? Or might some ferocious fish come along and rip the sack and make a meal of the body before it had even left the upper waters and the region of light?

He pictures it now—the child being eaten. Not swallowed whole as in the case of Jonah but chewed into bits as he himself would chew a tasty chunk from a boiled sheep. But there is the matter of a soul. The soul leaves the body at the moment of death. But from which part of the body does it leave? The best guess seems to be that it emerges with the last breath, having been hidden somewhere in the chest, around the place of the heart and the lungs. Though Walter has heard a joke they used to tell about an old fellow in the Ettrick, to the effect that he was so dirty that when he died his soul came out his arsehole, and was heard to do so with a mighty explosion.

This is the sort of information that preachers might

be expected to give you—not mentioning anything like an arsehole, of course, but explaining something of the proper location and exit. Yet they shy away from it. Also they cannot explain—at least, he has never heard one explain—how the souls maintain themselves outside of bodies until the Day of Judgment and how on that day each one finds and recognizes the body that is its own and reunites with it, though it be not so much as a skeleton at that time. *Though it be dust.* There must be some who have studied enough to know how all this is accomplished. But there are also some—he has learned this recently—who have studied and read and thought till they have come to the conclusion that there are no souls at all. No one cares to speak about these people, either, and indeed the thought of them is terrible. How can they live with the fear—indeed, the certainty—of Hell before them?

On the third day aboard ship Old James gets up and starts to walk around. After that, he stops and speaks to anybody who seems ready to listen. He tells his name, and says that he comes from Ettrick, from the Valley and Forest of Ettrick, where the old kings of Scotland used to hunt.

"And on the field at Flodden," he says, "after the battle of Flodden, they said you could walk up and down among the corpses and pick out the men from the Ettrick, because they were the tallest and the strongest and the finest-looking men on the ground. I have five sons and they are all good strong lads, but only two of them are with me. One of my sons is in Nova Scotia. The last I heard of him he was in a place called Economy, but we have not had any word of him since and I do not know whether he is alive or dead. My eldest son went off to work in the Highlands, and the son that is next to the youngest took it into his head to go off there, too, and I will never see either of them again. Five sons and, by the mercy of God, all grew to be men, but it was not the Lord's will that I should keep them with me. A man's life is full of sorrow. I have a daughter as well, the oldest of them all, but she is nearly a dwarf. Her mother was chased by a ram when she was carrying her."

On the afternoon of the 14th a wind from the North and the ship began to shake as if every board

that was in it would fly loose from every other. The buckets overflowed from the people that were sick and vomiting and there was the contents of them slipping all over the deck. All people were ordered below but many of them crumpled up against the rail and did not care if they were washed over. None of our family was sick however and now the wind has dropped and the sun has come out and those who did not care if they died in the filth a little while ago have got up and dragged themselves to be washed where the sailors are splashing buckets of water over the decks. The women are busy too washing and rinsing and wringing out all the foul clothing. It is the worst misery and the suddenest recovery I have seen ever in my life.

A young girl ten or twelve years old stands watching Walter write. She is wearing a fancy dress and bonnet and has light-brown curly hair. Not so much a pretty face as a pert one.

"Are you from one of the cabins?" she says.

Walter says, "No. I am not."

"I knew you were not. There are only four of them, and one is for my father and me and one is for the captain and one is for his mother, and she never comes out, and one is for the two ladies. You are not supposed to be on this part of the deck unless you are from one of the cabins."

"Well, I did not know that," Walter says, but does not bestir himself to move away.

"I have seen you before writing in your book."

"I haven't seen you."

"No. You were writing, so you didn't notice. I haven't told anybody about you," she adds carelessly, as if that were a matter of choice and she might well change her mind.

When she leaves, Walter adds a sentence.

And this night in the year 1818 we lost sight of Scotland.

The words seem majestic to him. He is filled with a sense of grandeur, solemnity, and personal importance.

16th was a very windy day with the wind coming out of the SW the sea was running very high and the ship got her gib-boom broken on account of the violence of the wind. And our sister Agnes was taken into the cabin.

"Sister," he has written, as if she were all the same to him as poor Mary, but that is not the case. Agnes is a tall well-built girl with thick dark hair and dark eyes. The flush on one of her cheeks slides into a splotch of pale brown as big as a handprint. It is a birthmark, which people say is a pity, because without it she would be handsome. Walter can hardly bear looking at it, but this is not because it is ugly. It is because he longs to touch it, to stroke it with the tips of his fingers. It looks not like ordinary skin but like the velvet on a deer. His feelings about her are so troubling that he can speak to her only unpleasantly, if he speaks at all. And she pays him back with a good seasoning of contempt.

Agnes thinks that she is in the water and the waves are heaving her up and slamming her down. Every time they slap her down it is worse than the time before, and she sinks farther and deeper, the moment of relief passing before she can grab it, for the next wave is already gathering its power to hit her.

Then sometimes she knows that she is in a bed, a strange bed and strangely soft, but it is all the worse for that because when she sinks down there is no resistance, no hard place where the pain has to stop. People keep rushing back and forth in front of her. They are all seen sideways and all transparent, talking very fast so she can't make them out, and maliciously taking no heed of her. She sees Andrew in the midst of them, and two or three of his brothers. Some of the girls she knows are there, too—the friends she used to lark around with in Hawick. And they do not give a poor penny for the plight she is in now.

She never knew before that she had so many enemies. They are grinding her down and pretending they don't even know it. Their movement is grinding her to death.

Her mother bends over her and says in a drawling, cold, lackadaisical voice, "You are not trying, my girl. You must try harder." Her mother is all dressed up and talking fine, like some Edinburgh lady.

Evil stuff is poured into her mouth. She tries to spit it out, knowing it is poison.

I will just get up and get out of this, she thinks. She

starts trying to pull herself loose from her body, as if it were a heap of rags on fire.

She hears a man's voice, giving some order. "Hold her," he says, and she is split and stretched wide open to the world and the fire.

"Ah—ah—anh," the man says, panting as if he had been running in a race.

Then a cow that is so heavy, bawling heavy with milk, rears up and sits down on Agnes's stomach.

"Now. Now," the man says, and he groans at the end of his strength as he tries to heave it off.

The fools. The fools, ever to have let it in.

She was not better till the 18th when she was delivered of a daughter. We having a surgeon on board nothing happened. Nothing occurred till the 22nd this was the roughest day we had till then experienced. Agnes was mending in an ordinary way till the 29th we saw a great shoal of porpoises and the 30th (yesterday) was a very rough sea with the wind blowing from the west we went rather backwards than forwards.

"In the Ettrick there is what they call the highest house in Scotland," Old James says, "and the house that my grandfather lived in was a higher one than that. The name of the place is Phauhope—they call it Phaup. My grandfather was Will O'Phaup, and fifty years ago you would have heard of him if you came from any place south of the Forth and north of the Debatable Lands."

There are people who curse to see him coming, but others who are glad of any distraction. His sons hear his voice from far away, amid all the other commotion on the deck, and make tracks in the opposite direction.

For the first two or three days, Young James refused to be unfastened from Mary's hip. He was bold enough, but only if he could stay there. At night he slept in her cloak, curled up beside her, and she wakened aching along her left side, because she had lain stiffly all night so as not to disturb him. Then in the space of one morning he was down and running about and kicking at her if she tried to hoist him up.

Everything on the ship calls out for his attention. Even at night he tries to climb over her and run away in the dark. So she gets up aching not only from her position but from lack of sleep altogether. One night she drops off and the child gets loose, but most fortunately stumbles against his father's body in his bid for escape. Henceforth, Andrew insists that he be tied down every night. He howls, of course, and Andrew shakes him and cuffs him and then he sobs himself to sleep. Mary lies by him softly explaining that this is necessary so that he cannot fall off the ship into the ocean, but he regards her at these times as his enemy, and if she puts out a hand to stroke his face he tries to bite it with his baby teeth. Every night he goes to sleep in a rage, but in the morning when she unties him, still half asleep and full of his infant sweetness, he clings to her drowsily and she is suffused with love.

Then one day he is gone. She is in the line for wash water and she turns around and he is not beside her. She was just speaking a few words to the woman ahead of her, answering a question about Agnes and the infant, she had just told the woman its name—Isabel—and in that moment he got away.

Everything in an instant is overturned. The nature of the world is altered. She runs back and forth, crying out James's name. She runs up to strangers, to sailors who laugh at her as she begs them, "Have you seen a little boy? Have you seen a little boy this high, he has blue eyes?"

"I seen fifty or sixty of them like that in the last five minutes," a man says to her. A woman trying to be kind says that he will turn up, Mary should not worry herself, he will be playing with some of the other children. Some women even look about, as if they would help her search, but of course they cannot, they have their own responsibilities.

This is what Mary sees plainly in those moments of anguish: that the world which has turned into a horror for her is still the same ordinary world for all these other people and will remain so even if James has truly vanished, even if he has crawled through the ship's railings—she has noticed everywhere the places where this would be possible—and been swallowed by the ocean.

The most brutal and unthinkable of all events, to her, would seem to most others like a sad but not extraordinary misadventure. It would not be unthinkable to them.

Or to God. For in fact when God makes some rare and remarkable, beautiful human child is He not particularly tempted to take His creature back, as if the world did not deserve it?

Still, she is praying to Him all the time. At first she only called on the Lord's name. But as her search grows more specific and in some ways more bizarre—she is ducking under clotheslines that people have contrived for privacy, she thinks nothing of interrupting folk at any business, she flings up the lids of their boxes and roots in their bedclothes, not even hearing them when they curse her—her prayers also become more complicated and audacious. She tries to think of something to offer, something that could equal the value of James's being restored to her. But what does she have? Nothing of her own—not health or prospects or anybody's regard. There is no piece of luck or even a hope that she can offer to give up. What she has is James.

And how can she offer James for James?

This is what is knocking around in her head.

But what about her love of James? Her extreme and perhaps idolatrous, perhaps wicked love of another creature. She will give up that, she will give it up gladly, if only he isn't gone.

If only he can be found. If only he isn't dead.

She recalls all this an hour or two after somebody has noticed the boy peeping out from under a large empty bucket, listening to the hubbub. And she retracts her vow at once. Her understanding of God is shallow and unstable, and the truth is that, except in a time of terror such as she has just experienced, she does not really care. She has always felt that God or even the idea of Him was more distant from her than from other people. There is a stubborn indifference in her that nobody knows about. In fact, everybody may imagine that she clings secretly to religion because there is so little else available to her. They are quite wrong, and now that she has James back she gives no thanks but thinks what a fool she was and how she could not give up her love of him any more than stop her heart beating.

After that, Andrew insists that James be tied down not only by night but also by day, to the post of the bunk or to their clothesline on the deck. Andrew has trounced his son for the trick he played, but the look in James's eyes says that his tricks are not finished.

Agnes keeps asking for salt, till they begin to fear that she will fuss herself into a fever. The two women looking after her are cabin passengers, Edinburgh ladies, who took on the job out of charity.

"You be still now," they tell her. "You have no idea what a fortunate lassie you are that we had Mr. Suter on board."

They tell her that the baby was turned the wrong way inside her, and they were all afraid that Mr. Suter would have to cut her, and that might be the end of her. But he had managed to get it turned so that he could wrestle it out.

"I need salt for my milk," says Agnes, who is not going to let them put her in her place with their re-proaches and their Edinburgh speech. They are idiots, anyway. She has to explain to them how you must put a little salt in the baby's first milk, just place a few grains on your finger and squeeze a drop or two of milk onto it and let the child swallow that before you put it to the breast. Without this precaution there is a good chance that it will grow up half-witted.

"Is she even a Christian?" one of them says to the other.

"I am as much as you," Agnes says. But to her own surprise and shame she starts to weep aloud, and the baby howls along with her, out of sympathy or hunger. And still she refuses to feed it.

Mr. Suter comes in to see how she is. He asks what all the grief is about, and they tell him the trouble.

"A newborn baby to get salt in its stomach—where did she get the idea?"

He says, "Give her the salt." And he stays to see her squeeze the milk on her salty finger, lay the finger to the infant's lips, and follow it with her nipple.

He asks her what the reason is and she tells him.

"And does it work every time?"

She tells him—a little surprised that he is as stupid as they are, though gentler—that it works without fail.

"So where you come from they all have their wits about them? And are all the girls strong and good-looking like you?"

She says that she would not know about that.

Sometimes visiting young men, educated men from the town, used to hang around her and her friends, complimenting them and trying to work up a conversa-tion, and she always thought that any girl who allowed it was a fool, even if the man was handsome. Mr. Suter is far from handsome—he is too thin, and his face is badly pocked, so that at first she took him for an old fellow. But he has a kind voice, and if he is teasing her a little there is no harm in it. No man would have the nature left to deal with a woman after looking at her spread wide, her raw parts open to the air.

"Are you sore?" he asks, and she believes there is a shadow on his damaged cheeks, a slight blush rising. She says that she is no worse than she has to be, and he nods, picks up her wrist, and bows over it, strongly pressing her pulse.

"Lively as a racehorse," he says, with his hands still above her, as if he did not know where to put them next. Then he decides to push back her hair and press his fingers to her temples, as well as behind her ears.

She will recall this touch, this curious, gentle, tingling pressure, with an addled mixture of scorn and longing, for many years to come.

"Good," he says. "No sign of a fever."

He watches, for a moment, the child sucking.

"All's well with you now," he says, with a sigh. "You have a fine daughter, and she can say all her life that she was born at sea."

Andrew arrives later and stands at the foot of the bed. He has never looked on her in such a bed as this (a regular bed, even though bolted to the wall). He is red with shame in front of the ladies, who have brought in the basin to wash her.

"That's it, is it?" he says, with a nod—not a glance—at the bundle beside her.

She laughs in a vexed way and asks what did he think it was. That is all it takes to knock him off his unsteady perch, to puncture his pretense of being at ease. Now he stiffens up, even redder, doused with fire. It isn't just what she said. It is the whole scene—the smell of the infant and the milk and the blood, and most of all the basin, the cloths, the women standing by, with their proper looks that might seem to a man both admonishing and full of derision.

He looks as if he can't think of another word to say, so she has to tell him, with rough mercy, to get on his way, there's work to be done here.

Some of the girls used to say that when you finally gave in and lay down with a man—even granting he was not the man of your first choice—it gave you a helpless but calm and even sweet feeling. Agnes does not recall that she felt that with Andrew. All she felt was that he was an honest lad and the right one for her in her circumstances, and that it would never occur to him to run off and leave her.

Walter has continued to go to the same private place to write in his book and nobody has caught him there. Except the girl, of course. One day he arrives at the place and she is there before him, skipping with a red-tasselled rope. When she sees him she stops, out of breath. And no sooner does she catch her breath than she begins to cough, so that it is several minutes before she can speak. She sinks down against the pile of canvas that conceals the spot, flushed, her eyes full of bright tears from the coughing. He simply stands and watches her, alarmed at this fit but not knowing what to do.

"Do you want me to fetch one of the ladies?"

He is on speaking terms with the Edinburgh women now, on account of Agnes. They take a kind interest in the mother and baby and Mary and Young James, and think that the old father is comical. They are also amused by Andrew and Walter, who seem to them so bashful.

The coughing girl is shaking her curly head violently.

"I don't want them," she says, when she can gasp the words out. "I have never told anybody that you come here. So you mustn't tell anybody about me."

"Well, you are here by rights."

She shakes her head again and gestures for him to wait till she can speak more easily.

"I mean that you saw me skipping. My father hid my skipping rope but I found where he hid it."

"It isn't the Sabbath," Walter says reasonably. "So what is wrong with you skipping?"

"How do I know?" she says, regaining her saucy tone. "Perhaps he thinks I am too old for it. Will you swear not to tell anyone?"

What a queer, self-important little thing she is, Walter thinks. She speaks only of her father, so he thinks it likely that she has no brothers or sisters and—like himself—no mother. That condition has probably made her both spoiled and lonely.

The girl—her name is Nettie—becomes a frequent visitor when Walter tries to write in his book. She always says that she does not want to disturb him, but after keeping ostentatiously quiet for about five minutes she interrupts him with some question about his life or a bit of information about hers. It is true that she is motherless and an only child. She has never even been to school. She talks most about her pets—those dead and those living at her house in Edinburgh—and a woman named Miss Anderson, who used to travel with her and teach her. It seems that she was glad to see the back of this woman, and surely Miss Anderson, too, was glad to depart, after all the tricks that were played on her—the live frog in her boot and the woollen but lifelike mouse in her bed.

Nettie has been back and forth to America three times. Her father is a wine merchant whose business takes him to Montreal.

She wants to know all about how Walter and his people live. Her questions are, by country standards, quite impertinent. But Walter does not really mind. In his own family he has never been in a position that allowed him to instruct or teach or tease anybody younger than himself, and it gives him pleasure.

What does Walter's family have for supper when they are at home? How do they sleep? Are animals kept in the house? Do the sheep have names, and what are the sheepdogs' names, and can you make pets of them? What is the arrangement of the scholars in the school-room? Are the teachers cruel? What do some of his words mean that she does not understand, and do all the people where he is from talk like him?

"Oh, aye," Walter says. "Even His Majesty the Duke does. The Duke of Buccleuch."

She laughs and freely pounds her little fist on his shoulder.

"Now you are teasing me. I know it. I know that Dukes are not called Your Majesty. They are not."

One day she arrives with paper and drawing pencils. She says that she has brought them to keep herself busy, so she will not be a nuisance to him. She offers to teach him to draw, if he wants to learn. But his attempts make her laugh, and he deliberately does worse and worse, till she laughs so hard she has one of her coughing fits. Then she says that she will do some drawings in the back of his notebook, so that he will have them to remember the voyage by. She draws the sails up above and a hen that has somehow escaped its cage and is trying to travel like a seabird over the water. She sketches from memory her dog that died. And she makes a picture of the icebergs she saw, higher than houses, on one of her past voyages with her father. The setting sun shone through these icebergs and made them look—she says—like castles of gold. Rose-colored and gold.

Everything that she has drawn, including the icebergs, has a look that is both guileless and mocking, peculiarly expressive of herself.

"The other day I was telling you about that Will O'Phaup that was my grandfather, but there was more to him than I told you. I did not tell you that he was the last man in Scotland to speak to the fairies. It is certain that I have never heard of any other, in his time or later."

Walter is sitting around a corner, near some sailors who are mending the torn sails, but by the sounds that are made throughout the story he can guess that the out-of-sight audience is mostly women.

There is one tall well-dressed man—a cabin passenger, certainly—who has paused to listen within Walter's view. There is a figure close to this man's other side, and at one moment in the tale this figure peeps around to look at Walter and he sees that it is Nettie. She seems about to laugh, but she puts a finger to her lips as if warning herself—and Walter—to keep silent.

The man must, of course, be her father. The two of them stand there listening quietly till the tale is over. Then the man turns and speaks directly, in a familiar yet courteous way, to Walter. "Are you writing down what you can make of this?" the man asks, nodding at Walter's notebook.

Walter is alarmed, not knowing what to say. But Nettie looks at him with calming reassurance, then drops her eyes and waits beside her father as a demure little miss should.

"I am writing a journal of the voyage," Walter says stiffly.

"Now, that is interesting. That is an interesting fact, because I, too, am keeping a journal of this voyage. I wonder if we find the same things worth writing of."

"I only write what happens," Walter says, wanting to make clear that this is a job for him and not an idle pleasure. Still, he feels that some further justification is called for. "I am writing to keep track of every day so

that at the end of the voyage I can send a letter home."

The man's voice is smoother and his manner gentler than any address Walter is used to. He wonders if he is being made sport of in some way. Or if Nettie's father is the sort of person who strikes up an acquaintance in the hope of getting hold of your money for some worthless investment.

Not that Walter's looks or dress would mark him out as a likely prospect.

"So you do not describe what you see? Only what, as you say, is happening?"

Walter is about to say no, and then yes. For he has just thought, if he writes that there is a rough wind, is that not describing? You do not know where you are with this kind of person.

"You are not writing about what we have just heard?"

"No."

"It might be worth it. There are people who go around now prying into every part of Scotland and writing down whatever these old country folk have to say. They think that the old songs and stories are disappearing and that they are worth recording. I don't know about that—it isn't my business. But I would not be surprised if the people who have written it all down will find that it was worth their trouble—I mean to say, there will be money in it."

Nettie speaks up unexpectedly.

"Oh, hush, Father. The old fellow is starting again."

This is not what any daughter would say to her father in Walter's experience, but the man seems ready to laugh, looking down at her fondly.

And indeed Old James's voice has been going this little while, breaking in determinedly and reproachfully on those of his audience who might have thought it was time for their own conversations.

"And still another time, but in the long days in the summer, out on the hills late in the day but before it was well dark…"

Walter has heard the stories his father is spouting, and others like them, all his life, but the odd thing is that until they came on board this ship he had never heard them from his father. The father he knew until a short while ago would, he is certain, have had no use for them.

"This is a terrible place we live in," his father used to

say. "The people is all full of nonsense and bad habits, and even our sheep's wool is so coarse you cannot sell it. The roads are so bad a horse cannot go more than four miles an hour. And for plowing here they use the spade or the old Scotch plow, though there has been a better plow in other places for fifty years. 'Oh, aye, aye,' they say when you ask them. 'Oh, aye, but it's too steep hereabouts, the land is too heavy.'

"To be born in the Ettrick is to be born in a backward place," he would say, "where the people is all believing in old stories and seeing ghosts, and I tell you it is a curse to be born in the Ettrick."

And very likely that would lead him on to the subject of America, where all the blessings of modern invention were put to eager use and the people could never stop improving the world around them.

But hearken at him now.

"You must come up and talk to us on the deck above," Nettie's father says to Walter when Old James has finished his story. "I have business to think about and I am not much company for my daughter. She is forbidden to run around, because she is not quite recovered from the cold she had in the winter, but she is fond of sitting and talking."

"I don't believe it is the rule for me to go there," Walter says, in some confusion.

"No, no, that is no matter. My girl is lonely. She likes to read and draw, but she likes company, too. She could show you how to draw, if you like. That would add to your journal."

So they sit out in the open and draw and write. Or she reads aloud to him from her favorite book, which is "The Scottish Chiefs."[1] He already knows the story—who does not know about William Wallace?[2]—but she reads smoothly and at just the proper speed and makes some things solemn and others terrifying and others comical, so that soon he is as much in thrall to the book as she is. Even though, as she says, she has read it twelve times already.

He understands a little better now why she has so many questions to ask him. He and his folk remind her of the people in her book, such people as there were out on the hills and in the valleys in the olden times. What would she think if she knew that the old fellow, the old tale-spinner spouting all over the boat and penning people up to listen as if they were sheep—what would she think if she knew that he was Walter's father?

She would be delighted, probably, more curious about Walter's family than ever. She would not look down on them, except in a way that she could not help or recognize.

> We came on the fishing bank of Newfoundland on the 12th of July and on the 19th we saw land and it was a joyful sight to us. It was a part of Newfoundland. We sailed between Newfoundland and St. Paul's Island and having a fair wind both the 18th and the 19th we found ourselves in the river on the morning of the 20th and within sight of the mainland of North America. We were awakened at about 1 o'clock in the morning and I think every passenger was out of bed at 4 o'clock gazing at the land, it being wholly covered with wood and quite a new sight to us. It was a part of Nova Scotia and a beautiful hilly country.

This is the day of wonders. The land is covered with trees like a head with hair and behind the ship the sun rises, tipping the top trees with light. The sky is clear and shining as a china plate and the water playfully ruffled with wind. Every wisp of fog has gone and the air is full of the resinous smell of the trees. Seabirds are flashing above the sails all golden like creatures of Heaven, but the sailors fire a few shots to keep them from the rigging.

Mary holds Young James up so that he may always remember this first sight of the continent that will be his home. She tells him the name of this land—Nova Scotia.

"It means New Scotland," she says.

Agnes hears her. "Then why doesn't it say so?"

Mary says, "It's Latin, I think."

Agnes snorts with impatience. The baby was woken early by all the hubbub and celebration, and now she is miserable, wanting to be on the breast all the time, wailing whenever Agnes tries to take her off. Young James, observing all this closely, makes an attempt to get on the other breast, and Agnes bats him off so hard that he staggers.

---

[1] *The Scottish Chiefs*   An historical novel by Jane Porter (1809).

[2] *William Wallace*   Great Scottish hero (c. 1270–1305).

"Suckie-laddie," Agnes calls him. He yelps a bit, then crawls around behind her and pinches the baby's toes.

Another whack.

"You're a rotten egg, you are," his mother says. "Somebody's been spoiling you till you think you're the Laird's arse."

Agnes's roused voice always makes Mary feel as if she were about to catch a blow herself.

Old James is sitting with them on the deck, but pays no attention to this domestic unrest.

"Will you come and look at the country, Father?" Mary says uncertainly. "You can have a better view from the rail."

"I can see it well enough," Old James says. Nothing in his voice suggests that the revelations around them are pleasing to him.

"Ettrick was covered with trees in the old days," he says. "The monks had it first and after that it was the Royal Forest. It was the King's forest. Beech trees, oak trees, rowan trees."

"As many trees as this?" Mary says, made bolder than usual by the novel splendors of the day.

"Better trees. Older. It was famous all over Scotland. The Royal Forest of Ettrick."

"And Nova Scotia is where our brother James is," Mary continues.

"He may be or he may not. It would be easy to die here and nobody know you were dead. Wild animals could have eaten him."

Mary wonders how her father can talk in this way, about how wild animals could have eaten his own son. Is that how the sorrows of the years take hold of you—turning your heart of flesh to a heart of stone, as it says in the old song? And if it is so, how carelessly and disdainfully might he talk about her, who never meant to him a fraction of what the boys did?

Somebody has brought a fiddle onto the deck and is tuning up to play. The people who have been hanging on to the rail and pointing out to one another what they can all see on their own—likewise repeating the name that by now everyone knows, Nova Scotia—are distracted by these sounds and begin to call for dancing. Dancing, at seven o'clock in the morning.

Andrew comes up from below, bearing their supply of water. He stands and watches for a little, then sur-

prises Mary by asking her to dance.

"Who will look after the boy?" Agnes says immediately. "I am not going to get up and chase him." She is fond of dancing, but is prevented now not only by the nursing baby but by the soreness of the parts of her body that were so battered in the birth.

Mary is already refusing, saying she cannot go, but Andrew says, "We will put him on the tether."

"No. No," Mary says. "I've no need to dance." She believes that Andrew has taken pity on her, remembering how she used to be left on the sidelines in school games and at the dancing, though she can actually run and dance perfectly well. Andrew is the only one of her brothers capable of such consideration, but she would almost rather he behaved like the others and left her ignored as she has always been. Pity galls her.

Young James begins to complain loudly, having recognized the word "tether."

"You be still," his father says. "Be still or I'll clout you."

Then Old James surprises them all by turning his attention to his grandson.

"You. Young lad. You sit by me."

"Oh, he will not sit," Mary says. "He will run off and then you cannot chase him, Father. I will stay."

"He will sit," Old James says.

"Well, settle it," Agnes says to Mary. "Go or stay."

Young James looks from one to the other, cautiously snuffling.

"Does he not know even the simplest word?" his grandfather says. "Sit. Lad. Here."

Young James lowers himself, reluctantly, to the spot indicated.

"Now go," Old James says to Mary. And all in confusion, on the verge of tears, she is led away.

People are dancing not just in the figure of the reel but quite outside of it, all over the deck. They are grabbing anyone at all and twirling around. They are even grabbing some of the sailors, if they can get hold of them. Men dance with women, men dance with men, women dance with women, children dance with one another or all alone and without any idea of the steps, getting in the way—but everybody is in everybody's way already and it is no matter.

Mary has caught hands with Andrew and is swung around by him, then passed on to others, who bend to her and fling her undersized body about. She dances down at the level of the children, though she is less bold and carefree. In the thick of so many bodies she is helpless, she cannot pause—she has to stamp and wheel to the music or be knocked down.

"Now, you listen and I will tell you," Old James says. "This old man, Will O'Phaup, my grandfather—he was my grandfather as I am yours—Will O'Phaup was sitting outside his house in the evening, resting himself. It was mild summer weather. All alone, he was. And there was three little lads hardly bigger than you are yourself, they came around the corner of Will's house. They told him good evening. 'Good evening to you, Will O'Phaup,' they says. 'Well, good evening to you, lads. What can I do for you?' 'Can you give us a bed for the night or a place to lie down?' they says. And 'Aye,' he says. 'Aye, I'm thinking three bits of lads like yourselves should not be so hard to find room for.' And he goes into the house with them following and they says, 'And by the bye, could you give us the key, too, the big silver key that you had of us?' Well, Will looks around, and he looks for the key, till he thinks to himself, What key was that? For he knew he never had such a thing in his life. Big key or silver key, he never had it. 'What key are you talking about?' And turns himself around and they are not there. Goes out of the house, all around the house, looks to the road. No trace of them. Looks to the hills. No trace. Then Will knew it. They was no lads at all. Ah, no. They was no lads at all."

James has not made any sound. At his back is the thick and noisy wall of dancers, to the side his mother, with the small clawing beast that bites into her body. And in front of him is the old man with his rumbling voice, insistent but remote, and his blast of bitter breath.

It is the child's first conscious encounter with someone as perfectly self-centered as he is.

He is barely able to focus his intelligence, to show himself not quite defeated. "Key," he says. "Key?"

Agnes, watching the dancing, catches sight of Andrew, red in the face and heavy on his feet, linked arm to arm with various jovial women. There is not one girl whose looks or dancing gives Agnes any worries. Andrew never gives her any worries, anyway. She sees Mary tossed around, with even a flush of color in her cheeks—

though she is too shy, and too short, to look anybody in the face. She sees the nearly toothless witch of a woman who birthed a child a week after her own, dancing with her hollow-cheeked man. No sore parts for her. She must have dropped the child as slick as if it were a rat, then given it to one or the other of her weedy-looking daughters to mind.

She sees Mr. Suter, the surgeon, out of breath, pulling away from a woman who would grab him, ducking through the dance and coming to greet her.

She wishes he would not. Now he will see who her father-in-law is; he may have to listen to the old fool's gabble. He will get a look at their drab, and now not even clean, country clothes. He will see her for what she is.

"So here you are," he says. "Here you are with your treasure."

It is not a word that Agnes has ever heard used to refer to a child. It seems as if he is talking to her in the way he might talk to a person of his own acquaintance, some sort of a lady, not as a doctor talks to a patient. Such behavior embarrasses her and she does not know how to answer.

"Your baby is well?" he says, taking a more down-to-earth tack. He is still catching his breath from the dancing, and his face is covered with a fine sweat.

"Aye."

"And you yourself? You have your strength again?" She shrugs very slightly, so as not to shake the child off the nipple.

"You have a fine color, anyway. That is a good sign."

He asks then if she will permit him to sit and talk to her for a few moments, and once more she is confused by his formality but tells him that he may do as he likes.

Her father-in-law gives the surgeon—and her as well—a despising glance, but Mr. Suter does not notice it, perhaps does not even realize that the old man and the fair-haired boy who sits straight-backed facing the old man have anything to do with her.

"What will you do in Canada West?" he asks.

It seems to her the silliest question. She shakes her head—what can she say? She will wash and sew and cook and almost certainly suckle more children. Where that will be does not much matter. It will be in a house, and not a fine one.

She knows now that this man likes her, and in what

way. She remembers his fingers on her skin. What harm can happen, though, to a woman with a baby at her breast? She feels stirred to show him a bit of friendliness.

"What will you do?" she says.

He smiles and says that he supposes he will go on doing what he has been trained to do, and that the people in America—so he has heard—are in need of doctors and surgeons, just like other people in the world.

"But I do not intend to get walled up in some city. I'd like to get as far as the Mississippi River, at least. Everything beyond the Mississippi used to belong to France, you know, but now it belongs to America and it is wide open—anybody can go there, except that you may run into the Indians. I would not mind that, either. Where there is fighting with the Indians, there'll be all the more need for a surgeon."

She does not know anything about this Mississippi River but she knows that Mr. Suter does not look like a fighting man himself—he does not look as if he could stand up in a quarrel with the brawling lads of Hawick, let alone red Indians.

Two dancers swing so close to them as to put a wind into their faces. It is a young girl, a child, really, whose skirts fly out—and who should she be dancing with but Agnes's brother-in-law Walter. Walter makes some sort of silly bow to Agnes and the surgeon and his father, and the girl pushes him and turns him around and he laughs at her. She is dressed like a young lady, with bows in her hair. Her face is lit up with enjoyment, her cheeks are glowing like lanterns, and she treats Walter with great familiarity, as if she had got hold of a large toy.

"That lad is your friend?" Mr. Suter says.

"No. He is my husband's brother."

The girl is laughing quite helplessly, as she and Walter—through her heedlessness—have almost knocked down another couple in the dance. She is not able to stand up for laughing, and Walter has to support her. Then it appears that she is not laughing but coughing. Walter is holding her against himself, half carrying her to the rail.

"There is one lass that will never have a child to her breast," Mr. Suter says, his eyes flitting to the sucking child before resting again on the girl. "I doubt if she will live long enough to see much of America. Does she not

have anyone to look after her? She should not have been allowed to dance."

He stands up so that he can keep the girl in view as Walter holds her by the rail.

"There, she has stopped," he says.

"No hemorrhaging. At least not this time."

Agnes can see that he takes a satisfaction in the verdict he has passed on this girl. And it occurs to her that this must be because of some condition of his own—that he must be thinking that he is not so bad off by comparison.

There is a cry at the rail, nothing to do with the girl and Walter. Another cry, and many people break off dancing and rush to look at the water. Mr. Suter rises and goes a few steps in that direction, following the crowd, then turns back.

"A whale," he says. "They are saying there is a whale to be seen off the side."

"You stay here!" Agnes shouts in an angry voice, and he turns to her in surprise. But he sees that her words are meant for Young James, who is on his feet.

"This is your lad, then?" Mr. Suter exclaims, as if he had made a remarkable discovery. "May I carry him over to have a look?"

And that is how Mary—happening to raise her face in the crush of passengers—beholds Young James, much amazed, being carried across the deck in the arms of a hurrying stranger, a pale and determined dark-haired man who is surely a foreigner. A child stealer, or child murderer, heading for the rail.

She gives so wild a shriek that anybody would think she was in the Devil's clutches herself, and people make way for her as they would for a mad dog.

"Stop, thief! Stop, thief!" she is crying. "Take the boy from him. Catch him. James! James! Jump down!"

She flings herself forward and grabs the child's ankles, yanking him so that he howls in fear and outrage. The man bearing him nearly topples over but doesn't give him up. He holds on and pushes at Mary with his foot.

"Take her arms," he shouts to those around them. He is short of breath. "She is in a fit."

Andrew has pushed his way in, through people who are still dancing and people who have stopped to watch the drama. He manages somehow to get hold of Mary and Young James and to make clear that one is his son and the other his sister and that it is not a question of fits.

All is shortly explained with courtesies and apologies from Mr. Suter.

"I had just stopped for a few minutes' talk with your wife, to ask her if she was well," the surgeon says. "I did not take time to bid her goodbye, so you must do it for me."

Mary remains unconvinced by the surgeon's story. Of course he would have to say to Agnes that he was taking the child to look at the whale. But that does not make it the truth. Whenever the picture of that devilish man carrying Young James flashes through her mind, and she feels in her chest the power of her own cry, she is astonished and happy. It is still her belief that she has saved him.

> We were becalmed the 21st and 22nd but we had rather more wind the 23rd but in the afternoon were all alarmed by a squall of wind accompanied by thunder and lightning which was very terrible and we had one of our mainsails that had just been mended torn to rags again with the wind. The squall lasted about 8 or 10 minutes and the 24th we had a fair wind which sent us a good way up the River, where it became more strait so that we saw land on both sides of the River. But we becalmed again till the 31st when we had a breeze only two hours.

Nettie's father's name is Mr. Carbert. Sometimes he sits and listens to Nettie read or talks to Walter. The day after the dancing, when many people are in a bad humor from exhaustion and some from drinking whiskey, and hardly anybody bothers to look at the shore, he seeks Walter out to talk to him.

"Nettie is so taken with you," he says, "that she has got the idea that you must come along with us to Montreal."

He gives an apologetic laugh, and Walter laughs, too.

"Then she must think that Montreal is in Canada West," Walter says.

"No. No. I am not making a joke. I looked out for you on purpose when she was not with me. You are a fine companion for her and it makes her happy to be with you. And I can see that you are an intelligent lad

and a prudent one and one who would do well in my office."

"I am with my father and my brother," Walter says, so startled that his voice has a youthful yelp in it. "We are going to get land."

"Well, then. You are not the only son your father has. There may not be enough good land for all of you. And you may not always want to be a farmer."

Walter tells himself that this is true.

"My daughter, now, how old do you think she is?"

Walter cannot think. He shakes his head.

"She is fourteen, nearly fifteen," Nettie's father says. "You would not think so, would you? But it does not matter—that is not what I am talking about. Not about you and Nettie, anything in years to come. You understand that? There is no question of years to come. But I would like for you to come with us and let her be the child that she is and make her happy now with your company. Then I would naturally want to repay you, and there would also be work for you in the office, and if all went well you could count on advancement."

Both of them at this point notice that Nettie is coming toward them. She sticks out her tongue at Walter, so quickly that her father apparently does not notice.

"No more now. Think about it and pick your time to tell me," her father says. "But sooner rather than later would be best."

Walter does not take long to make up his mind. He knows enough to thank Mr. Carbert, but says that he has not thought of working in an office, or at any indoor job. He means to work with his family until they are set up with land to farm and then when they do not need his help so much he thinks of being a trader to the Indians, a sort of explorer. Or a miner for gold.

"As you will," Mr. Carbert says. They walk several steps together, side by side. "I must say I had thought you were rather more serious than that. Fortunately, I said nothing to Nettie."

But Nettie has not been fooled as to the subject of their talks together. She pesters her father until he has to let her know how things have gone and then she seeks out Walter.

"I will not talk to you anymore from now on," she says, in a more grownup voice than he has ever heard from her. "It is not because I am angry but just because if I go on talking to you I will have to think all the time about how soon I'll be saying goodbye to you. But if I stop now I will have already said goodbye, so it will all be over sooner."

She spends the time that is left walking sedately with her father, in her finest clothes.

Walter feels sorry to see her—in these fine cloaks and bonnets she looks more of a child than ever, and her show of haughtiness is touching—but there is so much for him to pay attention to that he seldom thinks of her when she is out of sight.

Years will pass before she will reappear in his mind. But when she does he will find that she is a source of happiness, available to him till the day he dies. Sometimes he will even entertain himself with thoughts of what might have happened had he taken up the offer. He will imagine a radiant recovery, Nettie's acquiring a tall and maidenly body, their life together. Such foolish thoughts as a man may have in secret.

> Several boats from the land came alongside of us with fish, rum, live sheep, tobacco, etc. which they sold very high to the passengers. The 1st of August we had a slight breeze and on the morning of the 2nd we passed by the Isle of Orleans and about six in the morning we were in sight of Quebec in as good health I think as when we left Scotland. We are to sail for Montreal tomorrow in a steamboat.

> My brother Walter in the former part of this letter has written a large journal which I intend to sum up in a small ledger. We have had a very prosperous voyage being wonderfully preserved in health. We can say nothing yet about the state of the country. There is a great number of people landing here but wages is good. I can neither advise nor discourage people from coming. The land is very extensive and very thin-peopled. I think we have seen as much land as might serve all the people in Britain uncultivated and covered with wood. We will write you again as soon as settled.

When Andrew has added this paragraph, Old James is persuaded to add his signature to those of his two sons before the letter is sealed and posted to Scotland from Quebec. He will write nothing else, saying, "What does

it matter to me? It cannot be my home, it can be nothing to me but the land where I will die."

"It will be that for all of us," Andrew says. "But when the time comes we will think of it more as a home."

"Time will not be given to me to do that."

"Are you not well, Father?"

"I am well and I am not."

Young James is now paying occasional attention to the old man, sometimes stopping in front of him and looking straight into his face, with a sturdy insistence.

"He bothers me," Old James says. "I don't like the boldness of him. He will go on and on and not remember a thing of Scotland, where he was born, or the ship he travelled on. He will get to talking another language the way they do when they go to England, only it will be worse than theirs. He looks at me with the kind of look that says he knows that me and my times is all over with."

"He will remember plenty of things," Mary says. Since the dancing and the incident of Mr. Suter she has grown more forthright within the family. "And he doesn't mean his look to be bold," she says. "It is just that he is interested in everything. He understands what you say, far more than you think. He takes everything in and he thinks about it."

Her eyes fill with tears of enthusiasm, but the others look down at the child with sensible reservations.

Young James stands in the midst of them—bright-eyed, fair, and straight. Slightly preening, somewhat wary, unnaturally solemn, as if he had indeed felt descend upon him the burden of the future.

The adults, too, feel the astonishment of the moment. It is as if they had been borne for these past six weeks not on a ship but on one great wave, which has landed them with a mighty thump on this bewildering shore. Thoughts invade their heads, wheeling in with the gulls' cries, their infidel commotion.

Mary thinks that she could snatch up Young James and run away into some part of the strange city of Quebec and find work as a sewing woman (talk on the boat has made her aware that such work is in demand). Then she could bring him up all by herself, as if she were his mother.

Andrew thinks of what it would be like to be here as a free man, without wife or father or sister or children, without a single burden on his back. What could he do then? He tells himself that it is no harm, surely, it is no harm to think about it.

Agnes has heard women on the boat say that the officers you see in the street here are surely the best-looking men anywhere in the world, and that they are ten or twenty times more numerous than the women. Which must mean that you can get what you want out of them—that is, marriage. Marriage to a man with enough money that you could ride in a carriage and send presents to your mother. If you were not married already and dragged down with two children.

Walter thinks that his brother is strong and Agnes is strong—she can help him on the land while Mary cares for the children. Who ever said that he should be a farmer? When they get to Montreal he will go and attach himself to the Hudson's Bay Company and they will send him to the frontier, where he will find riches as well as adventure.

Old James has sensed defection and begins to lament openly, "How shall we sing the Lord's song in a strange land?"

These travellers lie buried—all but one of them—in the graveyard of Boston Church, in Esquesing, in Halton County, Ontario, almost within sight, and well within sound, of Highway 401, which at that spot, just a few miles from Toronto, may be the busiest road in Canada.

Old James is here. And Andrew and Agnes. Nearby is the grave of Mary, married after all and buried beside Robert Murray, her husband. Women were scarce and so were prized in the new country. She and Robert did not have any children together, but after Mary's early death he married another woman and with her he had four sons who lie here, dead at the ages of two, and three, and four, and thirteen. The second wife is here, too. Her stone says "Mother." Mary's says "Wife."

Agnes is here, having survived the births of many children. In a letter to Scotland, telling of the death of Old James in 1829 (a cancer, not much pain until near the end, though "it eat away a great part of his cheek and jaw"), Andrew mentions that his wife has been feeling poorly for the past three years. This may be a roundabout way of saying that during those years she bore her sixth, seventh, and eighth children. She must have recovered her health, for she lived into her eighties.

Andrew seems to have prospered, though he spread himself less than Walter, who married an American girl from Montgomery County, in New York State. Eighteen when she married him, thirty-three when she died after the birth of her ninth child. Walter did not marry again, but farmed successfully, educated his sons, speculated in land, and wrote letters to the government complaining about his taxes. He was able, before he died, to take a trip back to Scotland, where he had himself photographed wearing a plaid and holding a bouquet of thistles.

On the stone commemorating Andrew and Agnes there appears also the name of their daughter Isabel, who, like her mother, died an old woman.

Born at Sea.

Here, too, is the name of Andrew and Agnes's firstborn child, Isabel's elder brother.

Young James was dead within a month of the family's landing at Quebec. His name is here, but surely he cannot be. They had not yet taken up their land when he died; they had not even seen this place. He may have been buried somewhere along the way from Montreal to York or in that hectic new town itself. Perhaps in a raw temporary burying ground now paved over, perhaps without a stone in a churchyard, where other bodies would someday be laid on top of his. Dead of some mishap in the busy streets, or of a fever, or dysentery, or any of the ailments, the accidents, that were the common destroyers of little children in his time.

—2005

Ngũgĩ wa Thiong'o
b. 1938

Novelist, playwright, essayist, and lecturer, Kenyan author Ngũgĩ (pronounced "Nn-goog-y") wa Thiong'o is one of East Africa's most important voices. Most of Ngũgĩ's fiction and non-fiction deals with African history and human rights issues; two acclaimed early novels, *Weep Not, Child* (1964) and *A Grain of Wheat* (1967), are sympathetic accounts of the Mau Mau uprisings of the 1950s that determined Kenya's future. These works have been followed by numerous novels, stories, essays, and plays that deal with colonialism and neo-colonialism—that state of oppression, according to Ngũgĩ, which is "nurtured in the womb of colonialism," leaving economic and spiritual control in the hands of the colonists long after they have departed. Passionate about the state of the African people's identity, Ngũgĩ has written extensively about the need to preserve African cultures and languages. He dedicated *Decolonising the Mind* (1986) "to all those who write in African languages, and to all those who over the years have maintained the dignity of the literature, culture, philosophy, and other treasures carried by African languages." For the past three decades has written all of his creative work in Gikuyu, his native tongue.

Ngũgĩ was born to Thiong'o wa Nducu and and Wanjika wa Ngũgĩ, in Kamiriithu, Kenya, in 1938. His was a large peasant family composed of his father, his mother, who was one of his father's

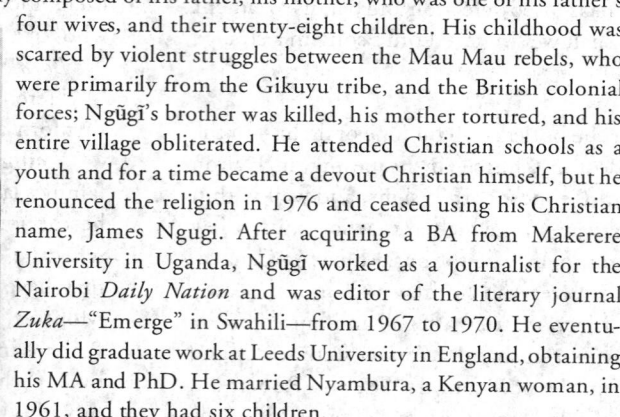

four wives, and their twenty-eight children. His childhood was scarred by violent struggles between the Mau Mau rebels, who were primarily from the Gikuyu tribe, and the British colonial forces; Ngũgĩ's brother was killed, his mother tortured, and his entire village obliterated. He attended Christian schools as a youth and for a time became a devout Christian himself, but he renounced the religion in 1976 and ceased using his Christian name, James Ngugi. After acquiring a BA from Makerere University in Uganda, Ngũgĩ worked as a journalist for the Nairobi *Daily Nation* and was editor of the literary journal *Zuka*—"Emerge" in Swahili—from 1967 to 1970. He eventually did graduate work at Leeds University in England, obtaining his MA and PhD. He married Nyambura, a Kenyan woman, in 1961, and they had six children.

Ngũgĩ's own literary career began in 1963 (coincidentally, the year in which Kenya achieved independence from Britain) with the successful production of his first play, *The Black Hermit*. His first novel, *The River Between* (1965), is still widely regarded as a classic of African and English literature. It is a finely observed and deeply compassionate novel of the tension between the traditional ways of rural Kenya and those of Christianity and of the modern world (including such highly charged issues as those surrounding the practice of female circumcision). *The River Between* was written in English, as were *A Grain of Wheat* (1967) and *Weep Not, Child* (1976). The popularity of Ngũgĩ's 1977 play *Ngaahika Ndeenda (I Will Marry When I Want)*, co-written with Ngũgĩ wa Mirii, led to his exile from Kenya. Working class people and farmers were so enamored of the play and its themes of empowerment and land rights that the government feared an uprising and banned the production. Soon afterward Ngũgĩ was imprisoned for political dissent, an experience he recounts in 1981's *Detained: A Writer's Prison Diary*. He was not reinstated in his post at the University of Nairobi after his detainment, and he left the country in 1982. In 1987 he wrote

Matigari Ma Njiruungi, based on a Gikuyu fable about a freedom fighter; again the Kenyan government reacted in fear and anger, issuing another warrant for his arrest.

The 1977 novel *Petals of Blood* marked Ngũgĩ's "farewell to the English language as a vehicle of my writing of plays, novels and short stories," and *Decolonising the Mind* was his farewell to non-fiction writing in English. "From now on," he said, "it is Gikuyu and Kiswahili all the way." By going back to his original language, especially after having succeeded in eliminating the University of Nairobi's English Department while he was Chair, he worked to end "the domination of the mental universe of the colonised." *Petals of Blood* also marked a change in the focus of his work, from themes of colonialism to those of neo-colonialism. For Ngũgĩ, the problems in Africa did not begin, nor did they end, with the slave trade. According to him, in order to control the native people of Africa, colonizers set out to obliterate African independence both by destroying African culture and by superimposing their own culture and languages. Ngũgĩ has said that neo-colonialism continues long after the colonizers have departed, with first-world countries exploiting African goods and services, keeping the economy "still in the hands of the imperialist bourgeoisie." *Caitaani Mutharabaini*, or *Devil on the Cross* (1982), was written soon after *Petals of Blood* (while he was in a Nairobi prison) and, according to the author, is one of his most important novels.

In a 2004 interview Ngũgĩ said: "In a spiritual sense I have never left Kenya. Kenya and Africa are always in my mind. But I look forward to a physical reunion with Kenya, my beloved country," and soon afterward he made his long-awaited return. Crowds of people celebrated his homecoming, but tragedy followed in the form of an assault upon Ngũgĩ and Njeeri, his second wife (whom he married after Nyambura's death). The couple and their two children fled the country the following day.

Ngũgĩ has taught at universities in New Zealand and Germany, as well as at New York University, Yale, and Smith in the U.S.A. Most of his writing in the past fifteen years has focused on cultural theory, such as the 1993 volume *Moving the Centre: The Struggle for Cultural Freedom*. He currently works at the University of California, Irvine, as Director of the International Center for Writing and Translation, and Distinguished Professor.

⌘ ⌘ ⌘

from *Decolonising the Mind*

CHAPTER 3

I was born into a large peasant family: father, four wives and about twenty-eight children. I also belonged, as we all did in those days, to a wider extended family and to the community as a whole.

We spoke Gĩkũyũ as we worked in the fields. We spoke Gĩkũyũ in and outside the home. I can vividly recall those evenings of storytelling around the fireside. It was mostly the grown-ups telling the children but everybody was interested and involved. We children would re-tell the stories the following day to other children who worked in the fields picking the pyrethrum flowers, tea-leaves or coffee beans of our Euro-pean and African landlords.

The stories, with mostly animals as the main characters, were all told in Gĩkũyũ. Hare, being small, weak but full of innovative wit and cunning, was our hero. We identified with him as he struggled against the brutes of prey like lion, leopard, hyena. His victories were our victories and we learnt that the apparently weak can outwit the strong. We followed the animals in their struggle against hostile nature—drought, rain, sun, wind—a confrontation often forcing them to search for forms of co-operation. But we were also interested in their struggles amongst themselves, and particularly between the beasts and the victims of prey. These twin struggles, against nature and other animals, reflected real-life struggles in the human world.

Not that we neglected stories with human beings as

the main characters. There were two types of characters in such human-centred narratives: the species of truly human beings with qualities of courage, kindness, mercy, hatred of evil, concern for others; and a man-eat-man two-mouthed species with qualities of greed, selfishness, individualism and hatred of what was good for the larger co-operative community. Co-operation as the ultimate good in a community was a constant theme. It could unite human beings with animals against ogres and beasts of prey, as in the story of how dove, after being fed with castor-oil seeds, was sent to fetch a smith working far away from home and whose pregnant wife was being threatened by these man-eating two-mouthed ogres.

There were good and bad story-tellers. A good one could tell the same story over and over again, and it would always be fresh to us, the listeners. He or she could tell a story told by someone else and make it more alive and dramatic. The differences really were in the use of words and images and the inflexion of voices to effect different tones.

We therefore learnt to value words for their meaning and nuances. Language was not a mere string of words. It had a suggestive power well beyond the immediate and lexical meaning. Our appreciation of the suggestive magical power of language was reinforced by the games we played with words through riddles, proverbs, trans-positions of syllables, or through nonsensical but musically arranged words. So we learnt the music of our language on top of the content. The language, through images and symbols, gave us a view of the world, but it had a beauty of its own. The home and the field were then our pre-primary school but what is important, for this discussion, is that the language of our evening teach-ins, and the language of our immediate and wider community, and the language of our work in the fields were one.

And then I went to school, a colonial school, and this harmony was broken. The language of my educa-tion was no longer the language of my culture. I first went to Kamaandura, missionary run, and then to another called Maanguu̅u̅ run by nationalists grouped around the Gĩkũyũ Independent and Karinga Schools[1] Association. Our language of education was still Gĩkũyũ. The very first time I was ever given an ovation

for my writing was over a composition in Gĩkũyũ. So for my first four years there was still harmony between the language of my formal education and that of the Limuru[2] peasant community.

It was after the declaration of a state of emergency over Kenya in 1952 that all the schools run by patriotic nationalists were taken over by the colonial regime and were placed under District Education Boards chaired by Englishmen. English became the language of my formal education. In Kenya, English became more than a language: it was *the* language, and all the others had to bow before it in deference.

Thus one of the most humiliating experiences was to be caught speaking Gĩkũyũ in the vicinity of the school. The culprit was given corporal punishment—three to five strokes of the cane on bare buttocks—or was made to carry a metal plate around the neck with inscriptions such as I AM STUPID or I AM A DONKEY. Sometimes the culprits were fined money they could hardly afford. And how did the teachers catch the culprits? A button was initially given to one pupil who was supposed to hand it over to whoever was caught speaking his mother tongue. Whoever had the button at the end of the day would sing who had given it to him and the ensuing process would bring out all the culprits of the day. Thus children were turned into witch-hunters and in the process were being taught the lucrative value of being a traitor to one's immediate community.

The attitude to English was the exact opposite: any achievement in spoken or written English was highly rewarded; prizes, prestige, applause; the ticket to higher realms. English became the measure of intelligence and ability in the arts, the sciences, and all the other branch-es of learning. English became *the* main determinant of a child's progress up the ladder of formal education.

As you may know, the colonial system of education in addition to its apartheid racial demarcation had the structure of a pyramid: a broad primary base, a narrow-ing secondary middle, and an even narrower university apex. Selections from primary into secondary were through an examination, in my time called Kenya African Preliminary Examination, in which one had to pass six subjects ranging from Maths to Nature Study and Kiswahili.[3] All the papers were written in English.

---

[1]   *Karinga Schools*   Run by the Orthodox and Pentecostal churches.

[2]   *Limuru*   Located in the Nairobi region.

[3]   *Kiswahili*   Swahili language.

Nobody could pass the exam who failed the English language paper no matter how brilliantly he had done in the other subjects. I remember one boy in my class of 1954 who had distinctions in all subjects except English, which he had failed. He was made to fail the entire exam. He went on to become a turn boy in a bus company. I who had only passes but a credit in English got a place at the Alliance High School, one of the most elitist institutions for Africans in colonial Kenya. The requirements for a place at the University, Makerere University College, were broadly the same: nobody could go on to wear the undergraduate red gown, no matter how brilliantly they had performed in all the other subjects unless they had a credit—not even a simple pass!—in English. Thus the most coveted place in the pyramid and in the system was only available to the holder of an English language credit card. English was the official vehicle and the magic formula to colonial elitedom.

Literary education was now determined by the dominant language while also reinforcing that dominance. Orature (oral literature) in Kenyan languages stopped. In primary school I now read simplified Dickens and Stevenson alongside Rider Haggard. Jim Hawkins, Oliver Twist, Tom Brown[1]—not Hare, Leopard and Lion—were now my daily companions in the world of imagination. In secondary school, Scott and G.B. Shaw vied with more Rider Haggard, John Buchan, Alan Paton, Captain W.E. Johns. At Makerere I read English: from Chaucer to T.S. Eliot with a touch of Grahame Greene.

Thus language and literature were taking us further and further from ourselves to other selves, from our world to other worlds.

What was the colonial system doing to us Kenyan children? What were the consequences of, on the one hand, this systematic suppression of our languages and the literature they carried, and on the other the elevation of English and the literature it carried? To answer those questions, let me first examine the relationship of language to human experience, human culture, and the human perception of reality.

---

[1] *Jim Hawkins ... Tom Brown* Characters in Robert Louis Stevenson's *Treasure Island*, Charles Dickens's *Oliver Twist*, and Thomas Hughes's *Tom Brown's Schooldays* respectively.

CHAPTER 4

Language, any language, has a dual character: it is both a means of communication and a carrier of culture. Take English. It is spoken in Britain and in Sweden and Denmark. But for Swedish and Danish people English is only a means of communication with non-Scandinavians. It is not a carrier of their culture. For the British, and particularly the English, it is additionally, and inseparably from its use as a tool of communication, a carrier of their culture and history. Or take Swahili in East and Central Africa. It is widely used as a means of communication across many nationalities. But it is not the carrier of a culture and history of many of those nationalities. However in parts of Kenya and Tanzania, and particularly in Zanzibar, Swahili is inseparably both a means of communication and a carrier of the culture of those people to whom it is a mother-tongue.

Language as communication has three aspects or elements. There is first what Karl Marx once called the language of real life, the element basic to the whole notion of language, its origins and development: that is, the relations people enter into with one another in the labour process, the links they necessarily establish among themselves in the act of a people, a community of human beings, producing wealth or means of life like food, clothing, houses. A human community really starts its historical being as a community of co-operation in production through the division of labour; the simplest is between man, woman and child within a household; the more complex divisions are between branches of production such as those who are sole hunters, sole gatherers of fruits or sole workers in metal. Then there are the most complex divisions such as those in modern factories where a single product, say a shirt or a shoe, is the result of many hands and minds. Production is co-operation, is communication, is language, is expression of a relation between human beings and it is specifically human.

The second aspect of language as communication is speech and it imitates the language of real life, that is communication in production. The verbal signposts both reflect and aid communication or the relation established between human beings in the production of their means of life. Language as a system of verbal signposts makes that production possible. The spoken word is to relations between human beings what the hand is to the relations between human beings and nature. The hand through tools mediates between human beings and nature and forms the language of real life: spoken words mediate between human beings and form the language of speech.

The third aspect is the written signs. The written word imitates the spoken. Where the first two aspects of language as communication through the hand and the spoken word historically evolved more or less simultaneously, the written aspect is a much later historical development. Writing is representation of sounds with visual symbols, from the simplest knot among shepherds to tell the number in a herd or the hieroglyphics among the Agĩkũyũ gicaandi singers and poets of Kenya, to the most complicated and different letter and picture writing systems of the world today.

In most societies the written and the spoken languages are the same, in that they represent each other: what is on paper can be read to another person and be received as that language, which the recipient has grown up speaking. In such a society there is broad harmony for a child between the three aspects of language as communication. His interaction with nature and with other men is expressed in written and spoken symbols or signs which are both a result of that double interaction and a reflection of it. The association of the child's sensibility is with the language of his experience of life.

But there is more to it: communication between human beings is also the basis and process of evolving culture. In doing similar kinds of things and actions over and over again under similar circumstances, similar even in their mutability, certain patterns, moves, rhythms, habits, attitudes, experiences and knowledge emerge. Those experiences are handed over to the next generation and become the inherited basis for their further actions on nature and on themselves. There is a gradual accumulation of values which in time become almost self-evident truths governing their conception of what is right and wrong, good and bad, beautiful and ugly, courageous and cowardly, generous and mean in their internal and external relations. Over a time this becomes a way of life distinguishable from other ways of life. They develop a distinctive culture and history. Culture embodies those moral, ethical and aesthetic values, the set of spiritual eyeglasses, through which they

come to view themselves and their place in the universe. Values are the basis of a people's identity, their sense of particularity as members of the human race. All this is carried by language. Language as culture is the collective memory bank of a people's experience in history. Culture is almost indistinguishable from the language that makes possible its genesis, growth, banking, articulation and indeed its transmission from one generation to the next.

Language as culture also has three important aspects. Culture is a product of the history which it in turn reflects. Culture in other words is a product and a reflection of human beings communicating with one another in the very struggle to create wealth and to control it. But culture does not merely reflect that history, or rather it does so by actually forming images or pictures of the world of nature and nurture. Thus the second aspect of language as culture is as an image-forming agent in the mind of a child. Our whole conception of ourselves as a people, individually and collectively, is based on those pictures and images which may or may not correctly correspond to the actual reality of the struggles with nature and nurture which produced them in the first place. But our capacity to confront the world creatively is dependent on how those images correspond or not to that reality, how they distort or clarify the reality of our struggles. Language as culture is thus mediating between me and my own self; between my own self and other selves; between me and nature. Language is mediating in my very being. And this brings us to the third aspect of language as culture. Culture transmits or imparts those images of the world and reality through the spoken and the written language, that is through a specific language. In other words, the capacity to speak, the capacity to order sounds in a manner that makes for mutual comprehension between human beings is universal. This is the universality of language, a quality specific to human beings. It corresponds to the universality of the struggle against nature and that between human beings. But the particularity of the sounds, the words, the word order into phrases and sentences, and the specific manner, or laws, of their ordering is what distinguishes one language from another. Thus a specific culture is not transmitted through language in its universality but in its particularity as the language of a specific community with a specific history. Written literature and orature are the main means by which a particular language transmits the images of the world contained in the culture it carries.

Language as communication and as culture are then products of each other. Communication creates culture: culture is a means of communication. Language carries culture, and culture carries, particularly through orature and literature, the entire body of values by which we come to perceive ourselves and our place in the world. How people perceive themselves affects how they look at their culture, at their politics and at the social production of wealth, at their entire relationship to nature and to other beings. Language is thus inseparable from ourselves as a community of human beings with a specific form and character, a specific history, a specific relationship to the world.

CHAPTER 5

So what was the colonialist imposition of a foreign language doing to us children?

The real aim of colonialism was to control the people's wealth: what they produced, how they produced it, and how it was distributed; to control, in other words, the entire realm of the language of real life. Colonialism imposed its control of the social production of wealth through military conquest and subsequent political dictatorship. But its most important area of domination was the mental universe of the colonised, the control, through culture, of how people perceived themselves and their relationship to the world. Economic and political control can never be complete or effective without mental control. To control a people's culture is to control their tools of self-definition in relationship to others.

For colonialism this involved two aspects of the same process: the destruction or the deliberate undervaluing of a people's culture, their art, dances, religions, history, geography, education, orature and literature, and the conscious elevation of the language of the coloniser. The domination of a people's language by the languages of the colonising nations was crucial to the domination of the mental universe of the colonised.

Take language as communication. Imposing a foreign language, and suppressing the native languages as spoken and written, were already breaking the harmony previously existing between the African child and the three aspects of language. Since the new language as a means of communication was a product of and was reflecting the "real language of life" elsewhere, it could never as spoken or written properly reflect or imitate the real life of that community. This may in part explain why technology always appears to us as slightly external, *their* product and not *ours*. The word "missile" used to hold an alien far-away sound until I recently learnt its equivalent in Gĩkũyũ, *ngurukuhĩ* and it made me apprehend it differently. Learning, for a colonial child, became a cerebral activity and not an emotionally felt experience.

But since the new, imposed languages could never completely break the native languages as spoken, their most effective area of domination was the third aspect of language as communication, the written. The language of an African child's formal education was foreign. The language of the books he read was foreign. The language of his conceptualisation was foreign. Thought, in him, took the visible form of a foreign language. So the written language of a child's upbringing in the school (even his spoken language within the school compound) became divorced from his spoken language at home. There was often not the slightest relationship between the child's written world, which was also the language of his schooling, and the world of his immediate environment in the family and the community. For a colonial child, the harmony existing between the three aspects of language as communication was irrevocably broken. This resulted in the disassociation of the sensibility of that child from his natural and social environment, what we might call colonial alienation. The alienation became reinforced in the teaching of history, geography, music, where bourgeois Europe was always the centre of the universe.

This disassociation, divorce, or alienation from the immediate environment becomes clearer when you look at colonial language as a carrier of culture.

Since culture is a product of the history of a people which it in turn reflects, the child was now being exposed exclusively to a culture that was a product of a world external to himself. He was being made to stand outside himself to look at himself. *Catching Them Young* is the title of a book on racism, class, sex, and politics in children's literature by Bob Dixon. "Catching them young" as an aim was even more true of a colonial child. The images of his world and his place in it implanted in a child take years to eradicate, if they ever can be.

Since culture does not just reflect the world in images but actually, through those images, conditions a child to see that world a certain way, the colonial child was made to see the world and where he stands in it as seen and defined by or reflected in the culture of the language of imposition.

And since those images are mostly passed on through orature and literature it meant the child would now only see the world as seen in the literature of his language of adoption. From the point of view of alienation, that is of seeing oneself from outside oneself as if one was another self, it does not matter that the imported literature carried the great humanist tradition of the best Shakespeare, Goethe, Balzac, Tolstoy, Gorky, Brecht, Sholokhov, Dickens. The location of this great mirror of imagination was necessarily Europe and its history and culture and the rest of the universe was seen from that centre.

But obviously it was worse when the colonial child was exposed to images of his world as mirrored in the written languages of his coloniser. Where his own native languages were associated in his impressionable mind with low status, humiliation, corporal punishment, slow-footed intelligence and ability or downright stupidity, non-intelligibility and barbarism, this was reinforced by the world he met in the works of such geniuses of racism as a Rider Haggard or a Nicholas Monsarrat; not to mention the pronouncement of some of the giants of western intellectual and political establishment, such as Hume ("... The negro is naturally inferior to the whites ..."), Thomas Jefferson ("... The blacks ... are inferior to the whites on the endowments of both body and mind ..."), or Hegel with his Africa comparable to a land of childhood still enveloped in the dark mantle of the night as far as the development of self-conscious history was concerned. Hegel's statement that there was nothing harmonious with humanity to be found in the African character is representative of the racist images of Africans and Africa such a colonial child was bound to encounter in the literature of the colonial languages. The results could be disastrous.

—1986

ANGELA CARTER
1940 — 1992

Fiction writer Angela Carter spent much of her life out of step with dominant literary trends, creating works that both fascinated and baffled her readers. Carter (whom Margaret Atwood described as "born subversive") liked to disrupt conventions and deny expectations. Her writing inhabits a gray area between the fantastic and the real, and makes innovative use of numerous familiar genres—most of which (Gothic, fantasy, science fiction, magic realism) are somewhat outside the literary mainstream. Her unusually dense, allusive texts revel in linguistic play as they combine material from a myriad of sources, including folklore, tabloid headlines, French surrealism, Hollywood movies, and eighteenth-century allegorical fiction. Since her death, appreciation for her inventiveness and for the originality of her artistic vision has continued to grow; she is one of the most widely taught British writers of fiction.

Carter was born Angela Olive Stalker in Sussex in 1940. Much of her early childhood was spent with her grandmother in industrial Yorkshire, to which she and her brother had been evacuated to escape war-time bombings. After she finished high school,

Carter's father, a journalist, got her a job as a reporter for a south London paper. Direct, factual reporting of events was not her forte, however, and in 1960 she left that job to follow her new husband, Paul Carter, to Bristol. There she entered Bristol University, where she studied medieval literature.

Her first published novel, *Shadow Dance* (1966), marked the beginning of a fertile creative period; two more novels, *The Magic Toyshop* (1967) and *Several Perceptions* (1968) quickly followed. Though many of her early works are set in the Bristol of her youth, they are permeated with elements of the Gothic fairy tale and an underlying threat of violence, while distinctions between reality and daydream are often blurred.

Several Perceptions won the prestigious Somerset Maugham award; the £500 prize enabled Carter to depart for Japan, where she lived for two years, leaving her husband behind. In Japan, Carter began what she referred to as an apprenticeship in signs. She had gone seeking a culture that had never been Judeo-Christian, and in attempting to interpret such an utterly foreign culture—with no knowledge of the language—she was forced to rely on a heightened awareness of visual social cues, observing how roles (particularly those of gender) and customs were created and maintained. After her return to Britain in 1972, the new, radical self-awareness that resulted from her life in Japan led her to examine her own social and cultural heritage aggressively from her newly gained viewpoint of an outsider.

The Sadeian Woman (1979), her first book of nonfiction and one of her most controversial works, attacks the prestige she sees as often being accorded to the suffering of women, and criticizes portrayals of women as blameless victims. These strategies, she believes, only valorize the role of the powerless outsider. *The Sadeian Woman* also stated Carter's particular aims for her narratives, which she believed should provide means of exploring ideas and serve as arguments, presented in fictional terms, for the ways in which we should interpret and respond to the world around us. As she says, "Fine art, that exists for itself alone, is art in a final state of impotence. If nobody, including the artist, acknowledges art as a means of *knowing* the world, then art is relegated to a kind of rumpus room of the mind."

Published in the same year as the *Sadeian Woman*, Carter's collection of short fiction *The Bloody Chamber* (1979) takes characters from stories such as "Red Riding Hood" (Carter's version of which, "The Company of Wolves," was made into a successful film), "Sleeping Beauty," "Beauty and the Beast," and "Bluebeard," and brings them to life in a contemporary setting. Carter claimed she was interested in myths "because they are extraordinary lies designed to make people unfree," and by opening up the timeless realms of these myths to historical consciousness, she demonstrated how she believed they can—and should—end differently.

Carter's fiction from this period relies heavily on allegory, and also makes use of many elements of science fiction and magic realism. *The Infernal Desire Machine of Doctor Hoffman* (1972), in particular, is often classified as science fiction, though it also draws heavily on the picaresque. This novel has remained one of her most controversial, frequently criticized for an alleged male chauvinistic viewpoint that seems to celebrate the pornographic. With Carter's use of multiple voices and ever-shifting narrative positions, however, it is sometimes difficult to tell whether she is embracing or parodying the gender roles she sets out.

In the late 1970s and early 1980s, Carter's work began to be more favorably reviewed, and she took on a demanding lecturing and teaching schedule that saw her traveling around the world. In 1983 she also began a family, giving birth to a son, Alexander, with Mark Pearce, whom she married in 1991. Despite her busy schedule, Carter produced her longest novel, *Nights at the Circus*, in 1984. This story about a Cockney trapeze artist with wings has often been compared to Gabriel Garcia Marquez's *One Hundred Years of Solitude* (1967)—a comparison that brought Carter more into the mainstream than she had perhaps ever been. This and her final novel, *Wise Children* (1991), were both very well received, and when Carter died of lung cancer in 1992, she was mourned as a central literary figure of her day.

Many lamented that her obituary notices spoke of her work more generously than most of her reviews had. But critical acceptance had never been a goal of Carter's; she was always suspicious of critical consensus of any kind. Indeed, her writing seeks to provoke those whose opinions are widely accepted, and, in doing so, to produce fruitful critical debate. As one of her critics said, "I'll please no one, least of all her, by trying to say she's not offensive."

⌘ ⌘ ⌘

The Bloody Chamber[1]

I remember how, that night, I lay awake in the wagon-lit[2] in a tender, delicious ecstasy of excitement, my burning cheek pressed against the impeccable linen of the pillow and the pounding of my heart mimicking that of the great pistons ceaselessly thrusting the train that bore me through the night, away from Paris, away from girlhood, away from the white, enclosed quietude of my mother's apartment, into the unguessable country of marriage.

And I remember I tenderly imagined how, at this very moment, my mother would be moving slowly about the narrow bedroom I had left behind for ever, folding up and putting away all my little relics, the tumbled garments I would not need any more, the scores for which there had been no room in my trunks, the concert programmes I'd abandoned; she would linger over this torn ribbon and that faded photograph with all the half-joyous, half-sorrowful emotions of a woman on her daughter's wedding day. And, in the midst of my bridal triumph, I felt a pang of loss as if, when he put the gold band on my finger, I had, in some way, ceased to be her child in becoming his wife.

---

[1]   *The Bloody Chamber*   Cf. Charles Perrault's "La Barbe Bleue" ("Bluebeard"), 1697.

[2]   *wagon-lit*   French: sleeping coach (on a train).

Are you sure, she'd said when they delivered the gigantic box that held the wedding dress he'd bought me, wrapped up in tissue paper and red ribbon like a Christmas gift of crystallized fruit. Are you sure you love him? There was a dress for her, too; black silk, with the dull, prismatic sheen of oil on water, finer than anything she'd worn since that adventurous girlhood in Indo-China, daughter of a rich tea planter. My eagle-featured, indomitable mother; what other student at the Conservatoire could boast that her mother had outfaced a junkful[1] of Chinese pirates, nursed a village through a visitation of the plague, shot a man-eating tiger with her own hand and all before she was as old as I?

"Are you sure you love him?"

"I'm sure I want to marry him," I said.

And would say no more. She sighed, as if it was the reluctance that she might at last banish the spectre of poverty from its habitual place at our meager table. For my mother herself had gladly, scandalously, defiantly beggared herself for love; and, one fine day, her gallant soldier never returned from the wars, leaving his wife and child a legacy of tears that never quite dried, a cigar box full of medals and the antique service revolver that my mother, grown magnificently eccentric in hardship, kept always in her reticule,[2] in case—how I teased her—she was surprised by footpads[3] on her way home from the grocer's shop.

Now and then a starburst of lights spattered the drawn blinds as if the railway company had lit up all the stations through which we passed in celebration of the bride. My satin nightdress had just been shaken from its wrappings; it had slipped over my young girl's pointed breasts and shoulders, supple as a garment of heavy water, and now teasingly caressed me, egregious, insinuating, nudging between my thighs as I shifted restlessly in my narrow berth. His kiss, his kiss with tongue and teeth in it and a rasp of beard, had hinted to me, though with the same exquisite tact as this nightdress he'd given me, of the wedding night, which would be voluptuously deferred until we lay in his great ancestral bed in the sea-girt, pinnacled domain that lay, still, beyond the grasp of my imagination … that magic place, the fairy castle whose walls were made of foam, that legendary habitation in which he had been born. To which, one day, I might bear an heir. Our destination, my destiny.

Above the syncopated roar of the train, I could hear his even, steady breathing. Only the communicating door kept me from my husband and it stood open. If I rose up on my elbow, I could see the dark, leonine shape of his head and my nostrils caught a whiff of the opulent male scent of leather and spices that always accompanied him and sometimes, during his courtship, had been the only hint he gave me that he had come into my mother's sitting room, for, though he was a big man, he moved as softly as if all his shoes had soles of velvet, as if his footfall turned the carpet into snow.

He had loved to surprise me in my abstracted solitude at the piano. He would tell them not to announce him, then soundlessly open the door and softly creep up behind me with his bouquet of hot-house flowers or his box of marrons glacés,[4] lay his offering upon the keys and clasp his hands over my eyes as I was lost in a Debussy[5] prelude. But that perfume of spiced leather always betrayed him; after my first shock, I was forced always to mimic surprise, so that he would not be disappointed.

He was older than I. He was much older than I; there were streaks of pure silver in his dark mane. But his strange, heavy, almost waxen face was not lined by experience. Rather, experience seemed to have washed it perfectly smooth, like a stone on a beach whose fissures have been eroded by successive tides. And sometimes that face, in stillness when he listened to me playing, with the heavy eyelids folded over eyes that always disturbed me by their absolute absence of light, seemed to me like a mask, as if his real face, the face that truly reflected all the life he had led in the world before he met me, before, even, I was born, as though that face lay underneath this mask. Or else, elsewhere. As though he had laid by the face in which he had lived for so long in order to offer my youth a face unsigned by the years.

And, elsewhere, I might see him plain. Elsewhere. But, where?

In, perhaps, that castle to which the train now took us, that marvellous castle in which he had been born.

Even when he asked me to marry him, and I said:

---

[1]   *junk*   Common Chinese boat with a flat bottom and square prow.

[2]   *reticule*   Handbag.

[3]   *footpads*   Thieves.

[4]   *marrons glacés*   Chestnuts glazed with icing sugar.

[5]   *Debussy*   French composer Claude Achille Debussy (1862–1918).

"Yes," still he did not lose that heavy, fleshy composure of his. I know it must seem a curious analogy, a man with a flower, but sometimes he seemed to me like a lily. Yes. A lily. Possessed of that strange, ominous calm of a sentient vegetable, like one of those cobra-headed, funereal lilies whose white sheaths are curled out of a flesh as thick and tensely yielding to the touch as vellum. When I said that I would marry him, not one muscle in his face stirred, but he let out a long, extinguished sigh. I thought: Oh! how he must want me! And it was as though the imponderable weight of his desire was a force I might not withstand, not by virtue of its violence but because of its very gravity.

He had the ring ready in a leather box lined with crimson velvet, a fire opal the size of a pigeon's egg set in a complicated circle of dark antique gold. My old nurse, who still lived with my mother and me, squinted at the ring askance: opals are bad luck, she said. But this opal had been his own mother's ring, and his grandmother's, and her mother's before that, given to an ancestor by Catherine de Medici[1] … every bride that came to the castle wore it, time out of mind. And did he give it to his other wives and have it back from them? asked the old woman rudely; yet she was a snob. She hid her incredulous joy at my marital coup—her little Marquise—behind a façade of fault-finding. But, here, she touched me. I shrugged and turned my back pettishly on her. I did not want to remember how he had loved other women before me, but the knowledge often teased me in the threadbare self-confidence of the small hours.

I was seventeen and knew nothing of the world; my Marquis had been married before, more than once, and I remained a little bemused that, after those others, he should now have chosen me. Indeed, was he not still in mourning for his last wife? Tsk, tsk, went my old nurse. And even my mother had been reluctant to see her girl whisked off by a man so recently bereaved. A Romanian countess, a lady of high fashion. Dead just three short months before I met him, a boating accident, at his home, in Brittany. They never found her body but I rummaged through the back copies of the society magazines my old nanny kept in a trunk under her bed and tracked down her photograph. The sharp muzzle of

a pretty, witty, naughty monkey; such potent and bizarre charm, of a dark, bright, wild yet worldly thing whose natural habitat must have been some luxurious interior decorator's jungle filled with potted palms and tame, squawking parakeets.

Before that? *Her* face is common property; everyone painted her but the Redon[2] engraving I liked best, *The Evening Star Walking on the Rim of Night*. To see her skeletal, enigmatic grace, you would never think she had been a barmaid in a café in Montmartre until Puvis de Chavannes[3] saw her and had her expose her flat breasts and elongated thighs to his brush. And yet it was the absinthe doomed her, or so they said.

The first of all his ladies? That sumptuous diva; I had heard her sing Isolde,[4] precociously musical child that I was, taken to the opera for a birthday treat. My first opera; I had heard her sing Isolde. With what white-hot passion had she burned from the stage! So that you could tell she would die young. We sat high up, halfway to heaven in the gods, yet she half-blinded me. And my father, still alive (oh, so long ago), took hold of my sticky little hand, to comfort me, in the last act, yet all I heard was the glory of her voice.

Married three times within my own brief lifetime to three different graces, now, as if to demonstrate the eclecticism of his taste, he had invited me to join this gallery of beautiful women, I, the poor widow's child with my mouse-coloured hair that still bore the kinks of the plaits from which it had so recently been freed, my bony hips, my nervous, pianist's fingers.

He was rich as Croesus.[5] The night before our wedding—a simple affair, at the Mairie,[6] because his countess was so recently gone—he took my mother and me, curious coincidence, to see *Tristan*. And, do you know, my heart swelled and ached so during the Liebestod[7] that I thought I must truly love him. Yes. I did. On his arm, all eyes were upon me. The whispering

---

[1] *Catherine de Medici* Queen of France; wife of King Henry II (1519–89).

[2] *Redon* French painter and lithographer Odilon Redon (1840-1916).

[3] *Puvis de Chavannes* French painter (1824–98).

[4] *Isolde* I.e., in composer Richard Wagner's opera *Tristan und Isolde* (first performed 1865).

[5] *Croesus* Sixth-century BCE king of Lydia, famous for his wealth.

[6] *Mairie* French: town hall, mayor's residence.

[7] *Liebestod* Aria describing the suicide of lovers.

crowd in the foyer parted like the Red Sea to let us through. My skin crisped at his touch.

How my circumstances had changed since the first time I heard those voluptuous chords that carry such a charge of deathly passion in them! Now, we sat in a loge,[1] in red velvet armchairs, and a braided, bewigged flunkey brought us a silver bucket of iced champagne in the interval. The froth spilled over the rim of my glass and drenched my hands, I thought: My cup runneth over. And I had on a Poiret[2] dress. He had prevailed upon my reluctant mother to let him buy my trousseau;[3] what would I have gone to him in, otherwise? Twice-darned underwear, faded gingham, serge skirts, hand-me-downs. So, for the opera, I wore a sinuous shift of white muslin tied with a silk string under the breasts. And everyone stared at me. And at his wedding gift.

His wedding gift, clasped round my throat. A choker of rubies, two inches wide, like an extraordinarily precious slit throat.

After the Terror, in the early days of the Directory,[4] the aristos who'd escaped the guillotine had an ironic fad of tying a red ribbon round their necks at just the point where the blade would have sliced it through, a red ribbon like the memory of a wound. And his grandmother, taken with the notion, had her ribbon made up in rubies; such a gesture of luxurious defiance! That night at the opera comes back to me even now … the white dress; the frail child within it; and the flashing crimson jewels round her throat, bright as arterial blood.

I saw him watching me in the gilded mirrors with the assessing eye of a connoisseur inspecting horseflesh, or even of a housewife in the market, inspecting cuts on the slab. I'd never seen, or else had never acknowledged, that regard of his before, the sheer carnal avarice of it; and it was strangely magnified by the monocle lodged in his left eye. When I saw him look at me with lust, I dropped my eyes but, in glancing away from him, I caught sight of myself in the mirror. And I saw myself, suddenly, as he saw me, my pale face, the way the muscles in my neck stuck out like thin wire. I saw how much that cruel necklace became me. And, for the first time in my innocent and confined life, I sensed in myself a potentiality for corruption that took my breath away.

The next day, we were married.

The train slowed, shuddered to a halt. Lights; clank of metal; a voice declaring the name of an unknown, never-to-be visited station; silence of the night; the rhythm of his breathing, that I should sleep with, now, for the rest of my life. And I could not sleep. I stealthily sat up, raised the blind a little and huddled against the cold window that misted over with the warmth of my breathing, gazing out at the dark platform towards those rectangles of domestic lamplight that promised warmth, company, a supper of sausages hissing in a pan on the stove for the station master, his children tucked up in bed asleep in the brick house with the painted shutters … all the paraphernalia of the everyday world from which I, with my stunning marriage, had exiled myself.

Into marriage, into exile; I sensed it, I knew it—that, henceforth, I would always be lonely. Yet that was part of the already familiar weight of the fire opal that glimmered like a gypsy's magic ball, so that I could not take my eyes off it when I played the piano. This ring, the bloody bandage of rubies, the wardrobe of clothes from Poiret and Worth,[5] his scent of Russian leather— all had conspired to seduce me so utterly that I could not say I felt one single twinge of regret for the world of tartines[6] and maman that now receded from me as if drawn away on a string, like a child's toy, as the train began to throb again as if in delighted anticipation of the distance it would take me.

The first grey streamers of the dawn now flew in the sky and an eldritch half-light seeped into the railway carriage. I heard no change in his breathing but my heightened, excited senses told me he was awake and gazing at me. A huge man, an enormous man, and his eyes, dark and motionless as those eyes the ancient Egyptians painted upon their sarcophagi, fixed upon

---

[1] *loge* Opera-house box.

[2] *Poiret* Dressmaker Paul Poiret (1879–1944).

[3] *trousseau* Bride's collection of clothing and linens.

[4] *Terror … Directory* Reign of Terror, during the French Revolution (1793–94), during which thousands of people, considered by the political regime to be enemies of the state, were executed; *Directory* I.e., the *Directoire*, the period at the end of the French Revolution during which five Directors shared executive power over the state.

[5] *Worth* Charles Frederick Worth (1825–95), British and French fashion designer and founder of Maison Worth.

[6] *tartines* Slices of bread with butter or jam; a child's meal.

me. I felt a certain tension in the pit of my stomach, to be so watched, in such silence. A match struck. He was igniting a Romeo y Julieta[1] fat as a baby's arm.

"Soon," he said in his resonant voice that was like the tolling of a bell and I felt, all at once, a sharp premonition of dread that lasted only as long as the match flared and I could see his white, broad face as if it were hovering, disembodied, above the sheets, illuminated from below like a grotesque carnival head. Then the flame died, the cigar glowed and filled the compartment with a remembered fragrance that made me think of my father, how he would hug me in a warm fug[2] of Havana, when I was a little girl, before he kissed me and left me and died.

As soon as my husband handed me down from the high step of the train, I smelled the amniotic salinity of the ocean. It was November; the trees, stunted by the Atlantic gales, were bare and the lonely halt was deserted but for his leather-gaitered chauffeur waiting meekly beside the sleek black motor car. It was cold; I drew my furs about me, a wrap of white and black, broad stripes of ermine and sable, with a collar from which my head rose like the calyx of a wildflower. (I swear to you, I had never been vain until I met him.) The bell clanged; the straining train leapt its leash and left us at that lonely wayside halt where only he and I had descended. Oh, the wonder of it; how all that might of iron and steam had paused only to suit his convenience. The richest man in France.

"Madame."

The chauffeur eyed me; was he comparing me, invidiously, to the countess, the artist's model, the opera singer? I hid behind my furs as if they were a system of soft shields. My husband liked me to wear my opal over my kid glove, a showy, theatrical trick—but the moment the ironic chauffeur glimpsed its simmering flash he smiled, as though it was proof positive I was his master's wife. And we drove towards the widening dawn, that now streaked half the sky with a wintry bouquet of pink of roses, orange of tiger-lilies, as if my husband had ordered me a sky from a florist. The day broke around me like a cool dream.

Sea; sand; a sky that melts into the sea—a landscape of misty pastels with a look about it of being continu-

ously on the point of melting. A landscape with all the deliquescent harmonies of Debussy, of the études[3] I played for him, the reverie I'd been playing that afternoon in the salon of the princess where I'd first met him, among the teacups and the little cakes, I, the orphan, hired out of charity to give them their digestive of music.

And, ah! his castle. The faery solitude of the place; with its turrets of misty blue, its courtyard, its spiked gate, his castle that lay on the very bosom of the sea with seabirds mewing about its attics, the casements opening on to the green and purple, evanescent departures of the ocean, cut off by the tide from land for half a day … that castle, at home neither on the land nor on the water, a mysterious, amphibious place, contravening the materiality of both earth and the waves, with the melancholy of a mermaiden who perches on her rock and waits, endlessly, for a lover who had drowned far away, long ago. That lovely, sad, sea-siren of a place!

The tide was low; at this hour, so early in the morning, the causeway rose up out of the sea. As the car turned on to the wet cobbles between the slow margins of water, he reached out for my hand that had his sultry, witchy ring on it, pressed my fingers, kissed my palm with extraordinary tenderness. His face was as still as ever I'd seen it, still as a pond iced thickly over, yet his lips, that always looked so strangely red and naked between the black fringes of his beard, now curved a little. He smiled; he welcomed his bride home.

No room, no corridor that did not rustle with the sound of the sea and all the ceilings, the walls on which his ancestors in the stern regalia of rank lined up with their dark eyes and white faces, were stippled with refracted light from the waves which were always in motion; that luminous, murmurous castle of which I was the chatelaine,[4] I, the little music student whose mother had sold all her jewellery, even her wedding ring, to pay the fees at the Conservatoire.

First of all, there was the small ordeal of my initial interview with the housekeeper, who kept this extraordinary machine, this anchored, castellated ocean liner, in smooth running order no matter who stood on the bridge; how tenuous, I thought, might be my authority here! She had a bland, pale, impassive, dislikeable face

---

[1] *Romeo y Julieta* Brand of Havana cigar.

[2] *fug* Thick, close atmosphere.

[3] *études* Class of musical compositions.

[4] *chatelaine* Mistress.

beneath the impeccably starched white linen head-dress of the region. Her greeting, correct but lifeless, chilled me; daydreaming, I dared presume too much on my status ... briefly wondered how I might install my old nurse, so much loved, however cosily incompetent, in her place. Ill-considered schemings! He told me this one had been his foster mother; was bound to his family in the utmost feudal complicity, "as much part of the house as I am, my dear." Now her thin lips offered me a proud little smile. She would be my ally as long as I was his. And with that, I must be content.

But, here, it would be easy to be content. In the turret suite he had given me for my very own, I could gaze out over the tumultuous Atlantic and imagine myself the Queen of the Sea. There was a Bechstein[1] for me in the music room and, on the wall, another wedding present—an early Flemish primitive of Saint Cecilia[2] at her celestial organ. In the prim charm of this saint, with her plump, sallow cheeks and crinkled brown hair, I saw myself as I could have wished to be. I warmed to a loving sensitivity I had not hitherto suspected in him. Then he led me up a delicate spiral staircase to my bedroom; before she discreetly vanished, the housekeeper set him chuckling with some, I dare say, lewd blessing for newlyweds in her native Breton. That I did not understand. That he, smiling, refused to interpret.

And there lay the grand, hereditary matrimonial bed, itself the size, almost, of my little room at home, with the gargoyles carved on its surfaces of ebony, vermilion lacquer, gold leaf; and its white gauze curtains, billowing in the sea breeze. Our bed. And surrounded by so many mirrors! Mirrors on all the walls, in stately frames of contorted gold, that reflected more white lilies than I'd ever seen in my life before. He'd filled the room with them, to greet the bride, the young bride. The young bride, who had become that multitude of girls I saw in the mirrors, identical in their chic navy blue tailor-mades, for travelling, madame, or walking. A maid had dealt with the furs. Henceforth, a maid would deal with everything.

"See," he said, gesturing towards those elegant girls. "I have acquired a whole harem for myself!"

I found that I was trembling. My breath came

thickly. I could not meet his eye and turned my head away, out of pride, out of shyness, and watched a dozen husbands approach me in a dozen mirrors and slowly, methodically, teasingly, unfasten the buttons of my jacket and slip it from my shoulders. Enough! No; more! Off comes the skirt; and, next, the blouse of apricot linen that cost more than the dress I had for First Communion. The play of the waves outside in the cold sun glittered on his monocle; his movements seemed to me deliberately coarse, vulgar. The blood rushed to my face again, and stayed there.

And yet, you see, I guessed it might be so—that we should have a formal disrobing of the bride, a ritual from the brothel. Sheltered as my life had been, how could I have failed, even in the world of prim bohemia in which I lived, to have heard hints of *his* world?

He stripped me, gourmand that he was, as if he were stripping the leaves off an artichoke—but do not imagine much finesse about it; this artichoke was no particular treat for the diner nor was he yet in any greedy haste. He approached his familiar treat with a weary appetite. And when nothing but my scarlet, palpitating core remained, I saw, in the mirror, the living image of an etching by Rops[3] from the collection he had shown me when our engagement permitted us to be alone together ... the child with her sticklike limbs, naked but for her button boots, her gloves, shielding her face with her hand as though her face were the last repository of her modesty; and the old, monocled lecher who examined her, limb by limb. He in his London tailoring; she, bare as a lamb chop. Most pornographic of all confrontations. And so my purchaser unwrapped his bargain. And, as at the opera, when I had first seen my flesh in his eyes, I was aghast to feel myself stirring.

At once he closed my legs like a book and I saw again the rare movement of his lips that meant he smiled.

Not yet. Later. Anticipation is the greater part of pleasure, my little love.

And I began to shudder, like a racehorse before a race, yet also with a kind of fear, for I felt both a strange, impersonal arousal at the thought of love and at the same time a repugnance I could not stifle for his white, heavy flesh that had too much in common with the armfuls of arum lilies that filled my bedroom in great

---

[1] *Bechstein* Type of piano created by Carl Bechstein in 1853.

[2] *Saint Cecilia* Patron saint of music and musicians.

[3] *Rops* Belgian artist Félicien Rops (1833–98).

glass jars, those undertakers' lilies with the heavy pollen that powders your fingers as if you had dipped them in turmeric. The lilies I always associate with him; that are white. And stain you.

This scene from a voluptuary's life was now abruptly terminated. It turns out he has business to attend to; his estates, his companies—even on your honeymoon? Even then, said the red lips that kissed me before he left me alone with my bewildered senses—a wet, silken brush from his beard; a hint of the pointed tip of the tongue. Disgruntled, I wrapped a négligé of antique lace around me to sip the little breakfast of hot chocolate the maid brought me; after that, since it was second nature to me, there was nowhere to go but the music room and soon I settled down at my piano.

Yet only a series of subtle discords flowed from beneath my fingers: out of tune ... only a little out of tune; but I'd been blessed with perfect pitch and could not bear to play any more. Sea breezes are bad for pianos; we shall need a resident piano-tuner on the premises if I'm to continue with my studies! I flung down the lid in a little fury of disappointment; what should I do now, how shall I pass the long, sea-lit hours until my husband beds me?

I shivered to think of *that*.

His library seemed the source of his habitual odour of Russian leather. Row upon row of calf-bound volumes, brown and olive, with gilt lettering on their spines, the octavo[1] in brilliant scarlet morocco. A deep-buttoned leather sofa to recline on. A lectern, carved like a spread eagle, that held open upon it an edition of Huysmans's *Là-bas*,[2] from some over-exquisite private press; it had been bound like a missal,[3] in brass, with gems of coloured glass. The rugs on the floor, deep, pulsing blues of heaven and red of the heart's dearest blood, came from Isfahan and Bokhara;[4] the dark panelling gleamed; there was the lulling music of the sea and a fire of apple logs. The flames flickered along the spines inside a glass-fronted case that held books still

crisp and new. Eliphas Levy;[5] the name meant nothing to me. I squinted at a title or two: *The Initiation, The Key of Mysteries, The Secret of Pandora's Box*, and yawned. Nothing, here, to detain a seventeen-year-old girl waiting for her first embrace. I should have liked, best of all, a novel in yellow paper;[6] I wanted to curl up on the rug before the blazing fire, lose myself in a cheap novel, munch sticky liqueur chocolates. If I rang for them, a maid would bring me chocolates.

Nevertheless, I opened the doors of that bookcase idly to browse. And I think I knew, I knew by some tingling of the fingertips, even before I opened that slim volume with no title at all on the spine, what I should find inside it. When he showed me the Rops, newly bought, dearly prized, had he not hinted that he was a connoisseur of such things? Yet I had not bargained for this, the girl with tears hanging on her cheeks like stuck pearls, her cunt a split fig below the great globes of her buttocks on which the knotted tails of the cat were about to descend, while a man in a black mask fingered with his free hand his prick, that curved upwards like the scimitar he held. The picture had a caption: "Reproof of curiosity." My mother, with all the precision of her eccentricity, had told me what it was that lovers did; I was innocent but not naive. *The Adventures of Eulalie at the Harem of the Grand Turk* had been printed, according to the flyleaf, in Amsterdam in 1748, a rare collector's piece. Had some ancestor brought it back himself from that northern city? Or had my husband bought it for himself, from one of those dusty little bookshops on the Left Bank where an old man peers at you through spectacles an inch thick, daring you to inspect his wares ... I turned the pages in the anticipation of fear; the print was rusty. Here was another steel engraving: "Immolation of the wives of the Sultan." I knew enough for what I saw in that book to make me gasp.

There was a pungent intensification of the odour of leather that suffused his library; his shadow fell across the massacre.

"My little nun has found the prayerbooks, has she?" he demanded, with a curious mixture of mockery and relish; then, seeing my painful, furious bewilderment, he

---

[1] *octavo* Book size. The pages of an octavo are produced by folding a standard-sized printing sheet three times to form eight leaves.

[2] *Huysmans's Là-bas* 1891 novel by French novelist Joris Karl Huysmans.

[3] *missal* Prayer book; contains the service of the Mass for the liturgical year.

[4] *Isfahan and Bokhara* Cities in Iran and Uzbekistan.

[5] *Eliphas Levy* Pseudonym of French magician Alphonse Louis Constant (1810–75).

[6] *novel in yellow paper* I.e., a popular novel.

laughed at me aloud, snatched the book from my hands and put it down on the sofa.

"Have the nasty pictures scared Baby? Baby mustn't play with grownups' toys until she's learned how to handle them, must she?"

Then he kissed me. And with, this time, no reticence. He kissed me and laid his hand imperatively upon my breast, beneath the sheath of ancient lace. I stumbled on the winding stair that led to the bedroom, to the carved, gilded bed on which he had been conceived. I stammered foolishly: We've not taken luncheon yet; and, besides, it is broad daylight …

All the better to see you.

He made me put on my choker, the family heirloom of one woman who had escaped the blade. With trembling fingers, I fastened the thing about my neck. It was cold as ice and chilled me. He twined my hair into a rope and lifted it off my shoulders so that he could the better kiss the downy furrows below my ears; that made me shudder. And he kissed those blazing rubies, too. He kissed them before he kissed my mouth. Rapt, he intoned: "Of her apparel she retains/Only her sonorous jewellery."

A dozen husbands impaled a dozen brides while the mewing gulls swung on invisible trapezes in the empty air outside.

I was brought to my senses by the insistent shrilling of the telephone. He lay beside me, felled like an oak, breathing stertorously, as if he had been fighting with me. In the course of that one-sided struggle, I had seen his deathly composure shatter like a porcelain vase flung against a wall; I had heard him shriek and blaspheme at the orgasm; I had bled. And perhaps I had seen his face without its mask; and perhaps I had not. Yet I had been infinitely dishevelled by the loss of my virginity.

I gathered myself together, reached into the cloisonné[1] cupboard beside the bed that concealed the telephone and addressed the mouthpiece. His agent in New York. Urgent.

I shook him awake and rolled over on my side, cradling my spent body in my arms. His voice buzzed like a hive of distant bees. My husband. My husband, who, with so much love, filled my bedroom with lilies until it looked like an embalming parlour. Those

somnolent lilies, that wave their heavy heads, distributing their lush, insolent incense reminiscent of pampered flesh.

When he'd finished with the agent, he turned to me and stroked the ruby necklace that bit into my neck, but with such tenderness now, that I ceased flinching and he caressed my breasts. My dear one, my little love, my child, did it hurt her? He's so sorry for it, such impetuousness, he could not help himself; you see, he loves her so … and this lover's recitative of his brought my tears in a flood. I clung to him as though only the one who had inflicted the pain could comfort me for suffering it. For a while, he murmured to me in a voice I'd never heard before, a voice like the soft consolations of the sea. But then he unwound the tendrils of my hair from the buttons of his smoking jacket, kissed my cheek briskly and told me the agent from New York had called with such urgent business that he must leave as soon as the tide was low enough. Leave the castle? Leave France! And would be away for at least six weeks.

"But it is our honeymoon!"

A deal, an enterprise of hazard and chance involving several millions, lay in the balance, he said. He drew away from me into that waxworks stillness of his; I was only a little girl, I did not understand. And, he said unspoken to my wounded vanity, I have had too many honeymoons to find them in the least pressing commitments. I know quite well that this child I've bought with a handful of coloured stones and the pelts of dead beasts won't run away. But, after he'd called his Paris agent to book a passage for the States next day—just one tiny call, my little one—we should have time for dinner together.

And I had to be content with that.

A Mexican dish of pheasant with hazelnuts and chocolate; salad; white, voluptuous cheese; a sorbet of muscat grapes and Asti spumante. A celebration of Krug exploded festively. And then acrid black coffee in precious little cups so fine it shadowed the birds with which they were painted. I had Cointreau, he had cognac in the library, with the purple velvet curtains drawn against the night, where he took me to perch on his knee in a leather armchair beside the flickering log fire. He had made me change into that chaste little Poiret shift of white muslin; he seemed especially fond of it, my breasts showed through the flimsy stuff, he

[1] *cloisonné* Enamel.

said, like little soft white doves that sleep, each one, with a pink eye open. But he would not let me take off my ruby choker, although it was growing very uncomfortable, nor fasten up my descending hair, the sign of a virginity so recently ruptured that still remained a wounded presence between us. He twined his fingers in my hair until I winced; I said, I remember, very little.

"The maid will have changed our sheets already," he said. "We do not hang the bloody sheets out of the window to prove to the whole of Brittany you are a virgin, not in these civilized times. But I should tell you it would have been the first time in all my married lives I could have shown my interested tenants such a flag."

Then I realized, with a shock of surprise, how it must have been my innocence that captivated him—the silent music, he said, of my unknowingness, like *La Terrasse des audiences au clair de lune*[1] played upon a piano with keys of ether. You must remember how ill at ease I was in that luxurious place, how unease had been my constant companion during the whole length of my courtship by this grave satyr who now gently martyrized my hair. To know that my naivety gave him some pleasure made me take heart. Courage! I shall act the fine lady to the manner born one day, if only by virtue of default.

Then, slowly yet teasingly, as if he were giving a child a great, mysterious treat, he took out a bunch of keys from some interior hidey-hole in his jacket—key after key, a key, he said, for every lock in the house. Keys of all kinds—huge, ancient things of black iron; others slender, delicate, almost baroque; wafer-thin Yale keys for safes and boxes. And, during his absence, it was I who must take care of them all.

I eyed the heavy bunch with circumspection. Until that moment, I had not given a single thought to the practical aspects of marriage with a great house, great wealth, a great man, whose key ring was as crowded as that of a prison warder. Here were the clumsy and archaic keys for the dungeons, for dungeons we had in plenty although they had been converted to cellars for his wines; the dusty bottles inhabited in racks all those deep holes of pain in the rock on which the castle was built. These are the keys to the kitchens, this is the key to the picture gallery, a treasure house filled by five

centuries of avid collectors—ah! he foresaw I would spend hours there.

He had amply indulged his taste for the Symbolists, he told me with a glint of greed. There was Moreau's great portrait of his first wife, the famous *Sacrificial Victim* with the imprint of the lacelike chains on her pellucid skin. Did I know the story of the painting of that picture? How, when she took off her clothes for him for the first time, she fresh from her bar in Montmartre, she had robed herself involuntarily in a blush that reddened her breasts, her shoulders, her arms, her whole body? He had thought of that story, of that dear girl, when first he had undressed me … Ensor, the great Ensor, his monolithic canvas: *The Foolish Virgins*. Two or three late Gauguins, his special favourite the one of the tranced brown girl in the deserted house which was called: *Out of the Night We Come, Into the Night We Go*. And, besides the additions he had made himself, his marvellous inheritance of Watteaus, Poussins and a pair of very special Fragonards, commissioned for a licentious ancestor who, it was said, had posed for the master's brush himself with his own two daughters … He broke off his catalogue of treasures abruptly.

Your thin white face, chérie; he said, as if he saw it for the first time. Your thin white face, with its promise of debauchery only a connoisseur could detect.

A log fell in the fire, instigating a shower of sparks; the opal on my finger spurted green flame. I felt as giddy as if I were on the edge of a precipice; I was afraid, not so much of him, of his monstrous presence, heavy as if he had been gifted at birth with more specific *gravity* than the rest of us, the presence that, even when I thought myself most in love with him, always subtly oppressed me … No. I was not afraid of him; but of myself. I seemed reborn in his unreflective eyes, reborn in unfamiliar shapes. I hardly recognized myself from his descriptions of me and yet, and yet—might there not be a grain of beastly truth in them? And, in the red firelight, I blushed again, unnoticed, to think he might have chosen me because, in my innocence, he sensed a rare talent for corruption.

Here is the key to the china cabinet—don't laugh, my darling; there's a king's ransom in Sèvres in that closet, and a queen's ransom in Limoges.[2] And a key to

---

[1] *La Terrasse des audiences au clair de lune*   Piano solo by Claude Debussy (1912–13).

[2] *Sèvres … Limoges*   Fine china.

the locked, barred room where five generations of plate[1] were kept.

Keys, keys, keys. He would trust me with the keys to his office, although I was only a baby; and the keys to his safes, where he kept the jewels I should wear, he promised me, when we returned to Paris. Such jewels! Why, I would be able to change my earrings and necklaces three times a day, just as the Empress Josephine used to change her underwear. He doubted, he said, with that hollow, knocking sound that served him for a chuckle, I would be quite so interested in his share certificates although they, of course, were worth infinitely more.

Outside our firelit privacy, I could hear the sound of the tide drawing back from the pebbles of the foreshore; it was nearly time for him to leave me. One single key remained unaccounted for on the ring and he hesitated over it; for a moment, I thought he was going to unfasten it from its brothers, slip it back into his pocket and take it away with him.

"What is *that* key?" I demanded, for his chaffing had made me bold. "The key to your heart? Give it me!"

He dangled the key tantalizingly above my head, out of reach of my straining fingers; those bare red lips of his cracked sidelong in a smile.

"Ah, no," he said. "Not the key to my heart. Rather, the key to my enfer."[2]

He left it on the ring, fastened the ring together, shook it musically, like a carillon. Then threw the keys in a jingling heap in my lap. I could feel the cold metal chilling my thighs through my thin muslin frock. He bent over me to drop a beard-masked kiss on my forehead.

"Every man must have one secret, even if only one, from his wife," he said. "Promise me this, my whey-faced piano-player; promise me you'll use all the keys on the ring except that last little one I showed you. Play with anything you find, jewels, silver plate; make toy boats of my share certificates, if it pleases you, and send them sailing off to America after me. All is yours, everywhere is open to you—except the lock that this single key fits. Yet all it is is the key to a little room at the foot of the west tower, behind the still-room, at the end of a dark little corridor full of horrid cobwebs that

would get into your hair and frighten you if you ventured there. Oh, and you'd find it such a dull little room! But you must promise me, if you love me, to leave it well alone. It is only a private study, a hideaway, a 'den,' as the English say, where I can go, sometimes, on those infrequent yet inevitable occasions when the yoke of marriage seems to weigh too heavily on my shoulders. There I can go, you understand, to savour the rare pleasure of imagining myself wifeless."

There was a little thin starlight in the courtyard as, wrapped in my furs, I saw him to his car. His last words were, that he had telephoned the mainland and taken a piano-tuner on to the staff; this man would arrive to take up his duties the next day. He pressed me to his vicuna[3] breast, once, and then drove away.

I had drowsed away that afternoon and now I could not sleep. I lay tossing and turning in his ancestral bed until another daybreak discoloured the dozen mirrors that were iridescent with the reflections of the sea. The perfume of the lilies weighed on my senses; when I thought that, henceforth, I would always share these sheets with a man whose skin, as theirs did, contained that toad-like, clammy hint of moisture, I felt a vague desolation that within me, now my female wound had healed, there had awoken a certain queasy craving like the cravings of pregnant women for the taste of coal or chalk or tainted food, for the renewal of his caresses. Had he not hinted to me, in his flesh as in his speech and looks, of the thousand, thousand baroque intersections of flesh upon flesh? I lay in our wide bed accompanied by a sleepless companion, my dark newborn curiosity.

I lay in bed alone. And I longed for him. And he disgusted me.

Were there jewels enough in all his safes to recompense me for this predicament? Did all that castle hold enough riches to recompense me for the company of the libertine[4] with whom I must share it? And what, precisely, was the nature of my desirous dread for this mysterious being who, to show his mastery over me, had abandoned me on my wedding night?

Then I sat straight up in bed, under the sardonic

---

[1] *plate*   I.e., silver dishes and utensils.

[2] *enfer*   French: Hell.

[3] *vicuna*   Fine, silky wool made from the coat of a South American animal of the same name.

[4] *libertine*   Immoral, dissolute man.

masks of the gargoyles carved above me, riven by a wild surmise. Might he have left me, not for Wall Street but for an importunate mistress tucked away God knows where who knew how to pleasure him far better than a girl whose fingers had been exercised, hitherto, only by the practice of scales and arpeggios? And, slowly, soothed, I sank back on to the heaping pillows; I acknowledged that the jealous scare I'd just given myself was not unmixed with a little tincture of relief.

At last I drifted into slumber, as daylight filled the room and chased bad dreams away. But the last thing I remembered, before I slept, was the tall jar of lilies beside the bed, how the thick glass distorted their fat stems so they looked like arms, dismembered arms, drifting drowned in greenish water.

Coffee and croissants to console this bridal, solitary waking. Delicious. Honey, too, in a section of comb on a glass saucer. The maid squeezed the aromatic juice from an orange into a chilled goblet while I watched her as I lay in the lazy, midday bed of the rich. Yet nothing, this morning, gave me more than a fleeting pleasure except to hear that the piano-tuner had been at work already. When the maid told me that, I sprang out of bed and pulled on my old serge skirt and flannel blouse, costume of a student, in which I felt far more at ease with myself than in any of my fine new clothes.

After my three hours of practice, I called the piano-tuner in, to thank him. He was blind, of course; but young, with a gentle mouth and grey eyes that fixed upon me although they could not see me. He was a blacksmith's son from the village across the causeway; a chorister in the church whom the good priest had taught a trade so that he could make a living. All most satisfactory. Yes. He thought he would be happy here. And if, he added shyly, he might sometimes be allowed to hear me play ... for, you see, he loved music. Yes. Of course, I said. Certainly. He seemed to know that I had smiled.

After I dismissed him, even though I'd woken so late, it was still barely time for my "five o'clock."[1] The housekeeper, who, thoughtfully forewarned by my husband, had restrained herself from interrupting my music, now made me a solemn visitation with a lengthy menu for a late luncheon. When I told her I did not need it, she looked at me obliquely, along her nose. I understood at once that one of my principal functions as chatelaine was to provide work for the staff. But, all the same, I asserted myself and said I would wait until dinner-time, although I looked forward nervously to the solitary meal. Then I found I had to tell her what I would like to have prepared for me; my imagination, still that of a schoolgirl, ran riot. A fowl in cream—or should I anticipate Christmas with a varnished turkey? No; I have decided. Avocado and shrimp, lots of it, followed by no entree at all. But surprise me for dessert with every ice-cream in the ice box. She noted all down but sniffed; I'd shocked her. Such tastes! Child that I was, I giggled when she left me.

But, now ... what shall I do, now?

I could have spent a happy hour unpacking the trunks that contained my trousseau but the maid had done that already, the dresses, the tailor-mades hung in the wardrobe in my dressing room, the hats on wooden heads to keep their shape, the shoes on wooden feet as if all these inanimate objects were imitating the appearance of life, to mock me. I did not like to linger in my overcrowded dressing room, nor in my lugubriously lily-scented bedroom. How shall I pass the time?

I shall take a bath in my own bathroom! And found the taps were little dolphins made of gold, with chips of turquoise for eyes. And there was a tank of goldfish, who swam in and out of moving fronds of weeds, as bored, I thought, as I was. How I wished he had not left me. How I wished it were possible to chat with, say, a maid; or, the piano-tuner ... but I knew already my new rank forbade overtures of friendship to the staff.

I had been hoping to defer the call as long as I could, so that I should have something to look forward to in the dead waste of time I foresaw before me, after my dinner was done with, but, at a quarter before seven, when darkness already surrounded the castle, I could contain myself no longer. I telephoned my mother. And astonished myself by bursting into tears when I heard her voice.

No, nothing was the matter. Mother, I have gold bath taps.

I said, gold bath taps!

No; I suppose that's nothing to cry about, Mother.

The line was bad, I could hardly make out her congratulations, her questions, her concern, but I was a little comforted when I put the receiver down.

---

[1]   "five o'clock"   Late afternoon tea.

Yet there still remained one whole hour to dinner and the whole, unimaginable desert of the rest of the evening.

The bunch of keys lay, where he had left them, on the rug before the library fire which had warmed their metal so that they no longer felt cold to the touch but warm, almost, as my own skin. How careless I was; a maid, tending the logs, eyed me reproachfully as if I'd set a trap for her as I picked up the clinking bundle of keys, the keys to the interior doors of this lovely prison of which I was both the inmate and the mistress and had scarcely seen. When I remembered that, I felt the exhilaration of the explorer.

Lights! More lights!

At the touch of a switch, the dreaming library was brilliantly illuminated. I ran crazily about the castle, switching on every light I could find—I ordered the servants to light up all their quarters, too, so the castle would shine like a seaborne birthday cake lit with a thousand candles, one for every year of its life, and everybody on shore would wonder at it. When everything was lit as brightly as the café in the Gare du Nord, the significance of the possessions implied by that bunch of keys no longer intimidated me, for I was determined, now, to search through them all for evidence of my husband's true nature.

His office first, evidently.

A mahogany desk half a mile wide, with an impeccable blotter and a bank of telephones. I allowed myself the luxury of opening the safe that contained the jewellery and delved sufficiently among the leather boxes to find out how my marriage had given me access to a jinn's[1] treasury—parures,[2] bracelets, rings ... While I was thus surrounded by diamonds, a maid knocked on the door and entered before I spoke; a subtle discourtesy. I would speak to my husband about it. She eyed my serge skirt superciliously; did madame plan to dress for dinner?

She made a moue[3] of disdain when I laughed to hear that, she was far more the lady than I. But, imagine—to dress up in one of my Poiret extravaganzas, with the jewelled turban and aigrette[4] on my head, roped with pearl to the navel, to sit down all alone in the baronial dining hall at the head of that massive board at which King Mark[5] was reputed to have fed his knights ... I grew calmer under the cold eye of her disapproval. I adopted the crisp inflections of an officer's daughter. No, I would not dress for dinner. Furthermore, I was not hungry enough for dinner itself. She must tell the housekeeper to cancel the dormitory feast I'd ordered. Could they leave me sandwiches and a flask of coffee in my music room? And would they all dismiss for the night?

Mais oui, madame.

I knew by her bereft intonation I had let them down again but I did not care; I was armed against them by the brilliance of his hoard. But I would not find his heart amongst the glittering stones; as soon as she had gone, I began a systematic search of the drawers of his desk.

All was in order, so I found nothing. Not a random doodle on an old envelope, nor the faded photograph of a woman. Only the files of business correspondence, the bills from the home farms, the invoices from tailors, the billets-doux from international financiers. Nothing. And this absence of the evidence of his real life began to impress me strangely; there must, I thought, be a great deal to conceal if he takes such pains to hide it.

His office was a singularly impersonal room, facing inwards, on to the courtyard, as though he wanted to turn his back on the siren sea in order to keep a clear head while he bankrupted a small businessman in Amsterdam or—I noticed with a thrill of distaste —engaged in some business in Laos that must, from certain cryptic references to his amateur botanist's enthusiasm for rare poppies, be to do with opium. Was he not rich enough to do without crime? Or was the crime itself his profit? And yet I saw enough to appreciate his zeal for secrecy.

Now I had ransacked his desk, I must spend a coolheaded quarter of an hour putting every last letter back where I had found it, and, as I covered the traces of my visit, by some chance, as I reached inside a little drawer that had stuck fast, I must have touched a hidden spring, for a secret drawer flew open within that drawer

---

[1] *jinn* Shape-changing demon of Islamic folklore; a genie.

[2] *parures* Sets of several pieces of jewelry.

[3] *moue* Pout.

[4] *aigrette* Spray of jewels.

[5] *King Mark* Of Arthurian legend.

itself; and this secret drawer contained—at last!—a file marked: *Personal.*

I was alone, but for my reflection in the uncurtained window.

I had the brief notion that his heart, pressed flat as a flower, crimson and thin as tissue paper, lay in this file. It was a very thin one.

I could have wished, perhaps, I had not found that touching, ill-spelt note, on a paper napkin marked *La Coupole*, that began: "My darling, I cannot wait for the moment when you may make me yours completely." The diva had sent him a page of the score of *Tristan*, the Liebestod, with the single, cryptic word: "Until …" scrawled across it. But the strangest of all these love letters was a postcard with a view of a village graveyard, among mountains, where some black-coated ghoul enthusiastically dug at a grave; this little scene, executed with the lurid exuberance of Grand Guignol,[1] was captioned: "Typical Transylvanian Scene—Midnight, All Hallows." And, on the other side, the message: "On the occasion of this marriage to the descendant of Dracula—always remember, 'the supreme and unique pleasure of love is the certainty that one is doing evil.' Toutes amitiés,[2] C."

A joke. A joke in the worst possible taste; for had he not been married to a Romanian countess? And then I remembered her pretty, witty face, and her name— Carmilla. My most recent predecessor in this castle had been, it would seem, the most sophisticated.

I put away the file, sobered. Nothing in my life of family love and music had prepared me for these grown-up games and yet these were clues to his self that showed me, at least, how much he had been loved, even if they did not reveal any good reason for it. But I wanted to know still more; and, as I closed the office door and locked it, the means to discover more fell in my way.

Fell, indeed; and with the clatter of a dropped canteen of cutlery, for, as I turned the slick Yale lock, I contrived, somehow, to open up the key ring itself, so that all the keys tumbled loose on the floor. And the very first key I picked out of that pile was, as luck or ill

fortune had it, the key to the room he had forbidden me, the room he would keep for his own so that he could go there when he wished to feel himself once more a bachelor.

I made my decision to explore it before I felt a faint resurgence of my ill-defined fear of his waxen stillness. Perhaps I half-imagined, then, that I might find his real self in his den, waiting there to see if indeed I had obeyed him; that he had sent a moving figure of himself to New York, the enigmatic, self-sustaining carapace[3] of his public person, while the real man, whose face I had glimpsed in the storm of orgasm, occupied himself with pressing private business in the study at the foot of the west tower, behind the still-room. Yet, if that were so, it was imperative that I should find him, should know him; and I was too deluded by his apparent taste for me to think my disobedience might truly offend him.

I took the forbidden key from the heap and left the others lying there.

It was now very late and the castle was adrift, as far as it could go from the land, in the middle of the silent ocean where, at my orders, it floated, like a garland of light. And all silent, all still, but for the murmuring of the waves.

I felt no fear, no intimation of dread. Now I walked as firmly as I had done in my mother's house.

Not a narrow, dusty little passage at all; why had he lied to me? But an ill-lit one, certainly; the electricity, for some reason, did not extend here, so I retreated to the still-room and found a bundle of waxed tapers in a cupboard, stored there with matches to light the oak board at grand dinners. I put a match to my little taper and advanced with it in my hand, like a penitent, along the corridor hung with heavy, I think Venetian, tapestries. The flame picked out, here, the head of a man, there, the rich breast of a woman spilling through a rent in her dress—the Rape of the Sabines,[4] perhaps? The naked swords and immolated horses suggested some grisly mythological subject. The corridor wound down-

---

[1] *Grand Guignol* Drama dealing with macabre subject matter and containing graphic violence. Originally, the name of a Paris theater that shocked its audience members in the early twentieth century with the graphic nature of its performances.

[2] *Toutes amitiés* French: all the best.

[3] *carapace* Shell.

[4] *Rape … Sabines* Legendary event in early Roman history, in which young Roman men abducted and raped large numbers of women from neighboring Sabine in order to try to quicken the growth of the population of early Rome. The scene has been widely depicted in works of art, including paintings by Rubens, Poussin, and David.

wards; there was an almost imperceptible ramp to the thickly carpeted floor. The heavy hangings on the wall muffled my footsteps, even my breathing. For some reason, it grew very warm; the sweat sprang out in beads on my brow. I could no longer hear the sound of the sea.

A long, a winding corridor, as if I were in the viscera of the castle; and this corridor led to a door of worm-eaten oak, low, round-topped, barred with black iron. And still I felt no fear, no raising of the hairs on the back of the neck, no prickling of the thumbs.

The key slid into the new lock as easily as a hot knife into butter.

No fear; but a hesitation, a holding of the spiritual breath.

If I had found some traces of his heart in a file marked: *Personal*, perhaps, here, in his subterranean privacy, I might find a little of his soul. It was the consciousness of the possibility of such a discovery, of its possible strangeness, that kept me for a moment motionless, before, in the foolhardiness of my already subtly tainted innocence, I turned the key and the door creaked slowly back.

"There is a striking resemblance between the act of love and the ministrations of a torturer," opined my husband's favourite poet;[1] I had learned something of the nature of that similarity on my marriage bed. And now my taper showed me the outlines of a rack. There was also a great wheel, like the ones I had seen in woodcuts of the martyrdoms of the saints, in my old nurse's little store of holy books. And—just one glimpse of it before my little flame caved in and I was left in absolute darkness—a metal figure, hinged at the side, which I knew to be spiked on the inside and to have the name: the Iron Maiden.

Absolute darkness. And, about me, the instruments of mutilation.

Until that moment, this spoiled child did not know she had inherited nerves and a will from the mother who had defied the yellow outlaws of Indo-China. My mother's spirit drove me on, into that dreadful place, in a cold ecstasy to know the very worst. I fumbled for the matches in my pocket; what a dim, lugubrious light they gave! And yet, enough, oh, more than enough, to see a

room designed for desecration and some dark night of unimaginable lovers whose embraces were annihilation.

The walls of this stark torture chamber were the naked rock; they gleamed as if they were sweating with fright. At the four corners of the room were funerary urns, of great antiquity, Etruscan, perhaps, and, on three-legged ebony stands, the bowls of incense he had left burning which filled the room with a sacerdotal[2] reek. Wheel, rack, and Iron Maiden were, I saw, displayed as grandly as if they were items of statuary and I was almost consoled, then, and almost persuaded myself that I might have stumbled only upon a little museum of his perversity, that he had installed these monstrous items here only for contemplation.

Yet at the centre of the room lay a catafalque,[3] a doomed, ominous bier of Renaissance workmanship, surrounded by long white candles and, at its foot, an armful of the same lilies with which he had filled my bedroom, stowed in a four-foot-high jar glazed with a sombre Chinese red. I scarcely dared examine this catafalque and its occupant more closely; yet I knew I must.

Each time I struck a match to light those candles round her bed, it seemed a garment of that innocence of mine for which he had lusted fell away from me.

The opera singer lay, quite naked, under a thin sheet of very rare and precious linen, such as the princes of Italy used to shroud those whom they had poisoned. I touched her, very gently, on the white breast; she was cool, he had embalmed her. On her throat I could see the blue imprint of his strangler's fingers. The cool, sad flame of the candles flickered on her white, closed eyelids. The worst thing was, the dead lips smiled.

Beyond the catafalque, in the middle of the shadows, a white, nacreous glimmer; as my eyes accustomed themselves to the gathering darkness, I at last—oh, horrors!—made out a skull; yes, a skull, so utterly denuded, now, of flesh, that it scarcely seemed possible the stark bone had once been richly upholstered with life. And this skull was strung up by a system of unseen cords, so that it appeared to hang, disembodied, in the still, heavy air, and it had been crowned with a wreath of white roses, and a veil of lace, the final image of his bride.

---

[1] *There is ... poet* Unidentified.

[2] *sacerdotal* Belonging to the priesthood.

[3] *catafalque* Decorative platform for a coffin.

Yet the skull was still so beautiful, had shaped with its sheer planes so imperiously the face that had once existed above it, that I recognized her the moment I saw her; face of the evening star walking on the rim of night. One false step, oh, my poor, dear girl, next in the fated sisterhood of his wives; one false step and into the abyss of the dark you stumbled.

And where was she, the latest dead, the Romanian countess who might have thought her blood would survive his depredations? I knew she must be here, in the place that had wound me through the castle towards it on a spool of inexorability. But, at first, I could see no sign of her. Then, for some reason—perhaps some change of atmosphere wrought by my presence—the metal shell of the Iron Maiden emitted a ghostly twang; my feverish imagination might have guessed its occupant was trying to clamber out, though, even in the midst of my rising hysteria, I knew she must be dead to find a home there.

With trembling fingers, I prised open the front of the upright coffin, with its sculpted face caught in a rictus[1] of pain. Then, overcome, I dropped the key I still held in my other hand. It dropped into the forming pool of her blood.

She was pierced, not by one but by a hundred spikes, this child of the land of the vampires who seemed so newly dead, so full of blood … oh God! how recently had he become a widower? How long had he kept her in this obscene cell? Had it been all the time he had courted me, in the clear light of Paris?

I closed the lid of her coffin very gently and burst into a tumult of sobbing that contained both pity for his other victims and also a dreadful anguish to know I, too, was one of them.

The candles flared, as if in a draught from a door to elsewhere. The light caught the fire opal on my hand so that it flashed, once, with a baleful light, as if to tell me the eye of God—his eye—was upon me. My first thought, when I saw the ring for which I had sold myself to this fate, was, how to escape it.

I retained sufficient presence of mind to snuff out the candles round the bier with my fingers, to gather up my taper, to look around, although shuddering, to ensure I had left behind me no traces of my visit.

I retrieved the key from the pool of blood, wrapped it in my handkerchief to keep my hands clean, and fled the room, slamming the door behind me. It crashed to with a juddering reverberation, like the door of hell.

I could not take refuge in my bedroom, for that retained the memory of his presence trapped in the fathomless silvering of his mirrors. My music room seemed the safest place, although I looked at the picture of Saint Cecilia with a faint dread; what had been the nature of her martyrdom? My mind was in a tumult; schemes for flight jostled with one another … as soon as the tide receded from the causeway, I would make for the mainland—on foot, running, stumbling; I did not trust that leather-clad chauffeur, nor the well-behaved housekeeper, and I dared not take any of the pale, ghostly maids into my confidence, either, since they were his creatures, all. Once at the village, I would fling myself directly on the mercy of the gendarmerie.[2]

But—could I trust them, either? His forefathers had ruled this coast for eight centuries, from this castle whose moat was the Atlantic. Might not the police, the advocates, even the judge, all be in his service, turning a common blind eye to his vices since he was milord whose word must be obeyed? Who, on this distant coast, would believe the white-faced girl from Paris who came running to them with a shuddering tale of blood, of fear, of the ogre murmuring in the shadows? Or, rather, they would immediately know it to be true. But were all honour-bound to let me carry it no further.

Assistance. My mother. I ran to the telephone; and the line, of course, was dead.

Dead as his wives.

A thick darkness, unlit by any star, still glazed the windows. Every lamp in my room burned, to keep the dark outside, yet it seemed still to encroach on me, to be present beside me but as if masked by my lights, the night like a permeable substance that could seep into my skin. I looked at the precious little clock made from hypocritically innocent flowers long ago, in Dresden; the hands had scarcely moved one single hour forward from when I first descended to that private slaughter-house of his. Time was his servant, too; it would trap me, here, in a night that would last until he came back to me, like a black sun on a hopeless morning.

And yet the time might still be my friend; at that

---

[1]   *rictus* Gape.

[2]   *gendarmerie* French: police force.

hour, that very hour, he set sail for New York.

To know that, in a few moments, my husband would have left France calmed my agitation a little. My reason told me I had nothing to fear; the tide that would take him away to the New World would let me out of the imprisonment of the castle. Surely I could easily evade the servants. Anybody can buy a ticket at a railway station. Yet I was still filled with unease. I opened the lid of the piano; perhaps I thought my own particular magic might help me, now, that I could create a pentacle[1] out of music that would keep me from harm for, if my music had first ensnared him, then might it not also give me the power to free myself from him?

Mechanically, I began to play but my fingers were stiff and shaking. At first, I could manage nothing better than the exercises of Czerny but simply the act of playing soothed me and, for solace, for the sake of the harmonious rationality of its sublime mathematics, I searched among his scores until I found *The Well-Tempered Clavier*. I set myself the therapeutic task of playing all Bach's equations, every one, and, I told myself, if I played them all through without a single mistake—then the morning would find me once more a virgin.

Crash of a dropped stick.

His silver-headed cane! What else? Sly, cunning, he had returned; he was waiting for me outside the door!

I rose to my feet; fear gave me strength. I flung back my head defiantly.

"Come in!" My voice astonished me by its firmness, its clarity.

The door slowly, nervously opened and I saw, not the massive, irredeemable bulk of my husband but the slight, stooping figure of the piano-tuner, and he looked far more terrified of me than my mother's daughter would have been of the Devil himself. In the torture chamber, it seemed to me that I would never laugh again; now, helplessly, laugh I did, with relief, and, after a moment's hesitation, the boy's face softened and he smiled a little, almost in shame. Though they were blind, his eyes were singularly sweet.

"Forgive me," said Jean-Yves. "I know I've given you grounds for dismissing me, that I should be crouching outside your door at midnight ... but I heard you walking about, up and down—I sleep in a room at the

foot of the west tower—and some intuition told me you could not sleep and might, perhaps, pass the insomniac hours at your piano. And I could not resist that. Besides, I stumbled over these—"

And he displayed the ring of keys I'd dropped outside my husband's office door, the ring from which one key was missing. I took them from him, looked round for a place to stow them, fixed on the piano stool as if to hide them would protect me. Still he stood smiling at me. How hard it was to make everyday conversation.

"It's perfect," I said. "The piano. Perfectly in tune."

But he was full of the loquacity of embarrassment, as though I would only forgive him for his impudence if he explained the cause of it thoroughly.

"When I heard you play this afternoon, I thought I'd never heard such a touch. Such technique. A treat for me, to hear a virtuoso! So I crept up to your door now, humbly as a little dog might, madame, and put my ear to the keyhole and listened, and listened—until my stick fell to the floor through a momentary clumsiness of mine, and I was discovered."

He had the most touchingly ingenuous smile.

"Perfectly in tune," I repeated. To my surprise, now I had said it, I found I could not say anything else. I could only repeat: "In tune ... perfect ... in tune," over and over again. I saw a dawning surprise in his face. My head throbbed. To see him, in his lovely, blind humanity, seemed to hurt me very piercingly, somewhere inside my breast; his figure blurred, the room swayed about me. After the dreadful revelation of that bloody chamber, it was his tender look that made me faint.

When I recovered consciousness, I found I was lying in the piano-tuner's arms and he was tucking the satin cushion from the piano-stool under my head.

"You are in some great distress," he said. "No bride should suffer so much, so early in her marriage."

His speech had the rhythms of the countryside, the rhythms of the tides.

"Any bride brought to this castle should come ready dressed in mourning, should bring a priest and a coffin with her," I said.

"What's this?"

It was too late to keep silent; and if he, too, were one of my husband's creatures, then at least he had been kind to me. So I told him everything, the keys, the

---

[1] *pentacle* Magic symbol enclosed in a circle.

interdiction, my disobedience, the room, the rack, the skull, the corpses, the blood.

"I can scarcely believe it," he said, wondering. "That man ... so rich; so well-born."

"Here's proof," I said and tumbled the fatal key out of my handkerchief on to the silken rug.

"Oh God," he said. "I can smell the blood."

He took my hand; he pressed his arms about me. Although he was scarcely more than a boy, I felt a great strength flow into me from his touch.

"We whisper all manner of strange tales up and down the coast," he said. "There was a Marquis, once, who used to hunt young girls on the mainland; he hunted them with dogs, as though they were foxes. My grandfather had it from his grandfather, how the Marquis pulled a head out of his saddle bag and showed it to the blacksmith while the man was shoeing his horse. 'A fine specimen of the genus, brunette, eh, Guillaume?' And it was the head of the blacksmith's wife."

But, in these more democratic times, my husband must travel as far as Paris to do his hunting in the salons. Jean-Yves knew the moment I shuddered.

"Oh, madame! I thought all these were old wives' tales, chattering of fools, spooks to scare bad children into good behaviour! Yet how could you know, a stranger, that the old name for this place is the Castle of Murder?"

How could I know, indeed? Except that, in my heart, I'd always known its lord would be the death of me.

"Hark!" said my friend suddenly. "The sea has changed key; it must be near morning, the tide is going down."

He helped me up. I looked from the window, towards the mainland, along the causeway where the stones gleamed wetly in the thin light of the end of the night and, with an almost unimaginable horror, a horror the intensity of which I cannot transmit to you, I saw, in the distance, still far away yet drawing moment by moment inexorably nearer, the twin headlamps of his great black car, gouging tunnels through the shifting mist.

My husband had indeed returned; this time, it was no fancy.

"The key!" said Jean-Yves. "It must go back on the

ring, with the others. As though nothing had happened."

But the key was still caked with wet blood and I ran to my bathroom and held it under the hot tap. Crimson water swirled down the basin but, as if the key itself were hurt, the bloody token stuck. The turquoise eyes of the dolphin taps winked at me derisively; they knew my husband had been too clever for me! I scrubbed the stain with my nail brush but still it would not budge. I thought how the car would be rolling silently towards the closed courtyard gate; the more I scrubbed the key, the more vivid grew the stain.

The bell in the gatehouse would jangle. The porter's drowsy son would push back the patchwork quilt, yawning, pull the shirt over his head, thrust his feet into his sabots ... slowly, slowly; open the door for your master as slowly as you can ...

And still the bloodstain mocked the fresh water that spilled from the mouth of the leering dolphin.

"You have no more time," said Jean-Yves. "He is here. I know it. I must stay with you."

"You shall not!" I said. "Go back to your room, now. Please."

He hesitated. I put an edge of steel in my voice, for I knew I must meet my lord alone.

"Leave me!"

As soon as he had gone, I dealt with the keys and went to my bedroom. The causeway was empty; Jean-Yves was correct, my husband had already entered the castle. I pulled the curtains close, stripped off my clothes and pulled the bedcurtains round me as a pungent aroma of Russian leather assured me my husband was once again beside me.

"Dearest!"

With the most treacherous, lascivious tenderness, he kissed my eyes, and, mimicking the new bride newly wakened, I flung my arms around him, for on my seeming acquiescence depended my salvation.

"Da Silva of Rio outwitted me," he said wryly. "My New York agent telegraphed Le Havre and saved me a wasted journey. So we may resume our interrupted pleasures, my love."

I did not believe one word of it. I knew I had behaved exactly according to his desires; had he not bought me so that I should do so? I had been tricked into my own betrayal to that illimitable darkness whose source I had been compelled to seek in his absence and, now that I had met that shadowed reality of his that came to life only in the presence of its own atrocities, I must pay the price of my new knowledge. The secret of Pandora's box;[1] but he had given me the box, himself, knowing I must learn the secret. I had played a game in which every move was governed by a destiny as oppressive and omnipotent as himself, since that destiny was himself; and I had lost. Lost at that charade of innocence and vice in which he had engaged me. Lost, as the victim loses to the executioner.

His hand brushed my breast, beneath the sheet. I strained my nerves yet could not help but flinch from the intimate touch, for it made me think of the piercing embrace of the Iron Maiden and of his lost lovers in the vault. When he saw my reluctance, his eyes veiled over and yet his appetite did not diminish. His tongue ran over red lips already wet. Silent, mysterious, he moved away from me to draw off his jacket. He took the gold watch from his waistcoat and laid it on the dressing table, like a good bourgeois; scooped out his rattling loose change and now—oh God!—makes a great play of patting his pockets officiously, puzzled lips pursed, searching for something that has been mislaid. Then turns to me with a ghastly, a triumphant smile.

"But of course! I gave the keys to you!"

"Your keys? Why, of course. Here, they're under the pillow; wait a moment—what—Ah! No … now, where can I have left them? I was whiling away the evening without you at the piano, I remember. Of course! The music room!"

Brusquely he flung my négligé of antique lace on the bed.

"Go and get them."

"Now? This moment? Can't it wait until morning, my darling?"

I forced myself to be seductive. I saw myself, pale, pliant as a plant that begs to be trampled underfoot, a dozen vulnerable, appealing girls reflected in as many mirrors, and I saw how he almost failed to resist me. If he had come to me in bed, I would have strangled him, then.

But he half-snarled: "No. It won't wait. Now."

The unearthly light of dawn filled the room; had only one previous dawn broken upon me in that vile place? And there was nothing for it but to go and fetch the keys from the music stool and pray he would not examine them too closely, pray to God his eyes would fail him, that he might be struck blind.

When I came back into the bedroom carrying the bunch of keys that jangled at every step like a curious musical instrument, he was sitting on the bed in his immaculate shirtsleeves, his head sunk in his hands.

And it seemed to me he was in despair.

Strange. In spite of my fear of him, that made me whiter than my wrap, I felt there emanate from him, at that moment, a stench of absolute despair, rank and ghastly, as if the lilies that surrounded him had all at once begun to fester, or the Russian leather of his scent were reverting to the elements of flayed hide and excrement of which it was composed. The chthonic[2] gravity of his presence exerted a tremendous pressure on the room, so that the blood pounded in my ears as if we had been precipitated to the bottom of the sea, beneath the waves that pounded against the shore.

I held my life in my hands amongst those keys and, in a moment, would place it between his well-manicured fingers. The evidence of that bloody chamber had showed me I could expect no mercy. Yet, when he raised his head and stared at me with his blind, shuttered eyes as though he did not recognize me, I felt a terrified pity for him, for this man who lived in such strange, secret places that, if I loved him enough to follow him, I should have to die.

The atrocious loneliness of that monster!

The monocle had fallen from his face. His curling mane was disordered, as if he had run his hands through it in his distraction. I saw how he had lost his impassivity and was now filled with suppressed excitement. The hand he stretched out for those counters in his game of love and death shook a little; the face that turned towards me contained a sombre delirium that seemed to me compounded of a ghastly, yes, shame but also of a terrible, guilty joy as he slowly ascertained how I had sinned.

That tell-tale stain had resolved itself into a mark the shape and brilliance of the heart on a playing card. He disengaged the key from the ring and looked at it for a while, solitary, brooding.

[1] *Pandora's box* In Greek myth, a box that contained all human evils, said to have been opened by a girl named Pandora.

[2] *chthonic* Dwelling below the earth's surface.

"It is the key that leads to the kingdom of the unimaginable," he said. His voice was low and had in it the timbre of certain great cathedral organs that seem, when they are played, to be conversing with God.

I could not restrain a sob.

"Oh, my love, my little love who brought me a white gift of music," he said, almost as if grieving. "My little love, you'll never know how much I hate daylight!" Then he sharply ordered: "Kneel!"

I knelt before him and he pressed the key lightly to my forehead, held it there for a moment. I felt a faint tingling of the skin and, when I involuntarily glanced at myself in the mirror, I saw the heart-shaped stain had transferred itself to my forehead, to the space between the eyebrows, like the caste mark of a brahmin woman. Or the mark of Cain. And now the key gleamed as freshly as if it had just been cut. He clipped it back on the ring, emitting that same, heavy sigh as he had done when I said that I would marry him.

"My virgin of the arpeggios, prepare yourself for martyrdom."

"What form shall it take?" I said.

"Decapitation," he whispered, almost voluptuously. "Go and bathe yourself; put on that white dress you wore to hear *Tristan* and the necklace that prefigures your end. And I shall take myself off to the armoury, my dear, to sharpen my great-grandfather's ceremonial sword."

"The servants?"

"We shall have absolute privacy for our last rites; I have already dismissed them. If you look out of the window you can see them going to the mainland."

It was now the full, pale light of morning; the weather was grey, indeterminate, the sea had an oily, sinister look, a gloomy day on which to die. Along the causeway I could see trouping every maid and scullion, every pot-boy and pan-scourer, valet, laundress and vassal who worked in that great house, most on foot, a few on bicycles. The faceless housekeeper trudged along with a great basket in which, I guessed, she'd stowed as much as she could ransack from the larder. The Marquis must have given the chauffeur leave to borrow the motor for the day, for it went last of all, at a stately pace, as though the procession were a cortège and the car already bore my coffin to the mainland for burial.

But I knew no good Breton earth would cover me,

like a last, faithful lover; I had another fate.

"I have given them all a day's holiday, to celebrate our wedding," he said. And smiled.

However hard I stared at the receding company, I could see no sign of Jean-Yves, our latest servant, hired but the preceding morning.

"Go, now. Bathe yourself; dress yourself. The lustratory ritual and the ceremonial robing; after that, the sacrifice. Wait in the music room until I telephone for you. No, my dear!" And he smiled, as I started, recalling the line was dead. "One may call inside the castle just as much as one pleases; but, outside—never."

I scrubbed my forehead with the nail brush as I had scrubbed the key but this red mark would not go away, either, no matter what I did, and I knew I should wear it until I died, though that would not be long. Then I went to my dressing room and put on that white muslin shift, costume of a victim of an auto-da-fe,[1] he had bought me to listen to the Liebestod in. Twelve young women combed out twelve listless sheaves of brown hair in the mirrors; soon, there would be none. The mass of lilies that surrounded me exhaled, now, the odour of their withering. They looked like the trumpets of the angels of death.

On the dressing table, coiled like a snake about to strike, lay the ruby choker.

Already almost lifeless, cold at heart, I descended the spiral staircase to the music room but there I found I had not been abandoned.

"I can be of some comfort to you," the boy said. "Though not much use."

We pushed the piano stool in front of the open window so that, for as long as I could, I would be able to smell the ancient, reconciling smell of the sea that, in time, will cleanse everything, scour the old bones white, wash away all the stains. The last little chambermaid had trotted along the causeway long ago and now the tide, fated as I, came tumbling in, the crisp wavelets splashing on the old stones.

"You do not deserve this," he said.

"Who can say what I deserve or no?" I said. "I've done nothing; but that may be sufficient reason for condemning me."

"You disobeyed him," he said. "That is sufficient reason for him to punish you."

---

[1]   *auto-da-fe* Public burning of heretics by the Spanish Inquisition.

"I only did what he knew I would."

"Like Eve," he said.

The telephone rang a shrill imperative. Let it ring. But my lover lifted me up and set me on my feet; I knew I must answer it. The receiver felt heavy as earth.

"The courtyard. Immediately."

My lover kissed me, he took my hand. He would come with me if I would lead him. Courage. When I thought of courage, I thought of my mother. Then I saw a muscle in my lover's face quiver.

"Hoofbeats!" he said.

I cast one last, desperate glance from the window and, like a miracle, I saw a horse and rider galloping at a vertiginous speed along the causeway, though the waves crashed, now, high as the horse's fetlocks. A rider, her black skirts tucked up around her waist so she could ride hard and fast, a crazy, magnificent horsewoman in widow's weeds.

As the telephone rang again.

"Am I to wait all morning?"

Every moment, my mother drew nearer.

"She will be too late," Jean-Yves said and yet he could not restrain a note of hope that, though it must be so, yet it might not be so.

The third, intransigent call.

"Shall I come up to heaven to fetch you down, Saint Cecilia? You wicked woman, do you wish me to compound my crimes by desecrating the marriage bed?"

So I must go to the courtyard where my husband waited in his London-tailored trousers and the shirt from Turnbull and Asser,[1] beside the mounting block, with, in his hand, the sword which his great-grandfather had presented to the little corporal, in token of surrender to the Republic, before he shot himself. The heavy sword, unsheathed, grey as that November morning, sharp as childbirth, mortal.

When my husband saw my companion, he observed: "Let the blind lead the blind, eh? But does even a youth as besotted as you are think she was truly blind to her own desires when she took my ring? Give it me back, whore."

The fires in the opal had all died down. I gladly slipped it from my finger and, even in that dolorous place, my heart was lighter for the lack of it. My husband took it lovingly and lodged it on the tip of his little finger; it would go no further.

"It will serve me for a dozen more fiancées," he said. "To the block, woman. No—leave the boy; I shall deal with him later, utilizing a less exalted instrument than the one with which I do my wife the honour of her immolation; for do not fear that in death you will be divided."

Slowly, slowly, one foot before the other, I crossed the cobbles. The longer I dawdled over my execution, the more time it gave the avenging angel to descend …

"Don't loiter, girl! Do you think I shall lose appetite for the meal if you are so long about serving it? No; I shall grow hungrier, more ravenous with each moment, more cruel … Run to me, run! I have a place prepared for your exquisite corpse in my display of flesh!"

He raised the sword and cut bright segments from the air with it, but still I lingered although my hopes, so recently raised, now began to flag. If she is not here by now, her horse must have stumbled on the causeway, have plunged into the sea … One thing only made me glad; that my lover would not see me die.

My husband laid my branded forehead on the stone and, as he had done once before, twisted my hair into a rope and drew it away from my neck.

"Such a pretty neck," he said with what seemed to be a genuine, retrospective tenderness. "A neck like the stem of a young plant."

I felt the silken bristle of his beard and the wet touch of his lips as he kissed my nape. And, once again, of my apparel I must retain only my gems; the sharp blade ripped my dress in two and it fell from me. A little green moss, growing in the crevices of the mounting block, would be the last thing I should see in all the world.

The whizz of that heavy sword.

And—a great battering and pounding at the gate, the jangling of the bell, the frenzied neighing of a horse! The unholy silence of the place shattered in an instant. The blade did *not* descend, the necklace did *not* sever, my head did *not* roll. For, for an instant, the beast wavered in his stroke, a sufficient split second of astonished indecision to let me spring upright and dart to the assistance of my lover as he struggled sightlessly with the great bolts that kept her out.

The Marquis stood transfixed, utterly dazed, at a loss. It must have been as if he had been watching his beloved *Tristan* for the twelfth, the thirteenth time and

---

[1] *Turnbull and Asser*   Exclusive British tailor.

Tristan stirred, then leapt from his bier in the last act, announced in a jaunty aria interposed from Verdi[1] that bygones were bygones, crying over spilt milk did nobody any good and, as for himself, he proposed to live happily ever after. The puppet master, open-mouthed, wide-eyed, impotent at the last, saw his dolls break free of their strings, abandon the rituals he had ordained for them since time began and start to live for themselves; the king, aghast, witnesses the revolt of his pawns.

You never saw such a wild thing as my mother, her hat seized by the winds and blown out to sea so that her hair was her white mane, her black lisle legs exposed to the thigh, her skirts tucked round her waist, one hand on the reins of the rearing horse while the other clasped my father's service revolver and, behind her, the breakers of the savage, indifferent sea, like the witnesses of a furious justice. And my husband stood stock-still, as if she had been Medusa,[2] the sword still raised over his head as in those clockwork tableaux of Bluebeard that you see in glass cases at fairs.

And then it was as though a curious child pushed his centime into the slot and set all in motion. The heavy, bearded figure roared out aloud, braying with fury, and, wielding the honourable sword as if it were a matter of death or glory, charged us, all three.

On her eighteenth birthday, my mother had disposed of a man-eating tiger that had ravaged the villages in the hills north of Hanoi. Now, without a moment's hesitation, she raised my father's gun, took aim and put a single, irreproachable bullet through my husband's head.

We lead a quiet life, the three of us. I inherited, of course, enormous wealth but we have given most of it away to various charities. The castle is now a school for the blind, though I pray that the children who live there are not haunted by any sad ghosts looking for, crying for, the husband who will never return to the bloody chamber, the contents of which are buried or burned, the door sealed.

I felt I had a right to retain sufficient funds to start a little music school here, on the outskirts of Paris, and we do well enough. Sometimes we can even afford to go to the Opera, though never to sit in a box, of course. We know we are the source of many whisperings and much gossip but the three of us know the truth of it and mere chatter can never harm us. I can only bless the—what shall I call it?—the *maternal telepathy* that sent my mother running headlong from the telephone to the station after I had called her, that night. I never heard you cry before, she said, by way of explanation. Not when you were happy. And who ever cried because of gold bath taps?

The night train, the one I had taken; she lay in her berth, sleepless as I had been. When she could not find a taxi at that lonely halt, she borrowed old Dobbin from a bemused farmer, for some internal urgency told her that she must reach me before the incoming tide sealed me away from her for ever. My poor old nurse, left scandalized at home—what? interrupt milord on his honeymoon?—she died soon after. She had taken so much secret pleasure in the fact that her little girl had become a marquise; and now here I was, scarcely a penny the richer, widowed at seventeen in the most dubious circumstances and busily engaged in setting up house with a piano-tuner. Poor thing, she passed away in a sorry state of disillusion! But I do believe my mother loves him as much as I do.

No paint nor powder, no matter how thick or white, can mask that red mark on my forehead; I am glad he cannot see it—not for fear of his revulsion, since I know he sees me clearly with his heart—but, because it spares my shame.

—1979

---

1 *Verdi* Italian opera composer Guiseppe Verdi (1813–1901).
2 *Medusa* Powerful female from Greek myth, a look at whose face would turn one to stone.

JOHN CLEESE AND GRAHAM CHAPMAN
1939 –, and 1941 – 1989

Graham Chapman and John Cleese were the founders of the influential British comedy troupe Monty Python's Flying Circus. Their work with fellow Pythons Michael Palin (1943–), Eric Idle (1943–), Terry Jones (1942–), and Terry Gilliam (1940–) attracted huge followings not just in Britain but also throughout the English-speaking world. In 2000, the British Film Institute named their television series, *Monty Python's Flying Circus*, number five in their listing of the top 100 greatest British television programs.

John Cleese was born on 27 October 1939 in Weston-Super-Mare, Somerset, England. He studied at Clifton College, Bristol, and then at Cambridge University's Downing College, where he completed a degree in law. He began working in comedy as part of the Cambridge Footlights Revue, an amateur theatrical club run by students. It was here that he met Graham Chapman.

Chapman was born in Leicester on 8 January 1941. As a schoolboy, he participated in school productions, including plays by Shakespeare and Gilbert and Sullivan, and revue shows. In 1959, he was admitted to Emmanuel College at Cambridge University, where he studied medicine. He eventually qualified as a doctor at St. Bartholomew's Hospital Medical College, London.

Like Cleese, Chapman joined the Cambridge Footlights Revue and toured to New Zealand and New York. Upon returning in 1965, Cleese and Chapman wrote and performed in various British radio and television comedy series, including *The Dick Emery Show* (1965–84), *Doctor in the House* (1969–70), *At Last the 1948 Show* (1967), and *I'm Sorry, I'll Read That Again* (1964–72). When the two were hired to write for *The Frost Report* (1966–67), a BBC comedy/variety series, they were introduced to Eric Idle, Terry Jones, and Michael Palin. It was here that the future colleagues developed their trademark comedy style.

In 1969, Chapman and Cleese were offered their own television series. Their partnership was not an easy one; Chapman had developed a drinking problem, and Cleese found himself bearing most of the burden of the show. As a result, Cleese invited Palin, Idle, Jones, and Terry Gilliam (an American animator he had met while in New York) to work on the show, and the Monty Python troupe was born. Their television show, *Monty Python's Flying Circus,* ran between 1969 and 1974. The show's humor was quirky and irreverent, featuring cartoonish authority figures, strange satirical takes on the idiosyncrasies of British life, and frequent references to philosophers, literary figures, and famous works of art.

The troupe produced 45 episodes of *Monty Python's Flying Circus*, in four series. They also made five films: *And Now for Something Completely Different* (1971), a collection of re-filmed sketches from the television show; *Monty Python and the Holy Grail* (1974), a spoof of the Arthurian legends; *Monty Python's Life of Brian* (1979), a controversial send-up of organized religion and epic Bible movies; *Monty Python Live at the Hollywood Bowl* (1982), a live film of a public performance; and *Monty Python's The Meaning of Life* (1983), a darkly comic philosophical meditation.

Cleese left the show after its third series, unhappy with the strain of working with the alcoholic Chapman. He went on to co-write and star as Basil Fawlty in the very popular television series *Fawlty Towers* and to continue making films, most notably *A Fish Called Wanda* (1988), one of the most financially successful British films in history. Graham Chapman's career faltered after Monty Python. He gave up drinking in 1977, but his only solo film project, *Yellowbeard* (1983), suffered both critically and commercially. In late 1988, Chapman was diagnosed with throat cancer, which quickly spread to his spine. He died on 4 October 1989.

⌘ ⌘ ⌘

from *Monty Python's Flying Circus*

DEAD PARROT SKETCH[1]

THE CAST:
PRALINE: John Cleese
SHOPKEEPER: Michael Palin
PORTER: Terry Jones

PRALINE.   Hello, I wish to register a complaint. … Hello? Miss?

SHOPKEEPER.   What do you mean, miss?

PRALINE.   Oh, I'm sorry, I have a cold. I wish to make a complaint.

SHOPKEEPER.   Sorry, we're closing for lunch.

PRALINE.   Never mind that my lad, I wish to complain about a parrot what I purchased not half an hour ago from this very boutique.

SHOPKEEPER.   Oh yes, the Norwegian Blue. What's wrong with it?

PRALINE.   I'll tell you what's wrong with it. It's dead, that's what's wrong with it.

SHOPKEEPER.   No, no it's resting look!

PRALINE.   Look my lad, I know a dead parrot when I see one and I'm looking at one right now.

SHOPKEEPER.   No, no sir, it's not dead. It's resting.

PRALINE.   Resting?

SHOPKEEPER.   Yeah, remarkable bird the Norwegian Blue, beautiful plumage, innit?[2]

PRALINE.   The plumage don't enter into it—it's stone dead.

SHOPKEEPER.   No, no—it's just resting.

PRALINE.   All right then, if it's resting I'll wake it up. (*Shouts in into cage.*) Hello Polly! I've got a nice cuttlefish for you when you wake up, Polly Parrot!

SHOPKEEPER.   (*Jogging cage.*) There it moved.

PRALINE.   No he didn't. That was you pushing the cage.

SHOPKEEPER.   I did not.

PRALINE.   Yes, you did. (*Takes parrot out of cage, shouts.*) Hello Polly, Polly. (*Bangs it against the counter.*) Polly Parrot, wake up. Polly. (*Throws it in the air and it lands on the floor.*) Now that's what I call a dead parrot.

SHOPKEEPER.   No, no it's stunned.

PRALINE.   Look my lad, I've had just about enough of this. That parrot is definitely deceased. And when I bought it not half an hour ago, you assured me that its lack of movement was due to it being tired and shagged out after a long squawk.

SHOPKEEPER.   It's probably pining for the fjords.

PRALINE.   Pining for the fjords, what kind of talk is that? Look, why did it fall flat on its back the moment I got it home?

SHOPKEEPER.   The Norwegian Blue prefers kipping[3] on its back. Beautiful bird, lovely plumage.

PRALINE.   Look, I took the liberty of examining the parrot, and I discovered that the only reason that it had been sitting on its perch in the first place was that it had been nailed there.

SHOPKEEPER.   Well of course it was nailed there. Otherwise it would muscle up to those bars and voom.

PRALINE.   Look matey (*Picks up parrot.*) this parrot wouldn't go voom if I put four thousand volts through it. It's bleeding demised.

SHOPKEEPER.   It's not. It's pining.

PRALINE.   It's not pining, it's passed on. This parrot is no more. It has ceased to be. It's expired and gone to meet its maker. This is a late parrot. It's a stiff. Bereft of life, it rests in peace. If you hadn't nailed it to the perch, it would be pushing up the daisies. It's rung down the curtain and joined the choir invisible. This is an ex-parrot.

SHOPKEEPER.   Well I'd better replace it then.

PRALINE.   (*To camera.*) If you want to get anything done in this country you've got to complain till you're blue in the mouth.

SHOPKEEPER.   Sorry guv, we're right outa parrots.

PRALINE.   I see. I see. I get the picture.

SHOPKEEPER.   I've got a slug.

PRALINE.   Does it talk?

SHOPKEEPER.   Not really, no.

PRALINE.   Well, it's scarcely a replacement, then is it?

SHOPKEEPER.   Listen, I'll tell you what, (*Handing over a card.*) tell you what, if you go to my brother's pet shop in Bolton[4] he'll replace your parrot for you.

PRALINE.   Bolton eh?

SHOPKEEPER.   Yeah.

PRALINE.   All right.

---

[1]   *Dead Parrot Sketch*   From *Monty Python's Flying Circus*, Episode 9.

[2]   *innit*   I.e., Isn't it.

[3]   *kipping*   Sleeping.

[4]   *Bolton*   Town near Manchester in northern England.

(*He leaves, holding the parrot.*
Caption: "A similar pet shop in Bolton, Lancs"[1]
Close-up of sign on door reading: "Similar Pet Shops Ltd."
Pull back from sign to see same pet shop. Shopkeeper now
has a moustache. Praline walks into the shop. He looks
around with interest, noticing the empty parrot cage on the
floor.)

PRALINE.   Er, excuse me. This is Bolton, is it?

80 SHOPKEEPER.   No, no it's, er, Ipswich.[2]

PRALINE.   (*To camera,*) That's Inter-City Rail for you.

(*Leaves.*)
(*Man in porter's outfit standing at complaints desk for*
railways. Praline approaches.)

PRALINE.   I wish to make a complaint.

PORTER.   I don't have to do this, you know.

PRALINE.   I beg your pardon?

85 PORTER.   I'm a qualified brain surgeon. I only do this
because I like being my own boss.

PRALINE.   Er, excuse me, this is irrelevant, isn't it?

PORTER.   Oh yeah, it's not easy to pad these out in thirty
minutes.

90 PRALINE.   Well I wish to make a complaint. I got on to
the Bolton train and found myself deposited here in
Ipswich.

PORTER.   No, this is Bolton.

PRALINE.   (*To camera.*) The pet shop owner's brother was
95 lying.

PORTER.   Well you can't blame British Rail for that.

PRALINE.   If this is Bolton, I shall return to the pet shop.

(*Caption: "A Little Later Ltd"*
Praline walks into the shop again.)

PRALINE.   I understand this *is* Bolton.

SHOPKEEPER.   Yes.

100 PRALINE.   Well, you told me it was Ipswich.

SHOPKEEPER.   It was a pun.

PRALINE.   A pun?

SHOPKEEPER.   No, no, not a pun, no. What's the other
thing which reads the same backwards as forwards?

105 PRALINE.   A palindrome?

SHOPKEEPER.   Yes, yes.

PRALINE.   It's not a palindrome. The palindrome of
Bolton would be Notlob. It don't work.

SHOPKEEPER.   Look, what do you want?

110 PRALINE.   No, I'm sorry, I'm not prepared to pursue my
line of enquiry any further as I think this is getting too
silly.

—1969

PET CONVERSION[3]

THE CAST:

MAN: John Cleese
SHOPKEEPER: Michael Palin
HARRY: Graham Chapman

(*Superimposed caption: A Pet Shop Somewhere Near*
Melton Mowbray.[4])

MAN.   Good morning, I'd like to buy a cat.

SHOPKEEPER.   Certainly sir. I've got a lovely terrier.
(*Indicates a box on the counter.*)

MAN.   (*Glancing in box.*) No, I want a cat really.

5 SHOPKEEPER.   (*Taking box off counter and then putting it*
back on counter as if it is a different box.) Oh yeah, how
about that?

MAN.   (*Looking in box.*) No, that's the terrier.

SHOPKEEPER.   Well, it's as near as dammit.

10 MAN.   Well what do you mean? I want a cat.

SHOPKEEPER.   Listen, tell you what. I'll file its legs down
a bit, take its snout out, stick a few wires through its
cheeks. There you are, a lovely pussy cat.

MAN.   It's not a proper cat.

15 SHOPKEEPER.   What do you mean?

MAN.   Well it wouldn't miaow.

SHOPKEEPER.   Well it would howl a bit.

MAN.   No, no, no, no. Er, have you got a parrot?

SHOPKEEPER.   No, It's afraid not actually guv, we're
20 fresh out of parrots. I'll tell you what though ... I'll lop
its back legs off, make good, strip the fur, stick a couple
of wings on and staple on a beak of your own choice.
(*Taking small box and rattling it.*) No problem. Lovely
parrot.

---

[1] *Lancs* Lancashire, a county in the north of England.

[2] *Ipswich* County town in East Anglia, in the east of England, 390
kilometers (243 miles) from Bolton.

[3] *Pet Conversion* Featured in *Monty Python's Flying Circus*, Episode
10.

[4] *Melton Mowbray* Town in county Leicestershire.

25 MAN. And how long would that take?

SHOPKEEPER. Oh, let me see … er, stripping the fur off, no legs … (*Calling.*) Harry … can you do a parrot job on this terrier straight away?

HARRY. (*Off screen.*) No, I'm still putting a tuck in the
30 Airedale, and then I got the frogs to let out.

SHOPKEEPER. Friday?

MAN. No I need it for tomorrow. It's a present.

SHOPKEEPER. Oh dear, it's a long job. You see parrot conversion … Tell you what though, for free, terriers
35 make lovely fish. I mean I could do that for you straight away. Legs off, fins on, stick a little pipe through the back of its neck so it can breathe, bit of gold paint, make good …

MAN. You'd need a very big tank.
40 SHOPKEEPER. It's a great conversation piece.

MAN. Yes, all right, all right … but, er, only if I can watch.

—1969

DIRTY HUNGARIAN PHRASEBOOK[1]

THE CAST:

HUNGARIAN: John Cleese
TOBACCONIST: Terry Jones
POLICEMAN: Graham Chapman

(*Set: A tobacconist's shop.*)

(*Roller caption: In 1970, the British Empire lay in ruins, and foreign nationalists frequented the streets—many of them Hungarians [not the streets—the foreign nationals]. Anyway, many of these Hungarians went into tobacconists' shops to buy cigarettes …*)

(*Enter Hungarian gentleman with phrase book. He is looking for the right phrase.*)

HUNGARIAN. I will not buy this record. It is scratched.

TOBACCONIST. Sorry?

HUNGARIAN. I will not buy this record. It is scratched.

TOBACCONIST. No, no, no. This … tobacconist's.
5 HUNGARIAN. Ah! I will not buy this tobacconist's. It is scratched.

TOBACCONIST. No, no, no … tobacco … er, cigarettes?

HUNGARIAN. Yes, cigarettes. My hovercraft is full of eels.
10 TOBACCONIST. What?

HUNGARIAN. (*Miming matches.*) My hovercraft is full of eels.

TOBACCONIST. Matches, matches?

HUNGARIAN. Yah, yah. (*He takes cigarettes and matches
15 and pulls out loose change; he consults his book.*) Er, do you want … do you want to come back to my place, bouncy bouncy?

TOBACCONIST. I don't think you're using that thing right.
20 HUNGARIAN. You great pouf.[2]

TOBACCONIST. That'll be six and six,[3] please.

HUNGARIAN. If I said you had a beautiful body, would you hold it against me? I am no longer infected.

TOBACCONIST. (*Miming that he wants to see the book; he
25 takes the book.*) It costs six and six … (*Mumbling as he searches*) Costs six and six … Here we are … Yandelvayasna grldenwi stravenka.

(*Hungarian hits him between the eyes. Policeman walking along street suddenly stops and puts his hand to his ear. He starts running down the street, round corner and down another street, round yet another corner and down another street into the shop.*)

POLICEMAN. What's going on here then?

HUNGARIAN. (*Opening book and pointing at
30 Tobacconist.*) You have beautiful thighs.

POLICEMAN. What?

TOBACCONIST. He hit me.

HUNGARIAN. Drop your panties, Sir William, I cannot wait till lunchtime.
35 POLICEMAN. Right! (*Grabs him and drags him out.*)

HUNGARIAN. My nipples explode with delight.

(*Cut to a courtroom.*)

CAST:

JUDGE: Terry Jones
CLERK: Eric Idle
LAWYER: John Cleese
POLICEMAN: Graham Chapman (still)
YAHLT: Michael Palin

---

[1] *Dirty Hungarian Phrasebook* Featured in *Monty Python's Flying Circus*, Episode 25.

[2] *pouf* Derogatory British slang for gay man.

[3] *six and six* Six shillings and sixpence.

CLERK. Call Alexander Yahlt!

VOICES. Call Alexander Yahlt. Call Alexander Yahlt. Call Alexander Yahlt.

(*They do this three times, finishing with harmony.*)

40 MAGISTRATE. Oh, shut up.

(*Alexander Yahlt enters. He is not Hungarian but an ordinary man in a mac.*)[1]

CLERK. (*To publisher.*) You are Alexander Yahlt?

YAHLT. (*Derek Nimmo's[2] voice dubbed on.*) Oh, I am.

CLERK. Skip the impersonations. You are Alexander Yahlt?

45 YAHLT. (*Normal voice.*) I am.

CLERK. You are hereby charged that on the 28th day of May 1970 you did wilfully, unlawfully, and with malice aforethought publish an alleged English-Hungarian phrase book with intent to cause a breach of the peace.

50 How do you plead?

YAHLT. Not guilty.

CLERK. You live at 46, Horton Terrace?

YAHLT. I do live at 46 Horton Terrace.

CLERK. You are the director of a publishing company?

55 YAHLT. I am the director of a publishing company.

CLERK. Your company publishes phrasebooks?

YAHLT. My company does publish phrasebooks.

CLERK. You did say 46, Horton Terrace did you?

YAHLT. Yes.

(*He claps his hand to his mouth; gong sounds—general applause.*)

60 CLERK. Ha, ha, ha, I got him.

MAGISTRATE. Get on with it! Get on with it!

CLERK. Yes, m'lud,[3] on the 28th of May you published this phrasebook.

YAHLT. I did.

65 CLERK. I quote one example. The Hungarian phrase meaning "Can you direct me to the station?" is translated by the English phrase, "please fondle my bum."

YAHLT. I wish to plead incompetence.

(*The Policeman stands up.*)

POLICEMAN. Please may I ask for an adjournment, m'lud?

70 MAGISTRATE. An adjournment? Certainly not.

(*The Policeman sits down; there is a loud raspberry;[4] the policeman goes bright red.*)

Why on earth didn't you say *why* you wanted an adjournment?

POLICEMAN. I didn't know an acceptable legal phrase, m'lud.

75

(*Cut to stock film of Women's Institute[5] applauding. Cut back to the magistrate.*)

MAGISTRATE. If there's any more stock film of women applauding I shall clear the court.
—1970

SPAM[6]

THE CAST:

MR. BUN: Eric Idle
MRS. BUN: Graham Chapman
WAITRESS: Terry Jones
HUNGARIAN: John Cleese
HISTORIAN: Michael Palin

(*Scene: A cafe. All the customers are Vikings. Mr. and Mrs. Bun enter—downwards, on wires.*)

MR. BUN. Morning.

WAITRESS. Morning.

MR. BUN. What have you got, then?

WAITRESS. Well there's egg and bacon; egg sausage and
5 bacon; egg and spam; egg, bacon and spam; egg, bacon, sausage and spam; spam, bacon, sausage and spam; spam, egg, spam, spam, bacon and spam; spam, spam, spam, egg and spam; spam, spam, spam, spam, spam, spam, baked beans, spam, spam, spam, and spam; or
10 lobster thermidor aux crevettes with a mornay sauce

---

1 *mac* I.e., mackintosh, a raincoat.

2 *Derek Nimmo* British comedic actor and BBC Radio game show panelist who had a distinctive, aristocratic voice.

3 *m'lud* I.e., my lord.

---

4 *raspberry* Rude sound, generally made with the lips and tongue. Here, denotes flatulence.

5 *Women's Institute* Organization for women in England and Wales.

6 *Spam* Featured in *Monty Python's Flying Circus*, Episode 25.

garnished with truffle pâté, brandy and a fried egg on top and spam.

MRS. BUN.   Have you got anything without spam in it?

WAITRESS.   Well, there's spam, egg, sausage and spam. That's not got *much* spam in it.

MRS. BUN.   I don't want *any* spam.

MR. BUN.   Why can't she have egg, bacon, spam and sausage?

MRS. BUN.   That's got spam in it!

MR. BUN.   Not as much as spam, egg, sausage and spam.

MRS. BUN.   Look, could I have egg, bacon, spam and sausage without the spam.

WAITRESS.   Uuuuuuggggh!

MRS. BUN.   What do you mean uuugggh! I don't like spam.

VIKINGS.   (*Singing.*) Spam, spam, spam, spam, spam … spam, spam, spam, spam … lovely spam, wonderful spam …

(*Brief stock shot of a Viking ship.*)

WAITRESS.   Shut up! Shut up! Shut up! You can't have egg, bacon, spam and sausage without the spam.

MRS. BUN.   (*Shrieks.*) I don't like spam!

MR. BUN.   Don't make a fuss, dear. I'll have your spam. I love it. I'm having spam, spam, spam, spam, spam …

VIKINGS.   (*Singing.*) Spam, spam, spam, spam …

MR. BUN.   … baked beans, spam, spam and spam.

WAITRESS.   Baked beans are off.

MR. BUN.   Well can I have spam instead?

WAITRESS.   You mean spam, spam, spam, spam, spam, spam, spam, spam, spam?

VIKINGS.   (*Still singing.*) Spam, spam, spam, spam … (*etc.*)

MR. BUN.   Yes.

WAITRESS.   Arrggh!

VIKINGS.   … lovely spam, wonderful, spam.

WAITRESS.   Shut up! Shut up!

(*The Vikings shut up momentarily. Enter the Hungarian.*)

HUNGARIAN. Great boobies, honeybun, my lower intestine is full of spam, egg, spam, bacon, spam, tomato, spam …

VIKINGS.   (*Starting up again.*) Spam, spam, spam, spam …

WAITRESS.   Shut up.

(*A policeman rushes in and bundles the Hungarian out.*)

HUNGARIAN.   My nipples explode …

(*Cut to a historian. Superimposed caption: "A HISTORIAN."*)

HISTORIAN.   Another great Viking victory was at the Green Midget café at Bromley. Once again the Viking strategy was the same. They sailed from these fiords here (*indicating map with arrows on it*), assembled at Trondheim and waited for the strong north-easterly winds to blow their oaken galleys to England whence they sailed on May 23rd. Once in Bromley they assembled at the Green Midget café and spam selecting a spam particular spam item from the spam menu would spam, spam, spam, spam, spam …

(*The backdrop behind him rises to reveal the café again. The Vikings start singing again and the historian conducts them.*)

VIKINGS.   (*Singing.*) Spam, spam, spam, spam, spam, lovely spam, wonderful spam. Lovely spam, wonderful spam …

(*Mr. and Mrs. Bun rise slowly in the air.*)

—1970

SALMAN RUSHDIE
b. 1947

Salman Rushdie has become recognized as one of the key figures of postmodernist fiction, and of postcolonial writing of all sorts. He has been honored with many prestigious awards and has helped to shape an entire generation of Indian writing in English. But his achievements were for many years overshadowed by a furor created by the violent opposition of Islamic fundamentalists to his novel, *The Satanic Verses* (1988); this became one of the major artistic and religious controversies of the twentieth century.

Born Ahmed Salman Rushdie to devout Muslim parents in Bombay (now Mumbai), India, he was educated at the Cathedral School in Bombay, and then moved to England at age 14, where he attended Rugby School, one of England's most prestigious boarding schools. It was far from an entirely pleasant experience; Rushdie has recounted how he was the object of racially motivated attacks by white students. He moved back to Bombay after graduating, but returned to England to attend Cambridge University's King's College, where he studied history and joined a student theater group. After earning his BA in 1968, Rushdie worked in television in Pakistan for several years, and then returned to England to become a copywriter for an advertising agency.

In his first novel, *Grimus* (1975), Rushdie concocted a literary mixture of fantasy and realism of a sort that would become characteristic of his work. An adaptation of an old Sufi poem, *Grimus* is a fantastical work that borders on science fiction. It met with little success. But his next novel, *Midnight's Children* (1981), catapulted Rushdie to the top of the English-language literary world. *Midnight's Children* presents the life of its protagonist, a pickle-factory worker named Saleem Sinai who was born (like Rushdie) at the time of India's independence from Britain, as an allegory for the history of post-colonial India. The tone of the novel again partakes both of realism and of fantasy—as its famous first sentence signals: "I was born in the city of Bombay … once upon a time. No, that won't do, there's no getting away from the date: I was born in Doctor Narlikar's Nursing Home on August 15th, 1947." The novel was very much in tune with its age. In the literary world, this was the dawn of literary postmodernism, and writers of fiction were increasingly interested in self-conscious or ironic explorations of the play of illusion and reality. And in the world of literary theory and criticism, works on post-colonial themes were coming more and more to be considered central to the literature of the English-speaking world; from this angle too, *Midnight's Children* was of intense interest. In 1981 the novel won the prestigious Booker Prize for Fiction, and in 1993 it won the Booker of Bookers' Prize for the novel deemed to have been the best of all those awarded the Booker in the award's first twenty-five years.

His next work was a short novel, *Shame* (1983), in which Rushdie shifted his focus to neighboring Pakistan. His treatment of the rulers of Pakistan, particularly former Prime Minister Zulfikar Ali Bhutto and General Muhammad Zia-ul-Haq, explored the connection between shame and violence. This novel was also shortlisted for the Booker Prize.

In 1988 Rushdie published a novel that was to change the course of his life. Like *Midnight's Children* and *Shame*, *The Satanic Verses* was critically acclaimed (it won the Whitbread Novel Award in 1988), and like them it featured elements that hover between fantasy and reality. But to some it was altogether too real; the novel was condemned by a number of prominent Muslim leaders on the grounds that the book's unflattering portrayal of the prophet Mohammed was blasphemous; it was banned in eleven countries, and was the subject of violent protests. The controversy over the book escalated on 14 February 1989, when Iran's spiritual and political leader, the Ayatollah Ruhollah Khomeini, issued a *fatwa* (or legal pronouncement) calling for Rushdie's death. Ten days later Khomeini placed a $3 million (U.S.) bounty on Rushdie's head (the amount was doubled in 1997). Rushdie went into hiding, under the protection of British authorities. The Japanese translator of the book was murdered in Toyko in 1991. Other translators were attacked and harassed. In 1998 the Iranian government made a public pledge not to carry out the death sentence against Rushdie. Nevertheless, the *fatwa* still stands.

While in hiding, Rushdie published a children's book, *Haroun and the Sea of Stories* (1990), an allegory for India and Pakistan's dispute over the State of Kashmir. The book also contains harsh criticisms of literary censorship. He followed up with a book of essays, entitled *Imaginary Homelands: Essays and Criticism 1981–1991* (1991), from which the essay below is taken.

Rushdie's later work expands his artistic vision to treat the intersection of Indian culture with western cultures. In *The Moor's Last Sigh* (1995) Rushdie explores the connection between descendants of Portuguese settlers and their Indian neighbors. The novel won the Whitbread Novel Award in 1995. *The Ground Beneath Her Feet* (1999), a variation on the Greek Orpheus myth, deals with the influence of American rock and roll music on Indian culture. His 2001 novel, *Fury*, is set in New York, and features a transplanted Bombay-born intellectual as its protagonist. *Shalimar the Clown* (2005) returns to the Indian subcontinent for its subject matter, telling the story of two Kashmiri villages whose inhabitants get caught up in a cycle of escalating violence.

Rushdie is Honorary Professor in the Humanities at the Massachusetts Institute of Technology (MIT), and a Fellow of Britain's Royal Society of Literature. He continues to live in hiding in New York City.

⌘ ⌘ ⌘

Is Nothing Sacred?[1]

I grew up kissing books and bread. In our house, whenever anyone dropped a book or let fall a chapati or a "slice," which was our word for a triangle of buttered leavened bread, the fallen object was required not only to be picked up but also kissed, by way of apology for the act of clumsy disrespect. I was as careless and butter-fingered as any child and, accordingly, during my childhood years, I kissed a large number of "slices" and also my fair share of books.

Devout households in India often contained, and still contain, persons in the habit of kissing holy books. But we kissed everything. We kissed dictionaries and atlases. We kissed Enid Blyton novels and Superman comics. If I'd ever dropped the telephone directory I'd probably have kissed that, too.

All this happened before I had ever kissed a girl. In fact it would almost be true, true enough for a fiction writer, anyhow, to say that once I started kissing girls, my activities with regard to bread and books lost some of their special excitement. But one never forgets one's first loves.

---

[1] *Is Nothing Sacred?* This essay was the Herbert Read Memorial Lecture for 1990, delivered at the Institute of Contemporary Arts in London on 6 February 1990. It was read by playwright Harold Pinter. Rushdie himself was for many years prevented from making public appearances by the widely publicized call for his death issued by Iran's Ayatollah Khomeini.

Bread and books: food for the body and food for the soul—what could be more worthy of our respect, and even love?

It has always been a shock to me to meet people for whom books simply do not matter, and people who are scornful of the act of reading, let alone writing. It is perhaps always astonishing to learn that your beloved is not as attractive to others as she is to you. My most beloved books have been fictions, and in the last twelve months I have been obliged to accept that for many millions of human beings, these books are entirely without attraction or value. We have been witnessing an attack upon a particular work of fiction that is also an attack upon the very ideas of the novel form, an attack of such bewildering ferocity that it has become necessary to restate what is most precious about the art of literature—to answer the attack, not by an attack, but by a declaration of love.

Love can lead to devotion, but the devotion of the lover is unlike that of the True Believer in that it is not militant. I may be surprised—even shocked—to find that you do not feel as I do about a given book or work of art or even person; I may very well attempt to change your mind; but I will finally accept that your tastes, your loves, are your business and not mine. The True Believer knows no such restraints. The True Believer knows that he is simply right, and you are wrong. He will seek to convert you, even by force, and if he cannot he will, at the very least, despise you for your unbelief.

Love need not be blind. Faith must, ultimately, be a leap in the dark.

The title of this lecture is a question usually asked, in tones of horror, when some personage or idea or value or place held dear by the questioner is treated to a dose of iconoclasm. White cricket balls for night cricket? Female priests? A Japanese takeover of Rolls-Royce cars?

Is nothing sacred?

Until recently, however, it was a question to which I thought I knew the answer. The answer was No.

No, nothing is sacred in and of itself, I would have said. Ideas, texts, even people can be made sacred—the word is from the Latin *sacrare,* "to set apart as holy"— but even though such entities, once their sacredness is established, seek to proclaim and to preserve their own absoluteness, their inviolability, the act of making sacred

is in truth an event in history. It is the product of the many and complex pressures of the time in which the act occurs. And events in history must always be subject to questioning, deconstruction, even to declarations of their obsolescence. To respect the sacred is to be paralysed by it. The idea of the sacred is quite simply one of the most conservative notions in any culture, because it seeks to turn other ideas—Uncertainty, Progress, Change—into crimes.

To take only one such declaration of obsolescence: I would have described myself as living in the aftermath of the death of God. On the subject of the death of God, the American novelist and critic William H. Gass had this to say, as recently as 1984:

> The death of god represents not only the realization that gods have never existed, but the contention that such a belief is no longer even irrationally possible: that neither reason nor the taste and temper of the times condone it. The belief lingers on, of course, but it does so like astrology or a faith in a flat earth.

I have some difficulty with the uncompromising bluntness of this obituary notice. It has always been clear to me that God is unlike human beings in that it can die, so to speak, in parts. In other parts, for example India, God continues to flourish, in literally thousands of forms. So that if I speak of living after this death, I am speaking in a limited, personal sense—my sense of God ceased to exist long ago, and as a result I was drawn towards the great creative possibilities offered by surrealism, modernism and their successors, those philosophies and aesthetics born of the realization that, as Karl Marx said, "all that is solid melts into air."

It did not seem to me, however, that my ungodliness, or rather my post-godliness, need necessarily bring me into conflict with belief. Indeed, one reason for my attempt to develop a form of fiction in which the miraculous might coexist with the mundane was precisely my acceptance that notions of the sacred and the profane both needed to be explored, as far as possible without pre-judgement, in any honest literary portrait of the way we are.

That is to say: the most secular of authors ought to be capable of presenting a sympathetic portrait of a devout believer. Or, to put it another way: I had never felt the need to totemize my lack of belief, and so make it something to go to war about.

Now, however, I find my entire world-picture under fire. And as I find myself obliged to defend the assumptions and processes of literature, which I had believed that all free men and women could take for granted, and for which all unfree men and women continue every day to struggle, so I am obliged to ask myself questions I admit to finding somewhat unnerving.

Do I, perhaps, find something sacred after all? Am I prepared to set aside as holy the idea of the absolute freedom of the imagination and alongside it my own notions of the World, the Text and the Good? Does this add up to what the apologists of religion have started calling "secular fundamentalism"? And if so, must I accept that this "secular fundamentalism" is as likely to lead to excesses, abuses and oppressions as the canons of religious faith?

A lecture in memory of Herbert Read is a highly appropriate occasion for such an exploration, and I am honoured to have been asked to deliver it. Herbert Read, one of the leading British advocates of the modernist and surrealist movements, was a distinguished representative of the cultural values closest to my heart. "Art is never transfixed," Read wrote. "Change is the condition of art remaining art." This principle is also mine. Art, too, is an event in history, subject to the historical process. But it is also *about* that process, and must constantly strive to find new forms to mirror an endlessly renewed world. No aesthetic can be a constant, except an aesthetic based on the idea of inconstancy, metamorphosis, or, to borrow a term from politics, "perpetual revolution."

The struggle between such ideas and the eternal, revealed truths of religion is dramatized this evening, as I hope I may be excused for pointing out, by my absence. I must apologize for this. I did, in fact, ask my admirable protectors how they would feel if I were to deliver my text in person. The answer was, more or less, "What have we done to deserve this?" With regret, I took the point.

It is an agony and a frustration not be able to re-enter my old life, not even for such a moment. However, I should like to thank Harold Pinter, through his own mouth, for standing in my place. Perhaps this event could be thought of as a form of secular revela-

tion: a man receives a text by mysterious processes from Elsewhere—above? below? New Scotland Yard?[1]—and brings it out before the people, and recites ...

More than twenty years ago, I stood packed in at the back of this theatre, listening to a lecture by Arthur Koestler.[2] He propounded the thesis that language, not territory, was the prime cause of aggression, because once language reached the level of sophistication at which it could express abstract concepts, it acquired the power of totemization; and once peoples had erected totems, they would go to war to defend them. (I ask pardon of Koestler's ghost. I am relying on an old memory, and that's an untrustworthy shoulder to lean on.)

In support of his theory, he told us about two tribes of monkeys living on, I think, one of the northern islands of Japan. The two tribes lived in close proximity in the woods near a certain stream, and subsisted, not unusually, on a diet of bananas. One of the tribes, however, had developed the curious habit of washing its bananas in the stream before eating them, while the other tribe continued to be non-banana-washers. And yet, said Koestler, the two tribes continued to live contentedly as neighbours, without quarrelling. And why was this? It was because their language was too primitive to permit them to totemize either the act of banana-washing or that of eating bananas unwashed. With a more sophisticated language at their disposal, both wet and dry bananas could have become the sacred objects at the heart of a religion, and then, look out!—Holy war.

A young man rose from the audience to ask Koestler a question. Perhaps the real reason why the two tribes did not fight, he suggested, was that there were enough bananas to go round. Koestler became extremely angry. He refused to answer such a piece of Marxist claptrap. And, in a way, he was right. Koestler and his questioner were speaking different languages, and their languages were in conflict. Their disagreement could even be seen

---

[1] *New Scotland Yard* Headquarters for the metropolitan police force of Greater London.

[2] *Arthur Koestler* Hungarian-born novelist (1905–83), political activist, and social philosopher, whose most famous work, *Darkness at Noon* (1940), depicts extremes of censorship and oppression under a Soviet-style Marxist dictatorship.

as the proof of Koestler's point. If he, Koestler, were to be considered the banana-washer and his questioner the dry-banana man, then their command of a language more complex than the Japanese monkeys' had indeed resulted in totemizations. Now each of them had a totem to defend: the primacy of language versus the primacy of economics: and dialogue therefore became impossible. They were at war.

Between religion and literature, as between politics and literature, there is a linguistically based dispute. But it is not a dispute of simple opposites. Because whereas religion seeks to privilege one language above all others, one set of values above all others, one text above all others, the novel has always been *about* the way in which different languages, values and narratives quarrel, and about the shifting relations between them, which are relations of power. The novel does not seek to establish a privileged language, but it insists upon the freedom to portray and analyse the struggle between the different contestants for such privileges.

Carlos Fuentes has called the novel "a privileged *arena.*" By this he does not mean that it is the kind of holy space which one must put off one's shoes to enter; it is not an arena to revere; it claims no special rights *except the right to be the stage upon which the great debates of society can be conducted.* "The novel," Fuentes writes, "is born from the very fact that we do not understand one another, because unitary, orthodox language has broken down. Quixote and Sancho, the Shandy brothers, Mr. and Mrs. Karenin:[1] their novels are the comedy (or the drama) of their misunderstandings. Impose a unitary language: you kill the novel, but you also kill the society."

He then poses the question I have been asking myself throughout my life as a writer: *Can the religious mentality survive outside of religious dogma and hierarchy?* Which is to say: Can art be the third principle that mediates between the material and spiritual worlds; might it, by "swallowing" both worlds, offer us something new—something that might even be called a secular definition of transcendence?

I believe it can. I believe it must. And I believe that, at its best, it does.

---

[1] *Quixote ... Karenin* Characters from Cervantes's *Don Quixote*, Laurence Sterne's *Tristam Shandy*, and Tolstoy's *Anna Karenina*, respectively.

What I mean by transcendence is that flight of the human spirit outside the confines of its material, physical existence which all of us, secular or religious, experience on at least a few occasions. Birth is a moment of transcendence which we spend our lives trying to understand. The exaltation of the act of love, the experience of joy and very possibly the moment of death are other such moments. The soaring quality of transcendence, the sense of being more than oneself, of being in some way joined to the whole of life, is by its nature short-lived. Not even the visionary or mystical experience ever lasts very long. It is for art to capture that experience, to offer it to, in the case of literature, its readers; to be, for a secular, materialist culture, some sort of replacement for what the love of god offers in the world of faith.

It is important that we understand how profoundly we all feel the needs that religion, down the ages, has satisfied. I would suggest that these needs are of three types: firstly, the need to be given an articulation of our half-glimpsed knowledge of exaltation, of awe, of wonder; life is an awesome experience, and religion helps us understand why life so often makes us feel small, by telling us what we are *smaller than;* and, contrariwise, because we also have a sense of being special, of being *chosen,* religion helps us by telling us what we have been chosen by, and what for. Secondly, we need answers to the unanswerable: How did we get here? How did "here" get here in the first place? Is this, this brief life, all there is? How can it be? What would be the point of that? And, thirdly, we need codes to live by, "rules for every damn thing." The idea of god is at once a repository for our awestruck wonderment at life and an answer to the great questions of existence, and a rule book, too. The soul needs all these explanations—not simply rational explanations, but explanations of the heart.

It is also important to understand how often the language of secular, rationalist materialism has failed to answer these needs. As we witness the death of communism in Central Europe, we cannot fail to observe the deep religious spirit with which so many of the makers of these revolutions are imbued, and we must concede that it is not only a particular political ideology that has failed, but the idea that men and women could ever define themselves in terms that exclude their spiritual needs.

It seems obvious, but relevant, to point out that in all the countries now moving towards freedom, art was repressed as viciously as was religion. That the Czech revolution began in the theatres and is led by a writer is proof that people's spiritual needs, more than their material needs, have driven the commissars from power. What appears plain is that it will be a very long time before the peoples of Europe will accept any ideology that claims to have a complete, totalized explanation of the world. Religious faith, profound as it is, must surely remain a private matter. This rejection of totalized explanations is the modern condition. And this is where the novel, the form created to discuss the fragmentation of truth, comes in. The film director Luis Buñuel used to say: "I would give my life for a man who is looking for the truth. But I would gladly kill a man who thinks he has found the truth." (This is what we used to call a joke, before killing people for their ideas returned to the agenda.) The elevation of the quest for the Grail over the Grail itself, the acceptance that all that is solid has melted into air, that reality and morality are not givens but imperfect human constructs, is the point from which fiction begins. This is what J.-F. Lyotard called, in 1979, *La Condition Postmoderne.* The challenge of literature is to start from this point, and still find a way of fulfilling our unaltered spiritual requirements.

Moby Dick meets that challenge by offering us a dark, almost Manichean vision[1] of a universe (the *Pequod*)[2] in the grip of one demon, Ahab, and heading inexorably towards another; namely the Whale. The ocean always was our Other, manifesting itself to us in the form of beasts—the worm Ouroboros, Kraken, Leviathan.[3] Herman Melville delves into these dark waters in order to offer us a very modern parable: Ahab, gripped by his possession, perishes; Ishmael, a man without strong

feeling or powerful affiliations, survives. The self-interested modern man is the sole survivor; those who worship the Whale—for pursuit is a form of worship—perish by the Whale.

Joyce's wanderers, Beckett's tramps, Gogol's tricksters, Bulgakov's devils, Bellow's[4] high-energy meditations on the stifling of the soul by the triumphs of materialism; these, and many more, are what we have instead of prophets and suffering saints. But while the novel answers our need for wonderment and understanding, it brings us harsh and unpalatable news as well.

It tells us there are no rules. It hands down no commandments. We have to make up our own rules as best we can, make them up as we go along.

And it tells us there are no answers; or, rather, it tells us that answers are easier to come by, and less reliable, than questions. If religion is an answer, if political ideology is an answer, then literature is an inquiry; great literature, by asking extraordinary questions, opens new doors in our minds.

Richard Rorty, in *Philosophy and the Mirror of Nature,* insists on the importance of historicity, of giving up the illusions of being in contact with Eternity. For him, the great error is what he calls "foundationalism," which the theologian Don Cupitt, commenting on Rorty, calls "the attempt, as old as (and even much older than) Plato, to give permanence and authority to our knowledge and values by purporting to found them in some unchanging cosmic realm, natural or noumenal, outside the flux of our human conversation." It is better, Cupitt concludes, "to be an adaptable pragmatist, a nomad."

Michel Foucault, also a confirmed historicist, discusses the role of the author in challenging sacralized absolutes in his essay, "What is an Author?" This essay argues, in part, that "texts, books and discourses really began to have authors ... to the extent that authors became subject to punishment, that is, to the extent that discourses could be transgressive." This is an extraordinary, provocative idea, even if it is stated with Foucault's characteristic airiness and a complete absence of supporting evidence: *that authors were named only when it*

---

[1] *Manichean vision* Form of dualism, in which the world is seen to be determined by the tension between the forces of good and evil.

[2] *the Pequod* Captain Ahab's ship (in Herman Melville's novel *Moby Dick* [1851]).

[3] *Ouroboros ... Leviathan* Ouroboros is an ancient symbol from many cultures that depict a snake or a dragon devouring itself. The Kraken is an enormous sea monster said to be living in the ocean between Norway and Iceland. Leviathan is a sea monster referred to in various places in the Bible.

[4] *Joyce ... Bellow* Authors James Joyce (1882–1941), Samuel Beckett (1906–89), Nikolai Gogol (1809–52), Mikhail Bulgakov (1891–1940), and Saul Bellow (b. 1915).

was necessary to find somebody to blame. Foucault continues:

> In our culture (and doubtless in many others), discourse was not originally a product, a thing, a kind of goods; it was essentially an act—an act placed in the bipolar field of the sacred and the profane, the licit and the illicit, the religious and the blasphemous. Historically it was a gesture fraught with risks …

In our beginnings we find our essences. To understand a religion, look at its earliest moments. (It is regrettable that Islam, of all religions the easiest to study in this way, because of its birth during the age of recorded history, has set its face so resolutely against the idea that it, like all ideas, is an event inside history.) And to understand an artistic form, too, Foucault suggests, look at its origins. If he is right about the novel, then literature is, of all the arts, the one best suited to challenging absolutes of all kinds; and, because it is in its origin the schismatic Other of the sacred (and authorless) text, so it is also the art mostly likely to fill our god-shaped holes.

There are other reasons, too, for proposing the novel as the crucial art form of what I can no longer avoid calling the post-modern age. For one thing, literature is the art least subject to external control, because it is made in private. The act of making it requires only one person, one pen, one room, some paper. (Even the room is not absolutely essential.) Literature is the most low-technology of the art forms. It requires neither a stage nor a screen. It calls for no interpreters, no actors, producers, camera crews, costumers, musicians. It does not even require the traditional apparatus of publishing, as the long-running success of samizdat literature[1] demonstrates. The Foucault essay suggests that literature is as much at risk from the enveloping, smothering forces of the market economy, which reduces books to mere products. This danger is real, and I do not want to seem to be minimizing it. But the truth is that of all the forms, literature can still be the most free. The more money a piece of work costs, the easier it is to control it.

Film, the most expensive of art forms, is also the least subversive. This is why, although Carlos Fuentes cites the work of film-makers like Buñuel, Bergman and Fellini as instances of successful secular revolts into the territory of the sacred, I continue to believe in the greater possibilities of the novel. Its singularity is its best protection.

Among the childhood books I devoured and kissed were large numbers of cheap comics of a most unliterary nature. The heroes of these comic books were, or so it seemed, almost always mutants or hybrids or freaks: as well as the Batman and the Spiderman there was Aquaman, who was half-fish, and of course Superman, who could easily be mistaken for a bird or a plane. In those days, the middle 1950s, the super-heroes were all, in their various ways, hawkish law-and-order conservatives, leaping to work in response to the Police Commissioner's Bat-Signal, banding together to form the Justice League of America, defending what Superman called "truth, justice and the American way." But in spite of this extreme emphasis on crime-busting, the lesson they taught children—or this child, at any rate—was the perhaps unintentionally radical truth that exceptionality was the greatest and most heroic of values; that those who were unlike the crowd were to be treasured the most lovingly; and that this exceptionality was a treasure so great and so easily misunderstood that it had to be concealed, in ordinary life, beneath what the comic books called a "secret identity." Superman could not have survived without "mild-mannered" Clark Kent; "millionaire socialite" Bruce Wayne made possible the nocturnal activities of the Batman.

Now it is obviously true that those other freakish, hybrid, mutant, exceptional beings—novelists—those creators of the most freakish, hybrid and metamorphic of forms, the novel, have frequently been obliged to hide behind secret identities, whether for reasons of gender or terror. But the most wonderful of the many wonderful truths about the novel form is that the greater the writer, the greater his or her exceptionality. The geniuses of the novel are those whose voices are fully and undisguisably their own, who, to borrow William Gass's[2] image, *sign every word they write.* What draws us to an author is his or her "unlikeness," even if the

---

[1] *samizdat literature* Underground, self-published literature, originally created in the Soviet Union to undermine the system of state censorship.

[2] *William Gass* American novelist, essayist and critic.

apparatus of literary criticism then sets to work to demonstrate that he or she is really no more than an accumulation of influences. Unlikeness, the thing that makes it impossible for a writer to stand in any regimented line, is a quality novelists share with the Caped Crusaders of the comics, though they are only rarely capable of leaping tall buildings in a single stride.

What is more, the writer is there, in his work, in the reader's hands, utterly exposed, utterly defenceless, entirely without the benefit of an alter ego to hide behind. What is forged, in the secret act of reading, is a different kind of identity, as the reader and writer merge, through the medium of the text, to become a collective being that both writes as it reads and reads as it writes, and creates, jointly, that unique work, "their" novel. This "secret identity" of writer and reader is the novel form's greatest and most subversive gift.

And this, finally, is why I elevate the novel above other forms, why it has always been, and remains, my first love: not only is it the art involving least compromises, but it is also the only one that takes the "privileged arena" of conflicting discourses *right inside our heads*. The interior space of our imagination is a theatre that can never be closed down; the images created there make up a movie that can never be destroyed.

In this last decade of the millennium, as the forces of religion are renewed in strength and as the all-pervasive power of materialism wraps its own weighty chains around the human spirit, where should the novel be looking? It seems clear that the renewal of the old, bipolar field of discourse, between the sacred and the profane, which Michel Foucault proposes, will be of central importance. It seems probable, too, that we may be heading towards a world in which there will be no real alternative to the liberal-capitalist social model (except, perhaps, the theocratic, foundationalist model of Islam). In this situation, liberal capitalism or democracy or the free world will require novelists' most rigorous attention, will require reimagining and questioning and doubting as never before. "Our antagonist is our helper," said Edmund Burke, and if democracy no longer has communism to help it clarify, by opposition, its own ideas, then perhaps it will have to have literature as an adversary instead.

I have made a large number of sweeping claims for literature during the course of this piece, and I am aware of a slightly messianic tone in much of what I've written. The reverencing of books and writers, by writers, is nothing particularly new, of course. "Since the early 19th century," writes Cupitt, "imaginative writers have claimed—have indeed enjoyed—a guiding and representative role in our culture. Our preachers are novelists, poets, dramatists, film-makers and the like, purveyors of fiction, ambiguous people, deceivers. Yet we continue to think of ourselves as rational."

But now I find myself backing away from the idea of sacralizing literature with which I flirted at the beginning of this text; I cannot bear the idea of the writer as secular prophet; I am remembering that one of the very greatest writers of the century, Samuel Beckett, believed that all art must inevitably end in failure. This is, clearly, no reason for surrender. "Ever tried. Ever failed. Never mind. Try again. Fail better."

Literature is an interim report from the consciousness of the artist, and so it can never be "finished" or "perfect." Literature is made at the frontier between the self and the world, and in the act of creation that frontier softens, becomes permeable, allows the world to flow into the artist and the artist to flow into the world. Nothing so inexact, so easily and frequently misconceived, deserves the protection of being declared sacrosanct. We shall just have to get along without the shield of sacralization, and a good thing, too. We must not become what we oppose.

The only privilege literature deserves—and this privilege it requires in order to exist—is the privilege of being the arena of discourse, the place where the struggle of languages can be acted out.

Imagine this. You wake up one morning and find yourself in a large, rambling house. As you wander through it you realize it is so enormous that you will never know it all. In the house are people you know, family members, friends, lovers, colleagues; also many strangers. The house is full of activity: conflicts and seductions, celebrations and wakes. At some point you understand that there is no way out. You find that you can accept this. The house is not what you'd have chosen, it's in fairly bad condition, the corridors are often full of bullies, but it will have to do. Then one day you enter an unimportant-looking little room. The room is empty, but there are voices in it, voices that seem to be whispering just to you. You recognize some of the voices, others are completely unknown to you. The voices are talking about the house, about everyone in it, about everything that is happening and has happened and should happen. Some of them speak exclusively in obscenities. Some are bitchy. Some are loving. Some are funny. Some are sad. The most interesting voices are all these things at once. You begin to go to the room more and more often. Slowly you learn that most of the people in the house use such rooms sometimes. Yet the rooms are all discreetly positioned and unimportant-looking.

Now imagine that you wake up one morning and you are still in the large house, but all the voice-rooms have disappeared. It is as if they have been wiped out. Now there is nowhere in the whole house where you can go to hear voices talking about everything in every possible way. There is nowhere to go for the voices that can be funny one minute and sad the next, that can sound raucous and melodic in the course of the same sentence. Now you remember: there is no way out of this house. Now this fact begins to seem unbearable. You look into the eyes of the people in the corri-

dors—family, lovers, friends, colleagues, strangers, bullies, priests. You see the same thing in everybody's eyes. *How do we get out of here?* It becomes clear that the house is a prison. People begin to scream, and pound the walls. Men arrive with guns. The house begins to shake. You do not wake up. You are already awake.

Literature is the one place in any society where, within the secrecy of our own heads, we can hear *voices talking about everything in every possible way.* The reason for ensuring that that privileged arena is preserved is not that writers want the absolute freedom to say and do whatever they please. It is that we, all of us, readers and writers and citizens and generals and godmen, need that little, unimportant-looking room. We do not need to call it sacred, but we do need to remember that it is necessary.

"Everybody knows," wrote Saul Bellow in *The Adventures of Augie March,* "there is no fineness or accuracy of suppression. If you hold down one thing, you hold down the adjoining."

Wherever in the world the little room of literature has been closed, sooner or later the walls have come tumbling down.

—1990

KAZUO ISHIGURO
b. 1954

Kazuo Ishiguro is best known for his Booker Prize-winning novel *The Remains of the Day* (1989), but his other novels have also received extraordinary international acclaim. He has been hailed—along with writers such as Salman Rushdie, Michael Ondaatje, Vikram Seth, and Timothy Mo—as part of a new movement of "world fiction." Like these writers, he writes in English but is of non-Anglo-Saxon ancestry, and often depicts characters and settings which differ from those traditionally found in English literature. With influences that include Japanese pop culture of the 1940s and 1950s, nineteenth-century American writers, and Russian authors Dostoevski and Chekhov, Ishiguro often produces work that challenges his readers' expectations.

Ishiguro was born in Nagasaki, Japan, in 1954. When he was five his father accepted a one-year research position at the National Institute of Oceanography in Britain, and the family left for England. Ishiguro's parents educated him in the expectation that the family would return to Japan—providing him with Japanese magazines, books, and movies—but their return continued to be postponed, and eventually they became permanent British residents. Ishiguro studied English and philosophy at the University of Kent at Canterbury, where he received his B.A. He went on to a Master's degree in Creative Writing at the University of East Anglia in Norwich, where he was a member of a postgraduate class directed by Malcolm Bradbury.

Ishiguro, who for several years had attempted unsuccessfully to become a singer/songwriter, enjoyed almost immediate success as a writer of fiction. His first two novels, *A Pale View of Hills* (1982) and *An Artist of the Floating World* (1986), won prestigious literary awards in England and established him as an important new novelist. Both these early novels are set in Japan, although Ishiguro would not make his first return to Japan until 1989; Ishiguro has said that the Japan of these novels is one of his own personal imagination, constructed on a foundation of childhood memories.

Throughout his life Ishiguro has retained something of the outsider's perspective. When he began writing he realized he "wasn't a very English Englishman, and [he] wasn't a very Japanese Japanese either." This unique perspective enables him to pinpoint and dissect cultural myths, norms, and stereotypes—indeed, Ishiguro believes one of an artist's most important jobs is to "tackle and rework myths." Lurking behind the faintly comic resolution of *An Artist of the Floating World* is Ishiguro's knowledge that many Western readers—familiar only with stereotypes of Japanese society—would expect at the novel's end the cultural cliché of the protagonist's ritual suicide by *seppuku*.

The Remains of the Day is widely regarded as one of the most accomplished works of fiction of the twentieth century. Its story concerns Stevens, an aging butler who looks back in the summer of 1956 on the events of his life—in particular, on the great events that had transpired in his presence in the mid-1930s when his employer, Lord Darlington, had been organizing clandestine support in Britain for Germany's Nazi government; and on the unacknowledged love that had existed over the same period between himself and the housekeeper at Darlington Hall, Miss Kenton. The story is told in Stevens's voice; from between the lines of the butler's spare and formal narrative the reader is led to piece together a tale of misplaced loyalty, lost opportunity, and almost unbearable sadness.

Ishiguro has been compared to novelist Graham Swift in his intertwining of personal and world histories. His novels often center on characters who attempt to cope with traumatic events of history, but he has little interest in investigating the historic events themselves. *The Remains of the Day* looks back from the 1950s to the impending Nazi threat of the 1930s, with barely a glance at its culmination during World War II; similarly, although *A Pale View of Hills* is set in Nagasaki in the late 1940s, no mention is ever made of the atomic bomb, the effects of which permeate every aspect of the protagonist's life. As Ishiguro says, this is because he is "more interested in what people tell themselves happened … than what actually happened." Often recounted in the first person by an unreliable narrator who is haunted by events in his or her past, Ishiguro's narratives frequently center on distortions of perception or of memory. His very writing style mimics the workings of memory, moving fluidly across time and through tangentially connected episodes.

Ishiguro's settings are often loosely defined, as is the case in "A Village After Dark" (2001) or in *The Unconsoled* (1995), which could be set in any European city. Whether they take place in Japan, England, or Shanghai—the setting of *When We Were Orphans* (2002)— there is often a somewhat unsettling universality to the experiences described; the locations are important only in that they provide backdrops for, and insights into, Ishiguro's characters. As a result, Ishiguro's fiction—which has been printed in over thirty languages—is well suited for translation.

Never Let Me Go (2005) has been widely praised as Ishiguro's most accomplished work since *The Remains of the Day*. Set largely in a boarding school where the atmosphere is at once warmly familiar and deeply disturbing, the novel explores against a futuristic dystopian background the roots of social exclusion, the sometimes frightening conjunction of medical science and human notions of progress, the nature of love, and the shadow cast by death on human existence.

Ishiguro lives with his wife and daughter in London.

⌘⌘⌘

A Village After Dark

There was a time when I could travel England for weeks on end and remain at my sharpest—when, if anything, the travelling gave me an edge. But now that I am older I become disoriented more easily. So it was that on arriving at the village just after dark I failed to find my bearings at all. I could hardly believe I was in the same village in which not so long ago I had lived and come to exercise such influence.

There was nothing I recognized, and I found myself walking forever around twisting, badly lit streets hemmed in on both sides by the little stone cottages characteristic of the area. The streets often became so narrow I could make no progress without my bag or my elbow scraping one rough wall or another. I persevered nevertheless, stumbling around in the darkness in the hope of coming upon the village square— where I could at least orient myself—or else of encountering one of the villagers. When after a while I had done neither, a weariness came over me, and I decided my best course was just to choose a cottage at random, knock on the door, and hope it would be opened by someone who remembered me.

I stopped by a particularly rickety-looking door, whose upper beam was so low that I could see I would have to crouch right down to enter. A dim light was leaking out around the door's edges, and I could hear voices and laughter. I knocked loudly to insure that the occupants would hear me over their talk. But just then someone behind me said, "Hello."

I turned to find a young woman of around twenty, dressed in raggedy jeans and a torn jumper, standing in the darkness a little way away.

"You walked straight past me earlier," she said, "even though I called to you."

"Did I really? Well, I'm sorry. I didn't mean to be rude."

"You're Fletcher, aren't you?"

"Yes," I said, somewhat flattered.

"Wendy thought it was you when you went by our cottage. We all got very excited. You were one of that lot, weren't you? With David Maggis and all of them."

"Yes," I said, "but Maggis was hardly the most important one. I'm surprised you pick him out like that. There were other, far more important figures." I reeled off a series of names and was interested to see the girl nodding at each one in recognition. "But this must have all been before your time," I said. "I'm surprised you know about such things."

"It was before our time, but we're all experts on your lot. We know more about all that than most of the older ones who were here then. Wendy recognized you instantly just from your photos."

"I had no idea you young people had taken such an interest in us. I'm sorry I walked past you earlier. But you see, now that I'm older, I get a little disoriented when I travel."

I could hear some boisterous talk coming from behind the door. I banged on it again, this time rather impatiently, though I was not so eager to bring the encounter with the girl to a close.

She looked at me for a moment, then said, "All of you from those days are like that. David Maggis came here a few years ago. In '93, or maybe it was '94. He was like that. A bit vague. It must get to you after a while, travelling all the time."

"So Maggis was here. How interesting. You know, he wasn't one of the really important figures. You mustn't get carried away with such an idea. Incidentally, perhaps you could tell me who lives in this cottage." I thumped the door again.

"The Petersons," the girl said. "They're an old house. They'll probably remember you."

"The Petersons," I repeated, but the name meant nothing to me.

"Why don't you come to our cottage? Wendy was really excited. So were the rest of us. It's a real chance for us, actually talking to someone from those days."

"I'd very much like to do that. But first of all I'd better get myself settled in. The Petersons, you say."

I thumped the door again, this time quite ferociously. At last it opened, throwing warmth and light out into the street. An old man was standing in the doorway. He looked at me carefully, then asked, "It's not Fletcher, is it?"

"Yes, and I've just got into the village. I've been travelling for several days."

He thought about this for a moment, then said, "Well, you'd better come in."

I found myself in a cramped, untidy room full of rough wood and broken furniture. A log burning in the fireplace was the only source of light, by which I could make out a number of hunched figures sitting around the room. The old man led me to a chair beside the fire with a grudgingness that suggested it was the very one he had just vacated. Once I sat down, I found I could not easily turn my head to see my surroundings or the others in the room. But the warmth of the fire was very welcome, and for a moment I just stared into its flames, a pleasant grogginess drifting over me. Voices came from behind me, inquiring if I was well, if I had come far, if I was hungry, and I replied as best I could, though I was aware that my answers were barely adequate. Eventually, the questions ceased, and it occurred to me that my presence was creating a heavy awkwardness, but I was so grateful for the warmth and the chance to rest that I hardly cared.

Nonetheless, when the silence behind me had gone unbroken for several minutes, I resolved to address my hosts with a little more civility, and I turned in my chair. It was then, as I did so, that I was suddenly seized by an intense sense of recognition. I had chosen the cottage quite at random, but now I could see that it was none other than the very one in which I had spent my years in this village. My gaze moved immediately to the far corner—at this moment shrouded in darkness—to the spot that had been *my* corner, where once my mattress had been and where I had spent many tranquil hours browsing through books or conversing with whoever happened to drift in. On summer days, the windows, and often the door, were left open to allow a refreshing breeze to blow right through. Those were the days when the cottage was surrounded by open fields and there would come from outside the voices of my friends, lazing in the long grass, arguing over poetry or philosophy. These precious fragments of the past came back to me so powerfully that it was all I could do not to make straight for my old corner then and there.

Someone was speaking to me again, perhaps asking another question, but I hardly listened. Rising, I peered through the shadows into my corner, and could now make out a narrow bed, covered by an old curtain, occupying more or less the exact space where my mattress had been. The bed looked extremely inviting, and I found myself cutting into something the old man was saying.

"Look," I said, "I know this is a bit blunt. But, you see, I've come such a long way today. I really need to lie down, close my eyes, even if it's just for a few minutes. After that, I'm happy to talk all you like."

I could see the figures around the room shifting uneasily. Then a new voice said, rather sullenly, "Go ahead then. Have a nap. Don't mind us."

But I was already picking my way through the clutter toward my corner. The bed felt damp, and the springs creaked under my weight, but no sooner had I curled up with my back to the room than my many hours of travelling began to catch up with me. As I was drifting off, I heard the old man saying, "It's Fletcher, all right. God, he's aged."

A woman's voice said, "Should we let him go to sleep like that? He might wake in a few hours and then we'll have to stay up with him."

"Let him sleep for an hour or so," someone else said. "If he's still asleep after an hour, we'll wake him."

At this point, sheer exhaustion overtook me.

It was not a continuous or comfortable sleep. I drifted between sleep and waking, always conscious of voices behind me in the room. At some point, I was aware of a woman saying, "I don't know how I was ever under his spell. He looks such a ragamuffin now."

In my state of near-sleep, I debated with myself whether these words applied to me or, perhaps, to David Maggis, but before long sleep engulfed me once more.

When I next awoke, the room appeared to have grown both darker and colder. Voices were continuing behind me in lowered tones, but I could make no sense of the conversation. I now felt embarrassed at having gone to sleep in the way I had, and for a few further moments remained motionless with my face to the wall. But something about me must have revealed that I was awake, for a woman's voice, breaking off from the general conversation, said, "Oh, look, look." Some whispers were exchanged, then I heard the sound of someone coming toward my corner. I felt a hand placed gently on my shoulder, and looked up to find a woman

kneeling over me. I did not turn my body sufficiently to see the room, but I got the impression that it was lit by dying embers, and the woman's face was visible only in shadow.

"Now, Fletcher," she said. "It's time we had a talk. I've waited a long time for you to come back. I've thought about you often."

I strained to see her more clearly. She was somewhere in her forties, and even in the gloom I noticed a sleepy sadness in her eyes. But her face failed to stir in me even the faintest of memories.

"I'm sorry," I said. "I have no recollection of you. But please forgive me if we met some time ago. I do get very disoriented these days."

"Fletcher," she said, "when we used to know one another, I was young and beautiful. I idolized you, and everything you said seemed like an answer. Now here you are, back again. I've wanted to tell you for many years that you ruined my life."

"You're being unfair. All right, I was mistaken about a lot of things. But I never claimed to have any answers. All I said in those days was that it was our duty, all of us, to contribute to the debate. We knew so much more about the issues than the ordinary people here. If people like us procrastinated, claiming we didn't yet know enough, then who was there to act? But I never claimed I had the answers. No, you're being unfair."

"Fletcher," she said, and her voice was oddly gentle, "you used to make love to me, more or less every time I wandered in here to your room. In this corner, we did all kinds of beautifully dirty things. It's odd to think how I could have once been so physically excited by you. And here you're just a foul-smelling bundle of rags now. But look at me—I'm still attractive. My face has got a bit lined, but when I walk in the village streets I wear dresses I've made specially to show off my figure. A lot of men want me still. But you, no woman would look at you now. A bundle of stinking rags and flesh."

"I don't remember you," I said. "And I've no time for sex these days. I've other things to worry about. More serious things. Very well, I was mistaken about a lot in those days. But I've done more than most to try and make amends. You see, even now I'm travelling. I've never stopped. I've travelled and travelled trying to undo what damage I may once have caused. That's more than can be said of some others from those days. I bet

Maggis, for instance, hasn't worked nearly as hard to try and put things right."

The woman was stroking my hair.

"Look at you. I used to do this, run my fingers through your hair. Look at this filthy mess. I'm sure you're contaminated with all sorts of parasites." But she continued slowly to run her fingers through the dirty knots. I failed to feel anything erotic from this, as perhaps she wished me to do. Rather, her caresses felt maternal. Indeed, for a moment it was as though I had finally reached some cocoon of protectiveness, and I began once more to feel sleepy. But suddenly she stopped and slapped me hard on the forehead.

"Why don't you join the rest of us now? You've had your sleep. You've got a lot of explaining to do." With that she got up and left.

For the first time, I turned my body sufficiently to survey the room. I saw the woman making her way past the clutter on the floor, then sitting down in a rocking chair by the fireplace. I could see three other figures hunched around the dying fire. One I recognized to be the old man who had opened the door. The two others—sitting together on what looked like a wooden trunk—seemed to be women of around the same age as the one who had spoken to me.

The old man noticed that I had turned, and he indicated to the others that I was watching. The four of them proceeded to sit stiffly, not speaking. From the way they did this, it was clear that they had been discussing me thoroughly while I was asleep. In fact, as I watched them I could more or less guess the whole shape their conversation had taken. I could see, for instance, that they had spent some time expressing concern for the young girl I had met outside, and about the effect I might have on her peers.

"They're all so impressionable," the old man would have said. "And I heard her inviting him to visit them."

To which, no doubt, one of the women on the trunk would have said, "But he can't do much harm now. In our time, we were all taken in because all his kind—they were young and glamorous. But these days the odd one passing through from time to time, looking all decrepit and burned out like that—if anything, it goes to demystify all that talk about the old days. In any case, people like him have changed their position so much these days. They don't know themselves what they believe."

The old man would have shaken his head. "I saw the way that young girl was looking at him. All right, he looks a pitiful mess over there just now. But once his ego's fed a little, once he has the flattery of the young people, sees how they want to hear his ideas, then there'll be no stopping him. It'll be just like before. He'll have them all working for his causes. Young girls like that, there's so little for them to believe in now. Even a stinking tramp like this could give them a purpose."

Their conversation, all the time I slept, would have gone something very much like that. But now, as I observed them from my corner, they continued to sit in guilty silence, staring at the last of their fire. After a while, I rose to my feet. Absurdly, the four of them kept their gazes averted from me. I waited a few moments to see if any of them would say anything. Finally, I said, "All right, I was asleep earlier, but I've guessed what you were saying. Well, you'll be interested to know I'm going to do the very thing you feared. I'm going this moment to the young people's cottage. I'm going to tell them what to do with all their energy, all their dreams, their urge to achieve something of lasting good in this world. Look at you, what a pathetic bunch. Crouching in your cottage, afraid to do anything, afraid of me, of Maggis, of anyone else from those times. Afraid to do anything in the world out there, just because once we made a few mistakes. Well, those young people haven't yet sunk so low, despite all the lethargy you've been preaching at them down the years. I'll talk to them. I'll undo in half an hour all of your sorry efforts."

"You see," the old man said to the others. "I knew it would be this way. We ought to stop him, but what can we do?"

I crashed my way across the room, picked up my bag, and went out into the night.

The girl was still standing outside when I emerged. She seemed to be expecting me and with a nod began to lead the way.

The night was drizzly and dark. We twisted and turned along the narrow paths that ran between the cottages. Some of the cottages we passed looked so decayed and crumbling that I felt I could destroy one of them simply by running at it with all my weight.

The girl kept a few paces ahead, occasionally glancing back at me over her shoulder. Once she said, "Wendy's going to be so pleased. She was sure it was you when you went past earlier. By now, she'll have guessed she was right, because I've been away this long, and she'll have brought the whole crowd together. They'll all be waiting."

"Did you give David Maggis this sort of reception, too?"

"Oh, yes. We were really excited when he came."

"I'm sure he found that very gratifying. He always had an exaggerated sense of his own importance."

"Wendy says Maggis was one of the interesting ones, but that you were, well, important. She thinks you were really important."

I thought about this for a moment.

"You know," I said, "I've changed my mind on very many things. If Wendy's expecting me to say all the things I used to all those years ago, well, she's going to be in for a disappointment."

The girl did not seem to hear this, but continued to lead me purposefully through the clusters of cottages.

After a little while, I became aware of footsteps following a dozen or so paces behind us. At first, I assumed this was just some villager out walking and refrained from turning round. But then the girl halted under a street lamp and looked behind us. I was thus obliged also to stop and turn. A middle-aged man in a dark overcoat was coming toward us. As he approached, he held out his hand and shook mine, though without smiling.

"So," he said, "you're here."

I then realized I knew the man. We had not seen each other since we were ten years old. His name was Roger Button, and he had been in my class at the school I had attended for two years in Canada before my family returned to England. Roger Button and I had not been especially close, but, because he had been a timid boy, and because he, too, was from England, he had for a while followed me about. I had neither seen nor heard from him since that time. Now, as I studied his appearance under the street lamp, I saw the years had not been kind to him. He was bald, his face was pocked and lined, and there was a weary sag to his whole posture. For all that, there was no mistaking my old classmate.

"Roger," I said, "I'm just on my way to visit this young lady's friends. They've gathered together to receive me. Otherwise I'd have come and looked you up straightaway. As it was, I had it in my mind as the next thing to do, even before getting any sleep tonight. I was just thinking to myself, However late things finish at the young people's cottage, I'll go and knock on Roger's door afterward."

"Don't worry," said Roger Button as we all started to walk again. "I know how busy you are. But we ought to talk. Chew over old times. When you last saw me—at school, I mean—I suppose I was a rather feeble specimen. But, you know, that all changed when I got to fourteen, fifteen. I really toughened up. Became quite a leader type. But you'd long since left Canada. I always wondered what would have happened if we'd come across each other at fifteen. Things would have been rather different between us, I assure you."

As he said this, memories came flooding back. In those days, Roger Button had idolized me, and in return I had bullied him incessantly. However, there had existed between us a curious understanding that my bullying him was all for his own good; that when, without warning, I suddenly punched him in the stomach on the playground, or when, passing him in the corridor, I impulsively wrenched his arm up his back until he started to cry, I was doing so in order to help him toughen up. Accordingly, the principal effect such attacks had on our relationship was to keep him in awe of me. This all came back to me as I listened to the weary-looking man walking beside me.

"Of course," Roger Button went on, perhaps guessing my train of thought, "it might well be that if you hadn't treated me the way you did I'd never have become what I did at fifteen. In any case, I've often wondered how it would have been if we'd met just a few years later. I really was something to be reckoned with by then."

We were once again walking along the narrow twisted passages between cottages. The girl was still leading the way, but she was now walking much faster. Often we would only just manage to catch a glimpse of her turning some corner ahead of us, and it struck me that we would have to keep alert if we were not to lose her.

"Today, of course," Roger Button was saying, "I've let myself go a bit. But I have to say, old fellow, you seem to be in much worse shape. Compared with you, I'm an athlete. Not to put too fine a point on it, you're just a filthy old tramp now, really, aren't you? But, you know, for a long time after you left I continued to idolize you. Would Fletcher do this? What would Fletcher think if he saw me doing that? Oh, yes. It was only when I got to fifteen or so that I looked back on it all and saw through you. Then I was very angry, of course. Even now, I still think about it sometimes. I look back and think, Well, he was just a thoroughly nasty so-and-so. He had a little more weight and muscle at that age than I did, a little more confidence, and he took full advantage. Yes, it's very clear, looking back, what a nasty little person you were. Of course, I'm not implying you still are today. We all change. That much I'm willing to accept."

"Have you been living here long?" I asked, wishing to change the subject.

"Oh, seven years or so. Of course, they talk about you a lot around here. I sometimes tell them about our early association. 'But he won't remember me,' I always tell them. 'Why would he remember a skinny little boy he used to bully and have at his beck and call?' Anyway, the young people here, they talk about you more and more these days. Certainly, the ones who've never seen you tend to idealize you the most. I suppose you've come back to capitalize on all that. Still, I shouldn't blame you. You're entitled to try and salvage a little self-respect."

We suddenly found ourselves facing an open field, and we both halted. Glancing back, I saw that we had walked our way out of the village; the last of the cottages were some distance behind us. Just as I had feared, we had lost the young woman; in fact, I realized we had not been following her for some time.

At that moment, the moon emerged, and I saw we were standing at the edge of a vast grassy field—extending, I supposed, far beyond what I could see by the moon.

Roger Button turned to me. His face in the moonlight seemed gentle, almost affectionate.

"Still," he said, "it's time to forgive. You shouldn't keep worrying so much. As you see, certain things from the past will come back to you in the end. But then we can't be held accountable for what we did when we were very young."

"No doubt you're right," I said. Then I turned and looked around in the darkness. "But now I'm not sure where to go. You see, there were some young people waiting for me in their cottage. By now they'd have a warm fire ready for me and some hot tea. And some home-baked cakes, perhaps even a good stew. And the moment I entered, ushered in by that young lady we were following just now, they'd all have burst into applause. There'd be smiling, adoring faces all around me. That's what's waiting for me somewhere. Except I'm not sure where I should go."

Roger Button shrugged. "Don't worry, you'll get there easily enough. Except, you know, that girl was being a little misleading if she implied you could walk to Wendy's cottage. It's much too far. You'd really need to catch a bus. Even then, it's quite a long journey. About two hours, I'd say. But don't worry, I'll show you where you can pick up your bus."

With that, he began to walk back toward the cottages. As I followed, I could sense that the hour had got very late and my companion was anxious to get some sleep. We spent several minutes walking around the cottages again, and then he brought us out into the village square. In fact, it was so small and shabby it hardly merited being called a square; it was little more than a patch of green beside a solitary street lamp. Just visible beyond the pool of light cast by the lamp were a few shops, all shut up for the night. There was complete silence and nothing was stirring. A light mist was hovering over the ground.

Roger Button stopped before we had reached the green and pointed.

"There," he said. "If you stand there, a bus will come along. As I say, it's not a short journey. About two hours. But don't worry, I'm sure your young people will wait. They've so little else to believe in these days, you see."

"It's very late," I said. "Are you sure a bus will come?"

"Oh, yes. Of course, you may have to wait. But eventually a bus will come." Then he touched me reassuringly on the shoulder. "I can see it might get a little lonely standing out here. But once the bus arrives your spirits will rise, believe me. Oh, yes. That bus is always a joy. It'll be brightly lit up, and it's always full of cheerful people, laughing and joking and pointing out the window. Once you board it, you'll feel warm and comfortable, and the other passengers will chat with you, perhaps offer you things to eat or drink. There may even be singing— that depends on the driver. Some drivers encourage it, others don't. Well, Fletcher, it was good to see you."

We shook hands, then he turned and walked away. I watched him disappear into the darkness between two cottages.

I walked up to the green and put my bag down at the foot of the lamppost. I listened for the sound of a vehicle in the distance, but the night was utterly still. Nevertheless, I had been cheered by Roger Button's description of the bus. Moreover, I thought of the reception awaiting me at my journey's end—of the adoring faces of the young people—and felt the stirrings of optimism somewhere deep within me.

—2001

CAROL ANN DUFFY
b. 1955

As the British newspaper *The Guardian* has put it, "in the world of British poetry, Carol Ann Duffy is a superstar." Lauded by reviewers and by academic critics, her work has also been enormously popular with the general public; perhaps not since Philip Larkin's *High Windows* became a bestseller in the mid-1970s has a British poet simultaneously enjoyed such high levels of critical esteem and such a broad readership. Duffy first made her mark in the 1980s as a writer of dramatic monologues, many of them poems of controlled edginess (such as "Stealing") that give voice to tough, working class personae. She has since become equally well known for tightly crafted lyrics of concentrated emotional force, especially on the themes of love and loss.

The eldest child of five, Duffy was born in Glasgow to an Irish mother and Scottish father, and raised largely in the north Midlands town of Stafford, where her father became a member of the local council and was a Labour Party candidate for Parliament. She attended St. Joseph's Convent School and Stafford Girls High School before studying philosophy at Liverpool University. She then worked for some years in London, where she was editor of the poetry magazine *Ambit*. In 1996 Duffy moved to Manchester, and since then she has taught at Manchester Metropolitan University, where in 2005 she was appointed Creative Director of the Writing School.

With her early collections—most notably her first book, *Standing Female Nude* (1985)—Duffy established a reputation as a powerful feminist voice, as a poet of considerable versatility, and as an entertainer, as capable of writing in a comic as in a dramatic or lyric mode. In *Mean Time* (1993), the emotional as well as technical range of her work broadened, as can be seen in poems such as "Nostalgia," "The Good Teachers," and "Crush." Her 1999 book *The World's Wife* is a striking *tour de force* in which each poem is written in the persona of a wife, sister, or lover of a famous man from history or mythology, from "Mrs. Faust" and "Anne Hathaway" to "Mrs. Lazarus." Her 2005 collection *Rapture* is also a unified work, though of a very different sort; here she presents a chronologically-ordered series of poems that trace the emotional trajectory of a relationship of love—poems, as Duffy puts it in the sonnet from which the book takes its title, of "desire and passion on the thinking air." *Rapture* is confessedly autobiographical, but in the only interview on the collection that Duffy consented to give, she declined to discuss any specifics: "I could not feel more deeply than I have in these poems," she said, "but these are not journals or diaries or letters, they are works of art. A transformation takes place—it has to, if the feeling is to be revealed to others."

Though Duffy's poetry often bristles with contemporaneity in its tone and subject matter, it also exhibits a remarkable range of formal accomplishment; many of her poems follow accentual-syllabic metrical patterns, and many use rhyme extensively. It is perhaps more a reflection on reading habits that took root in the second half of the twentieth century than it is on Duffy's work itself that as formal patterns of rhythm and rhyme began to play a larger and larger role in her work, some began to wonder, in Jeannette Winterson's words, "whether Duffy had lost her balance. Had she stopped writing poetry and slopped into verse?" Unlike many poets who are inclined toward formal complexity, Duffy eschews unusual diction: as she has put it, "I'm not interested, as a poet, in words like 'plash'—Seamus Heaney words, interesting words. I like to use simple words but in a complicated way."

Among lesbian writers, Duffy is noteworthy for her rejection of any exceptionalist status. "I'm not a lesbian poet, whatever that is. If I am a lesbian icon and a role model, that's great, but if it is a word that is used to reduce me, then you have to ask why.... I define myself as a poet and a mother—that's all." Duffy's daughter Ella was born in 1995.

Duffy has written or edited over thirty books, including several plays, collections of poetry for children, and a variety of edited volumes. Among the many awards she has received are the 2003 Forward Poetry Prize, the 2003 Whitbread Poetry Award (for *Mean Time*), and the 2005 T.S. Eliot Prize (for *Rapture*). She was appointed an Officer of the British Empire in 1993 and a Commander of the British Empire in 2001.

⌘⌘⌘

Stealing

The most unusual thing I ever stole? A snowman.
Midnight. He looked magnificent; a tall, white
    mute
beneath the winter moon. I wanted him, a mate
with a mind as cold as the slice of ice
5   within my own brain. I started with the head.

Better off dead than giving in, not taking
what you want. He weighed a ton; his torso,
frozen stiff, hugged to my chest, a fierce chill
piercing my gut. Part of the thrill was knowing
10   that children would cry in the morning. Life's tough.

Sometimes I steal things I don't need. I joy-ride cars
to nowhere, break into houses just to have a look.
I'm a mucky ghost, leave a mess, maybe pinch a
    camera.
I watch my gloved hand twisting the doorknob.
15   A stranger's bedroom. Mirrors. I sigh like this—Aah.

It took some time. Reassembled in the yard,
he didn't look the same. I took a run
and booted him. Again. Again. My breath ripped out
in rags. It seems daft now. Then I was standing
20   alone among lumps of snow, sick of the world.

Boredom. Mostly I'm so bored I could eat myself.
One time, I stole a guitar and thought I might
learn to play. I nicked[1] a bust of Shakespeare once,

flogged[2] it, but the snowman was the strangest.
25   You don't understand a word I'm saying, do you?
—1987

Adultery

Wear dark glasses in the rain.
Regard what was unhurt
as though through a bruise.
Guilt. A sick, green tint.

5   New gloves, money tucked in the palms,
the handshake crackles. Hands
can do many things. Phone.
Open the wine. Wash themselves. Now

you are naked under your clothes all day,
10   slim with deceit. Only the once
brings you alone to your knees,
miming, more, more, older and sadder,

creative. Suck a lie with a hole in it
on the way home from a lethal, thrilling night
15   up against a wall, faster. Language
unpeels to a lost cry. You're a bastard.

Do it do it do it. Sweet darkness
in the afternoon; a voice in your ear
telling you how you are wanted,
20   which way, now. A telltale clock

---

[1] *nicked* Slang for stole.

[2] *flogged* Slang for sold.

wiping the hours from its face, your face
on a white sheet, gasping, radiant, yes.
Pay for it in cash, fiction, cab-fares back
to the life which crumbles like a wedding-cake.

25 Paranoia for lunch; too much
to drink, as a hand on your thigh
tilts the restaurant. You know all about love,
don't you. Turn on your beautiful eyes

for a stranger who's dynamite in bed, again
30 and again; a slow replay in the kitchen
where the slicing of innocent onions
scalds you to tears. Then, selfish autobiographical sleep

in a marital bed, the tarnished spoon of your body
stirring betrayal, your heart over-ripe at the core.
35 You're an expert, darling; your flowers
dumb and explicit on nobody's birthday.

So write the script—illness and debt,
a ring thrown away in a garden
no moon can heal, your own words
40 commuting to bile in your mouth, terror—

and all for the same thing twice. And all
for the same thing twice. You did it.
What. Didn't you. Fuck. Fuck. No. That was
the wrong verb. This is only an abstract noun.
—1993

The Good Teachers

You run round the back to be in it again.
No bigger than your thumbs, those virtuous
      women
size you up from the front row. Soon now,
Miss Ross will take you for double History.
5 You breathe on the glass, making a ghost of her, say
South Sea Bubble Defenestration of Prague.[1]

You love Miss Pirie. So much, you are top
of her class. So much, you need two of you

to stare out from the year, serious, passionate.
10 The River's Tale by Rudyard Kipling[2] by heart.
Her kind intelligent green eye. Her cruel blue one.
You are making a poem up for her in your head.

But not Miss Sheridan. Comment vous appelez.[3]
But not Miss Appleby. Equal to the square
15 of the other two sides. Never Miss Webb.
Dar es Salaam. Kilimanjaro.[4] Look. The good teachers
swish down the corridor in long, brown skirts,
snobbish and proud and clean and qualified.

And they've got your number. You roll the waistband
20 of your skirt over and over, all leg, all
dumb insolence, smoke-rings. You won't pass.
You could do better. But there's the wall you climb
into dancing, lovebites, marriage, the Cheltenham
and Gloucester,[5] today. The day you'll be sorry one
      day.
—1993

Drunk

Suddenly the rain is hilarious.
The moon wobbles in the dusk.

What a laugh. Unseen frogs
belch in the damp grass.

5 The strange perfumes of darkening trees.
Cheap red wine

and the whole world a mouth.
Give me a double, a kiss.
—1993

---

[1] *South Sea ... Prague* Two unconnected historical incidents.

[2] *Rudyard Kipling* English novelist, poet and short-story writer who was born in Bombay (1865–1936).

[3] *Comment vous appelez* French: what do you call.

[4] *Dar es Salaam. Kilimanjaro* The largest city and the tallest mountain, respectively, in Tanzania.

[5] *Cheltenham and Gloucester* The name of a commercial bank in the United Kingdom.

Mean Time

The clocks slid back an hour
and stole light from my life
as I walked through the wrong part of town,
mourning our love.

5   And, of course, unmendable rain
fell to the bleak streets
where I felt my heart gnaw
at all our mistakes.

If the darkening sky could lift
10   more than one hour from this day
there are words I would never have said
nor have heard you say.

But we will be dead, as we know,
beyond all light.
15   These are the shortened days
and the endless nights.
—1993

Mrs. Lazarus[1]

I had grieved. I had wept for a night and a day
over my loss, ripped the cloth I was married in
from my breasts, howled, shrieked, clawed
at the burial stones till my hands bled, retched
5   his name over and over again, dead, dead.

Gone home. Gutted the place. Slept in a single cot,
widow, one empty glove, white femur
in the dust, half. Stuffed dark suits
into black bags, shuffled in a dead man's shoes,
10   noosed the double knot of a tie round my bare neck,

gaunt nun in the mirror, touching herself. I learnt
the Stations of Bereavement, the icon of my face
in each bleak frame; but all those months
he was going away from me, dwindling
15   to the shrunk size of a snapshot, going,

going. Till his name was no longer a certain spell
for his face. The last hair on his head
floated out from a book. His scent went from the
      house.
The will was read. See, he was vanishing
20   to the small zero held by the gold of my ring.

Then he was gone. Then he was legend, language;
my arm on the arm of the schoolteacher—the shock
of a man's strength under the sleeve of his coat—
along the hedgerows. But I was faithful
25   for as long as it took. Until he was memory.

So I could stand that evening in the field
in a shawl of fine air, healed, able
to watch the edge of the moon occur to the sky
and a hare thump from a hedge; then notice
30   the village men running towards me, shouting,

behind them the women and children, barking dogs,
and I knew. I knew by the sly light
on the blacksmith's face, the shrill eyes
of the barmaid, the sudden hands bearing me
35   into the hot tang of the crowd parting before me.

He lived. I saw the horror on his face.
I heard his mother's crazy song. I breathed
his stench; my bridegroom in his rotting shroud,
moist and dishevelled from the grave's slack chew,
40   croaking his cuckold name, disinherited, out of his
      time.
—1999

[1] *Mrs. Lazarus*   In the story recounted in John 11.41–44, "a man named Lazarus" is sick; his sisters Martha and Mary send for Jesus asking for help. Jesus sends a reply asserting that "the sickness will not end in death," but does not come at once to help. When he does arrive a few days later Lazarus is dead and has been entombed for four days, but when Jesus has the stone covering the entrance to the tomb rolled back, Lazarus emerges in his grave-cloths. There is no mention of Lazarus's wife in the Biblical account.

Wish

But what if, in the clammy soil, her limbs
grew warmer, shifted, stirred, kicked off
the covering of earth, the drowsing corms,[1]
the sly worms, what if her arms reached out
5   to grab the stone, the grooves of her dates
under her thumb, and pulled her up? I wish.
Her bare feet walk along the gravel path
between the graves, her shroud like washing
blown onto the grass, the petals of her wreath
10   kissed for a bride. Nobody died. Nobody
wept. Nobody slept who couldn't be woken
by the light. If I can only push open this heavy door
she'll be standing there in the sun, dirty, tired,
wondering why do I shout, why do I run.
—2002

Rapture

Thought of by you all day, I think of you.
The birds sing in the shelter of a tree.
Above the prayer of rain, unacred blue,
not paradise, goes nowhere endlessly.
5   How does it happen that our lives can drift
far from our selves, while we stay trapped in time,
queuing[2] for death? It seems nothing will shift
the pattern of our days, alter the rhyme
we make with loss to assonance with bliss.
10   Then love comes, like a sudden flight of birds
from earth to heaven after rain. Your kiss,
recalled, unstrings, like pearls, this chain of words.
Huge skies connect us, joining here to there.
Desire and passion on the thinking air.
—2005

---

[1]   *corms* Bulbs.

[2]   *queuing* Lining up.

READING POETRY

WHAT IS A POEM?

Most of us know what a poem is when we see one. Still, even poets find it difficult to define a poem, or poetry. In a lecture on "The Name and Nature of Poetry" (1933), the English poet A.E. Housman stated that he could "no more define poetry than a terrier can define a rat"; however, he added, "we both recognize the object by the symptoms which it provokes in us." Housman knew he was in the presence of poetry if he experienced a shiver down the spine, or "a constriction of the throat and a precipitation of water to the eyes." Implicit in Housman's response is a recognition that we have to go beyond mere formal characteristics—stanzas, rhymes, rhythms—if we want to know what poetry is, or why it differs from prose. Poetry both represents and *creates* emotions in a highly condensed way. Therefore, any definition of the genre needs to consider, as much as possible, the impact of poetry on us as readers or listeners.

Worth consideration too is the role of the listener or reader not only as passive recipient of a poem, but also as an active participant in its performance. Poetry is among other things the locus for a communicative exchange. A section below deals with the sub-genre of performance poetry, but in a very real sense all poetry is subject to performance. Poems are to be read aloud as well as on the page, and both in sensing meaning and in expressing sound the reader plays a vital role in bringing a poem to life, no matter how long dead its author may be; as W.H. Auden wrote memorably of his fellow poet W.B. Yeats, "the words of a dead man / Are modified in the guts of the living."

For some readers, poetry is, in William Wordsworth's phrase, "the breath and finer spirit of all knowledge" ("Preface" to the *Lyrical Ballads*). They look to poetry for insights into the nature of human experience, and expect elevated thought in carefully-wrought language. In contrast, other readers distrust poetry that seems moralistic or didactic. "We hate poetry that has a palpable design upon us," wrote John Keats to his friend J.H. Reynolds; rather, poetry should be "great & unobtrusive, a thing which enters into one's soul, and does not startle it or amaze it with itself but with its subject." The American poet Archibald MacLeish took Keats's idea a step further: in his poem "Ars Poetica" he suggested that "A poem should not mean / But be." MacLeish was not suggesting that a poem should lack meaning, but rather that meaning should inhere in the poem's expressive and sensuous qualities, not in some explicit statement or versified idea.

Whatever we look for in a poem, the infinitude of forms, styles, and subjects that make up the body of literature we call "poetry" is, in the end, impossible to capture in a definition that would satisfy all readers. All we can do, perhaps, is to agree that a poem is a discourse that is characterized by a heightened attention to language, form, and rhythm, by an expressiveness that works through figurative rather than literal modes, and by a capacity to stimulate our imagination and arouse our feelings.

THE LANGUAGE OF POETRY

To speak of "the language of poetry" implies that poets make use of a vocabulary that is somehow different from the language of everyday life. In fact, all language has the capacity to be "poetic," if by poetry we understand a use of language to which some special importance is attached. The ritualistic utterances of religious ceremonies sometimes have this force; so do the skipping rhymes of children in the schoolyard. We can distinguish such uses of language from the kind of writing we find in, say, a computer user's manual: the author of the manual can describe a given function in a variety of ways, whereas the magic of the skipping rhyme can be invoked only by getting the right words in the right order. So with the poet: he or she chooses particular words in a particular order; the *way* the poet speaks is as important to our understanding as what is said. This doesn't mean that an instruction manual couldn't have poetic qualities—indeed, modern poets have created "found" poems from even less likely materials—but it does mean that in poetry there is an intimate relation amongst language, form, and meaning, and that the writer deliberately structures and manipulates language to achieve very particular ends.

THE BEST WORDS IN THE BEST ORDER

Wordsworth provides us with a useful example of the way that poetry can invest quite ordinary words with a high emotional charge:

> No motion has she now, no force,
> She neither hears nor sees;
> Rolled round in earth's diurnal course
> With rocks, and stones, and trees.

To paraphrase the content of this stanza from "A Slumber Did My Spirit Seal," "she" is dead and buried. But the language and structures used here give this prosaic idea great impact. For example, the regular iambic meter of the two last lines conveys something of the inexorable motion of the earth and of Lucy embedded in it; the monosyllabic last line is a grim reminder of her oneness with objects in nature; the repeated negatives in the first two lines drive home the irreparable destructiveness of death; the alliteration in the third and fourth lines gives a tangible suggestion of roundness, circularity, repetition in terms of the earth's shape and motion, suggesting a cycle in which death is perhaps followed by renewal. Even the unusual word "diurnal" (which would not have seemed so unusual to Wordsworth's readers) seems "right" in this context; it lends more weight to the notion of the earth's perpetual movement than its mundane synonym "daily" (which, besides, would not scan here). It is difficult to imagine a change of any kind to these lines; they exemplify another attempted definition of poetry, this time by Wordsworth's friend Samuel Taylor Coleridge: "the best words in the best order" (*Table Talk*, 1827).

POETIC DICTION AND THE ELEVATED STYLE

Wordsworth's diction in the "Lucy" poem cited above is a model of clarity; he has chosen language that, in its simplicity and bluntness, conveys the strength of the speaker's feelings far more strongly than an elaborate description of grief in more conventionally "poetic" language might have done. Wordsworth, disturbed by what he felt was a deadness and artificiality in the poetry of his day, sought to "choose incidents and situations from common life" and to describe them in "a selection of language really used by men" ("Preface" to *Lyrical Ballads*). His plan might seem an implicit reproach of the "raised" style, the elevated diction of epic poetry we associate with John Milton's *Paradise Lost*:

> Anon out of the earth a fabric huge
> Rose like an exhalation, with the sound
> Of dulcet symphonies and voices sweet,

Built like a temple, where pilasters round
Were set, and Doric pillars overlaid
With golden architrave; nor did there want
Cornice or frieze, with bossy sculptures graven;
The roof was fretted gold.

              (*Paradise Lost* I.710–17)

At first glance this passage, with its Latinate vocabulary and convoluted syntax, might seem guilty of inflated language and pretentiousness. However, Milton's description of the devils' palace in Hell deliberately seeks to distance us from its subject in order to emphasize the scale and sublimity of the spectacle, far removed from ordinary human experience. In other words, language and style in *Paradise Lost* are well adapted to suit a particular purpose, just as they are in "A Slumber Did My Spirit Seal," though on a wholly different scale. Wordsworth criticized the poetry of his day, not because of its elevation, but because the raised style was too often out of touch with its subject; in his view, the words did not bear any significant relation to the "truths" they were attempting to depict.

"PLAIN" LANGUAGE IN POETRY

Since Wordsworth's time, writers have been conscious of a need to narrow the apparent gap between "poetic" language and the language of everyday life. In much of the poetry of the past century, especially free verse, we can observe a growing approximation to speech—even to conversation—in the diction and rhythms of poetry. This may have something to do with the changed role of the poet, who today has discarded the mantle of teacher or prophet that was assumed by poets of earlier times, and who is ready to admit all fields of experience and endeavor as appropriate for poetry. The modern poet looks squarely at life, and can often find a provoking beauty in even the meanest of objects.

We should not assume, however, that a greater concern with the "ordinary," with simplicity, naturalness, and clarity, means a reduction in complexity or suggestiveness. A piece such as Stevie Smith's "Mother, Among the Dustbins," for all the casual and playful domesticity of some of its lines, skilfully evokes a range of emotions and sense impressions defying simple paraphrase.

IMAGERY, SYMBOLISM, AND FIGURES OF SPEECH

The language of poetry is grounded in the objects and phenomena that create sensory impressions. Sometimes the poet renders these impressions quite literally, in a series of *images* that seek to recreate a scene in the reader's mind:

Only a man harrowing clods
In a slow silent walk
With an old horse that stumbles and nods
Half asleep as they stalk.

Only thin smoke without flame
From the heaps of couch-grass;
Yet this will go onward the same
Though Dynasties pass.

> Yonder a maid and her wight
> Come whispering by:
> War's annals will cloud into night
> Ere their story die.
>
> (Thomas Hardy, "In Time of 'The Breaking of Nations'")

Here, the objects of everyday life are re-created with sensory details designed to evoke in us the sensations or responses felt by the speaker viewing the scene. At the same time, the writer invests the objects with such significance that the poem's meaning extends beyond the literal to the symbolic: that is, the images come to stand for something much larger than the objects they represent. Hardy's poem moves from the presentation of stark images of rural life to a sense of their timelessness. By the last stanza we see the ploughman, the burning grass, and the maid and her companion as symbols of recurring human actions and motives that defy the struggles and conflicts of history.

IMAGISM

The juxtaposition of clear, forceful images is associated particularly with the Imagist movement that flourished at the beginning of the twentieth century. Its chief representatives (in their early work) were the American poets H.D. and Ezra Pound, who defined an image as "that which represents an intellectual and emotional complex in an instant of time." Pound's two-line poem "In a Station of the Metro" provides a good example of the Imagists' goal of representing emotions or impressions through the use of concentrated images:

> The apparition of these faces in the crowd,
> Petals on a wet, black bough.

As in a Japanese *haiku*, a form that strongly influenced the Imagists, the poem uses sharp, clear, concrete details to evoke both a sensory impression and the emotion or the atmosphere of the scene. Though the Imagist movement itself lasted only a short time (from about 1912 to 1917), it had a far-reaching influence on modern poets such as T. S. Eliot, and William Carlos Williams.

FIGURES OF SPEECH

Imagery often works together with figurative expression to extend and deepen the meaning or impact of a poem. "Figurative" language means language that is metaphorical, not literal or referential. Through "figures of speech" such as metaphor and simile, metonymy, synecdoche, and personification, the writer may alter the ordinary, denotative meanings of words in order to convey greater force and vividness to ideas or impressions, often by showing likenesses between unlike things.

With *simile*, the poet makes an explicit comparison between the subject (called the *tenor*) and another object or idea (known as the *vehicle*), using "as" or "like":

> It is a beauteous evening, calm and free,
> The holy time is quiet as a Nun
> Breathless with adoration. …

In this opening to a sonnet, Wordsworth uses a visual image of a nun in devout prayer to convey in concrete terms the less tangible idea of evening as a "holy time." The comparison also introduces an emotional dimension, conveying something of the feeling that the scene induces in the poet. The simile can thus illuminate and expand meaning in a compact way. The poet may also extend the simile to elaborate at length on any points of likeness.

In *metaphor*, the comparison between tenor and vehicle is implied: connectives such as "like" are omitted, and a kind of identity is created between the subject and the term with which it is being compared. Thus in John Donne's "The Good-Morrow," a lover asserts the endless joy that he and his beloved find in each other:

> My face in thine eye, thine in mine appears,
> And true plain hearts do in the faces rest;
> Where can we find two better hemispheres,
> Without sharp north, without declining west?

Here the lovers are transformed into "hemispheres," each of them a half of the world not subject to the usual natural phenomena of wintry cold ("sharp north") or the coming of night ("declining west"). Thus, they form a perfect world in balance, in which the normal processes of decay or decline have been arrested. Donne renders the abstract idea of a love that defies change in pictorial and physical terms, making it more real and accessible to us. The images here are all the more arresting for the degree of concentration involved; it is not merely the absence of "like" or "as" that gives the metaphor such direct power, but the fusion of distinct images and emotions into a new idea.

Personification is the figure of speech in which the writer endows abstract ideas, inanimate objects, or animals with human characteristics. In other words, it is a type of implied metaphorical comparison in which aspects of a non-human subject are compared to the feelings, appearance, or actions of a human being. In the second stanza of his ode "To Autumn," Keats personifies the concept of autumnal harvesting in the form of a woman, "sitting careless on a granary floor, / Thy hair soft-lifted by the winnowing wind." Personification may also help to create a mood, as when Thomas Gray attributes human feelings to a hooting owl in "Elegy Written in a Country Church-Yard"; using such words as "moping" and "complain," Gray invests the bird's cries with the quality of human melancholy:

> … from yonder ivy-mantled tow'r
> The moping owl does to the moon complain
> Of such, as wand'ring near her secret bow'r,
> Molest her ancient solitary reign.

In his book *Modern Painters* (1856), the English critic John Ruskin criticized such attribution of human feelings to objects in nature. Calling this device the "pathetic fallacy," he objected to what he saw as an irrational distortion of reality, producing "a falseness in all our impressions of external things." Modern criticism, with a distrust of any notions of an objective "reality," tends to use Ruskin's term as a neutral label simply to describe instances of extended personification of natural objects.

Apostrophe, which is closely related to personification, has the speaker directly addressing a non-human object or idea as if it were a sentient human listener. Blake's "The Sick Rose," Shelley's "Ode to the West Wind" and his ode "To a Sky-Lark" all employ apostrophe, personifying the object addressed. Keats's "Ode on a Grecian Urn" begins by apostrophizing the urn ("Thou still unravish'd bride of quietness"), then addresses it in a series of questions and reflections through which the speaker attempts to unravel the urn's mysteries.

Apostrophe also appeals to or addresses a person who is absent or dead. W. H. Auden's lament "In Memory of W. B. Yeats" apostrophizes both the earth in which Yeats is to be buried ("Earth, receive an honoured guest") and the dead poet himself ("Follow, poet, follow right / To the bottom of the night ..."). Religious prayers offer an illustration of the usefulness of apostrophe, since they are direct appeals from an earth-bound supplicant to an invisible god. The suggestion of strong emotion associated with such appeals is a common feature of apostrophe in poetry also, especially poetry with a religious theme, like Donne's "Holy Sonnets" (e.g., "Batter My Heart, Three-Personed God").

Metonymy and *synecdoche* are two closely related figures of speech that further illustrate the power of metaphorical language to convey meaning more intensely and vividly than is possible with prosaic statement. *Metonymy* (from the Greek, meaning "change of name") involves referring to an object or concept by substituting the name of another object or concept with which it is usually associated: for example, we might speak of "the Crown" when we mean the monarch, or describe the U.S. executive branch as "the White House." When the writer uses only part of something to signify the whole, or an individual to represent a class, we have an instance of *synecdoche*. T. S. Eliot provides an example in "The Love Song of J. Alfred Prufrock" when a crab is described as "a pair of ragged claws." Similarly, synecdoche is present in Milton's contemptous term "blind mouths" to describe the "corrupted clergy" he attacks in "Lycidas."

Dylan Thomas employs both metonymy and synecdoche in his poem "The Hand That Signed the Paper":

The hand that signed the paper felled a city;
Five sovereign fingers taxed the breath,
Doubled the globe of dead and halved a country;
These five kings did a king to death.

The mighty hand leads to a sloping shoulder,
The finger joints are cramped with chalk;
A goose's quill has put an end to murder
That put an end to talk.

The hand that signed the treaty bred a fever,
And famine grew, and locusts came;
Great is the hand that holds dominion over
Man by a scribbled name.

The five kings count the dead but do not soften
The crusted wound nor stroke the brow;
A hand rules pity as a hand rules heaven;
Hands have no tears to flow.

The "hand" of the poem is evidently a synecdoche for a great king who enters into treaties with friends and foes to wage wars, conquer kingdoms, and extend his personal power—all at the expense of his suffering subjects. The "goose quill" of the second stanza is a metonymy, standing for the pen used to sign the treaty or the death warrant that brings the war to an end.

Thomas's poem is an excellent example of the power of figurative language, which, by its vividness and concentrated force, can add layers of meaning to a poem, make abstract ideas concrete, and intensify the poem's emotional impact.

THE POEM AS PERFORMANCE: WRITER AND PERSON

Poetry is always dramatic. Sometimes the drama is explicit, as in Robert Browning's monologues, in which we hear the voice of a participant in a dialogue; in "My Last Duchess" we are present as the Duke reflects on the portrait of his late wife for the benefit of a visitor who has come to negotiate on behalf of the woman who is to become the Duke's next wife. Or we listen with amusement and pity as the dying Bishop addresses his venal and unsympathetic sons and tries to bargain with them for a fine burial ("The Bishop Orders His Tomb at St. Praxed's"). In such poems, the notion of a speaking voice is paramount: the speaker is a personage in a play, and the poem a means of conveying plot and character.

Sometimes the drama is less apparent, and takes the form of a plea, or a compliment, or an argument addressed to a silent listener. In Donne's "The Flea" we can infer from the poem the situation that has called it forth: a lover's advances are being rejected by his beloved, and his poem is an argument intended to overcome her reluctance by means of wit and logic. We can see a similar example in Marvell's "To His Coy Mistress": here the very shape of the poem, its three-paragraph structure, corresponds to the stages of the speaker's argument as he presents an apparently irrefutable line of reasoning. Much love poetry has this kind of background as its inspiration; the yearnings or lamentations of the lover are part of an imagined scene, not merely versified reflections about an abstraction called "love."

Meditative or reflective poetry can be dramatic too. Donne's "Holy Sonnets" are pleas from a tormented soul struggling to find its god; Tennyson's "In Memoriam" follows the agonized workings of a mind tracing a path from grief and anger to acceptance and renewed hope.

We should never assume that the speaker, the "I" of the poem, is simply a voice for the writer's own views. The speaker in W. H. Auden's "To an Unknown Citizen," presenting a summary of the dead citizen's life, appears to be an official spokesperson for the society which the citizen served ("Our report on his union"; "Our researchers …" etc.). The speaker's words are laudatory, yet we perceive immediately that Auden's own views of this society are anything but approving. The speaker seems satisfied with the highly regimented nature of his society, one in which every aspect of the individual's life is under scrutiny and subject to correction. The only things necessary to the happiness of the "Modern Man," it seems, are "A phonograph, a radio, a car, and a frigidaire." The tone here is subtly ironic, an irony created by the gap between the imagined speaker's perception and the real feelings of the writer.

PERFORMANCE POETRY

Poetry began as an oral art, passed on in the form of chants, myths, ballads, and legends recited to an audience of listeners rather than readers. Even today, the dramatic qualities of a poem may extend beyond written text. "Performance poets" combine poetry and stagecraft in presenting their work to live audiences. Dramatic uses of voice, rhythm, body movement, music, and sometimes other visual effects make the "text" of the poem multi-dimensional. For example, Edith Sitwell's poem-sequence *Façade* (1922) was originally set to music: Sitwell read from behind a screen, while a live orchestra played. This performance was designed to enhance the verbal and rhythmic qualities of her poetry:

Beneath the flat and paper sky
The sun, a demon's eye
Glowed through the air, that mask of glass;
All wand'ring sounds that pass

Seemed out of tune, as if the light
Were fiddle-strings pulled tight.
The market-square with spire and bell
Clanged out the hour in Hell.
    (from *Façade*)

By performing their poetry, writers can also convey cultural values and traditions. The cultural aspect of performance is central to Black poetry, which originates in a highly oral tradition of folklore and storytelling. From its roots in Africa, this oral tradition has been manifested in the songs and stories of slaves, in spirituals, in the jazz rhythms of the Twenties and the Thirties and in the rebelliousness of reggae and of rap. Even when it remains "on the page," much Black poetry written in the oral tradition has a compelling rhythmic quality. The lines below from Linton Kwesi Johnson's "Mi Revalueshanary Fren," for example, blur the line between spoken poetry and song. Johnson often performs his "dub poetry" against reggae or hip-hop musical backings.

yes, people powa jus a showa evry howa
an evrybady claim dem democratic
but some a wolf an some a sheep
an dat is problematic

The chorus of Johnson's poems, with its constant repetitions, digs deeply into the roots of African song and chant. Its performance qualities become clearer when the poem is read aloud:

Husak
e ad to go
Honnicka
e ad to go
Chowcheskhu
e ad to go
Just like apartied
will av to go

To perform a poem is one way to see and hear poetry as multi-dimensional, cultural, historical, and often also political. Performance is also another way to discover how poetic "meaning" can be constructed in the dynamic relation between speaker and listener.

TONE: THE SPEAKER'S ATTITUDE

In understanding poetry, it is helpful to imagine a poem as having a "voice." The voice may be close to the poet's own, or that of an imagined character, a *persona* adopted by the poet. The tone of the voice will reveal the speaker's attitude to the subject, thus helping to shape our understanding and response. In speech we can indicate our feelings by raising or lowering our voices, and we can accompany words with physical actions. In writing, we must try to convey the tonal inflections of the speaking voice through devices of language and rhythm, through imagery and figures of speech, and through allusions and contrasts.

THE IRONIC TONE

Housman's poem "Terence, This Is Stupid Stuff" offers a useful example of ways in which manipulating tone can reinforce meaning. When Housman, presenting himself in the poem as "Terence," imagines himself to be criticized for writing gloomy poems, his response to his critics takes the form of an ironic alternative: perhaps they should stick to drinking ale:

> Oh, many a peer of England brews
> Livelier liquor than the Muse,
> And malt does more than Milton can
> To justify God's ways to man.

The tone here is one of heavy scorn. The speaker is impatient with those who refuse to look at the realities of life and death, and who prefer to take refuge in simple-minded pleasure. The ludicrous comparisons, first between the brewers who have been made peers of England and the classical Muse of poetry, then between malt and Milton, create a sense of disproportion and ironic tension; the explicit allusion to *Paradise Lost* ("To justify God's ways to man") helps to drive home the poet's bitter recognition that his auditors are part of that fallen world depicted by Milton, yet unable or unwilling to acknowledge their harsh condition. The three couplets that follow offer a series of contrasts: in each case, the first line sets up a pleasant expectation and the second dashes it with a blunt reminder of reality:

> Ale, man, ale's the stuff to drink
> For fellows whom it hurts to think:
> Look into the pewter pot
> To see the world as the world's not.
> And faith, 'tis pleasant till 'tis past:
> The mischief is that 'twill not last.

These are all jabs at the "sterling lads" who would prefer to lie in "lovely muck" and not think about the way the world is. Housman's sardonic advice is all the more pointed for its sharp and ironic tone.

POETIC FORMS

In poetry, language is intimately related to form, which is the structuring of words within identifiable patterns. In prose we speak of phrases, sentences, and paragraphs; in poetry, we identify structures by lines, stanzas, or complete forms such as the sonnet or the ode (though poetry in complete or blank verse has paragraphs of variable length, not formal stanzas: see below).

   Rightly handled, the form enhances expression and meaning, just as a frame can define and enhance a painting or photograph. Unlike the photo frame, however, form in poetry is an integral part of the whole work. At one end of the scale, the term "form" may describe the *epic,* the lengthy narrative governed by such conventions as division into books, a lofty style, and the interplay between human and supernatural characters. At the other end lies the *epigram*, a witty and pointed saying whose distinguishing characteristic is its brevity, as in Alexander Pope's famous couplet,

> I am his Highness' dog at Kew;
> Pray tell me sir, whose dog are you?

Between the epic and the epigram lie many other poetic forms, such as the sonnet, the ballad, or the ode. "Form" may also describe stanzaic patterns like *couplets* and *quatrains*.

"FIXED FORM" POEMS

The best-known poetic form is probably the sonnet, the fourteen-line poem inherited from Italy (the word itself is from the Italian *sonetto*, little song or sound). Within those fourteen lines, whether the poet chooses the "Petrarchan" rhyme scheme or the "English" form (see below in the section on "Rhyme"), the challenge is to develop an idea or situation that must find its statement and its resolution within the strict confines of the sonnet frame. Typically, there is an initial idea, description, or statement of feeling, followed by a "turn" in the thought that takes the reader by surprise, or that casts the situation in an unexpected light. Thus in Sonnet 130, "My Mistress' Eyes Are Nothing Like the Sun," William Shakespeare spends the first three quatrains apparently disparaging his lover in a series of unfavorable comparisons—"If snow be white, why then her breasts are dun"—but in the closing couplet his point becomes clear:

> And yet, by heaven, I think my love as rare
> As any she belied with false compare.

In other words, the speaker's disparaging comparisons have really been parodies of sentimental clichés which falsify reality; his mistress has no need of the exaggerations or distortions of conventional love poetry.

Other foreign forms borrowed and adapted by English-language poets include the *ghazal* and the *pantoum*. The *ghazal*, strongly associated with classical Urdu literature, originated in Persia and Arabia and was brought to the Indian subcontinent in the twelfth century. It consists of a series of couplets held together by a refrain, a simple rhyme scheme (a/a, b/a, c/a, d/a...), and a common rhythm, but only loosely related in theme or subject. Some English-language practitioners of the form have captured the epigrammatic quality of the ghazal, but most do not adhere to the strict pattern of the classical form.

The *pantoum*, based on a Malaysian form, was imported into English poetry via the work of nineteenth-century French poets. Typically it presents a series of quatrains rhyming *abab*, linked by a pattern of repetition in which the second and fourth lines of a quatrain become the first and third lines of the stanza that follows. In the poem's final stanza, the pattern is reversed: the second line repeats the third line of the first stanza, and the last line repeats the poem's opening line, thus creating the effect of a loop.

Similar to the pantoum in the circularity of its structure is the *villanelle*, originally a French form, with five *tercets* and a concluding *quatrain* held together by only two rhymes (aba, aba, aba, aba, aba, abaa) and by a refrain that repeats the first line at lines 6, 12, and 18, while the third line of the first tercet reappears as lines 9, 15, and 19. With its interlocking rhymes and elaborate repetitions, the villanelle can create a variety of tonal effects, ranging from lighthearted parody to the sonorous and earnest exhortation of Dylan Thomas's "Do Not Go Gentle Into That Good Night."

STANZAIC FORMS

Recurring formal groupings of lines within a poem are usually described as "stanzas." Both the recurring and the formal aspects of stanzaic forms are important; it is a common misconception to think that any group of lines in a poem, if it is set off by line spaces, constitutes a stanza. If such a group of lines is not patterned as one of a recurring group sharing similar formal characteristics, however, then it may be more appropriate to refer to such irregular groupings in the way we do for prose—as paragraphs. A ballad is typically divided into stanzas; a prose poem or a poem written in free verse, on the other hand, will rarely be divided into stanzas.

A stanza may be identified by the number of lines and the patterns of rhyme repeated in each grouping. One of the simpler traditional forms is the *ballad stanza*, with its alternating four and three-foot lines and its *abcb* rhyme scheme. Drawing on this form's association with medieval ballads and legends, Keats produces the eerie mystery of "La Belle Dame Sans Merci":

> I saw pale kings and princes too,
> Pale warriors, death-pale were they all;
> They cried—"La Belle Dame sans Merci
> Hath thee in thrall!"

Such imitations are a form of literary allusion; Keats uses a traditional stanza form to remind us of poems like "Sir Patrick Spens" or "Barbara Allen" to dramatize the painful thralldom of love by placing it within a well-known tradition of ballad narratives with similar forms and themes.

The four-line stanza, or *quatrain*, may be used for a variety of effects: from the elegiac solemnity of Gray's "Elegy Written in a Country Churchyard" to the apparent lightness and simplicity of some of Emily Dickinson's poems. Tennyson used a rhyming quatrain to such good effect in *In Memoriam* that the form he employed (four lines of iambic tetrameter rhyming *abba*) is known as the "In Memoriam stanza."

Other commonly used forms of stanza include the *rhyming couplet, terza rima, ottava rima, rhyme royal,* and the *Spenserian stanza*. Each of these is a rhetorical unit within a longer whole, rather like a paragraph within an essay. The poet's choice among such forms is dictated, at least in part, by the effects that each may produce. Thus the *rhyming couplet* often expresses a complete statement within two lines, creating a sense of density of thought, of coherence and closure; it is particularly effective where the writer wishes to set up contrasts, or to achieve the witty compactness of epigram:

> Of all mad creatures, if the learn'd are right,
> It is the slaver kills, and not the bite.
> A fool quite angry is quite innocent:
> Alas! 'tis ten times worse when they repent.
>
> (from Pope, "Epistle to Dr. Arbuthnot")

Ottava rima, as its Italian name implies, is an eight-line stanza, with the rhyme scheme *abababcc*. Like the sonnet, it is long enough to allow the development of a single thought in some detail and complexity, with a concluding couplet that may extend the central idea or cast it in a wholly unexpected light. W.B. Yeats uses this stanza form in "Sailing to Byzantium" and "Among Schoolchildren." Though much used by Renaissance poets, it is particularly associated with George Gordon, Lord Byron's *Don Juan*, in which the poet exploits to the full its potential for devastating irony and bathos. It is long enough to allow the development of a single thought in some detail and complexity; the concluding couplet can then, sonnet-like, turn that thought upon its head, or cast it in a wholly unexpected light:

Sagest of women, even of widows, she
    Resolved that Juan should be quite a paragon,
And worthy of the noblest pedigree
    (His sire was of Castile, his dam from Aragon).
Then for accomplishments of chivalry,
    In case our lord the king should go to war again,
He learned the arts of riding, fencing, gunnery,
And how to scale a fortress—or a nunnery.

(Don Juan I.38)

FREE VERSE

Not all writers want the order and symmetry—some might say the restraints and limitations—of traditional forms, and many have turned to *free verse* as a means of liberating their thoughts and feelings. Deriving its name from the French "vers libre" made popular by the French Symbolistes at the end of the nineteenth century, free verse is characterized by irregularity of metre, line length, and rhyme. This does not mean that it is without pattern; rather, it tends to follow more closely than other forms the unforced rhythms and accents of natural speech, making calculated use of spacing, line breaks, and "cadences," the rhythmic units that govern phrasing in speech.

Free verse is not a modern invention. Milton was an early practitioner, as was Blake; however, it was the great modern writers of free verse—first Walt Whitman, then Pound, Eliot, and William Carlos Williams (interestingly, all Americans, at least originally)—who gave this form a fluidity and flexibility that could free the imagination to deal with any kind of feeling or experience. Perhaps because it depends so much more than traditional forms upon the individual intuitions of the poet, it is the form of poetic structure most commonly found today. The best practitioners recognize that free verse, like any other kind of poetry, demands clarity, precision, and a close connection between technique and meaning.

PROSE POETRY

At the furthest extreme from traditional forms lies poetry written in prose. Contradictory as this label may seem, the two have much in common. Prose has at its disposal all the figurative devices available to poetry, such as metaphor, personification, or apostrophe; it may use structuring devices such as verbal repetition or parallel syntactical structures; it can draw on the same tonal range, from pathos to irony. The difference is that prose poetry accomplishes its ends in sentences and paragraphs, rather than lines or stanzas. First given prominence by the French poet Charles Baudelaire (*Petits Poèmes en prose*, 1862), the form is much used to present fragments of heightened sensation, conveyed through vivid or impressionistic description. It draws upon such prosaic forms as journal entries, lists, even footnotes. Prose poetry should be distinguished from "poetic prose," which may be found in a variety of settings (from the King James Bible to the fiction of Jeanette Winterson); the distinction—which not all critics would accept—appears to lie in the writer's intention.

Christan Bok's *Eunoia* is an interesting example of the ways in which a writer of prose poetry may try to balance the demands of each medium. *Eunoia* is an avowedly experimental work in which each chapter is restricted to the use of a single vowel. The text is governed by a series of rules described by the author in an afterword; they include a requirement that all chapters "must allude to the art of writing. All sentences must accent internal rhyme through the use of syntactical parallelism. The text must exhaust the lexicon for each vowel, citing at least 98% of the available repertoire...." Having imposed such constraints upon the language and form of the work, Bok then sets himself the task of showing that "even under such improbable conditions of duress, language can still express an uncanny, if not sublime, thought." The result is a surrealistic narrative that blends poetic and linguistic devices to almost hypnotic effect.

THE POEM AS A MATERIAL OBJECT

Both free verse and prose poetry pay attention in different ways to the poem as a living thing on the printed page. But the way in which poetry is presented in material form is an important part of the existence of almost any form of poetry. In the six volumes of this anthology the material form of the poem is highlighted by the inclusion of a number of facsimile reproductions of poems of other eras in their earliest extant material form.

RHYTHM AND SCANSION

When we read poetry, we often become aware of a pattern of rhythm within a line or set of lines. The formal analysis of that rhythmic pattern, or "metre," is called *scansion*. The verb "to scan" may carry different meanings, depending upon the context: if the *critic* "scans" a line, he or she is attempting to determine the metrical pattern in which it is cast; if the *line* "scans," we are making the observation that the line conforms to particular metrical rules. Whatever the context, the process of scansion is based on the premise that a line of verse is built on a pattern of stresses, a recurring set of more or less regular beats established by the alternation of light and heavy accents in syllables and words. The rhythmic pattern so distinguished in a given poem is said to be the "metre" of that poem. If we find it impossible to identify any specific metrical pattern, the poem is probably an example of free verse.

QUANTITATIVE, SYLLABIC, AND ACCENTUAL-SYLLABIC VERSE

Although we owe much of our terminology for analyzing or describing poetry to the Greeks and Romans, the foundation of our metrical system is quite different from theirs. They measured a line of verse by the duration of sound ("quantity") in each syllable, and by the combination of short and long syllables. Such poetry is known as *quantitative* verse.

Unlike Greek or Latin, English is a heavily accented language. Thus poetry of the Anglo-Saxon period, such as *Beowulf*, was *accentual:* that is, the lines were based on a fixed number of accents, or stresses, regardless of the number of syllables in the line:

> Oft Scyld Scefing   sceapena þreatum
> monegum maegþum   meodosetla ofteah.

Few modern poets have written in the accentual tradition. A notable exception was Gerard Manley Hopkins, who based his line on a pattern of strong stresses that he called "sprung rhythm." Hopkins experimented with rhythms and stresses that approximate the accentual quality of natural speech; the result is a line that is emphatic, abrupt, even harsh in its forcefulness:

> I caught this morning morning's minion, kingdom of daylight's dauphin, dapple-dawn-drawn
>   Falcon, in his riding

> Of the rolling level underneath him steady air ....
>
> (from "The Windhover")

Under the influence of French poetry, following the Norman invasion of the eleventh century, English writers were introduced to *syllabic* prosody: that is, poetry in which the number of syllables is the determining factor in the length of any line, regardless of the number of stresses or their placement. A few modern writers have successfully produced syllabic poetry.

However, the accentual patterns of English, in speech as well as in poetry, were too strongly ingrained to disappear. Instead, the native accentual practice combined with the imported syllabic conventions to produce the *accentual-syllabic* line, in which the writer works with combinations of stressed and unstressed syllables in lines of equal syllabic length. Geoffrey Chaucer was the first great writer to employ the accentual-syllabic line in English poetry:

> Ther was also a Nonne, a Prioresse,
> That of hir smiling was ful simple and coy.
> Hir gretteste ooth was but by sainté Loy,
> And she was clepéd Madame Eglantine.
>
> (from *The Canterbury Tales*)

The fundamental pattern here is the ten-syllable line (although the convention of sounding the final "e" at the end of a line in Middle English verse sometimes produces eleven syllables). Each line contains five stressed syllables, each of which alternates with one or two unstressed syllables. This was to become the predominant metre of poetry in English until the general adoption of free verse in the twentieth century.

IDENTIFYING POETIC METER

Conventionally, meter is established by dividing a line into roughly equal parts, based on the rise and fall of the rhythmic beats. Each of these divisions, conventionally marked by a bar, is known as a "foot," and within the foot there will be a combination of stressed and unstressed syllables, indicated by the prosodic symbols / (stressed) and x (unstressed).

> I know | that I | shall meet | my fate
> Somewhere | among | the clouds | above ...
>
> (from Yeats, "An Irish Airman Foresees His Death")

To describe the meter used in a poem, we must first determine what kind of foot predominates, and then count the number of feet in each line. To describe the resultant meter we use terminology borrowed from classical prosody. In identifying the meter of English verse we commonly apply the following labels:

iambic (x /): a foot with one weak stress followed by one strong stress

> ("Look home | ward, Ang | el, now, | and melt | with ruth")

trochaic (/ x): strong followed by weak

> ("Ty | ger! Ty | ger! bur | ning bright")

anapaestic (x x /): two weak stresses, followed by a strong

   ("I have passed | with a nod | of the head")

dactylic (/ x x): strong stress followed by two weak

   ("Hickory | dickory | dock")

spondaic (/ /): two strong stresses

   ("If hate | killed men,| Brother | Lawrence,
    God's blood,| would not | mine kill | you?")

We also use classical terms to describe the number of feet in a line. Thus, a line with one foot is *monometer*; with two feet, *dimeter*; three feet, *trimeter*; four feet, *tetrameter*; five feet, *pentameter*; and six feet, *hexameter*.

Scansion of the two lines from Yeats's "Irish Airman" quoted above shows that the predominant foot is iambic (x /), that there are four feet to each line, and that the poem is therefore written in *iambic tetrameters*. The first foot of the second line, however, may be read as a trochee ("Somewhere"); the variation upon the iambic norm here is an example of *substitution*, a means whereby the writer may avoid the monotony that would result from adhering too closely to a set rhythm. We very quickly build up an expectation about the dominant meter of a poem; the poet will sometimes disturb that expectation by changing the beat, and so through substitution create a pleasurable tension in our awareness.

The prevailing meter in English poetry is iambic, since the natural rhythm of spoken English is predominantly iambic. Nonetheless, poets may employ other rhythms where it suits their purpose. Thus W.H. Auden can create a solemn tone by the use of a trochaic meter(/ x):

   Earth, receive an honoured guest;
   William Yeats is laid to rest:
   Let the Irish vessel lie
   Emptied of its poetry.

The same meter may be much less funereal, as in Ben Jonson's song *"To Celia"*:

   Come, my Celia, let us prove,
   While we may, the sports of love.
   Time will not be ours forever;
   He, at length, our good will sever.

The sense of greater pace in this last example derives in part from the more staccato phrasing, and also from the greater use of monosyllabic words. A more obviously lilting, dancing effect is obtained from anapaestic rhythm (x x /):

   I sprang to the stirrup, and Joris, and he;
   I galloped, Dirck galloped, we galloped all three.
   "Good speed!" cried the watch, as the gatebolts undrew;
   "Speed!" echoed the wall to us galloping through.
      (from *Browning*, "How They Brought the Good News from Ghent to Aix")

Coleridge wittily captured the varying effects of different meters in "Metrical Feet: Lesson for a Boy," which the poet wrote for his sons, and in which he marked the stresses himself:

> Trochee trips from long to short;
> From long to long in solemn sort
> Slow Spondee stalks; strong foot! yet ill able
> Ever to come up with Dactyl trisyllable.
> Iambics march from short to long:—
> With a leap and a bound the swift Anapaests throng....

A meter which often deals with serious themes is unrhymed iambic pentameter, also known as *blank verse*. This is the meter of Shakespeare's plays, notably his great tragedies; it is the meter, too, of Milton's *Paradise Lost*, to which it lends a desired sonority and magnificence; and of Wordsworth's "Lines Composed a Few Miles above Tintern Abbey," where the flexibility of the meter allows the writer to move by turns from description, to narration, to philosophical reflection.

RHYME, CONSONANCE, ASSONANCE, AND ALLITERATION

Perhaps the most obvious sign of poetic form is rhyme: that is, the repetition of syllables with the same or similar sounds. If the rhyme words are placed at the end of the line, they are known as *end-rhymes*. The opening stanza of Housman's "To an Athlete Dying Young" has two pairs of end-rhymes:

> The time you won your town the *race*
> We chaired you through the market-*place*;
> Man and boy stood cheering *by*,
> And home we brought you shoulder-*high*.

Words rhyming within a line are *internal rhymes*, as in the first and third lines of this stanza from Coleridge's "The Rime of the Ancient Mariner":

> The fair breeze *blew*, the white foam *flew*
> The furrow followed free;
> We were the *first* that ever *burst*
> Into that silent sea.

When, as is usually the case, the rhyme occurs in a stressed syllable, it is known as a *masculine rhyme*; if the rhyming word ends in an unstressed syllable, it is referred to as *feminine*. The difference is apparent in the opening stanzas of Alfred Tennyson's poem "The Lady of Shalott," where the first stanza establishes the basic iambic meter with strong stresses on the rhyming words:

> On either side the river *lie*
> Long fields of barley and of *rye*,
> That clothe the wold and meet the *sky*;
> And through the field the road runs *by*
> To many-towered Camelot ...

In the second stanza Tennyson changes to trochaic lines, ending in unstressed syllables and feminine rhymes:

> Willows whiten, aspens *quiver*,
> Little breezes dusk and *shiver*
> Through the wave that runs *forever*
> By the island in the *river*
> Flowing down to Camelot.

Not only does Tennyson avoid monotony here by his shift to feminine rhymes, he also darkens the mood by using words that imply a contrast with the bright warmth of day—"quiver," "dusk," "shiver"—in preparation for the introduction of the "silent isle" that embowers the Lady.

NEAR RHYMES

Most of the rhymes in "The Lady of Shalott" are exact, or "*perfect*" rhymes. However, in the second of the stanzas just quoted, it is evident that "forever" at the end of the third line is not a "perfect" rhyme; rather, it is an instance of "*near*" or "*slant*" rhyme. Such "*imperfect*" rhymes are quite deliberate; indeed, two stanzas later we find the rhyming sequence "early," "barley," "cheerly," and "clearly," followed by the rhymes "weary," "airy," and "fairy." As with the introduction of feminine rhymes, such divergences from one dominant pattern prevent monotony and avoid a too-mechanical sing-song effect.

More importantly, near-rhymes have an oddly unsettling effect, perhaps because they both raise and frustrate our expectation of a perfect rhyme. Their use certainly gives added emphasis to the words at the end of these chilling lines from Wilfred Owen's "*Strange Meeting*":

> For by my glee might many men have laughed,
> And of my weeping something had been left,
> Which must die now. I mean the truth untold,
> The pity of war, the pity war distilled.
> Now men will go content with what we spoiled,
> Or, discontent, boil bloody, and be spilled.

CONSONANCE AND ASSONANCE

In Owen's poem, the near-rhymes "laughed / left" and "spoiled / spilled" are good examples of *consonance*, which pairs words with similar consonants but different intervening vowels. Other examples from Owen's poem include "groined / groaned," "hall / Hell," "years / yours," and "mystery / mastery."

Related to consonance as a linking device is *assonance*, the echoing of similar vowel sounds in the stressed syllables of words with differing consonants (lane/hail, penitent/reticence). A device favored particularly by descriptive poets, it appears often in the work of the English Romantics, especially Shelley and Keats, and their great Victorian successor Tennyson, all of whom had a good ear for the musical quality of language. In the following passage, Tennyson makes effective use of repeated "o" and "ow" sounds to suggest the soft moaning of the wind as it spreads the seed of the lotos plant:

> The Lotos blooms below the barren peak,
> The Lotos blows by every winding creek;

> All day the wind breathes low with mellower tone;
> Through every hollow cave and alley lone
> Round and round the spicy downs the yellow Lotos dust is blown.

(from "The Lotos-Eaters")

ALLITERATION

Alliteration connects words which have the same initial consonant. Like consonance and rhyme, alliteration adds emphasis, throwing individual words into strong relief, and lending force to rhythm. This is especially evident in the work of Gerard Manley Hopkins, where alliteration works in conjunction with the heavy stresses of *sprung rhythm*:

> Brute beauty and valour and act, oh, air, pride, plume, here
> Buckle! AND the fire that breaks from thee then, a billion
> Times told lovelier, more dangerous, O my chevalier!

(from "The Windhover")

Like assonance, alliteration is useful in descriptive poetry, reinforcing an impression or mood through repeated sounds:

> Thou on whose stream, 'mid the steep sky's commotion,
> Loose clouds like Earth's decaying leaves are shed,
> Shook from the tangled boughs of Heaven and Ocean ....

(from Percy Shelley, "Ode to the West Wind")

The repetition of "s" and "sh" sounds conveys the rushing sound of a wind that drives everything before it. This effect is also an example of *onomatopoeia*, a figure of speech in which the sound of the words seems to echo the sense.

RHYME AND POETIC STRUCTURE

Rhyme may play a central role in the structure of a poem. This is particularly apparent in the *sonnet* form, where the expression of the thought is heavily influenced by the poet's choice of rhyme-scheme. The "English" or "Shakespearean" sonnet has three quatrains rhyming *abab, cdcd, efef,* and concludes with a rhyming couplet, *gg*. This pattern lends itself well to the statement and restatement of an idea, as we find, for example, in Shakespeare's sonnet "That time of year thou mayst in me behold." Each of the quatrains presents an image of decline or decay—a tree in winter, the coming of night, a dying fire; the closing couplet then relates these images to the thought of an impending separation and attendant feelings of loss.

The organization of the "Italian" or "Petrarchan" sonnet, by contrast, hinges on a rhyme scheme that creates two parts, an eight-line section (the *octave*) typically rhyming *abbaabba*, and a concluding six-line section (the *sestet*) rhyming *cdecde* or some other variation. In the octave, the writer describes a thought or feeling; in the sestet, the writer may elaborate upon that thought, or may introduce a sudden "turn" or change of direction. A good example of the Italian form is Donne's "Batter My Heart, Three-Personed God."

The rhyming pattern established at the beginning of a poem is usually followed throughout; thus the opening sets up an expectation in the reader, which the poet may sometimes play on by means of an unexpected or surprising rhyme. This is especially evident in comic verse, where peculiar or unexpected rhymes can contribute a great deal to the comic effect:

> I shoot the Hippopotamus
> with bullets made of platinum,
>   Because if I use leaden ones
> his hide is sure to flatten 'em.
>   (Hilaire Belloc, "The Hippopotamus")

Finally, one of the most obvious yet important aspects of rhyme is its sound. It acts as a kind of musical punctuation, lending verse an added resonance and beauty. And as anyone who has ever had to learn poetry by heart will testify, the sound of rhyme is a powerful aid to memorization and recall, from helping a child to learn numbers—

> One, two,
> Buckle my shoe,
> Three, four,
> Knock at the door—

—to selling toothpaste through an advertising jingle in which the use of rhyme drives home the identity of a product:

> You'll wonder where the yellow went,
> When you brush your teeth with Pepsodent.

OTHER FORMS WITH INTERLOCKING RHYMES

Other forms besides the sonnet depend upon rhyme for their structural integrity. These include the *rondeau*, a poem of thirteen lines in three stanzas, with two half lines acting as a refrain, and having only two rhymes. The linking effect of rhyme is also essential to the three-line stanza called *terza rima*, the form chosen by Shelley for his "Ode to the West Wind," where the rhyme scheme (*aba, bcb, cdc* etc.) gives a strong sense of forward movement. But a poet need not be limited to particular forms to use interlocking rhyme schemes.

THE POET'S TASK

The poet's task, in Sir Philip Sidney's view, is to move us to virtue and well-doing by coming to us with

> words set in delightful proportion, either accompanied with, or prepared for, the well-enchanting skill of music; and with a tale forsooth he cometh unto you, with a tale which holdeth children from play, and old men from the chimney corner; and pretending no more,

doth intend the winning of the mind from wickedness to virtue: even as the child is often brought to take most wholesome things by hiding them in such other as have a pleasant taste.

(The Defence of Poesy, 1593)

Modern poets have been less preoccupied with the didactic or moral force of poetry, its capacity to win the mind to virtue; nonetheless, like their Renaissance counterparts, they view poetry as a means to understanding, a point of light in an otherwise dark universe. To Robert Frost, a poem "begins in delight and ends in wisdom":

It begins in delight, it inclines to the impulse, it assumes direction with the first line laid down, it runs a course of lucky events, and ends in a clarification of life—not necessarily a great clarification, such as sects and cults are founded on, but in a momentary stay against confusion.

("The Figure a Poem Makes," *Collected Poems,* 1939)

Rhyme and metre are important tools at the poet's disposal, and can be valuable aids in developing thought as well as in creating rhythmic or musical effects. However, the technical skills needed to turn a good line or create metrical complexities should not be confused with the ability to write good poetry. Sidney wryly observes in his *Defence of Poesy* that "there have been many excellent poets that never versified, and now swarm many versifiers that need never answer to the name of poets....it is not rhyming and versing that maketh a poet, no more than a long gown maketh an advocate." Technical virtuosity may arouse our admiration, but something else is needed to bring that "constriction of the throat and ... precipitation of water to the eyes" that A.E. Housman speaks about. What that "something" is will always elude definition, and is perhaps best left for readers and listeners to determine for themselves through their own encounters with poetry.

MAPS

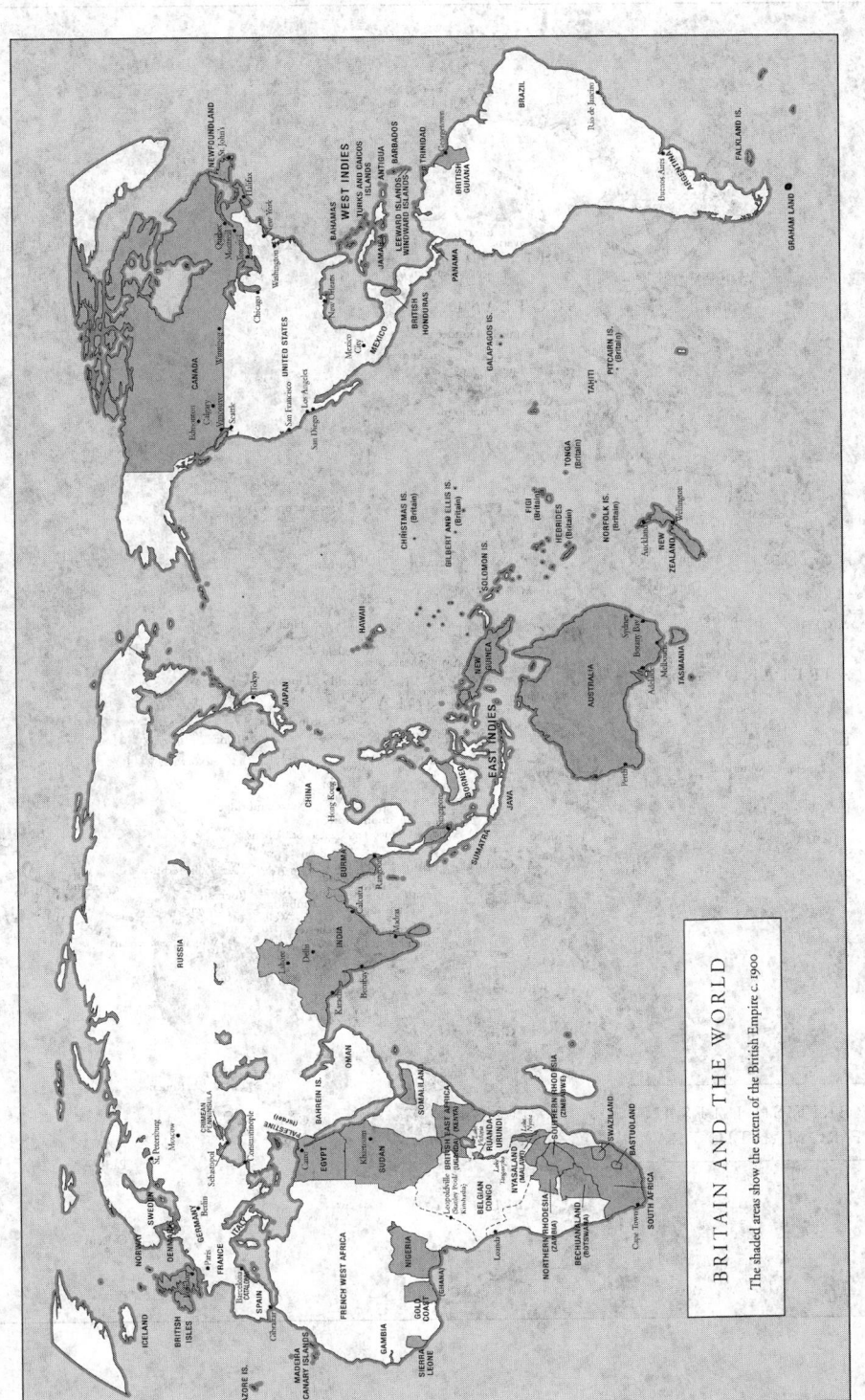

BRITAIN AND THE WORLD

The shaded areas show the extent of the British Empire c. 1900

THE BRITISH ISLES IN
THE ROMANTIC ERA

THE BRITISH ISLES IN
THE VICTORIAN ERA

THE BRITISH ISLES IN THE
TWENTY-FIRST CENTURY

COUNTIES
OF BRITAIN
AND IRELAND

GREATER LONDON
Finchley
Tottenham
Harrow
EPPING FOREST
Hampstead Heath
Wembley
Islington
Twyford Abbey
West Ham
London
Tower
Millenium Dome
Westminster
Fulham
Chelsea
Woolwich
Greenwich
Heathrow Airport
Battersea
Richmond
Deptford
Twickenham
Wandsworth
Dartford
Crystal Palace
Kingston
Wimbledon
Sydenham
Hampton Court
Merton
Bromley
Croydon

CENTRAL LONDON
1 Lambeth Palace
2 Westminster Bridge
3 Westminster Abbey
4 Whitehall
5 Tyburn
6 Covent Garden
7 The Temple
8 Blackfriar's Bridge
9 Swan Theatre
10 Bear Garden
11 Globe Theatre
12 London Bridge
13 St. Paul's Cathedral
14 Fortune Theatre
15 The Theatre
16 Bethlehem Hospital ("Bedlam")
17 The Tower
18 Tower Bridge
19 Waterloo Station
20 Houses of Parliament
21 Tate Gallery
22 Vauxhall Bridge
23 Victoria Station
24 Buckingham Palace
25 Royal Albert Hall
26 Kensington Palace
27 Paddington Station
28 Trafalgar Square
29 British Museum
30 Euston Station
31 St. Pancras Station
32 King's Cross Station
City Rd.
Edgeware Rd.
Gray's Inn Rd.
Tottenham Court Rd.
Aldersgate
Bishopsgate
Marylebone Rd.
Holborn
Oxford St.
Drury Lane
Fleet St.
Cheapside
Thames St.
Strand
Thames
Hyde Park
Piccadilly
Pall Mall
Green Park
St. James's Pk
Kensington Rd.
Chelsea Rd.
Lambeth
Chelsea
Thames
Vauxhall

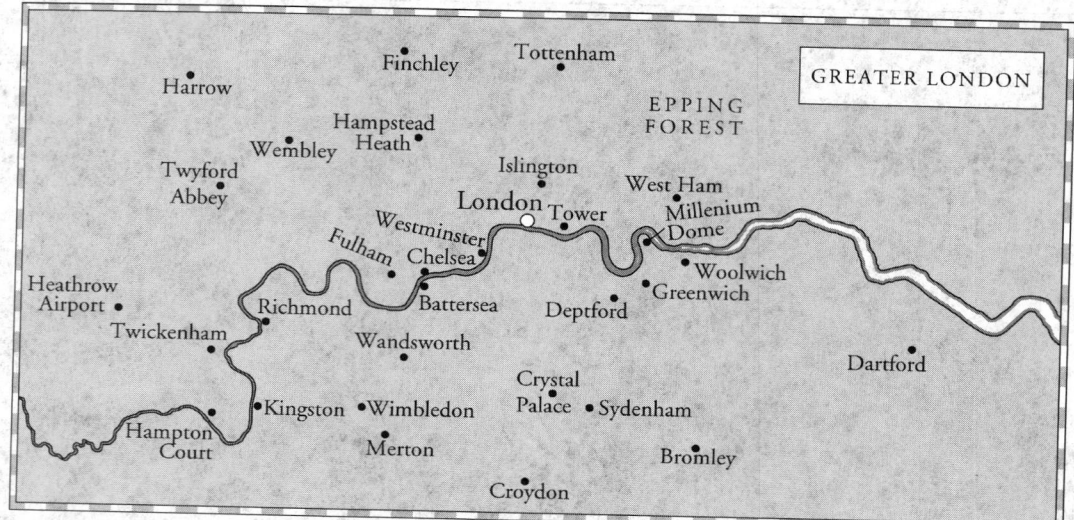

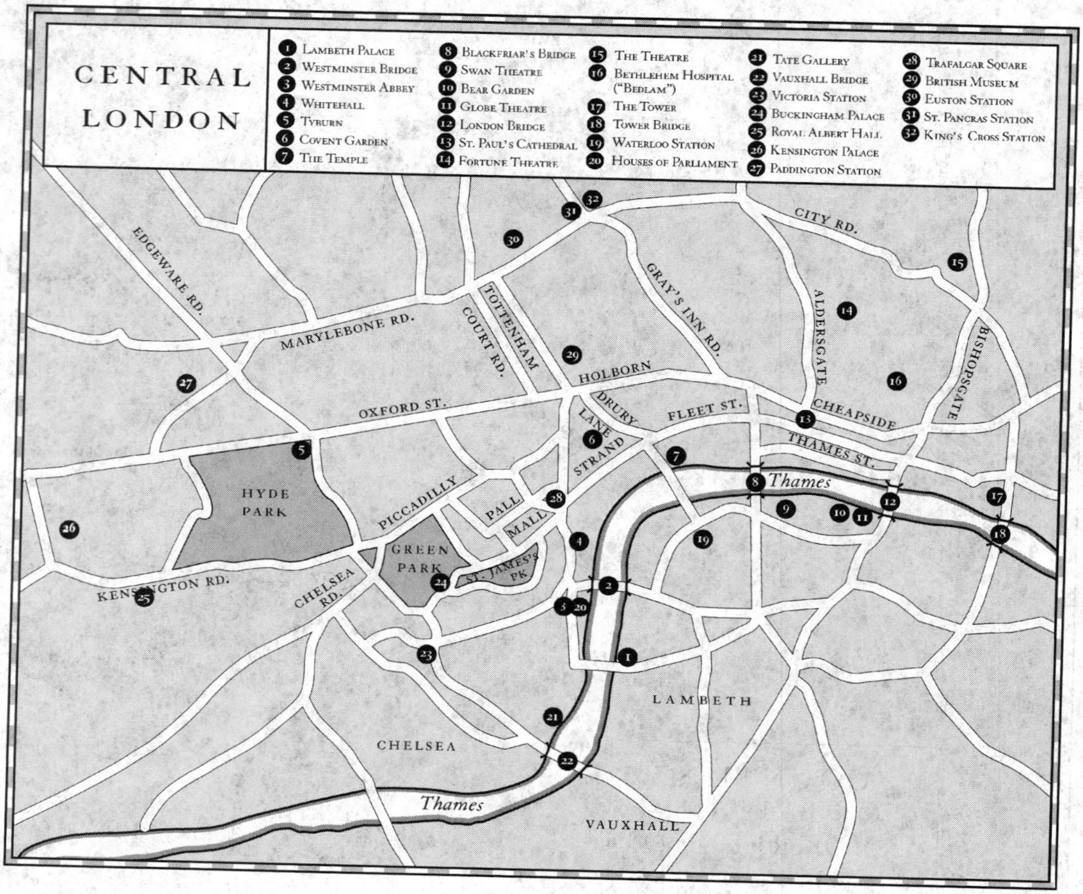

MONARCHS AND PRIME MINISTERS
OF GREAT BRITAIN

MONARCHS

HOUSE OF WESSEX

Egbert (Ecgberht)	829–39
Æthelwulf	839–58
Æthelbald	858–60
Æthelbert	860–66
Æthelred I	866–71
Alfred the Great	871–99
Edward the Elder	899–924
Athelstan	924–40
Edmund I	940–46
Edred (Eadred)	946–55
Edwy (Eadwig)	955–59
Edgar	959–75
Edward the Martyr	975–78
Æthelred II (the Unready)	978–1016
Edmund II (Ironside)	1016

DANISH LINE

Canute (Cnut)	1016–35
Harold I (Harefoot)	1035–40
Hardecanute	1040–42

WESSEX LINE, RESTORED

Edward the Confessor	1042–66
Harold II	1066

NORMAN LINE

William I (the Conqueror)	1066–87
William II (Rufus)	1087–1100
Henry I (Beauclerc)	1100–35
Stephen	1135–54

MONARCHS

PLANTAGENET,
ANGEVIN LINE

Henry II	1154–89
Richard I (Coeur de Lion)	1189–99
John (Lackland)	1199–1216
Henry III	1216–72
Edward I (Longshanks)	1272–1307
Edward II	1307–27
Edward III	1327–77
Richard II	1377–99

PLANTAGENET,
LANCASTRIAN LINE

Henry IV	1399–1413
Henry V	1413–22
Henry VI	1422–61

Henry VIII

PLANTAGENET,
YORKIST LINE

Edward IV	1461–83
Edward V	1483
Richard III	1483–85

HOUSE OF TUDOR

Henry VII	1485–1509
Henry VIII	1509–47
Edward VI	1547–53
Mary I	1553–58
Elizabeth I	1558–1603

HOUSE OF STUART

James I	1603–25
Charles I	1625–49

Mary I

(The Commonwealth)	1649–60
Oliver Cromwell	1649–58
Richard Cromwell	1658–59

MONARCHS		PRIME MINISTERS	

George III

MONARCHS

HOUSE OF STUART, RESTORED
Charles II	1660–85
James II	1685–88

HOUSE OF ORANGE AND STUART
William III and Mary II	1689–94
William III	1694–1702

HOUSE OF STUART
Anne	1702–14

HOUSE OF BRUNSWICK, HANOVER LINE
George I	1714–27
George II	1727–60
George III	1760–1820

George, Prince of Wales,
Prince Regent

PRIME MINISTERS

Sir Robert Walpole (Whig)	1721–42
Earl of Wilmington (Whig)	1742–43
Henry Pelham (Whig)	1743–54
Duke of Newcastle (Whig)	1754–56
Duke of Devonshire (Whig)	1756–57
Duke of Newcastle (Whig)	1757–62
Earl of Bute (Tory)	1762–63
George Grenville (Whig)	1763–65
Marquess of Rockingham (Whig)	1765–66
William Pitt the Elder (Earl of Chatham) (Whig)	1766–68
Duke of Grafton (Whig)	1768–70
Frederick North (Lord North) (Tory)	1770–82
Marquess of Rockingham (Whig)	1782
Earl of Shelburne (Whig)	1782–83
Duke of Portland	1783
William Pitt the Younger (Tory)	1783–1801
Henry Addington (Tory)	1801–04
William Pitt the Younger (Tory)	1804–06
William Wyndham Grenville (Baron Grenville) (Whig)	1806–07

MONARCHS

George, Prince of Wales, Prince Regent	1811–20
George IV	1820–30
William IV	1830–37
Victoria	1837–1901

Victoria

HOUSE OF SAXE-COBURG-GOTHA

Edward VII	1901–10

HOUSE OF WINDSOR

George V	1910–36

PRIME MINISTERS

Duke of Portland (Whig)	1807–09
Spencer Perceval (Tory)	1809–12
Earl of Liverpool (Tory)	1812–27
George Canning (Tory)	1827
Viscount Goderich (Tory)	1827–28
Duke of Wellington (Tory)	1828–30
Earl Grey (Whig)	1830–34
Viscount Melbourne (Whig)	1834
Sir Robert Peel (Tory)	1834–35
Viscount Melbourne (Whig)	1835–41
Sir Robert Peel (Tory)	1841–46
Lord John Russell (later Earl) (Liberal)	1846–52
Earl of Derby (Con.)	1852
Earl of Aberdeen (Tory)	1852–55
Viscount Palmerston (Lib.)	1855–58
Earl of Derby (Con.)	1858–59
Viscount Palmerston (Lib.)	1859–65
Earl Russell (Liberal)	1865–66
Earl of Derby (Con.)	1866–68
Benjamin Disraeli (Con.)	1868
William Gladstone (Lib.)	1868–74
Benjamin Disraeli (Con.)	1874–80
William Gladstone (Lib.)	1880–85
Marquess of Salisbury (Con.)	1885–86
William Gladstone (Lib.)	1886
Marquess of Salisbury (Con.)	1886–92
William Gladstone (Lib.)	1892–94
Earl of Rosebery (Lib.)	1894–95
Marquess of Salisbury (Con.)	1895–1902
Arthur Balfour (Con.)	1902–05
Sir Henry Campbell-Bannerman (Lib.)	1905–08
Herbert Asquith (Lib.)	1908–15
Herbert Asquith (Lib.)	1915–16

MONARCHS		PRIME MINISTERS	
		Andrew Bonar Law (Con.)	1922–23
		Stanley Baldwin (Con.)	1923–24
		James Ramsay MacDonald (Labour)	1924
		Stanley Baldwin (Con.)	1924–29
		James Ramsay MacDonald (Labour)	1929–31
		James Ramsay MacDonald (Labour)	1931–35
		Stanley Baldwin (Con.)	1935–37
Edward VIII	1936	Neville Chamberlain (Con.)	1937–40
George VI	1936–52	Winston Churchill (Con.)	1940–45
		Winston Churchill (Con.)	1945
		Clement Attlee (Labour)	1945–51
		Sir Winston Churchill (Con.)	1951–55
Elizabeth II	1952–	Sir Anthony Eden (Con.)	1955–57
		Harold Macmillan (Con.)	1957–63
		Sir Alex Douglas-Home (Con.)	1963–64
		Harold Wilson (Labour)	1964–70
		Edward Heath (Con.)	1970–74
		Harold Wilson (Labour)	1974–76
		James Callaghan (Labour)	1976–79
		Margaret Thatcher (Con.)	1979–90
		John Major (Con.)	1990–97
		Tony Blair (Labour)	1997–

GLOSSARY OF TERMS

Accent: the natural emphasis (stress) speakers place on a syllable.

Accentual Verse: poetry in which a line is measured only by the number of accents or stresses, not by the number of syllables.

Accentual-Syllabic Verse: the most common metrical system in traditional English verse, in which a line is measured by the number of syllables and by the pattern of accented (stressed) and unaccented (unstressed) syllables.

Aesthetes: members of a late nineteenth-century movement that valued "art for art's sake"—for its purely aesthetic qualities, as opposed to valuing art for the moral content it may convey, for the intellectual stimulation it may provide, or for a range of other qualities.

Alexandrine: a line of verse that is 12 syllables long. In English verse, the alexandrine is always an iambic hexameter: that is, it has six iambic feet. The most-often quoted example is the second line in a couplet from Alexander Pope's "Essay on Criticism" (1711): "A needless Alexandrine ends the song / That, like a wounded snake, drags its slow length along." See also *Spenserian stanza*.

Allegory: a narrative with both a literal meaning and secondary, often symbolic meaning or meanings. Allegory frequently employs personification to give concrete embodiment to abstract concepts or entities, such as feelings or personal qualities. It may also present one set of characters or events in the guise of another, using implied parallels for the purposes of satire or political comment, as in John Dryden's poem "Absalom and Achitophel."

Alliteration: the grouping of words with the same initial consonant (e.g., "break, blow, burn, and make me new"). The repetition of sound acts as a connector. See also *assonance* and *consonance*.

Alliterative Verse: poetry that employs alliteration of stressed syllables in each line as its chief structural principle.

Allusion: a reference, often indirect or unidentified, to a person, thing, or event. A reference in one literary work to another literary work, whether to its content or its form, also constitutes an allusion.

Ambiguity: an "opening" of language created by the writer to allow for multiple meanings or differing interpretations. In literature, ambiguity may be deliberately employed by the writer to enrich meaning; this differs from any unintentional, unwanted, ambiguity in non-literary prose.

Amphibrach: a metrical foot with three syllables, the second of which is stressed: x / x (e.g., sensation).

Analogy: a broad term that refers to our processes of noting similarities among things or events. Specific forms of analogy in poetry include *simile* and *metaphor* (see below).

Anapaest: a metrical foot containing two unstressed syllables followed by one stressed syllable: xx / (e.g., underneath, intervene).

Anglican Church / Church of England: formed after Henry VIII's break with Rome in the 1530s, the Church of England had acquired a permanently Protestant cast by the 1570s. There has remained considerable variation within the Church, however, with distinctions often drawn among High Church, Broad Church, and Latitudinarian. At one extreme High Church Anglicans (some of whom prefer to be known as "Anglo-Catholics") prefer relatively elaborate church rituals not dissimilar in form to those of the Roman Catholic Church and place considerable emphasis on church hierarchy, while in the other direction Latitudinarians prefer relatively informal religious services and tend far more towards egalitarianism.

Antistrophe: from Greek drama, the chorus's countermovement or reply to an initial movement (strophe). See *ode* below.

Apostrophe: a figure of speech (a trope; see figures of speech below) in which a writer directly addresses an object—or a dead or absent person—as if the imagined audience were actually listening.

Archetype: in literature and mythology, a recurring idea, symbol, motif, character, or place. To some scholars and psychologists, an archetype represents universal human thought-patterns or experiences.

Assonance: the repetition of identical or similar vowel sounds in stressed syllables in which the surrounding consonants are different: for example, "shame" and "fate"; "gale" and "cage"; or the long "i" sounds in "Beside the pumice isle..."

Aubade: a lyric poem that greets or laments the arrival of dawn.

Ballad: a folk song, or a poem originally recited to an audience, which tells a dramatic story based on legend or history.

Ballad Stanza: a quatrain with alternating four-stress and three-stress lines, rhyming *abcb*. A variant is "common measure," in which the alternating lines are strictly iambic, and rhyme *abab*.

Ballade: a fixed form most commonly characterized by only three rhymes, with an 8-line stanza rhyming *ababbcbc* and an envoy rhyming *bcbc*. Both Chaucer and Dante Gabriel Rossetti ("Ballad of the Dead Ladies") adopted this form.

Baroque: powerful and heavily ornamented in style. "Baroque" is a term from the history of visual art and of music that is sometimes also used to describe certain literary styles, such as that of Richard Crashaw.

Bathos: an anticlimactic effect brought about by a writer's descent from an elevated subject or tone to the ordinary or trivial.

Benedictine Rule: set of instructions for monastic communities, composed by Saint Benedict of Nursia (died c. 457).

Blank Verse: unrhymed lines written in iambic pentameter, a form introduced to English verse by Henry Howard, Earl of Surrey, in his translation of parts of Virgil's *Aeneid* in 1547.

Bombast: inappropriately inflated or grandiose language.

Broadside: individual sheet of paper printed on only one side. From the sixteenth through to the eighteenth centuries broadsides of a variety of different sorts (e.g., ballads, political tracts, short satires) were sold on the streets.

Broken Rhyme: in which a multi-syllable word is split at the end of a line and continued onto the next, to allow an end-rhyme with the split syllable.

Burlesque: satire of a particularly exaggerated sort, particularly that which ridicules its subject by emphasising its vulgar or ridiculous aspects.

Caesura: a pause or break in a line of verse occurring where a phrase, clause, or sentence ends, and indicated in scansion by the mark II. If it occurs in the middle of the line, it is known as a "medial" caesura.

Canon: in literature, those works that are commonly accepted as possessing authority or importance. In practice, "canonical" texts or authors are those that are discussed most frequently by scholars and taught most frequently in university courses.

Canto: a sub-section of a long (usually epic) poem.

Canzone: a short song or poem, with stanzas of equal length and an envoy.

Carpe Diem: Latin (from Horace) meaning "seize the day." The idea of enjoying the moment is a common one in Renaissance love poetry. See, for example, Marvell's "To His Coy Mistress."

Catalexis: the omission of unstressed syllables from a line of verse (such a line is referred to as "catalectic"). In iambic verse it is usually the first syllable of the line that is omitted; in trochaic, the last. For example, in the first stanza of Housman's "To an Athlete Dying Young" the third line is catalectic: i.e., it has dropped the first, unstressed syllable called for by the poem's iambic tetrameter form: "The time you won your town the race / We chaired you through the market-place; / Man and boy stood cheering by, / And home we brought you shoulder-high."

Catharsis: the arousal through the performance of a dramatic tragedy of "emotions of pity and fear" to a point where "purgation" or "purification" occurs and the feelings are released or transformed. The concept was developed by Aristotle in his *Poetics* from an ancient Greek medical concept, and adapted by him into an aesthetic principle.

Chiasmus: a figure of speech (a scheme) that reverses word order in successive parallel clauses. If the word order is A-B-C in the first clause, it becomes C-B-A in the second: for example, Donne's line "She is all states, and all princes, I" ("The Sun Rising") incorporates this reversal (though with an ellipsis).

Classical: originating in or relating to ancient Greek or Roman culture. As commonly conceived, *classical* implies a strong sense of formal order. The term *neoclassical* is often used with reference to literature of the Restoration and eighteenth century that was strongly influenced by ancient Greek and Roman models.

Closet Drama: a play (typically in verse) written for private performance. The term came into use in the first half of the nineteenth century.

Colored Narrative: alternative term for *free indirect discourse*.

Comedy: as a literary term, used originally to denote that class of ancient Greek drama in which the action ends happily. More broadly the term has been used to describe a wide variety of literary forms of a more or less light-hearted character.

Commedia dell'arte: largely improvised comic performances conducted by masked performers and involving considerable physical activity. The genre of *commedia dell'arte* originated in Italy in the sixteenth century; it was influential throughout Europe for more than two centuries thereafter.

Commonwealth: from the fifteenth century, a term roughly equivalent to the modern "state," but tending to emphasize the commonality of interests among all citizens. In the seventeenth century Britain was named a commonwealth under Oliver Cromwell. In the twentieth century, the term came to be applied to associations of many nations; the British Commonwealth became the successor to the British Empire.

Conceit: an unusually elaborate metaphor or simile that extends beyond its original tenor and vehicle, sometimes becoming a "master" analogy for the entire poem (see, for example, Donne's "The Flea," and Robert Frost's sonnet "She is as in a field a silken tent"). Ingenious or fanciful images and comparisons were especially popular with the metaphysical poets of the seventeenth century, giving rise to the term "metaphysical conceit."

Concrete Poetry: an experimental form, most popular during the 1950s and 60s, in which the printed type itself forms a visual image of the poem's key words or ideas. See also *pattern poetry, assonance*.

Connotation: the implied, often unspoken meaning(s) of a given word, as distinct from its denotation, or literal meaning. Connotations may have highly emotional undertones and are usually culturally specific.

Conservative Party: See *Political Parties*.

Consonance: the pairing of words with similar initial and ending consonants, but with different vowel sounds (live/love, wander/wonder). See also *alliteration*.

Convention: aesthetic approach, technique, or practice accepted as characteristic and appropriate for a particular form. It is a convention of certain sorts of plays, for example, that the characters speak in blank verse, of other sorts of plays that characters speak in rhymed couplets, and of still other sorts of dramatic performances that characters frequently break into song to express their feelings.

Couplet: a pair of rhyming lines, usually in the same meter. If they form a complete unit of thought and are grammatically complete, the lines are known as a closed couplet. See also *heroic couplet* below.

Dactyl: a metrical foot containing one strong stress followed by two weak stresses: / xx (e.g., muttering, helplessly). A minor form known as "double dactyls" makes use of this meter for humorous purposes, e.g., "Jiggery pokery" or "Higgledy Piggledy."

Denotation: See *connotation* above.

Devolution: process through which a degree of political power was transferred in the late twentieth and early twenty-first centuries from the British government to assemblies in Scotland and in Wales.

Dialogue: words spoken by characters to one another. (When a character is addressing him or her self or the audience directly, the words spoken are referred to as a *monologue*.)

Diction: word choice. Whether the diction of a literary work (or of a literary character) is colloquial, conversational, formal, or of some other type contributes significantly to the tone of the text as well as to characterization.

Didacticism: aesthetic approach emphasizing moral instruction.

Dimeter: a poetic line containing two metrical feet.

Dirge: a song or poem that mourns someone's death. See also *elegy* and *lament* below.

Disestablishmentarianism: movement opposing an official state-supported religion, in particular the Church of England in that role.

Dissonance: harsh, unmusical sounds or rhythms which poets may use deliberately to achieve certain effects.

Dramatic Irony: this form of irony occurs when the audience's reception of a speech by a character on the stage is affected by the possession by the audience of information not available to the character.

Dramatic Monologue: a lyric poem that takes the form of an utterance by a single person addressing a silent listener. The speaker may be an historical personage (as in some of Robert Browning's dramatic monologues), a figure drawn from myth or legend (as in some of Tennyson's), or an entirely imagined figure, as in Webster's "A Castaway."

Dub Poetry: a form of protest poetry originating in Jamaica, with its roots in dance rhythms, especially reggae, and often accompanied in performance by drums and music. See also *rap* and *hip-hop*.

Duple Foot: A duple foot of poetry has two syllables. The possible duple forms are iamb (in which the stress is on the second of the two syllables), trochee (in which the stress is on the first of the two syllables), spondee (in which both are stressed equally), and pyrrhic (in which both syllables are unstressed).

Eclogue: now generally used simply as an alternative name for a pastoral poem. In classical times and in the early modern period, however, an *eclogue* (or *idyll*) was a specific type of pastoral poem—a dialogue or dramatic monologue involving rustic characters. (The other main sub-genre of the pastoral was the *georgic*.)

Elegiac Stanza: a quatrain of iambic pentameters rhyming *abab*, often used in poems meditating on death or sorrow. The best-known example is Thomas Gray's "Elegy Written in a Country Churchyard."

Elegy: a poem which formally mourns the death of a particular person (e.g., Tennyson's "In Memoriam") or in which the poet meditates on other serious subjects (e.g., Gray's "Elegy"). See also *dirge*.

Elision: omitting or suppressing a letter or an unstressed syllable at the beginning or end of a word, so that a line of verse may conform to a given metrical scheme. For example, the three syllables at the beginning of Shakespeare's sonnet 129 are reduced to two by the omission of the first vowel: "Th' expense of spirit in a waste of shame." See also *syncope*.

Ellipsis: the omission of a word or words necessary for the complete grammatical construction of a sentence, but not necessary for our understanding of the sentence.

End-Rhyme: See *rhyme*.

End-stopped: a line of poetry is said to be end-stopped when the end of the line coincides with a natural pause in the syntax, such as the conclusion of a sentence; e.g., in this couplet from Pope's "Essay on Criticism," both lines are end-stopped: "A little learning is a dangerous thing; / Drink deep, or taste not the Pierian spring." Compare this with *enjambement*.

Enjambement: the "running-on" of the sense from one line of poetry to the next, with no pause created by punctuation or syntax. (The more commonly found alternative is referred to as an *end-stopped line*.)

Envoy (Envoi): a stanza or half-stanza that forms the conclusion of certain French poetic forms, such as the *sestina* or the *ballade*. It often sums up or comments upon what has gone before.

Epic: a lengthy narrative poem, often divided into books and sub-divided into cantos. It generally celebrates heroic deeds or events, and the style tends to be lofty and grand. Examples in English include Spenser's *The Faerie Queene* and Milton's *Paradise Lost*.

Epic Simile: an elaborate simile, developed at such length that the vehicle of the comparison momentarily displaces the primary subject with which it is being compared.

Epigram: a very short poem, sometimes in closed couplet form, characterized by pointed wit.

Epigraph: a quotation placed at the beginning of a discourse to indicate or foreshadow the theme.

Epiphany: a moment at which matters of significance are suddenly illuminated for a literary character (or for the reader), typically triggered by something small and seemingly of little import. The term first came into wide currency in connection with the fiction of James Joyce.

Episodic Plot: plot comprising a variety of episodes that are only loosely connected by threads of story material (as opposed to plots that present one or more continually unfolding narratives where successive episodes build one on another).

Epithalamion: a poem celebrating a wedding. The best-known example in English is probably Edmund Spenser's "Epithalamion" (1595).

Eulogy: text expressing praise, especially for a distinguished person recently deceased.

Euphemism: mode of expression through which aspects of reality considered to be vulgar, crudely physical, or unpleasant are referred to indirectly rather than named explicitly. A variety of euphemisms exist for the processes of urination and defecation; *passed away* is often used as a euphemism for *died*. (The word *euphemism* has the same root as *Euphuism* (see below), but has taken on a different meaning.)

Euphony: pleasant, musical sounds or rhythms—the opposite of dissonance.

Euphuism: In the late sixteenth century John Lyly published a prose romance, *Euphues*, which employed a style that featured long sentences filled with balanced phrases and clauses, many of them adding little to the content. This highly mannered style was popular in the court of Elizabeth I for a few years following the publication of Lyly's famous work, and the style became known as *Euphuism*.

European Union: (EU) Group of nations formed in 1993 as the successor to the European Economic Community (Common Market). Britain first applied for membership in the latter in 1961; at first its efforts to join were blocked by the French government, but in 1973 Prime Minister Edward Heath successfully negotiated Britain's entry into the group. Britain has resisted some moves towards full integration with the European community, in particular retaining its own currency when other European nations adopted the Euro on 1 January 2002.

Exchequer: In earlier eras, the central royal financial office, responsible for receiving and keeping track of crown revenues. In later eras, part of the bureaucracy equivalent to the Ministry of Finance in Canada or the Treasury in the United States (the modern post of Chancellor of the Exchequer is equivalent to the American post of Secretary of the Treasury, the Canadian post of Minister of Finance or the Australian post of Treasurer).

Exposition: the setting out of material in an ordered form, either in speech or in writing. In a play those parts of the action that do not occur on stage but are rather recounted by the characters are frequently described as being presented in exposition. Similarly, when the background narrative is filled in near the beginning of a novel, such material is often described as having been presented in exposition. Somewhat confusingly, however, the term "expository prose" is usually used with reference not to fiction but to the setting forth of arguments or descriptions in the context of essays or other works of prose non-fiction.

Eye-Rhyme: See *rhyme* below.

Feminine Ending: the ending of a line of poetry on an "extra," and, especially, on an unstressed syllable. See, for example, the first line of Keat's "Ode on a Grecian Urn": "A thing of beauty is a joy forever," a line of iambic pentameter in which the final foot is an amphibrach rather than an iamb.

Feminine Rhyme: See *rhyme* below.

Figures of Speech: deliberate, highly concentrated uses of language to achieve particular purposes or effects on an audience. There are two kinds of figures: schemes and tropes. Schemes involve changes in word-sound and word-order, such as *alliteration* and *chiasmus*. Tropes play on our understandings of words to extend, alter, or transform meaning, as in *metaphor* and *personification*.

First-Person Narrative: narrative recounted using *I* and *me*. See also *narrative perspective*.

Fixed Forms: the term applied to a number of poetic forms and stanzaic patterns, many derived from French models, such as *ballade, rondeau, sestina, triolet,* and *villanelle*. Other "fixed forms" include the *sonnet, rhyme royal, haiku,* and *ottava rima*.

Folio: largest of several sizes of book page commonly used in the first few centuries after the introduction of the printing press. A folio size results from sheets of paper of at least 14 inches by 20 inches being folded in half (a folio page size will thus be at least 7 inches by 10 inches). When the same sheet is folded twice a quarto is produced, and when it is folded 3 times an octavo.

Foot: a unit of a line of verse which contains a particular combination of stressed and unstressed syllables. Dividing a line into metrical feet (*iambs, trochees,* etc.), then counting the number of feet per line, is part of *scansion*. See also *meter*.

Franklin: in the late medieval period, a landholder of free status, but ranking below the gentry.

Free Indirect Discourse: in prose fiction, commentary in which a seemingly objective and omniscient narrative voice assumes the point of view of one or more characters. When we hear through the third person narrative voice of Jane Austen's *Pride and Prejudice*, for example, that Mr. Darcy "was the proudest, most disagreeable man in the world, and every body hoped that he would never come there again," the narrative voice has assumed the point of view of "every body" in the community; we as readers are not meant to take it that Mr. Darcy is indeed the most disagreeable man in the world. Similarly, in the following passage from the same novel, we are likely to take it to read it as being the view of the character Charlotte that marriage is "the only honourable provision for well-educated young women of small fortune," not to take it to be an objective statement of perceived truth on the part of the novel's third person narrative voice:

> [Charlotte's] reflections were in general satisfactory. Mr. Collins to be sure was neither sensible nor agreeable; his society was irksome, and his attachment to her must be imaginary. But still he would be her husband. Without thinking highly either of men or of matrimony, marriage had always been her object; it was the only honourable provision for well-educated young women of small fortune, and however uncertain of giving happiness, must be their pleasantest preservative from want.

The term free indirect discourse may also be applied to situations in which it may not be entirely clear if the thoughts expressed emanate from the character, the narrator, or some combination of the two. (In the above-quoted passage expressing Charlotte's thoughts, indeed, some might argue that the statement concerning marriage should be taken as the expression of a belief that the narrative voice shares, at least in part.)

Free Verse: poetry that does not follow any regular meter, line length, or rhyming scheme. In many respects, though, free verse follows the complex natural "rules" and rhythmic patterns (or cadences) of speech.

Gaelic: Celtic language, variants of which are spoken in Ireland and Scotland.

Genre: a particular literary form. The concept of genre may be used with different levels of generality. At the most general, poetry, drama, and prose fiction are distinguished as separate genres. At a lower level of generality various sub-genres are frequently distinguished, such as (within drama) comedy and tragedy, or, at a still lower level of generality, Elizabethan domestic tragedy, Edwardian drawing-room comedy, and so on.

Georgic: (from Virgil's *Georgics*) a poem that celebrates the natural wealth of the countryside and advises how to cultivate and live in harmony with it. Pope's *Windsor Forest* and James Thomson's *Seasons* are classed as georgics. They were often said to make up, with eclogues, the two alliterative forms of pastoral poetry.

Ghazal: derived from Persian and Indian precedents, the ghazal presents a series of thoughts in closed couplets joined by a simple rhyme-scheme: *ab bb cb eb fb*, etc.

Gothic: in architecture and the visual arts, a term used to describe styles prevalent from the twelfth to the fourteenth centuries, but in literature a term used to describe work with a sinister or grotesque tone that seeks to evoke a sense of terror on the part of the reader or audience. Gothic literature originated as a genre in the eighteenth century with works such as Horace Walpole's *The Castle of Otranto*. To some extent the notion of the medieval itself then carried with it associations of the dark and the grotesque, but from the beginning an element of intentional exaggeration (sometimes verging on self-parody) attached itself to the genre. The Gothic trend of youth culture that began in the late twentieth century is less clearly associated with the medieval, but shares with the various varieties of Gothic literature (from Walpole in the eighteenth century, to Bram Stoker in the early twentieth, to Stephen King and Anne Rice in the late twentieth) a fondness for the sensational and the grotesque, as well as a propensity to self-parody.

Guilds: non-clerical associations that arose in the late Anglo-Saxon period, devoted both to social purposes (such as the organization of feasts for the members) and to piety. In the later medieval period guilds developed strong associations with particular occupations.

Haiku: a Japanese form, using three unrhymed lines of five, seven, and five syllables. Conventionally, it uses precise, concentrated images to suggest states of feeling.

Heptameter: a line containing seven metrical feet.

Heroic Couplet: a pair of rhymed iambic pentameters, so called because the form was much used in seventeenth and eighteenth-century poems and plays on heroic subjects.

Hexameter: a line containing six metrical feet.

Home Rule: movement dedicated to making Ireland politically independent from Britain.

Horatian Ode: inspired by the work of the Roman poet Horace, an ode that is usually calm and meditative in tone, and homostrophic (i.e., having regular stanzas) in form. Keats's odes are English examples.

House of Commons: elected legislative body, in Britain currently consisting of six hundred and fifty-nine members of Parliament. See also *Parliament*.

House of Lords: the "Upper House" of the British Houses of Parliament. Since the nineteenth century the House of Lords has been far less powerful than the elected House of Commons. The House of Lords is currently made up of both hereditary peers (Lords whose title is passed on from generation to generation) and life peers. As a result of legislation enacted by the Labour government of Tony Blair, the role of hereditary peers in Parliament is being phased out.

Humors: The four humors were believed in until the sixteenth and seventeenth centuries to be elements in the makeup of all humans; a person's temperament was thought to be determined by the way in which the humors were combined. When the *choleric* humor was dominant, the person would tend towards anger; when the *sanguine* humor was dominant, towards pleasant affability; when the *phlegmatic* humor was dominant, towards a cool and calm attitude and/or a lack of feeling or enthusiasm; and when the *melancholic* humor was dominant, towards withdrawal and melancholy.

Hymn: a song whose theme is usually religious, in praise of divinity. Literary hymns may praise more secular subjects.

Hyperbole: a *figure of speech* (a trope) that deliberately exaggerates or inflates meaning to achieve particular effects, such as the irony in A.E. Housman's claim (from "Terence, this is stupid stuff") that "malt does more than Milton can / To justify God's ways to man."

Iamb: the most common metrical foot in English verse, containing one unstressed syllable followed by a stressed syllable: x / (e.g., between, achieve).

Idyll: traditionally, a short pastoral poem that idealizes country life, conveying impressions of innocence and happiness.

Image: the recreation in words of objects perceived by the senses, sometimes thought of as "pictures," although other senses besides sight are involved. Besides this literal application, the term also refers more generally to the descriptive effects of figurative language, especially in *metaphor* and *simile*.

Imagism: a poetic movement that was popular mainly in the second decade of the twentieth century. The goal of Imagist poets (such as H.D. and Ezra Pound in their early work) was to represent emotions or impressions through highly concentrated imagery.

In Memoriam Stanza: a four-line stanza in iambic tetrameter, rhyming *abba*: the type of stanza used by Tennyson in *In Memoriam*.

Incantation: a chant or recitation of words that are believed to have magical power. A poem can achieve an "incantatory" effect through a compelling rhyme scheme and other repetitive patterns.

Interlocking Rhyme: See *rhyme*.

Internal Rhyme: See *rhyme*.

Irony: a subtle form of humor in which a statement is understood to convey a quite different (and often entirely opposite) meaning. A writer achieves this by carefully making sure that the statement occurs in a context which undermines or twists the statement's "literal" meaning. *Hyperbole* and *litotes* are often used for ironic effect. *Sarcasm* is a particularly strong or crude form of irony (usually spoken), in which the meaning is conveyed largely by the tone of voice adopted; something said sarcastically is meant clearly to imply its opposite.

Labour Party: See *Political Parties*.

Lament: a poem which expresses profound regret or grief either because of a death, or because of the loss of a former, happier state.

Language Poetry: a movement that defies the usual lyric and narrative conventions of poetry, and that challenges the structures and codes of everyday language. Often seen as both politically and aesthetically subversive, its roots lie in the works of modernist writers like Ezra Pound and Gertrude Stein.

Liberal Party: See *Political Parties*.

Litotes: a *figure of speech* (a trope) in which a writer deliberately uses understatement to highlight the importance of an argument, or to convey an ironic attitude.

Liturgical Drama: drama based on and/or incorporating text from the liturgy—the text recited during religious services.

Lollard: member of the group of radical Christians that took its inspiration from the ideas of John Wyclif (c. 1330–84). The Lollards, in many ways precursors of the Protestant Reformation, advocated making the Bible available to all, and dedication to the principles of evangelical poverty in imitation of Christ.

Luddites: protestors against the mechanization of industry on the grounds that it was leading to the loss of employment and to an increase in poverty. In the years 1811 to 1816 there were several Luddite protests in which machines were destroyed.

Lyric: a poem, usually short, expressing an individual speaker's feelings or private thoughts. Originally a song performed with accompaniment on a lyre, the lyric poem is often noted for musicality of rhyme and rhythm. The lyric genre includes a variety of forms, including the *sonnet*, the *ode*, the *elegy*, the *madrigal*, the *aubade*, the *dramatic monologue*, and the *hymn*.

Madrigal: a lyric poem, usually short and focusing on pastoral or romantic themes. A madrigal is often set to music.

Masculine Ending: a metrical line ending on a stressed syllable. *Masculine Rhyme*: see *rhyme*.

Masque: an entertainment typically combining music and dance, with a limited script, extravagant costumes and sets, and often incorporating spectacular special effects. Masques, which were performed before court audiences in the early seventeenth century, often focused on royal themes and frequently drew on classical mythology.

Mass: Within Christianity, a church service that includes the sacrament of the Eucharist (Holy Communion), in which bread and wine are consumed which are believed by those of many Christian denominations to have been transubstantiated into the body and blood of Christ. Anglicans (Episcopalians) are more likely to believe the bread and wine merely symbolizes the body and blood.

Melodrama: originally a term used to describe nineteenth-century-plays featuring sensational story lines and a crude separation of characters into moral categories, with the pure and virtuous pitted against evil villains. Early melodramas employed background music throughout the action of the play as a means of heightening the emotional response of the audience. By extension, certain sorts of prose fictions or poems are often described as having melodramatic elements.

Metaphor: a *figure of speech* (in this case, a trope) in which a comparison is made or identity is asserted between two unrelated things or actions without the use of "like" or "as." The primary subject is known as the *tenor*; to illuminate its nature, the writer links it to wholly different images, ideas, or actions referred to as the *vehicle*. Unlike a *simile*, which is a direct comparison of two things, a metaphor "fuses" the separate qualities of two things, creating a new idea. For example, Shakespeare's "Let slip the dogs of war" is a metaphorical statement. The tenor, or primary subject, is "war"; the vehicle of the metaphor is the image of hunting dogs released from their leash. The line fuses the idea of war with the qualities of ravening bloodlust associated with hunting dogs.

Metaphysical Poets: a group of seventeenth-century English poets, notably Donne, Cowley, Marvell, and Herbert, who employed unusual difficult imagery and *conceits* (see above) in order to develop intellectual and religious themes. The term was first applied to these writers to mark as far-fetched their use of philosophical and scientific ideas in a poetic context.

Meter: the pattern of stresses, syllables, and pauses that constitutes the regular rhythm of a line of verse. The meter of a poem written in the English accentual-syllabic tradition is determined by identifying the stressed and unstressed syllables in a line of verse, and grouping them into recurring units known as feet. See *accent, accentual-syllabic, caesura, elision,* and *scansion*. For some of the better known meters, see *iamb, trochee, dactyl, anapaest,* and *spondee*. See also *monometer, dimeter, trimeter, tetrameter, pentameter,* and *hexameter*.

Methodist: Protestant denomination formed in the eighteenth century as part of the religious movement led by John and Charles Wesley. Originally a movement within the Church of England, Methodism entailed enthusiastic evangelism, a strong emphasis on free will, and a strict regimen of Christian living.

Metonymy: a *figure of speech* (a trope), meaning "change of name," in which a writer refers to an object or idea by substituting the name of another object or idea closely associated with it: for example, the substitution of "crown" for monarchy, "the press" for journalism, or "the pen" for writing. *Synecdoche* (see below) is a kind of metonymy.

Mock-heroic: a style applying the elevated diction and vocabulary of epic poetry to low or ridiculous subjects. An example is Alexander Pope's "The Rape of the Lock."

Monologue: words spoken by a character to him or herself or to an audience directly.

Monometer: a line containing one metrical foot.

Mood: This can describe the writer's attitude, implied or expressed, towards the subject (see *tone* below); or it may refer to the atmosphere that a writer creates in a passage of description or narration.

Motif: an idea, image, action, or plot element that recurs throughout a literary work, creating new levels of meaning and strengthening structural coherence. The term is taken from music, where it describes recurring melodies or themes. See also *theme*.

Narrative Perspective: in fiction, the point of view from which the story is narrated. A first-person narrative is recounted using *I* and *me*, whereas a third person narrative is recounted using *he, she, they*, and so on. When a narrative is written in the third person and the narrative voice evidently "knows" all that is being done and thought, the story is typically described as being recounted by an "omniscient narrator."

Neoclassical: adapted from or substantially influenced by the cultures of ancient Greece and Rome. The term *neoclassical* is often used to describe the ideals of Restoration and eighteenth-century writers and artists who looked to ancient Greek and Roman civilization for models.

Nobility: privileged class, the members of which are distinguished by the holding of titles. Dukes, Marquesses, Earls, Viscounts, and Barons (in that order of precedence) are all holders of hereditary titles—that is to say, in the British patrilineal tradition, titles passed on from generation to generation to the eldest son. The title of Baronet, also hereditary, was added to this list by James I. Holders of non-hereditary titles include Knights and Dames.

Nonconformist: general term used to describe one who does subscribe to the Church of England.

Nonsense Verse: light, humorous poetry which contradicts logic, plays with the absurd, and invents words for amusing effects. Lewis Carroll is one of the best-known practitioners of nonsense verse.

Octave: also known as "octet," the first eight lines in an Italian/Petrarchan sonnet, rhyming *abbaabba*. See also *sestet* and *sonnet*.

Octosyllabic: a line of poetry with eight syllables, as in iambic tetrameter.

Ode: originally a classical poetic form, used by the Greeks and Romans to convey serious themes. English poetry has evolved three main forms of ode: the Pindaric (imitative of the odes of the Greek poet Pindar); the Horatian (modeled on the work of the Roman writer Horace); and the irregular ode.

The Pindaric ode was an irregular stanza in English, has a tripartite structure of "strophe," "antistrophe," and "epode" (meaning turn, counterturn, and stand), modeled on the songs and movements of the Chorus in Greek drama. The Horatian ode is more personal, reflective, and literary, and employs a pattern of repeated stanzas. The irregular ode, as its name implies, avoids a recurrent stanza pattern, and is sometimes irregular in line length also (see, for example, Wordsworth's "Ode: Intimations of Immortality").

Onomatopoeia: a *figure of speech* (a scheme) in which a word "imitates" a sound, or in which the sound of a word seems to reflect its meaning.

Ottava Rima: an 8-line stanza, usually in iambic pentameter, with the rhyme scheme *abababcc*. For an example, see Byron's *Don Juan*, or Yeats's "Sailing to Byzantium."

Oxymoron: a *figure of speech* (a trope) in which two words whose meanings seem contradictory are placed together, a paradox: for example, the phrase "darkness visible," from Milton's *Paradise Lost*.

Paean: a triumphant, celebratory song, often associated with a military victory.

Pale: in the medieval period, term for a protective zone around a fortress. As of the year 1500 three of these had been set up to guard frontiers of territory controlled by England—surrounding Calais in France, Berwick-upon-Tweed on the Scottish frontier, and Dublin in Ireland. The Dublin Pale was the largest of the three, and the term remained in use for a longer period there.

Pantoum: a poem in linked quatrains that rhyme *abab*. The second and fourth lines of one stanza are repeated as the first and third lines of the stanza that follows. In the final stanza the pattern is reversed: the second line repeats the third line of the first stanza, the fourth and final line repeats the first line of the first stanza.

Parliament: in Britain, the legislative body, comprising both the House of Commons and the House of Lords. Since the eighteenth century, the most powerful figure in the British government has been the Prime Minister rather than the monarch, the House of Commons has been the dominant body in Parliament, and members of the House of Commons have been organized in political parties. Since the mid-nineteenth century the effective executive in the British Parliamentary system has been the Cabinet, each member of which is typically in charge of a department of government. Unlike the American system, the British Parliamentary system (sometimes called the "Westminster system," after the location of the Houses of Parliament) brings together the executive and legislative functions of government, with the Prime Minister leading the government party in the House of Commons as well as directing the cabinet. By convention it is understood that the House of Lords will not contravene the wishes of the House of Commons in any fundamental way, though the "Upper House," as it is often referred to, may sometimes modify or reject legislation.

Parody: a close, usually mocking imitation of a particular literary work, or of the well-known style of a particular author, in order to expose or magnify weaknesses. Parody is a form of satire—that is, humor that may ridicule and scorn its object.

Pastiche: a discourse which borrows or imitates other writers' characters, forms, style, or ideas. Unlike a parody, a pastiche is usually intended as a compliment to the original writer.

Pastoral: in general, pertaining to country life; in prose, drama, and poetry, a stylized type of writing that idealizes the lives and innocence of country people, particularly shepherds and shepherdesses. Also see *eclogue, georgic, idyll,* above.

Pastoral Elegy: a poem in which the poet uses the pastoral style to lament the death of a friend, usually represented as a shepherd. Milton's "Lycidas" provides a good example of the form, including its use of such conventions as an invocation of the muse and a procession of mourners.

Pathetic Fallacy: a form of personification in which inanimate objects are given human emotions: for example, rain clouds "weeping." The word "fallacy" in this connection is intended to suggest the distortion of reality or the false emotion that may result from an exaggerated use of personification.

Pathos: the emotional quality of a discourse; or the ability of a discourse to appeal to our emotions. It is usually applied to the mood conveyed by images of pain, suffering, or loss that arouse feelings of pity or sorrow in the reader.

Pattern Poetry: a predecessor of modern concrete poetry, in which the shape of the poem on the page is intended to suggest or imitate an aspect of the poem's subject. George Herbert's "Easter Wings" is an example of pattern poetry.

Penny Dreadful: Victorian term for a cheap and poorly produced work of short fiction, usually of a sensational nature.

Pentameter: a line of verse containing five metrical feet.

Performance Poetry: poetry composed primarily for oral performance, often very theatrical in nature. See also *dub poetry* and *rap.*

Persona: the assumed identity or "speaking voice" that a writer projects in a discourse. The term "persona" literally means "mask." Even when a writer speaks in the first person, we should be aware that the attitudes or opinions we hear may not necessarily be those of the writer in real life.

Personification: a *figure of speech* (a trope), also known as "prosopopoeia," in which a writer refers to inanimate objects, ideas, or animals as if they were human, or creates a human figure to represent an abstract entity such as Philosophy or Peace.

Petrarchan Sonnet: the earliest form of the sonnet, also known as the Italian sonnet, with an 8-line octave and a 6-line sestet. The Petrarchan sonnet traditionally focuses on love and descriptions of physical beauty.

Phoneme: a linguistic term denoting the smallest unit of sound that it is possible to distinguish. The words *fun* and *phone* each have three phonemes, though one has three letters and one has five. (Each makes up a single syllable.)

Pindaric: See *ode.*

Plot: the organization of story materials within a literary work. The order in which story material is presented (especially causes and consequences); the inclusion of elements that allow or encourage the reader or audience to form expectations as to what is likely to happen; the decision to present some story material through exposition rather than in more extended form as part of the main action of the narrative—all these are matters of plotting.

Political Parties: The party names "Whig" and "Tory" began to be used in the late seventeenth century; before that time members of the House of Commons acted individually or through shifting and very informal factions. At first the Whigs and Tories had little formal organization either, but by the mid-eighteenth century parties had acknowledged leaders, and the leader of the party with the largest number of members in the House of Commons had begun to be recognized as the Prime Minister. The Tories evolved into the modern Conservative Party, and the Whigs into the Liberal Party. In the late nineteenth century the Labour Party was formed in an effort to provide better representation in Parliament for the working class, and since the 1920s Labour and the Conservatives have alternated as the party of government, with the Liberals reduced to third-party status. (Since 1988, when the Liberals merged with a breakaway faction from Labour known as the Social Democrats, this third party has been named the Liberal Democrats.)

Pre-Raphaelites: originally a group of Victorian artists and writers, formed in 1848. Their goal was to revive what they considered the simpler, fresher, more natural art that existed before Raphael (1483-1520). The poet Dante Gabriel Rossetti was one of the founders of the group.

Presbyterian: term applied to a group of Protestants (primarily English and Scottish) who advocated replacing the traditional hierarchical church in which bishops and archbishops governed lower level members of the clergy with a system in which all presbyters (or ministers) would be equal. The Presbyterians, originally led by John Knox, were strongly influenced by the ideas of John Calvin.

Prose Poem: a poetic discourse that uses prose formats (e.g., it may use margins and paragraphs rather than line breaks or stanzas) yet is written with the kind of attention to language, rhythm and cadence that characterizes verse.

Prosody: the study and analysis of meter, rhythm, rhyme, stanzaic pattern, and other devices of versification.

Protagonist: the central character in a literary work.

Prothalamion: a wedding song; a term coined by the poet Edmund Spenser, adapted from "epithalamion" (see above).

Public School: See *schools* below.

Pun: a play on words, in which a word with two or more distinct meanings, or two words with similar sounds, may create humorous ambiguities. Also known as *paranomasia*.

Puritan: term, originally applied only in a derogatory fashion but later widely accepted as descriptive, referring to those in England who favored religious reforms that went beyond those instituted as part of the Protestant Reformation, or, more generally, who were more forceful and uncompromising in pressing for religious purity both within the Church and in society as a whole.

Pyrrhic: a metrical foot containing two weak stresses: xx.

Quadrivium: group of four academic subjects (arithmetic, astronomy, geometry, and music) that made up part of the university coursework in the Middle Ages. There were studied after the more basic subjects of the *Trivium*.

Quantitative Meter: a metrical system used by Greek and Roman poets, in which a line of verse was measured by the "quantity," or length of sound of each syllable. A foot was measured in terms of syllables classed as long or short.

Quantity: duration of syllables in poetry. The line "There is a Garden in her face" (the first line from the poem of the same name by Thomas Campion) is characterized by the short quantities of the syllables. The last line of Thomas Hardy's "During Wind and Rain" has the same number of syllables as the line by Campion, but the quantities of the syllables are much longer—in other words, the line take much longer to say: "Down their carved names the rain drop ploughs."

Quatrain: a four-line stanza, usually rhymed.

Quintet: a five-line stanza. Sometimes given as *quintain*.

Rap: originally coined to describe informal conversation, "rap" now usually describes a style of performance poetry in which a poet will chant rhymed verse, sometimes improvised and usually with musical accompaniment that has a heavy beat.

Realism: as a literary term, the presentation through literature of material closely resembling real life. As notions both of what constitutes "real life" and of how it may be most faithfully represented in literature have varied widely, "realism" has taken a variety of meanings. The term *naturalistic* has sometimes been used a synonym for *realistic*; *naturalism* originated in the nineteenth century as a term denoting a form of realism focusing in particular on grim, unpleasant, or ugly aspects of the real.

Refrain: one or more words or lines repeated at regular points throughout a poem, often at the end of each stanza or group of stanzas. Sometimes a whole stanza may be repeated to create a refrain, like the chorus in a song.

Reggae: a style of heavily-rhythmic music from the West Indies with lyrics that are colloquial in language and often anti-establishment in content and flavor. First popularized in the 1960s and 1970s, reggae has had a lasting influence on performance poetry, rap, and dub.

Rhetoric: in classical Greece and Rome, the art of persuasion and public speaking. From the Middle Ages onwards, the study of rhetoric gave greater attention to style, particularly figures of speech. Today in poetics, the term rhetoric may encompass not only figures of speech, but also the persuasive effects of forms, sounds and word choices.

Rhyme: the repetition of identical or similar sounds, usually in pairs and generally at the ends of metrical lines.

End-rhyme: a rhyming word or syllable at the end of a line.

Eye Rhyme: rhyming that pairs words whose spellings are alike but whose pronunciations are different: for example, though/slough.

Feminine Rhyme: a two-syllable (also known as "double") rhyme. The first syllable is stressed and the second unstressed: for example, hasty/tasty. See also *triple rhyme* below.

Interlocking Rhyme: the repetition of rhymes from one stanza to the next, creating links that add to the poem's continuity and coherence. Examples may be found in Shelley's use of *terza rima* in "Ode to the West Wind" and in Dylan Thomas's villanelle "Do Not Go Gentle Into That Good Night."

Internal Rhyme: the placement of rhyming words within lines so that at least two words in a line rhyme with each other.

Masculine Rhyme: a correspondence of sound between the final stressed syllables at the end of two or more lines, as in grieve/leave, arr-ive/sur-vive.

Slant Rhyme: an imperfect or partial rhyme (also known as "near" or "half" rhyme) in which the final consonants of stressed syllables match but the vowel sounds do not. E.g., spoiled / spilled, taint / stint.

Triple Rhyme: a three-syllable rhyme in which the first syllable of each rhyme-word is stressed and the other two unstressed (e.g., lottery / coterie).

True Rhyme: a rhyme in which everything but the initial consonant matches perfectly in sound and spelling.

Rhyme Royal: a stanza of seven iambic pentameters, with a rhyme-scheme of *ababbcc*. This is also known as the Chaucerian stanza, as Chaucer was the first English poet to use this form. See also *septet*.

Rhythm: in speech, the arrangement of stressed and unstressed syllables creates units of sound. In song or verse, these units usually form a regular rhythmic pattern, a kind of beat, described in prosody as *meter*.

Romanticism: a major social and cultural movement, originating in Europe, that shaped much of Western artistic thought in the late eighteenth and nineteenth centuries. Opposing the ideal of controlled, rational order of the Enlightenment, Romanticism emphasizes the importance of spontaneous self-expression, emotion, and personal experience in producing art. In Romanticism, the "natural" is privileged over the conventional or the artificial.

Rondeau: a fifteen-line poem, generally octosyllabic, with only two rhymes throughout its three stanzas, and an unrhymed refrain at the end of the ninth and fifteenth lines, repeating part of the opening line.

Sarcasm: See *irony*.

Satire: literary work designed to make fun of or seriously criticize its subject. According to many literary theories of the Renaissance and neoclassical periods, the ridicule through satire of a certain sort of behavior may function for the reader or audience as a corrective of such behavior.

Scansion: the formal analysis of patterns of rhythm and rhyme in poetry. Each line of verse will have a certain number of fairly regular "beats" consisting of alternating stressed and unstressed syllables. To "scan" a poem is to count the beats in each line, to mark stressed and unstressed syllables and indicate their combination into "feet," to note pauses, and to identify rhyme schemes with letters of the alphabet.

Scheme: See *figures of speech.*

Schools: In the sixteenth and seventeenth centuries the different forms of school in England included Cathedral schools (often founded with a view to the education of members of the choir); grammar schools (often founded by towns or by guilds, and teaching a much broader curriculum than the modern sense of "grammar" might suggest, private schools, operated by private individuals out of private residences; and public schools, which (like the private schools and the grammar schools) operated independent of any church authority, but unlike the grammar schools and private schools were organized as independent charities, and often offered free education. Over the centuries certain of these public schools, while remaining not-for-profit institutions, began to accept fee-paying students and to adopt standards that made them more and more exclusive. In the eighteenth and nineteenth century attendance at such prestigious public boarding schools as Eton, Westminster, and Winchester had become almost exclusively the preserve of the upper classes; by the nineteenth century such "public" schools were the equivalent of private schools in North America. Though a few girls attended some early grammar schools, the greater part of this educational system was for boys only. Though a number of individuals of earlier periods were concerned to increase the number of private schools for girls, the movement to create a parallel girls' system of public schools and grammar schools dates from the later nineteenth century.

Septet: a stanza containing seven lines.

Serf: in the medieval period, a person of unfree status, typically engaged in working the land.

Sestet: a six-line stanza that forms the second grouping of lines in an Italian / Petrarchan sonnet, following the octave. See *sonnet* and *sestina.*

Sestina: an elaborate unrhymed poem with six 6-line stanzas and a 3-line envoy.

Shire: originally a multiple estate; since the late medieval period a larger territory forming an administrative unit—also referred to as a county.

Simile: a *figure of speech* (a trope) which makes an explicit comparison between a particular object and another object or idea that is similar in some (often unexpected) way. A simile always uses "like" or "as" to signal the connection. Compare with *metaphor* above.

Sonnet: a highly structured lyric poem, which normally has fourteen lines of iambic pentameter. We can distinguish four major variations of the sonnet.

Italian/Petrarchan: named for the 14th-century Italian poet Petrarch, has an octave rhyming *abbaabba*, and a sestet rhyming *cdecde*, or *cdcdcd* (other arrangements are possible here). Usually, a turn in argument takes place between octave and sestet.

Miltonic: developed by Milton and similar to the Petrarchan in rhyme scheme, but eliminating the turn after the octave, thus giving greater unity to the poem's structure of thought.

Shakespearean: often called the English sonnet, this form has three quatrains and a couplet. The quatrains rhyme internally but do not interlock: *abab cdcd efef gg*. The turn may occur after the second quatrain, but is usually revealed in the final couplet. Shakespeare's sonnets are the best-known examples of this form.

Spenserian: after Edmund Spenser, who developed the form in his sonnet cycle *Amoretti*. This sonnet form has three quatrains linked through interlocking rhyme, and a separately rhyming couplet: *abab bcbc cdcd ee*.

Speaker: in the late medieval period, a member of the Commons in Parliament who spoke on behalf of that entire group. (The Commons first elected a Speaker in 1376.) In later eras the role of Speaker became one of chairing debates in the House of Commons and arbitrating disputes over matters of procedure.

Spenserian Stanza: a nine-line stanza, with eight iambic pentameters and a concluding alexandrine, rhyming *ababbcbcc*.

Spondee: a metrical foot containing two strong stressed syllables: // (e.g., blind mouths).

Sprung Rhythm: a modern variation of accentual verse, created by the English poet Gerard Manley Hopkins, in which rhythms are determined largely by the number of strong stresses in a line, without regard to the number of unstressed syllables. Hopkins felt that sprung rhythm more closely approximated the natural rhythms of speech than did conventional poetry.

Stanza: any lines of verse that are grouped together in a poem and separated from other similarly-structured groups by a space. In metrical poetry, stanzas share metrical and rhyming patterns; however, stanzas may also be formed on the basis of thought, as in irregular odes. Conventional stanza forms include the *tercet*, the *quatrain*, *rhyme royal*, the *Spenserian stanza*, the *ballad stanza*, and *ottava rima*.

Stream of Consciousness: narrative technique that attempts to convey in prose fiction a sense of the progression of the full range of thoughts and sensations occurring within a character's mind. Twentieth-century pioneers in the use of the stream of consciousness technique include Dorothy Richardson, Virginia Woolf, and James Joyce.

Stress: See *accent*.

Strophe: the first stanza in a Pindaric ode. This is followed by an *antistrophe* (see above), which presents the same metrical pattern and rhyme scheme, and finally by an *epode*, differing in meter from the preceding stanzas. Upon completion of this "triad," the entire sequence can recur. *Strophe* may also describe a stanza or other subdivision in other kinds of poem.

Sublime: a concept, most popular in eighteenth-century England, of the qualities of grandeur, power, and awe that may be inherent in or produced by undomesticated nature or great art. The sublime was thought of as higher and loftier than something that is merely beautiful.

Subplot: a line of story that is subordinate to the main storyline of a narrative. (Note that properly speaking a subplot is a category of story material, not of plot.)

Substitution: a deliberate change from the dominant pattern of stresses in a line of verse to create emphasis or variation. Thus the first line of Shakespeare's sonnet "'Shall I compare thee to a summer's day?' is decidedly iambic in meter (x / x / x / x / x /), whereas the second line substitutes a trochee (/ x) in the opening foot: "Thou art more lovely and more temperate."

Subtext: implied or suggested meaning of a passage of text, or of an entire work.

Syllabic Verse: poetry in which the length of a line is measured solely by the number of syllables, regardless of accents or patterns of stress.

Syllable: vocal sound or group of sounds forming a unit of speech; a syllable may be formed with a single effort of articulation. Some syllables consist of a single phoneme (e.g., the word *I*, or the first syllable in the word *u-ni-ty*) but others may be made up of several phonemes (as with one-syllable words such as *lengths*, *splurged*, and *through*). By contrast, the much shorter words *ago*, *any*, and *open* each have two syllables.

Symbol: a word, image, or idea that represents something more, or other, than for what it at first appears to stand. Like metaphor, the symbol extends meaning; but while the tenor and vehicle of metaphor are bound in a specific relationship, a symbol may have a range of connotations. For example, the image of a rose may call forth associations of love, passion, transience, fragility, youth and beauty, among others. Depending upon the context, such an image could be interpreted in a variety of ways, as in Blake's lyric, "The Sick Rose." Though this power of symbolic representation characterizes all language, poetry most particularly endows the concrete imagery evoked through language with a larger meaning. Such meaning is implied rather than explicitly stated; indeed, much of the power of symbolic language lies in the reader's ability to make meaningful sense of it.

Syncope: in poetry, the dropping of a letter or syllable from the middle of a word, as in "trav'ler." Such a contraction allows a line to stay within a metrical scheme. See also *catalexis* and *elision*.

Synecdoche: a kind of *metonymy* in which a writer substitutes the name of a part of something to signify the whole: for example, "sail" for ship or "hand" for a member of the ship's crew.

Tercet: a group, or stanza, of three lines, often linked by an interlocking rhyme scheme as in *terza rima*. See also *triplet*.

Terza Rima: an arrangement of tercets interlocked by a rhyme scheme of *aba bcb cdc ded*, etc., and ending with a couplet that rhymes with the second-last line of the final tercet (for example, *efe, ff*). See, for example, Percy Shelley's "Ode to the West Wind."

Tetrameter: a line of poetry containing four metrical feet.

Theme: the governing idea of a discourse, conveyed through the development of the subject, and through the recurrence of certain words, sounds, or metrical patterns. See also *motif*.

Third-Person Narrative: See *narrative perspective*.

Tone: the writer's attitude toward a given subject or audience, as expressed though an authorial persona or "voice." Tone can be projected through particular choices of wording, imagery, figures of speech, and rhythmic devices. Compare *mood*.

Tories: See *Political Parties*.

Tragedy: in the traditional definition originating in discussions of ancient Greek drama, a serious narrative recounting the downfall of the protagonist. More loosely, the term has been applied to a wide variety of literary forms in which the tone is predominantly a dark one and the narrative does not end happily.

Transcendentalism: a philosophical movement that influenced such Victorian writers as Thomas Carlyle and Robert Browning. Also a mode of Romantic thought, Transcendentalism places the supernatural and the natural within one great Unity and believes that each individual person embodies aspects of the divine.

Trimeter: a line of poetry containing three metrical feet.

Triolet: a French form in which the first line appears three times in a poem of only eight lines. The first line is repeated at lines 4 and 7; the second line is repeated in line 8. The triolet has only two rhymes: *abaaabab*.

Triple Foot: poetic foot of three syllables. The possible varieties of triple foot are the anapest (in which two unstressed syllables are followed by a stressed syllable), the dactyl (in which a stressed syllable is followed by two unstressed lines), and the mollossus (in which all three syllables are stressed equally). English poetry tends to use duple rhythms far more frequently than triple rhythms.

Triplet: a group of three lines with the same end-rhyme, much used by eighteenth-century poets to vary or punctuate the flow of couplets. See also *tercet*.

Trivium: group of three academic subjects (dialectic, grammar, and rhetoric) that were part of the university curriculum in the Middle Ages. Their study precedes that of the more advanced subjects of the *quadrivium*.

Trochee: a metrical foot containing one strong stress followed by one weak stress: / x (heaven, lover).

Trope: any figure of speech that plays on our understandings of words to extend, alter, or transform "literal" meaning. Common tropes include *metaphor, simile, personification, hyperbole, metonymy, oxymoron, synecdoche,* and *irony.* See also *figures of speech,* above.

Turn (Italian "volta"): the point in a *sonnet* where the mood or argument changes. The turn may occur between the octave and sestet, i.e., after the eighth line, or in the final couplet, depending on the kind of sonnet.

Unities: Many literary theorists of the late sixteenth through late eighteenth centuries held that a play should ideally be presented as representing a single place, and confining the action to a single day and a single dominant event. They disapproved of plots involving gaps or long periods of time, shifts in place, or subplots. These concepts, which came to be referred to as the unities of space, time, and action, were based on a misreading of classical authorities (principally of Aristotle).

Vers de societé: French: literally, "verse about society." The term originated with poetry written by aristocrats and upper-middle-class poets that specifically disavows the ambition of creating "high art" while treating the concerns of their own group in verse forms that demonstrate a high degree of formal control (e.g., artful rhymes, surprising turns of diction).

Vers libre (French): See *free verse* above.

Verse: a general term for works of poetry, usually referring to poems that incorporate some kind of metrical structure. The term may also describe a line of poetry, though more frequently it is applied to a stanza.

Villanelle: a poem usually consisting of 19 lines, with five 3-line stanzas (tercets) rhyming *aba*, and a concluding quatrain rhyming *abaa*. The first and third lines of the first tercet are repeated at fixed intervals throughout the rest of the poem. See, for example, Dylan Thomas's "Do Not Go Gentle Into That Good Night."

Whigs: See *Political Parties*.

Workhouse: public institution in which the poor were provided with a minimal level of sustenance and with lodging in exchange for work performed. Early workhouses were typically administered by individual parishes. In 1834 a unified system covering all of England and Wales was put into effect.

Zeugma: a *figure of speech* (trope) in which one word links or "yokes" two others in the same sentence, often to comic or ironic effect. For example, a verb may govern two objects, as in Pope's line "Or stain her honour, or her new brocade."

Permissions Acknowledgments

Duffy, Carol Ann. "Stealing," from SELLING MANHATTAN. London: Anvil Press Poetry, 1987; "Adultery," "The Good Teachers," "Drunk" and "Mean Time," from MEAN TIME. London: Anvil Press Poetry, 1993. Reprinted by permission of the publisher; "Wish" "Mrs. Lazarus," from THE WORLD'S WIFE. London: Faber, 1999. Reprinted by permission of Macmillan, London, UK; "Rapture," from RAPTURE. London: Picador, 2005. Reprinted by permission of Pan Macmillan, London, UK.

Eliot, T.S. "Journey of the Magi," "Marina" and "Burnt Norton," from COMPLETE POEMS AND PLAYS, 1909-1950. New York: Harcourt, 1952. Reprinted by permission of Faber and Faber Ltd.

Graves, Robert. Excerpts from GOODBYE TO ALL THAT by Robert Graves. Doubleday Anchor Books, Garden City, New York (1929, renewed in US 1957), pages 182 – 189. Reprinted by permission of Carcanet Press Limited.

Heaney, Seamus. "Digging," Thatcher," "The Wife's Tale," "The Grauballe Man," "Punishment," "Casualty" and "Seeing Things," from OPENED GROUND: SELECTED POEMS, 1966-1996. New York: Farrar, Straus & Giroux, 1999. Copyright © 1998 by Seamus Heaeney. Reprinted by permission of Faber and Faber Ltd; Excerpts from "Englands of the Mind," from PREOCCUPATIONS: SELECTED PROSE 1968-1978. New York: Farrar, Straus & Giroux, 1999. Copyright © 1980 by Seamus Heaney. Reprinted by permission of the publisher.

Housman, A.E. "The Chestnut Casts His Flambeaux" and "Epitaph on an Army of Mercenaries," from COMPLETE POEMS OF A.E. HOUSMAN. New York: Henry Holt, 1959.

Hughes, Ted. "The Thought Fox," "Pike," "Wodwo," "Theology," "A Childish Prank," "The Seven Sorrows" and "Heptonstall Old Church," from COLLECTED POEMS OF TED HUGHES. London: Faber, 2005. Reprinted by permission of Faber and Faber Ltd; "You Hated Spain" and "Daffodils," from BIRTHDAY LETTERS. New York: Farrar, Straus & Giroux, 1999. Copyright © 1998 by Seamus Heaney. Reprinted by permission of the publisher and of Faber and Faber Ltd.

Ishiguro, Kazuo. "A Village After Dark." Originally published in *The New Yorker*, 21 May 2001. Copyright © 2001 by Kazuo Ishiguro. Reproduced by permission of the author c/o Rogers, Coleridge & White Ltd., 20 Powis Mews, London W11 1JN.

Larkin, Phillip. "Church Going," from THE LESS DECEIVED. Yorkshire: Marvel Press, 1955; "Talking in Bed," from THE WHITSUN WEDDINGS. 1960. New York: Random House, 1964; "Days," "Dockery and Son," "Annus Mirabilis," "High Window," "This Be The Verse," "Vers de Société," "The Old Fools" and "Aubade," from COLLECTED POEMS. London: Faber, 2003. Copyright © 1988, 2003 by the Estate of Philip Larkin. Reprinted by permission of Faber and Faber Ltd and of Farrar, Straus & Giroux, LLC.

Lawrence, D.H. "Tortoise Shout" and "Bavarian Gentians," from THE COMPLETE POEMS OF D.H. LAWRENCE. Eds. Vivian De Sola Pinto and Warren Roberts. New York: Penguin, 1964. Reproduced by permission of Pollinger Limited and the proprietor; "Snake," from BIRDS, BEASTS AND FLOWERS: POEMS BY D.H. LAWRENCE. New York: Haskell House Publishers Ltd., 1974. Reproduced by permission of Pollinger Limited and the proprietor.

Mitchell, John. "Reply to Flanders Fields," from THE BEST LOVED POEMS OF THE AMERICAN PEOPLE. Ed. Hazel Felleman. New York: Doubleday, 1936.

Munro, Alice. "The View from Castle Rock." Originally published in *The New Yorker*, 29 August 2005. Copyright © 2005 Alice Munro. Reprinted by permission of William Morris Agency, LLC on behalf of the Author.

Orwell, George. Excerpts from HOMAGE TO CATALONIA. New York: Harvest, 1969. Copyright © 1937 by George Orwell, 1952 and renewed 1980 by Sonia Brownell Orwell. Reprinted by permission of the publisher and Bill Hamilton as the Literary Executor of the Estate of the Late Sonia Brownell Orwell and Martin Secker & Warburg Ltd; "Politics and the English Language" and "Shooting an Elephant," from SHOOTING AN ELEPHANT AND OTHER ESSAYS. New York: Harvest, 1984. Copyright © 1936 and 1946 respectively by George Orwell, 1950 by the publisher, and renewed 1979 by Sonia Brownell Orwell. Reprinted by permission of the publisher and Bill Hamilton as the Literary Executor of the Estate of the Late Sonia Brownell Orwell and Martin Secker & Warburg Ltd.

Palmer, Vance. "The Farmer Remembers the Somme," from THE PENGUIN BOOK OF AUSTRALIAN VERSE. Victoria: Penguin, 1972.

Rhys, Jean. "Let Them Call it Jazz," from TIGERS ARE BETTER-LOOKING: WITH A SELECTION FROM THE LEFT BANK. London: Penguin, 1972. Copyright © Jean Rhys 1972. Reproduced by permission of Penguin Books Ltd.

Rushdie, Salman. "Is Nothing Sacred?," from IMAGINARY HOMELANDS. New York: Viking, 1991. Copyright © Salman Rushdie 1991. Used by permission of Viking Penguin, a division of Penguin Group (USA) Inc.

Sassoon, Siegfried. "They," "Glory of Women" and "Everyone Sang," from COLLECTED POEMS OF SIEGFRIED SASSOON by Siegfried Sassoon, copyright © 1918, 1920 by E.P. Dutton. Copyright © 1936, 1946, 1947, 1948 by Siegfried Sassoon. Used by permission of Viking Penguin, a division of Penguin Group (USA) Inc; Excerpts from "Part II," from MEMOIRS OF AN INFANTRY OFFICER. London: Faber, 1930. Copyright © Siegfried Sassoon by kind permission of George Sassoon.

Shaw, Bernard. "Mrs. Warren's Profession," from PLAYS UNPLEASANT. London: Penguin, 1988. By permission of the Society of Authors, on behalf of the Bernard Shaw Estate. Copyright © 1898, 1913, 1926, 1930, 1933, 1941, George Bernard Shaw. Copyright © 1905, Bretano's. Copyright © 1957, The Public Trustee as Executor for the Estate of Bernard Shaw.

Thomas, Dylan. "The Force That Through the Green Fuse Drives the Flower," from THE POEMS OF DYLAN THOMAS, copyright © 1939 by New Directions Publishing Corp. Reprinted by permission of New Directions Publishing Corp; "Fern Hill" and "A Refusal to Mourn the Death, by Fire, of a Child in London," from THE POEMS OF DYLAN THOMAS, copyright © 1945 by the Trustees for the Copyrights of Dylan Thomas. Reprinted by permission of New Directions Publishing Corp; "Do Not Go Gentle Into That Good Night," from THE POEMS OF DYLAN THOMAS, copyright © 1952 by Dylan Thomas. Reprinted by permission of New Directions Publishing Corp.

ILLUSTRATION CREDITS

Tate Gallery, London/Art Resource, NY; "Will you Answer the Call?" [The Art Archive/Imperial War Museum/Eileen Tweedy]; "Dig for Victory," Bridgeman Art Library; "Kendal Street," by Sirkka-Liisa Konttinen, 1969; "The Lambeth Walk," Bill Brandt Photography; Jacket cover of the Macmillan edition of JOURNEY WITHOUT MAPS by Graham Greene, reprinted by permission of Macmillan, London, UK; Jacket cover of THE VAN, reprinted by permission of The Random House Group Ltd; Jacket cover of NEVER LET ME GO, reprinted by permission of Random House Inc; "Peel Square," Tim Smith Photos; "Notting Hilll Carnival" David Hoffman Photo Library. Page 1009: Bill Brandt Photography. Page 1010: AP/Wide World Photos. Page 1011: Front cover of BRIGHTON ROCK by Graham Greene (Penguin Books 1943). Reproduced by permission of Penguin Books Ltd. Page 1015: Reprinted with the permission of Atheneum Books for Young Readers, an imprint of Simon & Schuster Children's Publishing Division from THE WIND IN THE WILLOWS by Kenneth Grahame, illustrated by Ernest H. Shepard. Copyright 1933 Charles Scribner's Sons; copyright renewed © 1961 Ernest H. Shepard. Page 1017: (bottom right) Getty Images. Page 1018: (top right) Getty Images. Page 1020: Getty Images. Page 1023: Front cover of MAJOR BARBARA by George Bernard Shaw (Penguin Books 1946). Reproduced by permission of Penguin Books, Ltd; Page 1025: Getty Images. Page 1027: United Press International. Page 1028: BRAVE NEW WORLD by Aldous Huxley, published by Chatto & Windus, 1932. Reprinted by permission of The Random House Group Ltd. Page 1029: Jacket Cover from THE RAZOR'S EDGE by W. Somerset Maugham. Used by permission of Doubleday, a division of Random House, Inc. Page 1071: Reproduced by permission of the National Portrait Gallery, London. Page 1108: Reproduced by permission of the National Portrait Gallery, London. Page 1113: Reproduced by permission of the National Portrait Gallery, London. Page 1117: Reproduced by permission of the National Portrait Gallery, London. Page 1122: Bridgeman Art Library. Page 1125: used with permission of the Trustees of the Imperial War Museum, London. Page 1126: used with permission of the Trustees of the Imperial War Museum, London. Page 1128: used with permission of the Trustees of the Imperial War Museum, London. Page 1131: Australian War Memorial. Page 1140: Reproduced by permission of the National Portrait Gallery, London. Page 1169: Reproduced by permission of the National Portrait Gallery, London. Page 1216: Reproduced by permission of the National Portrait Gallery, London. Page 1218: Sylvia Beach Papers. Manuscripts Division. Department of Rare Books and Special Collections. Princeton University Library. Page 1272: Reproduced by permission of the National Portrait Gallery, London. Page 1298: Reproduced by permission of the National Portrait Gallery, London. Page 1314: Reproduced by permission of the National Portrait Gallery, London. Page 1349: Reproduced by permission of the National Portrait Gallery, London. Page 1359: Reproduced by permission of the National Portrait Gallery, London. Page 1378: Portrait by Lisa Brawn. Page 1385: Reproduced by permission of the National Portrait Gallery, London. Page 1401: (bottom) Getty Images. Page 1403: The Press Association. Page 1404: from Political Spider by Ulli Beier. Reprinted by permission of Harcourt Education. Page 1405: (Left) Getty Images; (Right): Tom Hollyman. Page 1410: Getty Images. Page 1417: Reproduced by permission of the National Portrait Gallery, London. Page 1421: Portrait by Lisa Brawn. Page 1428: Portrait by Lisa Brawn. Page 1432: Photograph by Fay Godwin/Collections. Page 1435: Photo courtesy of Don Hamerman. Page 1444: © The Nobel Foundation. Reprinted by permission. Page 1459: Photograph by Derek Shapton. Page 1476: Reprinted by permission. Page 1483: Portrait by Lisa Brawn. Page 1511: Portrait by Lisa Brawn. Page 1522: Portrait by Lisa Brawn. Page 1528: Reprinted by permission of Anvil Press Poetry.

The publisher has endeavored to contact rights holders of all copyright material and would appreciate receiving any information as to errors or omissions.

INDEX OF FIRST LINES

Index of Authors and Titles